Interconnection Networks for High-Performance Parallel Computers

Interconnection Networks for High-Performance Parallel Computers

Isaac D. Scherson and Abdou S. Youssef

 IEEE COMPUTER SOCIETY PRESS

 THE INSTITUTE OF ELECTRICAL AND
ELECTRONICS ENGINEERS, INC.

Interconnection Networks for High-Performance Parallel Computers

Isaac D. Scherson
Abdou S. Youssef

IEEE Computer Society Press
Los Alamitos, California

Washington • Brussels • Tokyo

Library of Congress Cataloging-in-Publication Data

Interconnection networks for high-performance parallel computers /
    [edited by] Isaac D. Scherson, Abdou S. Youssef.
        p.   cm.
    Includes bibliographical references.
    ISBN 0-8186-6197-6 (case). — ISBN 0-8186-6196-8 (fiche)
    1. Parallel computers.   2. Computer networks.
    I. Scherson, Isaac D.   II. Youssef, Abdou S.
    QA76.58.I495   1994
    004'.35 — dc20   94-29120
                                                                     CIP

Published by the
IEEE Computer Society Press
10662 Los Vaqueros Circle
P.O. Box 3014
Los Alamitos, CA 90720-1264

IEEE Computer Society Press Order Number 6197-01
IEEE Catalog Number EH0405-1
Library of Congress Number 94-29120
ISBN 0-8186-6196-8 (microfiche)
ISBN 0-8186-6197-6 (case)

Additional copies can be ordered from

IEEE Computer Society Press	IEEE Service Center	IEEE Computer Society	IEEE Computer Society
Customer Service Center	445 Hoes Lane	13, avenue de l'Aquilon	Ooshima Building
10662 Los Vaqueros Circle	P.O. Box 1331	B-1200 Brussels	2-19-1 Minami-Aoyama
P.O. Box 3014	Piscataway, NJ 08855-1331	BELGIUM	Minato-ku, Tokyo 107
Los Alamitos, CA 90720-1264	Tel: (908) 981-1393	Tel: +32-2-770-2198	JAPAN
Tel: (714) 821-8380	Fax: (908) 981-9667	Fax: +32-2-770-8505	Tel: +81-3-3408-3118
Fax: (714) 821-4641			Fax: +81-3-3408-3553
Email: cs.books@computer.org			

Technical Editor: Dhiraj Pradhan
Copy Editor: Phyllis Walker
Production Editor: Lisa O'Conner
Printed in the United States of America by Braun-Brumfield, Inc.

The Institute of Electrical and Electronics Engineers, Inc.

Contents

Preface

This book is a continuation of the 1984 IEEE publication, *Tutorial: Interconnection Networks for Parallel and Distributed Processing*, by Chuan-lin Wu and Tse-yun Feng. Their book thoroughly covered developments in the field, from the very early papers to the then-recent works by Batcher, Parker, Pease, Siegel, and many others. By concentrating on papers published after 1984, we intend for our book to provide a companion volume to Wu and Feng's. All of the papers we selected were published between 1985 and 1993, with the exception of one important earlier paper, published in 1984, that they did not include.

The analysis of certain aspects of interconnection network technology cannot be tracked with known mathematical tools; many processes are stochastic, and results can be predicted only via simulation. Therefore, we balanced our selection of papers between those that are theoretical and those that are experimental. In addition, because the field of interconnection networks is changing so rapidly, the selected papers cover only what we believe are important research and pedagogical contributions.

Isaac D. Scherson
Abdou S. Youssef
August 1994

Chapter 1: Introduction

One of the most viable methods of developing very high performance computers uses many processors in parallel. The field of parallel processing has generated a great deal of research in a wide variety of computer science areas. Since communications overhead is one of the most important factors affecting the performance of parallel computer systems, the study of interconnection networks has become one of the most popular research areas in parallel processing. In essence, the basic problem to be solved is extremely simple: Given a set of processor nodes, define a set of *links* (or *connections*) between them such that all nodes can communicate at minimum cost. Obviously, such an oversimplification of the basic problem may not do justice to the field; however, its solution domain has spawned much investigation in the past 30 years. "Communicate" may mean many different things, depending on the application at hand. For instance, the communications requirements of a network of workstations are quite different from those imposed by permutation patterns needed in the computation of, say, fast Fourier transforms.

Stringent requirements are imposed on a network used in a parallel-processing system. The issues affecting its cost-effectiveness, which are too numerous to list, depend strongly on both the type of parallel system considered — namely, single-instruction, multiple-data (SIMD) or multiple-instruction, multiple-data (MIMD) — and the degree of parallelism.

In this book, we include a selection of recent papers (published from 1984 to 1993) that together address the main problems encountered in the design, analysis, use, and reliability of interconnection networks. Below, we list these problems separately, detailing how this book addresses each of them.

(1) *Design*. Design requirements and available design tools must be understood before the design process is begun. Moreover, knowing what is already available, as well as knowing how what is available can be changed to fit the design requirements, is important. The fundamental questions of network structure, description, and construction are addressed in Chapter 2, which includes papers presenting a mixture of theoretical and experimental analyses. Chapter 3 shows the importance of choosing a well-behaved rule for connecting nodes and illustrates how other constructs may have advantages over the binary hypercube, although many of the most popular networks in use today are derivatives of the cube. This chapter includes a collection of papers introducing novel, interesting interconnection topologies.

(2) *Analysis*. Because interconnection networks are used for communications between processing elements, routing is probably the most important problem in analyzing interconnection networks. The types of routing requirements imposed by the applications running in a parallel computer vary widely. We have identified four main classes of routing — permutation routing, nonuniform routing, deadlock-free routing, and multicasting — which are discussed in Chapters 4 through 6. Because some of the problems encountered in routing do not have a nice, closed, analytical solution, an entire chapter — Chapter 7 — is devoted to performance evaluation techniques. The techniques are illustrated by example, using a number of well-known networks. Each class of techniques represents a research area in its own right. The papers included in Chapter 7 define the set of important parameters to use in the analysis of how "good" networks are.

(3) *Use*. For a network to be useful, it must accommodate a large class of applications. The mapping (or embedding) problem, discussed in Chapter 8, deals with how an application's communication requirements can be satisfied by the connections established by the network. This problem is essentially one of network emulation. If we consider the application's requirements as a network definition, the computer must be

capable of emulating such a network with minimum time and space costs. Because applications may have different communication requirements and because embeddings may be more or less efficient, time sharing of resources may be advisable in order to increase system utilization and throughput. However, to do this, the system must be partitionable at the network level. Hence, different applications could concurrently use different partitions in the system. Partitioning is the subject of Chapter 9.

(4) *Reliability*. As the complexity of parallel systems grows, so does the probability of failure. Transient or permanent faults may occur with higher probability in larger systems. Tolerating faults is the key to system survival. To achieve fault tolerance, networks must be capable of preserving certain properties, even when faults occur. Chapter 10 — devoted to the subject of fault tolerance — addresses the issue of survivability achieved by both hardware and software techniques. For fault tolerance to exist in a parallel system, methods to diagnose failures must be implemented. Fault diagnosis in interconnection networks is a relatively new area, and important results are given in the papers that are included in Chapter 11, the last chapter of this book.

It is important to note that a prior IEEE book on interconnection networks was published in 1984: *Tutorial: Interconnection Networks for Parallel and Distributed Processing*, by Chuan-lin Wu and Tse-yun Feng.[1] This book, which became a classic, contains many of the groundbreaking papers in this important field. The collection of papers in our book concentrates on the years after 1984. Therefore, our collection forms a companion book to Wu and Feng's, and many of the papers included here cite papers that appeared there. The reader may find it useful to consult the early works prior to, or concurrently with, the study of the recent papers we have selected.

Perhaps today's most representative commercially available machines are the CM-5, by Thinking Machines Corporation, and the MP-2, by MasPar Computer Corporation. The former represents the MIMD parallel-processing environment, while the latter is a data-parallel SIMD engine. It is extremely interesting to note the differences in basic design philosophy between these computers. Thinking Machines' CM-5 is based on commercially available processor nodes interconnected by a message-passing network introduced in 1985 by Leiserson[2] (see Chapter 3) — namely, a fat-tree. On the other hand, MasPar's MP-2 is based on custom very large scale integration (VLSI) processors with an X-net (eight-neighbor mesh) for local routing and a circuit-switched global router for random communication patterns.

Like many impatient readers, we begin our "story" at the end, presenting two of the more recent papers first. These papers, by Leiserson et al. (1992) and Alleyne and Scherson (1992), describe the CM-5 and the MP-2 networks, respectively. We hope that the reader will find starting at "The End" interesting and will be motivated to find out "what happened" to get there.

Happy reading!!!

References

Papers marked with an asterisk are included as reprints in this book.

1. C. Wu and T. Feng, *Tutorial: Interconnection Networks for Parallel and Distributed Processing*, IEEE CS Press, Los Alamitos, Calif., 1984.

*2. C.E. Leiserson, "Fat-Trees: Universal Networks for Hardware-Efficient Supercomputing," *IEEE Trans. Computers*, Vol. C-34, No. 10, Oct. 1985, pp. 892–901.

The Network Architecture of the Connection Machine CM-5

(Extended Abstract)

Charles E. Leiserson,[*] Zahi S. Abuhamdeh, David C. Douglas, Carl R. Feynman, Mahesh N. Ganmukhi,
Jeffrey V. Hill, W. Daniel Hillis, Bradley C. Kuszmaul,[†] Margaret A. St. Pierre, David S. Wells,
Monica C. Wong, Shaw-Wen Yang, and Robert Zak

Thinking Machines Corporation
Cambridge, Massachusetts 02142

May 5, 1992

Abstract

The Connection Machine Model CM-5 Supercomputer is a massively parallel computer system designed to offer performance in the range of 1 teraflops (10^{12} floating-point operations per second). The CM-5 obtains its high performance while offering ease of programming, flexibility, and reliability. The machine contains three communication networks: a data network, a control network, and a diagnostic network. This paper describes the organization of these three networks and how they contribute to the design goals of the CM-5.

1 Introduction

In the design of a parallel computer, the engineering principle of *economy of mechanism* suggests that the machine should employ only a single communication network to convey information among the processors in the system. Indeed, many parallel computers contain only a single network: typically, a hypercube or a mesh. The Connection Machine Model CM-5 Supercomputer has three networks, however, and none is a hypercube or a mesh. This paper describes the architecture of each of these three networks and the rationale behind them.

Figure 1 shows a diagram of the the CM-5 organization. The machine contains between 32 and 16,384 *processing nodes*, each of which contains a 32-megahertz SPARC processor, 32 megabytes of memory, and a 128-megaflops vector-processing unit capable of processing 64-bit floating-point and integer numbers. System administration tasks and serial user tasks are executed by a collection of *control processors*, which are Sun Microsystems workstation computers. There are from 1 to several tens of control processors in a CM-5, each configured with memory and disk according

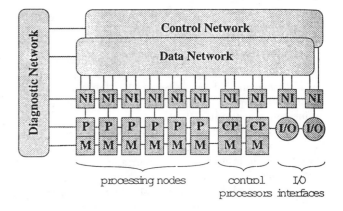

Figure 1: The organization of the Connection Machine CM-5. The machine has three networks: a data network, a control network, and a diagnostic network. The data and control networks are connected to processing nodes, control processors, and I/O channels via a network interface.

to the customer's preference. Input and output is provided via high-bandwidth *I/O interfaces* to graphics devices, mass secondary storage, and high-performance networks. Additional low-speed I/O is provided by Ethernet connections to the control processors. The largest machine, configured with up to 16,384 processing nodes, occupies a space of approximately 30 meters by 30 meters, and is capable of over a teraflops (10^{12} floating-point operations per second).

The processing nodes, control processors, and I/O interfaces are interconnected by three networks: a data network, a control network, and a diagnostic network. The data network provides high-performance point-to-point data communications between system components. The control network provides cooperative operations, including broadcast, synchronization, and *scans* (parallel prefix and suffix). It also provides system management operations, such as error reporting. The diagnostic network allows "back-door" access to all system hardware to test system integrity and to detect and isolate errors.

The system operates as one or more user *partitions*. Each partition consists of a control processor, a collection of processing nodes, and dedicated portions of the data and control networks. Access to system functions is classified as either *privileged* or *nonprivileged*. All nonprivileged system functions, including access to the data and control networks, can be executed directly by user code without system calls. Con-

---

[*]Charles E. Leiserson is a Corporate Fellow of Thinking Machines Corporation and Professor of Computer Science and Engineering in the MIT Laboratory for Computer Science.

[†]Bradley C. Kuszmaul is a consultant to Thinking Machines Corporation and a graduate student in the MIT Laboratory for Computer Science.

"The Network Architecture of the Connection Machine CM-5" by C.E. Leiserson et al. from *Proc. Fourth Ann. ACM Symp. Parallel Algorithms and Architectures,* 1992, pp. 272-285. Copyright 1992, Association for Computing Machinery, Inc., reprinted with permission.

sequently, network communication within a user task occurs without operating system overhead. Access to the diagnostics network, to shared system resources (such as I/O), and to other partitions is privileged and must be accomplished via system calls. Protection and addressing mechanisms ensure that no user can interfere with the function or performance of another user in another partition. If the system administrator so desires, a single partition can be timeshared among a group of users, where each user gets a fair portion of the available time and cannot otherwise be interfered with by any other user.

Further details about the CM-5 system can be found in the CM-5 Technical Summary [23].

When we first set about designing the CM-5, we established engineering goals that went beyond mere performance specifications. We thought hard about issues of *scalability*: making a machine whose size would be limited only by the dollars a customer could spend, not by any architectural or engineering constraint. We thought hard about system issues, including timesharing, I/O, and user protection. We thought hard about reliability, since we were designing a machine which, in its largest configuration, would have well over 10 times the electronics of our previous supercomputer, the Connection Machine Model CM-2 Supercomputer.

The following goals drove our network designs:

- The networks must deliver high performance to the users. We wanted the users to be easily able to program the networks to get good performance. We did not want to force the users to worry constantly about pathological worst cases, and we wanted the best cases to run well without the user needing to do anything special.

- The networks must scale up to a very large size. We wanted the logical design of the networks to scale up to a million processing nodes. We wanted to build SUPER-computers.

- The networks should efficiently support the data-parallel programming model (see Section 5), but should be flexible enough to allow us to support other parallel programming models as well. The data-parallel programming model was used extensively on the CM-2, and we wanted to be able to transport our existing high-level programming environments (Fortran90, *Lisp, and C*) to the CM-5. We also wanted to be able to run codes written for other machines competitively.

- The networks must be highly reliable and highly available. The system must notice whenever part of a network fails, be able to isolate the failure quickly, and be able to quickly reconfigure the networks around the failure. It was desired that even if part of a network has failed, the rest of the network should be able to function correctly with only a small degradation in performance.

- The networks must work in a spaceshared environment. We wanted a user's network traffic to be insulated from other users and I/O in other partitions.

- The networks must work in a timeshared environment. A timeshared user must get a fair share of network bandwidth. Users must be able to be context-swapped quickly. Privileged system software must be able to seize control of a user's task.

- The networks must be operational as soon as possible. Time to market was of the essence. Chips and systems needed to work the first time. We wanted the networks to be simple enough to engineer quickly, robust enough to respond to last-minute design changes, and easily verifiable. Consequently, we opted for conservative technology, for example, copper wires rather than optical fibers. We chose to use CMOS in order to minimize the risk associated with new technology. We chose standard-cell technology in order to be able to make extensive use of the wide variety of available design tools (such as timing verifiers and automatic test generators). To achieve high performance with this conservative technology, we incorporated custom macro cells for circuits on the critical path. Our attitude was that there was more performance to be gained by architectural improvements than by eking out extra nanoseconds in technology. Conservative technologies, with their well-developed computer-aided design tools, would allow us to make many more architectural improvements during the design.

- The chips used to build the networks must be organized in a way to allow technological or architectural improvements to be easily incorporated in subsequent revisions of the CM-5 system. On the CM-2, both processors and communication were implemented on the same chip, which made it difficult to incorporate advanced technology in one area without impacting the other. We wanted to be able to incorporate any advances without having to reengineer a major piece of the system.

- The networks should embody both economy of mechanism and single-minded functionality. We wanted the networks to be lean and mean. Whenever anyone suggested anything complicated, we viewed it with suspicion. For example, the job of the data network is to deliver messages, nothing else. But it delivers both user messages and messages to I/O devices using the same mechanisms. The data network does not combine messages, duplicate messages, or acknowledge delivery of messages. It just focuses on moving data as fast as possible.

We ended up designing two networks visible to the user and a network interface that provides an abstract view of them. We also designed a diagnostic network to provide "back-door" access to the system. This paper describes the three networks, the network interface, and how we engineered them to meet our goals. The reader should be aware that the performance specifications quoted in this paper apply only to the initial release of the CM-5 system. Because of our ability to reengineer pieces of the system easily, these numbers represent only a snapshot of an evolving implementation of the architecture.

The remainder of this paper is organized as follows. To begin, Section 2 describes the network interface which provides the user's view of the data and control networks. Section 3 then describes the data network. A justification for having both a data and control network is provided in Section 4. The control network is then described in Section 5, and Section 6 describes the diagnostic network. The paper closes with Section 7, which gives a short history of our development project.

2 The CM-5 Network Interface

Early on in the design of the CM-5, we decided to specify an interface between the processing nodes and the networks that isolates each from the details of the other. This interface provides three features. First, the interface gives the processors a simple and uniform view of the networks (and the networks get a simple and uniform view of the processors). Second, the interface provides support for time-sharing, space-sharing, and mapping out of failed components. Third, the interface provides a contract for the implementors which decouples the design decisions made for the networks from those of the processors.

The processor's view of the interface is as a collection of memory-mapped registers. By writing to or reading from fixed physical memory addresses, data is transferred to or from the networks, and the interface interprets the particular address as a command.

A memory mapped interface allows us to use many of the memory-oriented mechanisms found in off-the-shelf processors to deal with network interface issues. To access the network, a user or compiler reads from or writes to locations in memory. We regarded the prospect of executing a system supervisor call for every communication as unacceptable, in part because we wished to support the fine-grain communication needs of data-parallel computation. A memory-mapped interface allows the operating system to deny users access to certain network operations by placing the corresponding memory-mapped registers on protected pages of the processor's address space. The processor's memory management unit enforces protection without any additional hardware.

The interface is broadly organized as a collection of memory-mapped FIFO's. Each FIFO is either an *outgoing* FIFO to provide data to a network, or an *incoming* FIFO to retrieve data from a network. Status information can be accessed through memory-mapped registers. For example, to send a message over a network, a processor pushes the data into an outgoing FIFO by writing to a suitable memory address. When a message arrives at a processor, the event is signaled by interrupting the processor, or alternatively, the processor can poll a memory-mapped status bit. The data in the message can then be retrieved by reading from the appropriate incoming FIFO. This paradigm is identical for both the data and control networks.

The network interface provides the mechanisms needed to allow context switching of user tasks. Each user partition in the CM-5 system can run either batch jobs or a time-sharing system. When a user is swapped out during time-sharing, the processors must save the computation state. Some of this state information is retrieved from the network interface, and the rest is garnered from the networks. The context-switching mechanism also supports automatic checkpointing of user tasks.

The interface provides processor-address mapping so that the user sees a 0-based contiguous address space for the processor numbers within a partition. Each processor can be named by its *physical* address or by its *relative* address within the partition. A physical address is the actual network address as interpreted by the hardware inside the networks. A relative address gives the index of a processor relative to the start of a user partition, where failed processors are mapped out. All processor addresses in user code are relative addresses. To specify physical addresses requires supervisor privileges. Relative addresses are bounds checked, so that user code cannot specify addresses outside its partition.

The user's view of the networks is independent of a network's topology. Users cannot directly program the wires of the networks, as they could on our previous machine, the CM-2. The reason is simple: the wires might not be there! Because the CM-5 is designed to be resilient in the presence of faults, we cannot allow the user to rely on a specific network topology. One might think topology independence would hurt network performance, but we found this presumption to be less true than we initially imagined. Because we did not provide the user with access to the wires of the network, we were able to apply more resources to generic network capabilities. A further advantage of topology independence is that the network technology becomes decoupled from processor technology. Any future network enhancements are independent of user code and processor organization.

An important ramification of the decoupling of the processors from the networks is that the networks must assume full responsibility for performing their functions. The data network, for example, does not rely on the processors to guarantee end-to-end delivery. The processors assume that delivery is reliable; nondelivery implies a broken system, since there is no protocol for retransmission. By guaranteeing delivery, additional error-detection circuitry must be incorporated into the network design, which slightly reduces its performance, but since the processor does not need to deal with possible network failures, the overall performance as seen by a user is much better.

The CM-5 network interface is implemented in large measure by a single 1-micron standard-cell CMOS chip, with custom macro cells to provide high-performance circuits where needed. The interface chip is clocked by both the 32-megahertz processor clock and the 40-megahertz networks clock. Asynchronous arbiters synchronize the processor side of the interface with the network side.

Choosing to build a separate network interface allowed the processor designers to do their jobs and the network designers to do theirs with a minimum of interference. As a measure of its success in decoupling the networks from the processor organization, the same interface chip is used to interface the network to I/O channels, of which there are many types, including CMIO, VME, FDDI, and HIPPI.

3 The CM-5 Data Network

The basic architecture of the CM-5 data network is a *fat-tree* [8, 15]. Figure 2 shows a binary fat-tree. Unlike a computer scientist's traditional notion of a tree, a fat-tree is more like a real tree in that it gets thicker further from the leaves. Processing nodes, control processors, and I/O channels are located at the leaves of the fat-tree. (For convenience, we shall refer to all of these network addresses simply as processors.)

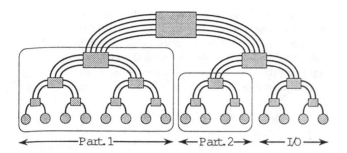

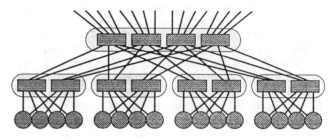

Figure 2: A binary fat-tree. Processors are located at the leaves, and the internal nodes are switches. Unlike an ordinary binary tree, the channel capacities of a fat-tree increase as we ascend from leaves to root. The hierarchical nature of a fat-tree can be exploited to give each user partition a dedicated subnetwork which cannot be interfered with by any other partition's message traffic. The CM-5 data network uses a 4-ary tree instead of a binary tree.

Figure 3: The interconnection pattern of the CM-5 data network. The network is a 4-ary fat-tree in which each internal node is made up of several router chips. Each router chip is connected to 4 child chips and either 2 or 4 parent chips.

A user partition corresponds to a subtree in the network. Messages local to a given partition are routed within the partition's subtree, thereby requiring no bandwidth higher in the tree. Access to shared system resources, such as I/O, is accomplished through the part of the fat-tree not devoted to any partition. Thus, message traffic within a partition, between a partition and an I/O device, or between I/O devices does not affect traffic within any other partitions. Moreover, since I/O channels can be addressed just like processing nodes, the data network becomes a true "system bus" in which all system components have a unique physical address in a single, uniform name-space.

Of critical importance to the performance of a fat-tree routing network is the communication bandwidth between nodes of the fat-tree. Most networks that have been proposed for parallel processing, such as meshes and hypercubes, are inflexible when it comes to adapting their topologies to the arbitrary bandwidths provided by packaging technology. The bandwidths between nodes in a fat-tree, however, are not constrained to follow a prescribed mathematical formula. A fat-tree can be adapted to effectively utilize whatever bandwidths make engineering sense in terms of cost and performance. No matter how the bandwidths of the fat-tree are chosen, provably effective routing algorithms exist [8, 14] to route messages near-optimally. The underlying architecture and mechanism for addressing is not affected by communication bandwidths: to route a message from one processor to another, the message is sent up the tree to the least common ancestor of the two processors, and then down to the destination.

Because of various implementation trade-offs—including the number of pins per chip, the number of wires per cable, and the maximum cable length—we designed the CM-5 data network using a 4-ary fat-tree, rather than a binary fat-tree. Figure 3 shows the interconnection pattern. The network is composed of router chips, each with 4 *child* connections and either 2 or 4 *parent* connections. Each connection provides a link to another chip with a raw bandwidth of 20 megabytes/second in each direction. (Some of this bandwidth is devoted to addressing, tags, error checking, and congestion.) By selecting at each level of the tree whether 2 or 4 parent links are used, the bandwidths between nodes

in the fat-tree can be adjusted. Flow control is provided on every link.

Based on technology, packaging, and cost considerations, the CM-5 bandwidths were chosen as follows. Each processor has 2 connections to the data network, corresponding to a raw bandwidth of 40 megabytes/second in and out of each processing node. In the first two levels, each router chip uses only 2 parent connections to the next higher level, yielding an aggregate bandwidth of 160 megabytes/second out of a subtree with 16 processing nodes. All router chips higher than the second level use all 4 parent connections, which, for example, yields an aggregate bandwidth of 10 gigabytes/second, in each direction, from one half of a 2K-node system to the other. The bandwidth continues to scale linearly up to 16,384 nodes, the largest machine that Thinking Machines can currently build. (The architecture itself scales to over one million nodes.) In larger machines, transmission-line techniques are used to pipeline bits across long wires, thereby overcoming the bandwidth limitation that would otherwise be imposed by wire latency. The machine is designed so that network bandwidth can be enhanced in future product revisions without affecting the architecture.

The network design provides many comparable paths for a message to take from a source processor to a destination processor. As it goes up the tree, a message may have several choices as to which parent connection to take. This decision is resolved by pseudorandomly selecting from among those links that are unobstructed by other messages. After the message has attained the height of the least common ancestor of the source and destination processors, it takes the single available path of links from that chip down to its destination. The pseudorandom choice at each level balances the load on the network and avoids undue congestion caused by pathological message sets. (Many naive algorithms for routing on mesh and hypercubic networks suffer from having specific message patterns that do not perform well, and the user is left to program around them.) The CM-5 data network routes all message sets nearly as well as the chosen bandwidths allow.

A consequence of the automatic load balancing within the data network is that users can program the network in a straightforward manner and obtain high performance. Moreover, an accurate estimate of the performance of routing a set of messages through the network can be predicted by using a relatively simple model [16]. One determines the load of messages passing through each arm of the fat-tree and divides this value by the available bandwidth. The worst-case such ratio, over all arms of the fat-tree, provides the estimate.

On random permutations, each processor can provide data into, and out of, the network at a rate in excess of 4 megabytes/second. When the communication pattern is more local, such as nearest neighbor within a regular or irregular two- or three-dimensional grid, bandwidths of 15 megabytes/second per processor are achievable. The network latency ranges between 3 and 7 microseconds, depending on the size of the machine. All of these empirical values include the time required for processors to execute the instructions needed to put messages into and take messages out of the network.

The data network is currently implemented from 1-micron standard-cell CMOS chips, with custom macro cells to provide high-performance circuits where needed. Each chip has an 8-bit-wide bidirectional link (4 bits of data in each direction) to each of its 4 child chips lower in the fat-tree, and 4 8-bit-wide bidirectional links to its parent chips higher in the fat-tree. The data-router chip can be viewed as a crossbar connecting the 8 input ports to the 8 output ports, but certain input/output connections are impossible due to the nature of the routing algorithm. For example, we never route a message from one parent port to another. When a message is blocked from its desired output port, it is buffered. Flow control information is passed in the reverse direction of message traffic to prevent buffer overflow. When multiple messages compete for the same output port, the arbitration is fair and prevents any link from being starved. We designed only one chip to do message routing, and we use the same chip for communication between chips on the same circuit board as between chips that are in different cabinets.

Interchip data is sent on differential pairs of wires, which increases the pin count of the chips, but which provides outstanding noise immunity and reduces overall power requirements. We rejected using separate transceivers at the packaging boundaries, because it would have increased power consumption, board real estate, and the number of different chips we would have needed to design, debug, test, stock, etc. The diagnostics can independently test each conductor of each differential signal, because differential signals are so immune to noise that they sometimes work even with broken wires.

The first 2 levels of the data network are routed through backplanes. The wires on higher levels are run through cables, which can be either 9 or 26 feet in length. The longer cables maintain multiple bits in transit. The wires in cables are coated with expanded Teflon, which has a very low dielectric constant. The cables reliably carry signals in excess of 90 percent of the speed of light.

The data network chips are clocked synchronously by a 40-megahertz clock. The clock is distributed with very low skew—even for the biggest machines—by locally generating individual clocks and adjusting their phases to be synchronous with a centrally broadcast clocking signal.

Messages routed by the data network are formatted as shown in Figure 4. The beginning of the message contains routing instructions that tell how high the message is to go

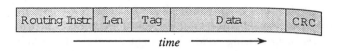

Figure 4: The format of messages in the data network. Each message contains routing instructions, a length field that indicates how many data words are in the message, a tag field that indexes an interrupt vector in the processor, data words, and a cyclic redundancy check.

in the tree and then the path it is to follow downward after it reaches its zenith. The routing instructions are chip-relative instructions that allow each chip to make a simple, local decision on how to route the message. Following the routing instructions is a field that indicates the length of the data in 32-bit words. Currently, the CM-5 network interface allows between 1 and 5 words. Longer messages must be broken into smaller pieces. Following the length field is a 4-bit tag field that can be used to distinguish among various kinds of messages in the system. The network interface interprets some of these tags as system messages, and the rest are available to the user. When a message arrives at a processor, the tag indexes a 16-bit mask register in the network interface, and if the corresponding mask bit is 1, the processor is interrupted. After the tag comes the data itself, and then a field that provides an integrity check of the message using a cyclic redundancy code (CRC).

Because we desired to build very large machines, we deemed it essential to monitor and verify the data network dynamically, because the chances of a component failure increase with the size of the system. Message integrity is checked on every link and through every switch. If a message is found to be corrupted, an error is signaled. Messages snake their way through the switches in a manner similar to cut-through [13] or worm-hole [3, 4] routing, and so by the time that a data-router chip has detected an error, the head of the message may have traveled far away. To avoid an avalanche of errors, the complement of a proper CRC is appended to the message. Any chip that discovers the complement of a proper CRC signals a secondary error. Thus, a typical error causes one chip to signal a primary error with a trail of chips reporting secondary errors, although there is some positive probability that a primary error is reported as a secondary error. Diagnostic programs can easily isolate the faulty chip or link based on this information, which is accessible through the diagnostic network. Lost and replicated messages can be detected by counters on each chip and in the network interfaces that maintain the number of messages that pass on each link. Using a variation on Kirchoff's current law, the number of messages entering any region of the network, including the entire network or a single chip, must eventually equal the number of messages leaving the region. This condition is checked for the entire data network by the control network (see Section 5).

Once a faulty processor node, network chip, or interconnection link has been identified, the fault is mapped out of the system and quarantined. The network interface allows for mapping faulty processing nodes out of the network address space. The rest of the control network ignores all signals from the mapped-out portion, thereby allowing the system to remain functional while servicing and testing the mapped-out portion.

When a chip or link in the data network fails, there are two mechanisms to map around the fault. Either the network can be configured to route messages away from the failure, or processing nodes that might use the chip or link can be mapped out. By picking the better of the two alternatives, the system can guarantee either that at most 6 percent of the network is lost or that at most 1/64 of the processing nodes are mapped out.

The network has a contract with processors that guarantees all messages are delivered. The contract says, *"The data network promises to eventually accept and deliver all messages injected into the network by the processors as long as the processors promise to eventually eject all messages from the network when they are delivered to the processors."* The data network is acyclic from inputs to outputs, which precludes deadlock from occurring if this contract is obeyed. To send a message, a processor writes the destination processor address and data to be sent to a memory-mapped outgoing FIFO in its network interface. The processor then checks whether the message was accepted by the network. If not, which may occur because flow control information indicates that the network has not removed enough of a previous message from the outgoing FIFO, the processor can try again later. The processor may not block or spin when attempting to put a message into the network, however, because that would violate the contract. Instead, the processor must attempt to receive any messages that have arrived. In the current implementation, the processor is involved in all transactions with the network.

Although the simple contract above can implement the sending of data through the network in a deadlock-free manner, it is not strong enough to allow some communication protocols to be implemented straightforwardly. For example, suppose each processor wishes to fetch a value from another processor, and the processors have finite buffer space. The message traffic for this protocol corresponds to a round trip in the network: a request from one processor to another, followed by a response from the other to the one. In this scenario, one processor may receive requests for data from many processors, but unfortunately, be unable to send responses because its outgoing FIFO to the data network is busy. The outgoing FIFO will eventually free, according to the contract, but only if the processor continues to accept delivery of messages from the network. With finite buffer space, however, there is a limit to how many requests it can handle. When it runs out of buffer space, the processor will be forced to refuse delivery, thereby breaking the contract, and deadlock may result.

With buffer space proportional to the number of processors in the system, it is possible to construct a "round-trip" protocol that precludes deadlock. The key idea is to have at most a bounded number of messages outstanding between any two processors at a time. A processor X does not attempt to send a message to another processor Y until Y informs X that it has room to handle the message. This protocol, which has been implemented on some parallel computing systems, including the CM-5, requires substantial bookkeeping.

The CM-5, however, provides another way to solve the round-trip problem in a simple fashion requiring no bookkeeping and only constant buffer space. Each processor has 2 outgoing and 2 incoming FIFO's in its interface to the data network: a *left* port and a *right* port. The topology of the network is such that all links reachable from the left port are unreachable from the right port and vice versa. Thus, the data network is really two independent, interleaved networks. To implement the round-trip protocol, requests can be sent on the left side of the network, and responses returned on the right side. If a processor cannot send a response on the right side and his constant-size buffer is full, he stops receiving on the left side. Since any processor requesting data has a place to put it, however, the processors can satisfy the contract on the right side and the responses will eventually clear out. Because the responses on the right side will eventually clear out, a processor can always eventually accept every request that arrives on the left side, and thus the processors satisfy the contract on the left side. Consequently, deadlock cannot occur.

In fact, deadlock cannot occur even if responses are sent on both sides of the data network, as long as requests are sent on one side only. The data network requires no more than two sides, even when there are many intermediate destinations, because such a communication pattern can be broken into a collection of round trips.

The CM-5 programming systems (Fortran90, C*, and *Lisp) never allow a user to deadlock, because they implement deadlock-free protocols for communication. Deadlock can occur, however, if a programmer chooses to program the individual processing nodes directly. All he need do is break the contract that the processing nodes have with the data network: he writes code that sends messages but never attempts to receive them. This danger may seem quite alarming, but it is no more alarming than the danger that a user writes an infinite loop. On the CM-5, the user can send and receive messages without executing a system call, as is required on many other systems. By giving the user direct access to the network, the user can in some circumstances obtain greater efficiency than he could obtain with the communication routines available in the standard system libraries. If he does deadlock himself, or write an infinite loop, he does not affect any other user.

Each user partition in the CM-5 system is capable of being run in either a batch or a timesharing mode. The requirement for timesharing raises the issue of what should be done with messages that are in transit in the routing network when a user's timeslice has expired and another user must be given access to the partition. The system cannot afford to wait until the user completes his communication, since the communication may not terminate for a very long time, and it in fact may not ever complete if the user has deadlocked himself.

We considered several solutions to the problem of swapping users. For example, we considered entering a special routine that would pull messages out of the router and discard them. This solution was considered too expensive, because the user would be constantly forced to checkpoint the computation so that the discarded messages could be reconstructed. Moreover, if the user fills the network with messages that are all addressed to the same processing node, then the time to empty the router would be proportional to the machine size, which was deemed unacceptably long.

This problem of swapping users is solved in the CM-5 by putting the data network into *all-fall-down* mode. Instead of trying to route messages to their destinations, the network misroutes each one down through the network so they are distributed evenly among the processing nodes. In the worst case, no node receives only a small number of misdirected messages, even if all were headed for the same destination processor. The all-fall-down messages are then saved in memory with the user's state. When the user's task is resumed, the system resends them to their true destinations. Even if a timeshared user deadlocks, this context-switching mechanism precludes him from unduly affecting the other users who are sharing his partition.

In summary, the CM-5 data network provides fast point-to-point communication of data, but as importantly, it provides a flexible solution to many system problems.

4 Synchronized MIMD

The CM-5 is a *synchronized MIMD* machine. Whereas the data network in the CM-5 is responsible for moving data efficiently between pairs of processors, the CM-5's control network provides an infrastructure for the coordination and synchronization of an entire set of processors. Much as a conventional microprocessor is divided into control and datapath [10, Chapter 5], we found that partitioning communication into a control network and a data network led to a simpler, more efficient design. This section discusses why we adopted a synchronized MIMD execution model for the CM-5.

A major design goal of the CM-5 was to support the *data-parallel* programming model [2, 11] efficiently. The basic idea of data parallelism is that processing large amounts of data usually implies that the same operations are performed on all elements of large sets of data. Consequently, these operations can be performed in parallel. For example, an operation might be specified for all pixels of digitized image, in which case it can be performed in parallel on each of the pixels. Data-parallel languages—such as Fortran90, C*, and *Lisp—allow the programmer to express such operations naturally. The programmer applies parallel operations to an entire *set* of data simultaneously, and the system efficiently multiplexes the computation onto the processing nodes of the machine.

Traditionally, the data-parallel model has been supported by so-called *single instruction stream, multiple data stream* (SIMD) parallel computers, such as our previous machine, the Connection Machine CM-2. SIMD machines typically have two networks. Besides a message-routing network, these machines employ a *broadcast* network over which a front-end processor distributes instructions to the individual processing nodes in the system. All processing nodes receive and execute the same instruction at the same time. Based on data in its memory, however, a processor may decline to execute an instruction and sit idle instead. In machines like the CM-2, the broadcast network is embellished with an OR network, which can compute a logical OR of boolean values,

one value per processing node, and distribute the result back to the processing nodes.

There are many advantages of using a SIMD architecture to execute data-parallel code. When a parallel operation is applied to a large set of data, each processor receives can receive the same instructions and execute the same code, thereby causing the operation to be applied to each of the individual elements. Since SIMD machines are highly synchronized, it is also easy to coordinate processors to perform cooperative actions. Moreover, all processors are doing much the same thing, and thus the broadcasting of instructions saves the need to implement instruction-fetch units in all of the processing nodes.

SIMD machines are less efficient, however, when different processors wish to execute different sections of code. The machine must step through each section of code serially while processors not interested in the particular section of code being executed sit idle. This loss of efficiency limits the flexibility of SIMD machines.

In contrast with the SIMD machine organization is the *multiple instruction stream, multiple data stream* (MIMD) organization of a parallel computer. In a MIMD machine, each processor executes its own instruction stream, and thus there is no loss of efficiency when processors execute different code. Typically, processors in MIMD machines communicate among themselves using message-passing techniques [18, 19] or through shared memory [6, 7], but there is little or no architectural support for coordinating and synchronizing sets of processors. A programmer must synthesize aggregate operations himself, resulting in considerable code complexity and loss in performance. Thus, the greater flexibility of MIMD comes at a great cost.

In the CM-5, we abandoned the SIMD architecture of its predecessor, the CM-2, in favor of a MIMD execution model, but we salvaged SIMD's best attributes: the ability to share data among processors efficiently and the ability to quickly synchronize sets of processors. To support the sharing of data, the control network provides a fast broadcast mechanism. To support the synchronization of sets of processors, the control network provides fast "barrier synchronization." These two mechanisms allow data-parallel code to be executed efficiently on what is otherwise a MIMD machine. We now briefly discuss how each of these mechanisms supports the data-parallel programming model.

To execute a data-parallel program on the CM-5, the control processor broadcasts a section of the data-parallel program to the processing nodes, rather than broadcasting the entire instruction stream, as in a typical SIMD machine. The idea of distributing a single program to multiple processors has been dubbed "SPMD," for *single-program, multiple data* [5]. Unlike shared-memory machines, in which processors must individually fetch the program from a central memory, however, in the CM-5, the control processor broadcasts the program to the processing nodes over the control network, and then the processors execute the program locally.

As long as a processor in a data-parallel programming environment does not communicate with other processors, it can execute code without worrying where in the code the other processors are. When processors communicate, however, program correctness often demands that processors know when it is safe to proceed to code after the communication step. In particular, a processor may not know for a given communication pattern whether it will receive zero, one, or more messages, and thus it cannot determine whether it can proceed without some knowledge of whether other processors still have messages to send it. Consequently, the CM-5 provides a synchronization mechanism to inform all processors of the termination of message routing on the data network.

The CM-5 provides *barrier synchronization* (see, for example, [12, 20, 5]) via its control network. In barrier synchronization, a point in the code is designated as a barrier. No processor is allowed to cross the barrier until all processors have reached the barrier. In addition, the barrier mechanism in the CM-5 can check whether message routing is complete in the data network. By providing barrier synchronization in hardware, we avoided the complicated protocols that users often implement by hand on MIMD machines that are not synchronized. Since our mechanism is a parallel one, we also avoid the performance problems endemic in machines that support barriers through the use of shared semaphores.

We discovered four implementation advantages of synchronized MIMD over SIMD. First, the bandwidth in and out of a processing node is a critical resource. A program is typically much shorter than the instruction stream it generates. By broadcasting a program to the processing nodes, rather than sending its entire instruction stream, less of the bandwidth into a node is required for instructions, and hence more is available for communicating the user's data. Second, since processing nodes fetch their instructions locally, we were able to build the CM-5 from standard microprocessors rather than having to design our own. At the time of this decision, high-performance RISC microprocessors were just becoming available. We decided they were a good technology curve to "ride" and would allow us to focus more of our internal effort on networks and vector units, the bread and butter of high-performance computing. Third, the implementation of a control network gave us a platform to solve other system coordination problems. For example, if a user hangs up one or all of his processors, the operating system can broadcast a message that causes the processors to trap to supervisor code. Fourth, our synchronized MIMD architecture can execute more traditional MIMD code. For example, we have been able to port message-passing applications from other MIMD machines, and in many cases, simplified them considerably by replacing their elaborate protocols with simple uses of our control network.

To summarize, the synchronized MIMD architecture of the CM-5 simply and efficiently provides the flexibility of MIMD and the SIMD ability to coordinate sets of processors.

5 The CM-5 Control Network

There are three general classes of operations on the control network: broadcasting, combining, and global operations. Separate FIFO's in the network interface correspond to each type of control-network function. A processor pushes a message into one of the outgoing FIFO's, and shortly after all processors have pushed messages, the result becomes available to all processors as messages in their respective incoming FIFO's.

Every operation on the control network potentially involves every processing node. Broadcast messages from the control processor are replicated at nodes in the tree and distributed to the subtrees. Other operations, such as scans (parallel prefix), require input from all processors and provide output to all processors. The control network is pipelined, so that several messages can be sent before any are received. To provide further flexibility, each processing node can set up the network interface to abstain from certain control-network operations. These operations complete as if the abstaining processors had provided "identity" data, but without making them waste processing cycles. Overall, the control network is designed to support cooperative functions that require little bisection bandwidth, and hence, which can be implemented efficiently on a simple tree.

Broadcasting

A processor may broadcast a message through the control network to all other processors in its partition. The control network supports four kinds of broadcasting: user broadcast, supervisor broadcast, interrupt broadcast, and utility broadcast. User and supervisor broadcasts are essentially identical, except that supervisor broadcasts are privileged operations. These broadcast operations can be used to download code and to distribute data. An interrupt broadcast is a privileged operation that causes every processor to receive an interrupt. Interrupt broadcasts provide the ability to "grab the attention" of all processors in the user partition, which is especially useful for implementing operating system functions, such as swapping timeshared users. The utility broadcast is used by the operating system to configure partitions and to perform other sorts of system operations.

Only one processor may broadcast at a time, but broadcasts are pipelined so that the broadcasting processor can fully utilize the broadcast bandwidth of the network. If, while one processor is broadcasting, another processor sends a broadcast message, the control network signals an error when the competing messages collide. The number of simultaneous pipelined broadcasts supported by the control network depends upon the height of the network partition. The current implementation of the CM-5 provides the user with up to 8 words in a broadcast and the supervisor with up to 4 words.

Combining

The control network supports four different types of combining operations: reduction, forward scan (parallel prefix), backward scan (parallel suffix), and router done.

Reduction combines messages from each processor with one of five operators on 32-bit words: bitwise logical OR, bitwise logical XOR, signed maximum (which also works for IEEE floating-point numbers), signed addition, and unsigned addition. (The two addition operators differ in how overflow is reported.) A reduction operation combines the values provided by all processors and delivers a copy of the result to all processors. Reductions over other commonly occurring operators (such as bitwise logical AND) can be easily synthesized from these and local processor operations.

A forward scan operation delivers to the ith processor the result of applying one of the five reduction operators to the values in the preceding $i - 1$ processors (in the linear order given by data network address). For example, a forward scan of the vector $\langle 3, 2, 0, 4, 2, 6, 5, 8 \rangle$ with the operator $+$ yields the vector $\langle 0, 3, 5, 5, 9, 11, 17, 22 \rangle$. A backward scan provides similar functionality in the reverse direction. Scans can be segmented: if a "segment start" bit in the network interface is set, the scan starts over at that point. An excellent discussion of scans can be found in [2].

Early on in the design of the CM-5, we decided to support scans in hardware. Our experience with the CM-2 showed that many high-performance data-parallel algorithms—including both combinatorial and numerical algorithms—make extensive use of scans. The operations that were selected (OR, XOR, etc.) reflect a compromise between making the hardware fast and simple and providing sufficient building blocks out of which other operations could be constructed. For instance, OR can be used to implement AND (DeMorgan's law), so there is no need to implement both. As a more sophisticated example, segmented reductions, which are not provided directly by the hardware, can be implemented by using two segmented scans, one forward and one backward. Since the control network is pipelined, the overhead of doing both is minimal.

The router-done operation is a specialized reduction that lets the processors know when communications involving the data network are complete. In the data-parallel programming model, this operation is often required so that processors know when it is safe to proceed to the next data-parallel operation.

The basic idea behind the implementation of router-done is "Kirchoff's current law." When all processors have completed sending their messages and the number of messages that entered the data network equals the number that have left, the routing cycle is complete. The network interfaces keep track of the number of messages that enter and leave the data network. After a processor has completed sending all its messages, it pushes a message into the outgoing router-done FIFO. When all processors have sent messages into their outgoing FIFO's, the control network continually monitors the difference between the total number of messages put into the data network and the number removed from the data network. When this number becomes zero, each processor receives a message in its incoming router-done FIFO informing it that the data network is done routing messages. Using this "Kirchoff" method has the additional benefit that if a hardware error causes messages to be lost or created, the error can be detected and signaled, either by a failure of the router-done operation to complete on the one hand or by the unexpected arrival of a message after the router-done operation has completed on the other.

Global operations

The global operations supported by the CM-5 control network include one synchronous OR operation and two identical asynchronous OR operations. The synchronous OR is similar to an OR reduction, except that a processor's input and output each consist of only a single bit. Each asynchronous OR operates continuously without waiting for all processors to participate. Processors are free to change their inputs at any time and sample the output. The asynchronous OR can be used for signaling conditions and exceptions. The transition of an asynchronous OR from 0 to 1 can be used to signal an interrupt. One of the two asynchronous OR's is privileged, and the other is nonprivileged.

The synchronous OR or any of the various combining operations can be used to implement *split-phase* barrier synchronization [22]. (In independent work [9], this type of synchronization has been called a *fuzzy barrier*.) In a split-phase barrier, the barrier is a region of code with an entry and an exit. (If the region is empty, an ordinary barrier results.) When a processor enters the split-phase barrier, it pushes an input message into an appropriate outgoing FIFO. Shortly after all other processors have pushed their messages, they all receive messages from the corresponding incoming FIFO, and each can infer that all have entered the barrier. The advantage of a split-phase barrier over an ordinary barrier is that the processor can execute code while waiting for the barrier to complete. Thus, just as the instruction following a delayed branch in a RISC architecture can compensate for the latency of the branch, the code between barrier entry and exit can compensate for the latency of synchronization. The router-done operation couples barrier synchronization with the test of whether routing on the data network has completed, so that no processor abandons its effort to receive messages until all processors are done sending them.

At the end of a user's timeslice during timesharing, the control network can be flushed in a manner similar to a broadcast operation, aborting any user-level control-network operations in progress. The network interfaces retain the values that the user has pushed into the control network until the corresponding operation has completed, however. These values are saved as part of the user's state. When the user's task is resumed, the saved values can be used to reinitiate the control-network operations.

The control network also detects certain kinds of communication errors and distributes them throughout the system. For example, if two processors attempt to perform different combining operations, an error is signaled. More importantly, hard errors detected by the data network and the network interfaces are collected by the control network. These error signals are combined using a logical OR and are redistributed to all the processors so that the operating system can isolate them and recover if possible.

Organization of the control network

The architecture of the control network is that of a complete binary tree with processing nodes, control processors, and I/O channels at the leaves. When a CM-5 system is configured, each user partition is assigned to a subtree of the network. Processing nodes are located at the leaves of the subtree, and a control processor is mapped into the partition as an additional leaf.

The control network is implemented using a 1-micron CMOS standard-cell chip that contains custom macro cells

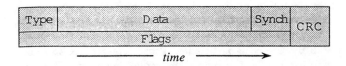

Figure 5: The format of messages in the control network. Each message contains a field that indicates the type of message, a 32-bit word of data, some synchronization bits, and various other flags. The message is checked using a cyclic redundancy code.

to implement high-performance circuitry. Like the data network chip, it uses a 40-megahertz clock. Three binary-tree nodes are packaged on each chip. There are 4 11-bit-wide bidirectional links (6 bits in the up direction and 5 bits in the down direction) to 4 child chips lower in the tree and 1 11-bit-wide bidirectional link to a parent. As in the data network, interchip signals are sent on differential pairs of wires.

Unlike data network packets, control network packets have a fixed length of 65 bits. (There is actually, in addition, a 5-bit packet used during system initialization to align the 65-bit packet boundaries so that a node can process the same fields in arriving messages at the same time.) The general format is illustrated in Figure 5. It is broken into two parallel streams, a major stream and a minor stream. The minor stream contains a variety of control bits, including various error and status flags, several flow-control bits, and a bit to implement segmented scans. The major stream begins with a packet description field, which defines the packet type—*single-source*, *multiple-source*, *idle*, or *abstain*—as well as the specific operation—user broadcast, supervisor broadcast, interrupt, scan (including combiner), reduce, etc. Then comes a 32-bit word of data. The major stream ends with a field containing the global synchronization bits. The entire packet is checked using a cyclic redundancy code (CRC), which is the last information in the packet to be transmitted.

The four packet types are processed differently by the control network. Whereas single-source packets are used to implement broadcasting, scans and reductions employ multiple-source packets. Idle packets are used as "filler" and are sent when a control network node has nothing better to ship. The abstain packet allows a control network node to proceed when it would otherwise wait for a multiple-source packet.

When a processor initiates a broadcast or interrupt through the control network, its network interface inserts a single-source message into the tree at a leaf. This message proceeds up to the root node of the user's tree, where it is turned around and distributed to all the processors in the partition. An error is signaled if two single-source packets from different sources meet at a control network node. If it meets with other kinds of packets, a single-source packet has priority. There is no buffering for single-source packets. Flow control for single-source packets is implemented by the network interface on an end-to-end basis.

Processing multiple-source packets is more involved. When a processor initiates a cooperative operation such as a scan, the network interface inserts a multiple-source message into the tree. At each internal node, a multiple-source message waits until its sibling's message has arrived. While a message is waiting, the node sends idle messages up the tree. When the sibling's message arrives, arithmetic or logical operations combine the two messages into one, which is sent up the tree. To implement scans, the message or its sibling may be put aside in another buffer to combine later with a value coming from the node's parent. When a multiple-source message finally reaches the root, it is sent downward. As it reencounters the internal nodes of the tree, it is replicated or further combined with waiting messages. (A good overview of the implementation of scans can be found in [2].)

While a multiple-source packet is waiting for a sibling or a parent, other packets arriving on the same input can be processed. If the newly arriving packet is a single-source packet, it proceeds ahead of the waiting packet, thereby giving priority, for example, to supervisor broadcasts and interrupts. If the new packet is another multiple-source packet, it is queued in the buffer behind the packets already waiting. Multiple-source packets thus maintain a consistent order, which allows two or more combining operations on the control network to be pipelined properly. Flow control in the network precludes buffers from overflowing.

An important requirement of the control network was that it be able to connect a control processor to each user partition. The control processor executes the scalar part of the data-parallel code, while the processing nodes execute the parallel part. We considered having scalar code executed by one or all of the processing nodes, but eventually decided that having a control processor associated with each partition would simplify matters. First, since the system cost of the control processor is very low compared with the multitude of processing nodes, we can afford to run it with large amounts of memory and with additional architectural features to enhance its performance. Consequently, the control processor is able to more efficiently execute scalar code than can a processing node. Second, the data-parallel code that runs on the earlier CM-2 machine is already split into scalar and parallel parts. Porting this code to the CM-5 was easier, since we could maintain the same split. Finally, since the control processor has a connection to an Ethernet, the user partition can run a standard Unix which communicates across the attached Ethernet.

In case of a fault in a CM-5 processing node, network chip, or interconnection link, the control network—like the data network—can be configured to map the fault out of the system. The diagnostic network (see Section 6) can set internal switches within the control network to map out parts of the control network. Since the computations performed by the control network depend only on the control network being a binary tree, and not on its being a *complete* binary tree, computations within the control network can safely ignore the mapped-out portions of the system.

In addition, the control network has some additional switching capability to map around faults in the control network itself and to be able to connect any of the control processors to any partition. This additional switching capability is implemented as follows. Conceptually, each switch of the control network has 2 parents and 4 children and contains two binary-tree nodes which can be statically configured so that either can connect to any pair of children. By connecting these chips in a manner similar to the data network fat-tree, any control processor can be connected to any partition, subject to the availability of bandwidth. For example, if there are only 4 control network channels into a subtree, one cannot connect 5 control processors to 5 partitions in the subtree. Short of this bandwidth restriction, however, any connection of control processors to legal partitions can be implemented using an off-line routing algorithm similar to that in [15, Theorem 1].

In summary, the CM-5 control network provides the mechanisms to allow data-parallel code to be executed efficiently, as well as allowing more general kinds of parallel models to be implemented. Its structure as a binary tree provides an inexpensive way to provide the advantages of both traditional SIMD and traditional MIMD architectures.

6 The CM-5 Diagnostic Network

During the design of the CM-5, great emphasis was placed on system availability. Despite conservative design techniques and the use of proven circuit and interconnect technologies, the sheer size of the largest CM-5 systems forced us to abandon any attempt to achieve high availability by depending solely on inherent component reliability. Instead, our strategy relies on two architectural features of the machine: diagnosability which allows missing or broken hardware to be detected and isolated; and configurability, which allows most of the machine to operate when portions are broken or being serviced. This section shows how this strategy is implemented on the CM-5 through the use of a diagnostic network, the one network in the system that the user never sees.

One strategy to diagnose a parallel computer is to create diagnostic programs running on the processor nodes that exercise the processor nodes and various communications networks. When some part of the system fails to function correctly—for example, the data router fails to deliver a message or the control network produces the wrong answer for a combine operation, the diagnostic program itself may fail, because its correctness depends on the correct functioning of the system. We call such diagnostic programs *functionality dependent*. Our experience with the CM-1 and CM-2 exposed many of the limitations of functionality-dependent diagnostics. They are exceedingly difficult to write, they have nebulous coverage, and they lack precision in reporting the root cause of error conditions.

In contrast, diagnostics that are *functionality independent* rely on specific test structures, rather than the failure of normal system operation, to detect faults in the system. Using this kind of design-for-testability strategy, it becomes possible to view the CM-5 (or *any* sequential machine, for that matter) in terms of registers connected by combinational logic and wires. This change in perspective permits commercially available software tools to be used to generate high-coverage tests automatically for chips, boards, and the wiring that connects them. Moreover, when these tests fail, they provide specific information on the location and extent of the failure.

In the CM-5, design for testablity starts at the chip level.

All CM-5 VLSI components support the IEEE 1149.1 testability architecture standard [1], also known as JTAG, for the Joint Test Action Group which originated the standard.[1] At the system level, the CM-5 diagnostic network provides parallel access to all system components from a *diagnostic processor*. The JTAG standard and the diagnostic network combine to form a diagnostic system which can quickly perform an in-system check of the integrity (over 99 percent single stuck-at fault coverage) of all CM-5 chips that support the JTAG standard and all networks.

Let us briefly review the JTAG interface standard. The JTAG standard provides a 4-pin interface for each chip in a system. On each chip, two pins provide input and output, respectively, for a selectable scan chain within the chip.[2] The standard specifies the *boundary scan register* (BSR) which connects all I/O pads in the chip into a bit-serial shift register. Two other pins serve as clock and control inputs. By scanning data in and out of chips, the BSR can be used to apply stimulus to the chip core for chip tests, or to monitor inputs and control outputs of the chip for connectivity tests.

In the CM-5, we extended the JTAG standard to include full internal scan in all proprietary chips. Details of this design are described in [24]. The use of a full internal scan allows software for automatically generating test patterns to generate a set of scan vectors with very high fault coverage. The vectors can be applied through the JTAG interface to test individual chips when they are manufactured and packaged. Later, when the chips are assembled into a system, the same tests can be applied through the diagnostic network.

The JTAG interface is designed to extend to multichip systems. When more than one chip is incorporated in a system, the scan paths are linked together in series by connecting the output from one scan path to the input of the next in a daisy-chain fashion. The clock and control pins are connected in parallel so that these signals can be broadcast to all chips in the chain.

Previous designs have focused on reducing the length of very long scan chains by placing scan-controllable bypass elements in the scan chain [21]. Unfortunately, testing all the chips in the system still requires serial access to each one. Even with ideally short test times on the order of seconds per device, this method would be unacceptably slow for an entire 16,384-node CM-5 comprising many tens of thousands of devices. Moreover, this method fails to take advantage of the inherent parallelism that can be achieved by testing large numbers of identical system components. For these reasons, it was evident early on in the design of the CM-5 that we needed a parallel strategy for supporting scan-based diagnostics.

The CM-5 diagnostic network provides simple and reliable access to the system components of the CM-5. It provides scan access to all chips supporting the JTAG standard, and programmable *ad hoc* access to non-JTAG chips. The

---

[1] In the current implementation of the CM-5 architecture, neither the SPARC processor nodes nor the DRAM chips support the JTAG interface. Given the growing acceptance of JTAG standard, however, it is likely that off-the-shelf processors and memory will support the standard in the near future. The CM-5 architecture is designed to incorporate these JTAG-supporting chips when they become available.

[2] This use of the term "scan" has nothing whatsoever to do with parallel prefix and suffix computations, as discussed in Section 5.

diagnostic network itself is completely testable and diagnosable. The diagnostic network is able to map out and ignore parts of the machine that are faulty or powered down. It can be partitioned consistently with user partitions. The network is able to select and access groups of system chips in parallel, including:

- a single chip;
- a single type of chip;
- the chips within a user partition;
- the chips associated with a geographical portion of the system, *e.g.*, a given board, backplane, cabinet, etc.; and
- unions and intersections of previously specified sets of chips.

The diagnostic network is organized as a (not necessarily complete) binary tree, at the root of which sit one or more diagnostic processors, and at the leaves of which are *pods*. Each pod is a physical subsystem, such as a board, which directly supports the JTAG interface. At any given time, a single diagnostic processor controls the diagnostic network. From the root of the tree, an individual pod can be addressed by giving a binary number, each bit of which corresponds to a level in the tree and specifies a path from the root to the leaf: bit i of the address specifies whether the addressed leaf is in the left or right subtree of the node at level i. If the height of the tree is h, then h bits are sufficient to specify any leaf.

The diagnostic network allows groups of pods to be addressed according to a "hypercube address" scheme. For a tree of height h, a *diagnostic virtual address* is an h-digit number in which each digit is a 0, 1 or B. The B ("both") digit is a "wild-card" that matches both 0 and 1. For example, in a height-6 tree, the address 00B10B addresses the set {000100, 000101, 001100, 001101}, or {4, 5, 12, 13}. The addressing scheme can also be used to address the internal nodes of the diagnostic network by specifying addresses with fewer than h digits.

The decoding logic to implement the diagnostic virtual addressing scheme is based on the notion of steering "tokens" down the tree, as is illustrated in Figure 6. The mechanism works as follows. A token is inserted at the root of the tree together with a diagnostic virtual address, which is piped digit-serially into the root of the tree, high-order digit first. The root selects its right, its left, or both of its subtrees based on the high-order digit. If both subtrees are selected, the token splits into two tokens. Subsequent digits then steer the tokens and subsequent digits down the selected paths. When the end of the address is encountered, the nodes holding tokens are considered to be selected, and nodes on paths from them to the root provide the conduit for control.

Tokens and their paths from the root stay in place until a subsequent address erases them or until they are explicitly erased. This feature can be employed to combine two sets of selected nodes. For conceptual simplicity, suppose each of the two sets of nodes is in a separate subtree of the root. First, the left set is selected using a 0 as the high-order digit and pushing a token down the appropriate paths. Next, the right set is selected using a 1 as the high-order digit and pushing a token down the appropriate paths. The left set

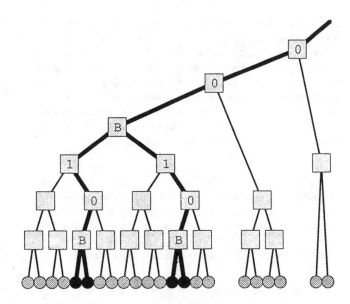

Figure 6: Steering a token down the diagnostic network. The address is decoded digit-serially, where each digit is , , or , representing a selection of the left subtree, right subtree, or both subtrees, respectively. The example shows the selection made by the address

remains intact, but is temporarily inaccessible from the root because the right set is being selected. Finally, we push another token with an address of B to select the root itself and cause it to enable both its children, thereby merging the two sets. More complicated set unions are possible using this basic mechanism.

Most of this mechanism is hidden from the diagnostic engineer. Software extends the diagnostic virtual address within pods to address individual chips. Software also converts between the diagnostic network addresses and two other kinds of addresses: *geographical addresses*, which specify cabinets, backplane, slot type, slots, etc.; and *network addresses*, which give the locations of components according to the data and control networks' view of the machine. In general, important subsets of geographical addresses can be specified with one diagnostic virtual address. Important subsets of network addresses—for example, all data network chips at a given height in the machine, or all boards containing processing nodes in some contiguous range—typically take a combination of at most h diagnostic virtual addresses, where h is the number of bits in the address. The most important aspect of the addressing scheme, however, is that the time to access the various subsets does not grow by more than a small additive amount when the size of the machine doubles.

Having addressed a subset of the pods in the system, scan vectors can be applied in parallel to detect errors. JTAG serial data and control inputs are broadcast to all selected pods. Each pod provides a scan output signal that can be OR'ed or AND'ed with the corresponding signals from the other selected pods. The choice of an OR or AND combiner depends on what the diagnostic processor is expecting for a scan result. If the expected bit is a 1, the AND combiner is chosen. The result of the combining will be a 1 if and only if all selected pods assert a 1. Similarly, if the expected output is a 0, the OR combiner is chosen. The result of the combining will be a 0 if and only if all selected pods assert a 0. If an error is detected in a group of selected pods, the offending pod can be isolated either by addressing each pod in the group individually one at a time, or by a divide-and-conquer methodology. Within a pod, standard techniques for finding errors within a serial chain of JTAG interfaces are used to isolate the error to the chip level.

Since the diagnostic network is a tree, it is relatively easy to make it self diagnosing. Each level beneath the root can be tested by the levels above. Moreover, since there is not much logic in the diagnostic network, the probability of the network itself failing is much less than the probability that other parts of the system fail. Moreover, since the network is a tree, most of its logic is near the leaves, so that when a part of the diagnostic network does fail, only a small part of the tree is likely to be isolated. We did not mind relying on relatively few components near the root, since any small set of components is quite reliable—it is only large aggregates which have a high probability of failing.

The current implementation of the diagnostic network uses essentially two off-the-shelf chips. The address decoding of a binary node is implemented with a P22V10 24-pin PAL, and the finite-state control of a node is implemented with a P18V8 20-pin PAL. The chips can be clocked at any speed up to about 1 megahertz. In some places in the system, to save chips, address decoding of a 4-ary or 8-ary node is implemented directly as a single-chip PAL, rather than by using several separate binary-node PAL's.

7   Conclusion

We conclude this paper with a brief history of our implementation effort.

Work on the CM-5 architecture was begun in the latter part of 1987. We performed network simulations that led us, by January 1988, to choose a fat-tree architecture for the data network. By May 1988, most of the data network logic had been designed and verified, although several changes were implemented during the summer of 1988. A register-transfer-level (RTL) description of the data network chip was completed in early 1989, and the data network architecture was frozen. A gate-level description of the data network chip was completed by the early summer of 1989. The JTAG diagnostic interface was debugged using the data network chip design as a framework. The data network chip also served as the guinea pig for system and chip timing software. The chip was submitted for fabrication in May 1990.

The MIMD-plus-control-network design was proposed in early 1988, but we did not officially decide to use it until May 1989. Until then, we maintained other potential design alternatives. Work on the control network chip and the network interface proceeded concurrently. By the end of summer 1989, RTL models of both were simulating successfully. Gate-level models were implemented by the end of December 1989, and the control network architecture and network interface were frozen shortly thereafter. In May 1990, both the control network chip and the interface chip were submitted for fabrication.

The strategy of the diagnostic network was laid out in 1988, but work did begin on it in earnest until the fall of 1989. Most of the work involved implementing the JTAG interface on the various chips. The design of the diagnostic network itself took only a few months, but considerable effort in 1990 and 1991 went into diagnostic software.

In the latter part of 1990, our attention turned to system integration. We received and tested the data network chips in July 1990, the control network chips in August, and the interface chips in September. Within two days after the interface chips arrived, we had assembled the networks for a 2-node machine and powered it up, a feat due in large measure to our functional verification methodology [17]. That same day, the operating system—which had been developed on a simulator—functioned correctly on the machine. By year's end, we had successfully constructed several small machines, including a 64-node machine, some of which were dedicated to software development.

The year 1991 began with an effort to build a 256-node machine using a completely new mechanical design. Initially, it had been more important to make machines available to our software engineers than to construct a large machine. To test the limits of our physical design, however, we needed to build large machines. The 256-node machine was begun in February, and finished in March. The time frame was dominated by the build time in manufacturing. In May, we built a 544-node machine, which was shipped in August to the Minnesota Supercomputer Center on behalf of the Army High Performance Computer Research Center.

In October 1991, the Connection Machine Model CM-5 Supercomputer was publicly announced.

Acknowledgments

The CM-5 project was managed by Rolf-Dieter Fiebrich. Many others at Thinking Machines contributed to its success, but space does not permit us to thank them all individually. Of special mention, however, are Pam Chulada-Smith, for keeping our systems running; Ken Crouch, for helping to design and test the data network protocols; Rick Epstein, who managed the hardware design of boards; Don Moodie, who engineered the mechanical design; Sami Nuwayser, for his system administration and chip-design talents; Dave Patterson, for encouraging us to resurrect our MIMD-plus-control-network design; David Potter, who led the electrical and packaging effort; Linda Simko, whose administrative talents saved us from needing to have any; Cindy Spiller, for writing the initial system code and helping to verify the system; Guy Steele, for insights into the linguistic implications of the network architecture, and John Wade, who contributed to the design of the differential pads and system clocking.

In addition, we would like to thank Keira Bromberg, Dan Cassiday, Chung Der, John Devine, John Earls, Jamie Frankel, Steve Goldhaber, Harold Hubschman, Jim Lalone, Don Newman, Ralph Palmer, Gary Sabot, Soroush Shakibnia, Craig Stanfill, John Sullivan, Lew Tucker, Bob Vecchioni, Charlie Vogt and Bruce Walker for their contributions. We also thank the representatives from our chip vendors—Mark O'Brien, Curt Dicke, Laura Le Blanc,

Jerome Li, and Shabnam Zarrinkhameh of LSI Logic; and Jerry Frenkil, Frank Kelly, Marc Corbacho, Paul Pinelle, and George Wall, of VLSI Technology, Inc.—for their help in producing the network chips.

References

[1] IEEE Std 1149.1-1990. IEEE standard test access port and boundary-scan architecture, 1990.

[2] G. E. Blelloch. *Vector Models for Data-Parallel Computing*. The MIT Press, 1990.

[3] W. J. Dally. Wire-efficient VLSI multiprocessor communication networks. In Paul Losleben, editor, *Proceedings of the 1987 Stanford Conference on Advanced Research in VLSI*, pages 391–415, Cambridge, MA, 1987. The MIT Press.

[4] W. J. Dally and C. L. Seitz. Deadlock-free message routing in multiprocesor interconnection networks. *IEEE Transactions on Computers*, C-36(5):547–553, May 1987.

[5] F. Darema-Rogers, D. A. George, V. A. Norton, and G. F. Pfister. A single-program-multiple-data computational model for EPEX/FORTRAN. Research Report RC 11552, Computer Sciences Department, IBM T. J. Watson Research Center, Yorktown Heights, NY, November 1986.

[6] M. Dubois and S. Thakkar, editors. *Cache Architectures in Tightly Coupled Multiprocessors*. IEEE Computer Society, June 1990. Special Issue of *Computer*, Volume 23, Number 6.

[7] A. Gottlieb, R. Grishman, C. P. Kruskal, K. P. McAuliffe, L. Rudolph, and M. Snir. The NYU ultracomputer — designing a MIMD, shared-memory parallel machine. *IEEE Transactions on Computers*, C-32(2):175–159, February 1983.

[8] R. I. Greenberg and C. E. Leiserson. Randomized routing on fat-trees. *Advances in Computing Research*, 5:345–374, 1989.

[9] R. Gupta. The fuzzy barrier: A mechanism for high speed synchronization of processors. In *Third International Conference on Architectural Support for Programming Languages and Operating Systems*, pages 54–63, Boston, Massachusetts, 1989.

[10] J. L. Hennessy and D. A. Patterson. *Computer Architecture A Quantitative Approach*. Morgan Kaufmann, 1990.

[11] W. D. Hillis and G. L. Steele, Jr. Data parallel algorithms. *Communications of the ACM*, 29(12):1170–1183, December 1986.

[12] H. F. Jordan. A multi-microprocessor system for finite element structural analysis. In A. K. Noor and Jr. McComb, H. G., editors, *Trends in Computerized Structural Analysis and Synthesis*, pages 21–29. Pergamon Press Ltd, 1978. Published as a special issue of *Computers & Structures*, Volume 10, Numbers 1–2.

[13] P. Kermani and L. Kleinrock. Virtual cut-through: A new computer communication switching technique. *Computer Networks*, 3:267–286, 1979.

[14] F. T. Leighton, B. Maggs, and S. Rao. Universal packet routing algorithms. In *29th Annual IEEE Symposium on Foundations of Computer Science*, pages 256–271, 1988.

[15] C. E. Leiserson. Fat-trees: Universal networks for hardware-efficient supercomputing. *IEEE Transactions on Computers*, C-34(10):892–901, October 1985.

[16] C. E. Leiserson and B. M. Maggs. Communication-efficient parallel algorithms for distributed random-access machines. *Algorithmica*, 3:53–77, 1988.

[17] M. St. Pierre, S.-W. Yang, and D. Cassiday. Functional VLSI design verification methodology for the CM-5 massively parallel supercomputer. In *International Conference on Computer Design*, October 1992. To appear.

[18] C. L. Seitz. The cosmic cube. *Communications of the ACM*, 28(1):22–23, January 1985.

[19] C. L. Seitz, W. C. Athas, W. J. Dally, R. Faucette, A. J. Martin, S. Mattisson, C. S. Steele, and W.-K. Su. *Message-Passing Concurrent Computers: Their Architecture and Programming*. Addison-Wesley, Reading, MA, 1986.

[20] P. Tang and P.-C. Yew. Processor self-scheduling for multiple-nested parallel loops. In K. Hwang, S. M. Jacobs, and E. E. Swartzlander, editors, *Proceedings of the 1986 International Conference on Parallel Processing*, pages 528–535, August 1986.

[21] Texas Instruments. *SN54ACT8997, SN74ACT8997 Scan Path Linker With 4-bit Identification Bus*, April 1990. Product Preview.

[22] Thinking Machines Corporation, applicant. W. Daniel Hillis, inventor. European Patent Application Serial Number 89 902 461.6, priority date of February 2, 1988, entitled *Method and Apparatus For Aligning The Operation Of A Plurality Of Processors*. Also International Application Number WO 89/07299 (Published under the Patent Cooperation Treaty), Publication Date 10 August 1989.

[23] Thinking Machines Corporation, 245 First Street, Cambridge, MA 02154-1264. *The Connection Machine CM-5 Technical Summary*, October 1991.

[24] R. Zak and J. Hill. An IEEE 1149.1 compliant testability architecture with internal scan. In *International Conference on Computer Design*, October 1992. To appear.

EXPANDED DELTA NETWORKS FOR VERY LARGE PARALLEL COMPUTERS *†

Brian D. Alleyne

Dept. of Elect. Eng.

Princeton University

Princeton, NJ 08544

Isaac D. Scherson

Dept. of ICS

University of California

Irvine, CA 92717

Abstract

Expanded Delta Networks are a generalization of Patel's well-known delta network. In general, EDNs provide multiple paths which can be exploited to reduce contention and hence increasing network performance. EDNs are analyzed with respect to their routing capabilities in SIMD models of computation. The concepts of *capacity* and *clustering* are also addressed as solutions to network I/O constraints. A Restricted Access Expanded Delta Network, of which the MasPar MP-1 router network is an example, is introduced and analyzed.

Keywords: interconnection networks, delta networks, crossbar, hyperbar, clustering, capacity, MIMD, SIMD.

1 Introduction

Multistage interconnection networks extensively investigated over the past 40 years have included the "Omega network" [11], the "Delta network" [18], and variants of the "Multistage cube" networks [21, 1]. Many of these networks were eventually incorporated into MIMD and SIMD parallel computers. Examples of these include the Maspar MP-1 [15] the IBM RP-3 [19], the NYU Ultracomputer [6] and the GP1000 by BBN Advanced Computers Inc. [3]. This paper analyzes the *Expanded Delta Network* (EDN), a generalization of the traditional delta network introduced by Patel [18]. EDNs share the digit controlled routing strategy of delta networks so that no global controller is necessary. Unlike delta networks, EDNs contain multiple paths (multipath) between any input and output. This fact can be used to reduce conflicts or Non Uniform Traffic Spots (NUTS) [10] that occur within the network.

The concept of capacity (defined later) is similar to the concept of "dilation" [22] in that the networks are "multipath". However, the number of wires between stages in a d-dilated network is d times the number of wires of the equivalent stage of an EDN with the same number of inputs, resulting in a much less space efficient network.

In Section 2, the Expanded Delta Network is defined and some of its properties are described. Section 3 deals with the general performance of the EDN. Section 4 expands the analysis to that of SIMD systems.

2 Expanded Delta Networks

The MP-1 massively parallel processor, produced by Maspar Corporation, uses a *hyperbar* switch in its router network [5]. The generalized version of this switch [14] is the main building block for the Expanded Delta Network.

---

*We gratefully acknowledge Tom Blank and Russ Tuck, of Maspar Corporation, for sharing with us the inner works of the MP-1 router network.

†This research was supported in part by the Air Force Office of Scientific Research under grant number F49620-92-J-0126, by the NSF under grant number MIP-9106949, and by NASA under grant number NAG 5-1897.

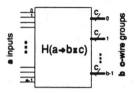

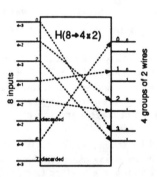

Figure 1: A $H(a \to b \times c)$ hyperbar

Definition 1 *A hyperbar switch $H(a \to b \times c)$ connects a inputs labeled $0, 1, 2, \cdots, a-1$ to $b \times c$ outputs labeled $0, 1, 2, \cdots, (b \times c) - 1$. Every group of c outputs has a label in the range $[0$ to $b-1]$. There are b output groups (or buckets) each with capacity c. Each input indicates to which of the b output groups it should be connected by supplying a base-b digit d. If more than c inputs request connections to a particular output group, c are accepted randomly and the rest are rejected (See Figure 1).*

$H(a \to b \times 1)$ is a traditional $a \times b$ crossbar. In Figure 1, we also show a $H(8 \to 4 \times 2)$ hyperbar with a sample switch routing where some of the inputs have to be discarded since their destination buckets were already full. For simplicity, and without loss of generality, we shall assume that a, b and c are all powers of 2.

Definition 2 *An $EDN(a,b,c,l)$ is an $(l+1)$ stage interconnection network. The first $0 \cdots (l-1)$ stages consist of $H(a \to b \times c)$ hyperbar switches, and the last stage consists of $c \times c$ crossbar (or $H(c \to c \times 1)$) switches. The connectivity rule between hyperbar stages is specified by the permutation $\gamma_{j,k}^n(y)$ defined on an n-bit label y as follows:*

1) Fix the j least significant bits of the label

2) Left cyclic shift by k the remaining $(n-j)$ bits

The function $\gamma_{j,k}^n(y)$ is related to the "segment shuffle" defined by Lenfant [13]. $\gamma_{0,1}^n(0 \le i < 2^n)$ is the well-known shuffle of 2^n labels. $\gamma_{0,\log_2(q)}^n(0 \le i < 2^n)$ is a q-shuffle of 2^n objects defined by Patel [18]. $\gamma_{n,0}^n(0 \le i < 2^n)$ is the identity permutation.

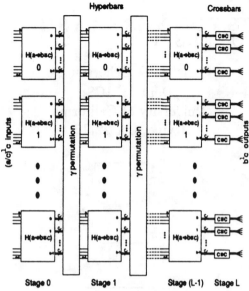

Figure 2: An EDN(a,b,c,l)

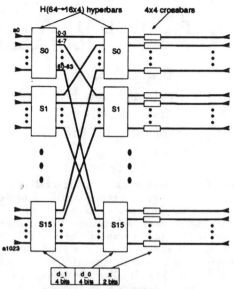

Figure 3: An EDN(64,16,4,2)

An EDN network will have $(a/c)^l c$ inputs and $b^l c$ outputs. The ith stage has $(a/c)^{l-i} b^{i-1}$ hyperbars, and the $l + 1$ stage has b^l crossbars. Let the switches be named $0, 1, 2, \cdots$ from top to bottom (Figure 2).

At the output of stage i and the input of stage $(i + 1)$, there are $w_i = (a/c)^{l-i} b^i c$ wires. Let y be any output of stage i, $y \in \{0, 1, 2, \cdots, (a/c)^{l-i} b^i c\}$, and let y be represented by a binary string of length $\log_2((a/c)^{l-i} b^i c)$. Then y is connected to input z of stage $(i + 1)$ if and only if

$$z = \gamma_{j,k}^n(y); \quad n = \log_2(w_i), \quad j = \log_2(c), \quad k = \log_2(a/c) \quad (1)$$

The generalized EDN is shown in Figure 2, and a specific instance is shown in Figure 3. Note that at the lth stage, each of the b^l buckets are sent directly to a $c \times c$ crossbar.

A $(l \times \log_2(b) + \log_2(c))$ destination tag is used for routing. At each hyperbar stage, $log_2(b)$ bits are used for routing, and at the final $c \times c$ crossbar stage, $\log_2(c)$ bits are used. Let the destination tag be written as $D = d_{l-1} d_{l-2} \cdots d_0 x$ where the d_i's are digits in a base-b system, and x is a digit in a base-c system. After the destination tags pass through the network, some sources are connected to some destinations and data is transmitted.

Routing in the EDN is performed as follows:

1. At stage i, $(1 \leq i \leq l)$, digit d_{l-i} of the destination tag $D = d_{l-1} d_{l-2} \cdots d_0 x$ determines which of the output buckets of a hyperbar a message should be connected to. Since each d_{l-i} is used once during the routing and is never considered again, we liken this to "retiring" and say that digit d_{l-i} of D is "retired" at stage i.

2. At stage (l), messages are input to a $c \times c$ crossbar. At this point digit x of the routing tag $D = d_{l-1} d_{l-2} \cdots d_0 x$ is used to determine the output the message is to be routed to.

Theorem 1 *[Connectivity] An EDN(a,b,c,l) can connect any source S to any destination $D = d_{l-1} d_{l-2} \cdots d_0 x$ by retiring d_{l-i} of D at stage i ($0 \leq i \leq l$) and by retiring x at stage l.*

Proof: This is quite obvious from the relationship to Delta networks. A similar approach to that used by Patel

[18] to prove that a delta network can connect any source to any destination is applied for this proof.

Corollary 1 *A renaming, or permuting of the inputs of an EDN does not prevent a source from connecting to a destination $D = d_{l-1} d_{l-2} \cdots d_0 x$.*

Proof: By Theorem 1, an EDN(a,b,c,l) is always connected and a path exists from which we can connect source to destination $D = d_{l-1} d_{l-2} \cdots d_0 x$ according to the routing algorithm irrespective of where the message originated. $\Box Q.E.D.$

Corollary 2 *If the digits of $D = d_{l-1} d_{l-2} \cdots d_0 x$ are retired in an order given by a digit-permutation $F(D)$, then the source with D is routed to $F(D)$.*

Proof: The proof of this Corollary is obvious and hence omitted. The following is an important observation.

Remark: To retire the digits in a different order, while preserving the destination $D = d_{l-1} d_{l-2} \cdots d_0 x$, the permutation F^{-1} must be performed at the output of the network. $\Box Q.E.D.$

To illustrate the usefulness of Corollary 2, consider the EDN(64,16,4,2) shown in Figure 3. This network is incapable of performing the identity permutation in one pass. However, by retiring the digits of the routing tag in a different order, and then adding an additional permutation stage to compensate, the modified EDN in Figure 4 is obtained. It should be noted that these networks will perform identically in the average case, while very differently for *specific* permutations.

Theorem 2 *[Multiple Paths] An EDN(a,b,c,l) has c^l different paths from any input to any output.*

Proof: At each stage i, digit d_{l-i} in $D = d_{l-1} d_{l-2} \cdots d_0 x$ only determines to which bucket the source is switched. Thus, there are c alternate paths that the source can be switched to at each stage. Since this occurs in l stages, there are c^l possible paths any source can take to any one output. $\Box Q.E.D.$

There are two special cases of EDNs worthy of mention. An EDN(a,b,1,1) is an $a \times b$ crossbar. An EDN(a,b,1,l) is an $a^l \times b^l$ delta network [18]. In both of these cases, $c = 1$ and so by Theorem 2 there is a unique path from any input to any output.

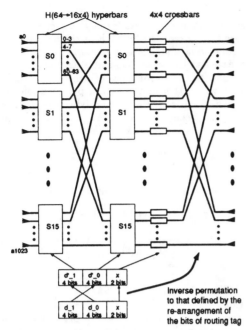

Figure 4: An EDN(64,16,4,2) modified to perform the identity permutation

3 General Analysis of EDNs

The number of crosspoint switches ($C_s(a, b, c, l)$) required to build the network is a possible measure of the cost of the EDN(a,b,c,l) since the number of crosspoints give an idea of the layout area necessary.

$$C_s(a, b, c, l) = \frac{(a/c)^l - b^l}{(a/c) - b} abc + b^l c^2 \quad (a/c) \neq b \quad (2)$$
$$= lb^{l+1}c + b^l c^2 \quad (a/c) = b$$

Another measure of cost of the EDN(a,b,c,l) is the wire cost $C_w(a, b, c, l)$ which provides an estimate of PC board area, the number of pins and, in some cases, the number of connections needed across a backplane.

$$C_w(a, b, c, l) = \frac{(a/c)^l - b^l}{(a/c) - b} bc$$
$$+ (a/c)^l c + b^l c \quad (a/c) \neq b \quad (3)$$
$$= (l + 2)b^l c \quad (a/c) = b$$

Let us now consider the average routing performance of EDNs. Theorem 1 showed that an EDN(a,b,c,l) is capable of routing any input to any output. However, if many inputs require to be routed simultaneously, there is the possibility that some of the inputs will not be routed. Two or more inputs may contend for the same output in which case all but one of these inputs will be blocked. Even if there is no contention for an output, an input may be blocked as it makes its way through the network itself.

A cycle is defined as the time required for a request at any input to propagate through the network (if not blocked), plus the time for the corresponding message to propagate through the network. It is assumed that the network is circuit-switched, so there are no queues in the network. At the beginning of each cycle, the network attempts to accommodate all the requests presented at the inputs. Some of the requests are blocked, and so the number of requests actually satisfied is a fraction of the requests issued. For the purpose of analysis, the following assumptions are made about the nature of the requests generated:

1. inputs are uniformly and independently distributed over the outputs.
2. At the beginning of each cycle, the probability that there is a request on an input line is r.
3. The requests which are blocked are ignored, and do not affect the requests generated at the next cycle.

Let us consider a hyperbar $H(a \to b \times c)$, in which the requests are independently and uniformly distributed over the output buckets and for each of the a inputs of the hyperbar, the probability that there is a request is r. The probability of exactly n requests for any bucket is

$$\binom{a}{n} \left(\frac{r}{b}\right)^n \left(1 - \frac{r}{b}\right)^{a-n} \quad \text{for } n \leq a$$
$$0 \quad \text{for } n > a$$

Since each bucket has a capacity of c, requests beyond c will be discarded. Thus the expected number of requests accepted per bucket is

$$E(r) = \sum_{n=1}^{c} n \binom{a}{n} \left(\frac{r}{b}\right)^n \left(1 - \frac{r}{b}\right)^{a-n}$$
$$+ \sum_{n=1}^{c} c \binom{a}{n} \left(\frac{r}{b}\right)^n \left(1 - \frac{r}{b}\right)^{a-n}$$

which simplifies to:

$$c \left(1 - \left(1 - \frac{r}{b}\right)^a\right) + \sum_{n=1}^{c} (n - c) \binom{a}{n} \left(\frac{r}{b}\right)^n \left(1 - \frac{r}{b}\right)^{a-n}$$

Therefore probability that there is a request at an output of the hyperbar is $E(r)/c$.

If r_{in} is the request rate at the inputs of any stage of hyperbars and r_{out} is the request rate at the outputs, then $r_{out} = E(r_{in})/c$ and in particular, $r_{i+1} = E(r_i)/c$ for $0 \leq i < l$, $r_0 = r$ except for the final stage where r_l is the input to the $c \times c$ crossbar stage of the network yielding $r_{final} = 1 - (1 - r_l/c)^c$.

The probability of acceptance P_A is defined as the ratio of the expected number of requests routed per cycle ((number of outputs $\times r_{final}) = b^l c \times r_{final}$) to the expected number of requests generated per cycle ((number of inputs $\times r) = (a/c)^l c \times r$). Thus

$$P_A(r) = \frac{b^l c \times r_{final}}{(a/c)^l c \times r} = \left(\frac{bc}{a}\right)^l \frac{r_{final}}{r} \quad (4)$$

$$\text{where } r_0 = r \quad \text{and for } 0 \leq i < l$$
$$r_{i+1} = \left(1 - \left(1 - \frac{r_i}{b}\right)^a\right)$$
$$+ \sum_{n=1}^{c} \left(\frac{n}{c} - 1\right) \binom{a}{n} \left(\frac{r_i}{b}\right)^n \left(1 - \frac{r_i}{b}\right)^{a-n}$$
$$r_{final} = 1 - (1 - r_l/c)^c$$

In Figures 5 and 6 representative plots are given to compare the performance of various EDNs. The performance of a crossbar network is also included as reference. EDNs generated with 8 input/8 output hyperbars are featured in Figure 5 while in Figure 6 EDNs generated with 16 input/16 output hyperbars are featured. As expected, the EDN(8,8,1,*) and EDN(16,16,1,*) which correspond to delta networks perform the worse in each family. For a given switch size, if the capacity is increased, the performance increases, and for a given capacity, if the switch size is increased the performance also improves.

In the following section we turn our attention to SIMD computing systems in which EDNs are likely to be embedded. The MIMD case will not be addressed as the methods described in [9] can be applied for the analysis.

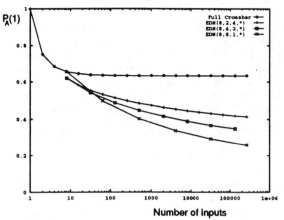

Figure 5: Performance of EDNs with 8 input/output hyperbars

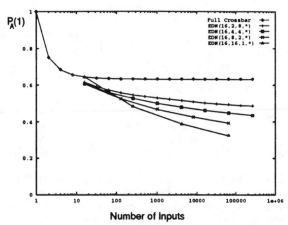

Figure 6: Performance of EDNs with 16 input/output hyperbars

4 Analysis of the EDNs in SIMD Computers

Currently available Massively Parallel computers such as Thinking Machine's CM-1&2 [8], MasPar's MP-1 [15] and AMT's DAP [17] have proven the feasibility of systems in which there are more than 4K processing elements (PEs). In MIMD architectures, different processors may require communication at different times. Therefore the "goodness" of the network is based on degree, diameter and bandwidth. In a SIMD system all (or at least a good portion) of the processors usually want to communicate at the *same* time. Hence the goal of the router is to route an arbitrary permutation in a reasonable time.

4.1 Permutation Routing

Let us now assume that the input requests to the EDN form a permutation on the outputs of the network.

Lemma 1 *If the input requests to an EDN form a permutation, there will be no blocking in the final two stages.*

Proof: Since the input requests form a permutation, there will never be a contention for an output of the network. Thus there will be no conflicts in the final stage of the network. Each of the b output groups of the second-to-last stage is connected directly to a $c \times c$ crossbar switch which is connected directly to c outputs of the network. There

are never more than c requests for any $c \times c$ crossbar and so never more than c requests to each of the b output groups of the second-to-last stage. All requests can therefore be accommodated at the second-to-last stage. $\square Q.E.D.$

Let us denote the probability of acceptance P_A in the special case where the inputs form a permutation as P_{Ap}. P_{Ap} can be derived from P_A by modifying the equation for P_A to take into account that there will be no blocking in the last two stages by Lemma 1. Thus

$$P_{Ap}(r) = \frac{b^{l-1}c \times r_{final}}{(a/c)^{l-1}c \times r} = \left(\frac{bc}{a}\right)^{l-1}\frac{r_{l-1}}{r} \qquad (5)$$

where $r_0 = r$ and for $0 \le i < l-2$

$$r_{i+1} = \left(1 - \left(1 - \frac{r_i}{b}\right)^a\right)$$

$$+ \sum_{n=1}^{c}(\frac{n}{c} - 1) \left(\begin{array}{c} a \\ n \end{array}\right) \left(\frac{r_i}{b}\right)^n \left(1 - \frac{r_i}{b}\right)^{a-n}$$

4.2 Restricted Access EDNs

The Connection Machine CM-1 [8] and the Maspar MP-1 [15] have chips containing 16 or 32 processing elements respectively. With the ability to pack more and more processing elements per processing chip, the I/O bottleneck between processing elements and the interconnection network is only aggravated. As the number of processing elements continues to grow, it will most certainly be impractical (or impossible) to build interconnection networks where the network size is equal to the number of PEs. One solution to this problem is clustering, which is used in the architecture of the MasPar MP-1 system, in thinking Machine's CM-1&2, and the proposed P^3 system [2]. In clustering, a restricted access network is used where a group of processing elements (a cluster), as opposed to a single processing element, has access to the network at any given time. This has been studied in the case where the interconnection network is a crossbar, Clos or Benes Network[24]. Much research has been done on permutation routing on multistage networks [4, 11, 12, 21] as well as on static networks [7, 16, 20, 23] but all these research efforts assume that the network size (i.e., the number of its input terminals) is equal to the number of processors in the system.

We will refer to a system consisting of p clusters connected by an EDN of size p as a restricted access expanded delta network or $RA-EDN$. Since the number of inputs and outputs of the EDN must be the same, the EDN used can be represented as EDN(bc,b,c,l), with $p = b^l c$. Each cluster labeled $0, 1, ..., p-1$ has q processing elements locally labeled $0, 1, ..., q-1$. Every processor in the system is globally labeled with two digits $\overline{xy}$ indicating that it is processor y in cluster x, where $0 \le x \le p-1$ and $0 \le y \le q-1$. A $RA-EDN$ system thus parameterized and labeled is denoted $RA-EDN(b,c,l,q)$ (Figure 7).

Routing a permutation f of the set $S_N = \{0, 1, ..., N-1\}$ in a system of N processors $(0, 1, ..., N-1)$ consists of delivering a message from processor i to processor $f(i)$ for every $i = 0, 1, ..., N-1$. In RA-EDN(b,c,l,q), at most one message from each cluster can be sent at every network cycle and as there are q processors (and thus messages) in every cluster, routing f requires at least q network cycles.

At any cycle, a processor with an undelivered message is selected randomly per cluster. The selected processor in every cluster is connected to the network through a q-to-1 multiplexor and the destination address of the selected pro-

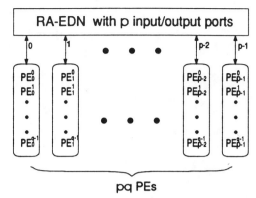

Figure 7: Restricted access RA-EDN System

cessor is expressed in its 2-digit form (say $\overline{u_i v_i}$). The (u_i)'s are used to establish a path between the inputs and outputs of the network of $RA-EDN(b,c,l,q)$ and v_i is used to select the local processor of global label $u_i v_i$ through a 1-to-q multiplexor. At this point a path exists between certain selected processors and their destinations, and messages can be forwarded to their final destinations. If there are conflicts in the network, then some messages will not be delivered and will have to wait for a subsequent cycle. These cycles are repeated until there are no undelivered messages. Conflicts only occur through the EDN, and not after an input has arrived at the destination cluster. Thus the trailer v_i need not be considered in the analysis.

We are interested in the average number of cycles required to perform a typical permutation between the pq processors. Let r_i be the request rate to the EDN after i cycles. The expected number of inputs presented to the network is $r_i \times p$. For some i, say I, $(r_I \times p) < 1$ at which point that all requests are assumed routed. Let $a^i(j)$ represent the probability that after i cycles exactly j messages have been delivered from a cluster. Initially $a^0(0) = 1, a^0(j) = 0$; $j \neq 0$. Then

$$r_i = \sum_{n=0}^{q-1} a^i(n)$$
$$a^{i+1}(0) = (1 - P_A(r_i))a^i(0)$$
$$a^{i+1}(j) = P_A a^i(j-1) + (1 - P_A(r_i))a^i(j) \quad (0 < j < q)$$
$$a^{i+1}(q) = P_A a^i(q-1) + a^i(q)$$

The MasPar MP-1 router is similar to a RA-EDN(16,4,2,16) system with the following differences. The embedded EDN is modified (Corollary 2) to allow the identity permutation. In event of conflict, inputs are prioritized according to input label, and a processor with an undelivered message is not chosen randomly in each cluster, but according to its label.

References

[1] G.B. Adams III and H.J. Siegel, *The extra stage cube: a fault-tolerant interconnection network for supersystems*, IEEE Transactions on Computers, Vol. C-31, No. 5, pp. 443–454, May 1982.

[2] B.D. Alleyne, David A. Kramer and Isaac D. Scherson, *A bit-Parallel, word-Parallel, massively Parallel Processor for Scientific Computing*, Frontiers of Massively Parallel Processing, pp. 176-185, 1990.

[3] *Inside the GP1000* (Cambridge, Massachusetts: BBN Advanced Computers Inc., 1988)

[4] V. E. Benes, *Mathematical theory on connecting networks and telephone traffic*, Academic Press, New York, 1965.

[5] T. Blank, R. Tuck, *Personal Communications*, MasPar Computer Corporation, 1991.

[6] A. Gottlieb et al., *The NYU Ultracomputer – Designing an MIMD shared-memory parallel computer*, IEEE Transactions on Computers, Vol. c-32, No. 2, pp. 175–189, February 1983.

[7] A. Gottlieb and C. P. Kruskal, *Complexity Results for Permuting Data and Other Computations on Parallel Processors*, Journal of the ACM, Vol. 31, No. 2, pp. 193–209, April 1984.

[8] D. Hillis, *The Connection Machine*, MIT Press, Cambridge, Mass., 1986.

[9] K. Hwang and F.A. Briggs, *Computer Architecture and Parallel Processing*, Chapter 7, Section 7.2.4, McGraw-Hill Press, 1984.

[10] T. Lang and L. Kurisaki, *Nonuniform Traffic Spots (NUTS) in Multistage Interconnection Networks*, Proceedings of the International Conference on Parallel Processing, pp. 191–195, August 1988.

[11] D. K. Lawrie, *Access and Alignment of Data in an Array Processor*, IEEE Transactions on Computers, C-24, pp. 1145, 1155, Dec. 1975.

[12] K. Y. Lee, *A New Benes Network Control Algorithm*, IEEE Transactions on Computers, C-36, pp. 768–772, May 1987.

[13] J. Lenfant, *Parallel Permutations of Data: A Benes Network Control Algorithm for Frequently Used Permutations*, IEEE Transactions on Computers, C-27, pp. 637–647, July 1987.

[14] S. Liew and K. Lu, *Performance Analysis of Asymmetric Packet Switch Modules with Channel Grouping*, Frontiers of Massively Parallel Processing, pp. 668-676, 1990.

[15] MasPar Computer Corporation, *MasPar Parallel Application Language (MPL) Users Guide, Software Version 2.0* , MasPar Computer Corporation, Sunnyvale California, 1991.

[16] D. Nassimi and S. Sahni, *An Optimal Routing Algorithm for Mesh-Connected Parallel Computers*, J. ACM, Vol. 27, No. 1, pp. 6-29, Jan. 1980.

[17] D. Parkinson, D.J. Hunt, K.S. MacQueen, *The ATM DAP 500*, Proceedings of the thirty-third IEEE Computer Society International Conference, pp. 196-199, 1988.

[18] J.H. Patel, *Performance of Processor-Memory Interconnections for Multiprocessors* IEEE Transactions on Computers, Vol. C-30, No. 10, pp. 771–780, October 1981.

[19] G.F. Pfister at al., *The IBM Research Parallel Processor Prototype (RP3): introduction and architecture*, 1985 International Conference on Parallel Processing, pp. 764-771,August 1985.

[20] C. S. Raghavendra and V. K. Prasanna Kumar, *Permutations on Illiac IV-Type Networks*, IEEE Transactions on Computers, Vol. C-35, No. 7, pp. 662–669, July 1986.

[21] H.J. Siegel, *Interconnection Networks for Large-Scale Parallel Processing*, Lexington Books, 1985.

[22] T.H. Szymanski and V.C. Hamacher, *On the Universality of Multipath Multistage Interconnection Networks*, Journal of Parallel and Distributed Computing, Vol. 7, No. 3, pp. 541–569, December 1989.

[23] L. G. Valiant, *A Scheme for Fast Parallel Communication*, SIAM Journal on Computers, Vol. 11, No. 2, pp. 350–361, May 1982.

[24] A. Youssef, B.D. Alleyne, I.D. Scherson, *Permutation Routing in Restricted Access Networks*, 6th International Parallel Processing Symposium, pp. 403–406, March 1992.

Chapter 2: Foundations

Many interconnection networks were proposed in the early days of parallel processing. Probably the seminal work was that done by Stone[1] on the shuffle-exchange network. A number of derivatives of the shuffle-exchange, such as the flip network[2] and the generalized cube,[3] were introduced later. Seemingly different, they were studied in the light of their connectivity and permutational capabilities. However, in their now-classic paper, Wu and Feng[4] showed the topological equivalences of certain multistage interconnection networks. Then, because of the introduction of novel network configurations, additional fundamental work was needed: in particular, theoretical developments that would explain the differences and similarities between interconnection structures such as blocking and nonblocking networks.

The papers included in this chapter present fundamental work on interconnection networks. The first two papers, by Kruskal and Snir (1986) and Scherson (1991), show equivalences between networks due to their common construction rules. Akers and Krishnamurthy (1989) address a class of mathematically founded topologies — namely, Cayley graphs. The paper by Szymanski and Hamacher (1989) shows the characteristics of multipath networks due to multiple wires per switch channel. Feldman, Friedman, and Pippenger (1988) develop an important theoretical result that in 1988 answered a question related to wide-sense nonblocking networks (as opposed to strictly nonblocking networks) that was first posed in 1962 by Benes.[5] The paper by Lee (1985) presents a proof on the rearrangeability of $2(\log_2 N)-1$ stage networks. Finally, Fiduccia (1992) examines pin-optimal bused hypercubes.

References

1. H.S. Stone, "Parallel Processing with the Perfect Shuffle," *IEEE Trans. Computers*, Vol. C-20, No. 2, Feb. 1971, pp. 153–161.

2. K.E. Batcher, "The Flip Network in Staran," *Proc. Int'l Conf. Parallel Processing*, IEEE CS Press, Los Alamitos, Calif., 1976, pp. 65–71.

3. H.J. Siegel and S.D. Smith, "Study of Multistage SIMD Interconnection Networks," *Proc. Fifth Ann. Symp. Computer Architecture*, IEEE CS Press, Los Alamitos, Calif., 1978, pp. 223–229.

4. C. Wu and T. Feng, "On a Class of Multistage Interconnection Networks," *IEEE Trans. Computers*, Vol. C-29, No. 8, Aug. 1980, pp. 694–702.

5. V.E. Benes, "Heuristic Remarks and Mathematical Problems Regarding the Theory of Switching Systems," *Bell System Tech. J.*, Vol. 41, No. 4, July 1962, pp. 1201–1247.

A UNIFIED THEORY OF INTERCONNECTION NETWORK STRUCTURE*

Clyde P. KRUSKAL
Department of Computer Science, University of Maryland, College Park, MD 20742, U.S.A.

Marc SNIR
Institute of Mathematics and Computer Science, Hebrew University, Jerusalem 91904, Israel

Communicated by E. Shamir
Received October 1983
Revised March 1984, June 1986

Abstract. The relationship between the topology of interconnection networks and their functional properties is examined. Graph-theoretical characterizations are derived for delta networks, which have a simple routing scheme, and for bidelta networks, which have the delta property in both directions. Delta networks are shown to have a recursive structure. Bidelta networks are shown to have a unique topology. The definition of bidelta network is used to derive in a uniform manner the labelling schemes that define the omega networks, indirect binary cube networks, flip networks, baseline networks, modified data manipulators and two new networks; these schemes are generalized to arbitrary radices.

The labelling schemes are used to characterize networks with simple routing. In another paper (Kruskal/Snir, 1984), we characterize the networks with optimal performance/cost ratio. Only the multistage shuffle-exchange networks have both optimal performance/cost ratio and simple routing. This helps explain why few fundamentally different geometries have been proposed.

Key words. Banyan network, baseline network, bidelta network, capacity, delay, delta network, flip network, indirect binary cube network, interconnection network, isomorphism, multistage network, omega network, packet-switching network, routing, topological equivalence.

1. Introduction

There has been large amount of research on multistage interconnection networks for parallel processing (see, for example, [4, 6, 15, 17]). Nevertheless, there seems to be a surprisingly small number of basic designs for interconnection networks

* This work was supported in part by the Applied Mathematical Sciences Program of the U.S. Department of Energy under contract No. DE-AC02-76ER03077, in part by the National Science Foundation under Grant Nos. NSF-MCS79-21258 and NSF-MCS81-05896, and in part by a grant from IBM. The work was done while the first author was at the University of Illinois, Urbana, IL 61801, U.S.A. and the second author was at the Courant Institute, New York University, New York, NY 10012, U.S.A. Some of this material appeared in the *Proc. 1982 Conf. on Information Sciences and Systems*, Princeton University, March 1982.

that recur under many disguises. A particularly ubiquitous geometry is the 'multistage shuffle-exchange network' [1, 2, 5, 7, 11, 12, 14, 16, 19]. This geometry provides good performance and 'simple' message routing (or control). Given the paucity of other network geometries, one is tempted to conjecture that these networks are in some sense optimal. In this paper, we shall characterize the networks with simple message routing. In another paper [10], we characterize the geometries that provide optimal performance/cost ratio. The multistage shuffle-exchange networks are the unique networks with both simple routing and optimal performance/cost ratio. This helps explain why few fundamentally different geometries have been proposed.

The approach followed in this paper differs from that followed in most of the literature on interconnection networks. Most research concentrates on the properties of specific networks. In this paper we shall start from a set of desired properties and obtain a complete description of the networks having those properties. Starting from a functional definition for 'delta' networks [13], i.e., networks in which routing is done according to the successive bits of the destination, we obtain a complete description of the possible geometries for such networks. The geometry of 'bidelta' networks, i.e., networks in which the delta property holds in both directions, is shown to be unique. The labelling schemes that define omega networks, indirect binary cube networks, flip networks, baseline networks, reverse baseline networks, modified data manipulators, and two new networks are derived in a uniform manner.

2. Definitions

An (M, N)-*network* G is a directed graph whose nodes include a set I of M distinguished *input* nodes and a set O of N distinguished *output* nodes. We shall use *switch* as a synonym for node. We assume, without loss of generality, that for each node u of G there is a directed path connecting some input to u and a directed path connecting u to some output. The *indegree* of a node is the number of edges leading into it, and the *outdegree* of a node is the number of edges leading out of it.

A network with a unique path from each input to each output is called a *banyan network* [7]. A banyan network is *layered* if the nodes can be arranged in successive layers, with inputs at the first layer, outputs at the last layer, and edges connecting nodes from one layer to nodes at the next layer. A layered network with n stages of nodes is called an *n-stage network*. A *rectangular banyan network of degree k* is a layered banyan network where all nodes (with the exception of inputs) have indegree exactly k, and all nodes (with the exception of outputs) have outdegree exactly k. A rectangular banyan network has $n + 1$ layers, each consisting of k^n nodes.

Components of a network must be labelled in order for routing of messages to be possible: the outputs of the network need to be labelled by distinct *addresses*; the edges going out of each node have to be distinguished by a numbering scheme; and if the network is centrally controlled, each node has to carry a distinct label.

We shall assume that if a node has k outgoing edges, then these edges are numbered from 0 to $k-1$.

Two networks are *topologically equivalent* if their underlying graphs are isomorphic; they are *isomorphic* if there exists a label-preserving graph isomorphism between them. The two networks in Fig. 1 are topologically equivalent since, ignoring labels, they look exactly alike; but the networks are not isomorphic.

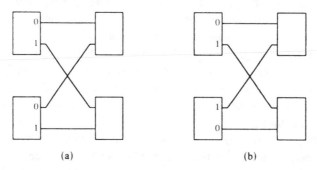

(a)   (b)

Fig. 1. Two networks that are topologically equivalent but not isomorphic.

A path from an input to an output can be described by the sequence of labels that label the successive edges on this path. We shall call this string the *path descriptor*. In a message-switching network with nonadaptive routing, the path descriptor may be used as a header for routing a message: each successive node uses the first element of the string to route the message, and then discards it.

3. Delta networks

What labelling scheme will simplify routing? In a general network, the paths leading from different input nodes to the same output node may have different path descriptors. Thus, a routing table, containing a path descriptor for each output node, is needed at each input node. It is convenient to have all these tables identical. Then we can take the path descriptor associated with paths leading to the output node s to be the *address* of s, and the unique information needed to route a packet to an output node is the address of that node.

Extending the original definition of Patel [13], we define a *digit controlled* or *delta network* to be a network with the following properties:

(1) there is a path from each input node to each output node;

(2) the path descriptors associated with paths leading to the same output node are identical.

The second condition implies that there is at most one path from an input to an output since two different paths from the same input have different descriptors. This, along with the first condition, implies that delta networks are banyan networks, i.e., there is exactly one path from each input to each output. The second condition also implies that all the paths leading from the inputs to any particular node in the network have the same length. In particular, the nodes of a delta network can be arranged by stages so that the input nodes are all at stage 1, and edges connect nodes at stage i only to nodes at stage $i+1$. Note, however, that the output nodes of a delta network need not all be at the same stage—see Fig. 2. Delta networks in which all outputs are at the same stage are layered banyan networks (according to the definition given in Section 2).

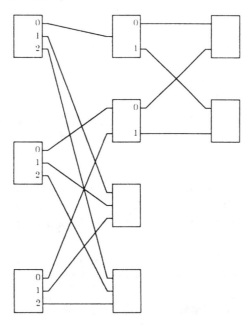

Fig. 2. Delta network.

Let $G = \langle V, E \rangle$ be a network with inputs I and outputs O, and let S be a subset of nodes from G. The *subnetwork $G' = \langle V', E' \rangle$ spanned by S* is the network whose graph consists of all nodes and edges reachable by some (directed) path starting from any node in S (including the nodes in S). A node $i \in V'$ is an input node of G' if no edge of E' enters i; a node $o \in V'$ is an output node of G' if no edge of E' exits o. (Input nodes of G' will be nodes from S; output nodes of G' will be nodes from O.)

If G is a delta network, then a delta network structure is induced on 'reasonable' subnetworks of G. The concept of a 'reasonable' subnetwork is embodied by the conditions of the following lemma.

Lemma 3.1. *Let G be a delta network, and let G' be the subnetwork spanned by a set S of nodes in G. Then G' is a delta network if it fulfills the following two conditions:*
 (1) *there exists a path from each input to each output in G';*
 (2) *all the inputs of G' are nodes from the same stage of G.*

Proof. Suppose G' fulfills both conditions. Condition (1) is the first condition definining delta networks, so G' is a delta network if the path descriptors associated with paths leading to the same output are identical. Let p and p' be descriptors for paths from two distinct inputs s and s' of G' to the same output t of G'. Let q and q' be descriptors of paths leading from inputs of G to s and s' in G, and let $|q|$ and $|q'|$ be their lengths. Then $qp = q'p'$, and $|q| = |q'|$, so that $p = p'$. $\square$

The last lemma implies an alternative, recursive definition of delta networks.[1]

Theorem 3.2. *A delta network G either consists of a unique node, or consists of one stage of nodes all with same outdegree k, followed by k (disjoint) delta networks $G_0, \dots, G_{k-1}$; each node in the first stage is connected to an input of G_i via an edge with label i, for $i = 0, \dots, k-1$.*

Proof. Let u be a node of the delta network G. All paths connecting inputs of G to u have the same path descriptor: indeed, let i and i' be two inputs connected to u by paths with descriptors α and α', respectively; let u be connected to an output o via a path with descriptor β. Then $\alpha\beta = \alpha'\beta$ so that $\alpha = \alpha'$.

Let G_i be the subgraph induced by the set of nodes in the network that are reached by paths starting with label i (Fig. 3). The previous remark implies that these subgraphs are disjoint; by Lemma 3.1, they are delta networks. $\square$

Conversely, it is easy to see that any network that can be recursively decomposed as specified in Theorem 3.2 is a delta network. We have thus achieved a geometric (recursive) definition of delta networks.

Not every rectangular banyan network admits a decomposition of the form given above and, therefore, not every rectangular banyan network can be labelled to be a delta network (for example, see Fig. 4). On the other hand, it immediately follows

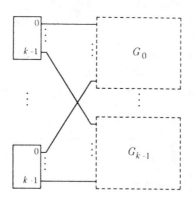

Fig. 3. Recursive structure of delta network.

[1] This theorem was independently proved by Dias [3], and by Kruskal and Snir [9].

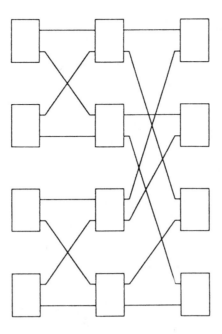

Fig. 4. Nondelta rectangular banyan network.

from the recursive definition that for each k and n there exists an n-stage rectangular delta network of degree k. This rectangular delta network is not unique: Figure 5 shows two 3-stage rectangular delta networks of degree 2 that are not even topologically equivalent.

4. Bidelta networks

In many applications, traffic through the network is bidirectional. It is convenient then that the traffic in the reverse direction also traverses a delta network—especially if the 'output' nodes can initiate requests. The *reversal* G^R of the network G is the network obtained from G by reversing the direction of each edge, and replacing each input by an output and each output by an input. We assume that the reverse network G^R is labelled or, equivalently, that the inputs of G carry distinct addresses, and that each edge of G carries two numbers, one associated with each of the two incident nodes.

A network G is a *bidelta network* if both G and G^R are delta networks. In a bidelta network all paths connecting inputs to outputs have the same length, all paths leading from inputs to a given node have the same length and the same path descriptor, and all reverse paths leading from outputs to the same node have the same length and the same path descriptor—see Fig. 6. We use the term *multistage*

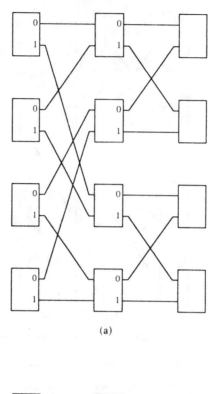

(a)

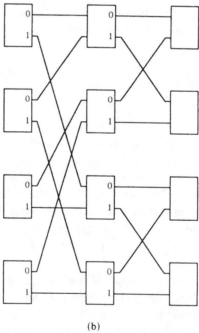

(b)

Fig. 5. Two 3-stage delta networks of degree 2 that are not topologically equivalent.

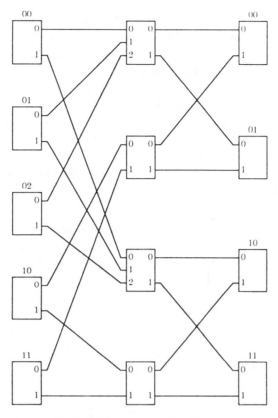

Fig. 6. Bidelta network with addresses.

shuffle-exchange network for any *n*-stage bidelta network of degree *k* (although in the literature the term often refers only to networks of degree 2).

In packet-switching networks, when messages are sent from inputs to outputs, replies are often returned to the sender. We remark, in passing, that in a packet-switching network that has labels on both the input edges and the output edges, a message need not (initially) carry the sender address [8, 18]. Rather, this address can be created on the fly when the message is routed: whenever one digit from the 'forward' path descriptor is discarded, it is replaced by one digit that identifies the edge through which the message has arrived. When the message arrives at its destination, it carries a path descriptor for the reverse path to the sender; in a bidelta network this is the address of the sender.

Two bidelta networks are isomorphic if there is a label-preserving graph isomorphism between them (labels for both directions are preserved). Now we achieve at last our hope of having a functional description that defines a unique network[2]

---

[2] This theorem was independently proved by Dias [3], and by Kruskal and Snir [9].

Theorem 4.1. *Any two n-stage bidelta networks of degree k are isomorphic.*

Proof. The claim is trivial for $n = 1$. Assume it holds for $n - 1$, and let G and G' be two n-stage bidelta networks of degree k. As G^R and G'^R are bidelta networks, they both admit a decomposition of the form illustrated in Fig. 7, where G_i^R ($G_i'^R$), $i = 0, \ldots, k - 1$, are $(n - 1)$-stage delta networks of degree k, and each output of G_i (G_i') is connected to an output of G (G') in the last stage via an edge labelled at its head with i. Since G is a delta network, the k edges connected to the same output of G (G') have the same label at their tails. By Lemma 3.1, each network G_i, G_i' is a delta network. It follows that each of them is an $(n - 1)$-stage bidelta network, and therefore, all of them are isomorphic. The claim now follows. $\square$

The theorem can be extended to nonrectangular bidelta networks: for any tuple $\langle 0 = p_1, q_1, p_2, q_2, \ldots, p_{n-1}, q_{n-1}, p_n, q_n = 0 \rangle$ there exists, up to isomorphism, a unique bidelta network consisting of n stages of nodes, where nodes at stage i have indegree p_i and outdegree q_i. Thus, the functional properties of bidelta networks

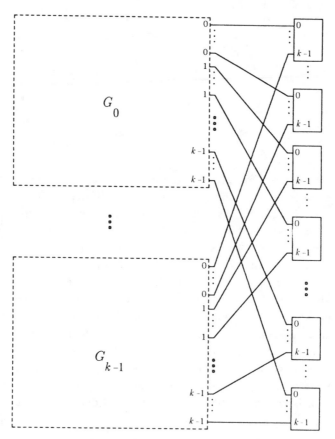

Fig. 7. Decomposition of reverse bidelta network.

uniquely determine the structure of such networks once the size of the network and the indegree and outdegree of the nodes at each stage are fixed.

5. Node numbering scheme

In bidelta networks, the path descriptors on both directions can be used to uniquely identify any node in the network. For each node s of G, denote by $\vec{\alpha}(s)$ the path descriptor of the paths connecting inputs to s, and denote by $\tilde{\alpha}(s)$ the path descriptor of the reverse paths connecting outputs to s. (We omit s when it can be inferred from the context.)

Lemma 5.1. *Let G be a bidelta network. Node $s = s'$ iff $\vec{\alpha}(s) = \vec{\alpha}(s')$ and $\tilde{\alpha}(s) = \tilde{\alpha}(s')$.*

Proof. Suppose $\vec{\alpha}(s) = \vec{\alpha}(s')$ and $\tilde{\alpha}(s) = \tilde{\alpha}(s')$. Let u and u' be inputs connected to s and s', respectively, and let v and v' be outputs connected to s and s', respectively. The path connecting u' to v has the same path descriptor as the path connecting u to v. This path descriptor starts with $\vec{\alpha}(s)$, which is also a descriptor for the path from u' to s'. The path from u' to v passes, therefore, through s'. A similar argument shows that the reverse path connecting v' to u passes through s'. Node u is connected to v by a path that passes through s', as well as by a path that passes through s (see Fig. 8). Thus, $s = s'$.

The converse implication is immediate. $\square$

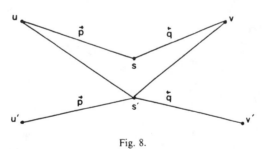

Fig. 8.

The last result implies that the following naming convention can be used to uniquely identify each node in a bidelta network G: associate with each node s of G an address $\alpha(s) = \vec{\alpha}(s)\tilde{\alpha}(s)$ obtained by concatenating the path descriptor of the paths connecting inputs to s and the path descriptor of the reverse paths connecting outputs to s. Note that this naming convention is consistent with the scheme previously introduced to label output (input) nodes. The naming scheme is precisely that which describes the structure of the *baseline network* [19]. It is illustrated in Fig. 9(a) for nodes with indegree and outdegree two.

There are five other (full labelled) networks that are known to be isomorphic to baseline networks. These are the reverse baseline networks [19], the omega networks [11], the flip networks [1], the modified data manipulators [5], and the indirect binary cube networks [14]. (See [12, 16, 19] for a proof of their isomorphism.)

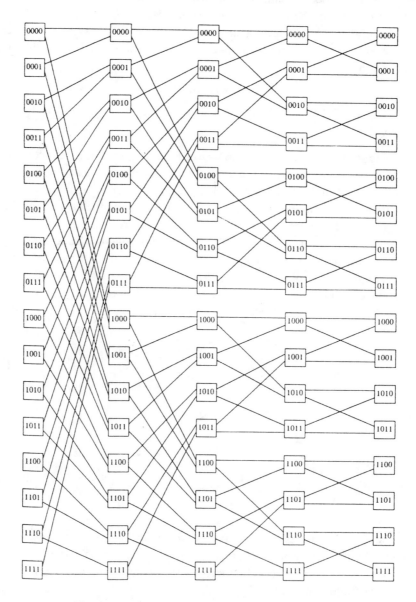

Fig. 9(a). Baseline network; forward path descriptor first.

It turns out that these networks are obtained by slightly varying the naming scheme that yields the baseline network: the two address parts may be exchanged, and each of them may be reversed (Figs. 9(b)–(f)). If a node s is connected to a node s' via an edge that has label δ at its tail and label ε at its head, then $\vec{\alpha}(s') = \vec{\alpha}(s)\delta$ and $\tilde{\alpha}(s) = \tilde{\alpha}(s')\varepsilon$.

(a) The baseline naming scheme associates to each switch the address $\vec{\alpha}\tilde{\alpha}$. Thus, in the baseline network, a node u at stage i with label $\alpha_1, \ldots, \alpha_{n-2}, \varepsilon$ is connected

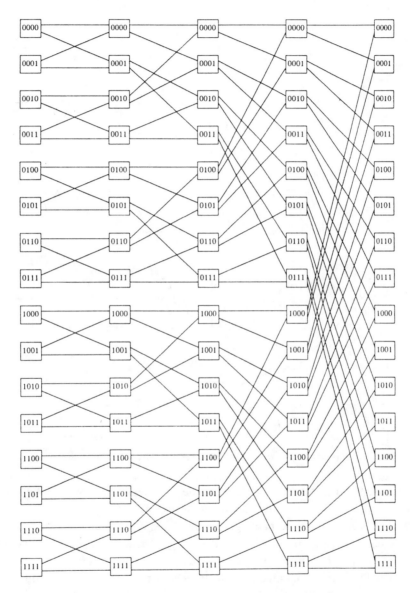

Fig. 9(b). Reverse baseline network; back path descriptor first.

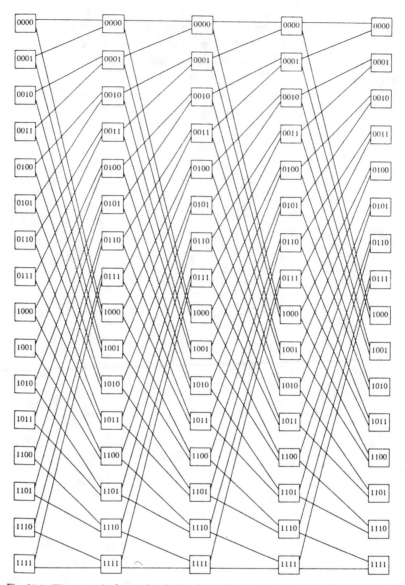

Fig. 9(c). Flip network; forward path descriptor first, forward path descriptor reversed.

via an edge with labels δ, ε to a node at stage $i+1$ with label $\alpha_1, \ldots, \alpha_{i-1}, \delta, \alpha_i, \ldots, \alpha_{n-2}$, for $\delta = 0, \ldots, \text{outdegree}(u) - 1$.

(b) The reverse baseline naming scheme associates to each switch the address $\tilde{\alpha}\vec{\alpha}$. Nodes at stage i with label $\alpha_1, \ldots, \alpha_{n-i-1}, \varepsilon, \alpha_{n-i+1}, \ldots, \alpha_{n-1}$, are connected to nodes at stage $i+1$ with labels $\alpha_1, \ldots, \alpha_{n-i-1}, \alpha_{n-i+1}, \ldots, \alpha_{n-1}, \delta$.

(c) The flip network naming scheme associates to each switch the address $\vec{\alpha}^R\tilde{\alpha}$. Nodes at stage i with labels $\alpha_1, \ldots, \alpha_{n-2}, \varepsilon$ are connected to nodes at stage $i+1$ with labels $\delta, \alpha_1, \ldots, \alpha_{n-2}$.

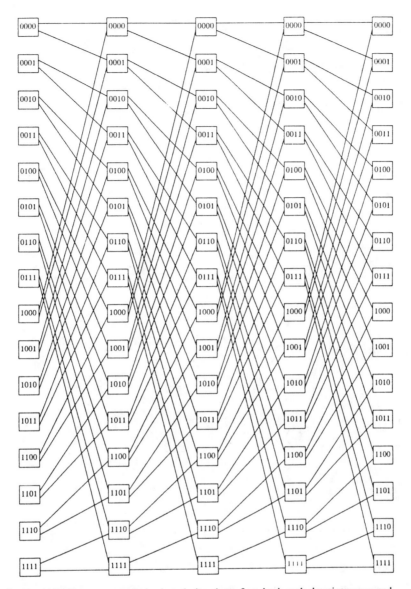

Fig. 9(d). Omega network; back path descriptor first, back path descriptor reversed.

(d) The omega network naming scheme associates to each switch the address $\bar{\alpha}^R \vec{\alpha}$. Nodes at stage i with labels to $\varepsilon, \alpha_2, \ldots, \alpha_{n-1}$ are connected with nodes at stage $i+1$ with labels $\alpha_2, \ldots, \alpha_{n-1}, \delta$.

(e) The modified data manipulator naming scheme associates to each switch the address $\vec{\alpha}\bar{\alpha}^R$. Nodes at stage i with label $\alpha_1, \ldots, \alpha_{i-1}, \varepsilon, \alpha_{i+1}, \ldots, \alpha_{n-1}$ are connected with nodes at stage $i+1$ with labels $\alpha_1, \ldots, \alpha_{i-1}, \delta, \alpha_{i+1}, \ldots, \alpha_{n-1}$.

(f) The indirect binary cube naming scheme associates to each switch the address $\bar{\alpha}\vec{\alpha}^R$. Nodes at stage i with labels $\alpha_1, \ldots, \alpha_{n-i-1}, \varepsilon, \alpha_{n-i+1}, \ldots, \alpha_{n-1}$ are connected to nodes at stage $i+1$ with labels $\alpha_1, \ldots, \alpha_{n-i-1}, \delta, \alpha_{n-i+1}, \ldots, \alpha_{n-1}$.

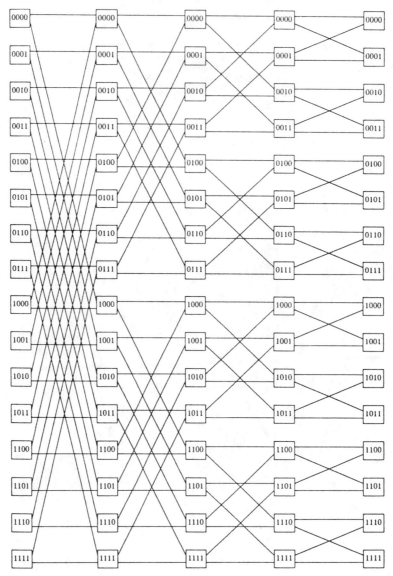

Fig. 9(e). Modified data manipulator network; forward path descriptor first, back path descriptor reversed.

These define the six networks mentioned in [12, 16, 19]. There are two additional networks of the same form, which, alas, remain nameless (Figs. 9(g) and (h)):

(g) If we associate with each switch the address $\vec{\alpha}^R \tilde{\alpha}^R$, then a node at stage i with label $\alpha_1, \ldots, \alpha_{i-1}, \varepsilon, \alpha_{i+1}, \ldots, \alpha_{n-1}$ is connected at stage $i+1$ to the nodes with labels $\delta, \alpha_1, \ldots, \alpha_{i-1}, \alpha_{i+1}, \ldots, \alpha_{n-1}$.

(h) Finally, if we associate with each switch the address $\tilde{\alpha}^R \vec{\alpha}^R$, then a node at stage i with address $\varepsilon, \alpha_2, \ldots, \alpha_{n-1}$ is connected at stage $i+1$ to the nodes with labels $\alpha_2, \ldots, \alpha_{n-i}, \delta, \alpha_{n-i+1}, \ldots, \alpha_{n-1}$.

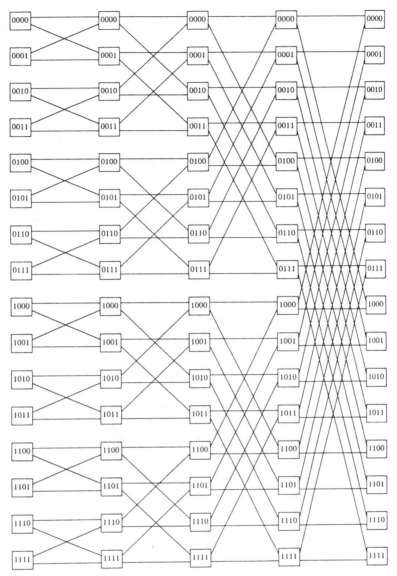

Fig. 9(f). Indirect binary cube network; back path descriptor first, forward path descriptor reversed.

While our Figs. 9(a)-(h) illustrate these eight networks for nodes with indegree and outdegree of two, the definitions are valid for arbitrary indegrees and outdegrees, and even for indegree and outdegree that varies from stage to stage. This immediately extends the definitions of the eight basic networks to arbitrary radix notation.

5.1. Circuit switching

The general node-numbering scheme allows us to uniformly derive the control mechanism for all eight networks when they are used for circuit switching. Given

39

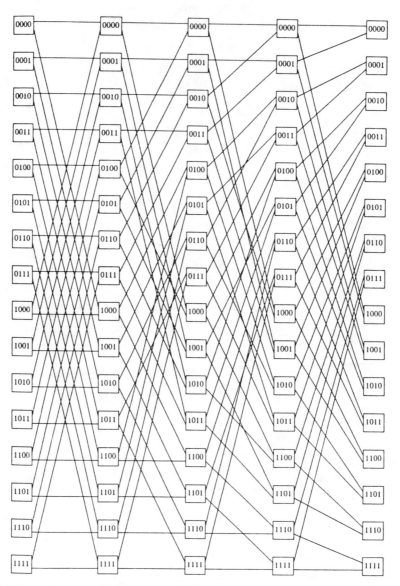

Fig. 9(g). Forward path descriptor first, forward path descriptor reversed, back path descriptor reversed.

a set of input-output connections, one has to determine if the connections do not conflict and, if so, to compute the setting of each switch. If a switch has indegree and outdegree two, then it has two states: 0 (straight) and 1 (cross).

It is convenient to assume that an n-stage network of degree 2 has 2^n input nodes of outdegree 1 and 2^n output nodes of indegree 1, which are not considered switches, and inbetween n stages of switches. This way, all of the switches on a path will be given a setting. Note that the input and output nodes must be appropriately numbered according to the numbering scheme.

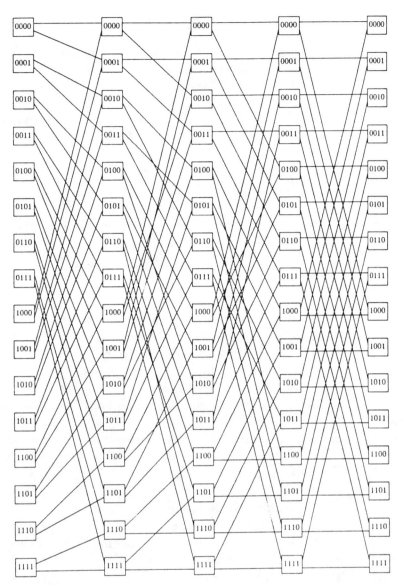

Fig. 9(h). Back path descriptor first, forward path descriptor reversed, back path descriptor reversed.

Suppose that input $\alpha_1, \ldots, \alpha_n$ is connected to output $\beta_1, \ldots, \beta_n$. At stage i, the path crosses the switch with forward path descriptor $\beta_1, \ldots, \beta_{i-1}$ and backward path descriptor $\alpha_1, \ldots, \alpha_{n-i+1}$; it enters the switch via the input labelled with α_{n-i+1} and leaves the switch via the output labelled β_i. If switches of indegree and outdegree 2 are used, then the switch control setting is $\alpha_{n-i+1} \oplus \beta_i$, where $\oplus$ is exclusive-OR.

This can now be used for deriving the control function for each of the previously described eight networks. In each case, a conflict occurs if an attempt is made to set a switch to two distinct states.

(a) Baseline network: at stage i, switch $\beta_1, \ldots, \beta_{i-1}, \alpha_1, \ldots, \alpha_{n-i}$ is set to $\alpha_{n-i+1} \oplus \beta_i$.

(b) Reverse baseline network: at stage i, switch $\alpha_1, \ldots, \alpha_{n-i}, \beta_1, \ldots, \beta_{i-1}$ is set to $\alpha_{n-i+1} \oplus \beta_i$.

(c) Flip network: at stage i, switch $\beta_{n-i+2}, \ldots, \beta_n, \alpha_1, \ldots, \alpha_{n-i}$ is set to $\alpha_{n-i+1} \oplus \beta_{n-i+1}$.

(d) Omega network: at stage i, switch $\alpha_{i+1}, \ldots, \alpha_n, \beta_1, \ldots, \beta_{i-1}$ is set to $\alpha_i \oplus \beta_i$.

(e) Modified data manipulator network: at stage i, switch $\beta_1, \ldots, \beta_{i-1}, \alpha_{i+1}, \ldots, \alpha_n$ is set to $\alpha_i \oplus \beta_i$.

(f) Indirect binary cube network: at stage i, switch $\alpha_1, \ldots, \alpha_{n-i}, \beta_{n-i+2}, \ldots, \beta_n$ is set to $\alpha_{n-i+1} \oplus \beta_{n-i+1}$.

(g) At stage i, switch $\beta_{n-i+2}, \ldots, \beta_n, \alpha_{i+1}, \ldots, \alpha_n$ is set to $\alpha_i \oplus \beta_{n-i+1}$.

(h) At stage i, switch $\alpha_{i+1}, \ldots, \alpha_n, \beta_{n-i+2}, \ldots, \beta_n$ is set to $\alpha_i \oplus \beta_{n-i+1}$.

6. Summary and conclusion

We have presented in this paper a geometrical theory of multistage interconnection networks. We considered labelling schemes for networks. A natural requirement on the labelling scheme, namely that routing be controlled by the successive digits of the address on both directions, was shown to enforce a unique geometry. In this respect, the isomorphism of the omega network, baseline network, flip network, etc., is no mere coincidence, but a result of the functional properties of these networks.

The labelling schemes for the six known bidelta networks and two new ones were derived in a simple, uniform manner. This immediately yielded the algorithms used to control these networks when circuit switching is used.

The following further result shows the close resemblance between delta networks and Benes networks: a network is a Benes network iff it consists of a rectangular delta network G of degree 2 followed by its reversal G^R, where each switch in the last stage of G is identified with the corresponding switch in the first stage of G^R. The proof immediately follows from the recursive characterization of delta networks and from the definition of Benes networks.

This unified theory can be further applied to simplify other results concerning similar interconnection networks, e.g., testing procedures. We hope that this paper will help to prevent the confusion created by the multiplication of notations in this area, and will prevent the duplication of results for these closely related networks.

References

[1] K.E. Batcher, The flip network in STARAN, *Proc. 1976 Internat. Conf. Parallel Processing*, Detroit, MI (1976) 65-71.

[2] L.N. Bhuyan and D.P. Agrawal, Design and performance of a general class of interconnection networks, *Proc. 1982 Internat. Conf. on Parallel Processing*, Columbus, OH, U.S.A.

[3] D.M. Dias, Packet communication in delta and related networks, Ph.D. Thesis, 1981, Rice University, Houston, TX, U.S.A.

[4] D.M. Dias and J.R. Jump, Packet switching interconnection networks for modular systems, *Computer* **14** (1981) 43-54.

[5] T.-Y. Feng, Data manipulating functions in parallel processors and their implementations, *IEEE Trans. Comput.* **C-23** (1974) 309-318.

[6] T.-Y. Feng, A survey of interconnection networks, *Computer* **14** (1981) 12-27.

[7] C.R. Goke and G.J. Lipovski, Banyan networks for partitioning multiprocessor systems, *1st Ann. Symp. on Computer Architecture*, Florida, U.S.A. (1973) 21-28.

[8] A. Gottlieb, R. Grishman, C.P. Kruskal, K.P. McAuliffe, L. Rudolph and M. Snir, The NYU Ultracomputer—designing an MIMD, Shared-Memory Parallel Machine, *IEEE Trans. Comput.* **C-32** (1983) 75-89.

[9] C.P. Kruskal and M. Snir, Some results on multistage interconnection networks for multiprocesors, *Proc. 1982 Conf. on Information Sciences and Systems*, Princeton University, 1982.

[10] C.P. Kruskal and M. Snir, Optimal interconnection networks for parallel processors: The importance of being square, in: Y. Yemini, ed., *Current Advances in Distributed Computing and Communications* (Computer Science Press, Rockville, MD, 1987); see also *Proc. 11th Ann. Internat. Symp. on Computer Architecture*, Ann Arbor, MI, U.S.A. (1984) 91-98.

[11] D.H. Lawrie, Access and alignment of data in an array processor, *IEEE Trans. Comput.* **C-24** (1975) 1145-1155.

[12] D.S. Parker, Jr., Notes on shuffle/exchange-type switching networks, *IEEE Trans. Comput.* **C-29** (1980) 213-222.

[13] J.A. Patel, Performance of processor-memory interconnections for multiprocessors, *IEEE Trans. Comput.* **C-30** (1981) 771-780.

[14] M.C. Pease, The indirect binary n-cube microprocessor array, *IEEE Trans. Comput.* **C-26** (1977) 458-473.

[15] H.J. Siegel, Interconnection networks for SIMD machines, *Computer* **12** (1979) 57-65.

[16] H.J. Siegel and S.D. Smith, Study of multistage SIMD interconnection networks, *Proc. 5th Ann. Symp. on Computer Architecture*, California, U.S.A. (1978) 223-229.

[17] J.J. Siegel, *Interconnection Networks for Large-Scale Parallel Processing: Theory and Case Studies* (Lexington Books, Lexington, MA, 1985).

[18] B.W. Weide, A flexible packet-switching chip and its applications, *Proc. 19th Allerton Conf. on Communication, Control, and Computing*, Urbana, IL, U.S.A. 1981.

[19] C.L. Wu and T-Y. Feng, On a class of multistage interconnection networks, *IEEE Trans. Comput.* **C-29** (1980) 694-702.

Orthogonal Graphs for the Construction
of a Class of Interconnection Networks

Isaac D. Scherson, *Member, IEEE*

Abstract—A graph theoretical representation for a class of interconnection networks is suggested. The idea is based on a definition of orthogonal binary vectors and leads to a construction rule for a class of orthogonal graphs. An orthogonal graph is first defined as a set of 2^m nodes, which in turn are linked by 2^{m-n} edges for every *link mode* defined in an integer set Q^*. The degree and diameter of an orthogonal graph are determined in terms of the parameters n, m, and the number of link modes defined in Q^*. Routing in orthogonal graphs is shown to reduce to the *node covering* problem in bipartite graphs. The proposed theory is applied to describe a number of well-known interconnection networks such as the binary m-cube and spanning-bus meshes. Multidimensional access (MDA) memories are also shown as examples of orthogonal shared memory multiprocessing systems. Finally, orthogonal graphs are applied to the construction of multistage interconnection networks. Connectivity and placement rules are given and shown to yield a number of well-known networks.

Index Terms—Hypercubes, multidimensional access memories, multistage interconnection networks, orthogonal graphs, orthogonal interconnection networks, routing.

I. INTRODUCTION

IN RECENT years, two research groups introduced a multiprocessing architecture in which p processors could gain conflict-free access to a $p \times p$ array of memory modules [6], [9], [48]. Access was defined by either rows or columns and hence the name orthogonal multiprocessor (OMP). The architecture was applied to a number of vector processing problems which were reported in detail in [16], [33], and [36]. Alnuweiri and Kumar called this architecture reduced mesh of trees (RMOT) and developed optimal algorithms for a number of applications including image processing and graph problems [1], [2]. A successful attempt was made by Hwang and Kim to generalize the concept for massively parallel computations [15]. In their paper, Hwang and Kim generalize OMP to higher dimensions and present a construction technique for the generation of radix r orthogonal systems. They show that such technique leads to generalized hypercubes as defined in [7].

The author of this paper was motivated by the same questions as Hwang and his group. Is the OMP a really novel architecture with applications to a wide variety of scientific problems? or is it a subset of some well-known class of systems? Furthermore, is OMP a feasible architecture given that it requires p^2 memory modules for p processors? and what is the generalized idea in the light of higher dimensional systems, say 3 or 4? In the search for the answers to these basic questions, the theory of orthogonal graphs was developed. Although still in its early stages, and with more and more questions arising as new results are discovered, it provides a thorough understanding of OMP

Manuscript received November 24, 1989; revised May 2, 1990. This work was supported in part by the Air Force Office of Scientific Research under Grant AFOSR-90-0144.

The author is with the Department of Information and Computer Science, University of California, Irvine, CA 92717.

IEEE Log Number 9040806.

and its generalizations to higher dimensional systems. In fact, it shows that an orthogonal multiprocessing system is actually defined by 2^n processors and 2^m memory modules which can be accessed in a number of different modes. Among other things, it is shown in this paper that OMP is a particular case of multidimensional access (MDA) memories like the one designed by Batcher for STARAN [4]. In turn, it will be seen that MDA memories are a subset of the hypercube interconnection rule [3].

Mapping orthogonal graphs as switching networks leads to the generation of multistage interconnection networks (MIN's). These networks have been widely studied and numerous papers have been published on this subject [17], [18], [45]. Some excellent studies address the topological properties and/or the permutational capabilities of these networks [30], [51]. The simplicity of the graph construction rule permits the description of well-known networks as well as the understanding of their differences and similarities.

The importance of the proposed description relies on the fact that hypercube-like machine equivalences are easily stated using the theory of orthogonal graphs. In this light, the relationship between the binary m-cube [40] (the functionally complete orthogonal architecture), and its subsets MDA and OMP becomes surprisingly clear.

For completeness, and to motivate the development of the orthogonal graph construction rule, let us briefly review the basic characteristics of OMP. Recall that in OMP, p processors, P_k, can access p^2 memory modules M_{ij} by either rows or columns. The access rule is given by

$$P_k \text{ accesses } M_{ij} \begin{cases} \text{by rows if} & k = i \quad \forall j \\ \text{by columns if} & k = j \quad \forall i. \end{cases}$$

An obvious generalization of this concept would be to organize the memory modules in a higher dimensional array and define the access rule by equating the processor index to either one of the indexes of memory modules. Thus, the number of access modes defined is the same as the number of indexes used to identify memory modules. The main disadvantage of this approach is that the interconnection network becomes extremely complex as processors need to connect to modules organized in a higher dimensional Euclidean structure.

The problem can be simplified by associating just one index with each memory module. Consider the two-dimensional case above. Let us denote by x the n-bit binary expansion of the processor index and let

$$y = 2^n \sum_{l=0}^{n-1} i_l + \sum_{l=0}^{n-1} j_l$$

be the $2n$-bit binary concatenation of the memory index pair ij. OMP's access rule can now be recast in terms of the indexes x and y as follows:

$$P_x \text{ accesses } M_y \begin{cases} \text{by rows if} & \sum_{l=0}^{n-1} x_l \oplus y_{l+n} = 0 \\ \text{by columns if} & \sum_{l=0}^{n-1} x_l \oplus y_l = 0 \end{cases}$$

where $\oplus$ stands for the Boolean Exclusive-OR and Σ is the standard integer sum. A generalization of this access rule can now be given. Rather than assuming that the memory indexes are $2n$ bits long for n-bit processor indexes, assume that memory indexes are defined with m bits for some integer $m > n$. Let q be some integer in the interval $[0, m-1]$, the generalized *orthogonal access rule* is now given by

P_x accesses M_y in access mode q

$$\Leftrightarrow \sum_{l=0}^{n-1} x_l \oplus y_{(l+q) \bmod m} = 0.$$

Because the above expression is reminiscent of the inner product of vectors whose coordinates are 0 or 1, and the inner product is equated to 0 for the access rule, we shall refer to them as *orthogonal binary vectors*. In Section II, a class of orthogonal graphs, whose definition is based on the formal definition of inner product and orthogonality of binary vectors, will be given. The graphs are characterized by providing expressions for their degree and diameter. A theorem is given to single out those graphs in which a path is guaranteed to exist between any pair of nodes and the routing problem is discussed. Orthogonal graphs are then used to define either MIMD or SIMD arrays of loosely or tightly coupled parallel processing systems.

In Section V, orthogonal graphs are used to generate multistage interconnection networks. Well-known networks such as the generalized cube, the SW-banyan, and the baseline network, among others, are shown to fall within the framework of the theory of orthogonal graphs.

II. Orthogonal Graphs

The concept of orthogonal interconnection networks is based on the definition of inner product and the orthogonality of binary vectors. A number of basic concepts needs to be introduced before formal definitions are given. We start by defining two operations on sets of binary vectors. Properties of these operations lead to the definition of a set as a linear span of some basis. Most of the ideas presented in the following paragraphs are known from set theory and Boolean algebra. They are given here for completeness and to establish the nomenclature and notation used in the remainder of this work.

Let Y_m be the set of all binary vectors of length m and let $Q = \{0, \cdots, m-1\}$ be an ordered set. Define the operations $\oplus$ and $\bullet$ on Y_m as follows:

$\oplus : Y_m \times Y_m \rightarrow Y_m,$

$\quad \forall\, y, y' \in Y_m, y \oplus y' = (y_{m-1} \oplus y'_{m-1}, \cdots, y_0 \oplus y'_0)$

$\bullet : Q \times Y_m \rightarrow Y_m, \quad \forall\, q \in Q,$

$\quad \forall\, y \in Y_m, q \bullet y = y', y'_i = y_{(i-q) \bmod m}.$

$\oplus$ is the bitwise Boolean Exclusive OR operation while $\bullet$ is a left cyclic shift of the vector y by the number of bit positions given by the integer q. It is obvious that the set Y_m is an abelian group with respect to $\oplus$. The operation $\bullet$ satisfies the following two properties.

- $\square$ $\exists\, 0 \in Q$ such that $\forall\, y \in Y_m, \quad 0 \bullet y = y$
- $\square$ $\forall\, q \in Q$ and $\forall\, y_1, y_2 \in Y_m, q \bullet (y_1 \oplus y_2) = q \bullet y_1$
  $\oplus\, q \bullet y_2.$

These properties allow the description of the set Y_m as a *linear span* of certain sets $B_m \subseteq Y_m$. The idea is to write every vector in Y_m as the Exclusive OR of elements in B_m shifted cyclically by a

number of bit positions given by coefficients $q_i \in Q$. The obvious basis that spans the set Y_m is $B_m = \{(000 \ldots 01)\}$. In this basis, the coordinates of vector $y \in Y_m$ become $\{q_l \mid 0 \leq l \leq m-1\}$ such that for every bit $y_i = 1$ we define a $q_l = i$. Writing the vector y in terms of its *coordinates* with respect to the basis $\{(000 \ldots 01)\}$ is just a matter of stating which bit positions contain a 1. The only exception is the vector $0 = 00 \ldots 0$ whose coordinates are $\{0, 0\}$. As a simple example, consider Y_4, with $Q = \{0, 1, 2, 3\}$, which is a linear span of $B_4 = \{(0001)\}$. The vector (0110) can be expressed as

$$(0110) = 1 \bullet (0001) \oplus 2 \bullet (0001).$$

With respect to the basis $B_4 = \{(0001)\}$, the vector (0110) has coordinates $\{1, 2\}$. It is important to note that if $y = \{q_l\}$ and $y' = \{q'_l\}$, the bitwise Exclusive OR of the two vectors has coordinates

$$(\{q_l\} \cup \{q'_l\}) - (\{q_l\} \cap \{q'_l\}).$$

To define the operation $\bullet$ in terms of coordinates, we use integer addition modulo m as follows:

$\forall\, y = \{q_l\} \in Y_m,$

$\quad \forall\, q \in Q, q \bullet y = \{(q + q_l) \bmod m\}, 0 \leq l \leq m-1.$

It is clear that any m-bit vector which contains a single 1-bit in any bit position is a basis for the set Y_m. We shall refer to these elements as *atomic vectors*. With respect to the atom $(00 \ldots 01)$, coordinates can be thought of as the *minterm* description of the Boolean function y. We shall use these ideas later on in this section to discuss the routing problem in orthogonal graphs.

Consider now an element $z_n \in Y_m$ such that, for some integer $n < m$

$$z_i = \begin{cases} 1 & \text{if } 0 \leq i \leq n-1 \\ 0 & \text{otherwise.} \end{cases}$$

The formal definition of *inner product mode q* and the *orthogonality* of binary vectors is akin to the inner product of vectors in a Cartesian vector space.

Definition 1: The *inner product mode q* of vectors y and $y' \in Y_m$ is a mapping $\star_q$ from $Y_m \times Y_m$ onto the set $\{0, 1, 2, \cdots, n\} \subseteq Q$ such that

$$y \star_q y' = |(y \oplus y') \wedge (q \bullet z_n)| = \sum_{i=q}^{(q+n-1) \bmod m} y_i \oplus y'_i$$

where $\wedge$ stands for the bitwise Boolean AND and Σ is the standard integer sum.

Definition 2: Two vectors y and $y' \in Y_m$ are said to be *orthogonal mode q* if and only if $y \star_q y' = 0$. We denote this symbolically as $y \perp_q y'$.

The element z_n is a mask which allows us to extract a subset $Y_n \subset Y_m$ such that

$$Y_n = \{y_n \mid y_n = y \wedge z_n, \quad \forall\, y \in Y_m\}$$

where $\wedge$ stands for the bitwise Boolean AND.

Let X_n be the set of all binary vectors of length n. A cast operation is defined to map elements $x \in X_n$ as elements of $Y_n \subset Y_m$ such that cast(x) is the m-bit vector $0 \ldots 0 x_{n-1} \ldots x_0$. Because cast$(X_n) \subset Y_m$, an inner product and orthogonality between n-bit and m-bit vectors can also be introduced. We shall

45

say that two vectors x and y are orthogonal mode q if and only if

$$q \bullet \text{cast}(x) \perp_q y \Leftrightarrow \sum_{i=0}^{n-1} x_i \oplus y_{(i+q)\bmod m} = 0.$$

This is the same generalized OMP access rule given in the Introduction.

Based on these concepts, we formally introduce a class of graphs whose construction rule is the orthogonality of binary vectors.

Definition 3: An orthogonal graph $G(n, m, Q*)$, where $Q* \subseteq Q$, is an undirected graph with 2^m nodes. A link (edge) exists between two distinct nodes y and y' if and only if there exists a $q \in Q*$ such that $y \perp_q y'$.

Fig. 1 illustrates an 8-node and a 16-node orthogonal graph. Let an edge be denoted by the pair of nodes it links. The set of $2^{m-n} - 1$ edges defined for every node y and for every mode $q \in Q*$ is then given by

$$E_q = \{(y, y_i) \mid y_i \perp_q y \quad \forall i = 0, \cdots, 2^{m-n} - 1\}.$$

This set E_q will be labeled with the pair (x, q) where $\text{cast}(x) = (m - q) \bullet (y \wedge (q \bullet z_n))$.

It is clear that an orthogonal graph as defined above is a *regular* graph. To determine its degree, we need to give an expression which defines the number of neighbors for every node in the graph. By definition, for every $q \in Q*$, a cluster of $2^{m-n} - 1$ neighbors is defined for any node y. Let $N(q)$ be the number of nearest neighbors linked under mode q (the number of elements in E_q) and let $N(q_1, q_2, \cdots)$ be the number of neighbors in common defined under modes $q_1, q_2 \cdots$ (the number of elements in $E_{q1} \cap E_{q2} \cap \cdots$). The principle of inclusion and exclusion is used to enumerate the total number of neighbors for a given node.

Theorem 1 (Degree): The degree of a graph $G(n, m, Q*)$ is given by

$$\begin{aligned} d = \; & N(q_1) + N(q_2) + \cdots + N(q_{\#Q*}) \\ & - N(q_1, q_2) - N(q_1, q_3) - \cdots - N(q_{\#Q*-1}, q_{\#Q*}) + \cdots \\ & + (-1)^{\#Q*-1} N(q_1, q_2, \cdots, q_{\#Q*}) \end{aligned}$$

where $\#Q*$ denotes the cardinality of $Q*$.

Proof: Follows from the principle of inclusion and exclusion. □

The number of elements $N(q_1, q_2, \cdots)$ is easily computed as $N(q_1, q_2, \cdots) = 2^t - 1$ where $t = m - |(q_1 \bullet z_n) \vee (q_2 \bullet z_n) \vee \cdots|$, and $\vee$ stands for the bitwise Boolean OR. Note that if $\forall q_i, q_j \in Q*(i \neq j), q_i \bullet z_n \vee q_j \bullet z_n = 1$, then $N(q_1, q_2, \cdots) = 0$. We shall say that $Q*$ is a *set of disjoint modes*. An interesting result arises for graphs defined with a set $Q*$ of disjoint modes.

Corollary 1: The degree of an orthogonal graph $G(n, m, Q*)$ such that $Q*$ is a set of disjoint modes is given by

$$d = (2^{m-n} - 1) \times \#Q*.$$

Proof: Follows by direct substitution of the values of $N(q_1, \cdots)$ in Theorem 1. □

In addition to the degree d of a graph, it is also important to determine its diameter k. Recall that the distance between nodes of a graph is the minimum number of edges traversed to go from a source to a destination node. In the case of orthogonal graphs, a path between any pair of nodes is a sequence of nodes $\{y_p\}$ such that

$$\forall y_p, y_{p+1}, \quad \exists q_p \in Q* \text{ such that } y_p \perp_{q_p} y_{p+1}.$$

Clearly, the existence of a path between two nodes depends on n and on the available values of $q \in Q*$. The following theorem guarantees the existence of a path between any two nodes in an orthogonal graph (i.e., the graph is connected).

Theorem 2 (Connectivity): An orthogonal graph $G(n, m, Q*)$, where $Q* = \{q_0, q_1, \cdots, q_l\}$, $l < m$, is connected if and only if $q_0 \bullet z_n \wedge q_1 \bullet z_n \cdots \wedge q_l \bullet z_n = 0$.

Proof: From any source node, only the $m - n$ contiguous bit positions given by 0's in $q \bullet z_n$ can be altered under mode q. To guarantee a path between any two nodes, the maximum Hamming distance m needs to be *covered*. That is, for any bit position i, $0 \leq i \leq m - 1$, there must exist a $q \in Q*$ such that the ith bit of $q \bullet z_n$ is 0. The theorem follows. □

If $G(n, m, Q*)$ is connected, $Q*$ will be called a *complete set of modes*.

The proof above tells us that we could change at most $m - n$ contiguous bits between two consecutive nodes in the path from y to y'. In other words, given any source label y, to reach a destination label y' we need to compute the bit positions in which source and destination differ and modify the bits of the source in groups of at most $m - n$ contiguous bits. This routing problem can be stated in terms of mask coverage by means of a bipartite graph shown in Fig. 2. The nodes on the left correspond to the m bits of node labels while the nodes on the right represent the modes in $Q*$ (q-nodes). The top bipartite graph shows the coverage defined by every mask $q \bullet z_n$. The routing problem reduces then to finding a set of q-nodes whose edges cover all 1-bits in $y \oplus y'$. An example is given in the bottom graph of Fig. 2. The *coordinates* of $y \oplus y'$ are circled on the left and possible coverage sets are indicated. Note that the solution is not unique, as shown by different sets of *routing masks*. Also, there is no predefined order in which routing masks need to be applied.

A better understanding of the complexity of this problem can be gained by using the concept of *coordinates* with respect to the atomic vector $(000 \ldots 001)$ introduced earlier. Let $y \oplus y' = \{q_l\}$ and consider a connected orthogonal graph $G(n, m, Q*)$. A bipartite graph can be built such that the nodes on the left are labeled with the coordinates $\{q_l\}$ while the nodes on the right are all q's in $Q*$. A coverage set can be found in linear time by scanning the left nodes from top to bottom. However, such coverage is not unique and does not necessarily lead to a shortest path. This general problem of finding a minimal coverage set is the same as the one of minimization of Boolean functions [24], [31], [32]. Think of coordinates of $y \oplus y' = \{q_l\}$ as minterms and masks $q \bullet z_n$ as prime implicants. This procedure then results in the determination of the minimum number of prime implicants which cover all minterms $\{q_l\}$. It is well known that such a procedure requires an exhaustive search in the worst case.

Continuing the analogy with Boolean minimization, if some bit position 0 through $m - 1$ is covered by one and only one $q \in Q*$, we shall refer to that q as an *essential mode*. If $Q*$ is a set of disjoint modes, all q's are essential and scanning coordinates to determine coverage yields a unique solution which defines also a shortest path. A case like this is exemplified in Fig. 3. In the next section, it is shown that an orthogonal graph, such that $m - n = 1$, and $Q*$ is a complete set of disjoint modes, defines the well-known binary m-cube. The scanning procedure outlined above is the standard routing mechanism used in hypercube machines.

To provide full coverage of the maximum Hamming distance between any two nodes in the graph, it is enough to define the set $Q*$ such that every mask $q \bullet z_n$ covers a distinct set of bits. That is, all q's in $Q*$ are essential but not necessarily disjoint.

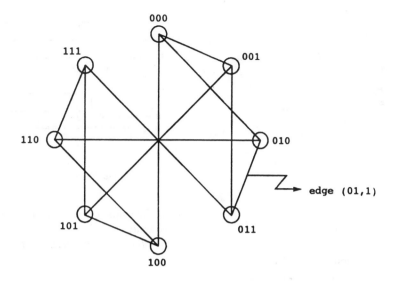

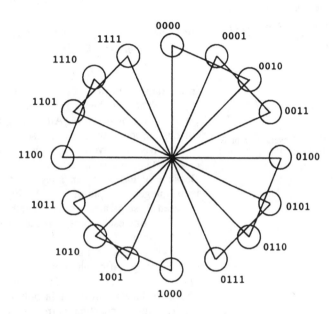

Fig. 1. Top: The graph of $(2, 3, \{0, 1, 2\})$. Bottom: The graph of $(3, 4, \{0, 2\})$.

The following theorem provides an upper and lower bound on sets of modes such that all modes are essential.

Theorem 3: Let $G(n, m, Q*)$ be a connected orthogonal graph such that each mode in $Q*$ uniquely covers at least one bit position 0 through $m - 1$. The cardinality of $Q*$ is k such that

$$\left\lceil \frac{m}{m-n} \right\rceil \le k \le 2 \left\lfloor \frac{m}{m-n+1} \right\rfloor + \left\lfloor \frac{m \bmod (m-n+1)}{m-n} \right\rfloor.$$

Proof: The lower bound $\lceil m/(m-n) \rceil$ is obvious. For the upper bound, because each member of $Q*$ must uniquely cover at least one bit position 0 through $m - 1$, no bit position can be covered by more than two q's. In the worst case, to construct $Q*$, in each group of $m - n + 1$ bits we can place two q's. Hence, the first term $2\lfloor m/(m-n+1) \rfloor$. After choosing the above coverage, exactly $m - n$ or fewer bits remain to be covered. When 0 bits remain, $Q*$ is a maximum. If $m - n$ bits remain, only one q can be added for connectivity. When 1 to $m - n - 1$ bits remain, elements in $Q*$ can be rearranged to cover all bits. Hence, zero or one additional q needs to be added. □

For a connected graph with a disjoint set of modes, the minimum number of modes needed to guarantee full coverage is $k = m/(m-n)$. k in Theorem 3 above shows the minimum number of q's in $Q*$ which allows the definition of a path between any two nodes of an orthogonal graph. For each q, we may alter at most $m - n$ bits of the current source node in the path sequence. Because the Hamming distance between two node labels is at most m, k in Theorem 3 is the diameter of $G(n, m, Q*)$.

In this section, the definition and characterization of orthogonal graphs has been presented. There are a number of open questions which are still to be addressed. For the remainder of this paper, only the case of connected orthogonal graphs with a disjoint set of modes will be further studied. These graphs are called omega graphs and are introduced formally in the next section.

III. THE CLASS OF OMEGA GRAPHS

The generation of connected orthogonal graphs with disjoint sets of modes requires that we choose m and n such that m is an

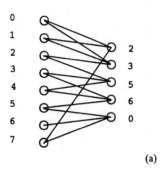

(a)

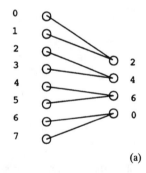

Routing masks 1 = (3,2)

Routing masks 2 = (3,0)

Routing masks 3 = (2,3)

Routing masks 4 = (2,5)

(b)

Fig. 2. The routing problem in an orthogonal graph. (a) Coverage graph for $(5, 8, \{0, 2, 3, 4, 6\})$ (b) Routing graph for path from 01101011 to 1110100.

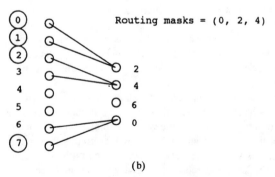

(a)

Routing masks = (0, 2, 4)

(b)

Fig. 3. Routing in an orthogonal graph with a set of disjoint modes. (a) Coverage graph for $(6, 8, \{0, 2, 4, 6\})$. (b) Routing graph for path from 01101011 to 11101100.

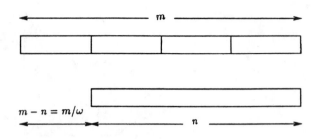

Fig. 4. The relation between m, n, and ω.

integer multiple of $m - n$ and $Q*$ contains modes spaced $m - n$ units apart.

Definition 4: An omega graph is a graph $G(n, m, Q*)$ such that

$$m = \omega(m - n) \Leftrightarrow m = \frac{\omega n}{\omega - 1}$$

for some integer $\omega \geq 2$, and an ordered set of integers $Q* \subseteq Q$ such that $\forall\ q_{i+1}, q_i \in Q*,\ (q_{i+1} - q_i) \bmod m = m - n$ and $\#Q* = \omega$.

The choice of $Q*$ is not unique. By setting q_0 to some value in the range 0 to $m - n - 1$, the remaining modes are uniquely defined. There is then a family of $m - n$ graphs defined for a given choice of *n* and *m*. All these graphs are isomorphic and, for our purposes, we shall choose $Q*$ such that $q_0 = 0$.

It is trivial to verify that the diameter of these graphs is $\omega = \#Q*$. We shall denote an omega graph by $\omega G(n, m)$. Because *m* has to be an integer, either $\omega = 2$ for all *n* or *n* is an integer multiple of $(\omega - 1)$. Fig. 4 shows the relationship between these parameters. The length *m* is divided into ω groups of $m - n$ bits each. Thus, *n* is the length of *m* minus the length of one group.

As a first important example of an ω-graph, consider the case of the orthogonal graph $G(n, m, Q*)$ such that $m - n = 1$ and $Q* = \{0, 1, \cdots, m - 1\}$. This is an ω-graph $mG(m - 1, m)$. The node labels will differ in only one bit position ($m - n = 1$). The interconnection corresponds to a structure in which nearest neighbors are logically adjacent and every node has *m* nearest neighbors. Such is the case of the binary *m*-cube connection, also known as the hypercube [40]. For the hypercube shown in Fig. 5 ($m = 4$, $n = 3$), edges that correspond to different link modes (q) are indeed orthogonal. The top graph in Fig. 1 is also a binary hypercube.

In Fig. 6, the graph $2G(2, 4)$ is shown. It is a 16-node hypercube with full connections on the parallel horizontal faces of the external and internal 3-cubes. Those faces are linked by full connections on the diagonal planes. To better understand this topology, consider a fully connected face as a set of nodes linked by a single *spanning bus*. Each face collapsed into a spanning bus will be labeled (x, q) where *x* is orthogonal mode *q* to all node labels in the face. Such a transformation is illustrated in Fig. 7 and the resulting spanning bus graph is shown in Fig. 8. This graph is the loosely coupled equivalent of the shared memory OMP suggested in [16], [33], and [36]. Fig. 9 shows the ω-graph $3G(4, 6)$.

Referring again to Fig. 4, another way to look at ω-graphs is to label nodes with m/ω indexes, which range from 0 to $2^{m-n} - 1$, and define spanning buses which connect all nodes with the same contiguous $\omega - 1$ indexes. The resulting interconnection is a Cartesian array of $2^{m-n} \times 2^{m-n} \times 2^{m-n} \cdots$ nodes of dimension ω.

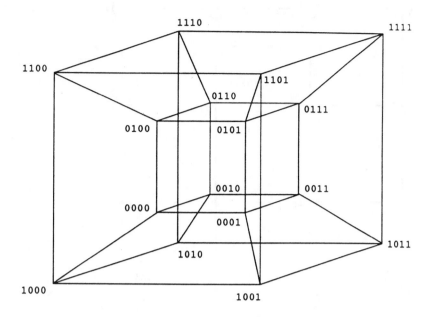

Fig. 5.　The graph of $4G(3,4)$.

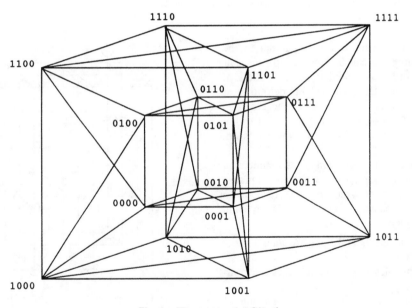

Fig. 6.　The graph of $2G(2,4)$.

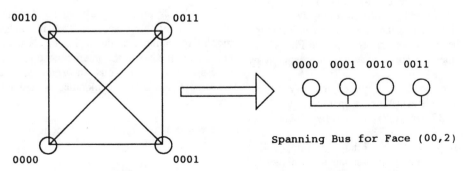

Spanning Bus for Face (00,2)

Fig. 7.　Transformation of a fully connected face into a spanning bus.

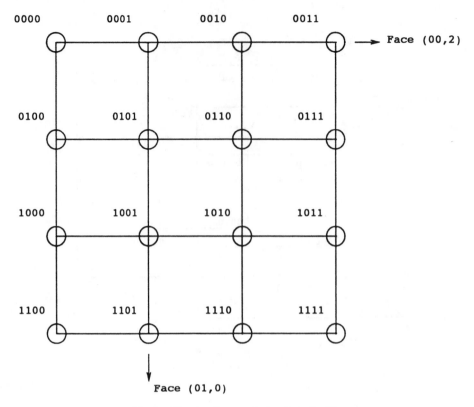

0000   0001   0010   0011

                                      → Face (00,2)

0100   0101   0110   0111

1000   1001   1010   1011

1100   1101   1110   1111

Face (01,0)

Fig. 8. Spanning bus graph for $(2, 4, \{0, 2\})$.

Spanning buses are defined in every direction parallel to the Cartesian axes. Each spanning bus can be labeled with the pair (x, q) where $x \in X_n$ is orthogonal mode q to the labels of the nodes connected by the bus. Observe that this definition of ω-graphs leads to the generalization of the OMP access rule. Hwang and his group [16] discovered this same idea but generalized it to indexes in a range 0 to $r - 1$, where r is not necessarily a power of 2.

The application of ω-graphs to the definition of interconnection networks for parallel processing structures now becomes a matter of mapping nodes and links of the graph onto corresponding computing devices and interconnection elements. Three main cases can be identified, namely:

1) Nodes are computing elements and links are interconnection wires.
2) Nodes are memory modules and spanning buses are computing element buses.
3) Spanning buses correspond to switching boxes capable of permuting their 2^{m-n} inputs (nodes on the bus).

The first case above is a direct mapping of an orthogonal graph to the definition of a loosely coupled multiprocessing system. The main example of such a system is the binary m-cube. Spanning bus hypermeshes are the next extension as shown in Figs. 8 and 9. Generalized hypercubes [7] are also ω-graphs as shown by Hwang and Kim [16].

The second class corresponds to a shared memory system in which each processing element owns a spanning bus. Such a case is discussed in [37] and [38] and briefly reviewed in Section IV.

The third class corresponds to the orthogonal rule applied to the definition of multistage interconnection networks. Such a case deserves close attention and is discussed in Section V.

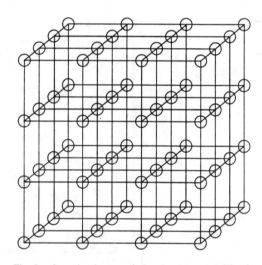

Fig. 9. Spanning bus graph for the ω-graph $3G(4, 6)$

IV. ORTHOGONAL SHARED MEMORY MULTIPROCESSORS

Consider 2^n processing elements (P_x) and 2^m memory modules (M_y). In this case, we associate nodes of an orthogonal graph with memory modules. The edges are associated with processing elements and the interconnection is defined for different access modes in $Q*$. Thus, an *orthogonal interconnect* between processors and memory modules is defined by the following access rule,

P_x has access to M_y, in access mode q,

if and only if $x \perp_q y$.

Think of edges in the orthogonal graph as buses of processing elements (spanning bus) which span each direction of the array

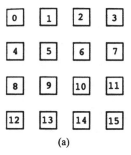

(a)

(b)   (c)

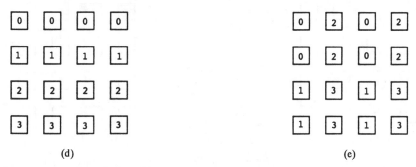

(d)   (e)

Fig. 10. A multidimensional access memory $(2, 4, \{0, 1, 2, 3\})$. (a) Labeling of 4×4 array of memory modules. (b) $q = 0$. (c) $q = 1$. (d) $q = 2$. (e) $q = 3$.

of memory modules for each *access mode* $q \in Q*$. Hence, an orthogonal shared-memory architecture will be given by a triplet $(n, m, Q*)$ where the set $Q* \subseteq Q$ is an ordered set which contains admissible values of q. For each value of $q \in Q*$ an access mode is defined.

As a typical example of a shared memory architecture, consider the multidimensional-access (MDA) memory designed by Batcher for the STARAN associative computer [4]. Recall that an MDA memory allows 2^n processors to access a $2^n \times 2^n$ array of memory cells by rows, columns, or stencils (2^{n-k} cells every 2^k rows). In terms of orthogonal graphs, an MDA memory is defined by the triplet $(n, 2n, \{0, 1, \cdots, 2n - 1\})$. For $q = 0$, all modules in a column can be accessed by a processor. For $q = n$, processors can access all modules in a row. Intermediate values of q define stencils. Fig. 10 shows an MDA with 4 processors and 16 memory modules, that is, a system $(2, 4, \{0, 1, 2, 3\})$. For access mode 0, conflict-free access is by columns of the 4×4 array of memory modules, while for access mode 2, the access

is by rows. This is the OMP architecture given in [48], [16], [9], [33], and [36]. OMP is thus a particular case of an MDA given by the triplet $(n, 2n, \{0, n\})$, which defines only two access modes, namely by rows or by columns.

The OMP is the minimum ω-graph which is a subset of STARAN's MDA. It provides only two access modes as opposed to $2n$ for Batcher's MDA. Seemingly, such an enhanced OMP should be capable of additional computational capabilities. However, the additional access modes do not add to speed up the running time of applications on the OMP. Alnuweiri and Kumar have shown optimal techniques to perform permutations on their RMOT [1]. Thus, a system $(n, 2n, \{0, n\})$ will perform as well as a system $(n, 2n, \{0, 1, \cdots, 2n - 1\})$. Their results confirm the performance analysis presented in [36] for OMP running parallel unrestricted algorithms. Optimal and near-optimal sorting algorithms for OMP can be found in [35].

In Fig. 11, an MDA $(3, 4, \{0, 1, 2, 3\})$ is illustrated. It shows how the original MDA proposed by Batcher can be generalized

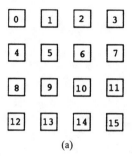

(a)

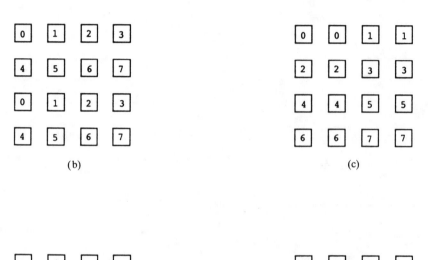

(b)   (c)

(d)   (e)

Fig. 11. A multidimensional access memory $(3, 4, \{0, 1. 2, 3\})$. (a) Labeling of 4×4 array of memory modules. (b) $q = 0$. (c) $q = 1$. (d) $q = 2$. (e) $q = 3$.

to include the cases other than the n-PE structure accessing an $n \times n$ array of storage cells. This architecture is one in which nodes of a binary m-cube correspond to memory modules while the links are processing elements which can access the memories in orthogonal directions depending upon the access mode q. This is an important result because it reiterates the well-known fact that *an MDA is a particular case of the hypercube* (which also contains the OMP). Fig. 11 depicts the hypercube interconnect applied to a shared memory system.

It is interesting to further analyze Batcher's MDA in light of the fact that it corresponds to the general orthogonal graph $G(n, 2n, \{0, 1, \cdots, 2n - 1\})$. It can easily be seen that for $q \in [0, n - 1]$, processors gain access to 2^q memory modules every 2^q rows of the $2^n \times 2^n$ array. For $q \in [n, 2n - 1]$, the same result applies to the columns of the memory array. Therefore, the following lemma is derived and illustrated in Fig. 12.

Lemma 1 (MDA Access): Multidimensional access memories, defined by $(n, 2n, \{0, 1, \cdots, 2n - 1\})$ are accessed along columns such that each processor connects to 2^q memory elements

every 2^q rows for all $q \in [0, n - 1]$. For $q' \in [n, 2n - 1]$, the access pattern is the transpose of access mode q if and only if $q' = q \bmod n$.

V. ORTHOGONAL MULTISTAGE INTERCONNECTION NETWORKS

Multistage interconnection networks have been widely studied and reported in the technical literature [17], [18], [45]. Some excellent studies address the topological properties and also permutational capabilities of these networks [30], [51]. At the end of Section III, it was suggested that ω-graphs could be mapped into switching networks by replacing every spanning bus by a $2^{m-n} \times 2^{m-n}$ switch capable of permuting the nodes on the bus. Let us illustrate the application of the theory of orthogonal graphs to the construction of multistage interconnection networks by means of example. Consider the orthogonal ω-graph $(3, 4, \{0, 1, 2, 3\}) = 4G(3, 4)$ which has been shown to correspond to the binary 4-cube (Fig. 5). Recall that each $q \in Q*$ defines all parallel links in a single given direction.

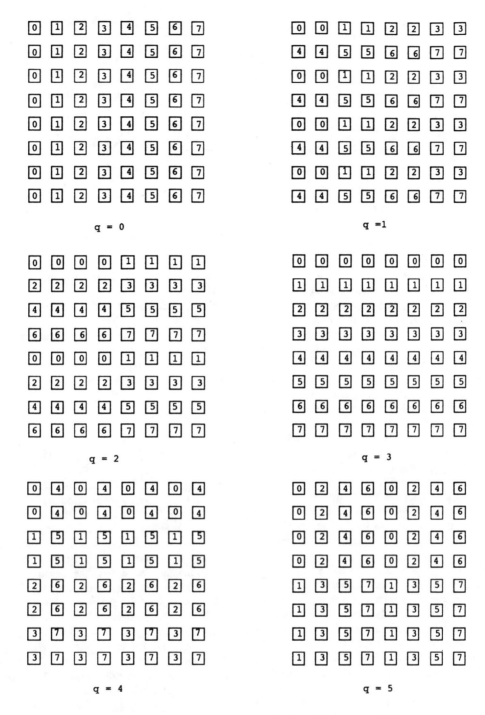

Fig. 12. A multidimensional access memory $(3, 6, \{0, 1, 2, 3, 4, 5\})$

Let us associate a $2^{m-n} \times 2^{m-n}$ switch with every link defined for a direction $q_s \in Q*$. In the particular case of the binary 4-cube, sets of $2^3 = 8$ 2×2 switches will be associated with each one of the directions $\{0, 1, 2, 3\}$ (not necessarily in that order). Thus, for each $q_s \in Q*$ we define one stage of an OMIN as a set of switches labeled x. A connection exists between an input labeled y and a switch if and only if $q_s \bullet \text{cast}(x) \perp_{q_s} y$. Fig. 13 shows a 2×2 switch for $m - n = 1$ and a 4×4 switch for $m - n = 2$.

To label each input to a switch x, we define a set of m-bit binary vectors

$$B_{m-n} = \{b_{m-n} \mid b_{m-n} = 00 \ldots 0x..xx\}$$

where $x..xx$ stands for any $m - n$ bit string. Hence, the labeling scheme used in Fig. 13. Note that, for labeling purposes, it is assumed that the switch performs an identity permutation and outputs are labeled the same as their corresponding inputs. We shall also use an m-bit mask z_{m-n} (akin to z_n) such that only the $m - n$ least significant bits are 1. We do this for convenience as $z_{m-n} = (m - n) \bullet \bar{z}_n$, where $\bar{z}_n$ is the bitwise complement of z_n.

When defining one stage for each $q_s \in Q*$ for the OMIN corresponding to the graph $4G(3, 4)$ and connecting the stages as defined above, the top OMIN shown in Fig. 14 is obtained. Note that it is nothing but the famous generalized multistage cube [45]. The bottom OMIN in the same Fig. 14 corresponds to the

53

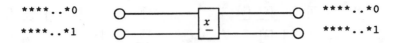

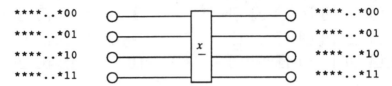

Fig. 13. Switches for the construction of OMIN's corresponding to ω-graphs.

graph $2G(2,4)$ which is the equivalent multistage OMP.

The switches in all stages of the networks shown in Fig. 14 have been labeled in the natural order. Suppose now that we allow a different labeling of switches at different stages. This would lead to a repositioning of the switches in the basic generalized cube network. Other well-known networks are thus derived. This placement of switches in the network stems from an indexing scheme applied to the traversal of the links of the corresponding orthogonal graph. We conclude that to define different multistage interconnection networks two rules are of importance. First is the connectivity rule outlined above. Next, a switch placement rule needs to be defined corresponding to an indexing function which defines the edge traversal scheme used to map the orthogonal graph into a multistage network. The permutation of the natural switch order should lead to a characterization of the permutational capabilities of a network. This question is beyond the scope of this paper and is left as an open problem. We are now in a position to generalize these ideas and formally define multistage interconnection networks using the theory of orthogonal graphs.

An OMIN consists of 2^m inputs and $\#Q*$ stages of $2^n 2^{m-n} \times 2^{m-n}$ switches each. Every stage is labeled with a $q_s \in Q*$ and each switch will correspond to a spanning bus in the direction q_s. It can easily be seen that an OMIN can be viewed as a two-dimensional array of switches where each entry corresponds to a spanning bus. The entries are arranged such that each column in the array corresponds to all spanning buses in a given direction $q_s \in Q*$. The order in which the entries are organized in each column is referred to as the *placement rule*. Therefore, to build an OMIN, we need to give the connectivity rule and a switch placement rule. If we use m-bit and n-bit binary numbers to label inputs and switches, respectively, the following rules define the construction of an OMIN:

- *Connectivity:* A node labeled y connects to a switch x at stage q_s if and only if $q_s \bullet \text{cast}(x) \perp_{q_s} y$. The line labeled y connects to input b where $b = [(m - n - q_s) \bullet y] \wedge z_{m-n}$. Conversely, output b of switch x is labeled $y = q_s \bullet [(n \bullet b) \oplus \text{cast}(x)]$.
- *Placement:* An indexing function $f(x)$ which defines how the basic natural order is altered to define a different switch permutation at each stage q_s.

The switch placement rule can be stated in terms of the $\bullet$ operation as shown in Table I for the networks shown in Figs. 15, 16, and 17. Starting with the natural order in the first stage, switches in the same row of each stage are obtained by a q-shuffle of their binary indexes. In this case, the placement defines

the entries of each column in terms of the entries in the prior column.

For the baseline network or modified data manipulator [51], [10], shown in Fig. 20, the placement rule is recursive. Let us pause to define the power of an ω-graph and derive the recursive rule for these networks.

Let $\omega G(n, m)$ be an ω-graph, the power of G is defined as

$$\omega G^2(n, m) = (\omega + 1)G(m, 2m - n).$$

Conversely, if $\omega' G(n', m')$ is the power of a graph $\omega G(n, m)$, then

$$\omega' G^{1/2}(n', m') = (\omega' - 1)G(2n' - m', n').$$

In Fig. 18 the application of the rule above is illustrated to build the well-known baseline network [51]. We start by defining one stage of the network corresponding to $\omega G(m - 1, m)$ and feed the outputs into two identical networks $(\omega - 1)G(m - 2, m - 1)$. Each one of the latter networks is built in the same manner and the recursion terminates with the basic 2×2 switch. Conversely, the construction can be carried out starting at the last stage as illustrated in Fig. 19. The basic 2×2 switch is viewed as a network $1G(0, 1)$ (the only link mode is $q = 0$). The network $1G^2(0, 1)$ is obtained next and the link modes correspond to $q_s = 0$ and $q_{s-1} = (q_s - 1) \bmod m$. At each stage to the left, the switches are labeled in the natural order and the stages to the right relabeled according to the connectivity rule. To better understand this construct, let us pause to summarize a number of properties in terms of the operations $\oplus$, $\bullet$, and cast.

1) A switch x in stage s receives input y if and only if

$$[q_s \bullet \text{cast}(x) \oplus y] \wedge (q_s \bullet z_n) = 0.$$

2) Switch x at stage s produces outputs

$$y = q_s \bullet [(n \bullet b) \oplus \text{cast}(x)].$$

3) An input labeled y connects to a switch x_s if and only if

$$\text{cast}(x_s) = [(m - q_s) \bullet y] \wedge z_n.$$

4) The outputs of switch x_{s-1} feed the inputs of switch x_s if and only if

$$\text{cast}(x_s) = z_n \wedge [(m - (q_s - q_{s-1})) \\ \bullet ([n \bullet b] \oplus \text{cast}(x_{s-1}))].$$

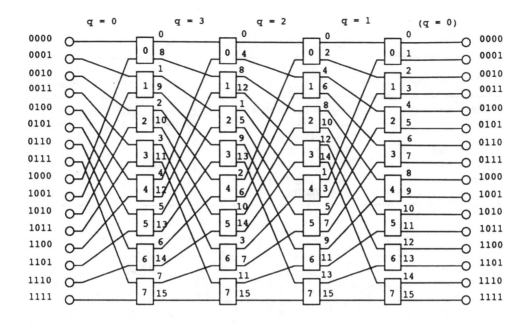

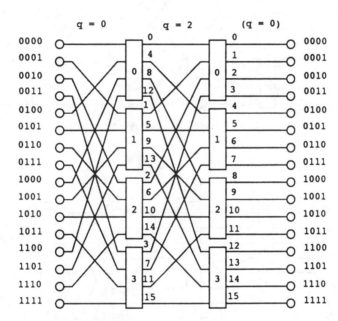

Fig. 14. Top: A generalized-cube $(3, 4, \{0, 3, 2, 1\})$. Bottom: An OMIN $(2, 4, \{0, 2\})$.

5) Similarly, an inverse network can be obtained by defining the switches in stage q_{s-1} fed by switches in stage q_s.

$$\text{cast}(\boldsymbol{x}_{s-1}) = \boldsymbol{z}_n \wedge [(m - (q_{s-1} - q_s)) \bullet [n \bullet b] \oplus \text{cast}(\boldsymbol{x}_s))].$$

Using properties 4 and 5 above, forward or backward labeling of the different edges and switches in the baseline network becomes apparent.

The theory of orthogonal graphs has helped us provide a construction rule for most of the well-known networks derived from the binary hypercube. The network built with 4×4 switches shown in Fig. 14 corresponds to the now well-known OMP. One now asks what other networks can be built by varying the parameters n, m, and $Q*$. This question is being addressed by

the author and his group. A new class of networks was already characterized and reported in [39].

VI. Conclusion

Motivated by the power of the orthogonal multiprocessing system (OMP), a graph theoretical framework was developed to better understand the architecture, its extensions, and its computational power. This paper reports the seminal work thus far and opens new questions, the answer to which should provide a unified description of a number of well-known interconnection networks for multiprocessing systems.

In this paper, orthogonal graphs were introduced as a tool for the description and analysis of hypercube-based structures

TABLE I
KNOWN OMIN'S AND THEIR PARAMETERS

Network	Reference	Q^* $(m - n = 1)$	Placement
Generalized Cube	Siegel and Smith 1978 [42]	$\{0, m-1, \cdots, 1\}$	$x_{s+1} = 0 \bullet x_s$
Omega	Lawrie 1975 [22]	$\{0, m-1, \cdots, 1\}$	$x_{s+1} = 0 \bullet x_s$
Flip	Batcher 1976 [3]	$\{1, \cdots, m-1, 0\}$	$x_{s+1} = 0 \bullet x_s$
Indirect Cube	Pease 1977 [28]	$\{1, \cdots, m-1, 0\}$	$x_{s+1} = 2 \bullet x_s$
SW-Banyan ($S = F = 2$)	Goke and Lipovsky 1973 [11]	$\{1, \cdots, m-1, 0\}$	$x_{s+1} = 2 \bullet x_s$
Baseline	Wu and Feng 1980 [51]	$\{1, \cdots, m-1, 0\}$	Recursive
Modified Data Manipulator	Feng 1974 [10]	$\{1, \cdots, m-1, 0\}$	Recursive

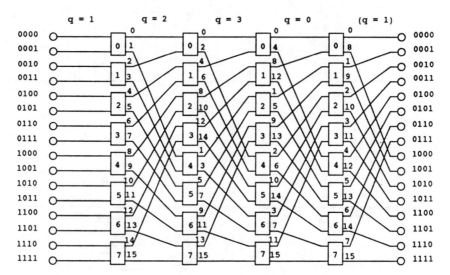

Fig. 15. The flip network $(3, 4, \{1, 2, 3, 0\})$.

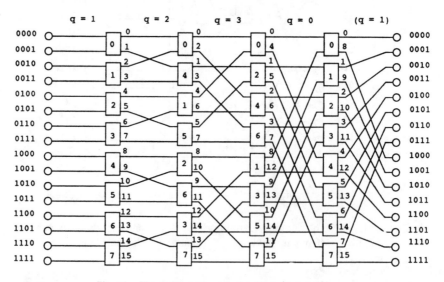

Fig. 16. The indirect binary cube $(3, 4, \{1, 2, 3, 0\})$.

such as the binary m-cube, STARAN's MDA memory, and OMP. Orthogonal graphs can also be applied to the definition of several multistage interconnection networks.

Formal algorithm mapping onto orthogonal computing structures is still an open problem. The feasibility of such a mapping has already been proven by Hwang, Alnuweiri and Kumar, Sen, Ma, and the author of this paper, and many others.

The theoretical framework is by no means complete. However, the ideas presented here are sufficient for the description and analysis of a large class of multiprocessing systems. It is conjectured that, by studying other possible combinations of the parameters which define orthogonal graphs, new structures may be discovered. Of particular importance is the study of reliable systems. These might be generated in a formal manner by adding

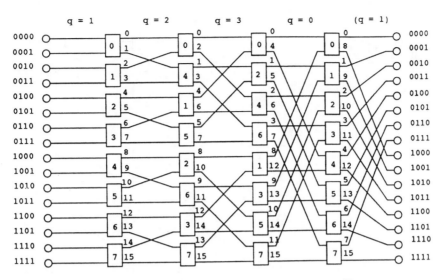

Fig. 17. The SW-banyan $(S = F = 2)(3, 4, \{1, 2, 3, 0\})$.

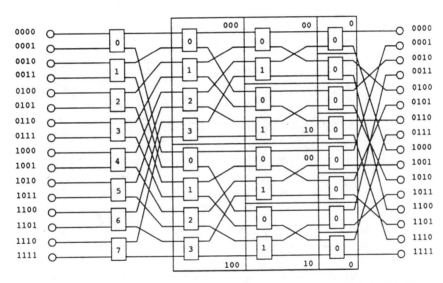

Fig. 18. Recursive placement for the baseline interconnection network $(3, 4, \{1, 2, 3, 0\})$.

link modes to the set $Q*$. A systematic methodology might then be found which yields the degree of fault tolerance desired based on formal parameters to define the multiprocessing system.

ACKNOWLEDGMENT

I am indebted to T. Lang, who spent precious weekends reading, correcting, and criticizing this work, to M. Malek for valuable discussions and advice, and to the anonymous reviewers who did an exemplary job in reviewing this paper. Also my gratitude goes to P. Corbett (for his contribution to Theorem 3) and other EE graduate students at Princeton University who shared my excitement over this work.

REFERENCES

[1] H. M. Alnuweiri and V. K. P. Kumar, "A reduced mesh of trees organization for efficient solution to graph problems," in *Proc. 22nd Annu. Conf. Inform. Sci. Syst.*, Mar. 1988.

[2] ——, "Optimal image computations on reduced VLSI architectures," *IEEE Trans. Circuits Syst.*, Sept. 1989.

[3] K. E. Batcher, "The Flip network in STARAN," in *Proc. 1976 Int. Conf. Parallel Processing*, 1976, pp. 65–71.

[4] ——, "The multidimensional access memory in STARAN," *IEEE Trans. Comput.*, vol. C-26, no. 2, pp. 172–177, Feb. 1977.

[5] ——, "Design of a massively parallel processor," *IEEE Trans. Comput.*, vol. C-29, no. 9, pp. 836–840, Sept. 1980.

[6] R. E. Buehrer *et al.*, "The ETH multiprocessor EMPRESS: A dynamically reconfigurable MIMD system," *IEEE Trans. Comput.*, vol. C-31, no. 11, pp. 1035–1044, Nov. 1982.

[7] L. N. Bhuyan and D. P. Agrawal, "Generalized hypercube and hyperbus structures for a computer network," *IEEE Trans. Comput.*, vol. C-33, no. 4, pp. 323–333, Apr. 1984.

[8] P. Chen, D. Lawrie, P. Yew, and D. A. Padua, "Interconnection networks using shuffles," *IEEE Comput. Mag.*, vol. 14, no. 12, pp. 55–64, Dec. 1981.

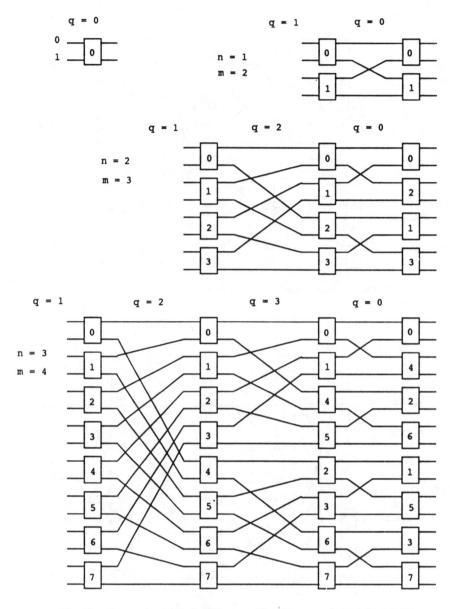

Fig. 19. Construction of the baseline interconnection network $(3, 4, \{1, 2, 3, 0\})$.

[9] G. Ezer, B. Hoyt, S. Sen, J. S. Sreekant, and I. D. Scherson, "A parallel processing architecture for image generation and processing," Tech. Rep. ECE 84-20, Dep. ECE, Univ. of California, Santa Barbara, Aug. 1984.

[10] T. Y. Feng, "Data manipulating functions in parallel processors and their implementations," *IEEE Trans. Comput.*, vol. C-23, no. 3, pp. 309–318, Mar. 1974.

[11] L. R. Goke and G. J. Lipovski, "Banyan networks for partitioning multiprocessor systems," in *Proc. First Annu. Symp. Comput. Architecture*, 1973, pp. 21–28.

[12] A. Gottlieb *et al.*, "The NYU Ultracomputer—Designing an MIMD shared memory parallel computer," *IEEE Trans. Comput.*, vol. 32, no. 2, pp. 175–189, Feb. 1983.

[13] R. P. Grimaldi, *Discrete and Combinatorial Mathematics. An Applied Introduction.* Reading, MA; Addison-Wesley, 1989.

[14] F. Harary, *Graph Theory.* Reading, MA: Addison-Wesley, 1969.

[15] K. Hwang and D. Kim, "Generalization of orthogonal multiprocessor for massively parallel computation," in *Proc. Frontiers 88, 2nd Symp. Frontiers Massively Parallel Computat.*, pp. 391–398.

[16] K. Hwang, P. S. Tseng, and D. Kim, "An orthogonal multiprocessor for large-grain scientific computations," *IEEE Trans. Comput.*, vol. C-38, no. 1, pp. 47–61, Jan. 1989.

[17] IEEE Computer Magazine, Special Issue on Interconnection Networks, C-l. Wu, Ed., Dec. 1981.

[18] IEEE Computer Magazine, Special Issue on Interconnection Networks for Parallel and Distributed Computing, L. N. Bhuyan, Ed., June 1987.

[19] Z. Kohavi, *Switching and Finite Automata Theory.* New York: McGraw-Hill, 1978.

[20] T. Lang and H. S. Stone, "A shuffle-exchange network with simplified control," *IEEE Trans. Comput.*, vol. C-25, no. 1, pp. 55–65, Jan. 1976.

[21] T. Lang, "Interconnections between processors and memory modules using the shuffle-exchange network," *IEEE Trans. Comput.*, vol. C-25, no. 5, pp. 496–503, May 1976.

[22] D. H. Lawrie, "Access and alignment of data in an array processor," *IEEE Trans. Comput.*, vol. C-24, no. 12, pp. 1145–1155, Dec. 1975.

[23] D. H. Lawrie and D. A. Padua, "Analysis of message switching with shuffle-exchanges in multiprocessors," in *Proc. Workshop Interconnection Networks for Parallel and Distributed Processing*, 1980, pp. 116–123.

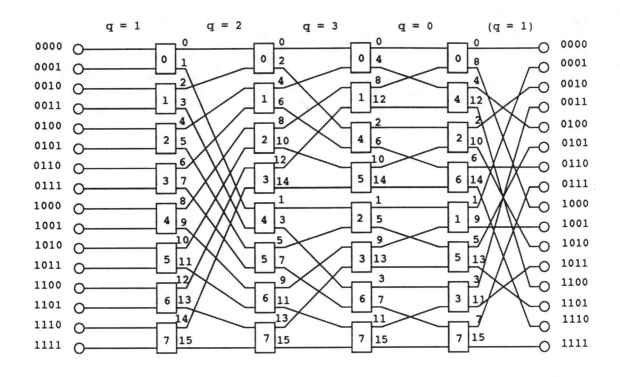

Fig. 20. The baseline and the modified data manipulator $(3, 4, \{1, 2, 3, 0\})$

[24] E. J. McCluskey, "Minimization of Boolean functions," *Bell Syst. Tech. J.*, vol. 35, no. 6, pp. 1417–1444, Nov. 1956.

[25] G. Memmi and Y. Raillard, "Some new results about the (d, k) graph problem," *IEEE Trans. Comput.*, vol. C-31, no. 8, pp. 784–791, Aug. 1982.

[26] D. Nath, S. N. Maheshwary, and P. C. Bhatt, "Efficient VLSI networks for parallel processing based on orthogonal trees," *IEEE Trans. Comput.*, vol. C-32, no. 6, pp. 569–581, June 1983.

[27] D. S. Parker, "Notes on shuffle/exchange-type networks," *IEEE Trans. Comput.*, vol. C-29, no. 3, pp. 213–222, Mar. 1980.

[28] M. C. Pease, "The indirect binary *n*-cube microprocessor array," *IEEE Trans. Comput.*, vol. C-26, no. 5, pp. 458–473, May 1977.

[29] G. F. Pfister *et al.*, "The IBM research parallel processor prototype (RP3): Introduction and architecture," in *Proc. 1985 Int. Conf. Parallel Processing*, 1985, pp. 764–771.

[30] D. K. Pradhan and K. L. Kodandapani, "A uniform representation of single- and multistage interconnection networks used in SIMD machines," *IEEE Trans. Comput.*, vol. C-29, no. 9, pp. 777–791, Sept. 1980.

[31] W. V. Quine, "The problem of simplifying truth functions," *Amer. Mathematics Monthly*, vol. 59, no. 8, pp. 521–531, Oct. 1952.

[32] ——, "A way to simplify truth functions," *Amer. Mathematics Monthly*, vol. 62, no. 9, pp. 627–631, Nov. 1955.

[33] I. D. Scherson and Y. Ma, "Vector computations in an orthogonal memory access multiprocessing system," in *Proc. 8th Symp. Comput. Arithmetic*, May 1987, pp. 28–37, Feb. 1989, pp. 238–249.

[34] I. D. Scherson, S. Sen, and Y. Ma, "Two nearly optimal sorting algorithms for mesh-connected processor arrays using shear-sort," *J. Parallel Distributed Comput.*, vol. 6, no. 1, pp. 151–165, Feb. 1989.

[35] I. D. Scherson and S. Sen, "Parallel sorting in two-dimensional VLSI models of computation," *IEEE Trans. Comput.*, vol. C-38, no. 2, pp. 238–249, Feb. 1989.

[36] I. D. Scherson and Y. Ma, "Analysis and applications of the orthogonal access multiprocessor," *J. Parallel Distributed Comput.*, vol. 7, no. 2, pp. 232–255, Oct. 1989.

[37] I. D. Scherson, "A theory for the description and analysis of a class of interconnection networks," Princeton Univ. Tech. Rep. CE-S89-002.

[38] ——, "Definition and analysis of a class of spanning bus orthogonal multiprocessing systems," in *Proc. 1990 ACM Comput. Sci. Conf.*, Feb. 19–22, 1990, Washington, DC, pp. 194–200.

[39] I. D. Scherson, P. F. Corbett, and T. Lang, "An analytical characterization of generalized shuffle-exchange networks," in *Proc. INFOCOM'90*, June 1990.

[40] C. L. Seitz, "The Cosmic Cube," *Commun. ACM*, vol. 28, no. 1, pp. 22–33, Jan. 1985.

[41] H. J. Siegel, "Analysis techniques for SIMD machine interconnection networks and the effects of processor address masks," *IEEE Trans. Comput.*, vol. C-26, no. 2, pp. 153–161, Feb. 1977.

[42] H. J. Seigel and S. D. Smith, "Study of a multistage SIMD interconnection networks," in *Proc. Fifth Annu. Symp. Comput. Architecture*, Apr. 1978, pp. 223–229.

[43] H. J. Siegel, "The theory underlying the partitioning of permutations networks," *IEEE Trans. Comput.*, vol. C-29, no. 9, pp. 791–801, Sept. 1980.

[44] H. J. Siegel and R. J. McMillen, "The multistage cube: A versatile interconnection network," *IEEE Comput. Mag.*, vol. 14, no. 12, pp. 65–76, Dec. 1981.

[45] H. J. Siegel, *Interconnection Networks for Large Scale Parallel Processing: Theory and Case Studies*. 2nd Ed. New York: McGraw-Hill, 1990.

[46] H. S. Stone, "Parallel processing with the perfect shuffle," *IEEE Trans. Comput.*, vol. C-20, no. 2, pp. 153–161, Feb. 1971.

[47] ——, *High Performance Computer Architecture*. Reading, MA: Addison-Wesley, 1987.

[48] P. S. Tseng, K. Hwang, and P. K. Kumar, "A VLSI-based multiprocessor architecture for implementing parallel algorithms," in *Proc. 13th Int. Conf. Parallel Processing*, Aug. 1985.

[49] A. Tucker, *Applied Combinatorics*. New York: Wiley, 1980.

[50] L. D. Wittie, "Communication structures for large networks of microcomputers," *IEEE Trans. Comput.*, vol. C-30, no. 4, pp. 264–273, Apr. 1981.

[51] C. L. Wu and T. Y. Feng, "On a class of multistage interconnection networks," *IEEE Trans. Comput.*, vol. C-29, no. 8, pp. 694–702, Aug. 1980.

[52] ——, "The universality of the shuffle-exchange network," *IEEE Trans. Comput.*, vol. C-30, no. 5, pp. 324–332, May 1981.

Isaac D. Scherson (S'81–M'83) was born in Santiago, Chile, on February 12, 1952. He received the B.S.E.E. and M.S.E.E. degrees from the National University of Mexico (UNAM) and the Ph.D. degree in computer science from the Weizmann Institute of Science, Rehovot, Israel.

He served as an Assistant Professor in the Department of Electrical and Computer Engineering of the University of California, Santa Barbara (1983–1987), and in the Department of Electrical Engineering at Princeton University (1988–1990). He is currently Associate Professor of Information and Computer Science at the University of California, Irvine. His research interests include massively parallel computer architectures, interconnection networks, associative memory and processing, computer graphics, algorithms and their complexity, and VLSI.

Dr. Scherson was a member of the Technical Program Committee for Computer Graphics International, 1987, and for the IEEE Symposium on the Frontiers of Massively Parallel Computation, 1990, and the Guest Editor of the Special Issue of *The Visual Computer* on Foundations of Ray Tracing (June 1990). He is also a member of the IEEE Computer Society, the ACM SIGGARCH and SIGGRAPH, and of the Eta Kappa Nu Electrical Engineering Honor Society.

A Group-Theoretic Model for Symmetric Interconnection Networks

SHELDON B. AKERS, FELLOW, IEEE, AND BALAKRISHNAN KRISHNAMURTHY, SENIOR MEMBER, IEEE

Abstract—Symmetric graphs, such as the ring, the *n*-dimensional Boolean hypercube, and the cube-connected cycles, have been widely used as processor/communication interconnection networks. The performance of such networks is often measured through an analysis of their degree, diameter, connectivity, fault tolerance, routing algorithms, etc. In this paper, we develop a formal group-theoretic model, called the *Cayley graph* model, for designing, analyzing, and improving such networks. We show that this model is universal and demonstrate how the networks mentioned above can be concisely represented in this model.

More importantly, we show that this model enables us to design new networks based on representations of finite groups. We can then analyze these networks by interpreting the group-theoretic structure graph theoretically. Using these ideas, and motivated by certain well-known combinatorial problems, we develop two new classes of networks, called the *star graphs* and the *pancake graphs*. These networks are shown to have better performance, as measured by the parameters mentioned above, than the popular *n*-cubes.

Index Terms—Cayley graphs, interconnection networks, *n*-cubes.

I. Introduction

A processor/communication interconnection network is often modeled as an undirected graph, in which the vertices correspond to processor/communication ports, and the edges correspond to communication channels. Communication over such a network is achieved by a message passing protocol, and the delay in communication is measured by the number of edges traversed. Some of the key features of interest in such an interconnection network are its degree, diameter, congestion, symmetry, connectivity, routing algorithms, and structure.

A number of interconnection network topologies have been suggested in the literature which address one or more of the above features ([12]–[14], [16]–[19]). These range from simple graphs, such as cycles, complete graphs and stars to more sophisticated graphs such as shuffle-exchange graphs, *n*-dimensional Boolean cubes, and cube-connected cycles. Since there is no single measure to compare these networks, each of the above examples has been justified for one application or another.

A special class of networks, called *symmetric interconnection networks,* has the property that the network viewed from any vertex of the network looks the same. In such a network, congestion problems are minimized since the load will be distributed uniformly through all the vertices. Moreover, this symmetry allows for identical processors at every vertex with identical routing algorithms. It is also very useful in designing algorithms that exploit the structure of the network. It is this class of networks that we address in this paper. With the exception of the star network and the shuffle-exchange graphs, all of the networks mentioned above are symmetric networks.

In designing symmetric interconnection networks, the overall objective has been to construct large vertex symmetric graphs with small degree and diameter, high connectivity, and offering simple routing algorithms.[1] One attractive network that offers all these properties together with a good degree and diameter is the *n*-cube, which is a network of 2^n vertices, with degree *n* and diameter *n*. Thus, the *n*-cube will be used as a standard against which to compare many of the networks constructed in this paper.

Specifically, we shall present a group-theoretic model for designing, analyzing, and improving symmetric interconnection networks. We show that most symmetric interconnection networks can be represented using this model, and that *every* symmetric interconnection network can be represented by a simple extension of this model. This allows us to provide an algebraic representation of each of the symmetric networks mentioned above. More importantly, this group-theoretic model enables us to start with an arbitrary finite group and construct a symmetric network using that group as the algebraic model. This, in conjunction with the vast literature on finite groups, allows us to construct a variety of new interconnection networks.

Another advantage of analyzing such networks in this algebraic setting is that many properties of these networks can be proved for the class as a whole, instead of proving that property for each network independently. For example, all networks derived from a finite group are necessarily vertex symmetric, i.e., the network viewed from any vertex in the network looks the same. We prove a number of other such properties of these networks. Furthermore, even for specific networks constructed using this algebraic model we can often derive properties algebraically and interpret the properties

Manuscript received August 28, 1986; revised June 24, 1987.

S. B. Akers is with the Department of Electrical and Computer Engineering, University of Massachusetts, Amherst, MA 01003.

B. Krishnamurthy is with the Computer Research Laboratory, Tektronix Laboratories, Beaverton, OR 97077.

IEEE Log Number 8825673.

[1] We point out that the problem of constructing large graphs of a given degree and diameter—known as the (*d*, *k*) graph problem—is a well-studied extremal graph theory problem. However, solutions to the (*d*, *k*) graph problem often ignore the more subjective parameters of this problem, such as symmetry, ease of routing, and the structure of the graph, which are essential for the design of efficient algorithms on these networks.

Reprinted from *IEEE Trans. Computers,* Vol. 38, No. 4, Apr. 1989, pp. 555–566. Copyright © 1989 by The Institute of Electrical and Electronics Engineers, Inc. All rights reserved.

graph theoretically. We will repeatedly use this technique in this paper.

Apart from the algebraic model suggested in this paper, we also offer two specific classes of networks that are especially attractive for distributed processing. We call these the *star graphs* and the *pancake graphs*. We describe these networks in some detail and compare them to the *n*-cubes.

The paper is organized into eight sections. In the second section, we define the algebraic model, called the *Cayley graph* model and provide a number of examples as well as some new networks. In Section III, we prove certain general properties of Cayley graphs. In Section IV, we define *transposition trees* which is a level of abstraction beyond Cayley graphs. A specific Cayley graph resulting from a specific transportation tree, called the *star graph,* is investigated in Section V. In Section VI, we present some preliminary ideas on designing algorithms on another class of such graphs, called *pancake graphs*. In Section VII, we compose Cayley graphs using a variety of group-theoretic operations and study the resulting graphs. The concluding Section VIII again emphasizes that this group-theoretic model is a fertile source of new interconnection networks.

In the remainder of this section, we will state the group-theoretic and graph-theoretic terminology that we will use in this paper. We will assume basic knowledge of elementary group theory and graph theory. The reader is referred to [9] and [5] for an elementary exposition of the relevant terminology in group theory and graph theory, respectively. Since we will only be considering finite groups, we will represent our groups as permutation groups. We will represent the cyclic group on *n* symbols by Z_n and the symmetric group on *n* symbols by S_n. In addition, we will represent the trivial identity group consisting of the identity permutation on *n* symbols by I_n. We will be using the notion of a direct product of two groups and will define the wreath product of two permutation groups.

Much of the work reported in this paper involves permutations. We will be using a one-row representation for permutations. Thus, the permutation whose cycle representation is (12)(345) will be represent by us as 21453. Recall that transpositions are permutations with exactly one cycle of length 2 and all other cycles of length 1. Our descriptions of permutations will be quite informal. Thus, we will view a transportation as *swapping* a pair of symbols. We will denote the number of cycles (including the invariances) in a permutation π by $\eta(\pi)$ and the number of invariances in π by $\Psi(\pi)$.

As we mentioned in the beginning of the section, we will view interconnection networks as an undirected[2] graph. Thus, in the remainder of the paper we will use the term *graph* in place of *interconnection network*. Our graphs will be finite, undirected, loop-free, and devoid of multiple edges. We will make special use of cycles, complete graphs, trees, and stars. Graphs of particular interest are the *vertex symmetric graphs*, which we formally define as the following.

Definition: A graph is said to be *vertex symmetric* if for

every pair of vertices, *a* and *b*, there exists an automorphism of the graph that maps *a* into *b*. A graph is said to be *edge symmetric* if for every pair of edges, *a* and *b*, there exists an automorphism of the graph that maps *a* into *b*.

II. THE CAYLEY GRAPH MODEL

Given a set of generators for a finite group *G*, we can draw a graph, called the *Cayley graph,* in which the vertices correspond to the elements of the group *G* and the edges correspond to the action of the generators. That is, there is an edge from an element *a* to an element *b* iff there is a generator *g* such that *ag = b* in the group *G*. We require that the set of generators be closed under inverses so that the resulting graph can be viewed as being undirected.

Let us illustrate Cayley graphs with a few examples which will make these ideas clearer. First, we point out that since we will be considering permutation groups the generators are themselves permutations. We will be representing permutations using the symbols $1, 2, 3, \cdots, n$. For example, consider the generators 1324, 2143, and 4321. Since these generators are permutations of four symbols, they must generate either S_4 (which itself consists of 24 permutations) or a subgroup[3] of S_4. In this case, the subgroup generated by these three generators consists of the eight permutations: 1234, 2143, 2413, 4231, 4321, 3412, 3142, and 1324. The corresponding Cayley graph arising from the above generators is shown in Fig. 1. The reader can easily convince himself that the edges of this graph correspond to the action of the generators.

As another example, consider the generators 213456, 124356, and 123465. The group generated by these generators again contains eight permutations. These permutations and the corresponding Cayley graph are shown in Fig. 2. This is, of course, the familiar three-dimensional cube. Figs. 3 and 4 show two additional examples of Cayley graphs, where we have only shown the permutations at a few selected vertices. In Fig. 4 we have also shown the generators as labels on the edges. Observe that Fig. 3 is a three-dimensional cube-connected cycle [14], i.e., a three-dimensional cube with its corners truncated. Fig. 4 is an example of a star graph that we will discuss later in this paper.

The reader might have observed that all the Cayley graphs shown so far are vertex symmetric. In fact,

Theorem 1: Every Cayley graph is vertex symmetric.

Proof: We need to show that given any two vertices in the Cayley graph there exists an automorphism of the graph that maps one vertex into the other. Let *a* and *b* be the permutations corresponding to the two vertices. Consider the transformation on the group that maps an arbitrary permutation *x* into $ba^{-1}x$. Clearly, this maps *a* into *b*. Furthermore, this transformation is an automorphism of the graph. For, if two permutations *x* and *y* were connected by an edge in the graph, then there is a generator *g* such that *xg = y*. Then the images of the two permutations, $ba^{-1}x$ and $ba^{-1}y$, are connected by an edge since $ba^{-1}xg = ba^{-1}y$. Hence, the proof. ☐

As mentioned in Section I, an attractive feature of vertex

---

[2] The techniques of this paper can also be used for directed graphs. However, we will limit our attention to undirected graphs.

[3] The reader unfamiliar with LaGrange's theorem would find it useful to know that in a finite group the order of any subgroup (the number of elements in it) always divides the order of the group.

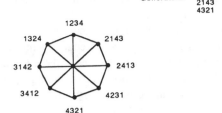

Generators: 1324
2143
4321

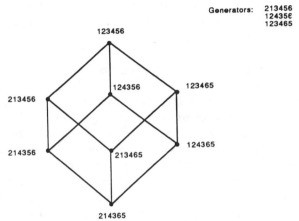

Fig. 1. A simple Cayley graph.

Generators: 213456
124356
123465

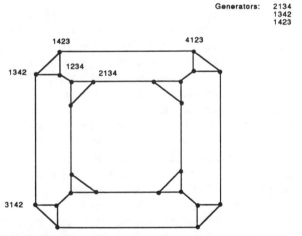

Fig. 2. Three-cube as a Cayley graph.

Generators: 2134
1342
1423

Fig. 3. Three-dimensional cube-connected cycles as a Cayley graph.

Generators: 2134 (1)
3214 (2)
4231 (3)

Fig. 4. An example of a star graph.

symmetric graphs is that routing between two arbitrary vertices reduces to routing from an arbitrary vertex to a special vertex. We can now state this more formally. First, observe that in a Cayley graph a path from one vertex to another can be represented by a sequence of generators $g_1, g_2, \cdots, g_p$, where each g_i is a generator of the Cayley graph. Now if $g_1, g_2, \cdots, g_p$ is a path from x to y, then it is also a path from $y^{-1}x$ to I, the identity permutation. Thus, if we want to find a route from x to y we can instead find a route from $y^{-1}x$ to I. Consequently the problem of routing becomes that of sorting.

We can now describe a class of Cayley graphs, which we will call the *bubble sort graphs*. Recall that a Cayley graph is completely specified by providing the set of generators. The generators for the nth bubble sort graph is the set of $n - 1$ transpositions of the n symbols $1, 2, \cdots, n$ that transpose ad-

jacent symbols. Thus, for $n = 4$ the generators are 2134, 1324, and 1243. Notice that a path in this graph is a sequence of adjacent transpositions. Thus, finding a route from a given permutation to the identity permutation can be accomplished by sorting the given permutation using the familiar bubble sort algorithm. The reader can verify that the group generated by this set of generators is the symmetric group S_n. Consequently, the corresponding Cayley graph has $n!$ vertices. Furthermore, it is easily shown that the corresponding Cayley graph has degree $n - 1$ and diameter $\binom{n}{2}$.

As a second example of a family of Cayley graphs, we consider an old combinatorial problem, called the *pancake flipping problem* [1]. The problem is to sort a stack of n pancakes of different sizes by repeatedly flipping top substacks with a spatula. For example, consider an arrangement of five pancakes represented by the permutation 23514. Let us adopt the convention that the left end of the permutation is the top of the stack. Thus, the sorted stack would look like the identity permutation 12345. If we apply a 3-flip, i.e., flip the top (left) three pancakes with the spatula, the 23514 permutation will be transformed into 53214. Notice that such a 3-flip is equivalent to multiplying on the right by 32145. We give below a sequence of flips to sort the given permutation:

$$23514 \rightarrow 53214 \rightarrow 12354 \rightarrow 45321 \rightarrow 54321 \rightarrow 12345.$$

We model the pancake flipping problem as a class of Cayley graphs using generators representing the pancake flips. Thus, flipping the top i of n pancakes with a spatula gives rise to the generator $i(i - 1) \cdots 321(i + 1)(i + 2) \cdots n$. Clearly, there are $(n - 1)$ generators, one for each value of $i, 1 < i \leq n$. It is easy to show that the corresponding Cayley graph has $n!$ vertices each with degree $(n - 1)$. Finding the diameter of the *pancake graph* is equivalent to finding the maximum number of pancake flips one would need to sort an arbitrary stack of pancakes. This problem is still open, and the best known results can be found in [8].

For this paper, we will give a simple routing algorithm that routes in at most $(2n - 3)$ steps. Recall that instead of finding a path between two arbitrary permutations, it suffices to find a path from one permutation to the identity, i.e., to sort a given permutation. In one step we can bring the symbol n to the leftmost position using an appropriate flip (generator). In one more step, we can bring n to the nth position using the n-flip. Thereafter, we can ignore the symbol n and sort the remainder of the permutation, recursively. This yields a route of $2n$ steps. We can slightly improve this by observing that the last two symbols, i.e., the symbols 1 and 2, do not require two steps each. In fact, when we have moved all the other symbols to their place, 1 and 2 would require at most one more flip. Hence, the $(2n - 3)$ result. Note that we have in effect proved a $(2n - 3)$ upper bound on the diameter of this Cayley graph. We will point out that in contrast to the n-cubes, whose diameter and degree grow logarithmically as a function of the number of vertices, the n-pancake graphs have degree and diameter that grow slower than logarithmically as a function of its size.

Before we offer a picture of the pancake graph for a small value of n, we will first mention some elementary properties of Cayley graphs. This will allow us to use the underlying group-theoretic structure of these graphs in analyzing them.

III. PROPERTIES OF CAYLEY GRAPHS

A Cayley graph is completely specified by a set of d permutations as generators. The degree of the graph will, of course, be d. We have already shown in Theorem 1 that every Cayley graph is vertex symmetric. As we had mentioned in Section I, a vertex symmetric graph has the desirable property that the communication load is uniformly distributed on all the vertices so that there is no point of congestion. Recall that a stronger notion of symmetry, called *edge symmetry*, requires that every edge in the graph looks the same. Such a symmetry would ensure that the communication load is uniformly distributed over all the communication links, so that there is no congestion at any one link. We show the following condition for a Cayley graph to be edge symmetric.

Theorem 2: Consider a Cayley graph defined by a set of d generators on n symbols $\{1, 2, 3, \cdots, n\}$. The Cayley graph is edge symmetric if and only if for every pair of generators g_1 and g_2 there exists a permutation of the n symbols that maps the set of generators into themselves, and, in particular, maps g_1 into g_2.

Proof: The necessity of the condition follows directly from the definition of edge symmetry. To show that it is sufficient, we need to show that under the stated conditions, for every pair of edges (u, v) and (u', v'), there exists an automorphism of the Cayley graph that maps the edge (u, v) into (u', v'). We will show this in two stages. First we claim that if the two edges correspond to the same generator, then the very transformation used in the proof of Theorem 1 will suffice here. Second, if the two edges correspond to different generators, then the transformation used in Theorem 1 will map (u, v) into (u', v''), i.e., an incident at u' but not connecting it to v' as desired, but rather to some other vertex v''. We then need to compose this transformation with another transformation that corresponds to interchanging the action of

the generators. Such a transformation is guaranteed by the hypothesis of the theorem. ☐

As a consequence of the above theorem, we can conclude that the graphs of Figs. 2 and 4 are edge symmetric.

Apart from the symmetry properties of these Cayley graphs there is a very useful decomposition of these graphs that can be seen using elementary group theory. First, we observe that one of the attractive features of the n-cube is its recursive decomposition into smaller cubes. Thus, an n-cube can be viewed as consisting of two $(n - 1)$-cubes, interconnected by edges that are said to lie in the nth dimension. We will now show that this property can be abstracted as a group-theoretic property and is possessed by a number of different Cayley graphs.

Consider the four-pancake graph defined by the three generators 2134, 3214, and 4321 on four symbols. Let us examine the subgraph of the four-pancake graph consisting of those vertices (i.e., permutations) that fix the symbol 4 in the fourth position. Clearly, there are 3! such permutations and thus six vertices in this subgraph. Furthermore, the only edges that connect these vertices in this subgraph are those that correspond to the first two generators, since the last generator will move the symbol 4 from the fourth position. Consequently, this subgraph is identical to a three-pancake graph (on the symbols $\{1, 2, 3\}$), with the symbol 4 being affixed at the end of each permutation.

More interestingly, let us now examine the subgraph of the four-pancake graph consisting of the six permutations that fix the symbol 3 in the last position. Once again we will find the subgraph is identical to the three-pancake graph, but this time on the symbols $\{1, 2, 4\}$, with the symbol 3 being affixed at the end of each permutation. In this manner, we can identify four mutually disjoint subgraphs of the four-pancake graph, each of size $3! = 6$, with each subgraph being a copy of the three-pancake graph. These four copies of the three-pancake graph are then interconnected by edges that correspond to the fourth generator, i.e., the generator corresponding to a flip of all four pancakes. We can now offer the informative picture of Fig. 5 illustrating the four-pancake graph.

Finally we make the trivial observation that the three-pancake graph itself (i.e., the hexagon) is made up of three copies of the two-pancake graph which is itself a line. More generally, an n-pancake graph can be viewed as n copies of $(n - 1)$-pancake graphs that are interconnected by edges corresponding to the n-flip. Furthermore, this decomposition can be carried out recursively, so that each of the $(n - 1)$-pancake graphs in turn is made up of $n - 1$ copies of $(n - 2)$-pancake graphs, and so on.

We can now ask which Cayley graphs have this recursive decomposition property. Notice that in the four-pancake graph we used the property that the 4-flip cannot be obtained through any combination of 2- and 3-flips. That is, the permutation corresponding to the 4-flip, i.e 4321, is outside the subgroup generated by the 2- and 3-flips. In fact, that is the only requirement that is needed for such a decomposition. Thus, for convenience we will define a Cayley graph to be *hierarchical*, if its generators can be ordered as $g_1, g_2, \cdots, g_d$, such that for each $i, 1 < i \le d, g_i$ is outside the subgroup generated by

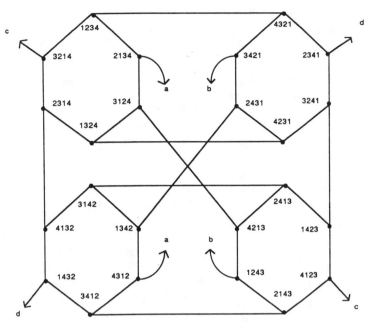

Generators: 2134
3214
4321

Fig. 5. The four-pancake graph.

by the first $i - 1$ generators. Under this definition, every hierarchical Cayley graph has such a recursive decomposition structure.

Some Cayley graphs (particularly, the edge symmetric Cayley graphs) are hierarchical under any ordering of the set of generators. We call such a Cayley graph *strongly hierarchical*. The three-cube shown in Fig. 2 as well as its obvious generalization to the n-cube is strongly hierarchical. So is the four-star graph shown in Fig. 4. However, the pancake graphs are not strongly hierarchical. A strongly hierarchical graph has the additional property that it can be recursively decomposed using the generators in any order. Thus, for example, the n-cube can be decomposed into two $(n - 1)$-cubes along any one of its n dimensions. We will show in Section V that the star graphs are strongly hierarchical.

Another important property of interconnection networks is their fault tolerance. The *fault tolerance* of a graph is better defined through the graph-theoretic property, called *connectivity*. The *connectivity* of a graph is the minimum number of vertices that need to be removed to disconnect the graph. The fault tolerance is then one less than the connectivity and indicates the maximum number of vertices that can be removed and still have the graph remain connected. Clearly, any graph can be disconnected by removing all the vertices adjacent to a given vertex. Thus, its connectivity can be at most its degree. It has been shown [2] that hierarchical Cayley graphs (with an additional size requirement) are *maximally fault tolerant*. That is, their fault tolerance is exactly one less than their degree.

The last property we will mention in this section is the universality of this model for symmetric graphs. Can every vertex symmetric graph be represented as a Cayley graph? For example, the n-cube can be represented as a Cayley graph by generalizing the example shown in Fig. 2. We will offer a

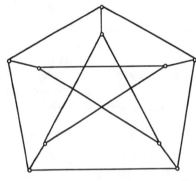

Fig. 6. Petersen graph—an example of a vertex symmetric graph that is not a Cayley graph.

more formal representation of the n-cube in Section VII. We will also provide in that section a representation of the cube-connected cycles as Cayley graphs. While most symmetric networks considered in the literature can be viewed as Cayley graphs, it remains that there are certain vertex symmetric graphs that cannot be represented as Cayley graphs. A prime example is the Petersen graph [4], shown in Fig. 6.

However, one can extend the Cayley graph model to the *quotient graph* of two finite groups. In this paper, we will merely give a brief definition of the quotient and state (without proof) a theorem that establishes the universality of this model. To define the quotient graph of two groups we select a subgroup H of a finite group G generated by a given set of generators. We then identify the subgroup H and all its left cosets as subgraphs of the Cayley graph of G, as defined by the chosen set of generators. The quotient graph is obtained by reducing these subgraphs to vertices and connecting two such vertices iff there existed an edge between elements of the corresponding subgraphs. A fundamental theorem originally shown in [15] states the following.

Theorem 3: Every vertex symmetric graph can be represented as the quotient of two Cayley graphs.

Finally, we mention an interesting open conjecture. Recall that a *Hamiltonian path* is a path that visits every vertex exactly once. A *Hamiltonian cycle* is a cycle that forms a Hamiltonian path.

Conjecture: Every Cayley graph is Hamiltonian, i.e., has a Hamiltonian cycle. Furthermore, every vertex symmetric graph has a Hamiltonian path.

This conjecture has remained open in the sense that neither has it been proven nor has a Cayley graph been shown to violate it. For a specific Cayley graph, it is often easy to establish that it is Hamiltonian. For example, the Hamiltonian property of the *n*-cubes is demonstrated by Gray codes. The Hamiltonian property of the *n*-pancake graphs has been shown in [20]. The reader will note that the claim for a vertex symmetric graph is weaker than that for a Cayley graph. We will point out that the Petersen graph, shown in Fig. 6, which is a vertex transitive graph but not a Cayley graph, has a Hamiltonian path but not a Hamiltonian cycle.

As we have mentioned, most symmetric interconnection networks that have been suggested in the literature can be represented as Cayley graphs. However, we offer this group-theoretic model not only to capture existing networks, but also to design new networks. It is in this vein that we suggest the pancake graphs. We have already pointed out how their degree and diameter (as a function of its size) are more attractive than the *n*-cubes. Later, in Section VI, we will show how we can design some fundamental computational algorithms on the pancake graphs. But first, we will show how even better graphs can be designed using the Cayley graph model.

IV. Transposition Trees

Again we recall that a Cayley graph is completely specified by providing a set of *d* permutations as generators. We do point out a requirement that this set of permutations be closed under inverses. In the examples of Cayley graphs given above, we have not explicitly shown to have met this condition since the generators that we have used have often been involutions, i.e., self-inverses. A specific class of involutions are the transpositions—permutations that swap two symbols. For example, 12435 is a transposition that swaps the symbols 3 and 4. All the generators of the bubble sort graphs are transpositions. In this section we provide a model for representing a set of $(n-1)$ transpositions as generators.

Consider a tree on *n* vertices. We can label the vertices of this tree with the symbols $\{1, 2, 3, \cdots, n\}$ and interpret the edges as transpositions. For example, the tree on six vertices shown in Fig. 7 gives rise to five transpositions: 321456, 132456, 124356, 123546, and 123654. Thus, we can interpret a tree as a set of transpositions, which in turn gives rise to a Cayley graph. We call such a tree, a *transposition tree*. As another example, the path on *n* vertices gives rise to the bubble sort graph. The following general theorem about Cayley graphs of transposition trees is an indication of the symmetry and structure underlying these graphs that can be readily uncovered by a simple group-theoretic analysis.

Theorem 4: Let Γ be a Cayley graph of a transposition tree

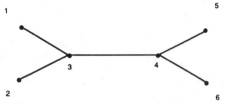

Fig. 7. An example of a transposition tree.

of order *n*. Then,

1) Γ has *n*! vertices.

2) the vertex connectivity of Γ is maximal, i.e., equal to its degree

3) Γ is bipartite, and hence its chromatic number is 2

4) the chromatic index of Γ is equal to its degree

5) the edges of the transposition tree can be ordered appropriately so as to render Γ a hierarchical Cayley graph. Thus, Γ can be represented as an interconnection of *n* identical copies of a Cayley graph of a transposition tree of order $n-1$.

Proof: Property 1 follows from a result in [3]. Property 5 (and, in particular, the transposition tree) can be obtained by successive additions of terminal edges. Property 2 follows from Properties 1 and 5 and a result in [2]. To establish Property 3, observe that all edges in Γ are between odd and even permutations. Property 4 follows trivially by edge coloring Γ with the corresponding generators. □

We can view the Cayley graph of a transposition tree as the state diagram of a puzzle. Consider the vertices of the transposition tree to be labeled as suggested above. Now place *n* markers, each labeled with a symbol from $\{1, 2, 3, \cdots, n\}$, at the vertices of the tree in any arbitrary way. The puzzle is to move the markers to their appropriate positions by moves consisting of interchanging the markers at the ends of an edge in the transposition tree. The Cayley graph is then the state diagram of such a puzzle. That is, the vertices of the Cayley graph are the possible arrangement of markers at the vertices of the tree. The edges of the Cayley graph correspond to the permissible moves in this puzzle. Finding a path in the Cayley graph corresponds to sorting a permutation, which in turn corresponds to solving this puzzle. And, consequently, the maximum number of moves required to solve the puzzle is, in fact, the diameter of the Cayley graph. The next theorem provides an upper bound for the number of moves required to solve this puzzle. The proof, which provides an actual algorithm for solving the puzzle, is given in the Appendix. Recall that $\eta(\pi)$ is the number of cycles in π.

Theorem 5: Let *T* be a transportation tree on *n* vertices. Given an assignment of markers as a permutation π of the vertices of *T*, π can be sorted in

$$\eta(\pi) - n + \sum_{i=1}^{n} \delta(i, \pi(i))$$

where, $\delta(i, j)$ is the distance between vertices *i* and *j* in *T*.

We remark that the above bound on the diameter of the Cayley graph conforms to the diameter of the bubble sort graph. In fact,

Theorem 6: Of all trees on *n* vertices, the path yields a Cayley graph (i.e., the bubble sort graph) of maximum diameter.

66

Proof: Follows by induction on n by noting that in any tree on n vertices a marker corresponding to a leaf can be positioned in at most $n - 1$ steps, after which that leaf of the tree can be ignored. $\square$

In this section, we have shown that a class of Cayley graphs can be concisely described using transposition trees. Just as a set of generators succinctly describes a large Cayley graph by exploiting the symmetries of the graph, a transposition tree succinctly describes a set of generators by exploiting the symmetries within the generators. Thus, by analyzing a tree on n vertices, we can describe properties of a much larger graph, the Cayley graph, on $n!$ vertices. In the next section, we do precisely this for a specific transposition tree.

V. The Star Graph

Motivated by Theorem 6, we consider the other extreme tree, namely the star, as a transposition tree. The resulting Cayley graph is called the *star graph*. Since this turns out to be an especially attractive alternative to the n-cube, we provide an informal description of this graph. The vertices of the graph are labeled by permutations of 1 though n. A permutation is connected to every other permutation that can be obtained from it by interchanging the first symbol with any of the other symbols. Thus, clearly the degree of the graph is $n - 1$. An illustration of the four-star graph was given in Fig. 4.

Let us examine how we might route within this graph. Recall that routing between two vertices in a Cayley graph is equivalent to sorting a permutation. So we need to ask how we might sort a given permutation by exchanging the first symbol with any of the other symbols. For example, consider the permutation 64725831. Let us employ a greedy algorithm where we observe that the symbol in the first position, namely 6, can be moved to its correct position by exchanging 6 and 8. This gives us the permutation 84725631. Again, a greedy move gives us 14725638. Now we are stuck, since 1 is already at its own position. We now must waste one step and move 1 into any position not occupied by the correct symbol. In this case, we could interchange 1 and 4 yielding the permutation 41725638. Now following the greedy approach gives us 21745638 and subsequently 12745638. Again we need to waste a step and insert 1 into a position not occupied by the correct symbol. Thus, interchanging 1 with 7 gives 72145638. Returning back to the greedy step gives 32145678 and the final move to 12345678. Notice that we took eight moves to sort this permutation. That means that in the Cayley graph we have shown a path of length 8 between 64725831 and the identity.

Lemma 1: Using the generators of the star graph, any permutation π can be sorted in the following number of steps.[4]

$$n + \eta(\pi) - 2\Psi(\pi) - \begin{cases} 2 & \text{if } \pi(1) \neq 1 \\ 1 & \text{otherwise.} \end{cases}$$

Proof: Follows from the routing algorithm described above. $\square$

[4] The number of cycles in a permutation includes the number of invariances.

Theorem 7: The diameter of the n-star graph is $\lfloor \frac{3(n-1)}{2} \rfloor$.

Proof: Note that when n is odd the expression in Theorem 7 becomes $3((n - 1)/2)$ and when n is even, $1 + (3(n - 2)/2)$. We shall now show two permutations which require precisely these numbers of steps. When n is odd consider: $13254 \cdots (n)(n - 1)$. Note that for any swap, one and only one position (other than the first) is involved. Now it is easily confirmed that to move 3 and 2 (currently in the second and third positions, respectively) to their correct positions, at least *three* swaps each involving the second or third position will be required. Since there are $(n - 1)/2$ such pairs, the above diameter follows. Likewise, when n is even, consider: $214365 \cdots (n)(n - 1)$. We can position 2 with one swap, but the remaining $(n - 2)/2$ pairs again each require three. Thus, the indicated diameter again follows. $\square$

Let us compare this network against the n-cube. Recall that the n-cube interconnects 2^n vertices with degree n and diameter n. In contrast, the n-star graph interconnects $n!$ vertices with degree $n - 1$ and diameter $\lfloor \frac{3(n-1)}{2} \rfloor$. Notice that both the degree and diameter of the star graph grows slower than a logarithmic function of its size. Thus, asymptotically, the star graphs offer a network with less interconnecting edges and smaller communication delays than the n-cubes. Even from a practical point of view, it is evident from Table I that purely based on the degree and diameter requirements, the star graph is superior. Table I provides a comparison of various n-cubes against comparable n-star graphs.

Of course, the degree and the diameter are not the only considerations for choosing a specific network. Let us examine some of the other relevant properties. The connectivity of the n-cube is n, indicating that up to $n - 1$ vertices can fail without disrupting the network. Recall that the connectivity is at most equal to the degree of the graph. In the case of the n-star graph, the degree is $n - 1$, and, indeed, its connectivity is also $n - 1$. So it is maximally fault tolerant. This is a result from [2]. Actually, such a worst case fault tolerance measure does not really reflect the practical fault tolerance of the network. Even though the n-cube has a connectivity of n, the only way to remove n vertices and disconnect the graph is by removing all the n neighbors of any one vertex—a very unlikely event. Likewise, even though the connectivity of the n-star graph is $n - 1$ the only way to remove $n - 1$ vertices and disconnect the graph is to remove all the $n - 1$ neighbors of any one vertex. In general, both these networks can tolerate a much higher failure.

With regard to symmetry considerations, we recall that the n-cube is both vertex and edge symmetric. This alleviates any congestion problems. We know that the star graphs, being Cayley graphs, are vertex symmetric. Furthermore, it follows from Theorem 2 that the star graph is edge symmetric. Finally, it follows from Theorem 4 that star graphs are hierarchical. In fact, the edge symmetric property implies that they are strongly hierarchical.

In this section, we have tried to make a case for the star graphs by comparing them to the n-cubes. We believe that the Cayley model extracts the attractive properties of the n-cubes and formulates it in an abstract setting. This allows us to design other networks that possess similar properties. the

TABLE I
A COMPARISON

	n-cube				n-star graph		
n	Size 2^n	Degree n	Diameter n	n	Size $n!$	Degree $n-1$	Diameter $\left\lfloor \frac{3}{2}(n-1) \right\rfloor$
7	128	7	7	5	120	4	6
8	256	8	8	6	720	5	7
9	512	9	9	6	720	5	7
10	1024	10	10	7	5040	6	9
11	2048	11	11	7	5040	6	9
12	4096	12	12	7	5040	6	9

star graphs being a prime example. An issue that we have not addressed in this section is how one uses the interconnection structure of these Cayley graphs to develop specific computational algorithms that can be executed on these networks. We address that in the next section using the pancake graphs as our example.

VI. ALGORITHMS ON THE PANCAKE GRAPHS

Recall that the n-pancake graphs are obtained using the $n-1$ possible pancake flips, which will denote by $f_2, f_3, \cdots, f_n$, as generators. The ith pancake flip, f_i, is a permutation that reverses the prefix of i symbols in the identity permutation. In Section II, we analyzed the degree and diameter of these graphs and also their recursive decomposition structure.

In this section, we show how we might implement certain fundamental algorithms on such a network. First, we should recount similar algorithms on the n-cube. Suppose we wish to find the maximal element among 2^n elements distributed among 2^n processors located at the vertices of an n-cube. A straightforward algorithm involves n time steps. At the ith step every processor communicates with the processor connected to it along the ith dimension and compares notes on the maximal element that it has encountered so far. We then claim that at the end of the n steps every processor knows the value of the maximal element. The proof of the claim goes as follows. Let d_i represent the edge along the ith dimension and let a word of the form d_2, d_4, d_3 represent a path in the n-cube starting from a specified vertex. Using these conventions, consider the word $d_1, d_2, \cdots, d_n$. It is easy to see that given any two vertices on the cube, there is a subsequence[5] of the above word that forms a path from the first to the second. Consequently, for every vertex a of the n-cube there is a subsequence of the above word that forms a path from the vertex containing the maximal element to a. This establishes the claim that the processor at every vertex knows the maximal element.

[5] A subsequence need not necessarily be a contiguous subsequence.

The reason for detailing the above algorithm is to establish the background necessary to implement a similar algorithm on interconnection networks. Thus, a general algorithm for finding the maximum of N elements distributed at the N vertices of some interconnection network can be viewed as a word over an alphabet of colors used to edge color the graph. The word is interpreted as was in the preceding paragraph, and the (parallel) time complexity of the algorithm is the length of the word. The correctness of the algorithm is established by demonstrating that for every pair of vertices, a and b, of the graph there is a subsequence of the word that forms a path from a to b.

Under this model, to establish an algorithm for finding the maximum of $n!$ elements distributed over the vertices of the n-pancake graph, what we need is a word on the alphabet of the generators $\{f_i\}$, such that given any two vertices in the pancake graph there exists a subsequence of the suggested word that forms a path between the two vertices. Actually, it is sufficient to show that we can sort an arbitrary permutation. We provide precisely that. First, we point out that in an algorithm such as the one suggested above for the n-cube, each processor communicates with only one other processor at each time step. Consequently, the number of processors that know the value of the maximal element can only double at each step. Thus, any such algorithm must take at least as many steps as the logarithm[6] of the number of vertices. In the case of the n-pancake graphs, which contain $n!$ vertices, this lower bound is $\Omega(n \log n)$.

Consider the following word (a single word of 21 symbols broken up into many lines) on the generators of an eight-pancake graph:

$$f_7 f_4 f_2 \quad f_8$$
$$f_6 f_4 f_2 \quad f_7$$
$$f_5 f_4 f_2 \quad f_6$$
$$f_4 f_2 \quad f_5$$
$$f_3 f_2 \quad f_4$$
$$f_2 \quad f_3$$
$$f_2.$$

The above word has been broken up into many lines to emphasize the block structure of the word, and the groupings within each block have been appropriately indicated.

We claim that for every permutation there is a subsequence of the above word that forms a path to the identity, i.e., sorts the given permutation. To sort the permutation we first bring the largest symbol, namely 8, to the first position. This is done using a subsequence of the first three letters in the word (grouped together to indicate that). It should be clear that we can bring 8 to the first position no matter where 8 starts out. Having done that we take 8 to the last position using f_8. Thus, the first block of the word is sufficient to position 8 in the correct place. As the reader might have guessed, the subsequent blocks of the word are each sufficient to position

[6] All logarithms are in base 2.

68

each of the remaining symbols in their correct places. We have proved the following general theorem.

Theorem 8: There is an $O(n \log n)$ algorithm to find the maximal element among $n!$ elements distributed among $n!$ processors located at the vertices of an n-pancake graph.

Proof: It should be clear how to generalize the word suggested above for the eight-pancake graph into a general word for the n-pancake graph. Furthermore, we can also similarly prove that every permutation of n symbols can be sorted by a subsequence of that word. The algorithm, then, is merely to execute one letter of that word at each time step. Executing a letter requires that every vertex communicate with the vertex connected to it along the edge corresponding to that generator and compare notes on the maximal element that it has encountered so far. Thus, the (parallel) time taken by this algorithm is exactly the length of the word. It is easy to see that the length of the word is $O(n \log n)$. □

In fact, we can use the above technique to construct a binary tree of depth $O(n \log n)$ over the $n!$ vertices of the pancake graph. Every edge of this tree is an edge of the pancake graph. Thus, we can simulate a binary tree. Once we do that, we can perform any computation for which an effective solution can be simulated on a binary tree. For example, the following theorem states, we can compute prefixes over an arbitrary associative binary operation.

Theorem 9: Given any associative binary operation $*$ and an assignment of values x_i to each of the $n!$ processors located at the vertices of an n-pancake graph, there is an $O(n \log n)$ algorithm that computes (in parallel) the prefix $x_1 * x_2 * \cdots * x_i$ at processor i. (The $n!$ vertices must be numbered appropriately.)

Proof: Follows from the construction for $P_0(n)$ given in [11]. □

The prefix computation problem is interesting because it is a general formulation of a class of problems. For example, the problem of computing the maximal element can be viewed as the prefix computation problem over the associative binary operation MAX. Other trivial applications include computing an n-ary associative operation, such as summation. Nontrivial applications include addition of binary numbers (particularly, computing the carry bits), simultaneous evaluation of polynomials, and other related problems (see [6]). The prefix computation is merely an example of how we might design algorithms on the pancake graphs. Clearly, there is considerable scope for further work in this area.

In the last two sections, we have described some of the attractive features of two new interconnection networks: the star graphs and the pancake graphs. We have shown how they compare against the n-cubes. We have used the n-cubes as our basis for comparison since (we believe) it is the most widely studied nontrivial interconnection network. However, the n-cubes themselves are Cayley graphs, as we mentioned in Section I. Even some of the variants of the n-cubes, such as the cube-connected cycles, can be abstracted as Cayley graphs. However, such an abstraction requires that we develop an interesting connection between group-theoretic products and graph-theoretic products. We do this in the next section.

VII. Products of Groups and Graphs

We now concentrate on the construction and representation of graphs as products of Cayley graphs. We might point out that our objective in this section is to present the cubes and the cube-connected cycles in the Cayley graph setting. As a consequence of that exercise, we also develop certain generic algebraic constructions that motivate the development of a class of graphs, that we call the *burnt pancake graphs*. However, most of the material in this section has less of a practical implication than the previous material presented in this paper. Furthermore, to develop the required construction we turn to some additional group-theoretic background. For the sake of brevity, some of the results in this section will be stated informally.

Recall that the direct product of two groups is a group on the ordered pairs with componentwise multiplication. Let G_1 and G_2 be two permutation groups and let $\{g_i^1\}$ and $\{g_i^2\}$ be sets of generators for these groups, respectively. Let Γ_1 and Γ_2 be the corresponding Cayley graphs and let $\Gamma_1 \times \Gamma_2$ represent their Cartesian product (see [5]). We now construct a Cayley graph for the direct product of G_1 and G_2. To do this we must choose an appropriate set of generators. (Note that by varying the choice of generators we can obtain different graphs for the same group.) Our choice of generators corresponds to the union of the generators for the constituent groups, i.e., $\{g_i^1\} \cup \{g_i^2\}$. However, note that the generators $\{g_i^1\}$ belong to the group G_1 and not to the direct product of G_1 and G_2. To account for this we use the identity elements e_1 and e_2 of the two group G_1 and G_2, respectively. Using these identities our choice of generators for the direct product of G_1 and G_2 is the set $\{(g_i^1, e_2)\} \cup \{(e_1, g_i^2)\}$. The following theorem and the subsequent corollary are immediate consequences of the above explanation.

Theorem 10: The Cayley graph of the direct product of G_1 and G_2 using the generators corresponding to $\{g_i^1\} \cup \{g_i^2\}$ is $\Gamma_1 \times \Gamma_2$.

Corollary 1: The n-cube is the Cayley graph of the nth direct product of S_2.

Definition: If G is a permutation group of order M on m symbols and H is a permutation group of order N on n symbols, the *wreath product $G \wr H$* is a permutation group of order $N \cdot M^n$ on $m \cdot n$ symbols. For each symbol i used in the group H we construct a copy G_i of G using m new symbols. For every permutation h in H we construct a set of permutations in $G \wr H$ by replacing each symbol i in h by a permutation from G_i in every possible way. An element of the wreath product is represented as $(g_1, g_2, \cdots, g_n, h)$, where $g_1, g_2, \cdots, g_n$ are group elements of G and h is a group element of H. The multiplication in $G \wr H$ is given by

$$(g_1, g_2, \cdots, g_n, h) * (g_1', g_2', \cdots, g_n', h')$$

$$= (g_{h(1)}g_1', g_{h(2)}g_2', \cdots, g_{h(n)}g_n', hh').$$

A proof that the wreath product indeed forms a group can be found in [10]. In fact, a more intuitive definition of a wreath product involves representing the elements as a two-level rooted ordered tree. The first level consists of vertices corresponding to the symbols of H. Each vertex at the first level contains a second level representing the specific permutation that has been chosen from G. Thus, the element $(g_1, g_2, \cdots, g_n, h)$ of $G \wr H$ is represented by a tree whose first level is the permutation h. Each symbol i of this permutation has a second level representing the permutation g_i.

As a concrete example, consider $S_2 \wr Z_3$. Here G is a group of two elements and H is a group of three elements on three symbols. Thus, $S_2 \wr Z_3$ contains 24 vertices. A typical element is (21, 12, 21, 231). This element will be represented as a tree as shown in Fig. 8. The action of this element of the wreath product can be viewed as follows. Consider the (obvious) identity tree. Apply the permutation 231 to the first level of the tree. Then apply the permutation 21, 12, and 21 to the first, second, and third subtrees. Clearly, this will result in precisely the tree shown in Fig. 8. The advantage of this view is that the product of two elements in the wreath product can now be defined as performing the action of each of the two elements successively. We leave it to the reader to verify that this definition of the wreath product is identical to the one given earlier.

Consider, again the group $S_2 \wr Z_3$. Let us identify three generators for this group, namely (12, 12, 12, 231), (12, 12, 12, 312), and (21, 12, 12, 123). Notice that the first two generators cyclically rotate the first level of the tree in each of the two directions. The third generator rotates the first subtree. The reader should convince himself that each of the 24 elements of $S_2 \wr Z_3$ can be generated using these generators. We are now ready to show how to interpret an element of this group as a vertex of a three-dimensional cube-connected cycles graph, shown in Fig. 3. As the reader might have guessed, the three subtrees correspond to the cube vertex and the first level of the tree indicates the position in the cycle. It then follows that the three chosen generators correspond to the three edges incident at that vertex: two edges along the cycle and an edge along the cube. We have thus shown that the Cayley graph of $S_2 \wr Z_3$ using the prescribed set of generators is the three-dimensional cube-connected cycles graph.

In fact, it follows from a generalization of the above argument that:

Theorem 11: The Cayley graph of $G \wr H$ under the prescribed generator set is the composition [7] of the Cayley graph of the nth direct product of G, and the Cayley graph of H.

Corollary 2: The n-dimensional cube-connected cycles is the Cayley graph of $S_2 \wr Z_n$ under the prescribed generator set.

Observe that $S_2 \wr I_n$, where I_n is the identity group on n symbols, is once again the n-cube! This prompts us to look at $S_2 \wr G$ for various other groups G and choices of generators. For example, $S_2 \wr S_2$ taken n times represents the symmetries of a complete binary tree of depth n. We can derive general results for computing the diameter of the wreath product, and tight results for the diameter of the Cayley graph of $\wr^n S_2$. It should be pointed out that the choice of an appropriate set of generators is critical for deriving the diameter of the Cayley graph.

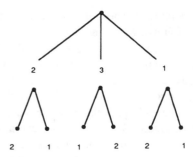

Fig. 8. An element of a wreath product.

As a final example of an interesting group-theoretic product, consider the Cayley graphs of $S_2 \wr S_n$, with the pancake generators for S_n. We can interpret this wreath product as the *burnt pancake flipping problem,* in which the pancakes are not only of different sizes, but are all consistently burnt on one side. The vertices of the Cayley graph are all possible arrangements of n burnt pancakes. Clearly, such an arrangement is uniquely specified by a permutation of n symbols and an n-bit vector.

Thus, an element of the wreath product will consist of a permutation (corresponding to the pancake arrangement) at the first level of the tree, and n independent elements of S_2 as the second level. Applying an i-flip using the spatula amounts to not only reversing the left i symbols of the first level of the tree, but also rotating the first i subtrees, since each of the first i pancakes would reverse sides. These spatula actions are captured by the following generators in the case of $n = 5$.

$$(21, 12, 12, 12, 12, 12345)$$

$$(21, 21, 12, 12, 12, 21345)$$

$$(21, 21, 21, 12, 12, 32145)$$

$$(21, 21, 21, 21, 12, 43215)$$

$$(21, 21, 21, 21, 21, 54321).$$

We state the following theorem without proof.

Theorem 12: The Cayley graph of $S_2 \wr P_n$, with the prescribed set of n generators, is the graph of the burnt pancake flipping problem.

We state the following theorem without proof.

Theorem 13: A stack of n burnt pancakes of different sizes can be sorted with at most $2n$ spatula flips.

Corollary 3: The Cayley graph of $S_2 \wr P_n$ has $n!2^n$ vertices with degree n and diameter $2n$.

In this section, we have indicated how the powerful techniques of algebraic products can be used to develop new and intricate interconnection networks. In particular, we showed that the familiar n-cubes and the cube-connected cycles can be represented as Cayley graphs by considering appropriate direct and wreath products of some well-known groups.

VIII. Conclusion

The main conclusion of this paper is that this group-theoretic view of symmetric interconnection networks not only abstracts the structure and symmetry properties that make the

---

[7] The composition of two graphs is informally defined as replacing vertices of one graph by copies of the other graph. Certain degree and size restrictions apply.

n-cubes so attractive, but also offers a fertile source of other promising topologies. We can now bring to bear the algebraic tools in analyzing such symmetric networks.[8] The universality of this model, indicated by Theorem 3, allows us to present all symmetric networks in a uniform and comparable framework.

Some of the immediate advantages of using Cayley graphs as a tool for modeling interconnection networks is the conciseness with which a symmetric network can be specified, i.e., by providing the set of generators for the Cayley graph. Furthermore, casting such a network as a Cayley graph immediately allows one to infer all the generic properties of Cayley graphs.

Aside from representing known interconnection networks as Cayley graphs, we have pointed out how this model offers a rich source of new topologies. In particular, the ability to start from a finite group and construct a Cayley graph is particularly attractive. We believe that we have hardly made a dent in the possible topologies that one could investigate. And even with such a limited investigation we have uncovered many topologies that compare favorably against the *n*-cubes.

The *n*-cubes have a number of attractive features. But many of these features can be interpreted as symmetry properties that many other Cayley graphs could well possess. We have indicated this at many places during the course of our presentation. A case in point is the recursive decomposition structure of Cayley graphs. That is really an analysis of the cosets of the group with respect to a given subgroup.

Finally, we have made an initial attempt at showing how we might design certain fundamental algorithms on such networks as the pancake graphs. We believe that the design of algorithms on such networks could conceivably use the algebraic properties of these graphs. There are definitely many open problems along these lines.

There are also many other features of an interconnection network that we have not at all addressed in this paper. For example, what are the issues involved in laying out these graphs? Can the *n*-star graphs be laid out at least as efficiently as the comparable *n*-cubes? We do conjecture that the *n*-star graphs can be laid out on a surface of genus $(n - 2)$.

In summary, we have offered a unified view of symmetric interconnection networks and suggested some new networks—the star graphs and the pancake graphs. We believe that we have done little more than scratch the surface of an obviously fertile field.

Appendix

Proof of Theorem 5: Denote the sum term by S, the number of cycles by c, and the number of moves (transpositions) by M. For any marker i, if $i = \pi(i)$, i will be said to be *homed*. Note that each homed marker contributes one (self-loop) cycle. Clearly if all markers are homed, $S = 0$ and $c = n$. Hence. $M = c - n + S$ will be 0.

If m markers are not homed, then $S \geq m$ and $c \geq n - m + 1$. Hence, M will positive. We shall show that M can be reduced to 0 with at most M transpositions.

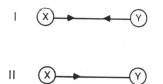

Fig. 9.   A case analysis.

Consider any unhomed marker x. There will be one and only one edge e, which leads from x's position to $\pi(x)$. We denote this fact by directing an arrow along e towards $\pi(x)$. We do this for all unhomed markers. Now it follows that we can always find an edge between (say) markers x and y—such that either x and y both want to move toward each other, (Case I in Fig. 9) or, x wants to move towards y and y is homed (Case II). Now it will be shown that in either case transposing x and y will reduce M.

First we note that if x and y are in the same cycle then transposing them will result in two cycles; and conversely that if they are in two cycles then one will result. Now consider Case I. Clearly, transposing x and y will reduce S by 2 since each marker goes in its desired direction. Thus, even if x and y are in the same cycle, c will increase by at most 1 and hence M will decrease.

Finally, in Case II x moves towards its desired position but y moves away. Thus, S does not change. However, since x and y are in different cycles (y is in a self-loop), c and hence M must decrease.

References

[1] *Amer. Math. Monthly,* vol. 82, no. 1, p. 1010, 1975.

[2] S. B. Akers and B. Krishnamurthy, "Group graphs as interconnection networks," in *Proc. 14th Int. Conf. Fault Tolerant Comput.,* 1984, pp. 422–427.

[3] C. Berge, in *Principles of Combinatorics.* New York: Academic, 1971, p. 141.

[4] N. L. Biggs, *Algebraic Graph Theory.* Cambridge, MA: Cambridge University Press, 1974.

[5] J. A. Bondy and U. S. R. Murty, *Graph Theory with Applications.* New York: North Holland, 1979.

[6] F. E. Fich, "New bounds for parallel prefix circuits," in *Proc. 15th Annu. ACM Symp. Theory Comput.,* 1983, pp. 100–109.

[7] E. Fuller and B. Krishnamurthy, "Symmetries in graphs: An annotated bibliography," Tektronix Lab. Tech. Rep. CR-86-03, 1986.

[8] W. H. Gates and C. H. Papadimitriou, "Bounds for sorting by prefix reversal," *Discrete Math,* vol. 27, pp. 47–57, 1979.

[9] I. N. Herstein, *Topics in Algebra.* Blaisdel, 1964.

[10] C. Hoffman, *Group Theoretic Algorithms and Graph Isomorphism.* New York: Springer-Verlag, 1982.

[11] R. E. Ladner and M. J. Fischer, "Parallel prefix computation," *J. ACM,* vol. 27, pp. 831–838, 1980.

[12] F. T. Leighton, *Complexity Issues in VLSI: Optimal Layouts for Shuffle Exchange Graphs and Other Networks.* Cambridge, MA: MIT Press, 1983, pp. 76–93.

[13] M. C. Pease, "The indirect binary *n*-cube microprocessor array," *IEEE Trans. Comput.,* vol. C-26, pp. 458–473, 1977.

[14] F. P. Preparata and J. Vuillemin, "The cube-connected cycles: A versatile network for parallel computation," *Commun. ACM,* vol. 24, no. 5, pp. 300–309, 1981.

[15] G. Sabidussi, "Vertex transitive graphs," *Monatsh. Math.* vol. 68, pp. 426–438, 1968.

[16] M. R. Samatham and D. K. Pradhan, "A multiprocessor network suitable for single-chip VLSI implementation," in *Proc. 11th Int. Symp. Comput. Architecture,* 1984, pp. 328–337.

[17] C. L. Seitz, "Concurrent VLSI architectures," *IEEE Trans. Comput.,* pp. 1247–1265, 1984.

[8] An extensive survey of the literature on the use of group-theoretic techniques in analyzing symmetries in graphs can be found in [7].

[18] H. S. Stone, "Parallel processing with the perfect shuffle," *IEEE Trans. Comput.*, vol. C-20, pp. 153–161, 1971.

[19] J. D. Ullman, *Computational Aspects of VLSI*. Rockville, MD: Computer Science Press, 1984, pp. 209–243.

[20] S. Zaks, "A new algorithm for generation of permutations," Tech. Rep. 220, Technion–Israel Instit. Technol., 1981.

Sheldon B. Akers (SM'62–F'75) was born in Washington, DC. He received the B.S. degree in electrical engineering and the M.A. degree in mathematics from the University of Maryland, College Park, in 1948, and 1952, respectively.

He is currently a Professor in the Department of Electrical and Computer Engineering, University of Massachusetts, Amherst. Prior to this, he was employed by the General Electric Company for 28 years, primarily at the Electronics Laboratory, Syracuse, NY. He was an Adjunct Professor at Syracuse University from 1973–1985 and a Visiting Professor in 1980. He has published a number of papers in the areas of switching theory, Boolean difference, placement and routing, test generation, binary decision diagrams, and self-testing.

Mr. Akers is a member of Pi Delta Epsilon, Omicron Delta Kappa, Sigma Xi, and the Mathematical Association of America. He has held a number of positions with the Technical Committees on Fault-Tolerant Computing and the Mathematical Foundations of Computing. He has served as a Distinguished Visitor for the Computer Society and received the Society's Honor Roll Award. He was a contributor to *Design Automation of Digital Systems* (Englewood Cliffs, NJ; Prentice-Hall, 1972) and an Associate Editor of the *Journal of Digital Systems*. He was a Guest Editor of the April 1986 IEEE TRANSACTIONS ON COMPUTERS Special Issue on Fault-Tolerant Computing.

Balakrishnan Krishnamurthy (M'85–SM'86) received the M.Sc. degree in mathematics from Birla Institute of Technology and Science, India, in 1976, and the M. S. and Ph.D. degrees in computer science from the University of Massachusetts, Amherst, in 1978 and 1981, respectively.

From 1981 to 1984 he was at various research centers of General Electric Company. He is currently at Tektronix Labs where he is the Director of their Computer Research Laboratory. His research interests include combinatorial algorithms particularly for design automation, digital testing, and parallel computation. He has held Adjunct Faculty positions at Rensselaer Polytechnic Institute and Oregon Graduate Center.

Dr. Krishnamurthy is a member of the Association for Computing Machinery.

On the Universality of Multipath Multistage Interconnection Networks[*]

T. H. SZYMANSKI

*Department of Electrical Engineering and Center for Telecommunications Research,
Columbia University, New York, New York 10027*

AND

V. C. HAMACHER

*Electrical Engineering and Computer Science Departments and Computer Systems Research
Institute, University of Toronto, Toronto, Ontario, Canada*

Received August 23, 1986

An analytic approximation for the blocking probability of a circuit-switched, multipath multistage interconnection network when it is required to perform arbitrary permutations under local control is presented. An analytic approximation for the expected number of conflict-free permutations realizable by a network in one pass under local control is also presented. In addition, an analytic approximation for the expected number of passes through a network required to realize an arbitrary permutation under local control is presented. These models give a quantitative measure of a network's ability to perform arbitrary permutations and of the inherent blocking in a network. These models are used to analyze two variations of banyan networks that have been discussed in the literature: dilated and augmented banyan networks. It is shown that these networks can be designed with very low blocking probabilities under permutation request patterns, and that they can be designed to realize almost all permutations in one pass under local control. © 1989 Academic Press, Inc.

LIST OF SYMBOLS

pb blocking probability of an interconnection network

$k^n \times k^n$ banyan   a banyan network with k^n inputs and k^n outputs, made with n stages of $k \times k$ crossbar switches, with k^{n-1} switches per stage

[*] This research was supported by NSERC (Canada) under Grant A-5192 and by the Center for Telecommunications Research at Columbia University under NSF Grant CDR-88-11111.

p-path $k^n \times k^n$ a banyan network, as specified above, with p physical links
   banyan   replacing each original link in the network
E_c the expected number of cycles required to realize a permu-
                        tation

1. Introduction

An $N \times N$ *multistage interconnection network* (MIN) is typically used to interconnect a set of N *input terminals* and a set of N *output terminals* using multiple stages of small, fixed-size crossbar switches. A *banyan* MIN is any MIN in which there is a unique path between each input and each output. A *multipath* MIN is any MIN that has a multiplicity of possible paths between some (or all) inputs and outputs.

In the circuit-switched mode of operation, each input receives a *call* (or *request*) for one particular output. The network is used to establish a *connection* (i.e., a circuit-switched path) between the input and the output specified by its call, over which data may be transferred.

A *permutation* is defined as a set of N simultaneous calls such that there is a one-to-one mapping of inputs onto outputs. A *nonblocking* network is defined as a network which can realize a call between any idle input and any idle output without disturbing any existing calls. Clearly, a nonblocking $N \times N$ network can realize any of the $N!$ permutations. A *rearrangeable* network is one in which a call between any idle input and any idle output can always be established, although some existing calls may have to be "rearranged" in order to make room for the new call.

The majority of networks examined in the literature are *blocking*, i.e., they cannot realize all $N!$ permutations. A number of quantitative performance measures have been defined for blocking networks. Beneš has defined the *combinatorial power* of a circuit-switched $N \times N$ network as the fraction of the $N!$ permutations that it can realize in "one pass" [4]. It is generally assumed that *global routing algorithms* are used in this definition, since a global routing algorithm can make optimal decisions when determining the routing of the permutation through the network.

When a network is blocking, it is still possible to realize a particular permutation of data by repeated passes of the data through the network. The *universality* of a network has been traditionally defined as the number of passes through the network required to realize an arbitrary permutation [41]. Typically, each pass through the network performs some admissible permutation of the data, until finally all data arrive at their intended destinations simultaneously. Global control is assumed in order to minimize the number of passes required.

The determination of the routing of a given permutation through a banyan network is simple since there is only one possible path through the network for each call. However, due to the unique path property banyan networks exhibit large inherent blocking probabilities and hence they can realize very few of the $N!$ permutations in one pass. The determination of the number of conflict-free permutations in a banyan network is also relatively simple since each distinct network state in which no blocking occurs realizes a distinct permutation [37].

Beneš has observed that the exact number of conflict-free permutations in an arbitrary network is a combinatorial property of the network, and that the determination of the optimal routing of a permutation through an arbitrary network is similar to the problem of packing objects into a knapsack in an optimal manner [4]. Most routing algorithms for permutation networks transform the routing problem into one of finding the edge coloring of a certain graph [30, 48]. Thus, the determination of the combinatorial power or universality of a multipath network (i.e., see [39]) are usually nontrivial combinatorial problems.

To date no simple techniques for estimating the combinatorial power or the universality of a network have been presented. The assumption that global routing algorithms are used in the previous definitions is responsible for the combinatorial nature of the analysis. If a simple distributed routing algorithm is assumed then the determination of these quantities is made considerably easier. Recently, a simple technique that yields an analytic approximation for the blocking probability of generalized multistage networks when they are required to perform arbitrary permutations under local control has been presented [44, 45, 47]. Using this quantity, it is shown that the fraction of conflict-free permutations and the universality, both under local control, can also be computed easily.

In this paper, a simpler but slightly less accurate analytic approximation for the blocking probability of generalized unique path and multipath multistage networks under permutations is presented, and a simple technique for estimating the number of conflict-free permutations in a multipath network under local control is developed. Since local control will perform no better than global control, then the fraction of conflict-free permutations under local control is a lower bound on the combinatorial power as defined by Beneš.

A simple technique for estimating the number of passes required to realize an arbitrary permutation through a multipath network under local control is also presented. Again, since local control will perform no better than global control, the number of passes required under local control is a lower bound on the number of passes required under global control. The proposed modeling techniques are general and they should be applicable to other multipath networks.

Currently, many of the networks studied in the literature have been examined for use in both telephone switching networks and parallel processors. In both applications, a network's ability to realize arbitrary permutations is an important consideration since it is a quantitative measure of the inherent blocking in the network (there are no output port conflicts when a network performs a permutation). The inherent blocking of a network gives a measure of the efficiency of the use of crosspoints in the design of a network. The techniques proposed in this paper are used to evaluate two variations of multipath networks that have been presented in the literature previously—dilated and augmented banyan networks. It has been shown that dilated banyans can be designed to have extremely low blocking probabilities under permutations [47]. In this paper, it is shown that these networks can be designed to realize almost all of the $N!$ permutations in one pass under local control.

Section 2 includes the necessary background and definitions. Section 3 presents a simple analytic model for the blocking probability of MINs under arbitrary permutations and local control. Section 4 presents an analytic approximation for the expected number of conflict-free permutations realizable by a multipath MIN under local control. Section 5 presents an analytic approximation for the expected number of network passes required to realize an arbitrary permutation under local control, which will be defined as the universality of a network under local control. Section 6 presents a performance comparison of various MINs under arbitrary permutations. Section 7 summarizes the paper and contains some concluding remarks.

2. Background

In this section, banyan MINs and the two multipath MINs derived from banyan MINs that are considered in the paper are reviewed. The traditional definition of the universality of a network (under global control) and our definition (under local control) are also given.

2.1. Interconnection Networks

The crossbar network is nonblocking, i.e., it can realize all $N!$ permutations under local control. However, this network requires $O(N^2)$ crosspoints [11] and large crossbars are impractical to build. There has been a considerable amount of research on networks with reasonable (i.e., $O(N \log N)$) crosspoint complexities whose performance under permutations approaches that of a crossbar.

A *banyan* network is defined as any network with a unique path between each input/output pair [15]. Multistage banyans (called *delta* networks in [37]) are constructed with multiple stages of switches. A square $k^n \times k^n$ SW-banyan [15] network of size N consists of $n = \log_k N$ stages, where each stage consists of N/k crossbar switches of size $k \times k$, as shown in Fig. 1a. Each switch is said to be of degree k. A topologically equivalent network called the *omega* network [23] is shown in Fig. 1b. These *banyan* networks have a number of desirable features; their cost is $O(N \log N)$ crosspoints and they use simple, distributed routing algorithms (i.e., they use *local control*). However, due to the unique path property these networks exhibit large inherent blocking probabilities. Under arbitrary permutations, the blocking probability of a banyan is a measure of the inherent blocking within the network, since there are no output port conflicts in a permutation.

The routing algorithm for multistage banyan networks is as follows [15]. (Assume 2×2 switches; the algorithm easily generalizes to larger switches.)

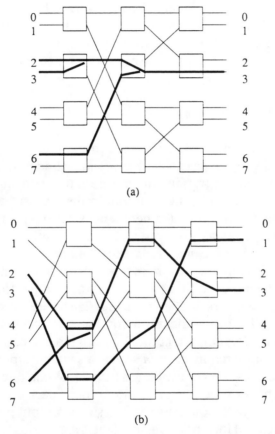

(a)

(b)

FIG. 1. (a) A $2^3 \times 2^3$ SW-banyan network connecting eight inputs $(0 \cdots 7)$ and eight outputs $(0 \cdots 7)$. Attempted routing from 2 to 3, 3 to 1, and 6 to 2 is shown by the thick lines. Link contention occurs in the first and second stages. (b) A topologically equivalent network called the omega network with different link contention for the same three requests.

Each request contains an n-bit destination *tag* equal to the binary address of the requested output port. In the mth stage, a switch that receives a request examines the mth most significant bit in the destination tag and selects an output port based on the value of the bit. If the bit is a 0 the upper output port is selected, and if the bit is a 1 the lower output port is selected. If only one request selects a particular output port, it is forwarded on the single output link. When two requests arrive at one switch and select the same output port, *link contention* has occurred. One request is selected randomly and forwarded, and the other is *blocked*. Figure 1 shows the attempted routing for requests from 2 to 3, 3 to 1, and 6 to 2. Two requests are involved in link contention in the first stage and only one request is forwarded. The winner of that contention is also involved in link contention in the second stage.

In general, the introduction of multiple paths between input/output pairs increases the fault tolerance of a network and it may lead to performance improvements as well. (Note that such a network is by definition no longer a banyan network due to the path multiplicity.) In this paper, our analytic models will be applied to two multipath variations of banyans that have been described in the literature previously—dilated and augmented banyan networks.

2.1.1. *Dilated Banyan Networks*

A *d-dilated* banyan network is obtained from an unmodified (1-dilated) banyan network by replacing each link by d independent links [21] (also see [20]). For example, one way in which a d-dilated banyan can be implemented is by space multiplexing each link in the regular banyan so that it can support up to d connections (rather than just one connection). Call each link in the regular (1-dilated) banyan a "logical" link, and call each of the d links that replace it a link. Since each logical link in a 1-dilated banyan network is effectively replaced by d independently controllable links, the network's fault tolerance to link failures is improved considerably. A 2-dilated SW-banyan network is shown in Fig. 2a, where all of the links are shown explicitly. The routing algorithm for these networks is a simple generalization of that used in unipath networks. Each request carries an n-bit destination tag, and a switch in stage m selects a switch output port based on the mth most significant bit of the tag (as before). When one or two requests arrive at a switch and select the same output port, each request can be forwarded. If three or more requests arrive at a switch output port, then two are randomly selected and forwarded and the others are *blocked*. Figure 2a shows the routing for the same requests as those used in Fig. 1. Observe that in a 2-dilated $2^n \times 2^n$ network, the first stage does not block any requests ever (assuming that each network input receives just one request per cycle), and the last stage does not block any requests destined for distinct outputs.

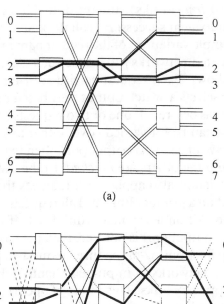

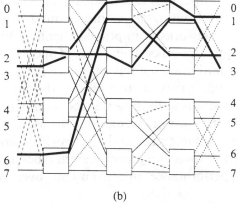

Fig. 2. (a) A 2-dilated $2^3 \times 2^3$ SW-banyan network. (b) A 2-augmented $2^3 \times 2^3$ SW-banyan network. Possible routings for requests from 2 to 3, 3 to 1, and 6 to 2 are shown by the thick lines.

2.1.2. Augmented Networks

Each logical link in a 1-dilated banyan is treated as d-independent links in a d-dilated banyan. However, each of these links shares the same source switch and the same destination switch. It is possible to distribute each set of d links among a number of the switches in the next stage as a means of achieving much greater fault tolerance to node failures. These networks are called *augmented* networks [40]. In a 2-augmented banyan network, one link leads to the same switch that it would lead to in the unmodified banyan network, and the other link leads to a functionally equivalent switch (two switches that are functionally equivalent have the same successors in the next stage). A 2-augmented SW-banyan network is shown in Fig. 2b. The solid lines represent links leading to the same successor that they normally would lead to (call these *primary* links), and the dotted lines represent links leading to functionally equivalent successors (call these *secondary* links).

A number of simple variations of the regular banyan routing algorithm can be used in augmented networks [40]. One such algorithm for 2-augmented networks is as follows. Each request carries an n-bit destination tag, and a switch in stage m selects a switch output port based on the mth most significant bit of the tag (as before). If one or two requests arrive at a switch output port, each request can be forwarded (over either available link). If three or more requests arrive at a switch output port, then two are randomly selected and forwarded, and the others are *blocked*. In the last stage of the network, the following restriction also applies. All requests that arrive on a primary link must also exit on a primary link, and all requests that arrive on a secondary link must also exit on a secondary link [40]. If the appropriate link in the selected switch output port is not free, then the request is blocked. Figure 2b shows one possible routing of the three requests used in Fig. 1. (The performance of these networks is improved slightly when processors submit their requests on primary links. This mode of operation is assumed.)

The primary contributions of this paper are the modeling techniques for the ability of a multipath network to perform arbitrary permutations. Dilated and augmented networks were chosen as the multipath MINs to be analyzed in this paper for the following reasons. First, the use of dilations or augmentations increases the fault tolerance of the network considerably. Second, these multipath networks exhibit very low inherent blocking and hence they may offer significant performance improvements over conventional banyan networks.

2.2. Cost and Delay Modeling Assumptions

Throughout this paper it is assumed (unless otherwise stated) that all switches are built on a single integrated circuit (IC) and that all switches in any one network are of the same size. In a comparison of the delays of networks built with switches of different sizes, some normalization is required [13]. Due to pin limitations on each IC, it is usually assumed that each IC has a fixed amount of total I/O bandwidth. Assuming that the bandwidth is evenly distributed over all incident links, the bandwidth of a link is proportional to the degree of the switch. Hence, the delay in propagating a fixed amount of data between two switches over a link is proportional to the degree of the switches. It is often assumed that the delay of a network is equal to the degree of its switches times the length of a path (in the number of links) through the network [18]. (Note that this simple delay measure does not consider queuing delays due to external or internal blocking in the networks.) This assumption is made for the circuit-switched networks considered in this paper. Under this assumption, the delay of a d-dilated (or d-augmented) MIN is d times the delay of a 1-path MIN.

One possible implementation of a d-dilated banyan network is to allow the space multiplexing of d paths onto each link of the regular banyan. In this case the cost (in the number of ICs or logical links) of a d-dilated banyan network is identical to the cost of an unmodified (i.e., a 1-dilated) banyan network. (Assume that the extra control logic overhead can be easily realized on the VLSI IC.) However, as a result of this multiplexing the bandwidth of each circuit-switched path is decreased by a factor of d. (The same effect is true for packet-switched versions of these networks.)

A 2-augmented network will have a more complex wiring pattern than the unmodified network, since the physical links now go to different switches in general. Cost estimates of the augmented networks must consider the effects of the wiring.

Throughout this paper, we do not distinguish between dilated and augmented networks since their performances are similar. Each of these multipath networks will be denoted as a p-path MIN, where p is the path multiplicity per stage. Note that using this notation, a p-path MIN will have k^{n+1} paths that differ by at least one link between any input/output pair.

2.3. The Universality of a Network

The universality of a network has been defined as the maximum number of passes through a network required to realize an arbitrary permutation. Global control is usually assumed in order to minimize the number of passes. It has been shown that under global control, three passes through the omega (or equivalently $3 \cdot \log_2 N$ passes through the single stage Shuffle Exchange Network (SEN)) are sufficient to realize any permutation [35]. It has also been shown that under global control $3 \log_2 N - 1$ [51], $3 \log_2 N - 3$ [19], and $3 \log_2 N - 4$ [39] passes through the single stage SEN are sufficient to realize any permutation. It has been shown that under local control $6 \log_2 N$ passes through the omega network are sufficient to realize any permutation [43].

The definition of the universality used in this paper is slightly different from the traditional definition. Here it is assumed (1) that local control is used, and (2) that a request is removed as soon as it reaches its destination. Under local control, the expected number of passes through the network required to realize an arbitrary permutation is the desired performance measure. Note that each request is removed as soon as it reaches its destination, and that any requests that are blocked in one cycle are resubmitted during the next cycle.

3. THE PERMUTATION CAPABILITY OF MULTISTAGE INTERCONNECTION NETWORKS

Our analytic approximations for the number of conflict-free permutations in a network and for the universality of a network under local control will make use of the blocking probability of the network under arbitrary permutations and local control. It has been shown previously that accurate analytic approximations for the blocking probability of a network under arbitrary permutations and local control can be obtained from an analytic model for the blocking probability of the same network under random and uniform requests and local control through a simple modification of biasing probabilities [47]. The same technique will be used in this paper to generate a simpler (and slightly less accurate) analytic approximation for the blocking probability of dilated/augmented networks under arbitrary permutations and local control.

It is first necessary to derive an analytic model for the blocking probability of p-path $k^n \times k^n$ MINs under the assumption of random, uniform request patterns. This model is then modified (in the next subsection) to yield the blocking probability under the assumption of permutation request patterns (or simply under permutations).

3.1. Analysis of Multistage Interconnection Networks under Random Request Patterns

In this section, an approximate analytic model for the blocking probability of generalized p-path $k^n \times k^n$ MINs under random request patterns is presented. This analysis is simpler but slightly less accurate than the exact analysis for dilated banyans presented in [47].

The assumptions for the analysis are as follows: (1) During the beginning of each cycle every processor issues a single request with probability u_0; (2) requests are randomly and uniformly distributed among the memories; and (3) unsatisfied requests in any cycle are ignored, and a new set of requests is issued during the next cycle subject to (1) and (2).

Assume that any physical link between stages i and $i + 1$ carries one request with probability u_i, the aggregate link utilization. Hence, the probability that a switch in a particular stage receives i requests can be modeled by a simple binomial distribution. Since each p-path $k \times k$ switch has pk inputs, the probability that i requests arrive at the switch in stage $m + 1$ is given by

$$\binom{pk}{i} u_m^i (1 - u_m)^{pk-i}.$$

The probability that j of these requests select a particular logical output port is given by

$$\binom{i}{j}\left(\frac{1}{k}\right)^{j}\left(1-\frac{1}{k}\right)^{i-j}.$$

Since each processor submits at most one request by assumption, then due to path multiplicity the first f stages will not block, where f is given by

$$f = \lfloor \log_k p \rfloor.$$

The aggregate link utilization u_f after stage f is simply u_0/p.

In general, after any stage $m + 1$ we are interested in $p(i)$, the probability that a logical link carries i requests. The $p(i)$, for $0 \leqslant i \leqslant p$, can be calculated as follows:

For $j < p$:

$$p(j) = \sum_{i=j}^{pk} \binom{pk}{i} u_m^i (1 - u_m)^{pk-i} \binom{i}{j}\left(\frac{1}{k}\right)^{j}\left(1-\frac{1}{k}\right)^{i-j}. \tag{1.1}$$

For $j = p$:

$$p(j) = \sum_{i=p}^{pk} \binom{pk}{i} u_m^i (1 - u_m)^{pk-i} \sum_{t=p}^{i} \binom{i}{t}\left(\frac{1}{k}\right)^{t}\left(1-\frac{1}{k}\right)^{i-t}. \tag{1.2}$$

After each stage $m + 1$, the aggregate link utilization u_{m+1} is computed as

$$u_{m+1} = \sum_{i=0}^{p} \frac{p(i)\cdot i}{p}. \tag{1.3}$$

The blocking probability of a network of size $N \geqslant 2^{f+1}$ (assuming each memory services at most one request in each cycle) is then

$$pb = 1 - \frac{p(0)}{u_f}. \tag{1.4}$$

Figure 3a illustrates the analytic results and simulations for various augmented and dilated networks. The model is exact for unipath networks, but is only an approximation for multipath networks.

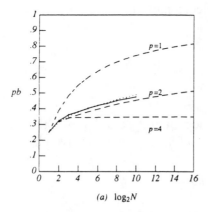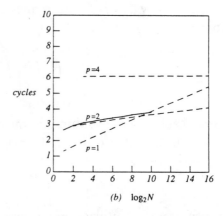

FIG. 3. (a) Blocking probability of p-path $2^n \times 2^n$ banyans under random distributions. (b) Expected service time in cycles for an individual (random) request at 100% utilization (normalized w.r.t. unipath network cycle time). Solid curves are simulations for augmented networks, dotted curves are simulations for dilated networks, and dashed curves are analytic.

The expected number of cycles required to satisfy an individual request (when all requests are random and independent from cycle to cycle) is given by

$$(1 - pb) \cdot 1 + pb(1 - pb) \cdot 2 + pb^2(1 - pb) \cdot 3 + \cdots \approx \frac{1}{1 - pb}.$$

In a comparison of the delays through networks built with different sizes of switches, some normalization is required. According to the delay assumptions discussed in Section 2, the delay through a p-path network built with $k \times k$ switches is equal to p times the delay through a 1-path network built with $k \times k$ switches. The normalized expected service time expressed in 1-path network cycle times, for a single (random) request, is shown in Fig. 3b. From Fig. 3b, it is clear that when the network is fully saturated, a synchronously circuit-switched 2-dilated (or 2-augmented) banyan network outperforms the corresponding unipath banyan network for large enough N.

The preceding discussion indicates that in many practical designs, a 2-dilated (or 2-augmented) banyan network may be preferable to a unipath banyan network based on performance considerations alone (when requests are random and independent). Since these multipath MINs offer significant fault tolerance improvements as well, they may be viable alternatives to unipath MINs in many practical applications. It will also be shown that multipath MINs offer significant performance improvements when the requests submitted to the network are permutations.

3.2. Analysis of Multistage Interconnection Networks under Permutation Request Patterns

The previous model for the blocking probability under random requests can be adapted to yield the blocking probability of the network under arbitrary partial or complete permutations, using the technique presented in [47]. The blocking probability under arbitrary permutations is the probability that an issued request will block in the network given that the set of requests forms a randomly selected partial or complete permutation.

The assumptions for the analysis are as follows: (1) During the beginning of each cycle every processor issues a request with probability u_0; (2) each memory module is requested by at most one processor and the requests are uniformly distributed over the memories; and (3) unsatisfied requests in any cycle are ignored, and a new set of requests is issued during the next cycle subject to (1) and (2).

Consider the $2^3 \times 2^3$ SW-banyan network shown in Fig. 1b. An output link from the first stage can reach four different memories, and a switch in the first stage can reach eight different memories. The first request arriving at a switch in the first stage selects an output link with probability $4/8$. A second request arriving at the same switch selects the same output link with probability $3/7$, and selects the other output link with probability $4/7$.

The preceding technique can be generalized; consider the probabilities of requests selecting outputs at a particular p-path $k \times k$ crossbar switch in stage m of any multipath, multistage banyan network. Each output link leads to k^{n-m} memory modules. The first request selects a particular output link with probability k^{n-m}/k^{n-m+1}. Given that the first request selects a particular output link, the second request selects that same output link with probability $(k^{n-m} - 1)/(k^{n-m+1} - 1)$.

As a notational convenience, define function $p\_s(s, r, m)$ as the exact probability that a request at a switch in stage m will select a particular output link given that s requests have already selected that link, and that r requests have already selected other links.

$$p\_s(s, r, m) = \begin{cases} \dfrac{k^{n-m} - s}{k^{n-m+1} - s - r}, & \text{for} \quad s < k^{n-m}, \quad r + s < k^{n-m+1} \\ 0, & \text{otherwise.} \end{cases}$$

The exact probability that j requests select a particular output link leading to k^{n-m} memories in stage m is given by

$$\prod_{s=0}^{j-1} p\_s(s, 0, m) = \binom{k^{n-m}}{j} \bigg/ \binom{k^{n-m+1}}{j}.$$

In a similar manner, define function $p\_ns(s, r, m)$ as the exact probability that a request at a switch in stage m will not select a particular output link given that s requests have already selected that link, and that r requests have already selected other links.

$$p\_ns(s, r, m)$$

$$= \begin{cases} \dfrac{(k-1)k^{n-m} - r}{k^{n-m+1} - s - r}, & \text{for} \quad r < (k-1)k^{n-m}, \quad s + r < k^{n-m+1} \\[2ex] 0, & \text{otherwise.} \end{cases}$$

The exact probability that $i - j$ requests do not select a particular output link leading to k^{n-m} memories in stage m, given that j requests already have selected that output link, is given by

$$\prod_{r=0}^{i-j-1} p\_ns(j, r, m) = \binom{(k-1)k^{n-m}}{i-j} \bigg/ \binom{k^{n-m+1} - j}{i-j}.$$

Assuming that the events occurring at the inputs of each switch in stage $m + 1$ of the banyan network are independent (which is the primary source of error in the analytic model and which will result in a slightly pessimistic blocking probability), the probability that i requests arrive on pk input links of a switch in stage $m + 1$ is given by

$$\binom{pk}{i} u_m^i (1 - u_m)^{pk-i}.$$

Given that i requests arrive at a switch in stage $m + 1$, the exact probability that j of these requests select a particular output and that $i - j$ of these requests do not select that same output is given by

$$\binom{i}{j} \prod_{s=0}^{j-1} p\_s(s, 0, m) \prod_{r=0}^{i-j-1} p\_ns(j, r, m)$$

or equivalently

$$\binom{i}{j} \frac{\dbinom{k^{n-m}}{j} \cdot \dbinom{(k-1)k^{n-m}}{i-j}}{\dbinom{k^{n-m+1}}{j} \cdot \dbinom{k^{n-m+1} - j}{i-j}}.$$

Hence, Eq. (1.1) can be modified easily to yield an accurate approximation of the blocking probability of generalized p-path $k^n \times k^n$ banyans under permutation requests. With the assumptions, the first f stages will not block, where f is given by

$$f = \lfloor \log_k p \rfloor.$$

Under permutation requests, the last l stages will not block, where l is given by

$$l = \lfloor \log_k p \rfloor + 1.$$

The aggregate utilization u_f on links leaving stage f must be computed; since the first f stages did not block, let $u_f = u_0/p$. In general, after any stage $m + 1$ the value of $p(i)$, the probability that a logical link carries i requests, is required. The $p(i)$, for $0 \le i \le p$, can be calculated as follows:

For $j < p$:

$$p(j) = \sum_{i=j}^{pk} \binom{pk}{i} u_m^i (1 - u_m)^{pk-i} \cdot \binom{i}{j} \prod_{x=0}^{j-1} p\_s(x, 0, m) \prod_{x=0}^{i-j-1} p\_ns(i, x, m).$$

$$(2.1)$$

For $j = p$:

$$p(j)$$

$$= \sum_{i=p}^{pk} \binom{pk}{i} u_m^i (1 - u_m)^{pk-i} \cdot \sum_{t=p}^{i} \binom{i}{t} \prod_{x=0}^{j-1} p\_s(x, 0, m) \prod_{x=0}^{i-t-1} p\_ns(i, x, m),$$

$$(2.2)$$

which can also be expressed as

For $j < p$:

$$p(j) = \sum_{i=j}^{pk} \binom{pk}{i} u_m^i (1 - u_m)^{pk-i} \cdot \binom{i}{j} \frac{\binom{k^{n-m}}{j} \cdot \binom{(k-1)k^{n-m}}{i-j}}{\binom{k^{n-m+1}}{j} \cdot \binom{k^{n-m+1}-j}{i-j}}.$$

$$(2.3)$$

For $j = p$:

$$p(j) = \sum_{i=p}^{pk} \binom{pk}{i} u_m^i (1 - u_m)^{pk-i} \cdot \sum_{t=p}^{i} \binom{i}{t} \frac{\binom{k^{n-m}}{t} \cdot \binom{(k-1)^{n-m}}{i-t}}{\binom{k^{n-m+1}}{t} \cdot \binom{k^{n-m+1}-t}{i-t}}.$$

$$(2.4)$$

After each stage $m + 1$, the aggregate link utilization u_m leaving stage m is computed as

$$u_m = \sum_{i=0}^{p} \frac{p(i) \cdot i}{p}.$$
(2.5)

The blocking probability of the network is then

$$pb = 1 - \frac{u_{n-l}}{u_f}.$$
(2.6)

This model is compared with simulations in the next subsection.

3.2.1. *Comparison of Model with Simulations*

This analytic model is compared with a number of simulations, for various unipath and multipath MINs. Figure 4 illustrates the blocking probabilities for various augmentations of $k^n \times k^n$ banyans of size N under permutation requests. (The pb of dilated and augmented networks, with the same path multiplicity, differ by only a few percent; these simulations happen to be for augmented networks, although the model is more accurate for dilated networks.) These figures indicate that the model is reasonably accurate. The $p = 1$ curve in (a) is very close to the simulation results reported by Franklin [12]. The $p = 4$ curves are very close to zero and are not easily visible. The $p = 8$ networks exhibit very low blocking probabilities (typically less than 10^{-6}) and their curves are not visible on this scale.

The simulation results were obtained as follows. First, a permutation is selected at random (using a standard pseudorandom number generator). This permutation is submitted to the network, the network is simulated, and the number of blocked requests is recorded as one observation. This procedure is repeated until the 95% confidence intervals of the average observed blocking probability are less than 1%. The simulations typically sampled 500 randomly selected permutations for each network of size N. While 500 is a vanishingly small number compared to the $N!$ possible permutations for large N, the 95% confidence intervals obtained from these samples are very small and they are not easily visible on these graphs.

There are two major sources of error in this model. First, the analytic model for the pb under the assumption of random, independent requests is itself only an approximation and has an error of a few percent. (More detailed analyses for the blocking probability have been presented in [47].) Second, when the model is adapted for permutation requests, the assumption that requests arriving at the inputs of a switch are statistically indepen-

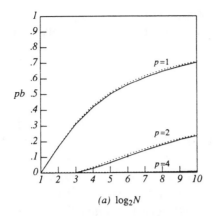 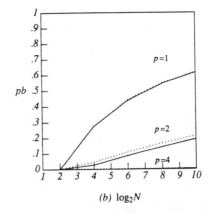

FIG. 4. (a) *pb* for various augmentations of $2^n \times 2^n$ networks with N sources under permutation requests. (b) *pb* for various augmentations of $4^n \times 4^n$ networks with N sources under permutation requests. (Solid curves are simulations with very small 95% confidence intervals; dotted curves are analytic.)

dent introduces some small inaccuracies. However, more refined analyses can take these considerations into account (see [47]).

The techniques presented here are general, and models for the blocking probability of other multipath MINs under the assumptions of arbitrary permutations should be easily created from their analytic models for their blocking probability under the assumption of random requests using the same technique.

4. ON THE EXPECTED NUMBER OF CONFLICT-FREE PERMUTATIONS IN MULTIPATH MINS

A simple technique for determining the exact number of conflict-free permutations in unipath $2^n \times 2^n$ MINs has been presented in [1, 9, 35, 37]. An analysis that was extended to $k^n + k^n$ banyans was also presented in [9]. A similar analysis for $k^n \times k^n$ multistage banyans is presented here.

In a unipath MIN with N processors and N memories, there are exactly N links between stages. If a permutation (of N requests) is conflict-free, then every link must carry one request. Hence, each $k \times k$ switch will have k requests arriving at its inputs and it must have k requests leaving on its outputs (so that no requests block). Each switch can therefore perform $k!$ mappings of its inputs to its outputs, i.e., there are $k!$ distinct settings for each switch. Since the network has a unique path between each input/output pair, each output link leads to distinct outputs. Therefore every distinct switch state must result in a different mapping for at least one input. The number of distinct permutations is therefore equal to the number of distinct network states. Since there are N/k switches per stage, and $\log_k N$ stages, the exact number of conflict-free permutations in a unipath network is simply

$$(k!)\exp\left(\frac{N}{k} \cdot \log_k N\right). \tag{1}$$

In a multipath network, the analysis is much more difficult. Since there are more than N links between each stage, each link does not necessarily carry a request, and each switch does not necessarily have k requests arriving at its inputs. Furthermore, each distinct switch state does not necessarily lead to a distinct permutation. Therefore, the number of distinct permutations is not necessarily equal to the number of distinct network states. Equation (1) can be adapted to estimate the number of distinct switch settings in a multi-path MIN [36]; however, this estimate "does not come close to estimating the number of permutations realizable by the [gamma] network. Estimating the actual number of permutations seems to be much harder" [36]. In this section, an approximate analytic model for the expected number of conflict-free permutations in multipath MINs under local control is presented.

Let X be the random variable denoting the number of requests that block in one cycle, given that N requests which form a permutation are submitted initially. In this section, we wish to find an analytic model for the probability distribution function pdf [6] of X, denoted pdf(X), for $0 \leqslant X \leqslant N$.

The simplest approach is to hypothesize that all requests are statistically identical and independent, and that pdf(X) is simply binomially distributed;

$$\text{Prob}(X = i) = \binom{N}{i} pb^i (1 - pb)^{N-i}. \tag{2}$$

Equation (2) gives an estimate for the Prob($X = i$) when each of the N processors submits a request. In general, the value Prob($X = i$) when only j of the processors submit requests will also be of interest. This situation occurs when a partial permutation consisting of j requests is submitted to the network. Assuming that the j processors issuing the requests are randomly distributed over the inputs of the network, and that the requests are randomly distributed over the memories such that no memory is requested by more than one processor, an expression for the Prob($X = i$) is simply

$$\text{Prob}(X = i) = \binom{j}{i} pb^i (1 - pb)^{j-i}. \tag{3}$$

Figure 5 illustrates the observed pdf(X) versus the hypothesized values for various networks. (Note that the pb obtained from simulations was used in computing the hypothesized pdf's.) From Fig. 5, observe that the independence assumption is very accurate for the multipath banyans, and reasonably close for the unipath banyans. The hypothesized pdf (given by Eq. (2)) can be compared to the observed pdf and the quality of the "fit" can be determined by using the χ^2 *goodness of fit* test [6]. At a 5% level of significance, the hypothesis is rejected for most unipath networks and accepted for all multipath networks that were simulated. (The hypothesis is accepted when there are no significant statistical differences between the hypothesized pdf and the observed pdf.)

Given that the pdf(X) is reasonable for multipath networks, an accurate estimate of the number of conflict-free permutations in these networks N_p is as follows. There are $N!$ permutations of N elements, and the probability that all N requests in a permutation are accepted is simply $(1 - pb)^N$. Hence, N_p is given by

$$N_p \approx N! \cdot (1 - pb)^N. \qquad (4)$$

Note that Eq. (4) is valid as long as the independence assumption behind Eq. (3) is valid, whether the network is unique path or multipath. Our simulations indicate that for unipath networks the hypothesized pdf is less accurate, primarily because the independence assumption is not valid. A more complicated multinomial distribution that models the effects of the statistical dependence explicitly is required for the hypothesized pdf of unipath networks.

Equation (4) yields an estimate for the fraction of conflict-free permutations in a network under local control. Since global control will always perform as well as or better than local control, the fraction of conflict-free permutations under local control is a lower bound for Beneš' combinatorial power. Conversely, the combinatorial power is an upper bound for the number of conflict-free permutations under local control. (In general, Eq. (2.6) gives a reasonably accurate estimate of pb, which can be used in Eq. (4).)

Using Eq. (4), the number of conflict-free permutations in 2-path, 4-path, and 8-path multistage banyans can be estimated. The results of a comparison between some well-known networks are shown in Table I. The results for the 2-, 4-, and 8-path banyans were obtained by using the analytic model for the blocking probability. Recall from Fig. 4 that the analytic blocking probability is slightly higher than the simulated values. Hence, the estimate for the number of conflict-free permutations may be pessimistic for the multipath banyans. The results for the 1-path omega can be computed using Eq. (1). The results for the ADM/IADM networks and the Beneš network were taken from Leland's Ph.D. thesis [27]. Note that the Beneš network can realize all $N!$ permutations, and hence the values under the Beneš column are also approximations for $N!$.

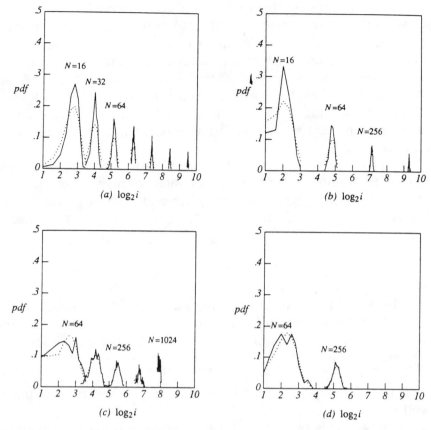

FIG. 5. (a) pdf(X) for unipath $2^n \times 2^n$ banyans. (b) pdf(X) for unipath $4^n \times 4^n$ banyans. (c) pdf(X) for 2-augmented $2^n \times 2^n$ banyans. (d) pdf(X) for 2-augmented $4^n \times 4^n$ banyans. (solid curves are simulations; dotted curves are analytic.)

An interesting observation is that the number of conflict-free permutations in the 2-path banyan is significantly higher than that of the ADM/IADM network. It is often assumed in the computer literature that the ADM network is much more powerful than the banyan networks due to its path multiplicity. However, a 2-path banyan appears to be more powerful than the ADM.

Observe that a dilation of 4 or 8 is sufficient to reduce the network blocking probability to an extremely small value (typically smaller than 10^{-6}) for networks of reasonable sizes, and hence they can realize almost all permutations in one pass.

5. THE EXPECTED NUMBER OF NETWORK PASSES REQUIRED TO REALIZE AN ARBITRARY PERMUTATION

In this section, an approximate analytic model for the expected number of network passes required to realize an arbitrary permutation under local

TABLE I

APPROXIMATE NUMBER OF CONFLICT-FREE PERMUTATIONS IN VARIOUS NETWORKS

N	1-path MIN	2-path MIN	4-path MIN	8-path MIN	ADM/IADM	Beneš
4	16	24	24	24	24	24
8	4096	40320	40320	40320	26496	40320
16	$\sim 10^9$	$\sim 10^{12}$	$\sim 10^{13}$	$\sim 10^{13}$	$\sim 10^{12}$	$\sim 10^{13}$
32	$\sim 10^{24}$	$\sim 10^{32}$	$\sim 10^{33}$	$\sim 10^{33}$	$\sim 10^{31}$	$\sim 10^{33}$
64	$\sim 10^{58}$	$\sim 10^{86}$	$\sim 10^{89}$	$\sim 10^{89}$	$\sim 10^{75}$	$\sim 10^{89}$
128	$\sim 10^{135}$	$\sim 10^{205}$	$\sim 10^{215}$	$\sim 10^{215}$	$\sim 10^{178}$	$\sim 10^{215}$
256	$\sim 10^{308}$	$\sim 10^{474}$	$\sim 10^{497}$	$\sim 10^{497}$	$\sim 10^{409}$	$\sim 10^{497}$
512	$\sim 10^{893}$	$\sim 10^{1102}$	$\sim 10^{1166}$	$\sim 10^{1166}$	$\sim 10^{925}$	$\sim 10^{1166}$
1024	$\sim 10^{1541}$	$\sim 10^{2516}$	$\sim 10^{2636}$	$\sim 10^{2639}$	$\sim 10^{1957}$	$\sim 10^{2639}$

control is developed. This quantity will be defined as the universality of a network under local control. The universality of various networks has been examined by numerous researchers. Under global control, the universalities of some networks have been established, and upper or lower bounds for others have been established. Under local control, the only results to date are for the universality of some networks [27, 53].

5.1. *An Upper Bound for the Universality*

A proof for an upper bound for the number of passes required to realize any arbitrary permutation in unipath $2^n \times 2^n$ banyans has been presented in [2]. The basic idea was to count the number of requests that must use a specific link in the network in the worst case; i.e., if the worst-case permutation requires m requests to use a specific link, then the upper bound for the number of passes is m. The upper bound on the number of passes in a $2^n \times 2^n$ banyan was shown to be $2^{\lfloor n/2 \rfloor}$. An identical bound has been derived (but using a slightly different technique) in [48].

However, the implied assumption in this bound is that the critical link will be utilized by a request in each pass, and that the request that used it will indeed be established. To ensure this assumption would require precomputed routing for each individual permutation to optimally schedule requests over the critical link.

If the usual simple, distributed banyan routing algorithm is used, this upper bound does not apply (it will be exceeded occasionally). This situation occurs when a request uses the critical link during a pass and is blocked at a later stage in the same pass, hence requiring the use of the critical link again. Numerous examples of this situation can be found for networks of size $N \geqslant 8$.

The correct upper bound (under local control) must also consider the conflicts that may occur at the switch after the critical link, and it is at least $2 \cdot 2^{\lfloor n/2 \rfloor}$ [45].

5.2. Analysis for the Universality of MINs

In this section, an analytic model for the expected number of (synchronous, circuit-switched) network passes required to realize an arbitrary permutation is presented. The accuracy of this model depends on the accuracy of the $pdf(X)$. As will be shown, the model is very accurate for multipath networks and optimistic for unipath networks (based on comparisons with our simulations).

The approximate analytic model consists of a discrete time Markov chain with $N + 1$ states, denoted i, for $0 \leqslant i \leqslant N$, as shown in Fig. 6. The probability of state i at time t is denoted by $S_{i,t}$. Each state i represents the probability that i requests are still unsatisfied after t passes, and these requests must be resubmitted in the next network pass. This chain has one source state, N, and one sink state, 0. Initially, all N requests in a permutation are unsatisfied, so $S_{N,0} = 1$, and all other states $S_{i,0}$ are 0.

For each network pass, every state probability is updated as follows. Consider updating state i at time t; this state is the probability that i requests remain unsatisfied after the tth pass, and this state can be reached from any state j, where $j > i$ and where $S_{j,t-1} > 0$. The physical events that correspond to this state transition are simple; the processor array submits a partial permutation consisting of j requests in one pass, i of the requests are blocked, and the rest are accepted. The blocking probability of the network, when j requests that form a partial permutation are submitted, can be computed from Eq. (2.6). The probability that i of these requests are blocked (given that j requests were submitted) can be computed from Eq. (3). Hence, the state transition probabilities for the Markov chain can be computed easily.

The Markov model can be solved with the usual iterative algorithm. After a number of iterations (say $t = MAX\_TIME$), the model will converge to a stable state (in absence of numeric errors, the steady state will have $S_{0,t} = 1$, and all other states equaling 0). After the state vector converges the average number of passes required to realize a permutation, denoted E_c, is simply

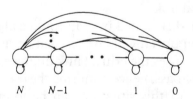

$$N \qquad N-1 \qquad \qquad 1 \qquad \qquad 0$$

FIG. 6. Discrete time Markov chain for an $N \times N$ MIN.

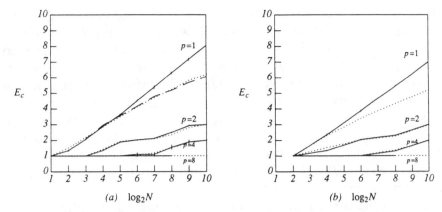

FIG. 7. (a) E_c for various p-path $2^n \times 2^n$ banyans. The dashed curve is simulation results from Leland's Ph.D. thesis [27]. (b) E_c for various p-path $4^n \times 4^n$ banyans. (Solid curves are simulations with 95% confidence intervals shown; dotted curves are analytic.)

$$E_c = \sum_{t=1}^{MAX\_TIME} (S_{0,t} - S_{0,t-1}) \cdot t.$$

Figure 7 illustrates the analytic results and simulations for various networks. The simulation results were obtained as follows. First a permutation is randomly selected. The network is then simulated for a number of passes until all requests in the permutation are satisfied. The number of passes required to realize that randomly selected permutation is recorded as one observation. Then another arbitrary permutation is selected and the network simulation is repeated. After a number of observations, typically between 500 and 1000, the desired results along with 95% confidence intervals are computed.

Figure 7 indicates that the model is very accurate for multipath networks, and optimistic for large unipath networks. However, most practical networks will likely have some path multiplicity, hence these models can be used.

Simulations for the universality of the unipath $2^n \times 2^n$ omega network have been presented in Leland's Ph.D. thesis [27]. The regular banyan routing algorithm was slightly modified; requests which could not be routed properly in one pass still were routed completely through the network, arriving at incorrect destinations. In the next pass(es), any data at incorrect destinations are routed from there to the correct destinations (or possibly to another incorrect destination . . .).[1] The simulations presented in [27] are almost identical to our analytic results for the unipath $2^n \times 2^n$ networks. This

[1] This mode of operation requires that the network output i be connected directly to the network input i, so that incorrectly routed data arriving at output i can be resubmitted to the network at input i in the next pass.

observation explains the discrepancies of our simulations and analytic results. Using the mode of operation in [27], when $j < N$ processors submit requests to the network, these processors tend to be randomly distributed over the N processors (since these resubmitted requests were routed to incorrect memories which are more or less randomly distributed). Such an assumption is necessary for Eq. (3) to be accurate. In our mode of operation, this assumption is not valid. Consider the case when $N/2$ processors submit requests in our mode of operation. These $N/2$ processors are not randomly distributed over the N processors, but are more likely to be separated by idle processors; i.e., at a 50% utilization, it is highly likely that one processor per switch submits a request.

When a partial permutation consisting of j requests is submitted in one pass, a more refined pdf model should account for the distribution of the requesting processors, the statistical dependencies between links arriving at one switch, and the statistical dependencies between switches in the same stage (particularly in the last few stages).

6. Comparisons of the Universality of P-Path MINs

The true performances of p-path networks must reflect on the bandwidth of the links used in the network, as discussed in Section 2. Consider a network of size $N = 1024$ made with 2×2 switches. The unipath network will require about eight passes to realize an arbitrary permutation, and the 2-path network will require about three passes (each requiring about twice as much time) to realize an arbitrary permutation. From Fig. 7 it is clear that a 2-path network actually outperforms a unipath network by about 25% when the bandwidth of each network is considered.

In addition to offering performance improvements for large network sizes (when the realization of arbitrary permutations through circuit-switched networks is the performance criterion), the 2-path network is also significantly more fault tolerant.

Solutions of this Markov model indicate that the expected number of passes through an 8-path $2^n \times 2^n$ network required to realize an arbitrary permutation is only very slightly greater than 1 for $N \leqslant 1K$. The solution of this Markov model required excessive computational resources for larger N. (A Monte Carlo algorithm that yields efficient approximate solutions for chains of this type was presented in [46]. This algorithm can be used to obtain accurate approximate solutions for much larger network sizes.)

The 8-path networks have a cost of $O(N \log N)$ switches (crosspoints), they use local control, and they have a very high degree of fault tolerance (assuming that link failures are the predominant failure mechanism). In one of many possible implementations, an 8-dilated banyan can be implemented from an unmodified (1-dilated) banyan by allowing the multiplexing of up to eight requests onto a single logical link. In this case, the 8-dilated network has the same cost as the unmodified (1-dilated) banyan network. However, as a result of the multiplexing the bandwidth available to each connection in this implementation is one-eighth of the logical link's original bandwidth and hence one pass through this network is about eight times as long as one pass through a 1-path network (according to the delay assumptions discussed in Section 2).

If the network's bandwidth is sufficiently large that the bandwidth of a connection through a dilated network is acceptable, then dilations may offer attractive solutions to the large inherent blocking in unipath banyans.

Otherwise, in order to increase the bandwidth of a dilated network connection the total bandwidth of each logical link must be increased. For example, if another possible implementation each d-dilated $k \times k$ switch can be implemented by a number of replicated d-dilated $k \times k$ switches (each on a single IC) operating in parallel and in synchronization. By replicating each switch r times, this implementation effectively increases each logical link's bandwidth by a factor of r. (Franklin *et al.* [13] have shown that the best implementation of a unique path banyan would use the largest possible $k \times k$ crossbars that fit on a single IC. To increase the bandwidth of a connection, each $k \times k$ switch could then be implemented by a number of ICs operating in parallel and in synchronization. The same concept can be used to increase the bandwidth of dilated banyans.) Letting $r = d$, the bandwidth of each connection in a d-dilated network is restored to the same value as that in the unmodified (1-dilated) banyan. However, this implementation would require more hardware than the unmodified banyan (d times as many ICs) and the network performance would have to be compared with the performance of other networks with comparable cost. (It has been shown that dilated banyan networks have much lower inherent blocking when compared to unsynchronized replications of a banyan operating in parallel [47]. They also have much greater fault tolerance under certain assumptions. Hence, the approach of dilations appears to be more cost effective than the approach of replications [47].)

An alternative approach to improving the bandwidth of a logical link is to use a faster technology for the network/links so that the bandwidth of each connection through a dilated/augmented network is increased. Again, this approach should be compared with other network architectures also using the faster technology.

7. CONCLUSIONS

A simple analytic approximation for the blocking probability of multistage networks when they are required to perform arbitrary permutations with local control has been presented. The model yields accurate approximate solutions for generalized multistage interconnection networks with varying degrees of path multiplicity per stage. Such a model is obtained by modifying an analytic model of the network's blocking probability under random traffic, and hence models for other types of multipath networks should be easy to create. Other than in [44, 45, 47], no such general technique has been presented in the literature.

A simple analytic approximation for the expected number of conflict-free permutations in multipath MINs under local control has been presented. The number of conflict-free permutations realizable by a MIN under local control is a lower bound for the combinatorial power of a network, and it gives a quantitative measure of the efficiency of the use of crosspoints in a network [4]. The technique used is general and it should be applicable to other multipath networks. No such general technique for estimating the fraction of conflict-free permutations in a network has been presented in the literature previously, although lower and upper bounds on the number of conflict-free permutations realizable in certain MINs under global control have been presented [1] and in one case an exact analysis for the ADM network has been presented [27, 28]. (An exact analysis for the extra stage multistage networks which ultimately relies on an enumeration method has also been presented [14].)

A simple approximate analytic model for the expected number of passes required to realize an arbitrary permutation in a multipath MIN under local control has been presented. This quantity was defined as the universality of a network under local control. The technique used is general and it should be applicable to other multipath networks. No such general technique for estimating the universality of a network under local control has been presented previously.

It was shown that variations of banyan networks can be designed to have very low blocking probabilities when they are required to realize arbitrary permutations. The 8-path banyan network has a very low blocking probability for networks of reasonable sizes and it can realize most permutations in one pass for reasonable network sizes. Further work would be comparing the performance of these multipath networks with other network architectures in specific operating environments and using specific cost comparisons. Kruskal and Snir have previously made some comparisons of buffered versions of these networks under randomly distributed traffic in [21] (also see [20]). Simulations of the ability of these networks to supply data vectors to vector processors with a prime number of memory modules have been presented in [45].

REFERENCES

1. Adams, G. B., III, and Siegel, H. J., On the number of permutations performable by the augmented data manipulator. *IEEE Trans. Comput.* **C-31** (Apr. 1982), 270–277.
2. Agrawal, D. P. Graph theoretical analysis and design of multistage interconnection networks. *IEEE Trans. Comput.* **C-32**, (July 1983), 637–648.

3. Barnes, G. H., and Lundstrom, S. F. Design and validation of a connection network for many-processor multiprocessor systems. *IEEE Comput.* (Dec. 1981), 31–41.

4. Beneš, V. E. *The Mathematical Theory of Connecting Networks and Telephone Traffic.* Academic Press, San Diego, CA, 1965.

5. Bhuyan, L. N., and Agrawal, D. P. Design and performance of generalized interconnection networks. *IEEE Trans. Comput.* **C-32** (Dec. 1983), 1081–1090.

6. Blake, I. F. *An Introduction to Applied Probability.* Wiley, New York, 1979.

7. Budnick, P., and Kuck, D. J. The organization and use of parallel memories. *IEEE Trans. Comput.* **C-20,** 12 (Dec. 1971), 1566–1569.

8. Cantor, D. G. On nonblocking switching networks. *Networks* **1,** 4 (Winter 1971), 367–377.

9. Cherkassky, V., and Malek, M. On the permuting properties of regular rectangular SW-banyans. *IEEE Trans. Comput.* **C-34,** 6 (June 1985), 542–546.

10. Ciminiera, L., and Serra, A. A connecting network with fault tolerance capabilities. *IEEE Trans. Comput.* **C-35,** 6 (June 1986), 578–580.

11. Clos, C. A study of nonblocking switching networks. *Bell System Tech. J.* (Mar. 1953), 406–424.

12. Franklin, M. A. VLSI performance comparison of banyan and crossbar communications networks. *IEEE Trans. Comput.* **C-30,** 4 (Apr. 1981), 283–290.

13. Franklin, M. A., Wann, D. F., and Thomas, W. J. Pin limitations and partitioning of VLSI interconnection networks. *IEEE Trans. Comput.* **C-31,** 11 (Nov. 1982), 1109–1116.

14. Gazit, I., and Malek, M. On the number of permutations performable by extra stage multistage interconnection networks. *Proc. International Conference on Parallel Processing,* IEEE, 1987, pp. 461–470.

15. Goke, G. R., and Lipovski, G. J. Banyan networks for partitioning multiprocessor systems. *Proc. 1st Annual Symposium on Computer Architecture,* 1973, pp. 21–28.

16. Gottlieb, A., and Kruskal, C. P. Complexity results for permuting data and other computations on parallel processors. *J. Assoc. Comput. Mach.* **31,** 2 (Apr. 1984), 193–209.

17. Gottlieb, A., and Schwartz, J. T. Networks and algorithms for very-large-scale parallel computation. *IEEE Comput.* (Jan. 1982), 27–36.

18. Hwang, K., and Ghosh, J. Hypernet: A communication-efficient architecture for constructing massively parallel computers. *IEEE Trans. Comput.* **C-36,** 12 (Dec. 1987), 1450–1466.

19. Huang, S-T., and Tripathi, S. K. Finite state model and compatibility theory: New analysis tools for permutation networks. *IEEE Trans. Comput.* **C-35,** 7 (July 1986), 591–601.

20. Kumar, M., and Jump, J. R. Generalized delta networks. *Proc. International Conference on Parallel Processing,* IEEE, 1983, pp. 10–18.

21. Kruskal, C. P., and Snir, M. The performance of multistage interconnection networks for multiprocessors. *IEEE Trans. Comput.* **C-32,** 12 (Dec. 1983), 1091–1098.

22. Lang, T. Interconnections between processors and memory modules using the shuffle-exchange network. *IEEE Trans. Comput.* **C-25,** 5 (May 1976), 496–503.

23. Lawrie, D. H. Access and alignment of data in an array processor. *IEEE Trans. Comput.* **C-24,** 12 (Dec. 1975), 1145–1155.

24. Lawrie, D. H. The prime memory system for array access. *IEEE Trans. Comput.* **C-31,** (May 1982), 435–442.

25. Lee, K. Y. On the rearrangeability of $2(\log_2 N) - 1$ stage permutation networks. *IEEE Trans. Comput.* **C-34,** 5 (May 1985), 412–425.

26. Leiserson, C. E. Fat-trees: Universal networks for hardware efficient supercomputing. *IEEE Trans. Comput.* **C-34,** 10 (Oct. 1985), 892–901.

27. Leland, M-D. P. Properties and comparisons of multistage interconnection networks for SIMD machines. Ph.D. thesis, University of Wisconsin, Madison, 1983.

28. Leland, M-D. P. On the power of the augmented data manipulator network. *Proc. International Conference on Parallel Processing*, IEEE, 1985, pp. 74–78.

29. Lenfant, J. Parallel permutations of data: A Benes network control algorithm for frequently used permutations. *IEEE Trans. Comput.* **C-27,** 7 (July 1978), 637–647.

30. Lev, G. F., Pippenger, N., and Valiant, L. G. A fast parallel algorithm for routing in permutation networks. *IEEE Trans. Comput.* **C-30** (Feb. 1981), 93–100.

31. Masson, G. M., Gingher, G. C., and Nakamura, S. A sampler of circuit switching networks. *IEEE Comput.* (June 1979), 32–48.

32. Nassimi, D., and Sahni, S. A self-routing Benes network and parallel permutation algorithms. *IEEE Trans. Comput.* **C-30,** 5 (May 1981), 332–340.

33. Opferman, D. C., and Tsao-Wu, N. T. On a class of rearrangeable switching networks. *Bell System Tech. J.* **50** (May–June 1971), 1579–1600.

34. Padmanabhan, K., and Lawrie, D. H. A class of redundant path multistage interconnection networks. *IEEE Trans. Comput.* **C-32,** 12 (Dec. 1983), 1099–1108.

35. Parker, D. S. Notes on shuffle/exchange-type switching networks. *IEEE Trans. Comput.* **C-29,** 3 (Mar. 1980), 213–222.

36. Parker, D. S., and Raghavendra, C. S. The gamma network: A multiprocessor interconnection network with redundant paths. *Proc. 9th Annual Symposium on Computer Architecture*, 1982, pp. 73–80.

37. Patel, J. H. Performance of processor-memory interconnections for multiprocessors. *IEEE Trans. Comput.* **C-30,** 10 (Oct. 1981), 771–780.

38. Raghavendra, C. S., and Prasanna Kumar, V. K. Permutations on Illiac IV-type networks. *IEEE Trans. Comput.* **C-35,** 7 (July 1986), 662–669.

39. Raghavendra, C. S., and Varma, A. Rearrangeability of the 5-stage shuffle/exchange network for N = 8. *Proc. International Conference on Parallel Processing*, IEEE, 1986, pp. 119–122.

40. Reddy, S. M., and Kumar, V. P. On fault-tolerant multistage interconnection networks. *Proc. International Conference on Parallel Processing*, IEEE, 1984, pp. 155–164.

41. Seigel, H. J. On the universality of various types of SIMD machine interconnection networks. *Proc. 4th Annual International Symposium on Computer Architecture*, 1977, pp. 70–79.

42. Siegel, H. J. Analysis techniques for SIMD machine interconnection networks and the effects of processor address masks. *IEEE Trans. Comput.* **C-26,** 2 (Feb. 1977), 153–161.

43. Steinberg, D. Invariant properties of the shuffle-exchange and a simplified cost-effective version of the omega network. *IEEE Trans. Comput.* **C-32** (May 1983), 444–450.

44. Szymanski, T. H. On the universality of multistage interconnection networks. *Proc. International Conference on Parallel Processing*, IEEE, 1986, pp. 316–323.

45. Szymanski, T. H. On interconnection networks for parallel processors. Ph.D. thesis, Department of Electrical Engineering, University of Toronto, Jan. 1988.

46. Szymanski, T. H. Interconnection network modelling using Monte Carlo methods, Markov chains and performance Petri nets. In Iazeollo, G., Courtois, P. J., and Boxma, O. J. (Eds.). *Computer Performance and Reliability*. North-Holland, Amsterdam, 1988, pp. 259–274.

47. Szymanski, T. H., and Hamacher, V. C. On the permutation capability of multistage interconnection networks. *IEEE Trans. Comput.* **C-36,** 7 (July 1987), 810–822.

48. Varma, A., and Raghavendra, C. S. Realization of permutations on generalized Indra networks. *Proc. International Conference on Parallel Processing*, IEEE, 1985, pp. 328–333.

49. Waksman, A. A permutation network. *J. Assoc. Comput. Mach.* **15** (Jan. 1968), 159–163.

50. Wu, C-L., and Feng, T-Y. The reverse-exchange interconnection network. *IEEE Trans. Comput.* **C-29**, 10 (Sept. 1980), 801–811.

51. Wu, C-L., and Feng, T-Y. The universality of the shuffle-exchange network. *IEEE Trans. Comput.* **C-30**, 5 (May 1981), 324–331.

52. Wu, C-L., and Feng, T-Y. *Tutorial: Interconnection Networks for Parallel and Distributed Processing.* IEEE Comput. Soc. Press, Los Angeles, CA, 1984, pp. 1–647.

53. Yew, P-C. On the design of interconnection networks for parallel and multiprocessor systems. Ph.D. thesis, University of Illinois at Urbana–Champaign, 1981.

TED H. SZYMANSKI received the B.A.Sc. degree in engineering science in 1980 and the M.A.Sc. degree in electrical engineering in 1982 from the University of Toronto. During 1983–1984 he was a consultant to a number of firms in the Toronto area. During 1984–1987 he was working on his Ph.D. degree at the University of Toronto. Since August 1987 he has been an assistant professor in the Department of Electrical Engineering at Columbia University, where he is also a member of the Center for Telecommunications Research. His research interests include interconnection networks, communications networks, VLSI and optical networks, network performance analysis, and parallel computer architecture.

V. CARL HAMACHER was born in London, Canada, in 1939. He received the B.A.Sc. degree in engineering physics in 1963 from the University of Waterloo, Waterloo, Canada; the M.Sc. degree in electrical engineering in 1965 from Queen's University, Kingston, Canada; and the Ph.D. degree in electrical engineering in 1968 from Syracuse University, Syracuse, New York. Since then he has been at the University of Toronto, Toronto, Canada, where he is a professor in the Departments of Electrical Engineering and Computer Science. He held the position of director for the Computer Systems Research Institute during 1984–1988, and is currently chairman of the Division of Engineering Science, both at Toronto. His current interests include local area computer networks, multiprocessors, and real-time computer systems. During 1978–1979, he was a visiting scientist at the IBM Research Laboratory in San Jose, California; and during 1986–1987 he was a research visitor at the Laboratory for Circuits and Systems associated with the University of Grenoble in France. He is a co-author of the textbook *Computer Organization,* published by McGraw-Hill in 1984. Dr. Hamacher is a senior member of the IEEE, and a member of ACM, Sigma Xi, and the Association of Professional Engineers of Ontario.

WIDE-SENSE NONBLOCKING NETWORKS*

PAUL FELDMAN†, JOEL FRIEDMAN‡, AND NICHOLAS PIPPENGER§

Abstract. A new method for constructing wide-sense nonblocking networks is presented. Application of this method yields (among other things) wide-sense nonblocking generalized connectors with n inputs and outputs and size $O(n \log n)$, and with depth k and size $O(n^{1+1/k}(\log n)^{1-1/k})$.

Key words. nonblocking network, connection network, concentrator, generalizer

AMS(MOS) subject classifications. 94C15, 68E10, 05C35

1. Introduction. In this introductory section, we shall give an informal account of our results. More precise definitions will be given in later sections.

Informally, a "network" is an acyclic directed graph that allows connections to be made between "inputs" and "outputs." A "nonblocking" network is one that allows connections to be created and destroyed dynamically, with each request for creation being satisfied without disturbing other previously established connections.

Given a network, we may consider a game between two players, the "blocker" (representing the collective activity of the users interconnected by the network) and the "router" (representing the activity of the controller of the network). The positions in this game are the states of the network, and the initial position is the state in which no connections are established. The players move alternately, starting with the blocker. The blocker moves by making a request to create or destroy a connection, and the router responds by satisfying this request (if possible). The goal of the blocker is to make a request that cannot be satisfied, and the goal of the router is to avoid this by satisfying every request. Roughly speaking, a "wide-sense" nonblocking network is one in which the router can indefinitely avoid losing. (In addition to wide-sense nonblocking networks, there are "strictly" nonblocking networks and "rearrangeable" networks. We do not need these notions to formulate our results, but we shall occasionally need them to discuss other results in the literature.)

The main contribution of this paper is a new principle, according to which certain "expanding graphs" are shown to be "generalized concentrators" (a special case of which are "concentrators"). For these networks, inputs request connection to one or more outputs, without specifying to which output they are to be connected. This principle will be presented in § 2.

In § 3, we apply the results of § 2 to construct "generalized connectors" (a special case of which are "connectors"). For these networks, inputs request connection to one or more specified outputs. Our results in this section, taken together with results of Friedman [F], show that wide-sense nonblocking connectors can have smaller size than strictly nonblocking connectors with the same number of inputs and outputs and the same depth. This answers a question that has been open since the distinction between "wide-sense" and "strictly" nonblocking networks was introduced by Beneš in 1962 [B1] (see also [B2], [B3]).

In § 4, we apply the results of § 2 to construct "bi-generalized connectors." This new type of network provides greater interconnection facility than most other types

---

* Received by the editors June 17, 1987; accepted for publication (in revised form) November 6, 1987.

† Massachusetts Institute of Technology, Cambridge, Massachusetts 02139.

‡ Princeton University, Princeton, New Jersey 08544.

§ IBM Almaden Research Center, San Jose, California 95120-6099.

considered in the literature, and it serves as a natural setting to display the power of the new principle.

The results of §§ 3 and 4 concern networks with "limited depth," in which the length of the routes from inputs to outputs is constrained. In § 5 we apply the results of § 2 to construct networks of "unlimited depth," in which only the "size" (corresponding to the number of switches in the network) is to be minimized. Our results in this section, taken together with results of Shannon [S], show that wide-sense nonblocking generalized connectors need be larger than wide-sense nonblocking connectors by only a constant factor. The corresponding result for "rearrangeable" rather than "wide-sense nonblocking" networks has been known since the work of Ofman [O] in 1965. The corresponding result for "strictly nonblocking" rather than "wide-sense nonblocking" networks does not hold (see Bassalygo and Pinsker [BP2]).

A preliminary account of some of these results appears in our earlier paper [FFP].

2. Generalized concentrators. In this section we shall define networks precisely and present the principle on which most of the results of this paper are based. We shall base our formulation of a "network" on a directed graph with "inputs" and "outputs." There is an alternative formulation based on an undirected graph with "terminals." Our choice for this paper is technically simpler, though our results hold (with obvious modifications) for either formulation.

A *network* is an acyclic directed graph with a set of distinguished vertices called *inputs* and a disjoint set of distinguished vertices called *outputs*. A vertex that is neither an input nor an output will be called a *link*. We shall use the prefix "(n, m)-" to the term "network" (and later to other nouns) to indicate that there are n inputs and m outputs; we shall use the prefix "n-" in these cases in place of "(n, n)-."

A *route* in a network is a directed path from an input to an output. The *size* of a network is the number of edges in it. The *depth* of a network is the maximum number of edges in a route in it.

Two routes are *compatible* if their intersection is an initial segment (possibly empty) of both of them. A *state* of a network is a set of pairwise compatible routes. (A state may be regarded as a forest of vertex-disjoint trees, with their roots at the inputs and their leaves at the outputs. This alternative viewpoint is taken in many papers on networks with "generalized" properties.) The states of a network are partially ordered by inclusion, and we shall use the terms *above* and *below* to refer to this partial order. A vertex or edge is *busy* in a state if it appears in some route of that state; otherwise, it is *idle*.

A *concentration request* in a network is an input of the network. A concentration request is *satisfied* by a route if the route originates at the input of the request. A *generalized concentration assignment* is a multiset of concentration requests. A generalized concentration assignment is *realized* by a state if each request is satisfied in the state by a number of routes equal to its multiplicity.

A generalized concentration assignment is (a, r)-*limited* if each request has multiplicity at most r and the sum of the multiplicities is at most a. A state is (a, r)-*limited* if the generalized concentration assignment it realizes is (a, r)-*limited*. A concentration request is (a, r)-*limited* in a state if the generalized concentration assignment obtained by adjoining the request to the generalized concentration assignment realized by the state is (a, r)-*limited*.

A *wide-sense nonblocking* (a, r)-*limited generalized concentrator* is a network for which there exists a set of distinguished states, called the *safe* states, with the following properties: (1) the empty state is safe; (2) any state below a safe state is itself safe; and (3) given any safe state and any (a, r)-limited concentration request in that state, there exists a safe state above the given state containing another route satisfying the given request. (In our previous paper [FFP], "generalized concentrators" were called "generalizers." This change has been adopted to increase the uniformity of our terminology.)

A *wide-sense nonblocking a-limited concentrator* is a wide-sense nonblocking $(a, 1)$-limited generalized concentrator. When discussing concentrators, we shall use the adjective "a-limited" in place of "$(a, 1)$-limited."

The key to the results of this paper is the following proposition.

PROPOSITION 1. *If F is a network of depth one in which every set of x inputs, where $1 \leq x \leq 2a$, has at least $(r + s)x$ neighbors, then F is a wide-sense nonblocking (as, r)-limited generalized concentrator.*

Proof. Let $F = (V, W, E)$ be a network of depth one, with inputs V, outputs W, and edges E. Suppose that if $X \subseteq V$, with $|X| = x$ and $1 \leq x \leq 2a$, then $|E(X)| \geq (r + s)x$. (Here $E(X)$ denotes the set of neighbors of X, and $|Y|$ denotes the cardinality of Y.) We shall show that F is a wide-sense nonblocking (as, r)-limited generalized concentrator.

The first step of the proof is the definition of the set of safe states; for this we shall need some auxiliary definitions. Let X be a set of inputs. We shall define the *assets* of X in S, $A_S(X)$, to be the number of idle neighbors of X in S. Let v be an input in V. We shall define the *liabilities* of v in S, $B_S(v)$, to be r minus the number of busy edges directed out of v in S. We shall define the *liabilities* of X in S, $B_S(X)$, to be the sum of $B_S(v)$ over inputs v in X. We define the *balance* of X in S, $C_S(X)$, to be $A_S(X) - B_S(X)$. We shall say that X is *solvent* in S if $C_S(X) \geq 0$, that X is *critical* in S if $C_S(X) = 0$, and that X is *bankrupt* in S if $C_S(X) < 0$. Finally, we shall say that S is *safe* if, for every $X \subseteq V$ with $|X| = x$ and $1 \leq x \leq 2a$, X is solvent in S.

Let O denote the empty state. We shall show that O is safe. Let X be a set of inputs with $|X| = x$ and $1 \leq x \leq 2a$. By the hypothesis on F, $|E(X)| \geq (r + s)x \geq rx$. Since all vertices are idle in O, $A_O(X) \geq rx$. Since $B_O(X) = rx$, X is solvent, and thus O is safe.

Let S be a state, let (v, w) be a route not in S, and suppose that $T = S \cup \{(v, w)\}$ is a safe state. We shall show that S is safe. We observe that (1) $A_T(X) = A_S(X) - 1$ if $w \in E(X)$, otherwise $A_T(X) = A_S(X)$; and (2) $B_T(X) = B_S(X) + 1$ if $v \in X$, otherwise $B_T(X) = B_S(X)$. Since $v \in X$ implies $w \in E(X)$, $C_S(X) \geq C_T(X) \geq 0$, and thus S is safe.

Finally, let S be a safe state and let v be an (as, r)-limited concentration request in S. We shall show that for some idle neighbor w of v in S, the state $S \cup \{(v, w)\}$ is safe. Suppose, to obtain a contradiction, that for every idle neighbor w of v, the state $S \cup \{(v, w)\}$ is unsafe. Then for every idle neighbor w of v, there is a set of inputs X_w with $|X_w| \leq 2a$ such that X_w is bankrupt in $S \cup \{(v, w)\}$. Of course, since S is safe, for every w, X_w is solvent in S. From these conditions, and from observations (1) and (2) above, it is easy to see that for every idle neighbor w of v we have (i) w belongs to $E(X_w)$, but v does not belong to X_w, and (ii) X_w is critical in S. We shall need the following lemmas concerning critical sets.

LEMMA 1.1. *If X is critical in S, then $|X| < a$.*

Proof. Suppose, to obtain a contradiction, that X with $|X| = x$ and $a \leq x \leq 2a$ is unsafe in S. By the hypothesis on F, $|E(X)| \geq (r + s)x$. Since the request v is (as, r)-limited in S, fewer than sa outputs are busy in S, so $A_S(X) > (r + s)x - sa$. Since $B_S(X) \leq B_O(X) = rx$ and $x \geq a$, we have $C_S(X) > 0$, contradicting the assumption that X is critical in S. $\square$

LEMMA 1.2. *For any state S, $C_S(X)$ is submodular in X; that is, $C_S(X \cup Y) + C_S(X \cap Y) \leq C_S(X) + C_S(Y)$.*

Proof. Since $B_S(X)$ is defined by a sum over the inputs in X, it is *modular* in X; that is, $B_S(X \cup Y) + B_S(X \cap Y) \leq B_S(X) + B_S(Y)$. Thus it remains to show that $A_S(X)$

is submodular in X. This follows from the relations $E(X \cup Y) = E(X) \cup E(Y)$ and $E(X \cap Y) \subseteq E(X) \cap E(Y)$, and the identity $|X \cup Y| + |X \cap Y| = |X| + |Y|$. $\quad\square$

LEMMA 1.3. *If S is a safe state, $|X|$, $|Y| \leq 2a$, and X and Y are critical in S, then $|X \cup Y| \leq 2a$ and $X \cup Y$ is critical in S.*

Proof. Since X and Y are critical for S, Lemma 1.1 implies $|X|$, $|Y| < a$, and thus $|X \cup Y| \leq 2a$. Thus it remains to show that $X \cup Y$ is critical in S. Since X and Y are critical, $C_S(X) + C_S(Y) = 0$. By Lemma 1.2, $C_S(X \cup Y) + C_S(X \cap Y) \leq 0$. Since S is safe and $|X \cap Y| < a$, $X \cap Y$ is solvent. Thus $X \cup Y$ is critical. $\quad\square$

Returning to the proof of Proposition 1, let the set of inputs X be the union of X_w over all idle neighbors w of v. Since each X_w is critical in S, Lemma 1.3 implies that X is critical in S, and Lemma 1.1 implies $|X| < a$. Now consider the set $X \cup \{v\}$. Since S is safe and $|X \cup \{v\}| \leq a$, $X \cup \{v\}$ is solvent in S. On the other hand, (i) and (ii) above imply that every idle neighbor of v belongs to $E(X)$, but v does not belong to X. Thus $A_S(X \cup \{v\}) = A_S(X)$ and, since the request v is (as, r)-limited in S,

$$B_S(X \cup \{v\}) = B_S(X) + 1.$$

Thus, since X is critical in S, $X \cup \{v\}$ is bankrupt in S. This contradiction completes the proof of Proposition 1. $\quad\square$

The argument used in the proof of Proposition 1 has also found application to some combinatorial problems concerning fault-tolerant networks (see Friedman and Pippenger [FP]) and processor-interconnection networks (see Peleg and Upfal [PU]). This argument suffers the defect that it provides no efficient algorithm for finding safe routes. Indeed, determining the solvency of a state is a minor variant of a co-**NP**-complete problem (see Blum et al. [BKVPY]). We shall present some results (Theorems 4 and 6) that avoid this defect; it is avoided in another way in the work of Peleg and Upfal [PU].

A wide-sense nonblocking (a, r)-limited generalized concentrator remains one if any number of inputs (together with the edges incident with them) are deleted and any number of outputs (with no incident edges) are added.

If F is an (n, m)-network and G is an (m, l)-network, let $F \circ G$ denote a network obtained by identifying the outputs of F with the inputs of G in any one-to-one fashion. If F is an n-network, define $F^{\circ k}$ by letting $F^{\circ 1} = F$ and $F^{\circ k} = F \circ F^{\circ (k-1)}$ for $k \geq 2$.

PROPOSITION 2. *If F is a wide-sense nonblocking (a, r)-limited generalized m-concentrator and G is a wide-sense nonblocking (a, s)-limited generalized m-concentrator, then $F \circ G$ is a wide-sense nonblocking (a, rs)-limited generalized m-concentrator.*

Proof. Let the safe states of $F \circ G$ be those in which the induced states of F and G are safe. Clearly, the empty state is safe and any state below a safe state is itself safe. Let S be a safe state and let v be an (a, rs)-limited concentration request in S. Let $S(F)$ be the state of F induced by S and let $S(G)$ be the state of G induced by S.

Since v is (a, rs)-limited, S contains at most $a - 1$ routes, at most $rs - 1$ of which are from v. Thus either (1) there are routes in $S(F)$ from v to at most $r - 1$ outputs of F, or (2) there is a route in $S(F)$ from v to some output w of F and there are routes in $S(G)$ from w to at most $s - 1$ outputs of G.

In case (1), the concentration request v is (a, r)-limited in $S(F)$, so there is a safe state $T(F)$ above $S(F)$ containing a route from v to some output w of F that is idle in $S(F)$. The concentration request w is then (a, s)-limited in $S(G)$, so there is a safe state $T(G)$ above $S(G)$ containing a route from w to some output of G that is idle in $S(G)$. Then the state obtained by adjoining to S the concatenation of the route from v to w in $T(F)$ with the route from w in $T(G)$ is a safe state above S containing a route from v to an output of $F \circ G$ that is idle in S.

In case (2), the concentration request w is (a, s)-limited in $S(G)$, so there is a safe state $T(G)$ above $S(G)$ containing a route from w to an output of G that is idle in $S(G)$. Then the state obtained by adjoining to S the concatenation of the route from v to w in $S(F)$ with the route from w in $T(G)$ is a safe state above S containing a route from v to an output of $F \cdot G$ that is idle in S. $\quad\square$

3. Generalized connectors. In this section we shall use Proposition 1 to construct wide-sense nonblocking generalized connectors. Our first goal is to define these networks.

A *connection request* in a network is an ordered pair comprising an input and an output. A connection request is *satisfied* by a route if the route originates at the input of the request and terminates at the output of the request. A *generalized connection assignment* is a set of connection requests, no two of which have an output in common. A generalized connection assignment is *realized* by a state if each request of the generalized connection assignment is satisfied by some route of the state.

A generalized connection assignment is (a, r)-*limited* if it contains at most a requests, of which at most r have an input in common. Observe that a state is (a, r)-limited if the generalized connection assignment that it realizes is (a, r)-limited. A connection request is (a, r)-*limited* in a state if (1) the output of the request is idle in the state and (2) the generalized connection assignment obtained by adjoining the connection request to the generalized connection assignment realized by the state is (a, r)-limited.

A *wide-sense nonblocking* (a, r)-*limited generalized connector* is a network for which there exists a set of distinguished states, called the *safe* states, with the following properties: (1) the empty state is safe; (2) any state below a safe state is itself safe; and (3) given any safe state and any (a, r)-limited connection request in that state, there exists a safe state above the given state containing a route satisfying the given request.

A *wide-sense nonblocking* a-*limited connector* is a wide-sense nonblocking $(a, 1)$-limited generalized connector. When discussing (ungeneralized) connectors, we shall use the term "connection assignment" in place of "generalized connection assignment" and the adjective "a-limited" in place of "$(a, 1)$-limited." We shall also use the term "connector" in place of "∞-limited connector."

Our main result in this section is the following.

THEOREM 3. *For every fixed $k \geq 1$ and $n \to \infty$, a wide-sense nonblocking generalized n-connector exists with depth k and size $O(n^{1 + 1/k}(\log n)^{1 - 1/k})$.*

The bound of Theorem 3 is almost the best possible; Pippenger and Yao [PY] have shown that size $\Omega(n^{1 + 1/k})$ is necessary (even for networks satisfying a much weaker property, that of being "rearrangeable n-shifters" with depth k).

The previously best upper bound for wide-sense nonblocking generalized connectors was obtained from a construction due to Pippenger [P1] and Nassimi and Sahni [NS]. It yields wide-sense nonblocking generalized connectors with depth $j^2 - 3j + 3$ and size $O(n^{1 + 2/j})$. The special case of depth three and size $O(n^{5/3})$ was given (using a different method) by Masson and Jordan [MJ].

The construction of Pippenger [P1] and Nassimi and Sahni [NS] requires wide-sense nonblocking (ungeneralized) connectors as components. The previously best upper bound for these networks was obtained from constructions due to Clos [Cl], Cantor [Ca], and Pippenger [P2]. It yields networks of depth $2j - 1$ and size $O(n^{1 + 1/j})$. (These networks satisfy a stronger property, that of being "strictly nonblocking n-connectors" with depth $2j - 1$.)

The best upper bound for wide-sense nonblocking connectors is now given by Theorem 3. The best upper bound for "rearrangeable generalized connectors" is also now given by Theorem 3 (the previously best bound was $O((n \log n)^{1 + 1/k})$, due to Dolev et al. [DDPW]). Indeed, the bound of Theorem 3 is not much larger than the currently best bound of $O(n^{1+1/k}(\log n)^{1/k})$ for "rearrangeable connectors," due to Pippenger and Yao [PY].

The lower bound of $\Omega(n^2)$ (for any depth) due to Bassalygo and Pinsker [BP2] shows that Theorem 3 cannot be extended to "strictly nonblocking generalized connectors." The lower bound of $\Omega(n^{1+1/(k-1)})$ (for depth k) due to Friedman [F] shows that it cannot even be extended to "strictly nonblocking connectors."

We need the following lemma for the proof of Theorem 3.

LEMMA 3.1. *For every n and a, there exists a network of depth one with n inputs and $8a$ outputs in which (1) every input has $d = \lceil \log_2 (2n^3) \rceil$ neighbors, and (2) every set of x inputs with $1 \leq x \leq 2a$ has at least $2x$ neighbors.*

Proof. Consider a random graph in which each input has a randomly chosen set of d outputs as neighbors, with all sets of d outputs being equally likely and with the random choices for distinct inputs being independent. Clearly (1) is satisfied; it remains to show that the probability that (2) is satisfied is strictly positive. The probability that (2) fails is at most

$$\sum_{1 \leq x \leq 2a} \binom{n}{x}\binom{8a}{2x}\left(\binom{2x}{d} \Big/ \binom{8a}{d}\right)^x.$$

Using the estimates

$$\binom{n}{x}\binom{8a}{2x} \leq n^{3x}$$

and

$$\binom{2x}{d} \Big/ \binom{8a}{d} \leq \left(\frac{2x}{8a}\right)^d \leq \left(\frac{1}{2}\right)^d,$$

we see that this probability is at most $\sum_{1 \leq x \leq 2a}(1/2)^x < 1$. $\square$

A wide-sense nonblocking (a, r)-limited generalized connector remains one if any number of inputs and outputs (together with the edges incident with them) are deleted.

The following propositions and their subsequent use are the counterparts for wide-sense nonblocking generalized connectors of a method used by Pippenger [P1] for "strictly nonblocking generalized connectors" and by Nassimi and Sahni [NS] for "rearrangeable generalized connectors."

PROPOSITION 3.2. *If F is a wide-sense nonblocking a-limited (n, m)-concentrator and G is a wide-sense nonblocking (a, r)-limited generalized (m, l)-connector, then $F \cdot G$ is a wide-sense nonblocking (a, r)-limited generalized (n, l)-connector.*

Proof. Let the safe states of $F \cdot G$ be those in which the induced states of F and G are safe. Clearly, the empty state is safe and any state below a safe state is itself safe. Let S be a safe state and let (v, w) be an (a, r)-limited connection request in S. Let $S(F)$ be the state of F induced by S and let $S(G)$ be the state of G induced by S. Either (1) v is idle in S, or (2) S contains a route originating at v.

In case (1), the concentration request v is a-limited in $S(F)$, so there is a safe state $T(F)$ above $S(F)$ containing a route from v to an output u of F that is idle in $S(F)$. The connection request (u, w) is (a, r)-limited in $S(G)$, so there is a safe state $T(G)$ above $S(G)$ containing a route from u to w. Then the state obtained by adjoining to S the concatenation of the route from v to u in $T(F)$ with the route from u to w in $T(G)$ is a safe state above S containing a route from v to w.

In case (2), the route originating at v passes through some link u that is an input of G. The connection request (u, w) is (a, r)-limited in $S(G)$, so there is a safe state $T(G)$ above $S(G)$ containing a route from u to w. Then the state obtained by adjoining to S the concatenation of the route from v to u in $S(F)$ with the route from u to w in $T(G)$ is a safe state above S containing a route that from v to w. $\square$

If F is an (n, m)-network and G is an (n, l)-network, let $F \vdash G$ denote an $(n, m + l)$-network obtained by identifying the inputs of F with the inputs of G in any one-to-one fashion. If F is any network, define $F^{\vdash t}$ by letting $F^{\vdash 1} = F$ and $F^{\vdash t} = F \vdash F^{\vdash (t-1)}$ for $t \geq 2$.

PROPOSITION 3.3. *If F is a wide-sense nonblocking (a, r)-limited generalized (n, m)-connector and G is a wide-sense nonblocking (a, r)-limited generalized (n, l)-connector, then $F \vdash G$ is a wide-sense nonblocking (a, r)-limited generalized $(n, m + l)$-connector.*

Proof. Let the safe states of $F \vdash G$ be those that induce safe states of F and G. Clearly, the empty state is safe and any state below a safe state is itself safe. Let S be a safe state and let the connection request (v, w) be (a, r)-limited in S. Without loss of generality, we may suppose that w is an output of F.

Let $S(F)$ be the state of F induced by S. The connection request (v, w) is (a, r)-limited in $S(F)$, so there is a safe state $T(F)$ above $S(F)$ containing a route from v to w. Then the state obtained by adjoining this route to S is a safe state above S containing a route from v to w. $\square$

Proof of Theorem 3. We proceed by induction on k. For $k = 1$, the conclusion is trivial. For $k \geq 2$, take $a = \lceil n^{1 - 1/k}(\log n)^{1/k} \rceil$ in Lemma 3.1 and $r = s = 1$ in Proposition 1 to obtain a wide-sense nonblocking concentrator F with n inputs, $8a$ outputs, depth one, and size $O(n \log n)$. By inductive hypothesis, there exists a wide-sense nonblocking generalized $(8a)$-connector G with depth $k - 1$ and size

$$O(a^{1 + 1/(k-1)}(\log a)^{1 - 1/(k-1)}) = O(n \log n).$$

By Proposition 3.2, $H = F \circ G$ is a wide-sense nonblocking generalized $(n, 8a)$-connector with depth k and size $O(n \log n)$. Let $t = \lceil n/8a \rceil = O(n^{1/k}/(\log n)^{1/k})$. By Proposition 3.3, $H^{\vdash t}$ is a wide-sense nonblocking generalized $(n, 8at)$-connector with depth k and size $O(n^{1 + 1/k}(\log n)^{1 - 1/k})$. Deleting all but n outputs of this network completes the proof. $\square$

The networks of Theorem 3 are obtained by the nonconstructive Lemma 3.1; moreover, since they rely on Proposition 1, no efficient algorithm is known for finding safe routes. The following remaining results of this section mitigate these defects in some special cases.

THEOREM 4. *Wide-sense nonblocking generalized n-connectors can be explicitly constructed with depth two and size $O(n^{5/3})$, and with depth three and size $O(n^{11/7})$.*

For the proof of Theorem 4 we shall need the following lemma.

LEMMA 4.1. *For every prime power q, a (q^3, q^2)-network with depth one can be explicitly constructed in which every input has q neighbors and every pair of distinct inputs has at most two common neighbors.*

Proof. Let GF (q) be the field with q elements. Let the inputs be the elements of GF $(q)^3$ and let the outputs be the elements of GF $(q)^2$. Let the input (a, b, c) have the output (x, y) as a neighbor if and only if $ax^2 + bx + c = y$ (where all arithmetic is in GF (q)).

Every input has q neighbors, one for each possible value of x. If (x, y) is a common neighbor of (a, b, c) and (a', b', c'), then $ax^2 + bx + c = y$ and $a'x^2 + b'x + c' = y$. Subtracting these equations, we have $(a - a')x^2 + (b - b')x + (c - c') = 0$. If (a, b, c) is distinct from (a', b', c'), the coefficients of this quadratic equation do not all vanish, and thus it can be satisfied by at most two values of x. Thus this pair of inputs can have at most two common neighbors, one for each of these values of x. □

Let $F(q)$ denote the network constructed in the proof of Lemma 4.1.

PROPOSITION 4.2. *The network $F(5^\lambda)$ is a wide-sense nonblocking $(2 \cdot 5^{2\lambda-2})$-limited concentrator.*

Proof. Let the safe states be those in which every input has at most $3 \cdot 5^{\lambda-1}$ neighbors that terminate routes originating at other inputs. Clearly, the empty state is safe and any state below a safe state is itself safe. Consider a safe state S in which some concentration request v cannot be satisfied. We shall show that at least $2 \cdot 5^{2\lambda-2}$ outputs are busy in S.

Since v is idle in S, v has at most $3 \cdot 5^{\lambda-1}$ busy neighbors in S. Thus it has at least $2 \cdot 5^{\lambda-1}$ idle neighbors in S. Say that an output w is *critical* if w is a neighbor of v, w is idle in S, and $S \cup \{(v, w)\}$ is not safe. Then there are at least $2 \cdot 5^{\lambda-1}$ critical outputs.

Say that an input u is *critical* if u is distinct from v and u has $3 \cdot 5^{\lambda-1}$ neighbors that terminate routes that originate at inputs other than u. Each critical output w must be the neighbor of some critical input, else $S \cup \{(v, w)\}$ would be safe. Each critical input u can have at most two critical outputs as neighbors, else the distinct inputs v and u would have more than two common neighbors. Thus there must be at least $5^{\lambda-1}$ critical inputs.

Let X be a set of $5^{\lambda-1}$ critical inputs. Each critical input in X has at least $3 \cdot 5^{\lambda-1}$ busy neighbors. Furthermore, each of the $\binom{5^{\lambda-1}}{2}$ pairs of distinct critical inputs in X has at most two busy neighbors in common. Thus there are at least

$$5^{\lambda-1}(3 \cdot 5^{\lambda-1}) - \binom{5^{\lambda-1}}{2} \cdot 2 \geqq 2 \cdot 5^{2\lambda-2}$$

busy outputs in S. □

Proof of Theorem 4. To prove the first assertion, we may assume that $n = 5^{3\lambda}$ for some integer $\lambda \geqq 1$. Let $q = 5^\lambda$ and $a = 2 \cdot 5^{2\lambda-2}$. Let G be a wide-sense nonblocking generalized (q^2, a)-connector with depth one and size $q^2 a = O(n^{4/3})$ (in which each input is joined by an edge to each output). By Proposition 3.2, $H = F(q) \circ G$ is a wide-sense nonblocking generalized (n, a)-connector with depth two and size $O(n^{4/3})$. Let $t = \lceil n/a \rceil = O(n^{1/3})$. By Proposition 3.3, H^{+t} is a wide-sense nonblocking generalized (n, at)-connector with depth 2 and size $O(n^{5/3})$. Deleting all but n outputs completes the proof of the first assertion.

To prove the second assertion, we may assume that $n = 5^{7\mu}$ for some integer $\mu \geqq 1$. Let $q = 5^{3\mu}$ and $a = 2 \cdot 5^{6\mu-2}$. By deleting all but n inputs from $F(q)$, we obtain a wide-sense nonblocking a-limited (n, q^2)-concentrator F' with depth one and size $O(n^{10/7})$. Let G' be a wide-sense nonblocking generalized (q^2, a)-connector with depth two and size $O(n^{10/7})$ constructed by taking $\lambda = 2\mu$ in the proof of the first assertion and deleting all but a outputs. By Proposition 3.2, $H = F' \circ G'$ is a wide-sense nonblocking generalized (n, a)-connector with depth three and size $O(n^{10/7})$. Let $t = \lceil n/a \rceil = O(n^{1/7})$. By Proposition 3.3, H^{+t} is a wide-sense nonblocking generalized (n, at)-connector with depth three and size $O(n^{11/7})$. Deleting all but n outputs completes the proof of the second assertion. □

We could extend Theorem 4 to yield size $O(n^{23/25})$ for depth four, and so forth. As $k \to \infty$, the sequence of exponents approaches, but remains greater than, $3/2$. In the following section, however, we shall obtain size $O(n^{3/2})$ for depth four, so this extension is of little interest.

4. Bi-generalized connectors. Our efforts to replace the probabilistic argument of the preceding section by an explicit construction lead naturally to consideration of the best currently known explicit constructions for expanding graphs, due to Lubotzky, Phillips, and Sarnak [LPS] and Margulis [M2]. The networks produced with the aid of these constructions have greater size than those produced in the preceding section; they possess, however, a stronger property than that of being generalized connectors. We shall call them "bi-generalized connectors." Our next goal is to define these networks.

Two routes are *bi-compatible* if their intersection is an initial segment or a final segment (possibly empty) of both of them. A *bi-state* is a set of pairwise bi-compatible routes. (A bi-state may be regarded as two forests with their leaves identified, one with its roots at the inputs and the other with its roots at the outputs.)

A *bi-generalized connection assignment* is a set of connection requests. A bi-generalized connection assignment is *realized* by a bi-state if each request of the assignment is satisfied by some route of the bi-state.

A bi-generalized connection assignment is *a-limited* if it contains at most a connection requests. A bi-state is *a-limited* if the bi-generalized connection assignment it realizes is a-limited. A connection request is *a-limited* in a bi-state if the bi-generalized connection assignment obtained by adjoining the connection request to the bi-generalized assignment realized by the bi-state is a-limited.

A *wide-sense nonblocking a-limited bi-generalized connector* is a network for which there exists a set of distinguished bi-states, called the *safe* bi-states, with the following properties: (1) the empty bi-state is safe; (2) any bi-state below a safe bi-state is itself safe; and (3) given any safe bi-state and any a-limited connection request in that bi-state, there exists a safe bi-state above the given bi-state and containing a route satisfying the given request.

We shall use the term "bi-generalized connector" in place of "bi-generalized ∞-limited connector."

Our main result in this section is the following.

THEOREM 5. *For every fixed $k \geq 2$ and $n \to \infty$, a wide-sense nonblocking bi-generalized n-connector can be explicitly constructed with depth k and size $O(n^{1 + 2/k})$.*

For the proof of Theorem 5 we shall need the following lemma.

LEMMA 5.1. *Let p and q be distinct primes congruent to one modulo four. Then a $(q + 1)$-network of depth one can be explicitly constructed in which every input has $p + 1$ outputs as neighbors, every output is a neighbor of $p + 1$ inputs and every set of x inputs with $1 \leq x \leq 12(q + 1)/(p + 1)$ has at least $x(p + 1)/16$ neighbors.*

Proof. By the results of Lubotzky, Phillips, and Sarnak [LPS], an undirected graph G can be explicitly constructed in which there are $q + 1$ vertices, $p + 1$ edges incident with each vertex and in which the adjacency matrix $M(G)$ of G has $p + 1$ as a simple eigenvalue and has all other eigenvalues at most $2p^{1/2}$ in absolute value. Let the network F be the double cover of G; that is, let the inputs and outputs of F each correspond to the vertices of G and let the input v have the output w as a neighbor if and only if the vertices of G corresponding to v and w are adjacent. Clearly F is a $(q + 1)$-network of depth one in which every input has $p + 1$ neighbors and every output is a neighbor of $p + 1$ inputs. Let $M(F)$ denote the matrix whose rows are indexed by inputs of F, whose columns are indexed by outputs of F and whose (v, w) entry is the number of edges from v to w. Then $M(F)^T M(F) = M(G)^2$ has $(p + 1)^2$ as a simple eigenvalue and all other eigenvalues at most $4p$ in absolute value. Let $\varepsilon = 4p/(p + 1)^2$ and let $f(\xi) = \xi/(\xi + \varepsilon(1 - \xi))$. By the result of Tanner [T], if X is a set of inputs and $F(X)$ is the set of neighbors of X, then $|F(X)|/(q + 1) \geq f(|X|/(q + 1))$. Let $\delta = 4/(p + 1)$. Then $\varepsilon \leq \delta$ and $f(3\delta) \geq 3/4$. Since f is concave, if $|X| \leq 3\delta(q + 1)$, then $|F(X)| \geq (q + 1)f(|X|/(q + 1)) \geq (|X|/3\delta)f(3\delta) \geq |X|/4\delta$. $\square$

A wide-sense nonblocking bi-generalized a-limited connector remains one if any number of inputs and outputs (together with the edges incident with them) are deleted.

A *t-approximate a-limited m-junctor* is an m-network in which, given any $(a - 1)$-limited bi-state S, any set V containing t inputs and any set W containing t outputs, there exists a route ρ from some $v \in V$ to some $w \in W$ such that $S \cup \{\rho\}$ is a bi-state.

A t-approximate a-limited junctor remains one if any number of inputs and outputs (together with the edges incident with them) are deleted.

If F is an (n, m)-network, let F^* denote the (m, n)-network obtained by reversing the edges and exchanging the inputs and outputs of F. Clearly, $F^{**} = F$.

If S is a bi-state of F, let S^* denote the bi-state of F^* obtained by reversing the routes of S. Clearly, $S^{**} = S$.

Two routes are *anti-compatible* if their intersection is a final segment (possibly empty) of both of them. An *anti-state* is a set of pairwise anti-compatible routes. Clearly, if S is a state, then S^* is an anti-state.

PROPOSITION 5.2. *Let F be a wide-sense nonblocking $(a - 1 + t, t)$-limited generalized (n, m)-concentrator and let G be an t-approximate a-limited m-junctor. Then $F \circ G \circ F^*$ is a wide-sense nonblocking a-limited bi-generalized n-connector.*

Proof. Let S be a bi-state of $F \circ G \circ F^*$. Say that S is safe if (1) S induces a safe state $S(F)$ of F and (2) S induces an anti-state $S(F^*)$ of F^* and $S(F^*)^*$ is a safe state of F. Clearly, the empty bi-state is safe and any bi-state below a safe bi-state is itself safe. Let S be a safe bi-state of $F \circ G \circ F^*$ and let (v, w) be an a-limited connection request in S. Since (v, w) is a-limited, S contains at most $a - 1$ routes.

The concentration request v is (a, t)-limited in $S(F)$, so there is a safe state $T(F)$ above $S(F)$ in which v has routes to all the outputs in some set V of t outputs of F. Similarly, there is an anti-state $T(F^*)$ above $S(F^*)$ in which all the inputs in some set W of t inputs of F^* have routes to w and such that $T(F^*)^*$ is a safe state for F.

The bi-state $S(G)$ of G induced by S contains at most $a - 1$ routes. Since G is a t-approximate a-limited m-junctor, there is a bi-state $T(G)$ above $S(G)$ containing a route from some $v' \in V$ to some $w' \in W$. Let the route ρ be the concatenation of the route from v to v' in $T(F)$, the route from v' to w' in $T(G)$, and the route from w' to w in $T(F^*)$. Then $S \cup \{\rho\}$ is a safe bi-state above S containing a route from v to w. $\square$

PROPOSITION 5.3. *Let F be an m-network with depth one in which every set of t inputs has at least $\lceil (m + a)/2 \rceil$ neighbors. Then $F \circ F^*$ is a t-approximate a-limited m-junctor.*

Proof. Let S be an $(a - 1)$-limited bi-state of $F \circ F^*$. If V is a set of t inputs, then V has as neighbors all the outputs of F in some set V' of $\lceil (m + a)/2 \rceil$ outputs. Similarly, if W is a set of t outputs, then W has as neighbors all the inputs of F^* in some set W' of $\lceil (m + a)/2 \rceil$ inputs. Then $V' \cap W'$ contains at least $\lceil (m + a)/2 \rceil + \lceil (m + a)/2 \rceil - m \geq a$ links between F and F^*. Since S is $(a - 1)$-limited, at most $a - 1$ links can be busy. Thus there is some idle link u in $V' \cap W'$. The link u has as neighbors some input v in V and some output w in W. Let ρ be the route from v through u to w in $F \circ F^*$. Then $S \cup \{\rho\}$ is a bi-state above S containing a route from $v \in V$ to $w \in W$. $\square$

COROLLARY 5.4. *Let q be a prime congruent to one modulo four with $32n \leq q + 1 \leq 128n$. For every $t \leq n$, a t-approximate n-limited $(q + 1)$-junctor can be explicitly constructed with depth 2 and size $O(n^2/t)$.*

Proof. Let p be the smallest prime congruent to one modulo four such that $p + 1 \geq 12(q + 1)/t$. Then $p + 1 = O(n/t)$. Let F be the network constructed in the proof of Lemma 5.1. Then F has depth one and size $O(n^2/t)$. Furthermore, every set of t inputs has at least $3(q + 1)/4$ neighbors. It follows from Proposition 5.3 that F is a t-approximate n-limited $(q + 1)$-junctor. $\square$

111

Proof of Theorem 5 for k even. For $k = 2$, the claim is trivial, so suppose $k \geq 4$.

Let q be a prime congruent to one modulo four such that $32n \leq q + 1 \leq 64n$. Let p be a prime congruent to one modulo four such that $32n^{2/k} \leq p + 1 \leq 64n^{2/k}$. Let F be the network constructed in the proof of Lemma 5.1.

Let $r = \lceil (p + 1)/32 \rceil$ and $a = \lfloor 6(q + 1)/(p + 1) \rfloor$. Then $ar \geq 2n$. By Lemma 5.1, every set of x inputs with $1 \leq x \leq 2a$ has at least $2rx$ neighbors. Then by Proposition 1 with $s = r$, F is a wide-sense nonblocking $(2n, r)$-limited generalized $(q + 1)$-concentrator.

Let $j = (k - 2)/2$ and $t = \lceil n^{1 - 2/k} \rceil$. Since $r \geq n^{2/k}$, $r^j \geq t$. By Proposition 2, $H = F^{\circ j}$ is a wide-sense nonblocking $(2n, t)$-limited generalized $(q + 1)$-concentrator.

By Corollary 5.4, a t-approximate n-limited $(q + 1)$-network G can be explicitly constructed with depth two and size $O(n^2/t) = O(n^{1 + 2/k})$. By Proposition 5.2, $H \cdot G \cdot H^*$ is a wide-sense nonblocking n-limited bi-generalized $(q + 1)$-connector with depth k and size $O(n^{1 + 2/k})$. Deleting all but n inputs and n outputs from this network completes the proof. □

COROLLARY 5.5. *Let q be a prime congruent to one modulo four with $32n \leq q + 1 \leq 128n$. For every $t \leq n$, a t-approximate n-limited $(q + 1)$-junctor can be explicitly constructed with depth one and size $O(n^3/t^2)$.*

Proof. In the network constructed in Corollary 5.4, replace each route of length two by a route of length one, then delete all links and edges incident with them. The resulting network is clearly a t-approximate n-limited $(q + 1)$-junctor with depth one. Since in the original network each of the $(q + 1)$ links has $O(n/t)$ inputs and $O(n/t)$ outputs as neighbors, the resulting network has size $O(n^3/t^2)$. □

Proof of Theorem 5 for k odd. For $k = 1$, the claim is trivial, so suppose $k \geq 3$.

Let q be a prime congruent to one modulo four such that $32n \leq q + 1 \leq 64n$. Let p be a prime congruent to one modulo four such that $32n^{2/k} \leq p + 1 \leq 64n^{2/k}$. Let F be the network constructed in the proof of Lemma 5.1.

Let $r = \lceil (p + 1)/32 \rceil$ and $a = \lfloor 6(q + 1)/(p + 1) \rfloor$. Then $ar \geq 2n$. By Lemma 5.1, every set of x inputs with $1 \leq x \leq 2a$ has at least $2rx$ neighbors. Then by Proposition 1 with $s = r$, F is a wide-sense nonblocking $(2n, r)$-limited generalized $(q + 1)$-concentrator.

Let $j = (k - 1)/2$ and $t = \lceil n^{1 - 1/k} \rceil$. Since $r \geq n^{2/k}$, $r^j \geq t$. By Proposition 2, $H = F^{\circ j}$ is a wide-sense nonblocking $(2n, t)$-limited generalized $(q + 1)$-concentrator.

By Corollary 5.4, a t-approximate n-limited $(q + 1)$-network G can be explicitly constructed with depth one and size $O(n^3/t^2) = O(n^{1 + 2/k})$. By Proposition 5.2, $H \cdot G \cdot H^*$ is a wide-sense nonblocking n-limited bi-generalized $(q + 1)$-connector with depth k and size $O(n^{1 + 2/k})$. Deleting all but n inputs and n outputs from this network completes the proof. □

Since the networks constructed in Theorem 5 rely on Proposition 1, no efficient algorithm is known for finding safe routes. The remaining results of this section mitigate this defect in some special cases.

THEOREM 6. *Wide-sense nonblocking bi-generalized n-connectors can be explicitly constructed with depth three and size $O(n^{5/3})$, and with depth four and size $O(n^{3/2})$.*

For the proof of Theorem 6 we shall need the following lemma.

LEMMA 6.1. *For every prime power q, a (q^3)-network of depth one can be explicitly constructed in which every input has q^2 neighbors and any two distinct inputs have at most q common neighbors.*

Proof. Let GF (q) be the field with q elements. Let the outputs correspond to the q^3 points in the three-dimensional affine space over GF (q). Let the inputs correspond to any q^3 planes in this space. (There are $q^3 + q^2 + q$ planes in the space.) Let the input v have the output w as a neighbor if the plane corresponding to v contains the point corresponding to w. Clearly, each plane contains q^2 points and any two distinct planes have at most the q points of a line in common. □

Let $F_3(q)$ denote the network constructed in the proof of Lemma 6.1.

PROPOSITION 6.2. *The network $F_3(2^\lambda)$ is a wide-sense nonblocking $(2^{3\lambda-5}, 2^{2\lambda-1})$-limited generalized concentrator.*

Proof. Let the safe states be those in which every input has at most $2^{2\lambda-2}$ neighbors that terminate routes originating at other inputs. Clearly the empty state is safe, and any state below a safe state is itself safe. Let S be a safe state, let v be a $(2^{3\lambda-5}, 2^{2\lambda-1})$-limited concentration request in S, and suppose that there is no safe state above S containing a route from v to an output that is idle in S. We shall derive a contradiction.

Since v is $(2^{3\lambda-5}, 2^{2\lambda-1})$-limited in S, there are routes from v to at most $2^{\lambda-1}$ neighbors of v. Since S is safe, at most $2^{2\lambda-2}$ other neighbors of v are busy. Say that an output w is *critical* if w is a neighbor of v, w is idle in S and $S \cup \{(v, w)\}$ is not safe. Then there are at least $2^{2\lambda} - 2^{2\lambda-1} - 2^{2\lambda-2} = 2^{2\lambda-2}$ critical outputs.

Say that an input is *critical* if u is distinct from v and $2^{2\lambda-2}$ neighbors of u terminate routes that originate at inputs other than u. Each critical output w must be the neighbor of some critical input, else $S \cup \{(v, w)\}$ would be safe. Each critical input u can have at most 2^λ critical outputs as a neighbor, else the distinct inputs v and u would have more than 2^λ common neighbors. Thus there must be at least $2^{\lambda-2}$ critical inputs.

Let X be a set of $2^{\lambda-2}$ critical inputs. Each critical input in X has at least $2^{2\lambda-2}$ busy neighbors. Furthermore, each of the $\binom{2^{\lambda-2}}{2}$ pairs of distinct critical inputs in X has at most 2^λ busy neighbors in common. Thus there are at least

$$2^{\lambda-2} \cdot 2^{2\lambda-2} - \binom{2^{\lambda-2}}{2} \cdot 2^\lambda \geqq 2^{3\lambda-5}$$

busy outputs in S. This contradicts the assumption that v is $(2^{3\lambda-5}, 2^{2\lambda-1})$-limited in S. $\square$

Proof of the first assertion of Theorem 6. We may assume that $n = 2^{3\lambda-6}$ for some integer $\lambda \geqq 3$. Let $t = 2^{2\lambda-1} = O(n^{2/3})$. Let F be the network obtained by deleting all but n inputs from $F_3(2^\lambda)$. By Proposition 6.2, F is a wide-sense nonblocking $(2n, t)$-limited generalized $(n, 64n)$-concentrator with depth one and size $O(n^{5/3})$.

Let q be a prime congruent to one modulo four with $64n \leqq q + 1 \leqq 128n$. By Corollary 5.5, a t-approximate n-limited $(q + 1)$-junctor can be explicitly constructed with depth one and size $O(n^3/t^2) = O(n^{5/3})$. Let G be the network obtained by deleting all but $64n$ inputs and $64n$ outputs from this network. By Proposition 5.2, $F \circ G \circ F^*$ is a wide-sense nonblocking bi-generalized n-connector with depth three and size $O(n^{5/3})$, which completes the proof of the first assertion. $\square$

To prove the second assertion we shall need the following lemma.

LEMMA 6.3. *For every prime power q, a (q^2)-network of depth one can be explicitly constructed in which every input has q neighbors and any two distinct inputs have at most one common neighbor.*

Proof. Let GF (q) be the field with q elements. Let the outputs correspond to the q^2 points in the affine plane over GF (q). Let the inputs correspond to any q^2 lines in this plane. (There are $q^2 + q$ lines in the plane.) Let the input v have the output w as a neighbor if the line corresponding to v contains the point corresponding to w. Clearly, each line contains q points and any two distinct lines have at most one point in common. $\square$

Let $F_2(q)$ denote the network constructed in the proof of Lemma 6.3.

PROPOSITION 6.4. *The network $F_2(2^\lambda)$ is a wide-sense nonblocking $(2^{2\lambda-5}, 2^{\lambda-1})$-limited generalized concentrator.*

Proof. Let the safe states be those in which every input has at most $2^{\lambda-2}$ neighbors that terminate routes originating at other inputs. Clearly the empty state is safe, and any state below a safe state is itself safe. Let S be a safe state, let v be a $(2^{2\lambda-5}, 2^{\lambda-1})$-limited concentration request in S, and suppose that there is no safe state above S containing a route from v to an output that is idle in S. We shall derive a contradiction.

Since v is $(2^{2\lambda-5}, 2^{\lambda-1})$-limited in S, there are routes from v to at most $2^{\lambda-1}$ neighbors of v. Since S is safe, at most $2^{\lambda-2}$ other neighbors of v are busy. Say that an output w is *critical* if w is a neighbor of v, w is idle in S and $S \cup \{(v, w)\}$ is not safe. Then there are at least $2^{\lambda} - 2^{\lambda-1} - 2^{\lambda-2} = 2^{\lambda-2}$ critical outputs.

Say that an input u is *critical* if u is distinct from v and $2^{\lambda-2}$ neighbors of u terminate routes that originate at inputs other than u. Each critical output w must be the neighbor of some critical input, else $S \cup \{(v, w)\}$ would be safe. Each critical input u can have at most one critical output as a neighbor, else the distinct inputs v and u would have more than one common neighbor. Thus there must be at least $2^{\lambda-2}$ critical inputs.

Let X be a set of $2^{\lambda-2}$ critical inputs. Each critical input in X has at least $2^{\lambda-2}$ busy neighbors. Furthermore, each of the $\binom{2^{\lambda-2}}{2}$ pairs of distinct critical inputs in X has at most one busy neighbor in common. Thus there are at least

$$2^{\lambda-2} \cdot 2^{\lambda-2} - \binom{2^{\lambda-2}}{2} \cdot 1 \geqq 2^{2\lambda-5}$$

busy outputs in S. This contradicts the assumption that v is $(2^{2\lambda-5}, 2^{\lambda-1})$-limited in S. $\square$

Proof of the second assertion of Theorem 6. We may assume that $n = 2^{2\lambda-6}$ for some integer $\lambda \geqq 4$. Let $t = 2^{\lambda-1} = O(n^{1/2})$. Let F be the network obtained by deleting all but n inputs from $F_2(2^{\lambda})$. By Proposition 6.4, F is a wide-sense nonblocking $(2n, t)$-limited generalized $(n, 64n)$-concentrator with depth one and size $O(n^{3/2})$.

Let q be a prime congruent to one modulo four with $64n \leqq q + 1 \leqq 128n$. By Corollary 5.4, a t-approximate n-limited $(q + 1)$-junctor can be explicitly constructed with depth two and size $O(n^2/t) = O(n^{3/2})$. Let G be the network obtained by deleting all but $64n$ inputs and $64n$ outputs from this network. By Proposition 5.2, $F \circ G \circ F^*$ is a wide-sense nonblocking bi-generalized n-connector with depth four and size $O(n^{3/2})$, which completes the proof of the second assertion. $\square$

5. Networks with unlimited depth. In previous sections we have used Proposition 1 to construct various networks with limited depth. In this section we shall use it in situations where depth is not constrained. We shall show that wide-sense nonblocking generalized n-connectors and bi-generalized n-connectors can be constructed with size $O(n \log n)$. That these results are best possible (to within constant factors) is shown by a result of Shannon [S] to the effect that even "rearrangeable n-connectors" require size $\Omega(n \log n)$. (Indeed, Pippenger and Valiant [PV] have shown that even networks satisfying a still weaker property, that of being "rearrangeable n-shifters," must have size $\Omega(n \log n)$.)

The previously best upper bound for wide-sense nonblocking generalized connectors was $O(n(\log n)^2)$, due to Pippenger [P1]. This construction requires wide-sense nonblocking (ungeneralized) connectors as components. That size $O(n \log n)$ is sufficient for these networks (and indeed, even for networks that satisfy a stronger property, that of being "strictly nonblocking connectors") is due to Bassalygo and Pinsker [BP1]. The proof of Bassalygo and Pinsker is nonconstructive (in the same sense as Lemma 3.1), but subsequent results by others ([M1], [GG], [JM], [LPS], [M2]) yield an explicit construction (see Pippenger [P3] for details).

That our results cannot be extended to "strictly nonblocking generalized connectors" is shown by the lower bound of $\Omega(n^2)$, due to Bassalygo and Pinsker [BP2].

The key to our results in this section is the following proposition.

PROPOSITION 7. *A wide-sense nonblocking generalized* $(n, 18n)$-*concentrator can be explicitly constructed with depth* $O(\log n)$ *and size* $O(n \log n)$.

This proposition has the following immediate corollary.

COROLLARY 7.1. *A wide-sense nonblocking generalized n-connector can be explicitly constructed with depth* $O(\log n)$ *and size* $O(n \log n)$.

To prove Corollary 7.1 we shall need the following proposition.

PROPOSITION 7.2. *Let* F *be a wide-sense nonblocking* (a, r)-*limited generalized* (n, m)-*concentrator and let* G *be a wide-sense nonblocking* (m, n)-*connector. Then* $F \cdot G$ *is a wide-sense nonblocking* (a, r)-*limited generalized n-connector.*

Proof. Let the safe states of $F \cdot G$ be those that induce safe states of F and G. Clearly, the empty state is safe and any state below a safe state is itself safe. Let S be a safe state of $F \cdot G$ and let the connection request (v, w) be (a, r)-limited in S.

The concentration request v is (a, r)-limited in $S(F)$, so there exists a safe state $T(F)$ above $S(F)$ containing a route from v to an output u of F that is idle in $S(F)$. The connection request (u, w) is a-limited in $S(G)$, so there exists a safe state $T(G)$ above $S(G)$ containing a route from u to w.

The state obtained by adjoining to S the concatenation of the route from v to u in $T(F)$ with the route from u to w in $T(G)$ is a safe state above S containing a route from v to w. $\square$

Proof of Corollary 7.1. Let F be the network constructed in the proof of Proposition 7, and let G be an explicitly constructed nonblocking $(18n, n)$-connector with depth $O(\log n)$ and size $O(n \log n)$ (see [P3] for a construction). By Proposition 7.2, $F \cdot G$ satisfies the claim. $\square$

We can also extend the foregoing corollary to bi-generalized connectors.

COROLLARY 7.3. *A wide-sense nonblocking bi-generalized n-connector can be explicitly constructed with depth* $O(\log n)$ *and size* $O(n \log n)$.

To prove Corollary 7.3 we shall need the following proposition.

PROPOSITION 7.4. *Let* F *be a wide-sense nonblocking* (a, a)-*limited generalized* (n, m)-*concentrator and let* G *be a wide-sense nonblocking* a-*limited m-connector. Then* $F \cdot G \cdot F^*$ *is a wide-sense nonblocking bi-generalized n-connector.*

Proof. Let S be a bi-state of $F \cdot G \cdot F^*$. Say that S is safe if (1) S induces a safe state $S(F)$ of F; (2) S induces a safe state $S(G)$ of G; and (3) S induces an anti-state $S(F^*)$ of F^* and $S(F^*)^*$ is a safe state of F. Clearly, the empty bi-state is safe and any bi-state below a safe bi-state is itself safe. Let S be a safe bi-state of $F \cdot G \cdot F^*$ and let the connection request (v, w) be a-limited in S.

The concentration request v is a-limited in $S(F)$, so there exists a safe state $T(F)$ above $S(F)$ containing a route from v to an output v' of F that is idle in $S(F)$. Similarly, there is an anti-state $T(F^*)$ above $S(F^*)$ containing a route from an input w' of F^* that is idle in $S(F^*)$ to w and such that $T(F^*)^*$ is a safe state for F. The connection request (v', w') is a-limited in $S(G)$, so there exists a safe state $T(G)$ above $S(G)$ containing a route from v' to w'.

Let the route ρ be the concatenation of the route from v to v' in $T(F)$, the route from v' to w' in $T(G)$, and the route from w' to w in $T(F^*)$. Then $S \cup \{\rho\}$ is a safe bi-state above S containing a route from v to w. $\square$

Proof of Corollary 7.3. Let F be the network constructed in the proof of Proposition 7, and let G be an explicitly constructed nonblocking $(18n)$-connector with depth $O(\log n)$ and size $O(n \log n)$ (see [P3] for a construction). By Proposition 7.4, $F \cdot G \cdot F^*$ satisfies the claim. $\square$

Proof of Proposition 7. Let $p = 53$ and let q be a prime congruent to one modulo four with $9n \leq q + 1 \leq 18n$. Let F be the network of depth one and size $O(n)$ constructed in the proof of Lemma 5.1. Then every set of x inputs with $1 \leq x \leq 2n$ has at least $3x$ neighbors in F. By Proposition 1 with $r = 2$ and $s = 1$, F is a wide-sense nonblocking $(n, 2)$-limited generalized $(q + 1)$-concentrator.

Let $k = \lceil \log_2 n \rceil$. By Proposition 2, F^{*k} is a wide-sense nonblocking (n, n)-limited generalized $(q + 1)$-concentrator. Deleting all but n inputs and adding $18n - (q + 1)$ isolated outputs completes the proof. $\square$

The results of this paper that rely on Proposition 1 do not provide efficient algorithms for finding safe routes. In special cases (Theorems 4 and 6) we have been able to avoid this defect. It may be possible to extend the methods used in these special cases to obtain a version of Proposition 1 that allows an efficient algorithm for finding safe routes, but such an extension has eluded our efforts thus far.

REFERENCES

[B1]   V. E. BENEŠ, *Heuristic remarks and mathematical problems regarding the theory of switching systems*, Bell System Tech. J., 41 (1962), pp. 1201–1247.

[B2]   ———, *Semilattice characterization of nonblocking networks*, Bell System Tech. J., 52 (1973), pp. 697–706.

[B3]   ———, *Blocking states in connecting networks made of square switches arranged in stages*, Bell System Tech. J., 60 (1981), pp. 511–521.

[BKPVY]   M. BLUM, R. M. KARP, C. H. PAPIDIMITRIOU, O. VORNBERGER, AND M. YANNAKAKIS, *The complexity of superconcentrators*, Inform. Process. Lett., 13 (1981), pp. 164–167.

[BP1]   L. A. BASSALYGO AND M. S. PINSKER, *Complexity of an optimum nonblocking switching network without reconnections*, Problems Inform. Transmission, 9 (1974), pp. 64–66.

[BP2]   ———, *Asymptotically optimal networks for generalized rearrangeable switching and generalized switching without rearrangement*, Problemy Peredachi Informatsii, 16 (1980), pp. 94–98.

[Ca]   D. G. CANTOR, *On non-blocking switching networks*, Networks, 1 (1971), pp. 367–377.

[Cl]   C. CLOS, *A study of non-blocking switching networks*, Bell System Tech. J., 32 (1953), pp. 406–424.

[DDPW]   D. DOLEV, C. DWORK, N. PIPPINGER, AND A. WIDGERSON, *Superconcentrators, generalizers and generalized connectors with limited depth*, ACM Symposium on Theory of Computing, 15 (1983), pp. 42–51.

[F]   J. FRIEDMAN, *A lower bound for strictly non-blocking networks*, Combinatorica, to appear.

[FFP]   P. FELDMAN, J. FRIEDMAN, AND N. PIPPENGER, *Non-blocking networks*, ACM Symposium on Theory of Computing, 18 (1986), pp. 247–254.

[FP]   J. FRIEDMAN AND N. PIPPENGER, *Expanding graphs contain all small trees*, Combinatorica, 7 (1987), pp. 71–76.

[GG]   O. GABBER AND Z. GALIL, *Explicit construction of linear-sized superconcentrators*, J. Comput. System Sci., 22 (1981), pp. 407–420.

[JM]   S. JIMBO AND A. MARUOKA, *Expanders obtained from affine transformations*, ACM Symposium on Theory of Computing, 17 (1985), pp. 88–97.

[LPS]   A. LUBOTZKY, R. PHILLIPS, AND P. SARNAK, *Explicit expanders and the Ramanujan conjectures*, ACM Symposium on Theory of Computing, 18 (1986), pp. 240–246.

[M1]   G. A. MARGULIS, *Explicit constructions of concentrators*, Problems Inform. Transmission, 9 (1973), pp. 325–332.

[M2]   ———, *Arithmetic groups and graphs without short cycles*, Problemy Peredachi Informatsii, to appear.

[MJ]   G. M. MASSON AND B. W. JORDAN, JR., *Generalized multi-stage connection networks*, Networks, 2 (1972), pp. 191–209.

[NS]   D. NASSIMI AND S. SAHNI, *Parallel permutation and sorting algorithms and a new generalized connection network*, J. Assoc. Comput. Mach., 29 (1982), pp. 642–667.

[O]   YU. P. OFMAN, *A universal automaton*, Trans. Moscow Math. Soc., 14 (1965), pp. 200–215.

[P1]   N. PIPPENGER, *The complexity theory of switching networks*, Ph.D. thesis, Department of Electrical Engineering, Massachusetts Institute of Technology, Cambridge, MA, 1973.

[P2]   ——, *On rearrangeable and nonblocking switching networks*, J. Comput. System Sci., 17 (1978), pp. 145–162.

[P3]   ——, *Telephone switching networks*, AMS Proc. Symposium on Applied Mathematics, 26 (1982), pp. 101–133.

[PU]   D. PELEG AND E. UPFAL, *Constructing disjoint paths on expander graphs*, ACM Symposium on Theory of Computing, 19 (1987), pp. 264–273.

[PV]   N. PIPPENGER AND L. G. VALIANT, *Shifting graphs and their applications*, J. Assoc. Comput. Mach., 23 (1976), pp. 423–432.

[PY]   N. PIPPENGER AND A. C.-C. YAO, *Rearrangeable networks with limited depth*, SIAM J. Algebraic Discrete Methods, 3 (1982), pp. 411–417.

[S]   C. E. SHANNON, *Memory requirements in a telephone exchange*, Bell System Tech. J., 29 (1950), pp. 343–349.

[T]   R. M. TANNER, *Explicit construction of concentrators from generalized N-gons*, SIAM J. Algebraic Discrete Methods, 5 (1984), pp. 287–293.

On the Rearrangeability of $2(\log_2 N) - 1$ Stage Permutation Networks

KYUNGSOOK YOON LEE

Abstract —For any parallel computer systems which consist of many processing elements and memories, interconnection networks provide communication paths among processing elements and memories. Both the rearrangeability proof and the control algorithm are well known for the Benes network, which is intrinsically symmetric. However, there has been little progress for the case of nonsymmetric networks of similar hardware requirements.

We provide a new proof on the rearrangeability of a $2(\log_2 N) - 1$ stage network. The proof does not depend on the symmetry of the network and can be applied to nonsymmetric as well as symmetric networks. We develop a global approach, one advantage of which is that it leads naturally to the idea of the rearrangeability proof and a control algorithm. For ease of understanding and presentation, the reduced $\Omega_N \Omega_N^{-1}$ (the last switching stage of Ω_N removed together with more redundant switches) is chosen to show the proof method. The Ω_N^{-1}-passable permutations are first characterized, and the bit control algorithm emerges as the "natural" control algorithm for such permutations. By a simple reinterpretation of the Ω_N^{-1}-passable condition into Ω_N, a unique control algorithm for the reduced Ω_N to transform an arbitrary permutation into an Ω_N^{-1}-passable permutation is obtained.

The hardware requirement of the reduced $\Omega_N \Omega_N^{-1}$ is $N(\log_2 N) - N + 1$ switches, which is the lower bound for rearrangeable networks. Although our algorithm has the same time complexity of $O(N \log_2 N)$ for single control and $O(N)$ for multiple control as the looping algorithm of the Benes network, it is simpler because calculations of inverse mappings are not required, and it is easier to understand because the switches are set stage by stage. It is also general enough to be useful for any $2(\log_2 N) - 1$ stage rearrangeable network.

Index Terms —Control algorithm, hardware redundancy, hardware requirement, interconnection network, multistage networks, passable permutations, permutation, rearrangeability.

I. INTRODUCTION

AS a way of achieving high computing power, computer systems built upon a large number of processing elements and memory modules are becoming increasingly important. Interconnection networks provide the communication paths among processing elements and memories.

An interconnection network is rearrangeable if its permitted states realize any one-to-one assignment of input points to output points [1]. The Benes binary network, a member of Clos' type networks [4], is a rearrangeable network which

Manuscript received January 23, 1984; revised July 20, 1984. This work was supported in part by the National Science Foundation under Grant US NSF MCS80-01561, and in part by the University of California under Grant US DOE SBC UCAL 5498609.

The author is with the Department of Computer and Information Science, The Ohio State University, Columbus, OH 43210.

requires near-optimum hardware [5], [14]. The control algorithm which sets switching elements of an interconnection network to realize any requested input–output connection was well defined for the Benes network [8]. Some researchers devised parallel versions of this basic looping algorithm [15], [16], while some others worked on fast, tailored control algorithms for limited but useful subsets of all the possible permutations [17].

While the Benes network was proven to be a rearrangeable network long ago [1], very little has been known about the rearrangeability of the multistage networks of the same hardware complexity. The Benes network is a symmetric network; the left half and the right half of the network are the mirror images of each other, with the center stage as the plane of symmetry. On the other hand, the multistage networks can be nonsymmetric. The Slepian–Duguid theorem [2], [3], on which the rearrangeability of the Benes network is founded, inherently applies only to symmetric networks.

Slepian–Duguid Theorem

The symmetric three-stage network of square switches, in which switches on adjacent stages are connected by exactly one link, is rearrangeable and corresponds to a factorization

$$S_{nr} = (S_n)^r \phi^{-1}(S_r)^n \phi(S_n)^r$$

where S_{nr} is a permutation of $n \times r$ numbers, $(S_n)^r$ are r independent permutations of n numbers, and ϕ and ϕ^{-1}, which are inverse to each other, are fixed connections represented as permutations. This theorem can be depicted as in Fig. 1.

In this paper, we provide a new method to understand and prove the rearrangeability (or the universality [12]) of $2(\log_2 N) - 1$ stage rearrangeable networks. Although our primary concern is $(N \times N)$ networks with $N = 2^n$, the results can easily be generalized for the case of $N = p^n$, $p > 2$. In the new method, the first $(\log_2 N) - 1$ stages, first half (FH), and the last $(\log N)$ stages, last half (LH), of the network are controlled by two different control algorithms. All the permutations realizable on LH are characterized in terms of residue classes regarding the input permutation as an ordered set. LH is controlled by the usual destination tag method [6], [10]. To transform an arbitrary permutation into an LH-passable permutation, FH is controlled by a proper residue class partitioning. Although a symmetric network $\Omega_N \Omega_N^{-1}$ will be used in the proof for ease of understanding and presentation, the proof does not depend on the symmetry of the network. It will also be shown that the last switching stage of Ω_N is redundant. Thus, the resulting network,

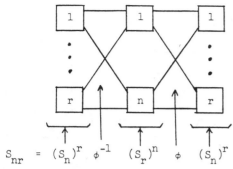

$$S_{nr} = (S_n)^r \quad \phi^{-1} \quad (S_r)^n \quad \phi \quad (S_n)^r$$

Fig. 1. A Clos network illustrating the result of the Slepian–Duguid theorem.

called the reduced $\Omega_N \Omega_N^{-1}$, is a rearrangeable network with $2(\log_2 N) - 1$ stages. The proof automatically yields a control algorithm. Asymmetric networks (e.g., baseline network followed by Ω^{-1}) might as well have been used for the illustration of the proof method. However, those networks require more notations.

Notations and definitions are given in Section II. The Ω_N^{-1}-passable permutations are defined in terms of set properties concerning residue classes in Section III. In Section IV, it is shown that an arbitrary permutation can be transformed into an Ω_N^{-1}-passable permutation via the reduced Ω_N (the last switching stage removed from Ω_N). Thus, Sections III and IV constitute the rearrangeability proof of a $2(\log_2 N) - 1$ stage permutation network.

The control algorithm for the reduced $\Omega_N \Omega_N^{-1}$ and the hardware redundancy presented implicitly in the proof are summarized in Section V. The number of switches for the reduced $\Omega_N \Omega_N^{-1}$ is the same as the number of switches for the reduced Benes network [5], [14], which is a lower bound for rearrangeable networks.

The proof method suggests a uniform control scheme for any $2(\log_2 N) - 1$ or $2 \log_2 N$ stage rearrangeable network. The control scheme and its time complexity are also described in Section V, and conclusions are given in Section VI.

II. Notations and Definitions

We begin this section by definitions of two key concepts used throughout this paper. Here, by a residue class mod m, we mean an equivalence class obtained by the remainder when m divides into a number.

Definition [9]

A *complete residue system modulo m* [CRS(mod m)] is a set of m integers which contains exactly one representative of each residue class mod m.

Thus, if we divide m into every element of a CRS(mod m), we get one each of the possible remainder values 0 through $(m - 1)$. Observe that any consecutive 2^n numbers form a CRS(mod 2^n). Next we define a partitioning operation on a CRS.

Definition

A complete residue partition (CRP) is a partition of a CRS(mod 2^k) into two CRS's(mod $2^{(k-1)}$), $k \geq 1$.

A CRS(mod 2^k) consists of 2^k numbers which yield each remainder $0 - (2^k - 1)$ when divided by 2^k. If the same numbers are divided by $2^{(k-1)}$ instead, these will yield pairs of each remainder $0 - (2^{(k-1)} - 1)$. In other words, a CRS(mod 2^k) contains two representatives of each residue class mod $2^{(k-1)}$. A CRP is a function which partitions a CRS(mod 2^k) into two CRS's(mod $2^{(k-1)}$). As there are two ways to choose each representative mod $2^{(k-1)}$, there are $2^{2^{(k-1)}}/2$ different ways to perform a CRP. So a CRP is not a unique function.

Examples

1) CRP($\{7, 6, 0, 1, 3, 4, 5, 2\}$) = $\{7, 1, 4, 2\}$, $\{6, 0, 3, 5\}$(or $\{7, 5, 4, 2\}$, $\{6, 0, 3, 1\}$, etc.)
   CRS(mod 8)   CRS's(mod 4).
2) CRP($\{7, 1, 4, 2\}$) = $\{7, 4\}$, $\{1, 2\}$ (or $\{7, 2\}$, $\{1, 4\}$)
   CRS(mod 4)   CRS's(mod 2).
3) CRP($\{6, 0, 3, 5\}$) = $\{6, 3\}$, $\{0, 5\}$ (or $\{6, 5\}$, $\{0, 3\}$)
   CRS(mod 4)   CRS's(mod 2).

Throughout this paper, $\{\}$ denotes a set, while $()$ denotes an ordered set. In example 1), a set of numbers 0–7 is a CRS(mod 8). When a CRP is performed on this set, two CRS's(mod 4) are obtained. The set $\{7, 1, 4, 2\}$ contains 3, 1, 0, 2 residue classes mod 4, and thus a CRS(mod 4). The remaining set $\{6, 0, 3, 5\}$ contains 2, 0, 3, 1 residue classes mod 4, and also a CRS(mod 4). Likewise, the set $\{7, 5, 4, 2\}$ contains 3, 1, 0, 2 residue classes mod 4, and the set $\{6, 0, 3, 1\}$ contains 2, 0, 3, 1 residue classes mod 4. Both are CRS's(mod 4). The original set $\{7, 6, 0, 1, 3, 4, 5, 2\}$ can be partitioned into two CRS's(mod 4) in $2^4/2 = 8$ different ways. In addition to the two ways shown above, the other six possible ways are

$\{0, 1, 2, 3\}\{4, 5, 6, 7\}$, $\{4, 1, 2, 3\}\{0, 5, 6, 7\}$,
$\{0, 5, 2, 3\}\{4, 1, 6, 7\}$, $\{4, 5, 2, 3\}\{0, 1, 6, 7\}$,
$\{0, 5, 6, 3\}\{4, 1, 2, 7\}$, and $\{4, 5, 6, 3\}\{0, 1, 2, 7\}$.

As far as a CRP is concerned, it is of no interest which particular four numbers are chosen to form a CRS(mod 4) as long as the set of chosen four numbers is a CRS(mod 4).

In example 2), a CRP is performed on the set $\{7, 1, 4, 2\}$, resulting in two CRS's(mod 2) $\{7, 4\}$ and $\{1, 2\}$. This partition could have been done in another way to yield $\{7, 2\}$ and $\{1, 4\}$. A CRS(mod 2) consists of an even number and an odd number. If the least significant bit of an input number is the control bit for a (2×2) switch, a CRS(mod 2) input to a switch ensures a distinct pair of control bit values, and thus a conflict-free state of the switch. As will be seen later for Ω_N^{-1}, a CRS(mod 2^i) property of the original input set ensures no conflict state at the switching stage $(i - 1)$. Thus, CRS properties are directly related to a conflict-free state of an interconnection network, and therefore can be used to define the characteristics of permutations realizable on a given interconnection network.

A CRP is a partitioning function operated on a CRS so that the two subsets of an equal size obtained by the partition preserve CRS properties for the smaller set size. It will be used as the basic function for a new network control algorithm.

Consider an $N = 2^n$ input/output interconnection network

Γ_N, consisting of $n = \log_2 N$ switching stages where each switching stage has $N/2$ (2×2) switching elements. Γ_N can be represented as

$$\Gamma_N = C^0 E^0 \cdots C^{(n-1)} E^{(n-1)} C^n$$

where C denotes a fixed connection, E denotes a switching stage, and the superscript i specifies the ith stage. In particular, the inverse omega network Ω_N^{-1} [6] can be represented as

$$\Omega_N^{-1} = E^0 \sigma^{-1} E^1 \sigma^{-1} \cdots E^{(n-1)} \sigma^{-1}$$

where σ^{-1} is an unshuffle connection. The effect of a switching stage E is an exchange permutation. Let $x = (x_{n-1}, x_{n-2}, \cdots, x_1, x_0)$ be an ordered set of n numbers. Then

$$E(x) = (\{x_{(n-1)}, x_{(n-2)}\}, \cdots, \{x_1, x_0\})$$

which indicates possible pairwise reordering by (2×2) switches. An unshuffle is the inverse of the perfect shuffle σ [13]. The effects of a shuffle and an unshuffle are a circular left shift and a circular right shift, respectively.

$$\sigma(x) = (x_{(n-2)}, x_{(n-3)}, \cdots, x_0, x_{(n-1)})$$

$$\sigma^{-1}(x) = (x_0, x_{(n-1)}, \cdots, x_2, x_1) .$$

An unshuffle can also be viewed as dividing a card deck into two halves by taking the top card from the original deck and placing the card at the bottom of two decks alternatively. An Ω_8^{-1} is shown in Fig. 2. In the same way, the omega network Ω_N [6] can be represented as

$$\Omega_N = \sigma E^0 \sigma E^1 \cdots \sigma E^{(n-2)} \sigma E^{(n-1)} .$$

Definition

The reduced Ω_N is Ω_N with the last switching stage $E^{(n-1)}$ removed. An Ω_8 is shown in Fig. 3. When the last switching stage in dashed lines is removed, we obtain the reduced Ω_8.

We shall use A^i to denote an ordered set of N input numbers $(a_0^i, \cdots, a_{(N-1)}^i)$, which is the input to the switching stage E^i of an Ω_N^{-1}. To be able to denote the subsets of A^i, we define the following. In this notation, $A_{j,k}^i$ represents the kth partition of size 2^j which is input to switching stage i.

Definition — Partitions of A^i

$$A_{0,k}^i = \{a_k^i\}, \qquad 0 \le k < 2^n$$

$$A_{j,k}^i = A_{(j-1),2k}^i \cup A_{(j-1),(2k-1)}^i,$$

$$0 \le k < 2^{(n-j)}, 1 < j \le n .$$

Thus, $A_{0,k}^i$ is simply the kth input number to switching stage i. Given the partitions of size $2^{(j-1)}$, the partitions of size 2^j are obtained by pairwise combination of two adjacent groups of size $2^{(j-1)}$. These partitions of A^i for $n = 3$ are shown in Fig. 4. In other words, $A_{j,k}^i$ is a partition performed by grouping 2^j contiguous numbers as one subset. There are $2^{(n-j)}$ such subsets which are denoted by k. Generalizing the second definition above, which shows pairwise grouping of partitions of size $2^{(j-1)}$ to form partitions of size 2^j, we obtain (1):

$$A_{j,k}^i = \bigcup_m \{A_{(j-s),(2^s k+m)}^i \,|\, 0 \le m < 2^s\}, \qquad 0 \le s < j . \quad (1)$$

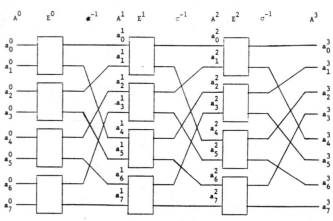

Fig. 2. An Ω_8^{-1} network.

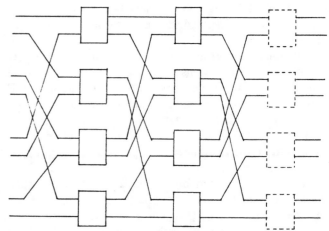

Fig. 3. An Ω_8 network. (Remove the last switching stage in dashed lines to obtain the reduced Ω_8.)

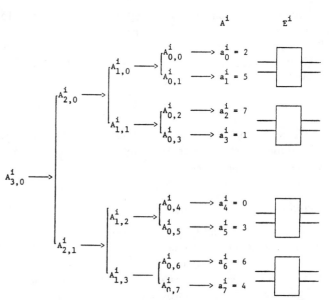

Fig. 4. Partitions of A^i, $A_{j,k}^i$ for $n = 3$.

Equation (1) shows that a partition of size 2^j can be obtained from combining 2^s consecutive partitions of size $2^{(j-s)}$. For example, in Fig. 4, $A_{2,0}^i$ is the union of $A_{0,0}^i$, $A_{0,1}^i$, $A_{0,2}^i$, and $A_{0,3}^i$ where $j = 2$ and $s = 2$.

The relation between A^i and $A^{(i+1)}$ is decided by the effects of E and σ^{-1}. By $A^{(i+1)} = A^i E \sigma^{-1}$, we mean that $A^{(i+1)}$ is obtained from A^i permuted by E, then by σ^{-1}. If

$$A^{(i+1)} = A^i E \sigma^{-1} = (A^i E) \sigma^{-1},$$

then by a switching permutation E,

$$(a_{2k}^i E, a_{(2k+1)}^i E) = \{a_{2k}^i, a_{(2k+1)}^i\},$$

and by an unshuffle,

$$(a_k^{(i+1)}, a_{(k+2^{(n-1)})}^{(i+1)}) = (a_{2k}^i E, a_{(2k+1)}^i E),$$

and so

$$\{a_k^{(i+1)}, a_{(k+2^{(n-1)})}^{(i+1)}\} = \{a_{2k}^i, a_{(2k+1)}^i\}, \qquad 0 \le k < 2^{(n-1)}. \quad (2)$$

An example of this relation for $n = 3$ is given in Fig. 5. The heavy lines show that $\{a_0^{(i+1)}, a_4^{(i+1)}\}$ is the same set as $\{a_0^i, a_1^i\}$, and the dashed lines show that $\{a_2^{(i+1)}, a_6^{(i+1)}\}$ is the same set as $\{a_4^i, a_5^i\}$. Thus, if

$$A^{(i+1)} = A^i E \sigma^{-1}, \qquad 0 \le i < n,$$

then

$$A_{j,k}^i = A_{(j-1),k}^{(i+1)} \cup A_{(j-1),(k+2^{(n-j)})}^{(i+1)},$$
$$1 \le j < n, 0 \le k < 2^{(n-j)}. \quad (3)$$

This is the relation between the different partitions of input numbers on subsequent stages caused by an unshuffle. It states that an unshuffle splits a partition of size 2^j in one stage into two partitions of size $2^{(j-1)}$ in the subsequent stage, and the two resulting partitions are apart from each other by a distance of $2^{(n-j)}$. As an example, see Fig. 6 for $n = 3$. The heavy lines indicate $A_{2,0}^i$ to form $A_{1,0}^{(i+1)}$ and $A_{1,2}^{(i+1)}$ after an unshuffle. Likewise, the dashed lines indicate $A_{2,1}^i$ to form $A_{1,1}^{(i+1)}$ and $A_{1,3}^{(i+1)}$ after an unshuffle. If we repeat the relation given by (3) s times, we obtain the following relation among different partitions of A^i and $A^{(i+s)}$ after s unshuffles. Equation (4) states that after s unshuffles, a partition of size 2^j results in 2^s partitions of size $2^{(j-s)}$ which are separated by the distance $2^{(n-j)}$.

$$A_{j,k}^i = \bigcup_m \{A_{(j-s),(k+m*2^{(n-j)})}^{(i+s)} \mid 0 \le m < 2^s\},$$
$$1 \le j < n, 0 \le k < 2^{(n-j)}, 0 \le s < j. \quad (4)$$

In particular, we are interested in the relation between partitions of the original input A^0 and partitions of the input to an intermediate stage A^i. From (4) with $i = 0$, $s = i$, and $j = (i + j)$,

$$A_{(i+j),k}^0 = \bigcup_m \{A_{j,(k+m*2^{(n-i-j)})}^i \mid 0 \le m < 2^i\},$$
$$0 \le i < n, (1 - i) \le j \le (n - i), 0 \le k < 2^{(n-i-j)}. \quad$$

So

$$A_{(i+j),k}^0 \supseteq A_{j,k}^i. \quad (5)$$

Equation (5) says that a partition of size 2^j at stage i is a proper subset of a partition of size $2^{(i+j)}$ at the first stage. Equation (5) is very useful for determining the Ω_N^{-1}-passable permutations in terms of set properties (CRS properties). First we state formally what is an Ω_N^{-1}-passable permutation.

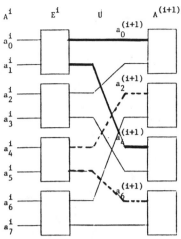

Fig. 5. Effect of an unshuffle. $\{a_0^{(i+1)}, a_4^{(i+1)}\} = \{a_0^i, a_1^i\}$, $\{a_2^{(i+1)}, a_6^{(i+1)}\} = \{a_4^i, a_5^i\}$, etc.

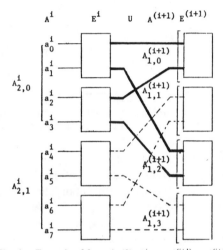

Fig. 6. Example of formula (3). $A_{2,0}^i = A_{1,0}^{(i+1)} \cup A_{1,2}^{(i+1)}$, $A_{2,1}^i = A_{1,1}^{(i+1)} \cup A_{1,3}^{(i+1)}$, etc.

Definition

An input sequence $A^0 = (a_0^0, a_1^0, \cdots, a_{(N-1)}^0)$ is an Ω_N^{-1}-passable permutation if $a_k^n = k$, $0 \le k < N$ when $A^n = A^0 \Omega_n^{-1}$.

This implies that regarding the Ω_N^{-1} as a sorting network, the input permutations that can be sorted by Ω_N^{-1} are said to be Ω_N^{-1}-passable.

The Ω_N^{-1}-control algorithm is as follows: each switch setting in the ith stage is controlled by the ith bit of the binary representation of the upper input number. If the control bit is "0," then the switch is set straight. If the control bit is "1," then the switch is set cross (Fig. 7). To avoid a conflict, the corresponding bit of the lower input should be the complement of the control bit. An example of the Ω_8^{-1}-control algorithm for the permutation $(2, 5, 0, 7, 1, 6, 3, 4)$ is shown in Fig. 8.

Through Lemmas 1 and 2 in the next section, we shall see that the Ω_N^{-1}-control algorithm is a "natural" control algorithm in the sense that it realizes all and only Ω_N^{-1}-passable permutations. A permutation can be realized by an Ω_N^{-1} if there is no conflict state in any switch; the control bits of two input numbers to a switch should be an odd–even pair for an Ω_N^{-1}-passable permutation. This implies the importance of

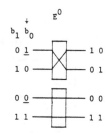

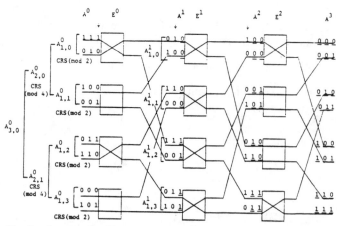

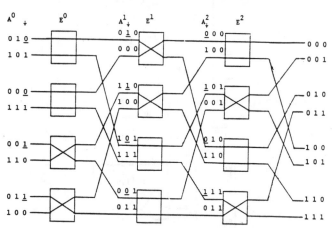

Fig. 7. The bit b_i of the upper input number to a switch controls the switch setting for the ith stage E^i. The control bits are underlined.

Fig. 8. Control algorithm for Ω_8^{-1} for the permutation (2, 5, 0, 7, 1, 6, 3, 4). The control bits are underlined.

Fig. 9. An example of Lemma 1 for $n = 3$. The lower i bits of A^i are sorted in ascending order by the Ω^{-1}-control algorithm. ($\rightarrow$ indicates the control bit.)

partitions of size 2^1, $A_{1,k}^i$. By (5), $A_{1,k}^i$ in turn implies the importance of partitions of size $2^{(i+1)}$ of the original input A^0. This intuitive argument is the basis of Theorem 1 on Ω_N^{-1}-passability in the next section.

By $A = \{x, y\} \equiv p, q \pmod{m}$, we mean that A consists of two elements x and y, congruent to p and $q \pmod{m}$, respectively.

III. Ω_N^{-1}-PASSABILITY

Ω_N^{-1}-Passable Permutations

In this section, we shall prove Theorem 1 on Ω_N^{-1}-passability. Theorem 1 defines the condition of the input permutation to be Ω_N^{-1}-passable. The proof is done by the use of Lemmas 1 and 2. Lemma 1 describes a characteristic of the Ω_N^{-1}-control algorithm. The Ω_N^{-1}-control algorithm works by sorting bits; if certain input conditions are satisfied, the lower i bits of the input numbers to the ith switching stage E^i are in ascending order, and moreover, the $(i+1)$st bits of two input numbers that share a switch are distinct. An example of Lemma 1 is shown in Fig. 9 for $n = 3$. The proofs for Lemmas 1 and 2 and Theorem 1 are given in the Appendix.

Lemma 1

If $A_{j,k}^0$ is a CRS(mod 2^j), $1 \le j < n$, $0 \le k < 2^{(n-j)}$ and $A^{(i+1)} = A^i E^i \sigma^{-1}$, $0 \le i < n$ where E^i is controlled by the Ω_N^{-1}-control algorithm, then

$$A_{1,k}^i \equiv \{p, p + 2^i\} \pmod{2^{(i+1)}}$$

$$\text{for any } A_{1,k}^i \subset A_{(n-i),p}^i, \ 0 \le p < 2^i, \ 1 \le i < n.$$

Lemma 2 states that for any input sequence that is Ω_N^{-1}-passable, the lower i bits of the input numbers are in ascending order and the $(i+1)$st bits of the two numbers that share a switch are distinct for all the intermediate stages i regardless of the particular switch setting of E^i. This indicates, together with Lemma 1, that the Ω_N^{-1}-control algorithm is the "natural" control algorithm for Ω_N^{-1}-passable permutations.

Lemma 2

If $a_k^n = k$, $0 \le k < 2^n$ and $A^i = A^{(i-1)}E^{(i-1)}\sigma^{-1}$, then regardless of the particular switch setting of E^i,

$$A_{1,k}^i \equiv \{p, p + 2^i\} \pmod{2^{(i+1)}}$$

$$\text{for any } A_{1,k}^i \subseteq A_{(n-i),p}^i, \ 0 \le p < 2^i \quad \text{and} \quad 1 \le i < n.$$

Theorem 1: Ω_N^{-1}-Passability

An input sequence $A^0 = (a_0^0, a_1^0, \cdots, a_{(N-1)}^0)$ is Ω_N^{-1}-passable iff $A_{j,k}^0$ is a CRS(mod 2^j), $1 \le j < n$ and $0 \le k < 2^{(n-j)}$.

Intuitively, CRS(mod 2) ensures no conflict state in the switching stage E^0, and CRS(mod 2^2) ensures no conflict state in the switching stage E^1, i.e., CRS(mod $2^{(j+1)}$) ensures no conflict state in the switching stage E^j.

As an example of Theorem 1, consider a permutation (3, 4, 5, 6, 7, 8, 9, 10, 11, 12, 13, 14, 15, 0, 1, 2), which is a uniform shift of distance 3. It is Ω_{16}^{-1}-passable because

(3, 4, 5, 6, 7, 8, 9, 10, 11, 12, 13, 14, 15, 0, 1, 2)

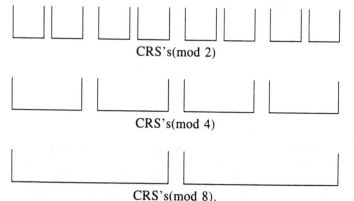

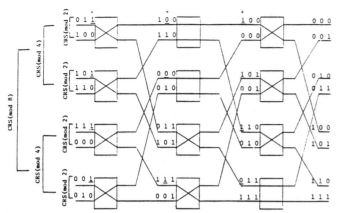

Fig. 10. An example of Theorem 1 for $N = 8$. A uniform shift of distance 3 (3, 4, 5, 6, 7, 0, 1, 2) is Ω_8^{-1}-passable. ($\rightarrow$ indicates the control bit.)

The switch settings for the same permutation for $n = 3$ are shown in Fig. 10. As another example of Theorem 1, a shuffle permutation (0, 8, 1, 9, 2, 10, 3, 11, 4, 12, 5, 13, 6, 14, 7, 15) is not Ω_{16}^{-1}-passable because

$$(0,8, \quad 1,9, \quad 2,10, \quad 3,11, \quad 4,12, \quad 5,13, \quad 6,14, \quad 7,15)$$

all of them not CRS(mod 2).

So the shuffle permutation has conflicts at the very first stage. In fact, it has conflicts at every stage.

Observe that given a permutation, it is very easy to determine whether or not it is Ω_N^{-1}-passable. We use the residue classes of input numbers rather than the bit relations among source tags and destination tags [6], [11].

We shall name the condition of Theorem 1 in the following definition.

Definition

The Ω_N^{-1}-*passable condition* for an input permutation $A^0 = (a_0^0, a_1^0, \cdots, a_{(N-1)}^0)$ is that $A_{j,k}^0$ is a CRS(mod 2^j) for $1 \leq j < n$ and $0 \leq k < 2^{(n-j)}$.

The Ω_N^{-1}-passable condition which is defined over the original input sequence A^0 can be transformed into a condition for the intermediate input sequences A^i in the following way. First remember that CRS(mod $2^{(i+1)}$) in A^0 plays the critical role to ensure no conflict state in E^i. Also note that in the original input sequence A^0, $2^{(i+1)}$ numbers of each subset $A_{(i+1),k}^0$, which form a CRS(mod $2^{(i+1)}$), are contiguous. By the time the input sequence reaches E^i, the original input sequence A^0 has gone through i unshuffles, and the originally contiguous $2^{(i+1)}$ numbers of $A_{(i+1),k}^0$ have been split into i groups of size 2 separated by a fixed distance $2^{(n-i-1)}$ as shown in (4). This motivates another way of partitioning A^i so that we can group a set of pairs of numbers which are separated from each other by a fixed distance.

Let

$$B_{j,k}^i = \bigcup_m \{A_{1,(k+m*2^{(n-j)})}^i \mid 0 \leq m < 2^{(j-1)}\}$$

$$= \bigcup_m \{a_{2(k+m*2^{(n-j)})}^i, a_{2(k+m*2^{(n-j)})+1}^i \mid 0 \leq m < 2^{(j-1)}\},$$

$$0 \leq k < 2^{(n-j)}, 1 \leq i \leq n. \quad (6)$$

Thus, $B_{j,k}^i$, in addition to $A_{j,k}^i$, provides another $2^{(n-j)}$ partition of A^i. In contrast to $A_{j,k}^i$, which consists of 2^j contiguous numbers, $B_{j,k}^i$ consists of $2^{(j-1)}$ pairs of numbers, with each pair separated from the subsequent pair by the distance of $2^{(n-j)}$. Refer to Fig. 11. $A_{j,k}^i$ is obtained by dividing A^i into $2^{(n-j)}$ subsets, each with 2^j numbers, and by naming them serially from 0 to $(2^{(n-j)} - 1)$, which is k.

On the other hand, $B_{j,k}^i$ is obtained by dividing A^i into $2^{(j-1)}$ groups, each with $2^{(n-j)}$ pairs of numbers, and then taking the kth pair from each group to form the kth subset of 2^j numbers. Naturally, there are $2^{(n-j)}$ such subsets.

In effect, this new way of partitioning incorporates the effect of i unshuffles occurring between A^0 and A^i. The $2^{(i+1)}$ contiguous numbers of $A_{(i+1),k}^0$ become separated by i unshuffles to form $B_{(i+1),k}^i$. Thus, $A_{(i+1),k}^0$ and $B_{(i+1),k}^i$ consist of identical numbers. We are ready to state the following lemma.

Lemma 3

The Ω_N^{-1}-passable condition is equivalent to the condition that each $B_{(i+1),k}^i$ is a CRS(mod $2^{(i+1)}$), $0 \leq k < 2^{(n-i-1)}$, $0 \leq i < n$.

Proof: By (4) and (6),

$$A_{(i+1),k}^0 = \bigcup_m \{A_{1,(k+m*2^{(n-i-1)})}^i \mid 0 \leq m < 2^i\} = B_{(i+1),k}^i.$$

Q.E.D.

Number of Ω_N^{-1}-Passable Permutations

Usually a network-passable condition has been defined in terms of the bit relations between the source tags and the destination tags. In Theorem 1, the Ω_N^{-1}-passable condition for an input permutation is given in terms of CRS, which is an easier tool to deal with. We can see easily why permutations such as identity and uniform shift are Ω_N^{-1}-passable, while permutations such as shuffle, unshuffle, and bit reversal are not Ω_N^{-1}-passable. Clearly, the identity permutation satisfies the CRS properties of Theorem 1, and the uniform shift preserves the CRS properties, while shuffle, unshuffle, and bit reversal violate the CRS properties inherently. Given a permutation, it is easy to decide whether it is Ω_N^{-1}-passable or not by Theorem 1. According to Theorem 1, an input permutation $A_N = (a_0, a_1, \cdots, a_{(N-1)})$ is Ω_N^{-1}-passable iff $A_{j,k}$ is a CRS(mod 2^j) for all possible values of j and k.

As another example of the application of Theorem 1, the number of Ω_N^{-1}-passable permutations among $N!$ possible permutations can be calculated. Let $Q(N)$ be the number of Ω_N^{-1}-passable permutations. As there are $n * (N/2)$ switches which can have two input numbers, we know that

$$Q(N) \leq 2^{n(N/2)} = N^{(N/2)}.$$

We compute $Q(N)$ by counting the permutations that satisfy Theorem 1 as follows. There are $2^n * 2^{(n-1)}$ ways of choosing a_0 and a_1 since they must come from the distinct (mod 2) equivalence classes. Now a_2 and a_3 must come from the distinct (mod 2^2) equivalence classes which contain neither a_0 nor a_1. There are only two such equivalent classes, each with $2^{(n-2)}$ numbers, and we can choose a_2 and a_3 in

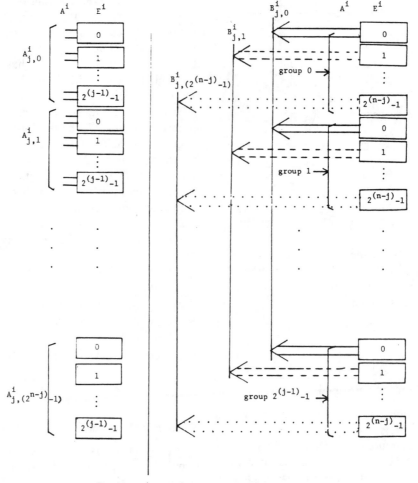

Fig. 11. $A_{j,k}^i$ and $B_{j,k}^i$: two different partitions of A^i.

$(2 * 2^{(n-2)}) * 2^{(n-2)} = 2^{(n-1)} * 2^{(n-2)}$ different ways. Continuing this, we obtain

$$Q(N) = (2^n)(2^{(n-1)})(2^{(n-1)} * 2^{(n-2)})$$
$$\cdot (2^{(n-1)} * 2^{(n-2)} * 2^{(n-2)} * 2^{(n-3)})$$
$$\cdots (2^{(n-1)} * 2^{(n-2)} \cdots * 2^{(n-n)}) = 2^{s_n}$$

where

$$s_0 = n,$$
$$s_1 = n + (n - 1),$$
$$s_2 = n + (n - 1) + \{(n - 1) + (n - 2)\},$$
$$\cdots$$
$$s_k = 2 * s_{(k-1)} - 2^{(k-1)}, \qquad n \geq k > 1.$$

Thus,

$$s_n = 2 * s_{(n-1)} - 2^{(n-1)}$$
$$= 2^2 * s_{(n-2)} - 2 * 2^{(n-1)}$$
$$\cdots$$
$$= 2^n * s_0 - n * 2^{(n-1)}$$
$$= n * 2^{(n-1)}$$

and

$$Q(N) = 2^{n*2^{(n-1)}} = N^{(N/2)}.$$

The fact that $Q(N)$ is the maximum possible number obtainable means that the Ω_N^{-1}-control algorithm is a "natural" control algorithm.

The probability $P(N)$ of a permutation to be Ω_N^{-1}-passable is

$$P(N) = N^{N/2}/N!.$$

For $N = 2^3 = 8$, $Q(8) = 8^4$ and $p(8) = 8^4/8! = 4096/40320 \approx 0.10$. When N becomes larger, the Ω_N^{-1}-passable probability approaches zero very fast.

IV. REARRANGEABILITY OF THE REDUCED $\Omega_N \Omega_N^{-1}$

If we can show that a network Γ_N can transform an arbitrary permutation into an Ω_N^{-1}-passable permutation defined in the previous section, then the network formed by concatenating Γ_N and Ω_N^{-1} is rearrangeable. In this section, we show that the reduced Ω_N can transform an arbitrary permutation into an Ω_N^{-1}-passable permutation, and thus the reduced $\Omega_N \Omega_N^{-1}$ is rearrangeable. First we show that Ω_N can do the necessary transformation and then show that the last switching stage of Ω_N is redundant.

When we reverse the direction of input and output in Ω_N^{-1}, Ω_N^{-1} can be considered as Ω_N with input A^n and output A^0 (see Fig. 12). We preserve the superscript labels for A^i and E^i so

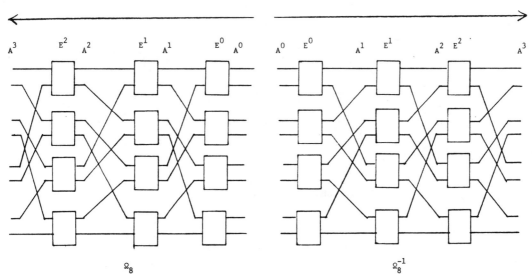

Fig. 12. By reversing the direction of input and output, an Ω_8^{-1} can be viewed as an Ω_8.

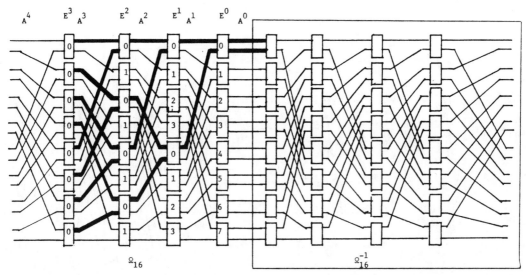

Fig. 13. Implication of the Ω-control to transform an arbitrary input sequence into an Ω^{-1}-passable sequence. Dark lines show a CRS which should be formed at each stage.

that we can use all the relations among A^i derived in the previous section without any change for Ω_N. Notice that for the middle stages of Ω_N, A^i is the output sequence (rather than the input sequence) for the switching stage E^i. By Theorem 1, the output A^0 from Ω_N is Ω_N^{-1}-passable iff $A_{j,k}^0$ is a CRS(mod 2^j) for all possible values of j and k. Restated by Lemma 3, this is the same condition as each $B_{(i+1),k}^i$ of Ω_N being a CRS(mod $2^{(i+1)}$). As shown in Fig. 13, this means that the output number set (and thus the input number set) from the switches in each stage, which are marked with the same number, form a group which should be a CRS(mod $2 * s$) where s is the number of switches in the group. Thus, the input numbers to the eight switches marked with "0" in E^3 should form a CRS(mod 2^4). Naturally, this is true for any input sequence consisting of 16 consecutive numbers. Likewise, the input numbers to the four switches marked with "0" ("1") in E^2 should be a CRS(mod 2^3), and

the input numbers to the two switches marked with "0"("1," "2," "3") in E^1 should be a CRS(mod 2^2). Finally, two input numbers to each switch in E^0 should be a CRS(mod 2). Intuitively from Fig. 13, we can see what function each switching stage has to perform. E^3 should do a CRP on a CRS(mod 2^4) so that two resulting CRS's(mod 2^3) reside on the upper and the lower output ports. These two CRS's(mod 2^3) are then guaranteed to be input to switches marked as "0" and "1," respectively, by a shuffle. The heavy lines between E^3 and E^2 show that the upper output ports of E^3 are linked to switches "0" in E^2. For E^2, we need two identical CRP's working separately on two CRS's(mod 2^3) of E^2, i.e., switches marked with "0" and "1," so that again, two CRS's(mod 2^2) from each CRP reside in the upper and lower output ports of corresponding switches. Only the formation of one CRS(mod 2^2) in the upper output ports of "0" in E^2 is shown as heavy lines between E^2 and E^1. But if we had four colors,

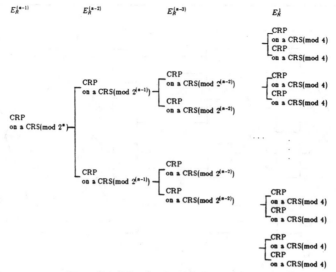

Fig. 14. A CRPT: a full binary tree of CRP's.

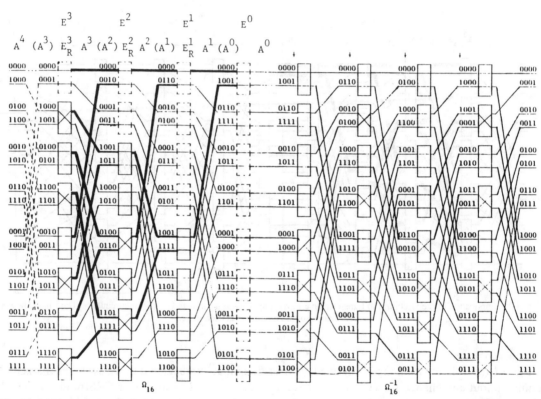

Fig. 15. A bit reversal on $\Omega_{16}\Omega_{16}^{-1}$. The reduced $\Omega_{16}\Omega_{16}^{-1}$ is drawn in solid lines. ($\rightarrow$ indicates the control bit and dark lines show a CRS partitioning.)

we could color these four CRS's(mod 2^2) differently to indicate that each CRS requires an independent CRP on the subsequent stage E^1.

To summarize the above process, a *full binary tree of CRP's, CRPT,* is the function that should be performed by Ω_N to transform an arbitrary input sequence into an Ω_N^{-1}-passable sequence. A CRPT is shown in Fig. 14.

At this point, two facts remain to be formalized.

1) A subset of the $B_{i,k}^{(i-1)}$ partition of the input sequence to the switching stage $E^{(i-1)}$ consists of a CRS(mod 2^i) on the upper (lower) output ports of some switches in the previous stage E^i followed by a shuffle.

2) A CRP on a CRS(mod 2^m) is realizable by $2^{(m-1)}$ switches so that the resulting two CRS's(mod $2^{(m-1)}$) reside on the upper and the lower output ports of the switches.

For 1), yet another $2^{(n-j)}$ partition of A^i, in addition to $A_{j,k}^i$ and $B_{j,k}^i$, has to be defined.

Definition

$$C_{j,k}^i = \bigcup_m a_{(k+m*2^{(n-j)})}^i,$$
$$0 \le k < 2^{(n-j)}, \ 0 \le m < 2^j, \ 1 \le i \le n. \quad (7)$$

The heavy lines (regular lines) for A^3 of Ω_{16} in Fig. 15 are an example of $C_{3,0}^3$ ($C_{3,1}^3$). The heavy lines for A^2 of Ω_{16} in

126

Fig. 15 are an example of $C_{2,0}^2$. Note that a subset of $C_{j,k}^i$ has all 2^j numbers from either the upper output ports or the lower output ports. We will show in Lemma 4, as a formalization of 1), that $C_{(i+1),k}^{(i+1)}$ after a shuffle forms $B_{(i+1),k}^i$. (As we are concerned only with a set property, here we denote both the input and output sequence of E^i as A^i; see Fig. 15.)

Lemma 4

$$B_{(i+1),k}^i \equiv C_{(i+1),k}^{(i+1)}\sigma.$$

Proof: We shall show that $C_{(i+1),k}^{(i+1)}$ is obtained from $B_{(i+1),k}^i$ by an unshuffle.

By the definition of $B_{j,k}^i$ in (6),

$$B_{(i+1),k}^i = \bigcup_m \{a_{2(k+m*2^{(n-i-1)})}^i, a_{2(k+m*2^{(n-i-1)})+1}^i \mid 0 \leq m < 2^i\}.$$

By an unshuffle, the effect of which is given in (2),

$$B_{(i+1),k}^i\sigma^{-1} = \bigcup_m \{a_{(k+m*s^{(n-i-1)})}^{(i+1)}, a_{(k+m*2^{(n-i-1)}+2^{(n-1)})}^{(i+1)} \mid 0 \leq m < 2^i\}$$
$$\equiv \bigcup_m \{a_{(k+m*2^{(n-i-1)})}^{(i+1)} \mid 0 \leq m < 2^{(i+1)}\}.$$

By the definition of $C_{j,k}^i$ in (7),

$$B_{(i+1),k}^i\sigma^{-1} \equiv C_{(i+1),k}^{(i+1)}$$

or

$$B_{(i+1),k}^i \equiv C_{(i+1),k}^{(i+1)}\sigma.$$

Q.E.D.

The last remaining point 2), which states in essence that a CRP is an exchange permutation and can be realized on a set of switches, is formalized in Lemma 5.

Lemma 5

Consider

$(a_k, b_k), 0 \leq k < 2^{(i-1)}$ and $\{a_k, b_k \mid 0 \leq k < 2^{(i-1)}\}$
$$= \text{CRS}(\text{mod } 2^i).$$

Then there is a permutation E such that $\{a_k E, b_k E\} = \{a_k, b_k\}$ for each k (i.e., E is an exchange permutation), and such that $\{a_k E \mid 0 \leq k < 2^{(i-1)}\}$ is a CRS(mod $2^{(i-1)}$).

Proof: By construction.

Let $a_k \equiv p_k (\text{mod } 2^{(i-1)})$, $b_k \equiv q_k (\text{mod } 2^{(i-1)})$, $0 \leq k < 2^{(i-1)}$. Every number between 0 and $(2^{(i-1)} - 1)$ occurs twice among the p_k and q_k. Rearrange the pairs into groups in such a way that in each group with more than one pair, any two adjacent pairs have a number in common and the first and the last pairs have a number in common. In such a group, if the common number of the first and the second pairs occurs in the same position of each pair, then exchange the positions of the two numbers of the second pair. By repeating this process between the second and the third pairs, and so on, we obtain (p_k', q_k')s such that $(p_k', q_k') = \{p_k, q_k\}$, $0 \leq k < 2^{(i-1)}$, and all p_k' are distinct.

Set

$$(a_k E, b_k E) = (a_k, b_k) \quad \text{if } p_k' = p_k,$$
$$= (b_k, a_k) \quad \text{otherwise}.$$

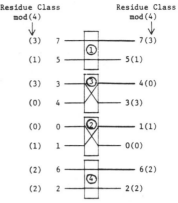

Fig. 16. An example of Lemma 4: a CRP can always be realized on a set of switches. (Circled numbers show the order of the switch setting. Input CRS(mod 8) {7, 5, 3, 4, 0, 1, 6, 2} is partitioned to two CRS's(mod 4), {7, 4, 1, 6} and {5, 3, 0, 2}.)

Then by construction,

$$a_k E = p_k' (\text{mod } 2^{(i-1)}), \quad 0 \leq k < 2^{(i-1)} \quad \text{and}$$
$$\{a_k E \mid 0 \leq k < 2^{(i-1)}\} \text{ is a CRS}(\text{mod } 2^{(i-1)}).$$

Q.E.D.

Note that in the exchange processes in the proof, one pair of numbers does not need an exchange, indicating the redundancy of a switch in each CRP. An example of Lemma 5 is given in Fig. 16.

Lemmas 4 and 5 lead us to Theorem 2. First we define an exchange permutation E_R^i.

Definition

An exchange permutation E_R^i is defined as: if $A^i = (A^{(i+1)}\sigma)E_R^i$ and if every $C_{(i+1),k}^{(i+1)}$ is a CRS(mod $2^{(i+1)}$), then every $C_{i,k}^i$ is a CRS(mod 2^i).

E_R^i is then just a set of $2^{(n-i-1)}$ CRP's, each of which is shown to be realizable in Lemma 5. E_R^i is the one and only control for the stage E^i of Ω_N. In other words, $\{E_R^i \mid 0 < i < n\}$ is a CRPT to control the Ω_N.

Theorem 2

$\{E_R^i \mid 0 < i < n\}$ is the one and only kind of control to transform an arbitrary permutation $A^n = (a_0^n, a_1^n, \cdots, a_{(N-1)}^n)$ into an Ω_N^{-1}-passable permutation $A^0 = (a_0^0, a_1^0, \cdots, a_{(N-1)}^0)$ via the reduced Ω_N.

Proof: Since $A^n \equiv C_{n,0}^n$ is always a CRS(mod 2^n), by the definition of E_R^i, it follows that each $C_{i,k}^i$, $0 \leq k < 2^{(n-i)}$, $1 \leq i \leq n$ is a CRS(mod 2^i) when $A^i = (A^{(i+1)}\sigma)E_R^i$. Hence, by Lemmas 3 and 4, $A^0 = (a_0^0, a_1^0, \cdots, a_{(N-1)}^0)$ is an Ω_N^{-1}-passable permutation. Conversely, any such control must be E_R^i at stage i by Theorem 1, Lemmas 3 and 4, and (8). The fact that $1 \leq i < n$, not $0 \leq i < n$, means that the Ω_N^{-1}-passable condition is satisfied already for the input to E^0. Thus, the switches of the last stage E^0 of Ω_N are redundant, leaving us with the reduced Ω_N.

Q.E.D.

An example of Theorem 2 is shown in Fig. 17. The input sequence (7, 5, 0, 1, 3, 4, 6, 2) is not Ω_8^{-1}-passable. But by setting the switches E^i by $\{E_R^i \mid 0 < i < 3\}$ and the redundant switches E^0 straight, the output (7, 2, 0, 5, 3, 4, 6, 1) is

127

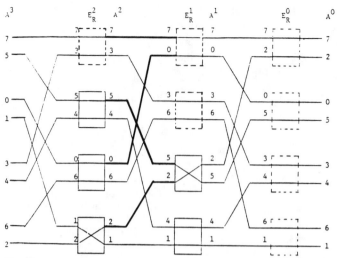

Fig. 17. An example of Theorem 2: an arbitrary permutation can be transformed to meet the Ω_N^{-1}-passable condition via the reduced Ω_N. $A^3 =$ (7, 5, 0, 1, 3, 4, 6, 2) is not Ω_8^{-1}-passable, but $A^0 =$ (7, 2, 0, 5, 3, 4, 6, 1) is. (Redundant switches are drawn in dashed lines.)

Ω_8^{-1}-passable. In other words, one CRP is performed for E_R^2, and two CRP's are performed independently for E_R^1 (one for switches with dark input lines and another for the remaining switches). As noted earlier, E_R^0 is redundant.

In conclusion, the concatenation of the reduced Ω_N and Ω_N^{-1}, called the reduced $\Omega_N \Omega_N^{-1}$, is a 2($\log_2 N$) − 1 stage rearrangeable network.

Theorem 3

The reduced $\Omega_N \Omega_N^{-1}$ is a rearrangeable network.
Proof: By Theorems 1 and 2.

Q.E.D.

V. THE REDUCED $\Omega \Omega_N^{-1}$-CONTROL ALGORITHM AND THE HARDWARE REDUNDANCY

In this section, we summarize the reduced $\Omega_N \Omega_N^{-1}$-control algorithm which has been described in the previous sections. A CRPT is a full binary tree of (n − 1) levels whose root node on level (n − 1) is a CRP on a CRS(mod 2^n), and the two sons of a node are two CRP's on the two CRS's produced by the parent node. Observe that E_R^i in the previous section corresponds to the (i + 1)st level of a CRPT.

The reduced $\Omega_N \Omega_N^{-1}$-control algorithm includes the following.

1) The reduced Ω_N is controlled by a CRPT.
2) Ω_N^{-1} is bit controlled by the Ω_N^{-1}-control algorithm.

Examples of the reduced $\Omega_N \Omega_N^{-1}$-control algorithm are shown in Fig. 18 for the permutation (6, 7, 0, 4, 1, 5, 3, 2) and in Fig. 15 for a bit reversal permutation.

We discussed earlier, in the proof of Theorem 2, the redundancy of the last switching stage of Ω_N by which we obtained the reduced Ω_N. Further redundancy in switches was mentioned after Lemma 5; one switch in each CRP is redundant. The number of the CRP's in a CRPT is

$$1 + 2 + \cdots + 2^{(n-2)} = 2^{(n-1)} - 1 = (N/2 - 1).$$

Thus, the number of necessary switches in the reduced $\Omega_N \Omega_N^{-1}$ is

$$(2n - 1) * N/2 - (N/2 - 1) = N(\log_2 N) - N + 1.$$

This is exactly the same as the number of switches required for the reduced Benes binary network [5], [14], and it matches the lower bound for the rearrangeable networks.

The control by a CRPT requires $O(N \log_2 N)$ time steps, and the Ω_N^{-1}-control requires $O(\log_2 N)$ time steps. Therefore, the time complexity of the reduced $\Omega_N \Omega_N^{-1}$-control algorithm is $O(N \log_2 N)$. When more hardware is available for the control, the CRP's on the same level of a CRPT can be done in parallel, reducing the CRPT control time and thus the overall control time to

$$O(N + N/2 + \cdots + 2) = O(N).$$

These control time complexities are of the same order of magnitude as those of the looping algorithm for the Benes network [8]. But our algorithm is simpler as inverse mappings are not needed, and it is easier to understand as the switches are set stage by stage. It is also expected to be faster because the last n stages are bit controlled.

A characteristic of a CRPT control is that any fixed connection at the beginning of a rearrangeable network is redundant. Therefore, the first shuffle of the reduced $\Omega_N \Omega_N^{-1}$ can be removed, and the resultant network is still rearrangeable.

VI. CONCLUSIONS

A new proof method on the 2($\log_2 N$) − 1 stage rearrangeability was developed. The proof method does not rely on the recursiveness or symmetry of the network topology. Thus, it can be used for any multistage network, and it helps for better understanding of the many multistage networks proposed in the literature. In essence, it showed for the first time that the Benes network is not the only rearrangeable network with minimum hardware requirement, but that many networks can

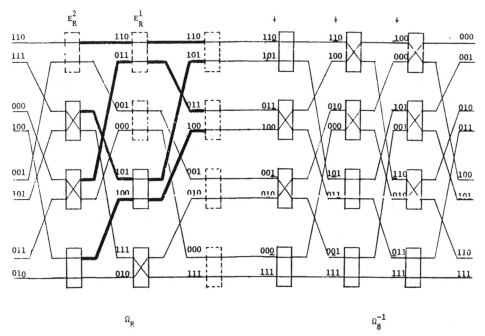

Fig. 18. (6, 7, 0, 4, 1, 5, 3, 2) on the reduced $\Omega_8\Omega_8^{-1}$. ($\rightarrow$ indicates the control bit and dashed switches are redundant.)

be built that require the same number of switches. The proof method also showed a uniform control scheme for all these networks. By applying the control scheme to the Benes network, a new Benes network control algorithm can be obtained [7]. This control algorithm sets the switches stage by stage, and the last n stages of the network are bit controlled. Thus, it is simpler and easier than the Opferman and Tsao–Wu looping algorithm. All the results obtained for $N = 2^n$ networks can be generalized to $N = p^n$ networks $p > 2$ in a natural way [7].

APPENDIX
PROOFS FOR LEMMAS 1 AND 2 AND THEOREM 1

Lemma 1

If $A_{j,k}^0$ is a CRS(mod 2^j), $1 \leq j < n$, $0 \leq k < 2^{(n-j)}$ and $A^{(i+1)} = A^i E^i U$, $0 \leq i < n$ where E^i is controlled by the Ω_N^{-1}-control algorithm, then $A_{1,k}^i \equiv \{p, p + 2^i\} \,(\mathrm{mod}\ 2^{(i+1)})$ for any $A_{1,k}^i \subset A_{(n-i),p}^i$, $0 \leq p < 2^i$, $1 \leq i < n$.

Proof: By induction on i.

Suppose that

$$A_{1,m}^i \equiv \{q, q + 2^i\} \,(\mathrm{mod}\ 2^{(i+1)}), \qquad \text{for any } A_{1,m}^i \subset A_{(n-i),q}^i.$$

Let

$$A_{1,k}^{(i+1)} \subset A_{(n-(i+1)),p}^{(i+1)}.$$

Then

$$2^{(n-(i+1)-1)} * p \leq k < 2^{(n-(i+1)-1)} * (p + 1),$$

$$0 \leq p < 2^{(i+1)}.$$

Case 1. $0 \leq k < 2^{(n-2)}$:

$$2^{(n-(i+1)-1)} * p < 2^{(n-2)}, \quad \text{and so } p < 2^i.$$

$$A_{1,k}^{(i+1)} = \{a_{2(2k)}^i E^i, a_{2(2k+1)}^i E^i\},$$

$$2^{(n-i-1)} * p \leq 2k, (2k + 1) < 2^{(n-i-1)} * (p + 1).$$

Hence,

$$A_{1,2k}^i, A_{1,(2k+1)}^i \subset A_{(n-i),p}^i$$

and so

$$A_{1,2k}^i, A_{1,(2k+1)}^i \equiv \{p, p + 2^i\} \,(\mathrm{mod}\ 2^{(i+1)}).$$

Thus,

$$a_{2(2k)}^i E^i \equiv a_{2(2k+1)}^i E^i \equiv p \,(\mathrm{mod}\ 2^{(i+1)}) \qquad (\text{since } p < 2^i).$$

However, they must be distinct (mod $2^{(i+2)}$) since

$$A_{1,k}^{(i+1)} \subset (A_{1,2k}^i \cup A_{1,(2k+1)}^i) = A_{2,k}^i \subset A_{(i+2),k}^0 \quad \text{by (5)}.$$

As $A_{(i+2),k}^0$ is a CRS(mod $2^{(i+2)}$),

$$A_{1,k}^{(i+1)} \equiv \{p, p + 2^{(i+1)}\} \,(\mathrm{mod}\ 2^{(i+2)}).$$

Case 2. $2^{(n-2)} \leq k < 2^{(n-1)}$:

$$2^{(n-2)} < 2^{(n-(i+1)-1)} * (p + 1), \quad \text{and so } 2^i \leq p < 2^{(i+1)}.$$

$$A_{1,k}^{(i+1)} = \{A_{(2(2k')+1)}^i E^i, a_{(2(2k'+1)+1)}^i E^i\}$$

$$\text{where } 2k' = 2k - 2^{(n-1)}.$$

$$2^{(n-i-1)} * (p - 2^i) \leq 2k',$$

$$(2k' + 1) < 2^{(n-i-1)} * (p - 2^i + 1)$$

$$A_{1,2k'}^i, A_{1,(2k'+1)}^i \subset A_{(n-i),(p-2^i)}^i.$$

Therefore,

$$A_{1,2k'}^i, A_{1,(2k'+1)}^i \equiv \{p - 2^i, p\} \,(\mathrm{mod}\ 2^{(i+1)}).$$

Thus,

$$a^i_{(2(2k')+1)}E^i \equiv a^i_{(2(2k'+1)+1)}E^i \equiv p \,(\mathrm{mod}\ 2^{(i+1)})$$

(since $p - 2^i \leq 2^i$ and $2^i \leq p < 2^{(i+1)}$).

Again,

$$A^{(i+1)}_{1,k} \subset (A^i_{1,2k'} \cup A^i_{1,(2k'+1)}) = A^i_{2,k'} \subset A^0_{(i+2),k'},$$

and as $A^0_{(i+2),k'}$ is a CRS(mod $2^{(i+2)}$),

$$A^{(i+1)}_{1,k} \equiv \{p, p + 2^{(i+1)}\} \,(\mathrm{mod}\ 2^{(i+2)}).$$

Since it can be shown in the same way as above that

$$A^1_{1,k} \equiv \{p, p + 2\} \,(\mathrm{mod}\ 2^2)$$

$$\text{for any } A^1_{1,k} \subset A^1_{(n-1),p}, \qquad 0 \leq p < 2$$

as the induction basis, the lemma is proved.

Q.E.D.

Lemma 2

If $a^n_k = k$, $0 \leq k < 2^n$ and $A^i = A^{(i-1)}E^{(i-1)}\sigma^{-1}$, then regardless of the particular switch setting of E^i,

$$A^i_{1,k} \equiv \{p, p + 2^i\} \,(\mathrm{mod}\ 2^{(i+1)})$$

for any $A^i_{1,k} \subset A^i_{(n-i),p}$, $0 \leq p < 2^i$ and $1 \leq i < n$.

Proof: By induction on i. Note that

$$A^{(n-1)}_{1,k} = \{a^n_k, a^n_{(k+2^{(n-1)})}\} \equiv \{k, k + 2^{(n-1)}\} \,(\mathrm{mod}\ 2^n).$$

Suppose that

$$A^{(i+1)}_{1,m} \equiv \{q, q + 2^{(i+1)}\} \,(\mathrm{mod}\ 2^{(i+2)})$$

$$\text{for any } A^{(i+1)}_{1,m} \subset A^{(i+1)}_{(n-(i+1)),q}.$$

Let

$$A^i_{1,k} \subset A^i_{(n-i),p}.$$

Then

$$2^{(n-i-1)} * p \leq k < 2^{(n-i-1)} * (p+1), \qquad 0 \leq p < 2^i.$$

Now

$$A^i_{1,k} = \{a^i_{2k}, a^i_{(2k+1)}\} = \{a^{(i+1)}_k, a^{(i+1)}_{(k+2^{(n-1)})}\},$$

$$a^{(i+1)}_k \in A^{(i+1)}_{1,m} \quad \text{and} \quad a^{(i+1)}_{(k+2^{(n-1)})} \in A^{(i+1)}_{1,(m+2^{(n-2)})}$$

where m is given by $k \in \{2m, 2m+1\}$.

Since

$$2^{(n-(i+1)-1)} * p \leq m < 2^{(n-(i+1)-1)} * (p+1),$$

$$2^{(n-(i+1)-1)} * (p+2^i) \leq l + 2^{(n-2)}$$

$$< 2^{(n-(i+1)-1)} * (p + 2^i + 1),$$

therefore

$$A^{(i+1)}_{1,m} \subset A^{(i+1)}_{(n-(i+1)),p} \quad \text{and} \quad A^{(i+1)}_{1,(m+2^{(n-2)})} \subset A^{(i+1)}_{(n-(i+1)),(p+2^i)}.$$

Hence, by the induction hypothesis,

$$A^{(i+1)}_{1,m} \equiv \{p, p + 2^{(i+1)}\} \,(\mathrm{mod}\ 2^{(i+2)})$$

and

$$A^{(i+1)}_{1,(m+2^{(n-2)})} \equiv \{p + 2^i, p + 2^i + 2^{(i+1)}\} \,(\mathrm{mod}\ 2^{(i+2)}),$$

and so

$$a^{(i+1)}_k \equiv p \,(\mathrm{mod}\ 2^{(i+1)}) \quad \text{and} \quad a^{(i+1)}_{(k+2^{(n-1)})} \equiv p + 2^i \,(\mathrm{mod}\ 2^{(i+1)}).$$

Thus,

$$A^i_{1,k} \equiv \{p, p + 2^i\} \,(\mathrm{mod}\ 2^{(i+1)}).$$

Q.E.D.

Theorem 1: Ω_N^{-1}-Passability

An input sequence $A^0 = (a^0_0, a^0_1, \cdots, a^0_{(N-1)})$ is Ω_N^{-1}-passable iff $A^0_{j,k}$ is a CRS(mod 2^j), $1 \leq j < n$ and $0 \leq k < 2^{(n-j)}$.

Proof:

If:

We use the Ω_N^{-1}-control algorithm for switch settings. Then by Lemma 1,

$$A^{(n-1)}_{1,k} = \{a^{(n-1)}_{2k}, a^{(n-1)}_{(2k+1)}\} = \{k, k + 2^{(n-1)}\}, \qquad 0 \leq k < 2^{(n-1)}.$$

Hence,

$$(a^n_k, a^n_{(k+2^{(n-1)})}) = (a^{(n-1)}_{2k}E^{(n-1)}, a^{(n-1)}_{(2k+1)}E^{(n-1)}) = (k, k + 2^{(n-1)}),$$

$$0 \leq k < 2^{(n-1)}.$$

Thus, $a^n_k = k$, $0 \leq k < 2^n$ and the input sequence is Ω_N^{-1}-passable.

Only If: By Lemma 2,

$$A^i_{1,k} = \{p, p + 2^i\} \,(\mathrm{mod}\ 2^{(i+1)})$$

for any $A^i_{1,k} \subset A^i_{(n-i),p}$, $0 \leq p < 2^i$ and $1 \leq i < (n-2)$.

Consider $A^0_{1,k} = \{a^1_k, a^1_{(k+2^{(n-1)})}\}$.

$$a^1_k \in A^1_{1,m}, a^1_{(k+2^{(n-1)})} \in A^1_{1,(m+2^{(n-2)})}$$

$$\text{with } m \text{ given by } k \in \{2m, 2m+1\}.$$

Then

$$0 \leq m < 2^{(n-2)} \qquad (\text{since } k < 2^{(n-1)}) \quad \text{and}$$

$$A^1_{1,m} \subset A^1_{(n-1),0}, A^1_{1,m} \equiv \{0, 2\} \,(\mathrm{mod}\ 2^2)$$

and

$$A^1_{1,(m+2^{(n-2)})} \subset A^1_{(n-1),1}, A^1_{1,(l+2^{(n-2)})} \equiv \{1, 1 + 2\} \,(\mathrm{mod}\ 2^2).$$

Thus,

$$a^1_k \equiv 0 \,(\mathrm{mod}\ 2), \qquad a^1_{(k+2^{(n-1)})} \equiv 1 \,(\mathrm{mod}\ 2)$$

and $A^0_{1,k}$ is a CRS(mod 2).

For $j > 1$,

$$A^0_{j,k} = \bigcup_m \{A^{(j-1)}_{1,p(m)} \mid 0 \leq m < 2^{(j-1)}\},$$

$$p(m) = k + m * 2^{(n-j)}, \qquad 0 \leq k < 2^{(n-j)}.$$

Since

$$2^{(n-(j-1)-1)} * m \leq p(m) < 2^{(n-(j-1)-1)} * (m+1),$$

$$A^{(j-1)}_{1,p(m)} \subset A^{(j-1)}_{n-(j-1),m} \quad \text{and} \quad A^{(j-1)}_{1,p(m)} \equiv \{m, m + 2^{(j-1)}\} \,(\mathrm{mod}\ 2^j)$$

it follows that

$$A^0_{j,k}, \quad \text{for } j > 1, \text{ is a CRS(mod } 2^j).$$

Q.E.D.

Acknowledgment

The author is grateful to Prof. D. J. Kuck, who introduced her to this interesting research topic, and provided her with constant support and advice.

References

[1] V. E. Benes, "Permutation groups, complexes, and rearrangeable connecting networks," *Bell Syst. Tech. J.*, vol. 43, pp. 1619–1640, July 1964.

[2] ——, *Mathematical Theory of Connecting Networks and Telephone Traffic*. New York: Academic, 1965.

[3] B. E. Benes, "Proving the rearrangeability of connecting networks by group calculations," *Bell Syst. Tech. J.*, vol. 54, pp. 421–434, Feb. 1975.

[4] C. Clos, "A study of non-blocking switching networks," *Bell Syst. Tech. J.*, vol. 32, pp. 406–424, Mar. 1953.

[5] A. E. Joel, "On permutation switching networks," *Bell Syst. Tech. J.*, vol. 47, pp. 813–822, May–June 1968.

[6] D. H. Lawrie, "Access and alignment of data in an array processing," *IEEE Trans. Comput.*, vol. C-25, pp. 1145–1155, Dec. 1976.

[7] K. Y. Lee, "Interconnection networks and compiler algorithms for multiprocessors," Ph.D. dissertation, Dep. Comput. Sci., Univ. Illinois, Urbana-Champaign, Rep. 83-1125.

[8] D. C. Opferman and N. T. Tsao-Wu, "On a class of rearrangeable switching networks, Part I: Control algorithm," *Bell Syst. Tech. J.*, vol. 50, pp. 1579–1600, May–June 1971.

[9] A. A. Gioia, *The Theory of Numbers*. Chicago, IL: Markham, 1970.

[10] J. H. Patel, "Processor-memory interconnections for multiprocessors," in *Proc. 6th Annu. Symp. Comput. Architecture*, New York, NY, Apr. 1979, pp. 168–177.

[11] M. C. Pease, "The indirect binary *n*-cube microprocessor array," *IEEE Trans. Comput.*, vol. C-26, pp. 458–473, May 1977.

[12] H. J. Siegel, "The universality of various types of SIMD machine interconnection networks," in *Proc. 4th Annu. Symp. Comput. Architecture*, Mar. 1977, pp. 70–79.

[13] H. S. Stone, "Parallel processing with the perfect shuffle," *IEEE Trans. Comput.*, vol. C-20, pp. 153–161, Feb. 1971.

[14] A. Waksman, "A permutation network," *J. ACM*, vol. 15, pp. 159–163, Jan. 1968.

[15] D. Nassimi and S. Sahni, "Parallel algorithms to set up the Benes permutation network," *IEEE Trans. Comput.*, vol. C-31, pp. 148–154, Feb. 1982.

[16] G. P. Lev, N. Pippenger, and L. G. Valiant, "A fast parallel algorithm for routing in permutation networks," *IEEE Trans. Comput.*, vol. C-30, pp. 93–100, Feb. 1981.

[17] J. Lenfant, "Parallel permutations of data: A Benes network control algorithm for frequently used permutations," *IEEE Trans. Comput.*, vol. C-27, pp. 637–647, July 1978.

Kyungsook Yoon Lee received the B.S. degree in chemistry from the Sogang University, Seoul, Korea, in 1970, the M.S. degree in computer science from the University of Utah, Salt Lake City, in 1976, and the Ph.D. degree in computer science from the University of Illinois, Urbana-Champaign, in 1983.

Since 1983 she has been an Assistant Professor in the Department of Computer and Information Science, the Ohio State University, Columbus. Her research interests include interconnection networks, vectorizing compilers, and parallel computer architectures.

Bused Hypercubes and Other Pin-Optimal Networks

Charles M. Fiduccia

Abstract—**Pin minimization is an important issue for massively parallel architectures because the number of processing elements that can be placed on a chip, board, or chassis is often pin limited. A new d-dimensional bused hypercube interconnection network is presented that allows nodes to simultaneously (in one clock tick) exchange data across any dimension using only $d + 1$ ports per node rather than $2d$. Despite this near two-to-one reduction, the network also allows nodes that are two dimensions apart to simultaneously exchange data; as a result, certain routings can be performed in nearly half the time. The network is shown to be a special case of a general construction in which any set of d permutations can be performed, in one clock tick, using only $d + 1$ ports per node. A lower-bound technique is also presented and used to establish the optimality of the network, as well as that of several other new bused networks.**

Index Terms—**Binary cubes, buses, designs, difference covers, hypergraphs, interconnection networks, massive parallelism, parallel processing, permutations networks, pin minimization, SIMD architectures.**

I. INTRODUCTION

THE conventional d-dimensional binary hypercube Q_d is an undirected *graph* [4] consisting of $n = 2^d$ nodes joined by $nd/2$ edges. The nodes may be numbered from 0 to $2^d - 1$, in a natural way, by labeling each node with the bit-vector $v \in \{0, 1\}^d$ that represents that node's position in the d-dimensional unit cube. Each node v has degree d and is adjacent to d neighbors: those nodes whose labels u differ from v in exactly one bit. If each node is viewed as a site for a processing element and each edge is viewed as a communication link, the hypercube can serve as an interconnection network [9], [10].

Many parallel algorithms for hypercubes require that nodes exchange data values across each one of the d dimensions [8]. Such an exchange requires that each edge along that dimension carry two values, one in each direction. In Q_d this can only be done in two clock ticks, by using the edge once in each direction. A directed version $\vec{Q}_d$ of Q_d can be easily constructed that can perform the exchange *in one clock tick*. This is done by simply replacing each edge of Q_d with two parallel arcs (directed edges) going in opposite directions; unfortunately, this doubles the number of ports per node from d to $2d$. In this paper, we show how the nd arcs of $\vec{Q}_d$ can be combined to form n buses, each bus running along d edges of Q_d. The result is a network (hypergraph) that has only $d + 1$ ports per node yet allows nodes to exchange values across any one dimension *in one clock tick*.

Our use of the phrase "in one clock tick" is meant to capture the fact that the indivisible action of moving a data value, from one node to another, has no intermediate states. Each bus moves a data value *directly*, from source to target, without passing through any other intermediate nodes. Any two nodes connected to a bus are one clock tick apart, no matter how the bus is depicted. This is important to keep in mind since we draw buses along the edges of Q_d to maintain a sense of geometry.

The essential idea of our construction is to give each of the n nodes of the bused hypercube, henceforth denoted Q_d^*, its own bus through which it can communicate with its d cube neighbors. Each node uses one port to connect to its own bus plus d additional ports to connect to the buses of its d cube neighbors, for a total of $d + 1$ ports per node. Each of the resulting n buses thus has $d + 1$ ports and connects a node to its d cube neighbors. Fig. 1 depicts Q_3^*. Nodes are drawn as large squares, ports are drawn as dark numbered dots, in or on the boundary of a node, and buses are drawn as sets of edges incident on ports. The bus owned by node 000 is highlighted to show the "shape" of a typical net. The significance of the port numbers is explained in Section II.

We note that, for our purposes, a *bus* (net, hyperedge) is simply a *maximal subset of node–port pairs that are connected together* (in the electrical sense). In particular, we assume that the wires (edges) that connect the node–port pairs of a bus are capable of carrying data values in either direction. This allows a data value, which is placed at any node–port pair of a bus, to propagate to all other node–port pairs of that bus, in one clock tick. At the end of Section III we discuss how this requirement might be relaxed, thus allowing unidirectional wires to be used.

There are many ways of depicting (wiring) bus connections, and this is an important implementation consideration; however, the depiction in no way affects the algebraic properties of the buses it represents. Here, we confine our attention to these properties.

The bused network Q_d^* is a highly-symmetric structure in which nodes (processors) and hyperedges (buses) play dual roles. The similarity between such networks and combinatorial block designs [6] or finite geometries has been previously noted [1], [7]. We note that Q_d^* is not a block design, when $d \geq 3$, since every pair of nodes need *not* share a bus. It has recently been established [5] that networks such as Q_d^* can be described in terms of *difference covers*. Indeed, the network Q_d^* was independently obtained [5] using a product construction different from the one presented here. In this paper, we also show that, in addition to being able to perform simultaneous exchanges across any one dimension of Q_d, the bused network Q_d^* can also perform, in one clock tick,

Manuscript received February 20, 1990; revised January 31, 1991.
The author is with the Supercomputing Research Center, Bowie, MD 20715.
IEEE Log Number 9102440.

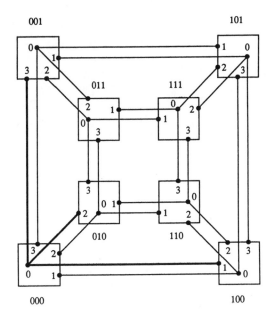

Fig. 1. The four-pin three-dimensional bused hypercube Q_3^*.

simultaneous exchanges of n data values across any *two* dimensions of Q_d.

In Section II, we explain our SIMD interconnection model; this model was introduced by the author [2] in 1984 as part of the GE/MIT massively parallel computer, known as the *Cross-Omega Machine*, and later described in [3]. In Section III, we give the construction of the bused hypercube Q_d^* and prove that it can swap across any one dimension in one clock tick. In Section IV, we prove that Q_d^* can also swap across any two dimensions in one clock tick. In Section V, we show that the method used to construct Q_d^* is general and that it works for any set of permutations. In Section VI, we cover several examples. In Section VII, we develop a lower-bound technique and then use it to establish the optimality of Q_d^* and several other bused networks.

II. THE NETWORK MODEL

Once the network Q_d^* has been constructed, its nodes and buses can be *used* in many different ways. In this paper, we confine our attention to a very specific mode of operation by assuming that the network operates in a single-instruction multiple-data (SIMD) mode, a mode that is especially attractive for massively parallel architectures. We assume that at each clock tick a global command can be issued that instructs all nodes to participate in a particular global permutation of n data values currently residing (one per node) at the n nodes. The network performs a permutation of these values, *in one clock tick*, by having each of the n nodes send its current data value, via a bus, directly to another node (possibly itself). The permutation is accomplished in an orderly manner (without contention) by broadcasting two global quantities to every node. These are the local port i to which it will write its current data value, and the local port j from which it will read its new data value. All nodes are assumed to be identical, each having p ports labeled with the same p global labels. These labels are used only for port identification within a node, so that no meaning is generally attached to their values.

In this model, we ignore the additional ports needed to connect each node to the global instruction bus, clock, power supply, etc., and concentrate strictly on the node-to-node connections. These connections are achieved in a particularly simple manner. The ports of the nodes, henceforth called *node–port pairs* to distinguish them from port labels, are simply connected together (in the electrical sense) to form buses; this uses no extra hardware outside of the nodes. A particular communication pattern is then achieved, in one clock tick, by simply writing to the buses and simultaneously reading from them. These patterns are thus *hard-wired* into the network. Other patterns are achieved, in multiple clock ticks, under software control.

The only communication primitive is (**write** i, **read** j). This parameterized global command causes every node to simultaneously write to its ith port, read from its jth port, and ignore all of its other ports. This is typically achieved with two multiplexors per node. By using the network in this mode, a node never uses more than two ports per clock tick. It is this property that we will exploit to reduce the number of ports per node; however, one should not take this to mean that two ports per node are sufficient. Far from it. Indeed, in Section VII, we prove that Q_d^* needs $d + 1$ ports per node and is therefore optimal.

A network is thus defined by how its node–port pairs are connected. Any network whose node–port pairs are connected in such a way as to allow more than one node–port pair to write to the same bus, for some i and j in (**write** i, **read** j), is considered to be *invalid* and is said to have *write conflicts*. Our solution to this problem is to guarantee validity by prohibiting the construction of any bus that would connect two or more node–port pairs with the same port label: *If (x, i) and (y, j) are two distinct node–port pairs on the same bus, we require that $i \neq j$.*

In the sequel, when we refer to a SIMD network, we will mean a network within the above conflict-free class, used in the above manner. Such a network is completely specified by a $p \times p$ write–read table, where p is the number of ports per node and the ijth entry of the table is the (possibly partial) node-to-node permutation performed by the command (**write** i, **read** j). Note that, for every i, (**write** i, **read** i) performs the identity permutation, so that the diagonal of the table is "wasted," and that (**write** i, **read** j) performs the *inverse* of (**write** j, **read** i), so that the table is *skew symmetric*.

A network N is said to *perform* a permutation π, in one clock tick, if π appears in its write–read table. The set of all permutations that N can perform will be denoted by $P(N)$. We say that N performs a set A of permutations if $A \subseteq P(N)$. Thus, if N performs A then N also performs any subset $B \subseteq A$.

The best we can expect from using p ports per node is to perform a maximum of $p(p - 1)$ nontrivial permutations. Any network with this property will be called *perfect*. Skew symmetry implies that perfection cannot be achieved if some off-diagonal entry is its own inverse, for then, that entry and its inverse are identical. Any network that achieves the maximum allowed under this restriction, namely, $p(p-1) - s$, where s is the number of nontrivial entries that are self-inverse, will be called *quasi-perfect*. For example, the bused hypercube Q_d^* will be shown to have this property, with $s = p(p-1)/2$.

Since the identity occupies the p locations on the diagonal and the s nontrivial self-inverses occupy $2s$ off-diagonal locations, if the network is to be quasi-perfect, it must be the case that $p^2 = p + 2s + (n - 1 - s)$, where $n = |P(N)|$ is the total number of permutations that N can perform (including the identity), so that $n - 1 - s$ is the number of nontrivial permutations that are not self-inverse. It follows that: *A network is quasi-perfect iff $n + s - 1 = p(p-1)$.*

In general, the goal is not to construct perfect networks but networks that perform a desired set of permutations using the fewest number of ports per node. Such networks are said to be *optimal for* that set of permutations. A network that is optimal for a set of permutations need not be perfect. A network can be optimal for one set and nonoptimal for another; although optimality is clearly monotonic with respect to set inclusion: *If a network N can perform a set of permutations A and is optimal for a subset $B \subseteq A$, then N is also optimal for A.* Monotonicity raises the question of whether a network N is optimal for the set $P(N)$ of all permutations that N can perform in one clock tick. A network N that is optimal for $P(N)$ will simply be called *optimal*. An optimal network N is clearly *not* optimal for every subset $B \subseteq P(N)$. Any *quasi-perfect network is necessarily optimal*, since no other network with fewer ports per node could perform as many permutations; moreover: *A network N that is not optimal cannot be optimal for any set $B \subseteq P(N)$*, since any other network N', with fewer ports per node, that performs $P(N)$ would also perform B.

It follows that, in our search for networks that are optimal for a desired set of permutations A, we can restrict ourselves to optimal networks. By looking at its write–read table, it is a trivial matter to determine if a network is either perfect or quasi-perfect—optimality is much more difficult.

III. Construction of the Bused Hypercube

To obtain the bused hypercube network Q_d^*, we will modify the hypercube graph Q_d so that it can perform a *swap* across any one of its d dimensions in one clock tick. The swap across dimension k is formally defined by the permutation $\sigma_k(v) = v \oplus e_k$, where $e_k \in \{0,1\}^d$ is the unit d-vector with 1 in its kth coordinate and 0 elsewhere, and $\oplus$ is the binary operation that performs bit-wise addition modulo 2. Since $(v \oplus e_k) \oplus e_k = v$, we see that σ_k swaps the value in node v with that of its neighbor $v \oplus e_k$ across dimension k of Q_d. The $n/2$ individual exchanges (cycles of the permutation σ_k), from one half of Q_d to the other, do not interfere with each other because they take place along different edges (one-dimensional subcubes of Q_d). This is a direct consequence of the fact [4] that $Q_d = Q_{d-1} \times Q_1$.

Of course, Q_d cannot perform σ_k in one clock tick, because the single edge between v and $v \oplus e_k$ cannot simultaneously carry two data values in opposite directions. The following modification rectifies this weakness.

Construction of Q_d^*: Start with the n isolated nodes of Q_d, each with $d+1$ ports labeled $0, 1, \cdots, d$. For each node v, form a bus b_v by connecting port 0 of v to port k of $v \oplus e_k$, for each $k = 1, \cdots, d$. That is to say, for each v, form the subset of node–port pairs $b_v = \{(v, 0), (v \oplus e_1, 1), \cdots, (v \oplus e_d, d)\}$.

The resulting network Q_d^* has n nodes, n buses, $d+1$ ports per node, and $d+1$ ports per bus. From Fig. 1, we see that each edge of Q_d is covered by *two* buses of Q_d^*. The result is the same as if:

- Each edge of Q_d had been replaced by two parallel arcs, one in each direction.
- Each node v formed its own bus b_v by combining the tails of its d outgoing arcs into a single port.
- The directions on all arcs were erased.

Proposition 1: For any $k \in \{1, \cdots, d\}$, the bused hypercube Q_d^* can perform the permutation $\sigma_k(v) = v \oplus e_k$ in one clock tick. Moreover, σ_k can be performed by either (**write** 0, **read** k) or (**write** k, **read** 0).

Proof: We first establish that Q_d^* has no write conflicts and that it has a sufficient number of buses. By construction, the node–port pair $(v, 0)$ appears only in bus b_v; thus, port 0 establishes a bijection (one-to-one and onto map) between the n nodes and the n buses. We need to show that this is also the case for every other port $k \in \{1, \cdots, d\}$. This follows from the fact that σ_k is a bijection, so that the pair $(\sigma_k(v), k)$ appears only in b_v. Thus, each port $i \in \{0, 1, \cdots, d\}$ connects each node to a unique bus; that is to say, Q_d^* has no write conflicts and contains enough buses so that, using any fixed port i, all n nodes can simultaneously write or read their n data values to or from the n distinct buses.

Now consider the command (**write** 0, **read** k). By definition of b_v, each node v writes its current data value to bus b_v via port 0, and, in the same clock tick, that value is read by node $v \oplus e_k$ via port k. In this way, the data value in node v moves to node $v \oplus e_k = \sigma_k(v)$ without passing through any other node; thus, (**write** 0, **read** k) makes the network perform the permutation σ_k.

In a similar way, the command (**write** k, **read** 0) causes the data value in node $v \oplus e_k$ to move to node v, and thus makes the network perform the inverse of the permutation σ_k. Since $(v \oplus e_k) \oplus e_k = v$, σ_k is its own inverse, so that (**write** k, **read** 0) also makes the network perform σ_k. In the next section we show that the write–read table for Q_d^* is in fact symmetric. $\qquad\square$

For the network Q_d^*, each permutation σ_k is its own inverse, so that both (**write** 0, **read** k) and (**write** k, **read** 0) perform σ_k. This redundancy cannot be "optimized out" of any network that performs σ_k. In our SIMD model, (**write** j, **read** i) performs the inverse of (**write** i, **read** j); thus, *any permutation that is its own inverse must be performed by both commands and so must occupy both the ijth and the jith locations of the write–read table.*

The fact that Q_d^* can perform every σ_k by uniformly choosing either $i = 0$ or $j = 0$ in (**write** i, **read** j) is of considerable technological importance. Rather than building buses that are symmetric, with respect to all their ports, we might treat port 0 of each bus as a *transmitter* and ports 1 through d as *receivers*, or vice versa. This interpretation of the buses may be especially useful in technologies where these communication terms make sense, such as optical or radio frequency systems. If Q_d^* is used in this very restricted mode, unidirectional communication lines will suffice.

Holding port 0 fixed throughout all the commands (**write** 0, **read** k) can also be interpreted to mean that port 0 of each node is constantly supplying that node's value to its bus. In that case, (**write** 0, **read** k) could be replaced by the simpler command (**read** k). Indeed, any subset of the ports 1 through d can then read from a node's output bus. In particular, this allows a node's value to be broadcast to any subset of its d neighbors.

Still another interpretation of a bus is possible if we adopt the view that port 0 is used only for input and ports 1 through d are used only for output. Port 0 of a node might then be viewed as a d-input AND gate, say, by allowing the d output ports of its neighbors to logically *pull down* on it. Alternatively, port 0 might be viewed as an *analog summing junction*. In these interpretations, one must be careful to *isolate*, within each node, the source of a data value from the buses that it feeds, lest *sneak paths* be introduced, which will short out these buses. Note that, in this scenario, the *sum* computed by each bus is available to all the nodes that have ports on that bus; thus, because of the required *internal* isolation between ports and sources at each node, the value at an output port of a node is not determined by just that node, but by all nodes on that bus.

These are merely several suggestions for other possible interesting *uses* of bused networks, such as Q_d^*; they are not part of our present SIMD model and will not be pursued further in this paper.

IV. Crossing Two Dimensions at a Time

Now that we have established that Q_d^* can perform any of the d swaps σ_k, we show that it is quasi-perfect and that it can also perform, in one clock tick, any of the $d(d-1)/2$ swaps $\sigma_{ij}(v) = \sigma_i(\sigma_j(v)) = v \oplus e_{ij}$, for $1 \leq i < j \leq d$, where $e_{ij} = e_i \oplus e_j$. This of course does not mean that Q_d^* can simultaneously perform both σ_i and σ_j, nor that σ_i and σ_j are performed in two clock ticks. The claim is that Q_d^* can perform the product $\sigma_i\sigma_j$ in just one clock tick. Of course, Q_d^* can perform this product in two clock ticks; the point is that it can also do it in one. The general phenomenon is explained in Section V.

To visualize the action of σ_{ij}, consider node $v = 0$. Bus b_0 connects port 0, of v, to ports 1 through d, of nodes e_1 through e_d, respectively. Each bus b_v may thus be depicted to resemble the origin and the d coordinate axes of d-dimensional space, thus shedding some light on why Q_d^* has $d+1$ ports per node. The three-dimensional case of this may be seen in the lower left corner of Fig. 1, by concentrating on b_0. Visualize the node–port pair $(000, 0) \in b_0$ as "the origin;" the horizontal segment of b_0, connecting node–port pair $(000, 0)$ to node–port pair $(100, 1) \in b_0$, as "the x_1 axis;" the segment connecting $(000, 0)$ to $(010, 2)$ as "the x_2 axis;" and the segment connecting $(000, 0)$ to $(001, 3)$ as "the x_3 axis."

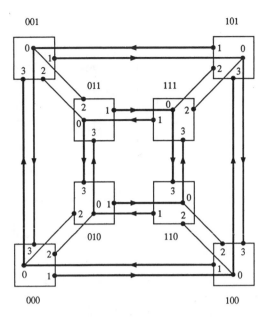

Fig. 2. Crossing dimensions one and three: $x \mapsto x \oplus 101$ of Q_3^*, in one clock tick, using the command (**write** 1, **read** 3).

If we issue the command (**write** i, **read** j), node e_i will write its data value x, say, to bus b_0, and that value will be read by node e_j, during the same clock tick. Although x also appears at port 0 of node 0, node 0 plays no role in moving x, since it is busy tending its own ports i and j and is ignoring port 0.

While x is moving from node e_i to e_j, the data value y, say, from node e_j, is also moving, via the bus connected to port 0 of node $u = e_j \oplus e_i$, to node $u \oplus e_j = e_i$. Thus, in one clock tick, nodes e_i and e_j exchange their data values x and y. During this same clock tick, nodes 0 and e_{ij} also exchange their data values.

Just as the $n/2$ individual cycles of the permutation σ_k take place on the $n/2$ one-dimensional subcubes along dimension k of Q_d, the $n/2$ cycles of σ_{ij} take place (in pairs) on the $n/4$ two-dimensional subcubes associated with dimensions i and j of Q_d. As a direct consequence of the fact that $Q_d = Q_{d-2} \times Q_2$, these subcubes do not interfere with each other.

In general, for every pair $1 \leq i < j \leq d$, there are 2^{d-2} such subcubes, each consisting of a set of four nodes v, $v \oplus e_i$, $v \oplus e_j$, and $v \oplus e_{ij}$. Each of these subcubes acts as an isolated copy of Q_2^* and allows v to swap with $v \oplus e_{ij}$ and $v \oplus e_i$ to swap with $v \oplus e_j$. This is shown in Fig. 2. Fig. 3 gives the entire write–read table for Q_3^* in two forms: In the first, each permutation is written as a the product of its cycles; whereas, in the second, it is written as a translation $v \mapsto v \oplus e_{ij}$ and only the constant e_{ij} is entered as the ijth entry of the table.

Noting that σ_{ij} is its own inverse, this characterizes all the remaining permutations that Q_d^* can perform in one clock tick:

Propositon 2: For any pair of ports $1 \leq i < j \leq d$, the bused hypercube Q_d^* can perform the $d(d-1)/2$ permutations $\sigma_{ij}(v) = v \oplus e_{ij} = v \oplus e_i \oplus e_j$ in one clock tick. Moreover, σ_{ij} can be accomplished by either (**write** i, **read** j) or (**write** j, **read** i), so that Q_d^* is quasi-perfect.

W \ R	0	1	2	3
0	( ) 000	(0 4)(1 5)(2 6)(3 7) 100	(0 2)(1 3)(4 6)(5 7) 010	(0 1)(2 3)(4 5)(6 7) 001
1	(0 4)(1 5)(2 6)(3 7) 100	( ) 000	(0 6)(1 7)(2 4)(3 5) 110	(0 5)(1 4)(2 7)(3 6) 101
2	(0 2)(1 3)(4 6)(5 7) 010	(0 6)(1 7)(2 4)(3 5) 110	( ) 000	(0 3)(1 2)(4 7)(5 6) 011
3	(0 1)(2 3)(4 5)(6 7) 001	(0 5)(1 4)(2 7)(3 6) 101	(0 3)(1 2)(4 7)(5 6) 011	( ) 000

Fig. 3. The write–read table for Q_3^*, in both the product-of-cycles form and the translation form.

Note that unlike the permutations $\sigma_k(v) = v \oplus e_k$, in Proposition 1, those in Proposition 2 require that ports 1 through d be used as both input and output ports. No additional nontrivial permutations can be performed by Q_d^* in one clock tick; Propositions 1 and 2 exhaust $P(Q_d^*)$. The full set $P(Q_d^*)$ of $(d+1)d/2 = d(d-1)/2 + d$ swaps that can be performed by Q_d^*, in one clock tick, can be summarized by its $(d+1) \times (d+1)$ *translation table*. Since every permutation performed by Q_d^* is a translation, of the form $v \mapsto v \oplus c_{ij}$, for some constant c_{ij} in $\{0,1\}^d$, the (i,j)th entry can be completely specified by simply entering the constant c_{ij}, in the table, rather than the permutation σ_{ij} itself. The translation table is thus nothing more than an abbreviated form of the write–read table and works for translations over arbitrary groups.

Write–read tables are always skew symmetric because (**write** j, **read** i) performs the inverse of the permutation performed by (**write** i, **read** j). For Q_d^*, the table turns out to be *symmetric* because every σ_i and every σ_{ij} is its own inverse.

We now consider how many clock ticks it takes Q_d^* to accomplish an arbitrary translation of the form $\sigma_c(v) = v \oplus c$. This is a well-posed question, since any constant $c \in \{0,1\}^d$ can be expressed as the sum of vectors of the form e_{ij} and e_i. Define $|c|$, the *weight* of c, to be the number of nonzero bits in c. By deleting two nonzero bits at a time, c can be expressed as the sum of $\lceil |c|/2 \rceil$ of the e_{ij} and e_i. This fact, combined with Propositions 1 and 2, establishes the following result.

Theorem 1: For any constant $c \in \{0,1\}^d$, the bused hypercube Q_d^* can accomplish the permutation $\sigma_c(v) = v \oplus c$ in $\lceil |c|/2 \rceil$ clock ticks.

We note in passing that the bused hypercube Q_d^* can also be obtained directly from the hypercube graph Q_{d+1} by 2-coloring its nodes; this can be done for any d because the neighbors of a node in Q_d have different parity from that node. If we use the two colors, "processor" and "bus," half of the nodes of Q_{d+1} become the processor nodes of Q_d^*, and the other half become the buses of Q_d^*. This construction points out the duality between nodes and buses and immediately explains why each has $d + 1$ ports. Fig. 4 shows Q_2^* as a 2-coloring of Q_3. This view of bused networks, as 2-colorable (bipartite) *multigraphs*, is entirely general and will be considered in a forthcoming paper.

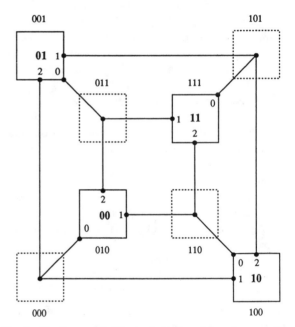

Fig. 4. The hypergraph Q_2^* as a 2-coloring of the cube graph Q_3.

V. GENERAL BUSED PERMUTATION NETWORKS

The hypercube graph Q_d is a special case of the d-dimensional $m_1 \times \cdots \times m_d$ hypertorus $T_d = T_d(m_1, \cdots, m_d)$, in which each node v is adjacent to the nodes $v \pm e_k$, for $k = 1, \cdots, d$, addition being done in the abelian group $\mathbf{Z}_{m_1} \times \cdots \times \mathbf{Z}_{m_d}$. That is to say, in the sum $u = v \pm w$, the components are defined by $u_k = v_k \pm w_k \pmod{m_k}$, for $k = 1, \cdots, d$. Note that, unlike the hypercube Q_d, each node of T_d generally has *two* edges along each dimension k, unless $m_k = 2$.

In T_d, we wish to perform each of the d permutations (cyclic shifts) $\sigma_k(v) = v + e_k$. Their d inverses $\sigma_{-k}(v) = v - e_k$ come free, because of the skew symmetry of the write–read table. The $d + 1$ ports per node construction, used to obtain the bused hypercube Q_d^*, can be easily generalized to T_d to obtain T_d^*; however, rather than proving a specific result for T_d, we establish a generic result that shows how to construct a $d + 1$ port network for *any* set of d permutations of any set S.

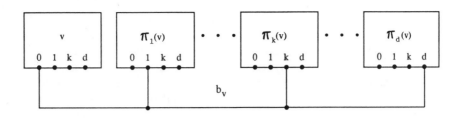

Fig. 5. The bus $b_v = \{(v, 0), (\pi_1(v), 1), \cdots, (\pi_k(v), k), \cdots, (\pi_d(v), d)\}$.

Let $\Pi = \{\pi_k : S \to S | k \in K\}$ be any set of permutations, of a (possibly infinite) set S, indexed by a set K. We wish to construct a permutation network $N(\Pi)$ that has a node v for each element of S and which can perform each of the permutations π_k, in one clock tick, via a SIMD command (**write** i, **read** j). We show that $N(\Pi)$ can always be constructed using $|\Pi| + 1$ ports per node, rather than the obvious $2|\Pi|$ ports per node. In addition to using K as the set of port labels, we will need an additional label 0, say, for the extra port. We assume that $0 \notin K$ and henceforth denote the complete set of port labels by $K_0 = K \cup \{0\}$.

Construction of $N(\Pi)$: Start with $|S|$ isolated nodes, each labeled with a unique element of S, and give each node $|\Pi|+1$ ports, each labeled with a unique element from K_0. For each node $v \in S$ construct a bus $b_v = \{(v, 0)\} \cup \{(\pi_k(v), k) | k \in K\}$, as shown in Fig. 5.

The resulting network clearly has $|S|$ nodes, each with $|\Pi| + 1$ ports. Since a bus is a *maximal* set of connected node−port pairs, we need to prove that b_v does in fact represent a bus with $|\Pi|+1$ node−port pairs and that $N(\Pi)$ does in fact have $|S|$ buses. This is critical. If what appear to be two buses have a nonempty intersection, "they" are in fact portions of a single bus and writing to them would create a write conflict.

Lemma 1: The family of subsets $\{b_v | v \in S\}$ forms a partition of the set $S \times K_0$ of all node−port pairs of the network $N(\Pi)$. This partition has $|S|$ blocks, each of cardinality $|K_0|$. In every block b_v, each element of K_0 appears exactly once as the second component of a node−port pair.

Proof: We first establish that each node−port pair in $S \times K_0$ is contained in one, and only one, set b_v. A pair takes one of two forms: If it has the form $(v, 0)$, it is contained only in b_v, because $0 \notin K$ by construction. If it has the form $(\pi_k(v), k) \in b_v$, suppose that it is also contained in b_u. Then $\pi_k(v) = \pi_k(u)$ and so $u = v$, because π_k is injective (one-to-one). Thus, the pair $(\pi_k(v), k)$ is contained only in b_v. This shows that $\{b_v | v \in S\}$ forms a partition of $S \times K_0$, in which each element of K_0 appears exactly once in each block, as the second component of some node−port pair, so that each block b_v may be properly viewed as a bus.

From the definition of the subsets b_v, $v \in S$, it is clear that there are *at most* $|S|$ blocks, and that each block has cardinality *at most* $|\Pi| + 1$. The fact that $(v, 0)$ is contained only in b_v shows that there are *at least* $|S|$ blocks, while the fact that the second component of the pairs in each block ranges over K_0 shows that the each block b_v has cardinality *at least* $|\Pi|+1$. □

It is important to note that the set of values $\{v\} \cup \Pi(v)$, in the first component of the node−port pairs in a block b_v,

need *not* be distinct. Except for v, the remaining values are determined entirely by Π and are therefore arbitrary. Although it does not occur in the bused hypercube Q_d^*, what this means is that a bus *can* be connected to more than one port of a node v. Indeed, this must be the case if $\pi_k(v) = v$ for some $\pi_k \in \Pi$. A simple natural example of this arises in Section VI.

Having established that the network $N(\Pi)$ has enough buses to permute $|S|$ data values, in one clock tick, we now show that it has no write conflicts. That is to say, for each port $k \in K_0$, each node v is connected, via port k, to a different bus.

Toward this end, define, for each $k \in K_0$, a *node-to-bus map* β_k, where $\beta_k(u) = b_v$ if the node−port pair (u, k) is in bus b_v. This map is well defined, because by Lemma 1 a pair (u, k) is contained in one, and only one, bus. The informal notion that *the network $N(\Pi)$ has no write conflicts* is then equivalent to the formal condition that: *Every map β_k, $k \in K_0$, is injective.* In fact, $N(\Pi)$ satisfies the following stronger condition.

Lemma 2: For every port $k \in K_0$, the node-to-bus map β_k is a bijection. Indeed, $\beta_k(u) = b_v$, where $v = \pi_k^{-1}(u)$, and π_0 is defined to be the identity.

Proof: By definition, $\beta_k(u) = b_v$ if $(u, k) \in b_v$. From the definition of b_v and the fact that bus b_v is a block of the above partition, the only such pair in b_v is $(\pi_k(v), k)$, so that $v = \pi_k^{-1}(u)$. Since π_k is a bijection, so is β_k. Indeed, if b_v were identified with its index v, so that bus b_v were simply called bus v, then β_k would *be* precisely π_k^{-1}. The reason for the inversion will become apparent shortly. □

Up to now, the command (**write** i, **read** j) has been intuitively described by explaining its action. Every node v puts its current data value on the bus connected to its ith port and gets its new data value from the bus connected to its jth port. In this way, the data value at node v of a network N is moved to node $u = N_{ij}(v)$, where N_{ij} is the ijth entry of the write−read table for N. For an arbitrary SIMD network N, the node-to-node mapping N_{ij} is generally only a *partial* injection, because the network may have more buses than nodes. Because the node-to-bus maps of our $N(\Pi)$ *are* bijections, each of its N_{ij} also turns out to be a node-to-node bijection. *We henceforth assume that this is the case.* The map $N_{ij} : S \to S$ can be visualized by noting that (**write** i) uses β_i in the *forward* direction (moving data from nodes to buses), whereas (**read** j) uses β_j in the *reserve* (inverse) direction (moving data from buses to nodes).

Formally, (**write** i, **read** j) causes the network $N(\Pi)$ to perform, in one clock tick, a node-to-node bijection N_{ij} that can be expressed as a *difference*, in the multiplicative sense [5]. In the sequel, the multiplication of permutations is treated as function composition with arguments placed to the right: $(fg)(x) = f(g(x))$.

Theorem 2 [5]: For any two ports $i, j \in K_0$, the permutation N_{ij} performed by the network $N(\Pi)$, in one clock tick, in response to the SIMD command (**write** i, **read** j), is the difference $N_{ij} = \beta_j^{-1}\beta_i$.

An important consequence of this result is that the write–read table of a network is not just an ad hoc tabulation of the permutations it can perform, but an algebraic object, namely, a difference table. This means that, if we use $\beta_1, \cdots, \beta_p$, as the labels for the rows and columns of the $p \times p$ table, then the entry N_{ij}, in row i column j, is the (left) difference $N_{ij} = \beta_j^{-1}\beta_i$; the order appears reversed because we apply functions on the left and view multiplication of permutations as function composition.

By construction of $N(\Pi)$, we arranged the buses b_v, $v \in S$, so that the primary purpose of the network was to perform the permutations $\pi_k \in \Pi$, where π_k is performed by (**write** 0, **read** k). This is formally expressed by the following result.

Proposition 3: For any port $k \in K$, the network $N(\Pi)$ can perform the permutation π_k, or its inverse, in one clock tick. Moreover, $\pi_k = N_{0k}$ and its inverse is N_{k0}.

Proof: By Theorem 2, $N_{0k}(v) = \beta_k^{-1}(\beta_0(v))$. By Lemma 2, $\beta_0(v) = b_v$, so that $\beta_k^{-1}(b_v) = \pi_k(v)$. Since this is true for all v, we have $N_{0k} = \pi_k$. Similarly, N_{k0} is the inverse. □

Proposition 3 is the generic version of Proposition 1, where the set of permutations Π is now completely arbitrary. The observations made about the bused hypercube Q_d^*, at the end of Section III, also apply to the bused network $N(\Pi)$.

The following generic version of Proposition 2 shows that the network $N(\Pi)$ can also combine two permutations and perform their difference in one clock tick. Since each permutation in Π need not be its own inverse, as was the case for the bused hypercube Q_d^*, it is not surprising that inverses appear in the general case.

Proposition 4: For any two ports $i, j \in K_0$, the network $N(\Pi)$ can perform the permutation $N_{ij} = \pi_j\pi_i^{-1}$ in one clock tick.

Proof: By Theorem 2, $N_{ij}(v) = \beta_j^{-1}(\beta_i(v))$. By Lemma 2, $\beta_i(v) = b_u$, where $u = \pi_i^{-1}(v)$. Applying β_j^{-1} to b_u gives $N_{ij}(v) = \pi_j(\pi_i^{-1}(v))$. Since this is true for all v, we have $N_{ij} = \pi_j\pi_i^{-1}$. □

Using the terminology of difference covers [5] and recalling that π_0 denotes the identity permutation, the last two propositions are equivalent to the following statement.

For any set of permutations Π, of a set S, the differences of the set $\Pi \cup \{\pi_0\}$ consist precisely of every permutation in Π, the inverse of every permutation in Π, and the difference of every ordered pair of permutations in Π.

Combining these results, $N(\Pi)$ can thus be characterized as follows:

Theorem 3: For any set of permutations Π, of any set S, the network $N(\Pi)$, has $|S|$ nodes, $|S|$ buses, $|\Pi| + 1$ ports per node, and $|\Pi| + 1$ ports per bus. A permutation can be performed by $N(\Pi)$, in one clock tick, if and only if it is a permutation $\pi_k \in \Pi$, the inverse π_k^{-1} of a permutation in Π, or the difference $\pi_j\pi_i^{-1}$ of a pair of permutations in Π.

Note that $|\Pi| + 1$ is a *uniform* upper bound on the number of ports per node that are needed in a network $N(\Pi)$. It holds for any Π, regardless of its structure. For best results, one should not apply this upper bound blindly. Since "inverses are free," one should first remove from Π the inverse of any element that is also in Π. Since "the identity is free," one should make certain that it does not appear in Π. In practice, removal of inverses may reduce the number of ports per node by nearly a factor of two. This is especially true in networks obtained from undirected graphs, such as T_d, since one typically wishes to communicate over an edge in either direction.

VI. EXAMPLES

A. The Bused d-Dimensional Mesh

Let $\mathbf{Z}^d$ be the infinite group of all d-tuples of integers under component-wise addition. The d-dimensional mesh consists of the locally finite, regular graph M_d, say, of degree $2d$, whose nodes are the elements of $\mathbf{Z}^d$ and whose edges connect each node x to the $2d$ nodes $x \pm e_k$, where $e_1 = (1, 0, \cdots, 0)$ through $e_d = (0, \cdots, 0, 1)$ are the unit vectors in $\mathbf{Z}^d$.

In M_d, each node has $2d$ ports, which may be used in many different ways to communicate between nodes. Suppose that we wish to use M_d in a SIMD mode and that the only global communication commands to all nodes are: **Shift**(k, b), for $k = 1, \cdots, d$ and for $b = 1, -1$. For any dimension k, the command **Shift**$(k, 1)$ makes every node x send its current data value to node $x + e_k$, and therefore simultaneously receive a new data value from node $x - e_k$. Thus, in one clock tick, the command **Shift**$(k, 1)$ performs the permutation $\sigma_k(x) = x + e_k$. Similarly, **Shift**$(k, -1)$ performs the inverse permutation $\sigma_k^{-1}(x) = x - e_k$.

By taking $\Pi = \{\sigma_1, \cdots, \sigma_d\}$ and applying our construction, we will obtain a perfect bused version $M_d^* = N(\Pi)$ of M_d, with $p = d + 1$ ports per node, which can perform any one of the translations $x \mapsto x + t$, where t ranges over the set of differences $T = \{\pm e_k | k = 1, \cdots, d\} \cup \{e_i - e_j | i, j = 1, \cdots, d\}$ of the set $\{0, e_1, \cdots, e_d\}$. Since the only duplicated differences are along the diagonal of the table: $e_i - e_i = 0$, $(i = 1, \cdots, d)$, T has maximal cardinality $|T| = (d+1)^2 - d = d(d+1) + 1$. Each node of M_d^* thus has the *maximal number of neighbors* that a node with $p = d + 1$ ports can have in our SIMD model, namely $p(p-1) = (d+1)d$. This means that there is a unique command (**write** i, **read** j) for each nontrivial translation $x \mapsto x + t$; so that M_d^* is perfect.

Although natural, the choice $\sigma_k(x) = x + e_k$, in the definition of M_d^*, is somewhat arbitrary. We could just as well have chosen $\sigma_k(x) = x \pm e_k$. In this way, we obtain 2^d variations of M_d^*, all essentially equivalent. As shown below, we can subsume *all* of these if we are willing to use more ports per node.

Since T does not contain the sums $e_i + e_j$, the neighborhood $\{x + t | t \in T\}$ of a node x of M_d^* is not geometrically symmetric. A larger symmetric neighborhood can be obtained at the expense of d additional ports per node. If we simply take $\Pi' = \{\sigma_1, \sigma_1^{-1}, \cdots, \sigma_d, \sigma_d^{-1}\}$, so that it also includes the inverse of each σ_k, the resulting bused network $N(\Pi') = B_d^*$, say, will have $2d+1$ ports per node and the property that: *The neighbors $x + t$, of a node x, where t ranges over the nonzero differences of $\{0, \pm e_1, \cdots, \pm e_d\}$, consist precisely of all those nodes that are at most two edges away from x, in the graph M_d.* This is the closed l^1 (Manhattan distance) *ball* of radius 2 centered at x.

Fig. 6 shows a finite 5×5 section of the infinite two-dimensional case B_2^*. Note how, for any d, each bus has $2d+1$ ports and that its "shape" can be obtained by connecting the origin 0, of d-dimensional space, to the $2d$ lattice points $\pm e_1, \cdots, \pm e_d$. In view of this, a natural numbering for the ports of each nodes is $0, \pm 1, \pm 2, \cdots, \pm d$. Port 0 then connects each node x to the "center" of its "own" bus, port k connects x to the bus owned by node $x + e_k$, and port $-k$ connects x to the bus owned by node $x - e_k$. An equally good case can be made for replacing $\pm k$ by $\mp k$. Only the pins of the five buses connected to the (typical) central node have their ports numbered, to show which ports are connected to this node. In addition, the central bus is highlighted to show the shape of the typical bus.

Fig. 7 shows the 12 neighbors of the (typical) central node of the infinite network B_2^*. The circles around the eight surrounding neighbors indicate that each of these occurs twice in the translation table. In this way, we account for all 20=12+8 off-diagonal entries in the translation table given in Fig. 6. The three-dimensional diagram for B_3^* is also given to show the trend of where the $2d(d + 1)$ neighbors of a typical node are located in the general case. In the two-dimensional case, neighbors that are circled can be reached, from the center, via two different buses and thus appear twice in the table. The central node can of course reach *itself* five different ways, via each of its five pins. Thus, if multiplicity is taken into account, there is a correspondence between the p^2 entries of a $p \times p$ write–read table and the multiset of p^2 points in the neighborhood diagram. In the three-dimensional case, the seven buses connected to the central node are shown along with all the nodes connected to those buses. By definition, this *is* the neighborhood of the central node. Note that the figure consists of nothing more than the (highlighted) bus "owned" by the central node, plus the six buses "owned" by the nodes $x \pm e_1$, $x \pm e_2$, and $x \pm e_3$. With a bit of patience, one can see the radius-1 and radius-2 "layers" of the three-dimensional l^1 ball; each has the shape of an octahedron.

Although B_d^* is geometrically symmetric, it is not perfect, since the maximal number of neighbors with $p = 2d + 1$ is $p(p-1) = 4d^2 + 2d$, whereas the l^1 ball of radius 2, excluding the center, contains only $2d(d + 1) = 2d^2 + 2d$ nodes. The factor-of-two loss stems from the fact that, except for the $2d$ neighbors of the form $x \pm 2e_k$, all other neighbors of x can be reached in two different ways. Thus, $e_k = 0 - (-e_k) = e_k - 0$. Moreover, for $i \neq j$ and $a_i, b_j \in \{1, -1\}$, we have $a_i e_i - b_j e_j = (-b_j)e_j - (-a_i)e_i$. Each of these equations can be interpreted to mean that two different commands cause the network to perform the same permutation. This can be easily verified for B_2^* in Figs. 6 and 7.

In addition to its symmetry, the network B_d^* also has another desirable property. If we take the idea of a node "owning" the

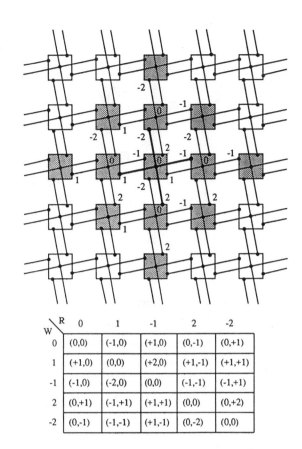

W \ R	0	1	-1	2	-2
0	(0,0)	(-1,0)	(+1,0)	(0,-1)	(0,+1)
1	(+1,0)	(0,0)	(+2,0)	(+1,-1)	(+1,+1)
-1	(-1,0)	(-2,0)	(0,0)	(-1,-1)	(-1,+1)
2	(0,+1)	(-1,+1)	(+1,+1)	(0,0)	(0,+2)
-2	(0,-1)	(-1,-1)	(+1,-1)	(0,-2)	(0,0)

Fig. 6. A 5×5 section of the infinite five-pin two-dimensional bused ball B_2^* together with the 5×5 finite translation table of B_2^*. The highlighted nodes comprise the neighborhood of the node at the center.

bus connected to its port 0 seriously, we can use B_d^* in the **read-only** mode discussed at the end of Section II. Each node x simply makes its data value *always available on its own bus*, thus allowing its $2d$ neighbors $x \pm e_k$ $(k = 1, \cdots, d)$ to read it at will. Under this restriction, which is equivalent to turning the d edges of each bus into d arcs directed *away* from port 0, a node can no longer communicate directly with nodes that are at distance 2, even though they are still directly connected to it via buses owned by other intermediate nodes. This can be seen in Fig. 6.

Both of the above bused mesh networks M_d^* and B_d^* can of course be made finite, along any subset of its d dimensions, by wraparound. Indeed, the bused hypercube Q_d^* is the result of wrapping all d dimensions of M_d^* into cycles of length two.

B. Networks from Matchings

One should not get the impression that bused networks are only good for *local* communications, as is the case for the bused meshes, or that they are *point symmetric*, so that every node looks like every other node. Since any d permutations of any set X can be used to construct a network, with $|X|$ nodes, the closest we come to anything that remotely sounds geometric is to possibly view the network as a d-dimensional structure, in which the kth permutation plays the role of the kth dimension, so that all the neighbors of a node are "next" to it. At the other extreme, any network can be viewed as a

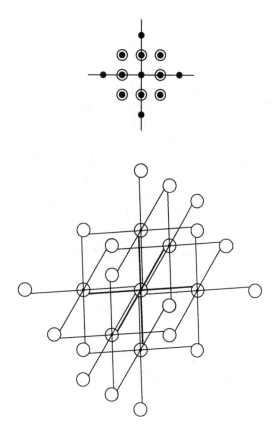

Fig. 7. The $2d(d+1)$ neighbors of a typical (central) node in the bused balls B_2^* and B_3^*, where the l^1 ball of radius 2, centered at a point x, in the lattice of points $\mathbb{Z}^d$, consists of all points y such that $\Sigma_1^d |y_i - x_i| \leq 2$. The circled nodes in B_2^* can be reached two different ways from the central node.

for $k = 1, \cdots, d$, are the set of edges along the kth dimension of the hypercube Q_d.

Fig. 8 shows a small example K_3^*—with fixed points—obtained from the three maximal matchings of the triangle graph $G = K_3$; these yield the three transpositions $\Pi = \{(12), (13), (23)\}$. By constructing the 4×4 write−read table for $N(\Pi)$, one finds that it can perform, in one clock tick, not only Π, but *all* permutation in the symmetric group S_3.

Although clearly not perfect, this network is optimal; indeed, it is *optimal for* S_3, because the set $P(K_3^*)$ of all permutations it performs is S_3. To prove optimality, suppose there were a solution with $p = 3$ ports per node. Its 3×3 write−read table would have only six off-diagonal positions, because the diagonal is wasted on the identity. Three of these positions would have to be occupied by the three transpositions (1 2), (2 3), and (1 3). Since these are their own inverses, the three remaining positions would also have to be occupied by these same three transpositions. This would leave no room for the two remaining elements (1 2 3) and (1 3 2) of S_3. Thus, no such 3×3 table exists; so that four ports per node are necessary and sufficient in any network that performs S_3.

There is no quasi-perfect network for S_3. Using the $n + s - 1 = p(p - 1)$ criterion for quasi-perfection, we see that $n = |S_3| = 6$ and $s = 3$; so that $n + s - 1 = 8$, which is not of the form $p(p - 1)$. Thus, a 3×3 table is too small and a 4×4 table is too large.

A more detailed algebraic analysis, based on Theorem 3, shows that three ports per node are also not enough to perform just the subset $\Pi \subseteq S_3$. Thus, K_3^* *is also optimal for the subset* $\Pi = \{(1\ 2), (2\ 3), (1\ 3)\}$.

Note that a matching M is perfect if and only if σ_M has no fixed points, and that M is empty if and only if σ_M is the identity permutation. Any node x that is a fixed point of some nonperfect matching M will thus have at least two distinct ports connected to some bus because, in our SIMD model, fixed points are handled as nodes that *send to themselves*. Thus, to avoid wasting ports in this manner, one would most likely not use this technique if the matchings $M_1, \cdots, M_d$ were small, relative to $|X|/2$, such as if $G = (X, E)$ were a tree with several nodes of high degree. In the extreme case, in which each matching is just one edge of G, corresponding to a transposition, it is clear that a *single bus would suffice*, given a more powerful write−read control strategy for the network; on the other hand, in our SIMD network model, it is always the case that: *There are at least as many buses as there are nodes*.

In general, except for loops arising from fixed points, the bused network obtained from matchings $M_1, \cdots, M_d$ of a graph $G = (X, E)$ resembles the subgraph $(X, M_1 \cup \cdots \cup M_d)$, where the number of buses that run along a given edge e is equal to twice the number of matchings that contain e. It is worth noting that: *The ports of a node that belong to a given bus cannot be combined into a single port* (thus deleting loops and reducing the number of ports per node), because there is no uniform way of labeling the ports, at all nodes, to comply with our SIMD requirement that all nodes be identical and respond to (**write** i, **read** j) in a uniform way. The optimality proof for $K_3^* = N(\{(1\ 2), (1\ 3), (2\ 3)\})$ confirms this; otherwise, we would obtain a three-port solution, which we proved does

one-dimensional structure, by simply arranging the elements of X on the line, in which each node has neighbors that can be arbitrarily "far" from it. Such comparisons simply point out the difference between the notions of a *shortest path* between two nodes and the *distance* between them in an *embedding* of the network into some metric space. Although the latter cannot be pragmatically ignored, the former is generally the more appropriate algorithmic measure, since it determines how many clock ticks are needed for two nodes to communicate.

An interesting class of "swap networks" can be derived from graph matchings, the hypercube Q_d being one of them.

Let $G = (X, E)$ be a simple, locally finite, undirected graph with node set X and edge set E. If $M \subseteq E$ is a *matching* (set of nonadjacent edges) in G, we can associate with M the permutation (involution) σ_M of X that has as fixed points those nodes of G that are unmatched by M and swaps across every edge of M. This transforms each edge of M into a 2-cycle of σ_M. Formally, $\sigma_M(x) = y$ and $\sigma_M(y) = x$, if the edge $\{x, y\} \in M$, else $\sigma_M(x) = x$. Note that, as in all swaps, σ_M is its own inverse.

To any d matchings $M_1, \cdots, M_d$ in G we can thus associate d permutations $\sigma_1, \cdots, \sigma_d$ of X and then construct the $d + 1$-ports per node bused network $N(\sigma_1, \cdots, \sigma_d)$. *Perfect matchings* appear to be particularly attractive for this purpose since each one partitions the nodes into two blocks of equal size. For example, the hypercube Q_d is a special case of this since the d perfect matchings $M_k = \{\{x, x \oplus e_k\} | x \in \{0, 1\}^d\}$,

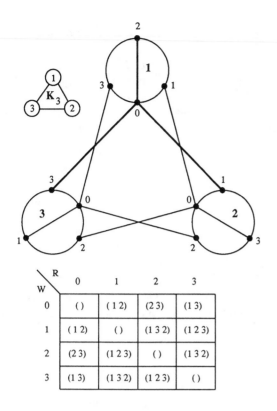

W \ R	0	1	2	3
0	( )	(1 2)	(2 3)	(1 3)
1	(1 2)	( )	(1 3 2)	(1 2 3)
2	(2 3)	(1 2 3)	( )	(1 3 2)
3	(1 3)	(1 3 2)	(1 2 3)	( )

Fig. 8. The optimal four-pin bused triangle K_3^* for the symmetric group S_3 and its write–read table in cycle form.

not exist. More powerful SIMD models, which maintain the (**write** i, **read** j) paradigm and permit port labels to be *sets* or use lookup tables, are being considered to address this issue.

VII. OPTIMALITY

In this section, we show that the uniform upper bound of $|\Pi| + 1$ ports per node cannot be improved without additional knowledge about Π. That is to say, there exist sets of permutations of cardinality d that *cannot* be performed by any SIMD network with fewer than $d+1$ ports per node. In fact, we show that the bused hypercube Q_d^* is such a case. The lower-bound technique used to establish this result is general and can be applied to other networks.

Theorem 4: Let A be a subset of an abelian group G. To each $t \in A$, associate the permutation $\pi_t(x) = x + t$ of G, called translation by t, and let $\Pi = \{\pi_t | t \in A\}$. If A contains r elements $t_1, \cdots, t_r$ such that $c_1 t_1 + \cdots + c_r t_r \neq 0$, for every nonzero $(c_1, \cdots, c_r) \in \{0, 1, -1\}^r$, then $r+1$ ports per node are necessary, and $|A|+1$ are sufficient, in any SIMD network that performs each permutation in Π in one clock tick.

Proof: Suppose there exists a network N, with r ports per node and node-to-bus maps $\beta_1, \cdots, \beta_r$, that performs each permutation in Π in one clock tick. If we let π_k denote π_{t_k}, for $k = 1, \cdots, r$, there exists some command (**write** i, **read** j) such that $\pi_k = \beta_j^{-1} \beta_i$. We now show how to eliminate $\beta_1, \cdots, \beta_r$ from these r equations to obtain an equation among $t_1, \cdots, t_r$ that contradicts the hypothesis of the theorem.

Construct a directed graph $G(N)$ with r vertices labeled $\beta_1, \cdots, \beta_r$, and r arcs labeled $\pi_1, \cdots, \pi_r$. The arc π_k goes from vertex β_j to vertex β_i to express the equation $\beta_i = \beta_j \pi_k$.

Since $G(N)$ has more than $r - 1$ edges, it cannot be a tree, or a forest, and so *must have at least one undirected cycle.* Such a cycle can be used to eliminate the β's from the subset of equations it represents. Indeed, if we go around a cycle, starting at any vertex, and compose the permutations on the arcs, using π_k when the direction of the cycle matches that of the arc and π_k^{-1} when the directions differ, the resulting product is the identity permutation. If we then make the substitution $\pi_k(x) = x + t_k$, and appeal to the fact that G is abelian to rearrange terms, we will obtain a nontrivial sum of the t_k that *is* equal to zero. This contradiction proves that $r + 1$ ports are necessary. Theorem 3 shows that $|A| + 1$ ports are sufficient. $\square$

It is important to note that the $r + 1$ lower bound holds simply because the network needs to perform the r permutations in Π corresponding to $t_1, \cdots, t_r$. The remaining permutations performed by the network are of no consequence and *do not* account for the lower bound.

By taking the group G to be a direct sum of cyclic groups, we can capture the fact that bused networks that simulate d-dimensional "toroidal meshes" cannot be constructed with fewer than (the worst case) $d + 1$ ports per node.

Corollary 1: Let $G = G_1 \oplus \ldots \oplus G_d$ be the direct sum of d nontrivial cyclic groups. Let $e_k = (0, \cdots, 1_k, 0, \cdots, 0) \in G$, for $k = 1, \cdots, d$, where 1_k is a generator of G_k, and let $\sigma_k(x) = x + e_k$, for $k = 1, \cdots, d$, be a translation of G. Then $d + 1$ ports per node are necessary and sufficient for any SIMD network that performs each of the translations $\sigma_1, \cdots, \sigma_d$ in one clock tick.

Proof: $c_1 e_1 + \cdots + c_r e_r = 0$ holds in G if and only if $c_k 1_k = 0$ holds in G_k, for $k = 1, \cdots, r$. Setting $c_k = 1$ and $c_k = -1$, respectively, gives $1_k = 0$ and $-1_k = 0$. This contradicts the fact that 1_k is the generator of a nontrivial cyclic group; so $c_k = 0$ for all k. Theorem 4 thus applied, with $A = \{e_1, \cdots, e_d\}$, so that $r = d = |A|$. $\square$

Example: For any $d \geq 1$, $d+1$ ports per node are necessary and sufficient in any SIMD network that performs, in one clock tick, each of the d orthogonal shifts $\sigma_k(x) = x + e_k$, for $k = 1, \cdots, d$, of the infinite d-dimensional mesh $\mathbf{Z}^d$, where $\mathbf{Z}$ is the group of integers under addition. Thus, M_d^* is optimal for these shifts.

Example: For any $d \geq 1$, $d + 1$ ports per node are necessary and sufficient for any SIMD network that performs, in one clock tick, each of the d cyclic shifts $\sigma_k(x) = x + e_k \bmod m_k$, for $k = 1, \cdots, d$, on the d-dimensional hypertorus $T_d(m_1, \cdots, m_d)$.

Corollary 2: Let A be a subset of a vector space V. For $t \in A$, define a permutation (translation) $\pi_t(x) = x + t$ of V and let $\Pi = \{\pi_t | t \in A\}$. If A contains r linearly independent elements, then $r + 1$ ports per node are necessary and $|A| + 1$ are sufficient in any SIMD network that performs Π.

Proof: A vector space V, over any field, is an abelian group. Any linearly independent subset of r elements clearly satisfy the condition of Theorem 4. $\square$

We are now in a position to show that the bused hypercube Q_d^* is *optimal* with respect to being able to swap across each of its d dimensions. This follows from the above corollary, or the fact that $Q_d = T_d(2, 2, \cdots, 2)$. This is a rather strong result, since it means that the lower bound for Q_d^* matches the uniform $d+1$ upper bound obtained from Theorem 4. Because each of the d swaps $\sigma_k(x) = x \oplus e_k$ is its own inverse, any write–read table for Q_d^* must be symmetric; moreover, its diagonal entries are all the identity permutation. Despite this "waste," such a $p \times p$ table would still have $p(p-1)/2$ locations to accommodate $\sigma_1, \cdots, \sigma_d$. Thus, there is no *a priori* reason to suspect that $p \approx \sqrt{2d}$ ports per node are not enough. This is the *best* we can expect, while Theorem 4 shows that $p = d+1$ is the *worst* we can expect. Alas, the latter is the case:

Corollary 3: For any $d \geq 1$, $d + 1$ ports per node are necessary and sufficient for any SIMD network that performs, in one clock tick, each of the d permutations $\sigma_k(x) = x \oplus e_k$, for $k = 1, \cdots, d$, of the $n = 2^d$ nodes of the d-dimensional hypercube Q_d. Thus, the bused hypercube Q_d^* is optimal for $\{\sigma_1, \cdots, \sigma_d\}$

Proof: In the vector space $V = \mathbf{Z}_2^d$, over the field $GF(2)$, the set $A = \{e_1, \cdots, e_d\}$, consisting of the d unit vectors, is a basis and clearly satisfies the conditions of Theorem 4. $\square$

VIII. CONCLUSION

We have presented a technique for constructing bused networks that are designed to perform, in one clock tick, any desired set Π of d node-to-node permutations, using only $d+1$ ports per node, rather than the obvious $2d$ ports per node. There is a kind of double savings involved, since the network also performs the inverses of elements in Π, and these are generally as desirable as those in Π. Whether or not we want them, the network also performs the difference $\pi_i \pi_j^{-1}$ of any two elements in Π. This means that using $d+1$ ports per node, the network can perform $O(d^2)$ useful permutations. Of course, the real design problem is to find a network that performs Π using the smallest number of ports per node, possibly as small as $p = \sqrt{d}$.

The lower-bound technique we have presented shows that the $\sqrt{d}$ goal is totally hopeless for networks that are essentially multidimensional meshes. It is not clear whether this means that such networks are, in some sense, *powerful* or that our SIMD network model is *weak*. Naturally, we prefer to think that the former is the case.

Although simple, our uniform $2d$ to $d + 1$ port-reduction procedure cannot be improved without taking into account the algebraic properties of Π. The design problem for such permutation networks is essentially that of finding minimal difference covers for a given subset of a group. There is no known polynomial-time algorithm for this problem. The author has developed a reasonably fast search algorithm for the pin-minimization problem. The lower-bound technique can be also be generalized to arbitrary (nonabelian) groups. These techniques will be the topics of a future paper.

An avenue of research that we have not explored at all, in this paper, concerns how the resulting networks could be used if we were to drop the rather strong SIMD restriction that we use only global commands of the form (**write** i, **read** j).

We must make a distinction between *what* the network is and how it is *used*. Particularly in the case of the bused hypercube Q_d^*, one should not overlook the fact that the network is a finely-balanced symmetric structure that has $n = 2^d$ buses, each available to $d + 1$ nodes, and that each node has $d + 1$ ports that give it access to $d + 1$ buses. That sounds like a powerful combination worthy of further consideration.

ACKNOWLEDGMENT

A significant portion of this work was performed while the author was on the staff of the Computer Science Branch at the General Electric Corporate Research and Development Center, Schenectady, NY. The optimality of bused hypercubes arose from an initial conjecture based on unsuccessful attempts to find better solutions, for small hypercubes, using a pin-minimization algorithm developed by the author. D. O'Halloran was kind enough to code the algorithm in the programming language C. His assistance is much appreciated.

REFERENCES

[1] J. C. Bermond, J. Bond, and J. F. Sacle, "Large hypergraphs of diameter 1," in *Graph Theory and Combinatorics*, B. Bollobas, Ed. London, England: Academic, 1984.
[2] C. M. Fiduccia, "Local interconnection scheme for parallel processing architectures," U.S. Patent 4739476, Apr. 1988.
[3] ——, "A bussed hypercube and other optimal permutation networks," GE Res. Develop. Center, Rep. 88CRD255, presented at the Fourth SIAM Conf. Discrete Math., San Francisco, CA, June 1988.
[4] F. Harary, *Graph Theory*. Reading, MA: Addison-Wesley, 1972.
[5] J. Kilian, S. Kipnis, and C. E. Leiserson, "The organization of permutation architectures with bussed interconnections," in *Proc. 28th Annu. Symp. Foundations Comput. Sci.*, IEEE, Oct. 1987.
[6] E. S. Lander, *Symmetric Designs: An Algebraic Approach*. New York: Cambridge University Press, 1983.
[7] M. D. Mickunas, "Using projective geometry to design bus connection networks," in *Proc. Workshop Interconnection Networks for Parallel and Distributed Processing*, ACM/IEEE, Apr. 1980.
[8] F. P. Preparata and J. Vuillemin, "The cube-connected cycles: A versatile network for parallel computation," *Commun. ACM*, pp. 300–309, May 1981.
[9] H. J. Siegel, *Interconnection Networks for Large-Scale Parallel Processing*. Lexington, MA: Lexington Books, 1985.
[10] C. Wu and T. Feng, *Interconnection Networks for Parallel and Distributed Processing*, IEEE, 1984.

Charles M. Fiduccia received the B.S. degree from the Newark College of Engineering, Newark, NJ, in 1966 and the Ph.D. degree from Brown University, Providence, RI, in 1973.

He was on the faculty of the Computer Science Department at the State University of New York, Stony Brook, from 1971 to 1978. During the next ten years, he was a member of the technical staff in the Computer Science Branch at the General Electric Corporate Research and Development Center, Schenectady, NY. In 1989, he joined the technical staff of the Supercomputing Research Center, Bowie, MD, where he is currently a member of the Algorithms Group. His research interests include interconnection networks, parallel algorithms, massive parallelism, and computational complexity.

Dr. Fiduccia is a member of the IEEE Computer Society, the Association for Computing Machinery, and the Society for Industrial and Applied Mathematics.

Chapter 3: Topologies

A network is usually modeled by a graph, called the *network topology*, where the edges represent communication links and the nodes represent either processors or switches. A network is either *static* or *dynamic*. In a static (or fixed) network, the nodes represent processors. Examples of static networks include rings, trees, meshes, tori, and hypercubes. In a dynamic (or reconfigurable) network, the nodes represent switches. Multistage interconnection networks are prime examples of dynamic networks and include the omega, inverse omega, indirect binary n-cube, and baseline networks.

In the design of static networks, the various considerations that must be weighed include those listed below.

- The node degree, which represents the number of I/O ports per processing node, should be small.
- The diameter and the average distance, which represent the worst-case and average-case node-to-node communication delay in packet-switched systems, respectively, should be kept minimal.
- The network topology should be rich enough to efficiently embed several frequently used topologies that model the communication patterns of parallel algorithms.
- The topology should be regular to allow for fast distributed routing.

Other aspects that may be considered include

- the partitionability of the network into subnetworks for the support of multiusers and multitasking,
- the network fault-tolerance capabilities essential to system reliability, and
- the VLSI implementation cost.

In the design of dynamic networks, similar considerations, listed below, must be taken into account.

- The routing control complexity, the communication latency, and the hardware cost measured in numbers of switches or in VLSI area should all be minimal.
- The communication capabilities, expressed in both the type and number of realizable permutations in synchronous systems and the bandwidth in asynchronous systems, should be high.
- Partitionability and good fault-tolerance capabilities are desirable.

In the 1960s, and especially in the 1970s and the early 1980s, many static and dynamic topologies — such as the ones mentioned above — were introduced and studied.[1] In the last several years, new networks have appeared. These networks have the following three distinctive characteristics:

- For the most part, the new networks are static.
- Many of the new networks are enhanced versions, generalizations, or syntheses of old topologies.
- Several large network classes have been introduced that encompass old and new networks and are underpinned by well-founded, unified mathematical theories.

The papers included in this chapter feature a representative selection of new networks. The first three papers, by Akers, Harel, and Krishnamurthy (1987), Samatham and Pradhan (1989), and Leiserson (1985), present three topologies: the star graph, the De Bruijn network, and the fat-tree. The final three papers, by Youssef and Narahari (1990), Kilian, Kipnis, and Leiserson (1990), and Dally (1991), introduce and study synthesized networks.

Reference

1. C. Wu and T. Feng, *Tutorial: Interconnection Networks for Parallel and Distributed Processing*, IEEE CS Press, Los Alamitos, Calif., 1984.

The Star Graph: An Attractive Alternative to the n-Cube

Sheldon B. Akers
Dept. of Elec. & Comp. Engr.
University of Massachusetts
Amherst, MA 01003

Dov Harel
Computer Research Lab.
Tektronix Laboratories
Beaverton, OR 97077

Balakrishnan Krishnamurthy
Computer Research Lab.
Tektronix Laboratories
Beaverton, OR 97077

ABSTRACT

In this paper we present a new interconnection topology, the *star graph*, and compare it to the widely used n-cube. Like the n-cube, the star graph is shown to possess rich structure and symmetry properties as well as many desirable fault tolerant characteristics. In addition, with regard to the important properties of degree and diameter the star graph is shown to be markedly superior. A number of optimal algorithms on the star graph, which exploit its versatility, are presented and analyzed. Finally the inherent simplicity of the n-cube is weighed against the indicated advantages of the star graph.

1. Introduction

In the design of a large multi-processor computing system one of the primary design decisions involves the topology of the communication structure amongst the processors. In the past designers have restricted their attention to simple interconnection topologies such as linear arrays (vector machines), two dimensional arrays (Goodyear's MPP) and circular rings (a distributed network over an ethernet). More recently, with the advent of VLSI, a number of projects have been initiated to design large multi-processor systems with more sophisticated interconnection topologies. In fact, with the availability of faster processors and larger memories on a single chip, such multi-processor systems using non-trivial topologies and off the shelf components are now commercially available. In this paper a new sophisticated topology will be described.

The most popular non-trivial topology currently in use is the Boolean n-cube [3, 15, 17]. Its popularity stems from the fact that a large number of processors (2^n processors) can be interconnected using a small number of communication links (n links per processor) while at the same time keeping the communication delay between processors at a minimum. In addition the n-cube is a completely symmetric topology and, consequently, minimizes congestion problems. It also permits the use of identical processors since every vertex plays an identical role in the topology. The n-cube has a very simple and optimal routing algorithm that routes messages between processors along a shortest path. This enables the design of low-cost routing hardware. Other attractive features of the n-cube includes our familiarity and understanding of the topology, particularly the recursive decomposition structure of the n-cube into successive cubes of lower dimensions.

There are also a number of other fault tolerant properties of the n-cube that make it very attractive. Due to the multitude of paths between vertices the n-cube not only possesses optimal fault tolerance properties but provides little or no degradation of performance in the presence of (a tolerable number of) faults. Even when an intolerable number of failures do occur, causing the topology to become disconnected, we are guaranteed to find a large segment of the n-cube still intact. Additionally a number of algorithms have been designed to run on the n-cube. These algorithms have demonstrated the usefulness of the structure and symmetry properties inherent in the graph and how they may be exploited.

Considering this list of attractive properties of the n-cube its popularity is not surprising. However, in [1] it was pointed out that many of these properties of the n-cube are, in fact, group theoretic properties possessed by a large class of networks called Cayley graphs [1, 7]. In fact, it was shown that some Cayley graphs not only possess all these properties but even offer a better degree and diameter than the n-cube. One such graph is the *star graph*.

In this paper we will define the star graph and exploit the rich symmetry in the star graph to demonstrate many of its attractive properties. In particular, we shall examine routing techniques, algorithm implementation procedures and fault tolerance considerations. Finally, we will compare the star graph with the n cube and argue that the star graph is an attractive alternative.

2. Background

Throughout this paper we will view an interconnection network as an undirected graph. The vertices of the graph correspond to processors and the edges of the graph correspond to communication links between processors. A graph is *regular* if the degree of every vertex in the graph is the same. The *degree of a regular graph* is then the degree of any of its vertices. The *diameter* of a graph is the maximum distance between any pair of vertices in the graph. Clearly, the degree of a graph is a measure of the cost of the interconnection network and the diameter is a measure of the communication delay. Consequently, it is desirable to construct a large graph with small degree and small diameter.

A graph is *vertex symmetric* if the graph looks the same from each of its vertices. More formally, given any two vertices a and b there is an automorphism of the graph that maps a to b. Similarly, a graph is *edge symmetric* if every edge looks the same, i.e., given any two edges x and y there is an automorphism of the graph that maps x to y. Such symmetry properties of a graph are very important when viewed as an interconnection network. For example, a vertex symmetric graph allows for all the processors to be identical. Similarly, a vertex/edge symmetric graph minimizes vertices/edges of congestion when messages are routed in the graph.

As mentioned, we will also be concerned with the fault tolerance properties of these networks. Consequently, we must define the fault tolerance of a graph. A graph is said to be f-*fault tolerant* if whenever f or fewer vertices are removed from the graph the remaining graph always remains connected. The *fault tolerance* of a graph is defined to be the largest f for which it is f-fault tolerant. The reader familiar with the notion of connectivity in graph theory will observe that the fault tolerance of a graph is precisely one less than its connectivity. Let us observe that if all the neighbors of a chosen vertex in a graph are removed then the chosen vertex will be disconnected from the remainder of the graph. Thus, the fault tolerance of a graph can at most be $d-1$, where d is the degree of the graph. A graph whose fault tolerance is exactly $d-1$ is said to be *maximally fault tolerant*.

When a graph is used as an interconnection network it is essential that we have a simple routing algorithm to route messages from one vertex to another. In fact, it is desirable that this routing algorithm produce a path of minimal length between the two vertices. In addition, if the fault tolerance properties of the graph are to be effectively utilized then we must also have a fault tolerant routing algorithm. That is, an algorithm that, in the presence of at most f faults (where f is the fault tolerance of the graph), will find a path between two non-faulty vertices. The *fault diameter* of a graph G with fault tolerance f is the maximum diameter of any graph obtained from G by deleting at most f vertices. Clearly, if the fault diameter of G is very close to its normal diameter then the performance of G, in terms of the communication delay, does not drastically worsen in the presence of a tolerable number of faults. Motivated by this observation, a family of graphs G_n is defined to be *strongly resilient* (see [11]) if the fault diameter of G_n is at most $k_n + c$, where k_n is the normal diameter of G_n and c is a fixed constant independent of n.

Having defined all these terms for a general family of graphs, let us look specifically at the n-cube. Recall that the n-cube is a graph on 2^n vertices each labeled by an n-bit vector. It is a regular graph of degree n and diameter n. Observe that the degree and diameter are both logarithmic in the size of the graph. It is easily seen that the n-cube is both vertex and edge symmetric. Thus, it provides for uniform congestion on both the vertices and the edges. It is well known that the connectivity of the n-cube is also n. Thus, its fault tolerance is $n-1$, and hence it is maximally fault tolerant. Further, it has been shown in [11] that the fault diameter of the n-cube is $n+1$. Therefore, the n-cubes, as a family of graphs, is strongly resilient.

In the next section we will define the star graph and address similar properties of that graph.

3. The Star Graph

Consider the following puzzle: Five markers labeled A, B, C, D and E are placed arbitrarily on the five numbered vertices (one marker per vertex) of the tree shown in Figure 1. Through a series of interchanges of adjacent markers we are to bring the markers to their respective positions, i.e., marker A to vertex 1, marker B to vertex 2, etc. Can this always be done? How many moves would it take in the worst case?

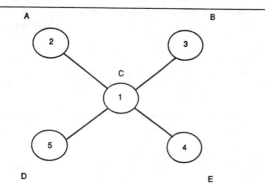

Figure 1: A Star Tree.

Before we examine these questions let us point out that the initial configuration of the 5 markers, (or, for that matter, any intermediate configuration of the 5 markers) can be viewed as a permutation of the symbols A, B, C, D and E. For example the initial configuration shown in Figure 1 is $CABED$. Correspondingly, the desired final configuration of the 5 markers is the *identity permutation* (or, the sorted permutation) $ABCDE$. Thus, we wish to find a minimal sequence of permutations starting with $CABED$ and ending with $ABCDE$, such that every intermediate permutation is obtained from the previous one by interchanging the first symbol with any one of the other four symbols.

Observe that this problem readily generalizes to n markers. The state of the puzzle will be represented by a permutation on n symbols. We will use the symbols A, B, C, etc. as the symbols being permuted. Since we will need to refer to the last symbol we will use Z to mean the last symbol (not necessarily the 26th symbol). Thus, the identity permutation on n symbols is $ABC \cdots Z$. The permissible moves of the general puzzle corresponds to interchanging the symbol in the first position with any one of the other symbols. Thus, any permutation can be transformed into any one of $n-1$ permutations in one move.

The n-star graph, S_n, is obtained by drawing the state transition graph for the puzzle with n markers. That is, S_n has $n!$ vertices corresponding to the $n!$ permutations of the n symbols. There is an edge from one permutation to another if and only if there is a move of the puzzle that will take that one permutation into the other. (Note that these edges are undirected.) Clearly, every vertex has $n-1$ incident edges, corresponding to the $n-1$ symbols that the symbol in the first position can interchange with. Thus, S_n is regular of degree $n-1$. In fact, it has been shown in [1] that S_n is

vertex symmetric as well as edge symmetric. Furthermore, since each edge connects an odd permutation with an even permutation, S_n is bipartite. The reader is encouraged to convince himself of these facts. The graph S_3 is shown in Figure 2.

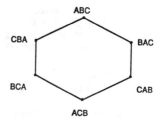

Figure 2: The 3-Star: A Hexagon

Now let us return to the problem posed in the beginning of this section. The maximum number of moves that any permutation will take is the distance of the furthest vertex from the identity vertex in S_n. But since S_n is vertex symmetric, this is exactly the diameter of S_n. We will find not only the diameter of S_n but will also show an optimal routing algorithm for S_n.

Let us examine how we might route within S_n. As noted, it is sufficient to route from an arbitrary permutation to the identity permutation, i.e., to sort an arbitrary permutation. For example, consider the permutation $FDGBEHCA$ on 8 symbols. Let us employ a greedy algorithm where we observe that the symbol in the first position, namely F, can be moved to its correct position by interchanging F with H. This gives us the permutation $HDGBEFCA$. Again, a greedy move gives us $ADGBEFCH$. Now we are stuck, since A is already at its own position. Accordingly, we must now take an extra step to move A into any position not occupied by the correct symbol. In this case we could interchange A with D yielding the permutation $DAGBEFCH$. Now again following the greedy approach we obtain $BAGDEFCH$ and subsequently $ABGDEFCH$. Once again we need to take an extra step to insert A into a position not occupied by the correct symbol. Thus, interchanging A with G gives $GBADEFCH$. Returning back to the greedy step gives $CBADEFGH$ and the final move to $ABCDEFGH$. Notice that we took 8 moves to sort this permutation. That means that in the graph S_n we have shown a path of length 8 between $FDGBEHCA$ and the identity permutation.

Of course, this does not establish the diameter of S_n. For that we must find the permutation that requires the maximum number of steps to sort. But first we will compute the exact number of steps needed to sort an arbitrary permutation and show that this is an optimal routing algorithm. We do this in the next section.

4. Routing on the Star Graph

Note that just two rules were involved in finding this path:

1. if A is first, move it to any position not occupied by the correct symbol, and
2. if X (i.e., any symbol other than A) is first, move it to its position.

Not only will these rules insure a minimum length path, but they will also allow us to calculate the length of this path by simply examining the permutation involved.

Recall that any permutation can be viewed as a set of cycles - i.e., cyclically order sets of symbols with the property that each symbol's desired position is that occupied by the next symbol in the set. The permutation, $FDGBEHCA$, considered above, for example, consists of the cycles: (FHA), (DB), (GC), and (E). Note that any symbol already in the correct position (e.g., E) appears as a 1-cycle.

Now for a given permutation, π let c denote the number of cycles of length at least 2, and m the total number of symbols in these cycles – i.e., the number of symbols not in their correct positions. The minimum distance $d(\pi)$, from π to the identity permutation will be given by:

Theorem 1: The minimum distance $d(\pi)$, from π to the identity permutation is given by:

$$d(\pi) = c + m - \begin{cases} 0 \text{ if } A \text{ is first} \\ 2 \text{ if } A \text{ is not first} \end{cases}$$

With the previous permutation, for example, $c=3$ and $m=7$ (with F first) giving $3+7-2=8$ steps, as already seen. The proof of this theorem follows form Table I which summarizes the basic routing rules and shows how c, m and d change for the various cases. (M is used to denote any symbol not in the correct position; Y is a symbol other than X or A.) Note that when X is in the first position, we do not necessarily have to use the *greedy* approach of taking X immediately to its desired position. We can in fact interchange it with any M not in its cycle. This turns out to be an especially useful rule when routing in the presence of faults.

Before turning to a consideration of the diameter of the star graph, it may be instructive to restate Theorem 1 in terms which are more familiar to the group theorist. In particular, for a given permutation, π, let $\psi(\pi)$ be the total number of invariances (i.e., symbols in the correct position) and $\eta(\pi)$ be the total number of cycles - including invariances. It then follows that for m and c as defined above, $m = n - \psi(\pi)$ and $c = \eta(\pi) - \psi(\pi)$. Substituting into Theorem 1 gives:

Theorem 2:

$$d(\pi) = n + \eta(\pi) - 2\psi(\pi) - \begin{cases} 0 \text{ if } A \text{ is first} \\ 2 \text{ if } A \text{ is not first} \end{cases}$$

Now let us consider the diameter, k_n, of the star graph. As already noted this will be simply the maximum value obtainable by $d(\pi)$. Examining Theorem 1, we see that when A is first, it follows that $m \le n - 1$ and $c \le (n-1)/2$ so that $d \le \left\lfloor \dfrac{3(n-1)}{2} \right\rfloor$. With X first, $m \le n$ and $c \le n/2$ so that $d \le \left\lfloor \dfrac{3n-4}{2} \right\rfloor$. Thus the worst case occurs with permutations having A first giving:

Theorem 3: The diameter k_n of the star graph S_n is $\left\lfloor \dfrac{3(n-1)}{2} \right\rfloor$.

Symbol in First Position	Rule	New Symbol in First Position	Δc	Δm	Δd
A	Swap A with any M	X	0	+1	−1
X	(1) Swap X to its position	A	−1	−2	−1
X	(1) Swap X to its position	Y	0	−1	−1
X	(2) Swap X with M in another cycle	Y	−1	0	−1

Table 1. Star Graph Routing Rules

Using Theorem 2 we can also obtain the average distance between two randomly chosen vertices in S_n. A proof of this theorem can be found in [1].

Theorem 4: The average distance $\hat{k}_n$ of the star graph S_n is $n + \dfrac{2}{n} + H_n - 4$, where H_n is the n-th Harmonic number, i.e., $H_n = \sum_{i=1}^{n} \dfrac{1}{i}$.

It is interesting to compare the degree and diameter of the n-star graph against that of an appropriate n-cube. Whereas the n-cube interconnects 2^n vertices using a degree of n and providing a diameter of n, the n-star graph interconnects $n!$ vertices using a degree of $n-1$ and yielding a diameter of $\left\lfloor \dfrac{3}{2}(n-1) \right\rfloor$. In other words, whereas the degree and diameter of the n-cube is logarithmic in the size of the n-cube, the degree and diameter of S_n is sub-logarithmic in its size. Thus, asymptotically, the star graph offers a network with less interconnecting edges and smaller communication delays than the n-cube. Looking ahead, Table 2 provides a comparison of various n-cubes against comparable n-star graphs. Even from a practical point of view, it is evident from Table 2 that purely based on the degree and diameter requirements the star graph is superior.

5. Structure of the Star Graph

Let us now look more closely at the structure of the n-star graph. Observe that if the symbol in the last position is held fixed, say with the last symbol, i.e., Z, then there are $(n-1)!$ permutations and they with all the other permissible interchanges will constitute an $(n-1)$-star graph. In fact, if the symbol in the last position is held fixed with any symbol whatsoever we will still get $(n-1)!$ permutations that are interconnected in a manner identical to an $(n-1)$-star graph. Thus, the vertices of S_n can be partitioned into n groups, each containing $(n-1)!$ vertices, based on the symbol in the last position. Each such group will be isomorphic to S_{n-1}. These groups will be interconnected by edges corresponding to interchanging the symbol in the first position with the symbol in the last position. A representation of S_4 as 4 interconnected copies of S_3 is shown in Figure 3. We might point out that in that figure as well as others in this paper we have indicated certain edges by labeled arrows. Edges connecting pairs of vertices with similarly labeled arrows are intended.

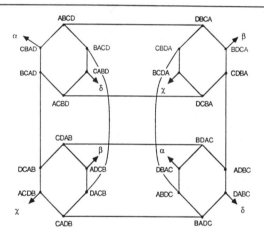

Figure 3: The 4-Star: 4 Interconnected Hexagons

The reader familiar with group theory will observe that the permutations in S_{n-1} form a subgroup of the permutations in S_n. Correspondingly, the n copies of S_{n-1} that we find within S_n are merely the subgroup and its cosets. The fact that the cosets are isomorphic to the subgroup itself is easily seen group theoretically. A more detailed account of such a group theoretic view can be found in [1].

Recall that the n-cube can be viewed as 2 interconnected copies of $(n-1)$-cubes. Our decomposition of S_n into n interconnected copies of S_{n-1} is very analogous. In fact, like the n-cube S_n can be decomposed into S_{n-1}'s along any one of its dimensions. That is, instead of fixing the symbol in the last position we could fix the symbol in any position 2 through n. Let us denote by E_3 the induced subgraph consisting of all the permutations containing E in the third position. More generally, we will denote by X_i the induced subgraph consisting of all the permutations that contain X

in the i-th position. It is easily seen that for $2 \leq i \leq n$ the subgraph X_i is isomorphic to S_{n-1}. Thus, for each of the $n-1$ values of i we can get a decomposition of S_n by looking at the $(n-1)$-star graph defined by the symbol in the i-th position. Thus, the decomposition based on the symbol in the last position partitions the vertices of S_n into $A_n, B_n, \cdots Z_n$. Notice that this decomposition can be carried on recursively, again as in the n-cube.

Let us now look at an orthogonal partition of the vertices of S_n. This time we will partition them into $A_1, A_2, \cdots A_n$. As observed earlier, the subgraphs $A_2 \cdots A_n$ will each be isomorphic to S_{n-1}. However, it is somewhat surprising to note that A_1 is a collection of $(n-1)!$ isolated vertices! This is because for any permutation in A_1 an interchange of the symbol in the first position with any other symbol will necessarily result in a permutation outside A_1. More strikingly, every vertex in A_1 is connected to a vertex in each of the sets $A_2 \cdots A_n$. Thus, the vertices of A_1 can be viewed as *stars* with $n-1$ edges leading to the $n-1$ satellites. A representation of S_4 in this view is provided in Figure 4. Note the three hexagons interconnected by a set of six independent vertices at the center.

Once again, this orthogonal decomposition can be achieved using any symbol, not necessarily A. Thus, the decomposition of S_n into $X_1, X_2 \cdots X_n$ will result in the same picture, but with a different grouping. Incidentally, it is worth noting that X_1 forms both a *maximal independent set* as well as a *minimal dominating set* for S_n. The flexibility in decomposing the star graph along any one of its dimensions in one of two orthogonal ways is due to the rich symmetry present in the definition of the star graph. This flexibility has been used extensively in demonstrating fault tolerant properties in the star graph, which we do in the next section.

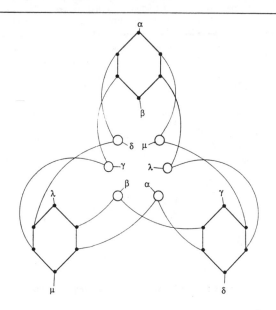

Figure 4: The 4-Star: 3 Interconnected Hexagons and a Dominating Set

6. Fault Tolerance of the Star Graph

A vital consideration in the analysis of any large interconnection network is its fault tolerance - i.e., its ability to function effectively in the presence of various faults which may appear. As noted earlier, this in fact is one of the especially significant features of the n-cube. Accordingly, if the star graph is to be considered as a viable alternative to the n-cube, it is certainly necessary that its corresponding fault tolerant properties be discussed. In [2] a number of these properties have been formally derived and examined, so that here we shall simply enumerate these findings with particular emphasis on their relation to corresponding properties of the n-cube.

Underlying almost all fault tolerant considerations is of course the basic notion of *connectivity*. Given that various faults are present, do the non-faulty processors become isolated from one another or can they continue to operate in a coherent fashion? As already defined in Section 2, the notion of maximal fault tolerance quantifies this concept. Like the n-cube, the star graph is also maximally fault tolerant. (In fact it is one of the large class of *hierarchical* graphs which all possess this important feature.) Moreover, the above routing rules can be easily modified to accommodate this faulty situation. (In [2] both *static* and *dynamic* routing strategies are given - i.e., procedures for routing when either global or only local knowledge of the faults is available.)

Likewise, the star graph is *strongly resilient* as defined earlier. Specifically, it is shown in [2] that its diameter increases by at most 3 (and we suspect less). Thus, even when faults are present in a star graph its increased (fault) diameter may still be better than the fault-free diameter of an n-cube of comparable size. (See Table 2, for example.)

Of equal interest, of course, is the performance of a network when the number of faults increases beyond the *optimally fault tolerant* case discussed above. What claims can be made when f is $\geq d-1$? Does the network essentially *fall apart* or can we still expect a large number of non-faulty processors to remain connected. With the star graph, S_n, it has been found that as long as f remains less than $(n-1)(n-2)$ then at most $3f$ vertices will become disconnected from the rest of the graph. In other words, the graph, whose original size was $n!$, now *degrades gracefully* into a non-faulty component of at least $n!-3f$ vertices.

While even one fault in an n-star will degrade its overall performance, there will remain embedded within the n-star a myriad of "sub-stars" which are still individually fault-free. Accordingly, it is of interest to examine not only the number of such structures, but also their susceptibility to various faults. As observed earlier, if in S_n we limit our attention to only those vertices in which a specific symbol (say E) is fixed in a specific position other than the first (say the third), then these E_3-vertices and their shared edges will constitute and $(n-1)$-star. Since there are n symbols and $n-1$ positions, it follows that any n-star contains $n(n-1)$ copies of S_{n-1}.

Figure 5 shows a drawing of the 4-star in which all 12 3-stars (i.e., hexagons) are identified. Observe that 7 of the 12 hexagons appear intact in Figure 5 while the remaining 5 seem to appear in pieces since many of the edges have not been drawn in. Notice that the permutation associated with any vertex can be identified by considering the three hexagons incident at that vertex, since each hexagon contains all 6 permutations that fix a specific symbol in a specific position. Thus, for example, the identity permutation, $ABCD$ lies at the meeting of the B_2, C_3 and D_4 hexagons.

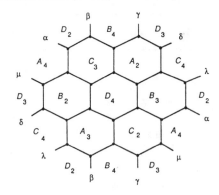

Figure 5: The 4-Star: 12 Embedded Hexagons

By an argument similar to the above we see that if p symbols are fixed then an $n-p$ star results. Clearly, the p positions can be chosen in $\binom{n-1}{p}$

different ways and the p symbols in $\frac{n!}{(n-p)!}$ different ways. Thus, the number of $(n-p)$-stars in an S_n is:

$$\binom{n-1}{p} \frac{n!}{(n-p)!}$$

Given that an n-star contains f faults, what can we say about the number of these *sub-stars* which will also be faulty - i.e., will contain one or more of the f faulty vertices? Becker and Simon [5] have addressed this problem for the n-cube. Using their notation, we will define $f(n,p)$ to be the minimum number of faults necessary to make every $(n-p)$-star faulty.

In other words, the existence of a fault-free $(n-p)$-star is guaranteed as long as the number of faults remains below $f(n,p)$. Using the above formula, for the number of $(n-p)$-stars, a lower bound on $f(n,p)$ is easily obtained. We have only to observe that any single fault - i.e., a faulty vertex, appears in precisely $\binom{n-1}{p}$ $(n-p)$-stars. Thus it follows that

Theorem 5: $f(n,p) \geq \dfrac{n!}{(n-p)!}$

Thus we see that if we view an n-star – not as an entity unto itself – but rather as an interconnection network for a large set of sub-stars, then the fault tolerance of this structure could be quite significant.

7. Algorithms on the Star Graph

A processor interconnection network would be of little value if we could not run algorithms whose computation is distributed over the vertices of the network. Of course, some algorithms rely primarily on the existence of short paths between vertices. For such algorithms any graph that has a small diameter (or average distance) will suffice. Clearly, the star graph is not only a prime candidate, but even shines over the n-cube. More interestingly, other algorithms exploit the structure and symmetry properties of the graph. In this section we will develop such algorithms for some fundamental problems. In fact, the algorithms that we will show all rely on a binary tree that we will indicate in the star graph. But first let us establish the framework for describing parallel algorithms on a general graph.

Consider an undirected graph whose edges are edge-colored[1] from an alphabet of colors. A parallel algorithm on this graph consists of a sequence of colors together with a sequential algorithm to be executed by each processor at each time step. The execution of the parallel algorithm will take as many time steps as the length of the sequence of colors. At each time step, i, each processor will execute the sequential algorithm which might involve communicating with its neighboring processor along the edge colored with the i-th color in the sequence. Of course, the sequential algorithm to be executed at each time step must involve a bounded amount of computation.

Let us illustrate the above view of a parallel algorithm by a well known example on the n-cube. Consider the *broadcasting problem* which consists of broadcasting a piece of information resident at one processor on the cube to all other processors on the cube. Let the cube be edge-colored in the natural way, with the color i, $1 \leq i \leq n$, used for the edges along the i-th dimension of the cube, i.e., that change the i-th bit. Consider the sequence $1\ 2\ 3\ \cdots\ n$. At the i-th time step each processor communicates with its neighbor along the i-th dimension and compares notes on whether either of them have received the information that is being broadcasted. If neither has so far received it then no information is exchanged. If one has received it and the other has not then the information is relaid to the uninformed processor. We claim that at the end of the parallel algorithm (i.e., after n time steps) all the processors will have received the broadcasted information. To establish this observe that given any two vertices on the n-cube, there is a subsequence[2] of the above sequence that forms a path

from the first to the second. Consequently, for every processor a of the n-cube there is a subsequence of the above sequence that forms a path from the processor originating the broadcast to the processor a. That establishes the claim for the n-cube.

In fact, we can prove a general theorem:

Theorem 6: Consider a graph whose edges are edge-colored. A sequence σ constitutes a broadcasting algorithm if and only if for every pair of vertices there exists a subsequence that forms a path from one vertex to the other.
Proof: If the sequence has the stated property then it forms a broadcasting algorithm by an argument similar to the one above. Conversely, if the sequence constitutes a broadcasting algorithm then for any two vertices we can always find a subsequence that forms a path between them by broadcasting from one vertex and analyzing how the information arrived at the other vertex. □

We are now ready to describe a similar algorithm on the star graph S_n. Our first order of business is to edge-color S_n. We choose the natural coloring involving the $n-1$ colors $2, 3, \ldots, n$. An edge corresponding to an interchange of the i-th symbol in the permutation with the first symbol is colored with the color i. The reader will note that this is indeed an edge-coloring.

We now need to construct a sequence σ with the property stated in Theorem 6. In fact, we need not consider every pair of vertices. We can exploit the vertex symmetry of S_n to argue that it suffices to show that for any permutation a there is a subsequence of σ that sorts a. For then, we would have established a path from the arbitrary vertex a to the identity, and by symmetry we can claim a path from a to any other vertex.

Let us suggest one such sequence albeit somewhat long. Consider a sequence that enumerates the alphabet of colors, in any order, as many times as the diameter of S_n. Thus, the sequence would look like

$$2\ 3\ \cdots\ n\ 2\ 3\ \cdots\ n\ \cdots\ 2\ 3\ \cdots\ n \quad (k_n \text{ times}).$$

Clearly, any permutation can be sorted by a subsequence (of length at most k_n). We can trivially improve this algorithm to yield

$$2\ 3\ \cdots\ n\ (n-1)(n-2)\ \cdots\ 3\ 2\ 3\ 4\ \cdots\ n\ (n-1)(n-2)\ \cdots\ (k_n \text{ times}).$$

In either case this sequence yields an $O(n^2)$ algorithm, since the (parallel) time complexity of the algorithm is proportional to the length of the sequence.

At this point we observe:

Theorem 7: Any broadcasting algorithm on a graph on N vertices must require a sequence of length $\log N$.
Proof: Note that by the nature of the algorithm at every time step the number of processors that have received the information being broadcasted can at most double. The theorem follows. □

By the above theorem the suggested algorithm on the n-cube is optimal but the above algorithm on S_n is not optimal. In order to find an optimal broadcasting algorithm on S_n we must find an $O(n \log n)$ sequence σ such that every permutation can be sorted by a subsequence of σ.

Let us digress to establish a connection with a classical problem in permutation networks. We first observe that a path of the form $3\ 4\ 3$ in S_n leads from one permutation to another in which only the symbols in the third and fourth positions have been interchanged. More generally, any pair of symbols within a permutation can be interchanged using at most three star operations. Consequently, if we can find a sequence τ, using pairwise interchanges of symbols, that meets the conditions of Theorem 6 then we can emulate τ using a sequence σ of star operations, whose length is at most three times that of τ.

Motivated by this, we consider a *permutation network* (see [8, 19]) — a directed acyclic graph with n sources, n sinks and a collection of 2-input, 2-output binary switches as internal vertices[3]. By setting the switches in different ways one can achieve a permutation of the n inputs at the n outputs. In fact, the definition requires that in a permutation network each of the $n!$ permutations is achievable by an appropriate setting of the

---

[1] An edge-coloring requires that two edges incident at a vertex be colored with distinct colors.

[2] A subsequence need not necessarily be a contiguous subsequence.

switches. A 4-input permutation network is shown in Figure 6 and is taken from [9].

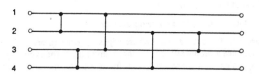

Figure 6: A 4-input Sorting Network.

Returning to the sequence that we wished to construct, the network of Figure 6 yields a sequence τ (of pairwise interchanges of symbols) of length 5:

$$(1,2)\ (3,4)\ (1,3)\ (2,4)\ (2,3)$$

This sequence yields the sequence σ on the original alphabet of colors:

$$2\ \ 3\,4\,3\ \ 3\ \ 2\,4\,2\ \ 2\,3\,2$$

We have indicated the grouping of elements in the above sequence to indicate its relationship to the previous sequence. Note that (in general) each element of the τ sequence, such as the (3,4) interchange, gives rise to three elements in the σ sequence, namely 3 4 3. However, the interchanges with the symbol in the first position, such as (1,2), in τ are themselves edges in S_n, and hence can be emulated in σ using a single element, namely 2. We can optimize this sequence by observing the *idempotency rule* that two consecutive occurrence of any symbol can be replaced by one occurrence of that symbol[4] There are two places in the above sequence where this rule can be applied, giving the 9 element sequence σ

$$2\,3\,4\,3\,2\,4\,2\,3\,2$$

The diligent reader can convince himself by examining Figure 3 that for every permutation there is a subsequence of the 9 element sequence σ given above that sorts that permutation, i.e., provides a path to the identity element. Hence, σ constitutes a broadcasting algorithm for S_4.

From the above example it is easily seen that an $O(n \log n)$ permutation network will provide an $O(n \log n)$ broadcasting algorithm for S_n. We can now appeal to the construction of such $O(n \log n)$ permutation networks reported in [4,6]. For the sake of completeness we provide such a network, together with a proof.

Consider the switching network of Figure 7 on 8 inputs. This network has been drawn indicating the cross connections of the switches, instead of the switches as boxes as in Figure 6. A generalization of this network to any power of 2 is readily seen, and we will call the network with n inputs T_n. Thus, Figure 7 shows T_8. Note that T_8 has 20 switches. In general, it is easily seen:

Theorem 8: T_n has $n \log n - \frac{n}{2}$ switches.

We now show:

Theorem 9: For every n which is a power of 2, every permutation of n elements can be sorted through an appropriate setting of the switches in T_n.

Proof: By induction on n. The basis step ($n=2$) consists of a single switch and requires no proof. Inductively, let T_{n-1} have the stated property. Let the n inputs to the network be a permutation of the numbers 0 through $n-1$ and the desired n outputs to be the sorted permutations with the smaller numbers on top. Observe that the first stage of T_n consists of $\frac{n}{2}$ switches connecting the 0-th input with the $(\frac{n}{2})$-th input, the 1-st input with the

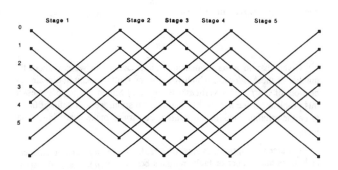

Figure 7: An *n log n* Switching Network.

$(\frac{n}{2}+1)$-th input, etc. We will call these pairs of numbers *conjugate pairs*. Note that the $\log n - 1$ least significant bits in the binary representation of conjugate pairs are always the same.

Our first claim is that using these $\frac{n}{2}$ switches we can switch any set of inputs so that every conjugate pair is distributed with one element in the top half and the other in the bottom half. To show this let us simply show an algorithm. Consider the element 0. Having determined which half it is in, check to see if its conjugate is in the opposite half. If not switch the conjugate to the opposite half and consider the other number that automatically got switched. Proceeding along in this manner the algorithm must come to a situation where the conjugate of an element being considered is in the correct half. At that point we have reduced the number of elements yet to be considered and we can recursively apply the algorithm.

The above claim ensures that after the first stage of T_n we can consider two sub-problems each of $\frac{n}{2}$ in size, one in the top half and the other in the bottom half. Further the numbers in each half can be viewed to range from 0 to $\frac{n}{2}-1$ by considering only the $\log n - 1$ least significant bits. Thus, by the inductive hypothesis we can sort each sub-problem using the second through the last but one stage. Observe that having done that not only will each conjugate pair be in the two different halves, they will in fact line up with each other, i.e., they will either be in their right places or will be in each other's places. Consequently the last stage is then sufficient to complete the sorting of the n elements. $\square$

We now resort to the construction of σ from this switching network analogous to our construction using the sorting networks. We write the set of switches for T_n in a linear order. (Any topological ordering of the switches will do.) This gives us a sequence τ. We then emulate every element of this sequence using (up to) three of the star moves to get the sequence σ. This gives us the following theorem:

Theorem 10: There is a sequence of length at most $3(n \log n - \frac{n}{2})$ that constitutes a broadcasting algorithm on S_n.

Proof: We have shown this result for values of n that are powers of 2. For other values of n it suffices to draw the switching network described above for the next power of 2 and delete from that network all those switches that involve elements beyond the first n. We leave it to the reader to verify that the resulting network will sort any input permutation. It is easily seen that the bound on the number of switches also holds. $\square$

Let us illustrate this with an example. Consider the 6-star graph S_6. We use the network T_8 (shown in Figure 7) and delete the switches involving elements other than the first 6. The resulting linear list of the remaining switches gives the following sequence τ of 11 elements corresponding to the 11 remaining switches:

$$(1,5)\ (2,6)\ (1,3)\ (2,4)\ (1,2)\ (3,4)\ (5,6)\ (1,3)\ (2,4)\ (1,5)\ (2,6)$$

---

[3] These are distinct from *sorting networks* (see [9] pp.220-235) where comparators are used in place of the switches and consequently provide less flexibility.

[4] There are other optimization techniques, such as replacing any occurrence of $i\ j\ i$ by $j\ i\ j$, that we will not discuss or employ here.

Replacing the switches by star operations we get the following sequence σ of 23 elements:

5 262 3 242 2 343 565 3 242 5 262

Applying the idempotency rule mentioned above we get the reduced sequence σ of 22 elements:

5 2 6 2 3 2 4 2 3 4 3 5 6 5 5 3 2 4 2 5 2 6 2

The above sequence constitutes a broadcasting algorithm for S_6.

In the beginning of the section we mentioned that we will exploit the ability to construct a binary tree on the star graph to develop efficient algorithms for a variety of problems. We claim that the broadcasting algorithm mentioned above has, in effect, constructed a binary tree on the $n!$ vertices of S_n. It is the depth of that binary tree that yields the $O(n \log n)$ bound on the length of the sequence. However, space constraints restrict an explicit exposition of the tree.

Instead, we will show similar algorithms for two other problems. The broadcasting algorithm can be directly used to compute the maximum of $n!$ numbers distributed at the vertices of S_n. Here we use the same sequence, but the sequential algorithm executed by each processor at each step is slightly different. Instead of comparing notes and relaying the information being broadcasted as in the broadcasting algorithm, here the two processors compare notes and determine the largest number that has been encountered between the two of them. It is easy to see that once again we will obtain an equally short algorithm as the broadcasting algorithm.

Generalizing this notion, we can compute the product of any associative operation on $n!$ elements distributed over the vertices of S_n, using a similar algorithm (see [12]). In fact, we can compute all the products of prefixes of a linearly ordered list of $n!$ elements distributed over S_n. In other words, suppose $n!$ numbers $X_1, X_2, \ldots, X_{n!}$ are distributed on the vertices of S_n, with processor i holding X_i. We require processor i to compute the sum of $X_1, X_2, \ldots, X_i$. To do this we will have to run the broadcasting sequence twice, once forward and once backward. It would amount to going up the tree and then down. We leave the (non-trivial) details of this algorithm to the inquisitive reader.

8. Conclusion and Open Problems

In this paper we have examined a new network interconnection topology - the star graph - and have compared its basic properties with those of the ubiquitous n-cube. Like the n-cube, the star graph has been shown to be vertex symmetric, edge symmetric, bipartite, strongly hierarchical, maximally fault tolerant, and strongly resilient. In addition, both topologies exhibit graceful degradation as well as other attractive fault tolerant properties.

Many of these properties of both the n-cube and the star graph result from their symmetry and structure properties. The recursive decomposition of the n-cube is instrumental in proving many of its attractive properties. We have shown in this paper that, likewise, the star graph also has an abundance of hierarchical structure. The three different representations of S_4 presented in Figures 3, 4 and 5 are illustrative of this fact.

Beyond sharing these important network characteristics with the n-cube, the star graph has the additional virtue of having significantly less interconnections (i.e., degree) and smaller delays (i.e., average distance and diameter) when compared with n-cubes of comparable numbers of vertices. (Table 2 shows three typical comparisons.) Particularly, for larger networks (say $N > 10000$) the superiority of the star graph in this regard becomes quite pronounced.

Of course, an outstanding virtue of the n-cube is the basic simplicity of its definition which leads to quite simple routing procedures and associated algorithms. As such it is especially easy to understand and analyze by anyone with a background in binary numbers. On the other hand, it can be argued that the underlying definition of the n-star is of nearly comparable simplicity - the only real difference seems to be that with the n-cube *binary numbers* are involved rather than the less familiar *permutations*

associated with the n-star. The n-cube also enjoys the literature that has accumulated over the years on exploring and designing various algorithms tailored for it. But, again, we would like to argue that the reader will be significantly motivated by the richness of the star graph to contribute to a similar repertoire of techniques for it as well.

Clearly, there are many open problems on the star graphs that need to be resolved. While we have indicated algorithms that involve binary trees, we have not addressed other classical problems. Sorting, for example, is a fundamental problem whose solution could well be useful in a variety of applications. Formally, given $n!$ numbers distributed over the vertices of S_n find an algorithm (a sequence together with a sequential algorithm) that will sort the $n!$ numbers. Of course, that requires that we have somehow ordered all the vertices in some predetermined order in which the sorted

	Vertices	Degree	Diameter	Average Distance	Fault Diameter
5-star	120	4	6	3.7	≤ 9
7-cube	128	7	7	3.5	8
7-star	5040	6	9	5.9	≤ 12
12-cube	4096	12	12	6	13
9-star	362880	8	12	8.1	≤ 15
18-cube	262144	18	18	9	19

Table 2. A Comparison of star graphs and n-cubes

data is to result. This ordering is significant since it can be shown that a necessary condition for the existence of a sorting algorithm is that this ordering forms a Hamiltonian path. So, the first order of business is to determine a Hamiltonian path. We have shown that the star graph has a Hamiltonian cycle[5] The Hamiltonian property of the n-cube has been known for quite some time, and has been established in more ways than one. Using such a Hamiltonian path sorting algorithms have been constructed for the n-cube (see [18]) whose (parallel) time complexity is $O(2^n)$, i.e., proportional to the number of vertices. Correspondingly the target for a sorting algorithm on S_n should be one whose complexity is $O(n!)$. We have not yet constructed a comparable sorting algorithm on the star graph.

Another class of algorithms of wide interest (particularly, in image processing) involves the construction of multi-dimensional (usually 2-dimensional) grids on the original network. Such constructions are quite elementary on the n-cube. On the star graph the $n!$ number of vertices does not readily lend itself to convenient grid. However, recent results of [10] indicate that if we can construct an $(n-1)$-dimensional grid of size $2 \times 3 \times \cdots \times n$ then we can emulate any two dimensional grid without too much loss in the emulation.

Other interesting open questions involve layout considerations. As is well known the n-cube cannot be laid out very efficiently ([13]). In fact,

---

[5] A famous conjecture in algebraic graph theory [14, 16] states that every Cayley graph is Hamiltonian, i.e., has a Hamiltonian cycle. Recall that the star graph is a Cayley graph [1].

it is the very reason for its short diameter. The star graph is not going to be any simpler. While we do not have any significant insight to offer on how the star graph might be laid out, we do conjecture that the genus of S_n is $n-3$. The interested reader will observe that while S_3 (the hexagon) is planar S_4 requires a torus (see Figure 5). This trend seems to continue.

Thus, a number of questions remain to be resolved before the universal applicability of the star graph can be meaningfully assessed. In the meanwhile, it remains as an interesting and significant challenger to the n-cube. Particularly, for general purpose processor interconnection topology, where degree, distance and diameter are of primary concern the star graph is clearly superior.

References

1. Akers, S.B. and Krishnamurthy, B., "A Group Theoretic Model for Symmetric Interconnection Networks," *Proc. Intl. Conf. Parallel Processing*, pp. 216-223, 1986.

2. Akers, S.B. and Krishnamurthy, B., "The Fault Tolerance of Star Graphs," *2nd Intl. Conf. on Supercomputing*, 1987 (to appear).

3. Armstrong, J.R. and Gray, F.G., "Fault Diagnosis in Boolean n-Cube Array of Microprocessors," *IEEE Trans. Comput.*, vol. C-30, pp. 587-590, 1981.

4. Batcher, K.E., "Sorting Networks and Their Applications," *AFIPS Conf. Proc.*, vol. 32, pp. 297-314, Atlantic City, NJ, 1968.

5. Becker, B. and Simon H.U., "How Robust is the n-Cube?," *Proc. Symp. Foundations of Comp. Sci.*, pp. 283-291, 1986.

6. Benes, V.E., "Optimal Rearrangeable Multistage Connecting Networks," *Bell System Technical Journal*, vol. 43 , no. (4), pp. 1641-1656, July 1964.

7. Biggs, N.L., *Algebraic Graph Theory*, Cambridge University Press, 1974.

8. Joel, A.E., "On Permutation Switching Networks," *Bell System Technical Journal*, pp. 813-822, May-June 1968.

9. Knuth, D.E., *The Art of Computer Programming*, 1, Addison Wesley, 1973.

10. Kosaraju, S.R. and Atallah, M.J., "Optimal Simulations Between Mesh-Connected Arrays of Processors," *Proc. Symp. on Theory of Comput.*, pp. 264-272, 1986.

11. Krishnamoorthy, M.S. and Krishnamurthy, B., "Fault Diameter of interconnection Networks," *Computers and Math. with Applications (to appear)*.

12. Ladner, R.E. and Fischer, M.J., "Parallel Prefix Computation," *JACM*, vol. 27, pp. 831-838, 1980.

13. Leighton, F.T., *Complexity Issues in VLSI: Optimal Layouts for Shuffle Exchange Graphs and Other Networks*, pp. 76-93, The MIT Press, 1983.

14. Marusic, D., "Hamiltonian Circuits in Cayley Graphs," *Discrete Math*, pp. 49-54, 1983.

15. Pease, M.C., "The Indirect Binary n-Cube Microprocessor Array," *IEEE Trans. Comput.*, vol. C-26, pp. 458-473, 1977.

16. Sabidussi, G., "Vertex Transitive Graphs," *Monatsh. Math.*, vol. 68, pp. 426-438, 1968.

17. Seitz, C.L., "Concurrent VLSI Architectures," *IEEE Trans. Comput.*, pp. 1247-1265, 1984.

18. Ullman, J.D., *Computational Aspects of VLSI*, pp. 209-243, Computer Science Press, 1984.

19. Waksman, A., "A Permutation Network," *JACM*, vol. 15 , no. (1), pp. 159-163, 1968.

The De Bruijn Multiprocessor Network: A Versatile Parallel Processing and Sorting Network for VLSI

MAHESWARA R. SAMATHAM, MEMBER, IEEE, AND DHIRAJ K. PRADHAN, FELLOW, IEEE

Abstract—It is shown that the binary de Bruijn multiprocessor network (BDM) can solve a wide variety of classes of problems. The BDM admits an N-node linear array, and N-node ring, $(N - 1)$-node complete binary trees, $((3N/4) - 2)$-node tree machines, and an N-node one-step shuffle-exchange network, where $N(= 2^k$, k is an integer) is the total number of nodes.

The de Bruijn multiprocessor networks are proven to be fault tolerant, as well as shown to be extensible. A tight lower bound of the VLSI layout area of the BDM is derived; a procedure for an area-optimal VLSI layout is also described. It is demonstrated, too, that the BDM is more versatile than the shuffle-exchange (SE) and the cube-connected cycles (CCC).

Recent work has classified sorting architectures into 1) sequential input/sequential output, 2) parallel input/sequential output, 3) parallel input/parallel output, 4) sequential input/parallel output, 5) hybrid input/hybrid output. Such a classification is based not only on the I/O method, but also on the interconnection network, the sorting algorithm, and the type of keys used. Demonstrated here is that the de Bruijn multiprocessor networks (DM) can sort data items in all of the above-mentioned categories. No other network which can sort data items in all the categories is known. Sorting algorithms and time complexities which correspond to each of these categories are given here, as well. Also, it is proven that DM's work as sorting networks, even in the presence of some faults.

Index Terms—Bisection width, complete binary tree, fault tolerance, fault-tolerant sorting network, Hamiltonian path, sorting network, multiprocessor network, parallel algorithm, parallel sorting network, undirected de Bruijn graph, VLSI layout.

I. INTRODUCTION

THE SEARCH for computationally efficient multiprocessor architectures that are suitable for VLSI has spawned an increasingly important research area. Several parallel architectures which solve a wide variety of problems have been proposed. These include the linear array [2], [5], the ring [6], the complete binary tree (CBT) [7]–[9], the tree machine (TM) [10], the shuffle-exchange (SE) [11], [14], the cube-connected cycles (CCC) [15], the two-dimensional mesh [16], the even double-exchange [17], the orthogonal trees [18], and the doubly-twisted torus [19].

Manuscript received August 15, 1985; revised December 7, 1986. This work was supported in part by AFOSR 88-0205, as well as in part by NSF MIP 88-05586.

M. R. Samatham is with the Department of Electrical Engineering and Computer Science, Northwestern University, Evanston, IL 60201.

D. K. Pradhan is with the Department of Electrical and Computer Engineering, University of Massachusetts, Amherst, MA 01003.

IEEE Log Number 8823538.

Certain of the real-life problems that must be accommodated have been successfully grouped into various classes [1], [4], [15], [28], [32]. These classifications are important, because statements such as, "all problems in this class have this complexity," inform much more than statements like "this problem is of this complexity" [28]. Included among these classifications are the *pipeline class* [4], the *multiplex class* [32], the *NP-complete class* [24], the *ASCEND* and *DESCEND* classes [15], as well as the *decomposable searching class* [28].

First, problems in the *pipeline class* can be efficiently solved in a pipe (linear array). Depending on the problem, data may flow in one direction or in both directions simultaneously. Matrix–vector multiplication is a typical example of those problems that can be solved by one-way pipeline algorithms [4]. Band matrix–vector multiplication, recurrence evaluation, and priority queues are good representations of problems that can be solved by two-way pipeline algorithms [4].

The *multiplex class* covers a range of problems characterized by [32]: 1) operation on N data operands to produce a single result. 2) Evaluation that can be described by a tree. Evaluation of general arithmetic expressions, polynomial evaluation, etc., is included in this category. The natural computation graph for this paradigm is a tree, whose nodes correspond to operations, and whose edges correspond to data flow between operations. The CBT (complete binary tree) can be used to solve the problems inherent in this class.

Another important class of problems is the NP-complete class [24]. For this class, the CBT can efficiently implement exhaustive search algorithms [1]. Here, time complexity still is exponential.

ASCEND and *DESCEND classes* are comprised of highly parallel algorithms [15]. Here, the paradigm of the algorithms is the iterative rendition of a divide-and-conquer scheme. The input and output are each a vector of $N(= 2^k)$ data items; "divide" refers to two subproblems of equal size, where the "marry step" combines the results of two subproblems consisting of the execution of a single operation on the corresponding pairs of data items. That is: assume that input data $D_0, D_1, \cdots, D_{N-1}$ are stored, respectively, in storage location $T[0], T[1], \cdots, T[N - 1]$. An algorithm in the DESCEND class performs a sequence of basic operations on pairs of data successively $2^{k-1}, 2^{k-2}, \cdots, 2^1, 2^0$ locations apart. In terms of the above divide-and-conquer model, the marry step involves pairs of 2^0 locations apart. On the other hand, in the

Reprinted from *IEEE Trans. Computers*, Vol. 38, No. 4, Apr. 1989, pp. 567-581.

dual class (the ASCEND class), basic operations are performed on the data that are successively $2^0, 2^1, \cdots, 2^{k-1}$ locations apart; the marry step involves pairs of 2^{k-1} locations apart, problems which can be solved in the SE [11] and the CCC [15].

Problems in the *decomposable searching class* can be described as illustrated below [28]. Preprocess a set, F, of N objects into a data structure D such that certain kinds of queries about F can be answered quickly. A searching problem is decomposable if the response to a query Q asking the relation of an object z to the set F can be written as $Q(z, F) = \Delta q(z, f)$, for all f in F, where f is an element in F; Δ is a binary operator which is associative, commutative, and has an identity; and where q is the query asking the relation of the object z to the element f. The TM described in [10] solves this large class of searching problems. This paper demonstrates that multiprocessor networks based on binary de Bruijn graphs referred to as binary de Bruijn multiprocessor (BDM) and general de Bruijn graphs referred to as de Bruijn multiprocessors (DM) can solve all of the above classes of problems efficiently. Specifically, it is shown that these multiprocessor networks can be used as versatile sorting networks.

Sorting is a theoretically interesting problem with a great deal of practical significance [46]. The sorting problem as defined in [42] is described below. We are given N items

$$D_1, D_2, D_3, \cdots, D_{N-1}, D_n$$

to be sorted; we shall call them data items (or records). Each data item D_j has a key K_j which governs the sorting process. The object of such sorting is to determine a permutation $p(1)p(2) \cdots p(N)$ of the data items, which puts the keys in nondecreasing order

$$D_{p(1)} \leq D_{p(2)} \leq \cdots \leq D_{p(N)}.$$

Usually, we output the sorted sequence or the ith smallest item is placed in the ith processor.

A classification method for sorting architectures was presented by Winslow and Chow [47]. The sorters have been classified into the following categories:

1) sequential input/sequential output (SI/SO)
2) parallel input/sequential output (PI/SO)
3) parallel input/parallel output (PI/PO)
4) sequential input/parallel output (SI/PO)
5) hybrid input/hybrid output (HI/HO)

all of which are illustrated in Fig. 1. Note that the classification is based, not only on the I/O method, but also on the interconnection network, the sorting algorithm, and the type of keys used.

This paper demonstrates that the de Bruijn multiprocessor networks can be used to sort elements in all of the five categories. The main advantages are fourfold in having an interconnection network which can sort data items in all of the categories, as the following situations can be handled.

1) Although it is theoretically possible to load the data items in parallel, the number of ports available for I/O may be limited.

2) Even though the I/O ports are available, it may not be

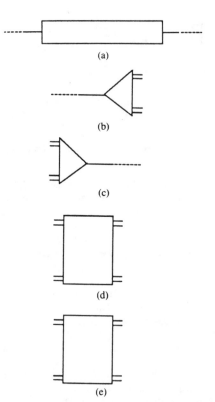

Fig. 1. Categories of sorter architectures (a) Sequential input/sequential output. (b) Sequential input/parallel output. (c) Parallel input/sequential output. (d) Parallel input/parallel output. (e) Hybrid input/hybrid output.

possible to load the data items, from the secondary storage, in parallel.

3) Different sets of data may have different types of keys.

4) In practice, there may be faults in the network.

For each of these categories, time complexity and size complexity is given in this paper. The *time complexity* is the worst case time required to sort the data items. The *size complexity* is the number of data items that can be sorted.

The multiprocessor networks based on undirected binary de Bruijn graphs presented here can solve *all* the above-mentioned classes of problems. Also, these networks are shown to be suitable for VLSI implementation. What follows is organized into five sections. Section II describes the binary de Bruijn multiprocessor network (BDM). Section III shows that the BDM admits many basic networks.

The characteristics of both fault tolerance and extensibility for these networks are examined in Section IV. In Section V, a lower bound of the layout area on a VLSI chip, for the BDM, is obtained and a procedure for an area-optimal layout is given. Section VI presents the BDM as a versatile sorting network. Specifically, Section VI describes how the BDM can be used as an SI/SO, PI/SO, and PI/PO sorter. It also describes how the DM can be used as an SI/PO and HI/HO sorter. Finally, Section VII concludes with a demonstration that the BDM is more versatile than the SE and the CCC.

II. THE DE BRUIJN MULTIPROCESSOR NETWORKS

A graph is a widely-used model for a multiprocessor network, the nodes of the graph being the processors, the edges being the existing communication links between the processors. The following related definitions and notations are used throughout.

Definitions: The length of a path between two nodes is the number of edges encountered in the path. The *distance* between two nodes is the length of a shortest path between these two nodes. The *diameter* of a network is the largest distance between any two nodes. The degree of a node is the number of edges connected to that node. The *degree* of a network is the largest degree of all the nodes in that network.

Notations: Any vertex (edge) set and its cardinality are represented by $V(E)$ and $|V|$ ($|E|$), respectively. The edge between two vertices, v_1 and v_2, is denoted by $\langle v_1, v_2 \rangle$. Let $SE\{V, E\}$ be the N-node shuffle-exchange graph, where $N = |V|(= 2^k)$. Let $SH(a_{k-1} \cdots a_1 a_0) = (a_{k-2} \cdots a_0 a_{k-1})$ and $EX(a_{k-1} \cdots, a_1, a_0) = (a_{k-1} \cdots, a_1, \bar{a}_0)$ be the shuffle and exchange operations, respectively, where $a_i \in \{0, 1\}, 0 \leq i \leq k - 1$, and $\bar{a}_i$ is the complement of a_i.

Any node whose binary representation is f-bits of y followed by g-bits of $\bar{y}$, followed by h-bits of x, where $y \in \{0, 1\}, \bar{y}$ is the complement of y, and x is a DON'T CARE will be represented as $(y^f \cdot (\bar{y})^g \cdot x^h)$.

A. Undirected de Bruijn Graphs

The undirected de Bruijn graph denoted as [20], [23] $DG(d, k)$ has $N = d^k$ nodes with diameter k and degree $2d$. This corresponds to the state graph of a shift register of length k using d-ary digits. A shift register changes a state by shifting in a digit in the state number in one side, and then shifting out one digit from the other side. If we represent a node by $d_{k-1} d_{k-2} \cdots d_1 d_0$, where $d_j \in \{0, 1, \cdots, (d - 1)\}, 0 \leq j \leq (k - 1)$, then its neighbors are represented by $d_{k-2} d_{k-3} \cdots d_0 p$ and $p d_{k-1} d_{k-2} \cdots d_2 d_1$, where $p = 0, 1, \cdots (d - 1)$. The multiprocessor network based on the $DG(d, k)$ is called de Bruijn multiprocessor network denoted by $DM(d, k)$, and referred to simply as DM.

B. Undirected Binary de Bruijn Graphs

The $DG(2, k)$ can be obtained as follows. If we represent a node i by a k-bit binary number, say, $i = a_{k-1} a_{k-2} \cdots a_1 a_0$, then its neighbors can be represented as

$$a_{k-2} a_{k-3} a_{k-4} \cdots a_1 a_0 a_{k-1}(i_1) \qquad (1)$$

$$a_0 a_{k-1} a_{k-2} \cdots a_2 a_1 (i_2) \qquad (2)$$

$$a_{k-2} a_{k-3} a_{k-4} \cdots a_1 a_0 \bar{a}_{k-1}(i_3) \qquad (3)$$

$$\bar{a}_0 a_{k-1} a_{k-2} \cdots a_2 a_1 (i_4). \qquad (4)$$

The multiprocessor network based on the $DG(2, k)$ is called binary de Bruijn multiprocessor network denoted by $BDM(k)$ and referred to simply as BDM.

Example 2.1: The BDM (3) is shown in Fig. 2.

Neighbors i_1 and i_2 are obtained by a shift-end-around (SEA) operation on i; hence, i_1 and i_2 are called SEA neighbors. Neighbors i_3 and i_4 are obtained by a shift-end-around-complement operation on i; hence, i_3 and i_4 are called SEAC neighbors.

Let $SEA(i)$ represent the shift-end-around operation on i

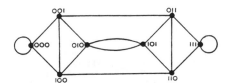

Fig. 2. The DG(2, 3).

and $SEA^{-1}(i)$ represent the inverse shift-end-around operation on i. Similarly let $SEAC(i)$ represent the shift-end-around-complement operation on i and $SEAC^{-1}(i)$ represent the inverse operation. Note that $SEA(SEA^{-1}(i)) = i$ and $SEAC(SEAC^{-1}(i)) = i$.

The neighbor i_3 is obtained by a shift-end-around-complement (SEAC) operation on i; hence, i_3 and i are called SEAC neighbors. In particular, we denote the above four neighbors of i_1, i_2, i_3, and i_4 as $SEA(i), SEA^{-1}(i), SEAC(i)$, and $SEAC^{-1}(i)$, respectively.

An edge $\langle i, j \rangle$ is called an SEA edge if $j = SEA(i)$ or $j = SEA^{-1}(i)$. Similarly, an edge $\langle i, j \rangle$ is called an SEAC edge if $j = SEAC(i)$ or $j = SEAC^{-1}(i)$.

C. The Proposed Architecture

The BDM is organized as a message-passing network of processors, as opposed to shared memory multiple processors. The proposed BDM, like the cosmic cube [33], therefore employs no switching network between the processors and the memories. Instead, each node has local memory. There are several advantages of the message-passing machine [33], the most important of which is found in the separation of engineering concerns into processor-memory communication and interprocessor communication. The former is reduced because of the close proximity. Also, message-passage machines are simpler as well as more economical than shared-memory machines. Importantly, the greater the number of processors, the greater this advantage becomes. Such an organization is obviously preferred for systems with hundreds of thousands of processing elements.

Also, because the processors are identical, the proposed multiprocessor architecture is regular. Possessing a versatile topology, it is capable of realizing many basic networks, as explained in Section III. Precisely the node architectures required to realize these basic networks is described below.

A block diagram of a processor in the BDM is given in Fig. 3. Each processor has four input/output registers, one for each neighbor. We designate these registers as R(NEIGHBOR), where NEIGHBOR can be SEA, SEA^{-1}, SEAC, or $SEAC^{-1}$. The processors communicate with their neighbors through these registers; the communication is assumed to be bidirectional. Each processor has an I/O port to communicate with the external world. These ports are used only when the data are available in parallel. When the data are available in serial, it is input and output through the processors 0 and $N - 1$.

The complexity of a processing element (PE) depends on the type of applications for which the network is designed. For example, if the network (BDM) is intended to compute only FFT, the PE will only have a multiply-add unit to calculate

155

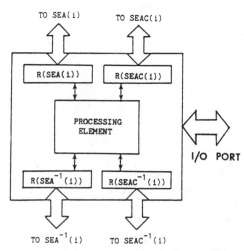

Fig. 3. Block diagram of a processor in the BDM.

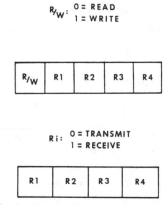

Fig. 4. Format of the control instructions.

weighted sums, and a small local memory to store the weights [38].

All of the processors can work in synchronization with a common clock, called the system clock, or they may work asynchronously. Data movement between the input/output registers and the PE can be synchronized and easily implemented. One possible implementation, illustrated in Fig, 4, requires only 5 bits to specify the operation read/write from/to any combination of registers. For example, 10101 indicates the write operation and that the registers are 2 and 4. Similarly, data movement between the processors can also be achieved easily, by specifying the 4 bits to select the direction of each of the four registers. A bit value, 1, may be used to indicate the receive mode; a value, 0, indicates the transmit mode. For example, 1010 indicates that the registers 1, 3 are in the receive mode and 2, 4 are in the transmit mode. The above-mentioned data movements can be implemented by simple microcode, residing within each processor. The next section depicts the many basic networks embedded in the BDM.

III. Basic Networks in the BDM

In this section, it is demonstrated that the BDM admits many computationally important networks. Specifically, it is shown that it has N-node ring, N-node linear array, $(N - 1)$-node CBT's, $((3N/4) - 2)$-node TM's, and N-node one-step shuffle-exchange network.

A. A Ring

Definition 3.1: A Hamiltonian cycle is a cycle passing through all the nodes in the graph exactly once.

It is well-known that the BDM has a Hamiltonian cycle. This cycle corresponds to the maximal length shift register sequence [25].

B. A Linear Array

Definition 3.2: A Hamilitonian path is defined as a path passing through all the nodes in the graph exactly one. There are several Hamiltonian paths in the BDM [25].

C. Complete Binary Trees

The directed DG has a tree structure in it [20], [23]. A systematic procedure is given here to construct various CBT's in the BDM.

The BDM has at least four CBT's of height $\log_2 N$. Root nodes of these trees are $y^{k-1} \cdot \bar{y}$ and $\bar{y} \cdot y^{k-1}$, where y is either 0 or 1. The complete binary tree for the root node $y^{k-1} \cdot \bar{y}(\bar{y} \cdot y^{k-1})$ is denoted as CBT $[y^{k-1} \cdot \bar{y}]$(CBT $[\bar{y} \cdot y^{k-1}]$). The following algorithm describes the construction of the CBT $[y^{k-1} \cdot \bar{y}]$.

Algorithm 3.1:

$t := 0$ *Initialization*

Step 1: Let $j := (y)^{k-1-t} \cdot \bar{y} \cdot (x)^t$.

Compute the following: left child of $j := (y)^{k-1-(t+1)} \cdot \bar{y} \cdot (x)^t \cdot 0$, and right child of $j := (y)^{k-1-(t+1)} \cdot \bar{y} \cdot (x)^t \cdot 1$.

Step 2: Repeat step 1 for all possible values of $(x)^t$. There are 2^t possible values of $(x)^t$.

Step 3: If $t = k - 1$ then STOP; otherwise increment t and go to Step 1. *end of the algorithm.*

The CBT $[0^3 \cdot \bar{0}]$ and CBT $[1^3 \cdot \bar{1}]$ are shown in Fig. 5(a) and (b), respectively. Similarly, the CBT $[\bar{y} \cdot y^{k-1}]$ can be constructed by replacing step 1 in Algorithm 3.2 by the following:

Step 1a: Let $j := (x)^t \cdot \bar{y} \cdot (y)^{k-1-t}$ Compute the following: left child of $j := 0 \cdot (x)^t \cdot \bar{y} \cdot y^{k-1-(t+1)}$, and right child of $j := 1 \cdot (x)^t \cdot \bar{y} \cdot y^{k-1-(t+1)}$.

end of the Step 1a.

D. Tree Machines

A tree machine (TM) of $(3 \cdot 2^{k-1} - 2)$ nodes is obtained by connecting a $(2^k - 1)$-node CBT and a $(2^{k-1} - 1)$-node CBT back to back. The $(3 \cdot 2^3 - 2)$-node tree machine is shown in Fig. 6.

There are at least four TM's, one for each of the root nodes of input tree $y^{k-1} \cdot \bar{y}$ and $\bar{y} \cdot y^{k-1}$, where y is either 0 or 1 in the BDM(k). The TM for the root node of the input tree $y^{k-1} \cdot \bar{y}(\bar{y} \cdot y^{k-1})$ is denoted by TM$[y^{k-1} \cdot \bar{y}]$(TM$[\bar{y} \cdot y^{k-1}]$). The construction of TM $[y^{k-1} \cdot \bar{y}]$ is described by the following algorithm.

Algorithm 3.2:

Step 1: Construct the CBT $[y^{k-1} \cdot \bar{y}]$ up to the level of $k - 1$.

run Algorithm 3.1 by replacing $t = k - 1$ with $t = k - 2$ in step 3.

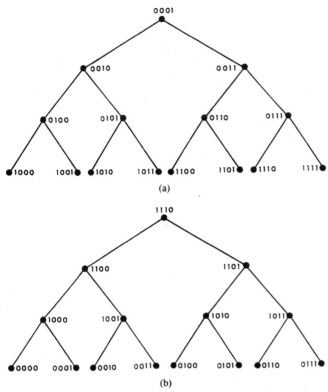

(a)

(b)

Fig. 5.   (a) The CBT $(0^3 \cdot \bar{0})$. (b) The CBT $(1^3 \cdot \bar{1})$.

ROOT NODE OF THE
INPUT TREE

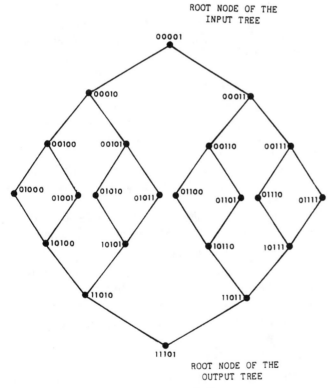

ROOT NODE OF THE
OUTPUT TREE

Fig. 6.   The TM$(0^4 \cdot \bar{0})$.

Step 2: $t := 0$

Initialization

Step 3: The nodes of the form $(\bar{y}^t \cdot y) \cdot (x)^{k-2-t} \cdot 0$ and $(\bar{y}^t \cdot y) \cdot (x)^{k-2-t} \cdot 1$ are connected to a node of the form $(\bar{y})^{t+1} \cdot y \cdot (x)^{k-2-t}$.

Step 4: Repeat step 3 for all possible values of $(x)^{k-2-t}$. There are 2^{k-2-t} possible values of $(x)^{k-2-t}$.

Step 5: If $t = k - 2$ then STOP; otherwise increment t and go to Step 3.

end of the algorithm.

Note that the root node of the output tree is in the form $(\bar{y}^{k-1} \cdot y)$. The TM $[0^4 \cdot \bar{0}]$ is shown in Fig. 6. Similarly we can obtain the TM$[\bar{y} \cdot y^{k-1}]$.

E. One-Step Shuffle-Exchange Network

One can note that the SEA operation is the same as the SH operation, and the SEAC operation is the SH operation followed by the EX operation. Therefore, the BDM can emulate the SE graph. The eight-node shuffle-exchange graph is given in Fig. 7.

Results reported in this section are summarized in Fig. 8. The next section describes that the BDM is fault tolerant and extensible.

IV. Fault Tolerance and Extensibility

A. Fault Tolerance

It has been shown in several instances that these networks have good fault tolerance and self-diagnosability. Some of their characteristics are 1) in the event of a single faulty node, only four additional hops are required to detour around the fault [21], 2) the control information for the bypassing of a faulty node can be incorporated locally with the neighbors of the faulty node [23], 3) the network admits simple distributed fault diagnosis techniques [23].

A different type of fault tolerance question is addressed here: "If there is a fault in a Class 1 graph, can a Class 2 graph or a smaller sized Class 1 graph be extracted?" [31]. The following results for the BDM are obtained from this fault-tolerance point of view.

Lemma 4.1: The CBT$[0^{k-1} \cdot \bar{0}]$ and the CBT$[1^{k-1} \cdot \bar{1}]$ are edge disjoint.

Proof: This is a proof by contradiction. Suppose an edge $\langle i, j \rangle$ exists in both the trees. Let i and j be represented as $(a^i_{k-1} a^i_{k-2} \cdots a^i_0)$ and $(a^j_{k-1} a^j_{k-2} \cdots a^j_0)$, respectively.

From the construction of the CBT's given in Section III-C, leaf nodes of the CBT$[0^{k-1} \cdot \bar{0}]$ are of the form $\bar{0} \cdot x^{k-1}$ and those of the CBT$[1^{k-1} \cdot \bar{1}]$ are of the form $\bar{1} \cdot x^{k-1}$. Furthermore, the nonleafs of CBT$[0^{k-1}\bar{0}]$(CBT$[1^{k-1}\bar{1}]$) are *not* of the form $\bar{0} \cdot x^{k-1}(\bar{1} \cdot x^{k-1})$. First note that i (equally j) must be a leaf of one of the trees, because if i is a nonleaf of CBT$[0^{k-1} \cdot \bar{0}]$ (equally CBT$[1^{k-1} \cdot \bar{1}]$), then to be in CBT$[1^{k-1} \cdot \bar{1}]$ it must be a leaf of CBT$[1^{k-1} \cdot \bar{1}]$. Also, i and j cannot be leaf nodes in the same tree because there is no edge between two leaf nodes. Without loss of generality, assume that i is a leaf node in the CBT$[0^{k-1} \cdot \bar{0}]$ and j is a leaf node in the CBT$[1^{k-1} \cdot \bar{1}]$.

Looking in the CBT$[0^{k-1} \cdot \bar{0}]$, we can conclude that j must be of the form $0 \cdot a^i_{k-1} \cdots a^i_1$, i.e.,

$$a^j_{k-1} a^j_{k-2} \cdots a^j_0 = 0 \cdot a^i_{k-1} a^i_{k-2} \cdots a^i_1. \quad (5)$$

Similarly looking in the CBT$[1^{k-1} \cdot \bar{1}]$, i must be of the

157

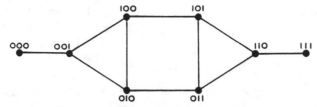

Fig. 7. The eight-node shuffle-exchange graph.

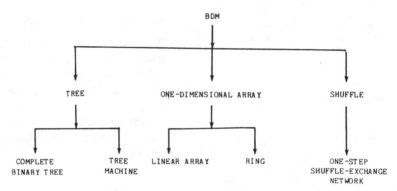

Fig. 8. Various topologies in the BDM.

form $1 \cdot a_{k-1}^j \cdots a_1^j$, i.e.,

$$a_{k-1}^i a_{k-2}^i \cdots a_0^i = 1 \cdot a_{k-1}^j a_{k-2}^j \cdots a_1^j. \qquad (6)$$

From (1) and (2), we can further conclude that $i(j)$ must be of the form $1010 \cdots (0101 \cdots)$, i.e., alternate 1's and 0's starting with 1 (0). However, there are two parallel edges between such nodes. Therefore, the two trees are edge disjoint. Q.E.D.

Corollary 4.1: CBT$[\bar{0} \cdot 0^{k-1}]$ and CBT$[\bar{1} \cdot 1^{k-1}]$ are edge disjoint.

Theorem 4.1: When an edge fails, the BDM will have a fault-free CBT.

Proof: Immediate from Lemma 4.1. Q.E.D.

Lemma 4.2: When a processor fails, the BDM can be configured into a linear array of $N - 1$ nodes.

Proof: Since the BDM has a Hamiltonian cycle, even when a processor fails, it has a Hamiltonian path of the remaining fault-free $(N - 1)$ nodes. Q.E.D.

Corollary 4.2: Even when an edge fails, the BDM can still be configured as a fault-free linear array. Q.E.D.

Lemma 4.3: When a processor fails, the BDM can still be configured as a complete binary tree of height $(k - 1)$.

Proof: When a node of the form $0 \cdot X$, where X is any $(k - 1)$-bit binary number, fails, the BDM has a fault-free CBT$[1^{k-1} \cdot \bar{1}]$ of height $k - 1$. Similarly, if the failed node is of the form $1 \cdot X$, it has a fault-free CBT$[0^{k-1} \cdot \bar{0}]$ of height $k - 1$. Q.E.D.

Lemma 4.4: The DM(d, k) has $\binom{d}{e}$ DM(e, k) graphs in it, where $2 \le d$.

Proof: All the nodes which are represented by only e digits out of d digits form a DM(e, k). There are $\binom{d}{e}$ selections of e digits out of d digits. Q.E.D.

Example 4.1: The DM$(3, k)$ has $\binom{3}{2} = 3$ BDM(k) graphs in it.

Lemma 4.5: Every node i, in the DM(d, k) is in $\binom{d-j}{e-j}$

DM(e, k) graphs, where $j(\le e)$ is the number of different digits in the d-ary digit representation of i.

Proof: A node i is in all those DM(e, k) graphs that are represented by these j digits out of e digits. By fixing these j digits, the remaining $(e - j)$ digits out of the rest of the $(d - j)$ digits can be selected in $\binom{d-a}{e-j}$ ways. Q.E.D.

Lemma 4.6: Let $M(i)$ be the number of different DM(e, k) graphs (of the form in the proof of Lemma 4.4) in which the node i is present. $M(u, u, \cdots, u) > M(i)$, for all $i, i \ne (u, u, \cdots, u)$ and $0 \le u \le (d - 1)$.

Proof: This follows from Lemma 4.5. In the node $(u, u, \cdots, u)$, the value of j is equal to 1. Therefore, this node is in $\binom{d-1}{e-1}$ different DM(e, k) graphs. In all the other nodes, the value of j is greater than 1. Q.E.D.

Let $Z = \binom{d}{e} / \binom{d-1}{e-1} = d/e$ and let $F = \lceil Z - 1 \rceil$.

Theorem 4.2: The DM(d, k) has a fault-free DM(e, k), even if any F nodes (or edges) fail.

Proof: By Lemma 4.5, each node of the form $(u, u, \cdots, u)$ is in $\binom{d-1}{e-1}$ DM(e, k) graphs. This means that a failed node can eliminate at the most $\binom{d-1}{e-1}$ DM(e, k) graphs. But, by Lemma 4.4, there are a total of $\binom{d}{e}$ DM(e, k) graphs. Therefore, F failure will leave at least one fault-free DM(e, k). Q.E.D.

Results obtained in this section are summarized in Table I.

B. Extensibility

Extensibility is an important property which facilitates constructing large-sized systems out of small-sized systems. Here it is shown that the de Bruijn multiprocessor network (DM) is extensible.

There are two methods of extending a DM(d, k) to a DM$(d + 1, k)$. In the first method, extra $[(d + 1)^k - d^k]$ processors are added to the original DM(d, k). In the second method, $\binom{d+1}{d}$ different DM(d, k) are interconnected to ob-

TABLE I
FAULT-TOLERANCE RESULTS FOR THE DM

Before the fault	Type of fault	After the fault
BDM(k)	A Communication link	$(2^k - 1)$-node CBT
BDM(k)	A Processor (or a communication link)	$(2^k - 1)$-node linear array
BDM(k)	A Processor (or communication link)	$(2^{k-1} - 1)$-node CBT
DM(d,k)	F Processor	DM(e,k)

tain a DM$(d + 1, k)$, provided $d \geq k$. These two methods are described by the following algorithms.

Algorithm 4.1:

Step 1: Represent the processors of the original DM(d, k) with k-digit d-ary numbers, where the d digits are $0, 1, \cdots, (d - 1)$.

Step 2: Add $[(d + 1)^k - d^k]$ processors, and represent each of these with k-digit $(d + 1)$-ary number such that at least one of the k digits is d.

Step 3: Add communication links which satisfy the adjacency relation of the DM$(d + 1, k)$.

end of Algorithm 4.1.

Example 4.2: Extension of the DM(2, 2) to the DM(3, 2) using Algorithm 4.1 is shown in Fig. 9. In this figure, the original DM(2, 2) network is indicated by solid lines, processors and communication links that are added are shown by dashed lines.

Algorithm 4.2:

Step 1: Add d more DM(d, k)'s.

Step 2: Represent the processors in all the DM(d, k)'s with k-digit $(d + 1)$-ary numbers in such a way that the processors in the same DM(d, k) are represented with the same set of d digits.

Step 3: Treat the processors with the same k-digit representation as a single processor.

Step 4: Add communication links which satisfy the adjacency relation of the DM$(d + 1, k)$.

end of algorithm 4.2.

Example 4.3: Extension of the DM(2, 2) to the DM(3, 2) using Algorithm 4.2 is shown in Fig. 10.

The next section presents an area-optimal Thompson model layout for the BDM.

V. OPTIMAL VLSI LAYOUT

In this section, an asymptotically optimal-area layout of the BMD is presented. Here the layout model proposed by Thompson [26] is used. In this model, the chip is divided into a grid of vertical and horizontal tracks, spaced apart by unit intervals. Processors are assumed to occupy unit area and can be located only at the intersections of grid tracks. Wires are routed through the tracks in order to connect pairs of processors. Although a wire in a horizontal track is allowed to cross a wire in a vertical track, pairs of wires are not allowed to overlap any processor to which they are not linked. The layout area is the product of the number of the vertical and the number of the horizontal tracks in the layout.

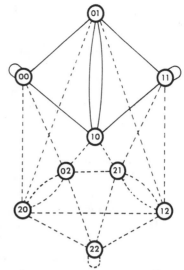

Fig. 9. Extension of the DM(2, 2) to the DM(3, 2) using Algorithm 4.1.

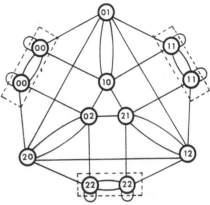

Fig. 10. Extension of the DM(2, 2) to the DM(3, 2) using Algorithm 4.2.

A. Lower Bound on Area

First, a lower bound of the layout area is derived.

Lemma 5.1: If the distance between two nodes, v_1 and v_2, in the SE is greater than 2, then $\langle v_1, v_2 \rangle \notin E$, where E is the edge set of the BDM.

Definition 5.1: A bisection of a graph $G = \{V, E\}$ is the subset B of E and a partition of V into two sets, V_1 and V_2, such that $|V_1| = |V_2|$; B contains all the edges of G connecting the vertices in V_1 with the vertices in V_2. The width of a bisection is $|B|$ and the minimum bisection width of a graph is the least width of any bisection of the graph denoted by $|B|_{\min}$.

Lemma 5.2: $|B|_{\min}$ of the BDM is $\Theta(N / \log N)$.

Proof: Any N-node graph which can compute an N-point FFT in $O(\log N)$ steps has a $|B|_{\min}$ of $\Omega(N / \log N)$ [26]. The BDM can compute an N-point FFT in $O(\log N)$ steps [38]. Therefore, $|B|_{\min}$ of the BDM is $\Omega(N / \log N)$. Next it is shown that $|B|_{\min}$ of the BDM is $O(N / \log N)$.

Consider the minimum bisection of the SE. Let $v_{11}, v_{12}, \cdots, v_{1(N/2)}$ be the vertices in V_1, and $v_{21}, v_{22}, \cdots, v_{2(N/2)}$ be the vertices in V_2. It may be noted that since the bisection width of the SE is $\Theta(N / \log N)$ both N and m are integers equal to $c \cdot (N / \log N)$, c is a constant greater than 0. The vertices in V_1 can be placed into three levels as follows:

$$V_{1(\text{LEVEL0})} = \{v_{11}, v_{12}, \cdots v_{1m}\} \qquad (7)$$

$$V_{1(\text{LEVEL1})} = \{v_{1i} : \langle v_{1j}, v_{1i}\rangle \in E, i > m \text{ and } j \leq m\} \qquad (8)$$

$$V_{1(\text{LEVEL2})} = \{v_{1i} : \langle v_{1j}, v_{1i}\rangle \notin E, i > m \text{ and } j \leq m\}. \qquad (9)$$

Similarly, the vertices in V_2 can be partitioned into $V_{2(\text{LEVEL0})}$, $V_{2(\text{LEVEL1})}$, $V_{2(\text{LEVEL2})}$. The following can be concluded: 1) $|V_{1(\text{LEVEL0})}|$, $|V_{2(\text{LEVEL0})}| = c \cdot (N \log N)$, since the $|B|_{\min}$ of the SE is $O(N \log N)$. 2) $|V_{1(\text{LEVEL1})}| \leq 2 \cdot c \cdot (N \log N)$ and $|V_{2(\text{LEVEL1})}| \leq 2 \cdot c \cdot (N \log N)$, since the degree of vertices in SE is less than or equal to 3.

Now, the BDM is considered with the above partition of vertices. By Lemma 5.1, the edges in the BDM which connect a node in V_1 and a node in V_2 exist only between the vertices $V_{1(\text{LEVEL0})} \cup V_{1(\text{LEVEL1})}$ and the vertices in $V_{2(\text{LEVEL0})} \cup V_{2(\text{LEVEL1})}$. Since the degree of each vertex in BDM is four, $|B|_{\min}$ of the BDM is $O(N/\log N)$. Therefore, $|B|_{\min}$ of the BDM is $\Theta(N/\log N)$. Q.E.D.

Theorem 5.1: Any VLSI layout of the BDM requires at least $\Omega(N^2/\log^2 N)$ area.

Proof: Thompson [26] has proved that the layout area of any graph is $\Omega(|B|_{\min}^2)$. The theorem follows from the Lemma 5.2. Q.E.D.

B. Optimal-Area VLSI Layout

It is shown here that any layout procedure for the SE network may be used to layout the BDM network in comparable area. An asymptotically optimal layout for the SE network is given in [14]. This yields an asymptotically optimal layout for the BDM network. The following algorithm lays out BDM(k).

Algorithm 5.1
Step 1: Layout the 2^{k+1}-node SE network in $O([2^{k+1}/(k+1)]^2)$ area.
Step 2: Double the lengths and widths of all nodes and edges, so each node occupies a 2×2 area and double the length of all edges.
Step 3: Duplicate each EX edge.
Step 4: For each node labeled $X^k \cdot 1$, replace the node with connections between the two EX edges and the two SEA edges.
Step 5: Strip off the last (bit a_0) from the labels of all nodes.
end of the algorithm.

Example 5.1: Fig. 11(a) shows a fragment of a 32-node SE network. Fig. 11(b) shows the layout after applying step 3 of Algorithm 5.1. Fig. 11(c) shows the final product of Algorithm 5.1.

Example 5.2: Fig. 12 shows a layout for the 16-node SE network. Applying Algorithm 5.1 to this layout yields the layout in Fig. 13 for the BMD (3) network.

Theorem 5.2: For the BDM (k), when k is large, Algorithm 5.1 gives an area-optimal layout.

Proof: Kleitman [14] gives a layout for the SE network

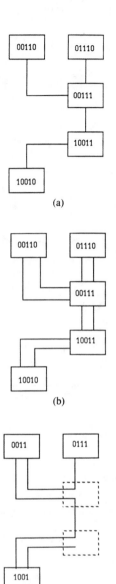

Fig. 11.   Application of Algorithm 5.1.

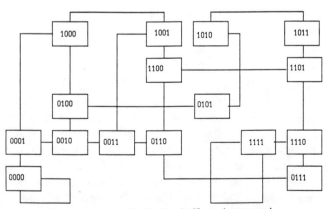

Fig. 12.   Layout of 16-node shuffle-exchange graph.

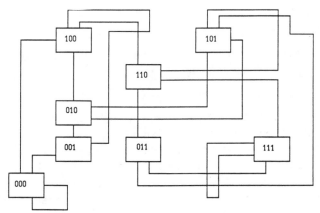

Fig. 13. Layout of eight-node de Bruijn graph.

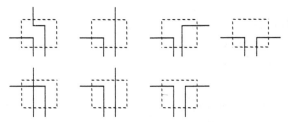

Fig. 14. Substitution of edges for a node in step 4.

bounded by $c \cdot N^2/\log^2 N$, for some constant c. Step 1 requires the layout for a $2N$-node SE network. This occupies area $\leq c \cdot (2N)^2/\log^2 (2N) \leq 4c \cdot N^2/\log^2 N$. Step 2 increases the area by a factor of two in both dimensions, so the area used is $\leq 16c \cdot N^2/\log^2 N$, which is $O(N^2/\log^2 N)$. The area does not increase with any further step. The connections made in step 4 can be made in the 2×2 area of a node. All cases (ignoring symmetric cases) are shown in Fig. 14.

The layout method of Algorithm 5.1 is very crude, but much of the area wasted could be recovered by fine tuning using a plowing variety of program. Furthermore, the algorithm's output could be "shaken" and annealed to obtain a compact layout.   Q.E.D.

VI. The De Bruijn Multiprocessor Network as a Sorting Network

A. The BDM as SI/SO Sorter

The ladder sorter, introduced by Chen *et al.* [41], is a typical example of an SI/SO sorter, consisting of a chain of shift registers with comparators between links in the chain. Data items are loaded sequentially; as the items are loaded, they are interchanged among the shift registers so that as soon as the last item is loaded, the sorted data begin emerging sequentially from the ladder. The size of the ladder and the sorting time, which includes the time for loading, are both $O(N)$.

The SI/SO sorter can be further classified as 1) two port, and 2) single port. In a two-port SI/SO sorter, data items are input through one port, and output through some other port. In a single-port SI/SO sorter, data items are input as well as output through only one port. Interestingly, the BDM can realize both a two-port SI/SO and a single-port SI/SO sorter.

B. The BDM as a Two-Port SI/SO Sorter

As shown earlier, the BDM has a Hamiltonian path between the processors 0 and $(N - 1)$.

Definition: The right (left) neighbor of a node i is the node which is on the right (left) side of the node i, in the Hamiltonian path from the node 0 to $N - 1$ (node 0 on the left and node $N - 1$ on the right) and is denoted by $R(i)$ $(L(i))$.

If each processor has a comparator which can compare two data items, and executes the following algorithm, it works as a two-port SI/SO sorter. The main idea behind the following algorithm is that whenever a processor i has two data items, it sends the smaller of the two data items to $R(i)$. If this processor has only one data item and it has not received another item from $L(i)$ then it sends this item to $R(i)$.

Algorithm for Processor i
Start:Count1: = 0
       Count2: = 0
Initializations

Count1 keeps track of how many data items have passed through this processor and Count2 keeps track of how many data items are now with this processor

Loop:**IF** *a* data item is received from $L(i)$
           then begin
               Count1: = Count1 + 1
               Count2: = Count2 + 1
               end
           end if
If Count2 = 2 **then begin**
           send smaller of the data items to $R(i)$
           Count2: = Count2 - 1
           end
end if
If (Count1 = N and Count2 = 1) **then begin**
           send the data item to $R(i)$
               goto Start
               end
           else goto loop
end if
end of algorithm.

Lemma 6.1: The worst case time required to sort N data items is $3N - 1$, which includes loading and unloading time.

Proof: The loading phase requires N time units; the worst case time to receive the smallest item at the output port is N. The remaining $N - 1$ data items can be received in $N - 1$ time units.   Q.E.D.

Example 6.1: The sorting of four data items by the BDM as a two-port SI/SO sorter is shown in Table II.

Note that the above sorter is different from the sorter presented in [48]; there, a global bus is used to pass data to each cell, whereas ours uses none.

C. The BDM as a Single-Port SI/SO Sorter

The BDM was shown earlier to contain a Hamiltonian cycle. If each processor has a comparator, and executes the following algorithm, it works as a single-port SI/SO sorter.

TABLE II
SORTING OF FOUR DATA ITEMS USING TWO-PORT SI/SO SORTER

Time Unit	Input	Contents of the Processors				Output
		Proc. # 0	Proc. # 1	Proc. # 2	Proc. # 3	
t_1	1,2,3	4				
t_2	1,2	3,4				
t_3	1	2,4	3			
t_4		1,4	2,3			
t_5		4	1,3	2		
t_6			4,3	1,2		
t_7			4	3,2	1	
t_8				4,3	2,1	
t_9				4	3,2	1
t_{10}					4,3	2,1
t_{11}					4	3,2,1
t_{12}						4,3,2,1

Algorithm 6.1:

Step 1: Each processor executes the algorithm given in Section VI-B to load a maximum of $2N$ data items. (After the loading phase, each processor has two data items.)

Step 2: Each processor sends the larger of the two elements to $L(i)$.

Step 3: Repeat step 2 until all the processors are empty.
end of algorithm.

Lemma 6.2: The worst case time to sort N data items is $3N$ time units, and that to sort $2N$ data items is $4N$ time units.

Proof: Sorting N data items is similar to that of the two-port SI/SO, except that the last data item has to go through one additional processor.

In the case of $2N$ data items, loading the data requires $2N$ time units. Odd–even transposition sorting requires N time units; unloading the data requires $2N$ time units.

D. The BDM as PI/SO Sorter

The tree sorter is a typical example of the PI/SO sorter, developed by Song [8]. Parallel data are fed to the leaves of a binary tree; pairs of leaves are compared simultaneously and the larger (or smaller) of the two sons is propagated to the father node. Continuing in this fashion, after $\log_{2N}$ time units, the sorted sequence starts emerging from the root of the tree. The size and time complexity are $O(N)$ and $O(N + \log_2 N)$, respectively.

The BDM has four complete binary trees, CBT[$y^{k-1} \cdot \bar{y}$] and CBT[$\bar{y} \cdot y^{k-1}$], where y is either 0 of 1. If each processor of the BDM has a comparator which can compare two data items and executes the following algorithm, it works as a PI/SO sorter. Data items are input through the processors, i, $N/2 \le i \le (N-1)$. Initially, each of these processors contains two data items.

Algorithm for Processor i: $i = a_{k-1}a_{k-2} \cdots a_1a_0$
begin

If a processor receives a request from its parent, **then** send the requested data items to its parent.

If a processor has two data items, send the smaller key value to its parent.

If a processor has one or no data items, compare the keys of its sons and request for the data item which has a smaller key value.

end.
end of algorithm

Lemma 6.3: The size and time complexity of the above sorter are N and $N + \log_2 N$, respectively.

E. The BDM as PI/PO Sorter

Stone [11] has given an $O(\log_2 N)$ time algorithm to execute Batcher's bitonic sorting method [11] on a perfect shuffle interconnection network. The following is an adaptation of the algorithm given in [40]. The key difference is that the algorithm given here is distributed in the sense that each processor, i, $0 \le i \le (N-1)$, executes the algorithm without the use of a centralized controller.

Algorithm for Processor i:
$i = a_{k-1}a_{k-2} \cdots a_0$
begin
Procedure Shuffle1 (R)
    begin
        send R to SEA(i)
    end;
end of procedure Shuffle 1
Procedure Shuffle2 (Data)
begin
    send Data to SEA(i) and SEAC(i)
end;
end of procedure Shuffle 2
Procedure Compare–Exchange
    begin
    Min := minimum of $\{R(\text{SEA}^{-1}(i)), R(\text{SEAC}^{-1}(i))\}$
    Max := maximum of $\{R(\text{SEA}^{-1}(i)), R(\text{SEAC}^{-1}(i))\}$
    if Mask := 0 **then if** $a_0 = 0$ **then** Data := Min
            else Data := Max
            else if $a_0 = 0$ **then** Data := Max
            else Data := Min
    end if;
end;
end of procedure Compare–Exchange
Main program begins
    $R := a_0$
a_0 is the least significant bit of i
    Mask := R
Mask bit determines the behavior of Compare-Exchange operation
    For $j :=$ 1 **to** k **do**
    begin
        Mask := Mask $\oplus R$
        Shuffle1 (Mask)
    end
    Shuffle2 (Data)
    Compare–Exchange
    For $j :=$ 1 **to** $k - 1$ **do**
    begin
    Shuffle (R)
    Mask := Mask $\oplus R$
    For $l :=$ 1 **to** $k - 1 - j$ **do**
    Shuffle1 (Mask)
    Shuffle2 (Data)

For $l := k - j$ to $k - 1 - j$ do
begin
       Shuffle1 (Mask)
       Shuffle2 (Data)
       Compare–Exchange
   end
end.
end of the algorithm.

Lemma 6.4: The size and time complexities of the above sorter are N and $O((\log_2 n)^2)$, respectively.

F. The BDM as $O(\log^2 N)$-Time PI/PO Sorter

Examples of the PI/PO sorters are the network sorters proposed by Batcher [40]. These networks include the merge sorter and the bitonic sorter. Both sorters require $N \log_2^2 N$ comparators and $O(\log_2^2 N)$ time units. Muller and Preparata [44] have shown the sorting times of $O(\log_2 N)$ are possible for PI/PO sorters, if $O(N^2)$ comparators are used. Recently, Leighton [43] provided a construction of a bounded-degree $O(N)$-node network that sorts N numbers in $O(\log N)$ steps. An example of the SI/PO is the distributed tree sorter [47]. It is shown that by replacing the comparators by distributors it is possible to improve the sorting time [47]. A tree of distributors can be constructed by placing one distributor at the root of the tree, d distributors at level one of the tree, and so forth, with d^p distributors at level p of the tree. A data item is inserted at the root and passed down the levels until it reaches the output level. The result is an SI/PO sorter with size and time complexities of $O((N-1)/(d-1))$ and $O(N + \log_d N)$, respectively.

Nassimi and Sahni [45] have given an $O(p \cdot \log N)$ algorithm to sort N data items, on perfect shuffle computers, with $N^{(1+1/p)}$ processing elements, $1 \le p \le \log N$. This algorithm can be easily adapted to execute on the BDM. This means that the BDM of N^2 processors can sort N data items in $O(\log N)$ time.

Even though the works of Ajtai, Komlos, and Szemeridi [39] and Leighton [43] are milestones in the history of sorting, the constants involved in their results are quite high. Therefore, because of this, we conclude that for the reasonable values of N the BDM of N processors may sort data items faster than those that are given in [39] and [43].

G. The DM as a SI/PO Sorter

The DM of $N(= d^k)$ processors has d-ary trees of height $\log_d N$ [23]. We are interested in the tree whose root node is $(0, 0, 0, \cdots 0)$. The DM as a tree for the root node $(0, 0, \cdots, 0)$ is shown in Table II.

Definition: The jth neighbor of a node i is the node which is obtained by shifting digit j into the most significant digit and by omitting the least significant digit of i.

In this tree, the children of the node i are all jth neighbors, $j = 0, 1, \cdots, (d - 1)$. There are $(d - 1)$ processors in level 2, $d(d - 1)$ processors in level 3 and so on, $d^{k-1}(d - 1)$ processors in level k. If each processor in the DM has a distributor and executes the algorithm given below, it works as an SI/PO sorter.

The level of node i denoted by LEVEL(i), in the above-mentioned trees, can be expressed as LEVEL(i) = $k + 2 - \text{POSITION}(i)$, where $k = \log_d N$ and POSITION(i) is the position where the first nonzero digit exists when counted from right to left in i, represented by a k-digit d-ary number.

Example: POSITION$(000 \cdots 00) = k + 1$ and POSITION$(XX \cdots X1) = 1$, where X is a DON'T CARE.

We make the following assumptions.
1) There are N data items.
2) All the keys are represented by k-digit d-ary numbers.
3) No two keys have the same value.

Algorithm for Processor i
begin
      Determine the level, LEVEL(i)
      Initialization
      Whenever a data item is received **do**
      begin
      If ((LEVEL(i) = $k + 1$) OR (key value = i))
      then retain this item
      else
             begin
                  Determine the digit value, D(key), of the key in the position LEVEL(i) starting from the right, when the key is represented by a k-digit d-ary number

                  Send data item to D(key)th neighbor.
             end if
end.
    end of algorithm

The output is received from all the nodes in parallel. The data item with key (X) will appear at the node (X).

Lemma 6.5: The size and time complexities are N and $N + \log_d N$, respectively.

H. The DM as an HI/HO Sorter

The parallel balanced tree sorter (PBT), described in [47], is an example of an HI/HO sorter. In a balanced tree (BT), all subtrees have the same height. Each node in a balanced tree contains $(d - 1)$ values and the "nearest" value is used to determine which son node is used for the next comparison node. Sooner or later, it reaches a node where a match is found, or it reaches the bottom of the tree. If we have SBT sorters working in parallel, each sorting a separate subtree, the sort time should be divided by S.

Implementations of BT and PBT sorters are described in [47]. Now, a brief description of the workings of the DM as a balanced tree (BT) sorter is given below.

Conceptually, a BT sorter consists of a base d comparator (the design given in [23]), and a set of buckets. The base d comparator inputs an item, compares the item to all $(d - 1)$ node values simultaneously, determines the "nearest" node value, and assigns the item to a bucket which is associated with the node value.

In the DM, if each processor has a base d comparator and executes the algorithm described below, it works as a BT sorter. The following assumptions are made.

1) The total of data items is N

2) The exact node values ($d - 1$ in number) of each processor are known and these values are selected so that the tree is always balanced. Let these values for processor i be $D_j(i), 1 \le j \le (d - 1)$.

3) Data items are input through the node $(0, 0, \cdots 0)$, adjacent to the root and each data item is output through the corresponding node.

Algorithm for Processor i
> **begin**
>> Procedure d-Compare (data)
>> **begin**
>>> **CASE** key (data) **of:**
>>> **begin**
>>>> $D_j(i) \le$ key (data) $\le D_{j+1}(i), 1 \le j \le (d - 1)$; send data to jth neighbor.
>>>> key (data) $\le D_{d-1}(i)$: send data to 0th neighbor.
>>>> key (data) $> D_{d-1}(i)$: send data to $(d - 1)$st neighbor.
>>> **end CASE**
>> **end**
> *end of procedure d-Compare (data)*
>> **Whenever** a data item is received **do**
>>> If POSITION $(i) \ne 1$ **then** d-compare (data)
>>>> **else stop**
>>> **end if**
>> **end**
> *end of algorithm.*

The size and time complexities of the above sorter are N and $(N + \log_d N)$, respectively. In the above sorter, it is assumed that leaf nodes can sort incoming data.

I. The DM as PBT Sorter

Theoretically, if we have d BT sorters working in parallel, each sorting a separate subtree, the sort time should be divided by d. The problem is to store the subtrees in separate memories and to avoid conflicts during the first pass. In the DM, this can be achieved by inputing the data through processors at level $2((d - 1)$ processors) and by arranging the memory in the root node $(0, 0, \cdots 0)$ into $2(d - 1)$ separate memory banks. The reason for using $2(d - 1)$ memory banks is explained in [47]. The memories are assumed to have multiple ports, one port for each processor at level 2. The size of the memory unit is selected so that there will not be any overflow. Two consecutive memory banks constitute a memory unit. The jth data item in the lth memory unit is denoted by $M(l, j), 1 \le l \le (d - 1), l \le j \le (N/(d - 1))$.

The DM works as a PBT in two passes. In the first pass, as the data items are input through the processors in level 2, they are sent to one of the memories in the root node, after comparing to each of its node values ($2(d - 1)$ in number). These node values are selected so that in the second pass, the tree remains balanced.

In the second pass, the root node sends the corresponding data items to all of the nodes in level 2, in parallel. The algorithm executed by the root node, in the second pass, is given below. All of the processors, except the root node and

the leaf nodes, execute the algorithm given in the case of the BT sorter. The base d comparator hardware in the leaf nodes is used to sort the incoming data items as they are loaded into the comparator. A hybrid output of d data items from each processor is yielded. Note that $(d - 1)$ data items are input in parallel.

Algorithm for the Root Node:
> **begin**
>> **for** $j := 1$ to N **do**
>>> **for** $l := 1$ to d **in parallel do**
>>>> Send $M(l, j)$ to $(l - 1)$st neighbor
> **end**.

Lemma 6.6: The size and time complexities of the above sorter are N and $2(N/d) + \log_d N + c$, respectively, where c is a variable which depends on the queueing time of the multiport memory.

The results obtained in this section are summarized in Table III.

J. The DM as a Sorting Network Under Faults

This section shows that the de Bruijn multiprocessor network works as a sorting network even in the presence of some faults. First, we study the BDM.

K. The BDM as a Sorting Network Under Faults

Here, assuming that the BDM is capable of sorting in PI/PO mode when there are no faults, we obtain the following results.

Theorem 6.3: When a communication link fails, the BDM can still be used as a PI/SO sorter.

Proof: Proof follows from the Lemma 6.1.   Q.E.D.

Theorem 6.4: When a processor fails, the BDM can be used as a PI/SO sorter of size complexity 2^{k-1}.

Proof: Even if a processor fails, a complete binary tree of height k has a complete binary tree of height $k - 1$.Q.E.D.

Theorem 6.5: When a node fails, the BDM can be used as a two-port SI/SO sorter.

Proof: Since the BDM has a Hamiltonian cycle, when a processor fails, it will have a Hamiltonian path of length $(N - 1)$.   Q.E.D.

L. The DM as a Sorting Network Under Faults

Here, we present some results for the general de Bruijn multiprocessor networks.

Theorem 6.6: The SI/SO sorter of size complexity d^k can be used as an SI/PO sorter of size e^k, even when there are F faults, where F is as defined in Section IV-A.

Proof: Proof follows from the Theorem 2.   Q.E.D.

Theorem 6.7: When $p, 1 \le p \le (d - 1)$, processors fail, the faulty DM can be used as a BT sorter.

Proof: The PBT sorter is essentially d BT sorters working in parallel. When $(d - 1)$ processors fail, still we have a BT sorter.   Q.E.D.

These results are summarized in Table IV.

VII. Comparison and Conclusions

It is shown here that the BDM admits 1) an N-node ring, 2) an N-node linear array, 3) $(N - 1)$-node CBT's, 4)

TABLE III
SIZE AND TIME COMPLEXITIES OF THE DM AS A
SORTING NETWORK

Category	Size complexity	Time complexity
A. SI/SO		
(a) Two port	N	$3N$
(b) Single port	N	$3N$
	$2N$	$4N$
B. PI/SO		
	N	$N + \log_2 N$
C. PI/PO		
(a) N Processor	N	$0((\log_2 N)^2)$
(b) N^2 Processor	N	$0(\log_2 N)$
D. SI/PO	N	$N + \log_d N$
E. HI/HO	N	$2(N/d) + \log_d N + c$

TABLE IV
THE DM AS A SORTING NETWORK UNDER FAULTS

Before the fault			After the fault	
Sorter	Size Complexity	Type of Fault	Sorter Complexity	Size
PI/PO	2^k	A communication link	PI/SO	2^k
PI/PO	2^k	a processor	PI/SO	2^{k-1}
PI/PO	2^k	a processor	SI/SO	$2^k - 1$
SI/PO	d^k	F processors	SI/PO	n^k
HI/HO	d^k	(d-1) processors	SI/PO	e^{k-1}

$((3N/4) - 2)$-node TM's, and 5) an N-node one-step shuffle-exchange network. Thus, the BDM is quite useful for constructing a processor network that performs computations for 1) the pipeline class, 2a) the multiplex class, 2b) the NP-complete class, 3) the decomposable searching class, and 4) the ASCEND and DESCEND classes of problems. The BDM can also be used as an efficient VLSI dictionary machine [37], since it has a complete binary tree. A tight lower bound of the VLSI layout area of the BDM is given, and a procedure for an area-optimal VLSI layout is derived, as well. It is also shown that the de Bruijn multiprocessor network is fault tolerant in its ability to gracefully degrade in the event of certain faults, and these networks are shown to be extensible.

In comparing the BDM to the SE and the CCC, the following may be observed. Although the BDM is similar to the SE, the former is twice as fast as the latter in executing the ASCEND and DESCEND classes, the multiplex class, the NP-complete class, and the decomposable searching class of problems. This is chiefly because the BDM is obtained by a one-step shuffle-exchange (SEAC) operation. Since in VLSI the communication is costly, this will substantially improve performance. Even more importantly, the SE does not have a Hamiltonian cycle, and it is not even known whether it can have a Hamiltonian path. Consequently, the pipeline class of algorithms cannot be executed on the SE. It is also not known whether the CCC can be used to efficiently solve pipeline, NP-complete, or decomposable searching classes of problems, because it is not known whether the CCC has a linear array, a complete binary tree, or a tree machine. Interestingly, in the case of the ASCEND and DESCEND classes, the BDM can be as much as 2 times faster than the CCC. This is due to the fact that in the case of simple algorithms [15] for example, the CCC requires $O(k - r) + O(2^r)$ steps, where r is the smallest integer for which $k \leq (r + 2^r)$ and

2^k is the total number of processors in the network. But 2^r is approximately equal to k.

It can be noted that one possible shortcoming of the BDM, as compared to the CCC, is that the Thompson model layout of the BDM is not as regular as that of the CCC. In practice, though, one has to introduce some fault tolerance (like spare processors, buses, switches) into the network [27], [36]. This factor may minimize the significance of the regularity of the layout of the original interconnection network.

In comparing the BDM to the binary cube network [33], it may be noted that it is known [49] that the cube network can emulate linear arrays, meshes, and binary trees (if we allow one of the nodes used as a connecting node). However, it appears that the cube network cannot embed or emulate the shuffle-exchange network easily. One of the useful networks that the cube can emulate is the mesh of trees [50]. At this time it is not known whether the BDM can also emulate the mesh of trees. The advantage the BDM has over the cube is that the number of connections per node does not grow with the size of the network.

In summary, the conclusion is that the BDM can be effectively used as a general purpose parallel processing network for VLSI. It can also be used as a fault-tolerant add-on processor, for execution of multiple applications, since the network can be dynamically restructured to fit the applications.

Furthermore, this paper has shown that the architectures based on the DG's can be used to sort data items in 1) sequential input/sequential output, 2) parallel input/sequential output, 3) parallel input/parallel output, 4) sequential input/parallel output, and 5) hybrid input/hybrid output modes. Sorting algorithms that correspond to each of these categories are given. The algorithms are distributed in the sense that these are executed by individual processors without any centralized controller.

Time complexities and size complexities that correspond to each of the categories are tabulated in Table III. It can be concluded that the architectures based on the DG's achieve the previously known best upper bound times. Also these networks are shown to be fault-tolerant sorting networks. Finally, a comparison of binary cube and de Bruijn graph is illustrated in Table V.

Finally we pose an open question: "Is it possible to sort N data items in $O(\log N)$ time in the BDM of N (or $N \log N$) processors?"

TABLE V
DE BRUIJN GRAPHS— AN ATTRACTIVE ALTERNATIVE TO THE BINARY CUBE

	Binary-Cube	Binary-DeBruijn Graph
Number of Nodes	2^n	2^n
Number of Connections Per Node	n	4
Node Size	Grows with the Size of the Network	Constant
Longest Path Length	n	n
Routing	Easy Self-Routing	Easy Self-Routing
Fault-Tolerance	Yes	Yes
Routing with Node/Link Fault	Easy	Easy
Longest Path Length with Single Fault	At Most $(n+1)$	At Most $(n+4)$
Allows Easy Detours Around Faults	No	Yes
Extensibility	Difficult	Difficult
Emulation of: Binary Tree	Difficult	Easy (even w/faults)
Tree Machine (Back to Back Binary Tree)	Not Known	Easy
Shuffle-Exchange	Not Possible	Easy
Linear Array	Easy	Easy (even w/faults)
Mesh	Yes (even w/faults)	Not Known

ACKNOWLEDGMENT

The authors wish to thank F. T. Leighton of M.I.T., V. K. P. Kumar of U.S.C., and F. Meyer of the University of Massachusetts for helpful suggestions and useful hints in obtaining proofs.

REFERENCES

[1] C. Mead and L. Conway, *Introduction to VLSI Systems.* Reading, MA: Addison-Wesley, Oct. 1980.

[2] H. T. Kung and C. E. Leiserson, "Systolic arrays for VLSI," in *Introduction to VLSI Systems,* C. Mead and L. Conway, Eds. Reading, MA: Addison-Wesley.

[3] R. P. Brent and H. T. Kung, "Systolic VLSI arrays for polynomial GCD computation," Tech. Rep., Carnegie-Mellon Univ., Mar. 1982.

[4] H. T. Kung, "The structures of parallel algorithms" in *Advances in Computers, Vol. 19.* New York: Academic, 1980, pp. 65–112.

[5] P. E. Danielsson, "Serial/parallel convolvers," *IEEE Trans. Comput.,* vol. C-33, pp. 652–667, July 1984.

[6] H. T. Kung and M. S. Lam, "Fault-tolerant and two-level pipelining in VLSI systolic arrays," in *Proc. MIT Conf. Advance Res. VLSI,* Jan. 1984.

[7] S. A. Browning, "The tree machine: A highly concurrent computing environment," Ph.D. dissertation, Dep. Comput. Sci., California Instit. Technol., Jan. 1980.

[8] S. W. Song, "A highly concurrent tree machine for data base applications," in *Proc. 1980 Int. Conf. Parallel Processing,* Aug. 1980, pp. 259–268.

[9] E. Horowitz and A. Zorat, "The binary tree as an interconnection network: Applications to multiprocessor systems and VLSI," *IEEE Trans. Comput.,* vol. C-30, pp. 247–253, Apr. 1981.

[10] J. Bently and H. T. Kung, "A tree machine for searching problems," in *Proc. 1979 Int. Conf. Parallel Processing,* Aug. 1979, pp. 257–266.

[11] H. S. Stone, "Parallel processing with the perfect shuffle," *IEEE Trans. Comput.,* vol. C-20, pp. 153–161, Feb. 1971.

[12] T. Lang, "Interconnection between processing and memory modules using the shuffle-exchange network," *IEEE Trans. Comput.,* vol. C-25, pp. 55–66, Jan. 1976.

[13] D. S. Parker, "Notes on shuffle-exchange type switching networks," *IEEE Trans. Comput.,* vol. C-29, pp. 213–222, Mar. 1980.

[14] D. Kleitman, F. T. Leighton, M. Lepley, and G. L. Miller, "New layouts for the shuffle-exchange graph," in *Proc. 13th Annu. ACM Symp. Theory Comput.,* May 1981, pp. 278–292.

[15] F. P. Preparata and J. E. Vuillemin, "The cube-connected-cycles: A versatile network for parallel computation," *Commun. ACM,* pp. 300–309, May 1981.

[16] C. D. Thompson and H. T. Kung, "Sorting on a mesh-connected parallel computer," *Commun. ACM,* vol. 20, pp. 263–271, 1977.

[17] W. E. Leland, "Density and reliability of interconnection topologies for multicomputers," Ph.D. dissertation, Univ. Wisconsin, Madison, May 1982.

[18] D. D. Nath, S. N. Maheshwari, and P. C. P. Bhatt, "Efficient VLSI networks for parallel processing based on orthogonal trees," *IEEE Trans. Comput.,* vol. C-32, pp. 569–581, June 1983.

[19] C. H. Sequin, "Doubly twisted torus networks for VLSI processor arrays," in *Proc. 8th Annu. Int. Symp. Comput. Architecture,* 1981, pp. 471–480.

[20] N. G. de Bruijn, "A combinatorial problem," Koninklijke Netherlands: Academe Van Wetenschappen, *Proc. Vol. 49,* part 20, 1946, pp. 758–764.

[21] M. L. Schlumberger, "de Bruijn communications networks," Ph.D. dissertation, Dep. Comput. Sci. Stanford Univ., 1974.

[22] M. Imase and M. Itoh, "Design to minimize diameter on building-block networks," *IEEE Trans. Comput.,* vol. C-30, pp. 439–443, June 1981.

[23] D. K. Pradhan and S. M. Reddy, "A fault-tolerant communication architecture for distributed systems," *IEEE Trans. Comput.,* vol. C-31, pp. 863–870, Sept. 1982.

[24] M. R. Garey and D. S. Johnson, *Computers and Intractability—A Guide to the Theory of NP-Completeness.* San Francisco, CA: Freeman, 1979.

[25] T. Etzion and A. Lempel, "Algorithms for the generation of full-length shift-register sequences," *IEEE Trans. Inform. Theory,* vol. IT-30, pp. 244–251, May 1984.

[26] C. D. Thompson, "A complexity theory for VLSI," Ph.D. dissertation, Carnegie-Mellon Univ., Dep. Comp. Sci., Aug. 1980.

[27] L. Synder, "Introduction to the configurable highly parallel computer," *IEEE Computer,* pp. 47–56, Jan. 1982.

[28] J. L. Bentley, "Decomposable searching problem," *Inform. Processing Lett.,* vol. 8, pp. 244–251, June 1979.

[29] H. T. Kung, "Let's design algorithms for VLSI systems," in *Proc. Conf. Very Large Scale Integration: Architecture, Design and Fabrication, at California Institute of Technology,* Jan. 1979.

[30] L. Haynes, R. Lau, D. Siewiorek, and D. Mizell, "A survey of highly parallel computing," *IEEE Computer,* pp. 9–24, Jan. 1982.

[31] F. T. Leighton and C. E. Leiserson, "Wafer-scale integration of systolic arrays," in *Proc. 23rd IEEE Symp. Foundations Comput. Sci.,* pp. 297–311.

[32] P. Banerjee and J. A. Abraham, "Fault-secure algorithms for multiprocessor system," in *Proc. 11th Int. Symp. Comput. Architecture,* June 1986, pp. 279–287.

[33] C. L. Seitz, "The cosmic cube," *Commun. ACM,* vol. 28, pp. 22–33, Jan. 1985.

[34] A. Esfahanaian and S. L. Hakimi, "Fault-tolerant routing in the de Bruijn communication networks," *IEEE Trans. Comput.,* vol. C-34, pp. 777–788, Sept. 1985.

[35] F. T. Leighton, "Optimal layouts for the shuffle-exchange graph and lower bound techniques for VLSI," Ph.D. dissertation, M.I.T., Aug. 1981.

[36] J. I. Raffel *et al.,* "a wafer-scale integrator," in *Proc. Int. Conf. Comput. Design,* Oct. 1984, pp. 212–126.

[37] A. K. Somani and V. K. Agarwal, "An efficient VLSI dictionary machine," in *Proc. Int. Conf. Comput. Architecture,* June 1984, pp. 142–150.

[38] M. R. Samatham and D. K. Pradhan, "A multiprocessor network suitable for single-chip VLSI implementation," in *Proc. 11th Symp. Comput. Architecture,* June 1984, pp. 328–337.

[39] M. Ajtai, J. Komlos, and E. Szemeredi, "An $O(N \log N)$ sorting networks," in *Proc. 15th ACM Symp. Theory Comput.,* 1983, pp. 1–9.

[40] K. E. Batcher, "Sorting networks and their applications," in *Proc. 1968 SJCC,* AFIPS, vol. 32, 1968, pp. 307–314.

[41] T. C. Chen, V. Y. Lum, and C. Tung, "The rebound sorter: An efficient sort engine for large files," in *Proc. 1978 Int. Conf. Very Large Data Bases,* 1978, pp. 312–318.

[42] D. E. Knuth, "Sorting and searching," *The Art of Computer Programming, Vol. 3.* Reading, MA: Addison-Wesley, 1973.

[43] F. T. Leighton, "Tight bounds on the complexity of parallel sorting," in *Proc. 16th ACM Symp. Theory Comput.,* 1984, pp. 71–80.

[44] D. E. Muller and F. P. Preparata, "Bounds to complexities of networks for sorting and switching," *J. ACM,* vol. 22, pp. 196–201, 1975.

[45] D. Nassimi and S. Sahni, "Parallel permutation and sorting algorithms and a new generalized connection network," *J. ACM,* vol. 29, pp. 642–667, July 1982.

[46] C. D. Thompson, "The VLSI complexity of sorting," *IEEE Trans. Comput.,* vol. C-32, Dec. 1983.

[47] L. E. Winslow and Y.-C. Chow, "The analysis and design of some new sorting machines," *IEEE Trans. Comput.,* vol. C-32, pp. 677–683, July 1983.

[48] H. Yasuura, N. Takagi, and S. Yajima, "The parallel enumeration sorting scheme for VLSI," *IEEE Trans. Comput.,* vol. C-31, pp. 1192–1201, Dec. 1982.

[49] F. T. Leighton, private communication.

[50] M. R. Samatham and D. K. Pradhan, "De Bruijn multiprocessor network: A versatile sorting network," in *Proc. 12 Int. Symp. Comput. Architecture,* 1985, pp. 360–367.

Maheswara R. Samatham (S'82–M'85) was born in Vijayawada, India in December 1956. He received the B.Tech. degree in electronics and communication engineering from Jawaharlal Nehur Technological University, the M.Tech. degree in electrical engineering from the Indian Institute of Technology, Kanpur, and the Ph.D. degree in electrical and computer engineering from the University of Massachusetts, Amherst.

Since January 1986, he has been with Northwestern University, Evanston, IL, as an Assistant Professor in the Department of Electrical Engineering and Computer Science. His current research interests include computer architecture, parallel processing, VLSI/WSI computation, and fault-tolerant computing.

Dr. Samatham is a member of the IEEE Computer Society, the Association for Computing Machinery, and Tau Beta Pi.

Dhiraj K. Pradhan (S'70–M'72–SM'80–F'88), for a photograph and biography, see p. 365 of the March 1989 issue of this TRANSACTIONS.

Correction to "The De Bruijn Multiprocessor Network: A Versatile Parallel Processing and Sorting Network for VLSI"[2]

M.R. Samatham and D.K. Pradhan

(The following corrections to the galley proof were inadvertently omitted.)

- The following is the missing paragraph after the first paragraph.

   In this paper, we develop VLSI architectures based on De Bruijn Graphs. De Bruijn graphs as a candidate for VLSI architecture was first proposed in Pradhan [51] and developed later in [52] and [38]. This work has found application in NASA's Galileo project in that a large VLSI De Bruijn network is being built which uses the architectural concepts similar to those developed earlier by us in [51], [52], and [38]. This De Bruijn VLSI network by NASA consists of 8192 nodes and is an application-specific architecture scheduled for completion by 1995. (See missing references [51] and [52] given below.)

- Page 568: Column 1: Para. 3–Line 4: The last subscript should be N instead of n.
- Page 569: Section B Lines 4–8 delete i_j at the end and replace j by i_j; therefore, for example $a_{k-2}, a_{k-3} \cdots, a_1, a_0, a_{k-1}$ (i) (1) should be replaced by $a_{k-2}, a_{k-3}, \cdots, a_1, a_0, a_{k-1}$ (i).
- Page 570: "one" replaced by once.
- Page 571: Column 2: Line 7: The line should begin with $\left(y^{k-2} \cdot y \right)$ instead of $\left(y^{k-1} \cdot y \right)$.
- Page 572: Column 2: Line 6: The term $\begin{pmatrix} d-a \\ e-j \end{pmatrix}$ should actually be $\begin{pmatrix} d-j \\ e-j \end{pmatrix}$.
- Page 573: Algorithm 4.2 Step 4 is erroneous and should read: "Add all additional nodes that may be necessary to have all $(d+1)^k$ nodes of DM$(d+1, k)$. Then add all links necessary to satisfy adjacency relationship of DM$(d+1, k)$."
- Page 575: The time complexity given in Lemma 6.1 should be $3N$, not $(3N - 1)$, and the proof should be modified accordingly.

- Page 576: Column 1: Line 15: The words "Odd–even transposition sorting requires N time units" should be removed.
- Page 576: Column 2: Line 6: The term $O(\log_2 N)$ should be $O\left(\log_2^2 N\right)$.
- Page 576: Column 2: Make all words "procedure" into bold face.
- Page 576: Column 2: Insert a "begin" just after *Main program begins* (approximately 20 lines from the bottom).
- Page 576: Column 2: Insert a "begin" after the "For . . . ", line 3 from bottom.
- Page 576: Column 2: Add a line "end" at the end of the column.
- Page 576: The algorithm for Processor i given under E needs the following correction: Line 5 from the bottom should be shuffle1(R) instead of simply shuffle(R).
- Page 576: Column 2: The last line should be "shuffle1(Data)" instead of "shuffle2(Data)."
- Page 577: The last sentence, third paragraph from the bottom on the left-hand column, should read: "The DM as a tree for the root node $(0, 0, \cdots, 0)$ is shown in Fig. 15." (see attached missing Figure).
- Page 578: Column 2: Para. 6: In the title K. should be replaced by J.1.
- Page 578: Column 2: Para. 11: In the title L. should be replaced by J.2.
- Page 578: Theorem 6.6 and corresponding entry in Table IV are erroneous. Theorem 6.6 should read: "With up to $F = [d/e - 1]$ faults the SI/PO sorter of size complexity d^k can be used as an SI/PO sorter of size e^k where e divides d.

   In Table IV, the entry for SI/PO in the last column should be e^k instead of n^k.

- Missing references:

[51] D. K. Pradhan, "Interconnection topologies for fault-tolerant parallel and distributed architectures," in *Proc. 10th Int. Conf. Parallel Processing*, Aug. 1981, pp. 238–242.

[52] —— "Dynamically restructurable fault-tolerant processor network architectures," *IEEE Trans. Comput.*, vol. C-34, no. 5, pp. 434–440, May 1985.

[1] S. Saxena, P. C. P. Bhatt, and V. C. Prasad, *IEEE Trans. Comput.*, vol. 39, no. 3, pp. 400–404, Mar. 1990.

[2] M. R. Samantham and D. K. Pradhan, *IEEE Trans. Comput.*, vol. 38, no. 4, pp. 567–581, Apr. 1989.

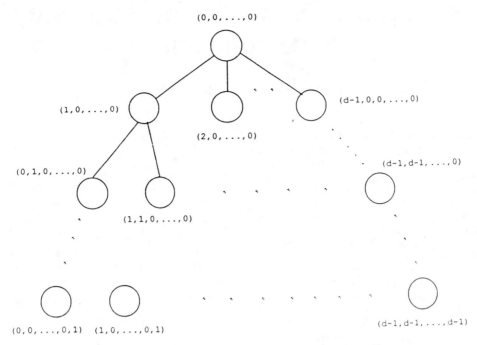

Fig. 15. The DM as a tree for the root node $(0, 0, 0, \cdots, 0)$

Fat-Trees: Universal Networks for Hardware-Efficient Supercomputing

CHARLES E. LEISERSON, MEMBER, IEEE

Abstract — **This paper presents a new class of universal routing networks called *fat-trees*, which might be used to interconnect the processors of a general-purpose parallel supercomputer. A fat-tree routing network is parameterized not only in the number of processors, but also in the amount of simultaneous communication it can support. Since communication can be scaled independently from number of processors, substantial hardware can be saved over, for example, hypercube-based networks, for such parallel processing applications as finite-element analysis, but without resorting to a special-purpose architecture.**

Of greater interest from a theoretical standpoint, however, is a proof that a fat-tree of a given size is nearly the best routing network of that size. This *universality theorem* is proved using a three-dimensional VLSI model that incorporates wiring as a direct cost. In this model, hardware size is measured as physical volume. We prove that for any given amount of communications hardware, a fat-tree built from that amount of hardware can simulate every other network built from the same amount of hardware, using only slightly more time (a polylogarithmic factor greater). The basic assumption we make of competing networks is the following. In unit time, at most $O(a)$ bits can enter or leave a closed three-dimensional region with surface area a. (This paper proves the universality result for *off-line* simulations only.)

Index Terms — **Fat-trees, interconnection networks, parallel supercomputing, routing networks, universality, VLSI theory.**

I. INTRODUCTION

MOST routing networks for parallel processing supercomputers have been analyzed in terms of performance and cost. Performance is typically measured by how long it takes to route permutations, and cost is measured by the number of switching components and wires. This paper presents a new routing network called fat-trees, but analyzes it in a somewhat different model. Specifically, we use a three-dimensional VLSI model in which *pin boundedness* has a direct analog as the bandwidth limitation imposed by the surface of a closed three-dimensional region. Performance is measured by how long it takes to route an arbitrary set of messages, and cost is measured as the volume of a physical implementation of the network. We prove a *universality* theorem which shows that for a given volume of hardware, no network is much better.

Unlike a computer scientist's traditional notion of a tree, fat-trees are more like real trees in that they get thicker further from the leaves. In physical structure, a fat-tree resembles, and is based on, the *tree of meshes* graph due to Leighton [12], [14]. The processors of a fat-tree are located at the leaves of a complete binary tree, and the internal nodes are switches. Going up the fat-tree, the number of wires connecting a node with its father increases, and hence the communication bandwidth increases. The rate of growth influences the size and cost of the hardware as well.

Most networks that have been proposed for parallel processing are based on the Boolean hypercube, but these networks suffer from wirability and packaging problems and require nearly order $n^{3/2}$ physical volume to interconnect n processors. In his influential paper on "ultracomputers" [27], Schwartz demonstrates that many problems can be solved efficiently on a supercomputer-based on a shuffle network [28]. But afterwards, Schwartz comments, "The most problematic aspect of the ultracomputer architecture suggested in the preceding section would appear to be the very large number of intercabinet wires which it implies." Schwartz then goes on to consider a "layered" architecture, which seems easier to build, but which may not have all the nice properties of the original architecture.

On the other hand, there are many applications that do not require the full communication potential of a hypercube-based network. For example, many finite-element problems are planar, and planar graphs have a bisection width of size $O(\sqrt{n})$, as was shown by Lipton and Tarjan [19]. Moreover, any planar interconnection strategy requires only $O(n)$ volume. Thus, a natural implementation of a parallel finite-element algorithm would waste much of the communication bandwidth provided by a hypercube-based routing network.

Fat-trees are a family of general-purpose interconnection strategies which effectively utilize any given amount of hardware resource devoted to communication. This paper proves that for a given physical volume of hardware, no network is much better than a fat-tree. Section II introduces fat-tree architectures and gives the logical structure of one feasible implementation. Section III shows how communication on a fat-tree can be scheduled off-line in a near-optimal fashion. Section IV defines the class of *universal* fat-trees and investigates their hardware cost in a three-dimensional VLSI model. Section V contains several combinatorial theorems concerning the recursive decomposition of an arbitrary routing network, and Section VI uses these results to demonstrate that fat-trees are indeed a class of hardware-efficient universal routing networks. Finally, Section VII offers some remarks about the practicality of fat-trees.

Manuscript received February 1, 1985; revised May 30, 1985. This work was supported in part by the Defense Advanced Research Projects Agency under Contract N00014-80-C-0622. A preliminary version of this paper was presented at the IEEE 1985 International Conference on Parallel Processing, St. Charles, IL, Aug. 1985.

The author is with the Laboratory for Computer Science, Massachusetts Institute of Technology, Cambridge, MA 02139.

Reprinted from *IEEE Trans. Computers,* Vol. C-34, No. 10, Oct. 1985, pp. 892-901. Copyright © 1985 by The Institute of Electrical and Electronics Engineers, Inc. All rights reserved.

II. Fat-Trees

This section introduces fat-trees as a routing network for parallel computation. The parallel computer based on fat-trees that we present is somewhat arbitrary and is influenced by the various connection machine projects [5], [9], [11] conceived at M.I.T. The computational model is not meant to be exclusive—the results in this paper undoubtedly apply to more general models. Moreover, arbitrary "engineering design decisions," which may not be the best choices from either a practical or a theoretical perspective, have been made in this description of fat-trees. Most of the choices influence the results by only a logarithmic factor, however, and do not affect the overall thrust of the paper—the universality theorem in Section VI.

The intuitive model for parallel computation that we use is a parallel computation engine composed of a set of processors interconnected by a *routing network*. The processors share no common memory, and thus they must communicate through the routing network, using *messages*. The job of the routing network is to see that all messages eventually reach their destinations as quickly as possible.

A fat-tree FT is a routing network based on a complete binary tree. (See Fig. 1.) A set P of n processors is located at the leaves of the fat-tree. Each edge of the underlying tree corresponds to two *channels* of the fat-tree: one from parent to child, the other from child to parent. Each channel consists of a bundle of wires, and the number of wires in a channel c is called its *capacity*, denoted by cap(c). The capacities of channels in the routing network are determined by how much hardware we can afford, a topic to be discussed in Section IV. The channel leaving the root of the tree corresponds to an interface with the external world. Each (internal) node of the fat-tree contains circuitry that switches messages between incoming channels and outgoing channels.

Messages produced by processors are *batched* into *delivery cycles*. During a delivery cycle, a processor may send messages through the network to other processors. Some messages may be lost in the routing network during a delivery cycle. Thus, in general, at the end of the delivery cycle, acknowledgments are sent from the destination processor back to the source processor. Messages that are not delivered must be sent again in subsequent delivery cycles.

The nodes of the fat-tree accomplish most of the switching. In order to understand their function, one must first understand how the routing of messages is accomplished. A *message set M* $\subseteq P \times P$ is a set of *messages* (i, j). If $(i, j) \in M$, then processor i has a message to be sent to processor j. (We omit details concerning the contents of messages and the handling of messages routed to and from the external interface.) Routing in the fat-tree is basically easy since every message has a unique path in the underlying complete binary tree. A message going from processor i to processor j goes up the tree to their least common ancestor and then back down according to the least significant bits of j. Notice that at any node of the fat-tree, there are only two choices for the routing of a message. If it comes into a node from a left subtree, for example, it can only go up or down to the right. Thus, a bit

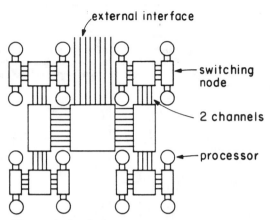

Fig. 1.   The organization of a fat-tree. Processors are located at the leaves, and the internal nodes contain concentrator switches. The capacities of channels increase as we go up the tree.

string of length at most $2 \lg n$ is sufficient to represent the destination of any message.[1]

We shall consider communication through the fat-tree network to be synchronous and bit serial. Messages snake through the tree with leading bits of a message establishing a path for the remainder to follow. Since some of the paths through the tree are longer than others, synchronization of the departures and arrivals of messages can be a bit tricky. Buffering of messages by the sending processors is one solution to this problem. (As was mentioned before, there are many other engineering alternatives that lead to the same kinds of theoretical results reported here.) The differing lengths of paths in the fat-tree are actually a major advantage of the network because messages can be routed locally without soaking up the precious bandwidth higher up in the tree, much as telephone communications are routed within an exchange without using more expensive trunk lines.

The messages in the network obey the bit-serial protocol shown in Fig. 2. The first bit is the *M bit*, which tells whether the remaining bits actually contain a message. Next come the *address* bits, which name the destination processor. The final field in the message format is the data themselves. As messages are routed through the network, each node uses the M bit to identify whether a wire carries a message, and it uses the first address bit to make a routing decision. A path is established through the node for a new M bit and the remaining message bits to follow. The address bits are stripped off one by one as the message establishes a path through the network.

A fat-tree node has three input ports, U_I, L_I, and R_I, and three output ports, U_O, L_O, and R_O, connected in the natural way to the wires in the channels. Messages entering input port L_I will go either to output port U_O or to output port R_O. The logic of the switching circuitry in a node consists of three similar portions, shown in Fig. 3. A wire from an input port is fanned out towards the two opposite output ports. The M bit of each wire is then examined to determine whether the wire has a message. On the next clock tick, the first address bit is examined on both branches of the input wire. By ANDing

[1]We use the notation $\lg n$ to mean max$\{1, \log_2 n\}$.

171

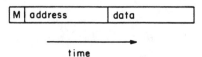

M	address		data

time

Fig. 2. The format of bit-serial messages. The first bit that a switch sees is the M bit, which indicates whether an input wire actually contains a message. The address bits arrive bit-serially in subsequent time steps, and the message contents are last.

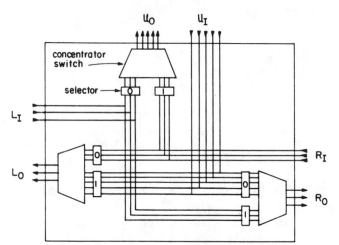

Fig. 3. The internal structure of a fat-tree node. A selector determines which messages are destined for an output port, and then a concentrator switch establishes disjoint electrical paths for as many of those messages as possible.

the M bit with either the address bit or its complement, an M bit is determined for each branch by a *selector*. Next, the messages destined for an output port, which currently occupy many wires, are switched onto fewer wires by a *concentrator switch*.

The job of the concentrator switch is to create electrical paths from those input wires that carry messages to fewer output wires. Obviously, if there are more input messages than output wires, some messages will be lost. In this case we shall say that the output channel is *congested*. We have already mentioned an acknowledgment mechanism that detects when messages are lost due to congestion.

For the time being, we shall assume that the concentrator switch has the following property. If there is no congestion — that is, the number of input messages does not exceed the number of output wires — then no messages are lost. The concentrator switch that we shall present in Section IV is a *partial concentrator* and does not have exactly this property, but it makes little difference to the theoretical results. This circuit has $O(m)$ components if there are a total of m incident wires, and it switches in constant time. Thus, the time required for an entire delivery cycle in a fat-tree of n processors is $O(\lg n)$.

Although we have described the general setting as an *on-line* switching environment, this paper makes the simplifying assumption that the fat-tree nodes contain *off-line* circuitry, in that the switches, although dynamically set, have their settings predetermined by an off-line scheduling algorithm. Naturally, it would be better to dynamically determine the settings themselves in real time, and indeed, it is possible to build such on-line switches, but these results will be reported elsewhere [8]. We have chosen here to prove the weaker off-line results so as to simplify the presentation of the universality theorem in Section VI.

There are several consequences of the off-line assumption that bear mention, however. For example, the results apply to practical situations when the settings of switches can be "compiled," as when simulating a large VLSI design or emulating a fixed-connection network. Also, some of the mechanisms — such as acknowledging the receipt of messages, which is necessary in an on-line environment — can be omitted from the off-line hardware structure, thereby reducing the complexity of the design.

III. OFF-LINE SCHEDULING ON FAT-TREES

The concentrator switches in the nodes of a fat-tree routing network guarantee that no messages are lost unless there is congestion. This section gives an algorithm for scheduling the delivery of an arbitrary set of messages so that all messages will be delivered. We give a simple value, called the *load factor* of a set of messages, which provides a lower bound on how quickly the messages can be delivered. We show that for an arbitrary message set, off-line scheduling can be done optimally to within a logarithmic factor of the number of processors.

Let us be more precise about the off-line scheduling problem. Let FT be a fat-tree on n processors, and let C be the set of channels in FT. For any channel $c \in C$, the capacity $\mathrm{cap}(c)$, which is the number of wires in the channel, is also the maximum number of simultaneous messages the channel can support because we are assuming bit-serial communication. Since each message between two processors determines a unique path in the underlying complete binary tree, we can define $\mathrm{load}(M, c)$ to be the total number of messages in a message set M that must go through channel c. We call M a *one-cycle* message set if $\mathrm{load}(M, c) \leq \mathrm{cap}(c)$ for all channels $c \in C$. If all capacity constraints are met, a fat-tree with ideal concentrator switches can route every message in one delivery cycle.

A *schedule* of a message set M is a partition of M into one-cycle message sets $M_1, M_2, \cdots, M_d$ where d is the total number of delivery cycles. A simple lower bound on d for an arbitrary message set M is $d \geq \max_c(\mathrm{load}(M, c)/\mathrm{cap}(c))$, which leads to the following definition.

Definition: Let M be a message set, and let $c \in C$ be a channel in a fat-tree. The *load factor* $\lambda(M, c)$ of a channel c due to M is

$$\lambda(M, c) = \frac{\mathrm{load}(M, c)}{\mathrm{cap}(c)},$$

and the *load factor* of the entire fat-tree due to M is

$$\lambda(M) = \max_{c \in C} \lambda(M, c).$$

A message set M is a *one-cycle* message set if $\lambda(M) \leq 1$.

The simple lower bound on the number d of delivery cycles required for any schedule of M can now be reexpressed as $d \geq \lambda(M)$. The next theorem shows that this lower bound can be achieved to within a logarithmic factor of n.

Theorem 1: Let FT be a fat-tree on n processors, and let C be the set of channels in FT. Then for any message set M

with $\lambda(M) > 1$, there is an off-line schedule $M_1, M_2, \cdots, M_d$ such that $d = O(\lambda(M) \lg n)$.

Proof: The idea is to partition the messages going from left to right through the root of the fat-tree into at most $2\lambda(M)$ one-cycle message sets, to do the same for the messages going from right to left, and then to recursively partition the messages in the two subtrees of the root. Let Q_1 be the subset of M consisting of those messages that must go through the root from left to right. The scheduling algorithm will begin by partitioning Q_1 into two message sets Q_2 and Q_3. It then iteratively refines each Q_k into Q_{2k} and Q_{2k+1}, until each Q_k, $k = r, \cdots, 2r - 1$ is a one-cycle message set for some $r \le 2\lambda(M)$. The r message sets $Q_r, \cdots, Q_{2r-1}$ form the initial sequence of the schedule.

The algorithm similarly partitions the message set consisting of messages going from right to left in the fat-tree and adds them to the schedule. (Each of these message sets can, in fact, be routed at the same time as one of the Q_k.) Finally, the algorithm recursively partitions the messages remaining within the two subtrees of the root. The upper bound of $2\lambda(M)$ one-cycle message sets holds for all messages routed through the root of a subtree. But since all subtrees with roots at the same level can be routed at the same time, the total number of delivery cycles required is at most the height of the fat-tree times the time for one level, which yields $d = O(\lambda(M) \lg n)$.

It remains to show that the message sets can be partitioned effectively. Consider once again the message set Q_1 of messages going left to right through the root of the fat-tree. We now show that each message set Q_k, $k = 1, 2, \cdots, r - 1$, can be partitioned into Q_{2k} and Q_{2k+1} so that for every channel $c \in C$, the messages of Q_k that go through c are split exactly evenly, that is, so that $\text{load}(Q_{2k}, c) \le \lceil (1/2) \text{load}(Q_k, c) \rceil$ and $\text{load}(Q_{2k+1}, c) \le \lceil (1/2) \text{load}(Q_k, c) \rceil$. The partitioning consists of two parts, matching and tracing, and is reminiscent of switch setting in a Benes network [34] and the Eulerian tour routing algorithm from [10].

First, do the matching. Consider each message in Q_k as being a string with two ends: a source end and a destination end. Within each processor, match as many pairs of string ends as possible until at most one message of Q_k is unmatched within each processor. Notice that source ends are matched only with source ends and destination ends only with destination ends because all messages in Q_k go left to right through the root. Then consider two-leaf subtrees. If each of the two leaves has one unmatched string end, match the ends. Continue matching the unmatched string ends in four-leaf subtrees, and so on up the fat-tree. At every level of the fat-tree, at most one string end is unmatched in each of the two subtrees of a node. At the root, at most one string end from each side will be unmatched (when there is an odd number of messages going from left to right through the root).

Now the tracing phase begins. If there is an unmatched string end in the left subtree, start with it. Otherwise, pick a string end arbitrarily from the left subtree. Put the corresponding message into Q_{2k}, and follow the string to the right subtree. Find the mate of the string end on the right side, and put the corresponding message into Q_{2k+1}. Follow this new string back to the left side, find its mate, and put the corre-

sponding message into Q_{2k}. In general, when traversing a string left to right, put the corresponding message into Q_{2k}. When traversing right to left, put the message into Q_{2k+1}. If we discover that a string end has no mate, or that the message corresponding to the mate has already been assigned, we have either found the (one) unmatched string end on the right or completed a cycle. In either event, pick another string end arbitrarily and continue until all messages in Q_k have been assigned either to Q_{2k} or to Q_{2k+1}.

To see that this algorithm evenly splits the messages of Q_k in every channel c, observe that the number of times we enter a subtree of the fat-tree is equal to the number of times we leave, unless we are tracing the one possible string end matched outside the subtree. Since the split is even in every channel, the partitioning of Q_1 into one-cycle message sets $Q_r, \cdots, Q_{2r-1}$ will be achieved when

$$r \le 2 \max_c \frac{\text{load}(Q_1, c)}{\text{cap}(c)}$$

$$\le 2 \max_c \frac{\text{load}(M, c)}{\text{cap}(c)}$$

$$\le 2\lambda(M),$$

which completes the proof. ∎

For the special case when $\text{cap}(c) > a \lg n$, for some $a > 1$, the logarithmic factor in the upper bound of Theorem 1 can be removed. Thus, under these conditions, the lower bound of the load factor can be met almost exactly.

Corollary 2: Let FT be a fat-tree on n processors, let C be the set of channels in FT, and suppose that there is a constant $a > 1$ such that $\text{cap}(c) \ge a \lg n$ for all $c \in C$. Then for any message set M, there is an off-line schedule $M_1, M_2, \cdots, M_d$ such that $d = O((a/a - 1)\lambda(M))$.

Proof: For each channel $c \in C$, define a set of *fictitious capacities* $\text{cap}'(c) = \text{cap}(c) - \lg n$. The fat-tree with the fictitious capacities has a load factor $\lambda'(M) \le (a/a - 1)\lambda(M)$. Now use the scheduling algorithm of Theorem 1, but during the recursion on lower levels of the tree, rather than using new message sets, simply reuse the $2\lambda'(M)$ message sets produced by partitioning the messages through the root.

The bisections at a given level produce partitions of the set of messages that are equal to within one, and this error can accumulate in a single channel as we go down the tree. The largest value of the error can be as much as $\lg n$, but the actual capacities are never exceeded, and so each of the $2\lambda'(M)$ message sets will be routable in one delivery cycle. ∎

Thus, for example, if the capacities are each at least $2 \lg n$, the number of delivery cycles is not worse than $4\lambda(M)$. (In fact, the divide-and-conquer partitioning of messages can be improved to $2\lambda(M) + o(\lambda(M))$.)

IV. The Hardware Requirements of Fat-Trees

This section investigates the amount of hardware required by a fat-tree. We give a precise description of how the switches in the nodes of a fat-tree might be implemented and determine how much hardware a node requires. We then define the channel capacities of *universal* fat-trees. Finally, we determine the amount of hardware required to build universal fat-trees.

The model for hardware that we use is an extension of Thompson's two-dimensional VLSI model [29] by making the natural extension to three dimensions. In this model, wires occupy volume and have a minimum cross-sectional area. Similar three-dimensional models have been studied by Rosenberg [26] and Leighton and Rosenberg [16].

We first present an implementation of a fat-tree node. As was shown in Fig. 3, most of the switching components are contained in the three concentrator switches. According to the three-dimensional VLSI model, however, we must also be concerned with the amount of wire consumed by the interconnection of the components. We shall show that a fat-tree node with m incident wires can be built with $O(m)$ components in a box whose side lengths are $O(h\sqrt{m})$, $O(h\sqrt{m})$, and $O(\sqrt{m}/h)$, for any $1 \leq h \leq \sqrt{m}$. The node requires constant time to route its inputs.

We shall need some definitions. An (r, s) *concentrator graph* [21] is a directed acyclic graph with r inputs and $s \leq r$ outputs such that any $k \leq s$ inputs can be simultaneously connected to some k outputs by vertex-disjoint paths. An (r, s, α) *partial concentrator graph* is a directed acyclic graph with r inputs and $s \leq r$ outputs and a constant $0 < \alpha < 1$ such that any $k \leq \alpha s$ inputs can be simultaneously connected to some k outputs by vertex-disjoint paths.

Pinsker [21] and Pippenger [22] showed that (r, s) concentrator networks can be built with $O(r)$ components using probabilistic constructions, but they do not bound the depth of the graph, which we wish to be constant. Pippenger [23], however, uses another probabilistic argument to construct (r, s, α) partial concentrator graphs for sufficiently large r where $s = 2r/3$ and $\alpha = 3/4$. The partial concentrator graphs are bipartite (no intermediate vertices between inputs and outputs), every input has degree at most 6, and every output has degree at most 9. By pasting several of these graphs together, outputs to inputs, any constant ratio of concentration can be obtained in constant depth. For a given set of inputs, the paths through the graph can be set up in polynomial time using network flow techniques or by performing a sequence of matchings on each level of the graph.

We use a partial concentrator graph to construct a good concentrator switch. We simply make switching decisions at the inputs to each level. These decision bits can be interleaved with the address bits that specify the path of a message through the fat-tree. In order to use the off-line routing results from Section III, we treat the actual capacity of a channel as α times the number of wires, which changes the results by only a constant factor.

We now turn our attention to the physical structure of a fat-tree node. A node with m incident wires contains $O(m)$ components. The next theorem gives the physical volume necessary to wire the components.

Lemma 3: A set of m components and external wires can be wired together according to an arbitrary interconnection pattern to fit in a box whose side lengths are $O(h\sqrt{m})$, $O(h\sqrt{m})$, and $O(\sqrt{m}/h)$, for any $1 \leq h \leq \sqrt{m}$.

Proof: We need to use the fact that in two dimensions,

any permutation of m inputs and m outputs can be routed in $O(m^2)$ area, which can be seen by considering a "crossbar" layout. Thus, in two dimensions, the wiring of the components and external wires can be accomplished by laying all components and external wires along a line and routing the permutation dictated by the interconnection.

The construction in three dimensions is essentially that of Leighton and Rosenberg [16]. In three dimensions, the external wires and components lie on a face of a box. Any permutation of m inputs and m outputs can be routed in a box of $O(m^{3/2})$ volume where each side has length $O(\sqrt{m})$. This proves the result of the theorem for constant h.

To extend the result, we use a result of Thompson [29] on converting a layout of height h into a layout of height 2. Consider slicing the box into slices of height h, and consider one such slice. If we expand each of the other two dimensions by a factor of h, the h layers can be superimposed, slightly offset from one another. Since this can be done with each of the slices simultaneously, the theorem follows. ∎

We are now in a position to ascertain the cost of a fat-tree implementation based on the capacities of its channels. If the capacities of the fat-tree channels are determined arbitrarily, the analysis could be messy. For the fat-trees that will be used in universality results of Section VI, however, the channel capacities can be characterized by the capacity at the root. This section defines the channel capacities of a *universal* fat-tree and evaluates the hardware costs of an implementation. Without loss of generality, and for simplicity, we assume in this section that the number of connections to each processor in the fat-tree is 1.

Let FT be a fat-tree on n processors, and let C be the set of channels in FT. Consider each node to have a level number that is its distance to the root, and give each channel $c \in C$ the same level number as the node beneath it. Thus, for example, the root and the channel between the root and the external interface are both at level 0. The processors and the channels leaving them are at level $\lg n$. If the channel at level 0 has capacity w, then we say that FT has *root capacity w*.

Definition: Let FT be a fat-tree on n processors with root capacity w where $n^{2/3} \leq w \leq n$. Then if each channel $c \in C$ at level k satisfies

$$\text{cap}(c) = \min\left\{ \left\lceil \frac{n}{2^k} \right\rceil, \left\lceil \frac{w}{2^{2k/3}} \right\rceil \right\},$$

we call FT a *universal fat-tree*.

The capacities of the channels of a universal fat-tree grow exponentially as we go up the tree from the leaves. Initially, the capacities double from one level to the next, but at levels closer than $3 \lg(n/w)$ to the root, the channel capacities grow at the rate of $\sqrt[3]{4}$.

We can now determine the hardware required by a universal fat-tree.

Theorem 4: Let FT be a universal fat-tree on n processors with root capacity w where $n^{2/3} \leq w \leq n$. Then there is an implementation of FT in a cube of volume $v = O((w \lg(n/w))^{3/2})$ with $O(n \lg(w^3/n^2))$ components.

Proof: We first establish the component count. For a node at level $k \leq 3 \lg(n/w)$, the number of components in the node is $O(w/2^{2k/3})$, and the number of nodes at level k is 2^k. Thus, the number of components in all levels between 0 and $3 \lg(n/w)$ is

$$\sum_{k=0}^{3\lg(n/w)} 2^k O(w/2^{2k/3}) = w \sum_{k=0}^{3\lg(n/w)} O(2^{k/3})$$
$$= O(n)$$

since the largest term of the geometric series occurs when $k = 3 \lg(n/w)$. Nearer the leaves, each level has about the same number of components. The total number in the levels between $3 \lg(n/w)$ and $\lg n$ is

$$\sum_{k=3\lg(n/w)}^{\lg n} 2^k O(n/2^k) = O(n \lg(w^3/n^2)) .$$

Thus, the number of components nearer the leaves of the fat-tree dominates.

The volume bound is somewhat more intricate to establish, but is essentially the unrestricted three-dimensional layout construction given by Leighton and Rosenberg [16]. The interested reader is referred to their paper. Similar divide-and-conquer layout strategies for two dimensions can be found in [3], [12], [14], [17], [18], [32]. ∎

Theorem 4 gives the volume of a fat-tree in terms of its root capacity. For the universality results of Section VI, we shall be interested in the reverse.

Definition: Let FT be a universal fat-tree that occupies volume v and has root capacity $\Theta(v^{2/3}/\lg(n/v^{2/3}))$. Then FT is a *universal fat-tree of volume v.*

Remark: A universal fat-tree on n processors of volume v must satisfy $v = \Omega(n \lg n)$ and $v = O(n^{3/2})$ to be well defined. By modifying the definition of a universal fat-tree, the lower bound can be relaxed to $\Omega(n)$, which results in minor changes to the bounds quoted in the universality theorem of Section VI.

V. Decomposition Trees

The physical implementation of a routing network constrains the ability of processors in a parallel supercomputer to communicate with one another. The universality theorem from Section VI makes essentially one assumption about competing networks: at most $O(a)$ bits can pass through a surface of area a in unit time. This assumption can be brought to bear on an arbitrary portion of a routing network implementation through the use of *decomposition trees,* a refinement of the graph-theoretic notion of *separators* [19]. Similar results can be found in the VLSI theory literature. The results presented here generalize and greatly simplify some of the constructions in the literature, notably those in [3], [4], and [13]. The generalizations are necessary for the proof of the universality theorem.

A routing network R interconnecting a set P of processors has a $[w_0, w_1, \cdots, w_r]$ *decomposition tree* if the amount of information that can enter or leave the set P of processors from the outside world is at most w_0 bits per unit time; P can be partitioned into two sets P_0 and P_1 such that the amount of information that can enter or leave each set is at most w_1 bits

per unit time; each of P_0 and P_1 can be partitioned into two sets such that the bandwidth to and from each of the four sets is at most w_2; and so on, until every set at the rth level has either zero or one processors in it. When the bandwidth decreases by a constant amount from one level to the next, we shall adopt a shorthand notation. We shall say that R has a (w, α) decomposition tree for $1 < \alpha \leq 2$ if it has a $[w, w/\alpha, w/\alpha^2, \cdots, O(1)]$ decomposition tree. (For VLSI graph layouts, there is a similar notion called *bifurcators* [3], [13].)

Theorem 5: Let R be a routing network that occupies a cube of volume v. Then R has an $(O(v^{2/3}), \sqrt[3]{4})$ decomposition tree.

Proof: The cube has side length $\sqrt[3]{v}$ and surface area $6v^{2/3}$. Imagine a rectilinearly oriented plane that splits the cube into two equal boxes, each occupying volume $v/2$. This cutting plane naturally partitions the processors into two sets. Partition each of the two boxes by repeating this procedure with a plane perpendicular to the first. Continuing now in the third dimension yields eight cubes. Repeat this procedure until each box contains either zero or one processors.

The volume of each of the 2^i boxes generated by the ith cut is $v/2^i$, and the surface area is at most $4\sqrt[3]{4}(v/2^i)^{2/3}$. Let γ be the constant factor by which the bandwidth of information transfer differs from the surface area. Then the routing network R has a $(4\sqrt[3]{4}\gamma v^{2/3}, \sqrt[3]{4})$ decomposition tree. ∎

A decomposition tree generated by the cutting plane method can be unbalanced in the sense that the number of processors lying on either side of a given cut may be unequal. Following the approach of Bhatt and Leighton [3], we define a *balanced decomposition tree* to be a decomposition tree in which the number of processors on either side of a given partition is equal, to within one. We shall show that a balanced decomposition tree can be produced from an unbalanced one.

First, however, we shall need two combinatorial lemmas. The first, which deals with the partitioning of strings of pearls, is typical of lemmas proved in the VLSI theory literature.

Lemma 6: Consider any two strings composed of even numbers of black and white pearls. By making at most two cuts, the pearls can be divided into two sets, each containing at most two strings, such that each set has exactly half the pearls of each color.

Proof:[2] Call the strings L and S for "long" and "short." We use a continuity argument to show that two sets A and $\overline{A}$ satisfying the conditions of the lemma can always be produced. Place the strings L and S end-to-end in a circle, as is illustrated in Fig. 4(a). Let A be the set of pearls comprising the shaded half of the circle in Fig. 4(b), and let $\overline{A}$ be the set of pearls in the other half. Suppose without loss of generality that the set A contains too many black pearls and set $\overline{A}$ contains too few. We shall show how to transform set A so that it occupies the initial position of set $\overline{A}$. The transformation consists of a sequence of moves such that for each

---

[2]Thanks to G. Miller of USC, who provided this argument, which is simpler than our original algebraic proof.

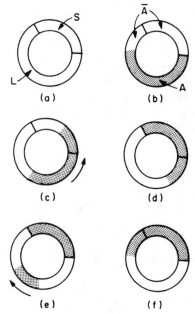

Fig. 4. The partitioning argument. (a) The two strings *L* and *S* laid end-to-end in a circle. (b) The initial position of set *A*. (c)–(f) The transformation of *A* into $\bar{A}$.

move, the number of blacks within set *A* changes by at most one. Since set *A* starts out with too many black pearls and ends with too few, by continuity there will be a position in the middle where *A* has exactly half the black pearls. Furthermore, because *A* has half the total number of pearls, it will also have half the white pearls.

The transformation begins by rotating set *A* counterclockwise, as shown in Fig. 4(c), until it reaches the position shown in Fig. 4(d). Then, set *A* is broken into two pieces and the tailing piece is rotated clockwise until it meets up with the leading piece on the other side, shown in Fig. 4(e) and (f). The position of set *A* is now the initial position of set $\bar{A}$. As can be verified, at all times during the transformation, sets *A* and $\bar{A}$ each contain at most two strings. ∎

Lemma 7: Let T be a complete binary tree drawn in the natural way with leaves on a straight line, and consider any string s of k consecutive leaves. Then there exists a forest F of complete binary subtrees of T such that 1) the leaves of F are precisely the leaves in s, 2) there are at most two trees of any given height, and 3) the height of the largest tree is at most lg k.

Proof: The forest is constructed from the maximal complete subtrees of *T* whose leaves lie only in *s*. ∎

Theorem 8: Let R be a routing network on n processors that has a $[w_0, w_1, \cdots, w_r]$ decomposition tree T. Then R has a $[w_0', w_1', \cdots, w_{\lceil \lg n \rceil}']$ balanced decomposition tree T' where

$$w_i' = 4 \sum_{k=i}^{r} w_k.$$

Proof: Draw the decomposition tree *T* in the natural way with the 2^r leaves on a line. Each leaf either contains a processor or else is empty. If the leaf contains a processor, color it black; otherwise, color it white. Considering the line

of processors as a string of black and white pearls, as in Lemma 6, we can cut the string in at most two places such that the pearls are divided into two sets, each containing at most two strings, such that each set has exactly half the pearls of each color. This partition represents the first level in the balanced decomposition tree *T'*.

Recursively partition each of the two sets using Lemma 6. At each step, the number of black pearls (processors) is split evenly in a set, and each set contains at most two strings (consecutive leaves from the decomposition tree *T*). Thus, at level $\lceil \lg n \rceil$, each set (leaf of *T'*) contains at most one processor.

It remains to prove the bound on the rates w_i' of information transfer in and out of each subtree of the balanced decomposition tree *T'*. Each subtree of *T'* corresponds to at most two strings of leaves from the original decomposition tree *T*. From Lemma 7, these two strings correspond to a forest of complete binary trees with at most four trees of a given height. All external communication of a complete binary subtree of a decomposition tree occurs through the surface corresponding to its root. Thus, the external communication per unit time of a subtree of *T'* is bounded by the sum of bandwidths from the roots of the corresponding complete binary subtrees of *T*. ∎

Corollary 9: Let R be a routing network that has a (w, a) decomposition tree for $1 < \alpha \le 2$. Then S has a $(4(\alpha/\alpha - 1)w, \alpha)$ balanced decomposition tree.

Proof: The summation in Theorem 8 becomes a geometric series. ∎

VI. Universality of Fat-Trees

We now show that a fat-tree is universal for the amount of interconnection hardware it requires in the sense that any other routing network of the same volume can be efficiently simulated. From a theoretical point of view, we define "efficiently" as meaning at most polylogarithmic slowdown. Polylogarithmic time in parallel computation corresponds to polynomial time for sequential computation.

Some may argue that polylogarithmic slowdown may not be efficient if the exponent of the logarithm is large. The ability of one parallel computer to simulate another, however, merely gives confidence in the general-purpose nature of the computer. The loss of efficiency in the simulation is not felt if the parallel computer is programmed directly.

Many of the networks currently being built are not universal (for example, two-dimensional arrays, simple trees, or multigrids). These networks exhibit polynomial slowdown when simulating other networks. Thus, they have no theoretical advantage over a sequential computer which can easily simulate a network with polynomial slowdown. Interestingly, hypercube-based networks are universal for volume $\Theta(n^{3/2})$, but as we have observed, they do not scale down to smaller volumes.

Theorem 10: Let FT be a universal fat-tree on a set of n processors that occupies a cube of volume v, and let R be an arbitrary routing network on a set of n processors that also occupies a cube of volume v. Then there is an identification

176

of the processors in FT with the processors of R with the following property. Any message set M that can be delivered in time t by R can be delivered by FT (off-line) in time $O(t \lg^3 n)$.

Proof: By Theorem 5, the routing network R has an $(O(v^{2/3}), \sqrt[3]{4})$ decomposition tree, and hence by Corollary 9, it also has an $(O(v^{2/3}), \sqrt[3]{4})$ balanced decomposition tree. Identify the processors at the leaves of the balanced decomposition tree of R in the natural way, with the processors at the leaves of the fat-tree FT.

By assumption, routing network R can deliver all the messages in a message set M in time t. In unit time, at most $O(v^{2/3}/2^{2k/3})$ messages can enter or leave a subtree rooted at level k in R's balanced decomposition tree. Thus, in t time, the total number of messages that can enter or leave a subtree rooted at level k is $O(tv^{2/3}/2^{2k/3})$.

There is a second bound on the transfer of information in and out of a subtree of the balanced decomposition tree of R. The number of messages that can enter or leave a single processor in time t is $O(t)$ since the number of connections to a processor is constant. Since there are at most $n/2^k$ processors in a subtree rooted at level k, the total number of messages that can enter or leave this subtree in t time is $O(tn/2^k)$.

We now compute an upper bound on the load factor $\lambda(M)$ that M puts on the fat-tree FT. Let c be a channel at level k in FT. We have just seen that the number load(M, c) of messages of M that must go through c is $O(tv^{2/3}/2^{2k/3})$ and $O(tn/2^k)$. Since FT is a universal fat-tree with root capacity $\Theta(v^{2/3}/\lg(n/v^{2/3}))$, the capacity of c is

$$\text{cap}(c) = \min\left\{ \left\lceil \frac{n}{2^k} \right\rceil, \Theta\left(\frac{v^{2/3}}{2^{2k/3} \lg(n/v^{2/3})} \right) \right\}.$$

Thus, the load factor on c due to M is

$$\lambda(M, c) = O(t \lg(n/v^{2/3})),$$

and the load factor on the whole fat-tree is

$$\lambda(M) = O(t \lg(n/v^{2/3})).$$

The off-line routing result from Theorem 1 says that $O(t \lg(n/v^{2/3}) \lg n)$ delivery cycles are sufficient to route all the messages in M. Since the fat-tree can execute an off-line delivery cycle in $O(\lg n)$ time, the result follows. ∎

The $O(\lg^3 n)$ factor lost in simulation is attributable to the channel capacities, the routing algorithm, and the switching. Of these three, only the last, the $O(\lg n)$ switching time for a delivery cycle, seems to be a necessary cost.

The first $O(\lg n)$ factor (actually $O(\lg(n/v^{2/3}))$) is because a fat-tree of volume v has a root capacity of $O(v^{2/3}/\lg(n/v^{2/3}))$. This logarithmic factor vanishes for the simulation of networks that have only slightly less $(O(v/\lg^{3/2}(n/v^{2/3})))$ volume. We have chosen to put all the simulation expense in time so that the comparison will be equal hardware versus equal hardware.

The second $O(\lg n)$ factor is lost by the off-line routing algorithm. In fact, we have recently discovered [8] that off-line routing in $O(\lambda(M) + \lg n \lg \lg n)$ delivery cycles is always possible. Moreover, if we assume that each processor has $\Theta(\lg n)$ connections, as is required by a Boolean hypercube, and each channel has capacity $\Omega(\lg n)$, Corollary 2 from Section III allows us to route in $O(\lambda(M))$ delivery cycles.

An important application of the universality of fat-trees is to the simulation of *fixed-connection networks,* that is, networks that have direct connections between processors. Here we relax the technical assumption in the definition of a universal fat-tree to allow the processors to have a given number d of connections to the routing network, instead of 1. Such a universal fat-tree of volume $O(v \lg^{3/2}(n/v^{2/3}))$ on n processors can simulate an arbitrary degree d fixed-connection network of volume v on n processors with only $O(\lg n)$ time degradation. The idea is that the channel capacities of the universal fat-tree are sufficiently large that the connections implied by the network can be represented as a one-cycle message set, which requires $O(\lg n)$ time to be delivered.

High-volume universal fat-trees can be compared to classical permutation networks, which all require $\Omega(n^{3/2})$ volume. A universal fat-tree on n processors with $O(n^{3/2})$ volume can route an arbitrary permutation off-line in time $O(\lg n)$. Up to constant factors, this is the best possible bound (assuming bounded-degree processors), but it is also achievable, for instance, by Benes networks [2], [34] or by on-line sorting networks [1], [15].

A natural extension to the off-line routing results presented here, and indeed, the one that motivates the entire paper, is the problem of on-line routing in fat-trees. Not surprisingly, there are universal fat-trees for on-line routing. In results to be reported elsewhere [8] we have discovered a randomized routing algorithm that delivers all messages in $O(\lambda(M) + \lg n \lg \lg n)$ delivery cycles with high probability [8], but the nodes of the fat-tree have somewhat different structure from the design given here. Using this result and essentially the construction given in this paper, one can obtain an on-line analog to Theorem 10, except with an $O(\lg^3 n \lg \lg n)$ time degradation. We anticipate further research will improve this bound.

VII. Concluding Remarks

Universality has been studied more generally in the parallel computation literature. Valiant [33] and Valiant and Brebner [31] have discovered universal routing schemes for large-volume networks. Galil and Paul [7] have proposed a general-purpose parallel processor based on the cube-connected-cycles network [25] that can simulate any other parallel processor with only a logarithmic loss in efficiency. Valiant [30] has shown that there are classes of universal Boolean circuits. A universal circuit of a given size can be programmed to simulate any circuit whose size is only slightly smaller. Fiat and Shamir [6] have proposed a universal architecture for systolic array interconnections.

Universal fat-trees are parameterized not only in the number of processors, but also in volume, which is indirectly a measure of communication potential. By considering arbitrary networks in terms of these two parameters, we have seen that the one fat-tree architecture is near-optimal throughout the entire range of the parameters. For communication-limited engineering situations, one need not necessarily retreat to special-purpose devices in order to compute efficiently in parallel.

Fat-trees have the advantage that they are a robust engineering structure. In principle, one need not worry about the exact capacities of channels as long as the capacities exhibit reasonable growth as we go up the tree. As a practical matter, one should build the biggest fat-tree that one can afford, and the architecture automatically ensures that communication bandwidth is effectively utilized. Another feature of fat-trees is that algorithms are the same no matter how big the fat-tree is. Code is portable in that it can be moved between an inexpensive computer and a more expensive one. Finally, the root channel offers a natural high-bandwidth external connection.

Although universal fat-trees have many desirable properties, there are many issues in the design of a routing network that we have not faced directly. For example, despite our concern for wirability, we have not presented a practical packaging scheme. Possibly, the packaging techniques for trees from [4] and [18] can be exploited. The constraints to be faced in packaging, however, will only be more stringent than the surface area constraint given in Assumption L3. We have attempted to deal with "pin boundedness" in a simple mathematical model, and our results should generalize to more complicated packaging models.

Another issue that we have not addressed is how messages should be sent in the network. The choice of the bit-serial approach in Section II has the advantage that the hardware is cheaper, but we may be paying in the performance of the routing algorithm. We also assumed the architecture was synchronized by delivery cycle. Presumably, fat-tree architectures can be built with different design decisions.

Whether the notion of universal parallel supercomputers is consistent with engineering reality, however, remains an open question. Independent of routing network issues, there are many other problems that must be solved if abstract n-processor parallel supercomputers are to become a reality. For example, problems of maintenance, fault tolerance, clock distribution, and reliable power supply must be solved. The hardware mechanisms needed for synchronization and instruction distribution, which are simple for single-processor machines, may be sufficiently complicated to overwhelm the advantages of having many processors.

But the largest problem that must be solved in parallel supercomputing seems to us to be the problem of programming the system with the concerns of both programming abstraction and algorithmic integrity (computational resources are not free). A supercomputer should not be a mere supercalculator (good at one restricted algorithm). It should have the power to efficiently execute many different parallel algorithms and to easily combine the results of separate parallel computations. A universal machine has the power, not just of any other machine, but of all other machines.

ACKNOWLEDGMENT

T. Knight of the M.I.T. Artificial Intelligence Laboratory inspired the author with many discussions about connection machine architectures, which led him towards the ideas in this paper. He is to blame for the name "fat-tree." Thanks to R. Greenberg of the M.I.T. Laboratory for Computer Science for finding many bugs in various versions of the paper. Thanks also to A. Bawden, T. Bui, B. Chor, T. Cormen, O. Goldreich, A. Ishii, T. Leighton, B. Maggs, M. Maley, G. Miller, C. Phillips, R. Rivest, and P. Shor for their helpful comments and technical assistance.

REFERENCES

[1] M. Ajtai, J. Komlos, and E. Szemeredi, "Sorting in $c \log n$ parallel steps," *Combinatorica*, vol. 3, no. 1, pp. 1–19, 1983.
[2] V. E. Benes, *Mathematical Theory of Connecting Networks and Telephone Traffic.* New York: Academic, 1965.
[3] S. N. Bhatt and F. T. Leighton, "A framework for solving VLSI graph layout problems," *J. Comput. Syst. Sci.*, vol. 28, no. 2, pp. 300–343, Apr. 1984.
[4] S. N. Bhatt and C. E. Leiserson, "How to assemble tree machines," in *Advances in Computing Research, Vol. 2.* Greenwich, CT: Jai Press, 1984, pp. 95–114.
[5] S. Fahlman, *NETL: A System for Representing and Using Real-World Knowledge.* Cambridge, MA: M.I.T. Press, 1979.
[6] A. Fiat and A. Shamir, "Polymorphic arrays: A novel VLSI layout for systolic computers," in *Proc. IEEE 25th Annu. Symp. Foundations Comput. Sci.*, Oct. 1984, pp. 37–45.
[7] Z. Galil and W. J. Paul, "An efficient general-purpose parallel computer," *J. ACM*, vol. 30, no. 2, pp. 360–387, Apr. 1983.
[8] R. I. Greenberg and C. E. Leiserson, "Randomized routing on fat-trees," in *Proc. IEEE 26th Annu. Symp. Foundations Comput. Sci.*, Nov. 1985, to appear.
[9] W. D. Hillis, "The connection machine," Artif. Intell. Lab., Mass. Inst. Technol., Tech. Memo. 646, Sept. 1981.
[10] R. M. Karp, F. T. Leighton, R. L. Rivest, C. D. Thompson, U. Vazirani, and V. Vazirani, "Global wire routing in two-dimensional arrays," in *Proc. IEEE 24th Annu. Symp. Foundations Comput. Sci.*, Nov. 1983, pp. 453–459.
[11] T. F. Knight, "The cross-omega router," Mass. Inst. Technol., Cambridge, unpublished manuscript, 1984.
[12] F. T. Leighton, "New lower bound techniques for VLSI," *Math. Syst. Theory*, vol. 17, no. 1, pp. 47–70, Apr. 1984.
[13] ——, "A layout strategy for VLSI which is provably good," in *Proc. 14th Annu. ACM Symp. Theory Comput.*, May 1982, pp. 85–98.
[14] ——, *Complexity Issues in VLSI.* Cambridge, MA: M.I.T. Press, 1983.
[15] ——, "Tight bounds on the complexity of parallel sorting," *IEEE Trans. Comput.*, vol. C-34, pp. 344–354, Apr. 1985.
[16] F. T. Leighton and A. L. Rosenberg, "Three dimensional circuit layouts," Lab. Comput. Sci., Mass. Inst. Technol., Tech. Rep. MIT-LCS-TM-262, June 1984.
[17] C. E. Leiserson, "Area-efficient graph layouts (for VLSI)," in *Proc. IEEE 21st Annu. Symp. Foundations Comput. Sci.*, Oct. 1980, pp. 270–281.
[18] ——, *Area-Efficient VLSI Computation.* Cambridge, MA: M.I.T. Press, 1983.
[19] R. J. Lipton and R. E. Tarjan, "A planar separator theorem," *SIAM J. Appl. Math.*, vol. 36, no. 2, pp. 177–189, Apr. 1979.
[20] C. A. Mead and L. A. Conway, *Introduction to VLSI Systems.* Reading, MA: Addison-Wesley, 1980.
[21] M. S. Pinsker, "On the complexity of a concentrator," in *Proc. 7th Int. Teletraffic Conf.*, Stockholm, Sweden, June 1983, pp. 318/1–318/4.
[22] N. J. Pippenger, "The complexity theory of switching networks," Ph.D. dissertation, Dep. Elec. Eng. Comput. Sci., Mass. Inst. Technol., Cambridge, Aug. 1973.
[23] ——, "Superconcentrators," *SIAM J. Comput.*, vol. 6, no. 2, pp. 298–304, June 1977.

[24] ——, "Parallel communication with limited buffers," in *Proc. IEEE 25th Annu. Symp. Foundations Comput. Sci.*, Oct. 1984, pp. 127–136.

[25] F. P. Preparata and J. E. Vuillemin, "The cube-connected cycles: A versatile network for parallel computation," *Commun. ACM*, vol. 24, no. 5, pp. 300–309, May 1981.

[26] A. L. Rosenberg, "Three-dimensional integrated circuitry," in *Proc. CMU Conf. VLSI Syst. Comput.*, H. T. Kung, R. Sproull, and G. Steele, Eds., Oct. 1981, pp. 69–79.

[27] J. T. Schwartz, "Ultracomputers," *ACM Trans. Programming Lang. Syst.*, vol. 2, no. 4, pp. 484–521, 1980.

[28] H. S. Stone, "Parallel processing with the perfect shuffle," *IEEE Trans. Comput.*, vol. C-20, pp. 153–161, Feb. 1971.

[29] C. D. Thompson, "A complexity theory for VLSI," Ph.D. dissertation, Carnegie-Mellon Univ., Pittsburgh, PA, 1980.

[30] L. G. Valiant, "Universal circuits," in *Proc. 8th Annu. ACM Symp. Theory Comput.*, May 1976, pp. 196–203.

[31] L. G. Valiant and G. J. Brebner, "Universal schemes for parallel communication," in *Proc. 13th Annu. ACM Symp. Theory Comput.*, May 1981, pp. 263–277.

[32] L. G. Valiant, "Universality considerations in VLSI circuits," *IEEE Trans. Comput.*, vol. C-30, pp. 135–140, Feb. 1981.

[33] ——, "A scheme for fast parallel communication," *SIAM J. Comput.*, vol. 11, no. 2, pp. 350–361, May 1982.

[34] A. Waksman, "A permutation network," *J. ACM*, vol. 15, no. 1, pp. 159–163, Jan. 1968.

Charles E. Leiserson (M'83) received the B.S. degree in computer science and mathematics from Yale University, New Haven, CT, in 1975 and the Ph.D. degree in computer science from Carnegie-Mellon University, Pittsburgh, PA, in 1981.

He is currently an Associate Professor of Computer Science and Engineering at the Massachusetts Institute of Technology (M.I.T.), Cambridge. In 1981 he joined the faculty of the Theory of Computation Group in the M.I.T. Laboratory for Computer Science. His expertise includes parallel computation, VLSI architectures, graph theory, digital circuit timing, analysis of algorithms, computer-aided design, placement and routing, wafer-scale integration, layout compaction, and most recently, parallel supercomputing. His principal interest is in the theoretical foundation of parallel computation, especially as it relates to engineering reality.

Prof. Leiserson has authored over 20 papers on the theory of VLSI and parallel algorithms. As a graduate student at Carnegie-Mellon he wrote the first paper on systolic architectures with H. T. Kung, for which they received a U.S. patent. His Ph.D. dissertation, "Area-Efficient VLSI Computation," which deals with the design of systolic systems and with the problem of determining the VLSI area of a graph, won the first ACM Doctoral Dissertation Award. He was awarded a Presidential Young Investigator Award in 1985. He is a member of the ACM, and he serves on the ACM General Technical Achievement Award Committee, which selects the Turing Award winner.

The Banyan-Hypercube Networks

ABDOU S. YOUSSEF AND BHAGIRATH NARAHARI, MEMBER, IEEE

Abstract—Some of the desirable network features of parallel general-purpose machines are partitionability and the support of some common topological structures. The hypercube is among the networks that have been proposed and studied. It is partitionable, has a small diameter, and embeds rings, meshes, and trees efficiently. It can also be viewed as a hierarchy of levels where each level is a subcube. The number of levels is limited to a power of two, and the interlevel interconnection is a hypercube structure which is not highly suitable for the embedding of pyramids. This paper introduces a new family of networks that are a synthesis of banyans and hypercubes called the *banyan-hypercubes* (BH). They combine the advantageous features of banyans and hypercubes and thus have better communication capabilities. These networks can be viewed as a scheme of interconnecting hypercubes. We shall show that many hypercube features can be incorporated into BH's in routing, embedding of rings and meshes, and partitioning, and that new improvements over the hypercube are made. In particular, we shall show that BH's have better diameters and average distances than hypercubes, and embed pyramids and multiple pyramids with dilation cost 1. We also give an optimal routing algorithm for BH's and an efficient partitioning strategy.

Index Terms—Banyan, diameter, embedding, hypercube, interconnection networks, partitioning, routing.

I. INTRODUCTION

THE PERFORMANCE of parallel systems is governed by many factors such as the underlying communication networks and the matching of algorithm characteristics with the network structure. Therefore, some of the desirable network features of parallel machines are efficient routing and the capability of embedding some common topological structures. These structures have emerged in major application areas such as image processing and scientific computing, and include rings, meshes, trees, and hierarchical structures such as pyramids and multiple pyramids [3], [10], [19], [12]. Another desirable network feature is partitionability in order to support multitasking in general-purpose multitasking parallel machines.

Several fixed as well as multistage networks have been proposed and studied [5], [8], [11], [18], [19], [21]. Banyans [4], [6], [8], [15] and hypercubes [5], [7], [16], [19] are among the networks that have received a lot of attention. Banyan networks are partitionable and have easy routing. In addition to the above features, the hypercube has point-to-point interconnections and a small diameter, and embeds rings, meshes, and trees efficiently. It can also be viewed as a hierarchy of levels where each level is a subcube. The number of levels is

limited to a power of two, and the interlevel interconnection is a hypercube structure. In particular, the interconnections between successive levels are mere straight lines which are not highly suitable for the embedding of pyramids and multipyramids. A better interlevel interconnection is the banyan.

This paper introduces a new family of hierarchical, partitionable networks that are a synthesis of rectangular banyans and hypercubes, called the *banyan-hypercubes* (BH). A BH(h, k, s) network is constructed by initially taking the first h levels (from the base) of a $(k + 1)$-level rectangular banyan of spread (outdegree) and fan-out (indegree) equal to s, where s is a power of 2. Each level has s^k nodes representing processing elements, labeled from 0 to $s^k - 1$ in binary, and *interconnected* as a hypercube. A hypercube is a BH($1, k, s$) network and hence a special case.

BH networks will be shown to combine the advantageous features of banyans and hypercubes and thus have better communication capabilities. In particular, many hypercube features in routing, embedding, and partitioning will be incorporated into banyan-hypercubes and new gains will be achieved in diameter, average distance, embedding efficiency, partitioning flexibility, and lower cost extendability.

The next section defines banyan-hypercubes more formally, exposes their highly recursive structure, and shows how they can be easily extended with a low cost in most cases. Section III presents some fundamental properties of BH networks such as their degrees, diameters, and average distances. In Section IV BH networks are shown to be self-routed and an optimal routing algorithm is developed. In Section V embeddings with dilation cost one on BH networks are constructed for rings, meshes, pyramids, and multipyramids, using Gray codes. Full binary trees are embedded in BH(h, k, s) with dilation cost $h/4$ which is small for practical values of h. Section VI shows how BH networks can be partitioned vertically and horizontally into subnetworks of the same structure (i.e., BH's). Finally, Section VII gives some concluding remarks for our future research.

II. BANYAN-HYPERCUBES

In this section banyan-hypercube networks are defined. Rectangular banyans are reviewed first. For a thorough treatment of banyan networks the reader is referred to [6] and [8].

A *banyan* graph is a Hasse diagram of a partial ordering where there is a unique path from every base to every apex. A base is any vertex having no arcs incident into it, and an apex is any node having no arcs incident out from it. An *L-level* banyan is a banyan whose nodes can be arranged into L levels so that the arcs are only between adjacent levels. A *regular*

Manuscript received April 21, 1989; revised November 10, 1989.
The authors are with the Department of Electrical Engineering and Computer Science, The George Washington University, Washington, DC 20052.
IEEE Log Number 8934118.

Reprinted from *IEEE Trans. Parallel and Distributed Systems,* Vol. 1, No. 2, Apr. 1990, pp. 160-169. Copyright © 1990 by The Institute of Electrical and Electronics Engineers, Inc. All rights reserved.

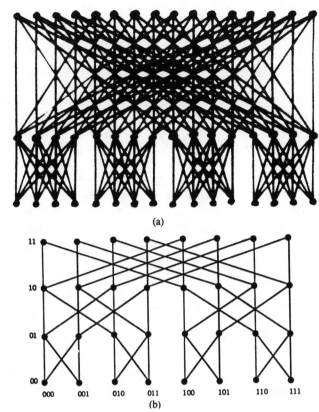

(a)

(b)

Fig. 1. Two banyan networks.

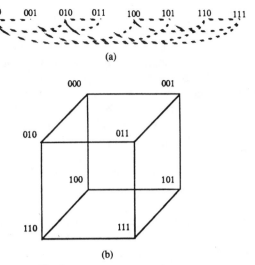

(a)

(b)

Fig. 2. Two layouts of the 3-cube.

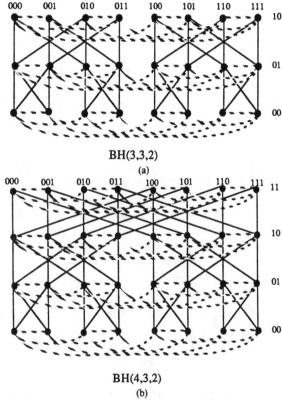

BH(3,3,2)

(a)

BH(4,3,2)

(b)

Fig. 3. Banyan-hypercubes.

banyan is an L-level banyan where all the nodes except the bases have the same indegree F called the *fanout* and all the nodes except the apexes have the same outdegree S called the *spread*. A *rectangular* banyan is a regular banyan where $S = F$. In this case, all the levels have the same number of nodes, which is S^{L-1}. Fig. 1 shows a rectangular banyan of spread 2 and another of spread 4.

Normally the base nodes represent system resources such as memory modules and processors, while the other nodes are switching elements. In this paper all the nodes of a banyan will represent processing elements, and the arcs will be treated as undirected edges representing bidirectional links. The spread will be assumed to be a power of two so that each level has a power of two number of nodes and can be interconnected in a hypercube structure.

A hypercube of dimension k, or a k-cube, is a graph of 2^k nodes labeled in k-bit binary labels such that there is an edge between every two nodes that differ by exactly one bit. Fig. 2 shows a 3-cube.

A *banyan-hypercube* BH(h, k, s), where $h \leq k + 1$ and s is a power of two ($s = 2^r$ for some r), is a graph of h levels of nodes where each level has s^k nodes interconnected in a hypercube structure and the interlevel edges form the first h levels (from the base) of a $(k + 1)$-level rectangular banyan of spread s. The nodes in each level are labeled in binary from 0 to $s^k - 1$ and the levels are numbered from 0 to $h - 1$ from the base to the top. Every node is then uniquely identified by a pair (L, X) of its level number L and its cube label X. The label X can be viewed as $x_{k-1} \cdots x_1 x_0$ in the number system of base s where each x_i is an s-ary digit, or as a binary label of $k \log s$ bits $t_{kr-1} \cdots t_0$ such that $x_i = t_{(i+1)r-1} \cdots t_{ir+1} t_{ir}$.

Clearly the total number of nodes is $N = hs^k$. Fig. 3 shows two banyan-hypercube networks.

BH(h, k, s) can be specified more formally in graph theoretical terms as follows. The h levels and the nodes of all the levels are labeled as above. For every level L, each node (L, X) in level L, where $X = x_{k-1} \cdots x_1 x_0$ in base system s, is adjacent to the following s nodes in level $L + 1$: $(L + 1, x_{k-1} \cdots x_{L+1} a x_{L-1} \cdots x_0)$ for $a = 0, 1, \cdots s - 1$ if $L < h$, and to the following s nodes in level $L - 1$: $(L - 1, x_{k-1} \cdots x_L a x_{L-2} \cdots x_0)$ for $a = 0, 1, \cdots, s - 1$ if $L > 0$. It is also adjacent to the $k \log s$ nodes (L, Y) in the same level where Y differs from X in exactly one bit when both X and Y are expressed in binary.

Another useful way of viewing these networks is as recursive structures. $BH(1, 0, s)$ is the smallest banyan-hypercube and consists of one node only. $BH(h, k, s)$ can be viewed as constructed from s copies of $BH(h, k - 1, s)$ in the following way if $h < k + 1$. Label these networks by $0, 1, \cdots, s - 1$ in s-ary and transform the label of each node (L, X) in the ith network to (L, iX) (iX is the concatenation of the s-ary digit i and the s-ary label X). Two nodes (L, iX) and (L, jX) in network i and j, respectively, are called *siblings*. These siblings are afterwards interconnected in an s-cube, that is, any two nodes (L, iX) and (L, jX) become adjacent if i and j differ in only one bit when expressed in binary. This is done at every level.

Similarly, $BH(h, k, s)$ can be constructed from $BH(h - 1, k, s)$ by adding a new level (labeled h) of s^k nodes, and then making every node $(h - 1, x_{k-1} \cdots x_0)$ of level $h - 1$ adjacent to all the s nodes $(h, x_{k-1} \cdots x_{L+1} a x_{L-1} \cdots x_0)$ of the new level for $a = 0, 1, \cdots, s - 1$. Therefore, $BH(k + 1, k, s)$ can for example be constructed from $BH(k, k, s)$ which in turn is constructed from s $BH(k, k - 1, s)$.

This recursive structure will prove useful in routing as well as partitioning. It also shows how to extend these networks. $BH(h, k, s)$ can be extended to $BH(h + 1, k, s)$ with a fraction of the cost (as opposed to hypercube extension) by adding a new level and without changing the degree. Extending $BH(h, k, s)$ to $BH(h, k + 1, s)$ is harder however because it requires s copies of the old network and a change in degree as is the case in hypercubes.

When $h = k + 1$, the network $BH(h, k, s)$ is said to be *full*. The reason for not always taking all the levels of the rectangular banyan when constructing $BH(h, k, s)$ is to have more partitioning flexibility and uniformity as will be seen later. Moreover, the analysis of these networks is often the same whether the network is full or not.

Although most of the study carried out in this paper applies to BH's for any values of s, in practice s is preferred to be 2 or 4 because the resulting banyan-hypercube meets all the requirements of partitioning and embedding without incurring a high-degree cost. In particular, the optimal mapping of pyramids and multiple pyramids is possible when $s = 4$ while the embedding of all the other topological structures mentioned earlier is the same for all values of s.

It should be noted at this point that many networks have been or can be synthesized with the hypercube. Examples include hypertrees [9] and cube-connected cycles [14]. Hypertrees are full binary trees where the nodes at each level are interconnected using a subset of cube connections. Hypertrees can be easily shown to be subgraphs of the banyan-hypercubes. The cube-connected cycles are derived from n-cubes by replacing every node by a cycle of n nodes. Both hypertrees and cube-connected cycles have the great advantage of a small, constant degree, but that very advantage makes them harder to route, partition, and embed various common topological structures. The banyan-hypercubes, on the other hand, will be shown to have efficient routing, partitioning, and embedding capabilities. A detailed comparison between the banyan-hypercube synthesis and these other syntheses falls outside the scope of this paper. However, as

banyan-hypercubes can be viewed as a scheme of interconnecting or augmenting hypercubes, a comparison will be made between the hypercube and the banyan-hypercube to point out the advantages and disadvantages of this scheme.

It should also be noted that many multistage networks that have the banyan property (i.e., unique path between every source and every destination) can be synthesized with the hypercube. These networks include the omega network [11], the baseline network [20], the indirect binary n-cube [13], and several others. They can be synthesized with hypercubes by replacing the crossbar switches by nodes and interconnecting the nodes of each level by a hypercube as in the case of the BH. As the aforementioned networks are topologically equivalent [20], it can be shown that they remain topologically equivalent after they are synthesized with hypercubes, and therefore, they share with the banyan-hypercube the same topological properties in diameter, average distance, routing, embedding and partitioning. For this reason, we limit the discussion to the banyan-hypercube.

III. PROPERTIES OF THE BANYAN-HYPERCUBES

In this section the degree, diameter and average distance of BH networks are computed. The degree of $BH(h, k, s)$ can be easily seen to be $2s + k \log s$, the sum of the degree $2s$ of the banyan of spread s and the degree $k \log s$ of the hypercube of s^k nodes. The degree of the hypercube of hs^k nodes (when h is a power of two) is $\log hs^k$ which is equal to $\log h + k \log s$. Therefore, the degree of the hypercube is asymptotically larger than that of the banyan-hypercube of the same size, assuming fixed s and increasing k and h. However, for practical values of s (2 or 4) and k (less than 16 when $s = 2$ and at most 8 when $s = 4$), the degree of the BH is slightly larger. The corresponding extra hardware cost is nevertheless justified by the smaller diameter and average distance of the banyan-hypercube, as well as its added embedding capabilities.

The diameter of $BH(k + 1, k, s)$ is shown next to be k when $s = 2$ and $2k$ when $s = 4$, using the recursive structure of $BH(k + 1, k, s)$.

Theorem 3.1: The diameter of $BH(k + 1, k, s)$ is $k \log s$ for $s = 2$ and $s = 4$, and $2k$ for $s > 4$.

Proof: For the case $s = 2$ or 4, the proof is by induction on k. The basis step where $k = 0$ is trivial because the network is just a single node whose diameter is 0. For the induction step, assume that the diameter of $BH(k, k - 1, s)$ is $(k - 1) \log s$. Let x and y be two nodes in $BH(k + 1, k, s)$. If x and y are both in one of the constituent $BH(k - 1, k, s)$'s, then $d(x, y) \leq (k - 1) \log s$. If the two nodes are both in the top level, then their distance is $\leq$ the diameter of the hypercube in that level, that is, $\log s^k = k \log s$. If x is in one $BH(k, k - 1, s)$ and y in the top level, then $d(x, y) \leq d(x, y') + d(y', y) \leq (k - 1) \log s + 1 \leq k \log s$ where y' is a node of the top level of $BH(k - 1, k, s)$ that is adjacent to y. Finally, if x is in one $BH(k, k - 1, s)$ and y in another, then let y' be the sibling node of y in the $BH(k, k - 1, s)$ where x belongs. Clearly, $d(x, y) \leq d(x, y') + d(y', y) \leq (k - 1) \log s + \log s = k \log s$. Thus, in all cases the distance between x and y is $\leq k \log s$. To finish the proof, note that the distance between the node $00 \cdots 0$ and the node $11 \cdots 1$ of the base level is the diameter $k \log s$ of the base hypercube because using banyan edges would not shorten the path between these two nodes when $s = 2$ or 4 (for more details on this point, refer to the next section on routing). It follows then that the diameter is $k \log s$.

For the case where $s > 4$, the distance between any two nodes is at most their distance in pure banyan (i.e., using only banyan links) and thus $\leq 2k$. The distance between $00 \cdots 0$ and $11 \cdots 1$ in the base level is $2k$ since any shortest path between them must go to the apex level and back to the other node. Thus, the diameter is $2k$. ∎

Corollary 3.2: The diameter of BH(h, k, s) is $k \log s$ for $s = 2, 4$.

Proof: From the proof of the last theorem it can be seen that one shortest path between any node in level i and any node in level j can use only nodes from the levels that fall in between these two levels. Thus, the distance between any two nodes in BH(h, k, s) is the same as their distance in BH$(k+1, k, s)$, and the corollary follows. ∎

The diameter of the hypercube of the same number of nodes hs^k as BH(h, k, s) is $\log hs^k = \log h + k \log s$. Therefore, BH$(h, k, s)$ has a smaller diameter than the hypercube of the same size. Note that the comparison is valid only when h is a power of two.

As the diameter reflects only the worst case communication time, the average distance conveys better in practice the actual performance of the network. The next theorem gives the average distance of BH$(k + 1, k, s)$ for $s = 2$ or 4.

Theorem 3.3: The average distance of BH$(k + 1, k, 2)$ is $k(4k + 5)/6(k + 1)$ and that of BH$(k + 1, k, 4)$ is k.

Proof: Let S_k be the sum of all distances in BH$(k + 1, k, s)$. The average distance is S_k divided by the square of the number of nodes of BH$(k + 1, k, s)$. The recursive structure of banyan-hypercubes will be exploited to get the following recurrence relation:

$$S_k = s^2 S_{k-1} + \left[\left(\frac{\sigma_s}{s^2} + \frac{\log s}{2} + 1 \right) k^2 + k \right] s^{2k} \quad (1)$$

where $\sigma_s = 2$ if $s = 2$, and 16 if $s = 4$.

The recurrence relation can then be solved using standard linear recurrence relations techniques and the average distance will follow.

To derive relation (1), let L be the set of nodes in level k (i.e., top level) of BH$(k + 1, k, s)$, T the set of nodes of BH(k, k, s), and D the set of nodes of the whole network BH$(k + 1, k, s)$. Let also x and y represent two arbitrary nodes in BH$(k + 1, k, s)$, and $d(x, y)$ the distance between x and y.

$$S_k = \Sigma_{(x, y) \in D \times D} d(x, y)$$

$$S_k = \Sigma_{(x, y) \in T \times T} d(x, y) + \Sigma_{(x, y) \in L \times L} d(x, y)$$

$$+ \Sigma_{(x, y) \in L \times T} d(x, y) + \Sigma_{(x, y) \in T \times L} d(x, y)$$

$$S_k = \Sigma_{(x, y) \in T \times T} d(x, y) + \Sigma_{(x, y) \in L \times L} d(x, y)$$

$$+ 2 \Sigma_{(x, y) \in L \times T} d(x, y).$$

As $L \times D = L \times L \cup L \times T$, it follows that

$$S_k = \sum_{(x, y) \in T \times T} d(x, y) + 2 \sum_{(x, y) \in L \times D} d(x, y)$$

$$- \sum_{(x, y) \in L \times L} d(x, y).$$

Let A be the first sum, B the second sum, and C the third sum. To compute A, recall that BH(k, k, s) is constructed by having s BH$(k, k - 1, s)$ networks and connecting each s sibling nodes in a hypercube. It can be shown that if G and G' are two graphs of n and n' nodes, respectively, and if GG' denotes the graph derived by having n' copies of G and connecting each n' sibling nodes into a graph structure G', then $S(GG') = n'^2 S(G) + n^2 S(G')$ where S indicates the sum of all the distances in the corresponding graph. Therefore,

$$A = s^2 S_{k-1} + (ks^{k-1})^2 \sigma_s$$

where σ_s is the sum of distances of the hypercube of s nodes, which is 2 if $s = 2$, and 16 if $s = 4$.

C is the sum of all distances in the hypercube of s^k nodes. The average distance of a hypercube of N nodes is $\log N/2$, and therefore, the sum of all distances in such a hypercube is $N^2 \log N/2$. It follows that

$$C = s^{2k} k \frac{\log s}{2}.$$

To compute B, let $a_k = \Sigma_{(x, y) \in L \times D} d(x, y)$, that is, $a_k = B$.

$$a_k = \Sigma_{(x, y) \in L \times D} d(x, y) = \Sigma_{(x, y) \in L \times L} + \Sigma_{(x, y) \in L \times T} d(x, y)$$

$$a_k = s^{2k} k \frac{\log s}{2} + \Sigma_{(x, y) \in L \times T} d(x, y).$$

Let D' be the set of nodes of BH$(k, k - 1, s)$ and L' the level just below level L.

$\Sigma_{(x, y) \in L \times T} d(x, y) = s \Sigma_{(x, y) \in L \times D'} d(x, y)$ due to the symmetry of the s BH$(k, k - 1, s)$'s with respect to L.
$\Sigma_{(x, y) \in L \times T} d(x, y) = s \Sigma_{(x', y) \in L' \times D'} s(1 + d(x', y))$ because each node x' in L' has s neighbors in L.
$\Sigma_{(x, y) \in L \times T} d(x, y) = s^2 \Sigma_{(x', y) \in L' \times D'} (1 + d(x', y))$
$\Sigma_{(x, y) \in L \times T} d(x, y) = s^2 |L'| \times |D'| + s^2 \Sigma_{(x', y) \in L' \times D'} d(x', y)$
$\Sigma_{(x, y) \in L \times T} d(x, y) = ks^{2k} + s^2 a_{k-1}.$

Consequently,

$$a_k = ks^{2k} \left(1 + \frac{\log s}{2} \right) + s^2 a_{k-1}. \quad (2)$$

Letting $b_k = a_k/s^{2k}$ transforms (2) to $b_k = b_{k-1} + k(1 + \log s/2)$. This recurrence relation is linear and its solution is $(1 + \log s/2)k(k + 1)/2$, making use of the initial value $a_0 = 0$. Therefore, the solution to (2) is

$$a_k = s^{2k} \left(1 + \frac{\log s}{2} \right) \frac{k(k + 1)}{2}.$$

Replacing A, B, and C by their values leads to the recurrence

183

relation (1). Again taking $t_k = S_k/s^{2k}$ results in a linear relation. Solving that relation in t_k and using $S_k = s^{2k}t_k$ and $S_0 = 0$, we get

$$S_k = s^{2k}\left[\left(\frac{\sigma_s}{s^2} + \frac{\log s}{2} + 1\right)\right.$$
$$\left.\cdot \frac{k(k+1)(2k+1)}{6} + \frac{k(k+1)}{2}\right].$$

The average distance of BH$(k+1, k, s)$ is then $S_k/((k+1)s^k)^2$. When $s = 2$, $\sigma_s = 2$ and the average distance of BH$(k+1, k, 2)$ is

$$\text{AVG} - \text{DIST}(\text{BH}(k+1, k, 2)) = \frac{k(4k+5)}{6(k+1)}$$

and when $s = 4$, $\sigma_s = 16$, and thus the average distance of BH$(k+1, k, 4)$ is

$$\text{AVG} - \text{DIST}(\text{BH}(k+1, k, 4)) = k.$$

∎

Corollary 3.4: The average distance of BH$(h, k, 2)$ is $k/2 + (h^2 - 1)/6h$, and that of BH$(h, k, 4)$ is k.

Proof: It was pointed out in the proof of the previous theorem that $S(GG') = n'^2 S(G) + n^2 S(G')$ where $S(G)$ is the sum of all the distances of G. It follows then that the average distance of GG' is the sum of the average distances of G and G'. It can be seen that BH$(h, k, s) =$ BH$(h, h-1, s)G_s$ where G_s is a hypercube of s^{k-h+1} nodes. Thus,

$$\text{AVG-DIST}(\text{BH}(h, k, s)) = \text{AVG}$$
$$-\text{DIST}(\text{BH}(h, h-1, s)) + \text{AVG-DIST}(G_s).$$

Using the previous theorem, we get

$$\text{AVG-DIST}(\text{BH}(h, h-1, 2)) = \frac{(h-1)(4h+1)}{6h} \text{ and}$$
$$\text{AVG-DIST}(\text{BH}(h, h-1, 4)) = h - 1.$$

Since

$$\text{AVD-DIST}(G_s) = \frac{\log s^{k-h+1}}{2} = \frac{(k-h+1)\log s}{2},$$

it follows that

$$\text{AVG-DIST}(\text{BH}(h, k, 2)) = \frac{(h-1)(4h+1)}{6h}$$
$$+\frac{(k-h+1)\log 2}{2} = \frac{k}{2} + \frac{h^2 - 1}{6h}.$$

Similarly,

$$\text{AVG-DIST}(\text{BH}(h, k, 4)) = h - 1 + \frac{(k-h+1)\log 4}{2}$$
$$= h - 1 + k - h + 1 = k.$$

∎

The average distance of the hypercube of the same number of nodes hs^k as BH(h, k, s) is $\log hs^k/2 = \log h + k \log s/2$.

TABLE I

DIAMETER, AVERAGE DISTANCE, AND DEGREE OF HYPERCUBES AND BANYAN-HYPERCUBES OF THE SAME SIZE

	Banyan-Hypercube			Hypercube		
Net-Size	Diameter	Ave. Dist.	Degree	Diameter	Ave. Dist.	Degree
4	1	0.75	3	2.	1.0	2
32	3	1.41	7	5	2.5	5
1024	7	4.67	11	10	5.0	10
2^{19}	15	10.15	19	19	9.5	19

Therefore, the average distance k of BH$(h, k, 4)$ is always smaller than the average distance $k + \log h/2$ of the hypercube of the same size. For the case $s = 2$, Table I presents some actual values of the diameter, average distance and degree of BH$(k+1, k, 2)$'s and the hypercubes of the same number of nodes. The table clearly shows the improvement in diameter and average distance of BH's over hypercubes for practical sizes, and also shows the somewhat larger node degree of the BH. For $h \leq 8$ and for any $k \geq h - 1$, BH$(h, k, 2)$ can be shown to have better average distance than the hypercube of the same number of nodes.

IV. ROUTING

An optimal routing algorithm in any network would route messages from their source to their destination along a shortest path such that every intermediary node finds the next node on the path in constant time. To be optimal in space too, it is preferable if the information needed at every node is just the destination address. An example of such routing is hypercube routing.

Due to the highly recursive structure of the banyan-hypercubes and the exchange interconnections between the levels, the routing turns out to be simple and doable in optimal time and space. The main idea is to view routing a message from a source node to a destination node as a sequence of communication steps equivalent to a sequence of changes made to the source address label to become the destination address label. This is presented in more detail next.

Let (L, X) be the address label of a node holding a message to be routed to the destination (L', D) where $X = x_{k-1}\cdots x_1 x_0$ and $D = d_{k-1}\cdots d_1 d_0$. Since the interconnections at all the levels are parallel, the message can be sent first to the level of the destination node using banyan edges and then to the destination itself using hypercube edges in the same level, without incurring any unnecessary communication steps. In label terms, this corresponds to increasing L (if $L' > L$) or decreasing it (if $L' < L$) by one every time the message is sent to a new level, and then X is transformed to D bit by bit using hypercube routing. On the way from level L to level L' the bits of X that differ from the corresponding bits of D can be changed to agree with those of D if their positions lie between L and $L' - 1$ if $L' > L$ or between L' and $L - 1$ if $L' < L$. Specifically, if $L' > L$ and x_L differs from d_L, then the message can be sent to node $(L+1, x_{k-1}\cdots x_{L+1}d_L x_{L-1}\cdots x_0)$ in one step since a direct edge exists between the two nodes as explained in the definition of BH. Similarly, if $L' < L$ and x_{L-1} differs from d_{L-1}, then the message should be sent to node $(L - 1, x_{k-1} \cdots x_L d_{L-1} x_{L-2} \cdots x_0)$. Note that if these bits do not differ, then the message is sent through the straight edge. Note also that when the new node receives the message, it will follow the same routing policy, that is, it can view itself as a new source. This makes the routing algorithm uniform in the sense that all the nodes run the same algorithm when they forward a message.

The above outlined routing policy routes along shortest paths when $s = 2$ or 4. To show this, it is enough to argue that when the source and destination are in the same level, one shortest path can be found in the level without using interlevel edges. In the case $s = 2$, using an interlevel edge would change at most one bit but incur two extra communication steps to come back to the same level. Similarly, in the case $s = 4$, using an interlevel edge would change at most two binary bits but incur two extra communication steps to come back to the same level. Thus, using interlevel edges in either case would not gain us any communication speedup.

Consequently, the following routing algorithm which implements the above routing policy routes messages from sources to destinations along shortest paths when executed by every node. The time spent at every node is constant and the information needed is just the destination address. Hence, this algorithm is optimal.

Route from Current node X with address $(L, x_{k-1} \cdots x_1 x_0)$ to
Destination Node D with address $(L', d_{k-1} \cdots d_1 d_0)$
Algorithm Route(X,D);
begin
    Case:
      $L' > L$: /* go up */
        Send to $(L + 1, x_{k-1} \cdots x_{L+1} d_L x_{L-1} \cdots x_0)$
      $L' < L$: /* go down */
        Send to $(L - 1, x_{k-1} \cdots x_L d_{L-1} x_{L-2} \cdots x_0)$
      $L' = L$: /* horizontally */
      Route in Hypercube
    End Case
end

Routing Algorithm for the Banyan-Hypercube

V. EMBEDDING ON THE BANYAN-HYPERCUBES

Several topological structures are commonly used in various applications such as image processing and scientific computing. Among the most common structures are rings, meshes of various dimensions, full binary trees, pyramids, and multiple pyramids. In order for algorithms of one of these structures to have efficient communication time, the underlying network should embed these structures efficiently. The efficiency is defined in terms of the dilation cost. The dilation cost of an embedding of a guest graph on a host graph is the largest distance between nodes in the host graph which correspond to neighboring nodes in the guest graph. Clearly, the shorter the dilation, the better the embedding.

The embedding problem has received a lot of attention in recent years [3], [5], [6], [7], [10]. The hypercube is known to embed rings and meshes of powers of two dimensions with dilation cost 1. It also embeds full binary trees and pyramids with dilation cost 2. Embedding multiple pyramids on the hypercube is more difficult and would require a larger dilation cost.

This section incorporates the hypercube embedding of rings and meshes to embed these structures in the banyan-hypercubes with dilation cost 1. Full binary trees will be embedded on BH(h, k, s) with dilation cost $h/4$ by showing that twisted cubes [7] are subgraphs of BH's and by using the dilation one embedding of trees in twisted cubes [7]. Such dilation is better than that of the tree embedding on the hypercube for $h < 4$ and is equal to it for $h = 8$, which is a practical value of h for $s = 4$. Pyramids and multiple pyramids will be reviewed and optimally embedded on BH networks with dilation cost 1.

A. Ring Embedding

Rings are embedded on hypercubes using binary-reflected Gray codes [10]. A Gray code is a sequence of binary labels such that any two successive labels differ by only one bit. A binary-reflected Gray code G_k is a recursively defined Gray code of 2^k k-bit binary labels as follows. $G_1 = (0, 1)$, and $G_k = (0G_{k-1}, 1G_{k-1}^r)$ for $k > 1$ where G_{k-1}^r is G_{k-1} backward. For example, $G_2 = (00, 01, 11, 10)$ and $G_3 = (000, 001, 011, 010, 110, 111, 101, 100)$. Note that the last label and the first label differ by one bit only. Therefore, to embed a ring in k-cube using all the nodes, list the nodes in a binary-reflected Gray code. This embedding is obviously of dilation 1.

We incorporate the embedding of rings on cubes into the embedding of rings on banyan-hypercubes. The next theorem shows that such embedding can be done with dilation 1. The proof provides a constructive embedding.

Theorem 5.1: A BH(h, k, s) embeds a ring of all the nodes with dilation cost 1.

Proof: To embed a ring in a BH(h, k, s) using all the nodes, a Gray code is used in each level, and the levels are linked by the interlevel straight edges as follows. To distinguish between the various Gray codes corresponding to various levels, a Gray code G_i in level L is denoted $[L, G_i]$. Now it can be easily seen that the following sequence of nodes forms a full ring:

$$([0, 1G_{k-1}^r], [1, 1G_{k-1}], [2, 1G_{k-1}^r], [3, 1G_{k-1}],$$
$$\cdots [h - 1, G_{k-1}], [h - 1, 0G_{k-1}^r], [h - 2, 0G_{k-1}],$$
$$\cdots [1, 0G_{k-1}^r], [0, 0G_{k-1}])$$

when h is even,

and

$$([0, 1G_{k-1}^r], [1, 1G_{k-1}], [2, 1G_{k-1}^r], [3, 1G_{k-1}],$$
$$\cdots [h - 1, 1G_{k-1}^r], [h - 1, 0G_{k-1}], [h - 2, 0G_{k-1}],$$
$$\cdots [1, 0G_{k-1}^r], [0, 0G_{k-1}])$$

when h is odd. ∎

185

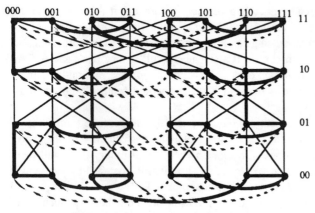

(a) Embedding a Ring on BH(4,3,2)

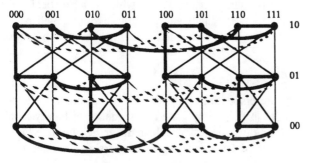

(b) Embedding a Ring on BH(3,3,2)

Fig. 4.   Ring embedding.

Fig. 4 shows an example of ring embedding for each case.

B. Mesh Embedding

The embedding of meshes is done in a similar manner (using Gray codes) [10], [3]. First note that if G_i and G_j are two Gray codes, then G_iG_j, the cross product or concatenation, is a matrix of $(i+j)$-bit labels where each row and each column is a Gray code. The corresponding nodes in a k-cube, where $k \geq i+j$, form a $2^i \times 2^i$ mesh. More generally, if G_{i_1}, G_{i_2}, $\cdots$, G_{i_l} are l Gray codes, then the multidimensional table $G_{i_1}G_{i_2} \cdots G_{i_l}$ corresponds to $2^{i_1} \times 2^{i_2} \times \cdots 2^{i_l}$ mesh in a k-cube where $k \geq i_1 + i_2 + \cdots + i_l$. Note that this embedding is of dilation 1. Note also that if all the nodes of a k-cube are to be used to embed a mesh, the dimensions have to be powers of two.

It follows that if a $2^{i_1} \times \cdots \times 2^{i_l}$ mesh is embedded at every level of BH(h, k, s) and the interlevel straight edges are used to link all these level meshes, a new $h \times 2^{i_1} \times \cdots \times 2^{i_l}$ mesh is embedded in BH(h, k, s) with dilation cost 1. Note that h can be anywhere between 1 and $k + 1$, and thus the mesh has more flexibility in one dimension.

We note that any two dimensional $n \times m$ mesh, where $n = h \times 2^{i_1} \cdots \times 2^{i_p}$ and $m = 2^{i_{p+1}} \times \cdots \times 2^{i_l}$, can be embedded in the above specified mesh with dilation 1 [3]. It can therefore be embedded in BH(h, k, s) with the same dilation.

C. Tree Embedding

Full binary trees of $2^n - 1$ nodes have been shown to be embeddable with dilation 1 in an $(n+1)$-cube and with dilation two in a n-cube [1]. However, they cannot be embedded with

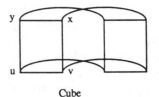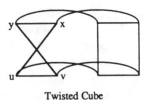

Fig. 5.   Cubes and twisted cubes.

dilation 1 in an n-cube. Twisted n-cubes of 2^n nodes were shown to embed full binary trees of $2^n - 1$ nodes with dilation 1 [7]. A twisted n cube is constructed from the n-cube by taking an arbitrary four-node cycle u, v, x, y of the cube and reconnect it to the new cycle u, x, v, y, as shown in Fig. 5.

The embedding of the full binary tree can be done such that u is the root and y is the idle remaining node (or vice versa). We will show that every two successive levels of BH(h, k, s) have a twisted cube as a subgraph and can thus embed a tree of $2s^k - 1$ nodes with dilation 1. Then a larger full binary tree can be embedded in any four successive levels with dilation 1. Embedding of full binary trees onto BH(h, k, s) is later carried out for any $h > 4$ with dilation $h/4$ which is small in practice. Note that to be able to embed a Full binary tree with minimum remaining idle nodes, hs^k has to be a power of two, and hence h itself has to be a power of two. So in the following discussion, h is assumed to be a power of two. In case it is not, only the largest power of two number of levels are taken from BH(h, k, s) to embed the tree.

Lemma 5.2: Every two consecutive levels of BH(h, k, s) embed a twisted cube of $2s^k$ nodes with dilation cost 1.

Proof: To see that every two successive levels L and $L+1$ of BH(h, k, s) can be configured as a twisted cube, note first that the two levels form a new cube since the two levels are parallel cubes and the corresponding nodes are connected by direct edges (the straight vertical edges). Observe also that the node $u = (L, 0\cdots0)$ is adjacent to some node $x = (L + 1, X)$ and the node $y = (L + 1, 0\cdots0)$ is adjacent to the node $v = (L, X)$, such that there is a cube edge between $(L, 0\cdots0)$ and (L, X), and between $(L + 1, 0\cdots0)$ and $(L + 1, X)$. Clearly, u, v, x, y form a cycle in the cube of the two levels. In Fig. 3, for example, the cycle u, v, x, y in the bottom two levels is the leftmost "square." It can be seen that a twisted cube is embedded in the two levels by ignoring the edges (u, y) and (v, x), and considering the edges (u, x) and (v, y). ∎

Consequently, a full binary tree of $2s^k - 1$ nodes can be embedded in the two levels with dilation 1, where the root is node $u = (L, 0\cdots0)$ and the idle node is $y = (L + 1, 0\cdots0)$. This is generalized next in the following theorem and its constructive proof.

Theorem 5.3: For any power of two $h \geq 4$, BH(h, k, s) embeds a full binary tree of $hs^k - 1$ nodes with dilation cost $h/4$.

Proof: BH$(4, k, s)$ is first shown to embed a full tree with $4s^k - 1$ nodes. Embed a full tree of $2s^k - 1$ nodes in levels 0 and 1, and another one in levels 2 and 3. The root of the first tree is $(0, 0\cdots0)$ and the corresponding idle node is $(1, 0\cdots0)$. The root of the second tree is node $(2, 0\cdots0)$ and the corresponding idle node is $(3, 0\cdots0)$. Make node $(1,$

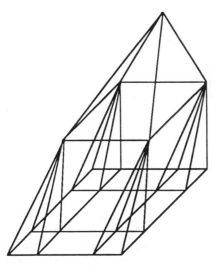

Fig. 6. A pyramid with a 4×4 base.

$0 \cdots 0$) a new root whose children are the old roots, which are adjacent to it in BH. Thus, the embedding is of dilation 1.

For $h > 4$, the embedding can be done recursively. Assume that an embedding of a full tree of $hs^k - 1$ nodes can be done on h levels with dilation $h/4$ (for $h = $ a power of two) such that the idle node is in the top leftmost node and the root is the leftmost node of the level that is $h/2$ steps away from the idle node. A similar embedding of the next larger full tree can be constructed from $2h$ levels. Embed a full tree in the bottom h levels and another full tree in the top h levels as just explained. Take the idle node of the first embedding to be the new root whose children are the old roots. Clearly, each of the old roots are $h/2$ (that is $2h/4$) steps away from the new root. Also the remaining idle node is the top leftmost node (in level $2h$) and the new root is h (that is $2h/2$) steps away from the idle node. This proves our claim inductively and constructively. ∎

D. Embedding of Pyramids

Pyramids are very useful data structures in image processing and scientific multigrid computations [3], [19]. Therefore, it is desirable to have an efficient embedding of pyramids on the underlying network of a given architecture. The embedding of pyramids in hypercubes has been shown to have dilation cost 2 and cannot be done in dilation 1 [3], [19]. We will show that $BH(k + 1, k, 4)$ networks have pyramids as subgraphs and can thus embed them with dilation 1.

A pyramid with an $n \times n$ base, where n is a power of two, has $\log n + 1$ levels of nodes where the base level (called level 0) is a $n \times n$ mesh, and each level i is an $n/2^i \times n/2^i$ mesh such that each node is the parent of four nodes in the level below (see Fig. 6). The top level has only one node called the apex.

Theorem 5.4: A pyramid with a $2^k \times 2^k$ base is a subgraph of $BH(k+1, k, 4)$, that is, can be embedded in it with dilation 1.

Proof: If a breadth first search is carried out from node $(k, 0 \cdots 0)$ down to the base level of $BH(k + 1, k, 4)$, the resulting tree along with all the edges between its nodes form a pyramid. This can be proved by induction on k by exploiting

the recursive structure of banyan-hypercubes. If $k = 0$, it is trivial as both the corresponding BH and pyramid are a single node. Assume that a pyramid can be embedded in $BH(k, k - 1, 4)$ as outlined earlier. Recall that $BH(k + 1, k, 4)$ is constructed by taking four $BH(k, k - 1, 4)$'s and a new level of 4^k nodes, connecting every four siblings in a cube, and finally connecting each node $(L + 1, x_{x-1} \cdots x_0)$ to the four nodes $(L, ax_{k-2} \cdots x_0)$ for $a = 0, 1, 2, 3$. By the inductive hypothesis, a pyramid of a $2^{k-1} \times 2^{k-1}$ base is embedded in the ath $BH(k, k - 1, 4)$ where the apex is node $(L, a0 \cdots 0)$, for $a = 0, 1, 2, 3$. At each level, the nodes of the four meshes of the four pyramids are respective siblings, and hence connected in cubes of four nodes. Out of these cube edges the four meshes can be linked together to form a new mesh of four times the size. Moreover, the node $(k + 1, 0 \cdots 0)$ is adjacent to the four apexes of those pyramids (connected in a cube of four nodes or a 2×2 mesh). The resulting subgraph is clearly the pyramid sought, which proves that such a pyramid can be embedded with dilation 1. ∎

Note that in $BH(h, k, 4)$, where $h < k + 1$, several smaller pyramids can be embedded, one in each of the $4^{k-(h-1)}$ $BH(h, h - 1, 4)$'s which are subgraphs of $BH(h, k, 4)$.

E. Embedding of Multiple Pyramids

A multiple pyramid of degree d is a graph made of d pyramids that have the same base but otherwise are disjoint. Such topological structures are useful in image processing where an image, stored at the base, has multiple objects of interests that can be processed simultaneously (by different pyramids), or different image processing tasks are to be done on the same image [12].

The above embedding of pyramids can be extended to embed multiple pyramids of degree 4 on $BH(k + 1, k, 4)$ with dilation 1. The embedding can be accomplished by tracing down each of the four nodes $(k+1, 0 \cdots 00)$, $(k+1, 0 \cdots 01)$, $(k+1, 0 \cdots 10)$, and $(k+1, 0 \cdots 011)$ in a breadth first search manner all the way to the base level. The same proof above can be applied to show that that search results in four pyramids that overlap at the base. These pyramids can also be shown to be disjoint above the base in a straightforward way by similar induction.

In general, a multiple pyramid of degree s can be embedded with dilation 1 in $BH(k + 1, k, s)$. However, no multiple pyramid with degree $d > s$ can be embedded with dilation 1 because in such a multiple pyramid each node at the base has d parents while in $BH(k + 1, k, s)$ each base node has only s adjacent nodes in the level above.

We plan to investigate the embedding of other topological structures (e.g., meshes of trees and hypernets) in the future. The rich and recursive structure of banyan-hypercubes may allow us to embed many more useful topological structures.

VI. Partitioning the Banyan-Hypercubes

Network partitionability is an essential feature of parallel machines which support multitasking to serve several users or to run multiple tasks of the same algorithm simultaneously. To run multiple tasks in parallel, where each task can itself be parallel, the machine is partitioned into independent parts,

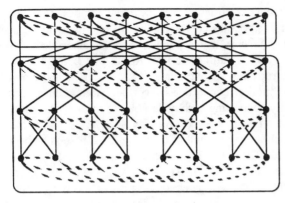

BH(4,3,2) ---> BH(3,3,2) & BH(1,3,1)

Fig. 7.   Horizontal partitioning.

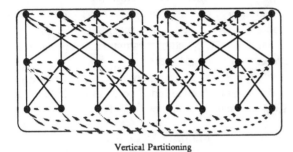

Vertical Partitioning

BH(3,3,2) ---> BH(3,2,2) & BH(3,2,2)

Fig. 8.   Vertical partitioning.

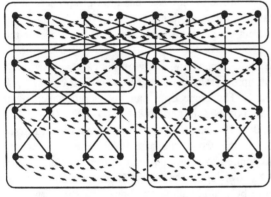

Horizontal Partitioning gives: BH(4,3,2) ⟶ BH(3,3,2) & BH(1,3,2)

Vertical Partitioning gives: BH(3,3,2) ⟶ BH(3,2,2) & BH(3,2,2)

Horizontal Partitioning gives: BH(3,2,2) ⟶ BH(2,2,2) & BH(1,2,2)

Fig. 9.   Mixed partitioning.

and to support the communication of each part, the network has to be partitioned into independent subnetworks. One desirable property of partitionability is to have the partitions (i.e., subnetworks) have the same topology as the original network [18]. The reason is that such property enables the system to use the same algorithms for routing, embedding, and partitioning on each partition.

The hypercube is partitionable into smaller subcubes. Banyans are also partitionable due to their recursive structure [8]. In this section, banyan-hypercubes are shown to be highly partitionable into BH subnetworks due to their recursive structure and the flexibility of allowing the number of levels to vary between 1 and $k + 1$. The recursive structure

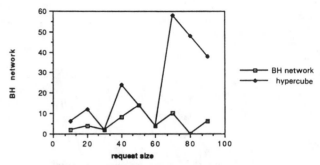

Fig. 10.   Comparison of internal fragmentations.

allows for *vertical partitioning* and the flexibility of having a variable number of levels allows for *horizontal partitioning*.

Horizontal partitioning consists of separating the top level from the remaining levels of BH(h, k, s) and getting a BH(1, k, s) and a BH($h - 1, k, s$). Recall that the top level is a hypercube of s^k nodes and that such a hypercube is BH(1, k, s). Fig. 7 shows an example of such a partitioning.

If BH(h, k, s) is not full, that is, $h < k + 1$, then the network is vertically partitionable into s BH($h, k - 1, s$) networks. This is a direct consequence of the recursive definition of BH(h, k, s). Fig. 8 shows an example of vertical partitioning.

A combination of horizontal and vertical partitioning is possible, thus leading to smaller and smaller partitions. Fig. 9 shows an example of mixed partitioning.

Note that horizontal partitioning results in hypercubes of various dimensions. The vertical partitioning of these cubes amounts to the buddy strategy of partitioning in [5]. This makes it easy to grant requests of rings, meshes, and trees by partitioning the cube BH(1, k, s) and mapping these structures onto the partitions (i.e., cubes). That is done when the requests are of sizes (i.e., number of nodes) smaller than the size of BH(1, k, s). If, on the other hand, the size of a request is larger than that of BH(1, k, s), then a number of horizontal partitionings are performed on BH(h, k, s) to get enough levels from the top to satisfy the request. If also the request is a pyramid or a multiple pyramid, then a BH with several levels is needed and consequently, a number of vertical and horizontal partitionings should be performed till a BH partition that best fits the request size is formed. Here too it can be seen that banyan-hypercubes are an enhancement over hypercubes in the sense that partitioning the former subsumes partitioning of the latter, and that many requests can be granted by partitioning the hypercube subnetwork, while other requests can be better served by a BH than by a hypercube.

A measure that shows the partitioning improvement of BH's over hypercubes is internal fragmentation. It measures the number of nodes that have to remain idle when various requests are granted in both networks. Each request in a hypercube system is fit in the smallest subcube that can accommodate the request, while in a BH system, the request is fit in the smallest BH partition. Fig. 10 gives a plot of internal fragmentation in both networks for a range of request sizes. It clearly indicates the advantage of the banyan-hypercubes due to the fact that partition sizes need not be powers of two.

We are developing algorithms and data structures to partition banyan-hypercubes efficiently as requests for topologies arrive to the system, and also to keep track of all the free and busy partitions of the network.

VII. Conclusion

This paper defined and studied a new family of networks called the banyan-hypercubes. These networks were shown to incorporate many hypercube features in routing, partitioning, and embedding of rings, meshes, and trees. They were also shown to offer an improvement over hypercubes in diameter, average distance, embedding of hierarchical structures, extendability cost, and flexibility in partitioning.

A useful way of viewing banyan-hypercubes is as a method of connecting various hypercubes with rich interlevel interconnections of the banyan without much limitation on the number of levels, and with a small increase in degree. This resulting hierarchical structure allowed for better embedding of pyramids and multiple pyramids. The flexibility of the number of levels offered better extendibility and more flexible partitioning.

Further extensions can be made in embedding and partitioning. Future work will investigate the embedding of additional topological structures, efficient partition allocation algorithms, and data structures to keep track of all the busy and free partitions. To allow for better partition management, the definition of BH's can be extended to be any number of successive levels between level i and level j in $BH(k+1, k, s)$. These levels can be shown to be isomorphic to the $j - i + 1$ bottom levels of $BH(k+1, k, s)$. Another extension is to allow the number of levels to grow beyond $k + 1$ levels. This involves defining new interlevel interconnections in such a way that all the previous properties of $BH(h, k, s)$ for $h \leq k + 1$ are preserved. Such an extension, if possible, can have many positive implications on extendibility cost, added partitioning flexibility, and perhaps embedding.

References

[1] S. N. Bhatt and C. F. Ipsen, "How to embed trees in hypercubes," Res. Rep. YALEU/DCS/RR-443, Dep. Comput. Sci., Yale University, New Haven, CN, Dec. 1985.

[2] V. Cantoni and S. Levialdi, "PAPIA: A case history," in *Parallel Computer Vision*, L. Uhr, Ed. New York: Academic, 1987, pp. 3–14.

[3] T. F. Chan and Y. Saad, "Multigrid algorithms on the hypercube multiprocessor," *IEEE Trans. Comput.*, vol. C-35, pp. 969–977, Nov. 1986.

[4] S. Cheemalavagu and M. Malek, "Analysis and simulation in Banyan interconnection networks with 2×2, 4×4, 8×8 switching elements," in *Proc. 1982 Real-Time Syst. Symp.*, Dec. 1982, pp. 83–89.

[5] M. Chen and K. G. Shin, "Processor allocation in an n-cube multiprocessor using Gray codes," *IEEE Trans. Comput.*, vol. C-36, pp. 1396–1407, Dec. 1987.

[6] D. DeGroot, "Mapping communication structures into SW-Banyan networks," Ph.D. dissertation, Univ. Texas, Austin, 1981.

[7] A. Esfahanian, L. M. Ni, and B. E. Sagan, "On enhancing hypercube multiprocessors," in *Proc. 1988 Int. Conf. Parallel Processing.*, Aug. 1988, pp. 86–89.

[8] R. L. Goke, "Banyan networks for partitioning multiprocessor systems," Ph.D. dissertation, Univ. Florida, Gainesville, 1976.

[9] J. R. Goodman and C. H. Sequin, "Hypertree: A multiprocessor interconnection topology," *IEEE Trans. Comput.*, vol. C-30, pp. 923–933, Dec. 1981.

[10] S. L. Johnsson, "Communication efficient basic linear algebra computations on hypercube architectures," *J. Parallel Distribut. Comput.*, no. 4, pp. 133–172, 1987.

[11] D. H. Lawrie, "Access and alignment of data in an array processor," *IEEE Trans. Comput.*, vol. C-24, pp. 1145–1155, Dec. 1976.

[12] R. Miller and Q. F. Stout, "Simulating essential pyramids," *IEEE Trans. Comput.*, vol. 37, pp. 1642–1648, Dec. 1988.

[13] M. C. Pease, "The indirect binary n-cube microprocessor array," *IEEE Trans. Comput.*, vol. C-26, pp. 458–473, May 1977.

[14] F. P. Preparata and J. E. Vuillemin, "The cube-connected cycles: A versatile network for parallel computation," in *Proc. 20th Symp. Foundations Comput. Sci.*, 1979, pp. 140–147.

[15] R. M. Jenevein and T. Mookken, "Traffic analysis of rectangular SW-Banyan networks," presented at The 15th Annu. Int. Symp. Comput. Architect., *Comput. Architect. News*, vol. 16, no. 2, May 30–June 2, 1988, pp. 333–342.

[16] C. Seitz, "The cosmic cube," *Commun. ACM*, vol. 28, pp. 22–33, Jan. 1985.

[17] M. Sejnowski et al., "An overview of the Texas reconfigurable array computer," in *Proc. AFIPS Conf.*, vol. 49, NCC, 1980, pp. 631–641.

[18] H. J. Siegel, *Interconnection Networks for Large-Scale Parallel Processing*. Lexington Books, 1985.

[19] Q. F. Stout, "Hypercubes and pyramids," in *Pyramidal Systems for Computer Vision*, V. Cantoni and S. Levialdi, Eds. Berlin: Springer, 1986.

[20] C. L. Wu and T. Y. Feng, "On a class of multistage interconnection networks," *IEEE Trans. Comput.*, vol. C-29, pp. 694–702, Aug. 1980.

[21] A. Youssef, "Properties of multistage interconnection networks," Ph.D. dissertation, Princeton Univ., Princeton, NJ, 1988.

Abdou S. Youssef was born on January 12, 1960. He received the B.S. degree in mathematics from the Lebanese University, Lebanon, in 1981, the M.A. and Ph.D. degrees from Princeton University, Princeton, NJ, in 1985 and 1988, respectively.

He taught for a year in 1982 at the Institute of Applied Sciences, The Lebanese University. He has been an Assistant Professor in the Department of Electrical Engineering and Computer Science at The George Washington University, Washington, DC, since 1987. His research interests include interconnection networks, parallel processing, computer architecture, and algorithms.

Dr. Youssef is a member of the Association of Computing Machinery.

Bhagirath Narahari (M'88) was born on August 24, 1960. He received the B.E. degree in electronics and electrical engineering from the Birla Institute of Technology and Science in 1982, and the M.S.E. and Ph.D. degrees from the University of Pennsylvania, Philadelphia, in 1984 and 1987, respectively.

He has been an Assistant Professor in the Department of Electrical Engineering and Computer Science at The George Washington University, Washington, DC, since 1987. His research interests include parallel algorithms, reconfigurable parallel architectures, interconnection networks, and theory of computation.

Dr. Narahari is a member of The Association of Computing Machinery and the IEEE Computer Society.

The Organization of Permutation Architectures with Bused Interconnections

Joe Kilian, Shlomo Kipnis, *Student Member, IEEE,* and Charles E. Leiserson, *Member, IEEE*

Abstract—This paper explores the problem of efficiently permuting data stored in VLSI chips in accordance with a predetermined set of permutations. By connecting chips with shared bus interconnections, as opposed to point-to-point interconnections, we show that the number of pins per chip can often be reduced. For example, for infinitely many n, we exhibit permutation architectures with $\lceil \sqrt{n} \rceil$ pins per chip that can realize any of the n cyclic shifts on n chips in one clock tick. When the set of permutations forms a group with p elements, any permutation in the group can be realized in one clock tick by an architecture with $O(\sqrt{p \lg p})$ pins per chip. When the permutation group is abelian, $O(\sqrt{p})$ pins suffice. These results are all derived from a mathematical characterization of *uniform permutation architectures* based on the combinatorial notion of a *difference cover*. We also consider uniform permutation architectures that realize permutations in several clock ticks, instead of one, and show that further savings in the number of pins per chip can be obtained.

Index Terms—Barrel shifter, bused interconnections, cyclic shifter, difference cover, difference set, group theory, permutation architecture, projective plane, special-purpose architecture, uniform architecture.

I. Introduction

THE organization of communication among chips is a major concern in the design of an electronic system. Because of the costs associated with wiring and packaging, it is generally desirable to minimize the number of wires and the number of pins per chip in an architecture. This paper investigates how buses (multiple-pin wires) can be employed to efficiently implement various communication patterns among a set of chips. Other theoretical studies of bused interconnections can be found in [1], [3]–[5], [7], [12], [21], [24], [25], and [29].

Perhaps the simplest example of the advantage of bused interconnections is the use of a single shared bus to communicate between any pair of chips connected to the bus in one clock tick. Communicating between any pair of chips in one clock tick can be implemented with two-pin wires, but any such scheme requires $\binom{n}{2}$ wires and $n - 1$ pins per chip.[1] Of course, a two-pin interconnection scheme may be able to implement more communication patterns, but if we are only interested in communication between individual pairs, the additional power, which comes at a high cost, is wasted.

Manuscript received April 4, 1988; revised January 6, 1989. This work was supported in part by the Defense Advanced Research Projects Agency under Contract N00014-80-C-0622. J. Kilian was supported in part by a Fannie and John Hertz Foundation Fellowship. C. E. Leiserson was supported in part by an NSF Presidential Young Investigator Award with matching funds provided by AT&T Bell Laboratories, IBM Corporation, and Xerox Corporation.

The authors are with the Laboratory for Computer Science, Massachusetts Institute of Technology, Cambridge, MA 02139.

IEEE Log Number 9038759.

[1] Unless otherwise specified, we count only data pins in our analysis and omit consideration of the pins for control, clock, power, and ground since they are needed by all implementations.

An example that better illustrates the ideas in this paper comes from the problem of building a fast *cyclic shifter* (sometimes called a *barrel shifter*) on n chips. Initially, each chip c contains a one-bit value ϵ_c. The function of the shifter is to move each bit ϵ_c to chip $c + s \pmod{n}$ in one clock tick, where s can be any value between 0 and $n - 1$.

Any cyclic shifter that uses only two-pin wires requires at least $\binom{n}{2}$ wires and $n - 1$ pins per chip in order to shift in one clock tick because each chip must be able to communicate directly with each of the other $n - 1$ chips. Using buses, however, we can do much better. Fig. 1 gives an architecture for a cyclic shifter on 13 chips which uses 13 buses and only 4 pins per chip. To realize a shift by 8, for example, each chip writes its bit to pin 3 and reads from pin 1. The reader may verify that all other cyclic shifts among the chips are possible in one clock tick. (In Section IV, we give a general method for constructing such cyclic shifters based on finite projective planes.)

The cyclic shifter of Fig. 1 has the advantage of uniformity. All chips have exactly the same number of pins, and to accomplish each of the 13 permutations specified by the problem, all chips write to (and read from) pins with identical labels. For all buses, the number of pins per bus is 4, which is the same as the number of pins per chip. Moreover, the connections between chips and buses follow a periodic pattern. The uniformity of the architecture leads to simplicity in the control of the system. Four control wires from a central controller are sufficient to determine each of the 13 shifts—two wires for specifying the number of the pin on which to write, and two for the pin to read—which is the minimum possible. Thus, our control scheme uses the minimum number of control pins, and the on-chip decoding logic is straightforward and identical for all the chips.

Cyclic shifters for general n can be constructed using an idea from combinatorial mathematics related to difference sets [18, p. 121]. (See also [6], [14], [16], [22], [26].)

Definition 1: A subset $D \subseteq Z_n$ of the integers modulo n is a *difference cover for* Z_n if for all $s \in Z_n$, there exist d_i, $d_j \in D$ such that $s = d_i - d_j \pmod{n}$.

That is, every integer in Z_n can be represented as the difference modulo n of two integers in D. For example, the set $D = \{0, 1, 3, 9\}$ is a difference cover for Z_{13}, since

$$0 = 0 - 0$$
$$1 = 1 - 0$$
$$2 = 3 - 1$$
$$3 = 3 - 0$$
$$4 = 0 - 9$$
$$5 = 1 - 9$$
$$6 = 9 - 3$$
$$7 = 3 - 9$$

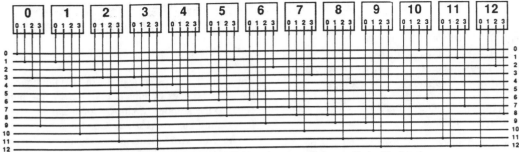

Fig. 1. A cyclic shifter on 13 chips that uses 13 buses. Each chip has 4 pins, and each bus has 4 chips connected to it. This cyclic shifter is based on the difference cover {0, 1, 3, 9} for Z_{13}.

$$8 = 9 - 1$$
$$9 = 9 - 0$$
$$10 = 0 - 3$$
$$11 = 1 - 3$$
$$12 = 0 - 1$$

where all subtractions are performed modulo 13.

Given a difference cover for Z_n with k elements, a cyclic shifter on n chips with n buses and k pins per chip can be constructed. Suppose $D = \{d_0, d_1, \cdots, d_{k-1}\}$ is a difference cover for Z_n. In the cyclic shifter, chip c connects via its pin i to bus $c + d_i$ (mod n), for all $c = 0, 1, \cdots, n - 1$ and $i = 0, 1, \cdots, k - 1$. To see that any cyclic shift on the n chips can be uniformly realized, consider a cyclic shift by s. Since D is a difference cover for Z_n, there exist $d_i, d_j \in D$ such that $s = d_i - d_j$ (mod n). To realize the shift by s, each chip writes to pin i and reads from pin j. Chip c therefore writes onto bus $c + d_i$, and bus $c + d_i$ is read by chip $(c + d_i) - d_j = c + s$. No collisions occur because each bus has exactly one pin labeled i and one pin labeled j connected to it, as can be verified.

The remainder of this paper explores permutation architectures, the properties of multiple-pin interconnections, and related combinatorial mathematics. In Section II we define a permutation architecture, introduce the notion of uniformity, and prove some basic properties of architectures that employ buses to realize arbitrary sets of permutations. Section III defines the notion of a difference cover for a set of permutations, relates it to the notion of a uniform permutation architecture, and proves some properties of difference covers. In Section IV, we show how to build cyclic shifters that are provably efficient. Section V investigates how to design small difference covers for any set of permutations that forms a finite group. In Section VI, we extend the discussion to uniform architectures that realize permutations in more than one clock tick. We present a variety of extensions to the results of the paper in Section VII. Finally, in Section VIII we discuss questions left open by our research. An Appendix of standard notations and definitions is included for reference. Notations and definitions more specific to the content of the paper are provided in context.

II. Permutation Architectures

In this section, we formally define the notion of a permutation architecture, and we make precise the notion of uniformity. We also prove some basic properties of permutation architectures that realize arbitrary sets of permutations. The definitions in this section are somewhat intricate and tedious, and are indicative of the difficulties faced in the design of efficient permutation architectures. In the next section, however, we use these definitions

to show that reasoning about uniform permutation architectures is essentially equivalent to reasoning about difference covers, a simpler and more elegant mathematical notion. The remainder of the paper then uses the simpler notion.

For convenience, we adopt a few notational conventions. We use multiplicative notation to denote composition of permutations. The inverse of a permutation π is denoted by π^{-1}. Composition of functions is performed in right-to-left order, so that $\pi_1 \pi_2$ is defined by $\pi_1 \pi_2 x = \pi_1(\pi_2(x))$. The identity permutation on n elements is denoted by I_n, or by I if the number of elements is unimportant. For a permutation set Φ, we denote by Φ^{-1} the set of all the inverses of the permutations of Φ, i.e., $\Phi^{-1} = \{\phi^{-1} : \phi \in \Phi\}$. For two permutation sets Φ and Ψ, the notation $\Phi\Psi$ is used to denote the permutation set $\{\phi\psi : \phi \in \Phi \text{ and } \psi \in \Psi\}$. We use the notation $[n]$ to denote the set of n integers $\{0, 1, \cdots, n - 1\}$.

We first define the notion of a permutation architecture.

Definition 2: A *permutation architecture* is a 6-tuple $\mathscr{A} = \langle C, B, P, \text{CHIP}, \text{BUS}, \text{LABEL} \rangle$ as follows.

1) C is a set of *chips*;
2) B is a set of *buses*;
3) P is a set of *pins*;
4) CHIP is a function CHIP: $P \rightarrow C$;
5) BUS is a function BUS: $P \rightarrow B$;
6) LABEL is a function LABEL: $P \rightarrow N$, where if $x, y \in P$, $x \neq y$, and CHIP(x) = CHIP(y), then LABEL(x) $\neq$ LABEL(y).

The set C contains all the chips in the architecture, and the set B contains all the buses. Which chips are connected to which buses is determined by the pins they have in common; the set P contains all the pins. The function CHIP determines which chip a given pin is on. Similarly, the function BUS determines which bus is connected to a given pin. The function LABEL names the pins on the chips by natural numbers such that all pins on a given chip have distinct labels, which we shall sometimes call pin numbers.

Our formal definition of a permutation architecture omits several subsystems that technically should be included, but whose inclusion is not germane to our study. These subsystems include a control network that specifies what permutation is to be performed and clocking circuitry for synchronization. Our focus is on the structure of the bused interconnections for permuting the data, and thus our definition encompasses only this aspect of the architecture.

We now define what it means for a permutation architecture to realize a permutation.

Definition 3: A permutation architecture $\mathscr{A} = \langle C, B, P, \text{CHIP}, \text{BUS}, \text{LABEL} \rangle$ *realizes* a permutation $\pi : C \rightarrow C$ if there exist two functions $\text{WRITE}_\pi : C \to P$ and $\text{READ}_\pi : C \to P$, such that for any chips c, c_1, $c_2 \in C$, we have

1) $\text{CHIP}(\text{READ}_\pi(c)) = \text{CHIP}(\text{WRITE}_\pi(c)) = c$;
2) $\text{BUS}(\text{WRITE}_\pi(c)) = \text{BUS}(\text{READ}_\pi(\pi(c)))$;
3) $c_1 \neq c_2$ implies $\text{BUS}(\text{WRITE}_\pi(c_1)) \neq \text{BUS}(\text{WRITE}_\pi(c_2))$.

The architecture *uniformly realizes* π if, in addition:

4) $\text{LABEL}(\text{WRITE}_\pi(c_1)) = \text{LABEL}(\text{WRITE}_\pi(c_2))$;
5) $\text{LABEL}(\text{READ}_\pi(c_1)) = \text{LABEL}(\text{READ}_\pi(c_2))$.

We say a permutation architecture *realizes* a set Π of permutations if it realizes every permutation in Π. We say it *uniformly realizes* Π if it uniformly realizes every permutation in Π.

Intuitively, for a permutation π, the functions WRITE_π and READ_π identify the *write pin* and the *read pin* for each chip. Condition 1 makes sure that each chip writes and reads pins that are connected to it. Condition 2 ensures that the bus to which chip c writes is read by chip $\pi(c)$. Condition 3 guarantees that no collisions occur, that is, no two data transfers use the same bus. The architecture uniformly realizes a permutation (Conditions 4 and 5) if all chips write to pins with the same pin number and read from pins with the same pin number, as in the cyclic shifter from Fig. 1.

Our definition of a permutation architecture implies that "complete" permutations are to be realized, that is, every chip sends exactly one datum and receives exactly one datum. Moreover, an interconnection is required even when a chip sends a datum to itself. Since no collisions occur, the number of buses in the architecture must be at least the number of chips. This observation leads directly to the following theorem.

Theorem 1: In any permutation architecture that realizes some nonempty permutation set Π, the average number of pins per bus is at most the average number of pins per chip.

Proof: Let $\mathscr{A} = \langle C, B, P, \text{CHIP}, \text{BUS}, \text{LABEL} \rangle$ be a permutation architecture for Π. The average number of pins per chip is $|P|/|C|$, and the average number of pins per bus is $|P|/|B|$. Condition 3 of Definition 3 says that for any permutation $\pi \in \Pi$, any two distinct chips are mapped to distinct buses. Consequently, we get that $|B| \geq |C|$, which proves the theorem. ∎

Under the assumption that no interconnection is needed for a chip to send data to itself, Theorem 1 is no longer applicable. A similar theorem can be proved for this model, however, which involves the number of fixed points in the permutations realized by the architecture. Specifically, suppose the architecture realizes a set Π of permutations. Define the *rank* of a permutation $\pi \in \Pi$ as $\text{RANK}(\pi) = |\{c \in C : \pi(c) \neq c\}|$, and define the rank of the permutation set Π as $\text{RANK}(\Pi) = \max_{\pi \in \Pi} \text{RANK}(\pi)$. The analogue to Theorem 1 states that the ratio between the average number of pins per bus and the average number of pins per chip is at most $|C|/\text{RANK}(\Pi)$.

In any architecture $\mathscr{A}$ that uniformly realizes a permutation set Π, the number of pins that are actually used to uniformly realize Π is the same for all chips, and additional pins on a chip are unused. Furthermore, the number of buses used in realizing any permutation $\pi \in \Pi$ is equal to the number of chips. These observations lead to the following definition of a uniform architecture.

Definition 4: A *uniform permutation architecture* for a permutation set Π is a permutation architecture $\mathscr{A} = \langle C, B, P, \text{CHIP}, \text{BUS}, \text{LABEL} \rangle$ such that

1) $\mathscr{A}$ uniformly realizes Π;

2) $|\{x \in P : \text{CHIP}(x) = c_1\}| = |\{x \in P : \text{CHIP}(x) = c_2\}|$ for any two chips c_1, $c_2 \in C$;
3) $|B| = |C|$;
4) if $x \neq y$ and $\text{LABEL}(x) = \text{LABEL}(y)$, then $\text{BUS}(x) \neq \text{BUS}(y)$.

Thus, all the chips in a uniform permutation architecture have the same number of pins (Condition 2), the number of buses is equal to the number of chips (Condition 3), and the labels of the pins of any bus are distinct (Condition 4).

The following theorem demonstrates that any permutation architecture that uniformly realizes some permutation set Π can be made into a uniform architecture.

Theorem 2: Let $\mathscr{A} = \langle C, B, P, \text{CHIP}, \text{BUS}, \text{LABEL} \rangle$ be a permutation architecture that uniformly realizes the permutation set Π, and let k be the smallest number of pins on any chip in C. Then there is a uniform architecture $\mathscr{A}' = \langle C', B', P', \text{CHIP}', \text{BUS}', \text{LABEL}' \rangle$ for Π with at most k pins per chip.

Proof: We construct the uniform architecture $\mathscr{A}'$ from the permutation architecture $\mathscr{A}$ in two steps. First, we construct an intermediate permutation architecture $\mathscr{A}'' = \langle C'', B'', P'', \text{CHIP}'', \text{BUS}'', \text{LABEL}'' \rangle$ by removing extraneous pins from chips in $\mathscr{A}$ such that all chips end up with the same number of pins per chip and such that each pin plays a role in uniformly realizing Π. Then, the buses of $\mathscr{A}''$ are reorganized to produce the architecture $\mathscr{A}'$ in such a way that the number of buses in $\mathscr{A}'$ is equal to the number of chips. We assume that the permutation set Π is nonempty, since otherwise the theorem is trivial.

In the first step, we remove pins that are unused in uniformly realizing Π. Since $\mathscr{A}$ uniformly realizes Π, each permutation $\pi \in \Pi$ can be associated with a distinct pair (i, j) of pin labels corresponding to the labels that all chips write to and read from in order to realize π. A pin is unused if its label does not appear in any of these $|\Pi|$ pairs. Removing the unused pins results in the architecture $\mathscr{A}''$ in which all chips have the same number of pins, since each chip has exactly one pin for each label used in uniformly realizing Π. The permutation architecture $\mathscr{A}''$ uniformly realizes Π, and furthermore, each pin is used in uniformly realizing some $\pi \in \Pi$. If we let s denote the number of pins per chip in $\mathscr{A}''$, then we have $s \leq k$, since originally at least one chip had k pins and no pins were added.

In the second step, we reorganize the buses of $\mathscr{A}''$ to produce the uniform architecture $\mathscr{A}'$ in which the number of buses is equal to the number of chips. For any permutation architecture that realizes a nonempty permutation set, the number of buses is never smaller than the number of chips. Assume without loss of generality that $C'' = [n]$, $B'' = [m]$, and $\text{range}(\text{LABEL}'') = [s]$. The theorem is proved if the architecture $\mathscr{A}''$ uses only $n = |C''|$ buses, but in general, the architecture might use $m > n$ buses.

We define a collection of mappings $\Psi = \{\psi_0, \psi_1, \cdots, \psi_{s-1}\}$, where for each $0 \leq i \leq s - 1$, the mapping $\psi_i : [n] \to [m]$ is defined to be $\psi_i(c) = b$ if and only if chip $c \in C''$ is connected via its pin number i to bus $b \in B''$. The elements of Ψ are indeed mappings since each chip has a pin numbered i for each $0 \leq i \leq s - 1$. The mappings are injective (one-to-one), since otherwise two pins with the same pin number would be connected to the same bus, and both pins could not be used to uniformly realize permutations, thereby violating the construction of $\mathscr{A}''$ in the first step. The collection Ψ is a multiset, since it may be that two different pin numbers $i \neq j$ define the same mapping (i.e., $\psi_i = \psi_j$). The key idea is that any permutation is implemented by each chip writing to pin i and reading from pin

j, thereby employing the mapping ψ_i to write data from the n chips to n distinct buses, and the inverse of the mapping ψ_j to read data from the same n buses back to the n chips.

We now show how to reorganize the buses of $\mathscr{A}''$ in order to construct a uniform architecture $\mathscr{A}'$. We partition Ψ into l equivalence classes $\Psi_0 \cup \Psi_1 \cup \cdots \cup \Psi_{l-1}$ such that ψ_i and ψ_j are in the same equivalence class Ψ_r, if and only if range$(\psi_i) = $ range(ψ_j). This partitioning has the property that if $\pi \in \Pi$, then there exists an r such that $\pi = \psi_j^{-1}\psi_i$ where ψ_i, $\psi_j \in \Psi_r$. (Recall that the inverse of an injective mapping $\psi:[n] \to [m]$ is defined as the mapping $\psi^{-1}:$range$(\psi) \to [n]$ such that if $\psi(c) = b$, then $\psi^{-1}(b) = c$.) For each $0 \le r \le l - 1$, pick a bijection (one-to-one, onto) $f_r:$range$(\psi) \to [n]$, where ψ is any mapping in Ψ_r. (We can pick a bijection, since ψ is injective, which implies $|$range$(\psi)| = n$.) We define the architecture $\mathscr{A}'$ by $C' = C''$, $B' = [n]$, $P' = P''$, CHIP$' = $ CHIP$''$, LABEL$' = $ LABEL$''$, and for any pin $x \in P'$ such that $\psi_{\text{LABEL}'(x)} \in \Psi_r$, we define BUS$'(x) = f_r(BUS''(x))$.

The architecture $\mathscr{A}'$ has exactly s pins per chip and satisfies $|B'| = |C'| = n$, thereby satisfying Conditions 2 and 3 of Definition 4. We show Condition 4 holds by considering any two pins x and y with LABEL$'(x) = $ LABEL$'(y) = i$. We have BUS$'(x) = f_r($BUS$''(x))$ and BUS$'(y) = f_r($BUS$''(y))$ for some f_r as defined in the previous paragraph. Since f_r is an injective mapping and because Condition 4 of Definition 4 holds for $\mathscr{A}''$, we then have $x \ne y$ implies BUS$'(x) \ne $ BUS$'(y)$.

It remains to show that Condition 1 of Definition 4 holds, that is, that $\mathscr{A}'$ uniformly realizes Π. Consider any permutation $\pi \in \Pi$. Since $\mathscr{A}''$ uniformly realizes Π, there exists a pair of pin labels (i, j) such that π is realized in $\mathscr{A}''$ by each chip writing to its pin numbered i and reading from its pin numbered j. We use the same pin labels (i, j) to realize the permutation π in $\mathscr{A}'$. Conditions 1, 4, and 5 of Definition 3 are immediately satisfied. To verify Conditions 2 and 3 we use the following observation. In architecture $\mathscr{A}''$ chip c is connected via its pin labeled h to bus $\psi_h(c)$, while in architecture $\mathscr{A}'$ it is connected to bus $f_r(\psi_h(c))$, where $\psi_h \in \Psi_r$. Condition 2 now holds since $\pi = \psi_j^{-1}\psi_i = (f_r\psi_j)^{-1}(f_r\psi_i)$. Condition 3 holds since $f_r\psi_i$ is a permutation on $[n]$. We therefore conclude that $\mathscr{A}''$ is a uniform architecture for Π with at most k pins per chip. ∎

The next theorem provides a lower bound on the number of pins per chip in any uniform architecture for a permutation set Π. (A related theorem due to Fiduccia appears in [20, p. 308].)

Theorem 3: Let $\mathscr{A} = \langle C, B, P, $ CHIP, BUS, LABEL$\rangle$ be a uniform permutation architecture for a permutation set Π. Then the number of pins per chip in $\mathscr{A}$ is at least $\sqrt{|\Pi|}$.

Proof: Because architecture $\mathscr{A}$ realizes Π uniformly, we can associate each $\pi \in \Pi$ with a pair (i, j) of pin numbers such that π is realized by each chip writing to its pin labeled i and reading from its pin labeled j. Since $\mathscr{A}$ is uniform, each chip has exactly $|P|/|C|$ pins, and the number of such pairs is $(|P|/|C|)^2$. No two permutations can be associated with the same pair, and thus, we have $(|P|/|C|)^2 \ge |\Pi|$ or $|P|/|C| \ge \sqrt{|\Pi|}$. ∎

A permutation architecture can often nonuniformly realize many more permutations than the square of the number of pins per chip. As an example, consider a "crossbar" architecture of n chips and n buses where each chip is connected to each bus. This architecture can nonuniformly realize all $n!$ permutations, which is much greater than n^2, the square of the number of pins per chip. In Section VII, we discuss some of the capabilities of nonuniform permutation architectures.

III. DIFFERENCE COVERS

In this section, we present our main theorems which establish the relationship between difference covers for permutation sets and uniform permutation architectures. We also prove some lemmas concerning difference covers for Cartesian products of permutation sets. Finally, we present an alternative representation for difference covers called substring covers based on similar notions in the literature of difference sets.

We first provide a generalization of Definition 1 to arbitrary sets of permutations.

Definition 5: A *difference cover* for a permutation set Π is a set $\Phi = \{\phi_0, \phi_1, \cdots, \phi_{k-1}\}$ of permutations such that for each $\pi \in \Pi$ there exist ϕ_i, $\phi_j \in \Phi$ such that $\pi = \phi_j^{-1}\phi_i$.

Equivalently, we can use our product-of-sets notation to say that Φ is a difference cover for Π if $\Phi^{-1}\Phi \supseteq \Pi$.

The following two theorems show how difference covers and uniform architectures are related. Theorem 4 describes how to design a uniform architecture for a permutation set Π when a difference cover for Π is given. Theorem 5 presents a construction of a difference cover for a permutation set Π from a uniform architecture for Π.

Theorem 4: Let Π be a permutation set, and let Φ be a difference cover for Π such that $|\Phi| = k$. Then there exists a uniform architecture for Π with k pins per chip.

Proof: Let $\Phi = \{\phi_0, \phi_1, \cdots, \phi_{k-1}\}$, and assume that Π is a set of permutations on n objects. We construct a permutation architecture for Π with n buses and k pins per chip. We name the chips and buses of the architecture by natural numbers, and the pins by pairs of natural numbers. The architecture $\mathscr{A} = \langle C, B, P, $ CHIP, BUS, LABEL$\rangle$ is defined as $C = [n]$, $B = [n]$, $P = [n] \times [k]$, CHIP$(c, i) = c$, LABEL$(c, i) = i$, and BUS$(c, i) = \phi_{\text{LABEL}(c, i)}($CHIP$(c, i)) = \phi_i(c)$. That is, chip c is connected via its pin number i to bus $\phi_i(c)$.

To see formally that this architecture uniformly realizes Π, let $\pi \in \Pi$ be a permutation, and let ϕ_i, $\phi_j \in \Phi$ be elements of the difference cover for Π such that $\pi = \phi_j^{-1}\phi_i$. Define the write function for π as WRITE$_\pi(c) = (c, i)$ and define the read function for π as READ$_\pi(c) = (c, j)$. (Note that i and j are always in the range 0 through $k - 1$.) We now verify that the five Conditions of Definition 3 are satisfied. Condition 1 holds since for any chip $c \in C$ we have CHIP(WRITE$_\pi(c)$) $=$ CHIP$(c, i) = c$, and CHIP(READ$_\pi(c)$) $=$ CHIP$(c, j) = c$. Condition 2 is satisfied since for any chip $c \in C$ we have

$$\text{BUS}\big(\text{WRITE}_\pi(c)\big) = \text{BUS}(c, i)$$
$$= \phi_i(c)$$
$$= \phi_j\phi_j^{-1}\phi_i(c)$$
$$= \phi_j\big(\pi(c)\big)$$
$$= \text{BUS}\big(\pi(c), j\big)$$
$$= \text{BUS}\big(\text{READ}_\pi(\pi(c))\big).$$

Condition 3 holds because if BUS(WRITE$_\pi(c_1)$) $=$ BUS(WRITE$_\pi(c_2)$) for any two chips c_1, $c_2 \in C$, then we have $\phi_i(c_1) = \phi_i(c_2)$, which implies that $c_1 = c_2$, since ϕ_i is invertible. Conditions 4 and 5 both hold since LABEL(WRITE$_\pi(c)$) $= i$ and LABEL(READ$_\pi(c)$) $= j$ for all chips $c \in C$. We therefore conclude that the architecture $\mathscr{A}$ uniformly realizes Π. The architecture is uniform, but Theorem 2 obviates the need to show this fact. ∎

Given a difference cover of small cardinality, Theorem 4 says we can construct a uniform architecture with few pins per chip. In fact, the reverse is true as well, as the following theorem shows.

Theorem 5: Let Π be a permutation set, and let $\mathcal{A}$ be a uniform architecture for Π with k pins per chip. Then Π has a difference cover Φ such that $|\Phi| \leq k$.

Proof: Given a uniform architecture $\mathcal{A} = \langle C, B, P, \text{CHIP}, \text{BUS}, \text{LABEL} \rangle$ for the permutation set Π, where k is the number of pins on each chip, we construct a difference cover Φ for Π as follows. Assume without loss of generality that $C = B = [n]$ and range(LABEL) $= [k]$. For each pin number i, where $i = 0, 1, \cdots, k-1$, we define ϕ_i by $\phi_i(c) = b$ if and only if chip c is connected via its pin number i to bus b. We now define the difference cover Φ to be the set $\Phi = \{\phi_0, \phi_1, \cdots, \phi_{k-1}\}$. (The set Φ may have less than k elements, since some permutations may be repeated among the ϕ_i's.)

To see that Φ is a difference cover for Π, consider any permutation $\pi \in \Pi$. Since $\mathcal{A}$ uniformly realizes π, there exists a pair of pin labels (i, j) such that π is realized by each chip writing to its pin numbered i and reading from its pin numbered j. The labels i and j satisfy $i = \text{LABEL}(\text{WRITE}_\pi(c))$ and $j = \text{LABEL}(\text{READ}_\pi(c))$ for all chips $c \in C$, as follows from Conditions 4 and 5 of Definition 3. Conditions 1 and 3 of Definition 3 imply that ϕ_i and ϕ_j are both permutations, and therefore there are $\phi_h, \phi_l \in \Phi$ such that $\phi_h = \phi_i$ and $\phi_l = \phi_j$. Finally, Condition 2 of Definition 3 implies that $\pi = \phi_j^{-1}\phi_i = \phi_l^{-1}\phi_h$, which proves that Φ is indeed a difference cover for Π. ∎

Theorems 4 and 5 show that uniform architectures and difference covers are very closely related. Thus, when designing a uniform permutation architecture for a set of permutations, it suffices to focus on the problem of constructing a good difference cover for that set.

The structure of a permutation set can be helpful in obtaining a difference cover for it. In Sections IV and V, we investigate the construction of difference covers for cyclic groups of permutations and for groups in general. Here, we examine permutation sets formed by Cartesian products.

Definition 6: Let Π_1 be a set of permutations on X_1, and let Π_2 be a set of permutations on X_2. The *Cartesian product* $\Pi = \Pi_1 \times \Pi_2$ is the set of permutations from $X_1 \times X_2$ to $X_1 \times X_2$ defined as $\Pi = \{(\pi_1, \pi_2): \pi_1 \in \Pi_1, \pi_2 \in \Pi_2\}$. Operations on the elements of Π are performed componentwise.

The Cartesian product $\Pi_1 \times \Pi_2$ is isomorphic to the Cartesian product $\Pi_2 \times \Pi_1$. If Π_1 and Π_2 are both nonempty, then the Cartesian product $\Pi = \Pi_1 \times \Pi_2$ is an abelian permutation set if and only if both Π_1 and Π_2 are abelian permutation sets.

The next two lemmas provide bounds on the size of difference covers for Cartesian products of permutation sets. (Similar lemmas hold for composition products of permutation sets.)

Lemma 6: Let Π_1 be a permutation set on n_1 objects, and let Π_2 be a permutation set on n_2 objects. Then the Cartesian product $\Pi = \Pi_1 \times \Pi_2$, which is a permutation set on $n_1 \cdot n_2$ objects, has a difference cover of size $|\Pi_1| + |\Pi_2|$.

Proof: Let Φ be the union of $\{(\pi_1^{-1}, I_{n_2}): \pi_1 \in \Pi_1\}$ and $\{(I_{n_1}, \pi_2): \pi_2 \in \Pi_2\}$. Each permutation $\pi = (\pi_1, \pi_2) \in \Pi$, can be represented as $(\pi_1, \pi_2) = (\pi_1^{-1}, I_{n_2})^{-1} \cdot (I_{n_1}, \pi_2)$, where both (π_1^{-1}, I_{n_2}) and (I_{n_1}, π_2) are in Φ. Thus, Φ is a difference cover for Π, and the size of Φ is exactly $|\Pi_1| + |\Pi_2|$. ∎

Lemma 7: Let Π_1 be a permutation set on n_1 objects with a difference cover Φ_1, and let Π_2 be a permutation set on n_2 objects with a difference cover Φ_2. Then the Cartesian product $\Phi = \Phi_1 \times \Phi_2$ is a difference cover for $\Pi = \Pi_1 \times \Pi_2$.

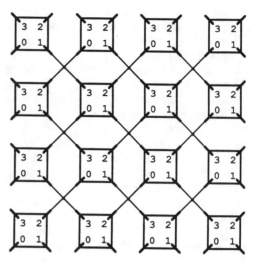

Fig. 2. A uniform architecture due to Fiduccia [10] based on the difference cover {S, SE, E, I} for the permutation set $\Pi = $ {I, N, E, S, W, NE, SE, NW, SW}.

Proof: For each $\pi = (\pi_1, \pi_2) \in \Pi$, there exist $\phi_{i_1}, \phi_{j_1} \in \Phi_1$ such that $\pi_1 = \phi_{j_1}^{-1}\phi_{i_1}$, and there exist $\phi_{i_2}, \phi_{j_2} \in \Phi_2$ such that $\pi_2 = \phi_{j_2}^{-1}\phi_{i_2}$. We then have $(\pi_1, \pi_2) = (\phi_{j_1}^{-1}\phi_{i_1}, \phi_{j_2}^{-1}\phi_{i_2}) = (\phi_{j_1}, \phi_{j_2})^{-1}(\phi_{i_1}, \phi_{i_2})$, where both (ϕ_{i_1}, ϕ_{i_2}) and (ϕ_{j_1}, ϕ_{j_2}) are in $\Phi = \Phi_1 \times \Phi_2$, and hence Φ is a difference cover for Π. ∎

To demonstrate both the use of difference covers and Lemma 7, we present in Fig. 2 a uniform permutation architecture due to Fiduccia [10] for realizing shifts in a two-dimensional array. The architecture uniformly realizes the permutation set $\Pi = $ {I, N, E, S, W, NE, SE, NW, SW} of eight compass directions plus the identity I. We introduce two permutation sets $\Pi_1 = $ {I, N, S}, $\Pi_2 = $ {I, E, W}, and corresponding difference covers $\Phi_1 = $ {I, S} and $\Phi_2 = $ {I, E}. The Cartesian product $\Pi_1 \times \Pi_2$ is Π, and the set of permutations $\Phi = \Phi_1 \times \Phi_2 = $ {S, SE, E, I} is a difference cover for Π.

We conclude this section by defining the notion of a substring cover for a permutation set Π, which is equivalent to the notion of a difference cover. (A similar notion for difference sets is well known in the literature [6], [26].)

Definition 7: An ordered list $\Sigma = \langle \sigma_0, \sigma_1, \cdots, \sigma_{k-1} \rangle$ of permutations is a *substring cover* for a permutation set Π if

1) $\sigma_0 \sigma_1 \cdots \sigma_{k-1} = I$, and

2) for all $\pi \in \Pi$, there exist $0 \leq i, j \leq k-1$ such that $\pi = \sigma_i \sigma_{i+1} \cdots \sigma_j$, where the arithmetic in the indexes is performed modulo k.

The substring cover Σ is a list of permutations such that all the permutations in Π can be represented as a composition of a substring of permutations of Σ. The following two theorems show that the notions of a substring cover and a difference cover are equivalent.

Theorem 8: Let Π be a permutation set on n elements, and let Σ be a k-element substring cover for Π. Then Π has a difference cover Φ with at most k elements.

Proof: Given a k-element substring cover $\Sigma = \langle \sigma_0, \sigma_1, \cdots, \sigma_{k-1} \rangle$ for Π, a difference cover Φ with at most k elements can be constructed. For each $0 \leq i \leq k-1$ we define $\phi_i = \sigma_0 \sigma_1 \cdots \sigma_i$. If a permutation π can be represented as $\pi = \sigma_i \sigma_{i+1} \cdots \sigma_j$, then $\pi = \phi_{i-1}^{-1}\phi_j$. By construction, the difference cover Φ has at most k elements. ∎

Theorem 9: Let Π be a permutation set on n elements, and let Φ be a k-element difference cover for Π. Then Π has a substring cover Σ with k elements.

Proof: Given a k-element difference cover $\Phi = \{\phi_0, \phi_1, \cdots, \phi_{k-1}\}$ for Π, we build a substring cover Σ for Π by defining $\sigma_i = \phi_{i-1}^{-1}\phi_i$ for all $0 \le i \le k - 1$. The product $\sigma_0\sigma_1 \cdots \sigma_{k-1}$ yields the identity permutation. For each $\pi \in \Pi$, if $\pi = \phi_i^{-1}\phi_j$, then $\pi = \sigma_{i+1}\sigma_{i+2} \cdots \sigma_j$. Therefore, Σ is a substring cover for Π with k elements. ∎

Referring back to the example of the eight compass directions, we present a substring cover for the permutation set $\Pi = \{$I, N, E, S, W, NE, SE, NW, SW$\}$. The substring cover $\Sigma = \langle$S, E, N, W$\rangle$ is constructed from the difference cover $\Phi = \{$S, SE, E, I$\}$ that was used in the architecture of Fig. 2. Each of the eight compass directions can be realized as a substring of the list $\Sigma = \langle$S, E, N, W$\rangle$.

As another example, consider the permutation set $\Pi = \{$I, N, E, S, W$\}$ of the shifts in a two-dimensional array corresponding to the four compass directions. This permutation set has a difference cover $\Phi = \{$N, E, I$\}$ and a corresponding substring cover $\Sigma = \langle$N, SE, W$\rangle$. Consequently, there is a uniform architecture for realizing the four compass directions with three pins per chip, as has been observed by Feynman [15, pp. 437–438]. Fig. 3 presents a uniform architecture based on the difference cover $\Phi = \{$N, E, I$\}$ for the permutation set $\Pi = \{$I, N, E, S, W$\}$.

IV. Cyclic Shifters

This section describes uniform architectures for realizing cyclic shifts among n chips in one clock tick. We first present a difference cover of size $O(\sqrt{n})$ for the set of all n cyclic shifts on n elements, and we give an area-efficient layout for the corresponding permutation architecture suitable for implementation as a printed-circuit board. When n can be expressed as $n = q^2 + q + 1$, where q is a power of a prime, we improve the bound on the size of a difference cover for all cyclic shifts on n elements to the optimal value of $\lceil \sqrt{n} \rceil$. Finally, we prove that for any cyclic shifter that operates in one clock tick (even a nonuniform one), the average number of pins per chip is at least $\lceil \sqrt{n} \rceil$.

The first permutation architecture for cyclic shifters that we present is based on the construction in the following simple theorem.

Theorem 10: The set of n cyclic shifts on n elements has a difference cover of size at most $2\lceil \sqrt{n} \rceil - 1$.

Proof: Since the set of n cyclic shifts on n elements forms a group, and since this group is isomorphic to the group Z_n, we shall construct a difference cover D for Z_n. For convenience, let $m = \lceil \sqrt{n} \rceil$. Define two sets $A = \{0, 1, \cdots, m - 1\}$ and $B = \{0, m, 2m, \cdots, (m - 1)m\}$, and let the difference cover D be defined by $D = A \cup B$. Each element $s \in Z_n$ can be realized as $s = b - a \pmod{n}$, where $a \in A$ and $b \in B$ by taking $a = m - (s \bmod m)$ and $b = \lceil s/m \rceil \cdot m$, as can be verified. The size of the difference cover D is $2m - 1 = 2\lceil \sqrt{n} \rceil - 1$, since the element 0 occurs in both A and B. ∎

The difference cover constructed in the proof of Theorem 10 corresponds to an architecture with a regular, area-efficient layout, as shown in Fig. 4. The n chips of the architecture are laid out in an array consisting of $m = \sqrt{n}$ rows, each containing $\sqrt{n}$ chips. (For simplicity, we assume that n is a square.) Each chip has pins $0, 1, \cdots, m - 1$ on the top side, and pins $m, m + 1, \cdots, 2m - 1$ on the left side. Each bus consists of one vertical segment and one or two horizontal segments. Each wiring channel consists of $m = \sqrt{n}$ tracks, where each track is

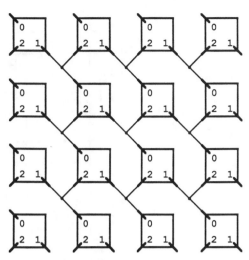

Fig. 3. A uniform architecture due to Feynman [15] based on the difference cover $\{$N, E, I$\}$ for the permutations set $\Pi = \{$I, N, E, S, W$\}$.

used to lay out segments of buses. When n is not a square, a cyclic shifter on n chips can be laid out in a similar fashion, with each wiring channel having at most $2\lceil \sqrt{n} \rceil$ tracks. The side of the layout is therefore $O(n)$, since there are $\lceil \sqrt{n} \rceil$ chips and $\lceil \sqrt{n} \rceil$ wiring channels along the side. The area of the layout is $O(n^2)$, which is asymptotically optimal since any architecture that can realize any of the cyclic-shift permutations in one clock tick requires area $\Omega(n^2)$ [30, p. 56].

Remark: The bound of $2\lceil \sqrt{n} \rceil - 1$ pins per chip can be improved to $(\sqrt{2} + o(1))\sqrt{n}$. See Section VIII.

Occasionally, it is desirable to implement a subset of the cyclic shifts on n elements. The following corollary to Theorem 10 shows that when the shift amounts form an arithmetic sequence, a small difference cover exists.

Corollary 11: Let a, b, and p be integers modulo n. For each $r \in [p]$, define π_r to be the permutation on $[n]$ that maps each $c \in [n]$ to $c + a + rb \pmod{n}$. Then the permutation set $\{\pi_r : r \in [p]\}$ has a difference cover of size $2\lceil \sqrt{p} \rceil$.

Proof: As in the proof of Theorem 10, we construct two sets A and B whose union is the desired difference cover. The sets are $A = \{0, b, 2b, \cdots, (m - 1)b\}$ and $B = \{a, a + mb, a + 2mb, \cdots, a + (m - 1)mb\}$, where $m = \lceil \sqrt{p} \rceil$. ∎

Returning to the problem of implementing all n cyclic shifts on n elements, the following theorem demonstrates that for certain values of n, the optimal $\lceil \sqrt{n} \rceil$ bound can be obtained.

Theorem 12: The set of n cyclic shifts on n elements has a difference cover of size $\lceil \sqrt{n} \rceil$ if $n = q^2 + q + 1$, where q is a power of a prime.

Proof: As in the proof of Theorem 10, the problem is equivalent to that of constructing a difference cover D for Z_n. When n is the size of a projective plane ($n = q^2 + q + 1$, where q is a power of a prime), this problem is equivalent to the problem of constructing a difference set. The difference set we give is due to Singer; a proof of its correctness is given in Hall [18, p. 129]. Let x be a primitive root of the Galois field $GF(q^3)$, and let $F(y)$ be any irreducible cubic polynomial over the Galois field $GF(q)$. We construct a difference cover D for Z_n from the set $[n]$ by choosing those $i \in [n]$ such that the power x^i can be written in the form $x^i = ax + b \pmod{F(x)}$ for some $a, b \in GF(q)$. ∎

The construction of a uniform architecture based on a projective plane can be interpreted as follows. The n points of the projective plane correspond to the n chips, and the n lines of the

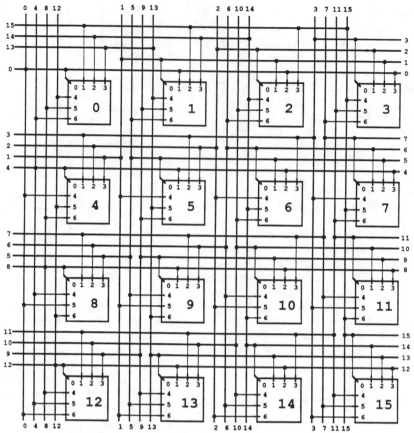

Fig. 4. A layout for a cyclic shifter with $n = 16$ chips. Each chip and each bus has 7 pins. Each bus is constructed of one vertical segment and either one or two horizontal segments.

projective plane correspond to the n buses. Each line contains $q + 1$ points, which means that each bus is connected to $q + 1$ chips. Each point is incident on $q + 1$ lines, which means that each chip is connected to $q + 1$ different buses through its $q + 1$ pins. For example, Fig. 1 demonstrates a uniform architecture based on the projective plane of size 13.

Theorems similar to Theorem 10 (but without application to architecture) appear in the combinatorics literature: see, for example, [22]. Bus connection networks based on projective planes have also been studied by Bermond, Bond, and Scalé [4] and by Mickunas [25], who observed that projective planes can be used to construct hypergraphs of diameter one.

Uniform architectures for cyclic shifters based on projective planes achieve the minimal number of pins per chip among all uniform cyclic shifters. We now prove a lower bound of $\lceil \sqrt{n} \rceil$ on the average number of pins per chip for any permutation architecture that realizes all the cyclic shifts. This lower bound applies to all permutation architectures, including nonuniform ones, and shows that uniform cyclic shifters based on projective planes are optimal among all cyclic shifters that operate in a single clock tick.

Theorem 13: Let $\mathscr{A} = \langle C, B, P, \text{CHIP}, \text{BUS}, \text{LABEL} \rangle$ be a permutation architecture for the n cyclic shifts on n chips. Then the average number of pins per chip is at least $\lceil \sqrt{n} \rceil$.

Proof: The average number of pins per chip is $|P|/n$. We shall prove that $|P| \geq n \lceil \sqrt{n} \rceil$ which implies the theorem. We adopt the following conventions for notational convenience:

1) The set of buses is $B = \{b_0, b_1, \cdots, b_{m-1}\}$. We denote by k_i the number of pins connected to bus b_i, that is, $k_i = |\{x \in P : \text{BUS}(x) = b_i\}|$.

2) The buses that have at least $\lceil \sqrt{n} \rceil$ pins each are indexed first, that is, if there are r buses with at least $\lceil \sqrt{n} \rceil$ pins each, then $k_i \geq \lceil \sqrt{n} \rceil$ for $i = 0, 1, \cdots, r - 1$ and $k_i < \lceil \sqrt{n} \rceil$ for $i = r, r + 1, \cdots, m - 1$.

The thrust of the proof is to count the number of distinct data transfers when the architecture realizes each of the $n - 1$ nontrivial shifts in turn. (The identity permutation is a trivial shift.) Each chip can be mapped to each other chip by one of the cyclic shifts, i.e., the cyclic shifts form a transitive group of permutations. Considering only the $n - 1$ nontrivial shifts, there are exactly $n(n - 1)$ distinct data transfers that must be implemented through interconnections in the architecture.

We compute an upper bound on the number of distinct data transfers that the buses can implement. Each of the first r buses $b_0, \cdots, b_{r-1}$ can be employed to realize at most one distinct data transfer in each of the $n - 1$ nontrivial shifts. Thus, at most $r(n - 1)$ distinct data transfers can be carried out by the first r buses. Any other bus b_i, where $r \leq i \leq m - 1$, can realize at most $k_i(k_i - 1)$ distinct nontrivial data transfers, since it has only k_i pins connected to it. Thus, the total number of distinct data transfers that the buses can realize is

$$r(n - 1) + \sum_{i=r}^{m-1} k_i(k_i - 1)$$

which must be larger than $n(n - 1)$ if all nontrivial shifts are to

196

be realized. Hence, we have

$$\sum_{i=r}^{m-1} k_i(k_i - 1) \geq (n-r)(n-1).$$

We can use this inequality to bound the number of pins on all buses with fewer than $\lceil \sqrt{n} \rceil$ pins. We have $k_i - 1 \leq \lceil \sqrt{n} \rceil - 2$ for $i = r, \cdots, m-1$, and thus

$$\sum_{i=r}^{m-1} k_i \geq \frac{1}{\lceil \sqrt{n} \rceil - 2} \sum_{i=r}^{m-1} k_i(k_i - 1)$$

$$\geq \frac{(n-r)(n-1)}{\lceil \sqrt{n} \rceil - 2}$$

$$\geq (n-r)\lceil \sqrt{n} \rceil.$$

We now bound the total number of pins in the architecture from below. We have

$$|P| = \sum_{i=0}^{m-1} k_i$$

$$= \sum_{i=0}^{r-1} k_i + \sum_{i=r}^{m-1} k_i$$

$$\geq r\lceil \sqrt{n} \rceil + (n-r)\lceil \sqrt{n} \rceil$$

$$= n\lceil \sqrt{n} \rceil,$$

which proves the theorem. ■

V. Difference Covers for Groups

In this section, we show that small difference covers for abelian and nonabelian permutation groups exist. Specifically, for any permutation group Π with p elements, we show how to construct a difference cover with $O(\sqrt{p \lg p})$ elements. In the case where Π is abelian, we apply the decomposition theorem for finite abelian groups and the results for cyclic shifters in Section IV to sharpen this bound to $O(\sqrt{p})$, which is optimal to within a constant factor.

As the first result of this section, we give a method for constructing a small difference cover for an arbitrary permutation group.

Theorem 14: Let Π be an arbitrary group with p elements. Then Π has a difference cover Φ of size at most $\sqrt{2p \ln p} + 1$.

Proof: We construct a difference cover incrementally starting with a partial difference cover $\Phi_1 = \{I\}$. At each step of the construction, we select an element $\phi_{i+1} \in \Pi$ such that $|\Phi_i^{-1}(\Phi_i \cup \{\phi_{i+1}\})|$ maximizes $|\Phi_i^{-1}(\Phi_i \cup \{\pi\})|$ over all $\pi \in \Pi$. We then define the new partial difference cover as $\Phi_{i+1} = \Phi_i \cup \{\phi_{i+1}\}$.

The analysis of this construction is in three parts. We first determine a lower bound on the number of elements of Π that are not covered by the partial difference cover Φ_i but are covered by Φ_{i+1}. We then develop a recurrence to upper bound the number of elements of the group Π that are not covered at the ith step. Finally, we solve the recurrence to determine that the number k of iterations needed to cover all elements in Π is at most $\sqrt{2p \ln p} + 1$.

We first determine how many new elements of Π are covered when Φ_i is augmented with ϕ_{i+1} to produce Φ_{i+1}, for $i \geq 1$. Let the set Δ_i be the set of elements that are not covered by the partial difference cover Φ_i, that is $\Delta_i = \Pi - \Phi_i^{-1}\Phi_i$. Consider triples of the form $\langle \phi, \delta, \pi \rangle$ such that $\phi \in \Phi_i$, $\delta \in \Delta_i$, $\pi \in \Pi$, and $\phi\delta = \pi$. Observe that for any fixed $\pi \in \Pi$ and $\delta \in \Delta_i$, there

is at most one triple of the form $\langle \phi, \delta, \pi \rangle$ in the set of triples, namely $\langle \pi\delta^{-1}, \delta, \pi \rangle$ when $\pi\delta^{-1} \in \Phi_i$. For a fixed π, the number of triples $\langle \phi, \delta, \pi \rangle$ in the set of triples is a lower bound on the number of elements covered by $\Phi_i \cup \{\pi\}$ but not by Φ_i, since we have $\delta = \phi^{-1}\pi$ and $\delta \in \Delta_i = \Pi - \Phi_i^{-1}\Phi_i$. For each $\phi \in \Phi_i$ and $\delta \in \Delta_i$, there is exactly one triple in the set of triples, and thus there are exactly $|\Phi_i| \cdot |\Delta_i|$ triples. Since there are at most $|\Pi|$ distinct permutations appearing as the third coordinate of a triple, the permutation ϕ_{i+1} that appears most often must appear at least $|\Phi_i| \cdot |\Delta_i| / |\Pi|$ times, and hence at least this many elements are covered by Φ_{i+1} that are not covered by Φ_i.

We can now bound the number of elements not covered by Φ_{i+1} in terms of the number of elements not covered by Φ_i by

$$|\Delta_{i+1}| \leq |\Delta_i| - \frac{|\Phi_i| \cdot |\Delta_i|}{|\Pi|}$$

$$= |\Delta_i|\left(1 - \frac{i}{p}\right)$$

$$= |\Delta_1| \prod_{j=1}^{i}\left(1 - \frac{j}{p}\right)$$

$$< p \prod_{j=1}^{i}\left(1 - \frac{j}{p}\right).$$

When we obtain $|\Delta_k| < 1$ for some k, the partial difference cover Φ_k is a difference cover for Π because Δ_k is empty. Thus, Φ_k is a difference cover when

$$p \prod_{j=1}^{k-1}\left(1 - \frac{j}{p}\right) \leq 1,$$

or equivalently, when

$$\ln p + \sum_{j=1}^{k-1} \ln\left(1 - \frac{j}{p}\right) \leq 0.$$

Using the inequality $\ln(1 + x) \leq x$, we have

$$\ln p + \sum_{j=1}^{k-1} \ln\left(1 - \frac{j}{p}\right) \leq \ln p - \sum_{j=1}^{k-1} \frac{j}{p}$$

$$= \ln p - \frac{1}{p}\sum_{j=1}^{k-1} j$$

$$\leq \ln p - \frac{(k-1)^2}{2p}$$

$$\leq 0.$$

Thus, Φ_k is a difference cover when $k \geq \sqrt{2p \ln p} + 1$. ■

This proof of Theorem 14 provides a construction which can be implemented as a deterministic, polynomial-time algorithm with $O(p^2 \lg p)$ algebraic steps. We could also have proved the theorem by relying on the result of Babai and Erdős [2] that any group has a small set of generators, but this method would have produced only an existential (nonconstructive) result.

We have shown that there are difference covers of size $O(\sqrt{p \lg p})$ for general permutation groups with p elements. We now show that if the group is abelian, difference covers of size $O(\sqrt{p})$ exist.

Theorem 15: For any abelian group Π with p elements, there exists a difference cover Φ of size at most $3\sqrt{p}$.

Proof: Assume without loss of generality that $p > 1$. By

the decomposition theorem for finite abelian groups [23, p. 133], any abelian group Π is isomorphic to a cross product of cyclic groups

$$\Pi \approx Z_{p_1} \times Z_{p_2} \times \cdots \times Z_{p_k}$$

where $p_1 p_2 \cdots p_k = p$, and each $p_j \geq 2$. Let i be the unique index such that $p_1 p_2 \cdots p_{i-1} \leq \sqrt{p}$ and $p_{i+1} p_{i+2} \cdots p_k < \sqrt{p}$, and let $m = \lceil \sqrt{p} / p_1 p_2 \cdots p_{i-1} \rceil$. Using the argument of Theorem 10, we first construct a difference cover for Z_{p_i} from the union of two sets A_i and B_i, where $|A_i| \leq m$ and $|B_i| \leq \lfloor p_i/m \rfloor$, such that each element of Z_{p_i} can be expressed in the form $b - a \pmod{p_i}$ or $a - b \pmod{p_i}$, where $a \in A_i$ and $b \in B_i$.

We now construct a difference cover for $\Pi \approx Z_{p_1} \times Z_{p_2} \times \cdots \times Z_{p_k}$ from the union of two sets A and B, where

$$A \approx Z_{p_1} \times Z_{p_2} \times \cdots \times Z_{p_{i-1}} \times A_i,$$

and

$$B \approx B_i \times Z_{p_{i+1}} \times Z_{p_{i+2}} \times \cdots \times Z_{p_k}.$$

That $A \cup B$ is a difference cover for Π follows from essentially the same argument as is used in Lemma 7.

The size of the difference cover $A \cup B$ is $|A| + |B|$. The size of A is

$$\begin{aligned}
|A| &= p_1 p_2 \cdots p_{i-1} |A_i| \\
&\leq p_1 p_2 \cdots p_{i-1} m \\
&\leq p_1 p_2 \cdots p_{i-1} \lceil \sqrt{p} / p_1 p_2 \cdots p_{i-1} \rceil \\
&\leq \sqrt{p} + p_1 p_2 \cdots p_{i-1} \\
&\leq 2\sqrt{p}.
\end{aligned}$$

Similarly, the size of B is

$$\begin{aligned}
|B| &= |B_i| \, p_{i+1} p_{i+2} \cdots p_k \\
&\leq \lfloor p_i/m \rfloor p_{i+1} p_{i+2} \cdots p_k \\
&\leq (p_i / \lceil \sqrt{p} / p_1 p_2 \cdots p_{i-1} \rceil) p_{i+1} p_{i+2} \cdots p_k \\
&\leq (p_1 p_2 \cdots p_i / \sqrt{p}) p_{i+1} p_{i+2} \cdots p_k \\
&= \sqrt{p}.
\end{aligned}$$

Consequently, the size of the difference cover for Π is at most $3\sqrt{p}$. ∎

VI. Multiple Clock Ticks

In this section, we discuss uniform permutation architectures that realize permutations in several clock ticks. By using more than one clock tick, further savings in the number of pins per chip can be obtained. We generalize the notion of a difference cover to handle multiple clock ticks, and describe a cyclic shifter on n chips with only $O(n^{1/2t})$ pins per chip that operates in t ticks.

We first generalize the notion of a difference cover to handle realization of permutations in $t \geq 1$ clock ticks.

Definition 8: A *t-difference cover* for a permutation set Π is a set Φ of permutations such that $(\Phi^{-1}\Phi)^t \supseteq \Pi$.

Using a t-difference cover Φ for the permutation set Π, any permutation $\pi \in \Pi$ can be expressed as the composition of t differences of permutations from Φ. The next lemma relates t-difference covers to permutation architectures that realize permutations in t clock ticks.

Lemma 16: Let Φ be a t-difference cover with k elements for a permutation set Π. Then there is a permutation architecture with k pins per chip that uniformly realizes Π in t clock ticks.

Proof: We define the permutation set $\Sigma = \Phi^{-1}\Phi$. Let $\mathcal{A} = \langle C, B, P, \text{CHIP}, \text{BUS}, \text{LABEL} \rangle$ be the permutation architecture, based on the difference cover Φ, that uniformly realizes Σ. Hence, the permutation architecture $\mathcal{A}$ can uniformly realize any $\sigma \in \Sigma$ in one clock tick. Each permutation $\pi \in \Pi$ can be expressed as $\pi = \sigma_{t-1}\sigma_{t-2} \cdots \sigma_0$, where $\sigma_i \in \Sigma$ for $0 \leq i \leq t - 1$, since we have $\Sigma^t = (\Phi^{-1}\Phi)^t \supseteq \Pi$. In order to realize π in t clock ticks, the permutation architecture $\mathcal{A}$ uniformly realizes σ_i in clock tick i for $0 \leq i \leq t - 1$. ∎

Lemma 16 claims that the problem of uniformly realizing a permutation set Π in t clock ticks can be reduced to finding a permutation set Σ such that $\Sigma^t \supseteq \Pi$, and then finding a difference cover for Σ. The great advantage of using more than one clock tick is in the further savings in the number of pins per chip. The following theorem, for example, describes a construction of a t-difference cover of size $O(n^{1/2t})$ for the set of cyclic shifts on n objects. This result can be used to build a uniform architecture on n chips with only $O(n^{1/2t})$ pins per chip that can realize any cyclic shift on the n chips in t clock ticks.

Theorem 17: For any $n \geq 1$ and $t \geq 1$, the permutation set of all the n cyclic shifts on n objects has a t-difference cover of size $O(n^{1/2t})$.

Proof: For the purpose of the proof, we denote the permutation set of all the n cyclic shifts on n objects by Π_n. (We remind that $\Pi_n \approx Z_n$.) We first treat the case for those n such that there exists an integer m satisfying $n^{1/t} \leq m \leq 4n^{1/t}$ and $\gcd(m, n) = 1$. We then use this case to extend the proof to all values of n.

Since $\gcd(m, n) = 1$, there exists an $m^{-1} \in Z_n$ such that $m \cdot m^{-1} = 1 \pmod{n}$. For each $r \in [m]$, define the permutation $\sigma_r : [n] \to [n]$ as $\sigma_r(c) = m^{-1}(c + r) \pmod{n}$, and define the permutation $\sigma_r' : [n] \to [n]$ as $\sigma_r'(c) = m^{t-1}(c + r) \pmod{n}$. Next define the permutation set $\Sigma = \{\sigma_r\} \cup \{\sigma_r'\}$. The set $\{\sigma_r\}$ is an arithmetic sequence of cyclic shifts on n elements (as in Corollary 11) followed by the fixed permutation corresponding to multiplication by m^{-1}, and thus $\{\sigma_r\}$ has a difference cover of size $O(\sqrt{m})$. Similarly, the set $\{\sigma_r'\}$ has a difference cover of size $O(\sqrt{m})$. Combining the two difference covers for $\{\sigma_r\}$ and $\{\sigma_r'\}$, we get a difference cover Φ of size $O(\sqrt{m}) = O(n^{1/2t})$ for Σ.

We now show the inclusion $\Sigma^t \supseteq \Pi_n$. Let $\pi \in \Pi_n$ be a permutation of a cyclic shift by s. We express the shift amount $s \in [n]$ as $s = s_0 + s_1 m + \cdots + s_{t-1} m^{t-1}$, where $s_i \in [m]$ for $0 \leq i \leq t - 1$. The permutation π can be described as

$$\begin{aligned}
\pi(c) &= c + s \pmod{n} \\
&= c + s_0 + s_1 m + \cdots + s_{t-1} m^{t-1} \pmod{n} \\
&= m^{t-1}(s_{t-1} + m^{-1}(s_{t-2} + \cdots + m^{-1}(s_0 + c))) \pmod{n} \\
&= \sigma_{s_{t-1}}' \sigma_{s_{t-2}} \cdots \sigma_{s_0}(c)
\end{aligned}$$

which proves that $\pi \in \Sigma^t$. Hence, we get the inclusion $\Sigma^t \supseteq \Pi_n$, which together with the fact that there is a difference cover Φ of size $O(n^{1/2t})$ for Σ, proves the theorem for the case when there exists an integer m satisfying $n^{1/t} \leq m \leq 4n^{1/t}$ and $\gcd(m, n) = 1$.

Such an m need not exist for every n and every t, however. We can overcome this difficulty by factoring $n = n_1 n_2$ such that n_1 consists of no even-indexed primes $(3, 7, 13, \cdots)$ and n_2

consists of no odd-indexed primes $(2, 5, 11, \cdots)$. Since we have $\gcd(n_1, n_2) = 1$, we can use the Chinese remainder theorem to express Z_n as a Cartesian product $Z_n \approx Z_{n_1} \times Z_{n_2}$. We let m_1 be the first even-indexed prime at least as large as $n_1^{1/t}$, and let m_2 be the first odd-indexed prime at least as large as $n_2^{1/t}$. Bertrand's postulate [19, p. 343] guarantees that for every x, there is a prime between x and $2x$, which means $m_j \in [n_j^{1/t}, 4n_j^{1/t}]$ for $j = 1, 2$. (Tighter bounds are possible.)

We can now use the previous construction to construct a t-difference cover Φ_1 of size $O(n_1^{1/2t})$ for Z_{n_1}, which is isomorphic to Π_{n_1}, and a t-difference cover Φ_2 of size $O(n_2^{1/2t})$ for Z_{n_2}, which is isomorphic to Π_{n_2}. Using the same technique as in the proof of Lemma 7, we can construct a t-difference cover of size $O(n_1^{1/2t}) \cdot O(n_2^{1/2t}) = O(n^{1/2t})$ for $Z_{n_1} \times Z_{n_2} \approx Z_n \approx \Pi_n$. ∎

One can rather straightforwardly use Corollary 11 to obtain a t-difference cover of size $O(tn^{1/2t})$. Based on the representation of the shift amount $s = s_0 + s_1 m + \cdots + s_{t-1}m^{t-1}$, one can come with t separate difference covers, each of size $O(n^{1/2t})$, for the t separate sequences of arithmetic shifts by $\{sm^i : s \in [m]\}$ for $0 \le i \le t - 1$. Theorem 17 avoids the extra factor of t by constructing only one such difference cover and using its elements for each one of the t differences.

VII. Extensions

This section contains some additional results on permutation architectures and difference covers. We describe efficient, uniform architectures that can realize the permutations implemented by various popular interconnection networks, including multidimensional meshes, hypercubes, and shuffle-exchange networks. We examine nonuniform permutation architectures, and adapt some combinatorial results in the literature to apply to permutation architectures. A result of de Bruijn leads to a nonuniform architecture with $O(\sqrt{n \lg n})$ pins per chip that can realize all $n!$ permutations on n chips.

A. Specific Networks

By using buses, many popular interconnection networks can be realized with fewer pins than conventionally proposed. Here, we mention a few.

The permutation architectures for realizing compass shifts on two-dimensional arrays can be extended in a natural fashion to d-dimensional arrays. For the d-dimensional analogue of the shifts $\{I, N, E, S, W\}$, there is a uniform architecture that uses only $d + 1$ pins per chip to implement the $2d + 1$ permutations. For the d-dimensional analogue of the shifts $\{I, N, E, S, W, NE, SE, NW, SW\}$, there is a uniform architecture that uses only 2^d pins per chip to implement the 3^d permutations. (These two results were independently discovered by Fiduccia [11], [12].)

A Boolean hypercube of dimension d is a degenerate case of a d-dimensional array. Only $d + 1$ pins per chip are required by a permutation architecture that uses buses, whereas $2d$ pins per chip are needed if point-to-point wires are used. (To realize a swap of information across a dimension in one clock tick, each chip requires two pins for that dimension: one to read and one to write.)

A permutation architecture that implements the permutations shuffle, inverse shuffle, and exchange can be constructed with three pins per chip instead of the usual four, and it can implement the shuffle-exchange and inverse shuffle-exchange permutations in one tick as well.

B. Average Number of Pins per Chip

Theorem 13 presents a lower bound on the average number of pins per chip in any cyclic shifter that operates in one clock tick. The following theorem is a natural extension of Theorem 13 for a general set of permutations.

Theorem 18: Let Π be a permutation set on n objects with p permutations and with a total of T nontrivial data transfers, and let $\mathscr{A} = \langle C, B, P, \text{CHIP}, \text{BUS}, \text{LABEL} \rangle$ be any permutation architecture for realizing Π. Then the average number of pins per chip is at least $T/n\sqrt{p}$.

Proof: As in the proof of Theorem 13, we prove that $|P| \ge T/\sqrt{p}$ which implies the theorem. We make similar notational conventions:

1) The set of buses is $B = \{b_0, b_1, \cdots, b_{m-1}\}$. We denote by k_i the number of pins connected to bus b_i.

2) The r buses that have at least $\sqrt{p}$ pins each are indexed first, that is $k_i \ge \sqrt{p}$ for $i = 0, \cdots, r - 1$ and $k_i < \sqrt{p}$ for $i = r, \cdots, m - 1$.

We count the number of distinct data transfers that can be accomplished by each bus. Each of the first r buses can be employed to realize at most p out of the T nontrivial data transfers, since it can be used at most once for each of the p permutations. Any other bus b_i, where $r \le i \le m - 1$, can realize at most $k_i(k_i - 1)$ out of the T nontrivial data transfers, since it has only k_i pins connected to it. We need to have $\sum_{i=r}^{m-1} k_i(k_i - 1) \ge T - rp$, which implies

$$\sum_{i=r}^{m-1} k_i \ge \frac{T - rp}{\sqrt{p}}$$
$$= \frac{T}{\sqrt{p}} - r\sqrt{p}.$$

The number of pins in the architecture can now be bounded as follows:

$$|P| = \sum_{i=0}^{m-1} k_i$$
$$= \sum_{i=0}^{r-1} k_i + \sum_{i=r}^{m-1} k_i$$
$$\ge r\sqrt{p} + \left(\frac{T}{\sqrt{p}} - r\sqrt{p}\right)$$
$$= \frac{T}{\sqrt{p}}. \quad \blacksquare$$

Theorem 18 demonstrates that uniform architectures can achieve the optimal number (to within a constant factor) of pins per chip for certain classes of permutation sets. When there are relatively few permutations that are responsible for many nontrivial data transfers, the average number of pins per chip is high. The set of cyclic shifts is an example of this kind of permutation set.

C. Nonuniform Architectures

When the uniformity condition on permutation architectures is dropped, one can do much better in terms of the number of pins per chip. The complexity of control may increase substantially, however, due to the irregular communication patterns and the number of possible permutations realizable for some of the architectures. Nevertheless, from a mathematical point of view, nonuniform architectures are quite interesting.

In fact, nonuniform architectures have been studied quite extensively in the mathematics literature in the guise of partitioning problems. For the problem of realizing all $n!$ permutations on n chips, a result due to de Bruijn, Erdös, and Spencer [31, p. 106–108] implies that $O(\sqrt{n} \lg n)$ pins per chip suffice. The nonuniform architecture that achieves this bound is constructed probabilistically, however. It is an open problem to obtain this bound deterministically. The best deterministic construction to date is due to Feldman, Friedman, and Pippenger [9] and uses $O(n^{2/3})$ pins per chip.

VIII. Further Research

In this section, we list a few of the problems that have been left open by our research. We also describe briefly some further work brought on by an earlier version [20] of our work.

In Section IV, we described a difference cover of size $2\lceil \sqrt{n} \rceil - 1$ for the cyclic group Z_n, and proved that when n is the order of a projective plane, there is a difference cover of size $\lceil \sqrt{n} \rceil$. It seems reasonable that any cyclic group Z_n might actually have a difference cover of size $\sqrt{n} + o(\sqrt{n})$, but we have been unable to prove or disprove this conjecture. Mills and Wiedemann [27] have computed a table of minimal difference covers for all the cyclic groups of cardinality up to 110. For any value of n up to 110, the difference cover they find has at most $\lceil \sqrt{n} \rceil + 2$ elements. They also provide [28] a "folk theorem" that establishes a stronger upper bound for the general case than $2\lceil \sqrt{n} \rceil - 1$.

Theorem 19: The set of n cyclic shifts on n elements has a difference cover of size $(\sqrt{2} + o(1))\sqrt{n}$.

Sketch of proof: [28] Let q be the smallest prime such that $l = q^2 + q + 1 \geq n/2$. We have $q = (1 + o(1))\sqrt{n/2}$, since for large x, there exists a prime between x and $x + o(x)$. Let $\{d_0, d_1, \cdots, d_q\}$ be a difference cover for Z_l chosen as in Theorem 12. It can be verified that the set $\{d_0, d_1, \cdots, d_q\} \cup \{d_0 + l, d_1 + l, \cdots, d_q + l\}$ forms a difference cover for Z_n. ∎

Another interesting problem related to cyclic shifters involves finding an area-efficient VLSI layout of the cyclic shifter based on projective planes. In Section IV, we presented an area-efficient layout using a difference cover whose size is twice the optimal size. Is there a good layout for the pin-optimal design?

In Section V, we showed that any abelian group of p elements has a difference cover of size $O(\sqrt{p})$, and we showed that any group of p elements has a difference cover of size $O(\sqrt{p} \lg p)$. Finkelstein, Kleitman, and Leighton [13] have recently improved our result for general groups to $O(\sqrt{p})$. Their proof uses a folk theorem [8] that every simple group of nonprime order p has a subgroup of size at least $\sqrt{p}$. The folk theorem is proved by checking each type of group in the classification theorem [17, pp. 135–136]. It would be interesting to know if there is a more direct proof that every group has a difference cover of size $O(\sqrt{p})$.

To implement cyclic shifters that operate in t clock ticks, we showed how to construct a t-difference cover for Z_n of size $O(n^{1/2t})$. A simpler construction achieves the bound $O(tn^{1/2t})$. Theorem 13 gives a lower bound of $\lceil \sqrt{n} \rceil$ on the average number of pins per chip for a cyclic shifter that operates in one clock tick. It may be possible to prove a lower bound of $\Omega(n^{1/2t})$ on the average number of pins per chip when an architecture operates in t clock ticks, but we were unable to extend the argument. We were also unable to extend either of these constructions to give good t-difference covers for groups, either general or abelian. It would be interesting to know

whether any abelian group of permutations with p permutations has a t-difference cover of size $O(tn^{1/2t})$, for any $t \geq 1$.

We have concentrated primarily on permutation sets that have good structure, specifically group properties. It would be interesting to identify other structural properties of permutation sets besides group properties that allow small difference covers to exist.

Appendix

For completeness, we include definitions of common mathematical notations and algebraic terms used in the paper. Definitions specific to the content of the paper are included in context.

We adopt the following notations:

- $|X|$ denotes the size of the set X.
- $[n]$ denotes the set of n integers $\{0, 1, \cdots, n-1\}$.
- $\lfloor x \rfloor$ (floor of x) denotes the largest integer that is smaller than or equal to x.
- $\lceil x \rceil$ (ceiling of x) denotes the smallest integer that is larger than or equal to x.
- $\lg x$ denotes $\log_2 x$.
- $\ln x$ denotes $\log_e x$.
- $\binom{n}{k}$ denotes $\dfrac{n!}{k!(n-k)!}$.

For two asymptotically positive functions $f(n)$ and $g(n)$, we write:

- $f(n) = o(g(n))$ if $\lim_{n \to \infty} f(n)/g(n) = 0$.
- $f(n) = O(g(n))$ if there exists $c > 0$ and n_0, such that $f(n) \leq cg(n)$ for all $n > n_0$.
- $f(n) = \Omega(g(n))$ if there exists $c > 0$ and n_0, such that $f(n) \geq cg(n)$ for all $n > n_0$.
- $f(n) = \Theta(g(n))$ if both $f(n) = O(g(n))$ and $f(n) = \Omega(g(n))$.

Let $f: A \to B$ be a function.

- f is *injective (one to one)* if $a \neq b$ implies $f(a) \neq f(b)$.
- f is *surjective (onto)* if for all $b \in B$, there exists some $a \in A$ such that $b = f(a)$.
- f is *bijective* if it is injective and surjective.

A *group* is a set of elements G with a binary operation $\oplus$, such that the following properties hold.

- *Closure*: For every $a, b \in G$, we have $a \oplus b \in G$.
- *Associativity*: For every $a, b, c \in G$, we have $a \oplus (b \oplus c) = (a \oplus b) \oplus c$.
- *Identity*: There exists an element $e \in G$ such that $a \oplus e = e \oplus a = a$ for all $a \in G$.
- *Inverse*: For every $a \in G$, there exists an element $a^{-1} \in G$ such that $a \oplus a^{-1} = a^{-1} \oplus a = e$.

An *abelian* group is a group G with an additional property:

- *Commutativity*: For every $a, b \in G$, we have $a \oplus b = b \oplus a$.

We often use the notations:

- ab to denote $a \oplus b$,
- a^k to denote $a \oplus a \oplus \cdots \oplus a$ (k times),
- a^{-k} to denote $(a^{-1})^k$.

A *cyclic group* G is a group in which there exists $a \in G$ such that $G = \{a^k : k \text{ integer}\}$. Cyclic groups are abelian. The notation Z_n denotes the cyclic group of residues modulo n, with modular addition as the group operation. A *permutation* on a set X is a bijective function from X to X. All the possible permutations on X form a group with functional composition as the group operation.

Acknowledgment

G. L. Steele, Jr. of Thinking Machines Corporation originally acquainted us with the problem of implementing cyclic shifters with buses. T. Leighton of MIT helped simplify our proof of Theorem 15 and acquainted us with references to relevant work in the combinatorics literature. N. Pippenger of the University of British Columbia referred us to the combinatorics results in Section VII-C. N. Alon of Tel Aviv University made the observation in Section V that the result of Babai and Erdös could be used to show the existence of a small difference cover for any group. C. Fiduccia of General Electric Research Center provided excellent comments and identified a few bugs in an early version of our paper. Dr. I. J. Matrix of the Massachusetts Institute of Theology acquainted us with his related work [14, pp. 65–67]. We thank these individuals for helpful discussions, as well as B. Chor, L. Fortnow, S. Goldwasser, P. Klein, and S.-M. Wu of MIT, and A. Odlyzko of AT&T Bell Laboratories. We would also like to thank the referees which provided excellent suggestions.

References

[1] A. Aggarwal, "Optimal bounds for finding maximum on array of processors with k global buses," *IEEE Trans. Comput.*, vol. C-35, no. 1, pp. 62–64, Jan. 1986.

[2] L. Babai and P. Erdös, "Representation of group elements as short products," *Ann. Discrete Math.*, vol. 12, pp. 27–30, 1982.

[3] J. C. Bermond, J. Bond, and C. Peyrat, "Interconnection network with each node on two buses," in *Proc. Int. Colloq. Parallel Algorithms Architectures*, Marseille Luminy, France, 1986, pp. 155–167.

[4] J. C. Bermond, J. Bond, and J. F. Scalé, "Large hypergraphs of diameter one," in *Graph Theory and Combinatorics, Proc. Coll. Cambridge, 1983*. London, England: Academic, 1984, pp. 19–28.

[5] Y. Birk, "Concurrent communication among multi-transceiver stations over shared media," Ph.D. dissertation, Stanford Univ., Mar. 1987.

[6] G. S. Bloom and S. W. Golomb, "Numbered complete graphs, unusual rulers, and assorted applications," in *Theory and Applications of Graphs*, Y. Alavi and D. R. Lick, Eds. New York: Springer-Verlag, 1978.

[7] S. H. Bokhari, "Finding maximum on an array processor with a global bus," *IEEE Trans. Comput.*, vol. C-33, no. 2, pp. 133–139, Feb. 1984.

[8] W. Feit, private communications, 1987.

[9] P. Feldman, J. Friedman, and N. Pippenger, "Wide-sense nonblocking networks," *SIAM J. Discrete Math.*, vol. 1, no. 2, pp. 158–173, May 1988.

[10] C. M. Fiduccia, public communication, MIT, 1984.

[11] ——; private communication, Apr. 1987.

[12] ——, "A bused hypercube and other optimal permutation networks," presented at the 4th SIAM Conf. Discrete Math., June 1988.

[13] L. Finkelstein, D. Kleitman, and T. Leighton, "Applying the classification theorem for finite simple groups to minimize pin count in uniform permutation architectures," in *VLSI Algorithms and Architectures*, Lecture Notes in Computer Science, Vol. 319, J. H. Reif, Ed. New York: Springer-Verlag, 1988, pp. 247–256.

[14] M. Gardner, *The Incredible Dr. Matrix*. New York: Scribner's, 1976.

[15] L. A. Glasser and D. W. Dobberpuhl, *The Design and Analysis of VLSI Circuits*. Reading, MA: Addison-Wesley, 1985.

[16] S. W. Golomb, "How to number a graph," in *Graph Theory and Computing*, R. C. Read, Ed. New York: Academic, 1972, pp. 23–37.

[17] D. Gorenstein, *Finite Simple Groups*. New York: Plenum, 1982.

[18] M. Hall, Jr., *Combinatorial Theory*. Waltham, MA: Blaisdell, 1967.

[19] G. H. Hardy and E. M. Wright, *An Introduction to the Theory of Numbers*. London, England: Oxford University Press, 1938.

[20] J. Kilian, S. Kipnis, and C. E. Leiserson, "The organization of permutation architectures with bused interconnections," in *Proc. 28th Annu. Symp. Foundations Comput. Sci.*, IEEE, Oct. 12–14, 1987, pp. 305–315.

[21] T. Lang, M. Valero, and M. A. Fiol, "Reduction of connections for multibus organization," *IEEE Trans. Comput.*, vol. C-32, no. 8, pp. 707–715, Aug. 1983.

[22] J. Leech, "On the representation of 1, 2, $\cdots$, n by differences," *J. London Math. Soc.*, vol. 31, pp. 160–169, 1956.

[23] D. J. Lewis, *Introduction To Algebra*. New York: Harper and Row, 1965.

[24] R. J. Lipton and R. Sedgewick, "Lower bounds for VLSI," in *Proc. 13th Annu. Symp. Theory Comput.*, ACM, May 11–13, 1981, pp. 300–307.

[25] M. D. Mickunas, "Using projective geometry to design bus connection networks," in *Proc. Workshop Interconnection Networks for Parallel and Distributed Processing*, ACM/IEEE, Apr. 21–22, 1980, pp. 47–55.

[26] J. C. P. Miller, "Difference bases, three problems in additive number theory," in *Computers in Number Theory*, A. O. L. Atkin and B. J. Birch, Eds. London, England: Academic, 1971, pp. 299–322.

[27] W. H. Mills and D. H. Wiedemann, "A table of difference coverings," unpublished abstract, Institute for Defense Analyses, Communications Research Division, Jan. 1988.

[28] D. H. Wiedemann, private communication, Nov. 1988.

[29] Q. F. Stout, "Meshes with multiple busses," in *Proc. 27th Annu. Symp. Foundations Comput. Sci.*, IEEE, Oct. 27–29, 1986, pp. 264–273.

[30] J. D. Ullman, *Computational Aspects of VLSI*. Rockville, MD: Computer Science Press, 1984.

[31] J. H. van Lint, "Solutions: Problem 350," *Nieuw Archief voor Wiskunde*, vol. 22, pp. 94–109, 1974.

Joe Kilian received the B.S. degree in mathematics and computer science from MIT in 1985 and the Ph.D. degree in mathematics from MIT in 1989.

His main interests are in cryptography and complexity theory.

Shlomo Kipnis (S'87) received the B.Sc. degree in mathematics and physics and the M.Sc. degree in computer science from the Hebrew University of Jerusalem, Israel, in 1983 and 1985, respectively.

He is currently working towards the Ph.D. degree in computer science at the Massachusetts Institute of Technology, Cambridge. His Ph.D. research is concentrating on parallel algorithms and architectures. Other interests include VLSI, digital signal processing, and computational geometry.

Mr. Kipnis is a member of the Association for Computing Machinery, the IEEE Computer Society, and SIAM.

Charles E. Leiserson (M'83) received the B.S. degree in computer science and mathematics from Yale University, New Haven, CT, in 1975 and the Ph.D. degree in computer science from Carnegie-Mellon University, Pittsburgh, PA, in 1981.

He is currently an Associate Professor of Computer Science and Engineering at the Massachusetts Institute of Technology, Cambridge. As a graduate student at Carnegie-Mellon, he wrote the first paper on systolic architectures with his advisor H. T. Kung, for which they received a U.S. patent. His Ph.D. dissertation "Area-Efficient VLSI Computation," which dealt with the design of systolic systems and with the problem of determining the VLSI area of a graph, won the first ACM Doctoral Dissertation Award. In 1981, he joined the faculty of the Theory of Computation Group in the Laboratory for Computer Science, Massachusetts Institute of Technology. He has authored or coauthored papers on systolic architectures, graph layout, digital circuit optimization, analysis of algorithms, computer-aided design, placement and routing, computer architecture, and parallel computation. His principal interest is in the theoretical foundation of parallel computation, especially as it relates to engineering reality.

Dr. Leiserson is a member of the Association for Computing Machinery and SIAM. In 1985 he received a Presidential Young Investigator Award from the National Science Foundation. He is coauthor of the popular textbook, *Introduction to Algorithms,* (MIT Press and Mc-Graw-Hill, 1990).

Express Cubes: Improving the Performance of k-ary n-cube Interconnection Networks

William J. Dally, *Member, IEEE*

Abstract—Express cubes are k-ary n-cube interconnection networks augmented by *express channels* that provide a short path for nonlocal messages. An express cube combines the logarithmic diameter of a multistage network with the wire-efficiency and ability to exploit locality of a low-dimensional mesh network. The insertion of express channels reduces the network diameter and thus the distance component of network latency. Wire length is increased allowing networks to operate with latencies that approach the physical speed-of-light limitation rather than being limited by node delays. Express channels increase wire bisection in a manner that allows the bisection to be controlled independent of the choice of radix, dimension, and channel width. By increasing wire bisection to saturate the available wiring media, throughput can be substantially increased. With an express cube both latency and throughput are wire-limited and within a small factor of the physical limit on performance. Express channels may be inserted into existing interconnection networks using *interchanges*. No changes to the local communication controllers are required.

Index Terms—Communication networks, concurrent computing, interconnection networks, multicomputers, packet routing, packet switching, parallel processing, topology.

I. INTRODUCTION

INTERCONNECTION networks are used to pass messages containing data and synchronization information between the nodes of concurrent computers [1], [2], [18], [19]. The messages may be sent between the processing nodes of a message-passing multicomputer [1] or between the processors and memories of a shared-memory multiprocessor [2].

An interconnection network is characterized by its topology, routing, and flow control [10]. The topology of a network is the arrangement of its nodes and channels into a graph. Routing determines the path chosen by a message in this graph. Flow control deals with the allocation of channel and buffer resources to a message as it travels along this path. This paper deals only with topology. Express cubes can be applied independent of routing and flow control strategies.

The performance of a network is measured in terms of its *latency* and its *throughput*. The latency of a message is the elapsed time from when the message send is initiated until the message is completely received. Network latency is the

Manuscript received October 14, 1989; revised April 27, 1990. This work was supported in part by the Defense Advanced Research Projects Agency under Contracts N00014-88K-0738 and N00014-87K-0825 and in part by a National Science Foundation Presidential Young Investigator Award, Grant MIP-8657531, with matching funds from General Electric Corporation and IBM Corporation.

The author is with the Artificial Intelligence Laboratory and the Laboratory for Computer Science, Massachusetts Institute of Technology, Cambridge, MA 02139.

IEEE Log Number 9101688.

average message latency under specified conditions. Network throughput is the number of messages the network can deliver per unit time.

Low-dimensional k-ary n-cube networks using *wormhole routing* have been shown to provide low latency and high throughput for networks that are wire-limited [4], [5], [9]. For $n \leq 3$, the k-ary n-cube topology is wire-efficient in that it makes efficient use of the available bisection width. This topology maps into the three physical dimensions in a manner that allows messages to use all of the available bandwidth along their path without ever having to double back on themselves. Also, low-dimensional k-ary n-cubes concentrate bandwidth into a few wide channels so that the component of latency due to message length is reduced. In most contemporary concurrent computers, this is the dominant component of latency. Because of their low-latency, high throughput, and affinity for implementation in VLSI, these k-ary n-cube networks with $n = 2$ or 3 have been used successfully in the design of several concurrent computers including the Ametek 2010 [19], the J-Machine [7], [8], and the Mosaic [20].

However, low-dimensional k-ary n-cube interconnection networks have two significant shortcomings:

- Because wires are short, node delays dominate wire delays and the distance related component of latency falls more than an order of magnitude short of speed-of-light limitations. In the J-Machine [7], for example, node delay is 50 ns while the longest wire is 225 mm and has a time-of-flight delay of 1.5 ns.
- The channel width of these networks is often limited by node pin count rather than by wire bisection. For example, the J-Machine channel width is limited to 9-bits by pin count limitations. In the physical node width of 50 mm, a six-layer printed circuit board can handle over four times this channel width after accounting for through holes and local connections.

In short, many regular k-ary n-cube interconnection networks are node-limited rather than wire-limited. In these networks, node delay and pin limitations dominate wire delay and wire density limitations. The ratios of node delay to wire delays and pin density to wire density cannot be balanced in a regular k-ary n-cube.

Express cubes overcome this problem by allowing wire length and wire density to be adjusted independently of the choice of radix k, dimension n, and channel width W. An express cube is a k-ary n-cube augmented by one or more levels of express channels that allow nonlocal messages to

Reprinted from *IEEE Trans. Computers*, Vol. 40, No. 9, Sept. 1991, pp. 1016-1023. Copyright © 1991 by The Institute of Electrical and Electronics Engineers, Inc. All rights reserved.

bypass nodes. The wire length of the express channels can be increased to the point that wire delays dominate node delays. The number of express channels can be adjusted to increase throughput until the available wiring media is saturated. This ability to balance node and wire limitations is achieved without sacrificing the wire-efficiency of k-ary n-cube networks. The number of channels traversed by a message in a hierarchical express cube grows logarithmically with distance as in a multistage interconnection network [12], [21]. The express cube, however, is able to exploit locality while in a multistage network all messages must traverse the diameter of the network. With an express cube, both latency and throughput are wire-limited and are within a small constant factor of the physical limit on performance.

The remainder of this paper describes the express cube topology and analyzes its performance. Section II summarizes the notation that will be used throughout the paper. Section III introduces the express cube topology in steps. Basic express cubes (Section III-A) reduce latency to twice the delay of dedicated wire for messages traveling long distances. Throughput can be increased to saturate the available wiring density by adding multiple express channels (Section III-B). With a hierarchical express cube (Section III-C), latency for short distances, while node-limited, is within a small constant factor of the best that can be achieved by any bounded degree network. Some design considerations for express cube interchanges are discussed in Section IV.

II. NOTATION

The following symbols are used in this paper. They are listed here for reference.

C, the set of channels in the network.

D, Manhattan distance traveled by a message, $|x_s - x_d| + |y_s - y_d| + |z_s - z_d|$, where the source is at (x_s, y_s, z_s) and the destination is at (x_d, y_d, z_d).

f_j, the fraction of traffic at level j in a hierarchical express cube.

H, *hops*, the number of nodes traversed by a message.

i, number of nodes between interchanges in an express cube.

k, the radix of the network—the length in each dimension.

l, the number of levels of hierarchy in a hierarchical express cube.

L, the message length in bits.

m_j, the number of multiple express channels at level j.

M, the number of express channels through each node.

n, the dimension of the network.

N, the set of nodes in the network. Where it is unambiguous, N is also used for the number of nodes in the network, $|N|$.

T_n, the latency of a node.

T_w, the latency of a wire that connects two physically adjacent nodes.

T_p, the pipeline period of a node.

W, the width of a channel in bits.

$\mathcal{W}$, the width of a node—the number of wires that may pass into a node in each dimension.

α, the ratio of node latency to wire latency, T_n/T_w.

β, the ratio of channel width to node width, $\mathcal{W}/W$.

An interconnection network consists of a set of nodes N that are connected by a set of channels, $C \subseteq N \times N$. Each channel is unidirectional and carries data from a source node to a destination node. For the purposes of this paper it is assumed that the network is bidirectional: channels occur in pairs so that $(n_1, n_2) \in C \Rightarrow (n_2, n_1) \in C$.

Communication between nodes is performed by sending *messages*. A message may be broken into one or more *packets* for transmission. A packet is the smallest unit that contains routing and sequencing information. Packets contain one or more flow control digits or *flits*. A flit is the smallest unit on which flow control is performed. A flit in turn is composed of one or more physical transfer units or *phits*.[1] A phit is W-bits, the size of the physical communication media.

The express cube topology is particularly suitable for use with wormhole routing, a flow-control protocol that advances each flit of a packet as soon as it arrives at a node (pipelining) and blocks packets in place when required resources are unavailable [4], [5], [9]. Wormhole routing is attractive in that 1) it reduces the latency of message delivery compared to store and forward routing, and 2) it requires only a few flit buffers per node. Wormhole routing differs from virtual cut-through routing [11] in that with wormhole routing it is not necessary for a node to allocate an entire packet buffer before accepting each packet. This distinction reduces the amount of buffering required on each node making it possible to build fast, inexpensive routers.

The *bisection width* of a network is the minimum number of channels that must be cut to partition the network into two equal halves. The *wire bisection* is the number of wires in this channel cutset. Bisection width gives a lower bound on *wire density*, the maximum number of wires that must cross a unit distance (2-D) or area (3-D).

III. EXPRESS CUBES

A. Express Channels Reduce Latency

Fig. 1 illustrates the application of express channels to a k-ary 1-cube or linear array. A regular k-ary 1-cube is shown in Fig. 1(a). The network is a linear array of k processing nodes, labeled N, each connected to its nearest neighbors by channels of width W. The delay of a phit propagating through a node is T_n. The delay of the wire connecting two nodes is T_w. Each channel can accept a new phit every T_p. The latency of a message of length L sent distance D is

$$T_a = HT_n + DT_w + \frac{L}{W}T_p. \tag{1}$$

---

[1] There is no constraint that the physical unit of transfer, phit, must be smaller than the flow control unit, flit. It is possible to construct systems with several flits in each phit.

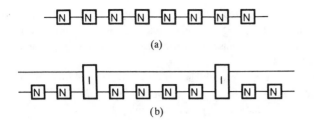

(a)

(b)

Fig. 1. Insertion of express channels reduces latency: (a) A regular k-ary 1-cube network may be dominated by node delay. (b) A k-ary 1-cube with express channels reduces the node delay component of latency.

Message latency is composed of three components as shown in (1).[2] The first component is the node latency, due to the number of hops H. The second component is the wire latency, due to the distance D. The third component is due to message length L.

For a conventional k-ary n-cube, $H = D$ giving

$$T_a = (T_n + T_w)D + \frac{L}{W}T_p. \qquad (2)$$

For most networks $T_n >> T_w$ so the node latency dominates the wire latency. Express cubes reduce the node latency by increasing wire length to reduce the number of hops H.

An express k-ary 1-cube is shown in Fig. 1(b). Express channels have been added to the array by inserting an interchange, labeled I, every i nodes. An interchange is not a processing node. It performs only communication functions and is not assigned an address. Each interchange is connected to its neighboring interchanges by an additional channel of width W, the express channel. When a message arrives at an interchange it is routed directly to the next interchange if it is not destined for one of the intervening nodes. To preserve the wire-efficiency of the network, messages are never routed past their destinations on the express channels even though doing so would reduce H in many cases.

The delay T_n, and throughput $1/T_p$, of an interchange are assumed to be identical to those of a node. The wire delay of the express channel is assumed to be iT_w. To simplify the following analysis, it is assumed that interchanges add no physical distance to the network. Assuming $i \mid D$, $H = D/i + i$ and insertion of express channels reduces the latency to

$$T_b = \left(\frac{D}{i} + i\right)T_n + T_wD + \frac{LT_p}{W}. \qquad (3)$$

In the general case, $i \nmid D$, an average message traversing D processing nodes travels over $H_i = (i+1)/2$ local channels to reach an interchange, $H_e = \lfloor D/i - 1/2 + 1/(2i) \rfloor$ express channels to reach the last interchange before the destination, and finally $H_f = (1 + (D - i/2 - 1/2) \bmod i)$ local channels to the destination. The total number of hops is $H = H_i + H_e + H_f$ giving a latency of

$$T_b = \left(\frac{i+1}{2} + \left\lfloor \frac{D}{i} - \frac{1}{2} + \frac{1}{2i} \right\rfloor\right.$$

$$+ \left(1 + \left(D - \frac{i}{2} - \frac{1}{2}\right) \bmod i\right)\right)T_n + DT_w$$

$$+ \frac{LT_p}{W}. \qquad (4)$$

For large distances, $D >> \alpha = T_n/T_w$, choosing $i = \alpha$ balances the node and wire delay. With this choice of i, the latency due to distance is approximately twice the wire latency, $T_D \approx 2T_wD$. The latency for large distances of an express channel network with $i = \alpha$ is within a factor of two of the latency of a dedicated Manhattan wire between the source and destination.[3]

For small distances or large α, the i term in the coefficient of T_n in (3) is significant and node delay dominates. For such networks, latency is minimized by choosing $i = \sqrt{D}$ resulting in $T_D \approx 2(\sqrt{D} - 1)T_n$. The use of hierarchical express channels (Section III-C) can further improve the latency for small distances.

B. Multiple Express Channels Increase Throughput to Saturate Wire Density

To first order, network throughput is proportional to wire bisection and hence wire density. If more wires are available to transmit data across the network, throughput will be increased provided that routing and flow control strategies are able to profitably schedule traffic onto these wires. Many regular network topologies, such as low-dimensional k-ary n-cubes, are unable to make use of all available wire density because of pin limitations. The wire bisection of an express cube can be controlled independent of the choice of radix k, dimension n, or channel width W by adding multiple express channels to the network to match network throughput with the available wiring density $\mathcal{W}$.

Fig. 2 shows two methods of inserting multiple express channels. Multiple express channels may be handled by each interchange as shown in Fig. 2(a). Alternatively, simplex interchanges can be interleaved as shown in Fig. 2(b).

In method (a), using multiple channel interchanges, an interchange is inserted every i nodes as above and each interchange is connected to its neighbors using m parallel express channels. Fig. 2(a) shows a network with $i = 4$ and $m = 2$. The interchange acts as a concentrator combining messages arriving on the m incoming express channels with nonlocal messages arriving on the local channel and concentrating these messages streams onto the m outgoing express channels. This method has the advantage of making better use of the express channels since any message can route on any express channel. Flexibility in express channel assignment is achieved at the expense of higher pin count and limited expansion.

With method (b), interleaving simplex interchanges, m simplex interchanges are inserted into each group of i nodes. Each interchange is connected to the corresponding interchange in the next group by a single express channel. All messages from the nodes immediately before an interchange will be routed on that interchange's express channels. Because load cannot

---

[2] Throughout this paper the term latency is used to refer to the latency of a single message in the absence of traffic. For a discussion of the effects of traffic on latency see [5] and [9].

[3] There is nothing special about the factor of two. By choosing $i = j\alpha$ the distance component of latency will be $(1 + 1/j)$ times the latency of a Manhattan wire.

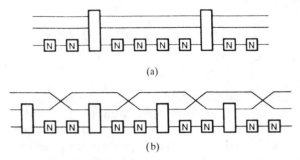

(a)

(b)

Fig. 2. Multiple express channels allow wire density to be increased to saturate the available wiring media. Express channels can be added using either (a) interchanges with multiple express channels, or (b) interleaved simplex interchanges.

be shared among interleaved express channels, an uneven distribution of traffic may result in some channels being saturated while parallel channels are idle. Method (b) has the advantage of using simple interchanges and allowing arbitrary expansion. In the extreme case of inserting an interchange between every pair of nodes the resulting topology is almost the same as the topology that would result from doubling the number of dimensions.

Both of the methods illustrated in Fig. 2 have the effect of increasing the wire density (and bisection) by a factor of $m + 1$. To first order, network throughput will increase by a similar amount. There will be some degradation due to uneven loading of parallel channels.

The use of multiple express channels offsets the load imbalance between express and local channels. If traffic is uniformly distributed, the average fraction of messages crossing a point in the center of the network on a local channel is $f_0 = 2i/k$ as compared to $f_1 = (k - 2i)/k$ crossing on an express channel. For large networks where $k >> i$, the bulk of the traffic is on express channels. Increasing the number of express channels applies more of the network bandwidth where it is most needed. The issue of allocating multiple express channels is discussed further in Section III-E.

Multiple express channels are an effective method of increasing throughput in networks where the channel width is limited by pinout constraints. For example, in the J-Machine the channel width $W = 9$ is set by pin limitations.[4] The printed-circuit board technology is capable of running $\mathcal{W} = 80$ wires in each dimension across the 50 mm width of a node. Even with many of these wires used for local connections, four parallel 15-bit (data + control) wide channels can be easily run across each node. A multiple express channel network with $m = 3$ could use this available wire density to quadruple the throughput of the network.

C. Hierarchical Express Cubes Have Logarithmic Node Delay

With a single level of express channels, an average of i local channels are traversed by each nonlocal message. The node delay on these local channels represents a significant component of latency and causes networks with short distances, $D \leq \alpha^2$,

[4] Each J-Machine node is packaged in a 168-pin pin-grid array. The six communication channels each require 9 data bits and six control bits consuming 90 of these pins. Power connections use 48 pins. The remaining 30 pins are used by external memory interface and control [16].

to be node limited. Hierarchical express cubes overcome this limitation by using several levels of express channels to make node delay increase logarithmically with distance for short distances.

The use of hierarchical express channels, shown in Fig. 3, reduces the latency due to node delay on local channels. With hierarchical express channels, there are l levels of interchanges. A first-level interchange is inserted every i nodes. A second-level interchange replaces every ith first level interchange, every i^2 nodes. In general, a jth level interchange replaces every ith $j - 1$st level interchange, every i^j nodes.[5] Fig. 3 illustrates a hierarchical express cube with $i = 2$, $l = 2$.

A jth level interchange has $j + 1$ inputs and $j + 1$ outputs. Arriving messages are treated identically regardless of the input on which they arrive. Messages that are destined for one of the next i nodes are routed to the local (0th) output. Those remaining messages that are destined for one of the next i^2 nodes are routed to the 1st output. The process continues with all messages with a destination between i^p and i^{p+1} nodes away, $0 \leq p \leq j - 1$, routed to the pth output. All remaining messages are routed to the jth output.

A message in a hierarchical express cube is delivered in three phases: ascent, cruise, and descent. In the ascent phase, an average message travels $(i + 1)/2$ hops to get to the first interchange, and $(i - 1)/2$ hops at each level for a total of $H_a = (i - 1)/2 + 1$ hops and a distance of $D_a = (i^l - 1)/2$. During the cruise phase, a message travels $H_c = \lfloor (D - D_a)/i^l \rfloor$ hops on level l channels for a distance of $D_c = i^l H_c$. Finally, the message descends back through the levels routing on each level, j, as long as the remaining distance is greater than i^j. For the special case where $i^l \mid D$, the descending message takes $H_d = (i - 1)l/2 + 1$ hops for a distance of $D_d = (i^l + 1)/2$. This gives a latency of

$$T_c = \left(\frac{D}{i^l} + (i - 1)l + 1 \right) T_n + T_w D + \frac{LT_p}{W}. \quad (5)$$

Choosing i and l so that $i^l = \alpha$ balances node and wire delay for large distances. With this choice, the delay due to local nodes is $(i - 1)l T_n = (i - 1) \log_i \alpha T_n$. Given that i is an integer greater than unity, this expression is minimized for $i = 2$. Choosing i to be a power of two facilitates decoding of binary addresses in interchanges. Networks with $i = 4$, $i = 8$, and $i = 16$ may be desirable under some circumstances.

In the general case, $i^l \nmid D$, the latency of a hierarchical express cube is calculated by representing the source and destination coordinates as $h = \log_i k$-digit radix-i numbers, $S = s_{h-1} \cdots s_0$, and $D = d_{h-1} \cdots d_0$. Without loss of generality we assume that $S < D$. During the ascent phase, a message routes from S to $s_{h-1} \cdots s_{l+1} 0 \cdots 0$ taking $H_a = \Sigma_{j=0}^{l-1} ((i - s_j) \mod i)$ hops for a distance of $D_a = \Sigma_{j=0}^{l-1} ((i - s_j) \mod i) i^j$. The cruise phase takes the message $H_c = \Sigma_{j=l}^{h-1} (d_j - s_j) i^{j-l}$ hops for a distance of $D_c = H_c i^l$. Finally, the descent phase takes the message from $d_{h-1} \cdots d_l 0 \cdots 0$ to D taking $H_d = \Sigma_{j=0}^{l-1} d_j$ hops for a distance of $D_d = \Sigma_{j=0}^{l-1} d_j i^j$.

[5] This construction yields a fixed-radix express cube, with radix i for each level. It is also possible to construct mixed-radix express cubes where the radix varies from level to level.

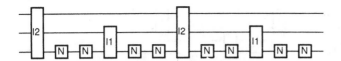

Fig. 3.   Hierarchical express channels reduce latency due to local routing.

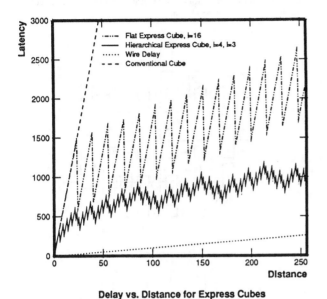

Delay vs. Distance for Express Cubes

Fig. 4.   Latency as a function of distance for a hierarchical express channel cube with $i = 4$, $l = 3$, $\alpha = 64$, and a flat express channel cube with $i = 16$, $\alpha = 64$. In a hierarchical express channel cube latency is logarithmic for short distances and linear for long distances. The crossover occurs between $D = \alpha$ and $D = i\alpha \log_i \alpha$. The flat cube has linear delay dominated by T_n for short distances and T_w for long distances.

For short distances the cruise phase will never be reached. The message will move from ascent to descent as soon as it reaches a node where all nonzero coordinates agree with D. The total latency for the general case is plotted as a function of distance in Fig. 4.

Fig. 5 shows how hierarchical interchanges can be implemented using pin-bounded modules. A level-j interchange requires $j + 1$ inputs and outputs if implemented as a single module as shown for a third level interchange in Fig. 5(a). A level-j interchange can be decomposed into $2j - 1$ level-one interchanges as shown for $j = 2$ in Fig. 5(b). A series of $j - 1$ ascending interchanges that route nonlocal traffic toward higher levels is followed by a top-level interchange and a series of $j - 1$ descending interchanges that allow local traffic to descend. With some degradation in performance, the ascending interchanges can be eliminated as shown in Fig. 5(c). This change requires extra hops in some cases as a message cannot skip levels on its way up to a high-level express channel. Each message must traverse at least one level $j - 1$ channel before being switched to a level-j channel. By restricting messages to also travel on at least one channel at each level as they descend, the descending interchanges can be eliminated as well leaving only the single top-level interchange as shown in Fig. 5(d).

D. Performance Comparison

Fig. 4 shows how latency varies with distance in hierar-

chical and flat express cubes and compares these latencies to the latency of a conventional k-ary 1-cube and of a direct wire. These curves assume that the message source is midway between two interchanges. The latencies are normalized to units of the wire delay between adjacent nodes. The latency of a conventional k-ary 1-cube is linear with slope α while the latency of a wire is linear with slope 1.

For short distances, until the first express channel is reached, a flat (nonhierarchical) express cube has the same delay as a conventional k-ary n-cube, $T_D = \alpha D$. Once the message begins traveling on express channels, latency increases linearly with slope $1 + \alpha/i$. This occurs at distance $D = 24$ in the figure. There is a periodic variation in delay around this asymptote due to the number of local channels being traversed, $D_{\text{local}} = (i + 1)/2 + ((D - i/2 + 1/2) \bmod i)$.

The hierarchical express cube has a latency that is logarithmic for short distances and linear for long distances. The latency of messages traveling a short distance, $D < \alpha$ is node limited and increases logarithmically with distance, $T_D \approx (i - 1) \log_i DT_n$. This delay is within a factor of $i - 1$ of the best that can be achieved with radix i switches. Long distance messages have a latency of $T_D \approx \left(1 + \alpha/i^l\right)T_w$. If $i^l = \alpha$, this long distance latency is approximately twice the latency of a dedicated Manhattan wire. In a hierarchical network, the interchange spacing i can be made small, giving good performance for short distances, without compromising the delay of long distance messages which depends on the ratio α/i^l. In a flat network with a single parameter i, it is not possible to simultaneously optimize performance for both short and long distances.

E. Area Tradeoffs

Assume that a node has a cross-sectional area that permits W wires to pass through in each dimension. W of these wires are used for a local channel. The remaining $W - W$ wires are allocated as $M = \lfloor \beta - 1 \rfloor$ W-wire channels since a narrower channel will form a bottleneck that will slow other channels. The M available channels should be divided among the levels in a hierarchical express cube in a manner that evenly balances the load.

Assuming random traffic, at each level j, from $j = 0$, local channels, to $j = l - 1$, the fraction of traffic carried at level j on a channel near the center of the machine is

$$f_j = \frac{2i^j}{k}. \qquad (6)$$

The fraction of traffic on the top-level channel is the remainder,

$$f_l = \frac{i^l - i}{1 - i}. \qquad (7)$$

To balance the load between levels of the express cube, m_j channels should be allocated to each level j of the cube in proportion to the fraction of traffic f_j at that level. In practice, M is not large enough to permit an exact balance. For example, in a cube with $k = 64$, $i = 2$, $l = 3$, and random traffic, the fractions, f_0 to f_3, are 0.0625, 0.125, 0.250, and 0.5625,

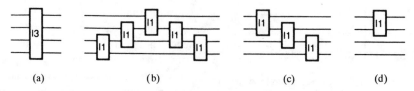

Fig. 5.   Hierarchical interchanges. (a) A third-level interchange. (b) A third-level interchange implemented from first-level interchanges. (c), (d) With a small performance penalty, ascending and/or descending interchanges can be eliminated.

respectively. If $M = 7$, a reasonable allocation to m_0 through m_3 is 1, 1, 2, and 4, respectively.

If there is considerable locality in the traffic pattern, more traffic will travel on the lower levels and additional channels should be allocated to these levels. It is better to overallocate channels to lower levels than to higher levels because the lower-level channels are more versatile. Long distance messages can make use of lower level channels with some increase in latency; however, local messages cannot make progress on high-level channels.

F. Express Channels in Many Dimensions

A multidimensional express cube may be constructed by inserting interchanges into each dimension separately as shown in Fig. 6(a). The figure shows part of a two-dimensional express cube with $i = 4$, $l = 1$. Interchanges have been inserted separately into the X and Y dimensions. A similar construction can be realized for higher dimensions and for hierarchical networks. With this approach interchange pincount is minimal as each interchange handles only a single dimension. Also, the design is easy to package into modules as the interchanges are located in regular rows and columns. This approach has the disadvantage that messages must descend to local channels to switch dimensions.

An alternate construction of a multidimensional express cube is to interleave multidimensional interchanges into the array as shown in Fig. 6(b) for $i = 4$, $l = 1$. This approach allows messages on express channels to change dimensions without descending to a local channel. It is particularly useful in networks that use adaptive routing [14], [15] as it provides alternate paths at each level of the network. The interleaved construction has the disadvantages of requiring a higher interchange pin count and being more difficult to package into modules.

G. Modularity

The interchanges in an express cube can be used to change wire density, speed, and signaling levels at module boundaries as shown in Fig. 7. Large networks are built from many modules in a physical hierarchy. A typical hierarchy includes integrated circuits, printed circuit boards, chassis, and cabinets. Available wire density and bandwidth change significantly between levels of the hierarchy. For example, a typical integrated circuit has a wire density of 250 wires/mm per layer while a printed circuit board can handle only 2 wires/mm per layer.[6] Interchanges placed at module boundaries as shown

---

[6]This integrated circuit wire density is typical of first-level metal in a 1 μm CMOS process. The printed circuit wire density is for a board with 8 mil wires and spaces. Both densities assume all area is available for wiring.

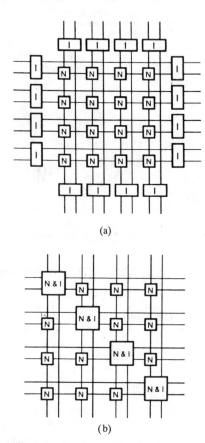

Fig. 6.   A multidimensional express cube may be constructed either by (a) inserting interchanges into each dimension separately, or (b) interleaving multidimensional interchanges into the array.

in Fig. 7 can be used to vary the number and width of express and local channels. These boundary interchanges may also convert internal module signaling levels and speeds to levels and speeds more appropriate between modules. Using express channels and boundary interchanges, the network can be adjusted to saturate the available wiring density even though this density is not uniform across the packaging hierarchy. To make use of the available bandwidth, computations running on the network must exploit locality.

IV. INTERCHANGE DESIGN

Fig. 8 shows the block diagram of a unidirectional interchange. A bidirectional interchange includes an identical circuit in the opposite direction. The basic design is similar to that of a router [17], [6], [3]. Two input latches hold arriving flits and two output latches hold departing flits. If additional buffering is desired, any of these latches may be replaced by a FIFO buffer. If a phit is a different size than a flit,

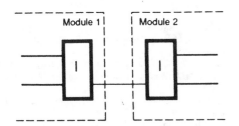

Fig. 7. Interchanges allow wire density, speed, and signaling levels to be changed at module boundaries.

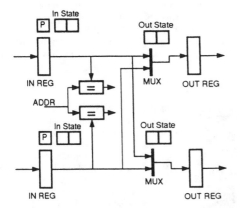

Fig. 8. Block diagram of an interchange. Two multiplexors perform switching between input and output registers based on a comparison of the high address bits in a message header.

multiplexing and demultiplexing is required between the flit buffers and the interchange pins. Associated with each output latch is a multiplexor that selects which input is routed to the latch. Routing decisions are made by comparing the address information in the head flit(s) of the message to the local address. If the destination lies within the next i nodes, the local channel is chosen, otherwise the express channel is chosen. If i is a power of two, interchanges are aligned, and absolute addresses are used in headers, the comparison can be made by checking all but the $l \log_2 i$ least significant bits for equality to the local address.

The interchange state includes presence bits for each register, an input state for each input, and an output state for each output. The presence bits are used for flit-level flow control. A flit is allowed to advance only if the presence bit of its destination register is clear (no data present), or if the register is to be emptied in the same cycle. The input state bits hold the destination port and status (empty, head, advancing, blocked) of the message currently using each input. The output state consists of a bit to identify whether the output is busy and a second bit to identify which input has been granted the output. The combinational logic to maintain these state bits and control the data path is straightforward.

V. CONCLUSION

Express cubes are k-ary n-cubes augmented by express channels that provide a short path for nonlocal messages. An express cube retains the wire efficiency of a conventional k-ary n-cube while providing improved latency and through-

put that are limited only by the wire delay and available wire density. For short distances, a hierarchical express cube has a latency that is within a small factor of the best that can be achieved with a bounded degree network. For long distances, the latency can be made arbitrarily close to that of a dedicated Manhattan wire. Multiple express channels can be used to increase throughput to the limit of the available wire density. The express cube combines the low diameter of multistage interconnection networks with the wire efficiency and ability to exploit locality of a low-dimensional mesh network. The result is a network with latency and throughput that are within a small factor of the physical limit.

Express channels are added to a k-ary n-cube by periodically inserting interchanges into each dimension. No modifications are required to the routers in each processing node; express channels can be added to most existing k-ary n-cube networks. Interchanges also allow wire density, speed, and signaling levels to be changed at module boundaries. An express cube can make use of all available wire density even if the wire density is nonuniform. This is often required as the wire density and speed may change significantly between levels of packaging.

Express cubes achieve their performance at the cost of adding interchanges, increasing the latency for some short-distance messages, and increasing the bisection width of the network. Each interchange adds a component to the system and increases the latency of local messages that cross an interchange but do not take the express channel by one node delay, $(T_n + T_w)$. Express channels increase the wire bisection by using available unused wiring capacity. In parts of the network that are already wire-limited the express and local channels can be combined as shown in Fig. 7.

As the performance of interconnection networks approaches the limits of the underlying wiring media their range of application increases. These networks can go beyond exchanging messages between the nodes of concurrent computers to serving as a general interconnection media for digital electronic systems. For distances larger than $D' = \alpha i \log_i \alpha$, the delay of a hierarchical express cube network is within a factor of three of that of a dedicated wire. The network may provide better performance than the wire because it is able to share its wiring resources among many paths in the network while a dedicated wire serves only a single source and destination. For distances smaller than D', dedicated wiring offers a significant latency advantage at the cost of eliminating resource sharing.

ACKNOWLEDGMENT

I thank C. Leiserson for pointing out the node-limited nature of most real k-ary n-cubes. Express cubes have been strongly influenced by his work on fat trees [13]. I thank S. Ward, A. Agarwal, and T. Knight for many helpful comments and suggestions about routing networks and their analysis. I thank C. Seitz for many helpful suggestions about networks, routers, and concurrent computers. I thank A. Chien and M. Noakes for their careful review of early drafts of this manuscript. Finally I thank all the members of the MIT Concurrent VLSI

Architecture group for their help with and contributions to this paper.

REFERENCES

[1] W. C. Athas and C. L. Seitz, "Multicomputers: Message-passing concurrent computers," *IEEE Comput. Mag.,* vol. 21, pp. 9–24, Aug. 1988.

[2] BBN Advanced Computers, Inc., "Butterfly parallel processor overview," BBN Rep. 6148, Mar. 1986.

[3] W. J. Dally and C. L. Seitz, "The torus routing chip," *J. Distributed Syst.,* vol. 1, no. 3, pp. 187–196, 1986.

[4] W. J. Dally, *A VLSI Architecture for Concurrent Data Structures.* Hingham, MA: Kluwer, 1987.

[5] ——, "Wire efficient VLSI multiprocessor communication networks," in *Proc. Stanford Conf. Advanced Res. VLSI,* P. Losleben, Ed. Cambridge, MA: MIT Press, Mar. 1987, pp. 391–415.

[6] W. J. Dally and P. Song, "Design of a self-timed VLSI multicomputer communication controller," in *Proc. Int. Conf. Comput. Design, ICCD-87,* 1987, pp. 230–234.

[7] W. J. Dally *et al.,* "The J-Machine: A fine-grain concurrent computer," in *Proc. IFIP Congress,* 1989.

[8] W. J. Dally, "The J-Machine: System support for actors," in *Actors: Knowledge-Based Concurrent Computing,* Hewitt and Agha, Eds. Cambridge, MA: MIT Press, 1991.

[9] ——, "Performance analysis of *k*-ary *n*-cube interconnection networks," *IEEE Trans. Comput.,* vol. 39, pp. 775-785, June 1990.

[10] ——, "Network and processor architecture for message-driven computing," in *VLSI and Parallel Processing,* R. Suaya and G. Birtwistle, Eds. Los Altos, CA: Morgan Kaufmann, 1990.

[11] P. Kermani and L. Kleinrock, "Virtual cut-through: A new computer communication switching technique," *Comput. Networks,* vol. 3, pp. 267–286, 1979.

[12] D. H. Lawrie, "Alignment and access of data in an array processor," *IEEE Trans. Comput.,* vol. C-24, pp. 1145–1155, Dec. 1975.

[13] C. E. Leiserson, "Fat-trees: Universal networks for hardware-efficient supercomputing," *IEEE Trans. Comput.,* vol. C-34, pp. 892–900, Oct. 1985.

[14] J. Mailhot, "A comparative study of routing and flow control strategies in *k*-ary *n*-cube networks," S.B. thesis, Massachusetts Instit. of Technol., May 1988.

[15] J. Ngai, "A framework for adaptive routing in multicomputer networks," Ph.D. dissertation, Caltech Computer Science Tech. Rep., Caltech-CS-TR-89-09, May 1989.

[16] M. O. Noakes and W. J. Dally, "System design of the J-Machine," in *Proc. Sixth MIT Conf. Advanced Res. VLSI,* MIT Press, 1990, pp. 179–194.

[17] P. R. Nuth, "Router protocol," MIT Concurrent VLSI Architecture Memo 23, Feb. 1989.

[18] C. L. Seitz, "The Cosmic Cube," *Commun. ACM,* vol. 28, pp. 22–23, Jan. 1985.

[19] C. L. Seitz *et al.,* "The architecture and programming of the Ametek Series 2010 Multicomputer," in *Proc. Third Conf. Hypercube Concurrent Comput. Appl.,* ACM, Jan. 1988, pp. 33–37.

[20] C. L. Seitz *et al.,* "Submicron systems architecture project semiannual technical report," Caltech Computer Science Tech. Rep., Caltech-CS-TR-88-18, p. 2 and pp. 11–12, Nov. 1988.

[21] C.-L. Wu and T. Feng, "On a class of multistage interconnection networks," *IEEE Trans. Comput.,* vol. C-29, pp. 694–702, Aug. 1980.

William J. Dally (S'78–M'86) received the B.S. degree in electrical engineering from Virginia Polytechnic Institute, the M.S. degree in electrical engineering from Stanford University, and the Ph.D. degree in computer science from Caltech.

He has worked at Bell Telephone Laboratories where he contributed to design of the BELLMAC-32 microprocessor. Later as a consultant to Bell Laboratories he helped design the MARS hardware accelerator. He was a Research Assistant and then a Research Fellow at Caltech where he designed the MOSSIM Simulation Engine and the Torus Routing Chip. He is currently an Associate Professor of Computer Science at the Massachusetts Institute of Technology where he directs a research group that is building the J-Machine, a fine-grain concurrent computer. His research interests include concurrent computing, computer architecture, computer-aided design, and VLSI design.

Chapter 4: Permutation Routing

Routing, the most fundamental function of networks, can be subdivided into two broad categories: *asynchronous routing* and *synchronous routing*. Asynchronous routing is used mainly in MIMD systems, while synchronous routing is used mainly in SIMD systems. Asynchronous routing is treated in later chapters. Synchronous routing, in its most standard form, is the subject matter of this chapter. In the most standard form of synchronous routing, every source sends at most one data item and every destination receives at most one data item. This routing is modeled by a (partial) permutation f, where $f(i) = j$ designates that source i sends a data item to destination j. The problem of routing a permutation f consists of determining and establishing the source-destination paths $i \rightarrow f(i)$ over which the data items are sent. In dynamic networks, this problem consists of appropriately setting the switches. In static networks, it consists of finding intermediary basic steps, with the communication in a basic step being between neighboring nodes. The concern in static networks is to develop routing algorithms that quickly compute the source-destination paths that involve a minimum number of basic communication steps. Another concern in static networks is the inherent complexity of data permuting; the first paper included in this chapter, by Gottlieb and Kruskal (1984), addresses this concern.

Routing algorithms can be *centralized* or *distributed*. A centralized routing algorithm is either run serially on a single processor to compute the source-destination paths or run in parallel on a number of processors. A distributed routing algorithm computes the source-destination paths by having the nodes (switches or processors) locally determine their configurations using minimum control information, such as the destination addresses. Distributed routing algorithms for delta multistage networks were developed early. However, these networks do not realize all permutations. This makes routing on the universal Benes and Clos networks very important. Serial centralized routing algorithms were initially designed for Benes and Clos networks, but they are too slow for real-time environments. To remedy this, parallel centralized routing algorithms and distributed routing algorithms have been developed in the last few years. The second paper included here, by Lee (1987), presents a parallel centralized routing algorithm for Benes networks. Next, Raghavendra and Boppana (1991) give a distributed routing algorithm for Benes networks that realizes a large subclass of permutations without conflict. The paper by Youssef and Arden (1990) presents a distributed approach to routing on three-stage Benes-Clos networks of arbitrary switch sizes. Finally, Mitra and Cieslak (1987) study a randomized distributed routing algorithm on an extended omega network. The algorithm and analysis apply to Benes networks as well.

Complexity Results for Permuting Data and Other Computations on Parallel Processors

ALLAN GOTTLIEB

New York University, New York, New York

AND

CLYDE P. KRUSKAL

University of Illinois at Urbana-Champaign, Urbana, Illinois

Abstract. For a wide class of problems, we obtain lower bounds for algorithms executed on certain parallel processors. These bounds show that for sufficiently large problems many known algorithms are optimal. The central result of the paper is the following sharper lower bound for permutation algorithms. Any permutation algorithm for N data items on a P processor parallel machine without shared memory requires time on the order of $N \log_K P/P$, where K is the maximum number of processors directly connected to a single processor. In particular, a speedup on the order of P is impossible if K is bounded.

Categories and Subject Descriptors: C.1.2 [**Processor Architectures**]: Multiple Data Stream Architecture—*parallel processors*; F.1.2 [**Computation by Abstract Devices**]: Modes of Computation—*parallelism*; F.2.2 [**Analysis of Algorithms and Problem Complexity**]: Nonnumerical Algorithm and Problems—*routing and layout, sorting and searching*

General Terms: Algorithms, Theory

Additional Key Words and Phrases: Lower bounds, parallel computation, permutations, routing, shuffle-exchange machine

1. *Introduction*

With the advent of large-scale integrated circuits, parallel computers consisting of thousands of processors will soon be feasible. We distinguish two classes of such machines. Members of the first class feature a shared central memory to which all processors have access, whereas members of the second class have local memories each accessed exclusively by one processor (or shared by a small number of processors). (See Gottlieb et al. [10] and the references therein for designs of the first class, and Schwartz [19] and the references therein for designs of the second

Part of this work was done while the first author was on leave from York College, CUNY, and while the second author was at New York University.

This work was supported in part by the Applied Mathematical Sciences Program of the U.S. Department of Energy under contract DE-AC02-76ER03077, and in part by the National Science Foundation under Grant NSF-MCS76-00116.

Authors' addresses: A. Gottlieb, Courant Institute, New York University, 251 Mercer Street, New York, NY 10012; C. P. Kruskal, Department of Computer Science, University of Illinois, 222 Digital Computer Laboratory, 1304 West Springfield, Urbana, IL 61801-2987.

"Complexity Results for Permuting Data and Other Computations on Parallel Processors" by A. Gottlieb and C.P. Kruskal from *J. Assoc. for Computing Machinery*, Vol. 31, No. 2, Apr. 1984, pp. 193-209. Copyright © 1984 Assoc. for Computing Machinery, Inc., reprinted with permission.

class.) To use the second class of machines effectively, it is necessary to be able to permute data items among local memories in a highly efficient manner. The present paper analyzes the complexity of this problem.

We model a parallel machine as a graph whose vertices correspond to processors (with private memories) and whose edges correspond to connections between processors. For example, a complete graph represents a parallel computer in which each processor is connected to every other.[1]

We show that for any initial distribution of N data items among P processors with each processor connected to at most K others, there exists a permutation requiring on the order of $N \log_K P/P$ data routing steps. In particular, if K does not grow with P, the maximum possible speedup is proportional to $P/\log P$. We also show that if the data items are distributed evenly among the processors, the latter bound is sharp by exhibiting an algorithm that achieves the necessary speedup for the *shuffle-exchange machine* ($K = 3$). This latter result is valid for arbitrary K (and large enough N) since an analogous algorithm exists for the K-*way shuffle-exchange machine*.

We also obtain general lower bounds that apply to many problems and, in an appendix, present tables showing, for several important problems, how these lower bounds compare to the performances attained by the fastest known algorithms.

Our general lower bound results should be compared with the work of Munro and Paterson [16], who consider only completely connected parallel processors but restrict the operations permitted. We, in contrast, permit restricted interconnection patterns, but allow arbitrary binary operations.

The following section gives the notation necessary for our analyses. Section 3 establishes the lower bounds. Section 4 presents and analyzes two permutation algorithms. Section 5 summarizes our results.

2. Definitions and Terminology

Throughout this paper we use *log* to denote a logarithm whose base is immaterial, *lg* to denote $\log_2$, and $log^k x$ to denote $(\log x)^k$. We follow Knuth's [13] usage of o, O, Θ, Ω, and ω to indicate asymptotic orders, and for the reader's convenience review these definitions. Let f and g be positive real-valued functions of a positive integer variable.[2] Then

$o(g)$ is the set of f such that f/g approaches 0; that is, $\forall \epsilon > 0 \; \exists N$ such that $\forall n \geq N f(n) < \epsilon g(n)$.

$O(g)$ is the set of f such that f/g is bounded above; that is, $\exists C$ such that $\forall n$ $f(n) < C g(n)$.

$\Theta(g)$ is the set of f such that f/g is bounded above and bounded away from zero, that is, $\exists C_1, C_2$ such that $\forall n \; 0 < C_1 g(n) < f(n) < C_2 g(n)$.

$\Omega(g)$ is the set of f such that f/g is bounded away from 0; that is, $\exists C$ such that $\forall n \; 0 < C g(n) < f(n)$.

$\omega(g)$ is the set of f such that f/g approaches infinity; that is, $\forall C \; \exists N$ such that $\forall n \geq N \; C g(n) < f(n)$.

Following Knuth, we often write $f = o(g)$ instead of $f \in o(g)$ and similarly for O, Θ, Ω, and ω.

---

[1] Such a fully connected machine with P processors would require on the order of P^2 wires. Often such machines are approximated by utilizing an interconnection network having on the order of $P \log P$ wires (see Lawrie [14] and Goke and Lipovski [9]).

[2] Knuth considers real-valued functions of real variables. We restrict the domains and ranges since the definitions are slightly easier and all functions we consider satisfy the restriction.

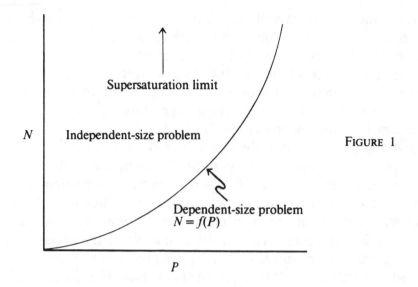

FIGURE 1

The *size of a parallel processor* is the number of processing elements (PEs) that it contains. We consistently denote processor size by P and number the processing elements: $PE_0, \ldots, PE_{P-1}$. We refer to the PEs connected to PE_i as its *neighbors*. The *degree of a PE* is the number of its neighbors. The *degree of a parallel processor* is the maximum degree of any PE. The *size of (an instance of) a problem* is the number of data items to be processed[3] and is denoted by N.

As will be seen, many of our estimates will be for "asymptotically large P and asymptotically much larger N" (defined below). We consider these estimates important because we expect large-scale machines to appear in the near future, and new more powerful machines have always given rise to problem instances that fill them to capacity (e.g., by solving partial differential equations (PDEs) with ever finer meshes).

It is likely that these machines will fall into "families," in which the family members have the same structure but differ in size (e.g., the family of binary tree machines). In Section 4, we give algorithms for one such family. Our lower bounds, however, depend only on the size and degree of a machine's underlying graph (and not on its topology).

The time complexity of a sequential algorithm (i.e., an algorithm for a single processor) is a function of one variable, the problem size, whereas the time complexity of a parallel algorithm is a function $T_P(N)$ of not only the problem size N but also the parallel processor size P. In a *dependent-size problem*, N is some specified function f of P; that is, the problem size varies with the parallel processor size. A *saturated problem* is a dependent-size problem with $f(P) = P$ and with the data items distributed one per PE. In an *independent-size problem*, N is independent of P. (See Figure 1.) A *dependent-size algorithm* solves a dependent-size problem, a *saturated algorithm* solves a saturated problem, and an *independent-size algorithm* solves an independent-size problem.

For example, consider the problem of summing N numbers. The obvious (and optimal) sequential algorithm has complexity $\Theta(N)$. For the saturated problem (i.e., when $N = P$), many parallel architectures can solve this problem in time $\Theta(\log P)$. To generalize this to an independent-size problem, we let N be independent of P. By letting each PE independently determine the sum of $\lceil N/P \rceil$ numbers and then using the saturated algorithm to determine the total sum of these local

---

[3] We assume that each item fits in one machine word.

sums, we can solve the independent-size problem in time

$$T_P(N) = \Theta\left(\frac{N}{P} + \log P\right).$$

For N large relative to P, this is $\Theta(N/P)$. To make this last statement precise, we introduce "supersaturation"-order notations, which describe asymptotic behavior of functions of two variables at an asymmetrical limit having one variable much larger than the other. Let f and g be functions of P and N.

Definition. $O_S(g)$ is the set of f such that there exist constants P_0 and c and a function $N_0(P)$ such that, for all $P \geq P_0$ and $N \geq N_0(P)$, $f \leq cg$. As above when $f \in O_S(g)$ we write $f = O_S(g)$ and say that f is of order g in the supersaturation limit.

Definition.   For f and g functions of P and N, $f = \Omega_S(g)$ if $g = O_S(f)$.

Definition.   For f and g functions of P and N, $f = \Theta_S(g)$ if $f = O_S(g)$ and $f = \Omega_S(g)$.

Intuitively, the supersaturation limit consists of taking asymptotically large P and asymptotically much larger N, and corresponds to first choosing an arbitrarily large parallel processor and then loading it arbitrarily heavily. We can now say that the independent-size summing algorithm requires time $\Theta(N/P + \log P) = \Theta_S(N/P)$. Other examples of supersaturation limits include $3NP = \Theta_S(NP)$ and $PN/(N + P\log P) = \Theta_S(P)$.

We now consider the question of how heavily loaded a parallel processor must be before the supersaturation limit behavior is attained. For example, in the summing algorithm, if we require that $N \geq N_0(P) = P\log P$,

$$T_P(N) = \Theta\left(\frac{N}{P} + \log P\right) = \Theta\left(\frac{N}{P}\right).$$

We summarize this behavior by saying that summing "supersaturates at" $N = P\log P$. More precisely, letting $g(P, N)$ be the formula describing the supersaturation limit behavior of f, a function of P and N, we say that f *supersaturates at* $N = N_0(P)$ if, in the region $N \geq N_0(P)$,

$$f = \Theta(g).$$

Of course many N_0's will satisfy this condition.

The *speedup* $S_P(N)$ of a parallel algorithm is defined to be the ratio

$$\frac{T_1(N)}{T_P(N)},$$

where $T_1(N)$ is the complexity of the fastest known sequential algorithm for the same problem.[4] It is well known that any such speedup S (for a "reasonable" parallel algorithm) must be between 1 and P.[5] To see this, note first that since a parallel processor can act as a sequential processor by utilizing just a single PE, a parallel processor is at least as fast as a sequential processor; and second that a

---

[4] Note that, by abuse of notation, the $T_1(N)$ appearing in the definition of speedup is not necessarily the value of $T_P(N)$ for $P = 1$. Moreover, speedup would be more naturally defined with respect to the fastest sequential algorithm (rather than just the fastest known), but in general this quantity is difficult to determine.

[5] Actually, the latter term may be slightly greater than P owing to bookkeeping overhead (see next note).

sequential processor can simulate a parallel processor at the cost of a time factor of P.[6] Thus $1 \leq S \leq P$ as desired.

The speedup of the saturated summing algorithm is

$$\frac{\Theta(P)}{\Theta(\log P)} = \Theta\left(\frac{P}{\log P}\right).$$

The speedup of the corresponding supersaturated algorithm is

$$\frac{\Theta(N)}{\Theta(N/P + \log P)} = \Theta\left(\frac{N}{N/P + \log P}\right) = \Theta\left(\frac{P}{1 + P\log P/N}\right) = \Theta_S(P).$$

N.B. The definition of "supersaturates at" given above is actually not well defined because it is relative to the choice of asymptotic formula in the supersaturation limit, for example, $N/P + \log P = \Theta_S(N/P)$ and $= \Theta_S(N/P + P)$ (among innumerable other possibilities) and these two choices lead to supersaturating at different loads, $\Theta(P \log P)$ and $\Theta(1)$, respectively. It is true that normally there is a clearly "simplest" choice of asymptotic behavior, namely, the former in the present example, but this "simplest" is not meaningfully distinguished. Nevertheless, the concept of speedup in the supersaturation limit does not usually suffer from a comparable ambiguity because being limited to the range from 1 to P it will not depend on N in a significant way. When we speak of the load at which some algorithm supersaturates, we really mean the load at which its speedup supersaturates.

The following cases of supersaturated speedup are particularly interesting.

(1) We say that a problem is *completely parallelizable* if some algorithm has maximal speedup in the supersaturation limit, that is, $S_P(N) = \Omega_S(P)$. A problem is *completely parallelizable at size* $N_0(P)$ if its speedup supersaturates at $N_0(P)$.

(2) We say that a problem is *completely unparallelizable* if the fastest algorithm in the supersaturation limit has minimal speedup, that is, $S_P(N) = O_S(1)$. Moreover, in analogy with the above, we introduce the notion of *completely unparallelizable at size* $N_0(P)$.

The basic idea behind our analyses is to take a dependent-size algorithm and generalize it to an independent-size algorithm. Many dependent-size algorithms, for example, the above summing algorithm, can be made independent-size by replacing each data item by L data items. We follow Schwartz [19] and say that the problem has been loaded to *level* L and note that a dependent-size algorithm for a problem of size $f(P)$, when loaded to level L, solves problems of size $Lf(P)$. In particular, if the original problem was saturated (so that $f(P) = P$), the resulting problem is of size LP. Therefore, for summing,

$$T_P(N) = \Theta(L + \log P) = \Theta_S(L).$$

---

[6] We note that Baudet [1] has given a parallel version of the α–β algorithm that, for small P and certain search trees, outperforms the sequential algorithm by a factor in excess of P. As just mentioned, we can use a sequential processor to simulate the parallel version of this algorithm. So even if we were to assume that Baudet's algorithm is efficient for all values of P and for all search trees, when compared with this sequential implementation of Baudet's α–β algorithm, the parallel version would have a speedup proportional to P (where the constant of proportionality represents the bookkeeping overhead of simulation alluded to in the previous note).

(3) We say that a dependent-size algorithm *scales up* if

$$S_P(M) = \Theta_S(S_P(N)) \qquad \text{for} \quad M = \Omega(f(P)).$$

Thus, an algorithm scales up if increasing the problem size beyond the dependent size does not change the speedup, that is, if the dependent size is large enough for the speedup to have already attained the supersaturation limit behavior.

3. *Lower Bounds*

3.1. An Abstract Model of Computation.

In proving lower bounds, it is often convenient to analyze "*P*-computations" (which are defined below) rather than algorithms. Munro and Paterson [16] have shown that any *P*-computation involving only addition, subtraction, multiplication, and division, producing a single result, and requiring $\Omega(N)$ steps on a sequential processor, requires $\Omega(N/P + \log N)$ steps on any parallel processor.[7] The restriction to arithmetic operations is necessary, since Valiant [21] has given a *P*-computation involving comparisons that finds the maximum of *P* items in $\Theta(\log\log P)$ steps.

Definition. A *P-computation* consists of a sequence of time steps during which each PE can effect one of the following actions:

(1) perform a binary operation on two local data items, creating a third data item;
(2) perform a binary test on two local data items creating a test result;
(3) receive some data item from a neighboring PE;
(4) receive some test result from a neighboring PE.

(Unary operations and tests are permitted as degenerate special cases of (1) and (2).) At the end of every time step, each PE individually decides, by inspecting the test results that it has established or received from neighboring PEs, which action to perform next.

A *P*-computation is essentially an algorithm in which we permit test results to be combined in zero time. Thus, lower bounds for the complexity of *P*-computations are lower bounds for algorithms.

3.2. General Lower Bounds.

In this section, we present some general lower bounds for *P*-computations on degree *K* parallel processor that hold for any initial distribution of the data items; in particular, each data item may be replicated in all the PEs. We shall show that on a bounded degree parallel processor the Munro–Paterson formula holds, up to a multiplicative constant, even when arbitrary binary operations are allowed. For example, a *P*-computation that calculates the maximum of *N* items requires $\Omega(N/P + \log N)$ steps. (Note that Valiant's *P*-computation requires an unbounded degree parallel processor.)

Note that the following simple result, which was shown in Section 2 for algorithms, holds for *P*-computations (by analogous proof).

LEMMA 1. *If the complexity of a problem on a sequential processor is $T(N)$, then its complexity on a parallel processor of size P is*

$$\Omega\left(\frac{T(N)}{P}\right).$$

Definition. A *degree K P-computation* is a *P*-computation on a degree *K* parallel processor (of size *P*).

---

[7] Actually, Munro and Paterson give exact lower bounds, not merely orders.

Definition. The computation of M output items $(y_1, \ldots, y_M)$ *depends on* N *input items* $(x_1, \ldots, x_N)$ if each x_i is required for at least one y_j; that is, $(y_1, \ldots, y_M) = f(x_1, \ldots, x_N)$ where f satisfies the following condition: For each $i = 1, 2, \ldots, N$, there exist a, b such that

$$f|_{x_i=a} \neq f|_{x_i=b}.$$

For the remainder of this section, we let $Q = \{PE_0, \ldots, PE_{P-1}\}$ be a degree K parallel processor.

Definition. Let $PE, PE' \in Q$. We denote by $d(PE, PE')$ the distance from PE to PE' (i.e., the minimum d such that there exists a sequence $PE = PE_0, PE_1, \ldots, PE_d = PE'$ where PE_i is a neighbor of PE_{i+1}). If no path exists, the distance from PE to PE' is defined to be infinite. We say that PE' is within distance d of PE if $d(PE, PE') \leq d$.

PROPOSITION 1 (cf. Gentleman [8]). *For each PE_i in a degree $K > 1$ parallel processor, the number of PEs within distance D of PE_i is less than or equal to $K^{D+1} - 1$.*

PROOF. For completeness, we prove a slightly sharper result from which the proposition follows immediately. □

LEMMA 2. *Let Z be the number of PEs within distance D of PE_i. Then $Z \leq 1 + \sum_{i=0}^{D-1} K(K-1)^i$. Thus, for $K=2$, $Z \leq 2D+1$ and for $K \geq 3$, $Z \leq (K(K-1)^D - 2)/(K-2)$.*

PROOF. Only PE_i itself is within distance 0 of PE_i, only PE_i's (at most) K neighbors can be at distance 1 from PE_i, each of PE_i's neighbors can have at most $K-1$ neighbors at distance 2 not counting PE_i, etc. Thus, in general, within distance D the number of PEs is at most

$$1 + K + K(K-1) + K(K-1)^2 + \cdots + K(K-1)^{D-1}. \quad \square$$

PROPOSITION 2. *Let $PE_i \in Q$ and let Z be a subset of Q. Then*

$$\max_{z \in Z} d(PE_i, z) \geq \log_K(|Z| + 1) - 1.$$

PROOF. We may assume that $K > 1$ since the proposition is trivially true otherwise. Let

$$M = \max_{z \in Z} d(PE_i, z);$$

that is, all $z \in Z$ are within M of PE_i. Hence, by Proposition 1,

$$K^{M+1} - 1 \geq |Z|,$$

or

$$(M+1)\log K \geq \log(|Z| + 1).$$

The result follows. □

COROLLARY 1. *A degree K parallel processor has diameter at least $\log_K(P+1) - 1$.*

COROLLARY 2. *Let Q be a degree K parallel processor, let $PE_i \in Q$, and let Z be a subset of Q. Then*

$$\max_{z \in Z} d(PE_i, z) = \Omega(\log_K |Z|).$$

THEOREM 1. *A degree K P-computation of a single item y depending on N given items requires time $\Omega(N/P + \log_K N)$ (where K is considered a third independent variable, subject to $1 < K < P$).*

PROOF. The first term N/P follows from Lemma 1; we now justify the second term. If any PE examines $\Omega(\log_K N)$ data items and test results, the theorem holds trivially. Thus we may assume that each PE examines $O(\log_K N)$ data items and test results and hence

$$\Omega\left(\frac{N}{\log_K N}\right).$$

PEs must communicate (directly or indirectly) with the PE that will eventually contain y. Since $\log(N/\log_K N) = \Omega(\log N)$, the result now follows from Corollary 2. □

COROLLARY 3. *A bounded degree P-computation of a single item y depending on N given items requires time $\Omega(N/P + \log N)$.*

The version of Corollary 3 to be used later is

COROLLARY 4. *A bounded degree P-computation of a single item y depending on $N \geq P$ items requires time $\Omega(N/P + \log P)$.*

3.3. A SHARPER LOWER BOUND FOR PERMUTATIONS. Suppose we are given a set of data items $W = \{w_0, \ldots, w_{N-1}\}$, distributed among the PEs with each item in only one PE, and a permutation π of $(0, \ldots, N-1)$. The permutation problem is to effect π, that is, to permute W according to π.

In this section, we provide an asymptotic lower bound on the complexity of an (independent-size) permutation algorithm for any parallel processor. Specifically, we show that a permutation algorithm for a degree K parallel processor requires time $\Omega(N \log_K P/P)$ (where K here and in the following is, as earlier, a third independent variable satisfying $1 < K < P$), and hence any permutation algorithm for a bounded degree parallel processor requires time $\Omega(N \log P/P)$. We shall see in Section 4 that the shuffle-exchange machine, a degree 3 parallel processor, achieves this latter bound.

The idea of the proof is as follows: We first apply Proposition 1 to establish that most pairs of PEs are separated by a distance at least logarithmic in the number of PEs. A theorem of Dirac on the existence of Hamiltonian cycles is then applied to find for each PE_i a distinct PE_j at least a logarithmic distance away. This "processor permutation" is applied to the data items, and the minimum complexity needed to achieve the resulting data permutation is estimated using a Lagrange multiplier argument.

Throughout this section, we continue to let $Q = \{PE_0, \ldots, PE_{P-1}\}$ be a degree K parallel processor of size P. The following lemma shows that most PEs are far away (at least a logarithmic distance) from any given PE.

LEMMA 3. *For each $g < 1$, there exists an $h > 0$ such that, for any nonempty subset R of Q and any $PE_i \in R$, the set*

$$S =_{def} \{PE_j \in R \mid d(PE_i, PE_j) > h \log|R|\}$$

has cardinality at least $\lfloor g|R| \rfloor + 1$. We may choose

$$h = \frac{1}{2(\log K - \log(1 - g))}.$$

PROOF. Let $r = |R|$ and let $s = |S|$. We may assume that $K > 1$ and $r > 1$ since the lemma holds trivially otherwise. By Proposition 1 (and the fact that r is an integer)

$$s \geq r - (K^{\lceil h \log r \rceil} - 1)$$
$$= (\lfloor gr \rfloor + 1) + (\lceil (1 - g)r \rceil - K^{\lceil h \log r \rceil}).$$

Thus, it suffices to choose h such that

$$K^{\lceil h \log r \rceil} \leq \lceil (1 - g)r \rceil$$

or

$$(h \log r + 1) \log K \leq \log(1 - g) + \log r$$

or

$$h \leq \left(\frac{\log(1 - g) + \log r}{\log K} - 1 \right) \Big/ \log r$$
$$= \left(1 + \frac{\log(1 - g)/K}{\log r} \right) \Big/ \log K.$$

So $h \leq 1/2 \log K$ suffices if $r \geq ((1 - g)/K)^{-2}$. But for any r, if $h < 1/\log r$, the lemma holds trivially, and thus $h \leq 1/\log((1 - g)/K)^{-2} = 1/2(\log K - \log(1 - g))$ suffices for $r < ((1 - g)/K)^{-2}$. Hence, choosing

$$h \leq \min \left(\frac{1}{2 \log K}, \frac{1}{2(\log K - \log(1 - g))} \right)$$
$$= \frac{1}{2(\log K - \log(1 - g))}$$

completes the proof. $\square$

Definition. A *processor permutation* is a bijection of a subset of Q (i.e., a permutation of some of the PEs constituting the parallel processor).

Definition. Given a subset R of the PEs in Q and a subset V of W (the items to be permuted) such that each PE of R contains exactly one $w \in V$, the *data permutation* π^D corresponding to the processor permutation π assigns the item initially in PE_i to $\pi(PE_i)$.

Definition. We say that a processor permutation π *moves a* $PE_i \in R$ *a distance* δ if

$$d(PE_i, \pi(PE_i)) = \delta.$$

This distance δ equals the minimum number of data transfers needed to move one item from PE_i to $\pi(PE_i)$; it measures the minimum number of steps needed to realize π^D on an item in PE_i.

Note that although we are specifying the distance between two PEs contained in a subset R of Q, the sequence of PEs used to measure the distance may be chosen from all of Q (i.e., the sequence of PEs is not restricted to R).

We will need the following theorem of Dirac on the existence of Hamiltonian cycles [6]; see also [12, p. 68].

THEOREM (Dirac). *If for all vertices v of a graph of size $P \geq 3$, the degree of v is at least $P/2$, then G contains a Hamiltonian cycle.*

PROPOSITION 3. *There exists an $h > 0$ such that, for any nonempty subset R of Q, there exists a processor permutation $\pi = \pi_R: R \to R$ moving each $PE_i \in R$ a distance $\delta > h \log|R|$. We may choose $h = 1/2(\log K + \log 2)$.*

PROOF. We may assume $|R| > 1$ since the proposition holds trivially otherwise. Let $g = \frac{1}{2}$ and apply Lemma 3. The resulting h may be chosen as $1/2(\log K + \log 2)$. Consider the graph whose set of vertices is R and set of edges is E, where $(PE_i, PE_j) \in E$ if $d(PE_i, PE_j) > h \log|R|$. By Lemma 3, every vertex has degree $\geq \lfloor |R|/2 \rfloor + 1 \geq |R|/2$ and thus Dirac's theorem guarantees that a Hamiltonian cycle C exists. Choosing an orientation for C and defining $\pi(PE_i)$ to be the successor of PE_i on C complete the proof. □

The essence of Proposition 3 is that any subset of the PEs can be permuted so that each PE is moved at least a logarithmic distance. We now wish to mimic this behavior for data items; that is, we wish to permute the items so that each one is sent to a PE at least a logarithmic distance away from the PE in which it initially resides. Were the items evenly distributed this would be trivial: Apply Proposition 3 with $R = Q$ and require that all items initially located in PE_i end up in $\Pi_Q(PE_i)$. For a general distribution of data items, this is impossible: If the number of items initially in PE_i exceeds the number of items initially in $\Pi_Q(PE_i)$, then no permutation can assign all the former to $\Pi_Q(PE_i)$. Instead, we shall first partition W, the set of N data items, into $W_1 \cup W_2 \cup \cdots \cup W_M$, where each W_i consists of one item from each PE in R_i, a subset of Q, and then apply Proposition 3 to each R_i individually.

We define R_i and W_i by the following greedy procedure that attempts to choose sets as large as possible subject to the constraint that W_i contains at most one element from any PE. Let $R_1 \subseteq Q$ be those PEs containing at least one data item and choose $W_1 \subseteq W$ consisting of one item from each PE in R_1. Replace W by $W - W_1$ and repeat the procedure obtaining R_2 and W_2. Replace W by $W - W_2$ and continue until W is empty. Thus

$$W = W_1 \cup \cdots \cup W_M,$$

where M is the maximum number of items in any one PE. Now apply Proposition 3 to each R_i obtaining the processor permutation $\Pi_{R_i}: R_i \to R_i$ and let $\Pi_{W_i}: W_i \to W_i$ be the corresponding data permutation. Finally, define $\Pi: W \to W$ by $\Pi|_{W_i} = \Pi_{W_i}$ (i.e., for $w \in W_i$, $\Pi(w) = \Pi_{W_i}(w)$).

PROPOSITION 4. *The number of cycles needed to achieve Π is at least*

$$h \left(\frac{N}{P} \right) \log \left(\frac{N}{M} \right)$$

where we may choose $h = 1/2(\log K + \log 2)$.

PROOF. By Proposition 3, the number of data transfers needed to move an item $w \in W_j$ to its destination $\Pi(w)$ is at least $h \log|W_j|$. Since at most P data transfers can occur during one cycle, the number of cycles needed to achieve Π is at least

$$\frac{1}{P} \sum_{j=1}^{M} h|W_j| \log|W_j| \qquad \text{where} \quad \sum_{j=1}^{M} |W_j| = N.$$

A simple Lagrange multiplier argument shows that the sum is minimized when $|W_j| = N/M$ for all j. The proposition follows. □

THEOREM 2. *Let $Q = \{PE_0, \ldots, PE_{P-1}\}$ be a degree K parallel processor of size P and let N data items be distributed without replication among the PEs. Then there exist $h > 0$ depending only on K and a data permutation Π such that at least $h(N/P)(\log P)$ cycles are required to achieve Π, where we may choose $h = 1/3(\log K + \log 2)$.*

PROOF. We may assume that $K > 1$ since the theorem holds trivially otherwise. By Proposition 4, we can find a data permutation Π_1 that requires at least $h_1(N/P)\log(N/M)$ cycles to achieve, where $h_1 = 1/2(\log K + \log 2)$ and M is the maximum number of items initially located in any one PE. But it is trivial to construct a data permutation Π_2 that requires M cycles to achieve (permute without fixed points the M items initially located in one PE). Thus letting Π be the more time-consuming of Π_1 and Π_2, we see that the number of cycles needed to achieve Π is at least

$$\max(h_1(N/P)\log(N/M), M).$$

It is straightforward to check that for $M = (2/3)h_1(N/P)\log P$, $h_1(N/P)\log(N/M) > M$. The theorem now follows with $h = (2/3)h_1$. □

COROLLARY 5. *Any (independent-size) permutation algorithm for a degree K parallel processor requires time $\Omega(N\log_K P/P)$.*

COROLLARY 6. *Any (independent-size) permutation algorithm for a bounded degree parallel processor requires time $\Omega((N/P)\log P)$.*

COROLLARY 7. *The permutation problem is not completely parallelizable on any degree $P^{o(1)}$ parallel processor.*

PROOF. By Corollary 5, the permutation problem is not completely parallelizable if

$$\frac{N\log_K P}{P} = \omega\left(\frac{N}{P}\right) \quad \text{or} \quad \log K = o(1)\log P \quad \text{or} \quad K = P^{o(1)}. \quad \square$$

COROLLARY 8. *The permutation problem is not completely parallelizable on any bounded degree parallel processor.*

4. Algorithms

In this section we show that the *shuffle-exchange machine*, a degree 3 parallel processor, can permute in time $\Theta_S(N\log P/P)$, providing the data are evenly distributed among the processors. Thus, the lower bound given in Corollary 6 is tight for balanced distributions. Clearly no degree 1 or 2 parallel processor can permute evenly distributed data in time $\Theta_S(N\log P/P)$, but the algorithms below do generalize to arbitrary $K \geq 3$: The *K-way shuffle machine*[8] can permute in time $O(N\log_K P/P)$ providing the data are evenly distributed, $K \geq 3$, and $N = \Omega(PK)$. This result shows that the cube-connected computer is an inefficient permutation engine since another $\log P$ degree machine, the $(\log P)$-way shuffle, can permute in $\Theta_S(N\log P/P\log\log P)$ steps, whereas the cube-connected computer requires $\Theta(N\log P/P)$ steps. (Valiant and Brebner [22] make a similar observation for probabilistic routing with exactly one item in each PE.)

---

[8] A *K-way shuffle machine* is defined for $P = K^p$ by specifying that PE_i is connected to PE_j if the first $p - 1$ K-ary digits of i equal the last $p - 1$ digits of j, or if the last $p - 1$ digits of i equal the first $p - 1$ digits of j.

We obtain an optimal algorithm for the "static" permutation problem (i.e., the problem in which the permutation to be effected is known in advance) by generalizing the saturated shuffle-exchange algorithm of Clos [5] and Benes [3]. An apparently more difficult variant of the permutation problem is to have the permutation to be effected presented at run time. We supply a shuffle-exchange algorithm for this "dynamic" permutation problem that also has complexity $\Theta_S(L \log P)$, but do not know of an independent-size dynamic permutation algorithm as fast as the static permutation algorithm for $N = o(P^{4.5}/\log P)$.

In our terminology, a shuffle-exchange machine [20] is a particular class of degree 3 parallel processors. We say $Q = \{PE_0, \ldots, PE_{P-1}\}$ is a shuffle-exchange machine provided that

(1) P is a power of 2, and
(2) PE_i is connected to $PE_{\epsilon(i)}$, $PE_{\sigma(i)}$, and $PE_{\sigma^{-1}(i)}$ where $\epsilon(i)$ is the *exchange* map defined by $\epsilon(i) = i + 1$ for i even and $\epsilon(i) = i - 1$ for i odd, and σ is the *shuffle* map defined by $\sigma(i) = 2i$ for $i < P/2$ and $\sigma(i) = 2i - P + 1$ for $i \geq P/2$.

Suppose that we are given $N = PL$ items, L in each PE, and wish to permute them according to a permutation π (given in advance). Clos [5], Benes [3], Opferman and Tsao-Wu [18], and Schwartz [19] have shown that, in the saturated case (i.e., $L = 1$) any such π can be factored into $O(\log P)$ shuffles, unshuffles, and transpositions, each of which may be effected in time $O(1)$. Since π is given in advance, the factorization may be precalculated so that the time required to effect Π is $O(\log P)O(1) = O(\log P)$.

To describe the independent-size algorithm, it is convenient to consider the data items as a $P \times L$ matrix $(w_{i,j})$ where $w_{i,j}$ is the jth data item in PE_i. By a well-known application of the Hall–Konig "matching" or "marriage" theorem (Waksman [23]), π can be factored as

$$\pi = \sigma \tau \sigma',$$

where σ and σ' are permuations that leave each row invariant and τ is a permutation that leaves each column invariant.

The algorithm correspondingly decomposes into three steps.

(1) Within each PE_i, perform the local permutation σ'_i, the restriction of σ' to row i.
(2) Apply the saturated permutation algorithm L times, once to each column of $(w_{i,j})$, to realize τ.
(3) In each PE_i, perform the local permutation σ_i, the restriction of σ to row i.

Steps (1) and (3) are sequential permutations, which can be performed in time $\Theta(L)$; step (2) consists of L applications of the saturated permutation algorithm, each of which can be performed in time $\Theta(\log P)$; thus, the entire algorithm can be performed in time

$$\Theta(L \log P) = \Theta_S(L \log P).$$

This is optimal (at all levels) by Corollary 3.6. The speedup is

$$\Theta\left(\frac{LP}{L \log P}\right) = \Theta\left(\frac{P}{\log P}\right) = \Theta_S\left(\frac{P}{\log P}\right).$$

Thus the saturated static permutation algorithm scales up.

Now suppose we are given as data a permutation π of $(0, 1, \ldots, N - 1)$ and a set $W = \{w_0, \ldots, w_{N-1}\}$ of $N = PL$ items, L in each PE, and wish to permute these items according to π. The saturated case of this problem can be solved via sorting in time $\Theta(\log^2 P)$, or if π is to be applied repeatedly it may be advantageous to factor π into shuffles, unshuffles, and transpositions and then use the static permutation algorithm. Nassimi and Sahni [17] and Schwartz [19] give procedures for calculating such factorizations in time $\Theta(\log^4 P)$ and Lev et al. [15] present a $\Theta(\log^2 P)$ procedure for a shared memory machine (which is easily converted to a $\Theta(\log^4 P)$ algorithm for a shuffle-exchange machine).

In order to realize π on W, each data item w_i must be sent to its destination processing element $\text{PE}_{d(i)}$. After this is accomplished, each PE merely performs a permutation of its local data. The algorithm for sending w_i to $\text{PE}_{d(i)}$ is as follows:

(1) Within each PE form the pairs $(w_i, d(i))$ and sort these pairs by the second components, thus grouping together pairs with the same destination.
(2) By the Hall–Koenig "matching" or "marriage" theorem (see [4, p. 134]), (nonempty) groups may be chosen, one from each PE, in such a way that each group has a distinct destination. These choices constitute a permutation σ of the PEs. Let S be the cardinality of the smallest chosen group.
(3) Factor σ as above and then permute S pairs from each group according to σ. The SP pairs transmitted are now in their correct PEs and are no longer considered for transmission. This eliminates (the nonempty set of) those chosen groups having minimal cardinality.
(4) Repeat steps (2) and (3) until no groups remain.

Initially, each PE contains at most P nonempty groups, all destination components are between 0 and $P - 1$, and the total number of items in each PE is L. Thus step (1) can be accomplished in time $\Theta(P + L)$.

The required matching in step (2) can be determined by finding a maximal matching in the bipartite graph (A, B, E), where $A = \{a_0, \ldots, a_{P-1}\}$ and $B = \{b_0, \ldots, b_{P-1}\}$ each represents the set of PEs in the shuffle-exchange computer and $(a_i, b_j) \in E$ if PE_i contains a group whose destination component is PE_j. This matching problem is solvable in time $\Theta(P^{2.5})$ [7]. Since, among all the PEs, there are at most P^2 groups and each iteration of steps (2) and (3) eliminates at least one group, step (2) is executed at most P^2 times. Thus the total time for step (2) is $\Theta(P^{4.5})$.

Step (3) is also executed P^2 times and each calculation of the control bits requires time $\Theta(\log^4 P)$; thus the total cost of calculating control bits is $\Theta(P^2 \log^4 P)$. During the P^2 executions of step (3), a total of L saturated permutations are effected. This requires time $\Theta(L \log P)$. The final step, local permutations of L items within each PE, requires time $\Theta(L)$.

The entire algorithm, therefore, requires time

$$\Theta(P + L + P^{4.5} + P^2 \log^4 P + L \log P + L)$$
$$= \Theta(P^{4.5} + L \log P) = \Theta_S(L \log P),$$

which is optimal by Corollary 6. The speedup is

$$\Theta\left(\frac{LP}{P^{4.5} + L \log P}\right) = \Theta_S\left(\frac{P}{\log P}\right).$$

The above supersaturation limits occur at level

$$L = \Omega\left(\frac{P^{4.5}}{\log P}\right).$$

Note that for $L = o(P^{4.5}/\log^2 P)$ the above algorithm is slower than sorting (see [2] and [11]), an alternative method for realizing permutations.

TABLE I. PERFORMANCE OF SEQUENTIAL AND DEPENDENT-SIZE ALGORITHM

| Problem | Sequential | | Dependent-size | | |
	Time $T_1(N)$	Size $N = f(P)$	Time bounds Lower	Time bounds Upper	Speedup $S_p(N)$
Summing	N	P	$\log P$	$\log P$	$\dfrac{P}{\log P}$
Permuting (static)	N	P	$\log P$	$\log P$	$\dfrac{P}{\log P}$
Packing	N	P	$\log P$	$\log P$	$\dfrac{P}{\log P}$
Sorting	$N \log N$	P	$\log P$	$\log^2 P$	$\dfrac{P}{\log P}$
Sorting (1 to N)	N	P	$\log P$	$\log^2 P$	$\dfrac{P}{\log^2 P}$
Merging	N	P	$\log P$	$\log P$	$\dfrac{P}{\log P}$
Permuting (dynamic)	N	P	$\log P$	$\log^2 P$	$\dfrac{P}{\log^2 P}$
Median	N	P	$\log P$	$\log^2 P$	$\dfrac{P}{\log^2 P}$
Median average case	N	P	$\log P$	$\log^2 P$	$\dfrac{P}{\log^2 P}$
Set and map operations	$N \log N$	P	$\log P$	$\log^2 P$	$\dfrac{P}{\log P}$
FFT	$N \log N$	P	$\log P$	$\log P$	P
Matrix mult[a] (naive)	$N^{1.5}$	$P^{2/3}$	$\log P$	$\log P$	$\dfrac{P}{\log P}$
Matrix mult[b] (Strassen)	$N^{0.5 \lg 7}$	$P^{2/\lg 7}$	$\log P$	$\log P \log \log P$	$\dfrac{P}{\log P \log \log P}$
Gauss elim[c] (complete pivoting)	$N^{1.5}$	P	$\sqrt{P}$	$\sqrt{P} \log P$	$\dfrac{P}{\log P}$
Odd–even reduction (tridiagonal)	N	P	$\log P$	$\log P$	$\dfrac{P}{\log P}$

[a] N is the number of items in the matrix. The speedup is relative to the naive (cubic in $\sqrt{N}$) algorithm (not the fastest known).

[b] N is the number of items in the matrix. The speedup is relative to Strassen's algorithm (not the fastest known).

[c] N is the number of items in the matrix.

5. Summary

We have shown that the permutation problem for arbitrarily distributed data is not completely parallelizable on any bounded degree parallel processor. Specifically, we have shown that permuting N items on a degree K machine of size P requires $\Omega(N \log_K P/P)$ data routing steps. Thus, if K does not grow with P, the complexity is $\Omega(N \log P/P)$.

We have shown that this last bound is sharp for evenly distributed data and a permutation given in advance by presenting an algorithm and proving that it attains the necessary speedup. We have also considered the dynamic permutation problem and presented an algorithm achieving the same speedup, but only in the supersaturation limit.

Appendix

This appendix summarizes, in tabular form, the analyses of the algorithms presented above, as well as several algorithms whose analyses are discussed in

TABLE II. PERFORMANCE OF INDEPENDENT-SIZE ALGORITHMS

Problem	Independent-size		
	Time bounds		Speedup
	Lower	Upper	
Summing	$L + \log P$	$L + \log P$	$\dfrac{LP}{L + \log P}$
Permuting (static)	$L \log P$	$L \log P$	$\dfrac{P}{\log P}$
Packing	$L + \log P$	$L \log P$	$\dfrac{P}{\log P}$
Sorting	$L \log(LP)$	$L \log L + L \log^2 P$	$\dfrac{P \log(LP)}{\log L + \log^2 P}$
Sorting (1 to N)	$L + \log P$	$L \log^2 P$	$\dfrac{P}{\log^2 P}$
Merging	$L + \log P$	$L \log P$	$\dfrac{P}{\log P}$
Permuting[a] (dynamic)	$L \log P$	$P^{4.5} + L \log P$	$\dfrac{LP}{P^{4.5} + L \log P}$
Median	$L + \log P$	$(1 + \lg L)\log^2 P + L \log P$	$\dfrac{LP}{(1 + \lg L)\log^2 P + L \log P}$
Median average case	$L + \log P$	$L \log P + \log^2 P$	$\dfrac{LP}{L \log P + \log^2 P}$
Set and map operations	$L \log(LP)$	$L \log L + L \log^2 P$	$\dfrac{P \log(LP)}{\log L + \log^2 P}$
FFT	$L \log(LP)$	$L \log(LP)$	P
Matrix mult[b] (naive)	$L^{1.5} + \log P$	$L^{1.5} + L \log P$	$\dfrac{P}{1 + L^{-0.5}\log P}$
Matrix mult[c] (Strassen)	$L^{0.5 \lg 7} + \log P$	$L \log P \log \log P + L^{0.5 \lg 7}$	$\dfrac{P}{1 + L^{1-0.5 \lg 7}\log P \log \log P}$
Gauss elim[d] (complete pivoting)	$L^{1.5}\sqrt{P}$	$L^{1.5}\sqrt{P} + L\sqrt{P} \log P$	$\dfrac{P}{1 + L^{-0.5}\log P}$
Odd–even reduction (tridiagonal)	$L + \log P$	$L + \log P$	$\dfrac{LP}{L + \log P}$

[a] A faster algorithm is known for $L = O(P^{4.5}/\log^2 P)$.
[b] N is the number of items in the matrix. The speedup is relative to the naive (cubic in $\sqrt{N}$) algorithm (not the fastest known).
[c] N is the number of items in the matrix. The speedup is relative to Strassen's algorithm (not the fastest known).
[d] N is the number of items in the matrix.

[11]. These tables show that for most of the algorithms considered, the speedup attained in the supersaturation limit significantly exceeds the dependent-size speedup, and for none of the algorithms considered does the reverse occur. In particular, several dependent-size algorithms that are not completely parallelizable become so in the supersaturation limit.

As above, P denotes the number of PEs and N denotes the number of data items. The lower bounds given are for a bounded degree parallel processor (and thus K does not appear), and the upper bounds are achievable on the shuffle-exchange machine ($K=3$).

Table I summarizes the performance of sequential and dependent-size algorithms, Table II does the same for independent-size algorithms,[9] and Table III

[9] The bounds given assume that the problem is at least as large as the corresponding dependent-size problem, that is, $N \geq f(P)$.

TABLE III. Supersaturation Limits of Algorithms

Problem	Supersaturation limits Time bounds Lower	Upper	$S_P(N)$	Remarks[a]
Summing	L	L	P	Optimal at all levels and CP at $L = \Omega(\log P)$
Permuting (static)	$L \log P$	$L \log P$	$\dfrac{P}{\log P}$	Optimal at all levels and scales up
Packing	L	$L \log P$	$\dfrac{P}{\log P}$	Scales up
Sorting	$L \log L$	$L \log L$	P	CP at $L = P^{\Omega(\log P)}$
Sorting (1 to N)	L	$L \log^2 P$	$\dfrac{P}{\log^2 P}$	Scales up
Merging	L	$L \log P$	$\dfrac{P}{\log P}$	Scales up
Permuting (dynamic)	$L \log P$	$L \log P$	$\dfrac{P}{\log P}$	Optimal at $L = \Omega\left(\dfrac{P^{4.5}}{\log P}\right)$
Median	L	$L \log P$	$\dfrac{P}{\log P}$	Supersaturates at $L = \Theta(\log P \log \log P)$
Median average case	L	$L \log P$	$\dfrac{P}{\log P}$	Supersaturates at $L = \Theta(\log P)$
Set and map operations	$L \log L$	$L \log L$	P	CP at $L = P^{\Omega(\log P)}$
FFT	$L \log L$	$L \log L$	P	CP at all levels
Matrix mult[b] (naive)	$L^{1.5}$	$L^{1.5}$	P	CP at $L = \Omega(\log^2 P)$
Matrix mult[c] (Strassen)	$L^{0.5 \lg 7}$	$L^{0.5 \lg 7}$	P	CP at $L = \Omega((\log P \log \log P)^\alpha)$, $\alpha = 1/(0.5 \lg 7 - 1)$
Gauss Elim[d] (complete pivoting)	$L^{1.5}\sqrt{P}$	$L^{1.5}\sqrt{P}$	P	CP at $L = \Omega(\log^2 P)$
Odd–even reduction (tridiagonal)	L	L	P	Optimal at all levels and CP at $L = \Omega(\log P)$

[a] CP = Completely parallelizable.
[b] N is the number of items in the matrix. The speedup is relative to the naive (cubic in $\sqrt{N}$) algorithm (not the fastest known).
[c] N is the number of items in the matrix. The speedup is relative Strassen's algorithm (not the fastest known).
[d] N is the number of itmes in the matrix.

shows the behavior of the latter algorithms at their supersaturation limits. The lower bounds given in Tables I, II, and III result from three considerations:

(1) Speedups cannot exceed $\Theta(P)$ (Lemma 1).
(2) "Most" problems require time $\Omega(L + \log P)$ (Corollary 4).
(3) Permuting requires time $\Omega(L \log P)$ (Corollary 6).

As above, these lower bounds are based on the fastest known sequential algorithm (rather than the fastest possible). The upper bounds are taken both from Section 4 and [11].

The "packing" problem consists of moving data to (low-numbered) consecutive PEs; "sorting (1 to N)" refers to sorting N (not necessarily distinct) integers in the range 1 to N; "set and map operations" include union, intersection, set difference, and map composition; and "odd–even reduction" is a method for solving a linear system whose matrix is in tridiagonal form.

ACKNOWLEDGMENTS. We thank Mark Fulk for help with the proof of Proposition 3 and Martin Kruskal, Larry Rudolph, Marc Snir, and J. T. Schwartz for reading preliminary versions of this paper and suggesting numerous technical improvements. We also thank the referees whose suggestions considerably improved the quality of the exposition.

REFERENCES

1. BAUDET, G. The design and analysis of algorithms for asynchronous multiprocessors. Ph.D. dissertation, Carnegie-Mellon Univ., Pittsburgh, 1978.
2. BAUDET, G., AND STEVENSON, D. Optimal sorting algorithms for parallel computers. *IEEE Trans. Comput. C-27* (1974), 84–87.
3. BENES, V.E. *Mathematical Theory of Connecting Networks and Telephone Traffic*. Academic Press, New York, 1965.
4. BERGE, C. *Graphs and Hypergraphs*. 2d ed. Elsevier North-Holland, New York, 1976.
5. CLOS, C. A study of nonblocking switching networks. *Bell Syst. Tech. J. 32* (1953), 406–424.
6. DIRAC, G.A. Some theorems on abstract graphs. *Proc. London Math. Soc.* (1952), 69–81.
7. EVEN, S. *Graph Algorithms*. Computer Science Press, Woodland Hills, Calif., 1979.
8. GENTLEMAN, W.M. Some complexity results for matrix computations on parallel processors. *J. ACM 25*, 1 (Jan. 1978), 112–115.
9. GOKE, L.R., AND LIPOVSKY, G.J. Banyan networks for partitioning multiprocessor systems. In *1st Annual Symposium on Computer Architecture* (Gainesville, Fla., Dec. 9–11). ACM, New York, 1973, pp. 21–28.
10. GOTTLIEB, A., GRISHMAN, R., KRUSKAL, C.P., MCAULIFFE, K.P., RUDOLPH, L., AND SNIR, M. The NYU ultracomputer—Designing an MIMD shared memory parallel computer. *IEEE Trans. Comput. 32* (Feb. 1983), 175–189.
11. GOTTLIEB, A., AND KRUSKAL, C.P. *Supersaturated Ultracomputer Algorithms*. Ultracomputer Note #11, Courant Institute, New York Univ., New York, 1980.
12. HARARY, F. *Graph Theory*. Addison-Wesley, Reading, Mass., 1972.
13. KNUTH, D.E. Big omicron, big omega, and big theta. *SIGACT News* (ACM) *8*, 2 (1976), 18–24.
14. LAWRIE, D. Access and alignment of data in an array processor. *IEEE Trans. Comput. 24* (1975), 1145–1155.
15. LEV, G., PIPPENGER, N., AND VALIANT, L.G. A fast parallel algorithm for routing in permutation networks. *IEEE Trans. Comput. C-30* (1981), 93–100.
16. MUNRO, I., AND PATERSON, M. Optimal algorithms for parallel polynomial evaluation. *J. Comput. Syst. Sci. 7* (1973), 189–198.
17. NASSIMI, D., AND SAHNI, S. Parallel algorithms to setup the benes permutation network. *IEEE Trans. Comput. C-31* (1982), 148–154.
18. OPFERMAN, D.C., AND TSAO-WU, N.T. On a class of rearrangeable switching networks. *Bell System Tech. J. 50* (1971), 1579–1618.
19. SCHWARTZ, J.T. Ultracomputers. *ACM Trans. Program. Lang. Syst. 2*, 4 (Oct. 1982), 484–521.
20. STONE, H.S. Parallel processing with the perfect shuffle. *IEEE Trans. Comput. C-20* (1971), 153–161.
21. VALIANT, L.G. Parallelism in comparison problems. *SIAM J. Comput. 4* (1975), 348–355.
22. VALIANT, L.G., AND BREBNER, G.J. Universal schemes for parallel processing. In *Proceedings of ACM 13th Annual Symposium on Theory of Computing* (Milwaukee, Wis., May 11–13). ACM, New York, 1981, 263–277.
23. WAKSMAN, A. A permutation network. *J. ACM, 15*, 1 (Jan. 1968), 159–163.

RECEIVED OCTOBER 1981; REVISED AUGUST 1983; ACCEPTED OCTOBER 1983

A New Benes Network Control Algorithm

KYUNGSOOK YOON LEE

Abstract—A new Benes network control algorithm is presented. Unlike the original looping algorithm, the new algorithm is not recursive. In this algorithm $(N \times N)$ Benes network is viewed as a concatenation of two subnetworks SN1 and SN2. The first $(\log N - 1)$ stages of a Benes network correspond to SN1, and the remaining $\log N$ stages correspond to SN2. SN1 is controlled by a full binary tree of set partitioning functions, called a Complete Residue Partition Tree, and SN2 is bit controlled. The new control algorithm sets switches one stage at a time, stage by stage.

Index Terms—Benes network, bit control, control algorithm, permutation, rearrangeable network, set partition, subnetwork.

I. INTRODUCTION

The Benes network [1], which is a member of Clos' type networks [2], is a well known rearrangeable network. An interconnection network (IN) is rearrangeable if its permitted states realize every input-to-output permutation. A control algorithm is described in [7] for the Benes network. This control algorithm, called the "looping algorithm," is based upon the recursive configuration of the Benes network. As shown in Fig. 1, an $(N \times N)$ Benes network with $N = p^n, p \geq 2$, consists of a switching stage, a $(p \times p^{(n-1)})$ unshuffle connection [8], followed by a stack of $(p^{(n-1)} \times p^{(n-1)})$ Benes networks as the middle stage, a $(p \times p^{(n-1)})$ shuffle connection [8], and a switching stage. The looping algorithm sets switches in the two outer switching stages, and recursively sets switches for smaller Benes networks of the middle stage. Thus, it works in the direction of outside-in toward the center stage working on two outer switching stages at a time until it reaches the single center stage consisting of $p^{(n-1)}$ copies of $(p \times p)$ switching elements.

In this paper we present a new Benes network control algorithm which is not recursive. The new control algorithm sets switches one stage at a time, starting from the leftmost stage heading for the rightmost stage. The stage-by-stage switch setting localizes the control information within a stage, as we do not need the knowledge on the switch setting of another stage. This is not the case for the looping algorithm, and can be an advantage for the VLSI implementation of the Benes network. It will reduce the interchip (or interboard) information transfer significantly. The time complexities of the new algorithm are $O(N \log N)$ for a serial control and $O(N)$ for a parallel control, which are the same as those of the looping algorithm. Throughout the paper, logarithm of base 2 is assumed.

The new Benes control algorithm is a direct consequence of the earlier work [4] in which a uniform rearrangeability proof method was developed for $(2 \log N - 1)$ stage permutation networks. As the proof was a constructive one, it also yielded a uniform control algorithm for $(2 \log N - 1)$ stage rearrangeable networks.

In the new Benes control algorithm two different control schemes are used for the first $(\log N - 1)$ stages (SN1) and the remaining log N stages (SN2). A residue set partitioning control is used for SN1, and a bit control is used for SN2. Thus, SN2 is controlled in real time, and the slow control remains only within SN1. This fact can be regarded as another advantage compared to the looping algorithm.

This paper consists of six sections. After an introduction in Section

Manuscript received October 8, 1984; revised September 10, 1985. This work was supported in part by the National Science Foundation under Grant US NSF MCS80-01561, and in part by the University of California under Grant US DOE SBC UCAL 5498609.

The author is with the Department of Computer and Information Science, The Ohio State University, Columbus, OH 43210.

IEEE Log Number 8613385.

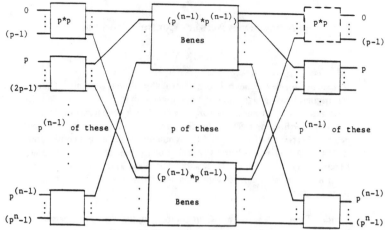

Fig. 1. A ($p^n \times p^n$) Benes network.

I, definitions are given in Section II. A new Benes network control algorithm is described in Section III for ($2^n \times 2^n$) Benes network. Hardware redundancy is discussed in Section IV. The results are generalized informally to ($p^n \times p^n$) case with $p > 2$ in Section V. Finally conclusions are drawn in Section VI.

II. DEFINITIONS

We define two key concepts used for the new control algorithm.

Definition 1: A *Complete Residue System modulo m, CRS-(mod m)*, is a set of m integers which contains exactly one representative of each residue class mod m.

Definition 2: A *Complete Residue Partition, CRP,* is a partition of a CRS(mod 2^k) into two CRS's(mod $2^{(k-1)}$), $k \geq 1$.

A CRP can be performed in many different ways. As it is the same problem as dividing a pile of 2^k objects consisting of pairs of $2^{(k-1)}$ distinct objects into two piles of $2^{(k-1)}$ distinct objects, there are $2^{(2^{(k-1)}-1)}$ different ways to perform a CRP.

As an example, $\{7, 5, 0, 1, 4, 6, 2, 3\}$ is a CRS(mod 8). When a CRP is performed on this set, we get two CRS's(mod 4), $\{7, 5, 0, 2\}$ and $\{1, 4, 6, 3\}$ (or $\{7, 5, 4, 2\}$ and $\{0, 1, 6, 3\}$, etc.) If we apply two independent CRP's on these two CRS's(mod 4), we have four CRS's(mod 2). In general starting from a CRS(mod 2^n), a full binary tree of CRP's, called a CRPT, generates a full binary tree of CRS's with the leaves being $2^{(n-1)}$ CRS's(mod 2).

Definition 3: A *Complete Residue Partition Tree, CRPT,* is a full binary tree of CRP's. The root node of a CRPT is a CRP on a CRS(mod 2^n), and two sons of a node are two CRP's on the two CRS's produced by the parent node. The leaves of a CRPT are $2^{(n-2)}$ CRP's each working on a CRS(mod 4) independently to create $2^{(n-1)}$ CRS's(mod 2).

A CRPT is shown in Fig. 2.

III. A NEW BENES NETWORK CONTROL ALGORITHM

For the new control algorithm an ($N \times N$) Benes network (BN) is regarded as a concatenation of two subnetworks, SN1 being the first ($\log N - 1$) stages of BN, and SN2 being the remaining $\log N$ stages. First the control algorithm will be described for $N = 2^n$ case where the basic elements of the network are (2×2) switches. It can be generalized easily for the $N = P^n$ case with ($p \times p$) switches, $p > 2$.

The BN can be represented as

$$BN = (E^0 \sigma_n^{-1} \cdot E^1 \sigma_{(n-1)-1}^{-1} \cdots E^{(n-2)} \sigma_2^{-1})$$
$$\cdot (E^0 \sigma_2 \cdot E^1 \sigma_3 \cdots E^{(n-2)} \sigma_n \cdot E^{(n-1)})$$
$$= SN1 \cdot SN2$$

where σ_k^{-1} and σ_k stand for a segment unshuffle connection and a segment shuffle connection with the segment size equal to 2^k, respectively, and E represents a switching stage.

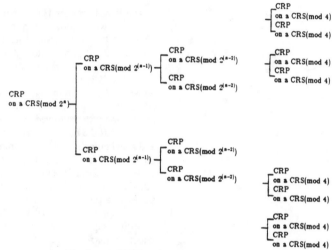

Fig. 2. A CRPT: a full binary tree of CRP's.

In the new control algorithm SN2 is bit controlled. Each of n destination tag bits is used once as a control bit. If the control bit of the upper input number is "0," the switch is set straight. If it is "1," the switch is set cross.

As pointed out in the earlier work [4], this kind of a bit control is a natural control for $\log N$ stage IN's; it realizes all permutations and only permutations that can pass through the network without a conflict. A formal proof of this fact is given in [4] for the inverse omega network [3]. An intuitive argument may be the fact that any $\log N$ stage IN in the literature can be viewed as N copies of 1-to-2^n demultiplexer trees overlaid in the certain manner [8], [10]. To reach an output point from an input point, we only have to follow the unique path decided by the demultiplexer tree with the input point as the root node. The bit control does this.

The selection of n control bits should be based on the particular configuration of the overlaid demultiplexer trees, and can be regarded as an important characteristic of an n stage IN. Refer to [5] for further elaboration on this point.

In this paper we state the following without a formal proof.

Control Bit Sequence for SN2 of the Benes Network

Let $b = b_{(n-1)}b_{(n-2)} \cdots b_0$ denote a destination tag. The control bit C_i for the ith switching stage E^i of SN2 should be the bit $b_{(n-1-i)}$ to realize all and only permutations that can pass through SN2 without a conflict.

$$C_i = b_{(n-1-i)}.$$

This is a direct consequence of the segment shuffles used as connection patterns in SN2.

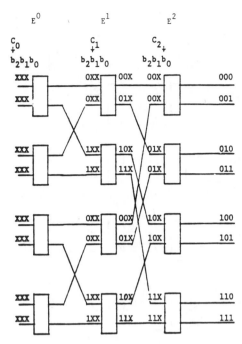

Fig. 3. The control bit selection for SN1 of a Benes network.

We can see the correctness of this control sequence intuitively in Fig. 3. To be connected to the output ports 000 through 111 for $N = 8$ case, the high order two bits of the input numbers to E^2 should have already been sorted in ascending order. The least significant bit b_0 can be in any order. When b_0 is used as the control bit C_2 for E^2, that bit is sorted by the bit control to reach the right output port. Similarly, the most significant bits of the input sequences to upper and lower halves of E^1 should be in ascending order. When b_1 is used as the control bit C_1 for E^1, the two high order bits of the output sequences will be in ascending order. In general $b_{(n-1-i)}$ should be used as C_i for E^i of SN2. The same bits are used as the control bits for the last n stages of the self-routing Benes network [6].

Now the SN2-passable condition for an input sequence to SN2 can be informally stated as follows.

SN2-Passable Condition

An input permutation is SN2-passable if and only if groups of 2^j consecutive input numbers form CRS's(mod 2^j) for the j control bits $C_{(j-1)}C_{(j-2)} \cdots C_0$, $n > j \geq 1$. In other words the groups of two input numbers should have ("0," "1,") pairs for C_0. The groups of four input numbers should have ("00," "01," "10," "11") quadruples for $C_1 C_0$, and so on.

The SN2-passable condition is given here very informally, just to convey the ideas and to avoid necessary formalization of notations. Readers interested in a more formal approach are referred to [4], [5].

As the SN2-passable condition has been defined now, we set the switches of SN1 to transform an arbitrary input permutation to an SN2-passable permutation. A CRPT is used to do this. It is shown in [4] how a group of $2^{(k-1)}$ switches can be set to perform a CRP on the 2^k input numbers which form a CRS(mod 2^k), so that the resulting two CRS's(mod $2^{(k-1)}$) are separated into the upper and the lower output ports. For the completeness of our discussion we cite an example from [4] and repeat it in Fig. 4. In this example a CRP is performed on a CRS(mod 8) by setting four switches in such a way that the resulting two CRS's(mod 4) from the CRP reside on the upper and the lower output ports. The switch marked as ① is set straight arbitrarily. By doing that we missed the residue class 1(mod 4) for the upper output port. So we find another residue class 1(mod 4) which is number 1 in the switch marked as ② and set the switch ② cross. By doing this we missed the residue class 0 for the upper output port. So we connect the switch marked as ③ cross, and so on.

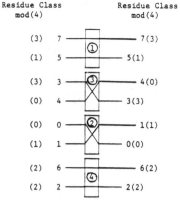

Fig. 4. A CRP can always be realized on a set of switches. (Circled numbers show a possible order of switch setting, where the input CRS(mod 8) {7, 5, 3, 4, 0, 1, 6, 2} is partitioned to two CRS's(mod 4), {7, 4, 1, 6} and {5, 3, 0 2}).

Observe that the switch ① is redundant, and the time complexity of a CRP control on N numbers is $O(N)$.

A CRPT Control for SN1

SN1 is controlled by a CRPT. For E^0, a CRP is needed to form two CRS's(mod $2^{(n-1)}$) for bits $b_1 b_2 \cdots b_{(n-1)}$. For E^1 two CRP's are needed to work on the two CRS's(mod $2^{(n-1)}$ for bits $b_1 b_2 \cdots b_{(n-2)} b_{(n-1)}$. Continuing this process we form a CRPT of $(n-1)$ levels, one level per switching stage.

We summarize the above discussion as follows.

A New Control Algorithm for the ($N \times N$) Benes Network, $N = 2^n$

1. The N numbers of the destination permutation in the binary representation are the input to the network.
2. Perform 2^i CRP's on the 2^i CRS's(mod $2^{(n-i)}$), formed by bits $b_i \cdots b_{(n-1)}$ for E^i of SN1 to get $2^{(i+1)}$ CRS's(mod $2^{(n-i-1)}$) on bits $b_{(i+1)} \cdots b_{(n-1)}$ for $0 \leq i \leq (n-2)$.
3. The remaining n switching stages are controlled by $b_{(n-1)}, b_{(n-2)}, \cdots, b_0$ used as control bits $C_0, C_1, \cdots, C_{(n-1)}$, respectively. If $C_i = 0$, set a switch in E^i of SN2 straight, else if $C_i = 1$ set it cross, $0 \leq i \leq (n-1)$.

An example of the new control algorithm is shown in Fig. 5 for the bit reversal permutation on (8×8) BN. For E^0 of SN1, we set the switches so that bits $b_1 b_2$ of four numbers on four upper (lower) output ports form a CRS(mod 4)—(000, 010, 101, 111) and (100, 110, 001, 011), respectively. For E^1 of SN1, we perform two CRP's independently on the two groups of switches marked 1 and 2 to form four CRS'(mod 2) for bit b_2 (000, 101), (010, 111), (100, 001), and (110, 011). SN2 is bit controlled. Another example is shown in Fig. 6 for a shuffle permutation on the (16×16) BN.

The time complexity of the SN1 control is $O(N \log N)$, since SN1 consists of $\log N - 1$ stages where each stage is controlled in $O(N)$ time required for the CRP control. The time complexity of the SN2 control is $O(\log N)$, since SN2 is bit controlled. Thus, the time complexity of the overall algorithm is $O(N \log N)$ for a single control. For a multiple control all the CRP's on the same stage can be done in parallel. Thus, the time complexity becomes $O(N)$.

Observe that the switches are set stage by stage starting from the leftmost stage of BN, and continuing to the rightmost stage. All the information required to set switches of each stage is contained within the input sequence and thus no other information exchange is necessary among stages. This property can be exploited to pipeline the switch settings for the consecutive permutations in MIMD environments to decrease the control time by a factor of $O(\log N)$. This is not the case for the looping algorithm. Also note that more than half of the network is bit controlled in real time. Thus, the bottleneck of the control time remains within SN1.

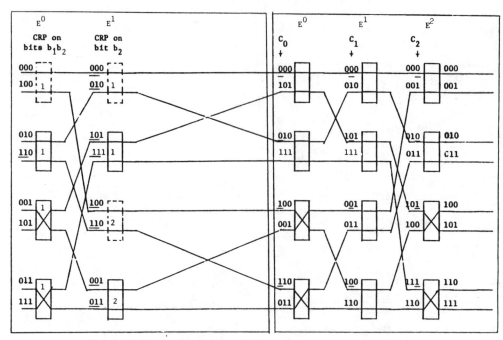

Fig. 5.   A bit reversal on (8 × 8) Benes network by the new control algorithm. (Dashed switches are redundant.)

SN1:   A CRPT Control   SN2:   Bit Control

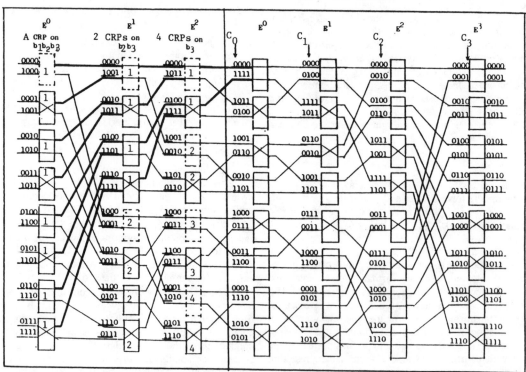

Fig. 6.   A shuffle permutation on (2^4 × 2^4) Benes network by the new control algorithm. (Dashed switches are redundant.)

IV. HARDWARE REDUNDANCY IN THE BENES NETWORK

As noted in the previous section one switch per CRP is redundant because we can set one switch arbitrarily. In a CRPT we have

$$1 + 2 + \cdots 2^{(n-2)} = 2^{(n-1)} - 1$$

$$= (N/2 - 1)$$

CRP's. Thus, $(N/2 - 1)$ switches of the BN is redundant, which means we have

$$(2n - 1)N/2 - (N/2 - 1) = (N \log N - N + 1)$$

switches in the BN. This matches the switch requirement given by Waksman [9]. In Figs. 5 and 6 redundant switches are marked with dashed lines.

V. Generalization to the $(p^n \times p^n)$ Benes Network, $p > 2$

The new control algorithm can be easily generalized for $N = p^n$ BN with $(p \times p)$ switches, $p > 2$. We need to generalize both CRP and the bit control to include a radix greater than 2.

Definition 4: A complete residue partition in radix r, CRP(r), is a partition of a CRS(mod r^k) into r CRS's(mod $r^{(k-1)}$).

Digit controlled switch setting sets a switch in such a way that the outcoming control digits are sorted in ascending order. It is a generalization of the bit control.

For $(p^n \times p^n)$ BN, SN1 is controlled by a CRPT consisting of CRP's(p), and SN2 is digit controlled. Refer to [5] for examples.

VI. Conclusions

Extending the earlier work [4] in which a general proof method for $(2 \log N - 1)$ stage rearrangeable networks was developed, a new Benes network control algorithm was presented. This new control algorithm does not view the Benes network as a recursive network, but rather as a concatenation of two subnetworks SN1 and SN2.

SN1 corresponds to the first $(\log N - 1)$ stages, and SN2 corresponds to the remaining $\log N$ stages of the Benes network. SN1 is controlled by a full binary tree of set partitioning functions, called a CRPT, and SN2 is bit controlled. Thus, the new control algorithm sets switches stage by stage.

The time complexity of the new control algorithm is the same as that of the looping algorithm. But it has some advantages compared to the looping algorithm. First, it sets switches stage by stage, one stage at a time. Thus, it eliminates the information exchange among different stages, making the pipelining of switch setting feasible for MIMD environments. Second, SN2 is bit controlled in real time, and the bottleneck remains only within SN1.

In the new algorithm one switch per CRP is redundant, which gives us exactly the same number of switch requirements of the reduced Benes network [9].

The new algorithm applies to any $(p^n \times p^n)$ Benes network for $p \geq 2$.

Acknowledgment

The author is grateful to Prof. D. Kuck. Without him this work would have not been possible.

References

[1] V. E. Benes, "Permutation groups, complexes, and rearrangeable connecting networks," *Bell. Syst. Tech. J.*, vol. 43, pp. 1619–1640, July 1964.

[2] C. Clos, A study of non-blocking switching networks," *Bell. Syst. Tech. J.*, vol. 32, pp. 406–424, Mar. 1953.

[3] D. H. Lawrie, "Access and alignment of data in an array processor," *IEEE Trans. Comput.*, vol. C-25, pp. 1145–1155, Dec. 1975.

[4] K. Y. Lee, "On the rearrangeability of a $(2 \log N - 1)$ stage permutation network," in *Proc. 1981 Int. Conf. Parallel Processing*, 1981, pp. 221–228; also in *IEEE Trans. Comput.*, vol. C-34, pp. 412–425, May 1985.

[5] ——, "Interconnection networks and compiler algorithms for multiprocessors," Ph.D. dissertation, Dep. Comput. Sci., Univ. Illinois, Urbana-Champaign, Rep. 83-1125, 1983.

[6] D. Nassimi and S. Sahni, "A self-routing Benes network and parallel permutation algorithms," *IEEE Trans. Comput.*, vol. C-30, pp. 332–340, May 1981.

[7] D. C. Opferman and N. T. Tsao-Wu, "On a class of rearrangeable switching networks, Part I: Control algorithm," *Bell. Syst. Tech. J.*, vol. 50, pp. 1579–1600, 1971.

[8] J. H. Patel, "Processor-memory interconnections for multiprocessors," in *Proc. 6th Ann. Symp. Comput. Architecture*, Apr. 1979, pp. 168–177.

[9] A. Waksman, "A permutation network," *J. Ass. Comput. Mach.*, vol. 15, pp. 159–163, Jan. 1968.

[10] C. L. Wu and T. Feng, "The reverse-exchange interconnection network," in *Proc. Int. Conf. Parallel Processing*, 1979; also in *IEEE Trans. Comput.*, vol. C-29, pp. 801–811, Sept. 1980.

On Self-Routing in Beneš and Shuffle-Exchange Networks

C. S. Raghavendra and Rajendra V. Boppana

Abstract—In this paper, we present self-routing algorithms for realizing the class of linear permutations in various multistage networks such as Beneš, $2n$-stage shuffle-exchange, etc. Linear permutations are useful in providing fast access of data arrays. In the first half of the network, switches are set by comparing the destination tags at their inputs, and, in the second half, switches are set using the Omega self-routing algorithm. We show that the comparison operations can be implemented in bit-serial networks without loss of time. In contrast, with the well-known Beneš network self-routing algorithm of Nassimi and Sahni [10], switches are set by giving priority to the destination tag at the upper input to them. Their algorithm routes many useful permutations but the class of linear permutations. The previously known techniques to realize linear permutations in multistage networks are not of the self-routing type. Hence, the algorithms presented are extremely useful in providing fast access of various data patterns using interconnection networks cheaper than crossbars.

Index Terms—Beneš network, interconnection networks, linear permutations, self-routing algorithms, shuffle-exchange networks.

I. Introduction

Typically, a parallel processor consists of a number of processors and an interconnection network for exchange of information among them as well as with memory units. In a processor–memory network model, any processor should be able to communicate with any memory unit, which is called full access. To keep the communication step overhead minimum, parallel algorithms are often designed with permutation (one-to-one) type data transfers. To support SIMD type computations, ideally one would like the network to be able to perform all the permutations that allow simultaneous use of the memory units. If the underlying network cannot support a required permutation function, then it has to be realized in multiple passes through it. To avoid this, crossbar networks or networks that are rearrangeable, for example, the Beneš network, can be used as interconnection networks. The advantages with rearrangeable networks are any permutation can be realized in one pass through the networks, and, if they are built using smaller switches such as 2×2 switches, then they are cheaper than crossbar networks. Therefore, rearrangeable networks are used in some parallel computer implementations (e.g., GF-11 [1]).

A well-known rearrangeable network is the Beneš network [2], which is built in a recursive manner using 2×2 switches. (An 8×8 Beneš network constructed recursively from two 4×4 Beneš networks is shown in Fig. 1.) In such networks, it takes some time to set up the switches to realize a given arbitrary permutation. For an $N \times N, N = 2^n$, Beneš network $\mathcal{B}_n$, determining the switch settings, to realize an arbitrary permutation, takes $O(nN)$ time on a uniprocessor computer [17]. Parallel algorithms to determine the switch settings require $O(n^2)$ or $O(n^4)$ time using, respectively, a completely interconnected computer or a shuffle-exchange computer [11]. Therefore, if the required permutations change frequently during a computation, the communication time may become the bottleneck.

Manuscript received September 12, 1988; revised July 13, 1990. This work was supported by the NSF Presidential Young Investigator Award MIP 8452003, DARPA/ARO Contract DAAG 29-84-k-0066, ONR Contract N00014-86-k-06062.

The authors are with the Department of EE–Systems, University of Southern California, Los Angeles, CA 90089.

IEEE Log Number 9042300.

Reprinted from *IEEE Trans. Computers,* Vol. 40, No. 9, Sept. 1991, pp. 1057-1064. Copyright © 1991 by The Institute of Electrical and Electronics Engineers, Inc. All rights reserved.

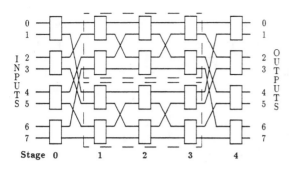

Fig. 1. An 8×8 Beneš network, $\mathcal{B}_3$. The dashed boxes indicate 4×4 Beneš networks.

Often, the above methods, which can realize arbitrary permutations in Beneš network, are unusable for the following reasons. The time to set up the network is large compared to the propagation delay of the network, which is $O(n)$. Since the status of each switch is decided elsewhere, for example, at a centralized network controller, and transmitted to the switches, excessive hardware costs and time delays are encountered with these methods. Also, these methods do not facilitate pipelining of data movement—desirable in reducing the overhead of communication by overlapping it with computations—in interconnection networks. Finally, due to the nature of techniques used in developing parallel algorithms, the permutations required are generally nice and regular and can be expressed as algebraic functions [8]. This motivates us to develop fast self-routing algorithms—which route permutations by setting up switches on-the-fly using only local information (source and destination information of the messages present) at each switch—for many useful permutations required in parallel processing, if not for all the $N!$ permutations.

Nassimi and Sahni [10] developed a self-routing algorithm to pass the class of the bit-permute-complement permutations in the Beneš network. Their algorithm also routes the Lenfant's FUB families [8], which are shown to occur in the execution of various parallel algorithms by Lenfant. Yew and Lawrie [18] adapted the Nassimi and Sahni's Beneš network routing algorithm to realize bit-permute-complement permutations in $2n$-stage shuffle-exchange network, $\prod_n$. Recently, Nassimi gave a generalized self-routing algorithm to realize bit-permute-complement permutations in a class of $(2n - 1)$-stage networks [9]. However, none of these methods realizes the linear class of permutations, which are useful in the parallel access of data arrays [4].

In this paper, we develop self-routing algorithms for routing the linear class of permutations on various interconnection networks. These algorithms are simple and route many other classes of permutations as well. Our algorithms differ from those of Nassimi and Sahni [10] and Yew and Lawrie [18] in giving priority to route messages, when there is contention for the output links of a switch. Our algorithms give priority, based on some type of comparison operation, to the smaller of the two whereas their algorithms give priority to the message at upper input line of the switch. We consider Beneš, $\prod$, and $(2n - 1)$-stage Shuffle-Exchange networks. Our results include simple routing algorithms for the classes of linear (we extend this class with complements of bits), Omega, and inverse Omega permutations on these networks. For other permutations one can use a general looping type algorithm or break the original permutation into multiple simpler permutations.

II. Preliminaries

Interconnection Networks: We consider $N \times N, N = 2^n$ with $n \geq 2$, Beneš, $\prod$, and $(2n - 1)$-stage Shuffle-Exchange networks

constructed of 2×2 crossbars (switches). These networks may be used for processor-to-processor or processor-to-memory interconnections. The $2n$-stage Shuffle-Exchange network, $\prod_n$, is a cascade of two copies of Lawrie's Omega network (Ω_n), the n-stage Shuffle-Exchange network. ($\prod_3$ is shown in Fig. 2.) The $(2n - 1)$-stage shuffle-exchange network is theoretically interesting due to the long standing conjecture about its rearrangeability [16].

The input ports, also the output ports, of a network are numbered $0, \cdots, N - 1$, top to bottom. The stages of a network of k stages are numbered, from left to right, $0, \cdots, k - 1$. Switch (i, j) is the jth switch, numbered top to bottom $0, \cdots, \frac{N}{2} - 1$, in ith stage. Addresses of lines within a network are assigned as follows. An input line to a switch in stage 0 has the same address as that of the network input port to which it is connected. If the upper and lower input lines of a switch are indexed a and b, respectively, then its upper and lower output lines are also indexed a and b, respectively. Interconnection patterns do not affect the addresses of lines. This numbering is illustrated in Fig. 2 for $\prod_3$.

The multistage networks we consider share a property. In a stage, addresses of inputs to each switch differ in exactly one common bit, called the *connecting* bit; the upper line address is smaller compared to the lower line address. For $\mathcal{B}_n$, connecting bits for stages $0, \cdots, n - 2, n, \cdots, 2n - 2$ are, respectively, $0, \cdots, n - 2, n - 1, n - 2, \cdots, 0$. And, for a k stage shuffle exchange network, the connecting bits are $n - 1, \cdots, n - k \pmod n$, for stages, respectively, $0 \cdots, k - 1$.

Notation: Each input (respectively, output) line is given a unique and distinct index $x, 0 \leq x < N$, which may be represented in binary form as $x_{n-1} \cdots x_0$ with x_{n-1} being the most significant bit (MSB). However, it is treated as an n-bit column vector $(x_0, \cdots, x_{n-1})^T$ (the superscript T indicates the matrix transpose operation) in the Boolean matrix-vector computations. Similarly, given an n-bit column vector $(y_0, \cdots, y_{n-1})^T$, its value is computed as $\sum_{i=0}^{n-1} y_i 2^i$. Given a Boolean matrix $Q = (q_{i,j})_{n \times n}$, the matrix-vector product Qx is the n-bit vector given below. Here "$\oplus$" indicates modulo 2 addition of bits.

$$
\begin{pmatrix}
x_0 q_{0,0} \oplus \cdots \oplus x_{n-1} q_{0,n-1} \\
\vdots \\
x_0 q_{n-1,0} \oplus \cdots \oplus x_{n-1} q_{n-1,n-1}
\end{pmatrix}.
$$

If the columns of Q are represented as $q_0, \cdots, q_{n-1}$, then $Q = (q_0, \cdots, q_{n-1})$ and $Qx = x_0 q_0 \oplus \cdots \oplus x_{n-1} q_{n-1}$. Here, $x_i q_i$ indicates the multiplication of each component of q_i with the scalar x_i, and $x_i q_i \oplus x_j q_j$ indicates componentwise module 2 addition of the vectors $x_i q_i$ and $x_j q_j$.

Linear permutations: Let $V = \{0, 1, \cdots, N - 1\}$. A linear permutation on V is a permutation that maps each $x \in V$ to some $y \in V$ such that each bit in the binary form of y is a linear combination of the bits of x. (Addition of bits is modulo 2.)

Definition 1: A permutation on V is said to be linear [13], if there exists an $n \times n$ binary matrix Q such that, for every $x \in V$, its image y is given by the following equation

$$
y = Qx. \tag{1}
$$

Note that Q is nonsingular by definition. If each bit of y is a linear combination of the bits of x and constant 1, then the resulting permutation is a linear-complement permutation. Formally, this is defined as follows.

Definition 2: A permutation on V is a linear-complement permutation, if there exists an $n \times n$ binary matrix Q and an n-bit column vector c such that, for every $x \in V$, its image y is given by the

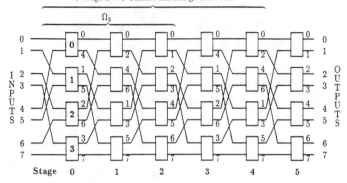

Fig. 2. A 6 stage 8×8 Shuffle-Exchange network. Numbers within a switch, shown only for stage 0, indicate its number in that stage. Numbers on the lines represent their addresses.

following equation.

$$y = Qx \oplus c. \qquad (2)$$

In the literature [3], [6], linear permutations are termed as the nonsingular linear transformations of the n-dimensional vector space over the field $GF(2)$ — the field consisting of two elements: 0 and 1.

The Boolean matrix Q in (2) is the important parameter of a linear-complement permutation. Any two linear-complement permutations with the same "Q" have similar properties. Given any $\pi_1, \pi_2 \in \mathcal{LC}_n$, $\pi_1^{-1} \in \mathcal{LC}_n$, and the composed permutation (right to left) $\pi_2 \pi_1 \in \mathcal{LC}_n$.

If Q is a nonsingular lower (respectively, upper) triangular matrix, then the corresponding permutation is called a lower (respectively, upper) triangular linear-complement permutation or simply a lower (respectively, upper) triangular linear permutation, for $c = 0$. If a permutation matrix—a nonsingular matrix with exactly one 1 in each row and column—is chosen as Q in (2), then the resulting linear-complement permutation is also a bit-permute-complement permutation [10]. For any $N = 2^n$, $n \geq 2$, the class of bit-permute-complement permutations ($\mathcal{BPC}_n$) is a special subclass of the class of linear-complement permutations ($\mathcal{LC}_n$). There are $n! \, N$ and $2^{n(n+1)/2} \prod_{i=1}^{n} (2^i - 1)$ permutations in $\mathcal{BPC}_n$ and $\mathcal{LC}_n$, respectively; for $N = 8$, $|\mathcal{BPC}_3| = 48$ and $|\mathcal{LC}_3| = 1344$, where $|X|$ is the cardinality of set X.

Definition 3: The class of permutations passable by Omega network is called the Omega class. And the class of inverse Omega passable permutations is called the inverse Omega class.

Lawrie [7] and Pease [13] characterized these two classes of permutations; a permutation is in Omega or inverse Omega class if and only if each bit of a tag (y) is a function of the bits of its input line (x) given by (3) or (4), respectively. Both these classes contain lower and upper triangular linear-complement permutations.

$$y_i = x_i \oplus f_i(y_{n-1}, \cdots, y_{i+1}, x_{i-1}, \cdots, x_0), \qquad 0 \leq i < n \qquad (3)$$
$$y_i = x_i \oplus f_i(y_{n-1}, \cdots, y_0, x_{n-1}, \cdots, x_{i+1}), \qquad 0 \leq i < n. \qquad (4)$$

Here, f_i's are arbitrary Boolean functions.

III. THE SELF-ROUTING ALGORITHMS

In permutation routing, each input of the network has the address of a unique and distinct output line, called the destination address or, simply, the tag. With a self-routing control algorithm, each switch in the interconnection network uses the tags at its inputs and sets itself appropriately using some simple logic.

The well-known bit-controlled (variously called, Omega, Delta, or digit-controlled) self-routing algorithm routes a tag as follows. If the ith bit is the connecting bit for a stage, then the ith bit of the tag, called *routing* bit, is used for routing it through that stage; it is routed to the upper (lower) output line of the switch, if the routing bit is 0 (1).

When the routing bits of both the tags at a switch are the same, there exists a conflict in setting up the switch since both of them specify the same output line. Some important permutations which exhibit switch conflicts are the bit reversal, shuffle, etc. Even though these permutations can be realized by Beneš and shuffle-exchange networks with at least $2n - 1$ stages, the simple bit-controlled algorithm cannot route them. Therefore, to route such permutations in Beneš or other networks, the above algorithm has to be modified suitably by giving priority to one of the input lines in setting up a switch whenever there is a conflict.

Nassimi and Sahni [10] proposed to resolve such conflicts by giving priority to the upper input line; that is, whenever there is a conflict in setting up a switch, the tag at the upper input line is routed to the output line specified by its routing bit and the tag at the lower input line is routed to the remaining output line. Their method is simple, yet very powerful; it can realize the important classes of bit-permute-complement permutations, inverse Omega permutations, and many others. However, the class of linear-complement permutations cannot be realized by their method.

Pease [13] showed that a given linear permutation can be realized in two passes through the indirect binary n-cube network (identical to inverse Omega network [12]), by decomposing it into two simpler permutations, each of which is realized by the network in a single pass. However, this is not a self-routing method, since it involves the factorization of the Boolean matrix Q corresponding to the linear permutation. Etzion and Lempel [5] describe a method to pass linear permutations in $(2n - 1)$-stage Shuffle-Exchange networks, but it is not of self-routing type and takes $O(n^2)$ time to set up the network.

Given below are simple methods to pass linear-complement permutations in Beneš and Shuffle-Exchange networks. They are quite powerful and realize many other permutations as well.

A. An Algorithm for the Beneš Network

Algorithm BL: For the first $(n - 1)$ stages of $\mathcal{B}_n$, switches are set up such that input line with smaller destination tag value is routed according to its routing bit. For the next n stages, switches are set up using the standard Omega self-routing algorithm. ∎

This algorithm is different from that of Nassimi and Sahni [10]. In case of conflict in setting up a switch, their algorithm gives priority

Fig. 3. An example showing switch settings done by Algorithm BL.

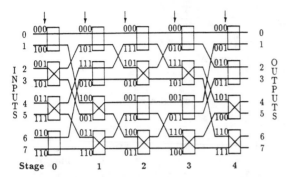

Fig. 4. Routing a linear permutation in $\mathcal{B}_3$ using Algorithm BL.

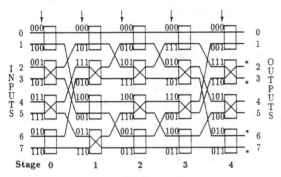

Fig. 5. The example linear permutation is incorrectly routed by Nassimi and Sahni's algorithm.

to the tag at the top input line, whereas Algorithm BL gives priority to the smaller tag.

A couple of examples of switch settings effected by Algorithm BL are shown in Fig. 3. For each switch, the destination tags at its inputs are shown, in binary form, and the routing bit is indicated by an arrow. In Fig. 3(a), the routing bit is 1 for both the tags; so there is a conflict in setting up the switch. This is resolved by comparing the destination tags and giving priority to the tag with smaller value, which, in this case, is at the lower input. The other tag is routed to the remaining output line. In Fig. 3(b), since the routing bits for two the tags are different each tag is routed according to its routing bit.

A complete example of this routing scheme is illustrated, using the linear permutation given by (5), in Fig. 4. Destination tags for each input line to a switch are given in the binary form. The routing bit for each stage is indicated by a downward arrow. Nassimi and Sahni's algorithm does not route this permutation. (See Fig. 5. Output ports with incorrect tags are marked with an asterisk.)

$$\begin{pmatrix} y_0 \\ y_1 \\ y_2 \end{pmatrix} = \begin{pmatrix} 0 & 1 & 1 \\ 0 & 0 & 1 \\ 1 & 0 & 0 \end{pmatrix} \begin{pmatrix} x_0 \\ x_1 \\ x_2 \end{pmatrix}. \tag{5}$$

In stage 0, the routing bit is the same for both tags to a switch. Each switch in this stage is set up to route the smaller tag; for example, switch $(0, 2)$ routes tag 011 to its lower output line as specified by the tag's 0th bit.

Due to its recursive construction, stages 1, 2, and 3 of $\mathcal{B}_3$ can be partitioned into top and bottom 4×4 Beneš networks, $\mathcal{B}_2$'s. (See Fig. 1.) The input addresses for these top and bottom $\mathcal{B}_2$'s are, respectively, $\{0, 2, 4, 6\}$ and $\{1, 3, 5, 7\}$. Notice that, after routing through stage 0, there exists a linear-complement permutation between y_2, y_1 of destination tags and x_2, x_1 of input lines for both the top and bottom $\mathcal{B}_2$'s given by equations, respectively, (6) and (7).

$$\begin{pmatrix} y_1 \\ y_2 \end{pmatrix} = \begin{pmatrix} 0 & 1 \\ 1 & 1 \end{pmatrix} \begin{pmatrix} x_1 \\ x_2 \end{pmatrix} \tag{6}$$

$$\begin{pmatrix} y_1 \\ y_2 \end{pmatrix} = \begin{pmatrix} 0 & 1 \\ 1 & 1 \end{pmatrix} \begin{pmatrix} x_1 \\ x_2 \end{pmatrix} \oplus \begin{pmatrix} 0 \\ 1 \end{pmatrix}. \tag{7}$$

There exists conflict in setting up switches in stage 1 of the network as well. Switches 0 and 3 are set up such that the smaller tags, which are at the upper inputs, are routed, correctly; the other two switches are set such that the smaller tags, which are at the lower inputs, are routed, correctly. Switches in the last three stages are set up without conflicts.

B. An Algorithm for the $2n$-Stage Shuffle-Exchange Network

Algorithm PL: For the first n stages of $\prod_n$, switches are set up such that the destination tag with smaller value, when compared after bit reversal of the destination tags of both the inputs to the switch, is routed according to its routing bit. For the next n stages, switches are set up using the standard Ω self-routing algorithm. ∎

The working of Algorithm PL is illustrated, using the example linear permutation given by (5), in Fig. 6. Routing bit at each stage is indicated by a downward arrow. This permutation is not realized by the $\prod_n$ self-routing algorithm of Yew and Lawrie [18]. Consider the tags 100 and 111 at switch $(0, 1)$ in Fig. 6. They compete for the lower output line; since 100 is smaller, the switch is set route it correctly. For switch $(0, 3)$, tag 110 (with bits reversed, has value 011) wins over tag 101 (with bits reversed, has value 101) and, hence, it is routed according to its routing bit (to the lower output line).

C. An Analysis of Algorithms BL and PL

First, we prove some results common to Algorithms BL and PL.

Consider a column (stage) of $N/2$ switches of size 2×2 with the ith bit as the routing bit; the upper input line to a switch has ith bit 0. At each input, there is a message with a destination address (tag). The relation between input line addresses and their tags is given by some permutation, $f \in \mathcal{LC}_n$. Then, f^{-1} is a linear-complement permutation giving the relation between the tags and input line addresses; it is expressed by a set of linear equations with each bit of x (line address) expressed as a linear combination of its y (tag) bits and the constant 1, if it is to be complemented.

Property 1: For any $\pi \in \mathcal{LC}_n$, let $\pi(x)$ denote the destination tag of any $x \in V$. Then, for any $a \in V$, $\pi(x)$ and $\pi(x \oplus a)$ differ in a bit if and only if, for all $x' \in V$, $\pi(x')$ and $\pi(x' \oplus a)$ differ in that bit.

For example, each pair of tags at the inputs of any switch, in the column described above, differ in the same bit positions. This can be readily shown using (2).

Let j be some bit position in which the destination tags to a switch differ. (If the destination tags to a switch differ in many bit positions, j could be any one of them.) Now, suppose the tags are routed through the column of switches using the following rule.

Routing rule: The destination tag with 0 as its jth bit is routed to the upper (respectively, lower) output line of the switch, if its ith bit is 0 (respectively, 1); the other tag is routed to the remaining output line. ∎

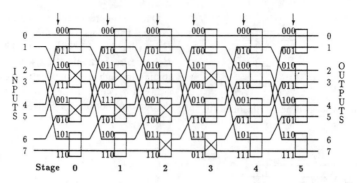

Fig. 6. Routing the example linear permutation in $\prod_3$ using Algorithm PL.

After routing, let g denote the relation from the line addresses to their corresponding tags, after routing. We prove the following results about g.

Lemma 1: The relation from line addresses to tags, after routing, is a linear-complement permutation.

 Proof: It is clear that this relation, g, is a permutation. To prove the lemma, it is sufficient to show that g^{-1}, the permutation from tags to output line addresses, is a linear-complement permutation.

Depending upon how a switch is set, the line address at which the tag is present after routing is different from that before routing in at most one bit, namely, bit i. Therefore, irrespective of how the switches are set, the rth bit equation, $0 \leq r < n$ and $r \neq i$, of g^{-1} is the same as that of f^{-1}.

We need to show that x_i also is a linear combination of y-bits. There are two cases to consider.

Case 1 (no conflict): ith bits of the destination tags to a switch differ. Then the effect of routing is such that tags match their line addresses in bit i. That is, $x_i = y_i$.

Case 2 (conflict): ith bits of the destination tags to a switch are the same. Then, the tag with 0 in its jth bit is routed to the output line that matches it in the ith bit, and the other tag (whose jth bit is 1) is routed to the other output line, which does not match it in the ith bit. That is, $x_i = y_i \oplus y_j$.

In either case, the bit equation of x_i is as follows.

$$x_i = y_i \oplus \lambda y_j \qquad (8)$$

where $\lambda = 0$ (for the "no conflict" case) or 1 (for the "conflict" case). ∎

As an example consider the routing of the example linear permutation, (5), by Algorithm BL (same as the routing rule with i and j being, respectively, 0 and 2) through stage 0 of $\mathcal{B}_3$. (See Fig. 4.) Here, f^{-1} and g^{-1} are given by, respectively, (9) and (10). Notice that g^{-1} is different from f^{-1} in only the bit equation for x_0.

$$\begin{pmatrix} x_0 \\ x_1 \\ x_2 \end{pmatrix} = \begin{pmatrix} 0 & 0 & 1 \\ 1 & 1 & 0 \\ 0 & 1 & 0 \end{pmatrix} \begin{pmatrix} y_0 \\ y_1 \\ y_2 \end{pmatrix} \qquad (9)$$

$$\begin{pmatrix} x_0 \\ x_1 \\ x_2 \end{pmatrix} = \begin{pmatrix} 1 & 0 & 1 \\ 1 & 1 & 0 \\ 0 & 1 & 0 \end{pmatrix} \begin{pmatrix} y_0 \\ y_1 \\ y_2 \end{pmatrix}. \qquad (10)$$

Lemma 2: Any two tags that differ in the ith bit only are routed such that one of them goes to the upper output line of some switch and the other goes to the lower output line of some switch.

 Proof: Clearly, for the "no conflict" case, the lemma holds. We prove the validity of the lemma for the other case, by contradiction.

Let two tags s and t, which differ only in bit i, be routed to some two upper output lines. (The following argument is essentially the same when s and t are both routed to lower output lines.)

Any tag y routed to an upper output line satisfies the identity: $y_j \oplus y_i = x_i = 0$.

Since s and t are routed to upper output lines, $s_j \oplus s_i = t_j \oplus t_i = 0$. Noting that $s_j = t_j$, we get $s_i = t_i$, a contradiction. ∎

Let $B = \{n-1, \cdots, 0\}$ be the set of all bit positions, and $B_i = \{n-1, \cdots, 0\} \setminus \{i\}$, the set of all bit positions except the bit position i. Also, let the relation from the set of line addresses with ith bit equal to 0 (respectively, 1) to their tags considering the bits in B_i be denoted g_0 (respectively, g_1). Then, g_0 and g_1 are said to be subrelations of g, when it is partitioned on bit i. In Lemma 3, we show that g_0, g_1 are indeed some permutations in $\mathcal{LC}_{n-1}$ and, hence, subpermutations of g, which is in $\mathcal{LC}_n$. For the above example, g is partitioned on bit 0 into g_0 and g_1 given by, respectively, (6) and (7).

Lemma 3: The relations g_0 and g_1 are some permutations in $\mathcal{LC}_{n-1}$.

 Proof: From Lemma 2, any two tags routed to the upper lines differ in one or more bits other than the ith bit and, hence, are distinct considering only the bits in B_i. So g_0 is a permutation. Therefore, g_1 also is a permutation. To complete the proof, we show that $g_0^{-1}, g_1^{-1} \in \mathcal{LC}_{n-1}$.

From Lemma 1, after routing, the ith bit equation of g^{-1} is $x_i = y_i \oplus \lambda y_j$, where $\lambda \in \{0, 1\}$ [(8)]. The rth bit equation of g^{-1}, $0 \leq r < n$ and $r \neq i$, can be rewritten by substituting the occurrences of y_i, if any, with $x_i \oplus \lambda y_j$.

The rth bit equation of $g_0^{-1} (g_1^{-1})$ is obtained from that of g^{-1} by replacing any occurrence of x_i, which is a constant for the set of line addresses of this permutation, with its value—0 for the set of upper line addresses and 1 for the set of lower line addresses. That is, each bit equation of $g_0^{-1} (g_1^{-1})$ is free of x_i and y_i. ∎

Observation 1: When expressed in the form of (2), g_0 and g_1 are given by the same $(n-1) \times (n-1)$ Boolean matrix, although they might differ in the "c" vector.

Corollary 2: Suppose a linear-complement permutation is to be routed through some k, $1 \leq k < n$, stages of switches according to the above routing rule using a distinct routing bit i_p in stage p, $1 \leq p \leq k$.

a) At any stage p, it is possible to select the "j" bit of the above routing rule, bit j_p in stage p, such that $j_p \notin \{i_1, \cdots, i_{p-1}\}$. (If $p = 1$, then $\{i_1, \cdots, i_{p-1}\}$ is the empty set.)

b) The relation from line addresses to tags after any stage p is a linear-complement permutation. Furthermore, it can be partitioned on bits $i_1, \cdots, i_p$ into 2^p subpermutations, each in $\mathcal{LC}_{n-p}$.

 Proof: Both parts can be proved by induction using Lemma 3, for $k = 1$, as the basis. ∎

All the results proved so far can be applied to Algorithms BL and PL due to the following claim.

Claim 4: a) The routing specified by Algorithm BL, in any of the first $n-1$ stages of $\mathcal{B}_n$, in realizing a linear-complement permutation is the same as that given by the rule using the most significant bit (MSB), in which the tags to a switch differ, to decide the priority of an input line.

b) The routing specified by Algorithm PL, in any of the first n stages of $\prod_n$, in realizing a linear-complement permutation is the same as that given by the rule using the least significant bit (LSB), in which the tags to a switch differ, to decide the priority of an input line.

Proof is trivial.

Theorem 1: Algorithm BL routes any permutation of $\mathcal{LC}_n$ in $\mathcal{B}_n$.

Proof: Induction is used. It is trivially true for $n = 1$, since $\mathcal{B}_1$ is a 2×2 switch. For induction hypothesis, assume that any permutation in $\mathcal{LC}_m$, $m < n$, is realized correctly by Algorithm BL in a $\mathcal{B}_m$.

Consider the routing of a permutation $f \in \mathcal{LC}_n$ by Algorithm BL in $\mathcal{B}_n$. After routing through stage 0, the permutation g at the outputs of stage 0 switches can be partitioned on the 0th bit (the routing bit) into two subpermutations $g_0, g_1 \in \mathcal{LC}_{n-1}$. (Lemma 3.) Due to the inverse shuffle connection between stages 0 and 1, g_0 and g_1 appear at the inputs of, respectively, the top and bottom subnetworks $\mathcal{B}_{n-1}$'s, which comprise the stages $1, \cdots, 2n - 3$ of $\mathcal{B}_n$. These subpermutations are correctly realized by Algorithm BL, in $\mathcal{B}_{n-1}$'s, by induction hypothesis. That is, after routing through stage $(2n - 3)$, tags match their line addresses in bits $n - 1, \cdots, 1$.

At the inputs of switches in stage $(2n - 2)$, the last stage: the tags at a switch differ in only in the 0th bit, LSB, since the input line addresses to a switch differ only in LSB and each tag matches its line address in bits $n - 1, \cdots, 1$. Hence, the switches in stage $(2n - 2)$ can be set such that each tag is routed to the correct destination. ∎

We now prove that Algorithm PL realizes linear-complement permutations correctly in $\prod$ networks.

Lemma 5: After routing a permutation in $\mathcal{LC}_n$ through the first n stages of $\prod_n$ using Algorithm PL, the relation between the line addresses and the tags is a lower triangular linear permutation.

Proof: First, we note that the relation between line addresses and tags after routing through a stage is some linear-complement permutation. (Corollary 2.) Let f_i denote the linear-complement permutation from line addresses to tags after routing through stage i, $0 \leq i < n$. We show that f_{n-1}^{-1} (hence, f_{n-1}) is a lower triangular linear permutation.

From Lemmas 1 and 3, after routing through stage $i, 0 \leq i < n-1$, the equation of bit $n - 1 - i$ for permutation f_i^{-1} is of the form $x_{n-1-i} = y_{n-1-i} \oplus \lambda_{n-1-i} y_j$, where $\lambda_{n-1-i} \in \{0, 1\}$ and $j < n - 1 - i$ (due to the comparison with *bits reversed*); furthermore, it is not changed later, since a bit equation in the permutation from tags to line addresses does not change, if that bit is not used for routing, and, of course, the ith bit is not used for routing again in the first half of $\prod_n$. After routing through stage $(n - 2)$, the two tags at lines with addresses x and $x \oplus 1$, for any $x \in V$, differ in the 0th bit, the only bit not yet used for routing. [Corollary 2a).] Since the tags at lines x and $x \oplus 1$ meet at a switch in stage $(n - 1)$, it can be set up without a conflict. Therefore, after routing through stage $(n - 1)$, each tag matches its line address in the 0th bit. In summary, f_{n-1}^{-1} is of the following form.

$$
\left.
\begin{aligned}
x_{n-1} &= y_{n-1} \oplus \lambda_{n-1} y_{j_{n-1}}, \quad j_{n-1} < n - 1 \\
&\vdots \\
x_1 &= y_1 \oplus \lambda_1 y_{j_1}, \qquad\qquad j_1 < 1 \\
x_0 &= y_0
\end{aligned}
\right\}.
\tag{11}
$$

It is clear that the above set of equations define a linear permutation with Boolean matrix in the lower triangular form. ∎

For the routing of the example linear permutation of (5), the permutation from line addresses to tags after stage 2 of $\prod_3$, "f_{n-1}",

is as follows. (See Fig. 6.)

$$
\begin{pmatrix} y_0 \\ y_1 \\ y_2 \end{pmatrix} = \begin{pmatrix} 1 & 0 & 0 \\ 0 & 1 & 0 \\ 1 & 0 & 1 \end{pmatrix} \begin{pmatrix} x_0 \\ x_1 \\ x_2 \end{pmatrix}.
$$

Theorem 2: Algorithm PL routes any permutation of $\mathcal{LC}_n$ in $\prod_n$.

Proof: From Lemma 5, after the first n stages of routing by Algorithm PL, the resulting permutation is some lower triangular linear permutation, which can be routed in Ω_n, formed by the remaining n-stages of $\prod_n$. ∎

Remarks:

1) Proof of Lemma 5 is very instructive in showing the effect of routing a linear-complement permutation by Algorithm PL in Ω_n. The effect of applying Algorithm BL to route a linear-complement permutation in Ω_n^{-1} is similar, except that the permutation from outputs to tags is an upper triangular linear permutation. (This can be shown readily by mimicking the proof of Lemma 5.) Thus, Algorithms BL and PL route linear-complement permutations by factorizing them into two simpler permutations, automatically. Lemma 5 shows the form of the "second" permutation, for the case of Algorithm PL. The "first" permutation is more complicated than the second one and is routed in the first half of the network. (This indeed is the approach discussed by Pease [13], although his treatment is not suitable for efficient routing.) Furthermore, after routing a given linear-complement permutation in Ω_n^{-1} (using Algorithm BL) or Ω_n (using Algorithm PL), the second permutation to be realized is simple enough to be realized by, for example, one of Steinberg's lower or upper triangular networks [15] or the second half of Waksman's network [17] (also, see Section IV-A).

2) Noting that $\mathcal{B}_n$ is simply Ω_n^{-1} followed by Ω_n with the last stage of Ω_n^{-1} identified with the first stage of Ω_n, an alternate proof for Theorem 1 can be given.

3) The effect of giving priority to the tag with larger value does not effect the correct routing of a linear-complement permutation by Algorithms BL and PL. However, the second permutation to be passed by the second half of the network is either an upper or a lower triangular linear-complement permutation. Now, the routing through a stage is described with the modified form of (8) of Lemma 1: $x_i = y_i \oplus \lambda y_j \oplus \lambda$.

4) If the bit used for resolving conflicts is already used in one of the earlier stages as routing bit, then the second permutation is neither an upper nor a lower triangular linear-complement permutation, but some linear-complement permutation simple enough to be passed by Ω_n or Ω_n^{-1} correctly. This can be observed, e.g., for Algorithm PL, by removing the restriction that $j_i < i, 0 < i < n - 1$, in (11). Note that $x_0 = y_0$ is still true for this second permutation but, to show it, Corollary 2 has to be proved without the restriction that $j_p \notin \{i_1, \cdots, i_{p-1}\}$. It is readily shown by noting that the linear equations defining a permutation are independent.

The drawbacks of choosing an already used routing bit for conflict resolution are: a) the second permutation is slightly more complicated and b) it precludes on-the-fly switch setting for bit-serial networks (see Section IV-C).

IV. Other Applications of Algorithms BL and PL

A. Routing Linear-Complement Permutations in Waksman's Network

Waksman's network, $\mathcal{W}_n$, is simply a $\mathcal{B}_n$ with some switches ($\frac{N}{2} - 1$, to be precise) permanently set straight (hence, removed); this network is shown by Waksman to be rearrangeable with (asymptotically) the minimum number switches [17]. $\mathcal{W}_n$ is obtained from

$\mathcal{B}_n$ by setting the switches, given below, straight.

$$\left\{\text{switch}\left(n+i, 2^{i+1}j\right) \mid 0 \le i \le n-2, 0 \le j < N/2^{i+2}\right\}.$$

For example, $\mathcal{W}_3$ is obtained from $\mathcal{B}_3$ by setting the switches $\{(3,0), (3,2), (4,0)\}$ straight permanently.

Theorem 3: Algorithm BL routes linear-complement permutations in $\mathcal{W}_n$.

Proof: First, we investigate the setting of switches in $\mathcal{B}_n$ by Algorithm BL.

It is easily seen that tags with value 0 and 1 go to, respectively, upper and lower $\mathcal{B}_{n-1}$'s after routing through state 0. So, routing is completed with switch $(2n-2, 0)$ set straight. Since the subpermutations to be routed in the top and bottom $\mathcal{B}_{n-1}$'s are in $\mathcal{LC}_{n-1}$ (Theorem 1), the above argument can be recursively applied. So, the very switches always set straight by Algorithm BL in routing linear-complement permutations in $\mathcal{B}_n$ are the ones permanently set straight in $\mathcal{W}_n$. ∎

B. An Algorithm for the $(2n-1)$-stage Shuffle-Exchange Network

Algorithm PL routes any $\pi \in \mathcal{LC}_n$ in $\prod_n$ with all the switches in the last stage are set straight, because $x_0 = y_0$ after the first n stages of routing [(11)]. See, for an example, Fig. 6. Therefore, we need only a $(2n-1)$-stage Shuffle-Exchange network followed by a perfect shuffle pattern (σ) to realize linear-complement permutations by Algorithm PL. Therefore, if we apply Algorithm PL to route π in $(2n-1)$-stage Shuffle-Exchange network, we actually route, $\sigma^{-1}\pi$, correctly, but not π. (Composition of permutations is right to left.)

For correct routing of π in $(2n-1)$-stage Shuffle-Exchange network, we modify Algorithm PL to treat destination tags as if a shuffle was performed on them; i.e., y_i is treated as $y_{i+1 (\mod n)}$. With this modification, Algorithm PL actually attempts to route $\pi' = \sigma\pi$. And $\left(\sigma^{-1}\pi'\right)$ is routed correctly, by Algorithm PL after $(2n-1)$ stages of Shuffle-Exchange. But, $\sigma^{-1}\pi' = \sigma^{-1}\sigma\pi = \pi$.

Theorem 4: With the above modification, Algorithm PL routes any permutation of $\mathcal{LC}_n$ in the $(2n-1)$-stage Shuffle-Exchange network.

Remark: The addresses of output lines of switches in the last stage of the $(2n-1)$-stage Shuffle-Exchange network do not match the network output port addresses. (This problem does not arise for $\mathcal{B}_n$ and $\prod_n$.) A perfect shuffle is required to match the output port addresses with the line addresses. This missing shuffle is compensated by treating the tags suitably. In general, if this "mismatch" is some $f \in \mathcal{BPC}_n$, then tags are processed with f before routing. If bit-controlled routing techniques are to be used, then f cannot be any other permutation.

C. Efficient Implementation of Algorithms BL and PL

Implementation of Algorithms BL and PL requires that the switches in the first half of the interconnection networks should be capable of comparing the tags. For the other half, since it is set using the Omega self-routing algorithm, extremely fast implementation techniques are known. In what follows, we discuss fast and efficient techniques for implementing the routing in the first half of the networks.

For word-parallel networks—each line of the network can carry one word at a time, this comparison operation represents additional time and hardware. However, with the current VLSI technology, comparison of two 32-bit words can be fast and, hence, the time penalty need not be severe. Since, with 32 bits, more than 4 billion lines can be indexed distinctly, for almost all networks of practical size, the routing overhead is manageable.

In bit-serial networks—each line in the network can carry one bit at a time, Algorithms BL and PL as stated appear inefficient, since switches in stage i, $1 \le i < n-1$, need $(n-i)$ tag bits from the previous stage to set themselves. However, the following observation allows an efficient implementation of the algorithms with switches set on-the-fly. Thus, the switch setup times are similar to those with, for example, Nassimi and Sahni's algorithm [10].

Consider the effect of routing $\pi \in \mathcal{LC}_n$ by Algorithm PL in Ω_n. If there is a conflict in setting up switches in stage i, then $y_{j_{n-1-i}}$, where $j_{n-1-i} < n-1-i$ and is the LSB in which the two tags at a switch differ, is used to decide the priority [(11)]. However, y_p, where $p < n-1-i$ and is the MSB in which the two tags at a switch differ, could have been used for conflict resolution. (Of course, it is possible that $p = j_{n-1-i}$.) Even then, after routing through the first half, the second permutation to be passed through the second half of $\prod_n$ is still a lower triangular linear permutation, albeit a different one.

A similar observation holds for Algorithm BL. (Here, "pth bit" corresponds to the LSB not yet used for routing and the two tags at a switch differ in that bit.) Note that these modifications do not affect the results about the algorithms, proved earlier.

We organize tags as follows. For Beneš network, the actual tag consists of a $(2n-1)$-bit-stream sent through the network in sequence $0, \cdots, n-2, n-1, n-2, \cdots, 0$. (Message bits follow the tag bits.) For $\prod_n$, the tag consists of a $2n$-bit-stream sent through the network in sequence (left to right) $n-1, \cdots, 0, n-1, \cdots, 0$. At each input of the network, a tag organized as above followed by its message is fed, one bit at a time.

A switch in stage i, $0 \le i < n$, of the network operates as follows. The first bit received is used as the routing bit. It examines the routing bits of its tags and removes them from their respective streams of bits. The remaining bits are sent to the next stage after setting itself as follows. It sets itself appropriately in the absence of conflicts and passes all the remaining bits it receives.

If there is a conflict, it sets itself straight or cross, depending on whether the routing bit value is 0 or 1, and send the incoming bit-streams to the outputs until they differ in a bit. (This is the "pth bit" of the above discussion.) If the bit at the upper input is 0, then the setting of the switch is not disturbed; otherwise, it is toggled—changed from cross to straight or vice versa. This bit and the following bits are sent to the switches in the next stage.

In the case of conflict, it does not matter how the switch is set, as long as both the incoming bits are the same. Once the streams differ in a bit, it can be set correctly. And conflict resolution is patterned after the above discussion. Hence, this implementation routes linear-complement permutations correctly.

D. Routing in Multistage Networks with Larger Size Switches

Algorithms BL and PL can be suitably modified to route linear-complement permutations in Beneš and $\prod$ networks constructed from $K \times K$ switches, $K = 2^k$ for $k \ge 1$. When N is not an integral power of K, switches in the middle stages can be of smaller size. An 8×8 Beneš network with 4×4 switches in the first and the last stages is shown in Fig. 7. We briefly sketch the modifications to the Algorithm BL, below. Similar modifications are applicable to Algorithm PL.

To set a $K \times K$, a group of k bits, which together form the routing digit, is used. In stage i, $0 \le i < \lfloor \log_K(N) \rfloor$, bits $(i+1)k-1, \cdots, ik$ are used to form the routing digit. Conflicts in setting up a switch are resolved as follows. Apply the tags of a $K \times K$ switch to an Ω_k, Ω_k^{-1}, or some similar network made up of 2×2 switches with routing bits that form the routing digit of the switch; for conflict resolution, if necessary, complete tag may be used. (For a switch in the first stage of the network in Fig. 7, the network shown within it could be used with tag bits $0, 1$ for routing.) Route the tags by applying Algorithm BL or PL, whichever is appropriate, in this network. Now set the $K \times K$ switch such that

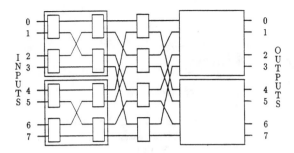

Fig. 7. A $\mathcal{B}_3$ with 4×4 switches in the first and last stages. The network within a switch in the first stage is used to determine its setting.

it simulates the routing specified by this $K \times K$ network built with 2×2 switches. There will not be any conflicts in routing through the remaining stages of the network.

V. CONCLUSIONS

In this paper, we have presented algorithms to route linear-complement permutations in Beneš, $\prod$, and $(2n-1)$ stage Shuffle-Exchange networks. The feature introduced by the algorithms is: when there are conflicts in setting up a switch, one of the tags is given priority based on some type of comparison operation. When there are no conflicts in setting up a switch, the routing is similar to the Omega self-routing algorithm. These algorithms can be efficiently implemented in bit-serial networks. For word-parallel networks, the overhead of comparison operation is reasonable for networks with, say up to 4 billion inputs and outputs.

Algorithm BL realizes the class of inverse Omega permutations in Beneš networks, since there will not be any conflicts in setting up the switches. Similarly, Algorithm PL realizes any Ω permutation in $2n$-stage Shuffle-Exchange networks. In fact, the classes of permutations realized by these algorithms are much larger than the linear class. It is interesting to note that Algorithm BL routes all permutations in $\mathcal{B}_2$. However, it does not route all Omega permutations in larger size Beneš networks. If a permutation is known to be in Omega class, then it can be realized in a Beneš network by setting the first $(n-1)$ stages of the network straight, as suggested by Nassimi and Sahni [10].

Using the analysis techniques presented, we have shown that the following classes of permutations are realized by Algorithm BL on $\mathcal{B}_n$ [14]. Similar results are shown for Algorithm PL. To pass these permutations, conflict resolution should be as given for the case of bit-serial networks.

1) Any permutation of the form πv, where v is an Omega admissible upper triangular permutation [15] and $\pi \in \mathcal{LC}_n$. These types of permutations are useful in parallel memory access of sub- and superdiagonals of data matrices [4].

2) Any permutation partitionable on the first k least significant bits into 2^k subpermutations—each may be distinct and similarly partitioned. Permutations of this type are useful in partitionable SIMD systems.

Further work in characterizing the classes of permutations realized by the proposed algorithms is needed. Another direction for further work is in developing simple control algorithms to route any permutation, specified as an algebraic function, since such types of permutations are used frequently in parallel processing.

REFERENCES

[1] J. Beetem, M. Denneau, and D. Weingarten, "The GF11 supercomputer," in *Proc. Int. Symp. Comput. Architecture,* 1985, pp. 108–115.

[2] V. E. Beneš, *Mathematical Theory of Connecting Networks and Telephone Traffic.* New York: Academic, 1965.

[3] G. Birkhoff and S. MacLane, *A Survey of Modern Algebra,* fourth ed. New York: Macmillan, 1977.

[4] R. V. Boppana and C. S. Raghavendra, "Generalized schemes for access and alignment of data in parallel processors with self-routing interconnection networks," *J. Parallel Distributed Comput.,* vol. 11, pp. 97–111, 1991.

[5] T. Etzion and A. Lempel, "An efficient algorithm for generating linear transformations in a shuffle exchange network," *SIAM J. Comput.,* vol. 15, no. 1, 1986.

[6] K. Hoffman and R. Kunze, *Linear Algebra,* second ed. Englewood Cliffs, NJ: Prentice-Hall, 1971.

[7] D. H. Lawrie, "Access and alignment of data in an array processor," *IEEE Trans. Comput.,* vol. C-24, no. 12, 1975.

[8] J. Lenfant, "Parallel permutations of data: A Beneš network control algorithm for frequently used permutations," *IEEE Trans. Comput.,* vol. C-27, 1978.

[9] D. Nassimi, "A fault-tolerant routing algorithm for BPC permutations on multistage interconnection networks," in *Proc. Int. Conf. Parallel Processing,* 1989, pp. 278–287.

[10] D. Nassimi and S. Sahni, "A self-routing Beneš network and parallel permutation algorithms," *IEEE Trans. Comput.,* vol. C-30, no. 5, 1981.

[11] ____, "Parallel algorithms to set up the Beneš permutation network," *IEEE Trans. Comput.,* vol. C-31, pp. 148–154, 1982.

[12] D. S. Parker, "Notes on shuffle/exchange-type switching networks," *IEEE Trans. Comput.,* vol. C-29, pp. 213–222, 1980.

[13] M. C. Pease, III, "The indirect binary n-cube microprocessor array," *IEEE Trans. Comput.,* vol. C-26, 1977.

[14] C. S. Raghavendra and R. V. Boppana, "An analysis of some self-routing schemes for multi-stage interconnection networks," Tech. Rep., Dep. EE–Systems, Univ. of Southern Cal., Univ. Park, Los Angeles, CA 90089-0781, June 1990.

[15] D. Steinberg, "Invariant properties of the shuffle-exchange and a simplified cost-effective version of the omega network," *IEEE Trans. Comput.,* vol. C-32, pp. 444–450, 1983.

[16] A. Varma and C. S. Raghavendra, "Rearrangeability of multistage shuffle/exchange networks," *IEEE Trans. Commun.,* vol. COM-36, no. 10, 1988.

[17] A. Waksman, "A permutation network," *J. ACM,* vol. 15, no. 1, 1968.

[18] P.-C. Yew and D. H. Lawrie, "An easily controlled network for frequently used permutations," *IEEE Trans. Comput.,* vol. C-30, no. 4, 1981.

A New Approach to Fast Control of $r^2 \times r^2$ 3-Stage Benes Networks of $r \times r$ Crossbar Switches

Abdou Youssef

Department of Elect. Eng. & Comput. Sci.
The George Washington University
Washington, DC 20052

Bruce Arden

College of Engineering and Applied Science
University of Rochester
Rochester, NY 14627

ABSTRACT

The routing control of Benes networks has proven to be costly. This paper introduces a new approach to fast control of $N \times N$ 3-stage Benes networks of $r \times r$ crossbar switches as building blocks, where $N = r^2$ and $r \geq 2$. The new approach consists of setting the leftmost column of switches to an apropriately chosen configuration so that the network becomes self-routed while still able to realize a given family of permutations. This approach requires that, for any given family of permutations, a configuration for the leftmost column be found. Such a family is called compatible and the configuration of the leftmost column is called the compatibility factor. In this paper, compabitibility is characterized and a technique to determine compatibility and the compatibility factor is developed. The technique is used to show the compatibility and find the compatibilty factor of Ω-realizable permutations, the permutations needed to emulate a hypercube, and the families of permutations required by FFT, bitonic sorting, tree computations, multidimensional mesh and torus computations, and multigrid computations. An $O(\log^2 N)$ time routing algorithm for the 3-stage Benes will also be developed. Finally, as only 3 compatibility factors are required by the above families of permutations, it will be proposed to replace the first column by 3 multiplexed connections yielding a self-routing network with strong communication capabilities.

§1. Introduction

Reconfigurable multistage interconnection networks have been the focus of intensive research due to their central role in the design and performance of large parallel processing systems [5], [6], [9], [18], [24]. The effectiveness of these networks depend on the efficiency of their routing control and the permutations they realize. Some of these networks, called banyan multistage networks, have efficient routing control but do not realize all permutations [1], [10], [14], [21], [23]. Benes networks, however, realize all permutations but have inefficient routing control [5], [16]. Controlling Benes networks involves either computing the switch configurations of permutations in advance and storing them, or computing them at run time. The first way is costly in space for large systems, while the second is costly in time as setting the switches to realize a given permutation takes $O(N \log N)$ sequential time [22] and $O(N)$ parallel time [11], where N is the number of input terminals of the network.

Two different approaches have been introduced to bypass this control complexity. The first, due to Nassimi and

Sahni [15], consists of using destination addresses in a specified manner, and allows for the realization of a subset of permutations in optimal time. The second, due to Lenfant [13], identifies families of frequently used permutations, and develops a specialized control algorithm for each family to realize the permutations of the family efficiently. The first approach produces optimal control but allows for the realization of only a small fraction of permutations. The second approach is limited to a few families.

This paper introduces a new approach to controlling 3-stage Benes networks of r^2 input terminals, r^2 output terminals and $r \times r$ crossbar switches, for arbitrary $r \geq 2$ (Fig. 1). These networks can have up to 1024 input/output terminals as the current technology can provide 32×32 crossbar switches. IBM's GF11 [4] is an example of a 3-stage benes-connected parallel system of 24×24 crossbar switches and 576 processors.

The new approach of routing control consists of setting the first stage of the network to a fixed configuration so that the remaining network can be <u>self-routed</u> and can realize a given family of permutations. This approach requires that, for a given family of permutations, the family be examined to determine if there exists a configuration to which the first column of the network can be set so that the remaining network realizes the family (such a family is said to be *compatible*). This approach combines the advantages of the aforementioned two approaches in having optimal control for numerous large families of permutations.

In this paper compatibility is characterized and a technique to determine compatibility is developed. The technique is used to show the compatibility of the families of permutations required by many interesting classes of problems such as FFT, bitonic sorting, tree computations, multidemensional mesh and torus computations, and multigrid computations. Additional useful families of permutations, such as the permutations realizable by the omaga network, are also shown to be compatible.

The rest of the paper is organized as follows. The next section gives some definitions and fundamental concepts. Compatibility is characterized in Section 3. Section 4 shows the compatibility of several families of permutations. Section 5 identifies the families of permutations required by several interesting classes of problems and shows their compatibility. Finally, Section 6 gives an implementation of the new control scheme and draws some conclusions

Reprinted from *Proc. 17 th Int'l Symp. Computer Architecture,* 1990, pp. 50-59.

regarding the possibility of replacing the leftmost column of the 3-stage Benes network with some fixed interconncetions which leads to self-routed networks of powerful communication capibilities.

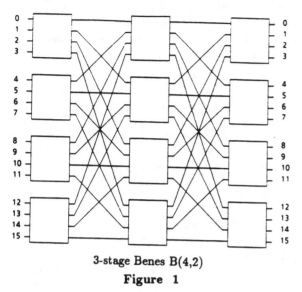

3-stage Benes B(4,2)

Figure 1

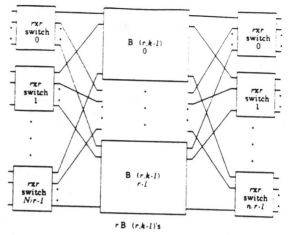

The recursive structure of the Benes network

Figure 2

§2. Definitions and Fundamental Concepts

A Benes network [5], denoted here $B(r,k)$, of r^k input terminals, r^k output terminals, and $r \times r$ crossbar permutation switches as building blocks (where $r \geq 2$), is defined recursively as shown in Fig. 2. For $k = 1$, the network is simply the $r \times r$ crossbar switch. For $k \geq 2$, the connectivity between the leftmost column and the middle $B(r, k-1)$ networks is a permutation that maps (i.e., links) the q-th output port of the p-th switch to the p-th input terminal of the q-th $B(r, k-1)$ for $q = 0, 1, ..., r-1$ and $p = 0, 1, ..., r^{k-1}-1$. The inverse of this permutation connects the output terminals of the middle $B(r, k-1)$ networks to the input ports of the rightmost column. Note that $B(r, k)$ has $2k-1$ columns of r^{k-1} crossbar switches each. An interesting special case is when $k = 2$. The network $B(r, 2)$ has then 3 columns as illustrated in Fig. 1.

The $B(r, 2)$ networks for arbitrary r are the focus of this paper and referred to as *3-stage Benes networks*. Let $N = r^2$ throughout this paper. The columns of $B(r, 2)$ are numbered 0, 1, 2 from left to right, and will often be referred to as left, middle and right column, respectively. Each column has r switches numbered $0, 1, ..., r-1$ from top to bottom. The ports of each column are numbered $0, 1, ..., N-1$, from top to bottom. The q-th port of the p-th switch in any column is then labeled $pr + q$. The connectivity between the left column and middle column is a permutation f where $f(pr+q) = qr+p$, for $p = 0, 1, ..., r-1$ and $q = 0, 1, ..., r-1$. The connectivity between the middle column and the right column is f^{-1} which happens to be equal to f.

Let $R_N = \{0, 1, ..., N-1\}$, $R_r = \{0, 1, ..., r-1\}$, and S_N be the set of permutations of R_N. Every number $x \in$ R_N is uniquely expressed as $pr + q$ for some p and q, where $0 \leq p \leq r-1$ and $0 \leq q \leq r-1$. Let H be the subset of permutations that are realizable by any column of switches of $B(r, 2)$. Observe that H is a subgroup of the symmetric group S_N, and $h \in H$ if $h(pr + q) = pr + q'$ for some q' function of p and q. Let then $q' = t(p, q) = h(pr + q)$ mod r. Denote by $t(p, .)$ the mapping from R_r to R_r such that $t(p, .)(q) = t(p, q)$. Clearly, $t(p, .)$ is a permutation of R_r.

If $h \in H$, a column of $B(r, 2)$ is said to be *set to* h if the switches are set so that input port $pr + q$ is connected to output port $h(pr + q)$. Equivalently, for $0 \leq p \leq r-1$, the p-th switch of the column is set in such a way that its q-th input port is connected to its $t(p, q)$-th output port.

A permutation ϕ in S_N is *realizable* by $B(r, 2)$ if the switches of $B(r, 2)$ can be set such that the input terminal i is connected to the output terminal $\phi(i)$, for $i = 0, 1, ..., N-1$. A permutation is said to be h-*realizable* for some h in H if it is realizable by $B(r, 2)$ with the left column set to h. A family of m permutations in S_N is said to be *compatible* if there is some permutation $h \in H$ such that all the permutations in the family are h-realizable. The permutation h is then called a *compatibility factor* of the family.

Every path from an input terminal s to an output terminal d in $B(r, 2)$, denoted $s \rightarrow d$, goes through six ports $(x_1, x_2, x_3, x_4, x_5, x_6)$, where $x_1 = s$, x_2 is an output port of the left column, x_3 is an input port of the middle column, and so on. Note that $x_3 = f(x_2)$ and $x_5 = f(x_4)$, and therefore, the path is fully decided by x_2 and x_4. Two paths $(x_1, x_2, x_3, x_4, x_5, x_6)$ and $(y_1, y_2, y_3, y_4, y_5, y_6)$ are said to *conflict* if $x_i = y_i$ for some i.

If the left column is set to some configuration h in H, where $h(pr + q) = pr + t(p, q)$, and if the path $(x_1, x_2, x_3, x_4, x_5, x_6)$ between an input terminal $s = x_1 = pr + q$ and an output terminal $d = x_6 = lr + n$ is realizable with the left column set to h, then $x_2 = h(x_1) = pr + t(p, q)$, $x_3 = f(x_2) = t(p, q)r + p$, $x_4 = t(p, q)r + p'$ for some $p' \in R_r$, and $x_5 = f(x_4) = p'r + t(p, q)$. As x_5

and x_6 are linked to the same switch in the right column, it follows that $p' = l$. Thus we have:

$$x_1 = pr + q, \ x_2 = pr + t(p,q),$$
$$x_3 = t(p,q)r + p, \ x_4 = t(p,q)r + l,$$
$$x_5 = lr + t(p,q), \text{ and } x_6 = d = lr + n.$$

Therefore, if the left column is set to some configuration h in H, there exists a unique path between every input terminal and every output terminal. That path can be determined using the output terminal address [12] as follows: Each switch in the middle column, when receiving a request to connect to some output terminal $lr + n$, links the incoming request to its l-th output port, and each switch in the right column links the incoming request to its n-th output port. Therefore, $B(r,2)$ becomes self-routed when the left column is set to a configuration h in H. Consequently, if a family of permutations is compatible, where one compatibility factor is some h in H, the left column of the 3-stage Benes network can be set to h and the resulting network can realize all the permutations of the family in a self-routed fashion. This is the primary motivation behind our approach.

The main focus of this paper is to determine if a given family of permutations is compatible, and if so, to find one compatibility factor. Compatibility is characterized and various families of permutations that arise from many important classes of problems are identified and shown compatible, and their compatibility factors are found. These compatibility factors (permutations) can then be stored.

When a 3-stage Benes-based computer system executes an algorithm whose communication requirements can be fulfilled by a compatible family of permutations, the left column is first set to the family's compatibility factor (if already found and stored) for the entire duration of the algorithm, allowing then for fast, self-routed realization of the permutations, and leading to speedy execution of the algorithm. Note that the amount of memory required to store the compatibilty factors is very small in comparison with the amount of memory needed to store the setting of the switches for all the $N!$ permutations.

§3. Characterization of Compatibility

In this section, necessary and sufficient conditions for a permutation to be h-realizabale will be given and then a compatibility characterization theorem is concluded which gives necessary and sufficient conditions for a given family of permutations to be compatible. This characterization will be used to show the compatibilty of several interesting families of permutations.

3.1 Lemma. *If the left column is set to some configuration $h \in H$, where $h(pr + q) = pr + t(p,q)$, and if s and s' are two distinct input terminals and d and d' two distinct output terminals, where $s = pr+q$, $s' = p'r+q'$, $d = lr+n$, and $d' = l'r + n'$, then the paths $s \to d$ and $s' \to d'$ conflict if and only if $t(p,q) = t(p',q')$ and $l = l'$.*

Proof. Let the path $(s \to d) = (x_1, x_2, x_3, x_4, x_5, x_6)$ and $(s' \to d') = (y_1, y_2, y_3, y_4, y_5, y_6)$. Since $x_1 \neq y_1$, it follows

that $h(x_1) \neq h(y_1)$ and $f(h(x_1)) \neq f(h(y_1))$, and hence $x_2 \neq y_2$ and $x_3 \neq y_3$. We have also $x_6 \neq y_6$. Therefore, the two paths conflict if and only if $x_4 = y_4$ or $x_5 = y_5$. As $x_5 = f(x_4)$ and $y_5 = f(y_4)$, we have $x_4 = y_4$ if and only if $x_5 = y_5$. So the two paths conflict if and only if $x_4 = y_4$. It was shown in the preceding section that $x_4 = t(p,q)r + l$, and $y_4 = t(p',q')r + l'$. Hence, $x_4 = y_4$ if and only if $t(p,q) = t(p',q')$ and $l = l'$. ∎

3.2 Theorem. *Let h be in H where $h(pr + q) = pr + t(p,q)$. Let also ϕ be a permutation in S_N, and $\alpha(p,q) = \lfloor \frac{\phi(pr+q)}{r} \rfloor$. ϕ is h-realizable if and only if for every two distinct input terminals $s = pr + q$ and $s' = p'r + q'$, $\alpha(p,q) = \alpha(p',q')$ implies that $t(p,q) \neq t(p',q')$.*

Proof. Let $s = pr + q$ and $s' = p'r + q'$ be two arbitrary distinct input terminals, and let $\phi(s) = d = lr + n$ and $\phi(s') = d' = l'r + n'$, where $l = \alpha(p,q)$ and $l' = \alpha(p',q')$. Clearly, $d \neq d'$. If ϕ is h-realizable, then the paths $s \to d$ and $s' \to d'$ do not conflict in $B(r,2)$ with the left column set to h. After the preceding lemma, we must have either $t(p,q) \neq t(p',q')$ or $l \neq l'$. Therefore, if $\alpha(p,q) = \alpha(p',q')$, then $t(p,q) \neq t(p',q')$.

Conversely, if for every two distinct input terminals $s = pr + q$ and $s' = p'r + q'$, $\alpha(p,q) = \alpha(p',q')$ implies that $t(p,q) \neq t(p',q')$, then by the preceding lemma, for every two distinct input terminals s and s', the paths $s \to \phi(s)$ and $s' \to \phi(s')$ do not conflict in $B(r,2)$ with the left column set to h. Consequently, ϕ is h-realizable. ∎

3.3 The Compatibility Characterization Theorem.

Let $\{\phi_1, \phi_2, ..., \phi_m\}$ be a family of permutations in S_N, and $\alpha_i(p,q) = \lfloor \frac{\phi_i(pr+q)}{r} \rfloor$, for $i = 1, 2, ..., m$. The family $\{\phi_1, \phi_2, ..., \phi_m\}$ is compatible if and only if there is a mapping $t: R_r \times R_r \to R_r$ such that:
(i) $t(p,.)$ is a permutation of R_r for every p in R_r.
(ii) If for some $p, p', q, q' \in R_r$ there exists i such that $\alpha_i(p,q) = \alpha_i(p',q')$ and $p \neq p'$, then $t(p,q) \neq t(p',q')$.

Proof. Assume first that $\phi_1, \phi_2, ..., \phi_m$ are compatible, and that h is a compatibility factor. Let t be such that $h(pr + q) = pr + t(p,q)$. Clearly, $t(p,.)$ is a permutation of R_r for every p. To show (ii), assume that for some p, p', q, q' in R_r there exists i such that $\alpha_i(p,q) = \alpha(p',q')$ and $p \neq p'$. Let $s = pr + q$ and $s' = p'r + q'$. Clearly $s \neq s'$ because $p \neq p'$. Since ϕ_i is h-realizable, $s \neq s'$ and $\alpha_i(p,q) = \alpha_i(p',q')$, it follows that $t(p,q) \neq t(p',q')$, after Theorem 3.2.

Conversely, assume that there is a mapping $t : R_r \times R_r \to R_r$ that satisfies (i) and (ii). Let h be the mapping from R_N to R_N such that $h(pr+q) = pr+t(p,q)$. Since $t(p,.)$ is a permutation of R_r for every p, h must a permutation in H. For every i, ϕ_i will be shown h-realizable using Theorem 3.2. Let $s = pr + q$ and $s' = p'r + q'$ such that $s \neq s'$ and $\alpha_i(p,q) = \alpha_i(p',q')$. Since $s \neq s'$, we have $p \neq p'$ or $q \neq q'$. If $p \neq p'$, it follows from (ii) that $t(p,q) \neq t(p',q')$. If $p = p'$, then $q \neq q'$ and therefore $t(p,q) \neq t(p,q')$ because $t(p,.)$ is a permutation. So in both cases $t(p,q) \neq t(p',q')$. After Theorem 3.2, ϕ_i is h-realizable. ∎

It can be seen from the proof of the previous theorem

that when there is a mapping t that satisfies the conditions (i) and (ii) of the theorem, one compatibility factor of the family is a permutation $h \in H$ where $h(pr+q) = pr + t(p,q)$.

It is worthwhile to note that Theorem 3.3 can be mapped into a graph-theoretic problem, namely, the node coloring problem. Let $\phi_1, \phi_2, ..., \phi_m$ be m permutations in S_N. Let $G = (V,E)$ be the following undirected graph: $V = R_r \times R_r$ and $E = \{((p,q),(p',q'))|p = p' \text{ or } (\exists i)(\alpha_i(p,q) = \alpha_i(p',q')\}$. The theorem can now be stated as follows: $\phi_1, \phi_2, ..., \phi_m$ are compatible if and only if G can be r-colored such that no two adjacent nodes have the same color. To prove this, let $t(p,q)$ be the color of node (p,q). It is clear that t satisfies condition (i) and (ii) of Theorem 3.3 if and only if t r-colors G in such a way that no two adjacent nodes have the same color.

The general coloring problem is NP-complete, but it remains open whether these graphs have any peculiarities that open the door to a fast (i.e., polynomial) algorithm to r-color them. Such an algorithm would automate deciding compatibility and finding a compatibility factor.

Using this graph formulation, it can be shown that not every family of permutations is compatible. Take for example $r = 2$, (and hence $N = 4$ and $R_r = \{0,1\}$), $\phi_1 = (0\ 1\ 2)(3)$ and $\phi_2 = (0)(1\ 2\ 3)$. It can be shown that $\alpha_1(0,0) = \alpha_1(1,0) = 0$, $\alpha_1(0,1) = \alpha_1(1,1) = 1$, $\alpha_2(0,0) = \alpha_2(1,1) = 0$, and $\alpha_2(0,1) = \alpha_2(1,0) = 1$. The corresponding graph G is depicted in Fig. 3. Since G has a 3-clique, it cannot be 2-colored and, therefore, ϕ_1 and ϕ_2 are not compatible.

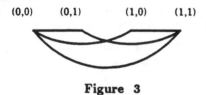

(0,0)   (0,1)   (1,0)   (1,1)

Figure 3

§4. Compatible Families of Permutations

Various families of permutations will be shown compatible in this section. In particular, two large families of permutations, namely, the family of *pseudo bit translations* and the *L-family*, will be defined and shown to be compatible. The permutations realizable by the omega network Ω_N will also be shown compatible. In the next section, the families of permutations required by many application areas will be shown to be subfamilies of these three families and hence compatible. In the remainder of the paper, r is assumed to be a power of two ($r = 2^k$), and therefore, $N = r^2 = 2^{2k}$.

Every number $x = pr + q$ in R_N can be expressed in binary as $x = x_{2k-1}x_{2k-2}...x_0$ and conveniently also as $x = p_{k-1}p_{k-1}...p_0q_{k-1}q_{k-2}...q_0$, where $p = p_{k-1}p_{k-2}...p_0$ and $q = q_{k-1}q_{k-2}...q_0$. The bit positions $0, 1, ..., k-1$ of x (i.e., the k least significant bits) are said to form the q-*wing* of x, and the bit positions $k, k+1, ..., 2k-1$ (i.e., the k most significant bits) the p-*wing* of x. For $i = 0, 1, ..., k-1$, bits p_i and q_i are called *siblings*. Also, p_i is the p-*sibling* of

q_i and q_i the q-*sibling* of p_i.

If π is a permutation of $\{0, 1, ..., 2k-1\}$, then f_π denotes a permutation in S_N, called a *bit permutation*, such that $f_\pi(x_{2k-1}x_{2k-2}...x_0) = x_{\pi(2k-1)}x_{\pi(2k-2)}...x_{\pi(0)}$. A bit permutation f_π manipulates the bits of its parameter x, moving the i-th bit of x to bit position $\pi^{-1}(i)$, for $i = 0, 1, ..., 2k-1$. A *pseudo bit translation* is a bit permutation f_π that satisfies the following condition: f_π moves a bit from the q-wing to the p-wing if and only if f_π moves the p-sibling of that bit to the q-wing.

4.1 Theorem. *All pseudo bit translations are compatible and their compatibility factor is h such that $h(pr+q) = pr + (p \oplus q)$, where $p \oplus q$ is the bitwise XOR of p and q.*
Proof. Let $t(p,q) = p \oplus q$. It is enough to show that t satisfies the conditions (i) and (ii) of Theorem 3.3.
(i) $t(p,.)$ is a permutation since $t(p,.)(q) = t(p,.)(q') \Rightarrow t(p,q) = t(p,q') \Rightarrow p \oplus q = p \oplus q' \Rightarrow q = q'$.
(ii) Assume that for some p, p', q, $q' \in R_r$ there is a pseudo bit translation ϕ such that $\alpha_\phi(p,q) = \alpha_\phi(p',q')$ and $p \neq p'$. We need to show that $t(p,q) \neq t(p',q')$.
Let E be the set of bit positions of the q-wing that are moved to the p-wing by ϕ. Since ϕ is a pseudo bit translation, E must also be the set of p-wing bit positions that move to the q-wing.
$\alpha_\phi(p,q) = \alpha_\phi(p',q') \Rightarrow [(\forall i \notin E)(p_i = p_i') \text{ and } (\forall i \in E)(q_i = q_i')] \Rightarrow q \oplus q'$ has 0's in all bit positions $i \in E$.
$p \neq p' \Rightarrow (\exists i_0)(p_{i_0} \neq p_{i_0}') \Rightarrow p \oplus p'$ has '1' in bit position i_0. Clearly $i_0 \in E$ because $\forall i \notin E$ we have $p_i = p_i'$. Therefore $(p \oplus p') \oplus (q \oplus q')$ has '1' in bit position i_0. Consequently, $t(p,q) \oplus t(p',q') = (p \oplus q) \oplus (p' \oplus q') = (p \oplus p') \oplus (q \oplus q') \neq 0$. Hence, $t(p,q) \neq t(p',q')$. ∎

Fig. 4-a shows the setting of the left column for pseudo bit translations.

Next we define the *L-family* and show it to be compatible. For every permutation ϕ in S_N, let $\alpha_\phi(p,q) = \lfloor \frac{\phi(pr+q)}{r} \rfloor$ = the leftmost k bits of $\phi(pr+q)$. The *L-family* of permutations in S_N is the set
$L = \{\phi \in S_N|$ if $\alpha_\phi(p,q) = \alpha_\phi(p',q')$ and $p \neq p'$, then p and p' agree in all but one bit position, and q and q' agree in at least one bit position$\}$

To show that the L-family is compatible, the set of switches of the left column (i.e., the set R_r of the switch labels) is partitioned into two subsets E_k and F_k, which will be defined recursively such that the binary representations of any two numbers in each subset disagree in at least two bit positions. Let $E_1 = \{0\}$, $F_1 = \{1\}$ and recursively $E_i = 0E_{i-1} \cup 1F_{i-1}$ and $F_i = 0F_{i-1} \cup 1E_{i-1}$, where $aE_{i-1} = \{ax_{i-2}...x_0 \mid x_{i-2}...x_0 \in E_{i-1}\}$ for $a = 0$ or 1, and aF_{i-1} is defined similarly. For example, $0E_1 = \{00\}$, $0F_1 = \{01\}$, $1E_1 = \{10\}$, $1F_1 = \{11\}$, and consequently, $E_2 = \{00, 11\}$ and $F_2 = \{01, 10\}$.

It can be easily shown by induction on $i = 1, 2, ..., k$ that $E_i \cup F_i = \{0, 1, ..., 2^i - 1\}$ (in decimal), $E_i \cap F_i = \emptyset$ and for $i > 1$, any two numbers in each of the sets E_i and F_i disagree in at least two bit positions. In particular, $E_k \cap F_k = \emptyset$ and $E_k \cup F_k = \{0, 1, ..., r-1\} = R_r$

4.2 Theorem. *The L-familiy is compatible and its compatibility factor is h such that $h(pr + q) = pr + q$ if $p \in E_k$ and $h(pr + q) = pr + \bar{q}$ if $p \in F_k$, where $\bar{q}$ is the bitwise complement of q.*

Proof. Let $t(p, q) = q$ if $p \in E_k$ and $t(p, q) = \bar{q}$ if $p \in F_k$. It will be shown that t satisfies the two conditions (i) and (ii) of Theorem 3.3.

(i) $t(p, .)$ is a permutation because $t(p, q) = t(p, q') \Rightarrow [q = q'$ or $\bar{q} = \bar{q'}] \Rightarrow q = q'$.

(ii) Assume that for some p, p', q, $q' \in R_r$ there is a permutation $\phi \in L$ such that $\alpha_\phi(p, q) = \alpha_\phi(p', q')$ and $p \neq p'$. By definition of L, it follows that p and p' agree in all but one bit position, and q and q' agree in at least one bit position. Consequently, p and p' cannot both be in the same E_k or F_k. Assume without loss of generality that $p \in E_k$ and $p' \in F_k$. Then $t(p, q) = q$ and $t(p', q') = \bar{q'}$. As q and q' agree in at least one bit position, q and $\bar{q'}$ must disagree in at least one bit position, and therefore, $t(p, q) \neq t(p', q')$. ∎

Fig. 4-b shows the setting of the left column for the L-family.

In addition to the above two families, two more families will be shown compatible, namely, the set H and the set of permutations realizable by the omega network Ω_N [10].

4.3 Theorem. *For every h and $g \in H$, g is h-realizable. In particular, H is compatible and its compatibilty factor can be any arbitrary permutation $h \in H$.*

Proof. Let h and g be two permutations in H, and let I

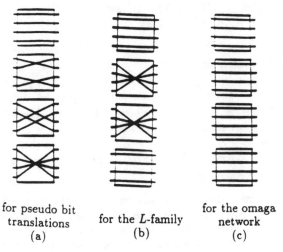

for pseudo bit
translations
(a)

for the L-family
(b)

for the omaga
network
(c)

The configurations of the left column
for various families

Figure 4

be the identity permutation which is also in H. As H is a subgroup of S_N, $h^{-1}g \in H$. Set the left column of $B(r, 2)$ to h, the middle column to I and the right column to $h^{-1}g$. This setting realizes the permutation $hfIfh^{-1}g$ which is equal to g (recall that $f = f^{-1}$ and hence $fIf = ff = I$). It follows that $B(r, 2)$ can realize g with its left column set

to h. ∎

4.4 Theorem. *The permutations realizable by the omega network Ω_N of N input terminals, N output terminals, and 2×2 crossbar switches as building blocks, are compatible and their compatibility factor is the identity permutation.*

Proof. Let $t(p, q) = q$. It will be shown that t satisfies conditions (i) and (ii) of Theorem 3.3.

(i) Since $t(p, .)(q) = t(p, q) = q$, $t(p, .)$ is the identity permutation of R_r.

(ii) Assume that for some p, p', q, and q' in H there is a permutation ϕ realizable by Ω_N such that $\alpha_\phi(p, q) = \alpha_\phi(p', q')$ and $p \neq p'$. It will be proved next that $t(p, q) \neq t(p', q')$. It was shown in [10] that a permutation ψ is realizable by Ω_N if and only if $(\forall s = s_{2k-1}s_{2k-2}...s_0 \in R_N)(\forall s' = s'_{2k-1}s'_{2k-2}...s'_0 \in R_N)(\forall l < \log N = 2k - 1)$ (if $s \neq s'$ and $d_{2k-1}d_{2k-2}...d_{l+1} = d'_{2k-1}d'_{2k-2}...d'_{l+1}$, then $s_l s_{l-1}...s_0 \neq s'_l s'_{l-1}...s'_0$), where $\psi(s) = d_{2k-1}d_{2k-2}...d_0$ and $\psi(s') = d'_{2k-1}d'_{2k-2}...d'_0$. This will be used to show that $t(p, q) \neq t(p', q')$.

Let $s = pr + q$, $s' = p'r + q'$ and $l = k - 1$. Thus $p = s_{2k-1}...s_k$, $q = s_{k-1}...s_0$, $p' = s'_{2k-1}...s'_k$ and $q' = s'_{k-1}...s'_0$. Let also $\phi(s) = d_{2k-1}d_{2k-2}...d_0$ and $\phi(s') = d'_{2k-1}d'_{2k-2}...d'_0$. Then $\alpha_\phi(p, q) = d_{2k-1}d_{2k-2}...d_k$ and $\alpha_\phi(p', q') = d'_{2k-1}d'_{2k-2}...d'_k$.

$\alpha_\phi(p, q) = \alpha_\phi(p', q') \Rightarrow d_{2k-1}d_{2k-2}...d_k = d'_{2k-1}d'_{2k-2}...d'_k$. $p \neq p' \Rightarrow s \neq s'$. As ϕ is realizable by Ω_N, it follows that $s_{k-1}s_{k-2}...s_0 \neq s'_{k-1}s'_{k-2}...s'_0$ which implies that $q \neq q'$, that is $t(p, q) \neq t(p', q')$.

Therefore, by Theorem 3.3, all the permutations realizable by Ω_N are h-realizable, where $h(pr + q) = pr + t(p, q) = pr + q$, that is, the identity permutation. ∎

Fig. 4-c shows the setting of the left column for the Ω_N-realizable permutations.

§5. Applications

In this section the families of permutations of several problems are identified and shown to be subfamilies of the families in the last section, and hence compatible.

5.1 The Fast Fourier Transform

To compute FFT in the way described in [19], two permutations are needed: The shuffle (S) and the exchange (E), where $S(x_{2k-1}x_{2k-2}...x_0) = x_{2k-2}...x_0 x_{2k-1}$ and $E(x_{2k-1}x_{2k-2}...x_0) = x_{2k-1}x_{2k-2}...x_1 \overline{x_0}$. However, at the end of the computation, the components of the resulting vector are in bit reversed order. To restore the order, the bit reversal permutation (ρ) is needed, where $\rho(x_{2k-1}x_{2k-2}...x_0) = x_0 x_1...x_{2k-2}x_{2k-1}$. Thus, the overall family of permutations needed by FFT is $\{S, E, \rho\}$.

5.1 Theorem. *The permutations needed by FFT are compatible.*

Proof. As $S(p_{k-1}p_{k-2}...p_0 q_{k-1}...q_0) = p_{k-2}...p_0 q_{k-1}...q_0 p_{k-1}$, it follows that S moves only one bit from the q-wing to the p-wing, namely, bit q_{k-1}, and only one bit from the p-wing to the q-wing, namely, p_{k-1}. As these two bits are siblings, S is a pseudo bit translation. The bit reversal ρ moves every bit of the q-wing to the p-wing and every bit of the p-wing to the q-wing. Therefore, ρ is trivially a pseudo bit translation. After Theorem 4.1, S and ρ are h-realizable where $h(pr + q) = pr + p \oplus q$. Since $E \in H$, E must be h-realizable for the same h, after Theorem 4.3. ∎

5.2 Bitonic Sorting

Although parallel sorting algorithms of $O(\log N)$ time have been found [2], they are not practical due to the extremely large multiplicative constant factor of $\log N$. Bitonic Sorting, though of time complexity $O(\log^2 N)$, is a practical parallel algorithm [19].

As shown in [19], N numbers can be sorted using a sorting network of $\frac{\log_2 N(\log_2 N+1)}{2}$ stages of comparison switches and based on Batcher's bitonic sorter [3]. Simulating this sorting network on 3-stage Benes networks involves realizing the interconnections (i.e., permutations) between the columns of the sorting network, as well as the columns of switches themselves.

Bitonic sorting and the sorting network based on the bitonic sorter are briefly reviewed next, and the permutations required to simulate the sorting network on $B(r,2)$ are identified and shown to be compatible.

A sequence of real numbers $a_0, a_1, \dots a_{N-1}$ is *bitonic* if (1) there exists i such that $\{a_0, a_1, \dots, a_i\}$ is increasing, and $\{a_{i+1}, \dots, a_{N-1}\}$ is decreasing; or if (2) the sequence can be shifted cyclically so that (1) is satisfied.

An $N \times N$ bitonic sorter is a recursive network where, for $N = 2$, it is a 2×2 comparison switch that takes two input numbers and puts the smaller in the upper output port and the larger in the lower output port (as in Fig. 5-a), or vice versa (as in Fig. 5-b), according to a control bit. For larger N, it is as depicted in Fig. 6. It is shown in [3] and [19] that if the input is a bitonic sequence, then this network sorts the input in increasing order. If the switches of the network of Fig. 6 are replaced by switches of the type in Fig. 5-b, the network sorts the bitonic input in decreasing order.

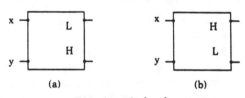

(a)   (b)

Bitonic switch, also a
2×2 bitonic sorter
Figure 5

A full sorting network that sorts any sequence of $N = 2^m$ numbers can be built in m steps, where the i-th step is a column of $\frac{N}{2^i}$ $2^i \times 2^i$ bitonic sorters as shown in Fig. 7. The network works as follows. The first step sorts pairs of numbers into alternately increasing and decreasing pairs so that each sequence of 4 numbers is bitonic. The second step sorts these bitonic sequences into alternately increasing and decreasing sequences so that each sequence of 8 numbers is bitonic. And so on to the last step which receives a bitonic

sequence of length N. Since the last step is an $N \times N$ bitonic sorter, it can sort the incoming sequence. Fig. 8 shows an 8×8 sorting network where the shaded switches place the larger item on the top output, and the blank switches place the smaller on top.

The operations of the sorting network can be viewed as a sequence of data permutations. First the items are permuted by the first column of comparison switches, second they are permuted by the interconnection between the first column and the second column, and then permuted by the second column of switches, and so on. Therefore, the simulation of the sorting network on $B(r,2)$ is done by executing the above sequence of permutations on $B(r,2)$ in order, assuming that the input and output terminals of $B(r,2)$ are N processing elements $pe_0, pe_1, \dots, pe_{N-1}$.

Note that when simulating a column of comparison switches (column j, say), more than permuting is required. Assume the numbers coming to this column are $b_0, b_1, \dots b_{N-1}$ from top to bottom. Then, in our simulation, these numbers are in $pe_0, pe_1, \dots pe_{N-1}$, respectively, when column j is due to be simulated. At comparison switch i of column j, the incoming numbers are b_{2i} and b_{2i+1}. Hence, in simulation, these numbers are in pe_{2i} and pe_{2i+1}, respectively. To be able to do comparison in the simulation, each of pe_{2i} and pe_{2i+1} must have both b_{2i} and b_{2i+1}, for $i = 0, 1, \dots, N - 1$. This can be accomplished by first executing the exchange permutation on the numbers, and then if switch i of the sorting network is in state (a) (as in Fig. 5-a), pe_{2i} keeps $\min(b_{2i}, b_{2i+1})$, while pe_{2i+1} keeps

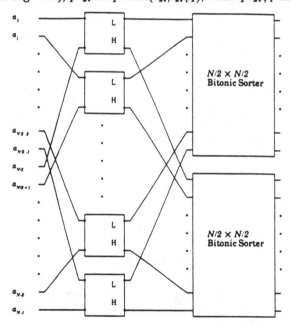

The structure of the bitonic sorter
Figure 6

$\max(b_{2i}, b_{2i+1})$. If the comparison switch is in state (b), the opposite is done. Note that the states of the comparison switches of the sorting network can be known *a priori*.

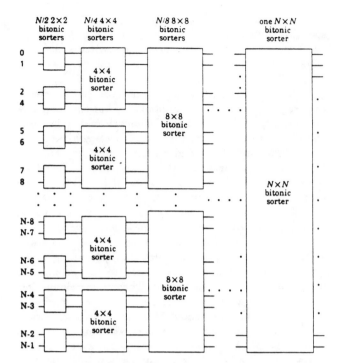

The general structure of the $N \times N$
sorting network based on bitonic sorters

Figure 7

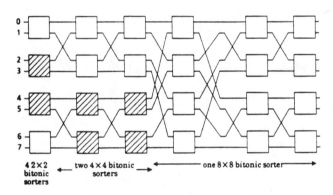

An 8×8 sorting network

Figure 8

The interconnection permutations between the successive columns of the sorting network are identified in the following lemma.

5.2 Lemma. *The inter-column interconnections of the sorting network form the set*

$$\{S_i | 0 \le i \le m - 2\} \cup \{U_i S_{i+1} | 0 \le i \le m - 2\}$$

where

$$S_i(x_{m-1}...x_0) = x_{m-1}...x_{m-i}x_{m-i-2}...x_0 x_{m-i-1}$$

and

$$U_i(x_{m-1}...x_1 x_0) = x_{m-1}...x_{m-i}x_0 x_{m-i-1}...x_1.$$

Proof. Observe first that S_0 is the perfect shuffle on $\{0, 1, \ .. \ , 2^m - 1\}$, S_1 is the perfect shuffle within two segments which are $\{0, 1, ..., 2^{m-1} - 1\}$ and $\{2^{m-1}, 2^{m-1} + 1, ..., 2^m - 1\}$, and in general, S_i is the perfect shuffle within 2^i contiguous segments of length 2^{m-i} each. Similarly, U_0 is the perfect unshuffle (i.e, the inverse of S_0) on $\{0, 1, ..., 2^m - 1\}$, and U_i is the perfect unshuffle (i.e, $U_i = S_i^{-1}$) within the same 2^i contiguous segments which S_i shuffles. A close inspection of the bitonic sorter in Fig. 6 shows that the leftmost interconnection is the perfect shuffle S_0, and the interconnection between the first column and the other $2 \frac{N}{2} \times \frac{N}{2}$ bitonic sortes is the unshuffle U_0. The leftmost interconnection of these $2 \frac{N}{2} \times \frac{N}{2}$ bitonic sorters must then be S_1. It follows then that the interconnection between the first two columns is $U_0 S_1$. It can be easily shown by induction that the remaining interconnections are $U_1 S_2, U_2 S_3, ... U_{m-2} S_{m-1}$, due to the recursive structure of the bitonic sorter.

As described earlier, the sorting network (Fig. 7) has at the i-th block (from the left) $\frac{N}{2^i} 2^i \times 2^i$ bitonic sorters, whose interconnections are then
$S_{m-i}, U_{m-i} S_{m-i+1}, U_{m-i+1} S_{m-i+2}, ..., U_{m-2} S_{m-1}$,
for $i = 2, 3, ..., m$. Note that the first block is just the first column of comparison switches and has no interconnections. It follows that the interconnections of the sorting network are

$$\cup_{2 \le i \le m} \{S_{m-i}, U_{m-i} S_{m-i+1}, U_{m-i+1} S_{m-i+2}, ... U_{m-2} S_{m-1}\}$$

which is equal to $\{S_i | 0 \le i \le m - 2\} \cup \{U_i S_{i+1} | 0 \le i \le m - 2\}$. ∎

5.3 Theorem. *The permutations required by bitonic sorting are compatible.*

Proof. Note that $m = 2k$ and that for $i \ge k$, $S_i(x)$ does not alter the k most significant bits of x, and therefore, S_i is in the set H. Note also that

$(x_{m-1}...x_0)U_i S_{i+1} = S_{i+1}(x_{m-1}...x_{m-i}x_0 x_{m-i-1}...x_1)$
$= x_{m-1}...x_{m-i}x_0 x_{m-i-2}...x_1 x_{m-i-1}$

and therefore $U_i S_{i+1}$ does not alter the k most significant bits if $i \ge k$. Hence, for $i \ge k$, $U_i S_{i+1} \in H$. The exchange permutation E needed to simulate the columns of the sorting network is also in H. After Theorem 4.3, H is compatible and its compatibility factor is arbitrary. Consequently, it suffices to show that the remaining permutations $S_0, S_1, ..., S_{k-1}, U_0 S_1, U_1 S_2, ..., U_{k-1} S_k$ are compatible. In fact, they will be shown to be in the L-family.

For all $i < k$, $S_i(p_{k-1}...p_0 q_{k-1}...q_0) =$
$p_{k-1}...p_{k-i}p_{k-i-2}...p_0 q_{k-1}...q_0 p_{k-i-1}$. Let $\alpha_i(p, q)$ be the leftmost bits of $S_i(p_{k-1}...p_0 q_{k-1}...q_0)$, that is, $\alpha_i(p, q) = p_{k-1}...p_{k-i}p_{k-i-2}...p_0 q_{k-1}$.

$[\alpha_i(p, q) = \alpha_i(p', q')$ and $p \ne p'] \Rightarrow [p$ and p' agree in all but bit position $k - i - 1$, and q and q' agree in at least bit position $k - 1] \Rightarrow S_i \in L$.

Similarly, for $i < k$, we have $(p_{k-1}...p_0 q_{k-1}...q_0)U_i S_{i+1} =$
$p_{k-1}...p_{k-i}q_0 p_{k-i-2}...p_0 q_{k-1}...q_1 p_{k-i-1}$.

248

Let $\alpha_i(p,q)$ be the k leftmost bits of

$$(p_{k-1}...p_0 q_{k-1}...q_0)U_i S_{i+1},$$

that is, $\alpha_i(p,q) = p_{k-1}...p_{k-i}q_0 p_{k-i-2}...p_0$.
$[\alpha_i(p,q) = \alpha_i(p',q')$ and $p \neq p'] \Rightarrow [p$ and p' agree in all but bit position $k-i-1$, and q and q' agree in at least bit position $0] \Rightarrow U_i S_{i+1} \in L$.
Therefore, all the permutations required by bitonic sorting are compatible and their compatibility factor is h of Theorem 4.2. ∎

5.3 Tree Computations

Many parallel computations require full binary tree structures. These include semigroup computations such as addition and multiplication of N numbers, finding the maximum or minimum of N numbers, logical *and* and logical *or* operations on N boolean values, and any other associative operators.

If these algorithms are to run on 3-stage Benes systems, then the tree communication structure has to be emulated by permutations as explained next. Assume a full binary tree of $N-1$ nodes, where $N = 2^{2k}$. The nodes are labeled by level in a standard way where the root is labeled 1 and every internal node i has node $2i$ as its left child and node $2i+1$ as its right child. In the top-down tree communication, each node may send data to its chidren. In the bottom-up communication. each node may send data to its parent. The top-down communication can be accomplished in two steps, where each step can be carried out on $B(r,2)$ by a permutation. In the first step the parents send data to their left children, and in the second step the parents send data to the right children. As the shuffle permutation S maps i to $2i$ for all $i \leq \frac{N}{2}-1$, S can then carry out the first step. In the second step, where every node $i \leq \frac{N}{2}-1$ may send to node $2i+1 = E(2i)$, the permutation SE, which is the composition of S and the exchange E, can carry out the communication because $(i)SE = E(S(i)) = E(2i) = 2i+1$.

Similarly, the bottom-up communication can be accomplished by two steps. where in the first step the left children send data to their parents, and in the second the right children send data to the parents. The first step can be carried out by the unshuffle permutation U, where $U(x_{2k-1}x_{2k-2}...x_1 x_0) = x_0 x_{2k-1}x_{2k-2}...x_1$ (in particular, $U(2i) = i$ for $i \leq \frac{N}{2}-1$). The second step where $2i+1$ has to map to $i = U(2i) = U(E(2i+1)) = (2i+1)EU$ can be done by the composition EU.

Therefore, the permutations required are
$$\{S, SE, U, EU\},$$
which will be shown to be in the L-family and hence compatible.

5.4 Theorem. *The permutations required by tree computations are compatible.*

Proof. From the definitions of S, SE, U and EU, it can be easily seen that $\alpha_S(p,q) = \alpha_{SE}(p,q) = p_{k-2}p_{k-3}...p_0 q_{k-1}$, $\alpha_U(p,q) = q_0 p_{k-1}p_{k-2}...p_1$, and $\alpha_{EU}(p,q) = \overline{q_0}p_{k-1}p_{k-2}...p_1$, where $p = p_{k-1}p_{k-2}...p_0$ and $q = q_{k-1}q_{k-2}...q_0$.

$\alpha_S(p,q) = \alpha_S(p',q')$ clearly implies that
$$p_{k-2}p_{k-3}...p_0 q_{k-1} = p'_{k-2}p'_{k-3}...p'_0 q'_{k-1}$$
and, therefore, p and p' agree in the right $k-1$ bit positions, and q and q' agree in bit position $k-1$. If in addition $p \neq p'$, then p and p' must agree in all but one position because they can disagree in only bit position $k-1$. Therefore, S is in L. As $\alpha_S(p,q) = \alpha_{SE}(p,q)$, it follows that SE is in L too.

Similarly, $\alpha_U(p,q) = \alpha_U(p',q')$ clearly implies that
$$q_0 p_{k-1}p_{k-2}...p_1 = q'_0 p'_{k-1}p'_{k-2}...p'_1$$
and, therefore, p and p' agree in the left $k-1$ bit positions, and q and q' agree in bit position 0. If in addition $p \neq p'$, then p and p' must agree in all but one position. Therefore, U is in L.

A similar proof would show that EU is in L. It follows then that all the four permutations are compatible after Theorem 4.2. ∎

5.4 Multidimensional Torus and Mesh Computations

Toruses and meshes are very useful structures in image processing and scientific computing. The permutations required to emulate these structures on $B(r,2)$ will be shown to be realizable by the omega network Ω_N and therefore compatible.

An n-dimensional $l_1 \times l_2 \times ... \times l_n$ mesh (resp. torus) is a graph where the set of nodes is $R_{l_1} \times R_{l_2} \times ... R_{l_n}$ (recall that $R_z = \{0, 1, ..., z-1\}$) and any two nodes $(x_1, x_2, ..., x_n)$ and $(x'_1, x'_2, ..., x'_n)$ form an edge if and only if there exists some j such that $(\forall i \neq j)(x_i = x'_i)$ and $x_j = x'_j + 1$ or $x_j = x'_j - 1$ (in the torus case, $+$ and $-$ are modulo l_j). Note that the only difference between meshes and toruses is that toruses have "wrap around" edges.

The communication in toruses and meshes is usually done along one dimension at a time, and also in the same direction. That is, in a communication step there exist some j and $a = 1$ or -1 such that every node $(x_1, x_2, ..., x_{j-1}, x_j, x_{j+1}, ..., x_n)$ may send data to node $(x_1, x_2, ..., x_{j-1}, x_j + a, x_{j+1}, ..., x_n)$, where in the case of torus the addition in the j-th dimension is modulo l_j. Therefore, a communication step in a mesh or torus can be carried out by a permutation $f_j^{(a)}$ such that $f_j^{(a)}(x_1, x_2, ..., x_n) = (x_1, x_2, ..., x_{j-1}, (x_j + a) \bmod l_j, x_{j+1}, ..., x_n)$, where $j = 1, 2, ..., n$ and $a = 1$ or -1.

These permutations will be shown to be realizable by Ω_N when each l_j is a power of two for all $j = 1, 2, ..., n$, and the number of nodes $l_1 \times l_2 \times ... \times l_n = N = 2^{2k}$. To do so we need the following two lemmas which are presented without proof because the first is straightforward and the second follows from the first. They will be used in the following subsection also.

5.5 Lemma. *Let m be a positive integer and $a = 2^i$ or -2^i, where $0 \leq i \leq m-1$. Let also x and x' be two m-bit binary numbers. If $(x + a) \bmod 2^m$ and $(x' + a) \bmod 2^m$ agree in the l most significant bits, then x and x' agree in the l most significant bits.*

5.6 Lemma. Let $m_1, m_2, ..., m_n$ be n positive integers, j an integer in $\{1, 2, ..., n\}$ and $a = 2^i$ or -2^i, where $0 \leq i \leq m_j - 1$. Let also $x = (x_1, x_2, ..., x_n)$ and $x' = (x'_1, x'_2, ..., x'_n)$ where $(\forall c = 1, 2, ..., n)(x_c$ and x'_c are m_c-bit binary numbers). View the binary representation of x (resp. x') as the concatenation of the binary representations of $x_1, x_2, ..., x_n$ (resp., $x'_1, x'_2, ..., x'_n$). If $(x_1, x_2, ..., x_{j-1}, (x_j + a) \bmod 2^{m_j}, x_{j+1}, ..., x_n)$ and $(x'_1, x'_2, ..., x'_{j-1}, (x'_j + a) \bmod 2^{m_j}, x'_{j+1}, ..., x'_n)$ agree in the most significant l bits, then x and x' agree in the most significant l bits.

5.7 Theorem. The permutations of multidimensional toruses and meshes of 2^{2k} nodes are compatible.

Proof. Assume the torus (or mesh) is an n-dimensional $2^{m_1} \times 2^{m_2} \times ... \times 2^{m_n}$ torus (or mesh), where $m_1 + m_2 + ...m_n = 2k$. It will be shown that $(\forall j = 1, 2, ..., n)(\forall a = -1, 1)(f_j^{(a)}$ is realizable by $\Omega_N)$. Using the characterization in [10] of permutations realizable by Ω_N, it is enough to show that for all j and a

$(\forall s, s' \in R_N)(\forall l = 1, 2..., 2k - 1)($ if $s \neq s'$ and $d_{2k-1}...d_{l+1} = d'_{2k-1}...d'_{l+1}$, then $s_l s_{l-1}...s_0 \neq s'_l s'_{l-1}...s'_0)$

where

$s = s_{2k-1}...s_0 = (x_1, x_2, ..., x_n),$
$s' = s'_{2k-1}...s'_0 = (x'_1, x'_2, ..., x'_n),$
$f_j^{(a)}(s) = d_{2k-1}...d_0$
$\quad = (x_1, ..., x_{j-1}, (x_j + a) \bmod 2^{m_j}, x_{j+1}, ..., x_n)$
$f_j^{(a)}(s') = d'_{2k-1}...d'_0$
$\quad = (x'_1, ..., x'_{j-1}, (x'_j + a) \bmod 2^{m_j}, x'_{j+1}, ..., x'_n).$

After Lemma 5.6, $d_{2k-1}...d_{l+1} = d'_{2k-1}...d'_{l+1}$ yields that $s_{2k-1}...s_{l+1} = s'_{2k-1}...s'_{l+1}$, which in turn implies that $s_l s_{l-1}...s_0 \neq s_l s_{l-1}...s_0$ because $s \neq s'$. ∎

5.5 Hypercube Computations

Hypercubes are a special case of multidimesional toruses. Specifically, a hypercube of dimension n is the n-dimensional $2 \times 2 \times ... \times 2$ torus. In particular, the node labels $(x_1, x_2, ..., x_n)$'s are binary and $(x_j + 1) \bmod 2 = (x_j - 1) \bmod 2 = \overline{x_j}$. Consequently, $f_j^{(a)}(x_1, x_2, ..., x_n) = (x_1, ...x_{j-1}, \overline{x_j}, x_{j+1}, ...x_n)$, whether $a = 1$ or -1.

5.8 Theorem. The permutations of the hypercube of dimension $2k$ are compatible.

Proof. Since the hypercube is a torus, the theorem follows from Theorem 5.7. ∎

5.6 Multigrid Computations

A grid is a two-dimensional mesh. Multigrid computations are common in image processing [20] and scientific computing [7], [8]. The communications in these computations are between nodes that differ in only one dimension by 2^i for $i = 0, 1, 2, ...$ In terms of permutations, the permutations required by a $2^k \times 2^k$ multigrid computations are: $f_{i,1}^{(1)}(x_1, x_2) = (x_1 + 2^i, x_2)$, $f_{i,1}^{(-1)}(x_1, x_2) = (x_1 - 2^i, x_2)$, $f_{i,2}^{(1)}(x_1, x_2) = (x_1, x_2 + 2^i)$, and $f_{i,2}^{(-1)}(x_1, x_2) = (x_1, x_2 - 2^i)$, for $i = 0, 1, 2, ..., k - 1$, where $+$ and $-$ are modulo 2^k.

5.9 Theorem. The permutations of $2^k \times 2^k$ multigrid computations are compatible.

Proof. The proof can be easily carried out using Lemma 5.6 and following the same line of reasoning as in Theorem 5.7. ∎

§6. Conclusions

A new approach to controlling 3-stage Benes networks has been developed. It consists of finding a configration to which the leftmost column can be set so that a given family of permutations can be realized in a self-routed fashion, leading to fast communication and speedy execution of algorithms. The speedup is high when the compatible family of permutations is large. Compatibility, that is, the existence of an appropriate configuration for the leftmost column, was characterized and a technique to show compatibility was derived from the characterization theorem. Various interesting families of permutations were shown compatible and an appropriate configuration of the leftmost column was found for each family. The unsolved case is how to proceed when the permutations cannot be functionally defined (as in FFT and bitonic sorting) but are irregular as in sparse linear systems. More generally, the problem of deciding compatibility in polynomial time remains open.

The implementation of the new approach of routing control is straightforward and can be integrated into the instruction set of the system. A one-bit flag is needed. For each known compatible family, its compatibilty factor h is stored in memory. Before a certain algorithm starts to run, if the family of permutations required by the algorithm is compatible, the compatibility factor is loaded to the leftmost column of the network and the flag is set to 1. Otherwise, the flag is set to 0. If the system has already an instruction REALIZE-PERM that takes a permutation (or a pointer to it) as operand and sets the network to it, then when the flag is set to 0, the same execution takes place; otherwise, the permutation is realized in the self-routed mode using destination addresses. This implementation shows the utility of the new control scheme when the algorithms require compatible permutations.

Among the families that were shown compatible was the family of permutations required by bitonic sorting. One consequence to this is a new $O(\log^2 N)$ routing control algorithm for 3-stage Benes networks: As sorting destination addresses brings the sources to their destinations, a permutation can be realized on the 3-stage Benes in as many passes as needed by bitonic sorting, that is $\frac{\log N(\log N + 1)}{2} = O(\log^2 N)$. Another consequence is that the leftmost column of the 3-stage Benes network can be replaced by the interconnection (i.e., configuration) that is the compatibility factor of the permutations of bitonic sorting. The resulting network is cheaper and self-routed, and realizes any permutation in $O(\log^2 N)$ passes. It also realizes the permutations of bitonic sorting and tree computations in a single pass.

Along the same lines, the leftmost column can be replaced by the three compatibility factors (i.e., interconnections) that have been identified as needed by many interesting problem areas. Some multiplexers can be added to choose one of the three interconnections as required. Then every one of the computation areas discussed in this paper and shown to need a compatible family of permutations can be run efficiently on the resulting self-routed network.

§7. References

[1] D. P. Agrawal and J. -S. Leu, "Dynamic accessibility testing and path length optimization of multistage interconnection networks," *IEEE Trans. Comput.*, C-34, pp. 255–266, Mar. 1985.

[2] M. Ajtai, J. Kanlos and E. Szemeredi, "Sorting in clog *n* parallel steps," *Combinatorica* 3, pp. 1-19, 1983.

[3] K. E. Batcher, "Sorting networks and their applications," *1968 Spring Joint Comput. Conf., AFIPS Conf.* Vol. 32, Washington, D.C.: Thompson, 1968, pp. 307–314.

[4] J. Beetem, M. Denneau, and D. Weingarten, "The GF11 Supercomputer," *The 12th ann. Int'l Sump. on Comp. Arch.*, 1985, pp. 108–113.

[5] V. E. Benes, *Mathematical theory on connecting networks and telephone traffic,* Academic Press, New York, 1965.

[6] L. N. Bhuyan and D. P. Agrawal, "Design and performance of generalized interconnection networks," *IEEE Trans. Comput.*, pp. 1081–1090, Dec. 1983.

[7] A. Brandt, "Multigrid Solvers on parallel computers," in *Elliptic Problem Solvers* (M. Schultz, ed.), New York, pp. 39–83, 1981.

[8] T. F. Chan and Y. Saad, "Multigrid algorithms on the Hypercube multiprocessor," *IEEE Trans. Comput.*, vol. C-35, pp. 969–977, Nov. 1986.

[9] T. Feng, "A survey of interconnection networks," *Computer*, Vol. 14, pp. 12–27, Dec. 1981.

[10] D. K. Lawrie, "Access and alignment of data in an arrary processor," *IEEE Trans. Comput.*, C-24, pp. 1145–1155, Dec. 1975.

[11] K. Y. Lee, "On the rearrangeability of $2(\log_2 N) - 1$ stage permutation networks," *IEEE Trans. Comput.*, C-34, pp. 412–425, May 1985.

[12] K. Y. Lee, "A Nerw Benes Network Control Algorithm," *IEEE Trans. Comput.*, C-36, pp. 768–772, May 1987.

[13] J. Lenfant, "Parallel permutations of data: A Benes network control algorithm for frequently used permutations," *IEEE Trans. Comput.*, C-27, pp. 637–647, July 1978.

[14] G. F. Lev, N. Pippenger and L. G. Valiant, "A fast parallel algorithm for routing in permutation networks," *IEEE Trans. Comput.*, C-,30 pp. 93–100, Feb. 1981.

[15] D. Nassimi ans S. Sahni, "A self-routing Benes network and parallel permutation algorithms," *IEEE Trans. Comput.*, C-30, pp. 332–340, May 1981.

[16] D. C. Opferman and N. T. Tsao-Wu, "On a class of rearrangeable switching networks, Parts I and II," *Bell Syst. Tech. J.*, pp. 1579–1618, May-June 1971.

[17] M. C. Pease, "The indirect binary n-cube multiprocessor array," *IEEE Trans. Comput.*, C-26, pp. 458–473, May 1976.

[18] H. J. Siegel and S. Smith, "Study of multistage interconnection networks," *Proc. Fifth Annual Symp. Comp. Arch.*, pp. 223–229, Apr. 1978.

[19] H. S. Stone, "Parallel processing with the perfect shuffle," *IEEE Trans. Comput.*, C-20, pp. 153–161, Feb. 1971.

[20] Q. F. Stout, "Hypercubes and Pyramids," in *Pyramidal Systems for Computer Vision*, edited by V. Cantoni and S. Levialdi, Springer-Verlag, Berlin, 1986.

[21] T. H. Szymanski and V. C. Hamacher, "On the permutation Capibility of multistage interconnection networks," *IEEE Trans. Comput.*, C-36, pp. 810–822, July 1987.

[22] A. Waksman, "A permutation network," *JACM*, Vol. 15, No. 1 pp. 159–163, Jan 1968.

[23] C. Wu and T. Feng, "On a class of multistage interconnection networks," *IEEE Trans. Comput.*, C-29, pp. 694–702, Aug. 1980.

[24] A. Youssef, *Properties of multistage interconnection networks,* Ph.D. dissertation, Princeton University, Feb. 1988.

Randomized Parallel Communications on an Extension of the Omega Network

DEBASIS MITRA

AT&T Bell Laboratories, Murray Hill, New Jersey

AND

RANDALL A. CIESLAK

University of California, Berkeley, California

Abstract. Parallel communication algorithms and networks are central to large-scale parallel computing and, also, data communications. This paper identifies adverse source-destination traffic patterns and proposes a scheme for obtaining relief by means of randomized routing of packets on simple extensions of the well-known omega networks. Valiant and Aleliunas have demonstrated randomized algorithms, for a certain context which we call nonrenewal, that complete the communication task in time $O(\log N)$ with overwhelming probability, where N is the number of sources and destinations. Our scheme has advantages because it uses switches of fixed degree, requires no scheduling, and, for the nonrenewal context, is as good in proven performance. The main advantage of our scheme comes when we consider the renewal context in which packets are generated at the sources continually and asynchronously. Our algorithm extends naturally from the nonrenewal context. In the analysis in the renewal context we, first, explicitly identify the maximum traffic intensities in the internal links of the extended omega networks over all source-destination traffic specifications that satisfy loose bounds. Second, the benefits of randomization on the stability of the network are identified. Third, exact results, for certain restricted models for sources and transmission, and approximate analytic results, for quite general models, are derived for the mean delays. These results show that, in the stable regime, the maximum mean time from source to destination is asymptotically proportional to $\log N$. Numerical results are presented.

Categories and Subject Descriptors: C.1.2. [**Processor Architectures**]: Multiple Data Stream Architectures—*interconnection architectures*; C.2.1. [**Computer-Communication Networks**]: Network Architecture and Design—*distributed networks*; D.4.8 [**Operating Systems**]: Performance—*queuing theory*; G.3 [**Mathematics of Computing**]: Probability and Statistics—*probabilistic algorithms* (*including Monte Carlo*)

General Terms: Algorithms, Design, Performance, Theory, Verification

Additional Key Words and Phrases: Asynchronous communications, renewal point processes, routing

1. Introduction

In parallel computing and in data communications an important cost in time and hardware is in the communication of packets from sources to destinations. In computing, these sources and destinations, of which we assume there are N each,

Partial results have been presented at the 1986 International Conference on Parallel Processing.

The research of R. A. Cieslak was supported by Joint Services Electronic Program contract F49620-79-C-0178 and Office of Naval Research contract N00014-80-C-0507.

Authors addresses: D. Mitra, AT&T Bell Laboratories, Room 2C 174, 600 Mountain Avenue, Murray Hill, NJ 07974-2070; R. A. Cieslak, Department of Electrical Engineering and Computer Sciences, University of California, Berkeley, Berkeley, CA 94720.

may be processors, as in message-passing architectures, or processors and memory modules, as in shared memory architectures [11]. In all of the above the communication medium is an interconnection network, for example, the hypercube, shuffle-exchange [3], or banyan [10], of which the omega [22] is a particular case. With the advent of very large parallel computers [8, 11, 27], there is a recurring concern that particular, not well-understood, source-destination traffic patterns may cause unbalanced usage of the internal links of the ierconnection network and thereby severely degrade its overall performance. This paper presents results that identify the effects of adverse traffic patterns and proposes a scheme for obtaining relief from randomized routing on networks that are simple extensions of the omega network. The biggest of the extended omega networks that we consider is termed the fully extended omega network, and it is less than twice as big as the omega network.

Randomized parallel communications were pioneered by Valiant [28, 32–34] who, in 1981, demonstrated, in a certain context that we call nonrenewal, a probabilistic algorithm that completed the communications task on the hypercube in time $O(\log N)$ with overwhelming probability. This performance was superior to any known before. However, the hypercube is complex hardware, since the degree of the switches used is $O(\log N)$ and therefore unbounded. For the same nonrenewal context, Aleliunas [1] in 1982 gave a randomized algorithm based on prioritized scheduling at each queue and showed, by elegant analysis, that it achieves the same performance on the shuffle-exchange network, which has switches of fixed degree.

The randomized algorithm that we propose requires no scheduling—the discipline throughout is first-come, first-served—and the extended omega networks use switches of fixed degree. For the fully extended omega network, and for the same nonrenewal context, we prove that our scheme has as good delay characteristics as have been proved for Valiant's scheme.

The main advantage of our scheme comes when we consider the renewal context in which packets are generated at the sources continually and asynchronously. In this context it is possible to investigate the stationary throughput-delay characteristics for various traffic patterns, and we believe these characteristics are of fundamental importance in communications. Now, Valiant's and Aleliunas's schemes have not been defined for this context, and there are difficult choices in making the transition. The scheme that we give carries over naturally from the nonrenewal context. It is important to note that schemes based on the shuffle-exchange network considered by Aleliunas cannot have throughput-delay performance comparable to our scheme simply because it lacks the pipeline that the extended omega networks offer. Correspondingly, our scheme is not tied exclusively to extensions of the omega network, which we have chosen so as to be specific, and any of the other pipelined networks to which it is isomorphic [26] can serve as well. We show, for the renewal context and various stochastic models for the sources and link transmission times, that the stationary expected time from source to destination is asymptotically proportional to $\log N$ on the fully extended omega network. The constant of proportionality remains fairly flat initially and then rapidly goes to ∞ as the traffic intensities at the sources approach a stability boundary.

Let us now be more specific, beginning with the hardware requirements for the extended omega network. The well-known [4, 10, 19, 22, 26] omega network allows switches of various fixed degrees, but we assume throughout that the switches have degree 2. All our results extend easily to the case of switches of degree k, where k is any fixed integer. We also assume $N = 2^n$. The omega networks typically have n stages, each stage consisting of $N/2$ switches and N links, each with a queue.

The wiring of links between consecutive stages is uniform across the network. The extended omega networks are obtained by simply concatenating r, $1 \leq r \leq n - 1$, additional stages to the n stages of the omega network; r is the degree of extension. The fully extended omega network corresponds to $r = n - 1$. Every route from a source to a destination uses $n + r$ switches and links, and redundancies in routing are introduced where none exists in the omega network.

The randomized routing algorithm requires each packet to be given a statistically independent scattering ticket. A *distributed switching* rule uses the ticket to implement the routing; the rule inherits the simplicity that switching in the omega network has. Details are provided in Section 2.3.

The specific communication tasks considered in the nonrenewal context are *partial h-relations* [34] in which initially each source has at most h packets, with no destination occurring on more than h packets. The task is completed when all packets are delivered to their correct destinations. The assumptions in the nonrenewal context are that all the link queues in the network are initially empty and that no packets arrive at the sources while the task is in progress; the assumptions may be relaxed but must ensure that no queuing delays are incurred by the packets participating in the task on account of any other packets. Our results for the nonrenewal context are given in Section 3.

In the renewal context we assume that the packets at each source form stationary renewal processes. The specific framework for the analysis is the *partial λ-relations* in which the intensity, or average rate, at each source is no more than λ and the intensity at each destination is no more than λ. Our results for the renewal context are given in Section 4.

In both the partial h-relations and the partial λ-relations there are no direct specifications on the traffic from particular sources to particular destinations. The delay analysis must, if only implicitly, identify and take into account those specifications that cause maximal delay. Theorem 2 in Section 4.1 gives an explicit characterization of the extremal traffic in the internal links of the extended omega networks.

The time to complete partial h-relations in the nonrenewal context are bounded by quantities that are proportional to h. The mean delay for partial λ-relations in the renewal context is nonlinear in λ and rapidly goes to ∞ as λ approaches the stability boundary. A single unstable link queue causes unbounded mean delay to packet classes with routes that include the affected link. Randomization has the effect of extending the region of stability. This is discussed in Section 4.2.

We have made an effort to give our results with regard to their dependence on the degree of randomization as measured by r. One reason for this is that a higher value of r also means, of course, an increased investment in hardware. A reasonable conclusion of this study is that the trade-off is tilted in favor of maximum randomization. It should be mentioned that this conclusion is derived from a worst-case analysis. An average-case analysis will give a different trade-off.

Section 5 concludes by giving some further directions of future investigations that appear important to us.

2. *The Extended Omega Network and Randomized Routing*

The omega network and indexing systems for its links are well known [26]. Nonetheless, in Section 2.1 we describe the specific indexing system that is followed here, since the subsequent traffic analysis makes frequent references to it. Section 2.2 is a brief introduction to congestion in the omega network. The

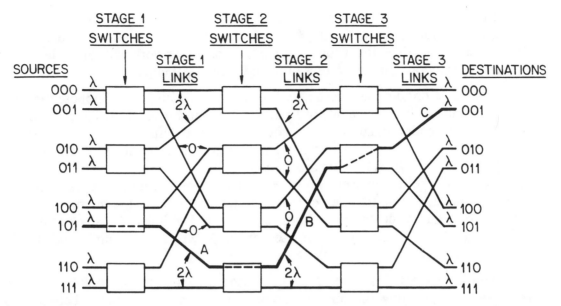

FIG. 1. An omega network, $n = 3$. The route from source 1, 0, 1 to destination 0, 0, 1 is shown by the thick line. Links A, B, C are, respectively, indexed $(1; 1, 1, 0)$, $(2; 0, 1, 1)$, $(3; 0, 0, 1)$. (For explanation of the inscriptions on the links, see Example 1, Section 2.2.)

extended omega network is described in Section 2.3, together with its indexing system, which is largely a carryover from the omega network. The implementation of randomized routing on it is described there.

2.1 THE OMEGA NETWORK. The omega network is a periodic structure of switches and links for connecting $N = 2^n$ sources to N destinations. There are n identical stages, numbered $1-n$ with stage 1 leftmost. (See Figure 1 for an example with $N = 8$.) The ports on both sides of each switch are addressed identically, as are the ports of switches in different stages, with all port addresses being n-bit binary sequences $a_n, \ldots, a_1$, with zero at the top. Once a particular switch has been identified, a shorthand convention for specifying its ports consists of calling the upper ports 0 and the lower ports 1, which are really the least significant bits of their full addresses. Such a shorthand specification is useful in describing the switching rules for packets. Packets entering a switch can be routed to either output port of the switch.

Each link is given an address with the format $(i; a_n, \ldots, a_1)$, where i denotes the stage to which it belongs and $a_n, \ldots, a_1$ is the address of the port in the switch at the $(i + 1)$th stage where the link terminates. The wiring in the omega network connects output ports $a_n, \ldots, a_1$ at the ith stage to the input port $a_1, a_n, \ldots, a_2$ at the $(i + 1)$th stage. The link that makes this connection is, by our previously stated rule, $(i; a_1, a_n, \ldots, a_2)$. The net effect is that a packet on link $(i; a_n, \ldots, a_1)$ on entering a switch in the $(i + 1)$th stage is switched to output port $b \in \{0, 1\}$, and leaves on the link $(i + 1; b, a_n, \ldots, a_2)$.

Each link is equipped with a queue at its originating port, which for the purposes of this paper is of unlimited capacity.

The routing in the network can now be described simply. A packet originating at source $s_n, \ldots, s_1$ with destination $d_n, \ldots, d_1$ is switched to output port d_i in the switch at stage i. This packet passes through the links $(0; s_n, \ldots, s_1) \rightarrow (1; d_1, s_n, \ldots, s_2) \rightarrow (2; d_2, d_1, s_n, \ldots, s_3) \rightarrow \cdots \rightarrow (n; d_n, \ldots, d_1)$.

2.2 CONGESTION IN THE OMEGA NETWORK. Large omega networks achieve massive concentrations of traffic in its internal links for certain source-destination traffic specifications. The following example for a small network will suffice here. Later results elaborate on the features observed here and their effects.

Example 1. Consider the omega network in Figure 1 with $N = 8$. Suppose each source transmits at the average rate of λ packets per unit time, and, on the average, source s_3, s_2, s_1 sends a fraction $\alpha(s_3, s_2)$ of its packets to destination s_1, s_2, s_3 and the remainder to $\bar{s}_1$, s_2, s_3, where the bar denotes bit reversal. The numbers $\alpha(0, 0)$, $\alpha(0, 1)$, $\alpha(1, 0)$, $\alpha(1, 1)$ are arbitrary in $[0, 1]$.

Note that each destination receives packets at the average rate of λ packets per unit time. The resulting intensities, or average rates, on traffic on the internal links of the network are as shown on the links in Figure 1. The links of stages 1 and 2 fall into one of two groups, one composed of links that carry no traffic and the remainder that have traffic intensity 2λ.

2.3 THE EXTENDED OMEGA NETWORK, SCATTERING TICKETS, AND ROUTING. We propose augmenting the omega network by a *scattering network* between the sources and the omega network. The scattering network is made of r stages, $1 \le r \le n - 1$, and the stages of the scattering network are identical to the stages of the omega network. At each stage of the scattering network, traffic entering a switch is, on the average, routed to each output port evenly. Scattering is accomplished by assigning a *scattering ticket* to each packet at the source. Each scattering ticket is a binary r-tuple $c_r, \ldots, c_1$, in which each element is obtained from the result of a completely independent trial with equiprobable outcomes. A packet with scattering ticket $c_r, \ldots, c_1$ is routed to output port c_i at the ith stage of the scattering network. Thereafter, the packet is routed through the omega network as before.

The *extended omega network* is obtained by concatenating the scattering network and the omega network. It consists of $n + r$ stages. Figure 2 shows such a network with $n = 3$, as in Figure 1, and $r = 1$.

The following fact follows directly from the description given earlier of a single stage of the network. Links in the extended omega network are defined as before.

FACT. Every packet with source $s_n, \ldots, s_1$, destination $d_n, \ldots, d_1$, and scattering ticket $c_r, \ldots, c_1$ is routed through the following links:

$$(i; c_i, c_{i-1}, \ldots, c_1, s_n, \ldots, s_{i+1}), \qquad 1 \le i \le r, \qquad (2.1a)$$

$$(i; d_{i-r}, \ldots, d_1, c_r, \ldots, c_1, s_n, \ldots, s_{i+1}), \qquad r + 1 \le i \le n - 1, \quad (2.1b)$$

$$(i; d_{i-r}, \ldots, d_1, c_r, \ldots, c_{i-n+1}), \qquad n \le i \le n + r - 1. \quad (2.1c)$$

Note that, if $r = n - 1$, then the set in (2.1b) is empty. The final link used is obviously

$$(n + r; d_n, \ldots, d_1). \qquad (2.1d)$$

We make use of the Fact on several occasions to infer the traffic carried by a particular link. The following equivalent repreesntation is also useful. For each packet, define

$$\mathbf{R} \triangleq d_n, \ldots, d_1, c_r, \ldots, c_1, s_n, \ldots, s_1. \qquad (2.2)$$

Now consider a window of width n, that is, it exposes n consecutive numbers of $\mathbf{R}$. The window therefore has $n + r + 1$ positions. Number these positions 0 to $n + r$,

SOURCES   DESTINATIONS

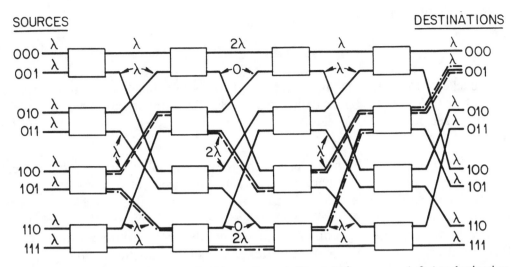

FIG. 2. An extended omega network with $n = 3$, $r = 1$. The path from source 1, 0, 1 to destination 0, 0, 1 of packets with scattering ticket $c_1 = 1$ is shown by chained line, and of packets with $c_1 = 0$ by dashed line. The inscriptions on links are their traffic intensities for Example 1 (see also Example 2, Section 4.1).

where position 0 is rightmost and an increment in position corresponds to sliding the window by one unit to the left. A statement equivalent to the Fact is: The link used by the packet at the ith stage, $1 \le i \le n + r$, has address given by the values in **R** that are exposed by the window at the ith position.

The above facts on link usage are consistent with the following switching rule that was mentioned earlier: While the packet is at the switch in the ith stage, route it to the output port

$$
\begin{aligned}
c_i, & \quad 1 \le i \le r, \\
d_{i-r}, & \quad r + 1 \le i \le n + r.
\end{aligned}
\tag{2.3}
$$

3. *Traffic Analysis: The Nonrenewal Case*

With randomized routing, as described above, in extended omega networks parameterized by r, the degree of extension, we consider the time to deliver packets from their sources to their respective destinations in the nonrenewal context. The probabilistic bound given here holds for *partial h-relations* in which initially each source has at most h packets, with no destination occurring on more than h packets. The analysis also makes use of *full h-relations*, in which initially there are exactly h packets at each source, with each destination occurring on h packets. The assumption is made in this section that each link transmits one packet in unit time.

3.1 NONREPEATING, NONOVERTAKING. The extended omega networks are *not* nonrepeating and *not* nonovertaking. (The nonrepeating and nonovertaking properties are identical. The former term is used in [34], while the latter is well established in the literature on network of queues [9, 14, 35].) That is, it is possible for two packets to use a common link at stage i_1, different links at stage i_2 and a common link at stage i_3, for some i_1, i_2, i_3 where $1 \le i_1 < i_2 < i_3$.

Note, however, that there is partial nonovertaking. To see this, split the extended omega network with $(n + r)$ stages into two halves. From the Fact in Section 2.3, it is easy to see that the isolated first half is nonovertaking. Likewise, the isolated second half is also nonovertaking.

Specificially, with

$$\hat{\imath} \triangleq \left\lfloor \frac{n+r}{2} \right\rfloor, \qquad (3.1)$$

each packet's transit through links in stages 1 to $\hat{\imath}$ is called its Phase 1 and its transit from stage $(\hat{\imath} + 1)$ to $(n + r)$ is called its Phase 2. The time to complete each phase by all packets in a partial h-relation is, in turn, bounded below with the help of the nonovertaking property in each phase.

3.2 BOUNDS. Consider first Phase 1; the results for Phase 2 are almost identical. The routes of two separate packets X and Y given, respectively, by $\mathbf{R}^X$ and $\mathbf{R}^Y$ (see (2.2)) are said to intersect in Phase 1 if at least one link in stages 1–$\hat{\imath}$ is common to both routes. Now let X be a marked packet and Y any other packet in a partial h-relation. In Appendix A it is shown that the two routes intersect in Phase 1 if and only if Y's scattering ticket $\mathbf{c}^Y$ belongs to the set $S(\mathbf{d}^Y, \mathbf{s}^Y, \mathbf{R}^X)$, which, as the notation implies, is defined by Y's destination and source, and X's route. A precise definition of the set may be found in Appendix A.

Fix the marked packet X *and* its route $\mathbf{R}^X$. For Y and Z, two distinct packets separate from X, we claim that the probability that Z's route intersects with that of X in Phase 1, conditional on the knowledge that Y's route does (or does not) intersect X's route in Phase 1 is the same as without the conditioning. That is, the two trials are independent. To see this, recall that each packet is given a scattering ticket in which each element is generated from the outcome of the toss of a memoryless coin. Hence,

$$\Pr[\mathbf{c}^Z \in S(\mathbf{d}^Z, \mathbf{s}^Z, \mathbf{R}^X) \,|\, \mathbf{c}^Y \in S(\mathbf{d}^Y, \mathbf{s}^Y, \mathbf{R}^X)] = \Pr[\mathbf{c}^Z \in S(\mathbf{d}^Z, \mathbf{s}^Z, \mathbf{R}^X)], \quad (3.2)$$

and the assertion is proved. Note that this holds regardless of the value of r.

It may be helpful to distinguish between the independence being asserted here and the dependence between "Y's route intersects X's route," "X's route intersects Z's route," and "Z's route intersects X's route." From the outcome of the first two trials it is possible to infer information on the coincidence of the scattering tickets of Y and Z, thus making these trials dependent.

Now consider the set of at most $(Nh - 1)$ trials, each trial corresponding to a distinct packet other than X in a partial h-relation, with success and failure as the possible outcomes of each trial, and success in a trial indicating that the route of the corresponding packet intersects the route of X in Phase 1. By the argument given above, the probability that a trial has a particular outcome conditioned on the outcome of all the remaining trials is the same as without the conditioning.

We thus have that the set of trials are Bernoulli trials, with possibly unequal probabilities of success in the trials. It is now convenient to inflate the number of Bernoulli trials to Nh by introducing dummy trials in each of which the probability of success is zero.

In Appendix A it is proved that among the packets other than X in a partial h-relation, the expected number of packets with routes that intersect the route of X in Phase 1 is at most $\sigma h/2$, where

$$\sigma = r - 1 + 2^{1 + \lfloor (n-r)/2 \rfloor}. \qquad (3.3)$$

Note that in the fully extended omega network $r = n - 1$ and $\sigma = n$.

Hence, in the context of the Bernoulli trials, the sum over all trials of the probability of success in each trial is at most $\sigma h/2$. From a result due to Hoeffding [13], which is quoted by Valiant and Brebner [34] and which applies to just such a set of Bernoulli trials with an accompanying bound on the sum of probabilities of success, for any $\Delta \geq \sigma h/2$,

$$\Pr[\text{Number of successes in } Nh \text{ trials} \geq \Delta] \leq B\left(\Delta, Nh, \frac{\sigma}{2N}\right), \quad (3.4)$$

where $B(m, M, p)$ is the probability of at least m successes in M Bernoulli trials with probability p of success in each trial.

Now, as a consequence of the nonovertaking property alluded to in Section 3.1, X's queuing delay in Phase 1 is at most equal to the number of packets that intersect its route in Phase 1. Hence,

$$\Pr[\{X\text{'s queuing delay in Phase 1}\} \geq \Delta] \leq B\left(\Delta, Nh, \frac{\sigma}{2N}\right), \quad (3.5)$$

for any $\Delta \geq \sigma h/2$.

Since there are at most Nh packets to consider, the probability that at least one of them suffers a queuing delay of at least Δ is bounded by Nh times the quantity on the right in (3.5). This is true even if the random variables denoting queuing delays are dependent. Finally, noting that for any packet the total time to complete Phase 1 is its queuing delay plus its own time for transmission, which is $\lfloor (n + r)/2 \rfloor$, we obtain

$$\Pr\left[\text{time to complete Phase 1} \geq \frac{n + r}{2} + \Delta\right] \leq Nh\, B\left(\Delta, Nh, \frac{\sigma}{2N}\right), \quad (3.6)$$

for any $\Delta \geq \sigma h/2$.

Now, Chernoff's bound [7] states that for $\Delta \geq \sigma h/2$,

$$B\left(\Delta, Nh, \frac{\sigma}{2N}\right) \leq \left(\frac{e\sigma h}{2\Delta}\right)^{\Delta} e^{-\sigma h/2}. \quad (3.7)$$

Hence, from (3.6) and (3.7), for any $\Delta \geq \sigma h/2$,

$$\Pr\left[\text{time to complete Phase 1} \geq \frac{n + r}{2} + \Delta\right] \leq Nh\left(\frac{e\sigma h}{2\Delta}\right)^{\Delta} e^{-\sigma h/2}. \quad (3.8)$$

An almost identical statement holds for Phase 2. However, when counting the number of intersections, as in (3.3), we exclude the final, $(n + r)$th, stage, since the delays encountered in this stage are more predictable and hence may be counted separately. For any $\Delta \geq \sigma h/2$, where σ is in (3.3),

$$\Pr\left[\text{time to complete Phase 2} \geq \frac{n + r + 1}{2} + h + \Delta\right] \leq Nh\left(\frac{e\sigma h}{2\Delta}\right)^{\Delta} e^{-\sigma h/2}. \quad (3.9)$$

Equations (3.8) and (3.9) represent our main result in the nonrenewal context and they hold for all values of N and r.

To obtain asymptotic (as $n \to \infty$) results, we distinguish between

$$r = n - 1$$

and

$$r = \gamma n, \quad \text{where } \gamma, \ \gamma < 1 \text{ is fixed.}$$

In the first case we have already noted that $\sigma = n$. In the second case, from (3.3), $\sigma = O(N^{(1-\gamma)/2})$.

In summary we obtain from (3.8) and (3.9) and appropriate selections of Δ:

THEOREM 1

(i) *For any $\Delta \geq \sigma h/2$, where σ is given in (3.3),*

$$Pr\left[\left\{time\ to\ complete\ each\ phase\right\} \geq \frac{n+r+1}{2} + h + \Delta\right] \leq Nh\left(\frac{e\sigma h}{2\Delta}\right)^{\Delta} e^{-\sigma h/2}.$$

(ii) *For $r = n - 1$, each phase in any partial h-relation is completed in time $O(\log N)$ with overwhelming probability. In particular, for any $K \geq e$,*

$$Pr\left[\left\{time\ to\ complete\ each\ phase\right\} \geq \frac{n+r+1}{2} + h + Khn\right] \leq hN^{-(Kh-1)}. \quad (3.10)$$

For $r = \gamma n$, γ fixed and less than unity, each phase in any partial h-relation is completed in time $O(N^{(1-\gamma)/2})$ with overwhelming probability.

4. Traffic Analysis: The Renewal Case

In the renewal context, at each source $s_n, \ldots, s_1$ the packets to be delivered to destination $d_n, \ldots, d_1$ form a stationary point process with mean rate, or intensity, $\lambda(s_n, \ldots, s_1 : d_n, \ldots, d_1)$. A particular case is Poisson processes at the sources. The collection of these traffic intensities over all sources and destinations constitute the *source-destination traffic specification*. At its source, each packet is given a scattering ticket and then routed through the extended omega network exactly as described in Section 2. Unlike the treatment in Section 3, here we allow for statistical fluctuations in the time required by each link to transmit a packet, although special consideration is given to the case of constant link transmission time. These fluctuations may be significant on account of the congestion dependence of the time for the protocol between the link's source and destination and for the acknowledgment of received packets, time-sharing of the switches' hardware between links, variations in actual transmission time and packet length, and variations in the time for queue management. We assume that when the link transmission times are random, they are, for all links and packets, mutually independent, independent of the traffic, and picked from a common distribution with mean 1.

Section 4.1 considers all source-destination traffic specifications that satisfy full λ-relations, which are the natural extensions to the renewal context of the full *h*-relations. A result there specifies the extremal traffic intensities that may be encountered in the various stages of a particular route, for various degrees of extensions of the omega network. Section 4.2 gives the condition on λ for the link queues to be stable over all source-destination traffic specifications satisfying the full λ-relations. Section 4.3 calculates the effect of r, the randomization parameter, on the maximum mean time from source to destination of packet classes, where the maximization is over all full λ-relations. However, in this section only Poisson sources and exponentially distributed link transmission times are allowed. For the case of the fully extended omega network, Section 4.4 gives a program for the approximate analysis of mean delays for general stationary renewal processes at the sources and general distributions of the link transmission times, including the special case of constant transmission time. Simple recursive formulas for the descriptors of the link traffic and their asymptotic (for large n) counterparts are obtained. The understanding thus gained is used to incorporate the results of simple simulations in calculations for the mean delay for large fully extended omega networks.

In a partial λ-relation

$$\sum_{d_n,\ldots,d_1} \lambda(s_n, \ldots, s_1; d_n, \ldots, d_1) \leq \lambda, \qquad \forall s_n, \ldots, s_1 \qquad (4.1a)$$

and

$$\sum_{s_n,\ldots,s_1} \lambda(s_n, \ldots, s_1; d_n, \ldots, d_1) \leq \lambda, \qquad \forall d_n, \ldots, d_1. \qquad (4.1b)$$

In full λ-relations, (4.1) holds with equality. Hereafter, in this section we exclusively consider full λ-relations, since the results on delay statistics for it are obvious bounds for the partial λ-relations. It should be noted that, although full λ-relations are analytically convenient, the practical situation is more likely to be described initially by partial λ-relations.

4.1 LINK TRAFFIC INTENSITIES. Here $t(i; a_n, \ldots, a_1)$ denotes the traffic intensity, that is, the mean number of carried packets per unit time, on link $(i; a_n, \ldots, a_1)$. Also, $T(\lambda, n, r)$ denotes the extremal traffic intensity over all links and all traffic specifications satisfying the full λ-relations; that is,

$$T(\lambda, n, r) \triangleq \max_{\text{full }\lambda\text{-relation}} \max_{i:1\leq i\leq(n+r)} \max_{a_n,\ldots,a_1} t(i; a_n, \ldots, a_1). \qquad (4.2)$$

We say that the traffic is *symmetric* if the traffic intensity is identical in all links of the network.

We find useful the notion of traffic class. Each traffic class is indexed by source, destination, and scattering ticket, that is, by the binary $(2n + r)$-tuple $(s_n, \ldots, s_1; d_n, \ldots, d_1; c_r, \ldots, c_1)$. Each packet that arrives at source $s_n, \ldots, s_1$, with destination $d_n, \ldots, d_1$, on being given its ticket $c_r, \ldots, c_1$ belongs to the obvious class for the duration of its transit through the extended omega network. Obviously, each class has its own unique route through the network.

Each traffic class has an associated traffic intensity, and quite obviously the traffic intensity of the class indexed by $s_n, \ldots, s_1; d_n, \ldots, d_1; c_r, \ldots, c_1$ is

$$\frac{1}{2^r} \lambda(s_n, \ldots, s_1; d_n, \ldots, d_1). \qquad (4.3)$$

The traffic intensity $t(i; a_n, \ldots, a_1)$ is obtained by summing the traffic intensity of all classes with routes that include the link $(i; a_n, \ldots, a_1)$. The Fact in Section 2.3 may be used to calculate this quantity.

The following theorem and its corollary are a summary of our results on the extremal link traffic intensities, both as seen by a packet following a specific route and as seen by an independent observer of traffic in the extended omega network.

THEOREM 2

(i) *for full λ-relations and for all binary n-tuples* $(a_n, \ldots, a_1)$,

$$t(i; a_n, \ldots, a_1) = \lambda, \qquad 1 \leq i \leq r \quad and \quad n \leq i \leq n + r - 1. \qquad (4.4)$$

If $r = n - 1$, *then the above specifies the traffic intensities on all links of the extended omega network. If* $r < n - 1$,

$$t(i; a_n, \ldots, a_1) \leq \lambda 2^{min(i-r,n-i)}, \qquad r + 1 \leq i \leq n - 1. \qquad (4.5)$$

(ii) *If* $r < n - 1$, *then there are source-destination traffic specifications satisfying the full λ-relations such that the traffic intensity on each of the links used in the*

261

route followed by a particular class is given by (4.4) *and* (4.5), *with equality holding in* (4.5).

The proof of Theorem 2 is in Appendix B. A corollary to the theorem is obtained by observing that

$$\max_{i:r+1 \le i \le n-1} 2^{\min(i-r,n-1)} = 2^{\lfloor(n-r)/2\rfloor}, \tag{4.6}$$

and that the stages where the link traffic intensity is maximum are

$$\hat{i} = \frac{n+r}{2} \qquad \text{if } (n+r) \text{ is even,} \tag{4.7a}$$

$$\hat{i}_{1,2} = \frac{n+r \mp 1}{2} \qquad \text{if } (n+r) \text{ is odd.} \tag{4.7b}$$

COROLLARY

(i)

$$T(\lambda, n, r) = \lambda 2^{\lfloor(n-r)/2\rfloor}. \tag{4.8}$$

(ii) *The traffic is symmetric for all source-destination traffic specifications satisfying the full λ-relations if and only if $r = n - 1$.*

Note that the above theorem applies as well to the nonrenewal case of Section 3 provided only that "traffic" replaces "traffic intensity." In particular, all the terms appearing on the right in (4.4) and (4.5) may be summed to give a bound, like the one given in (3.3), on the expected number of packets with routes that intersect the route of a particular packet in a full h-relation. However, this bound is worse by a factor of about 2 than the bound derived from (3.3).

Example 2. In Appendix B on the proof of Theorem 2, a class B of source-destination traffic specifications is defined to illustrate statement (ii) of the theorem. For these specifications, traffic classes have either zero traffic intensity or else use links that have the maximum traffic intensities allowed by statement (i). The source-destination traffic specification given in Example 1 in Section 2.2 is a member of the class B. The traffic intensities resulting from randomized routing for this specification are marked on the links in Figure 2.

4.2 STABILITY WITH RESPECT TO FULL λ-RELATIONS. The stability condition of interest here is that at each link the traffic intensity is less than the mean link transmission time of packets. When this time is constant or exponentially distributed, the condition is known to be equivalent to various natural definitions of stability, and recent results [6] suggest that this is also true for a broad class of distributions. Our primary interest is in *stability with respect to full λ-relations*, that is, stability for all source-destination traffic specifications that satisfy the full λ-relation. From the Corollary to Theorem 2, the condition for stability with respect to full λ-relations is

$$\lambda 2^{\lfloor(n-r)/2\rfloor} < 1. \tag{4.9}$$

For the omega network $r = 0$, and the stability condition is $\lambda < 1/\sqrt{N}$ if $\log_2 N$ is even, and $\lambda < \sqrt{2/N}$ if $\log_2 N$ is odd. For the fully extended omega network $r = n - 1$, and the stability condition is $\lambda < 1$.

4.3 MEAN DELAY FOR VARIOUS DEGREES OF EXTENSIONS OF THE OMEGA NETWORK. The object here is to use the results in Section 4.1 on link traffic intensities to obtain qualitative information on the mean delays seen by packets. We are, once again, primarily interested in the maximum mean class delays that are possible in full λ-relations, and the extent to which relief is gained from the combination of randomized routing and various degrees of extensions of the omega network. The dependence on λ is, of course, of interest.

Here we make the restrictive assumption that the packets at the sources form Poisson processes and that the link transmission times are random variables with exponential distributions. Any one distribution is hard to justify; the exponential has the advantage that exact delay statistics are simple to obtain. Also, we shall see that in the framework of Section 4.5, where these restrictive assumptions are removed, (i) the qualitative dependence of delays on λ is relatively insensitive to the transmission time distribution, and (ii) the exponential distribution gives delay statistics that are upper bounds on statistics for other distributions with coefficient of variation less than 1, which is more typical, for the case of Poisson sources.[1]

The well-known result [17] that makes the problem tractable is that, in equilibrium, the joint distribution of packets of all classes and in all links is of the same form as if the arrival processes to the links were Poisson. Therefore [17]

$$W(i; a_n, \ldots, a_1) = \text{mean queuing delay at link } (i; a_n, \ldots, a_1),$$

$$= \frac{1}{1 - t(i; a_n, \ldots, a_1)} - 1, \tag{4.10}$$

where $t(\ )$ is the traffic intensity on the link.

For each class, let

$$D(\text{class}) \triangleq \text{mean time from source to destination for class packets},$$

$$= \sum_{\text{link} \in \text{class route}} \{W(\text{link}) + 1\}. \tag{4.11}$$

As usual, we include the last link, that is, the $(n + r)$th link that connects to the destination, in the route. Finally, let

$$D \triangleq \max_{\text{full } \lambda\text{-relation}} \max_{\text{class}} D(\text{class}). \tag{4.12}$$

We know from statement (ii) of Theorem 2 that there exist traffic classes that use links having traffic intensities as high as that allowed by statement (i). Hence,

PROPOSITION. *With randomized routing in the extended omega network with $n + r$ stages, $1 \leq r \leq n - 1$,*

$$D = \frac{2r + 1}{1 - \lambda} + 2 \sum_{i=1}^{(n-r-1)/2} \frac{1}{1 - \lambda 2^i} \qquad \text{if } (n + r) \text{ is odd,}$$

$$= \frac{2r + 1}{1 - \lambda} + \frac{1}{1 - \lambda 2^{(n-r)/2}} + 2 \sum_{i=1}^{(n-r-2)/2} \frac{1}{1 - \lambda 2^i} \qquad \text{if } (n + r) \text{ is even.} \tag{4.13}$$

Figure 3 plots D against λ for various values of r when $n = 10$. This important figure indicates that, unless λ can be a priori restricted to be quite small, the worst-case analysis of this paper argues in favor of maximum randomization.

For the particular case of the fully extended omega network, (4.13) yields $D = (2n - 1)/(1 - \lambda)$, and thus also the logarithmic dependence of the mean delay on N.

---

[1] Related monotonicity properties of the delay, which are implied by convex orderings of the service time distributions, are proved for GI/GI/1 in [31].

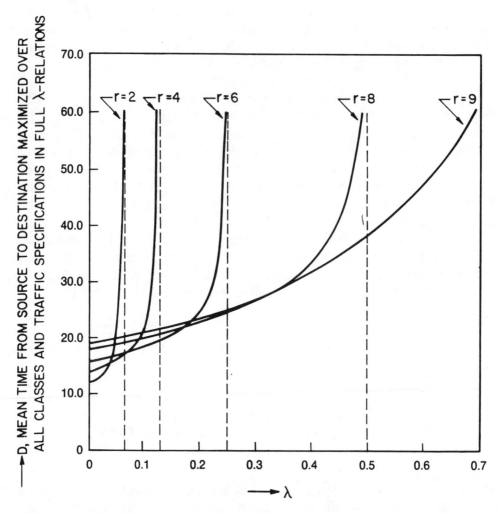

FIG. 3. Extended omega network, $n = 10$ and various values of r. Poisson processes at sources, exponentially distributed link transmission time.

One consequence of overtaking in the extended omega networks (see Section 3.1) is that the extraction of exact distributional information, other than the mean, of the source-to-destination delays by simple analytical means has to be ruled out. The partial nonovertaking property mentioned in Section 3.1 allows bounds on the delay distribution to be obtained, but we do not pursue this line in this paper.

4.4 APPROXIMATE ANALYSIS FOR GENERAL RENEWAL SOURCES AND GENERAL TRANSMISSION TIME DISTRIBUTIONS IN THE FULLY EXTENDED OMEGA NETWORK. Here we depart from the preceding treatment of the renewal case by assuming that the packets at the sources form general stationary renewal processes and that the distribution of the link transmission time is general. Poisson sources and constant link transmission time are, in particular, allowed. However, the analysis is approximate. The program that we follow is based on a proposal of Kuehn [20]. The program decomposes the network into GI/G/1 queues and relates the descriptors of the processes associated with each queue by using prior results on GI/G/1 queues, particularly the works of Kraemer and Langenbach-Belz [17] and Marshall [23]. In one important step (see (4.18)), we depart from Kuehn and use instead a relation proposed by Whitt [36], which, in our prior experience [29, 30], based on comparisons with simulations on general networks of queues, is

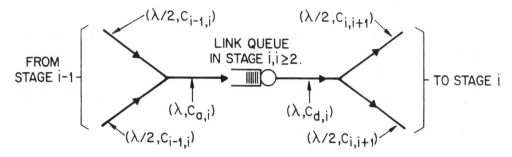

FIG. 4. The traffic descriptors and the splitting and superposition of processes.

generally robust and also simpler. More specifically, the program undertakes (i) the approximation of the departure process from each link queue as a stationary renewal process, and (ii) the description of each stationary renewal process by two moments, the mean (i.e., traffic) intensity and the coefficient of variation of the underlying interarrival distribution. In particular, the distribution of the link transmission time is specified by its mean, which is 1, and its coefficient of variation,

$$c_l^2 \triangleq \text{variance of link transmission time.} \qquad (4.14)$$

For constant transmission time $c_l = 0$ and for exponential distributions $c_l = 1$. Also, the stationary renewal processes at the sources are described by their mean λ, and the common coefficient of variation c_s,

$$c_s^2 \triangleq \frac{\text{variance of interarrival time of packets at source}}{\lambda^2}. \qquad (4.15)$$

For Poisson sources $c_s = 1$. We mention that a large body of validations and corroborations with analytic solutions and simulations have been reported [18, 20, 29, 30, 36, 37].

We only consider the fully extended omega network, that is, $r = n - 1$. The extensions of the formulas to be given below to the cases in which $r < n - 1$, while not hard to obtain, are full of diverting details that do not add significantly to the qualitative information contained in Section 4.3.

Two properties of the network of link queues distinguish it from general queuing networks: First, there is no feedback, that is, a packet on leaving a queue never returns; second, in the case being considered, namely, $r = n - 1$ and full λ-relations, all link queues in any particular stage have identical statistical behavior. Also, traffic is symmetric, that is, the traffic intensity in each link is λ. For these reasons we are able to obtain simple, explicit relations, in the form of recursions, for all traffic descriptors in the network, even when there are extremely large numbers of them.

For Poisson sources, the link queues in the first stage are M/G/1 [17], for which the Pollaczek–Khintchine formula [17] gives the mean queuing delay and an expression reported by Marshall [23] gives the coefficient of variation of the departing process. The formulas below reduce to these exact results.

Figure 4 is descriptive of the link queues at all subsequent stages, $i \geq 2$.

Figure 4 reflects the following features: (i) the approximation of the departing process from the link queue by a stationary renewal process with coefficient of variation $c_{d,i}$; (ii) the splitting of this process into two stationary renewal processes with means $\lambda/2$ and coefficient of variation $c_{i,i+1}$; (iii) the superposition of two processes described by $(\lambda/2, c_{i-1,i})$ to form the arrival process described by $(\lambda, c_{a,i})$.

We now give three relations to correspond to the above. Kraemer and Langenbach-Belz [18] have reported extensively to support an approximation, which in our case reduces to

$$c_{d,i}^2 = c_{a,i}^2 + 2\lambda^2 c_l^2 - \lambda^2(c_{a,i}^2 + c_l^2)g(\lambda, c_{a,i}^2, c_l^2), \qquad i \geq 1, \qquad (4.16a)$$

where

$$g(\lambda, c_{a,i}^2, c_l^2) = \exp\left\{\frac{-2(1 - \lambda)}{3\lambda}\frac{(1 - c_{a,i}^2)^2}{(c_{a,i}^2 + c_l^2)}\right\} \qquad \text{if} \quad c_{a,i} \leq 1, \qquad (4.16b)$$

$$= \exp\left\{-(1 - \lambda)\frac{(c_{a,i}^2 - 1)}{(c_{a,i}^2 + 4c_l^2)}\right\} \qquad \text{if} \quad c_{a,i} > 1. \qquad (4.16c)$$

Decomposition, or splitting, of renewal processes yields (see, e.g., Kuehn [20]) the following exact relation:

$$c_{i-1,i}^2 - 1 = \tfrac{1}{2}(c_{d,i-1}^2 - 1), \qquad i \geq 2. \qquad (4.17)$$

Finally, for the description of the superimposed renewal process we use the following approximation due to Whitt [36]:

$$c_{a,i}^2 - 1 = w(c_{i-1,i}^2 - 1), \qquad i \geq 2, \qquad (4.18a)$$

where

$$w = \frac{1}{1 + 4(1 - \lambda)^2}. \qquad (4.18b)$$

Also, there is the initial condition,

$$c_{a,i}^2 = c_s^2, \qquad i = 1, \qquad (4.18c)$$

where c_s (see (4.15)) characterizes the processes at the sources. Equations (4.16)–(4.18) define a complete recursive system that yields $\{c_{a,i}, c_{d,i}, c_{i,i+1}; i \geq 1\}$. Note that the dimension of the network given by n does not appear in the system.

We proceed to the mean queuing delay W_i for a link queue at stage i (queuing delay excludes transmission time). Marshall [23] has given an exact relation for GI/G/1 that relates W_i to $(c_{a,i}^2, c_{d,i}^2, c_l^2)$:

$$W_i \triangleq \text{mean queuing delay at a link in stage } i, \qquad i \geq 1,$$

$$= \frac{c_{a,i}^2 + 2\lambda^2 c_l^2 - c_{d,i}^2}{2\lambda(1 - \lambda)}. \qquad (4.19)$$

By Little's law

$$N_i \triangleq \text{mean total queue length, including packet in transmission,}$$
$$\text{at a link in stage } i, \qquad i \geq 1,$$
$$= \lambda(1 + W_i). \qquad (4.20)$$

Finally,

$$D \triangleq \text{mean time from source to destination}$$
$$= (2n - 1) + \sum_{i=1}^{2n-1} W_i. \qquad (4.21)$$

TABLE I. Statistics for Fully Extended Omega Network ($\gamma = n - 1$) and Source Destination Traffic Specifications That Satisfy Full λ-Relations, Calculated from (4.16)–(4.20)[a]

| Stage | $\lambda = 0.2$ | | $\lambda = 0.4$ | | $\lambda = 0.6$ | | $\lambda = 0.8$ | |
	Mean queuing delay	Mean total queue length	Mean queuing delay	Mean total queue length	Mean queuing delay	Mean total queue length	Mean queuing delay	Mean total queue length
1	0.125	0.225	0.333	0.533	0.750	1.050	2.000	2.400
2	0.124	0.224	0.322	0.528	0.667	1.000	1.448	1.958
3	0.124	0.224	0.320	0.528	0.648	0.988	1.345	1.876
4	0.124	0.224	0.319	0.527	0.643	0.986	1.327	1.861
5	0.124	0.224	0.319	0.527	0.642	0.985	1.324	1.859
6	0.124	0.224	0.319	0.527	0.642	0.985	1.324	1.859
$i, i > 6$	0.124	0.224	0.319	0.527	0.642	0.985	1.324	1.859

[a] Poisson processes of packets at sources and unit time for transmission of each packet across each link.

TABLE II. Statistics for Fully Extended Omega Network, Full λ-Relations, Calculated from (4.16)–(4.21)[a]

| | Mean time from source to destination | | | |
n	$\lambda = 0.2$	$\lambda = 0.4$	$\lambda = 0.6$	$\lambda = 0.8$
4	7.870	9.254	11.637	17.093
6	12.366	14.533	18.207	26.390
8	16.863	19.811	24.777	35.686
10	21.360	25.090	31.346	44.983
12	25.857	30.368	37.916	54.279
14	30.353	35.647	44.486	63.575

[a] Poisson packet traffic at sources and unit time for transmission of a pack across a link.

The first term is from the transmission time and the second is from the cumulative queuing delay. Note that (4.21) is the only point in the procedure where n is used. This completes the description of the analytic approximations.

Tables I and II give numerical values for the case of Poisson sources and constant link transmission time. Observe that for each λ, the queuing delay shrinks at the early stages before rather quickly reaching an asymptotic value. This is consistent with the coefficient of variation of the arrival processes to the links at the early stages shrinking before quickly leveling off.

For any fixed, positive λ, c_s^2, and c_l^2, the asymptotic values of $c_{a,i}^2$, $c_{d,i}^2$ and $c_{i-1,i}^2$, as $i \to \infty$, are obtained simply as fixed points of the recursions in (4.16)–(4.18). These may be substituted in (4.19) to obtain the asymptotic value $\bar{W}(\lambda, c_s^2, c_l^2)$, where $W_i \to \bar{W}(\lambda, c_s^2, c_l^2)$. From (4.21), as $n \to \infty$,

$$D \sim 2\{1 + \bar{W}(\lambda, c_s^2, c_l^2)\}n. \qquad (4.22)$$

This asymptotic result is noteworthy; it is consistent with the result in Theorem 1, Section 3, for the nonrenewal case. The last row of Table I gives the computed values of $\bar{W}(\lambda, 1, 0)$ for various values of λ.

The procedure based on (4.16)–(4.21), with $c_s = c_l = 1$, gives mean values that are the correct values for Poisson sources and exponentially distributed link transmission times. In this case, the mean queuing delay for stage i, W_i, is independent of i and equal to $\lambda/(1 - \lambda)$ (see (4.19)). Thus (4.22) holds with

$\overline{W} = \lambda/(1 - \lambda)$. The data given in Table II for the mean time from source to destination for unit link transmission time depart from the corresponding values for the exponentially distributed link transmission time by at most a factor of 2.1, and the latter is always greater. This factor is reached at $\lambda = 0.8$, whereas at the other extreme for small values of λ, not surprisingly, the difference vanishes. The numerical results for c_l in the range [0, 1] are bounded by the results for $c_l = 0$ and $c_l = 1$ in the case of Poisson sources.

The generalization of the procedure given here to the case of $k \times k$ switches is straightforward. Also, the given approximation applies regardless of the topology of the network, provided there are two input links to each switch and symmetric traffic.

4.4.1 *Accuracy of Approximation, Simulations.* The procedure in (4.16)–(4.21), based on a decomposition into renewal processes, is approximate, and the mean values obtained from it must be treated accordingly. However, the procedure has implied important qualitative information that may be combined with simple simulations to give more precise estimates. This is important because straightforward simulations of very large networks must be ruled out.

In the particular case of constant link transmission time and light traffic, that is, small λ, the decomposition is a poor one leading to overestimation by a factor of 2 of the queuing delay in all stages beyond the first (see Table I). (Results for stage 1 are exact.) The reason is that, in light traffic packets that meet one another in a link queue are highly unlikely to meet again in subsequent link queues—a distributional feature of the departure process, which is ignored in the decomposition. (Note that the essential argument on the nonrenewal context in Section 3 uses refinements of this argument. Generally, there are fundamental similarities between traffic in the nonrenewal context and light traffic in the renewal context.) On the other hand, empirical evidence indicates that the approximation is good in heavy traffic [16].

The net effect of the inaccuracies on what is arguably the topic of main interest, the mean time from source to destination in the fully extended omega network (see Table II), is not large. This is, of course, because in light traffic this time is dominated by the transmission time. Therefore, we expect, and indeed observe, the largest errors to occur at medium traffic, that is, at about $\lambda = 0.6$. Generally, the errors are smaller as we depart from constant link transmission time and add more variability.

As previously observed, the procedure in (4.16)–(4.21) yields, as reflected in Table I, mean queuing delays and statistics that converge quickly, with increasing stages, to asymptotic values. This important fact may be used to simplify simulations. Thus, an omega network of small dimension, say with four stages, may be simulated, and the mean delay observed for the final stage may be taken to apply to all subsequent stages in calculations for large extended omega networks.

We have undertaken the program just outlined. The results of the simulation of the four-stage omega network for Poisson sources and unit link transmission time are given in Table III. The results of the extrapolation to large, fully extended omega networks are given in Table IV, which should be considered a refinement of Table II.

Finally, we mention the recent work of Kruskal et al. [19] on the omega network for memoryless sources and clocked, that is, slotted, operations. A certain limit taken after rescaling time gives results corresponding to Poisson sources, unit transmission time and asynchronous operations, which is a case that we have

TABLE III. STATISTICS FROM SIMULATIONS OF OMEGA NETWORK WITH FOUR STAGES[a]

Stage	$\lambda = 0.2$ Mean queuing delay	$\lambda = 0.2$ Variance of queuing delay	$\lambda = 0.4$ Mean queuing delay	$\lambda = 0.4$ Variance of queuing delay	$\lambda = 0.6$ Mean queuing delay	$\lambda = 0.6$ Variance of queuing delay	$\lambda = 0.8$ Mean queuing delay	$\lambda = 0.8$ Variance of queuing delay
1	0.123	0.097	0.335	0.336	0.751	1.055	2.002	5.308
2	0.067	0.048	0.199	0.172	0.478	0.572	1.339	3.063
3	0.066	0.047	0.196	0.167	0.468	0.575	1.318	3.032
4	0.067	0.048	0.195	0.165	0.461	0.540	1.323	3.047

[a] Poisson packet traffic at sources and unit time for transmission of a packet across a link.

TABLE IV. STATISTICS EXTRAPOLATED FROM DATA IN TABLE III AS EXPLAINED IN SECTION 4.5.1 FOR FULLY EXTENDED OMEGA NETWORK AND FULL λ-RELATIONS—COMPARE WITH TABLE II[a]

	Mean time from source to destination			
n	$\lambda = 0.2$	$\lambda = 0.4$	$\lambda = 0.6$	$\lambda = 0.8$
4	7.529	8.512	10.544	16.954
6	11.801	13.292	16.390	26.249
8	16.072	18.073	22.235	35.544
10	20.344	22.854	28.081	44.839
12	24.615	27.635	33.927	54.134
14	28.887	32.416	39.772	63.428

[a] Poisson packet traffic at sources and unit time for transmission of a packet across a link.

considered. The appropriate results and simulation data in [19] corroborate the main points made above.

5. Conclusions

We mention four topics for future investigations.

(i) *Reordering Delays.* Randomized routing in the extended omega network allows overtaking (see Section 4.4), albeit of a restricted variety. We believe that this will also be true in the hypercube with renewal sources, unless costly steps are taken to synchronize operations. In certain applications, in voice-data communications [21], for example, a packet received at the destination is released only after all packets from the same source transmitted prior to it are released. Overtaking represents a hidden cost, since the effective delay is the sum of the delay encountered in the network and the time for reordering at the destination. Estimates of the reordering delay [2] will be useful, even in the case of symmetric traffic.

(ii) *Randomized Routing of Virtual Circuits.* The starting point here is the presence of messages, each constituted from a variable number of packets with a common source and destination. There are advantages to having all packets in each message follow the same route, a virtual circuit. One advantage, of course, is that there is no overtaking by packets in a message and hence no reordering delay—there is no need to reorder packets from different messages. We may implement randomized routing of virtual circuits in the extended omega network by giving each message an independent scattering ticket and having all packets in the message use the common scattering ticket. The degree of randomization is reduced relative to the scheme described here, and so is performance by an extent that is not known.

On parallel processors such as those proposed in [8], [11], and [27], a desirable property is that all packets originating at a particular processor and addressed to a particular memory location (not memory module) are received in the same order in which they are issued. Although this property is lost with unrestricted randomized routing, randomized virtual circuit routing as discussed above maintains the property.

(iii) *Finite Queues and Circuit Switching.* We have assumed unlimited capacity for the link queues. If, in fact, the capacities are small, then, in the renewal context, the source-to-destination delays are quite different, especially in heavy traffic. In the extreme case, when buffers are completely eliminated, the behavior approaches that of circuit switching, which is of independent interest. In this case the primary performance measure is the probability of blocking.[2] We mention that a randomization algorithm for a mesh without queues has been proposed in [24] and analyzed in [12].

(iv) *Closed Models.* In this paper the traffic intensities at the sources are considered given. But how are they to be obtained? It may be argued that parallel computing reality is closer to closed models in which the process by which traffic is generated at a source is coordinated with the arrival of packets at a corresponding destination. A model of this kind makes severe demands on the source model, but the latter may be forthcoming in some cases such, as sorting [5] and solution of recursions. An important decision that has to be made with respect to the source model is whether to include multiprogramming. An analysis of the closed model will yield the rate at which tasks of interest are performed.

Appendix A. Nonrenewal Traffic

A1. INTERSECTION OF A PAIR OF ROUTES. Let X be a marked packet with route $\mathbf{R}^X$ (see (2.2)), and Y another packet with route $\mathbf{R}^Y$. We find that the two routes intersect in Phase 1 if and only if Y's scattering ticket, $\mathbf{c}^Y$, belongs to a set $S(\mathbf{d}^Y, \mathbf{s}^Y, \mathbf{R}^X)$, which, as the notation implies, is defined in terms of Y's destination and source, and X's route. Two basic parameters of this set are A and B, where $(n - A)$ is the maximum number of most significant bits over which the addresses of the sources of X and Y coincide, that is,

$$s_i^Y = s_i^X, \qquad n \geq i \geq A + 1, \qquad \text{and} \qquad s_A^Y \neq s_A^X. \tag{A1}$$

Correspondingly, $(n - B)$ is the maximum number of least significant bits over which the addresses of the destination of X and Y coincide, that is,

$$d_i^Y = d_i^X, \qquad 1 \leq i \leq n - B, \qquad \text{and} \qquad d_{n-B+1}^Y \neq d_{n-B+1}^X. \tag{A2}$$

Let $A = 0$ ($B = 0$) if X and Y have the same source (destination).

The importance of these parameters is illustrated first for the case of $r = n - 1$. From the Fact in Section 2.3 it is clear that there can be no intersection of routes at stages 1 to $(A - 1)$ and that the first intersection that can possibly occur is at stage A. Such an intersection occurs if

$$c_i^Y = c_i^X, \qquad 1 \leq i \leq A. \tag{A3}$$

Moreover, if (A3) is not true, then no intersection occurs in Phase 1. (As shown below, adjustments have to be made to (A3) if $A = 0$ or $A = n$.)

---

[2] Some recent results on it may be found in [15], [25], and [38].

After filling in the details, we obtain the following condition for intersection. For A as defined in (A1), let

$$A^* = \begin{cases} 1 & \text{if } A = 0, \\ A & \text{if } 1 \le A \le r, \\ r & \text{if } r < A, \end{cases} \tag{A4}$$

and recall from (3.1) that the end stage of Phase 1 is $\hat{\imath} = \lfloor (n + r)/2 \rfloor$. Let

$$S(\mathbf{d}^Y, \mathbf{s}^Y, \mathbf{R}^X) \triangleq \begin{cases} \{\mathbf{c} \mid c_i = c_i^X, 1 \le i \le A^*\} & \text{if } (A + B \le n + r) \\ & \text{and } A \le \hat{\imath}, \\ \text{empty} & \text{if } (A + B > n + r) \\ & \text{or } A > \hat{\imath}. \end{cases} \tag{A5}$$

Now, packet Y's route intersects X's route in Phase 1 if and only if

$$\mathbf{c}^Y \in S(\mathbf{d}^Y, \mathbf{s}^Y, \mathbf{R}^X). \tag{A6}$$

A2. EXPECTED NUMBER OF PACKETS WITH ROUTES THAT INTERSECT A PARTICULAR ROUTE. We use notions introduced above to obtain a bound on the expected number of packets with routes that intersect the route of the marked packet X in Phase 1. We first consider full h-relations.

For $1 \le i \le \hat{\imath}$, let

$$F_i \triangleq \text{expected number of packets with routes that have} \tag{A7}$$
$$\textit{first} \text{ intersection with } X\text{'s route at stage } i.$$

Now,

$$F_i = \begin{cases} (\text{Number of packets with } A = 0 \text{ or } 1) \Pr[c_1 = c_1^X], & i = 1, \\ (\text{Number of packets with } A = i) \Pr[c_j = c_j^X, 1 \le j \le i], & 2 \le i \le r, \\ (\text{Number of packets with } A = i \text{ and } B \le n - i + r) \Pr[c_j = c_j^X, 1 \le j \le r], \\ \hspace{8cm} r + 1 \le i \le \hat{\imath}. \end{cases} \tag{A8}$$

Hence

$$F_1 = h, \tag{A9}$$

$$F_i = \frac{h}{2}, \quad 2 \le i \le r. \tag{A10}$$

Now,

$$\text{number of packets with } A = i \text{ and } B \le n - i + r$$
$$\le \text{number of packets with } A = i,$$
$$= h2^{i-1}, \quad \text{for } i \le \hat{\imath}.$$

Hence,

$$F_i \le h2^{i-r-1}, \quad r + 1 \le i \le \hat{\imath}. \tag{A11}$$

Hence, as claimed in (3.3),

expected number of packets with routes that intersect $\mathbf{R}^X$ over stages 1 to $\hat{\imath}$

$$= \sum_{i=1}^{\hat{\imath}} F_i \le \frac{h}{2} [r - 1 + 2^{1 + \lfloor (n-r)/2 \rfloor}]. \tag{A12}$$

For partial n-relations the only difference is that the values for F_1 and F_i, $2 \leq i \leq r$, in (A9) and (A10) are upper bounds. The final result in (A12) therefore remains intact.

Appendix B. Proof of Theorem 2

(i) Consider a link $(i; a_n, \ldots, a_1)$ for $1 \leq i \leq r$. From (2.1a), the traffic passing through this link consists of all packets such that (a) the packet originated at source $s_n, \ldots, s_1$ with $s_n, \ldots, s_{i+1} = a_{n-i}, \ldots, a_1$, and (b) the packet was assigned a scattering ticket $c_r, \ldots, c_1$ with $c_i, \ldots, c_1 = a_n, \ldots, a_{n-i+1}$. The traffic intensity of packets with property (a) is $\lambda 2^i$ in a full λ-relation, and since all scattering tickets have all components that are generated independently and with equal probabilities, $t(i; a_n, \ldots, a_1) = \lambda$ for all i such that $1 \leq i \leq r$. A similar argument yields $t(i; a_n, \ldots, a_1) = \lambda$ for $n \leq i \leq n + r$. It remains to consider the traffic intensity in the links $(i; a_n, \ldots, a_1)$ for $r + 1 \leq i \leq n - 1$. From (2.1b) the traffic intensity on such a link is a fraction $1/2^r$ of the total traffic intensity from sources $s_n, \ldots, s_1$ to destinations $d_n, \ldots, d_1$ where $s_n, \ldots, s_{i+1} = a_{n-i}, \ldots, a_1$ and $d_{i-r}, \ldots, d_1 = a_n, \ldots, a_{n-i+r+1}$. In a full λ-relation, the total traffic intensity from sources of this type cannot exceed $\lambda 2^i$, and the total traffic intensity to destinations of this type cannot exceed $\lambda 2^{n-i+r}$. Therefore,

$$t(i; a_n, \ldots, a_1) \leq \frac{\lambda}{2^r} \min(2^i, 2^{n-i+r}), \tag{B1}$$

and the proof of statement (i) is complete.

(ii) We introduce the class B of source-destination traffic specifications that, while not exhausting the specifications for which statement (ii) holds, is interesting because, for $r < n - 1$, the link usage is particularly unbalanced: at the middle of the networks. many links are not used at all, while the remainder are used maximally.

We assume $(n + r)$ is even, in which case $\hat{i}$ is as given in (4.7a). The reader may easily provide a similar account for the case $(n + r)$ odd.

Let B be the class of source-destination traffic specifications that satisfy the full λ-relations, and

$$\lambda(s_n, \ldots, s_1; d_n, \ldots, d_1) \geq 0 \quad \text{if} \quad (d_i = s_{n-i+1}, \, i = 1, 2, \ldots, \hat{i}),$$
$$= 0 \quad \text{otherwise.} \tag{B2}$$

That is, for each binary sequence of $\hat{i}$ bits define a block of $2^{(n-r)/2}$ sources, with the most significant bits of their addresses coinciding with the sequence, and a matching block of $2^{(n-r)/2}$ destinations, with the least significant bits of their addresses coinciding with the sequence in reversed order. Now, if each of the sources in any such source-block transmits only to destinations in the matching destination-block and the full λ-relations are satisfied, then the ensuing source-destination traffic specification belongs to class B.

Clearly, there is always one member in B, namely, the specification in which source $s_n, \ldots, s_1$ transmits only to destination $s_1, \ldots, s_n$. Example 1 in Section 2 gives for $n = 3$, $r = 1$ source-destination traffic specifications that are in B. Especially if $(n - r)$ is large, the class B admits a rich variety of traffic specifications.

Now consider the following set of links in the middle stage of the network:

$$(\hat{i}; a_1, \ldots, a_{(n-r)/2}, b_r, \ldots, b_1, a_{(n-r)/2}, \ldots, a_1), \tag{B3}$$

where $a_{(n-r)/2}, \ldots, a_1, b_r, \ldots, b_1$ are each either 0 or 1. There are 2^i such links. It is claimed that for traffic specifications in B, each such link carries traffic with intensity

$$\lambda 2^{\lfloor (n-r)/2 \rfloor}. \tag{B4}$$

All other links at stage $\hat{\imath}$, if there are any, carry no traffic. The proof follows by simply introducing (B2) in the argument that gave (B1).

Now consider any traffic class (specified by source, destination, and scattering ticket) with a positive traffic intensity that is obtained from a source-destination traffic specification in B. From (4.4) and (B4) it follows that each link in the route of such a traffic class carries traffic of intensity given on the right of (4.5).

Note that *all* traffic classes obtained from a source-destination traffic specification in B that have positive traffic intensities use links that have the stated maximal traffic intensities.

ACKNOWLEDGMENTS. It is with gratitude that D. Mitra acknowledges the benefit of discussions with colleagues at AT&T Bell Laboratories, specifically, Dr. P. Semal (visting from Philips Research Laboratory, Brussels), Dr. L. A. Shepp, and Dr. A. Weiss. The assistance of Dr. K. G. Ramakrishnan and Ms. J. B. Seery in the simulations is gratefully acknowledged.

REFERENCES

1. ALELIUNAS, R. Randomized parallel communication. In *Proceedings of the ACM SIGACT-SIGOPS Symposium on Principles of Distributed Computing* (Ottawa, Ont., Canada, Aug. 18–20). ACM, New York, 1982, pp. 60–72.
2. BACCELLI, F., GELENBE, E., AND PLATEAU, B. An end-to-end approach to the resequencing problem. *J. ACM 31*, 3 (July 1984), 474–485.
3. BATCHER, K. E. Sorting networks and their applications. In *AFIPS Spring Joint Computer Conference*, vol. 32. AFIPS Press, Reston, Va., 1968, pp. 307–314.
4. BHUYAN, L. N., AND LEE, C. W. An interference analysis of interconnection networks. In *Proceedings of the 1983 International Conference on Parallel Processing*. IEEE, New York, 1983, pp. 2–9.
5. BORODIN, A., AND HOPCROFT, J. E. Routing, merging and sorting on parallel models of computation. *J. Comput. Sci. Syst. Sci. 30* (1985), 130–145.
6. BOROVKOV, A. A. Talk at Oberwolfach Conference on Applied Stochastic Processes, Apr. 1985.
7. CHERNOFF, H. A measure of asymptotic efficiency for tests of a hypothesis based on the sum of observations. *Ann. Math. Statistics 23* (1952), 493–507.
8. COHN, L. A. A conceptual approach to general purpose parallel computer architecture. Ph.D. dissertation, Columbia Univ., New York, N.Y., 1983.
9. DADUNA, H. Passage times for overtake-free paths in Gordon–Newell networks. *Adv. Appl. Prob. 14* (1981), 672–686.
10. GOKE, G. R., AND LIPOVSKI, G. J. Banyan networks for partitioning multiprocessor system. In *Proceedings of the 1st Annual Symposium on Computer Architecture*. IEEE, New York, 1973, pp. 21–28.
11. GOTTLIEB, A., GRISHMAN, R., KRUSKAL, C. P., MCAULIFFE, K. P., RUDOLPH, L., AND SNIR, M. The NYU ultracomputer-designing an MIMD shared memory parallel computer. *IEEE Trans. Comput. C-32*, 2 (Feb. 1983), 175–189.
12. GREENBERG, A. G., AND GOODMAN, J. Sharp approximate analysis of adaptive routing in mesh networks. In *Teletraffic Analysis and Computer Performance Evaluation*, O. J. Boxma, J. W. Cohen, and H. C. Tijms, Eds. Elsevier (North-Holland), New York, 1986, pp. 225–270.
13. HOEFFDING, W. On the distribution of the number of successes in independent trials. *Ann. Math. Statistics 27* (1956), 713–721.
14. KELLY, F. P. The dependence of sojourn times in closed queueing networks. In *Mathematical Computer Performance and Reliability*, G. Iazeolla, P. J. Courtois, and A. Hordijk, Eds. Elsevier Science Publishers B. V. (North-Holland), New York, 1984, pp. 111–121.

15. KELLY, F. P.   Blocking probabilities in large circuit-switched networks. *Adv. Appl. Prob. 18* (1986), 473–505.

16. KINGMAN, J. F. C.   The heavy traffic approximation in the theory of queues. In *Proceedings of the Symposium on Congestion Theory*, W. Smith and W. Wilkinson, Eds. The University of North Carolina Press, Chapel Hill, N.C., pp. 137–159.

17. KLEINROCK, L.   *Queueing Systems*, vol. I and II. Wiley, New York, 1975.

18. KRAEMER, W., AND LANGENBACH-BELZ, M.   Approximate formulae for the delay in the queueing system GI/G/1. In *Congressbook of the 8th International Teletraffic Congress* (Melbourne, Australia). 1976, pp. 235–1/8.

19. KRUSKAL, C. P., SNIR, M., AND WEISS, A.   The distribution of waiting times in clocked multistage interconnection networks. *IEEE Trans. Comput.* To appear.

20. KUEHN, P. J.   Approximate analysis of general queueing networks by decomposition. *IEEE Trans. Commun. COM-27*, 1 (Jan. 1979), 113–126.

21. KULZER, J. J. AND MONTGOMERY, W. A.   Statistical switching architectures for future services. In *Proceedings of the International Switching Symposium* (Florence, Italy). AEI, Milano, Italy, Session 43A, May 1984.

22. LAWRIE, D. H.   Access and alignment of data in an array processor. *IEEE Trans. Comput. C-24* (1975), 1145–1155.

23. MARSHALL, K. T.   Some inequalities in queueing. *Oper. Res. 16* (1968), 651–665.

24. MAXEMCHUK, N.   Regular mesh topologies in local and metropolitan area networks. *AT&T Tech. J. 65*, 7 (Sept. 1985), 1659–1685.

25. MITRA, D.   Asymptotic analysis and computational methods for a class of simple, circuit-switched networks with blocking. *Adv. Appl. Prob. 19* (1987), 219–239.

26. PARKER, D. S., JR.   Notes on shuffle/exchange-type switching networks. *IEEE Trans. Comput. C-29* (1980), 213–222.

27. PFISTER, G. F., BRANTLEY, W. C., GEORGE, D. A., HARVEY, S. L., KLEINFELDER, W. J., MCAULIFFE, K. P., MELTON, E. A., NORTON, V. A., AND WEISS, J.   The IBM research parallel processor prototype (RP3): Introduction and architecture. In *Proceedings of the 1985 International Conference on Parallel Processing*. IEEE, New York, 1985, pp. 764–771.

28. PIPPENGER, N.   Parallel communication with limited buffers. In *Proceedings of the 16th Annual ACM Symposium on Theory of Computing* (Washington, D.C., Apr. 30–May 2). ACM, New York, 1984, pp. 127–136.

29. RAMAKRISHNAN, K. G., AND MITRA, D.   An overview of PANACEA, a software package for analyzing Markovian queueing networks. *Bell Syst. Tech. J. 61*, 10 (Dec. 1982), 2849–2872.

30. RAMAKRISHNAN, K. G., AND MITRA, D.   *A Short User's Manual for PANACEA* 4.1 (*Analytic Approximations*). AT&T Bell Laboratories memorandum, Jan. 1985.

31. STOYAN, D.   *Comparison Methods for Queues and Other Stochastic Models*. Wiley, New York, 1983.

32. UPFAL, E.   Efficient schemes for parallel communication. In *Proceedings of the ACM SIGACT-SIGOPS Symposium on Principles of Distributed Computing* (Ottawa, Ont., Canada, Aug. 18–20). ACM, New York, 1982, pp. 55–59.

33. VALIANT, L. G.   A scheme for fast parallel communication. *SIAM J. Comput. 11* (1982) 350–361.

34. VALIANT, L. G., AND BREBNER, G. J.   Universal schemes for parallel communication. In *Proceedings of the 13th Annual ACM Symposium on Theory of Computing* (Milwaukee, Wis., May 11–13). ACM, New York, 1981, pp. 263–277.

35. WALRAND, J., AND VARAIYA, P.   Sojourn times and the overtaking condition in Jacksonian networks. *Adv. Appl. Prob. 12* (1980), 1000–1018.

36. WHITT, W.   The queueing network analyzer. *Bell Syst. Tech. J. 62*, 9, part 1 (Nov. 1983), 2779–2816.

37. WHITT, W.   Performance of the queueing network analyzer. *Bell Syst. Tech. J. 62*, 9, Part 1 (Nov. 1983), 2817–2847.

38. WHITT, W.   Blocking when service is required from several facilities simultaneously. *AT&T Tech. J. 64*, 8 (Oct. 1985), 1807–1856.

RECEIVED MARCH 1986; REVISED NOVEMBER 1986; ACCEPTED JANUARY 1987

Chapter 5: Nonuniform Routing (Hot Spots)

The mode of routing in MIMD systems is *asynchronous routing*, where sources generate and send their messages independently of each other. The traffic pattern is either *uniform* or *nonuniform*. In uniform traffic, every source targets all the destinations uniformly — that is, all destinations are equally likely. In nonuniform traffic, certain destination(s) are targeted more often than others. Because of the simplicity of the uniform-traffic model, early studies[1] focused on the performance of networks under that model. However, out of the research on IBM RP3 came the pioneering paper by Pfister and Norton (1985) — the first paper included in this chapter. Pfister and Norton observed and studied what they called *hot spots*, which occur because of shared-memory variables such as shared locks and synchronization variables. The ubiquitous nature of hot spots in real applications generated much research activity into their effects and ways of handling them, mostly in buffered, omega-like multistage networks.

The papers included in this chapter address the various aspects of hot spots, depending on whether there is a single hot spot or multiple ones, whether all or some of the source contributes to the hot spot, and how the problem of hot spots can be alleviated or eliminated. The paper by Pfister and Norton (1985) that is mentioned above introduces the concept of hot spots, studies the saturation effect of a hot spot on the traffic in the network, and evaluates message combining as a hardware method of eliminating the effect of hot spots. The next paper, by Kumar and Pfister (1986), evaluates the time it takes for saturation to occur when there is a single hot spot. Lee (1985) studies the effect of a single hot spot when only a few sources contribute to the hot spot. Both of these papers study the pairwise combining of messages, whereas the paper by Lee, Kruskal, and Kuck (1986) studies other combining methods they have proposed for eliminating the effect of a hot spot. The paper by Yew, Tzeng, and Lawrie (1987) proposes and evaluates software methods for handling hot spots. Then, Lang and Kurisaki (1990) address multiple hot spots and the benefit of using multiple paths to reduce the effect of hot spots. Finally, the paper by Scott and Sohi (1990) proposes and studies a feedback method to handle tree saturation.

Reference

1. J.H. Patel, "Performance of Processor-Memory Interconnections for Multiprocessors," *IEEE Trans. Computers*, Vol. C-30, No. 10, Oct. 1981, pp. 771–780.

"Hot Spot" Contention and Combining in Multistage Interconnection Networks

GREGORY F. PFISTER, SENIOR MEMBER, IEEE, AND V. ALAN NORTON

Abstract — **The combining of messages within a multistage switching network has been proposed [1], [11], [14] to reduce memory contention in highly parallel shared-memory multiprocessors, especially for shared lock and synchronization data. This paper reports on a quantitative investigation of the performance impact of such contention, performed as part of the RP3 project [7]–[9] and the effectiveness of combining in reducing this impact. We investigated the effect of a nonuniform traffic pattern consisting of a single *hot spot* of higher access rate superimposed on a background of uniform traffic. The potential degradation due to even moderate hot spot traffic was found to be very significant, severely degrading all memory access, not just access to shared lock locations, due to an effect we call *tree saturation*. The technique of message combining was found to be an effective means of eliminating this problem if it arises due to lock or synchronization contention.**

Index Terms — **Concurrent computation, highly parallel systems, hot spots, message combining, multiprocessors, multistage interconnection networks, parallel processing.**

I. INTRODUCTION

IN proposed highly parallel multiprocessor systems, e.g., systems with 100 or more processors, contention for memory access is a potential bottleneck. At the same time, it is often proposed that access to a shared memory in such systems be provided by means of a message- or packet-switched multistage switching network, with topologies such as a tree [12], Omega network or variant [1], [9], binary N-cube [11], etc. Two projects in this area, the NYU Ultracomputer [1] and the Columbia CHoPP (or GEM) [11], [14], have proposed the technique of *message combining* within the switch to use its multistage nature to help alleviate potential memory access bottlenecks. This technique (described in more detail below) merges similar references into composite *combined* references at each stage of the network.

However, the proposers addressed neither the detailed hardware cost nor the benefit to be derived from this technique in a quantitative fashion. This paper addresses these issues.

The hardware needed to support this feature is quite costly. As part of the RP3 project [7]–[9], detailed cost and size estimates were made based on state-of-the-art silicon and packaging data. These indicated that message combining in-

creases the switch size and/or cost by a factor of between 6 and 32. The wide range is due to the variability of factors like circuit technology, packaging technology, and network topology.

To determine if this very significant added cost is worth the benefit derived, we performed a series of simulation experiments whose results are reported and interpreted in this paper. The following was determined.

1) A type of network traffic nonuniformity, a "hot spot," typically but not uniquely produced by global shared locks, can produce effects that severely degrade *all* network traffic, not just the traffic to shared locks. This effect, which we call *tree saturation,* has not previously been reported.

2) This effect is quite general. It is independent of network topology, switching mode (packet or circuit), or whether the network is used for memory access or message passing. It requires only a multistage network with distributed routing, and a network traffic pattern which, for any reason, exhibits "hot spot" nonuniformity.

3) Message combining, originally proposed to solve a different set of problems, is an effective technique for dealing with this problem when it arises due to global shared locks.

The technique of message combining is described below, along with the simulation experiments we performed and interpretation of the results.

We interpret these results as implying the need for message combining in any highly parallel multipurpose machine, such as RP3. The need for combining to avoid the effect of hot spots can be quantified; we in fact shall show that systems which do not employ message combining are limited by tree saturation in the degree of parallelism obtainable. How the results reported here are being applied in RP3 is also described.

It should be noted that message combining was proposed to solve problems different from those reported here. In [1], its justification is the elimination of serial bottlenecks in programs. In [11] and [14], its justification is broadcasting read-only data and reducing the latency of memory references in general memory traffic. While these claims may be true, we do not present evidence here to support them. In particular, we have, and presently know of, no quantitative evidence to support or deny the value of combining in general (i.e., not locking or synchronizing) memory traffic. Such information is difficult to obtain because it relies on the dynamic properties of large-scale parallelism, properties which are not observable without impractically detailed system-wide simulation. RP3 is itself intended to provide a

Manuscript received February 1, 1985; revised May 30, 1985. This paper appeared in the IEEE 1985 International Conference on Parallel Processing, St. Charles, IL, Aug. 1985.

The authors are with the IBM T. J. Watson Research Center, Yorktown Heights, NY 10598.

276

test environment to determine whether such combining is beneficial.

II. MESSAGE COMBINING

Message combining works by detecting the occurrence of memory request messages directed at identical memory locations as they pass through each switch node. Such messages are combined, at the switch node, into a single message. The fact that combining took place is recorded in a *wait buffer* in each switch node. When the reply to a combined message reaches a node where it was combined, multiple replies are generated to satisfy the multiple individual requests. Since in successive switch stages combined messages can themselves be combined, the generation of multiple replies produces the effect of a dynamically generated broadcast of data to multiple processors.

The form of message combining described above is that of the NYU Ultracomputer. The Columbia ChoPP/GEM scheme of "repetition filter memories" (RFM's) operates somewhat differently, acting more like a cache at each network node, and may catch more combinable references. However, it appears to be an even more complex design, and since it is usable only for read-only data, it cannot, as will be seen, address the problem we later present.

III. SIMULATED SWITCH

The specific method of combining investigated here uses a switch node that is a slight variation on the NYU Ultracomputer's. Its data flow is shown in Fig. 1. It is a two-way switch, and actually contains two separate switching nodes: one in the forward direction, which compares message addresses and performs combining, and one in the reply direction, which performs the required broadcasting.

The forward direction subnode is a standard 2×2 crossbar with output queues, with the following characteristics.

1) The output queues are used only when a succeeding stage indicates that it cannot accept a message. When not used, only a single stage of pipelining is seen by the message.

2) Comparisons are performed only between queued messages. Thus, no combining occurs if traffic is low enough that no queueing occurs.

3) The output queues can accept two messages simultaneously. This feature is used if two messages destined for the same output port arrive simultaneously under conditions where they must both be enqueued.

4) An additional buffer able to hold one complete message is associated with each input. It is used to hold a message in the event that the destined output queue is full. Without it, each node would have to signal to both its predecessors that it cannot accept input if either queue had less than two message slots free. With it, the signal that a message cannot be accepted on a given input is identical to that input's buffer being full. The buffer therefore allows greater output queue utilization; and since combining is done only in the output queues, this greater utilization implies that more opportuni-

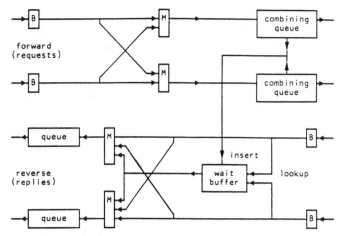

Fig. 1. Block diagram of the switch node used in simulation.

ties for combining are available. These additional buffers are not present in the NYU design.

5) A message can combine with only one other message in a given node. A combined message can combine again in a later node.

6) One "packet" of a message travels from one switch node to the other in a single switch clock cycle (e.g., with an 8 bit data path a 64 bit message requires 8 clock cycles to go from one node's queue to the next).

7) The entire operation is completely pipelined, so that when all arriving messages are combinable, the arrival of two messages can be overlapped with the departure of a third message formed as the combination of two prior messages.

Saved information about combinations made in both input queues is held in a single wait buffer. Replies arriving from either reverse-direction port are decombined using information in that wait buffer. The output queues in the reverse direction are assumed to be able to accept up to four inputs simultaneously: two messages from the two reverse-direction inputs and two "decombinations."

More detail about how the comparison and combining takes place is available in [1].

IV. THE EXPERIMENTS

Our network was configured as an omega network [13]. There were N processors, N memory modules, and the total switch contained $\log(N)$ ranks of $N/2$ switches with ranks connected by a shuffle-exchange connection. Our "processors" were simply generators of memory request messages. Our memories turned requests into replies in a single network cycle; this is unreasonably fast, but as will be seen it makes our results conservative.

Initially, we simulated a variety of network sizes ($4 \leq N \leq 64$) using the usual, analytically tractable, assumption that each source's memory references were independent and uniformly distributed across the entire address space. This was done to establish agreement with analytical models of switch performance (used in [8]), and to determine the queue length for which adequate performance was obtained (e.g., a length of four messages). Under those circumstances, virtually no combining occurred since the probability that references to exactly equal addresses are queued in the same switch node at the same time is negligible.

Independent uniformly distributed references are not, however, an adequate model in the presence of global locks, even if all nonlock references are uniformly distributed. Locking operations do not work unless directed at identical memory locations.

We therefore altered the address distribution to be a "flat" (uniform) distribution with a single "spike" or *hot spot*, i.e., a single location to which a specified fraction of the total memory references was directed. That fraction was varied from 0.5 to 32 percent.

The simulation results with combining disabled are shown in Fig. 2. With combining enabled, the same experiments produced the results of Fig. 3. These figures show the steady-state average response time for a memory request as a function of the total switch traffic. The response time is in units of network cycles, and the switch traffic is in units of packets per network cycle per input. The lowest dashed line shows the analytically predicted response time with a uniform address distribution and infinite queue sizes. The other lines indicate the response time with various hot spot percentages.

It is important to note that the response times of Fig. 2 and Fig. 3 average response time of *all* memory requests, *not* just requests to the single lock location. If the delays for the hot spot traffic and background traffic are plotted separately, they are found to exhibit essentially identical behavior (the hot spot traffic does show slightly more delay). By comparison, if hot spot and background traffic are plotted separately when combining is being used, additional overhead appears only for references to the hot spot.

Combining clearly has a very substantial effect in reducing the average memory response time. However, two questions can be asked.

1) Without combining, why do all memory requests, not just those to lock locations, exhibit increased latency as the percentage of lock references rises?

2) Is the situation modeled realistic, i.e., do any practical situations correspond to the events modeled here?

These questions are discussed below.

V. MODELING OF NONCOMBINING HOT SPOT TRAFFIC

This section addresses the reasons why nonlock memory requests are delayed. A cause — *tree saturation* — is described, and its effect with regard to system scaling is discussed.

A. Tree Saturation

Examining Fig. 2, one can notice that with a hot spot the latency climbs to an asymptote at the point where the total traffic and hot spot percentage combine to *saturate the weakest link* in the round trip from processor to memory and back.

More specifically, given that

p is the number of processors, and there are an equal number of memories

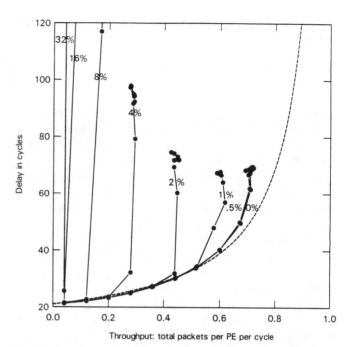

Fig. 2. Average memory latency in the presence of a hot spot, without combining, versus total network throughput for various percentages of network traffic referencing the hot spot. The switch nodes used had a queue size of four messages and a wait buffer size of six messages. The dashed line shows analytical estimates based on infinite queues.

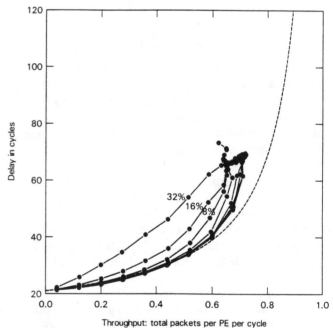

Fig. 3. The same experiments and conditions as shown in Fig. 2., but with combining used.

r is the number of network packets emitted per processor per switch cycle ($0 \leq r \leq 1$)

h is the fraction of memory references directed at the hot spot, i.e., each processor emits packets directed to the hot spot at a total rate of rh,

then the effective data rate into the "hot" memory module is $r(1 - h) + rhp$, i.e., the system attempts to send that many packets to the "hot" memory module every network cycle. The asymptote occurs when this value is equal to the capacity of the weakest link in the round trip between a processor and the "hot" memory. In general, since loads dominate over stores and the response to a load is generally larger than the load request itself, the weakest link will actually be the interface between the memory and the return-trip network. In our simulations, however, all requests and replies were the same size, and the memories cycled in one switch cycle. As a result, the links into and out of the hot memory should saturate at the same point, namely, when the above formula equals unity. This is in close agreement with the simulated results.

Saturating the capacity of the link into the hot memory causes the queues in the switch closest to that memory to fill; then the same happens to the two switches in the prior rank that feed that one; then the same happens to the four in the next prior rank; etc. Thus, a tree of switches rooted at the hot memory and extending to all the processors is saturated, i.e., all the queues in that tree are full.

Since the tree has a leaf at every processor, all memory references from any processor to any memory module must begin within it, and therefore, all memory references, whether involved with the lock or not, are delayed. The fact that some of the references cross only very few levels of the tree is counterbalanced by the fact that they cross levels further from the memory, whose queues are emptying most slowly. Since the memory is filling requests serially, any fair routing scheme will cause the rate of queue service to decrease exponentially with distance from the memories.

B. Effect of System Size on Tree Saturation

The effect of tree saturation as the number of processors is increased can be illustrated by noting that the asymptotically maximum network throughput is obtained when the expression derived above for the probability of reference to a hot memory module, $r(1 - h) + rhp$, equals 1. Thus, the asymptotically maximum value of the network throughput per processor, R, is defined by

$$R = \frac{1}{1 + h(p - 1)}.$$

More revealing is the expression

$$B = pR = \frac{p}{1 + h(p - 1)},$$

which gives the asymptotic limit of the total communication bandwidth available as a function of the number of processors and the hot spot percentage. This is plotted in Fig. 4 as a function of p for various values of h. The amount of computation a system can do is very strongly related to the available communication bandwidth for a fixed processor architecture (neglecting input and output). The graph of Fig. 4 therefore indicates how hot spot contention, in the absence of combining, limits the speedup achievable with a given number of processors. The limitation from this effect alone is quite significant for large systems: with 1000 processors, only 0.125 percent hot spot traffic limits the potential speedup to 500, i.e., 50 percent efficiency.

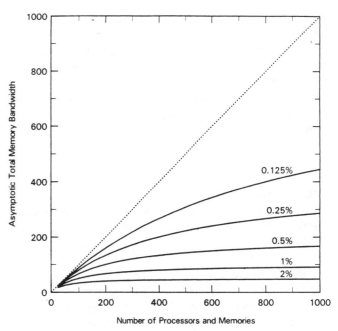

Fig. 4. Asymptotically maximum total network bandwidth as a function of the number of processors for various fractions of the network traffic aimed at a single hot spot.

VI. EVALUATION

The simulation and analysis above provides strong evidence that tree saturation is a significant problem. What we claim, however, is somewhat more, namely, the *need* for combining and other techniques to avoid tree saturation in *any* large-scale multiple-purpose parallel system. Because this is a phenomenon which cannot occur in serial machines or in small-scale parallelism, it is necessary to ask how pervasive the problem is, and whether it might yield to simpler or less costly solutions.

A. Generality

The tree saturation effect is not dependent on network topology for a multistage blocking network with distributed routing control. All such networks must contain trees from every sink to every source, which can become saturated and thereby delay all references. The existence of multiple paths through the network does not avoid the problem, even with dynamic rerouting. As congestion begins, the messages to the hot spot will themselves be rerouted and in the steady state will saturate all the alternate paths.

It is also clear that there is no requirement that the messages be memory references. Hot spot nonuniformity in the traffic through a purely message-based system can produce similar global degradation. It is in principle possible to use message combining in such systems, but doing so implies that the transport mechanism should be given some knowledge of the message semantics — specifically, how to combine them. How one does this has not been investigated.

An effect entirely analogous to tree saturation as presented here can also afflict circuit switching networks with distributed routing. In this case, there will of course be no effect on data transfer once it has begun, but the time required to complete a circuit prior to initiating the transfer will be affected. The exact manner in which tree saturation occurs depends on the distributed routing technique used.

While the presentation here implies that tree saturation is a result of finite queue lengths, a very similar effect—with somewhat different causes—can be shown to occur under the assumption of infinite queues. We do not discuss this (and the associated analytical model) here due to space limitations.

B. Realism

Whether the situation modeled is realistic can be divided into two questions.

1) Is there typically only one hot spot (or at most a small number)?

2) Is the traffic to the hot spots typically large enough to cause a problem?

The simulations performed on whole codes at NYU [2], [4], [5] did, in fact, typically contain only one or two hot spots at any given time during execution. We are beginning to augment such experimental results with our own traces of large parallel applications (not just kernels). The experience so far is that one or two hot spots are typical, although more can occur if cacheable data are not designated as such.

On the other hand, it may be argued that one application is not the right place to look for hot spot references, that the operating system will normally generate numerous such references during normal coordination because of the various central queues which are inherent in parallel systems. We therefore have also tested the effectiveness of combining with more hot spots, simulating, for example, five hot spots in separate memory modules. Essentially identical results were obtained; combining is still quite effective, and without it major degradation still occurs. (Were all the hot spots in the same memory module, identical results would be obtained, except that larger queues might be needed. Given more than 100 memory modules, address interleaving, and hashing, it is unlikely that more than one of a small number of hot spots will lie in the same module.)

For the NYU simulations, the percentage of total data requests to memory aimed at the hot spot was typically 1–2 percent [3]. This appears inconclusive since with 100 processors Fig. 4 indicates a maximum speedup of only 30–50 in this range of hot spot requests. But the situation is potentially much worse than that.

For performance reasons, a cache is usually interposed between the processors and the network, and other results indicate that approximately 80–90 percent of all data traffic can be intercepted by the cache. So the total network traffic, which is all we are concerned with, is 10–20 percent of the total data traffic. At the same time, none of the references to a globally accessed lock can be cached. So the 1–2 percent of total data traffic to the hot spot(s) represents 5–20 percent of the total network traffic. Under those conditions, Fig. 4 indicates that maximum performance is severely degraded: with 100 processors, the maximum speedup that can be attained is in the range of 5 to 20.

It can be argued that the NYU results are not representative. Indeed, they may not be since NYU developed this style of combining, was testing the concept, and certainly did not program with the intention of minimizing its use. A factor of 10 reduction in hot spot traffic might reasonably be obtained by coding that attempted to reduce that traffic.

In addition, there are a number of software techniques that can be used to reduce hot spot contention. For example, if a global sum is desired, creating it by filling in a tree of partial sums can, without combining, make the maximum contention a constant (equal to N for an N-ary tree of partial sums), rather than proportional to the number of processors, as would be the case if fetch-and-add were naively used. We are, however, unaware of any way to get the full effect of a combining fetch-and-add—including distribution of the incremental sums—by software alone, without combining, and we suspect it can be proved that this is impossible.

C. Pragmatic Considerations

The above discussion is inconclusive in the absence of a broader range of experience than is presently available; there will always be parallel applications which communicate or synchronize infrequently enough to not cause a problem, and there are applications which will consistently cause tree saturation. However, there are pragmatic points that must be considered.

Without combining, the potential major loss of efficiency that hot spot references can cause must be taken into account in all code written for a highly parallel system. We can scarcely afford to have this additional complexity permeate the programming task.

Furthermore, the running of multiple users in a multiprogramming environment on a highly parallel machine without combining has a serious flaw. Traffic to a single hot spot has a global effect. Therefore, it is possible for a *single* user with a highly parallel task that is not debugged, naive, or even malicious to degrade the *entire system's* performance via hot spot traffic. This is clearly an unacceptable situation. While it may be possible to avoid it by other means, the alternatives we are aware of impose more of a burden than the hardware cost of combining.

D. The RP3 Combining Network

In addition to the above considerations, the RP3 design is subject to the constraint that, given existing technology, it is physically unrealistic to build a combining network sufficiently fast to support all memory references of 512 processors. The speed required for efficient memory access implies that the network should be built in a bipolar technology. However, combining is a logic-intensive function which benefits greatly from the density available in MOSFET technology.

It is therefore planned to use two different networks in RP3:

1) a high-speed multistage noncombining network with sufficiently low latency to handle the normal memory references of 512 processors, built in bipolar technology;

2) a smaller, slower combining network with characteristics adequate to support the synchronization references of 512 processors, built in MOSFET technology.

The required separation of memory traffic is achieved by diverting synchronization references, such as fetch-and-op [1], test-and-set, etc., into the combining network. All other references will use the noncombining network. For experimental purposes it will be possible to divert all traffic into either network.

Software and hardware measures in RP3 are planned to minimize the potential of tree blockage in the noncombining network. For example, experiments with parallel memory reference traces and cache simulation show that the most common occurrence of hot spots in loads and stores results from not caching global data which could be cached, for example, shared "constants" which are stored only once and then fetched many times. RP3 hardware allowing dynamic control of cacheability can be used by software to alleviate such problems.

VII. CONCLUSION

By considering nonuniform *hot spot* memory reference patterns, we have demonstrated that multistage blocking networks have an unfortunate property. A sufficient concentration of references to one server — a "hot spot" — can degrade the response of the network to all references, not just those to the hot spot server, and the potential degradation is sufficient to cripple system performance. The "tree saturation" effect causing this requires only that the network be multistage, blocking, and controlled by distributed routing. Message combining is adequate to deal with this effect.

It is possible to avoid this problem in special-purpose systems, tailored to a particular application. Such systems can usually incorporate hardware that directly addresses this problem if it exists in their context.

It is also possible to avoid this problem in some multiple-purpose systems, if the application is carefully tailored to the communication topology and, by explicitly managing communication, happens to keeps the traffic completely uniform. This is the case, for example, with the "crystalline" mode of operation of the Cosmic Cube [10], the mode in which most of its applications have so far been run.

Message combining provides a solution to this problem. It requires no additional programming overhead, should be effective in a broad range of applications and environments, and should enable applications programmers to code without undue attention to excessive synchronization, with the additional assurance that no one user can degrade a multiuser system with his own excessive synchronization.

The additional cost of a combining network is outweighed by its potential advantages, and such advantages grow with the size of the parallel system. We consider the technique of message combining to be a required part of RP3, or of any other multiple-purpose parallel system of comparable size.

ACKNOWLEDGMENT

The authors would like to gratefully acknowledge the assistance of A. Gottlieb, who wrote the initial version of the two-way switch simulation code we used, and M. Wong, who performed numerous simulation experiments on the effects of hot spots and combining with a variety of switch designs.

REFERENCES

[1] A. Gottlieb *et al.*, "The NYU Ultracomputer — Designing an MIMD, shared memory parallel computer," *IEEE Trans. Comput.*, pp. 175–189, Feb. 1983.
[2] M. Kalos, "Scientific computations on the Ultracomputer," Courant Inst., New York Univ., New York, Ultracomputer Note 30, 1981.
[3] ——, Courant Inst., New York Univ., New York, private communication.
[4] M. Kalos, L. Gabi, and B. D. Lubachevsky, "Molecular simulation of equilibrium properties. Parallel implementation," Courant Inst., New York Univ., New York, Ultracomputer Note 27, 1981.
[5] D. Korn, "Timing simulations for elliptic PDE's run under washcloth," Courant Inst., New York Univ., New York, Ultracomputer Note 31, 1981.
[6] C. Kruskal and M. Snir, "The performance of multistage interconnection networks for multiprocessors," *IEEE Trans. Comput.*, vol. C-32, pp. 1091–1098, Dec. 1983.
[7] W. C. Brantley, K. P. McAuliffe, and J. Weiss, "The RP3 processor/memory element," in *Proc. IEEE 1985 Int. Conf. Parallel Processing*, St. Charles, IL, Aug. 1985.
[8] V. A. Norton and G. F. Pfister, "A methodology for predicting multiprocessor performance," in *Proc. IEEE 1985 Int. Conf. Parallel Processing*, St. Charles, IL, Aug. 1985.
[9] G. F. Pfister *et al.*, "The IBM Research Parallel Processor Prototype (RP3): Introduction and architecture," in *Proc. IEEE 1985 Int. Conf. Parallel Processing*, St. Charles, IL, Aug. 1985.
[10] C. S. Seitz, "The Cosmic Cube," *Commun. ACM*, vol. 28, no. 1, pp. 22–23, Jan. 1985.
[11] H. Sullivan, T. Bashkow, and D. Klappholtz, "A large scale homogeneous, fully distributed parallel machine," in *Proc. Fourth Annu. Symp. Comput. Architecture*, 1977, pp. 105–124.
[12] R. J. Swan, S. H. Fuller, and D. P. Siewiorek, "CM* — A modular, multimicroprocessor," in *Proc. AFIPS Conf.*, vol. 46, 1977, pp. 637–644.
[13] D. Lawrie, "Access and alignment of data in an array processor," *IEEE Trans. Comput.*, vol. C-24, pp. 1145–1155, 1975.
[14] L. A. Cohn, "A conceptual approach to general purpose parallel computer architecture," Ph.D. dissertation, Columbia Univ., New York, 1983.

Gregory F. Pfister (S'71–M'74–SM'85) was born in Detroit, MI, on November 29, 1945. He received the S.B., S.M., and Ph.D. degrees from the Massachusetts Institute of Technology, Cambridge, in 1967, 1969, and 1974, respectively, in electrical engineering.

He joined IBM in 1974, working between then and 1978 in several organizations on computer graphics software and remote software service. From 1975 to 1976 he was on the faculty of the Department of Electrical Engineering and Computer Science, University of California, Berkeley. In 1978 he joined the IBM Research Division, Yorktown Heights, NY, as a Research Staff Member. He was Manager of Software Support for the Yorktown Simulation Engine and is presently Manager of the Parallel Systems Architecture Group, in charge of RP3 architecture, performance evaluation, and software. His technical interests include parallel architectures, languages for parallel processing, VLSI design automation, and computer graphics.

Dr. Pfister is a member of Eta Kappa Nu, Tau Beta Pi, and Sigma Xi.

V. Alan Norton was born in Salt Lake City, UT, on August 20, 1947. He received the B.A. degree from the University of Utah, Salt Lake City, in 1968, and the Ph.D. degree from Princeton University, Princeton, NJ, in 1976, both in mathematics.

He was an Instructor at the University of Utah from 1976 to 1979 and an Assistant Professor at Hamilton College, Clinton, NY, from 1979 to 1980 before coming to IBM Research. Currently, he is a Research Staff Member at IBM, Yorktown Heights, NY, working on the Research Parallel Processing Prototype (RP3). His research interests include the performance analysis and architecture of parallel computer systems, parallel algorithms, fractals, and computer graphics.

Dr. Norton is a member of the Association for Computing Machinery and the American Mathematical Society.

The Onset of Hot Spot Contention

Manoj Kumar and Gregory F. Pfister

IBM T.J. Watson Research Center
Yorktown Heights, NY 10598

Abstract: Non-uniform traffic distributions in a multistage network characterized by "hot spots" — destinations getting more than their share of traffic—can cause dramatic reductions in the maximum throughput of the network. In this paper we develop an analytical model predicting how long a "hot spot" must be persist in shuffle/exchange networks before its its full effect is felt. The model predicts that hot spots will disrupt network traffic severely in a very short time: 10 to 50 instruction execution times in a shared-memory machine. This result, verified by simulation, leads to the conclusion that if stringent measures are not taken to ensure uniformity, the performance of large multistage networks will be substantially worse than has been previously predicted.

1.0   Introduction

Multistage interconnection networks with distributed routing have often been proposed as a means of connecting large parallel or distributed computing systems. However, for such networks it has been shown that statistically non-uniform traffic patterns—patterns containing a **hot spot** [6] that gets more than its share of the traffic—can cause severe performance degradation for all network traffic, not just traffic to the hot spot. For example, as little as 0.125% imbalance in a 1000-way network can limit network throughput to less than 50% of its maximum value.   This is independent of network topology, redundant paths, or mode of use of the network (e.g.: message passing, shared memory, circuit vs. packet switching, etc.). This effect was discovered in the IBM RP3 project [5,1,4], and first reported in [6]. It was also reported there that the technique of "combining" messages in the interconnection network could solve the problem for some cases of interest.

However, the analysis and simulation reported in [6] does not address a crucial issue: Over what time interval must a non-uniform pattern be sustained in order to reach tree saturation? This is important, because it is a critical measure of how uniform the traffic must be to avoid hot spot problems. Statistical uniformity is much more easily achieved when averaged over hours (for example) than when averaged over microseconds.

We address that issue here by developing a model, verified by simulation, of how long a hot spot must persist before its effects are fully felt. This provides a lower bound on the interval over which uniformity must be measured.

Unfortunately, the result is that the required interval is quite short indeed. For example, with a 1024-way network of 4-way switches containing 4-element queues, a 0.125% hot spot non-uniformity will have its full effect within (approximately) 10 to 50 times the minimum time to traverse the switch. (See Figure 4.)

We can only derive a crude lower bound for the time for a network to recover from a hot spot; that appears to be a more complex process. However, both that lower bound and our simulations demonstrate that the recovery time is much longer than the onset time.

Before deriving these results and comparing them with simulation, a brief overview of the hot spot effect will be given. A discussion of possible remedies, and of our conclusions, ends the paper.

2.0   Hot Spot Contention and Tree Saturation

Here we summarize the results presented in [6], with a slight addition.

Consider a two-sided packet-switched multistage network, with p ports on each side, connected to message sources on one side and message sinks on the other, such as the Omega network [3] illustrated in Figure 1.

Suppose the traffic pattern is initially uniform, with messages emitted from each source at a rate r ($0 \leq r \leq 1$). Then, at some time after a steady state has been achieved, the traffic pattern is altered to direct a fraction h, $0 \leq h \leq 1$, of all references are aimed at a specific sink: the **hot sink**. I.e., each source emits $r(1 - h)$ messages uniformly distributed, and rh messages to the hot sink. h is the hot spot rate. As a result, the hot sink receives two components of traffic: $r(1 - h)$ from the uniform background, and rhp from the hot spot.

If h is large enough, the rate into the hot sink will be unity due to the rhp term. If this happens, the queues in

Reprinted from *Proc. Int'l Conf. Parallel Processing*, 1986, pp. 28-34. Copyright © 1986 by The Institute of Electrical and Electronics Engineers, Inc. All rights reserved.

the network switch closest to that sink will fill. This causes the preceding switches' queues to fill; then the next preceding; etc. Finally, a tree of switches rooted at the sink and extending to every source is saturated. This is called **tree saturation**, and is illustrated by the marked switch queues in Figure 1.

Once tree saturation is in effect, every message from any source to any sink must cross the saturated tree and so is delayed. In effect, all the network traffic is gated by the speed at which the single hot sink can dispose of its messages. In the steady state, this occurs when the total traffic rate into the hot sink $(r(1 - h) + rhp)$ equals unity. In [6] it was shown that this has a dramatic effect as the system is scaled up in size, as noted in the examples cited in the present paper's introduction. In the steady state, hot spot effects are independent of network topology, finite queue size, etc. (However, the timing analysis presented here does depend on these factors.)

Beyond what was presented in [6], we note here that tree saturation is a finite queue effect. But in order to eliminate it, the queues in the final stage of the network must be large enough to accommodate the maximum hot spot traffic of the entire system. In other words, their size must be equal to $M \times$ the number of network ports, where M is the maximum number of messages that can be simultaneously outstanding from each source. Thus if queue sizes are taken into account, the total network size has another factor equal to the number of network ports.

This raises the network size to $O(M \times N^2 \log N)$, rather than the usually-cited $O(N \log N)$. The factor of N^2 negates any size advantage over a full crosspoint switch.

3.0 Modelled Behavior

The network behavior modelled here assumes that the network is initially in a steady state with uniformly distributed traffic flowing through it at a rate r. At time 0, all the sources simultaneously change their traffic patterns to include a hot spot. r does not change, but a fraction h of r sufficient to cause tree saturation is now directed at a hot sink. The throughput of the network now declines until at a time T it reaches a steady-state minimum caused by tree saturation. We wish to estimate T as a function of r, h, network size, etc.

Packet switching is assumed, with one packet per message. In the analysis, one time unit is required for a packet to move from one switch to the next. For reasons explained later, the results shown in the figures are scaled to be in units equal to the minimum time to traverse the switch.

4.0 Model of Onset

It is convenient to imagine the messages sent to the hot sink after time 0 as being colored red, and all other messages colored white. The total rate at which each source emits red messages is

$$R = rh + \frac{r(1 - h)}{p}$$

R is not simply rh because $1/p$ of the messages from the uniform background are sent to the hot sink, where p is the number of network ports.

Rather than dealing directly with the complex dynamics of message flow through the network, we will count the red messages in the network. On the one hand, the number N of red messages is a function of time and of their total arrival and departure rates from the network as a whole. On the other hand, when tree saturation is reached there is a steady-state number N of red messages in the network that is a function of the input traffic and the amount of buffering available. So equating N in both formulations can tell us how long it takes to reach saturation.

4.1 Arrival and Departure

To estimate the arrival and departure rates, we make a set of assumptions that, overall, amount to the general assumption that the onset of tree saturation happens fast and suddenly — too fast and suddenly for the internal dynamics of the network to have much effect on arrival and departure rates until the point of saturation is reached.

We assume that the total arrival rate of red messages is constant (i.e., is Rp) until tree saturation is reached; and then it drops instantly to the tree saturation value. Under this assumption, the number of red messages generated by time T is simply RpT. Our simulations do not verify a constant arrival rate: the input rate does decline with time. Nevertheless the final results are adequate.

For the departure rate, we assume the following:

At T, the first red messages enter the first switch stage. They make their way through the tree of switches that will be saturated, gradually becoming more and more concentrated, until they reach the hot sink. Then:

1. Until the hot sink is reached, there is no effect on the rate at which messages are transported. The first red messages reach the hot sink at a time $D(r)$ that equals the average delay through the network at a total input rate of r.

2. At $D(r)$, the concentration of red messages is immediately sufficient to saturate the hot output port; i.e., after $D(r)$ that port emits messages at a rate of unity.

3. After $D(r)$, all the messages emitted by the hot output port are red.

While somewhat unrealistic, these assumptions are conservative. They overestimate the departure rate, and thus indicate that the saturated tree fills with red messages sooner than it actually will.

With those assumptions, the number of messages that have left the network at time T is simply $T - D(r)$. Then, since the number of red messages arriving by time T is RpT, $N = RpT + T - D(r)$. Solving this for T yields

K is the size of each individual switch, i.e., number of input and output ports, so K^i is the number of switches at each stage that lie within the saturated tree. q is the size of each queue; $(K + q)$ is the total storage available for messages aimed at the hot spot in each switch stage. (The additional K is due an additional buffer on each input port used in the simulation; this is discussed later).

For each switch at stage i in the saturated tree, mix_i is the fraction of red messages in its queue during steady-state tree saturation:

$$mix_i = \frac{AR_i}{AR_i + AW_i}$$

AR_i and AW_i are respectively the arrival rates of red and white messages at stage i:

$$AR_i = R \times \frac{p}{K^i}$$

because p/K^i is the number of sources in the subtree leading to each switch in stage i.

$$AW_i = r(1 - h) \times \frac{K^i - 1}{K^i}$$

Recall that $r(1 - h)$ is the total rate of uniform background traffic, part of which is directed at the hot sink. Since there are K^i possible destinations for the cool traffic

$$T = \frac{N - D(r)}{Rp - 1}$$

The denominator becomes zero as the combinations of R and p reaches a point inadequate to sustain an output rate of unity. I.e., as that point is approached the time to saturation approaches infinity, which is expected.

To estimate $D(r)$ we use the well-known formula for the average queue length in a switch stage [2]:

$$B(r) = \frac{r}{2(1 - r)} \left(1 - \frac{1}{K} \right)$$

Where r is the steady state rate and K is the number of ports of each switch in the network. Then $D(r) = S(1 + B(r))$. Because it assumes infinite queues, $B(r)$ will again produce conservative results (faster transportation than reality) for high total rates r.

4.2   Steady-State Population

In the steady state of tree saturation, N is the sum of the number of red messages n_i at each network stage (we count stages from 0, starting at the stage closest to the sinks):

$$N = \sum_{i=0}^{S-1} K^i \times (K + q) \times mix_i$$

at stage i, and one of them is the hot sink, the fraction above follows.

If we substitute back into the expression for mix_i, substitute the original expression for R, and simplify, we obtain

$$mix_i = \frac{Hp + 1}{Hp + K^i}$$

where $H = h/(1 - h)$, the ratio of hot to cool packet generation.

Finally substituting back into T, with slight simplification, we get

$$T = \frac{\left((K + q) \sum_{i=0}^{S-1} K^i mix_i \right) - S(1 + B(r))}{Rp - 1}$$

5.0   Simulation

To verify the above model, we ran simulations of the situation described above for a number of cases. These results are plotted with the analytical predictions in Figure 2 through Figure 4.

The switches simulated had two non-standard characteristics that match those of [6], and serve to make the simulated network act more like the ideal network modelled:

1.   Each output queue can simultaneously accept K messages in one time unit. While fairly realistic for $K = 2$, this is undoubtedly unrealistic for larger switches.

2.   Each input port to a switch has an additional one-message lookaside buffer that is not counted in the queue size. This allows the queues to be more fully utilized, since without it there must be K empty positions in every queue of a switch for any of the switch's predecessors to be enabled to send messages. This is the source of the additional K buffers per switch that was included in the prior analysis.

A complication arose in deciding what to measure as the time at which the switch reaches saturation. Our formula effectively assumes that all the queues in the saturated tree fill up simultaneously, and this is clearly not the case. What we did was find, from the simulations, the average red message occupancy of the queues in steady-state tree saturation. Then the time to saturate was taken to be the time at which 80% of that steady-state value was reached. 80% was chosen because at approximately that value there is a single message slot unused in each queue.

All plotted points are the means of 200 simulation runs each.

6.0   Results

A surprisingly short amount of time is required to reach tree saturation.

Figure 2 shows the time to tree saturation as a function of the initial uniform background rate r for values of h ranging from 0.125% to 16% in factors of two. It assumes a 64-way Omega network where each 2-way switch has queues of size 4. The time unit is not T as derived above, but rather T/S, the minimum time required for a message to traverse the switch in one direction; in our formulation, that equals the the depth of the network. This unit was chosen for two reasons: First, it allows meaningful comparison across different network and switch sizes; it turns out that, when expressed in this unit, the time to saturate is relatively constant across network and switch sizes (10-50, for 4 element queues). Second, in a shared memory system, it is typically comparable to the time required to execute a single instruction in a processor. (It is not identical to the time required to perform a complete memory reference; that time includes two trips across the network—request and reply—as well as memory access time and other delays.)

The dotted lines at the top of the figure mark the minimum background rate below which each plotted hot spot rate will not cause tree saturation; this is equivalent to the maximum rate sustainable with the associated hot spot rate. Thus the graphs can be interpreted as follows: Pick a given initial background rate (point on the lower axis). Proceed vertically to the curve corresponding to the hot spot rate of interest. The time that curve indicates (shown on the vertical axis) is the amount of time required for that hot spot rate to drive the network throughput from the initial rate to the asymptote associated with the hot spot rate (dotted line).

Figure 3 shows the same information, but in this case for a 256-port network with 4-way switches. Figure 4 shows the predicted results for a large (1024 port) network; this was not simulated. As can be seen, the onset time is very short.

As can be seen, our predicted results match the simulated results reasonably well except for two situations: very high r in the 256-port network; and very low r in the 64-port network. At high r in the 256-port network we are pushing the actual maximum capacity of the network and would expect all the approximations we are using to break down. At low r in the 64-port network, there is a breakdown in our assumptions about total arrival and departure rates: Onset is a more diffuse process with more time for complex internal feedback effects. However, in this case our estimates are on the optimistic side.

7.0 Recovery Time

Figure 5 shows the throughput of a 64-way network as a hot spot of 16% is applied and then removed within a total background rate of 0.4. As can be seen, the recovery time is substantially longer than the onset time. A rationale for this follows.

Intuitively, many sources "cooperate" to saturate the tree; but only one sink (the hot one) operates to eliminate saturation. The time to recover "normal" traffic flow should be related to the time to remove all red messages from the switch after the sources stop generating them. If the hot output port runs at the maximum rate (unity), this time is simply equal to the steady-state count of red messages N during tree saturation, derived previously. This is longer than the time to saturation, since the onset time T is $(N - D(r))/(Rp - 1)$. One might imagine that after a time $2mix_{S-1}N/K$, for K-way switches, all the switches closest to the sources would be clear; so after that time, $1 - 1/K$ of the traffic would resume its normal rate. Then after an additional time equal to $2mix_{S-2}N/K$, $1 - 1/K^2$ of the traffic will resume its normal rate; etc. The slow rise of throughput shown in Figure 5 tends to indicate that something like this is occurring. However, we have not yet compared this to simulation results, and consider it unlikely to be correct, for the following reason: Until all the red packets are gone, they should tend to delay uniformly distributed messages that happen to be directed to the hot sink; and by filling queues, this will affect other messages. This may cause continued congestion even after all the red messages have left the network.

8.0 Discussion

The time required to reach tree saturation is distressingly short. What points of leverage can be used to improve the situation?

Increasing the switch size (K) actually makes the situation worse: Even when, as we have done, the units are the depth of the network—giving larger switches a large advantage—smaller switches saturate more slowly.

Increasing the queue size also helps. But the queue size is a linear factor in the total saturation time, so very large queues are necessary to make a substantial difference. E.g., to get saturation time up to the range of 100 switch traversals, queues on the order of 40 elements are needed. This is unreasonable with present technology.

The addition of redundant paths will also help, but only because the total queue storage available rises with the number of paths. So this decrease is also linear.

One thing that certainly can help is over-design, in the sense of using the network only at at traffic rates less than the rates where the expected hot spot activity will cause tree saturation. This adds significantly to the expense of the network. Furthermore, at present there is little experience available to define exactly what degree of non-uniformity to expect in general.

As discussed in [6], "combining" of identical messages within the switch nodes themselves can eliminate the problem completely. However, combining only works when the the hot spot is caused by references to identical entities at the sinks (e.g., identical memory locations).

When the hot spot occurs because many sources are accessing many different entities that happen to occupy the same sink, combining cannot help. What may help in that case are techniques to ensure that non-identical references are scattered uniformly among the destinations, such as the combination of interleaving and randomization used by RP3 [5]. How well this will work in practice is not yet known; if it does, simultaneously using both this technique and "combining" (also present in RP3) may solve the problem, at least for shared memory systems. It is not obvious at this time how to solve the problem for systems based on other computational models.

Global control over routing can avoid the problem completely, of course, as discussed in [6].

To summarize:

1. Very little perturbation, over a very short time, can drastically reduce network throughput.

2. Recovery after the perturbation takes much longer than than the onset of the problem.

This leads to the conclusion that multistage networks with distributed routing are unstable under non-uniform traffic loads, in the sense that they tend to "fall into" tree saturation easily. For large networks in particular, e.g., networks of size 512 or greater, if stringent measures are not taken to maintain a uniform traffic pattern, swift onset and slow recovery makes it very probable that at least partial tree saturation will always be present; and thus large multistage networks may not perform anywhere near as well as has previously been predicted.

References

[1] W.C. Brantley, K.P. McAuliffe, J. Weiss, "The RP3 Processor-Memory Element," *Proceedings of the 1985 International Conference in Parallel Processing*, August 1985, pp. 782-789.

[2] C. Kruskal and M. Snir, "The Performance of Multistage Interconnection Networks for Multiprocessors," *IEEE Trans. on Computers*, Vol. C-32(12), 1983, pp.1145-1155.

[3] D. Lawrie, "Access and Alignment of Data in an Array Processor", *IEEE Trans. on Computers*, No. C-24, 1975, pp. 1145-1155.

[4] V.A. Norton and G.F. Pfister, "A Methodology for Predicting Multiprocessor Performance," *Proceedings of the 1985 International Conference in Parallel Processing*, August 1985, pp. 772-781.

[5] G.F. Pfister, W.C. Brantley, D.A. George, S.L. Harvey, W.J. Kleinfelder, K.P. McAuliffe, E.A. Melton, V.A. Norton, J. Weiss, "The IBM Research Parallel Processor Prototype (RP3): Introduction and Architecture," *Proceedings of the 1985 International Conference in Parallel Processing*, August 1985, pp. 764-771.

[6] G.F. Pfister and V.A. Norton, "'Hot Spot' Contention and Combining in Multistage Interconnection Networks," *IEEE Trans. Comp.*, Vol. C-34, No. 10, October 1985, pp. 934-948; also *Proceedings of the 1985 International Conference in Parallel Processing*, August 1985, pp. 790-797.

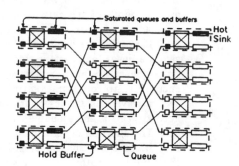

Figure 1 : An 8x8 shuffle-exchange network, depicting the saturation caused by a hot sink.

Figure 1. An 8-port Omega network. The marked switches are saturated, as discussed in the text.

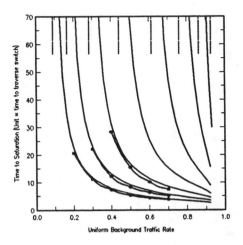

Figure 2.   Time required to saturate a 64-port Omega network: The switches have queue size 4, and 2 inputs and outputs. The solid curves are the predicted values for h ranging from 0.125% to 16% by factors of 2. the dots connected by dashed lines show simulation results. The dotted lines show the sustainable throughput after tree saturation for the values of h used.

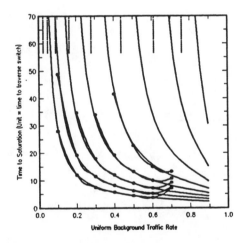

Figure 3.   Time to saturate a 256-port Delta network: The switches have queue size 4; other elements are the same as Figure 2.

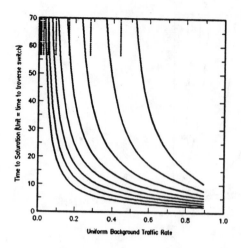

Figure 4.   Time to saturate a 1024-port Omega network: Information and are the same
as Figure 2.

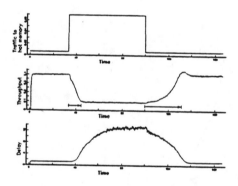

Figure 5.   Onset and Recovery from a Hot Spot: Hot spot percentage, throughput, and
delay as a function of time. The network is the same as Figure 2's, and the hot
spot is 16%. The arrows indicate the time for onset and recovery.

On "hot spot" contention

Rosanna Lee

Computer Science Laboratory, SRI International

333 Ravenswood Avenue, Menlo Park, CA 94025

November 13, 1985

Abstract

In a recent paper. Pfister and Norton[4] brought to our attention the potential degradation in performance of multi-stage interconnection networks in the presence of nonuniform traffic patterns. More specifically. they studied the effect of a single *hot spot* – a location that is accessed more frequently – in an otherwise uniform traffic environment. Their simulations assumed that *all* input lines contribute to the hot spot. Their results showed that the effect of hot spots drastically reduced the bandwidth of the network. In this note. we confirm Pfister and Norton's results and present supplemental data and arguments which illustrate other aspects of hot spot contention. In particular. we show that the performance improves when the source of the hot spot is more localized.

Introduction

Present day computer architecture places heavy emphasis on modularity and scalability. Multiprocessors designed with these goals in mind usually involve two components: processing elements/memory modules and a switching network that interconnects the modules. Buffered delta networks or similar multi-stage networks are usually chosen to be the switch because of their scalability in terms of cost (number of switching switching is $O(N \log N)$) and performance[1.2.3]. These performance studies. however. examined the switch under uniform traffic conditions. Recent results from Pfister and Norton[4] indicated that the performance degrades severely as hot spots are introduced into the traffic.

Pfister and Norton reported on simulation results of hot spot contention in multi-stage interconnection networks. They assumed an environment in which processors are on one side of the switch and memory modules are on the other. Memory references are uniformly distributed among the modules except for a single hot spot to which more requests are directed. The percentage of "extra" requests directed at the hot spot is referred to as the *hot spot percentage*. For example. a 2% hot spot means that 2% of all requests are directed at the hot spot. and the remaining 98% are directed to *all* locations. including the hot spot. They also assumed that the hot spots arise from globally shared locks and hence. *all* processors contribute to the hot spot percentage. We shall refer to the number of processors contributing to the hot spot. the *contribution percentage*. The shared lock case described above represents a contribution percentage of 100.

Pfister and Norton's simulation results (which are reproduced in Figure 1) indicated that hot spot contention limits the scalability of the switch by limiting the growth of the throughput capacity as the size of the switch (i.e. number of processors/memory modules) increases. As the size of the switch is increased. the throughput did not improve correspondingly: in fact. with a 2% hot spot. the throughput did not grow at all from a switch for 200 processors to that for 1000 processors. They explained the cause of this degradation in terms of the *tree saturation effect* in which the capacity of the links leading to the hot spot becomes saturated and the saturation propagates in a tree-like manner back to the input lines (see Figure 2).

Their solution to the problem (as caused by globally shared locks) was to combine. within the switch. messages destined for identical locations. in order to reduce contention. Combining would not be effective. however. if hot spots do not arise from shared locks but come about because of a few input lines that frequently use a particular output line – a more *localized* source. In such a case. combining provides no relief and buffers located along the routes from the source to the hot spot will become saturated.

In this note. we present simulation results that concur with Pfister and Norton's. We also exam-

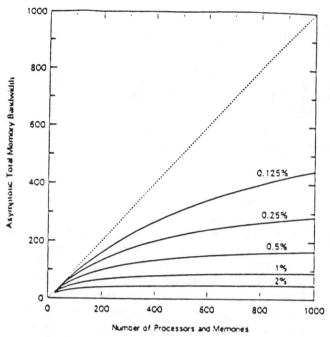

Fig. 1. Asymptotically maximum total network bandwidth as a function of the number of processors for various fractions of the network traffic aimed at a single hot spot.

Figure 1: Copy of Pfister and Norton's results[4]

ine the consequences of removing their assumption that the hot spot percentage stays constant as the number of processors is increased. The cause of the hot spot discussed by Pfister and Norton is just one case out of numerous examples in which hot spots may arise. For example, another interesting cause of a hot spot is a single point-to-point traffic overlay on top of an otherwise uniform distribution resulting from, say, a file transfer[5]. Yet another cause of hot spots would be a global variable that is shared among a fixed number of processors, regardless of the *total* number of processors present. By studying the effect of hot spots arising out of these scenarios, we can get a better picture of the effects of hot spot contention.

Assumptions

The switch being simulated is a buffered delta network[3] made up of 2-by-2 switching elements. It is a packet-switched, synchronous, pipelined network. A switching element can receive a packet from each of its input lines and output them within one cycle, in the absence of "conflicts." A pair of packets *conflict* if they both need the same output line. Conflicts are resolved by alternately choosing one of the

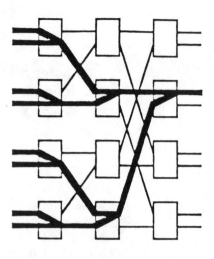

Figure 2: Tree saturation effect[4]

input lines. The packet left behind is resubmitted during the next cycle. Buffering is assumed to be done within one cycle, independent of the buffer size.

The destinations of the packets are randomly and uniformly distributed. Each packet has equal probability of going to any of the destinations regardless of which input line it came from. The exception is with hot spot runs. In hot spot runs, a number of input lines are destinated as "contributors" to the hot spot; this number is based on the contribution percentage (specified as a parameter of the run). For example, a 100% contribution means all input lines are contributors. A percentage of a contributor's packets are set aside for the hot spot (as determined by the *overall* hot spot percentage) and the rest are evenly distributed among all lines.

We are interested in the worse case, in terms of performance, that the switch can experience. This occurs when packets are being submitted to all lines of the switch every cycle; we refer to this as the "100% load" condition. All data presented were obtained under 100% load.

Results presented in this note are expressed in terms of *throughput percentage* and *absolute throughput*. Throughput percentage is the number of packets that passed through the switch divided by the total submitted. Absolute throughput, sometimes called *bandwidth*, is the number of packets that passed through the switch during a given period.

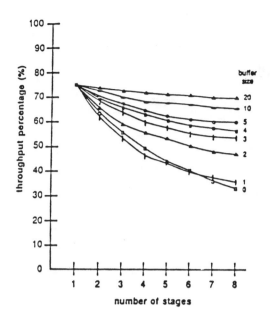

Figure 3: Uniform traffic: Throughput percentage vs switch size

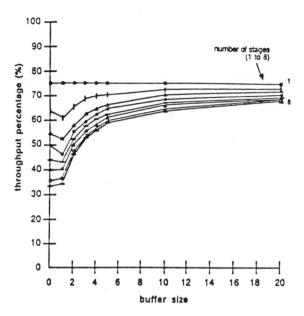

Figure 4: Uniform traffic: Throughput percentage vs buffer size

Uniform traffic

In order to have a point of reference for the performance of the switch with hot spots present, we first present statistics of the switch in uniform traffic. Figures 3 and 4 illustrate the relationship between the switch size (expressed in terms of the number of stages) and throughput percentage, and that between the buffer size and the throughput percentage, respectively. Figure 7 shows the absolute throughput.

The effect of increasing the switch size (the number of stages) on the performance of the switch determines its scalability. Our simulation results show that the throughput percentage decreases gradually as the number of stages is increased. As the number of stages increases, so does the number of input lines (number of stages = $\log_2$(number of input lines)) and hence the number of packets submitted. Thus, although the throughput percentage decreases, the bandwidth of the switch increases, as shown in Figure 7. Dias and Jump's analytical and simulation results[1] are different from ours in terms of absolute value, but follow a similar trend, especially for larger sized switches.

As the buffer size is increased, throughput is increased, with the *rate* of increase of throughput slowing down as the buffer size is increased. The growth in buffer size increases the throughput sub-

stantially for increases up to a buffer size of 5; switches with larger buffers bring in much less gains in throughput. Gottlieb et al.[2] reported that their simulations have shown that switches with queues of around size 8 give essentially the same performance as those with infinite queues. The results of Dias and Jump also showed a similar pattern.

All lines contributing to hot spot

Figures 5 and 6 show the throughput percentage of the switch with respect to the switch size and buffer size, with all input lines contributing to a 2% hot spot. Figure 7 shows the absolute throughput as the switch size is increased (linearly). Comparing these with Figures 3 and 4, we see that the throughput drops dramatically for the hot spot case, especially for larger switches. Smaller switches are also affected, but the effect is not as dramatic. For small switches, say an 8-input switch, 2% (of 8) is a very small number; for larger switches, say a 256-input switch, however, 2% is much more substantial. As the switch size is increased, the number of packets directed at the hot spot increases exponentially. Our results agree closely with those of Pfister and Norton.

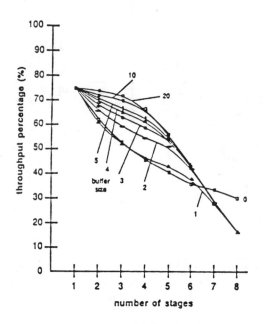

Figure 5: 2% hot spot: Throughput percentage vs switch size

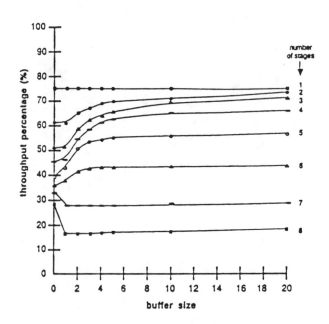

Figure 6: 2% hot spot: Throughput percentage vs buffer size

Figure 6 show that increasing the buffer size does not alleviate the situation (at least up to buffers of size 20). Buffers along the routes from the input lines to the hot spot output line of the switch back up and eventually block all input lines. Larger buffers only delay the effect because they eventually get filled up too. Examining Figures 3 and 5, we see that the unbuffered switches (with 0 buffer size) are not affected in the same way as buffered switches. Their degraded performance is a consequence of increased conflicts due to contention for the hot spot routes. An unbuffered switch is one example of *non-blocking* switches; only blocking switches are affected by this phenomenon, as pointed out by Pfister and Norton.

Some lines contributing to hot spot

The results for switch performance in the presence of a hot spot are obtained so far by making all input lines contribute to the hot spot percentage. By lowering the number of contributors but fixing the *overall* hot spot percentage, we can get a slight increase in throughput. Figure 8 shows the throughput percentage for a 256-input switch with an overall 1% hot spot and a varying number of lines contributing to that single percent. For example, 100% contri-

bution means that all 256 lines are contributing 1% of their packets to the hot spot (and the rest to all lines, as noted earlier). A 50% contribution means that 128 lines are contributing 2% of their packets to the hot spot, and so on.

The improvement is due to less routes being congested as a result of the hot spot. In other words, the "saturation tree" has a narrower span (of leaves). As the buffer size is increased, the effect of this tree on other routes is further mitigated.

Single line contributing to hot spot

We also measured the throughput with a *single* source contributing *all* of its packets to a single output line, with the remaining input lines sending uniformly and randomly to *all* lines. In other words, one input line sends 100% of its packets to the hot spot line, regardless of the switch size. This traffic pattern is referred to as a "point-to-point" hot spot[5]. By limiting the source of the hot spot to a single line, the *overall* hot spot percentage is lowered as the switch size is increased. The results are presented in Figure 9.

These results show that larger switches with large buffers actually outperform their correspond-

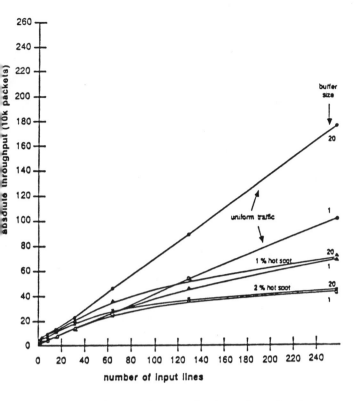

Figure 7: Comparisons: Absolute throughput vs switch size

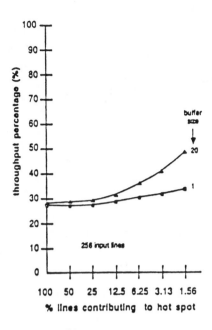

Figure 8: Fixed 1% hot spot and varying number of contributors

ing smaller counterparts. There are two opposing factors at work as the size of the switch is increased. First, as noted earlier, more conflicts occur with larger switches, and hence the percentage of throughput decreases. However, as the size of the switch increases, the *percentage* of packets directed at the hot spot decreases. With a 2-input switch, 1 line constitutes a 50% hot spot, whereas for a 256-input switch, 1 line is less than 0.4%. Therefore, the larger switches have more uniformly distributed destinations, which in turn improves the throughput. As the buffer size is increased, the effect of the hot spot for larger switches is further lessened because the small percentage of packets destined for the hot spot can be cushioned by the buffers. For the smaller switches, however, quite significantly larger buffers would be required before the percentage of packets to the hot spot can be buffered. Therefore, with large buffers, larger switches eventually outperform smaller switches.

Wu[5] analysed the effect of mixing a single "point-to-point" traffic with a background of uniform traffic for single-buffered banyan networks. He discovered that point-to-point traffic degrades the maximum throughput significantly, as we have discovered. However, he did not analysed the effect of buffer size. The solutions he proposed included the use of non-blocking networks and special routing strategies.

Summary

In this note, we reported on some simulation results for buffered delta networks in the presence of different types of hot spots. First, we presented data for the switches when the traffic is uniformly distributed to serve as reference. We then showed that, when all input lines contribute to the hot spot, the throughput percentage of larger switches is drastically decreased, confirming the results of Pfister and Norton[4]. Increasing the buffer size does not improve the throughput as it did for the uniform case. When fewer lines contribute to the (same) hot spot percentage, the throughput improves slightly, especially with larger buffers. Finally, when the source of the hot spot is reduced to a single line contributing 100% of its packets to the hot spot, the throughput is still adversely affected, but as the buffer size is increased, larger switches actually outperform smaller switches.

Acknowledgements

I would like to thank Ed Ashcroft, R. Jagannathan and Leah Jamieson for their valuable help. This work is funded by the Strategic Computing Program, through ONR contract N00014-85-C-0775.

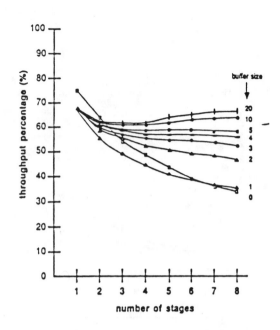

Figure 9: Single line contributes 100% to hot spot

References

1. D.M. Dias and J.R. Jump, "Analysis and simulation of buffered delta networks," *IEEE Transactions on Computer*, Vol. C-30, No. 4, pp 273-282, April 1981.

2. A. Gottlieb, R. Grishman, C.P. Kruskal, K.P. McAuliffe, L. Rudolph, and M. Snir, "The NYU Ultracomputer – designing an MIMD shared memory parallel computer," *IEEE Transactions on Computer*, Vol. C-32, No. 2, pp 175-189, Feb 1983.

3. J.H. Patel, "Processor-memory interconnections," In *Proceedings of the 6th Annual Symposium on Computer Architecture*, pp 168-177, April 1979.

4. G.F. Pfister and V.A. Norton ""Hot spot" contention and combining in multistage interconnection networks," *IEEE Transactions on Computer*, Vol. C-34, No. 10, pp 943-948, Oct 1985.

5. L.T. Wu, "Mixing traffic in a buffered banyan network," In *Proceedings of the 9th Data Communications Symposium*, pp 134-139, Sept 1985.

The Effectiveness of Combining in Shared Memory
Parallel Computers in the Presence of 'Hot Spots'

Gyungho Lee

Center for Supercomputing
Research and Development
University of Illinois
Urbana, IL. 61801

Clyde P. Kruskal

Department of Computer Science
University of Maryland
College Park, MD. 20742

David J. Kuck

Center for Supercomputing
Research and Development
University of Illinois
Urbana, IL. 61801

Abstract

Concurrent requests to a shared variable by many processors on a shared memory machine can create contention that will be serious enough to stall large machines. This idea has been formalized in the "hot spot" traffic model [PfNo85], where a fixed fraction of memory requests is for a single shared variable. "Combining," in which several requests for the same variable can be combined into a single request, has been suggested as an effective method of alleviating this contention. The NYU Ultracomputer [GGKM83] and the IBM RP3 [PBGH85] machine use "pairwise" combining, in which only two requests for the same variable can be combined at a switch. We study the effectiveness of combining. In particular, it turns out that pairwise combining cannot handle hot spots if the machine size is large enough. We suggest ways to overcome this weakness.

1. Introduction

The popularity of shared memory parallel computers, where processors and memory modules are interconnected through a multistage network, can be seen in several current projects, including the University of Illinois Cedar machine [GKLS83] [KDLS86], the NYU Ultracomputer [GGKM83] [EGKM85], and the IBM RP3 machine [PBGH85]. Sharing the memory in a parallel computer suggests that there is a possibility of many processors requesting the same variable at the same time (*concurrent requests*). This can create congestion in a machine, and the congestion becomes more serious as the number of processors in the machine (*machine size*) increases. To reduce congestion, when several requests directed at the same shared variable meet at a switch, they can be combined into a single request, which is forwarded toward the shared memory. When the response from the memory returns, the switch satisfies all of the requests, one at a time. The idea of reducing the congestion in this way, known as "combining," has been suggested as an effective way of allowing concurrent requests to a common location; combining can be found in the Columbia CHoPP [SuBK77], the NYU Ultracomputer, and most recently the IBM RP3 machine. (See [KrRS86] for a general discussion of what types of memory requests can be combined.)

This work was supported in part by the National Science Foundation under Grant No. US NSF DCR84-10110, and the U.S. Department of Energy under Grant No. US DOE DE-FG02-85ER25001. Part of this work was done while the second author was at the University of Illinois.

Pfister and Norton [PfNo85] suggested that the effectiveness of combining could be studied with the "hot spot" traffic model: a fixed fraction of the total memory traffic is concurrent requests to a single shared variable. Hot spots capture the effect of all of the processors continually accessing a common variable. Pfister and Norton argue that hot spots will seriously degrade the performance of any machine that lacks combining, and that this effect is quite general. They also discuss how well the hot spot model captures reality.

In this paper, we study the effectiveness of several different combining schemes. In particular, we will see that the pairwise combining scheme used in the NYU Ultracomputer and in the IBM RP3 machine is not powerful enough to handle hot spots. We suggest ways to modify their designs in order to overcome this weakness.

2. The Model

There have been many studies on the performance of multistage interconnection networks for processor-memory connection (see [Sieg85] and the references therein). One common traffic model for these studies is: A stream of memory requests from each processor is an independent, identically distributed random process; each processor's requests are uniformly distributed to all of the memory modules. This *uniform* traffic model does not capture the effect of traffic with requests to a single shared variable. To represent such traffic patterns, we use the *hot spot* model [PfNo85]: each request has a (finite) probability q of being headed to the same shared variable. The hot spot model is *nonuniform* in the sense that the requests are not uniformly distributed onto the memory modules. There are two types of request streams: the *noncombinables*, which are uniformly distributed to the memory modules as in the (usual) uniform model, and the *combinables*, which are headed to the same shared variable (and hence the same memory module).

We consider a buffered square banyan network [GoLi73] as the multistage network for interconnecting the processors and the memory modules. Square banyan networks include Omega networks [Lawr75] and Delta networks [Pate81]. (For details and general characteristics of multistage networks, see, for example, [Feng81], [KrSn82], [Sieg85].)

A network is composed of n stages of 2×2 (crossbar) switches with FIFO queues (i.e. buffers) at each output port. We assume that the network is packet-switched and synchronous, so that packets can be sent only at times $t_c, 2t_c, \cdots,$ where t_c is the *network cycle time*. Without loss of generality, we assume $t_c = 1$. We make the following further

Reprinted from *Proc. Int'l Conf. Parallel Processing*, 1986, pp. 35-41. Copyright © 1986 by The Institute of Electrical and Electronics Engineers, Inc. All rights reserved.

assumptions:

- Each request is a single packet.
- Each queue can accept at each cycle up to two distinct requests, one from each input port. If at some cycle a queue has only one free location and two requests are directed to it, the queue randomly accepts one of the two (the other request remains on the queue of the previous stage).
- The enqueuing process of a request and the dequeuing process are overlapped (i.e. while the request in front of the queue, if there is one, is being removed, other requests can be inserted onto the queue).
- The service time of a request in a queue is the same as the cycle time. So, the delay of a request at a switch is the number of requests ahead of it in the queue.
- Each processor has an infinite queue for requests. If a request is blocked from entering the first stage it is placed on the queue, and the processor continues issuing requests.

A square banyan network has a complete tree leading from the processors to each memory module (Figure 1). The tree that combinable requests traverse will be called the *fan-in tree*. Our main concern is with the average queuing delay in the fan-in tree.

Combining works as follows: When several combinable requests meet at a switch they are combined into a single request, which is forwarded toward the shared memory. A record of this is kept at the *wait buffer*. When the response from the memory returns, the switch satisfies all of the requests, one at a time (and the record is removed from the wait buffer). To concentrate our attention on queuing delays, we assume in Sections 2-6 that wait buffers have infinite size. Also, we will consider the delay of a request only from the processors to the memory modules, temporarily ignoring the delay on the return trip. Section 7 considers finite wait buffers, and their effect on the delay of a request in both directions of the network.

We will distinguish queue size and queue length. *Queue size* is the number of requests a queue can store at one time. We use *infinite queue* to mean that the queue size is infinite, and *finite queue* to mean that the queue size is finite. *Queue length* is the number of requests stored on a queue at some particular time. We will use equivalent definitions for wait buffer size and wait buffer length.

We consider several different combining schemes. In each case, we will consider what happens both with finite queues and with infinite queues. Infinite queues provide a nice yardstick to compare the more practical finite queue schemes. For finite queues, unless otherwise specified, we will always consider queue size four. This is large enough so that for the traffic loads considered, the performance under uniform traffic is almost as good as with infinite queues.

A network is *stable* if in steady state average delays in the network are uniformly bounded. This is an important property of a network. Under the *uniform* traffic model, buffered multistage interconnection networks are generally believed to be stable for "light" traffic (see [KrSn83],[KrSW86]).

We assume that at each cycle each processor issues a request with probability r, i.e. r is the rate of requests.

Each request has probability q of being a combinable request. Let r_c be the rate of combinables (i.e. hot spot requests), and r_n be the rate of noncombinables. Then

$$r_c = qr \qquad \text{and} \qquad r_n = (1-q)r \ .$$

Let r^i be the rate of requests at the stage i of the fan-in tree $(r^0 = r)$. Let r_c^i and r_n^i be the rate of combinable requests and noncombinable requests, respectively, at the stage i of the fan-in tree $(r_c^0 = r_c$ and $r_n^0 = r_n)$.

3. No Combining

In this section we will consider the performance of systems without combining. It is obvious that the combinables will create congestion in the network. The question is, how much will this degrade performance?

3.1. Infinite Queues

Assume the queues have infinite size and there is no combining. Recall that the rate of requests at the first stage is $r_n = r(1-q)$ and $r_c = rq$. Since there is no combining, the rate of combinable requests keeps doubling at each stage approaching the root of the fan-in tree. In particular, the rate of requests at stage i will be

$$r^i = r_n + 2^i r_c \ .$$

For any finite value of r_c, after several stages, the requests will be arriving at each queue at a greater rate than the queue can forward them. Networks large enough to see this effect will be unstable. For example, consider the case of $r = 0.25$ and $q = 0.01$. Even with q so small, by the ninth stage the arrival rate of the combinables alone will be $r_c = 1.28$, so the queuing delay will be unbounded.

In practice one expects short intensive periods of "hot spot" contention. If there are not too many stages of the fan-in tree in which the rate of requests is greater than one, the system may still provide acceptable performance. Only the combinable requests will suffer extraordinary delays, along with the relatively few noncombinable requests traversing the fan-in tree near its root.

3.2. Finite Queues

With finite queues the situation is worse. Pfister and Norton [PfNo85] noticed a very interesting phenomenon they call *tree saturation*. When the queue at the root of fan-in tree becomes full, the two queues feeding it can no longer send requests to it. They too will become full and stop the four queues feeding them from sending requests. Eventually the entire fan-in tree will consist of full queues. All of the queues at the same level of the fan-in tree can together satisfy combinables only at the same rate as the root satisfies them. In other words, at the ith level from the root, each queue can satisfy combinables only at a rate $1/2^i$ as fast as the root does. So, although each queue at this level has on average only $1/2^i$ as many combinables as the root, with respect to combinables the queues are not progressing any faster. Thus, progress of the whole system is governed by the service rate at the "hot spot"; noncombinables will suffer delay proportional to the queue size on each stage of the fan-in tree traversed.

Kumar and Pfister [KuPf86] have observed that a relatively short period of hot spot contention will produce tree saturation. Furthermore, after the processors stop issuing hot spot requests, the network takes a long time to return to normal.

4. Pairwise Combining

Ideally, one would like to combine all of the combinables that reside concurrently on a queue. This, however, makes the combining process complicated, and also creates congestion at a wait buffer when the response returns from memory. (To simplify the combining process and to avoid contention at the wait buffer, the NYU Ultracomputer and IBM's RP3 machine support combining only a pair of requests at a switch.) This section studies the effectiveness of such *pairwise* (or *two-way*) combining.

4.1. Infinite Queues

We did simulations to check the effectiveness of pairwise combining with infinite queues. Our concern is whether congestion at the hot spot still occurs. (Recall that r_c^i is the traffic load of combinables from each input port of a switch at stage i of the fan-in tree.) In our experiments, r_c^i increased rapidly until $r_n + r_c^i$ reached 1.0 (see Figure 2). This shows that with pairwise combining and infinite queues large networks are unstable.

The reason for congestion even with combining is that a combinable request does not always encounter another combinable request to combine with. Whenever a combinable request does not combine, it will be added to the traffic of the combinables coming out of the queue. Thus, the rate of combinables will necessarily increase towards the root of the fan-in tree. It is conceivable that this rate approaches some limit less than $1 - r_n$, in which case the network would be stable. However, our experiments show this simply does not happen: the rate of combinables increases without bound.

4.2. Finite Queues

It may seem *a priori* that finite queues will always provide worse performance than infinite queues, since infinite queues have more storage capacity. However, this is not necessarily so: Suppose at stage i of the fan-in tree, a queue becomes full. Then, the two queues at stage $i-1$ of the fan-in tree feeding this queue will become blocked (at least for requests destined to the full queue). This will increase the chances of these two queues becoming full, thereby blocking the queues at stage $i-2$ that feed them, and so on. Thus, if the rate of requests is large enough to create congestion at the root of the fan-in tree, the whole fan-in tree will tend to become congested. The overall affect on a message traversing the fan-in tree will be that its total delay will be fairly large at every stage, which contrasts with infinite queues where the delay is large only near the root. This means that combinables will spend more time near the leaves of the fan-in tree, and therefore have more chance of combining near the leaves. This will reduce the traffic rate of combinables which in turn will improve the overall performance of the network. (Recall that with pairwise combining, if a combinable traverses a stage without combining, it increases the rate of combinables for all later stages.)

We performed simulations on networks of nine stages with finite queues and pairwise combining. The queue size was assumed to be four. For the traffic of $r = 0.6$ and $q = 0.1$, we observed tree saturation: the average waiting times at each stage of the fan-in tree was approximately equal to the queue size. Waiting times of requests at each processor's queue seem to increase without bound as the number of network cycles simulated increased. Although we did not observe tree saturation for lower traffic loads, we expect that it would occur in larger machines. (See Figure 3.)

Since the probability of combining increases as a combinable request stays in a queue longer, larger sized queues should help combining, which in turn can help avoid tree saturation. One might think that the tree saturation reported here conflicts with the results of Pfister and Norton [PfNo85], where pairwise combining was effective in handling hot spots with queue sizes of only four. Although there were some minor differences in our two models, which could account for the different results, the main difference was that they were simulating a network with only six stages. We believe that adding a few more stages to their network would produce tree saturation and make their network unstable. Minor changes in switch design cannot overcome the inherent weakness of pairwise combining, at least not without making the delays at each stage of the fan-in tree unacceptably long.

5. Unbounded Combining

Unbounded combining allows any number of combinables to be combined into a single request at a queue. Although the combining of the Columbia CHoPP is very similar to unbounded combining, our study is not directly applicable CHoPP because of its "repetition filter memory", which allows the combining of incoming requests with requests already in the wait buffer.

We have done extensive simulations of networks with infinite queues and unbounded combining. The networks seem to be stable and provide reasonable delay irrespective of the machine size and the traffic load. The traffic of the combinables adds only slightly to the average queuing delay of the noncombinables alone. It seems that unbounded combining eliminates the contention on the fan-in tree because there can be at most only a single combinable request waiting in a queue at any given time.

Simulations show that with unbounded combining, finite queues provide only slightly larger delay than do infinite queues. When compared to infinite queues, delays are just about the same at the first few stages and slightly larger at all the later stages.

6. Bounded Combining

We have so far considered two extreme combining schemes: unbounded combining and pairwise combining. Unbounded combining provides good performance, but seems to be expensive (even to approximate); pairwise combining suffers from tree saturation, but is *relatively* easy to implement. We suggest a compromise scheme, *bounded* combining, where more than two, but at most a predetermined constant number of, combinables can be combined into a single request at a queue; in *k-way* combining the bound is k. Bounded combining is easier to implement than unbounded combining; the hope is that it will provide approximately the same performance. The question is, how large does k have to be?

In the experiments with unbounded combining, we observed that a combinable request coming out of the switches at the later stages represents on average only slightly more than two combinables. This suggests that *three-way combining*, i.e. at most three combinables can be combined into a single request at a queue, will be effective. Simulations show that three-way combining performs almost as well as unbounded combining for both finite and infinite queues (see Figure 4). This indicates that pairwise combining may be slightly too restrictive with respect to the number of combinables it supports.

7. Wait Buffers and Return Queues

Up until now we have considered the delay of a request only from the processors to the memory modules. For the return trip, there must be two *return queues* exiting each switch passing responses from the memory modules towards the processors. The performance of a network will be sensitive to the size of these return queues. We have assumed that the size of wait buffers is infinite. This is unrealistic in practice. The wait buffer size is an important factor for good performance, because combining cannot take place if the wait buffer is full.

A combining of k requests is represented as $k-1$ pairwise combinings, i.e. it uses $k-1$ wait buffer locations. When the response returns from memory, all $k-1$ locations are immediately freed and the k response messages are placed on the return queue.

This section considers the effect of wait buffer size and return queue size on queuing delay. Our main concern is to determine the proper size of wait buffers and return queues for three-way combining to obtain performance close to that of unbounded combining with infinite return queues and infinite wait buffers.

7.1. Infinite Queues, Returns Queues, and Wait Buffers

To get an idea of the appropriate size of wait buffers, we measured the average length of the buffers assuming infinite queues, return queues, and wait buffers. Although the unbounded and three-way combining schemes avoid congestion by inserting more combinables into the buffer at a time than pairwise combining, our simulations show that the average length of the buffers with pairwise combining is actually unbounded while it is quite moderate with three-way combining (see Figure 5). The reason for this is that the average length of the buffers is proportional to queuing delays.

Suppose combining takes place in a switch at stage i of an n-stage network. Then, a record of the combining will remain in the wait buffer until a response from the memory arrives at the switch some time later. So, the average length of the wait buffer is determined by the average number of combinings and the average number of cycles until the memory responds. Let c_i be the average number of combinings per cycle at the switch and t_i be the average response time from memory (to the switch) for a combinable request. Then, the wait buffer is a queuing system with arrival rate c_i and service rate $1/t_i$. The arrival rate c_i is determined by the traffic load and the position (i) of the switch in the network. The service rate is determined by the queuing delays at stage i and later stages. Given fixed traffic load and fixed network size, the average length of the wait buffer will be unbounded if there is severe enough congestion at later stages for $c_i \geq 1/t_i$.

Since the service rate $1/t_i$ is smaller for switches closer to processors, one may worry about the average length of the wait buffers at earlier stages. However, this is counterbalanced to some extent by the fact that there is less contention in the earlier stages so that fewer combinings take place. Notice that the wait buffer lengths become unbounded as the network size increases, for any fixed arrival rate c_i at the wait buffer, irrespective of the combining scheme. The wait buffer size needs to grow with the network size.

7.2. Finite Queues, Return Queues, and Wait Buffers

To see the effect of small wait buffer sizes, we did simulations with queues of size four, infinite return queues, and wait buffers of size six. As can be seen in Figure 6, three-way combining with "small" wait buffers performs as badly as pairwise combining does. The reason is that the buffers at the later stages are almost always nearly full, and three-way combining effectively changes to pairwise combining.

To see the effect of small return queue sizes, we did simulations with queues of size four and infinite wait buffers. It turns out that, for three-way combining, return queues of size four are not large enough to provide good performance. This may seem surprising, since (forward) queues of size four are sufficient, and the responses are just returning along the same path that the original request traversed. The reason is that on the return path combinables are returning in bursts, since a combinable response can split into two or three responses. Thus, each return queue in a switch is effectively a queuing system with the same traffic intensity as the (forward) queue in the same switch, but with fewer, larger-sized packets. The former system will provide worse performance and require larger queue sizes (see [KrSW86]). With three-way combining, return queues of size of ten obtained approximately the same performance as infinite return queues.

In our experiments for moderate traffic loads, return queues of size ten and wait buffers of size fifteen seem to be large enough to obtain performance close to that of unbounded combining with infinite sized queues and wait buffers (see Figure 7). Neither return queues of size eight and wait buffers of size fifteen nor return queues of size ten and wait buffers of size ten produced good performance.

8. Conclusion

Shared memory machines have the potential of congestion due to concurrent requests to a shared variable. Since hot spot contention becomes more serious as the machine size grows, congestion can severely degrade the performance of "large" machines. To avoid potentially serious congestion, pairwise combining was suggested in the NYU Ultracomputer and IBM RP3 machine as an effective way of eliminating congestion.

We studied the hot spot traffic model, where a fixed fraction of the total memory traffic is for a single shared variable. As observed by Pfister and Norton [PfNo85], large networks with finite queues and no combining suffer from tree saturation. With finite queues, even pairwise combining has the potential of tree saturation creating unbounded delay no matter how "light" the traffic load is, for large enough machines. If hot spots are a real-life phenomenon, pairwise combining as suggested for the NYU Ultracomputer and the IBM RP3 machine is too restrictive. Three-way combining resolves the congestion. It remains to be seen whether three-way combining can be realized efficiently in hardware.

A combining network must be carefully balanced. There are many parameters: the network size, the boundedness of the combining, the queue size, the wait buffer size, the queue size on the return path, etc. It is not obvious how any particular choice of these parameters will behave. For example, we have seen that changing finite queues to infinite queues, which one might expect would improve performance, can actually degrade performance.

One must be very careful in interpreting our results. We do not believe that processors are likely to concurrently access the same shared (synchronization) variable for extended periods of time. If hot spots are only transient, i.e. if there are short, intensive periods of hot spot contention, pairwise combining may very well combine enough to provide acceptable performance. One might consider the (steady state) hot spot model suggested by Pfister and Norton to be a conservative worst case scenario.

We have restricted our attention to square banyan networks composed of 2×2 switches, and to messages of length one. We believe our results generalize to other network topologies, other switch sizes, and other message size distributions. Any interconnection network will have to have a tree, maybe implicitly, leading from every processor to any given memory module. This will create the possibility of tree saturation when there are hot spots, but also the opportunity for combining. With $k \times k$ switches, it seems that k-way combining is not enough; some fraction slightly higher than that will be necessary. Longer messages seem to increase the amount of combining, but not enough to avoid tree saturation with only pairwise combining.

Acknowledgements

The authors thank Alan Norton and Greg Pfister for helpful comments.

References

[DiJu81]   D. M. Dias and J. R. Jump, "Packet Switching Interconnection Networks for Modular Systems", *IEEE Computer*, Vol.14 No.12 1981

[EGKM85] J. Edler, A.Gottlieb, C. P. Kruskal, K. P. McAuliffe, L. Rudolph, M. Snir, P. J. Teller, and J. Willson "Issues Related to MIMD Shared-Memory Computers: The NYU Ultracomputer Approach", *The 12th Annual International Symp. on Computer Architecture*, June, 1985, pp.126-135

[Feng81]   T. Y. Feng, "A Survey of Interconnection Networks", *IEEE Computer*, Dec. 1981

[GKLS83] D. D. Gajski, D. J. Kuck, D. Lawrie, and A. Sameh, "Cedar – A Large Scale Multiprocessors", *Proc. of the 1983 International Conf. on Parallel Processing*, Aug. 1983

[GoLi73]   G. R. Goke and G. J. Lipovski, "Banyan Networks for Partitioning Multiprocessor Systems", *The 1st Annual Symposium on Computer Architecture*, 1973

[GGKM83]A. Gottlieb, R. Grishman, C. P. Kruskal, K. M. McAuliffe, L. Rudolph, and M. Snir, "The NYU Ultracomputer - designing an MIMD shared memory parallel computer", *IEEE Trans. on Computers, Vol. C-32, No. 2, 1983*

[KrRS86] C. P. Kruskal, L. Rudolph, and M. Snir, "Efficient Synchronization on Multiprocessors with Shared Memory", *The 5th ACM SIGACT-SIGOPS Symp. on Principles of Distributed Computing*, Aug. 1986

[KrSn82]   C. P. Kruskal and M. Snir, "Some Results on Multistage Interconnection Networks for Multiprocessors", NYU Ultracomputer note 41; also in *Proc. 1982 Conf. Informat. Sci. Syst.*, Princeton Univ., Princeton, NJ, Mar. 1982

[KrSn83]   C. P. Kruskal and M. Snir, "The Performance of Multistage Interconnection Networks for Multiprocessors", *IEEE Trans. on Computers*, Vol. c-32, No. 12, Dec. 1983

[KrSW86] C. P. Kruskal, M. Snir, and A. Weiss, "The Distribution of Waiting Times in Clocked Multistage Interconnection Networks", *Proc. of the 1986 International Conf. on Parallel Processing*, Aug. 1986

[KDLS86] D. J. Kuck, E. S. Davidson, D. H. Lawrie, and A. H. Sameh, "Parallel Supercomputing Today and the Cedar Approach", *Science*, Vol. 281, Feb. 28, 1986

[KuPf86]   M. Kumar and G. Pfister, "The Onset of Hot Spot Contention", *Proc. of the 1986 International Conf. on Parallel Processing*, Aug. 1986

[Lawr75]   D. H. Lawrie, "Access and Alignment of Data in an Array Processor", *IEEE Trans. on Computers*, Vol. c-24, 1975

[Pate81]   J. A. Patel, "Performance of Processor-Memory Interconnections for Multiprocessors", *IEEE Trans. on Computers*, Vol. c-30, 1981

[PBGH85] G. F. Pfister, W. C. Brantley, D. A. George, S. L. Harvey, W. J. Kleinfelder, K. P. McAuliffe, E. A. Melton, V. A. Norton, J. Weiss, "The IBM Research Parallel Processor Prototype (RP3): Introduction and Architecture", *Proc. of the 1985 International Conf. on Parallel Processing*, Aug. 1985

[PfNo85]   G. F. Pfister and V. A. Norton, "'Hot Spot' Contention and Combining in Multistage Interconnection Networks", *IEEE Trans. on Computers*, Vol. c-34, No.10, 1985

[Schw80] J. T. Schwartz, "Ultarcomputers", *ACM TOPLAS*, 1980, pp. 484-521

[Sieg85]   Howard Jay Siegel, *Interconnection Networks for Large-Scale Parallel Processing, Theory and Case Studies*, Lexington Books. 1985

[SuBK77] H. Sullivan, T. Bashkow, and D. Klappholtz, "A Large Scale Homogeneous Fully Distributed Parallel Machine", *Proc. of the Fourth Symp. on Computer Architecture*, 1977

Figures

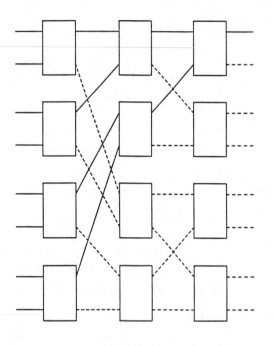

Figure 1. Fan-in Tree on a 3-stage Square Banyan Network

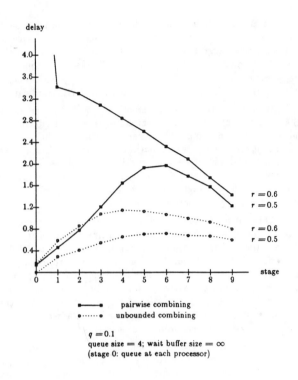

pairwise combining
unbounded combining

$q = 0.1$
queue size $= 4$; wait buffer size $= \infty$
(stage 0: queue at each processor)

Figure 3. Tree Saturation Effect with Pairwise Combining

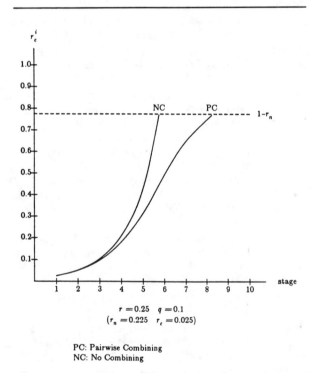

$r = 0.25 \quad q = 0.1$
$(r_n = 0.225 \quad r_c = 0.025)$

PC: Pairwise Combining
NC: No Combining

Figure 2. Traffic Load of the Combinables at Later Stages

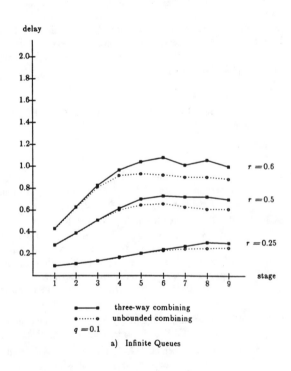

three-way combining
unbounded combining
$q = 0.1$

a) Infinite Queues

Figure 4. Delays with Bounded Combining

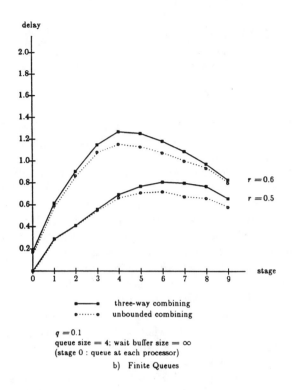

Figure 4. (Continued)

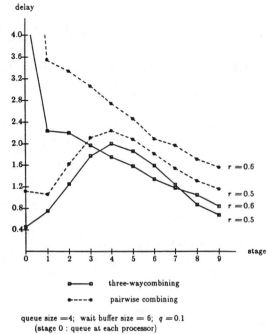

Figure 6. Effects of Small Sized Buffers

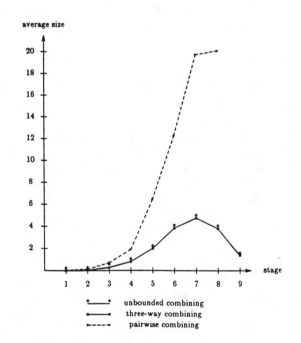

Figure 5. Average Length of Buffers ($r = 0.25$ and $q = 0.1$)

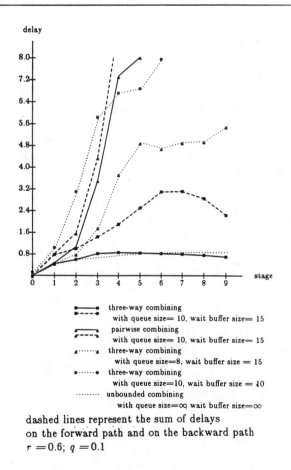

dashed lines represent the sum of delays
on the forward path and on the backward path
$r = 0.6$; $q = 0.1$

Figure 7. Performance of Bounded Combining

Distributing Hot-Spot Addressing in Large-Scale Multiprocessors

PEN-CHUNG YEW, MEMBER, IEEE, NIAN-FENG TZENG, MEMBER, IEEE, AND DUNCAN H. LAWRIE, FELLOW, IEEE

Abstract—When a large number of processors try to access a common variable, referred to as *hot-spot* accesses in [6], not only can the resulting memory contention seriously degrade performance, but it can also cause *tree saturation* in the interconnection network which blocks both hot and regular requests alike. It is shown in [6] that even if only a small percentage of all requests are to a hot-spot, these requests can cause very serious performance problems, and networks that do the necessary combining of requests are suggested to keep the interconnection network and memory contention from becoming a bottleneck.

Instead we propose a software combining tree, and we show that it is effective in decreasing memory contention and preventing tree saturation because it distributes hot-spot accesses over a software tree whose nodes can be dispersed over many memory modules. Thus, it is an inexpensive alternative to expensive combining networks.

Index Terms—Combining networks, hot-spot memory, memory bandwidth, memory contention, software combining tree, synchronization.

I. INTRODUCTION

A LARGE, shared-memory multiprocessor system such as Cedar [1], the NYU Ultracomputer [2] or IBM RP3 [3], may contain hundreds or even thousands of processors and memory modules. Multistage interconnection networks such as the Omega network [4] or its variations [5] are usually used to provide communication between these processors and memory modules.

In these systems, any variable shared by these processors will create memory contention at some memory modules. Those shared variables could be locks for process synchronization [15], loop index variables for parallel loops [12], etc. Even though accesses to these shared variables (called *hot-spot* accesses in [3] and [6]) may account for a very small percentage of the total data accesses to the shared memory (typically less than ten percent are observed in most applications), this memory contention can create a phenomenon called *tree saturation* [6], and can cause severe congestion in the interconnection network. It is shown [6], [14] that tree saturation due to hot-spot contention can seriously degrade the effective bandwidth of the shared memory system.

Various schemes like combining networks used in the IBM

Manuscript received September 3, 1986; revised November 23, 1986. This work was supported in part by the National Science Foundation under Grants US NSF DCR84-10110 and US NSF DCR84-06916, and by the Department of Energy under Grant DOE DE-FG02-85ER25001.

P.-C. Yew and D. H. Lawrie are with the Center for Supercomputing Research and Development, University of Illinois, Urbana, IL 61801.

N.-F. Tzeng is with AT&T Bell Laboratories, Columbus, OH 43213.

IEEE Log Number 8613051.

RP3 [3] and NYU Ultracomputer [2], or the repetition filter memory in the Columbia CHoPP [7] has been proposed to eliminate such memory contention. The basic idea of these schemes is to incorporate some hardware in the interconnection networks to trap and combine data accesses when they are fanning in to the particular memory module that contains the shared variable. Because data accesses can be combined in the interconnection network, it is hoped that memory contention at that memory module can be eliminated.

However, the hardware required for such schemes is extremely expensive. It is estimated [6] that the extra hardware increases the switch size and/or cost by a factor between 6 and 32, and this is only for combining networks consisting of 2×2 switches. With $k \times k$ switches ($k > 2$), the hardware cost will be even greater. The extra hardware also tends to add extra network delay which will penalize most of the regular data accesses that do not need these facilities, unless the combining network is built separately as in RP3 [6].

Furthermore, the effectiveness of the combining network depends very much on the extent to which such combining can be done. If such combining is restricted as described in [8], i.e., if the number of requests that can be combined is restricted to k in a $k \times k$ switch, then the effectiveness of the combining network can be limited. Unless this combining is unrestricted, tree saturation can still occur even in a combining network [8].

In this paper, we are studying this problem from a different perspective. We assume a shared memory multiprocessor system like Cedar [1] with a standard, buffered Omega network providing interconnection [9], and without expensive combining hardware. In addition we use a hardware facility in the shared memory modules to handle necessary indivisible synchronization operations for the shared variables [10]. Regular memory accesses bypass this hardware without delay and, hence, will not be penalized. Each memory module will handle memory accesses, including those memory accesses to shared variables, one at a time.

To eliminate memory contention due to the hot-spot variable, a software tree is used to do the combining. This idea is similar to the concept of a combining network, but it is implemented in software instead of hardware. We will show that this scheme can achieve quite satisfactory results as compared to more expensive hardware combining.

II. HOT SPOTS AND TREE SATURATION

The phenomenon of how hot-spot accesses can cause tree saturation is briefly described here. For a more detailed analysis and discussion, please refer to [6].

Reprinted from *IEEE Trans. Computers*, Vol. C-36, No. 4, Apr. 1987, pp. 388-395. Copyright © 1987 by The Institute of Electrical and Electronics Engineers, Inc. All rights reserved.

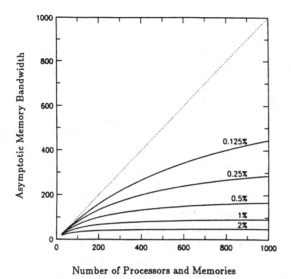

Fig. 1. Asymptotically maximum total network as a function of the number of processors for various fractions of the network traffic aimed at a single hot spot (results from [6]).

Assume N is the number of processors in the system, and there are also N memory modules in the shared memory system. Each processor issues r requests to the shared memory per network cycle ($0 \leq r \leq 1$). Among those requests, h percent of the requests are hot-spot requests. Thus, in each network cycle, there are Nrh hot-spot requests and $r(1 - h)$ normal requests directed to the "hot" memory module for a total of $Nrh + r(1 - h)$. If each memory module can accept 1 request per network cycle (i.e., the maximum rate), the maximum network throughput per processor is

$$H = 1/(1 + h(N-1)) \tag{A}$$

and the total effective memory bandwidth for the shared memory system is

$$B = N/(1 + h(N-1)). \tag{B}$$

Fig. 1 shows B as a function of N for various h. This clearly shows that in a system with 1000 processors, hot-spot traffic of only one percent can limit the total memory bandwidth B to less than ten percent.

Notice that this discussion assumes that hot-spot requests can continue to be issued from a processor even if that processor still has an unsatisfied hot-spot request pending in the network. In many applications this is not true, because hot-spot requests are usually related to some kind of synchronization operation: A processor usually has to wait for the outcome of the synchronization operation before it can issue another request to the synchronization variable. So, the issuing rate from a processor is inherently limited. We will address these issues in more detail in later sections.

III. SOFTWARE COMBINING TREE

To illustrate the principle of a software combining tree, let us assume that we have a variable whose value is N, and that we want each processor to decrement this variable so that when all processors are finished, the value will be zero. This is

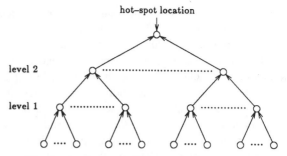

Fig. 2. A software combining tree with fan-in of 10.

a common way of making sure all processors are finished with a given task before proceeding with a new task, for example, and is one cause of hot-spot accesses. Now suppose that instead of one single variable, we build a tree of variables, assigning each to a different memory module, as shown in Fig. 2. If $N = 1000$ and assuming a fan-in of 10, we have 111 variables each with value 10. We partition the processors into 100 groups of ten, with each group sharing one of the variables at the bottom of the tree. When the last processor in each group decrements its variable to zero, it then decrements the value in the parent node. Thus, we have increased the total number of accesses from 1000 to 1110, but instead of having one hot spot with 1000 accesses, we have 111 hot spots with only 10 accesses each. It should be clear that this will result in a significant improvement in throughput rate and bandwidth, and the simulations we describe later verify that even if we account for the increase in total accesses, the improvement is still quite significant. It should also be clear that a three-level tree with fan-in equal to ten is not necessarily optimal, but that the optimal point depends on access times and on other factors.

Another basic operation that can be implemented with a software combining tree is *busy-wait*. Here it is assumed that processors are waiting for a shared variable to change in some way. Presumably some other processor will cause this change. We build a combining tree as before, this time assigning one processor to each node in the tree. Each processor monitors the state of its node by continually reading the node. When the processor monitoring the root node detects the change in its node, it in turn changes the state of its children's nodes, and so on until all processors have detected the change and are able to proceed with the next task.

This idea, in a sense, is not very different from a hardware combining tree built from 10×10 switches, except that the combining buffer that would be inside each switch now resides in a shared memory module in a software combining tree. One distinct advantage for a software combining tree is that we can tune performance by changing the fan-in of each node without incurring any hardware cost.

A. Modeling of Software Combining Tree

We will classify hot-spot accessing in two ways. First, accesses will be *limited* or *unlimited* depending on whether a given processor can have only one or more than one hot-spot request outstanding. We let η denote the number of outstanding hot-spot requests. Second, the number of accesses will be *fixed* or *variable* depending on whether the total number of accesses is fixed, or whether the total number varies depending on the number of conflicts or some other factor. For example, assume we are adding a vector of numbers to form a sum. Then each processor can have more than one outstanding request to add an element to the shared sum, but since we assume the addition is done indivisibly by logic in the memory, the total number of requests generated by all the processors is fixed. This case is *unlimited-fixed*. A case like the one described earlier, where processors are decrementing a counter to see which is the last processor, is *limited-fixed*. A third example is illustrated by *busy waiting* where the processors may all be waiting for one processor to complete some task. Each processor continually reads the value of a shared variable until the value changes, for example from zero to one. Thus, the number of requests to the hot-spot depends on how soon the variable gets reset, and this case is *limited-variable*. Notice that a barrier synchronization [11] can be implemented by a counter decrement (*limited-fixed*), followed by a busy wait (*limited-variable*) triggered by the final processor which decrements the counter.

When we implement combining trees for hot-spot accesses, it is important to minimize the possible memory contention, so it is preferable that all shared variables in a software combining tree (i.e., the nodes of the tree) reside in separate memory modules. The largest combining tree we can construct for a hot-spot is a tree with minimum fan-in, i.e., a fan-in of two. The total number of nodes in a combining tree with N leaves is $N/2 + N/4 + \cdots + 2 + 1 = N - 1$. Hence, it is always possible to spread those nodes across N separate memory modules. Our simulations in this study assume all of the nodes in a software tree to be in separate memory modules.

We also assume the following system configuration in our simulations.

1) There are two identical, back-to-back, unidirectional Omega networks: one is for traffic from processors to the shared memory; the other is for traffic from memory returning to the processors. Both networks are packet-switching, pipelined networks.

2) Each network consists of 2×2 switching elements with an output buffer of finite size at each output port of a switching element. The fan-in capability of each output port is two, i.e., it can accept two simultaneous requests from its two input ports. One request is forwarded to the next stage and the other is stored in the output buffer. If the output buffer is full, no more requests are accepted by the output port. In our simulations, we assume the size of the output buffer to be four.

3) There are many different algorithms to implement software combining trees for various types of shared variables [17]. It is beyond the scope of this paper to describe those algorithms. Instead, we used a very general and simplified model to simulate a software tree. Each node of a software tree contains a counter with an initial value of 0. In the limited-variable case, the counter is decremented to -1 by the first processor which visits the node. The rest of processors sharing the node will be busy-waiting whenever the counter value is -1. The extra delay for busy-waiting is accounted for in simulations. The first processor will visit its parent node and bring back a positive value equal to the fan-out of the node.

The counter is set to that value and the rest of processors can then decrement the counter and move on. The counter will eventually become 0 again and the whole process will repeat. This model is very similar to broadcasting a scalar to all processors through a software combining tree. The scalar may be updated from time to time. In the limited-fixed or the unlimited-fixed case, processors will increment the counter until it equals to the fan-out of a node. A representative is then chosen to reset the counter and also to increment the counter in its parent node. The whole process will repeat at the parent node. This model is very similar to the first part of a barrier synchronization where processors increment a counter to see if all of them have reached the barrier.

4) All requests are of the same length. In our simulations, we assume each request consists of only one packet.

5) The access time of a memory module is one network cycle, i.e., the time for a request to go through a switching element when no conflict exists.

B. Possible Overhead in a Software Combining Tree

As mentioned earlier, constructing a software combining tree creates many shared variables. Therefore, more hot-spot traffic is created even though that traffic generates less memory contention.

As before, let us assume that the hot-spot rate from a processor is $r \times h$, and the software combining tree has a fan-in of k for each node. For *fixed-type* access patterns, the fractional increase in hot-spot traffic will be

$$\sum_{l=1}^{\log_k N - 1} rh/k^l = rh \left(\frac{1 - (k/N)}{k - 1} \right).$$

When $k = 2$, the increased hot-spot traffic is $rh(1 - 2/N)$, which approximates the original hot-spot traffic for large N. This means that the hot-spot traffic cannot be more than doubled after all of the extra hot-spot traffic is included. As we will see later in our simulations, the decreased memory contention will more than offset the increased hot-spot traffic if h is less than 30 percent.

For *variable* access patterns, the additional accesses caused by the combining tree are difficult to quantify because the number of accesses is not fixed to begin with. In practice, since busy-waiting is often the cause of *variable* access patterns (with $\eta = 1$), and the number of accesses for a busy-wait operation depends on how quickly the state change is propagated to the children in the tree, the total number of accesses could even be less than that required by a single shared variable; the state change can be propagated more quickly by the combining tree than by N accesses to a single shared variable.

IV. Bounds on Bandwidth

A. Unlimited Hot-Spot Requests Per Processor

In a packet-switching Omega network, with finite buffers in each switching element and with hot-spot rate $h = 0$, we still cannot achieve 100 percent memory bandwidth because of conflicts in the network [9]. These conflicts are also possible if a crossbar switch is used. If we assume R to be the maximum request rate reaching a memory module when no hot spot exists, then in a steady state, R is also the maximum request rate allowed for a processor. Therefore, we can consider R to be an absolute upper bound on the bandwidth per processor.

The value of R depends on the network buffer size, the length of a request, and the network switch size, etc. [13]. However, as h increases, the request rate to the hot memory module, i.e., $r(1 - h) + rhk$, will increase from R to 1. Tree saturation will occur when the request rate to the hot memory module approaches 1, and the maximum processor request rate r will decrease. Hence, we have

$$R \leq r(1 - h) + rhk \leq 1.$$

By rearranging the above equation, we have the following:

$$R/(1 + h(k - 1)) \leq r \leq 1/(1 + h(k - 1)).$$

$1/1 + h(k - 1))$ is equal to 1 when h is 0. Since the absolute upper bound is $R (R \leq 1)$ as discussed before, we can have a tighter upper bound by using R, i.e.,

$$R/(1 + h(k - 1)) \leq r \leq R \tag{C}$$

Notice that (C) also shows a lower bound for the maximum processor request rate r when a software combining tree is used with a fan-in of k, and η is unlimited, i.e., even when η is unlimited, the maximum bandwidth cannot be worse than $NR/(1 + h(k - 1))$.

We obtained R from simulations, and in Fig. 3 we plot lower bounds for various system sizes with h varying from 0–32 percent. Notice that those curves are in a very narrow range, i.e., the lower bound in (C) seems to be tight at least for systems up to size 1024. The top dotted line in Fig. 3 shows R, the maximum bandwidth we can get when there are no hot-spot requests.

The degradation factor in (C) is $1 + h(k - 1)$. This degradation factor is independent of the system size and reaches a minimum when $k = 2$. Given unlimited hot-spot requests, i.e., $\eta \geq 1$, the optimal software combining tree for maximum memory bandwidth has a minimum fan-in of 2.

B. Single Hot-Spot Request Per Processor

If the hot-spot request rate is limited ($\eta = 1$), then there cannot be more than N hot-spot requests in the system at any time. For systems with instruction look-ahead or with data prefetching capability, regular requests still may be issued while a hot-spot request is pending. However, this case is not different from that of unlimited hot-spot requests with a very small h; when h is very small, it is unlikely that there will be more than one hot-spot request pending at any time.

Hence, when $\eta = 1$, we will only consider the case where no additional requests, hot or regular, are issued by the processor when there is a pending hot-spot request. Thus, the bandwidth depends on the delay of the hot-spot requests. The request rate from the processor is further restricted by any increased delay. If a software combining tree is used to

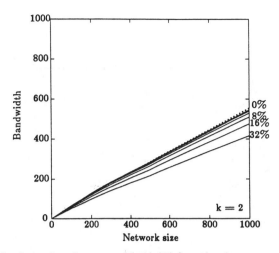

Fig. 3. Lower bounds on network bandwidth for various hot-spot rates ($\eta =$ unlimited).

eliminate the memory contention caused by the hot-spot requests, the limiting factor for the memory bandwidth will only be η; the inherent nature of the hot-spot that prohibits further processor requests.

During a long period of time T, there will be rT requests from a processor, among which rhT requests are hot-spot requests. The processor will be barred from issuing any request for a total period of $rhTC$ where C is the average round-trip delay for a hot-spot request. The processor can issue a request only for a total period of $T - rhTC$. Within that period, $r(1 - h)T$ regular requests are issued. Hence, the real issuing rate for regular requests is $r(1 - h)T/(T - rhTC)$. This rate cannot be greater than 1, i.e.,

$$r(1 - h)T/(T - rhTC) \leq 1.$$

This equation can be rearranged to obtain an upper bound for r

$$r \leq 1/(1 - h + hC). \tag{D}$$

As expected, the maximum rate of r is greatly dependent on the hot-spot delay C. This bound gets tighter as the hot-spot rate h gets larger. When $h = 1$, the equality in (D) will hold. Fig. 4 shows this upper bound for various hot-spot rates h with minimum hot-spot delay of $C = 2 \log_2 N$. For $N = 1000$ and $h = 8$ percent, the upper bound will be around 40 percent of the total bandwidth. Notice that *the upper bound in (D) is valid even for a hardware combining network* because it is a bound imposed by the inherent nature of the hot-spot request (i.e., $\eta = 1$).

V. Simulation Results

To study the effectiveness of a software combining tree, we performed several simulations for $N = 256$, with h varying from 0–32 percent. These simulations are based on the system models described in Section III-A. Fig. 5 shows the delay and maximum bandwidth when neither a software combining tree nor a hardware combining network is used. Following each curve from left to right, each point represents a larger value of r. As shown in [6], while r increases, bandwidth increases

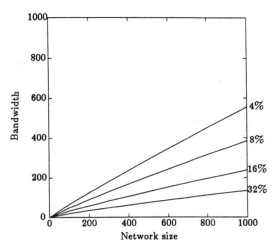

Fig. 4. Upperbounds on network bandwidth for various hot-spot rates ($\eta = 1$).

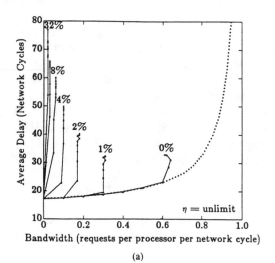

(a)

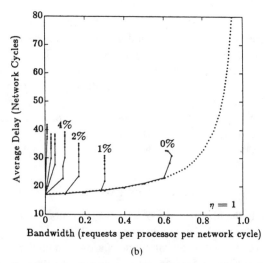

(b)

Fig. 5. Average network delay versus bandwidth for a network of size 256 (h varies from 0 to 32 percent).

while delay stays relatively constant up to a point of saturation. After the saturation point, bandwidth ceases to increase while delay gets worse. The results clearly show low bandwidth and increased average network delay results. The maximum bandwidth of $0.63N$ is achieved when $h = 0$.

Fig. 6 represents *fixed*-type access patterns with unlimited η, and shows the use of a software combining tree to reduce hot-spot contention. The fan-in's for the software combining trees are varied from $k = 16$ to 2. The improvement is quite significant compared to the result in Fig. 5(a). According to (C), the minimum degradation factor for the bandwidth can be obtained when the software combining tree has the minimum fan-in. In Fig. 6 we can see that when $k = 2$, the degradation is indeed the smallest.

As presented in Section III-B, the hot-spot traffic can be nearly doubled by the extra hot-spot traffic created by the software combining tree with the minimum fan-in $k = 2$. In Fig. 6, h is indicated as the original hot-spot request rate; the results shown there already include all extra hot-spot traffic. This shows that with an original hot-spot request rate of 16 percent, the degradation remains small. The elimination of the hot-spot contention, indeed, more than offsets the results of increased traffic.

We also simulate some cases for *fixed*-type access patterns with $\eta = 1$ (Fig. 7). If we take into account the fact that busy-waiting is not required in this kind of access pattern, we can see that the results are quite similar to those from our simulations of *variable*-type access patterns discussed above. In fact, the average hot-spot request delay, i.e., C in (D), is smaller in this case. Also, as shown in (D), we can expect an improved maximum rate r.

Fig. 8 represents *limited-variable* access patterns, wherein no additional requests are issued by a processor while it has a hot-spot request pending, but the total number of requests allowed over time is not fixed. The upper bound on the bandwidth given in (D) will depend on C, the average delay of the hot-spot requests. The value of delay C includes the overhead from traversing the software tree, busy waiting in the intermediate nodes, and the possible memory contention. From these figures, we can see that the optimal fan-in k for the software tree is no longer $k = 2$, but rather at around $k = 4$. The increased fan-in k allows for a lesser number of levels of nodes in the tree, thus reducing the time required for requests to traverse the tree.

Furthermore, when h increases, the upper bound in (D) becomes tighter. There is less traffic in the network due to the restriction that no more requests will be issued when a hot-spot request is pending. In this case, the turnaround time for a request can actually improve as Fig. 9 shows.

The lower dotted lines in Fig. 5 through Fig. 9 are the average delay of a request through the network assuming the buffer size in each switching element is unlimited. These values are calculated based on the analytical model in [16].

VI. DISCUSSION

Our simulations show that the software combining tree effectively eliminates tree saturation caused by hot-spot contention. However, the main purpose of the software

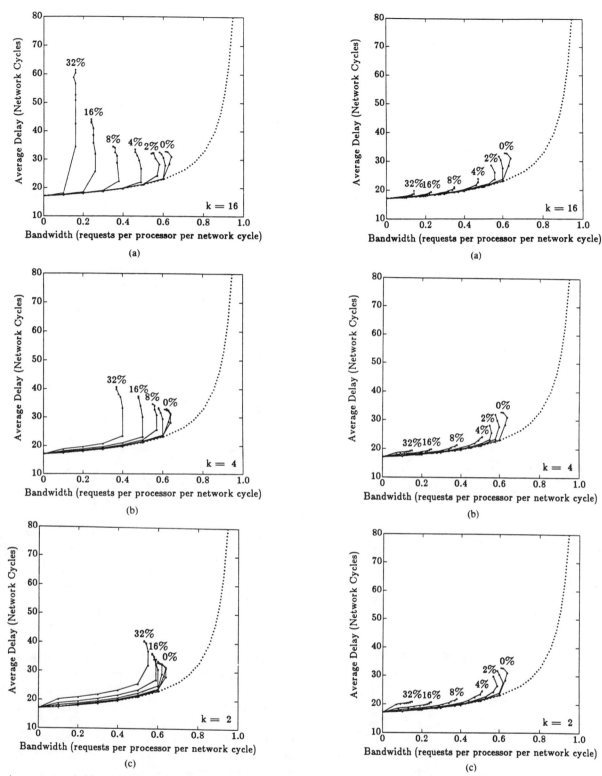

Fig. 6. Average network delay versus bandwidth for unlimited-fixed access patterns ($N = 256$, h varies from 0 to 32 percent).

Fig. 7. Average network delay versus bandwidth for limited-fixed access patterns ($N = 256$, h varies from 0 to 32 percent).

combining tree differs slightly from the original purpose of the hardware combining networks [2], [6].

Hardware combining networks were originally proposed to speedup hot-spot requests by combining those requests in the interconnection network and in this way eliminate memory contention at the hot memory module. Because such memory contention creates the serious side effect of tree saturation that

can adversely affect even regular requests [6], such requests must also be processed through the hardware combining network. Although it alleviates the problem of tree saturation, hardware combining can cause extra delay in processing regular requests.

Software combining trees seem to effectively relieve regular requests from the side effect of tree saturation, without the

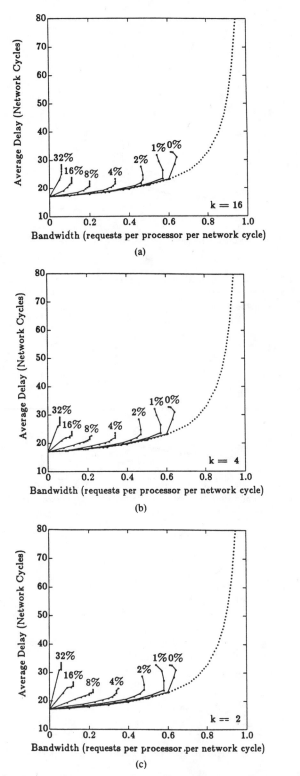

(a)

(b)

(c)

Fig. 8. Average network delay versus bandwidth for limited-variable access patterns ($N = 256$, h varies from 0 to 32 percent).

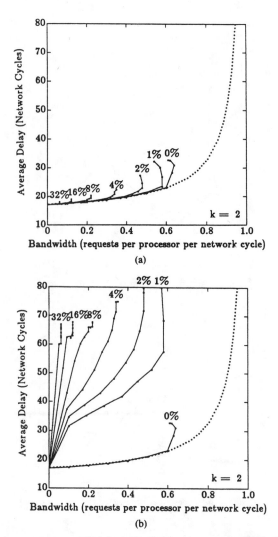

(a)

(b)

Fig. 9. (a) Average delay of regular requests versus bandwidth for limited-variable access patterns ($N = 256$, h varies from 0 to 32 percent). (b) Average delay of hot spot requests versus bandwidth for limited-variable access patterns ($N = 256$, h varies from 0 to 32 percent).

expense of hardware combining networks. The beneficial result from this scheme is that the service time of hot-spot requests decreases. Theoretically, this improvement cannot be as good as a hardware combining network with unrestricted combining capability: In a software combining tree, a hot-spot request must traverse the interconnection network $\log_k N$ times, whereas in a hardware combining network the request

must traverse the network only once. However, in a real implementation, unrestricted combining in a switch is impossible due to the complexity of the switches in a hardware combining network. This will inevitably hamper the effectiveness of a combining network [8], and also introduces increased delay due to the extra hardware. It is difficult to determine the system size requirements necessary to prove the hardware combining network to be the optimal method of speeding up hot-spot requests. The effect of the somewhat slower hot-spot requests on total system performance, if the rate is very small, also remains to be seen.

VII. CONCLUSIONS

When a large number of processors try to access a common variable, referred to as *hot-spot* accesses in [6], not only can the resulting memory contention seriously degrade performance, but it can also cause *tree saturation* in the interconnection network which blocks both hot and regular requests alike. It is shown in [6] that even if only a small percentage of all requests are to a hot spot, these requests can cause very serious performance problems, and networks that do the necessary combining of requests are suggested to keep the interconnection network and memory contention from becoming a bottleneck.

Instead we propose a software combining tree, and we show that it is effective in decreasing memory contention and preventing tree saturation because it distributes hot-spot accesses over a software tree whose nodes can be dispersed over many memory modules. Thus, it is an inexpensive alternative to expensive combining networks.

REFERENCES

[1] D. J. Kuck *et al.*, "Parallel supercomputing today and the Cedar approach," *Science*, vol. 21, pp. 967–974, Feb. 1986.

[2] A. Gottlieb *et al.*, "The NYU ultracomputer—Designing a MIMD, shared memory parallel machine," *IEEE Trans. Comput.*, vol. C-32, pp. 175–189, Feb. 1983.

[3] G. F. Pfister *et al.*, "The IBM research parallel processor prototype (RP3): Introduction and architecture," in *Proc. 1985 Int. Conf. Parallel Processing*, Aug. 1985, pp. 764–771.

[4] D. H. Lawrie, "Access and alignment of data in an array processor," *IEEE Trans. Comput.*, vol. C-24, pp. 1145–1155, Dec. 1975.

[5] C. L. Wu and T.-Y. Feng, "On a class of multistage interconnection networks," *IEEE Trans. Comput.*, vol. C-29, pp. 694–702, Aug. 1980.

[6] G. F. Pfister and V. A. Norton, " 'Hot-spot' contention and combining in multistage interconnection networks," *IEEE Trans. Comput.*, vol. C-34, pp. 943–948, Oct. 1985.

[7] H. Sullivan, T. Bashkow, and D. Klappholtz, "A large scale homogeneous, fully distributed parallel machine," in *Proc. Fourth Ann. Symp. Comput. Architect.*, June 1977, pp. 105–124.

[8] G. Lee, C. P. Kruskal, and D. J. Kuck, "The effectiveness of combining in shared memory parallel computer in the presence of 'hot spots'," in *Proc. 1986 Int. Conf. Parallel Processing*, Aug. 1986, pp. 35–41.

[9] D. M. Dias and J. R. Jump, "Analysis and simulation of buffered delta networks," *IEEE Trans. Comput.*, vol. C-30, pp. 273–282, Apr. 1981.

[10] C. Q. Zhu and P. C. Yew, "A synchronization scheme and its applications for larger multiprocessor systems," in *Proc. 4th Int. Conf. Distrib. Comput. Syst.*, May 1984, pp. 486–493.

[11] P. Tang and P. C. Yew, "Processor self-scheduling for multiple-nested parallel loops," in *Proc. 1986 Int. Conf. Parallel Processing*, Aug. 1986, pp. 528–535.

[12] E. L. Lusk and R. A. Overbeek, "Implementation of monitors with macros: A programming aid for the HEP and other parallel processors," Argonne Nat. Lab., Argonne, IL, Tech. Rep. ANL-83-97, Dec. 1983.

[13] P. Y. Chen, "Multiprocessor systems: Interconnection networks, memory hierarchy, modeling and simulations," Dep. Comput. Sci., Univ. Illinois, Urbana, Rep. UIUCDCS-R-82-1083, Jan. 1982.

[14] R. Lee, "On hot spot contention," *ACM SIG Comput. Architect.*, vol. 13, pp. 15–20, Dec. 1985.

[15] E. W. Dijkstra, "Solution of a problem in concurrent programming control," *Commun. Ass. Comput. Mach.*, vol. 8, pp. 569–569, Sept. 1965.

[16] C. P. Kruskal and M. Snir, "The performance of multistage interconnection networks for multiprocessors," *IEEE Trans. Comput.*, vol. C-32, pp. 1091–1098, Dec. 1983.

[17] P. Tang and P. C. Yew, "Algorithms for distributing hot-spot addressing in large multiprocessor systems," Center for Supercomputing R.&D., Univ. Illinois, Urbana, Cedar doc. 617, Dec. 1986.

Pen-Chung Yew (S'76–S'78–M'80–S'80–M'81) received the BSEE degree from National Taiwan University, Taiwan, in 1972, the M.S. degree in electrical and computer engineering from the University of Massachusetts, Amherst, 1977, and the Ph.D. degree in computer science from the University of Illinois, Urbana, in 1981.

He is currently an Assistant Professor in the Department of Computer Science and a Senior Computer Engineer in the Center for Supercomputing Research and Development, University of Illinois, Urbana. He has been working on the architecture and hardware design for the Cedar supercomputer since 1984. His current research interests are parallel processing, computer architecture, high-performance multiprocessor systems, and performance evaluation.

Nian-Feng Tzeng (S'85–M'87) was born on November 22, 1956 in Taichung, Taiwan, Republic of China. He received the B.S. degree in computer science from National Chiao Tung University, Taiwan, the M.S. degree in electrical engineering from National Taiwan University, Taiwan, and the Ph.D. degree in computer science from the University of Illinois, Urbana, in 1978, 1980, and 1986, respectively.

Currently, he is a member of the Technical Staff with AT&T Bell Laboratories, Columbus, OH. Prior to joining Bell Laboratories, he was a Research Assistant with the Center for Supercomputing Research and Development, University of Illinois, Urbana, where he had been involved in the Cedar supercomputer project for more than two years. His research interests include interconnection networks, fault-tolerant computings, distributed and parallel processings, and computer architectures.

Dr. Tzeng is a member of Tau Beta Pi.

Duncan H. Lawrie (S'66–M'73–SM'81–F'84) is currently Professor of Computer Science, Professor of Electrical and Computer Engineering, and Associate Director of the Center for Supercomputing Research and Development at the University of Illinois, Urbana. He has contributed to the design of several large computers including the Illiac IV where he designed and implemented Glypnir, the first high-level language for that machine, and the Burroughs Scientific Processor where he was a Principal Architect, specializing in the array memory system. He is currently a Principal Architect of the Cedar large-scale multiprocessor at the University of Illinois, and directs the compiler and operating systems development work for that machine. His main interest is in the area of design and evaluation of computer architecture, with specialization in the areas of high-speed algorithm design, communication networks, virtual memory performance, and the use of mass storage devices. He has been a consultant to industry and government in the areas of computer organization, local networking, and applications studies.

Dr. Lawrie was Chairman of the Symposium on High-Speed Computer and Algorithm Organization, Program Chairman of the Ninth International Conference on Parallel Processing, and General Chairman of the Fourth International Conference on Distributed Computing Systems. He has also served as Editor of the Computer Architecture and Systems Department of the *Communications of the ACM,* and was the Chairman for Conferences and Chairman for Tutorials of the Conferences and Tutorials Board as well as Acting Vice President for Publications of the IEEE Computer Society. He is a Member and Secretary of the IEEE Computer Society Governing Board (1986–1987), and is a member of the Association for Computing Machinery.

Nonuniform Traffic Spots (NUTS) in Multistage Interconnection Networks

TOMAS LANG AND LANCE KURISAKI

Computer Science Department, University of California, Los Angeles, Los Angeles, California 90024

The performance of multistage interconnection networks for multiprocessors is degraded when the traffic pattern produces nonuniform congestion in the blocking switches, that is, when there exist nonuniform traffic spots. For some specific patterns we evaluate this degradation in performance and propose modifications to the network organization and operation to reduce the degradation. Successful modifications are the use of diverting switches and the extension of the network with additional links. The use of these modifications makes the network more effective for a larger variety of traffic patterns. We also consider the case in which the network carries the superposition of two types of traffic. One type is the high throughput data and instruction traffic, while the other consists of control and I/O packets which are of low throughput but have severe real-time constraints. We conclude that diverting switches and networks with additional links are also suitable for assuring low latency for the real-time traffic, especially when using the displacing mode. © 1990 Academic Press, Inc.

1. INTRODUCTION

Multistage interconnection networks (MIN) are used in multiprocessor systems to connect processors with other processors or memory modules. These networks provide a compromise between networks of low latency and high cost, such as the crossbar, and networks of high latency and low cost, such as the shared bus. Moreover, MINs can be pipelined to provide a bandwidth comparable to that of the crossbar for suitable traffic patterns. In addition, the control of routing is simple. We are concerned here with networks which have inputs on one side and outputs on the other side—there are no sources or sinks at intermediate stages. A large body of work has been done on the structure, operation, and performance of these networks; a comprehensive reference is [23]. These networks were initially introduced for use in array computers of the SIMD type; in this context the interconnection networks are sometimes called permutation networks. More recently, they are being proposed and used in multiprocessors of the MIMD type, especially in those of the shared-memory variety [6, 7, 20, 25]. In this paper we are concerned with this second type of use.

MINs, in their basic form, provide a unique path between any source–destination pair. However, the paths for differ-ent pairs are not disjoint and, therefore, conflicts might occur when simultaneous communication is established between several source–destination pairs. The basic method used to handle this problem is to use a packet-switched type of operation and to buffer the packets in the switches. Blocking occurs whenever the buffers become full.

It has been shown that the performance of these networks is satisfactory for uniform traffic [4, 11, 19]. More recently, several studies [12, 17, 21] have indicated that the performance of the network is degraded significantly when the traffic includes hot-spot traffic, that is, when each source generates a larger fraction of the traffic to one particular destination. This type of traffic occurs because of access to shared variables, such as semaphores. To overcome this degradation, a network with combining switches has been proposed [21, 26].

The topic of this paper is a different type of nonuniform traffic, in which there is no concentration of the traffic to one destination, but the traffic is not uniformly distributed among the switches, as illustrated in Fig. 3. To differentiate this with the hot-spot case, we call these nonuniform traffic spots (NUTS). We illustrate some typical cases of this type of traffic and show the degradation in network performance produced by them. We then explore solutions to reduce this performance degradation.

Of course, in this case the use of combining switches is not a solution since the contention packets do not necessarily have the same destination. We show that randomization of the traffic, proposed for reducing contention in multicomputers, and networks with discarding switches are not suitable either. As positive alternatives to improve the performance, we consider the use of diverting switches, with several diverting policies, and networks with additional links to provide alternate paths. Because of the reduction in degradation produced, the proposed modifications to the basic network with blocking make the multistage network suitable for a larger variety of multiprocessor applications.

We also consider the case in which the network carries the superposition of two types of traffic. One type is the high throughput data and instruction traffic, while the other consists of control packets (for singularity conditions, errors, etc.) and I/O packets. In many instances, this second type is of low throughput but has severe real-time constraints. In such a case, it is necessary to assure low latency for these packets. In the sequel we will call the first type of traffic background traffic (bgt) and the second type real-time traffic (rtt). We consider strategies to control the network to achieve the low latency for rtt, especially in the case where the bgt has NUTS.

Three solutions to this situation come to mind. In the first, a separate network is used for the rtt, which would be designed to assure the low latency; the disadvantage of this is the cost of the additional network. A second solution is to share one network but to have separate buffers in the switches for each traffic; moreover, in case of conflicts for the switch output ports, priority is given to the rtt. Still, this solution has the additional cost of the buffers and is more complex to control, especially when blocking switches are used because of the need for additional full signals. Finally, it is possible to share the network and buffers and to develop control strategies to assure low latency for the rtt. Here we explore this third alternative.

We conclude that the diverting switches, which produce good performance for NUTS, are also suitable for assuring low latency for the rtt, especially when using the displacing mode (see Section 8). Moreover, we show that the network with additional links, which provides the highest throughput in the presence of NUTS, is also suitable for low latency rtt. We also conclude that even for uniform traffic it is not possible to assure low latency for the rtt when using blocking switches.

The performance of the proposed solutions is evaluated by simulation. The objective of this evaluation is to show that, under reasonable conditions, performance of the original network with blocking switches is badly degraded by the presence of NUTS and that the modifications proposed significantly reduce this degradation. On the other hand, it is not our objective to give an extensive set of graphs from which the performance of particular networks with specific traffic patterns can be determined. Consequently, we select a set of reasonable network parameters and traffic patterns and use these for the simulation. More detail can be found in [14].

2. MULTISTAGE NETWORK STRUCTURE AND OPERATION WITH BLOCKING AND DISCARDING SWITCHES

We now give a brief description of the structure of operation of the multistage network, emphasizing the assumptions we make. The definitions and terminology used here are the same as those used by Siegel [23]. The type of multistage interconnection network we are considering has $N = 2^n$ inputs (sources) and outputs (destinations). It consists of n stages of $N/2$ 2×2 switches, as shown in Fig. 1. The outputs of stage-i switches are connected to the inputs of stage-$(i - 1)$ switches, with the network inputs going to stage-$(n - 1)$ switches and the network outputs coming

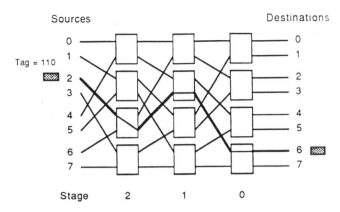

FIG. 1. An 8×8 Omega network.

from the stage-0 switches. This type of network has been referred to as a two-sided MIN [9].

Several specific multistage networks have been proposed, differing in the interconnection pattern between stages. Since the characteristics, in terms of type of operation and performance, are similar for all these different topologies, we consider here the Omega network [15], which has been extensively studied and is being used in several multiprocessor systems [7, 20, 25]. Previous studies dealing with uniform traffic show that these networks provide reasonable performance with very few buffers under a moderate traffic load [4, 11, 19].

The routing of packets in the network is unique since there is a single path from a specific source to a specific destination. The control of routing is done using a destination tag associated with each packet. At stage i, the routing depends only on the ith bit of the tag: if the bit has value 0(1), then the route is to the upper (lower) output of the switch.

The operation of the network is synchronous and pipelined. In its basic form, each switch has one register per output and in each cycle one packet is transferred from an output register in a switch of stage i to the corresponding output register of a switch of stage $i - 1$. This implies that the packets are all of the same size. If the packet is large, the above-mentioned cycle can be divided into several subcycles and a part of the packet transferred per subcycle. However, we are not concerned with this subdivision and use the packet as the basic unit of transfer and the time of this transfer as the unit of time (one cycle).

Since each output can send only one packet per cycle (the network is synchronous and pipelined), there is a conflict when both packets entering a switch in a cycle have to be routed to the same output. One solution to this conflict is to have a buffer for each output and to store the additional packet in such a buffer. Of course, these buffers are finite so it is necessary to have an operation policy when the buffer is full. The basic scheme used is a *blocking* policy in which the predecessor switches do not send packets to a full buffer. To support this policy it is necessary to have signals from a

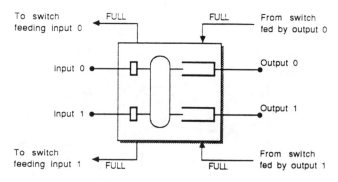

FIG. 2. Blocking switch with FULL control signals.

switch to its predecessors indicating that the corresponding buffer(s) is full (Fig. 2). The registers at the inputs of the switch serve to simplify the FULL signal generation and reduce the number of signals needed to one per input port.

An alternative policy to blocking when conflicts occur is to *discard* one of the packets, and have its source send it again at a later time. The retransmission may be initiated by the switches, by triggering an explicit signal when a discarding occurs, or by the sources, which buffer outstanding messages and retransmit them after a time-out period expires (we used the switch-initiated approach). This type of switch is used in the BBN Butterfly Parallel Processor [25].

Several variations on the basic switch buffer design are possible [10]. The switch can have a single buffer pool to service both inputs/outputs, which leads to the best buffer utilization. However, this requires that two packets be accepted and sent from the queue per cycle. Moreover, if a FIFO policy is used, a packet in the front of the queue can block the sending of another packet. The other possibility is to have dedicated buffers, either servicing one input or one output. Input buffers have the advantage of simplifying the generation of the full signal and receive at most one packet per cycle. However, arbitration is necessary to determine which packets are sent to the output and a FIFO policy leads to the same blocking characteristics as for the single buffer. Output buffers have to be able to receive two packets per cycle. Queue management policies can be FIFO or non-FIFO with some kind of priority scheme. More complex control algorithms are possible, leading to better utilization, but the cost and speed requirements of the switch limit the practicality of such complex algorithms. As technology improves, however, more options become available.

In this paper we do not evaluate the different buffering organizations and policies. The degradation produced by NUTS is inherent to the blocking operation of the network, which is present for any of the buffer organizations and policies. Moreover, the modifications we propose are applicable to all these organizations. Consequently, we perform our analysis using output buffers with FIFO policy.

As mentioned, the basic network is composed of 2×2

switches. However, generalizations are possible in which $k \times k$ switches are used. This has the advantage of reducing the number of stages to $\log_k N$, with the corresponding reduction in delay. In this paper, we only consider 2×2 switches, but the results should be equally applicable to the general case.

When processors send request packets to remote memory modules, traffic in the opposite direction is also generated. These return packets must traverse an analogous network to reach the processors. The analysis of this type of traffic is similar to the request traffic and is not considered here.

3. PERFORMANCE EVALUATION BY SIMULATION

We now describe the measures that we will use to evaluate the performance of the network. We also indicate the types of traffic and network parameters considered. As discussed in the Introduction, we select a reasonable set of parameters and perform simulations to compare the performance for the original network and for the modifications proposed.

Of importance in our study are the different traffic patterns used, since the degradation due to NUTS and the applicable solutions depend on the traffic patterns considered. In the next section we present the patterns used.

In addition to the traffic pattern, the traffic load is of importance. We distinguish two types of systems: open and closed systems. In an open system, each processor generates a packet every r cycles, so that the load is specified by the fraction $1/r$. In a closed system, on the other hand, the load is defined by the maximum number of outstanding packets per source. We have found that the results are qualitatively similar for both cases for the same total throughput. Consequently, to concentrate on significant parameters, we only report on results for open systems.

We evaluate the steady-state behavior of the system; that is, the traffic pattern under consideration is applied to the system for a period long enough to achieve this steady state before statistics are gathered.

The fundamental parameters for the network are its size and the size of the queues. We have found that the relative performance of the network remains essentially the same for different values of these parameters. Consequently, we report our results for a network of size 64 and queues of size 2, which are also convenient because they produce a relatively small delay.

In the simulations with real-time traffic, we consider a typical situation of 50% load on the network; that is, each input provides one packet per two cycles on average (if the corresponding first-stage buffer is not full in the blocking case, and if there are no packets to resend in the other cases). We assume that the rtt is of low throughput so that it alone does not produce congestion in the network. The total traffic is a mix of 95% bgt and 5% rtt. We are especially interested in cases in which the bgt has NUTS because these are the difficult cases and where there is a difference between alternative control mechanisms.

The main performance measures of interest are the throughput of the network in packets/cycle and the average delay of the packets. The maximum throughput is of N packets per cycle and the minimum delay is of n cycles. This performance is obtained when there is no buffer contention, that is, when in all cycles all switches received two packets and route one to each output. For other cases, the performance is shown by the function delay vs relative throughput (fraction of the maximum throughput).

In a parallel processing system, all processors cooperate in the execution of a task and must synchronize periodically. Consequently, it is convenient for all processors to advance at a uniform pace, so that fast processors do not have to wait unnecessarily for slower ones. The measure we use to evaluate the relative advance of the processors is the distribution of throughput among processors.

Since we are interested in providing a low latency for the rtt, we measure the distribution of delay for rtt packets. From this distribution we obtain as most significant measures the maximum delay of an rtt packet and the average delay of the slowest 10% of the rtt. The maximum delay shows the worst case and serves as an upper bound on the delay experienced by an rtt packet. Quite often, however, the maximum delay occurs for only very few packets. To get a better feel for the delay, we look at the slowest 10% of the packets.

For the simulations we built a network simulator using as a basis SIMON, a general-purpose multiprocessor simulator developed at the University of Utah [5].

Several studies have been reported on the performance of multistage interconnection networks with uniform traffic [4, 11, 19]. They generally find that a few buffers at each switch (1 or 2) are sufficient to give good performance at moderate traffic loads for a basic blocking, packet switching network. Since our purpose is to consider the performance for nonuniform traffic, we performed simulations for uniform traffic only to validate the simulator and to provide a reference point with which to compare to other traffic patterns. The results of our simulations for uniform traffic confirm what previous studies have indicated.

4. TRAFFIC PATTERNS PRODUCING NUTS

The evaluation studies that have been made for the "hot-spot" problem point to a related situation with nonuniform traffic. The same type of degradation should occur whenever the traffic is such that one or more switches carry a larger fraction of the total traffic than its share. This degradation is due to the same "tree saturation" effect observed in the hot-spot case [21]. In the context of the Omega network, switch i of stage j can carry all of the traffic going

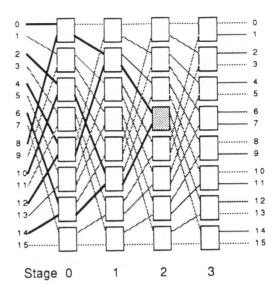

FIG. 3. A nonuniform traffic spot.

from a specific subset of 2^{j+1} sources to a specific subset of destinations. For example, in Fig. 3, the shaded switch could carry any subset of the traffic generated by even-numbered sources. Consequently, switch congestion occurs whenever this traffic is excessive. This can occur even in situations in which the fraction of traffic going to each destination is the same. The main objective of this research is to identify the traffic patterns that produce nonuniform traffic spots, to evaluate the degradation in performance, and to propose and evaluate solutions to this problem.

To study the influence of NUTS on performance we have considered two types of traffic as follows. These types are just examples to illustrate the problem and evaluate the solutions: they correspond to situations that could occur, but are not derived from any particular application.

Traffic of Type I

In the first type, each source issues all its requests to one destination and no pair of sources sends to the same destination. In the shared memory case, this type of pattern models a system in which each processor has a preferred memory module that contains both the code and the data for the processor. It might be argued that in such a case it would be better to assign to each processor a local memory module with direct access without going through the network (this is the scheme used, for example, in the BBN Butterfly). The local memory model is appropriate when memory referencing characteristics remain static. On the other hand, the use of the network to have a uniform access time from any processor to any memory module permits a flexible dynamic scheduling approach that is not possible in the local scheme. In this dynamic scheduling model, a processor can have its code/data in any memory module,

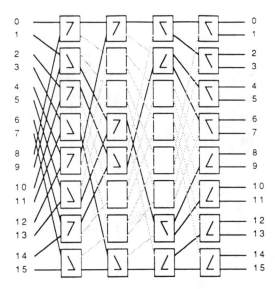

FIG. 4. Switch positions for the bit-reversal permutation.

and this module can vary with time. This type of traffic would also model situations in which the communication is among pairs of processors by choosing the appropriate permutation.

Some specific instances of this type of traffic patterns produce significant NUTS while others do not. We use two different instances for our study. In instance 1, we use a *bit-reversal* permutation which is known to produce a large contention in the Omega network as evident from the switch positions shown in Fig. 4. To model a more typical situation, as instance 2 we generate an *arbitrary* permutation with source–destination pairs produced at random.

Traffic of Type II

The second traffic pattern consists of requests going from even-numbered sources to destinations in the first half and from odd-numbered sources to destinations in the second half (*EFOS*) (Fig. 5). This pattern serves to illustrate a case

in which each source accesses a subset of destinations. In this case, there are also NUTS.

As one of the reviewers commented, these traffic patterns are quite static—an actual program would rarely be so rigid as to exhibit a single permutation over its entire lifetime. As we previously stated, however, these traffic patterns serve merely to illustrate the problem. Any NUTS effect might be less severe with traffic patterns that are more dynamic (closer to uniform), but all types of switches would benefit by such patterns.

The throughput–delay for these patterns is shown in Fig. 6. As can be seen, there is significant degradation in performance, as compared to the uniform traffic case.

Moreover, in the case of arbitrary permutation, there is a large variation between the throughput of the different processors (Fig. 7). As mentioned before, this is not desirable when the processors are cooperating on a single task.

We conclude from these simulations that the performance of the network is badly degraded by the NUTS, with respect to the performance for uniform traffic. We now explore ways to reduce this degradation.

5. UNSUCCESSFUL SOLUTIONS: RANDOMIZATION AND DISCARDING

We now report on randomization and discarding, two approaches for reducing the degradation due to NUTS which turned out to be unsuccessful.

Randomization

As a first solution to the degradation due to NUTS, we consider the use of *randomization* of the traffic. In this approach, proposed previously to handle load imbalances in the routing of multicomputers [18, 28], packets are first sent to random destinations and then rerouted to their final destinations (Fig. 8). These scheme has the effect of making the traffice pattern uniform and, therefore, of eliminating the added congestion of nonuniform traffic.

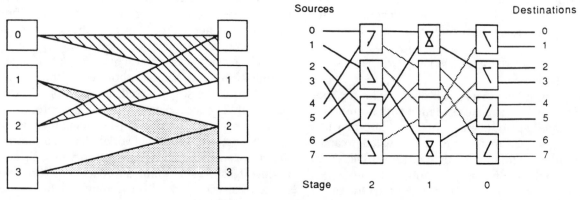

FIG. 5. The EFOS traffic pattern.

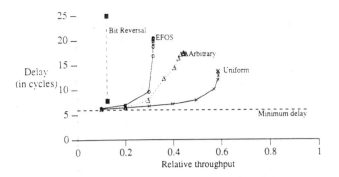

FIG. 6. Throughput–delay for blocking switches.

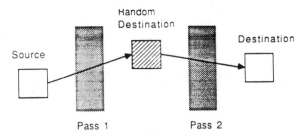

FIG. 8. Randomization.

In the context of multistage networks, the use of this scheme implies that all packets make two passes through the network and requires that the network have a wrapped-around organization. This has the two negative effects of doubling the minimum delay and reducing the effective throughput to half, because of the additional traffic through the net produced by rerouting. The results of simulations for the two types of traffic described in the previous section are shown in Fig. 9, which exhibits the expected throughput and delay. As seen from the figure, randomization produces a relatively small improvement for the extreme bit-reversal case, while it is detrimental for the others.

Discarding Switch

Another solution we considered was the use of discarding switches. Switches of this type resolve congestion by discarding overflow packets (Fig. 10). The original source of the packet is made aware of the status of the packet, through an explicit signal from the switch or a time-out mechanism, and retransmits it. No FULL signals are needed in this case, which simplifies the control logic. Note that this requires the source to buffer all outstanding packets until an acknowledgment is received from the destination. The switches also require the ability to signal the appropriate source that a particular packet was discarded. This requires additional interconnect and more complex control. This type of switch is used in the Butterfly Parallel Processor to deal with contention in the network and to avoid "tree saturation" [25].

The simulations show that, for the traffic patterns considered, there is no improvement with respect to the network with blocking switches. This can be explained by the fact that the discarded traffic is reissued by the same processor and, therefore, follows the same path leading to the NUTS.

6. DIVERTING SWITCH

In a *diverting switch* the packets in front of the buffers are always sent to the successors, irrespective of whether there is space for them in the corresponding destination buffers. If both packets that arrive to a switch go to the same output buffer and there is no space for both, then one of the packets is diverted to the other buffer of the switch (Fig. 11). Note that there is always space for at least one packet in each buffer since one packet departs from each buffer in every cycle. Of course, the diverted packet will go to a wrong destination (since there is just one path in the network for each source–destination pair); therefore, the packet will have to be resent into the network to the correct destination. Consequently, this mode of operation requires a connection between each network output and corresponding input (a wrapped-around organization).

Diversion has potentially better performance than discarding because the packets are rerouted from a source that is *different* from the original source. This makes it possible

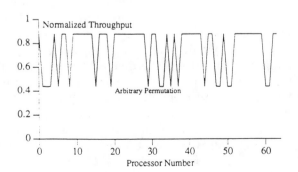

FIG. 7. Throughput distribution (arbitrary permutation traffic).

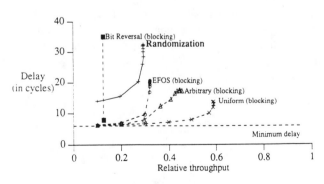

FIG. 9. Randomization simulation results.

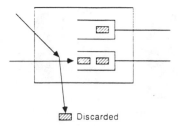

FIG. 10. A discarding switch.

for the packet to avoid the NUTS in the second pass (Fig. 12).

Since to obtain a good performance it is convenient to reduce the number of packets that are diverted, whenever a conflict occurs and one of the packets in the conflict has already been diverted (in that pass through the network) we give preference to the nondiverted packet (to go to the correct destination). Moreover, because of the diversions, a packet might traverse the network several times before getting to its destination. A problem with this form of operation is that it is not possible to assure that a particular packet will have a bounded delay. To deal with this and make the delay distribution more uniform, we give preference to older packets when their *DIVERTED* flags are equal. This age information is stored in each packet in the form of either a time stamp or a hop count (simulations used a time stamp).

It is also possible for packets to arrive at the destination out of order due to the diversions. If this is a problem, the destination node must buffer the out-of-order packets and do the resequencing. However, this might not be a problem in all instances. For example, if the packets correspond to requests for different cache lines, the order in which the requests are satisfied does not have to be preserved.

It is important to note that a diverting switch is never blocked, since it always sends a packet through each output port if there is one to be sent. This means that there are no FULL signals to arbitrate and generate. A diverting switch will, therefore, have fewer input/output lines and none of the logic associated with the FULL signals required by the blocking switch.

Similar techniques have been applied to conflict resolution in single-stage shuffle-exchange networks [16] and in fault-tolerant routing in multistage interconnection networks [29, 30].

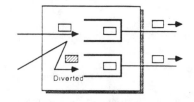

FIG. 11. Behavior of the diverting switch.

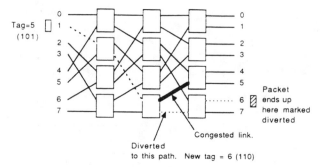

First pass through network

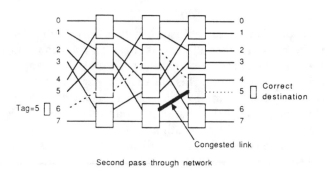

Second pass through network

FIG. 12. Diverting can avoid the NUTS in the second pass.

Diverting Policies

Once a packet is diverted, it cannot reach its desired destination during that pass; it has to go through the network again. This means that we now have a great deal of freedom in deciding where to route these diverted packets. The main goal is to route the diverted packet to an interim destination that has a "clear" path to the true destination, so that it will not be diverted again.

We have experimented with several diverting policies. We present here the results of two of them, to show that diverting produces an improvement in the performance and that the specific diverting policy has an impact.

We call the first diverting policy *direct diverting*. In it, the routing of the diverted packet continues using the destination tag; that is, each time the packet is diverted, the interim destination is wrong in the corresponding bit. As shown in Fig. 13 the performance is significantly better than with the blocking policy.

We call the second diverting policy *complement diverting*. In this case, once a packet is diverted, instead of using the destination tag for routing, it is routed using a tag corresponding to the complement of the source. On its next pass through the network, the original destination tag is again used. This policy has the advantage that it assures that the rerouted packet will avoid the NUTS where it was diverted in the first pass as illustrated in Fig. 12. The packet cannot reach the switch where it was diverted in the first pass since the low-order bits of the new source tag, which become the

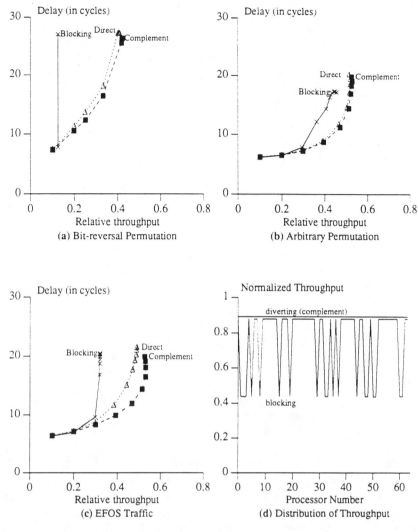

FIG. 13. Simulation results for diverting switches.

high-order bits at stage i, are the complement of the original source tag bits (Fig. 14). Of course, the packet can pass through some other NUTS.

Figures 13a–13c show the corresponding performance for the various traffic patterns. We see that this policy produces a somewhat better performance than the direct policy.

These simulation results indicate that the use of diverting switches improves the throughput–delay characteristic of the network when the traffic produces NUTS. Moreover, the use of diverting switches eliminates the unequal distribution of throughput experienced in blocking switches (Fig. 13d).

7. NETWORK WITH ALTERNATE PATHS

The MINs previously considered have the characteristic of a unique path between each source–destination pair. Sev-

eral reports [1, 13, 27] have described adding redundant paths to MINs to improve fault-tolerance characteristics. These alternate paths can also improve the performance of a fully functional network.

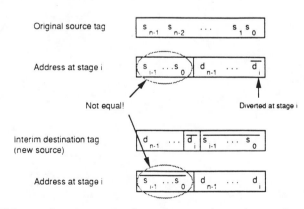

FIG. 14. Complement diverting avoids congestion on the second pass.

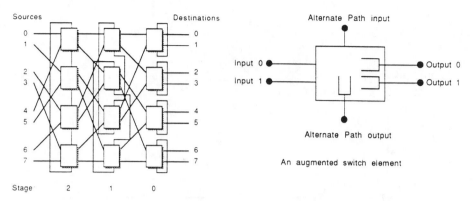

Sources   Destinations

Stage   2   1   0

Alternate Path input

Input 0   Output 0
Input 1   Output 1

Alternate Path output

An augmented switch element

FIG. 15.   An alternate path network and switch element.

In particular [13] and [27] propose the addition of links to connect switches in the same stage into rings such that any switch in a particular ring can reach the same subset of destinations. The application of this technique to the Omega network is illustrated in Fig. 15. If a packet entering a switch finds the desired output queue full, it can be rerouted to another switch in the same group via the alternate path link, and still be able to reach its true destination directly without a second pass through the network.

This modified Omega network requires augmented switches acting as a 3 × 3 crossbar, as shown in Fig. 15. The routing control is somewhat more complex than for the original 2 × 2 switch. We still use a diverting policy, since this has given better performance for the original network and no "full signals" are needed. Each cycle up to three packets enter the switch. They are placed in the output queues giving priority to the older packets that have not been diverted (in that pass). The highest priority packet is always placed in the correct queue, since there is always at least one space in each queue (because one packet leaves each queue each cycle). The next packet is placed in the

correct queue, if there is space, or in the alternate queue. Finally, the lowest priority packet is placed in the correct queue, in the alternate queue, or in the wrong queue (diverted).

Figure 16 shows the performance of the network with alternate paths for two of the traffic patterns. We can see that the introduction of alternate paths produces a significant reduction in the degradation due to NUTS.

8. STRATEGIES FOR LOW-LATENCY REAL-TIME TRAFFIC

We consider here the case in which the network carries the superposition of two types of traffic. One type is the high throughput data and instruction traffic, while the other consists of control packets (for singularity conditions, errors, etc.) and I/O packets. In many instances, this second type is of low throughput but has severe real-time constraints [24]. In such a case, it is necessary to assure low latency for these packets. In the sequel we will call the first type of traffic background traffic (bgt) and the second type real-time

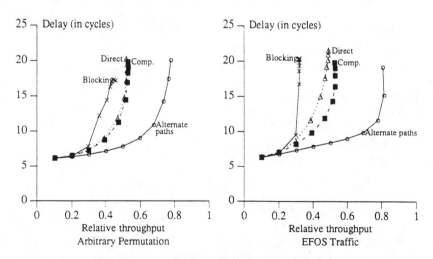

FIG. 16.   Throughput–delay graphs (alternate paths).

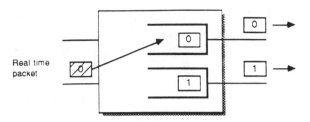

FIG. 17a. rtt to the back of the queue.

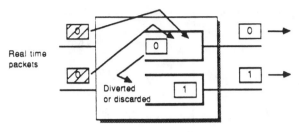

FIG. 17c. Displacing.

traffic (rtt). We consider strategies to control the network to achieve the low latency for rtt, especially in the case where the bgt has NUTS.

We now present the strategies we propose and evaluate to obtain low latency for the real-time traffic. For discarding and diverting switches the basic strategy we use to reduce the latency of the rtt is to give priority to packets of this traffic type when one of the two packets coming to a buffer has to be discarded or diverted (as previously noted, both packets never have to be discarded or diverted because there is always at least one space in each buffer, left by the departing packets). Specifically, when one of the packets coming to a buffer (with only one space) is of the bgt type, this is the one that is discarded/diverted. For obvious reasons, none of this applies to blocking switches.

On top of this basic strategy we consider the following three alternatives, as illustrated in Fig. 17. In the first, the rtt packets are placed at the back of the buffers, in the same way as the bgt packets (Fig. 17a). In the second alternative, the rtt are placed in front of the buffer, while the bgt packets are placed at the back (Fig. 17b). Finally, the third alternative always allows the placement of up to two rtt packets in the front of the buffer; if there is no space for both packets in the buffer, this requires the displacement of a packet from the end of the buffer (note that this displaced packet might be a bgt packet or a rtt packet). This displaced packet is discarded or diverted to another queue (this scheme does not apply to blocking switches) (Fig. 17c).

9. REAL-TIME TRAFFIC SIMULATION RESULTS

The simulation results are presented in the graphs of Figs. 18 and 19. As previously noted, we use a traffic mix of 5%

rtt and 95% bgt at a 50% load. Figure 18a shows the distribution of delay of the rtt packets for EFOS bgt and EFOS rtt with diverting switches; the results for the other types of traffic are very similar. We see that the policy with displacing provides the lowest delay for the rtt, followed by rtt to front and finally rtt to back. The zoom view shows the slowest 5% of the rtt packets for the two best policies. We see

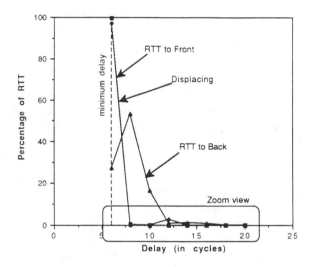

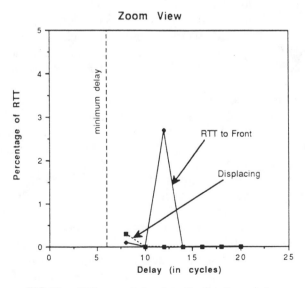

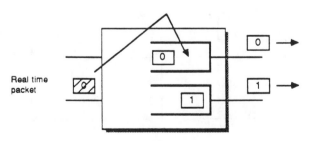

FIG. 17b. rtt to the front of the queue.

FIG.18a. Different switch policies for diverting switches.

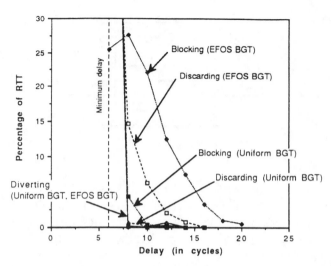

FIG.18b.   Effect of different background traffic (rtt to front. 50% load).

that rtt to front caused roughly 3% of the rtt packets to be diverted, requiring a second pass through the network (delay of 12 cycles), while displacing eliminates these diversions.

Figure 18b shows the effect of the bgt on the delay of the rtt. The simulations used uniform rtt and the rtt to front policy for different types of switches and bgt patterns. We see that with diverting switches, the bgt pattern has practically no effect on the delay of the rtt, while the effect is significant when blocking and discarding switches are used. It is because of this degradation that we conclude blocking and discarding switches are unable to assure low latency to rtt in the presence of NUTS.

Figure 19 shows the maximum delay experienced by the real-time traffic (in cycles) and the average delay of the slowest 10% of the real-time traffic for different policies with diverting and alternate path switches. The traffic used is a mix of 5% uniform rtt and 95% EFOS bgt. Since the simulated network has 6 stages, the minimum delay is 6 cycles. Data for blocking and discarding switches are not shown since we have previously concluded that both are unsuitable for rtt.

We conclude that for very low rtt latency the policy with displacing should be used, while for somewhat larger delay the policy rtt to front is acceptable for diverting and alternate paths. Also, the policy rtt to back produces a significant degradation in both cases.

It is important to note that the network with alternate paths carries a much higher total throughput than the diverting switch network (70% load versus 50% load for the diverting switch). Failure to notice this may lead one to falsely conclude that the added expense of alternate paths is of little value in this case. The difference in the throughput values makes it difficult to directly compare the delay of the different alternatives.

Similar results are obtained for other types of rtt and bgt. The pattern of the rtt is not very significant, since it is of very low rate. A small degradation occurs when the rtt has the same pattern as the bgt, because of the NUTS produced by the latter.

Finally, from the operation of the network, we see that if the rtt corresponds to nonintersecting paths (Fig. 20), the use of diverting switches with rtt to front produces the minimum delay of 6, since two rtt packets would never conflict. For this type of rtt there would be no need to use the somewhat more complicated policy of displacing.

10. CONCLUSIONS

We have shown several traffic patterns that produce NUTS in blocking multistage interconnection networks and therefore result in a degradation of performance. The randomization technique, proposed for eliminating imbalances of loading in multicomputers, is not appropriate in

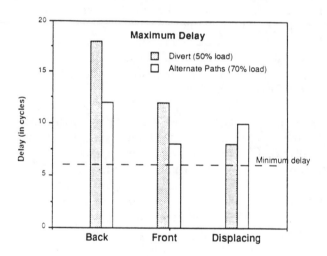

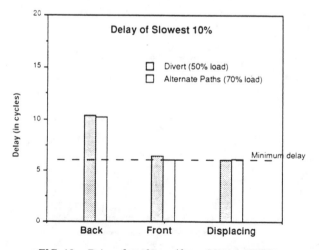

FIG. 19.   Delay of rtt (5%, uniform; 95% bgt. EFOS).

320

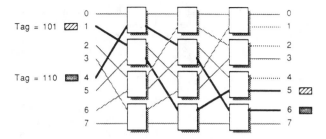

FIG. 20. Two nonintersecting paths.

this case because it increases the delay of each packet and the real traffic through the network. The use of discarding switches is not advantageous either because the discarded traffic has to be resent through the same congested path.

As positive solutions, we have shown that diverting switches produce a significant reduction in the degradation. Moreover, the control of congestion is simpler than that for blocking switches because no "full signals" are needed. However, to implement this policy, it is necessary to have a network with wrapped-around connections.

The performance is much better using networks with alternate paths. However, this network requires 3×3 switches instead of the basic 2×2, which complicates the implementation.

We have presented several strategies to assure low latency for low rate real-time traffic in the presence of high rate background traffic, even when there exist NUTS produced by the latter. For the basic network with a single path between any source–destination pair, the best strategy is to use diverting switches with displacing policy. The use of diverting switches provides a large throughput for background traffic producing NUTS, while this type of switches with displacing assures low latency for rtt. Discarding switches are not good because they have a significant degradation with NUTS and blocking switches degrade both types of traffic.

The application of these modifications to the basic blocking policy in the control of contention in multistage interconnection networks makes it possible to use the network effectively for a larger variety of traffic patterns.

The traffic patterns used in the simulations were static; as mentioned by one of the reviewers, the extension of this work to more dynamic (and realistic) patterns should prove interesting.

ACKNOWLEDGMENTS

This research was sponsored in part by the State of California MICRO program and Hughes Aircraft Co.

REFERENCES

1. Adams, G. B., and Siegel, H. J. The extra stage cube: A fault-tolerant interconnection network for supersystems. *IEEE Trans. Comput.* C-31, 5 (May 1982), 443–454.

2. Brantley, W. C., McAuliffe, K. P., and Weiss, J. RP3 processor-memory element. *Proc. 1985 International Conference on Parallel Processing.* IEEE Computer Society, Silver Spring, MD, Aug. 1985, pp. 782–789.

3. Chen, P., Lawrie, D., and Yew, P. Interconnection networks using shuffles. *Computer* (Dec. 1981), 55–64.

4. Dias, D., and Jump, R. Packet switching interconnection networks for modular systems. *Computer* (Dec. 1981), 43–54.

5. Fujimoto, R. M., and Swope, S. M. SIMON II kernel reference manual. Tech. Rep. UUCS-86-001, Computer Science Department, University of Utah, Mar. 1986.

6. Gajski, D. D., Kuck, D., Lawrie, D., and Sameh, A. Cedar—A large scale multiprocessor. *Proc. 1983 International Conference on Parallel Processing.* IEEE Computer Society, Silver Spring, MD, Aug. 1985, pp. 524–529.

7. Gottlieb, A., et al. The NYU ultracomputer—Designing an MIMD shared memeory parallel computer. *IEEE Trans. Comput.* C-32, 2 (1983), 175–189.

8. Hwang, K., and Briggs, F. *Computer Architecture and Parallel Processing.* McGraw–Hill, New York, 1984.

9. Jenevein, R. M., and Mookken, T. Traffic analysis of rectangular SW-Banyan networks. *Proc. 15th Annual Symposium on Computer Architecture,* 1988, pp. 333–342.

10. Karol, M. J., Hluchyj, M. G., and Morgan, S. P. Input vs. output queueing on a space-division packet switch. *IEEE Global Telecommunications Conference.* Houston, TX, Dec. 1986, pp. 659–665.

11. Krustal, C. P., and Snir, M. The performance of multistage interconnection networks for multiprocessors. *IEEE Trans. Comput.* 32, 12 (Dec. 1983), 1091–1098.

12. Kumar, M., and Pfister, G. The onset of hot spot contention. *Proc. 1986 International Conference on Parallel Processing.* IEEE Computer Society, Silver Spring, MD, Aug. 1986.

13. Kumar, V. P., and Reddy, S. M. Design and analysis of fault-tolerant multistage interconnection networks with low link complexity. *Proc. 12th Annual Symposium on Computer Architecture,* June 1985, pp. 376–386.

14. Lang, T., and Kurisaki, L. Nonuniform traffic spots (NUTS) in multistage interconnection networks. Tech. Rep. CSD-880001, University of California, Los Angeles, Jan. 1988.

15. Lawrie, D. H. Access and alignment of data in an array processor. *IEEE Trans. Comput.* C-24, 12 (Dec. 1975), 1145–1155.

16. Lawrie, D. H., and Padua, D. A. Analysis of message switching with shuffle-exchanges in multiprocessors. *Proc. Workshop on Interconnection Networks for Parallel and Distributed Processing,* Apr. 1980, pp. 116–123.

17. Lee, R. On hot spot contention. *Comp. Architecture News.* 13, 5 (Dec. 1985), 15–20.

18. Mitra, D. Randomized parallel communications. *Proc. 1986 International Conference on Parallel Processing.* IEEE Computer Society, Silver Spring, MD, Aug. 1986, pp. 224–230.

19. Patel, J. H. Performance of processor–memory interconnections for multiprocessors. *IEEE Trans. Comput.* (Oct. 1981), 771–780.

20. Pfister, G. F., Brantley, W. C., George, D. A., Harvey, S. L., Kleinfelder, W. J., McAuliffe, K. P., Melton, E. A., Norton, V. A., and Weiss, J. The IBM research parallel processor prototype (RP3): Introduction and architecture. *Proc. 1985 International Conference on Parallel Processing.* IEEE Computer Society, Silver Spring, MD, Aug. 1985, pp. 764–771.

21. Pfister, G. F., and Norton, V. A. Hot spot contention and combining in multistage interconnection networks. *IEEE Trans. Comput.* C-34, 10 (Oct. 1985), 943–948.

22. Rosenblum. D. S.. and Mayr. E. W. Simulation of an ultracomputer with several "hot spots." Tech. Rep. STAN-CS-86-1119, Stanford University. June 1986.

23. Siegel. H. J. *Interconnection Networks for Large-Scale Parallel Processing. Theory and Case Studies.* Lexington Books. Lexington, MA. 1985.

24. Tamir. Y.. and Frazier. G. Support for high-priority traffic in VLSI communication switches. *9th Real-Time Systems Symposium.* Dec. 1988. pp. 191–200.

25. Thomas. R. H. Behavior of the Butterfly Parallel Processor in the presence of memory hot spots. *Proc. 1986 International Conference on Parallel Processing.* IEEE Computer Society. Silver Spring, MD. Aug. 1986. pp. 46–50.

26. Tzeng. N. Design of a novel combining structure for shared-memory multiprocessors. *Proc. 1989 International Conference on Parallel Processing.* IEEE Computer Society. Silver Spring. MD. Aug. 1989. pp. I-1–I-8.

27. Tzeng. N.. Yew. P.. and Zhu. C. A fault-tolerant scheme for multistage interconnection networks. *12th Annual Symposium on Computer Architecture.* June 1985. pp. 368–375.

28. Valiant. L. G. A scheme for fast parallel communication. *SIAM J. Comput.* **11**, 2 (May 1982). 350–361.

29. Varma. A.. and Raghavendra. C. S. Fault-tolerant routing in multistage interconnection networks. *IEEE Trans. Comput.* (Mar. 1989). 385–393.

30. Varma. A.. and Rathi. B. D. A fault-tolerant scheme for unique-path multistage interconnection networks. IBM Res. Rep. RC 13441 (No. 60126). IBM Research Division. Watson Research Center, Jan. 21, 1988.

Received March 2, 1989

TOMAS LANG received the electrical engineering degree from the University of Chile in 1965. the master's degree from the University of California. Berkeley. in 1966, and the Ph.D. from Stanford University in 1974. He served as Professor of Electrical Engineering at the University of Chile from 1966 to 1973 and in 1974 joined the faculty of the Computer Science Department of the University of California. Los Angeles. From 1978 to 1981 he was Professor of Computer Science at the Universidad Politecnica de Barcelona. His research and teaching interests are computer architecture and design. At present, his research specializes in digital arithmetic, special-purpose systems for matrix computations, and interconnection networks for parallel computers.

LANCE KURISAKI received a B.S. in EECS from the University of California at Berkeley in 1983 and an M.S. in computer science from Stanford University in 1984. He is presently working toward a Ph.D. in computer science from the University of California at Los Angeles and is a member of technical staff at TRW Inc. in Redondo Beach. California. His research interests include networks and performance analysis. He is a member of the Eta Kappa Nu and Tau Beta Pi honorary societies.

The Use of Feedback in Multiprocessors and Its Application to Tree Saturation Control

Steven L. Scott, *Student Member, IEEE,* and Gurindar S. Sohi, *Member, IEEE*

Abstract—In this paper, we propose the use of feedback control schemes in multiprocessor systems. In a multiprocessor, individual processors do not have complete control over, nor information about, the overall state of the system. The potential exists, then, for the processors to unknowingly interact in such a way as to degrade the performance of the system. An example of this is the problem of tree saturation caused by hot spot accesses in multiprocessors using multistage interconnection networks. Tree saturation degrades the performance of all processors in the system, including those not participating in the hot spot activity.

We see that feedback schemes can be used to control tree saturation, reducing degradation to memory requests that are not to the hot spot, and thereby increasing overall system performance. As a companion to feedback schemes, damping schemes are also considered. Simulation studies presented in this paper show that feedback schemes can improve overall system performance significantly in many cases and with relatively little hardware cost. Damping schemes in conjunction with feedback are shown to further improve system performance.

Index Terms—Damping, feedback, hot spots, multistage interconnection networks, tree saturation control.

I. Introduction

ONE of the most important and widely used concepts in the design of engineering control systems is the concept of *feedback* [3]. Feedback is primarily used to prevent instability in a system and keep system outputs within a desired range. Fig. 1 illustrates how feedback works. Without feedback [Fig. 1(a)], the inputs of the system are independent of events that might be occurring in the system. Consequently, an unstable situation could arise in which system outputs take on undesired values. This is referred to as an open loop system. With feedback [Fig. 1(b)], the outputs of the system (and possibly other state values of the system) are fed back to the input generator. Based upon the feedback information, the system input generator tries to modify the system inputs to keep the system outputs at some set of desired values or within some set of desired ranges. This is referred to as a closed loop system.

Modern computing systems have evolved into large-scale parallel processors that consist of possibly hundreds of processors and memory modules interconnected together in some fashion. Fig. 2 illustrates a typical processing system based on a shared memory programming paradigm [1], [16]. The processing system consists of a set of processing elements, a set of memory modules, and an interconnection network. The interconnection network is logically broken into a forward network

Manuscript received September 8, 1989; revised March 14, 1990. S. L. Scott was supported by fellowships from the Wisconsin Alumni Research Foundation and the Fannie and John Hertz Foundation. G. S. Sohi was supported in part by National Science Foundation Grant CCR-8706722. A preliminary version of this paper appeared in the 16th International Symposium on Computer Architecture, Jerusalem, Israel, June 1989.

The authors are with the Computer Sciences Department, University of Wisconsin–Madison, Madison, WI 53706.

IEEE Log Number 9036058.

and a reverse network though it is possible that the two networks could be the same physical network (for example, a set of buses). It is important to realize that the overall performance of such a processing system is not determined solely by the performance of the individual components; it is affected by how the components interact dynamically.

Let us compare Figs. 1 and 2. If we assume that the forward interconnection network is the system, then the inputs to the system are the requests generated by the processors and the outputs of the system are the requests arriving at the memory modules. Let us consider, in particular, the *arrival rates* of the requests at the memory modules. The desired value for the arrival rate of requests to a memory module is the minimum of the rate at which the requests can be accepted by the memory module, and the aggregate access rate desired by the processors. If the arrival rate is lower than that desired by the processors, and lower than that which can be accepted by the memory module, then we are using system resources poorly by wasting memory module cycles. If the arrival rate is higher than that at which the requests can be accepted, then blockage occurs within the network. This blockage unnecessarily reduces the effective bandwidth of the entire system (interconnection network), as will be discussed in Section II.

For performance reasons, then, we want to maintain the desired arrival rates at all memory modules, a task that depends largely upon the input streams from the processors. Considering this dependence, and the resemblance between Figs. 1 and 2, we ask ourselves: 1) why has explicit feedback not been used thus far in the design of computing systems and 2) why might it be useful now?

The answers lie in the distributed nature of modern parallel processing systems. Traditionally, a computing system consisted of a single processor (system input generator). This processor generated requests to memory (there could be either a single or multiple outstanding requests) and had to wait for results back from the memory. This implicit feedback (waiting for the memory responses) sufficed to regulate the arrival rate of requests at the memory. In a multiprocessor system, however, many processors are generating requests without knowledge of the state of other components in the system. In such a processing system, it is possible that the collective input of the processors could interact in such a way as to cause unnecessary degradation of the network. This can occur if the arrival rate at any memory or intermediate point within the network is too high. The implicit feedback to processors (via memory responses) is not sufficient, as we shall see in Section IV, to convey enough information to correct the anomalous behavior. To provide enough information to correct the behavior, explicit feedback mechanisms may be warranted.

One could alter the processing system of Fig. 2 to resemble the system of Fig. 1(b) by providing explicit feedback from

Reprinted from *IEEE Trans. Parallel and Distributed Systems,* Vol. 1, No. 4, Oct. 1990, pp. 385-398. Copyright © 1990 by The Institute of Electrical and Electronics Engineers, Inc. All rights reserved.

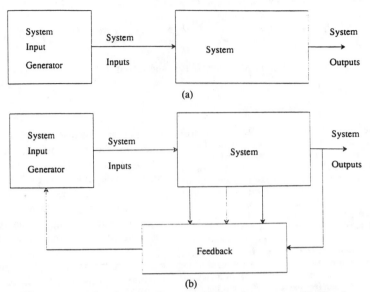

(a)

(b)

Fig. 1. An engineering control system. (a) Open-loop system. (b) Closed-loop (feedback) system.

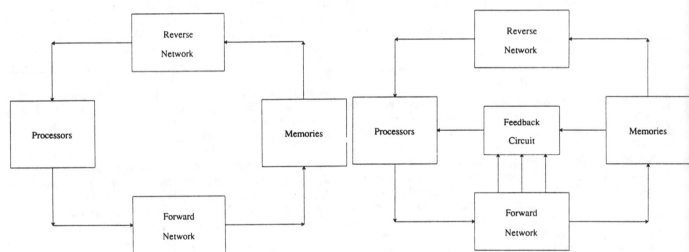

Fig. 2. A typical shared memory multiprocessing system.

Fig. 3. A shared memory multiprocessing system with feedback.

points within the forward interconnection network to the processors (see Fig. 3). This explicit feedback could then be used to detect congestion at points within the network and instruct the processors to modify their inputs to the network such that the congestion is relieved. By reducing congestion and blockages within the network, the overall performance of the system could be enhanced.

In this paper, we illustrate the use of feedback in computer systems design by targeting the problem of *tree saturation* in parallel computer systems that use buffered multistage interconnection networks (MIN's). Tree saturation is a special form of network congestion that can severely degrade the performance of MIN's [14]. We demonstrate how feedback concepts can be used to control tree saturation and reduce the performance degradation that it causes.

The remainder of this paper is as follows. In Section II, we consider the undesirable situation of tree saturation in multistage interconnection networks that use a distributed routing control. We point out that if tree saturation could be controlled, the overall bandwidth of the network (and consequently the throughput of the multiprocessor) could be improved in many cases. In Section III, we propose schemes for controlling tree saturation.

In Section IV, we present the results of a simulation analysis carried out to test the effectiveness of the tree-saturation-controlling mechanisms. In Section V, we present a discussion of the feedback concept in light of the results of Section IV, and in Section VI we present concluding remarks.

II. TREE SATURATION IN MULTISTAGE INTERCONNECTION NETWORKS

A widely proposed interconnection network for medium to large scale multiprocessors is a blocking, buffered $O(N \log N)$ multistage interconnection network with distributed routing control. An example of such a MIN is the Omega network [11]. An Omega network consists of $\log N$ stages of switching elements (or switches). Memory requests enter the network at the inputs to the first stage and proceed to the outputs of the last stage, one stage at a time. Routing decisions are made local to each switch. Since there is no global control mechanism, the state of any particular switch is unknown to other entities (processors, memories, other switches) in the multiprocessor, and a particular input request pattern to the network might cause the request arrival rate at some point to exceed the capacity with which that point can service requests.

A. Discussion of the Problem

The problem of *tree saturation* is the direct result of an arrival rate being too high. This problem was first observed by Pfister and Norton in conjunction with requests to a *hot spot* [14]. In their analysis, the hot spot was caused by accesses to a shared synchronization variable. When the average request rate to a *hot memory module* exceeds the rate at which the module services the requests, the requests will back up in the switch which connects to the hot module. When the queue in this switch is full, it will back up the queues in the switches that feed it. In turn, those switches will back up the switches feeding them. Eventually, a tree of saturated switches results. Depending upon the number of outstanding requests and the reference patterns of the various processors, this tree of saturated queues may extend all the way back to every processor. Any request which must pass through any of the switches in the saturated tree, whether to a hot module or not, must wait until the saturated queues are drained. Thus, even requests whose destinations are idle will be blocked for potentially long periods of time, leading to unnecessary degradation of the network bandwidth and increase in the latency through the network.

Since the problem of tree saturation (caused by hot spot activity or otherwise) can be catastrophic to the performance of systems such as the NYU Ultracomputer [6], Cedar [8], and the IBM RP3 [15], all of which use buffered MIN's, considerable effort has been devoted to studying the problem and suggesting solutions to it [1], [6], [12], [14], [18].

When the problem is caused by accesses to synchronization variables (or more generally, by accesses to the same memory location), *combining* can be used. *Hardware combining* uses special hardware in the network switches to combine requests destined to the same memory location [1], [6]. On the return trip, the response for the combined request is broken up (decombined) into responses for the individual requests. It is estimated that using combining hardware in the network switches would increase the hardware cost of a multistage interconnection network by a factor of 6 to 32 [14]. *Software combining* uses a tree of variables to effectively spread out access to a single, heavily-accessed variable [5], [18]. It is applicable only to known hot spot locations such as variables used for locking, barrier synchronization, or pointers to shared queues.

Since the overall bandwidth of the network is determined by the number (or equivalently the rate) of requests that have to be serviced by the hot module, combining can improve overall network bandwidth by reducing the rate at which requests are submitted to the hot module. Combining also improves the latency of memory requests that do not access the hot memory module since it alleviates tree saturation. Unfortunately, combining cannot alleviate the bandwidth degration or the tree saturation if the hot requests are to different memory locations within same memory module, that is, the entire memory module is hot. Such a situation could arise from a larger percentage of shared variables residing in a particular module, stride accesses that result in the nonuniform access of the memory modules, or temporal swings in which variables stored in a particular module are accessed more heavily. In these cases, one module will receive more requests than its uniform share, just as if it contained a single hot variable. Recognizing this problem, the RP3 researchers have suggested scrambling the memory to distribute memory locations randomly across the memory modules [2], [13]. With a scrambled distribution it is hoped that nonuniformities will occur less often though we are unaware of any hard data to support this fact.

Even though processor requests may be distributed uniformly among the memory modules, tree saturation can still occur if any of the switches in the network have a higher load (in the short term) than other switches at the same stage [10]. Alternate queue designs may improve the latency of memory requests that do not access the hot module, in the short term, but eventually tree saturation will occur even with alternate queue designs [17].

To alleviate the problem of tree saturation in general, we need a mechanism that detects the possibility of tree saturation and instructs the processors[1] to hold requests that might contribute to the tree saturation. If many of the problem-causing requests can be held outside the network, the severity of the problem can be reduced.

Before proceeding further, let us convince the reader that alleviating the congestion caused by tree saturation can indeed result in an increase in the overall performance of the system. We shall only consider hot requests that cannot be combined in this paper, since no solution to the problem of tree saturation is known in this case. We shall also restrict ourselves to $N \times N$ Omega networks though our results can easily be extended to other MIN's.

B. Bandwidth Degradation Due to Tree Saturation

Consider a processing situation in which a fraction f of the processors (the *hot processors*) are making requests to a hot module with a probability of h on top of a background of uniform requests to all memory modules, and the remaining processors (the *cold processors*) are making only uniform requests. Processors may have multiple outstanding requests. This is a likely scenario if more than one job is run on the multiprocessor. Let r_1 be the rate (requests per network cycle) at which the hot processors generate requests and let r_2 be the rate at which the cold processors generate requests. The number of requests per cycle that appear at the hot module is therefore

$$R_{\text{hot}} = fNr_1\left(h + \frac{(1-h)}{N}\right) + (1-f)Nr_2\left(\frac{1}{N}\right)$$

$$= fr_1(hN + (1-h)) + (1-f)r_2. \tag{1}$$

Since the hot module can service only one request in each memory cycle, the maximum value of R_{hot} is 1. Constraining the right-hand side of (1) to be less than or equal to 1 and rearranging terms, we get

$$r_1 \le \frac{1 - (1-f)r_2}{f(1 + h(N-1))}. \tag{2}$$

To calculate the overall bandwidth of the network, we observe that the fN hot processors require a bandwidth of r_1 and the $(1-f)N$ cold processors require a bandwidth of r_2. Therefore, the average bandwidth per processor is constrained by

$$\text{BW} = \frac{fNr_1 + (1-f)Nr_2}{N}$$

$$\le \frac{1 + (1-f)h(N-1)r_2}{1 + h(N-1)}. \tag{3}$$

---

[1] For the remainder of this paper, the words "processors" and "processors network interfaces (PNI's)" will be used interchangeably. For feedback schemes, the entities responding to the feedback information are actually the PNI's though for explanation purposes it is easier to talk of the "processors" using the feedback information to alter the request pattern into the network.

If there were no tree saturation in the network and the cold processors could proceed without *any* interference at all, they could achieve a *best-case* throughput of 1 request per cycle, i.e., $r_2 = 1$. Therefore, the best-case (or cutoff) per-processor bandwidth of the system would be

$$\mathrm{BW_{cut}} = \frac{1 + (1 - f)h(N - 1)}{1 + h(N - 1)} = 1 - \frac{fh(N - 1)}{1 + h(N - 1)}. \tag{4}$$

Unfortunately, tree saturation prevents the cold processors from proceeding without interference and achieving a throughput r_2 that is close to the best case. With tree saturation, cold processors as well as hot processors suffer degraded service. It does not matter which processors are responsible for the tree saturation, *all* processors are affected by it. Empirically, we have observed that in this case the system behaves as if all processors were participating in the hot spot activity. The rate at which hot requests are issued when fN processors have a hot rate of h is equal to the rate when all N processors have a smaller hot rate of fh. Thus, when hot requests are permitted to cause tree saturation, we have observed that the average cutoff bandwidth per processor can be estimated by the standard formula for a hot rate of fh:

$$\mathrm{BW_{cut}} = \frac{1}{1 + fh(N - 1)}. \tag{5}$$

Since (4) estimates the bandwidth of the system when the cold processors are not degraded by tree saturation and (5) estimates the bandwidth when they are, we can estimate the bandwidth improvement (if tree saturation is controlled and the cold processors allowed to proceed without any interference) by comparing (4) and (5).

Fig. 4 plots the bandwidths suggested by (4) and (5) as a function of f, for $h = 4\%$, and $N = 256$. These equations represent upper limits only, and in particular, for very small f, normal traffic contention will limit the bandwidth per processor to below 1. Simulation results presented in Section IV, however, confirm that the bandwidth degradation due to tree saturation (Fig. 6) closely corresponds to that predicted in (5), and that the relationship shown in Fig. 4(b) also occurs.

As can be seen from Fig. 4, it appears that the overall bandwidth of the network can be improved significantly if the problem of tree saturation is alleviated, allowing the cold processors to access the network without interference caused by the tree saturation. The bandwidth improvement is zero at the endpoints, i.e., all processors are making uniform requests ($f = 0$) and all processors making hot spot requests ($f = 1$), and the greatest when only half of the processors are making hot requests ($f = 1/2$). Our experimental results in Section IV will confirm this.

III. CONTROLLING TREE SATURATION

To alleviate the problem of tree saturation, requests that compound the problem must be prevented from entering the network until the problem has subsided. Ideally, requests to a hot module must be made to wait outside the network, at the processor–network interface (PNI), until the hot module is ready (or slightly before it is ready) to service them, and then enter the network at a rate at which they can be serviced by the hot module. If this can be done effectively, then tree saturation will be eliminated, and system throughput should increase as shown in Fig. 4. In practice, it is unlikely that tree saturation can be

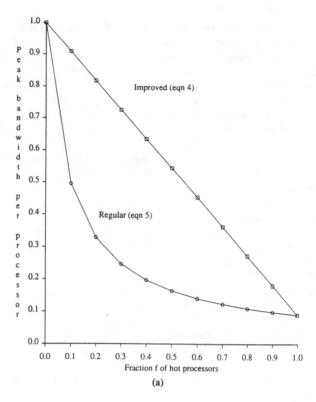

(a)

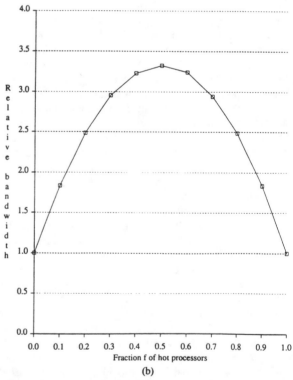

(b)

Fig. 4. Estimated peak bandwidth per processor with and without tree saturation control. (a) Estimated peak bandwidth per processor from (4) and (5). (b) Estimated bandwidth improvement [(4) relative to (5)].

completely eliminated with no side effects, but the closer we come to this goal, the better we can expect our performance to be. In Section III-A, we present a basic feedback scheme that attempts to achieve this goal, and in Section III-B we present extensions to this scheme that significantly improve its effectiveness.

A. The Basic Feedback Scheme

Fig. 3 presents a multiprocessing system with feedback. Select state information is tapped from the MIN and the memory modules and fed back to the PNI's. The PNI's use this information to modify their collective input to the network when it is causing state values of the system (in our case, the arrival rate of requests at the memory modules) to exceed their desired values. The feedback information therefore must indicate to the processors when such a performance-degrading situation is occurring.

Since tree saturation is caused by the arrival rate at the memory modules exceeding the rate at which the module can service requests, the difference between the arrival rate and module service rate is the state information that needs to be fed back to the processors. Unfortunately, the arrival rate by itself might be hard to measure. However, a good indication that the arrival rate at a module is too high, and that tree saturation might develop, is that the length of the queue feeding the module begins to grow. This queue length, then, would be a good candidate for use as state information to be fed back to the processors. As the queue length for a particular memory module grew, the PNI's could respond by reducing the rate at which requests to that module are submitted into the network. Tree saturation will not occur if the queues can be kept from overflowing.

The desired range for the length of a memory module queue is between one (zero if there are no outstanding requests for that memory module) and the capacity of the buffer used to contain the queue. If the queue becomes empty while the memory module is idle, and there are outstanding requests for that module, then we are making inefficient use of the memory module. If the queue overflows its capacity, then tree saturation begins to develop and can interfere with requests to other memory modules.

There is a considerable amount of freedom available in the feedback policy chosen to keep the queue lengths within the desired range. The scheme we have used in this paper is quite simple. We define a memory module to be hot if its queue length exceeds a certain threshold T, and define it to be cold otherwise. It is this binary value for each module that is fed back to the PNI's. The PNI's respond by allowing requests to cold modules to enter the network freely, while blocking requests to hot modules outside the network. This causes the arrival rate of requests at a hot module to drop sharply, shortly after the module becomes hot. By compensating for periods of high arrival rate with periods of low (or zero) arrival rate, it is hoped that average arrival rate will remain at its desired value and the queue length will remain within its desired range, thus avoiding the occurrence of tree saturation.

The choice of this simple feedback scheme allows for an implementation with very low hardware complexity. All that we need to do is monitor the size of the queue at each memory module and notify the processors when a module becomes hot (the size of the queue exceeds a predefined threshold T) and when a module becomes cold (the size of the queue falls below the threshold T). The most obvious way to do this is to have an N-bit feedback bus from the memory modules to all the processors. Memory module i sets the ith bit on the bus if it is hot. The processors can determine the status of each memory module simply by looking at the information on the bus.

As system size increases, distribution of a bus can become difficult. In this event, a fanout tree of buses can be used. This causes the latency of feedback to increase, but speed is not critical. It has been estimated [9] that the onset of tree saturation occurs as quickly as several network traversal times. Even using a fanout tree, feedback information can be supplied to the processors in less than a single network traversal time.

In addition, when the information content of the information being fed back to the PNI's is low, i.e., the number of modules that experience hot–cold or cold–hot transitions in a given cycle is low, alternate designs can be used for this feedback circuit. Preliminary experience shows that large scale parallel programs typically have only one or two hot spots at a time [7], [14]. In such cases, an N-bit feedback bus is clearly wasteful.

The feedback circuit that we use is a $\log_2 N + 2$ bit bus; $\log_2 N$ bits to indicate the module number and 2 control bits to indicate whether the module indicated by the $\log_2 N$ bits experienced a hot to cold, cold to hot, or no transition in the particular network cycle. As before, this bus can be implemented as a tree, if necessary. Since multiple transitions may take place in a single cycle, arbitration is required, and this may also be implemented as a tree for large systems. The hardware required for this feedback, while not trivial, is small in comparison to the MIN itself. In particular, due to the lenient speed requirements, the branching factor for a feedback tree would be quite large.

Each PNI maintains a lookup table in a fast memory. This table stores a single bit per memory module (indicating if the module is hot or cold), and is updated automatically from the transition messages on the feedback bus. When submitting a request into the network, the PNI checks the status of the request's destination module in the table and submits the request only if the destination module is cold. When a request is being held back at the PNI, the processor is stopped from making additional requests.

The feedback scheme outlined above prevents a hot module from causing full tree saturation because, as soon as the module becomes hot, requests to that module are stopped from entering the network. However, it has some problems analogous to the *undershoot* and *overshoot* problems in classical control systems theory [3].

First, let us examine undershoot and what might cause it. When a module becomes hot, requests in transit destined for that module continue while new requests destined for that module are held back. At some point in the future, the memory module will drain its queue beyond the threshold, the module will be declared cold again, and the requests to that module that were being held back in the PNI's will be released into the network. If the memory module consumes the rest of its queued requests before the newly released requests arrive, the module will become idle for one or more cycles. This is an especially inefficient use of resources given the fact that the hot module is a system bottleneck.

Now let us examine the more detrimental effect of overshoot in the simple feedback scheme. While a module is hot, requests to that module are held back at the PNI's. With a high hot rate, there may be requests waiting at the majority of the PNI's by the time the module becomes cold again. When the module becomes cold, all of the held back requests are released simultaneously. This can cause temporary overflow of the module's queue when the requests reach their destination, leading to partial tree saturation in the network.

While it has been estimated in the literature [9] that the onset of tree saturation occurs as quickly as several network traversal times (the time for a packet to traverse the network in one direction), the onset of this partial tree saturation can occur much more quickly due to the surge of traffic associated with overshoot. With no measures taken to prevent undershoot and overshoot, we would expect a system to oscillate between periods of partial tree saturation, and periods in which the hot module becomes idle. Thus, we must address both of these problems in order to minimize performance degradation.

The problem of undershoot can be dealt with in a rather straightforward way. Recall that the problem occurs when the number of requests in a hot module's queue falls to below its threshold, the module is declared cold, and new requests to that module can be released into the network. If the module consumes the rest of its queued requests before the newly submitted requests arrive, then it will become idle temporarily. The solution is to inform the PNI's sooner that they may resume submitting requests. This can be done by setting the feedback threshold to a sufficiently large number such that newly released requests will arrive before, or shortly after, the queue has been completely drained. Our simulation results in Section IV will confirm the effectiveness of this approach.

Unfortunately, the problem of overshoot is not dealt with as easily. The response to the signal that a hot module has become cold with the simple feedback scheme is simply too strong; nothing can prevent blockage with the network once all the previously held back requests are released. To reduce the response to the hot–cold transition, some form of *damping* needs to be introduced.

B. Using Damping with Feedback

To prevent overshoot, we need a method that gradually releases held back requests into the network, rather than letting them all go at once on a hot–cold transition. By preventing the sudden surge of hot spot traffic associated with overshoot, the feedback mechanism would have more time to detect impending queue overflow and instruct the processors to modify their inputs. As a result, queue overflow and the resulting partial tree saturation could be significantly reduced or eliminated completely. We will present two damping schemes which attempt to do this. The first is an idealized and very strong form of damping called *limiting,* which we include for purposes of comparison. While performing very well, limiting would be prohibitively expensive to build in a real system. The second is a more practical scheme that uses adaptive backoff techniques to dynamically alter its behavior based upon the intensity of the hot spot.

1) Limiting Damping: Limiting uses global arbitration to limit the number of requests that enter the network each cycle for each memory module. When a module is cold, we allow a maximum of two requests destined for that module to enter the network in a given cycle. This limits the rate at which the memory module queue can grow, giving the feedback mechanism time to signal the processors if the queue reaches its threshold and avoid any significant queue overflow. When a module is hot, we allow a maximum of one request destined for that module to enter the network in a given cycle. Allowing a single request to enter even when the module is hot makes it very unlikely that the module's queue will become empty.

This form of damping is quite strong and requires a significant hardware overhead. N arbiters are required (one for each memory module), each of which must be capable of arbitrating between N processors on every cycle. Clearly such hardware would carry a prohibitive cost, but, as mentioned earlier, the scheme is included as an example of a very strong form of damping for comparison purposes.

It is worth noting that global limiting alone (with no feedback mechanism) can be used to prevent tree saturation, but only at the expense of decreasing overall system bandwidth for normal traffic. By limiting the number of requests allowed into the network for each memory module to a maximum of one per cycle, no tree saturation is allowed to occur. However, this unnecessarily limits throughput for uniform traffic. The reason for this is that without the feedback information, the global limiting must be blindly applied to all requests. Thus, requests issued in the same cycle to the same memory module are *always* constrained to enter the network one at a time. When the destination module is cold, however, this constraint is unnecessary, as multiple requests could enter the network in the same cycle and proceed to the final stage of the network without hindering requests to other memory modules. In the final stage, they could queue up and be serviced one at a time.

2) Adaptive Backoff Damping: The motivation for our adaptive backoff damping scheme comes from a need to regulate the release of hot requests, as in the limiting scheme discussed above, but without paying the price of global arbitration mechanisms. We need a purely distributed scheme that tells us how long to hold a given hot request in the PNI before releasing it into the network after its destination module becomes cold. This is difficult to do in general because the period of time over which we should release the requests depends upon the number of requests being held back at all PNI's at the instant the destination module becomes cold, which is information that individual PNI's do not have. The more requests that are being held back, the longer the period of time over which we must release the requests in order to prevent a surge of traffic that causes tree saturation.

Our approach is to dynamically adapt the length of this release period for each memory module according to the intensity of the hot spot at that module. We can determine whether the current release period for a module is too long or too short, by monitoring the module's *cold time.* The cold time for a module is the time for which the module remained cold the last time it changed from hot to cold. If the cold time was too small (it became hot again quickly), it indicates that the release period last used was too small. If the cold time was very large (it took a long time to become hot again), it indicates that the release period last used was too large. By adjusting the release period appropriately, the PNI's can independently adapt their release schedules to the request rate for each memory module, and thus avoid the surges of traffic associated with overshoot.

The implementation we have used to filter the release of requests into the network is to require a match of the low b bits of the source PNI address and the current time. If $b = 1$, then requests at half of the PNI's will be eligible for release on a given cycle. If $b = 4$, then requests at one sixteenth of the PNI's will be eligible for release on a given cycle. If $b = \log_2 N$, then only the request at a single PNI will be eligible for release on a given cycle. Thus, for a given value of b, all held back requests will be released over a period of 2^b cycles. This filtering is done only for requests being held back at the time a hot module becomes cold; requests to other modules are not affected, and subsequent requests to this module (which is now cold) proceed without delay.

The current value of b is saved for each memory module in the lookup table proposed earlier for saving the hot/cold states of each module. In addition, we save the last hot–cold transition time for each module so that the cold time can be computed when the module next becomes hot. The value of b is initially set to 0 for all PNI's, and is incremented by some appropriate value (either positive, negative, or zero) on each hot–cold

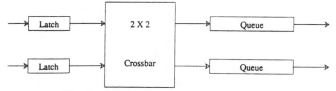

Fig. 5.   Switch used in model and simulations.

transition, based upon the value of cold time relative to the network traversal time. This allows b to become properly adjusted within 2 or 3 hot–cold transitions.

The cost of adding this damping scheme to the basic feedback scheme is increased PNI complexity, and storage required to save the hot–cold transition times and values of b for each memory in each PNI. Since b can take on values from 0 to $\log_2 N$, we need $\log_2 (\log_2 N)$ bits to represent a value of b (3 bits in a 256 processor system, 4 bits in a 64K processor system). To dynamically change b, we need to measure cold times up to a maximum of K network traversal times (in our simulations, K was 6). Thus, the number of bits needed for a hot–cold transition time is $\log_2 (K * \log_2 N)$ bits plus 2 bits to handle wraparound (8 bits in a 256 processor system, 9 bits in a 64K processor system). If we liberally allow 2 bytes for storing a (hold–cold transition time, b) pair, then we require 512 bytes per processor in a 256 processor system, and 128K bytes per processor in a 64K processor system. While still a small cost in relation to the MIN, this might be expensive.

An alternative to storing the complete table is to cache the information for recently hot modules. While assuming a full table for our simulations, we believe that caching would work quite well. When a hot module becomes cold, either its entry resides in the caches, or it is placed in the caches with b set to 0 (which is what b should be if the module has been cold for a long time). On subsequent hot–cold transitions, the entry should reside in the caches. If the number of active hot modules is low, then we should see very little contention and excellent temporal locality in the caches, allowing the size to be quite small. Caching the full table is a topic for further study.

IV. SIMULATION MODEL AND RESULTS

A. Network and Workload Model

For all our experiments we considered an $N \times N$ Omega network connecting N processors to N memory modules. A forward network carries requests from the processors to the memories and a reverse network is used for responses from the memory modules to the processors.

A 2×2 crossbar switching element (shown in Fig. 5) is used as the basic building block. The size of the queue at each output is Q requests and each queue can accept a request from both inputs simultaneously if it has room for the requests. The order in which multiple inputs are gated to the same output is chosen randomly.

Requests move from one stage of the network to the next in a single network cycle. Each memory module can accept a single request every network cycle and the latency of each memory module is one network cycle. Therefore, the best-case roundtrip time for a processor request is $2\log_2 N + 2$ network cycles [issue (1) + forward network hops ($\log_2 N$) + memory module service (1) + reverse network hops ($\log_2 N$)].

The workload model that we use is the same as the one that has been widely used in the hot spot literature [9], [10], [12], [14], [17]. In each network cycle, a processor makes a request

with a probability of r. A fraction f of the processors (the hot processors) make a fraction h of their requests to a hot memory module and the remaining $(1 - h)$ of their requests are distributed uniformly over all memory modules. The remaining fraction $(1 - f)$ of the processors (the cold processors) make uniform requests over all memory modules. A processor may have multiple outstanding requests, but is blocked from making further requests when its last request has not been accepted into the network by its PNI. This is due to the fact that there are no queues in the PNI's.

B. Simulation Results

The results presented in this section are for 256×256 ($N = 256$) Omega networks with queue sizes of 4 elements ($Q = 4$) at each switching element output, a main memory module latency of 1 network cycle, and no queues in the PNI's. We have also simulated 64×64, 128×128, and 512×512 Omega networks, each with varying queue sizes and memory latencies and with and without queues in the PNI's. The results follow a similar trend to the results we report for 256×256 networks with queue sizes of 4 and memory latencies of 1 and no queues in the PNI's, though the magnitude of the results are different. For reasons of brevity, we shall not present those results in this paper.

Five varieties of networks were simulated:

- regular Omega networks
- networks with simple feedback (threshold $T = 1, 2, 3,$ and 4 queue elements)
- networks with feedback ($T = 4$) and adaptive backoff damping
- networks with feedback ($T = 1$) and limiting damping
- networks with straight limiting (one request per module per cycle).

The choice of ($T = 4$) for feedback with adaptive backoff damping is to minimize undershoot. With limiting damping, undershoot is not a problem, and ($T = 1$) is used to maximize control of tree saturation.

1) Bandwidth Improvement: Fig. 6 plots the saturation bandwidth per processor for a regular Omega network (without feedback). Several hot rates h are considered, and f is varied from 0 to 1. The saturation bandwidth is calculated by offering the network a load of one (each processor makes one request per cycle), and measuring the realized throughput of the network after cold start effects have subsided. From Fig. 6 we see that as the fraction of processors making hot requests increases, the overall system bandwidth decreases. The higher the hot rate h, the faster the bandwidth drops off. When all processors are making hot requests, the bandwidth is severely affected by the hot rate.

The purpose of feedback schemes and limiting schemes is to control tree saturation and consequently improve overall network bandwidth. At the endpoints of each curve in Fig. 6, i.e., $f = 0$ and $f = 1$, feedback is of little use in improving the bandwidth (but as we shall see in Section IV-B2, it can still improve memory latency). This is because when all processors are making uniform requests ($f = 0$), little tree saturation occurs, and when all processors are making hot requests ($f = 1$), the bandwidth is limited by the rate at which the hot module can service requests and not by the tree saturation that is present. Overall bandwidth of the network can be improved by controlling tree saturation only when the tree saturation is actually limiting the bandwidth, i.e., f is between 0 and 1.

Now we consider the use of our basic feedback scheme of

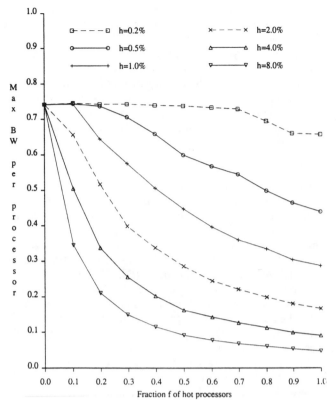

Fig. 6. Maximum bandwidth per processor with a regular Omega network ($N = 256$).

Section III-A. Fig. 7(a), (b), and (c) plots the bandwidth improvements for networks with feedback thresholds (T) of 1, 3, and 4, respectively. The bandwidth improvement is the bandwidth of the modified network (with feedback) divided by the bandwidth of a regular network with no feedback or limiting. A value of 1 for the improvement indicates that the two networks have the same bandwidth, a value greater than 1 indicates that the modified network has a higher bandwidth, and a value of less than 1 indicates that the modified network has a lower bandwidth.

From Fig. 7(a)–(c) we see that when f lies between 0 and 1, the use of feedback alleviates the tree saturation caused by the hot requests, allowing the processors making uniform requests to proceed with less interference, and increasing network bandwidth. The actual magnitude of the improvement is less than what is possible, since tree saturation has not been eliminated, but rather just reduced. Qualitatively, however, these simulation results confirm the predictions of Section II.

We can make two observations concerning the threshold values for feedback. The first observation is that under high hot rates, lower thresholds perform better than higher thresholds. This is due to the fact that lower thresholds prevent hot traffic from entering the network sooner and thus have less temporary hot module queue overflow and partial tree saturation. With a threshold $T = 1$, a hot module's queue can accept three more requests at the time it becomes hot, before overflowing and causing partial tree saturation. With a threshold, $T = 4$, the queue is already full by the time the module is declared hot and further requests to the module that are already in the network will cause partial tree saturation in earlier stages of the network.

The second and more striking observation is that using thresholds that are too small can limit the bandwidth of a network with feedback to *less* than the bandwidth of a regular network, for uniform and low hot-rate traffic. The smaller the threshold, the more likely a request is to be held back at the PNI even though the destination memory module of the request is receiving an average of less than one request per cycle. Networks with larger thresholds are less likely to restrict bandwidth unnecessarily due to temporal fluctuations in the traffic pattern. Another reason that smaller thresholds restrict bandwidth is that they allow the hot module's queue to become empty for longer periods of time (the undershoot problem, as discussed in Section III-A).

On closer look at Fig. 7(c), we see that even with a high feedback threshold ($T = 4$), the bandwidth is sometimes slightly less than the bandwidth of a regular network for low hot rates. This can be attributed to the problem of the hot module's queue occasionally becoming idle for a few cycles. When $f = 0$ (no hot spots) the relative bandwidth is unity. This indicates that normal traffic is not being restricted. If the queue sizes permitted a threshold equal to the number of stages in the network, the problem of a hot module's queues becoming idle could essentially be eliminated.

The higher the hot rate, the more the overall network bandwidth is improved by using even a simple feedback scheme. With a hot rate of 4 or 8%, significant increases in system bandwidth occur even with a small percentage of processors making hot requests. As systems become larger, the tree saturation caused by a given hot rate will become more severe, and the hot rate needed to cause a given level of tree saturation will decrease. In such cases, the need for feedback schemes is even more compelling.

Now let us consider the results of using the simple feedback scheme with an adaptive backoff damping strategy. Fig. 7(d) shows the relative bandwidth for a system which uses a high feedback threshold ($T = 4$), to minimize undershoot, and adaptive backoff damping to minimize overshoot. We see that the relative bandwidth does not fall appreciably below unity at any point, and the peak bandwidth improvement is significantly better than that obtained using simple feedback [Fig. 7(a)–(c)]. This demonstrates that the addition of damping to simple feedback is effective in reducing the amount of overshoot which occurs when a hot module becomes cold.

Now let us consider feedback with a limiting damping strategy. Since the damping mechanism prevents undershoot by allowing a single request for a module to enter each cycle when the module is hot, we can use a small feedback threshold ($T = 1$). Fig. 7(e) shows the relative bandwidth improvement when our strong form of limiting damping is used in conjunction with feedback. We can see that the results are quite good, controlling tree saturation even better than the adaptive backoff method. With 50% of the processors making requests with a hot rate of 8%, system bandwidth is improved by a factor of 4. It is worth noting here that since the feedback and limiting are not improving the bandwidth of the processors making hot requests (they cannot, since the bandwidth of the processors making hot requests is being limited by the number of requests to the hot module), and since the *average* bandwidth is increased by a factor of 4, then the bandwidth of the processors making uniform requests is actually being increased by a factor of 7.

Finally, Fig. 7(f) shows the use of limiting alone without any feedback information. We can see that performance is very good for high hot rates, but that bandwidth is significantly degraded for low hot rates. This agrees with the observations made in Section III-B. In the absence of feedback information, limiting must be applied to all references. While this prevents tree saturation from occurring, it also restricts normal traffic.

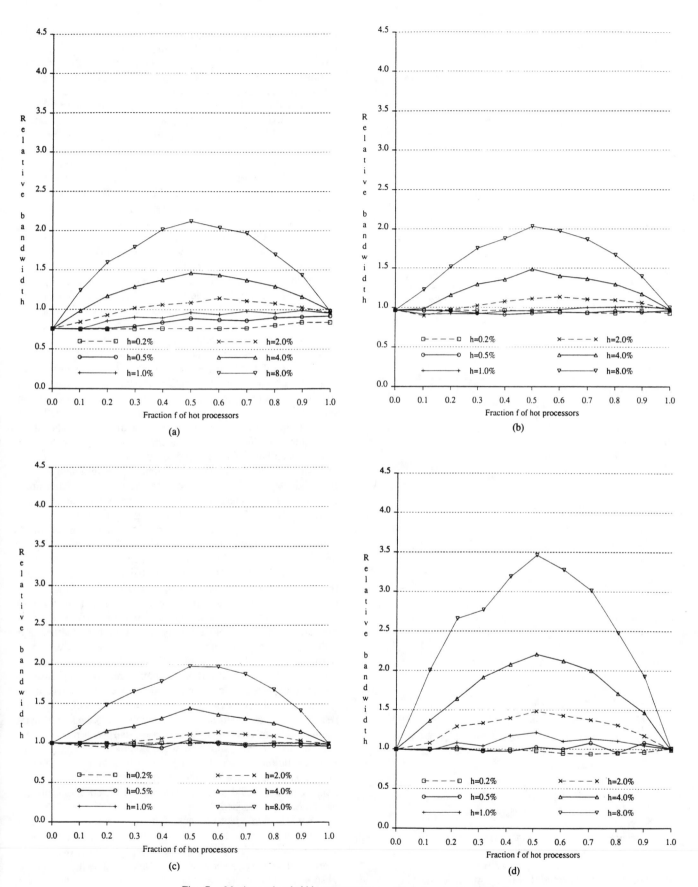

Fig. 7. Maximum bandwidth per processor with tree saturation control
mechanisms, relative to a regular Omega network ($N = 256$). (a) Feedback, $T = 1$. (b) Feedback, $T = 3$. (c) Feedback, $T = 4$. (d) Feedback
($T = 4$) with adaptive backoff damping.

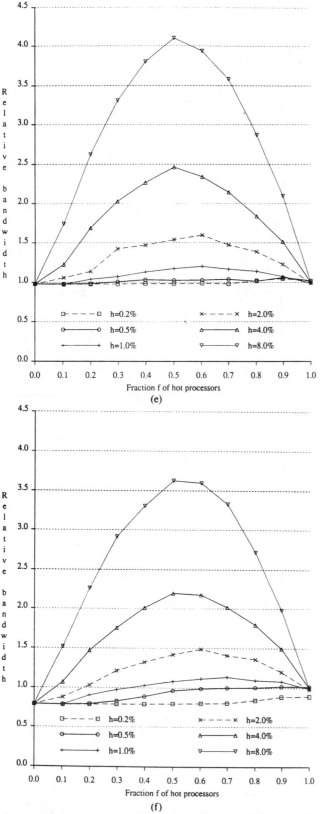

Fig. 7. (continued). (e) Feedback ($T = 1$) with limiting damping. (f) Plain limiting.

2) Latency Improvement:

So far we have seen how bandwidth can be improved when some processors are making hot requests and the rest are making uniform requests. The improvement stems from reducing the tree saturation that blocks the processors not participating in the hot spot activity. However,

for all schemes, no bandwidth improvement is obtained in the cases where all processors are making hot requests ($f = 1$). How can we be sure that tree saturation is being controlled even in this case (and in cases where little bandwidth improvement is obtained)? As we have noted before, the maximum bandwidth is inherently limited by the number of requests that must all go to the same module, and the only thing that can be done to improve the bandwidth is to cut down on the number of requests. However, the roundtrip latency experienced by the requests also gives us a good handle on the degree of tree saturation in the network. If tree saturation were being controlled, the latency experienced by cold requests should be considerably less than it would if tree saturation was present in the network. Furthermore, the latency of hot requests should not be significantly worse (and, as we shall see, might actually be better), as the hot requests will simply wait at the PNI rather than waiting within the network.

Fig. 8 shows the roundtrip latency of cold requests as a function of realized bandwidth for various values of h and the various networks. The latency is measured as the time taken by a request since its generation by the processor until the time the processor receives a response from the memory module (waiting times in all queues are included). The curves were generated by varying the offered load (requests per processor per cycle) from 0 to 1. In all cases, the realized bandwidth reaches some maximum less than one due to congestion in the network. As the offered load increases above this maximum realized bandwidth, latencies increase. All latencies reach a maximum value, however, due to the finite capacity of the queues; if the queues were infinite, then latency would tend to infinity.

Under uniform loading, the latency rises gradually as the bandwidth approaches saturation. In the presence of hot spots, however, latency increases sharply at the point that the maximum bandwidth is reached. This is due to the onset of tree saturation at this point, which quickly transforms a lightly loaded network into a very congested one. This phenomenon can be seen in Fig. 8(a) for a regular Omega network. The higher the hot rate, the lower the saturation bandwidth, and the higher the maximum (due to finite queues) roundtrip latency. This is consistent with the results reported by Pfister and Norton [14].

Fig. 8(b) shows the same curves for a network with simple feedback with $T = 4$. Note that the saturation bandwidths are no different than for the regular network, since all processors are participating in the hot spot activity ($f = 1$). We can see, however, that tree saturation is being reduced, because the latencies experienced are significantly lower than those in the regular network, especially with higher hot rates. We can also see that some tree saturation is still present, because the maximum latency of cold requests still rises sharply at the saturation bandwidths. If tree saturation were completely eliminated, the network buffers would be empty (except, of course, for the normal contention due to uniform traffic) and then the latency of cold requests would not increase at all when the saturation bandwidth was reached.

Feedback with adaptive backoff damping does a much better job of controlling the tree saturation, as can be seen in Fig. 8(c). As the saturation bandwidth for a given hot rate is reached, the latency of cold requests increases slightly, showing some congestion present in the network, but the amount is clearly quite small compared to the regular network and the network with simple feedback. The stronger limiting damping [Fig. 8(d)] can be seen to be even more effective in eliminating tree saturation. With this scheme, latency of cold requests is barely increased

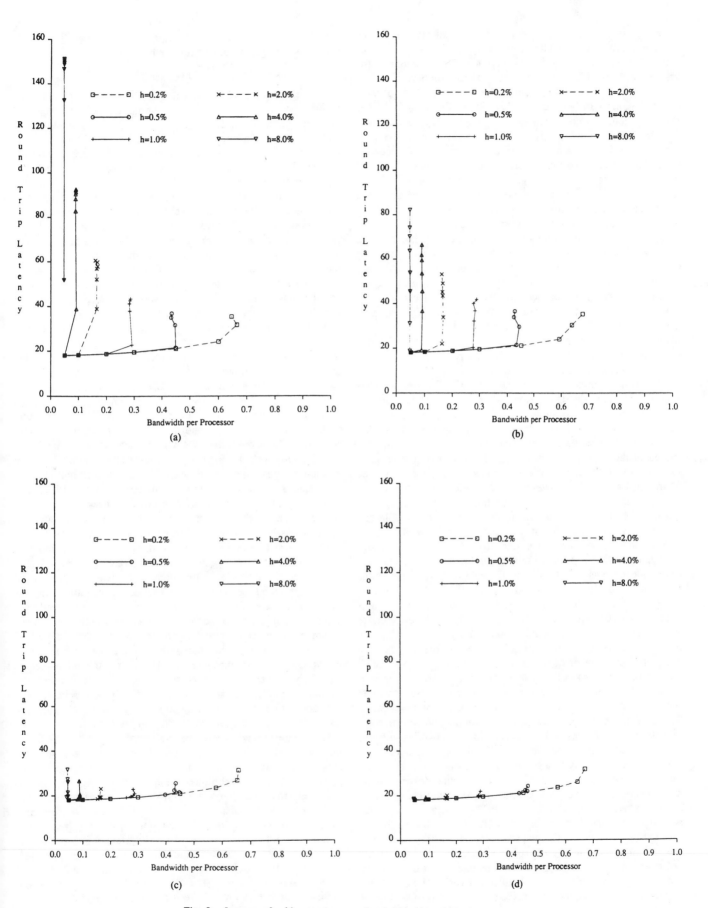

Fig. 8. Latency of cold requests versus bandwidth ($N = 256$, $f = 1$). (a) Regular Omega network. (b) Feedback, $T = 4$. (c) Feedback with adaptive backoff damping. (d) Feedback ($T = 1$) with limiting damping.

when the saturation bandwidth is reached indicating that tree saturation has been eliminated completely.

Fig. 9 presents latency curves for hot requests similar to the latency curves of Fig. 8 for cold requests. In comparing Figs. 8 and 9, several observations are in order. The first observation is that the latencies of hot requests (Fig. 9) are significantly higher than the latency of cold requests (Fig. 8), even in the case of a regular Omega network. (Note that the scale of the Y-axis is different for Figs. 8 and 9.) At first, this may seem incorrect since Pfister and Norton reported that the latencies of hot requests are degraded only slightly more than latencies of cold requests [14]. The difference, however, occurs because of a difference in the networks considered. In [14], processor requests are queued before entering the network, allowing the processors to continue making requests before their last requests have entered the network. In the presence of a hot spot, tree saturation reaches all the way up these queues to the processors, and all requests must wait in these queues until released into the network. Since these queues are the farthest from the hot module, they drain the slowest and the majority of a request's latency consists of waiting in its processor queue. For this reason, hot requests in [14] show only a slightly higher latency than cold requests. Our model, however, does not include queues between the processors and the network. A processor is blocked from submitting another request until its last request has entered the network. Thus, when a given request is made, it effectively starts out its journey at what would be the head of the queues used in [14]. Since half of the cold requests will be able to miss the tree saturation by being routed away from the hot module at the first switch, the average latency of cold requests is substantially lower than that of hot requests in our model. The saturation bandwidths, however, are not affected by this difference because, when $f = 1$, the saturation bandwidths are determined solely by the rate at which the hot memory module can service requests and not by other artifacts of the network.

A second observation is that, except for the highest hot rates, the tree saturation controlling schemes did not reduce the latency of the hot requests, as they did for the cold requests. This is due to the fact that the latencies of hot requests are determined by contention for the hot memory module, *not* by tree saturation or other contention within the network. It can be shown that, as long as the hot memory module remains busy, the average time taken for a hot request to be serviced by the hot memory module is equal to the number of outstanding hot requests (those issued, but not yet serviced) in the system at the time that the request is issued. Thus, only by reducing the number of outstanding hot requests, can the average latency of hot requests be reduced.

A final observation is that under the highest hot rates, some reduction in hot request latency *is* seen in the networks with tree saturation controlling mechanisms. As discussed above, however, this is due solely to a reduction in the number of outstanding hot requests in the system. The tree saturation controlling mechanisms detect the presence of a hot spot and cause subsequent hot requests to be held in the PNI's, blocking the processors from making further requests. This limits the number of outstanding hot requests to one per processor plus the number in the system at the time the hot spot was detected. For the higher hot rates, there would be more than this number of hot requests outstanding, on average, in a regular network. Thus, the tree saturation controlling mechanisms have the effect of reducing the number of outstanding hot requests and so reducing the average latency of hot requests. As in the case of cold requests, if queues existed between the processors and the network, this effect would not be seen, because blocking requests at the PNI would not inhibit the generation of further hot requests.

V. DISCUSSION

So far we have seen that using a simple feedback scheme, which results in the PNI's withholding requests to congested areas in the network, can lead to a reduction in tree saturation and improve overall network performance. By adding damping to the basic feedback system, performance can be improved even further. What other enhancements might we make to achieve further improvements?

One seemingly obvious improvement is to use large queues at the memory modules to increase the buffering of temporary tree saturation. Using larger queues toward the memory side of the network has already been proposed in [16] for general networks. This technique is particularly appropriate for networks with feedback. First, it allows for larger thresholds, as discussed in Section III-A. Recall from the simulation results that the larger the threshold, the less bandwidth was unnecessarily restricted (undershoot). If the threshold can be set sufficiently large such that when a module becomes cold its queue will not drain before new requests arrive, then undershoot can essentially be eliminated. Larger queues at the modules also buffer more of the overshoot tree saturation that occurs with feedback. We have simulated networks with larger queues at the memory modules and found a small, but noticeable, improvement.

Another possible way to improve upon a feedback scheme with damping would be to shorten the delay between inputs and feedback. This would involve taking feedback from points internal to the network. Performance would be enhanced by detecting possible congestion at earlier stages in the network and restricting requests that would aggravate this congestion until it clears. Alternately, mechanisms that fed information back *into* switches within the network could be constructed. The design of such mechanisms is the subject of further study.

Other possibilities include using different feedback information or different damping mechanisms. We have used only the binary value (hot/cold) for the memory module state that is fed back. Perhaps a scheme which fed back a "temperature" indication with greater granularity could be used. This might allow a subtler response on the part of the processors. Alternate damping mechanisms could also be considered. The adaptive backoff scheme presented in this paper does not adapt as quickly as might be desired. It takes a few cold–hot–cold transitions before the proper filtering value is settled upon. Furthermore, the simulation results indicate that our adaptive backoff scheme does not reduce tree saturation as much as the global limiting scheme does. This indicates room for further improvement.

In addition to asking how we can improve upon feedback, we may also ask if it is really needed. It is clear that for the experimental workload used in this paper, tree saturation does occur and feedback techniques are quite effective in its control. However, the assumption that processors pipeline requests and the lack of synchronization constraints between processes may overestimate the problem of tree saturation. But will tree saturation occur for actual workloads in real systems? The analysis in Section II indicates that tree saturation should become a problem with only slight imbalances in network traffic, and that the problem should become worse as system sizes grow. This would indicate that tree saturation from hot memory modules is likely to occur in actual large-scale systems. Moreover, researchers from the IBM RP3 project have verified the presence of significant tree saturation in a running 64-processor system [4]. Thus

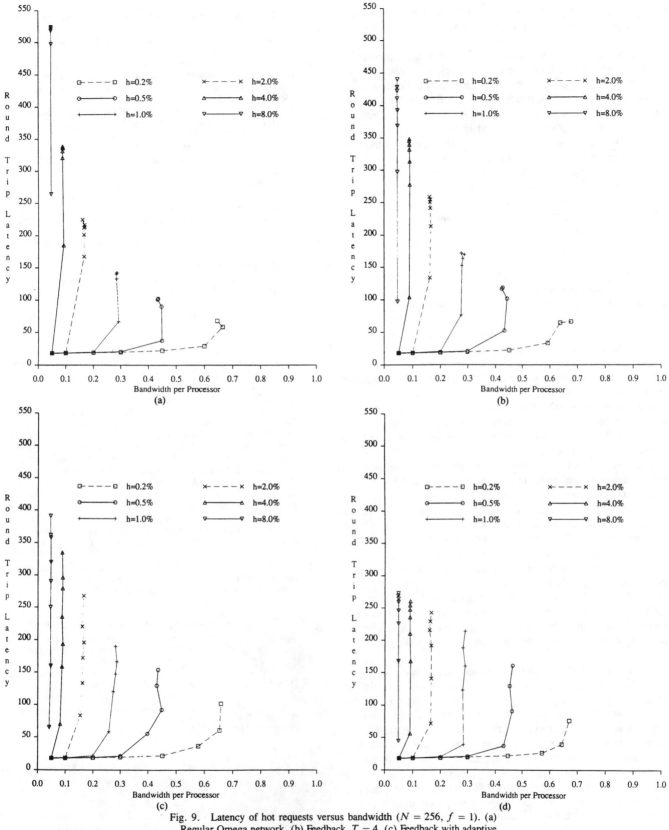

Fig. 9. Latency of hot requests versus bandwidth ($N = 256$, $f = 1$). (a) Regular Omega network. (b) Feedback, $T = 4$. (c) Feedback with adaptive backoff damping. (d) Feedback ($T = 1$) with limiting damping.

we can tentatively answer yes to the above question. The answer should become clearer as more experience is gained in this area. Feedback schemes offer a possible solution if the problem *does* exist. In any case, the cost of implementing a feedback scheme is low compared to the MIN, and, if properly designed, it should

have negligible effects on uniform traffic. Furthermore, a feedback mechanism such as the one proposed in this paper can be added to an existing design without changing of the network itself and with minimal additional logic in the memory queues and the PNI's. Because of its simplicity and potential payoff, a feedback scheme might be warranted to guard against the occurrence of tree saturation even if the possibility of it occurring is remote.

As stated in the Introduction, feedback is not a replacement for combining (either hardware or software), but rather a technique that can be applied where combining cannot. Feedback can be used to prevent tree saturation resulting from a hot module, rather than just from a hot memory location. As such, feedback could be used in conjunction with software or hardware combining to provide protection against hot spots that are not caused by access to synchronization variables. It also can prevent a single process from crippling the entire system by creating a hot spot. In addition, feedback, unlike combining, is not just useful for request–reply type networks. It can be used for networks routing information in one direction only, such as those that might exist in a dataflow machine or a simulation engine.

VI. Concluding Remarks

In this paper, we have proposed the use of feedback in multistage interconnection networks as an aid in the distributed routing process and evaluated the effectiveness of feedback mechanisms in controlling the tree saturation problem in such networks. We saw that, with feedback mechanisms, tree saturation can be limited. This is accomplished by detecting hot spots, and holding requests destined for these spots outside of the network until the congestion clears. This prevents these requests from waiting within the network where they would consume buffer space and block other requests that might otherwise be able to proceed. When tree saturation is limited, system bandwidth can be significantly improved in many cases, and the latency of requests reduced.

We have shown that a system using only simple feedback can exhibit behavior analogous to overshoot and undershoot in classical control theory. Two damping mechanisms, designed to reduce this behavior, were proposed. One of these mechanisms is feasible to implement, while the other was included as a basis for comparison. Both damping schemes significantly improve the performance of a simple feedback mechanism.

The hardware requirements of feedback are relatively modest. Feedback from the destinations to the sources requires no alteration of the interconnection network itself, and thus could be added to existing networks with minimal upheaval. The logic required for simple feedback is straightforward, and that for damping is still small compared to the interconnection network itself.

Feedback is general enough to find many applications in computer system design. It can be used in any parallel or distributed system in which a resource can be accessed without global control and in which contention for access to this resource can degrade the overall system. In the case of multistage interconnection networks, it provides distributed input sources with the information they need to avoid causing tree saturation. A network with feedback presents a promising alternative to a network with global control, which is expensive to implement, or a network with purely distributed routing control, which is prone to degradation due to nonuniform use of its resources.

References

[1] G. S. Almasi and A. Gottlieb, *Highly Parallel Computing.* Redwood City, CA: Benjamin/Cummings, 1989.

[2] W. C. Brantley, K. P. McAuliffe, and J. Weiss, "RP3 processor-memory element," in *Proc. 1985 Int. Conf. Parallel Processing,* Aug. 1985, pp. 782–789.

[3] W. L. Brogan, *Modern Control Theory.* New York: Quantum, 1974.

[4] R. Bryant, personal communication, IBM T. J. Watson Research Center, July 1989.

[5] J. R. Goodman, M. K. Vernon, and P. J. Woest, "A set of efficient synchronization primitives for a large-scale shared-memory multiprocessor," in *Proc. ASPLOS-III,* Boston, MA, Apr. 1989, pp. 64–73.

[6] A. Gottlieb *et al.,* "The NYU Ultracomputer—Designing a MIMD, shared memory parallel machine," *IEEE Trans. Comput.,* vol. C-32, pp. 175–189, Feb. 1983.

[7] M. Kalos *et al.,* "Scientific computations on the ultracomputer," Ultracomputer Note 27, Courant Institute, New York Univ., New York, NY.

[8] D. J. Kuck *et al.,* "Parallel supercomputing today and the Cedar approach," *Science,* vol. 21, pp. 967–974, Feb. 1986.

[9] M. Kumar and G. F. Pfister, "The onset of hot spot contention," in *Proc. 1986 Int. Conf. Parallel Processing,* Aug. 1986, pp. 28–34.

[10] T. Lang and L. Kurisaki, "Nonuniform traffic spots (NUTS) in multistage interconnection networks," in *Proc. 1988 Int. Conf. Parallel Processing,* Aug. 1988, pp. 191–195.

[11] D. H. Lawrie, "Access and alignment of data in an array processor," *IEEE Trans. Comput.,* vol. C-24, pp. 1145–1155, Dec. 1975.

[12] G. Lee, C. P. Kruskal, and D. J. Kuck, "The effectiveness of combining in shared memory parallel computers in the presence of 'hot spots'," in *Proc. 1986 Int. Conf. Parallel Processing,* Aug. 1986, pp. 35–41.

[13] A. Norton and E. Melton, "A class of Boolean linear transformations for conflict-free power-of-two access," in *Proc. 1987 Int. Conf. Parallel Processing,* Aug. 1987, pp. 247–254.

[14] G. F. Pfister and V. A. Norton, "'Hot-spot' contention and combining in multistage interconnection networks," *IEEE Trans. Comput.,* vol. C-34, pp. 943–948, Oct. 1985.

[15] G. F. Pfister, W. C. Brantley, D. A. George, S. L. Harvey, W. J. Kleinfelder, K. P. McAuliffe, E. A. Melton, V. A. Norton, and J. Weiss, "The IBM Research Parallel Processor Prototype (RP3): Introduction and architecture," in *Proc. 1985 Int. Conf. Parallel Processing,* Aug. 1985, pp. 764–771.

[16] H. S. Stone, *High-Performance Computer Architecture.* Reading, MA: Addison-Wesley, 1987.

[17] Y. Tamir and G. L. Frazier, "High-performance multi-queue buffers for VLSI communication switches," in *Proc. 15th Annu. Symp. Comput. Architecture,* Honolulu, HI, June 1988, pp. 343–354.

[18] P.-C. Yew, N.-F. Tzeng, and D. H. Lawrie, "Distributing hot-spot addressing in large scale multiprocessors," *IEEE Trans. Comput.,* vol. C-36, pp. 388–395, Apr. 1987.

Steven L. Scott (S'87) received the B.S. degree in electrical engineering in 1987 and the M.S. degree in computer science in 1988, both from the University of Wisconsin at Madison.

He is currently a Hertz Foundation fellow and Ph.D. candidate in computer science at the University of Wisconsin. His research interests include multiprocessor architectures and parallel programming.

Gurindar S. Sohi (S'85–M'85) received the B.E. (Hons.) degree in electrical engineering from the Birla Institute of Science and Technology, Pilani, India, in 1981 and the M.S. and Ph.D. degrees in electrical engineering from the University of Illinois, Urbana–Champaign, in 1983 and 1985, respectively.

Since September 1985, he has been with the Computer Sciences Department at the University of Wisconsin–Madison where he is currently an Assistant Professor. His interests are in computer architecture, parallel and distributed processing, and fault-tolerant computing.

Chapter 6: Deadlock-Free Routing and Multicasting

Unlike in feedforward, acyclic, dynamic multistage networks, routing in static networks can lead to *deadlock*. Particularly, deadlocks can occur in packet-switched networks of bounded buffers and in circuit-switched, unbuffered networks.

The papers included in this chapter present methods for preventing deadlocks. The paper by Gopal (1985) addresses deadlock prevention in store-and-forward, packet-switched, buffered networks. The next paper, by Dally and Seitz (1987), proposes and studies methods of deadlock-free routing in general circuit-switched, unbuffered networks that utilize wormhole routing; the wormhole routing considered is the model that has been implemented in recent parallel computers. In this model, routing follows unique, system-determined paths between every source and every destination. The paper by Linder and Harden (1991) studies deadlock-free, fault-tolerant routing in wormhole hypercubes where alternate, multiple paths between every source-destination pair can be chosen.

Besides permutation and point-to-point routing, several common routing patterns that deserve special attention include *broadcasting*, *multicasting* (in the strict sense), and *complete exchange*. In broadcasting, the problem is to deliver the same message from a given source node to all destination nodes in a minimum number of routing steps. In a modified version of broadcasting called *personalized communication,* a source node needs to deliver a distinct message to each destination node. In multicasting (in the strict sense), the problem is to deliver a message from a given source node to an arbitrary number of destination nodes in a minimum number of routing steps, such that the number of intermediary nondestination nodes is minimized. In complete exchange, the problem is for each node to send a distinct message to each other node in a minimum number of routing steps.

The remaining papers included in this chapter address these routing patterns. The paper by Johnsson and Ho (1989) treats broadcasting and personalized communication in hypercubes using the concept of *binomial trees*. The paper by Lan, Esfahanian, and Ni (1990) studies multicasting in message-passing hypercubes, while the paper by Lin and Ni (1991) examines multicasting in meshes and hypercubes that use wormhole routing. Lastly, Bokhari (1991) gives a complete-exchange algorithm for wormhole routing hypercubes.

Note that other routing patterns, such as trees, meshes, and multigrids, are worthy of consideration. They will be treated in Chapter 8, which covers mapping and embedding.

Prevention of Store-and-Forward Deadlock in Computer Networks

INDER S. GOPAL, MEMBER, IEEE

Abstract—Much previous work has been done on the prevention of store-and-forward deadlock in computer networks using buffer reservation. The emphasis has been on reducing the number of reserved buffers necessary in each node. In this paper, we propose a scheme that, for most networks, will guarantee deadlock freedom for any arbitrary routing with a third fewer reserved buffers than the best previously proposed scheme.

I. INTRODUCTION

STORE-and-forward deadlock (SFD) is a potentially catastrophic problem in packet-switched computer networks. If a "buffer" is defined to be a unit of storage large enough to accommodate a single packet, we can state that SFD occurs when a set of buffers exists such that each buffer within that set contains a packet that is destined for another buffer within that same set. Fig. 1 shows a typical example of *direct* SFD [4] with *A*'s buffers full of packets to send to *B* and *B*'s buffers full of packets to send to *A*. Fig. 2 shows an example of *indirect* SFD [4] with *A* full of packets destined for *B*, *B* full of packets for *C*, and *C* full of packets for *A*. Clearly, in both cases, none of the deadlocked buffers can be emptied and no useful network traffic can be transmitted.

Several techniques to resolve SFD exist [1]–[7]. The typical approach has been to institute some form of flow control based on buffer reservation. These solutions involve partitioning the buffer pool at a node into several classes and permitting only a restricted set of packets access to a given buffer class. Solutions proposed have included buffer reservation based on the number of hops [2], [4], [6], the number of "valleys" [4], [6], the route which the packet is traveling on [6], [7], etc.

The approach used in our paper will also make use of buffer reservation. There are several reasons why we restrict our attention to buffer reservation (BR) schemes. As will become apparent, BR schemes are "local" in nature and, thus, can be implemented very easily without the need for complex global synchronization mechanisms. In addition, BR schemes do not require exchange of special control information packets beyond the control packets that would usually be exchanged in the course of data transmission (ACK's, NAK's, etc.). Furthermore, their "local" nature ensures that transmissions over one link do not inhibit transmissions over any other link, thereby permitting high throughput in the network.

The problem with buffer reservation techniques, however, is that they require that a certain minimum number of buffers be present in some nodes. For example, the scheme based on the number of hops traveled cannot be guaranteed deadlock free if all the nodes contain fewer than $H + 1$ buffers, where H is the maximum number of hops that any packet in the network will have to travel. Even if we make the assumption

Paper approved by the Editor for Computer Communication of the IEEE Communications Society. Manuscript received August 1, 1984; revised March 1, 1985. This paper was presented at the IFIP International Symposium on Data Communication and Computer Networks, Madras, India, October 1984.

The author is with the IBM T. J. Watson Research Center, Yorktown Heights, NY 10598.

Fig. 1. Direct store-and-forward deadlock.

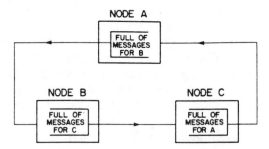

Fig. 2. Indirect store-and-forward deadlock.

that the routing used in the network is "loop-free," i.e., the same node is never visited more than once by a packet, then H may still be as large as $N - 1$ where N is the number of nodes in the network.

The minimum number of buffers necessary to guarantee deadlock freedom is of great importance in a network. This number determines the network "entry level" requirement for a node. Reducing this number permits nodes with limited storage capacity to be full participants in a network. The recent proliferation of mini and microcomputers and their need to interconnect has made this capability particularly important. Thus, in this paper, we shall focus on minimizing this number.

The network environment that we shall assume is one in which no *a priori* knowledge exists on the routing that is to be used between nodes. Thus, the emphasis is on designing a scheme which permits any route or routes to be chosen between any pair of nodes in the network. No such "arbitrary routing" scheme has been proposed that *guarantees* SFD freedom, even if every node in the network has fewer than $H + 1$ buffers. In this paper we propose, for a wide class of network topologies, such a scheme.

The paper is structured in the following fashion. In Section II we shall introduce preliminary concepts and formalize our problem definition. In Section III we define a flow control scheme which requires fewer that $H + 1$ buffers. In Section IV we relax the problem definition somewhat and propose a scheme that requires fewer buffers than the scheme suggested in Section III. Finally, in Section V we suggest some ways in which the schemes can be implemented in a distributed fashion.

II. PRELIMINARIES

We shall term the class of flow control schemes that we shall consider in this paper the *buffer reservation* (BR) flow control class. A BR scheme is implemented in the following manner (shown schematically in Fig. 3). Consider a situation

Reprinted from *IEEE Trans. Communications*, Vol. COM-33, No. 12, Dec. 1985, pp. 1258-1264. Copyright © 1985 by The Institute of Electrical and Electronics Engineers, Inc. All rights reserved.

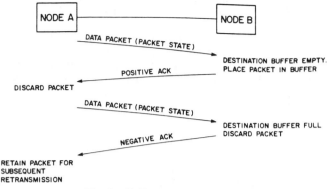

Fig. 3. Buffer reservation scheme.

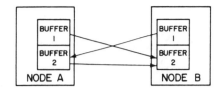

Fig. 4. Typical buffer graph.

with two nodes A and B directly connected to each other, and where A has a packet which it wishes to send to B. Under a BR flow control scheme, A would simply send B the packet with some "packet state" information included in the packet header. Node B, upon receiving the packet, would compute, based upon the packet state, which of its buffers that packet may be placed in. If one of these buffers is empty, B accepts the packet and sends to A a positive acknowledgment, whereupon A discards the packet from its own buffer. If none of the buffers is free, B rejects the packet and sends a negative acknowledgment to A. A then does not discard the packet from its buffer, but retains it and attempts to send it to B at some future time. Both of the above scenarios are shown in Fig. 3.

The packet state information contained in the packet must clearly be something that can be easily obtained. A reasonable packet state, and one that we shall assume for the rest of the paper, is the route that is taken by the packet. If the entire route is not known, then the sequence of nodes visited thus far comprises the packet state.

As mentioned in the previous section, we shall assume no *a priori* knowledge of the routing used in the network except the fact that the maximum number hops in any route is no larger than H. If we make the assumption that the routing used in the network is "loop-free," i.e., the same node is never visited more than once by a packet, then H is smaller than $N - 1$. Typically, H can be bounded even further.

Under this assumption, we seek to find a BR flow control scheme that guarantees deadlock freedom while minimizing the number of buffers needed in each node. However, rather than focusing on the average (or equivalently) the total number of buffers necessary in the network, we shall focus on the number of buffers necessary in the node that has the largest buffer requirement. The maximum captures the effectiveness of a scheme better than the average, as a small average may still imply that some nodes need to have an impossibly large number of buffers. In more formal terms, we define B_i to be the minimum number of buffers necessary to guarantee deadlock freedom with "arbitrary routing" in node i under the given scheme. We are seeking a scheme that minimizes the quantity $B_{max} = \max_i\{B_i\}$.

We now make some definitions which will enable us to define SFD freedom in more formal terms. A buffer graph G_B of a network under a given BR scheme is a graph with directed edges defined as follows. Each buffer in the network is represented by a vertex in G_B. Thus, a node with three buffers will be represented by three vertices. A directed edge is defined from vertex i to vertex j if, under the given scheme, it is possible for a packet to move from the buffer corresponding to vertex i to the buffer corresponding to vertex j. Fig. 4 shows an example of a typical buffer graph.

It has been shown in [4] that a necessary condition for SFD is that this buffer graph contains a directed cycle. Conversely,

to be SFD free, it is sufficient to construct a scheme whose buffer graph contains no directed cycles.

A simple BR flow control scheme that produces a buffer graph with no directed cycles is the hop count (HC) scheme [2], [4], [6]. One version of the scheme is the following. Each node contains a reserved buffer pool consisting of $H + 1$ buffers, making $B_{max} = H + 1$. The buffer pool is partitioned into $H + 1$ classes, labeled $0, 1, \cdots, H$. A buffer of class i is reserved for packets that have traveled i hops. Clearly, the number of hops is trivially obtained from the packet state. Thus, a packet traveling through the network would occupy the buffer of class 0 at its entry node, the buffer of class 1 after its first hop, and so on. Every edge in the buffer graph formed under this scheme would be between a buffer of class i and a buffer of class $i + 1$, $i = 0, 1, 2, \cdots, H - 1$. In order to see that the buffer graph is free of directed cycles, observe that a directed cycle forms a directed path from a buffer of a given class back to another buffer of the same class (i.e., itself). This implies that along this directed path, there must be some edges which either go between two buffers of the same class or from a buffer of higher class to a buffer of lower class. Neither possibility can occur, and therefore no directed cycles can occur, and consequently, the scheme is SFD free.

Several variations on this scheme have been proposed. These include permitting packets that have traveled i hops to use any buffer of class i or lower, having a different number of buffers in each class, etc. However, in terms of our cost function, all have the same requirement $B_{max} = H + 1$. Other schemes proposed, such as the valley count scheme, may provide $B_{max} < H + 1$ in some circumstances, but there is no guarantee that they will. The scheme that we shall propose in the next section does provide such a guarantee.

III. The Negative Hop Scheme

We have already seen how a simple BR scheme ensures SFD freedom. We now propose a better scheme, the negative hop (NH) scheme, that is slightly more complex.

The first step is to partition the nodes of the network into several subsets, such that each subset contains no two nodes that are mutually adjacent. This is the well-known coloring problem of graph theory. Let us assume that we have partitioned the network and have obtained M such subsets. Fig. 5 shows an example with $M = 3$.

We label the subsets $1, 2, \cdots, M$ and denote a node in subset with label i as a node of label i. We define a *negative hop* to be hop from a node with a higher label to a node with a lower label. (Note that hops between nodes with the same label are not possible.) The negative hop scheme is now simply defined. It is exactly the hop count scheme except that rather than counting hops, we count negative hops. Thus, the buffer of class i in a node is reserved for a packet that has traveled i negative hops. Fig. 6 shows a typical path taken by a packet.

The following observation follows directly from the structure of the buffer graph.

Observation 1: The buffer graph under the NH scheme contains no directed edges from a buffer of higher class to a buffer of lower class.

Note that, unlike in the hop count scheme, there are edges in the buffer graph between buffers of the same class.

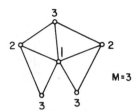

Fig. 5.   Network partitioning.

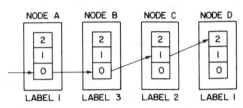

Fig. 6.   Typical path.

We now show that the negative hop scheme is deadlock free.

Theorem 1: The buffer graph produced under the NH scheme contains no directed cycles.

Proof: Assume that there exists a directed cycle. In order to form a cycle, the edges in the directed cycle must satisfy one of the following two properties.

i) One or more of the edges go from a buffer of higher class to a buffer of lower class. This is not possible by Observation 1.

ii) All edges go between buffers of the same class. Directed edges always go from a buffer in one node to a buffer in a neighboring node, as an edge goes between two buffers of the same class only if it is not traversing a negative hop. As links between nodes with the same label do not exist, all edges in the cycle traverse links that go from a lower label node to a node with a strictly higher label. Clearly, all edges in the cycle cannot have this property.

Thus, either property creates a contradiction, completing the proof. ∎

Having convinced ourselves of the scheme's deadlock freedom, we now proceed to show that it is better than the HC scheme. Let the maximum number of negative hops possible in any routing be H_n. Clearly, as in the HC case, the cost function B_{max} is given by $H_n + 1$. We know that the number of negative hops can be no greater than the number of hops, i.e., $H_n \leq H$. The next theorem states that it is usually possible to bound H_n to within some fraction of H.

Theorem 2:

$$H_n \leq \left\lceil \frac{(M-1)}{M} H \right\rceil.$$

Proof: Consider any route of h hops in the network. Consider the first M hops in this route. If all these hops were negative hops, this would mean that the first $M + 1$ nodes had strictly increasing labels, something that is not possible, as we have only M distinct labels. Thus, of the first M hops, at most $M - 1$ can be negative hops; similarly for the second M hops, the third M hops, and so on. If h is not exactly divisible by M, then the last $h \bmod M$ hops could all be negative. Putting all this together with the fact that $h \leq H$, we get

$$H_n \leq \left(\frac{M-1}{M} \right)(H - H \bmod M) + H \bmod M$$

$$= \left\lceil \frac{(M-1)}{M} H \right\rceil. \quad ∎$$

The above result shows us that if we can restrict M to small values, H_n could be substantially smaller than H. Fortunately, for a large class of computer networks, M is fairly small. Calling on the plethora of results on the coloring problem (see, for example, [9]), we can state the following results.

1) Degree Constrained Networks: If the maximum degree (the number of links incident on the node) of a node in the network is less than D, then $M \leq D + 1$ (see, for example, [9]). This gives that

$$B_{max} \leq \left\lceil \frac{D}{D+1} H \right\rceil + 1.$$

For networks with $D = 3$, this gives a scheme which is approximately 25 percent better than HC.

2) Planar Networks: The well-known four-color theorem states that, for planar graphs, $M = 4$. This provides a scheme that is again about 25 percent better than HC.

Numerous results on the value of M for other types of network structures abound in the literature. We spare the reader a repetition of these results here.

IV. The Improved Negative Hop Scheme

In this section we provide an improved negative hop (INH) scheme by relaxing some of the original problem constraints.

Recall that in the Introduction we had distinguished between direct and indirect SFD. In the HC and NH schemes, both kinds of SFD were prevented from occurring by the same scheme. In the INH scheme, we shall use different methods to cope with each kind. The method used to prevent indirect SFD is exactly the NH scheme, except that the technique used in the partitioning will be slightly different. The method used to prevent direct SFD is based on an "atomic exchange" idea similar to that proposed in [5].

The "atomic exchange" idea is the following. Assume that a direct SFD situation exists between node n and node m, with n having a packet in its buffer of class i to send to the buffer of class j in m and m having a packet in its buffer of class j to send to n's buffer of class i. Assume that n and m recognize this situation. The atomic exchange procedure would then be invoked. Node n would send its packet to node m. Node m would place the received packet in an "exchange" buffer, send its packet in buffer of class j to n, and then copy the packet in the exchange buffer into the buffer of class j. Node n, upon receiving the packet from m, would place it in its buffer of class i, discarding the packet that it had sent to m and completing the atomic exchange procedure. Notice that at the completion of the procedure nodes, n and m have successfully exchanged their packets and the exchange buffer used in the exchange is empty.

The INH scheme uses the atomic exchange procedure to cope with direct SFD. The first issue, however, is how nodes n and m detect a direct SFD situation. Assuming that all nodes use the same procedure to determine which buffer class an incoming packet can be placed in, a node can determine which buffer class any of the packets in its buffers are destined for and, conversely, which buffer class any received packet came from. Thus, upon receipt of a packet from node n, node m can determine which buffer class it came from, and if the buffer in which the packet is to be placed contains a packet destined for the same buffer class in node n. If so, then a possible direct SFD situation exists, and node m initiates the atomic exchange procedure and sends node n its packet with information in the packet header indicating that it is part of the atomic exchange procedure. Node n receives the packet, places it in the appropriate buffer, discards the original packet, and the procedure is complete. Fig. 7 shows the exchange of messages in detail. In order to prevent both n and m from initiating the atomic exchange procedure simultaneously, a further restriction may be placed, permitting a node to initiate the procedure

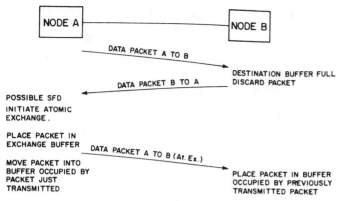

Fig. 7. The "atomic exchange" idea.

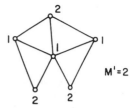

Fig. 8. The INH scheme.

only if the packet that is received is from a node with a lexicographically smaller name. In other words, m would initiate an atomic exchange procedure if it receives a packet from n, but not vice versa.

Clearly, as Figs. 3 and 7 indicate, the atomic exchange procedure does not increase the number of messages that need to be transmitted.

The method used to prevent indirect SFD is the NH scheme with the following modification. Instead of partitioning the nodes of the network into subsets that contain mutually nonadjacent nodes, we partition the nodes such that the subgraph induced by any subset (the subgraph consisting of all the nodes in the subset and all links that have both endpoints in the subset) contains no cycles. Recall that the network's links are not directed, and therefore, we are searching for undirected cycles. Fig. 8 shows the same network as Fig. 6 but partitioned into subgraphs with no cycles.

Observation 1 on the structure of the buffer graph still holds. We now proceed to show that the INH scheme is SFD free. In order to show this, we need only to show that indirect SFD cannot occur. Indirect SFD implies a directed cycle of three or more edges in the buffer graph.

Theorem 3: The buffer graph under the INH scheme contains no directed cycles consisting of three or more edges.

Proof: Again, the proof is by contradiction. Assume that we have a directed cycle of three or more edges. As in the proof of Theorem 1, one of the following two properties must hold for the directed cycle.

i) One or more of the edges go from a buffer of higher class to a buffer of lower class. As before, this is not possible by Observation 1.

ii) All edges go between buffers of the same class. As in the NH case, directed edges always go from a buffer in one node to a buffer in a neighboring node, and an edge goes between two buffers of the same class only if it is not traversing a negative hop. Without the presence of an edge that traverses a negative hop, it must be the case that all edges in the cycle traverse links that go between nodes with the same label. This would mean that the links joining the nodes form an undirected cycle of three or more edges, contradicting the premise that the network was partitioned into cycle free subsets.

Thus, either property creates a contradiction, completing the proof. ∎

Having proven deadlock freedom, let us examine how good the scheme is. Let M_i be the number of subsets in the partition. The cost function B_{max} is still directly related to the maximum number of negative hops in the network, H_n. However, because of the extra exchange buffer necessary to prevent direct SFD, the number of buffers is not $H_n + 1$ but $H_n + 2$. It is easily seen that Theorem 2, bounding H_n to a fraction of H, still holds with M being replaced by M_i. The next step,

therefore, is to examine what M_i is for typical network topologies.

A. Degree Constrained Networks

Lemma 4: If all nodes in the network have degree $\leq D$, then

$$M_i \leq \left\lceil \frac{D+1}{2} \right\rceil.$$

Proof: The proof is by induction on the number of nodes. Assume that for any $N - 1$ node network with the above property, the lemma holds. Consider an N node network. Remove any node and partition the remaining $N - 1$ node network into $\lceil (D + 1)/2 \rceil$ cycle-free subsets. Now add the previously removed node and all of its links.

We claim that there is at least one subset which has the property that it contains no more than one node that is adjacent to the newly added node. To see the validity of this claim, assume that it is false. Then each subset has two or more nodes with links to the new node. Thus, the degree of the new node is

$$\geq 2 \times \left\lceil \frac{D+1}{2} \right\rceil \geq D + 1.$$

We know, however, that the degree is $\leq D$, resulting in a contradiction.

Select one subset that satisifies the claim and add the new node to that subset. It cannot create any cycles, as links to at least two nodes are necessary for a cycle. Thus, we have constructed a partitioning of the N node network. This completes the induction. As the lemma holds trivially for $N = 1$, this completes the proof. ∎

The above lemma shows that for degree constrained networks, M_i is roughly half the value of M, resulting in a correspondingly lower value for B_{max}. For example, if $D = 3$, $M_i = 2$ and B_{max} is approximately 0.5 H.

B. Planar Networks

Lemma 5: For planar networks, $M_i \leq 3$.

Proof: Again, the proof is by induction. Assume that the lemma is true for any $N - 1$ node planar network. Consider an N node planar network. A well-known graph theory result [9] states that every planar graph contains at least one vertex of degree ≤ 5. Find such a node and remove it to obtain an $N - 1$ node network. Partition this network into three cycle-free subsets. Put back the previously removed node and all its links. In a manner analogous to Lemma 4, it can be shown that at least one of the three subsets has no more than one node with a link to the new node. Add the new node to this subset. As before, the new subset is cycle free, thereby completing the induction and the proof. ∎

This gives that B_{max} is approximately 0.67 H.

C. Networks with a Bounded Number of High Degree Nodes

Lemma 6: If no more than $D + 1$ nodes in the network

have degree $> D$, then

$$M_i \le \left\lceil \frac{D+1}{2} \right\rceil.$$

Proof: The proof is by induction on the number of nodes and is analogous to Lemmas 4 and 5. ∎

This result is essentially a stronger version of Lemma 4, saying that even if a small number of nodes in the network have high degree, it is still possible to achieve significant savings with the INH scheme. Lemmas 4 and 6 can be strengthened further by the observation that nodes of degree 1 never cause cycles and can effectively be ignored. Thus, even if the degree of a node is replaced (in the statement of the lemmas) by the degree minus the number of neighbors with degree of 1, the lemmas continue to hold.

The above results show that for most communication networks, guaranteed SFD freedom can be achieved with a third fewer buffers than the HC scheme with minimal additional complexity. Many other such results can be proven, but we present only one more.

D. Bidirectional Ring

An interesting special case is the ring topology. Here, previous results have shown that in the arbitrary routing case, with traffic flow permitted in both directions, deadlock freedom can be achieved with four buffers. Let us apply the INH scheme to this topology. We first partition the network into two subsets, with subset 1 consisting of a single node and subset 2 consisting of all the remaining nodes. Both subsets are cycle free. It is clear that for any loop-free route, the maximum number of negative hops is 1, thus providing a scheme to avoid SFD with three buffers.

V. Partitioning Techniques

We have seen how the appropriate partitioning of the network can result in the use of fewer buffers. Here, we discuss some issues which arise in the formation of the partition.

To find the true minimum values of M or M_i for a given network is NP-complete (see [8, ''Graph-Coloring'' and ''Partition Into Forests'']). Fortunately, as most communication networks are reasonably small, potentially exponential methods such as branch-and-bound work quite well, and optimal or near-optimal values of M or M_i can be found. In the previous sections we showed that if the underlying network has certain properties (planarity, bounded degree, etc.), then the optimal value of M or M_i can be upper bounded by a small value. However, even if it is not known that the network possesses any of these properties, experimental trials on some real network configurations indicate that M_i is typically not larger than 3, resulting in a savings of about 33 percent for the INH scheme over the HC scheme. For example, the 1983 ARPANET topology [10] can be partitioned with M_i equal to 2.

Thus, we envisage two possible scenarios for the implementation of the NH and INH schemes. The first scenario is the following. Prior to the startup of the network, the maximal network topology (i.e., the topology formed by all links and nodes that are or may potentially be in the network) is known. The partitioning of the network is then done in a centralized fashion on this maximal topology. Clearly, if the partitioned subsets have the desired property for the NH or INH scheme in the maximal topology, they will continue to possess the same property under any subset of the maximal topology. In other words, even if links or nodes fail and subsequently recover, no relabeling of the nodes will be necessary.

In most environments, the technique suggested above will be applicable. In some environments, however, the topology is too dynamic for this approach. In these environments a possibility is to perform a dynamic relabeling of nodes when a topology change which requires a relabeling occurs. For the case of the INH scheme, this occurs only when a link comes up between two nodes that have the same label and causes a cycle among nodes of that label. (We are assuming that a node coming up is equivalent to each one of its links coming up sequentially.) Thus, most topology changes will not require relabeling.

In the circumstance that relabeling is required, it can be performed in two ways. The first way is applicable in environments where every node maintains its own updated view of the topology of the network, as is done in ARPANET. In such cases, each node will individually detect the necessity for relabeling and will each run identical centralized partitioning algorithms to provide the new labeling. As long as all nodes eventually end up with the same view of the network topology, and as long as the partitioning algorithms are truly identical (including in the way they resolve ties), the relabeling procedure will function correctly.

In environments where each node does not maintain the network topology, more complex relabeling procedures are required. Even the detection of when relabeling is necessary is more of a problem. One possibility is to perform relabeling whenever a link comes up between two nodes that have the same label, and where each of those nodes already has another neighbor with the same label. This is a necessary but not sufficient condition for relabeling to be required, and therefore, some extra relabeling may occur. The advantage, however, is that this event can be easily detected by the two nodes.

The relabeling itself is accomplished by a distributed algorithm. For the remainder of the section, we discuss two such distributed algorithms. Both algorithms are for the INH scheme. We shall first describe the algorithms in an informal manner and then present a more formal description. We assume that the network is in the process of being ''brought up,'' i.e., all nodes are in the initialize state and are seeking to be assigned to a subset (to be labeled). It is the responsibility of the node that decides upon relabeling to ensure that all other nodes enter this initialize state. This can be done by the broadcast flooding of the network through a procedure such as the PI described in [11].

The first algorithm provides a good heuristic for general networks, although we can give no formal bound on the number of labels it will generate. For networks whose maximum degree is known, however, the algorithm is guaranteed not to require more labels than the upper bound of Lemma 4. The algorithm has two phases. The first phase consists of each node sending a message to each one of its neighbors, telling it of its unique node ID. This is done by means of an INTRODUCE(node__id) message (the information contained in the message is within the parentheses). Upon receipt of the INTRODUCE message from all neighbors, a node selects the label 1 for itself if its node__id is larger than the node__id of all of its neighbors, and then sends a LABELED(label) message to all neighbors informing them of the fact. If there are neighbors with higher node__id's, it waits until it receives a LABELED message from all such neighbors and then selects the smallest label which has the property that it has been chosen by no more than one neighbor of a higher node__id.

Algorithm to Partition Networks:

Types of messages:

INTRODUCE(node__id), LABELED(label,node__id)

Variables:

counter : keeps track of the number of INTRODUCE messages received

no___neighbors : number of neighbors
neighbor___id : vector of dimension no___neighbors to keep
track of node___id's
Reset upon receipt of LABELED messages
neighbor___label: vector of dimension no___neighbors to keep
track of neighbor's labels
my___label : label of node i

Algorithm executed at node i:

Procedure initialize:
    counter = 0;
    neighbor___id = neighbor___label = 0;
    send INTRODUCE(i) to all neighbors;

Procedure receive___INTRODUCE(node___id);
    counter = counter + 1;
    neighbor___id(counter) = node___id;
    if (counter = no___neighbors) then attempt ___labeling;
    end;

Procedure attempt___labeling;
    if (max(neighbor___id) $< i$) then do;
        my___label = select___from (neighbor ___label);
        send LABELED(my___label) to all neighbors;
        terminate algorithm;
        end;

Procedure receive___LABELED(label,node___id)
    index = find___index(node___id,neighbor___id)
    neighbor___id (index) = 0;
    neighbor___label (index) = label;
    attempt___labeling;
    end;

Function max (vector);
    /* returns maximum value in vector*/

Function select___from (vector)
    /* returns smallest positive integer that is not
    repeated twice or more in vector*/

Function find___index(value,vector)
    /* returns index of first occurrence of value in
    vector*/

We note that the above algorithm requires each node to send two messages over each link. Thus, the total number of messages sent in the algorithm is exactly four times the number of links. As mentioned previously, for degree constrained networks, the number of labels produced by the algorithm satisfies the bound of Lemma 4.

However, the algorithm is not guaranteed to satisfy the bound of Lemma 5 (i.e., use no more than three labels) if it is known that the network is planar. The following algorithm, however, is specifically designed for planar networks, and does satisfy that bound. It is also a two-phase algorithm but the phases are slightly more complex. The first phase consists of a node choosing a level as well as informing all its neighbors of its unique node ID. The level of a node is different from its label and is used to order the selection of labels among the nodes. The definition of the level of a node is the following. A node which chooses level i has the property that when nodes of level $i - 1, i - 2, \cdots, 0$ are removed from the network, the node has degree ≤ 5. Thus, nodes of level 0 have degree ≤ 5 in the original network, nodes of level 1 have degree ≤ 5 in the network without all nodes of level 0, and so on.

As in the previous algorithm, the first phase is accomplished by means of sending INTRODUCE(level,node___id) messages to all neighbors. However, a node sends such messages only when it has five or fewer neighbors that have not yet sent it INTRODUCE messages. Thus, nodes with degree ≤ 5 will send INTRODUCE messages immediately, while nodes of degree > 5

will have to wait until they receive some INTRODUCE messages from their neighbors. The level that a node selects is one larger than the largest level contained in an INTRODUCE message received prior to it itself sending INTRODUCE messages. Thus, a node has no more than five neighbors that have levels that are larger than or equal to itself.

After sending the INTRODUCE messages to its neighbors, a node waits until it in turn receives INTRODUCE messages from all of its neighbors and LABELED messages from all "superior" neighbors (neighbors that have a larger level or have the same level and larger node___id's). There can be at most five such superior neighbors. A node then selects the smallest label which has the property that it has been chosen by no more than one superior neighbor, and sends a LABELED message to all of its neighbors, informing them of the choice.

Algorithm to Partition Planar Networks:

Types of messages:

INTRODUCE(level,node___id), LABELED(label,node___id)

Variables:

counter : keeps track of the number of INTRODUCE messages received
no___neighbors : number of neighbors
neighbor___id : vector of dimension no___neighbors to keep
track of node___id's.
Reset upon receipt of LABELED messages
neighbor___label: vector of dimension no___neighbors to keep
track of neighbor's labels.
neighbor___level: vector of dimension no___neighbors to keep
track of node___levels.
Reset upon receipt of LABELED messages
neighbor___level: vector of dimension no___neighbors to keep
track of
my___label : label of node i
level___set : true if a level has been chosen

Algorithm executed at node i:

Procedure initialize;
    counter = 0;
    neighbor___id = neighbor___label = 0;
    level___set = .false.
    if(no___neighbors .le. 5) then do;
        my___label = 0;
        level___set = .true.
        send INTRODUCE(my___label,i) to all neighbors;
        end;
    end;

Procedure receive___INTRODUCE(level,node___id);
    counter = counter + 1;
    neighbor___level(counter) = level;
    neighbor___id(counter) = node___id;
    if((no___neighbors-counter).le. 5) & ¬ level___set then do;
        my___level = max(neighbor___level) + 1;
        level___set = .true.
        send INTRODUCE(my___level,i) to all neighbors;
        end;
    if (counter = no___neighbors) then attempt___labeling;
    end;

Procedure attempt___labeling;
    k = max(neighbor___level);
    l = node___label(find___index(k,neighbor___level))
    if (k.lt. my___level) or ((k = my___level) & (l.lt.i))
    then do;
        my___label = select___from (neighbor___label);

```
send LABELED(my__label,i) to all neighbors;
     terminate algorithm;
     end;
Procedure receive__LABELED(label,node__id)
     index = find__index(node__id,neighbor__id)
     neighbor__id (index) = neighbor__level(index) = 0;
     neighbor__label (index) = label;
     attempt__labeling;
     end;

Function max (vector);
     /* returns maximum value in vector */

Function select__from (vector)
     /* returns smallest positive integer that is not
        repeated twice or more in vector*/

Function find__index(value, vector)
     /* returns index of first occurrence of value in
        vector*/
```

As before, the algorithm requires each node to send two messages over each link, resulting in the total number of messages sent in the algorithm being exactly four times the number of links. Also, as mentioned above, the algorithm never uses more than three labels for planar networks.

VI. CONCLUSION

The NH and the INH techniques presented in this paper enable the prevention of SFD with fewer buffers than previously suggested schemes. They are also not significantly more complex in terms of implementation.

We note that the paper describes only the aspects of the schemes that are necessary in order to show the reduction in the number of buffers. We have ignored the possible impact on network performance (measured in terms of time delays and throughput) caused by the restrictions imposed on traffic flow. To alleviate the impact somewhat, there are some enhancements that can potentially improve the performance of our schemes. These enhancements are similar to those in [4] and include permitting a message destined for a buffer of class i to use any buffer of class i or *lower*, having a different number of buffers in each class, etc. It is easily seen that such enhancements can be applied to our schemes without affecting the property of SFD freedom.

However, there is still much that needs to be done to understand the performance impact of the traffic restrictions, and the effect of the various possible enhancements. To investigate the performance aspect further, including the schemes proposed in this paper as well as schemes proposed by other authors, remains a rich area for future work.

ACKNOWLEDGMENT

I would like to acknowledge G. Grover and A. Baratz for several stimulating and useful discussions on this subject.

REFERENCES

[1] S. Toueg, "Deadlock- and livelock-free packet switched networks," in *Proc. ACM Symp. Theory of Comput.*, 1980, pp. 94–99.
[2] S. Toueg and J. D. Ullman, "Deadlock-free packet switched networks," in *Proc. ACM Symp. Theory of Comput.*, 1979, pp. 89–98.
[3] D. Gelernter, "A DAG-based algorithm for prevention of store-and-forward deadlock in packet networks," *IEEE Trans. Comput.*, vol. C-30, pp. 709–715, Oct. 1981.
[4] K. D. Gunther, "Prevention of deadlocks in packet-switched data transport systems," *IEEE Trans. Commun.*, vol. COM-29, pp. 512–524, Apr. 1981.
[5] J. Blacewicz, D. P. Bouvet, and G. Gambosi, "Deadlock-resistant flow control procedures for store-and-forward networks," *IEEE Trans. Commun.*, vol. COM-32, pp. 884–887, Aug. 1984.
[6] P. M. Merlin and P. J. Schweitzer, "Deadlock avoidance in store-and-forward networks—I: Store-and-forward deadlock," *IEEE Trans. Commun.*, vol. COM-28, pp. 345–354, Mar. 1981.
[7] B. Gavish, P. M. Merlin, and P. J. Schweitzer, "Minimal buffer requirements for avoiding store-and-forward deadlock," IBM Res. Rep. RC6672, Aug. 9, 1977.
[8] M. R. Garey and D. S. Johnson, *Computers and Intractability—A Guide to the Theory of NP-Completeness.* San Francisco, CA: Freeman, 1979.
[9] C. Berge, *Graphs and Hypergraphs.* New York: North-Holland, 1973.
[10] P. E. Green, "Computer communications: Milestones and prophecies," *IEEE Commun. Mag.*, vol. 22, pp. 49–63, May 1984.
[11] A. Segall, "Distributed network protocols," *IEEE Trans. Inform. Theory*, vol. IT-29, pp. 23–35, Jan. 1983.

Inder S. Gopal (S'80–M'82), for a photograph and biography, see p. 501 of the June 1985 issue of this TRANSACTIONS.

Deadlock-Free Message Routing in Multiprocessor Interconnection Networks

WILLIAM J. DALLY, MEMBER, IEEE, AND CHARLES L. SEITZ, MEMBER, IEEE

Abstract—A deadlock-free routing algorithm can be generated for arbitrary interconnection networks using the concept of virtual channels. A necessary and sufficient condition for deadlock-free routing is the absence of cycles in a channel dependency graph. Given an arbitrary network and a routing function, the cycles of the channel dependency graph can be removed by splitting physical channels into groups of virtual channels. This method is used to develop deadlock-free routing algorithms for k-ary n-cubes, for cube-connected cycles, and for shuffle-exchange networks.

Index Terms—Communication networks, concurrent computation, graph model, interconnection networks, message passing multiprocessors, parallel processing.

I. INTRODUCTION

MESSAGE passing concurrent computers [13] such as the Cosmic Cube [11] consist of many processing nodes that interact by sending messages over communication channels between the nodes. Deadlock in the interconnection network of a concurrent computer occurs when no message can advance toward its destination because the queues of the message system are full [7]. Consider the example shown in Fig. 1. The queue of each node in the 4-cycle is filled with messages destined for the opposite node. No message can advance toward its destination; thus, the cycle is deadlocked. In this locked state, no communication can occur over the deadlocked channels until exceptional action is taken to break the deadlock.

In this paper we consider networks that use *wormhole* [12] rather than *store-and-forward* [16] routing. Instead of storing a packet completely in a node and then transmitting it to the next node, wormhole routing operates by advancing the head of a packet directly from incoming to outgoing channels. Only a few flow control digits (flits) are buffered at each node. A *flit* is the smallest unit of information that a queue or channel can accept or refuse.

As soon as a node examines the header flit(s) of a message, it selects the next channel on the route and begins forwarding flits down that channel. As flits are forwarded, the message

Manuscript received May 15, 1985; revised July 2, 1986. This work was supported in part by the Defense Advanced Research Projects Agency, ARPA Order 3771, and monitored by the Office of Naval Research under Contract N00014-79-0587, in part by a grant from Intel Corporation, and in part by an AT&T Ph.D. fellowship.

W. J. Dally is with the Department of Electrical Engineering and Computer Science, Massachusetts Institute of Technology, Cambridge, MA 02139.

C. L. Seitz is with the Department of Computer Science, California Institute of Technology, Pasadena, CA 91125.

IEEE Log Number 8713946.

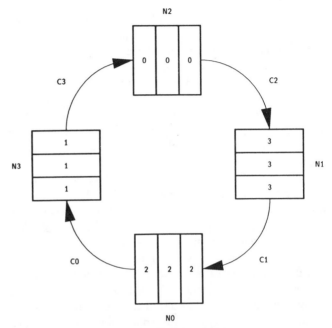

Fig. 1. Deadlock in a 4-cycle.

becomes spread out across the channels between the source and destination. It is possible for the first flit of a message to arrive at the destination node before the last flit of the message has left the source. Because most flits contain no routing information, the flits in a message must remain in contiguous channels of the network and cannot be interleaved with the flits of other messages. When the header flit of a message is blocked, all of the flits of a message stop advancing and block the progress of any other message requiring the channels they occupy.

A method similar to wormhole routing, called *virtual cut-through*, is described in [6]. Virtual cut-through differs from wormhole routing in that it buffers messages when they block, removing them from the network. The deadlock properties of cut-through routing are accordingly identical to those of store-and-forward routing. With wormhole routing, blocked messages remain in the network.

Many deadlock-free routing algorithms have been developed for store-and-forward computer communications networks [5], [9], [17], [18], [4]. These algorithms are based on the concept of a *structured buffer pool*. The message buffers in each node of the network are partitioned into classes, and the assignment of buffers to messages is restricted to define a partial order on buffer classes. The structured buffer pool

Reprinted from *IEEE Trans. Computers*, Vol. C-36, No. 5, May 1987, pp. 547-553.

method has in common with the virtual channel method that both prevent deadlock by assigning a partial order to resources. The two methods differ in that the structured buffer pool approach restricts the assignment of buffers to packets while the virtual channel approach restricts the routing of messages. Either method can be applied to store-and-forward networks, but the structured buffer pool approach is not directly applicable to wormhole networks, since the flits of a message cannot be interleaved the way that packets can. Once one flit of a message is accepted and assigned a buffer, the remaining flits must be accepted before the flits of any other message can be accepted by the channel. With wormhole routing, we cannot restrict buffer allocation to break deadlock. Instead, we must restrict routing.

Reliable concurrent computation requires a routing algorithm that is provably free of deadlock. In this paper we present a general method for constructing deadlock-free routing algorithms for arbitrary networks. In Section II we state our assumptions and develop the necessary and sufficient conditions on a *channel dependency graph* for a routing to be deadlock free. These conditions are used in Section III to develop a method of constructing deadlock-free algorithms for arbitrary networks. This method is based on the concept of virtual channels: groups of channels that share a physical channel but in which each virtual channel has its own queue. Using virtual channels, we develop deadlock-free routing algorithms for arbitrary *k*-ary *n*-cubes in Section IV, for cube-connected cycles in Section V, and for shuffle-exchange networks in Section VI. In each of these examples, physical channels belonging to cycles are split into a group of virtual channels. The virtual channels are ordered; routing is restricted to visit channels in decreasing order to eliminate cycles in the channel dependency graph.

II. DEADLOCK-FREE ROUTING

We assume the following.

1) A message arriving at its destination node is eventually consumed.

2) A node can generate messages destined for any other node.

3) The route taken by a message is determined only by its destination, and not by other traffic in the network (*deterministic or nonadaptive* routing).

4) A node can generate messages of arbitrary length. Packets will generally be longer than a single flit.

5) Once a queue accepts the first flit of a message, it must accept the remainder of the message before accepting any flits from another message.

6) An available queue may arbitrate between messages that request that queue space, but may not choose among waiting messages.

7) Nodes can produce messages at any rate subject to the constraint of available queue space (source queued).

The following definitions develop a notation for describing networks, routing functions, and configurations. A summary of notation is given below.

Definition 1: An *interconnection network I* is a strongly connected *directed* graph, $I = G(N, C)$. The vertices of the graph N represent the set of processing nodes. The edges of the graph C represent the set of communication channels. Associated with each channel, c_i, is a queue with capacity cap (c_i). The source node of channel c_i is denoted s_i and the destination node d_i.

Definition 2: A *routing function* $R:C \times N \mapsto C$ maps the current channel c_c and destination node n_d to the next channel c_n on the route from c_c to n_d, $R(c_c, n_d) = c_n$. A channel is not allowed to route to itself, $c_c \neq c_n$. Note that this definition restricts the routing to be memoryless in the sense that a message arriving in channel c_c has no memory of the route that brought it to c_c. However, this formulation of routing as a function from $C \times N$ to C has more memory than the conventional definition of routing as a function from $N \times N$ to C. Making routing dependent on the current channel rather than the current node allows us to develop the idea of channel dependence.

Definition 3: A *channel dependency graph D* for a given interconnection network I and routing function R, is a directed graph, $D = G(C, E)$. The vertices of D are the channels of I. The edges of D are the pairs of channels connected by R:

$$E = \{(c_i, c_j) \mid R(c_i, n) = c_j \text{ for some } n \in N\}. \quad (1)$$

Since channels are not allowed to route to themselves, there are no 1-cycles in D.

Definition 4: A *configuration* is an assignment of a list of nodes to each queue. The number of flits in the queue for channel c_i will be denoted size (c_i). If the first flit in the queue for channel c_i is destined for node n_d, then head $(c_i) = n_d$. A configuration is legal if

$$\forall c_i \in C, \text{ size } (c_i) \leq \text{cap } (c_i) \quad (2)$$

Definition 5: A *deadlocked configuration* for a routing function R is a nonempty legal configuration of channel queues $\ni$

$$\forall c_i \in C, \text{ (head } (c_i) \neq d_i \text{ and } c_j = R(c_i, n)$$
$$\Rightarrow \text{size } (c_j) = \text{cap } (c_j)). \quad (3)$$

In this configuration no flit is one step from its destination and no flit can advance because the queue for the next channel is full. A routing function R is *deadlock free* on an interconnection network I if no deadlock configuration exists for that function on that network.

Summary of Notation

I	interconnection network, a directed graph $I = G(N, C)$,
N	the set of nodes,
n_i	a node,
C	the set of channels,
c_i	a channel,
s_i	the source node of channel c_i,
d_i	the destination node of channel c_i,
cap (c_i)	the capacity of the queue of channel c_i,
size (c_i)	the number of flits enqueued for channel c_i,
head (c_i)	the destination of the head flit enqueued for channel c_i,

R a routing function $R: C \times N \mapsto C$,
D the channel dependency graph.

Theorem 1: A routing function R for an interconnection network I is deadlock free iff there are no cycles in the channel dependency graph D.

Proof: $\Rightarrow$ Suppose a network has a cycle in D. Since there are no 1-cycles in D, this cycle must be of length two or more. Thus, one can construct a deadlocked configuration by filling the queues of each channel in the cycle with flits destined for a node two channels away, where the first channel of the route is along the cycle.

$\Leftarrow$ Suppose a network has no cycles in D. Since D is acyclic, one can assign a total order to the channels of C so that if $(c_i, c_j) \in E$ then $c_i > c_j$. Consider the least channel in this order with a full queue c_l. Every channel c_n that c_l feeds is less than c_l and thus does not have a full queue. Thus, no flit in the queue for c_l is blocked, and one does not have deadlock. ∎

III. Constructing Deadlock-Free Routing Algorithms

Now that we have established this if-and-only-if relationship between deadlock and the cycles in the channel dependency graph, we can approach the problem of making a network deadlock free by breaking the cycles. We can break such cycles by splitting each physical channel along a cycle into a group of *virtual channels*. Each group of virtual channels shares a physical communication channel; however, each virtual channel requires its own queue.

Consider for example the case of a unidirectional four-cycle as shown in Fig. 2(a), $N = \{n_0, \cdots, n_3\}$, $C = \{c_0, \cdots, c_3\}$. The interconnection graph I is shown on the left and the dependency graph D is shown on the right. We pick channel c_0 to be the dividing channel of the cycle and split each channel into high virtual channels, $c_{10}, \cdots, c_{13}$, and low virtual channels, $c_{00}, \cdots, c_{03}$, as shown in Fig. 2(b).

Messages at a node numbered less than their destination node are routed on the high channels, and messages at a node numbered greater than their destination node are routed on the low channels. Channel c_{00} is not used. We now have a total ordering of the virtual channels according to their subscripts: $c_{13} > c_{12} > c_{11} > c_{10} > c_{03} > c_{02} > c_{01}$. Thus, there is no cycle in D and the routing function is deadlock free. In the next three sections we apply this technique to three practical communications networks. In each case we add virtual channels and restrict the routing to route messages in order of decreasing channel subscripts.

IV. k-ary n-cubes

The *e-cube* routing algorithm [15], [8] guarantees deadlock-free routing in binary n cubes. In a cube of dimension n, we denote a node as n_k where k is an n-digit binary number. Node n_k has n output channels, one for each dimension, labeled $c_{0k}, \cdots, c_{(n-1)k}$. The *e-cube* algorithm routes in decreasing order of dimension. A message arriving at node n_k destined for node n_l is routed on channel c_{ik} where i is the position of the most significant bit in which k and l differ. Since messages are routed in order of decreasing dimension, and hence decreasing

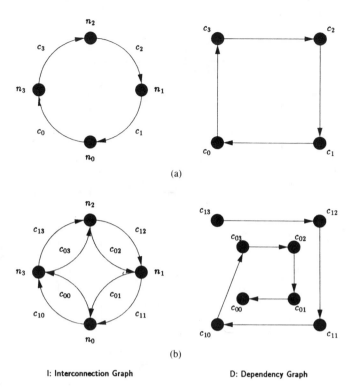

(a)

(b)

I: Interconnection Graph   D: Dependency Graph

Fig. 2.   Breaking deadlock by adding virtual edges.

channel subscript, there are no cycles in the channel dependency graph and e-cube routing is deadlock free.

Using the technique of virtual channels, this routing algorithm can be extended to handle all k-ary n-cubes: cubes with dimension n and k nodes in each dimension. Rings and toroidal meshes are included in this class of networks. This algorithm can also handle mixed radix cubes. Each node of a k-ary n-cube is identified by an n-digit radix k number. The ith digit of the number represents the node's position in the ith dimension. For example, the center node in the 3-ary 2-cube of Fig. 3 is n_{11}. The channels are identified by the number of their source node and their dimension. For example, the dimension 0 (horizontal) channel from n_{11} to n_{10} is c_{011}. To break cycles we divide each channel into an upper and lower virtual channel. The upper virtual channel of c_{011} will be labeled c_{0111}, and the lower virtual channel will be labeled c_{0011}. Virtual channel subscripts are of the form dvx where d is the dimension, v selects the virtual channel, and x identifies the source node of the channel. To assure that the routing is deadlock free, we restrict it to route through channels in order of descending subscripts.

As in the e-cube algorithm we route in order of dimension, most significant dimension first. In each dimension i, a message is routed in that dimension until it reaches a node whose subscript matches the destination address in the ith position. The message is routed on the high channel if the ith digit of the destination address is greater than the ith digit of the present node's address. Otherwise, the message is routed on the low channel. It is easy to see that this routing algorithm routes in order of descending subscripts, and is thus deadlock free.

Formally, we define the routing function.

347

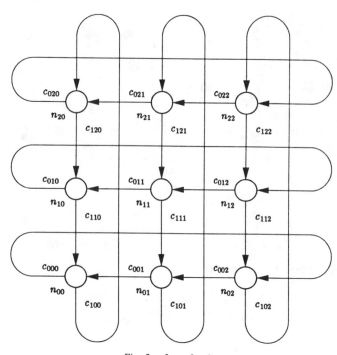

Fig. 3.   3-ary 2-cube.

$$R_{KNC}(c_{dvx}, n_j)$$

$$
= \begin{cases}
c_{d1(x-k^d)} \\
\quad \text{if } (\text{dig } (x, d) < \text{dig } (j, d)) \wedge (\text{dig } (x, d) \neq 0), \\
\\
c_{d0(x-k^d)} \\
\quad \text{if } (\text{dig } (x, d) > \text{dig } (j, d)) \vee (\text{dig } (x, d) = 0), \\
\\
c_{i1(x-k^d)} \\
\quad \text{if } (\forall k > i, \text{dig } (x, k) = \text{dig } (j, k)) \\
\quad \wedge (\text{dig } (n, i) \neq \text{dig } (j, i)).
\end{cases}
$$

$$(4)$$

Where dig (x, d) extracts the dth digit of x, and k is the radix of the cube. The subtraction, $x - k^d$, decrements the dth digit of x modulo k.

Assertion 1: The routing function R_{KNC} correctly routes messages from any node to any other node in a k-ary n-cube.

Proof: By induction on dimension d. For $d = 1$, a message, destined for n_j, enters the system at n_i. If $i < j$, the message is forwarded on channels, $c_{01i}, \cdots, c_{010}, c_{00k-1}, \cdots,$ $c_{00(j+1)}$ to node n_j. If $i > j$, the path taken is $c_{00i}, \cdots, c_{00(j+1)}$. In both cases the route reaches node n_j.

Assume that the routing works for dimensions $\leq d$. Then for dimension $d + 1$ there are two cases. If dig $(i, d) \neq$ dig (j, d), then the message is routed around the most significant cycle to a node $n_x \ni$ dig $(x, d) =$ dig (j, d), as in the $d = 1$ case above. If dig $(i, d) =$ dig (j, d), then the routing need only be performed in dimensions d and lower. In each of these cases, once the message reaches a node, $n_x, \ni$ dig $(x, d) =$ dig (j, d), the third routing rule is used to route the message to

a lower dimensional channel. The problem has then been reduced to one of dimension $\leq d$ and by induction the routing reaches the correct node. ∎

Assertion 2: The routing function R_{KNC} on a k-ary n-cube interconnection network I is deadlock free.

Proof: Since routing is performed in decreasing order of channel subscripts, $\forall c_i, c_j, n_c \ni R(c_i, n_c) = c_j, i > j$, the channel dependency graph, D is acyclic. Thus, by Theorem 1 the route is deadlock free. ∎

V. Cube-Connected Cycles

The cube-connected cycle (CCC) [10] is an interconnection network based on the binary n-cube. In the CCC, each node of a binary n-cube is replaced with an n-cycle, and the cube connection in the nth dimension is attached to the nth node in the cycle. A CCC of dimension 3 is shown in Fig. 4.

Each node in the CCC is labeled with the position of its cycle (an n-bit binary number), and its position within the cycle. For example, in Fig. 4, node 2 in cycle 111 is labeled n_{2111}. There are two channels out of each node: an in-cycle channel and an out-of-cycle channel. The in-cycle channel is split into three virtual channels. One set of virtual channels is used to rotate a message around the cycle to get to the most significant node in the cycle. These channels are labeled c_{2d0c} where d is the dimension of the node (its position in the cycle), and c is the cycle address. The next set of virtual channels is used to decrement the dimension during the e-cube routing of the message between cycles. These channels are labeled c_{1d0c}. The out-of-cycle channels, labeled c_{1d1c}, are used to toggle the bit of the current cycle address corresponding to dimension d. Note that the channels c_{1d1c} are actually physical channels. These connections are not shared with any other channels. The third set of virtual channels is used to rotate the message around the cycle to its destination once it is in the proper cycle. These channels are labeled c_{0d0c}. As above, we will restrict our routing to route through channels in order of descending subscripts.

The routing algorithm proceeds in three phases. During phase 1, messages are routed around the cycle using the first set of virtual channels until they reach a node with dimension greater than or equal to the position of the most significant bit in which the destination cycle address differs from the current cycle address. During phase 2 we route the message to the proper cycle using a variant of the e-cube algorithm. At each step of phase 2, we find the most significant dimension i in which the current cycle and destination cycle addresses differ. The message is routed around the current cycle until it reaches the node with dimension i and is then routed out of the cycle. When the message arrives in the destination cycle, it is routed around the cycle using the third set of virtual channels to reach its destination node. It is easy to see that routing is always performed in order of decreasing channel numbers, and thus the routing is guaranteed to be deadlock free.

While most cube-connected cycles are binary, this routing algorithm can be extended for k-ary cube-connected cycles, that is, cubes with k cycles in each dimension. The only modification required is to split each out-of-cycle channel into two virtual channels. For simplicity, however, we will analyze

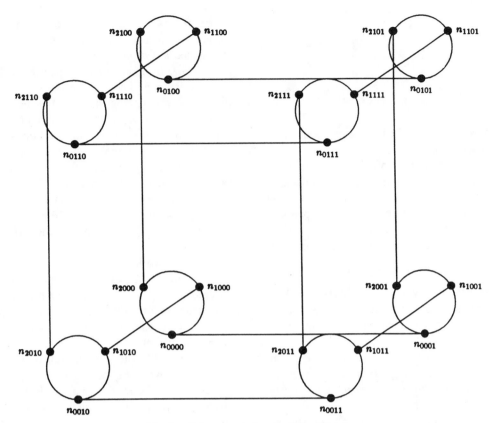

Fig. 4.   Cube connected cycle of dimension 3.

the routing for the binary case only. Formally, we define the routing function.

$$R_{CCC}(c_{vdxc}, n_{d'c'})$$

$$= \begin{cases} c_{2(d-1)0c} & \text{if } (v \geq 2) \wedge (d>0) \\ & \wedge (\exists i>d \quad \text{dig }(i, c) \neq \text{dig }(i, c')), \\ c_{1(d-1)1c} & \text{if } (v \geq 1) \wedge (x=0) \\ & \wedge (\forall i>d \text{ dig }(i, c) = \text{dig }(i, c')) \\ & \wedge (\text{dig }(d, c) \neq \text{dig }(d, c')), \\ c_{1(d-1)0c} & \text{if } (v \geq 1) \wedge (x=0) \\ & \wedge (\forall i \geq d \text{ dig }(i, c) = \text{dig }(i, c')), \\ c_{1d0(c-k^d)} & \text{if } (v=1) \wedge (x=1) \\ & \wedge (\forall i \geq d \text{ dig }(i, c) = \text{dig }(i, c')), \\ c_{1d1(c-k^d)} & \text{if } (v=1) \wedge (x=1) \\ & \wedge (\forall i>d \text{ dig }(i, c) = \text{dig }(i, c')) \\ & \wedge (\text{dig }(d, c) \neq \text{dig }(d, c')), \\ c_{0(d-1)0c} & \text{if } (x=0) \wedge (c=c') \wedge (d'<d), \\ c_{0(d)0c} & \text{if } (x=1) \wedge (c=c') \wedge (d'<d). \end{cases}$$

$$(5)$$

Assertion 3: $(v < 2) \Rightarrow \text{dig }(i, c) = \text{dig }(i, c') \; \forall i > d$.

Proof: The only way v can be decreased to less than 2 is for the right side of the assertion to hold. Initially $v = 3$. Then as long as $\exists i > d \ni \text{dig }(i, c) \neq \text{dig }(i, c')$, the first routing rule forwards the message along channels for which $v = 2$. When the arriving channel has $d = 0$, the current node has $d = n - 1$ (where n is the dimension of the CCC). In this case the first routing rule forwards the message along a channel for which $v = 1$. The assertion holds since there are only n digits in c and c', so there is no $i \geq n$ for which the ith digit of these two cycle addresses differ.

Once $v < 2$, the right side of the assertion continues to hold because of routing rules 2, 3, 4, and 5. We prove this by induction on d. For $d = n - 1$, the assertion holds as stated above. If we assume the assertion holds for $d = i$, then for $d = i - 1$ it also holds since routing rules 2 and 5 route the messages out-of-cycle to toggle the dth digit of n if the addresses disagree in that digit. ∎

Assertion 4: $(v = 0) \Rightarrow (c' = c) \wedge (d' < d)$.

Proof: The only way to decrease v to zero is by routing rules 6 and 7 which require the right side of the assertion. By Assertion 3, when $v < 2$ and $d = 0$, after one or two more traversals, the right side of the assertion will be met. Once $v = 0$, no out-of-cycle channels will be used so c does not change. ∎

Assertion 5: The routing function R_{CCC} correctly routes messages from any node to any other node in a k-ary cube-connected cycle.

Proof: Since there are only a finite number of channels, and R_{CCC} routes in order of decreasing channel subscripts, v will eventually be decreased to 0. Then by Assertion 4, $c' = c$

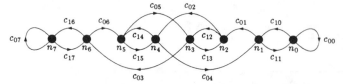

Fig. 5. Shuffle-exchange network, $N = 8$.

and $d' < d$, so the message will be rotated about the cycle until it reaches its destination. ∎

Assertion 6: The routing function R_{CCC} on a k-ary cube-connected cycle interconnection network I is deadlock free.

Proof: As in the case of k-ary n-cubes, since routing is performed in decreasing order of channel subscripts, $\forall c_i, c_j, n_c \ni R(c_i, n_c) = c_j, i > j$, the channel dependency graph, D is acyclic. Thus, by Theorem 1 the route is deadlock free. ∎

VI. SHUFFLE-EXCHANGE NETWORKS

The shuffle-exchange network [14], shown in Fig. 5, provides two channels out of each node: a shuffle channel and an exchange channel. The shuffle channel from node n_i has as its destination the node n_j where the binary representation of j is the left rotation of the binary representation of i, denoted here $j = \text{rol}(i)$. The exchange channel from n_i routes messages to n_k where the binary representations of k and i differ in the least significant bit.

The exchange channel out of n_i is labeled c_{1i}. The shuffle channel is labeled c_{0i}. For the shuffle-exchange network we split each channel into n virtual channels where $N = 2^n$. That is, we have one virtual channel for each bit of node address. Readers understanding the relationship between the binary n-cube and the shuffle [14] will find this assignment of virtual channels unsurprising since the shuffle is a uniform single stage of an n-stage indirect binary n-cube. The virtual channels are labeled c_{dxi}, where $0 \leq d \leq n - 1$, $x \in \{0, 1\}$, and $0 \leq i \leq N$.

The routing algorithm, like the e-cube algorithm, routes a message toward its destination one bit at a time beginning with the most significant bit. At the ith step of the route, the $n - i$th bit of the destination address is compared to the least significant bit of the current node address. If the two bits agree, the message is forwarded over the shuffle channel to rotate the node address around to the next bit. Otherwise, the message is forwarded over the exchange channel to bring the two bits into agreement and then over the shuffle channel to rotate the address. At the ith step messages are forwarded over channels with $d = n - i$. Since d is always decreasing and, during a single step, the exchange channel is used before the shuffle channel, messages are routed in order of decreasing virtual channel subscripts.

Formally, we define the routing function.

$$R_{SEN}(c_{dxi}, n_j)$$

$$= \begin{cases} c_{(d-1)0\,\text{rol}\,(i)} & \text{if } (x=0) \wedge (\text{dig}\,(d-1, i) = \text{dig}\,(0, j)), \\ c_{(d-1)1\,\text{rol}\,(i)} & \text{if } (x=0) \wedge (\text{dig}\,(d-1, i) \neq \text{dig}\,(0, j)), \\ c_{d0(i \oplus 1)} & \text{if } (x=1). \end{cases}$$

(6)

Assertion 7: If a message is routed on channel c_{d0i} destined for node n_j, then $\forall m \geq d$, $\text{dig}\,(m, j) = \text{dig}\,(m, k)$, where k is i rotated left d bits.

Proof: By induction on dimension d. For $d = n - 1$, a message is only routed on the shuffle connection, $x = 0$, of dimension $n - 1$ if $\text{dig}\,(n - 1, i) = \text{dig}\,(0, j) \Rightarrow \text{dig}\,(n - 1, i) = \text{dig}\,(n - 1, k)$ by the definition of k. Since there is only one possible value for m, the assertion is satisfied.

If the assertion is true for dimension d, then after routing on connection $c_{(d-1)0i}$, the assertion also holds for $d - 1$ by the same argument: a message is only routed on the shuffle connection, $x = 0$, of dimension $d - 1$ if $\text{dig}\,(d - 1, i) = \text{dig}\,(0, j) \Rightarrow \text{dig}\,(d - 1, i) = \text{dig}\,(d - 1, k)$. ∎

Assertion 8: The routing function R_{SEN} correctly routes messages from any node to any other node in a shuffle-exchange network.

Proof: From Assertion 7, after routing on channel c_{00i}, the message will be at its destination. It may reach its destination before this. Since the function routes in order of decreasing channel subscripts and there are a finite number of channels, messages will reach their destinations. ∎

Assertion 9: The routing function R_{SEN} on a shuffle-exchange network I is deadlock free.

Proof: Since routing is performed in order of decreasing channel numbers, D is acyclic and the routing is deadlock free. ∎

VII. CONCLUSION

We have shown how a deadlock-free routing algorithm can be constructed for an arbitrary communications network by introducing virtual channels. This technique has been applied to construct deadlock-free routing algorithms for k-ary n-cubes, for cube-connected cycles, and for shuffle-exchange networks.

The use of virtual channels to construct deadlock-free routing functions is motivated by the definition of a routing function that maps $C \times N$ to C, rather than the conventional definition of a routing function that maps $N \times N$ to C. By including C in the domain of the routing function, we explicitly define the dependencies between channels. These dependencies are represented by a channel dependency graph D. A necessary and sufficient condition for deadlock-free routing is that D be acyclic.

To generate a deadlock-free routing algorithm, we restrict the routing by removing edges from D to make D acyclic. If it is not possible to make D acyclic without disconnecting the network, we add edges to D by splitting physical channels into a group of virtual channels. Each group of virtual channels shares a single physical channel; however, each virtual channel requires its own queue. The additional edges provided by the virtual channels make it possible to make D acyclic while keeping I strongly connected.

To develop deadlock-free routing algorithms for specific networks we assign a subscript to each virtual channel using a mixed radix notation. Routing is performed in order of decreasing subscripts. Since the subscripts define a total order on the channels, there are no cyclic dependencies and the routing is deadlock free.

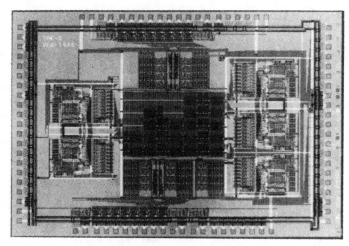

Fig. 6. Torus routing chip.

The cost of implementing virtual channels is small. Each virtual channel requires its own queue, but the queue size can be as small as a single flit.

To demonstrate the concept of virtual channels we have designed the Torus Routing Chip [3], [1], shown in Fig. 6. This chip implements the k-ary n-cube routing function R_{KNC} (4), in hardware. This self-timed VLSI circuit uses wormhole routing, virtual channels, and low-dimension network topology to achieve latencies several orders of magnitude lower than in previous systems.

The availability of deadlock-free routing algorithms encourages the investigation of different interconnection topologies. While $O(\log N)$ diameter networks such as the binary n-cube and the shuffle are attractive because of their richness of interconnection, these networks are almost always embedded in a grid for physical implementation. In keeping with the VLSI imperative of making form fit function, high bandwidth grid interconnections often turn out to be more attractive. Under constant wire bisection, for example, low-dimensional k-ary n-cube networks outperform binary n-cubes [2], [1].

ACKNOWLEDGMENT

The authors thank C. Steele for pointing out problems in an early version of this paper and the referees for their helpful suggestions.

REFERENCES

[1] W. J. Dally, "A VLSI architecture for concurrent data structures," Ph.D. dissertation, Dep. Comput. Sci., California Instit. Technol., Tech. Rep. 5209:TR:86, 1986.

[2] ——, "On the performance of k-ary n-cube interconnection networks," Dep. Comput. Sci., California Instit. Technol., Tech. Rep. 5228:TR:86, 1986.

[3] W. J. Dally and C. L. Seitz, "The torus routing chip," Distributed Comput., vol. 1, no. 3, 1986.

[4] D. Gelernter, "A DAG-based algorithm for prevention of store-and-forward deadlock in packet networks," IEEE Trans. Comput., vol. C-30, pp. 709–715, Oct. 1981.

[5] K. D. Gunther, "Prevention of deadlocks in packet-switched data transport systems," IEEE Trans. Commun., vol. COM-29, pp. 512–524, Apr. 1981.

[6] P. Kermani and L. Kleinrock, "Virtual cut-through: A new computer communication switching technique," Comput. Networks, vol. 3, pp. 267–286, 1979.

[7] L. Kleinrock, Queueing Systems, Vol. 2. New York: Wiley, 1976, pp. 438–440.

[8] C. R. Lang, "The extension of object-oriented languages to a homogeneous concurrent architecture," Ph.D. dissertation, California Instit. Technol., 5014:TR:82, pp. 118–124, 1982.

[9] P. M. Merlin and P. J. Schweitzer, "Deadlock avoidance in store-and-forward networks—I: Store-and-forward deadlock," IEEE Trans. Commun., vol. COM-28, pp. 345–354, Mar. 1980.

[10] F. P. Preparata and J. E. Vuillemin, "The cube-connected cycles: A versatile network for parallel computation," in Proc. 20th IEEE Symp. Foundations Comput. Sci., pp. 140–147.

[11] C. L. Seitz, "The cosmic cube," CACM, vol. 28, pp. 22–33, Jan. 1985.

[12] C. Seitz et al., Wormhole Chip Project Report, Winter 1985.

[13] C. L. Seitz, W. C. Athas, W. J. Dally, R. Faucette, A. J. Martin, S. Mattisson, C. S. Steele, and W.-K. Su, Message-Passing Concurrent Computers: Their Architecture and Programming. Reading, MA: Addison-Wesley, 1986.

[14] H. S. Stone, "Parallel processing with the perfect shuffle," IEEE Trans. Comput., vol. C-20, pp. 153–161, Feb. 1971.

[15] H. Sullivan and T. R. Brashkow, "A large scale homogeneous machine," in Proc. 4th Annu. Symp. Comput. Architecture, 1977, pp. 105–124.

[16] A. S. Tanenbaum, Computer Networks. Englewood Cliffs, NJ: Prentice-Hall, 1981.

[17] S. Toueg and J. D. Ullman, "Deadlock-free packet switching networks," in Proc. 11th ACM Symp. Theory Comput., 1979, pp. 89–98.

[18] S. Toueg, "Deadlock- and livelock-free packet switching networks," in Proc. 12th ACM Symp. Theory Comput., 1980, pp. 94–99.

William J. Dally (S'78–M'80) received the B.S. degree in electrical engineering from Virginia Polytechnic Institute, Blacksburg, in 1980, the M.S. degree in electrical engineering from Stanford University, Stanford, CA, in 1981, and the Ph.D degree in computer science from California Institute of Technology, Pasadena, in 1986.

From 1980 to 1982 he worked at Bell Telephone Laboratories where he contributed to the design of the BELLMAC-32 microprocessor. From 1982 to 1983 he worked as a consultant in the area of digital systems design. From 1983 to 1986 he was a Research Assistant and then a Research Fellow at Caltech. He is currently an Assistant Professor of Computer Science at the Massachusetts Institute of Technology, Cambridge. His research interests include concurrent computing, computer architecture, computer-aided design, and VLSI design.

Charles L. Seitz (S'68–M'69–M'82) received the B.S., M.S., and Ph.D. degrees from the Massachusetts Institute of Technology, Cambridge.

He is now a Professor of Computer Science at the California Institute of Technology, Pasadena, where his research and teaching activities are in the areas of VLSI architecture and design, concurrent computation, and self-timed systems. Prior to joining the Caltech faculty, he worked as a Consultant to Burroughs Corporation from 1972 to 1977, was an Assistant Professor of Computer Science at the University of Utah from 1970 to 1972, and was a member of the Technical Staff of the Evans and Sutherland Computer Corporation from 1969 to 1971. While at the Massachusetts Institute of Technology, he was an Instructor in Electrical Engineering.

Dr. Seitz is a member of the Association for Computing Machinery.

An Adaptive and Fault Tolerant Wormhole Routing Strategy for *k*-ary *n*-cubes

Daniel H. Linder, *Member, IEEE,* and Jim C. Harden, *Member, IEEE*

Abstract—The concept of virtual channels is extended to multiple, virtual communication systems that provide adaptability and fault tolerance in addition to being deadlock-free. A channel dependency graph is taken as the definition of what connections are possible and any routing function must use only those connections defined by it. Virtual interconnection networks allowing adaptive, deadlock-free routing are examined for three *k*-ary *n*-cube topologies: unidirectional, torus-connected bidirectional, and mesh-connected bidirectional.

Index Terms—Adaptive routing, concurrent computing, deadlock, fault-tolerant computing, message passing architecture, virtual channels, virtual networks, wormhole routing.

I. Introduction

THE interest in highly concurrent computers has led to much research in message passing architectures. Since shared memory is not used for communication in these architectures, the potential exists for scaling them to tens of thousands of processors [1], [2]. Instead of shared memory, all interprocessor communication occurs over high performance data channels linking the processors or *nodes*. Each node is a complete computer with its own local memory. Ideally, the communication system should allow messages to be quickly sent between any pair of nodes. The closer the system is to this ideal, the less cognizant the software need be of the actual topology of the channels. A direct channel between each pair of nodes would permit the fastest communication, but the cost would be prohibitive for large computers. A compromise topology is generally chosen with channels only between certain pairs of nodes. However, messages are then forced to travel through intermediate nodes to reach their destination. This concession can lead to a condition called deadlock.

Intuitively, deadlock occurs when messages traveling in the communication system develop *dependency loops* among themselves that prevent further movement. The possibility of deadlock is introduced when a message must travel through intermediate nodes because some portion of the message must always be stored at these nodes. Since this storage is finite, it may become filled. When this happens, new messages cannot enter the node until old messages start to leave.

Store-and-forward and *wormhole* routing are the two common message routing methods, and each uses different approaches to eliminate deadlock [3]–[6]. In store-and-forward routing, a message is treated as a packet that is transferred as a whole between each node along its path. Deadlock can be prevented if a pool of buffers is provided that is properly structured, but the

number of buffers necessary to maintain this structure tends to grow with the size of the network. This is not desirable for a computer with thousands of nodes.

With wormhole routing, a message is decomposed into words or *flits* (flow control digits), and the flits of one message may be spread out among several nodes as the message moves. The conceptual model for the communications portion of a node is a set of queues—one for each input channel. Instead of one channel dumping a message into a buffer and that buffer being emptied into another channel, the queue of an input channel is connected to an output channel, and the message flits flow through the connection until the entire message has passed. Then the connection can be broken and other connections made. Deadlock can be prevented by restricting the combinations in which the input and output channels are connected. Only wormhole routing is examined in this paper since the nodal storage requirements (i.e., number of queues) grows with the number of input and output channels and not the total number of nodes in the system. Also, if the message traffic is not heavy, the *message latency* (time spent in transit) is less due to the inherent pipelining effect when the flits are spread over several nodes.

Restricting the input channel connections can prevent deadlock for wormhole routing, but this has the undesirable effect of restricting the paths that a message can take between a particular pair of nodes. If a communication system can send messages along alternate paths between the same pair of nodes, it is called *adaptable*. An adaptable system has two distinct advantages: 1) if one path is crowded with message traffic, another path can be taken to reduce message latency, and 2) if one path has a faulty node, another path can be taken to preserve communication. Previous wormhole routing schemes have restricted message traffic to a single path between any pair of nodes [6]. The purpose of this paper is to present simple, deadlock-free, adaptable, and fault-tolerant wormhole routing techniques for a popular topology—the *k*-ary *n*-cube.

The *k*-ary *n*-cube topology has been used in several significant computers like the Cosmic Cube and the Connection Machine [2], [8], and has proven to be useful for general purpose processing. High radix (high *k*), low dimensional (low *n*) cubes are especially easy to construct and scale, and they exhibit low message latencies for important physical field simulations like CFD (computational fluid dynamics) [9]. There are three basic types of *k*-ary *n*-cube: 1) unidirectional, 2) torus-connected bidirectional, and 3) mesh-connected bidirectional. Examples of all three forms will be shown later as each is studied.

II. Virtual Communication Systems for *k*-ary *n*-cubes

As discussed earlier, the wormhole routing technique associates a queue with each communication channel. Let a physical channel be the actual interconnect between a pair of nodes. If only one queue is used for each physical channel, a unidirectional

Manuscript received May 16, 1988; revised February 15, 1989. This work was supported by the Defense Advanced Research Projects Agency under Contract DAAA15-86-K-0025, monitored by the Department of the Army. Additional support was provided by grants from Sun Microsystems, Inc.

The authors are with the Department of Electrical Engineering, Mississippi State University, Mississippi State, MS 39762.

IEEE Log Number 9040678.

Reprinted from *IEEE Trans. Computers,* Vol. 40, No. 1, Jan. 1991, pp. 2-12. Copyright © 1991 by The Institute of Electrical and Electronics Engineers, Inc. All rights reserved.

k-ary n-cube will not be deadlock-free regardless of how the input to output channel connections are restricted at each node. Although a mesh-connected k-ary n-cube can be made deadlock-free using only one queue for each physical channel, messages are constrained to travel through each dimension in a defined order. This allows for only one message path between each pair of nodes and provides no adaptability. To free the communication system from the constraints of a fixed physical topology, the concept of a *virtual network* is introduced.

Previous investigators have shown how *virtual channels* can be used to avoid deadlock in unidirectional k-ary n-cubes as well as a variety of other topologies [6]. Virtual channels are logical abstractions that share the same physical channel. Even though they are time multiplexed over a single physical channel, a separate queue must be maintained in the node for each virtual channel. This concept is extended here to multiple, virtual communication systems that provide adaptability and fault tolerance in addition to being deadlock-free.

Fig. 1 illustrates the concept of virtual communication systems underlying a single physical communication system. There is a mapping from the virtual nodes and channels to the physical nodes and channels although it is not necessarily one-to-one. The only restriction on the mapping is that nodes adjacent in the virtual systems map to nodes adjacent in the physical system. All virtual channels that map to a single physical channel are time multiplexed over the physical channel. The remainder of this paper will focus on describing various virtual communication systems for k-ary n-cubes. Some definitions are required, though, before precise descriptions can be given (several definitions are based closely on the work in [6]).

Definition 1: A *physical interconnection network*, PI, is a strongly connected directed graph, $\text{PI} = \text{PG}(\text{PN}, \text{PC})$. PN is a set of nodes representing processors, and PC is a set of edges representing actual physical channels connecting the processors. Let pn_i and pc_i be the ith node and channel, respectively. Also, the source node of pc_i is ps_i and the destination node is pd_i. Later the simple i subscripts will be expanded into several integers to indicate the relationships between nodes and channels.

Definition 2: A *virtual interconnection network*, VI_i, is a directed graph, $\text{VI}_i = \text{VG}_i(\text{VN}_i, \text{VC}_i)$. The subscript i is used because a single physical interconnection network could have several virtual interconnection networks mapped to it. VN_i is a set of virtual nodes that are mapped to PN by the function nmap: $\text{VN}_i \rightarrow \text{PN}$. VC_i is a set of edges representing virtual channels that are mapped to PC by the function cmap: $\text{VC}_i \rightarrow \text{PC}$. Let vc_{ij} be the jth virtual channel in the ith virtual interconnection network. Associated with each virtual channel, vc_{ij}, is a queue vq_{ij}. Also, the source node of vc_{ij} is vs_{ij} and the destination node is vd_{ij}. Later the simple i and j subscripts will be expanded into several integers to indicate the relationships between nodes and channels.

Definition 3: A *connection* exists from channel vc_{ij} to vc_{ik} if the flit at the head of vq_{ij} will be transferred to the tail of vq_{ik} when the space in vq_{ik} becomes available.

Definition 4: A *channel dependency graph*, D_i, for the virtual interconnection network VI_i is a graph $D_i = G_i(\text{VC}_i, E_i)$ where $E_i = \{(\text{vc}_{ij}, \text{vc}_{ik}) \mid \text{a connection can exist from } \text{vc}_{ij} \text{ to } \text{vc}_{ik}\}$. Thus, D_i is a graph with a node for every channel in VI_i and edges to define what connections can be made between the channels. A channel is not allowed to connect to itself, so there will be no 1-cycles in D_i.

Definition 5: A *routing function* $R_i : \text{VC}_{ij} \times \{\text{all possible states of } \text{VI}_i\} \rightarrow \text{VC}_{ik}$ for a virtual interconnection network VI_i maps a channel vc_{ij} and the present state of VI_i to another channel vc_{ik}. When the first flits of a message arrive at the head of some channel queue, vq_{ij}, the routing function determines the channel, vc_{ik}, that vc_{ij} should be connected to so that the flits in vq_{ij} can advance (possibly indirectly) toward their destination. The state of the network can encompass varying quantities of information about the network depending on how "smart" the routing should be. Simple routing may only care about the destination of the message in vq_{ij} while more complex routing may need to know the entire configuration of VI_i or even how long a message has traveled in the network and what its path was. Note that the definition of the routing function could be relaxed some to allow it to specify a set of channels where the channel finally taken would be the first one to become free. However, from the standpoint of deadlock, we must consider the worst case where a message can only go to a particular channel next.

Definitions 4 and 5 represent a subtle difference between the treatment given in this paper and earlier research. Previously, a routing function was defined for a virtual interconnection network, and then a channel dependency graph was derived from this routing function by using it as an implicit definition of all possible channel connections. In contrast, we take the channel dependency graph as the definition of what connections are possible, and any routing functions developed for the network are restricted to use only those connections. This approach highlights a separation between the structure of the virtual interconnection networks and the adaptive routing algorithms that indicate how messages will travel. Thus, instead of showing each new routing function is deadlock-free, the virtual interconnection network is shown to be deadlock-free for a given channel dependency graph, and then new routing functions are shown to obey the restrictions of the channel dependency graph. To illustrate these concepts, an analogy can be drawn between virtual interconnection networks and traffic systems. The virtual interconnection network is a map that tells what channels (roads) exist, and the channel dependency graph tells what connections (turns) are legal. Then, if all messages (cars) obey these restrictions and the restrictions were properly developed, no deadlock (accidents) should occur. A routing function (the driver) just guides a message from node A to node B while obeying all restrictions.

Deadlock results from flits waiting for other flits to move. If one flit is forced to wait on another to move, its motion is dependent on the motion of the other flit. That is why D_i, which specifies channel connections, is called a channel *dependency* graph. If a connection is possible from vc_{ij} to vc_{ik}, then the motion of flits in vc_{ij} may be dependent on the motion of flits in vc_{ik}. It is important that once VI_i is proven to be deadlock-free based on D_i, no other additional dependencies are introduced. These could result from the multiplexing of several virtual channels over a single physical channel. If queue space becomes available in channel vc_{ik} where $\text{vc}_{ik} = R_i(\text{vc}_{ij}, \text{state of } \text{VI}_i)$, then a flit at the head of vq_{ij} must be allowed to cross the physical channel $\text{cmap}(\text{vc}_{ik})$ within a finite time regardless of the flit traffic on any other virtual channel mapped to $\text{cmap}(\text{vc}_{ik})$. It is permissible to slow flits down while other flits finish transferring, but making a flit wait until other flits on different virtual networks have found queue space will create an additional dependency that may produce deadlock.

It was shown in [6] that deadlock is impossible if the channel dependency graph is acyclic (of course, in [6] it was proven that a *routing function* was deadlock free and not a *virtual network* but the same proof would apply). This result will be used in the

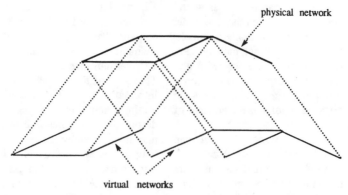

physical network

virtual networks

Fig. 1. Multiple virtual networks underlying a single physical network.

following sections to show that the proposed virtual networks are deadlock-free.

Before discussing the details of different interconnection networks, it is necessary to define two convenience functions. First, $\mathrm{mod}_k(\text{expression})$ is equal to the value of the expression calculated with modulo k arithmetic. Second, $\mathrm{dig}(N, d)$ is equal to the dth digit of N. For example, $\mathrm{mod}_4(2 + 3) = 1$, $\mathrm{mod}_4(2 - 3) = 3$, $\mathrm{dig}(567, 0) = 7$, and $\mathrm{dig}(567, 2) = 5$.

A. Unidirectional k-ary n-cubes

There is only one channel between adjacent nodes in a unidirectional k-ary n-cube. The physical interconnection network for a 4-ary 2-cube is shown in Fig. 2. The physical nodes are identified by a label pn_N (i has been replaced with a single integer N) where N is the *node position*. It is an n digit, radix k integer that indicates the node's position in each dimension, i.e., $\mathrm{dig}(N, d)$ is equal to the position of the node in dimension d.

The physical channels are identified by a label $\mathrm{pc}_{SC,\mathrm{DIM}}$ (i has been expanded into two integers) where SC is the node position N of the *physical source node of the channel*, i.e., the node where flits enter the channel. DIM is the *channel dimension*. This tells what dimension the channel lies in as it exits the node. That is, the node positions of nodes $\mathrm{ps}_{SC,\mathrm{DIM}}$ and $\mathrm{pd}_{SC,\mathrm{DIM}}$ differ in digit DIM. DIM is an integer with range 0 to $n-1$. The destination node of $\mathrm{pc}_{SC,\mathrm{DIM}}$ is $\mathrm{pd}_{SC,\mathrm{DIM}} = \mathrm{pn}_N$ where $\mathrm{dig}(N, \mathrm{DIM}) = \mathrm{mod}_k(\mathrm{dig}(SC, \mathrm{DIM}) - 1)$ and $\mathrm{dig}(N, d) = \mathrm{dig}(SC, d)$ for $d \neq \mathrm{DIM}$.

The end-around channels can lead to dependency loops and deadlock if only one queue is used per physical channel and message movement is unrestricted. This section describes a virtual interconnection network, UVI, for the unidirectional k-ary n-cube that is not only deadlock-free but also adaptable (UVI is substituted for the generic VI since several virtual interconnection networks are described in this paper).

The precise description of the virtual interconnection network has two components. First, the virtual topology will be defined by identifying the virtual nodes and channels that make up the network and specifying which nodes are the sources and destinations of each channel. For the unidirectional k-ary n-cube topology there will be only one virtual interconnection network mapped to the physical network so the i subscript used in the definitions of virtual objects will be dropped in this case. Second, the edges of the channel dependency graph will be listed to specify the connections that routing functions may use.

For any unidirectional k-ary n-cube, the virtual nodes in the single virtual interconnection network are identified by a label $\mathrm{vn}_{N,L}$ (i has been dropped, and j has been expanded into two

integers) where L is the *level number*. To eliminate deadlock due to the end-around connections, the physical network is split into multiple levels. Each time a flit travels through an end-around connection, it starts traveling in a new level (i.e., L is reduced by 1). L is an integer with a minimum range of 0 to n (this range is discussed shortly). Periodically moving to different sets of storage structures is reminiscent of previous store-and-forward buffer structuring methods [3]–[5]. A message always starts in a level $\geq m$ where m is the number of end-around channels it will move through. Each virtual node is mapped to the physical node with the same node position, i.e., $\mathrm{nmap}(\mathrm{vn}_{N,L}) = \mathrm{pn}_N$.

The virtual channels are identified by a label $\mathrm{vc}_{SC,\mathrm{DIM},L}$ (i has been dropped, and j has been expanded into three integers) where SC is the node position N of the *virtual source node of the channel*, i.e., the node where flits enter the channel. DIM is the *channel dimension*. This tells what dimension the channel lies in as it exits the node. That is, the node positions of nodes $\mathrm{vs}_{SC,\mathrm{DIM},L}$ and $\mathrm{vd}_{SC,\mathrm{DIM},L}$ differ in digit DIM. DIM is an integer with range 0 to $n-1$. The destination node of $\mathrm{vc}_{SC,\mathrm{DIM},L}$ is

$$\mathrm{vd}_{SC,\mathrm{DIM},L}$$
$$= \begin{cases} \mathrm{vn}_{N,L} & \text{if } \mathrm{vc}_{SC,\mathrm{DIM},L} \text{ is not an end-around channel} \\ \mathrm{vn}_{N,L-1} & \text{if } \mathrm{vc}_{SC,\mathrm{DIM},L} \text{ is an end-around channel} \end{cases}$$

where $\mathrm{dig}(N, \mathrm{DIM}) = \mathrm{mod}_k(\mathrm{dig}(SC, \mathrm{DIM}) - 1)$ and $\mathrm{dig}(N, d) = \mathrm{dig}(SC, d)$ for $d \neq \mathrm{DIM}$. Note that $\mathrm{vc}_{SC,\mathrm{DIM},L}$ is an end-around channel if $\mathrm{dig}(SC, \mathrm{DIM}) = 0$. Also, each virtual channel is mapped to the physical channel that is between the same nodes, i.e., $\mathrm{cmap}(\mathrm{vc}_{SC,\mathrm{DIM},L}) = \mathrm{pc}_{SC,\mathrm{DIM}}$.

Fig. 3 shows the virtual interconnection network for a 4-ary 2-cube. The number of levels depends on how many times a message might need to travel through end-around channels for a given routing function. The minimum number of levels for a message to be able to travel between any pair of nodes is $n+1$. For example, a message traveling from pn_{00} to pn_{11} travels through two end-around channels and thus, needs two extra levels in addition to the starting level.

The set of edges E in the channel dependency graph D is

$$E = \{(\mathrm{vc}_{SC1,\mathrm{DIM1},L1}, \mathrm{vc}_{SC2,\mathrm{DIM2},L2}) \mid \mathrm{vd}_{SC1,\mathrm{DIM1},L1}$$
$$= \mathrm{vs}_{SC2,\mathrm{DIM2},L2}\}.$$

That is, any channel with destination virtual node A can be connected to any channel with source virtual node A.

Note that the definition of the channel dependency graph is very simple only because the previous discussion has developed the concept of virtual nodes. Theoretically, virtual nodes could

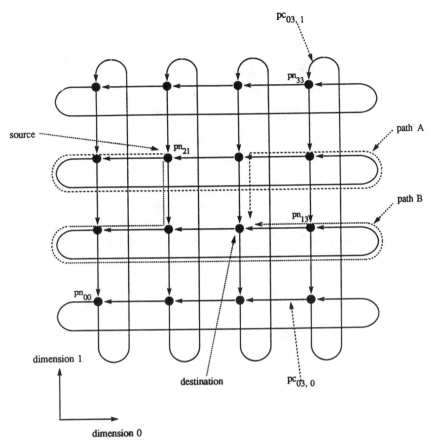

Fig. 2. Physical interconnection network for a unidirectional 4-ary 2-cube.

be eliminated leaving only virtual channels. The virtual channels would be defined by giving them distinct labels and mapping them to appropriate physical channels. Then the channel dependency graph would have the expanded task of defining the possible connections for this mass of channels so that the levels would be implied. We believe, however, that introducing virtual nodes as an intermediate step allows easier visualization of message traffic and thus aids the understanding and development of virtual topologies. It is the channel dependency graph, however, that gives the virtual nodes meaning and forces the additional constraints needed for the more complex systems to follow.

Before a virtual interconnection network with its associated channel dependency graph can be of any use, it must be shown to be deadlock-free.

Assertion 1: The virtual interconnection network, UVI, with its associated channel dependency graph D defined for a unidirectional k-ary n-cube is deadlock-free.

Proof: To show that UVI is deadlock-free, it must be proven that D has no cycles. By definition, D has no 1-cycles. It can be shown that if a number x can be assigned to each node in a graph such that an edge from node A to node B implies $x_A > x_B$, then the graph is acyclic [10]. Assign the number

$$x_{\text{SC,DIM},L} = (L \times k^n) + \sum_{i=0}^{n-1} [\text{dig}(\text{SC}, i) \times k^i]$$

to virtual channel $\text{vc}_{\text{SC,DIM},L}$. Now if $(\text{vc}_{\text{SC1,DIM1},L1}, \text{vc}_{\text{SC2,DIM2},L2})$ is an element of E, then there are two possible cases for the numbers assigned to these channels.

1) If $\text{vc}_{\text{SC1,DIM1},L1}$ is not an end-around channel, then $L2 = L1$ and $\text{dig}(\text{SC2, DIM1}) = \text{dig}(\text{SC1, DIM1}) - 1$. Thus,

$x_{\text{SC1,DIM1},L1} > x_{\text{SC2,DIM2},L2}$ since the summation is reduced by k^{DIM1}.

2) If $\text{vc}_{\text{SC1,DIM1},L1}$ is an end-around channel, then $L2 = L1 - 1$ and $\text{dig}(\text{SC2, DIM1}) = k - 1$. Thus, $x_{\text{SC1,DIM1},L1} > x_{\text{SC2,DIM2},L2}$ since $x_{\text{SC2,DIM2},L2}$ is increased by $(k-1)^{\text{DIM1}}$ but it is decreased by $k^n > (k-1)^n \geq (k-1)^{\text{DIM1}}$.

Either case yields $x_{\text{SC1,DIM1},L1} > x_{\text{SC2,DIM2},L2}$ so D is acyclic, and thus, UVI is deadlock-free. □

The key feature of UVI is the adaptability it provides for the physical network. Previous schemes have forced messages to move through the dimensions in a fixed order. Since, in UVI, a flit can exit a virtual node in any dimension, a message can move through dimensions at will. Fig. 2 shows a message taking two different paths, A and B, in the physical interconnection network. Fig. 3 illustrates this motion in UVI. These two paths are called *shortest paths* since they use the least number of channels in moving between the two nodes. UVI allows messages to take *any* shortest path between two nodes. However, a message can also take other paths as long as the number of end-around channels it travels through does not exceed the number of levels in UVI minus one. If very convoluted paths are desirable, then more levels can be added.

B. Torus-Connected Bidirectional k-ary n-cubes

There are two channels between adjacent nodes in a bidirectional k-ary n-cube—one for each direction. A bidirectional cube can take advantage of locality of communication. If two adjacent nodes need to exchange messages, the path is only one channel

355

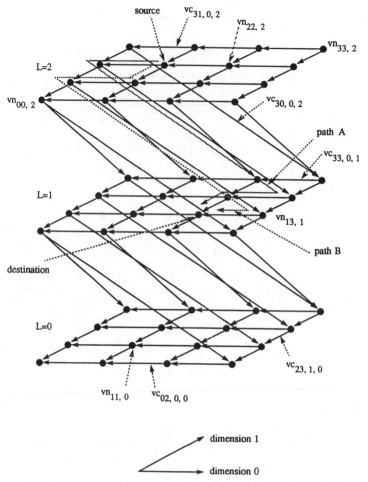

Fig. 3. Virtual interconnection network, UVI, for a unidirectional 4-ary 2-cube.

long for both messages. In a unidirectional cube, however, one path would be $k-1$ channels long. For bidirectional cubes, the end-around channels are not essential. If they are present, the cube is called torus connected, and if not, it is called mesh connected. It will be shown in Section II-C that eliminating the end-around channels greatly simplifies the virtual interconnection networks. The physical interconnection network for a torus-connected 4-ary 2-cube is shown in Fig. 4. The physical nodes are identified by a label pn_N (i has been replaced with a single integer N) where N is the same *node position* defined earlier.

The physical channels are identified by a label $pc_{SC,DIM,DIR}$ (i has been expanded into three integers) where DIR is the *channel direction*. DIR is 0 if the channel is in the direction of decreasing subscripts and 1 if the channel is in the direction of the increasing subscripts. The next equation states this more precisely. The destination node of $pc_{SC,DIM,DIR}$ is $pd_{SC,DIM,DIR} = pn_N$ where

$$\text{dig}(N, \text{DIM}) = \begin{cases} \text{mod}_k(\text{dig}(SC, \text{DIM}) - 1) & \text{if DIR} = 0 \\ \text{mod}_k(\text{dig}(SC, \text{DIM}) + 1) & \text{if DIR} = 1 \end{cases}$$

$$(1)$$

and $\text{dig}(N, d) = \text{dig}(SC, d)$ for $d \neq \text{DIM}$.

For this topology, there will be several virtual interconnection networks mapped to the physical network. Thus, the i subscript used in the definitions of virtual objects will not be dropped. Instead, i will be represented by an $n-1$ digit, binary integer VN which is called the *virtual network* of the object. VN is

defined as

$$\text{dig}(\text{VN}, d) = \begin{cases} 0 & \text{if the channels in dimension } d+1 \text{ of this} \\ & \text{network point exclusively in the direction} \\ & \text{of decreasing subscripts} \\ 1 & \text{if the channels in dimension } d+1 \text{ of this} \\ & \text{network point exclusively in the direction} \\ & \text{of increasing subscripts.} \end{cases}$$

That is, there will be 2^{n-1} virtual networks for a torus-connected k-ary n-cube identified by TVI_{VN} and each will have different restrictions on the directions of its channels. Levels will also be used here because the end-around channels are still present, but the bidirectional nature of the physical network presents a new source of the dependency loops—multidimensional loops. To eliminate this problem, we will split the bidirectional network into several virtual networks that are very similar to the unidirectional networks examined in Section II-A. Each network will have channels in only one direction in $n-1$ dimensions and both directions in the 0th dimension. Allowing the 0th dimension to be bidirectional while the rest are unidirectional will complicate our analysis, but it does result in reducing the number of virtual networks by half.

A message will use a particular network depending on where it wishes to go. For example, if the source node of a message traveling in a 5-ary 3-cube were at position 114 and the destination node were at position 341, the message would use the virtual network identified with VN = 10. That is, the message would want to move in the direction of increasing subscripts

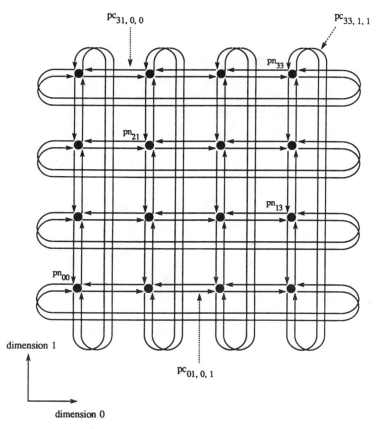

Fig. 4. Physical interconnection network for a torus-connected bidirectional 4-ary 2-cube.

(i.e., $1 \rightarrow 2 \rightarrow 3$) for dimension 2 (hence, $\mathrm{dig}(\mathrm{VN}, 1) = 1$ and the direction of decreasing subscripts (i.e., $1 \rightarrow 0 \rightarrow 4$) for dimension 1 (hence, $\mathrm{dig}(\mathrm{VN}, 0) = 0$.

For any torus-connected bidirectional k-ary n-cube, the virtual nodes in the virtual interconnection network $\mathrm{TVN}_{\mathrm{VN}}$ are identified by a label $\mathrm{vn}_{\mathrm{VN},N,L}$ (j has been expanded into two integers) where VN is the *virtual network* described above. Each virtual node is mapped to the physical node with the same node position, i.e., $\mathrm{nmap}(\mathrm{vn}_{\mathrm{VN},N,L}) = \mathrm{pn}_N$.

The virtual channels are identified by a label $\mathrm{vc}_{\mathrm{VN},\mathrm{SC},\mathrm{DIM},L,\mathrm{DIR}}$ (j has been expanded into four integers) where DIR is the *channel direction*. DIR is defined as

$$\mathrm{DIR} = \begin{cases} 0 & \text{if } \mathrm{DIM} \neq 0 \\ 0 & \text{if } \mathrm{DIM} = 0 \text{ and the channel points in the} \\ & \text{direction of decreasing subscripts} \\ 1 & \text{if } \mathrm{DIM} = 0 \text{ and the channel points in the} \\ & \text{direction of increasing subscripts.} \end{cases} \quad (2)$$

Thus, DIR has no meaning outside dimension 0 since these dimensions are unidirectional. In dimension 0, however, there are two channels originating at each node and they point in opposite directions. The destination node of $\mathrm{vc}_{\mathrm{VN},\mathrm{SC},\mathrm{DIM},L,\mathrm{DIR}}$ is

$$\mathrm{vd}_{\mathrm{VN},\mathrm{SC},\mathrm{DIM},L,\mathrm{DIR}} = \begin{cases} \mathrm{vn}_{\mathrm{VN},N,L} & \text{if } \mathrm{vc}_{\mathrm{VN},\mathrm{SC},\mathrm{DIM},L,\mathrm{DIR}} \text{ is} \\ & \text{not an end-around} \\ & \text{channel} \\ \mathrm{vn}_{\mathrm{VN},N,L-1} & \text{if } \mathrm{vc}_{\mathrm{VN},\mathrm{SC},\mathrm{DIM},L,\mathrm{DIR}} \text{ is} \\ & \text{an end-around channel} \end{cases}$$

where

$$\mathrm{dig}(N, \mathrm{DIM})$$

$$= \begin{cases} \mathrm{mod}_k(\mathrm{dig}(\mathrm{SC},\mathrm{DIM}) & \text{if } (\mathrm{DIM} \neq 0 \wedge \\ \quad -1) & \quad \mathrm{dig}(\mathrm{VN},\mathrm{DIM}-1)=0) \\ & \quad \vee (\mathrm{DIM}=0 \wedge \mathrm{DIR}=0) \\ \mathrm{mod}_k(\mathrm{dig}(\mathrm{SC},\mathrm{DIM}) & \text{if } (\mathrm{DIM} \neq 0 \wedge \\ \quad +1) & \quad \mathrm{dig}(\mathrm{VN},\mathrm{DIM}-1)=1) \\ & \quad \vee (\mathrm{DIM}=0 \wedge \mathrm{DIR}=1) \end{cases}$$

$$(3)$$

and $\mathrm{dig}(N, d) = \mathrm{dig}(\mathrm{SC}, d)$ for $d \neq \mathrm{DIM}$. Note that $\mathrm{vc}_{\mathrm{VN},\mathrm{SC},\mathrm{DIM},L,\mathrm{DIR}}$ is an end-around channel if it points in the direction of increasing subscripts and $\mathrm{dig}(\mathrm{SC},\mathrm{DIM}) = k - 1$ or it points in the direction of decreasing subscripts and $\mathrm{dig}(\mathrm{SC},\mathrm{DIM}) = 0$. Also, each virtual channel is mapped to the physical channel that is between the same nodes, i.e.,

$$\mathrm{cmap}(\mathrm{vc}_{\mathrm{VN},\mathrm{SC},\mathrm{DIM},L,\mathrm{DIR}})$$
$$= \begin{cases} \mathrm{pc}_{\mathrm{SC},\mathrm{DIM},\mathrm{DIR}} & \text{if } \mathrm{DIM} = 0 \\ \mathrm{pc}_{\mathrm{SC},\mathrm{DIM},\mathrm{dig}(\mathrm{VN},\mathrm{DIM}-1)} & \text{if } \mathrm{DIM} \neq 0. \end{cases} \quad (4)$$

Note that these equations show that the virtual interconnection networks, $\mathrm{TVI}_{\mathrm{VI}}$, are completely separate, i.e., have no channels in common. Thus, they can be treated separately for deadlock analysis.

Fig. 5 shows the two virtual interconnection networks, TVI_1 and TVI_0, for a 4-ary 2-cube. Again, the number of levels depends on how many times a message might need to travel through end-around channels for a given routing function (the minimum number of levels is $n + 1$).

The set of edges E_{VN} in the channel dependency graph D_{VN} for $\mathrm{TVI}_{\mathrm{VN}}$ is

$$E_{\mathrm{VN}} = \{(\mathrm{vc}_{\mathrm{VN},\mathrm{SC}1,\mathrm{DIM}1,L1,\mathrm{DIR}1}, \mathrm{vc}_{\mathrm{VN},\mathrm{SC}2,\mathrm{DIM}2,L2,\mathrm{DIR}2}) \mid$$
$$\mathrm{vd}_{\mathrm{VN},\mathrm{SC}1,\mathrm{DIM}1,L1,\mathrm{DIR}1}$$

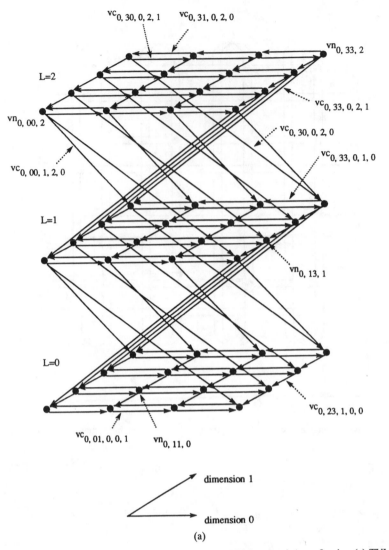

$vc_{0, 30, 0, 2, 1}$ $vc_{0, 31, 0, 2, 0}$

$vn_{0, 33, 2}$

L=2

$vn_{0, 00, 2}$

$vc_{0, 33, 0, 2, 1}$

$vc_{0, 00, 1, 2, 0}$

$vc_{0, 30, 0, 2, 0}$

$vc_{0, 33, 0, 1, 0}$

L=1

$vn_{0, 13, 1}$

L=0

$vc_{0, 23, 1, 0, 0}$

$vc_{0, 01, 0, 0, 1}$ $vn_{0, 11, 0}$

dimension 1

dimension 0

(a)

Fig. 5. Virtual interconnection network for a torus-connected bidirectional 4-ary 2-cube. (a) TVI_0. (b) TVI_1.

$$= vs_{VN, SC2, DIM2, L2, DIR2} \wedge$$
$$\text{if } DIM1 = DIM2 = 0 \text{ then } DIR1 = DIR2\}. \quad (5)$$

That is, any channel with destination virtual node A can be connected to any channel with source virtual node A with the restriction that the channels are not in opposite directions in dimension 0.

Assertion 2: The virtual interconnection network, TVI_{VN}, with its associated channel dependency graph D_{VN} defined for a torus-connected bidirectional k-ary n-cube is deadlock-free.

Proof: To show that TVI_{VN} is deadlock-free, it must be proven that D_{VN} has no cycles. By definition, D_{VN} has no 1-cycles. Following the proof used in assertion 1, assign the number

$$x_{VN, SC, DIM, L, DIR} = (L \times k^n)$$
$$+ \sum_{i=1}^{n-1} \begin{cases} \operatorname{dig}(SC, i) \times k^i & \text{if } \operatorname{dig}(VN, i-1) = 0 \\ [(k-1) - \operatorname{dig}(SC, i)] \times k^i & \text{if } \operatorname{dig}(VN, i-1) = 1 \end{cases}$$
$$+ \begin{cases} 0 & \text{if } DIM \neq 0 \\ \operatorname{dig}(SC, 0) \times 1 & \text{if } DIM = 0 \wedge DIR = 0 \\ [(k-1) - \operatorname{dig}(SC, 0)] \times 1 & \text{if } DIM = 0 \wedge DIR = 1 \end{cases}$$
$$(6)$$

to virtual channel $vc_{VN, SC, DIM, L, DIR}$. We have effectively defined new node position digits that always decrease in the direction of the channels. The only anomaly is that the 0th digit of the node position for channels not in dimension 0 is ignored. This is done because a channel in the 0th dimension must be able to enter a channel in another direction regardless of its position in the 0th dimension. Now, if $(vc_{VN, SC1, DIM1, L1, DIR1}, vc_{VN, SC2, DIM2, L2, DIR2})$ is an element of E_{VN}, there are several possible cases for the numbers assigned to these channels.

1) If $vc_{VN, SC1, DIM1, L1, DIR1}$ is not an end-around channel, then $L2 = L1$ and:

   a) If $(DIM1 \neq 0 \wedge \operatorname{dig}(VN, DIM1 - 1) = 0) \vee (DIM1 = DIM2 = 0 \wedge DIR1 = 0)$ then $\operatorname{dig}(SC2, DIM1) = \operatorname{dig}(SC1, DIM1) - 1$ which reduces the summation by k^{DIM1}. If the first channel is not in dimension 0 but the second is, there can also be a change in that part of the sum associated with the 0th digit of SC. However, the maximum increase would be $k - 1$ while the summation is reduced by $k^{DIM1} > k - 1$ if $DIM1 \neq 0$.

   b) If $(DIM \neq 0 \wedge \operatorname{dig}(VN, DIM1 - 1) = 1) \vee (DIM1 = DIM2 = 0 \wedge DIR1 = 1)$ then

358

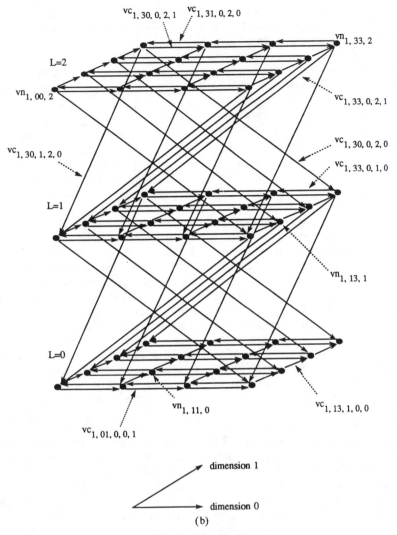

$vc_{1, 30, 0, 2, 1}$ $vc_{1, 31, 0, 2, 0}$

$vn_{1, 33, 2}$

L=2

$vn_{1, 00, 2}$

$vc_{1, 33, 0, 2, 1}$

$vc_{1, 30, 1, 2, 0}$

$vc_{1, 30, 0, 2, 0}$

$vc_{1, 33, 0, 1, 0}$

L=1

$vn_{1, 13, 1}$

L=0

$vn_{1, 11, 0}$

$vc_{1, 13, 1, 0, 0}$

$vc_{1, 01, 0, 0, 1}$

dimension 1

dimension 0

(b)

Fig. 5. (*Continued*)

$\mathrm{dig}(SC2, DIM1) = \mathrm{dig}(SC1, DIM1)+1$. Thus, $[(k-1)-\mathrm{dig}(SC1, DIM1)]-\{(k-1)-[\mathrm{dig}(SC1, DIM1)+1]\} = 1$ which reduces the summation by k^{DIM1}. If the first channel is not in dimension 0 but the second is, there can also be a change in that part of the sum associated with the 0th digit of SC. However, the maximum increase would be $k - 1$ while the summation is reduced by $k^{DIM1} > k-1$ if $DIM1 \neq 0$.

c) If $(DIM1 = 0 \land DIM2 \neq 0)$ then the part of the sum associated with the 0th digit of SC is 0. This reduces the total sum by at least 1 since if $\mathrm{dig}(SC1,0) = 0$ then $DIR1 = 1$ and if $\mathrm{dig}(SC1,0) = k - 1$ then $DIR1 = 0$.

2) If $vc_{VN, SC1, DIM1, L1, DIR1}$ is an end-around channel, then $L2 = L1 - 1$ and:

a) If $(DIM1 \neq 0 \land \mathrm{dig}(VN, DIM1-1) = 0) \lor (DIM1 = DIM2 = 0 \land DIR1 = 0)$ then $\mathrm{dig}(SC2, DIM1) = k - 1$. Since $\mathrm{dig}(SC1, DIM1) = 0$, the summation is increased by $(k - 1)k^{DIM1}$. If the first channel is not in dimension 0 but the second is, there can also be a change in that part of the sum associated with the 0th digit of SC. However, the maximum increase would

be $k - 1$; so the total increase in x would be no more than $(k - 1)k^{DIM1} + k - 1$.

b) If $(DIM \neq 0 \land \mathrm{dig}(VN, DIM1-1) = 1) \lor (DIM1 = DIM2 = 0 \land DIR1 = 1)$ then $\mathrm{dig}(SC2, DIM1) = 0$. Since $\mathrm{dig}(SC1, DIM1) = k - 1$, the summation is still increased by $(k - 1)k^{DIM1}$. If the first channel is not in dimension 0 but the second is, there can also be a change in that part of the sum associated with the 0th digit of SC. However, the maximum increase would be $k - 1$; so the total increase in x would be no more than $(k - 1)k^{DIM1} + k - 1$.

c) If $(DIM1 = 0 \land DIM2 \neq 0)$ then the part of the sum associated with the 0th digit of SC is 0. This does not increase the total sum.

Thus, $x_{VN, SC1, DIM1, L1, DIR1} > x_{VN, SC2, DIM2, L2, DIR2}$ since $x_{VN, SC2, DIM2, L2, DIR2}$ is increased by at most $(k - 1)k^{DIM1} + k - 1$ but it is decreased by $k^n = (k - 1)k^{n-1} + k^{n-1} > (k - 1)k^{DIM1} + k - 1$ if $n > 1$. If $n = 1$, the additional $k - 1$ term would never be present and the inequality would still hold. All the cases yield $x_{VN, SC1, DIM1, L1, DIR1} > x_{VN, SC2, DIM2, L2, DIR2}$ so D_{VN} is acyclic, and thus, TVI_{VN} is deadlock-free. $\qquad\Box$

As with the UVI, the key feature of the TVI_{VN} virtual interconnection networks is the adaptability they provide for the physical network. Since, in TVI_{VN}, a flit can exit a virtual node in any dimension, a message can move through dimensions at will taking any shortest path (other paths can be taken as long as the number of end-around channels it travels through does not exceed the number of levels minus one). In addition, since all the networks are complete unidirectional k-ary n-cubes, a message can travel to its destination in any of the virtual networks although some will allow shorter paths than others.

C. Mesh-Connected Bidirectional k-ary n-cubes

A bidirectional k-ary n-cube in which the end-around channels have been eliminated is called mesh connected. Unfortunately, the penalty for removing the end-around channels is that the longest path a message might have to travel is doubled (i.e., the *diameter* of the network is doubled) and symmetry is lost resulting in unevenly distributed traffic. The physical interconnection network for a mesh-connected 4-ary 2-cube is identical to the network in Fig. 4 except that the end-around connections are dropped. The physical nodes and channels are identified in the same manner as for the torus-connected cube. The destination node of $\text{pc}_{\text{SC,DIM,DIR}}$ is $\text{pd}_{\text{SC,DIM,DIR}} = \text{pn}_N$ where $\text{dig}(N, \text{DIM})$ is defined the same as in (1) except that the modulo functions are dropped since there are no end-around channels.

For this topology, there will be 2^{n-1} virtual networks for a mesh-connected bidirectional k-ary n-cube identified by MVI_{VN} and each will have different restrictions on the directions of its channels. These different networks are required to eliminate multidimensional loops, but each network is simplified because no levels are required to break up loops resulting from end-around channels. A message will still use a particular network depending on where it wishes to go. For example, if the source node of a message traveling in a 5-ary 3-cube were at position 114 and the destination node were at position 341, the virtual network identified with VN = 11 would be used.

For any mesh-connected bidirectional k-ary n-cube, the virtual nodes in the virtual interconnection network MVI_{VN} are identified by a label $\text{vn}_{\text{VN},N}$. Each virtual node is mapped to the physical node with the same node position, i.e., $\text{nmap}(\text{vn}_{\text{VN},N}) = \text{pn}_N$. The virtual channels are identified by a label $\text{vn}_{\text{VN,SC,DIM,DIR}}$ (j has been expanded into three integers) where DIR is defined the same as in (2). The destination node of $\text{vc}_{\text{VN,SC,DIM,DIR}}$ is $\text{vd}_{\text{VN,SC,DIM,DIR}} = \text{vn}_{\text{VN},N}$ where $\text{dig}(N, \text{DIM})$ is defined the same as in (3) except the modulo functions are dropped. Also, each virtual channel is mapped to the physical channel that is between the same nodes, i.e., $\text{cmap}(\text{vc}_{\text{VN,SC,DIM,DIR}})$ is defined the same as in (4).

Fig. 6 shows the two virtual interconnection networks, MVI_1 and MVI_0, for a 4-ary 2-cube. Note that the lack of levels greatly reduces the number of virtual channels. The set of edges E_{VN} in the channel dependency graph D_{VN} for MVI_{VN} is the same as (5) except the L subscripts are dropped.

Assertion 3: The virtual interconnection network, MVI_{VN}, with its associated channel dependency graph D_{VN} defined for a mesh-connected bidirectional k-ary n-cube is deadlock-free.

Proof: To show that MVI_{VN} is deadlock-free, it must be proven that D_{VN} has no cycles. By definition, D_{VN} has no 1-cycles. Following the procedure used in the proof of Assertion 1, assign the number $x_{\text{VN,SC,DIM,DIR}}$ to virtual channel $\text{vc}_{\text{VN,SC,DIM,DIR}}$ where $x_{\text{VN,SC,DIM,DIR}}$ is defined as in (6) except the term as-

sociated with L is dropped. The proof that $x_{\text{VN,SC1,DIM1,DIR1}} > x_{\text{VN,SC2,DIM2,DIR2}}$ is identical to case 1 of the proof for Assertion 2.

III. Fault Tolerance

A message passing communication system is fault tolerant if failures in some nodes do not prevent other nodes from communicating. The adaptability afforded by multiple paths is the key to fault tolerance when a node is truly unusable (i.e., there are no redundant nodes that can be "switched" in to replace the failed node). It may be inconvenient, however, to have some "global" controller in a network that is aware of all faults. A simpler and more distributed system would allow a message to start out along any path to its destination and then, route around faulted nodes as they are encountered. This section will describe additions to the virtual interconnection networks detailed in previous sections that allow them to be tolerant of at least one faulty node.

Consider first the unidirectional k-ary n-cube. Suppose the first flit of a message is presently at a node pn_{N1} and the destination is pn_{N2}. If $N1$ and $N2$ differ in more than one digit, then there is more than one dimension in which the flit can leave pn_{N1} to move toward its destination, and if one is blocked by failure, another can be used. If $N1$ and $N2$ differ in only one dimension, say DIM1, and the channel in this dimension is blocked by a failure in the adjacent node, then the flit will have to temporarily move away from its destination. That is, it can travel through one channel in some other dimension, say DIM2, and then finish its movement in dimension DIM1. To get to its destination, all it has to do is completely traverse dimension DIM2 using an end-around channel. Note that the message was "unaware" when it started that it would have to make an extra movement through an end-around channel in DIM2 to avoid a failed node. Thus, another level should be added to UVI so that a message can make an end-around movement in every dimension plus one more for fault tolerance.

The same fault-avoidance method applies to torus-connected bidirectional k-ary n-cubes. There is an additional method, however, if the dimension that is blocked, DIM, is not dimension 0. In this case, the message can travel through one channel in dimension 0, complete its motion in DIM, and then reach its destination by moving in the opposite direction in dimension 0.

For the mesh-connected bidirectional k-ary n-cubes, if the blocked dimension, DIM, is not dimension 0 then the method just discussed for the torus-connected cube applies. However, when DIM = 0, there is no end-around channel in some other dimension to use. One solution is to make dimension 1 bidirectional with special virtual channels that are switched on only if there is a fault. Fig. 7 illustrates one of these special channels, vc_1, (only dimensions 0 and 1 are shown). They were not considered in the proof of Assertion 3, so the question of deadlock arises. There were no cycles in the channel dependency graph before the special channel vc_1 was added; so if there is a cycle after it is added, the cycle must involve vc_1. We assume the routing system will only allow two new connections involving $\text{vc}_1 : \text{vc}_2$ to vc_1 and vc_1 to vc_3. If there is a cycle, then vc_3 must connect to some channel that connects to others that eventually connect to vc_2. This is impossible since a channel in dimension 0 cannot connect to another channel in dimension 0 that is in the opposite direction. Thus, any attempt to get back to vc_2 would require a movement in some dimension other than dimension 0, and since these are all unidirectional, there is no way to return by moving in the opposite direction. By limiting which channels connect to vc_1, deadlock is avoided.

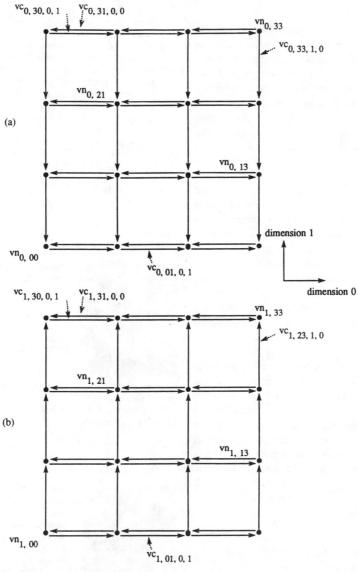

Fig. 6. Virtual interconnection network for a mesh-connected bidirectional 4-ary 2-cube. (a) MVI_0. (b) MVI_1.

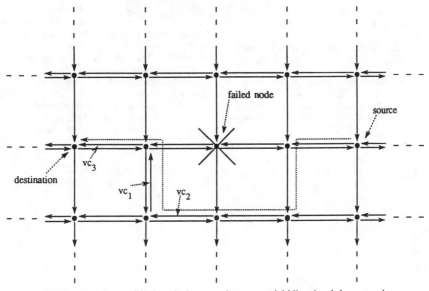

Fig. 7. Avoiding a failed node in a mesh-connected bidirectional k-ary n-cube.

IV. Conclusion

To escape the constraints of a fixed physical interconnection network, virtual interconnection networks can be created that are time multiplexed over the physical channels. Virtual interconnection networks have been described in this paper that provide for adaptability and fault tolerance. Other approaches to adaptability using an exchange model and prioritized messages are under development [12], [13]. These approaches are valid for general topologies but involve more complex decision processes. We believe that the virtual network scheme described here may lead to a simpler implementation for regular topologies like the k-ary n-cube.

Although the physical channels are shared by the virtual channels, virtual channels still have a cost in terms of queue space and switching mechanisms. The unidirectional k-ary n-cube cannot exploit locality of communication, so it is probably undesirable for most purposes. It was studied as an introduction to the more powerful, but complex bidirectional k-ary n-cube. With 2^{n-1} virtual interconnection networks, $n + 1$ levels per network, and k^n virtual channels per level for the bidirectional k-ary n-cube, the number of virtual channels rapidly increases with n. However, research has shown that low-dimensional cubes (i.e., $n = 2$ to 4) are likely to be the best networks for general purpose processing [13]. If the routing function and virtual queues were implemented in software, a bidirectional k-ary n-cube of low dimension would certainly be practical and would offer a great degree of adaptability and fault tolerance. The mesh-connected bidirectional k-ary n-cube, especially in two dimensions, costs very little and is probably best suited for hardware implementations of the routing function and virtual queues. Future research could involve the development of routing functions that examine the present state of the message traffic in the network and make optimum use of the adaptability and fault tolerance allowed by the virtual structures described in this paper.

References

[1] W. C. Athas and C. L. Seitz, "Multicomputers," Tech. Rep. 5244:TR:87, Dep. Comput. Sci., California Instit. Technol., 1987.
[2] C. L. Seitz, "The Cosmic Cube," *Commun. ACM,* vol. 28, pp. 22–23, Jan. 1985.
[3] I. S. Gopal, "Prevention of store and forward deadlock in computer networks," *IEEE Trans. Commun.,* vol. CO.,l-33, no. 12, pp. 1258–1264, Dec. 1985.
[4] K. D. Gunther, "Prevention of deadlocks in packet-switched data transport systems," *IEEE Trans. Comput.,* vol. C-29, no. 4, pp. 512–524, Apr. 1981.
[5] S. Toueg and J. D. Ullman, "Deadlock-free packet switching networks," *SIAM J. Comput.,* vol. 10, no. 3, pp. 594–611.
[6] W. J. Dally and C. L. Seitz, "Deadlock-free message routing in multiprocessor interconnection networks," *IEEE Trans. Comput.,* vol. C-36, no. 5, pp. 547–553, May 1987.
[7] *Submicron Systems Architecture Semiannual Technical Report,* Tech. Rep. 5235:TR:86, Dep. Comput. Sci., California Instit. Technol., 1986.
[8] W. D. Hillis, "The connection machine," *Scient. Amer.,* vol. 256, no. 6, pp. 108–115, June 1987.
[9] W. Welch, "Message-driven solver for Euler fluid dynamics equations," in *Proc. 1988 ACM Southeast Regional Conf.,* Apr. 1988.
[10] B. Carre', *Graphs and Networks.* Oxford, England: Clarendon, 1979, pp. 50–51.
[11] J. Blazewicz, J. Brzezniski, and G. Gambosi, "Time-stamp approach to store-and-forward deadlock prevention," *IEEE Trans. Commun.,* vol. COM-35, no. 5, pp. 490–495, May 1987.
[12] J. Y. Ngai and C. L. Seitz, "A framework for adaptive routing," Tech. Rep. 5246:TR:87, Dep. Comput. Sci., California Instit. Technol., 1987.
[13] W. J. Dally, *A VLSI Architecture for Concurrent Data Structures.* Boston, MA: Kluwer Academic, 1987, pp. 144–161.

Daniel H. Linder (M'89) was born in Baltimore, MD, on November 15, 1962. He received the B.S.E.E. and M.S.E.E. degrees from Mississippi State University, Mississippi State, in 1985 and 1987, respectively.

In 1988 he was employed in the aerospace processing group of Westinghouse, Baltimore, MD. He is presently a Research Engineer with the NSF Engineering Research Center for CFS at Mississippi State University. His research interests include concurrent computing, VLSI, and simulation.

Mr. Linder is a member of Phi Kappa Phi, Tau Beta Pi, and the IEEE Computer Society.

Jim C. Harden (S'82–M'85) was born in Cleveland, MS, on November 3, 1943. He received the B.S.E.E. degree from Mississippi State University, Mississippi State, in 1965, the M.S.E.E. degree from Georgia Institute of Technology, Atlanta, in 1966, and the Ph.D. degree in electrical engineering from Texas A&M University, College Station, in 1985.

Presently, he is an Associate Professor of Electrical Engineering at Mississippi State University. Prior to this appointment, he worked in the telemetry and data acquisition areas in industry, beginning in 1966 at Radiation (now Harris) and then at IBM Federal Systems Division, Huntsville, AL. Later as a founding member of Care Electronics (now Care Monitoring Systems) he was involved in the application of digital telemetric techniques to commercial cardiac monitoring. His current research interests include wafer scale integration, cellular computing structures, and real-time data acquisition systems.

Dr. Harden is a member of the IEEE Computer Society, Sigma Alpha Epsilon, Tau Beta Pi, and Eta Kappa Nu.

Optimum Broadcasting and Personalized Communication in Hypercubes

S. LENNART JOHNSSON MEMBER, IEEE, AND CHING-TIEN HO

Abstract—Effective utilization of communication resources is crucial for good overall performance in highly concurrent systems. In this paper, we address four different communication problems in Boolean n-cube configured multiprocessors: 1) one-to-all broadcasting: distribution of common data from a single source to all other nodes; 2) one-to-all personalized communication: a single node sending unique data to all other nodes; 3) all-to-all broadcasting: distribution of common data from each node to all other nodes; and 4) all-to-all personalized communication: each node sending a unique piece of information to every other node. Three new communication graphs for the Boolean n-cube are proposed for the routing, and scheduling disciplines provably optimum within a small constant factor are proposed. One of the new communication graphs consists of n edge-disjoint spanning binomial trees and offers optimal communication for case 1; a speedup with a factor of n over the spanning binomial tree for large data volumes. The other two new communication graphs are a balanced spanning tree and a graph composed of n rotated spanning binomial trees. With appropriate scheduling and concurrent communication on all ports of every processor, routings based on these two communication graphs offer a speedup of up to $n/2$, $n/2$, and $O(\sqrt{n})$ over the routings based on the spanning binomial tree for cases 2, 3, and 4, respectively. All three new spanning graphs offer optimal communication times for cases 2, 3, and 4 and concurrent communication on all ports of every processor. The graph consisting of n edge-disjoint spanning trees offers graceful degradation of performance under faulty conditions. Timing models and complexity analysis have been verified by experiments on a Boolean cube configured multiprocessor.

Index Terms—Balanced trees, Boolean cubes, broadcasting, binomial trees, multicast, personalized communication, routing.

I. INTRODUCTION

IN THIS paper, we investigate *broadcasting* and *personalized communication* on Boolean n-cube configured ensemble architectures. In *broadcasting*, a data set is copied from one node to all other nodes, or a subset thereof. In *personalized communication*, a node sends a unique data set to all other nodes, or a subset thereof. We consider broadcasting from a single source to all other nodes, *one-to-all broadcasting*, and concurrent broadcasting from all nodes to all other nodes, or *all-to-all broadcasting*. Broadcasting is used in a variety of linear algebra algorithms [10], [17], [19]

such as matrix–vector multiplication, matrix–matrix multiplication, LU-factorization, and Householder transformations. It is also used in database queries and transitive closure algorithms [4]. The reverse of the broadcasting operation is *reduction*, in which the data set is reduced by applying operators such as addition/subtraction or max/min.

For personalized communication, we consider *one-to-all personalized communication* and *all-to-all personalized communication*. Fundamentally, the difference between broadcasting and personalized communication is that in the latter no replication/reduction of data takes place. The bandwidth requirement is highest at the root and is reduced monotonically towards the leaves. Personalized communication is used, for instance in transposing a matrix, and the conversion between different data structures [17], [22]. Matrix transposition is useful in the solution of tridiagonal systems on Boolean cubes for certain combinations of machine characteristics [20], [23] and for matrix–vector and matrix–matrix [21] multiplications.

For single-source broadcasting and personalized communication, a *one-to-all communication graph* is required. Graphs of minimum height have minimum propagation time which is the overriding concern for small data volumes, or a high overhead for each communication action. For large data volumes, it is important to use the bandwidth of a Boolean cube effectively, in particular, if each processor is able to communicate on all its ports concurrently. We propose three new spanning graphs for Boolean n-cubes of $N = 2^n$ nodes: one consisting of n edge-disjoint binomial tree (nESBT); one that consists of n rotated spanning binomial trees (nRSBT); and one *balanced tree* (SBnT), i.e., a tree with fan-out n at the root and approximately N/n nodes in each subtree. We prove some of the critical topological properties of the new one-to-all communication graphs and compare them to Hamiltonian paths and binomial tree embeddings. For each of the communications we consider, we prove the lower bounds in Table I.

We generalize the one-to-all communication to all-to-all communications and study the interleaving of communications from different sources by defining *all-to-all communication graphs* as the union of *one-to-all communication graphs*. We define scheduling disciplines for the four different communications as follows: 1) *one-to-all broadcasting;* 2) *one-to-all personalized communication,* 3) *all-to-all broadcasting,* and 4) *all-to-all personalized communication.* We show that for communication restricted to one port at a time, our spanning binomial tree scheduling results in communication times within a factor of two of the best known lower bounds for communications 2, 3, and 4. For case 1, the

Manuscript received January 23, 1987; revised January 15, 1988. This work was supported in part by the Office of Naval Research under Contracts N00014-84-K-0043 and N00014-86-K-0564. This work was presented in part at the 1986 International Conference on Parallel Processing.

S. L. Johnsson is with the Department of Computer Science and Electrical Engineering, Yale University, New Haven, CT 06520 on leave at the Thinking Machine Corporation, Cambridge, MA 02142.

C.-T. Ho is with the Department of Computer Science, Yale University, New Haven, CT 06520.

IEEE Log Number 8928027.

TABLE I
LOWER BOUNDS FOR SOME BOOLEAN CUBE COMMUNICATIONS

Comm. model	Communication task	Lower bound
one-port	One-to-all broadcasting	$\max((M + n - 1)t_c, n\tau)$
	One-to-all personalized comm.	$\max((N - 1)Mt_c, n\tau)$
	All-to-all broadcasting	$\max((N - 1)Mt_c, n\tau)$
	All-to-all personalized comm.	$\max(\frac{nNM}{2}t_c, n\tau)$
n-port	One-to-all broadcasting	$\max((\frac{M}{n} + n - 1)t_c, n\tau)$
	One-to-all personalized comm.	$\max(\frac{(N-1)M}{n}t_c, n\tau)$
	All-to-all broadcasting	$\max(\frac{(N-1)M}{n}t_c, n\tau)$
	All-to-all personalized comm.	$\max(\frac{NM}{2}t_c, n\tau)$

scheduling we define for the n edge-disjoint spanning binomial trees completes within a factor of four of the best known lower bound, also for concurrent communication on all ports. For concurrent communication and *one-to-all personalized communication,* the schedules for both the n edge-disjoint and the rotated binomial trees are of optimal order, as are the schedules for the balanced graph. These graphs also yield *all-to-all* communication within a factor of two of the lower bound for arbitrary cube sizes and data volumes, except for the nESBT graph which allows optimum scheduling within a factor of 2 only asymptotically, Table XVI.

Communication in Boolean cubes has recently received significant interest due to the success of the Caltech Cosmic Cube project [30] and commercially available Boolean cube configured concurrent processors (from Intel, NCUBE [12], and Ametek, and cube-like architectures from Floating-Point Systems [11] and Thinking Machines Corporation [13]). Embedding of complete binary trees is treated in [33], [17], [29], [6], and [3]. Wu [33] also discusses the embedding of k-ary trees. Embedding of arbitrary binary trees is discussed in [3] and improved in [2]. Efficient routing using randomization for arbitrary permutations has been suggested by Valiant *et al.* [32]. Our algorithms attain a speedup of up to a factor of n for case 1 with *one-port* and *n-port* communication, and cases 2 and 4 with *n-port* communication over the best previously known algorithms [28]. For case 3 and *n-port* communication, the improvement is by a constant factor. Communication on hypercubes has also been studied independently by Fox and Furmanski [8] and Stout and Wager [31]. For case 1, the best algorithm in [8] is about a factor of two slower than the best algorithm presented here and in [14]. The best algorithm in [31] requires one less routing cycle. The nRSBT routing [24] for cases 2, 3, and 4 with *n-port* communication was discovered independently by Stout. However, the SBnT routing [14] described here performs better, or as well as the nRSBT routing. The nESBT routing degrades gracefully under faulty conditions. The analysis is compared to experimental data.

The outline of the paper is as follows. Notations, definitions, and general graph properties used throughout the paper are introduced in Section II. In Section III, one-to-all communication graphs are defined and characterized. Scheduling disciplines and associated complexity estimates are given in Section IV for *one-to-all broadcasting,* in Section V for *one-to-all personalized communication,* in Section VI for *all-to-all broadcasting,* and in Section VII for *all-to-all personalized communication.* Section VIII presents implementation results

for some of the communication algorithms on the Intel iPSC. Conclusion follows in Section IX.

II. PRELIMINARIES

In the following, node i has address $(i_{n-1}i_{n-2} \cdots i_0)$, and node s has address $(s_{n-1}s_{n-2} \cdots s_0)$. The bitwise Exclusive-OR operation is denoted $\oplus$, and throughout the paper $i \oplus s = c = (c_{n-1}c_{n-2} \cdots c_0)$ where $c_m = i_m \oplus s_m$. c is the *relative address* of node i with respect to node s. Address bits are numbered from 0 through $n - 1$ with the lowest order bit being the 0th bit. The mth bit corresponds to the mth dimension in a Boolean space. Caligraphic letters are used for sets. The set of *node* addresses is $\mathfrak{N} \equiv \{0, 1, \cdots, N - 1\}$, and the set of dimensions is $\mathfrak{D} \equiv \{0, 1, \cdots, n - 1\}$. $|\mathcal{S}|$ is used to denote the cardinality of a set $\mathcal{S}$. d or m is used to denote an arbitrary dimension, $d, m \in \mathfrak{D}$.

Definition 1: The *Hamming* distance between a pair of binary numbers, or nodes, i and j is $Hamming(i, j) = \sum_{m=0}^{n-1} (i_m \oplus j_m)$.

Definition 2: A *Boolean n-cube* is graph $B = (\mathcal{V}, \mathcal{E}^B)$ such that $\mathcal{V} = \mathfrak{N}$ and $\mathcal{E}^B = \{(i, j)|i \oplus j = 2^m, \forall m \in \mathfrak{D}, \forall i, j \in \mathfrak{N} \}$. An edge (i, j) such that $i \oplus j = 2^m$ is in dimension m, and nodes i and j are connected through the mth *port*.

An *edge* (i, j) is *directed* from node i to node j, and of unit length, i.e., $Hamming(i, j) = 1$. It is a $0 \to 1$ edge if the bit that differs in i and j is zero in i; otherwise, it is a $1 \to 0$ edge. In a directed graph, all edges are directed. A node with no edges directed to it is a *root (source)* node, and a node with no edges directed away from it is a *leaf (sink)* node. A node that is neither a leaf node nor a root node is an *internal* node. If (i, j) is a directed edge, then node i is the *parent* of node j, and j is a *child* of i.

Lemma 1 [18], [29]: A Boolean n-cube has $N = 2^n$ nodes, diameter n, $\binom{n}{x}$ nodes at Hamming distance x from a given node, and n edge-disjoint paths between any pair of nodes i and j. Of these n paths, $Hamming(i, j)$ are length $Hamming(i, j)$ and $n - Hamming(i, j)$ paths are of length $Hamming(i, j) + 2$. Every node has n edges directed to it and n edges directed away from it. The total number of (directed) communication links is nN.

Definition 3: With *rotation of a node* we mean a right cyclic rotation of its address, $\text{Ro}(i) = (i_0 i_{n-1} \cdots i_2 i_1)$. With *rotation of a graph* $G(\mathcal{V}, \mathcal{E})$ we mean a graph $\text{Ro}(G(\mathcal{V}, \mathcal{E})) = G(\text{Ro}(\mathcal{V}), \text{Ro}(\mathcal{E}))$, where $\text{Ro}(\mathcal{V}) = \{\text{Ro}(i)|\forall i \in \mathcal{V}\}$ and $\text{Ro}(\mathcal{E}) = \{(\text{Ro}(i), \text{Ro}(j))|\forall (i, j) \in \mathcal{E}\}$. Moreover, Ro^{-1} is left rotation and $\text{Ro}^k = \text{Ro} \circ \text{Ro}^{k-1}$ for all k.

The right rotation operation is also known as an *unshuffle* operation and the left rotation as a *shuffle* operation.

Definition 4: With *reflection of a node* we mean a bit-reversal of its address, $\text{Re}(i) = (i_0 i_1 \cdots i_{n-2} i_{n-1})$. With *reflection of a graph* $G(\mathcal{V}, \mathcal{E})$ we mean a graph $\text{Re}(G(\mathcal{V}, \mathcal{E})) = G(\text{Re}(\mathcal{V}), \text{Re}(\mathcal{E}))$, where $\text{Re}(\mathcal{V}) = \{\text{Re}(i) | \forall\, i \in \mathcal{V}\}$ and $\text{Re}(\mathcal{E}) = \{(\text{Re}(i), \text{Re}(j)) | \forall\, (i, j) \in \mathcal{E}\}$.

Definition 5: With *translation of a node i by s* we mean a bitwise Exclusive-or of the addresses, $\text{Tr}(s, i) = c$. With *translation of a graph* $G(\mathcal{V}, \mathcal{E})$ with respect to node s, we mean a graph $\text{Tr}(s, G(\mathcal{V}, \mathcal{E})) = G(\text{Tr}(s, \mathcal{V}), \text{Tr}(s, \mathcal{E}))$, where $\text{Tr}(s, \mathcal{V}) = \{\text{Tr}(s, i) | \forall\, i \in \mathcal{V}\}$ and $\text{Tr}(s, \mathcal{E}) = \{(\text{Tr}(s, i), \text{Tr}(s, j)) | \forall\, (i, j) \in \mathcal{E}\}$.

Lemma 2: Rotations, reflections, and translations of a graph preserve the Hamming distance between nodes. The *rotation* operation Ro^k maps every edge in dimension d to dimension $(d - k) \bmod n$, the *reflection* operation maps every edge in dimension d to dimension $n - 1 - d$, and the *translation* operation preserves the dimension of every edge. *Rotation* and *reflection* preserve the direction of every edge. *Translation* reverses the direction of all edges in the dimensions for which $s_m = 1$, $m \in \mathcal{D}$.

Corollary 1: The topology of a graph remains unchanged under *rotation*, *reflection*, and *translation*.

Definition 6: For binary number i the *period* of i, $P(i) = \min_{m>0} \text{Ro}^m(i) = i$. A binary number i is *cyclic* if $P(i) < n$; and *noncyclic*, otherwise. A *cyclic node* is a node with cyclic *relative* address.

The period of the number (011011) is 3. A cyclic node is defined only when the source node is given. Node (001000) is cyclic with respect the the source node (000001).

Definition 7: A *spanning tree* $T^{\text{id}}(s)$ rooted at node s of a Boolean cube is a tree containing all the nodes of the Boolean cube. id is used to identify different spanning trees. $T^{\text{id}}(s) = \text{Tr}(s, T^{\text{id}}(0))$.

Definition 8: For the Boolean n-cube a *one-to-all communication graph*, *o-graph*, with source node s is a connected, directed graph $G^{\text{id}}(s) = \text{Tr}(s, G^{\text{id}}(0))$ where $G^{\text{id}}(0)$ is either a spanning tree, $G^{\text{id}}(0) = T^{\text{id}}(0)$, or a composition of n distinctly rotated spanning trees, $G^{\text{id}}(0) = \cup_{d \in \mathcal{D}} \text{Ro}^d(T^{\text{id}'}(0))$. The weight of every edge in an *o-graph* is 1 if the graph is a tree; and $1/n$, otherwise. id$'$ identifies the generating spanning tree for the *o-graph*.

The weight $1/n$ is introduced to account for the data to be communicated being split into n pieces for an *o-graph* composed of n spanning trees. There exist n paths from the root to any other node. If no two edges $\text{Ro}^\alpha(T^{\text{id}'}(0))$ and $\text{Ro}^\beta(T^{\text{id}'}(0))$ are mapped to the same cube edge $\forall\, \alpha, \beta \in \mathcal{D}, \alpha \neq \beta$, then the paths of the *o-graph* are *edge-disjoint* and there is no contention problem.

The root of a spanning tree has *level* 0. The node i in a spanning tree has a level which is one more than the level of its parent. The height h of a tree is the largest level of all the nodes.

Definition 9: For an *o-graph* G^{id}, the total weight of the edges in dimension d between levels l and $l + 1$ is denoted $e^{\text{id}}(d, l)$, and the total weight of edges in dimension d is $E^{\text{id}}(d)$.

Lemma 3: Given an *o-graph* $G^{\text{id}}(s) = \text{Tr}(s, G^{\text{id}}(0))$ where $G^{\text{id}}(0) = \cup_{d \in \mathcal{D}} \text{Ro}^d(T^{\text{id}'}(0))$, then $E^{\text{id}}(d) = (N - 1)/n$ and $e^{\text{id}}(d, l) = (1/n) \Sigma_{d \in \mathcal{D}} e^{\text{id}'}(d, l)$.

Proof: The lemma follows from Definition 9 and the rotation property in Lemma 2. ∎

We define three basic spanning trees: a *Hamiltonian* path T^H, a *spanning binomial tree* T^{SBT}, and a *spanning balanced n-tree* T^{SBnT}. These trees are used to form composition graphs that provide multiple paths (not necessarily edge-disjoint) to all other nodes.

For the definition/implementation of *o-graph* we use distributed algorithms that for any node compute the addresses of its set of children nodes, if any, and the address of the parent node, except for the root node. A node has one parent and a set of children nodes for each spanning tree used for the composition.

Definition 10: The *children*$^{\text{id}}(i, s, k)$ function generates the set of children addresses of node i in the kth spanning tree of $G^{\text{id}}(s)$. The *parent*$^{\text{id}}(i, s, k)$ function generates the address of the parent of node i in the kth spanning tree of $G^{\text{id}}(s)$. For the G^{id} being a spanning tree we omit the last parameter.

Definition 11: A *greedy spanning tree* rooted at node s of a Boolean n-cube is a spanning tree such that $\forall\, i \in \mathcal{N}$, the level of node i is $\text{Hamming}(i, s)$. A *greedy o-graph* of a Boolean n-cube is a composition of greed spanning trees.

Lemma 4: A greedy *o-graph* contains only $0 \rightarrow 1$ edges "relative" to the root.

Lemma 5: A spanning tree is greedy iff $|\{i\,|\,\text{Hamming}(i, s) = l\}| = \binom{n}{l}$. A greedy *o-graph* is acyclic and of minimal height.

Corollary 2: If $G^{\text{id}}(0) = \cup_{d \in \mathcal{D}} \text{Ro}^d(T^{\text{id}}(0))$, and T^{id} is greedy, then $e^{\text{id}}(d, l) = (1/n)\binom{n}{l+1}$.

Lemma 5 follows from Definition 11 and Lemma 1. Corollary 2 follows from Lemmas 3 and 5.

Note that an *o-graph* of minimum height is not necessarily a greedy *o-graph*. In all-to-all personalized communication, only greedy *o-graphs* have scheduling disciplines that accomplish minimal data transfer time.

Definition 12: In *one-port* communication, a processor can only send *and* receive on one of its ports at any given time. The port on which a processor sends and receives can be different. In *n-port* communication, a processor can communicate on all its ports concurrently.

We also assume that there is an overhead, startup time τ, associated with each communication of B elements, each of which requires a transfer time t_c. B_{opt} denotes an optimal packet size. For the analysis, it is convenient to assume that communication takes place during distinct time intervals. The duration of a *routing cycle* is $\tau + B t_c$. Routing cycles are labeled from 0.

For *broadcasting*, the data are replicated $|children^{\text{id}}(i, s, k)|$ times in node i for spanning tree k of the *o-graph* $G^{\text{id}}(s)$. With *n-port* communication, and negligible time for replication, all ports are scheduled concurrently. With *one-port* communication, the order of communications on different ports is important.

In *personalized communication*, the source node sends a unique message to every other node. An internal node needs to receive and forward all the data for every node of the subtree of which it is a root. The ordering of data for a port is important for the communication time both for *one-port* and *n-port* communication.

The *scheluling discipline* defines the communication order for each port, and the order between ports for every nonleaf node. We assume the same data independent scheduling discipline for every node. The scheduling disciplines are completely specified later.

Definition 13: In a *reverse-breadth-first* scheduling discipline for *one-to-all personalized communication* based on an *o-graph* of height h, the root sends out the data for the nodes at level $h - p$ during the pth cycle, $0 \leq p < h$. The data received by an internal node are propagated to the next level during the next cycle, if the data are not destined for the node itself. In a *postorder* [1] scheduling discipline, each node sends out the entire data set to each of its children nodes before accepting its own data.

The analysis of the complexity of the one-to-all personalized communication is considerably simplified for *n-port* communication and *reverse-breadth-first* scheduling if the root dominates the communication (in sending out the data). The following lemma characterizes the spanning trees for which the "root-dominant" property exists.

Lemma 6: Given a spanning tree, let $\phi^{id}(i, x)$ be the number of nodes at distance x from node i in the subtree rooted at node i. If for any child of the root, say node i, we have $\phi^{id}(i, x) \geq \phi^{id}(j, x)$ for any child node j of node i for all x, then the data transfer time of *n-port* one-to-all personalized communication based on *reverse-breadth-first* ordering is dominated by the data transfer over the edges from the root.

Proof: The lemma follows from the fact that with *reverse-breadth-first* scheduling, the propagation time for the internal nodes is at most the same as the transmission time for the root during each routing cycle. ∎

Definition 14: An *all-to-all communication graph, a-graph,* $G^{id}(*) = \bigcup_{s \in \mathfrak{N}} G^{id}(s)$.

The quantities $v^{id}(d, l)$ and $u^{id}(d, l)$ defined next are useful in deriving the time complexity of *all-to-all personalized communication* for the *a-graph*.

Definition 15: Define $v^{id}(d, l)$ of an *o-graph* as the total weight of all edges within all subtrees rooted at level $l + 1$ of all spanning trees with subtree roots connected to a parent node through an edge in dimension d, inclusive of the edge to the parent node. Let $\mathbb{S}^{id}_d = \{j \mid j \in \mathcal{V}, (i, j) \in \mathcal{E}^{id}$ and $i \oplus j = 2^d\}$. Define $u^{id}(d, l)$ to be the total weight of edges terminating on all nodes k such that k is descendent of j at distance l, $\forall j \in \mathbb{S}^{id}_d$.

Lemma 7: $v^{id}(d, l) = u^{id}(d, l) = \sum_{x=l}^{h-1} e^{id}(d, x) = 1/n \sum_{x=l}^{h-1} \sum_{d \in \mathfrak{D}} e^{id'}(d, x), \forall l \in [0, h - 1], d \in \mathfrak{D}$ for an *o-graph* $G^{id}(0) = \bigcup_{d \in \mathfrak{D}} \mathrm{Ro}^d(T^{id'}(0))$, where h is the height of $T^{id'}$.

Proof: From the n distinct rotations and Lemma 2, it follows that $v^{id}(d, l) = 1/n \times$ (the sum of the number of nodes at levels x, $l + 1 \leq x \leq h$) of $T^{id'}$. Similarly, $u^{id}(d, l) = 1/n \times$ (the sum of the number of nodes at levels x, $l + 1 \leq x \leq h$) of $T^{id'}$. By Lemma 3, $e^{id}(d, l) = 1/n \times$ (the number of edges between levels l and $l + 1$) of $T^{id'} = 1/n \sum_{d \in \mathfrak{D}} e^{id'}(d, l)$. ∎

Corollary 3: If an *o-graph* $G^{id}(0) = \bigcup_{d \in \mathfrak{D}} \mathrm{Ro}^d(T^{id'}(0))$ and $T^{id'}$ is greedy, then $v^{id}(d, l) = u^{id}(d, l) = 1/n \sum_{i=l+1}^{n} \binom{n}{i}$.

Proof: The corollary follows from Lemma 7 and Corollary 2. ∎

Lemma 8: For an *a-graph* $G^{id}(*)$, the total weight of communication graph edges mapped to every cube edge in dimension d is $E^{id}(d)$. The total weight of communication graph edges between levels l and $l + 1$ in dimension d is $e^{id}(d, l)$.

Proof: Since $G^{id}(*) = \bigcup_{s \in \mathfrak{N}} G^{id}(s) = \bigcup_{s \in \mathfrak{N}} \mathrm{Tr}(s, G^{id}(0))$, every *o-graph* edge is mapped to a distinct cube edge in the same dimension through N distinct Exclusive-OR operations. Hence, the total weight of *a-graph* edges mapped to every cube edge in dimension d is $E^{id}(d)$. The bitwise Exclusive-OR operation preserves the topology of a spanning tree, and hence the number of edges at a given distance from the source node. ∎

III. SPANNING GRAPHS

A. Three Spanning Trees

1) A Hamiltonian Path: A Hamiltonian path H originating at node 0 is defined by traversing the nodes of the Boolean cube in a *binary-reflected* Gray code [27] order with starting address equal to 0. Let the n-bit code of 2^n integers be *Gray(n)*. Two definitions of the code that are convenient to use are the following.

Definition 16: The *binary-reflected Gray code* on n bits is defined recursively as follows. Let $Gray(n) = (\hat{G}_0, \hat{G}_1, \cdots, \hat{G}_{2^n-2}, \hat{G}_{2^n-1})$.

Then $Gray(n + 1) = (0\hat{G}_0, 0\hat{G}_1, \cdots, 0\hat{G}_{2^n-2}, 0\hat{G}_{2^n-1}, 1\hat{G}_{2^n-1}, 1\hat{G}_{2^n-2}, \cdots, 1\hat{G}_1, 1\hat{G}_0)$, or alternatively, $Gray(n + 1) = (\hat{G}_0 0, \hat{G}_0 1, \hat{G}_1 1, \hat{G}_1 0, \hat{G}_2 0, \hat{G}_2 1, \cdots, \hat{G}_{2^n-1} 1, \hat{G}_{2^n-1} 0)$.

The following alternative definition is also useful for distributed routing algorithms. Let $T(n) = (t_0, t_1, \cdots, t_{2^n-2})$ be the sequence of dimensions on which a transition takes place in proceeding from integer 0 to integer $2^n - 1$ in the n-bit Gray code with the most significant bit labeled $n - 1$.

Definition 17: Then the *binary-reflected Gray code* can be defined through the recursion

$$T(n) = (T(n-1), n-1, T(n-1)), \qquad T(1) = 0.$$

Note that t_i is also the lowest order dimension with a 0-bit in the binary encoding of i. Let the binary encoding of $i = (i_{n-1} i_{n-2} \cdots i_0)$ and the Gray code encoding be $\hat{G}_i = (g_{n-1} g_{n-2} \cdots g_0)$. Then the conversions between binary and Gray code encoding are defined by $g_m = i_m \oplus i_{m+1}$, and conversely $i_m = g_{m+1} \oplus g_{m+2} \oplus \cdots \oplus g_{n-1}$.

2) A Spanning Binomial Tree: A 0-level binomial tree has one node. An n-level binomial tree is constructed out of two $(n - 1)$-level binomial trees by adding one edge between the roots of the two trees and by making either root the new root [1], [7]. The familiar spanning tree rooted in node 0 of a Boolean n-cube generated by complementing leading zeros of the binary encoding of a processor address i [9], [17], [26], [28], [29] is indeed a *spanning binomial tree* (SBT).

Definition 18: The spanning binomial tree rooted at node s,

$T^{\text{SBT}}(s)$, is defined as follows. Let p be such that $c_p = 1$ and $c_m = 0$, $\forall\, m \in \{p+1, p+2, \cdots, n-1\} \equiv \mathfrak{M}^{\text{SBT}}(c)$ and let $p = -1$ if $c = 0$. The set $\mathfrak{M}^{\text{SBT}}(c)$ is the set of leading zeros of c. Then,

$$\text{children}^{\text{SBT}}(i, s) = \{(i_{n-1}i_{n-2} \cdots \bar{i}_m \cdots i_0)\},$$

$$\forall\, m \in \mathfrak{M}^{\text{SBT}}(c),$$

$$\text{parent}^{\text{SBT}}(i, s) = \begin{cases} \phi, & i = s; \\ (i_{n-1}i_{n-2} \cdots \bar{i}_p \cdots i_0), & i \neq s. \end{cases}$$

It is easy to verify that the parent and children functions are consistent, i.e., that node j is a child of node i iff node i is the parent of node j. Fig. 1 shows the $T^{\text{SBT}}(0)$ for a 4-cube.

Definition 19: Subtree k of the $T^{\text{SBT}}(s)$ consists of all nodes such that $c_k = 1$ and $c_m = 0$, $\forall\, m \in \{0, 1, \cdots, k-1\}$.

Lemma 9: There are 2^{n-k-1} nodes in subtree k, and the maximum degree of any node at level l in subtree k is $n-k-l$, $0 < l \leq n-k$.

Lemma 10: Let $\phi^{\text{SBT}}(i, s, x)$ be the number of nodes at distance x from node i in the subtree rooted at node i of the SBT rooted at node s. Then, $\phi^{\text{SBT}}(i, s, x) \geq \phi^{\text{SBT}}(j, s, x)$, if $j \in \text{children}^{\text{SBT}}(i, s)$.

Proof: From the definition of the SBT, the subtree rooted at node j is a connected subgraph of the subtree rooted at node i. ∎

3) A Spanning Balanced n-Tree and a Spanning Balanced Graph: In the *spanning balanced n-tree* [15], the node set is divided into n sets of nodes with approximately an equal number of nodes. Each such set forms a subtree of the source node. The maximum number of elements that needs to traverse any edge directed away from the source node is minimized for personalized communication.

Definition 20: Let $\mathcal{K}(i, s) = \{k_1, k_2, \cdots, k_m | 0 \leq k_1 < k_2 < \cdots < k_m < n\}$ be such that $\text{Ro}^{\alpha}(c) = \text{Ro}^{\beta}(c)$, $\forall\, \alpha, \beta \in \mathcal{K}(i, s)$, and $\text{Ro}^{\alpha}(c) < \text{Ro}^{\gamma}(c)$, $\forall\, \alpha \in \mathcal{K}(i, s)$, $\gamma \notin \mathcal{K}(i, s)$. Then $\text{base}^{\text{SBnT}}(i, s) = k_1$.

For example, $\text{base}^{\text{SBnT}}((011100), 0) = 2$ and $\text{base}^{\text{SBnT}}((110100), (000010)) = 1$. Note that $|\mathcal{K}(i, s)| = n/P(c)$ where $P(c)$ is the period of c. The value of the base equals the minimum number of right rotations that minimized the value of c. For noncyclic nodes $|\mathcal{K}(i, s)| = 1$, but for a cyclic node c, $P(c) < n$ and $|\mathcal{K}(i, s)| > 1$. The notion of $\text{base}^{\text{SBnT}}$ is similar to the notion of the distinguished node used in [25] in that $\text{base}^{\text{SBnT}} = 0$ distinguishes a node from a generator set (necklace). To simplify the notation, we omit the subscript on k in the following.

Definition 21: Subtree k of the *spanning balanced n-tree* rooted at node s consists of all nodes $i \neq s$ such that $\text{base}^{\text{SBnT}}(i, s) = k$.

Note that all nodes in subtree k have $c_k = 1$, but not all with $c_k = 1$ are in the kth subtree.

Definition 22: Let $\text{base}^{\text{SBnT}}(i, s) = k$. For $c = 0$ let $p = -1$, else if $c = (00 \cdots 01_k 0 \cdots 0)$, then $p = k$, else let p be the first bit cyclically to the right of bit k that is equal to 1 in c, i.e., $c_p = 1$, and $c_m = 0$, $\forall\, m \in \{(p+1) \bmod n, (p+2) \bmod n, \cdots, (k-1) \bmod n\} \equiv \mathfrak{M}^{\text{SBnT}}(i, s)$ with $k = n$ if c

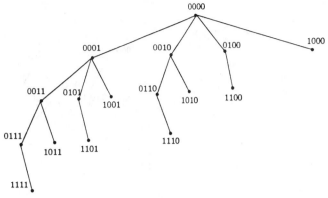

Fig. 1.   A spanning binomial tree in a 4-cube.

$= 0$. The spanning tree $T^{\text{SBnT}}(s)$ is defined through

$$\text{children}^{\text{SBnT}}(i, s)$$

$$= \begin{cases} \{(i_{n-1}i_{n-2} \cdots \bar{i}_m \cdots i_0)\}, \\ \quad \forall\, m \in \mathfrak{M}^{\text{SBnT}}(i, s), \quad \text{if } c = 0; \\ \{q_m = (i_{n-1}i_{n-2} \cdots \bar{i}_m \cdots i_0)\}, \\ \quad \forall\, m \in \mathfrak{M}^{\text{SBnT}}(i, s) \text{ and } \text{base}^{\text{SBnT}}(q_m, s) \\ \quad = \text{base}^{\text{SBnT}}(i, s), \quad \text{if } c \neq 0. \end{cases}$$

$$\text{parent}^{\text{SBnT}}(i, s) = \begin{cases} \phi, & \text{if } c = 0; \\ (i_{n-1}i_{n-2} \cdots \bar{i}_p \cdots i_0), & \text{otherwise.} \end{cases}$$

The $\text{parent}^{\text{SBnT}}$ function preserves the base, since for any node i with base k, c_p is the highest order bit of $\text{Ro}^k(c)$. Complementing this bit cannot change the base. It is also readily seen that the $\text{parent}^{\text{SBnT}}$ and $\text{children}^{\text{SBnT}}$ functions are consistent.

Theorem 1: The $\text{parent}^{\text{SBnT}}(i, s)$ function defines a spanning tree rooted at node s.

Proof: For every node i the $\text{parent}^{\text{SBnT}}(i, s)$ function generates a path to node s. Hence, the graph is connected. Moreover, the parent node of a node at distance l from node s is at distance $l - 1$ from node s, and each node only has one parent node. Hence, the graph is a spanning tree. ∎

Fig. 2 shows a spanning balanced 5-tree in a 5-cube.

Lemma 11: The SBnT is a greedy spanning tree.

Proof: From the definition of the $\text{parent}^{\text{SBnT}}(i, s)$ function, it follows that the distance from node i to node s is $Hamming(i, s)$. ∎

Lemma 12 [15]: Let $\phi^{\text{SBnT}}(i, s, x)$ be the number of nodes at distance x from node i in the subtree rooted at node i of the SBnT rooted at node s. Then, $\phi^{\text{SBnT}}(i, s, x) \geq \phi^{\text{SBnT}}(j, s, x)$, if $j \in \text{children}^{\text{SBnT}}(i, s)$.

Theorem 2: Excluding node $(\bar{s}_{n-1}\bar{s}_{n-2} \cdots \bar{s}_0)$, all the subtrees of the root of the SBnT are isomorphic, if n is a prime number. Furthermore, the kth subtree can be derived by $(k - j) \bmod n$ left rotation steps of each node of the jth subtree.

Proof: For n a prime number there are no cyclic nodes, except nodes with relative addresses $(00 \cdots 0)$ and $(11 \cdots 1)$. For all other nodes $|\mathcal{K}(i, s)| = 1$, and each generator set has n members. Any subtree has the same number of nodes as any other subtree at every level. It follows from the definition of

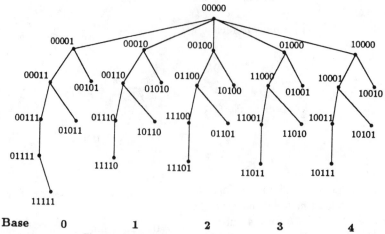

Fig. 2. A spanning balanced 5-tree in a 5-cube.

base^{SBnT} that if $j \in$ children$^{\text{SBnT}}(i, s)$, then Ro$^k(j) \in$ children^{SBnT} (Ro$^k(i), s) \; \forall \; k \in \mathfrak{D}$. ∎

If n is not a prime number, then some subtrees of the root of the SBnT will contain more nodes than others. It can be shown that the number of nodes in a subtree is of $O(\frac{N}{n})$ [15]. The imbalance is illustrated in Table II. This imbalance is important for personalized communication. The number of elements transferred over the edges can be perfectly balanced in the sense that the maximum at any level is minimized by allowing multiple paths to cyclic nodes. With multiple paths to cyclic nodes, the graph is no longer a tree. We call the SBnT so modified a *spanning balanced graph* (SBG). The SBG can be defined as a composition of n distinctly rotated SBnT's as follows.

Definition 23: Define $G^{\text{SBG}}(0) = \cup_{d \in \mathfrak{D}}$ Ro$^d(T^{\text{SBnT}}(0))$ and $G^{\text{SBG}}(s) = \text{Tr}(s, G^{\text{SBG}}(0))$. The number of different paths to a node i in an SBG rooted at node s is $n/P(i \oplus s)$ where $P(i)$ is the period of i.

B. Spanning Graphs Composed of n Spanning Trees

1) n Rotated Hamiltonian Paths:

Definition 24: The graph $G^{\text{nRH}}(s) = \text{Tr}(s, G^{\text{nRH}}(0))$, and $G^{\text{nRH}}(0) = \cup_{d \in \mathfrak{D}}$ Ro$^d(T^{\text{H}}(0))$.

The paths generated through n distinct rotations of the $G^H(s)$ path are not edge-disjoint, for $n > 2$. For instance, the edge $(2, 6)$ is used in two paths of the graph $G^{3RH}(0)$, and these paths are part of every graph $G^{\text{nRH}}(0)$ for $n > 3$.

Lemma 13: Path Ro$^k(T^H(s))$ and path Ro$^m(T^H(s))$ share $2^{n-\alpha-1} + 2^{n-\beta-1} - 2$ directed edges, where $\alpha = (k - m)$ mod n and $\beta = (m - k)$ mod n.

Each of the n cube edges $((00 \cdots 01_d 0 \cdots 0)$, $(00 \cdots 01_{(d+1)\bmod n}1_d 0 \cdots 0))$, $\forall \; d \in \mathfrak{D}$ are shared by $n - 1$ paths for $s = 0$. Fig. 3 shows the graph $G^{3H}(0)$. The fact that the paths are not edge-joint limits the potential for pipelining.

Lemma 14: In graph $G^{\text{nRH}}(s)$, the edges between nodes at distance l and distance $l + 1$ from the source node are edge-disjoint for $l \in \mathfrak{N}$.

Proof: By construction the edges are in different dimensions. ∎

Note that even though the n rotated Hamiltonian paths are not edge-disjoint it is possible to have edge-disjoint embeddings of several Hamiltonian paths generated in other ways.

TABLE II
A COMPARISON OF SUBTREE SIZES OF SBT AND SBnT. THE LAST COLUMN CONTAINS THE RATIO OF SBnT(max) TO $(N - 1)/n$

n	SBT(max)	SBnT(max)	SBnT(min)	$(N-1)/n$	factor
2	2	2	1	1.50	1.33
3	4	3	2	2.33	1.29
4	8	5	3	3.75	1.33
5	16	7	6	6.20	1.13
6	32	13	9	10.50	1.24
7	64	19	18	18.14	1.05
8	128	35	30	31.88	1.10
9	256	59	56	56.78	1.04
10	512	107	99	102.30	1.05
11	1024	187	186	186.09	1.00
12	2048	351	335	341.25	1.03
13	4096	631	630	630.08	1.00
14	8192	1181	1161	1170.21	1.01
15	16384	2191	2182	2184.47	1.00
16	32768	4115	4080	4095.94	1.00
17	65536	7711	7710	7710.06	1.00
18	131072	14601	14532	14563.50	1.00
19	262144	27595	27594	27594.05	1.00
20	524288	52487	52377	52428.75	1.00

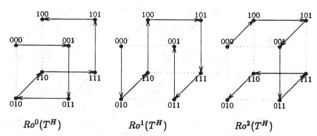

Fig. 3. Three rotated binary-reflected Gray code paths in a 3-cube.

Indeed, there exist n *undirected* edge-disjoint Hamiltonian cycles in a $2n$-cube [34]–[36]. Fig. 4 shows two of the four directed Hamiltonian cycles. The other two cycles are of a reversed direction.

2) n Rotated Spanning Binomial Trees:

Definition 25: The graph $G^{\text{nRSBT}}(s) = \text{Tr}(s, G^{\text{nRSBT}}(0))$, and $G^{\text{nRSBT}}(0) = \cup_{d \in \mathfrak{D}}$ Ro$^d(T^{\text{SBT}}(0))$.

Fig. 5 shows the nRSBT graph of a 3-cube. In general, a cube edge (i, j) is part of several rotated SBT's. The number on each cube edge in the figure shows the sum of the weights of the graph edges mapped onto it.

Lemma 15: For any node in the graph $G^{\text{nRSBT}}(0)$, except the root, the weight of the incoming cube edge in dimension d is

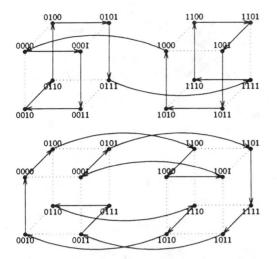

Fig. 4. Four directed edge-disjoint Hamiltonian cycles in a 4-cube. Only two cycles are shown. The other two are of a reversed direction.

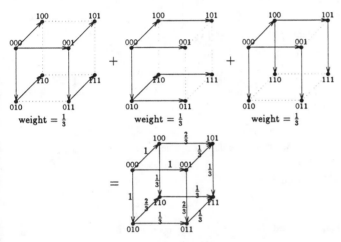

Fig. 5. Three rotated spanning binomial trees as an *o-graph* in a 3-cube.

$(p + 1)/n$, where p is the number of consecutive 0-bits immediately to the left of bit d.

Proof: A node in the SBT graph has an incoming edge in dimension d if the bit in dimension d is the highest order bit that is one. In the nRSBT graph, the number of incoming

in $\text{Ro}^m(G^{\text{SBT}}(0))$ for $m = \{d + 1, d + 2, \cdots, d + p + 1\}$ i.e., in these $p + 1$ SBT's, bit d is the last bit complemented in reaching node j. ∎

For instance, node (011001) has an incoming cube edge in dimension 0 with weight 1/2, an incoming edge in dimension 3 weighted 1/6, and an incoming edge in dimension 4 weighted 1/3.

Corollary 4: The sum of the weights of incoming edges is 1 for every node, except the source node.

Proof: From Lemma 15, the weight of an incoming edge is equal to the number of dimensions between the dimension considered and the next higher dimension with a 1-bit. ∎

Lemma 16: In any dimension, the edges of the nRSBT graph are only mapped to half of the cube edges.

Proof: Rotation does not change the direction of edges. ∎

3) n Edge-Disjoint Spanning Binomial Trees: The nESBT (n edge-disjoint spanning binomial trees) graph is composed of n SBT's with one tree rooted at each of the nodes adjacent to the source node. The SBT's are rotated such that the source node of the nESBT graph is in the smallest subtree of each SBT. The nESBT graph is then obtained by reversing the edges from the roots of the SBT's to the source node.

Definition 26: The nESBT graph $G^{\text{nESBT}}(s) = \text{Tr}(s, G^{\text{nESBT}}(0))$, where $G^{\text{nESBT}}(0) = \cup_{d \in \mathfrak{D}} T^{\text{SBT}d}(0)$, and $T^{\text{SBT}d}(0) = \text{Tr}(2^d, \text{Ro}^{n-d-1}(T^{\text{SBT}}(0)))$ (with the root being node 0 instead of node 2^d).

Fig. 6 shows an nESBT graph in a 3-cube. The nESBT graph is not a tree, and contains cycles. Every node appears in every subtree of the source node. The height of the nESBT graph is $n + 1$, since the source node is adjacent to all the roots of the SBT's used in the definition of the nESBT graph. The number of distinct edges in the n SBT's is $n(N - 1)$. An alternative definition of G^{nESBT} is through the functions children^{nESBT} and parent^{nESBT} below.

Definition 27: For a given k, let p be such that $c_p = 1$ and $c_m = 0, \forall m \in \{(p + 1) \bmod n, (p + 2) \bmod n, \cdots, (k - 1) \bmod n\}$. For $c = (00 \cdots 01_k 0 \cdots 0)$, $p = k$. Then $\mathfrak{M}^{\text{nESBT}}(i, s, k) = \{(p + 1) \bmod n, (p + 2) \bmod n, \cdots, (k - 1) \bmod n\}$. The children and parent of node i in the kth spanning tree, $T^{\text{SBT}k}(s)$, are

$$\text{children}^{\text{nESBT}}(i, s, k) = \begin{cases} \{(i_{n-1}i_{n-2} \cdots \bar{i}_k \cdots i_0)\}, & \text{if } c = 0; \\ \{(i_{n-1}i_{n-2} \cdots \bar{i}_m \cdots i_0)\}, \forall m \in \mathfrak{M}^{\text{nESBT}}(i, s, k) \cup \{k\}, & \text{if } c_k = 1, p \neq k; \\ \{(i_{n-1}i_{n-2} \cdots \bar{i}_m \cdots i_0)\}, \forall m \in \mathfrak{M}^{\text{nESBT}}(i, s, k), & \text{if } c_k = 1, p = k; \\ \phi, & \text{if } c_k = 0, c \neq 0. \end{cases}$$

$$\text{parent}^{\text{nESBT}}(i, s, k) = \begin{cases} \phi, & \text{if } c = 0; \\ (i_{n-1}i_{n-2} \cdots \bar{i}_k \cdots i_0), & \text{if } c_k = 0, c \neq 0; \\ (i_{n-1}i_{n-2} \cdots \bar{i}_p \cdots i_0), & \text{if } c_k = 1. \end{cases}$$

edges (i, j) to node j is equal to the number of graphs $\text{Ro}^m(G^{\text{SBT}}(0))$, $m \in \mathfrak{D}$ such that there exists an edge (i^m, j^m), where $i = \text{Ro}^m i^m$ and $j = \text{Ro}^m j^m$. Such an edge occurs

Dimension p is the first dimension to the right of dimension k, cyclically, which has a bit equal to one. All nodes with $c_k = 0$, except node s, are leaf nodes of the kth subtree (or kth

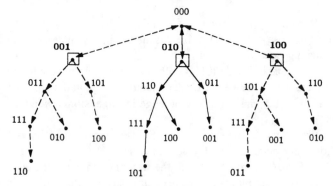

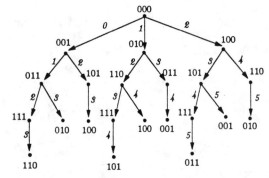

Fig. 6. Subtrees of an nESBT viewed as SBT's.

Fig. 7. Three edge-disjoint directed spanning trees in a 3-cube.

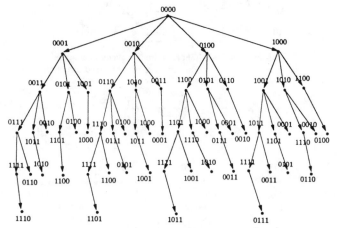

Fig. 8. Four edge-disjoint directed spanning trees in a 4-cube.

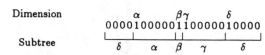

Fig. 9. Scheduling of broadcasting operations for a node with nESBT routing.

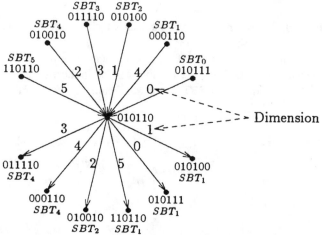

Fig. 10. Parents and children of a node in a 6-cube.

spanning tree). Conversely, all nodes with $c_k = 1$ are internal nodes of the kth subtree. The exceptional connection to node 0 is handled by the conditions on p. The first case defines the children for the source node, the second defines the set of children nodes of internal nodes of the kth subtree, except the node at level 1. The third case handles the node at level 1, and the last case handles the leaf nodes. Figs. 7 and 12 show that the three subtrees (spanning trees) of a 3ESBT graph are edge-disjoint. The lables on the edges will be used later. Fig. 8 shows a 4ESBT graph with source node 0. Every 1-bit in the node address divides the outgoing edges into distinct sets. The set of 0-bits to the right of 1-bit defines children nodes for a spanning subtree with the same index as the dimension of the 1-bit, Fig. 9.

Theorem 3: The n subtrees of the nESBT graph are edge-disjoint.

Proof: We only need to prove that for an arbitrary node the address of its parent node in each of the n subtrees is obtained by complementing a distinct bit.

From the definition of the children$^{nESBT}(i, s, k)$ [or parent$^{nESBT}(i, s, k)$] function, it is clear that a node is a leaf node of the kth subtree iff $c_k = 0$, with the exception of node s. If a node is a leaf node in a particular subtree, then its parent address in that subtree is obtained by complementing the corresponding bit in its address (bit k for the kth subtree). If a node is an internal node of the kth subtree, then the corresponding bit is 1, and the parent address is obtained by complementing the first bit cyclically to the right of the kth address bit that is equal to 1. Hence, the addresses of the parent nodes for all the subtrees of which the node is an internal node are also obtained by complementing distinct bits. ∎

Fig. 10 shows the parent and children of one node in a 6-cube. The numbers on the edges are the dimensions through which the node connects to its parents or children nodes in different subtrees. The labels on the nodes denote the subtree to which the parent and children nodes belong.

Corollary 5: There exists an edge-disjoint embedding of n spanning binomial trees in an n-cube.

Corollary 6: The nESBT graph for a Boolean n-cube is a directed graph, such that all directed cube edges, except those incident on the source node, appear precisely once in the nESBT graph.

Proof: Follows from Theorem 3. ∎

Corollary 7: The in-degree and the out-degree of any node

in an nESBT graph is n, with the exception that the source has in-degree 0 and all the neighbors of the source have out-degree $n - 1$.

Theorem 4: The height of the nESBT graph is minimal among all possible configurations of n edge-disjoint spanning trees.

TABLE III
SOME TOPOLOGICAL CHARACTERISTICS OF SOME *o-graphs*

Graph	$E(d)$	$e(d,l)$	$v(d,l)$	$u(d,l)$
G^H	2^{n-d-1}	0, $d \neq t_l$ or 1, o.w.	0, $d \neq t_l$ or $N-l-1$, o.w.	$\frac{N}{2^{d+1}} - \left\lceil \frac{l-2^d+1}{2^{d+1}} \right\rceil$
G^{nRH}	$\frac{N-1}{n}$	$\frac{1}{n}$	$\frac{1}{n}(N-l-1)$	$\frac{1}{n}(N-l-1)$
G^{SBT}	2^d	$\binom{d}{l}$	$\binom{d}{l}2^{n-d-1}$	$\binom{n-d-1}{l}2^d$
G^{nRSBT}	$\frac{N-1}{n}$	$\frac{1}{n}\binom{n}{l+1}$	$\frac{1}{n}\sum_{i=l+1}^{n}\binom{n}{i}$	$\frac{1}{n}\sum_{i=l+1}^{n}\binom{n}{i}$
G^{nESBT}	$\frac{N-1}{n}$	1, $l=0$; $n-1$, $l=1$; $\frac{1}{n}\binom{n}{l}$, $l \geq 2$	$N-1$, $l=0$; $N-2$, $l=1$; $\frac{1}{n}\sum_{i=l}^{n}\binom{n}{i}$, $l \geq 2$	$\frac{1}{n}\sum_{i=l+1}^{n}\binom{n}{i}$
G^{SBG}	$\frac{N-1}{n}$	$\frac{1}{n}\binom{n}{l+1}$	$\frac{1}{n}\sum_{i=l+1}^{n}\binom{n}{i}$	$\frac{1}{n}\sum_{i=l+1}^{n}\binom{n}{i}$

Proof: To prove that with n edge-disjoint spanning trees, the height $n + 1$ is minimal, we prove that n disjoint spanning trees with height n is impossible. The total number of directed edges in an n-cube is nN, but those n directed edges incident on the source node are not used. Each spanning tree has $N - 1$ edges. Hence, every eligible edge is used by the n edge-disjoint spanning trees. It follows that the edges directed out from the node with address $(\bar{s}_{n-1}\bar{s}_{n-2}\cdots\bar{s}_0)$ also must be used, and since this node is at distance n from the source node, the theorem follows. ∎

Lemma 17: The number of nodes at level l of a subtree of the nESBT graph is

$$\begin{cases} \binom{n-1}{l-1} + \binom{n-1}{l-2} = \binom{n}{l-1}, \\ \qquad \text{for } n+1 \geq l \geq 1,\ l \neq 2; \\ 1, \qquad \text{for } l = 0; \\ n-1, \qquad \text{for } l = 2. \end{cases}$$

Proof: Follows directly from the definition. ∎

Lemma 18: Let $\phi^{\text{nESBT}}(i, s, x)$ be the number of nodes at distance x from node i in the subtree rooted at node i of the nESBT rooted at node s. Then, $\phi^{\text{nESBT}}(i, s, x) \geq \phi^{\text{nESBT}}(j, s, x)$, if $j \in$ children$^{\text{nESBT}}(i, s)$.

Proof: By Definition 26, each subtree of the nESBT is an SBT with the smallest subtree removed. The lemma can be shown by Lemmas 10, 17, and 9. ∎

C. Summary of Topological Properties of the Communication Graphs

The topological characteristics used for the complexity analysis are summarized in Table III.

With respect to the entry for the SBT graph in Table III note that $\binom{x}{y} = 0$ if $x < y$. Moreover,

Lemmas 3 and 7, and the entries for the nRSBT graph proved using Definition 25, Corollaries 2, 3, and the fact that T^{SBT} is greedy. The nESBT properties can be proved using Definition 26 and Lemmas 3, 7, and 17.

IV. ONE-TO-ALL BROADCASTING

Lemma 19: A lower bound for *one-to-all broadcasting* with *one-port* communication is max $((M + n - 1)t_c, n\tau)$, and max $((\lceil M/n \rceil + n - 1)t_c, n\tau)$ for *n-port* communication.

Proof: The height of any *o-graph* is at least n. The root needs a time of Mt_c (or $\lceil M/n \rceil t_c$) to send out the data. An additional delay of at least $(n - 1)t_c$ is required to reach the node at maximum distance from the root. ∎

With $M = 1$ a tight lower bound is $n(t_c + \tau)$ both for *one-port* and *n-port* communication. This bound is realized by SBT routing and appropriate scheduling. In fact, it can be shown that with $M = 1$ and *one-port* communication, any routing for broadcasting that yields the lower bound is topologically equivalent to the graph G^{SBT}. With *n-port* communication any *o-graph* of height n can realize the lower bound communication for $M = 1$. The scheduling discipline we propose for the graph G^{nESBT} yields the lowest communication complexity of the broadcasting algorithms we consider, both for *one-port* and *n-port* communication, except $B_{\text{opt}} = M$ for *one-port* communication and $B_{\text{opt}} = M/n$ for *n-port* communication. For these two cases, our scheduling for the graph G^{nESBT} is inferior only by 1 routing cycle. With $1 < M \leq n$ and *n-port* communication, our scheduling for the graph G^{nRSBT} yields the lower bound, $n(t_c + \tau)$.

A. The Time Complexity of One-to-All Broadcasting

Table IV summarizes the routing algorithms and scheduling disciplines we have analyzed. The estimated communication times are summarized in Table V. For an *o-graph* composed of n spanning trees, the data set M is divided into n

$$\max_d v^{\text{SBT}}(d, l) = v^{\text{SBT}}(\min(2l, n-1), l) = \begin{cases} \binom{2l}{l} 2^{n-2l-1}, & \text{if } l \in \left\{0, \cdots, \left\lfloor \frac{n-1}{2} \right\rfloor\right\}; \\ \binom{n-1}{l}, & \text{if } l \in \left\{\left\lfloor \frac{n+1}{2} \right\rfloor, \cdots, n-1\right\}. \end{cases}$$

The entries in Table III for the SBG graph can be proved by Lemmas 3 and 11 and Corollaries 2 and 3. The characteristics for the nRH graph can be proved from Definition 24 and

approximately equal size subsets, and each such subset communicated by one of the spanning subtrees. If the trees are not edge-disjoint, we assume no pipelining.

TABLE IV
SCHEDULING DISCIPLINES FOR ONE-TO-ALL BROADCASTING

Comm.	Routing	Scheduling discipline
one-port	H	Pipeline.
	SBT	All data for a port at once. Tallest remaining subtree first.
	nRSBT	All data for the tallest remaining subtree of the spanning trees $0, 1, \ldots, p$ at once during routing cycle $p < n$, and all data for the tallest remaining subtrees of all spanning trees during cycles $n \leq p < 2n - 1$. For the source $B = \frac{p+1}{n} M$ for $p < n$, and $B = \frac{2n-p-1}{n} M$ for $n \leq p < 2n - 1$.
	nESBT	The source node sends to spanning trees $0, 1, \ldots, n - 1$ cyclically, i.e., pipeline among n spanning trees. The internal nodes always propagate (replicate) to the tallest subtree of the same spanning tree first.
n-port	SBT	Pipelining for each subtree, subtrees concurrently.
	nRSBT	All data at once for the tallest remaining subtree of every spanning tree. (The subtrees of each spanning tree are treated sequentially, and spanning trees concurrently.)
	nESBT	Pipelining for each subtree; subtrees and spanning trees concurrently.

TABLE V
THE COMPLEXITY OF ONE-TO-ALL BROADCASTING

Comm.	Routing	T	B_{opt}	T_{min}
one-port	H	$(M + (N - 2)B)t_c + (\lceil \frac{M}{B} \rceil + N - 2)\tau$	$\sqrt{\frac{M\tau}{(N-2)t_c}}$	$(\sqrt{Mt_c} + \sqrt{(N-2)\tau})^2$
	SBT	$Mnt_c + \lceil \frac{M}{B} \rceil n\tau$	M	$n(Mt_c + \tau)$
	nRSBT	$nMt_c + (2\sum_{i=1}^{n-1} \lceil \frac{M_i}{nB} \rceil + \lceil \frac{M}{B} \rceil)\tau$	M	$nMt_c + (2n - 1)\tau$
	nESBT	$(M + nB)t_c + (\lceil \frac{M}{B} \rceil + n)\tau$	$\sqrt{\frac{M\tau}{nt_c}}$	$(\sqrt{Mt_c} + \sqrt{n\tau})^2$
n-port	SBT	$(M + (n - 1)B)t_c + (\lceil \frac{M}{B} \rceil + n - 1)\tau$	$\sqrt{\frac{M\tau}{(n-1)t_c}}$	$(\sqrt{Mt_c} + \sqrt{(n-1)\tau})^2$
	nRSBT	$Mt_c + \lceil \frac{M}{nB} \rceil n\tau$	$\frac{M}{n}$	$Mt_c + n\tau$
	nESBT	$(\frac{M}{n} + nB)t_c + (\lceil \frac{M}{Bn} \rceil + n)\tau$	$\frac{1}{n}\sqrt{\frac{M\tau}{t_c}}$	$(\sqrt{\frac{Mt_c}{n}} + \sqrt{n\tau})^2$

For the graph G^{nRH}, the n paths are not edge-disjoint. But, all edges at a given distance from the source are mapped to different cube edges. Sending the entire data set M/n for each path concurrently is contention free. The data transfer time is an order of N/n higher than that of the H routing with pipelining. For nRSBT routing, the number of elements traversing every edge from the root is the same as in the SBT routing, and the transmission time is bounded from below by nMt_c with *one-port* communication. This time is an order of n higher than the lower bound.

Theorem 5: For a fixed packet size, the number of routing cycles to broadcast n packets by nRSBT routing is bounded from below by $2n - 1$ for *one-port* and n for *n-port* communication.

Proof: For *one-port (n-port)* communication, the root needs n (1) cycles to send out n packets, and the last packet has a latency of $n - 1$ cycles for a fixed packet size. ∎

With *one-port* communication, our scheduling discipline for the nRSBT routing completes in $2n - 1$ routing cycles for a packet size $B \geq M$. With *n-port* communication the scheduling of the data for each SBT used in the nRSBT graph is made as in the case of *one-port* communication for a single SBT. Since the SBT's are rotated, all ports of the root are used in every routing cycle until the last packet leaves the root. Data for the mth SBT is sent across dimension $(m + p) \bmod n$ during cycle p. There is no edge-conflict for this nonpipe-

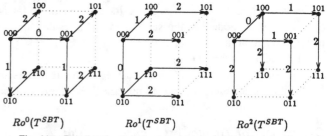

$Ro^0(T^{SBT})$ $\quad Ro^1(T^{SBT})$ $\quad Ro^2(T^{SBT})$

Fig. 11. Broadcasting based on three rotated SBT's in a 3-cube.

lined routing. Fig. 11 shows the routing of the three distinctly rotated SBT's in a 3-cube. The labels on the edges represent the routing cycle.

The number of routing cycles to broadcast n packets by nESBT routing is bounded from below by $2n$ for *one-port* and $n + 1$ for *n-port* communication, since the height of the graph is $n + 1$. The scheduling discipline for *one-port* communication and nESBT routing is defined by labeling the edges of the nESBT graph. The labels define the routing cycles during which the first packet arrives through that graph edge. We first define the edge label in the 0th spanning tree of the nESBT graph. Edges in dimension m are labeled m, except that the labels of the edges to the leaf nodes are labeled n. The labels of the edges in the kth spanning tree are defined by adding k to the label of the corresponding edges in the 0th spanning tree. Fig. 7 shows an nESBT graph for a 3-cube labeled by the

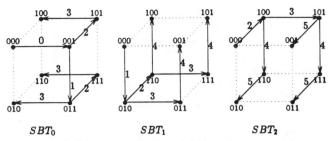

SBT₀   SBT₁   SBT₂

Fig. 12. Scheduling in an nESBT graph with *one-port* communication.

algorithm above. Fig. 12 shows a different view of the labels of the three composed spanning trees.

Theorem 6: For the nESBT graph, the scheduling discipline defined by the labeling scheme allows conflict-free *one-port* communication.

Proof: It follows from the labeling scheme that edges in dimension m are labeled $m \pmod n$. Also, for each spanning tree, the label of the outgoing edges of any node is greater than the label of the incoming edge. ∎

The largest label of all the input edges is $2n - 1$. Broadcasting the first n packets (one packet per subtree) can be done in $2n$ cycles. The complexity for *one-port* nESBT routing follows directly from the definition of the scheduling discipline, and the proof of it being contention free. For *n-port* communication, it is easy to determine the time of arrival of messages. The path length between nodes s and i in the kth spanning tree is equal to

$$\begin{cases} \|c\|, & \text{if } c_k = 1; \\ \|c\| + 2, & \text{if } c_k = 0, \end{cases}$$

where $\|c\|$ is the number of 1-bits in c. The input ports of node i that correspond to bits that are equal to 1 in the binary encoding of c receive the first element during the $(\|c\| - 1)$th routing cycle. The other input ports receive the first element during the $(\|c\| + 1)$th cycle.

B. Summary of One-to-All Broadcasting

In general, the data set to be broadcast is divided into a number of distinct packets. If the *o-graph* is a spanning tree, then every packet needs to be sent on every port of the root. The number of routing cycles required by the root to complete the communication of each distinct packet is summarized on the left of Table VI and the maximum propagation delay is summarized on the right.

In the nRSBT routing, every packet needs to be routed on every port because of the edge sharing. Note, that broadcasting by Hamiltonian path routing may be faster than by SBT routing depending on the values of M, t_c, τ and N. With *n-port* communication, the source can send out n distinct packets every cycle in the nESBT routing since the spanning trees are edge-disjoint, but only n packets every n cycles for the nRSBT routing.

For *n-port* communication, the data transmission time is reduced by a factor of approximately n for an arbitrary packet size in the SBT, nRSBT, and nESBT routings and the schedulings defined in Table IV. Optimizing the packet size makes the number of routing cyles proportional to the height of the *o-graph*. The data transmission times for the optimum packet sizes and *n-port* communication are approximately a

factor of n less than the transmission times for *one-port* communication with optimized buffer and an *o-graph* for which the root has degree n.

The nESBT routing always offers a reduction in bandwidth requirement for individual communication links by a factor of approximately n over the SBT and nRSBT routings. The nESBT routing offers a speedup of up to n over SBT and nRSBT routings for sufficiently large values of M, both for *one-port* and *n-port* communication. Communication complexities of broadcasting based on the H, SBT, and nRSBT algorithms are compared to that based on the nESBT in Table VII.

V. ONE-TO-ALL PERSONALIZED COMMUNICATION

In personalized communication, no replication of information takes place during distribution, nor is there any reduction during the reverse operation; the root has M elements for every node.

Lemma 20: The data transmission time for *one-to-all personalized communication* is bounded from below by $(N - 1)Mt_c$ for *one-port* communication, and by $((N - 1)M/n)t_c$ for *n-port* communication. A lower bound for the total time is $\max((N - 1)Mt_c, n\tau)$, and $\max(((N - 1)M/n)t_c, n\tau)$, respectively.

Proof: The root needs to send out $(N - 1)/M$ elements. ∎

In SBT routing for personalized communication the maximum number of nodes connected to the root through one of its edges is $NM/2$, and a data transmission time of the order given in the lemma is not achievable for *n-port* communication. In an SBnT graph, all edges of the root connect subtrees of approximately equal size. For the SBG, nRSBT, and nESBT graphs, all outgoing (cube) edges of the root transmit the same amount of data, $(N - 1)M/n$.

A. The Time Complexity of Personalized Communication

The general strategy for personalized communications is to schedule the data for the most remote nodes first. With *n-port* communication the ordering between ports is irrelevant, and a *reverse-breadth-first* ordering for each port of each node is the scheduling discipline. For *one-port* communication the scheduling disciplines depend on the *o-graph*, Table VIII.

Lemma 21: Scheduling nodes by complementing their binary addresses results in port communications in a binary-reflected Gray code order for *one-port* SBT routing.

Note that for *one-port* communication, scheduling the tallest remaining subtree first for each node recursively has the same complexity as the suggested discipline, but if certain

TABLE VI
NUMBER OF CYCLES PER DISTINCT PACKET (LEFT) AND PROPAGATION DELAY (RIGHT)

Routing	# of cyc. per pkt.		Propagation delay
	one-port	*n-port*	*one-* & *n-port*
H	1	1	$N - 1$
SBT	n	1	n
nRSBT	n	1	n
nESBT	1	$\frac{1}{n}$	$n + 1$

373

TABLE VII
RELATIVE COMPLEXITIES OF ONE-TO-ALL BROADCASTING

Communication model	Routing	One packet	$B = B_{opt}, \tau \gg M t_c$	$B = B_{opt}, n^2 \tau \ll M t_c$
one-port	H/nESBT	$\frac{N-1}{n+1}$	$\frac{N-2}{n}$	1
	SBT/nESBT	$\frac{n}{n+1}$	≈ 1	n
	nRSBT/nESBT	$\frac{n}{n+1}$	≈ 2	n
n-port	H/nESBT	$\frac{N-1}{n+1}$	$\frac{N-2}{n}$	n
	SBT,nRSBT/nESBT	$\frac{n}{n+1}$	≈ 1	n

Comm.	Routing	Scheduling discipline
one-port	H	Order nodes by decreased distance, pipeline.
	SBT	Order nodes by complementing their binary addresses.
	nESBT	All data for the tallest remaining subtree for each spanning tree.
	nRSBT	All data for the tallest remaining subtree of the spanning trees $0, 1, \ldots, p$ at once during routing cycle $p < n$, and all data for the tallest remaining subtrees of all spanning trees during cycles $n \leq p < 2n - 1$. For the source $B = N(1 - \frac{1}{2^{p+1}})\frac{M}{n}$ for $p < n$, and $B = N(\frac{1}{2^{p+1-n}} - \frac{1}{N})\frac{M}{n}$ for $n \leq p < 2n - 1$.
	SBG	Order nodes by decresing distance for each subtree. Order subtrees cyclically.
n-port	All	Order nodes in *reverse-breadth-first* order. All subtrees (spanning trees) are scheduled concurrently.

overlap between communications on different ports is possible, as on the Intel iPSC, then the discipline we adopt yields a lower time complexity if $M \geq B$.

B. Summary of One-to-All Personalized Communication

Tables IX and X summarize the communication complexities of personalized communication. For the SBT routing and *one-port* communication, our scheduling discipline yields a time complexity within a factor of two of the lower bound, providing the packet size is sufficiently large. The data transmission time of the nRSBT scheduling discipline is the same as the lower bound, $M(N - 1)t_c$; however, the minimum number of routing cycles is $2n - 1$. For the SBG routing and $B \geq (N - 1)M/n$, the root needs to perform only one communication per subtree, and completes the communication in time $T = (N - 1)Mt_c + n\tau$. But, an additional $n - 1$ routing cycles are needed to complete the communication. An upper bound on the time for personalized communication with unbounded packet size is $T = N(1 + (2 \log n)/n)Mt_c + (2n - 1)\tau$ for SBG routing [15]. The number of routing cycles is almost twice that of the SBT personalized communication and the total transfer time is higher by a lower order term. With a packet size of $(N - 1)M/n$, the number of routing cycles is approximately $2n$ for SBT, nESBT, nRSBT, and SBG communication. With *one-port* communication and a packet size $B \leq M$, the complexities of SBT, nRSBT, SBG, and H communications are approximately the same.

With *n-port* communication and *reverse-breadth-first* scheduling, the data transmission time of the SBT, nESBT, nRSBT, and SBG routings are all dominated by the root by Lemmas 6, 10, 12, and 18. The number of element transfers is approximately the same for all ports of the root except for the SBT communication. The number of routing cycles and the transmission time of the nESBT, SBG, and nRSBT communications are lower than that of the SBT by a factor of $1/2n$ for a packet size $B \leq M$. With a sufficiently large packet size all communications yield a minimum of n routing cycles, with the exception of the nESBT, which requires one more cycle. The optimum packet size for the nESBT, nRSBT, and SBG communications is $\sqrt{2/\pi}NM/n^{3/2}$, compared to $NM/\sqrt{2\pi(n-1)}$ for the SBT. The nRSBT routing is never of a lower complexity than the SBG routing, and of a higher complexity if n does not divide M. With $(M \bmod n) = k \neq 0$ a combination of *reflections* and *rotations* minimizes the maximum number of elements that need to be transferred over any cube edge. For k even $k/2$ distinct rotations should be used, and for every rotated graph a reflected graph is also used. For k even and optimally rotated SBT's the maximum number of elements transferred over a cube edge is $(N - 1)2^{(n/k)-1}/(2^{n/k} - 1)$ and for optimally reflected and rotated SBT's it is $(N - 1)(2^{(2n/k)-1} + 1)/(2^{2n/k} - 1)$.

VI. ALL-TO-ALL BROADCASTING

A. Time Bounds and Scheduling Disciplines

Theorem 7: A lower bound for all-to-all broadcasting is max $((N - 1)Mt_c, n\tau)$ for *one-port* communication and max $((N - 1)M/n)t_c, n\tau)$ for *n-port* communication.

Proof: Each node receives M elements from every other node, i.e., each node receives $(N - 1)M$ elements. Hence, for *one-port* communication a lower bound for the data

TABLE IX
THE COMPLEXITY OF ONE-TO-ALL PERSONALIZED COMMUNICATION

Comm.	Routing	T
one-port	H	$(N-1)Mt_c + \max(\lceil\frac{(N-1)M}{B}\rceil, N-1)\tau$
	SBT	$(N-1)Mt_c + \sum_{i=0}^{n-1}\lceil\frac{2^iM}{B}\rceil\tau$
	nESBT	$\frac{n+1}{n}(N-1)Mt_c + (n\lceil\frac{(N-1)M}{nB}\rceil + \sum_{i=0}^{n-1}\lceil\frac{2^iM}{nB}\rceil)\tau$
	nRSBT	$(N-1)Mt_c + (\sum_{i=1}^{n-1}\lceil\frac{(N-2^i)M}{nB}\rceil + \sum_{i=1}^{n}\lceil\frac{(2^i-1)M}{nB}\rceil)\tau$
n-port	SBT	$\frac{NM}{2}t_c + \sum_{i=0}^{n-1}\lceil\binom{n-1}{i}\frac{M}{B}\rceil\tau$
	nESBT	$\frac{(N-1)M}{n}t_c + (\lceil\frac{M}{nB}\rceil + \lceil\frac{(n-1)M}{nB}\rceil + \sum_{i=2}^{n}\lceil\frac{M}{nB}\binom{n}{i}\rceil)\tau$
	nRSBT	$\frac{(N-1)M}{n}t_c + \sum_{i=0}^{n-1}\lceil\binom{n}{i}\frac{M}{nB}\rceil\tau$
	SBG	$\frac{(N-1)M}{n}t_c + \sum_{i=0}^{n-1}\lceil\binom{n}{i}\frac{M}{nB}\rceil\tau$

TABLE X
THE OPTIMUM COMPLEXITY OF ONE-TO-ALL PERSONALIZED
COMMUNICATION

Comm.	Routing	B_{opt}	T_{min}
one-port	H	M	$(N-1)Mt_c + (N-1)\tau$
	SBT	$\frac{NM}{2}$	$(N-1)Mt_c + n\tau$
	nESBT	$\frac{(N-1)M}{n}$	$\frac{n+1}{n}(N-1)Mt_c + 2n\tau$
	nRSBT	$\frac{(N-1)M}{n}$	$(N-1)Mt_c + (2n-1)\tau$
	SBG	$\frac{(N-1)M}{n}$	$\le N(1+\frac{2\log n}{n})Mt_c + (2n-1)\tau$
n-port	SBT	$\frac{NM}{\sqrt{2\pi(n-1)}}$	$\frac{NM}{2}t_c + n\tau$
	nESBT	$\sqrt{\frac{2}{\pi}\frac{NM}{n^{3/2}}}$	$\frac{(N-1)M}{n}t_c + (n+1)\tau$
	nRSBT	$\sqrt{\frac{2}{\pi}\frac{NM}{n^{3/2}}}$	$\frac{(N-1)M}{n}t_c + n\tau$
	SBG	$\sqrt{\frac{2}{\pi}\frac{NM}{n^{3/2}}}$	$\frac{(N-1)M}{n}t_c + n\tau$

TABLE XI
SCHEDULING DISCIPLINE FOR ALL-TO-ALL BROADCASTING

Comm.	Scheduling discipline
one-port	1. For each spanning tree of the *a-graph*, the labels of the outgoing edges of any node are greater than the label of the incoming edge.
	2. All the edges with the same label in the *o-graph* are in the same dimension.
n-port	All data sent at once, spanning trees concurrently.

transfer time is $(N-1)Mt_c$, and with *n-port* communication the time is bounded by $((N-1)M/n)t_c$. ∎

Lemma 22: The data transfer time for *one-port* communication is minimized if one dimension is routed per cycle, and all nodes use the same scheduling discipline.

Proof: The number of elements transferred on every edge in the dimension subject to routing is the same, since the communication graphs for the different sources are translations of each other. ∎

For *one-port* all-to-all broadcasting it remains to define a scheduling discipline that minimizes the number of startups, preserving the minimum data transfer time. This can be accomplished implicitly by labeling the edges of the *o-graph* generating the *a-graph*. The label on the edge corresponds to the cycle during which the data are transferred across that edge. The rules are summarized in Table XI, which also gives the scheduling discipline for the *n-port* case. Rule 1 is obvious. Rule 2 is a sufficient conditon satisfying the *one-port* communication constraint. The labeling scheme is the same as the one used in the *one-port one-to-all personalized communication* based on the nESBT graph. The number of startups required for the broadcasting is equal to the maximum label plus 1 (the least label being 0). For a spanning tree of height h, the minimax label is at least $h-1$ by rule 1.

For the H path, we label the ith edge in the path i. The maximum label is $N-2$, which is a minimax label. For the SBT graph labeling edges in dimension i by i satisfies both rules. The maximum label is $n-1$, which is also a minimax label. For an *a-graph* based on the nESBT, nRSBT or SBG graphs, we first define the edge label in the 0th spanning tree of each such graph. Edges in dimension i are labeled i, except for the nESBT graph for which the labels of the edges to the leaf nodes (all in dimension 0) is n. The 0th subtree of the nESBT graph is equal to an n level SBT with the smallest subtree deleted. Hence, the minimax label is n for the 0th spanning tree of the nESBT graph. For the nESBT and nRSBT graphs, the labels of the edges in subtree j are defined by adding j to the label of the corresponding edges in subtree 0. The minimax label for the entire graph is equal to the minimax label of subtree 0 plus $n-1$. For the SBG graph, all the n composed SBnT's are labeled in the same way. By Theorem 2, it can be shown that the minimax label of the rotated SBnT

$R^d(G^{\mathrm{SBnT}})$, $d \in \mathfrak{D}$, is $2n - 2$ if $d = 1$; and $2n - 3$, otherwise. The minimax label of the nESBT, nRSBT, and SBG are $2n - 1$, $2n - 2$, and $2n - 2$, respectively. The labeling of the nESBT graph defined here is the same as the labeling for *one-port* one-to-all broadcasting, Fig. 12. The amount of data transferred during cycle i is equal to $M/n \times$ (number of edges labeled i). The maximum packet size and the number of startups can be derived easily from the labels of the edges.

Lemma 23: A lower bound for data transmission time of all-to-all broadcasting based on $G^{\mathrm{id}}(*)$ and "any" scheduling discipline is

$$\max_{\forall d \in \mathfrak{D}} E^{\mathrm{id}}(d)Mt_c.$$

Proof: $E^{\mathrm{id}}(d)M$ elements need to be sent across every cube edge in dimension d. ∎

Theorem 8: The communication time for all-to-all broadcasting based on $G^{\mathrm{id}}(*)$ of height h, *n-port* communication and the defined scheduling discipline requires a time of

$$T = \sum_{l=0}^{h-1} \left(Mt_c \times \max_{\forall d \in \mathfrak{D}} e^{\mathrm{id}}(d, l) + \left\lceil \frac{M}{B} \times \max_{\forall d \in \mathfrak{D}} e^{\mathrm{id}}(d, l) \right\rceil \tau \right).$$

If $B \geq \max_{0 \leq l \leq h-1, \ \forall d \in \mathfrak{D}} (M \times e^{\mathrm{id}}(d, l))$ then

$$T = \left(\sum_{l=0}^{h-1} \max_{\forall d \in \mathfrak{D}} e^{\mathrm{id}}(d, l) \right) Mt_c + h\tau.$$

Proof: Each node broadcasts its data set M according to its own *o-graph*. During the lth routing cycle all nodes at level $l + 1$ of each *o-graph* receive messages sent out from the roots during the 0th routing cycle. By Lemma 8, the amount of data contending for a communication link in dimension d is $M \times e^{\mathrm{id}}(d, l)$. ∎

Theorem 7 gives a lower bound for the communication time for any routing and scheduling discipline, and Lemma 23 gives a lower bound expressed in terms of an *a-graph*. Theorem 8 gives an upper bound. Next we give complexity estimates for some *a-graphs*, and show that broadcasting based on $G^{\mathrm{SBT}}(*)$ with the scheduling disciplines in Table XI is optimum within a factor of 2 for *one-port* communication, and that the schedulings of the $G^{\mathrm{SBG}}(*)$ and $G^{\mathrm{nRSBT}}(*)$ graphs are optimum within a factor of 2 for *n-port* communication.

Corollary 8: For a given *a-graph* satisfying $e^{\mathrm{id}}(x, l) = e^{\mathrm{id}}(y, l)$, $\forall x, y \in \mathfrak{D}$, and $0 \leq l < h$, the communication time for *all-to-all broadcasting* based on the graph $G^{\mathrm{id}}(*)$ of height h and *n-port* communication and the scheduling disciplines of Table XI is

$$T = \frac{(N-1)M}{n} t_c + h\tau, \qquad \text{if } B \geq \max_{0 \leq l < h} (M \times e^{\mathrm{id}}(d, l)).$$

Proof: The corollary follows from Theorem 8. ∎

From Table III and Corollary 8, the nRH, nRSBT, nESBT, and the SBG routings all yield the lower bound for the data transfer time with *n-port* communication. In fact, following Corollary 8, we have the following corollary.

Corollary 9: For $G^{\mathrm{id}}(*)$ with $G^{\mathrm{id}}(0)$ composed of n distinctly rotated spanning trees, the data transfer time for all-to-all broadcasting is minimun with *n-port* communication and the defined scheduling.

Routing according to a greedy *o-graph*, while it is a necessary condition for the *all-to-all personalized communication* to attain the minimum data transfer time, is not necessary for the *all-to-all broadcasting*. The nRSBT and the SBG both with minimum height also attain the minimum number of startups.

B. The Complexity of All-to-All Broadcasting

Tables XII and XIII summarize the complexity of all-to-all broadcasting.

The *one-port* $G^H(*)$ routing is employed in the matrix multiplication algorithm by Dekel [5], [21]. Messages with different source nodes are routed through different H paths. Messages are exchanged along a sequence of dimensions such as 0, 1, 0, 2, 0, 1, 0, 3, $\cdots$, etc. The SBT communication amounts to a single exchange per dimension [28].

With *one-port* communication SBT routing for all-to-all broadcasting is optimum within a factor of two. The H, nESBT, nRSBT, and SBG routings all have the minimum data transfer time. The number of startups is $(N - 1)$, $2n$, $2n - 1$ and $2n - 1$, respectively, with a packet size of $M(N - 2)/n$, $M(N - 1)/n$, and $M(N - 1)/n$, respectively. With a packet size of order MN/n, the number of startups for SBT, nESBT, nRSBT, and SBG routings are all comparable. Note that if the packet size is smaller than the data set to be broadcast, then the SBT routing is of the same complexity as the H routing. But, if $B \geq MN/2$ then $T_{\min} = (N - 1)Mt_c + n\tau$, which is optimum within a factor of 2. The startup time is reduced by a factor of $(N - 1)/n$ compared to the H routing.

With *n-port* communication the nRH, nESBT, nRSBT, and SBG routings achieve the lower bound transmission time for a sufficiently large packet size. Both the nRSBT and SBG routings also attain the minimum number of startups n with the same packet size $B \geq \sqrt{2/\pi} NM/n^{3/2}$. The nESBT routing has one more startup. The nRH routing, although optimum for data transfer time, has $N - 1$ startups. The SBT routing yields a slow-down of approximately $n/2$ for the data transfer time compared to the lower bound routing.

VII. ALL-TO-ALL PERSONALIZED COMMUNICATION

A. Time Bounds

Theorem 9: A lower bound for *one-port* all-to-all personalized communication is $\max((nNM/2)t_c, n\tau)$. The packet size must be at least $NM/2$ to attain this lower bound.

Proof: The bandwidth requirement for distributing personalized data from one node is

$$\sum_{i=0}^{n} i \binom{n}{i} M = \frac{nNM}{2}.$$

The total bandwidth requirement is $nN^2M/2$. During each cycle only N edges of the n-cube can communicate in the case of *one-port* communication; $nNM/2$ is the minimum number of element transfers in sequence. The number of startups is at

TABLE XII
THE COMPLEXITY OF ALL-TO-ALL BROADCASTING

Comm.	Routing	T
one-port	H	$(N-1)Mt_c + \lceil \frac{M}{B} \rceil (N-1)\tau$
	SBT	$(N-1)Mt_c + \sum_{i=0}^{n-1} \lceil \frac{2^i M}{B} \rceil \tau$
	nRSBT	$(N-1)Mt_c + (\sum_{i=0}^{n-1} \lceil \frac{(2^{i+1}-1)M}{nB} \rceil + \sum_{i=n}^{2n-2} \lceil \frac{(N-2^{i-n+1})M}{nB} \rceil)\tau$
	nESBT	$(N-1)Mt_c + (\sum_{i=0}^{n-1} \lceil \frac{2^i M}{nB} \rceil + \sum_{i=n}^{2n-2} \lceil \frac{(N-1-2^{i-n})M}{nB} \rceil)\tau$
n-port	nRH	$\frac{(N-1)M}{n}t_c + \lceil \frac{M}{nB} \rceil (N-1)\tau$
	SBT	$\frac{NM}{2}t_c + \sum_{i=0}^{n-1} \lceil \binom{n-1}{i} \frac{M}{B} \rceil \tau$
	nRSBT	$\frac{(N-1)M}{n}t_c + \sum_{i=1}^{n} \lceil \binom{n}{i} \frac{M}{nB} \rceil \tau$
	nESBT	$\frac{(N-1)M}{n}t_c + (\sum_{i=2}^{n} \lceil \binom{n}{i} \frac{M}{nB} \rceil + \lceil \frac{M}{nB} \rceil + \lceil \frac{(n-1)M}{nB} \rceil)\tau$
	SBG	$\frac{(N-1)M}{n}t_c + \sum_{i=1}^{n} \lceil \binom{n}{i} \frac{M}{nB} \rceil \tau$

TABLE XIII
THE OPTIMUM COMPLEXITY OF ALL-TO-ALL BROADCASTING

Comm.	Routing	B_{opt}	T_{min}
one-port	H	M	$(N-1)Mt_c + (N-1)\tau$
	SBT	$\frac{NM}{2}$	$(N-1)Mt_c + n\tau$
	nRSBT	$\frac{(N-1)M}{n}$	$(N-1)Mt_c + (2n-1)\tau$
	nESBT	$\frac{(N-2)M}{n}$	$(N-1)Mt_c + 2n\tau$
	SBG	$\frac{(N-1)M}{n}$	$(N-1)Mt_c + (2n-1)\tau$
n-port	nRH	$\frac{M}{n}$	$\frac{(N-1)M}{n}t_c + (N-1)\tau$
	SBT	$\frac{NM}{\sqrt{2\pi(n-1)}}$	$\frac{NM}{2}t_c + n\tau$
	nRSBT	$\sqrt{\frac{2}{\pi}\frac{NM}{n^{3/2}}}$	$\frac{(N-1)M}{n}t_c + n\tau$
	nESBT	$\sqrt{\frac{2}{\pi}\frac{NM}{n^{3/2}}}$	$\frac{(N-1)M}{n}t_c + (n+1)\tau$
	SBG	$\sqrt{\frac{2}{\pi}\frac{NM}{n^{3/2}}}$	$\frac{(N-1)M}{n}t_c + n\tau$

least n. The maximum packet size can be derived by dividing the total bandwidth requirement $nN^2M/2$ by the number of cycles n, and the number of directed edges that can be used in each routing cycle N. ∎

Theorem 10: A lower bound for *n-port* all-to-all personalized communication is max $((NM/2)t_c, n\tau)$. The packet size must be at least $NM/(2n)$ to attain this lower bound.

Proof: From Theorem 9 the total bandwidth requirement is $nN^2M/2$. During each routing cycle nN directed edges can communicate concurrently. The maximum packet size is derived by dividing the total bandwidth requirement by the number of cycles n and the total number of links nN. ∎

Theorem 11: The time for *n-port* all-to-all personalized communication based on $G^{id}(*)$ of height h and *postorder* scheduling is

$$T = \sum_{l=0}^{h-1} \left(Mt_c \times \max_{\forall d \in \mathfrak{D}} v^{id}(d, l) + \left\lceil \frac{M}{B} \times \max_{\forall d \in \mathfrak{D}} v^{id}(d, l) \right\rceil \tau \right).$$

If $B \geq \max_{0 \leq l \leq h-1, \forall d \in \mathfrak{D}} (M \times v^{id}(d, l))$ then

$$T = \left(\sum_{l=0}^{h-1} \max_{\forall d \in \mathfrak{D}} v^{id}(d, l) \right) Mt_c + h\tau.$$

Proof: For each $G^{id}(s)$, the total amount of data transmitted across all edges in dimension d during routing cycle l is $v^{id}(d, l) \times M$, $0 \leq l \leq h - 1$. For $G^{id}(*) = \bigcup_{s \in \mathfrak{N}} \mathrm{Tr}(s, G^{id}(0))$, each *a-graph* edge is mapped to N distinct cube edges with N distinct Exclusive-OR operations on both endpoints. The amount of data transmitted across each

cube edge in dimension d during routing cycle l is $v^{id}(d, l) \times M$. ∎

Theorem 12: The time for *n-port* all-to-all personalized communication based on $G^{id}(*)$ of height h and *reverse-breadth-first* scheduling is

$$T = \sum_{l=0}^{h-1} \left(Mt_c \times \max_{\forall d \in \mathfrak{D}} u^{id}(d, l) + \left\lceil \frac{M}{B} \times \max_{\forall d \in \mathfrak{D}} u^{id}(d, l) \right\rceil \tau \right)$$

If $B \geq \max_{0 \leq l \leq h-1, \forall d \in \mathfrak{D}} (M \times u^{id}(d, l))$ then

$$T = \left(\sum_{l=0}^{h-1} \max_{\forall d \in \mathfrak{D}} u^{id}(d, l) \right) Mt_c + h\tau.$$

Proof: Similar to the proof of Theorem 11. ∎

Theorem 13: The all-to-all personalized communication based on N translated *o-graphs* will attain the lower bound for the data transfer time iff the *o-graph* is greedy.

Proof: The bandwidth requirement for each node is

$$\sum_{l=0}^{h-1} \sum_{d=0}^{n-1} v^{id}(d, l) = \sum_{l=0}^{h-1} \sum_{d=0}^{n-1} u^{id}(d, l)$$

$$= \sum_{l=1}^{h} l \times (\text{the number of nodes at level } l).$$

Hence, nongreedy *o-graphs* require more data transfer than greedy *o-graphs*. ∎

Theorem 14: All-to-all personalized *n-port* communication based on $G^{id}(*)$ where $G^{id}(0) = \bigcup_{d \in \mathfrak{D}} \mathrm{Ro}^d(T^{id'}(0))$ and $T^{id'}(0)$ is greedy, can attain both the minimum data transmission time, $(NM/2)t_c$, and the minimum number of startups, n, for $B \geq (N - 1)M/n$ both for *postorder* and *reverse-breadth-first* schedulings.

Proof: From Theorem 11 and Corollary 3, the data transfer time is

$$\sum_{l=0}^{n-1} \sum_{i=l+1}^{n} \frac{M}{n} \binom{n}{i} t_c = \frac{NM}{2} t_c.$$

For the *postorder* scheduling, the packet size $(N - 1)M/n$ occurs during routing cycle 0. Similarly, the *reverse-breadth-first* scheduling discipline can be shown to be optimum, and has the same value of the maximum packet size. It occurs during the last routing cycle. ∎

TABLE XIV
THE COMPLEXITY OF ALL-TO-ALL PERSONALIZED COMMUNICATION

Comm.	Routing	T
one-port	H	$\frac{(N-1)NM}{2}t_c + \sum_{i=1}^{N-1}\lceil\frac{iM}{B}\rceil\tau$
	SBT	$\frac{nNM}{2}t_c + \lceil\frac{NM}{2B}\rceil n\tau$
	nRSBT	$\frac{nNM}{2}t_c + (\sum_{i=0}^{n-1}\lceil\frac{(i+1)NM}{2nB}\rceil + \sum_{i=n}^{i=2n-2}\lceil\frac{(2n-i-1)NM}{2nB}\rceil)\tau$
	nESBT	$(\frac{nN}{2}+N-2)Mt_c + (\sum_{i=0}^{n-1}\lceil(\frac{(i+2)N}{2}-1)\frac{M}{nB}\rceil + \sum_{i=1}^{n}\lceil(\frac{iN}{2}-1)\frac{M}{nB}\rceil)\tau$
	SBG	$\approx \frac{nNM}{2}t_c + \max(2n-1,\frac{nNM}{2B})\tau$
n-port	nRH	$\frac{(N-1)NM}{2n}t_c + \sum_{i=1}^{N-1}\lceil\frac{iM}{nB}\rceil\tau$
	SBT	$(\sum_{l=0}^{\lfloor\frac{n-1}{2}\rfloor}\binom{2l}{l}2^{n-2l-1} + \sum_{l=\lfloor\frac{n+1}{2}\rfloor}^{n-1}\binom{n-1}{l})Mt_c$ $+(\sum_{l=0}^{\lfloor\frac{n-1}{2}\rfloor}\lceil\binom{2l}{l}\frac{2^{n-2l-1}M}{B}\rceil + \sum_{l=\lfloor\frac{n+1}{2}\rfloor}^{n-1}\lceil\binom{n-1}{l}\frac{M}{B}\rceil)\tau$
	nRSBT	$\frac{NM}{2}t_c + \lceil\frac{NM}{2nB}\rceil n\tau$
	nESBT	$(\frac{N}{2}+\frac{N-2}{n})Mt_c + (\sum_{i=2}^{n}\lceil\sum_{j=i}^{n}\binom{n}{j}\frac{M}{nB}\rceil + \lceil\frac{(N-2)M}{nB}\rceil + \lceil\frac{(N-1)M}{nB}\rceil)\tau$
	SBG	$\frac{NM}{2}t_c + \sum_{i=1}^{n}\lceil\sum_{j=i}^{n}\binom{n}{j}\frac{M}{nB}\rceil\tau$

TABLE XV
THE OPTIMUM COMPLEXITY OF ALL-TO-ALL PERSONALIZED COMMUNICATION

Comm.	Routing	B_{opt}	T_{min}
one-port	H	$(N-1)M$	$\frac{(N-1)NM}{2}t_c + (N-1)\tau$
	SBT	$\frac{NM}{2}$	$\frac{nNM}{2}t_c + n\tau$
	nRSBT	$\frac{NM}{2}$	$\frac{nNM}{2}t_c + (2n-1)\tau$
	nESBT	$\frac{M}{n}(\frac{N(n-1)}{2}-1)$	$(\frac{nN}{2}+N-2)Mt_c + 2n\tau$
	SBG	$\frac{NM}{2}$	$\frac{nNM}{2}t_c + (2n-1)\tau$
n-port	nRH	$\frac{(N-1)M}{n}$	$\frac{(N-1)NM}{2n}t_c + (N-1)\tau$
	SBT	$\frac{NM}{2}$	$O(\sqrt{n})NMt_c + n\tau$
	nRSBT	$\frac{NM}{2n}$	$\frac{NM}{2}t_c + n\tau$
	nESBT	$\frac{(N-1)M}{n}$	$(\frac{N}{2}+\frac{N-2}{n})Mt_c + (n+1)\tau$
	SBG	$\frac{(N-1)M}{n}$	$\frac{NM}{2}t_c + n\tau$

Corollary 10: All-to-all personalized *n-port* communication based on $G^{\text{nRSBT}}(*)$ and $G^{\text{SBG}}(*)$ can attain the time $(NM/2)t_c + n\tau$, which is within a factor of 2 of the lower bound.

Notice that in *one-port* communication the data transfer time is always optimal if the routing is based on N translated greedy *o-graphs* and appropriate scheduling. But, not all greedy *o-graphs* have the same number of startups. Only the SBT graph allows a minimum of n startups for sufficiently large packet size. The minimum number of startups can be decided by the same labeling rules as were used in all-to-all broadcasting. The minimum number of startups is the same as for the all-to-all broadcasting. The difference is that the amount of data transferred during cycle i is equal to the sum of weighted subtree sizes with the root of each subtree connected through an edge labeled i to its parent.

B. The Complexity of All-to-All Personalized Communication

Tables XIV and XV summarize the complexity estimates.

With *one-port* communication and H routing, both the data transfer time and the startup times are off by a factor of N/n compared to the optimum for *one-port* communication. The complexity for *n-port* communication and nRH routing holds for both the *postorder* and *reverse-breadth-first* schedulings. The routing fully utilizes the cube bandwidth; however, much of the data transfer is not through the shortest path, i.e, nongreedy.

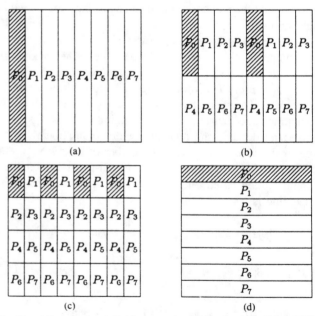

Fig. 13. All-to-all personalized communication in a 3-cube based on SBT's.

Fig. 13 shows all-to-all personalized communication on a 3-cube based on eight SBT's. The shaded area represents the portion of the data residing in processor 0 (denoted P_0). The task is to exchange the jth block of data of processor i with the ith block of processor j for any two distinct processors i and j.

378

If initially processor i owns the ith block column as in Fig. 13(a) then on completion of the all-to-all personalized communication processor i contains the ith block row as in Fig. 13(d).

Lemma 24: All-to-all personalized *one-port* communication based on $G^{SBT}(*)$ can be accomplished in time $(nNM/2)t_c + n\tau$, which is within a factor of 2 of the lower bound.

Proof: During the routing cycle 0, $NM/2$ data are exchanged along the lowest dimension. Then, the procedure is applied recursively with data set doubling for each cycle of the recursion and the dimension of the cube decreasing by 1. Let $T(i, M)$ be the time required by the stated personalized all-to-all routing algorithm with initially M data per node in an i-cube. Clearly, $T(n, M) = 2^{n-1}Mt_c + \tau + T(n - 1, 2M)$ and $T(1, M) = Mt_c + \tau$. Hence, $T(n, M) = (nNM/2)t_c + n\tau$. ∎

In the case of *n-port* communication, we can find the communication complexity from the previously derived formula. The interesting quantity for *postorder* scheduling is $\sum_{l=0}^{n-1} \max v^{id}(d, l)$.

$$\sum_{l=0}^{n-1} \max_d v^{SBT}(d, l) = \sum_{l=0}^{\lfloor (n-1)/2 \rfloor} \binom{2l}{l} 2^{n-2l-1}$$
$$+ \sum_{l=\lfloor (n+1)/2 \rfloor}^{n-1} \binom{n-1}{l}$$

which is of $O(\sqrt{n}N)$. Since $u^{SBT}(d, l) = v^{SBT}(n - d - 1, l)$, Table III, the *reverse-breadth-first* scheduling yields the same result.

The maximum packet size for nRSBT communication can be reduced from $(N - 1)M/n$ to $NM/(2n)$ by using a scheduling such that each SBT used in composing the nRSBT graph is the same as the scheduling for the SBT graph in *one-port one-to-all personalized communication*. The n SBT's are scheduled concurrently. Note that the same scheme, if applied to all-to-all broadcasting, will increase the maximum packet size from $\sqrt{2/\pi}NM/n^{3/2}$ to $NM/(2n)$. The time for nESBT communication is obtained from Theorems 11 and 12.

C. Summary of All-to-All Personalized Communication

With *one-port* communication, the SBT, nRSBT, SBG, and nESBT routings with *postorder* and *reverse-breadth-first* schedulings for all-to-all personalized communication are optimum within constant factors, Table XV. The SBT has the lowest complexity with a sufficiently large packet size. Only greedy *o-graphs* attain the optimum data transfer time. In fact, the optimum data transfer time can always be attained for the greedy *o-graphs* with appropriate scheduling. The number of startups is equal to the maximum edge label plus one for a graph labeling such that edges in the same dimension carry the same label, and outgoing edges always carry a higher label than incoming edges for the spanning trees making up the *o-graph*. Both the nRSBT and the SBG routings attain the optimum data transfer. The nESBT and H routings have a data transfer time that exceeds the lower bound by a factor of $(n + 2)/n$, and N/n. The number of routing cycles for the SBT communication is at least n, for the nRSBT and SBG

communications it is $2n - 1$ and for the nESBT communication it is $2n$.

With *n-port* communication, the nESBT, nRSBT, and SBG routings are optimum within a constant factor of ≈ 2 for *postorder* and *reverse-breadth-first* schedulings. Both the nESBT and nRH are nongreedy, but the extra distance of the edges from the root of the nESBT is constant. The SBT routing, although greedy, does not evenly utilize edges in the same dimension, and hence is nonoptimum. The data transfer time for the nESBT, the SBT, and the nRH routings are a factor of $n + 2/n$, $\sqrt{n}$, and N/n higher than the optimum time.

VIII. Experimental Results

Some of the communication algorithms presented here have been implemented on an Intel iPSC1 [16] with 128 nodes, connected as a seven-dimensional Boolean cube. It has a message passing programming model. Up to 16k bytes, an *external packet,* can be passed in each communicaton; however, the operating system subdivides messages into *internal packets* of size 1k bytes. There is a communication overhead (startup time) associated with each packet. For an external packet we recorded a startup time averaging 8 ms. For internal packets the startup time was approximately 6 ms (at the time our programs were tested). Interprocessor communication channels are 10 Mbit Ethernet channels. Although there are seven ports per processor, the storage bandwidth can only support 2–3 ports concurrently. However, we have effectively been unable to realize this potential with the available operating system. The concurrency in communication on different ports of the same processor amounts to an overlap of about 20 percent.

For *one-to-all broadcasting* the communication time increases almost linearly for external packet sizes below 1k bytes, Fig. 14. Fig. 15 shows the measured time of the SBT and nESBT communications for an external packet size of 1k bytes and for cube dimensions ranging from 2 to 6. As predicted, measured speedup is approximately n.

For *one-to-all personalized communication* based on SBT routing we schedule port communications in a *binary-reflected* Gray code order to take advantage of the partial overlap in communication on different ports. In the SBG routing, the root determines which node belongs to which subtree. If n is a prime number, the subtrees are isomorphic [excluding node $(\bar{s}_{n-1}\bar{s}_{n-2} \cdots \bar{s}_0)$] and the root only needs to keep one table of length $\approx N/n$ with each entry of size n bits. The order of the entries corresponds to the transmission order for each port. The table entries point to the messages transmitted over port 0. The pointers for the other ports are obtained by (right) cyclic shifts of the table entries. A one step cyclic rotation is used for port 1, two steps for port 2, etc. For n not a prime number there are also other cyclic nodes. The period $P(i)$ for each table entry needs to be found, and the message divided into $P(i)$ pieces. Our implementation uses a single path to every node (SBnT).

Internal nodes can either route according to the destination address if it is included, or use tables. If the destination is included, then a node first checks if it is the destination.

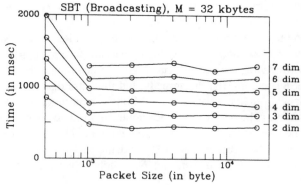

Fig. 14. One-to-all broadcasting for the SBT routing.

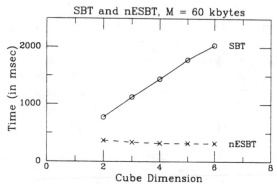

Fig. 15. One-to-all broadcasting for the SBT and nESBT routings.

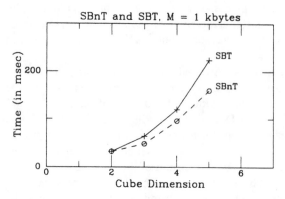

Fig. 16. One-to-all personalized communication for the SBnT and SBT routings.

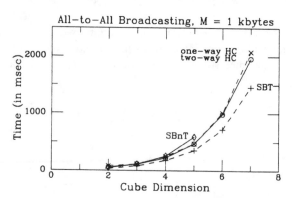

Fig. 17. All-to-all broadcasting on the Intel iPSC.

Otherwise, the output port is determined by finding the base from base^{SBnT} ((myaddress) $\oplus$ (source)) and then finding the first bit that is equal to 1 in ((myaddress) $\oplus$ (destination)) to the left (cyclically) of the bit corresponding to the base. If tables are used instead of a destination field, then for *postorder* scheduling it suffices that each internal node keeps a count for each port. Since the number of ports used in each subtree is at most $n - 3$ and the number of nodes in the entire subtree is approximately N/n, bound on the table size in each node is n^2 bits. A *reverse-breadth-first* scheduling can be implemented by internal nodes keeping a table of how many nodes there are at a given level in each of its subtrees. The table has at most n^2 entries. An upper bound for the number of nodes in a subtree at any level is $N/n^{3/2}$, and the total table size in a node is at most n^3 bits. Hence, without a more sophisticated encoding the *postorder* scheduling discipline requires less table space. It is used for the measurements presented in Fig. 16.

With *one-port* one-to-all personalized communication the expected time for SBT routing and SBG routing is the same for $B = M$. The observed advantage of the SBG over the SBT routing is due to the fact that the SBG can take better advantage of the overlap between communication on different ports. In the SBT case, even though messages were communicated over different ports in a binary-reflected Gray code order, the nodes adjacent to the root may not be finished with retransmitting the last packet received when a new packet arrives, in practice. In the SBG, a subtree receives a packet once every n cycles, and full advantage of the 20 percent overlap in communication actions is taken.

For *all-to-all broadcasting* the execution times are ex-

pected to be of the same order for all forms of all-to-all broadcasting on the Intel iPSC with $B = M$. The results of implementing the SBT, SBG, and two H routings are shown in Fig. 17.

We have also implemented the *all-to-all personalized communication* based on the SBT graph on the iPSC. The result is presented in [22].

IX. Summary and Conclusion

We have presented three new communication graphs for Boolean cubes and defined scheduling disciplines for 1) one-to-all broadcasting, 2) one-to-all personalized communication, 3) all-to-all broadcasting, and 4) all-to-all personalized communication, so that the communication tasks are completed within a small constant factor of the best known lower bounds. For each case we considered two communication models: communication restricted to one-port at-a-time for each processor; and concurrent communication on all ports of every processor. One of the new communication graphs consists of n edge-disjoint spanning binomial trees. Another is a balanced tree. Each subtree of the root of the balanced n-tree we define has approximately N/n nodes.

For communication restricted to *one-port at-a-time*, the nESBT routing is optimum for case 1 within a factor of 4 of the best known lower bound, a speedup of up to n over the SBT routing. For cases 2, 3, and 4, the SBT routings with appropriate scheduling are shown to be optimum within a factor of 2. The nESBT, nRSBT, and SBG routings are all optimum within a factor of 4. For *concurrent communication on all ports,* the nESBT routing is optimum within a

TABLE XVI
TIME COMPLEXITY OF COMMUNICATION ALGORITHMS. THE LAST
COLUMN SHOWS THE CONSTANT FACTORS AS COMPARED TO THE BEST
KNOWN LOWER BOUNDS

Comm.	Data distribution	Assumption	Routing	B_{opt}	T_{min}	Factor
one-port	One-to-all	$M=1$	SBT	1	$n(t_c+\tau)$	1
	Broadcasting	$M>1$	nESBT	$\sqrt{\dfrac{M\tau}{nt_c}}$	$(\sqrt{Mt_c}+\sqrt{n\tau})^2$	4
	One-to-all P.C.	$M\geq1$	SBT	$\dfrac{NM}{2}$	$(N-1)Mt_c+n\tau$	2
	All-to-all B.	$M\geq1$	SBT	$\dfrac{NM}{2}$	$(N-1)Mt_c+n\tau$	2
	All-to-all P.C.	$M\geq1$	SBT	$\dfrac{NM}{2}$	$\dfrac{nNM}{2}t_c+n\tau$	2
n-port	One-to-all	$M\leq n$	nRSBT	1	$n(t_c+\tau)$	1
	Broadcasting	$M>n$	nESBT	$\dfrac{1}{n}\sqrt{\dfrac{M\tau}{t_c}}$	$\left(\sqrt{\dfrac{Mt_c}{n}}+\sqrt{n\tau}\right)^2$	4
	One-to-all	$M\geq n$	nESBT	$\sqrt{\dfrac{2}{\pi}\dfrac{NM}{n^{3/2}}}$	$\dfrac{(N-1)M}{n}t_c+(n+1)\tau$	$\dfrac{2(n+1)}{n}$
	Personalized comm.	$M\geq1, M\geq n$	SBG, nRSBT	$\sqrt{\dfrac{2}{\pi}\dfrac{NM}{n^{3/2}}}$	$\dfrac{(N-1)M}{n}t_c+n\tau$	2
	All-to-all	$M\geq n$	nESBT	$\sqrt{\dfrac{2}{\pi}\dfrac{NM}{n^{3/2}}}$	$\dfrac{(N-1)M}{n}t_c+(n+1)\tau$	$\dfrac{2(n+1)}{n}$
	Broadcasting	$M\geq1, M\geq n$	SBG, nRSBT	$\sqrt{\dfrac{2}{\pi}\dfrac{NM}{n^{3/2}}}$	$\dfrac{(N-1)M}{n}t_c+n\tau$	2
	All-to-all	$M\geq n$	nESBT	$\dfrac{(N-1)M}{n}$	$\left(\dfrac{N}{2}+\dfrac{N-2}{n}\right)Mt_c+(n+1)\tau$	$\dfrac{2(n+2)}{n}$
	Personalized comm..	$M\geq1$	SBG	$\dfrac{(N-1)M}{n}$	$\dfrac{NM}{2}t_c+n\tau$	2
		$M\geq n$	nRSBT	$\dfrac{NM}{2n}$	$\dfrac{NM}{2}t_c+n\tau$	2

factor of 4 for case 1, a speedup of up to n over the SBT routing. For cases 2, 3, and 4, the nRSBT and SBG routings are optimum within a factor of 2. The nESBT routing is optimum within a factor of ≈2. The speedup of the data transmission time for the three routings over the SBT routing is $n/2$, $n/2$, and $O(\sqrt{N})$ for cases 2, 3, and 4 respectively. Table XVI summarizes the results.[1]

The SBG routing has the additional property that the order of the time complexity holds for any data volume, while this is not true for the routings using n paths to every node, such as the nESBT and nRSBT routings. The nESBT routing offers n edge-disjoint paths between the source and any destination node, and hence inherently has a good degree of fault tolerance with respect to communication links.

Routing for the four communication operations can also be based on two-rooted complete binary trees (TCBT) [3], [6]. Communication algorithms based on the TCBT may yield performance comparable to the algorithms presented here for *one-port* communication. For some such scheduling algorithms see [24].

The packet size is very important for the communication complexity. With *one-port* communication and a packet size less or equal to the data set to be communicated to every node, all considered routings have approximately the same complexity for one-to-all personalized communication and all-to-all broadcasting.

Experimental results on the Intel iPSC/d7 confirm the timing model and complexity analysis. The generic communications have been applied to matrix multiplication [21], matrix transpostion [22], and tridiagonal system solvers [23].

ACKNOWLEDGMENT

The authors would like to thank Q. Stout for his helpful comment on the lower bound in Lemma 20; A. Wagner for pointing out [34] and giving the construction of n (undirected) edge-disjoint Hamiltonian cycles in a $2n$-cube based on [34]; and referee D for making many helpful observations and suggestions that significantly improved the presentation.

[1] For the nESBT routing, T_{min} is valid only if $1\leq B_{opt}\leq M$ for *one-port* and $1\leq B_{opt}\leq M/n$ for *n-port* communication.

REFERENCES

[1] A. V. Aho, J. E. Hopcroft, and J. D. Ullman, *The Design and Analysis of Computer Algorithms.* Reading, MA: Addision-Wesley, 1974.
[2] S. N. Bhatt, F. R. K. Chung, F. T. Leighton, and A. L. Rosenberg, "Optimal simulations of tree machines," in *Proc. 27th IEEE Symp. Foundations Comput. Sci.*, 1986, pp. 274–282.
[3] S. N. Bhatt and I. I. F. Ipsen, "How to embed trees in hypercubes," Tech. Rep. YALEU/CSD/RR-443, Dept. Comput. Sci., Yale Univ., Dec. 1985.
[4] S. A. Browning, "The tree machine: A highly concurrent computing environment," Tech. Rep. 1980:TR:3760, Comput. Sci., California Instit. Technol., Jan. 1980.
[5] E. Dekel, D. Nassimi, and S. Sahni, "Parallel matrix and graph algorithms," *SIAM J. Comput.*, vol. 10, pp. 657–673, 1981.
[6] S. R. Deshpande and R. M. Jenevin, "Scaleability of a binary tree on a hypercube," in *Proc. Int. Conf. Parallel Processing*, 1986, pp. 661–668.
[7] M. J. Fischer, *Efficiency of Equivalence Algorithms.* New York: Plenum, 1972, pp. 153–167.
[8] G. C. Fox and W. Furmanski, "Optimal communication algorithms on hypercube," Tech. Rep. CCCP-314, California Instit. Technol., July 1986.
[9] G. C. Fox and D. Jefferson, "Concurrent processor load balancing as a statistical physics problem," Tech. Rep. CCCP-172, California Instit. Technol., May 1985.
[10] D. Gannon and J. Van Rosendale, "On the impact of communication complexity in the design of parallel numerical algorithms," *IEEE Trans. Comput.*, vol. C-33, pp. 1180–1194, Dec. 1984.
[11] J. L. Gustafson, S. Hawkinson, and K. Scott, "The architecture of a homogeneous vector supercomputer," in *Proc. 1986 Int. Conf. Parallel Processing*, 1986, pp. 649–652.
[12] J. P. Hayes, T. N. Mudge, Q. F. Stout, S. Colley, and J. Palmer, "Architecture of a hypercube supercomputer, in *Proc. 1986 Int. Conf. Parallel Processing*, 1986, 653–660.
[13] W. D. Hillis, *The Connection Machine.* Cambridge, MA: MIT Press, 1985.
[14] C. T. Ho and S. L. Johnsson, "Distributed routing algorithms for broadcasting and personalized communication in hypercubes," in *Proc. 1986 Int. Conf. Parallel Processing*, 1986, pp. 640–648. Tech. Rep. YALEU/DCS/RR-483, May 1986.
[15] ——, "Spanning balanced trees in Boolean cubes," Tech. Rep. YALEU/DCS/RR-508, Dept. Comput. Sci., Yale Univ., Jan. 1987.

[16] *Intel iPSC System Overview,* Intel Corp., Jan. 1986. *SIAM J. Sci. Stat. Comput.,* to be published.

[17] S. L. Johnsson, "Communication efficient basic linear algebra computations on hypercube architectures," *J. Parallel Distrib. Comput.,* vol. 4, pp. 133–172, Apr. 1987. Rep. YALEU/DCS/RR-361, Jan. 1985.

[18] ——, "Ensemble architectures and their algorithms: An overview," in *Proceedings* of the *IMA Workshop Numerical Algorithms Par. Comput. Architectures,* H. Schultz Ed., Berlin, Germany:Springer-Verlag, 1987. YALE/DCS/RR-580. Revision of YALE/DCS/RR-367, Feb. 1985.

[19] ——, "Odd-even cyclic reduction on ensemble architectures and the solution tridiagonal systems of equations," Tech. Rep. YALE/DCS/RR-339, Dep. Comput. Sci., Yale Univ., Oct. 1984.

[20] ——, "Solving tridiagonal systems on ensemble architectures," *SIAM J. Sci. Stat. Comp.,* vol. 8, pp. 354–392, May 1987; Rep. YALEU/DCS/RR-436, Nov. 1985.

[21] S. L. Johnsson and C. T. Ho, "Algorithms for multiplying matrices of arbitrary shapes using shared memory primitives on a Boolean cube," Tech. Rep. YALEU/DCS/RR-569, Dep. Comput. Sci., Yale Univ., Oct. 1987. Revision of YALEU/DCS/RR-530. Presented at the ARMY Workshop on Medium Scale Parallel Processors, Stanford Univ., Jan. 1986.

[22] ——, Matrix transposition on Boolean n-cube configured ensemble architectures," *SIAM J. Matrix Anal. Appl.,* vol. 9, pp. 415–454, July 1988. YALE/DCS/RR-572. rev. ed. YALEU/DCS/RR-494 Nov. 1986, to be published.

[23] ——, "Multiple tridiagonal systems, the alternating direction method, and Boolean cube configured multiprocessors," Tech. Rep. YALEU/DCS/RR-532, Yale Univ., June 1987. *SIAM J. Sci. Stat. Comput.,* to be published.

[24] ——, "Spanning graphs for optimum broadcasting and personalized communication in hypercubes," Tech. Rep. YALEU/DCS/RR-500, Dep. Comput. Sci., Yale Univ., Nov. 1986.

[25] F. T. Leighton, *Complexity Issues in VLSI: Optimal Layouts for the Shuffle-Exchange Graph and Other Networks.* Cambridge, MA: MIT Press, 1983.

[26] O. A. McBryan and E. F. Van de Velde, "Hypercube algorithms and implementations," *SIAM J. Scientif. Statist. Comput.,* vol. 8, pp. s227–s287, Mar. 1987.

[27] E. M. Reingold, J. Nievergelt, and N. Deo, *Combinatorial Algorithms.* Englewood Cliffs, NJ: Prentice-Hall, 1977.

[28] Y. Saad and M. H. Schultz, "Data communication in hypercubes," Tech. Rep. YALEU/DCS/RR-428, Dep. Comput. Sci., Yale Univ., Oct. 1985.

[29] ——, "Topological properties of hypercubes," Tech. Rep. YALEU/DCS/RR-389, Dep. Comput. Sci., Yale Univ., June 1985.

[30] C. L. Seitz, "The cosmic cube," *Commun. ACM,* vol. 28, pp. 22–33, 1985.

[31] Q. F. Stout and B. Wager, "Passing messages in link-bound hypercubes," in *Proc. 1986 Hypercube Conf.,* SIAM, 1987.

[32] L. Valiant and G. J. Brebner, "Universal schemes for parallel communication," in *Proc. 13th ACM Symp. Theory of Computat.,* ACM, 1981, pp. 263–277.

[33] A. Y. Wu, "Embedding of tree networks in hypercubes," *J. Parallel Distrib. Comput.,* vol. 2, pp. 238–249, 1985.

[34] J. Aubert and B. Schneider, "Decomposition de la somme cartesienne d'un cycle et de l'union de deux cycles hamiltoniens en cycles hamiltoniens," *Discrete Math.,* vol. 38, pp. 7–16, 1982.

[35] M. Foregger, "Hamiltonian decompositions of products of cycles," *Discrete Math.,* vol. 24, pp. 251–260, 1978.

[36] A. S. Wagner, personal communication, 1988.

S. Lennart Johnsson (M'87) received the M.S. and Ph.D. degees from Chalmers Institute of Technology, Gothenburg, Sweden, in 1967 and 1970, respectively.

He is director of Computational Sciences at Thinking Machines Corporation, and an Associate Professor of Computer Science and Electrical Engineering, Yale University, New Haven, CT. From 1970 to 1979 he was affiliated with the Central Research and Development Laboratories of ASEA AB, Sweden, first as a staff member and later as manager of Systems Engineering. He initiated and lead the development of large computer-based real-time computer systems for electric utilities, intelligent controllers, and mathematical software. From 1979 to 1983, he was a Senior Research Associate in computer science at the California Institute of Technology, where he taught VLSI design and started a course in scientific computing on parallel architectures. Since 1983 he has been with Yale University, where he has continued to teach courses on parallel algorithms and architectures. His current research interests include architecture, algorithms and software for high-performance parallel computers for the computational sciences, particularly the design of communication systems, graph embeddings, and the automatic mapping of data and control structures to parallel architectures, linear algebra, and fluid and solid mechanics applications. He has lead the development of scientific software for the Connection Machine at Thinking Machines Corporation since 1986. He has authored or co-authored over 50 publications in the areas of VLSI architecture and parallel scientific computing, and is an editor of the *Journal of Parallel and Distributed Computing.*

Dr. Johnsson is a co-recipient of the 1986 outstanding Paper Award of the International Conference of Parallel Processing, and he is a recipient of the John Ericson medal. He is a member of SIAM and ACM.

Ching-Tien Ho was born in Taiwan, on April 9, 1957. He received the B.S. degree in electrical engineering from National Taiwan University, Taiwan, in 1979 and the M.S. and M.Phil. degrees in computer science from Yale University, New Haven, CT, in 1985 and 1986, respectively.

He is currently pursuing a Ph.D. degree in computer science at Yale University, New Haven, CT. He has co-authored more than 10 papers. His primary research interests include routing algorithms for interconnection networks, graph embeddings, parallel algorithms and architectures.

Mr. Ho is a co-recipient of the 1986 Outstanding Paper Award of the International Conference on Parallel Processing. He is a student member of ACM and SIAM.

Multicast in Hypercube Multiprocessors

YOURAN LAN

Department of Computer Science, University of Missouri, Columbia, Missouri 65211

AND

ABDOL-HOSSEIN ESFAHANIAN AND LIONEL M. NI*

Department of Computer Science, Michigan State University, East Lansing, Michigan 48824-1027

An efficient interprocessor communication mechanism is essential to the performance of hypercube multiprocessors. All existing hypercube multiprocessors basically support one-to-one interprocessor communication only. However, multicast (one-to-many) communication is highly demanded in executing many data parallel algorithms. A multicast algorithm should attempt to inform each destination in a minimum number of time steps while generating a least amount of traffic. In this paper, we first propose a graph theoretical model, the *Optimal Multicast Tree* (OMT), for interprocessor communication in distributed-memory multiprocessors. The problem of finding an OMT is conjectured to be NP-hard even for hypercube multiprocessors. A heuristic Greedy multicast algorithm which guarantees a minimized message delivery time is proposed. Simulation results show that the performance of the Greedy algorithm is very close to the optimal solution. Routing of multicast messages is done in a distributed manner. The hardware design of a VLSI router which supports all types of communications is briefly discussed. © 1990 Academic Press, Inc.

1. INTRODUCTION

An *n-dimensional hypercube* (*n-cube*) multiprocessor consists of $N = 2^n$ processors constructed as follows: the processors are addressed distinctly by *n*-bit binary numbers, $b_{n-1}b_{n-2}\cdots b_j\cdots b_0$, from 0 to $2^n - 1$. Two processors are directly connected via a *link* (and hence become neighbors) if and only if their binary addresses differ in exactly one bit position. Thus, each processor has direct connection to *n* neighboring processors. The *distance* (the *length* of a shortest path, in number of links) between two processors is equal to the *Hamming distance* of their binary addresses.

Hypercube structure has been the subject of many research projects and it has been studied from different per-

spectives [7, 14, 16]. As a result, many topological properties of hypercube have been discovered. Regularity, symmetry, extensibility, small diameter, and the embeddability of many other topologies, such as ring, two- or higher-dimensional mesh, and tree are among many others. All these properties make hypercube multiprocessors suitable for a wide range of computational applications [1, 3]. Many hypercube multiprocessors are commercially available [15].

As a message passing system, the processors in a hypercube multiprocessor do not have shared memory. Message passing is the only means for interprocessor communication. In an *n*-cube, each node communicates directly only with its *n* neighboring nodes. Nonneighboring nodes have to communicate indirectly via other nodes. Thus, in general, a message may have to go through one or more intermediate nodes before reaching its destination(s). The message handling strategies and techniques, and how they are implemented, constitute the effectiveness of interprocessor communications. *Time* and *traffic* are the main parameters considered in adopting an interprocessor communication scheme.

Depending on the number of destinations, three types of interprocessor communications, namely, *one-to-one* (*unicast*), *one-to-many* (*multicast*), and *one-to-all* (*broadcast*), may be distinguished. A general purpose multiprocessor should directly support these types of communications as they usually arise in executing tasks on such systems. Furthermore, to reduce communication delay and overhead, communication services should be handled by hardware rather than software. These attributes are mostly lacked by the existing hypercube multiprocessors. One-to-one communication is the main service provided by these systems. In some systems, multicast communication is implemented by subroutine calls on top of one-to-one communication [10]. Such a scheme usually generates more traffic than required, which makes it inefficient even further.

* L. M. Ni was supported in part by the DARPA ACMP Project.

Since both one-to-one and broadcast communications were studied previously, this paper only studies the multicast communication. In fact, both one-to-one and broadcast are special cases of multicast communication. In Section 2, we first present our notation and terminologies, followed by a graph theoretical model which characterizes all three types of interprocessor communications. The main evaluation criterion considered is the one which minimizes time and traffic. For the case of multicast communication, the corresponding graph theoretical problem is known to be NP-hard in general [2]. This and the results presented in Section 3 have led us to conjecture that the multicast problem remains NP-hard even for the n-cube graph. After presenting an optimal solution for some special cases in Section 4, we present a suboptimal algorithm which is also distributed in the sense that the overall routing is not calculated solely by the source; instead, each intermediate node decides its own routing. A simulation result of the algorithm which attests to the efficiency of our algorithm is presented in Section 5. The hardware design of a VLSI router is briefly discussed in Section 6.

2. OPTIMAL MULTICAST TREE MODEL

We will closely follow the graph theoretical terminology and notation of [6]. Terms not defined here can be found in that book. Let $G(V, E)$ be a *graph* with the *node set* $V(G) = V$ and *edge set* $E(G) = E$. When G is known from the context, the sets $V(G)$ and $E(G)$ will be referred to by V and E, respectively. If an edge $e = (u, v) \in E$, then nodes u and v are said to be *adjacent* and edge e is said to be *incident* to these nodes. The *degree*, $\deg_G(v)$, of a node $v \in V$ is equal to the number of edges in G which are incident to v. We use *edge* and *link* interchangeably.

A *path* is an alternating sequence of nodes and edges, beginning and ending with nodes, in which all the nodes are distinct. A path p from node u_0 to node u_d is represented by an ordered sequence of nodes $(u_0, u_1, \ldots, u_d)$. The length of a path p is measured by the number of edges contained in the path. Therefore, the above path has length d. A path is *shortest* if there are no shorter paths between the two given nodes.

A graph is said to be *connected* if every pair of its nodes are joined by a path. A *tree* is a connected graph which contains no *cycles*. A graph $F(V, E)$ is a *subgraph* of another graph $G(V, E)$, if $V(F) \subseteq V(G)$ and $E(F) \subseteq E(G)$. When $V(F) = V(G)$, F is called a *spanning* subgraph. A subgraph which is a tree is referred to as a *subtree*. The *distance*, $d_G(u, v)$, between a pair of nodes u and v in G, is equal to the length (in number of edges) of a shortest path joining u and v.

The underlying topology of an n-dimensional hypercube multiprocessor is known as the *n-cube graph* $Q_n(V, E)$. For a vertex $v \in V(Q_n)$, $a(v)$ will represent the n-bit binary address of v; $\|a(v)\|$ will denote the number of 1's in binary number $a(v)$. Also, let $\oplus$ denote the *bitwise exclusive or* (XOR) operation on binary numbers. Then, $e = (u, v) \in E(Q_n)$ if and only if $\|a(u) \oplus a(v)\| = 1$. This implies that $\deg_{Q_n}(u) = n$ for every node $u \in V(Q_n)$. Furthermore, if $a(u) \oplus a(v) = 2^i$, edge e is said to be at dimension i. Also, $d_{Q_n}(u, v) = \|a(u) \oplus a(v)\|$ for every pair of nodes u, $v \in V(Q_n)$.

When considering communication issues at system level, the main problem is that of determining which path(s) should be used to deliver a message from a node (called *source*) to some destination(s). This path selection process is commonly referred to as *routing*. The two major routing design parameters are *time* and *traffic;* system load is another parameter; however, this parameter will not be considered in our study. Parameter *time* is measured in *time steps,* where a *time step* is the actual time needed to send a unit of information (message) from a node to one of its neighboring nodes. This time is assumed to be constant for all pairs of neighboring nodes. Furthermore, we assume that any node can inform any number of its neighboring nodes during a time step. This assumption is compatible with the current technology [13, 15]. Parameter *traffic* is quantified by the number of messages traversed in the communication links which are used to deliver the source message to its destination(s). Note that the number of time steps required to inform a destination is at least equal to the distance from the source to that destination. Also, the number of destinations gives a lower bound for the amount of traffic required to complete the communication. Clearly, it is desirable to develop a routing scheme that completes communication while minimizing both time and traffic. As will be seen shortly, these parameters, however, are not, in general, totally independent and therefore some ordering must be used for their minimization.

Another issue that arises when implementing a routing scheme is whether the source node should determine all the nodes which are needed to deliver its message to all destinations, or the source node only determines its neighboring nodes which are involved in message delivery. Then, these nodes will in turn figure out their neighbors which are needed for message delivery, and so on. The former method is referred to as *centralized* routing, whereas the latter one as *distributed* routing. The main disadvantage of centralized routing is that the address of all nodes involved in message delivery must be tagged with the source message, which may result in undesirable amount of message overhead.

Multicast communication refers to a type of interprocessor communication in which a source node wants to send its message to k distinct destination nodes. Clearly, this is the most general type of communication, and unicast ($k = 1$) and broadcast ($k = 2^n - 1$) are special cases of multicast. Multicast communication is highly demanded in many applications, such as simulation of logic circuits, modeling of mechanical engineering, and simulation of computer networks, in which the output of a component is usually connected to the input of several other components.

The multicast problem has not been studied previously. The problem is more difficult than the other two types of communications. One way of implementing multicast is by applying k one-to-one communications. This, in general, will create more traffic than needed. For example, consider multicast in a 4-cube in which node 0000 is the source, and nodes 1010 and 1100 are the destinations. If we apply two one-to-one communications by using paths $0000 \rightarrow 0010 \rightarrow 1010$ and $0000 \rightarrow 0100 \rightarrow 1100$, the amount traffic will be 4, whereas the source node could send its message to node 1000 and have that node send the message to nodes 1010 and 1100. This would, of course, generate 3 units of traffic.

Another difficulty in implementing multicast is that the two parameters, time and traffic, may no longer be independent. To illustrate, consider multicast in a 4-cube in which node 0000 is the source and nodes 0010, 1001, 1010, and 1011 are the destinations. Clearly, this communication will generate at least 4 units of traffic, and by using path $0000 \rightarrow 0010 \rightarrow 1010 \rightarrow 1011 \rightarrow 1001$, the source node can inform all its destinations while generating that minimum amount of traffic. However, node 1001 receives the source message after 4 time steps, whereas it could receive the message after 2 time steps if a shortest $(0000, 1001)$ path were used. It can be easily verified that there is no routing by which each of the destination nodes 0010, 1001, 1010, and 1011 can receive the source message in minimum number of time steps while generating 4 units of traffic. Thus, it will take at least 5 units of traffic in order to have each destination node receive the source message in minimum number of time steps. This can be accomplished by using paths $0000 \rightarrow 0010 \rightarrow 1010$ and $0000 \rightarrow 1000 \rightarrow 1001 \rightarrow 1011$.

From the above example we conclude that when doing multicast we should decide which of the two parameters, time or traffic, to minimize first. Considering a multiprocessor environment, our communication criterion will be to first minimize time and then traffic. By minimizing time we mean that each individual destination must receive the source message in a minimum number of time steps. This implies that for each destination node, the message should be delivered through a shortest path to that destination. Also note that to minimize traffic it suffices to minimize the number of intermediate nodes used to deliver the source message to all destinations. Using the above criterion, we now formulate the multicast communication problem as a graph theoretic problem.

A graph theoretical model for multicast communication in distributed memory multiprocessors can be formally defined as follows. Let $G(V, E)$ be a graph corresponding to the interconnection topology of a distributed memory multiprocessor under consideration and $D = \{u_1, u_2, \ldots, u_k\}$ $\subset V$ denote the set of k destination nodes in a multicast. The set $M = \{u_0\} \cup D$ is referred to as a *multicast set*, where node u_0 represents the source node. The multicast problem is the problem of finding a subtree $T(V, E)$ of $G(V, E)$, called the *Optimal Multicast Tree* (OMT), such that

(a) $M \subseteq V(T)$,

(b) $d_T(u_0, u_i) = d_G(u_0, u_i)$, for $1 \leq i \leq k$, and

(c) $|E(T)|$ is as small as possible,

where $E(T)$ and $V(T)$ are the edge set and vertex set of the tree $T(V, E)$, respectively. Note that condition (b) ensures a minimum number of time steps and condition (c) tries to reduce the traffic.

A subtree of G which satisfies conditions (a) and (b) above is referred to as a *multicast tree* (MT). In a multicast tree, a *leaf* node is a destination node of degree one, and all nonleaf nodes are referred to as *forward* nodes. Thus, an *intermediate* node refers to a nondestination forward node. In general, an OMT may not be unique.

In the next section, we study the OMT problem when $G(V, E)$ is the n-cube. Optimal algorithms for constructing OMT when the set M is small are given. In Section 4, we present a heuristic multicast algorithm which achieves condition (b) and may only compromise condition (c).

3. FINDING OMTs IN A HYPERCUBE

3.1. *Fundamentals*

Let $Q_n(V, E)$ be the topology of an n-dimensional hypercube multiprocessor, and node u_0 be the source node in a multicast. The node set V of Q_n can be partitioned into $n + 1$ disjoint subsets (or $n + 1$ *levels*), $V_0, V_1, \ldots, V_n$, with respect to node u_0, where $V_i = \{v \in V \mid d_{Q_n}(u_0, v) = i\}$.

The *level* of a node u, denoted by $\lambda(u)$, is equal to $d_{Q_n}(u_0, u)$. Of course, $\lambda(u_0) = 0$. From here on, we assume that the source node has address zero, i.e., $a(u_0) = 0$. If, however, $a(u_0) \neq 0$, then we can relabel the nodes by XORing all node addresses with the source address. Thus, if $u \in V_j$, then $\|a(u)\| = d_{Q_n}(u_0, u) = \lambda(u) = j$ (note that $a(u_0) = 0$). Furthermore, for simplicity of discussion, we assume that $\lambda(u_1) \leq \lambda(u_2) \leq \cdots \leq \lambda(u_k)$ for the nodes in the destination list $D = \{u_1, u_2, \ldots, u_k\}$.

DEFINITION. A node u is an *ancestor* of a node v (or v is a *descendant* of u) if and only if u is contained in a shortest path joining u_0 and v. Thus, $\lambda(u) \leq \lambda(v)$ and $\lambda(v) - \lambda(u) = d_{Q_n}(u, v)$. Note that u and v are not required to be distinct.

DEFINITION. Let $X \subseteq V - \{u_0\}$ be a nonempty set. Then, the *common ancestors* of X, the set $CA(X)$, is

$$CA(X) = \{u \in V \mid u \text{ is an ancestor of every node } v \in X\}.$$

Note that $CA(X)$ is not empty, since for any X, $u_0 \in CA(X)$. The *nearest common ancestor* of X, denoted by $NCA(X)$, is

$$NCA(X) = \{u \in V \mid u \in CA(X),$$

$$\text{and for every } v \in CA(X), \lambda(u) \geqslant \lambda(v)\}.$$

LEMMA 1. *Let* $X \subseteq V - \{u_0\}$ *and* $|X| = 2$. *Then* $NCA(X)$ *contains only one element. That is, the nearest common ancestor of any two nodes is unique. Furthermore, the address of this node can be calculated by bitwise ANDing the binary addresses of the two nodes.*

Proof. Let $X = \{u_1, u_2\}$, and "&" denote the bitwise AND operation on two or more binary numbers. For simplicity, denote $\lambda(u_i)$ by λ_i. Furthermore, let u_x be the node whose binary address $a(u_x)$ is given by

$$a(u_x) = a(u_1) \text{ \& } a(u_2). \tag{1}$$

This implies that

(A) $a(u_x)$ has value 1 at exactly λ_x bit positions and value 0 at the remaining $n - \lambda_x$ bit positions, and

(B) $a(u_1)$ and $a(u_2)$ have value 1 at the same λ_x bit positions as $a(u_x)$.

Furthermore, at each of the $n - \lambda_x$ bit positions, at least one of the two binary addresses $a(u_1)$ and $a(u_2)$ has value 0.

We first prove $u_x \in NCA(X)$. It is obvious from (1) that $u_x \in CA(X)$. In order to prove the *nearest* requirement, suppose there exists another node $u_y \in CA(X)$ with $\lambda_y > \lambda_x$. Without loss of generality, assume the only difference between $a(u_y)$ and $a(u_x)$ is that $a(u_y)$ has value 1 at one more bit position, say b_h, among those $n - \lambda_x$ bit positions. That is, $\lambda_y = \lambda_x + 1$. By condition (B), $a(u_y)$ differs from at least one of the two addresses $a(u_1)$ and $a(u_2)$, say $a(u_1)$, in one more bit position than $a(u_x)$ does. We then have $d_{Q_n}(u_y, u_1) = \lambda_1 - \lambda_x + 1$. However, $\lambda(u_1) - \lambda(u_y) = \lambda_1 - (\lambda_x + 1) = \lambda_1 - \lambda_x - 1$. Thus, $\lambda(u_1) - \lambda(u_y) \neq d_{Q_n}(u_y, u_1)$, which implies u_y is not an ancestor of u_1. Therefore, $u_y \notin CA(X)$, and λ_x is maximum. We conclude $u_x \in NCA(X)$.

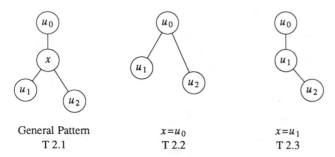

General Pattern
T 2.1

$x = u_0$
T 2.2

$x = u_1$
T 2.3

FIG. 1.   One-to-two multicast trees in hypercube.

Algorithm **One_to_Two_Multicast**

input: $a(u_0), a(u_1), a(u_2)$;

$a(x) := a(u_1) \text{ \& } a(u_2)$;

form a path between u_0 and x;

form a path between x and u_1;

form a path between x and u_2.

FIG. 2.   Multicast algorithm for the case of two destinations.

Now let us prove the uniqueness, that is, $NCA(X) = \{u_x\}$. Suppose there is another node $u_z \neq u_x$, such that $u_z \in NCA(X)$. Then, we must have $\lambda_z = \lambda_x$, which implies $\|a(u_z)\| = \|a(u_x)\|$. Without loss of generality, suppose $a(u_z)$ has a 0 at one of the λ_x bit positions, say b_g, and a 1 at one of the $n - \lambda_x$ bit positions, say b_h. Again, from condition (B), $a(u_z)$ differs from at least one of the two addresses $a(u_1)$ and $a(u_2)$, say $a(u_1)$, in *two* more bit positions than $a(u_x)$ does, i.e., $d_{Q_n}(u_z, u_1) = \lambda_1 - \lambda_x + 2$. However, $\lambda(u_1) - \lambda(u_z) = \lambda(u_1) - \lambda(u_x) = \lambda_1 - \lambda_x$. Thus, $\lambda(u_1) - \lambda(u_z) \neq d_{Q_n}(u_z, u_1)$, u_z is not an ancestor of u_1, and $u_z \notin NCA(X)$. Therefore, $NCA(X) = \{u_x\}$. $\blacksquare$

The argument presented in Lemma 1 can be easily generalized to the case of $|X| > 2$. Thus we have the following theorem.

THEOREM 1.   *Let* $X \subseteq V - \{u_0\}$ *and* $|X| = k$, $(2 \leqslant k \leqslant 2^n - 1)$. *Then* $NCA(X)$ *contains only one element. That is, the nearest common ancestor of any* k, $2 \leqslant k \leqslant 2^n - 1$, *nodes is unique. Furthermore, the address of this node can be calculated by bitwise ANDing the binary addresses of all the* k *nodes.* $\blacksquare$

3.2. OMT for $|M| = 3$

To better understand the multicast problem with arbitrary number of destinations, we first examine the solution space of this problem when the number of destinations is very small. In particular, we consider a two-destination multicast, that is, $M = \{u_0, u_1, u_2\}$.

All the possible patterns of OMTs for $|M| = 3$ are illustrated in Fig. 1. In the figure, circles denote nodes and lines denote shortest paths joining pairs of nodes. Observe that if T2.1 is the desired subtree, then node $x \in NCA(u_1, u_2)$. Similarly, if T2.2 is the desired subtree, we have $u_0 \in NCA(u_1, u_2)$. Finally, when T2.3 is the solution, $u_1 \in NCA(u_1, u_2)$. In fact, we may refer to T2.1 as the *general pattern* of the OMT when $|M| = 3$. This is because when $x = u_0$, we obtain subtree T2.2, and when $x = u_1$, we obtain subtree T2.3.

The above observations lead us to an algorithm for generating an OMT when $M = \{u_0, u_1, u_2\}$. The algorithm is listed in Fig. 2 as algorithm One_to_Two_Multicast.

In the One_to_Two_Multicast algorithm, to form a path between node u and node v implies that any shortest path between u and v is acceptable. If $u = v$, then no path has to be established. The validity of the above algorithm can be seen as follows. Denote the multicast tree found by the algorithm by $T(V, E)$. Let $UB = \|a(u_1)\| + \|a(u_2)\|$ (which is an upper bound of the traffic). In all three subtrees, $|E(T)| = UB - d(u_0, x)$. By Lemma 1, NCA(u_1, u_2) has the unique element x, which implies $d(u_0, x) = \lambda(x)$ is maximum. Thus, $|E(T)|$ is minimum.

3.3. OMT for $|M| = 4$

We now consider multicast with three destination nodes, i.e., $M = \{u_0, u_1, u_2, u_3\}$. Again, we investigate all possible subtree patterns, find a general pattern, and then give an optimal algorithm. The nine possible subtree patterns are shown in Fig. 3. Under the assumption that $\lambda(u_1) \leqslant \lambda(u_2) \leqslant \lambda(u_3)$, in Fig. 3, patterns having nodes labeled u_1, u_2, and u_3 represent distinct tree configuration. Each of the other patterns actually represents three *nonisomorphic* subtrees obtained by permuting i, j, and k, namely, $(i, j, k) \in \{(1, 2, 3), (1, 3, 2), (2, 3, 1)\}$. Observing the nine patterns, we can see that T3.1 is a general pattern. When $y = x_{12} = x_{23} = x_{13}$, T3.1 becomes T3.2, and when $x_{ij} \in \{u_1, u_2\}$, T3.1

becomes T3.3. When $y = u_0$ and $y = u_1$, the tree patterns in the first row correspond to the patterns in the second and third rows, respectively. Clearly, node y is in NCA(u_1, u_2, u_3). Also, node x_{ij} must satisfy

$$\lambda(x_{ij}) = \max\{\lambda(\mathrm{NCA}(u_1, u_2)), \lambda(\mathrm{NCA}(u_2, u_3)),$$
$$\lambda(\mathrm{NCA}(u_1, u_3))\}.$$

Since there is only one general pattern, we can again write a simple algorithm to solve the problem, which is listed in Fig. 4.

Denote the subtree found by the above algorithm by $T(V, E)$, and let

$$UB = \|a(u_1)\| + \|a(u_2)\| + \|a(u_3)\|.$$

It is not difficult to see that the following equation holds for every subtree pattern in Fig. 3:

$$|E(T)| = UB - 2d(u_0, y) - d(y, x_{ij}) = UB - 2\|a(y)\|$$
$$- (\|a(x_{ij})\| - \|a(y)\|) = UB - \|a(y)\| - \|a(x_{ij})\|.$$

Since UB is fixed, $a(y)$ is unique by Theorem 1. The maximum level number of $x_{\max}$ means $\|a(x_{ij})\|$ is maximum. Therefore, $|E(T)|$ is minimum. This establishes the validity of the above algorithm.

3.4. Four or More Destination Multicast

As we have seen, the possible configurations of the multicast trees grow dramatically when the number of destination nodes increases even from two to three. As the number of destinations increases from three to four, the problem becomes more complicated. The most important factor is that, in the case of four destinations, there is no unique general pattern; instead, there are two general patterns as shown in Fig. 5. If we want to write an optimal algorithm, we have to deal with the two general patterns separately, and then select the one having less intermediate nodes.

In general, if we have a k-destination multicast problem, one way of finding an OMT is to generate all the general patterns, consider each of them separately, and then select an optimal one. However, the number of general patterns grows very rapidly as the number of destinations increases. We have counted 3, 6, 11, and 23 general patterns for 5, 6, 7, and 8 destinations, respectively. We can see the trend of how rapidly the number of tree patterns and general patterns grows as the number of destinations increases. Also, the general patterns become more complicated.

Can we find an efficient algorithm to solve the OMT problem? For a general graph, the answer is *no*. In fact, it has been shown in [2] that the problem of finding an OMT for a general k is NP-hard even if $G(V, E)$ is *bipartite*. A problem which is very similar to the above problem is

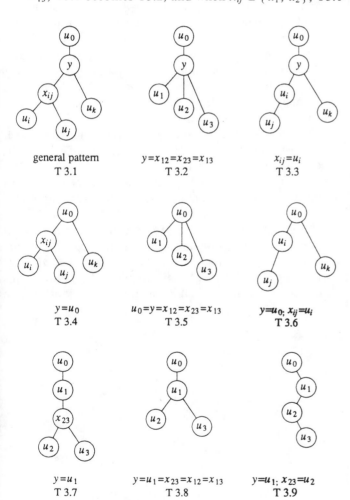

FIG. 3.   One-to-three multicast tree patterns.

Algorithm One_to_Three_Multicast

input: $a(u_0)$, $a(u_1)$, $a(u_2)$, $a(u_3)$;
$a(y) := a(u_1) \& a(u_2) \& a(u_3)$;
$a(x_{12}) := a(u_1) \& a(u_2)$, ;
$a(x_{23}) := a(u_2) \& a(u_3)$, $a(x_{13}) := a(u_1) \& a(u_3)$;
$x_{max} := x_{ij}$, such that $\lambda(x_{ij}) := \max \{\lambda(x_{12}), \lambda(x_{23}), \lambda(x_{13})\}$;
form a path between x_{max} and u_i;
form a path between x_{max} and u_j;
form a path between x_{max} and y;
form a path between y and u_k;   (* $k \neq i, j$ *)
form a path between y and u_0.

FIG. 4.   Multicast algorithm for the case of three destinations.

known as the *Steiner Tree* (ST) problem. It is the problem of finding the smallest subtree of a given graph, which contains a given subset of nodes [4]. It can be observed that if condition (b) in the definition of OMT is removed, the OMT problem becomes a ST problem. It has been shown that the ST problem is NP-complete even when $G(V, E)$ is the n-cube graph [5].

On the basis of the above observations, we conjecture that the OMT problem remains NP-hard even for hypercube topology. This prompted us to develop a heuristic algorithm for the multicast problem in hypercube multiprocessors.

4. A HEURISTIC ALGORITHM FOR MULTICAST

As discussed above, it is impractical to find an OMT when the number of destinations is large. Also, the optimal algorithms discussed so far are all centralized in the sense that they require the entire routing be handled solely by the source node. Subsequently, this approach requires the information about the entire paths be included in the message header, and thus increases the interprocessor communication overhead. In this section, we propose a distributed heuristic algorithm which has the following properties. First, the distance from the source node to each destination node in the multicast tree generated by the proposed algorithm is the same as that in an OMT. Second, the algorithm is simple and can be easily implemented in hardware. Third, it allows distributed routing. Finally, simulation results indicate that the traffic generated by the algorithm is very close to the optimal solution and is better than existing multidestination message delivery mechanisms.

4.1. Underlying Strategy in the Multicast Algorithm

Observe that in a multicast tree only forward nodes are involved in passing the multicast message to some other nodes in the multicast tree. Initially, a node, called the *source* node, decides to send its message to some number of other nodes; i.e., it issues a multicast message. By running the algorithm, the source node will decide which of its neighboring nodes should receive the message. A message

received by a node v includes the data unit, the address of the source node, and a list of destination nodes (destination list), which are descendants of node v in the multicast tree.

Each node, upon receiving a multicast message, will perform the following functions. First, it will compare its own address against the addresses in the destination list of the received message. If there is a match, that matched address will be removed from the destination list and a copy of the data field will be sent to the local processor. Then, if the destination list is empty, the node is a leaf node in the multicast tree and no message will be further forwarded. However, if the destination list is not empty (which implies the node is a forward node), the node will execute the algorithm to determine its descending neighbors in the multicast tree. Depending on the number of descending neighbors, say m, the forward node will split its destination list into m disjoint destination sublists, each consisting of destination nodes which are descendants of a particular descending neighbor. Each such destination sublist is put into a message header and sent to its corresponding descending neighbor.

Now the question is how each forward node decides which of its neighboring nodes to pass the received message. Consider a two-destination multicast, as shown in T2.1 (Fig. 1). In a hypercube environment, suppose the relative addresses of two destination nodes u_1 and u_2 have 1's at p common bit positions ($p \leq \lambda(u_1) \leq \lambda(u_2)$), which define the intermediate node x. For a message to go from node u_0 to x, it may traverse through these dimensions in any order (by changing the values at these p bit positions from 0 to 1, one at a time, in any order). There are $p!$ different paths between nodes u_0 and x. From the point of view of this message delivery, any of these paths has the same effect since they all require the same number of time steps and create the same amount of traffic.

Now, suppose that node u_0 wants to include an additional node, u_3, in its destination list. In this case, we have the situation of T3.1 (Fig. 3). Let $\lambda(y) = \|a(u_1) \& a(u_2) \& a(u_3)\| = q$, and $q < p$. In this situation, the q dimensions are a subset of the original p dimensions. Obviously, these

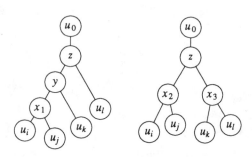

General Pattern 4.1   General Pattern 4.2

FIG. 5.   One-to-four general multicast tree patterns.

388

q dimensions have to be traversed first, and then those $p - q$ dimensions. Otherwise, NCA(u_1, u_2, u_3) will not contain y.

The above discussion suggests that each forward node can use the relative binary addresses of all its destination nodes to *vote* for preferred dimensions (bit positions). The process works as follows. Each of the n bit positions has a counter. For each destination, if its binary address has value 1 at c bit positions, the corresponding c counters are increased by 1. Then, if the counter of a particular bit position, say j, has the maximum number of 1's, the jth-dimensional neighbor of the forward node u_0 is selected. In case of a tie, select one of the tied bit positions at random. For simplicity, a lower bit position is selected in the actual implementation.

All the destination nodes whose binary addresses have value 1 at bit position j are selected to form a destination sublist in the message sent to the jth-dimensional neighbor. This implies that the neighbor is responsible for passing the message to all those destinations in the list. The same procedure continues for the remaining destinations which, of course, do not have 1 at their bit position j. Then we can find the second destination sublist if the set of the remaining destination nodes is not empty. This procedure is repeated until all destination nodes have been resolved.

4.2. The Greedy Multicast Algorithm

As mentioned earlier, our multicast algorithm is executed by each forward node. We now present a heuristic algorithm for the multicast. In the following algorithm, $a(u_s)$ and $a(u_0)$ represent the actual addresses of the source node and current forward node (which is currently executing the algorithm), respectively, and $a(u_1), a(u_2), \ldots, a(u_k)$ represent the actual addresses of the k destination nodes. For the algorithm to work, it is not necessary to sort the destination addresses according to their distances from the source, as this was previously assumed in order to simplify the explanation of the multicast problem. However, a forward node has to perform an XOR operation on its own address and the addresses of its descending destinations to change their actual addresses to relative addresses. The corresponding relative addresses are $r_0(u_0) = a(u_0) \oplus a(u_0) = 0$, and $r_0(u_i) = a(u_0) \oplus a(u_i)$, for $1 \leq i \leq k$. The listing of the heuristic algorithm is given in Fig. 6, followed by its proof of correctness. The algorithm is also called Greedy multicast algorithm, since it selects a dimension of maximum column-sum whenever it finds one.

LEMMA 2. *Given a source node u_s and a destination list $D = \{u_1, u_2, \ldots, u_i, \ldots, u_k\}$ in Q_n, the algorithm MULTICAST passes a message from u_s to every destination $u_i \in D$ through a shortest path between u_s and u_i.*

Proof. Let the path from u_s to u_i be $p = (u_s, v_1, \ldots, v_j, \ldots, v_{d-1}, u_i)$. It is implied that u_i is in the destination sublist received by every forward node v_j along the path. Assuming $a(v_j)$ and $a(v_{j+1})$ differ at bit position l, then u_i is included in the destination sublist sent from v_j to v_{j+1} only if $a(v_j)$ and $a(u_i)$ differ at bit position l. Also, $a(v_{j+1})$ and $a(u_i)$ must agree at bit position l. That is, each forward node passes messages to its descendant nodes only. Therefore, it is clear that for every destination u_i, if $\|a(u_s) \oplus a(u_i)\| = d$, then $\|a(v_j) \oplus a(u_i)\| = d - j$ holds for $1 \leq j \leq d - 1$. Starting from the source node u_s, after $d - 1$ steps, the message will travel to node v_{d-1}, whose address has only 1 bit position in difference from $a(u_i)$. The message then travels to u_i through the direct link between v_{d-1} and u_i. That is, the message travels from u_s to u_i in d steps if the addresses of u_s and u_i differ at d bit positions. The path is therefore a shortest one. ∎

LEMMA 3. *Given a source node u_s and a destination list $D = \{u_1, u_2, \ldots, u_i, \ldots, u_k\}$ in Q_n, by executing the algorithm MULTICAST at each forward node, every destination node $u_i \in D$ will receive the message exactly once.*

Proof. Lemma 2 has shown that each destination node receives a copy of the message through a shortest path. In the proof of Lemma 2, we have also shown that a message will travel from a forward node v_j to a destination u_i only when u_i is in the destination sublist received by v_j. We note that during the execution of the algorithm MULTICAST at forward node v_j, each destination node in the destination sublist is passed to one of v_j's descendant nodes only. This is true for every forward node. Also note that a message always travels from a node to its descendant node(s). Therefore, no two nodes at the same level (with respect to the source node) could have the same destination node in the destination sublist it receives. Therefore, only one copy of the message is received by each destination. ∎

THEOREM 2. *Given a source node u_s and a destination list $D = \{u_1, u_2, \ldots, u_i, \ldots, u_k\}$ in Q_n, the edges selected by the algorithm MULTICAST at each forward node induce a multicast tree.*

Proof. Let the subgraph formed by the edges selected by the algorithm MULTICAST be $T(V, E)$. It is obvious that T is a connected graph. We now show that there is no cycle in T. Note that if a node $u_x \notin D$ and u_x does not reside on a path from u_s to any $u_i \in D$, then $u_x \notin V(T)$. We now prove that the paths from u_s to each $u_i \in D$ do not form any cycle. We prove by contradiction. Assume there is a node $u_y \in V(T)$, such that there exist two paths from u_s to u_y in T. Clearly, it is impossible that $u_y \in D$, since Lemma 3 has shown that the path from u_s to every $u_i \in D$ is unique. Now suppose $u_y \notin D$, and the two paths from u_s to u_y are $p = (u_s, v_1, \ldots, v_j, \ldots, v_{y-1}, u_y)$ and $p' = (u_s, v'_1, \ldots, v'_j, \ldots, v'_{y-1}, u_y)$. Assume j is the smallest number such that $v'_j \neq v_j$. Also assume $a(v_{j-1})$ and $a(v_j)$ differ at bit position l, and $a(v_{j-1})$ and $a(v'_j)$ differ at bit position l'. Then $a(v_{j-1})$

Input: Local address: $a(u_0)$;
         Destination list: $D = \{a(u_1), a(u_2), \cdots, a(u_k)\}$.

Output: Destination sublist(s): $D_1, D_2, \cdots, D_g$
         where $D_i \subseteq D$, for $1 \leq i \leq g$; and $D_i \cap D_j = \varnothing$, for $i \neq j$.

Algorithm MULTICAST:

1.   (* Calculate relative addresses: *)
     $r_0(u_i) = b_{i(n-1)}b_{i(n-2)}..b_{ij}..b_{i0} \equiv a(u_0) \oplus a(u_i)$, for $1 \leq i \leq k$;
2.   (* if local processor is a destination, send a copy to it *)
     If $r_0(u_i) = 0$ for some $i \in [1,k]$, send the message to local processor;
3.   (* calculate column sums *)
     $c_j = \sum_{i=1}^{k} b_{ij}$, for $0 \leq j \leq n-1$;
4. $p = 0$;   (* start loop *)
5.   (* select a dimension with maximum column sum, *)
     (* lower dimension has higher priority in case of a tie *)
     Find smallest l, such that $c_l \geq c_j$ for all $0 \leq j \leq n-1$;
6.   If $c_l = 0$, stop.
7. $D_p = \varnothing$;
8.   (* form a new destination sublist, reset corresponding rows *)
     For each $r_0(u_i)$, $1 \leq i \leq k$, if $b_{il} = 1$, then
8.1. $D_p = D_p + \{r_0(u_i) \oplus a(u_0)\}$;
8.2.   Set $r_0(u_i) = 0$;
8.3. $c_j = c_j - b_{ij}$ for $0 \leq j \leq n-1$;
9.   Put destination sublist D_p into message header, send out the message at l-th dimension (to
     node $a(u_0) \oplus 2^l$);
10. (* start the selection of another dimension *)
     $p = p+1$; Goto step 5.

FIG. 6.   Greedy multicast algorithm.

and $a(u_y)$ must differ at both bit positions l and l'. If dimension l is selected first by the algorithm, then the addresses of all destination nodes in the destination sublist received by v_j differ from $a(u_y)$ at bit position l, while the addresses of all destination nodes in the destination sublist received by v'_j must agree with $a(u_y)$ at bit position l. Thus, the message passed to v'_j will never travel through dimension l and, therefore, will not reach node u_y. If dimension l' is selected first, the same situation will happen. Therefore, it is impossible that a cycle could exist in T, and thus T is a tree. Furthermore, Lemma 3 shows that every destination node receives a message through a unique shortest path; we conclude that T is a multicast tree. ∎

LEMMA 4.   *The multicast tree constructed by the algorithm MULTICAST is an optimal multicast tree when the number of destinations is less than 3.*

Proof.   When the number of destination is one, that is, in a unicast case, it is obvious that the multicast algorithm will generate a path from the source to the destination node exactly the same way as the unicast algorithm does. For the case of two-destination multicast, we show that the algorithm MULTICAST works in the same way as algorithm One_to_Two_Multicast (Fig. 2) does. Suppose $D = \{u_1, u_2\}$. We have $r_s(u_i) = a(u_s) \oplus a(u_i)$ $(1 \leq i \leq 2)$. Assuming $\| r_s(u_1) \& r_s(u_2) \| = m$, then when executing the algorithm at u_s to find column-sums, m column-sums will have value 2. The m dimensions will be selected by the multicast algorithm one by one from the lowest dimension to the highest dimension along the path. After m steps, the message will reach the NCA of u_1 and u_2, which is node u_x with $a(u_x) = a(u_1) \& a(u_2)$. The order of traversing the m dimensions is immaterial. At node u_x, all column-sums will be either 1 or 0. The message will travel to u_1 and u_2 through two separate paths. As detailed in the proof of algorithm One_to_Two_Multicast, it is optimal. ∎

The above discussions imply that our multicast algorithm is distributed in the sense that each forward node only decides to which of its neighboring nodes it should pass the message. Only the destination addresses are carried in the message header. No intermediate node addresses need to be carried. Also, each forward node will execute the same algorithm. The example in next section will make the idea clear, and show how a multicast tree is generated by the algorithm.

4.3. An Illustrative Example

In this section, we illustrate through an example how the Greedy multicast algorithm works. Consider a 5-cube in which node 00110 (6) wants to send a message to nodes $\{00111\ (7),\ 10100\ (20),\ 11101\ (29),\ 10010\ (18),\ 00001$ $(1),\ 00000\ (0)\}$. Initially, the source node 00110 is the only forward node which executes the Greedy algorithm (u_0 $=u_s$). The actual addresses of the source u_0, and destinations $u_1, \ldots, u_6$, are listed in Table I.

The actual addresses of all destination nodes are first XORed with the actual address of u_0. The resulting relative addresses are put into a binary reference array $A[1:k,\ 0:n-1]$. Initially, row i of array A corresponds to the relative address of destination $u_i\ (1 \leqslant i \leqslant k)$. The array is shown in Table II.

The number of 1's in each row of array A indicates the distance between that destination and the current node. The number of 1's in each column is counted to produce the vector column_sum, which has the values of $(3, 1, 3, 4, 3)$ in this example. Bit position 1 has the maximum value of 4. Thus, bit position 1 (i.e., dimension 1) is selected to receive the message. Rows 2, 3, 5, and 6 which have value 1 at bit position 1 are selected from a destination sublist. The corresponding descending neighbor, thus, is 00110 $\oplus$ 00010 = 00100, and the message sent to this node contains the following destination addresses: $a(u_2)$, $a(u_3)$, $a(u_5)$, and $a(u_6)$. These four rows (rows 2, 3, 5, and 6) in array A are then reset to all zeros. Array A now has new entries as shown in Table III.

Now, the new column_sum becomes $(1, 0, 1, 0, 1)$. Three bit positions, 4, 2, and 0 have the same maximum value of 1. Although any one may be selected, we assume that a lower bit position has a higher priority and thus bit position 0 is selected. As a result, destination address $a(u_1)$ forms another destination sublist included in the message sent to the descending neighbor 00110 $\oplus$ 00001 = 00111, which happens to be a destination node.

After row 1 is reset to zero, the only row left is row 4, as shown in Table IV. By repeating the same procedure, $a(u_4)$ = 10010 is the destination sublist to be included in the message sent to the descending neighbor 00010.

At this point, the multicast subtree with three descending

TABLE II
The Reference Array at Node 00110

	Reference array	
	4 3 2 1 0	Distances
$A[1, *]$	0 0 0 0 1	1
$A[2, *]$	1 0 0 1 0	2
$A[3, *]$	1 1 0 1 1	4
$A[4, *]$	1 0 1 0 0	2
$A[5, *]$	0 0 1 1 1	3
$A[6, *]$	0 0 1 1 0	2
column_sum	3 1 3 4 3	

neighbors, as shown in Fig. 7a, is formed. In this and the following figures, an arrow represents a link, and the number inside a small square by a link indicates at which step of executing the algorithm that dimension is determined. Also, a node marked by "*" means it is a destination node. The source node is marked by a "•".

Upon receiving a message from node 00110, node 00100 serves as a forward node. The corresponding multicast subtree of this node can be similarly generated and is shown in Fig. 7b.

By repeating this procedure at all forward nodes, the resulting complete multicast tree rooted at node 00110 is shown in Fig. 7c.

5. PERFORMANCE ANALYSIS

In this section, we first compute the time complexity of the Greedy multicast algorithm, and then compare the performance of the algorithm with the optimal solution and other alternative methods for multidestination message delivery.

We assume that the basic operations, such as addition, subtraction, comparison, and assignment, have time complexity $O(1)$. Let n be the dimension of the hypercube and

TABLE I
The Actual Addresses of Source (00110) and Destinations

	Actual addresses	
	$b_4\ b_3\ b_2\ b_1\ b_0$	Decimal
$a(u_0)$	0 0 1 1 0	6
$a(u_1)$	0 0 1 1 1	7
$a(u_2)$	1 0 1 0 0	20
$a(u_3)$	1 1 1 0 1	29
$a(u_4)$	1 0 0 1 0	18
$a(u_5)$	0 0 0 0 1	1
$a(u_6)$	0 0 0 0 0	0

TABLE III
The Reference Array after the First Run of the Algorithm

	Reference array	
	4 3 2 1 0	Distances
$A[1, *]$	0 0 0 0 1	1
$A[2, *]$	0 0 0 0 0	
$A[3, *]$	0 0 0 0 0	
$A[4, *]$	1 0 1 0 0	2
$A[5, *]$	0 0 0 0 0	
$A[6, *]$	0 0 0 0 0	
column_sum	1 0 1 0 1	

k be the number of destinations in the multicast. Then, in the algorithm, lines 1 and 2 have time complexity of $O(k)$; line 3 has $O(kn)$. The number of loops between lines 4 and 10 is at most n. Thus, we have $O(n^2)$ for line 5, $O(n)$ for lines 6 and 7, and $O(kn)$ for line 8. Lines 8.1 to 8.3 are executed at most k times regardless of the number of loops, which have the complexity of $O(3k + nk)$. Finally, we have $O(3n)$ for lines 4, 9, and 10. Therefore, the Greedy algorithm is of time complexity $O(4k + 3n + 3kn + n^2)$, or $O(nk + n^2)$ for large k and n.

In section 4, we have proven that the Greedy multicast algorithm guarantees a minimum message delivery time by providing shortest paths between source and each destination. Using the algorithm, the traffic generated for the multicast is also minimum when the number of destinations is less than 3. In general cases, the distribution of the destination nodes (the locality of information) has great effect on the traffic generated by the message delivery. Under the assumption of *uniform* routing distribution, the probability that node u_i sends a message to node u_j is the same for all $u_j \neq u_i$, u_i, $u_j \in V(Q_n)$. We have compared the performance of the Greedy algorithm with two other alternative approaches for multicasting, namely, multiple one-to-one and broadcast. Issuing k one-to-one message deliveries for a k-destination multicast is the actual approach used in the first generation hypercube multiprocessors. Implementing one-to-many using the broadcast communication, the router will not send the message to the local processor if the local address does not match any address in the destination list.

Figure 8 shows the amount of traffic generated by these different interprocessor communication methods in a 6-cube multiprocessor. A unit of traffic is measured as one message traversed over one link. In the figure, the number of destination nodes, k, is chosen within the range $[1, 63]$. For a given $k \in [1, 63]$, k destinations are selected at random (uniform distribution). Then, by executing a simulation program, the number of links involved in the message delivery is measured for each communication method. For each k, we have repeated the simulation 1000 times, and the amount of traffic generated for a given k is averaged over

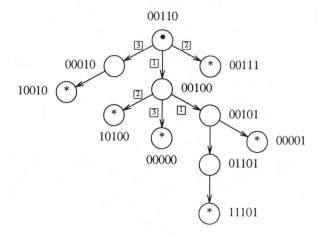

(a) The multicast subtree generated at node 00110

(b) The multicast subtree generated at node 00100

(c) The complete multicast tree

FIG. 7. A multicast tree in Q_5, where the number in each small square is the algorithm step which determined that link.

the 1000 runs. The dashed curve, solid curve, and dotted line show the results from multiple one-to-one, Greedy algorithm, and broadcast approach, respectively. The x-axis is the number of destinations, and the y-axis is the average traffic created by the message delivery. The Greedy multicast algorithm always generates the least amount of traffic compared with the other two approaches.

In the broadcast method, the traffic generated is independent of the number of destination nodes and is $2^6 - 1 = 63$. For multiple one-to-one message delivery, under the uniform routing assumption, $\binom{n}{i}$ destinations have distance i from the source. The total number of destinations is $2^n - 1$. Thus, the average distance between a source and a destination, under uniform distribution, is

TABLE IV

The Reference Array after the Second Run of the Algorithm

	Reference array	Distances
	4 3 2 1 0	
$A[1, *]$	0 0 0 0 0	
$A[2, *]$	0 0 0 0 0	
$A[3, *]$	0 0 0 0 0	
$A[4, *]$	1 0 1 0 0	2
$A[5, *]$	0 0 0 0 0	
$A[6, *]$	0 0 0 0 0	
column_sum	1 0 1 0 0	

$$d_{\mathrm{mean}} = \frac{1}{2^n - 1} \sum_{i=1}^{n} i \binom{n}{i} = n \times \frac{2^{n-1}}{2^n - 1}.$$

For the case of $n = 6$, $d_{\mathrm{mean}} = 3.05$. To send a message to a destination which is h hops away will create h units of traffic. Thus, the average traffic generated for k destinations using multiple one-to-one communication is $3.05k$ for uniform distribution. It follows that when the number of destination nodes is greater than 20, even broadcast approach performs better than the multiple one-to-one approach.

In order to better evaluate the performance of the Greedy algorithm, we also run simulation programs for an optimal algorithm and a multidestination routing algorithm, called *spare–global–send* algorithm, proposed by Moler and Scott [10]. The optimal solution is obtained by exhaustive searching and comparing of all possible paths for each given number of destinations (an exponential time complexity algorithm). The idea in the spare–global–send algorithm can be briefly described as follows. Given a local (forward) node and a destination list, the algorithm first searches the destination list and selects one which is *closest* to the local node, and a message is then sent to that node through a shortest path between the two nodes. Those destination nodes which are descendants of the selected node will receive the message through that node. The algorithm is repeated for the remaining nodes in the destination list until all destinations are dealt with. The algorithm is also distributed.

The results for the three algorithms are generated in a way similar to the curves in Fig. 8. Figure 9 shows the three curves, where the x-axis is the number of destinations and the y-axis is the traffic created by the message delivery; the upper dashed curve, solid curve, and lower dashed curve represent the result from spare–global–send, the Greedy multicast algorithm, and the optimal solution, respectively.

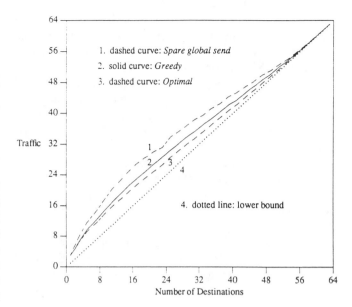

FIG. 9. Performance comparison of three multicast algorithms.

Also shown in Fig. 9 is the dotted line, which is a lower bound of the multicast. For k destinations, the theoretical lower bound of traffic generated is obviously k; i.e., no non-destination forward nodes are needed.

From the curves, we can see that the performance of the Greedy algorithm is better than the spare–global–send, and is very close to the optimal solution, especially when k is very small or very large. Note that it was proven in Section 4 that when $k < 3$, the performance of the Greedy algorithm is the same as that of the optimal algorithm. This can also be observed from the curves in Fig. 9.

A good scheduling algorithm in a hypercube multiprocessor should partition and map the data set to processors in a way that interprocessor communication is minimized. In other words, if the evaluation of one data partition requires information from another data partition, these two partitions should be allocated to adjacent processors [11]. In this case, those destination nodes are usually close to each other. *Decreasing-probability routing* is a good assumption for this situation [13]. Under this assumption, the probability that a node must send a message to a destination node which is d hops away decreases as the value d increases. In this case, the performance of the proposed algorithm will be better than that shown here [9].

6. CONCLUDING REMARKS

We have proposed a graph theoretical model, the OMT model, for interprocessor communication in distributed memory multiprocessors. Based on the model, a heuristic Greedy multicast algorithm for hypercube multiprocessors has been presented. For a given multicast message, the generation of the resulting multicast tree is fully distributed.

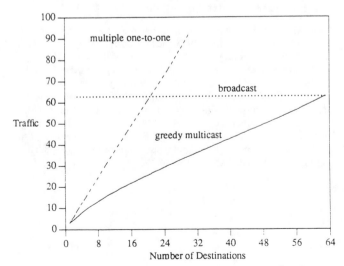

FIG. 8. Comparison of three communication methods in a Q_6.

The performance of the Greedy algorithm is shown to be very close to the optimal solution. When the number of destination nodes is less than 3, the Greedy multicast algorithm is able to provide an optimal solution.

A major advantage of the proposed algorithm is that it lends itself to an efficient hardware implementation, which is critical to the performance of a hypercube multiprocessor. Based on the proposed multicast algorithm, a prototype VLSI hardware router for a 3-cube was designed and fabricated [9]. The router has three input channels from its three neighbors, three output channels to the three neighbors, and one input connection and one output connection to the local nodal processor. In order to shorten the communication latency, a relay approach message routing based on the concept of *virtual cut-through* [8] is adopted. The chip has been fabricated by MOSIS based on a 3-μm CMOS technology. To shorten the design cycle, the control circuit is designed using a PLA approach. The cycle time is measured to be less than 1 μs.

In the theory part, we conjecture that the finding of an optimal solution in hypercube is NP-hard. Although an optimal algorithm is not important if it cannot be efficiently implemented, we are working on the proof of our conjecture to provide a solid theoretical foundation.

REFERENCES

1. Barhen, J., and Palmer, J. F. The hypercube in robotics and machine intelligence. *Comput. Mech. Engrg.* (Mar. 1986).

2. Choi, Y., Esfahanian, A. H., and Ni, L. M. One-to-k communication in distributed-memory multiprocessors. *Proc. 25th Annual Allerton Conference on Communication, Control, and Computing,* Sept. 1987, pp. 268–270.

3. Fox, G., and Otto, S. Algorithms for concurrent processors. *Phys. Today* **37**, 5 (May 1984), 50–59.

4. Garey, M. R., and Johnson, D. S. *Computers and Intractability: A Guide to the Theory of NP-Completeness.* Freeman, San Francisco, 1979.

5. Graham, R. L., and Foulds, L. R. Unlikelihood that minimal phylogenies for a realistic biological study can be constructed in reasonable computational time. *Math. Biosci.* **60** (1982), 133–142.

6. Harary, F. *Graph Theory.* Addison–Wesley, Reading, MA, 1972.

7. Hayes, J., Mudge, T., Stout, Q., Colley, S., and Palmer, J. Architecture of a hypercube supercomputer. *Proc. 1986 International Conference on Parallel Processing,* Aug. 1986, pp. 653–660.

8. Kermani, P., and Kleinrock, L. Virtual cut-through: A new computer communication switching technique. *Comput. Networks* **3** (1979), 267–286.

9. Ni, L. M., Lan, Y. and Esfahanian, A. H. A VLSI router design for hypercube multiprocessors. *INTEGRATION, the VLSI Journal,* Vol. 7, 1989, pp. 103–125.

10. Moler, C., and Scott, D. Communication utilities for the iPSC. iPSC *Tech. Rep.* No. 2, INTEL Scientific Computers, 1986.

11. Ni, L. M., King, C. T., and Prins, P. Parallel algorithm design considerations for hypercube multiprocessors. *Proc. 1987 International Conference on Parallel Processing,* 1987, pp. 717–720.

12. Peterson, J., Tuazon, J., Liberman, D., and Pniel, M. The MARK III hypercube-ensemble concurrent computer. *Proc. International Conference on Parallel Processing,* Aug. 1985, pp. 71–73.

13. Reed, D. A., and Fujimoto, R. M. *Multicomputer Networks: Message-Based Parallel Processing.* MIT Press, Cambridge, MA, 1987.

14. Saad, Y., and Schultz, M. Topological properties of hypercubes. *Research Rep. 389,* Department of Computer Science, Yale University, 1985.

15. Shih, Y., and Fier, J. Hypercube systems and key applications. In Hwang, K., and DeGroot, D. (Eds.). *Parallel Processing for Supercomputing and Artificial Intelligence.* McGraw–Hill, New York; 1988.

16. Sullivan, H., and Bashkow, T. A large scale, homogeneous, fully distributed parallel machine. I. *Proc. 4th Symposium on Computer Architecture,* 1977, pp. 105–117.

Received August 2, 1987; revised December 25, 1988

YOURAN LAN received the B.S. degree in electrical engineering from Tsinghua University, Beijing, China, in 1968, and the M.S. degree in electrical engineering and the Ph.D. degree in Computer Science from Michigan State University, East Lansing, Michigan, in 1983 and 1988, respectively. He is currently an assistant professor in the Department of Computer Science at the University of Missouri, Columbia. His research interests include advanced computer systems, parallel and distributed processing, and VLSI design. Dr. Lan is a member of IEEE Computer Society and the Association for Computing Machinery.

ABDOL-HOSSEIN ESFAHANIAN was born in Kashan, Iran, on July 16, 1954. He received the B.S. degree in electrical engineering and the M.S. degree in computer, information, and control engineering from the University of Michigan, Ann Arbor, in 1975, and 1977, respectively, and the Ph.D. degree in computer science from Northwestern University, Evanston, Illinois, in 1983. He has been an assistant professor of computer science at Michigan State University, East Lansing, since September 1983. His research interests include applied graph theory, computer networks, fault-tolerant computing, design and analysis of algorithms, and computational complexity. Dr. Esfahanian is a member of ACM and the Society for Industrial and Applied Mathematics.

LIONEL M. NI received the B.S. degree in electrical engineering from National Taiwan University in 1973, the M.S. degree in electrical and computer engineering from Wayne State University, Detroit, Michigan, in 1977, and the Ph.D. degree in electrical engineering from Purdue University, West Lafayette, Indiana, in 1980. In 1981 he joined the faculty of the Department of Computer Science, Michigan State University, East Lansing, where he is currently a professor. His research interests include parallel processing, distributed computing, VLSI design automation, and computer networks. A senior member of IEEE, Dr. Ni served as a Distinguished Visitor of the IEEE Computer Society from 1985 to 1988. He is a member of ACM and SIAM.

Deadlock-Free Multicast Wormhole Routing in Multicomputer Networks*

Xiaola Lin and *Lionel M. Ni*

Department of Computer Science
Michigan State University
East Lansing, MI 48824-1027

Abstract: Efficient routing of messages is the key to the performance of multicomputers. Multicast communication refers to the delivery of the same message from a source node to an arbitrary number of destination nodes. Wormhole routing is the most promising switching technique used in new generation multicomputers. In this paper, we present multicast wormhole routing methods for multicomputers adopting 2D-mesh and hypercube topologies. The dual-path routing algorithm requires less system resource, while the multipath routing algorithm creates less traffic. More importantly, both routing algorithms are deadlock-free, which is essential to wormhole networks.

1 Introduction

The performance of multicomputers is highly dependent on the underlying communication mechanism and the message routing scheme. *Multicast communication* refers to the delivery of the same message from one source node to an arbitrary number of destination nodes. This communication pattern is useful in many applications such as the simulation of computer network, circuit simulation and numerous parallel algorithms. A software approach for multicast communication in hypercube multicomputers was proposed in [1]. The Cosmic Environment, a popular message-based parallel programming language, developed at Caltech also supports multicast communication [2]. Although multicast communication can be implemented by multiple one-to-one or broadcast communications, these alternative methods create too much unnecessary traffic and are likely to cause message delay and network congestion, and even deadlock [3].

Various switching techniques have been used in multicomputers, which will affect the criteria in evaluating multicast schemes. All first generation hypercube multicomputers support the *store-and-forward* mechanism. Wormhole routing proposed in [4] has been adopted in more advanced multicomputers. In wormhole routing, a message consists of a sequence of *flits* (flow control digits). The header flit(s) of the message governs the route, and the remaining flits of the message follow in a pipeline fashion. The network latency for wormhole routing is

$$T_f D + L/B = (L_f/B)D + L/B,$$

where T_f is the delay of the individual routing nodes on the path, D is the number of nodes on the path (distance), and L/B is the time required for the message of length L to pass through the channels of bandwidth B, and L_f is the length of each flit. If $L_f << L$, the distance D has a negligible effect on the network latency. The other routing method, *virtual cut-through*, is similar to wormhole routing. Virtual cut-through, however, buffers blocked messages and thus removes them from the network, while blocked messages remain in the network in the wormhole routing. The routing criteria and the deadlock properties of wormhole routing are quite different from those of store-and-forward or virtual cut-through switching methods. Because wormhole routing has low network latency and requires small amount of dedicated buffers at each node, it becomes the most promising switching technology and has been adopted in Symult 2010, nCUBE-2, iWARP, and Intel's Touchstone project. It is also being used in some fine-grained multicomputers, such as MIT's J-machine [5] and Caltech's MOSAIC [6].

In multicomputer networks, communication channels and message buffers constitute the set of *permanent reusable resources*. The processors that send or receive

*This work was supported in part by the NSF grants ECS-8814027 and MIP-8811815

"Deadlock-Free Multicast Wormhole Routing in Multicomputer Networks" by X. Lin and L.M. Ni from *Proc. 18th Int'l Symp. Computer Architecture,* 1991, pp. 116-125. Copyright © 1991 Assoc. for Computing Machinery, Inc., reprinted with permission.

the messages compete for these resources. In short, messages are the entities that compete for these resources. Deadlock refers to the situation in which a set of messages each is blocked forever because each message in the set holds some resources also needed by the other. One solution to deadlock-free wormhole routing was proposed in [7] by dividing the physical channels into group of virtual channels and restricting the routing. The method deals with deadlock problems for one-to-one communications. As will be shown later, this method is difficult to be applied to the case of multicast communication.

Multicast communication has been studied in [8, 9], in which various graph models and multicast routing algorithms have been proposed. However, deadlock problem was not addressed in these papers. The multicast deadlock problem was studied in [10]. Three multicast protocols, *multi-unicast, resumable* and *restricted branch multicast* were presented to deal with the deadlock problem. However, it is based on virtual cut-through switching mechanism and no routing algorithms are proposed in the paper. In this paper, we study multicast communication in multicomputer networks adopting *wormhole* routing. In Section 2, we discuss why the tree-like routing scheme is not suitable for wormhole networks and propose a multicast star model for multicast wormhole routing. Our multicast wormhole routing algorithms are based on the concept of network partitioning which is described in Section 3. Two heuristic multicast routing algorithms are described in Section 4. The dual-path routing algorithm requires less message buffers at the source node, while the multi-path routing algorithm creates less channel traffic. Both routing algorithms are proved to be deadlock free. Some simulation results are presented in Section 5. Our concluding remarks will be given in Section 6.

2 Multicast Wormhole Routing Problem

An efficient multicast routing algorithm should be deadlock-free. Also it should transmit the source message to each destination node with as small transmission time and communication channels as possible. For a set of given destination nodes, the multicast routing algorithm might deliver the source messages along a common path as much as possible, then branch the messages to each destination node. This results in a tree-like routing pattern, as shown in Fig. 1 which actually shows a broadcast tree rooted at node (0000) in a 4-cube. The message shown in Fig. 1 consists of a sequence of flits. In wormhole routing, if the header flit is blocked in one channel in the routing process, for example suppose the header flit (flit number 1) is blocked due to a busy channel (0010, 0110) in Fig. 1, unlike store-and-forward or

virtual cut-through routing, node 0010 does not buffer the whole message. The message will still remain in the network. As a result, the progress of messages in the whole routing tree has to be stopped. Furthermore, when a message is blocked, all of its flits stop forwarding and remain in contiguous channels of the network, which in turn blocks the transmission of other messages requiring the channels they occupy. It will greatly increase the network congestion and degrade the performance of the multicomputer.

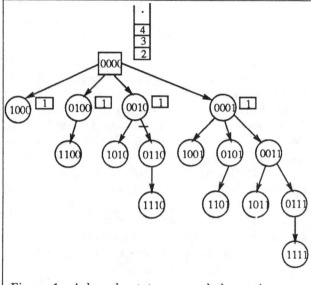

Figure 1. A broadcast tree wormhole routing pattern.

It is interesting to note that nCUBE-2 adopts wormhole routing [11]. Furthermore, it directly supports broadcast and special multicast in which the destination nodes form a subcube. For this purpose, nCUBE-2 supports tree-like wormhole routing as shown in Fig. 1. It will be interesting to see the performance degradation due to the contention of the channels. Furthermore, deadlock configuration has been found in the system [12].

A reasonable solution would be to prohibit the branch at each intermediate node and this leads to multicast path pattern [10, 9]. A *multicast path* for a multicast is a set of contiguous channels, starting from the source node and reaching each destination node in certain order. To reduce the length of the multicast path, we can divide the destination node set into several disjoint subsets and send the source messages down several separate multicast paths, each path for each subset of the destination nodes simultaneously.

A simple analysis can show that the probability a message is blocked in path-like routing is lower than that for tree-like routing. Suppose that the probability a message is blocked in each channel is p. Assuming at certain level of the tree-like routing the total number of branches is k, it requires all k channels available at the same time. The probability that a message is blocked at this level would be $1-(1-p)^k$. On the other hand, the block probability for path-like routing is p since each multicast path only requests one channel at one moment. Note that, when one path is blocked, it will not block the message delivery on the other paths. For example, suppose p is 0.1. In Fig. 1, the second level of the routing tree has 6 branches. The probability a message is blocked at this level is $1-(1-0.1)^6$, which is 0.47, while it is only 0.1 for path-like routing since the number of required channels at each step is always one.

Although in path-like routing, the average distance between the source and each destination is longer than that of tree-like routing, as indicated earlier, in wormhole routing the network latency is almost independent of the length of a path. In order to reduce the number of channels used for a given multicast, the subpath between the source and one of the destinations in a multicast path is not necessary a shortest path. The simulation study shown in [13] indicates that channel congestion becomes an important issue in affecting the network performance when the traffic is high. The simulation results presented in [10] also show that path-like model provides much better performance than the tree-like model when there is a contention in the network. Moreover, path-like routing does not need to replicate messages at each intermediate node.

The main problem here is that the methods for deadlock-free one-to-one wormhole routing cannot be employed for multicast path routing patterns. The e-cube routing algorithm for hypercube is not applicable. For example, in a 4-cube, node with address 0000 (we say node 0000) wants to send a message to both node 0101 and node 1010. In the multicast path routing pattern, the messages will be sent either to node 0101 then to node 1010, or first to node 1010 then 0101. In either order, it cannot keep routing in decreasing order of dimensions because the destination node that first received the messages will not buffer the entire message before sending them out toward the other destination node in wormhole routing.

A multiple multicast path routing model, namely *multicast star* (MS), is proposed in this paper to develop multicast routing algorithms. Apparently, for a given multicast set, it is desirable that the total number of the channels used by the multicast star can be minimized. However, this problem turns out to be computational intractable even for the popular 2D mesh and n-cube topologies. To better study the complexity of the optimal multicast routing problem and the deadlock properties, we use graph to model the underlying topologies of the multicomputers and the routing pattern.

Let graph $G(V, E)$ denote a graph with node set V and edge set E. For a pair of nodes u, v in $V(G)$, $d_G(u, v)$ denotes the length (the number of edges) of a shortest path from u to v in G. The interconnection topology of a multicomputer is denoted by a host graph $G(V, E)$, where each node in V corresponds to a processor and each edge in E corresponds to a communication channel. For a multicast communication, let u_0 denote the source node and $u_1, u_2, \ldots, u_k$ denote k destination nodes, where $k \geq 1$. The set $K = \{u_0, u_1, \ldots, u_k\}$ which is subset of $V(G)$ is called a *multicast set*. We can formulate multicast star problem as follows.

Definition 1 *A multicast star (MS) $S(V, E)$ of a host graph $G(V, E)$ for a multicast set K is a collection of several multicast paths. The i-th path starts from source node and reaches each destination in D_i, where $(\bigcup_{\forall j} D_j) \cup \{u_0\} = K$ and $D_i \cap D_j = \emptyset$ if $i \neq j$. An optimal MS (OMS) is a MS with a minimum length.*

The following two theorems are stated with their proofs shown in [14].

Theorem 1 *The OMS problem is NP-complete for 2D-mesh.*

Theorem 2 *The OMS problem is NP-complete for hypercube graph.*

Therefore, it is not practical to find an OMS in 2D mesh or hypercube topologies when the number of destinations is large, especially in a distributed manner. Heuristic routing algorithms will be developed for the MS model in the following sections.

3 Network Partitioning Strategies

Deadlock-free multicast routing algorithms are highly demanded for reliable and efficient parallel computations in multicomputers. In this section, we present network partitioning strategis, which are fundamental to the two heuristic deadlock-free multicast wormhole routing algorithms to be described in the next section. These algorithms can be applied to any multicomputer topologies which support Hamilton paths. A *Hamilton path* visits each node in the graph once and only once. Almost all topologies currently used in multicomputer networks, including 2D mesh and hypercube, have Hamilton paths. The proposed deadlock-free multicast routing algorithms assume that two neighboring nodes are connected by two opposite unidirectional channels. In practical design, these two unidirectional channels may share the same physical channel, which conforms current implementation of Ametek 2010 and nCUBE-2. Each unidirectional channel has its own flit buffer. A channel from node A to node B is the outgoing channel of node A and incoming channel of B. It is these channels that form the permanent reusable resources.

3.1 Partitioning of Channels

Each node, say node i, in a multicomputer is assigned with a label, $\ell(i)$. The assignment of the label to a node is based on the order of that node in a Hamilton path, where the first node in the path is assigned with label 0 and the last node in the path is assigned with label $m-1$ if there are m nodes in the network. Figure 2(a) and Figure 3(a) show a possible label assignment for a 4×3 mesh and a 3-cube multicomputer, respectively. Then we divide the network into two networks. The *high-channel network* contains all the channels which are from lower label nodes to higher label nodes, and the *low-channel network* contains all the channels from higher label nodes to lower label nodes. The corresponding high-channel and low-channel networks are also shown in Fig. 2 and Fig. 3.

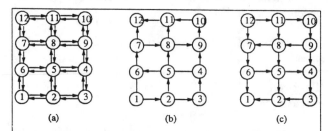

Figure 2. The label assignment and the corresponding high-channel and low-channel networks for a 4×3 mesh.

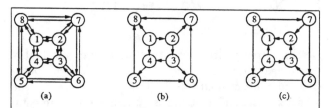

Figure 3. The label assignment and the corresponding high-channel and low-channel networks for a 3-cube.

First, let's consider the case of one-to-one communications. If the label of the destination node is greater than the label of the source node, the routing always takes place in the high-channel network; otherwise, it will take the low-channel network. Given a source and a destination node, it can be easily observed from Fig. 2 and Fig. 3 that there always exists a shortest path to deliver the message. Obviously, the performance of a

routing scheme is dependent on the selection of a Hamilton path. Figure 4 shows the label assignment for a 4×3 mesh based on a different Hamilton path and the corresponding high-channel and low-channel networks. Under such a label assignment, the routing paths between the node with label 4 and node with label 8 take 4 channels in either direction (see Fig. 4(b-c)) rather than a shortest path which should take only two channels.

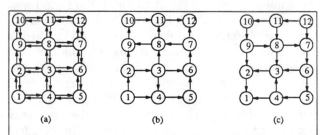

Figure 4. The other label assignment and channel partitioning for a 4×3 mesh.

In the following sections, we will propose label assignment schemes for both 2D-mesh and hypercube topologies and prove that these assignment schemes will provide a shortest routing path for any given pair of source and destination nodes.

3.2 Label Assignment

Suppose the address of a node in 2D mesh is represented by its integer coordinate (x, y), where the lower left node is $(0,0)$. The label assignment function ℓ for a $m \times n$ mesh can be expressed as

$$\ell(x, y) = \begin{cases} y * n + x & \text{if } y \text{ is even} \\ y * n + n - x - 1 & \text{if } y \text{ is odd} \end{cases}$$

For an n-cube, the label assignment function ℓ for a node with address $d_{n-1} d_{n-2} \ldots d_0$ is

$$\ell(d_{n-1} d_{n-2} \ldots d_0) = \sum_{i=0}^{n-1} (c_i \overline{d_i} 2^i + \overline{c_i} d_i 2^i),$$

where $c_{n-1} = 0, c_{n-j} = d_{n-1} \oplus d_{n-2} \oplus \ldots \oplus d_{n-j+1}$ for $1 < j \leq n$. It is straightforward to check that for two arbitrary nodes u and v in both 2D-mesh and n-cube, $\ell(u) \neq \ell(v)$ if $u \neq v$.

Let N be the node set of the 2D mesh or n-cube. We define a routing function $R, R : N \times N \rightarrow N$, as $R(u, v) = w$, such that w is the neighboring node of u, and

$\ell(w) = \max\{ \ell(p) : \ell(p) \leq \ell(v)$ and p is a neighboringnode of u } if $\ell(u) < \ell(v)$, or

$\ell(w) = \min\{ \ell(p) : \ell(p) \geq \ell(v)$ and p is a neighboringnode of u } if $\ell(u) > \ell(v)$.

For two arbitrary nodes u and v, a path from u to v can be selected by the routing function R as

$(v_1, v_2, \ldots, v_k)$, where $v_1 = u, v_i = R(v_{i-1}, v), 1 < i \leq k$, and $v_k = v$. The path is a partial order preserved for assignment ℓ if $\ell(v_i) < \ell(v_{i+1})$ for $1 \leq i < k$ (i.e., in the high-channel network), or $\ell(v_i) > \ell(v_{i+1})$ for $1 \leq i < k$ (i.e., in the low-channel network). We have the following important lemmas.

Lemma 1 *For two arbitrary nodes u and v in a 2D mesh, the path selected by the routing function R is a shortest path from u to v, and it is a partial order preserved for the label assignment function ℓ.*

Proof: Since u and v are two arbitrary nodes in a 2D mesh, without loss of generality, we can assume that $\ell(u) < \ell(v)$. We prove the lemma by induction on the distance $d(u, v)$.

Basis $(d(u,v)=1)$: It is easy to check that $R(u, v) = v$ and $\ell(u) < \ell(v)$.

Induction: Assume the hypothesis is true for k $(d(u, v) = k)$. We will prove that it is true for $d(u, v) = k + 1$. Suppose $u = (x_0, y_0)$ and $v = (x, y)$, and $w = R(u, v)$.

Case $y_0 = y$: By the definition of ℓ, $x > x_0$ if y is even, and $x < x_0$ if y is odd. We have $w = (x_0 + 1, y_0)$ for $x > x_0$, and $w = (x_0 - 1, y_0)$ for $x < x_0$ by the definition of routing function R. Again, by the definition of ℓ, $\ell(u) < \ell(w) \leq \ell(v)$. Obviously, $d(w, v) = d(u, v) - 1 = k$ and $\ell(w) < \ell(v)$ since $w \neq v$.

Case $y_0 < y$: By the definition of ℓ and R, when $y = y_0 + 1$, if y_0 is even and $x > x_0$ we have $w = (x_0 + 1, y_0)$, if y_0 is odd and $x < x_0$, then $w = (x_0 - 1, y_0)$. Otherwise $w = (x_0, y_0 + 1)$. In all cases, we have $d(w, v) = d(u, v) - 1 = k$ and $\ell(u) < \ell(w) < \ell(v)$.

By the definition of ℓ for 2D mesh, it is impossible to have $y_0 > y$ since $\ell(u) < \ell(v)$.

By the assumption of the induction, the path selected by routing function R for w and v, say $(w, u_1, \ldots, u_{k-1}, v)$, is a shortest path and a partial oreder preserved for ℓ with length k. Thus $(u, w, u_1, \ldots, u_{k-1}, v)$ is also such a path with length $k + 1$. The proof of this lemma is completed by the principle of induction. □

Lemma 2 *For two arbitrary nodes u and v in an n-cube, the path selected by the routing function R is a shortest path from u to v, and it is a partial order preserved for the label assignment function ℓ.*

Proof: Again, we assume that $\ell(u) < \ell(v)$, and prove by induction on the distance $d(u, v)$.

For $d(u,v)=1$, we have $R(u, v) = v$ and $\ell(u) < \ell(v)$. Assume that it is true for $k, (d(u, v) = k)$. Now, consider the case of $d(u, v) = k + 1$. Suppose the j-th bit (from left to right) is the first bit that u and v differ.

1. Suppose that u is $a_{n-1} \ldots a_{n-j+1} 0 b_{n-j-1} \ldots b_0$ and v is $a_{n-1} \ldots a_{n-j+1} 1 c_{n-j-1} \ldots c_0$.

(a) Consider node $a_{n-1} \ldots a_{n-j+1} 1 b_{n-j-1} \ldots b_0$, if $\ell(a_{n-1} \ldots a_{n-j+1} 1 b_{n-j-1} \ldots b_0) < \ell(a_{n-1} \ldots a_{n-j+1} 1 c_{n-j-1} \ldots c_0)$, then $R(u, v) = w$, where $w = a_{n-1} \ldots a_{n-j+1} 1 b_{n-j-1} \ldots b_0$ by the definition of R. We have $d(w, v) = d(u, v) - 1 = k$, and $\ell(u) < \ell(w) < \ell(v)$ by the definition of ℓ for n-cube. By the hypothesis of the induction, there is a shortest path selected by routing function R, say $(w, u_1, \ldots, u_{k-1}, v)$, which is a partial order preserved for ℓ with length k. Clearly, $(u, w, u_1, \ldots, u_{k-1}, v)$ is also such a path with length $k + 1$.

(b) If $\ell(a_{n-1} \ldots a_{n-j+1} 1 b_{n-j-1} \ldots b_0) > \ell(a_{n-1} \ldots a_{n-j+1} 1 c_{n-j-1} \ldots c_0)$, assume that p is the first bit that $a_{n-1} \ldots a_{n-j+1} 1 b_{n-j-1} \ldots b_0$ and $a_{n-1} \ldots a_{n-j+1} 1 c_{n-j-1} \ldots c_0$ differ (from left to right), and $p > j$. Let $a_{n-1} \ldots a_{n-j+1} 1 b_{n-j-1} \ldots b_0$ be $a_{n-1} \ldots a_{n-j+1} 1 c_{n-j-1} \ldots c_{n-p+1} \overline{c_{n-p}} b_{n-p-1} \ldots b_0$. Consider node s, where $s = a_{n-1} \ldots a_{n-j+1} 0 c_{n-j-1} \ldots c_{n-p+1} \overline{c_{n-p}} b_{n-p-1} \ldots b_0$. Since

$\ell(a_{n-1} \ldots a_{n-j+1} 1 c_{n-j-1} \ldots c_{n-p+1} \overline{c_{n-p}} b_{n-p-1} \ldots b_0)$
$= \ell(a_{n-1} \ldots a_{n-j+1} 1 b_{n-j-1} \ldots b_0) >$
$\ell(a_{n-1} \ldots a_{n-j+1} 1 c_{n-j-1} \ldots c_{n-p+1} \overline{c_{n-p}} b_{n-p-1} \ldots b_0)$,
and $a_{n-1} \oplus \ldots \oplus a_{n-j+1} \oplus 0 \oplus c_{n-j-1} \oplus \ldots \oplus c_{n-p+1}$
$= a_{n-1} \oplus \ldots \oplus a_{n-j+1} \oplus 1 \oplus c_{n-j-1} \oplus \ldots \oplus c_{n-p+1}$, we
have $\ell(u) = \ell(a_{n-1} \ldots a_{n-j+1} 0 b_{n-j-1} \ldots b_0) = \ell(a_{n-1} \ldots a_{n-j+1} 0 c_{n-j-1} \ldots c_{n-p+1} \overline{c_{n-p}} b_{n-p-1} \ldots b_0)$
$< \ell(a_{n-1} \ldots a_{n-j+1} 0 c_{n-j-1} \ldots c_{n-p+1} \overline{c_{n-p}} b_{n-p-1} \ldots b_0)$
$= \ell(s)$, by the definition of ℓ for n-cube. Note that $R(s, v) = v$, and $d(u, s) = d(u, v) - 1 = k$ and $\ell(u) < \ell(s) < \ell(v)$. Again, by the assumption of the induction, the path selected by R, say $(u, u_1, \ldots, u_{k-1}, s)$, is a shortest path and a partial order preserved for ℓ with length k. Hence, the path $(u, u_1, \ldots, u_{k-1}, s, v)$ selected by R is also such a path with length $k + 1$.

2. Suppose that u is $a_{n-1} \ldots a_{n-j+1} 1 b_{n-j-1} \ldots b_0$ and v is $a_{n-1} \ldots a_{n-j+1} 0 c_{n-j-1} \ldots c_0$. It is symmetric to the proof of part 1. □

3.3 Distributed Multicast Routing

Depending on which node(s) determines the routing path, either *centralized routing* or *distributed routing* may be adopted. In centralized routing, the source node determines all the nodes that will be involved in delivering its message to all the destinations. Thus, the routing information will be carried in the message itself. With distributed routing, the source node determines only to which of its neighboring nodes the source message will be sent. These nodes will repeat the procedure in turn. In this approach, the destination field in the message only carries the destination addresses.

The main drawback of centralized routing is that the addresses of all the intermediate nodes must be carried in the source message, which will create extra message overhead. In distributed routing, on the other hand, since the routing decision is made in each intermediate node, the routing algorithm should be simple enough to achieve a low overall message transmission time. All commercially available multicomputers support distributed routing for one-to-one communications. However, obtaining an efficient multicast routing algorithm is not an easy task in a distributed manner [9].

Two heuristic multicast algorithms are described in the next section. Both algorithms support distributed routing. The address field of each multicast message carries the addresses of the intended destination nodes. Note that nCUBE-2 does support multiple node addresses in the address field, and the message transmission has to follow the order of addresses specified in the address field [11].

For each multicast communication, the source node has to prepare the address field information for each message. This is referred to as *message preparation*. The message preparation overhead is dependent on the routing algorithm and may involve some computation, such as sorting of destination addresses. However, for most of the parallel algorithms which require multicast communication, the set of destination nodes is known in advance. Thus, message preparation for each set of destination nodes only needs to be computed once. In other words, the overhead incurred in message preparation should not be contributed to the overhead in performing the actual message routing.

4   Deadlock-Free Multicast Wormhole Routing

Two heuristic multicast wormhole routing algorithms based on the multicast star model are described in this section. The dual-path routing method allows up to two paths, while the multi-path routing method allows up to d paths, where d is the maximum number of outgoing channels in the source node.

4.1   Dual-Path Multicast Routing

The first heuristic routing algorithm divides the the destination node set into two subsets, D_H and D_L, where each destination node in D_H has a higher assigned label than that of the source node, and D_L contains the rest of the destination nodes, i.e., the node with assigned label lower than that of the source node. The source messages will be sent to the destination nodes in D_H using the high-channel network, while it uses the low-channel network to deliver the source messages to the destination nodes in D_L. The routing pattern is a multicast star with only two separate multicast paths. Thus, it is called *dual-path* routing algorithm. As can be shown later, the routing scheme is deadlock-free.

The message preparation in the source node of the

dual-path routing algorithm is given in Fig. 5, and the dual-path routing algorithm is shown in Fig. 6. In Fig. 5, the source node divides the destination node set into two subsets: D_H and D_L. Then, D_H and D_L are sorted in ascending order and descending order, respectively, with the assigned label as the sorting key. For each path, the message carries the corresponding sorted D in its address field.

Algorithm: Message preparation for the dual-path routing algorithm
  Input: Multicast set K, local address u_0, and node label assignment function ℓ;
  Output: Two sorted lists of destination nodes: D_H and D_L.
  Procedure:

1. Divide $K - \{u_0\}$ into two sets D_H and D_L such that D_H contains all the destination nodes with higher ℓ value than $\ell(u_0)$ and D_L the node with lower ℓ value than $\ell(u_0)$.

2. Sort the destination nodes in D_H and D_L using the ℓ value as the key, respectively. Put these sorted nodes in list D_H in ascending order and D_L in descending order, respectively.

Figure 5. Message preparation for the dual-path routing algorithm.

Each node upon receiving the message sends the message toward the first destination node in the address field of the message through a shortest path defined by the routing function R. For example, consider a 4-cube with node 1100 as the source as shown in Fig. 7. The number outside a node in the figure is the assigned label of the node. Suppose the destination nodes are 0100, 0011, 0111, 1010 and 1111. Clearly, $D_L=\{0100, 0111, 0011\}$ and $D_H=\{1111, 1010\}$. For D_H, the source node will send the message first to node 1111, the first destination node in D_H through the high-channel network. Based on the label assignment scheme, node 1100 has three outgoing channels reaching nodes 1000, 1101, and 111, respectively. According to the routing function R, node 1101 will be selected to forward the message. By repeating the same procedure for each node receiving the message, we get the routing pattern shown in Fig. 7.

The label assignment is based on a Hamilton path. Therefore, for any two nodes in the multicomputer, there is at least one path from a node with lower label to node with higher label, and there is also at least another path from the high label node to lower one since

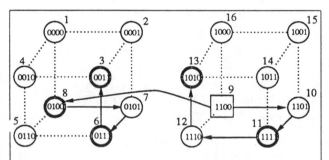

Figure 7. A 4-cube with node 1100 as the source.

we assume that there are two opposite unidirectional channels between two connected nodes. Since each destination can only be put in either D_H or D_L, it can be easily shown that the source message can be sent to each destination node once and only once.

Note that the label assignment function ℓ can be determined in advance for a given multicomputer. Thus, the label in Fig 5 and Fig. 6 for each node can be obtained in $O(1)$ time. Step 1 and Step 2 can be merged by using some well known sorting algorithm such as quick sort algorithm with time complexity $O(k \log k)$, where $k = |K|$. In the message routing part, both Step 1 and Step 2 take a constant time if we don't consider the time for message coping. Step 3 can be done in $O(d)$ time where d is the maximum number of outgoing channels of the node. For example, the maximum outdegree for a node is 4 in 2D mesh and n in n-cube. Thus we have established the following lemma and theorem.

Lemma 3 *The message preparation complexity for the*

dual-path routing algorithm is $O(|K| \log |K|)$, where K is the multicast set.

Theorem 3 *The dual-path routing algorithm for a multicast set K sends the source message to each destination node in K once and only once. The time complexity for each node is $O(d)$, where d is the maximum number of outgoing channels of the node.*

Corollary 1 *The dual-path multicast routing algorithm is deadlock-free.*

Proof: To show that the dual-path routing algorithm is deadlock-free, we need to prove that there is no cycle dependency of the channels, because the cycle dependency of the resource is the necessary condition of the deadlock situation. The two high-channel and low-channel networks each has separate sets of channels in the multicomputer. By the definition of channel partitioning scheme, it is easy to see that there is no cycle in each network. The path selected by the routing function R is a partial order preserved for the label assignment function ℓ by Lemma 1 and Lemma 2. Thus, no cycle dependency of the channels can be created. $\square$

The performance of the dual-path routing algorithm is dependent on the location distribution of destination nodes. Consider the example shown in Fig. 8 for a 6×6 mesh topology. The total number of channels used to deliver that message is 33 (18 in the high-channel network and 15 in the low-channel network). In order to reduce the average length of multicast paths and the number of the channels used for a multicast, a multi-path multicast routing algorithm is proposed below. In that algorithm, we relax the restriction of having at most two paths.

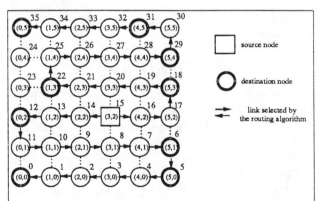

Figure 8. An example of dual-path routing in a 6×6 mesh.

4.2 Multi-Path Multicast Routing

If the outgoing degree of a node is q, obviously, up to q paths (or q copies of the message) can be used to deliver the message. The only difference between the dual-path routing and the multi-path routing is in the message preparation part. Figure 9 shows the message preparation of the multi-path routing algorithm, in which we use a simple greedy method to further partition the destination sets D_H and D_L of the dual-path algorithm for multiple multicast paths.

For the simple multicast example shown in Fig. 8, the destination set is first divided into two sets D_H and D_L at source node $(3,2)$, $D_H = \{$ $(5,3)$, $(1,3)$, $(5,4)$, $(4,5)$, $(0,5)$ $\}$ and $D_L = \{$ $(0,2)$, $(5,1)$, $(5,0)$, $(0,0)$ $\}$. Then D_H can be further divided into two subsets D_{H1} and D_{H2} at Step 3, $D_{H1} = \{$ $(5,3)$, $(5,4)$, $(4,5)$ $\}$ and $D_{H2} = \{$ $(1,3)$, $(0,5)$ $\}$. D_L can also be divided into $\{$ $(5,1)$, $(5,0)$ $\}$ and $\{$ $(0,2)$, $(0,0)$ $\}$. The multicast will be performed by four multicast paths as shown in Fig. 10. Note that the multi-path routing takes only 20 channels in the example.

Suppose that q is the maximun number of outgoing channels of the multicomputer. In the multi-path routing algorithm, Step 1 and Step 2 are exactly the same as those in dual-path algorithm. The two steps need $O(|K| \log |K|)$ time. In Step 3, we need to check at most p queues, $p \le q$, for each destination node in D_H, $|D_H| < K$, it takes $O(q|K|)$ time. Step 4 is symmetric to Step 3, it also requires $O(q|K|)$ time. The follow lemma is established.

Lemma 4 *The time complexity of message preparation of the multi-path routing algorithm is* $\max\{O(|K| \log |K|), O(q|K|)\}$, *where K is the multicast set and q is the maximum number of outgoing channels of the node.*

Following the same argument as in Corollary 1, we have the following corollary.

Corollary 2 *The multi-path multicast routing is deadlock-free.*

5 Performance Study

The performance of both dual-path and multi-path routing algorithms is studied. Since the message transmission time is almost independent of the length between the source and destination nodes, we only measure the average number (i.e., traffic) of channels used for multicast communication with different number of destinations. Our simulation program measures the channel traffic for both 8×8 mesh and 6-cube topologies.

For a given k, the number of the destination nodes in a multicast, a random number generates k integers within the rang $[0, 63]$ that represents k destination addresses. The amount of traffic generated by each algorithm is averaged over 1000 runs for each k. Figure 11 and Figure 12 show the average amount of additional

---

Algorithm: Message preparation for the multiple-path routing algorithm

Input: Multicast set K, local address u_0, and node assignment ℓ;

Output: Sorted destination node lists $D_1, D_2, \ldots, D_q$ for q multicast paths.

Procedure:

1. Divide $K - \{u_0\}$ into two sets D_H and D_L such that D_H contains all the destination nodes with higher ℓ value than $\ell(u_0)$ and D_L the nodes with lower ℓ value than $\ell(u_0)$.

2. Sort the destination nodes in D_H and D_L using the ℓ value as the key, respectively. Put these sorted nodes in list D_H in ascending order and D_L in descending order, respectively.

3. (Divide D_H, assume u_0 has p neighboring nodes, $v_1, v_2, \ldots, v_p$, each of which has ℓ label greater than $\ell(u_0)$.)

   (a) For $i = 1, 2, \ldots, p$ do
       i. $qhead[i] = v_i$.
       ii. $D_i \leftarrow \emptyset$.

   (b) $D \leftarrow D_H$.

   (c) (construct output queues $D_1, D_2, \ldots, D_p$) While $D \ne \emptyset$, do suppose u_j is in the head of D, find m, $1 \le m \le p$ such that $\ell(u_j) > \ell(qhead[m])$, and $d(u_j, qhead[m])$ $= \min_{1 \le t \le p}\{d(u_s, qhead[t])\}$

   (d) $D_m \leftarrow D_m \cup \{u_j\}$; $D \leftarrow D - \{u_j\}$; $qhead[m] \leftarrow u_j$.

4. (Divide D_L, it is symmetric to Step 3. This step constructs $D_{p+1}, \ldots, D_q$.)

Figure 9. Message preparation for the multi-path routing algorithm.

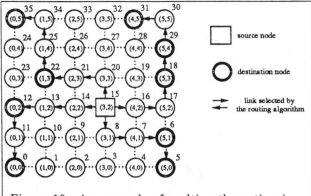

Figure 10. An example of multi-path routing in a 6 × 6 mesh.

traffic generated by both algorithms in 8 × 8 mesh and 6-cube topologies, respectively. For a multicast with k destination nodes, it requires at least k units of traffic [8]. The average additional traffic (AAT) in Fig. 11 and Fig. 12 is defined as the total amount of traffic minus k. As mentioned before, multicast can be implemented by multiple one-to-one or broadcast communications. Both heuristic routing algorithms create much less amount of traffic compared with multiple one-to-one or broadcast communications on both mesh and hypercube.

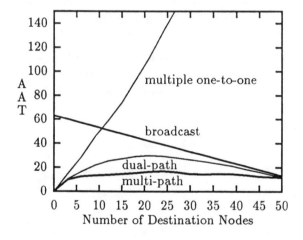

Figure 11. Performance of different multicast methods on a 8 × 8 mesh.

It is not difficult to see that the number of channels simultaneously required in both heuristic multicast algorithms generally is much smaller than that in broadcast. Hence, the contention of network is relatively low. The traffic generated by the dual-path algorithm for mesh or hypercube is higher than that generated by the multipath algorithm due to the small number of multicast

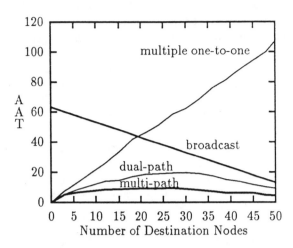

Figure 12. Performance of different multicast methods on a 6-cube.

paths.

Although the multi-path routing requires less number of channels than that of dual-path routing, it is more expensive in terms of hardware implementation. Each multicast path needs to buffer the complete message in the souce node, and the buffer cannot be released until the last flit is transmitted. Furthermore, for simultaneous transmission of multiple multicast paths, the bandwidth between the local processor and router may become a bottleneck. This router-to-processor channel bottleneck has already been observed in Symult 2010 [13].

The performance of the proposed multicast routing algorithms are dependent on the efficient implementation of of the routing function R. The complexity analysis shown in Section 4 is based on a software approach. It has been shown in [15] that with some special hardware design tricks, the routing decision making time can be significantly reduced. If the number of nodes is not very large, an associate memory can be used to implement the routing function; otherwise, a high speed SRAM may be used.

6 Concluding Remarks

It is observed that tree-like routing model is not suitable for multicast routing in wormhole networks. We have presented a multicast star wormhole routing model for multicast communications. Two multicast wormhole routing schemes under this model have been proposed, which are able to greatly reduce the communication traffic and to guarantee deadlock-free. Both routing algorithms can be applied to any multicomputer networks that have Hamilton paths. The performance of the routing scheme is dependent on the selection of a good Hamilton path. For 2D-mesh and hypercube topologies, we proposed methods to select such a Hamilton path so that for any given two nodes, there exists a shortest routing path between them.

The multi-path routing algorithm creates less traffic than that of dual-path routing algorithm because it can use multiple multicast paths to deliver the messages. However, it requires more hardware support and the channel between the processor and router in the source node may become a bottleneck. The routing scheme is dependent on the number of unidirectional channels between two connected nodes. If the concept of *virtual channels* [7] is used, two connected nodes may support many virtual channels. Here, each virtual channel should have its own dedicated flit buffer. Instead of partitioning the network into high-channel and low-channel networks, the network may be partitioned into many sub-networks. The set of destination nodes then may be distributed to different sub-networks to support multiple multicast paths. The issue will be how many virtual channels are required and how the destination nodes should be partitioned. This is an interesting issue and deserves further study.

References

1. C. Moler and D. Scott, "Communication utilities for the iPSC," iPSC Technical Report No. 2, Intel Scientific Computers, 1986.

2. C. L. Seitz, J. Seizovic, and W.-K. Su, "The C programmer's abbreviated guide to multicomputer programming," Tech. Rep. Caltech-CS-TR-88-1, Department of Computer Science, California Institute of Technology, Jan. 1988.

3. L. M. Ni, "Communication issues in multicomputers," in *Proceedings of the First Workshop on Parallel Processing*, (Taiwan, ROC), pp. 52–64, Dec. 1990.

4. W. J. Dally and C. L. Seitz, "The torus routing chip," *Journal of Distributed Computing*, vol. 1, no. 3, pp. 187–196, 1986.

5. W. J. Dally, "The J-machine: System support for Actors," in *Actors: Knowledge-Based Concurrent Computing* (Hewitt and Agha, eds.), MIT Press, 1989.

6. W. C. Athas and C. L. Seitz, "Multicomputers: Message-passing concurrent computers," *IEEE Computer*, pp. 9–25, Aug. 1988.

7. W. J. Dally and C. L. Seitz, "Deadlock-free message routing in multiprocessor interconnection networks," *IEEE Transactions on Computers*, vol. C-36, pp. 547–553, May 1987.

8. Y. Lan, A. H. Esfahanian, and L. M. Ni, "Multicast in hypercube multiprocessors," *Journal of Parallel and Distributed Computing*, pp. 30–41, Jan. 1990.

9. X. Lin and L. M. Ni, "Multicast communication in multicomputers networks," in *Proceedings of the 1990 International Conference on Parallel Processing*, pp. III–114–III–118, Aug. 1990.

10. G. T. Byrd, N. P. Saraiya, and B. A. Delagi, "Multicast communication in multiprocessor systems," in *Proceedings of the 1989 International Conference on Parallel Processing*, pp. I–196 – I–200, 1989.

11. NCUBE Company, *NCUBE 6400 Processor Manual*, 1990.

12. X. Lin, P. K. McKinley, and L. M. Ni, "Performance study of multicast wormhole routing in 2D-mesh multicomputers," Tech. Rep. MSU-CPS-ACS-33, Department of Computer Science, Michigan State University, Feb. 1991.

13. S. Chittor and R. Enbody, "Performance evaluation of mesh-connected wormhole-routed networks for interprocessor communication in multicomputers," in *Proceedings of Supercomputing'90*, pp. pp. 647 – 656, Nov. 1990.

14. X. Lin and L. M. Ni, "Deadlock-free multicast wormhole routing in in multicomputer networks," Tech. Rep. MSU-CPS-ACS-28, Department of Computer Science, Michigan State University, Oct. 1990.

15. Y. Lan, L. M. Ni, and A. H. Esfahanian, "A VLSI router design for hypercube multiprocessors," *Integration: The VLSI Journal*, vol. 7, pp. 103–125, 1989.

Multiphase Complete Exchange on a Circuit Switched Hypercube

Shahid H. Bokhari

Department of Electrical Engineering, University of Engineering & Technology,
Lahore, Pakistan

Abstract—For a circuit switched hypercube of dimension d ($n = 2^d$), two algorithms for achieving complete exchange are known. These are (1) the Standard Exchange approach that employs d transmissions of size 2^{d-1} blocks each and is useful for small block sizes, and (2) the Optimal Circuit Switched algorithm that employs $2^d - 1$ transmissions of 1 block each and is best for large block sizes.

A unified multiphase algorithm that includes these two algorithms as special cases is described. The complete exchange on a hypercube of dimension d and block size m is achieved by carrying out k partial exchanges on subcubes of dimension d_i, $\sum_{i=1}^{k} d_i = d$ and effective block size $m_i = m2^{d-d_i}$. When $k = d$ and all $d_i = 1$, this corresponds to algorithm (1) above. For the case of $k = 1$ and $d_1 = d$, this becomes the circuit switched algorithm (2). Changing the subcube dimensions d_i varies the effective block size and permits a compromise between the data permutation and block transmission overhead of (1) and the startup overhead of (2).

For a hypercube of dimension d, the number of possible combinations of subcubes is $p(d)$, the number of partitions of the integer d. This is an exponential but very slowly growing function (e.g. $p(7) = 15, p(10) = 42$) and it is feasible to enumerate over these partitions to discover the best combination for a given message size. The multiphase approach has been analysed for, and implemented on, the Intel iPSC-860 hypercube.

Introduction

On a distributed memory parallel computer system, the complete exchange communication pattern requires each of n processors to send a different m byte block of data to each of the remaining $n - 1$ processors. This communication pattern arises in many important applications such as matrix transpose, matrix-vector multiply, 2-dimensional FFTs, distributed table look-ups etc. It is also important in its own right since, being equivalent to a complete directed graph, it is the densest communication requirement that can be imposed on an interconnection network. The time required to carry out the complete exchange is an important measure of the power of a distributed memory parallel computer system.

There are two algorithms for complete exchange on circuit switched hypercubes like the Intel iPSC-2, Intel iPSC-

860, and Ncube-2. The first is the Standard Exchange algorithm: for an d-dimensional hypercube, this algorithm uses d transmissions of 2^{d-1} blocks each. On circuit switched machines this algorithm is useful for small block sizes ($< \approx 200$ bytes, on the iPSC-860). The second is the Optimal Circuit Switched algorithm, that uses $2^d - 1$ transmissions of 1 block each: the transmissions are carefully scheduled to avoid link contention.

We describe a unified multiphase algorithm that carries out the complete exchange on a hypercube of dimension d as set of k "partial" exchanges on subcubes of dimensions d_i, $\sum_{i=1}^{k} d_i = d$ with effective block size $m_i = m2^{d-d_i}$. The motivation here is to reduce the time required for the complete exchange by compromising between the data permutation and block transmission overhead of the Standard Exchange algorithm and the startup overhead of the Optimal algorithm.

For a hypercube of dimension d there are $p(d)$ possible generalised algorithms, where $p(d)$ is the number of partitions of the integer d. Although $p(d)$ is an exponential function, it grows very slowly. For example, $p(7) = 15$, $p(10) = 42$, and $p(20) = 672$. It is thus quite feasible to enumerate over all partitions to find the algorithm best suited for a given block size.

For the case where $k = d$ and each $d_i = 1$, the unified algorithm degenerates into the Standard Exchange algorithm. When $k = 1$ and $d_1 = d$, it becomes the Optimal algorithm. The unified algorithm thus includes the two known algorithms as special (although extreme) cases.

Measurements on the Intel iPSC-860 show that the multiphase approach can substantially improve performance for block sizes in the 0–160 byte range. This range corresponds to 0–40 floating point numbers and is commonly encountered in practical numeric applications. While our measurements are for the Intel iPSC-860, our techniques are applicable to all circuit switched hypercubes that use the common 'e-cube' routing strategy. The Intel iPSC-2 and the Ncube-2 are examples of such machines.

Circuit Switched Hypercubes

Circuit-switched communications distinguish the new hypercubes, (Intel iPSC-2, -860, and Ncube-2) from older machines. In these machines, a dedicated path is set up between two processors when communication is desired. Messages then flow through this path without involving intervening processors. The path between source and destination is determined by repeatedly applying the the 'e-cube' routing rule until destination is reached.

Research supported by the National Aeronautics and Space Administration under NASA contract NAS1-18605 while the author was in residence at the Institute for Computer Applications in Science & Engineering, Mail Stop 132C, NASA Langley Research Center, Hampton, VA 23665-5225.

e-cube rule: Starting with the right hand side of the binary label of the source, move to the processor whose label more closely matches the label of the destination.

The user has no control over *how* a message is routed between two processors. The fixed routing algorithm completely determines this path. Because of this, we can encounter *edge* and *node* contention. Edge contention is the sharing of an edge (i.e. a communication link) by two or more paths. Similarly, node contention is the sharing of a node. Measurements on the iPSC-860 [1] reveal that edge contention has a disastrous impact on communication time, while node contention has no measurable effect.

Since circuit switching provides very fast communications, it is generally felt that it eliminates most, if not all, of the inefficiencies caused by communication overhead. In particular, it is a common belief that programmers can ignore the details of the interconnection network, since communication overhead is negligible. This is false: as we shall see in this paper, very careful consideration of the interconnection network is necessary if the full power of the machine is to be utilised.

Algorithms for Complete Exchange

Of the two algorithms for complete exchange that are currently in use, Standard Exchange[5] is well known, while the Optimal Circuit Switched algorithm[7, 9] is a recent development. The former requires only $\log n$ transmissions of $n/2$ blocks each and has better performance for small block sizes. The latter uses $n - 1$ transmissions of 1 block each and has better performance for large block sizes. Both algorithms completely avoid edge contention.

The Standard Exchange Algorithm

The Standard Exchange algorithm [5] uses $\log n$ transmissions of size $n/2$ blocks each. All transmissions are along paths of length 1, thus there is no contention. This algorithm incurs overhead because of the shuffling of blocks and because it transmits $\frac{n}{2}\log n$ blocks instead of the optimal number, $n - 1$. It is, nevertheless, competitive for small block sizes. This is because there are only $\log n$ transmissions (as opposed to $n - 1$ for the algorithm discussed below) and thus the overhead of starting up a message is not incurred as frequently.

```
procedure Standard_Exchange;
  for j = d - 1 downto 0 do
    if (bit j of mynumber = 0) then
      message = blocks n/2 to n - 1
    else
      message = blocks 0 to n/2 - 1;
    send_message_to_processor((mynumber) ⊕ (2^j));
    shuffle blocks;
  end;
end;
```

The Optimal Circuit Switched Algorithm

For complete exchange, each processor must send its ith block to processor i, but is free to schedule its transmissions to avoid edge contention. Of the many possible schedules[2] that completely avoid contention, we use the one developed by Schmiermund and Seidel[7]. This has the property that the entire communication pattern is decomposed into a sequence of pairwise exchanges. This is very useful on the Intel iPSC-2 and iPSC-860 because of certain idiosyncrasies of their communication hardware.

```
procedure Optimal_Circuit_Switched;
  for i = 1 to n - 1 do
    send_block_to_processor((mynumber) ⊕ (i));
  end;
```

Analysis of Run Times

Let us define the following performance parameters of our hypercube. Transmission: τ μsec. per byte, data permutation: ρ μsec. per byte, startup(latency): λ μsec., distance impact: δ μsec. per dimension. The time taken by a message of size m bytes to cross d dimensions is $\lambda + \tau m + \delta d$; the time to shuffle m bytes of data within memory is ρm.

In Standard Exchange, d transmissions of $m2^{d-1}$ bytes each over dimension 1, take $d(\lambda + \tau m2^{d-1} + \delta)$ seconds. There are d shuffles on 2^d blocks of m bytes each, taking $d(\rho m2^d)$ seconds. The total time is thus $d(\lambda + (\tau + 2\rho)m2^{d-1} + \delta)$.

For the Optimal Circuit Switched algorithm there are $2^d - 1$ transmissions of blocks of m bytes. At each step, all pairs of processors are at identical distances from each other. Thus the overall distance impact equals the average path length in a hypercube, which is $d2^{d-1}/(2^d - 1)$. The total time is $(2^d - 1)(\lambda + \tau m + \delta \frac{d2^{d-1}}{2^d - 1})$.

Standard is better than Optimal whenever

$$m < \frac{(2^d - d - 1)\lambda + d(2^{d-1} - 1)\delta}{(d2^{d-1} - 2^d + 1)\tau + d2^d\rho}$$

For a hypothetical machine of dimension 6 with $\tau = \rho = 1$, $\lambda = 200$ and $\delta = 20$, Standard Exchange is better for $m < 30$.

The Multiphase Approach

In our multiphase approach the complete exchange is carried out as a set of two or more "partial" exchanges. This permits us to use the Circuit Switched algorithm for block sizes for which it is ordinarily inefficient and provides significant performance gains. In fact our multiphase approach is a unified algorithm that *includes* the Standard Exchange and Circuit Switched algorithms as special cases.

Motivation and Example

Given that the Standard Exchange algorithm is competitive for small message sizes and the Circuit Switched algorithm performs best at large message sizes, it is possible to combine these algorithms to obtain performance better than either. Recall that we have $n = 2^d$ nodes on our hypercube. Ordinary complete exchange is based on the exchange of sets of n blocks per processor. We can envisage a "partial" exchange that is carried out simultaneously on all subcubes of dimension $d_1 < d$ but based on $n = 2^d$ blocks (not 2^{d_1} blocks) per processor. By carefully permuting our data blocks, we can then execute another partial exchange on all subcubes of dimension $d_2 = d - d_1$, again with 2^d blocks and not 2^{d_2} blocks. The end result will be that a complete exchange on the hypercube of dimension d is carried out in two phases, using messages that are longer than the messages that would have been used if a single phase approach had been employed. What we have achieved here is an effective "lengthening" of messages that lets us take advantage of the Circuit Switched algorithm for message sizes for which it is normally unsuited. The price paid is the overhead of data permutation, which is required to align blocks to that they finish up in the correct position. Figure 1 illustrates this approach for a dimension 3 hypercube.

An example. Suppose we have to carry out the complete exchange of block size 24 on our hypothetical 6-d hypercube with $\tau = \rho = 1, \lambda = 200$ and $\delta = 20$. We have seen that Standard Exchange is best on this machine for blocksizes of less than 30 bytes. For 24 bytes the Standard algorithm takes 15144μsec. Let us see what happens if we carry out this exchange in two phases of dimension 2 and 4 respectively. The first phase on dimension 2 subcubes with an effective block size of $24 \times 2^{6-2} = 384$ bytes takes 1832μsec. using the Circuit Switched algorithm. The next exchange on dimension 4 subcubes with effective block size $24 \times 2^{6-4} = 160$ bytes takes 6040μsec., again using the Circuit Switched algorithm.

To this must be added the overhead of shuffling data, which is $\rho m 2^d$ per phase. This totals 3072μsec. The total time for the two phase approach is thus 10944μsec., which is substantially faster than the Standard algorithm.

General Algorithm

A complete exchange on a hypercube of dimension d with $n = 2^d$ processors and block size m is done using a set of partial exchanges $\mathcal{D} = \{d_1, d_2, \cdots, d_k\}$, where each d_i specifies a subcube dimension. Obviously $|\mathcal{D}| = k, 1 \leq k$, and $\Sigma_{i=1}^k d_i = d$. The jth partial exchange is done on the set of subcubes determined by bits $\Sigma_{i=1}^j d_i - d_j$ to $\Sigma_{i=1}^j d_i$ of the hypercube node labels.

In a partial exchange 2^d blocks of size m each are exchanged, regardless of cube dimension. Hence the time required for the ith phase is obtained from (1) or (2) with m replaced by $m 2^{d-d_i}$ bytes (the *effective block size*).

```
procedure Multiphase;
{ d:     dimension of the hypercube
  k:     number of phases (subcubes) in partition D
  d_i:   dimension of the ith subcube in partition D
  start: starting bit of subcube label
  stop:  ending bit of subcube label }
```

```
start = d - 1;
for i = 1 to k do {Partial exchange}
    stop = start - d_i + 1;
    compute effective blocksize;
    for j = 1 to (2^(start-stop+1) - 1) do
        send effective_block_to_processor
            ((mynumber) ⊕ (j2^stop));
    shuffle blocks d_i times;
    start = stop - 1;
end;
end;
```

When $k = d$, all d_is are 1 and the outer i loop is executed k times with $start = stop = d - 1, d - 2, \cdots, 1, 0$. The inner j loop is executed only once for each i and Multiphase degenerates into Standard Exchange. When $k = 1$ and thus $d_1 = d$, the outer loop is executed only once. $stop$ always equals 0, j takes on the values $1, 2, \cdots, 2^d - 1$ and Multiphase becomes Optimal Circuit Switched.

Minimizing the Execution Time

Given a hypercube of dimension d, there are many different combinations of subcube dimensions and algorithms that can be used to obtain a multiphase algorithm. The sequence of dimensions is unimportant, as long as the shuffles are carried out correctly. The optimal set can be obtained by enumerating over all the partitions of d. For each partition $\mathcal{D} = \{d_1, d_2, \cdots, d_k\}$ we select the best algorithm at each phase. This procedure is not as expensive as it appears at first sight, since we are enumerating over the partitions of hypercube *dimension* and not *size*. It is a classical result [4] that the number of partitions of an integer d is $p(d) \sim \frac{1}{4\sqrt{3}d} e^{\pi \sqrt{2/3} \sqrt{d}}$. Exact values can easily be calculated. Some values of interest are: $p(5) = 7, p(7) = 15, p(10) = 42, p(15) = 176, p(20) = 627$. Thus for a thousand node hypercube (the largest commercially available in 1990) we need to enumerate only 42 partitions—a trivial number.

Implementation on the iPSC-860

We have implemented the Multiphase algorithm on the Intel iPSC-860 hypercube. Complete details of our implementation may be found in [3].

For efficiency, we use FORCED message types and employ the *Pairwise Synchronized Exchange* technique of [6, 7, 8]. We use FORCED types for "pairwise synchronisation" messages as well as for the actual data transfers. We post all receives for all messages before a global synchronisation.

Measured Performance Characteristics

As discussed above, the time for a message of size m bytes to cross d dimensions is $\lambda + \tau m + \delta d$. When messages of the FORCED type are used and all receives are posted before transmission begins, the values λ and τ are 95.0μsec. and 0.394μsec./byte, respectively. The value of δ is 10.3μsec.

per dimension. The λ for a zero byte message is significantly better, being 82.5μsec. When using these measured parameters to predict the time required by the multiphase algorithm, we must remember that each pairwise exchange is preceded by an exchange of zero byte synchronization messages. Thus we have the *effective* values of $\lambda = 177.5\mu$sec. and $\delta = 20.6\mu$sec./dimension.

The time for global synchronization on a cube of dimension d has been measured at 150$d\mu$sec. The time for data permutation (shuffling) is $\rho = 0.54\mu$sec./byte. This is slower than the time to transmit data because of the overhead of computing the permutation. This occurs because we have implemented our algorithm in C using a compiler that does not take many of the powerful features of the iPSC-860 into account. It should be possible to significantly improve this figure by using assembly language and/or an optimizing compiler. This will change our final measured timings somewhat, but will not affect our overall approach, which is valid even if the cost of permutation is zero.

The time for a partial exchange on a subcube of dimension d_i within a hypercube of dimension d is thus $(2^{d_i-1} - 1) \cdot (177.5 + 0.394m + 20.6\frac{d2^{d_i-1}}{2^{d_i}-1} + 0.54 \cdot 2^d m) + 150d$. When $d_i = d$, the shuffling can be omitted, since d-shuffles of 2^d blocks are equivalent to the identity permutation.

Evaluation of Multiphase Algorithm

Measured timings for the Multiphase algorithm on an Intel iPSC-860 hypercube of dimension 7 are shown in Figure 2[2] Each combination is denoted by its set of subcubes. In particular, the Standard Exchange algorithm is denoted by $\{1,1,1,1,1,1,1\}$ and the Optimal Circuit Switched Algorithm by $\{7\}$. For dimension 7, the number of combinations are 15. Although we have measured the performance of all combinations, to avoid congested plots we show only those combinations that form the hull of optimality (i.e. only the best combination for every blocksize). The only exception is the Standard Exchange Algorithm ($\{1,1,\cdots\}$), which is shown for purposes of comparison, even though it is never optimal on the iPSC-860 for dimension 7. Dashed lines on our plots indicate predicted values and solid lines show actual measurements.

As expected, the Optimal Circuit Switched algorithm is always optimal for large enough block size. There are three optimal combinations in all: $\{2,2,3\}$, $\{3,4\}$ and $\{7\}$. $\{7\}$ (Optimal Circuit Switched) is optimal beyond 160 bytes and $\{2,2,3\}$ optimal for 0 to 12 bytes. The combination $\{3,4\}$ leads to a factor of two improvement over both the Standard Exchange and Optimal Circuit Switched Algorithms at blocks of 40 bytes. There is good agreement between the predicted and observed run times.

Conclusions

Circuit switched machines have only recently made an appearance as commercial products. These machines provide powerful communication mechanisms but, as the results of this paper show, very careful algorithm design is required to optimize performance.

We have addressed the implementation of complete exchange and have described a multiphase algorithm that unifies two previously known algorithms and yields performance better than either over some ranges of message sizes. Similar techniques can be applied to other communication patterns. Since complete exchange is the most demanding pattern, the time taken by our multiphase algorithm is an upper bound on any communication requirement.

Acknowledgements– I am indebted to my colleagues at ICASE, NASA-Langley and NASA-Ames for their generous assistance.

References

[1] S. H. Bokhari. Communication overheads on the Intel iPSC-860 hypercube. ICASE Interim Report 10, May 1990.

[2] S. H. Bokhari. Complete exchange on the Intel iPSC-860 hypercube. Technical Report 91-4, ICASE, January 1991.

[3] S. H. Bokhari. Multiphase complete exchange on a circuit switched hypercube. Technical Report 91-5, ICASE, January 1991.

[4] Emil Grosswald. *Topics from the Theory of numbers.* Birkhäuser, Boston, 1984.

[5] S. Lennart Johnsson and Ching-Tien Ho. Matrix transposition on boolean n-cube configured ensemble architectures. *SIAM J. Matrix Anal. Appl.*, 9(3):419–454, July 1988.

[6] Ming-Horng Lee and Steve R. Seidel. Concurrent communication on the Intel iPSC/2. Technical Report CS-TR 9003, Dept. of Computer Science, Michigan Tech. Univ., July 1990.

[7] Thomas Schmiermund and Steve R. Seidel. A communication model for the Intel iPSC/2. Technical Report CS-TR 9002, Dept. of Computer Science, Michigan Tech. Univ., April 1990.

[8] Steve Seidel, Ming-Horng Lee, and Shivi Fotedar. Concurrent bidirectional communication on the Intel iPSC/860 and iPSC/2. In *Proceedings of the Sixth Distributed Memory Computing Conference*, April 1991.

[9] Steve R. Seidel. Circuit switched vs. store-and-forward solutions to symmetric communication problems. In *Proc. 4th. Conf. Hypercube Concurrent Computers and Applications*, volume 1, pages 253–255, 1989.

---

[2]Timings for dimension 5 & 6 are reported in [3].

Figure 1

Figure 1 is a rotated (landscape) table showing a Multiphase Exchange. For each operation the left group of columns is the state **before** the operation and the right group is the state **after**. Columns are labelled by the binary processor labels `000 … 111`; the eight rows in each group are the eight data-block slots.

Block 1 — Partial Exchange, bits 2,1

Before:

000	001	010	011	100	101	110	111
0:0	1:0	2:0	3:0	4:0	5:0	6:0	7:0
0:1	1:1	2:1	3:1	4:1	5:1	6:1	7:1
0:2	1:2	2:2	3:2	4:2	5:2	6:2	7:2
0:3	1:3	2:3	3:3	4:3	5:3	6:3	7:3
0:4	1:4	2:4	3:4	4:4	5:4	6:4	7:4
0:5	1:5	2:5	3:5	4:5	5:5	6:5	7:5
0:6	1:6	2:6	3:6	4:6	5:6	6:6	7:6
0:7	1:7	2:7	3:7	4:7	5:7	6:7	7:7

After (Partial Exchange, bits 2,1):

000	001	010	011	100	101	110	111
0:0	1:0	0:2	1:2	0:4	1:4	0:6	1:6
0:1	1:1	0:3	1:3	0:5	1:5	0:7	1:7
2:0	3:0	2:2	3:2	2:4	3:4	2:6	3:6
2:1	3:1	2:3	3:3	2:5	3:5	2:7	3:7
4:0	5:0	4:2	5:2	4:4	5:4	4:6	5:6
4:1	5:1	4:3	5:3	4:5	5:5	4:7	5:7
6:0	7:0	6:2	7:2	6:4	7:4	6:6	7:6
6:1	7:1	6:3	7:3	6:5	7:5	6:7	7:7

⇑

Block 2 — 2-Shuffle

Before:

000	001	010	011	100	101	110	111
0:0	1:0	0:2	1:2	0:4	1:4	0:6	1:6
0:1	1:1	0:3	1:3	0:5	1:5	0:7	1:7
2:0	3:0	2:2	3:2	2:4	3:4	2:6	3:6
2:1	3:1	2:3	3:3	2:5	3:5	2:7	3:7
4:0	5:0	4:2	5:2	4:4	5:4	4:6	5:6
4:1	5:1	4:3	5:3	4:5	5:5	4:7	5:7
6:0	7:0	6:2	7:2	6:4	7:4	6:6	7:6
6:1	7:1	6:3	7:3	6:5	7:5	6:7	7:7

After (2-Shuffle):

000	001	010	011	100	101	110	111
0:0	1:0	0:2	1:2	0:4	1:4	0:6	1:6
2:0	3:0	2:2	3:2	2:4	3:4	2:6	3:6
4:0	5:0	4:2	5:2	4:4	5:4	4:6	5:6
6:0	7:0	6:2	7:2	6:4	7:4	6:6	7:6
0:1	1:1	0:3	1:3	0:5	1:5	0:7	1:7
2:1	3:1	2:3	3:3	2:5	3:5	2:7	3:7
4:1	5:1	4:3	5:3	4:5	5:5	4:7	5:7
6:1	7:1	6:3	7:3	6:5	7:5	6:7	7:7

⇑

Block 3 — Partial Exchange, bit 0

Before:

000	001	010	011	100	101	110	111
0:0	1:0	0:2	1:2	0:4	1:4	0:6	1:6
2:0	3:0	2:2	3:2	2:4	3:4	2:6	3:6
4:0	5:0	4:2	5:2	4:4	5:4	4:6	5:6
6:0	7:0	6:2	7:2	6:4	7:4	6:6	7:6
0:1	1:1	0:3	1:3	0:5	1:5	0:7	1:7
2:1	3:1	2:3	3:3	2:5	3:5	2:7	3:7
4:1	5:1	4:3	5:3	4:5	5:5	4:7	5:7
6:1	7:1	6:3	7:3	6:5	7:5	6:7	7:7

After (Partial Exchange, bit 0):

000	001	010	011	100	101	110	111
0:0	0:1	0:2	0:3	0:4	0:5	0:6	0:7
1:0	1:1	1:2	1:3	1:4	1:5	1:6	1:7
4:0	4:1	4:2	4:3	4:4	4:5	4:6	4:7
5:0	5:1	5:2	5:3	5:4	5:5	5:6	5:7
2:0	2:1	2:2	2:3	2:4	2:5	2:6	2:7
3:0	3:1	3:2	3:3	3:4	3:5	3:6	3:7
6:0	6:1	6:2	6:3	6:4	6:5	6:6	6:7
7:0	7:1	7:2	7:3	7:4	7:5	7:6	7:7

⇑

Block 4 — 1-Shuffle

Before:

000	001	010	011	100	101	110	111
0:0	0:1	0:2	0:3	0:4	0:5	0:6	0:7
1:0	1:1	1:2	1:3	1:4	1:5	1:6	1:7
4:0	4:1	4:2	4:3	4:4	4:5	4:6	4:7
5:0	5:1	5:2	5:3	5:4	5:5	5:6	5:7
2:0	2:1	2:2	2:3	2:4	2:5	2:6	2:7
3:0	3:1	3:2	3:3	3:4	3:5	3:6	3:7
6:0	6:1	6:2	6:3	6:4	6:5	6:6	6:7
7:0	7:1	7:2	7:3	7:4	7:5	7:6	7:7

After (1-Shuffle):

000	001	010	011	100	101	110	111
0:0	0:1	0:2	0:3	0:4	0:5	0:6	0:7
1:0	1:1	1:2	1:3	1:4	1:5	1:6	1:7
2:0	2:1	2:2	2:3	2:4	2:5	2:6	2:7
3:0	3:1	3:2	3:3	3:4	3:5	3:6	3:7
4:0	4:1	4:2	4:3	4:4	4:5	4:6	4:7
5:0	5:1	5:2	5:3	5:4	5:5	5:6	5:7
6:0	6:1	6:2	6:3	6:4	6:5	6:6	6:7
7:0	7:1	7:2	7:3	7:4	7:5	7:6	7:7

Figure 1: A Multiphase Exchange on a hypercube of dimension 3. The first row gives the binary labels of processors. Data blocks are arranged in columns. The first partial exchange is on the 2 subcubes of dimension 2 determined by bits 2 and 1; data are moved in superblocks of size 2. This is followed by a 2-shuffle. The second partial exchange is on the 4 subcubes of size 4 determined by bit 0; data are moved in superblocks of size 4.

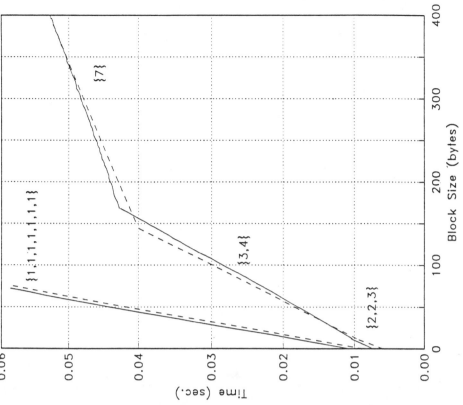

Figure 2: Performance of the Multiphase algorithm for a 128 node ($d = 7$) Intel iPSC-860. Three partitions are optimal in this case: $\{2,2,3\}$, $\{3,4\}$ and $\{7\}$. For block size 40 bytes, the time taken by the Standard Algorithm $\{1,1,1,1,1,1,1\}$ equals the time taken by the Optimal Circuit Switched Algorithm $\{7\}$ and is 0.037 sec. The time taken by the Multiphase algorithm $\{3,4\}$ is 0.016 sec, which is more than twice as fast.

Chapter 7: Performance Evaluation

Performance evaluation of networks involves

- the hardware cost,
- the potential for fault tolerance,
- the embedding capability,
- the partitioning capability,
- the message delay, and
- the network throughput.

In static networks, the hardware cost is expressed in terms of the number of links and the node degree, which represents the number of I/O ports per processor. In multistage networks, the hardware cost is expressed in terms of the number and complexity of switches. The potential for fault tolerance is measured by the *connectivity* of the network (that is, the number of elements that can fail without the network becoming disconnected or, equivalently, the number of node-disjoint paths between source-destination pairs). The embedding capability is the ability of a network to efficiently emulate other topological structures. The partitioning capability is the ability of a network to subdivide into subgraphs of identical topological structures. (Later chapters address the topics of embedding and partitioning.) The message delay is expressed theoretically by the network diameter and the average distance, although — in circuit-switched networks — these metrics are not very relevant. In practice, the message delay is expressed by the average latency of messages between the time of their departure from their source and the time of their arrival at their destination. The network throughput is measured by the average number of delivered messages per unit time.

This chapter includes a selection of papers that evaluate the performance of networks with respect to some or all of the performance evaluation criteria described above. The first paper, by Reed and Grunwald (1987), studies the performance of static networks in general. The next two papers, by Dally (1990) and Agarwal (1991), analyze the performance of k-ary hypercubes. Attallah (1988) and Scherson and Corbett (1991) study the performance of multidimensional meshes. Kurisaki and Lang (1989) study the traffic performance of link-enhanced multistage networks. The next two papers, by Kruskal, Snir, and Weiss (1988) and Yoon, Lee, and Liu (1990), analyze the traffic performance of buffered, packet-switched multistage interconnection networks. Dally (1992) studies the traffic performance of multistage interconnection networks using the concept of virtual channels. Tamir and Frazier (1988) give a detailed design and performance analysis of multiqueue switches. Finally, the paper by Nanda and Bhuyan (1993) describes multistage networks that support cache coherence.

The Performance of Multicomputer Interconnection Networks

Daniel A. Reed and Dirk C. Grunwald, University of Illinois

You cannot find an interconnection network optimal for *all* applications but, by employing the methods described here, you can choose one that fits the requirements of certain classes of applications well.

> The most constant difficulty in contriving the engine has arisen from the desire to reduce the time in which the calculations were executed to the shortest which is possible.
> —Charles Babbage (1837)

The spectrum of parallel processor designs can be divided into three sections according to the number and complexity of the processors. At one end there are simple, bit-serial processors. Any one of these processors is of little value, but when it is coupled with many others, the aggregate computing power can be large. This approach to parallel processing can be likened to a colony of termites devouring a log. The most notable examples of this approach are the NASA/Goodyear Massively Parallel Processor,[1] which has 16K one-bit processors, and the Thinking Machines Connection Machine,[2] which has 64K one-bit processors.

At the other end of the spectrum, a small number of processors, each built using the fastest available technology and the most sophisticated architecture, are combined. An example of this approach is the Cray X-MP. This type of parallel processing is akin to four woodmen attacking the log with chainsaws.

The middle approach is analogous to a small army of hungry beavers. It combines a large number of microprocessors. Within the last ten years, several groups have advocated such an approach to parallel processing, one based on large networks of interconnected microcomputers.[3-7] Each node in these multicomputer networks contains a processor with some locally addressable memory, a communication controller capable of routing messages without delaying the processor, and a small number of connections to other nodes.

The applications suggested for multicomputer networks are diverse—they include finite-element problem analysis, partial differential equation solving, linear algebra, physics problem solving, game tree searches, and functional programming. The cooperating tasks of a parallel algorithm for solving one of these problems will execute asynchronously on different nodes and communicate via message passing.

Because its nodes do not share any memory, the multicomputer interconnection network must efficiently support message passing. Typically, multicomputer networks provide datagram message transmission rather than virtual circuits.

Reprinted from *Computer*, Vol. 20, No. 6, June 1987, pp. 63-73.

Because of the high latency for message transmission, compared to a memory access, optimization of message traffic patterns is crucial. Methods for evaluating the performance of network alternatives are our subject here.

Commercial multicomputer networks. Recent advances in VLSI have finally made large multicomputer networks both technically and economically feasible. For example, a collaborative project at the California Institute of Technology produced the Cosmic Cube, a multicomputer network based on a hypercube interconnection. A hypercube is a generalization of a cube to D dimensions, where each of the 2^D cube vertices is a multicomputer node. If the hypercube nodes are numbered, beginning with zero, then node i is connected to the D other nodes whose numbers are obtained by negating one bit of the binary representation of i. Figure 1 illustrates the three-dimensional case.

In 1985 Intel announced the iPSC,[8] a commercial version of the Cosmic Cube containing up to 128 nodes. Each iPSC node contains 512K bytes of memory, an Intel 80286 microprocessor, an Intel 80287 floating-point coprocessor, and seven Ethernet transceiver chips to manage internode contains 512K bytes of memory, an Intel 80286 microprocessor, an Intel 80287 similar design.

Both the Intel iPSC and Ametek System/14 require many chips per node and one board for each node, limiting the maximum feasible system size. In contrast, each node of the NCube/ten hypercube[9] contains only seven chips: a custom 32-bit microprocessor with both on-chip floating-point and hardware communication support and six memory chips. Sixty-four nodes occupy a single board, and a fully configured system contains 1024 nodes.

Although the hypercube interconnection matches the communication patterns of many common algorithms, its primary disadvantage is that it requires a logarithmic increase in node connectivity as the number of nodes increases. Moreover, the limited interconnection afforded by VLSI node implementations suggests that other interconnection networks may be more appropriate for large numbers of nodes. Hence, we consider techniques for evaluating network performance.

Overview. Several different characterizations of network performance have been suggested.[4,6,7] However, repeated studies have shown that a system's performance is maximized when all the components are balanced (i.e., when there is no single system bottleneck).[10] Multicomputers are no different; optimizing performance requires a judicious combination of node computation speed and message transmission latency. The rate at which a network routes messages and the rate at which nodes perform computations are intimately related.

Here we examine the interdependency of nodes and multicomputer interconnection networks using simple "back of the envelope" calculations based on the asymptotic properties of queueing networks. Although the interaction of communication and computation can be examined analytically, time-varying behavior and the idiosyncrasies of system software can only be captured by observation and measurement. Thus, we also show how analytic models can be extended to benchmark existing interconnection networks such as the hypercube connection of the Intel iPSC.[8] Before beginning discussion of analytic models, however, we must first define several important terms and concepts used to quantify the performance of networks.

Definitions and background

The maximum internode distance, often referred to as the *diameter* of the interconnection network, places a lower bound on the delay required to propagate information throughout the network. It is simply the maximum number of communication links that must be traversed to transmit a message to any node along a shortest path.

In contrast, the mean internode distance is the expected number of link traversals a "typical" message needs to reach its destination. The mean internode distance is a better indicator of average message delay than the network diameter, but as we shall see, it too fails to completely capture the relative communication capacity of different interconnection networks.

Unlike the network diameter, the mean internode distance depends on the message routing distribution. This routing distribution specifies the probability that different network nodes exchange messages, and it ultimately depends on the communication requirements of the application and system programs as well as on the mapping of these programs onto the network.

In its most general form, the mean internode distance (the number of link visits, or LV) is given by

$$LV = \sum_{l=1}^{lmax} l \cdot \Phi(l) \qquad (1)$$

where $\Phi(l)$ is the probability of an arbitrary message crossing l communication links (i.e., the routing distribution), and $lmax$ is the network diameter. Different choices for $\Phi(l)$ lead to different message routing distributions and, in turn, different mean internode distances. In the following, we consider three different message routing distributions for which it is possible to obtain closed forms for the mean internode distance. To do this, however, we must first distinguish between two types of interconnection networks: symmetric and asymmetric.

In a symmetric interconnection network there exists an isomorphism that maps any node of the network graph onto any other node. Thus, all nodes possess the same view of the network. A bidirectional ring network is a simple example of a symmetric interconnection network because two nodes are always reachable by crossing any given number of communication links, and a simple node renumbering suffices to map any node onto any other. An asymmetric interconnection network is any network that is not symmetric (e.g., a tree). Here, we consider only symmetric networks; for an analysis of asymmetric networks, see Reed and Fujimoto.[11]

Uniform message routing. A message routing distribution is said to be uniform if the probability of node i sending a message to node j is the same for all i and j, $i \neq j$. Because we are interested in message transfers that use the network, we exclude the case of nodes sending messages to themselves.

Uniform routing distribution is appealing because it makes no assumptions about the type of computation generating the messages; this is also its greatest liability. However, because most computations should exhibit some measure of communication locality, it provides what is likely to be an upper bound on the mean internode message distance.

Sphere of locality. Suppose the uniform message routing assumption were relaxed. We would expect any reasonable mapping of a distributed computation onto a multicomputer network to place those tasks

413

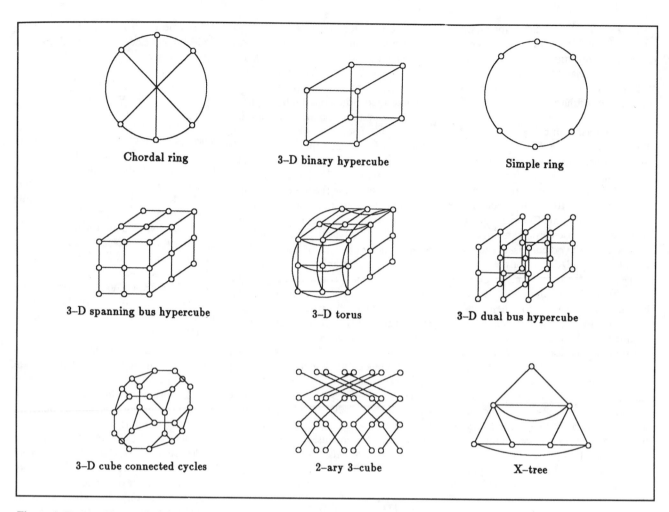

Figure 1. Representative interconnection networks.

that exchange messages with high frequency in close physical proximity. One abstraction of this idea places each node at the center of a sphere of locality with radius L, measured in hops. A node sends messages to the other nodes inside its sphere of locality with some (usually high) probability ϕ, and to nodes outside the sphere with probability $1 - \phi$. This model reflects the communication locality typical of many programs (e.g., the nearest-neighbor communication typical of iterative partial differential equation solvers coupled with global communication for convergence checking[9]).

Decreasing probability message routing. The previous definition of locality is useful if the probability of visiting the locality is high and the size of the locality is small compared to the size of the network. There are, however, many cases in which this is not an appropriate abstraction. An alternate, intuitively appealing notion of

locality is that the probability of sending a message to a node decreases as the distance of the destination node from the source node increases. The distribution function $\Phi(l) = Decay\,(d, lmax\,) \cdot d^l$ $0 < d < 1$, where $lmax$ is the network diameter and d is a locality parameter, is particularly attractive. Here, $Decay\,(d, lmax)$ is a normalizing constant for the probability Φ, chosen such that the probabilities sum to one. As d approaches one, the cumulative distribution function of Φ approximates a linearly increasing function of the distance from the source node. Conversely, as d approaches zero, the cumulative distribution function of Φ approaches a nearest-neighbor communication pattern. Small values of d mean that messages travel only small distances (i.e., that locality exists), whereas larger d values mean that messages can travel larger distances.

These three message routing distributions—uniform, sphere of locality,

and decreasing probability—can be used to calculate mean internode distances. However, the mean internode distance does not reflect link utilization. For this, we must define visit ratios.

Visit ratios. Each time a node sends a message to another node, the message must cross some communication links and pass through intermediate nodes before reaching its destination node. At the destination, it causes some computation to take place. This datagram model of communication accurately reflects a variety of multicomputer applications, including solution of partial differential equations and functional programming.

Each link crossing and destination node computation constitutes a *visit* to that link or processing element. If all possible source/destination pairs and the probabilities that they exchange messages are considered, the number of visits to each communication link and node by an average message can be calculated. Now consider such an average message and an arbitrary device i (either a node or a link). The average message will visit device i a certain number of times. This mean number of visits is called the visit ratio of device i and is denoted by V_i.[10]

By analogy, imagine that each message deposits a "token" at a device during each visit. After observing the system of nodes and links for some "reasonably long" interval, we can obtain the visit ratios by normalizing the token counts at each device (i.e., by dividing the number of tokens at that device by the total number of token-depositing messages that were created during the observation period). As we shall see, visit ratios can be used to locate those devices in a network that most limit performance—the bottlenecks.

Under the uniform message routing distribution discussed earlier, the visit ratios for all network nodes must be the same. In other words, the probability of visiting for each destination node is the same, and V_{PE}, the visit ratio for the nodes, is

$$V_{PE} = \frac{1}{K} \qquad (2)$$

when there are K nodes.

Somewhat surprisingly, the node visit ratios are also given by Equation 2 when the two proposed nonuniform message routing distributions are considered. This follows from two features of the networks and the routing distributions: network symmetry and similar message routing behavior at all nodes. That is, if all nodes behave similarly and the network is symmetric, each node is equally likely to be visited.

As we saw earlier, the mean internode distance LV represents the average number of visits to all communication links by a message. Dividing this number by the number of communication links yields the communication link visit ratios

$$V_{CL} = \frac{LV}{Numlinks\,(K,\,Net-type)} \qquad (3)$$

This quantity can be viewed as a measure of the message intensity supported by a single link. If V_{CL} is near one, then nearly all messages must cross each link at some point along the paths to their respective destinations. Unfortunately, this simple definition is accurate only if the interconnection network contains just one type of communication link (e.g., a ring). In a binary tree one would expect the commu-

nication traffic on the links at each tree level to be different, leading to different link visit ratios for each level.

Proposed interconnection networks

A plethora of interconnection network proposals have appeared in the research literature, and an enormous amount of research has centered on the design and analysis of these networks. Among the proposed interconnection networks are several that serve as useful points of reference or have particularly attractive features: the single bus, the complete connection, the simple ring, the chordal

---

A single bus joins all nodes and uses a contention resolution protocol to resolve simultaneous requests

---

ring,[3] the spanning bus hypercube,[7] the dual-bus hypercube,[7] the torus,[7] generalized hypercubes,[4] the cube-connected cycles,[12] the R-ary N-cube,[13] the lens,[6] the X-tree,[5] and the B-ary tree. Figure 1 illustrates a subset of these networks.

A single bus joins all nodes and uses a contention resolution protocol to resolve simultaneous requests for the bus. Although inexpensive, it can efficiently support only a modest number of nodes. In contrast, the complete connection directly connects each node to all other nodes. Its cost rises quadratically with the number of nodes, although its performance is the best achievable. These two networks, the bus and the complete connection, bound the spectrum of price and performance for all practical multicomputer networks.

The single ring is a modest improvement over a bus, but it too can efficiently support only a small number of nodes. The chordal ring introduces cross or chordal link connections between nodes on opposite sides of the simple ring, reducing the maximum number of links that must be traversed to reach a destination node.

The spanning bus hypercube is a D-dimensional lattice of width w in each dimension. Each node is connected to D buses, one in each of the orthogonal dimensions; w nodes share a bus in each dimension.

The dual-bus hypercube was proposed to bound the number of connections to each node. It is obtained by pruning $D-2$ bus connections from each network node. In particular, one dimension, the 0th dimension, is distinguished, and all nodes are connected to a 0th-dimension bus. In each $D-1$ hyperplane orthogonal to the 0th dimension, all nodes have a second connection to buses spanning the same dimension. The second bus direction differs from hyperplane to hyperplane but repeats if the width w of a dimension exceeds $D-2$. Figure 1 shows a three-dimensional dual-bus hypercube with width 3; the vertical direction is the distinguished dimension.

The torus is identical to the spanning bus hypercube except that it replaces the bus connecting each group of w nodes with a ring of point-to-point connections, improving the performance at an associated cost. As we shall see, the torus is a generalization of the binary hypercube used in the current generation of multicomputer networks. The performance motivations for this choice will become clear shortly.

Generalized hypercubes use a mixed radix numbering to obtain networks containing any number of nodes, in contrast to the limited expansion increments of traditional hypercubes.

The cube-connected cycles was also proposed to limit the number of connections to each node. This network replaces each node of a D-dimensional cube (i.e., of a binary hypercube) with a ring of D nodes. Each ring node connects to one of the D links incident on the vertex, fixing the node connectivity at three.

The bus-connected lens network proposed by Finkel and Solomon is created using a recursive construction algorithm.[6] In this network, an n-level lens contains $n(n-1)^n$ nodes, each connected to b buses.

The R-ary N-cube is a generalization of the indirect binary n-cube originally proposed by Pease.[13] In this network, N is the number of levels and R^N is the number of nodes on each level. The network contains NR^N nodes, each connected to $2R$ other nodes. Unlike Pease's original proposal, the cube is closed (i.e., the top and bottom rows shown in Figure 1 are the same).

An X-tree is a simple binary tree with all nodes at each level connected in a ring, reducing the communication bottleneck near the tree root.

Each of these networks can be analyzed to determine its network diameter and mean internode distance. These analyses are detailed, lengthy, and somewhat tedious. (The interested reader can find details in Reed and Fujimoto.[11]) In spite of this, these analyses have intrinsic value for two reasons. First, they represent the application of a uniform methodology to several networks. Second, many of the techniques embodied in the analyses are generally applicable to other networks and will likely be helpful when analyzing networks emerging in the future. To illustrate their application, we consider the torus, a generalization of the binary hypercube. Following this example, we show how the results of the analysis can be used to predict performance.

Analyzing the torus: An example

A *D*-dimensional torus—a *D*-dimensional lattice of width *w*—connects each of its w^D nodes to a ring of size *w* in each of the *D* orthogonal dimensions (see Figure 1). As its name implies, this interconnection network is topologically equivalent to a torus constructed in *D*-space. Because each of the w^D nodes is connected to *D* rings, there are $2Dw^D$ total link connections to the Dw^D communication links.

Message routing is easy if source and destination addresses are viewed as *D*-digit, base *w* numbers. Each digit represents a ring of *w* nodes, and a message is routed to its destination by successively sending the message to the correct location on each of the *D* rings. Consequently, the network diameter is just $D\lfloor w/2 \rfloor$, *D* times the maximum internode distance in any dimension using that dimension's ring. ($\lfloor x \rfloor$ denotes the integer portion of *x*—i.e., the largest integer less than *x*.)

When *w* = 2, this reduces to *D*, the binary hypercube case discussed earlier. If *w* is fixed and *D* increases, the network diameter increases only logarithmically with the number of nodes. This is the primary advantage of binary hypercubes. The offsetting disadvantage is that the number of connections per node also must increase with the network size. This means

that the maximum network size must be predetermined, when the nodes are designed.

It initially appears that for a torus the mean internode distance under the uniform message routing assumption is also simply *D* times that for a simple ring. However, this is incorrect. In the torus, some dimensions need no address resolution; that is, the source and destination nodes share the same address on that ring. For these cases, the approach overestimates the mean path length. Instead, we must include the case of zero moves in each dimension and scale the sum of the moves in each dimension to obtain the true mean path length. Thus, the average distance moved in each dimension is

$$LV^{uniform}_{one\ dimension} = \frac{\sum_{k=0}^{w-1} \min\left\{k,\ w-k\right\}}{w}$$

$$= \frac{w^2 - 1}{4w} \quad w\ odd$$

The minimum function in the sum reflects the routing of messages along the shorter of the two potential paths in the ring. Because the dimensions are independent, the true mean path length is *D* times this distance scaled to exclude nodes routing messages to themselves:

$$LV^{uniform}_{torus} = D\left(\frac{w^D}{w^D - 1}\right) LV^{uniform}_{one\ dimension}$$

Network symmetry and the existence of only one type of communication link allow us to immediately obtain the link visit ratios:

$$V^{uniform}_{CL} = \frac{LV^{uniform}_{torus}}{Dw^D}$$

$$= \frac{w^2 - 1}{4w(w^D - 1)} \quad w\ odd \qquad (4)$$

The derivation of mean path lengths and visit ratios for nonuniform message routing distributions, though conceptually straightforward, is computationally difficult. To simplify exposition, we consider only the case in which *w* is odd. The motivation for this is simple: for *w* odd, we can, without loss of generality, assume the source node is at the center of a *D*-dimensional hyperspace. Specifically, we can assume it is at the center of a (*D* − 1)-dimensional hyperplane and has $\lfloor w/2 \rfloor$ (*D* − 1)-dimensional hyperplanes "above" and "below" it. Suppose a message is sent

to the *l* links above or below the hyperplane containing the source node, and the message is permitted to cross a maximum of *L* links. Then only those nodes within *L* − *l* links of the point of origin in the destination hyperplane can be reached. This view of message routing leads to the recurrence

$$Reach(L,D,w) =$$
$$\begin{cases} 1 & L = 0 \\ 2 & D = 1\ and\ 0 < L \le \left\lfloor \frac{w}{2} \right\rfloor \\ 0 & D = 1\ and\ L > \left\lfloor \frac{w}{2} \right\rfloor \\ \min\left\{l, \left\lfloor \frac{w}{2} \right\rfloor\right\} \\ 2 \sum_{l=1} Reach(L-l, D-1, w) \\ \quad otherwise \\ \quad + Reach(L, D-1, w) \end{cases}$$

where $Reach(L, D, w)$ is the number of nodes exactly *L* links from a source node in a *D*-dimensional torus of width *w*. The first term in the last equation above contains a factor of two because a message can, by symmetry, go "up" or "down" from the source node. The second term in the last equation is the number of nodes reachable in the hyperplane in which the source node lies. This recurrence can be easily solved and a closed form for $Reach(L, D, w)$ can be obtained (though the symbol manipulation is arduous). Given the closed form, one can then easily obtain the number of nodes in the sphere of locality, the mean internode distance, and the link visit ratios.

Similarly, given the network diameter $D\lfloor w/2 \rfloor$, one can easily obtain the mean message-path-length visit ratios for the decaying probability message routing distribution.

Finally, the torus, with its lattice structure, has expansion increments of $w^D(w - 1)$ when *D*, the dimension, is increased and $(w + 1)^D - w^D$ when *w*, the width, is increased. Because expanding the number of dimensions requires two additional link connections per node, it will usually be necessary to rewire the entire interconnection network if this method of expansion is chosen.

Network performance bounds

In the formulation of message routing we have described, a message leaves a

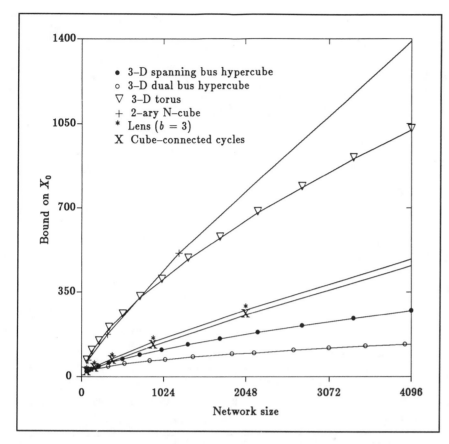

Figure 2. Upper bound on message completion rate with uniform routing.

source node, crosses some communication links to reach its destination, and causes some computation to take place there. After normalization, the visit ratio V_i can be interpreted as the average number of visits made to device i, a node or link, by a message. Suppose we define S_i as the average amount of service required by a message during each visit to device i. The product V_iS_i is the total amount of service required by an average message at device i, and the sum

$$\sum_i V_i S_i$$

is the total amount of service required by an average message at all nodes and links.

If the average number of messages circulating in the network is steadily increased, the utilization of at least one device must approach unity. Which device will saturate first? Because V_iS_i represents the average amount of service required at device i, the device with the maximum value of V_iS_i will first limit the message circulation rate. If X_0 denotes the rate at which a network can route messages from

source to destination, an absolute upper bound on X_0 is given by

$$X_0 \le \frac{1}{V_b S_b}$$

where

$$V_b S_b = \max_i V_i S_i$$

This technique, called asymptotic or bottleneck analysis in its most general form,[10] applies to any closed network in a steady state (that is, to any closed network in which the message arrival rate at each device equals the message departure rate). No assumptions about service time or queueing distributions are necessary. This simplicity allows one to make minimal assumptions about network behavior and, consequently, leads to conclusions applicable to a wide range of intended network environments.

To simplify comparison of networks, we assume that the mean time between message transmissions, S_{PE}, is the same at all nodes, and that all links require time S_{CL} to transmit an average message. We

emphasize that this assumption is not required. The succeeding discussion can be applied in its entirety, albeit involving somewhat more arduous symbol manipulation, if each device has a distinct service time.

If there are T distinct link visit ratios, the bound on X_0, the network message completion rate, is

$$X_0 < \frac{1}{\max\{V_{PE}S_{PE},\ V_{CL}^1 S_{CL}, \ldots, V_{CL}^T S_{CL}\}} \quad (5)$$

Through analysis similar to that for the torus, we can derive values for V_{PE} and V_{CL} for many networks. Using these analyses, Figure 2 illustrates the bounds on the message completion rate for the uniform message routing distribution. Figure 3 shows the effect of locality on the message completion rate. In both cases, unit node and link service times are assumed. However, other parameters can be used.

In the uniform routing case, the torus and R-ary N-cube have the highest message completion rate, followed by the lens, spanning bus hypercube, and cube-connected cycles. A comparison of the mean internode distances for the same networks is decidedly different (Figure 4). Although there is a correlation between the mean internode distance and the bound on the message passing rate, it is not direct. The mean internode distance does not reflect the intensity of traffic on the links; the performance bounds do.

Although increased message routing locality obviously increases the message completion rate, the many different parameterizations of the locality distributions make it exceedingly difficult to draw conclusions without knowledge of some specific application area. However, constraints on the regions of feasible computation can be obtained.

Feasible computation quanta. In addition to providing bounds on the maximum rate of message transfer, the visit ratios can also be used to determine appropriate granules of computation, given the relative speeds of processors and communication links.

If K is the number of network nodes, the amount of service required at an average node is $V_{PE}S_{PE} = S_{PE}/K$. A linear increase in the message completion rate can be expected only if the communication links' VS products are no larger than this value. That is, increased parallelism is effective only if communication delays do not dominate. As prior figures have shown, the message completion rate is not, in general, such a linear function, implying that communication delays are limiting the message completion rate. Other than changing the message routing distribution, one can only adjust the ratio S_{PE}/S_{CL} to ensure that communication is not the performance-limiting factor. Inspecting Equation 5 shows that the minimum ratio of computation to communication, where communication delays are not dominant, is

$$\frac{S_{PE}}{S_{CL}} = \frac{\max\{V_{CL}^1,\ldots,V_{CL}^T\}}{V_{PE}}$$

$$= K \cdot \max\{V_{CL}^1,\ldots,V_{CL}^T\} \quad (6)$$

In essence, the ratio of computation time to communication time for a message must be at least K times the maximum link visit ratio if the maximum computation rate is not to be limited by communication delays.

As an example, consider the torus again. The communication link visit ratios for uniform message routing are given by Equation 4, and the number of nodes is w^D. Applying Equation 6 yields

$$\frac{S_{PE}}{S_{CL}} = \frac{w^{D-1}(w^2-1)}{4(w^D-1)} \approx \frac{w}{4}$$

If communication delays are not to dominate performance, the ratio of computation time to communication time must increase linearly with w if the dimension of the torus is fixed. Simply put, larger granules of computation are needed for a wider torus. Conversely, increasing the dimension of the torus D does not require any increase in the ratio. This is the performance motivation for binary hypercubes: w is fixed at 2, only the dimension D grows, and the granule of computation is constant.

The lesson for designers of parallel algorithms is immediate and striking: the smallest feasible quantum of parallelism is dictated by the communication patterns of the algorithm *and* the network topology. At best, excessive parallelism leads to negligible performance gains. At worst, performance can decrease due to increased overhead.

Network selection. Situations do arise in which factors intrinsic to an intended application dictate the use of a specific ratio of computation to communication time for messages. When this occurs, the

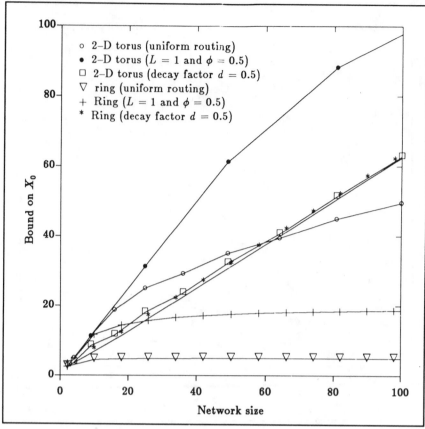

Figure 3. Upper bound on message completion rate with locality.

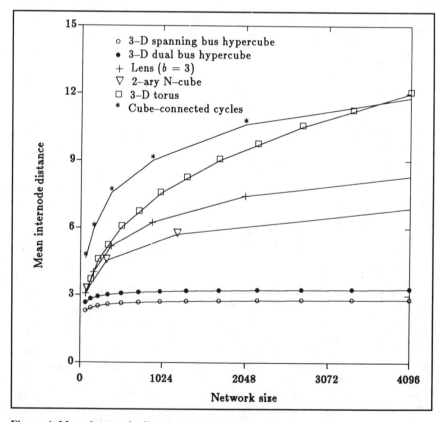

Figure 4. Mean internode distance with uniform routing.

designer must realize that the range of optimality for a specific network does *not* span the entire spectrum of network sizes. This is clearly illustrated by the crossing of the bounds on message completion rate in Figure 3. Thus, one may be justified in using one interconnection for ten nodes and a different one for one hundred nodes. One can analytically or numerically determine where the bounds for two networks cross by equating the *VS* products for the limiting devices, either nodes or links, and solving for the network size where they are equal.

Benchmarking multicomputer networks

Analytic models can capture the average, steady-state behavior of multicomputer networks, but they cannot easily reflect the time-varying behavior of real systems. Moreover, the idiosyncrasies of system software can be captured only through observation and measurement. For example, some commercial hypercubes such as the Ametek System/14 support only synchronous communication between directly connected nodes; others such as the Intel iPSC provide asynchronous transmission with routing. The effects of these differences are very difficult to model, but they can be measured easily.

Although analytic models cannot reflect all details of real systems, they do provide a framework for testing. For systems that support routing and asynchronous transmission, one can develop synthetic communication benchmarks that reflect communication patterns in both time *and* space. These benchmarks are based on the message routing distributions described earlier.

As analysis has just shown, binary hypercubes have attractive performance characteristics. To confirm this analysis and to highlight the interaction between analytic models and benchmarking, we examined the communication performance of two commercial hypercubes, the Intel iPSC and Ametek System/14. As shown in Table 1, both of these machines are based on the 16-bit Intel 80286 microprocessor. As noted earlier, the Intel iPSC uses Ethernet transceiver chips to manage internode communication. In contrast, the Ametek System/14 uses an Intel 80186 microprocessor to control internode communication via direct memory access.

Simple communication benchmarks. Data transfer time between two directly connected nodes is perhaps the simplest measure of communication network performance. Although independent of the type of interconnection network, this measure provides the value S_{CL} that is the basis for all network analysis.

If the messages transmitted between nodes are not broken into packets, message transmission time S_{CL} can be modeled as

$$S_{CL} = t_l + Nt_c \qquad (7)$$

where t_l is the communication latency (i.e., the startup time for a transmission), t_c is the transmission time per byte, and N is the number of bytes in the message. Figure 5 shows the measured values of S_{CL} for both the Intel iPSC and Ametek System/14. Statistically, the linear model in Equation 7 is a good fit to experimental data on both hypercubes. Table 2 shows the result of a least-squares fit of the data to this linear model. The Ametek System/14 has a lower latency than the Intel iPSC, but the higher bandwidth of the Intel iPSC yields smaller total communication time for messages of more than approximately 150 bytes.

We emphasize that extrapolating general communication performance from single link tests is fallacious. Such simple tests highlight only link-level characteristics. More general benchmarks are needed to investigate routing and buffering behavior; this is the motivation for the synthetic communication benchmarks presented below.

Synthetic communication benchmarks. Application programs can be used to study hypercube communication performance, but because each program occupies only a small portion of the space of potential communication behaviors, a large number of application programs are needed to achieve adequate coverage. To study hypercube performance under a variety of communication traffic patterns, we have developed a model of communication behavior. Each hypercube node executes a copy of the model, generating network traffic that reflects some pattern of both *temporal* and *spatial* locality. Temporal locality defines the pattern of internode communication in time. An application with high temporal locality exhibits communication affinity among a subset of network nodes. However, these nodes need not be near one another in the network. Physical proximity is determined by spatial locality.

Table 1. Hypercube hardware characteristics.

	Intel iPSC	Ametek S/14
Processor	8-MHz 80286	8-MHz 80286
Floating point	6-MHz 80287	8-MHz 80287
I/O procesor	none	10-MHz 80186
Minimum memory	0.5M bytes	1M byte
Maximum memory	4.5M bytes	1M byte
Channels per node	7	8
Peak bandwidth	10M bits/s	3M bits/s

Table 2. Hypercube communication comparison.

	Intel iPSC	Ametek System 14
Latency (seconds)	1.7×10^{-3}	5.5×10^{-4}
Transmission time (sec/byte)	2.83×10^{-6}	9.53×10^{-6}
Bandwidth (M bits/s)	2.8	0.84

Temporal locality. Our implementation of temporal locality is based on a *least recently used stack model*, or LRUSM, originally used to study management schemes for paged virtual memory[14]; other models are possible. When used in the memory management context, the *stack* after memory reference $r(t)$ (i.e., the reference at time t) contains the n most recently accessed pages, ordered by decreasing recency of reference. The stack distance $d(t)$ associated with reference $r(t)$ is the position of $r(t)$ in the stack defined just after memory reference $r(t-1)$ occurs. These distances are assumed to be independent random variables such that *Probability* $[d(t) = i] = b_i$ for all t. For example, if $b_1 = 0.5$, there is a 50-percent chance that the next page referenced will be the same as the one just referenced.

In our adaptation of LRUSM to network traffic, each node has its own stack containing the n nodes that were most recently sent messages. In other words, destination nodes in the network are analogous to pages in the address space of a process for the LRUSM model of memory reference patterns. Parameters given to the model include the stack reference probabilities b_i and the stack size n.

We emphasize that the sum of the probabilities b_i is normally less than 1. Consequently, it is possible for the condition $d(t) > n$ to occur. In this case, a stack *miss* occurs. This corresponds to a page fault in the virtual memory context. In our model, a stack miss means that a new node not currently in the stack is chosen as the destination of the next transmission. This selection is based on a *spatial* locality model. This, in turn, is simply one of the message routing distributions discussed earlier: uniform, sphere of locality, or decreasing probability.

Experimental results. Figure 6 shows the mean time for a 16-node Intel iPSC to transmit 3000 messages whose length was drawn from a negative exponential distribution with a mean of 512 bytes. The horizontal line denotes the uniform message routing distribution. This provides a point of reference for the decreasing probability and sphere of locality routing distributions.

In Figure 6, $\phi = 1$ for the sphere of locality distribution. This means that all messages generated will be sent to destinations within the radius. Thus, the expected execution time approaches that of the uniform routing distribution as the radius

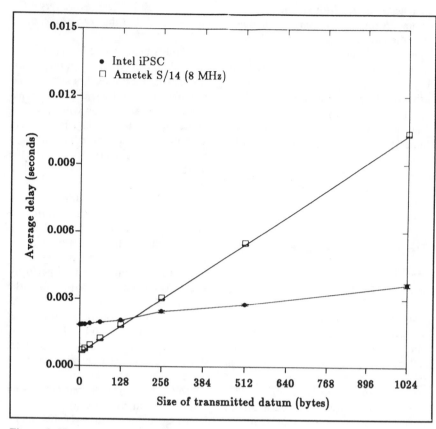

Figure 5. Hypercube data transfer benchmark.

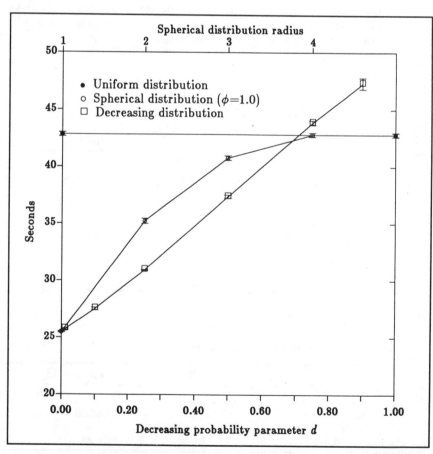

Figure 6. Spatial communication locality.

420

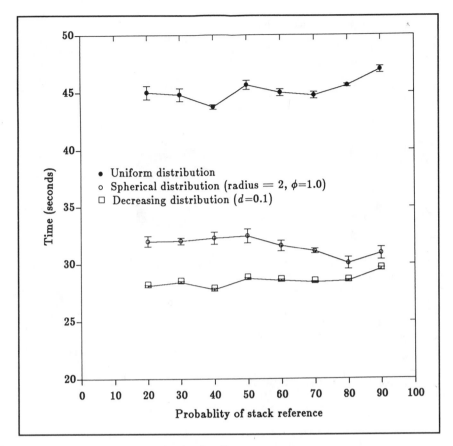

Figure 7. Temporal communication locality.

approaches the network diameter. With the decreasing probability distribution, increasing d means that a larger fraction of all messages are sent to distant nodes. For large enough values of d, the decreasing probability distribution is *anti-local*. Specifically, the mean internode distance is larger than that of the uniform routing distribution.

Figure 7 shows the effect of varying the temporal locality of the three spatial locality distributions, using the same number and type of messages as in Figure 6. In the figure, the temporal stack has a depth of one. This means that the number of messages sent to the node in the stack is the mean of a binomial distribution with parameter p, the probability of referencing the stack. Thus, there are "runs" of consecutive messages sent to a single destination node.

The most striking feature of Figure 7 is the small variation in the time needed to complete the suite of message transmissions. One would expect the temporal locality and its associated message runs to induce transient queues of outstanding messages on one link of each hypercube node. This phenomenon should manifest itself as increased delays as the probability of a stack reference increases. However, the variations shown in Figure 7 are not statistically significant. Why? Suppose the rate at which each node generated messages were perfectly balanced with the transmission capacity of each of the node's communications links. In this case, no message queues would form. Now suppose temporal locality were introduced. The presence of stack runs would induce an imbalance, a queue would form for at least one link, and messages would be delayed. This phenomenon does *not* occur in Figure 7, due to an imbalance of computation and communication speeds on the Intel iPSC. Nodes can generate messages faster than they can be transmitted by the communication links. Thus, queues develop for *all* links, independent of the presence of temporal locality, and these queues mask its effects.

Observations. Computation speeds, communication capacity, and communi-

cation patterns, both in time and space, interact in subtle ways. By using a synthetic benchmark that provides a broad spectrum of communication patterns, one can systematically and formally explore these interactions. This knowledge can be used to guide system design.

Could one analytically obtain the results shown in Figure 6? Yes, the analytic models do predict the observed behavior. However, predicting the specific crossing points and delay values requires knowledge of the node processing overhead and link transmission costs. Benchmarking is the only way to obtain these values. Thus, analysis and benchmarking are both important. One provides insight; the other provides concrete data.

Selecting an interconnection network suitable for all applications is difficult, if not impossible. However, a careful comparison of networks does show that there are classes of networks with ranges of performance. Among these, networks such as the torus and the R-ary N-cube seem most promising. As noted earlier, the binary hypercube is a special case of the torus.

When a network suitable for a specific class of applications is needed, a systematic approach based on a study of the most important applications in that class can expose the expected traffic patterns and computation requirements. Using these and the derived visit ratios, one can easily compare networks using asymptotic bounds.

A systematic approach is imperative. With such an approach, one can effectively compare new network topologies to existing ones and select networks suitable for specific application classes. □

We think there remains much detail to be worked out, and possibly some further invention needed, before the design can be brought into a state in which it would be possible to judge whether it would really so work.

—Committee examining Babbage's Analytical Engine

Acknowledgments

This work was supported in part under NSF Grant Number DCR 84-17948 and NASA Contract Number NAG-1-613 and by the Jet Propulsion Laboratory.

References

1. K.E. Batcher, "MPP—A Massively Parallel Processor," *Proc. Int'l Conf. Parallel Processing*, Computer Society Press, Washington, D.C., Aug. 1979, p. 249.

2. D. Hillis, *The Connection Machine*, MIT Press, Cambridge, Mass., 1985.

3. B.W. Arden and H.Lee, "Analysis of Chordal Ring Network," *IEEE Trans. Computers*, Apr. 1981, pp. 291-295.

4. L.N. Bhuyan and D.P. Agrawal, "Generalized Hypercube and Hyperbus Structures for a Computer Network," *IEEE Trans. Computers*, Apr. 1984, pp. 323-333.

5. A.M. Despain and D.A. Patterson, "X-TREE: A Tree Structured Multiprocessor Computer Architecture," *Proc. Fifth Ann. Symp. Computer Architecture*, in *ACM Sigarch Newsletter*, Apr. 1978, pp. 144-151.

6. R.A. Finkel and M.H. Solomon, "The Lens Interconnection Strategy," *IEEE Trans. Computers*, Dec. 1981, pp. 960-965.

7. L.D. Wittie, "Communication Structures for Large Multimicrocomputer Systems," *IEEE Trans. Computers*, Apr. 1981, pp. 264-273.

8. J. Rattner, "Concurrent Processing: A New Direction in Scientific Computing," *AFIPS Conf. Proc.*, Vol. 54, 1985 NCC, pp. 157-166.

9. M.T. Heath, *Hypercube Multiprocessors 1986*, Society for Industrial and Applied Mathematics, Philidelphia, 1986.

10. P.J. Denning and J.P. Buzen, "The Operational Analysis of Queueing Network Models," *Computing Surveys*, Sept. 1978.

11. D.A. Reed and R.M. Fujimoto, *Multicomputer Networks: Message-Based Parallel Processing*, MIT Press, Cambridge, Mass., to appear in Sept. 1987.

12. F.P. Preparata and J. Vuillemin, "The Cube-Connected Cycles: A Versatile Network for Parallel Computation," *Comm. ACM*, May 1981, pp. 300-309.

13. M.C. Pease, "The Indirect Binary *n*-cube Microprocessor Array," *IEEE Trans. Computers*, May 1977, pp. 458-473.

14. P.J. Denning, "Working Sets Past and Present," *IEEE Trans. Software Engineering*, Jan. 1980, pp. 64-84.

Daniel A. Reed is an assistant professor in the Department of Computer Science at the University of Illinois at Urbana-Champaign, where he was the recipient of an NSF Presidential Young Investigator Award. He also holds an appointment in the Center for Supercomputing Research and Development, where he is participating in the design of Faust, a programming environment for the Cedar shared memory multiprocessor. His interests include the design of parallel algorithms and software for message-based parallel processors. He is currently directing the design of Picasso, a hypercube operating system.

Reed received his BS, summa cum laude, in computer science from the University of Missouri—Rolla in 1978 and his MS and PhD, also in computer science, from Purdue University in 1983.

Dirk C. Grunwald is currently completing the requirements for the PhD degree at the University of Illinois at Urbana-Champaign. His interests are in multicomputer systems, operating systems and concurrent languages for ensemble machines, compiler design for vector and multicomputer systems, and concurrent algorithms. He received his BS and MS in 1983 and 1985 from the University of Illinois. He has been a summer intern with IBM-Boca Raton, DEC's Eastern Research Lab, and the hypercube concurrent computation project at the Jet Propulsion Laboratory. He is a member of IEEE and ACM.

Readers may write Reed at the Department of Computer Science, University of Illinois, 1304 West Springfield Ave., Urbana, IL 61801.

Performance Analysis of k-ary n-cube Interconnection Networks

WILLIAM J. DALLY, MEMBER, IEEE

Abstract—VLSI communication networks are wire-limited. The cost of a network is not a function of the number of switches required, but rather a function of the wiring density required to construct the network. This paper analyzes communication networks of varying dimension under the assumption of constant wire bisection. Expressions for the latency, average case throughput, and hot-spot throughput of k-ary n-cube networks with constant bisection are derived that agree closely with experimental measurements. It is shown that low-dimensional networks (e.g., tori) have lower latency and higher hot-spot throughput than high-dimensional networks (e.g., binary n-cubes) with the same bisection width.

Index Terms—Communication networks, concurrent computing, interconnection networks, message-passing multiprocessors, parallel processing, VLSI.

I. INTRODUCTION

THE critical component of a concurrent computer is its communication network. Many algorithms are communication rather than processing limited. Fine-grain concurrent programs execute as few as ten instructions in response to a message [7]. To efficiently execute such programs the communication network must have a latency no greater than about ten instruction times, and a throughput sufficient to permit a large fraction of the nodes to transmit simultaneously. Low-latency communication is also critical to support code sharing and garbage collection across nodes.

As the grain size of concurrent computers continues to decrease, communication latency becomes a more important factor. The diameter of the machine grows, messages are sent more frequently, and fewer instructions are executed in response to each message. Low latency is more difficult to achieve in a fine-grain machine because the available wiring space grows more slowly than the expected traffic. Since the machine must be constructed in three dimensions, the bisection area grows only as $N^{2/3}$ while traffic grows at least as fast as N, the number of nodes.

Manuscript received September 3, 1987; revised March 28, 1988. This work was supported in part by the Defense Advanced Research Projects Agency under Contracts N000014-80-C-0622 and N00014-85-K-0124 and in part by a National Science Foundation Presidential Young Investigator Award with matching funds from General Electric Corporation. A preliminary version of this paper appeared in the Proceedings of the 1987 Stanford Conference on Advanced Research in VLSI [10].

The author is with the Artificial Intelligence Laboratory and the Laboratory for Computer Science, Massachusetts Institute of Technology, Cambridge, MA 02139.

IEEE Log Number 9034541.

VLSI systems are wire-limited. The cost of these systems is predominantly that of connecting devices, and the performance is limited by the delay of these interconnections. Thus, to achieve the required performance, the network must make efficient use of the available wire. The topology of the network must map into the three physical dimensions so that messages are not required to *double back* on themselves, and in a way that allows messages to use all of the available bandwidth along their path.

This paper considers the problem of constructing *wire-efficient* communication networks, networks that give the optimum performance for a given wire density. We compare networks holding wire bisection, the number of wires crossing a cut that evenly divides the machine, constant. Thus, we compare low-dimensional networks with wide communication channels against high-dimensional networks with narrow channels. We investigate the class of k-ary n-cube interconnection networks and show that low-dimensional networks outperform high-dimensional networks with the same bisection width.

The remainder of this paper describes the design of wire-efficient communication networks. Section II describes the assumptions on which this paper is based. The family of k-ary n-cube networks is described in Section II-A. We restrict our attention to k-ary n-cubes because it is the dimension of the network that is important, not the details of its topology. Section II-B introduces *wormhole routing* [20], a low-latency routing technique. Network cost is determined primarily by wire density which we will measure in terms of bisection width. Section II-C introduces the idea of *bisection width*, and discusses delay models for network channels. A performance model of these networks is derived in Section III. Expressions are given for network latency as a function of traffic that agree closely with experimental results. Under the assumption of constant wire density, it is shown that low-dimensional networks achieve lower latency and better hot-spot throughput than do high-dimensional networks.

II. PRELIMINARIES

A. k-ary n-cubes

Many different network topologies have been proposed for use in concurrent computers: trees [6], [15], [21], Benes networks [4], Batcher sorting networks [2], shuffle exchange networks [23], *Omega* networks [14], *indirect* binary n-cube or *flip* networks [3], [22], and direct binary n-cubes [19], [17], [24]. The binary n-cube is a special case of the family of k-

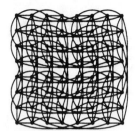

Fig. 1. A binary 6-cube embedded in the plane.

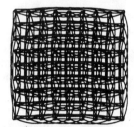

Fig. 2. A ternary 4-cube embedded in the plane.

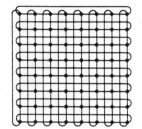

Fig. 3. An 8-ary 2-cube (torus).

ary n-cubes, cubes with n dimensions and k nodes in each dimension.

Most concurrent computers have been built using networks that are either k-ary n-cubes or are isomorphic to k-ary n-cubes: rings, meshes, tori, direct and indirect binary n-cubes, and Omega networks. Thus, in this paper we restrict our attention to k-ary n-cube networks. We refer to n as the *dimension* of the cube and k as the *radix*. Dimension, radix, and number of nodes are related by the equation

$$N = k^n, \ (k = \sqrt[n]{N}, \ n = \log_k N). \tag{1}$$

It is the dimension of the network that is important, not the details of its topology.

A node in the k-ary n-cube can be identified by n-digit radix k address, $a_0, \cdots, a_{n-1}$. The ith digit of the address, a_i, represents the node's position in the ith dimension. Each node can forward messages to its upper neighbor in each dimension, i, with address $a_0, \cdots, a_i + 1 (\mathrm{mod}\ k), \cdots, a_{n-1}$.

In this paper, we assume that our k-ary n-cubes are unidirectional for simplicity. We will see that our results do not change appreciably for bidirectional networks. For an actual machine, however, there are many compelling reasons to make our networks bidirectional. Most importantly, bidirectional networks allow us to exploit locality of communication. If an object A sends a message to an object B, there is a high probability of B sending a message back to A. In a bidirectional network, a roundtrip from A to B can be made short by placing A and B close together. In a unidirectional network, a roundtrip will always involve completely circling the machine in at least one dimension.

Figs. 1–3 show three k-ary n-cube networks in order of decreasing dimension. Fig. 1 shows a binary 6-cube (64 nodes). A 3-ary 4-cube (81 nodes) is shown in Fig. 2. An 8-ary 2-cube (64 nodes), or torus, is shown in Fig. 3. Each line in Fig. 1 represents two communication channels, one in each direction, while each line in Figs. 2 and 3 represents a single communication channel.

B. Wormhole Routing

In this paper, we consider networks that use *wormhole* [20] rather than *store-and-forward* [25] routing. Instead of storing a packet completely in a node and then transmitting it to the next node, wormhole routing operates by advancing the head of a packet directly from incoming to outgoing channels. Only a few flow control digits (flits) are buffered at each node. A *flit* is the smallest unit of information that a queue or channel can accept or refuse.

As soon as a node examines the header flit(s) of a message, it selects the next channel on the route and begins forwarding flits down that channel. As flits are forwarded, the message becomes spread out across the channels between the source and destination. It is possible for the first flit of a message to arrive at the destination node before the last flit of the message has left the source. Because most flits contain no routing information, the flits in a message must remain in contiguous channels of the network and cannot be interleaved with the flits of other messages. When the header flit of a message is blocked, all of the flits of a message stop advancing and block the progress of any other message requiring the channels they occupy.

A method similar to wormhole routing, called *virtual cut-through*, is described in [13]. Virtual cut-through differs from wormhole routing in that it buffers messages when they block, removing them from the network. With wormhole routing, blocked messages remain in the network.

Fig. 4 illustrates the advantage of wormhole routing. There are two components of latency, distance and message aspect ratio. The distance D is the number of *hops* required to get from the source to the destination. The message aspect ratio (message length L normalized to the channel width W) is the number of channel cycles required to transmit the message across one channel. The top half of the figure shows store-and-forward routing. The message is entirely transmitted from node N_0 to node N_1, then from N_1 to N_2 and so on. With store-and-forward routing, latency is the product of D and L/W.

$$T_{\mathrm{SF}} = T_c \left(D \times \frac{L}{W} \right). \tag{2}$$

The bottom half of Fig. 4 shows wormhole routing. As soon as a flit arrives at a node, it is forwarded to the next node. With wormhole routing, latency is reduced to the sum of D and L/W.

$$T_{\mathrm{WH}} = T_c \left(D + \frac{L}{W} \right). \tag{3}$$

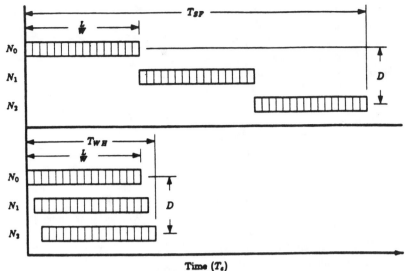

Fig. 4.   Latency of store-and-forward routing (top) versus wormhole routing
(bottom).

In both of these equations, T_c is the channel cycle time, the amount of time required to perform a transaction on a channel.

C. VLSI Complexity

VLSI computing systems [16] are wire-limited; the complexity of what can be constructed is limited by wire density, the speed at which a machine can run is limited by wire delay, and the majority of power consumed by a machine is used to drive wires. Thus, machines must be organized both logically and physically to keep wires short by exploiting locality wherever possible. The VLSI architect must organize a computing system so that its form (physical organization) fits its function (logical organization).

Networks have traditionally been analyzed under the assumption of constant channel bandwidth. Under this assumption each channel is one bit wide ($W = 1$) and has unit delay ($T_c = 1$). The constant bandwidth assumption favors networks with high dimensionality (e.g., binary n-cubes) over low-dimensional networks (e.g., tori). This assumption, however, is not consistent with the properties of VLSI technology. Networks with many dimensions require more and longer wires than do low-dimensional networks. Thus, high-dimensional networks cost more and run more slowly than low-dimensional networks. A realistic comparison of network topology must take both wire density and wire length into account.

To account for wire density, we will use bisection width [26] as a measure of network cost. The bisection width of a network is the minimum number of wires cut when the network is divided into two equal halves. Rather than comparing networks with constant channel width W, we will compare networks with constant bisection width. Thus, we will compare low-dimensional networks with large W with high-dimensional networks with small W.

The delay of a wire depends on its length l. For short wires, the delay t_s is limited by charging the capacitance of the wire and varies logarithmically with wire length.

$$t_s = \tau_{\text{inv}} e \, \log_e Kl \tag{4}$$

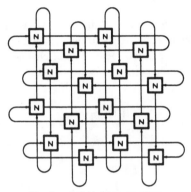

Fig. 5.   A folded torus system.

where τ_{inv} is the inverter delay, and K is a constant depending on capacitance ratios. For long wires, delay t_l is limited by the speed of light.

$$t_l = \frac{l \sqrt{\epsilon_r}}{c}. \tag{5}$$

In this paper, we will consider three delay models: constant delay T_c independent of length, logarithmic delay $T_c \propto \log l$, and linear delay $T_c \propto l$. Our main result, that latency is minimized by low-dimensional networks, is supported by all three models.

III. Performance Analysis

In this section, we compare the performance of unidirectional k-ary n-cube interconnection networks using the following assumptions.

• Networks must be embedded into the plane. If a three-dimensional packaging technology becomes available, the comparison changes only slightly.

• Nodes are placed systematically by embedding $n/2$ logical dimensions in each of the two physical dimensions. We assume that both n and k are even integers. The long end-around connections shown in Fig. 3 can be avoided by folding the network as shown in Fig. 5.

• For networks with the same number of nodes, *wire density is held constant*. Each network is constructed with the same bisection width B, the total number of wires crossing the midpoint of the network. To keep the bisection width constant, we vary the width W of the communication channels. We normalize to the bisection width of a bit-serial ($W = 1$) binary n-cube.

• The networks use *wormhole* routing.

• Channel delay T_c is a function of wire length l. We begin by considering channel delay to be constant. Later, the comparison is performed for both logarithmic and linear wire delays; $T_c \propto \log l$ and $T_c \propto l$.

When k is even, the channels crossing the midpoint of the network are all in the highest dimension. For each of the $\sqrt{N}$ rows of the network, there are $k^{((n/2)-1)}$ of these channels in each direction for a total of $2\sqrt{N}k^{((n/2)-1)}$ channels. Thus, the bisection width B of a k-ary n-cube with W-bit wide communication channels is

$$B(k, n) = 2W\sqrt{N}k^{((n/2)-1)} = \frac{2WN}{k}. \quad (6)$$

For a binary n-cube, $k = 2$, the bisection width is $B(2, n) = WN$. We set B equal to N to normalize to a binary n-cube with unit width channels, $W = 1$. The channel width $W(k, n)$ of a k-ary n-cube with the same bisection width B follows from (6):

$$\frac{2W(k, n)N}{k} = N,$$

$$W(k, n) = \frac{k}{2}. \quad (7)$$

The peak wire density is greater than the bisection width in networks with $n > 2$ because the lower dimensions contribute to wire density. The maximum density, however, is bounded by

$$\begin{aligned}
D_{\max} &= 2W\sqrt{N}\sum_{i=0}^{\frac{n}{2}-1} k^i = k\sqrt{N}\sum_{i=0}^{\frac{n}{2}-1} k^i \\
&= k\sqrt{N}\left(\frac{k^{n/2}-1}{k-1}\right) \\
&= k\sqrt{N}\left(\frac{\sqrt{N}-1}{k-1}\right) < \left(\frac{k}{k-1}\right)B. \quad (8)
\end{aligned}$$

A plot of wire density as a function of position for one row of a binary 20-cube is shown in Fig. 6. The density is very low at the edges of the cube and quite dense near the center. The peak density for the row is 1364 at position 341. Compare this density to the bisection width of the row, which is 1024. In contrast, a two-dimensional torus has a wire density of 1024 independent of position. One advantage of high-radix networks is that they have a very uniform wire density. They make full use of available area.

Each processing node connects to $2n$ channels (n input and n output) each of which is $k/2$ bits wide. Thus, the number

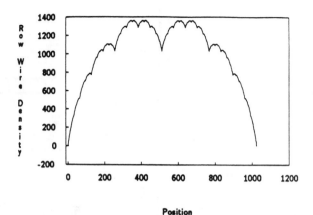

Fig. 6. Wire density versus position for one row of a binary 20-cube.

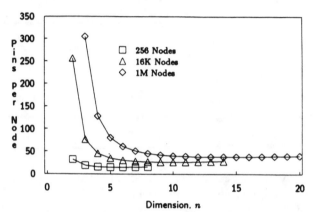

Fig. 7. Pin density versus dimension for 256, 16K, and 1M nodes.

of pins per processing node is

$$N_p = nk. \quad (9)$$

A plot of pin density as a function of dimension for $N = 256$, 16K, and 1M nodes[1] is shown in Fig. 7. Low-dimensional networks have the disadvantage of requiring many pins per processing node. A two-dimensional network with 1M nodes (not shown) requires 2048 pins and is clearly unrealizable. However, the number of pins decreases very rapidly as the dimension n increases. Even for 1M nodes, a dimension 4 node has only 128 pins. All of the configurations that give low latency also give a reasonable pin count.

A. Latency

Latency T_l is the sum of the latency due to the network and the latency due to the processing node,

$$T_l = T_{\text{net}} + T_{\text{node}}. \quad (10)$$

In this paper, we are concerned only with T_{net}. Techniques to reduce T_{node} are described in [7] and [11].

If we select two processing nodes, P_i, P_j, at random, the average number of channels that must be traversed to send a message from P_i to P_j is given by

$$D = \left(\frac{k-1}{2}\right)n. \quad (11)$$

[1] 1K=1024 and, 1M=1K×1K=1048576.

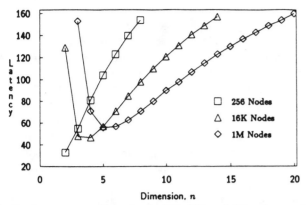

Fig. 8. Latency versus dimension for 256, 16K, and 1M nodes, constant delay.

The average latency of a k-ary n-cube is calculated by substituting (7) and (11) into (3)

$$T_{net} = T_c \left(\left(\frac{k-1}{2} \right) n + \frac{2L}{k} \right). \quad (12)$$

Fig. 8 shows the average network latency T_{net} as a function of dimension n for k-ary n-cubes with 2^8 (256), 2^{14} (16K), and 2^{30} (1M) nodes.[2] The left most data point in this figure corresponds to a torus ($n = 2$) and the rightmost data point corresponds to a binary n-cube ($k = 2$). This figure assumes constant wire delay T_c and a message length L of 150 bits. This choice of message length was based on the analysis of a number of fine-grain concurrent programs [7]. Although constant wire delay is unrealistic, this figure illustrates that even ignoring the dependence of wire delay on wire length, low-dimensional networks achieve lower latency than high-dimensional networks.

The latency of the tori on the left side of Fig. 8 is limited almost entirely by distance. The latency of the binary n-cubes on the right side of the graph is limited almost entirely by aspect ratio. With bit serial channels, these cubes take 150 cycles to transmit their messages across a single channel.

In an application that exploits locality of communication, the distance between communicating objects is reduced. In such a situation, the latency of the low-dimensional networks, dominated by distance (the left side of Fig. 8) is reduced. High-dimensional networks, on the other hand, cannot take advantage of locality. Their latency, because it is dominated by message length, will remain high.

In applications that send short messages, the component of latency due to message length is reduced resulting in lower latency for high-dimensional networks (the right side of Fig. 8).

For the three cases shown in Fig. 8, minimum latencies are achieved for $n = 2$, 4, and 5, respectively. In general, the lowest latency is achieved when the component of latency due to distance D and the component due to message length L/W

[2] For the sake of comparison, we allow radix to take on noninteger values. For some of the dimensions considered, there is no integer radix k that gives the correct number of nodes. In fact, this limitation can be overcome by constructing a *mixed-radix cube* [5].

are approximately equal, $D \approx L/W$. The following assertion makes this statement more precise.

Assertion: Minimum latency T_{net} occurs at a dimension $n \leq n_x$, where n_x is the dimension for which $D = L/W$.

Proof: Differentiating (12) with respect to n gives

$$\frac{\partial T_{net}}{\partial n} = \frac{k-1-k \log k}{2} + \frac{2L \log^2 k}{k \log N}. \quad (13)$$

For $n = n_x$, substituting $D = L/W$ into (7) and (11) gives

$$4L = nk(k-1) = \frac{k(k-1) \log N}{\log k}. \quad (14)$$

Substituting into the derivative (13) gives

$$\left. \frac{\partial T_{net}}{\partial n} \right|_{n=n_x} = \frac{k-1-k \log k}{2} + \frac{(k-1) \log k}{2}$$
$$= \frac{k-1-\log k}{2}. \quad (15)$$

For all $k \geq 2$, $(\partial T_{net}/\partial n)|_{n=n_x} \geq 0$. The derivative is monotonically increasing for $n \leq n_x$. Thus, the minimum latency $(\partial T_{net}/\partial n = 0)$ occurs for $n < n_x$. $\square$

Empirically, for all networks with $N < 2^{20}$ and integral valued k and n the minimum latency occurs when k and n are chosen so that $|D - (L/W)|$ is minimized.

The longest wire in the system becomes a bottleneck that determines the rate at which each channel operates, T_c. The length of this wire is given by

$$l = k^{(n/2)-1}. \quad (16)$$

If the wires are sufficiently short, delay depends logarithmically on wire length. If the channels are longer, they become limited by the speed of light, and delay depends linearly on channel length. Substituting (16) into (4) and (5) gives

$$T_c \propto \begin{cases} 1 + \log_e l = 1 + \left(\frac{n}{2} - 1 \right) \log_e k & \text{logarithmic delay} \\ l = k^{(n/2)-1} & \text{linear delay.} \end{cases} \quad (17)$$

We substitute (17) into (12) to get the network latency for these two cases:

$$T_l \propto \begin{cases} \left(1 + \left(\frac{n}{2} - 1 \right) \log_e k \right) \left(\left(\frac{k-1}{2} \right) n + \frac{2L}{k} \right) \\ \quad \text{logarithmic delay} \\ \left(k^{(n/2)-1} \right) \left(\left(\frac{k-1}{2} \right) n + \frac{2L}{k} \right) \\ \quad \text{linear delay.} \end{cases} \quad (18)$$

Fig. 9 shows the average network latency as a function of dimension for k-ary n-cubes with 2^8 (256), 2^{14} (16K), and 2^{20} (1M) nodes, assuming logarithmic wire delay and a message length, L, of 150. Fig. 10 shows the same data assuming linear wire delays. In both figures, the leftmost data point corresponds to a torus ($n = 2$) and the rightmost data point corresponds to a binary n-cube ($k = 2$).

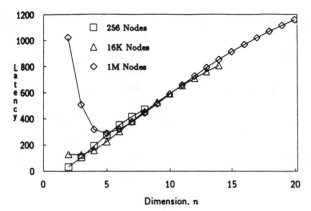

Fig. 9. Latency versus dimension for 256, 16K, and 1M nodes, logarithmic delay.

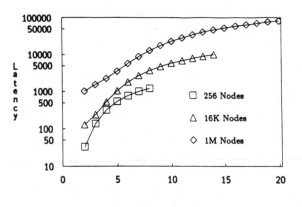

Fig. 10. Latency versus dimension for 256, 16K, and 1M nodes, linear delay.

In the linear delay case, Fig. 10, a torus ($n = 2$) always gives the lowest latency. This is because a torus offers the highest bandwidth channels and the most direct physical route between two processing nodes. Under the linear delay assumption, latency is determined solely by bandwidth and by the physical distance traversed. There is no advantage in having long channels.

Under the logarithmic delay assumption, Fig. 9, a torus has the lowest latency for small networks ($N = 256$). For the larger networks, the lowest latency is achieved with slightly higher dimensions. With $N = 16K$, the lowest latency occurs when n is three.[3] With $N = 1M$, the lowest latency is achieved when n is 5. It is interesting that assuming constant wire delay does not change this result much. Recall that under the (unrealistic) constant wire delay assumption, Fig. 8, the minimum latencies are achieved with dimensions of 2, 4, and 5, respectively.

The results shown in Figs. 8–10 were derived by comparing networks under the assumption of constant wire cost to a binary n-cube with $W = 1$. For small networks it is possible to construct binary n-cubes with wider channels, and for large networks (e.g., 1M nodes) it may not be possible to construct a binary n-cube at all. The available wiring area grows as $N^{2/3}$ while the bisection width of a binary n-cube grows as N. In the case of small networks, the comparison

---

[3] In an actual machine, the dimension n would be restricted to be an even integer.

---

against binary n-cubes with wide channels can be performed by expressing message length in terms of the binary n-cube's channel width, in effect decreasing the message length for purposes of comparison. The net result is the same: lower dimensional networks give lower latency. Even if we perform the 256 node comparison against a binary n cube with $W=16$, the torus gives the lowest latency under the logarithmic delay model, and a dimension 3 network gives minimum latency under the constant delay model. For large networks, the available wire is less than assumed, so the effective message length should be increased, making low-dimensional networks look even more favorable.

In this comparison, we have assumed that only a single bit of information is in transit on each wire of the network at a given time. Under this assumption, the delay between nodes T_c is equal to the period of each node T_p. In a network with long wires, however, it is possible to have several bits in transit at once. In this case, the channel delay T_c is a function of wire length, while the channel period $T_p < T_c$ remains constant. Similarly, in a network with very short wires we may allow a bit to ripple through several channels before sending the next bit. In this case, $T_p > T_c$. Separating the coefficients T_c and T_p, (3) becomes

$$T_{\text{net}} = \left(T_c D + T_p \frac{L}{W} \right). \tag{19}$$

The net effect of allowing $T_c \neq T_p$ is the same as changing the length L by a factor of $\frac{T_p}{T_c}$ and does not change our results significantly.

When wire cost is considered, low-dimensional networks (e.g., tori) offer lower latency than high-dimensional networks (e.g., binary n-cubes). Tori outperform binary n-cubes because they better match form to function. The logical and physical graphs of the torus are identical; thus, messages always travel the minimum distance from source to destination. In a binary n-cube, on the other hand, the fit between form and function is not as good. A message in a binary n-cube embedded into the plane may have to traverse considerably more than the minimum distance between its source and destination.

B. Throughput

Throughput, another important metric of network performance, is defined as the total number of messages the network can handle per unit time. One method of estimating throughput is to calculate the capacity of a network, the total number of messages that can be in the network at once. Typically the maximum throughput of a network is some fraction of its capacity. The network capacity per node is the total bandwidth out of each node divided by the average number of channels traversed by each message. For k-ary n-cubes, the bandwidth out of each node is nW, and the average number of channels traversed is given by (11), so the network capacity per node Γ is given by

$$\Gamma \propto \frac{nW}{D} \propto \frac{n\left(\dfrac{k}{2}\right)}{\left(\dfrac{k-1}{2}\right)n} \approx 1. \tag{20}$$

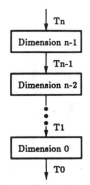

Fig. 11. Contention model for a network.

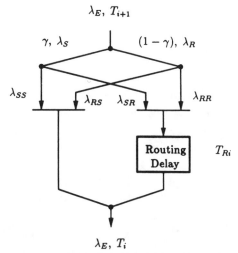

Fig. 12. Contention model for a single dimension.

The network capacity is independent of dimension. For a constant wire density, there is a constant network capacity.

Throughput will be less than capacity because contention causes some channels to block. This contention also increases network latency. To simplify the analysis of this contention, we make the following assumptions.

• Messages are routed using e-cube routing (in order of decreasing dimension) [8]. That is, a message at node $a_0, \cdots, a_{n-1}$ destined for nodes $b_0, \cdots, b_{n-1}$ is first routed in dimension $n-1$ until it reaches node $a_0, \cdots, a_{n-2}, b_{n-1}$. The message is then routed in dimension $n-2$ until it reaches node $a_0, \cdots, a_{n-3}, b_{n-2}, b_{n-1}$, and so on. As shown in Fig. 11, this assumption allows us to consider the contention in each dimension separately.

• The traffic from each node is generated by a Poisson process with arrival rate λ (bits/cycle).

• Message destinations are uniformly distributed and independent.

The arrival rate of λ(bits/cycle) corresponds to $\lambda_E = (\lambda/L)$(messages/cycles). At the destination, each flit is serviced as soon as it arrives, so the service time at the sink is $T_0 = L/W = 2L/k$. Starting with T_0 we will calculate the service time seen entering each preceding dimension.

For convenience, we will define the following quantities as illustrated in Fig. 12:

$\gamma = \dfrac{1}{k}$ probability that a message *skips* (does not route in) a dimension,

$\lambda_S = \gamma\lambda_E$ rate of traffic that skips the previous dimension, $i+1$, ($\frac{\text{messages}}{\text{cycle}}$),

$\lambda_R = (1-\gamma)\lambda_E$ rate of traffic that routes in the previous dimension, $i+1$, ($\frac{\text{messages}}{\text{cycle}}$),

$\lambda_{SS} = \gamma^2\lambda_E$ rate of traffic that skips both the previous dimension, $i+1$, and the current dimension i, ($\frac{\text{messages}}{\text{cycle}}$),

$\lambda_{SR} = \gamma(1-\gamma)\lambda_E$ rate of traffic that skips the previous dimension, $i+1$, and routes in the current dimension, i ($\frac{\text{messages}}{\text{cycle}}$),

$\lambda_{RS} = \gamma(1-\gamma)\lambda_E$ rate of traffic that routes in the previous dimension, $i+1$, and skips the current dimension i, ($\frac{\text{messages}}{\text{cycle}}$),

$\lambda_{RR} = (1-\gamma)^2\lambda_E$ rate of traffic that routes in both the previous dimension $i+1$, and the current dimension i, ($\frac{\text{messages}}{\text{cycle}}$).

$$(21)$$

Consider a single dimension i of the network as shown in Fig. 12. All messages incur a latency due to contention on entering the dimension. Those messages that are routed incur an additional latency T_{Ri} due to contention during routing. The rate λ_E message stream entering the dimension is composed of two components: a rate λ_S stream that skipped the previous ($i+1$st) dimension, and a rate λ_R stream that was routed in the previous dimension. These two streams are in turn split into components that will skip the ith dimension (λ_{SS} and λ_{RS}) and components that will be routed in the ith dimension (λ_{SR} and λ_{RR}). The entering latency seen by one component (say λ_{SS}) is given by multiplying the probability of a collision (in this case $\lambda_{RS}T_i$) by the expected latency due to a collision [in this case $(T_i/2)$]. The components that require routing must also add the latency due to contention during routing, T_{Ri}. Adding up the four components with appropriate weights gives the following equation for T_{i+1}.

$$T_{i+1} = T_i + (1-\gamma)T_{Ri} + \gamma(1-\gamma)^3\lambda_E(T_i + T_{Ri})^2 + \gamma^3(1-\gamma)\lambda_E T_i^2. \quad (22)$$

The first term of (22) is the latency seen entering the next dimension. The second term accounts for the routing latency T_{Ri} incurred by messages routing in this dimension (λ_{SR} and λ_{RR}). The entering latency due to contention when the two routing streams merge is given by the third term. The final term gives the entering latency for the messages that skip the dimension.

For large k, γ is small and the latency is approximated by $T_{i+1} \approx T_i + T_{Ri}$. For $k=2$ (binary n-cubes), $T_{Ri} = 0$; thus, $T_{i+1} = T_i + (\lambda_E T_i/8)$.

To calculate the routing latency T_{Ri} we use the model shown in Fig. 13. Messages enter the dimension with rate λ_R, route

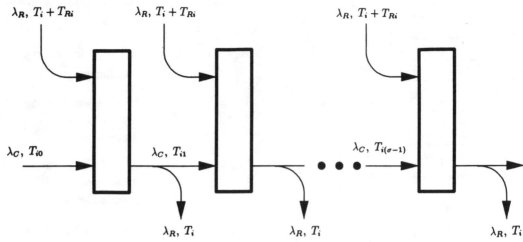

Fig. 13. Contention model for routing latency.

through a number of stages, denoted by boxes, and exit the dimension. The latency due to contention in the stages sums to T_{Ri}. Given that a message is to be routed in a dimension, the expected number of channels traversed by the message is $(k/2)$, one entering channel and $\sigma = (k-2)/2$ continuing channels. Thus, the *average* message rate on channels continuing in the dimension is $\lambda_C = \sigma \lambda_R$.

Using the average message rate to calculate latency is an approximation. The symmetry of the network assures that the traffic on physical channels is uniform. However, using virtual channels and *e*-cube routing [8] results in logical channels that form a spiral. Traffic on the *j*th channel on this spiral is given by $\lambda_{Cj} = (j - (i^2 + i)/2k)\lambda_R$. Using the uniform physical message rate results in a slightly pessimistic estimate of latency since contention for the physical channel occurs on flit boundaries while contention for the logical channel occurs on message boundaries.

To compute T_{Ri} we work backwards from the output. The service time in the last continuing channel in dimension *i* is $T_{i(\sigma-1)} = T_i$. Once we know the service time for the *j*th channel, T_{ij}, the additional service time due to contention at the $j-1$st channel is given by multiplying the probability of a collision $\lambda_R T_{i0}$ by the expected waiting time for a collision $T_{i0}/2$. Repeating this calculation σ times gives us T_{i0}.

$$T_{i(j-1)} = T_{ij} + \frac{\lambda_R T_{i0}^2}{2},$$

$$T_{i0} = T_i + \frac{\sigma \lambda_R T_{i0}^2}{2} = T_i + \frac{\lambda_C T_{i0}^2}{2},$$

$$= \frac{1 - \sqrt{1 - 2\lambda_C T_i}}{\lambda_C}. \tag{23}$$

Equation (23) is valid only when $\lambda_C < T_i/2$. If the message rate is higher than this limit, there is no steady-state solution and latency becomes infinite. There are two solutions to (23). Here we consider only the smaller of the two latencies. The larger solution corresponds to a state that is not encountered during normal operation of a network.

To calculate T_{Ri} we also need to consider the possibility of a collision on the entering channel.

$$T_{Ri} = T_{i0}\left(1 + \frac{\lambda_C T_{i0}}{2}\right) - T_i. \tag{24}$$

If sufficient queueing is added to each network node, the service times do not increase, only the latency and (24) and (22) become

$$T_{Ri} = \left(\frac{T_i}{1 - \frac{\lambda_C T_0}{2}}\right)\left(1 + \frac{\lambda_C T_0}{2}\right) - T_i, \tag{25}$$

$$T_{i+1} = T_i + (1 - \gamma)T_{Ri} + (\gamma(1 - \gamma)^3 + \gamma^3(1 - \gamma))\lambda_E T_0. \tag{26}$$

To be effective, the total queueing between the source and destination should be greater than the expected increase in latency due to blocking. Two flits of queueing per stage are sufficient when $\lambda < 0.3$ and $L < 200$. Longer messages result in a longer service time T_0 and require additional queueing. The analysis here is pessimistic in that it assumes no queueing.

Using (22), we can determine 1) the maximum throughput of the network and 2) how network latency increases with traffic.

Figs. 14 and 15 show how latency increases as a function of applied traffic for 1K node and 4K node *k*-ary *n*-cubes. The vertical axis shows latency in cycles. The horizontal axis is traffic per node, λ, in bits/cycle. The figures compare measurements from a network simulator (points) to the latency predicted by (24) (lines). The simulation agrees with the prediction within a few percent until the network approaches saturation.

For 1K networks, a 32-ary 2-cube always gives the lowest latency. For 4K networks, a 16-ary 3-cube gives the lowest latency when $\lambda < 0.2$. Because latency increases more slowly for two-dimensional networks, a 64-ary 2-cube gives the lowest latency when $\lambda > 0.2$. At the left side of each graph ($\lambda = 0$), latency is given by (12). As traffic is applied to the

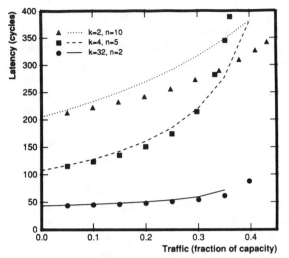

Fig. 14. Latency versus traffic (λ) for 1K node networks: 32-ary 2-cube, 4-ary 5-cube, and binary 10-cube, $L = 200$ bits. Solid line is predicted latency, points are measurements taken from a simulator.

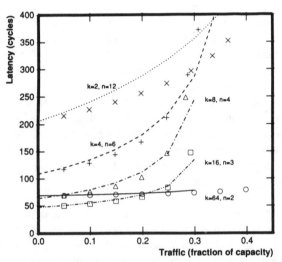

Fig. 15. Latency versus traffic (λ) for 4K node networks: 64-ary 2-cube, 16-ary 3-cube, 8-ary 4-cube, 4-ary 6-cube, and binary 12-cube, $L = 200$ bits. Solid line is predicted latency, points are measurements taken from a simulator.

network, latency increases slowly due to contention in the network until saturation is reached. Saturation occurs when λ is between 0.3 and 0.5 depending on the network topology. Networks should be designed to operate on the flat portion of the curve ($\lambda < 0.25$).

When the network saturates, throughput levels off as shown in Figs. 16 and 17. These figures show how much traffic is delivered (vertical axis) when the nodes attempt to inject a given amount of traffic (horizontal axis). The curve is linear (actual = attempted) until saturation is reached. From this point on, actual traffic is constant. This plateau occurs because 1) the network is source queued, and 2) messages that encounter contention are blocked rather than aborted. In networks where contention is resolved by dropping messages, throughput usually decreases beyond saturation.

To find the maximum throughput of the network, the source service time T_0 is set equal to the reciprocal of the message rate, λ_E, and (22), (23), and (24) are solved for λ_E. At this

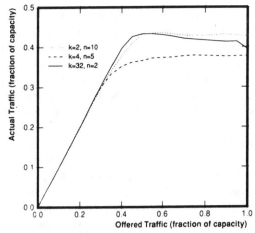

Fig. 16. Actual traffic versus attempted traffic for 1K node networks: 32-ary 2-cube, 4-ary 5-cube, and binary 10-cube, $L = 200$ bits.

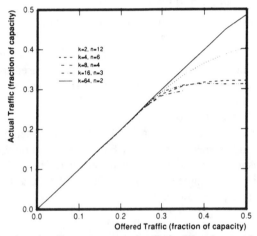

Fig. 17. Actual traffic versus attempted traffic for 4K node networks: 64-ary 2-cube, 16-ary 3-cube, 8-ary 4-cube, 4-ary 6-cube, and binary 12-cube, $L = 200$ bits.

TABLE I
MAXIMUM THROUGHPUT AS A FRACTION OF CAPACITY AND BLOCKING LATENCY IN CYCLES

Parameter	1K Nodes			4K Nodes				
Dimension	2	5	10	2	3	4	6	12
radix	32	4	2	64	16	8	4	2
Max Throughput	0.36	0.41	0.43	0.35	0.31	0.31	0.36	0.41
Latency $\lambda = 0.1$	46.1	128.	233.	70.7	55.2	79.9	135.	241.
Latency $\lambda = 0.2$	50.5	161.	269.	73.1	70.3	112.	181.	288.
Latency $\lambda = 0.3$	59.3	221.	317.	78.6	135.	245.	287.	357.

operating point the network can accept no more traffic. Messages are being offered as fast as the network can deliver them. The maximum throughput as a fraction of capacity for k-ary n-cubes with 1K and 4K nodes is tabulated in Table I. Also shown is the total latency for $L = 200$ bit messages at several message rates. The table shows that the additional latency due to blocking is significantly reduced as dimension is decreased.

In networks of constant bisection width, the latency of low-dimensional networks increases more slowly with applied traffic than the latency of high-dimensional networks. At $\lambda = 0.2$, the 32-ary 2-cube has $\approx\frac{1}{5}$ the latency of the binary 10-cube. At this point, the additional latency due to contention in the 32-ary 2-cube is $7T_c$ compared to $64T_c$ in the binary 10-cube.

Low-dimensional networks handle contention better because they use fewer channels of higher bandwidth and thus get better queueing performance. The shorter service times, L/W, of these networks results in both a lower probability of collision, and a lower expected waiting time in the event of a collision. Thus, the blocking latency at each node is reduced quadratically as k is increased. Low-dimensional networks require more hops, $D = (n(k-1)/2)$, and have a higher rate on continuing channels, λ_C. However, messages travel on the continuing channels more frequently than on the entering channels, thus most contention is with the lower rate channels. Having fewer channels of higher bandwidth also improves hot-spot throughput as described below.

C. Hot-Spot Throughput

In many situations traffic is not uniform, but rather is concentrated into *hot spots*. A *hot spot* is a pair of nodes that accounts for a disproportionately large portion of the total network traffic. As described by Pfister [18] for a shared-memory computer, hot-spot traffic can degrade performance of the entire network by causing congestion.

The *hot-spot throughput* of a network is the maximum rate at which messages can be sent from one specific node P_i to another specific node P_j. For a k-ary n-cube with deterministic routing, the hot-spot throughput, Θ_{HS}, is just the bandwidth of a single channel W. Thus, under the assumption of constant wire cost we have

$$\Theta_{HS} = W = k - 1. \tag{27}$$

Low-dimensional networks have greater channel bandwidth and thus have greater hot-spot throughput than do high-dimensional networks. Low-dimensional networks operate better under nonuniform loads because they do more resource sharing. In an interconnection network the resources are wires. In a high-dimensional network, wires are assigned to particular dimensions and cannot be shared between dimensions. For example, in a binary n-cube it is possible for a wire to be saturated while a physically adjacent wire assigned to a different dimension remains idle. In a torus all physically adjacent wires are combined into a single channel that is shared by all messages that must traverse the physical distance spanned by the channel.

IV. Conclusion

Under the assumption of constant wire bisection, low-dimensional networks with wide channels provide lower latency, less contention, and higher hot-spot throughput than higher-dimensional networks with narrow channels. Minimum network latency is achieved when the network radix k and dimension n are chosen to make the components of latency due to distance D and aspect ratio L/W approximately equal. The minimum latency occurs at a very low dimension, 2 for up to 1024 nodes.

Low-dimensional networks reduce contention because having a few high-bandwidth channels results in more resource sharing and thus better queueing performance than having many low-bandwidth channels. While network capacity and worst-case blocking latency are independent of dimension, low-dimensional networks have a higher maximum throughput and lower average blocking latency than do high-dimensional networks. Improved resource sharing also gives low-dimensional networks higher hot-spot throughput than high-dimensional networks.

The results of this paper have all been made under the assumption of constant channel delay, independent of channel length. The main result, that low-dimensional networks give minimum latency, however, does not change appreciably when logarithmic or linear delay models are considered. In choosing a delay model one must consider how the delay of a switching node compares to the delay of a wire. Current VLSI routing chips [9] have delays of tens of nanoseconds, enough time to drive several meters of wire. For such systems a constant delay model is adequate. As chips get faster and systems get larger, however, a linear delay model will more accurately reflect system performance.

Fat-tree networks have been shown to be universal in the sense that they can *efficiently* simulate any other network of the same volume [15]. However, the analysis of these networks has not considered latency. k-ary n-cubes with appropriately chosen radix and dimension are also universal in this sense. A detailed proof is beyond the scope of this paper. Intuitively, one cannot do any better than to fill each of the three physical dimensions with wires and place switches at every point of intersection. Any point-to-point network can be embedded into such a 3-D mesh with no more than a constant increase in wiring length.

This paper has considered only *direct* networks [19]. The results do not apply to *indirect* networks. The depth and the switch degree of an indirect network are analogous to the dimension and radix of a direct network. However, the bisection width of an indirect network is independent of switch degree. Because indirect networks do not exploit locality it is not possible to trade off diameter for bandwidth. When wire density is the limiting resource, a high-bandwidth direct network is preferrable to an indirect network.

The low-dimensional k-ary n-cube provides a very general communication media for digital systems. These networks have been developed primarily for message-passing concurrent computers. They could also be used in place of a bus or indirect network in a shared-memory concurrent computer, in place of a bus to connect the components of a sequential computer, or to connect subsystems of a special purpose digital system. With VLSI communication chips, the cost of implementing a network node is comparable to the cost of interfacing to a shared bus, and the performance of the network is considerably greater than the performance of a bus.

The networks described here have been demonstrated in the laboratory and incorporated into commercial multiprocessors. The Torus Routing Chip (TRC) is a VLSI chip designed to implement low-dimensional k-ary n-cube interconnection networks [9]. The TRC performs wormhole routing in arbitrary k-ary n-cube interconnection networks. A single TRC provides 8-bit data channels in two dimensions and can be cascaded to add more dimensions or wider data channels. A TRC network can deliver a 150-bit message in a 1024 node 32-ary 2-cube with an average latency of 7.5 μs, an order of magnitude better performance than would be achieved by a binary n-cube with bit-serial channels. A new routing chip, the Network Design Frame (NDF), improves the latency to ≈ 1 μs [12]. The Ametek 2010 uses a 16-ary 2-cube (without end around connections) for its interconnection network [1].

Now that the latency of communication networks has been reduced to a few microseconds, the latency of the processing nodes T_{node} dominates the overall latency. To efficiently make use of a low-latency communication network we need a processing node that interprets messages with very little overhead. The design of such a *message-driven processor* is currently underway [7], [11].

The real challenge in concurrent computing is software. The development of concurrent software is strongly influenced by available concurrent hardware. We hope that by providing machines with higher performance internode communication we will encourage concurrency to be exploited at a finer grain size in both system and application software.

Acknowledgment

I thank C. Seitz of Caltech for his many helpful suggestions during the early stages of this research.

References

[1] Ametek Corporation, Ametek 2010 product announcement, 1987.
[2] K. E. Batcher, "Sorting networks and their applications," in *Proc. AFIPS FJCC*, vol. 32, 1968, pp. 307–314.
[3] K. E. Batcher, "The Flip network in STARAN," in *Proc. 1976 Int. Conf. Parallel Processing*, pp. 65–71.
[4] V. E. Benes, *Mathematical Theory of Connecting Networks and Telephone Traffic*. New York: Academic, 1965.
[5] L. N. Bhuyan and D. P. Agrawal, "Generalized hypercube and hyperbus structures for a computer network," *IEEE Trans. Comput.*, vol. C-33, no. 4, pp. 323–333, Apr. 1984.
[6] S. Browning, "The tree machine: A highly concurrent computing environment," Dep. Comput. Sci., California Instit. Technol., Rep. 3760, 1980.
[7] W. J. Dally, *A VLSI Architecture for Concurrent Data Structures*. Hingham, MA: Kluwer, 1987.
[8] W. J. Dally and C. L. Seitz, "Deadlock-free message routing in multiprocessor interconnection networks," *IEEE Trans. Comput.*, vol. C-36, no. 5, pp. 547–553, May 1987.
[9] ——, "The torus routing chip," *J. Distributed Syst.*, vol. 1, no. 3, pp. 187–196, 1986.
[10] W. J. Dally, "Wire efficient VLSI multiprocessor communication networks," in *Proc. Stanford Conf. Advanced Res. VLSI*, Losleben, Ed. Cambridge, MA: MIT Press, Mar. 1987, pp. 391–415.
[11] W. J. Dally *et al.*, "Architecture of a message-driven processor," in *Proc. 14th ACM/IEEE Symp. Comput. Architecture*, June 1987, pp. 189–196.
[12] W. J. Dally and P. Song, "Design of a self-timed VLSI multicomputer communication controller," in *Proc. IEEE Int. Conf. Comput. Design*, 1987.
[13] P. Kermani and L. Kleinrock, "Virtual cut-through: A new computer communication switching technique," *Comput. Networks*, vol. 3, pp. 267–286, 1979.
[14] D. H. Lawrie, "Alignment and access of data in an array processor," *IEEE Trans. Comput.*, vol. C-24, no. 12, pp. 1145–1155, Dec. 1975.
[15] C. L. Leiserson, "Fat trees: Universal networks for hardware-efficient supercomputing," *IEEE Trans. Comput.*, vol. C-34, no. 10, pp. 892–901, Oct. 1985.
[16] C. A. Mead and L. A. Conway, *Introduction to VLSI Systems*. Reading, MA: Addison-Wesley, 1980.
[17] M. C. Pease, III, "The indirect binary n-cube microprocessor array," *IEEE Trans. Comput.*, vol. C-26, no. 5, pp. 458–473, May 1977.
[18] G. F. Pfister and V. A. Norton, "Hot spot contention and combining in multistage interconnection networks," *IEEE Trans. Comput.*, vol. C-34, no. 10, pp. 943–948, Oct. 1985.
[19] C. L. Seitz, "Concurrent VLSI architectures," *IEEE Trans. Comput.*, vol. C-33, no. 12, pp. 1247–1265, Dec. 1984.
[20] C. L. Seitz *et al.*, "The hypercube communications chip," Dep. Comput. Sci., California Inst. Technol., Display File 5182:DF:85, Mar. 1985.
[21] C. H. Sequin, "Single chip computers, The new VLSI building block," in *Proc. Caltech Conf. VLSI*, C. L. Seitz, Ed., Jan. 1979, pp. 435–452.
[22] H. J. Siegel, "Interconnection network for SIMD machines," *IEEE Comput. Mag.*, vol. 12, no. 6, pp. 57–65, June 1979.
[23] H. S. Stone, "Parallel processing with the perfect shuffle," *IEEE Trans. Comput.*, vol. C-20, no. 2, pp. 153–161, Feb. 1971.
[24] H. Sullivan and T. R. Bashkow, "A large scale homogeneous machine," in *Proc. 4th Ann. Symp. Comput. Architecture*, 1977, pp. 105–124.
[25] A. S. Tanenbaum, *Computer Networks*. Englewood Cliffs, NJ: Prentice-Hall, 1981.
[26] C. D. Thompson, "A complexity theory of VLSI," Dep. Comput. Sci., Carnegie-Mellon Univ., Tech. Rep. CMU-CS-80-140, Aug. 1980.

William J. Dally (S'78–M'86) received the B.S. degree in electrical engineering from Virginia Polytechnic Institute, Blacksburg, in 1980, the M.S. degree in electrical engineering from Stanford University, Stanford, CA, in 1981, and the Ph.D. degree in computer science from Caltech in 1986.

From 1980 to 1982, he worked at Bell Telephone Laboratories where he contributed to the design of the BELLMAC-32 microprocessor. From 1982 to 1983 he worked as a consultant in the area of digital systems design. From 1983 to 1986 he was a Research Assistant and then a Research Fellow at Caltech. He is currently an Associate Professor of Computer Science at the Massachusetts Institute of Technology. His research interests include concurrent computing, computer architecture, computer-aided design, and VLSI design.

Limits on Interconnection Network Performance

Anant Agarwal, *Member, IEEE*

Abstract—As the performance of interconnection networks becomes increasingly limited by physical constraints in high-speed multiprocessor systems, the parameters of high-performance network design must be reevaluated, starting with a close examination of assumptions and requirements. This paper models network latency, taking both switch and wire delays into account. A simple closed form expression for contention in buffered, direct networks is derived and is found to agree closely with simulations. The model includes the effects of packet size and communication locality. Network analysis under various constraints (such as fixed bisection width, fixed channel width, and fixed node size) and under different workload parameters (such as packet size, degree of communication locality, and network request rate) reveals that performance is highly sensitive to these constraints and workloads. A two-dimensional network has the lowest latency only when switch delays and network contention are ignored, but three or four dimensions are favored otherwise. However, two-dimensional networks regain their advantage if communication locality exists. Communication locality decreases both the base network latency and the network bandwidth requirements of applications. We show that a much larger fraction of the resulting performance improvement arises from the reduction in bandwidth requirements than from the decrease in latency.

Index Terms— Communication locality, interconnection networks, message-passing, multistage networks, parallel processing, performance analysis, shared-memory multiprocessors.

I. INTRODUCTION

AN efficient communication network for high-performance multiprocessors must provide low latency memory access and message transmission. While some communication latency can be tolerated by overlapping computation with communication, latency imposes fundamental limits on the effectiveness of multiprocessors. Communication latency depends not only on the properties of the network, such as dimension, channel width, node delay, and wire delay, but on the communication patterns of parallel computations as well. This paper analyses the contribution of these factors to the latency of direct networks.

In a direct network [24], the processing nodes communicate directly with each other over a set of point-to-point links. The point-to-point interconnections between processors distinguish direct networks from indirect networks (or multistage networks) [27], such as the Omega [19] and the Delta [22] networks. An indirect network does not integrate processors and switches. Consequently, processors cannot communicate directly with each other, but must do so through a set of intervening switching nodes. Because they allow the exploitation of communication locality, direct networks are becoming increasingly popular for interconnections in large-scale concurrent computers. Examples of machines that use direct networks include the Caltech Cosmic Cube [25] and the Connection Machine [13].

We will focus on the general class of direct networks called k-ary n-cubes [28]. A k-ary n-cube is a network with n dimensions having k nodes in each dimension. For example, a 100 processor array has $n = 2$ and $k = 10$. Given N processors, the relationship $N = k^n$ holds between the dimension n and the radix k. For planar mappings, two or three-dimensional networks are favored because they scale better than high-dimensional networks, they are modular, and they are easy to implement. Examples of machine designs that use such networks are the MuNet [12], Ametek 2010 [26], the Caltech Mosaic [3], the MIT J-machine [9], and the CMU–Intel iWarp [4]. Some recent distributed shared-memory designs are also planning to use low-dimensional direct networks, e.g., HORIZON [18], the Stanford DASH Multiprocessor [20], and the MIT Alewife machine [2], [6].

The choice of the optimal network for a multiprocessor is highly sensitive to the assumptions about system parameters and the constraints that apply on the design. System parameters include, among other factors, message size and the degree of communication locality; design constraints include limits on bisection width, node size, and channel width. Bisection width is defined as the minimum number of wires that must be cut to separate the network into two equal halves [29]. A bisection width constraint is tantamount to an area constraint. A constraint on the node size is assumed to limit the number of pins on the node. Assuming a constraint on the bisection width, Dally [7], [8] analyzed the performance of k-ary n-cube networks implemented in two-dimensional space, using constant, logarithmic, and linear wire delay models. The analysis suggests that a two-dimensional network yields the lowest latency with a linear wire delay model. Node delays, however, were ignored (although the constant wire delay model does indicate the results when node delays are dominant), and message lengths used in obtaining the results were 150 and 200 bits, which are large for shared-memory machines, but typical for message passing multicomputers.

Node delays cannot be ignored with current technology. When node delays (or switch delays) are neglected and a constant bisection width is assumed, a network of lower dimension has lower latency for two reasons: 1) it has wider channels, resulting in smaller message sizes, and 2) it has shorter wires, resulting in faster packet transfer between switches. However, a lower-dimensional network forces a message to traverse more nodes. Because the effective network latency depends on both the node delay and the wire delay, longer wire delays might not be harmful if the node delays dominate. With current

Manuscript received August 14, 1990; revised February 13, 1991. This work was supported by DARPA Contract N00014-87-K-0825.

The author is with the Laboratory for Computer Science, Massachusetts Institute of Technology, Cambridge, MA 02139.

IEEE Log Number 9102437.

technology, this is indeed the case. For example, assuming an aggressive 10 ns switch delay, it takes a wire length of about 10 ft for the wire delay to equal switch delay. Our results suggest that although two-dimensional networks have the lowest latency ignoring switch delay, three-dimensional networks are superior when switch delays are four times the wire delay of a two-dimensional network, and four-dimensional networks are best when the corresponding switch delays are 16 times greater.

Smaller messages diminish the relative advantage of networks with lower dimensions. When message sizes are small, wider channels—an advantage of low-dimensional networks—are less useful. Messages are expected to be smaller in a shared-memory multiprocessor (about 100 bits on average [5]) than in a message passing multicomputer. In addition, as observed in Section III-C, small messages suffer less contention delay than large messages per unit volume of data transferred. Our analysis shows that small messages favor three-dimensional networks for large networks (greater than 1K nodes).

If bisection width is fixed to be the same as that of a unit-channel-width binary n-cube network with a 1000 nodes, a two-dimensional network is clearly superior [see Fig. 11(c)]. However, if the node size is constrained to that of a two-dimensional network with 32 bit channels, a three-dimensional network is optimal [see Fig. 11(d)], while a four-dimensional network is slightly better than others when wire delays are the only constraining factor [see Fig. 11(b)]. Furthermore, in the previous two cases, higher dimensions are favored on account of their greater bandwidth, as the load on the network increases.

We show that communication locality in the application significantly improves both throughput and latency of direct networks, with a relative impact that increases with network load. We say a program running on a parallel machine displays *communication locality* (or memory reference locality) if the probability of communication (or access) to various nodes decreases with physical distance. Communication locality in parallel programs depends on the algorithms used as well as on the partitioning and placement of data and processes. When communication locality exists, low-dimensional networks outperform networks with higher dimensions. We compare the performance of direct and indirect networks under a node size constraint and show that low-dimensional direct networks do better than indirect networks only when communication locality exists.

Our analysis will examine network design based on several possible constraints. Technological constraints limit the wire density; we therefore assume a fixed wire density. Similarly, fundamental physical limitations on signal propagation speeds on wires will be maintained. Constant bisection width, however, is a potential limit imposed by cost, power, size, and other factors. Because bisection width is not a fundamental physical limit, this assumption will not always be made in this analysis. Instead, we will analyze networks under the following constraints:

- constant channel widths
- constant bisection width

- constant node size.

We develop a model for buffered low-dimensional direct networks that yields a simple closed form expression for network contention. (See [1] for a model of binary n-cube networks for unit packet sizes.) The model is thoroughly validated through measurements taken from a simulator. Although the assumptions made by the model are tailored to networks with high radices, in practice we have found that the model is accurate for low radix (e.g., $k = 4$) networks as well. Simple extensions to the model include the effects of packet size, multicycle pipelined switches, and communication locality.

We begin by presenting expressions for the base network latency that represent the effects of switch and wire delays in Section II. The *base network latency* is the latency of an unloaded network. Section III derives a model for contention in buffered k-ary n-cube networks and validates it through simulations. Section IV analyzes the effect of fixed channel widths, fixed bisection width, and fixed node size on the base network latency. Section V extends the analyses to include network contention and communication locality, and Section VI summarizes the chief results of the paper.

II. NODE DELAYS VERSUS WIRE DELAYS

As advances in technology make the fabrication of ever-faster switches feasible, while wire speeds remain roughly constant, it is inevitable that wire delays will dominate switch delays. However, switches and wires of similar dimensions will have comparable delays because the same physical limits that govern wire speeds will also limit switch speeds. Therefore, our analysis includes the effect of both switch and wire delays.

The following argument describes the tradeoff that must be made in choosing a network topology. Assume that the clock cycle is chosen to be the sum of the switch delay and the wire delay in a synchronous system, making each network hop cost a cycle. (Other models could also be chosen to account for multicycle pipelined switches, or pipelined transmission channels.) The latency is a product of the clock cycle and the number of hops a message traverses. A higher-dimensional network mapped onto a plane has longer wires, causing longer transmission times over each wire, but results in fewer hops.

A. Notation and Assumptions

Let message length in bits be L, network dimension be n, the radix be k, channel width in bits be W, and the number of nodes be N. Then, $N = k^n$, and message length in flits is L/W. In this paper, a flit is equal to the number of bits of data transferred over a channel in a clock cycle. Let T_b denote the base network latency (when contention is not considered), and let T_c denote the latency taking contention into account.

Message destinations are randomly chosen from all the nodes in the network unless specified otherwise. Although many network evaluation studies make this simplifying assumption, it is rarely true in practice. However, several software practices, such as memory interleaving, uniform distribution of parallel data structures, and distributed software combining tree implementations of barrier synchronizations, tend to spread accesses uniformly over all nodes. On the other hand, when software techniques are employed to enhance communication locality, nonuniform access patterns result; such inhomogeneous access distributions are considered in Section V-A.

Let wire delay be denoted $T^w(n)$ and switch delay T^s. We assume that switch delay is a constant over various network topologies. This assumption is largely true for low-dimensional networks where a relatively large fraction of switch delay arises from factors such as chip crossings. For high-dimensional networks, the increased logic complexity will make switch delays sensitive to n, which makes the case for low-dimensional networks even more compelling. Of course, a more detailed analysis might assume that T^s is some function of the switch dimension. We will also assume a linear wire delay model. The switches are pipelined (i.e., switches use wormhole routing [7], which is a variant of cut-through routing [14]). As mentioned before, the clock cycle is the sum of the switch delay and the delay due to the longest wire in the synchronous network.

Our study assumes that the networks are embedded in a plane. A similar analysis for mapping in three-dimensional space can be also be carried out, and we will suggest the changes needed when appropriate. We will consider networks with unidirectional channels and end-around connections. We will suggest the modifications necessary in the analyses to account for other topologies, such as networks with bidirectional channels, with and without end-around connections. We have analyzed these alternate cases and we shall indicate instances where the results differ substantially from the network topologies considered in this paper. Additional assumptions required for our contention analyses will be mentioned in Section III.

B. Deriving the Base Network Latency

The latency through the network without considering contention (T_b) is simply the product of the time through one node, and the sum of the nodes and the message length. The time through one node is the clock cycle time, which is the the sum of the switch and wire delay. That is,

$$T_b = (T^s + T^w(n))\left(\text{hops}(n) + \frac{L}{W}\right).$$

As a base time period, let us denote the delay of a wire in a two-dimensional network as $T^w(2)$. Let the switch delay T^s be greater than this wire speed by some constant factor s. Then,

$$T_b = T^w(2)\left(s + \frac{T^w(n)}{T^w(2)}\right)\left(\text{hops}(n) + \frac{L}{W}\right).$$

With randomly chosen message destinations, the average distance (k_d) a message must travel in each dimension in a network with unidirectional channels and end-around connections is given by

$$k_d = \frac{k-1}{2}. \tag{1}$$

Therefore, for an n-dimensional network, $\text{hops}(n) = n(k-1)/2$. If there are bidirectional channels in a network with end-around connections, k_d is $k/4$ when k is even, and $(k-1/k)/4$

when k is odd. The average distance in a dimension is $(k-1/k)/3$ when the end-around connections do not exist.

We determine the length of the longest wire from an embedding of the n-dimensional network in a plane. The mapping is achieved by embedding $n/2$ dimensions of the network in each of two physical dimensions. Each added dimension of the network increases the number of nodes in the network by a factor k (recall $N = k^n$), and contributes to a $\sqrt{k}$ factor increase in the number of nodes in each physical dimension of space. If the distance between the centers of physically-adjacent nodes remains fixed, each additional dimension also increases the length of the longest wire by a $\sqrt{k}$ factor. (In practice, if the wire widths are nonnegligible, the distance between adjacently-placed nodes may also increase in high-dimensional networks.) Let the length of wires in a two-dimensional mesh $T^w(2)$ be measured as the distance between the centers of adjacent nodes. Then the length of the longest wire relative to the wire length in a two-dimensional network is given by

$$\frac{T^w(n)}{T^w(2)} = \sqrt{k}^{n-2} = k^{\frac{n}{2}-1}.$$

The corresponding wire length for implementing the network in z-dimensional space is $k^{\frac{n}{z}-1}$. For example, given unit-length wires in two-dimensional networks mapped onto a plane, the length of the longest wire in three-dimensional networks is $\sqrt{k}$. As stated before, this length determines the frequency at which packets can be sent over the wires. We note that the influence of long wires on the clock can be mitigated by allowing multiple clocks for transmission on long wires, or by allowing multiple bits to be in flight on the wire at any given time.

Substituting for the wire length, we now have

$$T_b = T^w(2)\left(s + k^{\frac{n}{2}-1}\right)\left(n\frac{k-1}{2} + \frac{L}{W}\right).$$

Replacing k with $N^{1/n}$, the latency equation becomes

$$T_b = T^w(2)\left(s + N^{\frac{1}{2}-\frac{1}{n}}\right)\left(n\frac{N^{\frac{1}{n}}-1}{2} + \frac{L}{W}\right). \tag{2}$$

In the above equation the channel width is chiefly affected when constraints on the bisection width or node size are applied. Our results will be normalized to a wire delay, $T^w(2)$, of 1.

III. A CONTENTION MODEL FOR BUFFERED DIRECT NETWORKS

This section derives a contention model for high-radix direct networks and validates it through simulations. The derivation proceeds like the buffered-indirect-network analysis of Kruskal and Snir [16]. Our contention model assumes buffered networks as well. Simulation experiments by Kruskal and Snir show that as few as four packet buffers at each switch node can approach infinite buffer performance, with uniform traffic. A buffer is associated with each output port of a switching node. If multiple packets request a given output port in a cycle, then we assume all but one packet are queued in the output buffer. We will derive network latency as a function of the channel utilization in the network.

Let us first derive an expression for the delay in a switching node with unit sized packets, and then extend the analysis to include larger packets. In an n-dimensional direct network, each switch has n network inputs and n network outputs, and a port leading to the processor connected to the node. The queue corresponding to each network output port can be treated as a queueing server, with v_i packets joining the queue during a cycle i. v_i is a random variable that can take on values ranging from 0 through $n + 1$, corresponding to the n channels from the network and one from the processor. The v_i for different values of i are assumed to be independent random variables; let their expectation be E and variance be V. (In the future, we will drop the use of the subscript on v.) E is the expected number of arrivals in any given cycle. As shown in [16], the average waiting time w for a packet in such a unit cycle-time system can be derived from the set of equations that result from an M/G/1 queueing system [15], as

$$w = \frac{V}{2E(1 - E)} - \frac{1}{2}. \tag{3}$$

A. Deriving the Distribution of v

To compute E and V we need the distribution of the random variable v. In an indirect network, v has a simple binomial distribution because a packet from any input channel is steered toward an output queue with equal probability. In low-dimensional, high-radix, direct networks that route packets completely in one dimension before the next, this is not the case. (See [28] for such a routing scheme. This routing scheme is commonly used in contemporary direct networks. We will comment on the performance tradeoffs in routing schemes that generate a more uniform distribution.) In such routing methods, the packets have a high probability of continuing in the same dimension when the network radix k is large yielding a more complicated distribution for v.

The distribution of v depends on k_d, the average number of hops taken by a packet in a dimension. Recall that for a network with unidirectional channels and end-around connections, $k_d = (k - 1)/2$. For a network with a high value of k_d, a packet at an entering channel in a switch will choose to continue along an outbound channel in the same dimension with a high probability. Similarly, a packet at an entering channel in a switch will tend to change dimensions with a low probability; the lower the dimension of an outgoing channel, the lower the probability a message from a given high dimension will switch to that channel [7], [1].

We assume the routing probability of an incoming packet at a channel in a given dimension is nonnegligible only for the continuing channel in that dimension, and for the channel

corresponding to one lower dimension. We will also assume that incoming packets from the processing node are steered randomly to one of the output ports. In other words, our analysis ignores the contribution to contention at an output channel of a switch of all but two incoming *network* channels—one incoming channel corresponding to the same dimension as the output channel, and the other incoming channel from one higher dimension—and the processor port. Making the above assumption allows us to obtain a simple closed form expression for the distribution of packets joining a queue. We will analyze these assumptions through detailed simulations in Section III-C, where we will find that the assumptions yield accurate statistics even when k is small and n is large.

Let the probability of a packet arriving at an incoming channel be ρ (which is the channel utilization given our initial assumption of unit-sized packet). We can determine ρ as follows. Let the probability of a network request on any given cycle from a processor be m. The packet must travel k_d hops in each of n dimensions on the average, for a total of nk_d hops. Because each switch has n associated channels, the channel capacity consumed, or the channel utilization, is given by

$$\rho = \frac{mnk_d}{n} = mk_d. \tag{4}$$

For networks with separate channels in both directions $\rho = \frac{mk_d}{2}$. The network bandwidth per node, or the message rate for which the network reaches saturation is obtained by setting $\rho = 1$.

To model contention in the switch, the packet probability ρ in a channel along a given dimension is composed of three components:

ρ_c: packets continuing along the same dimension through the switch

ρ_s: packets that switched to this dimension in the switch

ρ_i: packets injected into this dimension from the processing node at the switch (ρ_i packets on average from each channel also exit the network at a switch).

These switching probabilities are depicted in Fig. 1 and are computed as follows. The probability a packet is generated by the processing node attached to the switch in any cycle is m, and the probability this packet routes to a given output channel in the switch is $1/n$, yielding $\rho_i = m/n = \rho/nk_d$.

Because the probability a packet exits the network from a channel is ρ_i, the probability it stays in the network is $\rho - \rho_i$. Since a packet switches dimensions once every k_d hops on average, the probability it will switch to one lower dimension in any given cycle is $\rho_s = (\rho - \rho_i)/k_d$.

Similarly, its probability of continuing along the same dimension is $(\rho - \rho_i)(1 - 1/k_d)$, or, $\rho_c = (\rho - \rho_i)(k_d - 1)/k_d$.

We can now write the distribution of v as

$$p(v) = \begin{cases} (1 - \rho_s)(1 - \rho_c)(1 - \rho_i) & v = 0 \\ \rho_c(1 - \rho_s)(1 - \rho_i) + \rho_s(1 - \rho_c)(1 - \rho_i) + \rho_i(1 - \rho_c)(1 - \rho_s) & v = 1 \\ \rho_c\rho_s(1 - \rho_i) + \rho_s\rho_i(1 - \rho_c) + \rho_i\rho_c(1 - \rho_s) & v = 2 \\ \rho_c\rho_s\rho_i & v = 3 \\ 0 & v > 3 \end{cases}$$

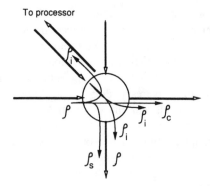

Fig. 1. Channel utilizations at a switch. ρ is the probability of a packet at an input port of the switch from the network, ρ_c is the probability of continuing along the same dimension, ρ_s is the probability of switching dimensions, and ρ_i is the probability of entering the network into this channel from the processing node.

Note that the above distribution yields $p(v) = 0$ for $v > 3$ in networks with three or more dimensions because of our assumption that only two dimensions contribute to contention. The distribution including the contribution due to all the channels could also be derived along the same vein, but the analysis would be more complicated.

The expectation and variance of the number of packets joining a queue are

$$E = \rho_c + \rho_s + \rho_i = \rho$$
$$V = \rho + 2\rho_c\rho_s + 2\rho_s\rho_i + 2\rho_i\rho_c - \rho^2$$
$$\approx \rho - \rho^2 + 2\rho^2 \frac{(k_d - 1)}{k_d^2}\left(1 + \frac{1}{n}\right). \quad (5)$$

In the above equation for V we ignore higher order terms in $1/k_d$ in the expression within the rightmost parentheses. (As we see in our validation experiments, neglecting these terms does not appreciably change the results even for networks with a small radix, say $k = 4$.) Substituting the expressions for E and V in (3) we get the average delay cycles through a switch

$$w = \frac{\rho}{(1 - \rho)} \frac{(k_d - 1)}{k_d^2}\left(1 + \frac{1}{n}\right). \quad (6)$$

It is useful to note that the $1/n$ term corresponds to the contention arising from the message component from the processing node.

B. Including the Effect of Packet Size

We now extend the model to include nonunit-sized packets. The effect of increasing the packet size to B flits can be approximated by increasing the delay through the switch by a factor B to reflect the increase in the service time of each packet, as would be the case in a system with synchronized message arrivals at a switch. Kruskal and Snir [16] made the same approximation in their analysis of buffered, indirect networks. We experimented with a wide range of networks and packet sizes to assess the validity of this approximation and found that it is indeed justified. (For example, the results of simulations with packet sizes 2 through 12 are depicted in Fig. 5.) With B-flit packets, the channel utilization also increases

by a factor B, yielding

$$\rho = mBk_d. \quad (7)$$

The contention delay through a switch is

$$w = \frac{\rho B}{(1 - \rho)} \frac{(k_d - 1)}{k_d^2}\left(1 + \frac{1}{n}\right) \quad (8)$$

and when $k_d \gg 1$ further simplifies to

$$w = \frac{\rho B}{(1 - \rho)} \frac{n + 1}{nk_d}. \quad (9)$$

The average transit time T_c through the network taking into account contention can now be computed in terms of the channel utilization. For pipelined switches (switches that use cut-through routing) with single cycle transit time through a switch, the average delay through a switch is thus $(1 + w)$. Given that the total number of network links traversed is nk_d, we have

$$T_c = \left[1 + \frac{\rho B}{(1 - \rho)} \frac{(k_d - 1)}{k_d^2}\left(1 + \frac{1}{n}\right)\right] nk_d + B. \quad (10)$$

In the above equation, $nk_d + B$ is the minimum latency suffered by a request. As stated previously, $k_d = (k - 1)/2$. The message size in flits is $B = L/W$, where L is message length in bits and W is channel width. Note that if the switch has a pipeline latency of p cycles, the switch delay will be p plus the contention component. When $k_d \gg 1$, the transit time including contention is approximately

$$T_c = nk_d + B + \frac{\rho B(n + 1)}{(1 - \rho)}. \quad (11)$$

C. Validation of the Model

We validated the model through simulations against several network types with a variety of workload parameters. In any given cycle, each node in the simulator generates a packet of size B with probability m to a randomly chosen destination node. The simulator routes messages through the network in the order of decreasing dimensions, and generates statistics such as average channel utilization in each dimension, average message latency, and observed message rates. Each simulation was run until the network reached steady state, that is, until a further increase in simulated network cycles did not change the measured channel utilization appreciably.

Fig. 2 compares the network latency predicted by our model (10), and through simulations for a 1K-node network with $k = 10$ and $n = 3$ for several packet sizes. Fig. 3 displays corresponding results for a two-dimensional 100 node network with $k = 10$. We can see that our simple model predicts network latency with remarkable accuracy even at high loads.

The model overestimates the latency for large packet sizes, but underestimates it slightly at high loads. Let us examine the causes of these discrepancies. We believe the packet-size-related errors are due to the assumption of synchronized message arrivals at a switch. The difference at high loads can be attributed to the routing preference of messages injected into the network by the processing nodes. Our network simulator routes packets highest-dimension first in

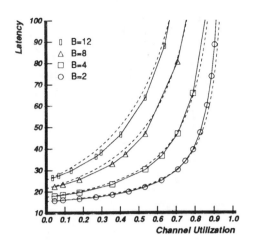

Fig. 2. Comparing the direct network model with simulations for $n = 3$ and $k = 10$. Dashed lines correspond to model predictions.

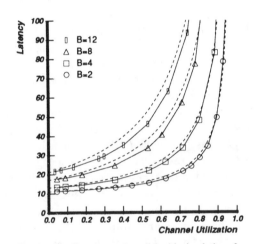

Fig. 3. Comparing the direct network model with simulations for $n = 2$ and $k = 10$. Dashed lines correspond to model predictions.

decreasing order of dimensions (see [28] for such a routing scheme). Such an ordered routing scheme allows deadlock-free routing in networks with finite-size buffers without end-around connections, and our general purpose simulator employs the same routing order for other networks as well. We verified in the simulations that the packets suffer higher-than-average delays in the higher dimensions.

We also modeled networks with separate channels in both directions without end-around connections. For such networks, $k_d = (k - 1/k)/3$, and $\rho = mBk_d/2$. The model's predictions were accurate for low to moderate loads, but the simulation latencies were higher than those of the model when the channels were heavily loaded. The higher simulated latencies result from the nonuniform channel loading within each dimension: the missing end-around connections caused higher channel loads in the middle regions of each dimension.

It is interesting to see that routing packets in the order of decreasing dimensions causes uneven probabilities of packet arrivals from various dimensions to an output switch channel, and results in low contention until a high network utilization [notice the $1/k_d$ factor in the expression for the contention in (9)]. This effect becomes more significant as k_d increases. This

uneven probability results in a low value for the variance V in (3). Note that V achieves its maximum value when $\rho_c = \rho_s$. The skew in the arrival distribution increases with network radix. Similar results were observed in buffered, binary n-cube networks by Abraham and Padmanabhan [1] and in unbuffered, direct networks by Dally [7].

We experimented with the model's predictive capabilities for low values of the radix k. Comparisons of the model and simulations for networks with $k = 4$ and $n = 2$, 3, and 4, are shown in Fig. 4. In general, we see that the model is robust; its predictions remain accurate even for low values of k, although as before, the model underestimates latency as the network approaches saturation. (The complete expression for V in (5) yields virtually the same curves.) The simulation curves are higher than those of the model at high loads in Fig. 4 than in Figs. 3 and 2; this is an artifact of nonnegligible switching probabilities from several lower dimensions when k is small. These switching probabilities could be safely ignored at high values of k.

Fig. 5 illustrates how packet size affects network contention. We derive network latency as a function of packet size, given a fixed number of bits transferred (mB), for several values of n and k. The request rates m are adjusted to achieve the same throughput ($\rho = 0.4$) for various packet sizes. For example, the request rate needed to achieve a 0.4 channel utilization for packet size B is given by $m = 0.4/(Bk_d)$. It is clear from the model (and confirmed by our simulations) that increasing packet size (for the same number of bits transferred) results in a proportional increase in network contention. The good correspondence between the model and simulations for the various network types validates our packet size extension to the contention model. As stated before, the model's overestimation of latency for large packets results from our assumption of simultaneous message arrivals at a switch.

We also see that the network can be operated without significant loss of performance at higher capacities when the packet size is small (see Figs. 2 and 3). That is, smaller packets allow the network to be operated closer to the network's theoretical peak bandwidth, without significant degradation in latency. Conversely, for a given channel utilization, smaller messages result in lower latency (see Fig. 5). Kruskal and Snir's indirect network model predicted a similar dependence of latency on blocksize, prompting Norton and Pfister to consider splitting messages into multiple smaller ones in the RP3 [21]. However, splitting long messages into multiple smaller ones with back to back transmission may not realize the higher predicted throughput because of the destination correlation of these submessages and the relatively high packet overhead. The node must also be able to support multiple outstanding submessages in the network. We believe higher throughput might be achieved with splitting if some delay is introduced between sending the submessages at the source, or by randomizing the routes taken by the submessages. We are currently investigating the potential performance benefits of such methods.

The contention, switch, and wire delay components of the latency [from (2) and (10)] can be combined to yield the

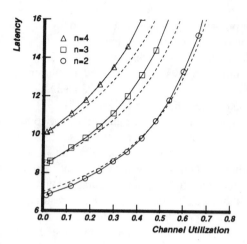

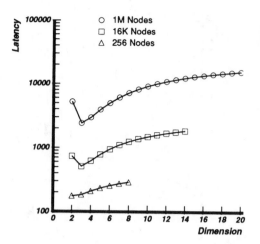

Fig. 4. Comparing the direct network model with simulations for small values of the radix. Radix $k = 4$, $B = 4$, and $n = 2, 3,$ and 4. Solid lines are measurements from a simulator, dashed lines correspond to predictions by the model.

Fig. 6. Latency for systems with 256, 16K, and 1M nodes assuming node to base wire delay ratio to be 4.0. Channel widths W are fixed at 8 bits. Message lengths (L/W) are assumed to be 20 flits.

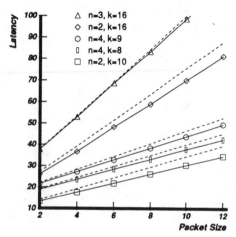

Fig. 5. Assessing the effect of packet size. Dashed lines correspond to model predictions. Channels are operated at a utilization of 0.4.

effective network delay:

$$T_c = T^w(2)\left(s + N^{\frac{1}{2} - \frac{1}{n}}\right)\left[nk_d(1+w) + \frac{L}{W}\right] \quad (12)$$

where w is contention delay per node.

IV. ANALYSIS OF BASE NETWORK LATENCY

The next three subsections analyze network performance using the base network latency (ignoring contention) with different constraints. To enable a comparison, the Appendix presents network latency results when node delays are ignored and bisection width is fixed. An analysis of networks including contention effects and communication locality will follow here. Our results assume $T^w(2)$ is normalized to 1.

A. Keeping Channel Widths Fixed

The base network latency T_b is derived using (2). Let us start with no constraints on the bisection width or node size to allow a constant channel width over networks of all dimensions [i.e.,

W is held constant in (2)]. Keeping channel widths fixed allows boundless system size increase for high dimensions and is impractical when the number of processors is large, but it allows us to reflect on fundamental constraints imposed by signal propagation delays alone.

We plot latency as a function of network dimension in Fig. 6 for several system sizes if switch delays also contribute to latency. Message length L/W is assumed to be 20 flits. Note that the Y axes in the graphs use a logarithmic scale and small relative differences in the curves can be significant. The graph in Fig. 6 shows that for 16K and 1M nodes, a three-dimensional topology is superior to a two-dimensional topology. This is in contrast to previous results in [7] where the linear wire delay model yielded the lowest latency for two-dimensional networks when the switch delay was ignored and the bisection width was held constant.

A more important point is that physical limitations favor low-dimensional networks, even when bisection width is unconstrained, because of the rapid increase in wire length as n is increased. If the number of dimensions is increased from n to $n + 1$ for the same total number of processors N, the wire length increases by a factor of $N^{\frac{1}{n(n+1)}}$.

Fig. 7(a) evaluates the effect of relative switch delay on network latency for 1M-node systems. As expected, the dimension of the best latency network shifts toward greater dimensions as the switch delay increases in proportion to the base wire delay. With zero switch delay, the two-dimensional network is indeed the best choice for message length L/W equal to 20 flits, with switch delays 2 through 8, the three-dimensional network is optimal, while a relative switch delay of 16 suggests that four dimensions are best.

Fig. 7(b) shows that larger message lengths favor networks with a lower dimensionality. The reason is that the number of hops in the latency equation becomes dominated by the message traversal time for long messages, making the gains because of fewer hops in a high-dimensional network less useful. Only when messages are exceedingly long (say, 3200 bits) does a two-dimensional network have the lowest latency.

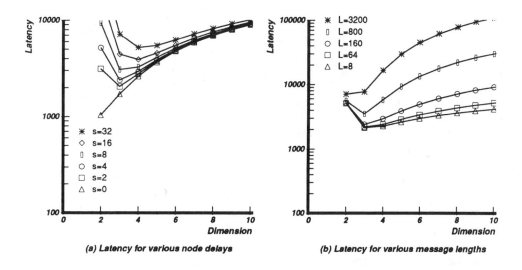

(a) Latency for various node delays   **(b) Latency for various message lengths**

Fig. 7.   Latency for 1M-node systems fixing only channel widths. (a) Varying node delays. Node to base wire delay ratio s ranging from 0 through 32. Message lengths (L/W) are assumed to be 20 flits. (b) Varying message lengths, with $s = 4.0$. Message lengths L/W range from 1 through 400 flits ($W = 8$).

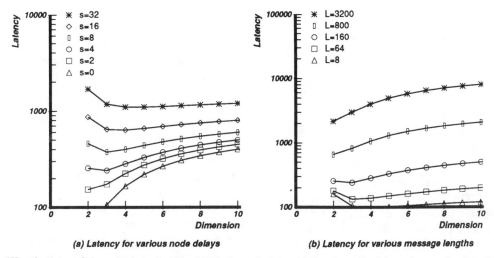

(a) Latency for various node delays   **(b) Latency for various message lengths**

Fig. 8.   Latency for 1K-node systems fixing only channel widths. (a) Varying node delays. Node to base wire delay ratio s ranging from 0 through 32. Message lengths (L/W) are assumed to be 20 flits. (b) Varying message lengths, with $s = 4.0$. Message lengths L/W range from 1 through 400 flits ($W = 8$).

The effect of switch delay and message length on networks with 1K nodes is shown in Fig. 8. For a fewer number of processors, the effect of wire delays is less pronounced when switch delays are greater than four times the wire delay. In this case, three-dimensional networks become favorable only when switch delays exceed 4. Most practical message lengths favor three-dimensional networks.

The analysis presented in this section made several different assumptions from those made in previous studies. First, we assumed that the bisection width is not a constraint. Second, we separately included switch delays and wire delays. Third, we explored the effect of smaller message sizes. Allowing greater bisection widths for networks with higher dimensions allowed the channel widths to remain the same for all network topologies. Modeling switch delays separately made the effect of longer wires less severe. Finally, we saw that smaller messages make the number of network hops traveled more significant in comparison with the pipeline delay of a message.

These inclusions tend to favor the choice of networks with higher dimensionality.

B. Keeping Bisection Width Fixed

In general, the bisection width cannot be increased arbitrarily. Because this width imposes bounds on the minimum layout area [29], allowable system size, switch node size, cost, and power considerations will limit this width. In such cases, the bisection width can be held constant at some limit, which directly affects the channel width and hence the average message length. The optimal value of n can then be derived.

For a fixed bisection size, channel widths become smaller with increasing n. We must also point out that if bisection width is a design constraint, then the *wire width* must surely be significant. For now, we do not model the increase in wire lengths as n is increased due to nonnegligible wire widths; we will touch on this issue later in this section.

The bisection width can be easily computed for a network with n dimensions and radix k. Adding an extra dimension to a network with $n-1$ dimensions requires the addition of an extra channel to each of the k^{n-1} nodes, which results in k^{n-1} channels in the highest dimension in the new n-dimensional network. These channels contribute to the bisection width. Thus, the bisection width for a k-ary n-cube with W-bit channels is $2Wk^{n-1}$ (the factor 2 accounts for the end-around channels). If N is the number of nodes, the bisection width is $2WN/k$. For example, in a linear array of processors, the bisection width is $2W$. The bisection width becomes $2Wk$ when each row of processors is replicated k times, and becomes $2Wk^2$ when this 2-D array is replicated k times for a 3-D network.

We will normalize bisection widths to that of a binary n-cube with unit-width channels. The bisection width of a binary n-cube with unit-width channels is N; consequently, the channel width W of a k-ary n-cube is derived as $k/2$. For example, in a 256 node system, if the binary 8-cube has unit-width channels, the corresponding mesh network ($n=2$) has $W=8$.

The normalization to the unit-channel-width binary n-cube is rather arbitrary, but it is easy to carry out a similar analysis using a different bisection width, obtained using some realistic cost constraint.

We derive the corresponding latency by substituting $W = k/2 = N^{\frac{1}{n}}/2$ in (2), as

$$T_b = T^w(2)\left(s + N^{\frac{1}{2}-\frac{1}{n}}\right)\left(n\frac{N^{\frac{1}{n}}-1}{2} + 2\frac{L}{N^{1/n}}\right).$$

Fig. 9 shows the latencies as a function of dimensions for various system sizes. The chief difference between the results here and those when the bisection is unconstrained is that the latency for large values of n is much larger, which results from smaller channel widths in addition to longer wire delays. As mentioned earlier, adding a network dimension with the same total number of nodes increases wire delays by a factor of $N^{\frac{1}{n(n+1)}}$, and increases message length in flits by the same factor. This result makes a stronger case for low-dimensional networks when bisection width is fixed.

The relative shapes of the curves for a 1M-node system with varying switch speed and message length (not shown here) are similar to those in Fig. 7. The primary result is that the network dimension that yields the minimum latency for various system sizes, switch-to-wire delays, and message lengths, is generally the same as the best dimension when the bisection width is not constrained.

The tradeoffs are slightly different in smaller systems. Fig. 10(a) and (b) analyzes latency for a 1K-node system with different switch-to-wire delays and message lengths, respectively. When bisection width is fixed, we see that the two-dimensional network is generally the best. In 1K-node systems, the relative impact of longer messages caused by narrowing channels is more significant than reducing the number of hops.

Our assumption in Section II-B of a fixed distance between physically-adjacent nodes implies that decreasing W does not

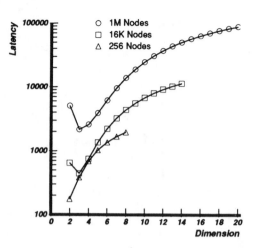

Fig. 9. Latency for systems with 256, 16K, and 1M nodes assuming node to base wire delay ratio s to be 4.0. Message lengths (L) are assumed to be 160 bits. Bisection is normalized to a binary n-cube with unit-width channels.

impact either the length of the longest wire or the switch delay. Alternatively, we can assume that the distance between adjacent nodes is proportional to the channel width W. In this context, let our normalization factor $T^w(2)$ represent the wire length in a unit-channel-width 2-D mesh network. Therefore, in a k-ary n-cube, the delay due to the longest wire is proportional to

$$WN^{\frac{1}{2}-\frac{1}{n}}.$$

Interestingly, with the above dependence on W, the length of the longest wire in a bisection-constrained network turns out to be a constant for all n. With the bisection normalized to a binary n-cube with $W=1$, the channel width can be written as $W = N^{\frac{1}{n}}/2$. The resulting wire delay is proportional to $N^{\frac{1}{2}}/2$, which is a constant for all n.

In this analysis, because bisection width is normalized to a binary n-cube, the channel widths of smaller-dimensional networks appear to be impractically large. Node size limitations will often be the constraining factor, and an analysis using pin-limited nodes is presented next.

C. Keeping Node Size Fixed

In practical systems, node sizes often constrain channel widths rather than bisection width. For example, pin limitations in VLSI switches allow channel widths of 8 or 16 bits for three-dimensional networks, with separate channels for each direction, or 16 or 32 bits without separate channels. This section fixes the total number of wires emanating from a switch. When n increases, for a fixed node size, the effective message length in flits increases because W must decrease.

Let us analyze networks with node sizes normalized to that of a 2-D mesh network with channel width $W = 32$. These widths yield 128 signal wires per node (not counting wires to the processor, power, and ground lines) assuming unidirectional channels. Such a node can be integrated into a single VLSI chip with current technology. The channel width of a n-dimensional network is then $W = 64/n$. As before, the default message length is 160 bits. Substituting in (2), the

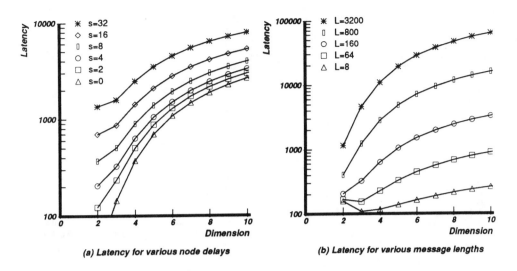

(a) Latency for various node delays   **(b) Latency for various message lengths**

s. 10. Latency for 1K-node systems fixing bisection width. Bisection width is normalized to a binary n-cube with unit channel width. (a) Varying node delays. Node to base wire delay ratio s ranging from 0 through 32. Message lengths (L) are fixed at 160 bits. (b) Varying message lengths, with $s = 4.0$. Message lengths range from 8 through 3200 bits.

base network latency becomes

$$T_b = T^w(2)\left(s + N^{\frac{1}{2}-\frac{1}{n}}\right)\left(n\frac{N^{\frac{1}{n}}-1}{2} + \frac{Ln}{64}\right).$$

The latency curves for various system sizes are similar in nature to those in Fig. 6 because W has a lower sensitivity to n, and because the normalization was done with respect to a 2-D mesh with $W = 32$. For the same reasons, the curves for various switch speeds and various message lengths are similar in nature to those in Figs. 7 and 8, respectively. That is, as switch speeds are increased from $s = 2$ to $s = 32$, the optimal n shifts from 2 to 4, and as message lengths are increased from 8 bits to 3200 bits, the most desirable value of n shifts from 3 to 2.

V. EFFECT OF NETWORK CONTENTION

This section explores the effect of the available network bandwidth in various networks using the contention model derived in Section III. We use the following constraints:

- ignore wire delays, with constant channel widths
- include wire delays, with constant channel widths
- include wire delays, with fixed bisection width
- include wire delays, with constant node size.

We consider networks with $N = 1K$ nodes, and $n = 2$, 3, 4, and 5. We assume switch delay $s = 4$, message length $L = 128$, and normalize channel widths to a network with $n = 2$ and $W = 32$.

When channel widths are held constant, low-dimensional networks have a smaller capacity than networks with more dimensions. Recall that channel utilization $\rho = m\frac{L}{W}k_d$ [from (7)]. The theoretical network-capacity limit is reached when the product of the request rate m and message size in flits L/W is $2/(k-1)$.

In general we found that the variability in network latency for different constraints is much greater than when network contention is ignored. Fig. 11(a) shows the effective network

latency when wire delay is ignored. As expected, the higher-dimensional networks have lower latencies for a given request rate. Clearly, the two-dimensional network lacks the bandwidth to support a request rate of more than about 0.015 (solving $mL/W = 2/(k-1)$, yields $m = 1/64$), while the three-dimensional network can support a request rate of up to about 0.05.

Fig. 11(b) shows the corresponding network latency when wire delays are included. Here we see that the performance of higher-dimensional networks is significantly hurt by wire delay. For low request rates, when bandwidth requirements do not dominate, networks with $n = 2$, 3, 4, and 5 perform similarly and are clearly superior to the two-dimensional network. Our base latency analysis yields similar conclusions (see Fig. 8).

Limiting the bisection width dramatically changes the relative standing of the low and high-dimensional networks. The constrained bisection results in narrower channels for higher dimensions, which not only increases the base latency, but also reduces the available network bandwidth. Fig. 11(c) shows the network latency when bisection is constrained, and when switch delays and wire delays are included. We normalize the bisections to that of a two-dimensional network with 32 bit channels. That is, $W = 32$ for $n = 2$ and $N = 1K$. This constraint is reflected in the value of the channel width W for the various networks. In (12), with the above bisection constraint, $W = k = N^{\frac{1}{n}}$. Thus, for a five-dimensional network $W = 8$, which yields 16-flit messages for $L = 128$. Here we see that the higher-dimensional networks suffer much higher delays, and we obtain results similar to those in [8]. With fixed bisection, the two-dimensional network outperforms the rest.

Fig. 11(d) plots network latency when the node size is fixed, and normalized to that of the two-dimensional network with $W = 32$. When node size is constrained, the two-dimensional network performs poorly at high loads (when $m > 0.01$) because it suffers significant contention; its performance is reasonable at low loads.

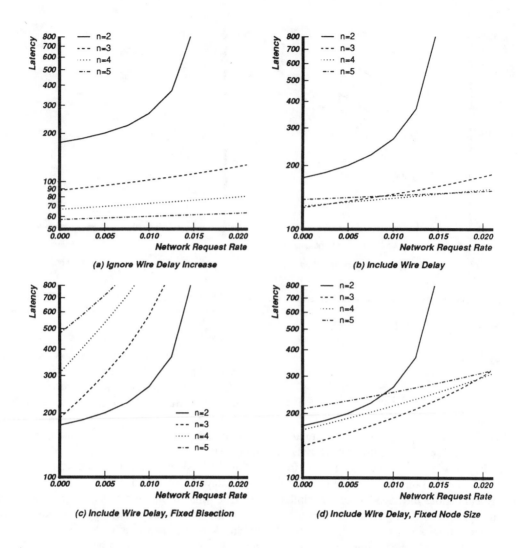

Fig. 11. Effect of contention on network latency with 1K nodes, $L = 128$, and $s = 4$. (a) Ignore increase in wire delay (assume unit wire delay), and $W = 32$. (b) Include wire delay $W = 32$. (c) Include wire delay and fix bisection (normalize to network with $n = 2$ and $W = 32$). (d) Include wire delay and fix node size (normalize to network with $n = 2$ and $W = 32$).

A. Communication Locality

Direct networks can take advantage of communication locality in parallel applications. Informally, we say that communication locality exists when the likelihood of communication (or access) to various nodes decreases with distance. Packets destined for neighboring nodes not only travel fewer hops, but also consume a smaller fraction of the network bandwidth. This section analyzes the effect of communication locality on network throughput and latency.

Our model can be easily extended to account for communication locality using the following simple locality model. Let us define the *locality fraction* l as the fraction of all processors that are potential candidates to receive a message from a source node. Furthermore, for a given source node, let message destinations be chosen randomly from the n-dimensional subcube with $N \times l$ processors centered at the source node. For example, let us consider an N-processor torus in which nodes are represented by their x and y coordinates. Given a locality fraction l, destination nodes for messages originating from source node (i, j) are randomly chosen from

the set of nodes with coordinates $(x | i \le x \le i + \sqrt{lN} - 1, \; y | j \le y \le j + \sqrt{lN} - 1)$. (Other forms of communication locality could also be realized by using some probability function to represent higher than average access likelihoods to nearby nodes, or to favor straight through paths over paths that require turns.)

With the above locality model, a packet travels an average distance of k_{dl} in each dimension, for a total of $n k_{dl}$ hops from source to destination. The average distance traversed in a dimension can be expressed as

$$k_{dl} = ((lN)^{1/n} - 1)/2 = (l^{1/n}k - 1)/2.$$

The average latency can be derived by replacing k_d in (10) with k_{dl}. The same substitution is necessary in (7) to compute ρ. Destinations chosen randomly over the entire machine correspond to $l = 1$.

Locality increases the effective throughput and decreases the latency of the network. The network reaches full capacity when all channels are fully utilized, that is, when $\rho = mBk_d = 1$ (although this ideal throughput is hard to achieve

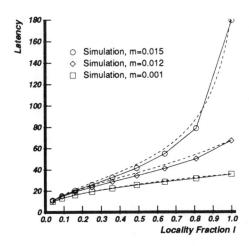

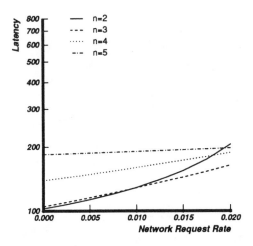

Fig. 12. Effect of communication bandwidth and latency reduction due to locality, with $N = 1K$, $n = 2$, $k = 32$, and $B = 4$. The locality fraction l is the fraction of all processors that can potentially receive a message from a given node. Dashed lines correspond to model predictions and points are taken from a simulator.

Fig. 13. Assessing the relative effect of communication locality on networks with various dimensions. Communication locality parameter $l = 0.3$, $N = 1K$ nodes, $L = 128$ bits, and $s = 4$. Include wire delay and fix node size (normalize to network with $n = 2$ and $W = 32$).

in practice owing to contention). The peak network throughput in messages per cycle per node is $1/Bk_d$, and is $1/k_d$ in flits per cycle per node. However, when communication locality exists, the throughput increases to $1/k_{dl}$ flits per cycle per node. Similarly, the base network latency of $nk_d + B$ hops decreases to $nk_{dl} + B$ when locality exists. In other words, locality increases throughput by a factor $1/l^{1/n}$, and decreases base network latency by the same factor (when $nk_d \gg B$).

Locality improves latency because it reduces both the number of hops per packet and average contention delays. As displayed in Fig. 12, with a light load of $m = 0.001$, latency reduction is largely due to the fewer number of hops. At light loads, latency is linearly related to k_{dl} or to $l^{1/n}$, which is clear from (10) when the contention component is ignored. For example, when $m = 0.001$, for a 1K-node machine ($n = 2$ and $k = 32$), the average latency for randomly selected destinations is roughly 35. When the average distance in a dimension decreases by 10% ($l^{1/2} = 0.9$), the latency decreases by the same fraction to 31.

The impact of locality is much more significant when contention is high. In this case, the latency reduction due to locality is largely due to a reduction in the bandwidth requirement. The latency at high loads is proportional to $1/(1 - mBk_{dl})$. For example, the average latency drops by over 25% (from 67 to 50) for the higher load of $m = 0.012$, when $l^{1/2} = 0.9$. Of this decrease, over 19% is due to the reduced bandwidth consumed, while less than 6% is due to the fewer number of hops. Thus, we see that communication locality has a much stronger effect on network performance through its reduction of bandwidth consumed than through its reduction of base network latency. The proportional impact of locality is even more significant at higher loads.

Communication locality makes low-dimensional networks more competitive with other networks. Although low-dimensional networks have shorter wires and smaller bisections, their lower available bandwidth and higher base latencies reduce their effectiveness. Locality mitigates these negative

aspects of low-dimensional networks by reducing the effective distance a message travels, consequently decreasing bandwidth requirements and the base latency. For example, compare the performance of the two-dimensional network relative to other networks in Fig. 13, which assumes a communication locality fraction of $l = 0.3$, with that in Fig. 11(d), which assumes no locality. We see that communication locality has a larger relative effect on the two-dimensional network.

B. Direct Versus Indirect Networks

In the past, shared-memory multiprocessors (e.g., the Ultra-computer [11], RP3 [23], Cedar [10], and BBN Butterfly) have generally employed indirect networks. These networks provide uniform-cost access to remote memory modules, and have a high bandwidth, but they do not allow the exploitation of locality in the communication patterns of parallel applications. Because they can exploit locality, distributed shared-memory multiprocessors based on direct networks can scale to a large number of processors for computations that exhibit locality.

This section compares the latency of direct networks with that of indirect networks under various constraints and workload conditions, for varying degrees of communication locality. Indirect networks for N processors are made up of n stages of $k \times k$ crossbar switches, where $N = k^n$. The indirect network forces each request to travel the n stages to its destination.

We will compare the latency of direct and indirect networks under a node-size constraint. The length of the longest wire in a planar mapping of an indirect network can be derived by noting that the indirect binary n-cube network is isomorphic to the direct binary n-cube [27]. The latency for an n-stage indirect network with $k \times k$ switches can be written as

$$T_c = \left\lceil n(1 + w) + \frac{L}{W} \right\rceil. \tag{13}$$

Kruskal and Snir [16] derived the contention delay w per switch stage for buffered indirect networks as[1]

---

[1] Kruskal, Snir, and Weiss derive more accurate formulas in [17], but this is sufficient for our purposes.

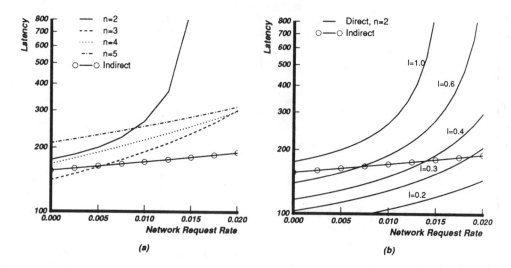

Fig. 14. Comparing direct network latency with indirect networks for 1K processors and message length $L = 128$. Switching node sizes normalized to direct network with $n = 2$ and $W = 32$. (a) No communication locality. (b) With communication locality, $n = 2$.

$$w = \frac{\rho B}{2(1-\rho)}\left(1 - \frac{1}{k}\right) \qquad (14)$$

where the message length in flits $B = L/W$ and the channel utilization $\rho = mB$. The derivation of the contention component in indirect networks differs from direct networks in the computation of $p(v)$, which is the distribution of the number of packets joining an output queue of a switch (see Section III). Because packets from k input ports in the indirect network are steered toward an output queue with equal probability, the distribution of $p(v)$ is binomial and results in a much simpler form of w [compare with the expression for w for direct networks in (8)]. Kruskal and Snir have validated this model for various networks and message rates; we verified the accuracy of this simple model for several packet sizes by comparing its predictions with simulations.

Let us analyze the latency of 1K-processor networks with $L = 128$ bits. Fig. 14(a) compares the latency of indirect networks with several direct networks as a function of network load. In this graph, the destinations are assumed to be randomly chosen. With 4×4 switches, ($k = 4$ and $n = 5$) the 1K-node indirect network has roughly the same number of switches as the direct network (1280 versus 1024) making a comparison based on pin constraints meaningful. The number of pins per switch is fixed at 128. Therefore, the torus network has $W = 32$ ($128/2n$), and the indirect network has $W = 16$ ($128/2k$).

When locality is not taken into account, the indirect network has the lowest latency and the highest bandwidth of all the networks shown. A three-dimensional direct network reaches saturation when the message rate $m = 2/B(k-1) = 0.037$ messages per cycle; the indirect network has a saturation message rate of $m = 1/B = 0.125$.

Direct networks can take advantage of communication locality. Fig. 14(b) compares the performance of the indirect network with a two-dimensional direct network for varying degrees of locality. Recall that locality reduces the number of potential destination nodes for a given source node by a frac-

tion l. The figure shows that the latencies of the two networks are comparable for low message rates when $l < 0.6$, and at high loads when $l < 0.3$. Thus, we see that communication locality can make low-dimensional direct networks perform as well as—or even better than—indirect networks, even though indirect networks have a greater bisection width.

VI. CONCLUSIONS

The performance of multiprocessor interconnection networks is influenced by switch delays and wire delays. This paper analyzed the relative effect of switch and wire delays under various constraints such as fixed bisection width, fixed channel widths, and fixed node sizes. We derived a simple model for contention in buffered direct networks and assessed its impact on network performance for the above constraints.

Under the constraint of constant wire density and constant bisection width, previous results for network embedding in a plane showed that a two-dimensional mesh yields the lowest latency. However, when node delays are taken into account, we showed that the best network has a moderately high dimension.

Message length plays an important role in the tradeoff between low and high-dimensional networks. Longer messages (such as those in message passing machines) make the relative effect of network distance from source to destination less important, while the lower expected message lengths in shared memory machines increase the relative influence of network distance, and tend to favor networks with more dimensions.

We introduced a contention model for buffered, direct networks to estimate the effect of network bandwidth. We validated the model through simulations, and demonstrated its robustness over a wide range of radices and dimensions. We evaluated the performance of networks including contention with constraints such as fixed bisection width and fixed node size. An interesting finding of this analysis is that the relative standing of networks is strongly dependent on the constraints chosen and on the expected workload parameters. In contrast, the results showed much less variance when bandwidth considerations were ignored. While it is true that lower-dimensional networks have a lower bandwidth than higher-dimensional networks, the higher-dimensional networks suffer when wire delays are included and the bisection size is constrained. However, when the less stringent limit of a fixed node size was applied, the situation is completely reversed: at low loads three-dimensional networks have the lowest latency, and at high loads four-dimensional networks are superior.

Direct networks can exploit communication locality; locality improves both network throughput and latency. At low loads, communication latency decreases linearly with the average distance traversed in each dimension. The relative decrease in latency is even more significant when network load is high, owing to a reduction in the bandwidth requirements of the application.

Communication locality enhances the attractiveness of low-dimensional networks. Although low-dimensional networks have shorter wires and smaller bisection widths than other networks, their lower available bandwidth and higher base latencies reduce their effectiveness. Locality mitigates these negative aspects of low-dimensional networks by reducing the effective distance a message travels, consequently decreasing bandwidth requirements and the base latency.

Communication locality depends on several factors including the architecture of the multiprocessor, the compiler and run-time systems, and the characteristics of parallel applications. If the communication locality of parallel applications can be enhanced through better algorithms and systems architectures, parallel machines with significantly higher performance can be built without incurring the high cost of expensive networks.

APPENDIX
KEEPING BISECTION WIDTH FIXED AND IGNORING NODE DELAYS

The analysis in this section keeps bisection width fixed, and assumes node delay is zero, as in [7]. Graphs are presented here for comparison with the case when switch delays are significant. With bisection width normalized to that of a binary n-cube with $W = 1$, the latency is given by

$$T_b = T^w(2)N^{\frac{1}{2} - \frac{1}{n}}\left(n\frac{N^{\frac{1}{n}} - 1}{2} + \frac{2L}{N^{1/n}}\right).$$

Figs. 15 and 16 compare latencies for various system sizes and various message lengths, respectively, when switch delays are insignificant. It is clear that ignoring node delays favors low-dimensional networks.

ACKNOWLEDGMENT

My gratitude to B. Dally, K. MacKenzie, G. Maa, S. Ward, T. Knight, D. Nussbaum, T. Leighton, and C. Leiserson for all the interesting discussions that fueled this research. I would also like to thank the referees for their constructive suggestions. D. Chaiken, B. Dally, B.-H. Lim, K. Johnson, and P. Nuth provided feedback on a draft of this paper. G. Maa wrote the Alewife network simulator and helped validate the network model.

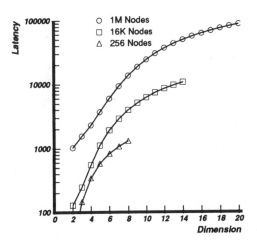

Fig. 15. Latency for systems with 256, 16K, and 1M nodes assuming zero node delay ($s = 0$). Message lengths (L) are assumed to be 160 bits. Bisection width is normalized to a binary n-cube with unit-width channels.

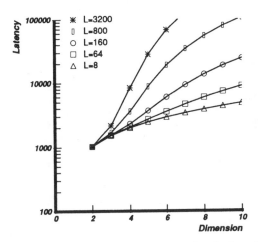

Fig. 16. Latency for 1M node systems with message lengths L ranging from 8 through 3200 bits. Bisection width is normalized to a binary n-cube with unit-width channels.

REFERENCES

[1] S. Abraham and K. Padmanabhan, "Performance of the direct binary n-cube network for multiprocessors," *IEEE Trans. Comput.*, vol. 38, pp. 1000–1011, July 1989.

[2] A. Agarwal, B.-H. Lim, D. A. Kranz, and J. Kubiatowicz, "APRIL: A processor architecture for multiprocessing," in *Proc. 17th Annu. Int. Symp. Comput. Architecture*, June 1990, pp. 104–114.

[3] W. C. Athas and C. L. Seitz, "Multicomputers: Message-passing concurrent computers," *IEEE Comput. Mag.*, vol. 21, pp. 9–24, Aug. 1988.

[4] S. Borkar *et al.*, "iWarp: An integrated solution to high-speed parallel computing," in *Proc. Supercomput. '88*, Nov. 1988.

[5] D. Chaiken, C. Fields, K. Kurihara, and A. Agarwal, "Directory-based cache-coherence in large-scale multiprocessors," *IEEE Comput. Mag.*, vol. 23, pp. 41–58, June 1990.

[6] D. Chaiken, J. Kubiatowicz, and A. Agarwal, "LimitLESS directories: A scalable cache coherence scheme," in *Proc. Fourth Int. Conf. Architectural Support for Programming Languages Oper. Syst. (ASPLOS IV)*, ACM, Apr. 1991.

[7] W. J. Dally, *A VLSI Architecture for Concurrent Data Structures.* New York: Kluwer, 1987.

[8] ———, "Performance analysis of k-ary n-cube interconnection networks," *IEEE Trans. Comput.*, vol. 39, pp. 775–785, June 1990.

[9] W. J. Dally *et al.*, "The J-Machine: A fine-grain concurrent computer," in *Proc. IFIP Congress*, 1989.

[10] D. Gajski, D. Kuck, D. Lawrie, and A. Saleh, "Cedar—A large scale multiprocessor," in *Proc. Int. Conf. Parallel Processing*, Aug. 1983, pp. 524–529.

[11] A. Gottlieb, R. Grishman, C. P. Kruskal, K. P. McAuliffe, L. Rudolph, and M. Snir, "The NYU Ultracomputer—Designing a MIMD shared-memory parallel machine," *IEEE Trans. Comput.*, vol. C-32, pp. 175–189, Feb. 1983.

[12] R. Halstead and S. Ward, "The MuNet: A scalable decentralized architecture for parallel computation," in *Proc. 7th Annu. Symp. Comput. Architecture*, May 1980, pp. 139–145.

[13] W. D. Hillis, *The Connection Machine.* Cambridge, MA: M.I.T. Press, 1985.

[14] P. Kermani and L. Kleinrock, "Virtual cut-through: A new computer communication switching technique," *Comput. Networks*, vol. 3, pp. 267–286, Oct. 1979.

[15] L. Kleinrock, *Queueing Systems.* New York: Wiley, 1975.

[16] C. P. Kruskal and M. Snir, "The performance of multistage interconnection networks for multiprocessors," *IEEE Trans. Comput.*, vol. C-32, pp. 1091–1098, Dec. 1983.

[17] C. P. Kruskal, M. Snir, and A. Weiss, "The distribution of waiting times in clocked multistage interconnection networks," *IEEE Trans. Comput.*, vol. 37, pp. 1337–1352, Nov. 1988.

[18] J. T. Kuehn and B. J. Smith, "The HORIZON supercomputing system: Architecture and software," in *Proc. Supercomputing '88*, Nov. 1988.

[19] D. H. Lawrie, "Access and alignment of data in an array processor," *IEEE Trans. Comput.*, vol. C-24, pp. 1145–1155, Dec. 1975.

[20] D. Lenoski, J. Laudon, K. Gharachorloo, A. Gupta, J. Hennessy, M. Horowitz, and M. Lam, "Design of the Stanford DASH multiprocessor," Comput. Syst. Lab. TR 89-403, Stanford Univ., Dec. 1989.

[21] A. Norton and G. F. Pfister, "A methodology for predicting multiprocessor performance," in *Proc. ICPP*, Aug. 1985, pp. 772–781.

[22] J. H. Patel, "Performance of processor–memory interconnections for multiprocessors," *IEEE Trans. Comput.*, vol. C-30, pp. 771–780, Oct. 1981.

[23] G. F. Pfister, W. C. Brantley, D. A. George, S. L. Harvey, W. J. Kleinfelder, K. P. McAuliffe, E. A. Melton, A. Norton, and J. Weiss, "TheIBM Research Parallel Processor Prototype (RP3): Introduction and architecture," in *Proc. ICPP*, Aug. 1985, pp. 764–771.

[24] C. L. Seitz, "Concurrent VLSI architectures," *IEEE Trans. Comput.*, vol. C-33, pp. 1247–1265, Dec. 1984.

[25] ——, "The Cosmic Cube," *Commun. ACM*, vol. 28, no. 1, pp. 22–33, Jan. 1985.

[26] C. L. Seitz *et al.*, "The architecture and programming of the Ametek Series 2010 multicomputer," in *Proc. Third Conf. Hypercube Concurrent Comput. and Appl.*, Jan. 1988.

[27] H. J. Siegel, *Interconnection Networks for Large-Scale Parallel Processing*, 2nd ed. New York: McGraw-Hill, 1990.

[28] H. Sullivan and T. R. Bashkow, "A large scale, homogeneous, fully distributed parallel machine," in *Proc. 4th Annu. Symp. Comput. Architecture*, Mar. 1977, pp. 105–117.

[29] C. D. Thompson, "A complexity theory for VLSI," Ph.D. dissertation, Dep. Comput. Sci., Carnegie-Mellon Univ., 1980.

Anant Agarwal (S'83–M'89) received the B.Tech. degree in electrical engineering from the Indian Institute of Technology, Madras, in 1982, and the M.S. and Ph.D. degrees in electrical engineering from Stanford University, Stanford, CA, in 1984 and 1987, respectively.

Since January 1988, he has been with the Laboratory for Computer Science at the Massachusetts Institute of Technology, Cambridge, as an Assistant Professor of Electrical Engineering and Computer Science. At Stanford, he participated in the MIPS and MIPS-X projects. He initiated the ALEWIFE project at M.I.T., which is aimed at the design and implementation of a large-scale cache-coherent multiprocessor. His current research interests include the design of scalable multiprocessor systems, VLSI processors, compilation and run-time technologies for parallel processing, and performance evaluation.

On Multidimensional
Arrays of Processors

MIKHAIL J. ATALLAH

Abstract—We investigate the relationship between an arbitrary d-dimensional mesh of n processors, and one all of whose dimensions have equal length. We give asymptotically optimal simulation algorithms between these two models.

Index Terms—Analysis of algorithms, graph embeddings, mesh-connected processor arrays, parallel computation, simulations

I. Introduction

The d-dimensional mesh of processors is one of the most popular models of parallel computation, and researchers have designed an impressive number of algorithms for solving various problems on this

Manuscript received August 12, 1985; revised November 14, 1986. This work was supported by the Office of Naval Research under Grants N00014-84-K-0502 and N00014-86-K-0689, and the National Science Foundation under Grant DCR-8451393, with matching funds from AT&T.

The author is with the Department of Computer Sciences, Purdue University, West Lafayette, IN 47907.

IEEE Log Number 8717707.

Reprinted from *IEEE Trans. Computers,* Vol. 37, No. 10, Oct. 1988, pp. 1306-1309. Copyright © 1988 by The Institute of Electrical and Electronics Engineers, Inc. All rights reserved.

model (e.g., [1], [2], [5]–[9], see [10] for a more complete bibliography). Most of these algorithms were designed for a mesh all of whose d dimensions have equal length, i.e., a d-dimensional cube (for convenience, we henceforth say that such a mesh is *square*, even when $d > 2$). Note that every side of such a square mesh has length $n^{1/d}$. (The known algorithms for a square mesh typically run in $O(n^{1/d})$ time.) A d-dimensional mesh which is not square is said to be *rectangular*. Rectangular meshes occur quite naturally in a number of settings. In [2], we ended up working with rectangular meshes even though we started out initially with a square one (this happened because we could not fit our subproblems into subsquares of the original square, and we had to settle for "packing" them into rectangular submeshes of the original square mesh). Also note that a $(d - k)$-dimensional square mesh is just a special case of a d-dimensional rectangular mesh, one where k of the dimensions have length 1 and the remaining $d - k$ dimensions have equal length.

The purpose of this paper is to investigate the relationship between a rectangular mesh and a square one. In the rest of this section, we introduce some terminology, state our results and discuss their significance, and (at the end of the section) briefly review the definition of the d-dimensional mesh. We leave the simulation algorithms that prove our results for Sections II and III. Section IV concludes.

Definition 1.1: Throughout this paper, when a mesh U can simulate every step of another mesh W with $O(h)$ of its own steps, then we say that U h-*simulates* W.

Note that if U h-simulates W, then any problem that W solves in time T can be solved by U in time $O(h \cdot T)$.

Definition 1.2: Throughout this paper, S will denote a square d-dimensional mesh of n processors, i.e., S is an $n^{1/d} \times \cdots \times n^{1/d}$ mesh. R will denote a rectangular d-dimensional mesh of n processors, i.e., R is an $l_1 \times l_2 \times \cdots \times l_d$ mesh where $\prod_{i=1}^{d} l_i = n$. The dimension d is assumed to be a constant, i.e., $d = O(1)$.

Theorem 1: Mesh R can $(\max_i l_i)/n^{1/d}$-simulate mesh S.

(The proof of the above theorem is given in Section II of this paper.)

Corollary 1.1: Any problem which S solves in time T can be solved by R in time $O(T \cdot (\max_i l_i)/n^{1/d})$.

Note that if S solves a certain problem in time $O(n^{1/d})$, then the above result implies that R can solve that same problem in time $O(\max_i l_i)$. This shows that Theorem 1 is essentially optimal, since any nontrivial computation on R requires $\Omega(\max_i l_i)$ time.

Except for the trivial case of $d = 2$, we find it quite surprising that only the largest of the l_i's is relevant to how well R simulates S.

The next corollary is obtained from Theorem 1 by setting $l_1 = l_2 = \cdots = l_{d-k} = n^{1/(d-k)}$ and $l_{d-k+1} = \cdots = l_d = 1$.

Corollary 1.2: An n-processor $(d - k)$-dimensional square mesh can $n^{k/d(d-k)}$-simulate an n-processor d-dimensional square mesh.

The simulation result of Theorem 1 is quite useful because it allows us to avoid designing algorithms for rectangular meshes and concentrate on designing algorithms for square meshes instead, a much more pleasant task (designing algorithms for rectangular meshes can be quite awkward, especially recursive algorithms where we want each of the "quadrants" to recursively solve a smaller subproblem). Probably the best way to design an $O(\max_i l_i)$ time algorithm running on R is to actually first design an $O(n^{1/d})$ time algorithm running on S and then use Theorem 1. (In general, algorithm designers prefer square meshes where $n^{1/d}$ is a power of two.)

Of course, our result also implies that all the known algorithms for a square mesh immediately imply corresponding algorithms for rectangular meshes of various shapes. We therefore automatically have $O(\max_i l_i)$ time algorithms for solving a large number of problems on rectangular mesh R.

Finally, it is natural to consider the simulation of rectangular mesh R by square mesh S. The next theorem settles this issue.

Theorem 2: Mesh S can 1-simulate mesh R.

(The proof of the above theorem is given in Section III of this paper.)

In other words, whatever the problem being solved, S is at least as good as R. The optimality of Theorem 2 can best be seen by noting that there are problems whose time complexity is $\Theta(n)$ on both mesh S and mesh R. One such problem is that of computing $a_1 \oplus (a_2 \oplus (\cdots \oplus (a_n))) \cdots)$ where $\oplus$ is not associative. This last example shows that it is impossible to guarantee that S will be faster than R for *all* problems; however, it does not rule out that S will be faster for *some* problems.

To make the paper self-contained, we end this section by reviewing the definition of a d-dimensional mesh of processors (the reader familiar with this model should skip this and go directly to Section II). The processors, which operate synchronously, are positioned on an $l_1 \times \cdots \times l_d$ grid, one processor per grid point. A processor is denoted by its position in the grid, e.g., processor $(i_1, \cdots, i_d)$ where $1 \leq i_k \leq l_k$ for every $k \in \{1, \cdots, d\}$. Processor $(i_1, \cdots, i_d)$ is a *neighbor* of processor $(j_1, \cdots, j_d)$ if and only if, for some $k \in \{1, \cdots, d\}$, we have $|i_k - j_k| = 1$, and $i_s = j_s$ for every $s \neq k$. We then say that these two processors are *neighbors along dimension k*. Note that a processor can have no more than $2d$ neighbors (processors at the boundary have less). A *step* of such a mesh consists either of each processor communicating with a neighbor by sending/receiving the contents of a register (a *data movement* step), or of each processor performing a computation within its own registers (a *computation* step). A *data movement* is a sequence of one or more data movement steps. A processor has a fixed [i.e., $O(1)$] number of storage registers. Some papers in the literature assume that a register can store up to $\log n$ bits, while other papers limit the size of a register to $O(1)$ bits: our results hold for either model.

II. PROOF OF THEOREM 1

Recall that we want to prove that R can $(\max_i l_i)/n^{1/d}$-simulate S, where S and R are as in Definition 1.2. Before giving the proof of this, we need the following two rather straightforward lemmas.

Lemma 2.1: Let U be a $u_1 \times \cdots \times u_d$ mesh of n processors, and let W be a $(d - 1)$-dimensional n-processor mesh which is obtained from U by replacing two of the dimensions of U by a dimension whose length is the product of their two lengths, while leaving the other $d - 2$ dimensions of U unchanged. In other words W is a $u_1 \times \cdots \times u_{d-2} \times (u_{d-1} \cdot u_d)$ mesh (we chose to multiply u_{d-1} and u_d purely for notational convenience, and we could have chosen any u_i and u_j instead). Then U can 1-simulate W.

Proof: Fig. 1 illustrates, for the case $d = 3$, how the new dimension in W [Fig. 1(a)] is 1-simulated by the two old ones in U [Fig. 1(b)]: we just embed linear chains of length $l_2 \cdot l_3$ (in W) into $l_2 \times l_3$ rectangles (in U), by "snaking" them as depicted in Fig. 1 (in that figure there are actually l_1 such chains, even though only one is shown). In general, there would be $l_1 \cdot l_2 \cdots l_{d-2}$ such chains, each of which is of length $l_{d-1} \cdot l_d$ and is snaked in an $l_{d-1} \times l_d$ rectangle. $\square$

The previous lemma will be used in the inductive step of the proof of Theorem 1. The next lemma provides the basis for the induction.

Lemma 2.2: Let U be an $l_1 \times l_2$ mesh of n processors. Let W be a $\sqrt{n} \times \sqrt{n}$ mesh. Then U can $\max(l_1, l_2)/\sqrt{n}$-simulate W.

Proof: Without loss of generality, assume that $l_1 \geq \sqrt{n} \geq l_2$. Think of W as consisting of $\sqrt{n}$ adjacent columns of length $\sqrt{n}$ each [see Fig. 2(a)].

Now, snake these columns one after the other in U, as depicted in Fig. 2(b). Note that each such snaked column occupies a width of $\sqrt{n}/l_2$ ($= l_1/\sqrt{n}$) along the l_1 direction of U (see the note following this proof). A data movement step between adjacent processors in the same column of W can clearly be simulated in $O(1)$ steps on U. It is trivial to design a data movement taking $O(l_1/\sqrt{n})$ on U and which simulates a data movement step between adjacent processors on the same row of W. $\square$

Note: In the above proof, it may seem at first glance that we might run out of space in U before having embedded all of W, because $l_1/\sqrt{n}$ is generally not an integer and therefore some columns of U are only partially used [see Fig. 2(b)]. This poses no problem since we can then "bounce back" at the last column of U and start embedding backward (i.e., right to left) until we have embedded all of W. This

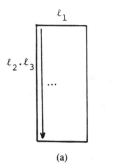

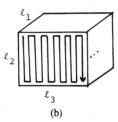

Fig. 1. Illustrating how a column of W is embedded into U. (a) W. (b) U.

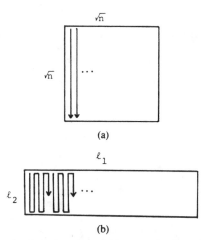

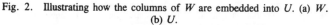

Fig. 2. Illustrating how the columns of W are embedded into U. (a) W. (b) U.

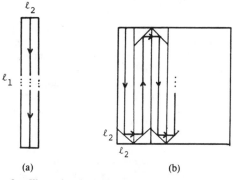

Fig. 3. Illustrating the basis of the induction. (a) R. (b) S.

may result in some processors of U having to simulate two processors of W, but this is acceptable. Actually, Definition 1.1 implies that we can "stretch" the dimensions of a mesh by a constant factor without changing its computational power (in the O sense), i.e., an $l_1 \times l_2$ mesh and a $(c \cdot l_1) \times l_2$ mesh can 1-simulate each other if c is a constant. In the rest of the paper, we avoid elaborating on such fine details, and concentrate on conveying to the reader the main ideas.

The above lemma (2.2) was so easy because choosing l_1 automatically determines l_2. This is no longer the case for $d \geq 3$, so the above proof does not directly generalize to higher dimensions. Instead we have to use induction on d, with Lemma 2.2 providing us with the basis of our induction. The rest of this section gives the inductive step of the proof of Theorem 1.

Inductive Step: Without loss of generality, assume that R is such that $l_1 \geq l_2 \geq \cdots \geq l_d$. Note that $l_1 \geq n^{1/d} \geq l_d$. Now, divide R along its first dimension into $n^{1/d}$ consecutive submeshes (which we call R *chunks*) each of which is an $(l_1/n^{1/d}) \times l_2 \times \cdots \times l_d$ mesh of $n^{1-1/d}$ processors. Similarly divide S along (say) its first dimension into $n^{1/d}$ submeshes (which we call S *chunks*) each of which is a $1 \times n^{1/d} \times \cdots \times n^{1/d}$ mesh of $n^{1-1/d}$ processors. From here on we ignore the first dimension (of length 1) of an S chunk, i.e., we consider it to be a $(d-1)$-dimensional square mesh of $n^{1-1/d}$ processors. Now, use each R chunk to simulate an S chunk. Of course, for this simulation, the S chunks are assigned to the R chunks in consecutive order. Before continuing with how an R chunk simulates an S chunk, let us pause to observe that two processors of S that are neighbors along S's first dimension are in two consecutive S chunks, and that one data movement step in S between such processors can be simulated in R by a data movement taking time O (width of an R chunk along its first dimension), i.e., $O(l_1/n^{1/d})$ (as in Lemma 2.2, we omit the detailed specification of this easy data movement). We still need to show that a data movement step of S along its second, or third, $\cdots$, or dth dimension, can also be simulated by $O(l_1/n^{1/d})$ steps of R. Since each such data movement is between processors in the same S chunk, it suffices to show that an

R chunk can $l_1/n^{1/d}$ simulate an S chunk. We cannot yet use the induction hypothesis because S chunks are $(d-1)$ dimensional while R chunks are d dimensional. This is where Lemma 2.1 comes in. Let C be an $(l_d \cdot l_1/n^{1/d}) \times l_2 \times \cdots \times l_{d-1}$ mesh, and observe that (by Lemma 2.1) an R chunk can 1-simulate C. Therefore, it suffices to show that C can $l_1/n^{1/d}$-simulate an S chunk. But C and an S chunk satisfy the induction hypothesis, and therefore C can max $(l_1 \cdot l_d/n^{2/d}, l_2/n^{1/d})$ simulate an S chunk. If $l_2/n^{1/d} \geq l_1 \cdot l_d/n^{2/d}$ then C can $l_2/n^{1/d}$-simulate an S chunk, and since $l_1 \geq l_2$ it follows that C can $l_1/n^{1/d}$-simulate an S chunk. If, on the other hand, $l_2/n^{1/d} < l_1 \cdot l_d/n^{2/d}$, then C can $l_1 \cdot l_d/n^{2/d}$ simulate an S chunk. Since $l_d/n^{1/d} \leq 1$, this implies that C can $l_1/n^{1/d}$ simulate an S chunk. $\qquad \square$

This completes the proof of Theorem 1.

III. PROOF OF THEOREM 2

Recall that we want to prove that S can 1-simulate R, where S and R are as in Definition 1.2. The proof is by induction on d. Throughout the proof, we assume, without loss of generality, that $l_1 \geq l_2 \geq \cdots \geq l_d$.

Basis of Induction: If $d = 2$, then embed R in S as follows. Partition S into $\sqrt{n}/l_2 (= l_1/\sqrt{n})$ rectangular slabs of dimensions $l_2 \times \sqrt{n}$ each, and then snake R through these slabs in the manner depicted in Fig. 3. Note that because of the way R moves from one slab of S to the next, some of the processors of S are idle (those in the empty triangular regions), while other processors of S are each simulating two of R's processors. It is obvious that this embedding enables S to simulate one step of R with $O(1)$ of its own steps. *Note:* The basis of the induction also follows from [3].

Inductive Step: Think of l_1 as being the *depth* of R, and $l_2 \times \cdots \times l_d$ as being its *base*. Let θ be the number of processors of R's base, i.e., $\theta = \Pi_{i=2}^{d} l_i (= n/l_1)$. Observe that $\theta \leq n^{1-1/d}$. Partition the $(d-1)$-dimensional, $n^{1-1/d}$-processor square determined by the last $d-1$ dimensions of S into $n^{1-1/d}/\theta$ $(d-1)$-dimensional squares of θ processors each. Fig. 4 illustrates for the case $d = 3$.

This partition induces a partition of S itself into $n^{1-1/d}/\theta$ rectangular *slabs* each having a depth of $n^{1/d}$ along S's first dimension, and a $(d-1)$-dimensional square base of θ processors (i.e., each slab is an $n^{1/d} \times \theta^{1/(d-1)} \times \cdots \times \theta^{1/(d-1)}$ rectangle). Now, embed the base of R into the base of a "corner" slab in S [e.g.,

451

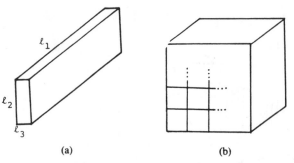

Fig. 4. The small $\sqrt{l_2 \cdot l_3} \times \sqrt{l_2 \cdot l_3}$ squares in (b) are the bases of the slabs. (a) R. (b) S.

into the lowest leftmost small square in Fig. 4(b)]. By the induction hypothesis, this can be done such that the base of the slab 1-simulates the base of R. Next, with its own base embedded in that of a slab, snake R back and forth through the slabs of S until it is completely embedded in S. We do not elaborate on this since it is an obvious generalization of the snaking done in Fig. 3(b). However, there is one point worth mentioning about the above embedding process. It is crucial that the depth of a slab ($= n^{1/d}$) is no smaller than the length of a base's side ($= \theta^{1/(d-1)}$) in order for R to shift smoothly from one slab to another (this condition was satisfied in Fig. 3(b) since we had $l_2 \leq \sqrt{n}$). A data movement step in R along its first dimension can obviously be simulated in $O(1)$ time in S. A data movement step along any of the remaining $d - 1$ dimensions of R can also be simulated in $O(1)$ time in S, because (by the induction hypothesis) the base of a slab can 1-simulate the base of R. □

IV. CONCLUDING REMARKS

We gave essentially optimal simulation results between an n-processor, d-dimensional mesh which is square and one which is rectangular. As corollaries to our results, we obtained simulations between d-dimensional square meshes and $(d - k)$-dimensional square meshes.

In general, simulation results between various networks of processors are not only interesting but also quite useful, since they enable us to design algorithms on the network we feel more comfortable with (e.g., the square mesh) in spite of the fact that the actual machine on which these algorithms will run is different (e.g., a rectangular mesh). In collaboration with S. R. Kosaraju, we have recently discovered new, more general simulation results (preliminary results of this ongoing research can be found in [4]).

REFERENCES

[1] M. J. Atallah and S. R. Kosaraju, "Graph problems on a mesh-connected processor array," *J. ACM*, vol. 31, pp. 649–667, July 1984.
[2] M. J. Atallah and S. E. Hambrusch, "Solving tree problems on a mesh-connected processor array," in *Proc. 26th Annu. IEEE Symp. Foundations Comput. Sci. (FOCS)*, Portland, OR, Oct. 1985, pp. 222–231; *Inform. Contr.*, vol. 69, pp. 168–187, 1986.
[3] R. Aleliunas and A. L. Rosenberg, "On embedding rectangular grids in square grids," *IEEE Trans. Comput.*, vol. C-31, pp. 907–913, Sept. 1982.
[4] S. R. Kosaraju and M. J. Atallah, "Optimal simulations between mesh-connected arrays of processors," Purdue CS Tech. Rep. 561 (a preliminary version appeared in *Proc. 18th Annu. ACM Symp. Theory Comput.*, Berkeley, CA, May 1986, pp. 264–272).
[5] S. R. Kosaraju, "Speed of recognition of context-free languages by array automata," *SIAM J. Comput.*, pp. 331–340, Sept. 1975.
[6] ——, "Fast parallel processing array algorithms for some graph problems," in *Proc. 11th Annu. ACM Symp. Theory Comput.*, 1979, pp. 231–236.
[7] D. Nassimi and S. Sahni, "Finding connected components and connected ones on a mesh-connected parallel computer," *SIAM J. Comput.*, pp. 744–757, 1980.
[8] ——, "Data broadcasting in SIMD computers," *IEEE Trans. Comput.*, pp. 101–106, 1981.
[9] C. Thompson and H. Kung, "Sorting on a mesh-connected parallel computer," *Commun. ACM*, pp. 263–271, 1977.
[10] J. D. Ullman, *Computational Aspects of VLSI.* Rockville, MD: Computer Science Press, 1984.

Communications Overhead and the Expected Speedup of Multidimensional Mesh-Connected Parallel Processors

Isaac D. Scherson and Peter F. Corbett

Department of Electrical Engineering, Princeton University, Princeton, New Jersey 08540

Incorporation of the effects of communications overhead in an expression for the maximum expected speedup of a parallel processing system provides a more accurate indication of potential system performance and considers both architectural and algorithmic effects. The measure of communications overhead in parallel processing systems is defined as a function of the algorithm and the architecture. Its dependence on the topology of the interconnection network is illustrated by computation of communication overhead and maximum speedup in an n^k-processor mesh-connected system with and without wraparound. The binary hypercube is a typical example ($n = 2$). The derived expression is applied to reported parallel algorithm results.

© 1991 Academic Press, Inc.

1. INTRODUCTION

The question of how much speedup is achievable in parallel processing systems is of interest as more and larger parallel processing systems are proposed and built. With a few exceptions, it is conceded that even linear speedup is difficult or impossible to obtain. It is rare to find practical applications which exhibit speedups close to N in an N-processor system. A primary cause of this loss of possible speedup is accounted for in Amdahl's law [1], which describes the limits on expected speedup in a system where part of the problem is inherently sequential.

That Amdahl's law is insufficient as an evaluation or even as a bound on performance is evident from the existence of parallel systems giving speedups greater than N. These superunitary speedups fall into several categories as described by Helmbold and McDowell [7]. The first is the demonstration of superunitary speedups on actual systems or in detailed system simulations. Here, the higher speedup is due to the effects of some factors not considered by Amdahl's law, such as memory size and paging requirements [11, 13]. The second category is superunitary speedups in the expected running time of parallel copies of randomized algorithms to solve NP-hard problems [12, 16]. Finally, constraining the sequential algorithm to a nonoptimal form may yield superunitary speedup under some conditions [10]. In all cases, the basic assumptions of Amdahl's law are violated. These assumptions are that the total amount of processing remains constant with the number of processors, and that at all times either the serial portion of the algorithm or the parallel portion of the algorithm is being executed.

Recently, a group of researchers at the Sandia National Laboratories reported speedups close to N for practical problems in a 1024-element hypercube [4]. In that article, the author suggested that Amdahl's law be recast to reflect the scaling of the problem to the architecture as opposed to the scaling of the architecture to the problem. In a recent letter to *Communications of the ACM* [6], Heath and Worley further discuss this issue. Both Amdahl's and Gustafson's formulations are sound. However, they are both overly simplistic in that they do not account for several factors which impose limits on the expected speedup of parallel processing systems. Significant among these factors is the communications overhead incurred when a number of processors need to communicate during the execution of an algorithm. Worley provides substantial insight into the problem in a thorough discussion comparing speedup for three common scientific problems using three different constraints [17, 18]. One is the fixed problem size constraint, which corresponds to Amdahl's law. The other two constraints that he applies are useful to formulate scaled speedup results. These constraints are fixed execution time and fixed memory per processor.

To examine the effects of communications overhead in a parallel processing system, we must first make some assumptions about the type of system with which we are dealing. In this paper, discussion focuses on those multiprocessors that consist of many homogeneous processors connected to each other by a point-to-point interconnection network. Communication is by message passing between adjacent processors. In general, the interconnection network among the processors will not be complete, but all processor pairs will be able to communicate by sending messages via as many intermediate processors as necessary.

Following Hoshino's formulation for the classes of problems suitable for implementation in a parallel processing environment [9] (also in [15]), we distinguish two main modes of computation, namely the continuum mode and the particle mode. In the former, data transfers occur between

"Communications Overhead and the Expected Speedup of Multidimensional Mesh-Connected Parallel Processors" by I.D. Scherson and P.F. Corbett from *J. Parallel and Distributed Computing*, Vol. 11, 1991, pp. 86-96. Copyright © 1991 by Academic Press, Inc., reprinted with permission.

nearest neighbors in the processor network, while in the latter, data transfers may occur between distant nodes. Nearest neighbors can be defined as two nodes which can exchange information in one basic communication step of the interconnection network. These modes of computation are a result of the mapping of problems and parallel algorithms onto the processor network. A problem that requires data transfers between distant particles may cause a significant decrease in multiprocessor performance. An object of this paper is to measure the communications overhead in the parallel solution of particle problems for a class of parallel processing architectures. For continuum problems, the communications overhead may not be as significant. It also should be noted that while a problem may map adjacent calculations into adjacent processors in one system, thus behaving according to the continuum model, it may also map into distant processors in a system with less extensive interconnections, thus behaving as a particle problem. An example is the one-dimensional elliptic problem reported by Worley [18].

In this paper, we first incorporate a communications overhead factor into an expression for the maximum expected speedup of multiprocessors on the basis of Amdahl's and Gustafson's formulations. We then derive a general measure of communications overhead that describes overhead in terms of expected communication distances in arbitrary multiprocessors. Closed form solutions are then given for the specific cases of multidimensional mesh-connected multiprocessors with and without wraparound, assuming a uniform distribution of communicating pairs. This assumption corresponds to the most tractable cases of particle problems. Multidimensional meshes can be described by two parameters: the number of dimensions (k) and the number of processors arrayed in any dimension (n). (All symbols used are listed in the Appendix at the end of the paper.) The total number of processors in the multidimensional mesh is therefore $N = n^k$. Processors are connected, with or without wraparound, by links parallel to each of the k axes. The derivation of communications overhead for multidimensional meshes is illustrative of a typical methodology for the analysis of average distance given a distribution of communicating pairs. Finally, the expression for maximum expected speedup with communications overhead is applied to several members of the multidimensional mesh class.

2. EXPECTED SPEEDUP OF PARALLEL PROCESSORS

It was our desire to enhance Amdahl's and Gustafson's expressions for maximum expected speedup of parallel systems by incorporating the effect of communications overhead into them. Thus, three factors were taken into account: parallel data processing steps, data transfer steps, and the serial part of the algorithm which cannot be broken into parallel tasks. Following the notation in [4], Amdahl's law can be expressed as

$$S = \frac{s + p}{s + p/N},$$ (1)

where s is the time spent in serial parts of the algorithm and p is the time spent by a sequential computer in those parts of the problem which can be divided among N processors of a parallel processing machine. Note that if s and p are expressed as fractions of the total time, $s + p = 1$ and speedup becomes

$$S = \frac{1}{s + (1 - s)/N} = \frac{N}{1 + s(N - 1)}.$$ (2)

Observe that if s is sufficiently small, Amdahl's law points to a potential speedup approaching N.

The above formulation implies that an architecture is scaled to fit a problem size. In [4], a form of the maximum expected speedup expression is suggested that reflects "fitting" the problem size to the available resources. In this case, p is defined as the total time spent by a parallel processing system in solving the parallel tasks. Therefore, the time required to execute the same tasks in a serial computer becomes pN. The resulting measure for speedup has been called "scaled speed-up" [4], and is given by

$$S = \frac{s + pN}{s + p}.$$ (3)

Again, letting $s + p = 1$, Eq. (3) can be rewritten as

$$S = s + pN = N - s(N - 1),$$ (4)

which again shows maximum expected speedups as high as N for very small values of s. This formulation is equivalent to normalizing Amdahl's expression with respect to the parallel processing system. That is, in Eq. (1), let $s + p/N = 1$. Accounting for the change in the definition of p, the resulting equation then becomes the same as Eq. (4) for scaled speedup.

A shortcoming of both Amdahl's and Gustafson's formulations is that they do not consider the communications overhead incurred when an algorithm is executed in a particular architecture. We now develop an expression for maximum expected speedup that includes communications overhead. We first derive expressions on the basis of Gustafson's formulation of scaled speedup; equivalent expressions using Amdahl's formulation are given later. Table I compares the results for the two formulations.

If the total time spent in the parallel part of the program is defined as p_T, then the communications overhead c is the fraction of p_T spent performing communications, and

TABLE I

Comparison of Amdahl's and Gustafson's
Speedup Formulations

Formulation	Amdahl	Gustafson
Total processing steps	$s + p$	$s + Np$
Maximum speedup	$\dfrac{N}{Ns + 1 - s}$	$N - s(N - 1)$
Maximum speedup with overhead	$\dfrac{(1 - c)N}{(1 - c)Ns + 1 - s}$	$(1 - c)N - s(N - 1 - c)$
Maximum speedup $s = 0$	$(1 - c)N$	$(1 - c)N$

$$p = (1 - c)p_T. \qquad (5)$$

In the case where processors can overlap some communications and computation, c is the fraction of p_T spent performing communications that are not overlapped with computation.

Following the same formulation as that given in [4], it is clear that a serial processor will execute the same algorithm in time $s + pN$. Let $s + p_T = 1$. The maximum expected speedup of the N-processor ensemble is therefore

$$S = \frac{s + pN}{s + p_T} = s + pN = (1 - c)N - s(N - 1 - c), \quad (6)$$

which is the same as Eq. (4), but now includes c factors affecting both the N term and the s term, thus incorporating the effect of communications overhead on the maximum attainable speedup.

In Eq. (6), if s is sufficiently small, the speedup will be determined by N and c. Thus, even in problems where the serial portion of the algorithm is small, speedup may be drastically reduced from N by communications overhead. If $N \geqslant 2$, which is always the case in multiprocessors, the second term in Eq. (6) is always positive. Ignoring the effects of the serial portion of the algorithm, an upper bound on the maximum expected speedup is

$$S \leqslant (1 - c)N. \qquad (7)$$

Now consider Amdahl's formulation. Again, letting $s + p = 1$, and with $p_T = (1 - c)p$, we get

$$S = \frac{1}{s + (1 - s)/(1 - c)N} = s + pN$$

$$= \frac{(1 - c)N}{(1 - c)Ns + 1 - s}. \qquad (8)$$

Again, if s is small the speedup is limited by

$$S \leqslant (1 - c)N. \qquad (9)$$

3. A MEASURE OF COMMUNICATIONS OVERHEAD

The time spent communicating between processors relative to the total time spent performing parallel computations is called the communications overhead c and is a quantity which depends on both the multiprocessor interconnection network architecture and the implemented algorithm.

Distributed memory multiprocessors may operate in either Single Instruction, Multiple Data (SIMD) or Multiple Instruction, Multiple Data (MIMD) fashion. Data communication patterns in an SIMD machine are predetermined by matching the algorithm to the multiprocessor topology, and synchronous communication mechanisms are most often used. In contrast, communication patterns in an MIMD environment typically are more random, and asynchronous mechanisms are more often used. We make no assumption about whether the multiprocessor runs in SIMD or MIMD fashion. The assumptions we do make will hold for algorithms running on either type of machine. However, it is likely that a larger set of MIMD machines and algorithms fit the assumptions.

On any processor, processing time can be separated into computation and communication steps. We make a first assumption that all processors require the same ratio of computation to communication steps. Since we are interested in an upper bound, we ignore the deleterious effects of blocking, contention, and deadlock in the network. Finally, we assume that routing time is a function only of the distance in hops between two processors. This is true of packet switching networks, where the store and forward mechanism is used [3] and packets are small. It is also true of circuit switching networks, where the packets are small and the packet transmission time is small relative to the channel setup time.

If the distance between any pair of processors on a network is defined as the minimum number of basic network hops necessary to move a data element from one processor to another, the diameter of the network is the maximum distance among all pairs of processors. For example, the diameter of an $n \times n$ mesh-connected network without wraparound is $2n - 2$. For networks without path conflicts, the shorter the diameter the less the system will suffer from high communication requirements. For a given interconnection scheme, the communications overhead may increase with the diameter, hence, in most cases, with the number of processors.

Assume that for a particular algorithm A, the processors need to do x data transfers and p parallel computational steps. After a finite number of transfer steps, processors have access to their operands to carry out their next computational step. For a particular machine M, let p_{ij} be the probability that a particular communication step is a data transfer from processor i to processor j. Also, let t_{ij} be the time it takes to transfer data from i to j, and let d_{ij} be the distance between i and j. Therefore, the expected time for a single communications step is

$$E(t) = \sum_{i=1}^{N} \sum_{j=1}^{N} t_{ij} p_{ij}. \qquad (10)$$

If we assume that t_{ij} and p_{ij} are both functions only of the distance d_{ij}, then Eq. (10) becomes

$$E(t) = \sum_{i=1}^{N} \sum_{j=1}^{N} t(d_{ij}) p(d_{ij}). \qquad (11)$$

The average fractional communications overhead for A is the ratio of communications time to total parallel processing and communications time:

$$c(A, M) = \frac{xE(t)}{p + xE(t)}. \qquad (12)$$

c is the fraction of total parallel processing time spent on communications. It should be noted that in the case of scaled speedup, the ratio of communication to computation steps may not remain constant. In fact, as pointed out by Worley [18], many algorithms actually require more communication as the size of the problem increases. In such cases, the upper bound performances that we indicate through application of communications overhead to the expressions for scaled speedup are overly optimistic, and the communications overhead must be expressed as an increasing function of problem size for the scaled speedup cases.

Note that computation and communication requirements depend on the algorithm alone, while $E(t)$ depends on both the algorithm and the topology of the interconnection network. Equation (12) is the general formulation for communications overhead. This expression can be substituted into Eqs. (6) and (7) to give expressions for the maximum expected speedup of arbitrary multiprocessors.

Reexamining our assumptions, we can see that in multiprocessors employing store and forward or circuit switching communication mechanisms with small packets, it is reasonable to assume that the communication time between two processors is proportional to the number of hops between them. If this is the case, then $t(d_{ij}) = Kd_{ij}$. Here, K is the scale factor between a communication step and a processing step. In a large number of MIMD systems, and in many SIMD systems, a reasonable assumption is that all processors are equally likely to communicate. If this is the case, then $p(d_{ij}) = 1/N^2$, and Eq. (11) becomes

$$E(t) = \frac{K}{N^2} \sum_{i=1}^{N} \sum_{j=1}^{N} d_{ij}. \qquad (13)$$

Thus $E(t) = Kd$, where d is the average distance between processors. Equation (12) becomes

$$c(A, M) = \frac{xKd}{p + xKd}. \qquad (14)$$

We can now normalize with respect to the number of processing steps to give

$$c(A, M) = \frac{\rho d}{1 + \rho d}, \qquad (15)$$

where $\rho = xK/p$ and is a constant for a given algorithm. Here ρ is analogous to $R/(C + R)$, with R/C as defined by Stone in [15] for MIMD multiprocessors.

4. COMMUNICATIONS OVERHEAD IN MULTIDIMENSIONAL MESH-CONNECTED MULTIPROCESSORS

To illustrate the application of this concept of communications overhead to a well-known class of parallel processing systems, consider the family of multidimensional mesh-connected parallel processors described above with $N = n^k$ processors arrayed in k orthogonal dimensions. The diameter of such a parallel processor is $k(n - 1)$. We want to determine the average distance spanned by a communication between two processors in the array. The distance between any two processors is measured as the minimum number of discrete hops that are necessary to get from one processor to another. This distance is bounded above by the diameter of the array. If the system is solving a continuum problem, communication is between nearest neighbors only, and $d = 1$. The c value for this case then becomes a measure of how efficient the link is between processors versus the computational power of the processors themselves. For the case of a mesh-connected architecture solving a particle problem, with uniform communication distribution, we need to evaluate the average distance d.

We derive an expression for the average communication distance between processors, assuming that any processor in the mesh is equally likely to communicate with any other processor. This is the situation in particle problems matched to the processor topology where the data flow in the problem is uniformly distributed among the operations to be performed and is not localized. Furthermore, this is a reasonable assumption to make in the case of large problems mapped onto smaller SIMD meshes, even when the distribution of likelihoods of communication is distance dependent, if the problem is mapped onto the mesh in a locally parallel, globally serial fashion. In this scheme, the entire large problem is decomposed into smaller problems that fit into the multiprocessor, the smaller problems being formed from contiguous sections of the large problem. These small problems are then executed serially in the multiprocessor. This is because the folding of the communication probability distribution onto the space of the processor array will tend to even out the likelihood of communications between any pairs of processors. Finally, this is a reasonable assumption to make in MIMD systems, where tasks are dynamically allocated to processors and interprocessor communication is asynchronous.

We express the identity of a processor by its address in k-space, specified by a k-tuple with each element being an integer from 0 to $n - 1$. Each pair of distinct processors in the mesh must differ in at least one address location.

We first consider the case of a multidimensional mesh without wraparound. There are two possible cases with the assumptions given here. These cases arise from including or not including a given processor in the set of processors it is likely to communicate with. We perform two separate derivations covering each case.

First, consider the case where a processor can communicate with itself. This is the most likely case in MIMD systems, as individual processors will often be assigned more than one task at a time. In the derivation, we allow processors to communicate with themselves at zero cost. To derive the expected orthogonal distance between any two processors randomly and uniformly chosen from a k-dimensional array of processors, we first must find the expected distance between two processors in one dimension, i.e., the expected distance between any two processors randomly and uniformly chosen from a linear array of processors. This can be determined by dividing the total distance between each possible pair of processors by the number of such pairs. The result is

$$d_1 = \frac{1}{n^2} \sum_{i=0}^{n-1} \sum_{j=0}^{n-1} |j - i| = \frac{2}{n^2} \sum_{i=0}^{n-1} \sum_{j=i+1}^{n-1} (j - i)$$
$$= \frac{n(n^2 - 1)/6}{n^2/2} = \frac{n^2 - 1}{3n}. \tag{16}$$

Since the distance in each dimension is independent, the total expected distance between processors is simply

$$d = \frac{(n^2 - 1)k}{3n}. \tag{17}$$

The case where a processor is excluded from communicating with itself is more complex. We first determine the expected distance between a pair of distinct processors randomly and uniformly selected from a one-dimensional array of processors:

$$d_1 = \frac{1}{\binom{n}{2}} \sum_{i=0}^{n-1} \sum_{j=i+1}^{n-1} (j - i) = \frac{n(n^2 - 1)/6}{n(n - 1)/2} = \frac{n + 1}{3}. \tag{18}$$

Now, in a multidimensional mesh-connected array of size $N = n^k$, the distance in a given dimension will be either 0, if the processors do not differ in that dimension, or have expected value $d_1 = (n + 1)/3$. Also, the distances between processors in each dimension in which their addresses differ are independent. The total expected orthogonal distance between any pair of processors is thus the sum of the expected distances between the processors in each dimension in which their addresses differ:

$$d = \sum_{i=1}^{k} id_1 p_i, \tag{19}$$

where i is the number of dimensions in which the addresses of the two processors differ and p_i is the probability of finding two processors which differ in i address dimensions.

It can be shown that

$$p_i = \binom{k}{i} \frac{(n - 1)^i}{n^k - 1}, \tag{20}$$

where $\binom{k}{i}$ is the number of ways to choose i differing dimensions from among k, $(n - 1)^i$ is the size of the hypermesh of processors that differ in i address dimensions from a selected processor, and $n^k - 1 = N - 1$ is the total number of processors available to pair with a selected processor.

Therefore,

$$d = \sum_{i=1}^{k} i \frac{(n + 1)}{3} \binom{k}{i} \frac{(n - 1)^i}{n^k - 1}$$
$$= \frac{(n + 1)}{3(n^k - 1)} \sum_{i=1}^{k} i \binom{k}{i} (n - 1)^i. \tag{21}$$

The summation can be evaluated by replacing the lone i term by $(\partial e^{yi}/\partial y)|_{y=0}$. The summation can then be put into the form of the binomial expansion, the derivative taken, and the result evaluated at $y = 0$, to give

$$d = \frac{(n + 1)}{3(n^k - 1)} k(n - 1)n^{k-1} = \frac{(n^2 - 1)kn^{k-1}}{3(n^k - 1)}. \tag{22}$$

The expressions in Eqs. (17) and (22) converge quickly to each other for any reasonably large values of n. They can be evaluated for a few common cases. In the Massively Parallel Processor [2], $k = 2$, $n = 128$, and $d \approx 85.3$. Furthermore, in meshes with moderately large n, $d \approx kn/3$. In hypercubes, $n = 2$ for all cases and $d \approx k/2$. For the 1024-

node hypercube used in [4], $k = 10$ and the expected distance is about 5.

For a two-dimensional mesh-connected array, using Eq. (15) and either (17) or (22), the communications overhead becomes

$$c(A, 2Dmesh) = \frac{\rho d}{1 + \rho d} \approx \frac{2\rho n}{3 + 2\rho n}. \qquad (23)$$

If the number of communication steps required is a large fraction of the number of computation steps, then $c(A, 2Dmesh)$ approaches 1 even for moderate values of n (and N), which means that this type of machine can be heavily loaded by communications overhead.

For a binary hypercube, the communications overhead becomes

$$c(A, hypercube) = \frac{\rho d}{1 + \rho d} = \frac{\rho k}{2 + \rho k}. \qquad (24)$$

Here again, $c(A, hypercube)$ approaches 1 for moderate values of k (and N), if a relatively large amount of communications steps are required. Thus, the hypercube can also be heavily burdened by communications overhead requirements.

We now consider the case of multidimensional meshes with wraparound. The analysis remains much the same. The only change is in the expected distance between two arbitrarily selected processors in one dimension. In the case where self-communication is allowed, by rotating one of the selected pair of processors to the center of a linear array of processors not connected by wraparound, this distance can be shown to be

$$d_1 = \begin{cases} \dfrac{n^2 - 1}{4n} & \text{if } n \text{ odd} \\[2ex] \dfrac{n}{4} & \text{if } n \text{ even} \end{cases}$$

or

$$d_1 \geq \frac{n^2 - 1}{4n}. \qquad (25)$$

Equation (17) then becomes, for the wraparound case,

$$d \geq \frac{k(n^2 - 1)}{4n}. \qquad (26)$$

Now, for the case where processors are restricted from communicating with themselves, we first find the expected distance between two unique randomly and uniformly placed processors in a one-dimensional array of processors with wraparound. Again rotating one processor to the center of an array without wraparound gives an equivalent situation:

$$d_1 = \begin{cases} \dfrac{n + 1}{4} & \text{if } n \text{ odd} \\[2ex] \dfrac{n^2}{4(n - 1)} & \text{if } n \text{ even} \end{cases}$$

or

$$d_1 \geq \frac{n + 1}{4}. \qquad (27)$$

For the wraparound case, Equation (22) becomes

$$d \geq \frac{(n^2 - 1)kn^{k-1}}{4(n^k - 1)}. \qquad (28)$$

Thus, wraparound will decrease the expected distance between processors in the array by a factor of $\frac{4}{3}$ and give a corresponding increase in performance. We do all subsequent analysis for the case without wraparound, keeping in mind that the performance of the multidimensional array can be improved by a constant factor if wraparound is employed. The results of this section are summarized in Table II.

5. APPLYING COMMUNICATIONS OVERHEAD TO MAXIMUM EXPECTED SPEEDUP

Now that we have an expression for the communications overhead in multidimensional mesh-connected parallel processors, it is possible to use this result to derive bounds on the speedup available in such processors. Let us consider an $n \times n$ (i.e., $N = n^2$) two-dimensional mesh-connected system without wraparound solving a particle problem. Using Eq. (7) and Eq. (23), we can write the expected speedup

$$S(2Dmesh, particle) \leq \frac{n^2}{1 + (\frac{2}{3})\rho n} < \frac{3n}{2\rho} = \frac{3N^{1/2}}{2\rho}. \qquad (29)$$

TABLE II
Approximate Communication Overhead Factors

Topology	No wraparound	Wraparound
2Dmesh	$\dfrac{2\rho n}{3 + 2\rho n}$	$\dfrac{\rho n}{2 + \rho n}$
Binary hypercube	$\dfrac{\rho k}{2 + \rho k}$	$\dfrac{\rho k}{2 + \rho k}$
Large n	$\dfrac{\rho k n}{3 + \rho k n}$	$\dfrac{\rho k n}{4 + \rho k n}$

458

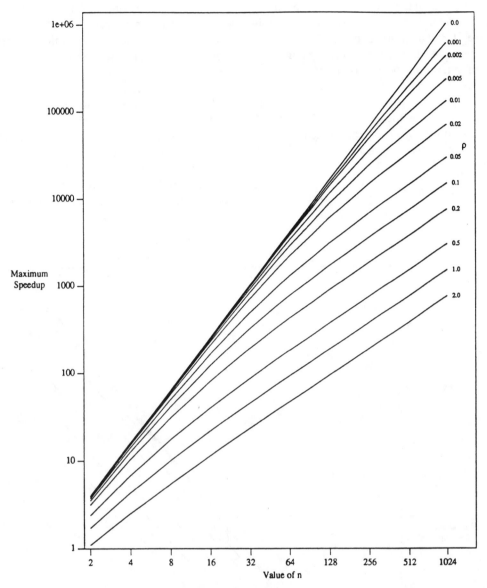

FIG. 1. Maximum speedup in two-dimensional meshes.

As N becomes large, a very poor maximum speedup can be realized on the mesh for this kind of problem. In Fig. 1, the relationship between the maximum speedup attainable and the size of the network is given. The various curves are for different values of ρ. Note that the dependency of maximum speedup on n (where $N = n^2$) is slightly sublinear, and that the speedup falls off rapidly with increasing ρ. The $\rho = 0.0$ line is simply a plot of N and therefore represents the ideal maximum attainable speedup.

On the other hand, if a continuum problem is considered, $d = 1$ and a linear speedup can be realized:

$$S(2\,Dmesh,\ continuum) \leqslant \frac{n^2}{1+\rho} = \frac{N}{1+\rho}. \quad (30)$$

The case of a one-dimensional mesh, the linear array of processors, shows even poorer speedup. For large N, this speedup approaches a constant value of $3/\rho$. Thus, adding processors is of no benefit, even when the entire algorithm is parallelizable and has no serial component.

Now consider a k-dimensional binary hypercube ($N = 2^k$) solving a particle problem. Using Eqs. (7) and (24), we can write the expected speedup as follows:

$$S(hypercube,\ particle) \leqslant \frac{2^k}{1 + \frac{1}{2}\rho k} = \frac{N}{1 + \frac{1}{2}\rho k}. \quad (31)$$

This equation shows that communication overhead is a much less significant factor in the hypercube than it is in the two-dimensional mesh for large N, even when a particle problem is being solved. Figure 2 shows the maximum speedup attainable in binary hypercubes of various sizes. Again, several curves are plotted for different values of ρ. The dependency of maximum speedup on k (where $N = 2^k$) is approximately exponential, and, as expected due to the higher connectivity of the network, the speedup is less sensitive to increasing ρ than was the two-dimensional mesh.

For the case of the continuum problem on the hypercube, the upper bound on the speedup is again

$$S(hypercube, continuum) \leqslant \frac{2^k}{1 + \rho} = \frac{N}{1 + \rho}. \quad (32)$$

The speedup in a continuum problem is a function only of the ratio of communication to computation steps ρ (along with their relative step times) and is not sensitive to the network topology. However, in a particle problem, ρ will also depend on the network topology as a particle algorithm may map onto some topologies better than others.

The above expressions indicate that the maximum speedup achievable in a mesh-connected network depends on how well the algorithm is mapped onto the architecture. The expected distance d is dependent both on the architecture itself and on the quality of the mapping of the algorithm onto the architecture. To achieve speedups close to N, as reported in [4], it is necessary for three conditions to coexist.

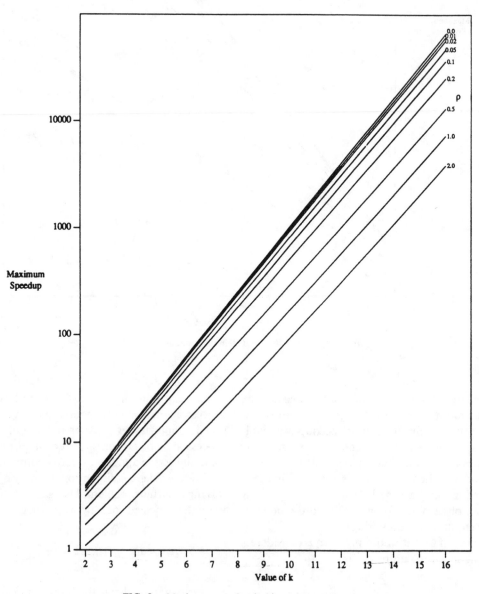

FIG. 2. Maximum speedup in binary hypercubes.

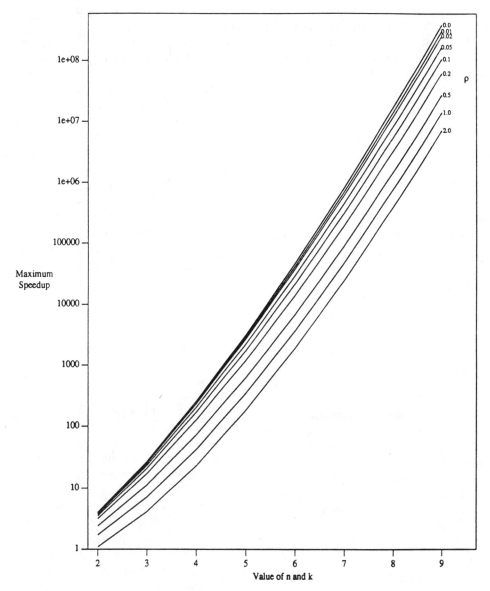

FIG. 3. Maximum speedup in hypermeshes with $n = k$.

One is that the actual serial portion of the algorithm must be small and increase in execution time slowly relative to the size of the parallel part of the algorithm. Another condition is that d must be small, as is the case in a continuum problem, or alternatively, as can be the case in a very highly connected network. Finally, the amount of communication required must be small compared to the amount of computation in the parallel part of the algorithm. The experiments referred to in [4] and described in detail in [5] were performed on a 1024 MIMD Binary Hypercube Multiprocessor. The computer was used to solve large scientific problems: wave mechanics, fluid dynamics, and structural analysis. As a binary hypercube, the system was subject to Eq. (32), which allows a speedup approaching N. It is also worth noting that in a practical multiprocessor running an algo-

rithm with a high degree of synchronized activity, it may be possible to perform communication and computation simultaneously in a given processor node, if this node has separate subsystems for each of these functions. Thus, in such a system, much of the communications overhead may be masked by simultaneous computational activity. However, this will not change the form of the results, as individual communications generally take much longer than computations, and processors must spend some time waiting for communications to complete before continuing computations.

As an example of the effect of network topology on speedup, consider the one-dimensional elliptic problem discussed by Worley [18]. The speedup and the scaled speedup have been computed here for the case of both a binary hypercube and a linear mesh of processors. In agreement with the results presented here for the binary hypercube, speedup increases as a linear function of N for both the time constrained and the memory constrained cases. When the problem is attempted on a one-dimensional mesh of processors, however, the scaled speedup is quickly limited to a constant value in both cases, as predicted by the bounds presented herein.

Let us now return to Eq. (7). For a speedup, we require

$$1 < S \le (1 - c)N = \frac{N}{1 + \rho d}, \tag{33}$$

which can be arranged to express the upper bound on the ratio of communication to processing that will achieve a speedup:

$$\rho < \frac{N - 1}{d}. \tag{34}$$

Note that for algorithms where more communication is required than processing ($\rho > 1$), network topologies with large average communication distances between processors will be slower than a uniprocessor system.

Finally, Fig. 3 shows the expected maximum speedup of topologies with $n = k$ (i.e., $N = n^n = k^k$). These form a family of multiprocessors with connectivity intermediate to the binary hypercubes and the two-dimensional meshes. Here the increase in performance is slightly superexponential in n. Also, for a given number of processors, the effect of the ratio of communications to computations ρ in meshes with $n = k$ is comparable to its effect in the binary hypercubes. This suggests that networks with lower levels of interconnection than those found in binary hypercubes may give comparable performance.

6. CONCLUSIONS

Communications overhead in parallel processing systems was incorporated in the expressions for the maximum expected speedup of multiprocessing systems. The expression for communications overhead reflects both its system architecture and its algorithm dependence. We derived closed form analytical expressions of average distance in multidimensional meshes of n^k processors with and without wraparound. The communications overhead and the maximum expected speedup of these multiprocessors were then derived using the distance expressions, with the assumption that communicating pairs were uniformly distributed and that communication time is directly proportional to the distance between the communicating processors. The problem of extracting the exact communications overhead for an algorithm is still very difficult. However, for some well-behaved mappings, the problem can be approximated, and maximum po-

tential speedups can be computed using the approach outlined in this paper.

We derived our speedup expressions assuming no blocking, contention, or deadlock. It would be interesting to explore the effects of these factors in further reducing the upper bounds on maximum speedup. An interesting result of this paper is that structures with lower connectivity than that of the binary hypercubes may have performance as measured by speedup comparable to that of the binary hypercube. This is a significant result as it indicates that high performance multiprocessor systems can be constructed at a cost lower than that required by binary hypercubes [14]. The maximum speedup expressions can be used to compare the potential performance of multiprocessor networks, as long as they behave according to the assumptions given. The specific cases of multidimensional mesh-connected networks presented here cover a large set of both current and proposed multiprocessor architectures.

APPENDIX: NOMENCLATURE

k number of dimensions of multiprocessor
n number of processors in each dimension
N total number of processors
S speedup
s serial fraction of total work
p parallel fraction of total work
p_T time in parallel part of algorithm
c fraction of p_T in communications
p_{ij} probability of communication between processors i and j
t_{ij} time for communication between processors i and j
d_{ij} distance between processors i and j
x number of data transfers
ρ normalized communication time
d_1 expected distance between two processors in one dimension
d expected distance between two processors

ACKNOWLEDGMENTS

The authors acknowlege the valuable discussions and correspondence of Niraj K. Jha and Andre B. Bondi that contributed to an early draft of this work.

REFERENCES

1. Amdahl, G. M. Validity of the single processor approach to achieving large scale computing capabilities. *AFIPS Conference Proceedings.* AFIPS Press, Reston, VA, 1967, Vol. 30, pp. 483–485.

2. Batcher, K. E. Design of a massively parallel processor. *IEEE Trans. Comput.* C-29 (Sept. 1980), 836–840.

3. Bhuyan, L. N. Interconnection networks for parallel and distributed processing. *IEEE Comput.* 20, 6 (June 1987), 9–12.

4. Gustafson, J. L. Reevaluating Amdahl's Law. *Comm. ACM* **31**, 5 (May 1988), 532–533.

5. Gustafson, J. L., Montry, G. R., and Benner, R. E. Development of parallel methods for a 1024-processor hypercube. *SIAM J. Sci. Statis. Comput.* **9**, 4 (July 1988), 609–638.

6. Heath, M., and Worley, P. Once again, Amdahl's law. *Comm. ACM* **32**, 2 (Feb. 1989), 262–263.

7. Helmbold, D. P., and McDowell, C. E. Modeling speedup (n) greater than N. *Proc. 1989 International Conference on Parallel Processing,* Aug. 1989, Vol. 3, pp. 219–225.

8. Ho, H. F., Chen, G. H., Lin, S. H., and Sheu, J. P. Solving linear programming on fixed sized hypercubes. *Proc. 1988 International Conference on Parallel Processing,* Aug. 1988, Vol. 3, pp. 112–116.

9. Hoshino, T. Invitation to the world of Pax. *IEEE Comput.* **19**, 5 (May 1986), 68–79.

10. Lai, T. H., and Sahni, S. Anomalies in parallel branch and bound algorithms. *Comm. ACM* **27**, 6 (June 1984), 594–602.

11. Li, K. IVY: A shared virtual memory system for parallel computing. *Proc. 1988 International Conference on Parallel Processing,* Aug. 1988, Vol. 2, pp. 94–101.

12. Mehrotra, R., and Gehringer, E. F. Superlinear speedup through randomized algorithms. *Proc. 1985 International Conference on Parallel Processing,* 1985, pp. 291–300.

13. Preiss, B. R., and Hamacher, V. C. Semi-static dataflow. *Proc. 1988 International Conference on Parallel Processing,* Aug. 1988, Vol. 2, pp. 127–134.

14. Shih, Y., and Kernek, A. A new generation in parallel processing systems. *Supercomputing* (Winter 1988), 5–28.

15. Stone, H. S. *High Performance Computer Architecture.* Addison–Wesley, Reading, MA, 1987.

16. Weide, B. W. Modeling unusual behavior of parallel algorithms. *IEEE Trans. Comput.* **C31**, 11 (Nov. 1982), 1126–1130.

17. Worley, P. H. Limits on parallelism in the numerical solution of linear PDEs. Tech. Rep. ORNL TM-10945, Oak Ridge National Laboratory, Oak Ridge, TN, Oct. 1988.

18. Worley, P. H. The effect of time constraints on scaled speed-up. Tech. Rep. ORNL TM-11031, Oak Ridge National Laboratory, Oak Ridge, TN, Jan. 1989.

Received October 30, 1989; revised April 23, 1990; accepted May 24, 1990

ISAAC D. SCHERSON was born in Santiago, Chile, on February 12, 1952. He received B.S. and M.S. degrees in electrical engineering from the National University of Mexico (UNAM) and a Ph.D. in computer science from the Weizmann Institute of Science, Rehovot, Israel. In the fall of 1983, he joined the faculty of the Department of Electrical and Computer Engineering of the University of California at Santa Barbara. He is currently an assistant professor in the Department of Electrical Engineering at Princeton University. His research interests include interconnection networks, shared memory multiprocessing, associative memory and processing, parallel algorithms, and computer graphics. Dr. Scherson is a member of Eta Kappa Nu, ACM, and IEEE.

PETER F. CORBETT was born in Sault Ste. Marie, Canada in 1959. He received B.A.Sc. (1983) and M.A.S. (1985) degrees in electrical engineering from the University of Waterloo, Waterloo, Canada. He spent two years at the General Electric Corporate Research and Development Center in the VLSI Simulation and Synthesis Group, where he worked on the design of the Parsifal Digit Serial Silicon Compiler. From 1987 to 1990, he has been a Ph.D. student in the computer engineering group of the Department of Electrical Engineering at Princeton University. Peter expects to join the research staff of the Prototype Design and Analysis Group of the IBM T. J. Watson Research Center in late 1990. His research interests include high performance parallel computer architecture, interconnection networks, parallel and systolic algorithms, VLSI design, and silicon compilation. Peter is a member of the IEEE.

MULTISTAGE NETWORKS INCLUDING TRAFFIC WITH REAL-TIME CONSTRAINTS

Lance Kurisaki and Tomas Lang

Computer Science Department
School of Engineering and Applied Science
University of California
Los Angeles, California 90024

Abstract

In this paper we investigate the performance of a multistage interconnection network (MIN) which carries the superposition of two types of traffic. One type is the high rate data and instruction traffic, while the other consists of control packets (for singularity conditions, errors, etc.) and I/O packets. In many instances, this second type is of low rate but has real-time constraints. We consider strategies to control the network to achieve low latency for real-time traffic (rtt), especially in the case where the background traffic produces nonuniform traffic spots (NUTS).

We evaluate the performance by simulations and conclude that diverting switches, which produce good performance for NUTS, are suitable for assuring low latency for the real-time traffic, especially when using the displacing mode. Moreover, we show that the network with additional links, which provides the highest throughput in the presence of NUTS, is also suitable for low latency rtt. Additionally, we conclude that it is not possible to assure low latency for the rtt when using blocking switches -- even under uniform traffic conditions.

Key words: Multiprocessors, Multistage networks, Nonuniform traffic spots, Real-time traffic, Diverting switches.

1. Introduction

Multistage interconnection networks (MIN) are used in multiprocessor systems to connect processors with other processors or with memory modules. These networks provide a compromise between networks of low latency and high cost, such as the crossbar, and networks of high latency and low cost, such as the shared bus. Moreover, MINs can be pipelined to provide a bandwidth comparable to that of the crossbar for suitable traffic patterns. In addition, the control of routing is simple. A large body of work has been done on the structure, operation, and performance of these networks; a comprehensive reference is [14]. These networks were initially introduced for use in array computers of the SIMD type; in this context the interconnection networks are sometimes called permutation networks. More recently, they are being proposed and used in multiprocessors of the MIMD type, especially of the shared-memory variety [4,5,12,15]. In this paper we are concerned with this second type of use.

In their basic form, these multistage networks provide a unique path between any source-destination pair. However, the paths for different pairs are not disjoint and, therefore, conflicts might occur when simultaneous communication is established between several source-destination pairs. The basic method used to handle this problem is to use a packet-switched type of operation and to buffer the packets in the switches. Blocking occurs whenever the buffers become full.

It has been shown that the performance of these networks is satisfactory for uniform traffic [2,6], that is, for traffic in which the destinations are generated by a random variable with uniform distribution. In [9] we have discussed the effect of nonuniform traffic spots (NUTS) and determined by simulations that the throughput is badly degraded when blocking switches are used. Moreover, we showed that the use of diverting switches improves the performance and that adding links to provide alternate paths produces the best throughput. This work has been motivated by earlier research in the area of "hot spot" contention in multistage networks [7,13].

In this paper we extend our work on multistage networks with NUTS to the case in which the network carries the superposition of two types of traffic. One type is the high rate data and instruction traffic, while the other consists of control packets (for singularity conditions, errors, etc.) and I/O packets. In many instances, this second type is of low rate but with real-time constraints. In such a case, it is necessary to assure low latency for these packets. In the sequel we will call the first type of traffic background traffic (bgt) and the second type real-time traffic (rtt). We consider here strategies to control the network to achieve the low latency for rtt, especially in the case where the bgt has nonuniform traffic spots (NUTS).

Three solutions to this situation come to mind. In the first, a separate network is used for the rtt, which would be designed to assure the low latency; the disadvantage of this is the cost of the additional network. A second solution is to share one network but have separate buffers in the switches for each traffic; moreover, in case of conflicts for the switch output ports, priority is given to the rtt. Still, this solution has the additional cost of the buffers and is more complex to control, especially when blocking switches are used because of the need for additional full signals. Finally, it is possible to share network and buffers and develop control strategies to assure low latency for the rtt. Here we explore this third alternative.

We evaluate the performance by simulations. Since the objective is to explore alternative switch control strategies, we use a small set of traffic patterns that produce NUTS to compare the alternatives. We expect that similar results would be obtained for other patterns; however, for specific values of throughput and delay, simulations should be done for the particular traffic.

2. Multistage Network Structure and Operation

To make this paper relatively self-contained, we present a brief description of the structure and operation of the multistage network, emphasising the assumptions made in [9]. A more detailed discussion can be found in [14]. The type of multistage interconnection network we are considering has $N = 2^n$ inputs (sources) and outputs (destinations), both labeled from 0 to $N-1$. It consists of n stages of $N/2$ 2×2 switches, as shown in Figure 1. The outputs of stage-i switches are connected to the inputs of stage-$(i-1)$ switches, with the network inputs going to stage-$(n-1)$ switches and the network outputs coming from the stage-0 switches.

Several specific multistage networks have been proposed, differing in the interconnection pattern between stages. Since the characteristics, in terms of type of operation and performance, are similar for all these different topologies, we consider here the Omega network [11], which has been extensively studied [1] and is being used in several multiprocessor systems. In this network, the interconnection pattern between stages corresponds to the perfect shuffle connection, as shown in Figure 1.

The routing of packets in the network is unique since there is a single path between specific source-destination pairs. The control of routing is done using a destination tag that is associated with the message as part of each packet. At stage i, the routing depends only on the ith bit of the tag; if the bit has value 0(1), route to the upper(lower) output of the switch.

The operation of the network is synchronous and pipelined. In its basic form, each switch has one register per output and each cycle one packet is transferred from an output register in a

"Multistage Networks Including Traffic with Real-Time Constraints" by L. Kurisaki and T. Lang from *Proc. Int'l Conf. Parallel Processing*, Vol. 1, 1989, pp. 19-22. Copyright © 1989 by The Pennsylvania State University. Reproduced by permission of the publisher.

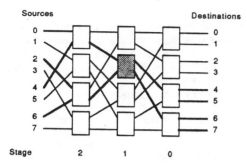

Stage   2   1   0

Figure 1. An 8×8 Omega network.

switch of stage i to the corresponding output register of a switch of stage $i-1$. This implies that the packets are all of the same size. If the packet is large, the above mentioned cycle can be divided into several subcycles and a part of the packet be transferred per subcycle. However, we will not be concerned with this subdivision and will use the packet as the basic unit of transfer and the time of this transfer as the unit of time (one cycle).

Since each output register can receive only one packet per cycle, there is a conflict when both packets entering a switch in a cycle have to be routed to the same output. One solution to this conflict is to have a buffer for each output and to store the additional packet in such a buffer. Of course, these buffers are finite so it is necessary to have an operation policy when the buffer is full. The basic scheme used is a blocking policy in which the predecessor switches do not send packets to a full buffer. To support this policy it is necessary to have signals from a switch to its predecessors indicating that the corresponding buffer(s) is full (Figure 2a).

To control contention it is also possible to use discarding and diverting switches, as shown in Figures 2b and 2c. In such cases, the packets are always sent to the successor switch but are discarded (and resent from the original source) or diverted to a wrong destination (and resent from the intermediate destination) when the buffers are full. It is important to note that in these cases, since packets always advance, there is at least one space in each output buffer so that at most one packet needs to be discarded or diverted per switch cycle, and no full signals are needed.

In [9] we showed that for traffic patterns that produce NUTS the diverting switches result in a larger throughput than either the blocking or the discarding switches.

To reduce further the contention it is possible to add intrastage links which produce alternate paths for the packets [8,16] (Figure 2d). Consequently, overflow packets can be routed through the additional link and still be able to reach the desired destination in a single pass through the network. This, of course, requires an augmented 3×3 switch with more complex control. We combine this alternate path configuration with diverting control to obtain the best throughput [9].

In this paper we do not evaluate different buffer organizations and policies. A more detailed discussion can be found in [10]. The degradation produced by NUTS is inherent to the blocking operation of the network, which is present for any switch design. Moreover, the modifications we propose are applicable to all organizations. Consequently, we perform our analysis using output buffers with FIFO policy.

3. Strategies for low-latency real-time traffic

We now present the strategies we propose and evaluate to obtain low latency for the real-time traffic (rtt).

For discarding and diverting switches the basic strategy we use to reduce the latency of the rtt is to give priority to packets of this traffic type when one of the two packets coming to a buffer has to be discarded or diverted (as previously noted, both packets never have to be discarded/diverted because there is always at least

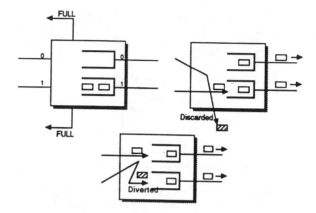

Figures 2a-c. Blocking, Discarding and Diverting Switches.

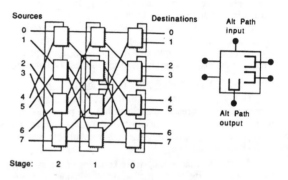

Figure 2d. Alternate Path Network and Switch Element.

one space in each buffer, left by the departing packets). Specifically, when one of the packets coming to a buffer is of the bgt type, this is the one discarded/diverted.

On top of this basic strategy we consider the following three alternatives, as illustrated in Figure 3:

- RTT to Back: rtt packets are placed at the back of the buffer, just as bgt packets (Figure 3a). However, rtt packets are given priority over bgt when there is one space in a buffer, so they are less likely to be diverted/discarded. An rtt packet will be diverted/discarded only when two rtt packets enter a switch at the same cycle, both are bound for the same output port, and the corresponding buffer has only one space available.

- RTT to Front: rtt packets are placed in the front of the buffer, while bgt packets are placed at the back (Figure 3b). Like the previous case, rtt packets are given priority over bgt packets when contending for buffer space.

- Displacing: this third alternative always allows the placement of up to two rtt packets in the front of the buffer. If two rtt packets enter the switch bound for the same buffer and there is only one space available, the packet currently at the end of the buffer will be displaced to make room (Figure 3c). This displaced packet is discarded or diverted (displacing does not apply to blocking switches). Note that the displaced packet might be either rtt or bgt.

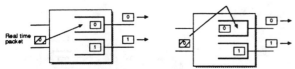

Figures 3a-b. RTT to Back, RTT to Front.

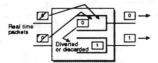

Figure 3c. Displacing Mode.

These policies can be easily extended to a 3×3 switch for a network with alternate paths. Rtt to front and rtt to back behave as expected in a 3×3 switch, placing the rtt traffic in the front or back of the buffer. In the displacing mode, up to two packets may be displaced if all three packets entering the switch are rtt. We also have a choice as to which queue we place the displaced packet. An intelligent choice could be made considering whether the displaced packet is already diverted (and from where), and how many real-time packets have entered the switch during the current cycle. Since simultaneous arrivals of real-time packets are assumed to be an infrequent event, a simple and fast decision is adequate. We currently put the displaced packet into the shortest available queue.

4. Performance evaluation by simulation

To study the performance of the network using the alternative control policies presented in Section 3, we performed simulations. For this, we built a network simulator using as a basis SIMON, a general-purpose multiprocessor simulator developed at the University of Utah [3].

We evaluate the **steady-state** behavior of the system, that is, we assume that the traffic pattern under consideration remains for a period long enough to achieve this steady state.

The fundamental parameters for the network are its size and the size of the buffers. We have found that the relative performance of the network remains essentially the same for different values of these parameters. Consequently, we report our results for a network of size 64×64 and buffer of size 2; this buffer size is convenient because it produces a relatively small delay. These parameters are the same as in [9], where more detail can be found.

We consider the worst case situation of maximum load on the network, that is, each input provides one packet per cycle (if the corresponding first-stage buffer is not full in the blocking case and if there are no packets to resend in the other cases). Finally, the total traffic is a mix of 95% of bgt and 5% of rtt.

We choose traffic patterns to illustrate different types of behavior and show the effect in performance between the alternative ways of controlling contention. We are especially interested in cases in which the bgt has NUTS because these are the difficult cases and where there is a difference between alternative control mechanisms. We assume that the rtt is of low throughput so that it alone does not produce congestion in the network.

To allow for adequate analysis, we use a set of three traffic patterns that produce contention, along with uniform traffic for comparison; we expect that the behavior will be similar for other patterns. More detail about the traffic patterns used can be found in [9].

The first type of traffic is produced when the even numbered sources send to the first half of the destinations, and odd sources send to the second half (EFOS). This pattern serves to illustrate a case in which each source accesses a subset of destinations.

The other two types of traffic are permutations. We use the **bit reversal** permutation since it is known to produce high

contention in an Omega network. As a more typical case, we also use a precomputed randomly generated **arbitrary** permutation.

To study both the effect of the bgt pattern and of the rtt pattern, we simulate two mixes: either the rtt is of the same pattern as the bgt or the rtt is uniform.

Since we are interested in providing low latency for the rtt, we measure the distribution of delay for rtt packets. From this distribution we obtain the delay of the slowest rtt packet and the average latency of the slowest 10% of the rtt. Moreover, since the network should carry the highest possible amount of bgt, we also show the total relative throughput.

5. Simulation Results

The simulation results are presented in the graphs of Figure 4 and in Table 1.

Figure 4a shows the distribution of delays of rtt packets for one type of traffic (EFOS) and with diverting switches; the graphs for other types of traffic are similar. The zoom view shows the slowest 5% of the rtt packets. We see that the displacing policy is best followed by rtt to front. Rtt to back performs poorly because rtt packets must often wait for bgt packets ahead of them in the queue.

Figure 4b shows the effect of the bgt pattern on the delay of the rtt (for rtt to front policy). We see that with diverting switches there is practically no effect while the effect is significant when blocking switches are used. Moreover, we see that blocking switches have a much larger percentage of slow rtt packets.

Table 1 shows the maximum latency experienced by the real-time traffic (in cycles) and the average delay of the slowest 10% of the real-time traffic. Since the simulated network has 6 stages, the minimum delay is 6 cycles.

The table shows the effect of the switch type when both types of traffic are EFOS. We conclude that to achieve very low rtt latency the policy with displacing should be used, while for somewhat larger delay the policy rtt to front is acceptable for discarding, diverting or alternate paths. Blocking switches are not suitable to assure a low latency for rtt -- even under uniform traffic conditions. Also, the policy rtt to back produces a significant degradation. Notice that the networks with diverting switches and alternate paths carry a much higher total throughput than either blocking or discarding switches (note a). Similar conclusions are obtained for the other patterns of real-time and background traffic.

The pattern of the rtt is not very significant, since it is of very low rate. A small degradation occurs when the rtt has the same pattern as the bgt, because of the NUTS produced by the latter.

Finally, from the operation of the network, we see that if the rtt pattern corresponds to nonintersecting paths, the use of diverting switches with rtt to front produces the minimum delay, since two rtt packets would never conflict. For this type of rtt there would be no need to use the somewhat more complicated displacing policy.

6. Conclusions

We have presented several strategies to assure low latency for low rate real-time traffic in the presence of high rate background traffic, even when there exist NUTS produced by the latter. For the basic network with a single path between any source-destination pair, the best strategy is to use diverting switches with the displacing policy. The use of diverting switches provides a large throughput for background traffic producing NUTS, while this type of switches with displacing assures the low latency for rtt. Discarding switches are not good because they have a significant degradation with NUTS [9] and blocking switches degrade both types of traffic.

| Switch Type | RTT: EFOS(5%)/BGT: EFOS(95%) | | | | | | Total Relative Throughput |
| | RTT to Back | | RTT to Front | | Displacing | | |
	Max	Top 10%	Max	Top 10%	Max	Top 10%	
Blocking	28	20.5	26	16.3	*	*	.32
Discarding	18	10.4	10	6.4	8	6.0	.35
Diverting	22	13.6	20	8.0	8	6.1	.53 (a)
Alternate Paths	14	12.1	8	6.1	8	6.3	.81

Table 1. Delay of RTT for Different Types of Switches.

Extension of the network obtained by adding intrastage links enhance even further the throughput of the bgt while having still a low latency for the rtt. The disadvantage of this type of extension is that it requires 3×3 switches which are somewhat more complex than the basic 2×2 type.

Acknowledgement

This research was sponsored in part by the State of California MICRO program and Hughes Aircraft Co.

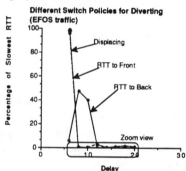

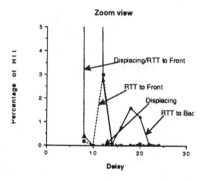

Figure 4a. Different Switch Policies for Diverting Switches.

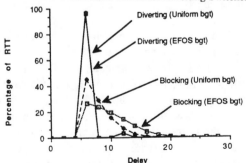

Figure 4b. Effect of Different Background Traffic (rtt to Front).

7. References.

[1] P. Chen, D. Lawrie, and P. Yew, ''Interconnection Networks Using Shuffles'', Computer , December 1981, pp. 55-64.

[2] D. Dias and R. Jump, ''Packet Switching Interconnection Networks for Modular Systems'', Computer , December 1981, pp. 43-54.

[3] R. M. Fujimoto, The CSIMON Interface , Computer Science Department, University of Utah, 1986.

[4] A. Gottlieb, et al. ''The NYU Ultracomputer--Designing an MIMD Shared Memory Parallel Computer'', IEEE Transactions on Computers , Vol. C-32, No. 2, pp. 175-189.

[5] K. Hwang and F. Briggs, Computer Architecture and Parallel Processing , McGraw Hill, 1984.

[6] C. P. Krustal and M. Snir, ''The Performance of Multistage Interconnection Networks for Multiprocessors'', IEEE Transactions on Computers , Vol. 32, No. 12, December 1983, pp. 1091-1098.

[7] M. Kumar and G. F. Pfister, ''The Onset of Hot Spot Contention'', Proceedings of the 1986 International Conference on Parallel Processing , August 1986.

[8] V. P. Kumar and S. M. Reddy, ''Design and Analysis of Fault-Tolerant Multistage Interconnection Networks With Low Link Complexity'', 12th Annual Symposium on Computer Architecture, pp. 376-386 (June 1985).

[9] T. Lang and L. Kurisaki, ''Nonuniform Traffic Spots (NUTS) In Multistage Interconnection Networks'', Proceedings of the 1988 International Conference on Parallel Processing , August 1988, pp. 191-195.

[10] T. Lang and L. Kurisaki, Nonuniform Traffic Spots (NUTS) In Multistage Interconnection Networks , UCLA Technical Report CSD-880001, January 1988.

[11] D. H. Lawrie, ''Access and Alignment of Data in an Array Processor'', IEEE Transactions on Computers , Vol. C-24, No. 12, Dec. 1975, pp. 1145-1155.

[12] G. F. Pfister, W. C. Brantley, D. A. George, S. L. Harvey, W. J. Kleinfelder, K. P. McAuliffe, E. A. Melton, V. A. Norton, J. Weiss, ''The IBM Research Parallel Processor Prototype (RP3): Introduction and Architecture'', Proceedings of the 1985 International Conference on Parallel Processing , August 1985, pp. 764-771.

[13] G. F. Pfister and V. A. Norton, ''Hot Spot Contention and Combining in Multistage Interconnection Networks'', IEEE Transactions on Computers , Vol. C-34, No. 10, October 1985, pp. 943-948.

[14] H. J. Siegel, Interconnection Networks for Large-Scale Parallel Processing, Theory and Case Studies , Lexington Books, 1985.

[15] R. H. Thomas, ''Behavior of the Butterfly Parallel Processor in the Presence of Memory Hot Spots'', IEEE Parallel Processing , 1986.

[16] N. Tzeng, P. Yew, and C. Zhu, ''A Fault-Tolerant Scheme for Multistage Interconnection Networks'', 12th Annual Symposium on Computer Architecture , pp. 368-375 (June 1985).

The Distribution of Waiting Times in Clocked Multistage Interconnection Networks

CLYDE P. KRUSKAL, MARC SNIR, AND ALAN WEISS

Abstract—We analyze the random delay experienced by a message traversing a buffered, multistage packet-switching banyan network. We find the generating function for the distribution of waiting time at the first stage of the network for a very general class of traffic, assuming messages have discrete sizes. For example, traffic can be uniform or nonuniform, messages can have different sizes, and messages can arrive in batches. For light-to-moderate loads, we conjecture that delays experienced at the various stages of the network are nearly the same and are nearly independent. This allows us to approximate the total delay distribution. Better approximations for the distribution of waiting times at later stages of the network are attained by assuming that in the limit a sort of spatial steady state is achieved. Extensive simulations confirm the formulas and conjectures.

Index Terms—Banyan networks, discrete networks, interconnection networks, parallel processing, performance analysis, queueing theory.

I. INTRODUCTION

BUFFERED interconnection networks are receiving increasing consideration for use in parallel computers. They are integral components of several machines currently under development, including the Cedar machine at the University of Illinois, the NYU Ultracomputer at New York University [8], and the RP3 machine [16] at IBM, where they are used to interconnect processors to shared memory. In order to study the multitude of options available in actually building a machine, it is extremely useful to have formulas that approximate the performance of an interconnection network. In fact, formulas derived in a previous paper by two of the authors [11] have been heavily used in designing both the NYU Ultracomputer [8] and RP3 [14]. While simulation results are often more accurate, they are time consuming and expensive. In this paper, we analyze the random delay experienced by a message traversing a buffered, multistage packet-switching banyan network, for a very general class of traffic. For example, traffic can be uniform or nonuniform, messages can have different sizes, and messages can arrive in batches.

Interconnection networks connect processing elements to memory modules through stages of switches (Fig. 1). Early work in describing these networks was done by Goke and Lipovski [7], Lawrie [13], and Patel [15], among others. For fuller explanations of interconnection networks see [6] or [17], for example. There have been a number of performance analyses of interconnection networks (e.g., [4], [5], [11], [12]).

The basic building block of an interconnection network is a k-input, s-output ($k \times s$) buffered switch (Fig. 2). Each input port can accept one packet per clock cycle, and route it to the appropriate output port. Each output port has a FIFO buffer. Conflicts between messages simultaneously routed to the same output port are resolved by queueing the messages. We idealize this structure by assuming that the output buffers have infinite length. While this is clearly infeasible in practice, it is well known that for light-to-moderate loads, moderate-sized buffers provide approximately the same performance as infinite buffers. We also assume that each output port buffer can accept any number of messages from the input ports in a clock cycle, and that arriving messages do not interfere with departing messages. Each output port can be viewed as a discrete queueing system.

We make the following probabilistic assumptions concerning traffic at the first stage of a network.

1) The number of messages arriving at successive cycles to an output port are independent, identically distributed random variables. These random variables may have a different distribution at different ports, and are clearly dependent from port to port.

2) The service requirements (the number of cycles required to forward a packet) for successive messages at an output port are independent, identically distributed random variables. This distribution may vary from port to port.

Constant service time is usually the appropriate assumption for interconnection networks realized with synchronous logic.

Assuming that the traffic is uniform (e.g., each request is equally likely to go to every output node) and that at each cycle a packet arrives at an input node with a fixed probability p, the expected delay has been computed [11]. This analysis is based on Little's identity, and it is not obvious that it can be extended to obtain more information about the delay distribution, such as the variance. Such information is quite important for two reasons. First, to obtain good performance on a parallel machine, it is not sufficient to have a low expected memory access time; high variance will impede performance, as it is often the case that the speed of the slowest processor dictates the system speed. Second, as we discuss in Section V, the

Manuscript received March 17, 1986; revised December 16, 1987. C. P. Kruskal was supported in part by a grant from IBM and in part as a visitor to AT&T Bell Laboratories.

C. P. Kruskal is with the Department of Computer Science, Institute for Advanced Computer Studies, University of Maryland, College Park, MD 20742.

M. Snir is with the IBM Thomas J. Watson Research Center, Yorktown Heights, NY 10598.

A. Weiss is with the AT&T Bell Laboratories, Murray Hill, NJ 07974.

IEEE Log Number 8820883.

Reprinted from *IEEE Trans. Computers,* Vol. 37, No. 11, Nov. 1988, pp. 1337-1352. Copyright © 1988 by The Institute of Electrical and Electronics Engineers, Inc. All rights reserved.

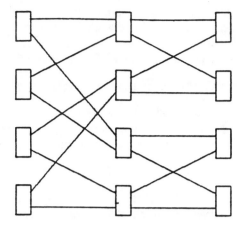

Fig. 1. Interconnection network.

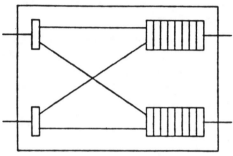

Fig. 2. 2 × 2 switch.

variance can be used to obtain an approximate formula for the waiting time distribution of a message through the entire network.

Exact formulas for both the average and variance of the waiting time at the first stage when all messages take a single cycle to service were obtained in a previous paper [12]. This was used to obtain approximate formulas for longer messages of constant size. Using stronger methods, we obtain in this paper exact formulas for the average and variance of the waiting time at the first stage for long messages of constant size; in fact, we obtain the entire distribution of waiting times for any discrete service time distribution. In the previous paper [12], we also suggested a method for analyzing the waiting time at later stages of the network, by assuming that the output of a queue can be modeled by a Markov process; the approximations were in practice hard to obtain and not very accurate. This paper gives an alternative method for approximating the waiting time at later stages; it is easy to use and provides extremely good approximations, as evidenced by comparison to simulation results.

In Section II, we analyze the performance of the first stage of an interconnection network, by calculating the z transform of the distribution of waiting times. This enables us to compute higher moments of that distribution. In particular, we present explicit formulas for the expected value and variance. In Section III, the formulas are used to find the expected value and variance of the waiting time under various standard assumptions. For light-to-moderate loads, we conjecture that waiting times experienced at the later stages of the network are nearly the same as for the first stage. In Section IV, we obtain

better approximations for the waiting time at the later stages. In Section V, we discuss how to analyze the total delay through the network. Section VI gives some concluding remarks.

II. ANALYSIS

Our model for the first stage of switching comes under the general rubric of a discrete time queueing system. We compute in this section the z transform for the waiting time, and use it to derive the expectation and variance of the waiting time, for general discrete service and arrival distributions. The solution method we use was indicated by Kobayashi and Konheim [10]. We are not, however, aware of a complete solution to this problem in the literature. As will be seen in the remainder of this paper, for the queueing systems we are interested in, it is useful to carry out the calculations in their entirety.

We start with some definitions. Let

$$\lambda = \text{average number of arrivals at any cycle}$$

and

$$m = \text{average service time of a message.}$$

The *traffic intensity* is then

$$\rho = m\lambda.$$

Let

$$f_j = \text{probability that } j \text{ messages arrive at any cycle}$$

and

$$R(z) = \sum_{j=0}^{\infty} f_j z^j.$$

Then

$$R'(1) = \lambda.$$

Let

$$g_j = \text{probability that a message requires } j \text{ time units to serve}$$

and

$$U(z) = \sum_{j=0}^{\infty} g_j z^j.$$

Then

$$U'(1) = m.$$

Theorem 1: Let w be the steady-state waiting time for a message. The z transform of the waiting time distribution of an output queue is

$$t(z) = \mathrm{E}(z^w) = \Psi(z)\phi(U(z))$$

$$= \frac{1-m\lambda}{\lambda} \frac{1-z}{R(U(z))-z} \frac{1-R(U(z))}{1-U(z)}. \tag{1}$$

Proof: Let s_n be the unfinished work at the end of the nth cycle, a_n be the number of messages arriving at the nth cycle, and c_n be the total service time for messages arriving at the nth cycle. Let s, a, and c be the steady-state variables corresponding to s_n, a_n, and c_n. Note that

$$E(z^a) = E(z^{a_n}) = R(z),$$

$$E(z^c) = \sum_{j=0}^{\infty} E(z^c | a=j) f_j = \sum_{j=0}^{\infty} (U(z))^j f_j = R(U(z)),$$

and

$$s_n = \max(0, s_{n-1} + c_n - 1).$$

Since c_n is independent of s_{n-1}, we obtain the identity

$$\begin{aligned}
E(z^s) &= E(z^{s+c-1} | s>0) P(s>0) \\
&\quad + E(z^{c-1} | s=0, c>0) P(s=0, c>0) \\
&\quad + E(z^0 | s=0, c=0) P(s=0, c=0) \\
&= E(z^c) E(z^{s-1} | s>0) P(s>0) \\
&\quad + E(z^{c-1} | c>0) P(s=0) P(c>0) \\
&\quad + P(s=0) P(c=0).
\end{aligned}$$

Let

$$\Psi(z) = \sum_{j=0}^{\infty} h_j z^j = E(z^s).$$

The previous identity implies

$$\begin{aligned}
\Psi(z) &= R(U(z)) \frac{(\Psi(z) - h_0)}{z} \\
&\quad + h_0 \frac{R(U(z)) - R(U(0))}{z} + h_0 R(U(0)),
\end{aligned}$$

so that

$$\Psi(z) = \frac{h_0 (1-z) R(U(0))}{R(U(z)) - z}.$$

We compute, using L'Hospital's rule

$$\Psi(1) = 1 = \frac{h_0 R(U(0))}{1 - m\lambda},$$

Since the arrival process is memoryless, arriving batches see the steady-state unfinished work distribution s. Thus $w = s + w'$, where w' is the steady-state service time for messages arriving at the same cycle, but served first. We have

$$E(z^w) = E(z^s) E(z^{w'}) = \Psi(z) E(z^{w'}).$$

Let d be the steady-state number of messages that arrive at the same cycle with any message, but are served before it; let $\phi(z) = E(z^d)$. Then, using the same derivation as before, we get

$$E(z^{w'}) = \phi(U(z)).$$

We shall now compute $\phi(z)$. The probability that any message arrives in a batch of j messages is equal to jf_j/λ. Thus,

$$\begin{aligned}
P(d=j) &= \sum_{k=j+1}^{\infty} P(d=j \,|\, \text{message arrives in a} \\
&\qquad \text{batch of } k \text{ messages}) \, k f_k / \lambda \\
&= \sum_{k=j+1}^{\infty} \frac{1}{k} (k f_k / \lambda),
\end{aligned}$$

so that

$$\begin{aligned}
\phi(z) &= \frac{1}{\lambda} \sum_{j=0}^{\infty} \sum_{k=j+1}^{\infty} f_k z^j \\
&= \frac{1}{\lambda} \sum_{k=1}^{\infty} f_k \sum_{j=0}^{k-1} z^j = \frac{1}{\lambda(z-1)} \sum_{k=1}^{\infty} f_k (z^k - 1) \\
&= \frac{R(z) - 1}{\lambda(z-1)}.
\end{aligned}$$

The z transform of the waiting time distribution is

$$\begin{aligned}
t(z) &= E(z^w) = \Psi(z) \phi(U(z)) \\
&= \frac{1-m\lambda}{\lambda} \frac{1-z}{R(U(z)) - z} \frac{1 - R(U(z))}{1 - U(z)}.
\end{aligned}$$

In principle, this gives the complete distribution of the waiting time. Differentiating $t(z)$, we obtain

$$t'(z) = E'(z^w)$$

$$= \frac{1-m\lambda}{\lambda} \frac{-R'(U(z)) U'(z)[1 - U(z)][1-z]^2 + [1 - U(z)][1 - R(U(z))]^2 + [R(U(z)) - z][1-z][1 - R(U(z))] U'(z)}{[R(U(z)) - z]^2 [1 - U(z)]^2}.$$

so that

$$h_0 = \frac{1 - m\lambda}{R(U(0))},$$

and

$$\Psi(z) = \frac{(1-z)(1 - m\lambda)}{R(U(z)) - z}.$$

Taking the limit as z approaches 1 (by applying L'Hospital's rule four times), we get

$$t'(1) = E(w) = \frac{m R''(1) + \lambda^2 U''(1)}{2\lambda(1 - m\lambda)}. \tag{2}$$

A formula for the second moment (and variance) is derived by looking at the second derivative of $t(z)$:

$$t''(1) = E(w(w-1)) = E''(z^w)|_{z=1}$$

$$= \frac{(2R'''(1)m^2 + 2\lambda^2 U'''(1))(1-m\lambda) + 3R''(1)^2 m^3 + 3\lambda^3 U''(1)^2 + 3R''(1)U''(1) + 3R''(1)U''(1)m\lambda}{6\lambda(1-m\lambda)^2}$$

which yields

$\text{Var}(w)$

$$= E(w(w-1)) + E(w)(1-E(w))$$

$$= \frac{(6m\lambda R''(1) + 4m^2\lambda R'''(1) + 6\lambda^3 U''(1) + 4\lambda^3 U'''(1))(1-m\lambda) - 3m^2 R''(1)^2(1-2m\lambda) + 3\lambda^4 U''(1)^2 + 6\lambda R''(1)U''(1)}{12\lambda^2(1-m\lambda)^2}.$$

$$\tag{3}$$

(The derivation of $t''(1)$ used six applications of L'Hospital's rule, and took Macsyma all night on a minicomputer.)

III. Examples

We now apply the above formulas to derive the expected value and the variance of the waiting time for messages in several standard and important queueing systems. Note that the expected value formulas only give the waiting time of a message. To obtain the *delay* of a message in a queue, one must add to these formulas the service time. For the queueing systems in this section, message arrivals are independent of queue length. Thus, the variance of the delay of a message in a queue is simply the sum of the variance of the waiting time and the variance of the service time.

A. Service Time One

Suppose that all messages take exactly one unit of time to be serviced. Then $m = 1$ and $U(z) = z$. Thus,

$$U'(z) = 1$$

and

$$U''(z) = U'''(z) = 0.$$

Substituting into (1), we obtain

$$t(z) = E(z^w) = \frac{1-\lambda}{\lambda} \frac{1-R(z)}{R(z)-z}.$$

Substituting into (2), we get

$$E(w) = \frac{R''(1)}{2\lambda(1-\lambda)} \tag{4}$$

and substituting into (3), we get

$\text{Var}(w)$

$$= \frac{2(3R''(1) + 2R'''(1))\lambda(1-\lambda) - 3(1-2\lambda)(R''(1))^2}{12\lambda^2(1-\lambda)^2}. \tag{5}$$

We analyze some special cases of this for k-input, s-output ($k \times s$) switches.

1) Uniform Traffic, Single Arrivals: Suppose that each input port has a probability p of receiving one message at each unit of time, and that each incoming message has an equal chance of going to any of the output ports. Then

$$f_j = \binom{k}{j}\left(\frac{p}{s}\right)^j \left(1-\frac{p}{s}\right)^{k-j}.$$

This quickly yields

$$R(z) = \left(1 - \frac{p}{s} + \frac{pz}{s}\right)^k$$

so that

$$R'(1) = \lambda = \frac{kp}{s},$$

$$R''(1) = k(k-1)\left(\frac{p}{s}\right)^2 = \lambda^2\left(1 - \frac{1}{k}\right),$$

and

$$R'''(1) = k(k-1)(k-2)\left(\frac{p}{s}\right)^3 = \lambda^3\left(1-\frac{1}{k}\right)\left(1-\frac{2}{k}\right).$$

Hence, substituting into (4) and (5),

$$E(w) = \frac{\left(1-\frac{1}{k}\right)\lambda}{2(1-\lambda)} \tag{6}$$

and

$$\text{Var}(w) = \frac{\left(1-\frac{1}{k}\right)\lambda\left[6 - 5\lambda\left(1+\frac{1}{k}\right) + 2\lambda^2\left(1+\frac{1}{k}\right)\right]}{12(1-\lambda)^2}. \tag{7}$$

2) Bulk Arrivals: In many systems, the size of a message exceeds the size of a transmission packet; a message is transmitted in several packets. These packets arrive at the first stage of the network in one bulk. This can be modeled as in the previous example, except arrivals at input ports are in batches.

Assuming a constant batch size of b messages,

$$R(z) = \left(1 - \frac{p}{s} + \frac{pz^b}{s}\right)^k .$$

Thus,

$$R'(1) = \lambda = \frac{kbp}{s},$$

$$R''(1) = \frac{bkp}{s}\left(b - 1 + \frac{b(k-1)p}{s}\right)$$

$$= \lambda\left(b - 1 + \left(1 - \frac{1}{k}\right)\lambda\right),$$

and

$$R'''(1) = \frac{bkp}{s}\left((b-1)(b-2) + \frac{3b(b-1)(k-1)p}{s}\right.$$

$$\left. + \frac{b^2(k-1)(k-2)p^2}{s^2}\right)$$

$$= \lambda\left((b-1)(b-2) + 3\lambda(b-1)\left(1 - \frac{1}{k}\right)\right.$$

$$\left. + \lambda^2\left(1 - \frac{1}{k}\right)\left(1 - \frac{2}{k}\right)\right).$$

Using (4) and (5), this gives

$$E(w) = \frac{(b-1) + \left(1 - \frac{1}{k}\right)\lambda}{2(1-\lambda)}$$

and

$$\text{Var}(w) = \frac{b^2 - 1 + 2\lambda\left(b^2 + 2 - \frac{3b}{k}\right) - 5\lambda^2\left(1 - \frac{1}{k^2}\right) + 2\lambda^3\left(1 - \frac{1}{k^2}\right)}{12(1-\lambda)^2} .$$

These agree with our previous formulas for the case $b = 1$.

3) *Nonuniform Traffic:* In many practical situations, each input is likely to have a distinct favorite output port (e.g., the output port connecting a processor to its private memory—see [1]). We assume that $k = s$. (It is not hard to generalize this for $k \neq s$, but the equations become quite lengthy.) We do assume bulk arrivals. Each input port sends arriving messages to its favorite output port with probability q, and sends them with probability $(1 - q)/k$ to each output port (including its favorite output). The distribution of messages at the output ports is the product of two terms: the first term accounts for normal messages and is essentially the same as given in Section III-A-2, with p replaced by $p(1 - q)$; the second term accounts for favored messages. We get

$$R(z) = \left(1 - p\frac{1-q}{k} + p\frac{1-q}{k}z^b\right)^{k-1}$$

$$\cdot \left(1 - p\left(q + \frac{1-q}{k}\right) + p\left(q + \frac{1-q}{k}\right)z^b\right).$$

Thus,

$$R'(1) = \lambda = bp,$$

$$R''(1) = bp\left(bp\left(1 - \frac{1}{k}\right)(1 - q^2) + (b-1)\right)$$

$$= \lambda\left(\lambda\left(1 - \frac{1}{k}\right)(1 - q^2) + b - 1\right),$$

and

$$R'''(1)$$

$$= bp\left(b^2p^2\left(1 - \frac{1}{k}\right)\left(1 - \frac{2}{k}\right)(1 - 3q^2 + 2q^3)\right.$$

$$+ 3b(b-1)p\left(1 - \frac{1}{k}\right)(1 - q^2) + (b-1)(b-2)\bigg)$$

$$= \lambda\left(\lambda^2\left(1 - \frac{1}{k}\right)\left(1 - \frac{2}{k}\right)(1 - 3q^2 + 2q^3)\right.$$

$$+ 3\lambda(b-1)\left(1 - \frac{1}{k}\right)(1 - q^2) + (b-1)(b-2)\bigg).$$

Substituting into (4),

$$E(w) = \frac{\lambda(1-q^2)\left(1 - \frac{1}{k}\right) + b - 1}{2(1-\lambda)} .$$

Note that for $q = 1$, we get $E(w) = 0$, and for $q = 0$ we obtain the same formula as in Section III-A-1 (with $k = s$), as it should be.

The general formula for the variance is quite lengthy. For $b = 1$,

$$\text{Var}(w) = \frac{\left(1 - \frac{1}{k}\right)p(1-q)}{12(1-p)^2}$$

$$\cdot \left[\left(6 - 5\left(1 + \frac{1}{k}\right)p + 2\left(1 + \frac{1}{k}\right)p^2\right)\right.$$

$$+ \left(6 - 5\left(1 + \frac{1}{k}\right)p + 2\left(1 + \frac{1}{k}\right)p^2\right)q$$

$$+ \left(-\left(5 - \frac{13}{k}\right)p + 2\left(1 - \frac{5}{k}\right)p^2\right)q^2$$

$$+ \left(3\left(1 - \frac{1}{k}\right)p - 6\left(1 - \frac{1}{k}\right)p^2\right)q^3\right].$$

472

B. Geometric Service Distribution

Suppose that service times are geometrically distributed. Let the distribution of service times be $g_j = \mu(1-\mu)^{j-1}$, $j = 1, 2, \cdots$, where μ is a constant, $0 < \mu \le 1$. Then

$$U(z) = \sum_{j=0}^{\infty} z^j \mu (1-\mu)^{j-1} = \frac{\mu z}{1 - z(1-\mu)}$$

so

$$U'(1) = m = \frac{1}{\mu},$$

$$U''(1) = \frac{2(1-\mu)}{\mu^2},$$

and

$$U'''(1) = \frac{6(1-\mu)^2}{\mu^3}.$$

For the case of individual arrivals and balanced traffic, as in Section III-A-1 above, we have

$$R(z) = \left(1 - \frac{p}{s} + \frac{pz}{s}\right)^k,$$

$$R'(1) = \lambda = \frac{kp}{s},$$

$$R''(1) = k(k-1)\left(\frac{p}{s}\right)^2 = \lambda^2\left(1 - \frac{1}{k}\right),$$

and

$$R'''(1) = k(k-1)(k-2)\left(\frac{p}{s}\right)^3 = \lambda^3\left(1 - \frac{1}{k}\right)\left(1 - \frac{2}{k}\right).$$

Recall that the traffic intensity is

$$\rho = m\lambda = \frac{kp}{\mu s}.$$

Substituting into (2) and (3), we obtain

$$E(w) = \frac{\rho\left(2 - \left(1 + \frac{1}{k}\right)\mu\right)}{2\mu(1-\rho)}$$

and

C. M/M/1 Queues

An M/M/1 queueing system can be thought of as the continuous time limit of systems with geometric service times. Suppose we scale time so that there are n cycles per time unit. Consider uniform traffic, single arrivals (as in Section III-B); let the geometric distribution approach the continuous, exponentially distributed, limit by replacing μ by mu/n, and letting n tend to infinity. (This gives the same average service time in unscaled units.) Replace the arrival probability p by p/n to maintain the same traffic intensity ρ. Then as $n \to \infty$, the queue becomes an M/M/1 queue with arrival rate $\lambda = pk/s$ and service time $m = 1/\mu$.

We can see this formally as a consequence of our results by computing the limiting distribution of the waiting time.

$$R(z) = \left(1 - \frac{p}{ns} + \frac{pz}{ns}\right)^k$$

$$\approx 1 + \frac{pk}{ns}(z-1)$$

and

$$U(z) - 1 = \frac{z-1}{1 - z\left(1 - \frac{\mu}{n}\right)},$$

which yields

$$t(z) \approx (1-\rho)\frac{1}{1 - \rho\dfrac{1}{1 - z\left(1 - \dfrac{\mu}{n}\right)}}.$$

Now scale time by replacing z by $z^{1/n}$, and change the z transform to a Laplace transform by introducing the variable $s = -\log z$. This gives the Laplace transform of waiting time as

$$\frac{1-\rho}{1 - \rho\dfrac{\mu}{\mu+s}},$$

which is the well-known transform of the M/M/1 waiting time distribution (see [9, Section 5.12]). So, in particular,

$$E(w) = \lim_{n\to\infty}\frac{1}{n}\frac{\rho\left(2 - \left(1 + \frac{1}{k}\right)\frac{\mu}{n}\right)}{2\frac{\mu}{n}(1-\rho)} = \frac{1}{\mu}\frac{\rho}{1-\rho}.$$

$$\mathrm{Var}(w) = \frac{6\rho\left(4 - 4\mu\left(1 + \frac{1}{2k}\right) + \mu^2\left(1 + \frac{1}{k}\right)\right) - \rho^2\left(12 - 12\mu + 5\mu^2\left(1 - \frac{1}{k^2}\right)\right) - 2\rho^3\left(6 - 12\mu + 5\mu^2\left(1 + \frac{1}{5k^2}\right)\right)}{12\mu^2(1-\rho)^2}.$$

These reduce to the equations in Section III-A-1 when $\mu = 1$.

This is the waiting time for an M/M/1 queue, as it should be. A similar derivation will show that the variance we obtained for geometric distribution converges to the variance of an M/M/1 queue.

D. Constant Service Times

We now consider the situation when messages can have one of several constant service times. We will only consider uniform traffic, single arrivals. Thus, as in Section III-A-1,

$$R(z) = \left(1 - \frac{p}{s} + \frac{pz}{s}\right)^k,$$

$$R'(1) = \lambda = \frac{kp}{s},$$

$$R''(1) = k(k-1)\left(\frac{p}{s}\right)^2 = \lambda^2\left(1 - \frac{1}{k}\right),$$

and

$$R'''(1) = k(k-1)(k-2)\left(\frac{p}{s}\right)^3 = \lambda^3\left(1 - \frac{1}{k}\right)\left(1 - \frac{2}{k}\right).$$

1) Single Size: First, suppose that each message takes exactly m units of time to transmit. This will occur, for instance, when each message is composed of an equal number (m) of packets, and the constituent packets of a message are transmitted at consecutive cycles. Then

$$U(z) = z^m,$$

so that

$$U'(1) = m,$$

$$U''(1) = m(m-1),$$

and

$$U'''(1) = m(m-1)(m-2).$$

The traffic intensity is now

$$\rho = \frac{mpk}{s}.$$

Substituting into (2) and (3), we obtain

$$E(w) = \frac{\rho\left(m - \frac{1}{k}\right)}{2(1-\rho)} \tag{8}$$

and

These coincide, for $m = 1$, with the equations of Section III-A-1.

2) Multiple Sizes: Now suppose there are n service times $m_1, \cdots, m_n$, and service time m_i occurs with probability g_i. This will occur when there are different kinds of requests. For example, read requests are likely to have different sizes than write requests.

We get

$$U(z) = \sum_{i=1}^{n} g_i z^{m_i},$$

so that

$$U'(1) = \sum_{i=1}^{n} m_i g_i$$

and

$$U''(1) = \sum_{i=1}^{n} m_i(m_i - 1)g_i.$$

Thus,

$$\rho = \frac{kp}{s} \sum_{i=1}^{n} m_i g_i.$$

Substituting into (2), we obtain

$$E(w) = \frac{\lambda \sum_{i=1}^{n} m_i\left(m_i - \frac{1}{k}\right)g_i}{2(1-\rho)} = \frac{\rho \sum_{i=1}^{n} m_i\left(m_i - \frac{1}{k}\right)g_i}{2(1-\rho)\sum_{i=1}^{n} m_i g_i}.$$

The formula for the variance could also be obtained, but it is quite lengthy and not particularly enlightening.

IV. LATER STAGES

We do not know how to analyze the later stages exactly as the inputs at successive cycles are not independent. We have, however, developed some very useful approximate formulas for the average and variance of the waiting time. These are based on two observations. First, as we progress through the network, the waiting time statistics quickly approach a limiting distribution. Second, nearly every waiting time distribution in queueing theory has an average on the order of $1/(1 - \rho)$ as ρ tends to one; that is, if $w_i(\rho)$ is the average waiting time at the ith stage, and $w_\infty(\rho)$ is the limit as i gets large, we expect $\lim_{\rho \to 1} (1 - \rho)w_\infty(\rho)$ to exist. We calculated $w_1(\rho)$ exactly in Section III, and we expect $w_1(\rho)$ and $w_\infty(\rho)$ to have similar qualitative properties, i.e., they should depend on most

$$\text{Var}(w) = \frac{\rho\left(\left(1 - \frac{1}{k}\right)\left[6m - 5\rho\left(1 + \frac{1}{k}\right) + 2\rho^2\left(1 + \frac{1}{k}\right)\right] + (m-1)[2(2m-1) - \rho(m+1)]\right)}{12(1-\rho)^2}. \tag{9}$$

parameters in roughly the same way. Hence, it seems reasonable to estimate

$$r(\rho) \overset{\text{def}}{=} \frac{w_\infty(\rho)}{w_1(\rho)}.$$

It seems clear that, for uniform traffic with unit service time, $r(0) = 1$. We use simulations to estimate $r(1/2)$, and then simply linearly interpolate to obtain a value a such that

$$r(\rho) \approx 1 + a\rho. \qquad (10)$$

Then

$$w_\infty(\rho) \approx (1 + a\rho) w_1(\rho).$$

We will also generalize the formulas to take into account the dependence of $w_i(\rho)$ on the stage, the switch size, and the message size distribution. This method of interpolation was previously applied to queueing systems by Burman and Smith [3] using light and heavy traffic theory. The light traffic limit exists in our case. We do not have a heavy traffic analysis for our process, so we rely on simulation instead.

Using the same ideas, we can obtain an approximation for the variance. Let v_i be the variance of the waiting time at stage i, and v_∞ be the variance in the limit. Since the formulas for variance have one higher power of ρ, we expect a good approximation of $v_\infty(\rho)/v_1(\rho)$ to contain (at least) one higher power of ρ, i.e., we obtain a quadratic interpolation for the variance. The variance after several stages can be approximated by

$$v_\infty \approx (1 + a\rho + b\rho^2) v_1$$

where a and b are constants to be determined.

In the remainder of this section, we obtain our expression for the waiting time and variance in step-by-step generalizations. We first estimate them for uniform traffic when messages have size one, then size m, and then general size. Finally, we consider nonuniform traffic.

A. Service Time One

Consider service time one, 2×2 switches, single arrivals, and uniform traffic. For $p = 0.5$, $w_1 = 0.25$ [see (6)], and, from the simulations in Table I, w_∞ seems to be about 0.3. Substituting into (10) and solving for a gives $a \approx 2/5$. Thus, we find $r(\rho) \approx 1 + 2p/5$, so the waiting time

$$w_\infty \approx \left(1 + \frac{2p}{5}\right) \frac{p}{4(1-p)}.$$

Table I compares the simulation results to our formulas. The waiting time values in the ANALYSIS row are from the exact formula for the first stage [see (6) and (7)], and the waiting time values in the ESTIMATE row are from the above approximation for the waiting time in the limit. Note that the approximation seems to be slightly low for p small and slightly high for p large. More complete simulation results (not included for brevity) show that $r(\rho)$ is actually slightly concave. An even better estimate could be obtained by using a quadratic approximation.

Using the same technique for 4×4 and 8×8 switches

TABLE I
WAITING TIMES AND VARIANCES: p VARYING ($k = 2$, $m = 1$, AND $q = 0$)

	$p = 0.2$		$p = 0.5$		$p = 0.8$	
	E	Var	E	Var	E	Var
ANALYSIS	0.0625	0.0602	0.2500	0.2500	1.0000	1.6000
SIMULATION						
1st stage	0.0625	0.0602	0.2501	0.2503	0.9987	1.5986
2nd stage	0.0657	0.0639	0.2809	0.3042	1.1964	2.4148
3rd stage	0.0670	0.0656	0.2929	0.3267	1.2569	2.7238
4th stage	0.0676	0.0663	0.2970	0.3359	1.2818	2.8490
5th stage	0.0676	0.0663	0.2985	0.3391	1.2907	2.9224
6th stage	0.0675	0.0662	0.2992	0.3409	1.2971	2.9305
7th stage	0.0679	0.0667	0.2997	0.3428	1.2935	2.9076
8th stage	0.0682	0.0669	0.2996	0.3410	1.2964	2.9347
9th stage	0.0681	0.0669	0.2997	0.3431	1.2968	2.9440
10th stage	0.0680	0.0667	0.2999	0.3422	1.3014	3.0016
11th stage	0.0680	0.0668	0.2999	0.3428	1.2980	2.9449
12th stage	0.0681	0.0669	0.3002	0.3431	1.2974	2.9656
ESTIMATE	0.0675	0.0656	0.3000	0.3438	1.3200	2.9440

TABLE II
WAITING TIMES AND VARIANCES: k VARYING ($p = 0.5$, $m = 1$, AND $q = 0$)

	$k = 2$		$k = 4$		$k = 8$	
	E	Var	E	Var	E	Var
ANALYSIS	0.2500	0.2500	0.3750	0.4375	0.4375	0.5469
SIMULATION						
1st stage	0.2501	0.2502	0.3740	0.4350	0.4371	0.5465
2nd stage	0.2812	0.3048	0.4005	0.4941	0.4532	0.5848
3rd stage	0.2928	0.3258	0.4060	0.5055	0.4559	0.5934
4th stage	0.2977	0.3372	0.4067	0.5112	0.4562	0.5934
ESTIMATE	0.3000	0.3438	0.4125	0.5195	0.4597	0.5982

gives a a bit less than 0.2 and a a bit less than 0.1, respectively (see (6) and Table II). This suggests that the above formula can be (crudely) extended to $k \times k$ switches by linearly including k as a parameter. This gives the waiting time

$$w_\infty \approx \left(1 + \frac{4p}{5k}\right) \frac{\left(1 - \frac{1}{k}\right)p}{2(1-p)}. \qquad (11)$$

Table II compares the simulation results to our formulas.

In Tables I and II it looks as if w_i approaches w_∞ geometrically. This suggests a formula of the form $r_i(\rho) = 1 + (1 - \alpha^{i-1})(r(\rho) - 1)$ for some $\alpha < 1$, yielding

$$w_i \approx \left(1 + \frac{4p}{5k}(1 - \alpha^{i-1})\right) \frac{\left(1 - \frac{1}{k}\right)p}{2(1-p)} \qquad (12)$$

as the expected waiting time at the ith stage. Looking once again at the formula for $k = 2$ and $p = 0.5$ (Table I), gives $\alpha = 2/5$ as a good approximation. It turns out that this value of α works reasonably well for general k and p. For brevity, we do not explicitly compare this formula to the simulations (although the interested reader can easily do the calculations). It is by no means surprising that, for a given p and k, w_i approaches w_∞ geometrically; what is perhaps surprising is that a single value of α works well for all p and k.

Applying the same techniques to variance, we find that a reasonable formula for the variance after several stages is

$$v_\infty \approx \left(1 + \frac{p}{2k} + \frac{2p^2}{k}\right)$$
$$\cdot \frac{\left(1 - \frac{1}{k}\right)p\left[6 - 5p\left(1 + \frac{1}{k}\right) + 2p^2\left(1 + \frac{1}{k}\right)\right]}{12(1-p)^2}. \qquad (13)$$

Since this is only an approximation and since the simulation results do not give exact answers, there is quite a bit of freedom in choosing coefficients a and b for the p and p^2 terms. Other choices will surely work just as well or better. We can also estimate the variance at stage i to be

$$v_i \approx \left(1 + \left(\frac{p}{2k} + \frac{2p^2}{k}\right)(1 - \alpha^{i-1})\right)$$

$$\cdot \frac{\left(1 - \frac{1}{k}\right)p\left[6 - 5p\left(1 + \frac{1}{k}\right) + 2p^2\left(1 + \frac{1}{k}\right)\right]}{12(1-p)^2} \quad (14)$$

where $\alpha = 2/5$.

B. Single Service Time

Consider the case when messages have a single constant size. Our model of the first stage is not a particularly good model for the later stages. At the first stage, a source after sending a message can send a new message on the next or any later cycle. At later stages, since sources are outputs from queues, once a source sends a message, that source will not send a message for at least m cycles. This will tend to reduce queueing delays at the later stages.

Later stages can be better modeled by assuming that messages take one cycle to be processed, but the cycle time is m times as long. Following [11], we use the formula for service time one (11), and, for a fixed p, multiply the time to process a message by a factor m, and also multiply the average number of packets per cycle by m. In other words, for a fixed traffic intensity ρ, the cycle time is m times as large. This gives the average waiting time

$$w_\infty \approx \left(1 + \frac{4mp}{5k}\right)\frac{\left(1 - \frac{1}{k}\right)m^2 p}{2(1 - mp)}. \quad (15)$$

For $m \geq 2$, this formula is a reasonable approximation at all stages after the first, and, of course, we have an exact formula for the first stage. Table III compares the simulation results to our formulas.

Let us examine the behavior of the interior stages in light traffic. Reasoning as in Section III-C, if we allow m to increase and p to decrease with $mp = \rho$ constant, then in time scaled by m, the first stage output queues become M/D/1 queues with arrival rate ρ and service time 1. (Actually, the well-known waiting time statistics of M/D/1 queues can be obtained as limits of (8) and (9).) Now the interior stages are not precisely M/D/1 queues in this scaling, because the packets output from previous stages must be spaced by at least m time units. Nevertheless, it is clear that in light traffic the interior stages will resemble M/D/1 queues, but the congestion will be lower than at the first stage, since packets will be very unlikely to collide with other packets from the same source. That is, the congestion will be as if the arrival rate were $(1 - 1/k)\rho$. Using the M/D/1 light traffic results,

$$E(w) = \frac{\left(1 - \frac{1}{k}\right)\rho}{2} + O(\rho^2)$$

TABLE III
WAITING TIMES AND VARIANCES: p AND m VARYING WITH $\rho = 0.5$
($k = 2$ AND $q = 0$)

	$m = 2$ $p = 1/4$		$m = 4$ $p = 1/8$		$m = 8$ $p = 1/16$		$m = 16$ $p = 1/32$	
	E	Var	E	Var	E	Var	E	Var
ANALYSIS	0.750	1.500	1.750	7.500	3.750	33.50	7.750	141.50
SIMULATION								
1st stage	0.749	1.500	1.750	7.535	3.752	33.68	7.791	142.58
2nd stage	0.588	1.158	1.203	4.708	2.435	19.23	4.889	77.35
3rd stage	0.592	1.186	1.198	4.710	2.412	18.81	4.815	74.71
4th stage	0.601	1.217	1.200	4.718	2.402	18.77	4.807	75.27
5th stage	0.603	1.230	1.203	4.736	2.402	18.81	4.772	73.90
6th stage	0.601	1.224	1.206	4.800	2.401	18.77	4.788	74.72
7th stage	0.600	1.219	1.200	4.754	2.399	18.79	4.773	73.78
8th stage	0.603	1.234	1.204	4.777	2.396	18.73	4.778	74.35
ESTIMATE	0.600	1.167	1.200	4.667	2.400	18.67	4.800	74.67

and

$$\text{Var}(w) = \frac{\left(1 - \frac{1}{k}\right)\rho}{3} + O(\rho^2).$$

Our approximations should have these properties, too. Equation (15) does satisfy this.

To obtain an approximation for the variance, we argue as before: start with the formula for the variance at the first stage for unit size messages (7), multiply by m^2, change p to mp, and then use the light traffic analysis and the simulations to interpolate. Our heuristic formula is [see (13)]

$$v_\infty \approx \left(\frac{2}{3} + \frac{C_1\rho}{k} + \frac{C_2\rho^2}{k}\right)$$

$$\cdot \frac{\left(1 - \frac{1}{k}\right)m^3 p\left[6 - 5mp\left(1 + \frac{1}{k}\right) + 2(mp)^2\left(1 + \frac{1}{k}\right)\right]}{12(1 - mp)^2},$$

where 2/3 was obtained from light traffic analysis. Light traffic analysis is a limiting case for m large; in practice, we found that 7/10 works better than 2/3 for small and moderate message sizes. We match the constants C_1 and C_2 to simulation results, giving

$$v_\infty \approx \frac{7}{10}\left(1 + \frac{2mp}{3k} + \frac{4(mp)^2}{k}\right)$$

$$\cdot \frac{\left(1 - \frac{1}{k}\right)m^3 p\left[6 - 5mp\left(1 + \frac{1}{k}\right) + 2(mp)^2\left(1 + \frac{1}{k}\right)\right]}{12(1 - mp)^2}. \quad (16)$$

This approximation is still slightly low for m small, as can be seen in Table III. Better approximations can be obtained for each individual value of m; in particular, (13) is a much better approximation for $m = 1$. As with waiting times, for $m \geq 2$, this formula can be used to approximate variances for all stages after the first.

C. Multiple Service Times

As in Section III-D-2, suppose there are n service times $m_1, \cdots, m_n$, and service time m_i occurs with probability g_i.

TABLE IV

WAITING TIMES AND VARIANCES: $m_1 = 4$; $m_2 = 8$; AND p, g_1, AND g_2 VARYING WITH $\rho = 0.5$ ($k = 2$ AND $q = 0$)

	$g_1 = 0.0$ $g_2 = 1.0$ $p = 1/16$		$g_1 = 0.25$ $g_2 = 0.75$ $p = 1/14$		$g_1 = 0.5$ $g_2 = 0.5$ $p = 1/12$		$g_1 = 0.75$ $g_2 = 0.25$ $p = 1/10$		$g_1 = 1.0$ $g_2 = 0.0$ $p = 1/8$	
	E	Var	E	Var	E	Var	E	Var	E	Var
ANALYSIS	3.750	33.50	3.464	29.30	3.083	23.94	2.550	16.94	1.750	7.50
SIMULATION										
1st stage	3.752	33.77	3.461	29.16	3.092	24.11	2.552	16.98	1.749	7.46
2nd stage	2.454	19.53	2.255	16.64	2.039	13.72	1.706	9.87	1.199	4.67
3rd stage	2.417	18.95	2.235	16.43	2.010	13.48	1.691	9.67	1.197	4.70
4th stage	2.405	18.88	2.241	16.45	2.018	13.51	1.689	9.75	1.204	4.76
5th stage	2.392	18.73	2.256	16.83	2.025	13.58	1.696	9.89	1.193	4.68
6th stage	2.409	18.09	2.249	16.64	2.023	13.65	1.691	9.78	1.202	4.76
7th stage	2.408	18.01	2.249	16.62	2.016	13.50	1.690	9.71	1.199	4.76
8th stage	2.396	18.68	2.238	16.41	2.023	13.70	1.695	9.78	1.196	4.70
ESTIMATE	2.400	18.67	2.238	16.58	2.018	13.84	1.700	10.08	1.200	4.67

TABLE V

WAITING TIMES AND VARIANCES: q VARYING ($p = 0.5$, $k = 2$, AND $m = 1$)

	$q = 0.0$		$q = 0.25$		$q = 0.50$		$q = 0.75$	
	E	Var	E	Var	E	Var	E	Var
ANALYSIS	0.2500	0.2500	0.2344	0.2344	0.1875	0.1875	0.1094	0.1094
SIMULATION								
1st stage	0.2501	0.2502	0.2341	0.2340	0.1886	0.1890	0.1093	0.1089
2nd stage	0.2811	0.3047	0.2598	0.2771	0.2041	0.2136	0.1138	0.1157
3rd stage	0.2919	0.3240	0.2683	0.2934	0.2087	0.2218	0.1174	0.1200
4th stage	0.2967	0.3330	0.2730	0.3036	0.2116	0.2275	0.1171	0.1200
5th stage	0.2983	0.3387	0.2741	0.3050	0.2117	0.2275	0.1172	0.1209
6th stage	0.2992	0.3399	0.2739	0.3030	0.2108	0.2265	0.1160	0.1185
7th stage	0.2998	0.3436	0.2754	0.3069	0.2100	0.2256	0.1163	0.1190
8th stage	0.3000	0.3426	0.2748	0.3079	0.2085	0.2228	0.1162	0.1195
ESTIMATE	0.3000	0.3438	0.2695	0.3003	0.2063	0.2227	0.1148	0.1196

The average service time is $m = \sum_{i=1}^{n} g_i m_i$. To obtain an approximate formula for the average waiting time, replace the size of all messages by their average size m and use the approximate waiting time formula from the previous section (15). This gives the average waiting time

$$w_\infty \approx \left(1 + \frac{4mp}{5k}\right) \frac{\left(1 - \frac{1}{k}\right) m^2 p}{2(1 - mp)} .$$

The values obtained from this formula tend to be a bit low. The reason is that we are approximating multiple size messages by their average size. Since we are able to calculate everything at the first stage exactly, we know how much off such an assumption would be at the first stage: simply the ratio of the actual expected waiting time and the waiting assuming all messages have their average size. Assuming this ratio is fairly constant at the different stages, multiplying the above formula by this ratio gives a very good approximation:

$$w_\infty \approx \left(1 + \frac{4mp}{5k}\right) \frac{\left(1 - \frac{1}{k}\right) mp \sum_{i=1}^{n} m_i \left(m_i - \frac{1}{k}\right) g_i}{2(1 - mp)\left(m - \frac{1}{k}\right)} .$$

An approximate formula for the variance v_∞ could be obtained similarly, but, as with the variance formula for the first stage, it is quite lengthy. We have, however, obtained numerical values from both variance formulas, i.e., for v_1 and v_∞. Table IV compares the simulation results to our formulas.

D. Nonuniform Traffic

We can also obtain approximate formulas when each input has a distinct favorite output port. Our form for w_∞ is a linear function of q multiplied by the exact formula for the first stage. For $m = 1$, the coefficients of the linear function were found by starting with (11) (the $q = 0$ case) and comparing to the simulation results. The average waiting time in the limit can be approximated as

$$w_\infty \approx \left(1 + \frac{4(1-q)p}{5k}\right) \frac{(1 - q^2)\left(1 - \frac{1}{k}\right) p}{2(1 - p)} .$$

Similarly, the variance v_∞ can be approximated as a linear function of q multiplied by the exact formula for the variance at the first stage. Starting with (13) and comparing to simulation results gives

$$v_\infty \approx \left(1 + \left(\frac{p}{2k} + \frac{2p^2}{k}\right)(1 - q)\right)$$

$$\cdot \frac{\left(1 - \frac{1}{k}\right) p \left[6 - 5p\left(1 + \frac{1}{k}\right) + 2p^2\left(1 + \frac{1}{k}\right)\right]}{12(1 - p)^2} .$$

Table V compares the simulation results to our formulas. It is not hard to generalize these to obtain formulas for w_i and v_i.

We can approximate the average waiting time for message sizes greater than one. Using the general techniques in Section

TABLE VI
CORRELATIONS OF WAITING TIMES BETWEEN STAGES: ($k = 2$, $p = 0.5$, AND $m = 1$)

stage	1	2	3	4	5	6	7	8
1	1.0000	0.1098	0.0391	0.0153	0.0065	0.0030	0.0007	0.0002
2		1.0000	0.1179	0.0435	0.0184	0.0080	0.0040	0.0018
3			1.0000	0.1222	0.0446	0.0191	0.0080	0.0042
4				1.0000	0.1231	0.0460	0.0184	0.0082
5					1.0000	0.1241	0.0452	0.0197
6						1.0000	0.1228	0.0467
7							1.0000	0.1236
8								1.0000

IV-B, gives

$$w_\infty \approx \left(1 + \frac{4mp}{5k}\right) \frac{(1-q^2)\left(1-\frac{1}{k}\right)m^2p}{2(1-mp)}.$$

This is a good approximation for the average waiting time at all stages after the first ($m \geq 2$). The variance can be approximated similarly.

V. Total Delay

Once we have formulas for the expected value and variance of the waiting time at each stage, these can be used to obtain approximations for the total waiting time. The expected value of the total waiting time is simply the sum of the average waiting times at the different stages. In particular, for messages of size one, summing the w_i in (12) approximates the total waiting time for an n-stage network as

$$n\left(1 + \frac{4p}{5k}\left(1 - \frac{1-\alpha^n}{n(1-\alpha)}\right)\right) \frac{\left(1-\frac{1}{k}\right)p}{2(1-p)}$$

where $\alpha = 2/5$. For $m > 1$, the average total waiting time can be approximated as the average waiting time from the first stage [see (8)] plus $n - 1$ times the waiting time as the later stages [see (15)], which is

$$\frac{\left(m-\frac{1}{k}\right)mp}{2(1-mp)} + (n-1)\left(1 + \frac{4mp}{5k}\right)\frac{\left(1-\frac{1}{k}\right)m^2p}{2(1-mp)}.$$

If the waiting times from stage to stage were independent, as is the case with Poisson arrivals and exponential service times, the variance of the total waiting time would simply be the sum of the variances at the different stages. Table VI shows the correlation of waiting times between stages for $k = 2$, $p = 0.5$, and $m = 1$. Note that waiting times at neighboring stages have fairly low correlation, and the correlation seems to drop geometrically as stages become further apart. Thus, summing the variances should be a good approximation. In particular, for messages of size one, summing the v_i in (14) approximates the total variance for an n-stage network as

$$n\left(1 + \left(\frac{p}{2k} + \frac{2p^2}{k}\right)\left(1 - \frac{1-\alpha^n}{n(1-\alpha)}\right)\right)$$

$$\cdot \frac{\left(1-\frac{1}{k}\right)p\left[6 - 5p\left(1+\frac{1}{k}\right) + 2p^2\left(1+\frac{1}{k}\right)\right]}{12(1-p)^2}$$

where $\alpha = 2/5$. For $m \geq 2$, the variance can be approximated as the variance for the first stage [see (7)] plus $n - 1$ times the variance at the later stages [see (16)].

To obtain a better approximation, note that the total variance is actually the sum of the covariances between stages. Let v_{ij} be the covariance between stage i and stage j. Covariances seem to drop geometrically as stages become further apart. In particular, the v_{ij} can be approximated as follows: $v_{ii} = v_i$, $v_{i,i+1} \approx av_i$, $v_{i,i+2} \approx abv_i$, $v_{i,i+3} \approx ab^2v_i$, $v_{i,i+4} \approx ab^3v_i$, $\cdots$, where $a = (1 - (2mp/5))3mp/5k$ and $b = (1 - 2mp/5)/k$. Now summing all of the covariances approximates the total variance as

$$\sum_{i=1}^{n}\left(1 + \frac{2a(1-b^{n-i})}{1-b}\right)v_i.$$

For $m = 1$, we use the v_i from (14). For $m > 1$, v_1 is the true variance for the first stage [see (9)], and v_i, $i > 1$, can be approximated by the formula for v_∞ [see (16)]. Tables VII–XII compare the simulation results to our formulas.

The distribution of waiting times seems to be about the same for all stages. If the distributions were independent, by the central limit theorem, the total waiting times for a large number of stages could be approximated by a (truncated) normal distribution, whose sum is the sum of the expected values and whose variance is the sum of the variances. The central limit theorem actually holds under much weaker hypotheses than independence (see, for example, [2]), and we expect it essentially to apply here. For only a few stages, however, a normal approximation may not be very accurate at the tails. Typically in queueing systems, the distribution of waiting times has an exponential or geometric tail, so we expect a gamma distribution with the proper expected value and variance to be a good approximation for even small networks.

We have simulated networks of $n = 3, 6, 9, 12$ stages for service times $m = 1, 4$ and traffic intensities $\rho = 0.2, 0.5, 0.8$. The histograms in Figs. 3–8 show for each simulation the probability that a message has a given total waiting time. (Note that a message can have waiting time zero, since the delay does not include the service time of the message itself.) For each figure, the smooth curve is the gamma distribution with the expected value and variance as *estimated* in Tables VII–XII. The figures show an incredibly good match between the estimated and the observed distributions, especially at the tails. In practice, the expected value, the variance, and the tail of the waiting time distribution are the quantities of interest; we believe our formulas are accurate enough for all practical purposes.

TABLE VII
COMPARISON OF PREDICTIONS TO SIMULATIONS: ($k = 2$, $p = 0.2$, AND $m = 1$)

	ESTIMATE		SIMULATION	
	E	Var	E	Var
3 stages	0.195	0.200	0.195	0.199
6 stages	0.397	0.432	0.399	0.422
9 stages	0.599	0.668	0.603	0.647
12 stages	0.802	0.905	0.807	0.873

TABLE VIII
COMPARISON OF PREDICTIONS TO SIMULATIONS: ($k = 2$, $p = 0.05$, AND $m = 4$)

	ESTIMATE		SIMULATION	
	E	Var	E	Var
3 stages	0.978	3.152	0.983	3.250
6 stages	1.788	5.939	1.798	6.181
9 stages	2.598	8.730	2.613	9.103
12 stages	3.408	11.521	3.429	12.042

TABLE IX
COMPARISON OF PREDICTIONS TO SIMULATIONS: ($k = 2$, $p = 0.5$, AND $m = 1$)

	ESTIMATE		SIMULATION	
	E	Var	E	Var
3 stages	0.822	1.037	0.824	1.013
6 stages	1.717	2.438	1.717	2.362
9 stages	2.617	3.877	2.616	3.759
12 stages	3.517	5.321	3.516	5.160

TABLE X
COMPARISON OF PREDICTIONS TO SIMULATIONS: ($k = 2$, $p = 0.125$, AND $m = 4$)

	ESTIMATE		SIMULATION	
	E	Var	E	Var
3 stages	4.15	20.47	4.14	20.67
6 stages	7.75	40.06	7.73	41.16
9 stages	11.35	59.66	11.32	61.90
12 stages	14.95	79.26	14.92	82.67

TABLE XI
COMPARISON OF PREDICTIONS TO SIMULATIONS: ($k = 2$, $p = 0.8$, AND $m = 1$)

	ESTIMATE		SIMULATION	
	E	Var	E	Var
3 stages	3.46	8.65	3.45	8.22
6 stages	7.39	21.43	7.32	20.90
9 stages	11.35	34.60	11.21	34.08
12 stages	15.31	47.80	15.10	47.57

TABLE XII
COMPARISON OF PREDICTIONS TO SIMULATIONS: ($k = 2$, $p = 0.125$, AND $m = 4$)

	ESTIMATE		SIMULATION	
	E	Var	E	Var
3 stages	17.56	201.90	17.49	201.61
6 stages	33.40	406.37	33.08	412.18
9 stages	49.24	610.98	48.66	622.27
12 stages	65.08	815.60	64.23	833.60

So far we have obtained formulas for the total waiting time. In order to obtain the *total delay* in the network, one has to add to the total waiting time the total service time. If service time is one, then the total service time is simply the number of stages. In general, it is the sum of service times at the successive stages.

The waiting time at one stage may depend on service time at a previous stage. However, the correlation is weak, so that these random variables are stochastically nearly independent. Thus, the variance of the total delay is approximately the variance of the total waiting time plus the sum of the variances of the service times. If the service times are constant, then their variances are zero, so the variance of the total delay is exactly the variance of the total waiting time. In general, the distribution of the total delay can easily be approximated by looking at the distributions of individual service times and the distribution of the total waiting time.

Note that constant service time greater than one was used to model a network in which messages are transmitted in several consecutive packets. In such situations, waiting (or service) at one stage can start before service at the previous stage has terminated; the total service time in the network is $n + m - 1$, where n is the number of stages, and m is the number of packets per message.

VI. CONCLUSION

We have analyzed the delay experienced by a message in a buffered, multistage, packet-switching banyan network. For the first stage, we were able to derive the complete distribution of the delay for a very general class of distributions, assuming messages have discrete sizes. This was used to determine exactly the average and variance of the delay for several commonly considered distributions. The formulas can be easily applied to other distributions. Using the delay formulas for the first stage, we developed extremely good approximations for the average and variance of the delay at later stages. Finally, this allowed us to obtain good approximations for the full distribution of the total delay of a message through the entire network.

In order to approximate the delay after the first stage, it was essential to have good formulas for the delay at the first stage. It was only by building on them that we were able to make educated guesses as to the delays at later stages.

One aspect of our results that is worth stressing is the dependency of waiting time on the message size m. For a *fixed* traffic intensity ρ, the average waiting time increases linearly in m [see (8) and (15)], and the variance increases quadratically in m [see (9) and (16)]. Thus, while using larger messages may save the overhead of duplicating the same routing information over several packets, it may dramatically increase delays in all but very lightly loaded networks. This point has already been made in [11], [12], and [8], but does not seem to be widely appreciated.

We believe that our techniques for obtaining approximations can be usefully extended in several ways. For example, better and more extensive simulations would allow the approximate formulas to be improved. Although it may not be tractable to analyze the delay at later stages exactly or even asymptotically, it might be possible to obtain a heavy traffic analysis. This would provide an exact value for $\lim_{\rho \to 1} r(\rho)$, and would simplify the task of obtaining good approximations for w_∞ and v_∞. Given our formulas for infinite buffer delays, along with some simulation results for finite buffers, it is possible that one could develop good approximate formulas for finite buffer delays.

Finally, while our simulations seem to indicate clearly that average waiting time at successive stages converges, it would be nice to be able to prove this result formally, i.e., to show

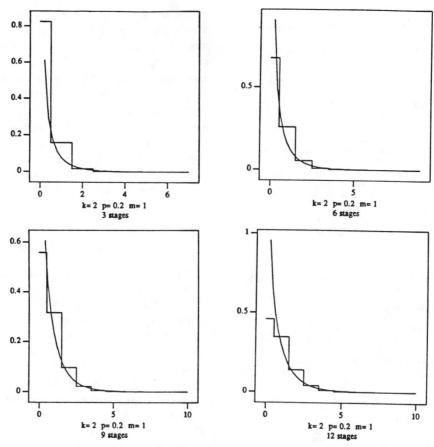

Fig. 3. Distribution of waiting times—simulation and prediction.

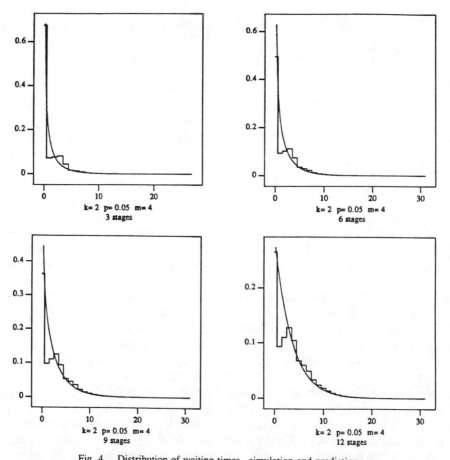

Fig. 4. Distribution of waiting times—simulation and prediction.

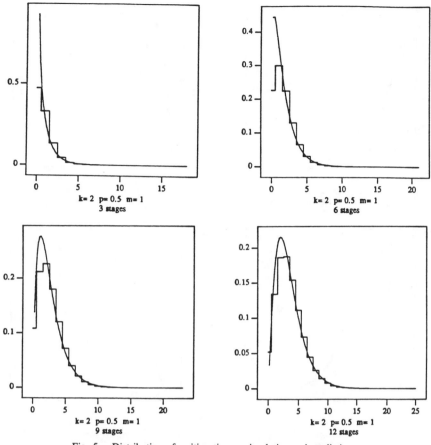

Fig. 5. Distribution of waiting times—simulation and prediction.

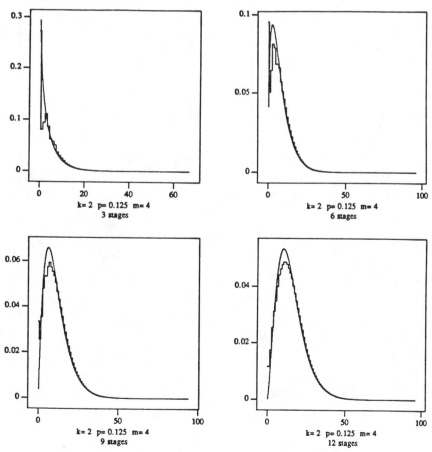

Fig. 6. Distribution of waiting times—simulation and prediction.

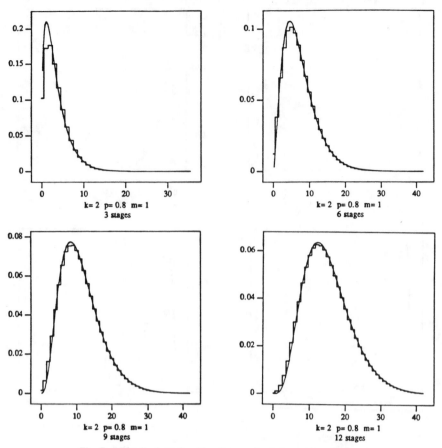

Fig. 7.   Distribution of waiting times—simulation and prediction.

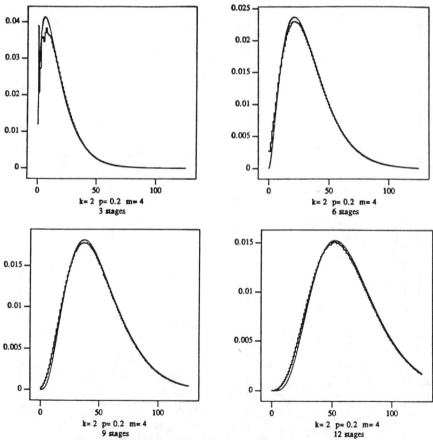

Fig. 8.   Distribution of waiting times—simulation and prediction.

that average delay at successive stages can be bounded, independently of the network size.

ACKNOWLDEGMENT

The authors thank S. Abraham, I. Mitrani, and B. Muchmore for their help.

REFERENCES

[1] L. N. Bhuyan and C. W. Lee, "An interference analysis of interconnection networks," in *Proc. 1983 Int. Conf. Parallel Processing*, pp. 2-9.

[2] J. Blum, H. Chernoff, M. Rosenblatt, and H. Teicher, "Central limit theorems for interchangeable processes," *Canadian J. Math.*, vol. 10, pp. 222-229, 1958.

[3] D. Y. Burman and D. R. Smith, "Asymptotic analysis of a queueing model with bursty traffic," *Bell Syst. Tech. J.*, vol. 62, pp. 1433-1453, July 1983.

[4] S. Cheemalavagu and M. Malek, "Analysis and simulation of Banyan interconnection networks with 2 × 2, 4 × 4, and 8 × 8 switching elements," in *Proc. Real-Time Syst. Symp.*, Dec. 1982, pp. 83-89.

[5] D. M. Dias and J. R. Jump, "Packet switching interconnection networks for modular systems," *IEEE Computer*, vol. 14, pp. 43-54, Dec. 1981.

[6] T-Y. Feng, "A survey of interconnection networks," *IEEE Computer*, vol. 14, pp. 12-27, Dec. 1981.

[7] G. R. Goke and G. J. Lipovski, "Banyan networks for partitioning multiprocessor systems," in *Proc. 1st Annu. Symp. Comput. Architecture*, 1973, pp. 21-28.

[8] A. Gottlieb, R. Grishman, C. P. Kruskal, K. P. McAuliffe, L. Rudolph, and M. Snir, "The NYU Ultracomputer—Designing an MIMD shared memory parallel computer," *IEEE Trans. Comput.*, vol. C-32, pp. 175-189, Feb. 1983.

[9] L. Kleinrock, *Queueing Systems, Vol. 1.* New York: Wiley, 1975.

[10] H. Kobayashi and A. G. Konheim, "Queueing models for computer communications system analysis," *IEEE Trans. Commun.*, vol. COM-25, pp. 2-29, 1977.

[11] C. P. Kruskal and M. Snir, "The performance of multistage interconnection networks for multiprocessors," *IEEE Trans. Comput.*, vol. C-32, pp. 1091-1098, Dec. 1983.

[12] C. P. Kruskal, M. Snir, and A. Weiss, "On the distribution of delays in buffered multistage networks for uniform and nonuniform traffic (extended abstract)," in *Proc. 1984 Int. Conf. Parallel Processing*, pp. 215-219.

[13] D. H. Lawrie, "Access and alignment of data in an array processor," *IEEE Trans Comput.*, vol. C-24, pp. 1145-1155, 1975.

[14] A. Norton and G. Pfister, "A methodology for predicting multiprocessor performance," in *Proc. 1985 Int. Conf. Parallel Processing*, pp. 772-781.

[15] J. A. Patel, "Performance of processor-memory interconnections for multiprocessors," *IEEE Trans. Comput.*, vol. C-30, pp. 771-780, 1981.

[16] G. Pfister, W. C. Brantley, D. A. George, S. L. Harvey, W. J. Kleinfelder, K. P. McAuliffe, E. A. Melton, V. A. Norton, and J. Weiss, "The IBM Research Parallel Processor Prototype (RP3): Introduction and architecture," in *Proc. 1985 Int. Conf. Parallel Processing*, pp. 764-771.

[17] H. J. Siegel, *Interconnection Networks for Large-Scale Parallel Processing: Theory and Case Studies.* Lexington, MA: Lexington Books, 1985.

Clyde P. Kruskal was born on May 25, 1954. He received the A.B. degree in mathematics and computer science from Brandeis University, Waltham, MA, in 1976, and the M.S. and Ph.D. degrees in computer science from the Courant Institute of New York University, New York, NY, in 1978 and 1981, respectively.

He was an Assistant Professor in Computer Science at the University of Illinois, Urbana, from 1981 to 1985. Since 1985, he has been on the faculty at the University of Maryland, College Park and is now an Associate Professor. His research interests include the analysis of sequential and parallel algorithms and the design of parallel computers.

Marc Snir received the B.Sc. degree in 1972 and the Ph.D. degree in 1979, both in mathematics, from the Hebrew University of Jerusalem, Jerusalem, Israel.

He is currently at the IBM T. J. Watson Research Center, on leave from the Hebrew University of Jerusalem. From 1979 to 1980 he held a visiting position at the University of Edinburgh. From 1980 to 1982 he was Assistant Professor at New York University, were he worked on the design of the NYU Ultracomputer, a large-scale parallel computer. Since 1982 he has been a Senior Lecturer in the Department of Computer Science of the Hebrew University. In addition to interconnection networks, his current research interests include parallel computer architectures, parallel algorithms, resource management in parallel computers, parallel programming languages, and complexity theory.

Dr. Snir is a member of IEEE Computer Society and of the Association for Computing Machinery.

Alan Weiss was born on December 5, 1955. He received the B.S. degree in both mathematics and physics from Case Western Reserve University, Cleveland, OH, in 1976, and the M.S. and Ph.D. degrees in mathematics from the Courant Institute of New York University, New York, NY, in 1979 and 1981, respectively.

Since 1981 he has been a member of the Technical Staff in the Mathematical Sciences Research Center at AT&T Bell Labs, Murray Hill, NJ. His research interests include the theory of large deviations, stochastic processes, and equations of evolution.

Performance Analysis of Multibuffered Packet-Switching Networks in Multiprocessor Systems

HYUNSOO YOON, KYUNGSOOK Y. LEE, AND MING T. LIU, FELLOW, IEEE

Abstract—We present a new analytic model and analytic results for the performance of multibuffered packet-switching interconnection networks in multiprocessor systems. Previous analyses of buffered interconnection networks in the literature have assumed either single or infinite buffers at each input (or output) port of a switch. As far as multibuffered interconnection networks are concerned, only some simulation results for delta networks have been known [1].

We first model single-buffered delta networks using the state transition diagram of a buffer. We then extend the model to account for multiple buffers.

The analytic results of multibuffered delta networks are compared to simulation results. We also analyze the performance of multibuffered data manipulator networks to demonstrate the generality of the model.

Index Terms—Buffer size, multibuffered delta networks, multibuffered PM2I networks, performance analysis, uniform traffic model.

I. INTRODUCTION

PACKET-SWITCHING multistage interconnection networks (MIN's) can be used for interconnecting a large number of processors and memory modules in multiprocessor systems, or for the resource arbitration and token distribution in the data flow computers [2]. They can also be used as a switching fabric of a packet switch for the high-speed packet-switching computer communications [3]–[5]. Since MIN's play a critical role in the overall performance of such systems, extensive studies have been done on characterizing their performance behavior.

MIN's can be categorized into two groups: unbuffered MIN's and buffered MIN's, depending on whether there are buffer(s) at each switching node. In unbuffered MIN's, whenever a path conflict occurs at a switch among competing packets, only one packet can take the resource and others are discarded. With buffer(s) at each switch, as in buffered networks, the packets, which would be lost otherwise, can be stored as long as buffers are available when a conflict occurs.

Manuscript received August 14, 1987; revised September 22, 1988 and July 3, 1989. H. Yoon and M. T. Liu were supported by the U.S. Army CECOM, Ft. Monmouth, NJ, under Contract DAAB07-88-K-A-003. The views, opinions, and/or findings contained in this paper are those of the authors and should not be construed as an official Department of the Army position, policy, or decision.

H. Yoon is with the Korea Advanced Institute of Science and Technology, Korea.

K. Y. Lee and M. T. Liu are with the Department of Computer and Information Science, The Ohio State University, Columbus, OH 43210.

IEEE Log Number 8932908.

A good body of performance analysis work exists both for unbuffered ([6]–[10] and references therein) and buffered MIN's [1], [11], [3], [7]. For the performance analyses of buffered networks, either a single buffer or infinite buffers at each input (or output) port of a switch have previously been considered. Dias and Jump [1], [11] analyzed the performance of delta networks with single buffers based on the timed Petri-net model. Jenq [3] analyzed the performance of a packet switch based on single-buffered banyan networks, while the performance of banyan networks with infinite buffers was studied by Kruskal and Snir [7].

The performance of multibuffered MIN's (multiple but finite buffers at each input port of a switch) has only partially been known through simulations [1], [11], [12]. In addition to the restriction in the number of buffers (either single or infinite), earlier performance analyses have considered only banyan (delta) networks based on (2×2) crossbar switches. These networks are unique-path networks, which provide a unique path for each input–output connection. Recently, the performance of single-buffered delta networks constructed from switching elements (SE's) of arbitrary sizes and the performance of single-buffered multiple-path networks (plus–minus-2^i networks) have been analytically studied by us [13].

In this paper, we present a simple analytic model, which can be used to analyze multibuffered packet-switching MIN's constructed from SE's of an arbitrary size and type (crossbar or bus). Jenq's elegant analytic model for single-buffered banyan networks [3] laid the ground work for our model.

This paper is organized as follows. Delta networks are briefly introduced in Section II. In Section III, a new analytic model is used to analyze the performance of single-buffered delta networks. The model is generalized for multibuffered delta networks in Section IV. The analytic results are presented and compared to simulation results in Section V. To demonstrate the generality of the model, multibuffered plus–minus-2^i (PM2I) networks are analyzed in Section VI. Conclusions are given in Section VII.

II. DELTA NETWORKS

An $(N \times N)$ delta network consists of n stages of N/a $(a \times a)$ crossbar switches, where $N = a^n$. A packet movement through the network can be controlled locally at each SE by a single base-a digit of the destination address of the packet. Delta networks are chosen in this paper because they are very general, i.e., they are a subclass of banyan net-

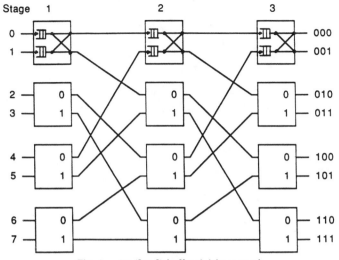

Fig. 1.   An (8 × 8) buffered delta network.

works which encompass all the useful unique path MIN's. Delta networks include the cube, omega, indirect binary n-cube, and baseline network [6], [1]. An example of an (8 × 8) buffered delta network is given in Fig. 1. For a detailed description of delta networks, refer to [6].

III. PERFORMANCE ANALYSIS OF SINGLE-BUFFERED DELTA NETWORKS

We analyze the network under the uniform traffic model as in [6], [1], [11], [3], [7], [9], [10], and [13], i.e., the following is assumed.

- Packets are generated at each source node with equal probability.
- Packets are of a fixed size and are directed uniformly over all of the network outputs.
- The routing logic at each SE is *fair*, i.e., conflicts are randomly resolved.

These assumptions imply that, for each switching stage of the network, the pattern of packet distribution is identical and statistically independent for all the SE's. Therefore, each switching stage can be characterized by a single SE, and this fact makes the analysis of the network very simple.

For the operation of single-buffered networks we assume the following as in [1], [11], and [3].

• Each input port of an SE has a single buffer to accommodate a single packet.

• A buffered network operates synchronously at a rate of τ (called *stage cycle*), which consists of two phases.

— In the first phase, the availability of the buffer space at the subsequent stage along the destined path of a packet in the current buffer is determined; the packet is informed whether it may go to the next stage or should stay in the current buffer.

— In the second phase, packets may move forward one stage.

• A packet is able to move forward only if it is selected (among competing packets) by the routing logic of the current

SE, *and* either the buffer of the SE it is destined to go to at the next stage is empty *or* the packet in that buffer is able to move forward.

Two important performance measures for buffered networks are throughput and delay. The *throughput* of a network is defined as the average number of packets passed by the network per stage cycle. The *delay* is the average number of stage cycles required for a packet to pass through the network.

We first define the following variables in the same manner as in [3], and derive a set of state equations relating these variables.

n = number of switching stages.

$p_0(k, t)$ = probability that a buffer of an SE at stage k is empty at the beginning of the tth stage cycle.

$p_1(k, t) = 1 - p_0(k, t)$: probability that a buffer of an SE at stage k is full at the beginning of the tth stage cycle.

$q(k, t)$ = probability that a packet is *ready to come* to a buffer of an SE at stage k during the tth stage cycle.

$r(k, t)$ = probability that a packet in a buffer of an SE at stage k is *able to move forward* during the tth stage cycle, *given that there is a packet in that buffer*.

S = normalized throughput (throughput normalized with respect to the network size N; the average number of packets passed by the network per output link).

d = normalized delay (delay normalized with respect to the number of switching stages, i.e., average number of stage cycles taken for a packet to pass a single stage).

Next, we derive relations among these variables. The $q(k, t)$, probability that a packet is ready to come to a buffer of an SE at stage k during the tth stage cycle, is related to the number of packets at the beginning of the tth stage cycle in the buffers of a switch in stage $k - 1$ feeding the buffer under consideration (see Fig. 2), and the destinations of those packets. Derivation of the following three equations for $q(k, t)$, $r(k, t)$, and $r'(k, t)$ assumes the independence of packets in different buffers, i.e., uniformity in destination of these packets, as in [3]. This is an optimistic assumption since these packets may not have been generated during the same stage cycle at the source nodes. As we will see later in Section V, this assumption leads to optimistic analytic results compared to simulation results.

The probability that an $(a \times a)$ SE at stage $k - 1$ has a total of j packets in its "a" single buffers at the beginning of the tth stage cycle is $\binom{a}{j} p_1(k, t)^j p_0(k, t)^{a-j}$. The probability that at least one of j packets is destined to the buffer in stage k under consideration is $[1 - (1 - 1/a)^j]$.[1] Then $q(k, t)$ is the sum over all possible numbers of buffered packets, of the product of these two probabilities.

$$q(k, t) = \sum_{j=0}^{a} \binom{a}{j} p_1(k - 1, t)^j p_0(k - 1, t)^{a-j}$$

$$\cdot [1 - (1 - 1/a)^j] = 1 - [1 - p_1(k - 1, t)/a]^a.$$

[1] This equation was given by Patel [6].

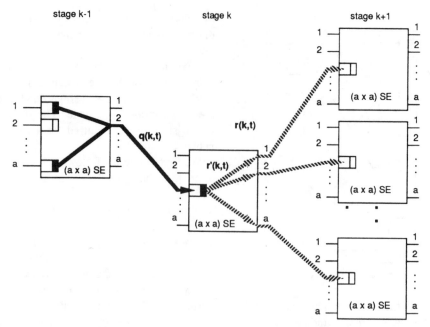

Fig. 2. The illustration $q(k, t)$, $r_1(k, t)$, and $r(k, t)$.

Now, let $r'(k, t)$ be the probability that a packet in a buffer of an SE at stage k is able to pass that SE to the desired output port of that SE during the tth stage cycle by winning the contention among competing packets, given that there is a packet in that buffer. That particular packet in stage k is able to move forward if it can pass the SE and if there is an available buffer at its next stop in stage $k + 1$. The buffer in stage $k + 1$ is available if it is empty or if it is full and the packet in that buffer (in stage $k + 1$) is able to move forward to stage $k + 2$ (see Fig. 2). Thus, $r(k, t)$ can be expressed as following.

$$r(k, t) = r'(k, t)[p_0(k + 1, t) + p_1(k + 1, t)r(k + 1, t)].$$

A packet in a buffer of an SE at stage k is able to pass that SE to the destined output port if it wins the contention among competing packets if any. Since the remaining $a - 1$ buffers may contain j packets, $0 \leq j \leq a - 1$, and the probability that the given packet is chosen out of $j + 1$ packets is $1/(j+1)$, and the destination of this particular packet can be any one of the "a" output ports, $r'(k, t)$ can be expressed as the following.

$$r'(k, t) = \sum_{j=0}^{a-1} \binom{a - 1}{j} p_1(k, t)^j p_0(k, t)^{a-1-j}$$

$$\left[1 - \left(1 - \frac{1}{a}\right)^{j+1}\right] \frac{1}{j + 1} \binom{a}{1}$$

Since $\binom{a - 1}{j} \binom{a}{1} / (j + 1) = \binom{a}{j + 1}$, $r'(k, t)$ can be simplified to $q(k+1, t)/p_1(k, t)$ after some manipulations. In summary, the following set of state equations hold for single-buffered delta networks.

$$q(k, t) = 1 - [1 - p_1(k - 1, t)/a]^a, \qquad 2 \leq k \leq n \quad (1)$$

$$r(k, t) = [q(k + 1, t)/p_1(k, t)]$$
$$\cdot [p_0(k + 1, t) + p_1(k + 1, t)r(k + 1, t)],$$
$$1 \leq k \leq n - 1 \qquad (2)$$

$$r(n, t) = [1 - \{1 - p_1(n, t)/a\}^a]/p_1(n, t) \qquad (3)$$

$$p_0(k, t + 1) = [1 - q(k, t)][p_0(k, t) + p_1(k, t)r(k, t)],$$
$$1 \leq k \leq n \quad (4)$$

$$p_1(k, t + 1) = 1 - p_0(k, t + 1), \qquad 1 \leq k \leq n. \quad (5)$$

Equation (3) assumes that if a packet is available at a network output at the beginning of a stage cycle, it is removed during that stage cycle.

We note that (1)–(5) reduce to Jenq's equations [3] when $a = 2$. To solve this set of equations iteratively, initial conditions need to be defined. We assume that initially at time $t = 0$, all the buffers of the network are empty. We also assume that $q(1, t)$ is the load applied to the network. With these initial conditions, the above set of equations can be solved iteratively to get the time-independent steady-state values.

As an example, Table I shows, for $n = 4$ and $q(1, t) = 1.0$, how $p_1(k, t)$, $q(k, t)$, and $r(k, t)$ change over successive stage cycles and converge to steady-state values. Denoting the $x(k, t)$ in the steady-state as $x(k)$, the normalized throughput (S) and the normalized mean delay (d) can be obtained by the following equations.

$$S = p_1(n)r(n) \qquad (6)$$

$$d = \frac{1}{n} \sum_{k=1}^{n} \frac{1}{r(k)}. \qquad (7)$$

Equation (7) is due to the fact that the stage delay encountered by a packet is the reciprocal of the probability that the packet is able to pass the stage.

TABLE I
VALUES OF $p_1(k, t)$, $q(k, t)$, AND $r(k, t)$ DURING SUCCESSIVE STAGE CYCLES FOR $n = 4$ AND $q(1, t) = 1.0$

	$t=0$	$t=1$	$t=2$	$t=3$	$t=4$	$t=5$	$t=6$	$t=7$	$t>7$
$p_1(1,t)$	0.00	1.00	1.00	1.00	1.00	1.00	1.00	1.00	1.00
$q(1,t)$	1.00	1.00	1.00	1.00	1.00	1.00	1.00	1.00	1.00
$r(1,t)$	0.00	0.75	0.65	0.59	0.56	0.54	0.54	0.53	0.53
$p_1(2,t)$	0.00	0.00	0.75	0.79	0.80	0.81	0.82	0.82	0.82
$q(2,t)$	0.00	0.75	0.75	0.75	0.75	0.75	0.75	0.75	0.75
$r(2,t)$	0.00	0.00	0.81	0.73	0.68	0.66	0.65	0.65	0.65
$p_1(3,t)$	0.00	0.00	0.00	0.61	0.67	0.70	0.71	0.71	0.72
$q(3,t)$	0.00	0.00	0.61	0.63	0.64	0.65	0.65	0.65	0.65
$r(3,t)$	0.00	0.00	0.00	0.85	0.78	0.76	0.75	0.74	0.74
$p_1(4,t)$	0.00	0.00	0.00	0.00	0.52	0.58	0.61	0.62	0.63
$q(4,t)$	0.00	0.00	0.00	0.52	0.56	0.57	0.58	0.59	0.59
$r(4,t)$	0.00	0.00	0.00	0.00	0.87	0.85	0.85	0.84	0.84

Fig. 3. The state transition diagram of a single buffer. q and r denote $q(k, t)$ and $r(k, t)$, respectively.

Before we generalize (1)–(7) for multibuffered networks in the next section, we note that (4) and (5) can be rewritten as follows, where $\bar{z}(k, t)$ is defined as $1.0 - z(k, t)$ for any variable z.

$$p_0(k, t+1) = p_0(k, t)\bar{q}(k, t) + p_1(k, t)\bar{q}(k, t)r(k, t) \tag{8}$$

$$p_1(k, t+1) = p_0(k, t)q(k, t)$$
$$+ p_1(k, t)[q(k, t)r(k, t) + \bar{r}(k, t)]. \tag{9}$$

Note that in single-buffered networks, a buffer has two possible states: the empty state (state 0) and the full state (state 1). In (8) and (9), we can interpret p_i as the probability that a buffer is in state i, and all other terms as transition probabilities of moving from one state to another. Then (8) and (9) can be represented by the state transition diagram of a single buffer in Fig. 3. This interpretation lends itself easily to the generalization of the single-buffered network analysis for multibuffered networks, as can be seen in the next section.

IV. PERFORMANCE ANALYSIS OF MULTIBUFFERED DELTA NETWORKS

In this section, we consider multibuffered delta networks. In a multibuffered network, each input port of every SE has a finite number of buffers so that multiple packets can be placed. (As before, one buffer can hold a single packet.) For some discussions in this section, we need to distinguish between the buffers for an input port of an SE as a whole and an individual buffer slot. We shall refer to the former as a "buffer module," and the latter as a "buffer" in this section. We shall also denote a buffer module of size m as an m-buffer.

In a multibuffered network, a packet is able to move forward one stage if either there is at least one empty buffer at the next stage, or a packet in the full buffer module at the next stage is able to move forward. We note that a packet in an infinite-buffered network is always able to move forward regardless of the status of the buffer module at the next stage, rendering the analysis much simpler than the one for finite-buffered networks. We have already introduced the new variable m to denote the size of a buffer module. The variables n, $q(k, t)$, S, and d defined in the previous section for single-buffered networks remain the same for multibuffered networks. The earlier definitions of p and r need to be modified to reflect multiple buffers.

m = buffer module size (number of buffers at each input port of an SE).

$p_j(k, t)$ = probability that there are j packets in a buffer module of an SE at stage k at the beginning of the tth stage cycle, $0 \leq j \leq m$ and $\sum_{j=0}^{m} p_j(k, t) = 1.0$ (e.g., p_0, $\bar{p}_0$, p_m, and $\bar{p}_m$ are the probabilities that a buffer module is empty, not empty, full, and not full, respectively).

$r(k, t)$ = probability that a packet in a buffer of an SE at stage k is able to move forward during the tth stage cycle, given that there is at least one packet in the buffer module (i.e., the buffer module is not empty).

With multiple buffers at an input port of each switch, $q(k, t)$, probability that a packet is ready to come to a buffer of an SE at stage k during the tth stage cycle, is related to the number of input ports with nonempty buffer modules at the beginning of the tth stage cycle, of a switch in stage $k - 1$ feeding the buffer module under consideration. By a similar reasoning for (1) and (2), $q(k, t)$ and $r(k, t)$ for an m-buffer can be expressed as follows. As for single-buffered networks, the following three equations for multibuffered networks assume the independence of packets in different buffer modules as well as within a buffer module. As can be seen later in Section V, quite interestingly, this independence assumption for multibuffered networks holds much better than the case of single-buffered networks.

$$q(k, t) = 1 - [1 - \bar{p}_0(k-1, t)/a]^a, \qquad 2 \leq k \leq n$$

$$r(k, t) = [q(k+1, t)/\bar{p}_0(k, t)][\bar{p}_m(k+1, t)$$
$$+ p_m(k+1, t)r(k+1, t)], \qquad 1 \leq k \leq n - 1.$$

Likewise, $r(n, t)$ can be expressed as

$$r(n, t) = q(n+1, t)/p_0(n, t).$$

The major difference between a single-buffer and an m-buffer is in the different possible number of buffer states. While a single-buffer can have only two possible states, full or empty, an m-buffer can be in one of $m + 1$ possible states, containing j packets (state j) with the probability $p_j(k, t)$, for $0 \leq j \leq m$. Since only a single packet may be transmitted between stages per stage cycle, an m-buffer can change its state only among adjacent neighbor states (-1 or $+1$) plus the old state itself as can be seen in Fig. 4. Thus, a nonboundary state j (neither full or empty) can be reached from three previous states, $j - 1$, j, $j + 1$. State 0 does not have -1 neighbor state, whereas state m does not have $+1$ neighbor state. The transition probabilities of moving from one state to another can be obtained by considering the ways in which one could move between the two states and the associated probabilities for movements. For example, a buffer module remains in the

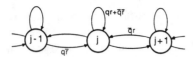

Fig. 4. The state transition diagram of a buffer module of size m in an intermediate state j, $1 < j < m$.

Fig. 5. The complete state transition diagram of a buffer module of size m.

old state j, if there is one departure and one arrival (with the probability $q \cdot r$), or no departure and no arrival (with the probability $\bar{q} \cdot \bar{r}$).

In general, the probability $p_j(k, t+1)$ that a buffer module is in a nonboundary state j at the beginning of stage cycle $t+1$ is the sum of the (mutually exclusive) probabilities that the same buffer module was in state $j-1$, j, or $j+1$ during stage cycle t, each multiplied by the transition probability to state j. We thus have for a nonboundary state j,

$$p_j(k, t+1) = p_{j-1}(k, t)q(k, t)\bar{r}(k, t)$$
$$+ p_j(k, t)[q(k, t)r(k, t) + \bar{q}(k, t)\bar{r}(k, t)]$$
$$+ p_{j+1}(k, t)\bar{q}(k, t)r(k, t).$$

The complete state transition diagram of an m-buffer is given in Fig. 5.

In summary, the following set of state equations holds for m-buffered delta networks, where m is the size of the buffer module at each input port.

$$q(k, t) = 1 - [1 - \bar{p}_0(k-1, t)/a]^a, \qquad 2 \leq k \leq n \tag{10}$$

$$r(k, t) = [q(k+1, t)/\bar{p}_0(k, t)][\bar{p}_m(k+1, t) + p_m(k+1, t)r(k+1, t)], \qquad 1 \leq k \leq n-1 \tag{11}$$

$$r(n, t) = q(n+1, t)/\bar{p}_0(n, t) \tag{12}$$

$$p_j(k, t+1) = q(k, t)[p_{j-1}(k, t)\bar{r}(k, t) + p_j(k, t)r(k, t)]$$
$$+ \bar{q}(k, t)[p_j(k, t)\bar{r}(k, t) + p_{j+1}(k, t)r(k, t)],$$
$$2 \leq j \leq m-1, 1 \leq k \leq n \tag{13}$$

$$p_0(k, t+1) = \bar{q}(k, t)[p_0(k, t) + p_1(k, t)r(k, t)],$$
$$1 \leq k \leq n \tag{14}$$

$$p_1(k, t+1) = q(k, t)[p_0(k, t) + p_1(k, t)r(k, t)]$$
$$+ \bar{q}(k, t)[p_1(k, t)\bar{r}(k, t) + p_2(k, t)r(k, t)],$$
$$1 \leq k \leq n \tag{15}$$

$$p_m(k, t+1) = q(k, t)[p_{m-1}(k, t)\bar{r}(k, t) + p_m(k, t)r(k, t)]$$
$$+ p_m(k, t)\bar{r}(k, t), \qquad 1 \leq k \leq n. \tag{16}$$

From (14)–(16), it can be verified that the probability of an m-buffer module being in any one of the possible $m+1$ states, $\sum_{j=0}^{m} p_j(k, t+1)$, is 1.0.

In the steady-state, a packet arrives at an output port of the network with probability $\bar{p}_0(n)r(n)$, which is the normalized throughput S.

$$S = \bar{p}_0(n)r(n). \tag{17}$$

Let $R(k)$ be the average probability that a packet in the buffer of an SE in stage k is able to move forward. Then the normalized delay d can be given as

$$d = \frac{1}{n} \sum_{k=1}^{n} \frac{1}{R(k)},$$

$$\text{where } R(k) = r(k) \sum_{i=1}^{m} [p_i(k)/\bar{p}_0(k)]\frac{1}{i}. \tag{18}$$

Note that (10)–(18) reduce to (1)–(7) when m is 1.

V. PERFORMANCE RESULTS AND COMPARISONS

Analytic Results

Equations (10)–(18) for m-buffered networks of the previous section are very powerful, in that they can be used to determine the normalized throughput and the normalized delay of buffered delta networks with the following four parameters:

1) $a = $ SE size,
2) $n = $ number of stages $= \log_a N$ ($N = $ network size),
3) $m = $ buffer size, i.e., the size of the buffer at each input port of an SE,
4) $q(1) = $ input load applied to the network.

Among the many possible variations of the parameters, the most interesting cases are computed and plotted in Figs. 6–12. Figs. 6 and 7 show normalized throughput versus network size, and normalized delay versus network size, respectively, for various buffer sizes. It is seen that the normalized throughput decreases as the network size increases, and also as the buffer size decreases. The normalized delay decreases as the network size increases, and as the buffer size decreases. However, we observe that the normalized delay of single-buffered delta networks slightly increases as the network size increases. (For the detailed analytic results of single-buffered networks, refer to [1], [11], [3], and [13].)

Figs. 8 and 9 show normalized throughput versus buffer size, and normalized delay versus buffer size, respectively, for various network sizes. The normalized throughput reaches the saturation point very quickly after the buffer size of six. The increase in normalized throughput is very significant up to the buffer size of 3–4. The normalized delay increases almost linearly with the buffer size, especially for not very large networks. These results confirm the well-known observation from simulations [1], [11], "Adding buffers to a packet switching networks can increase throughput. A word of warning—don't make them too large. For most application, the number of buffers should be limited to one, two, or three."

Fig. 10 plots normalized throughput versus switch size for various buffer sizes for multibuffered (4096 × 4096) delta networks. Notice that the throughput does not increase monoton-

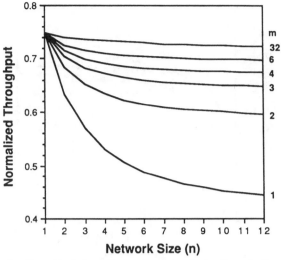

Fig. 6. Normalized throughput versus network size for m-buffered delta networks ($a = 2$, $q(1) = 1.0$).

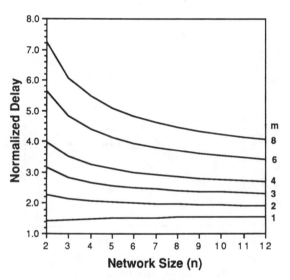

Fig. 7. Normalized delay versus network size for m-buffered delta networks ($a = 2$, $q(1) = 1.0$).

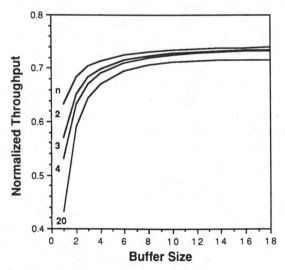

Fig. 8. Normalized throughput versus buffer size for buffered delta networks ($a = 2$, $q(1) = 1.0$).

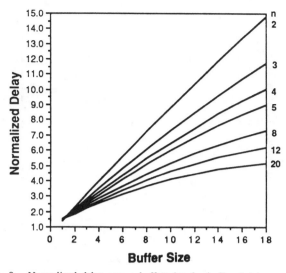

Fig. 9. Normalized delay versus buffer size for buffered delta networks ($a = 2$, $q(1) = 1.0$).

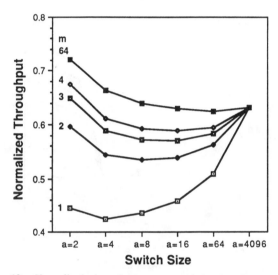

Fig. 10. Normalized throughput versus switch size for m-buffered (4096×4096) delta networks ($q(1) = 1.0$).

ically with the size of SE as in unbuffered networks. This phenomenon has also been observed in [12] by simulations.

Finally, for (1024×1024) delta networks, normalized throughput versus input load, and normalized delay versus input load are shown in Figs. 11 and 12, respectively. The effects of buffer size on the normalized throughput and also on the normalized delay become apparent only after the input load reaches 0.6–0.7.

Simulation Results

In order to validate the analysis presented in the previous section, we did some simulations of multibuffered delta networks. The basic assumptions for the analysis were implemented in the simulator as follows.

• The N processors generate packets at each stage cycle with probability $q(1)$ (input load).

• The destination of each packet generated at each stage cycle by processors is set randomly by a random number generator (one out of 0 to $N - 1$), to simulate uniform traffic.

• If there is a conflict among packets within an SE, one

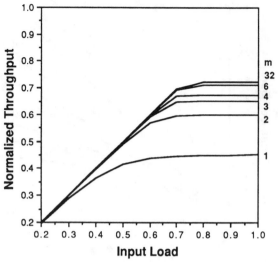

Fig. 11. Normalized throughput versus input load ($q(1)$) for m-buffered (1024×1024) delta networks ($a = 2$).

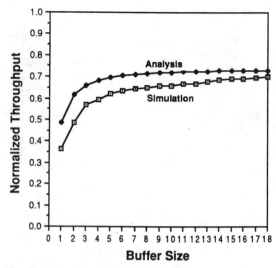

Fig. 13. Normalized throughput versus buffer size for buffered delta networks ($a = 2$, $q(1) = 1.0$, $n = 6$).

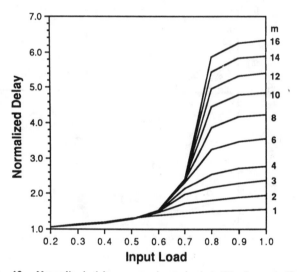

Fig. 12. Normalized delay versus input load ($q(1)$) for m-buffered (1024×1024) delta networks ($a = 2$).

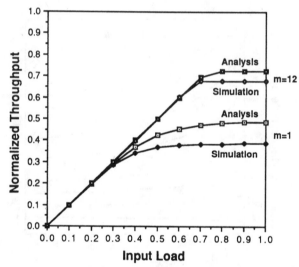

Fig. 14. Normalized throughput versus input load ($q(1)$) for 1-buffered and 12-buffered delta networks ($a = 2$, $n = 6$).

packet is selected randomly again by another random number generator.

• The throughput and the delay are measured at each output port of the network, and averaged over the network size and simulation time span to get the normalized throughput and the normalized delay of the network. In addition, in the simulator, first-in-first-out (FIFO) policy was used for each buffer module.

Sample simulation results are shown in Figs. 13 and 14. Fig. 13 shows normalized throughput versus buffer size for a (64×64) multibuffered delta network based on (2×2) SE's with the input load of 1.0. Fig. 14 plots normalized throughput versus input load for the same network for the buffer size of 1 and of 12.

Analytic results are more optimistic than simulation results. We believe that this is the effect of the highly idealistic uniform traffic model for the analysis. It is well known that a network performs better for uniform traffic than for nonuniform traffic, since with uniform traffic, network load is well distributed resulting in fewer path conflicts.

The analysis is based on several uniformity (or randomness) and independence assumptions. It is those assumptions that make the analysis simple, easy to understand, and easy to compute the result. Some important assumptions are that the packets arriving at each input port of the network are destined uniformly (or randomly) for all output links of the network, the "a" buffer modules in the same ($a \times a$) switch are statistically independent, and packets in a buffer module are independent. However, these assumptions are highly idealistic, and thus the analysis always produces the optimal or upper bound results.

In practice, the uniform traffic assumption is very hard to satisfy in a strict sense for several reasons. First, even though a source node does generate uniform destination requests, some requests may not be able to enter the network (and dropped) when the buffer at the first stage to which the source is connected is full. This disturbs the uniform traffic assumption, and will be more significant as the input load increases. This fact explains some of the observations we can make from Fig. 14. Notice that with single-buffers, there is no difference in normalized throughput between analysis and simulation until the input load reaches 0.3. For the 12-buffered network, no difference is observed until the input load reaches 0.7. Differences increase as the input load increases, and more significantly so for the single-buffered network. Of course, these are also due to the fact that lower input loads inherently create less conflicts in the network compared to higher input loads.

Second, even if the packets are uniform in their destination requests when they enter the network, they may experience somewhat different queueing delays depending upon destined paths and the state of the network. Thus, the head buffers of different buffer modules at each stage may contain requests generated at different stage cycles by source nodes, again disturbing the uniformity.

On a positive note, Figs. 13 and 14 indicate that the independence assumption of multiple buffers for an input port of an SE is indeed reasonable. Although we present results in Fig. 14 on only two different buffer sizes for the clarity of the graph, we have observed that the differences between analytic results and simulation results monotonically decrease as the buffer size increases. This can also be clearly seen in Fig. 13. In addition to the validity of the independence assumption among multiple buffers at each input port of an SE, another reason may well be that the traffic uniformity is less disturbed when more buffers are available, since less packets are dropped in that case. For the simulation, we used the network size of 64. The computing time for larger network sizes was simply overwhelming.

VI. APPLICATION TO NETWORKS OF A DIFFERENT TYPE

In this section, we illustrate the generality of our analytic model of multibuffered delta networks by applying it to multibuffered networks of a different type. For this purpose, multibuffered plus–minus–2^i (PM2I) networks are chosen.

PM2I networks include the augmented data manipulator (ADM), the inverse ADM (IADM), and the gamma network, which are described in detail in [14]–[18]. The $(N \times N)$ ADM consists of $(\log_2 N) + 1$ stages, and each stage contains (3×3) SE's except for the first and last stages. The first stage consists of (1×3) SE's, and the last stage (3×1) SE's. The (3×3) SE is not a crossbar but a multiplexer–demultiplexer pair (or a bus with three inputs/outputs), which accepts only one input at a time and directs it to one of three possible outputs. The IADM network is identical to the ADM except that the stages are traversed in reverse order, and the gamma network is identical to the IADM except that each bus switch is replaced by a (3×3) crossbar switch. The (8×8) IADM network (or gamma network) is shown in Fig. 15.

By noting the differences between delta and PM2I networks in the type and size of an SE and the number of switching stages, the following set of state equations can be formulated for multibuffered PM2I networks. Note that for PM2I networks, stages are numbered from 0 to n (unlike from 1 to n for delta networks in previous sections). So the input load applied to a network is $q(0, t)$.

$$q(1, t) = \bar{p}_0(0, t)/3 \tag{19}$$

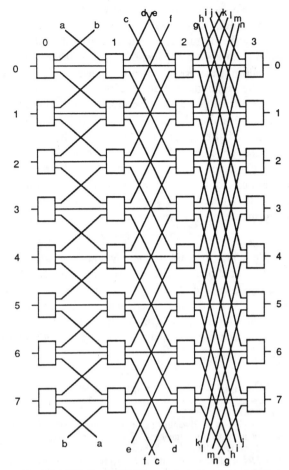

Fig. 15. The (8×8) IADM network (or gamma network).

$$q(k, t) = \begin{cases} 1 - [1 - \bar{p}_0(k-1, t)/3]^3 & : \quad \text{Gamma} \\ [1 - p_0(k-1, t)^3]/3 & : \quad \text{ADM/IADM,} \end{cases}$$
$$2 \leq k \leq n \tag{20}$$

$$r(0, t) = \bar{p}_m(1, t) + p_m(1, t)r(1, t) \tag{21}$$

$$r(k, t) = [q(k+1, t)/\bar{p}_0(k, t)][\bar{p}_m(k+1, t)$$
$$+ p_m(k+1, t)r(k+1, t)], \quad 1 \leq k \leq n-1 \tag{22}$$

$$r(n, t) = [1/3 - p_0(n, t)^3/3]/\bar{p}_0(n, t). \tag{23}$$

Eqs. (14)–(16) for

$$p_j(k, t+1), \quad 0 \leq j \leq m, \quad 0 \leq k \leq n \tag{24}$$

$$S = \bar{p}_0(0)r(0) \tag{25}$$

$$d = \frac{1}{n+1} \sum_{k=0}^{n} \frac{1}{R(k)},$$

$$\text{where } R(k) = r(k) \sum_{i=1}^{m} [p_i(k)/\bar{p}_0(k)]\frac{1}{i}. \tag{26}$$

VII. CONCLUSIONS

We introduced a new model for the performance analyses of buffered packet-switching networks in a multiprocessor environment. We used the model to analyze the performance of multibuffered delta networks.

Previously the performance behavior of multibuffered networks had been known for limited cases only through simulations except for the boundary cases (either single or infinite buffers). We compared the analytic results to simulation results, and verified that they agree closely with each other.

The analytic model is general enough to handle networks with arbitrary buffer sizes and switch sizes. It is simple yet powerful enough to be applicable to other types of networks as well. We illustrated the generality of the model by applying it to multibuffered PM2I networks which are multiple-path networks. Previously no attempt had been made to estimate the performance of such networks.

ACKNOWLEDGMENT

We would like to thank the anonymous referees for their constructive comments which helped us to significantly improve this paper, and Y. Kim for lending us his simulation program of buffered banyan networks. Y.-C. Jenq deserves credit for his elegant analytic model of single-buffered banyan networks, which served as the basis of our work reported herein.

REFERENCES

[1] D. M. Dias and J. R. Jump, "Analysis and simulation of buffered delta networks," *IEEE Trans. Comput.*, vol. C-30, no. 4, pp. 273–282, Apr. 1981.

[2] C. Y. Chin and K. Hwang, "Packet switching networks for multiprocessors and data flow computers," *IEEE Trans. Comput.*, vol. C-33, no. 11, pp. 991–1003, Nov. 1984.

[3] Y. C. Jenq, "Performance analysis of a packet switch based on single-buffered banyan network," *IEEE J. Select. Areas Commun.*, vol. SAC-3, no. 6, pp. 1014–1021, Dec. 1983.

[4] J. S. Turner, "Design of an integrated services packet network," *IEEE J. Select. Areas Commun.*, vol. SAC-4, no. 8, pp. 1373–1380, Nov. 1986.

[5] ——, "Design of a broadcast packet switching network," in *Proc. IEEE INFOCOM*, Apr. 1986, pp. 667–675.

[6] J. H. Patel, "Performance of processor–memory interconnections for multiprocessors," *IEEE Trans. Comput.*, vol. C-30, no. 10, pp. 771–780, Oct. 1981.

[7] C. P. Kruskal and M. Snir, "The performance of multistage interconnection networks for multiprocessors," *IEEE Trans. Comput.*, vol. C-32, no. 12, pp. 1091–1098, Dec. 1983.

[8] M. Lee and C. L. Wu, "Performance analysis of circuit switching baseline interconnection networks," in *Proc. 11th Annu. Comput. Architecture Conf.*, 1984, pp. 82–90.

[9] M. Kumar and J. R. Jump, "Performance of unbuffered shuffle-exchange networks," *IEEE Trans. Comput.*, vol. C-35, no. 6, pp. 573–578, June 1986.

[10] A. Varma and C. S. Raghavendra, "Performance analysis of a redundant-path interconnection network," in *Proc. 1985 Int. Conf. Parallel Processing*, 1985, pp. 474–479.

[11] D. M. Dias and J. R. Jump, "Packet switching interconnection networks for module systems," *IEEE Comput. Mag.*, vol. 14, no. 12, pp. 43–53, Dec. 1981.

[12] R. G. Bubenik and J. S. Turner, "Performance of a broadcast packet switch," Tech. Rep. WUCS-86-10, Washington Univ., Comput. Sci. Dep., June 1986.

[13] H. Yoon, K. Y. Lee, and M. T. Liu, "Performance analysis and comparison of packet switching interconnection networks," in *Proc. 1987 Int. Conf. Parallel Processing*, Aug. 1987, pp. 542–545.

[14] T. Feng, "Data manipulating functions in parallel processors and their implementations," *IEEE Trans. Comput.*, vol. C-30, no. 3, pp. 309–318, Mar. 1974.

[15] H. J. Siegel and S. D. Smith, "Study of multistage SIMD interconnection networks," in *Proc. 5th Symp. Comput. Architecture*, Apr. 1978, pp. 223–229.

[16] H. J. Siegel, "Interconnection networks for SIMD machines," *IEEE Comput. Mag.*, no. 12, pp. 57–65, June 1979.

[17] S. D. Smith, H. J. Siegel, R. J. McMillen, and G. B. Adams III, "Use of the augmented data manipulator multistage network for SIMD machines," in *Proc. Int. Conf. Parallel Processing*, Aug. 1980, pp. 75–78.

[18] D. S. Parker and C. S. Raghavendra, "The gamma network," *IEEE Trans. Comput.*, vol. C-33, no. 4, pp. 367–373, Apr. 1984.

Hyunsoo Yoon received the B.S. degree in electronics engineering from the Seoul National University, Seoul, Korea, in 1979, the M.S. degree in computer science from the Korea Advanced Institute of Science and Technology, in 1981, and the Ph.D. degree in computer and information science from the Ohio State University, Columbus, in 1988.

From 1978 to 1980, he was with the Tongyang Broadcasting Company, Korea, from 1980 to 1984, with the Computer Division of the Samsung Electronics Company, Korea, and from 1988 to 1989, with the AT&T Bell Laboratories as a member of the Technical Staff. He is currently an Assistant Professor at the Korea Advanced Institute of Science and Technology. His main research interests include parallel computer architectures and communication protocols.

Kyungsook Y. Lee received the B.S. degree in chemistry from the Sogang University, Seoul, Korea, in 1970, the M.S. degree in computer science from The University of Utah, Salt Lake City, in 1976, and the Ph.D. degree in computer science from the University of Illinois at Urbana–Champaign, in 1983.

Since 1983 she has been an Assistant Professor in the Department of Computer and Information Science, The Ohio State University. Her research interests are in parallel computing, parallel computer architecture, and communication networks.

Ming T. (Mike) Liu (M'65-SM'82-F'83) received the B.S.E.E. degree from the National Cheng Kung University, Tainan, Taiwan, in 1957, and the M.S.E.E. and Ph.D. degrees from the Moore School of Electrical Engineering, University of Pennsylvania, Philadelphia, in 1961 and 1964, respectively.

Since 1969 he has been with The Ohio State University, Columbus, where he is currently Professor of Computer and Information Science. Since 1974 he has been actively involved in research and development of computer networking and distributed computing, and has published over 100 technical papers in this and related areas.

Dr. Liu has received several awards for his technical contributions and for his dedicated services to the IEEE Computer Society. He was Program Co-Chair of the 1981 International Conference on Parallel Processing; Distinguished Visitor of the IEEE Computer Society from 1981 to 1984; Chairman of the Technical Committee on Distributed Processing from 1982 to 1984; Program and General Chairman of the Fifth and Sixth International Conference on Distributed Computing Systems, respectively; Chairman of the ACM/IEEE Eckert-Mauchly Award Committee for 1984–1985; Computer Society's Vice President for Membership and Information in 1986; and a member of the IEEE Fellow Committee from 1986 to 1988, among others. Since 1982 he has served as Guest Editor, Editor, and Editor-in-Chief of the IEEE TRANSACTIONS ON COMPUTERS. Three times he was elected a member of the Computer Society's Governing Board (1984–1990). Currently, he also serves as Chairman of the Steering Committee for the International Conference on Distributed Computing Systems, and Program Chairman for the Sixth International Conference on Data Engineering. He is also a member of the Association for Computing Machinery and Sigma Xi.

Virtual-Channel Flow Control

William J. Dally, *Member, IEEE*

Abstract—Network throughput can be increased by dividing the buffer storage associated with each network channel into several virtual channels [11]. Each physical channel is associated with several small queues, virtual channels, rather than a single deep queue. The virtual channels associated with one physical channel are allocated independently but compete with each other for physical bandwidth. Virtual channels decouple buffer resources from transmission resources. This decoupling allows active messages to pass blocked messages using network bandwidth that would otherwise be left idle. This paper studies the performance of networks using virtual channels using both analysis and simulation. These studies show that virtual channels increase network throughput, by a factor of 4 for 10-stage networks, and reduce the dependence of throughput on the depth of the network.

Index Terms—Communication networks, concurrent computing, flow control, interconnection networks, multicomputers, multiprocessors, packet routing, parallel processing, virtual channels, wormhole routing.

I. INTRODUCTION

Interconnection Networks

THE processing nodes of a concurrent computer exchange data and synchronize with one another by passing messages over an interconnection network [1], [2], [13], [4], [9], [24], [23]. The interconnection network is often the critical component of a large parallel computer because performance is very sensitive to network latency and throughput and because the network accounts for a large fraction of the cost and power dissipation of the machine.

An interconnection network is characterized by its topology, routing, and flow control [6]. The topology of a network is the arrangement of nodes and channels into a graph. Routing specifies how a packet chooses a path in this graph. Flow control deals with the allocation of channel and buffer resources to a packet as it traverses this path. This paper deals only with flow control. It describes a method for allocating resources to packets using virtual channels [11]. This method can be applied to any topology and routing strategy.

Manuscript received January 15, 1991; revised May 24, 1991. This work was supported in part by the Defense Advanced Research Projects Agency under Contracts N00014-88K-0738 and N00014-87K-0825 and in part by a National Science Foundation Presidential Young Investigator Award Grant MIP-8657531, with matching funds from General Electric Corporation and IBM Corporation. A preliminary version of this paper appeared in the proceedings of the 17th International Symposium on Computer Architecture [8].

The author is with the Artificial Intelligence Laboratory and Laboratory for Computer Science, Massachusetts Institute of Technology, Cambridge, MA 02139.

IEEE Log Number 9105524.

The Problem

The throughput of interconnection networks is limited to a fraction (typically 20%–50%) of the network's capacity [7] because of coupled resource allocation.

Interconnection networks are composed of two types of resources: buffers and channels. Typically, a single buffer is associated with each channel. Once a packet A is allocated a buffer b_i, no other packet B can use the associated channel c_i until A releases b_i. In networks that use flit[1]-level flow control [11], [1], [23], [9], packet A may be blocked due to contention elsewhere in the network while still holding b_i. In this case, channel c_i is idled even though there may be other packets in the network, e.g., packet B, that can make productive use of the channel.

This situation is illustrated in Fig. 1. In the figure, a fragment of a network is depicted with a rounded box denoting a node, a solid arrow a channel between two nodes, and a box denoting a flit buffer. Shaded arrows denote routes that are in progress. Packet A is blocked holding buffers 3E (east side of node 3) and 4S. Packet B is unable to make progress even though all physical channels it requires, (1E to 2W) through (4E to 5W), are idle because packet A holds buffer 3E which is coupled to channel (3E to 4W).

This problem of idling channels due to resource coupling is unique to interconnection networks that perform flow control at the flit-level. Most modern multicomputer networks that use circuit switching or wormhole routing [7] fall into this class. The problem does not occur in traditional packet-switched networks that perform flow control at the packet level since such networks never block a partially transmitted packet.

Virtual Channel Flow Control

A virtual channel consists of a buffer that can hold one or more flits of a packet and associated state information [11]. Several virtual channels may share the bandwidth of a single physical channel.[2]

Virtual channels decouple allocation of buffers from allocation of channels by providing multiple buffers for each channel in the network. If a blocked packet A holds a buffer b_{i0} associated with channel c_i, another buffer b_{i1} is available allowing other packets to pass A. Fig. 2 illustrates the addition of virtual channels to the network of Fig. 1. Packet A remains blocked holding buffers 3E.1 and 4S.1. In Fig. 2, however,

---

[1]A *flit* is a flow-control digit. See Section II-C for a more complete description.

[2]Virtual channels should not be confused with virtual circuits (named connections in a connection-oriented network [26], [3]) or with virtual cut-through (a packet-level flow-control technique [15]).

Reprinted from *IEEE Trans. Parallel and Distributed Systems,* Vol. 3, No. 2, Mar. 1992, pp. 194-205. Copyright © 1992 by The Institute of Electrical and Electronics Engineers, Inc. All rights reserved.

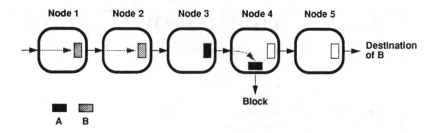

Fig. 1.   Packet B is blocked behind packet A while all physical channels remain idle.

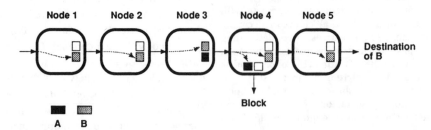

Fig. 2.   Virtual channels provide additional buffers allowing packet B to pass blocked packet A.

Packet B is able to make progress because buffer 3E.2 is available allowing it access to channel (3E to 4W).

Adding virtual channels to an interconnection network is analogous to adding lanes to a street network. A network without virtual channels is composed of one-lane streets. In such a network, a single blocked packet blocks all following packets. Adding virtual channels to the network adds lanes to the streets allowing blocked packets to be passed.

In addition to increasing throughput, virtual channels provide an additional degree of freedom in allocating resources to packets in the network. This flexibility permits the use of scheduling strategies, such as routing the oldest packet first, that reduce the variance of network latency.

The most costly resource in an interconnection network is physical channel (wire) bandwidth. The second most costly resource is buffer memory. Adding virtual channel flow control to a network makes more effective use of both of these resources by decoupling their allocation. The only expense is a small amount of additional control logic.

Background

The use of virtual channels for flow control builds on previous work in using virtual channels for deadlock avoidance and in using output queueing or split input queues for partial resource decoupling. Virtual channels were introduced in [11] for purposes of deadlock avoidance. A cyclic network can be made deadlock-free by restricting routing so there are no cycles in the channel dependency graph and then adding virtual channels to reconnect the network. Virtual channels were first implemented for this purpose in the torus routing chip [10].

The network design frame [12] and the J-Machine network [9] use virtual channels to provide two logical networks on a single physical network. The iWARP processing element [4], [5] uses virtual channels (called logical channels in [4]) primarily to guarantee bandwidth to virtual circuits. iWARP virtual channels are sufficiently general that they can be used to decouple resource allocation as described in this paper.

A single stage of resource decoupling is provided by output queueing [14]. By performing the queueing in the output of a switch rather than the input, arriving packets are able to pass blocked messages arriving on the same input. Tamir [25] has shown how to achieve the same single-stage resource decoupling by partitioning the switch's input queue. This single stage resource decoupling is effective only if an entire packet fits in a single node. As shown in Fig. 3, When a packet too long to fit entirely in one input queue is blocked, it backs up into the output stage of the previous node preventing any following packet from passing it. With output queueing, there is still only a single output buffer associated with each physical channel. If a packet blocks while holding this output buffer, the channel is idled.

Our network analysis builds on the work of Patel [22] and of Kruskal and Snir [18] in analyzing unbuffered networks. We also build on the work of Kermani and Kleinrock [16] in analyzing buffered circuit switched, packet switched, and cut through networks without virtual channels. The analysis here extends this previous work by modeling the effect of virtual channels and by modeling networks with fixed sized buffers where packets are blocked (delay model) rather than dropped (loss model) when contention occurs.

Summary

The next section introduces the notation and assumptions that will be used throughout this paper. Section III describes virtual channel flow control in detail. An analysis of network performance is given in Section IV. The results of simulating networks using virtual channel flow control are described in Section V.

II. PRELIMINARIES

A. Topology

An interconnection network consists of a set of *nodes*, N and a set of *channels*, $C \subseteq N \times N$. Each channel

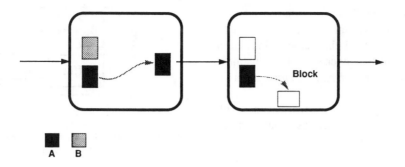

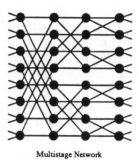

Fig. 3. Output queueing or partitioned input queues provide one stage of decoupling. However, long packets (such as packet A) continue to couple resources and cannot be passed.

is unidirectional and carries data from a source node to a destination node. A bidirectional network is one where $(n1, n2) \in C \Rightarrow (n2, n1) \in C$.

We have analyzed the performance of virtual channel flow control on multistage, k-ary n-fly, networks and have simulated the use of virtual channels on both multistage, networks and direct, k-ary n-cube, networks.

Multistage (k-ary n-fly) networks have k^n inputs connected to k^n outputs by n-stages of $k^{n-1} k \times k$-switches. For example, a 2-ary 4-fly is shown in Fig. 4.

A k-ary n-cube mesh network consists of k^n nodes arranged in an n-dimensional grid. Each node is connected to its Cartesian neighbors in the grid. For example, a 16-ary 2-cube is shown in Fig. 5.

The use of virtual channel flow control is in no way restricted to these two classes of networks. It is equally applicable to other topologies including trees, sorting networks, and irregular structures.

B. Routing

A packet is assigned a route through the network according to a *routing relation*, $R \subseteq C \times N \times C$, given the channel occupied by the head of the packet and the destination node of the packet, the routing relation specifies a (possibly singleton) set of channels on which the packet can be routed.

C. Flow Control

Communication between nodes is performed by sending *messages*. A message may be broken into one or more *packets* for transmission. A packet is the smallest unit of information that contains routing and sequencing information. A packet contains one or more flow control digits or *flits*. A flit is the smallest unit on which flow control is performed. Information is transferred over physical channels in physical transfer units or *phits*. A phit is usually the same size or smaller than a flit.

The flow control protocol of a network determines 1) how resources (buffers and channel bandwidth) are allocated and 2) how packet collisions over resources are resolved. A resource collision occurs when a packet P is unable to proceed because some resource it needs (usually a buffer) is held by another packet. Collisions may be resolved by 1) blocking P in place, 2) buffering P in a node prior to where the collision occurs, 3) dropping P, or 4) misrouting P to a channel other than the one

Fig. 4. A 2-ary 4-fly network.

Fig. 5. A 16-ary 2-cube network.

it requires. The technique described in this paper is applicable to all of these flow control strategies but is most appropriate for networks that use blocking or limited buffering to resolve collisions.

The flow control strategy allocates buffers and channel bandwidth to flits. Because flits have no routing or sequencing information, the allocation must be done in a manner that keeps the flits associated with a particular packet together. This may be done by associating a set of buffers and some control state together into a virtual channel. A virtual channel is allocated to a packet and the buffers of the virtual channel are allocated in a FIFO manner to the flits of that packet. In the remainder of this paper, the terms *lane* and *virtual channel* are used interchangeably.

Most networks associate only a single virtual channel with each physical channel. This paper describes a method for improving the performance of networks by associating several virtual channels with each physical channel. This method makes no assumptions about how wires are allocated.

D. Wormhole Routing

The technique described here is particularly suitable for use in networks that use wormhole routing [7]. Wormhole routing refers to a flow-control protocol that advances each flit of a packet as soon as it arrives at a node (pipelining) and blocks packets in place when required resources are unavailable. Wormhole routing is attractive in that 1) it reduces the latency of message delivery compared to store and forward routing, and 2) it requires only a few flit buffers per node. Wormhole routing differs from virtual cut-through routing [15] in that with wormhole routing it is not necessary for a node to allocate an entire packet buffer before accepting each packet. This distinction reduces the amount of buffering required on each node making it possible to build fast, inexpensive routers.

III. VIRTUAL CHANNEL FLOW CONTROL

A. Structure

Each node of an interconnection network contains a set of buffers and a switch.[3] In this paper, we assume that the buffers are partitioned into sets associated with each input channel, an input-buffered node, as shown in Fig. 6. An output-buffered switch [14], [25] can be considered to be an input buffered switch with a nonblocking first stage by associating the buffers on the output of each stage with the inputs of the next stage.

A conventional network organizes the flit buffers associated with each channel into a first-in, first-out (FIFO) queue as shown in Fig. 7(a). This organization restricts allocation so that each flit buffer can contain only flits from a single packet. If this packet becomes blocked, the physical channel is idled because no other packet is able to acquire the buffer resources needed to access the channel.

A network using virtual channel flow control organizes the flit buffers associated with each channel into several lanes as shown in Fig. 7(b). The buffers in each lane can be allocated independently of the buffers in any other lane. This added allocation flexibility increases channel utilization and thus throughput. A blocked message, even one that extends through several nodes, holds only a single lane idle and can be passed using any of the remaining lanes.

[3] Each node also contains driver and receiver circuits to communicate across the physical wires and control logic.

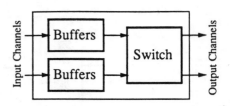

Fig. 6. Node organization. Each network node contains a set of buffers for each input channel and a switch.

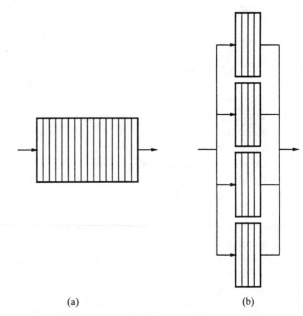

(a)   (b)

Fig. 7. (a) Conventional nodes organize their buffers into FIFO queues restricting routing. (b) A network using virtual-channel flow control organizes its buffers into several independent lanes.

B. Operation

In a network using virtual channel flow control, flow control is performed at two levels. Virtual channel assignment is made at the packet level while physical channel bandwidth is allocated at the flit level. When a packet arrives at a node, it is assigned (according to the routing algorithm) to an output virtual channel. This assignment remains fixed for the duration of the packet. The virtual channels associated with a physical channel arbitrate for physical channel bandwidth on a flit-by-flit basis.

Fig. 8 illustrates the hardware required to support virtual channel flow control on one physical channel. The transmitting node (node A) contains a status register for each virtual channel that contains the state of the lane buffer on the receiving node (node B). This state information includes: a bit to indicate if the lane is free, a count of the number of free flit buffers in the lane, and optionally the priority of the packet occupying the lane. node B contains a lane buffer and a status register for each virtual channel. The status maintained on node B includes input and output pointers for each lane buffer and the state of the channel: free, waiting (to be assigned an output), and active.

Lane assignment for physical channel P is performed by node A. When a packet arrives in an input buffer on node A (not shown), it is assigned a particular output channel based on its destination, the status of the output channels, and the routing algorithm in use. The flow-control logic then assigns this packet to any free lane of the selected channel. If all lanes are in use, the packet is blocked in the waiting state until a lane is available. Maintaining lane state information on the transmitting end of the channel allows lane assignment to be performed on a single node. No additional internode communication is required to maintain this information as it is already required for flit-level flow control.

Once a lane is assigned to a packet, flit-level flow control is used to advance the packet across the switch and physical channel. To advance from an input buffer on the node A to an input buffer on node B, a flit must gain access to 1) a path through the switch to reach the output of node A, and 2) the physical channel to reach the input of node B. Typically either the switch is nonblocking, and thus always available (see Section III-D), or a few optional flit buffers are provided at the output of node A so that switch and channel resources do not have to be allocated simultaneously.

When the last flit of a message (the tail flit) leaves a node the lane assigned to that packet is deallocated and may be reassigned to another packet.

The status register storage required to implement virtual channel flow control for one physical channel, S_{vc} is shown below in terms of the number of lanes, l, the total number of flit buffers in the receiver, b, and the number of bits used to encode priority, pri. Setting $l = 1$ and pri $= 0$ gives the status register storage required by a conventional channel, S_{conv}. The first term of the expression corresponds to the storage on node A while the second term describes the storage on node B. For typical values of $b = 16$, $l = 4$, and pri$= 0$, S_{vc} is 36 bits compared with 17 bits for S_{conv}. This overhead is small compared to the storage required for the lane buffers, 512 bits if the flit size is 32 bits.

$$S_{vc} = l\left(\lg\left(\frac{b}{l}\right) + 1 + \text{pri}\right) + l\left(2\lg\left(\frac{b}{l}\right) + 2\right). \quad (1)$$

C. Allocation Policies

Flit-level flow control across the physical channel involves allocating channel bandwidth among lanes that 1) have a flit ready to transmit and 2) have space for this flit at the receiving end. Any arbitration algorithm can be used to allocate this resource including random, round-robin, or priority. For each physical channel, the arbitration algorithm is implemented as combinational logic that operates on the contents of the status registers and picks the highest priority lane that has space available at the receiving end. For random and round-robin arbitration schemes, priority information is generated by logic based on the lane's position and the previous state. For priority based schemes, priority information is stored in the status register for each lane.

Deadline scheduling [20] can be implemented by allocating channel bandwidth based on a packet's deadline or age—earliest deadline or oldest age first. Scheduling packets by age reduces the variance of message latency. Deadline scheduling provides several classes of delivery service and reduces the variance within each class.

D. Implementation Issues

Virtual channel flow control can be integrated into existing switch designs by replacing FIFO buffers with multilane buffers. When this replacement is made, however, the switch must be modified to deal with a larger number of inputs and outputs, and the flow control protocol between nodes must be modified to identify lanes.

Increasing the number of virtual channels multiplexed on each physical channel increases the number of inputs and outputs that must be switched at each node. If the switch handles each of these inputs and outputs separately as shown in Fig. 9(a), the switch complexity will increase significantly. Increasing the switch complexity is not required, however. The average data rate out of the set of lanes associated with a given physical channel is limited to the bandwidth of the channel. Thus it is sufficient to provide a single switch input for each physical input and output channel as shown in Fig. 9(b). With this organization, a small (one or two flit) output buffer is desirable to decouple switch allocation from physical channel allocation. Individual lanes are multiplexed onto the single path through the switch in the same manner that they are multiplexed over the single physical channel between the nodes.

An intermediate organization, shown in Fig. 9(c), is to provide a switch with separate inputs and multiplexed outputs. This configuration has the advantage of simple arbitration. An input virtual channel competes only for switch output ports. It need not simultaneously arbitrate for both input and output ports as is required for a fully multiplexed switch.

Any network that uses blocking or buffering flow control must, for each channel, send information in the reverse direction to indicate the availability of buffering on the receiving node. These acknowledgment signals can be transmitted on separate wires [12] or, in a bidirectional network, they can be transmitted out-of-band on a channel in the opposite direction [19].

In a network using multilane buffers, two effects increase the acknowledgment traffic. First, a few bits must be added to each acknowledgment signal to identify the lane being acknowledged. Second, because a lane buffer is typically smaller than a channel FIFO, the use of block acknowledgments to amortize the cost of the signal over several flits is restricted.[4]

Even with these effects, acknowledgment signal bandwidth is still a small fraction of forward bandwidth. In a network with 32-bit flits, 15 lanes per channel, and no block acknowledgment, 4 bits must be sent along the reverse channel for each flit transmitted along the forward channel, a 12.5% overhead. An additional 12.5% overhead is required to identify the lane associated with each flit sent in the forward direction. Such a scheme could be realized by a physical channel consisting of a 9-bit forward path (8-bit phits) and a 1-bit reverse path. Every four channel cycles a 32-bit flit is transmitted over the

---

[4] A block acknowledgment signals the availability of a block (several flits) of storage in a single action rather than signaling each flit separately

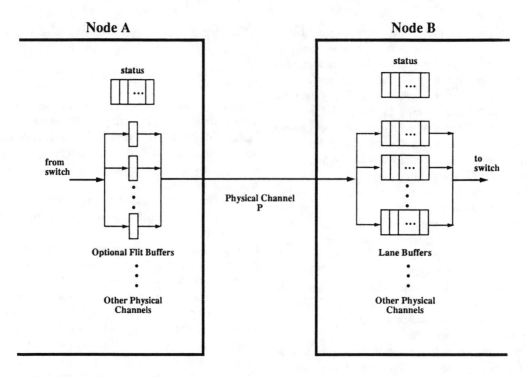

Fig. 8. Logic associated with one physical channel P to support virtual channel flow control. The transmitting node (node A) includes status registers for each virtual channel and optional flit buffers. The receiving node (node B) contains buffers and status registers.

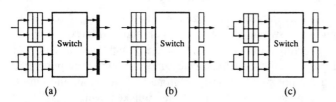

Fig. 9. (a) Adding virtual channels increases switch complexity if a complete switch is used. (b) Using a multiplexed switch leaves switch complexity unchanged. (c) Multiplexing only switch outputs give intermediate complexity and results in simpler arbitration than (b).

forward path along with its 4-bit lane identifier and a 4-bit acknowledgment code is transmitted over the reverse path.

IV. ANALYSIS

This section develops an analytical performance model for k-ary n-fly networks that use virtual channel flow control.

For convenience, the following is a summary of the notation used in this section.

$b_{i,j}$ The probability that all occupied virtual channels are blocked in stage i when j virtual channels are occupied.

j_{avg} The expected number of virtual channels sharing a physical channel–averaged over packets.

l Number of virtual channels per physical channel.

L Message length in bits.

λ The offered traffic rate.

$\lambda_{\max}$ Network throughput, the maximum rate for which a steady state solution exists.

n Number of stages in the network.

$p_{i,j}$ The probability that j virtual channels are occupied in stage i.

$q_{i,j}$ An intermediate variable used in the calculation of $p_{i,j}$.

t_0 The service time at the destination.

$t_{i,j}$ The effective service time out of stage i when j virtual channels are occupied.

T Network latency.

T_d Time required for a flit to propagate through one node.

w_i The average total amount of time spent acquiring virtual channels between stage i and the destination inclusive.

W Channel width in bits.

x_i The average amount of time spent waiting to acquire a virtual channel at stage i.

We make the following assumptions

1) Packet destinations are uniformly randomly distributed.
2) A packet that arrives at its destination is consumed without waiting.
3) All packets are of length L.
4) At each source packets are created by a Poisson process with rate λ.
5) Each virtual channel is associated with a single flit buffer.
6) Packet blocking probabilities are independent.

The analysis considers a single path through the network. Our analysis starts at the destination and works back to the source. Network stages are numbered starting from the destination. The final stage is stage 0. The stage connected to the source is stage $n - 1$.

The destination, stage 0, is always able to accept a packet, so the service time seen by a packet in the final stage is $t_0 = L/W$ which we will normalize to be unit time, $t_0 = 1.0$.

The service time at internal stages is increased because a channel may be idled when all of the virtual channels at a subsequent stage of the network are occupied. The average

498

amount of time that a packet waits to acquire a virtual channel at stage i of the network, x_i, is given by the product of the probability of all virtual channels in stage i being occupied, $p_{i,l}$, and the average waiting time, $t_{j,l}/2$.

$$x_i = \frac{p_{i,l}t_{j,l}}{2}. \tag{2}$$

The total time spent waiting to acquire virtual channels between stage i and the network output is the summation of the acquisition delays at each stage.

$$w_i = \sum_{j=0}^{i} x_j. \tag{3}$$

If j virtual channels at stage i are occupied, the total time required to service all j channels with no idling is jt_0. Each channel is individually blocked for a total time of w_{i-1}, so the probability of an individual channel being blocked is approximately[5] w_{i-1}/jt_0. Assuming that the blocking probabilities are independent, the probability of the channel being idled because all virtual channels are blocked, $b_{i,j}$, is the product of the individual probabilities.

$$b_{i,j} = \left(\frac{w_{i-1}}{jt_0}\right)^j. \tag{4}$$

Assuming independence of channel blocking probabilities is an approximation that slightly underestimates $b_{i,j}$. There is some dependence between blocking probabilities as it is possible for two packets to be blocked waiting on the same channel. This approximation, however, is justified because 1) it gives a result that agrees closely with experiment and 2) a calculation of $b_{i,j}$ that accounted for dependence did not give appreciably different results.

The effective service time seen by a packet at stage i with j virtual channels occupied, $t_{i,j}$, is thus

$$t_{i,j} = t_0(1 + b_{i,j}). \tag{5}$$

Equation (2) uses the probability of all l virtual channels being occupied. We calculate the occupancy probabilities for the virtual channels in a stage, i, using a Markov model as illustrated in Fig. 10. State S_j corresponds to j virtual channels being occupied. This state transitions to $j+1$ at rate λ, and to state $j-1$ at rate $1/t_{i,j}$. The rate out of the last stage is reduced to account for the arrival of packets while the stage is in this state. Solving this model for the steady state probabilities gives

$$q_{i,j} = \begin{cases} 1 & \text{if } j = 0 \\ q_{i,j-1}\lambda t_{i,j} & \text{if } 0 < j < l \\ q_{i,l-1}\frac{\lambda}{\frac{1}{t_{i,l}}-\lambda} & \text{if } j = l \end{cases} \tag{6}$$

$$p_{i,j} = \begin{cases} \frac{1}{\sum_{m=0}^{l} q_{i,m}} & \text{if } j = 0 \\ p_{i,j-1}\lambda t_{i,j} & \text{if } 0 < j < l \\ p_{i,l-1}\frac{\lambda}{\frac{1}{t_{i,l}}-\lambda} & \text{if } j = l. \end{cases} \tag{7}$$

[5]This is a slight overestimate as we are not considering the increase in effective service time due to blockage. The actual expression should be $w_{i-1}/(jt_0(1 + b_{i,j}))$ which results in a set of equations that cannot be solved in closed form for $j > 3$.

Network latency has four components as shown in (8).

$$T = \frac{L}{W}\left(j_{\text{avg}} + w_n + \frac{\lambda(t_0 + x_{n-1})^2}{2(1 - \lambda(t_0 + x_{n-1}))}\right) + T_d n. \tag{8}$$

The first term accounts for multiplexing delay due to virtual channels. If in the most congested stage j_{avg} virtual channels are occupied on average, a packet takes $j_{\text{avg}}L/W$ time to entirely traverse one channel. As the first stage, stage $n-1$, is always the most congested, j_{avg} can be calculated by

$$j_{\text{avg}} = \frac{\sum_{j=1}^{l} j^2 p_{n-1,j}}{\sum_{j=1}^{l} j p_{n-1,j}}. \tag{9}$$

The second term, $w_n L/W$, is the time spent waiting to acquire virtual channels.

The third term is the queueing delay in the source which is that of an M/D/1 queue with utilization $\rho = \lambda(t_0 + x_{n-1})$ and average service time $\overline{x} = L/W(t_0 + x_{n-1})$ [17]. For heavily loaded networks this term is the most significant. Modeling the source queue as M/D/1 is a slight approximation since even though message length is fixed the service time seen by the source has nonzero variance.

The final term, $T_d n$, is the time one flit of a packet spends traversing the n stages of the network in the absence of contention.

Fig. 11 shows the latency predicted by (8) as a function of offered traffic, λ, for a 2-ary 8-fly network. The figure shows that the addition of virtual channels greatly increases the traffic that can be offered to the network before saturation occurs. The figure also indicates that adding lanes has little effect on latency below saturation throughput. The curves lie on top of each other until traffic approaches saturation throughput.

Using virtual channel flow control increases saturation throughput because it decreases both waiting time and physical channel idle time. Waiting time, w_{n-1} (3), is reduced because a packet waits only when all l virtual channels are occupied. In a conventional network, $l = 1$, the blocking probability $p_{i,l}$ is much larger and w_{n-1} is increased proportionally. Waiting time is particularly important since it determines the service time seen by the source queue and hence the source queueing delay.

Physical channel idle time is reduced because a physical channel idles only when all of its virtual channels are blocked. Because virtual channels make this blocking probability, $b_{i,j}$ (4), small, the effective service time increases more slowly with traffic than in a conventional network.

The throughput λ_{max} of a multistage network using virtual channels can be determined by solving the equation

$$\lambda_{\text{max}} = \frac{1}{t_0 + x_{n-1}}. \tag{10}$$

Fig. 12 shows the throughput of several multistage networks as a function of the number of virtual channels, l. The figure shows that adding a small number of virtual channels causes a large increase in throughput with diminishing returns as more channels are added. The data suggests that four to eight lanes per physical channel is adequate for most networks. For all of

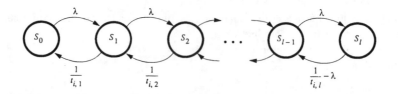

Fig. 10. Virtual channel occupancy probabilities are calculated using a Markov model. State S_j corresponds to j virtual channels being occupied.

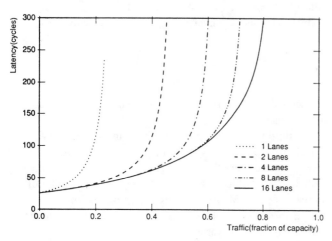

Fig. 11. Latency as a function of offered traffic as predicted by analysis for a 2-ary 8-fly network with 1, 2, 4, 8, and 16 virtual channels per physical channel.

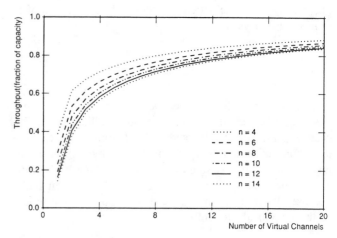

Fig. 12. Throughput of 2-ary n-cube networks with virtual channels as a function of the number of virtual channels.

the networks shown, eight lanes per physical channel results in at least 80% of the throughput as a network with 20 lanes.

Adding virtual channels to a network also reduces the dependence of throughput on the number of stages in the network. For conventional networks, $l = 1$ on the left side of the figure, there is a large difference in throughput with network size. Conventional networks with four and fourteen stages have throughputs of 0.39 and 0.14, respectively. With 18 virtual channels, the difference is narrowed to 6%, 0.83 versus 0.88. The effect of the number of stages on throughput is reduced by virtual channels because the reduction in waiting time and channel idle time reduce the rate at which service time increases with stage number.

V. EXPERIMENTAL RESULTS

To measure the effect of virtual channel flow control on network performance (throughput and latency), we have simulated a number of k-ary n-cube and k-ary n-fly networks. These simulations serve to check our analytical model, presented in Section IV, and to measure the performance of networks not covered by our model.

Our analytical model is limited to networks where lanes have unit depth independent of the number of virtual channels. We have simulated networks where the total buffer storage per physical channel is held constant constant while varying the number of lanes per channel. If lanes are added, the depth of each lane is proportionally reduced. These simulations compare the effect of increasing the number of virtual channels with increasing the depth of each virtual channel.

We have also simulated k-ary n-cube networks with virtual channels, a topology not covered by our analytic model, and networks employing deadline and priority scheduling.

The simulator is a 3000 line C program that simulates interconnection networks at the flit-level. A flit transfer between two nodes is assumed to take place in one time unit. The network is simulated synchronously moving all flits that have been granted channels in one time step and then advancing time to the next step. The simulator is programmable as to topology, routing algorithm, and traffic pattern.

The simulations were run with packet length fixed at 20 flits and uniformly distributed random packet destinations. Except where otherwise noted, channel bandwidth was allocated randomly to lanes.

Each simulation was run for a total of 30 000 flit times. Statistics gathering was inhibited for the first 10 000 flit times to avoid distortions due to the startup transient. For a typical test, ($\lambda = 0.4$, $n = 8$), measurements were taken for 100 000 packets. The standard deviation of both latency and throughput measurements for an individual packet is $\approx$ 30% of the mean value. Assuming that these values are independent and normally distributed, the standard deviation of the ensemble average measurements reported below is $\approx$ 0.1% of the mean value.

A. Throughput

Throughput is measured by applying to each network input a saturation source that injects a new packet into the network whenever a lane is available on its input channel. Throughput is given as a fraction of network capacity. A uniformly loaded network is operating at capacity if the most heavily loaded channel is used 100% of the time.

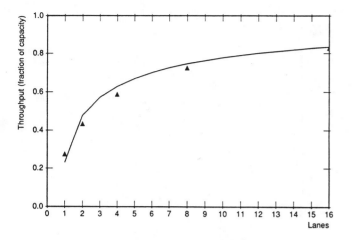

Fig. 13. Comparison of predicted (solid line) and measured (points) throughput for radix-2 eight stage networks.

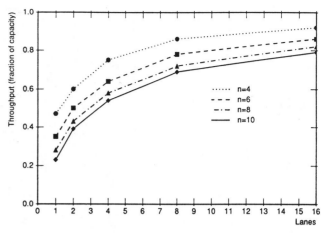

Fig. 14. Throughput versus number of lanes for radix-2 multistage networks holding the amount of storage per physical channel constant at 16 flits.

Fig. 13 compares the throughput predicted by the analytic model of Section IV with measurements from the simulator. The figure shows the throughput of 2-ary 8-fly networks with a single flit buffer per virtual channel as the number of virtual channels (lanes) per physical channel are varied. There is close agreement between the predicted and measured data.

To compare the effect of adding lanes to the network with adding depth to each lane, networks with equal storage were simulated. Each network simulated has 16 flits of storage per physical channel. The number of lanes per channel was varied from 1 (conventional network) to 16 in powers of two. The results of these simulations are shown in Fig. 14. The figure shows the saturation throughput versus the number of lanes per channel for radix-2 multistage networks (2-ary n-flys). Data are shown for networks with dimensions of 4, 6, 8, and 10. The data show that given a fixed amount of storage, adding lanes gives a far greater throughput improvement than does increasing the total amount of buffering with a single lane (see [21]).

B. Latency

Latency is measured by applying a constant rate source with exponentially distributed interarrival times to each input and measuring the time from packet creation until the last flit of the packet is accepted at the destination. Source queueing time is included in the latency measurement.

Fig. 15 compares the latency predicted by the model of Section IV with measurements from the simulator. The figure shows the latency of a 2-ary 8-fly network with four virtual channels per physical channel. Each virtual channel has a single flit buffer. As with the throughput comparison shown in Fig. 13, the latency measurements are in close agreement with the value predicted by analysis.

Fig. 16 shows latency results for 2-ary 8-fly networks with equal storage. Each network simulated has 16 flits of storage per physical channel. The number of lanes per node was varied from 1 to 16 in powers of two. As with the throughput results, Fig. 16 shows that adding lanes to a network is a more effective use of storage than adding depth to a lane. However, with

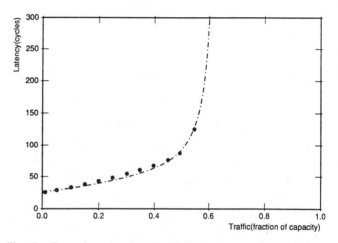

Fig. 15. Comparison of predicted (solid line) and measured (points) latency for a 2-ary 8-fly network with four lanes.

storage held constant, there is a small latency penalty (as much as 7%) at mid to high traffic rates associated with the shorter buffers that result when more virtual channels are used. For example, the curve for eight lanes drops below the curve for 16 lanes until it nears its saturation throughput.

Adding lanes is more effective in increasing throughput than adding depth for two reasons. First, adding lanes reduces the channel blocking probability exponentially, (4), while adding depth has a very small effect on blocking probability. Second, adding a single flit virtual channel buffer allows one packet to pass another. This has an effect on waiting time comparable to increasing the depth of a buffer by the packet length.

C. Scheduling Algorithm

Fig. 17 shows the effect of the channel scheduling algorithm on latency. The figure shows two latency histograms, one for a random assignment of channel bandwidth to packets, and the other for oldest-packet-first channel bandwidth allocation (deadline scheduling). Both curves are for 2-ary 6-fly networks with random traffic operating at 50% capacity. The histograms have been truncated at 140 cycles latency.

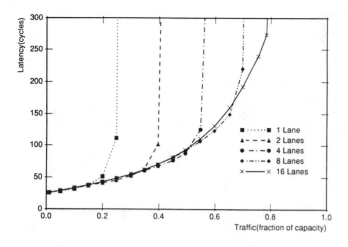

Fig. 16. Simulated latency versus offered traffic for 2-ary 8-fly networks with 16 flits of storage per physical channel.

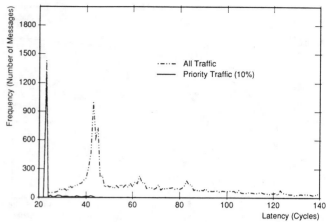

Fig. 18. Latency histogram for a 2-ary 6-fly network with random traffic at 50% capacity where 10% of the traffic is marked high-priority and scheduled by age. 80% of the high-priority traffic is delivered with the minimum latency.

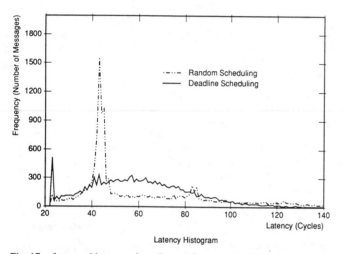

Latency Histogram

Fig. 17. Latency histogram for a 2-ary 6-fly network with random traffic at 50% capacity using deadline (oldest first) and random scheduling of physical channels. The histogram for deadline scheduling has a very sharp peak at 24 and a broad peak at 57. The curve for random scheduling shows a peak at 44.

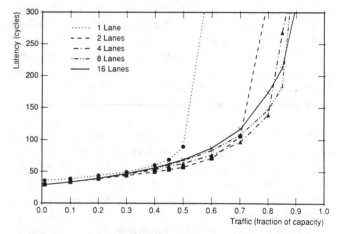

Fig. 19. Latency versus offered traffic for 16-ary 2-cube mesh networks under random traffic. As with the butterfly networks, adding lanes to a network has little effect on latency below the saturation throughput for a single lane. Adding a lane dramatically increases throughput at first with diminishing returns for 8 and 16 lanes.

The use of deadline scheduling reduced the average packet latency from 75.1 cycles to 62.2 cycles and reduced the standard deviation of packet latency by a factor of two. The deadline curve shows a sharp peak at 24 cycles latency, the minimum latency required to traverse the network, and a broad peak at 57 cycles. The random curve shows peaks at 44 and 84 cycles. The data suggest that deadline scheduling can be useful in reducing average message latency and in making message latency more predictable.

Fig. 18 shows how virtual channel scheduling can be used to provide different classes of service. The figures shows the result of an experiment where a network was loaded with 90% standard traffic and 10% priority traffic. The standard traffic was scheduled randomly, the priority traffic took precedence over standard traffic and was scheduled by age—oldest packet first. The figure shows that 80% of the priority traffic is delivered with the minimum latency (24 cycles). This type of scheduling would be useful, for example, in a switch that handles both voice and data where the voice traffic has a tight deadline and should be dropped if it cannot make its deadline.

D. k-ary n-cube Simulations

Fig. 19 shows average packet latency as a function of offered traffic for radix-16, dimension-2 mesh networks (16-ary 2-cubes). Each network simulated has 32 flits of storage per physical channel. The number of lanes per channel was varied from 1 to 16 in powers of two. The simulated network uses deterministic dimension-order routing.

The figure shows that adding lanes has little effect on latency below the saturation throughput for a single lane while it greatly increases the saturation throughput of the network. With a single lane, the network saturates at 50% capacity while with 16-lanes throughputs of 90% capacity are achievable. Most of the throughput gain is realized with four lanes. Adding additional lanes yields diminishing returns and actually increases latency by as much as 20%. As with the k-ary n-fly, latency in the mid to high traffic range is increased slightly by adding lanes. We suspect that this increase occurs because adding lanes while holding storage constant increases buffer utilization.

Direct, k-ary n-cube, networks using dimension-order routing require fewer virtual channels than multistage networks because most contention in these networks occurs when packets enter a new dimension. For purposes of analyzing contention, each dimension of a direct network is analogous to a stage of a multistage network. With few dimensions, there are fewer opportunities for blocking and fewer lanes are required to pass blocked packets.

VI. CONCLUSION

The performance of interconnection networks can be improved by organizing the buffers associated with each network channel into several lanes or virtual channels rather than a single FIFO queue. Associating several lanes with each physical channel decouples the allocation of virtual channels to packets from the allocation of physical channel bandwidth to flits. This decoupling allows active messages to pass blocked messages dramatically improving network throughput.

The use of virtual channel flow control also allows flexibility in allocating physical channel bandwidth. By decoupling resource allocation, a channel's bandwidth need not be allocated to the "next packet in line." Instead, this bandwidth may be allocated on the basis of packet type, age, or deadline. The use of deadline scheduling may be particularly important in networks where one class of packets must be delivered in a bounded amount of time.

This paper has developed a model for the performance of k-ary n-fly networks with virtual channels. This model can be used to calculate the latency and throughput of these networks. The model shows that adding virtual channels to a network greatly improves network throughput with little effect on latency at low traffic rates. For a 2-ary 10-fly network (1024 input butterfly), the throughput with 16 lanes per channel is 4 times the throughput with a single lane. The use of virtual channels also reduces the dependence of throughput on the number of stages in a network. Without virtual channels, throughput asymptotically varies as the inverse of the number of stages [18]. With virtual channels, throughput remains relatively constant as stages are added.

Several indirect (k-ary n-fly) and direct (k-ary n-cube) networks have been simulated to validate our model and to study networks not covered by the model. Simulation results agree closely with the values predicted by our model. Simulations also show that with the total amount of buffer storage per node held constant, adding lanes to a network is a significantly more effective use of storage than adding depth to a channel FIFO. The use of deadline scheduling reduces average latency by a small amount and makes latency much more predictable.

The critical resources in an interconnection network are wire bandwidth and buffer memory. Virtual channel flow control is a method for allocating these critical resources in a more efficient manner. With network switches constructed using VLSI circuits, the cost of adding the small amount of control state and logic required to implement multiple lanes per channel is well worth the cost.

ACKNOWLEDGMENT

I thank S. Ward, A. Agarwal, T. Knight, and C. Leiserson for many discussions about interconnection networks and their analysis. I thank all the members of the MIT Concurrent VLSI Architecture group and especially S. Wills, D. Chaiken, W. Horwat, and H. Aoki for their help with and contributions to this paper. L. Sardegna deserves thanks for preparing several of the illustrations in this paper. I thank the editor, B. Buckles, for arranging a speedy review of this manuscript and the referees (especially referee 4) for many helpful comments and suggestions.

REFERENCES

[1] R. Arlauskas, "iPSC/2 system: A second generation hypercube," in *Proc. Third Conf. Hypercube Concurrent Comput. and Appl.*, ACM, 1988, pp. 33–36.
[2] W. C. Athas and C. L. Seitz, "Multicomputers: Message-passing concurrent computers," *IEEE Comput. Mag.*, vol. 21, pp. 9–24, Aug. 1988.
[3] D. Bertsekas and R. Gallager, *Data Networks*. Englewood Cliffs, NJ: Prentice-Hall, 1987.
[4] S. Borkar, R. Cohn, G. Cox, S. Gleason, T. Gross, H. T. Kung, M. Lam, B. Moore, C. Peterson, J. Pieper, L. Rankin, P. S. Tseng, J. Sutton, J. Urbanski, and J. Webb, "iWARP: An integrated solution to high-speed parallel computing," in *Proc. Supercomput. Conf.*, IEEE, Nov. 1988, pp. 330–338.
[5] S. Borkar *et al.*, "Supporting systolic and memory communication in iWarp," in *Proc. 17th Int. Symp. Comput. Architecture*, May 1990, pp. 70–81.
[6] W. J. Dally, "Network and processor architecture for message-driven computers," in *VLSI and Parallel Computation*, Suaya and Birtwhistle, Eds. Los Altos, CA: Morgan Kaufmann, 1990.
[7] ——, "Performance analysis of k-ary n-cube interconnection networks," *IEEE Trans. Comput.*, vol. 39, June 1990. Also appears as a chapter in *Artificial Intelligence at MIT, Expanding Frontiers*, edited by P. H. Winston, with Sarah A. Shellard, vol. 1. Cambridge, MA: MIT Press, 1990, pp. 548–581.
[8] ——, "Virtual-channel flow control," in *Proc. 17th Annu. Int. Symp. Comput. Architecture*, Los Alamitos, CA, IEEE Computer Society Press, May 1990, pp. 60–68.
[9] W. J. Dally *et al.*, "The J-Machine: A fine-grain concurrent computer," in *Proc. IFIP Congress*, G. X. Ritter, Ed. New York: North-Holland, Aug. 1989, pp. 1147–1153.
[10] W. J. Dally and C. L. Seitz, "The torus routing chip," *Distributed Comput.*, vol. 1, pp. 187–196, 1986.
[11] ——, "Deadlock free message routing in multiprocessor interconnection networks," *IEEE Trans. Comput.*, vol. C-36, pp. 547–553, May 1987, VLSI memo 87–417.
[12] W. J. Dally and P. Song, "Design of a self-timed VLSI multicomputer communication controller," in *Proc. Int. Conf. Comput. Design*, IEEE Computer Society Press, Oct. 1987, pp. 230–234.
[13] BBN Advanced Computers Inc., "Butterfly parallel processor overview," BBN Rep. 6148, Mar. 1986.
[14] M. Karol, M. G. Hluchyj, and S. P. Morgan, "Input versus output queueing on a space-division packet switch," *IEEE Trans. Commun.*, vol. COM-35, Dec. 1987.
[15] P. Kermani and L. Kleinrock, "Virtual cut through: A new computer communication switching technique," *Comput. Networks*, vol. 3, pp. 267–286, 1979.
[16] ——, "A tradeoff study of switching systems in computer communication networks," *IEEE Trans. Comput.*, vol. C-29, pp. 1052–1060, Dec. 1980.
[17] L. Kleinrock, *Queueing Systems, Vol. 1: Theory*. New York: Wiley, 1975.
[18] C. P. Kruskal and M. Snir, "The performance of multistage interconnection networks for multiprocessors," *IEEE Trans. Comput.*, vol. C-32, pp. 1091–1098, Dec. 1983.
[19] InMOS Ltd., *IMS T424 Reference Manual*, Order Number 72 TRN 006 00, Nov. 1984.
[20] C. L. Liu and J. W. Layland, "Scheduling algorithms for multiprogramming in a hard-real-time environment," *J. ACM*, vol. 20, no. 1, pp. 46–61, Jan. 1973.
[21] J. N. Mailhot, "Routing and flow control strategies in multiprocessor networks," S.B. thesis, May 1988.

[22] J. H. Patel, "Performance of processor-memory interconnections for multiprocessors," *IEEE Trans. Comput.*, vol. C-30, pp. 771–780, 1981.

[23] C. L. Seitz *et al.*, "The architecture and programming of the Ametek Series 2010 multicomputer," in *Proc. Third Conf. Hypercube Concurrent Comput. and Appl.*, ACM, 1988, pp. 33–36.

[24] C. L. Seitz, "The Cosmic Cube," *Commun. ACM*, vol. 28, pp. 22–33, Jan. 1985.

[25] Y. Tamir and G. L. Frazier, "High-performance multi-queue buffers for VLSI communication switches," in *Proc. 15th Annu. ACM/IEEE Int. Symp. Comput. Architecture*, June 1988, pp. 343–354.

[26] A. S. Tanenbaum, *Computer Networks*, second ed. Englewood Cliffs, NJ: Prentice-Hall 1988.

William J. Dally (S'78–M'86) received the B.S. degree in electrical engineering from Virginia Polytechnic Institute, the M.S. degree in electrical engineering from Stanford University, and the Ph.D. degree in computer science from Caltech.

He has worked at Bell Telephone Laboratories where he contributed to the design of the BELLMAC-32 microprocessor. Later as a consultant to Bell Laboratories he helped design the MARS hardware accelerator. He was a Research Assistant and then a Research Fellow at Caltech where he designed he MOSSIM Simulation Engine and the Torus Routing Chip. He is currently an Associate Professor of Computer Science at the Massachusetts Institute of Technology, Cambridge, where he directs a research group that is building the J-Machine, a fine-grain concurrent computer. His research interests include concurrent computing, computer architecture, computer aided design, and VLSI design.

HIGH-PERFORMANCE MULTI-QUEUE BUFFERS FOR VLSI COMMUNICATION SWITCHES†

Yuval Tamir and Gregory L. Frazier
Computer Science Department
University of California
Los Angeles, California 90024
U.S.A.

Abstract

Small $n \times n$ switches are key components of multistage interconnection networks used in multiprocessors as well as in the communication coprocessors used in multicomputers. The design of the internal buffers in these switches is of critical importance for achieving high throughput low latency communication. We discuss several buffer structures and compare them in terms of implementation complexity and their ability to deal with variations in traffic patterns and message lengths. We present a new design of buffers that provide non-FIFO message handling and efficient storage allocation for variable size packets through the use of linked lists managed by a simple on-chip controller. We evaluate the new buffer design by comparing it to several alternative designs in the context of a multi-stage interconnection network. Our modeling and simulations show that the new buffer outperforms its "competition" and can thus be used to improve the performance of a wide variety of systems currently using less efficient buffers.

I. Introduction

Multiprocessors and multicomputers have the potential for achieving very high performance at a relatively low cost by exploiting parallelism. The speed at which processors can communicate with each other is a critical factor in determining the effectiveness of multiprocessor and multicomputer systems. Multiprocessors with a large number of nodes (e.g. greater than 64) use multistage interconnection networks composed of a large number of small $n \times n$ switches (typically, $2 \leq n \leq 10$) for communication [1,4]. Similarly, communication through point-to-point dedicated links in multicomputers [12, 16] relies on communication coprocessors with a small number of ports [2, 13] that basically function as small $n \times n$ switches with $n-1$ ports connected to other nodes, and one bidirectional port connected to the local application processor. The design of high-performance small $n \times n$

switches is thus of critical importance to the success of multiprocessor and multicomputer systems. Since many of these $n \times n$ switches are needed in a large system, there is strong motivation to implement each switch as a single VLSI chip.

This paper deals with the design and implementation of a small $n \times n$ VLSI communication switch, focusing on the design of its internal buffers. A switch's job is to take packets arriving at its input ports and route them to its output ports. As long as only one packet at a time arrives for a given output port, there will be no conflict, and the packets are routed with a minimum latency. Unfortunately, as the throughput goes up, so does the probability of conflict. When two packets destined for the same output port arrive at different input ports of a switch at approximately the same time, they cannot both be forwarded immediately. Only one packet can be transmitted from an output port at a time, and hence one of the two packets must be stored at the node for later transmission. The maximum throughput at which the switch can operate depends directly on how efficient the switch is at storing the conflicting packets and forwarding them when the appropriate output port is no longer busy.

An ideal switch has infinite buffer space, but will only buffer (keep) a packet as long as the output port to which the packet is destined is busy. Such a switch can handle n incoming packets while transmitting n packets and can receive and forward the first byte of a packet in a single cycle [6]. In a real single-chip implementation, buffers are finite and have a finite bandwidth. This can result in conflicts due to attempted simultaneous accesses to a shared buffers and in messages that cannot be received due to lack of buffer space. Packets ready to be transmitted may be blocked behind packets waiting for their output port to free up, and significant delays may be introduced by complex memory allocation schemes required to handle variable length packets.

The results reported in this paper were produced as part of the UCLA ComCoBB project. The goal of the ComCoBB (**Communication Coprocessor Building-Block**) project is to design and implement a single-chip

---

† This research is supported by Rockwell International and the State of California MICRO program.

505

Reprinted from *Proc. 15th Ann. Symp. Computer Architecture*, 1988, pp. 343-354. Copyright © 1988 by The Institute of Electrical and Electronics Engineers, Inc. All rights reserved.

high-performance communication coprocessor for use in VLSI multicomputer systems. The ComCoBB chip is, in part, a small $n \times n$ switch, and the problem of designing an efficient buffering scheme for it had to be faced early on in the project. As a result, we have developed a new type of buffer for small $n \times n$ switches, called a *dynamically allocated multi-queue* (DAMQ) buffer, which will be described and evaluated in this paper. While this buffer was originally developed for use in a multicomputer communication coprocessor, it is equally useful for multi-stage networks and it is in that context (of multi-stage network) that the buffer will be evaluated.

In the next section we will discuss some of the issues in designing a real $n \times n$ switch which is as close as possible to the ideal, yet implementable in current technology. Several alternative approaches will be described and the choice of the DAMQ buffer as a critical building block will be explained. The design and micro architecture of the DAMQ switch (a switch which uses the DAMQ buffer) will be described in Section 3. This description will include detailed timing of the buffer in the context of the ComCoBB chip and the use of virtual circuits [3] and virtual cut through routing [6]. In Section 4 the DAMQ switch is evaluated in the context of a multi-stage interconnection network by comparing it to three alternative designs using Markov analysis and simulations. One of the results described in Section 4 is that a multi-stage interconnection network implemented using 4×4 DAMQ switches can achieve maximum throughput which is *forty percent* higher than a network using FIFO (first-in-first-out) switches with the same number of storage cells in their buffers.

II. Designing a Switch for a Packet Switching Network

In an $n \times n$ switch packets that cannot be immediately forwarded to an output port need to be buffered within the switch. The buffers must be able to accept simultaneous arrival of packets from all of the input ports, while at the same time transmitting packets through all of the output ports. The buffers should be organized in such a way that if there is an available output port and there is a packet destined for that port, that packet will be sent there without having to wait for packets that need to be sent through other ports. Communication efficiency can be increased significantly if *virtual cut-through* [6] is supported so that there is no need to wait for a complete packet to arrive before beginning to forward it out of the switch through an available output port. Given the requirement of single-chip implementation, the buffering scheme must result in efficient use of available storage. When variable length packets are used, wasted memory due to internal and/or external fragmentation must be minimized.

Buffering may be done by centralized buffers, independent buffers at each input port, or independent buffers at each output port. Intuitively, complete sharing of available storage by all communication ports appears to be more efficient than statically partitioning the buffer storage between ports. However, central buffer pools have drawbacks, both in performance and in implementation. Simulation studies have shown that with complete sharing a single congested output port may "hog" most of the available storage in a centralized buffer pool, thus impeding all other communication through the switch [3, 10]. This, in turn, can cause the neighbors, which cannot transmit packets to the full switch's node, to have their buffer fill up, thus converting a single "hogged" buffer into a system-wide problem. The need to limit the buffer space used by any single port increases the implementation complexity [3, 10].

Implementation of a centralized buffer pool is difficult since, in order to achieve high performance, multiple high-bandwidth communication ports must be able to access the buffer pool simultaneously. Furthermore, the bandwidth of the interconnection between the buffer pool and the ports must be approximately equal to the sum of the bandwidths of all the ports. Multiport memory is undesirable since its implementation is expensive (in area) and leads to poor performance (long access times). By making the interconnection (e.g. a bus) to the buffer pool and the buffer memory itself wide enough, it is possible to achieve the requires bandwidth without using multiport memory [13]. However, the need to "assemble" bytes into wide words before transmission increases communication latency and some of the available bandwidth is wasted when transmitting blocks smaller than the width of the bus. With variable length packets, it is difficult to implement control circuitry that can quickly (within one or two cycles) make memory allocation decisions and minimize internal and external fragmentation.

The next option is to place the buffers at the output ports. According to Karol et al [5], the mean queue length of systems with output port buffering is always shorter than the mean queue length of equivalent systems with input port buffering. The reason for this is that with buffers at the input ports, packets destined for output ports which are idle may be queued behind packets whose output port is busy, and thus cannot be transmitted. The problem with implementing output port buffering is that either the switch must operate as fast as the sum of the speeds of its input ports, or the buffers must have as many write ports as there are input ports to the switch, to be able to handle simultaneous packet arrivals. Implementing buffers with multiple write ports increases their size and reduces their performance. Furthermore, if more than one write can occur at a time there is again, as was the case with centralized buffers, a difficult problem of allocating the buffer resources efficiently for variable size packets.

The remaining option is to implement buffering at the input ports. The advantage of input port buffering is that only one packet at a time arrives at the input port so that the buffer needs only a single write port. Furthermore, if the buffer is managed as a FIFO (first-in-first-out) queue, it is very easy to deal with variable length packets and avoid the memory management problems mentioned above. For these reasons many existing switches use FIFO queues at the input ports [2, 11]. The problem with FIFO buffers at the input ports is that a single packet at the head of the queue whose destination output port is busy can block all other packets in that queue from being transmitted even if their destination output ports are idle. Our design attempts to capture the advantages of input FIFO queues but avoid this very important disadvantage.

In the process of designing and evaluating the dynamically allocated multi-queue buffer we have experimented with several other buffer types. The "control" in our experiments was a buffer with a single write port and a single read port which treats packets in a first-in, first-out manner. We shall refer to this as a FIFO buffer. A simple switch with four input and four output ports using FIFO input buffers is shown in Figure 1a. The buffers are connected to the output ports by a four-by-four crossbar. It should be noted that the dual-ported storage cells are needed for virtual cut through and must be used for all buffer types [15].

As mentioned earlier, with FIFO input buffers it is quite likely that output ports will be idle even though there are packets in the switch waiting to be transmitted through those ports. In order to utilize the output ports more efficiently, and thus increase the switch's throughput, packets must somehow be segregated according to the output port to which they have been routed. One way to do this would be to implement separate FIFO buffers for each of the output ports at each of the input ports. In the case of a four-port switch, this amounts to sixteen separate buffers. Since there are multiple buffers at the same input port, a simple four-by-four crossbar will not accommodate all of the possible ways in which packets can be transmitted. Instead, this scheme requires a sixteen-by-four crossbar or, as we have shown in Figure 1b, four four-by-one switches. We

call this switch a *statically allocated, fully connected* (SAFC) switch, and the buffers are SAFC buffers. The name stems from the fact that the input ports have separate lines to each of the output ports (fully connected), and the storage in each input buffer is statically partitioned between queues to the output ports.

There are several problems with this design. First, it incurs a large amount of overhead. Four separate switches must be controlled, as opposed to a single crossbar. While it is much simpler to control a four-by-one switch than it is to control a four-by-four crossbar, using four of them will require replicating the same hardware four times. In addition, each input port will require four separate buffers and buffer controllers. In a VLSI implementation, with chip area at a premium, replicating control hardware is not an efficient use of a scarce resource.

Another problem is that the utilization of the available storage cells in the SAFC switch is not as good as in the FIFO switch. The available buffer space at each input port is *statically* partitioned so that, for a 4×4 switch, only one quarter of the input buffer space is available as potential storage for any given packet. This is in contrast to the FIFO buffers where the entire storage at the input port is available for all arriving packets. Thus, if traffic is not completely uniform, the FIFO buffer will "adapt" to it better than the SAFC buffers. With the SAFC buffers, packets may be rejected by an input port due to lack of buffer space even though there are some empty buffers at that port for other output ports.

Difficulties in implementing flow control is another problem with SAFC buffers. When an input port's buffer fills up, the opposite output port must be notified that it cannot transmit any more messages until some buffer space frees up. With four separate buffers at each input port, information about each of these buffers must be conveyed to the opposite output port. This is four times the amount of information that is necessary for the flow control of a FIFO buffer. More importantly, if an output port is notified that one of the opposite input port's buffers is full, it must pre-route packets to determine which of the buffers the packet is to be stored in before transmitting it. While pre-routing is possible, it increases the complexity of the routing hardware and causes routing decisions to be made based on information that may be out of date. An alternative flow control mechanism may be to avoid the use of pre-routing and discard a packet if there is no space for it. Such a scheme would require additional hardware to store unacknowledged packets and be able to retransmit discarded packets. It should be noted that pre-routing is necessary not only for flow control but also in order to

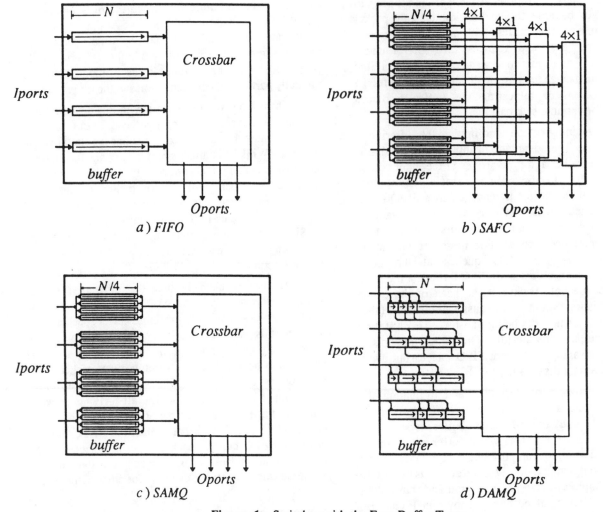

Figure 1: Switches with the Four Buffer Types

determine where to store the packet as it arrives at the input port. Without pre-routing incoming packets would have to be stored in a "staging buffer" until the routing decision is made. This again will add to communication latency as well as circuit complexity.

A way to simplify the SAFC is to implement the four separate buffers at each input port as a single buffer whose space is divided into four separate queues. This does not reduce the rate at which the buffers can receive packets, since there is only a single input port supplying all four queues, but it reduces the number of packets which can be read from the queues associated with input port (assuming that the buffer has a single read port and a single write port). This switch is shown in Figure 1c. It is called a *statically allocated multi-queue* (SAMQ) switch and the buffers are called SAMQ buffers. The space for the output ports is allocated statically, but it is implemented as multiple queues within a single buffer. Since only one packet can be read from a buffer at a

time, the interconnection network is a 4×4 crossbar. This eliminates some of the overhead associated with the SAFC switch. However, the problems caused by the need to pre-route packets and the inefficiency of statically partitioning the available buffer storage are the same as in the SAFC switch.

What is needed is a buffer which can access the packets destined for each of the output ports separately, but which can apply its free space to any packet. This is the buffer which we have designed, and we call it the dynamically allocated, multi-queue buffer (DAMQ). Dynamically allocated, because the space within the buffer is not statically partitioned between the output ports, but is allocated on the basis of each packet received. Multi-queue, because within each buffer there are separate FIFO queues of packets destined for each output port (Figure 1d).

III. Dynamically Allocated Multi-Queue Buffers

In this section we describe the design and micro architecture of the dynamically allocated, multi-queue buffer, as it is used in the ComCoBB chip. It should be noted that an almost identical design can be used for DAMQ buffers in a switch of a multistage interconnection network [1, 4]. To understand some of the design decisions in the DAMQ buffer, it is necessary to be familiar with a few details regarding the ComCoBB chip. The communications coprocessor being designed in the ComCoBB project has four input ports, four output ports, and a processor interface, all connected via a 5x5 crossbar switch. Each port is autonomous, and independently handles receiving and transmitting packets, so that all nine ports can be active at the same time. Each input port has associated with it a buffer and a router, and input and output ports are paired such that there are two unidirectional links between each pair of neighboring processing nodes. The links are eight bits wide and transfer data at a raw bandwidth of 20 Mbytes per second. The input port used a packet-level synchronizer that adjusts the receiving clock for each packet to minimize the probability of synchronization failures [15]. The packets in the ComCoBB system are of variable length, from one to thirty-two bytes long, and messages can be made up of multiple packets.

A. Buffer Organization

Multiple queues of packets are maintained within a DAMQ buffer in linked lists. In order to manage linked lists of variable size packets, the buffer is partitioned into eight-byte blocks. Each packet occupies from one to four blocks (the set of blocks which hold a packet is referred to as that packet's *slot* within the buffer). For each buffer block there is a pointer register, which points to the next block in the list (*Pointer Registers*, in Figure 2). The links in the linked list are stored in a separate storage array so that they can be accessed simultaneously with accessing the "data" in the buffer. There are five linked lists in each buffer: a list of packets destined for each of the three output ports with which the input port is not paired, a list of packets destined for the processor interface, and a list of free (currently unused) buffer blocks. Note that there is no linked list for the output port which is associated with the input port - in the ComCoBB, no packet is routed immediately back to the node from which it just came.

When a packet arrives at an input port, a block is removed from the free list and used to store the first eight bytes of the packet. The block is then linked to the rear of the list for the output port to which the packet is routed. When a packet is transmitted through the crossbar switch from the input buffer to an output port,

the blocks it occupies are returned to the free list so that they can be used again. To manage the linked lists, each buffer has five *head* and *tail* registers, as is shown in Figure 2. The head register points to the first block of the first packet of its linked list, and the tail register points to the last block of the last packet in the list. All the hardware required to implement dynamic buffer allocation and multiple queues as described above, except for the buffer storage array and the control finite state machine, is contained within the box marked 'B' in Figure 2. The functional blocks within 'A', on the other hand, are necessary for low latency handling of virtual circuits and variable length packets. The hardware in 'A' is independent of the DAMQ buffer, and would accompany any other buffer configuration.

B. Packet Reception and Transmission

The actions required to receive, forward, and transmit a packet depend on the packet format and basic protocol of the ComCoBB system. Packets consist of a *header byte*, a *length byte* if the packet is the first packet of a message, and then from one to thirty-two bytes of data. The *router* (shown as a "black box" in figure 2) uses the header byte to determine the packet's output port and new header (and length, if this is not the first packet in the message). The ComCoBB uses a form of virtual circuits [3, 10] to perform the routing. Each packet is preceded by a "start-bit", which is used for synchronization [15]. The header byte is transmitted in the clock cycle immediately following the start-bit, and the rest of the packet is transmitted at a byte per clock cycle following that.

Packet Reception. Because each byte of the packet must pass through the *synchronizer* before entering the buffer, there is a full clock cycle delay between the signaling of packet arrival (SB0 and SB1 in figure 2) and the actual arrival of the header byte, with the packet following in the succeeding clock cycles. While the router is dealing with the header byte, the first byte(s) of the packet are stored in the block which is at the head of the free block list. As the packet is being stored in the first free block, the router stores the packet's length in a length register associated with that block (and into the write counter), and notifies the buffer controller which of the output ports the packet is destined for. In addition, the router creates a new header byte for the packet and stores it in another register associated with the packet's first block.

Once the buffer controller is notified of the linked list into which the packet should be placed, it sets the pointer register of the block currently pointed to by the tail register of that linked list to point to the first block of

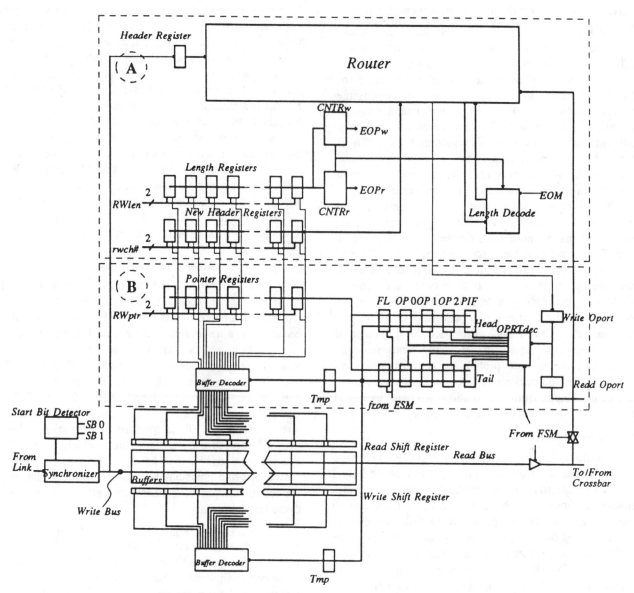

Figure 2: The Dynamically Allocated, Multi-Queue Buffer

the current packet. It then sets the tail register to point to the packet's first block. When the transmission reaches eight bytes, and the first block is filled, the next block in the free list (not necessarily adjacent within the buffer) is used to store the next eight bytes. The same sequence as given above is used to place the packet's second block at the end of the queue, and to point the tail of the list at that block. The end of the packet (EOP) is detected when the write counter reaches zero.

Packet Transmission and Virtual Cut Through.
The crossbar is controlled by a central arbiter which determines which buffers are to be connected to which output ports. It makes this decision based upon data it receives from each of the buffers, so that a buffer is never connected to an output port for which it does not

have any data. When a buffer is connected to an output port through the crossbar, it uses the head register of that output port's linked list to locate the first block to be transmitted. The first byte transmitted is the new header byte (the start bit is generated automatically by the output port). While the length of the packet is loaded into the read counter, the head register of that list is set to the value stored in the pointer register associated with the first block. The packet is transmitted until the read counter reaches zero, using the pointer registers associated with each block to find the next block to be transmitted. The list's head register always points to the next block to be transmitted, or to the first block in the free list if its linked list is empty.

Virtual cut through [6] is a switching method in

Cycle	Phase	Action
0		The start bit arrives in either phase 0 or phase 1. The start bit detector notifies the synchronizer of the proper phase in which to receive packets and notifies the FSM controlling the buffer that a packet is arriving.
1		The header byte arrives in the synchronizer in either phase 0 or phase 1, but is not yet available.
2	0	The synchronizer releases the header byte, which is latched by the header register, for use by the router. The rest of the packet will be released from the synchronizer a byte at a time, at phase 0 of each clock cycle.
2	1	The router determines the output port the packet is to be sent using a local table, and sends this information to to both the arbitrator (for access to the crossbar) and the controlling FSMs. The router also generates a new header for the packet, which is stored in a register associated with the packet's slot.
3	0	The byte specifying the length of the message is released from the synchronizer. It is loaded into the router, using the header byte to index a table contained within the router.
3	1	Latch the result of the crossbar arbitration. The packet's length is passed through the length decoder, and latched into the length register associated with the packet's slot and into the write counter.
4	0	The synchronizer releases the first byte of the packet itself, which is stored in the buffer. If the packet is only a single byte long, the write counter signals EOP. The new packet header is transmitted across the crossbar to be latched at the output port, and the output port generates a start-bit.
4	1	The output port latches the new packet header. The bit in the write address shift register is shifted up a location.
5	0	The output port transmits the header byte to the next switch. The packet's length is sent through the crossbar, and is also loaded into the read counter. The second byte of the packet is written into the buffer slot.
5	1	The output port latches the packet length. The bit in the write address shift register is shifted up a location. An on-bit is loaded into the read address shift register, at the beginning of the packet's slot, prepared to read the packet's first byte for transmission across the crossbar on the next clock cycle.

* The new start bit is generated here; thus, four cycle turn-around time.

Table 1: Virtual Cut Through in Four Clock Cycles

which the switch begins to forward a packet before it has completely received it. The amount of delay a packet experiences at each switch using virtual cut through depends on the availability of the output port and the speed with which the packet is routed - it is independent of the packet's length. We refer to this latency as the "turn-around" time: the time from the arrival of the start bit until the time that the switch transmits the start bit for the same packet to the next switch. Since the buffers can handle simultaneous reads and writes and the header and length registers are stored in a separate memory, the turn-around time can be as low as four cycles (see Table 1).

One of the critical factors that facilitates the short turn-around time is the fact that, when a linked list is empty, its head register is set to point to the first block of the free list. The only time a packet is "cut through" the buffer is when the linked list to the appropriate output port is empty and that output port is currently idle. When a packet arrives at an input port and it can be cut through, the head register for the appropriate linked list is already pointing to the correct block. Thus the process of receiving can be overlapped with the process of transmitting, resulting in a fast cut through.

Buffer Implementation. Our buffer design is driven by the high bandwidth of the ports. The links between ComCoBB chips consist of eight wires, each capable of transmitting at 20 Mbits per second (one bit per clock cycle), for a total bandwidth of 20 Mbytes per second. We achieve this high rate of transfer by using packet-level synchronized communication [15]. In order to achieve high transfer rates, address decode time is eliminated by using shift registers to address the storage cells instead of traditional addressing mechanisms [15]. The buffer pool is an $8 \times n$ array of dual ported static memory cells, where n is a multiple of eight (since the buffer must contain an integer number of blocks). Two eight-bit buses traverse the memory array: one carries data from the synchronizer (*write bus*), and one transmits data to the crossbar (*read bus*). We expect the size of the buffer to be between 64 and 128 bytes.

Using a shift register to address the buffer differentiates this memory from a normal RAM. Along both sides of the static cell array are a series of eight-bit shift registers, one shift register for each buffer block. There are separate shift registers for reading from and writing to the buffer, making the two operations completely independent. For either reading or writing, there is never more than a single shift register enabled at a time, and never more than a single bit of that shift register which is "on". It is the "on" bit of the enabled shift register which addresses the buffer, enabling the eight static cells associated with it to read/write their data. To write into the buffer, the "on" bit is set to the first byte of the initial buffer block in which we will receive the packet, and then each cycle a byte of the packet is written into the buffer, and the bit is shifted to receive the next byte. When the last byte of a block is used, the shift register associated with that block is disabled, and the shift register associated with the next block is enabled, with its "on" bit pointing to the first byte of the block [15].

As mentioned earlier, in order to efficiently handle variable length packets, the buffer is partitioned into eight-byte blocks. Support for the linked list organization is provided by a pointer register which is associated with each block. The value of the pointer register is the number of the next block in the list. One important design parameter is the size of the blocks. At one extreme, a block can be the size of the largest possible packet (32 bytes). This choice would result in inefficient utilization of the buffer memory since small packets (e.g. four bytes) would use up an entire block, wasting large amounts (e.g. twenty-eight out of thirty-two bytes) of memory. On the other hand, the blocks should not be too small since there is some overhead associated with each block. For each block there is a pointer register (for the linked lists) as well as a length register and a new header register (to facilitate fast virtual cut through) because any block can be the first block of a packet. Thus, smaller blocks require more chip area for the same amount of buffer space. Smaller blocks also require more processing by the receiving and transmitting finite state machines for pointer manipulation. As a compromise between the overhead of small blocks and the internal fragmentation in large blocks, we decided to use eight-byte blocks.

The buffers are locally controlled, to allow the ports to operate concurrently and independently. Each input port has three finite state machines associated with

it, each FSM handling a separate facet of the buffer management. The first is the *buffer manager*, which handles receiving new packets and assigning them to free buffers. Second, there is the router, which does the routing and updates the routing information. Finally, there is the *transmission manager*, which, when notified by the arbiter that the buffer has been connected to an output port, transmits the packets and returns the freed blocks to the free list. Because these state machines exist as separate entities, interacting via registers and a few shared signals, each buffer can both receive and transmit packets simultaneously at the highest bandwidth possible. The FSMs maintain the organization within the buffer via the head and tail registers of the five linked lists and the pointer registers associated with each block. The FSMs are synchronized so that they will not attempt to read/write to/from the same register or use the same bus simultaneously, and they will never read and write to/from the same byte of memory at the same time.

IV. Buffer Performance Evaluation

In our performance evaluation of the different buffer types we considered both *discarding switches*, which discard packets that attempt to enter a full buffer [1], and *blocking switches* which block the transmitter from sending to a full buffer [3,4]. In order to evaluate the DAMQ buffer, we compared its performance to that of the three alternative buffer designs previously discussed: FIFO, SAMQ and SAFC. Markov models were used to evaluate two-by-two discarding switches. For the four-by-four switches, the state space was too large for Markov modeling, so the evaluation was done using event-driven simulation [14].

A. Analysis Using Markov Chains

Markov chains were used to model a single two-by-two switch. This was done because of the intractable number of states in a model of a network of switches. Several simplifying assumptions were made: we assumed fixed length packets and a "long clock," so that packets either completely arrive or completely depart in a single clock cycle. Since we assume a uniform packet size, the packet slots are made up of a constant number of blocks, and will therefore be used as the unit of buffer storage.

We performed the Markov analysis on all four switch types, varying the network traffic and amount of buffer space on chip. The arbitration used to determine which packets were transmitted was to send two packets if at all possible, or to send a packet from the longest queue if not. The traffic level corresponds directly to the probability of a packet arriving at an input port, i.e. a network operating at 70% of the link capacity is modeled by a switch for which each input port has a probability of

Switch	Space at each Iport	Rate of Traffic (percent of link capacity)							
		25%	50%	75%	80%	85%	90%	95%	99%
FIFO	2	0^+	0.005	0.074	0.104	0.138	0.174	0.212	0.242
	3	0^+	0^+	0.049	0.084	0.126	0.169	0.211	0.242
	4	0^+	0^+	0.037	0.077	0.123	0.169	0.211	0.242
	5	0^+	0^+	0.030	0.074	0.123	0.169	0.211	0.242
	6	0^+	0^+	0.026	0.072	0.122	0.169	0.211	0.242
DAMQ	2	0^+	0.001	0.022	0.034	0.049	0.070	0.095	0.119
	3	0^+	0^+	0.003	0.006	0.014	0.028	0.050	0.076
	4	0^+	0^+	0^+	0.001	0.004	0.012	0.030	0.055
	5	0^+	0^+	0^+	0^+	0.001	0.005	0.018	0.042
	6	0^+	0^+	0^+	0^+	0^+	0.002	0.012	0.033
SAMQ	2	0.009	0.040	0.095	0.108	0.122	0.137	0.152	0.164
	4	0^+	0.001	0.016	0.025	0.037	0.052	0.071	0.089
	6	0^+	0^+	0.003	0.006	0.012	0.022	0.039	0.058
SAFC	2	0.009	0.039	0.092	0.105	0.120	0.135	0.150	0.163
	4	0^+	0^+	0.010	0.016	0.024	0.036	0.052	0.067
	6	0^+	0^+	0.001	0.003	0.007	0.014	0.026	0.041

Table 2: Probability for Discarding - Markov Analysis

0.70 of having a packet arrive each long clock cycle. From our model we could determine the probability that a given packet arriving at a switch will be discarded for a given level of traffic. The results are presented in Table 2. Since the SAMQ and SAFC switches statically allocate buffer space to each of the output ports, they can only have an even number of packet slots in each buffer.

As shown in Table 2, the switch with DAMQ buffers performs better (lower probability of discarding) than any of the other switches with the same amount of storage at any rate of traffic. It should be noted that a DAMQ switch with space for two packets per input buffer discards as few or fewer packets than the FIFO switch with space for up to six packets for all traffic rates. Furthermore, the DAMQ switch performs *significantly better* than the FIFO switch for high traffic rates. The savings in chip area for this dramatic decrease in storage requirements to achieve a given level of performance is expected to be many times greater than the area for the extra control circuitry for the DAMQ (ten head/tail registers, one pointer register per block, and a more complex FSM).

For light traffic and only two slots per buffer, the FIFO switch performs better than the SAMQ and SAFC switches. Under these conditions the probability of discarding is determined by available storage and the FIFO buffer, having a single pool of slots instead of statically partitioned storage, delivers better performance. This effect is overshadowed by contention for output ports when the traffic rate is high or when

there are more than four slots per buffer. In general, the SAMQ buffer performs almost as well as the SAFC buffer, indicating that the additional throughput provided by fully connecting the inputs with the outputs does not provide a significant boost in performance for uniform traffic.

The benefits of non-FIFO access to the buffers are demonstrated by the fact that the FIFO buffers perform significantly worse than the three other buffer types for traffic rates above 80% and a wide range of buffer sizes. Furthermore, the performance of the FIFO buffers cannot be improved by simply increasing the buffer size as demonstrated by, for example, observing that increasing the FIFO buffer size from three to six slots does not improve performance for a traffic rate of 90%. Thus, it is not always possible to tradeoff implementation and control complexity for increased storage. FIFO buffers perform poorly at high traffic rates *regardless of their size*.

We have previously described the benefits of the DAMQ buffer over the SAMQ and SAFC buffers in the areas of implementation, flow control, and routing. The performance advantage of the DAMQ compared with the SAMQ and SAFC buffers is based on more efficient use of storage. This effect becomes more pronounced as total buffer size decreases and as the partitioning of SAMQ and SAFC buffer increases (i.e., for $n \times n$ switches with larger n).

B. Omega Network Simulation

We have simulated communication on a 64×64 Omega network [7] constructed from three stages of 4×4 switches. The network connects sixty-four processors (message generators) to sixty-four memory modules (message receivers). In our simulation we assumed synchronized message transmissions, where packets are transmitted/received instantaneously once every twelve clock cycles (eight cycles to transmit and four cycles to route). Fixed length packets are assumed. Simulations were performed using the four switch types (DAMQ, FIFO, SAMQ and SAFC), with both a blocking protocol and a discarding protocol. The network was simulated under two different types of traffic: uniformly distributed traffic and traffic in which five percent of the messages are sent to a single common destination ("hot spot") [8].

Two different schemes for arbitrating the crossbar were used: *smart* and *dumb*. To arbitrate the crossbar, the switches' buffers were examined, one at a time, transmitting packets from the longest unblocked queue in the buffer. To enforce fairness, the priority in which buffers are examined should not be fixed. Dumb arbitration uses a round robin fairness scheme on the buffers, where in successive "rounds" each buffer in turn is the first buffer to be examined. Smart arbitration also uses a round robin fairness scheme, but does not "count" (change which buffer has the highest priority) the times a buffer does not trasmit any packets despite having top priority. With smart arbitration the round robin will not "advance" if, for example, a buffer happens to be the first buffer examined, but the destinations of all of the packets held in its slots are full. When the round robin does not advance, the buffer with the top priority maintains its priority for the next time. In order to maintain fairness within the buffers, smart arbitration also uses a stale count [13] to determine which queues within a buffer have held packets for a long period of time and should therefore get top priority.

Table 3 shows the results of simulating the network using a discarding protocol with uniform traffic. Each input buffer has four packet slots. The results show that with the DAMQ switch the percentage of packets discarded is dramatically smaller than it is with the other buffers. Furthermore, the maximum achievable throughput is significantly higher with the DAMQ switch. The FIFO switch performed consistently *better* than the SAMQ and SAFC switches due to the four-way static partitioning of the buffer space in the SAMQ and SAFC buffers. This is a clear demonstration of the shortcomings of SAMQ and SAFC buffers. The percentage of packets discarded for the dumb arbitration with a throughput of 0.50 is approximately the same as

Table 3: Discarding switches. Percentage of packets discarded for given *input* throughput. Uniform traffic. Four slots per buffer. In "over capacity" the output throughput is significantly lower than the input throughput (due to discarding).

Buffer Type	Throughput				Dumb Arb.
	Smart Arbitration				
			Over Cap. Input		
	0.25	0.50	perc. disc.	thpt.	0.50
FIFO	0.02	3.14	21.72	0.56	3.17
SAMQ	0.08	8.69	22.44	0.42	8.63
SAFC	0.07	8.05	20.55	0.44	8.04
DAMQ	0^+	0.22	5.37	0.69	0.22

the percentage of packets discarded for the smart arbitration at the same throughput. We found this to be generally true, that there is very little difference between the performance of smart and dumb arbitrations, so the remainder of the tables show only the results of smart arbitration.

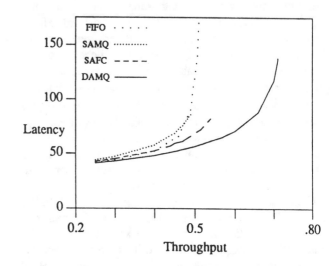

Figure 3: Latency vs. throughput. Blocking switches. Four packet slots per buffer. Uniform traffic.

A multistage interconnection network can be characterized by the relationship between latency and throughput. In general, as throughput increases, so does the latency. For low throughputs, before the network approaches saturation, latency grows very slowly with increasing throughput. As the throughput increases towards saturation latency begins to increase substantially. Near saturation, small increases in throughput imply dramatic changes in latency. Graphs of this relationship between latency and throughput are shown in Figure 3 and elsewhere [8]. We have compared the latencies of networks operating at the same throughputs which are less than either of the networks' saturation levels. We have also compared the throughputs at which the networks do saturate.

Some of the simulation results for blocking switches are presented in Table 4. As shown in the table, a network composed of DAMQ switches with four slots per input buffer can achieve a maximum throughput which is at least 30% higher than any of the other three switches. At a throughput of 0.50, the DAMQ network significantly outperforms the other three networks (i.e., it results in significantly lower latency). This difference in latency is due to the fact that the other switches are at or near their saturation throughputs. At lower throughputs (at or below 0.40) the average latencies with all the switches are almost identical. Hence, the major advantage of the DAMQ switches is their ability to provide good performance for high throughput rates.

While Table 4 shows that for low throughput rates the switch type does not matter, Table 5 indicates that for particular buffer type, as long as the throughput is well below saturation, the buffer size does not have a significant effect on performance. It should be noted that increasing the buffer size results in only moderate increases in the saturation throughput. For a high-throughput system, it is more beneficial to allocate hardware resources to the more complex control of the DAMQ buffer than to use these resources for additional buffer space.

Table 4: Average latencies for given throughputs. Four packet slots per buffer. Uniform traffic.

Buffer Type	Throughput					
	0.25	0.30	0.40	0.50	sat.	sat. thpt.
FIFO	41.47	43.62	51.89	89.94	169.77	0.51
DAMQ	41.09	42.90	47.97	56.24	117.25	0.70
SAFC	42.59	45.02	52.33	63.71	82.12	0.54
SAMQ	43.62	46.82	57.39	75.61	94.62	0.50

A sample of our simulation results with hot spot traffic are presented in Table 6. We have discovered that with hot spot traffic, the buffer type does not matter. Below saturation, the switches display almost equal latencies, just as they did with uniform traffic. However, unlike the situation with uniform traffic the switches all reach saturation at the same throughput, just under 0.25.

With hot spot traffic (Table 6), the saturation throughput for all switches is significantly lower than

Table 5: Average latencies for given throughput. Varying number of slots. Uniform traffic.

Buffer Type	Slots per Buffer	Throughput			
		0.25	0.50	saturated	sat. thpt.
FIFO	3	41.4	96.5	142.4	0.48
	4	41.5	89.9	169.8	0.51
	8	41.4	74.2	284.6	0.56
DAMQ	3	41.1	57.3	109.9	0.63
	4	41.1	56.2	117.3	0.70
	8	41.1	56.2	108.5	0.74

Table 6: Average latencies for given throughputs. Four slots per buffer. 5% hot spot traffic.

Buffer Type	Throughput			
	0.125	0.20	saturated	sat. thpt.
FIFO	38.50	42.82	129.62	0.24
SAMQ	39.51	44.53	68.46	0.24
SAFC	39.32	43.87	66.43	0.24
DAMQ	38.41	41.82	168.27	0.24

with uniform traffic (Table 4). This is caused by the increased probability of contention within each switch for the output port on the path to the hot spot. With FIFO buffers, when there is contention for an output port only one packet from one of the contending input ports is forwarded. All the other contending input ports are idle. Thus, within a short period of time, all of the switches which are on the path to the hot spot have a high probability of having packets destined for the hot spot at the head of their buffers, and of having their buffers completely full. Pfister and Norton [8] call this effect "tree saturation," because it spreads from the hot spot as its root through all of the switches which are on the path between the hot spot and the senders. Since there is a path from every sender (processor) to each receiver (memory bank), when a hot spot tree saturates, the traffic backs up to block every single sender.

Unfortunately, tree saturation occurs with DAMQ switches as well as FIFO switches. The DAMQ switches easily pass all of the non hot spot traffic, but cannot easily pass the hot spot traffic because it contends at the output ports. This causes the buffers to fill up with hot spot traffic. Once that happens, the DAMQ buffer is likely to be dominated by a queue to the output port on the path to the hot spot and the network becomes saturated just like a network with FIFO switches. With the SAMQ and SAFC switches buffer space cannot become completely occupied by hot spot traffic since it is statically partitioned. However, the blocked hot spot traffic at the inputs to the network quickly block all non hot spot traffic attempting to enter the network, thus leading to saturation at the same levels as the other switches. These results reinforce the decision of the designers of the RP3 multiprocessor [9] to use two separate networks: one being for general traffic and the second being a combining network [4] for hot spot traffic caused by semaphores, etc. In a system such as this, the hot spot traffic would not interfere with the uniform memory accesses, so significant performance gains would be made by using the DAMQ buffer instead of the FIFO in the general traffic network.

V. Summary and Conclusions

The potential of large multiprocessors and multicomputers to achieve high performance can only be realized if they are provided with high-throughput low-latency communication. Fast small $n \times n$ switches with routing and buffering capabilities are critical components for achieving high-speed communication. The structure of the buffers in the $n \times n$ switches is one of the most important factors in determining their performance.

We have developed a new type of buffer, called a *dynamically allocated multi-queue* buffer, for use in $n \times n$ switches. This buffer provides efficient handling of variable length packets and the forwarding of packets in non-FIFO order. We have described the micro architecture of a DAMQ buffer and its controller in the context of the ComCoBB communication coprocessor for multicomputers. The DAMQ buffer can be efficiently implemented in VLSI to support packet transmission and reception at the rate of one byte per clock cycle. With a "hardwired" linked list manager and a fast routing mechanism, the ComCoBB chip will support virtual cut through of messages with a latency of four cycles.

We have evaluated the DAMQ buffer by comparing its performance with that of three alternative buffers in the context of a multistage interconnection network. Our modeling and simulations show that for uniform traffic the DAMQ buffer results in significantly lower latencies and higher maximal throughput than other designs with the same total buffer storage capacity. Conversely, the DAMQ buffer uses chip area more efficiently since for a given performance level it requires less total buffer storage. In our modeling and simulations we have not considered variable length packets for which the DAMQ buffer is specifically designed. We believe that the DAMQ buffer will outperform its competition by an even wider margin for the more realistic case of variable length packets which arrive at the inputs of the switch asynchronously.

Acknowledgements

Discussions with T. Lang throughout this project have been extremely helpful. The SIMON simulator was provided by R. Fujimoto. Our simulation studies using SIMON were possible due to the work of T. Frazier, M. Huguet, and L. Kurisaki.

References

1. W. Crowther, J. Goodhue, R. Gurwitz, R. Rettberg, and R. Thomas, "The Butterfly Parallel Processor," *IEEE Computer Architecture Newsletter*, pp. 18-45 (September/December 1985).
2. W. J. Dally and C. L. Seitz, "The Torus Routing Chip," *Journal of Distributed Computing* 1(4) (1986).
3. R. M. Fujimoto, "VLSI Communication Components for Multicomputer Networks," CS Division Report No. UCB/CSD 83/136, University of California, Berkeley, CA (1983).
4. A. Gottlieb, R. Grishman, C. Kruskal, K. McAuliffe, L. Rudolph, and M. Snir, "The NYU Ultracomputer - Designing an MIMD Shared Memory Parallel Computer," *IEEE Transactions on Computers* C-32(2), pp. 175-189 (February 1983).
5. M. J. Karol, M. G. Hluchyj, and S. P. Morgan, "Input vs. Output Queueing on a Space-Division Packet Switch," *IEEE Global Telecommunications Conference*, Houston, TX, pp. 659-665 (December 1986).
6. P. Kermani and L. Kleinrock, "Virtual Cut Through: A New Computer Communication Switching Technique," *Computer Networks* 3(4), pp. 267-286 (September 1979).
7. D. H. Lawrie, "Access and Alignment of Data in an Array Processor," *IEEE Transactions on Computers* C-24(12), pp. 1145-1155 (December 1975).
8. G. F. Pfister and V. A. Norton, "'Hot Spot' Contention and Combining in Multistage Interconnection Networks," *IEEE Transactions on Computers* C-34(10), pp. 943-948 (October 1985).
9. G. F. Pfister, W. C. Brantley, D. A. George, S. L. Harvey, W. J. Kleinfelder, K. P. McAuliffe, E. A. Melton, V. A. Norton, and J. Weiss, "The IBM Research Parallel Processor Prototype (RP3): Introduction and Architecture," *IEEE Transactions on Computers* C-34(10), pp. 943-948 (October 1985).
10. D. A. Reed and R. M. Fujimoto, *Multicomputer Networks: Message-Based Parallel Processing*, The MIT Press (1987).
11. Y. Rimoni, I. Zisman, R. Ginosar, and U. Weiser, "Communication Element for the Versatile MultiComputer," *15th IEEE Conference in Israel* (April 1987).
12. C. L. Seitz, "The Cosmic Cube," *Communications of the ACM* 28(1), pp. 22-33 (January 1985).
13. K. S. Stevens, S. V. Robinson, and A. L. Davis, "The Post Office - Communication Support for Distributed Ensemble Architectures," *The 6th International Conference on Distributed Computing Systems*, Cambridge, MA, pp. 160-166 (May 1986).
14. S. M. Swope and R. M. Fujimoto, "Simon II Kernel Reference Manual," Technical Report UUCS 86-001, University of Utah, Salt Lake City, UT (March 1986).
15. Y. Tamir and J. C. Cho, "Design and Implementation of High-Speed Asynchronous Communication Ports for VLSI Multicomputer Nodes," *International Symposium on Circuits and Systems*, Espoo, Finland (June 1988). To appear.
16. C. Whitby-Strevens, "The Transputer," *12th Annual Symposium on Computer Architecture*, pp. 292-300 (June 1985).

Design and Analysis of Cache Coherent Multistage Interconnection Networks

Ashwini K. Nanda, *Member, IEEE*, and Laxmi N. Bhuyan, *Senior Member, IEEE*

Abstract— **Multistage Interconnection Networks (MIN's) are known to be highly scalable structures for large multiprocessor interconnections. But the conventional MIN's do not support many cache coherence protocols efficiently due to the lack of a fast broadcasting medium. In this paper, first we introduce a directory of state information into a MIN switch and develop a multiple copy cache coherence protocol. We also demonstrate that the multiple copy protocol is better than a single copy protocol on this MIN with Directories (MIND) scheme. Next, a new network called the Multistage Bus Network (MBN) is presented which introduces a bus and multiple snoopers into the switches of a MIN. The snooping buses form multiple trees with the memories at the roots and the processors at the leaves. Each switch contains directories to hold state information on the shared blocks that is used to filter the coherence traffic from one level to another. The shared requests pass through the directories whereas the private requests pass directly from the bus in one level to the bus in the next level. Analytical and simulation models for these multistage cache coherent architectures are developed. Both the MIND and the MBN schemes are studied with a simple multiple copy protocol, and the results are compared with those for a conventional directory scheme. The results show that the MBN scheme performs better than the other schemes.**

Index Terms— **Cache coherence protocols, multiprocessors, multistage interconnection networks, performance evaluation, queueing models.**

I. Introduction

SHARED memory multiprocessors offer a simple programming model and have gained widespread popularity for general purpose programming needs. However, interconnecting a large number of processors and memory modules becomes a major problem for the designer of a shared memory multiprocessor system. When the interconnection network (IN) becomes more complex, the memory access time increases and severely degrades the system performance. A large amount of research has been done on the design of efficient IN's for such multiprocessors. Among various IN's, the hierarchical buses [25] and Multistage Interconnection Networks (MIN's) [7] show a good promise for use in the future. These networks usually operate under synchronous packet switched environments [7] with buffers. When a system becomes large, the top level buses (the buses closer to the memory) in the hierarchical architectures form a bottleneck. In case of MIN's, however, the bandwidth remains the same across all the stages,

making them very appropriate for a large scale multiprocessor. Several commercial machines and research projects are based on such MIN's [6], [11], [14], [23]. Putting private cache memories near the processors further improves the efficiency of a multiprocessor. However they create a coherence problem for the shared writable data.

The issue of cache coherence in shared memory multiprocessors has been widely studied [4], [13], [24], [25]. This problem arises because there can be copies of the same data block in the memory as well as in different private caches. Modification of a shared block by any processor in its local cache will make the copies in other caches and in the memory obsolete. Hence proper consistency action must be taken in order to prevent stale data from being used by the other processors. The hardware solutions that have been devised to alleviate the cache coherence problem can be grouped into two categories: the global directory schemes and bus based snooping schemes. In global directory schemes there is a directory in the main memory that keeps the states of all the shared blocks in the system [1], [3], [9], [24], [27]. Sequential access to the directory for every consistency action and the process of invalidations cause a substantial amount of performance degradation. On the other hand, snoopy bus schemes take a decentralized approach based on a single snooping bus [4], [13], [26]. In these protocols each cache has a snooper that monitors the transactions over the bus and prompts appropriate action in the local cache. Fast broadcasting and distributed control of coherence actions make the snoopy protocols quite efficient. However, a multiprocessor built with these protocols is not scalable because of the limited bandwidth of the single bus.

Since MIN's do not contain buses, the snoopy protocols are not appropriate for MIN based multiprocessors. Mizrahi *et al.* [19] have proposed a Memory Hierarchical Network (or MHN) for avoiding the cache coherence problem in MIN based systems. The MHN scheme uses a special network of switches for handling shared data and a separate MIN for moving private data. The special MHN switches contain directories for the shared blocks. This scheme allows only single copies of shared read/write blocks in the private caches in order to avoid the consistency actions that would be required for maintaining multiple copies. It was shown that the MHN scheme works better than the directory schemes [19]. But it should be noticed that not allowing multiple copies will give rise to poor hit ratios on shared data references and will degrade the overall performance.

In this paper we present a design where a directory is put inside a conventional, crossbar based MIN switch for keeping

Manuscript received March 22, 1991; revised December 12, 1991. This work was supported by NSF Grant MIP-9002353.

The authors are with the Computer Science Department, Texas A&M University, College Station, TX 77843-3112.

IEEE Log Number 9207200.

state information on shared blocks. This MIN with Directory (MIND) scheme is similar to the MHN design in the sense that both have a directory in the switch. However the MIND scheme has provision to handle both the private and shared requests in the same network in contrast to the two separate networks used in the MHN scheme. We develop a simple multiple copy protocol on the MIND network and compare its performance with the single copy protocol implemented on the same network. It is found that the multiple copy protocol performs better than the single copy protocol for a wide range of parameters. This fact motivated us to look for new ways to modify the conventional switch design so that multiple copy protocols can be efficiently supported in MIN based systems. In order to support multiple copies efficiently, one needs a medium for fast broadcasting of the invalidation packets or the write update packets. Snooping bus schemes are good in this regard as all the devices on a bus can listen to every transaction on it simultaneously and take actions in parallel.

A conventional MIN switch is built using a crossbar design. In a multiprocessor environment where a processor waits for a memory request to be satisfied before submitting another request, the individual switches in the MIN are grossly underutilized [8], [16]. When private caches are used near the processors, the overall traffic in the network reduces further as most of the memory references get satisfied in the local caches. We show in this paper that the individual link utilizations of the MIN in such systems is often less than 10%. The situation can be improved with the use of a serial data transfer as in Butterfly [6] or by using a cluster of processors at an input of the MIN as in Cedar [11] and RP3 [23]. Since the complex crossbar design is an overkill for a MIN switch, there is a need to go for simpler link designs. A single bus would be an economical alternative to the crossbar in the above situation. In addition, bus based switch designs will facilitate the use of snooping cache protocols in multistage networks as explained below.

We present a new cache coherent network architecture which consists of multiple stages of buses connected in the form of a conventional MIN. A switch in this Multistage Bus Network (MBN) contains a snooping bus and the associated coherence controllers. The switches are bidirectional so that there is no need for separate forward and backward networks as required in a conventional MIN environment. As the name suggests, the MBN scheme takes advantage of the high memory bandwidth of MIN's and the snooping and broadcasting capability of buses. The bus network handles both the shared memory traffic and the regular private memory traffic. The controllers at various levels of the bus hierarchy contain directories for shared data in order to help maintain cache coherence. The coherence related traffic passes through the directory whereas the private data and replies to shared data requests pass directly from one bus to another bus. Once the snooping capability and the directory are provided, many different types of protocols can be designed to maintain cache coherence. The simple multiple copy protocol, designed for the MIND scheme, is used to study the behavior of the new network. The performance of the MBN scheme is compared with that of the MIND scheme and is shown to be better. It is also shown that both these schemes perform better than the conventional directory schemes.

The rest of the paper is organized as follows. The crossbar based MIND switch design is presented in Section II and a simple multiple copy protocol is described. The new MBN architecture and the design of an MBN switch are presented in Section III. A general analytical technique, developed for the multistage schemes, is presented in Section IV. Section IV also contains the description of a simulation model used for verifying the analytical results presented in this paper. Section V discusses the performance results for the various schemes and compares them with a conventional directory scheme. Finally, Section VI concludes the paper.

II. THE MIN WITH DIRECTORIES (MIND) ARCHITECTURE

A multiprocessor architecture, shown in Fig. 1, consists of a number of processors connected to a number of memory modules through a multistage interconnection network (MIN). The connections for a memory module to all the processors form a tree as shown in bold dotted lines in Fig. 1. Each processor has a private cache memory associated with it. An $N * N$ MIN consists of $\log_k(N)$ stages of $k * k$ crossbar switches with N/k such switches per stage [7]. An MIND switch design is shown in Fig. 2(a), where a *coherence controller* containing a directory is introduced into a conventional crossbar based MIN switch. A somewhat similar switch design was used in the MHN scheme [19] which employed different networks for private and shared requests. However, in the MIND scheme the same network handles both types of requests. As shown in Fig. 2(a), a switch in the MIND network has two functional modules, the *link controller* module and the *coherence controller* module. The link controller basically routes the requests from the input ports to the output ports. The coherence controller module holds a directory of state information on the shared blocks with respect to the local caches of the processors connected through that switch. The coherence controller module takes action on the shared requests depending on the rules of the protocol being implemented and then passes the request to an appropriate port. It should be noted that the coherence controller may obtain multiple requests from various inputs of the switch simultaneously. In case of multiple requests, the requests are queued in the buffers inside the coherence controller and served one by one.

The operation of the link controller module in a 4*4 MIND switch is illustrated in Fig. 2(b). Each upper and lower port is a bidirectional link capable of transmitting data both into and out of the switch. There is an output buffer for each link that holds the packets that are to be transmitted over that link. Private requests are passed from a lower port to an upper port and memory responses are passed vice versa using the self routing techniques of MIN's [7]. The arbiter takes the link request signals from various ports as input and generates the enable signals for the different tristate gates depending on the type and destination of a request. The coherence traffic (shared data requests, invalidations, etc.) passes between the coherence controller and the links through gates that are also controlled

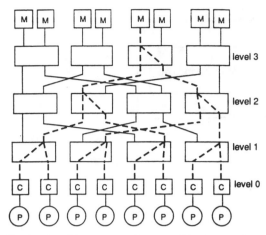

Fig. 1. A multiprocessor architecture with private caches.

by the arbiter. In the following subsection, we describe two cache coherence protocols and organization of the directory in a MIND switch for supporting these protocols.

A. Cache Coherence Protocols

We will define a few terminologies that will be used while describing the protocols. It must be noted that the connection from a memory module to the processors through a MIN, forms a tree with the memory at the *top* (root), the switches at the intermediate nodes, and the processors at the *bottom* (leaves). The tree connection is shown in Fig. 1 with bold dotted lines. The degree of the tree equals to the input/output size of a switch. A block is located in a particular memory module. All the requests or replies for that block will travel along a tree where that particular memory module is the root and the requesting processors are at the leaves. As a result, the cache coherence protocols can be described in terms of a hierarchy of levels of a tree that also correspond to the stages of the MIN.

The processors and their associated caches are at *level* 0. The first stage of switches in the MIND are at *level* 1, second stage of switches are at *level* 2, etc. The upper ports of a switch at level i are connected to the lower ports of switches at level $i + 1$. A switch at *level* i is closer to the processors than a switch at *level* $i + 1$. A switch is an *ancestor* of a processor if a memory request from the processor passes through that switch. A processor or a cache is *below* a switch, if the switch is an ancestor of that processor. If a processor is not below a switch, then it is *above* the switch. The *level* i switches that are connected to a *level* $i + 1$ switch are called the *children* of the *level* $i + 1$ switch. While describing the movement of a shared block, we will follow the above terms that pertain to the tree with the memory module containing that block at the root.

A Single Copy Protocol: A single copy protocol similar to the MHN/1/∞ protocol [19] is designed for our MIND architecture. The single copy protocol allows only a single copy of a shared block to be present in the entire system at any given time. A shared block can be in *present below* state or *not present below* state with respect to a switch at a given level as shown in Fig. 3(a). The present below state means a processor located below the switch has a copy of the block.

Not present below means the block is either present in another processor or in the memory. If present below, the directory in the switch keeps the information regarding the child to be searched for getting a copy of the shared block. If not present below, the request passes upwards (toward the memory) as per the tag bits of the address. The processor finally reaches the current owner of the block through the directories in the switches, loads the block, and becomes the new owner. Thus every read or write reference to the block from a different processor involves a data movement from the current owner to that processor.

A Simple Multiple Copy Protocol: A simple multiple copy cache coherence protocol is designed for testing the feasibility of the MIND scheme, and the MBN scheme discussed in the next section. The protocol described here allows multiple copies of shared blocks in the system and is based on write invalidation. Similar protocols can also be designed based on write update. A cache block can be in one of the following three states: *invalid below*, *valid below*, and *exclusive below*, with respect to a local cache or intermediate level switches. The meaning of the states with respect to the level i switch or local caches is as follows. Invalid below means the block is not present in any of the caches which are below the switch. Valid below means the block is present in valid state in one or more caches below the switch. Exclusive below means the block is in exclusive state in a cache below this switch. The state transition diagram for a shared block with respect to a level i switch or local cache is shown in Fig. 3(b). The actions taken by the coherence controllers at various levels can be described in terms of a read miss, a write hit, and a write miss on a shared block. In case of a read hit, the local cache supplies the block and no further action is necessary. All blocks are marked invalid in the caches and switches at all levels in the beginning. The actions taken by the protocol in case of various events are outlined in the following paragraphs. The details of the protocol are given in [20].

In case of a read miss on a shared request in the local cache, the request is passed on to the level 1 switch which is the parent of that cache with respect to the missed block. If the level 1 switch shows the block in valid below or exclusive below state, a copy is fetched from the level 0 cache having the copy and is supplied to the requester. If it is in exclusive below state, the memory is also updated according to write back policy by the replier cache. If invalid below, the request passes to the higher level switches till the state of the block is found to be either valid below or exclusive below at some level. If the block is in valid state in a higher level switch beyond level 1, the block is fetched from the main memory through the higher level switches. In case of exclusive, the block is always supplied by the cache having the exclusive copy. If the block is invalid below at all levels, it is fetched from the main memory. The switches on the reply path change the block's state to valid below, in their local directories.

If there is a write hit on an exclusive below block in the local cache, the block is written immediately and no coherence action is needed. For a write hit on a valid block, an invalidation signal is sent to the higher level switches. The invalidation signal passes up to the topmost level to change the

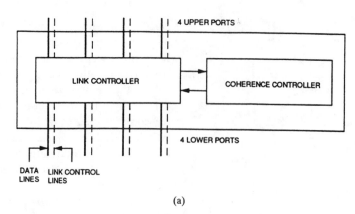

(a)

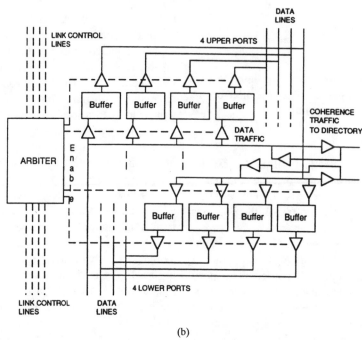

(b)

Fig. 2.   A 4*4 MIND switch. (a) 4*4 MIND switch functional modules. (b) Link controller operation of a 4*4 MIND switch.

state of the block to exclusive below in the switches along the path. At the same time, level i switch passes an invalidation signal below to the level $i - 1$ switch only if the block is in valid below state in that switch. Finally, all the level 0 caches having a valid copy of the block invalidate their copies and send an invalidation acknowledgment back to the level 1 switches following the same path. The intermediate level switches collect these signals and after all the signals are received, pass one acknowledgment upward. All the switches in the invalidation path change the block's state to invalid below. Finally the requester receives the acknowledgement, changes the state of the block to exclusive below, and resumes operation. The ancestor switches of the requester change the block's state to exclusive below.

On a write miss in the local cache, the request passes upward till it reaches a switch having the block either in valid below or exclusive below state. If the block is in valid below state in a switch, an invalidation signal is sent to the upper and lower level switches. The signal propagates as in the write hit case. The caches having a valid copy change the block's state to invalid. The block is fetched from the main memory through

the upper level switches and loaded in exclusive below state. If the block is in exclusive below state in the switch then the cache having the copy sends the block to the requester. The supplier cache and its ancestor switches change the block's state to invalid below. The requester and all its ancestors change the block's state to exclusive below.

B. Directory Organization

Two types of memory references exist in multiprocessor systems, *private* references, and *shared* references. The private requests include the instruction references, references to private data, and references to read-only shared data [10]. The shared references are the references to the shared read-write memory locations. The cache coherence problem and the related overheads concern only the shared references. It is suggested in [17] that the compiler tags a memory reference as private or shared depending on the type declaration of a variable in the program. In [22], the private and shared blocks are dynamically marked so using the broadcast capability of the system bus. In [15] and [19], it is assumed that the compiler distinguishes between private and shared data so that they are

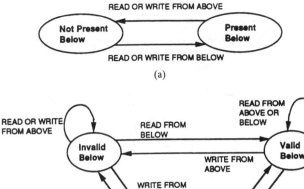

(a)

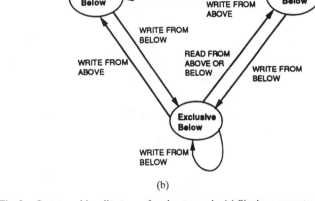

(b)

Fig. 3. State transition diagrams of cache protocols. (a) Single copy protocol. (b) Multiple copy protocol.

A : number of bits in physiacal address

s : number of bits to address a shared block

b : number of bits to address a word inside a block

Fig. 4. An example of physical address configuration.

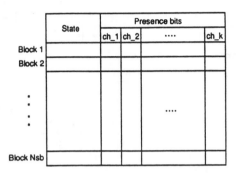

Fig. 5. Directory organization in an MIND switch.

held in different memory modules. Our cache organization is based on the same assumption.

We assume that the number of shared blocks, N_{sb}, in the system is fixed and the shared blocks are distributed across the memory modules. The compiler detects these data items and puts them in appropriate places. Let A be the total number of bits in the physical address of a memory location. Out of this we need b bits to address a word inside a memory block. Thus $A - b$ bits are used to address a memory block, private and shared. Since we have N_{sb} number of shared blocks, we need $s = \log_2 N_{sb}$ bits to distinguish among the shared blocks. A typical memory address configuration is shown in Fig. 4. When the most significant $(A - s - b)$ bits are 000..00 through 111...10, the address is to a private block. When these bits are all 1's, the address is to a shared block. In the configuration of Fig. 1, if the memory modules are low order interleaved, the N_{sb} shared blocks are equally divided among all memory modules and are placed toward the end of each module. Other distributions are also possible by reorganizing the "s" bits in a different manner.

The cache controller can thus distinguish a shared block easily by decoding a few bits of the address. In the typical example, cited above, only one bit [$(s + b + 1)$th] needs to be decoded. The cache controller enables a control line indicating that the address is to a shared block. This control line is passed to the switches in the MIND network as a part of the address lines. The directories in the network use this information to distinguish between private and shared blocks. The bits in the s field in Fig. 4 are then used to address a shared block uniquely in the directory. The above scenario, adopted in our paper, is easy to implement because the type of a variable is declared at the beginning of a program.

The directory in an MIND switch is organized as shown in Fig. 5. The directory size is fixed and it can contain information on N_{sb} number of shared blocks. The state field in a directory entry stores the state of the shared memory block. For the multiple copy protocol, shown in Fig. 3(b), only two bits are needed to encode the state informations. The presence bits field stores the information on the block with respect to the k children of the switch (k is the number of inputs to the switch). If the state field says the block is invalid below, all the presence bits are 0. If the state field says the block is exclusive below, one and only one of the presence bits, corresponding to the child where the block is exclusive below, is set to 1. If the state is valid below, all the presence bits corresponding to the children where the block is valid are 1, and others are 0. It may be observed that the directory keeps the state information only on its *children*, and not on all processors below it. This allows the word length of a directory entry to be short and uniform across all levels. Since the switch directory organization is similar to that of a cache memory, and the directory size in terms of bits is much smaller than a cache, the switch directory will be at least as fast as a cache controller. A more complex design of a MIN switch directory with request combining has appeared recently in [12].

In Section V we will observe that the multiple copy protocol yields better hit ratio on shared data than the single copy protocol does. The overall performance of the multiple copy protocol is also better than that of the single copy protocol for a wide range of system and workload parameters. In the next section we will present the design of a new Multistage Bus Network that will support the multiple copy protocol more efficiently than the MIND.

III. THE MULTISTAGE BUS NETWORK

A Multistage Bus Network (MBN) [8] that interconnects 16 processors to 16 memory modules, using 4*4 switches, is

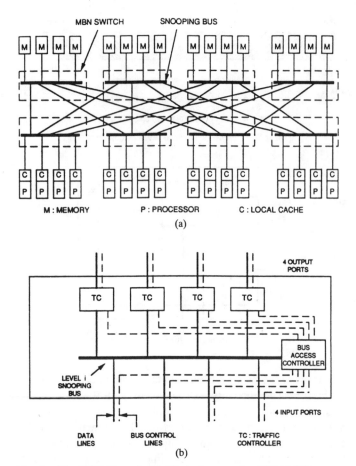

M : MEMORY   P : PROCESSOR   C : LOCAL CACHE

(a)

(b)

Fig. 6. The MBN Network. (a) Block diagram of a 16*16 MBN system using 4*4 switches. (b) Block diagram of a 4*4 MBN switch.

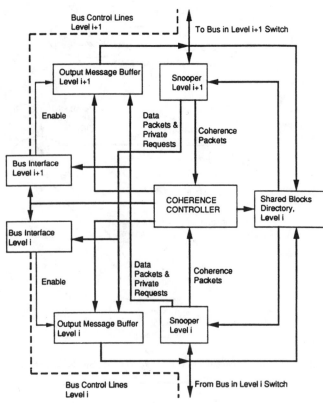

Fig. 7. Traffic Controller (TC) block diagram.

shown in Fig. 6(a). The MBN network is similar in structure to a regular multistage interconnection network (MIN), but is built using the special MBN switches. The major difference between an MBN switch and a MIN switch is that the former is a bus-based design as opposed to a crossbar-based design in the later. It has been shown in [8] that because a processor must wait for the memory access to complete, a bus-based design approach is more than adequate in meeting the bandwidth requirements in a multiprocessor.

The MBN switch can be designed to support cache coherence. The internal construction of a 4*4 MBN switch is shown in Fig. 6(b). The switch consists of a snooping bus, a Bus Access Controller (BAC), and a Traffic Controller (TC) corresponding to each upper port. The block diagram of a Traffic Controller (TC) is shown in Fig. 7. The TC's in the MBN switches keep a directory of state information on all the shared blocks in the system that would pass through them according to the switch connections, but they do not keep any information on the private blocks. The directory organization is similar to that of the MIND switch, discussed earlier. The TC in a level i switch uses the directory information to filter the requests from the level $i + 1$ bus to the level i bus and vice versa.

The outputs from the TC's are connected to the buses at the next higher level following the same connection patterns as a conventional MIN. The access to the snooping bus is controlled by a Bus Access Controller (BAC). The BAC receives bus request signals from the TC's connected to the bus and enables bus grant signals to the requesters following some arbitration policy. Each individual cache near the processors contains its own cache controller and a directory. As shown in Fig. 6(a), a number of processors form a cluster and are connected to a level 1 bus (in the stage 1 switch). The level 1 buses are connected to the level 2 buses through the TC's. In general, a group of level i buses are connected to a level $i + 1$ bus through individual level i TC's. The topmost level TC's are connected directly to the corresponding memory modules. The cache controllers in the processors snoop on the level 1 buses. A processor submits a memory request to its cache. If it is a private request and is a hit, then the block is supplied immediately. If it is a miss for the private request then the request is forwarded to the appropriate memory module through the MBN. The TC handles the private requests separately so that they are not subject to coherence actions. For the shared blocks, multiple copies are allowed to exist in different local caches and cache coherence is maintained by using the multiple copy protocol described in Section II.

The function of the various submodules in the TC in an MBN switch, shown in Fig. 7, are as follows. Each TC contains two snoopers. The *snoopers* at level i and level $i + 1$ snoop on their respective buses. Their job is to watch all the transactions going on the bus and take appropriate action. If the request is for a private block that has to pass through that particular TC as determined by the tag bits, then the snooper passes the request to the upper output message buffer. If the request is for a shared block, it reads the directory to determine if a coherence action is to be taken, and passes the request to the coherence controller if required. The particular coherence action depends on the state of the block in that switch as explained while describing the multiple copy protocol in the previous section. If it is a reply for a block read from the memory or from another cache, then the snooper directly sends the packet to the lower output message buffer. The *coherence controller* takes the actions required to implement a given cache protocol. It modifies the TC directory as necessary according to the received input message and the rules of the protocol, and transmits a message to the next level if required. The *Bus Interfaces* manage the accesses to the respective buses. When there is a message in an output queue to be transmitted to a bus, the interface sends a bus request signal to the BAC, and after getting ownership of the bus it enables the output buffer to put the message on the bus.

A. Comparison of MBN and MIND Switches

There are two major differences between the MBN switch and the MIND switch in how they handle a request at each level. One difference is that, all the input ports in an MBN switch are connected to the same bus and hence only one of the requests can pass at a time. On the other hand each individual link in the MIND switch can pass a request simultaneously with a transfer on another link because of the crossbar connection. The other difference is that, since there are no snoopers connected to the individual links in the MIND switch, all the coherence requests travel up to the coherence controller (see Fig. 2) and only the coherence controller can decide whether to take an action or not. In case of the MBN switches, however, the snoopers filter the requests from the bus itself and pass them to the coherence controllers only if an action needs to be taken in that switch. Thus a coherence controller in the MBN switch handles less traffic than the coherence controller in a MIND switch. Moreover, the MIND switch has only one directory to handle the shared requests. The MBN switch has a directory associated with each traffic controller (TC).

It is thus easy to see that the MIND provides more bandwidth compared to the MBN for private requests, where as the MBN provides more bandwidth than MIND for shared requests. Because the number of private requests at any time is limited to the number of processors in the system, the MBN bandwidth is adequate. The overall performance of the MBN will be better due to the efficient handling of coherence traffic. A crossbar is known to be more complex then a bus in terms of number of connections. We define the *cost* of a switch as the number of connections required in that switch [8]. The cost of a crossbar is $k \cdot k$ and that of a bus in an MBN switch is $2 \cdot k$, for a $k * k$ switch. When directories and snoopers are introduced into the switches, it becomes difficult to have a quantitative comparison of cost between the two switches unless a detailed hardware design is carried out. The complexity of a TC in an MBN is similar to the coherence controller in an MIND. Thus, when the directory size is small, the MBN switch may be comparable in cost to a MIND switch. For bigger directories (larger N_{sb}), the MBN would cost more since it uses multiple directories for snooping.

For a conventional MIN switch of size $k * k$, the number of I/O pins per switch is proportional to $2k$. In contrast, all the inputs to an MBN switch are connected to the same bus as can be seen in Fig. 6(b). Only one input connection per switch is sufficient which can be distributed to the different input ports via a printed circuit board (the bus control lines will be separate for centralized bus arbitration). Therefore the number of I/O pins required by an MBN switch is proportional to $k+1$, that is almost half the pin count of a conventional MIN switch of the same size. This saving in I/O pins is important for single chip implementations.

IV. PERFORMANCE EVALUATION TECHNIQUE

Both analytical and simulation methods were developed for evaluating the various multistage network architectures discussed in this paper. The simulations take enormous amount of time to run compared to the analysis. In view of this tremendous speed advantage analytical methods are preferred over detailed simulations when they are reasonably correct. However, a new analysis technique must always be verified against a detailed simulation of the system in order to gain credibility. Therefore we developed a simulation program and ran extensive experiments for verifying the results of the analysis developed here. In this section, we first describe the system and workload models, and then we describe the analysis and simulation methodologies.

A. The System Workload Model

The systems discussed in this paper are assumed to be synchronous and packet switched. The bus service time or the link service time to transfer a block of data forms the basis of the system cycle time. The service times of the caches, TC's, buses, crossbar MIN switches, and the memories are assumed to be integral multiples of this system cycle time. The processors are represented as delay centers; in a given cycle, they submit memory requests to their caches with some given probability. All kinds of requests, viz., read, write, and invalidation are assumed to have identical service demands at various centers although the invalidation requests should have shorter demands in practice. For the systems under consideration, we will define a *cluster* to consist of the group of processors connected to a level 1 switch. The various system parameters are defined below. The values used for these parameters for the performance evaluation will be discussed in Section V.

N: number of processors in the system

L: number of levels in the multistage network

g: number of groups or clusters

c_i: number of processors below a level i switch

$k * k$: size of the MIND or MBN switches

t_b: bus or link service time

t_c: cache cycle time or TC cycle time

t_s: crossbar MIN switch service time

t_m: memory service time

p: probability that a processor submits a memory request in a given cycle

P_u: processor utilization.

The processors submit memory requests to their private caches. The cache controllers take appropriate actions depending on the type of memory requests as discussed in the previous sections. The request then travels to a variable number of stages in the network depending on the type of request and the state of the block in the system. A processor waits till its memory access is successfully completed, and then submits a new request after doing some amount of computation. The delays encountered by a request in the various queueing centers will be calculated using the technique presented in Section IV-B.

In the absence of measurement data on the memory reference patterns in large multiprocessors, one has to resort to some kind of synthetic patterns while analyzing such systems. The workload model used for this analysis is an extension of the workload developed in [10]. The memory reference string of a processor consists of two streams, *private requests* and *shared requests*. A given memory request is to a shared block with probability q_s and to a private block with probability $1 - q_s$. The parameter q_s indicates how intensively the processors use the shared variables. When $q_s = 0$, there are no accesses to shared blocks and hence there is no overhead of cache coherence. As q_s increases the cache coherence overhead also increases and the performance is affected to a greater extent. A private request is a hit in the local cache with probability h and a miss with probability $1 - h$. The handling of private requests by the cache controllers is amply discussed in the literature [10], and hence only the handling of shared requests will be elaborated here. The number of shared blocks in a system, N_{sb}, is assumed to be fixed.

In large multiprocessor systems it is highly likely and advantageous for interacting parallel subtasks to be scheduled to groups (clusters) of processors such that the processors in the group are physically close to each other and they can communicate faster among themselves. This has been observed in many previous works including [19] and [25]. In our design the processors connected to level 1 switch form a cluster. Thus, the processors within a cluster are likely to share a group of data more often than other groups of shared data. We will call this group of data the *favorite* group of the cluster. For the $g(= N/k)$ number of clusters in the system there will be g such groups of shared data each having N_{sb}/g number of shared blocks. For any cluster, there is one favorite group and $(g - 1)$ nonfavorite groups. A processor accesses a block in its favorite group with probability q_f and a block in any nonfavorite group with probability $(1 - q_f)/(g - 1)$. Once a group is chosen, any of the N_{sb}/g blocks in the group is accessed with equal probability. When $q_f = 1/g$, all the shared blocks in the system are accessed with equal probability. A memory request is a write with probability f_w and a read with probability $f_r = 1 - f_w$. In invalidation based cache coherence protocols, the parameter f_w plays a major role. When $f_w = 0$, there are no writes and therefore there is no invalidation traffic. As f_w increases, the number of write requests increases and the invalidation traffic also increases causing performance degradation of the system. For a shared request the protocol takes appropriate actions depending on a read or a write, as has been described earlier. The various workload parameters are summarized below.

N_{sb}: number of shared blocks in the system

q_s: probability that a request is to a shared block (probability for a private block is $1 - q_s$)

q_f: probability that a request is to the favorite group

f_w: probability that a request is write ($f_r = 1 - f_w$)

h: probability that a private request is a hit in the cache.

The parameters q_s, f_w, and h are well known. The measured range of values for them are widely reported in the literature [2], [5] and are used in our analysis. Although measured values for the parameter q_f are not available, one can gain insight into its effect on the system behavior by varying its value over a wide range. It may be noted that although the above workload represents some important program behaviors, the actual reference patterns of different applications vary so much that it is impossible to frame a general workload model satisfying all applications.

B. An Analytical Technique

At any point of time a processor is either busy doing some internal computations or is waiting for the response to a memory request. If it is busy, it submits a memory request to its cache in a cycle with probability p. In case of a private request, the block is immediately supplied if it is a hit. If it is a miss, then the block is supplied by the memory through the multistage network with the same amount of delay for both a read and a write. In case of a shared request, the required consistency action is taken by the coherence controllers in the network switches and the request is satisfied with a variable amount of delay depending on whether it is a read or a write request and in which level the request is satisfied. The processor utilization can then be expressed in terms of these delays. If we define

d_p: delay due to private requests

d_r: delay due to shared read requests

d_w: delay due to shared write requests,

then P_u will be given by

$$P_u = \frac{1}{1 + p \cdot ((1 - q_s) \cdot d_p + q_s \cdot f_r \cdot d_r + q_s \cdot f_w \cdot d_w)}$$

The *processing power* defined as NP_u, will be used as the performance measure in our study. The delays d_p, d_r and d_w will depend on the amount of traffic in the network, which in turn is a function of P_u itself. Thus we get a nonlinear equation with P_u as the single variable, that can be solved by using iteration techniques. The rest of this subsection briefly describes the relationship of d_p, d_r, and d_w with P_u and other system parameters. The details are contained in [20].

In order to make the analysis simpler, each level in the network is considered in isolation from the other levels. The values of d_p, d_r, and d_w will be the aggregated delays across all the levels. If we assume a symmetrical system where all processors have similar memory reference patterns and devices in the same level have similar behavior, then all the service centers in a given level can be represented by the behavior of any single center in that level. We will assume infinite buffers for holding requests in the queue at the input of every service center.

The effect of replacements on the protocol are neglected by assuming a sufficiently large local cache. However, the protocol can easily accommodate the effect of replacements by suitable extensions. We make an additional assumption that two processors do not access a particular shared block simultaneously. In case this happens, the protocol should take extra coherence action that gives priority to one request while holding the other. However the simulation results suggest that this kind of simultaneous requests are rare, and hence their effects will be disregarded to facilitate our analysis. In the absence of block contention, the various request rates at lower levels can be added up to give the request rates at the higher levels.

Our analytical technique is similar to the one developed in [26]. Using the workload parameters described in the previous sections we can determine the steady state rates at which a block moves from one state to another following the coherence protocol (Fig. 3) at level i. The transition rates at a level depend on the number of processors below that level, the read and write fractions, shared access fraction, the processor utilization, and the request probability. These rates will be different for the blocks that are favorite in the clusters below the corresponding level and the blocks that are nonfavorite. By solving the flow balance equations we can determine the steady state probabilities of a block being in a given state (valid below, exclusive below or invalid below) [20], [26]. The routing behavior of a shared request in the switch hierarchy will depend on these probabilities.

The buses, TC's, caches, MIND links, and the memories are represented as individual queueing centers which receive requests from a number of inputs, service them and then send them to the appropriate output queues. The probability that there is a request at an input to a queue at a given cycle can be calculated by using the workload parameters and the state probabilities at different levels as mentioned above. Once the request probabilities are calculated, the delay at a queueing center can be determined by using the P-K formula [18]. For the shared requests, first we determine the level at which a request is satisfied by using the state probabilities at various levels. Then the overheads are calculated depending on where the request is satisfied. The overall delays d_p, d_w, and d_r are the sum of these delay overheads across all the levels. The details of the derivations are given in [20].

Having found the relations between P_u and various delays, we can employ any standard iterative technique to solve the equation for P_u. A higher order iteration would give faster convergence. Usually the speed of convergence also depends on the initial value. With some experimentation, $P_u = 1/N$ was found to be a good initial value for this problem and usually the convergence occurred in 2 to 5 iterations.

C. Simulation and Verification

An event driven simulation model similar to the one in [4] was developed for the multistage schemes. Event driven simulations are becoming popular in recent times due to the difficulties in obtaining traces for different applications running on large multiprocessors. Moreover, the results obtained from the trace driven simulations are unlikely to be accurate for other architectures and applications. In our event driven simulation, a central clock was maintained to take care of the synchronous behavior of the system. The processors were modeled as delay centers which submit a memory request after some amount of processing and then wait till the request is satisfied before submitting another request. The other service centers were assumed to have unlimited buffer size at their inputs and they receive and send requests only at the beginning of a system cycle. The invalidation signals are given priority over other types of requests. Initially all the shared memory blocks are marked invalid in the caches and the TC's.

We define an *event* as the arrival or completion of a request at a service center. The simulation program consists of five basic modules to handle these events and gather information from them. The *random number generator* module generates the random service times for various service centers. The *event generator* module looks for the processors that have completed a previous request and then prepares them for the next request by introducing new events in the *event queue*. The event queue is maintained by the *scheduler* module. The scheduler scans the event queue to determine the events being completed at the end of the current clock cycle and submits them to the *router* module. The router module decides where the requests should go in the next cycle and then puts them in the appropriate queues. Whenever a service center finishes servicing a request it takes another request from its input queue for service and the event generator inserts a corresponding completion event in the event queue. The system clock is incremented at the end of each cycle. The *statistics collector* module updates the busy time for each service center every time the center finishes servicing a request. The utilization of a service center is calculated as the ratio of its total busy time to the total observed system time at the end of the simulation.

The utilizations of all the service centers and the processors were calculated from the statistics accumulated during the simulation. The processing power was calculated as the sum of the processor utilizations. Simulation experiments were run for 100 000 to 500 000 processor request completions depending on the number of processors in the system. A number of experiments were conducted and the results were matched with analytical results for a wide range of workload parameters and system size. As an example, Fig. 8 plots the results of two representative experiments comparing the analytical and simulation models. The experiment was conducted for a 1024*1024 network using 4*4 switches. Other parameters are given in the figures. The maximum error observed between the analytical and simulation results is 5%. Hence, we will choose the analytical model as our evaluation technique in this paper due to its close correspondence with the simulation results, and the associated run time advantages.

V. PERFORMANCE RESULTS

In this section the analytical results of the various architectures are presented. The bus service time and the link service time for transferring a block of data form the basis of the system cycle time and are assumed to be one cycle each. The

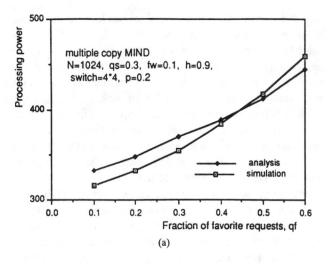

(a)

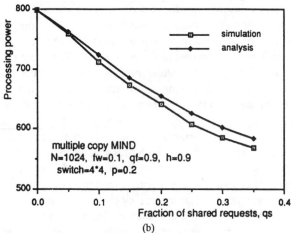

(b)

Fig. 8. Comparison of analytical and simulation results. (a) Multiple copy MIND, varying q_f. (b) Multiple copy MIND, varying q_s.

cache controller and coherence controller service times are also assumed to be one cycle. The memory service time is assumed to be 4 cycles in the following discussions. However, higher or lower values of memory service times can be used depending on a particular system design. Although we have assumed the same service time for data transfer and coherence actions for the sake of simplicity, actually the coherence packets need less time than the data packets. Therefore, our analysis will give a rather conservative estimate of the performance of the systems under consideration.

A. Comparison of Single Copy and Multiple Copy Protocols

The state diagrams of Fig. 3 were used to calculate the probabilities of a shared block being in a given state [20], [26]. Since we do not assume any replacements, any shared block not present in a cache is in invalid state, because a block is marked invalid initially. We define the *shared miss ratio* as the probability that a shared block is in state *invalid* in a local cache. A large number of experiments were conducted to compare the performance of single copy and multiple copy protocols on an MIND architecture. The multiple copy protocol was found to give consistently better performance. We will present two interesting curves as examples here.

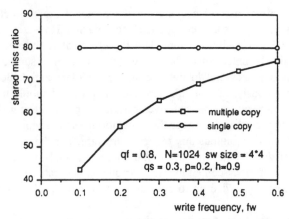

Fig. 9. Shared miss ratio as a function of f_w.

The shared miss ratios of the single copy and multiple copy protocols on the MIND architecture are compared in Fig. 9 while varying the fraction of write requests, f_w. In case of the single copy protocol, a shared block is moved out of the local cache for every read or write reference by a different processor which results in a poor hit ratio in the local cache. Since the multiple copy protocol moves a block out of the cache only in case of a write from a different processor but not for a read, the block is more likely to be present in the local cache when needed. In case of a write the multiple copy protocol incurs more overhead than the single copy protocol because of invalidations. Hence the shared miss ratio of the multiple copy protocol increases with increase in write frequency in Fig. 9 whereas it remains same for the single copy protocol.

Fig. 10 shows the relative performance, in terms of Processing Power, of the two protocols in the MIND architecture while varying the fraction of shared requests, q_s. We chose processing power as a performance measure because it indicates the average number of processors doing useful work. For a broad range of values of q_s, the multiple copy protocol performs better than the single copy protocol. The frequent block movements of the single copy protocol for both reads and writes involve more degradation in performance. Because the multiple copy protocol performs better than the single copy protocol on MIND, we will only consider the former while comparing the MIND scheme with the MBN scheme.

B. Comparison of MBN and MIND with a Conventional Directory Scheme

The conventional directory schemes for bus based systems are described in detail and compared in [1]. They are also suitable for MIN based systems. The directory scheme proposed by Tang [24] and Censier and Feautrier [9] outperforms the other directory schemes. In this scheme, called the $dir N$ scheme in [1], the directories keep the state information on all the blocks in all the caches. Unlike the MIND or the MBN systems, the directories in the $dir N$ scheme are associated with the memory modules. On a shared block miss in a MIN based multiprocessor, each request travels all the way to the directory in the memory, through the MIN. On a write hit or write miss on a shared block, the memory controller sends invalidation signals to the caches having a copy of the block,

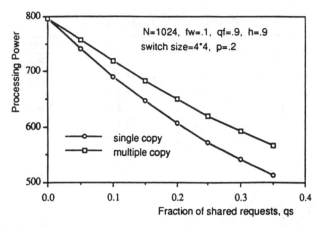

Fig. 10.   Comparison of single copy and multiple copy protocols, varying q_s.

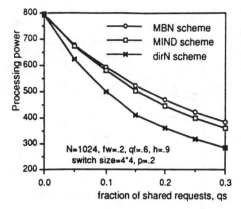

Fig. 11.   Comparison of various schemes, varying q_s.

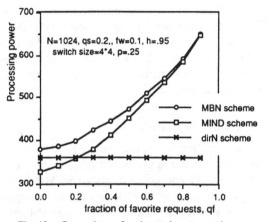

Fig. 12.   Comparison of various schemes, varying q_f.

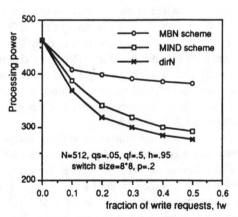

Fig. 13.   Comparison of various schemes, varying f_w.

if any. In the following paragraphs, the results for the MBN and MIND schemes are presented and compared with those of a $dirN$ scheme. In [20] and [21] we have developed an analytical model for the conventional directory based cache coherence protocols for multiprocessors with a MIN as the interconnection. The evaluation of the $dirN$ scheme is based on parameter values similar to the MIND scheme.

The effect of the shared reference ratio, q_s, on the performance of the various schemes is shown in Fig. 11. The system size is 1024 and the switch size is 4*4. The MBN performs better than MIND when q_s is larger, corroborating our earlier discussion that the MBN switch handles the coherence traffic better than the MIND switch. However, both the schemes are superior to the $dirN$ scheme, since both the schemes filter the requests at the intermediate level switches. The $dirN$ scheme has to go all the way to the memory for each miss on a shared block and hence incurs more delay.

Fig. 12 shows the effect of the ratio of favorite requests on performance. For smaller values of q_f, there are more requests for nonfavorite blocks resulting in lower hit ratios. Hence there is more traffic in the coherence controllers and the MIND switch is overloaded giving very low performance. The MBN switches can handle this traffic efficiently and hence perform better than the MIND and $dirN$ schemes. For low values of q_f, the $dirN$ scheme also performs better than the MIND scheme because of the load on the directories in the MIND switches. For higher values of q_f the requests mostly get satisfied in the local cache or in a neighbor cache (connected directly to the level 1 switch). There is less shared request traffic in the network and the switches in both MIND and MBN systems are lightly loaded. Therefore the gap in performance between the two schemes decreases, the MBN architecture still being superior. The performance of $dirN$ remains constant for all values of q_f, since for all misses (favorite or otherwise), the requests have to go to the directories in the memory modules.

Fig. 13 shows the effect of the write frequency f_w on the performance of the various schemes. These curves are drawn for a system size of 512 using 8*8 switches. For low f_w, the performance of all schemes is almost the same since there is negligible coherence traffic in the network. For higher values of f_w, the invalidation traffic is more. Due to efficient broadcasting and snooping the MBN switches can handle this traffic

better than the MIND switch, because the single coherence controller in an MIND switch gets saturated. However, both these schemes perform better than the $dirN$ scheme.

Fig. 14 shows the performance curves for different values of the private reference hit ratio, h. A fairly large system with 4096 processors and 8*8 switches is used in this experiment. When h is low, there are more misses on private requests and the load on the MBN buses is more compared to that on the MIND links. Hence the MIND architecture performs better than the MBN architecture. When h increases, the load on the buses decreases and the performance of MBN rises. The

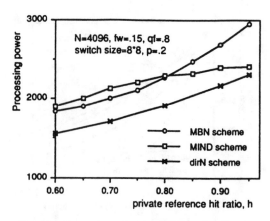

Fig. 14. Comparison of various schemes, varying h.

TABLE I
LINK UTILIZATION OF VARIOUS NETWORKS

h	MIN	MIND	MBN
50%	5.1%	10%	38%
60%	4.8%	9.5%	36%
70%	4.4%	8.7%	33%
80%	3.8%	7.4%	28%
90%	2.6%	5.1%	20%

switch size = 4*4 $q_s = 0.0$ $p = 0.4$

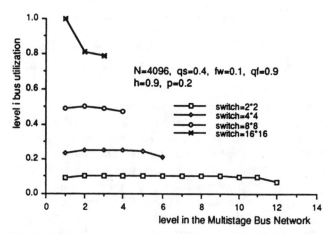

Fig. 15. Effect of switch size on bus utilization at various levels of MBN.

snooping capability of the buses and the multiple TC's make the MBN architecture perform much better than the MIND switch when h is more than 0.8. Since private hit ratios are higher than 0.9 in practice, MBN will be evidently superior to MIND. Again, as is clear from the figure, these two schemes perform better than the $dirN$ scheme.

C. Switch Utilization in MBN

Earlier we mentioned that the conventional MIN switches are highly underutilized in practice. Table I shows the utilization of the links in conventional MIN and MIND switches and the bus utilization in an MBN switch for a request rate p of 0.4. The switch size used in this table is 4*4 for all the three networks. The conventional MIN is assumed to have a forward and a backward network. The link utilization (fraction of time a link of a switch is busy) in the conventional MIN is observed to be less than 5%. Even though the MIND links are bidirectional, the link utilization is less than 10% for an unlikely low private hit ratio h of 50%. However, the buses in the MBN switches serve multiple upper and lower ports and are therefore reasonably well utilized around 20% to 38%. The above figures show that complex crossbar designs are not really necessary for MIN switches.

Fig. 15 plots the bus utilizations at various levels of the MBN scheme for a large number of processors (N=4096) and $q_s = 0.4$ with different switch sizes. Level 1 corresponds to the switches near the processors and level L corresponds to the switches near the memory. The number of levels (L) is given by $\log_k(N)$, where $k*k$ is the switch size. For smaller switch sizes, the buses are underutilized and the utilization is comparable across the levels. The higher levels tend to be less utilized due to some requests being satisfied in the lower levels. As the switch size increases, the bus utilization increases at all levels. However, until 8*8, the utilization is less than 50% and does not degrade the system performance. At 16*16, the bus utilization at level 1 is more than 98%, and at other levels about 80%. The saturation of level 1 bus is more than the other levels because there are more processors connected to it and due to the high value of q_f used in this experiment most of the requests get satisfied in the first level. For smaller values of q_f, the utilization at all levels will be comparable, but still will be very high.

VI. CONCLUSION

In this paper we showed that keeping multiple copies of shared blocks in a system gives better performance than keeping only single copies. Two switch designs for supporting multiple copy protocols in Multistage Interconnection Networks (MIN's) were presented. The first architecture, MIND, introduces a directory into a conventional crossbar based MIN switch for keeping state information on the shared blocks. It was found that the single coherence controller gets overloaded without snooping capability. The second design, Multistage Bus Network (MBN), has multiple snoopers in a switch and uses a bus instead of a crossbar as the transmission medium. A simple multiple copy protocol was designed for examining the feasibility of the two architectures. Analytical and simulation techniques were developed to estimate the performance of the new schemes. It was shown that the MBN architecture gives superior performance compared to the MIND architecture for a wide range of system and workload parameters. The multiple snoopers and the broadcasting capability of the buses in the switches make this performance improvement possible. It is also shown that both the schemes presented in this paper are superior to a conventional directory scheme due to the filtering of requests at the intermediate levels.

ACKNOWLEDGMENT

The authors are grateful to the referees for their detailed comments and helpful suggestions which improved the clarity of the paper to a large extent.

REFERENCES

[1] A. Agarwal, R. Simoni, J. Henesy, and M. Horowitz, "An evaluation of

directory schemes for cache coherence," in *Proc. 15th Annu. Int. Symp. Comput. Architecture*, June 1988, pp. 280–289.

[2] A. Agarwal and A. Gupta, "Memory reference characteristics of multiprocessor applications under Mach," in *Proc. Conf. ACM SIGMETRICS*, 1988, pp. 215–225.

[3] J. Archibald and J. L. Baer, "An economical solution to the cache coherence problem," in *Proc. 11th Annu. Int. Symp. Comput. Architecture*, June 1984, pp. 355–362.

[4] ———, "Cache coherence protocols: Evaluation using multiprocessor simulation model," *ACM Trans. Comput. Syst.*, pp. 273–298, Nov. 1986.

[5] S. J. Baylor and B. D. Rathi, "A study of the memory reference behavior of engineering/scientific applications in parallel processors," in *Proc. 1989 Int. Conf. Parallel Processing*, 1989.

[6] BBN Laboratories Inc., "Butterfly parallel processor overview," Dec. 19, 1985.

[7] L. N. Bhuyan, Q. Yang, and D. P. Agarwal, "Performance of multiprocessor interconnection networks," *IEEE Comput. Mag.*, Feb. 1989.

[8] L. N. Bhuyan and A. K. Nanda, "Multistage Bus Network (MBN): An interconnection network for cache coherent multiprocessors," in *Proc. 3rd IEEE Symp. Parallel Distributed Syst.*, Dallas, Dec. 1991.

[9] L. M. Censier and P. Feautrier, "A new solution to coherence problems in multicache systems," *IEEE Trans. Comput.*, pp. 1112–1118, Dec. 1978.

[10] M. Dubois and F. A. Briggs, "Effect of cache coherency in multiprocessors," *IEEE Trans. Comput.*, pp. 1083–1099, Nov. 1982.

[11] D. D. Gajski et al., "Cedar—A large scale multiprocessor," in *Proc. 1983 Int. Conf. Parallel Processing*, pp. 524–529.

[12] K. Ghose and S. Simhadri, "A cache coherency mechanism with limited combining capabilities for MIN-based multiprocessors," in *Proc. 1991 Int. Conf. Parallel Processing*, pp. I-296–300.

[13] J. R. Goodman, "Using cache memory to reduce processor-memory traffic," in *Proc. 10th Annu. Int. Symp. Comput. Architecture*, June 1983, pp. 124–132.

[14] A. Gotlieb et al., "The NYU Ultracomputer—Designing an MIMD shared memory parallel processor," *IEEE Trans. Comput.*, pp. 175–189, Feb. 1983.

[15] K. Hwang and F. A. Briggs, *Computer Architecture and Parallel Processing*. New York: McGraw-Hill, 1984, ch. 2.

[16] H. Jiang and L. N. Bhuyan, "MVAMIN: Mean value analysis algorithms for Multistage Interconnection Networks," *J. Parallel Distributed Comput.*, vol. 12, pp. 189–201, 1991.

[17] R. H. Katz et al., "Implementing a cache consistency protocol," in *Proc. 12th Annu. Int. Symp. Comput. Architecture*, June 1985, pp. 276–283.

[18] L. Kleinrock, *Queueing Systems Vol. 1, Theory*. New York: Wiley-Interscience 1975.

[19] H. E. Mizrahi et al., "Introducing memory into the switch elements of multiprocessor interconnection networks," in *Proc. 16th Annu. Int. Symp. Comput. Architecture*, June 1989.

[20] A. K. Nanda, "Design and application of cache coherent multiprocessors," Ph.D. dissertation under preparation at Texas A&M University.

[21] A. K. Nanda and H. Jiang, "Analysis of directory based cache coherence schemes with multistage networks," in *Proc. ACM Comput. Sci. Conf.*, Mar. 1992.

[22] M. Papamarcos and J. Patel, "A low overhead coherence solution for multiprocessors with private cache memories," in *Proc. 11th Annu. Int. Symp. Comput. Architecture*, 1984, pp. 348–354.

[23] G. F. Pfister et al., "The IBM Research Parallel Processor Prototype (RP3): Introduction and architecture," in *Proc. 1985 Int. Conf. Parallel Processing*, pp. 764–771.

[24] C. K. Tang, "Cache system design in tightly coupled microprocessor systems," in *AFPIS Proc., Nat. Comput. Conf.*, 1976, pp. 749–753.

[25] A. W. Wilson, "Hierarchical cache/bus architecture for shared memory multiprocessors," in *Proc. 14th Annu. Int. Symp. Comput. Architecture*, June 1987, pp. 244–252.

[26] Q. Yang, L. N. Bhuyan, and B. C. Liu "Analysis and comparison of cache coherence protocols for a packet switched multiprocessor," *IEEE Trans. Comput.*, pp. 1143–1153, Aug. 1989.

[27] W. C. Yen et al., "Data coherence problem in a multicache system," *IEEE Trans. Comput.*, pp. 56–65, Jan. 1985.

Ashwini K. Nanda (S'89 – M'92) received the B.Sc (Eng.) degree from Sambalpur University, India, and the M.Tech. degree in electrical engineering from Indian Institute of Technology, Madras. Currently he is pursuing the Ph.D. degree in computer science at Texas A&M University, College Station.

In the past he has worked for Wipro Information Technology, Bangalore, and Center for Development of Advanced Computing (CDAC), Pune, India. His research interests include parallel processing architectures and distributed computing.

Laxmi N. Bhuyan (S'81 – M'82 – SM'87) received the M.Sc. degree in electrical engineering from Sambalpur University, India, in 1979, and the Ph.D. degree in computer engineering from Wayne State University, Detroit, MI, in 1982.

At present, he is a Professor in Computer Science at Texas A&M University, College Station. Previously he was with the Center for Advanced Computer Studies at the University of Southwestern Louisiana. His research interests are in the areas of computer architecture, parallel and distributed computing, and performance evaluation.

Dr. Bhuyan currently serves on the Editorial Boards of *Computer* magazine and *Parallel Computing* journal. He was a Distinguished Visitor of the IEEE Computer Society and is an ACM Lecturer. He is a senior member of the IEEE Computer Society and a member of the Association for Computing Machinery.

Chapter 8: Mapping and Embedding

The mapping (or embedding) problem, introduced in 1981 by Bokhari,[1] has received considerable attention. It concerns *mapping* (or assigning) the nodes of a *guest graph* — which models the communication needs of a parallel algorithm — to the nodes of a *host graph* — which models a static network. The nodes in the guest graph represent the processes of a parallel task and the edges represent the need for data communication between the corresponding nodes. The purpose of mapping is to minimize the communication overhead of parallel algorithms. The ideal situation occurs when the guest graph is a subgraph of the host graph. However, this is rarely the case, because the only host graph that has every possible guest graph as a subgraph is the *complete graph*, which is prohibitively costly. Therefore, it is essential to construct efficient mappings for guest graphs onto buildable host networks such as meshes and hypercubes.

The most commonly used measure of the efficiency of mappings is the *dilation cost*, which is the maximum distance (in the host graph) between all pairs of nodes that host neighboring guest nodes. The problem of constructing a minimum-dilation mapping of a general guest graph to a general host graph is known to be NP-complete. However, for common guest graphs — such as linear arrays, trees, meshes, and multigrids — and for common host graphs — such as meshes and hypercubes — optimal mappings have been constructed.

This chapter includes several papers that show such optimal mappings. The first two papers, by Wu (1985) and Deshpande and Jenevein (1986), give mappings of trees onto hypercubes. The paper by Ho and Johnsson (1987) gives mappings of arbitrary meshes on hypercubes. Chan and Saad (1986) show how to embed multigrid algorithms on the hypercube, where the communicating nodes in a multigrid are the mesh nodes that are a power-of-two number of steps apart in any dimension. The paper by Ma and Tao (1993) presents embeddings of meshes and tori onto meshes and tori. Finally, Melhem and Hwang (1990) construct embeddings of rectangular meshes onto square meshes.

Reference

1. S.H. Bokhari, "On the Mapping Problem," *IEEE Trans. Computers*, Vol. C-30, No. 3, Mar. 1981, pp. 207–214.

Embedding of Tree Networks into Hypercubes*

Angela Y. Wu[†]

*Department of Mathematics, Statistics
and Computer Science,
The American University,
Washington, D.C. 20016*

The hypercube is a good host graph for the embedding of networks of processors because of its low degree and low diameter. Graphs such as trees and arrays can be embedded into a hypercube with small dilation and expansion costs, but there are classes of graphs which can be embedded into a hypercube only with large expansion cost or large dilation cost. © 1985 Academic Press, Inc.

1. Introduction

In the study of parallel computing, networks of processors are often organized into various configurations such as trees, pyramids, and mesh arrays [1–15]. These configurations can be represented as graphs. If the properties and structures of the underlying graph are used effectively, the computation and communication speeds can often be improved.

A hypercube of degree d has 2^d nodes and each node has exactly d neighbors. The distance between any two nodes is less than or equal to d. Both the diameter of the hypercube and the degree of the nodes grow very slowly (logarithmically) with respect to the number of nodes in the hypercube. The hypercube and hypercube-like networks such as the shuffle–exchange [12] and butterfly networks [14] are especially suited for sorting and computing the fast Fourier transform efficiently, among other tasks [11–15]. The hypercube configuration can transmit a large number of data quickly. This makes the hypercube potentially a more useful interconnection network than networks such as trees and rectangular grids [15].

Over the years, many parallel algorithms have been designed to solve different problems on various networks. It would be of interest to be able to execute these algorithms in a hypercube network. To do this, we need to map

*Research sponsored by the Air Force Office of Scientific Research (AFSC), under Contract F49620-83-C-0082. The U.S. Government's right to retain a nonexclusive royalty-free license in and to the copyright covering this paper, for governmental purposes, is acknowledged.

[†]The author wishes to thank Azriel Rosenfeld for suggesting the problem, and Janet Salzman for preparing this paper.

the algorithms' underlying network structure into the hypercube. This paper studies the mapping of different network configurations into a hypercube network. In other words, it studies the one-to-one association of the processors of a network with the processors of a hypercube network and the costs of such mappings. The costs considered are the distances of images of adjacent processors and the size of the hypercube with respect to the number of processors in the given network. The process can be viewed as embedding of a graph (the underlying structure of the network) into a hypercube and the dilation and expansion costs of the embedding [16, 17].

Graph embedding problems have applications in a wide variety of computational situations [17–22]. For example, the flow of information in a parallel algorithm defines a program graph, and embedding this into a network tells us how to organize the computation on the network. Other problems that can be formulated as graph embedding problems are laying out circuits on chips, representing data structures in computer memory, and finding efficient program control structures. Embedding of graphs into trees and some other issues of graph embedding have been studies by Rosenberg *et. al.* in [17, 23–25]. In this paper, the host graph in the embedding is always a hypercube. Section 2 defines and discusses some of the basic properties of hypercubes and graph embeddings. Sections 3 and 4 study embedding of trees in hypercubes. In Section 5, embedding of general graphs is discussed.

2. Hypercubes and Graph Embeddings

A hypercube of degree d has 2^d nodes and each node has d neighbors. The distance between any two nodes is less than or equal to d. The nodes in a hypercube may be labeled with binary numbers of length d. Two nodes $a_1 a_2 \ldots a_d$ and $b_1 b_2 \ldots b_d$ are adjacent to each other if and only if $\sum_{i=1}^{d} |a_i - b_i| = 1$.

A degree $d + 1$ hypercube C_{d+1} can be viewed as two degree d hypercubes $0C_d$ and $1C_d$ such that every node $0a_1 a_2 \ldots a_d$ in $0C_d$ is adjacent to one and only one node $1a_1 a_2 \ldots a_d$ in $1C_d$. Equivalently, given two degree d hypercubes, they can be combined into a degree $d + 1$ hypercube by making the appropriate connections. Moreover, we can specify how the two hypercubes are to be combined as long as the conditions specified are consistent in the sense that it is possible to relabel one of the hypercubes so that all the neighbor relations are preserved. This is the same as applying a sequence of rigid transformations of rotations and reflections to a hypercube. For example, one can specify which node in $1C_d$ is to become the neighbor of the node A in $0C_d$ and also how the neighbors of A are to be mapped into neighbors of this node in $1C_d$.

Another property of the hypercube which is useful in later sections is that it is Hamiltonian. This can easily be proved by induction and using the fact that C_{d+1} is obtained from two C_d's with the appropriate connections.

An embedding f of a graph $G = (V, E)$ in a graph $G' = (V', E')$ is a one-to-one function $f: V \rightarrow V'$. The cost of an embedding f is max{distance $(f(A), f(B))|(A, B) \in E}$, i.e., the largest distance in G' between the images of neighboring nodes of G. An embedding is said to preserve adjacency if its cost is 1. In the terminology of Rosenberg *et at.* [17] this is called the dilation cost. The expansion cost is the ratio of the number of nodes in V' to the number of nodes in V. Whenever no confusion can arise, we will refer to f as a function from G to G', and the image of a node A of G in G' will simply be identified as the node A in G'.

3. EMBEDDING OF BINARY TREES IN HYPERCUBES

We first consider a complete binary tree where each nonleaf node has two children. A complete binary tree T_d of height d has $2^d - 1$ nodes. The smallest hypercube large enough to house T_d is of degree d. However, this embedding of T_d into C_d cannot preserve adjacency.

PROPOSITION 1. *A complete binary tree of height $d > 2$ cannot be embedded in a hypercube of degree $\leq d$ such that adjacency is preserved. In other words, a complete binary tree cannot be embedded in a hypercube with a dilation cost of 1 and an expansion cost less than 2.*

Proof. A hypercube of degree $<d$ has fewer nodes than T_d; hence T_d cannot be embedded. Consider a mapping f of nodes T_d into a hypercube C_d of degree d. Suppose the nodes of C_d are labeled with binary numbers between 0 and 2^d as in Section 2. Without loss of generality, we may assume that the root of T_d (at level 0) is mapped onto node 0 in C_d. Note that if the image of a level k node N of T_d has t 1's in its label, the images of node N's children at level $k + 1$ have $t + 1$ or $t - 1$ 1's in their labels. Since f (level 0 node) has no 1's in its label, the following are true:

(1) f (level i node) has no more than i 1's in its label.
(2) f (odd level node) has an odd number of 1's in its label.
(3) f (even level node) has an even number of 1's in its label.

Case 1. *d is even.* The number of binary numbers of length d with an odd number of 1's is $\Sigma_{\text{odd } i} \binom{d}{i} = 2^{d-1}$.[1] The number of odd level nodes in T_d is $2 + 2^3 + 2^5 + \cdots + 2^{d-1} = \frac{2}{3}(2^d - 1)$. But $2^{d-1} < \frac{2}{3}(2^d - 1)$ if and only if $d > 2$. This shows that if d is even and $d > 2$, there are not enough nodes in C_d with an odd number of 1's in their labels to be the images of the odd level nodes of T_d.

Case 2. *d is odd.* The number of binary numbers of length d with an even number of 1's is $\Sigma_{\text{even } i} \binom{d}{i} = 2^{d-1}$. The number of even level nodes in T_d is

---

[1] $(x + y)^r = \Sigma_{i=0}^r \binom{r}{i} x^i y^{r-i}$. Let $x = -1$, $y = 1$; then we have $0 = \Sigma_{i=0}^r \binom{r}{i}(-1)^i = \Sigma_{\text{even } i} \binom{r}{i} - \Sigma_{\text{odd } i} \binom{r}{i}$, and $\Sigma_{\text{even } i} \binom{r}{i} = \Sigma_{\text{odd } i} \binom{r}{i} = \frac{1}{2} \Sigma_{i=0}^r \binom{r}{i} = \frac{1}{2} \cdot 2^r = 2^{r-1}$.

$2^0 + 2^2 + 2^4 + \cdots + 2^{d-1} = (2^{d+1} - 1)/3$. But $2^{d-1} < (2^{d+1} - 1)/3$ if and only if $d > 1$. This shows that if d is odd and $d > 1$, there are not enough nodes in C_d with an even number of 1's in their labels to be the images of the even label nodes of T_d. ∎

For $d > 2$, there is no adjacency-preserving embedding of T_d into C_d. However, Proposition 2 will show that if we allow a larger hypercube (one with twice as many nodes as necessary) as the target graph, then there is an adjacency-preserving embedding of T_d into it. In other words, there is an embedding with a dilation cost of 1 and an expansion cost of approximately 2. On the other hand, Proposition 3 will show that there is an embedding of T_d into C_d with a dilation cost of 2 and an expansion cost of approximately 1.

PROPOSITION 2. *A complete binary tree T_d of height d (for $d > 0$) can be embedded in a hypercube C_{d+1} of degree $d + 1$, in such a way that the adjacencies of nodes T_d are preserved.*

Proof. (by induction). Figure 1 shows how T_1, T_2, and T_3 can be embedded in C_2, C_3, and C_4 with adjacency preserved (cost = 1). Let $f_i\colon T_i \rightarrow C_{i+1}$ be an embedding of T_i into C_{i+1}. Suppose $f_{d-1}\colon T_{d-1} \rightarrow C_d$ preserves adjacency and (C_d, f_{d-1}) has the following property which we will refer to as the

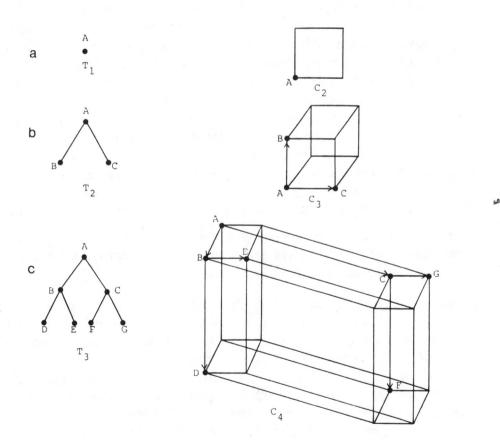

FIG. 1. Embeddings of T_1, T_2, T_3 into C_2, C_3, C_4.

"free-free neighbor" property: $R = f_{d-1}$ (root of T_{d-1}) has a free neighbor A and A has a free neighbor $B \neq R$, i.e., $\{A, B\} \not\subseteq \{f_{d-1}(N)|N$ a node of $T_{d-1}\}$. Note that (C_4, f_3) has the "free-free neighbor" property.

Given a complete binary tree T_d of height d, its left subtree can be embedded by f_{d-1} in $0C_d$ of C_{d+1}, such that $0L = f_{d-1}$ (root) has a free neighbor $0A$ which has a free neighbor $0B$. The right subtree can also be embedded in a degree d hypercube, call it C_d', using f_{d-1}' such that $R' = f_{d-1}'$ (root of right subtree) has a free neighbor A' which has a free neighbor B' in C_d'. We can now apply a rigid transformation $T: C_d' \rightarrow 1C_d$ such that $T(R')$ is the neighbor of $0A$ in $1C_d$ and $T(A')$ is the neighbor of $0B$ in $1C_d$. This is the same as forming a degree $d + 1$ hypercube from two degree d hypercubes by making sure that they are oriented properly using rotation and reflection so that a node (R') and its neighbor (A') in one hypercube match two specific neighbor nodes $(0A, 0B)$ in the other hypercube. This can always be done since $d \geq 3$. Now the embedding f_d of T_d into C_{d+1} can be defined: f_d (root of T_d) $= 0A$, $f_d|$left subtree $= f_{d-1}$, $f_d|$right subtree $= T(f_{d-1}')$. Distances between $0A$ and the images of the left and right children of the root are both 1. Moreover, the free-free neighbor property is satisfied by (C_{d+1}, f_d) since $0A$ has a free neighbor $0B$, and $0B$ has a free neighbor $T(A')$. See Fig. 2. By induction, the above construction shows that a complete binary tree of height d ($d \geq 0$) can be embedded in a hypercube of degree $d + 1$ with adjacency preserved. ∎

Intuitively, the embedding is built up from the smaller subtree's. Each of the root's subtrees is embedded in one smaller hypercube, the root is mapped into a free neighbor of its left child's image, the right subtree's image hypercube is oriented in such a way that the image of the right subtree's root is a neighbor of the root's image. The free-free neighbor property ensures that a free neighbor is available in the embedding of a taller tree.

This embedding has the property that each subtree is embedded with adjacency preserved in a hypercube which has about twice the number of nodes of the subtree. The above construction also does not completely restrict how the other nodes of the two degree d hypercubes are to be matched.

PROPOSITION 3. *A complete binary tree T_d of height d ($d > 0$) can be embedded in a hypercube C_d of degree d with cost $= 2$; i.e., neighbors in T_d are mapped into nodes of at most distance 2 away in C_d.*

Proof. Figures 1a and b and Fig. 3 show that T_1, T_2, and T_3 can be embedded in C_1, C_2, and C_3 in this way. Suppose T_{d-1} can be embedded in C_{d-1} by g_{d-1} and g_{d-1} (root of T_{d-1}) $= A$ and its left and right children are L, R; (C_{d-1}, g_{d-1}) has the cost 2 property, i.e., distance $(A, L) = 2$ and distance $(A, R) = 1$; and (g_{d-1}, C_{d-1}) also has the following property which we will refer to as the free neighbor property: the only free node in C_d is a neighbor of the root A. Figure 3 shows that (C_3, g_3) has cost 2 and the free neighbor property. We can embed T_d into C_d by first embedding the left subtree (height $d - 1$) into the $0C_{d-1}$ hypercube with $0A$ the root and $0B$ the

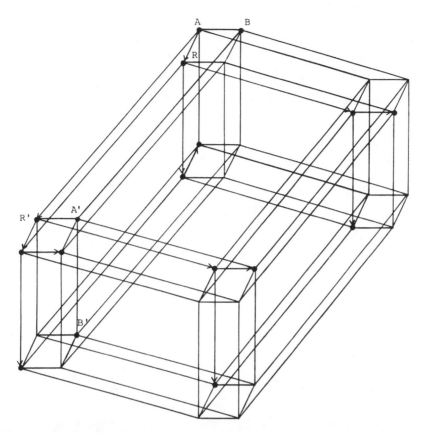

FIG. 2. The free-free-neighbor property. In C_4, A is a free neighbor of R (image of root of T_3); B is a free neighbor of A. In C'_4, A' is a free neighbor of R' (image of root of T'_3); B' is a free neighbor of A'. T_3 and T'_3 are the subtrees of T_4. In C_5, A becomes the new root of T_4, B is a free neighbor of A, A' is a free neighbor of B.

free neighbor of $0A$, then embedding the right subtree (height $d - 1$) into the $1C_{d-1}$ hypercube with $1A$ the root, $1B$ the free neighbor of $1A$, and $0A$, $1A$ are neighbors, $0B$, $1B$ are neighbors; finally, the root is mapped to $1B$. Clearly, distance $(g_d(\text{root}), g_d(\text{left child})) = $ distance $(1B, 0A) = 2$, distance $(g_d(\text{root}), g_d(\text{right child})) = 1$, the free node $0B$ is a neighbor of the root $1B$. By induction, T_d can be embedded in C_d with cost $= 2$. ∎

The above construction shows that every node in T_d is mapped into a node distance 2 away from its left son's image and distance 1 away from its right son's image. We can also specify a symmetric embedding so that for $d > 3$ the left and right subtrees of T_d are mapped into $0C_{d-1}$ and $1C_d$ in the same way so that the nodes in the same relative positions in the left and right subtrees of any node are neighbors of each other. More specifically, we can use a string S of length i in $\{L, R\}^*$ to denote a label i node $(0 < i < d)$ in T_d; this string S gives the path from the root to the node. For example, LR is a level 2 node which is the right child of the left child of the root. $S_1 L S_2$ and $S_1 R S_2$ $(S_1, S_2 \in \{L, R\}^*)$ are in the same relative positions in the left and right trees of the node denoted by S_1, and $g(S_1 L S_2)$ and $g(S_1 R S_2)$ are neighbors of each other. See Fig. 4.

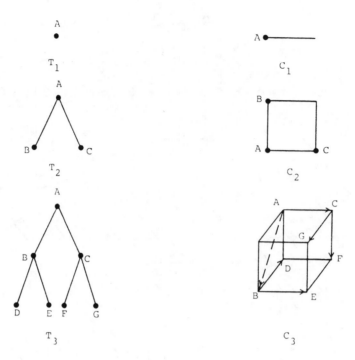

FIG. 3. Embeddings of T_1, T_2, T_3 into C_1, C_2, C_3 with dilation costs of 2. In C_3, the dotted line indicates that the distance between A and B is 2.

Let $A = a_1 a_2 \ldots a_i$, $B = b_1 b_2 \ldots b_i$ be the level i nodes in T_d, a_j, $b_j \in \{L, R\}$, $1 \le j \le i$. Suppose, at positions $p_1 \le p_2 \le \ldots \le p_t$ $(t \le i)$, $a_{p_j} \ne b_{p_j}$; then $g(A) = g(a_1 a_2 \ldots a_{p_1 - 1} a_{p_1} a_{p_1 + 1} \ldots a_i)$, $g(a_1 \ldots a_{p_1 - 1} b_{p_1}$
$a_{p_j} \ne b_{p_j}$; then $g(A) = g(a_1 a_2 \ldots a_{p_1 - 1} a_{p_1} a_{p_1 + 1} \ldots a_i)$, $g(a_1 \ldots a_{p_1 - 1} b_{p_1}$
$\ldots, g(a_1 \ldots b_{p_1} \ldots b_{p_2} \ldots b_{p_t} \ldots a_i) = g(B)$ is a path of length t in

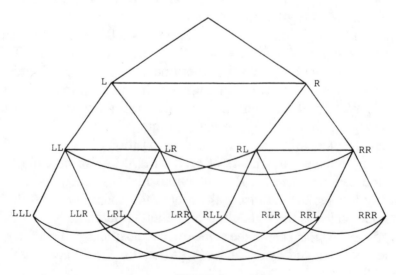

FIGURE 4

the hypercube C_d. Therefore, in this embedding the distance between two level i nodes is at most i.

The above propositions show how a complete binary tree can be embedded in a hypercube without greatly increasing the dilation cost or the expansion cost. If a binary tree is not complete, we can first complete the tree with imaginary nodes and then embed it in a hypercube. This in general is not economical because often a smaller hypercube can house the incomplete binary tree.

If we are interested in an adjacency-preserving embedding of an incomplete binary tree, we can construct an embedding using the same principles as in the proofs of Propositions 2 and 3. We start with a leaf node at the highest level, map it into a hypercube of degree 1, and continue to put its ancestor node which has only one child in the same hypercube if possible. We go to a larger size hypercube if needed and always try to have the free neighbor property (as defined in the proof of Propostion 3) satisfied (the free-free neighbor property as defined in the proof of Proposition 2 if possible). When we reach a node A whose parent P has another child B, then we can try to put B's subtree in the same hypercube if it can be done easily, say, if it has only 3 or 4 nodes; otherwise, we embed B's tree in another hypercube, making sure that *one* of A's or B's embeddings satisfies the free neighbor property (go to a higher-dimensional hypercube if necessary). Then P can be mapped into the free neighbor in the hypercube with the free neighbor property. Of course, if one of the cubes has the free-free neighbor property, then P should be mapped into that cube. The free-free neighbor and the free neighbor properties ensure that there is a free node in the cube for the root of the taller subtree. In general, the hypercube (and embedding) that results from this method is smaller than the one obtained from completing the incomplete binary tree. For example, a subtree which is a single branch of length m can be embedded in a hypercube of degree $\lceil \log_2 m \rceil$ since hypercubes are Hamiltonian. The free-neighbor property is satisfied if the hypercube is of degree $\lceil \log_2(m + 1) \rceil$. The free-free neighbor property is satisfied if the cube is of degree $\lceil \log_2(m + 1) \rceil$.

4. k-ARY TREES

A k-ary tree can be turned into a binary tree by adding $\lceil \log_2 k \rceil - 1$ levels of nodes, i.e., at most $2^{\lceil \log_2 k \rceil} - 2$ nodes between a node and its k children. See Fig. 5 for an example. A k-ary tree of height d becomes an equivalent binary tree of height $d + (d - 1)(\lceil \log_2 k \rceil - 1) = \lceil \log_2 k \rceil d - \lceil \log_2 k \rceil + 1$. The number of new nodes needed is $2^{(\lceil \log_2 k \rceil d - \lceil \log_2 k \rceil + 1)} - 1 -$ number of nodes in the k-ary tree. This distance between two adjacent nodes of the k-ary tree is $\lceil \log_2 k \rceil$ in the binary tree. This binary tree can be embedded in a hypercube as in Proposition 3 and we have proved the following:

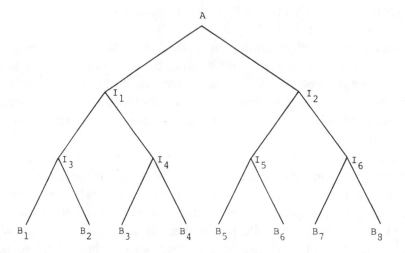

FIG. 5. $B_1, B_2, \ldots, B_8$ are the children of node A in an 8-ary tree. $I_1, I_2, \ldots, I_6$ are the nodes inserted to convert the 8-ary tree to a binary tree.

PROPOSITION 4. *A k-ary tree K_d of height d can be embedded in a hypercube of degree $(d - 1)\lceil log_2 k\rceil + 1$ such that the distance between the images of adjacent nodes of K_d is at most $2 * \lceil log_2 k\rceil$.*

If the k-ary tree K_d is complete and $k = 2^m$ for some m then the equivalent binary tree (and thus the hypercube) has less than twice the number of nodes in K_d and the cost of the embedding is $2\lceil log_2 k\rceil$, which is small in comparison with log_2(number of nodes in K_d). Again, if the k-ary tree is not complete, we can construct the embedding using the same principle as in the incomplete binary tree case and the images of the imaginary nodes added to form the equivalent binary tree can be used as images of real nodes in the k-ary tree.

5. GRAPHS

A graph G with n nodes can be embedded in a hypercube of degree $\lceil log_2 n\rceil$ by simply associating nodes of the structures in any one-to-one fashion. This embedding uses the smallest size hypercube needed, but the dilation cost can be as high as $\lceil log_2 n\rceil$. Another embedding method uses the spanning tree of the graph.

A graph $G = (V, E)$ of degree k and diameter d has a breadth-first spanning tree S which is k-ary with height d. An edge in E which is not an edge in S must connect only nodes in adjacent levels of S by the breadth-first construction. Thus a graph can be considered as a k-ary tree with additional edges joining nodes whose levels differ by at most one.

For any graph G, we can construct an embedding by first constructing its breadth-first spanning tree S, extending this k-ary tree into a binary tree T, and then embedding the binary tree in a hypercube C using the method described in Section 3. This hypercube has degree $(d - 1)\lceil\log_2 k\rceil + 1$ and $2^{(d-1)\lceil\log_2 k\rceil + 1}$ nodes. The cost of this embedding is $(d-1)\lceil\log_2 k\rceil + 1$, since adjacent nodes in G can be mapped into two leaf nodes of T which are distance = (height of $T-1$) apart.

For a graph which is a k-ary tree with each leaf node connecting to k other leaf nodes, the costs of the embedding resulting from the above methods are almost identical and the cost is high. However, in both of these methods, the graph structure was not examined nor used. By examining the structure, one can usually get better embedding schemes with smaller costs. For example, a $2^n \times 2^m$ array can be embedded in a hypercube of degree $n + m$ with adjacency preserved in a natural way: (a) First, embed each row i ($1 \leq i \leq 2^n$) in a hypercube $C_m^{(i)}$ of degree m; this can be done since hypercubes are Hamiltonian; (b) then combine $C_m^{(2j-1)}$ and $C_m^{(2j)}$ ($1 \leq j \leq 2^{n-1}$) into hypercube $C_{m+1}^{(j)}$ so that hypercube nodes representing array nodes in the same column are connected; then combine C_{m+1}^{2k-1} and C_{m+1}^{2k} ($1 \leq k \leq 2^{n-2}$) into hypercube C_{m+2}^k, again making sure that hypercube nodes representing array nodes at adjacent rows and same column are connected; continuing in this way, a hypercube C_{m+n} results and all adjacencies are preserved (cost = 1). If the embedding methods for general graphs were used, the cost could be as high as $m + n$ because the spanning tree of the $2^n \times 2^m$ array is of height $n + m$ and quite skewed.

On the other hand, there are graphs that cannot be embedded into a hypercube with adjacency preserved no matter how large the hypercube is. For example, any graph which contains a cycle with length $2i + 1$ for some $i > 0$ cannot have an adjacency-preserving (cost = 1) embedding. A complete graph of n nodes is another example. However, we can have a cost 2 embedding if we use a hypercube of degree $n - 1$. As a matter of fact, it is easy to see that any graph with n nodes can be embedded into a hypercube of degree $n - 1$ so that adjacent nodes are mapped into nodes distance 2 apart.

6. CONCLUDING REMARKS

The hypercube is a good host graph for the embedding of networks of processors because of its low degree and low diameter. Graphs such as trees and arrays can be embedded into a hypercube with small costs. The design of the embedding mappings makes use of the structures of these graphs. In general, there is a trade-off between the dilation cost and the expansion cost. Rosenberg et at. [17] illustrates how one of these costs can be minimized only at the expense of a dramatic increase in the other cost in three situations where binary trees are the host graphs. This paper has shown that there is no embedding of a complete binary tree into a hypercube with dilation cost of 1 and expansion cost less than 2. But there is an embedding with dilation cost

1 and expansion cost approximately 2, and there is an embedding with dilation cost 2 and expansion cost approximately 1. For embedding of general graphs, if the size of the hypercube is minimal, then the dilation cost of the embedding may be as large as log(number of nodes in the graph). On the other hand, there is always an embedding of an n node graph into a degree $n - 1$ hypercube (very high expansion cost) with a dilation cost of 2. We have also shown that there are classes of graphs which cannot have adjacency-preserving (dilation cost $= 1$) embeddings into hypercubes of any size.

REFERENCES

1. Duff, M. J. B. CLIP4: A large scale integrated circuit array parallel processor. *Proc. Third IJCPR*, pp. 728–733.

2. *Batcher, K. E. Design of a massively parallel processor. IEEE Trans. Comput.* **29** (1980), 836–840.

3. Bouknight, W., *et. al.* The ILLIAC IV System. *Proc. IEEE 60*, 1972, pp. 369–388.

4. Reeves, A. P. A systematically designed binary array processor. *IEEE Trans. Comput.* **29** (1980), 278–287.

5. Kuck, D. A survey of parallel machine organization and programming. *Comput. Surveys* **9** (1977), 29–59.

6. Uhr, L. Layered "recognition cone" networks that preprocess, classify and describe. *IEEE Trans. Comput.* **21** (1972), 758–768.

7. Dyer, C. R. A quadtree machine for parallel image processing. Tech. Rep. KSL 51, University of Illinois at Chicago Circle, 1981.

8. Tanimoto, S. Towards hierarchical cellular logic: Design considerations for pyramid machines. Department of Computer Science Tec. Rep. 81–02–01, University of Washington, 1981.

9. Hanson, A. R., and Riseman, E. M. Processing cones: A computational structure for image analysis. In Tanimoto, S., and Klinger, A. (Eds.). *Structured Computer Vision*, Academic Press, New York, 1980.

10. Wu, A., and Rosenfeld, A. Cellular graph automata, I, II. *Inform. and Control* **42** (1979), 305–329, 330–353.

11. Pease, M. C., III. The indirect binary n-cube microprocessor array. *IEEE Trans. Comput.* **26** (1977), 458–473.

12. Stone, H. S. Parallel processing with the perfect shuffle. *IEEE Trans. Comput.* **20** (1971), 153–161.

13. Preparata, F. P., and Vuillemin, J. E. The cube-connected cycles: A versatile network for parallel computation. *Proc. Twentieth IEEE Symposium on Foundations of Computer Science*, 1979, pp. 140–147.

14. Wise, D. S. Compact layouts of banyan/FFT networks. In Kung, Sproull, and Steele (Eds.). *VLSI Systems and Computations*. Computer Science Press, Rockville, Md., 1981, pp. 186–195.

15. Ullman, J. D. *Computational Aspects of VLSI*. Computer Science Press, Rockville, Md., 1984.

16. Rosenberg, A. L. Data encodings and their costs. *Acta Inform.* **9** (1978), 273–292.

17. Hong, J. W., Mehlhorn, K., and Rosenberg, A. L. Cost trade-offs in graph embeddings, with applications. *J. Assoc. Comput. Mach.* **30** (1983), 709–728.

18. DeMille, R. A., Eisenstat, S. C., and Lipton, R. J. On small universal data structures and related combinatorial problems. *Proc. Johns Hopkins Conf. on Information Sciences and Systems*, Baltimore, Md., 1978, pp. 408–411.

19. Lipton, R. J., Eisenstat, S. C., and DeMille, R. A. Space and time hierarchies for collections of control structures and data structures. *J. Assoc. Comput. Mach.* **23** (1976), 720–732.

20. Valient, L. G. Universality considerations in VLSI circuits. *IEEE Trans. Comput.* **30** (1981), 135–140.

21. Kung, H. T. and Stevenson, D. A software technique for reducing the routing time on a parallel computer with a fixed interconnection network. In Kuck, D. J., Lawrie, D. H., and Sameh, A. H. (Eds.). *High Speed Computer and Algorithm Optimization*. Academic Press, New York, 1977, pp. 423–433.

22. Rosenberg, A. L., Three dimensional VLSI: A case study. *J. Assoc. Comput. Mach.* **30** (1983), 397–416.

23. Rosenberg, A. L., Encoding data structures in trees. *J. Assoc. Comput. Mach.* **26** (1979), 668–689.

24. Hong, J. W., and Rosenberg, A. L. Graphs that are almost binary trees. *SIAM J. Comput.* **11** (1982), 227–242.

25. Rosenberg, A. L. Issues in the study of graph embeddings. In Noltemeier, H. (Ed.). *Graph-theoretic Concepts in Computer Science*. Springer-Verlag, New York, 1981, pp. 150–176.

Scalability of a Binary Tree on a Hypercube

Sanjay R. Deshpande and Roy M. Jenevein

Department of Electrical and Computer Engineering
University of Texas at Austin
Austin, Texas 78712.

Abstract

The concept of scalability is important for the next generation of super-multiprocessors. Two aspects of scalability of an architecture are *resource scalability* and *application scalability*. Both types of scalabilities are qualitative measures of goodness of an inductive architecture [4]. The application scalability measures the utilization of resources and the efficiency of execution of application. The resource scalability is a measure of growth rate of architectural properties.

In this paper, the resource scalability characteristics of the hypercube architecture are assessed and the concept of application scalability is applied to it in the context of a binary tree structured application graph. The criterion used is the utilization of processing nodes. Results are also derived for a modification of the application graph. A logN[1] time complexity distributed algorithm that can be used to set up the modified structure is outlined. This algorithm is shown to be useful for handling a single node fault in the architecture as well.

1 Introduction

An important consideration in designing an architecture for a super-multiprocessor system is its scalabilities [4,5]. We recognize two types of scalabilities: resource scalability and application scalability.

By resource scalability we imply the asymptotic growth rates of architectural properties and their associated costs. The smaller the cost, the better scalable is the architecture. For example, the multistage interconnection networks such as the omega, the banyan and the baseline are preferred for multiprocessor systems over the crossbar for the reason that these networks scale better than the crossbar. The hardware cost increases as NlogN for these networks compared to N^2 for the crossbar, for N interconnected resources.

Application scalability is a measure of utilization of architectural resources and efficiency of execution for a par-

ticular application under asymptotic growth in their size. In other words, it is a measure of optimality of mapping between the application and the architecture for all sizes. This concept is of relevance for inductive architectures [4], which are regular in structure and have the number of processing resources as a parameter. Some examples of inductive architectures are TRAC [13], PASM [14], Hypercube [3], CHiP [15] etc.. For these, the mappings can be evaluated as a function of size. By evaluating their application scalability, we can predict the asymptotic execution behavior of an application.

Consider an application mapped on a given architecture. The mapping results in certain utilization of resources and execution efficiency. If, when the architecture and the application are equally increased in size, the same utilization and execution efficiency is achieved, the architecture is considered to be well scalable with respect to that application. Of course, in some cases, a drop in execution efficiency can be allowed if it is the result of increased hardware delays.

It is not sufficient for a super-multiprocessor architecture to have good resource scalability; it must also have good application scalability for a number of applications. For instance, a bus oriented architecture has excellent resource scalability, but its bandwidth is exceeded for even modest communication requirements per processor, as the number of processors is increased beyond a certain value. The evaluation process should therefore account for architectural constructs embedded in software as well as hardware. These include, but are not limited to, software communication switches, polling routines, priority encoders, data translators, etc.. If these constructs are not accounted for, they may result in bottlenecks and degraded performance as the application grows in size.

The evaluation of application scalability of an architecture involves mapping of an application graph on the architectural topology. Conventionally, the mapping implies embedding of an application graph within the resource graph of the supporting architecture. The mapping problem arises because the two graphs are topologically non-isomorphic [6]. The solution results in assignment of one or more computation nodes of the application graph to a processing node in the system such that the processing and storage requirements are satisfied.

---

[1]Throughout this paper, unless otherwise specified, logN is used as short for $\log_2 N$.

Reprinted from *Proc. 15th Int'l Conf. Parallel Processing*, 1986, pp. 661-668. Copyright © 1986 by The Institute of Electrical and Electronics Engineers, Inc. All rights reserved.

We have chosen an application graph which has the structure of a balanced binary tree. Binary tree graphs are fundamental structures and appear in several computation graphs. They naturally result from *divide and conquer* methodology of formulating parallel algorithms for sorting, merging and min-max problems. A binary tree based algorithm is used for the recursive doubling method of computing a global histogram [7]. The Dictionary Machine of Atallah and Kosaraju uses a binary tree structured machine architecture [8]. Binary tree structures result from search trees in inference systems. Horowitz and Zorat suggest application of binary tree shaped interconnection networks for multiprocessor systems [9]. It would therefore be interesting to see how such an important computational topology is supported on a popular architecture.

Recently, substantial attention has been given to the hypercube architecture for multiprocessors [1, 2]. Many applications have been successfully implemented on it and impressive speed-ups have been obtained [3]. Most previous architectures have failed to furnish respectable speed-ups for more than just a few applications. On the other hand, the hypercube architecture seems to have lived up to its promise of being a good supporting architecture for a wide variety of application areas. This effectiveness of the hypercube architecture is seen to derive from the rich internode connection topology afforded by the underlying graph. But, before hypercube topology can be considered as a defining topology for a future generation super-multiprocessor, its resource scalability should be evaluated. Also of consequence to its applicability for a dedicated high performance computing engine is its application scalability for the targeted use. Binary tree structured algorithms being so common in the area of parallel processing, we focus here on their scalability on the hypercube.

2 Resource Scalability of Hypercube Architectures

A boolean or binary hypercube graph of order n (alternately called n-cube) has 2^n nodes connected with edges as defined in Appendix I. Figure 1 shows an example of a hypercube of order 3. In a hypercube based multiprocessor, nodes of the graph are occupied by independent processing elements. The edges between the nodes represent the point-to-point communication links between the processors. Each link or edge is dedicated to the corresponding node-pair. In some architectures, like the Intel's iPSC System, there is a separate processor called the Cube Manager to coordinate the parallel execution of a job [10]. The Cube Manager is connected to the processors in the cube by a broadcast bus for global communication, I/O and control. However, the concepts of Cube Manager and the global bus are not inherent to the hypercube architecture, and we will therefore ignore them. We will use the well-known rectangular, multistage, single-sided interconnection networks (MSINs) such as banyan, omega and baseline as a reference when comparing properties. These networks have been shown to be topologically isomorphic in [18]. We assume in this paper that the MSINs have logN stages of N/2 switches

each, and that switches allow "turn-around". Thus a message going from one processor to another travels a certain number of levels into the network and then turns around and travels to the destination in the reverse direction.

2.1 Communication Interface Costs

Each processing element in an n-cube has communication links to n other processors. If we focus on the number of processors, $N = 2^n$, in the cube, then there are logN communication interfaces on each processor. Thus the total communication interface cost of the network is NlogN. This is the same as the cost of the MSINs, although there is one minor difference: when the size of the hypercube is doubled, each of the original nodes has to be modified to allow one more communication link. The nodes of the original cube could be provided with ports for extra links, and when the cube is doubled, one of these could be utilized. However, it is important to remember that modification is necessary throughout the original system in the case of hypercube; whereas in the multistage network architectures, the modifications are localized to the boundary of the original system.

2.2 Communication Reliability

The communication reliability of the hypercube (n $\geq$ 3) is better than that of the MSINs. For them, unless extra stages are specifically provided for [16, 17], there are a constant number of disjoint paths (= out-degree of a node) between two processing nodes. On the other hand, in the hypercube architecture, there are (logN) disjoint paths available for any given pair of nodes [11].

Note that, in the hypercube architecture, the number of contingent paths and the reliability of interprocessor communication increases with logN, while those for the MSINs remain constant. Thus for the hypercube architecture, the communication reliability also scales better than that for the multistage networks.

2.3 Interprocessor Distance

The diameter of a network can be defined as that of the underlying graph structure in which the processing resources and switches are represented as nodes and the communication paths are represented as edges. For a graph, the diameter is the maximum distance between any pair of nodes. For the MSINs, the diameter is equal to twice the number of stages in the network; that is 2logN. For a hypercube network, the message passes at most logN links before reaching the destination [12], since for any given node, there is one node which is at distance logN from it. So for the hypercube, the diameter scales as logN.

It can be shown that the average distance from a given node, of all nodes including itself, is 2(logN-1) + 2/N, for MSINs. The same is logN/2 for a hypercube. Thus, under asymptotic growth, although both scale as logN, the hypercube has a better scaling coefficient[2].

3 Application Scalability for a Binary Tree

For the sake of this analysis, we will assume that the binary tree application is the sole task being executed in the system. Under this condition, we would like to execute the largest possible size of the application. Ideally, we would like to utilize the hypercube architecture fully, so that when the architecture and the application are scaled, no wastage results. If that is not possible, a constant resource overhead is allowable since the percentage of overhead would diminish with equal increase in the application size and architecture. The overhead that grows linearly with the number of nodes in the hypercube is unacceptable.

Let us consider mapping a binary tree on an order n hypercube. A balanced binary tree with n levels of nodes (called in this paper an n level tree), has a total of N-1 nodes of which N/2 are at the leaf level. It should therefore be possible to map an n level binary tree on an n-cube. This would result in all but one of the nodes being utilized and would represent constant under-utilization. If such mapping is possible for all n, the binary tree application could be considered well-scalable on a hypercube architecture. We ask precisely this question: Is such mapping possible?

It is possible to map a two-level binary tree on a 2-cube that has a square topology (See Figure 2). For all $n \geq 3$, it is impossible to map an n level binary tree on a hypercube of order n. Appendix I contains the proof for this result. For $n \geq 3$, the largest sized binary tree that can be mapped on an n-cube is of n-1 levels. Thus the tree occupies only about half (2^{n-1}-1) nodes out of the 2^n available. Resultant under-utilization of computing resources is $2^{n-1}+1$ nodes, which is slightly more than 50%. In terms of the total computing resource available in the system, the overhead is linear and therefore unacceptable.

Proof that an n-1 level binary tree can be mapped on an n-cube forms a part of Appendix II. In fact, two n-1 level binary trees can be simultaneously mapped on an n-cube.

The result obtained in Appendix I tends to question the suitability of hypercube topology for super-multiprocessor architecture on the grounds that it cannot support the scaling of a fundamental application. A question we may ask is: Is it possible to modify the application graph such that the new structure scales well on the hypercube architecture without introducing overheads that grow inordinately?

Appendix II shows that it is indeed possible to slightly modify the original tree graph and make it well-scalable on the cube. That is, a modified n level tree is optimally map-

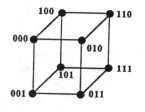 

Figure 1.   Figure 2.

pable on an n-cube. By the introduction of a single two-degree node as a son of its root, and thereby *stretching* (or equivalently double-rooting) it, the tree can be made to utilize the cube completely (see Figure 3b). The extra node so introduced is used only for communication between the root and one of its sons. It is interesting to note that only one such node is required for any n. This node therefore represents a constant overhead for all $n \geq 3$ which diminishes in percentage as n becomes larger.

Since each processing node in the cube accommodates a single computation node of the tree, equal increase in sizes of both application and architecture does not change the computational load on an individual processor. Upon scaling, the links between the processors continue to correspond to edges between neighboring nodes in the tree on a one-to-one basis and handle the same level of traffic as before. This ensures that the computational efficiency of the application too does not drop significantly, although a constant time is added because of the communication through the spacer node.

4 A Distributed Tree Set-Up Algorithm

In the previous section we saw that an n level stretched binary tree can be mapped onto a hypercube of order n. In order to prove that result, we have introduced transformations of the node labels. It is possible to use these transformations, namely FT3 and BT3, to obtain a distributed algorithm to set up the referred mapping. This algorithm has practical importance for executing a binary tree shaped application on a hypercube. It is used first to set up the communication topology among the processors of the cube, and then the application is executed. The algorithm does not require that the entire system be configured as a tree. It works as well within any subcube of the overall system. The algorithm is explained below.

The algorithm is executed by each processor in the hypercube. It is divided into two phases; namely compute and distribute. During the first phase, the nodes of the cube compute the loci of the mapped trees as they are transformed and merged to form larger trees. In the second phase, the port configurations of the nodes forming the final tree are sent to the appropriate nodes of the cube.

The algorithm starts by setting up initial 2^{n-3} three level trees having a predetermined configuration. That is,

---

[2]Certain other multi-tree networks, like the KYKLOS [19], are known to offer average interprocessor distances which are better than that for the MSINs.

every node in the cube is a member of a three-level tree; its position in the tree is determined by the least significant three bits of its ID. Each three-level tree is defined over a set of eight nodes which have identical n-3 most significant bits. The configuration of these trees are shown in Figure 5. The labels of the nodes of these mapped trees are henceforth referred to as *virtual addresses*. At each successive iteration of the algorithm, trees are merged to form larger trees until eventually the final tree is attained. These intermediate trees are not realized by activating links between appropriate nodes in the cube. However, the cumulative information available in the cube is sufficient to make this possible.

At the outset, the virtual address of a tree node corresponds to the label of the physical node in the cube to which it is mapped. After this, the physical nodes compute the loci in the n-cube of these initial tree nodes as the mappings are transformed and merged to form larger trees. At the end of the compute phase of the algorithm, each physical node holds the node label to which the virtual address would eventually be mapped, and also the port assignments required at this final node to configure the tree properly. These port assignments are relayed to the final node during the distribution phase of the algorithm.

For an n level tree in an n-cube, O(logN) iterations are required, and if we assume no collisions during the distribution phase, it too is O(logN) long, since each node in the cube emits one message. It therefore implies that the algorithm is of O(logN) time complexity. The algorithm is given in Appendix III.

5 Tree Mapping in Presence of a Node Fault

We consider here the mapping of a stretched binary tree topology in presence of single node faults. We make an assumption while formulating the strategies: the knowledge of this failure is global. That is, all processing nodes know before hand the label or Id of the failed node. This prior knowledge is not essential, and an algorithm to distribute the labels of the failed nodes can be formulated if necessary.

We will first consider a multiple step approach where each step represents one mapping of a portion of the computation graph and its subsequent execution. Clearly, an n-1 level sub-tree with a spacer node occupies 2^{n-1} nodes and thus is mappable into half of a hypercube of order n. By utilizing this partitioning of the cube, the corresponding computational graph must be segmented into three components: the root, the left sub-tree and the right sub-tree. In this way, each sub-tree segment of the graph can be mapped onto the valid half partition of the cube in which no nodes are faulty, while the faulty node is isolated to the other half.

Because the proof in Appendix II works inductively for successively higher order cubes, the reverse fragmentation to lower cubes follows directly, provided the cube partition is done on a dimensional boundary. Remembering that each successively higher order cube adds one bit to the node addresses, a mapping partition can consist of all nodes whose high order bit is the complement of that of the faulty node. In this way the problem is reduced to that of mapping a sub-tree to a subcube. Figure 6 shows the valid half of the cube as those nodes with the high order bit in their labels to be 1 since it is assumed that the faulty node has a 0 as the high order bit of its label.

The disadvantage with this approach, however, is that it may lead to a three-step process of map-and-execute (left tree, right tree and then root), and additionally, because of a single faulty node, $2^{n-1}-1$ nodes are left unutilized. This seems a high price to pay to avoid a fault. We now address the question of whether one can map-and-execute in a single step.

A three-level tree with the spacer node is shown in Figure 5. In this figure, we can see that the root of the tree occupies physical node ID 000 and the spacer node ID is 100. After mapping, only one node within the cube has no corresponding computational requirement in the stretched tree. We observe that the spacer node (S100 in Figure 4a) has as its only responsibility, the communication of results from the right sub-tree to the root. Certainly, this communication is an essential part of the computation graph. But, S100 is not the only node linking S000 and S110 within the hypercube, and because the node S010 likewise links them, it could be used instead.

Let us assume for the moment that we have a means to "force" the faulty node to be S100. In this way, all computation nodes are mapped to working processors and S010 doubles as both a computation node and an alternate link from the right sub-tree to the root (see Figure 9). In all of the tree algorithms discussed, at the time when this communication is needed all members of the right sub-tree have completed their computation and gone idle. This implies that no timing conflict arises as a result of this dual role for S010.

The remaining open question concerns the ability to "force" the faulty node to the spacer node. We answer this question via an example of a 3-cube. The method can be extended easily to an n-cube.

We will assume a single fault at node 001, which according to the mapping in Figure 7, is a computational node. We assume that the faulty node address (001) is available to all nodes in the cube. We now provide a means to remap the initial three level tree such that the fault will map to a logical node 100 and all other nodes will be transformed through three dimensional space conserving their adjacency relationships.

Figure 8 shows that an XOR bit mask controls the reflection or non-reflection of each bit in the node label. If the bit in the mask is 0, no reflection occurs; but if it is a 1, then a pair of node labels are swapped in that dimension.

Thus, a remapping of the labels occurs, but adjacency is preserved. This mask can be generated by taking the exclusive OR(XOR) between the fault node id and the spacer id (100). The XOR of this mask and each node id create virtual addresses which force the fault to be mapped to the spacer node as shown in Figure 9.

The above method can be extended to an n-cube if we can designate a particular label as that of the spacer node. The tree set-up algorithm of Appendix III always produces a spacer node at S100, where S is a string of n-3 zeros. Thus, in the case of an n-cube, all nodes use their own physical labels as virtual addresses to start with. Subsequent to the tree set-up algorithm, the resultant virtual addresses are XORed with the mask to obtain an appropriate tree with a spacer node mapped onto the faulty physical node.

6 Summary and Conclusions

In this paper the concept of application scalability was introduced and applied to an example of a hypercube architecture and a binary tree application. For inductive architectures like the hypercube, application scalability is an indicator of how well a given application will be supported with increasing sizes. The parameters of interest, while evaluating application scalability, are utilization of hardware resources and efficiency of execution. The first of the parameters is evaluated by mapping a maximum sized application graph onto the architecture graph and performing a calculation of the utilization as a function of size. The second is analyzed by measuring the growth of computation and communication delays as a function of size.

It was concluded that a balanced binary tree is not well scalable on a hypercube. It was also proved that a stretched binary tree results in a scalable mapping giving near 100% utilization of processing resource in the architecture. In addition, an O(logN) distributed algorithm was derived to generate a stretched binary tree in the hypercube. The tree construction algorithm was also shown to be adaptable to generate a mapping in presence of a single node fault by augmenting it with a subsequent fault-avoidance step.

Of the two approaches evaluated for executing the tree application in the presence of a single node fault, one provides complete utilization of fault-free nodes for an n level tree in an order n hypercube. Thus, even with single node fault, the binary tree application can be mapped and run with virtually no degradation in performance.

Acknowledgements

This research was supported by AFOSRF49620-84-C-0020, DCR-8116099, DE-AS05-81ER-10987 and Space and Naval Warfare Systems Command Contract N00039-86-C-0167. The authors would like to thank Prof. J. C. Browne, Matt Sejnowski and Ashok Adiga for their insightful comments.

Appendix I

Definition: A hypercube of order n (an n-cube) is an undirected graph with 2^n vertices labelled 0 through 2^n-1. There is an edge between a given pair of vertices if, and only if, the binary representation of their labels differ by one and only one bit. Hypercube of order 3 is shown in Figure 1.

Definition: Parity of a node is odd or even and is determined by the number of 1's in the label of the node.

Lemma 1: If nodes a and b are connected by an edge, a and b have opposite parities.

If we try to map a binary tree on a hypercube, we can observe the following lemma:

Lemma 2: The node parities alternate over the levels of a mapped binary tree.

We now count the number of odd and even nodes necessary to map a binary tree, and the number of odd and even nodes available in a hypercube:

By symmetry, the number of odd and even nodes available in the hypercube is the same and is half the total number of nodes, that is $\frac{1}{2}(2^n) = 2^{n-1}$. For a binary tree, we get the following values:

Case 1: n is even.

Number of even nodes $= 2^0 + 2^2 + ... + 2^{n-2} = \frac{1}{3}(2^n - 1)$

Number of odd nodes $= 2^1 + 2^3 + ... + 2^{n-1} = \frac{2}{3}(2^n - 1)$

Case 2: n is odd.

Number of even nodes $= 2^0 + 2^2 + ... + 2^{n-1} = \frac{1}{3}(2^{n+1} - 1)$

Number of odd nodes $= 2^1 + 2^3 + ... + 2^{n-2} = \frac{2}{3}(2^{n-1} - 1)$

In both cases the number of even and odd nodes required by the tree do not match those of the cube. This completes the proof.

Appendix II

Figure 3a shows a binary tree of n=3. The figure also shows the even and odd levels of the tree, assuming level 0 of the tree is at an even level. Figure 3b shows the construction of a 4-level tree out of two 3-level trees using an extra node at level 1 of the right hand subtree. The resultant tree has equal number of odd and even nodes which can be matched by those in a 4-cube. The following is a constructive proof that such a mapping is possible for n $\geq$ 3.

Definition: An n-cube is said to be k-dimensionally transformed when k bits in the label of each node of the cube are transformed according to a transformation. (Note that the bits undergoing transformation need not be contiguous.)

We define two 3-dimensional transformations, FT3 and BT3, as shown in Table 1. The x_i, x_j and x_k are the original values of the bits, and y_i, y_j and y_k are the corresponding resultant values.[3]

Definition: Distance between a pair of nodes in a graph is the minimum number of edges that have to be traversed when going from one node to the other. For an n-cube, this is also equal to the number of bits by which the binary representations of labels of the two nodes differ [11]. The *adjacency* in an n-cube is the distance relationship of a node with the rest of the nodes in the cube.

We state the following two theorems proved in [12].

Theorem 1: The FT3 preserves cube adjacency.

Theorem 2: The BT3 preserves cube adjacency.

We can now state the following corollaries:

Corollary 1: Nodes with distinct labels map to distinct resultant labels.

Corollary 2: If two nodes are neighbors and thus have labels differing in one bit position, their new labels after the transformations also differ in one bit position. Thus, neighborhood between the two nodes is preserved.

Theorem 3: A graph G mapped on an n-cube remains unchanged in structure after the transformations.

Proof: The proof follows as a direct consequence of corollaries 1 and 2, and is given in [12].

We can therefore state the following corollary:

Corollary 3: The transformations FT3 and BT3 preserve a tree structure mapped on an n-cube.

Theorem 4: A stretched binary tree (of the form shown in Figure 3b) of n levels can be mapped on an n-cube, for $n \geq 2$.

Proof: The case for n=2 is trivial. The case of n=3 is shown in Figure 5. The construction of a four level tree from a pair of 3-cubes can be found in [12]. We will now describe the inductive step. We assume that an n level stretched binary tree, as shown in Figure 4a, is mapped on an n-cube. To obtain an n+1 level tree in an n+1-cube:

- Duplicate the cube and the mapping. See Figure 4b.

---

[3]The two transformations define two of the many *rigid* transformations of a 3-cube. The rigid transformations include rotations and reflections of the original cube structure which preserve the adjacency between its nodes.

- Apply FT3 to the duplicate mapping using bit-2 as x_i, bit-1 as x_j and bit-0 as x_k to obtain a new mapping as in Figure 4c.
- Form an n+1-cube by connecting the nodes with like labels in the two n order subcubes. Append a 0 to the left of labels in the original subcube and a 1 to the left of those in the duplicate subcube (see Figure 4d).
- Deallocate links: 0S100-0S110 and 1S100-1S000, and allocate links: 0S000-1S000, 0S110-1S110 and 0S100-1S100. See Figure 4e.
- Apply the BT3 to the n+1 cube to obtain an n+1 level stretched binary tree rooted at 0S000. While applying the BT3, use the most significant bit as x_i, the third least significant bit (bit-2) as x_j, and the least significant bit (bit-0) as x_k. Replace the string 0S by S' to obtain a structure similar to the base structure we started with. See Figures 4f and 4g.

Appendix III

The tree set-up algorithm uses the following variables:

current-port: Every node in the cube has logN ports, each corresponding to a bit position. This variable keeps a running pointer to the current bit position being considered.
physical-id: Original label of a node.
current-id: A node label during current iteration.
port-relation(1..logN): An array of values specifying the current active connections of a node. All are initialized to "null" (inactive).

Following values are assigned to *port-relation(i)* variable:

"null":	No active connection.
"f":	Connection to "father" node.
"s":	Connection to "son" node.

The following is the compute phase of the tree set-up algorithm. This is followed by a distribution phase during which the connectivity information is sent to the appropriate physical node specified by the *current-id* variable.

```
for-all nodes do
  begin
  current-id = physical-id;
  {Set up 2^(n-3), 3 level trees.}
  case current-id( bits: 2..0) of
      0:   port-relation(0) = port-relation(2) = "s";
      1:   port-relation(0) = "f";
           port-relation(1) = port-relation(2) = "s";
      2:   port-relation(2) = "f";
      3:   port-relation(1) = "f";
      4:   port-relation(1) = "s";
           port-relation(2) = "f";
      5:   port-relation(2) = "f";
      6:   port-relation(0) = port-relation(2) = "s";
           port-relation(1) = "f";
      7:   port-relation(0) = "f";
```

```
end-case
for current-port = 3 to logN-1 do
  begin
  {Form larger trees iteratively.}
  if (current-id(current-port) = 1) then
  begin
  Apply FT3 to current-id's bits 2, 1 and 0;
  end
  if (Bits 3 through current-port-1 are 0) then
  begin
      case current-id( bits: current-port, 2, 1, 0 ) of
      0:   port-relation(2) = "f";
           port-relation(current-port) = "s";
      4:   port-relation(2) = "s";
           port-relation(current-port) = "s";
           port-relation(1) = "null";
      6:   port-relation(1) = "null";
           port-relation(current-port) = "f";
      8:   port-relation(2) = "null";
           port-relation(current-port) = "f";
      12:  port-relation(2) = "null";
           port-relation(current-port) = "f";
      14:  port-relation(current-port) = "s";
      end-case
  end
  Apply BT3 to bits current-port, 2 and 0 of current-id;
  end
end
```

References

[1] "The Mark III Hypercube-Ensemble Concurrent Computer"; J. C. Peterson et al., *ICPP* 1985.

[2] "The Cosmic Cube"; C. Seitz, *CACM*, January 1985.

[3] "CALTECH/JPL Mark II Hypercube Concurrent Processor"; J. Tuazon et al., *ICPP* 1985.

[4] "Inductive Computer Architectures: A Class of Supercomputer Architectures"; G. J. Lipovski, M. Malek and J. C. Browne, MCC Report, Parallel Processing Group, Microelectronic and Computer Technology Corporation, Austin, Texas.

[5] "Microprocessors: Architecture and Applications"; P. C. Patton, *IEEE Computer*, June 1985.

[6] "On the Mapping Problem"; S. Bokhari, *IEEE Transactions on Computers*, March 1981.

[7] Introduction to Computer Architecture; Editor: H. Stone, Science Research Associates Inc., 1975.

[8] "A Generalized Dictionary Machine for VLSI"; M. J. Atallah and S. R. Kosaraju, *IEEE Transaction on Computers*, February 1985.

[9] "The Binary Tree As An Interconnection Network: Applications to Multiprocessor Systems and VLSI"; E. Horowitz and A. Zorat, *IEEE Transactions on Computers*, April 1981.

[10] iPSC System Overview; Intel Corporation, October 1985.

[11] "Topological Properties of Hypercubes"; Y. Saad and M. H. Schultz, Research Report YALEU/DCS/RR-389, June 1985.

[12] "Scalability of a Binary Tree on a Hypercube"; S. R. Deshpande, Department of Computer Sciences Technical Report TR-86-01, University of Texas at Austin.

[13] "An Overview of the Texas Reconfigurable Array Computer"; M. C. Sejnowski et al, *Proc. of AFIPS NCC Conference*, 1980.

[14] "PASM: A Partitionable SIMD/MIMD System for Image Processing and Pattern Recognition"; H. J. Siegel, *IEEE Transactions on Computers*, December 1981.

[15] "Introduction to the Configurable, Highly Parallel Computer"; *IEEE Computer*, January 1982.

[16] "Reliability and Fault Diagnosis Analysis of Fault-Tolerant Multistage Interconnection Networks"; V. Cherkassky et al, *FTCS*, 1984.

[17] "The extra stage cube: a fault-tolerant interconnection network for supersystems"; G. B. Adams III and H. J. Siegel, *IEEE Transactions on Computers*, May, 1982.

[18] "On a Class of Multistage Interconnection Networks"; C. L. Wu and T. Y. Feng, *IEEE Transactions on Computers*, August, 1980.

[19] "KYKLOS: A Linear Growth Fault-Tolerant Interconnection Network"; B. L. Menezes and R. M. Jenevein, *ICPP*, 1985.

FT3						BT3					
x_i	x_j	x_k	y_i	y_j	y_k	x_i	x_j	x_k	y_i	y_j	y_k
0	0	0	1	0	0	0	0	0	0	0	1
0	0	1	0	0	0	0	0	1	1	0	1
0	1	0	1	0	1	0	1	0	0	0	0
0	1	1	0	0	1	0	1	1	1	0	0
1	0	0	1	1	0	1	0	0	0	1	1
1	0	1	0	1	0	1	0	1	1	1	1
1	1	0	1	1	1	1	1	0	0	1	0
1	1	1	0	1	1	1	1	1	1	1	0

Table 1.

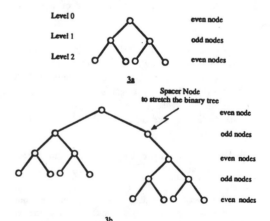

Figure 3.

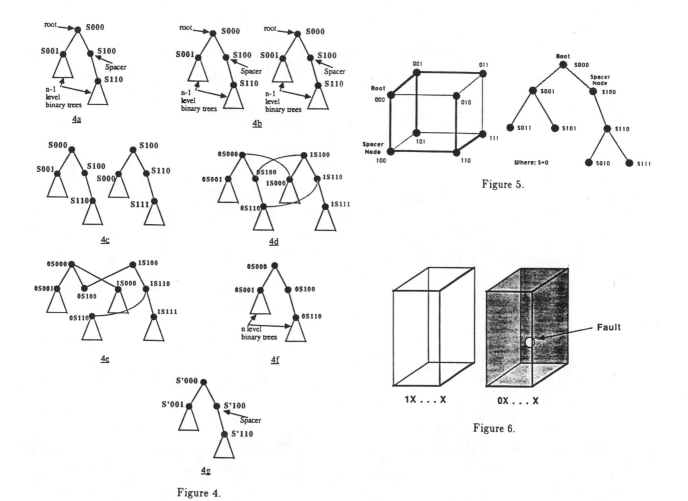

Figure 4.

Figure 5.

Figure 6.

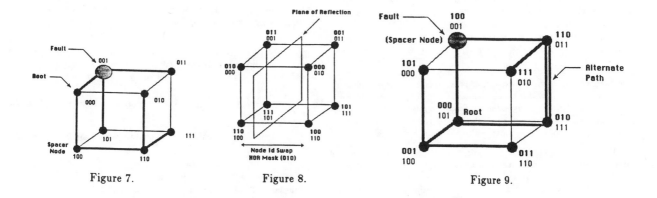

Figure 7.

Figure 8.

Figure 9.

On the Embedding of Arbitrary Meshes in Boolean Cubes with Expansion Two Dilation Two

Ching-Tien Ho and S. Lennart Johnsson
Department of Computer Science
Yale University
New Haven, CT 06520

Abstract   An embedding based on a binary-reflected Gray code [4] encoding of the mesh points in each dimension attains the minimum dilation, but the expansion of a d-dimensional mesh may be close to 2^d. A direct mapping method that yields dilation 2 and minimum expansion embeddings for most aspect ratios of two-dimensional meshes is presented. The average edge dilation asymptotically approaches one. The direct mapping method is also applied to higher dimensional meshes with preserved dilation.

1   Introduction

Processor utilization and communication time are two important considerations in selecting data structures and algorithms for *Ensemble Architectures*, i.e., architectures assembled out of a large number of identical parts. Communication is one of the most expensive resources in such an architecture, and its efficient utilization is imperative. In studying the efficient utilization of the communication system the communication needs of the computations are modeled by a graph, which we refer to as the *guest graph*. This graph discloses the interaction between the data elements of the computation. Similarly, the topology of the ensemble architecture is captured by a graph, the *host graph*. Each vertex represents a processor with local storage and each edge a communications link between processors. The guest graph is embedded in the host graph for the execution.

The embedding function f maps each vertex in the guest graph $G = (V_G, E_G)$ into a unique vertex in the host graph $H = (V_H, E_H)$. V_G and V_H denote the node sets of the guest and host graphs respectively, and E_G and E_H the edge sets. $|V_G|$ denotes the cardinality of the set V_G. The *expansion* of the mapping is $\frac{|V_H|}{|V_G|}$, and the dilation of the mapping is $max(distance(f(i), f(j)), \forall (i, j) \in E_G$. The *edge dilation* of edge (i, j) is $distance(f(i), f(j))$ and the *average edge dilation* is $\frac{1}{|E_G|} \sum (distance(f(i), f(j)), \forall (i, j) \in E_G$.

If each node of the guest graph is mapped to a distinct node of the host graph, then the expansion is a measure of the processor utilization. The slow down due to nearest neighbor communication in the original graph being extended to communication along paths is a function of the dilation, edge dilation, or average dilation, or the edge load (number of edges mapped to the same host edge).

We consider the embedding of arbitrarily shaped multi-dimensional meshes in Boolean cubes. It is well known that a multi-dimensional array can be embedded in a Boolean cube with dilation 1 by employing a binary-reflected Gray code [4] encoding of the indices [3,2]. The expansion is 1 if and only if the number of nodes in each dimension of the array is a power of 2. With an arbitrary number of nodes in each dimension, the expansion can be nearly 2^d for a d-dimensional mesh (if the number of nodes in dimension i is $2^{n_i}+1$). Embedding with dilation 3 and expansion < 2 is possible for any shape of 2-dimensional meshes[1]. The fraction of all possible 2-dimensional meshes having an expansion greater than 2 when embedded by a binary-reflected Gray code is $\approx 2\log_e 2 - 1 \approx 0.38$. The *direct mapping* method offers expansion < 2 for about 70% of the meshes for which the Gray code embedding has an expansion > 2. The average edge dilation is 1, asymptotically.

The *direct mapping* method is described in the context of embedding 2-dimensional meshes, then generalized to multi-dimensional meshes. The dilation is the same as for the 2-dimensional mesh embedding. The generalization described here is limited to meshes of an even number of dimensions. Different embedding methods can be employed to different pairs of dimensions.

2   Lower Bounds for the Expansion of Dilation One Embeddings

In this section we prove that for *any dilation one embedding* of an $N_1 \times N_2$ mesh into an n-cube, $n \geq \lceil \log_2 N_1 \rceil + \lceil \log_2 N_2 \rceil$. Expansion 1 requires that both N_1 and N_2 are powers of two. We also prove that the number of cube dimensions n for any dilation one embedding of a d-dimensional mesh, $N_1 \times N_2 \times \cdots \times N_d$, has to satisfy the condition $n \geq \lceil \log_2 N_1 \rceil + \lceil \log_2 N_2 \rceil + \cdots + \lceil \log_2 N_d \rceil$. The expansion is $2^{\lceil \log_2 N_1 \rceil + \lceil \log_2 N_2 \rceil + \cdots + \lceil \log_2 N_d \rceil} / (N_1 N_2 \cdots N_d)$, which is in the range of 1 to 2^d depending on the values of the $N_i's$.

Each node of the n-cube is represented by an n-bit binary number. Each node of the $N_1 \times N_2$ mesh is represented by an address (i, j), where $0 \leq i \leq N_1 - 1$, $0 \leq j \leq N_2 - 1$. There is a one-to-one mapping from edges of the mesh to edges of the cube in a dilation one embedding. By "an edge in a cube is in dimension i" we mean that the addresses of the two end points differ in bit i. The most significant bit (*msb*) is bit $n - 1$ and the least significant bit (*lsb*) is bit 0. The label on an edge in the mesh represents the dimension of the corresponding edge in the cube.

Theorem 1 *If an $N_1 \times N_2$ mesh is embedded in an n-dimensional Boolean cube with dilation one, then $n \geq \lceil \log_2 N_1 \rceil + \lceil \log_2 N_2 \rceil$.*

Proof: Label each edge in the mesh with a number that represents the dimension of the corresponding edge in the cube. A legal labelling should satisfy the following two properties:

1. Any cycle in the mesh must contain any label an even number of times.

2. Any path in the mesh must contain some label an odd number of times.

Consider any cycle of length 4 in the mesh. The labels of the four edges form a sequence (p, q, p, q), where $p \neq q$, Figure 1-(a). By extending this argument, it follows that any vertical or horizontal cut will only cut edges having the same label, Figure 1-(b). Now consider the labels of any horizontal path connecting all the N_2 nodes of a row. Since the corresponding cube nodes are distinct and the longest node-disjoint path in an n-cube is $2^n - 1$, the number of distinct labels on the edges forming a row is at least $\lceil \log_2 N_2 \rceil$. The same argument applies to any vertical path. Moreover, the set of labels on the horizontal paths must be disjoint from the set of labels on the vertical paths; otherwise there exist two adjacent edges with the same label, Figure 1-(c). Hence, the minimum number of dimensions required is $\lceil \log_2 N_1 \rceil + \lceil \log_2 N_2 \rceil$. ∎

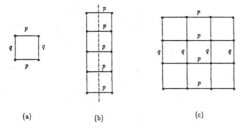

(a)   (b)   (c)

Figure 1: (a) Dimensions of a cycle of length 4. (b) Vertical or horizontal cuts. (c) The set of dimensions of vertical edges and the set of dimensions of horizontal edges are disjoint.

Theorem 2 *If an $N_1 \times N_2 \times \cdots \times N_d$ mesh is embedded in an n-cube with dilation one, then $n \geq \lceil \log_2 N_1 \rceil + \lceil \log_2 N_2 \rceil + \cdots + \lceil \log_2 N_d \rceil$.*

Proof: Since the set of cube dimensions used as labels for mesh edges in mesh dimension i is disjoint from the set of cube dimensions used as labels for mesh edges in dimension j, $i \neq j$, the proof follows that of theorem 1. ∎

3 Embedding Two-dimensional Meshes

3.1 Preliminaries

Let subcube 0 be the subcube that consists of all the nodes with the least significant bit of its address being 0. Subcube 1 is defined accordingly. An embedding of an $\alpha_1 N_1 \times \alpha_2 N_2$ mesh in an $(n_1 + n_2 + 1)$-cube, where $N_1 = 2^{n_1}$, $N_2 = 2^{n_2}$, $1 < \alpha_1, \alpha_2 < 2$ and $\alpha_1 \alpha_2 \leq 2$, is referred to as an (α_1, α_2)- embedding. All embeddings have dilation 2. $\alpha_i = \frac{\alpha_{ni}}{\alpha_{di}}$ with α_{ni} and α_{di} relatively prime, $1 \leq i \leq 2$. The values of (α_1, α_2) in this paper are $(\frac{5}{4}, \frac{3}{2})$, $(\frac{5}{4}, \frac{5}{4})^1$, $(\frac{11}{8}, \frac{11}{8})$ and $(\frac{9}{8}, \frac{7}{4})$. For the embeddings the mesh is partitioned into $\alpha_{n1} \times \alpha_{n2}$ blocks. The binary-reflected Gray code encoding is used for row and column indices for the upper left $N_1 \times N_2$ vertices, i.e., the vertices in the upper left $\alpha_{d1} \times \alpha_{d2}$ blocks[2]. The embedding of these nodes use all the nodes of subcube 0. Then we define the addresses of the remaining blocks by complementing the *msb* of the blocks defined in subcube 0. The addresses of the nodes in the block may require some transformation within the block such as V, H or O defined below in order to preserve the adjacency between blocks.

Definition 1 *The block at row r column c, $0 \leq r < \alpha_{d1}$, $0 \leq c < \alpha_{d2}$, is called block i, $i = (G(r)||G(c))$, $G(i)$ is the binary-reflected Gray code of i and '$||$' is the concatenation operator.*

Definition 2 *Let i be a block number, and define $C(i)$ as a function that complements the msb of each node address in the block.*

Definition 3 *Let i be a block number, and define $V(i)$ as the transformation function within block i that flips the block vertically and symmetrically around a horizontal line. Similarly define $H(i)$ as a function that flips the block horizontally, and symmetrically around a vertical line. Let $O(i)$ be the composed function $H \circ V(i)$ (or $V \circ H(i)$) that maps each node in i into a new node at the opposite position of the center of the block, called origin transformation. See Figure 2 for reference.*

Proving that the embedding is correct with dilation 2 is the same as proving the following properties:

---

[1] with better average edge dilation than $(\frac{5}{4}, \frac{3}{2})$-embedding.

[2] There is an exception in $(\frac{5}{4}, \frac{5}{4})$-embedding.

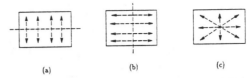

(a)   (b)   (c)

Figure 2: (a) Vertical Transformation. (b) Horizontal Transformation. (c) Origin Transformation.

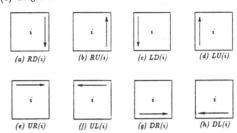

(a) RD(i) (b) RU(i) (c) LD(i) (d) LU(i)

(e) UR(i) (f) UL(i) (g) DR(i) (h) DL(i)

Figure 3: Eight directed boundary line of block i.

1. All the addresses of nodes in blocks mapped to subcube 1 are defined by one of $C(i)$, $H \circ C(i)$, $V \circ C(i)$ and $O \circ C(i)$ with distinct i, $0 \leq i < \alpha_{d1}\alpha_{d2}$.

2. The addresses of mesh nodes on boundaries of adjacent blocks, which are in subcube 0 and subcube 1, respectively, differ in at most two bits for each corresponding pair of nodes.

3. The addresses of boundary nodes of adjacent blocks, which are both in subcube 1, differ in at most two bits for each corresponding pair of nodes.

In the following, we use HC, VC and OC to represent the function compositions $H \circ C$, $V \circ C$ and $O \circ C$ respectively.

3.2 A $(\frac{5}{4}, \frac{3}{2})$-Embedding

Definition 4 *The Hamming distance of two directed lines, composed of the same number of vertices, is the maximum Hamming distance for each pair of corresponding vertices in the two directed lines.*

Definition 5 *Define RD, RU, LD, LU, UR, UL, DR and DL as the directed boundary lines of a given block as shown in Figure 3.*

To embed a $\frac{5}{4}N_1 \times \frac{3}{2}N_2$ mesh into an $(n_1 + n_2 + 1)$-cube, we use the mapping represented by Figure 4. In this figure, each block is of the size $\frac{N_1}{4} \times \frac{N_2}{2}$. Note that the '$*$' sign on the dashed line means that the Hamming distance of the mapped two boundary lines near the dashed line is 2. The Hamming distance of the ones mapped from other adjacent nodes in the mesh is always 1.

Lemma 1 *Figure 4 represents an embedding of a $\frac{5}{4}N_1 \times \frac{3}{2}N_2$ mesh into an $(n_1 + n_2 + 1)$-cube with dilation 2.*

Proof: To prove the embedding is correct and the dilation is 2, we prove the three properties mentioned above. Property 1 is obvious from the figure. To prove property 2, we prove that the Hamming distance of each of the 6 pairs of adjacent (in the mesh) boundary lines of subcube 0 and subcube 1, respectively, is at most 2. For instance,

$Hamming(RD(3), LD(OC(1)))$
$\leq Hamming(RD(3), RU(1)) + Hamming(RU(1), LD(OC(1))) = 2.$

$Hamming(DR(5), UR(OC(4)))$
$\leq Hamming(DR(5), DL(4)) + Hamming(DL(4), UR(OC(4))) = 2.$

0	1	C(0)
2	3	OC(1)
6	7	OC(3)
4	5	OC(7)
C(6)	OC(4)	OC(5)

Figure 4: Global view of $(\frac{5}{4}, \frac{3}{2})$-embedding.

000r0c	000r1c	100r0c
001r0c	001r1c	100r1c
011r0c	011r1c	101r1c
010r0c	010r1c	111r1c
111r0c	110r0c	110r1c

Figure 5: Block addresses of the $(\frac{5}{4}, \frac{3}{2})$-embedding.

000000	000001	000011	000010	100000	100001
000100	000101	000111	000110	100100	100101
001100	001101	001111	001110	100110	100111
001000	001001	001011	001010	100010	100011
011000	011001	011011	011010	101010	101011
011100	011101	011111	011110	101110	101111
010100	010101	010111	010110	111110	111111
010000	010001	010011	010010	111010	111011
111000	111001	110001	110000	110010	110011
111100	111101	110101	110100	110110	110111

Figure 6: Embedding of a 10×6 mesh into a 6-cube.

Note that $LD(OC(1)) = RU(C(1))$ and $UR(OC(4)) = DL(C(4))$ in the above expression. The rest of the proofs are similar. Property 3 can be shown similarly. For instance,

$Hamming(DR(C(0)), UR(OC(1))) = Hamming(DR(0), DL(1)) = 1.$

$Hamming(LD(OC(4)), RD(C(6))) = Hamming(RU(4), RD(6)) = 1.$

∎

Figure 5 shows the block addresses, i.e., nodes in the same block share some common bits. Figure 6 shows the embedding of a 10×6 mesh into a 6-cube.

The mapping function f, translating the mesh addresses to the cube addresses, can be derived from Figure 4. Let $R = (i_{n_1} i_{n_1-1} \ldots i_0)$, $C = (j_{n_2} j_{n_2-1} \ldots j_0)$, $R_g = (i_{n_1-1} i_{n_1-2})$, $C_g = (j_{n_2-1})$, $R_l = (i_{n_1-3} i_{n_1-4} \ldots i_0)$, $C_l = (j_{n_2-2} j_{n_2-3} \ldots j_0)$, $\hat{R}_g = i_{n_1} \| R_g$, $\hat{C}_g = j_{n_2} \| C_g$ and $G_k(i)$ be the binary-reflected Gray code of i in the k-bits form. Then

$$f(R,C) = \begin{cases} 0\|G_{n_1}(R)\|G_{n_2}(C), & \text{if } \hat{R}_g = 0xx, \hat{C}_g = 0x; \\ 1\|G_{n_1}(R)\|G_{n_2}(C), & \text{if } \hat{R}_g = 000, \hat{C}_g = 10; \\ 1\|G_{n_1}((R_g - 1)\|\overline{R_l})\|G_{n_2}((C_g - 1)\|\overline{C_l}), & \\ \qquad \text{if } \hat{R}_g = 100, \hat{C}_g = 01 \text{ or } \hat{R}_g \neq 000, \hat{C}_g = 10; \\ 1\|G_{n_1}((R_g - 2)\|R_l)\|G_{n_2}(C), & \text{if } \hat{R}_g = 100, \hat{C}_g = 00. \end{cases}$$

Here the first line describes blocks marked with 0 to 7, the second line describes block $C(0)$, the third line describes the rest of the blocks except block $C(6)$, which is described by the last line. Note that the dilation 2 of the embedding can also be proved by

$$Hamming(f(R,C), f(R-1,C)) \le 2, \quad \forall 0 < R < \frac{5}{4}N_1, 0 \le C < \frac{3}{2}N_2$$

and

$$Hamming(f(R,C), f(R,C-1)) \le 2, \quad \forall 0 \le R < \frac{5}{4}N_1, 0 < C < \frac{3}{2}N_2$$

3.3 Discussion

The number of edges with dilation 2 in the $(\frac{5}{4}, \frac{3}{2})$-embedding is $N_1 + N_2$ and the total number of edges is $\frac{1}{4}(15N_1N_2 - 5N_1 - 6N_2)$, as summarized in Table 1. As both N_1 and N_2 increase, the average edge dilation approaches 1. The table also contains figures for the embedding of meshes with three other aspect ratios.

Figure 7 shows a $(\frac{5}{4}, \frac{5}{4})$-embedding. The proofs of correctness and dilation 2 are similar to that in the $(\frac{5}{4}, \frac{3}{2})$-embedding. The $(\frac{5}{4}, \frac{5}{4})$-embedding achieves lower average edge dilation than the $(\frac{5}{4}, \frac{3}{2})$-embedding. In the embedding, the number of edges with dilation 2 is $\frac{1}{2}(N_1 + N_2)$.

Figure 8 shows the $(\frac{11}{8}, \frac{11}{8})$-embedding, and Figure 9 the $(\frac{9}{8}, \frac{7}{4})$-embedding.

Figure 10 shows the union of the set of pairs for which one dimension can be saved by the direct mapping method. The ratio of

Embed-ding	# of Edges w. Dil. 2	Average Dilation	Max Avg Dilation
$(\frac{5}{4}, \frac{3}{2})$	$N_1 + N_2$	$1 + \frac{4(N_1+N_2)}{15N_1N_2 - 5N_1 - 6N_2}$	1.3
$(\frac{5}{4}, \frac{5}{4})$	$\frac{1}{2}(N_1 + N_2)$	$1 + \frac{8(N_1+N_2)}{25N_1N_2 - 10N_1 - 10N_2}$	1.1
$(\frac{11}{8}, \frac{11}{8})$	$\frac{5}{8}N_1 + 2N_2$	$1 + \frac{20N_1+64N_2}{121N_1N_2 - 44N_1 - 44N_2}$	1.1
$(\frac{9}{8}, \frac{7}{4})$	$\frac{3}{8}N_1 + N_2$	$1 + \frac{12N_1+32N_2}{63N_1N_2 - 36N_1 - 56N_2}$	1.2

Table 1: Summary of embeddings for various aspect ratios.

the number of these pairs to the total number of pairs is $\approx \frac{1}{4}$, independent of the range of n_1, n_2. Hence, a total of $\approx 87\%$ of all meshes can be embedded with expansion < 2, and dilation 2 with either the binary-reflected Gray code embedding, or the direct embedding described here. The worst-case expansion using the direct mapping methods is about 2.4. The average edge dilation of the direct mapping is asymptotically 1.

4 Embedding of Multi-dimensional Arrays

We only consider multi-dimensional meshes with an even number of dimensions. For such meshes the dilation remains the same as for the 2-dimensional mesh embedding. Different embedding methods can be applied to different pairs of dimensions with the overall dilation being the maximum of all the dilations.

Theorem 3 *Given an embedding function f_2 which maps a guest mesh G_i into a host cube of dimension $dim(f_2, G_i)$ with dilation δ, then there exists an embedding function which maps a 2d-dimensional array of form $G_1 \times G_2 \times \cdots \times G_d$ into a cube of dimension $\sum_{i=1}^{d} dim(f_2, G_i)$ with dilation δ.*

Proof: Define the new mapping function f_{2d} as follows:

$$f_{2d}(a_1, b_1, a_2, b_2, ..., a_d, b_d) = f_2(a_1, b_1)\|f_2(a_2, b_2)\|\cdots\|f_2(a_d, b_d)$$

where (a_i, b_i) is a vertex in mesh G_i. From the mapping function f_{2d} it follows that any two adjacent vertices in the $2d$ dimensional array are mapped to nodes with addresses differing in exactly one of the d groups of bits, since the dimension of the mesh in which the nodes are adjacent belong to precisely one of the embedded 2-dimensional meshes. Since the dilation in any 2-dimensional mesh embedding is δ the dilation of the mapping function f_{2d} is also δ. ∎

Corollary 1 *Given an embedding function f_{2_i} which maps a guest mesh G_i into a host cube of dimension $dim(f_{2_i}, G_i)$ with dilation δ_i, then there exists an embedding function which maps a 2d-dimensional array of form $G_1 \times G_2 \times \cdots \times G_d$ into a cube of dimension $\sum_{i=1}^{d} dim(f_{2_i}, G_i)$ with dilation $\max(\delta_1, \delta_2, ..., \delta_d)$.*

0	1	3	2	HC(2)
4	5	7	6	HC(6)
12	13	15	14	HC(14)
8	9	11	OC(15)	OC(13)
VC(8)	VC(9)	VC(11)	OC(7)	OC(5)

Figure 7: Global view of $(\frac{5}{4}, \frac{5}{4})$-embedding.

0	1	3	2	6	7	5	4	HC(4)	HC(5)	HC(7)
8	9	11	10	14	15	13	12	HC(12)	HC(13)	HC(15)
24	25	27	26	30	31	29	28	HC(28)	HC(29)	HC(31)
16	17	19	18	22	23	21	20	HC(20)	HC(21)	HC(23)
48	49	51	50	54	55	53	52	HC(52)	HC(53)	HC(55)
56	57	59	58	62	63	61	60	HC(60)	HC(61)	HC(63)
40	41	43	42	46	47	45	44	HC(44)	HC(45)	HC(47)
32	33	35	34	38	39	37	36	HC(36)	HC(37)	HC(39)
C(40)	C(41)	C(43)	C(42)	OC(34)	OC(35)	OC(33)	OC(32)	C(48)	C(49)	C(51)
C(56)	C(57)	C(59)	C(58)	OC(50)	VC(2)	VC(3)	VC(1)	VC(0)	C(17)	C(19)
C(24)	C(25)	C(27)	C(26)	OC(18)	VC(10)	VC(11)	VC(9)	VC(8)	OC(16)	VC(22)

Figure 8: Global view of the $(\frac{11}{8}, \frac{11}{8})$-embedding.

0	1	3	2	HC(2)	HC(3)	HC(1)
4	5	7	6	HC(6)	HC(7)	HC(5)
12	13	15	14	HC(14)	HC(15)	HC(13)
8	9	11	10	HC(10)	HC(11)	HC(9)
24	25	27	26	HC(26)	HC(27)	HC(25)
28	29	31	30	HC(30)	HC(31)	HC(29)
20	21	23	22	HC(22)	HC(23)	HC(21)
16	17	19	18	C(16)	OC(20)	C(4)
C(0)	VC(17)	VC(19)	VC(18)	C(24)	OC(28)	C(12)

Figure 9: Global view of the $(\frac{9}{8}, \frac{7}{4})$-embedding.

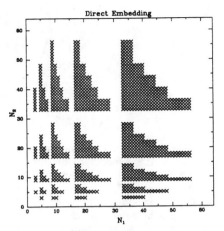

Figure 10: The aspect ratios for which one dimension can be saved by the direct mapping method.

There exist many choices in pairing the $2d$ dimensions into d pairs. Different pairings may result in different expansions. Let $N_i = \alpha_i 2^{n_i}$, $1 \leq \alpha_i < 2$ be the number of mesh points in dimension i. In order to minimize the expansion, pairs should be chosen such that the maximum number of pairs have a product for which a direct embedding exists.

5 Summary

The binary-reflected Gray code embedding of two-dimensional meshes yields dilation 1, and expansion of less than 2 for about 62% of all possible aspect ratios. For 70% of the remaining 38% the direct embedding method yields a dilation 2, expansion 2 embedding. Generalizing the direct embedding to multi-dimensional arrays yields embeddings with the same dilation as in the two-dimensional case. The average edge dilation for the direct mapping method asymptotically approaches 1. The direct embedding method generalizes to end-around meshes.

Acknowledgement Thanks go to Chris Hatchell for his assistance with the manuscript. This work has been supported in part by the Office of Naval Research under Contracts N00014-84-K-0043 and N00014-86-K-0564.

References

[1] D.S. Greenberg. *Optimum Expansion Embeddings of Meshes in Hypercubes.* Technical Report YALEU/CSD/RR-535, Yale University, Dept. of Computer Science, in preparation 1987.

[2] S.L. Johnsson. Communication efficient basic linear algebra computations on hypercube architectures. *Journal of Parallel and Distributed Computing*, 1986. Report YALEU/CSD/RR-361, January 1985, Dept. of Computer Science, Yale University.

[3] S.L. Johnsson and P. Li. *Solutionset for AMA/CS 146.* Technical Report 5085:DF:83, California Institute of Technology, May 1983.

[4] E.M. Reingold, J. Nievergelt, and N. Deo. *Combinatorial Algorithms.* Prentice Hall, 1977.

Multigrid Algorithms on the Hypercube Multiprocessor

TONY F. CHAN AND YOUCEF SAAD

Abstract—This paper examines several ways of implementing multigrid algorithms on the hypercube multiprocessor. We consider both the standard multigrid algorithms and a concurrent version proposed by Gannon and Van Rosendale. We present several mappings of the mesh points onto the nodes of the cube. The main property of these mappings, which are based on binary reflected Gray codes, is that the distance between neighboring grid points remains constant from one grid level to another. This results in a communication effective implementation of multigrid algorithms on the hypercube multiprocessor.

Index Terms—Gray codes, hypercube multiprocessor, multigrid algorithms, partial differential equations, parallel computing.

I. INTRODUCTION

IN recent years there has been a growing interest in the design of parallel algorithms for solving various mathematical problems that arise in scientific computing. One of the major objectives is to construct algorithms, either by restructuring existing ones designed for sequential machines or by inventing new algorithms, that can efficiently exploit the parallelism available in a given machine architecture. This task is often complicated by the need for efficient communication between the processors in a parallel architecture. This communication overhead, which is absent in analyses of sequential algorithms, can be a bottleneck if not handled efficiently. Thus, a successful implementation of an algorithm in a parallel architecture must not only decompose a given problem into appropriate smaller tasks for each of the individual processors to perform, but also must arrange this assignment so that the communication overhead is kept at a minimum.

In this paper, we study in detail a particular algorithm–architecture combination: the implementation of the class of multigrid algorithms for solving elliptic partial differential equations on hypercube multiprocessors. Multigrid algorithms are among the most efficient methods for solving partial differential equations. In addition to their immediate effects on applications, multigrid algorithms are also of theoretical interest because it can be proven that they can compute a solution to truncation error accuracy in time proportional to the number of unknowns. This optimality result, together with the fact that many aspects of the multigrid algorithms are highly parallelizable, makes it natural to consider parallel implementation of multigrid algorithms. There have been a few papers published on this optic: Grosch [5], [6], Brandt [2], Gannon and Van Rosendale [4], and Chan and Schreiber [3].

The hierarchy of grids in multigrid algorithms presents a special challenge in minimizing the communication overhead in a parallel implementation. For even though it is possible to map the grid points of the finest grid onto many architectures such that neighboring grid points are mapped into neighboring processors, it is generally much more difficult to preserve this proximity property for the coarser grids required in the multigrid algorithms. Grosch [6] asserts that a perfectly shufled nearest neighbor array is a suitable architecture. Gannon and Van Rosendale [4] propose a concurrent variation of the standard multigrid algorithms and consider implementations on mesh-connected arrays, permutation networks and direct VLSI imbeddings. In this paper, we consider the hypercube multiprocessor [12]. Of the many parallel architectures that have been proposed in the past few years, the hypercube multiprocessor is one of a few that is commercially available and one for which there has been some experience in its usage. We show that the hypercube architecture is also ideally suited to the implementation of multigrid algorithms, especially regarding the communication overhead.

In Section II, we briefly describe the architecture of the hypercube and in Section III we describe the essential features of the multigrid algorithms with regard to their parallel implementations. In Section IV, we consider various mappings of the grid structures behind the multigrid algorithms into the nodes of the hypercube in a communication-effective way. In Section V, we briefly analyze the arithmetic and communication complexity of the proposed parallel algorithms and we present some concluding remarks in Section VI.

II. THE HYPERCUBE PARALLEL PROCESSOR

Hypercubes are multiprocessor arrays with powerful interconnection features introduced under different names (Cosmic cube, Boolean n-cube, n-cube, etc. See [1], [7], and [12] for references). An n-cube consists of 2^n nodes that are numbered by n-bit binary numbers, from 0 to $2^n - 1$ and interconnected so that there is a link between two processors if and only if their binary representation differs by one and only one bit. For the case $n = 3$, the 8 nodes can be represented as the vertices of a three-dimensional cube, see Fig. 1.

Manuscript received March 12, 1985; revised April 2, 1986. This work was supported in part by the Office of Naval Research under Grant N00014-82-K-0184, by IBM/Kingston under a joint study grant, by the Department of Energy under Contract DE-AC02-81ER10996, and by the Army Research Office under Contract DAAG-83-0177.

The authors are with the Department of Computer Science, Yale University, New Haven, CT 06520.

IEEE Log Number 8610930.

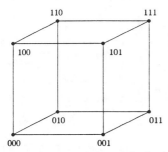
Fig. 1. 3-dimensional view of the 3-cube.

There are many reasons for the recent growing interest in the hypercube configuration. One of them, perhaps the most important, is that the hypercube imbeds many of the classical topologies such as two-dimensional or three-dimensional meshes (in fact arbitrary dimension meshes can be embedded) [11], [12]. The diameter of an n-cube is n: to reach a node from any other node one needs to cross at most n interprocessor connections. Another appealing feature of the hypercube is its homogeneity and symmetrical properties. Unlike many other ensemble architectures, such as tree or shuffle-exchange structures, no node plays a particular role. This facilitates algorithm design as well as programming. On the other hand, each node has a fan-out of n, a logarithmically increasing function of the total number of processors, and so with increasing n, there will be increasing hardware difficulties to fabricate each of these nodes.

Seitz [12] describes a real hypercube machine which is utilized at Caltech, and for the first time presents some details on software and applications of a machine based on the hypercube architecture. Saad and Schultz [11] analyze the intrinsic topological properties of the hypercube regarded as a graph, and propose several algorithms for transferring data between its nodes [10]. A generalization of the hypercube topology has been proposed by Bhuyan and Agrawal [1].

III. Multigrid Algorithms

In this section, we describe briefly the essential features of the multigrid algorithms that are relevant to their implementation on the hypercube.

Multigrid algorithms are generally used to solve continuous problems defined by differential or integral equations on a given region in space. To facilitate our presentation, we restrict our attention to the important case of the solution of linear elliptic differential equation

$$Lu = f$$

on a d-dimensional square in R^d. Such problems are usually solved approximately by discretizing the problem via a d-dimensional grid, say with m grid points in each coordinate direction. After applying an appropriate discretization technique (e.g., finite difference or finite element), the differential equation is transformed into a set of linear algebraic equations of size m^d. Many different methods can be used to solve this set of algebraic equations, e.g., Gaussian elimination or conjugate gradient methods. The class of multigrid methods is distinguished from others by their use of a hierarchy of coarser grids, in addition to the one on which the solution is sought, in order to improve efficiency. The basic idea is that if an iterative method (such as the Gauss–Seidel relaxation method) is used on the finest grid, convergence usually slows down after the high-frequency components of the error have been annihilated. Thus, by transferring the problem onto a coarser grid, the lower frequencies become the high frequencies of the coarser grid, and therefore can be annihilated more rapidly than on the fine grid. Employing this idea recursively, one eventually arrives at a grid that is coarse enough that the problem can be solved completely by either direct or iterative methods.

To describe the method more precisely, we denote the hierarchy of grids by G^i, with G^1 being the coarsest grid, the discretization of the elliptic operator on G^i by L^i and the corresponding solution and right-hand side by u^i and f^i, the operation of projection from G^i onto a coarser grid G^{i-1} by P^i and the interpolation back onto G^i from a coarser grid G^{i-1} by I^i. With this notation, the classical multigrid algorithm can now be described succintly as

Algorithm MG (L^i, f^i, u^i)
   Comment: Solve $L^i u^i = f^i$.
     if G^i is the coarsest grid **then**
       Solve $L^i u^i = f^i$ exactly.
     else
       Perform s smoothing iterations.
       Compute the residual:
         $r^i := f^i - L^i u^i$.
       Project the residual onto the next coarser grid:
         $g^{i-1} := P^i r^i$.
       Solve the coarse grid problem $L^{i-1} v^{i-1} = g^{i-1}$ recursively by c iterations of **MG**, i.e., repeat c times:
         MG$(L^{i-1}, g^{i-1}, v^{i-1})$, starting with $v^{i-1} := 0$.
       Interpolate the correction from G^{i-1} back to G^i:
         $u^i := u^i + I^i v^{i-1}$.
    endif.

The parameter c controls the flow of the algorithm, in particular the frequency with which the various grids are visited. The larger c is, the more time the algorithm spends on the coarser grids. The most common cases of $c = 1$ and $c = 2$ are often referred to as the V cycle and the W cycle, respectively.

There are many variants of the above multigrid algorithms, with different numerical properties, e.g., ones more suitable for nonlinear problems. The major steps, however, remain the same as in the above algorithm. In particular, the computations on a given grid and the transfers between neighboring grids as illustrated in the algorithm are typical. It is therefore sufficient, for the purpose of implementation on parallel systems, to consider the above algorithm.

IV. Paralellism in Multigrid Algorithms

Now we consider implementation on a parallel machine. The major steps of Algorithm MG are

  1) smoothing;
  2) computation of the residual;
  3) projection onto a coarser grid;
  4) interpolation from a coarser grid.

The first two are *intra*-grid operations while the last two are *inter*-grid ones. There are generally two opportunities for exploiting parallelism: performing operations on a given grid in parallel and performing operations on all grids in parallel. The first approach is more straightforward. Since the operator L^i is usually a local operator, both the smoother (e.g., Jacobi or red-black SOR) and the computation of the residual can be computed in parallel. Similarly, the operators P^i and I^i are also local operators and thus the projection and interpolation steps can also be performed in parallel. Such parallel multigrid algorithms have been considered by Grosch [5], [6], Brandt [2], and Chan and Schreiber [3]. The major drawback of this class of parallel multigrid methods is that at any given instance, only one grid is active, and therefore, the processors assigned to the other grids are idle. In order to have more efficient processor utilization, Gannon and Van Rosendale [4] considered a *concurrent* multigrid algorithm in which all processors on all grids are active all the time. Note that this approach represents a deviation from the standard multigrid algorithm and the extra operations must be designed carefully so as to improve and not diminish the rate of convergence.

For simplicity, we assume throughout this paper that the number of grid points in each coordinate direction on G^i, denoted by m_i, is given by $m_i = 2^{i-1}m_1$ and that the L^i's are nearest-neighbor stencils (e.g., the standard second order centered difference stencil for the Laplacian). For such problems, the natural architecture for the multigrid algorithm is the *pyramid*, a one-dimensional version of which is shown in Fig. 2. The "$\cdot$" points correspond to the coarsest level, the "x" points to the second level and the "o" points to the third and finest level. This topology completely describes the communication pattern between each grid point in the grid hierarchy. In other words, each connection in the pyramid represents a data flow path required by the algorithm. Unfortunately, for two- or three-dimensional elliptic problems, the corresponding pyramid is three-dimensional, and therefore cannot be easily implemented in two-dimensional architectures without creating long communication delays. For example, long wires are required in a direct VLSI implementation.

In this paper we are primarily interested in ensemble architectures consisting of a large number of identical processors interconnected to one another according to some convenient pattern. There is no global memory and no global bus. Although some designs may incoporate a global bus this does not constitute the main way of intercommunication. One advantage of such types of architectures is the simplicity of their design. The nodes are identical and can be produced at relatively low cost. Communication in ensemble architectures is done by message passing; data or code are transferred from Processor A to Processor B by traveling across a sequence of nearest neighbor nodes starting with node A and ending with B. For a given mapping of the pyramid onto the ensemble architecture, grid points that are direct neighbors on the pyramid may be assigned to processors that are far away from each other which may result in an increase in communication overhead. Therefore, given a machine on which the multigrid algorithm is to be implemented, the first task is to map the

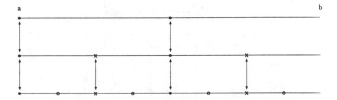

Fig. 2. One-dimensional pyramid.

pyramid architecture into the architecture of the given machine in such a way that the communication paths represented in the pyramid are as *short* as possible on the machine. Notice that these communication paths involve both grid points on the same grid and on other grids. While preserving locality on the finest grid for the *intragrid* communications is relatively easy on many parallel architectures, the *intergrid* communications and the need to preserve locality on coarser grids often present difficulties because neighboring grid points on the coarser grids may not be mapped onto neighboring processors. Grosch [5], [6] proposes a perfectly shuffled nearest-neighbor array to handle this problem. Gannon and Van Rosendale [4] consider a concurrent multigrid algorithm and suggested mappings for various parallel architectures, such as the nearest-neighbor mesh-connected arrays, the mesh-shuffle connected network and the omega network, but most of their mappings do not succeed in preserving the locality of coarser grids communication paths in the pyramid. In the next section, we will consider mappings of the pyramid onto the hypercube and show that it is possible to map the pyramid into the hypercube so that all communication paths in the pyramid are mapped into communication paths in the hypercube with length bounded by 2.

In designing such mappings, it is important to note that if the concurrent multigrid algorithm is to be implemented, then each grid point of the pyramid must be mapped into distinct processors. If only the standard multigrid algorithm is to be implemented, then points on different grids can be mapped into the same processor. This consideration may impose different constraints on the mapping.

V. Mesh to Hypercube Mappings

In this section, we are concerned with the problem of mapping general grids in 1-D, 2-D, or 3-D into the hypercube. Clearly there are numerous ways to map grid points into the 2^n processors in general. For reasons of communication efficiency we are interested in those mappings that have the property that any two neighboring points of the grid belong to neighboring processors. This is a fairly easy problem to which we will bring a solution in Section IV-A.

As mentioned in the introduction, a more critical requirement for the multigrid algorithms is that two grid points that are neighbors in the finer grid should remain either neighbors or close to each other when they are considered as grid points of a coarse grid. In other words, it should not only be inexpensive to access a neighboring point of the same grid but also a neighboring point of a grid of a different level.

A. One-Dimensional Meshes and Gray Codes

Consider the problem of assigning $N = 2^n$ mesh points which discretize some real interval, into an n-cube in such a way as to preserve the proximity property, i.e., so that any two neighboring mesh points belong to neighboring nodes. Another way of viewing the problem is that we are seeking a path of length $N = 2^n$ that crosses each node once and only once. In graph theory terminology, we are looking for a Hamiltonian path.

If we number the nodes of the hypercube according to its definition, i.e., so that two neighboring nodes differ by one and only one bit, a Hamiltonian path simply represents a sequence of n-binary numbers such that any two successive numbers have only one different bit and such that all n-bit binary numbers are represented in the sequence. Binary sequences with these properties are called Gray codes, and have been extensively studied in coding theory [9].

One of the simplest methods for generating Gray codes is as follows. Let $G_i = \{g_0, g_2, \cdots, g_{2i-1}\}$ be the i-bit Gray code, with $G_1 \equiv \{0, 1\}$ and denote by G_i^R the sequence obtained from G_i by reversing its order, and by $0G_i$ (respectively, $1G_i$) the sequence obtained from G_i by prefixing a zero (respectively, a one) to each element of the sequence. Then Gray codes of arbitrary order can be generated by the recursion

$$G_{i+1} = \{0G_i, 1G_i^R\} \quad i = 1, \cdots. \quad (5.1)$$

For example,

$$G_2 = \{00, 01, 11, 10\}$$

$$G_3 = \{000, 001, 011, 010, 110, 111, 101, 100\}. \quad (5.2)$$

There are many possible Gray codes; the particular one generated by the above algorithm is called a *binary reflected Gray code*.

We now describe a second algorithm for generating the binary reflected Gray code which will turn out to be more useful later. Given the n-bit binary reflected Gray code

$$G_n = \{g_0, g_1, \cdots g_{2^n-1}\}$$

one can generate the $(n + 1)$-bit Gray-code as follows:

$$G_{n+1} = \{g_0 0, g_0 1, g_1 1, g_1 0, g_2 0, g_2 1,$$
$$g_3 1, g_3 0, \cdots g_i 0, g_i 1, g_{i+1} 1, g_{i+1} 0, \cdots \}.$$

In other words, the general pattern for generating G_{n+1} is to expand any two successive nodes a, b of G_n into the nodes $a0$, $a1$, $b1$, $b0$. It can be proved that this algorithm indeed generates the binary reflected Gray code [9].

We now return to our original problem of assigning the $N = 2^n$ mesh-points of a discretized interval to the 2^n nodes of an n-cube. A desirable property is that the mesh points are assigned to neighboring processors, in order to achieve locality in communication. According to our previous discussion on Gray codes, it is clear that the solution is to assign successive nodes of the mesh to the successive nodes of a Gray code sequence, i.e., to the nodes of the cube whose binary numbers form a Gray code sequence. Thus, if there are 8 grid points numbered from 0 to 7 such that

$$x_0 < x_1 < x_2 < x_3 < x_4 < x_5 < x_6 < x_7$$

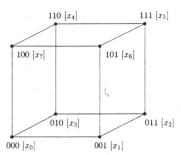

Fig. 3. Grid point assignment for a one-dimensional mesh of 8 points

can be assigned successively to the nodes of the sequence in Section V-B in that order; see Fig. 3.

B. Meshes in Higher Dimensional Spaces

One of the most attractive properties of the hypercube as a network, is that it can imbed meshes of arbitrary dimensions. This may in fact be the main reason for the success of the hypercube as a multiprocessor. Consider an $m_1 \times m_2 \cdots \times m_d$ mesh in the d-dimensional space R^d and assume that the mesh size in each direction is a power of 2, i.e., it is such that $m_i = 2^{p_i}$. Let $n = p_1 + p_2 + \cdots p_d$ and consider the problem of mapping the mesh points into the n-cube, one mesh point per node. Observe that we have just enough nodes to accomodate one mesh point per node. We show next how to extend the ideas of the previous section to more than one dimension.

This is best illustrated by an example. Consider an 8×4 mesh of a 2-dimensional problem, i.e., $d = 2$, $p_1 = 3$, $p_2 = 2$, $n = p_1 + p_2 = 5$. A binary number A of any node of the 5-cube can be regarded as consisting of two parts: its first three bits and its last two bits, which we write in the form

$$A = b_1 b_2 b_3 c_1 c_2$$

where b_i and c_j are binary bits. It is clear from the definitions of an n-cube that when the last two bits are fixed, the resulting 2^{p_1} nodes form a p_1-cube (with $p_1 = 3$). Likewise, whenever we fix the first three bits we obtain a p_2-cube. The mapping then becomes clear. Choosing a 3-bit Gray code for the x direction and a 2-bit Gray code for the y direction, the point (x_i, y_j) of the mesh is assigned to the node $b_1 b_2 b_3 c_1 c_2$ where $b_1 b_2 b_3$ is the 3-bit Gray code for x_i while $c_1 c_2$ is the 2-bit Gray code for y_j. We refer to the mapping $(x_i, y_j) \rightarrow b_1 b_2 b_3 c_1 c_2$ as the *cross product* of the two mappings $x_i \rightarrow b_1 b_2 b_3$ and $y_j \rightarrow c_1 c_2$. This mapping is illustrated in Fig. 4 where the binary node number of any grid-point is obtained by concatenating its binary x coordinate and its binary y coordinate. Note that any one column of grid points forms a Gray code and any one row of nodes forms a Gray code.

Generalizations to higher dimensions are straightforward. We can state the following general theorem.

Theorem 5:1: Any $m_1 \times m_2 \cdots \times m_d$ mesh in the d-dimensional space R^d where $m_i = 2^{p_i}$, can be mapped into an n-cube where $n = p_1 + p_2 + \cdots p_d$, with the proximity property preserved. The mapping of the grid points is the cross product $G_1 \times G_2 \times \cdots \times G_d$ where G_i is any one-dimensional Gray code mapping of the m_i points in the ith coordinate direction.

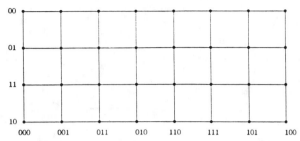

Fig. 4. Two dimensional Gray code for an 8 × 4 grid.

C. One-Dimensional Hierarchical Gray Codes for Standard Multigrid Methods

In the previous sections we have not addressed some of the important aspects of multilevel meshes that appear in multigrid methods. In particular, a crucial issue we would like to examine in this section is to find an efficient mapping of the mesh points of the different levels of refinement into a cube. In this section we consider only the classical multigrid approach. The concurrent approach will be examined in the next section.

As an illustration, consider a one-dimensional mesh on the interval $[a, b]$ with the periodic boundary condition $u(b) = u(a)$ as is illustrated in Fig. 2, which shows three different levels of meshes discretizing the interval, starting with two points. It is desirable to assign the mesh points of the finest mesh so that not only are its neighboring points assigned to neighboring processors but also so that the points of the coarser meshes are not too far from each other. The reason for this is clear: we wish to minimize the intercommunication not only when iterating at the finest level but at the coarser levels as well.

For example, we would wish to map the 8 points of the bottom mesh of Fig. 2 into a 3-cube so that the points of the submeshes shown in levels 1 and 2 remain not too far from each other. Ideally, we would like them to be neighbors. However, this turns out to be impossible. This is easy to see because the binary representations of both x_0 and x_2 must differ from that of x_1 in one bit. Since x_0 and x_2 are distinct nodes, the bit in which they differ from x_1 must be different and therefore the distance between x_0 and x_2 is bigger than 1. More generally, if it were possible to find such a mapping it would mean that there are odd cycles in an n-cube, which is impossible [11]. For example, if we could have a connection between the nodes containing x_0 and x_2 we would have the cycle x_0, x_1, x_2, x_0 which is of length 3.

The next best distance we can hope for is two. Observe that in order for the nearest-neighbor mesh connections to be maintained on the finest level, the node assignment of the finest mesh must be a Gray code. A Gray code which has the desired property that the distance between any neighboring points of coarser submeshes is constant and equal to two will be referred to as a *hierarchical* Gray code.

It is important to note that not every Gray code is hierarchical. Consider the following Gray code (obtained from the crossproduct of two 2-bit Gray codes).

{0000, 0001, 0011, 0010, 0110, 0111, 0101, 1101,

1111, 1110, 1010, 1011, 1001, 1000, 1100, 0100}.

For this Gray code, the coarsest submesh would be assigned to the nodes {0000, 1111} which are at a distance of 4 from one another.

Fortunately, the binary reflected Gray code described in Section V-A is hierarchical. More precisely one can prove the following property of the binary reflected Gray codes.

Theorem 5.2: Let $G_n \equiv (g_0, g_1, \cdots, g_{2^n-1})$ be the sequence of n-bit binary numbers of the binary reflected Gray code. Then g_i and g_{i+2^j} differ in exactly two bits for all $j > 0$ such that $i + 2^j \leq 2^n - 1$.

Proof: See [9] and [7]. ∎

We note that a similar problem was considered by L. Johnsson [7] in the context of odd-even cyclic reduction for solving tridiagonal systems.

As a consequence of the above theorem, if we map the mesh onto the cube using the binary reflected Gray code, the distance between neighboring mesh points at the finest level is one, while if we work on the coarser levels the distance is exactly two. The important fact here is that when we change levels we will not pay a heavy overhead in communication as is the case in schemes which do not preserve proximity. This can be easily verified for an 8-point grid on the 3-cube as is illustrated in Fig. 3. As a further illustration, if the total number of mesh points of the finest level is 16, we should assign the points

$$x_0 < x_2 < \cdots < x_{15}$$

successively to the nodes

0000, 0001, 0011, 0010, 0110, 0111, 0101, 0100,

1100, 1101, 1111, 1110, 1010, 1011, 1001, 1000.

We can verify in this example that the 8 points of the next coarser level (i.e, the points)

$$x_0, x_2, x_4, x_6, \cdots x_{14}$$

are assigned to nodes that are distant by two, namely the nodes

0000, 0011, 0110, 0101, 1100, 1111, 1010, 1001.

The same property can again be verified for the next level.

D. An Exchange Algorithm

Although it is satisfactory that the distance between neighboring mesh points at any level does not exceed two, it would be a nonnegligible gain to bring that distance from two to one by some exchange operation. When we pass to another level, we can exchange the data of some nodes, so as to make the mesh points of that level reside in neighboring processors. Relaxation on this level is then performed with improved efficiency since communication costs are divided by two. After the sweeps are done we can permute the data back to their initial assignments. This is effective if a sufficient number of relaxation sweeps on each level are performed in order to pay off for the initial and the final data exchanges.

To explain how the exchange will be done, we need to use the second algorithm for generating the binary reflected Gray code described in Section IV-A. Let us start with the n-bit binary reflected Gray code

$$G_n = \{g_0, \ g_1, \ \cdots \ g_{2^n-1}\}$$

and generate the $(n + 1)$-bit Gray code as follows:

$$G_{n+1} = \{g_0 0, \ g_0 1, \ g_1 1, \ g_1 0, \ g_2 0, \ g_2 1,$$

$$g_3 1, \ g_3 0, \ \cdots \ g_i 0, \ g_i 1, \ g_{i+1} 1, \ g_{i+1} 0, \ \cdots \}.$$

Recall that the general pattern for generating G_{n+1} is from any two successive nodes a, b to insert $a0$, $a1$, $b1$, $b0$. Consider now every other node, which corresponds to the next coarser grid. We get the sequence

$$\{g_0 0, \ g_1 1, \ g_2 0, \ g_3 1, \ \cdots \ g_{i-1} 0, \ g_i 1, \ g_{i+1} 0, \ \cdots \}. \quad (5.3)$$

As shown before, every two successive nodes differ by two bits: the last bit and the bit that differs between g_i and g_{i+1}. Now suppose that in the sequence G_{n+1} we permuted the pairs of the form $g_i 1$, $g_i 0$ wherever they occur (these occur only for i odd). We get the transformed sequence

$$\hat{G}_{n+1} = \{g_0 0, \ g_0 1, \ g_1 0, \ g_1 1, \ g_2 0, \ g_2 1, \ g_3 0,$$

$$g_3 1, \ \cdots \ g_i 0, \ g_i 1, \ g_{i+1} 0, \ g_{i+1} 1, \ \cdots \}.$$

In other words the general pattern is now $a0$, $a1$, $b0$, $b1$ where a and b are two successive elements of G_n. Taking every other node of $\hat{G}_{n+1}$, we get precisely the subsequence of G_{n+1} terminating with a zero, i.e.,

$$\hat{G}_n = \{g_0 0, \ g_1 0, \ g_2 0, \ \cdots g_i 0 \cdots g_{2^n-1} 0\}$$

which apart from the last bit is the n-bit Gray code. Therefore, if we send the data (i.e., the residual) in processor $g_i 1$ for i odd, to its neighbor $g_i 0$ before we visit a coarser grid, all neighboring grid points of the next coarser grid will then reside in neighboring processors. Finally, to show that this property is still true at even coarser levels, observe that the mesh-node assignment represented by $\hat{G}_n$ can be considered as the binary reflected Gray code G_n applied to an n-dimensional subcube—the half of the $(n + 1)$-cube whose node labels have 0 in the last bit of its binary representation. Therefore, by removing the last zero bit of $\hat{G}_n$ the argument used for G_{n+1} can be used recursively to show that by similar exchanges of data prior to visiting coarser meshes, all neighboring grid points on all levels are mapped to neighboring processor nodes.

Note that a similar exchange also occurs in the reverse direction when coming back from a coarse grid to the next finer grid. This time the correction is sent instead of the residual.

Numbering the levels by l, $l = 0, 1, \cdots$ starting from the finest to coarsest level, we can summarize the property of our algorithm in the following proposition.

Proposition 5.1: By transferring the residual from the nodes $g_i 1 0^l$, i odd, of level l to the node $g_i 0^{l+1}$, and the correction in the reverse direction, relaxation sweeps only require communication between neighboring nodes.

This exchange method is illustrated in Fig. 5.

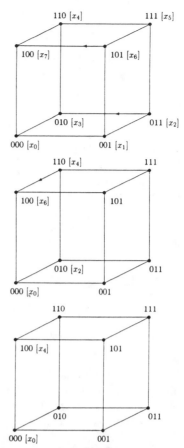

Fig. 5. The exchange algorithm. The picture shows the transfers from fine to coarse grids only.

E. One-Dimensional Hierarchical Gray Codes for Concurrent Algorithms

As was mentioned earlier, the previous parallel implementation of the standard multigrid algorithm leaves many nodes inactive during coarse grid relaxations. In fact, as is shown in [3], the *efficiency* of the standard algorithm decreases at the rate of $(\log_2 m)^{-1}$ as the grid size m increases. An intuitive reason for this is that while the finer grids get a higher proportion of the available processors, they are not proportionally active more often than the coarser grids. Therefore, a natural strategy is to assign the mesh points of different levels to different nodes and have the relaxation sweeps proceed at all levels in parallel. There are two types of communication for such a concurrent algorithm. The first is as before between the nodes containing the mesh points of the same level. Since there must be interaction between the mesh points of different levels, another type of communication is between the nodes holding data of different levels. We would like the two types of communication to be fast if possible.

Consider the example of Fig. 2 where we have a total a 14 points, 8 for the finest (third) level, 4 for the second level and, 2 for the coarsest level, to assign to the 16 nodes of a 4-cube. Note that more generally the total number of mesh points at all levels is of the form $(2^{n+1} - 1)m_1$ where m_1 is the number of points of the coarsest level and n is the number of refinements. We would like to assign these points to the 2^{n+1} nodes of an $(n + 1)$-cube. The 4-cube is split in two subcubes of lower dimensions, as represented in Fig. 6. The first subcube,

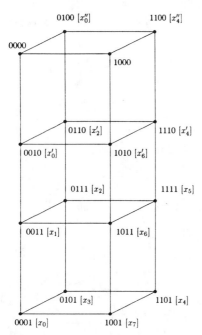

Fig. 6. Mapping of three levels of grid points into a 4-cube. The links between the nodes of the lower and upper horizontal planes are omitted.

consisting of all the nodes whose labels have the bit one as their last bit, will contain the 8 points of the finest mesh. For the purpose of having neighboring mesh points assigned to neighboring nodes, we will assign the points

$$x_0 \leq x_1 \leq \cdots \leq x_{2^n - 1}$$

successively to the nodes numbered $g_i 1$ where g_i, $i = 0, \cdots 2^n - 1$, is the sequence of the binary reflected n-bit Gray code.

Let the x'_{2i}, $i = 0, 1, \cdots 2^{n-1} - 1$ denote the grid points of the next coarser grid. Note that we use the same subscript but the prime indicates that the same physical point is now represented by two different points on the pyramid, namely x_{2i} in the fine level and x'_{2i} in the coarse level. The problem at this point is to assign the coarse mesh points x'_{2i}, $i = 0, 1, \cdots 2^{n-1} - 1$, so that

- the interlevel communication is inexpensive
- the grid points of the same level are held in neighboring nodes.

Note that the remaining points, i.e., the grid points of all the coarser levels, will now be assigned to the nodes of the form $g_i 0$ where again g_i, $i = 0, 1 \cdots 2^n - 1$, is the n-bit binary reflected Gray code. We assign the points of the next coarse grid successively to the nodes $g'_i 10$ where g'_i, $i = 0, 1, \cdots, 2^{n-1} - 1$, is the sequence of $(n - 1)$-bit binary reflected Gray code. This is illustrated in Fig. 6 for $n = 4$ where we have assigned the 14 points of the example of Fig. 2.

Consider the sequence of every other node in the finest grid:

$$g_0 1, \ g_2 1, \ g_4 1, \ \cdots .$$

The points x_0, x_2, x_4 $\cdots$ held by these nodes correspond physically to the same points as the coarse points $x'_0, x'_2, x'_4 \cdots$ that are held by the nodes

$$g'_0 10, \ g'_1 10, \ g'_2 10 \cdots .$$

Therefore, we want the distance between the nodes $g'_i 10$ and $g_{2i} 1$ to be small. In fact, we now show this distance alternates between one and two. To prove this, we need to use the second algorithm for generating binary reflected Gray codes, described in Section V-A. Appending the bit one to the sequence g_i of the n-bit Gray code obtained by that algorithm from the $(n - 1)$-bit Gray code sequence g'_i, we find the sequence

$$g'_0 01, \ g'_0 11, \ g'_1 11, \ g'_1 01, \ g'_2 01, \ g'_2 11, \ g'_3 11,$$
$$g'_3 01, \ \cdots, \ g'_i 01, \ g'_i 11, \ g'_{i+1} 11, \ g'_{i+1} 01, \ \cdots .$$

This is precisely the Gray code for the finest mesh. Therefore the subsequence of every other node, i.e., the sequence of nodes of the finest level which hold the points x_{2i}, $i = 0, 2, \cdots 2^{n-1}$, is

$$g'_0 01, \ g'_1 11, \ g'_2 01, \ g'_3 11, \ \cdots, \ g'_i 01, \ g'_{i+1} 11, \ \cdots .$$

The nodes $g'_i 11$ are directly connected to their counterparts $g'_i 10$ containing the points x'_{2i} of the coarser grid, i.e., the distance between them is one. However, the nodes of the form $g'_i 01$ are at distance 2 from their counterparts $g'_i 10$ containing the points x'_{2i} of the coarser grid, the path of length 2 being $g'_i 01 \rightarrow g'_i 11 \rightarrow g'_i 10$.

To assign the grid points x''_{4i}, $i = 0, 1, \cdots, 2^{n-2} - 1$, of the third level, observe that by removing the ending zeroes from the sequence $g'_i 10$ we are back to the previous situation with n replaced by $n - 1$. Hence, we assign the points of the third grid successively to the nodes $g''_i 100$, where $i = 0, 1, \cdots 2^{n-2} - 1$, is the $(n - 2)$-bit binary reflected Gray code. More generally, numbering the levels from finest to coarsest by $l = 0, 1, \cdots$, we assign the grid points of level number l successively to the nodes $g^{(l)}_i 10^l$ where the power refers to concatenation and where $g^{(l)}_i$, $i = 0, 1, \cdots 2^{n-l} - 1$, is the $(n - l)$-bit binary reflected Gray code. The proof that the distance between interlevel grid points are at distance one or two is straightforward.

Proposition 5.2: The mapping

$$x^{(l)}_{2^l i} \rightarrow g^{(l)}_i 10^l$$

is such that the distance between neighboring points on the same level is one and the distance between the grid points $x^{(l)}_{2^l i}$ of level number l and $x^{(l-1)}_{2^l i}$ of level number $(l - 1)$ is at most two.

F. Higher Dimensional Problems

As a result of Theorem 4.1, the mappings that we have introduced so far extend straightforwardly to higher dimensional problems. For mapping the grid of these problems, one uses cross products of one-dimensional binary reflected Gray code mappings. A higher dimensional submesh required by the multigrid algorithm is precisely the cross product of the corresponding one-dimensional submeshes. Therefore, the proximity preserving property of one-dimensional binary reflected Gray codes ensures that the same property holds for higher dimensional meshes.

However, there is a difficulty with the implementation of the *concurrent* algorithm. This stems from the fact that, for higher dimensional problems, the total number of points on the pyramid is not close to a power of 2. This misfit with the number of nodes in a cube leaves many nodes unassigned. To be specific, consider a d-dimensional problem whose finest grid has 2^n points to be assigned to the nodes of an $(n + 1)$-cube. The total number of points N_p on the pyramid is given by

$$N_p = 2^n + 2^{n-d} + \cdots + 1 = 2^n \left(\frac{1 - 2^{-nd}}{1 - 2^{-d}} \right) \approx \frac{2^n}{1 - 2^{-d}}.$$

Therefore, the fraction of the total number of nodes that are idle is

$$\frac{2^{n+1} - N_p}{2^{n+1}} \approx \frac{1 - 2^{-d+1}}{2 - 2^{-d+1}}.$$

Thus, for $d = 2$, a third of the nodes of the $(n + 1)$-cube is never used while for $d = 3$, this fraction becomes 3/7. This negates to some extent the advantage of being able to perform the concurrent iterations on different grid levels simultaneously.

The above discussions assumes that there are enough processors to accomodate the number of grid points. For higher dimensional problems, this may require more processors than are available. In such cases, it is natural to consider assigning each processor to more than just one grid point. For example, in a two-dimensional problem, each processor can hold a line of grid points in one coordinate direction. For the other coordinate direction, one can use the one-dimensional binary reflected Gray code for the mapping. The proximity preserving property obviously holds. Since the fine grids require fewer processors, such implementations can be more efficient in their usage of the available processors [3]. This is just a special case of the more general idea of *domain decomposition*. The idea is to decompose the finest grid into a collection of smaller domains, each assigned to a different processor. In other words, a particular level of the pyramid, not necessarily the finest, will get assigned one node per grid point. Processors are idle only when iterating on levels coarser than this selected level. This has the effect of increasing the efficiency of processor utilization [8].

VI. COMPLEXITY

In order to compare the performance of the three different algorithms described earlier, in this section we analyze their arithmetic and communication complexity. In this discussion we assume that each grid point is assigned to a different processor.

Let W_a denote the arithmetic complexity for the work performed per cycle in one single grid before a transfer to a different grid. Then W_a is given approximately by

$$W_a = (st_s + t_r + t_i)$$

where s denotes the total number of relaxation sweeps performed on that grid (before and after transferring to another grid), t_s denotes the time for performing one relaxation sweep, t_r denotes the time for computing, and projecting the residual and t_i denotes the time for performing the interpolation and correction. Note that W_a is the same for all three algorithms. For a general variable coefficient problem in d dimensions with a nearest-neighbor stencil discretization, injection of residuals and linear interpolation, we can estimate these times as follows:

$$t_s = \text{time of } [(2d + 1) \text{ multiplies} + (2d - 1) \text{ additions}]$$

$$t_r = \text{time of } [(2d + 1) \text{ multiplies} + 2d \text{ additions}]$$

$$t_i = \text{time of } [(2d - 1) \text{ additions}].$$

Next we consider the communication complexity of the algorithms. For simplicity, we assume that each node of the hypercube can send and receive data on all its data paths simultaneously. Let t_c denote the time it takes to send one floating point number from one node to its neighbor. For the standard algorithm with the binary reflected Gray code, we can estimate the communication complexity W_c^{st} on any grid as

$$W_c^{\text{st}} = (s + 2)2t_c$$

where the $(s + 2)$ term denotes the number of data transfers needed to perform the s relaxation sweeps and the computation of the residual and the interpolation; and the term $2t_c$ is a bound for the time it takes for each transfer. Similarly, the communication complexity W_c^{ex} for the standard algorithm with the exchange of data before transfer is estimated by

$$W_c^{\text{ex}} = (s + 2)t_c + 2t_c$$

because the exchange takes two extra data transfers, one before and one after transferring to a different grid, but afterwards each transfer takes only time t_c. Finally, the communication complexity W_c^{co} for the concurrent algorithm is estimated by

$$W_c^{\text{co}} = (s + 2)t_c + 4t_c$$

because the transfer between grids takes two data transfers each way.

One interesting point to note is that

$$W_c^{\text{ex}} < W_c^{\text{st}}.$$

In other words, the standard algorithm with exchange is always better than the standard algorithm without exchange, in terms of communication cost. Moreover, this advantage increases with increasing s, the number of relaxation sweeps. For this reason, it seems that the exchange algorithm is to be always preferred. Grosch [6] considers a similar strategy for his implementation of multigrid algorithms on the perfectly shuffled nearest-neighbor array. It is more difficult to compare the concurrent algorithm with the standard ones due to the difference in convergence rates. We only note that for large values of s, $W_c^{\text{co}} \approx W_c^{\text{ex}}$.

Finally, for small values of d and s, the number of arithmetic operations and data transfers are about the same order of magnitude and therefore communication should not become a bottleneck if the time it takes to send one floating point number is not much greater than the time it takes for one arithmetic operation.

VII. Concluding Remarks

The hypercube seems to be ideally suited for implementing the standard multigrid algorithm. A communication-efficient mesh-to-node mapping is possible via the binary reflected Gray codes and extends to higher dimensional meshes in a straightforward way. The concurrent algorithm, on the other hand, does not seem as well-suited to the hypercube for higher dimensional problems. The main problem is that in order to have each point on the pyramid mapped into distinct nodes, one has to use a hypercube of one higher dimension than that needed for just the fine mesh. As was shown in Section IV-F almost half of all the nodes are *never used*. For the concurrent algorithm to be cost-effective as compared to the standard algorithm, its convergence rate must be at least twice as fast. Unfortunately, very little is known about the convergence rate of the concurrent algorithm and experimental evidence indicates that the convergence rate *decreases* with increasing m [4]. Therefore, being able to perform the concurrent iterations on different grid levels simultaneously does not pay. The only way in which we can still achieve maximal use of the available processors for higher dimensional problems is by using each node of the one-dimensional pyramid to hold a line or a plane of unknowns, as discussed in Section IV-F.

When there are more than one problem to be solved on the same grid structure, the standard algorithm on the hypercube can be made more effective by pipelining these different problems. When the nodes assigned to a particular grid are inactive for one of the problems, they can be working on the other problems. The programming of the individual nodes may be more complicated, however.

It is interesting to note that the potential for a concurrent algorithm is there with the mapping described in Section IV-C for the standard algorithm. This is so because when the nodes assigned to a coarse grid are active, the other nodes, while not completely representing the inactive grids, can still be used to perform some sort of concurrent relaxation sweeps.

Finally, the mappings described in this paper, being dependent mainly on the grid structure, are useful for other variants of the standard multigrid algorithms, such as the nested iteration and the FAS algorithms [13].

References

[1] L. N. Bhuyan and D. P. Agrawal, "Generalized hypercube and hyperbus structures for a computer network," *IEEE Trans. Comput.*, vol. C-33, pp. 323–333, 1984.

[2] A. Brandt, "Multigrid solvers on parallel computers," in *Elliptic Problem Solvers*, M. H. Schultz Ed. New York: Academic, 1981, pp. 39–83.

[3] T. F. Chan and R. Schreiber, "Parallel networks for multigrid algorithms: Architecture and complexity," *SIAM J. Sci. Stat. Comput.*, vol. 6, pp. 698–711, July 1985.

[4] D. Gannon and J. Van Rosendale, "Highly parallel multigrid solvers for elliptic PDE's," ICASE, Tech. Rep. 82-36, 1984.

[5] C. E. Grosch, "Poisson solvers on large array computers," in *Proc. 1978 LASL Workshop Vector and Parallel Comput.*, 1978, pp. 98–132.

[6] ——, "Performance analysis of Poisson solvers on array computers," Old Dominion Univ., Norfolk, VA, Tech. Rep. TR 79-3, 1979.

[7] S. L. Johnsson, "Odd-even cyclic reduction on ensemble architectures," *SIAM J. Sci. Stat. Comput.*, 1986.

[8] J. M. Ortega and R. G. Voigt, "Solution of partial differential equations on vector and parallel computers," *SIAM Rev.*, vol. 27, pp. 149–240, 1985.

[9] E. M. Reingold, J. Nievergelt, and N. Deo, *Combinatorial Algorithms.* Englewood Cliffs, NJ: Prentice Hall, 1977.

[10] Y. Saad and M. H. Schultz, "Data communication in hypercubes," Dep. Comput. Sci., Yale Univ., New Haven, CT, Res. Rep. 428, 1985.

[11] ——, "Topological properties of hypercubes," Dep. Comput. Sci., Yale Univ., New Haven, CT, Res. Rep. 389, 1985.

[12] C. L. Seitz, "The cosmic cube," *CACM*, vol. 28, pp. 22–33, 1985.

[13] K. Stuben and U. Trottenberg, "Multi-grid methods: Fundamental algorithms, model problem analysis and applications," in *Multigrid Methods*, W. Hackbusch and U. Trottenberg, Eds. Berlin: Springer-Verlag, 1982.

Tony F. Chan, photograph and biography not available at the time of publication.

Youcef Saad received the Doctorat de troisieme cycle degree from the University of Grenoble, France, in 1974 and the Doctorat d'Etat degree from the Institute National Polytechnique de Grenoble in 1983.

He is currently a Senior Research Scientist in the Department of Computer Science, Yale University, New Haven, CT. He has held visiting positions at the University of Illinois, Urbana, in 1980 and at the University of California, Berkeley, in 1981. His research interests include numerical linear algebra, large-scale matrix problems, partial differential equations, and parallel algorithms.

Embeddings among Meshes and Tori*

Eva Ma

Department of Computing Science, University of Glasgow, Glasgow G12 8QQ, Scotland

AND

Lixin Tao

Department of Computer Science, Concordia University, Montreal, Quebec, Canada H3G 1M8

Given a d-dimensional mesh or torus G and a c-dimensional mesh or torus H of the same size, we study the problem of embedding G in H to minimize the dilation cost. We construct embeddings for increasing dimension cases ($d < c$) in which the shapes of G and H satisfy the condition of expansion, and for lowering dimension cases ($d > c$) in which the shapes of G and H satisfy the condition of reduction. We then use these results to construct embeddings for the cases in which G and H are square. The embeddings for square meshes and square tori are optimal for increasing dimension cases in which c is divisible by d, and optimal to within a constant multiplicative factor for fixed values of d and c for all lowering dimension cases.   © 1993 Academic Press, Inc.

1. INTRODUCTION

An embedding of a graph G in a graph H is an injection (one-to-one mapping) of the nodes in G to the nodes in H. The dilation cost of an embedding of G in H is the maximum distance in H between the images of any two neighboring nodes in G [15]. This cost gives a measure of the proximity in H of the neighboring nodes in G under an embedding. Graph embedding results have many important applications in parallel processing. They provide the theoretical foundation for studying the problem of matching the communication structure of a task to the communication support of a parallel system and, also, for studying the problem of evaluating the relative performance of two interconnection networks. In this paper, we study the embeddings among meshes and tori that are of the same size and of various dimensions and shapes to minimize the dilation costs. Meshes and tori represent

* This work was partially supported by National Science Foundation Grant DCR84-51408, an IBM research grant, an AT&T Information System research grant, National Science Foundation CER Grant MCS82-19196, Army Research Office Grant DAAG-29-84-K-0061, Canada NSERC Research Grant OGP0041648, and a British Science and Engineering Research Council visiting fellowship research grant.

the communication structures of many applications in scientific computations [10] as well as the topologies of many large-scale interconnection networks [10, 25].

All our embeddings are constructed from several basic results for embedding a line or a ring in a mesh or a torus. Let d and c be the dimensions of G and H, respectively. We construct embeddings for increasing dimension cases ($d < c$), in which the shapes of G and H satisfy the condition of expansion, and for lowering dimension cases ($d > c$), in which the shapes of G and H satisfy the condition of reduction. For expansion, the dilation costs of the embeddings are 1 or 2, depending on the types of graphs of G and H; except for the case in which G is a torus of even size and H is a mesh, these embeddings are optimal. For reduction, the dilation costs of the embeddings depend on the shapes of G and H; these embeddings are not optimal, in general.

By the embedding results for expansion and reduction, we construct embeddings, through one or more embedding steps, for the special cases in which both G and H are square. For increasing dimension cases in which the dimension of G is divisible by the dimension of H, the embeddings are all optimal, with dilation cost 2 if G is a torus of odd size and H is a mesh, and 1 otherwise. For lowering dimension cases, the embeddings are all optimal to within a constant multiplicative factor for fixed values of d and c, with dilation cost $2l^{(d-c)/c}$ if G is a torus and H is a mesh, and $l^{(d-c)/c}$ otherwise, where l is the length of the dimensions of G.

All the embedding functions presented in this paper have been implemented in the embedding kernel on the IBM Victor multiprocessor for the support of program mapping and network reconfiguration [17]. Using the embedding results derived in this paper, we have also studied the problem of simulating parallel neighboring communications among meshes and tori [23].

A few special cases of the embedding problem studied in this paper have been solved optimally in the literature: embedding a mesh (of size some power of 2) in a hypercube [6], embedding a two-dimensional square torus in a ring [18], embedding a two-dimensional mesh or a three-dimensional square mesh in a line [9], and embedding a hypercube in a line [12]. Other closely related results include the embedding of a two-dimensional square mesh in a line to minimize average proximity [7], the embedding of a finite array (mesh), a prism array, or an orthant array in a line to minimize proximity in various local and global senses [22], the embedding of a two-dimensional rectangular mesh in a two-dimensional square mesh to minimize the dilation cost while satisfying constraints on expansion costs [1, 8], the embeddings of a mesh in a hypercube with various expansion costs and dilation costs [11, 13, 2, 4, 5], and simulations between rectangular meshes [16]. (In a simulation of G in H, the size of H may be greater than the size of G, and a bounded number of nodes in G may be mapped into a single node in H.) With the exception of [16], in which the costs are expressed in terms of big O notation, the costs in the above cited papers and in this paper are all exact.

Section 2 defines the basic notations and terminologies; Section 3 presents the embeddings among general meshes; and Section 4 presents the embeddings among square meshes. The analyses of the other cases in which either (i) G is a torus or (ii) G is a mesh and H a torus, are similar to the analyses of the case for meshes G and H. We summarize the results for all cases in Section 5 and include the key analyses of the other cases not covered in Sections 3 and 4 in the Appendix. This paper is a revised and extended version of our earlier work [19, 20].

2. NOTATIONS AND TERMINOLOGIES

Unless stated otherwise, variables denote positive integers; graphs are undirected, and they are either meshes or tori. Given a positive integer n, $[n]$ denotes the set $\{0, 1, ..., n - 1\}$, and $[n]^+$ the set $\{1, 2, ..., n\}$. We use $(x_1, x_2, ..., x_p) \circ (y_1, y_2, ..., y_q)$ to denote the concatenation of the lists $(x_1, x_2, ..., x_p)$ and $(y_1, y_2, ..., y_q)$, which is $(x_1, x_2, ..., x_p, y_1, y_2, ..., y_q)$, and $f \circ g$ to denote the composition of the functions f and g: $(f \circ g)(x) = f(g(x))$ for all x in the domain of g. Given a positive integer k, a list $(i_1, i_2, ..., i_k)$, and a permutation $\pi : [k]^+ \rightarrow [k]^+$, $\pi((i_1, i_2, ..., i_k))$ denotes $(i_{\pi(1)}, ..., i_{\pi(k)})$. Given a rational number x, $\lfloor x \rfloor$ denotes the greatest integer less than or equal to x.

A *graph* $G = (V_G, E_G)$ is an ordered pair in which V_G is a set of nodes and E_G a set of edges. The size of G is $|V_G|$.

DEFINITION 1. An *embedding* f of a graph $G = (V_G, E_G)$ in a graph $H = (V_H, E_H)$ is an injection $f : V_G \rightarrow V_H$. The *dilation cost* of f is $\max_{\{i,j\} \in E_G}\{$distance between nodes $f(i)$ and $f(j)$ in $H\}$.

DEFINITION 2. Let d be a positive integer, and $l_1, l_2, ..., l_d$ integers greater than 1. Let $\mathcal{L} = (l_1, l_2, ..., l_d)$, $\Omega_{\mathcal{L}} =$

$\{(i_1, i_2, ..., i_d) \mid \forall k \in [d]^+, i_k \in [l_k]\}$, and $n = \Pi_{i \in [d]^+} l_i$. We call $\mathcal{L}$ a *shape* with *node set* $\Omega_{\mathcal{L}}$ and *size* n.

DEFINITION 3. Let $\Omega_{\mathcal{L}}$ be a node set, and $A = (i_1, i_2, ..., i_d)$ and $B = (i_1', i_2', ..., i_d')$ be two nodes in $\Omega_{\mathcal{L}}$. Two distance measures δ_m-distance and δ_t-distance are defined on $\Omega_{\mathcal{L}}$:

$$\delta_m(A, B) = \sum_{k=1}^{d} |i_k - i_k'|,$$

$$\delta_t(A, B) = \sum_{k=1}^{d} \min\{|i_k - i_k'|, l_k - |i_k - i_k'|\}.$$

The distance measures δ_m and δ_t are invariant under permutation: for any shape $\mathcal{L} = (l_1, l_2, ..., l_d)$ and any permutation $\pi : [d]^+ \rightarrow [d]^+$, the δ_m-distance and the δ_t-distance between any two nodes A and B in $\Omega_{\mathcal{L}}$ are the same as the δ_m-distance and the δ_t-distance between the nodes $\pi(A)$ and $\pi(B)$ in $\Omega_{\pi(\mathcal{L})}$, respectively.

DEFINITION 4. A *mesh* G_m of shape $\mathcal{L}$ is an ordered pair $(\Omega_{\mathcal{L}}, E_m)$, where

$$E_m = \{\{A, B\} \mid A \in \Omega_{\mathcal{L}}, B \in \Omega_{\mathcal{L}}, \delta_m(A, B) = 1\}.$$

DEFINITION 5. A *torus* G_t of shape $\mathcal{L}$ is an ordered pair $(\Omega_{\mathcal{L}}, E_t)$, where

$$E_t = \{\{A, B\} \mid A \in \Omega_{\mathcal{L}}, B \in \Omega_{\mathcal{L}}, \delta_t(A, B) = 1\}.$$

δ_m is the distance measure between nodes in a mesh, and δ_t the distance measure in a torus. Given a graph of shape $\mathcal{L} = (l_1, l_2, ..., l_d)$, d is its dimension; for all $j \in [d]^+$, l_j is the length of its jth dimension; and if $l_1 = l_2 = \cdots = l_d$, we say that the graph is *square*. A mesh of dimension 1 is a *line*, a torus of dimension 1 is a *ring*, and a mesh or torus with length 2 in each dimension is a *hypercube*. We call a graph of shape $\mathcal{L}$ an *$\mathcal{L}$-graph*. Figures 1 and 2 show a $(4, 2, 3)$-mesh and a $(4, 2, 3)$-torus, respectively; the distance between the nodes $(0, 0, 1)$ and $(3, 0, 0)$ is 4 in the mesh and 2 in the torus.

Let G, G', H, and H' be graphs of shapes $\mathcal{L}$, $\mathcal{L}'$, $\mathcal{M}$, and $\mathcal{M}'$, respectively, such that $\mathcal{L}' = \alpha(\mathcal{L})$ and $\mathcal{M}' = \beta(\mathcal{M})$ for some permutations α and β. Since δ_m-distance and δ_t-distance are invariant under permutations, if we have an embedding function $f : \Omega_{\mathcal{L}} \rightarrow \Omega_{\mathcal{M}}$ that embeds G in H with dilation cost ρ, then the function $\beta \circ f \circ \alpha^{-1}$ embeds G' in H' with the same dilation cost ρ.

DEFINITION 6. Given a shape $\mathcal{L}$ of size n and a bijection $f : [n] \rightarrow \Omega_{\mathcal{L}}$, we often call f a *sequence*, referring to $f(0), f(1), ..., f(n - 1)$, in which for all $i \in [n - 1]$, $f(i)$ and $f(i + 1)$ are taken to be successive elements. If $f(0)$ and $f(n - 1)$ are also taken to be successive, then we call

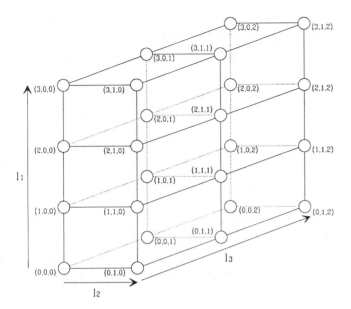

FIG. 1. A (4, 2, 3)-mesh.

i	0	1	2	3	4	5	6	7	8
$f(i)$	(0,0)	(0,1)	(0,2)	(2,2)	(2,1)	(2,0)	(1,0)	(1,1)	(1,2)

(a)

i	0	1	2	3	4	5	6	7	8
$\delta_m(f(i), f((i+1) \bmod 9))$	1	1	2	1	1	1	1	1	3
$\delta_t(f(i), f((i+1) \bmod 9))$	1	1	1	1	1	1	1	1	2

(b)

FIG. 3. A function f with $n = 9$ and $\mathscr{L} = (3, 3)$.

(same as the δ_m-spread in this case) is called a *Gray code* [21].

DEFINITION 7. Let $\mathscr{L} = (l_1, l_2, ..., l_d)$ be a shape of size n. We can view $\mathscr{L}$ as a radix-base, and $\Omega_{\mathscr{L}}$ the numbers in the radix-$\mathscr{L}$ numbering system. For all $i \in [d + 1]$, let $w_i = \Pi_{j=i+1}^{d} l_j$; $w_0, w_1, ..., w_d$ are the weights in the radix-$\mathscr{L}$ representation. Every integer x in $[n]$ has a unique radix-$\mathscr{L}$ representation $(\hat{x}_1, \hat{x}_2, ..., \hat{x}_d)$ in $\Omega_{\mathscr{L}}$ [24]; the correspondence is defined by the bijections $u_{\mathscr{L}} : [n] \to \Omega_{\mathscr{L}}$ and $u_{\mathscr{L}}^{-1} : \Omega_{\mathscr{L}} \to [n]$ such that for all $x \in [n]$,

$$u_{\mathscr{L}}(x) = (\hat{x}_1, \hat{x}_2, ..., \hat{x}_d),$$

where for all $j \in [d]^+$,

$$\hat{x}_j = \lfloor x/w_j \rfloor \bmod l_j,$$

and for all $(\hat{x}_1, \hat{x}_2, ..., \hat{x}_d) \in \Omega_{\mathscr{L}}$,

$$u_{\mathscr{L}}^{-1}((\hat{x}_1, \hat{x}_2, ..., \hat{x}_d)) = \sum_{k=1}^{d} \hat{x}_k w_k.$$

f a *cyclic sequence*. The δ_m-*spread* (δ_t-*spread*) of the sequence f is the maximum of the δ_m-distances (δ_t-distances) between all pairs of successive elements in f. The δ_m-spread and δ_t-spread of the cyclic sequence f are defined similarly.

Figure 3a gives a function $f : [9] \to \Omega_{(3,3)}$, and Fig. 3b gives the δ_m-distance and δ_t-distance between the pair $f(i)$ and $f((i + 1) \bmod 9)$, for all $i \in [9]$. For the sequence f, its δ_m-spread is 2 and its δ_t-spread is 1; for the cyclic sequence f, its δ_m-spread is 3 and its δ_t-spread is 2. If $\mathscr{L}$ is a shape of 2's, then a sequence f with unit δ_t-spread

3. EMBEDDING AMONG GENERAL MESHES

3.1. Embedding a Line in a Mesh

Let G be a line of size n and H an $\mathscr{L}$-mesh of the same size. The nodes in G are numbers in $[n]$ with neighbors corresponding to successive elements in the sequence $0, 1, ..., n - 1$. For any embedding $f : [n] \to \Omega_{\mathscr{L}}$ of G in H, its dilation cost is the same as the δ_m-spread of the sequence f.

Let P be the sequence $u_{\mathscr{L}}$, the numbers $0, 1, ..., n - 1$ in their radix-$\mathscr{L}$ representations. Every element in P has d components, of the form $(\hat{a}_1, \hat{a}_2, ..., \hat{a}_d)$, where $\hat{a}_i \in [l_i]$ for all $i \in [d]^+$. We can view P as comprising d separate sequences of natural numbers, $p_1, p_2, ..., p_d$, one for each of the d components of the elements in P. (Figure 4 shows the sequence P for $\mathscr{L} = (4, 2, 3)$.) From the properties of the radix-$\mathscr{L}$ representation of numbers, for all $i \in [d]^+$, the sequence p_i can be partitioned into n/w_{i-1} seg-

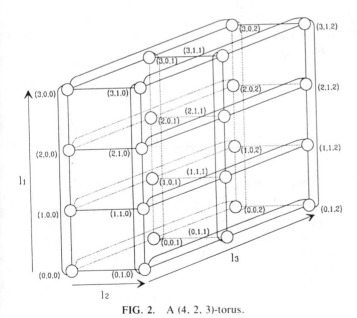

FIG. 2. A (4, 2, 3)-torus.

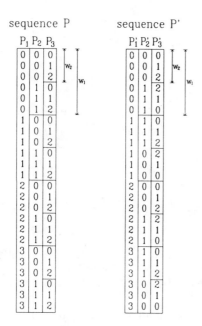

sequence P   sequence P'

P₁ P₂ P₃ ... P'₁ P'₂ P'₃

FIG. 4. Sequences P and P' for $\mathcal{L} = (4, 2, 3)$.

ments, numbered from 0 to $n/w_{i-1} - 1$ successively, each with w_{i-1} elements and of the form

$$\underbrace{0 \cdots 0}_{w_i} \underbrace{1 \cdots 1}_{w_i} \underbrace{(l_i - 1) \cdots (l_i - 1)}_{w_i};$$

the difference between two successive elements in p_i is at most 1 if they belong to the same segment in p_i, and is $l_i - 1$ otherwise. The δ_m-spread of the sequence P is greater than 1 for all $d > 1$.

Let P' be a sequence constructed from P: for all $i \in [d]^+$, reverse all odd-numbered segments of p_i and leave all even-numbered segments unchanged to produce the sequence p'_i. (Figure 4 shows the sequence P' for $\mathcal{L} = (4, 2, 3)$.) The difference between two successive elements in p'_i is at most 1 if they belong to the same segment, and is 0 otherwise. The sequence P' has unit δ_m-spread (Lemma 8). The function $f_{\mathcal{L}}$ given in Lemma 8 defines the sequence P'.

LEMMA 8. *Let $\mathcal{L} = (l_1, l_2, ..., l_d)$ be a shape of size n. Following the notations of Definition 7, let $f_{\mathcal{L}} : [n] \to \Omega_{\mathcal{L}}$ be the function such that for all $x \in [n]$, $f_{\mathcal{L}}(x) = (x_1, x_2, ..., x_d)$, where for all $i \in [d]^+$,*

$$x_i = \begin{cases} \hat{x}_i, & \text{if } \lfloor x/w_{i-1} \rfloor \text{ is even;} \\ l_i - \hat{x}_i - 1, & \text{if } \lfloor x/w_{i-1} \rfloor \text{ is odd.} \end{cases}$$

The function $f_{\mathcal{L}}$ is bijective, and the sequence $f_{\mathcal{L}}$ has unit δ_m-spread.

Proof. The proof is straightforward and contained in the technical report [19]. ∎

By the function $f_{\mathcal{L}}$, we can embed a line of size n in a mesh of shape $\mathcal{L}$ with unit dilation cost.

3.2. Embedding for Increasing Dimension

Given $\mathcal{A} = (a_1, a_2, ..., a_k)$, we use $\Pi\mathcal{A}$ to denote the product $a_1 a_2 \cdots a_k$.

DEFINITION 9. Let $\mathcal{L} = (l_1, l_2, ..., l_d)$ and $\mathcal{M} = (m_1, m_2, ..., m_c)$ be shapes for which $d < c$. $\mathcal{M}$ is an *expansion* of $\mathcal{L}$ if there exist d shapes $\mathcal{V}_1, \mathcal{V}_2, ..., \mathcal{V}_d$ such that for all $i \in [d]^+$, $\Pi \mathcal{V}_i = l_i$, and $\mathcal{M} = \mathcal{V}_1 \diamond \mathcal{V}_2 \diamond \cdots \diamond \mathcal{V}_d$. We call $\mathcal{V} = (\mathcal{V}_1, \mathcal{V}_2, ..., \mathcal{V}_d)$ the *expansion factor* of $\mathcal{L}$ into $\mathcal{M}$.

For example, $\mathcal{M} = (2, 3, 8, 4, 5, 4)$ is an expansion of $\mathcal{L} = (6, 8, 80)$ with $\mathcal{V} = ((2, 3), (8), (4, 5, 4))$.

THEOREM 10. *Let G and H be meshes of shapes $\mathcal{L}$ and $\mathcal{M}$, respectively, such that $\mathcal{M}$ is an expansion of $\mathcal{L}$ with expansion factor $\mathcal{V}$. Following the notations of Definition 9, let $\mathcal{F}_{\mathcal{V}} : \Omega_{\mathcal{L}} \to \Omega_{\mathcal{M}}$ be the function such that for all $(i_1, i_2, ..., i_d) \in \Omega_{\mathcal{L}}$.*

$$\mathcal{F}_{\mathcal{V}}((i_1, i_2, ..., i_d)) = f_{\mathcal{V}_1}(i_1) \diamond f_{\mathcal{V}_2}(i_2) \diamond \cdots \diamond f_{\mathcal{V}_d}(i_d).$$

Then G can be embedded in H with unit dilation cost by the function $\mathcal{F}_{\mathcal{V}}$.

Proof. For any two neighboring nodes $A = (i_1, i_2, ..., i_d)$ and $B = (i'_1, i'_2, ..., i'_d)$ in G, by the definition of a mesh, there exists exactly one index $k \in [d]^+$ such that $|i_k - i'_k| = 1$ and for all $j \in [d]^+$ such that $j \neq k$, $i_j = i'_j$. Since by Lemma 8 the sequences $f_{\mathcal{V}_1}, f_{\mathcal{V}_2}, ..., f_{\mathcal{V}_d}$ all have unit δ_m-spread, we have $\delta_m(f_{\mathcal{V}_k}(i_k), f_{\mathcal{V}_k}(i'_k)) = 1$, and for all $j \in [d]^+$ such that $j \neq k$, $\delta_m(f_{\mathcal{V}_j}(i_j), f_{\mathcal{V}_j}(i'_j)) = 0$. Thus $\mathcal{F}_{\mathcal{V}}(A)$ and $\mathcal{F}_{\mathcal{V}}(B)$ have unit δ_m-distance in $\Omega_{\mathcal{M}}$. Therefore, the function $\mathcal{F}_{\mathcal{V}}$ embeds G in H with unit dilation cost. ∎

3.3. Embeddings for Lowering Dimension

3.3.1. Simple Reduction

DEFINITION 11. Let $\mathcal{L} = (l_1, l_2, ..., l_d)$ and $\mathcal{M} = (m_1, m_2, ..., m_c)$ be shapes for which $d > c$. $\mathcal{M}$ is a *simple reduction* of $\mathcal{L}$ with *reduction factor* $\mathcal{V} = (\mathcal{V}_1, \mathcal{V}_2, ..., \mathcal{V}_c)$ if $\mathcal{L}$ is an expansion of $\mathcal{M}$ with expansion factor $\mathcal{V}$.

THEOREM 12. *Let G and H be meshes of shapes $\mathcal{L}$ and $\mathcal{M}$, respectively, such that $\mathcal{M}$ is a simple reduction of $\mathcal{L}$ with reduction factor $\mathcal{V}$. Following the notations of Definition 11, let $\mathcal{U}_{\mathcal{V}} : \Omega_{\mathcal{L}} \to \Omega_{\mathcal{M}}$ be the function such that for all $(i_1, i_2, ..., i_d) \in \Omega_{\mathcal{L}}$,*

$$\mathcal{U}_{\mathcal{V}}((i_1, i_2, ..., i_d)) = u_{\mathcal{V}_1}^{-1}(I_1) \diamond u_{\mathcal{V}_2}^{-1}(I_2) \diamond \cdots \diamond u_{\mathcal{V}_c}^{-1}(I_c),$$

where I_1, I_2, ..., I_c are partitions of $(i_1, i_2, ..., i_d)$ such that for all $k \in [c]^+$, $|I_k| = |\mathcal{V}_k|$, and $I_1 \diamond I_2 \diamond \cdots \diamond I_c = (i_1, i_2, ..., i_d)$; and $u_{\mathcal{V}_1}^{-1}$, $u_{\mathcal{V}_2}^{-1}$, ..., $u_{\mathcal{V}_c}^{-1}$ are the bijections given in Definition 7. Let v_i be the index in $[d]^+$ such that I_{v_i} is the first component in $\mathcal{V}_i$. Then G can be embedded in H with dilation cost $\max_{1 \leq i \leq c}\{m_i/l_{v_i}\}$ by the function $\mathcal{U}_{\mathcal{V}}$.

Proof. For all $k \in [c]^+$, $u_{\mathcal{V}_k}^{-1}$ maps the radix-$\mathcal{V}_k$ numbers to their corresponding integers in $[m_k]$; since $u_{\mathcal{V}_k}^{-1}$ is bijective, $\mathcal{U}_{\mathcal{V}}$ is also bijective. Let $A = I_1 \diamond I_2 \diamond \cdots \diamond I_k \diamond \cdots \diamond I_c$ and $B = I_1' \diamond I_2' \diamond \cdots \diamond I_k' \diamond \cdots \diamond I_c'$ be any two neighboring nodes in G. Let $q = |\mathcal{V}_k|$, and $(l_1', l_2', ..., l_q') = \mathcal{V}_k$, where $k \in [c]^+$. Without loss of generality, assume that A and B differ at the rth position in I_k, for some $r \in [q]^+$. Let i_r and i_r' denote the components of A and B at this position, respectively. The distance between $\mathcal{U}_{\mathcal{V}}(A)$ and $\mathcal{U}_{\mathcal{V}}(B)$ in H is $|u_{\mathcal{V}_k}^{-1}(I_k) - u_{\mathcal{V}_k}^{-1}(I_k')| = |i_r - i_r'| \prod_{j=r+1}^{q} l_j'$. Since $|i_r - i_r'| = 1$ and $m_k = \prod_{j=1}^{q} l_j'$, we have $\delta_m(\mathcal{U}_{\mathcal{V}}(A), \mathcal{U}_{\mathcal{V}}(B)) = m_k/\prod_{j=1}^{r} l_j' \leq m_k/l_1'$. Therefore, $\mathcal{U}_{\mathcal{V}}$ embeds G in H with dilation cost $\max_{1 \leq i \leq c}\{m_i/l_{v_i}\}$. ∎

3.3.2. General Reduction

Let G be a $(3, 3, 6)$-mesh and H a $(6, 9)$-mesh. We can view G as a $(3, 3)$-mesh of *supernodes*, each a line of length 6, and H a $(3, 3)$-mesh of *supernodes*, each a $(2, 3)$-mesh. (See Fig. 5.) With respect to supernodes, G and H have the same shape, a $(3, 3)$-mesh. We can embed neighboring supernodes of G in neighboring supernodes of H by the identity function, and embed the nodes belonging to a single supernode of G in the nodes belonging to the corresponding supernode of H by the function $f_{(2,3)}$. This embedding has dilation cost 3.

In general, given two meshes G and H whose shapes satisfy the condition of *general reduction*, G and H can be viewed as meshes of supernodes such that with respect to supernodes, G and H have the same shape, with the shape of H's supernodes being an expansion of the shape of G's supernodes. We can embed G in H by embedding neighboring supernodes of G in neighboring supernodes of H by the identity function, and embed the nodes belonging to a single supernode of G in the nodes belonging to the corresponding supernode of H by the embedding function for expansion.

Given $\mathcal{A} = (a_1, a_2, ..., a_k)$ and $\mathcal{B} = (b_1, b_2, ..., b_k)$, we use $\mathcal{A} \times \mathcal{B}$ to denote $(a_1 b_1, a_2 b_2, ..., a_k b_k)$, and $\mathcal{A} + \mathcal{B}$ to denote $(a_1 + b_1, a_2 + b_2, ..., a_k + b_k)$. We use $[\ ]$ for grouping.

DEFINITION 13. Let $\mathcal{L} = (l_1, l_2, ..., l_d)$ and $\mathcal{M} = (m_1, m_2, ..., m_c)$ be shapes for which $c < d < 2c$. $\mathcal{M}$ is a *general reduction* of $\mathcal{L}$ if there exist two shapes $\mathcal{L}'$ and $\mathcal{L}''$ of lengths c and $d - c$, respectively, such that $\mathcal{L} = \mathcal{L}' \diamond \mathcal{L}''$, and $d - c$ shapes $\mathcal{S}_1$, $\mathcal{S}_2$, ..., $\mathcal{S}_{d-c}$ such that $\mathcal{L}'' = (\Pi\mathcal{S}_1, \Pi\mathcal{S}_2, ..., \Pi\mathcal{S}_{d-c})$, $\tilde{\mathcal{S}} = \mathcal{S}_1 \diamond \mathcal{S}_2 ... \diamond \mathcal{S}_{d-c}$ has length b,

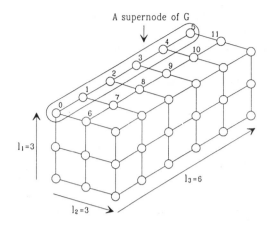

(a) $(3, 3, 6)$-mesh G

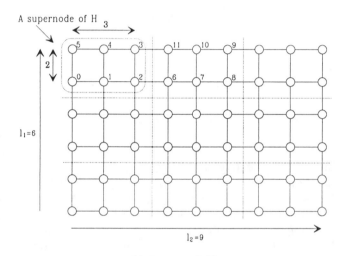

(b) $(6, 9)$-mesh H

FIG. 5. Supernode view.

where $d - c < b \leq c$, and $\mathcal{M} = [\tilde{\mathcal{S}} \diamond \mathcal{I}] \times \mathcal{L}'$, where

$$\mathcal{I} = \underbrace{(1, 1, ..., 1)}_{c-b}.$$

We call $\mathcal{S} = (\mathcal{S}_1, \mathcal{S}_2, ..., \mathcal{S}_{d-c})$ the *reduction factor* of $\mathcal{L}$ into $\mathcal{M}$, $\mathcal{L}'$ the *multiplicand sublist*, and $\mathcal{L}''$ the *multiplier sublist*.

For example, $\mathcal{M} = (10, 4, 18, 28, 3, 5)$ is a general reduction of $\mathcal{L} = (2, 2, 6, 4, 3, 5, 10, 21)$ with $\mathcal{L}' = (2, 2, 6, 4, 3, 5)$, $\mathcal{L}'' = (10, 21)$, $\mathcal{S} = ((5, 2), (3, 7))$, and $\mathcal{I} = (1, 1)$. By definition, if $\mathcal{M}$ is a general reduction of $\mathcal{L}$ with reduction factor $\mathcal{S} = (\mathcal{S}_1, \mathcal{S}_2, ..., \mathcal{S}_{d-c})$, then the shape $\tilde{\mathcal{S}} = \mathcal{S}_1 \diamond \mathcal{S}_2 \diamond \cdots \diamond \mathcal{S}_{d-c}$ is an expansion of $\mathcal{L}''$ with expansion factor $\mathcal{S}$.

THEOREM 14. *Let G and H be meshes of shapes $\mathcal{L}$ and $\mathcal{M}$, respectively, such that $\mathcal{M}$ is a general reduction of*

$\mathscr{L}$ with reduction factor $\mathscr{S}$. Following the notations of Definition 13, let $(s_1, s_2, ..., s_b) = \tilde{\mathscr{S}}$, and let $\mathscr{F}'_{\mathscr{G}} : \Omega_{\mathscr{S}} \to \Omega_{\mathscr{M}}$ be the function such that for all $(i_1, i_2, ..., i_d) \in \Omega_{\mathscr{S}}$,

$$\mathscr{F}'_{\mathscr{G}}((i_1, i_2, ..., i_d)) = [(s_1 i_1, s_2 i_2, ..., s_b i_b) + \mathscr{F}_{\mathscr{G}}((i_{c+1}, i_{c+2}, ..., i_d))] \circ (i_{b+1}, i_{b+2}, ..., i_c),$$

where $\mathscr{F}_{\mathscr{G}} : \Omega_{\mathscr{S}''} \to \Omega_{\mathscr{S}}$ is the function for expansion given in Theorem 10. Then G can be embedded in H with dilation cost $\max\{s_1, s_2, ..., s_b\}$ by the function $\mathscr{F}'_{\mathscr{G}}$.

Proof. For any node $(i_1, i_2, ..., i_d)$ in G, we have

$$\mathscr{F}'_{\mathscr{G}}((i_1, i_2, ..., i_d)) = [(s_1 i_1, s_2 i_2, ..., s_b i_b) + \mathscr{F}_{\mathscr{G}}((i_{c+1}, i_{c+2}, ..., i_d))] \circ (i_{b+1}, i_{b+2}, ..., i_c).$$

We call $(s_1 i_1, s_2 i_2, ..., s_b i_b)$ and $(i_{b+1}, ..., i_c)$ the *base*, and $\mathscr{F}_{\mathscr{G}}((i_{c+1}, i_{c+2}, ..., i_d))$ the *offset*. Let $\mathscr{F}_{\mathscr{G}}((i_{c+1}, i_{c+2}, ..., i_d)) = (e_1, e_2, ..., e_b)$. We can write $\mathscr{F}'_{\mathscr{G}}((i_1, i_2, ..., i_d))$ as $(s_1 i_1 + e_1, s_2 i_2 + e_2, ..., s_b i_b + e_b, i_{b+1}, ..., i_c)$.

Since $\mathscr{F}_{\mathscr{G}}$ is bijective, and for all $i \in [b]^+$, $0 \le e_i < s_i$, the function $\mathscr{F}'_{\mathscr{G}}$ is injective; since $|\Omega_{\mathscr{S}}| = |\Omega_{\mathscr{M}}|$, $\mathscr{F}'_{\mathscr{G}}$ is bijective. Let $A = (i_1, i_2, ..., i_d)$ and $B = (i'_1, i'_2, ..., i'_d)$ be any two neighboring nodes in G, and let $k = [d]^+$ be the index at which $|i_k - i'_k| = 1$. Let $A' = \mathscr{F}'_{\mathscr{G}}(A)$ and $B' = \mathscr{F}'_{\mathscr{G}}(B)$. If $k \in [c]^+$, then A' and B' have the same offset but different bases; the δ_m-distance between A' and B' is $|s_k i_k - s_k i'_k|$ if $k \in [b]^+$, and $|i_k - i'_k|$ if $k \in \{b+1, ..., c\}$. The distance between A' and B' in H is thus s_k if $k \in [b]^+$, and 1 if $k \in \{b+1, ..., c\}$. If $k \in \{c+1, ..., d\}$, then A' and B' have the same base but different offsets; since by the definitions of expansion and reduction, $\tilde{\mathscr{S}}$ is an expansion of $\mathscr{L}''$ with expansion factor $\mathscr{S}$, and since by Theorem 10, $\mathscr{F}_{\mathscr{G}}$ embeds the $\mathscr{L}''$-mesh in the $\tilde{\mathscr{S}}$-mesh with unit dilation cost, the distance between A' and B' in H is 1. Therefore, $\mathscr{F}'_{\mathscr{G}}$ embeds G in H with dilation cost $\max\{s_1, s_2, ..., s_b\}$. ∎

The condition of general reduction requires that the dimension of H is higher than half of the dimension of G. If this condition is not satisfied, an embedding of G in H can be constructed using the above results provided that there exists a sequence of intermediate graphs in which every pair of successive graphs have shapes satisfying the condition of general reduction. As to be shown in Section 4, if G and H are square, then either (i) their shapes satisfy the condition of simple reduction, or (ii) the sequence of intermediate graphs described above exists.

4. EMBEDDINGS AMONG SQUARE MESHES

4.1. A Lower Bound on Dilation Costs for Lowering Dimension Embeddings

In [22], Rosenberg studied the problem of embedding finite arrays (meshes), prism arrays, and orthant arrays in lines to minimize proximity in various local and global senses. Let t be an embedding of a d-dimensional mesh G in a line. For any positive integer k, the *diameter of preservation* σ_k is the smallest positive integer i such that for every node v in G, and for every pair of nodes u and w in G whose distances from v are no greater than k, $\delta_m(t(u), t(w)) < i$. Rosenberg proved that $\sigma_k > bk\mu^{d-1}$, where μ is the length of the shortest dimension of G, and b depends only on d and is a constant with respect to μ.

Let G and H be meshes of the same size and of dimensions d and c, respectively, such that $d > c$. By a straightforward modification of Rosenberg's proof for the lower bound on the diameter of preservation [22], we derive a lower bound on the dilation cost of any embedding of G in H. Given a node v in G and a positive integer k, let $Q(v, k)$ denote the set of nodes in G whose distances from v are no greater than k.

LEMMA 15 [22]. *Let G be a d-dimensional mesh. Let μ be the length of the shortest dimension of G. For any positive integer k such that $k < \mu$, $\max_{v \in G}|Q(v, k)| \ge \binom{k+d}{d} > bk^d$, where $b > 0$ is a constant with respect to k, and depends only on d.*

LEMMA 16. *Let G and H be meshes of the same size and of dimensions d and c, respectively. Let t be an embedding of G in H with dilation cost ρ. Then for any node v in G and any positive integer k, $|Q(v, k)| \le (2k\rho + 1)^c$.*

Proof. Let $p_1, p_2, ..., p_c$ be nonnegative integers. A set of lists is said to *lie within* a c-dimensional interval $[p_1, p_2, ..., p_c]$ if the lists are of the form $(i_1 + e_1, i_2 + e_2, ..., i_c + e_c)$, where for all $j \in [c]^+$, i_j is some fixed integer and $e_j \in [p_j]$. For any node v in G and any positive integer k, let $t(Q(v, k))$ be the set of images of the nodes in $Q(v, k)$ under the embedding t. We first show by induction on k that $t(Q(v, k))$ lies within a c-dimensional interval $[2k\rho + 1, 2k\rho + 1, ..., 2k\rho + 1]$.

Induction basis, $k = 1$. Let $q = |Q(v, 1)|$. Let $(a_1^1, a_2^1, ..., a_c^1), (a_1^2, a_2^2, ..., a_c^2), ..., (a_1^q, a_2^q, ..., a_c^q)$ denote the nodes in $t(Q(v, 1))$. For all $j \in [c]^+$, let $\alpha_j = \min\{a_j^1, a_j^2, ..., a_j^q\}$, and $\beta_j = \max\{a_j^1, a_j^2, ..., a_j^q\}$. Since for all $u, w \in Q(v, 1)$, $\delta_m(t(u), t(w)) \le \delta_m(t(u), t(v)) + \delta_m(t(v), t(w)) \le 2\rho$, we have for all $j \in [c]^+$, $|\alpha_j - \beta_j| \le 2\rho$. Therefore, $t(Q(v, 1))$ lies within a c-dimensional interval $[2\rho + 1, 2\rho + 1, ..., 2\rho + 1]$.

Induction hypothesis. Assume that for all $k \le k'$,

$t(Q(v, k))$ lies within a c-dimensional interval $[2k\rho + 1, 2k\rho + 1, ..., 2k\rho + 1]$.

Induction step, $k = k' + 1$. Since every node u in $Q(v, k' + 1)$ either belongs to $Q(v, k')$ or is a neighbor of some node w in $Q(v, k')$, the smallest c-dimensional interval containing $t(Q(v, k' + 1))$ contains at most 2ρ elements more in each of the c dimensions than the corresponding interval for $t(Q(v, k'))$. Therefore, by our induction hypothesis, $t(Q(v, k' + 1))$ must lie within a c-dimensional interval $[2\rho + 2k'\rho + 1, 2\rho + 2k'\rho + 1, ..., 2\rho + 2k'\rho + 1] = [2(k' + 1)\rho + 1, 2(k' + 1)\rho + 1, ..., 2(k' + 1)\rho + 1]$.

For any positive integer k, the maximum number of lists that can lie within a c-dimensional interval $[2k\rho + 1, 2k\rho + 1, ..., 2k\rho + 1]$ is $(2k\rho + 1)^c$. Since t is bijective, we have $|Q(v, k)| \le (2k\rho + 1)^c$. ∎

THEOREM 17. *Let G and H be meshes of the same size and of dimensions d and c, respectively, such that $d > c$. Let μ be the length of the shortest dimension of G. Then the dilation cost of any embedding of G in H is bounded from below by $b'\mu^{(d-c)/c}$, for some positive number b' that is a constant with respect to μ and depends only on d and c.*

Proof. Let ρ be the dilation cost of any embedding of G in H. By Lemmas 15 and 16, for any positive integer k such that $k < \mu$, $(2k\rho + 1)^c > bk^d$ for some positive number b that depends only on d. We thus have $\rho > (b^{1/c}/2)k^{(d-c)/c} - 1/2k \ge (b^{1/c}/2)k^{(d-c)/c}$. By letting $k = \mu - 1$, we have $\rho \ge (b^{1/c}/2)(\mu - 1)^{(d-c)/c}$. Since $\mu \ge 2$, $\mu - 1 \ge \mu/2$. Therefore $\rho \ge b'\mu^{(d-c)/c}$ for some b' that is a constant with respect to μ and depends only on d and c. ∎

4.2. Embeddings for Lowering Dimension

THEOREM 18. *Let G and H be square meshes of the same size and of dimensions d and c, respectively, such that $d > c$. Let l be the length of the dimensions of G. Assume that d is divisible by c. Then the shapes of G and H always satisfy the condition of simple reduction, and G can be embedded in H with dilation cost $l^{(d-c)/c}$; for fixed values of d and c this cost is optimal to within a constant multiplicative factor.*

Proof. Let $b = d/c$. Since d is divisible by c, b is an integer. Let m be the length of the dimensions of H. Since G and H are of the same size, we have $m^c = l^d$, and $m = l^b$. Hence, H is a simple reduction of G with reduction factor

$$((\underbrace{l, ..., l}_{b}), ..., (\underbrace{l, ..., l}_{b})).$$

By Theorem 12, G can be embedded in H with dilation cost $l^{(d-c)/c}$; the optimality condition of this cost follows from Theorem 17. ∎

The next lemma states a property of integers to be used in Theorem 20; this lemma in turn uses the following property of integers [3]:

Any positive integer $N > 1$ can be written uniquely in a *standard form* $N = p_1^{b_1}p_2^{b_2} \cdots p_r^{b_r}$ such that for all $i \in [r]^+$, b_i is a positive integer and each p_i is a prime with $1 < p_1 < \cdots < p_r$. $\quad$ (*)

LEMMA 19. *Let x be any integer greater than 1, and u and v any integers that are relatively prime. Assume that $x^{u/v}$ is an integer. Then $x^{1/v}$ is also an integer.*

Proof. Let $y = x^{u/v}$. By assumption, y is an integer. Furthermore, since x is an integer greater than 1, y is also an integer greater thn 1. By property (*) of integers, x can be written in its unique standard form $p_1^{b_1}p_2^{b_2} \cdots p_r^{b_r}$ in which $r, b_1, b_2, ..., b_r$ are positive integers and $p_1, p_2, ..., p_r$ are distinct primes with $p_1 < p_2 < \cdots < p_r$. Similarly, y can be written in its unique standard form $q_1^{c_1}q_2^{c_2} \cdots q_s^{c_s}$ in which $s, c_1, c_2, ..., c_s$ are positive integers and $q_1, q_2, ..., q_s$ are distinct primes with $q_1 < q_2 < \cdots < q_s$.

Since $y_v = x^u$, we have $q_1^{vc_1}q_2^{vc_2} \cdots q_s^{vc_s} = p_1^{ub_1}p_2^{ub_2} \cdots p_r^{ub_r}$. Since $q_1, q_2, ..., q_s$ are distinct primes with $q_1 < q_2 < ... < q_s$ and $p_1, p_2, ..., p_r$ are also distinct primes with $p_1 < p_2 < ... < p_r$, we have $r = s$ and for all $i \in [r]^+$, $q_i = p_i$ and $vc_i = ub_i$. Hence, for all $i \in [r]^+$, we have $ub_i/v = c_i$. Since c_i is an integer and u and v are relatively prime, b_i is divisible by v. It follows that $p_1^{b_1/v}p_2^{b_2/v} \cdots p_r^{b_r/v}$, which is $x^{1/v}$, must be an integer. ∎

THEOREM 20. *Let G and H be meshes of the same size and of dimensions d and c, respectively, such that $d > c$. Let l be the length of the dimensions of G. Assume that d is not divisible by c. Then there always exists a sequence of intermediate graphs in which the shapes of every pair of successive graphs satisfy the condition of general reduction, and G can be embedded in H with dilation cost $l^{(d-c)/c}$; for fixed values of d and c this cost is optimal to within a constant multiplicative factor.*

Proof. Let m be the length of the dimensions of H. Since G and H are of the same size, we have $m^c = l^d$, and $m = l^{d/c}$. Since m is an integer, $l^{d/c}$ is also an integer.

We first consider the simple case in which d and c are relatively prime. By the definition of meshes, $l > 1$, and hence by Lemma 19, $l^{1/c}$ is an integer. Let $I_0, I_1, ..., I_{d-c}$ be meshes such that for all $k \in [d - c + 1]$, I_k has dimension $d - k$ and shape

$$(\underbrace{l^{(c+k)/c}, ..., l^{(c+k)/c}}_{c}, \underbrace{l, ..., l}_{d-c-k}).$$

We have $I_0 = G$; $I_{d-c} = H$; $I_0, I_1, ..., I_{d-c}$ have the same size l^d; and, except for I_0 and I_{d-c}, none of the meshes I_1,

$I_2, ..., I_{d-c-1}$ is square. For all $k \in [d - c]$, the dimension of I_k is greater than the dimension of I_{k+1} by 1, and the shape of I_{k+1} is a general reduction of the shape of I_k with reduction factor

$$((\underbrace{l^{1/c}, ..., l^{1/c}}_{c})),$$

multiplicand sublist

$$(\underbrace{l^{(c+k)/c}, ..., l^{(c+k)/c}}_{c}, \underbrace{l, ..., l}_{d-c-k-1}),$$

and multiplier sublist (l). By Theorem 14 the mesh I_k can be embedded in I_{k+1} with dilation cost $l^{1/c}$. In the sequence of $d - c$ embedding steps, $G = I_0 \rightarrow I_1 \rightarrow \cdots \rightarrow I_{d-c-1} \rightarrow I_{d-c} = H$, each step has dilation cost $l^{1/c}$. This embedding of G in H thus has dilation cost at most $l^{(d-c)/c}$.

Let A and B be any two neighboring nodes along one of the first c dimensions of G, say, the jth, where $j \in [c]^+$. By the definition of the embedding function for general reduction given in Theorem 14, we can show by a simple induction that for all $k \in [d - c]^+$, the images of A and B in I_k differ only in the jth dimension by an amount exactly $l^{k/c}$. Thus the images of A and B in H are at distance exactly $l^{(d-c)/c}$. Therefore, the dilation cost of the embedding sequence is $l^{(d-c)/c}$.

Next we consider the case in which d and c are not relatively prime. Let a be the greatest common denominator of d and c, and let $u = d/a$ and $v = c/a$. Since d is not divisible by c, u and v are integers and relatively prime. We can write $l^{d/c}$ as $l^{u/v}$. Since $l^{u/v}$ is an integer and u and v are relatively prime, by Lemma 19 $l^{1/v}$ is an integer.

As in the preceding case, we can define a sequence of embeddings from G to H. This sequence consists of $u - v$ embedding steps; in each step the dimensions of the two corresponding graphs differ by a. Let $I_0, I_1, ..., I_{u-v}$ be meshes such that for all $k \in [u - v + 1]$, I_k has dimension $a(u - k)$ and shape

$$\mathcal{L}_k = (\underbrace{l^{(v+k)/v}, ..., l^{(v+k)/v}}_{av}, \underbrace{l, ..., l}_{a(u-v-k)}).$$

We have $I_0 = G$; $I_{u-v} = H$; $I_0, I_1, ..., I_{u-v}$ have the same size $l^{au} = l^d$; and, except for I_0 and I_{u-v}, none of the meshes $I_1, I_2, ..., I_{u-v-1}$ is square.

For all $k \in [u - v]$, let $\mathcal{L}'_k$ and $\mathcal{L}''_k$ be shapes of lengths $a(u - k - 1)$ and a, respectively, such that

$$\mathcal{L}'_k = (\underbrace{l^{(v+k)/v}, ..., l^{(v+k)/v}}_{av}, \underbrace{l, ..., l}_{a(u-v-k-1)}), \quad \mathcal{L}''_k = (\underbrace{l, ..., l}_{a}).$$

We have $\mathcal{L}_k = \mathcal{L}'_k \diamond \mathcal{L}''_k$. Let $\mathcal{R}_k = (\underbrace{l^{1/v}, ..., l^{1/v}}_{v})$ and $\mathcal{R}'_k =$

$\underbrace{\mathcal{R}_k \diamond \cdots \diamond \mathcal{R}_k}_{a}$. $\mathcal{R}'_k$ has length av, and $\mathcal{L}''_k = (\underbrace{\Pi \mathcal{R}_k, ..., \Pi \mathcal{R}_k}_{a})$. Further, since $\mathcal{L}_{k+1} = [\mathcal{R}'_k \diamond (\underbrace{1, ..., 1}_{a(u-v-k-1)})] \times \mathcal{L}'_k$, $\mathcal{L}_{k+1}$ is a general reduction of $\mathcal{L}_k$ with reduction factor $(\underbrace{\mathcal{R}_k, ..., \mathcal{R}_k}_{a})$. Therefore by Theorem 14, the mesh I_k can be embedded in the mesh I_{k+1} with dilation cost $l^{1/v}$.

In the sequence of $u - v$ embedding steps, $G = I_0 \rightarrow I_1 \rightarrow \cdots \rightarrow I_{u-v-1} \rightarrow I_{u-v} = H$, each step has dilation cost $l^{1/v}$; this embedding of G in H thus has dilation cost at most $l^{(u-v)/v} = l^{(d-c)/c}$. As in the preceding case, we can show that for any two neighboring nodes along one of the first c dimensions of G, the distance between the images in H is exactly $l^{(d-c)/c}$. Therefore, the dilation cost of the embedding sequence is $l^{(d-c)/c}$. In either case, the optimality condition of the cost follows from Theorem 17. ∎

In Theorems 18 and 20, the ratio of our dilation cost to the optimal dilation cost is bounded from above by $1/b$, for some positive number b that depends only on d and c. For fixed values of d and c, this upper bound on the ratio is a constant. Since in Theorems 18 and 20, an instance of G and H depends on d, c, and l (or, equivalently, on d, c, and m), we can fix the values of d and c without fixing an instance of G and H. For the special case in which G is a hypercube, Theorem 18 implies that G can be embedded in H with dilation cost $m/2$, where m is the length of the dimensions of H. For this special case, an instance of G and H depends, however, only on d and c (with $l = 2$ and $m = 2^{d/c}$), and thus fixing d and c fixes such an instance; therefore the upper bound $1/b$ on the ratio of our dilation cost to the optimal dilation cost varies with each problem instance.

4.3. Embeddings for Increasing Dimension

THEOREM 21. *Let G and H be square meshes of the same size and of dimensions d and c, respectively, such that $d < c$. Assume that c is divisible by d. Then G can be embedded in H with unit dilation cost.*

Proof. Let $a = c/d$. By the assumption of the theorem, a is an integer. Let l and m be the lengths of the dimensions of G and H, respectively, and $\mathcal{L}$ and $\mathcal{M}$ the shapes of G and H, respectively. We have $\mathcal{L} = (\underbrace{l, ..., l}_{d})$ and $\mathcal{M} = (\underbrace{m, ..., m}_{c})$. Since G and H have the same size, we have $l^d = m^c$ and $l = m^a$. Let $\mathcal{R} = (\underbrace{m, ..., m}_{a})$. Since $\Pi \mathcal{R} = l$ and $\mathcal{M} = \underbrace{\mathcal{R} \diamond \cdots \diamond \mathcal{R}}_{d}$, $\mathcal{M}$ is an expansion of $\mathcal{L}$ with expansion factor $(\underbrace{\mathcal{R}, \mathcal{R}, ..., \mathcal{R}}_{d})$. Therefore by Theorem 10, G can be embedded in H with unit dilation cost. ∎

TABLE I
Embeddings among General Meshes and General Tori

Condition	G	H	Other conditions	Function	Dilation cost
—	L	M or T	—	$f_{\jmath}$	1*
	R	M	Odd size	$g_{\jmath}$	2*
	R	M	Even size ($c > 1$)	$\pi^* \circ h_{\jmath^*}$	1*
	R	T	—	$h_{\jmath}$	1*
Expansion	M	M or T	—	$\mathscr{F}_{\gamma}$	1*
	T	T	—	$\mathscr{H}_{\gamma}$	1*
	T	M	Odd size	$\mathscr{G}_{\gamma}$	2*
	T	M	Even size	$\mathscr{G}_{\gamma}$	2†
	T	M	Even size and $\forall i, |\mathcal{V}_i| \geq 2$ with first component of $\mathcal{V}_i$ even	$\mathscr{H}_{\gamma}$	1*
—	M	H	—	$\mathscr{F}_{\gamma}$	1*
	T	H	—	$\mathscr{H}_{\gamma}$	1*
Simple reduction	T	M	—	$\mathscr{U}_{\gamma} \circ \mathscr{T}_{\tilde{v}}$	$2 \max_{1 \leq i \leq c}\{m_i/l_{v_i}\}$
	All others		—	$\mathscr{U}_{\gamma}$	$\max_{1 \leq i \leq c}\{m_i/l_{v_i}\}$
—	H	M or T	—	$\mathscr{U}_{\gamma}$	$\max_{1 \leq i \leq c} m_i/2$
General reduction	M	M or T	—	$\mathscr{F}'_{\jmath}$	$\max_{1 \leq i \leq b} s_i$
	T	T	—	$\mathscr{G}'_{\jmath}$	$\max_{1 \leq i \leq b} s_i$
	T	M	—	$\mathscr{G}''_{\jmath}$	$2 \max_{1 \leq i \leq b} s_i$

THEOREM 22. *Let G and H be square meshes of the same size and of dimensions d and c, respectively, such that $d < c$. Let l be the length of the dimensions of G, and a the greatest common divisor or c and d. Assume that c is not divisible by d. Then G can be embedded in H with dilation cost $l^{(d-a)/c}$.*

Proof. We first define an intermediate graph G' such that the shape of G' is an expansion of the shape of G and the shape of H is a general reduction of the shape of G'. Let m be the length of the dimensions of H. Let $u = d/a$, and $v = c/a$. Since u and v are relatively prime, and $l^{u/v} = m$ is an integer, by Lemma 19 $l^{1/v}$ is also an integer. Let G' be a square mesh of dimension vd and with the length of the dimensions equal to $l^{1/v}$. The mesh G' has the same size as G, and the shape of G' is an expansion of the shape of G with expansion factor $(\underbrace{\mathscr{R}, ..., \mathscr{R}}_{d})$, where $\mathscr{R} = (\underbrace{l^{1/v}, ..., l^{1/v}}_{v})$. By Theorem 10 the mesh G can be embedded in G' with unit dilation cost.

Since $vd = cu$ and $u > 1$, the dimension of G' is greater than and divisible by the dimension of H. By Theorem 18 G' can be embedded in H with dilation cost $(l^{1/v})^{(vd-c)/c} = l^{(d-a)/c}$, which is also the dilation cost of the embedding sequence $G \rightarrow G' \rightarrow H$. ∎

5. SUMMARY

In Table I we summarize the embedding results among general meshes and general tori, and in Table II the embedding results among square meshes and square tori. The analyses of the other cases of G and H are similar to the case in which G and H are both meshes; the keys of these analyses are included in the Appendix and the details can be found in the technical report [19]. In the table entries, we follow the same notations as in the corresponding theorems that state the embedding results for meshes G and H. The new embedding functions appeared in Table I are defined in the Appendix. We use M to denote a mesh, T a torus, L a line, R a ring, and H a hypercube. For any positive integers i and j, we use $i|j$ to mean that j is divisible by i, and $i{\not|}j$ to mean that j is not

TABLE II
Embeddings among Square Meshes and Square Tori

Condition	G	H	Other conditions	Embedding steps	Dilation cost
$d > c$, $c|d$	T	M	—	1	$2l^{(d-c)/c}$†
	All others		—	1	$l^{(d-c)/c}$†
$d > c$, $c{\not|}d$	T	M	—	$(d-c)/a$	$2l^{(d-c)/c}$†
	All others		—	$(d-c)/a$	$l^{(d-c)/c}$†
$d < c$, $d|c$	T	M	Odd size	1	2*
	T	M	Even size	1	1*
	All others		—	1	1*
$d < c$, $d{\not|}c$	T	M	Odd size	2	$2l^{(d-a)/c}$
	T	M	Even size	2	$l^{(d-a)/c}$
	All others		—	2	$l^{(d-a)/c}$

divisible by i. We label a dilation cost by a superscript $*$ if it is optimal, and by a superscript $\dagger$ if it is optimal, to within a constant multiplicative factor for fixed values of d and c.

Given any argument in the corresponding domain of an embedding function given in Table I, the number of operations needed to evaluate the function is proportionl to the maximum of the dimension of G and the dimension of H.

APPENDIX

6.1. The Embedding Function $g_{\mathcal{L}}$

Let G be a ring of size n, and H an $\mathcal{L}$-mesh of the same size. The nodes in G are numbers in $[n]$ with neighbors corresponding to successive elements in the cyclic sequence $0, 1, \ldots, n-1$. For any embedding $r: [n] \to \Omega_{\mathcal{L}}$ of G in H, its dilation cost is the same as the δ_m-spread of the cyclic sequence r. We number the elements in the sequence $f_{\mathcal{L}}$ successively from 0 to $n-1$. Let R' be the sequence of all even-numbered elements of $f_{\mathcal{L}}$ in the same order as they appear in $f_{\mathcal{L}}$, and R'' the sequence of all odd-numbered elements in $f_{\mathcal{L}}$ in the reverse order. Since the sequence $f_{\mathcal{L}}$ has unit δ_m-spread, both R' and R'' have δ_m-spread 2; and the cyclic sequence $R'R''$, the concatenation of R' and R'', also has δ_m-spread 2. The function $g_{\mathcal{L}}$ given in Lemma 23 defines the sequence $R'R''$.

LEMMA 23. *Let $\mathcal{L}$ be a shape of size n. Let $t_n : [n] \to [n]$ be the function such that for all $x \in [n]$:*

if n is even then

$$t_n(x) = \begin{cases} 2x, & \text{if } x < n/2; \\ n - 2(x - n/2) - 1, & \text{otherwise}; \end{cases}$$

if n is odd then

$$t_n(x) = \begin{cases} 2x, & \text{if } x < (n+1)/2; \\ n - 2(x - (n+1)/2) - 2, & \text{otherwise}. \end{cases}$$

Let $g_{\mathcal{L}} : [n] \to \Omega_{\mathcal{L}}$ be the function such that for all $x \in [n]$,

$$g_{\mathcal{L}}(x) = f_{\mathcal{L}}(t_n(x)).$$

Then $g_{\mathcal{L}}$ is bijective, and the cyclic sequence $g_{\mathcal{L}}$ has δ_m-spread 2.

The function $g_{\mathcal{L}}$ embeds a ring of size n in an $\mathcal{L}$-mesh of the same size with dilation cost 2.

6.2. The Embedding Function $h\mathcal{L}$

LEMMA 24. *Let $\mathcal{L} = (l_1, l_2)$ be a shape of size n. Then*

$$f_{\mathcal{L}}(n-1) = \begin{cases} (l_1 - 1, 0), & \text{if } l_1 \text{ is even}; \\ (l_1 - 1, l_2 - 1), & \text{otherwise}. \end{cases}$$

Proof. By definition, the radix-$\mathcal{L}$ representation of $n-1$ is $(l_1 - 1, l_2 - 1)$. Since $w_0 = n$, we have $\lfloor (n-1)/w_0 \rfloor = 0$, which is even. Since $n = l_1 l_2$ and $w_1 = l_2$, $\lfloor (n-1)/w_1 \rfloor = \lfloor l_1 - (1/l_2) \rfloor = l_1 - 1$, implying that $\lfloor (n-1)/w_1 \rfloor$ and l_1 have different parities. The lemma thus follows from the definition of $f_{\mathcal{L}}$. $\blacksquare$

Let $\mathcal{L} = (l_1, l_2)$ be a shape of size n. Let G be a ring of size n, and H a mesh or torus of shape $\mathcal{L}$. We assume the following coordinates: the origin of the graph H, $(0, 0)$, is at the lower left corner, with the first dimension increasing vertically upward and the second dimensions increasing horizontally to the right. Assume that $l_2 > 2$. We embed the nodes from the ring successively in the first column of H from top to bottom, and then by treating the remaining nodes in H as an $(l_1, l_2 - 1)$-graph, we embed the remaining nodes from the ring by the function $f_{(l_1, l_2 - 1)}$. In this embedding, the first node of the ring is embedded in node $(l_1 - 1, 0)$ in H, and by Lemma 24 the last node of the ring is embedded in node $(l_1 - 1, 1)$ if l_1 is even and in node $(l_1 - 1, l_2 - 1)$ if l_1 is odd. Thus if H is a mesh and l_1 is even, the embedding has unit dilation cost. If H is a torus, then nodes $(l_1 - 1, 0)$ and $(l_1 - 1, l_2 - 1)$ are also neighbors, and the embedding always has unit dilation cost.

For the case that $l_2 = 2$, we embed the nodes from the ring successively in the first column of H from top to bottom, and we embed the remaining nodes in the second column from bottom to top. This embedding has unit dilation cost for mesh or torus H. The function $r_{\mathcal{L}}$ given in Lemma 25 defines the above embeddings.

LEMMA 25. *Let $\mathcal{L} = (l_1, l_2)$ be a shape of size n. Let $r_{\mathcal{L}} : [n] \to \Omega_{\mathcal{L}}$ be the function such that for all $x \in [n]$:*

if $l_2 > 2$, then

$$r_{\mathcal{L}}(x) = \begin{cases} (l_1 - 1 - x, 0), & \text{if } x < l_1; \\ (x_1, x_2 + 1), \text{ where } (x_1, x_2) = \\ \qquad f_{(l_1, l_2 - 1)}(x - l_1), & \text{if } x \geq l_1; \end{cases}$$

if $l_2 = 2$, then

$$r_{\mathcal{L}}(x) = \begin{cases} (l_1 - 1 - x, 0), & \text{if } x < l_1; \\ (x - l_1, 1), & \text{if } x \geq l_1. \end{cases}$$

Then $r_{\mathcal{L}}$ is bijective; the cyclic sequence $r_{\mathcal{L}}$ always has unit δ_t-spread, and it has unit δ_m-spread if l_1 is even.

Let $\mathcal{L} = (l_1, l_2, ..., l_d)$ be a shape of size n with $d \geq 3$. Let $\mathcal{L}' = (l_1, l_2)$, $\mathcal{L}'' = (l_3, l_4, ..., l_d)$, and $m = \Pi_{i=3}^{d} l_i$. For all $i \in [m]$, let q_i be the sequence $r_{\mathcal{L}'}(0) \diamond f_{\mathcal{L}''}(i)$, $r_{\mathcal{L}'}(1) \diamond f_{\mathcal{L}''}(i)$, ..., $r_{\mathcal{L}'}(l_1 l_2 - 1) \diamond f_{\mathcal{L}''}(i)$. Since $r_{\mathcal{L}'} : [l_1 l_2] \to \Omega_{\mathcal{L}'}$ and $f_{\mathcal{L}''} : [m] \to \Omega_{\mathcal{L}''}$ are both bijective, each of these sequences consists of $l_1 l_2$ distinct elements in $\Omega_{\mathcal{L}}$. For all $i \in [m]$, let q_i' and q_i'' be two disjoint segments of q_i : q_i' consists of the first $l_1 l_2 - 1$ elements of q_i, with these elements in the same order as they appear in q_i if i is even and in the reverse order if i is odd; and q_i'' consists of the last element in q_i. Let $Q' = q_0' q_1' \cdots q_{m-1}'$, $Q'' = q_{m-1}'' q_{m-2}'' \cdots q_0''$, and $Q = Q'Q''$.

For any two successive elements in the sequence Q', if they belong to the same segment q_i', for some $i \in [m]$, then their rightmost $d - 2$ components are the same, and their leftmost two components correspond to successive elements in the sequence $r_{\mathcal{L}'}$. The δ_m-distance between them is 1. If they belong to different segments, then they have the same leftmost two components, and their rightmost $d - 2$ components correspond to successive elements in the sequence $f_{\mathcal{L}''}$. The δ_m-distance between them is also 1. The sequence Q' thus has unit δ_m-spread. For the sequence Q'', all its elements have the same leftmost two components, and for any two successive elements in Q'', their rightmost $d - 2$ components correspond to successive elements, in reverse order, in $f_{\mathcal{L}''}$. The sequence Q'' also has unit δ_m-spread.

We now analyze the *cyclic sequence* Q. Let y' and z' be the first and last elements of Q', and y'' and z'' be the first and last elements of Q''. Both z' and y'' come from the sequence q_{m-1}, with y'' being the last element in q_{m-1}, and depending on whether m is even or odd, z' being either the first or the second to last element in q_{m-1}. Assume that l_1 is even. Then by Lemma 25, the cyclic sequence $r_{\mathcal{L}'}$ has unit δ_m-spread. The δ_m-distance between z' and y'' is thus 1. For y' and z'', since they both come from the sequence q_0, with y' being the first element and z'' being the last, the δ_m-distance between y' and z'' is also 1. Therefore, the cyclic sequence Q has unit δ_m-spread if l_1 is even. By Lemma 25, the cyclic sequence Q always has unit δ_t-spread. For $d \geq 3$, the function $h_{\mathcal{L}}$ given in Lemma 26 defines the cyclic sequence Q.

LEMMA 26. *Let $\mathcal{L} = (l_1, l_2, ..., l_d)$ be a shape of size n. Let $h_{\mathcal{L}} : [n] \to \Omega_{\mathcal{L}}$ such that for all $x \in [n]$:*

if $d \geq 3$, then let $\mathcal{L}' = (l_1, l_2)$, $\mathcal{L}'' = (l_3, l_4, ..., l_d)$, $m = \Pi_{i=3}^{d} l_i$, $a = \lfloor x/(l_1 l_2 - 1) \rfloor$, $b = x \bmod (l_1 l_2 - 1)$, and

$$
h_{\mathcal{L}}(x) = \begin{cases}
r_{\mathcal{L}'}(b) \diamond f_{\mathcal{L}''}(a), \\
\qquad \text{if } x < m(l_1 l_2 - 1) \text{ and } a \text{ is even;} \\
r_{\mathcal{L}'}(l_1 l_2 - b - 2) \diamond f_{\mathcal{L}''}(a), \\
\qquad \text{if } x < m(l_1 l_2 - 1) \text{ and } a \text{ is odd;} \\
r_{\mathcal{L}'}(l_1 l_2 - 1) \diamond f_{\mathcal{L}''}(n - x - 1), \qquad \text{otherwise;}
\end{cases}
$$

if $d = 2$, then $h_{\mathcal{L}}(x) = r_{\mathcal{L}}(x)$; and
if $d = 1$, then $h_{\mathcal{L}}(x) = x$.

Then $h_{\mathcal{L}}$ is bijective; the cyclic sequence $h_{\mathcal{L}}$ always has unit δ_t-spread, and it has unit δ_m-spread if $d > 1$ and l_1 is even.

The function $h_{\mathcal{L}}$ embeds a ring in an $\mathcal{L}$-torus of the same size with unit dilation cost. Let $d > 1$ and $\mathcal{L} = (l_1, l_2, ..., l_d)$ be a shape of even size n. Let $\mathcal{L}^*$ be another shape and $\pi^* : [d]^+ \to [d]^+$ be a permutation such that the first component of $\mathcal{L}''$ is even and $\mathcal{L} = \pi^*(\mathcal{L}^*)$. Then the function $\pi^* \circ h_{\mathcal{L}^*}$ embeds a ring of size n in the $\mathcal{L}$-mesh with unit dilation cost.

6.3. The Embedding Functions $\mathcal{H}_V$ and $\mathcal{G}_V$

The functions $\mathcal{H}_V$ and $\mathcal{G}_V$ are defined in the same way as the function $\mathcal{F}_V$ except that for all $k \in [d]^+$ the component function f_{V_k} is replaced by g_{V_k} and h_{V_k}, respectively.

6.4. The Embedding Function $\mathcal{T}_{\mathcal{L}}$

LEMMA 27. *Let $\mathcal{L} = (l_1, l_2, ..., l_d)$ be a shape. Let $\mathcal{T}_{\mathcal{L}} : \Omega_{\mathcal{L}} \to \Omega_{\mathcal{L}}$ be the function such that for all $(x_1, x_2, ..., x_d) \in \Omega_{\mathcal{L}}$,*

$$\mathcal{T}_{\mathcal{L}}((x_1, x_2, ..., x_d)) = (t_{l_1}(x_1), t_{l_2}(x_2), ..., t_{l_d}(x_d)),$$

where the functions $t_{l_1}, t_{l_2}, ..., t_{l_d}$ are defined in Lemma 23. Then the function $\mathcal{T}_{\mathcal{L}}$ embeds a torus G in a mesh H of the same shape $\mathcal{L}$ with optimal dilation cost 2.

Let $\mathcal{L}$ and $\mathcal{M}$ be shapes of the same size. Assume that we have an embedding function r that embeds a mesh G' of shape $\mathcal{L}$ in a mesh H of shape $\mathcal{M}$ with dilation cost ρ. Then we can embed a torus G of shape $\mathcal{L}$ in the mesh H by the function $r \circ \mathcal{T}_{\mathcal{L}}$ with dilation cost at most 2ρ.

6.5. The Embedding Functions $\mathcal{G}_{\mathcal{L}}'$ and $\mathcal{G}_{\mathcal{L}}''$

Using the same notations as in Theorem 14, the functions $\mathcal{G}_{\mathcal{L}}'$ and $\mathcal{G}_{\mathcal{L}}''$ have the same domain and range as the function $\mathcal{F}_{\mathcal{L}}'$ such that

$$
\begin{aligned}
\mathcal{G}_{\mathcal{L}}'((i_1, i_2, ..., i_d)) = {}&[(s_1 i_1, s_2 i_2, ..., s_b i_b) \\
&+ \mathcal{G}_{\mathcal{L}}((i_{c+1}, i_{c+2}, ..., i_d))] \\
&\diamond (i_{b+1}, i_{b+2}, ..., i_c),
\end{aligned}
$$

$$
\begin{aligned}
\mathcal{G}_{\mathcal{L}}''((i_1, i_2, ..., i_d)) = {}&[(s_1 t_{l_1}(i_1), s_2 t_{l_2}(i_2), ..., s_b t_{l_b}(i_b)) \\
&+ \mathcal{G}_{\mathcal{L}}((i_{c+1}, i_{c+2}, ..., i_d))] \\
&\diamond (t_{l_{b+1}}(i_{b+1}), t_{l_{b+2}}(i_{b+2}) ..., t_{l_c}(i_c)).
\end{aligned}
$$

The function $\mathcal{G}_{\mathcal{L}}''$ embeds a torus G of shape $\mathcal{L}$ in a mesh H of shape $\mathcal{M}$ by first embedding the supernodes in G in the supernodes in H using the function $\mathcal{T}_{\mathcal{L}}$, and the embedding the nodes in the supernode of G in the nodes of the corresponding supernode of H using the function $\mathcal{G}_{\mathcal{L}}$.

ACKNOWLEDGMENTS

The authors are grateful to Dale Miller, Hungwen Li, and Ching-Tien Ho for their helpful discussions and suggestions to this paper.

REFERENCES

1. Aleliunas, R., and Rosenberg, A. L. On embedding rectangular grids in square grids. *IEEE Trans. Comput.* **C-31,** 9 (September 1982), 907–913.

2. Bettayeb, S., Miller, Z., and Sudborough, I. H. Embedding grids into hypercubes. In *Lecture Notes in Computer Science*, Vol. 319. Springer-Verlag, New York/Berlin, 1988, pp. 201–211. *Proc. 3rd Aegean Workshop on Computing, AWOC88, Corfu, Greece.*

3. Bunton, D. M. *Abstract and Linear Algebra.* Addison–Wesley, Reading, MA, 1972.

4. Chan, M. Y. Dilation-2 embeddings of grids into hypercubes. *Proceedings of International Conference on Parallel Processing, 1988,* pp. 295–298.

5. Chan, M. Y. Embeddings of 3-dimensional grids into optimal hypercubes. Technical Report UTDCS, 13-88. University of Texas at Dallas.

6. Chan, T. F., and Saad, Y. Multigrid algorithms on the hypercube miltiprocessor. *IEEE Trans. Comput.* **C-35,** 11 (November 1986), 969–977.

7. DeMillo, R. A., Eisenstat, S. C., and Lipton, R. J. Preserving average proximity in arrays. *Comm. ACM* **21,** 3 (March 1978), 228–231.

8. Ellis, J. A. Embedding rectangular grids into square grids. *IEEE Trans. Comput.* **C-40,** 1 (January 1991), 46–52.

9. FitzGerald, C. H. Optimal indexing of the vertices of graphs. *Math. Comp.* **28,** 127 (July 1974), 825–831.

10. Fox, G. C., Johnson, M. A., Lyzenga, G. A., Otto, S. W., Salmon, J. K., and Walker, D. W. *Solving Problems on Concurrent Processors, Vol. I. General Techniques and Regular Problems.* Prentice–Hall, Englwood Cliffs, NJ, 1988.

11. Greenberg, D. S. Optimum expansion embeddings of meshes in hypercubes. Technical Report YALEU/CSD/RR-535. Yale University, 1987.

12. Harper, L. H. Optimal numberings and isoperimetric problems on graphs. *J. Combin. Theory* **1** (1966), 385–393.

13. Ho, C. T., and Johnsson, S. L. On the embedding of arbitrary meshes in boolean cubes with expansion two dilation two. *Proceedings, International Conference on Parallel Processing, 1987,* pp. 188–191.

14. Hoffman, A. J., Martin, M. S., and Rose, D. J. Complexity bounds for regular finite difference and finite element grids. *SIAM J. Numer. Anal.* **10,** 2 (April 1973), 364–369.

15. Hong, J. W., Mehlhorn, K., and Rosenberg, A. L. Cost trade-offs in graph embeddings, with applications. *J. Assoc. Comput. Mach.* **30,** 4 (October 1983), 709–728.

16. Kosaraju, S. R., and Atallah, M. J. Optimal simulations between mesh-connected arrays of processors. *J. Assoc. Comput. Mach.* (July 1988).

17. Ma, E., and Shea, D. C. E-kernel—An embedding kernel on the IBM Victor multiprocessor for program mapping and network reconfiguration. IBM Research Report RC 16771 (#74236), April 1991.

18. Ma, E., Narahari, B., and Tao, L. Optimal embedding of 2-D torus into ring. *Inform. Process. Lett.* **41,** 4 (1992).

19. Ma, E., and Tao, L. Embeddings among toruses and meshes. Technical report MS-CIS-88-63, University of Pennsylvania, 1988.

20. Ma, E., and Tao, L. Embeddings among toruses and meshes. *Proceedings, International Conference on Parallel Processing, 1987,* pp. 178–187.

21. Reingold, E. M., Nievergelt, J., and Deo, N. *Combinatorial Algorithms.* Prentice–Hall, Englewood Cliffs, NJ, 1977.

22. Rosenberg, A. L. Preserving proximity in arrays. *SIAM J. Comput.* **4,** 4 (December 1975), 443–460.

23. Tao, L., and Ma, E. Simulating parallel neighboring communications among square meshes and square toruses. *J. Supercomputing* **5,** 1 (1991), 57–71.

24. Tremblay, J. P., and Manohar, R. *Discrete Mathematical Structures with Applications to Computer Science.* McGraw-Hill, New York, 1975.

25. Wilcke, W. W., Shea, D. G., Booth, R. C., Brown, D. H., Giampapa, M. E., Huisman, L., Irwin, G. R., Ma, E., Murakami, T. T., Tong, F. T., Varker, P. R., and Zukowski, D. J. The IBM Victor Multiprocessor Project. *Proceedings, 4th International Conference on Hypercubes, Vol. 1, 1989,* pp. 201–207.

Received February 5, 1991; accepted April 7, 1992

EVA MA received the B.A., M.S., and Ph.D. degrees from University of California, Berkeley in 1977, 1980, and 1981, respectively. She was an Assistant Professor at University of Pennsylvania from 1981 to 1988, a Visiting Scientist at IBM Thomas J. Watson Research Center from 1988 to 1990, and a Visiting Fellow at University of Glasgow, Scotland from 1990 to 1991. Her research interests include parallel processing, analysis of algorithms, and graph theory.

LIXIN TAO received his M.S.E. and Ph.D. degrees in Computer Science from University of Pennsylvania, Philadelphia, PA in 1985 and 1988, respectively. He is currently an Assistant Professor in the Department of Computer Science at Concordia University, Montreal. His current research interests include portable parallel programming systems, program mapping, and combinatorial optimization. He is a member of the Association for Computing Machinery and the IEEE Computer Society.

Embedding Rectangular Grids into Square Grids with Dilation Two

Rami G. Melhem, *Member, IEEE,* and Ghil-Young Hwang, *Member, IEEE*

Abstract—In this paper, a new technique, the multiple ripple propagation technique, is presented for mapping an $h \times w$ grid into a $w \times h$ grid such that the dilation cost is 2, i.e., such that any two neighboring nodes in the first grid are mapped onto two nodes in the second grid that are separated by a distance of at most 2. This technique is then used as a basic tool for mapping any rectangular source grid into a square target grid with the dilation two property preserved. The ratio of the number of nodes in the source grid to the number of nodes in the target grid, called the expansion cost, is shown to be always less than 1.2. This is a significant improvement over the previously suggested techniques, where the expansion cost could be bounded by 1.2 only if the dilation cost was allowed to be as high as 18.

Index Terms—Embeddings among grids, mapping onto meshes, minimizing the dilation cost, squaring up rectangular grids, theory of VLSI layout.

I. INTRODUCTION

IN THIS paper, we study the problem of squaring up a rectangular grid, that is, embedding an $h \times w$ rectangular grid into a $k \times k$ square grid, where $k \geq \lceil \sqrt{hw} \rceil$, and $\lceil \ \rceil$ is the ceiling function. The results of this research may be applied to the VLSI design of highly eccentric circuits that, without squaring up, would have to be laid out in a rectangular area with a height/width ratio deviating significantly from unity [7], [10]. They may also be applied to the mapping of toroidal [6] and rectangular problem domains [3], [8] onto mesh-connected architectures [1], [9]. Mapping of rectangular program graphs onto hypercube architectures may also benefit from this research. Specifically, it has been shown [5] that this mapping may be accomplished by embedding the graph into a square graph which is, then, mapped easily to the hypercube.

Two measures may be used to estimate the quality of an embedding. The first measure is the expansion cost E, which is the ratio of the number of nodes in the square target grid to the number of nodes in the source rectangular grid. That is $E = k^2/hw$. The other measure is the dilation cost D, which is a measure of the communication penalty that has to be paid due to the squaring up. More specifically, if a link λ in the source grid connects two neighboring nodes, say (i, j) and $(i, j + 1)$, and these two nodes are mapped to the nodes (i', j') and $(i' + c_i, j' + c_j)$ in the target grid, then the dilation of the edge λ after the embedding is defined by $D(\lambda) = |c_i| + |c_j|$. The dilation cost of the embedding is then given by $D = \max_\lambda D(\lambda)$.

The best known results for embedding an $h \times w$ grid into the smallest possible $k \times k$ grid are given in [2], where different embedding methods are suggested for different ranges of the eccentricity ratio $\rho = w/h$. Assuming that $h \geq 25$, all the methods suggested in [2] produce embeddings with expansion costs smaller than 1.2, and dilation costs ranging from 2 to 18, depending on the value of ρ. Specifically, the dilation cost is less than or equal to 3 if ρ is in one of the ranges (1, 2], (10/3, 4], (8, 9], or (155, ∞). Otherwise, the dilation cost is larger than 5.

In this paper, we first introduce, in Section II, the multiple ripple propagation technique which may be used to embed an $h \times w$ grid onto a $w \times h$ grid with expansion cost 1 and dilation cost 2. This basic technique is then used in Sections III and IV to embed any rectangular grid with $\rho \leq 4$ into a square grid. The idea is to apply the ripple propagation technique to carefully chosen subrectangles of the rectangular grid. For grids with $\rho > 4$, the ripple propagation technique may be combined with the technique of folding [2]. This is described and analyzed in Section V. Finally, in Section VI, we summarize our results and show that it is always possible to square up any rectangular grid at a dilation cost of 2 and an expansion cost less than 1.2. This is a clear improvement over the results given in [2].

II. A MULTIPLE RIPPLE PROPAGATION TECHNIQUE

The purpose of the technique described in this section is to map an $h \times w$ grid satisfying

$$h < w \leq 2h \tag{1}$$

onto a $w \times h$ grid with unity expansion cost and with dilation cost equal to 2. In order to accomplish that, the w nodes in each row in the original grid should be compressed to occupy only h columns. For this, we let $l = w - h$, and compress $2l$ nodes from each row into l columns by repeated rippling. The remaining $s = w - 2l = 2h - w$ nodes are left uncompressed. In Fig. 1(b), we show the grid of Fig. 1(a) after compressing each of its rows. As shown in the figure, the positions of the l ripples in each row are chosen as follows. In the first row, the l ripples are grouped to the right, and in the last row, the l ripples are grouped to the left. At each row, one of the ripples, that was grouped to the right in the previous row, starts its propagation to the left (moves one column). The propagation of that ripple continues at a rate of one column every row until it can no longer propagate. The propagation of the ripples is very similar to the motion of the legs of a walking worm.

Fig. 1(b) is laid out to occupy $w + s$ rows and h columns. However, it may be noticed that s positions in each column are not utilized. This allows for the compression of Fig. 1(b) into an $w \times h$ grid which has a dilation cost equal to 2 [see Fig. 1(c)]. In order to be more formal, we let $F(i, j) = (u(i, j), v(i, j))$ be the function which maps each point (i, j) in the source grid to a corresponding point $(u(i, j), v(i, j))$ in the target grid. Here, (1, 1) is the node at the top left corner of the grid. For any node $(1, j)$ in the first row of the source grid, the mapping function F

Manuscript received April 2, 1988; revised June 9, 1989. This work was supported in part by ONR Contract N00014-85-K-0339. A shorter version of this paper appeared in the Proceedings of the Allerton Conference on Computer, Control, and Communications, September 1988.

R. G. Melhem is with the Department of Computer Science, University of Pittsburgh, Pittsburgh, PA 15260.

G.-Y. Hwang is with the Sukus Computer Company, Seoul, Korea.

IEEE Log Number 9038763.

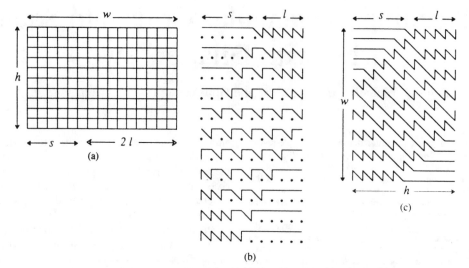

Fig. 1. Embedding an 11×16 grid into an 16×11 grid using multiple ripple propagation.

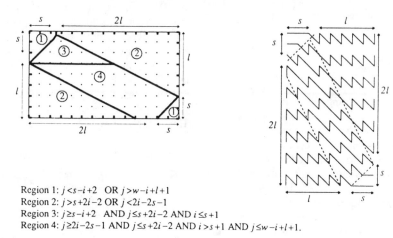

Region 1: $j < s-i+2$ OR $j > w-i+l+1$
Region 2: $j > s+2i-2$ OR $j < 2i-2s-1$
Region 3: $j \geq s-i+2$ AND $j \leq s+2i-2$ AND $i \leq s+1$
Region 4: $j \geq 2i-2s-1$ AND $j \leq s+2i-2$ AND $i > s+1$ AND $j \leq w-i+l+1$.

Fig. 2. Partitioning of the source grid for $s \leq l$.

is defined as follows:

$$u(1,j) = \begin{cases} 1 & \text{if } j = 1, \cdots, s \\ 1 + \text{rem}\left(\dfrac{j-s}{2}\right) & \text{if } j = s+1, \cdots, w \end{cases}$$

(2.a)

$$v(1,j) = \begin{cases} j & \text{if } j = 1, \cdots, s \\ s + \left\lceil \dfrac{j-s}{2} \right\rceil & \text{if } j = s+1, \cdots, w. \end{cases}$$

(2.b)

where rem( ) denotes the remainder of integer division. The function F may then be defined recursively such that, for any node (i, j) not in the first row, $F(i, j)$ is specified in terms of $F(i - 1, j)$. In order to simplify the recursive definition of F, we partition the source grid into four regions as shown in Figs. 2 and 3, and we use different recursive formulas for different regions. Specifically,

$$u(i,j) = \begin{cases} u(i-1,j) + 1 & \text{if } (i,j) \in \text{Region 1} \\ u(i-1,j) + 2 & \text{if } (i,j) \in \text{Region 2} \\ u(i-1,j) + \Delta_{u,3}(i,j) & \text{if } (i,j) \in \text{Region 3} \\ u(i-1,j) + \Delta_{u,4}(i,j) & \text{if } (i,j) \in \text{Region 4} \end{cases}$$

(3.a)

$$v(i,j) = \begin{cases} v(i-1,j) & \text{if } (i,j) \in \text{Region 1} \\ v(i-1,j) & \text{if } (i,j) \in \text{Region 2} \\ v(i-1,j) - \Delta_{v,3}(i,j) & \text{if } (i,j) \in \text{Region 3} \\ v(i-1,j) - \Delta_{v,4}(i,j) & \text{if } (i,j) \in \text{Region 4} \end{cases}$$

(3.b)

where $\Delta_{u,3}$ and $\Delta_{v,3}$ depend on the remainder $r(i, j) = \text{rem}((j - s + i - 1)/3)$. Specifically,

$$\Delta_{u,3} = \begin{cases} 0 & \text{if } r(i,j) = 2 \\ 2 & \text{otherwise} \end{cases}$$

$$\Delta_{v,3} = \begin{cases} 1 & \text{if } r(i,j) = 2 \\ 0 & \text{otherwise.} \end{cases}$$

Similarly, if $\bar{r}(i, j) = \text{rem}((j - 2i + 2s + 2)/3)$, then

$$\Delta_{u,4} = \begin{cases} 0 & \text{if } \bar{r}(i,j) = 2 \\ 2 & \text{otherwise} \end{cases}$$

$$\Delta_{v,4} = \begin{cases} 1 & \text{if } \bar{r}(i,j) = 2 \\ 0 & \text{otherwise.} \end{cases}$$

Given the above formulas, the following theorem proves that the dilation cost of the mapping F is at most two.

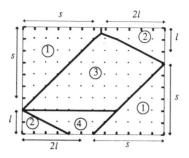
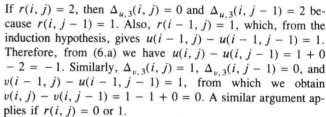

Region 1: $j < s - i + 2$ OR $j > w - i + l + 1$
Region 2: $j > s + 2i - 2$ OR $j < 2i - 2s - 1$
Region 3: $j \geq s - i + 2$ AND $j \leq s + 2i - 2$ AND $i \leq s + 1$ AND $j \leq w - i + l + 1$
Region 4: $j \geq 2i - 2s - 1$ AND $j \leq w - i + l + 1$ AND $i > s + 1$.

Fig. 3.   Partitioning of the source grid for $s > l$.

Theorem: For any (i, j), where $i, j > 1$, the following is true

$$|u(i, j) - u(i - 1, j)| + |v(i, j) - v(i - 1, j)| \leq 2 \quad (4.a)$$

and

$$|u(i, j) - u(i, j - 1)| + |v(i, j) - v(i, j - 1)| \leq 2. \quad (4.b)$$

That is, any two adjacent nodes in the source grid are mapped onto two nodes whose separation distance in the target grid is less than or equal to 2.

Proof: The proof of (4.a) is straightforward if (i, j) is in Region 1 or Region 2. If (i, j) is in region 3, then the left side of (4.a) reduces to $|\Delta_{u,3}(i, j)| + |\Delta_{v,3}(i, j)|$, which is equal to 1 if $r(i, j) = 2$, and to 2 otherwise. The case $(i, j) \in$ Region 4 is similar.

To prove (4.b) we use induction on i. For $i = 1$, the proof is by direct substitution from (2). Next, assuming that (4.b) holds for $i - 1$, we should show that it also holds for i. Again the inductive proof is straightforward if (i, j) is in Regions 1 or 2, and is similar if (i, j) is in Regions 3 and 4. For this reason we will consider in the rest of this proof only the case in which $(i, j) \in$ Region 3. For this case, we will prove, by induction, a more restrictive form of (4.b), namely

$$u(i, j) - u(i, j - 1) = \begin{cases} -1 & \text{if } r(i, j) = 2 \\ 1 & \text{if } r(i, j) = 0 \text{ or } 1 \end{cases} \quad (5.a)$$

$$v(i, j) - v(i, j - 1) = \begin{cases} 0 & \text{if } r(i, j) = 2 \\ 1 & \text{if } r(i, j) = 0 \text{ or } 1. \end{cases} \quad (5.b)$$

For $i = 2$, (5) is proved directly from (2) and (3). To prove the induction step, we notice that if (i, j) is in Region 3, then $(i, j - 1)$ is either in Region 3 or in Region 1. We first assume that $(i, j - 1)$ is in Region 3 and use (3) to obtain

$$u(i, j) - u(i, j - 1) = u(i - 1, j) - u(i - 1, j - 1) + \Delta_{u,3}(i, j) - \Delta_{u,3}(i, j - 1) \quad (6.a)$$

$$v(i, j) - v(i, j - 1) = v(i - 1, j) - v(i - 1, j - 1) - \Delta_{v,3}(i, j) + \Delta_{v,3}(i, j - 1). \quad (6.b)$$

If $r(i, j) = 2$, then $\Delta_{u,3}(i, j) = 0$ and $\Delta_{u,3}(i, j - 1) = 2$ because $r(i, j - 1) = 1$. Also, $r(i - 1, j) = 1$, which, from the induction hypothesis, gives $u(i - 1, j) - u(i - 1, j - 1) = 1$. Therefore, from (6.a) we have $u(i, j) - u(i, j - 1) = 1 + 0 - 2 = -1$. Similarly, $\Delta_{v,3}(i, j) = 1$, $\Delta_{v,3}(i, j - 1) = 0$, and $v(i - 1, j) - u(i - 1, j - 1) = 1$, from which we obtain $v(i, j) - v(i, j - 1) = 1 - 1 + 0 = 0$. A similar argument applies if $r(i, j) = 0$ or 1.

Finally, if $(i, j - 1)$ is in Region 1, then $j = s - i + 2$ and thus, $r(i, j) = 1$. From (3.a), we get $u(i, j) - u(i, j - 1) = u(i - 1, j) - u(i - 1, j - 1) + 2 - 1$ and from (3.b) we get $v(i, j) - v(i, j - 1) = v(i - 1, j) - v(i - 1, j - 1)$. But both $(i - 1, j)$ and $(i - 1, j - 1)$ are in Region 1, and thus $u(i - 1, j) = u(i - 1, j - 1)$, and $v(i - 1, j) = v(i - 1, j - 1) + 1$, which proves (5.a) and (5.b), respectively. □

The above theorem proves that it is possible to map an $h \times w$ grid, $h < w \leq 2h$, exactly into a $w \times h$ grid with dilation cost 2. It is also possible to concatenate the $w \times h$ target grid with its symmetric image (reflected across the line $v = h$) to obtain an exact embedding of an $h \times 2w$ grid into a $w \times 2h$ grid with dilation cost 2. Along the same line of thinking, an $h \times 2w + 1$ source grid may be divided into $h \times w + 1$ and $h \times w$ subgrids. These two subgrids may then be embedded into a $w + 1 \times h$ and a $w \times h$ grid, respectively, and by concatenating the former with the symmetric image of the latter, we may obtain a $w + 1 \times 2h$ target grid. The dilation cost at the line of concatenation may be shown to be at most two. Grid concatenations of the type described here will be used repeatedly and tacitly in the rest of this paper.

In the following sections, we apply the above technique to our original problem of mapping an $h \times \rho h$ rectangular grid (ρ is assumed to be greater than unity), into a square grid. First, two basic methods are introduced for grids with $\rho \leq 4$. These methods are then combined with folding and applied effectively to the embedding of any grid with $\rho > 4$.

III. The Method of Exact Row Fitting

Let k, $k \geq h$, be the dimension of the square grid (called the target grid) onto which a given $h \times \rho h$ grid (called the source grid) is to be mapped. Of course, it is desirable to choose the smallest possible k in order to minimize the expansion cost $E = k^2 / \rho h^2$. Given such a k, the method of exact row fitting assumes that the leftmost $h \times k$ subgrid of the source grid may be mapped exactly into the $k \times h$ leftmost subgrid of the target grid (see Fig. 4). This is possible if and only if condition (1) is

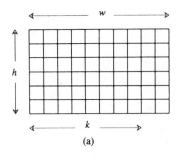
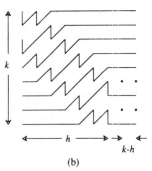

Fig. 4. Embedding a 7 × 11 grid into a 9 × 9 grid using the method of exact row fitting.

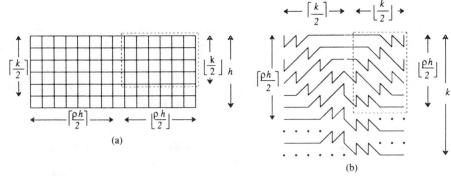

Fig. 5. Embedding a 7 × 15 grid into a 11 × 11 grid using exact column fitting.

satisfied. That is

$$h \leq k \leq 2h. \tag{7.a}$$

Moreover, if

$$k - h \geq \rho h - k \tag{7.b}$$

that is, the number of columns, $k - h$, remaining in the target grid is at least equal to the number of columns, $\rho h - k$, remaining in the source grid, then these columns may be mapped in a trivial way with dilation cost 2. In other words, the mapping may be completed with dilation cost 2 provided that the size of the target grid, k, satisfies the conditions (7.a/b).

The solution of inequalities (7.a/b) may be found by, first, computing the minimum k that satisfies (7.b), and then checking that this value is consistent with (7.a). Specifically, (7.b) is satisfied if

$$k = K_r = \left\lceil \frac{\rho + 1}{2} h \right\rceil. \tag{8}$$

It is straightforward to check that the value of k given by (8) satisfies (7.a) if $\rho \leq 3 - 1/h$. Hence, the method of exact row fitting may be applied only if $\rho \leq 3 - 1/h$. Noting that $K_r \leq ((\rho + 1)h + 1)/2$, we may obtain an upper bound on the expansion cost of the resulting embedding. Namely,

$$E_r = \frac{K_r^2}{\rho} \leq E_{r,\max} = \frac{\left(\rho + 1 + \frac{1}{h} \right)^2}{4\rho}. \tag{9}$$

The value of E_r increases monotonically with ρ for $\rho > 1 + 1/h$, and hence may exceed 1.2 for large values of ρ. For

examples, assuming $h = 12$, then $E_r > 1.2$ if $\rho \geq 2.06$. Moreover, if $\rho > 3 - 1/h$, the method may not be applied. In these cases, the method of exact column fitting, described in the following section, can be used.

IV. THE METHOD OF EXACT COLUMN FITTING

The embedding technique used in this section is based on the vertical dissection of both the source and the target grids, each into two subgrids which are as equal as possible. Each of the source subgrids is then embedded into the corresponding target subgrid in a way that ensures that all the columns of the target grid are efficiently used. In order to deal with the case of ρh being an odd integer, the number of columns in the two source subgrids is taken to be $\lceil \rho h/2 \rceil$ and $\lfloor \rho h/2 \rfloor$, respectively, where $\lfloor \ \rfloor$ is the floor function. For the same reason, the number of columns in the target subgrid is divided into $\lceil k/2 \rceil$ and $\lfloor k/2 \rfloor$ columns, respectively, (see Fig. 5).

The optimal size, $k = K_c$, of the target grid should be determined by the embedding of $h \times \lceil \rho h/2 \rceil \rightarrow k \times \lceil k/2 \rceil$ or the embedding $h \times \lfloor \rho h/2 \rfloor \rightarrow k \times \lfloor k/2 \rfloor$, whichever gives a more strict condition on k. It turns out that the latter embedding is more restrictive than the former, and hence, should be used to derive k. In the remainder of this section, we will denote the $h \times \lfloor \rho h/2 \rfloor$ grid by G_s, and the $k \times \lfloor k/2 \rfloor$ grid by G_t, and we will describe an embedding of G_s into G_t. The embedding of the other half of the source grid (the $h \times \lceil \rho h/2 \rceil$ subgrid) into the other half of the target grid (the $k \times \lceil k/2 \rceil$ subgrid) may be accomplished in a similar fashion.

Consider the upper $\lfloor k/2 \rfloor \times \lfloor h/2 \rfloor$ subgrid of G_s, and embed it into the upper $\lfloor \rho h/2 \rfloor \times \lfloor k/2 \rfloor$ subgrid of G_t using the ripple propagation technique of Section II. In order to

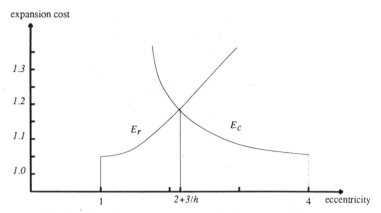

Fig. 6. Expansion cost versus eccentricity for $1 < \rho \le 4$ ($h = 20$).

accomplish this embedding we should have

$$\lfloor k/2 \rfloor \le h \qquad (10.a)$$

and condition (1) should be satisfied, namely

$$\lfloor k/2 \rfloor \le \lfloor \rho h/2 \rfloor \le 2 \lfloor k/2 \rfloor . \qquad (10.b)$$

With this, each of the remaining $h - \lfloor k/2 \rfloor$ rows in G_s may then be compressed to have the same pattern as the last row of the $\lfloor \rho h/2 \rfloor \times \lfloor k/2 \rfloor \to \lfloor k/2 \rfloor \times \lfloor \rho h/2 \rfloor$ embedding. This results in a dilation cost equal to 2 and requires $2(h - \lfloor k/2 \rfloor)$ additional rows in G_t. Thus, the following should be satisfied:

$$k - \lfloor \rho h/2 \rfloor \le 2(h - \lfloor k/2 \rfloor). \qquad (10.c)$$

Noting that $(x + 1)/2 \ge \lfloor x/2 \rfloor \ge (x - 1)/2$, we may calculate the minimum value of k which always satisfies (10.c). Namely,

$$k = K_c = \left\lceil \frac{\rho h/2 + 2h + 1}{2} \right\rceil . \qquad (11)$$

This value of K_c satisfies conditions (10.a) and (10.b) as long as $\rho \le 4$.

With the value of k given by (11), the two halves of the source grid may be successfully embedded into the two halves of the target grid with dilation cost 2. Noting that $\lceil x/4 \rceil \le (x + 3)/4$, it is possible to bound the expansion cost of the embedding as follows:

$$E_c \le E_{c,\max} = \frac{\left(\rho + 4 + \dfrac{5}{h}\right)^2}{16\rho}. \qquad (12)$$

For $1 < \rho \le 4$, the value of E_c is monotonically decreasing with ρ, which suggests the use of the method of fitting columns whenever the method of fitting rows fails to satisfy $E_r \le 1.2$ (see Fig. 6). The critical value of ρ that determines which of the two methods has a smaller expansion cost may be found by solving $E_{r,\max} = E_{c,\max}$. From (9) and (12), this gives $\rho = 2 + 3/h$. The expansion cost at this value of ρ is $(3h + 4)^2/(4h(2h + 3))$, which is always smaller than 1.2 if $h > 17$.

Hence, for $1 < \rho \le 4$, the most efficient embedding method depends on the value of ρ. Specifically, if $\rho \le 2 + 3/h$, then the methods of exact row fitting should be used, otherwise, the method of exact column fitting should be used. For values of ρ larger than four, the above methods can be combined with the known method of folding [2] as described in the next section.

V. Combining Ripple Propagation with Folding

If $\rho = (q + 1)^2$ for some integer $q \ge 1$, then the source grid may be folded $q + 1$ times to fit exactly an $(q + 1)h \times (q + 1)h$ target grid. In fact, it is easy to show that if

$$\frac{(q + 1)^2}{1.2} < \rho \le (q + 1)^2 \qquad (13.a)$$

for some integer $q \ge 1$, then folding the source grid into an $(q + 1)h \times (q + 1)h$ target grid will result in an expansion cost less than 1.2. In Fig. 7, we illustrate the technique of folding by an example. As clear from this figure, successive tracks (a track consists of h consecutive rows of the target grid) are joined by two $h \times h$ corner tiles that guarantee a dilation cost equal to two.

As described above, folding may result in few unused columns in the last track of the target grid, and condition (13.a) limits the number of these unused columns. It is also possible to apply folding and leave some rows of the target grid unused. More precisely, if the eccentricity of the source grid satisfies

$$q^2 \le \rho \le 1.2 q^2 \qquad (13.b)$$

then it is possible to fold this grid into an $\rho h/q \times \rho h/q$ target grid. This will leave $(\rho - q^2)h/q$ unused rows in the target grid, and condition (13.b) will guarantee that the number of unused rows does not exceed $0.2qh$. Thus, the expansion cost will be less than 1.2.

A. Combining Folding with Exact Row Fitting

Consider an $h \times \rho h$ source grid which satisfies $1.2q^2 < \rho < (q + 1)^2/1.2$. Clearly, folding this grid into a square grid is too expensive (expansion cost larger than 1.2) because neither (13.a) nor (13.b) is satisfied. In this section, we introduce a method which combines folding and exact row fitting. This method will be denoted by FR. In order to describe the FR method we assume that the source grid is to be embedded into a target grid of size k, where k satisfies $qh \le k \le (q + 1)h$. The embedding starts by folding the source grid into the target grid q times as shown in Fig. 8(a). Clearly, the rightmost $h \times (\rho h - qk)$ subgrid of the source grid will not fit into the target grid, and the last $k - qh$ rows of the target grid will be unused. The idea is to consider the last track resulting from the folding (an $h \times \rho h - (q - 1)k$ grid denoted by G_s), and to squeeze it into an $k - (q - 1)h \times k$ grid (denoted by G_t) that fits the target grid. The squeeze is performed by partitioning G_s vertically into P subgrids $G_{s,0}, \cdots, G_{s,P-1}$, and partitioning G_t vertically into

581

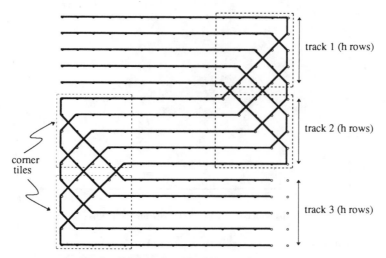

Fig. 7. Folding a 5 × 40 grid into a 15 × 15 grid.

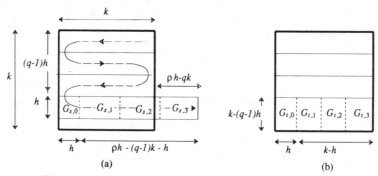

Fig. 8. Combining folding with exact row fitting ($q = 4$ and $P = 4$).

P subgrids, $G_{t,0}, \cdots, G_{t,P-1}$, and then mapping each $G_{s,i}$ into the corresponding $G_{t,i}$. The partitioning of G_s is such that $G_{s,0}$, is an $h \times h$ grid and each remaining $G_{s,i}$, $i = 1, \cdots, P-1$ is an $h \times \lceil (\rho h - (q-1)k - h)/(P-1) \rceil$ grid. Note that if $\rho h - (q-1)k - h$ does not divide $P - 1$ then $G_{s,P-1}$ will have few empty columns. Similarly, the partition of G_t is such that $G_{t,0}$ is a $k - (q-1)h \times h$ grid and each of the remaining $G_{t,i}$, $i = 1, \cdots, P-1$ is a $k - (q-1)h \times \lfloor (k-h)/(P-1) \rfloor$ grid.

The method of exact row fitting introduced in Section III is used to map each $G_{s,i}$, $i = 1, \cdots, q-1$, into the corresponding $G_{t,i}$. As for the mapping $G_{s,0} \rightarrow G_{t,0}$, it should ensure that the transition from track $q-1$ to track q does not increase the dilation cost beyond two. This may be accomplished by expanding the $h \times h$ corner tiles (see Fig. 7) into a $k - (q-1)h \times h$ pattern that fits $G_{t,0}$ such that the distribution of the h nodes in the last column of $G_{t,0}$ is similar to the distribution of the h nodes in the first column of $G_{t,1}$. This is always possible when exact row fitting is used to map $G_{s,1}$ to $G_{t,1}$. Specifically, as a result of exact row fitting, the nodes $n_1, \cdots, n_h$ in the first column of $G_{s,1}$ are mapped to the nodes $F(n_1), \cdots, F(n_h)$ in the first column of $G_{t,1}$ such that one of the following two conditions is satisfied for some integer z, $1 \le z \le h$:

1) the distance between $F(n_i)$ and $F(n_{i+1})$ is one, for $i = 1, \cdots, z-1$, and two, for $i = z, \cdots, h-1$.

2) the distance between $F(n_i)$ and $F(n_{i+1})$ is two, for $i = 1, \cdots, h-z$, and one, for $i = h-z+1, \cdots, h-1$.

For example, in the mapping of Fig. 4, $h = 7$, $z = 5$, and the second case applies. In general, using the notation in Fig. 4, the

value of z may be found from

$$z = 2h - k.$$

Because of the above property, it is straightforward to expand the $h \times h$ corner tile $G_{s,0}$ into $G_{t,0}$ such that the maximum dilation in $G_{t,0}$ is two and the node distribution in the last column of $G_{t,0}$ is identical to the node distribution in the first column of $G_{t,1}$. In Fig. 9, we show the expansion of a 7×7 corner tile to match the grid of Fig. 4(b).

In order to compute the optimum size k of the target grid, we follow the same reasoning as in Section III. Specifically, the method of exact row fitting may be used for mapping any $G_{s,i}$ into the corresponding $G_{t,i}$. For this, the following conditions should be satisfied (refer to Fig. 10):

$$h \le \left\lfloor \frac{k-h}{P-1} \right\rfloor \tag{14.a}$$

$$h \le k - (q-1)h \le 2h \tag{14.b}$$

$$\left\lfloor \frac{k-h}{P-1} \right\rfloor - h \ge \left\lceil \frac{(\rho-1)h - (q-1)k}{P-1} \right\rceil$$
$$- (k - (q-1)h). \tag{14.c}$$

In order to solve the above system of inequalities, we first find the minimum value of k which always satisfies (14.c). This value is

$$k = K_{fr} = \left\lceil \frac{(\rho + q(P-1))h + 2(P-2)}{q + P - 1} \right\rceil. \tag{15}$$

582

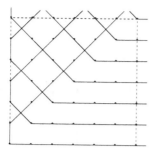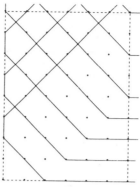

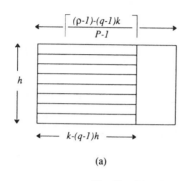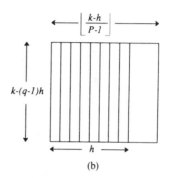

Fig. 9. Mapping a 7×7 corner tile into a 9×7 grid.

(a)

(b)

Fig. 10. Mapping $G_{s,i}$ into $G_{t,i}$ in the FR method.

By substituting (15) in (14.a) and (14.b), we conclude that these two conditions are satisfied, respectively, if

$$\rho \geq P^2 + q - P + \frac{(P + q - 3)(P - 2)}{h} \quad (16.a)$$

and

$$\rho \leq q(q + 1) + P - 1 - \frac{3P + q - 6}{h}. \quad (16.b)$$

Hence, given any rectangular grid, the method may be used if there exists a P that satisfies (16). The number of partitions P also affects the expansion cost. More precisely, from (15), we find that $K_{fr} \leq (\rho h + q(P - 1)h + 3P + q - 6)/(q + P - 1)$, which may be used to bound the expansion cost by

$$E_{fr} \leq E_{fr, \max} = \frac{\left(\rho + q(P - 1) + (3P + q - 6)/h\right)^2}{(P + q - 1)^2 \rho}. \quad (17)$$

The derivative $\partial E_{fr, \max}/\partial P$ is negative for $\rho \geq q^2$ which means that, from the point of view of minimizing E_{fr}, it is advantageous to find the maximum P which satisfies (16). For $P > q$, the two conditions (16.a) and (16.b) may not be satisfied simultaneously. If, however, ρ is in the range

$$q^2 + \frac{(q - 2)(2q - 3)}{h} \leq \rho \leq (q + 1)^2 - 2 - \frac{4q - 6}{h}, \quad (18)$$

then (16.a/b) are satisfied for $P = q$, and hence the embedding may be completed with q partitions in a target grid whose size is given by (15). The maximum expansion cost may then be found

by substituting $P = q$ in (17) to obtain

$$E_{fr} \leq E_{fr, \max} = \frac{\left(\rho + q(q - 1) + (4q - 6)/h\right)^2}{(2q - 1)^2 \rho}. \quad (19)$$

In Section VI, it will be shown that, for $q \geq 3$, E_{fr} is smaller than 1.2 for any ρ in the range specified by (18), and that, outside that range, ρ satisfies (13.a) or (13.b), which means that folding may be used with expansion cost less than 1.2. The case $q = 2$, however, is slightly more complicated. For instance, if $h \geq 20$, then, folding is too expensive in the range $5.85 \leq \rho \leq 7.5$ (expansion cost is larger than 1.2). Also, in that range, the FR method either does not apply (if $\rho > 6.9$) or gives $E_{fr} > 1.2$ (if $5.85 < \rho < 6.9$). In this case, combining folding with the method of exact column fitting (the FC method) turns out to be useful. Although we only need this combination for $q = 2$, the FC method will be described in the next section for general q. The reason for doing so is that for $q \geq 3$, although both the FC and the FR methods realize an expansion cost less than 1.2, it will be shown that the FC method gives better results than the FR method for some subranges of ρ.

B. Combining Folding with Exact Column Fitting

In this method, denoted from now on by FC, the source grid is folded into the target grid as described in the previous section, and also each of G_s and G_t is partitioned into P subgrids. The FC method is different from the FR method in that each subgrid $G_{s,i}$, $i = 1, \cdots, P - 1$, is mapped into the corresponding $G_{t,i}$ using the method of exact column fitting rather than exact row fitting.

The conditions that have to be satisfied in order to map $G_{s,i}$ into $G_{t,i}$ using exact column fitting are analogous to the conditions (10.a/b/c) of Section IV. Specifically, these conditions are

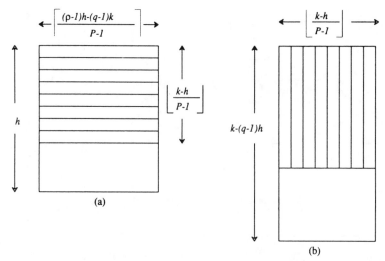

Fig. 11. Mapping $G_{s,i}$ into $G_{t,i}$ in the FC method.

(refer to Fig. 11):

$$\left\lceil \frac{(\rho - 1)h - (q - 1)k}{P - 1} \right\rceil \le k - (q - 1)h \quad (20.\text{a})$$

$$\left\lfloor \frac{k - h}{P - 1} \right\rfloor \le \left\lceil \frac{(\rho - 1)h - (q - 1)k}{P - 1} \right\rceil \le 2\left\lfloor \frac{k - h}{P - 1} \right\rfloor \quad (20.\text{b})$$

$$k - (q - 1)h - \left\lceil \frac{(\rho - 1)h - (q - 1)k}{P - 1} \right\rceil$$
$$\ge 2\left(h - \left\lfloor \frac{k - h}{P - 1} \right\rfloor \right). \quad (20.\text{c})$$

The same technique that was used in the last sections is applied to the solution of the above inequalities. From (20.c), the minimum size of the target grid is found to be

$$k = K_{fc} = \left\lceil \frac{(\rho + qP + P - q)h + 3(P - 2)}{P + q} \right\rceil. \quad (21)$$

By substituting (21) in (20.a) we obtain the condition

$$\rho \le P^2 - P + q + (P + q - 3)(P - 2)/h$$

which may be satisfied only if $P > q$. Also, by using (21) to compute the expansion cost E_{fc}, and then differentiating the resulting formula, we find that $\partial E_{fc}/\partial P$ is positive for $\rho \le P^2 - P + q$. This means that using $P = q + 1$ partitions will give the best expansion cost. Now using $P = q + 1$ in (21), and substituting the result in (20.a) and (20.b), we find that these conditions are satisfied if ρ lies in the following range

$$q^2 + 1 + \frac{3(q - 1)}{h} \le \rho \le (q + 1)^2 - 1 - \frac{(q - 1)^2}{qh}.$$
$$(22)$$

That is, the FC method may be applied if ρ satisfies (22). The expansion cost may then be computed from (21) with $P = q +$

1. The upper bound on this cost is given by

$$E_{fc} \le E_{fc,\max} = \frac{(\rho + q(q + 1) + 1 + (5q - 3)/h)^2}{(2q + 1)^2 \rho}.$$
$$(23)$$

VI. DISCUSSION AND CONCLUSION

Given an $h \times \rho h$ source grid, let q be the integer that satisfies $q^2 \le \rho < (q + 1)^2$. For $q = 1$, it has been shown in Sections III and IV that the mapping of the source grid into a square rectangular grid may be accomplished by using the method of exact row fitting if $\rho \le 2 + 3/h$, or the method of exact column fitting if $\rho > 2 + 3/h$. In both cases, the expansion cost is proven to be less than 1.2.

For $q \ge 2$, the FR or the FC methods described in Section V may be applied provided that $\rho_1 < \rho < \rho_2$, where the critical values ρ_1 and ρ_2 are specified from (18) and (22). Namely,

$$\rho_1 = q^2 + \frac{(q - 2)(2q - 3)}{h} \quad (24.\text{a})$$

$$\rho_2 = (q + 1)^2 - 1 - \frac{(q - 1)^2}{qh}. \quad (24.\text{b})$$

In order to determine which of the two methods gives a smaller expansion cost, we notice from (19) and (23) that, for $\rho > 0$, $E_{fr,\max}$ and $E_{fc,\max}$ intersect at only one point, namely

$$\rho_3 = q(q + 1) - \frac{1}{2} + \frac{2q^2 - 3q + 9}{2h}. \quad (24.\text{c})$$

We also observe that both $E_{fr,\max}$ and $E_{fc,\max}$ are of the form $f(\rho) = (\rho + a)^2/(b\rho)$, for some constants a and b. Given that, for $\rho > 0$, the function f has only one local minimum at $\rho = a$, we may determine that $E_{fr,\max}$ has its local minimum at $\rho_{fr} = q(q - 1) + (4q - 6)/h$, and $E_{fc,\max}$ has its minimum at $\rho_{fc} = q(q + 1) + 1 + (5q - 3)/h$. Clearly, ρ_{fr} is smaller than ρ_1 for $h > 4$, and ρ_{fc} lies between ρ_1 and ρ_2. This leads to the conclusion that $E_{fc,\max} < E_{fr,\max}$ if $\rho > \rho_3$ and $E_{fc,\max} > E_{fr,\max}$ if $\rho < \rho_3$. In Fig. 12, both $E_{fc,\max}$ and $E_{fr,\max}$ are plotted for $q = 2$, $h = 20$, and for $q = 4$, $h = 10$.

Hence, if ρ lies between ρ_1 and ρ_3, the FR method is

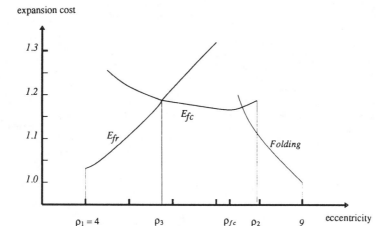

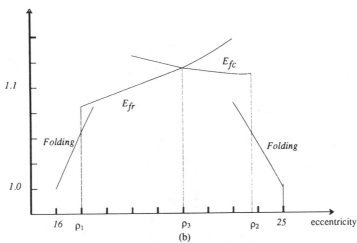

Fig. 12. Expansion cost for $q^2 \leq \rho < (q + 1)^2$, (a) $q = 2$, $h = 20$. (b) $q = 4$, $h = 10$.

recommended, and if ρ lies between ρ_3 and ρ_2, then the FC method is recommended. If this strategy is applied, then the largest expansion cost occurs at either $\rho = \rho_2$ or $\rho = \rho_3$. By direct substitution of (24.b) and (24.c) into (23), and after simple algebraic manipulation, it may be shown that, for $h \geq 18$, the value of $E_{fc, \max}$ is less than 1.2 at ρ_2 and ρ_3.

Neither the FR method nor the FC method may be applied if ρ is less than ρ_1 or larger than ρ_2. However, in these two cases, the expansion cost resulting from simple folding is low because ρ is close enough to q^2 and $(q + 1)^2$, respectively. In fact, if $\rho \leq \rho_1$, then $\rho < q^2(1 + 2/h)$, which satisfies (13.b) if $h > 10$. Also, if $\rho \geq \rho_2$, then $\rho \geq (q + 1)^2(1 - 1/qh) - 1$, which satisfies (13.a) if $h > 10$. In other words, the application of simple folding in these two regions will result in an expansion cost less than 1.2.

In brief, new techniques have been presented and analyzed in this paper, for embedding an $h \times \rho h$ rectangular grid into a square grid with dilation cost equal to two. The most appropriate technique for a given grid has been shown to depend on the size of that grid, that is on h and ρ. By adhering to the selection strategy suggested in the paper, the expansion cost is guaranteed to be smaller than 1.2 if h is larger than or equal to 18.

Finally, it should mentioned that, recently, the same problem of embedding rectangular grids into square grids has been studied independently by Ellis [4]. Specifically, it is shown in [4] that it is possible, with dilation at most three, to embed any $h \times w$ grid into a $k + 1 \times k + 1$ grid, where $k = \lceil \sqrt{hw} \rceil$.

REFERENCES

[1] L. Adams and R. Voigt, "Design, development and use of the finite element machine," in *Large Scale Scientific Computation*, S. Parter, Ed. New York: Academic, 1984, pp. 301–321.

[2] R. Aleliunas and A. Rosenberg, "On embedding rectangular grids in square grids," *IEEE Trans. Comput.*, vol. C-31, no. 9, pp. 907–913, 1982.

[3] S. Bokhary, "On the mapping problem," *IEEE Trans. Comput.*, vol. C-30, no. 3, pp. 207–214, 1981.

[4] J. Ellis, "Embedding rectangular grids into square grids," in *Proc. Aegean Workshop Comput.*, June 1988.

[5] S. L. Johnsson, "Communication efficient basic linear algebra computations on hypercube architectures," *J. Parallel Distributed Comput.*, vol. 4, pp. 133–172, 1987.

[6] Y. Ma and L. Tao, "Embedding among toruses and meshes," in *Proc. 1987 Int. Conf. Parallel Processing*, pp. 178–187.

[7] C. Mead and L. Conway, *Introduction to VLSI Systems*. Reading, MA: Addison-Wesley, 1980.

[8] P. Sadayappan and F. Ercal, "Nearest-neighbor mapping of finite element graphs onto processor meshes," *IEEE Trans. Comput.*, vol. C-36, no. 12, pp. 1408–1424, 1987.

[9] P. Tseng, K. Hwang, and P. Kumar, "A VLSI based multiprocessor architecture for implementing parallel algorithms," in *Proc. Int. Conf. Parallel Processing*, 1985, pp. 657–664.

[10] L. Valiant, ''Universality considerations in VLSI circuits,'' *IEEE Trans. Comput.*, vol. C-30, pp. 135–140, 1981.

Rami G. Melhem (S'82–M'84) was born in Cairo, Egypt, in 1954. He received the B.E. degree in electrical engineering from Cairo University in 1976, the M.A. degree in mathematics and the M.S. degree in computer science from the University of Pittsburgh in 1981, and the Ph.D. degree in computer science from the University of Pittsburgh in December 1983.

Since September 1989, he has been an Associate Professor of Computer Science at the University of Pittsburgh. Previously, he has been an Assistant Professor at Purdue University and at the University of Pittsburgh. His current research interests include fault-tolerant processor arrays, parallel algorithms, parallel architectures, and optical computing.

Dr. Melhem is a member of the Association for Computing Machinery, the IEEE Computer Society, and the International Society for Optical Engineering.

Ghil-Young Hwang (S'88–M'89) received the B.S. degree in physics from the Sogang University, Seoul, Korea, in 1981 and the M.S. degree in computer science from the University of Pittsburgh in 1985.

During 1986–1987, he conducted postgraduate studies at the University of Pittsburgh. His research interests include software engineering, parallel and distributed processing, and artificial intelligence. Currently, he is a Software Engineer at the Sukus Computer Company.

Mr. Hwang is a member of IEEE Computer Society.

Chapter 9: Partitioning

The ability to partition a parallel system into independent subsystems provides support for multitasking and for multiple users, improves system utilization, and even speeds up certain parallel algorithms. In order to use the same software, every subsystem should have the same (scaled-down) configuration as the parent system. Consequently, the underlying network in such systems should be partitionable into *subnetworks* (or subgraphs), with every subnetwork having the same topological structure as that of the parent network.

The three components of network partitioning are

- *splitting* (or subdividing),
- *merging* (or combining), and
- *compaction*.

Splitting is needed whenever a request for a given number of processors is made and the size of every available subnetwork is larger than the requested size. In this case, some subnetwork is subdivided into smaller subnetworks to obtain a subnetwork of the desired size, which is granted to the request. Merging is the opposite of splitting. Whenever a busy subnetwork becomes free, it should be merged with other subnetworks to form larger subnetworks for the purposes of minimizing system fragmentation and maximizing system throughput. Compaction is similar to garbage collection in memory systems. As subnetworks are granted and freed, the network may become very fragmented; that is, there may be many "holes" of uncombinable free subnetworks that are too small to satisfy requests. If and when such a situation arises, compaction may then be required in order to migrate the tasks to contiguous locations so that large subnetworks of free processors become available.

The metrics used to measure the efficiency of the partitioning process are

- the complexity of the partitioning process,
- the number of recognizable subnetworks,
- the system fragmentation, and
- the system throughput.

This chapter includes papers that propose partitioning strategies and analyze their performance with respect to these metrics. The first paper, by Krishnamurti and Ma (1988), studies the effect of partitioning on system throughput. The next three papers, by Chen and Shin (1990), Dutt and Hayes (1991), and Kim, Das, and Lin (1991), propose and evaluate various partitioning strategies on the hypercube. Cherkassky and Malek (1989) study partitioning properties of CC-banyan networks. Schwederski, Siegel, and Casavant (1990) study task migration in a multistage interconnection network. Finally, the paper by Li and Cheng (1989) addresses partitioning coupled with scheduling on the mesh.

The Processor Partitioning Problem
In Special-Purpose Partitionable Systems

Ramesh Krishnamurti
School of Computing Science
Simon Fraser University
Burnaby, B.C. V5A 1S6
Canada
(604) 291-4116

Eva Ma
Department of Computer Science
University of Pennsylvania
Philadelphia, PA 19104
(215) 898-8549

Abstract:

We address the problem of processor partitioning in partitionable systems used for special-purpose applications. We demonstrate that the partition size for a task should depend on the task characteristics, the workload, and the availability of resources. Thus, to maximize throughput, the partition sizes for a set of tasks should be determined at run time. Such an approach could be supported in special-purpose applications since the set of tasks the system needs to support are usually known in advance. We first show that given a set of tasks and their characteristics, the problem of determining the optimal partition sizes for the set of tasks is NP-Complete. We then present a polynomial time approximation algorithm for this problem. We also derive a worst-case bound on the solution obtained by the algorithm as compared to the optimal solution.

Section 1: Introduction

Partitionable architectures, also called Multiple SIMD-/MIMD architectures or MSIMD/MIMD architectures, consist of a set of processors and controllers [NUT77, PRE80, SIE81]. Such architectures can be partitioned into independent subsystems, each comprising of a variable number of processors and a controller assigned to the execution of a task. Each of these subsystems may either be in the SIMD or MIMD mode of computation. In addition to the flexibility of supporting both SIMD and MIMD modes, the ability to form multiple independent subsystems to execute several tasks in parallel provides such a system with the potential of achieving better utilization of processing resource.

An important problem that needs to be addressed in the partitioning of these systems is one of determining the number of processors allocated to each subsystem, that is, *the partition size* for each task. One possible approach to determining this size is to first derive the maximum degree of parallelism available in the program, and then choose the partition size to be either this maximum degree of parallelism or the maximum number of processors in the system that may be allocated to the task, whichever is smaller. Such an approach to determine the number of processors allocated to a task has been used widely in conventional SIMD and MIMD systems, and much work in the areas of programming languages and compiler design has been done to support this approach [KUC77].

Such an approach, however, may not be optimal from the standpoint of either minimizing the execution time for a task or the completion time for a set of tasks (we define completion time to be the least time by which all tasks in the set have completed execution). Since most parallel programs require communication among processors during their execution, for many parallel programs, the communication between processors may play a dominant role in the overall execution time with increasing partition size. As a result, the improvement in execution time may level off as the partition size increases. In other words, there is an effect of diminishing return in performance with larger partition sizes. Furthermore, beyond a certain partition size, the execution time may actually increase. The optimal partition size for a task depends on the computation and communication structure of the program, the size and values of the input data, and the computation and communication support of the system [LIN81, NIC87, MA87, MA88]. This size could be smaller than both the maximum degree of parallelism in the program and the maximum number of processors that may be allocated to the task.

In a partitionable system, due to the effect of diminishing return in performance with larger partition sizes, when there is a multiple number of tasks ready for execution, using a smaller partition size for each task and executing as many tasks in parallel as possible could lead to a shorter completion time than using the partition size that gives the minimum execution time for each individual task. For example, in a simulation study of a histogramming algorithm [KUE84], Kuehn and Siegel have shown that given a set of four histogramming tasks of the same size ready for exe-

This work has been supported by National Science Foundation Grant DCR84-51408, National Science Foundation CER Grant MCS82-19196, AT&T Information System Research Grant, Army Research Office Grant DAAG-29-84-K-0061, and the President's Research Grant at Simon Fraser University.

cution and a partitionable system of 256 processors, using a subsystem of 64 processors for each task and executing the four tasks in parallel gives a shorter completion time than using a partition of 256 processors for each task and executing the four tasks sequentially.

Given a set of tasks which are ready for execution, the optimal partition sizes for these tasks depend on the number of tasks in the set, their characteristics, and the amount of available resource. Since the information on what tasks are ready for execution, which we refer to as *workload*, and what resources are available for allocation cannot be determined until run time, the optimal partition sizes can be determined only at run time, and not at program design time or at compile time. Furthermore, in order to determine at run time the optimal partition sizes for a set of tasks, it is necessary for the system to know the characteristics of each individual task in the workload. Such characteristics, however, could be difficult to obtain for a system designed for general purpose application because the tasks the system needs to support may vary widely. But for a system designed for a special-purpose application, the tasks the system needs to support are relatively fixed and known in advance. For example, for the application of image processing, such tasks include FFT, Histogramming, Convolution and Image Smoothing. It is thus possible to pre-analyze the characteristics of the tasks and make them

available to the system. As a result, a partitionable system for special-purpose application can be designed with the ability to determine optimal partition sizes at run time. The feasibility and advantage of this approach is naturally determined by the overhead involved, which include the effort to pre-analyze the task characteristics, the storage required to record these characteristics in the system, and most importantly, the time it takes for the system to determine these partition sizes. In this paper, we focus on analyzing the time complexity of using such an approach to determining optimal partition sizes, assuming that the required information on task characteristics can be made available to the system. We show the problem of determining such optimal partition sizes to be NP-Complete; we also propose a polynomial time approximation algorithm for this problem and derive the performance bound for the algorithm.

In Section 2, we illustrate through a sequence of examples the impact of task characteristics and workload on optimal partition sizes. In Section 3, we formulate the processor partitioning problem, review the multiprocessor scheduling problems in the literature related to this problem, and establish the NP-completeness of this problem. In Section 4, we propose a polynomial time approximation algorithm for the partitioning problem and derive its performance bound. In Section 5, we apply the approximation algorithm on some examples to illustrate the possible reduction in completion time by using the partition sizes determined by the algorithm as opposed to using the partition sizes that minimize the execution time for each individual task.

Section 2: Impact of Task Characteristics and Workload on Optimal Partition Size

We illustrate the impact of task characteristics and workload on optimal partition sizes with some examples on the following model of a partitionable system. The system consists of 512 processors interconnected as a linear array. The links in the array are bidirectional. The system can be partitioned into several subsystems, each of which consists of a subset of consecutive processors in the linear array, operating in the SIMD mode. Furthermore, the time to communicate a data item between two adjacent processors equals the time to perform an arithmetic or logical operation over two data items. Note that the characteristics of the architecture, particularly those of the supporting interconnection network, have an important impact on task characteristics, and thus also affect the optimal partition sizes. More detailed analyses of the impact of the characteristics of tasks, workload, and system on optimal partition sizes are given in [MA88].

In the following examples, let N denote the number of data items for a task, and K denote the partition size allocated for the task. To simplify our presentation, we restrict K to be those integers such that N is divisible by K. Let T denote the completion time for a set of tasks executed by the system, which is the least time by which all tasks in the set have completed execution. If the set consists of only one task, then T is simply the execution time of the task, which is the sum of the computation and communication time for the execution of the task.

2.1: Impact of Task Characteristics on Optimal Partition Size

Example 1. Summing N Numbers

We use a recursive doubling algorithm to sum the N numbers. Initially all the processors are active, and each processor is assigned $\frac{N}{K}$ numbers. Each processor first forms the partial sum of $\frac{N}{K}$ numbers. These partial sums are then accumulated to form the final sum in $\log K$ iterations. In each iteration, starting from the leftmost active processor, every alternate processor sends its partial sum to the active processor immediately to its right. An active processor that receives a data forms a new partial sum by adding the received data to its own partial sum. At the end of an iteration, all the sending processors are disabled. This parallel algorithm takes $(\frac{N}{K} - 1) + \log K$ additions and $K - 1$ communication operations on the linear array. The completion time T is given by

$$T = \frac{N}{K} + K + \log K - 2.$$

For $1 \leq K \leq N$, the computation time, which is $\frac{N}{K} - 1 + \log K$, is a decreasing function of K, and the communication time, which is $K - 1$, is an increasing function of K; combining the effects of both, the execution time is concave upward with respect to K, with the minimum occuring at some K' between 1 and N. The variation between T and K for $N = 512$ is shown in Figure 1. For $N = 512$, the execution time has minimum at $K = 16$, and this is the optimal partition size for one summing task of size 512 on the given partitionable system. ∎

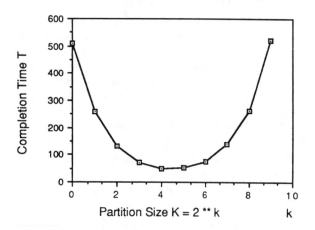

Figure 1 Summing 512 Numbers

Example 2. Sorting N Elements

We use the parallel algorithm given in [BAU78] to sort the N elements. The algorithm is a generalization of the odd-even transposition sort. Each processor is assigned $\frac{N}{K}$ elements. These elements are first sorted in each processor. The resulting subsequences are then merged and redistributed for K iterations to form the final sequence. For all odd iterations, processor $i + 1$, where $i = 1, 3, \ldots, 2\lfloor \frac{K}{2} \rfloor - 1$, first sends its subsequence to processor i, processor i then merges the two subsequences it has, retains the first half of the resulting subsequence (the $\frac{N}{K}$ smallest elements), and sends the second half of the subsequence (the $\frac{N}{K}$ largest elements) back to processor $i + 1$. For all even iterations, the same steps as the odd iterations are executed but for $i = 2, 4, \ldots, 2\lfloor \frac{K-1}{2} \rfloor$. After K such iterations, the final sorted sequence will be partitioned among the N processors, with each processor holding a subsequence of $\frac{N}{K}$ elements. These subsequences are in increasing order from processor 1 to processor N. Since the initial sorting takes $\frac{N}{K} \log \frac{N}{K}$ comparisons and each iteration takes $2\frac{N}{K}$ comparisons and $2\frac{N}{K}$ communication operations on the linear array, the overall completion time is given by $T = \frac{N}{K} \log \frac{N}{K} + 4N$.

For $1 \leq K \leq N$, the computation time, which is $\frac{N}{K} \log \frac{N}{K} + 2N$, is a decreasing function of K, and the communication time, which is $2N$, is a constant with respect to K; as a

result, the execution time is a decreasing function of K, with the minimum occuring at $K = N$. The variation between T and K for $N = 512$ is shown in Figure 2. For $N = 512$, the execution time has minimum at $K = 512$, and this is the optimal partition size for one sorting task of size 512 on the given partitionable system.

As illustrated in the above two examples, the optimal partition size for a task depends on the computation and communication requirements of a task, which in turn are determined by the characteristics of the corresponding program, input data, and supporting architecture. For the task of summing, the optimal partition size is smaller than the maximum degree of parallelism in the task, but for sorting, these two quantities are equal.

2.2: Impact of Workload on Optimal Partition Size

Due to the need for communication in most parallel programs, as we increase the number of processors allocated to a task by a factor of k, the execution time of the task is usually reduced by a factor less than k. For instance, for the summing task with $N = 512$ in Example 1, as the partition size increases from 1 to 16 by a factor of two each time (that is, from 1 to 2, 2 to 4, 4 to 8, and 8 to 16), the execution time decreases from 511 to 50 by factors of 1.988 (511 to 257), 1.947 (257 to 132), 1.808 (132 to 73), and 1.460 (73 to 50); when the partition size increases beyond 16, the execution time increases. For the sorting task with $N = 512$ in Example 2, as the partition size increases from 1 to 512 by a factor of two each time, the execution time decreases from 6656 to 2048 by factors of 1.625, 1.391, 1.210, 1.101, 1.046, 1.019, 1.008, 1.003, and 1.001. Due to such diminishing return in performance with larger partition sizes, when there are a multiple number of tasks ready for execution in a partitionable system, using a smaller partition size for each task and executing as many tasks in parallel as possible could lead to a shorter completion time than using the partition size that gives the minimum execution time for each task. We illustrate this impact of workload on optimal partition size in the next example.

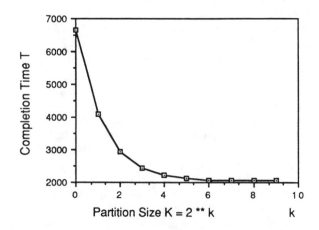

Figure 2 Sorting 512 Elements

Example 3. Multiple Sorting Tasks of N Elements

Suppose we have eight sorting tasks to be executed, with each task having to sort N elements. Assume that each task is allocated a partition of size K. Since there are 512 processors in the system, for $K \leq 64$ the eight sorting tasks can be executed in parallel, and the completion time T for these eight sorting tasks is the same as the execution time of one sorting task of size N using a partition of size K. However, for $K > 64$, the eight sorting tasks have to be executed in multiple batches, with each batch, except possibly the last, having $\lfloor \frac{512}{K} \rfloor$ tasks. The completion time T in this case is the product of $\lceil \frac{8K}{512} \rceil$ (the number of batches) and the execution time of one sorting task on a partition of size K. Figure 3 shows the variation between the completion time T and partition size K for $N = 512$. The least completion time for a set of eight tasks is obtained when $K = 64$, and this is the optimal partition size for each such task. The corresponding completion time T for the eight tasks is 2072. On the other hand, if we use a partition size of 512 for each of the eight tasks, which is the optimal partition size for the execution of one task, the completion time T is 16384 instead.

The least completion time for a set of sixteen tasks is obtained when $K = 32$, and this is the optimal partition size for each such task. The corresponding completion time T for the 16 tasks is 2112. If we use a partition size of 512 for each of the sixteen tasks, the completion time T is 32768 instead.

As illustrated in the above examples, determining the partition sizes at run time based on task characteristics, workload, and amount of resource available could provide higher throughput than determining such partition sizes at either the program design time or compile time. For a partitionable system designed for special purpose applications, since the set of tasks the system needs to support is usually known in advance, by pre-analyzing the characteristics of the tasks and making them available to the system, it is possible for it to determine the partition sizes at run time. The feasibility and advantage of such an approach is determined by the overhead involved. In the remainder of this

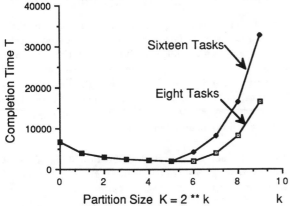

Figure 3 Multiple Sorting Tasks of Size 512

paper, we focus on analyzing the time complexity of the problem of determining optimal partition sizes at run time.

Section 3: The Processor Partitioning Problem

In multiprocessor scheduling problems, we are given a number of processors and a set of tasks, and the goal is to schedule the tasks on these processors such that some objective on the execution times of the tasks is optimized. These are variants of the general multiprocessor scheduling problem, and most of these problems are NP-Complete [GAR79]. In the following, we first review the general multiprocessor scheduling problem and two of its variants most related to our problem.

Let Z^+ denote the set of positive integers. Let n denote the number of processors and m the number of tasks, where n, $m \in Z^+$. For any positive integer k, we use $[k]$ to denote the set $\{1, \cdots, k\}$.

The general multiprocessor scheduling problem can be stated as follows [GAR79]: Given n processors and m tasks, where each task requires one processor for execution with a specific execution time and there is no precedence constraint among the tasks, the objective is to find a nonpreemptive schedule with the least completion time for all the tasks. This problem is NP-Complete in the strong sense for arbitrary n, but can be solved in pseudo-polynomial time for any fixed n. The problem remains NP-Complete for $n = 2$.

A variant of the general multiprocessor scheduling problem is the multiprocessor scheduling problem with nonfragmentable resource constraint [GAR75]. In a special-case of this problem, we are given n processors and m tasks, each task requiring one processor for execution with execution time equal to unity and no precedence constraints among the tasks. Further, we are given a resource R with a total amount B available, and a nonnegative resource requirement $R(i)$ for each task $i \in [m]$. The objective is to find a nonpreemptive schedule with the least completion time for all the tasks such that the sum of the resource requirements of all the tasks scheduled simultaneously does not exceed the total amount of the resource available. An important characteristic of the problem is that the resource does not have to be allocated in contiguous blocks since the resource does not suffer from fragmentation. This problem is shown to be NP-Complete by transforming the Three-Dimensional Matching problem to this problem [GAR75].

Yet another version of the scheduling problem is the multiprocessor scheduling problem with fragmentable resource constraint [BAK83]. In this, tasks share a resource such as memory, where such a resource may only be allocated in contiguous blocks. In this problem, we are given n processors and m tasks. We are also given a resource R with a total amount B available, and a nonnegative resource requirement $R(i)$ for each task $i \in [m]$. Once again, the objective is to find a nonpreemptive schedule with the least completion time for all the tasks such that the sum of the resource requirements of all the tasks scheduled simultaneously does not exceed the total amount of the resource available. The distinguishing characteristic between this problem and the earlier problem is that the resource may only be allocated in contiguous blocks since the resource is fragmentable. This problem is NP-Complete since it is equivalent to the 2-D bin packing problem.

In the processor partitioning problem, we are given n processors, r controllers, and m tasks among which there are no precedence constraints. Each task can be executed by a number of different partition sizes. The partitions may comprise of processors which need not be contiguous in any address space. The objective is to choose partition sizes for the tasks and to find a nonpreemptive schedule with the least completion time for all the tasks such that the maximum number of tasks scheduled simultaneously does not exceed the number of controllers r and the sum of the chosen partition sizes of all the tasks scheduled simultaneously does not exceed the total number of processors n. The above problem can be shown to be NP-Complete by transforming the multiprocessor scheduling problem with fragmentable resource constraint to a restricted version of the above problem. Details of the proof are omitted in this paper.

The processor partitioning problem that we study in the remainder of this paper is a special version of the problem stated above. In this version, we are given n processors, r controllers, and m tasks among which there are no precedence constraints, and each of which can be executed by a number of different partition sizes. The partitions may comprise of processors which need not be contiguous in any address space. For all $i \in [m]$, let q_i denote the total number of such partition sizes for task i, and let the functions $p_i : [q_i] \to [n]$ and $t_i : [q_i] \to Z^+$, define respectively the partition sizes and the corresponding execution times for task i. The functions p_i and t_i have properties such that for all $k, l \in [q_i]$ where $k < l$, we have the following:

(a) $p_i(k) < p_i(l)$ (the partition sizes defined by p_i are in increasing order)

(b) $t_i(k) > t_i(l)$ (the execution time of a task decreases as the partition size increases)

(c) $p_i(k) t_i(k) < p_i(l) t_i(l)$ (the execution time of a task using a larger partition size decreases by a factor which is less than the increase in partition size since $t_i(l)/t_i(k) > p_i(k)/p_i(l)$)

In addition, we have the assumption:

(∗) $m \leq r$ and $\sum_{i=1}^m p_i(1) \leq n$ (all the tasks available for execution can be executed in parallel when using the smallest partition sizes for these tasks).

The objective is to choose partition sizes (and their execution times, which obey the above three properties) for the tasks and to find a nonpreemptive schedule with the least completion time for all the tasks such that the maximum number of tasks scheduled simultaneously does not exceed the number of controllers r and the sum of the chosen partition sizes of all the tasks scheduled simultaneously does not exceed the total number of processors n. This problem can

also be shown to be NP-Complete by transforming the multiprocessor scheduling problem with fragmentable resource constraint to a restricted version of the above problem. Details of the proof are omitted in this paper.

In a partitionable system, properties (a) and (b) imply ordering the partition sizes in increasing order of index and selecting only that part of the task characteristics where the execution time continues to decrease with increasing partition size. For example, for the tasks of summing and sorting discussed in Section 2.1, we only include five partition sizes 1, 2, 4, 8, 16 for summing, while for sorting, we include all the ten partition sizes. Property (c) implies that speed-up in a parallel system is less than linear due to communication and control overhead. We make assumption (∗) to simplify the presentation of our solution to the problem. Our solution may be extended to the case where this assumption does not hold.

Section 4: Solution Techniques for the Processor Partitioning Problem

In this section, we first derive some lower bounds on the completion time for the processor partitioning problem. Using these lower bounds, we derive a condition on the processor partitioning problem under which optimal solutions can be determined easily. We then present a polynomial time approximation algorithm for the processor partitioning problem. We also derive a worst-case bound on the solution obtained by the algorithm and the conditions under which it gives optimal solutions.

Let S_o be an optimal schedule, and for each $i \in [m]$, let u_i denote the index for the partition size for task i in schedule S_o. Let T_o be the completion time for schedule S_o, which is the optimal completion time.

4.1: Lower Bounds on Completion Time

Lemma 1 provides us with a relation between the optimal completion time T_o and the partition sizes and respective execution times for the tasks in an optimal schedule S_o.

Lemma 1. $T_o \geq \sum_{i=1}^m p_i(u_i) t_i(u_i)/n$.

Proof. The term $\sum_{i=1}^m p_i(u_i) t_i(u_i)$ represents the total time units that the allocated processors are busy in schedule S_o. Since S_o is a feasible schedule, at any time instant, each of the n processors is allocated to at most one task. Thus each processor is busy for at most T_o time units. Since the total number of processors allocated at any instance is bounded by n, we have $\sum_{i=1}^m p_i(u_i) t_i(u_i) \leq n T_o$. The Lemma follows consequently. ∎

As per Property (c) stated in Section 3, in a partitionable system, as we transit from a given partition size to a higher partition size, the execution time decreases by a factor which is less than the increase in partition size. This property asserts that as we increase the partition size for a task, the time to execute on the new partition cannot decrease below a certain limit. Based on this relationship between partition sizes and execution times, Lemma 2 derives, under certain conditions, a lower bound on completion time for the special case where all the tasks to be executed are of the same type.

Lemma 2. *Assume that there are m tasks of the same type to be executed on an n processor system. Let q denote the number of possible partition sizes for this type of task. In addition, let the functions $p : [q] \to [m]$ and $t : [q] \to Z^+$ denote the partition sizes and the corresponding execution times respectively. Assume further that there exists some $l \in [q]$ such that $p(l) \geq \lceil \frac{n}{m} \rceil$. Let l^* be the smallest index in $[q]$ such that $p(l^*) \geq \lceil \frac{n}{m} \rceil$. Then $T_o \geq t(l^*)$.*

Proof. For each $i \in [m]$, let u_i be the index in $[q]$ such that $p(u_i)$ is the partition size for task i in some optimal schedule S_o. For each $i \in [m]$, the completion time for task i is $t(u_i)$. If for some $i \in [m]$, $u_i \leq l^*$ then $T_o \geq t(u_i) \geq t(l^*)$ from Property (b) and the lemma is trivially true. Thus assume that for every $i \in [m], u_i > l^*$. It follows from Property (c) that

$$\text{for every } i \in [m], \ p(l^*)t(l^*) < p(u_i)t(u_i).$$

The above implies that

$$m \, p(l^*)t(l^*) < \sum_{i=1}^{m} p(u_i)t(u_i).$$

Since $p(l^*) \geq \lceil \frac{n}{m} \rceil$, it follows that

$$m \lceil \frac{n}{m} \rceil t(l^*) < \sum_{i=1}^{m} p(u_i)t(u_i).$$

Since $\lceil \frac{n}{m} \rceil \geq \frac{n}{m}$, we have

$$t(l^*) < \sum_{i=1}^{m} p(u_i)t(u_i)/n.$$

Since the optimal schedule S_o has completion time T_o, from Lemma 1, we have $T_o > t(l^*)$. ∎

For the special case where all the tasks to be executed are of the same type, Theorem 3 states a condition under which a parallel schedule with $\frac{n}{m}$ processors in each partition has the least completion time.

Theorem 3. *Assume there are m tasks of the same type to be executed on an n processor system. Let q denote the number of possible partition sizes for this type of task. In addition, let the functions $p : [q] \to [m]$ and $t : [q] \to Z^+$ denote the partition sizes and the corresponding execution times respectively. Assume further that n is divisible by m and there exists some $l^* \in [q]$ such that $p(l^*) = \frac{n}{m}$. Then a parallel schedule with $\frac{n}{m}$ processors in each partition has the least completion time.*

Proof. Since the allocation is feasible, the theorem follows from Lemma 2. ∎

4.2: An Approximation Algorithm for Partitioning

We now present an approximation algorithm which runs in $O(\min\{n, \sum_{i=1}^{m} q_i\} \log m)$ time. This algorithm explores only parallel schedules and does not explore any serial-parallel schedules. By assumption (*), there always exists a feasible, parallel schedule for the given set of tasks. We first give an informal description of the algorithm below.

Initially, each task is allocated a number of processors equal to the smallest partition size for this task. By assumption (*), such an allocation is always possible. Then, the task with the longest execution time is selected. As many processors are allocated to this task as is neccessary to transit to the next larger partition size. This process is repeated until we run out of free processors.

Intuitively, the algorithm allocates processors to tasks in an efficient manner. To account for the effect of diminishing return with larger partition size, the algorithm starts with the smallest partition size for each task, and increases a partition size only if the execution time corresponding to such a partition size determines the completion time. Since the criterion to be minimized is completion time, the algorithm isolates the task with the longest execution time at every iteration, since this is what determines the completion time in a parallel schedule. It then allocates as many processors as is neccessary to reduce the execution time of this task so as to reduce the overall completion time. If this additional allocation results in a different task having the longest execution time, the algorithm allocates additional processors to this task. Thus, it provides processors to tasks that need them the most, in some sense. Given below is a more formal statement of the algorithm.

Approximation Algorithm: Partitioning

Input: n, m, for every $i \in [m]$, q_i, p_i, t_i.

Output: a set of indexes $\{l_i | l_i \in [q_i] \text{ for } i \in [m]\}$.

begin

    $remain := n$;

    for $i := 1$ **to** m **do**

    begin

        $l_i := 1$;

        $remain := remain - p_i(1)$

    end;

    $done := false$;

    while $(remain > 0)$ **and** $(not\ done)$ **do**

    begin

        find j such that $t_j(l_j) = max_{i \in \{1, \cdots, m\}} t_i(l_i)$;

        if $(l_j < q_j)$ **and** $(remain \geq p_j(l_j + 1)$

$$-p_j(l_j))$$

        then

```
begin
    l_j := l_j + 1;
    remain := remain - (p_j(l_j + 1) - p_j(l_j))
end
else
    done := true
end
end.
```

In the above algorithm, the *while loop* will be executed no more than $\min\{n, \sum_{i=1}^{m} q_i\}$. Inside the loop, we have to find the maximum of the t_i's, which can be done in time $O(\log m)$ if we use a priority queue to store the t_i's. The rest of the algorithm can be done in $O(m)$ time. Therefore, the approximation algorithm has complexity $O(\min\{n, \sum_{i=1}^{m} q_i\} \log m)$. Since $\sum_{i=1}^{m} p_i(l_i) \leq n$, the partition sizes chosen from the approximation algorithm allow a parallel schedule. In the next section, we derive some bounds on the performance of the algorithm.

4.3: Performance Analysis of the Approximation Algorithm

Let S_a be the schedule determined by the approximation algorithm. For each $i \in [m]$, let l_i denote the index for the partition size for task i in schedule S_a. Let T_a be the completion time for schedule S_a. By definition, we have the following set of inequalities: $T_o \leq T_a$, and for all $i \in [m]$, $t_i(u_i) \leq T_o$, $t_i(l_i) \leq T_a$.

Lemma 4 derives a relationship between partition sizes in the schedule S_a and partition sizes in a feasible schedule with completion time no greater than the completion time of S_a.

Lemma 4. *Let S_f be a feasible schedule. For all $i \in [m]$, let r_i denote the index for the partition size for task i in S_f. Let T_f denote the completion time due to schedule S_f. Assume that $T_f \leq T_a$. Then, for all $i \in [m], r_i \geq l_i$.*

Proof. Let i be an arbitrary element in $[m]$. We consider two cases.

a) $l_i = 1$. Since in any feasible schedule, every task needs at least as many processors as in the least-sized partition, we have $r_i \geq l_i$.

b) $l_i > 1$. In this case, we have $t_i(l_i - 1) > T_a$, otherwise the algorithm will not augment $l_i - 1$ to l_i. We thus have the following relationship:

$$t_i(r_i) \leq T_f \leq T_a < t_i(l_i - 1).$$

This implies that $r_i > l_i - 1$ from Property (b). Thus, $r_i \geq l_i$. ∎

Lemma 5 derives a lower bound on the optimal completion time T_o in terms of the partition sizes and the execution times of the tasks in the schedule S_a.

Lemma 5. $T_o \geq \sum_{i=1}^{m} p_i(l_i)t_i(l_i)/n$.

Proof. Since S_o is a feasible schedule and $T_o \leq T_a$, from Lemma 4, we have, for all $i \in [m], u_i \geq l_i$. Hence from Property (c), we have, for all $i \in [m]$,

$$p_i(u_i)t_i(u_i) \geq p_i(l_i)t_i(l_i).$$

Therefore,

$$\sum_{i=1}^{m} p_i(u_i)t_i(u_i) \geq \sum_{i=1}^{m} p_i(l_i)t_i(l_i).$$

From Lemma 1, we also have

$$nT_o \geq \sum_{i=1}^{m} p_i(u_i)t_i(u_i).$$

Thus, $T_o \geq \sum_{i=1}^{m} p_i(l_i)t_i(l_i)/n$. ∎

Theorem 6 derives a worst-case bound on the completion time T_a.

Theorem 6. *Let k be the index in $[m]$ such that task k is the one that determines the completion of T_a. Then $T_a \leq (n/p_k(l_k))T_o - (\sum_{\substack{1 \leq i \leq m \\ i \neq k}} p_i(l_i)t_i(l_i))/p_k(l_k)$.*

Proof. From Lemma 5, we have

$$\sum_{i=1}^{m} p_i(l_i)t_i(l_i) \leq nT_o.$$

Since $t_k(l_k) = T_a$, we can rewrite the above expression as

$$\sum_{\substack{1 \leq i \leq m \\ i \neq k}} p_i(l_i)t_i(l_i) + p_k(l_k)T_a \leq nT_o.$$

Thus, we have

$$T_a \leq nT_o/p_k(l_k) - \sum_{\substack{1 \leq i \leq m \\ i \neq k}} p_i(l_i)t_i(l_i)/p_k(l_k),$$

and the theorem follows. ∎

Theorem 7 proves that the schedule due to the approximation algorithm is an optimal schedule among all parallel schedules.

Theorem 7. *The completion time T_a due to the approximation algorithm is the optimal completion time among all parallel schedules.*

Proof. Assume to the contrary that there exists a parallel schedule S_p with completion time T_p such that $T_p < T_a$. For each $i \in [m]$, let v_i denote the index for the partition size for task i in S_p. Let k be the index in $[m]$ such that task k is the one that the approximation algorithm tries to increase the partition size of before it terminates (in case two or more tasks are tied in determining the task with the longest execution time). We have $t_k(l_k) = T_a$. From

Lemma 4, we have,

$$\text{for all } i \in [m], v_i \geq l_i.$$

Consequently, for each $i \in [m], p_i(v_i) \geq p_i(l_i)$.

Further, from our assumption that $T_p < T_a$, we get $t_k(v_k) < t_k(l_k)$. This implies that $v_k > l_k$, and hence $v_k \geq l_k + 1$. Therefore, $p_k(v_k) \geq p_k(l_k + 1)$. It follows that

$$\sum_{i=1}^{m} p_i(v_i) \geq \sum_{\substack{1 \leq i \leq m \\ i \neq k}} p_i(l_i) + p_k(l_k + 1).$$

Thus,

$$\sum_{i=1}^{m} p_i(v_i) \geq \sum_{i=1}^{m} p_i(l_i) + p_k(l_k + 1) - p_k(l_k). \quad (1)$$

When the algorithm terminates, the number of remaining processors is strictly less than $p_k(l_k + 1) - p_k(l_k)$ (task k determines the completion time). Otherwise, the algorithm would have reduced the completion time $T_a = t_k(l_k)$ by augmenting the partition size of task k from $p_k(l_k)$ to $p_k(l_k + 1)$. Thus, we have,

$$n - \sum_{i=1}^{m} p_i(l_i) < p_k(l_k + 1) - p_k(l_k).$$

This implies that

$$\sum_{i=1}^{m} p_i(l_i) + p_k(l_k + 1) - p_k(l_k) > n. \quad (2)$$

Combining inequalities (1) and (2), we have $\sum_{i=1}^{m} p_i(v_i) > n$, which is a contradiction since S_p is a parallel schedule and there are at most n processors. Thus, no parallel schedule S_p exists with completion time T_p such that $T_p < T_a$. The completion time due to the approximation algorithm is therefore optimal among all parallel schedules. ∎

Theorem 8 proves that the schedule due to the approximation algorithm is optimal under the condition that no processors remain to be allocated when the algorithm terminates, and in addition, the execution times of the tasks for the partition sizes allocated by the approximation algorithm are equal.

Theorem 8. *Assume that $\sum_{i=1}^{m} p_i(l_i) = n$ and for all $i \in [m], t_i(l_i) = T_a$. Then $T_a = T_o$.*

Proof. Assume to the contrary that $T_a > T_o$. From Lemma 5 we have

$$T_o \geq \sum_{i=1}^{m} p_i(l_i)t_i(l_i)/n.$$

By the assumption of the theorem, we have

$$T_o \geq \sum_{i=1}^{m} p_i(l_i)T_a/n.$$

Since $\sum_{i=1}^{m} p_i(l_i) = n$, the above implies that

$$T_o \geq T_a,$$

which is a contradiction. Thus, $T_a = T_o$. ∎

Corollary 9. *Assume there are m tasks of the same type to be executed on an n processor system, and n is divisible by m. Assume further that there exists some $l^* \in [q]$ such that $p(l^*) = \frac{n}{m}$. Then the approximation algorithm obtains an allocation with the optimal completion time, allocating partitions consisting of $\frac{n}{m}$ processors to each of the m tasks.*

Proof. When the approximation algorithm terminates, it allocates a partition of size $p(l_i) = \frac{n}{m}$, for each $i \in [m]$. Since every task is of the same type, $t(l_i) = T_a$, for each $i \in [m]$. Since $\sum_{i=1}^{m} p(l_i) = n$, the corollary follows from Theorem 8. ∎

The analyses in this subsection shows that under certain conditions (those stated in Theorem 8 and Corollary 9) the approximation algorithm produces an optimal schedule. Further, if we constrain ourselves to strictly parallel schedules, then the schedule due to the approximation algorithm is always optimal among all such schedules. In general, the performance of the schedule due to the approximation algorithm is always within the bound given in Theroem 6.

Section 5: Applications of the Approximation Algorithm

We now give an example of using the approximation algorithm in a typical application on the model of a partitionable system described in Section 2. The application we choose to illustrate the approximation algorithm is in the area of image processing. In image processing applications using stereo images, there is a need to compute the Histogram and perform Image Smoothing for a pair of images. Since both these computations may be carried out in parallel, the workload may then comprise of the following tasks: two Histogramming tasks and two Smoothing tasks (one for the right image, and one for the left image).

Assume that the image is a square of $\sqrt{N} \times \sqrt{N}$ pixels, where $\sqrt{N}$ is a positive integer. Let K denote the size of a partition, where $\sqrt{K}$ is a positive integer. Assume also that N is divisible by K.

We assume that the image is divided evenly over the K processors so that each processor has a square subimage of $\frac{N}{K}$ pixels. In computing the histogram of an image, the frequency count of each grey level is computed over the entire image. The final histogram is represented as an array of b elements, each element being a count of the number of pixels in the image with that grey level. Each processor first computes the histogram of the subimage local to it in time $\frac{N}{K}$. These partial histograms are then accumulated to form the total histogram in $\log K$ iterations using a recursive doubling algorithm similar to the one for the summing task given in Section 2, Example 1. Computing the new partial histogram in each iteration takes b time units since it amounts to a vector addition of b elements. Communication in the first iteration takes b time units since an array of b elements is sent to an adjacent processor. In general, for all $i = 1, \ldots, \log K$, communication in the ith iteration takes $b + 2^{i-1} - 1$ time units since an array of b elements is sent to a processor which is 2^{i-1} away, and the array of b elements can be sent in a pipelined fashion. The total number of computation operations is $\frac{N}{K} + b \log K$, and the total number of communication operations is $(b-1) \log K + K - 1$. The execution time for Histogram computation is given by

$$T = \frac{N}{K} + K - 1 + (2b - 1) \log_2 K.$$

For $N = 512 \times 512$, $b = 256$, and K varying from 1 to 4096 as squares of powers of two, the variation of the execution time T with partition size K is shown in Figure 4.

K	1	4	16	64	256	1024	4096
T	262144	66561	18443	7225	5367	6389	10291

Figure 4 Histogramming

In the problem of Image Smoothing, the grey value of each pixel in an image is averaged with the surrounding eight neighbouring points for a given number of iterations. In each iteration of the algorithm, each processor needs to perform $8\frac{N}{K}$ additions and $\frac{N}{K}$ divisions, and send a message to each of the eight processors operating on its surrounding subimages; four of these messages are of size $\sqrt{\frac{N}{K}}$ elements, and four of size one element. If the subimages are mapped row by row into the linear array, each processor has to communicate with two processors at a distance of one, two at a distance of $\sqrt{K}$, two at a distance of $\sqrt{K} + 1$, and two at a distance of $\sqrt{K} - 1$. The net communication time on the linear array is thus:

$$2\sqrt{\frac{N}{K}} + 2\sqrt{\frac{N}{K}}K + 2(\sqrt{K} - 1) + 2(\sqrt{K} + 1).$$

The total execution time for Smoothing is given by

$$T = 9\frac{N}{K} + 2\sqrt{\frac{N}{K}} + 2\sqrt{N} + 4\sqrt{K}.$$

For $N = 512 \times 512$, the variation of the execution time T with partition size K is shown in Figure 5.

K	1	4	16	64	256	1024	4096
T	2361348	591368	148752	38048	10368	3488	1872

Figure 5 Image Smoothing

Next we apply the approximation algorithm for the job mix of two Histogramming tasks and two Smoothing tasks, all of which are available for execution. The approximation algorithm stops after 18 iterations with a schedule whose overall completion time is 5367 time units. Table 6 shows the partition sizes for the tasks and the completion time. The table has one entry for every two iterations since the partition size has to increase for both Smoothing tasks or both Histogramming tasks to reduce completion time at each iteration.

Smooth Size	Hist Size	Comp Time
1	1	2361348
4	1	591368
16	1	262144
16	4	148752
64	4	66561
64	16	38048
256	16	18443
256	64	10368
1024	64	7225
1024	256	5367

Figure 6 Iterations in Approximation Algorithm

If we use the maximum partition size consisting of all 4096 processors for each task, and a strictly sequential schedule to execute the tasks, then the overall completion time is 24326 time units, implying a factor of 4.5 improvement in the overall completion time with the parallel schedule obtained by the approximation algorithm. If, on the other hand, we use the partition size with the least execution time for each task (the optimal partition size for the execution of a single task) and the best schedule possible to execute the tasks, then the overall completion time is 9111 time units, implying a factor of 1.6 improvement in the overall completion time with the parallel schedule obtained by the approximation algorithm.

Applying Theorem 6 to obtain a worst-case performance bound for the approximation algorithm in the above example, we get

$$T_a \leq \frac{4096}{256}T_o - \frac{2 \times 1024 \times 3488 + 256 \times 5367}{256},$$

which implies that

$$T_a \leq 16T_o - 33271,$$

from which we can infer that $T_o \geq 2415$. Using this bound, we can deduce that the approximation algorithm obtains a completion time which is less than 2.23 times the optimal completion time.

For this particular example, the schedule determined by

the approximation algorithm is actually optimal among all possible schedules, that is, $T_a = T_o = 5367$.

Section 6: Conclusion

In this paper, we address the problem of processor partitioning in partitionable architectures. We demonstrate the importance of determining the partition sizes based on task characteristics, workload, and availability of resources. An underlying assumption is that the task characteristics are available. For a system designed for a special-purpose application, it is possible to pre-analyze the characteristics of the tasks and make them available to the system since the set of tasks the system needs to support is usually known in advance. For such systems, we advocate determining the partition sizes at run time. To support such an approach, we investigate the design of an efficient approximation algorithm to determine the partition sizes based on task characteristics and workload. We derive the worst-case performance bound for the approximation algorithm, and conditions under which the algorithm is optimal.

Other important issues that may affect the feasibility of such an approach such as the overhead involved and the fragmentation of the processing resources in such systems will be studied in the future. The fragmentation of processors in such systems is influenced by the network interconnecting the processors in the system. We have preliminary analysis [KRI87] on the physical subset of processors that may comprise a partition in a partitionable system. We plan to investigate further these and related issues in the future.

Acknowledgements: The authors would like to thank the referees for carefully reading the paper and giving detailed comments that have helped improve the paper.

Bibliography

[BAK83] B. S. Baker, and J. S. Schwarz, "Shelf Algorithms for Two-dimensional Packing Problems," SIAM J. Comput. Vol. 12, No. 3, August 1983, pp. 508 - 525.

[BAU78] G. Baudet, and D. Stevenson, "Optimal Sorting Algorithms for Parallel Computers," IEEE Transactions on Computers, Vol. C-27, January 1978, pp. 84 - 87.

[GAR75] M. R. Garey, and D. S. Johnson, "Complexity Results for Multiprocessor Scheduling under Resource Constraints," SIAM J. Comput. Vol. 4, No. 4, December 1975, pp. 397 - 411.

[GAR79] M. R. Garey, and D. S. Johnson, Computers and Intractability: A Guide to the Theory of NP-Completeness, W. H. Freeman and Company, 1979.

[KRI87] R. Krishnamurti, "Reconfigurable Parallel Architectures for Special Purpose Computing," PhD thesis, Department of Computer and Information Science, University of Pennsylvania, Philadelphia, PA, 1987 (also available as Technical Report MS-CIS-87-81).

[KUC77] D. J. Kuck, "A Survey of Parallel Machine Organization and Programming," ACM Computing Surveys, Vol. 9, No. 1, March 1977, pp. 29 - 59.

[KUE84] J. T. Kuehn, and H. J. Siegel, "Simulation Studies of a Parallel Histogramming Algorithm for PASM," 7th International Conference on Pattern Recognition, 1984, pp. 646 - 649.

[LIN81] B. Lint, and T. Agerwala, "Communication Issues in the Design and Analysis of Parallel Algorithms," IEEE Transactions on Software Engineering, Vol. SE-7, March 1981, pp. 174 - 188.

[MA87] Y. W. Ma, R. Krishnamurti, L. Tao, D. G. Shea, B. Narahari, R. Varadarajan, "Reconfigurable Special-Purpose Computers," Second International Conference on Supercomputing, 1987, pp. 343 - 351.

[MA88] Y. W. Ma, and D. G. Shea, "Downward Scalability of Parallel Architectures," to appear in Third International Conference on Supercomputing, 1988.

[NIC87] D. M. Nicol, and F. H. Willard, "Problem Size, Parallel Architecture, and Optimal Speedup," Proceedings of 14th Annual International Symposium on Computer Architecture, June 1987, pp. 347 - 354.

[NUT77] G. J. Nutt, "Multiprocessor Implementation of a Parallel Processor", Proceedings of the Fourth Annual Symposium on Computer Architecture, 1977.

[PRE80] U. V. Premkumar, R. Kapur, M. Malek, G.J.Lipovski, and P.Horne, "Design and implementation of the Banyan Interconnection Network in TRAC," Proceedings of the National Computer Conference, 1980.

[SIE81] H. J. Siegel L. J. Siegel, F. C. Kemmerer, P. T. Mueller Jr., H. E. Smalley Jr., and S. D. Smith, "PASM: A Partitionable SIMD/MIMD System for Image Processing and Pattern Recognition," IEEE Transactions on Computers, Vol. C-30, December 1981, pp. 934 - 947.

Subcube Allocation and Task Migration in Hypercube Multiprocessors

MING-SYAN CHEN, MEMBER, IEEE, AND KANG G. SHIN, SENIOR MEMBER, IEEE

Abstract—This paper addresses two important issues in the management of processors in a hypercube: *subcube allocation* and *task migration* to eliminate the system fragmentation caused by allocation and deallocation of subcubes.

We prove that the subcube allocation strategy using a binary reflected Gray code (BRGC), called the *GC strategy*, possesses the best subcube recognition ability among all strategies that use sequential searches. A binary code (BC) is defined as the binary representation of a nonnegative integer, and an extended binary code (EBC) is the one obtained by permuting the bits of a BC. Similarly, an extended Gray code (EGC) is obtained from a BRGC. The subcube recognition ability of an allocation strategy using multiple EBC's is analyzed and compared to that using multiple EGC's. The minimal number of EBC's required for complete subcube recognition in an n-cube or Q_n is proved to be $C^n_{\lfloor n/2 \rfloor}$, where C^q_p stands for the number of combinations of choosing p out of q possibilities.

Allocation and deallocation of subcubes usually result in a fragmented hypercube, where even if a sufficient number of hypercube nodes are available, they do not form a subcube large enough to accommodate an incoming task. As the fragmentation in conventional memory allocation can be handled by memory compaction, the fragmentation problem in a hypercube can be solved by *task migration*, i.e., relocating tasks within the hypercube to remove the fragmentation. Note that the procedure for task migration is closely related to the subcube allocation strategy used, since active tasks must be relocated in such a way that the availability of subcubes can be detected by that allocation strategy. Specifically, we develop the task migration strategy for the GC strategy. A goal configuration (of destination subcubes) without fragmentation is determined first. Then, the node-mapping between the source and destination subcubes is derived. Finally, a routing procedure to obtain shortest deadlock-free paths for relocating tasks is developed.

Index Terms—Binary reflected Gray code (BRGC), deadlock, fragmentation, hypercube computers, stepwise adjoint, subcube recognition ability, task migration.

I. Introduction

OWING to their structural regularity and high potential for the parallel execution of various algorithms, hypercube computers have drawn considerable attention in recent years from both academic and industrial communities [1]–[6].

Each task arriving at the hypercube multiprocessor must be allocated to an unoccupied or available subcube for execution. Upon completion of the task, the subcube used for that task is released and made available for other tasks. More specifically, subcube allocation[1] in a hypercube multiprocessor consists of two steps: 1) *determination* of the dimension of a subcube required to execute each incoming task, and 2) *location* of a subcube of the dimension determined by step 1) within the hypercube. Various approaches have been developed to deal with the first step [4], [7]. The second step was addressed in [3], where a subcube allocation strategy was proposed based on a binary reflected Gray code (BRGC), called the *GC strategy*, as opposed to the one based on a binary code (BC), called the *buddy strategy* [8]. The former is shown to outperform the latter due mainly to its superiority in recognizing the existence of available subcubes within the hypercube.

Similarly to conventional memory management, the allocation and deallocation of subcubes usually results in a fragmented hypercube, where even if a sufficient number of nodes are available or unoccupied, they do not form a subcube large enough to accommodate an incoming task. Fig. 1 shows an example of a fragmented hypercube where four available nodes cannot form a 2-cube or Q_2; thus, if a task requiring a Q_2 arrives, it has to be either queued or rejected. As shown in the simulation results in [3], such fragmentation leads to poor utilization of hypercube nodes, and the improvement achieved by the GC strategy is thus limited. As the fragmentation problem in conventional memory allocation can be handled by memory compaction, the fragmentation problem in a hypercube can be solved by *task migration*, i.e., relocating and compacting active tasks[2] within the hypercube at one end so as to make large subcubes available at the other end. Note that the procedure for task migration depends strongly on the subcube allocation strategy used, since active tasks must be relocated in such a way that the availability of subcubes can be detected by that allocation strategy. For this reason, we shall in this paper address both the problems of subcube allocation and task migration.

We shall extend the results on subcube allocation in [3] significantly. To facilitate our discussion, the buddy and GC strategies introduced in [3] are described briefly. A BC is de-

Manuscript received December 11, 1987; revised September 15, 1988. This work was supported in part by the Office of Naval Research under Contracts N00014-85-K-0122 and N00014-85-K-0531.

M. S. Chen was with the Real-Time Computing Laboratory, Department of Electrical Engineering and Computer Science, The University of Michigan, Ann Arbor, MI 48109. He is now with the IBM Thomas J. Watson Research Center, Yorktown Heights, NY 10598.

K. G. Shin is with Real-Time Computing Laboratory, Department of Electrical Engineering and Computer Science, The University of Michigan, Ann Arbor, MI 48109.

IEEE Log Number 9037192.

---

[1] In view of the fact that each task is allocated to a subcube, we use the term *subcube allocation*, instead of processor allocation which was used in [3].

[2] Those tasks which are allocated to subcubes but not completed yet.

Reprinted from *IEEE Trans. Computers*, Vol. 39, No. 9, Sept. 1990, pp. 1146-1155. Copyright © 1990 by The Institute of Electrical and Electronics Engineers, Inc. All rights reserved.

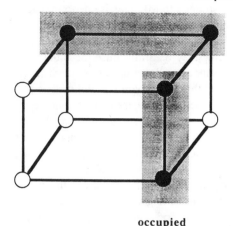

occupied

Fig. 1. An example of hypercube fragmentation.

0.	000		0.	000
1.	001		1.	100
2.	011		2.	101
3.	010		3.	001
4.	110		4.	011
5.	111		5.	111
6.	101		6.	110
7.	100		7.	010
	(a)			(b)

Fig. 2. Illustration of EGC's. (a) BRGC. (b) EGC with $\{g_1, g_2, g_3\} = \{3, 1, 2\}$.

fined as the binary representation of a nonnegative integer, and an extended binary code (EBC) is the one obtained by permuting the bits of a BC. Similarly, an extended Gray code (EGC) is defined as a code obtained by bit-permutation of a BRGC. The subcube recognition ability of an allocation strategy using multiple EBC's is analyzed and compared to that using multiple EGC's. Since, as will be proved later, no other strategy that involves a sequential search can recognize more subcubes than the GC strategy, we shall focus on the development of a task migration strategy under the GC strategy.

A collection of occupied subcubes is called a *configuration*. We first determine the goal configuration to which a given fragmented hypercube must change by relocating active tasks. Since the GC strategy is proved in [3] to be optimal for static allocation,[3] fragmentation can definitely be removed by task migration. When a task is allocated to a subcube, the portion of the task located in each node of this subcube is called a *task module*. The action for a node to move its task module to one of its neighboring nodes is called a *moving step*. The cost of each task migration is then measured in terms of the number of required moving steps while task migrations between different pairs of source and destination subcubes are allowed to be performed *in parallel*. Note that to move tasks in parallel, it is very important to avoid deadlocks during task migration. We not only formulate the node-mapping between each pair of source and destination subcubes in such a way that the number of required moving steps is minimized, but also develop a routing procedure to follow shortest deadlock-free paths for task migration.

The paper is organized as follows. Section II introduces the necessary definitions and notation. Some important results of subcube allocation strategies are presented in Section III. Our main results on task migration are given in Section IV. In three subsections are, respectively, presented the three steps for task migration under the GC strategy: 1) determination of a goal configuration, 2) determination of the node-mapping between the source and destination subcubes, and 3) determination of

---

shortest deadlock-free routing for moving task modules. The paper concludes with Section V.

II. PRELIMINARIES

An n-dimensional hypercube is defined as $Q_n = K_2 \times Q_{n-1}$, where K_2 is the complete graph with two nodes, Q_0 is a trivial graph with one node and $\times$ is the product operation on two graphs [9]. Let $\sum$ be the ternary symbol set $\{0, 1, *\}$, where $*$ is a DON'T CARE symbol. Every subcube in a Q_n can then be uniquely represented by a string of symbols in $\sum$. Such a string of ternary symbols is called the *address* of the corresponding subcube. For example, the address of the subcube Q_2 formed by nodes 0010, 0011, 0110, and 0111 in a Q_4 is $0*1*$. Also, the *Hamming distance* between two hypercube nodes is defined as follows.

Definition 1: The Hamming distance between two nodes with addresses $u = u_n u_{n-1} \cdots u_1$ and $w = w_n w_{n-1} \cdots w_1$ in a Q_n is defined as

$$H(u, w) = \sum_{i=1}^{n} h(u_i, w_i), \text{ where } h(u_i, w_i)$$

$$= \begin{cases} 1, & \text{if } u_i \neq w_i, \\ 0, & \text{if } u_i = w_i. \end{cases}$$

For convenience, the rightmost coordinate in the address of a subcube or a node will be referred to as *dimension 1*, the second to the rightmost coordinate as *dimension 2*, and so on. A formal definition for extended Gray codes (EGC's) was introduced in [3]. An EGC with parameters g_i, $i = 1, \cdots, n$, can be obtained by permuting the bits in the BRGC in such a way that dimension i of the BRGC becomes dimension g_i of the EGC. Fig. 2(a) gives an example of a BRGC which is also an EGC with parameters $\{g_1, g_2, g_3\} = \{1, 2, 3\}$, and Fig. 2(b) shows an EGC with parameters $\{g_1, g_2, g_3\} = \{3, 1, 2\}$. Similarly, an extended binary code (EBC) is defined as follows.

Definition 2: An EBC with parameters g_i, $i = 1, \cdots, n$, is a code resulting from permuting the bits in a BC in such a way that dimension i of the BC becomes dimension g_i of this EBC. (Recall that a BC is the binary representation of a nonnegative integer.)

Obviously, the BC is also an EBC with parameters $\{g_1, g_2, g_3\} = \{1, 2, 3\}$. Examples for the BC and the EBC with parameters $\{g_1, g_2, g_3\} = \{3, 1, 2\}$ are presented in Fig. 3. Also, a set of contiguous integers is called a *region* and let $\#[a, b] = \{k | a \leq k \leq b, k \in I^+\}$. *A coding scheme*

0. 000	0. 000
1. 001	1. 100
2. 010	2. 001
3. 011	3. 101
4. 100	4. 010
5. 101	5. 110
6. 110	6. 011
7. 111	7. 111
(a)	(b)

Fig. 3. Illustration of EBC's. (a) BC. (b) EBC with $\{g_1, g_2, g_3\} = \{3, 1, 2\}$.

0.	0000
1.	0001
2.	0011
3.	0010
4.	0110
5.	0111
6.	1111
7.	1110
8.	1100
9.	1000
10.	1010
11.	1011
12.	1001
13.	1101
14.	0101
15.	0100

Fig. 4. A coding scheme with 4 bits.

with n bits, denoted by C_n, is defined as a one-to-one mapping from a number within $\#[0, 2^n - 1]$ to a binary representation with n bits, and $C_n(m)$ denotes the representation of a number m with n bits under a given coding scheme. Note that an EGC with given parameters corresponds to some coding scheme, and so does an EBC. Figs. 2 and 3 are examples of coding schemes with 3 bits. Fig. 4 gives an example coding scheme with 4 bits which is neither an EGC nor an EBC. For convenience, let B_n and G_n denote n-bit coding schemes associated with the BC and a BRGC, respectively. For example, $B_3(5) = 101$, $G_3(5) = 111$, while $C_4(7) = 1110$ for the coding scheme in Fig. 4.

In addition, a *path* is defined as an ordered sequence of hypercube nodes in which any two consecutive nodes are physically adjacent to each other in the hypercube. Also, we assume that the hardware of the hypercube computer system under consideration is so designed that each hypercube node has separate input and output ports. Thus, each node can receive a task module while sending another task module to its next hop. Each moving step is assumed to take the same amount of time, which is defined as one time unit. $|S|$ denotes the cardinality of the set S and $\bar{b}$ denotes the complement of a bit $b \in \{0, 1\}$. Unless stated otherwise, a set is referred to as an unordered set, i.e., $\{a, b\} = \{c, d\}$ implies that ($a = c$ and $b = d$) or ($a = d$ and $b = c$).

III. Subcube Allocation Strategies

The results on subcube allocation in [3] are extended here and will later be applied to task migration. The subcube recog-

nition ability of the GC strategy was shown to be twice that of the buddy strategy in [3]. This is due to the fact that under the GC strategy the binary strings to be sequentially searched are ordered in a sequence different from those under the buddy strategy. One may naturally raise the following question: "Is there any subcube allocation strategy which can provide an even better subcube recognition ability than the GC strategy by ordering the binary strings to be searched in some other sequence?" To answer this question, we shall prove in Theorem 1 below that the GC strategy is optimal in the sense that no other strategy that involves a sequential search can recognize more subcubes than the GC strategy. By a "sequential search" we mean a search that checks the availability of each hypercube node in a given sequence until a set of consecutive unoccupied nodes forming a subcube of required size is encountered. The subcube recognition ability of an allocation strategy using multiple EBC's will also be analyzed and compared to that using multiple EGC's. The minimal number of EBC's required for complete subcube recognition in a Q_n is proved to be $C^n_{\lfloor n/2 \rfloor}$, whereas the number of EGC's required for complete subcube recognition is less than or equal to $C^n_{\lfloor n/2 \rfloor}$. Our results are shown to favor the use of the GC strategy over any other strategy based on a sequential search for subcubes.

A. Subcube Allocation Strategies Using a Single Code

Note that both the buddy and GC strategies are a first-fit sequential search. Node addresses under the buddy and GC strategies are ordered in a list according to the BC and the BRGC, respectively. Such a list is called an *allocation list*. Under each of these strategies, the availability of hypercube nodes is then kept track of by its allocation list. Suppose $k = |I_i|$ is the dimension of a subcube required to execute an incoming task I_i. The buddy strategy will search for a set of 2^k consecutive unoccupied nodes in its allocation list, say $B_n(p), B_n(p + 1), \cdots, B_n(p + 2^k - 1)$, under the constraint that p is a multiple of 2^k. On the other hand, the GC strategy searches for a set of 2^k consecutive unoccupied nodes in its allocation list, say $G_n(p), G_n(p + 1), \cdots, G_n(p + 2^k - 1)$, but in this case p only has to be a multiple of 2^{k-1}, instead of 2^k. A formal description of both strategies is given in Appendix A. Illustrative examples for the operations under both strategies can be found in Fig. 5.

It is proved in [3] that the GC strategy can recognize $2^{n-k+1} Q_k$'s for $1 \leq k \leq n - 1$, which is twice the number of subcubes recognizable by the buddy strategy. Moreover, we shall prove that the GC strategy is optimal insofar as the subcube recognition ability of a sequential search is concerned. To facilitate this proof, it is necessary to introduce the following lemma first.

Lemma 1: The intersection of two overlapping subcubes $\alpha = a_n a_{n-1} \cdots a_1$ and $\beta = b_n b_{n-1} \cdots b_1$ is a subcube with address $\gamma = c_n c_{n-1} \cdots c_1$, where

$$c_i = \begin{cases} *, & \text{if } a_i = b_i = *, \\ 0, & \text{if } a_i = b_i = 0 \text{ or } \{a_i, b_i\} = \{0, *\}, \\ 1, & \text{if } a_i = b_i = 1 \text{ or } \{a_i, b_i\} = \{1, *\}. \end{cases}$$

$|\mathbf{I}_1| = 0$ $|\mathbf{I}_3| = 0$ $|\mathbf{I}_5| = 1$

$|\mathbf{I}_2| = 2$ $|\mathbf{I}_4| = 0$

0. 0000 —	$\mathbf{I}_1$	
1. 0001 —	$\mathbf{I}_3$	
2. 0011 ⌐		
3. 0010		
4. 0110	$\mathbf{I}_2$	
5. 0111 ⌐		
6. 0101 —	$\mathbf{I}_4$	
7. 0100 ⌐		
8. 1100 ⌐	$\mathbf{I}_5$	
9. 1101		
10. 1111		
11. 1110		
12. 1010		
13. 1011		
14. 1001		
15. 1000		

0. 0000 —	$\mathbf{I}_1$	
1. 0001 —	$\mathbf{I}_3$	
2. 0010 —	$\mathbf{I}_4$	
3. 0011		
4. 0100 ⌐		
5. 0101	$\mathbf{I}_2$	
6. 0110		
7. 0111 ⌐		
8. 1000 ⌐	$\mathbf{I}_5$	
9. 1001 ⌐		
10. 1010		
11. 1011		
12. 1100		
13. 1101		
14. 1110		
15. 1111		

(a) (b)

Fig. 5. Example operations of both strategies. (a) GC strategy. (b) Buddy strategy.

Proof: Note that subcubes α and β are disjoint iff there exists a k such that $\{a_k, b_k\} = \{0, 1\}$. Therefore, the above equation includes all possible combinations of a_i and b_i, $\forall i$, since α and β are overlapping. It can be seen that nodes in γ are contained in both α and β.

On the other hand, suppose there is a node m with address $m_n m_{n-1} \cdots m_1$ that does not belong to γ. Then, there must exist a j such that $\{m_j, c_j\} = \{0, 1\}$. Without loss of generality, we can assume $m_j = 0$ and $c_j = 1$. Then, we have either $a_j = 1$ or $b_j = 1$, meaning that m is not contained in the intersection of α and β. Therefore, nodes in γ are the only nodes that are contained in both α and β, and thus this lemma follows. Q.E.D.

By Lemma 1, the intersection of two overlapping subcubes must be a subcube. This leads to the following important property of the BRGC.

Theorem 1: The BRGC is an optimal coding scheme as far as the subcube recognition ability of a sequential search is concerned.

Proof: Note that there are $2^{n-k+1} Q_k$'s recognizable by the BRGC. Suppose there exists a coding scheme that can recognize more than $2^{n-k+1} Q_k$'s. Then, there must exist two distinct integers i and j such that a) $|i - j| < 2^{k-1}$, b) nodes with addresses $C_n(p)$, $p \in \#[i, i+2^k -1]$, form a Q_k, and c) nodes with addresses $C_n(q)$, $q \in \#[j, j+2^k -1]$, form another Q_k. Thus, the cardinality of $\#[i, i+2^k -1] \cap \#[j, j+2^k -1]$ must be greater than 2^{k-1} since $|i-j| < 2^{k-1}$, and less than 2^k since $i \neq j$. However, this means that the intersection of these two regions does not form a subcube, a contradiction to Lemma 1. Q.E.D.

Notice that not only the BRGC but also each EGC has an optimal subcube recognition ability since each EGC can be obtained by permuting the bits of the BRGC.

B. Subcube Allocation Strategies Using Multiple Codes

In [3], we developed the following theorem to determine the subcube recognition ability of an EGC with given parameters.

Theorem 2 [3]: A subcube Q_k with the address $b_n b_{n-1} \cdots b_1$ can be recognized by an EGC with parameters g_i, $1 \leq i \leq n$, iff any of the following three conditions is satisfied:

a) $b_{g_i} = *$, $1 \leq i \leq k$.

b) $b_{g_i} = *$, $1 \leq i \leq k - 1$, and there exists an r such that $b_{g_{r-1}} = 1$, $b_{g_r} = *$, and $b_{g_s} = 0$, $k \leq s < r - 1$.

c) $b_{g_i} = *$, $1 \leq i \leq k - 1$, $b_{g_s} = 0$, $k \leq s \leq n - 1$, and $b_{g_n} = *$.

Similarly, the subcube recognition ability of an EBC with given parameters can be determined by the lemma below whose proof is trivial, and thus, omitted.

Lemma 2: A subcube Q_k with the address $b_n b_{n-1} \cdots b_1$ can be recognized by an EBC with parameters g_i, $1 \leq i \leq n$, iff $b_{g_i} = *$, for $1 \leq i \leq k$.

Let $R(n)$ denote the number of EBC's required for complete subcube recognition in a Q_n. We then obtain the following important result.

Theorem 3: $R(n) = C^n_{\lfloor n/2 \rfloor}$.

Proof: Note that there are $C^n_k 2^{n-k} Q_k$'s in a Q_n, and from Lemma 2, each EBC can only recognize $2^{n-k} Q_k$'s. Therefore, it requires at least C^n_k EBC's to recognize all Q_k's in a Q_n. However, $C^n_{\lfloor n/2 \rfloor} = \max_{0 \leq k \leq n} \{C^n_k\}$, leading to $R(n) \geq C^n_{\lfloor n/2 \rfloor}$.

The inequality $R(n) \leq C^n_{\lfloor n/2 \rfloor}$ can be proved in light of the Theorem of Matching [10] by using the same procedure as in the proof of Theorem 4 in [3]. Q.E.D.

Notice that the number of EGC's required for complete subcube recognition, as proved in [3], is less than or equal to $C^n_{\lfloor n/2 \rfloor}$. Naturally, this is due to the superiority of the subcube recognition ability of EGC's to that of EBC's. Following the same procedure as in the proof of Theorem 4 in [3], we obtain the parameters of those EBC's required for complete subcube recognition in a Q_5: $\{1, 2, 3, 4, 5\}$, $\{4, 5, 2, 1, 3\}$, $\{3, 5, 4, 1, 2\}$, $\{2, 5, 1, 3, 4\}$, $\{3, 4, 2, 5, 1\}$, $\{5, 1, 3, 2, 4\}$, $\{4, 1, 5, 2, 3\}$, $\{2, 4, 1, 5, 3\}$, $\{3, 1, 4, 5, 2\}$, $\{2, 3, 5, 1, 4\}$. Let B^i denote the ith EBC in the ten EBC's and $SB_k = \cup_{i=1}^k B^i$. The subcube recognition abilities of SB_h, $1 \leq h \leq 10$, are shown in Table I. For the comparison purpose, the subcube recognition ability of those EGC's with the same parameters is shown in Table II, where G^i is the ith EGC and $SG_k = \cup_{i=1}^k G^i$. The number of recognizable subcubes of each dimension with multiple EBC's and that with multiple EGC's are plotted in Fig. 6, where trivial cases for Q_0 and Q_5 are omitted. From Fig. 6, it is easy to see that the subcube recognition ability of EGC's is superior to that of EBC's.

IV. Task Migration under the GC Strategy

Due to similar reasons for the memory fragmentation in conventional memory allocation, allocation and deallocation of subcubes may result in a fragmented hypercube. As shown in the simulation results in [3], although the GC strategy outperforms the buddy strategy, the improvement achieved by using multiple codes is rather limited. This fact in turn implies that poor utilization of hypercube nodes is due mainly to system fragmentation, rather than the subcube recognition ability of an allocation strategy. Consequently, it is essential

TABLE I
THE NUMBER OF SUBCUBES RECOGNIZABLE BY SB_h, $1 \le h \le 10$

Q_k \ SB_h	h=1	h=2	h=3	h=4	h=5	h=6	h=7	h=8	h=9	h=10
k=0	32	32	32	32	32	32	32	32	32	32
k=1	16	32	48	64	64	80	80	80	80	80
k=2	8	16	24	32	40	48	56	64	72	80
k=3	4	8	12	16	20	24	28	32	36	40
k=4	2	4	6	8	10	10	10	10	10	10
k=5	1	1	1	1	1	1	1	1	1	1

TABLE II
THE NUMBER OF SUBCUBES RECOGNIZABLE BY SG_h, $1 \le h \le 10$

Q_k \ SG_h	h=1	h=2	h=3	h=4	h=5	h=6	h=7	h=8	h=9	h=10
k=0	32	32	32	32	32	32	32	32	32	32
k=1	32	57	72	79	79	80	80	80	80	80
k=2	16	32	47	58	65	71	75	78	79	80
k=3	8	16	22	25	31	34	37	38	39	40
k=4	4	8	10	10	10	10	10	10	10	10
k=5	1	1	1	1	1	1	1	1	1	1

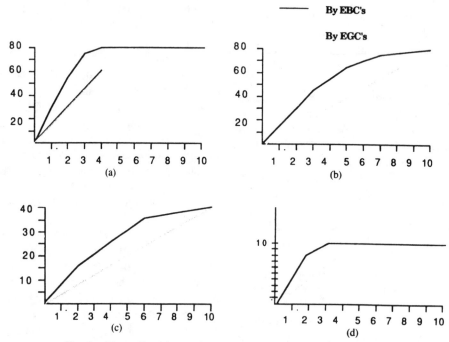

Fig. 6. The number of recognizable subcubes of each dimension. (a) One-dimensional cubes. (b) Two-dimensional cubes. (c) Three-dimensional cubes. (d) Four-dimensional cubes.

to develop an efficient procedure for task migration under the GC strategy, which relocates active tasks to eliminate the fragmentation. In the following three subsections, we shall determine, respectively, the goal configuration, the node-mapping between the source and destination subcubes, and shortest deadlock-free paths for task migration.

A. Determination of Goal Configuration

There are usually many ways to relocate active tasks and compact occupied subcubes. However, since it is desirable to perform task migration between each pair of subcubes in parallel, it is important to avoid any deadlock during the migration. Clearly, a deadlock might occur if there is a circular wait among the nodes involved. To prevent this, a linear ordering of hypercube nodes is established in such a way that each node can only move its task module to a node with a lower address, i.e., a node with address $G_n(p)$ sends its task module to another node with address $G_n(q)$, only if $p > q$. Since a node with a lower address never sends its task module to a node with a higher address, it is easy to see that the condition for any circular wait can be avoided by the above method. Thus, given a configuration of occupied subcubes, the goal configuration without fragmentation can be determined by the following algorithm.

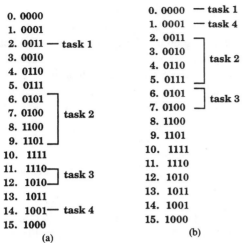

0. 0000	0. 0000	— task 1
1. 0001	1. 0001	— task 4
2. 0011 — task 1	2. 0011	
3. 0010	3. 0010	
4. 0110	4. 0110	task 2
5. 0111	5. 0111	
6. 0101	6. 0101	
7. 0100 task 2	7. 0100	task 3
8. 1100	8. 1100	
9. 1101	9. 1101	
10. 1111	10. 1111	
11. 1110 task 3	11. 1110	
12. 1010	12. 1010	
13. 1011	13. 1011	
14. 1001 — task 4	14. 1001	
15. 1000	15. 1000	
(a)	(b)	

Fig. 7. Task migration under the GC strategy. (a) Before. (b) After.

Algorithm A_1: Determination of the goal configuration:

Step 1. Label each task in the availability list with a distinct number in such a way that each task allocated to a subcube with a lower address is labeled with a smaller number.

Step 2. Relocate all tasks according to an increasing order of their labels.

For example, the goal configuration in Fig. 7(b) can be derived from the initial fragmented configuration in Fig. 7(a). It can be easily verified that by using algorithm A_1, each task will always be moved from a subcube with a higher address to a subcube with a lower address, while a task with a smaller label is not necessarily ahead of a task with a larger label in the goal configuration. An allocation strategy is said to be *statically optimal*, if a Q_n using the strategy can accommodate any input request sequence $\{I_i\}_{i=1}^k$ iff $\sum_{i=1}^k 2^{|I_i|} \leq 2^n$, where $|I_i|$ is the subcube dimension required by request I_i. As was proved in [3], the GC allocation strategy is statically optimal. This fact implies that fragmentation will definitely be removed by A_1.

B. Node-Mapping Between Source and Destination Subcubes

Once the goal configuration is determined, each active task will be moved from its current or source subcube to the destination subcube. The action for a node to move its task module to one of its neighboring nodes is called a *moving step*. To determine the number of moving steps for a task migration, we first define the *moving distance* of a task between two subcube locations as follows. As it will be shown in Theorem 4 below, the minimal number of moving steps required to move a task from one subcube location to another can be determined by the moving distance between the two subcube locations. Furthermore, as it will become clear later, when modules of a task are migrated in parallel, the moving distance between two subcube locations is equal to the number of moving steps required to move a task module from the source node to its destination node under the node mapping scheme described in Corollary 4.1.

Definition 3: The moving distance of a task between two subcube locations with addresses $\alpha = a_n a_{n-1} \cdots a_1$ and $\beta =$

$b_n b_{n-1} \cdots b_1$ in a Q_n is defined as

$$M(\alpha, \beta) = \sum_{i=1}^n m(a_i, b_i), \text{ where } m(a_i, b_i)$$

$$= \begin{cases} 1, & \text{if } \{a_i, b_i\} = \{0, 1\}, \\ 0, & \text{if } a_i = b_i, \\ \frac{1}{2}, & \text{otherwise.} \end{cases}$$

Then, we have the following theorem for the minimal number of moving steps required to move a task from one subcube location to another.

Theorem 4: Let $T(\alpha, \beta)$ be the minimal number of moving steps from a subcube location α to another location β. Then, $T(\alpha, \beta) = M(\alpha, \beta)2^{|\alpha|}$, where $|\alpha| = |\beta|$ is the dimension of the subcube.

To facilitate the proof of Theorem 4, it is necessary to introduce the following proposition whose proof can be found in [11].

Proposition 1: Given a node $u \in Q_n$, $\sum_{w \in Q_n} H(u, w) = n2^{n-1}$.

Proof of Theorem 4: We shall prove $T(\alpha, \beta) \geq M(\alpha, \beta)2^{|\alpha|}$ first. Suppose $\alpha = a_n a_{n-1} \cdots a_1$ and $\beta = b_n b_{n-1} \cdots b_1$. We define the *frontier subcube* of α towards β, denoted by $\sigma_{\alpha \to \beta}(\alpha) = f_n f_{n-1} \cdots f_1$, in such a way that, $\forall i, f_i = b_i$ if $a_i = {}^*$ and $b_i \in \{0, 1\}$, and $f_i = a_i$ otherwise. For example, if $\alpha = 00^{**}$ and $\beta = 1^*1^*$, then $\sigma_{\alpha \to \beta}(\alpha) = 001^*$ and $\sigma_{\beta \to \alpha}(\beta) = 101^*$. Clearly, $\sigma_{\alpha \to \beta}(\alpha)$ contains all the nodes in α which are closest to β. Besides, we define the Hamming distance between two subcubes as the shortest distance between any two nodes which, respectively, belong to the two subcubes, i.e., $H^*(\alpha, \beta) = \min_{u \in \alpha, w \in \beta} H(u, w)$. Since we align some bits of α with their corresponding bits of β to obtain $\sigma_{\alpha \to \beta}(\alpha)$, it is easy to see that $\forall u \in \alpha$ and $w \in \beta$, $H(u, w) \geq H^*(u, \sigma_{\alpha \to \beta}(\alpha)) + H^*(\sigma_{\alpha \to \beta}(\alpha), \sigma_{\beta \to \alpha}(\beta)) + H^*(\sigma_{\beta \to \alpha}(\beta), w)$.

Let $u' \in \beta$ denote the node to which the task module originally located at $u \in \alpha$ is to be moved. Notice that the number of moving steps required to move a task module from u to u' is greater than or equal to the Hamming distance between them, $H(u, u')$. Then, $T(\alpha, \beta) \geq \sum_{u \in \alpha} H(u, u')$. Moreover, from the above reasoning, we obtain

$$T(\alpha, \beta) \geq \sum_{u \in \alpha} H(u, u')$$

$$\geq \sum_{u \in \alpha} \{H^*(u, \sigma_{\alpha \to \beta}(\alpha))$$

$$+ H^*(\sigma_{\alpha \to \beta}(\alpha), \sigma_{\beta \to \alpha}(\beta))$$

$$+ H^*(\sigma_{\beta \to \alpha}(\beta), u')\}$$

$$= \sum_{u \in \alpha} H^*(u, \sigma_{\alpha \to \beta}(\alpha))$$

$$+ 2^{|\alpha|} H^*(\sigma_{\alpha \to \beta}(\alpha), \sigma_{\beta \to \alpha}(\beta))$$

$$+ \sum_{u \in \alpha} H^*(\sigma_{\alpha \to \beta}(\alpha), u').$$

Let r_1 be the number of dimensions in which $\{a_i, b_i\} = \{0, 1\}$, r_2 be the number of dimensions in which $a_i = b_i = {}^*$, r_3 be the number of dimensions in which $a_i = {}^*$ and $b_i \in \{0, 1\}$, and r_4 be the number of dimensions in which $b_i = {}^*$ and $a_i \in \{0, 1\}$. Clearly, $r_1 = H^*(\sigma_{\alpha \to \beta}(\alpha), \sigma_{\beta \to \alpha}(\beta))$, $r_2 + r_3 = |\alpha|$, $r_1 + r_3 = M(\alpha, \beta)$, and $r_3 = r_4$, because the addresses of α and β have the same number of *'s. Therefore,

$$
\begin{aligned}
T(\alpha, \beta) &\geq \sum_{u \in \alpha} H^*(u, \sigma_{\alpha \to \beta}(\alpha)) \\
&\quad + 2^{|\alpha|} H^*(\sigma_{\alpha \to \beta}(\alpha), \sigma_{\beta \to \alpha}(\beta)) \\
&\quad + \sum_{u \in \alpha} H^*(\sigma_{\alpha \to \beta}(\alpha), u') \\
&= 2^{|\alpha|} H^*(\sigma_{\alpha \to \beta}(\alpha), \sigma_{\beta \to \alpha}(\beta)) \\
&\quad + 2 \sum_{u \in \alpha} H^*(u, \sigma_{\alpha \to \beta}(\alpha)) \\
&= 2^{|\alpha|} r_1 + 2(2^{r_2} 2^{r_3 - 1} r_3)
\end{aligned}
$$

(From Proposition 1 and $r_2 = |\sigma_{\alpha \to \beta}(\alpha)|$.)

$$
= 2^{|\alpha|}(r_1 + r_3) = M(\alpha, \beta) 2^{|\alpha|}.
$$

Next, we prove the inequality $T(\alpha, \beta) \leq M(\alpha, \beta) 2^{|\alpha|}$ by showing the existence of a one-to-one mapping between nodes in α and β, and that the Hamming distance between each pair of mapping and mapped nodes is $M(\alpha, \beta)$. Suppose $p_1, p_2, \cdots, p_{r_3}$ are those dimensions in which $a_{p_i} \in \{0, 1\}$ and $b_{p_i} = {}^*$, and $q_1, q_2, \cdots, q_{r_4}$ are those dimensions in which $a_{q_i} = {}^*$ and $b_{q_i} \in \{0, 1\}$. Note that $r_3 = r_4$. Each node $u = u_n u_{n-1} \cdots u_1 \in \alpha$ can then be mapped to a node $w = w_n w_{n-1} \cdots w_1 \in \beta$ in such a way that when $i \neq p_j$ for any $1 \leq j \leq r_3$,

$$
w_i = \begin{cases} b_i, & \text{if } b_i \in \{0, 1\}, \\ u_i, & \text{if } a_i = b_i = {}^*, \end{cases}
$$

and when $i = p_j$ for some j, $1 \leq j \leq r_3$,

$$
w_{p_j} = \begin{cases} \overline{u_{p_j}}, & \text{if } w_{q_j} = u_{q_j}, \\ u_{p_j}, & \text{if } w_{q_j} \neq u_{q_j}. \end{cases}
$$

This is a one-to-one mapping, since the possibility of a many-to-one mapping is eliminated by different assignments of bits in the p_jth dimension, $1 \leq j \leq r_3$. Moreover, we have $H(u, w) = r_1 + r_3 = M(\alpha, \beta)$. By the above node-mapping, we can determine, for each source node in α, the corresponding mapped node in β, and the total number of moving steps is $M(\alpha, \beta) 2^{|\alpha|}$, thus satisfying $T(\alpha, \beta) \leq M(\alpha, \beta) 2^{|\alpha|}$. Q.E.D.

The above theorem proves that the minimal number of moving steps required to move a task from a subcube location α to another subcube location β as $M(\alpha, \beta) 2^{|\alpha|}$. There may be many ways to move a task from one subcube location to another, each having the same total number of moving steps. For example, we can move an active task from 10^*1 to 000^* by either a) $1011 \to 0000$ (3 hops) and $1001 \to 0001$ (1 hop), or b) $1011 \to 0001$ (2 hops) and $1001 \to 0000$ (2 hops). The total number of moving steps in either case is 4. However,

in order to exploit the inherent parallelism, we naturally want the total $M(\alpha, \beta) 2^{|\alpha|}$ moving steps to be equally distributed among all pairs of source and destination nodes such that every node u in α requires exactly $M(\alpha, \beta)$ moving steps to transfer its task module to the corresponding node in β. Clearly, this can be accomplished by the node-mapping scheme introduced in the proof of Theorem 4. Notice that the source and destination subcubes for tasks being migrated under a strategy must be recognizable by that strategy. In light of this fact, a simplified node-mapping scheme will be introduced in Corollary 4.1. However, it is necessary to introduce the following proposition first.

Proposition 2: Suppose $\alpha = a_n a_{n-1} \cdots a_1$ and $\beta = b_n b_{n-1} \cdots b_1$ are two k-dimensional subcubes recognizable by the GC strategy. Then, there is at most one dimension, say p, in which $a_p \in \{0, 1\}$ and $b_p = {}^*$.

Proof: From Theorem 2 and the fact that $g_i = i$, $1 \leq i \leq n$, for the BRGC, we know $a_i = {}^*$ and $b_i = {}^*$ for $1 \leq i \leq k - 1$. Since there are exactly k *'s in the address of a Q_k, this proposition follows. Q.E.D.

The node-mapping between two subcubes recognizable by the GC strategy can be determined as follows. Suppose $\alpha = a_n a_{n-1} \cdots a_1$ is the source subcube and $\beta = b_n b_{n-1} \cdots b_1$ is the destination subcube. Let p and q be the dimensions in which $a_p \in \{0, 1\}$ and $b_p = {}^*$, and $a_q = {}^*$ and $b_q \in \{0, 1\}$.

Corollary 4.1: Each source node $u = u_n u_{n-1} \cdots u_1 \in \alpha$ can be one-to-one mapped to a destination node $w = w_n w_{n-1} \cdots w_1 \in \beta$ in such a way that when $i \neq p$,

$$
w_i = \begin{cases} b_i, & \text{if } b_i \in \{0, 1\}, \\ u_i, & \text{if } a_i = b_i = {}^*, \end{cases}
$$

when $i = p$,

$$
w_p = \begin{cases} \overline{u_p}, & \text{if } w_q = u_q, \\ u_p, & \text{if } w_q \neq u_q, \end{cases}
$$

and $H(u, w) = M(\alpha, \beta)$.

For example, when $\alpha = 1^*1^*$, $\beta = 00^{**}$, and $u = 1110$, we have $p = 3$ and then $w = 0010$. It can be verified that every node in 1^*1^* will need exactly 2 moving steps to relocate its task module to the corresponding node in 00^{**}, i.e., 1010 $(12) \to 0000$ (0), 1011 $(13) \to 0001$ (1), 1110 $(11) \to 0010$ (3), and 1111 $(10) \to 0011$ (2). It is worth mentioning that the order of source nodes in the BRGC is not necessarily the same as that of their corresponding destination nodes after the node-mapping (see Fig. 7).

C. Determination of Shortest Deadlock-Free Routing

After the determination of the node-mapping, we now want to develop a routing method to move each task module from its source node to its destination node. As mentioned earlier, in order to avoid deadlocks, a linear ordering among hypercube nodes is enforced such that each node can only move its task module to a node with a lower address. More formally, we need the following definition.

Definition 4: A path is said to be *shortest deadlock-free* (SDF) with respect to a coding scheme if it is a shortest path from the source node to the destination node and the reverse

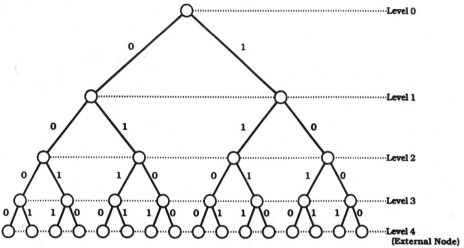

Fig. 8. The labeled complete binary tree for a BRGC.

order of nodes in that coding scheme is preserved in the node sequence of that path.

In other words, if $C_n(i)$ and $C_n(j)$ are two nodes in an SDF path, then $C_n(i)$ is ahead of $C_n(j)$ in the path iff $i > j$. For example, the path $[110, 010, 011]$ is an SDF path in G_3 of Fig. 2(a), whereas $[110, 111, 011]$ is not. A coding scheme C_n is said to be *SDF path preserving* if $\forall p < q$ there exists an SDF path from $C_n(q)$ to $C_n(p)$, i.e., there exists $[C_n(q), C_n(r_1), C_n(r_2), \cdots, C_n(r_{d-1}), C_n(p)]$, such that $q > r_1 > \cdots > r_{d-1} > p$.

Once the node-mapping between each pair of source and destination subcubes is determined, each source node appends to its task module the address of its destination node. Each node can then determine the next hop on which to route a task module by the following algorithm.

Algorithm A_2: Determination of an SDF path:

Step 1. Each node compares the destination address $d = d_n d_{n-1} \cdots d_1$ with its own address $s = s_n s_{n-1} \cdots s_1$ from left to right. Let the jth and kth dimensions be, respectively, the first and second dimensions in which they differ, i.e., $s_i = d_i$ for $j+1 \leq i \leq n$ and $k+1 \leq i \leq j-1$, and $s_j \neq d_j, s_k \neq d_k$.

Step 2. If $\sum_{i=k}^{j-1} s_i$ is even **then** send the task module to a neighboring node along the kth dimension **else** send the task module to a neighboring node along the jth dimension.

For example, suppose the source node is $G_4(12) = 1010$ and the destination node d is $G_4(1) = 0001$, then $j = 4$ and $k = 2$. The next node determined by A_2 is $G_4(3) = 0010$ since $\sum_{i=2}^{3} s_i$ is odd, and thus, the fourth dimension of 1010 is changed. Then, the next hop determined by the intermediate node $G_4(3) = 0010$ is $G_4(2) = 0011$, since we get $j = 2$ and $k = 1$ for $s = 0010$ and $d = 0001$. It can be verified that $[1010\ (12), 0010\ (3), 0011\ (2), 0001\ (1)]$ is an SDF path. Actually, this is not a coincidence. As it will be proved later, the paths determined by A_2 must be SDF. To facilitate the proof, it is necessary to introduce the following lemma which compares the order of two BRGC numbers.

Lemma 3: Let $G_n(p) = a_n a_{n-1} \cdots a_1$ and $G_n(q) = b_n b_{n-1} \cdots b_1$ be two BRGC numbers. Suppose the ith dimension is the first dimension in which $G_n(p)$ and $G_n(q)$ differ, when they are compared from left to right, i.e., $a_j = b_j$ for $n \geq j > i$ and $a_i \neq b_i$. Without loss of generality, we can assume $a_i = 1$ and $b_i = 0$. Then, $p > q$ iff $\sum_{j=i+1}^{n} a_j$ is even.

Proof: Consider the following procedure to generate the BRGC. Let $G_1 = \{0, 1\}$. Given a k-bit BRGC $G_k = \{d_0, d_1, \cdots, d_{2^k-1}\}$, a $(k+1)$-bit BRGC can be generated by

$$G_{k+1} = \{d_0 0, d_0 1, d_1 1, d_1 0, d_2 0, d_2 1, \cdots, d_{2^k-1} 1, d_{2^k-1} 0\}.$$

It is proved in [12] that this procedure indeed generates the BRGC. This procedure can be described by the complete binary tree in Fig. 8. As the number of bits in the BRGC increases, the corresponding tree grows. The address of every external node (leaf) is determined by the coded bits in the path from the root to the external node, and the BRGC is then obtained by the addresses of external nodes from left to right. It can be verified that every node which is reached from the root via an even number of links labeled with 1 has a 0 left-child and a 1 right-child. Note that an external node further to the right is associated with a larger number in the BRGC. Thus, it is proved that $p > q$ if $\sum_{j=i+1}^{n} a_j$ is even, and the fact that $p < q$ if $\sum_{j=i+1}^{n} a_j$ is odd follows similarly.   Q.E.D.

For example, in the 3-bit BRGC of Fig. 2(a), $G_3(3) = 010$ appears after $G_3(1) = 001$, since the number of 1's in the left of their first different bit position in $G_3(3)$ is zero which is even, whereas $G_3(4) = 110$ appears before $G_3(6) = 101$ since the number of 1's in the left of their first different bit position in $G_3(4)$ is one. With the aid of Lemma 3, the following important theorem can be derived.

Theorem 5: The path determined by A_2 is SDF.

Proof: Let $f(m)$ denote the number mapped into the binary string m in the BRGC, i.e., $p = f(m)$ iff $m = G_n(p)$. Since $f(s) > f(d)$, from Lemma 3 we know that $\sum_{i=j}^{n} s_i$ is odd. Let $u = u_n \cdots u_1$ denote the address of the next hop determined by A_2. Consider the case when $\sum_{i=k}^{j-1} s_i$ is even. Clearly, from Step 2 of A_2, $H(u, s) = 1$ and $H(u, d) = H(s, d) - 1$, since $u_i = s_i$ if $i \neq k$, and $u_k = \overline{s_k} = d_k$. Besides, we have $f(u) > f(d)$ since $\sum_{i=j}^{n} u_i = \sum_{i=j}^{n} s_i$ is odd, and $f(s) > f(u)$ since $\sum_{i=j}^{n} s_i + \sum_{i=k}^{j-1} s_i$ is odd.

On the other hand, in the case when $\sum_{i=k}^{j-1} s_i$ is odd, $H(u, s) = 1$ and $H(u, d) = H(s, d) - 1$, since $u_i = s_i$ if $i \neq j$, and $u_j = \overline{s_j} = d_j$. Also, $f(s) > f(u)$ since $\sum_{i=j}^{n} s_i$ is odd, and $f(u) > f(d)$ since $\sum_{i=k}^{n} u_i = \sum_{i=k}^{j-1} u_i + \sum_{i=j}^{n} u_i =$

$\sum_{i=k}^{j-1} s_i + \overline{s_j} + \sum_{i=j+1}^{n} s_i$ is odd. Therefore, in both cases, $H(u, d) = H(s, d) - 1$, $f(s) > f(u)$ and $f(s) > f(d)$. Since the above results hold for every intermediate node, this theorem follows.　　　　　　　　　　　　　　　　Q.E.D.

The above theorem shows that task migration under the GC strategy can be accomplished via SDF paths. Also, the following corollary results from Theorem 5.

Corollary 5.1: The BRGC is SDF path preserving.

Note that the BC is not SDF path preserving, neither is the coding scheme given in Fig. 4. For example, no SDF path exists from $B_3(2) = 010$ to $B_3(1) = 001$, and nor does from $C_4(9) = 1000$ to $C_4(1) = 0001$.

Furthermore, as it will be proved below, A_2 will not send any two modules of a task to the same next hop, implying that task migration can be performed in parallel. It was assumed in Section II that a hypercube node can send and receive task modules at the same time and each moving step takes one time unit. Let α be the source subcube and $S_1, S_2, \cdots, S_{2^{|\alpha|}}$ be the nodes of α. Suppose β is the destination subcube and $S_i(t)$ is the hypercube node which receives, via the path determined by A_2, the task module originally residing at S_i after t time units under the node-mapping scheme in Corollary 4.1. Thus, $S_i = S_i(0)$, $1 \leq i \leq 2^{|\alpha|}$, are the nodes of α, $S_i(M(\alpha, \beta))$, $1 \leq i \leq 2^{|\alpha|}$, are the nodes of β, and $[S_i(0), S_i(1), \cdots, S_i(M(\alpha, \beta))]$ is the path for moving a task module from S_i to its destination. Two paths $[S_i(0), S_i(1), \cdots, S_i(M(\alpha, \beta)]$ and $[S_j(0), S_j(1), \cdots, S_j(M(\alpha, \beta)]$ are said to be *stepwise disjoint*, if at any time t, the two corresponding task modules will not be sent to the same next hop, i.e., $S_i(t) \neq S_j(t)$, $\forall t \in [0, M(\alpha, \beta)]$. Then, we have the following corollary which states the impossibility for two task modules to compete for the same next hop during task migration, showing another advantage of using the GC strategy.

Corollary 5.2: Under the node-mapping scheme in Corollary 4.1, the paths determined by A_2 are stepwise disjoint.

Proof: Suppose $\alpha = a_n a_{n-1} \cdots a_1$ and $\beta = b_n b_{n-1} \cdots b_1$ are, respectively, the source and destination subcubes, and $|\alpha| = |\beta| = k$. From Proposition 2, we get $a_{k-1} = \cdots = a_1 = b_{k-1} = \cdots = b_1 = *$. From the node-mapping scheme in Corollary 4.1, it follows that for any pair of source node $u = u_n u_{n-1} \cdots u_1$ and destination node $w = w_n w_{n-1} \cdots w_1$, we have $u_{k-1} \cdots u_1 = w_{k-1} \cdots w_1$. This in turn implies that the path from u to w must be within subcube $*^{n-k+1} u_{k-1} \cdots u_1$.

Divide a Q_n into $2^{k-1} Q_{n-k+1}$'s, whose addresses are $*^{n-k+1} d_{k-1} \cdots d_1$, $d_i \in \{0, 1\}$, $1 \leq i \leq k - 1$. Call each of these Q_{n-k+1}'s a *partition*. From Proposition 2, it can be seen that each partition contains exactly two adjacent nodes in α. The entire paths for moving two task modules in a partition to their destination nodes will remain within the same partition. This means that task modules from different partitions will not collide with one another at any time. Moreover, since there is no cycle of an odd length in a Q_n, the two task modules originally residing at two adjacent nodes in the source subcube will not collide with each other at any time. This corollary thus follows.　　　　　　　　Q.E.D.

To illustrate the entire process of task migration, consider the fragmented configuration in Fig. 7(a). Using Al-gorithm A_1, we obtain the goal configuration in Fig. 7(b). By the node-mapping scheme developed in Section IV-B, we have $0011 \rightarrow 0000$ for task 1, $0101 \rightarrow 0011$, $0100 \rightarrow 0010$, $1100 \rightarrow 0110$, and $1101 \rightarrow 0111$ for task 2 (*10* $\rightarrow$ 0*1*), $1010 \rightarrow 0100$ and $1011 \rightarrow 0101$ for task 3 (101* $\rightarrow$ 010*), and $1001 \rightarrow 0001$ for task 4. (Note that the relative order of source nodes is changed during the node-mapping for task 3.) The SDF routing can then be determined by A_2 as follows:

Task 1: $0011 \rightarrow 0001 \rightarrow 0000$;

Task 2: $0101 \rightarrow 0111 \rightarrow 0011$, $0100 \rightarrow 0110 \rightarrow 0010$, $1100 \rightarrow 0100 \rightarrow 0110$ and $1101 \rightarrow 0101 \rightarrow 0111$;

Task 3: $1010 \rightarrow 1110 \rightarrow 1100 \rightarrow 0100$ and $1011 \rightarrow 1111 \rightarrow 1101 \rightarrow 0101$, and

Task 4: $1001 \rightarrow 0001$.

V. Conclusion

In this paper, we have derived several important results for the subcube allocation and task migration in a hypercube computer system. We first proved that the GC strategy is optimal in the sense of maximizing the subcube recognition ability of a sequential search. Also, the subcube recognition ability of an allocation strategy using multiple EBC's was analyzed and compared to that using multiple EGC's. The minimal number of EBC's required for complete subcube recognition in a Q_n was proved to be $C_{\lfloor n/2 \rfloor}^n$.

Furthermore, we have developed a procedure for task migration under the GC strategy to eliminate the system fragmentation, which consists of three steps. First, a goal configuration without fragmentation is determined in light of the static optimality of the GC strategy. Second, the node-mapping between the source and destination subcubes is determined. Finally, a routing procedure for obtaining shortest deadlock-free paths during task migration is derived. Moreover, the migrating paths determined by A_2 are proved to be stepwise disjoint, thus allowing for the full parallelism in task migration. Our results confirm the inherent superiority of the GC strategy over others.

Note that an active task has to be temporarily stopped when it is to be moved to another subcube location. The task will resume its execution once it reaches its destination subcube. Hence, task migration induces some operational overhead, degrading system performance. To optimize system performance, one has to determine an optimal threshold by striking a compromise between the system's task admissibility and the operational overhead caused by task migration. Derivation of such a threshold and a decision on when to perform task migration can be made by the host computer which keeps track of the status of every hypercube node. However, design of an optimal threshold depends strongly on the computing environment and the system objective under consideration, and may well vary from one hypercube to another.

Appendix A

Subcube Allocation Strategies

The Buddy Strategy

Subcube Allocation Using a BC:

Step 1. Set $k := |I_j|$, where $|I_j|$ is the dimension of a subcube required to accommodate the request I_j.

Step 2. Determine the least integer m such that all the allocation bits in the region $\#[m2^k, (m + 1)2^k - 1]$ are 0's, and set all the allocation bits in the region $\#[m2^k, (m + 1)2^k - 1]$ to 1's.

Step 3. Allocate nodes with addresses $B_n(i)$ to the request I_j, $\forall i \in \#[m2^k, (m + 1)2^k - 1]$.

Deallocation:

Reset every pth allocation bit to 0, where $B_n(p) \in q$ and q is the address of a released subcube.

The GC Strategy

Subcube Allocation Using a BRGC:

Step 1. Set $k := |I_j|$, where $|I_j|$ is the dimension of a subcube required to accommodate the request I_j.

Step 2. Determine the least integer m such that all $(i \bmod 2^n)$th allocation bits are 0's, where $i \in \#[m2^{k-1}, (m + 2)2^{k-1} - 1]$. Set all these 2^k allocation bits to 1's.

Step 3. Allocate nodes with addresses $G_n(i \bmod 2^n)$ to I_j, where $i \in \#[m2^{k-1}, (m + 2)2^{k-1} - 1]$.

Deallocation:

Reset every pth allocation bit to 0, where $G_n(p) \in q$, and q is the address of a subcube released.

Appendix B

List of Symbols

Q_n	A hypercube of dimension n.
C_n	An n-bit coding scheme.
G_n	An n-bit binary reflected Gray code (BRGC).
B_n	An n-bit binary code which converts a nonnegative integer to its binary representation.
$G_n(m)$	The n-bit BRGC representation of an integer m.
$B_n(m)$	The n-bit binary representation of an integer m.
$|\alpha|$	The dimension of a subcube α.
$H(u, w)$	The Hamming distance between two hypercube nodes.
$H^*(\alpha, \beta)$	The Hamming distance between two subcubes.
$M(\alpha, \beta)$	The moving distance between subcubes α and β.

References

[1] T. F. Chan and Y. Saad, "Multigrid algorithms on the hypercube multiprocessor," *IEEE Trans. Comput.*, vol. C-35, no. 11, pp. 969–977, Nov. 1986.

[2] Y. Saad and M. H. Schultz, "Topological properties of hypercubes," *IEEE Trans. Comput.*, vol. C-37, no. 7, pp. 867–872, July 1988.

[3] M.-S. Chen and K. G. Shin, "Processor allocation in an *N*-cube multiprocessor using Gray codes," *IEEE Trans. Comput.*, vol. C-36, no. 12, pp. 1396–1407, Dec. 1987.

[4] ——, "On relaxed squashed embedding of graphs a into hypercube," *SIAM J. Comput.*, vol. 18, no. 6, pp. 1226–1244, Dec. 1989.

[5] C. L. Seitz, "The Cosmic Cube," *Commun. ACM*, vol. 28, no. 1, pp. 22–23, Jan. 1985.

[6] N. Corp., *NCUBE/ten: An Overview*, Nov. 1985.

[7] S. L. Johnsson, "Communication efficient basic linear algebra computations on hypercube architectures," *J. Parallel Distributed Comput.*, pp. 133–172, 1987.

[8] K. C. Knowlton, "A fast storage allocator," *Commun. ACM*, vol. 8, no. 10, pp. 623–625, Oct. 1965.

[9] F. Harary, *Graph Theory*. Reading, MA: Addison-Wesley, 1969.

[10] C. L. Liu, *Introduction to Combinatorial Mathematics*. New York: McGraw-Hill, 1968.

[11] D. E. Knuth, *The Art of Computer Programming*, *Vol. 1*. Reading, MA: Addison-Wesley, 1968.

[12] E. M. Reingold, J. Nievergelt, and N. Deo, *Combinatorial Algorithm*. Englewood Cliffs, NJ: Prentice-Hall, 1977.

Ming-Syan Chen (S'87–M'88), for a photograph and biography, see the January 1990 issue of this Transactions, p. 18.

Kang G. Shin (S'75–M'78–SM'83), for a photograph and biography, see the January 1990 issue of this Transactions, p. 18.

Subcube Allocation in
Hypercube Computers

Shantanu Dutt and John P. Hayes

Abstract—In hypercube computers that support a multiuser environment, it is important for the operating system to be able to allocate subcubes of different dimensions. Previously proposed subcube allocation schemes, such as the buddy strategy, can fragment the hypercube excessively. We present a precise characterization of the subcube allocation problem and develop a general methodology to solve it. New subcube allocation and coalescing algorithms are described that have the goal of minimizing fragmentation. The concept of a maximal set of subcubes (MSS), which is useful in making allocations that result in a tightly packed hypercube, is introduced. The problems of allocating subcubes and of forming an MSS are formulated as decision problems, and shown to be NP-hard. We prove analytically that the buddy strategy is optimal under restricted conditions, and then show using simulation that its performance is actually poor under more realistic conditions. We suggest a heuristic procedure for efficiently coalescing a released cube with the existing free cubes. This coalescing approach is coupled with a simple best-fit allocation scheme to form the basis of a class of MSS-based strategies that give a substantial performance (hit ratio) improvement over the buddy strategy. Finally, we present simulation results comparing several different allocation and coalescing strategies, which show that our MSS-based schemes provide a marked performance improvement over previous techniques.

Index Terms—Allocation algorithms, coalescing algorithms, hypercube computers, hypercube fragmentation, multiprocessors, NP-complete problems, processor allocation, subcube packing.

Manuscript received March 29, 1988; revised July 1, 1989. This work was supported by the Office of Naval Research under Contract N00014-85-K-0531.

The authors are with the Advanced Computer Architecture Laboratory, Department of Electrical Engineering and Computer Science, University of Michigan, Ann Arbor, MI 48109.

IEEE Log Number 9040073.

I. INTRODUCTION

The hypercube architecture is becoming quite widely used in the design of distributed-memory multiprocessors. Its popularity stems from its attractive interconnection properties, which include a logarithmically-growing diameter and node degree, the isomorphic embeddability of useful structures like meshes, trees, rings of even length, etc., encountered in many computational processes, as well as its fault tolerance and modularity [1]. There are simple and efficient algorithms for node-to-node communication, broadcasting, and other forms of communication in the hypercube [2]. Several manufacturers including Intel, NCUBE, and Thinking Machines, have introduced commercial hypercube machines.

A particular advantage of hypercube computers is that they can support multiple users, each of which can be assigned an independent subcube of nodes (processors) by the operating system. In such an environment, especially one where requests for cubes of various dimensions arrive very frequently, it is of prime importance to make judicious allocations of subcubes so that the hypercube does not become badly fragmented. AXIS, the host operating system for the NCUBE hypercube series, for example, supports such a multiuser environment [3]. AXIS maintains a bit-vector for allocating the hypercube nodes, where a 0 (1) in position i means the node with address i is free (allocated). When a k-dimensional cube is requested, AXIS scans this bit-vector for the first integer m such that all nodes with addresses from $m \times 2^k$ to $(m + 1) \times 2^k$ are free; it then allocates the k-cube composed of these nodes. This "linear" strategy recognizes only a fraction of the total number of free subcubes and does not attempt to pack the hypercube tightly.

Fig. 1(a) illustrates how a sequence of allocations and releases is processed by the foregoing linear strategy applied to a 4-cube. In this and subsequent figures, allocated nodes are shown black, while free (unallocated) nodes are shown white. Here we have an instance [Step 5, Fig. 1(b)] where a request for a 3-cube has to be denied even though a free 3–cube ($* 1 * *$) is available, and another [Step 8, Fig. 1(c)] where a "bad" allocation fragments the hypercube, resulting in the denial of a request for a 3-cube in Step 9, which otherwise could have been granted. Suppose, however, that instead of $000*$, the 1-cube $111*$ [shown shaded in Fig. 1(c)] is allocated in Step 8. The 3-cube $0 * * *$ then remains free and can be allocated to the request made in Step 9. Thus, in a multiuser hypercube computer, it is desirable to handle streams of subcube requests and releases so that no user is denied a subcube due to preventable fragmentation of the hypercube.

An allocation scheme which is well-known in memory allocation, and also appears useful for subcube allocation, is the buddy strategy [4]. It is based on systematic halving and doubling of memory blocks whose sizes are powers of two; thus, it can be used to halve subcubes for allocation and double them when coalescing freed subcubes. In fact, the linear subcube allocation approach of AXIS can be regarded as a variation of the buddy strategy. Although the buddy system performs remarkably well with hit ratios of 95% for memory allocation [4], it does not, as we show here, perform as well for subcube allocation. Another strategy for subcube allocation has been proposed that uses single and multiple Gray codes for recognizing subcubes, and a first-fit scheme for allocating them [5]. This strategy recognizes more subcubes than the buddy scheme, but it does not significantly reduce the fragmentation of the hypercube. The fragmentation problem can be avoided entirely by compaction, where all allocated cubes are relocated from time to time so that they are contained within the smallest possible subcube. This solution, however, seems impractical due to the huge communication overhead involved; we shall therefore only be concerned with the use of allocation schemes to reduce fragmentation.

We distinguish between "on-line" and "off-line" allocation of subcubes. In off-line allocation, the operating system collects a sufficient number of requests before proceeding to allocate subcubes to them. We show that the decision problem corresponding to off-line allocation is NP-complete. In on-line allocation, each subcube

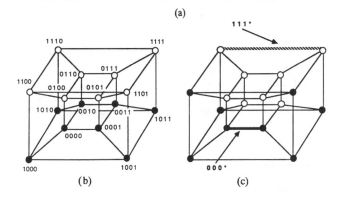

Step	Request	Allocated subcube	Released subcubes	Free subcubes	Comments
0	none	none	none	* * * *	All nodes initially free.
1	3-cube	0 * * *	none	1 * * *	
2	2-cube	1 0 * *	none	1 1 * *	
3	none	none	0 * * *	0 * * *, 1 1 * *	
4	2-cube	0 0 * *	none	0 1 * *, 1 1 * *	
5	3-cube	none	none	0 1 * *, 1 1 * *	Request denied as free 3-cube *1** not recognized.
6	1-cube	1 1 0 *	none	0 1 * *, 1 1 1 *	
7	none	none	0 0 * *, 1 0 * *	0 * * *, 1 0 * *, 1 1 1 *	
8	1-cube	0 0 0 *	none	0 1 * *, 0 0 1 *, 1 0 * * 1 1 1 *	Allocation fragments the hypercube badly.
9	3-cube	none	none	0 1 * *, 0 0 1 *, 1 0 * * 1 1 1 *	Request denied due to fragmentation in Step 8.

(a)

(b)   (c)

Fig. 1. (a) A sequence of subcube allocations and releases processed by linear allocation. (b) Step 5. (c) Step 8.

request is honored or denied immediately after it arrives, regardless of subsequent requests. It is desirable that any stream of satisfiable (one which can be satisfied by off-line allocation) subcube requests be allocated on-line. As we show, such an optimal on-line strategy is not computable, which gives some idea of the difficulty of the general subcube allocation problem. In general, on-line allocation is faster than off-line allocation, since the former processes each allocation request as soon as it comes in, and thus also has a smaller search space of allocation options. Moreover, most of the jobs submitted are on-line in nature, and require a fast allocation of a subcube. Consequently, all algorithms presented in this paper deal with on-line allocation only.

The concept of a maximal set of subcubes (MSS), which plays a fundamental role in on-line allocation, is introduced here. The consensus graph is then developed as a useful data structure that speeds up the formation of the MSS. Some interesting new properties of the consensus graph are also established. Efficient heuristic schemes for approximating the MSS, and for allocating and coalescing subcubes to maintain a good approximation of the MSS, are then discussed. These schemes form the basis of a class of MSS-based subcube allocation strategies, which we describe next. Finally, simulation results comparing the proposed MSS-based strategies to the buddy strategy are presented.

II. PROBLEM CHARACTERIZATION

Some notation and definitions needed in the sequel are introduced first. An n-dimensional hypercube Q_n is a graph with 2^n nodes, each of which can be labeled by a distinct n-bit Boolean vector, such that two nodes are joined by an edge iff their labels differ in exactly one bit. At any instant of time, a node may either be allocated or free (not allocated). A subcube of Q_n is free if all its nodes are free. Adopting some terminology from switching theory, the free nodes of Q_n are considered as the minterms of a Boolean function of n variables. The cube notation for Boolean functions [6] is also used to represent nodes and subcubes of Q_n. Subcubes are denoted by ternary strings in $\{0, 1, *\}^n$, where $*$ is the don't care symbol which can be replaced in the ternary string representation of the cube C by either a 1 or a 0 to obtain a subcube of C. Thus, the subcube formed by nodes 00000, 00001, 00010, and 00011 of Q_5 is denoted by $000**$. To denote a substring with k contiguous 0's, 1's, or *'s, the shorter forms 0^k, 1^k, or $*^k$, respectively, will be used. We shall use $\bar{x}$ to denote the Boolean complement of x, where $x = 0, 1, *$. Thus, $\bar{1} = 0$, $\bar{0} = 1$, and $\bar{*} = *$. Note that in the ternary representation of a subcube, the number of *'s is the subcube's dimension.

The dimension of a subcube C_1 of Q_n is denoted by $\dim(C_1)$; hence, $\dim(Q_n) = n$. The nodes (vertices) constituting subcube C_1 will be denoted by $V(C_1)$, and for a set S of cubes $V(S) = \cup_{C \in S} V(C)$; S is said to *contain* $V(S)$. The set of all free nodes of the hypercube is denoted by $V_f(Q_n)$. The *intersection* of two cubes C_1, C_2, denoted $C_1 \cap C_2$, is the set of nodes that are in both C_1, C_2, i.e., $C_1 \cap C_2 = V(C_1) \cap V(C_2)$. A cube C_2 *covers* a cube C_1 denoted $C_1 \subseteq C_2$, if $V(C_1) \subseteq V(C_2)$. The dimension indexes of a cube are listed in descending order, and $C_1[i]$ denotes the ith symbol from the right in the ternary string representation of C_1. The distance between two cubes C_1 and C_2, denoted $\text{dist}(C_1, C_2)$, is $\sum_{i=1}^{i=n} d(C_1[i], C_2[i])$, where $d(x, y) = 1$ if $x, y \neq *$ and $x = \bar{y}$; $d(x, y) = 0$ otherwise.

Definition 1: Two cubes C_1 and C_2 are *adjacent*, if $\dim(C_1) = \dim(C_2)$ and $\text{dist}(C_1, C_2) = 1$. If i is the dimension such that $d(C_1[i], C_2[i]) = 1$, then C_1 and C_2 are said to be *adjacent* along the ith dimension.

Definition 2: A cube C_1 is *prime* if $V(C_1) \subseteq V_f(Q_n)$ and there is no cube C_2 such that $V(C_2) \subseteq V_f(Q_n)$ and $C_1 \subset C_2$.

An *allocation request set* is a multiset $R = \{r_1, r_2, \cdots, r_k\}$ of nonnegative integers, where $k > 0$ and each r_i is the dimension of a subcube requested from Q_n.

Definition 3: An *allocation* from Q_n to an allocation request set R is a mapping $\phi : R \to 2^{V_f(Q_n)}$ such that for all i, $1 \leq i \leq |R|$, the graph induced in Q_n by $\phi(r_i)$ is a cube of dimension r_i. A *feasible allocation* from Q_n to R is a mapping $\tau : R \to 2^{V_f(Q_n)}$ such that τ is an allocation for R and for all $r_i, r_j \in R$, $\tau(r_i) \cap \tau(r_j) = \varnothing$, if $i \neq j$. An allocation request set for which there is a feasible allocation is a *feasible allocation request set*.

For the free (white) nodes of Q_4 shown in Fig. 1(c), $\{2, 1, 1\}$ and $\{1, 1, 1, 1\}$ are feasible allocation request sets, while $\{3\}$ is not.

Definition 4: An allocation request set R is said to be *grantable* if there is a feasible allocation from Q_n to R and there exists an online algorithm $\mathcal{A}$ that can satisfy each allocation request in R for any order of arrival of the requests. In such a case, $\mathcal{A}$ is said to *grant* R.

The decision problem corresponding to off-line allocation is stated as follows:

Problem 1: SUBCUBE ALLOCATION: Given a positive integer n, the set $\mathcal{P}$ of all prime cubes of $V_f(Q_n)$, and an allocation request set $R = \{r_1, \cdots, r_k\}$, is there a feasible allocation from Q_n to R?

In the remainder of this section we prove the NP-completeness of Problem 1 and various related decision problems. The relevant concepts from complexity theory can be found in [7].

Theorem 1: SUBCUBE ALLOCATION is NP-complete.

Proof: It is easy to see that *SUBCUBE ALLOCATION* is in NP, the set of problems that can be solved by a nondeterministic algorithm in polynomial time. We prove that *SUBCUBE ALLOCATION* is NP-hard by reducing the decision problem *INDEPENDENT SET*,[1] to it as follows. Label all the vertices of V in the input to *INDEPENDENT SET* from 1 to $|V|$. Then for each vertex i in V, form the ternary string representation for a cube PC_i as follows. For all $j \in \{1, 2, \cdots, |V|\}$, $\text{PC}_i[j] = 1$ if $i = j$, $\text{PC}_i[j] = *$ if $(i, j) \in E$, and $\text{PC}_i[j] = 0$ if $(i, j) \notin E$. Let l and s be the largest and smallest numbers of *'s, respectively, among all the cubes PC_i formed in this manner. (These are the largest and smallest degrees of the vertices in V.) Now extend the ternary notation for each cube PC_i as follows. Let h be the number of *'s already in PC_i. Then for all j in $\{|V| + 1, \cdots, |V| + l - s\}$, set $\text{PC}_i[j]$ to * if $j \leq |V| + l - h$; set

---

$\text{PC}_i[j]$ to 1 otherwise. It can be seen that each PC_i is an l-cube, and that PC_i and PC_j intersect if $(i, j) \in E$, and are disjoint otherwise. Let $\mathcal{P}$ be the set of all the PC_i's constructed in this manner. It is easy to show that $\mathcal{P}$ is the set of all prime cubes for the node set $\cup_{i=1}^{|V|} V(\text{PC}_i)$.

In addition to $\mathcal{P}$, let the value of the other inputs to *SUBCUBE ALLOCATION* be $n = |V| + l - s$ and $R =$ the multiset of k l's. This means that the question being asked in this instance of *SUBCUBE ALLOCATION* is whether there exist at least k disjoint cubes of dimension l in $\mathcal{P}$. It is easy to see that there is an independent set of size k in G iff there is a feasible allocation from Q_n to R. It should also be obvious that the above reduction is polynomial. As *INDEPENDENT SET* is NP-complete [7], so is *SUBCUBE ALLOCATION*. $\square$

Some criterion K is necessary for assessing how well the hypercube is being packed while allocations are made. An (on-line) allocation algorithm that maximizes or minimizes K can be said to *pack* the hypercube tightly with respect to K, and thus reduce fragmentation. We now introduce the concept of a maximal set of subcubes as a criterion for efficient packing of subcubes.

Definition 5: Let $\mathcal{A}$ and $\mathcal{B}$ be two sets of disjoint subcubes in Q_n. $\mathcal{A}$ is greater than $\mathcal{B}$, denoted $\mathcal{A} > \mathcal{B}$, if: a) $\mathcal{A}$ and $\mathcal{B}$ contain the same number of nodes; b) there exists an integer k, $0 \leq k \leq n$, such that for all m, $k < m \leq n$, $\mathcal{A}$ and $\mathcal{B}$ have equal numbers of subcubes of dimension m, and $\mathcal{A}$ has more subcubes of dimension k than $\mathcal{B}$. If condition a) is satisfied but not condition b), and $\mathcal{B}$ is not greater than $\mathcal{A}$, then $\mathcal{A}$ is *equal* to $\mathcal{B}(\mathcal{A} = \mathcal{B})$. If condition a) is satisfied for $\mathcal{A}$ and $\mathcal{B}$, then the expressions $\mathcal{A} \geq \mathcal{B}$ and $\mathcal{A} < \mathcal{B}$, have the usual meaning.

For example if $\mathcal{A} = \{00***, 10***, 010**, 001**, 1111*\}$ and $\mathcal{B} = \{11***, 10***, 000**, 001*, 010*1, 0111*\}$, then $\mathcal{A} > \mathcal{B}$ since $\mathcal{A}$ and $\mathcal{B}$ have the same number of 3-cubes, but $\mathcal{A}$ has more 2-cubes than $\mathcal{B}$.

Definition 6: A *maximal set of subcubes* (MSS) is a set of disjoint subcubes of $V_f(Q_n)$ that is greater than or equal to ($\geq$) all other sets of disjoint subcubes of $V_f(Q_n)$.

Note that the MSS need not be unique. Fig. 2 shows two MSS's $\{1*0*, 01**, 101*\}$ and $\{10**, *10*, 011*\}$ composed of the same set of free nodes. An MSS under consideration at any given time by the operating system will be called the *current* MSS. The notation $\text{MSS}(< k)$, $\text{MSS}(\geq k)$, etc., will be used to denote the set of cubes of dimension less than k, greater than or equal to k, etc., in the current MSS.

The goal of a "good" on-line allocation algorithm can now be stated simply as maintaining the greatest MSS after every allocation and release of a subcube. This is a reasonable goal for the following reasons. Consider the set S of all feasible allocation request sets, and the $\geq$ relation among these sets as defined by Definition 5. Then, constructing an MSS $\mathcal{M}$ (say in the form of a list of disjoint free cubes) guarantees that the allocation request set $\mathcal{G}$ in S, which is greater than or equal to all other sets in S, is grantable by using the following best-fit allocation algorithm BEST_FIT. Let k be the dimension of the subcube requested. If there is a k-cube available in $\mathcal{M}$, allocate it. Otherwise split an m-cube C in $\mathcal{M}$, where m is the dimension of the smallest cube in $\mathcal{M}(\geq k)$, into one cube of each of the dimensions $m - 1, \cdots, k + 1$ and two k-cubes. Allocate one of the k-cubes to the current request and reinsert the remaining $m - 1, \cdots, k$-dimensional subcubes of C in $\mathcal{M}$. We will subsequently also apply BEST_FIT to allocate cubes from any set of disjoint free subcubes, not necessarily an MSS.

Intuitively, the MSS obtained after going through a sequence of requests and releases is a measure of how tightly the cube is packed by the allocation process. If we maximize the MSS after each subcube allocation and form the MSS after each release of a subcube, then after each allocation or release step, the allocation request set $\mathcal{G}$ in S is the greatest among all such possible $\mathcal{G}$'s in all possible S's at that point. While the greatest allocation set $\mathcal{G}$ can be granted by BEST_FIT, there is no on-line algorithm that can grant all feasible allocation request sets in S, as shown by the following example.

Suppose that such an algorithm $\mathcal{A}$ exists. Consider Fig. 3, which

---

[1]Given a graph $G = (V, E)$ and a positive integer k, does there exist an independent set of size at least k in G, i.e., is there a subset V' of V such that $|V'| \geq k$ and no two vertices in V' have an edge between them [7]?

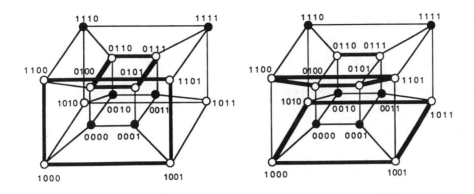

Fig. 2. Two different MSS's (heavy lines) for the same set of free nodes Q_4.

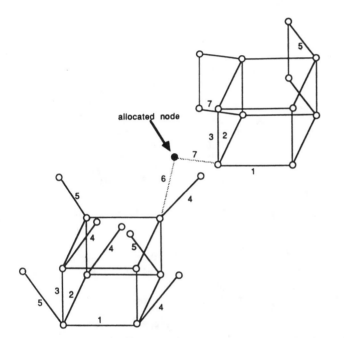

Fig. 3. The subgraph induced by the set of free nodes of Q_7.

shows all the free nodes and their induced subgraph in Q_7; for simplicity, the relevant edges of Q_7 are identified by numbers indicating the dimensions in which they lie. The two allocation request sets $R_1 = \{3, 2, 2, 2\}$ and $R_2 = \{3, 1, 1, 1, 1, 1, 1, 1, 1, 1, 1\}$ are both feasible. Suppose a request for a 3-cube arrives first; then to grant the sequence of requests from R_1, $\mathcal{A}$ will have to allocate the bottom left 3-cube, while to grant the sequence of requests from R_2 it should allocate the top right 3-cube. Thus, $\mathcal{A}$ can grant either R_1 or R_2 but not both, which contradicts our initial assumption that $\mathcal{A}$ can grant all feasible allocation request sets. The decision problem relating to MSS formation can now be stated.

Problem 2: MAXIMAL SET OF SUBCUBES: Given a positive integer n, the set $\mathcal{P}$ of all prime cubes of $V_f(Q_n)$, and an array A of $n + 1$ nonnegative integers denoted $A_0, \cdots, A_n$, then for each i from 0 to n, are there at least A_i i-cubes in an MSS for $V(\mathcal{P}) = V_f(Q_n)$ that are not subcubes of some higher dimensional cube in the MSS?

Theorem 2: MAXIMAL SET OF SUBCUBES is NP-hard.

Proof: The polynomial reduction from *INDEPENDENT SET* given in the proof of Theorem 1 is also applicable here, except that instead of R we construct the array A so that $A_l = k$, and for all $j \neq l$, $A_j = 0$, where l is as defined in the proof of Theorem 1. $\square$

```
Procedure FORM_MSS(Prime_Cubes)
/* Prime_Cubes is the set of all free prime cubes */
begin
    M := Largest_Sets(Prime_Cubes);
    /* Form all the largest sets Mᵢ of disjoint prime
    cubes of the highest dimension in Prime_Cubes */
    for all Mᵢ ∈ M do
    begin
        PC := New_Primes(Prime_Cubes, Mᵢ);
        /* Form the new set of prime cubes for
        the remaining free nodes not in Mᵢ */
        Setᵢ := FORM_MSS(PC) ∪Mᵢ ;
    end;
    return(MSS := Greatest_Set{Setᵢ : Mᵢ ∈ M });
    /* Return the greatest of all the sets Setᵢ */
end.
```

Fig. 4. Constructing a maximal set of subcubes.

Whenever there is an allocation request for a cube of dimension k, that k-cube should be allocated so that the resultant MSS is greater than or equal to all other MSS's obtainable after allocating any other k-cube. The decision problem corresponding to this can also be easily shown to be NP-hard. Thus, to reduce the complexity of the allocation problem, we use algorithm BEST_FIT for allocating subcubes. In this situation, it is of prime importance to maintain the MSS or a good approximation of it, in order to reduce fragmentation. We will subsequently show that BEST_FIT does in fact return a good approximation of the greatest MSS after an allocation.

III. FORMING A MAXIMAL SET OF SUBCUBES

In this section, we present an optimal algorithm FORM_MSS for constructing an MSS from $V_f(Q_n)$. We also introduce a data structure called the consensus graph that aids in quickly forming the new set of prime cubes required in every recursion of FORM_MSS. Finally, we give an approximate MSS formation scheme APPROX_MSS that uses this consensus graph technique, as well as a heuristic scheme for identifying a large set of disjoint cubes in a set of d-dimensional prime cubes.

FORM_MSS (Fig. 4) first selects the largest set $\mathcal{L} = M_i$ of disjoint prime cubes of the highest dimension in Prime_Cubes, which is the set of all prime cubes of $V_f(Q_n)$. Ties are broken by selecting that set $\mathcal{L}$ which yields the greatest MSS for the remaining free nodes not in $\mathcal{L}$. FORM_MSS then forms a new set of prime cubes for these remaining free nodes and recursively calls itself. The process terminates when no free nodes remain.

There are two high computation costs involved in the new prime cube formation procedure New_Primes, viz., identifying the remaining free nodes, i.e., the set $V_f(Q_n) - \mathcal{L}$, and constructing the set of prime cubes for this set. Since we already have the set of prime cubes of $V_f(Q_n)$, both of these steps can be carried out by modifying only those prime cubes that intersect the prime cubes in $\mathcal{L}$. These intersecting prime cubes can be identified efficiently with the help of a data structure called the consensus graph. This graph was originally suggested in the switching theory context [8] to identify prime implicants (cubes) for inclusion in the minimal disjunctive expression of a Boolean function. We have extended its use here for quickly forming a new set of prime cubes from the current one.

Following [8], the *sharp product* of two cubes C_1 and C_2, denoted $C_1 \# C_2$, is the set of nodes $V(C_1) - V(C_2)$. The *star product* of two cubes C_1 and C_2, denoted $C_1 \star C_2$, is the largest cube C_3 such that $V(C_3) \subseteq V(C_1) \cup V(C_2)$. (The symbol for the star product $\star$ should not be confused with the don't care symbol *.) C_3 is also called the *consensus* of C_1 and C_2, and C_3 is nonempty iff $\text{dist}(C_1, C_2) \leq 1$. If $\text{dist}(C_1, C_2) = 1$, and C_1 and C_2 differ in dimension j, then $C_3[j] = *$, while for all i other than j, if $C_2[i] = C_1[i]$ then $C_3[i] = C_1[i]$, otherwise $C_3[i] = C_k[i]$, where $C_k[i] \neq *$, $k = 1, 2$. If $\text{dist}(C_1, C_2) = 0$, then $C_3 = C_1 \cap C_2$. Note that the star product is not an associative operation. For example, $(10001 \star 10011) \star 10010 = 10001*$, while $10001 \star (10011 \star 10010) = 100*1$.

Definition 7: The *sharp prime cube set* $P(C_1, C_2)$ of a cube C_1 with respect to a cube C_2 is the set of all prime cubes in $C_1 \# C_2$. Each cube in $P(C_1, C_2)$ is called a sharp prime cube of C_1 with respect to C_2.

Thus, $P(100**, 1**00) = \{100*1, 1001*\}$ is the set of prime cubes for $100** \# 1**00 = \{10001, 10010, 10011\}$.

Definition 8: A *consensus graph* $G_c(V)$ of a set of nodes V of Q_n is a digraph with the following properties.

1) Its vertices are the prime cubes of V.
2) Its arcs are labeled as either "ancestor" (*a*) or "descendant" (*d*) arcs. If there is an ancestor (descendant) arc from C_1 to C_2 indicating that C_2 is an immediate ancestor (descendant) of C_1, then there is always a descendant (ancestor) arc from C_2 to C_1.
3) Any two prime cubes A and B that intersect correspond to vertices of $G_c(V)$ that either have arcs between them, or there exists a directed path $C_1 = A, C_2, \cdots, C_{k-1}, C_k = B$ from A to B such that every C_i in the path intersects A; there is a similar path from B to A.

We shall call property 3) the *intersection path* property, and any path defined as above is called an intersection path from A to B.

$G_c(V)$ can be created during the process of forming the set of prime cubes of V by a variation of the iterative consensus method [8]. In this method, whenever the consensus C of two cubes C_1 and C_2 is formed, ancestor arcs are inserted from C to C_1 and C_2, and descendant arcs are inserted from C_1 and C_2 to C. That is, C_1 and C_2 are made the immediate ancestors of C, and consequently C is made the immediate descendant of C_1 and C_2. A consensus graph for the free nodes of Fig. 5(a) is shown in Fig. 5(b). The heavy arcs in the figure indicate a traversal of the graphs, and are explained later.

Let S be the initial set of free cubes [which might be just the set $V_f(Q_n)$] that contains $V_f(Q_n)$. To obtain all the prime cubes of $V_f(Q_n)$ and its consensus graph, star products are formed by a variant of the iterative consensus method given in [8]. During this process, new vertices are created and some old ones deleted according to the rules given below. Let C be the new cube formed by taking the consensus of C_1 and C_2.

Consensus Graph Formation Rules (CGFR):

1) If C is covered by any other cube in the partially formed consensus graph G, then C is deleted from G. Otherwise the remaining rules are applied to C.
2) If C covers either C_1 or C_2, the immediate ancestors and descendants of the covered cubes become the immediate ancestors and descendants, respectively, of C. The covered cubes are deleted from G.
3) If C_1 is not covered by C, then C_1 becomes an immediate ancestor of C; similarly for C_2.

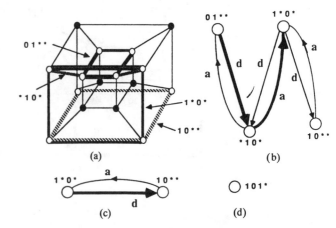

Fig. 5. Consensus graph and its application. (a) Free nodes and prime cubes of Q_4. (b) Consensus graph G for these free nodes. (c) Consensus graph G' after deleting $01**$ from G. (d) Consensus graph G'' after deleting $1*0*$ from G'.

Procedure VISIT_INTERSECTING_CUBES(C_2, C_1)
/* VISIT_INTERSECTING_CUBES finds all
descendants and ancestors of C_2 that intersect C_1 */
begin
    for all immediate ancestors C_3 of C_2 **do**
        if (C_3 intersects C_1 and has not already been visited) **then**
            VISIT_INTERSECTING_CUBES(C_3, C_1);
    for all immediate descendants C_3 of C_2 **do**
        if (C_3 intersects C_1 and has not already been visited) **then**
            VISIT_INTERSECTING_CUBES(C_3, C_1);
end.

Fig. 6. Finding prime cubes that intersect C_1.

4) If C covers some cube other than C_1 or C_2, then it inherits the immediate descendants of the covered cube. The covered cube is deleted from G.

The final graph resulting from the application of the above rules is a $G_c(V_f(Q_n))$.

Fig. 6 shows an algorithm VISIT_INTERSECTING_CUBES, which, when passed C_1 as both its parameters, visits every prime cube in $G_c(V)$ that intersects C_1. By forming $P(C_2, C_1)$ for every cube C_2 intersecting C_1, and identifying those cubes in $P(C_2, C_1)$ that are covered by some cube other than C_2 in $G_c(V)$, we obtain the new set of prime cubes of $V - V(C_1)$. To find the cubes in $P(C_2, C_1)$ that are covered by other cubes in $G_c(V)$, the cubes intersecting C_2 can be visited by calling VISIT_INTERSECTING_CUBES(C_2, C_2) and checking the cubes in $P(C_2, C_1)$ for containment. The cubes in $P(C_2, C_1)$ that are not covered by any cube in $G_c(V)$ other than C_2 will be denoted by $P_u(C_2, C_1)$. The following easily proven lemma provides a simple method for forming $P(C_2, C_1)$.

Lemma 1: Let C_1 and C_2 be two intersecting cubes, and let D be the set of dimensions in which C_2 has a * and C_1 has either a 1 or a 0. Then for each i in D, the cube P_i, where $P_i[i] = \overline{C_1[i]}$ and $P_i[j] = C_2[j]$ for all $j \neq i$, belongs to $P(C_2, C_1)$. No other cubes belong to $P(C_2, C_1)$.

For instance, if $C_1 = 01**1$ and $C_2 = 0*10*$, then $P(C_2, C_1) = \{0010*, 0*100\}$. As before, we denote by $\mathcal{L}$ the largest set of disjoint prime cubes that is selected at every recursion of FORM_MSS for inclusion in the MSS. If C_1 is a cube of $G_c(V)$ which is in $\mathcal{L}$, then it has to be deleted from $G_c(V)$ to form $G_c(V - V(C_1))$. The following theorem establishes that for each C_2 in $G_c(V)$ that intersects C_1, the cubes in $P_u(C_2, C_1)$ and the cubes in $G_c(V)$ disjoint from C_1, are all the prime cubes of $V - V(C_1)$.

Theorem 3: Let C_1 be a cube in $G_c(V)$, let I be the set of all cubes in $G_c(V)$ intersecting C_1, and let I' be the set of all cubes in

$G_c(V)$ disjoint from C_1. Then $(\cup_{C_2 \in I} P_u(C_2, C_1)) \cup I'$ is the set of all prime cubes of $V - V(C_1)$.

For example, we delete $C_1 = 01{*}{*}$ from the consensus graph G of Fig. 5(b), to obtain the consensus graph G' of Fig. 5(c). $*10*$ is the only prime cube intersecting $01{*}{*}$ in G; hence, $I' = \{1{*}0{*}, 10{*}{*}\}$. $P(*10*, 01{*}{*})$ contains a single cube $110*$, which is covered by the prime cube $1{*}0{*}$ in G. Thus, $P_u(*10*, 01{*}{*}) \cup I' = I'$, and as shown in G', I' is the set of all prime cubes for $V_f(Q_4) - V(C_1)$, where $V_f(Q_4)$ is the set of free nodes shown in Fig. 5(a).

$G_c(V - V(C_1))$ is generated from $G_c(V)$ by deleting C_1 from $G_c(V)$ and replacing each C_2 in $G_c(V)$ that intersects C_1 by the cubes in $P_u(C_2, C_1)$. This is done according to the following rules.

Consensus Graph Modification Rules (CGMR):

1) Let $(P_1, P_2, \cdots, P_q)$ be the cubes in $P(C_2, C_1)$ where P_i is as defined in Lemma 1. For each i from 1 to q, make P_i the immediate ancestor of all P_j's, where $i < j \leq q$.
2) Let C_3 be an immediate ancestor of C_2 other than C_1. If C_3 is disjoint from C_1 and intersects some P_i, make P_i C_3's immediate descendant. Otherwise let P_i be the cube such that $P_i[i] = \overline{C_1[i]}$. If $C_3[i] = *$, then there is a cube D_i in $P(C_3, C_1)$ such that $D_i[i] = \overline{C_1[i]}$. Make D_i the immediate ancestor of P_i.
3) If C_2 has an immediate descendant C_4 that is disjoint from C_1, then find a cube P_i in $P(C_2, C_1)$ that covers $C_2 \cap C_4$, and make C_4 an immediate descendant of P_i. If no such cube exists, then make C_4 the immediate descendant of all cubes in $P(C_2, C_1)$ that intersect it. If C_4 intersects C_1 then the required modification is done by applying rule 2 to $P(C_4, C_1)$.
4) When any cube P_i in $P(C_2, C_1)$ is found to be covered by some cube C_5 in $G_c(V)$, make all immediate ancestors and descendants of P_i other than C_5 the immediate ancestors and descendants, respectively, of C_5. Delete P_i from the consensus graph.

Referring to Fig. 5 again, suppose $\mathcal{L}$ is chosen to be $\{01{*}{*}, 1{*}0{*}\}$. Then we have to delete the cubes $01{*}{*}$ and $1{*}0{*}$ from the consensus graph G. Fig. 5(b) shows in heavy lines the paths traversed in G by VISIT_INTERSECTING_CUBES($01{*}{*}, 01{*}{*}$). $*10*$ is the only cube in the graph intersecting $\overline{0}1{*}{*}$, and $P(*10*, 01{*}{*}) = \{110*\}$. Since $1{*}0{*}$, an ancestor of $*10*$, does not intersect $01{*}{*}$, application of CGMR 2 makes it the ancestor of $110*$. However, $110*$ is covered by $1{*}0{*}$, and since $110*$ has no ancestor or descendant other than $1{*}0{*}$, on applying CGMR 4, $1{*}0{*}$ does not inherit any new ancestors or descendants from $110*$. The new consensus graph G' obtained by deleting the cube $01{*}{*}$ is shown in Fig. 5(c). Cube $1{*}0{*}$ has now to be deleted from G'. The only other cube in G' is $1{*}0{*}$'s descendant $10{*}{*}$ and on visiting it, the sharp prime cube set $P(10{*}{*}, 1{*}0{*}) = \{101*\}$ is formed. None of the CGMR's 1, 2, or 3 apply in this case, and $101*$ is not covered by any other cube in G'. It is thus incorporated in the new consensus graph G'' [Fig. 5(d)] obtained by deleting $1{*}0{*}$ from G'. Since G'' contains the single cube $101*$, it is included in the MSS. Thus, the MSS formed is $\{01{*}{*}, 1{*}0{*}, 101*\}$.

Theorem 4: Let C_1 be a cube in $G_c(V)$. Deleting C_1 from $G_c(V)$ and replacing each C_2 in $G_c(V)$ that intersects C_1 by the cubes in $P_u(C_2, C_1)$ according to the Consensus Graph Modification Rules above results in $G_c(V - V(C_1))$.

Proof outline: Let G' be the graph obtained by modifying $G_c(V)$ according to the CGMR's. By Theorem 3, the cubes in G' are all the prime cubes of $V - V(C_1)$. To see that the intersection path property holds in G', consider an intersection path $\mathcal{T}$: $D_1, D_2, \cdots, D_{k-1}, D_k$ from $A = D_1$ to $B = D_k$ in $G_c(V)$. For any cube D_j in $\mathcal{T}$ that intersects C_1, there is some cube in $P(D_j, C_1)$ that intersects A. Suppose first that D_{j-1} does not intersect C_1. If D_{j-1} is an immediate ancestor (descendant) of D_j in $G_c(V)$, then by CGMR 2 (3) some P_i in $P_u(D_j, C_1)$ that intersects A has D_{j-1} as an immediate ancestor (descendant) in G'. Similarly, if D_{j+1} does not intersect C_1, then some cube P_l in $P_u(D_j, C_1)$ that intersects A has D_{j+1} as either its immediate ancestor or descendant. Either $P_i = P_l$, or by CGMR 1, one is the immediate ancestor of the other. Thus, D_j is replaced in $\mathcal{T}$ by P_i and P_l to yield a new intersection path $\mathcal{T}'$ in G'. Now suppose D_{j-1} intersects C_1. Again by CGMR 2, a cube P_i in $P(D_j, C_1)$ that intersects A has a cube E_t as either an immediate ancestor or descendant (depending on whether C_{j-1} is an immediate ancestor or descendant of C_j), where E_t is a cube in $P(D_{j-1}, C_1)$ that intersects A. A similar situation occurs if D_{j+1} intersects C_1. Thus, every D_j in $\mathcal{T}$ intersecting C_1 is replaced by at most two cubes of $P(D_j, C_1)$ to form a new intersection path from A to B in G'. Consequently, the intersection path property holds in G'. □

```
Procedure APPROX_MSS(Prime_Cubes)
/* Prime_Cubes is the set of all free prime cubes */
begin
    L := Indep_Set(Prime_Cubes);
    /* Form a large set of disjoint prime cubes
    of the highest dimension in Prime_Cubes */
    PC := New_Primes(Prime_Cubes, L);
    /* Form the new set of prime cubes
    for the remaining free nodes not in L
    using the consensus graph technique */
    return(MSS := APPROX_MSS(PC) ∪ L) ;
end.
```

Fig. 7. Constructing an approximate MSS.

Note that the intersection path property is sufficient for VISIT_INTERSECTING_CUBES(C_1, C_1) to find all cubes in the consensus graph that intersect C_1.

We have presented a consensus graph modification method for generating the new set of prime cubes when deleting any cube C_1 from the original set of prime cubes. The procedure New_Primes can be implemented by iterating this consensus graph modification process for every cube in $\mathcal{L}$ to get the new set of prime cubes and a new consensus graph for the free nodes not contained in $\mathcal{L}$.

We now describe a heuristic Indep_Set to replace another source of high complexity, the procedure Largest_Sets, in FORM_MSS. Instead of identifying all the largest sets M_i of disjoint prime cubes as Largest_Sets does, Indep_Set identifies only one such "large" set $\mathcal{L}$. Let $\mathcal{C}$ be the set of k-dimensional prime cubes in Prime_Cubes, where k is the dimension of the largest cubes in Prime_Cubes. Form a graph G whose vertices correspond to the cubes in $\mathcal{C}$, and where two vertices are adjacent if the corresponding cubes intersect. It is easy to see that under this formulation, the problem of finding the largest maximal set of disjoint cubes in $\mathcal{C}$ reduces to that of finding the largest independent set in G, which is an NP-complete problem. We thus use the following approximate scheme for identifying a large independent set in G.

A vertex of G with the smallest degree is selected to be in $\mathcal{L}$. The selected vertex and all vertices adjacent to it are then deleted from G. This process is iterated until no vertices remain in G. Ties are broken by selecting a vertex v, the sum of the degrees of whose neighbors is a maximum. (This tie-breaking rule is basically a one-step look-ahead version of the main heuristic.) It is easy to show that forming the graph G requires time $O(nm^2)$, while finding a large independent set in it requires time $O(m^2)$, where m is the number of prime cubes in $\mathcal{C}$, and n is the dimension of the hypercube. Hence, the complexity of Indep_Set is $O(nm^2)$.

An approximate MSS formation scheme APPROX_MSS that uses Indep_Set is given in Fig. 7. Note that APPROX_MSS also avoids the additional complexity of FORM_MSS incurred in breaking ties between two or more largest sets of disjoint cubes M_i. In Section V, we describe an MSS-based subcube allocation scheme termed the MSS Strategy that uses APPROX_MSS to form approximations of the MSS.

IV. The Buddy Strategy

As pointed out earlier, the buddy strategy for memory allocation has been implicitly used for subcube allocation in AXIS, the host operating system for the NCUBE series of hypercubes [3]; the buddy approach has also been suggested in [5]. In this section, the buddy

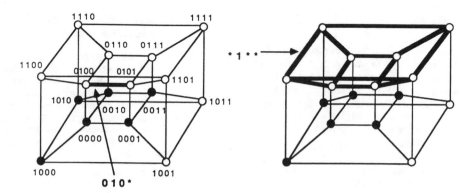

Fig. 8. A feasible expansion $*1**$ of $010*$ along $\{2, 4\}$.

allocation and coalescing strategy as applied to subcube allocation is formally described, and its optimality under certain restricted conditions is proven. However, simulation results derived under more realistic conditions will show that the buddy scheme performs quite poorly for subcube allocation. In the next section, we present two MSS-based strategies, which use BEST_FIT and a heuristic coalescing scheme HEURISTIC_COALESCE for coalescing released subcubes in order to maintain a good approximation of the MSS. Simulation results presented in the next section show that these MSS-based strategies perform very well in practice.

Definition 9: Let C be the free cube $c_n \cdots c_1$ where $c_i \in \{0, 1, *\}$, and let j be a dimension such that $c_j \neq *$. (Note that the dimension indexes are listed in descending order.) Then the *expansion* $\exp(C, j)$ of C along the jth dimension is the cube $c_n \cdots c_{j+1} * c_{j-1} \cdots c_1$. This is a *feasible expansion* if the cube adjacent to C along dimension j is free. Let $\mathcal{D}$ be a set of dimensions, and $(d_i, d_{i_2} \cdots d_{i_k})$ be an arbitrary ordering of all the dimensions of $\mathcal{D}$. An expansion of C along $\mathcal{D}$ is the cube C_k defined recursively as follows:

$$C_t = \exp(C_{t-1}, d_{i_t}), \qquad \text{for all } t, \qquad 1 \leq t \leq k,$$
$$\text{where } C_0 = C. \tag{9}$$

Each C_t is a feasible expansion if C_{t-1} is a feasible expansion and the cube adjacent to C_{t-1} along d_{i_t} is free.

Note that the expansion C_k of C along $\mathcal{D}$ is independent of the order in which the expansions are made along the dimensions in $\mathcal{D}$. Fig. 8 shows a feasible expansion $*1**$ of $010*$ along the dimensions $\{2, 4\}$ resulting in the 3-cube $*1**$ shown in heavy lines. Let S be a set of free subcubes, and let $C \in S$. A feasible expansion of C along a dimension d is called a 1-*expansion* (with respect to S) if there is a cube in S adjacent to C along d. A feasible expansion of C along a dimension d is called a 2-*expansion* (with respect to S) if there is a cube B in S such that $\dim(B) = \dim(C) + 1$, and B covers the cube adjacent to C along d.

The procedure BUDDY_STRATEGY for subcube allocation and coalescing is given in Fig. 9, and is self-explanatory. Note that BUDDY_STRATEGY maintains a set of (disjoint) free subcubes (SFS) S, which is organized as $n + 1$ lists of free subcubes, where the ith list contains i-dimensional free subcubes. This makes BUDDY_STRATEGY a more efficient adaptation of the buddy scheme for memory management than the linear approach of AXIS. In the linear approach, all nodes of Q_n are scanned until an appropriate set of free nodes forming a k-cube are found, while in BUDDY_STRATEGY lists of free cubes of different dimensions are maintained, which allow the requested k-cube to be found much faster.

The *buddy* of any i-dimensional cube C of the form $a_n a_{n-1} \cdots a_{i+1} *^i$, where the a_i's are either 1's or 0's, is the i-dimensional cube $a_n a_{n-1} \cdots \overline{a_{i+1}} *^i$, and is denoted by $\text{buddy}(C)$. $a_n a_{n-1} \cdots a_{i+1}$ is said to be the *address* of the i-cube $a_n a_{n-1} \cdots a_{i+1} *^i$. An allocation strategy is *optimal* if it can always allocate a k-cube when there are at least 2^k free nodes. It is *statically optimal* if it is always able to allocate a k-cube when at least 2^k free

nodes are available, under the condition that none of the allocated cubes are released.

Lemma 2: BUDDY_STRATEGY is optimal under LIFO release.

Proof: The proof is by induction on the number of cubes released. For no releases, optimality follows from the fact that BUDDY_STRATEGY is statically optimal [5]. Suppose the lemma holds for m releases. Between the mth and the $(m+1)$st release, there might be zero or more allocations. If there are $r > 0$ allocations, then by the induction hypothesis and its static optimality, BUDDY_STRATEGY remains optimal after each of the r allocations. Since the release order is LIFO, after the $(m+1)$st release the state of the system reverts to the one just before the rth allocation, for which, as we have just seen, the strategy is optimal.

Suppose there are no allocations between the mth and the $(m+1)$st releases. Consider the string of allocations and releases starting at time 0 and culminating in the $(m+1)$st release. As $m + 1 \geq 1$, there will be at least one situation where a release just following an allocation cancels out the allocation's effect, returning the system to the state just prior to the allocation. Consider the most recent such situation. If the corresponding allocation and release has not taken place, the current state of the system would have been unchanged, and the current $(m+1)$st release would be the mth release for this different history of allocations and releases. But by the induction hypothesis, the strategy is optimal just after the mth release, irrespective of its history. $\qquad \square$

Lemma 3: Under FIFO release of allocated subcubes, BUDDY_STRATEGY always forms an MSS when a subcube is released.

Proof: First note that in BUDDY_STRATEGY, any allocated or free cube of dimension i is of the form $a_n \cdots a_{i+1} *^i$ where the a_j's are either 1's or 0's. Also note that when BUDDY_ALLOCATE splits an m-cube to allocate a k-cube, where $k < m$, the k-subcube with the smallest address is allocated first. The proof is by induction on the number of releases. For no releases, since the allocation from the SFS S is best-fit, it is easy to see that S is an MSS. Assume that the lemma holds for t releases, i.e., after t releases S is an MSS for the current set of free nodes, and let the $(t+1)$st release be an i-cube $C_r = b_n \cdots b_{i+1} *^i$.

Case 1: $b_{i+1} = 0$. First suppose $\text{buddy}(C_r) = b_n \cdots b_{i+2} 1 *^i$ is allocated, which is consistent with the FIFO relinquishment order. Suppose also there is a free i-cube $C_k = b_n \cdots b_{k+1} \overline{b_k} b_{k-1} \cdots b_{i+2} 0 *^i$ adjacent to C_r along dimension k. If $b_k = 0$, then C_r is allocated before C_k, and to be consistent with FIFO release, C_k can be in the SFS when C_r is released only if it was never allocated. Furthermore, C_k can be in the SFS only if $\text{buddy}(C_k) = b_n \cdots b_{k+1} \overline{b_k} b_{k-1} \cdots b_{i+2} 1 *^i$ is allocated. But $\text{buddy}(C_k)$ is allocated only after C_k is allocated. We thus reach a contradiction. If $b_k = 1$, then C_r is allocated after both C_k and $\text{buddy}(C_k)$. Again, as C_k is in the SFS, $\text{buddy}(C_k)$ must still be allocated, as otherwise C_k and $\text{buddy}(C_k)$ would have been coalesced. But C_r being released before $\text{buddy}(C_k)$ is a violation of the FIFO release order. We thus reach another contradiction; hence, there are no cubes in S adjacent to C_r. However, it might be possible

Procedure HEURISTIC_COALESCE(C, S); /* C is the released cube, S is the current SFS */
begin
    D_{exp} := Expan_Dimen(C);
    /* Get all the dimensions along which C can be feasibly expanded */
    for all $i \in \{0, \ldots, n - dim(C)\}$ **do**
        $D_i := \{d_j : d_j \in D_{exp}$ and on expanding along d_j, C intersects a cube of dimension $dim(C) + i$ in $S\}$;
    X := EXPAND($C, 0$);
    /* X is an ordered set of dimensions along which C has feasible 1 or a 2-expansions */
    Expand C along the dimensions in X, splitting an intersected cube B in S into two equal subcubes
    whenever a 2-expansion with respect to S takes place;
end.

Procedure EXPAND(C_{exp}, k); /* C_{exp} is a feasible expansion of C, which has to be checked
for possible 1-expansions and 2-expansions with respect to S along D_k and D_{k+1} respectively */
begin
    if ($D_k = \emptyset$ AND $D_{k+1} = \emptyset$) **then**
        return($\emptyset$); /* There is neither a 1-expansion nor a 2-expansion of C_{exp} along D_k or D_{k+1} */
    else begin
        for all $d_i \in D_k \cup D_{k+1}$ **do**
        begin
            if (C_{exp} can be feasibly expanded along dimension d_i) **then begin**
                $X_i := \{d_i\} \cup$ EXPAND($exp(C_{exp}, d_i), k + 1$);
                /* X_i is the ordered set of dimensions along which C_{exp} is expanded starting with d_i */
            end;
            else $X_i := \emptyset$;
        end;
        Select an X_j that represents the most 1-expansions of C_{exp};
        /* This corresponds to the maximum improvement of the SFS */
        return(X_j);
    end;
end.

Fig. 10. Heuristic coalescing scheme.

to feasibly expand C_r along some of the dimensions in $\{i + 2, \cdots, n\}$, in which case the expansion of C_r contains noncontiguous *'s. To get an SFS greater than $S \cup \{C_r\}$, at least one expansion of C_r must be a 1-expansion. None of the free cubes have noncontiguous *'s, so this is impossible. Hence, by just including C_r in the current MSS S, we get an MSS for the new set of free nodes resulting from C_r's release.

Now suppose buddy(C_r) is also free (this is possible only if buddy(C_r) was never allocated), then C_r and buddy(C_r) will be coalesced to form a bigger cube. This new cube's buddy might also be free causing another coalescing to take place, and so on. Either a Q_n is formed, or the coalescings stop after l steps, producing the cube $C = b_n \cdots b_{l+i+1} *^{l+i}$ whose buddy is allocated. The same argument given for C_r when its buddy is allocated now holds for C. Thus, by including C in the SFS, we obtain an MSS.

Case 2: $b_{i+1} = 1$. buddy(C_r) has to be free, as it is allocated, and thus released, before C_r. This situation for buddy(C_r) is symmetric to the situation for C_r in Case 1 when buddy(C_r) is free. Thus, the sequence of one or more coalescings of buddy(C_r) will eventually yield an MSS. $\square$

V. MSS-Based Strategies

In spite of its optimality under restricted conditions, our simulation results will show that BUDDY_STRATEGY performs poorly under more realistic conditions. This is not unexpected, since 1) it recognizes only a small fraction $1/\binom{n}{k}$ of k-subcubes in an n-cube, and 2) it coalesces a released cube C only with its buddy, while there are $\Theta(n)$ other cubes with which C could possibly be coalesced to form a bigger free cube. We now present two MSS-based strategies, both of which maintain a current set of free subcubes (SFS) S that is an approximation of the MSS in the form of $n + 1$ lists of disjoint free subcubes, where the ith list contains i-dimensional subcubes. Both strategies use BEST_FIT for allocating subcubes, and a fast and efficient heuristic scheme HEURISTIC_COALESCE for coalescing released cubes; as we will show, these allocation methods perform much better than BUDDY_STRATEGY.

It is important to note here that starting from the initial state when the whole hypercube is free, it is trivial to allocate subcubes so that the resulting MSS is maximized as long as no allocated subcubes are released. It is the release of previously allocated subcubes that makes the allocation problem so hard to solve. The problem can be simplified if the released cubes are efficiently coalesced with the cubes in the current SFS S_1 (which is an approximation of the MSS) so that the new SFS S_2 is also a good approximation of the new MSS. If we coalesce a released cube C so that the largest free cube containing it is formed, we may be splitting a number of higher-dimensional cubes of S_1 in order to do so, and the SFS S_2 formed as a result may turn out to be a poor approximation of the new MSS. For example, let C be a 2-cube and let S_1 consist of one 4-cube B. Suppose that a 2-subcube of B is adjacent to C along d. If we expand C along d to form a 3-cube, this splits B and results in an SFS S_2 containing two 3-cubes and a 2-cube, which is less than even $S_1 \cup \{C\}$, the SFS obtained without coalescing C with any free cubes! To prevent such a situation, HEURISTIC_COALESCE performs expansions of C so that after each expansion, the new SFS is greater than or equal to the SFS before the expansion.

HEURISTIC_COALESCE is formally described in Fig. 10. Let $C_{\exp}$ be a feasible expansion of C along a set of dimensions $\mathcal{D}$, and let $d \notin \mathcal{D}$ be a dimension along which $C_{\exp}$ has a feasible expansion. We expand $C_{\exp}$ along d if

1) it is a 1-expansion with respect to the current SFS, or

2) it is a 2-expansion with respect to the current SFS.

Initially $C_{\exp} = C$, and the expansions of C are recursively formed according to the above conditions. Notice that in a 1-expansion of $C_{\exp}$, the SFS is always increased, i.e., if S_1 is the SFS before the expansion, and S_2 is the SFS obtained after a 1-expansion of $C_{\exp}$, then $S_2 > S_1$. In a 2-expansion we get an SFS $S_2 = S_1$. This is so, since we are just replacing a cube $C_{\exp}$ of dimension k and a $(k + 1)$-cube B by a cube of dimension $k + 1$ (the expansion of $C_{\exp}$ along d) and a cube of dimension k (the k-subcube of B not adjacent to $C_{\exp}$), to obtain S_2 from S_1. However, a 2-expansion of $C_{\exp}$ along d opens up the possibility of 1-expansions of the expanded cube $exp(C_{\exp}, d)$ along other dimensions. Such a situation is illustrated

Procedure BUDDY_STRATEGY(R);
/* R is either a request for or a release of a single cube */
begin
    if(R is a request for a k-cube) **then**
        BUDDY_ALLOCATE(k, S);
        /* S is the current set of free subcubes */
    else BUDDY_COALESCE(C, S);
        /* C is the released cube contained in R */
end.

Procedure BUDDY_ALLOCATE(k, S);
/* k is the dimension of the requested cube */
/* S is the current set of free subcubes */
begin
    if (a k-cube is available in S) **then**
        Allocate a k-cube in S with the smallest address;
    else begin
        $m :=$ dimension of the smallest cube in $S(\geq k)$;
        Find the m-dimensional cube $a_n \ldots a_{m+1} *^m$ in S
        with the smallest address, where $a_i \in \{0, 1\}$;
        $S := S - \{a_n \ldots a_{m+1} *^m\}$;
        for $i := 1$ **to** $m - k$ **do**
        /* Split this m-cube to allocate a k-cube from it */
        begin
            $C_1^{m-i} := a_n \ldots a_{m+1} 0^{i-1} 1 *^{m-i}$;
            $C_0^{m-i} := a_n \ldots a_{m+1} 0^i *^{m-i}$;
            $S := S \cup \{C_1^{m-i}\}$;
        end;
        Allocate C_0^k;
    end;
end.

Procedure BUDDY_COALESCE(C, S);
/* C is the released cube */
begin
    Let C be the cube $a_n \ldots a_{k+2} a_{k+1} *^k$.
    if ($buddy(C) = a_n \ldots a_{k+2} \overline{a_{k+1}} *^k$ is free) **then**
    begin
        $C := a_n \ldots a_{k+2} *^{k+1}$;
        $S := (S - \{buddy(C)\}) \cup \{C\}$;
        BUDDY_COALESCE(C, S);
    end;
    else $S := S \cup C$;
end.

Fig. 9. The buddy strategy for subcube allocation and coalescing.

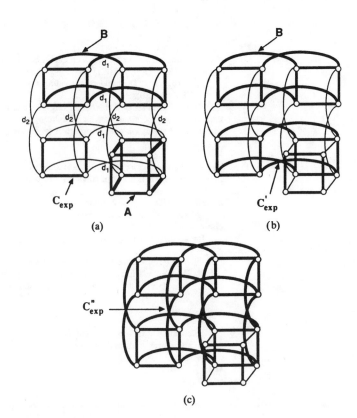

Fig. 11. Coalescing $C_{\exp}$ by HEURISTIC_COALESCE. (a) Before coalescing begins. (b) A 2-expansion $C'_{\exp}$ of $C_{\exp}$ that intersects B. (c) A 1-expansion $C''_{\exp}$ of $C'_{\exp}$.

in Fig. 11, where the cubes in each successive SFS generated by the expansions of $C_{\exp}$ are shown with heavy lines. $C_{\exp}$, a 2-cube, and A and B which are 3-cubes, are shown in Fig. 11(a). A 2-expansion of $C_{\exp}$ along d_1 results in the situation of Fig. 11(b), where the SFS is not improved. However, now the newly formed cube $C'_{\exp}$ can be 1-expanded along d_2 to coalesce with the 3-cube B, thus forming a 4-cube $C''_{\exp}$ [Fig. 11(c)]. This results in an improvement of the SFS.

Any expansion of C that is neither a 1-expansion nor a 2-expansion always results in an SFS that is less than the previous SFS. Of course, it is possible that after an initial deterioration of the SFS as a result of such an expansion, we might subsequently be able to improve the SFS dramatically by performing a number of 1-expansions. HEURISTIC_COALESCE does not consider such possibilities, and restricts itself to expansions that cause no deterioration of the SFS. In this sense, it is a hill-climbing approach to improving the SFS when a cube is released.

In procedure EXPAND, which is called by HEURISTIC_COALESCE, an expansion of $C_{\exp}$ along some dimension in D_k is a 1-expansion, and an expansion along a dimension in D_{k+1} is a 2-expansion. Note that the expansion $C'_{\exp}$ of $C_{\exp}$ along some dimension in either D_k or D_{k+1} might have a 1-expansion along some other dimension in D_{k+1}. Hence, at this point, EXPAND recursively calls itself with parameters $C'_{\exp}$ and $k + 1$.

We now consider the computational complexity of HEURISTIC_COALESCE. In addition to being stored in lists as mentioned earlier, the cubes in the current SFS S can also be organized as the leaves of a ternary tree to facilitate searching for free cubes with which C can be coalesced. In such a ternary tree, the ith level nodes represent the ith dimension, and three ternary subtrees S_0, S_1, and S_* containing free cubes with a 0, 1, and $*$, respectively, in the ith dimension, are rooted at each i-level node. Since all prime cubes of $V_f(Q_n)$ are not stored, a possible expansion of $C_{\exp}$ along some dimension may be missed, even though the required nodes are free. (The cube at a distance of one from $C_{\exp}$ along such a dimension may not be in the current SFS and is thus not explicitly stored.) Since only disjoint-free cubes are stored in this scheme, 2^n is an upper bound on the number of free cubes searched to find the set of dimensions $D_{\exp}$ along which C can be feasibly expanded. Let k_i be the cardinality of set D_i in EXPAND and, for simplicity, let there be $2t$ such sets for some $t > 0$. The worst case occurs when $k_{2i} = 0$, $0 \leq i \leq t$. In such a situation, the first expansion of $C_{\exp}$ along some dimension in D_{2i+1} is always a 2-expansion that is followed by a possible 1-expansion along another dimension of D_{2i+1}. Assuming each $k_{2i+1} > 1$, the worst case number of possible expansions tried is

$$T = \prod_{i=0}^{t-1} k_{2i+1}(k_{2i+1} - 1). \tag{10}$$

Again in the worst situation

$$\sum_{i=0}^{t-1} k_{2i+1} = n. \tag{11}$$

Setting

$$k_1 = n - \sum_{i=1}^{t-1} k_{2i+1} \tag{12}$$

we get

$$T = \left(n - \sum_{i=1}^{t-1} k_{2i+1}\right) \times \prod_{i=1}^{t-1} k_{2i+1}(k_{2i+1} - 1). \tag{13}$$

```
Procedure MSS_STRATEGY(R);
/* R is either a request for or a release of a single cube */
begin
    if(R is a request for a k-cube) then begin
        BEST_FIT(k, S); /* S is the current SFS */
        if (a k-cube cannot be allocated by BEST_FIT) then
            if (at least 2^k nodes are in S) then begin
                /* Form an approximate MSS for the set of free nodes in S */
                S := APPROX_MSS(S);
                /* Try again to allocate a k-cube */
                BEST_FIT(k, S);
            end;
    end
    else HEURISTIC_COALESCE(C, S);
    /* C is the released cube contained in R */
end.

Procedure FAST_MSS_STRATEGY(R);
/* R is either a request for or a release of a single cube */
begin
    if(R is a request for a k-cube) then
        BEST_FIT(k, S); /* S is the current SFS */
    else HEURISTIC_COALESCE(C, S);
    /* C is the released cube contained in R */
end.
```

Fig. 12. Two MSS-based subcube allocation and coalescing strategies.

Solving

$$\frac{\partial T}{\partial k_3} = \frac{\partial T}{\partial k_5} = \cdots = \frac{\partial T}{k_{2t-1}} = 0 \tag{14}$$

results in $k_1 = k_3 = \cdots = k_{2t-1} = n/t$, for which $T = \left(\frac{n}{t}\right)^{2t}$. $T = 2^n$ is its maximum value for $t = n/2$. Each computation step like checking whether there is a feasible expansion of $C_{\exp}$ along d takes time $O(n)$. Thus, the worst case complexity of HEURISTIC_COALESCE is $O(n2^n)$, which translates to $O(N \log N)$ in terms of the number $N = 2^n$ of nodes in Q_n.

Fig. 12 formally describes two MSS-based subcube allocation strategies MSS_STRATEGY and FAST_MSS_STRATEGY that use BEST_FIT and HEURISTIC_COALESCE. The primary difference between these two strategies is that when a k-cube cannot be allocated by BEST_FIT, and there are at least 2^k free nodes, MSS_STRATEGY forms an approximate MSS S, and again checks to see if there is a k-cube in S, while FAST_MSS_STRATEGY skips this step when a request cannot be allocated by BEST_FIT.

We now argue that the simple allocation scheme BEST_FIT is actually quite effective in returning a good approximation of the greatest MSS obtainable after an allocation.

Theorem 5: a) Any allocation of a k-cube from the current MSS to an incoming k-cube request yields the greatest MSS that can be obtained after allocating a k-cube.

b) If there are no k-cubes in the current MSS, and m is the dimension of the smallest cube in MSS($> k$), then no MSS obtained after allocating a k-cube by splitting an m-cube in the current MSS can have more than one cube of each of the dimensions $m - 1$, $m - 2, \cdots, k + 1$.

In case b) of Theorem 5, it is possible that the greatest MSS after allocation of a k-cube can contain more than one k-cube. When BEST_FIT is used to make allocations from an MSS in such a situation, it returns an SFS that has exactly one cube of each of the dimensions $m - 1, m - 2, \cdots, k$, which is thus a good approximation of the greatest MSS. For case a), BEST_FIT returns the greatest MSS possible. Extrapolating this argument, we can state that when BEST_FIT is used to make allocations from a good approximation S of the MSS, it always returns a good approximation of the greatest MSS obtainable after allocating a k-cube.

It is easy to see that the worst case time complexity of BEST_FIT is $O(n)$. Thus, the complexity of HEURISTIC_COALESCE is the dominating factor in FAST_MSS_STRATEGY, whose complexity is thus $O(n2^n)$. In practice, however, as we will shortly see, the

time taken by FAST_MSS_STRATEGY is reasonably small. The worst case complexity of MSS_STRATEGY is greater due to its use of APPROX_MSS; however, once more, as we will see, its actual execution time is small. It should be noted that the worst case complexity of BUDDY_STRATEGY and the single Gray code method [5] is $O(2^n)$, while that of the multiple Gray-code method [5] is $O\left(2^n \binom{n}{\lfloor n/2 \rfloor}\right)$. Furthermore, neither of these allocation strategies attempts to reduce fragmentation of the hypercube, whereas MSS_STRATEGY and FAST_MSS_STRATEGY implicitly do so, due to the fact that they always maintain a good approximation of the MSS.

VI. SIMULATION RESULTS

We now present the results of computer simulations carried out to compare the three subcube allocation and coalescing strategies: BUDDY_STRATEGY, MSS_STRATEGY, and FAST_MSS_STRATEGY, examined in the preceding sections. The various strategies were implemented in the C language and run on the VAX 11/780 computer. Simulations were performed assuming a Poisson arrival of allocation requests, uniform, Gaussian, and exponential distributions of request dimensions, and uniform and exponential distributions of allocation times, i.e., times for which a cube remains allocated. If a requested k-cube cannot be allocated in spite of the presence of at least 2^k free nodes, we regard this as a *miss*. An allocation request is termed *admissible* if the number of free nodes is at least 2^k, where k is the requested dimension. Note that a feasible allocation request is always admissible, but not vice versa.

The performance measure used for evaluating a strategy is the *miss percentage* M defined as

$$M = \sum_{\text{all misses}} 2^k \times 100 \div \sum_{\substack{\text{all admissible} \\ \text{requests}}} 2^k \tag{15}$$

where k is the requested dimension. The miss percentage M depends on two factors:

- How well the given allocation strategy packs the allocated cubes in Q_n, i.e., how low it keeps the level of fragmentation.
- The pattern of releases. If the release order is, say, LIFO, the hypercube fragmentation and hence M is very low. If, however, the release order is random, M is much higher.

As the release patterns are almost the same for all three strategies mentioned above, the value of M obtained in each case gives an estimate of how successful that strategy is in reducing fragmentation of the hypercube.

Fig. 13 shows M as a function of n (the hypercube dimension) for the three strategies considered, using various distributions of request dimension and allocation time. In all cases, there is a major performance gap ranging from 8% to 55% between BUDDY_STRATEGY and FAST_MSS_STRATEGY. MSS_STRATEGY has only a slightly better performance than FAST_MSS_STRATEGY, the largest and smallest gaps between them being 5% and 0.5%, respectively. Statistics collected also show that APPROX_MSS returns a greater SFS only 8% of the time that it is called by MSS_STRATEGY. These lead us to conclude that: 1) HEURISTIC_COALESCE returns a good approximation of the MSS when a cube is released, and 2) the full potential of the greatest MSS formation is not exploited in MSS_STRATEGY, since APPROX_MSS is invoked only when there is a miss.

Among all the distributions simulated, an allocation strategy is most severely tested by uniform distributions of request dimension and allocation time. As shown in Fig. 13(a), the largest variation in M among the three strategies is exhibited for this case. Understandably, M for all three strategies decreases as the request dimension distribution is changed from uniform to Gaussian to exponential, and the allocation time distribution is changed from uniform to exponential. The performance gap between BUDDY_STRATEGY and FAST_MSS_STRATEGY decreases in a similar manner, as the distributions are changed. The higher rate of decrease in M for

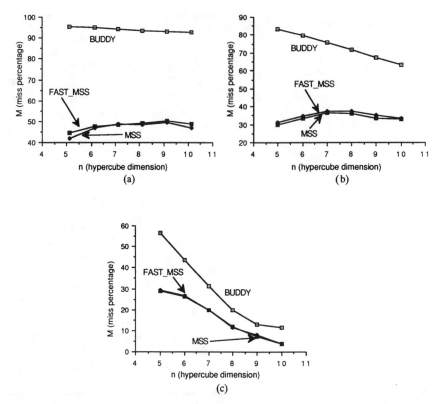

Fig. 13. Performance of three allocation strategies with (a) uniform distributions of request dimension and allocation time, (b) Gaussian distribution (mean $= n/2$) of request dimension and exponential distribution of allocation time, and (c) exponential distributions of request dimension and allocation time.

BUDDY_STRATEGY relative to the other two strategies, as the allocation time distribution is changed from uniform to exponential, can be explained by Lemma 3 and the fact that an exponential distribution of the allocation time closely approximates a FIFO release order.

Fig. 14 shows for each of the three strategies, the average CPU time T to make a successful allocation. FAST_MSS_STRATEGY has values of T that are at most two to three times those of BUDDY_STRATEGY. T is computed by dividing the total time to allocate and coalesce cubes during the simulation period, by the number of successful allocations. Thus, T is really the sum of the average coalescing and allocation times. The average response time is the same as the average allocation time, since a released cube can be coalesced in a background mode. Hence, the average response time is less than T. For FAST_MSS_STRATEGY, the average allocation/response time is a much smaller fraction of T than it is for BUDDY_STRATEGY; hence, from Fig. 14 it can be deduced that FAST_MSS_STRATEGY has a very fast response time, justifying its name.

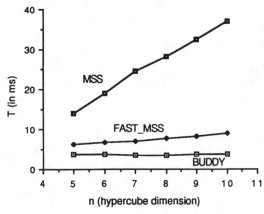

Fig. 14. Average computation (CPU) time T for a successful allocation as a function of the hypercube size n.

VII. Conclusions

We have presented a precise characterization of the subcube allocation problem for hypercube multiprocessors, and developed a methodology to solve it. We first showed that it is not possible to construct an on-line algorithm that guarantees to grant any sequence of allocation requests for which there exists a feasible allocation, i.e., which might otherwise be satisfied by an off-line algorithm. We then characterized on-line subcube allocation using the novel concept of a maximal set of subcubes (MSS), which helps in reducing fragmentation. We showed that the main allocation decision problems are either NP-hard or NP-complete, and thus demonstrated the necessity of using heuristics to solve them. The consensus graph was introduced as a speedup technique for MSS formation, and a fast coalescing scheme, HEURISTIC_COALESCE, which efficiently coalesces released cubes with other free cubes to obtain a good

approximation of the current MSS, was presented. Two MSS-based strategies, MSS_STRATEGY and FAST_MSS_STRATEGY, which use HEURISTIC_COALESCE for coalescing released cubes, and a best-fit allocation scheme BEST_FIT for allocating cubes, were described next. In spite of the simplicity of BEST_FIT and its low complexity, it was shown that it returns a good approximation of the greatest MSS after an allocation.

As shown in Fig. 13, the MSS-based strategies have a considerably higher performance than BUDDY_STRATEGY. The performance of the Gray-code first-fit strategy [5], on the other hand, provides only a small improvement over BUDDY_STRATEGY. FAST_MSS_STRATEGY achieves its performance improvement without sacrificing much in response speed to new allocation requests. Although BUDDY_STRATEGY was shown to be optimal under specific conditions, our simulation data show that it is not very cost-effective for more realistic conditions, and for large hypercubes.

The MSS-based strategy FAST_MSS_STRATEGY seems to be much better in such cases.

Another point to be noted is that the MSS-based algorithms are inherently fault tolerant. The situation where nodes become unusable due to faults can be easily dealt with by considering the faulty nodes as permanently allocated. On the other hand, the buddy and Gray-code methods [5] require the order in which they scan the nodes of the hypercube to be changed in the presence of faults. This is necessary, since most of the subcubes recognized by scanning the nodes in some fixed order, can be made faulty by a single fault.

REFERENCES

[1] F. Harary, J. P. Hayes, and H. J. Wu, "A survey of the theory of hypercube graphs," *Comput. Math. Appl.,* vol. 15, no. 4, pp. 277–289, 1988.

[2] Y. Saad and M. H. Schultz, "Data communications in hypercubes," Res. Rep. YALEU/DCS/RR-428, Yale Univ., Oct. 1985.

[3] J. P. Hayes *et al.,* "A microprocessor-based hypercube supercomputer," *IEEE Micro,* vol. 6, no. 5, pp. 6–17, Oct. 1986.

[4] D. Knuth, *The Art of Computer Programming—Vol. 1. Fundamental Algorithms.* Reading, MA: Addison-Wesley, 1969, pp. 422–445.

[5] M. S. Chen and K. G. Shin, "Processor allocation in an *n*-cube multiprocessor using Gray codes," *IEEE Trans. Comput.,* vol. C-36, pp. 1396–1407, Dec. 1987.

[6] D. L. Dietmeyer, *Logic Design of Digital Systems.* Boston, MA: Allyn and Bacon, 1979.

[7] M. R. Garey and D. S. Johnson, *Computers and Intractability: A Guide to the Theory of NP-Completeness.* San Francisco, CA: Freeman, 1979.

[8] M. R. Dagenais, V. K. Agarwal, and N. C. Rumin, "McBOOLE: A new procedure for exact logic minimization," *IEEE Trans. Comput.-Aided Design,* vol. CAD-5, pp. 229–237, Jan. 1986.

A Top-Down Processor Allocation Scheme for Hypercube Computers

Jong Kim, *Student Member, IEEE*, Chita R. Das, *Member, IEEE*, and Woei Lin, *Member, IEEE*

Abstract—This paper presents an efficient processor allocation policy for hypercube computers. The allocation policy is called *free list* since it maintains a list of free subcubes available in the system. An incoming request of dimension k (2^k nodes) is allocated by finding a free subcube of dimension k or by decomposing an available subcube of dimension greater than k. This free list policy uses a top-down allocation rule in contrast to the bottom-up approach used by the previous bit-map allocation algorithms. This allocation scheme is compared to the *buddy, gray code* (GC), and *modified buddy* allocation policies reported for the hypercubes. It is shown that the *free list* policy is not only statically optimal as the other policies but it gives better subcube recognition ability compared to the previous schemes in a dynamic environment. The performance of this policy, in terms of parameters such as average delay, system utilization, and time complexity, is compared to the other schemes to demonstrate its effectiveness. Finally, the extension of the algorithm for parallel implementation, noncubic allocation, and inclusion/exclusion allocation is also given.

Index Terms—Buddy strategy, free list, gray code, hypercube, modified buddy strategy, processor allocation, processor deallocation, subcube recognition.

I. INTRODUCTION

INCREASING interest in parallel computation has given impetus to the development of a variety of parallel computers (multiprocessors). One such multiprocessor that has received much attention in recent years is the hypercube system. A hypercube, also known as a binary n-cube, is a parallel computer with 2^n processors (nodes). Each node is located on one of the 2^n vertices of the n-cube. Research efforts on hypercube design aspects, performance evaluation, and other related areas have been addressed by several people [1]–[6]. The novelty of this architecture has resulted in several experimental and commercial products, such as the Intel iPSC [7], NCUBE/10 [8], Caltech/JPL [9], and the Connection Machine [10].

Processor allocation is an important issue for achieving high performance on a parallel machine in a multiuser environment. It involves two steps. The first one is to find the number of resources that should be allocated on a multiprocessor for running an application program. An application program/algorithm is represented by a number of interacting modules where each module can be assigned to a processing node of a hypercube. The number of nodes required for a task (job/algorithm) depends on the task flow graph. It has been reported that some regular interconnection topologies such as the ring, tree, and mesh can be embedded on a hypercube [11]. This implies that if we know

Manuscript received May 18, 1989; revised August 17, 1990. This work was supported in part by the National Science Foundation under Grant CCR-8810131. A preliminary version of this paper was presented at the 18th ICPP, August 1989.

J. Kim and C. R. Das are with the Department of Electrical and Computer Engineering, The Pennsylvania State University, University Park, PA 16802.

W. Lin is with the Department of Electrical Engineering, University of Hawaii at Manoa, Honolulu, HI 96822.

IEEE Log Number 9040814.

the size of a topology, the subcube size for accommodating the task is known. Moreover, Chen and Shin have presented a fast algorithm for determining the size of a subcube for a random graph under some relaxed restrictions on the module adjacency [5]. Hence, we assume that the first step of the allocation scheme, i.e., the size of the subcube for an incoming request is known.

The second step in the processor allocation is to locate and assign the required number of resources, as required by a task, on a multiprocessor. On a hypercube, this problem reduces to finding and allocating an appropriate subcube in the machine. This second step of the processor allocation scheme on a hypercube is addressed in this paper. Although this is the second part of the two-step process, we would call it "processor allocation" without loss of generality.

An efficient processor allocation scheme maximizes the resource utilization, reduces external as well as internal fragmentation, and finally improves system performance. An allocation policy is called *static* if the incoming requests are considered for allocation only at some specific time intervals. It does not consider deallocation (processor relinquishment) at any arbitrary time. On the other hand, a dynamic policy can handle processor allocation and deallocation at any time depending on the arrival and completion of jobs. A dynamic policy gives better utilization of resources than the static allocation. However, finding a perfect dynamic policy at minimal overhead is extremely hard. The problem that makes the allocation more difficult is to include some specific nodes for an allocation or/and to exclude some specific nodes for an allocation as the need arises. The inclusion situation occurs when some resources are reachable through specific nodes. The exclusion problem arises when some nodes are faulty or are designated for other purposes and, therefore, cannot be allocated.

Three subcube allocation policies have been reported in the literature using different bit-mapping schemes. A bit-mapping algorithm tries to find a k-cube with 2^k free nodes. The first one, called the *buddy strategy,* is based on the buddy system [12]. It is also implemented on a NCUBE/6 multiprocessor [13]. The second policy, known as the gray code strategy (*GC strategy*), was reported by Chen and Shin [14]. It was proved by these authors that the buddy policy is statically optimal. However, its subcube recognition ability is poor for dynamic allocation. Chen and Shin have shown that a single GC technique is statically optimal and also gives better subcube recognition ability than the first approach. However, a single GC cannot recognize all the subcubes in an n-cube. In view of this, the authors have proposed a multiple gray code scheme, where they use up to $\binom{n}{\lfloor n/2 \rfloor}$ gray codes for an n-cube for complete subcube recognition. It should be observed that the number of GC's required for perfect allocation increases with the increase in cube dimension. The time complexity of this policy, when implemented in a serial version, is high. Therefore, the authors have proposed a parallel implementation of the multiple GC strategy. The third policy proposed by Al-Dhelaan and Bose [15] is a modified buddy strategy that has improved subcube recognition ability. We will refer to this third strategy as the "modified buddy" strategy henceforth. This strategy outperforms the single GC strategy by $(n - k + 1)/2$ in cube recognition ability, where k is the size of the subcube requested by an incoming task. An extended version of the modified buddy scheme shows better performance than the single GC strategy by $(k(n - k) + 1)/2$ in cube recognition ability. But the implementation of the extended version is quite complex. Moreover, the modified buddy policy does not have a perfect subcube recognition ability compared to the multiple GC strategy. A common feature of these three schemes is that they use a "bottom-up" approach since a subcube is formed starting from the lowest dimension—individual nodes.

In this paper, we propose a new allocation strategy which has a perfect subcube recognition ability. It is called *"free list"* since it keeps a list of free cubes available in the n-cube. A task is allocated a proper subcube from this free list. This scheme differs from the previous schemes and also the usual prime implicant technique in that it uses a top-down approach for finding a required subcube. A similar type of approach has been used by Dutt and Hayes for the subcube allocation [16]. While both the schemes are based on the free list concept, our allocation and deallocation algorithms are different and are less complex than those given in [16]. Moreover, we have extended the idea of using the free list to cubic and noncubic allocations, parallel implementation, and to the inclusion and exclusion issues introduced before. Finally, the performance of all the allocation techniques are comparatively analyzed.

The rest of the paper is organized as follows. In Section II, we introduce the necessary definitions and notations. A brief description of the buddy, GC, and modified buddy strategies is given in Section III. The free list strategy is presented in Section IV. Extensions for the inclusion and exclusion problems are treated in Section V. The algorithm analysis and concluding remarks follow as Sections VI and VII.

II. DEFINITIONS AND NOTATION

Let Σ be a ternary symbol set $\{0, 1, x\}$, where x represents the don't care. Since an n-cube has n address bits, every subcubes of an n-cube can be uniquely represented by a sequence of ternary symbols in Σ, which is called the address of the corresponding subcube. The Hamming distance between two subcube addresses is defined as follows.

Definition 1 (Hamming distance): The Hamming distance, $H : \Sigma^k \times \Sigma^k \to I^+$, between two address strings $\alpha = a_1 a_2 \cdots a_k$ and $\beta = b_1 b_2 \cdots b_k$ in Σ^k for some integer k is defined as

$$H(\alpha, \beta) = \sum_{i=1}^{k} h(a_i, b_i)$$

where $h(a, b) = 1$ if $[a = 0$ and $b = 1]$ or $[a = 1$ and $b = 0]$, and $h(a, b) = 0$ otherwise.

Similarly, the exact distance $E : \Sigma^k \times \Sigma^k \to I^+$, between α and β is defined as

$$E(\alpha, \beta) = \sum_{i=1}^{k} e(a_i, b_i)$$

where $e(a, b) = 0$ if $[a = b]$, and $e(a, b) = 1$ otherwise. $\square$

The definition can be extended to multiple address strings. In the extended definition, $h(a_i, b_i, c_i, \cdots) = 1$ if none of the ith bit is x and at least two ith bits differ in the bit value. Otherwise,

$h(a_i, b_i, c_i, \cdots) = 0$. Similarly, $e(a_i, b_i, c_i, \cdots) = 0$ if all the ith bits have the same value, otherwise $e(a_i, b_i, c_i, \cdots) = 1$. For example, let us take $\alpha = 001x$ and $\beta = x001$. Then $H(\alpha, \beta) = 1$ and $E(\alpha, \beta) = 3$. Now if $\gamma = 101x$, then $H(\alpha, \beta, \gamma) = 1$ and $E(\alpha, \beta, \gamma) = 3$.

Definition 2 (Gray Code generation): Let G_n be the GC with parameters g_i, $1 \leq i \leq n$, where a sequence $\langle g_1, g_2, \cdots, g_n \rangle$ is a permutation of $Z_n = \{1, 2, \cdots, n\}$. Then, G_n is defined recursively as follows.

$$G_0 = \{\,\},$$
$$G_k = \{(G_{k-1})^{0 \backslash r_k}, (G_{k-1}^*)^{1 \backslash r_k}\}, \qquad 1 \leq k \leq n$$

where r_k is the partial ranking of g_k. $\square$

The definition of GC and partial ranking are explained in detail in [14]. However, for the completeness of definition, we summarize the generation of G_k from [14] here. Let $\langle g_1, g_2, \cdots, g_n \rangle$ be a sequence of distinct integers. The *partial ranking* r_i of g_i for $1 \leq i \leq n$ is defined as the rank of g_i in the partial set $\{g_1, g_2, \cdots, g_i\}$ when the set is arranged in ascending order. Let G be a sequence of binary strings of length $k - 1$, $k \geq 1$. Then a sequence of binary strings of length k denoted by $G^{b \backslash r_k}$, $b \in \{0, 1\}$, can be obtained by either inserting a bit b into the position immediately right of the r_kth bit from the right side of every string in G if $1 \leq r_k < k$, or by prefixing a bit b to every string in G if $r_k = k$. Also, let G^* denote a sequence of binary strings obtained from G by reversing the order of strings in G. The GC can be generated combining $(G_{k-1})^{0 \backslash r_k}$ and $(G_{k-1}^*)^{1 \backslash r_k}$. As an example, let us consider the generation of 3-bit GC code with parameters $\langle 3, 1, 2 \rangle$. The parameters have the partial ranking, $\langle 1, 1, 2 \rangle$. Then $G_1 = \{0, 1\}$, $G_2 = \{00, 10, 11, 01\}$, and $G_3 = \{000, 100, 101, 001, 011, 111, 110, 010\}$.

Definition 3 (Adjacent and Complementary Cubes): Two cubes α and β are adjacent if $H(\alpha, \beta) = 1$. A complement of cube α, is defined as $\bar{\alpha} = a_1 a_2 \cdots a_{j-1} b_j a_{j+1} \cdots a_n$ with bit j having any position between 1 and n, $a_j, b_j \in \{0, 1\}$, and $a_j \neq b_j$. A complement cube is a special case of adjacent cube where the two cubes differ exactly in one bit position. $\square$

For example, a cube $\{0x1x\}$ can have a complement cube $\{1x1x\}$ or $\{0x0x\}$.

Definition 4 (Bit Partner): The ith bit partner of integer α of bit length k, i.e., $\alpha^k = a_1 a_2 \cdots a_{i-1} a_i a_{i+1} \cdots a_k$, for any $1 \leq i \leq k$ is defined as

$$\alpha_i^k = \begin{cases} a_1 a_2 \cdots a_{i-1} 1 a_{i+1} \cdots a_k, & \text{if } a_i = 0, \\ \text{undefined} & \text{otherwise.} \end{cases} \square$$

For example, an integer $\alpha^3 = \{000\}$ has partners $\{001, 010, 100\}$, where each corresponds to α_1^3, α_2^3, and α_3^3.

III. PREVIOUS ALLOCATION SCHEMES

In this section, we describe the buddy, GC, and modified buddy strategies briefly before introducing the free list policy. This is because the free list strategy has also some similar features of those of the previous policies.

A. The Buddy Strategy

Since there are 2^n nodes in an n-cube, 2^n allocation bits are used to keep track of the availability of the nodes. A value 0 (1) in the allocation bit indicates the availability (unavailability) of the corresponding node.

Allocation:

Step 1: Set $k := |I_j|$, where $|I_j|$ is the dimension of a subcube required to accommodate the request I_j.

Step 2: Determine the least integer m such that all the allocation bits in the region $\#[m2^k, (m+1)2^k - 1]$ are 0's, and set all these allocation bits to 1's.

Step 3: Allocate nodes to the request I_j.

Relinquishment:

Step: Reset every pth allocation bit to 0, where p is the address of node that was released.

B. The GC Strategy

Similar to the buddy strategy, 2^n allocation bits are used to keep track of the availability of all nodes. But, the sequence of allocation bits follows the gray code pattern.

Allocation:

Step 1: Same as in Buddy.

Step 2: Determine the least integer m such that all the (i mod 2^n)th bits are 0's, where $i \in \#[m2^{k-1}, (m+2)2^{k-1} - 1]$, and set all these 2^k allocation bits to 1's.

Step 3: Allocate nodes to the request I_j.

Relinquishment:

Step: Same as in Buddy.

C. The Modified Buddy Strategy

Similar to the buddy strategy, 2^n allocation bits are used to keep track of the availability of all nodes. An integer α represented by m bits is regarded as free if $(\alpha^m)^{0\backslash 1}$ and $(\alpha^m)^{1\backslash 1}$ are free. For example, an integer three in 2 bits, i.e., 11, is free if integers six and seven in 3 bits are free. This notation implies the free subcubes of smaller dimension. Detailed description of the modified buddy strategy can be found in [15].

Allocation:

Step 1: Same as in Buddy.

Step 2: Determine the least integer α, $0 \leq \alpha \leq 2^{n-k+1} - 1$, such that α^{n-k+1} is free, and it has a pth partner, $1 \leq p \leq (n-k+1)$, α_p^{n-k+1} which is also free. Take p as small as possible.

Step 3: Allocate these processors to the request I_j and set their allocation bits to 1.

Relinquishment:

Step: Same as in Buddy.

D. Analysis of the Previous Strategies

Static allocation is concerned with the accommodation of the incoming requests without considering processor relinquishment. An allocation strategy is said to be statically optimal if an n-cube can accommodate any input request sequence $\{I_i\}_{i=1}^m$ iff $\sum_{i=1}^m 2^{|I_i|} \leq 2^n$, where $|I_i|$ is the dimension of a subcube required to accommodate request I_i. It has been proved that all the previous strategies are statically optimal [14], [15].

In a dynamic environment, when processor relinquishment is taken into consideration, the buddy strategy is shown to be poor because it generates more external fragmentation. It also cannot detect all available subcubes in an n-cube. For example, let us examine the following sequence of requests and relinquishment in a 4-cube system.

Example-1: Sequence

1) A request for a 2-cube (I_1),
2) A request for a 2-cube (I_2),
3) A request for a 2-cube (I_3),
4) A 2-cube relinquishment,
5) A request for a 3-cube.

The allocation of requests for a buddy strategy is shown by a K-map in Fig. 1(a). The last request for the 3-cube allocation can be accommodated immediately if the relinquished 2-cube is exactly the third 2-cube (I_3). Even though there is a 3-cube available when the second allocation (I_2) is relinquished, it cannot be detected using the buddy scheme. This is because the buddy strategy tries to allocate a 3-cube as shown in Fig. 1(b). Allocation of 2-cubes using GC strategy is shown in Fig. 1(c). The request for a 3-cube (sequence 5) can be accommodated using GC scheme if the relinquished 2-cube is either the first or the third one. Since the GC strategy has more subcube recognition ability, as shown in Fig. 1(d), it can detect a 3-cube when the first 2-cube (I_1) is also relinquished. Allocation of 2-cubes with the modified buddy strategy is the same as in Fig. 1(a), and the allocation strategy for the 3-cube request is the same as in Fig. 1(d). It can detect a 3-cube when the second request (I_2) or the third request (I_3) is relinquished.

The external fragmentation caused by the GC strategy is even less than that by the buddy strategy, since there is a tendency that the nodes allocated first are also released first for uniformly distributed service time. For example, there is an external fragmentation if the first 2-cube (I_1) is relinquished in the buddy and the modified buddy strategies. Release of the second 2-cube (I_2) results in external fragmentation in the GC scheme. Since it is likely that I_1 is released earlier than I_2, the buddy strategy is more susceptible to external fragmentation.

IV. Free List Strategy

The prime implicant method of finding a possible subcube is more complicated and computationally more expensive compared to the buddy and GC strategies. But the allocation would be easier than the former techniques if one maintains a list of available subcubes for task assignment. Since the scheme is based on the available cube list, it is called the "free list" strategy. The allocation and deallocation algorithms for the free list are discussed below.

A. Allocation Scheme

The free list consists of $n + 1$ independent lists, where the ith list corresponds to dimension i, for $0 \leq i \leq n$. The elements in the list are represented by their unique address—a sequence of n ternary symbols. An n-cube is represented as a sequence of n "x"s initially. When there is a request for a k-cube, for $k \leq n$, one of the nearest higher dimension subcubes is decomposed from the most significant bit side for finding a k-cube. Decomposition of the nearest higher dimension cube is not necessary if the free list has a subcube of dimension k. The requested k-cube is then assigned to the request. The remaining elements in the list are mutually disjoint. The formal procedure for the allocation is given below.

Allocation:

Step 1: Same as in Buddy.

Step 2: If there is an available subcube for the request size in the k-cube list, allocate it. Skip steps 3 and 4.

Step 3: If not, find the nearest higher dimension cube that is available. If there is no higher dimension cube in the list, then the request is kept in the waiting queue.

Step 4: Choose one of the nearest higher dimension cubes according to the selection rule (to be discussed below) and decompose it into two subcubes. Repeat this step until we reach the requested cube size. Allocate one k-cube.

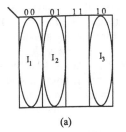 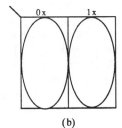 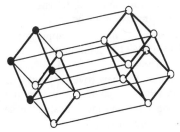

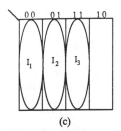 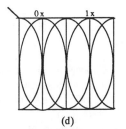

Fig. 1. (a) An allocated 2-cube under Buddy scheme. (b) Buddy strategy allocation rule for 3-cube. (c) An allocated 2-cube under GC scheme. (d) GC strategy allocation rule for 3-cube.

Fig. 2. A free 3-cube and 2-cube in a 4-cube system after a 2-cube is allocated.

The selection of a cube from the free list of cubes is determined using the same search technique used for the gray code. The search is based on the K-map adjacency rule. Let us assume that there is an available cube $\{01xxx\}$ and an outstanding 2-cube request in a 5-cube system. The selected 2-cube for the request is then $\{011xx\}$. This is because the previous allocations are part of the 3-cube $\{00xxx\}$ and we cannot find any more subcube in $\{00xxx\}$ that can accommodate a 2-cube. $\{011xx\}$ is the next available cube adjacent to $\{00xxx\}$. If no such adjacency exists, the first cube in the list is selected.

The decomposition always follows the adjacency rule. For the above example, the 4-cube $\{0xxxx\}$ is decomposed to two 3-cubes $\{00xxx, 01xxx\}$. The 2-cubes are allocated decomposing $\{00xxx\}$ first. The sequence of 2-cube allocations from $\{0xxxx\}$ is therefore $\{000xx\}$, $\{001xx\}$, $\{011xx\}$, and $\{010xx\}$.

The following example illustrates the process of free list allocation policy.

Example-2: Let us assume that there is a first request for a 2-cube in a 4-cube system. The initial free list is $\{\{xxxx\}\}$. After decomposition for finding a 2-cube, the free list changes to $\{\{1xxx\}, \{01xx\}\}$ (allocating 2-cube is $\{00xx\}$).

Note that all the cubes in the free list are mutually disjoint. The mutual disjoint property of the hypercube is pictorially given in Fig. 2 for example-2. The dark circles represent the allocated 2-cube. The following property of the subcubes is used in the allocation strategy.

Lemma 1: Let α, β be the two subcubes in an n-cube. These two cubes are mutually disjoint iff $H(\alpha, \beta) \neq 0$.

Proof: $\rightarrow$) Let $H(\alpha, \beta) \neq 0$. Then there is at least one bit position, say j, such that $a_j \neq b_j$, where a_j belongs to cube α, b_j belongs to cube β, and $a_j, b_j \in \{0, 1\}$. If we divide all the nodes of an n-cube using the value of the jth bit position, we get two mutually disjoint groups. Hence, all the nodes belonging to the cube α are disjoint to the nodes of the cube β.

$\leftarrow$) Let the two cubes be mutually disjoint. Then the Hamming distance between any two nodes belonging to different cubes is at least 1. Therefore, the Hamming distance cannot be 0 when the cubes are mutually disjoint. □

Theorem 1: The free list strategy is statically optimal.

Proof: Let $\mathcal{I} = \{I_1, I_2, \cdots, I_m\}$ be the set of requests such that $\sum_{i=1}^{m} 2^{|I_i|} \leq 2^n$ where n is the dimension of hypercube and $|I_i|$ represents the dimension of the request I_i. Assume that there is a sequence of requests $\mathcal{S} = \langle S_1, S_2, \cdots, S_m \rangle$ that cannot be accommodated by the free list scheme when $\mathcal{I}$ is mapped on to $\mathcal{S}$. Let S_j be the first request that cannot be accommodated from the request sequence $\mathcal{S}$. Since a request can be assigned if there exists a cube $C \geq |S_j|$, it is obvious that there is no cube larger than or equal to $|S_j|$ in the remaining free cubes. Let $\mathcal{R} = \{R_1, R_2, \cdots, R_k\}$ be the set of remaining free cubes after the allocation of requests up to S_{j-1}. None of these free cubes can accept the jth request. The free list strategy under static allocation can have at most *one* free cube for each dimension. Hence, all the free cubes are distinct from each other in terms of cube dimension. The total number of free nodes, $\sum_{i=1}^{k} 2^{|R_i|}$, is smaller than $2^{|S_j|}$. If we add all the allocated and free nodes, we must have $(\sum_{i=1}^{j-1} 2^{|S_i|} + \sum_{i=1}^{k} 2^{|R_i|}) = 2^n$. Since $\sum_{i=1}^{k} 2^{|R_i|} < 2^{|S_j|}$, $\sum_{i=1}^{j} 2^{|S_j|} > 2^n$, for $j \leq m$. It contradicts the assumption on the size of cubes, i.e., $\sum_{i=1}^{m} 2^{|S_i|} = \sum_{i=1}^{m} 2^{|I_i|} \leq 2^n$. Therefore, there is no sequence that cannot be accommodated if the total number of requested nodes is less than the number of nodes in the system, 2^n. Thus, the free list strategy is statically optimal. □

Dutt and Hayes have also used the free list concept for hypercube allocation [16]. The difference between the two methods in the allocation lies in the complexity and optimality. If there is a free cube in the list for the requested dimension k, both techniques assign the k-cube immediately. Our technique and that in [16] differ when there is no free cube of exact dimension k, but there are free cubes in the higher dimension list. We select the first free cube from the nearest higher dimension list for decomposition. In the other method, each free cube in the nearest higher dimension list is combined with free cubes of all lower dimensions to generate all possible k-cubes. Among the free cubes in the nearest higher dimension list, the one that generates the maximum number of k-dimension free cubes is selected for the decomposition. It should be observed that our allocation is simple and quick whereas the allocation scheme in [16] is optimal but time consuming.

B. Deallocation Scheme

After a task is completed, the corresponding subcube is deallocated and included in the free list. The list is then updated using the following deallocation algorithm.

Deallocation:

Step 1: Include the released k-cube in the corresponding k-cube list.

Step 2: Compare the released k-cube to all free cubes and form new cubes if possible.

Step 3: Do the following for all dimensions, starting from the lowest dimension in the list:

a: Generate the new (overlapping) i dimension cubes, if possible, by combining the cubes of the same dimension i.

b: Generate the new (overlapping) i or $(i+1)$ dimension cubes, if possible, by combining the cubes of dimension i and the cubes of the nearest nonempty higher dimension(s).

c: Combine two complement subcubes of dimension i if they exist and form an $(i+1)$-cube.

Step 4: Make the cubes (generated after step 3) mutually disjoint to each other as follows.

a: Select a cube from the highest dimension list and decompose all other same or lower dimension cubes that have a common node with the selected cube.

b: The cubes with a common node(s) with the selected cube are deleted from the list.

c: Repeat steps a and b for all the free cubes except the ones already selected.

Step 2 generates new overlapping cubes using the released k-cube. Step 3 also generates other cubes using the cubes of various dimensions. Part b of the step 3 combines cubes of dimension i with the cubes of nearest nonempty higher dimension, say j. If some of the i-cubes are not adjacent to the free j-cubes, they are passed to the next higher dimension for possible grouping. Once an i-cube is combined with a nearest higher dimension cube, it is not passed to other lists. Note that this technique is based on the Quine–McClusky algorithm for grouping disjoint subcubes [17].

Instead of passing an i-cube that cannot be combined with the next nonempty higher order cubes, we can modify step 3-b such that only cubes of dimension i are compared and coalesced with the nearest nonempty list. This modified deallocation procedure compares cubes of only two dimensions disregarding the possibility of combination. Let us call the free list with this changed deallocation as "modified free list." While this modified scheme reduces the time complexity, it does not generate all possible combinations. This is illustrated using the following situation in a 7-cube.

Example-3: Let us assume that all the nodes are allocated in the 7-cube at some point of time. Then the sequence of released cubes is $\mathcal{S} = \langle 0001xxx, 001x1xx, 01x01xx, 01x1x1x, 11000xx, 0000111, 0000110 \rangle$. It is possible to find a 4-cube from the released subcube, i.e., $\{0xxx11x\}$. If we follow the modified free list, step 2 generates the following 1-cubes after the released cube $\{0000110\}$: $\{000x110, 00x0110, 0x00110, 000011x\}$. The 1-cubes are combined with the nearest nonempty 2-cube $\{11000xx\}$ as for step 3-b of the modified scheme. But these 1-cubes cannot be combined with 2-cube $\{11000xx\}$ and hence a 4-cube cannot be obtained. Whereas using the original deallocation algorithm, the 1-cubes will also be compared to the 3-cubes for finally getting a 4-cube.

However, these types of situations are very rare. It will be shown in Section VI that the *modified free list* gives the same result as the original free list while reducing the deallocation complexity.

The deallocation algorithm uses the following lemmas to generate the same or higher dimension cubes.

Lemma 2: Let α, β be two cubes of dimension k. Then there is a cube δ of dimension k that only contains the nodes of α and β if $E(\alpha, \beta) = 3$ and $H(\alpha, \beta) = 1$.

Proof: Since cubes α and β differ exactly in three

positions $P(E(\alpha, \beta) = 3)$, let us assume that the positions are i, j, and l. Also, let i be the bit position that gives $H(\alpha, \beta) = 1$. Then, the possible combinations of i, j, l for the given condition are $(a_i \neq x, b_i \neq x)$, $(a_j = x, b_j \neq x)$, and $(a_l \neq x, b_l = x)$. Note that i, j, and l are interchangeable. Now, let us decompose the cube α into two $(k-1)$-cubes using the bit position j and decompose the cube β into two $(k-1)$-cubes using the bit position 1. This gives the following four $(k-1)$-cubes.

$$\alpha = \{\{a_1 a_2 \cdots a_i \cdots a_{j-1} 0 a_{j+1} \cdots a_l \cdots a_n\},$$
$$\{a_1 a_2 \cdots a_i \cdots a_{j-1} 1 a_{j+1} \cdots a_l \cdots a_n\}\}$$
$$\beta = \{\{b_1 b_2 \cdots b_i \cdots b_j \cdots b_{l-1} 0 b_{l+1} \cdots b_n\},$$
$$\{b_1 b_2 \cdots b_i \cdots b_j \cdots b_{l-1} 1 b_{l+1} \cdots b_n\}\}.$$

Choose the $(k-1)$-subcube of α that has the same bit value of b_j, and also choose the $(k-1)$-subcube of β that has the same value of a_l. Combine both these $(k-1)$-cubes and let it be γ. $\gamma = \{a_1 a_2 \cdots a_{i-1} x a_{i+1} \cdots a_{j-1} b_j a_{j+1} \cdots a_{l-1} a_l a_{l+1} \cdots a_n\}$. The dimension of γ is k since it is the combination of two $(k-1)$-cubes. □

Lemma 3: Let α, β be two disjoint subcubes of dimensions k and $k+s$, $s \geq 1$. Then there is a cube δ of size $(k+1)$ or k that only contains the nodes of α and β iff α and β are adjacent and $E(\alpha, \beta) = s+1$ for size $(k+1)$ or $E(\alpha, \beta) = s+2$ for size k.

Proof: $\rightarrow$) Since the cubes α and β differ exactly in $s+1$ bit positions for δ to be a $(k+1)$-cube ($s+2$ for the size k), let us assume that these positions are $i_0, i_1, \cdots, i_s$. One of these bit positions, say i_0, is such that $a_{i_0} \neq b_{i_0}$ and $a_{i_0}, b_{i_0} \in \{0,1\}$ since two cubes α and β are adjacent. For the remaining s positions, $a_{i_j} \neq x$ and $b_{i_j} = x$ because the size of α is k and β is $(k+s)$. Now, let us generate a cube $\delta = \{c_1, c_2, \cdots, c_n\}$ as follows: 1) $c_{i_0} = x$, 2) $c_j = a_j$ for any $j \neq i_0$. It is obvious that the overlapping cube δ contains the nodes of cubes α and β and its dimension is $(k+1)$. (For the proof of cube size k, assume one more position that is $a_{i_{s+1}} = x$ and $b_{i_{s+1}} \neq x$. For a cube δ, $c_{i_{s+1}} = b_{i_{s+1}}$. The rest of proof is the same.)

$\leftarrow$) Let δ be a cube that contains only the nodes of α and β. Then, δ should contain the same number of nodes from both the cubes. Let the common nodes (intersection) of α and δ be defined as a cube γ ($\alpha \cap \delta = \gamma$). Similarly, ω is the intersection of β and δ ($\beta \cap \delta = \omega$). γ and ω are complement cubes (hence adjacent) since they combine to form the cube δ. This adjacency property never changes with the growth of cubes γ and ω. Therefore, cubes α and β are also adjacent. If δ is a cube of size $(k+1)$, then γ and ω are cubes of size k and $\gamma = \alpha$. The cube ω should be a proper subset of cube β. It means that the address string of cube β has s x's, whereas the address string of cube ω does not have x in those positions. This gives the $E(\alpha, \beta) = s+1$. The same argument can be extended for $E(\alpha, \beta) = s+2$. □

The graphical illustrations of Lemmas 2 and 3 are given in Fig. 3. A simple example to explain the deallocation strategy is given below.

Example-4: Let the current free list have the elements $\{\{10xx\}, \{11x1\}, \{1110\}\}$, and assume that the released subcube is $\{1100\}$. The cube $\{1100\}$ is added to the 0-cube list $\{1110\}$. Step 2 of the deallocation algorithm generates three 1-cubes $\{11x0, 110x, 1x00\}$ when $\{1100\}$ is combined with cubes in the free list. The 1-cube list is updated as $\{11x1, 11x0, 110x, 1x00\}$. Using step 3, the same or higher dimension cubes are generated. First, the subcubes of dimension 1 are generated by comparing the lists of dimension 0 and 1. The generated subcube list of dimension 1 is $\{11x1, 11x0, 110x, 1x00, 111x\}$ including

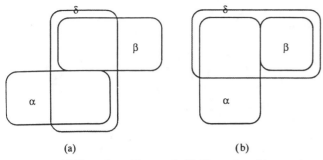

(a)　　　　　　　　　　(b)

Fig. 3. (a) Illustration of Lemma 2. (b) Illustration of Lemma 3.

the combination of cubes $\{1110, 1100\}$ that gives $\{11x0\}$. Second, the subcube list of dimension 2 is generated by combining cubes of dimensions 1 and 2. The 2-cube list becomes $\{10xx, 1x0x, 1xx1, 1x1x, 1xx0, 11xx\}$. Finally a 3-cube $\{1xxx\}$ is generated by combining the complement subcubes $\{10xx, 11xx\}$, $\{1x0x, 1x1x\}$, and $\{1xx1, 1xx0\}$. By step 4, the subcubes that have a common node with $\{1xxx\}$ are decomposed and removed. Since every cube in the list of dimensions 0, 1, and 2 is a subset of $\{1xxx\}$, all the smaller cubes are deleted from the list. The final free list is $\{\{1xxx\}\}$.

Theorem 2: The free list strategy can recognize any possible m-cube if it exists.

Proof: Without loss of generality, let us assume that there is no recognizable subcube larger than m. If a recognizable m-cube can be found after a k-cube $(k < m)$ is released, then there must be one s-cube, for $s \leq k$, in the released k-cube that is common to the recognizable m-cube. An s-cube that is a proper subset of an m-cube has $(m - s)$ neighboring s-cubes that are also proper subsets of the m-cube. This implies that at least $(m - s)$ cubes of different dimensions are generated by step 2 of the deallocation algorithm after the k-cube is released. Using step 3-a of the deallocation algorithm, these new cubes in the free list combine with adjacent cubes from the corresponding dimensions to generate overlapping cubes. Step 3-b combines the new cubes of dimension i $(1 \leq i \leq k + 1)$ with existing higher dimension lists to create new cubes and step 3-c combines complementary cubes to generate one higher dimension cube. In other words, each cube in the free list generates at least one subcube if an adjacent cube exists. Subcubes that include a subset of the m-cube generate new (overlapping) cubes since they can always find adjacent cubes. Hence, the cubes that are a proper subset of the m-cube are generated systematically in increasing size by step 3 until the final m-cube is obtained. Steps 2 and 3 thus find a recognizable m-cube if it exists. □

A striking advantage of the free list strategy compared to the others is its ability in recognizing quickly that there is no possible subcube available. It takes $O(n)$ time for the worst case. The GC, buddy, or modified buddy strategy needs to try every integer value m in the allocation step 2, and then decides that there is no available subcube. Some implementation technique as used in [15] can alleviate this problem for the previous strategies. In a multiple GC strategy, the search is also done over the complete 2^n bit-map.

The free list technique has nice parallel features. The parallel version of the free list is described next.

C. Parallelized Free List

It is assumed that the list for each dimension is kept on a separate node. Hence, $(n + 1)$ nodes of the hypercube are used for the parallel algorithm.

Parallel allocation:

Step 1: The host processor decides the cube size, i.e., k, for the request and broadcasts the size to the hypercube nodes that maintain a list of at least dimension k.

Step 2: All the nodes that have a free cube of dimension m, for $m \geq k$, respond to the request by sending the available cube to the host.

Step 3: The host selects the nearest higher dimension response, decomposes it if necessary (when $m > k$), and sends the decomposed subcubes to each corresponding node(s). It also sends a message to delete the cube m (since it was used for allocation) from the list to the node maintaining the list for dimension m.

Parallel deallocation:

Step 1: The released k-cube is added to the node that keeps the list of k-cubes.

Step 2: The host broadcasts the released k-cube to all the nodes. All the nodes generate possible subcubes by comparing their list to the released k-cube. The generated i-cubes are broadcasted to the node maintaining list size i.

Step 3: Each node sends a copy of its list to a node that has one higher dimension list. If the receiving node has an empty list, it redirects the message to the node that carries the next higher dimension list. At the same time each node generates overlapping subcubes using its original list and the subcubes received from the neighboring node. If an incoming cube cannot be combined with any of the cubes of the receiving node, the incoming cube is redirected to another node that has one higher dimension list. (This redirection is not necessary in the modified free list scheme.) The whole process works as a pipeline as shown in Fig. 4.

Step 4: From the node that has the highest dimension list, select one cube at a time and broadcast it to all other nodes. After the elements of highest dimension list are selected, the node that has the next lower dimension list repeats the same step. This process continues until it reaches the lowest dimension.

Step 5: Each participating node decomposes its own cubes that have a common node with the received cube. The common node cubes are deleted from the list and the decomposed smaller cubes are sent to the corresponding nodes for updating the list. Steps 4 and 5 can be done in parallel.

D. Noncubic Allocation

Up to this point we have assumed that the request size is always in a cubic form, i.e., 2^i nodes. This condition can be relaxed so that we need only y connected nodes where $y \neq 2^i$. This is called noncubic (NC) allocation. The advantage of the NC policy is that it can improve processor utilization and system throughput by reducing internal fragmentation. One possible approach to implement this allocation is to assign a large cube of dimension m that can accommodate the y nodes, i.e., $m \geq \lceil \log y \rceil$, and deallocate the unnecessary $(2^m - y)$ nodes. If a cube of dimension m does not exist, the request is delayed until further cubes are deallocated. An NC allocation can be handled by the free list alternatively as follows. First, the same strategy (finding an m-cube mentioned above) is applied. If an m-cube is not available, the number of nodes y is divided into smaller subcubes. For example, if a task needs 11 nodes, then

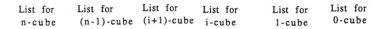

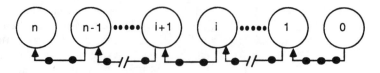

● : Free subcubes

Fig. 4. A pipelined generation of subcubes.

the request is divided into 8 and 4-node requests. The 8 nodes (3-cube) and the 4 nodes (2-cube) are allocated such that they are adjacent. Instead of allocating a 2-cube one can allocate a 1-cube and a 0-cube to make the number of nodes exactly 11. This exact allocation needs more time. The formal algorithm for the noncubic allocation is given below.

Allocation for Noncubic Request:

Step 1: Decide the cube size m that can accommodate the request size y.

Step 2: If an m-cube is found, deallocate the unused nodes and skip the remaining steps.

Step 3: Otherwise, decrease the cube size by 1, and try to allocate. If it succeeds, find another adjacent cube that can accommodate the remaining nodes.

Step 4: Repeat step 3 until it reaches the predetermined level. The level is related to the search depth of available cubes.

The deallocation algorithm is the same as the cubic policy given in Section IV-B.

V. Inclusion and Exclusion

A variation of the allocation problem is the inclusion or/and exclusion of specific nodes. There are many situations that typically resemble this case. In an inclusion case, a specific node can be a typical resource center. And in an exclusion problem, a specific node can be a faulty node. Let us assume that the number of nodes to be included or excluded is given as s different cubes. Deallocation algorithms for both cases are the same as the one in Section IV-B.

A. Inclusion

Problem statement: The incoming request for a dimension k requires that the s cubes should be included in the allocated m-cube such that $m \geq k$.

In some cases, the dimension of the cube that can include the s cubes is larger than the required size k. For example, we need the complete 4-cube $\{xxxx\}$ to cover the two nodes $\{0000, 1111\}$ in a 4-cube system [6].

Theorem 3: Let r be the number of bit positions where all the s cubes have "x." The number of m-cubes that can include the s cubes, $\alpha_1, \alpha_2, \cdots, a_s$ in $\sum^n$ is given by

$$\binom{n - E(\alpha_1, \alpha_2, \cdots, \alpha_s) - r}{m - E(\alpha_1, \alpha_2, \cdots, \alpha_s) - r} 2^{n-m}.$$

Proof: The number of m cubes in an n-cube is $\binom{n}{m}2^{n-m}$. The number of bit positions that should be used for an allocation to include the s cubes is $E(\alpha_1, \alpha_2, \cdots, \alpha_s) + r$. Hence, the remaining number of bit positions for an m-cube allocation is $m - E(\alpha_1, \alpha_2, \cdots, \alpha_s) - r$. But the total number of bit positions available in an n-cube is $n - E(\alpha_1, \alpha_2, \cdots, \alpha_s) - r$, since $E(\alpha_1, \alpha_2, \cdots, \alpha_s) + r$ bit positions are already reserved for the s cubes. □

Corollary 3-1: There is no possible subcube of dimension m if $m < E(\alpha_1, \alpha_2, \cdots, \alpha_s) + r$. □

Corollary 3-2: The smallest subcube that can accommodate $\{\alpha_1, \alpha_2, \cdots, \alpha_s\}$ is $E(\alpha_1, \alpha_2, \cdots, \alpha_s) + r$. □

We can decide whether a subcube of dimension m exists or not by Corollary 3-1. Corollary 3-2 helps to find the smallest cube that can accommodate the given s cubes.

Inclusion allocation:

Step 1: Determine the value r and the multiple exact distance E of the nodes to be included, and set $m := |I_j|$ where $|I_j|$ is the dimension of a subcube required to accommodate the request I_j. If m is less than $E(\alpha_1, \cdots, \alpha_s) + r$, set m to $E(\alpha_1, \cdots, \alpha_s) + r$.

Step 2: Follow step 3 of the free list deallocation strategy for creating all possible overlapping subcubes. Note that an m-cube is obtained combining smaller cubes. Step-3 of the deallocation algorithm finds all possible combinations. This increases the possibility of finding an m-cube.

Step 3: Allocate a subcube m if possible and decompose all the cubes that have common node(s) with the allocated cube. (This overlapping was done in step 2.) If there is no m-cube formed in step 2, wait for the release of other cubes.

Step 4: Follow step 4 of the deallocation strategy to make the cubes disjoint.

B. Exclusion

Problem statement: An incoming request for a subcube of dimension k requires that some s cubes should be excluded from the allocated k cube.

If we regard the cubes to be excluded as the cubes that are already allocated, the problem reduces to the simple free list allocation policy. The allocation strategy can be explained in three steps. First, we allocate the cubes to be excluded. Second, the request for dimension k is allocated. Finally, the nodes to be excluded are relinquished.

Exclusion allocation:

Step 1: Allocate all the s cubes to be excluded.

Step 2: Since the allocation of specific s cubes from the free list makes the lists internally fragmented, generate various subcubes in the same way used in the deallocation strategy (follow step 3 of deallocation strategy). Step 3 of the deallocation algorithm generates all possible combinations. This increases the possibility of finding a k cube.

TABLE I
SIMULATION RESULTS OF THE ALLOCATION SCHEMES ON A 5-CUBE
Scheduling discipline : FCFS

Distri-bution	T	delay(d_h)				Job Completion				Efficiency			
		Buddy	Gray	M. Bud.	Free	Buddy	Gray	M. Bud.	Free	Buddy	Gray	M. Bud.	Free
Case-1	100	7.43	7.20	7.15	6.84	77.74	78.54	78.57	79.35	76.344	77.094	77.156	78.000
	200	14.23	13.83	13.57	13.03	160.61	162.17	162.38	164.43	77.937	78.734	78.828	79.781
	300	21.29	20.32	20.32	19.29	243.94	246.96	246.97	250.01	78.500	79.427	79.418	80.437
Case-2	100	9.43	9.19	9.17	8.96	66.77	67.40	67.64	68.81	79.781	80.438	80.843	82.125
	200	19.93	19.69	19.59	19.18	137.31	138.08	138.92	140.92	81.219	81.166	82.234	83.359
	300	30.31	30.18	29.85	29.19	207.26	208.55	209.51	212.08	81.750	82.218	82.697	83.718
Case-3	100	8.54	8.24	8.38	8.11	67.14	68.00	67.23	68.73	74.813	75.719	75.031	76.531
	200	16.82	16.38	16.56	16.03	144.95	146.38	145.73	147.59	77.281	78.109	77.968	78.932
	300	25.70	24.85	25.28	24.02	220.80	224.46	224.41	227.81	78.323	79.239	79.114	80.396

Residence time dist.: Case-1: Uniform [3, 7], Case-2: Uniform [3.83, 7.83], Case-3: Uniform [8.36, 12.36].
Cube size dist.: Case-1: Uniform, Case-2, Normal,[1] Case-3: Biased Normal.[2]
1) $p_0 = p_4 = 0.098$, $p_1 = p_3 = 0.214$, $p_2 = 0.376$
2) $p_0 = 0.504$, $p_1 = 0.217$, $p_2 = 0.143$, $p_3 = 0.087$, $p_4 = 0.049$.

Step 3: Allocate the k-cube request, if possible.
Step 4: Deallocate all the s cubes of step 1 using the free list deallocation strategy.

VI. ALGORITHM ANALYSIS

A. Performance Comparison

The three bit-map allocation schemes [13]–[15] and the free list were simulated for comparison. Most of the assumptions used in the simulation were the same as in [14]. The assumptions are discussed below. An incoming request is assumed to arrive in every time unit. The generation is continued until the predetermined time T is reached. The dimensions of the subcubes required by the incoming requests are assumed to follow a given distribution. The residence times of the subcube are assumed to have uniform distribution. The request that was not satisfied upon arrival for the lack of an available subcube was queued until a subcube was available. The following statistics were collected and averaged over 100 independent runs.

Under the given condition, the following basic measures were taken.

T_c: Time when the last request was completed.
C_c: Number of requests that were completed in time T.
C_h: Number of requests that were assigned in time T.
D_h: Total delay until the last request was assigned.
U_t: Total utilization of the hypercube in time T. $U_t = \sum_{i=1}^{C_h} 2^{|I_i|} t_i$ where $|I_i|$ is the request size and t_i is the residence time until T of the request I_i.

From the above measures, the following system level measures were computed.

d_h: Average waiting delay per request given by D_h/T.
E: Efficiency of the strategy, given by $U_t/(2^n xT)$.

The results shown in Tables I and II are based on the following distributions of the incoming requests and an FCFS scheduling discipline. If there is a request in the queue, the new request is queued. The parameters compared in Table I are the average delay (d_h), the number of jobs completed in time T (C_c), and the system efficiency (E) of the buddy, single GC, modified buddy, and free list schemes. The parameter T represents the predetermined time interval for which the system was observed. It also gives the number of requests generated during T since a request was generated in every time unit. Two distributions (uniform and normal) were used for the cube size of incoming

TABLE II
COMPARISON OF THE FREE LIST AND MULTIPLE GC ON A 5-CUBE
Scheduling discipline : FCFS

	T	Buddy	Multiple Gray			M. Buddy	Freee
			#1	#5	#10		
delay(d_h)	100	3.73	3.70	3.39	3.32	3.67	3.22
	200	5.98	5.62	5.12	4.98	5.66	4.83
	300	7.89	6.75	6.23	5.93	7.70	5.73
Job comp.	100	84.53	84.72	85.56	85.61	84.91	85.83
	200	180.86	182.21	183.07	183.40	181.95	183.73
	300	278.61	281.19	282.26	282.88	280.76	282.87
Effi.	100	69.250	69.500	70.156	70.156	69.687	70.406
	200	71.625	72.297	72.625	72.734	72.078	72.890
	300	72.968	73.583	73.885	74.083	73.489	74.125

Residence time dist.: Uniform [4, 12].
Cube size dist.: Biased Normal.[1]
1) $p_0 = 0.45$, $p_1 = 0.25$, $p_2 = 0.15$, $p_3 = 0.10$, $p_4 = 0.05$.

requests. The job residence time was assumed to be uniformly distributed between the given time units. For example, in the first observation of Table I the time is distributed uniformly between 3 and 7. The p_i value denotes the probability that an incoming request needs a cube of size i, for $0 \leq i \leq 4$, ($p_1 = 0.2$ means that the probability that a new request needs a 1-cube is 0.2) such that $\sum p_i = 1$. It can be observed from Table I that the free list policy performs better than any other scheme in terms of average delay, number of jobs completed during a given time, and efficiency.

Table II compares the free list to the buddy, modified buddy, and the multiple GC using the same three parameters, d_h, C_c, and E. The residence times of the requests are uniformly distributed between 4 and 12 time units. The sequence of the multiple gray codes used in Table II is the same as given in [14]. The incoming request distribution is a biased normal. The probability of requests for different cube sizes is given in Table II. It should be observed that the free list is even slightly better than the multiple GC in a dynamic environment. The multiple GC for a 5-cube needs up to $\binom{5}{2} = 10$ gray codes.

Next, we changed the scheduling discipline to see if our earlier claim about the free list is valid. Table III is based on a modified FCFS policy—a request was scheduled upon arrival if a subcube was available disregarding whether there are requests in the queue or not. Also, requests in the middle of the queue were scheduled prior to the earlier requests in the front, which were not satisfied for the lack of available subcubes. The delay

TABLE III
Simulation Results of the Allocation Schemes on a 5-Cube
Scheduling discipline : Modified FCFS

Distri-bution	T	delay(d_p)				Job Completion				Efficiency			
		Buddy	Gray	M. Bud.	Free	Buddy	Gray	M. Bud.	Free	Buddy	Gray	M. Bud.	Free
Case-1	100	3.86	3.82	3.67	3.51	88.76	88.56	88.96	89.26	82.406	82.625	82.968	83.719
	200	5.91	5.85	5.67	5.34	185.66	185.68	185.90	186.34	86.062	86.484	86.531	87.281
	300	7.48	7.27	7.19	6.59	283.42	283.66	283.80	284.82	87.500	88.302	88.354	88.863
Case-2	100	6.16	6.42	6.20	5.99	81.92	80.95	81.64	81.85	86.969	87.031	86.437	88.156
	200	12.25	12.45	12.28	12.19	169.04	170.34	169.75	169.63	90.765	91.328	91.078	92.515
	300	21.28	18.91	18.28	18.26	260.54	256.44	257.78	258.28	92.823	93.562	93.250	94.239

Residence time dist.: Case-1: Uniform [3, 7], Case-2: Uniform [3.83, 7.83].
Cube size dist.: Case-1: Uniform, Case-2: Normal.[1]
1) $p_0 = p_4 = 0.098$, $p_1 = p_3 = 0.214$, $p_2 = 0.376$

TABLE IV
Results for Higher Dimension Cubes

Schesule	Dim.	Dist.	delay	Job comp.	Effciency
FCFS	8	Uniform[1]	1.44	193.05	59.912
	8	Normal[2]	13.79	161.46	83.232
	9	Uniform[3]	0.94	193.71	53.277
	9	Biased[4]	17.14	43.55	84.575
Mod. FCFS	8	Uniform[1]	0.62	194.28	60.002
	8	Normal[2]	6.62	182.24	90.029
	9	Uniform[3]	0.41	194.57	53.284
	9	Biased[4]	59.90	75.39	96.824

Time $T = 200$
1) Residence time dist.: Uniform [3, 7].
   $p_0 = p_1 = \cdots = p_7 = 0.125$.
2) Residence time dist.: Uniform [3.25, 7.25].
   $p_3 = p_7 = 0.098$, $p_4 = p_6 = 0.214$, $p_5 = 0.376$.
3) Residence time dist.: Uniform [3, 7].
   $p_0 = p_1 = \cdots = p_8 = 0.1111$.
4) Residence time dist.: Uniform [8.36, 12.36].
   $p_8 = 0.504$, $p_7 = 0.217$, $p_6 = 0.143$, $p_5 = 0.087$, $p_4 = 0.049$.

TABLE V
Comparison Between Noncubic and Cubic Allocation
Scheduling discipline : FCFS

Distri-bution			T				
			100	150	200	250	300
Case-1	total delay	Cubic	10.58	14.89	19.14	23.45	27.69
		N-Cubic	8.14	11.21	14.21	17.83	20.11
	Job comp.	Cubic	79.35	122.17	164.43	208.17	250.00
		N-Cubic	82.73	127.34	171.94	216.78	261.57
	Effi-ciency	Cubic	65.813	66.146	66.390	66.637	66.656
		N-Cubic	67.094	68.042	68.484	68.750	69.125
Case-2	total delay	Cubic	16.44	24.24	31.70	39.07	47.04
		N-Cubic	13.93	20.22	26.35	32.86	38.62
	Job comp.	Cubic	70.50	108.09	146.81	185.22	223.55
		N-Cubic	73.37	113.39	152.98	193.22	234.06
	Effi-ciency	Cubic	70.656	70.896	71.234	71.562	71.510
		N-Cubic	75.125	73.080	73.609	73.175	74.323

Residence time dist.: Case-1: Uniform [3, 7], Case-2: Uniform [3.83, 7.83].
Cube size dist.: Case-1: Uniform, Case-2: Normal.[1]
1) $p_0 = p_4 = 0.098$, $p_1 = p_3 = 0.214$, $p_2 = 0.376$

measured in Table III is different from those of Tables I and II. Since it is possible to allocate a request from the middle of the queue, some earlier requests may remain in the queue with a large potential delay when the clock reaches to the predetermined time T. The total delay can be determined by this potential delay of the requests remaining in the queue. The potential delay for each request in the queue was measured as $T - a_i$, where a_i is the arrival time of the ith request. After the clock reaches the predetermined time T, the potential delay of the requests in the queue was added to D_h. Table III shows that the modified FCFS discipline gives better performance compared to the FCFS scheduling of Table I. This is also confirmed from Table IV that gives the performance measures for higher dimension cubes.

We also simulated the modified free list policy that combines the i-cubes with *only* the members of the nearest nonempty higher dimension cube. The results were *exactly the same* as presented in all the tables using the original algorithm. This clearly shows that the modified deallocation scheme is quite efficient compared to other reported bit-map schemes. It even gives slightly better result than the multiple GC. The reason is that the multiple GC, with its perfect subcube recognition ability, finds a cube according a predetermined sequence of gray codes. In some cases, it splits a higher dimension cube even if there is an exact free cube available for a request. The allocation steps of the free list always preserve the higher dimension cubes if the allocation can be done without splitting. Hence, the free list can allocate a k-cube (if it exists) faster than the other schemes. This reduces the average queueing delay d_h and increases the number of jobs allocated in a given time T. Since the modified free list shows better results than the bit-map schemes, it can be concluded that a faster suboptimal algorithm is better than a perfect but slow algorithm.

Finally, Table V shows the effectiveness of the noncubic (NC) allocation. The algorithm discussed in Section IV-D was used for the NC allocation. First, we decide the cube size of a request according to a given distribution such as uniform or normal. This cube size is used for the cubic allocation. For the NC allocation, we find the exact number of nodes required by a task from the selected cube size assuming that each number in the same dimension has an equal probability. For example, if the selected cube size for the cubic allocation is 3, then one of node sizes 5, 6, 7, and 8 is chosen randomly for the NC request. The data for the cubic and NC schemes are generated using the free list algorithm. The delay used in the Table V is the total delay of all the requests until the last request is scheduled. The NC scheme shows a significant reduction in delay. It also completes more jobs and has better efficiency than the cubic allocation. These advantages of the NC would be more striking if one uses other cubic allocation schemes than the free list.

B. Time Complexity

The ability to have perfect subcube recognition makes the processor allocation scheme quite complex and thus increases the

TABLE VI
FREE LIST SIZE $(T = 300)$

	Cube size	Cube size for different dim.									
		0	1	2	3	4	5	6	7	8	9
Case-1	5	2.19	2.53	2.38	2.00	1.00	1.00				
Case-2	5	1.52	2.31	2.54	2.00	1.00	0.92				
Case-3	5	3.74	3.66	3.09	2.00	1.00	0.54				
Case-4	8	0.00	0.00	0.00	1.19	2.05	2.30	1.94	1.00	0.59	
Case-1	8	1.82	2.16	2.15	2.13	2.15	2.12	2.00	1.00	0.95	
Case-1	9	1.46	2.01	1.99	2.04	2.17	2.09	2.02	1.99	1.00	0.81

Residence time dist.: Case-1: Uniform $[3, 7]$, Case-2: Uniform $[3.83, 7.83]$,
Case-3: Uniform $[8.36, 12.36]$, Case-4: Uniform $[4, 12]$.
Cube size dist.: Case-1: Uniform, Case-2: Normal,[1] Case-3: Biased Normal,[2]
Case-4: Biased Normal.[3]
1) $p_0 = p_4 = 0.098$, $p_1 = p_3 = 0.214$, $p_2 = 0.376$
2) $p_0 = 0.504$, $p_1 = 0.217$, $p_2 = 0.143$, $p_3 = 0.087$, $p_4 = 0.049$
3) $p_3 = 0.45$, $p_4 = 0.25$, $p_5 = 0.15$, $p_6 = 0.10$, $p_7 = 0.05$.

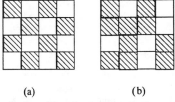

Fig. 5. (a) Distribution of free 0-cubes in a 4-cube system. (b) Distribution of free 1-cubes in a 4-cube system.

time complexity. The multiple GC scheme has time complexity $O\left(\binom{n}{\lfloor n/2 \rfloor} 2^n\right)$. This is because the time complexity of the single GC is $O(2^n)$. As one may need $\binom{n}{\lfloor n/2 \rfloor}$ different GC's for perfect subcube recognition, the worst case complexity becomes $O\left(\binom{n}{\lfloor n/2 \rfloor} 2^n\right)$. Dutt and Hayes proposed two deallocation algorithms [16]. One is a heuristic algorithm without perfect subcube recognition ability and the second algorithm is an optimal algorithm. The time complexity of these algorithms are $O(n2^n)$ and $O\left(2^{3^n}\right)$, respectively.

Now let us analyze the theoretical time complexity of the free list. This is related to the list size. The maximum number of *disjoint* subcubes for dimension i is less than or equal to $3 \times 2^{n-i-2} \cong 2^{n-i}$. Fig. 5 shows the possible free subcubes of dimensions 0 or 1 arranged like a mosaic in a 4-cube system. Addition of any other free cube would increase the free cube size in Fig. 5. Note that the list size for dimension i can grow as large as $O(2^{n-i})$ when all other lists are either empty or have very few free cubes. This is one of the worst case scenarios since almost all the free disjoint cubes are in one dimension. In particular, for dimension 0 or 1, the size becomes too large. If the requests are distributed evenly over many cubes, the free list size would decrease drastically. Now assuming that one of the lower dimension cubes has $O(2^{n-i})$ disjoint cubes and all other cubes are almost empty, step 3-a of the free list deallocation strategy may have $O(n2^{n-i})$ comparisons between cubes of dimension i.[1] Since all other cubes are either empty or have only few cubes, the overall complexity of the deallocation is $O(n2^n)$ for $i = 0$. The complexity of the free list allocation is $O(n)$.

The above timing analysis is mainly of theoretical interest. When the requests are distributed over many cubes, we would show that the deallocation complexity is $O(n^3)$. This argument is valid for most of the cases and gives the average deallocation time. The size of the list is really small, since the strategy always

combined cubes to form a large cube. Table VI shows the size of each list measured using simulation. For each experiment, the simulation finds the largest free list size for each dimension i in a given time frame T. The results are averaged over 100 experiments. The list size for all dimensions is measured after the allocation or deallocation is done. Therefore, the list size for the highest dimension n is not always 1. The various cases in Table VI represents the incoming cube size distribution of the requests. The requests are allocated on an FCFS basis. The results show that the list sizes for all dimensions are very small. Hence, in the following analysis we assume that the total list size is $h \cdot n$ for some constant h. Usually, the h is in the range 2 or 3.

The allocation time is only $O(n)$ because it needs to search for the availability of a k-cube from one of the lists i, for $k \leq i \leq n$. The time complexity of the deallocation algorithm is $O(h \cdot n^3)$. Step 2 of the algorithm takes $O(h \cdot n)$ time units for comparing the released k-cube to all the $O(h \cdot n)$ cubes in the list. Step 3 takes the maximum time since all subcubes (elements) in the free list of dimension i are compared to the elements of the same dimension and the higher dimension cubes, for all dimensions present in the free list. It was shown in Table VI that the total list size is $O(h \cdot n)$. Step 3-a of the deallocation algorithm generates all possible overlapping cubes of dimension i by comparing among themselves. The original h elements of ith cube may grow to $O(n)$ after step 3-a. Hence, the time required to generate the cubes from dimension i and the nearest nonempty higher dimensions is $O(h \cdot n^2)$. There can be n such comparisons for $(n + 1)$ lists maintained for the hypercube of dimension n. This gives the time complexity of step 3-b $O(h \cdot n^3)$. With h in the range 2 or 3, the total deallocation time complexity is $O(n^3)$. This timing analysis takes into consideration the possibility of passing an i-cube to more than one higher dimension cubes for combining.

Let us analyze the time complexity of the modified free list by restricting the comparison between two groups of cubes only. Since step 3-a generates $O(n)$ overlapping cubes, comparison between two adjacent dimensions takes $O(n^2)$ time. With $(n + 1)$ lists for the complete n-cube, there can be n such comparisons. This gives the time complexity $O(n^3)$.

The allocation time complexity of all the bit-map policies is $O(N)$ and deallocation time is $O(2^k)$ where k is the size of released cube. Therefore, under light and moderate load, the free list allocation is faster compared to the other policies. For $n \geq 10$, the $O(n^3)$ time complexity of the free list becomes less compared to $O(2^n)$. The parallel version of the free list can reduce the time complexity to $O(n^2)$, thereby making it more attractive.

[1] We assume that a comparison takes one time unit.

VII. Conclusions

Efficient processor allocation is essential for achieving high performance on a multiprocessor system. In this paper, a processor allocation scheme, based on the *free list policy*, is introduced for the hypercube computers. Using this policy, a requested subcube of dimension k is allocated from a free list of the available subcubes. The other known allocation policies [13]–[15] find a k-cube by combining 2^k free nodes (a bottom-up approach). Our policy differs from the others because of its top-down nature.

It is shown that this policy gives the better system utilization and less delay compared to the previous bit-map schemes. Multiple GC is the only other technique that gives close results to that of the free list. However, both the serial and parallel versions of the multiple GC are more complex than the corresponding free list versions. A slightly modified version of the free list gives the same performance at reduced complexity.

Another advantage of the free list scheme is its fast allocation ability. It takes $O(n)$ time to allocate a k-cube. The allocation time complexity of all other schemes is $O(2^n)$. Hence, if a subcube is already available, the free list can allocate it very fast. Specially, under light and moderate load on the system, it is likely that the system would have a lot of free nodes (assuming that the request sizes are smaller compared to hypercube dimension). The free list would give better results in these circumstances compared to others. If the request sizes are constant or do not have much variation, the complete n-cube would have lists only for those given dimensions. This would make the free list a very effective allocation scheme.

References

[1] E. Chow, H. Madan, *et al.*, "Hyperswitch network for the hypercube computers," in *Proc. 15th Int. Symp. Comput. Architecture,* June 1988, pp. 90–99.

[2] D. A. Reed and D. C. Grunwald, "The performance of multicomputer interconnection networks," *IEEE Comput. Mag.,* pp. 63–73, June 1987.

[3] L. N. Bhuyan and D. P. Agrawal, "Generalized hypercube and hyperbus structures for a computer network," *IEEE Trans. Comput.,* pp. 323–333, Apr. 1984.

[4] L. D. Wittie, "Communication structures for a large multicomputer system," *IEEE Trans. Comput.,* vol. C-30, pp. 264–273, Apr. 1981.

[5] M. S. Chen and K. G. Shin, "Embedding of interacting task modules into a hypercube," in *Proc. 2nd Hypercube Conf.,* Oct. 1986, pp. 122–129.

[6] B. Becker and H. U. Simon, "How robust is the n-cube?," in *Proc. 27th Annu. Symp. Foundations Comput. Sci.,* Oct. 1986, pp. 283–291.

[7] J. Rattner, "Concurrent processing: A new direction in scientific computing," in *AFIPS Conf. Proc.,* vol. 54, NCC, 1985, pp. 157–166.

[8] J. P. Hayes, T. N. Mudge, *et al.*, "Architecture of a hypercube supercomputer," in *Proc. Int. Conf. Parallel Processing,* Aug. 1986, pp. 653–660.

[9] J. C. Peterson *et al.*, "The Mark III hypercube ensemble concurrent processor," in *Proc. Int. Conf. Parallel Processing,* Aug. 1985, pp. 71–73.

[10] W. D. Hillis, *The Connection Machine.* Cambridge, MA: MIT Press, 1985.

[11] Y. Saad and M. H. Schultz, "Topological properties of hypercube," *IEEE Trans. Comput.,* vol. 37, pp. 867–872, July 1988.

[12] K. C. Knowlton, "A fast storage allocator," *Commun. ACM,* vol. 8, pp. 623–625, Oct. 1965.

[13] NCUBE Corp., "NCUBE/ten: An overview," Beaverton, OR, Nov. 1985.

[14] M. S. Chen and K. G. Shin, "Processor allocation in an *N*-cube multiprocessor using gray codes," *IEEE Trans. Comput.,* vol. C-36, pp. 1396–1407, Dec. 1987.

[15] A. Al-Dhelaan and B. Bose, "A new strategy for processors allocation in an *N*-cube multiprocessor," in *Proc. Int. Phoenix Conf. Comput. Commun.,* Mar. 1989, pp. 114–118.

[16] S. Dutt and J. P. Hayes, "On allocating subcubes in a hypercube multiprocessor," in *Proc. 3rd Conf. Hypercube,* Jan. 1988, pp. 801–810.

[17] E. J. McClusky, *Logic Design Principles.* Englewood Cliffs, NJ: Prentice-Hall, 1986.

Jong Kim (S'89) received the B.S. degree in electronic engineering from Hanyang University, Seoul, Korea, in 1981, and the M.S. degree in computer science from the Korea Advanced Institute of Science and Technology, Seoul, Korea, in 1983.

Since 1987, he has been working towards the Ph.D. degree in the Department of Electrical and Computer Engineering at The Pennsylvania State University. From 1983 to 1986, he was a system engineer in Korea Securities Computer Corporation, Seoul, Korea. His major areas of interest are fault-tolerant computing, performance evaluation, and parallel and distributed computing.

Chita R. Das (S'84–M'86) received the M.S. degree in electrical engineering from Regional Engineering College, Rourkela, Sambalpur University, India, in 1981, and the Ph.D. degree in computer science from the Center for Advanced Computer Studies, University of Southwestern Louisiana, Lafayette, in 1986.

He is currently an Assistant Professor in the Department of Electrical and Computer Engineering at The Pennsylvania State University. His main areas of interests are parallel and distributed computing, interconnection network, performance evaluation, and fault-tolerant computing.

Woei Lin (S'80–M'85) received the B.S. degree in control engineering from National Chiao-Tung University, Taiwan, in 1978, and the M.S. and the Ph.D. degree in electrical and computer engineering from the University of Texas at Austin, in 1982 and 1985, respectively.

He is currently an Associate Professor in the Department of Electrical Engineering, University of Hawaii at Manoa. Prior to joining the University of Hawaii, he was a faculty member at The Pennsylvania State University from 1985 to 1988. From 1978 to 1980, he served in the army in Taiwan as an officer partly for digital system maintenance. He was a Teaching Assistant from 1981 to 1984 and a Research Assistant from 1984 to 1985 in the University of Texas at Austin. His research interests include multiprocessor systems, parallel algorithms, interconnection networks, and parallel programming environments.

Partitioning and Permuting Properties of CC-Banyan Networks

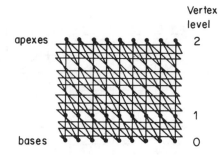

Fig. 1. A (3, 2) CC-banyan.

VLADIMIR CHERKASSKY AND MIROSLAW MALEK

Abstract—A multicomputer network, called rectangular CC-banyan, is presented and formally defined. A graph-theoretic approach is used to study this network's permuting and partitioning properties. It is shown that a CC-banyan has a modular structure and hence can be recursively defined. A method for evaluation of the total number of permutations in CC-banyans is presented. Using this method, we derive the analytical expressions for the number of permutations in CC-banyans with fan-outs two and three.

Index Terms—Banyan, graph modeling, multistage interconnection network, nonequivalent network, permutation, recursive network.

I. Introduction

There is a growing interest in multicomputer systems for increased performance and improved reliability. The operation of these systems is critically dependent on the interconnection network which connects system resources such as processors and memories (or computers). As a result of the rapid advances in LSI and VLSI technology, extensive research is being conducted on multicomputer systems [1]. Many of these systems are based on multistage interconnection networks (MIN's).

Various MIN's implemented with 2×2 switching elements, such as baseline, modified data manipulator, flip, omega, indirect binary n-cube, and regular rectangular SW-banyan ($s = f = 2$) are known to be topologically equivalent to each other [2], [3]. These equivalent networks possess a "buddy property," i.e., the outputs of two switching elements at stage i are connected as inputs to only two switching elements at the $(i + 1)$th stage [3].

Recent studies [1], [4] and the performance of the Texas Reconfigurable Array Computer (TRAC) [5] show that MIN's based on switching elements with fan-out and/or spread greater than two (e.g., banyans with f and s greater than two) could be more efficient and useful in many applications. Banyans [6] represent a large class of interconnection networks. An SW-banyan with fan-out two describes a class of equivalent MIN's implemented with 2×2 switching elements. Many nonequivalent MIN's [7] represent special cases of cylindrical cross-hatch (CC) banyans [6]. It has been shown in [8] that the so-called "nonequivalent" delta network [9] is isomorphic to a CC-banyan, and that the ADM network [10] can be viewed as two overlapping CC-banyans. Also, a CC-banyan with fan-out 4 and 3 stages is a barrel switch network [11].

Manuscript received August 1, 1984; revised October 30, 1987. This work was supported in part by the Graduate School at the University of Minnesota, IBM Corporation and the Office of Naval Research under Grant N0014-86-K-0554.

V. Cherkassky is with the Department of Electrical Engineering, University of Minnesota, Minneapolis, MN 55455.

M. Malek is with the Department of Electrical and Computer Engineering, University of Texas, Austin, TX 78712.

IEEE Log Number 8718955.

Permuting and partitioning properties of SW-banyans [6], [12], [13], and of equivalent MIN's [14]–[16], have been extensively studied with emphasis on formulating various conditions on classes of permutations (or partitionings) that can be supported by a given network. In this correspondence, we focus on nonequivalent networks. We analyze the recursive structure and evaluate the total number of permutations supported by a CC-banyan.

II. System Description

The system model is composed of the *resources* and the *interconnection network*. We use the rectangular CC-banyan interconnection network to study system mapping properties. This study is general and the results are applicable for any fan-out f and any number of levels L.

In the following, we give a brief description of CC-banyans. A banyan network is a network with a unique path from each source (input) to each sink (output) vertex. A multistage interconnection network is a network in which vertices can be arranged in stages, with all the source vertices at level 0, and all the outputs at stage i connected to inputs at stage $i + 1$. An L-stage banyan, or an L-stage MIN, is a network in which every path from any source (base) to any sink (apex) has length L. An (f, L) banyan is an L-stage banyan in which the in-degree (spread s) of every intermediate vertex equals its out-degree (fan-out f). Note that in this correspondence, the term "stage" is used to denote a level of edges. Thus, an (f, L) banyan has L stages (levels of edges) and $L + 1$ vertex levels (see Fig. 1).

(f, L) regular rectangular CC-banyan: An (f, L) banyan in which there is an edge from vertex i at vertex level $k + 1$ to a vertex j at vertex level k whenever $j = (i + mf^k) \bmod f^L$ for $m = 0, 1, 2, \ldots, f - 1, 0 \leqslant i, j \leqslant f^L - 1$ and $0 \leqslant k \leqslant L - 1$.

Examples of $(3, 2)$ and $(2, 3)$ regular rectangular CC-banyans are shown in Figs. 1 and 2, respectively. The vertex levels are numbered from bases (level 0) to apexes (level L). The interpretation of the network graph is the one commonly used with respect to banyan networks: a vertex represents a tie point and an edge represents a switch contact. According to this interpretation, connections through vertices in a banyan graph are *mutually exclusive*.

An example of a multicomputer system based on a rectangular CC-banyan network is shown in Fig. 2. In this system, each computer (processor with local memory) is attached to both sides of an (f, L) CC-banyan. There is a single path between each ordered pair of computers (without traversing through an intermediate third computer) and the communication through the network is *unidirectional*. The control of the system may be distributed (by the use of self-routing) or centralized, and is capable of executing one-to-one and one-to-many connections. The labeling and routing schemes for a system based on a rectangular CC-banyan are discussed in [17]. It is also worth noting that the routing scheme in CC-banyan uses relative addressing, based on the difference between destination and source address, in contrast to the systems based on SW-banyans which use absolute addressing.

Reprinted from *IEEE Trans. Computers*, Vol. 38, No. 2, Feb. 1989, pp. 274–278. Copyright © 1989 by The Institute of Electrical and Electronics Engineers, Inc. All rights reserved.

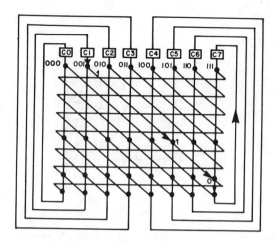

Fig. 2. Multicomputer system based on a (2, 3) CC-banyan with an example of routing from $C1$ to $C7$.

III. RECURSIVE STRUCTURE OF CC-BANYANS

Many known MIN's, such as baseline, SW-banyan, and Benes network, can be constructed recursively. This property enables the modular structure of MIN's and is useful in the analysis of partitioning and permuting properties.

Whereas the original definition of CC-banyans given in Section II is not recursive, it will be shown here that CC-banyans can be recursively defined. Conceptually, it is convenient to view an (f, L) rectangular CC-banyan as a union of L stages, where each stage represents a bipartite graph [7]. For example, three bipartite graphs for (2, 3) rectangular CC-banyan are shown in Fig. 3(a).

Theorem 1: In an (f, L) rectangular CC-banyan, a bipartite graph of stage $k(0 \leqslant k \leqslant L - 1)$ contains f^k components (disjoint subgraphs).

Proof: According to the definition of an (f, L) CC-banyan, there is an edge from vertex i at vertex level $k + 1$ to a vertex j at vertex level k if and only if

$$j = (i + mf^k) \bmod f^L \qquad \text{for } m = 0, 1, 2, \cdots, f-1.$$

Hence, the vertices number i and j, such that $i \neq j \bmod f^k$, belong to different components and the total number of components is f^k. [ ]

For example, components of stages of a (2, 3) CC-banyan are shown in Fig. 3(b).

Corollary 1: In an (f, L) rectangular CC-banyan, the bipartite graphs of all L stages are not isomorphic (to each other).

Proof: As follows from the proof of Theorem 1, bipartite graphs of different stages contain different numbers of components. Hence, they are not isomorphic. [ ]

Note that in the case of equivalent MIN's (e.g., SW-banyan, baseline, omega) the bipartite graphs of all stages are isomorphic, since these MIN's have the so-called "buddy property" [3], i.e., in the case of fan-out $f = 2$ each pair of vertices at level i is connected with only one pair of vertices at level $i + 1$.

Corollary 2: Each component of stage $k(0 \leqslant k \leqslant L - 1)$ has $2*f^{L-k}$ vertices.

Proof: In an (f, L) CC-banyan, there are f^L vertices at each vertex level and they belong to f^k different components. Hence, each stage-k component has $2*f^{L-k}$ vertices. [ ]

Corollary 3: In an (f, L) rectangular CC-banyan, the bipartite graph of stage 0, at the base side, contains one component; and the bipartite graph of stage $(L - 1)$, at the apex side, contains f^{L-1} components, which are $(f \times f)$ crossbar graphs.

Proof: The proof follows immediately from Theorem 1. [ ]

Before we proceed with the analysis of recursive structure of CC-banyans, note that the recursive decomposition of a CC-banyan into networks of smaller size may be only possible from the base side. This is due to the fact that the bipartite graph of stage 0, at the base

side, always contains one component, according to Corollary 3. In contrast to CC-banyans, rectangular SW-banyans and networks equivalent to them can be recursively decomposed from either side [3].

Theorem 2: An $(f, L + 1)$ CC-banyan can be recursively decomposed from the base side into f disjoint (f, L) CC-banyans.

Proof: Apply Theorem 1 successively to the kth stage of an $(f, L + 1)$ CC-banyan, for $k = 0, 1, \cdots, L - 1$. As follows from the definition of CC-banyan, the vertices numbered $(m + jf) \bmod f^{L+1}$, where $j = 0, 1, \cdots, f^L$, belong to the f disjoint (f, L) CC-banyans corresponding to different values of parameter $m = 0, 1, \cdots, f - 1$. [ ]

Based on the method used in the proof of Theorem 2, we give the following recursive definition of CC-banyans.

Definition: An $(f, 1)$ CC-banyan is simply an $(f \times f)$ crossbar graph. An $(f, L + 1)$ CC-banyan is constructed from f (f, L) CC-banyans by the following procedure:

1. Assign a number $m(m = 0, 1, \cdots, f - 1)$ to each (f, L) CC-banyan.
2. In the mth (f, L) CC-banyan, label the vertices at every vertex level by the numbers $m + jf$, where $j = 0, 1, 2, \cdots, f^L$ [see Fig. 4(a)].
3. Form stage 0 (base stage) of the composite $(f, L + 1)$ CC-banyan by connecting the bases numbered i ($i = 0, 1, \cdots, f^{L+1} - 1$) to the bases of the component (f, L) CC-banyans numbered $(i + mf) \bmod f^{L+1}$ for all $m = 0, 1, \cdots, f - 1$ [see Fig. 4(b)].
4. Rearrange the vertices of the composite $(f, L + 1)$ CC-banyan in the order of increasing label numbers, thus resulting in the conventional graphical representation for CC-banyans [see Fig. 4(c)]. [ ]

IV. PERMUTING PROPERTIES

In this section, we evaluate the number of various permutations performable by an (f, L) CC-banyan in one pass. We view an (f, L) rectangular CC-banyan as a permutation network that performs a one-to-one mapping (permutation) of a set of N apexes onto a set of N bases ($N = f^L$).

Since in an (f, L) regular rectangular (SW- or CC-) banyan network, every input–output connection, or base–apex path, is unique, the total number of distinct permutations is equal to the product of all permutations performable by each stage:

$$P = \prod_{k=0}^{L-1} P_k \qquad (1)$$

where P_k is the number of permutations performable at stage k.

According to Theorem 1, a bipartite graph of stage k contains f^k identical disjoint subgraphs. Let $C_{f,k}$ denote the number of permutations performable by each of f^k disjoint subgraphs of stage k. The indexes indicate that this number, generally, depends on both fan-out f and stage k. Therefore, expression (1) can be written as

$$P = \prod_{k=0}^{L-1} (C_{f,k})^{f^k}$$

where f^k is the number of disjoint subgraphs (components) at stage k (see Theorem 1).

In view of Corollary 3, the above expression can be simplified since stage $(L - 1)$ subgraphs (components) are $f \times f$ crossbar graphs, capable of $f!$ permutations:

$$P = (f!)^{f^{L-1}} * \prod_{k=0}^{L-2} (C_{f,k})^{f^k}. \qquad (2)$$

An exact analytical evaluation for $C_{f,k}$ does not seem to be feasible for an arbitrary fan-out f. However, we present a general approach which enables systematic enumeration of all permutations perform-

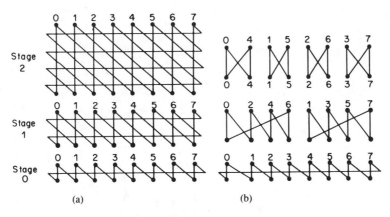

(a)

(b)

Fig. 3. Bipartite graphs (a) and disjoint subgraphs (b) of a (2, 3) CC-banyan.

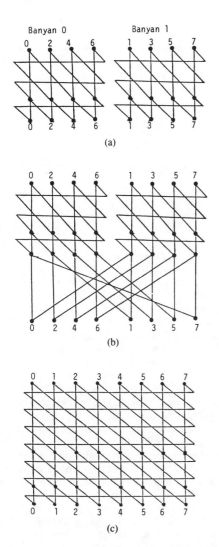

Banyan 0   Banyan 1

(a)

(b)

(c)

Fig. 4. Recursive construction of a (2, 3) CC-banyan.

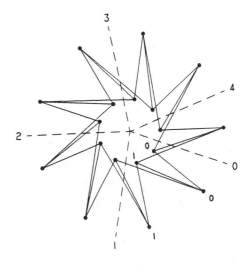

Fig. 5. Circular diagram of stage 0 of a (3, 2) CC-banyan.

able by a stage-k subgraph. Our analysis uses unconventional representation for a stage-k subgraph, in which the vertices of a bipartite subgraph are located on the two concentric circles corresponding to the vertex levels k and $k + 1$. An example of such symmetrical circular representation, or *circular diagram*, is shown in Fig. 5. Consider a circular diagram of a stage-k subgraph. As follows from Corollary 2, this subgraph performs permutations on f^{L-k} numbers. A permutation in this subgraph is a one-to-one mapping of its level-$(k + 1)$ vertices onto its level-k vertices. Every

permutation in a subgraph is uniquely defined by a set of f^{L-k} edges corresponding to this mapping. It is shown later in this section that due to a symmetric structure of circular diagrams, a set of edges corresponding to a permutation has some interesting invariant properties, which make possible the systematic enumeration of all permutations. Thus, our approach is to analyze the properties of circular diagrams corresponding to permutations in CC-banyans. Before we proceed with the analysis, we introduce several useful concepts related to circular diagrams.

A stage-k circular diagram may be divided into *radial sectors* of equal size $(f - 1)$ using *radial cuts* as shown in Fig. 5. The radial cuts and radial sectors are numbered clockwise from 0 to $(f^{L-k} - 1)/(f - 1)$, so that a radial sector m is formed by radial cuts m and $m + 1$, $m = 0, 1, \cdots, (f^{L-k} - 1)/(f - 1)$. Then each of the sectors has $(f - 1)$ vertices, and the last sector has only one vertex. Consider a set of edges corresponding to a permutation in a circular diagram. An edge corresponding to a permutation is called a *cross edge* if it crosses a radial cut in a circular diagram. Now we can state an important invariant property of permutations in CC-banyans.

Theorem 3: For any stage-k subgraph permutation in a circular diagram, all radial cuts have the same number of cross edges i ($0 \leqslant i \leqslant f - 1$).

Proof: Let i_m be the number of cross edges crossing radial cut m. Consider the radial sector of size $f - 1$ formed by radial cuts m and $m + 1$. In this sector, denote by j the number of "inner" edges that do not cross radial cuts. Then $f - 1$ vertices at vertex level k in this sector can be incident either to i_m cross edges or to j "inner" edges. Hence, $f - 1 = i_m + j$. Similarly, $f - 1$ vertices at vertex level $k + 1$ in this

633

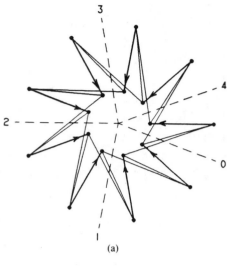

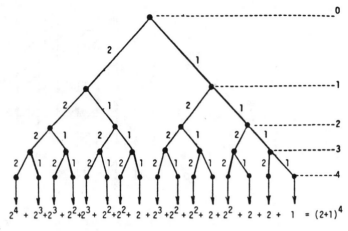

$$2^4 + 2^3+2^3 + 2^2+2^3 + 2^2+2^2 + 2 + 2^3+2^2 + 2^2+2 + 2 + 2^2 + 2 + 2 + 1 = (2+1)^4$$

Fig. 7. Decision tree to enumerate all permutations with the number of cross edges $i = 1$.

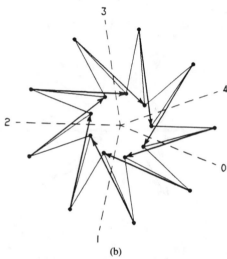

Fig. 6. Example of permutations in a circular diagram. (a) Identity permutation $v \to v$ (0 cross edges). (b) Cyclic shift $v \to v + 2$ (two cross edges).

sector can be incident either to i_{m+1} cross edges or to j ''inner'' edges, and $f - 1 = i_{m+1} + j$. Therefore, $i_m = i_{m+1}$. [ ]

An example of two different permutations and corresponding cross edges in a circular diagram is given in Fig. 6.

Theorem 4: In a circular diagram of a stage-k subgraph, there exists only one permutation corresponding to 0 or $(f - 1)$ cross edges; i.e., $C_{f,k}^0 = C_{f,k}^{f-1} = 1$.

Proof: The proof follows immediately from the structure of a circular diagram. Specifically, the identity permutation $v \to v$ corresponds to zero cross edges; and the cyclic shift permutation $v \to (v + f - 1) \bmod f^{L-k}$ corresponds to $(f - 1)$ cross edges (see Fig. 6). [ ]

Corollary 4: A stage-k subgraph of a CC-banyan with fan-out two can perform only two permutations, regardless of k: $C_{2,k} = 2$.

Proof: For CC-banyan with fan-out $f = 2$, the number of cross edges in a circular diagram may be only 0 or 1, since $f - 1 = 1$. According to Theorem 4, there are only two permutations. [ ]

Theorem 5: The total number of permutations performable by rectangular CC-banyan with fan-out $f = 2$ and number of stages L is

$$P_2 = 2^{2^L - 1}.$$

Proof: As follows from Corollary 4, $C_{2,k} = 2$, regardless of k. The total number of permutations immediately follows from (2):

$$P_2 = \prod_{k=0}^{L-1} 2^{2^k} = 2^{2^L - 1}. \qquad [\ ]$$

A systematic enumeration of all permutations in the case of arbitrary f uses a ''divide-and-conquer'' approach based on Theorems 1 and 3. In view of Theorem 3, the number of permutations performable by a stage-k subgraph can be expressed as

$$C_{f,k} = \sum_{i=0}^{f-1} C_{f,k}^i.$$

In view of Theorem 4, the above expression is simplified to

$$C_{f,k} = 2 + \sum_{i=1}^{f-2} C_{f,k}^i. \qquad (3)$$

The value of $C_{f,k}^i (1 \leqslant i \leqslant f - 2)$ can be found by enumeration of all permutations having the same number of cross edges i. A method for a systematic enumeration of such permutations is discussed below. Consider a set of permutations having the same number of cross edges $i (1 \leqslant i \leqslant f - 2)$. We may enumerate all permutations in a circular diagram by choosing, successively, i cross edges for every radial cut m, $m = 0, 1, 2, \cdots, (f^{L-k} - 1)/(f - 1)$. Since i cross edges in a radial cut $(m + 1)$ can be chosen independently from i cross edges in a preceding cut m, we can construct a tree of all possible outcomes (decision tree) for a systematic enumeration of all permutations.

We illustrate this method using an example of CC-banyan with fan-out $f = 3$. The only nontrivial case when the number of cross edges $i = 1$ has to be considered, since $C_{3,k}^0 = C_{3,k}^2 = 1$. We construct a decision tree to enumerate various possibilities for the choice of cross edges for all radial cuts for $i = 1$, as shown in Fig. 7. In this decision tree, a tree level corresponds to the radial cut number. Since every sector has $f - 1 = 2$ vertices, a stage-k vertex incident to a cross edge can be chosen in two different ways, and the decision tree fan-out is two. If the vertices in each sector are numbered from 0 to $f - 2$, as shown in Fig. 5, then the vertex v $(0 \leqslant v \leqslant f - 2)$ can be incident to $f - 1 - v = 2 - v$ cross edges. Therefore, two different choices of cross edges can be made in the case when vertex $v = 0$, and only one cross edge can be chosen if $v = 1$. Hence, we assign the weights 1 and 2 correspondingly to every ''right'' and ''left'' outgoing link in the decision tree. The total number of permutations can be found by adding the weights of all leaves of the tree, where the weight of each leaf is a product of all link weights along the path from root to this leaf (see Fig. 7). Since we may choose outgoing links (with weights 1 or 2) independently at every tree level, the total weight represents a binomial sum:

$$\sum_{j=0}^{h} \binom{h}{j} 2^j * 1^{h-j} = 3^h$$

where h is the decision tree height, or the number of radial cuts, whose i cross edges can be chosen independently:

$$h = (f^{L-k} - 1)/(f - 1).$$

Therefore, the number of permutations having the number of cross edges $i = 1$ in a stage-k subgraph of an $(3, L)$ CC-banyan is

$$C_{3,k}^1 = 3^{(3^{L-k}-1)/2}, \qquad 0 \leqslant k \leqslant L - 2. \tag{4}$$

Now we can evaluate the total number of permutations in CC-banyan with fan-out 3.

Theorem 6: The number of permutations in an (f, L) CC-banyan with fan-out $f = 3$ is

$$P = (3!)^{3^{L-1}} * \prod_{k=0}^{L-2} [2 + 3^{(3^{L-k}-1)/2}]^{3^k}.$$

Proof: The expression for the total number of permutations follows immediately from (2), (3), and (4). [ ]

The method of decision trees can also be used for enumeration of all permutations in the case of general fan-out f. We have been able to evaluate the number of permutations in CC-banyans with fan-out $f = 4$. However, the process of constructing decision trees becomes quite complex and elaborate for large values of f. This is due to the fact that the analysis of all possible permutations in a radial sector of size $(f - 1)$ becomes a complex combinatorial problem by itself, when f is large. Even so, for practical purposes, the number of permutations for larger fan-outs can be easily obtained by combining analytical expressions (2) and (3) with computer-generated exhaustive enumeration for $C_{f,k}^i$.

V. Conclusions

In this correspondence, we presented a graph-theoretic approach to the analysis of rectangular CC-banyan networks with an arbitrary fan-out f and an arbitrary number of stages L. It is shown that CC-banyans, like many other networks (e.g., SW-banyans, Benes networks) can be constructed recursively from the networks of smaller size. This recursiveness enables the modular structure of CC-banyans and can be used in the analysis of its partitioning properties.

We also presented a general approach to the analysis of permuting properties of CC-banyans. The analytical expressions for the number of permutations performable by CC-banyan with fan-outs 2 and 3 are derived. In the case of general fan-out f, we proposed a method, based on decision tree analysis, for a systematic enumeration of all permutations.

References

[1] G. J. Lipovski and M. Malek, *Parallel Computing.* New York: Wiley-Interscience, 1987.

[2] C. -L. Wu and T. Y. Feng, "On a class of multistage interconnection networks," *IEEE Trans. Comput.*, vol. C-29, pp. 694–702, Aug. 1980.

[3] D. P. Agrawal, "Graph theoretical analysis and design of multistage interconnection networks," *IEEE Trans. Comput.*, vol. C-32, pp. 637–648, July 1983.

[4] V. Cherkassky, "Performance of non-rectangular multistage interconnection networks," in *Proc. Int. Conf. Distribut. Comput. Syst.*, May 1986, pp. 2–7.

[5] U. V. Premkumar, R. Kapur, M. Malek, G. J. Lipovski, and P. Horne, "Design and implementation of the banyan interconnection network in TRAC," in *AFIPS Conf. Proc.*, vol. 49, NCC, Los Angeles, CA, 1980, pp. 643–653.

[6] L. R. Goke and G. J. Lipovski, "Banyan networks for partitioning multiprocessor system," in *Proc. 1st Annu. Symp. Comput. Architecture*, Dec. 1973, pp. 21–28.

[7] D. P. Agrawal and S.-C. Kim, "On non-equivalent multistage interconnection networks," in *Proc. 1981 Int. Conf. Parallel Processing*, Aug. 1981, pp. 234–237.

[8] V. Cherkassky and E. Opper, "Fault diagnosis and permuting properties of CC-banyan networks," in *Proc. Real-Time Syst. Symp.*, Dec. 1984, pp. 175–183.

[9] J. H. Patel, "Performance of processor–memory interconnections for multiprocessors," *IEEE Trans. Comput.*, vol. C-30, pp. 771–770, Oct. 1981.

[10] R. J. McMillen and H. J. Siegel, "Routing schemes for the augmented data manipulator network in MIMD system," *IEEE Trans. Comput.*, vol. C-31, pp. 1202–1214, Dec. 1982.

[11] G. H. Barnes, R. M. Brown, M. Kato, D. J. Kuck, D. L. Slotnik, and R. A. Stokes, "The ILLIAC IV computer," *IEEE Trans. Comput.*, vol. C-17, pp. 746–757, Aug. 1968.

[12] U. V. Premkumar and J. C. Browne, "Resource allocation in rectangular SW-banyans," in *Proc. 9th Annu. Symp. Comput. Architecture*, Apr. 1982, pp. 326–333.

[13] V. Cherkassky and M. Malek, "On permuting properties of regular rectangular SW-banyans," *IEEE Trans. Comput.*, vol. C-34, pp. 542–546, June 1985.

[14] H. J. Siegel, "The theory underlying the partitioning of permutation networks," *IEEE Trans. Comput.*, vol. C-29, pp. 791–801, Sept. 1980.

[15] C. Wu and T. Feng, "The reverse-exchange interconnection network," *IEEE Trans. Comput.*, vol. C-29, pp. 801–811, Sept. 1980.

[16] D. C. Opferman and N. T. Tsao-Wu, "On a class of rearrangeable switching networks, parts I and II," *Bell Syst. Tech. J.*, pp. 1579–1618, May–June 1971.

[17] E. Opper, M. Malek, and G. J. Lipovski, "Resource allocation in rectangular CC-banyans," in *Proc. 10th Annu. Symp. Comput. Architecture*, June 1983, pp. 178–184.

OPTIMIZING TASK MIGRATION TRANSFERS USING MULTISTAGE CUBE NETWORKS

Thomas Schwederski
Institute for Microelectronics Stuttgart
Allmandring 30a
D-7000 Stuttgart 80, West Germany

Howard Jay Siegel
hj@ecn.purdue.edu
Parallel Processing Laboratory
School of Electrical Engineering
Purdue University
West Lafayette, IN 47907, USA

Thomas L. Casavant
tomc@eng.uiowa.edu
Dept. of Electrical and Computer Engineering
University of Iowa
Iowa City, IA 52242, USA

Abstract -- As hardware and software technology progresses, the interest in large-scale parallel processing systems is increasing. Making such a system partitionable into independent subsystems has many advantages. To maximize these benefits, it may be necessary to move (migrate) a job from one submachine (partition) to another. Here, machines based on multistage cube networks are considered. Assume the task is to be migrated from a given set of K source PEs, P_s, to a given set of K destination PEs, P_d. A mapping to determine which PE in P_d is to receive data from each PE in P_s is given. It is proven that this mapping will allow the task migration to be performed in the minimum amount of time. An equation for determining this minimum time is derived. The results are shown for both packet- and circuit-switched multistage cube networks. The techniques presented can be used as part of a strategy for making decisions as to whether to migrate a task and which partitions to use as source and destination of the migration.

1. Introduction

This research builds on, but is distinct from, the work presented in [19]. The comments on motivation in this section, the qualitative discussion in Section 2, the model in Section 3, and the terminology in Section 4 are needed background material based on [19], and are included here so that this paper is self-contained. The results in Sections 5 and 6 are new and are the contributions of this paper.

As hardware and software technology progresses, the interest in large-scale parallel processing systems is increasing. Making such a system partitionable into independent subsystems has many advantages. These include exploitation of subtask parallelism, allowing multiple simultaneous users, and facilitating more efficient utilization of resources [22]. To maximize these benefits, it may be necessary to move (migrate) a job from one submachine (partition) to another. Here it is assumed that memory is physically distributed, i.e., each processor has some local memory associated with it, forming a **PE** (processing element), as is the case in most current large-scale parallel systems. Existing commercial and research distributed memory parallel machines that are partitionable to some degree (i.e., they can be subdivided into independent submachines, and each of these machines can perform a separate task) include the BBN Butterfly* [6], Connection Machine 2 [10, 24], IBM RP3* [16, 17], Intel iPSC/2 [13], NCube system [9], and PASM [22].

Task migration is the movement of a task (or subtask) executing on one **partition** (set of PEs) to another partition. The area of task migration in partitionable systems has received little attention because only recently have large-scale partitionable parallel systems become available. The overhead of task migration is studied here. In particular, the amount of time required to transfer data for the migration is investigated. This work builds on [19], deriving a new methodology that is proven optimal for both packet- and circuit-switched multistage cube networks. An equation for determining this minimum time is derived. The techniques presented can be used as part of a strategy for making decisions as to whether to migrate a task and which partitions to use as source and destination of the migration. These research results are applicable to MIMD, partitionable-SIMD, and partitionable-SIMD/MIMD systems that use multistage cube networks. This research is motivated by the study of the PASM parallel processing system [7, 22].

Partition restructuring, the movement of small tasks to make larger partitions available, is one motivation for task migration. In parallel processing systems with cube interconnection networks, the ways in which processors can be combined into independent submachines obey certain restrictions [20]. As a consequence, busy partitions and/or faulty PEs can cause a fragmentation problem that prohibits larger partitions from being formed. Depending on the situation, the migration of a task from one partition to another may make available a larger size partition.

This research was supported in part by the Office of Naval Research under grant no. N00014-90-J-1483, by the National Science Foundation under grant no. CCR-8809600 and CCR-8704826, and by the Naval Ocean Systems Center under the High Performance Computing Block, ONT.

*These machines can use a shared memory addressing scheme, but the memories are physically distributed with each memory associated with one local processor.

Consider a hypercube network with eight nodes, as illustrated in Fig. 1 (the situation is similar for a multistage cube network). If an independent partition with four nodes is desired, all four nodes must lie on the same surface of the cube. For example, nodes 1, 3, 5, and 7 can form a partition of size four. However, if two one-node tasks occupy nodes 0 and 7, each of the six surfaces contains one task. No size four partition can be formed, even though six nodes are available. By moving one task, e.g., by moving the task in node 0 to node 4, a size four partition becomes possible, consisting of nodes 0, 1, 2, and 3. This migration can result in an increase of the overall machine performance, or it can be used to meet real-time constraints that apply to the incoming task.

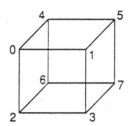

Fig. 1: Three-dimensional cube structure, with vertices labeled from 0 to 7 in binary.

A second motivation is load balancing [3]. Consider a parallel processing system that permits multiprocessing in its processors. For example, if a partition A shares its time between five tasks, while another partition B of the same size has only three tasks, migration of one task from A to B may represent a more favorable distribution of system load.

The task migration mechanism is also applicable to certain "fork" (spawning) situations. For example, if a task needs to spawn a copy of itself onto a partition of equal size, this is analogous to migrating the task.

Section 2 discusses the parameters of task migration qualitatively. The system model that is used to analyze task migration is presented in Section 3. In Section 4, terminology and parameters to describe task migration in multistage cube networks are defined. Section 5 derives the lower time bounds for task migrations. In Section 6, a mapping between source partition and destination partition PEs is given and proven to minimize task transfer time.

2. Qualitative Discussion of Task Migration Overhead

Several phases can be identified during the migration of a task from a source partition to a destination partition in a distributed memory machine. First, a decision must be made whether to migrate a task, and to which destination to migrate. In some situations, for this decision, the migration overhead must be known so that a task is migrated only if the migration cost is outweighed by the migration gain (this may require estimating the expected completion time of a task, techniques for which are outside of the scope of this paper). If a task can be migrated to one of several destinations, the cost of migration to each of these must be known so that the best choice can be made. Furthermore, there may be more than one task

which can be selected to be migrated. Making the migration decision might require computing resources. These are available, however, because a migration can be performed only if free resources (i.e., the potential destination of the migrating task) exist. The decision could be part of an overall automatic system reconfiguration scheme [4].

After the decision has been made, the task currently active in the source partition P_s must be suspended, and the destination partition P_d must be allocated. All necessary information must then be transferred from P_s through the interconnection network to P_d. The time to accomplish the data transfer depends on a combination of the amount of data to be transmitted, the location of source and destination partitions, which source PE is associated with each destination PE, the use of the network by other tasks, the type of interconnection network, and system implementation details. After the data transfer has been completed, the source partition is freed. The system controller can reassign it to a new task, usually as part of a larger partition. At P_d, the migrated task is resumed, and the migration process is completed. The components of the migration process are overviewed in [18].

In general, the data transfers will be the most significant component of the migration cost. Furthermore, it is relatively straightforward to determine the migration costs associated with the suspension and resumption of a task compared to the complexity of determining the cost of data transfers needed for migrating the task. This is a result of the fact that migration messages may conflict with one another in the network and with messages issued by other tasks. Here, only the transfer time of moving a task from a source partition to a destination partition is examined; interference from other tasks is not considered. This is because: (1) it is assumed that two simultaneous migrations would rarely occur, and, furthermore, two that would interfere with one another would be serialized, and (2) interference with normal inter-PE message traffic generated by task(s) executing in partition(s) that the task migration "passes through" is additive in nature and very limited relative to the task migration traffic. In contrast, poor task migration choices can increase transfer time by a multiplicative factor (e.g., by two in the example in Section 4). Migration time using multistage cube networks is studied here (hypercube systems were considered in [5]).

3. System Model

In this section, the model of parallel systems and multistage cube networks used here is briefly overviewed to define the terminology to be employed. It is assumed that the reader is familiar with the basic SIMD and MIMD models of parallelism [8], as well as with the multistage cube network [20, 21].

The **partitionable-SIMD/MIMD** machine organization shown in Fig. 2 is used as the general system model. It consists of $N = 2^n$ PEs numbered 0 through $N-1$. The binary representation of a PE number P is denoted $p_{n-1}p_{n-2}\cdots p_1 p_0$. PEs communicate with each other through an interconnection network. Sets of PEs can be grouped to form a partition; the ways in which partitions may be formed depends on the interconnection network and is described below. Each partition can operate in

SIMD or in MIMD mode and switch between modes. A **multiple-SIMD** machine is similar except MIMD operation is not permitted. The research described here is applicable to MIMD, multiple-SIMD, and partitionable-SIMD/MIMD machines; in all three classes PEs can be clustered together to form independent submachines (partitions).

The multistage cube network is part of a large topologically equivalent family of networks including baseline [25], delta (a=b=2) [14], flip [2], generalized cube [20], indirect binary n-cube [15], multistage shuffle-exchange [23], omega [11], and SW-banyan (with S=F=2) [12], and has been used or proposed for use in many machines (e.g., BBN Butterfly, IBM RP3, PASM) [21]. Therefore, the results presented here are directly applicable to physically distributed memory systems using these networks.

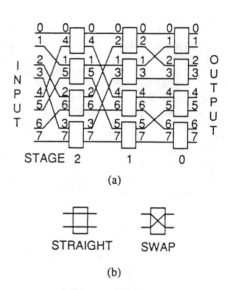

(a)

(b)

Fig. 3: (a) GC network topology for N=8.
(b) The states of an interchange box.

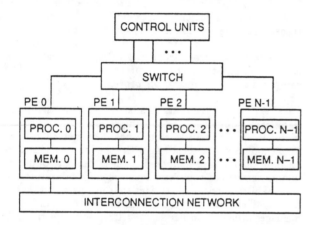

Fig. 2: Partitionable-SIMD/MIMD machine model.

The multistage cube interconnection network used in the analyses is a **Generalized Cube (GC)** network [20, 21]. This network can operate in the SIMD, multiple-SIMD, MIMD, and partitionable-SIMD/MIMD modes of parallelism. An N input/output GC network with N=8 is shown in Fig. 3a. It has $n = \log_2 N$ stages, where each stage consists of a set of N lines (**links**) connected to N/2 interchange boxes. Each **interchange box** is a two-input, two-output switch, and can be set to one of the states shown in Fig. 3b (broadcast (one-to-many) connections are not relevant to this study). The links are labeled from 0 to N−1. Links that differ only in bit position i are paired at interchange boxes in stage i. Each interchange box is controlled independently through the use of routing tags. PE i is connected to network input port i and output port i. In general, to go from a source $S = s_{n-1}...s_1 s_0$ to a destination $D = d_{n-1}...d_1 d_0$, the stage i box in the path from S to D must be set to swap if $s_i \neq d_i$ and to straight if $s_i = d_i$. There is only one path from a given source to a given destination, because only stage i can determine the i-th bit of the destination address.

One implementation aspect of all multistage networks is the way in which paths through the network are established and released [21]. A **packet-switched** network divides a message into a sequence of fixed-size packets, and each packet makes its way from stage to stage, releasing links and interchange boxes immediately after using them. Thus, a packet uses only one interchange box

at a time. Blocked packets can be stored in queues in interchange boxes. In a **circuit-switched** network, a complete circuit is established from the network input port to the desired network output port, and then data items are sent through the network. A total of n+1 links and n boxes are held for the duration of the transmission of the entire message. The simplifying assumption that if a path is blocked by another transmission, the blocked path is dropped and tried again later, is made.

The GC network control is distributed among the PEs by using a routing tag as a header on each packet in a packet-switched network and to establish each path in a circuit-switched network. Because each source PE generates its own tag, it is possible that a conflict will occur in the network, i.e., the messages at the two input links of a box both require the same box output link.

The **partitionability** of a GC interconnection network of size N is the ability to divide the network into independent subnetworks of different sizes (when a network of "size" N has N I/O ports) [20, 21]. Each subnetwork of size $N' < N$ must have all of the interconnection capabilities of a GC network originally built to be of size N'. The GC can be partitioned with the constraints that the size of each subnetwork must be a power of two, the physical addresses of the input/output ports of a subnetwork of size 2^k must all agree in some fixed set of n−k bit positions, and each input/output port can belong to at most one subnetwork. Each subnetwork forms a partition composed of the PEs associated with the input/output ports of the subnetwork, and within each partition, the PEs and input/output ports are logically numbered from 0 to $2^k - 1$.

4. Task Migration Using Multistage Cube Networks

Consider the analysis of moving task migration data through an interconnection network in a system of size $N = 2^n$ PEs. The numbers of all PEs in a partition of size $K = 2^k$ agree in n−k bit positions, and the other k bits assume all possible combinations. These k bits are called **partition bits**. It is assumed that all PEs in P_s must transfer the same amount of data, and P_s and P_d are of the same size (i.e., both contain k partition bits). Further, assume that logical PE i in the source partition transfers its data to logical PE i in the destination partition. However, logical labeling of PEs within a partition is restricted only by general constraints [20], and thus a partition bit in the source partition can correspond to any partition bit in the destination partition, or to its complement. This correspondence of partition bits is the **mapping** from the source partition to the destination partition. (The logical labelling of PEs within a partition may affect which paths through the network conflict when performing intra-partition transfers, but the number of conflict-free simultaneous paths does not change.)

As an example of a mapping, let $N = 32$,
$$P_s = \{17, 19, 21, 23, 25, 27, 29, 31\},$$
$$P_d = \{2, 6, 10, 14, 18, 22, 26, 30\}.$$
One possible mapping is to move the contents of PE:
$$s_4 s_3 s_2 s_1 s_0 = 1 X_2 \overline{X}_4 X_3 1 \text{ of } P_s$$

to PE:

$$d_4 d_3 d_2 d_1 d_0 = X_4 X_3 X_2 1 0 \text{ of } P_d,$$

where X_4, X_3, and X_2 are the partition bits; i.e, 21 to 2, 29 to 6, 23 to 10, ..., 27 to 30. Thus. s_3 maps to d_2, s_2 to d_4, and s_1 to d_3. Both PE $1 X_2 \overline{X}_4 X_3 1$ of P_s and PE of $X_4 X_3 X_2 1 0$ of P_d have the logical number $X_4 X_3 X_2$ within their respective partitions, as shown in Table 1.

Logical PE#	0	1	2	3	4	5	6	7
Physical PE# P_s	21	29	23	31	17	25	19	27
Physical PE# P_d	2	6	10	14	18	22	26	30

Table 1: Numbering for $N = 32$, $P_s = \{17, 19, 21, ..., 31\}$, $P_d = \{2, 6, 10, ..., 30\}$, and $X_4 X_3 X_2$ is the logical PE number corresponding to $1 X_2 \overline{X}_4 X_3 1$ in P_s and $X_4 X_3 X_2 1 0$ in P_d.

Fig. 4a shows an example of a task migration in a 16-PE system, where a two-PE task in PEs 5 and 7 migrates to PEs 13 and 15 with no conflicts. Fig. 4b shows an example where the two-PE task in PEs 5 and 7 migrates to PEs 8 and 9, and because there is a conflict and a link must be shared, the migration takes approximately twice as long as in the conflict-free case.

The utilization factor of a link was defined by Agrawal as the number of times a link must be used to pass a permutation [1]. In the context of task migration, the **utilization factor UF** of a link can be equivalently defined as the number of PEs that send data over that link to do the migration.

From properties of GC networks, a message from PE $s_{n-1}...s_0$ to PE $d_{n-1}...d_0$ enters stage i on a link whose label is $d_{n-1}...d_{i+1} s_i...s_0$ [20, 21]. Assume that the number of partition bits among the destination bits $d_{n-1}...d_{i+1}$ is k'_i, and that the number of partition bits among the source bits $s_i...s_0$ is k''_i. Further assume that q_i of the k''_i source partition bits in $s_i...s_0$ correspond (map) to q_i of the k'_i destination partition bits in $d_{n-1}...d_{i+1}$. Consider the example in Table 1, where data is moved from PE $s_4...s_0 = 1 X_2 \overline{X}_4 X_3 1$ to PE $d_4...d_0 = X_4 X_3 X_2 1 0$. When stage $i = 2$ is entered, the migration uses links $d_4 d_3 s_2 s_1 s_0$, where the destination partition bits $d_4 (= X_4)$ and

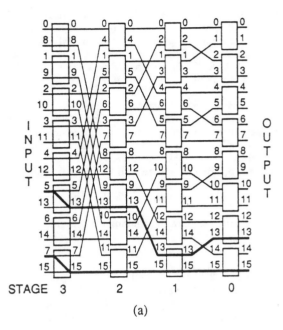

(a)

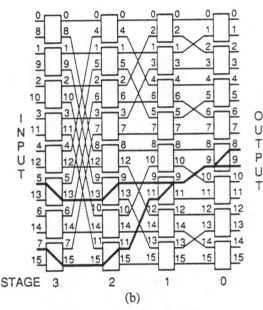

(b)

Fig. 4: Task migration in a system with 16 PEs.
(a) Migration from PEs 5 and 7 to 13 and 15.
(b) Migration from PEs 5 and 7 to 8 and 9.

$d_3 (= X_3)$ correspond to the source partition bits $s_2 (= \overline{X}_4)$ and $s_1 (= X_3)$, respectively. Hence, $k'_2 = k''_2 = q_2 = 2$. When stage $i = 1$ is entered, the migration uses links $d_4 d_3 d_2 s_1 s_0$, so $k'_1 = 3$, $k''_1 = 1$, and $q_1 = 1$.

The parameters k, k'_i, k''_i, and q_i are the same for all stage i links that are used during the migration. The utilization factor UF_i on each link used during the migration that connects a stage $i+1$ box to a stage i box is given by:

$$UF_i = 2^{k - k'_i - k''_i + q_i}$$

[19]. For a given P_s and P_d, different mappings of source partition bits to destination partition bits can result in different values of q_i, and hence in different utilization

factors. For the example in Table 1, the maximum UF_i occurs for UF_2, where $k'_2 = k''_2 = q_2 = 2$, so $UF_2 = 2$. If a different mapping which pairs bits d_4 and s_3, d_3 and s_2, and d_2 and s_1 (i.e., maps source PEs $1X_4X_3X_21$ to destination PEs $X_4X_3X_110$) is used, $UF_i = 1$ for all i, and the migration can be performed more quickly.

5. Lower Bounds of Migration Time

To determine whether or not the method of task migration presented in Section 6 is indeed an optimum one, a lower bound on the time required for migrating a task through a network has to be determined. For this reason, the **optimum utilization factor** is introduced:

$$UF_{opt} = \max_{i=0}^{n-1} 2^{k-k'_i-k''_i} = 2^u .$$

The **maximum utilization factor** for a migration is:

$$UF_{max} = \max_{i=0}^{n-1} (UF_i)$$

Because $UF_i = 2^{k-k'_i-k''_i+q_i}$, and $q_i \geq 0$, UF_{opt} is clearly a lower bound of the maximum utilization factor. From UF_{opt}, lower bounds of the migration time in packet-switched and circuit-switched GC networks can be derived.

Consider a packet-switched network first. Examine a link L between stage $i+1$ and i where $UF_i = UF_{max}$. Assume that each of the source PEs has to send M data packets during the migration, and let the **network cycle time** (i.e., the time to pass a single packet along a link (and its associated box circuitry)) be T_{NC}^P. Further, recall it is assumed that no conflicts with messages from other tasks interfere with the migration. Then link L must carry $M \times UF_{max}$ packets, because UF_{max} PEs use link L and each PE transfers M packets. A lower bound on the number of packets is given by using UF_{opt} as the lower bound for UF_{max}. That is, a lower bound on the number of packets that must traverse link L is $M \times UF_{opt}$. This will require time $T_{NC}^P \times M \times UF_{opt}$.

Each packet has not only to traverse link L, but must go from a source PE to the destination PE and traverse a total of $n+1$ links on the way (including the network input link). It is assumed that packets can be sent through one after another, i.e., can be "pipelined" through the network. Before the first packet reaches link L, it must traverse $n-i$ other links. After the last packet leaves link L, it must traverse i other links. Therefore, a lower bound of the migration time is given by:

$$T_{MIGR,PACK} = T_{NC}^P \times (M \times UF_{opt} + r) .$$

In a circuit-switched network, the data items must pass through link L as well, but in addition, a path through the network has to be established for each source PE sending to link L. Let the network cycle time (i.e., the time to pass a single word through the network) be T_{NC}^C. Assume that each of the source PEs has to send Y words during the migration, and that it takes S network cycles to establish a path. Recall that UF_{opt} is the minimum number of PEs that will need to use link L to perform the migration, and that blocked paths are dropped and tried again later (see Section 3). Each of the UF_{opt} PEs must establish the path that goes through link L and then send Y words through it. Therefore, the minimum migration time in circuit switched networks is given by:

$$T_{MIGR,CIR} = T_{NC}^C \times (S + Y) \times UF_{opt} .$$

6. Optimum Mapping Rule

Many alternatives to map source partition PEs to destination partition PEs exist. In the paper [19], one mapping was shown that was proven to result in the smallest possible utilization factor and avoid "dual conflicts." However, it was not shown that with this mapping the lower bound on migration time can be achieved. Here, a different mapping is presented that is proven to be optimum because it can be used to perform a migration in the smallest possible time. This mapping rule is now discussed.

Assume that a task with 2^k PEs must be migrated. The optimum utilization factor is $UF_{opt} = 2^u$; i.e., $u = \log_2 UF_{opt}$. First, map the highest (leftmost) u source partition bits to the u lowest (rightmost) destination partition bits in some arbitrary way. Then map the i-th highest remaining source partition bit to the i-th highest destination partition bit, for all remaining source partition bits.

This is illustrated by the following example. Consider a system with $N = 128$ PEs, and a task that needs a partition with $K = 16$ PEs ($k = 4$). Let the source partition be:

$$s_6 s_5 s_4 s_3 s_2 s_1 s_0 = X\,0\,X\,X\,1\,0\,X ,$$

and the destination partition be:

$$d_6 d_5 d_4 d_3 d_2 d_1 d_0 = 1\,X\,0\,0\,X\,X\,X ,$$

where X denotes a partition bit. UF_{opt} occurs for $i = 2$, when the link label is $d_6 d_5 d_4 d_3 s_2 s_1 s_0$, and where $k'_2 = 1$ (for d_5) and $k''_2 = 1$ (for s_0). Thus, $UF_{opt} = 2^{4-1-1} = 2^2 = 4$. The use of the optimum mapping rule is shown in Fig. 5.

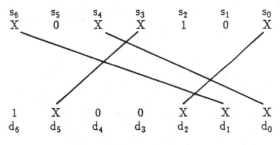

Fig. 5: Optimum mapping with $N = 128$, $K = 16$, and $UF_{opt} = 4$.

For the above example, $UF_{opt} = 4$, so $u = 2$. Therefore, the $u = 2$ highest source position bits, s_6 and s_4, map to the $u = 2$ lowest destination bits, d_1 and d_0. Then the i-th highest remaining source partition bit maps to the i-th highest remaining destination partition bit; i.e., s_3 maps to d_5, and s_0 maps to d_2.

The migration will be performed in UF_{opt} steps such that the u highest source partition bits are kept at a fixed value j during step j, $0 \leq j < UF_{opt}$. The remaining $k-u$ partition bits determine the set of PEs that is active during each step.

For the example above, the source partition PEs will be divided by fixing bit positions s_6 and s_4, and letting bit positions s_3 and s_0 vary. Thus, the $K = 16$ source partition PEs are divided into four subsets, each subset consisting of four PEs. At each step, one subset will transmit data. In step 0, $s_6 = s_4 = 0$, and source partition PEs $000X10X$ (i.e., 0000100, 0000101, 0001100, and 0001101) transmit data. In step 1, $s_6 = 0$, $s_4 = 1$, and source PEs $001X10X$ (i.e., 0010100, 0010101, 0011100, and 0011101) transmit data. In step 2, $s_6 = 1$, $s_4 = 0$, and source partition PEs $100X10X$ (i.e., 1000100, 1000101, 1001100, and 1001101) transmit data. Finally, in step 3, $s_6 = s_4 = 1$, and source partition PEs $101X10X$ (i.e., 1010100, 1010101, 1011100, and 1011101) transmit data.

It will be shown that the transfers performed by the PEs during each step do not interfere with each other. Because the overall migration process is performed in steps where only a specific subset of PEs is active, each step can be treated as a task migration by itself. For each of these **step task migrations** the utilization factor, denoted with an underscore as $\underline{UF}_i$, determines the amount of interference between migration messages in a step. Clearly, if the migration in each step is to be conflict-free, the utilization factor $\underline{UF}_i$ must be one for all stages and all steps. This is stated in Theorem 1. Lemma 1 is used in the proof of Theorem 1.

Lemma 1: Consider a source partition bit s_r that is one of the $k-u$ partition bits that vary during a migration step. Let s_r map to destination partition bit d_p. Then, because of the mapping rule, $p \geq r$.

Proof: The lemma is proven by contradiction. Assume that $p < r$, and consider the links that connect stage r with stage $r-1$. From Section 4, at these links, the bits $d_{n-1}...d_r$ contain k'_{r-1} destination partition bits, and the bits $s_{r-1}...s_0$ contain k'_{r-1} source partition bits. Because the highest u source partition bits are fixed during a step, only $k-u$ bits will vary. Therefore, $w_{r-1} = k-u-k''_{r-1}$ non-fixed source partition bits are in $s_{n-1}...s_r$. The rightmost of these source partition bits is s_r, and because $p < r$, this bit was not mapped to one of the k'_{r-1} destination partition bits in $d_{n-1}...d_r$. Recall from the mapping rule that the u highest source partition bits are mapped to the u lowest destination partition bits and that the next highest w_{r-1} source partition bits are mapped to the w_{r-1} highest destination bits. Because s_r is one of the w_{r-1} non-fixed source partition bits and does not map to one of the k'_{r-1} destination partition bits in $d_{n-1}...d_r$, it follows from the mapping rule that there must be at least k'_{r-1} non-fixed source partition bits in $s_{n-1}...s_{r+1}$ that do map to these destination partition bits. Thus, $w_{r-1} > k'_{r-1}$. Therefore,

$$k'_{r-1} < w_{r-1} = k - u - k'_{r-1} , \text{ or}$$

$$k - k'_{r-1} - k''_{r-1} > u .$$

However, in Section 5, u was defined to be the maximum value of $k - k'_{r-1} - k''_{r-1}$ for all r, and hence the lemma is proven by contradiction. $\quad\square$

Lemma 1 is now used to prove that each step migration can be done with no conflicts.

Theorem 1: If the above mapping rule is followed, the step utilization factor $\underline{UF}_i = 1$ for all steps and all stages.

Proof: Consider the migration performed in each step separately. For a given step task migration, the values for k', k'', and q will be distinguished by underscoring. Thus, the number of partition bits for the step task migration is $\underline{k} = k-u$, because u of the k partition bits are fixed during each step. Links connecting stage $b+1$ and stage b are numbered $d_{n-1}...d_{b+1}s_b...s_0$. In the step task migration, $d_{n-1}...d_{b+1}$ contain $\underline{k}'_b$ destination partition bits, and $s_b...s_0$ contain $\underline{k}''_b$ source partition bits. For the step task migration, neither $\underline{k}'_b$ nor $\underline{k}''_b$ contain any of the u fixed partition bits. The number of the $\underline{k}'_b$ destination partition bits in $d_{n-1}...d_{b+1}$ that correspond to any of the $\underline{k}''_b$ source partition bits in $s_b...s_0$ is $\underline{q}_b$. Let $\underline{w}_b = k - u - \underline{k}''_b$. Because of the mapping, each of the $\underline{k}'_b$ destination partition bits in $d_{n-1}...d_{b+1}$ must correspond to either one of the $\underline{k}''_b$ source partition bits in $s_b...s_0$ (exactly $\underline{q}_b$ do), or one of the $\underline{w}_b$ source partition bits in $s_{n-1}...s_{b+1}$. From Lemma 1, each of the $\underline{w}_b$ source partition bits in $s_{n-1}...s_{b+1}$ must correspond to one of the $\underline{k}'_b$ destination partition bits in $d_{n-1}...d_{b+1}$. Therefore, $\underline{k}'_b = \underline{w}_b + \underline{q}_b$. By definition, $\underline{w}_b = k - u - \underline{k}''_b$ and $\underline{k} = k - u$, so $\underline{w}_b = \underline{k} - \underline{k}''_b$. Thus,

$$\underline{k}'_b = \underline{w}_b + \underline{q}_b = \underline{k} - \underline{k}''_b + \underline{q}_b \Rightarrow$$

$$\underline{k} - \underline{k}'_b - \underline{k}''_b + \underline{q}_b = 0 .$$

Consequently, the step utilization factor is:

$$\underline{UF}_b = 2^{\underline{k} - \underline{k}'_b - \underline{k}''_b + \underline{q}_b} = 2^0 = 1$$

for all stages. $\quad\square$

Therefore, the migration can be performed in UF_{opt} steps, with no conflicts in any step. Theorem 2 proves that this implies the migration can be performed in the time given by the lower bounds in Section 5.

Theorem 2: If the step task migration approach described above is followed, the migration will be done in the minimum time possible.

Proof: The minimum migration times for packet- and circuit-switching were given in Section 5. First, consider packet-switching, then circuit switching.

From Theorem 1, each step of the migration is done with no conflicts. There are UF_{opt} steps. At each step, M data packets must be sent. Thus, a total of $M \times UF_{opt}$ packets must be sent (pipelined) through the network. Immediately (in the next network cycle) after one step task migration is completed, the next one is begun. Thus, when the last packets for step task migration i are in stage $n-2$, the first packets for step task migration $i+1$ are in stage $n-1$. Therefore, the total number of network cycles required is $M \times UF_{opt}$ for all the packets to enter the network (in a pipelined fashion), plus n more cycles for the last packet to exit the network. Hence, the total migration time is the lower bound:

$$T_{MIGR,PACK} = T_{NC}^P \times (M \times UF_{opt} + n) .$$

For the circuit-switched case, again from Theorem 1, each step of the migration can be done with no conflicts.

There are UF_{opt} step task migrations, each requiring time $T_{NC}^C \times (S + Y)$. Thus, the total migration time is the lower bound:

$$T_{MIGR,CIR} = T_{NC}^C \times (S+Y) \times UF_{opt} . \qquad \square$$

As an example of the use of this methodology, consider $N = 8$ and migrating a task from $P_s = \{0,2,4,6\}$ to $P_d = \{4,5,6,7\}$; i.e., $P_s = XX0$ and $P_d = 1XX$. $UF_{opt} = 2$, so $u = 1$ and using the mapping rule PE $X_0 X_1 0$ sends data to PE $1X_1 X_0$. This is done in two conflict-free steps using the step task migration approach: first X_0 is fixed at 0 and PEs 0 and 2 send data. and then X_0 is fixed at 1 and PEs 4 and 6 send data. This is shown in Fig. 6. Thus, if the network were circuit-switched, the migration time would be:

$$T_{NC}^C \times (S + Y) \times 2 .$$

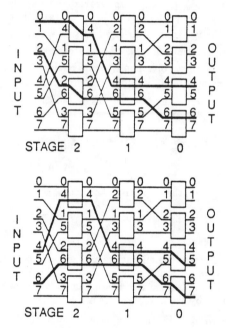

Fig. 6: Task migration from P_s $X_0 X_1 0$ to P_d $1X_1 X_0$ done in two steps.

Consider what would happen if, instead of using this methodology, PE $X_1 X_0 0$ sent data to PE $1X_1 X_0$ and all PEs attempted to send data simultaneously. Then PE 0 maps to 4, 2 to 5, 4 to 6, and 6 to 7. For both this mapping and the one above, $UF_1 = UF_0 = 2$. As shown in Fig. 7, if the 0 to 4 path is established first, it can cause the other paths to be blocked (depending on the timing of the other path establishment attempts). The 2 to 5 and 4 to 6 paths can next be established simultaneously, but they block the 6 to 7 path. Finally, the 6 to 7 path is established. Thus, three sets of transfers are needed: (1) from PE 0, (2) from PEs 2 and 4, and (3) from PE 6. Therefore, the migration time would be:

$$T_{NC}^C \times (S + Y) \times 3 ,$$

50% longer than the minimum, which is attainable with the mapping rule and step migration technique presented.

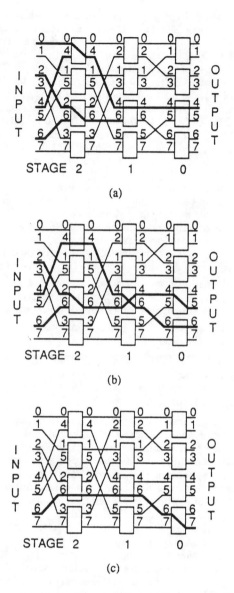

Fig. 7: Task migration for P_s $X_1 X_0 0$ to P_d $1X_1 X_0$ done in sets of transfers: (a) 0 to 4, (b) 2 to 5 and 4 to 6, and (c) 6 to 7.

7. Conclusions

A methodology for performing task migration transfers in the minimum possible time was presented. This methodology consisted of two components: a mapping of source partition PEs to destination partition PEs, and a way to group source PEs when data is transferred. The optimality of the methodology was proven correct under the assumptions of the model used.

The techniques and equations presented can be used to help determine if a given migration will save more time than it takes. For example, if a task is expected to complete is less time than it takes to migrate it, the migration should not be done.

These techniques can also be used to help select source and destination partitions. If the source partition is fixed, there may be a choice among several possible destination partitions. The optimum choice can be based solely on UF_{opt}, because the smallest UF_{opt} will require the shortest transfer time. If multiple destination partitions have the same smallest UF_{opt}, the choice between these can be made randomly, or other measures that take the effects of other tasks in the system into account can be employed [18].

If there are multiple possible source partitions in addition to multiple destinations, the amount of data that must be transmitted is, in general, different for every source partition. Therefore, UF_{opt} and the amount of data (M or Y) are used with the equations derived to determine the actual transfer time as a criterion for which source-destination partition pair to use.

In summary, as large-scale parallel processing systems become a reality, issues such as partitionability and task migration become important. The technique presented was proven to produce the minimum data transfer time for task migration using multistage cube networks.

Acknowledgement: The authors thank Mark A. Nichols for his comments.

References

[1]   D. P. Agrawal, "Graph theoretical analysis and design of multistage interconnection networks," *IEEE Trans. Computers*, v. C-32, July 1983, pp. 637-648.

[2]   K. E. Batcher, "The flip network in STARAN," *1976 Int'l Conf. Parallel Processing*, Aug. 1976, pp. 65-71.

[3]   T. L. Casavant and J. G. Kuhl, "A taxonomy of scheduling in general-purpose distributed computing systems," *IEEE Trans. Software Engineering*, Vol. SE-14, Feb. 1988, pp. 141-154.

[4]   C. H. Chu, E. J. Delp, L. H. Jamieson, H. J. Siegel, J. Weil, and A. B. Whinston, "A model for an intelligent operating system for executing image understanding tasks on a reconfigurable parallel architecture," *Journal of Parallel and Distributed Computing*, Vol. 6, June 1989, pp. 598-622.

[5]   G-I. Chen, and T-H. Lai, "Virtual subcubes and job migration in a hypercube," *1989 Int'l Conf. Parallel Processing, Vol. II*, Aug. 1989, pp. 73-76.

[6]   W. Crowther, J. Goodhue, R. Thomas, W. Milliken, and T. Blackadar, "Performance measurements on a 128-node butterfly parallel processor," *1985 Int'l Conf. Parallel Processing*, Aug. 1985, pp. 531-540.

[7]   S. A. Fineberg, T. L. Casavant, and H. J. Siegel, "Experimental analysis of a mixed-mode parallel architecture performing sequence sorting," *1990 Int'l Conf. Parallel Processing*, Aug. 1990, to appear.

[8]   M. J. Flynn, "Very high-speed computing systems," *Proceedings of the IEEE*, v. 54, Dec. 1966, pp. 1901-1909.

[9]   J. P. Hayes, T. N. Mudge, Q. F. Stout, and S. Colley, "Architecture of a hypercube supercomputer," *1986 Int'l Conf. Parallel Processing*, Aug. 1986, pp. 653-660.

[10]   W. D. Hillis, *The Connection Machine*, MIT Press, Cambridge, MA, 1985.

[11]   D. H. Lawrie, "Access and alignment of data in an array processor," *IEEE Trans. Computers*, Vol. C-24, Dec. 1975, pp. 1145-1155.

[12]   G. J. Lipovski and M. Malek, *Parallel Computing: Theory and Comparisons*, John Wiley & Sons, Inc., NY, NY, 1987.

[13]   S. F. Nugent, "The iPCS/2 direct-connect communications technology," *3rd Conf. Hypercube Computers and Applications*, Jan. 1988, pp. 51-60.

[14]   J. H. Patel, "Performance of processor-memory interconnections for multiprocessors," *IEEE Trans. Computers*, v. C-30, Oct. 1981, pp. 771-780.

[15]   M. C. Pease III, "The indirect binary n-cube microprocessor array," *IEEE Trans. Computers*, v. C-26, May 1977, pp. 458-473.

[16]   G. F. Pfister, W. C. Brantley, D. A. George, S. L. Harvey, W. J. Kleinfelder, K. P. McAuliffe, E. A. Melton, V. A. Norton, and J. Weiss, "The IBM Research Parallel Processor Prototype (RP3): introduction and architecture," *1985 Int'l Conf. Parallel Processing*, Aug. 1985, pp. 764-771.

[17]   G. F. Pfister and V. A. Norton, " 'Hot spot' " contention and combining in multistage interconnection networks," *1985 Int'l Conf. Parallel Processing*, Aug. 1985, pp. 790-797.

[18]   T. Schwederski, H. J. Siegel, and T. L. Casavant, "A model of task migration in partitionable parallel processing systems," *Frontiers '88: 2nd Symp. on the Frontiers of Massively Parallel Computation*, Oct. 1988, pp. 211-214.

[19]   T. Schwederski, H. J. Siegel, and T. L. Casavant, "Task migration transfers in multistage cube based parallel systems," *1989 Int'l Conf. Parallel Processing, v. I*, Aug. 1989, pp. 296-304.

[20]   H. J. Siegel, *Interconnection Networks for Large-Scale Parallel Processing: Theory and Case Studies, 2nd Edition*, McGraw-Hill, NY, NY, 1990.

[21]   H. J. Siegel, W. G. Nation, C. P. Kruskal, and L. M. Napolitano, Jr., "Using the multistage cube network topology in parallel supercomputers," *Proceedings of the IEEE*, v. 77, Dec. 1989, pp. 1932-1953.

[22]   H. J. Siegel, T. Schwederski, J. T. Kuehn, and N. J. Davis IV, "An overview of the PASM parallel processing system," in *Computer Architecture*, D. D. Gajski, V. M. Milutinovic, H. J. Siegel, and B. P. Furht, eds., IEEE Computer Society Press, Washington, DC, 1987, pp. 387-407.

[23]   S. Thanawastien and V. P. Nelson, "Interference analysis of shuffle/exchange networks," *IEEE Trans. Computers*, v. C-30, Aug. 1981, pp. 545-556.

[24]   L. W. Tucker and G. G. Robertson, "Architectures and applications of the Connection Machine," *Computer*, v. 21, Aug. 1988, pp. 26-38.

[25]   C.-L. Wu and T. Y. Feng, "On a class of multistage interconnection networks," *IEEE Trans. Computers*, v. C-29, Aug. 1980, pp. 694-702.

Complexity of Resource Allocation and Job Scheduling Problems in Partitionable Mesh Connected Systems *

Keqin Li and Kam Hoi Cheng
Computer Science Department
University of Houston
Houston, Texas 77204

Abstract

We consider the resource allocation and job scheduling problems in Partitionable Mesh Connected Systems (PMCS). These problems are first formally defined. We then show that the packability problem, a decision version of the resource allocation problem in PMCS, is NP-complete. Some special cases of the packability problem are also proved to be NP-complete. We then give a non-trivial polynomial time solvable case in which all jobs require submeshes with sizes being powers of 2. The job scheduling problem in PMCS is also shown to be NP-hard.

1. Introduction

With recent advances in VLSI technology, dramatic decrease in hardware implementation cost has made it possible to build very large scale parallel systems. It is not inconceivable that the size of a multiprocessor system is much larger than the size required by most applications, especially in systems which consist of very simple processors and interconnection pattern. For more than two decades, extensive research have been carried out to design various parallel architectures with numerous parallel algorithms developed for such systems.

In this paper, we consider the partitionable mesh connected system (PMCS). A PMCS consists of $p \times q \times c \times d$ processing elements (PEs) connected as a rectangular mesh. A mesh is a two dimensional arrangement of PEs with nearest neighbor connections as shown in Figure 1.1. For ease of implementation and system management, the smallest mesh that can be allocated is of size $c \times d$. Since this is a constant and does not affect problems that are considered, we treat a PMCS as having $p \times q$ PEs with the understanding that each unit actually contains $c \times d$ elements.

A PMCS may be used as a special VLSI device attached to the host computer. Independent subsystems of the PMCS are able to com-

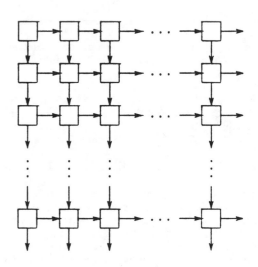

Figure 1.1

municate with the host directly as well as its neighboring subsystems. Responsibilities of the host computer include the development of user program, input/output handling and the management of the PMCS. An important feature of a PMCS is that it can be dynamically partitioned into many rectangular submeshes of different sizes. These submeshes can be assigned to independent jobs which may execute any parallel algorithm either in SIMD/MIMD manner or in systolic fashion. When a user program requires a rectangular mesh, the host computer either allocates a submesh of the required size to the job, or inserts

---
This research is based in part upon work supported by the Texas Advanced Research Program under Grant No.1028-ARP.

the job into a waiting list if no large enough subsystem is available. After completion of a job, the allocated submesh is reclaimed by the system for future use by other jobs. Thus a PMCS may be viewed as a shared resource just like the main memory in a multiprogramming system.

Mesh is chosen because of its simplicity, regularity, modularity and versatility. The orthogonal nearest neighbor interconnection pattern is simple and regular which is easy to implement by using VLSI technology. The modularity of a mesh allows easy expansion of the system and allows it to be partitionable. When multiple chips/systems of meshes are available, we are faced with the choice of implementing them as either many small independent systems or a large partitionable system. The reason which favors a large system is that a larger problem can be solved without the need to decompose the problem. A large system also allows a finer sampling grid that may not only improve the accuracy of the computation but may even improve the convergence speed of some numerical problems. However the price of a large system is a more complex resource management scheme.

The power of a mesh has long been recognised by many researchers. Work in cellular automata, which is concerned with computations distributed in a two-dimensional orthogonally connected array, is initiated by von Neumann [28]. A mesh-connected computer with end-around connections, ILLIAC-IV, has actually been built [3]. Detailed hardware implementation of MOPAC, a partitionable and reconfigurable mesh, is presented in [19]. Mesh may be used in many applications such as matrix computation [5], [6]; image processing [30]; sorting [18], [27]; graph theory [1], [20]; dictionary machine [9]; dynamic programming [12]; context-free language recognition [14] and computational geometry [24], [26]. Furthermore it is relatively easy to map other problem structures onto a mesh or reconfigure mesh into other structures. These structures include linear array and ring [16], multidimensional torus and mesh [33] and binary tree [11]. Thus all algorithms designed for these structures can also be run on a mesh.

There are many interesting and important problems that can be defined in a PMCS. In a large PMCS, most applications only require a small portion of the whole system. A

logical solution is to partition the system so that many jobs may be handled simultaneously. We will only be concerned with partitions that are independent subsystems, each having the properties of the whole system, i.e. a mesh connected system. Since the processor mesh is the only important resource in a PMCS, the resource allocation problem reduces to the system partitioning problem. The system partitioning problem is to determine how to partition the PMCS and how to combine idle submeshes into a larger system. A closely related problem is the packability problem which determines whether a given list of jobs can be done on a PMCS simultaneously. Another important problem is the job scheduling problem which determines how to schedule a given list of jobs so as to minimise the total processing time.

In this paper, we will only focus on these three problems. For each problem, first we formally define the problem, then a brief review on related research is presented, and finally its complexity is shown to be NP-hard.

2. The Packability Problem

Let $PMCS(p,q)$ denote a PMCS with size $p \times q$. A job J is specified as $J = (a,b)$ which means that job J requires a rectangular submesh of size $a \times b$, with a denoting the length of the horizontal edge and b the vertical edge. The packability problem is to determine whether a given job list $L = (J_1, J_2, \cdots, J_n)$ can be done on a $PMCS(p,q)$ simultaneously. It may be reformulated as the rectangle packing problem. Let $R(a,b)$ denote a rectangle of size $a \times b$. The rectangle packing problem is defined as follows:

Rectangle packing

Instance: A rectangle $R(p,q)$ and a list of rectangles $L = (R(a_1,b_1), R(a_2,b_2), \cdots, R(a_n,b_n))$.

Question: Can the list of rectangles L be packed into $R(p,q)$?

Note that the packing should be non-overlapping since no two jobs can share the same resource at the same time. We will only consider *orthogonal* packing where every edge of every rectangle is parallel to either the bottom edge or the vertical edge of the big rectangle (PMCS). It is not hard to realize that orthogonal packing always performs no worse than non-orthogonal packing when only rectangles are involved. An orthogonal packing is also *oriented* if a rotation of 90° is not allowed, i.e. a job $J=(a,b)$ should be assigned a sub-mesh of size a in the horizontal direction and b in the vertical direction. It is obvious that a non-oriented packing will result in a more compact packing and hence a more utilized system. However it will impose an additional requirement on the system to modify user's program and I/O direction so that a $b \times a$ mesh is sometimes allocated instead of a $a \times b$ mesh.

The rectangle packing problem that we have defined is actually the decision version of the two dimensional packing problem defined in [2], [8]. We will prove that the rectangle packing problem and some restricted versions are all NP-complete. In all our proofs, the packing is assumed to be orthogonal and oriented unless specified otherwise. Furthermore, sizes of all rectangles are assumed to be positive integers for obvious reasons.

Theorem 1. The rectangle packing problem is NP-complete.

Proof. It is easy to see that the problem is in NP, since a nondeterministic algorithm need only to guess the position of each rectangle and check in pairwise manner that no two rectangles overlap. The time needed is obviously polynomial in n.

To show that it is NP-hard, we reduce the known NP-hard *Partition* problem [13] to the rectangle packing problem. The partition problem is to determine whether a given set $S=\{a_1,a_2, \cdots ,a_n\}$ of n positive integers has a partition P such that $\sum_{a_i \in P} a_i = \sum_{a_i \in S-P} a_i$. Let S be an instance of the partition problem and $A=\frac{1}{2}\sum_{i=1}^{n} a_i$, an instance of the rectangle packing problem is constructed as follows:

$$L=(R(a_1,1),R(a_2,1), \cdots ,R(a_n,1)), R(A,2).$$

The transformation is obviously in polynomial time. If S has a partition P, then the corresponding packing is as shown in Figure 2.1. Conversely if L is packable into $R(A,2)$, since oriented packing is required and each rectangle is of height 1, the packing should be in two levels as in Figure 2.1. Thus we have a partition for S. $\square$

If for all i, $1 \le i \le n$, $a_i > 2$, even we allow the rectangles to rotate 90°, the packing problem is still NP-complete. This condition can be

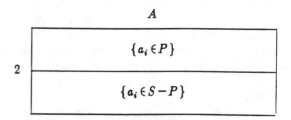

$$A$$

{$a_i \in P$}

2

{$a_i \in S-P$}

Figure 2.1

satisfied by multiplying all elements in S by a constant greater than 2 if there is some a_i in S which is not greater than 2. The modified set has the same partitionability as S. Hence we have the following.

Corollary 1. The rectangle packing problem is still NP-complete for non-oriented packing. $\square$

Not only is the general rectangle packing problem NP-complete, it remains NP-complete even by restricting its input. The proof that each of these restricted problems is in NP is the same as in the proof of Theorem 1. The proof of NP-hardness for each problem will be presented individually. The first special case of the rectangle packing problem is when the $PMCS(p,q)$ is a square mesh, i.e. $p = q$. The proof is based on the following lemmas which basically state that the packability of L into $R(p,q)$ is unchanged when all rectangles are scaled by a constant.

Lemma 1. For any positive integer m, $L=(R(a_1,b_1),R(a_2,b_2), \cdots ,R(a_n,b_n))$ can be packed into $R(p,q)$ if and only if $L'=(R(ma_1,b_1),R(ma_2,b_2), \cdots ,R(ma_n,b_n))$ can be packed into $R(mp,q)$. $\square$

Lemma 2. For any positive integer m, $L=(R(a_1,b_1),R(a_2,b_2), \cdots ,R(a_n,b_n))$ can be packed into $R(p,q)$ if and only if $L'=(R(a_1,mb_1),R(a_2,mb_2), \cdots ,R(a_n,mb_n))$ can be packed into $R(p,mq)$. $\square$

Theorem 2. The rectangle packing problem when restricted to $p = q$ is still NP-complete.

Proof. We reduce the rectangle packing problem to this restricted problem. For any given instance of the rectangle packing problem,

$$L = (R(a_1,b_1), \cdots ,R(a_n,b_n)), R(p,q),$$

we construct an instance of this problem,

$$L'=(R(qa_1,pb_1), \cdots ,R(qa_n,pb_n)), R(pq,qp).$$

According to Lemmas 1 and 2, L is packable into $R(p,q)$ if and only if L' is packable into $R(pq,qp)$. $\square$

Our next result is to show that when all rectangles in L are squares, i.e. all jobs require square submeshes, the problem is still NP-complete. We will use the NP-complete problem, *3-Partition* [10], in our proof.

3-Partition

Instance: A set of $3m$ ($m > 1$) positive integers $S = \{a_1, a_2, \cdots, a_{3m}\}$, a bound B, and for all i, $1 \le i \le 3m$, $B/4 < a_i < B/2$, and $\sum_{i=1}^{3m} a_i = mB$.

Question: Can S be partitioned into m disjoint sets $S_1, S_2, \cdots, S_m$ such that for each i, $1 \le i \le m$, the sum of all the elements in S_i is B? Note that the constraints in the instance require that each S_i should have exactly 3 elements of S.

Theorem 8. The rectangle packing problem remains to be NP-complete when all rectangles in L are squares.

Proof. Let $R(a)$ denote a square of size a. Given an instance I of the 3-partition problem,

$$S = \{a_1, a_2, \cdots, a_{3m}\},\ B,$$

we construct the corresponding instance I' of our packing problem as follows:

$$L = (R(A + a_1), \cdots, R(A + a_{3m})),\ R(p, q)$$

where $p = 3A + B$, $q = m\left(A + \dfrac{B}{2}\right)$, and $A > \dfrac{1}{4}(m-1)B$.

Suppose I has a partition, let $S_i = (a_{i1}, a_{i2}, a_{i3})$, $1 \le i \le m$. The corresponding packing is as shown in Figure 2.2.

Now suppose we have a packing for I', we note that at most m squares can be packed in the vertical dimension of length q. It is because the total height of $m+1$ squares is greater than $(m+1)\left(A + \dfrac{B}{4}\right)$ and

$$(m+1)\left(A + \frac{B}{4}\right) - q$$

$$= (m+1)\left(A + \frac{B}{4}\right) - m\left(A + \frac{B}{2}\right)$$

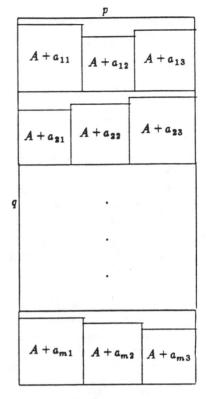

Figure 2.2

$$= A - \frac{1}{4}(m-1)B > 0.$$

It means that the total height of $m+1$ squares will exceed q. Similarly the horizontal dimension of length p can accomodate at most 3 squares. Otherwise the total width of 4 squares is greater than $4\left(A + \dfrac{B}{4}\right)$, while p is only $3A + B$. Since no overlap is allowed in the packing, the only packing that is possible will have exactly m levels of squares with 3 squares per level making a total of exactly $3m$ squares in the packing. If one level has less than 3 squares, then more than m levels of squares is required, a contradiction. Similarly if one column has less than m squares, then more than 3 squares is required for some level, which is again a contradiction. As a result, we can partition the $3m$ squares into m groups $G_1, G_2, \cdots, G_m$, where each group contains exactly 3 squares. Let G_i be represented by $G_i = (A + a_{i1}, A + a_{i2}, A + a_{i3})$, $1 \le i \le m$, then

$$3A + a_{i1} + a_{i2} + a_{i3} \le 3A + B$$

which implies that

$$a_{i1} + a_{i2} + a_{i3} \le B.$$

647

For each i, $1 \leq i \leq m$, the above inequalities must be equalities, otherwise we will have $\sum_{i=1}^{3m} a_i < B$, a contradiction. So $G_1, G_2, \cdots, G_m$ is a partition of the original instance I. $\square$

We would like to mention that the 3-partition problem is NP-complete in the strong sense, which means that there is no pseudo polynomial time algorithm to solve the problem if P$\neq$NP [10]. By Theorem 3, we know that the square packing into rectangle problem is also strongly NP-complete, so is the general rectangle packing problem.

Finally we consider the rectangle packing problem in which all jobs and the PMCS are restricted to be squares, i.e. the square packing into square problem. It is still an open question whether the problem is NP-hard or not. Intuitively the problem should be NP-hard since no necessary and sufficient condition has been found to determine the square packing problem. Some trivial necessary but not sufficient conditions are $\sum_{i=1}^{n} a_i^2 \leq p^2$ and $a_1 + a_2 \leq p$ where $a_1 \geq a_2 \geq \cdots \geq a_n$ are the sizes of square jobs and p is the size of the PMCS. A sufficient but not necessary condition [25] is $\sum_{i=1}^{n} a_i^2 \leq \frac{1}{2} p^2$. Obviously these conditions can easily be checked in polynomial time. However it is doubtful to find a polynomial time checkable necessary and sufficient condition for the square packing problem. Unfortunately there is still no formal proof that the problem is NP-hard. The next theorem shows that a restricted version of the square packing into square problem can actually be solved in polynomial time.

Theorem 4. A list of squares $L = (R(a_1), R(a_2), \cdots, R(a_n))$ where $a_i = 2^{e_i}$, $e_i \geq 0$, $1 \leq i \leq n$, can always be packed into a square $R(p)$ with $p = 2^N$ if and only if $\sum_{i=1}^{n} a_i^2 \leq p^2$.

Proof. The only if part is obvious. For the if part, the proof is by induction on $E(L) = \max(e_1, e_2, \cdots, e_n)$. When $E(L) = 0$, we have a set of unit squares, the result is trivial.

Suppose the statement is true for $E(L) = e < N$. When $E(L) = e+1$, without loss of generality, we may assume that

$$e_1 \leq e_2 \leq \cdots \leq e_r \leq e_{r+1} \leq \cdots \leq e_n = e+1$$

where $e_1 = e_2 = \cdots = e_r = 0$, $e_{r+1} > 0$, $r \geq 0$. This means that there are r unit squares. Since $\sum_{i=1}^{n} a_i^2 \leq p^2$ and unit squares can be put anywhere which is unoccupied, L can be packed into $R(p)$ if and only if

$$L' = (R(a_{r+1}), R(a_{r+2}), \cdots, R(a_n))$$

can be packed into $R(p)$. Note that by Lemmas 1 and 2, L' is packable into $R(p)$ if and only if

$$L'' = (R(\frac{a_{r+1}}{2}), R(\frac{a_{r+2}}{2}), \cdots, R(\frac{a_n}{2}))$$

can be packed into $R(\frac{p}{2})$. Since $E(L'') = e$ and

$$\sum_{i=r+1}^{n} \left(\frac{a_i}{2}\right)^2 = \frac{1}{4} \sum_{i=r+1}^{n} a_i^2 \leq \frac{1}{4} \sum_{i=1}^{n} a_i^2 \leq \left(\frac{p}{2}\right)^2$$

by the induction hypothesis, L'' can be packed into $R(\frac{p}{2})$, i.e. L can be packed into $R(p)$. $\square$

Theorem 4 has important practical implications because many parallel algorithms are designed for problems whose sizes are powers of 2. Note that the Theorem does not tell us how to pack L into $R(p)$. A solution to this problem is given in [21].

3. The System Partitioning Problem

The solution to the packability problem does not tell us how to partition a system even though a given job list can be packed into a PMCS. In addition it does not answer how to combine idle submeshes into larger ones. System partitioning can be classified as static and dynamic [34]. In static partitioning, the way to divide a system is fixed and is independent of the current job list. As a result, the problem of fragmentation arises as in segmented memory systems which results in a loss of the system computation power. Dynamic partitioning reconfigures a system based on the current job list and hence will result in a better utilization of the system.

A system partitioning scheme tells us how to partition a system and how to combine idle submeshes into larger ones. A good partitioning scheme may result in a highly utilized system, but the complexity for implementing it may be too high to be practical. On the other hand, a simple partitioning strategy may not fit all jobs into the system even though they have been proven to be packable. The system partitioning problem can therefore be expressed in another way: using a particular system partitioning scheme, what is the worst case utilisation of the system for all possible lists of jobs? The problem is formally defined as follows and it is actually an optimisation version of the packability problem and hence NP-hard for obvious reasons.

System partitioning

Instance: A PMCS(p,q) and a list of jobs $L=(J_1, J_2, \cdots, J_n)$ where $J_i=(a_i,b_i)$, $1\leq i\leq n$.

Problem: Pack L into PMCS(p,q) such that the utilisation of PMCS(p,q) is maximised.

The problem of partitioning multiprocessor system has received much attention recently. A multiprocessor system comprises a large number of resources such as processors, memory modules and interconnection networks, each of which may be partitioned to obtain better system utilisation. In [32], conditions that determine whether a network can be partitioned and the ways it can be partitioned are presented for the Cube, ILLIAC, PM2I and the Shuffle-Exchange networks. A survey on reconfiguring and partitioning multiprocessor system is presented in [34]. Quick algorithms for partitioning SW Banyan networks are discussed in [29]. Strategies for dynamically partitioning and combining subsystems in Hypercube and multistage cube connected networks can be found in [15].

Recently a dynamic system partitioning scheme called two dimensional buddy system (2DBS) is developed in [21] for resource management in a PMCS. A 2DBS is a generalisation of the classical one dimensional buddy system used in the management of the main memory. Detailed description of the 2DBS and its performance evaluation can be found in [21].

4. The Job Scheduling Problem

Let a job J be specified as $J=(a,b,t)$ which means that it requires a rectangular mesh of size $a\times b$ with processing time t. Given a list of jobs, even though a very good partitioning scheme is used, if they are not allocated in the correct order, the completion time of the given job list may not be short.

The job scheduling problem is to determine in what order jobs should be processed and to arrange jobs on the PMCS such that the total processing time is minimised. Jobs are assumed to be independent, i.e. there is nither communication nor precedence constraint among jobs. For each job J, a schedule specifies the location of the assigned submesh and the time interval during which J is executed. Since it is time consuming to suspend a job and resume it later on or even move a job to another part of the system, we will only consider non-preemptive scheduling, i.e. whenever a submesh is assigned to a job, the job will occupy the resource until it finishes.

For any job list $L=(J_1,J_2,\cdots,J_n)$, let f_i be the time at which job J_i is completed in a particular schedule. Then the total processing time of L under that schedule is

$$T(L) = \max(f_1, f_2, \cdots, f_n).$$

Now the job scheduling problem can be stated as follows:

Job scheduling in PMCS

Instance: A PMCS(p,q) and a list of jobs $L=(J_1, J_2, \cdots, J_n)$ where $J_i=(a_i,b_i,t_i)$, $1\leq i\leq n$.

Problem: Schedule L on the PMCS(p,q) to minimise the total processing time $T(L)$.

We can again abstract the problem in a more intuitive way. We use a rectangular box of size $a\times b\times t$ to represent a job $J=(a,b,t)$ where the bottom is of size $a\times b$ and the height is t. The system PMCS(p,q) is abstracted as a big box with infinite height and a bottom of size $p\times q$. Then the job scheduling problem becomes the problem of packing small boxes into a bigger one such that the total height is minimised. Here the packing is orthogonal and oriented in the time dimension.

Three dimensional packing

Instance: A list of rectangular boxes $L=(C_1,C_2,\cdots,C_n)$ where the size of C_i is $a_i\times b_i\times h_i$, $1\leq i\leq n$, and a big box C with infinite height and a bottom of size $p\times q$.

Problem: Pack L into C to minimise the total height.

Clearly the three dimensional packing problem is a generalisation of classical one [7] and two

[2] dimensional packing problems.

Most job scheduling problems are NP-hard [10], with only trivial cases as exceptions. Heuristic algorithms are presented in [31] to schedule tasks on supercomputers comprised of multiple pipelines and asynchronous multiple processors. Recently problems of scheduling multiprocessor jobs as well as time and resource constrained scheduling are considered in [4] and [35] respectively. Another related research can be found in [17] where the processor partitioning and scheduling problem is studied.

The job scheduling problem in PMCS is obviously NP-hard since it contains the multiprocessor scheduling problem [10] as a special case when each job only needs a unit square. The problem remains to be NP-hard even if p and q are known constants. We can also prove that the problem is NP-hard by reducing the rectangle packing problem to it. Specifically let all jobs in L have the same processing time t, then L is packable into PMCS(p,q) if and only if the total processing time is t. For the case when the PMCS is a square mesh or when all jobs need square submeshes, the job scheduling problem in PMCS remains to be NP-hard.

In addition to the NP-hardness of the problem, we have shown in [22] that if $P \neq NP$, then there does not exist a polynomial time approximation algorithm which, when given a job list L, can always produce a schedule with $T(L)$ less than twice the total processing time of the optimal schedule. In the same paper, we propose and analyze the performance of a heuristic algorithm which uses the longest-processing-time-first job scheduling policy and the layer-by-layer packing strategy. Results are to be reported in [23] about a new algorithm which employs the largest-job-first scheduling policy and the 2DBS system partitioning scheme.

Another performance measure, the *weighted mean finish time* of the schedule, can be defined as $\mathrm{WMFT}(L) = \frac{1}{n} \sum_{i=1}^{n} w_i f_i$ where w_i is the weight associated to J_i, $1 \leq i \leq n$. The non-preemptive scheduling problem with this measure remains to be NP-hard since its multiprocessor scheduling version is NP-hard [13].

5. Summary

We have introduced the Partitionable Mesh Connected System. The system is versatile, easily implementable and expandable. Resource allocation and job scheduling are important problems that need to be solved in order to use the PMCS efficiently. We have formalised these problems and proved that they are NP-hard even with some restrictions in the possible input. An open question remains to be answered is whether the square packing into square problem is NP-complete.

6. References

[1] M.J. Atallah and S.R. Kosaraju, *Graph Problems on a Mesh-Connected Processor Array*, Proc. 14th Annual ACM Symposium on the Theory of Computing, pp.345-353.

[2] B.S. Baker, E.G. Coffman, Jr. and R.L. River, *Orthogonal Packings in Two Dimensions*, SIAM J. Comput., Vol.9, Nov.1980, pp.846-855.

[3] G.H.Barnes, et al., *The ILLIAC IV Computer*, IEEE Trans. on Computers, August 1968, pp.746-757.

[4] J.Blazewicz, M.Drabowski and J.Weglarz, *Scheduling Multiprocessor Tasks to Minimize Schedule Length*, IEEE Trans. on Computers, May 1986, pp.389-393.

[5] P.R.Cappello, *A Mesh Automaton for Solving Linear Systems,* Int'l Conf. on Parallel Processing, 1985, pp.418-425.

[6] K.H.Cheng and S.Sahni, *VLSI Systems for Matrix Multiplication,* Foundations of Software Technology and Theoretical Computer Science Conference, New Delhi, India, Dec. 1985; Springer-Verlag Lecture Notes in Computer Science, 1985, pp.428-456.

[7] E.G. Coffman, Jr., J.Y.-T. Leung and D. Sluts, *On the Optimality of First-Fit and Level Algorithms for Parallel Machine Assignment and Sequencing,* Int'l Conf. on Parallel Processing, 1977, pp.95-99.

[8] E.G.Coffman,Jr., M.R.Garey, D.S.Johnson and R.E.Tarjan, *Performance Bounds for Level-Oriented Two-Dimensional Packing Algorithms,* SIAM J. Comput., Vol.9, Nov. 1980, pp.808-826.

[9] F.Dehne and N.Santoro, *Optimal VLSI Dictionary Machines on Meshes,* Int'l

Conf. on Parallel Processing, 1987, pp.832-840.

[10] M.R.Garey and D.S.Johnson, *Computers and Intractability: A Guide to the Theory of NP-completeness*, W.H.Freeman, San Francisco, 1979.

[11] D.Gordon, *Efficient Embeddings of Binary Trees in VLSI Arrays*, IEEE Trans. on Computers, Sept. 1987, pp.1009-1018.

[12] L.J.Guibas, H.T.Kung and C.D.Thompson, *Direct VLSI Implementation of Combinatorial Algorithms*, Caltech Conf. on VLSI, Jan. 1979, pp.509-525.

[13] E.Horowitz and S.Sahni, *Fundamentals of Computer Algorithms*, Computer Science Press, Inc., 1978.

[14] O.H. Ibarra, S.M. Kim and M.A. Palis, *Designing Systolic Algorithms Using Sequential Machines*, IEEE Trans. Computers, June 1986, pp.531-542.

[15] M.Jeng and H.J.Siegel, *Dynamic Partitioning in a Class Parallel Systems*, Int'l Conf. Distributed Comput. Sys., 1988, pp.33-40.

[16] I. Koren, *A Reconfigurable and Fault Tolerant VLSI Multiprocessor Array*, Annual Symposium on Computer Architecture, 1981, pp.425-442.

[17] R.Krishnamurti and E.Ma, *The Processor Partitioning Problem in Special Purpose Partitionable Systems*, Int'l Conf. on Parallel Processing, 1988, Vol.1, pp.434-443.

[18] H.-W. Lang, M.Schimmler, H.Schmeck and H.Schröder, *Systolic Sorting on a Mesh-Connected Network*, IEEE Trans. on Computers, July 1985, pp.652-658.

[19] W.H.Lee and M.Malek, *MOPAC: A Partitionable and Reconfigurable Multicomputer Array*, Int'l Conf. on Parallel Processing, 1983, pp.506-510.

[20] K.N. Levitt and W.T. Kautz, *Cellular Arrays for the Solution of Graph Problems*, CACM, Sept. 1972, pp.789-801.

[21] K.Li and K.H.Cheng, *A Two Dimensional Buddy System for Dynamic Resource Allocation in A Partitionable Mesh Connected System*, TR No. UH-CS-89-03, Computer Science Dept., Univ. of Houston, 1989.

[22] K.Li and K.H.Cheng, *Job Scheduling in Partitionable Mesh Connected Systems*. to be presented in Int'l Conference on Parallel Processing, August 1989.

[23] K.Li and K.H.Cheng, *Job Scheduling in PMCS using the 2DBS as a Partitioning Scheme*. Computer Science Dept., University of Houston, in preparation.

[24] M. Lu and P. Varman, *Mesh-Connected Computer Algorithms for Rectangle-Intersection Problems*, Int'l Conf. on Parallel Processing, 1986, pp.301-307.

[25] A. Meir and L. Moser, *On Packing of Squares and Cubes*, J. of Combinatorial Theory, 1968, pp.126-134.

[26] R.Miller and Q.F.Stout, *Mesh Computer Algorithms for Line Segments and Simple Polygons*, Int'l Conf. on Parallel Processing, 1987, pp.282-285.

[27] D.Nassimi and S.Sahni, *Bitonic Sort on a Mesh-Connected Parallel Computer*, IEEE Trans. on Computers, Jan.1979, pp.2-7.

[28] V. Neumann, *Theory of Self-Reproducing Automata*, (A.W.Burks Ed.), University of Illinois Press, Urbana, Illinois, 1966.

[29] U.V.Prekumar and J.C.Browne, *Resource Allocation in Rectangular SW Banyans*, 10th Int'l Conf. Computer Architecture, Oct.1982, pp.326-333.

[30] A.Rosenfeld, *Parallel Image Processing using Cellular Arrays*, Computer, January 1983, pp.14-20.

[31] S.Sahni, *Scheduling Multipipeline and Multiprocessor Computer*, IEEE Trans. on Computers, 1984, pp.637-645.

[32] H.J. Siegel, *The Theory Underlying the Partitioning of Permutation Networks*, IEEE Trans. on Computers, Sept.1980, pp.791-801.

[33] L. Tao and Y.-W.E. Ma, *Embeddings Among Multidimensional Toruses and Multidimensional Meshes*, Computer & Inf. Sci., University of Pennsylvania, 1988.

[34] S. Yalamanchili and J.K. Aggarwal, *Reconfiguration Strategies for Parallel Architectures*, Computer, Dec.1985, pp.44-61.

[35] W. Zhao, K. Ramamritham and J.A. Stankovic, *Preemptive Scheduling Under Time and Resource Constraints*, IEEE Trans. on Computers, August 1987, pp.949-960.

Chapter 10: Fault Tolerance

Fault-tolerant networks are essential to the reliability of parallel computer systems. A fault-tolerant network has the ability to route information even if certain network components (for example, processors, switches, and/or links) fail. The techniques often used for network fault tolerance are either software based or hardware based. Examples of software-based techniques are

- adaptive routing, which makes use of multiple source-destination paths to avoid faulty components, and
- multiple passes through the network (often used in omega-like multistage networks).

Examples of hardware-based techniques are

- enhancing the network with additional hardware (such as links and switches) and
- providing enough redundancy in the original network design to tolerate a certain number of faults.

The first paper included in this chapter, by Adams, Agrawal, and Siegel (1987), nicely surveys and compares fault-tolerant multistage interconnection networks. The next paper, by Esfahanian and Hakimi (1985), illustrates the use of software fault tolerance for routing in static networks. Then, Yeh and Feng (1991) give a software fault-tolerance scheme for rearrangeable multistage networks. The paper by Varma and Raghavendra (1989) first addresses the fault-tolerance capabilities of omega networks that have the ability to tolerate a number of faults by using multiple passes through the network; then, it presents multiple-pass routing algorithms. The next two papers, by Pradhan (1985) and Banerjee and Dugar (1989), study new network designs that achieve fault tolerance through hardware redundancy. Leighton and Maggs (1992) present fault-tolerant routing algorithms for multibutterflies and randomly wired splitter networks. Lastly, the paper by Kandlur and Shin (1992) shows how virtual cut-through can be used to decrease delays in fault-tolerant point-to-point networks.

Reprinted from *Computer,* Vol. 20, No. 6, June 1987, pp. 14-27.
Copyright © 1987 by The Institute of Electrical and Electronics
Engineers, Inc. All rights reserved.

A Survey and Comparison of

Fault-Tolerant Multistage Interconnection Networks

George B. Adams III, Research Institute for Advanced Computer Science

Dharma P. Agrawal, North Carolina State University

Howard Jay Siegel, Supercomputing Research Center*

Fault model and fault-tolerance criterion are essential metrics for any comparison of network fault-tolerance capabilities.

Today all branches of engineering and a multitude of other disciplines rely firmly and increasingly on computational support. However, each discipline has important problems that, to be solved feasibly, await our ability to field computers with orders of magnitude greater performance than currently available. Consequently, the need for very high performance computing is larger than ever and growing.

To date, high-performance computers have owed their speed primarily to advances in circuit and packaging technology. These technologies are subject to physical limits constraining the ultimate speed of a conventional uniprocessor computer. Parallel processing computers executing problem solutions expressed as parallel algorithms translated into parallel machine programs can exceed the single processor speed limit.

The means for communication among processors, memory modules, and other devices of a parallel computer is the interconnection network. Conventional von Neumann computers have relatively few subsystems to connect, yet a simple communication scheme such as a time-shared bus is an important system component. Large-scale multiprocessor computers have numerous communicating components, and therefore place great performance demands on an interconnection network.

Many interconnection networks for large-scale multiprocessor computer systems have been proposed.[1,2] Of these, *multistage interconnection networks* (MINs) compose a large subset, are well suited to communication among tightly coupled system components, and offer a good balance between cost and performance. For complex systems, assuring high reliability is a significant task. Thus, a crucial quality for MINs serving the communication needs of large-scale multiprocessor systems is fault-tolerance.

This article focuses on MINs that are intrinsically fault tolerant. Many have been proposed, and new ideas are published frequently. The survey herein, while not exhaustive due to space constraints, attempts to portray the diversity of fault-tolerant MINs and, through them, the scope of fault-tolerance techniques. The relative merits of fault-tolerant MINs can be difficult to assess. Therefore, once surveyed, the MINs are placed in perspective by defining a hypothetical MIN with ideal engineering characteristics and comparing the surveyed networks to this standard.

---

*This work was performed while Siegel was at the School of Electrical Engineering, Purdue University.

0-8186-6197-6/94 $4.00 © 1987 IEEE

Terminology

Figure 1 shows MIN hardware in the most general terms; dots indicate items that may repeat. MINs are comprised of a collection of *switches* and *links* between switches. A signal may enter or leave a network through a *port*. A network with A input ports and B output ports is an $A \times B$ network.

A switch may be viewed as a very simple network. Switches are multiport devices; the number of ports and the port-to-port connections supported within a switch vary among switch designs. A *crossbar* switch can simultaneously connect, in any pattern, a number of input/output port pairs equal to the minimum of the number of inputs and the number of outputs. A *selector* switch connects only one of its inputs to one of its outputs at a time.

The term *network component* may denote any element of the structure of a network. An interconnection network may consist of a single *stage*, or bank, of switches and may require that data pass through the network more than once to reach its destination.

A MIN is constructed from two or more stages of switches, and typically is designed so that data can be sent to the desired destination by one pass through the network.

A *fault-tolerant MIN* is one that provides service, in at least some cases, even when it contains a faulty component or components. A fault can be either permanent or transient; unless stated otherwise, we assume in this article that faults are permanent. Fault tolerance is defined only with respect to a chosen *fault-tolerance model*, which has two parts. The *fault model* characterizes all faults assumed to occur, stating the failure modes (if any) for each network component. The *fault-tolerance criterion* is the condition that must be met for the network to be said to have tolerated a given fault or faults.

Fault models may or may not correspond closely to predicted or actual experience with MIN hardware. In particular, a fault model may be chosen with characteristics that simplify reliability analysis, even if those characteristics depart widely from reality (such as assuming certain network components never fail). While fault-tolerance criteria typically closely reflect the normal (fault-free) operational capability of a network, this need not be so. The variability of fault-tolerance models hinders comparison of the engineering characteristics of fault-tolerant MINs.

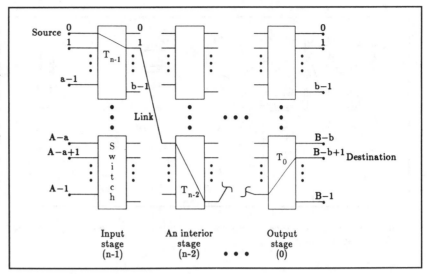

Figure 1. A generic MIN diagram detailing one path.

A network is *single-fault tolerant* if it can function as specified by its fault-tolerance criterion despite any single fault conforming to its fault model. More generally, if any set of i faults can be tolerated, then a network is *i-fault tolerant*. A network that can tolerate some instances of i faults is *robust* although not i-fault tolerant.

MINs can be considered from either a topological (graphical) or algebraic viewpoint. The *topology* of a network is the pattern of connections in its structure; the pattern can be represented by a graph. Topology is determined by switch design and the pattern of links. Different MINs are often compared graphically because comparison by topology is independent of hardware. When one network is said to be an instance of another, it is the network graphs being compared. Nodes in the graph of a MIN can be numbered, and then a MIN can be described in terms of the algebraic relations among the nodes. The algebraic model is useful in discussing control and communications routing strategy.

There are three basic forms of connection through a network. A *one-to-one connection* passes information from one network port, the *source*, to another network port, the *destination*. The exact route taken by the information is its *path*. Multiple one-to-one connections may be active simultaneously. A *permutation connection* is a set of one-to-one connections such that no two one-to-one connections have the same source or destination. Such connections are meaningful only in the context of

networks with an equal number of sources and destinations. Information flow from one source simultaneously to two or more destinations is supported by a *broadcast connection*, and the route taken is a *broadcast path*.

Routing tags are a way of describing a path through a network and providing for distributed network control. For MINs, tags often take the form of a multidigit integer, each successive digit encoding the setting for the switch in the next stage along a desired path. Control is distributed if devices using the network generate their own routing tags and network switches can set themselves based on tag information. Figure 1 shows a switch in stages $n-1$, $n-2$, and 0 being set, respectively, by tag digits T_{n-1}, T_{n-2}, and T_0. Routing tags are particularly important for fault-tolerant MINs since they should be able to specify a functioning path if one exists; tag limitations translate into fault-tolerance limitations.

There are three methods for sources to generate routing tags that specify a fault-free path. With *nonadaptive routing* a source learns of a fault only when the path it is attempting to establish reaches the faulty network component. Notice of the fault is sent to the source, which tries the next alternative path. This approach requires little hardware, but may have poor performance. There are two forms of *adaptive routing*. With *notification on demand* a source maintains a table of faults it has encountered in attempting to establish paths and uses this

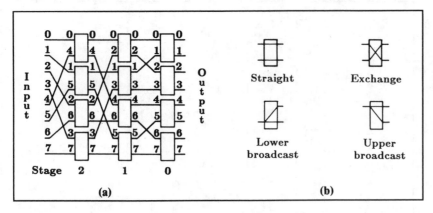

Figure 2. The generalized cube network for $N = 8$ (a) and four states of the generalized cube switching element (b).

Fault-tolerance issues

Fault tolerance can be achieved at various levels in a complex system. For example, when a process running on the TRAC[3] multiprocessor system encounters a fault in the portion of the TRAC MIN that links its set of system resources, it is dynamically rescheduled to another set of resources not affected by the MIN fault. The MIN subsystem is not itself intrinsically fault tolerant, but TRAC as a whole is, by allowing graceful degradation. Because fault-tolerant MINs are the focus of this article, we do not address fault tolerance of systems having embedded MINs.

Many fault-tolerant systems require fault diagnosis (detection and location) to achieve their fault tolerance. Techniques such as test patterns, dynamic parity checking, and write/read-back/verify for use in various MINs have been described. We assume fault diagnosis to be available as needed with respect to the surveyed MINs and do not discuss it further.

Techniques for fault-tolerant design can be categorized by whether they involve

information to guide future routing. With *broadcast notification* of a fault, all sources are notified of faulty components as they are diagnosed.

A fault-free path need not be specified by a source if routing tags can be modified in response to faults encountered as a path is followed or established. This *dynamic routing* can be accomplished in MINs constructed of switches capable of performing the necessary routing tag revisions.

modifying the topology (graph) of the system. Three well-known methods that do not modify topology are error-correcting codes, bit-slice implementation with spare bit slices, and duplicating an entire network (this changes the topology of the larger system using the network).

These approaches to fault tolerance can be applied to MINs. A number of techniques have also been developed tailored closely to the nature of MINs and their use. The following survey explores these methods in particular.

Survey

The surveyed networks are ordered roughly by the hardware modifications made to provide redundancy, from less to more extensive. Many possible techniques exist, including adding an extra stage of switches, varying switch size, adding extra links, and adding extra ports. (The technique of *chaining* switches within a stage so that data can sidestep a faulty switch is discussed in detail elsewhere in this issue.[4])

Extra stage cube and delta networks. The extra stage cube (ESC)[5,6] network derives from the generalized cube MIN.[7] The generalized cube is an $N \times N$ MIN, $N = 2^n$, with $n = \log_2 N$ stages, each stage consisting of N links connected to $N/2$ switches (see Figure 2a). The links connecting stage i switches to stage i-1 switches are stage i links. Each switch, called an *interchange box*, is 2×2, individually controlled, and can be set to one of four states (see Figure 2b). The upper I/O ports on any switch have the same numeric labels;

lower I/O ports also have the same labels. Upper and lower switch port labels in stage i differ only in the ith bit position.

The ESC is formed from the generalized cube by adding an extra stage to the input side of the network along with multiplexers and demultiplexers at the input and output stages, respectively. In addition, dual I/O links to and from the devices using the network are required. Stage n is connected like stage 0, that is, links that differ in the low order bit are paired. Figure 3 illustrates the ESC for $N = 8$.

Stage n and stage 0 can each be enabled or disabled (bypassed). A stage is *enabled* when its switches are being used to provide interconnection; it is *disabled* when its switches are being bypassed. Enabling and disabling in stages n and 0 are accomplished as shown in Figure 4. Having multiple ports per device using the ESC is equivalent to the input demultiplexer and output multiplexer arrangement originally described for the network.[5]

Normally, the network will be set so that stage n is disabled and stage 0 is enabled. The resulting structure matches that of the generalized cube. If a fault is found after running fault detection and location tests, the network is reconfigured. A fault in a stage n switch requires no change in network configuration; stage n remains disabled. If the fault occurs in stage 0, then stage n is enabled and stage 0 is disabled, i.e., stage n replaces the function of stage 0. For a fault in a link or in a switch in stages $n - 1$ to 1, both stages n and 0 will be enabled.

Enabling both stages n and 0 provides two distinct paths between any source and destination, at least one of which must be fault-free given any single fault in the network. ESC multiple-fault tolerance is enhanced by individually enabling and disabling stage n and 0 switches.[6]

The ESC fault model assumes that (1) any network component can fail, (2) faulty components are unusable, and (3) faults occur independently. The ESC fault-tolerance criterion is retention of the fault-free interconnection capability of a generalized cube MIN for one-to-one and broadcast connections. This corresponds to *full access*, the ability to connect any MIN input to any output. The ESC is single-fault tolerant and robust in the presence of multiple faults.

The ESC can be controlled by a simple extension of the routing tags used for the generalized cube. The tags are readily computed as the bit-wise Exclusive-OR of the number of the network input and output ports to be connected, perhaps modified by information as to the location of a fault (if any).

The augmented delta network[8] also utilizes an extra stage, without circuitry to enable and disable the input and output stages, to achieve fault tolerance. A delta, or *digit controlled*, network is an $a^w \times b^w$ network with w stages, each consisting of $a \times b$ crossbar switches, and with a link pattern between stages that provides a unique path of fixed length between any network input and output. Further, the link pattern is such that information can be routed from an input to an output using the switch output corresponding to a base-b digit in the base-b representation of the output number. The extra stage of N/b $b \times b$ switches results in b paths between any pair of network input/output ports. With a fault model assuming (1) any link and any interior switch can fail, (2) faulty components are unusable, and (3) faults occur independently, and a fault-tolerance criterion of retention of full access capability, an augmented delta network is $(b-1)$-fault tolerant.

Multipath omega network. The multipath omega network[9] derives from the omega MIN.[10] A $B^m \times B^m$ omega network consists of m stages of $B \times B$ crossbar switches linked by $(B*B^{m-1})$-shuffle interconnections, a generalized shuffle. If $B = 2$ and $m = \log_2 N$, the omega network is obtained; its topology is identical to that of the generalized cube. For the multipath omega network the fault model is the same as for the augmented delta; the fault-tolerance criterion is again full access.

Figure 5 shows one possible multipath omega network for $N = 16$. Its structure is described by the pseudofactorization $<4,2,2,4>$ of N. A *pseudofactorization* of N is an f-tuple $<B_1,B_2,...,B_f>$ of integers with $B_1*B_2*...*B_f = B$, such that B is a multiple of N. Let $B/N = R$, then an R-path multipath omega network corresponding to the pseudofactorization has f stages with stage i consisting of $B_i \times B_i$ crossbar switches. Links entering stage i switches implement the $\{k_i B_i * N/(k_i B_i)\}$-shuffle interconnection, where $k_i \geq 1$ and k_i is an integer chosen so that there are exactly R ways to connect any network input to any network output. For the network of Figure 5a, $k_1 = 1$, $k_2 = 1$, $k_3 = 8$, and $k_4 = 1$. The R paths in a multipath omega need not be distinct, hence, a single fault may affect more that one path. A multipath omega

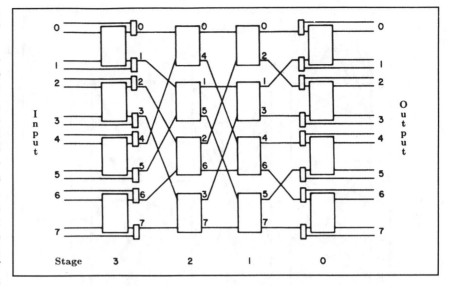

Figure 3. The extra stage cube network for $N = 8$.

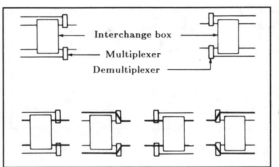

Figure 4. Detail of input stage switch with multiplexer for enabling and disabling (a), output stage switch with demultiplexer for enabling and disabling (b), input stage switch enabled (c), input stage switch disabled (d), output stage switch enabled (e), output stage switch disabled (f).

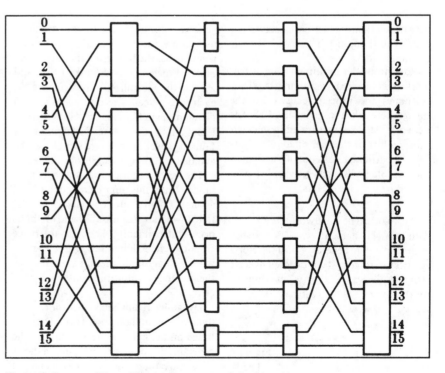

Figure 5. One possible multipath omega network for $N = 16$.

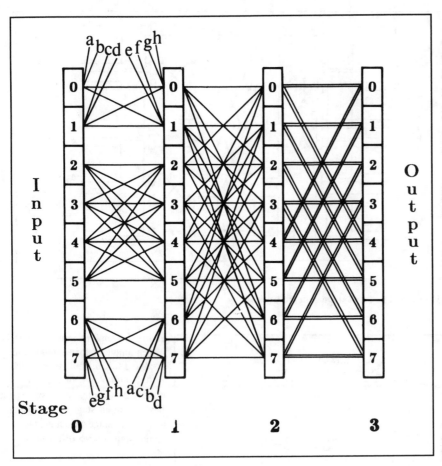

Figure 6. The F-network for $N = 8$.

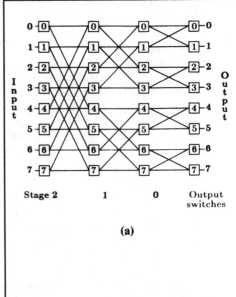

(a)

network with λ distinct paths between a source/destination pair is $(\lambda - 1)$-fault tolerant.

Routing in the multipath omega network is controlled by routing tags and resembles the procedure used for the omega network and generalized shuffle network. The destination address determines n bits of the tag; r additional bits select a particular path out of the R alternatives. Stage i switch settings are controlled by $b_i = \log_2 B_i$ bits.

F-network. The F-network[11] is $2^n \times 2^n$ with $n + 1$ stages of $N = 2^n$ switches each, that are, in general, 4×4 selectors. A switch in stage j, W_j, is denoted by a bit string $W_j = w_{n-1} \ldots w_1 w_0$. It connects to the stage $j + 1$ switches $W_{j+1} = w_{n-1} \ldots w_1 w_0$, $X_{j+1} = w_{n-1} \ldots w_{j+1}\overline{w_j}w_{j-1} \ldots w_1 w_0$, $Y_{j+1} = \overline{w_{n-1} \ldots w_{j+1}w_jw_{j-1} \ldots w_1 w_0}$, and $Z_{j+1} = \overline{w_{n-1} \ldots w_{j+1}}w_jw_{j-1} \ldots w_1 w_0$. Figure 6 shows the F-network for $N = 8$. The F-network contains the structure of the

generalized cube and can emulate it by using only the W_{j+1} and X_{j+1} connections. Thus, the fault tolerance approach of the F-network adds links (Y_{j+1} and Z_{j+1}) to the generalized cube structure. At each stage except the output stage, two different switches can be selected while maintaining the same destination. A faulty, as well as a busy, switch can be avoided by taking the appropriate path.

The F-network uses a yet less strict fault model than the augmented delta, and assumes (1) only interior switches fail, (2) failed switches are unusable, and (3) faults occur independently. The fault-tolerance criterion is retention of full access. The network is single-fault tolerant and robust in the presence of multiple faults.

Dynamic redundancy network. The dynamic redundancy network (DR)[12] is based on the graph representation of the generalized cube network. Figure 7a shows the graph representation of the generalized cube network of Figure 2a. Figure 7b

relates the graph and interchange box representations.

The DR network has $N + S$ I/O ports and $\log_2 N$ stages, each with $N + S$ switches followed by $3(N + S)$ links. There are $N + S$ output switches. Each switch j at stage i of the network has three links to stage $i - 1$. One is connected to switch $(j - 2^i) \bmod (N + S)$, the second to switch j, and the third to switch $(j + 2^i) \bmod (N + S)$. The DR output switches are its output ports. Figure 7c shows a DR network for $N = 8$ and $S = 2$. The S spare I/O ports allow S spares of the devices using the network, thus providing fault tolerance for devices.

A *row* of a DR network contains all the switches having the same address, all links incident out of them, and the associated network input and output links. A row has the same address as its switches. Two rows of the DR network are said to be *adjacent* if their addresses are consecutive (mod $N + S$).

The DR fault model is the same as for the ESC: any component may fail. Its fault tolerance criterion is retention of the ability to perform any set of simultaneous connections possible with the generalized cube. This is a stricter criterion than used for the ESC.

When there are no faults, rows 0 to $N - 1$ are used to emulate the generalized cube network. (For example, Figure 7a is a subgraph of rows 0 to 7 of Figure 7c.) If a component of row j is found to be faulty, the network is reconfigured so that the

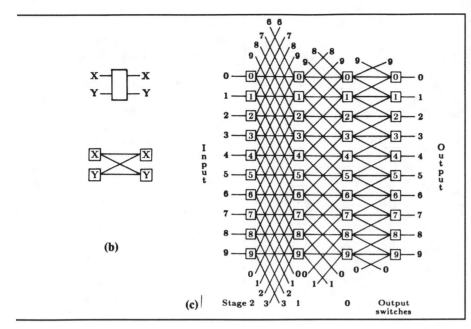

(b)

(c)

Stage 2   3   1   0   Output switches

Figure 7. Graphical representation of the generalized cube of Figure 2a (a), relationship between graphical representation and interchange box representation (b), and DR- network for $N = 8$ and $S = 2$ (c).

switches physically numbered p are logically renumbered $t(p)$, where $t(p) = (p - j - S) \, mod \, (N + S)$. As long as N adjacent rows remain, the DR network can contain the generalized cube subgraph and thus act as a fault-tolerant generalized cube.

Enhanced IADM network. As depicted in Figure 8, the IADM[13] consists of $n = \log_2 N$ stages each with N switches and $3N$ links, plus one column of output switches that are the network output ports. Each switch is a 3×3 selector. At stage i, $0 \leq i < n$, switch j, $0 \leq j < N$, is connected to switches $(j - 2^i) \, mod \, N$, j, and $(j + 2^i) \, mod \, N$ in stage $i + 1$. These links are known as the minus, straight, and plus links, respectively. Since $j - 2^{n-1} \equiv (j + 2^{n-1}) \, mod \, N$, there actually exist just two distinct logical data paths from each stage $n - 1$ switch.

Unlike the generalized cube, delta, and omega networks, the IADM can tolerate some faults (given a fault-tolerance criterion of full access) because of multiple paths between a source, S, and destination, D, if $S \neq D$. The nature of this native fault tolerance has been studied in detail for the closely related gamma network. The extra-stage gamma[14] is single-fault tolerant with respect to the fault model and fault-tolerance criterion of the augmented delta.

The enhanced IADM has the same fault model as the augmented delta network, as well as the same fault-tolerance criterion.

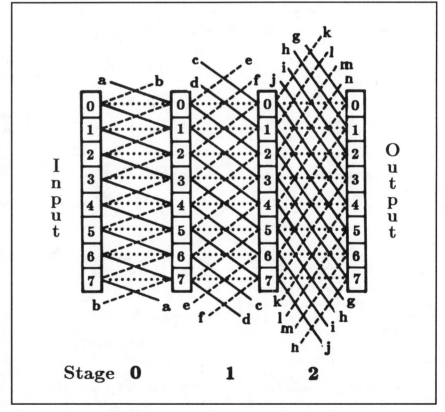

Figure 8. The inverse augmented data manipulator network for $N = 8$.

There are two forms of enhanced IADM. One version has redundant straight links. Faulty links can be avoided by using the second straight link, but switch faults cannot.[13] A second, more effective enhanced IADM adds *half links* to each of stages 1 through $n - 1$. Half links connect a switch m in stage i to switches

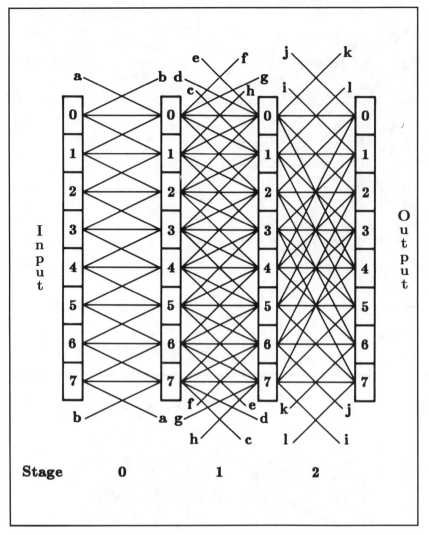

Figure 9. The enhanced inverse augmented data manipulator network with half links for N = 8.

$(m + 2^{i-1}) \bmod N$ and $(m - 2^{i-1}) \bmod N$ (see Figure 9).

Adding half links provides single-fault tolerance to any switch or link failure because at any switch (except those in stage $n - 1$, the last stage) there exist at least two (sometimes three) links leading to distinct switches in the successive stage, any of which can be used to satisfy the routing need. With a single-stage look-ahead technique and dynamic routing, the network is two-fault tolerant.[13] Each switch must have the ability to determine if the switches or links to which it connects are faulty and, if so, to modify routing tags to avoid a faulty component.

β-networks. A *β-network* results from simply interconnecting a set of β-elements;

no particular topology is specified.[15] A *β-element* is an interchange box that can perform only straight and exchange permutations.

The β-network fault model assumes (1) only switches fail, by becoming stuck in one of their two allowed states, (2) faulty switches are usable, and (3) faults occur independently. A β-network is said to tolerate a fault if the fault does not destroy dynamic full-access capability. A β-network is defined as having the *dynamic full-access* property if any given network input can be connected to any single network output in a finite number of passes through the network. Between passes it is assumed that each output can connect to its corresponding input (i.e., the input with the same number as the output) via a path

Augmented C-network. The augmented C-network (ACN)[16] fault-tolerance technique involves doubling the number of switch input and output ports, maintaining the same type switch function, and then adding links to connect selected pairs of switches in adjacent stages. The ACN derives from the C-network, an $N \times N$ MIN having an arbitrary number of stages of $N/2$ 2×2 crossbar switches each. Stages are numbered 0 to $m - 1$ from input to output.

Let one output of a switch be labeled 0 and the other, 1. For a switch P in stage i, i not the output stage, its *0-successor*, denoted $succ^0(P)$, is the switch in stage $i + 1$ connected to its 0 output. The *1-successor*, $succ^1(P)$, is the stage $i + 1$ switch connected to its 1 output.

The topology of a C-network is defined by the following relationship. For each switch P_j in stage i, $0 \le i < m - 1, 0 \le j < N/2$, there exists a switch P_k, $0 \le k < N/2$ and $k \ne j$, in stage i such that $succ^0(P_j) = succ^0(P_k)$ and $succ^1(P_j) = succ^1(P_k)$. Switches P_j and P_k are said to be *conjugate*, denoted $conj(P_j) = P_k$ and $conj(P_k) = P_j$. For example, in the generalized cube of Figure 2a the switch with labels 0 and 4 and the switch with labels 2 and 6 are conjugate.

The notion of conjugate switches has been discussed using the term *output buddies*.[17] The concept of *input buddies*, the 0- and 1-successors of both a switch and its conjugate, was also noted. A network in which two pairs of input buddies also constitute two pairs of output buddies, such as the generalized cube, has the *strict buddy* property. C-networks do not necessarily have this property.

A C-network with the additional property that $succ^0(P) \ne conj(succ^1(P))$ and $succ^1(P) \ne conj(succ^0(P))$, such as the generalized cube, provides the basis for the ACN. So that we can compare all networks in this survey on an equal basis, assume the C-network to have $\log_2 N$ stages. Beginning with such a C-network, an ACN is constructed by replacing all the 2×2 switches with 4×4 crossbar switches with inputs labeled 0, 1, $conj(0)$, and $conj(1)$. Switch outputs are labeled similarly. Those switch inputs and outputs labeled 0 and 1 are connected exactly as in the base C-network. The $conj(0)$ and $conj(1)$ ports are connected as shown in Figure 10.

One stringent ACN fault model is that

(1) any network component can fail, and (2) faulty components are unusable. Except for not specifying fault independence, this is the same stringent fault model used by the ESC. As does the ESC, the ACN requires dual I/O ports for each device using the network. The ACN fault-tolerance criterion is retention of full access capability. The ACN provides 2^n distinct paths between any source and destination (at each stage either switch i or switch $conj(i)$ can be used), but most of these paths are not disjoint. In general, there exist at least two switches at any stage and two links between stages by which a given source and destination can be joined. Thus, the ACN is single-fault tolerant to both switch and link failures.

Routing in the ACN is predicated on a routing tag scheme existing for the particular base C-network. We assume that a switch can determine when a successor switch is faulty. When no faults or busy switches occur, the tag is determined and interpreted by the ACN as it would be for the base C-network. Otherwise, two proposed routing strategies utilize both the standard path and conjugate path switches.[16]

Merged delta network. An $N \times N$ merged delta network (MDN)[16] results from cross-linking corresponding stages of C copies of an $N/C \times N/C$ delta network. An MDN denoted by C-MDN indicates explicitly the number of copies. The basic switch for the MDN is a $2C \times 2C$ crossbar, with $\log_2 N/C$ stages. The construction procedure used for MDNs works with any MIN; the delta was chosen by the MDN developers for its simple routing scheme.

Number the C copies of the delta network 0 to $C - 1$ and denote source S, destination D, and switch P associated with copy c, $0 \le c \le C - 1$, as (S, c), (D, c), and (P, c), respectively. Let $0 \le j \le N/2$. If source S connects to switch $P_{j,0}$ in the input stage of the delta network, then sources (S, c) connect to input stage switches $(P_{j,0}, c)$ in the MDN. If destination D connects to output stage switch $P_{j,n-1}$ in the delta network, then destinations (D, c) connect to switches $(P_{j,n-1}, c)$ in the MDN. Finally, if the outputs of stage i switch $P_{j,i}$ connect to stage $i + 1$ switches $P_{k,i+1}$ and $P_{m,i+1}$ in the delta network, then in the MDN each switch $P_{j,i}, c$ connects to switches $P_{k,i+1}, c$ and $P_{m,i+1}, c$. Figure 11 shows a 2-MDN ($C = 2$) for $N = 8$. Bold lines denote links from the replicated networks; light lines denote

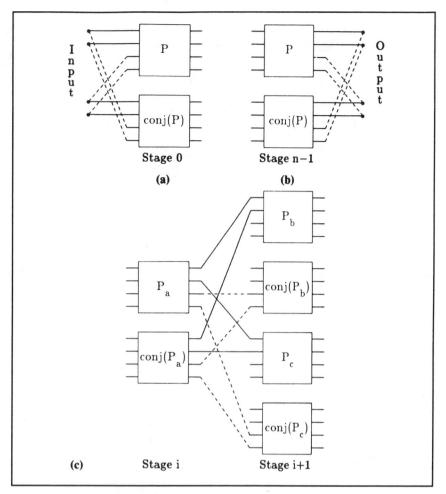

Figure 10. Connections to stage 0 switches in an ACN (a), connections from stage $n - 1$ in an ACN (b), connections from a conjugate switch pair in an ACN (c).

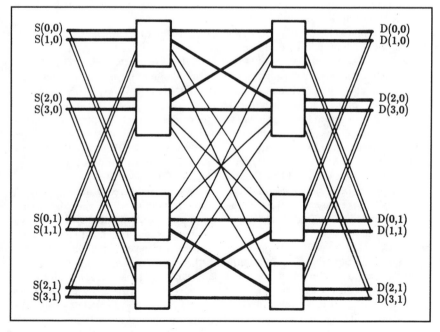

Figure 11. MDN for $N = 8$ and $C = 2$.

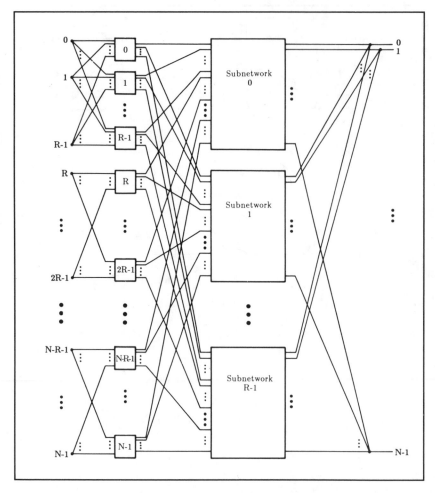

Figure 12. INDRA network shown as the union of R subnetworks.

links merging the two copies.

The MDN fault model assumes (1) only switches fail, and (2) faulty switches are unusable. The fault-tolerance criterion is full access. The MDN provides $C^{\log_2(N/C)}$ paths between any source and any destination (at each stage the corresponding switch in any of the C copies can be used). In general, there are at least C switches at any stage and C links between stages by which a given source and destination can join. Thus, the MDN is $(C - 1)$-fault tolerant to both switch and link failures (although the fault model assumes links never fail). Like the ESC and ACN, the MDN requires C I/O ports per device using the network.

MDN routing is based on the delta network routing procedure. Information is initially passed to a non-faulty switch in stage 0. From there, each switch in stage j forwards the information by choosing with equal probability one of the copies. If the

selected switch is faulty another copy is chosen. At stage $n - 1$ the switch output is chosen to reach the intended destination.

INDRA network. Interconnection networks designed for reliable architectures, or INDRA[18] networks, incorporate multiple copies of a basic network, typically the omega network, but preface the copies with a distribution stage of switches (see Figure 12). INDRA networks have $N = 2^m$ inputs and outputs with $\log_R N + 1$ stages of $R \times R$ switches. Stages are numbered 0 through n from input to output, where $n = \log_R N$, and each stage has N switches (typically N is a power of R, but it need not be). They are connected by links in an $R*(N/R)$-shuffle. Other link interconnection patterns, including the cube interconnections, are possible. As with the MDN, the construction technique used for INDRA networks can be applied to any MIN.

INDRA networks can be conceived as the union of R parallel networks each with $\log_R N$ stages of $R \times R$ switches, with an initial distribution stage at the input. Like the ESC, ACN, and MDN, the INDRA network requires C I/O ports per device using the network.

The INDRA network fault model matches that used for the MDN with the addition that faults are explicitly assumed to occur independently. The fault-tolerance criterion is the ability to perform any permutation in one pass that an omega network of size N with $R \times R$ switches can perform in one pass.

The INDRA network is digit-controlled in the same sense as delta networks and performs all omega network-performable permutations, as well as others. Without using the R redundant links to stage 0, there exist R paths between any source/destination pair. Using redundant links yields R^2 paths, although they are not all disjoint. In the case of a stage 0 switch fault, data can be routed through one of the alternate links from the input port. Other switch faults can be avoided by taking one of the R^2 paths that exist between any source and destination that does not include the faulty switch. This is always possible, as any faulty switch not in stage 0 lies within some subnetwork (see Figure 12), and a path exists between any source and destination that passes through some other subnetwork. Faults are avoided either by having sources keep track of failed switches and avoid them when generating routing tags, or by a form of *simulcasting*, whereby information is sent on multiple paths simultaneously to one destination.[18]

The INDRA network is $(R - 1)$-fault tolerant. Like the MDN, the INDRA network can tolerate link faults.

Comparison

Table 1 summarizes the network fault tolerance information presented in our survey. It lists: the possible faults that can occur in each network under the assumed fault model; whether or not faulty components are usable; the fault-tolerance criterion; the method by which the network copes with faults; whether the network is single-fault tolerant; and how the network performs with multiple faults. The phrase "interior switch only" used in the table is another way of saying input and output switches are assumed fault-free.

Table 1. Summary of fault tolerance information for the surveyed networks.

Network	Fault Model	Fault-Tolerance Criterion	Fault-Tolerance Method	Single-Fault Tolerant*	Multiple-Fault Tolerant*
Extra Stage Cube	Any component; unusable	Full access	Alternate route	Yes	Robust
Augmented Delta	Interior switch or link; unusable	Full access	Alternate route(s)	Yes	$(b-1)$-fault tolerant with $b \times b$ switches
Multipath Omega	Interior switch or link; unusable	Full access	Alternate route(s)	Yes	$(\lambda-1)$-fault tolerant
F-network	Interior switch only; unusable	Full access	Alternate routes	Yes	Robust
Extra Stage Gamma	Interior switch or link; unusable	Full access	Possible alternate route	No; only robust	Robust
Dynamic Redundancy	Any component; unusable	Full access	Alternate (spare)	Yes	Limited robustness
Enhanced IADM (half links)	Interior switch or link; unusable	Full access	Alternate routes	Yes	Two-fault tolerant with lookahead
β-networks	Switch stuck, but usable	Dynamic full access	Repeated passes	Depends on topology	Typically robust
Augmented C-network	Any component; unusable	Full access	Alternate routes	Yes	Robust
Merged Delta	Any switch; unusable	Full access	Alternate routes	Yes	$(C-1)$-fault tolerant
INDRA	Any switch; unusable	Ω permutation in one pass	Alternate routes	Yes	$(R-1)$-fault tolerant

*Using the fault model and fault-tolerance criterion defined for the network in question.

Table 2 summarizes structural characteristics of the networks. Switch type, number of stages of switches, number of switches per stage, and number of links between stages of switches are four parameters relevant to both implementation cost and achievable fault tolerance. Networks with high switch and link counts may require high package counts and hence cost more to produce than less complex structures. Networks with high package counts are, all other things equal, more likely to experience failure during a given period of time. The nature of real failures must be taken into account, along with expected reliability, package count, and network topology and operation protocol to estimate a cost/fault-tolerance performance ratio for a particular network.

Despite the growing research on fault-tolerant MINs, the results often have limitations, including unreasonably optimistic fault-tolerance models, and increased data routing complexity. To place the surveyed networks in perspective, we compare them to a hypothetical fault-tolerant MIN having the following ideal engineering characteristics:

(1) Fault model—any network component can fail, and failed components are unusable.
(2) Fault-tolerance criterion—full access.
(3) Routing complexity—as low as any surveyed network.
(4) Hardware complexity—as low as any surveyed network.
(5) Fault-tolerance capability—single-fault tolerant and robust with respect to multiple faults.

Table 3 summarizes the comparison in qualitative terms. For example, in the column on fault model the phrase "slightly less strict" generally means input and output stage switches are assumed fault-free, while the phrase "less strict" typically

Table 2. Summary of structural characteristics of the surveyed networks.

Network	Network Ports per Source or Destination	Switch Type*	Number of Stages	Number of Switches/Stage	Number of Links/Stage
Extra Stage Cube	2	Four-state interchange box	$1 + \log_2 N$	$N/2$	N
Augmented Delta	1	$a \times b$ crossbar	$i + \log_b N$, typically $i = 1$	N/b	N
Multipath Omega	1	$B_i \times B_i$ crossbar in stage i	f, selectable within constraints	n/B_i in stage i	N
F-network	1	4×4 mux/demux	$1 + \log_2 N$	N	$4N$
Extra Stage Gamma	1	3×3 crossbar	$2 + \log_2 N$	N	$3N$
Dynamic Redundancy	1	3×3 mux/demux	$\log_2 N$	$N + S$	$3(N + S)$
Enhanced IADM (half links)	1	5×5 mux/demux	$1 + \log_2 N$	N	$5N$ interior, $3N$ input stage, $4N$ output stage
β-networks	1	Two-state interchange box	Variable	Typically $N/2$†	Typically N†
Augmented C-network	2	4×4 crossbar	Same as underlying C-network	$N/2$	$2N$
Merged Delta	C	$2C \times 2C$ crossbar	$\log_2 (N/C)$	$N/(2C)$	CN
INDRA	R	$R \times R$ crossbar	$1 + \log_R N$	N	RN

*Input and output stage switches may differ; see text.
†Depends on specific instance of network topology.

includes the previous restriction and adds the assumption of fault-free links.

The choice of fault model and fault-tolerance criterion plays a key role in determining the fault-tolerance characteristics of a network. As seen from Table 3, the comparison fault model is stricter, and likely more realistic, than that for all but three of the networks: the ESC, DR, and ACN. The comparison fault-tolerance criterion is the same as that for most of the networks surveyed. Table 3 indicates the more strict fault-tolerance criteria of the DR and INDRA networks; each requires some permutation connection capability in addition to full access.

The fault-tolerance criterion used to study β-networks offers a much less strict test to pass. It requires only the ability to connect any input to any output in a finite number of passes through the network. Successive passes are performed by returning data from a network output to the same numbered input. Even a fault-free β-network may require multiple passes for data to reach its destination, so the chosen fault-tolerance criterion is appropriate. However, the breadth of the class of β-networks makes it important to note that this forgiving criterion may inflate the capabilities attributed to more complex β-networks.

For most of the networks, routing in the presence of faults is little more complex than in the absence of faults. The notable exception to this is β-networks. Once faults have been detected and located, considerable work remains to determine if dynamic full access has been retained. Agrawal and Leu have developed a specific testing technique.[19] Of course, we can precompute the network status for an assumed fault condition. Given an input and output to be connected, binary routing tags will suffice. However, the dynamic full access procedure requires choosing a set of intermediate outputs reachable consecutively. We do not know of a general solution to this problem. In a practical sense, this may result in delivered fault tolerance less than that theoretically available.

The hardware complexity of the networks varies significantly, as shown in Table 2. The hardware complexity entries

Table 3. Comparison of surveyed networks with hypothetical network of ideal engineering characteristics described in text. Entries give the relationship between the network in question and the hypothetical network as regards a particular attribute.

Network	Fault Model	Fault-Tolerance Criterion	Routing Complexity	Hardware Complexity	Fault-Tolerance Capability*
Extra Stage Cube	As strict	Same	Comparable	Slightly greater	Comparable
Augmented Delta	Slightly less strict	Same	Comparable	Same	Comparable
Multipath Omega	Slightly less strict	Same	Comparable to slightly greater	Same	Comparable to greater†
F-network	Less strict	Same	Comparable	Slightly greater	Comparable
Extra Stage Gamma	Slightly less strict	Same	Comparable	Greater	Comparable
Dynamic Redundancy	As strict	More strict	Comparable	Slightly greater	Less
Enhanced IADM (half links)	Slightly less strict	Same	Comparable; complexity hidden in switch	Greater	Greater if complex routing used
β-networks	Much less strict	Much less strict	Much higher	Less to greater†	Comparable to greater†
Augmented C-network	As strict	Same	Comparable; complexity hidden in switch	Much greater	Comparable
Merged Delta	Less strict	Same	Comparable; complexity hidden in switch	Much greater	Greater
INDRA	Less strict	More strict	Comparable	Much greater	Greater

*Using the fault model and fault-tolerance criterion defined for the network in question.
†Depends on specific instance of network topology.

of Table 3 are qualitative. The intent is to reflect a rough estimate of package count at various levels, specifically, the chip and board level or multiple-chip carrier level. However, hardware complexity and implementation cost may bear little relationship to each other; knowledge of implementation details arising from a hardware design study is necessary for high-confidence estimates of cost. VLSI technology often allows a large reduction in package count, for example. With this caveat, the hardware complexity data suits our comparison purposes.

The fault-tolerance capabilities of the networks are all quite similar, given the individual standards by which we measure each network. This is apparent in the column on fault-tolerance capabilities in Table 3. However, because we study each network using its own fault model and fault-tolerance criterion, significant differences in capabilities might appear if we adopted a common fault model and fault-tolerance criterion.

The fault model and fault-tolerance criterion of the hypothetical network can be applied to the surveyed networks to compare their fault tolerance. A common fault model and fault-tolerance criterion form a single scale by which we can measure any network. The results of this common measure appear in Table 4, Column I. Only the ESC, DR, ACN, merged delta, and INDRA networks are single-fault tolerant with respect to this fault model and fault-tolerance criterion. The DR network requires connections so that the N adjacent rows remain accessible regardless of the location of a failing row.

Many of the networks fail to be single-fault tolerant because they cannot tolerate an input or output switch fault, as can the above five networks. Thus many fault models refer only to interior switch faults. If we amend the hypothetical network fault model to assume fault-free switches in the input and output stages, some of the networks are by this measure single-fault tolerant (see Table 4, Column II). Alternatively, the MINs that become single-fault tolerant under the relaxed fault model could be fitted with input and output stage bypass circuitry and become

Table 4. Fault tolerance capabilities of the surveyed networks assuming a common network fault model and fault tolerance criterion. I. Single-fault tolerant using hypothetical network fault model and fault-tolerance criterion (see text). II. Single-fault tolerant if hypothetical network fault model is relaxed to assume input and output stage switches are fault-free.

Network	I	II
Extra Stage Cube	Yes	Yes
Augmented Delta	No	Yes
Multipath Omega	No	Yes*
F-network	No	Yes
Extra Stage Gamma	No	Yes
Dynamic Redundancy	Yes	Yes
Enhanced IADM (half links)	No	Yes
β-networks	No	Yes*
Augmented C-network	Yes	Yes
Merged Delta	Yes	Yes
INDRA	Yes	Yes

*Typically yes, but depends on specific instance of network topology.

single-fault tolerant under the more stringent conditions.

The ESC was designed with a fault model and fault-tolerance criterion identical to that of the hypothetical network. Its routing complexity is low, based on easily computed tags that specify one of two possible paths between a source and destination. The ESC incorporates slightly more hardware than the simplest of any of the surveyed networks (such as the augmented delta with $b = 2$), having enable/disable circuitry for the input and output stage switches.

A β-network is single-fault tolerant given the relaxed hypothetical fault model if it provides at least two paths that share no network components other than their first and last β-elements between any source and any destination. This restriction must hold for all passes through the network that may be required for the two paths.

The ACN network is single-fault tolerant under the hypothetical fault model and fault-tolerance criterion. However, this capability comes at the price of greater

hardware complexity. The ACN 4×4 crossbar switches are more complex than the switches of the hypothetical network and must have added circuitry in order to support the routing scheme. Further, the ACN has twice as many links as the hypothetical MIN.

The merged delta and INDRA networks are also single-fault tolerant under the assumptions made for Table 4. Again, this performance comes at the expense of hardware complexity. The MDN contains a total of $(N/(2C)) * \log_2(N/C)$ $2C \times 2C$ crossbar switches, each with significant routing support circuitry, and CN links. The INDRA network has $(1 + \log_R N)*N$ $R \times R$ crossbar switches and RN links. However, the MDN and INDRA networks provide C-fault and R-fault tolerance, respectively, and in the case of the INDRA network, with respect to a demanding fault-tolerance criterion. Given sufficiently high inherent component reliability, these networks may provide reliable interconnections in particularly demanding applications for which their probable high implementation costs can be justified.

W̲e have discussed eleven fault-tolerant MINs: the extra stage cube, augmented delta, multipath omega, F-network, extra stage gamma, dynamic redundancy, enhanced inverse augmented data manipulator, β-networks, augmented C-network, merged delta, and INDRA. The MIN characteristics described included fault model, fault-tolerance criterion, fault-tolerance method, single- and multiple-fault tolerance, routing complexity, and hardware complexity. Fault model and fault-tolerance criterion are essential metrics for any comparison of network fault-tolerance capabilities. Routing and hardware complexity are key data for engineering trade-off decisions. These networks represent the wide range of topologies, switch design, and data routing procedures proposed for fault-tolerance.

Error correcting codes, connecting redundant subsystems in parallel, and dividing a subsystem into identical parts connected in parallel are all venerable techniques for achieving fault tolerance. The surveyed networks serve to illustrate fault-tolerance techniques developed or employed for MINs. Those techniques independent of network topology discussed here are

(1) simulcasting (multiple transmission of

the same information on distinct paths) and
(2) dynamic full access (multiple passes through a MIN; used in β-networks).

Techniques that alter the topology of a MIN for better fault tolerance (and fault tolerant MINs embodying a given technique) are

(1) adding an extra stage with or without bypassing (ESC, augmented delta, extra stage gamma),
(2) adding extra links (F-network),
(3) increasing the number of network ports slightly (DR),
(4) completing inherent partial redundancy in a MIN (enhanced IADM),
(5) varying switch size and number of stages in an interrelated way (multipath omega),
(6) increasing switch size and adding corresponding links (ACN),
(7) replicating a MIN and cross-linking corresponding stages of switches (MDN), and
(8) replicating a MIN and adding an extra stage (INDRA).

We compared the surveyed networks by choosing a common fault model and fault-tolerance criterion based on the realistic representation of likely hardware failures rather than on easy analysis of reliability. The common fault model assumed that any network component could fail and, if faulty, was unusable. The fault-tolerance criterion specified that a network tolerated a fault only if it could still connect any one of its inputs to any one of its outputs.

Only five of the surveyed networks are single-fault tolerant under the stringent assumptions used for network comparison: the extra stage cube, dynamic redundancy, augmented C-network, merged delta, and INDRA. However, ACN, merged delta, and INDRA hardware complexity often results in a more complex and, hence, costly implementation than for the ESC. Data routing through these three networks is also more involved if their fault-tolerance capabilities are to be fully available. In their favor, all three are more tolerant of multiple faults. Finally, the dynamic redundancy network is most readily used in a system environment having spare processors to which processes can be rescheduled after failure blocks other processors from using the network.

Most of the other networks were single-fault tolerant if we relaxed the common fault model to assume perfectly reliable input and output stage switches. The ESC copes with input and output stage switch faults by having bypass circuitry that allows data to be routed past such faults when they occur. The ACN provides two links to two switches from each network input and two links to each output from two switches. The merged delta and INDRA networks each provide links to two or more switches from each network input and output. The other networks could achieve the same level of single-fault tolerance by either adding bypass circuitry in an appropriate way or including multiple connections between each network input and output port and network switches.

The field of fault-tolerant MINs is far from maturity. We can expect to see new fault-tolerant MINs and fault-tolerance techniques. Application of fundamental metrics such as fault model and fault-tolerance criterion will allow computer architects to continue to evaluate such networks when they are proposed. □

Acknowledgments

The authors thank G.J. Lipovski, M.R. Raugh, and D. Kaur for helpful discussions and comments.

This research was supported by Cooperative Agreement NCC 2-387 between the National Aeronautics and Space Administration and the Universities Space Research Association; the US Army Research Office, Dept. of the Army, under Contracts DAAG29-82-K-0101 and DAAG29-85-K-0236; the Rome Air Development Center, under Contract F30602-83-K-0119; and the National Science Foundation under Grant ECS 80-16580.

References

1. T.Y. Feng, "A Survey of Interconnection Networks," *Computer*, Dec. 1981, pp. 12-27.

2. H.J. Siegel, *Interconnection Networks for Large Scale Parallel Processing: Theory and Case Studies*, Lexington Books, Lexington, Mass., 1985.

3. M.C. Sejnowski et al., "An Overview of the Texas Reconfigurable Array Computer," *AFIPS 1980 NCC*, AFIPS Press, Montvale, N.J., 1980, pp. 631-641.

4. V.P. Kumar and S.M. Reddy, "A Fault-Tolerant Technique for Shuffle-Exchange Multistage Networks," *Computer*, this issue.

5. G.B. Adams III and H.J. Siegel, "The Extra Stage Cube: A Fault-Tolerant Interconnection Network for Supersystems," *IEEE Trans. Computers*, May 1982, pp. 443-454.

6. G.B. Adams III and H.J. Siegel, "Modifications to Improve the Fault Tolerance of the Extra Stage Cube Interconnection Network," *1984 Int'l Conf. Parallel Processing*, Computer Society Press, Silver Spring, Md., 1984, pp. 169-173.

7. H.J. Siegel and R.J. McMillen, "The Multistage Cube: A Versatile Interconnection Network," *Computer*, Dec. 1981, pp. 65-76.

8. D.M. Dias and J.R. Jump, "Augmented and Pruned *N*log*N* Multistage Networks: Topology and Performance," *1982 Int'l Conf. Parallel Processing*, Computer Society Press, Silver Spring, Md., 1982, pp. 10-11.

9. K. Padmanabhan and D.H. Lawrie, "A Class of Redundant Path Multistage Interconnection Networks," *IEEE Trans. Computers*, Dec. 1983, pp. 1099-1108.

10. D.H. Lawrie, "Access and Alignment of Data in an Array Processor," *IEEE Trans. Computers*, Dec. 1975, pp. 1145-1155.

11. L. Ciminiera and A. Serra, "A Connecting Network with Fault Tolerance Capabilities," *IEEE Trans. Computers*, June 1986, pp. 578-580.

12. M. Jeng and H.J. Siegel, "A Fault-Tolerant Multistage Interconnection Network for Multiprocessor Systems Using Dynamic Redundancy," *6th Int'l Conf. Distributed Computing Systems*, Computer Society Press, Silver Spring, Md., 1986, pp. 70-77.

13. R.J. McMillen and H.J. Siegel, "Performance and Fault Tolerance Improvements in the Inverse Augmented Data Manipulator Network," *9th Symp. Computer Architecture*, Apr. 1982, pp. 63-72.

14. K. Yoon and W. Hegazy, "The Extra Stage Gamma Network," *13th Symp. Computer Architecture*, Computer Society Press, Silver Spring, Md., 1986, pp. 175-182.

15. J.P. Shen and J.P. Hayes, "Fault-Tolerance of Dynamic-Full-Access Interconnection Networks," *IEEE Trans. Computers*, Mar. 1984, pp. 241-248.

16. S.M. Reddy and V.P. Kumar, "On Fault-Tolerant Multistage Interconnection Networks," *1984 Int'l Conf. Parallel Processing*, Computer Society Press, Silver Spring, Md., 1984, pp. 155-164.

17. D.P. Agrawal, "Graph Theoretical Analysis and Design of Multistage Interconnection Networks," *IEEE Trans. Computers*, July 1983, pp. 637-648.

18. C.S. Raghavendra and A. Varma, "INDRA: A Class of Interconnection Networks with Redundant Paths," *1984 Real-Time Systems Symp.*, Computer Society Press, Silver Spring, Md., 1984, pp. 153-164.

19. D.P. Agrawal and J.S. Leu, "Dynamic Accessibility Testing and Path Length Optimization of Multistage Interconnection Networks," *IEEE Trans. Computers*, Mar. 1985, pp. 255-266.

Readers may write to Adams at RIACS, M/S 230-5, NASA Ames Research Center, Moffett Field, CA 94035.

Readers may write to Agrawal at Dept. of Electrical and Computer Engineering, Box 7911, North Carolina State University, Raleigh, NC 27695.

Readers may write to Siegel at the Supercomputing Research Center, 4380 Forbes Blvd., Lanham, MD 20706.

George B. Adams III is a research engineer with the Research Institute for Advanced Computer Science (RIACS). His research interests include computer architecture, parallel computing, interconnection network design, and modeling and analysis of computer systems. He holds a patent with H.J. Siegel for the extra stage cube interconnection network.

Adams received the PhD degree in 1984 and the MSEE degree in 1980 from the School of Electrical Engineering, Purdue University. His BSEE degree, granted in 1978, is from Virginia Polytechnic Institute and State University.

Dharma P. Agrawal is a professor of electrical and computer engineering at North Carolina State University, Raleigh. He is the group leader for the B_Hive multicomputer project at NCSU. His research interests include both software and hardware aspects of parallel and distributed processing, computer architecture, and fault tolerant computing.

Agrawal is a fellow of the IEEE. He was awarded a "Certificate of Appreciation" by the Computer Society. He is an editor of *Computer* and the *Journal on Parallel and Distributed Computing*. He is the author of the tutorial text *Advanced Computer Architecture* published by the Computer Society of the IEEE.

Howard J. Siegel leads the PASM parallel processing system project at the Supercomputing Research Center in Lanham, Maryland. From 1976 to 1987, he was a professor at Purdue. He has consulted, given tutorials, and published over 120 papers about parallel processing. He authored the book *Interconnection Networks for Large-Scale Parallel Processing* and was a distinguished visitor of the Computer Society.

Siegel is general chairman of the 15th Computer Architecture Symposium to be held in 1988. He is also associate editor of the *Journal of Parallel and Distributed Computing*. He received degrees from MIT and Princeton and is a member of the Eta Kappa Nu and Sigma Xi honorary societies.

Fault-Tolerant Routing in DeBruijn Communication Networks

ABDOL-HOSSEIN ESFAHANIAN, MEMBER, IEEE, AND S. LOUIS HAKIMI, FELLOW, IEEE

Abstract — A class of communication networks which is suitable for "multiple processor systems" was studied by Pradhan and Reddy. The underlying graph (to be called Shift and Replace graph or SRG) is based on DeBruijn digraphs and is a function of two parameters r and m. Pradhan and Reddy have shown that the node-connectivity of SRG is at least r. The same authors give a routing algorithm which generally requires $2m$ hops if the number of node failures is $\leq (r - 1)$. In this paper we show that the node-connectivity of SRG is $(2r - 2)$. This would immediately imply that the system can tolerate up to $(2r - 3)$ node failures. We then present routing methods for situations with a certain number of node failures. When this number is $\leq (r - 2)$ our routing algorithm requires at most $m + 3 + \log_r m$ hops if $3 + \log_r m \leq m$. When the number of node failures is $\leq (2r-3)$ our routing algorithm requires at most $m + 5 + \log_r m$ hops if $4 + \log_r m \leq m$. In all the other situations our routing algorithm requires no more than $2m$ hops. The routing algorithms are shown to be computationally efficient.

Index Terms — Computer networks, connectivity of DeBruijn networks, fault-tolerant routing, multiple processor systems.

I. INTRODUCTION

THE advance in microtechnology on the one hand, and the increasing demand for reliable computing systems with high total computing power on the other hand, have intensified the research efforts in design of microcomputer systems [14], [17], [33], [34]. As a result, many architectural designs for such systems — each with its own taxonomy — have been suggested and some have been implemented [4], [16], [23], [25], [28], [32], [33]. Each design is particularly suitable for a certain application(s) and environment. The what, why, and when of such systems, and the different classifications pertinent to such systems have recently been surveyed and elaborated on by Fathi and Krieger [15]. In this paper, we are interested in a particular architecture. More specifically, we have under consideration a communication architecture which is suitable for "multiple processor systems."

A multiple processor system is a collection of linked autonomous processors where each processor has its own local memory [4], [5]. In such a system, processors communicate by transfer of data through system paths, where a path in the system is an alternating sequence of links (buses) and processors. As the processing resources, control, and data-base are distributed in these systems, they are naturally more reliable than centralized systems [29].

For diverse applications, it is desirable that a multiple processor system have the following characteristics.

1) The number of processors in the system must be large to accommodate the demand for high total computing power in applications such as database systems and interactive computing [25].

2) Since a microprocessor could be connected only to a small number of others, it is desirable to have a limited number of connections at each processing node. This would also minimize the switching logic required for each processor.

3) As the internal communication between processors for many applications does not always comply with the physical network, it is then desirable that the interprocessor distance be small [22], [25], [29]. Note that the above also implies that the system should allow ease of routing, i.e., the establishment of a communication path.

The above characteristics suggest that in the topological design of multiple processor systems, the underlying graph should have a large number of nodes, with few edges incident at each node, and a small diameter.

The above-mentioned graph design problem is known as the (Δ, D)-graph problem. In the construction of such graphs, there are three parameters of concern: the number of nodes, the maximum degree Δ, and the diameter D. These parameters are not totally independent, and specification of any two would set a bound on the third one. For instance, for given maximum degree Δ and diameter D there is a theoretical upper bound on the number of nodes in the graph. As this upper bound is generally not achievable, efforts have been made in closely approximating this bound [1], [6], [7], [11], [13], [18], [22], [24], [27], [30], [31].

The (Δ, D)-graph problem was first introduced by Elspas [13]. His work was followed by the work of Akers, Freidman, Korn, and Storwick in the 1970's [1], [13], [18], [24], [31]. More recently, the (Δ, D)-graph problem has received much attention because of its potential applications to the topological design of communication networks. The work of the above authors has been improved by Arden and Lee, Memmi and Raillard, Imase and Itoh, Leland *et al.*, Bermond *et al.*, and Reddy *et al.* [5], [7], [22], [26], [27], [30], [37].

If one, in addition to the above characteristics pertinent to MPS, is interested in fault tolerance, then the underlying graph should have high edge- and node-connectivities. Observe that such an attribute implies multiple disjoint communication paths between pairs of processors, which is also

Manuscript received August 3, 1983; revised April 15, 1985. This work was supported by the National Science Foundation under Grant ECS-8201387.

A.-H. Esfahanian is with the Department of Computer Science, Michigan State University, East Lansing, MI 48824.

S. L. Hakimi is with the Department of Electrical Engineering and Computer Science, Northwestern University, Evanston, IL 60201.

Reprinted from *IEEE Trans. Computers*, Vol. C-34, No. 9, Sept. 1985, pp. 777-788. Copyright © 1985 by The Institute of Electrical and Electronics Engineers, Inc. All rights reserved.

necessary for avoiding communication congestion.

Some work has been done in design of graphs with prescribed edge- and/or node-connectivity [3], [8]–[10], [19], [20], [35]. However, such graphs are not suitable for MPS because they generally lack some of the above essential characteristics for MPS. On the other hand, in the (Δ, D)-graph design problem the edge- and the node-connectivities are not design parameters. Consequently, the design of such graphs conveys little information about the connectivities of the designed graphs. To obtain the connectivities of the designed graphs, either analytical methods should be used or algorithms should be employed. Some authors had conjectured values for connectivities of their proposed graphs which later were proved by others [2], [27].

The Shift and Replace graph (SRG) is based on the De-Bruijn digraph, which in turn is a special case of a class of digraphs discovered by Imase and Itoh [12], [22], [29]. Until very recently, SRG was among the largest known (Δ, D)-graphs [27]. However, Bermond et al. and Reddy et al. have come up with graphs with a larger number of nodes than (Δ, D) SRG's [7], [30].

As it will be seen shortly, SRG is a very appropriate candidate for the topology of a multiple processor system. Pradhan and Reddy showed that the node-connectivity of SRG with $n = r^m$ nodes is at least r. They also proposed routing algorithms to be used in both nonfaulty and faulty environments.

In this paper we first review the SRG along with a summary of the results in [29]. In Section III, we prove that the node-connectivity of SRG with $n = r^m$ nodes is $(2r - 2)$, which is its maximum value. An upper bound for the diameter of SRG in case of node failures is also given in this section. Finally, in Section IV, we present routing algorithms which are suggested by our connectivity proof. Computational complexities of these algorithms are also given.

II. DEFINITIONS, NOTATIONS, AND SRG TOPOLOGY

Our notations will be a blend of notations used in [22] and [29]. Let $G(V, E)$ represent a graph (digraph) without loops or multiple edges, with node set V and edge set E. In the case of a graph, the degree $d(v)$ of node v is defined to be equal to the number of edges incident at node v, whereas in digraphs the in-degree (out-degree) $d_{in}(v)$ $(d_{out}(v))$ of node v is defined as the number of incoming (outgoing) directed edges to (from) node v. The distance $d(u - v)$ in G between two distinct nodes u and v is defined as the length of a shortest path (directed path in the case of digraph) from node u to node v, where the length of a path is equal to the number of edges in the path. In graph G the diameter is defined as $D(G) = \max\{d(u - v): \text{over all unordered pairs of } u \text{ and } v \text{ in } V\}$, whereas in digraph G the diameter is defined as $D(G) = \max\{d(u - v): (u - v) \in V \times V\}$. Let F be a subset of $V(G)$. By $G - F$ we mean the subgraph obtained from G by deleting the nodes in F together with their incident edges from G.

For graph $G(V, E)$, the node-connectivity $K(G)$ is defined as the minimum number of nodes whose removal would result in a disconnected or trivial graph [21]. By Menger's theorem, $K(G) = \min\{M(u - v): \text{over all } u \text{ and } v \text{ in } V\}$

where $M(u - v)$ is the maximum number of node-disjoint paths between nodes u and v in G [21]. Note that the higher the node-connectivity the more node-disjoint paths between the processors one would have, which can be used to reduce communication congestion and to increase reliability.

For given positive integers n and d, the digraph G^* proposed by Imase and Itoh in [22] is constructed as follows. Denote the nodes of G^* by $0, 1, 2, \cdots, n - 1$. Then there is a directed edge from node i to node j if and only $j = id + x(\text{mod } n)$ where $x = 0, 1, 2, \cdots, d - 1$. Clearly, for each node i in G^*, $d_{in}(i) = d_{out}(j) = d$. The same authors have shown that $D(G^*) = \lceil \log_d n \rceil$. An example of G^* with $n = 7$ and $d = 2$ [22] is given in Fig. 1.

For arbitrary values of n and d, G^* may not be a very suitable topology for multiple processor systems because, at this time, there is no known simple routing algorithm for G^*, nor is there any tight bound for the node-connectivity of G^*. For these reasons we shall primarily study the following special case of G^*.

Set $n = r^m$ and $d = r$ and construct G^* as above. The resulting digraph is known as a DeBruijn digraph [12]. The graph H^* obtained from DeBruijn digraph G^* by removing the directions of the edges in G^* and then eliminating the self-loops and the multiple edges is the topology studied by Pradhan and Reddy in [29]. Note that from the above discussion, $D(H^*) = m$. Also notice that when $m = 1$, H^* is a complete graph with r nodes; and when $r = 1$, H^* is a single node. Thus, interesting cases are when $m \geq 2$ and $r \geq 2$, and these are the cases which we will consider.

For an integer i, $0 \leq i \leq r^m - 1$, let $r(i) = (i_{m-1}, i_{m-2}, \cdots, i_1, i_0)$ be the radix-r representation of i. In H^*, a node i may also be referred to by $r(i)$. Doing so, it can be seen that in H^* node i is connected to node j, if $r(j) = (i_{m-2}, i_{m-3}, \cdots, i_0, x)$ or $r(j) = (x, i_{m-1}, i_{m-2}, \cdots, i_1)$ for $x = 0, 1, \cdots, r - 1$.

The graph H^* could be thought of as the state diagram of shift registers with alphabet size of r. The next states of the register containing $(i_{m-1}, i_{m-2}, \cdots, i_0)$ could be determined by left (or right) shifting of the register and replacing the least (most) significant digit by x, for $x = 0, 1, 2, \cdots, r - 1$, and thus the name Shift and Replace for H^*.

In [29] it is shown that H^* contains $n - r^2$ nodes of degree $2r$, r nodes of degree $2r - 2$, and $r^2 - r$ nodes of degree $2r - 1$.

We call a node j an R-neighbor of node i in H^* if $r(j) = (x, i_{m-1}, i_{m-2}, \cdots, i_2, i_1)$, and analogously, j is an L-neighbor of i if $r(j) = (i_{m-2}, i_{m-3}, \cdots, i_1, i_0, x)$ where $0 \leq x \leq r - 1$. We denote the sets consisting of R-neighbors, respectively, L-neighbors of node i by $R(i)$ and $L(i)$, and define $A(i) = R(i) \cup L(i)$. Also, it can readily be seen that $r - 1 \leq |R(i)| \leq r$, $r - 1 \leq |L(i)| \leq r$, and $|R(i) \cap L(i)| \leq 1$. In particular, $|R(i) \cap L(i)| = 1$ when $d(i) = 2r - 1$.

It can easily be seen that for an arbitrary distinct pair of nodes i and j in H^*, $|R(i) \cap L(j)| \leq 1$. In particular, $|R(i) \cap L(j)| = 1$ if and only if $(i_{m-1}, i_{m-2}, \cdots, i_2) = (j_{m-3}, \cdots, j_1, j_0)$. Also observe that either $|L(i) \cap L(j)| = 0$ or $|L(i) \cap L(j)| \geq r - 1$. Furthermore, $|L(i) \cap L(j)| \geq$

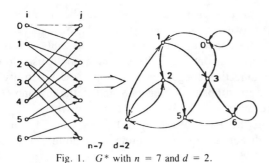

Fig. 1. G^* with $n = 7$ and $d = 2$.

TABLE I

$(i_{m-1}, i_{m-2}, i_{m-3}, \cdots, i_3, i_2, i_1, i_0)$		
path 0	path e	path (r-1)
$i_{m-2}, \cdots, i_0, 0$	$\cdots\cdots$ $i_{m-2}, \cdots, i_0, e$	$\cdots\cdots$ $i_{m-2}, \cdots\cdots, i_0, (r-1)$
$i_{m-3}, \cdots i_0, 0, 0$	$\cdots\cdots$ $i_{m-3}, \cdots, i_0, e, e$	$\cdots\cdots$ $i_{m-3}, \cdots, i_0, (r-1), (r-1)$
$\cdot$	$\cdot$	$\cdot$
$\cdot$	$\cdot$	$\cdot$
$\cdot$	$\cdot$	$\cdot$
$0, 0, \cdots, 0, 0$	$e, e, \cdots, e, e$	$(r-1), (r-1), \cdots, (r-1)$
$j_0, 0, \cdots, 0, 0$	$j_0, e, \cdots, e, e$	$j_0, (r-1), \cdots, (r-1)$
$\cdot$	$\cdot$	$\cdot$
$\cdot$	$\cdot$	$\cdot$
$\cdot$	$\cdot$	$\cdot$
$j_{m-3}, \cdots j_0, 0, 0$	$j_{m-3}, \cdots, j_0, e, e$	$j_{m-3}, \cdots, j_0, (r-1), (r-1)$
$j_{m-2}, \cdots, j_0, 0$	$j_{m-2}, \cdots, j_0, e$	$j_{m-2}, \cdots\cdots, j_1, j_0, (r-1)$

$(j_{m-1}, j_{m-2}, j_{m-3}, \cdots, j_3, j_2, j_1, j_0)$

TABLE II

$(i_{m-1}, i_{m-2}, i_{m-3}, \cdots, i_3, i_2, i_1, i_0)$		
path 0	path e	path (r-1)
$0, i_{m-1}, \cdots, i_1$	$\cdots\cdots$ $e, i_{m-1}, \cdots, i_1$	$\cdots\cdots$ $(r-1), i_{m-1}, \cdots\cdots, i_1$
$0, 0, i_{m-1}, \cdots, i_2$	$\cdots\cdots$ $e, e, i_{m-1}, \cdots, i_2$	$\cdots\cdots$ $(r-1), (r-1), i_{m-1}, \cdots, i_2$
$\cdot$	$\cdot$	$\cdot$
$\cdot$	$\cdot$	$\cdot$
$\cdot$	$\cdot$	$\cdot$
$0, 0, \cdots\cdots, 0$	$\cdots\cdots$ $e, e, \cdots\cdots, e$	$\cdots\cdots$ $(r-1), (r-1), \cdots, (r-1)$
$0, 0, \cdots, 0, j_{m-1}$	$\cdots\cdots$ $e, e, \cdots, e, j_{m-1}$	$\cdots\cdots$ $(r-1), \cdots\cdots, (r-1), j_{m-1}$
$\cdot$	$\cdot$	$\cdot$
$\cdot$	$\cdot$	$\cdot$
$\cdot$	$\cdot$	$\cdot$
$0, 0, j_{m-1}, \cdots, j_2$	$\cdots\cdots$ $e, e, j_{m-1}, \cdots, j_2$	$\cdots\cdots$ $(r-1), (r-1), j_{m-1}, \cdots, j_2$
$0, j_{m-1}, \cdots, j_1$	$\cdots\cdots$ $e, j_{m-1}, \cdots, j_1$	$\cdots\cdots$ $(r-1), j_{m-1}, \cdots\cdots, j_1$

$(j_{m-1}, j_{m-2}, j_{m-3}, \cdots, j_3, j_2, j_1, j_0)$

$r - 1$ if and only if $(i_{m-2}, i_{m-3}, \cdots, i_0) = (j_{m-2}, j_{m-3}, \cdots, j_0)$. Similar observations could be made about $|R(j) \cap L(i)|$ and $|R(i) \cap R(j)|$.

In H^* a path $v_0 - v_1 - v_2 - \cdots - v_{k-1} - v_k$, from node $i = v_0$ to node $j = v_k$, is said to be of type-R (type-L) path if for every p, $1 \leq p \leq k$, v_p is an R- (L-) neighbor of v_{p-1}. A path is said to be consistent if it is of type R or type L. Note that if $v_0 - v_1 - \cdots - v_{k-1} - v_k$ is a type-R path from node i to node j, then $v_1 \in R(i)$ and $v_{k-1} \in L(j)$. Similarly, if $v_0 - v_1 - \cdots - v_{k-1} - v_k$ is a type-L path from node i to node j, then $v_1 \in L(i)$ and $v_{k-1} \in R(j)$. We define $PR(i - j)$ as the shortest type-R path from node i to node j, and $PL(i - j)$ as the shortest type-L path from node i to node j. Observe that these paths are unique. Also note that $|PL(i - j)| \leq m$ and $|PL(i - j)| \leq m$ for any pair i and j where by $|P|$ we mean the length of the path P [22], [29].

In [29] it is shown that the node-connectivity of H^* is at least r by constructing r node-disjoint paths between an arbitrary pair of nodes $r(i) = (i_{m-1}, i_{m-2}, \cdots, i_0)$ and $r(j) = (j_{m-1}, j_{m-2}, \cdots, j_0)$ as depicted in Table I.

We note that in Table I, the first portion of the "eth path," $0 \leq e \leq r - 1$, i.e., the path from node i to node $(e, e, \cdots, e)$, is a type-L path; and the second portion of the eth path, i.e., the path from node $(e, e, \cdots, e)$ to node j, is of type R. Therefore, each of the above paths is composed of a type-L path followed by a type-R path.

Analogously, in Table II the r paths from node i to node j are node-disjoint paths where each path is composed of a type-R path followed by a type-L path.

Routing in H^* could be done by use of the shortest consistent path between a pair of nodes. In particular, given nodes i, $r(i) = (i_{m-1}, i_{m-2}, \cdots, i_1, i_0)$ and j, $r(j) = (j_{m-1}, j_{m-2}, \cdots, j_1, j_0)$, then the largest x such that $(i_{x-1}, \cdots, i_0) = (j_{m-1}, \cdots, j_{m-x})$ and the largest y such that $(j_{y-1}, \cdots, j_0) = (i_{m-1}, \cdots, i_{m-y})$ are found. Then, if $x > y$, the path

$$(i_{m-1}, i_{m-2}, i_{m-3}, \cdots\cdots\cdots\cdots\cdots\cdots, i_1, i_0)$$
$$(i_{m-2}, i_{m-3}, \cdots\cdots\cdots\cdots\cdots, i_0, j_{m-x-1})$$
$$(i_{m-3}, \cdots\cdots\cdots\cdots, i_0, j_{m-x-1}, j_{m-x-2})$$
$$\vdots$$
$$(i_{x+1}, i_x, \cdots\cdots, i_0, j_{m-x-1}, j_{m-x-2}, \cdots\cdots, j_2)$$
$$(i_x, i_{x-1}, \cdots\cdots\cdots, i_0, j_{m-x-1}, j_{m-x-2}, \cdots\cdots, j_1)$$
$$(j_{m-1}, j_{m-2}, j_{m-3}, \cdots\cdots\cdots\cdots\cdots\cdots, j_1, j_0)$$

would be $PL(i - j)$, the shortest consistent path (in this case type L) from node i to node j. If $y \leq x$, then the path

$$(i_{m-1}, i_{m-2}, \cdots\cdots\cdots\cdots\cdots\cdots, i_2, i_1, i_0)$$
$$(j_y, i_{m-1}, i_{m-2}, \cdots\cdots\cdots\cdots\cdots, i_2, i_1)$$
$$(j_{y+1}, j_y, i_{m-1}, \cdots\cdots\cdots\cdots\cdots, i_2)$$
$$\vdots$$
$$(j_{m-3}, \cdots\cdots, j_y, i_{m-1}, \cdots\cdots, i_{m-y+1}, i_{m-y})$$
$$(j_{m-2}, j_{m-3}, \cdots\cdots, j_y, i_{m-1}, \cdots\cdots, i_{m-y+1})$$
$$(j_{m-1}, j_{m-2}, \cdots\cdots\cdots\cdots\cdots\cdots, j_2, j_1, j_0)$$

would be $PR(i - j)$, the shortest consistent path (in this case type R) from node i to node j.

Since the node-connectivity of H^* is at least r, failures of up to $(r - 1)$ nodes could be tolerated, i.e., what remains of H^* is still connected. Given a set of faulty nodes F, where $|F| \leq r - 1$, routing for a pair of nonfaulty nodes could be done by choosing a path e in Table I (or in Table II) where e is not equal to the least (most) significant digit of radix-r representation of any node in F [29].

III. NODE-CONNECTIVITY OF SRG IS MAXIMUM

Let $H^*(V, E)$ be defined as before. In this section we will prove that $K(H^*) = 2r - 2$. We also give an upper bound for $D(H^*)$ in case of up to $(2r - 3)$ node failures. We begin with the following lemmas. A path P is said to avoid a set of nodes if it does not contain any member of that set. Unless otherwise specified, i and j are distinct nodes in H^* with $r(i) = (i_{m-1}, i_{m-2}, \cdots, i_1, i_0)$ and $r(j) = (j_{m-1}, j_{m-2}, \cdots, j_1, j_0)$.

Lemma 1: If $r(i) = (u, u, \cdots, u)$, $0 \leq u \leq r - 1$, and $j \notin A(i)$, then $L(i) \cap L(j) = \emptyset$ and $R(i) \cap R(j) = \emptyset$.

Proof: Assume otherwise, i.e., $L(i) \cap L(j) \neq \emptyset$. This means that $(i_{m-2}, \cdots, i_1, i_0) = (j_{m-2}, \cdots, j_1, j_0)$. As $(i_{m-1}, i_{m-2}, \cdots, i_1) = (u, u, \cdots, u) = (i_{m-2}, \cdots, i_1, i_0)$, we have $(i_{m-1}, i_{m-2}, \cdots, i_1) = (j_{m-2}, \cdots, j_1, j_0)$. But this implies that $j \in R(i) \subset A(i)$, a contradiction. By similar argument we also have $R(i) \cap R(j) = \emptyset$.

Lemma 2: Let $C = \{k \in V: k \in A(i), L(k) \cap L(j) = \emptyset$ and $R(k) \cap R(j) = \emptyset\}$. If $j \notin A(i)$, then $|C| \geq d(i) - 2$.

Proof: Let $C_1 = \{k_1 \in V: r(k_1) = (x, i_{m-1}, i_{m-2}, \cdots, i_1)$ where $0 \leq x \leq r - 1$ and $x \neq j_{m-1}\}$ and $C_2 = \{k_2 \in V: r(k_2) = (i_{m-2}, \cdots, i_1, i_0, y), 0 \leq y \leq r - 1$ and $y \neq j_0\}$. Note that $C_1 \subset R(i) \subset A(i)$ and $C_2 \subset L(i) \subset A(i)$. Furthermore, $|C_1| = |R(i)| - 1$ and $|C_2| = |L(i)| - 1$, and as $A(i) = R(i) \cup L(i)$ and $|R(i) \cap L(i)| \leq 1$, we have $|C_1 \cap C_2| \leq 1$, and consequently $|C_1 \cup C_2| \geq |A(i)| - 2 = d(i) - 2$. We want to show that for every $k_1 \in C_1$ and $k_2 \in C_2$ we have $R(k_1) \cap R(j) = \emptyset$, $L(k_1) \cap L(j) = \emptyset$, $R(k_2) \cap R(j) = \emptyset$, and $L(k_2) \cap L(j) = \emptyset$. To do this, assume that $L(k_1) \cap L(j) \neq \emptyset$. Thus $(i_{m-1}, i_{m-2}, \cdots, i_1) = (j_{m-2}, \cdots, j_1, j_0)$. But this implies that $j \in R(i)$, a contradiction as $R(i) \subset A(i)$. Now assume that $R(k_1) \cap R(j) \neq \emptyset$. This means that $(x, i_{m-1}, i_{m-2}, \cdots, i_2) = (j_{m-1}, j_{m-2}, \cdots, j_1)$, a contradiction as $x \neq j_{m-1}$. By the same token, $R(k_2) \cap R(j) = \emptyset$ and $L(k_2) \cap L(j) = \emptyset$. By letting $C = C_1 \cup C_2$ we have proved the lemma.

Hereafter, let F be a subset of $V(H^*)$ where $|F| = 2r - 3$. Denote the nodes in F by f^p with $r(f^p) = (f^p_{m-1}, f^p_{m-2}, f^p_{m-3}, \cdots, f^p_2, f^p_1, f^p_0)$ for $p = 1, 2, \cdots, (2r - 3)$. Let $H^*_f = H^* - F$. Note that any path in H^* which avoids F is also a path in H^*_f and vice versa. Also, let $MS(F) = \{e: 0 \leq e \leq r - 1, e = f^p_{m-1}$ for $p = 1, 2, \cdots, (2r - 3)\}$ and $LS(F) = \{e: 0 \leq e \leq r - 1, e = f^p_0$ for $p = 1, 2, \cdots, (2r - 3)\}$. Furthermore, define $CN = \{(u - v) \in V \times V: (u, v) \notin E, R(u) \cap R(v) = \emptyset$ and $L(u) \cap L(v) = \emptyset\}$. Remember that $\delta(H^*) = 2r - 2$ where $\delta(G)$ is the mini-

mum degree in G. This implies that $K(H^*) \leq 2r - 2$. Proving that $K(H^*) = 2r - 2$ is equivalent to showing that for any arbitrary F, and every pair of nodes i and j, i and $j \notin F$, i and j are joined by a path in H^*, which avoids F (in other words, H^*_f is connected). This is our strategy for proving that $K(H^*) = 2r - 2$. We first show that for particular F's, H^*_f is connected (Lemma 3). Then we show that for an arbitrary F, if certain pairs of nodes are connected by a path in H^*_f, then H^*_f is connected (Lemma 4). Theorem 1 will eventually lead us to prove that $K(H^*) = 2r - 2$. And now, the lemmas.

Lemma 3: If $|MS(F)| < r$ or $|LS(F)| < r$, then in H^* every pair of nodes i and j, i and $j \notin F$, is joined by a path which avoids F. Furthermore, the length of such a path is $\leq 2m$.

Proof: If $|MS(F)| < r$, then for each e, $e \notin MS(F)$, the path e in Table II is a path which joins i and j and avoids every node in F. Similarly, if $|LS(F)| < r$, then for each e, $e \notin LS(F)$, the path e in Table I is a path which joins i and j and avoids F, and hence the lemma. Also in this case, as any path in Table I or in Table II is of length $\leq 2m$, we have $D(H^*_f) \leq 2m$.

Lemma 4: Suppose every pair of nodes u and v, u and $v \notin F$, such that $(u - v) \in CN$, is joined in H^* by a path of length at most ω which avoids F. Then every pair of nodes i and j, i and $j \notin F$, such that $(i - j) \notin CN$, is joined by a path of length at most $(\omega + 1)$ in H^* which avoids F.

Proof: Observe that if $(i, j) \in E$, then we are done. Thus, we only consider the case that $(i, j) \notin E$. Moreover, we consider the case that $L(i) \cap L(j) \neq \emptyset$. The treatment of the case when $R(i) \cap R(j) \neq \emptyset$ is identical is thus omitted.

We prove the lemma by showing that if $L(i) \cap L(j) \neq \emptyset$, then there exists a node k_1, $k_1 \in A(i)$ and $k_1 \notin F$, such that $(k_1 - j) \in CN$. From the hypothesis, this would immediately imply the lemma. The argument goes as follows.

If $L(i) \cap L(j) \neq \emptyset$, then we have $(i_{m-2}, \cdots, i_1, i_0) = (j_{m-2}, \cdots, j_1, j_0)$. By Lemma 1, this means that $r(i) \neq (x, x, \cdots, x)$ and $r(j) \neq (y, y, \cdots, y)$ where $0 \leq x, y \leq r - 1$. This implies that $d(i) \geq 2r - 1$ and $d(j) \geq 2r - 1$.

Note that if node $(i_{m-2}, \cdots, i_1, i_0, j_0)$ is not in F, then the path $(i_{m-1}, i_{m-2}, \cdots, i_0) - (i_{m-2}, \cdots, i_1, i_0, j_0) - (j_{m-1}, j_{m-2}, \cdots, j_0)$ is a path from i to j which avoids F, and thus the lemma. Therefore, we need to consider only the case that $(i_{m-2}, \cdots, i_1, i_0, j_0)$ is in F.

Now, let the set $C = C_1 \cup C_2$ be as in the proof of Lemma 2. Note that the node $(i_{m-2}, i_{m-3}, \cdots, i_0, j_0)$ is *not* in C and $|C| \geq d(i) - 2$. As we are considering the case that $d(i) \geq 2r - 1$, we have $|C| \geq 2r - 3$. This implies that $|C - F| \geq 1$ because we are also assuming that $(i_{m-2}, i_{m-3}, \cdots, i_0, j_0) \in F$. Therefore, there exists at least one node $k_1 \in C$, and $k_1 \notin F$, where $L(k_1) \cap L(j) = \emptyset$ and $R(k_1) \cap R(j) = \emptyset$, and thus $(k_1 - j) \in CN$. Hence, the lemma holds.

Theorem 1: Let F, $MS(F)$, and $LS(F)$ be defined as above. Furthermore, let i and j, i and $j \notin F$, be a pair of distinct, nonadjacent nodes in H^*. Also, assume the following.

1) $|MS(F)| = r$ and $|LS(F)| = r$.
2) $(i - j) \in CN$.

Then, there exists a consistent path of length $\leq (2m - 1)$ from node i to node j which avoids F.

Proof: Before we proceed, let us consider the following points.

a) Observe that this theorem and Lemmas 3 and 4 imply that $K(H^*) = 2r - 2$ and also that $D(H_f^*) \leq 2m$.

b) For each k, $k = 0, 1, \cdots, (r - 1)$, let $M_k = \{r(f^p): f^p \in F, f_{m-1}^p = k\}$ and $L_k = \{r(f^p): f^p \in F, f_0^p = k\}$. It should not be difficult to see that assumption 1) in the statement of the theorem implies that $|M_k| \leq r - 2$ and $|L_k| \leq r - 2$. This is because if, for example, $|M_k| > r - 2$, then F contains at least $r - 1$ nodes with the same most significant digits (MSD's). As $|F| = 2r - 3$, this implies that the number of nodes in F having distinct MSD's is less than r, which contradicts assumption 1). We will make very much use of the above observation in our proof.

c) For a fixed but otherwise arbitrary pair of nodes i and j, let $\alpha = |F \cap L(i)|$ and $\beta = |F \cap R(j)|$. In our proof, we will need $\max_F(\alpha + \beta)$ and $\min_F(\alpha\beta)$. To find these numbers we first find an upper bound for $|F \cap (L(i) \cup R(j))|$. Without loss of generality, assume that $|F \cap (L(i) \cup R(j))| \leq |F \cap (R(i) \cup L(j))|$, because otherwise the role of i and j can be reversed. As it was mentioned in the previous section, for any node i in H^*, we have $|R(i) \cap L(i)| \leq 1$. In particular, only when $d(i) = 2r - 1$, we have $|R(i) \cap L(i)| = 1$. In this latter case let $R(i) = \{u_1, u_2, \cdots, u_r\}$ and $L(i) = \{v_1, v_2, \cdots, v_r\}$ with $u_1 = v_1$. Observe that, except when $d(i) = 2r - 1$, or $d(j) = 2r - 1$, we have $(R(i) \cup L(j)) \cap (R(j) \cup L(i)) = \emptyset$ (notice assumption 2) in the theorem). As $|F \cap (L(i) \cup R(j))| \leq |F \cap (R(i) \cup L(j))|$, this implies that $|F \cap (L(i) \cup R(j))| \leq \lfloor |F|/2 \rfloor = r - 2$. In order to show that $(r - 2)$ is also an upper bound for $|F \cap (L(i) \cup R(j))|$ when $d(i) = 2r - 1$, we consider a slight modification of the definition for $R(i)$ and $L(j)$ for node i if $d(i) = 2r - 1$ (and similarly for node j if $d(j) = 2r - 1$). Specifically, suppose we define $R(i) = \{u_1, u_2, \cdots, u_r\}$ and $L(i) = \{v_2, v_3, \cdots, v_r\}$. Then again, we would have $|F \cap (L(i) \cup R(j))| \leq |F \cap (R(i) \cup L(j))|$. This again implies that $|F \cap (L(i) \cup R(j))| \leq \lfloor |F|/2 \rfloor = r - 2$. Now, observe that $\alpha \leq r - 2$ and $\beta \leq r - 2$. In order to compute $\max(\alpha + \beta)$ and $\min(\alpha\beta)$, it is important to remember that for any distinct pair of nodes i and j in H^*, we have $|L(i) \cap R(j)| \leq 1$. Thus, we consider the following two cases: c1) $L(i) \cap R(j) = \emptyset$. Clearly, as we assume that i and j are such that $|F \cap (L(i) \cup R(j))| \leq |F \cap (R(i) \cup L(j))|$, then we have $\max(\alpha + \beta) = r - 2$ and $\min(\alpha\beta) = 0$. c2) $|L(i) \cap R(j)| = 1$. Let $v \in L(i) \cup R(j)$. If $v \notin F$, then we have $\max(\alpha + \beta) = r - 2$ and $\min(\alpha\beta) = 0$. Otherwise, we have $\max(\alpha + \beta) = r - 1$, and in this case, $\min(\alpha\beta) = r - 2$.

We prove the theorem by showing that there exists a node $b \notin F$ such that there is a type-L path from i to b which avoids F. And also, there is a type-L path from b to j which avoids F. This would immediately imply that i and j are joined by a type-L path in H_f^*.

Let $r(b) = (i_{m-x-1}, i_{m-x-2}, \cdots, i_0, b_{x-1}, b_{x-2}, \cdots, b_0)$ where $1 \leq x \leq m$ and $0 \leq b_k \leq r - 1$ for

$k = x - 1, x - 2, \cdots, 1, 0$. Define the path P from i to j as

$$(i_{m-1}, i_{m-2}, \cdots\cdots, i_{m-x}, i_{m-x-1}, i_{m-x-2}, \cdots\cdots, i_1, i_0)$$
$$(i_{m-2}, \cdots\cdots, i_{m-x}, i_{m-x-1}, i_{m-x-2}, \cdots\cdots, i_1, i_0, b_{x-1})$$
$$(i_{m-3}, \cdots, i_{m-x}, i_{m-x-1}, i_{m-x-2}, \cdots, i_0, b_{x-1}, b_{x-2})$$
$$\vdots$$
$$(i_{m-x}, i_{m-x-1}, i_{m-x-2}, \cdots\cdots, i_0, b_{x-1}, b_{x-2}, \cdots, b_1)$$
$$(i_{m-x-1}, i_{m-x-2}, \cdots\cdots, i_0, b_{x-1}, b_{x-2}, \cdots\cdots, b_0)$$
$$(i_{m-x-2}, i_{m-x-3}, \cdots, i_0, b_{x-1}, b_{x-2}, \cdots, b_0, j_{m-1})$$
$$(i_{m-x-3}, i_{m-x-4}, \cdots, i_0, b_{x-1}, b_{x-2}, \cdots, b_0, j_{m-1}, j_{m-2})$$
$$\vdots$$
$$(i_0, b_{x-1}, b_{x-2}, \cdots\cdots, b_0, j_{m-1}, j_{m-2}, \cdots\cdots, j_{x+1})$$
$$(b_{x-1}, b_{x-2}, \cdots\cdots, b_0, j_{m-1}, j_{m-2}, \cdots\cdots, j_x)$$
$$\vdots$$
$$(b_1, b_0, j_{m-1}, j_{m-2}, \cdots\cdots, j_2)$$
$$(b_0, j_{m-1}, j_{m-2}, \cdots\cdots, j_2, j_1)$$
$$(j_{m-1}, j_{m-2}, \cdots\cdots, j_1, j_0).$$

Observe that P is a type-L path from i to j via b, and also $|P| = x + m$. We will show that for some x, there exists a choice for $(b_{x-1}, b_{x-2}, \cdots, b_0)$ such that the path P avoids F. As mentioned earlier, we may refer to a node i in H^* by $r(i)$, the radix-r representation of i.

As each b_k, $k = x - 1, x - 2, \cdots, 2, 1, 0$, could take on any value between (and including) 0 and $r - 1$, there are r^x distinct choices for $(b_{x-1}, b_{x-2}, \cdots, b_0)$ and hence r^x candidates for $r(b)$. Of course, not every choice for $(b_{x-1}, b_{x-2}, \cdots, b_0)$ would lead to a satisfactory $r(b)$, i.e., the path P avoids F. Therefore, our goal is to find at least a choice (if indeed it exists) for $(b_{x-1}, b_{x-2}, \cdots, b_0)$ such that the path P avoids F. This task is accomplished by finding an upper bound for the number of choices for $(b_{x-1}, b_{x-2}, \cdots, b_0)$ which *are not* "allowable" because each choice may result in path P having at least one node in common with F. Denote by UC the number of unallowable choices. Note that if it turns out that UC $< r^x$, then there exists at least one choice for $(b_{x-1}, b_{x-2}, \cdots, b_0)$ and consequently one choice for $r(b)$ such that the path P avoids F. We proceed by examining closely each and every node in the path P and explore the nature of unallowable choices for $(b_{x-1}, b_{x-2}, \cdots, b_0)$.

As we assume that $i \notin F$, let us start with the first x nodes in the path P beyond node i. As a necessary condition for P to avoid F, for each k, $k = 1, 2, \cdots, x$ we must have

$$(i_{m-k-1}, i_{m-k-2}, \cdots, i_0, b_{x-1}, b_{x-2}, \cdots, b_{x-k})$$
$$\neq (f_{m-1}^p, f_{m-2}^p, f_{m-3}^p, \cdots, f_2^p, f_1^p, f_0^p)$$

for $p = 1, 2, \cdots, (2r - 3)$.

Thus, for each k, $k = 1, 2, \cdots, x$ we have $(2r - 3)$ relations to satisfy. However, for each k, those relations in which $(i_{m-k-1}, i_{m-k-2}, \cdots, i_0) \neq (f_{m-1}^p, f_{m-2}^p, \cdots, f_k^p)$ are already satisfied, implying that such relations do not restrict our choice for $(b_{x-1}, b_{x-2}, \cdots, b_0)$. Thus, we are only concerned about those relations in which $(i_{m-k-1}, i_{m-k-2}, \cdots, i_0) = (f^p_{m-1}, f^p_{m-2}, \cdots, f^p_k)$.

Formally, for each k, $k = 1, 2, \cdots, x$, define the sets: $Q_k = \{q: 1 \le q \le 2r - 3$ and $(f^q_{m-1}, f^q_{m-2}, \cdots, f^q_k) \ne (i_{m-k-1}, i_{m-k-2}, \cdots, i_0)\}$ and $S_k = \{(f^p_{m-1}, f^p_{m-2}, \cdots, f^p_1, f^p_0) \in F: p \notin Q_k\}$. Thus, $|\{p: p \notin Q_k\}| = |S_k|$. Before we go on, *it is important to observe that* $S_1 = F \cap L(i)$, *and thus* $|S_1| = \alpha$. Also note that for each k, those relations which correspond to those values of p with $p \in Q_k$ are already satisfied (and thus of no concern). And those relations which correspond to nodes in S_k will not be satisfied for some choices of $(b_{x-1}, b_{x-2}, \cdots, b_{x-k})$. In particular, for every $p \notin Q_k$, such a relation will not be satisfied if $(b_{x-1}, b_{x-2}, \cdots, b_{x-k}) = (f^p_{k-1}, f^p_{k-2}, \cdots, f^p_0)$. This means that each node in S_k makes r^{x-k} choices unallowable for $(b_{x-1}, b_{x-2}, \cdots, b_0)$ because $(b_{x-1}, b_{x-2}, \cdots, b_{x-k})$ must not be equal to $(f^p_{k-1}, f^p_{k-2}, \cdots, f^p_0)$ for $p \notin Q_k$.

Thus far we have explored the nature of unallowable choices for the first x nodes beyond i in the path P. Let us proceed with the middle $(m - x - 1)$ nodes.

Again, as a necessary condition for P to avoid F, we must have for each l, $l = 1, 2, \cdots, (m - x - 1)$:

$$(i_{m-x-l-1}, i_{m-x-l-2}, \cdots, i_0,$$
$$b_{x-1}, b_{x-2}, \cdots, b_0, j_{m-1}, j_{m-2}, \cdots, j_{m-l})$$
$$\ne (f^p_{m-1}, f^p_{m-2}, f^p_{m-3}, \cdots, f^p_2, f^p_1, f^p_0)$$
$$\text{for } p = 1, 2, \cdots, (2r - 3).$$

Once again, for each l, $l = 1, 2, \cdots, (m - x - 1)$ we have $(2r - 3)$ relations to satisfy. Observe that for each l, those relations for which we have $(i_{m-x-l-1}, i_{m-x-l-2}, \cdots, i_0) \ne (f^p_{m-1}, f^p_{m-2}, \cdots, f^p_{x+l})$ or $(j_{m-1}, j_{m-2}, \cdots, j_{m-l}) \ne (f^p_{l-1}, f^p_{l-2}, \cdots, f^p_0)$ are already satisfied and thus of no concern. For each l, $l = 1, 2, \cdots, (m - x - 1)$ define the sets: $Q''_l = \{q: 1 \le q \le 2r - 3$, either $(f^q_{m-1}, f^q_{m-2}, \cdots, f^q_{x+l}) \ne (i_{m-x-1-l}, i_{m-x-2-l}, \cdots, i_0)$ or $(f^q_l, f^q_{l-1}, \cdots, f^q_0) \ne (j_{m-1}, j_{m-2}, \cdots, j_{m-l})\}$ and $S''_l = \{(f^p_{m-1}, f^p_{m-2}, \cdots, f^p_1, f^p_0) \in F: p \notin Q''_l\}$. Thus, $|\{p: p \notin Q''_l\}| = |S''_l|$. It is not difficult to see that for each l, those relations which correspond to nodes in S''_l will not be satisfied if $(b_{x-1}, b_{x-2}, \cdots, b_0) = (f^p_{x+l-1}, f^p_{x+l-2}, \cdots, f^p_l)$ for some $p \notin Q''_l$. Thus, each node in S''_l makes only one choice unallowable for $(b_{x-1}, b_{x-2}, \cdots, b_0)$.

Now let us consider the last x nodes in the path P. Here again, as a necessary condition for P to avoid F, we must have for each k, $k = 1, 2, \cdots, x$:

$$(b_{x-k}, b_{x-k-1}, \cdots, b_0, j_{m-1}, j_{m-2}, \cdots, j_{x-k+1})$$
$$\ne (f^p_{m-1}, f^p_{m-2}, f^p_{m-3}, \cdots, f^p_2, f^p_1, f^p_0)$$
$$\text{for } p = 1, 2, \cdots, (2r - 3).$$

Here too, for each k, $k = 1, 2, \cdots, x$ we have $(2r - 3)$ relations to satisfy. However, for each k, those relations in which we have $(j_{m-1}, j_{m-2}, \cdots, j_{x-k+1}) \ne (f^p_{m-x+k-2}, f^p_{m-x+k-3}, \cdots, f^p_0)$ are already satisfied and thus of no concern. For each k, $k = 1, 2, \cdots, x$ define the sets: $Q'_k = \{q: 1 \le q \le 2r - 3, (f^q_{m-x+k-2}, f^q_{m-x+k-3}, \cdots, f^q_0) \ne (j_{m-1}, j_{m-2}, \cdots, j_{x-k+1})\}$ and $S'_k = \{(f^p_{m-1}, f^p_{m-2}, \cdots, f^p_0) \in F: p \notin Q'_k\}$. Thus, $|\{p: p \notin Q'_k\}| = |S'_k|$. *It is important to observe that* $S'_x = F \cap R(j)$, *and hence* $|S'_x| = \beta$. Also note

that those relations which correspond to nodes in S'_k will not be satisfied if $(b_{x-k}, b_{x-k-1}, \cdots, b_0)$ assumes values of the form $(f^p_{m-1}, f^p_{m-2}, \cdots, f^p_{m-x+k-1})$ for some $p \notin Q'_k$. This implies that each node in S'_k makes r^{k-1} choices unallowable for $(b_{x-1}, b_{x-2}, \cdots, b_0)$ as $(b_{x-k}, b_{x-k-1}, \cdots, b_0)$ must not assume $(f^p_{m-1}, f^p_{m-2}, \cdots, f^p_{m-x+k-1})$, $p \notin Q'_k$.

We summarize the above results in a tabular form. In Table III, on the left-hand side we have the nodes in the path P (excluding i and j). On the right-hand side, we have the "form" of unallowable choices for $(b_{x-1}, b_{x-2}, \cdots, b_0)$ corresponding to each node. Note that by $*$ we mean "don't care," i.e., any value for $*$, $0 \le * \le r - 1$, is acceptable.

We now proceed with computing an upper bound for unallowable choices (UC) for $(b_{x-1}, b_{x-2}, \cdots, b_0)$. Remember that for each k, $k = 1, 2, \cdots, x$ we have $|\{p: p \notin Q_k\}| = |S_k|$ and $|\{p: p \notin Q'_k\}| = |S'_k|$. Also, for each l, $l = 1, 2, \cdots, (m - x - 1)$ we have $|\{p: p \notin Q''_l\}| = |S''_l|$. In order to compute an upper bound for UC, we must first find an upper bound for $|S_k|$, $|S'_k|$, and $|S''_l|$. For this purpose we make use of the property of F, namely, $|MS(F)| = r$ and $|LS(F)| = r$. It is not difficult to see that these properties of F imply that $|S_k| \le r - 2$, $|S'_k| \le r - 2$, and $|S''_l| \le r - 2$ for $1 \le k \le x$ and $1 \le l \le (m - x - 1)$ (we refer the reader to comment 2) at the beginning of the theorem). In the computation of an upper bound for UC, we will use α and β for $|S_1|$ and $|S'_x|$, respectively. For all the other $|S_k|$, $|S'_k|$, and $|S''_l|$, we will use their upper bounds, i.e., $(r - 2)$. Now, let us proceed with counting the unallowable choices for $(b_{x-1}, b_{x-2}, \cdots, b_0)$.

Here by rows we mean the rows on the right-hand side of Table III. There are αr^{x-1} such choices in the first row, i.e., for $(f^0_0, *, *, \cdots, *)$; $(r - 2)r^{x-2}$ such choices in the second row; $(r - 2)r^{x-3}$ such choices in the third row; $\cdots$; $(r - 2)r$ such choices in the $(x - 1)$ row; and $(r - 2)$ such choices in the xth row. Also, there are $(r - 2)$ such choices for each of the middle rows, that is, rows $(x + 1)$ through $(m - 1)$. And finally, there are $(r - 2)$ such choices in the mth row; $(r - 2)r$ such choices in the $(m + 1)$ row; $(r - 2)r^2$ such choices in the $(m + 2)$ row; $\cdots$; $(r - 2)r^{x-2}$ such choices in the $(m + x - 1)$ row; and βr^{x-1} such choices in the last row. Adding these up we have

$$\text{UC} \le \alpha r^{x-1} + (r - 2)r^{x-2} + \cdots + (r - 2)r + (r - 2)$$
$$+ (r - 2)(m - x - 1) + (r - 2) + (r - 2)r$$
$$+ (r - 2)r^2 + \cdots + (r - 2)r^{x-2} + \beta r^{x-1}$$

or

$$\text{UC} \le (\alpha + \beta)r^{x-1} + 2(r - 2)(r^{x-1} - 1)/(r - 1)$$
$$+ (r - 2)(m - x - 1).$$

Although the above relation is an upper bound for UC, we can tighten this upper bound substantially as follows. Counting the unallowable choices as we did, many choices were counted more than once. Take, for example, the first and the last rows, namely, $(f^0_0, *, *, \cdots, *)$, $p \notin Q_1$ and $(*, *, \cdots, *, f^q_{m-1})$, $q \notin Q'_x$. The choices $(f^0_0, *, *, \cdots, *, f^q_{m-1})$ were counted twice. Thus, we could subtract $\alpha\beta r^{x-2}$ from the right-hand side of the above inequality, and this is

TABLE III

Nodes in the path P	Un-allowable choices for $(b_{x-1}, b_{x-2}, \ldots, b_0)$	
$(1_{m-2}, 1_{m-3}, \ldots, 1_{m-x-1}, \ldots, 1_0, b_{x-1})$	$(f_0^P, *, *, \ldots \ldots \ldots, *)$	$p \notin Q_1$
$(1_{m-3}, \ldots, 1_{m-x-1}, \ldots, 1_0, b_{x-1}, b_{x-2})$	$(f_1^P, f_0^P, *, *, \ldots \ldots, *)$	$p \notin Q_2$
.	.	.
.	.	.
$(1_{m-x}, \ldots, 1_0, b_{x-1}, b_{x-2}, \ldots, b_1)$	$(f_{x-2}^P, \ldots, f_1^P, f_0^P, *)$	$p \notin Q_{x-1}$
$(1_{m-x-1}, \ldots, 1_0, b_{x-1}, b_{x-2}, \ldots, b_0)$	$(f_{x-1}^P, f_{x-2}^P, \ldots, f_1^P, f_0^P)$	$p \notin Q_x$
$(1_{m-x-2}, \ldots, 1_0, b_{x-1}, \ldots, b_0, J_{m-1})$	$(f_x^P, f_{x-1}^P, \ldots, f_2^P, f_1^P)$	$p \notin Q_1''$
$(1_{m-x-3}, \ldots, 1_0, b_{x-1}, \ldots, b_0, J_{m-1}, J_{m-2})$	$(f_{x+1}^P, f_x^P, \ldots \ldots, f_2^P)$	$p \notin Q_2''$
.	.	.
.	.	.
$(1_0, b_{x-1}, \ldots, b_0, J_{m-1}, J_{m-2}, \ldots, J_{x+1})$	$(f_{m-2}^P, f_{m-3}^P, \ldots, f_{m-x-1}^P)$	$p \notin Q_{m-x-1}''$
$(b_{x-1}, \ldots, b_0, J_{m-1}, J_{m-2}, \ldots, J_x)$	$(f_{m-1}^P, f_{m-2}^P, \ldots, f_{m-x}^P)$	$p \notin Q_1'$
$(b_{x-2}, \ldots, b_0, J_{m-1}, J_{m-2}, \ldots, J_{x-1})$	$(*, f_{m-1}^P, \ldots, f_{m-x+1}^P)$	$p \notin Q_2'$
$(b_{x-3}, \ldots, b_0, J_{m-1}, J_{m-2}, \ldots, J_{x-2})$	$(*, *, f_{m-1}^P, \ldots, f_{m-x+2}^P)$	$p \notin Q_3'$
.	.	.
$(b_1, b_0, J_{m-1}, J_{m-2}, \ldots \ldots, J_2)$	$(*, *, \ldots, *, f_{m-1}^P, f_{m-2}^P)$	$p \notin Q_{x-1}'$
$(b_0, J_{m-1}, J_{m-2}, \ldots \ldots \ldots, J_1)$	$(*, *, \ldots \ldots, *, f_{m-1}^P)$	$p \notin Q_x'$

only when we consider the first and the last rows. Observing the same thing for the first row and the second-to-last row, namely, $(*, *, \ldots, *, f_{m-1}^q, f_{m-2}^q)$, $q \notin Q_{x-1}'$, the choices $(f_0^b, *, \ldots, *, f_{m-1}^q, f_{m-2}^q)$ have been counted twice, and thus we could subtract $\alpha(r - 2)r^{x-3}$ from the right-hand side. Continuing this process for all pairs of rows where such an observation is possible, we have

$$
\begin{aligned}
\text{UC} \leq{} & (\alpha + \beta)r^{x-1} + 2(r - 2)(r^{x-1} - 1)/(r - 1) \\
& + (r - 2)(m - x - 1) - \alpha\beta r^{x-2} \\
& - \alpha(r - 2)[r^{x-3} + r^{x-4} + \cdots + 1] \\
& - \beta(r - 2)[r^{x-3} + r^{x-4} + \cdots + 1] \\
& - (r - 2)^2 \sum_{k=1}^{x-3} k r^{x-k-3}
\end{aligned}
$$

or

$$
\text{UC} \leq (r - 1)^{-2}[(\alpha + \beta)g - \alpha\beta h + c]
$$

where

$$
g = (r - 1)^3 r^{x-2} + (r - 1)r^{x-2} + (r - 2)(r - 1)
$$

$$
h = (r - 1)^2 r^{x-2}
$$

$$
\begin{aligned}
c ={} & (r - 2)(2r^2 - 3r + 2)r^{x-2} + m(r - 2)(r - 1)^2 \\
& - x(r - 2)(r - 1) - (r - 2)(3r^2 - 7r + 5).
\end{aligned}
$$

Note that $g > 0$ and $h > 0$ for $r \geq 2$. This implies that we can compute an upper bound for UC by substituting $(\alpha + \beta)$ with its maximum and $\alpha\beta$ with its minimum. The theorem is proved if we can show that there exists an x such that for all $m, r \geq 2$ we have $\text{UC}_b < r^x$ where UC_b is the above upper bound for UC. Using the results we obtained for $\max(\alpha + \beta)$ and $\min(\alpha\beta)$, we have the following two cases to consider for finding UC_b.

Case 1: $\max(\alpha + \beta) = r - 2$ and $\min(\alpha\beta) = 0$.

We substitute $(\alpha + \beta) = r - 2$ and $(\alpha\beta) = 0$ in the expression for UC_b, which results in $\text{UC}_b = (r - 1)^{-2} \cdot [(r - 2)g + c]$. Thus, we need only to show that $(r - 1)^{-2}[(r - 2)g + c] < r^x$. Substituting for g and c their values, this inequality becomes

$$
\begin{aligned}
& -(r^2 - 2r + 2)r^{x-1} + m(r - 2)(r - 1)^2 \\
& \quad - x(r - 2)(r - 1) - (r - 2)(2r^2 - 4r + 3) < 0.
\end{aligned}
$$

We prove the validity of the above inequality by showing that $-(r^2 - 2r + 2)r^{x-1} + m(r - 2)(r - 1)^2 < 0$. Equivalently, we may write $(r^2 - 3r + 2)[m(r - 1) - r^{x-1}] - r^x < 0$. As $(r^2 - 3r + 2) \geq 0$ for integral values of $r > 0$, to prove the validity of the above inequality we need only show that $m(r - 1) - r^{x-1} \leq 0$ for integral values of $r > 0$. Clearly, if $x \geq \log_r m + \log_r(r - 1) + 1$, then the inequality $m(r - 1) - r^{x-1} \leq 0$ holds. Actually, we have $1 \leq x \leq m$. This implies that we must have $\lceil 1 + \log_r m \rceil \leq x \leq m$. Note that $\lceil 1 + \log_r m \rceil \leq m - 1$ for all $m \geq 5$, $r \geq 2$; and one can easily verify that for all $r \geq 2$, the original inequality (namely, $\text{UC}_b < r^x$) holds for $m = 2, 3$, and 4, if we let $x = m - 1$. Thus, by letting $x = \min(m - 1, \lceil 1 + \log_r m \rceil)$, we have chosen the smallest x such that the above inequality holds (the need for small x will be clear later). Hence, for this case there exists at least one choice for $(b_{x-1}, b_{x-2}, \cdots, b_0)$ and consequently one choice for $r(b)$ such that the path P avoids F. Notice that $|P| = m + x = m + \min(m - 1, \lceil 1 + \log_r m \rceil) \leq 2m - 1$ for this case.

Case 2: $\max(\alpha + \beta) = r - 1$ and $\min(\alpha\beta) = r - 2$.

Again, we substitute $(\alpha + \beta) = r - 1$ and $(\alpha\beta) = r - 2$ in the expression for UC_b, which results in $\text{UC}_b = (r - 1)^{-2}[(r - 1)g + (r - 2)h + c]$. Thus, again, we need to show that $(r - 1)^{-2}[(r - 1)g + (r - 2)h + c] < r^x$. Substituting for g, h, and c their values, the above inequality becomes

$$
\begin{aligned}
& -(r^2 - 3r + 3)r^{x-2} + m(r - 2)(r - 1)^2 \\
& \quad - x(r - 1)(r - 2) - (r - 2)(2r^2 - 5r + 4) < 0.
\end{aligned}
$$

Again, we prove the validity of the above inequality by showing that in fact $-(r^2 - 3r + 3)r^{x-2} + m(r - 2)(r - 1)^2 < 0$. Equivalently, we may write $(r^2 - 3r + 2)[m(r - 1) - r^{x-2}] - r^{x-2} < 0$. This implies that we need only show that $m(r - 1) - r^{x-2} \leq 0$ for integral values of $r > 0$. We again see that if $x \geq \log_r m + \log_r(r - 1) + 2$, then the above inequality holds. However, we have $1 \leq x \leq m$, and thus $\lceil 2 + \log_r m \rceil \leq x \leq m$. Again, observe that $\lceil 2 + \log_r m \rceil \leq m - 1$ for all $m \geq 6$, $r \geq 2$. And here too, one can easily verify that for all $r \geq 2$, the original inequality would hold for $m = 2, 3, 4$, and 5, if we let $x = m - 1$. Thus, by letting $x = \min(m - 1, \lceil 2 + \log_r m \rceil)$, we have chosen the smallest x such that the above inequality holds. Hence, for this case also there exists at least one choice for $(b_{x-1}, b_{x-2}, \cdots, b_0)$, and consequently one choice for $r(b)$ such that the path P avoids F. Notice that $|P| = m + x = m + \min(m - 1, \lceil 2 + \log_r m\rceil) \le 2m - 1$ for this case.

Therefore, by letting $x = \min(m - 1, \lceil 2 + \log_r m\rceil)$ we have chosen not only an x but also the smallest x such that there exists at least one choice for $(b_{x-1}, b_{x-2}, \cdots, b_0)$, which leads to a satisfactory $r(b)$, i.e., the path P avoids F. As we also have $|P| \le m + \min(m - 1, \lceil 2 + \log_r m\rceil) \le 2m - 1$, the theorem holds.

Theorem 2: Let $H^*(V, E)$, F, and H_f^* be defined as before. Then $K(H^*) = 2r - 2$. Furthermore, for any arbitrary F with $|F| \le 2r - 3$, $D(H_f^*) \le 2m$.

Proof: The fact that $K(H^*) = 2r - 2$ is implied by the results of Lemmas 3 and 4 and Theorem 1. We now show that if $|F| \le 2r - 3$, then every pair of nodes i and j in H^* is joined by at least one path of length $\le 2m$ which avoids F. If $|MS(F)| < r$ or $|LS(F)| < r$, then by Lemma 3, i and j are joined by at least one path as indicated in Table I or II. If $|MS(F)| = r$ and $|LS(F)| = r$, then by Theorem 1, those pairs of nodes i and j with $(i - j) \in CN$ are joined by a path P with $|P| = m + \min(m - 1, \lceil 2 + \log_r m\rceil) \le 2m - 1$. By Lemma 4, this implies that if $(i - j) \notin CN$, i and j are joined by a path of length $\le |P| + 1 \le 2m$. This completes the proof of the theorem.

The following theorem often gives a tighter upper bound for $D(H_f^*)$.

Theorem 3: Let H^*, F, and H_f^* be defined as before. Then for any arbitrary F with $|F| \le 2r - 3$, we have $D(H_f^*) \le m + \min(m, 5 + \log_r m)$.

Proof: Observe that when $5 + \log_r m > m$ the theorem is proved because by Theorem 2 we already know that $D(H_f^*) \le 2m$. Thus, we only need to show that when $5 + \log_r m \le m$, then we have $D(H_f^*) \le m + 5 + \log_r m$. We refer to those values of m for which "$5 + \log_r m \le m$" holds as "proper" values of m.

Let CN be defined as before. We prove the above by showing that for the proper values of m, an arbitrary pair of nodes i and j such that $i, j \notin F$ and $(i - j) \in CN$, is joined in H^* by a path of length $\le m + 4 + \log_r m$ which avoids F. By Lemma 4 this would immediately imply the desired result.

Let i and j be defined as above. Furthermore, without loss of generality, assume that $|F \cap (L(i) \cup R(j))| \le |F \cap (R(i) \cup L(j))|$, because otherwise the role of i and j could be reversed. Moreover, let the node b and the path P be defined as in proof of Theorem 1. Using the same technique as in the proof of Theorem 1, we show that for the proper values of m, when $x = 4 + \log_r m$, there exists at least one choice for $(b_{x-1}, b_{x-2}, \cdots, b_0)$, and consequently one choice for b such that the path P avoids F. Thus, without repeating the whole process of exploring the nature of unallowable choices for $(b_{x-1}, b_{x-2}, \cdots, b_0)$ we proceed with finding an upper bound for UC, the number of unallowable choices for $(b_{x-1}, b_{x-2}, \cdots, b_0)$. The main point of contrast between here and there is that except for $|S_1|$ and $|S_x'|$, here we have $|S_k| \le 2r - 3, |S_k'| \le 2r - 3$, and $|S_l''| \le 2r - 3$. This is because here we make no assumption about the size of the set $MS(F)$ or the size of the set $LS(F)$. Thus, in the process of finding an upper bound for UC we set $|S_1| = \alpha$ and $|S_x'| = \beta$. For all the other $|S_k|, |S_k'|$, and $|S_l''|$ we use their upper bounds $(2r - 3)$ (rather than $(r - 2)$, as was the case in Theorem 1). Doing so, we end up with Table IV.

Employing the same method of counting the unallowable choices for $(b_{x-1}, b_{x-2}, \cdots, b_0)$, we finally end up with the following expression for UC:

$$\text{UC} \le (r - 2)^{-2}[(\alpha + \beta)g' - \alpha\beta h' + c']$$

where

$$g' = (r - 1)(r - 2)r^{x-2} + (r - 1)^2 r^{x-2} + (r - 1)(r - 2)$$

$$h' = (r - 1)^2 r^{x-2}$$

$$c' = (2r - 3)(2r^2 - 4r + 3)r^{x-2} + m(2r - 3)(r - 1)^2 + x(2r - 3)(r^2 - 3r + 2) - (2r - 3)(5r^2 - 12r + 8).$$

Note that $g' > 0$ and $h' > 0$ for $r \ge 2$. Thus, we can compute an upper bound for UC as we did before. This leads us to consider the following two cases.

Case 1: $\max(\alpha + \beta) = r - 2$ and $\min(\alpha\beta) = 0$.

We substitute for $(\alpha + \beta) = r - 2$ and $(\alpha\beta) = 0$ in the expression for UC_b, which results in $\text{UC}_b = (r - 1)^{-2} \cdot [(r - 2)g' + c']$. Thus, we need only to show that for the proper values of m, and if $x = 4 + \log_r m$, then we have $(r - 1)^{-2}[(r - 1)g' + c'] < r^x$. Substituting for g' and c' their values, the above inequality becomes $-(r^2 - 3r + 3) \cdot r^{x-2} + m(2r - 3)(r - 1)^2 + x(2r - 3)(r^2 - 3r + 2) - (2r - 3)(4r^2 - 9r + 6) < 0$.

Before we prove the validity of the above inequality for the above value of x, let us point out that it is easy to see that for arbitrary m and r there may not exist an x, $1 \le x \le m$, such that the above inequality would hold. For example, when $m = 4$ and $r \ge 2$, the inequality does not hold for any x, $1 \le x \le 4$. This is why we could not prove Theorem 1 without assuming $|MS(F)| = r$ and $|LS(F)| = r$.

We now proceed to show the validity of the above inequality for the proper values of m and when $x = 4 + \log_r m$. Substituting $r^{x-2} = mr^2$, the above inequality becomes

$$-m(r^2 - 3r + 3)r^2 + m(2r - 3)(r - 1)^2 + x(2r - 3)$$
$$\cdot (r^2 - 3r + 2) - 2(2r - 3)(4r^2 - 9r + 6) < 0.$$

Observe that the condition that $1 \le x \le m$ is already satisfied because we are assuming that $5 + \log_r m \le m$. Hence, we prove the validity of the above inequality by showing the validity of the following inequality, which is the above inequality with $x = m$:

$$-m(r^2 - 3r + 3)r^2 + m(2r - 3)(r - 1)^2 + m(2r - 3)$$
$$\cdot (r^2 - 3r + 2) - 2(2r - 3)(4r^2 - 9r + 6)$$
$$= -m(r^4 - 7r^3 + 19r^2 - 21r + 9) - 2(2r - 3)$$
$$(4r^2 - 9r + 6) < 0.$$

One can easily verify that $(r^4 - 7r^3 + 19r^2 - 21r + 9) > 0$ for all $r \ge 2$. Thus, the above inequality holds for the proposed value of x.

Case 2: $\max(\alpha + \beta) = r - 1$ and $\min(\alpha\beta) = r - 2$.

We substitute $(\alpha + \beta) = r - 1$ and $(\alpha\beta) = r - 2$ in the

TABLE IV

Nodes in the path P	Un-allowable choices for $(b_{x-1}, b_{x-2}, \cdots \cdots, b_0)$	
$(i_{m-2}, i_{m-3}, \cdots \cdots, i_{m-x-1}, \cdots \cdots, i_0, b_{x-1})$	$(f_0^p, *, *, \cdots \cdots \cdots \cdots, *)$	$p \neq Q_1$
$(i_{m-3}, \cdots \cdots, i_{m-x-1}, \cdots \cdots, i_0, b_{x-1}, b_{x-2})$	$(f_1^p, f_0^p, *, *, \cdots \cdots, *)$	$1 \leq p \leq 2r-3$
.	.	.
.	.	.
.	.	.
$(i_{m-x}, \cdots \cdots, i_0, b_{x-1}, b_{x-2}, \cdots \cdots, b_1)$	$(f_{x-2}^p, \cdots \cdots, f_1^p, f_0^p, *)$	$1 \leq p \leq 2r-3$
$(i_{m-x-1}, \cdots \cdots, i_0, b_{x-1}, b_{x-2}, \cdots \cdots, b_0)$	$(f_{x-1}^p, f_{x-2}^p, \cdots \cdots, f_1^p, f_0^p)$	$1 \leq p \leq 2r-3$
$(i_{m-x-2}, \cdots \cdots, i_0, b_{x-1}, \cdots \cdots, b_0, j_{m-1})$	$(f_x^p, f_{x-1}^p, \cdots \cdots, f_2^p, f_1^p)$	$1 \leq p \leq 2r-3$
$(i_{m-x-3}, \cdots, i_0, b_{x-1}, \cdots, b_0, j_{m-1}, j_{m-2})$	$(f_{x+1}^p, f_x^p, \cdots \cdots, f_2^p)$	$1 \leq p \leq 2r-3$
.	.	.
.	.	.
$(i_0, b_{x-1}, \cdots, b_0, j_{m-1}, j_{m-2}, \cdots, j_{x+1})$	$(f_{m-2}^p, f_{m-3}^p, \cdots, f_{m-x-1}^p)$	$1 \leq p \leq 2r-3$
$(b_{x-1}, \cdots \cdots, b_0, j_{m-1}, j_{m-2}, \cdots \cdots, j_x)$	$(f_{m-1}^p, f_{m-2}^p, \cdots \cdots, f_{m-x}^p)$	$1 \leq p \leq 2r-3$
$(b_{x-2}, \cdots \cdots, b_0, j_{m-1}, j_{m-2}, \cdots, j_{x-1})$	$(*, f_{m-1}^p, \cdots \cdots, f_{m-x+1}^p)$	$1 \leq p \leq 2r-3$
$(b_{x-3}, \cdots \cdots, b_0, j_{m-1}, j_{m-2}, \cdots, j_{x-2})$	$(*, *, f_{m-1}^p, \cdots \cdots, f_{m-x+2}^p)$	$1 \leq p \leq 2r-3$
.	.	.
.	.	.
$(b_1, b_0, j_{m-1}, j_{m-2} \cdots \cdots \cdots \cdots, j_2)$	$(*, *, \cdots \cdots, *, f_{m-1}^p, f_{m-2}^p)$	$1 \leq p \leq 2r-3$
$(b_0, j_{m-1}, j_{m-2} \cdots \cdots \cdots \cdots, j_1)$	$(*, *, \cdots \cdots \cdots \cdots, *, f_{m-1}^p)$	$p \neq Q_x'$

expression for UC_b, which results in $UC_b = (r-1)^{-2} \cdot [(r-1)g' - (r-2)h' + c']$. Here again we need to show that $(r-1)^{-2}[(r-1)g' - (r-2)h' + c'] < r^x$ for the proper values of m and when $x = 4 + \log_r m$. Substituting for g', h', and c' their values, the above inequality becomes

$$-(r^2 - 2r + 2)r^{x-2} + m(2r-3)$$
$$\cdot (r-1)^2 + x(2r-3)(r^2 - 3r + 2) - (2r-3)$$
$$\cdot (4r^2 - 10r + 7) < 0.$$

Using the same method as in Case 1, one can readily verify that the above inequality holds for $x = 4 + \log_r m$ and proper values of m.

Thus, when $5 + \log_r m \leq m$, choosing $x = 4 + \log_r m$ implies that there exists at least one choice for $(b_{x-1}, b_{x-2}, \cdots, b_0)$, and consequently one choice for $r(b)$ such that the path P avoids F. As $|P| = m + x$ we have proved the theorem.

In summary, we have shown that $K(H^*) = 2r - 2$. Also, for an arbitrary F with $|F| \leq 2r - 3$, we have $D(H_f^*) \leq m + \min(m, 5 + \log_r m)$.

IV. Fault-Tolerant Routing in SRG

In a multiple processor system with $H^*(V, E)$ topology, let $F \subseteq V$ be the set of faulty nodes (processors). In Section II we reviewed the routing methods described in [29], which were mainly intended for situations in which we have $0 \leq |F| \leq r - 1$. As a result of the previous section, we have $K(H^*) = 2r - 2$. This implies that the system can tolerate up to $(2r - 3)$ processor failures without being dis-

connected. In this section we describe routing methods for the situations in which we have $1 \leq |F| \leq 2r - 3$.

Let F be defined as above. As mentioned in Section I, when $|F| = 0$, the routing method described in [29] is based on finding the shortest consistent (type-R or type-L) path between a pair of processors. We will refer to this method as *Algorithm 1*. When $1 \leq |F| \leq r - 1$, the routing method described in [29] is based on using a path in Table I or II as stated earlier. We refer to this method as *Algorithm 2*.

Clearly, in general, when $r \leq |F| \leq 2r - 3$, Algorithm 2 fails. For example, if $F = \{(x, x, \cdots, x) \in V: 0 \leq x \leq r - 1\}$, then every path in Tables I and II has a node in common with F, and thus it cannot be used. However, based on Lemma 3, in situations in which we have $|MS(F)| < r$ or $|LS(F)| < r$, the method described in [29] is still applicable and routing can be done by using the eth path in Table II or in Table I where $e \notin MS(F)$ or, respectively, $e \notin LS(F)$. We will refer to this method as *Algorithm 3*.

Our routing methods are primarily derived from our connectivity proof. Depending upon the value of m and the size of F, we describe different methods. However, in each case, for a given set of faulty nodes F, the routing for a pair of nonfaulty nodes i and j is done by finding a node b such that there is a path from i to j via b which avoids F. Thus, the major part of the computation in our methods will be due to finding such a node. As will be seen shortly, in most situations the computation for finding b is minimal. This is because such a computation is, for the most part, independent of i and j. We proceed with the following theorem.

Theorem 4: Let H^* and F with $|F| \leq r - 2$ be defined as before. Furthermore, for an arbitrary pair of nodes i and j such that $i, j \notin F$, let the node b and the path P be defined as in the proof of Theorem 1. Then, provided that $3 + \log_r m \leq m$, when $x = 3 + \log_r m$ there exists a particular choice for $(b_{x-1}, b_{x-2}, \cdots, b_0)$, and consequently node b such that the path P avoids F. Furthermore, the choice $(b_{x-1}, b_{x-2}, \cdots, b_0)$ is independent of i and j.

Proof: Using the same method as for the proof of Theorem 1, let us consider the first x nodes beyond i in the path P. As a necessary condition for the path P to avoid F, for each k, $k = 1, 2, \cdots, x$ we must have

$$(i_{m-k-1}, i_{m-k-2}, \cdots, i_0, b_{x-1}, b_{x-2}, \cdots, b_{x-k})$$
$$\neq (f_{m-1}^p, f_{m-2}^p, f_{m-3}^p, \cdots, f_2^p, f_1^p, f_0^p)$$
$$\text{for } p = 1, 2, \cdots, (r-2).$$

As we have no control on F, i, and j, to satisfy the above relations, for each k we must have

$$(b_{x-1}, b_{x-2}, \cdots, b_{x-k}) \neq (f_{k-1}^p, f_{k-2}^p, \cdots, f_0^p)$$
$$\text{for } 1 \leq p \leq r - 2.$$

Considering the middle $(m - x - 1)$ nodes in the path P, for each l, $l = 1, 2, \cdots, (m - x - 1)$ we must have

$$(i_{m-x-l-1}, i_{m-x-l-2}, \cdots, i_0,$$
$$b_{x-1}, b_{x-2}, \cdots, b_0, j_{m-1}, j_{m-2}, \cdots, j_{m-l})$$
$$\neq (f_{m-1}^p, f_{m-2}^p, f_{m-3}^p, \cdots, f_2^p, f_1^p, f_0^p)$$
$$\text{for } p = 1, 2, \cdots, (r-2).$$

Again, as we assume no control on F, i, and j, to satisfy the above relations, for each l we must have

$$(b_{x-1}, b_{x-2}, \cdots, b_0) \neq (f^p_{x+l-1}, f^p_{x+l-2}, \cdots, f^p_l)$$

$$\text{for } 1 \leq p \leq r - 2.$$

Finally, let us consider the last x nodes in the path P. As a necessary condition for path P to avoid F, for each k, $k = 1, 2, \cdots, x$ we must have

$$(b_{x-k}, b_{x-k-1}, \cdots, b_0, j_{m-1}, j_{m-2}, \cdots, j_{x-k+1})$$
$$\neq (f^p_{m-1}, f^p_{m-2}, f^p_{m-3}, \cdots, f^p_2, f^p_1, f^p_0)$$
$$\text{for } p = 1, 2, \cdots, (r - 2).$$

Here too, assuming no control on F, i, and j, to satisfy the above relations, for each k we must have

$$(b_{x-k}, b_{x-k-1}, \cdots, b_0) \neq (f^p_{m-1}, f^p_{m-2}, \cdots, f^p_{m-x+k-1})$$

$$\text{for } 1 \leq p \leq r - 2.$$

We summarize the above results in Table V. By this time the reader should not have difficulty in seeing that in Theorems 1, 3, and 4, the form of unallowable choices for $(b_{x-1}, b_{x-2}, \cdots, b_0)$, corresponding to each node in the path P, is the same. The main difference in each case is the number of choices having a particular form.

For the case under consideration, the number of choices having a particular form (i.e., rows of the above table) is exactly $(r - 2)$, the bound on $|F|$. Thus, using the same method of counting unallowable choices for $(b_{x-1}, b_{x-2}, \cdots, b_0)$, it is not difficult to see that one can come up with an upper bound for UC in this case by substituting $\alpha = r - 2$ and $\beta = r - 2$ in the expression for UC_b found in the proof of Theorem 1. Doing so, we have $\text{UC}_b \leq (r - 1)^{-2}[2(r - 2)g - (r - 2)^2h + c]$ where g, h, and c are as in the proof of Theorem 1. Thus, to prove the theorem we only need to show that $(r - 1)^{-2} \cdot [2(r - 2)g - (r - 2)^2h + c] < r^x$ for $x = 3 + \log_r m$ provided that $3 + \log_r m \leq m$. Substituting for g, h, and c their values, the above inequality becomes

$$-r^x + m(r - 2)(r - 1)^2 - x(r - 2)(r - 1)$$
$$- (r - 2)(r^2 - r + 1) < 0.$$

It is not difficult to verify that the above inequality indeed holds for $x = 3 + \log_r m$. As it is required that $1 \leq x \leq m$, we must have $3 + \log_r m \leq m$. The validity of this inequality is already assumed, thus the theorem.

Let us now consider how one can find a choice for $(b_{x-1}, b_{x-2}, \cdots, b_0)$ using each of Tables III–V. Clearly, a choice for $(b_{x-1}, b_{x-2}, \cdots, b_0)$ regarding a particular table could be found by sorting (according to their numerical values) all the unallowable choices of the forms in that table and then choosing a "missed" value as a choice for $(b_{x-1}, b_{x-2}, \cdots, b_0)$ where in a sorted array A, a missed value u is such that $A(k) < u < A(k + 1)$ for some k. However, it is important to observe that the unallowable choices in Table III depend on three parameters, namely, the end nodes i and j of the path P and the set of faulty nodes F. This is

TABLE V

Nodes in the path P	Un-allowable choices for $(b_{x-1}, b_{x-2}, \cdots, b_0)$	
$(i_{m-2}, i_{m-3}, \cdots, i_{m-x-1}, \cdots, i_0, b_{x-1})$	$(f^p_0, *, *, \cdots, *)$	$1 \leq p \leq r-2$
$(i_{m-3}, \cdots, i_{m-x-1}, \cdots, i_0, b_{x-1}, b_{x-2})$	$(f^p_1, f^p_0, *, *, \cdots, *)$	$1 \leq p \leq r-2$
.	.	.
.	.	.
.	.	.
$(i_{m-x}, \cdots, i_0, b_{x-1}, b_{x-2}, \cdots, b_1)$	$(f^p_{x-2}, \cdots, f^p_1, f^p_0, *)$	$1 \leq p \leq r-2$
$(i_{m-x-1}, \cdots, i_0, b_{x-1}, b_{x-2}, \cdots, b_0)$	$(f^p_{x-1}, f^p_{x-2}, \cdots, f^p_1, f^p_0)$	$1 \leq p \leq r-2$
$(i_{m-x-2}, \cdots, i_0, b_{x-1}, \cdots, b_0, j_{m-1})$	$(f^p_x, f^p_{x-1}, \cdots, f^p_2, f^p_1)$	$1 \leq p \leq r-2$
$(i_{m-x-3}, \cdots, i_0, b_{x-1}, \cdots, b_0, j_{m-1}, j_{m-2})$	$(f^p_{x+1}, f^p_x, \cdots, f^p_2)$	$1 \leq p \leq r-2$
.	.	.
.	.	.
.	.	.
$(i_0, b_{x-1}, \cdots, b_0, j_{m-1}, j_{m-2}, \cdots, j_{x+1})$	$(f^p_{m-2}, f^p_{m-3}, \cdots, f^p_{m-x-1})$	$1 \leq p \leq r-2$
$(b_{x-1}, \cdots, b_0, j_{m-1}, j_{m-2}, \cdots, j_x)$	$(f^p_{m-1}, f^p_{m-2}, \cdots, f^p_{m-x})$	$1 \leq p \leq r-2$
$(b_{x-2}, \cdots, b_0, j_{m-1}, j_{m-2}, \cdots, j_{x-1})$	$(*, f^p_{m-1}, \cdots, f^p_{m-x+1})$	$1 \leq p \leq r-2$
$(b_{x-3}, \cdots, b_0, j_{m-1}, j_{m-2}, \cdots, j_{x-2})$	$(*, *, f^p_{m-1}, \cdots, f^p_{m-x+2})$	$1 \leq p \leq r-2$
.	.	.
.	.	.
.	.	.
$(b_1, b_0, j_{m-1}, j_{m-2}, \cdots, j_2)$	$(*, *, \cdots, *, f^p_{m-1}, f^p_{m-2})$	$1 \leq p \leq r-2$
$(b_0, j_{m-1}, j_{m-2}, \cdots, j_1)$	$(*, *, \cdots, *, *, f^p_{m-1})$	$1 \leq p \leq r-2$

because Q's are found in terms of i, j, and F, whereas in Table IV, except for the unallowable choices in the first and the last rows, all the other rows depend only on F. In Table V the unallowable choices in all the rows depend only on F.

We now describe routing methods for a multiple processor system with H^* topology. Let F be the set of faulty nodes (processors). We consider the following cases.

Case 1: $|F| \leq r - 2$ and $3 + \log_r m \leq m$.

Our routing method for this case is based on Theorem 4. For a given set of faulty nodes F, a choice for $(b_{x-1}, b_{x-2}, \cdots, b_0)$ is found by using Table V. Then a pair of nonfaulty processors can converse using the path P where $P = PL(i - b) \cup PL(b - j)$. Observe that $|P| \leq m + 3 + \log_r m$.

Remember that the values in Table V are independent of the nodes i and j. Thus, for each set of faulty nodes F, it requires $O(r^x \log_2 r^x)$ with $x = 3 + \log_r m$ to find a choice for $(b_{x-1}, b_{x-2}, \cdots, b_0)$.

Case 2: $|F| \leq 2r - 3$ and $4 + \log_r m \leq m$.

The routing method in this case is based on Lemma 4 and Theorem 3. For a given F, all the unallowable choices in Table IV, except those involving the first and the last rows, are sorted in an array called sorted unallowable choices (SUC). Then a pair of nonfaulty processors i and j can converse as follows.

a) If $(i - j) \in CN$, then let Z be the sorted array composed of unallowable choices in the first and the last rows. Then do a mergesort on SUC and Z, and let T be the resulting array. Choose a missed value in T as a choice for $(b_{x-1}, b_{x-2}, \cdots, b_0)$. Then i can converse with j using the path $P = PL(i - b) \cup PL(b - j)$ if we have $|F \cap (L(i) \cup R(j))| \leq |F \cap (R(i) \cup L(j))|$. Otherwise, the path $P = PR(i - b) \cup PR(b - j)$ could be used. Thus, in what follows $(i - j) \notin CN$. Note that this implies either $R(i) \cap R(j) \neq \emptyset$ or $L(i) \cap L(j) \neq \emptyset$.

b) If $r(k_1) \notin F$ or $r(k_2) \notin F$, then i and j can converse using the path $P = i - r(k_1) - j$ or $P = i - r(k_2) - j$ where $r(k_1) = (i_{m-2}, i_{m-3}, \cdots, i_0, j_0)$ and $r(k_2) = (j_{m-1}, i_{m-1}, i_{m-2}, \cdots, i_1)$.

c) If both $r(k_1)$ and $r(k_2) \in F$, then choose a node k_3, $k_3 \in C - F$ where C is defined as in the proof of Lemma 3. Clearly, i can converse with k_3. Now let $i \leftarrow k_3$, and note that k_3 and j can converse as in step a). Stop.

To obtain a bound for the computational complexity in this case, first observe that the above algorithm establishes a communication path between i and j which is of length $\leq m + 5 + \log_r m$. Second, note that the major part of the computation in the above algorithm is due to creating the array T (finding a missed value can be embedded in the sorting algorithm). It can be seen that to create T takes $O(r^x) = O(mr^4)$ computational time. That is, having created SUC for a given set of faulty nodes F, then to converse between any pair of processors it requires $O(mr^4)$ additional computational time. Observe that for each set F, to find SUC it requires $O(r^x \log_2 r^x)$ with $x = 4 + \log_r m$, which is independent of i and j.

Case 3: $1 \leq |F| \leq 2r - 3$, and the above cases do not hold.

Our routing method for this case is based on Lemmas 3 and 4 and Theorem 1. A pair of nonfaulty processors can converse in this case as follows.

a) If $|MS(F)| < r$ or $|LS(F)| < r$, then i and j can converse using a path in Table II or in Table I according to Algorithm 3.

b) If $(i - j) \in CN$, then set $x = \min(m, 2 + \log_r m)$, and let T be the sorted array composed of all the unallowable choices in Table III. Choose a missed value in T as a choice for $(b_{x-1}, b_{x-2}, \cdots, b_0)$. If $|F \cap (L(i) \cup R(j))| \leq |F \cap (R(i) \cup L(j))|$, then i and j can converse using the path $P = PL(i - b) \cup PL(b - j)$. Otherwise, the path $P = PR(i - b) \cup PR(b - j)$ could be used.

c) If $r(k_1) \notin F$ or $r(k_2) \notin F$, then i and j can converse using the path $P = i - r(k_1) - j$ or $P = i - r(k_2) - j$ where $r(k_1) = (i_{m-2}, i_{m-3}, \cdots, i_0, j_0)$ and $r(k_2) = (j_{m-1}, i_{m-1}, i_{m-2}, \cdots, i_1)$.

d) Choose a node k_3, $k_3 \in C - F$ where C is defined as in the proof of Lemma 3. Clearly, i can converse with k_3. Now let $i \leftarrow k_3$ and go to step a). Stop.

Notice that the above algorithm establishes a communication path of length $\leq 2m$ between i and j. Also note that the major part of the computation in the above algorithm is due to creation of array T. It can readily be seen that this takes $O(r^x \log_2 r^x)$ computation where $x = \min(m, 2 + \log_r m)$.

Finally, after this paper was accepted for publication, a paper by Imase, Soneoka, and Okada [38] appeared in this TRANSACTIONS. In the Appendix of their paper [38], the above authors have proven a theorem (Theorem A) which implies that the node-connectivity of SRG is $2r - 2$, which is one of our results. However, to prove this result, these authors use Lemma A-1 (stated in the Appendix of their paper [38]), which is incorrect.

ACKNOWLEDGMENT

The authors gratefully acknowledge the help of Dr. H. Lee in the early stage of this work.

REFERENCES

[1] S. B. Akers, "On the construction of (d, k) graphs," *IEEE Trans. Electron. Comput.*, vol. EC-14, p. 488, June 1965.

[2] D. Amar, "On the connectivity of some telecommunication networks," *IEEE Trans. Comput.*, vol. C-32, pp. 512–519, May 1983.

[3] A. T. Amin and S. L. Hakimi, "Graphs with given connectivity and independence number," *IEEE Trans. Circuit Theory*, vol. CT-20, pp. 2–10, 1973.

[4] G. Anderson and E. D. Jensen, "Computer interconnection structure: Taxomony, characteristics, and examples," *ACM Comput. Surv.*, vol. 7, no. 4, Dec. 1975.

[5] B. W. Arden and H. Lee, "A multi-tree structure network," in *Proc. COMPCON '78 Fall*, Sept. 1978, pp. 201–210.

[6] E. Bannai and T. Ito, "On finite Moore graphs," *J. Fac. Sci. Univ. Tokyo*, pp. 191–208, 1973.

[7] J. C. Bermond, C. Delorme, and J. J. Quisquater, "Tables of large graphs with given degree and diameter," *Inform. Processing Lett.*, vol. 15, no. 1, pp. 10–13, Aug. 1982.

[8] F. T. Boesch and C. L. Suffel, "Realizability of p-point, q-line graphs with prescribed point connectivity, line connectivity, or minimum degree," *Networks*, vol. 12, pp. 341–350, 1982.

[9] ——, "Realizability of p-point graphs with prescribed minimum degree, maximum degree, and line-connectivity," *J. Graph Theory 4*, pp. 363–370, 1980.

[10] ——, "Realizability of p-point graphs with prescribed minimum degree, maximum degree, and point-connectivity," *Discrete Appl. Math. 3*, pp. 9–18, 1981.

[11] W. G. Bridges and S. Toueg, "On the impossibility of directed Moore graphs," *J. Combinatorial Theory (B)*, 1979.

[12] N. G. DeBruijn, "A combinatorial problem," in *Proc. Parallel Processing*, Aug. 1981, IEEE cal. 8ICHI634-5, pp. 238–242.

[13] B. Elspas, "Topological constraints on interconnection limited logic," in *Switching Circuit Theory Logic Des.*, pp. 133–147, Oct. 1964.

[14] P. H. Enslow, *Multiprocessors and Parallel Processing*. New York: Wiley, 1974.

[15] E. T. Fathi and M. Krieger, "Multiple microprocessor systems: What, why, and when," *IEEE Comput.*, vol. 16, pp. 23–35, Mar. 1963.

[16] R. A. Finkel and M. H. Solomon, "Processor interconnection strategies," Dep. Comput. Sci., Univ. Wisconsin–Madison, Madison, WI, Tech. Rep. CS-TR 301, July 1977.

[17] A. Frank et al., "Some architecture and system implications of local computer networks," in *Proc. COMPCON '79 Spring*, Feb. 1979, pp. 272–276.

[18] H. Freidman, "A design for (d, k) graphs," *IEEE Trans. Electron. Comput.*, vol. EC-15, pp. 253–254, Apr. 1966.

[19] S. L. Hakimi, "An algorithm for construction of the least vulnerable communication network for the graph with maximum connectivity," *IEEE Trans. Circuit Theory*, vol. CT-16, pp. 229–230, May 1969.

[20] F. Harary, "The maximum connectivity of a graph," *Proc. Nat. Acad. Sci.*, vol. 48, pp. 1142–1146, 1962.

[21] ——, *Graph Theory*. Reading, MA: Addison-Wesley, Oct. 1972, pp. 94–96.

[22] M. Imase and M. Itoh, "Design to minimize diameter on building-block networks," *IEEE Trans. Comput.*, vol. C-30, pp. 439–443, June 1981.

[23] R. M. Keller, G. Lindstrom, and S. Patil, "A loosely coupled applicative multiprocessing system," in *NCC 1979, AFIPS Conf. Proc.*, vol. 48, pp. 613–622.

[24] I. Korn, "On (d, k) graphs," *IEEE Trans. Electron. Comput.*, vol. EC-16, p. 90, Feb. 1967.

[25] H. Lee, "Modeling of multi-minicomputer networks," Ph.D. dissertation, Princeton Univ., Princeton, NJ, Nov. 1979.

[26] W. Leland et al., "High density graphs for processor interconnection," *Inform. Processing Lett.*, vol. 12, no. 3, pp. 117–120, June 1981.

[27] G. Memmi and Y. Raillard, "Some new result about the (d, k) graph problems," *IEEE Trans. Comput.*, vol. C-31, pp. 784–791, Aug. 1982.

[28] M. C. Pease, "The indirect binary n-cube microprocessor array," *IEEE Trans. Comput.*, vol. C-26, pp. 458–473, May 1977.

[29] D. K. Pradhan and S. M. Reddy, "A fault-tolerant communication architecture for distributed systems," *IEEE Trans. Comput.*, vol. C-31, pp. 863–870, Sept. 1982.

[30] S. M. Reddy *et al.*, "On digraphs with minimum diameter and maximum connectivity," in *Proc. 20th Annu. Allerton Conf. Commun. Contr., Comput.*, pp. 1018–1026, Oct. 1982.

[31] R. M. Storwick, "Improved construction technique for (d, k) graphs," *IEEE Trans. Electron. Comput.*, vol. EC-19, pp. 1214–1216, Dec. 1970.

[32] H. Sullivan and T. R. Bashkow, "A large scale, homogeneous, fully distributed, parallel machine: I," in *Proc. 4th Symp. Comput. Architecture*, 1977, pp. 105–117.

[33] K. J. Thurber, "Interconnection networks: A survey and assessment," in *NCC 1974, AFIPS Conf. Proc.*, vol. 43, pp. 909–919.

[34] K. J. Thurber and H. A. Freeman, "Local computer networks architecture," in *Proc. COMPCON '79 Spring*, Feb. 1979, pp. 256–261.

[35] R. S. Wilkov, "Analysis and design of reliable computer networks," *IEEE Trans. Commun.*, vol. COM-20, pp. 660–678, June 1972.

[36] C. Wu and T. Feng, "On a class of multistage interconnection networks," *IEEE Trans. Comput.*, vol. C-29, pp. 694–702, Aug. 1980.

[37] K. W. Doty, "New design for dense processor interconnection networks," *IEEE Trans. Comput.*, vol. C-33, pp. 447–450, May 1984.

[38] M. Imase, T. Soneoka, and K. Okada, "Connectivity of regular directed graphs with small diameter," *IEEE Trans. Comput.*, vol. C-34, pp. 267–274, Mar. 1985.

Abdol-Hossein Esfahanian (S'79–M'83) was born in Kashan, Iran, on July 16, 1954. He received the B.S. degree in electrical engineering and the M.S. degree in computer, information, and control engineering from the University of Michigan, Ann Arbor, in 1975 and 1977, respectively, and the Ph.D. degree in computer science from Northwestern University, Evanston, IL, in 1983.

He has been an Assistant Professor of Computer Science at Michigan State University, East Lansing, since September 1983. His research interests include graph theory, computer networks, design and analysis of algorithms, and computational complexity.

Dr. Esfahanian is a member of the ACM and the Society for Industrial and Applied Mathematics.

S. Louis Hakimi (S'56–M'59–SM'67–F'72) was born in Meshed, Iran, on December 16, 1932. He received the B.S. (Bronze Tablet), M.S., and Ph.D. degrees, all in electrical engineering, from the University of Illinois, Urbana, in 1955, 1957, and 1959, respectively.

He was an Assistant Professor of Electrical Engineering at the University of Illinois, Urbana, from February 1959 to August 1961. He came to Northwestern University, Evanston, IL, as an Associate Professor of Electrical Engineering in September 1961, and was promoted to Full Professor in September 1966. From September 1972 to September 1977 he served a five-year term as Chairman of the Electrical Engineering Department at Northwestern. He is now a Professor of Electrical Engineering and Computer Science, Industrial Engineering/Management Science, and Applied Mathematics. His research interests lie in applications of graph theory and combinatorics to circuits and network theory, coding theory, operations research, and computer science.

Dr. Hakimi has been a member of many national and regional committees. He served as a member of the Administrative Committee of the IEEE Circuits and Systems Society from 1966 to 1969. He was the Chairman of the Midwestern Electrical Engineering Department Heads from 1973 to 1975. He was an Associate Editor of the IEEE TRANSACTIONS ON CIRCUITS AND SYSTEMS from 1975 to 1977. He is an Associate Editor of the *Journal of Networks*. He was Co-Chairman of the National Science Foundation's Symposium on Large-Scale Networks held at Northwestern University in April 1974. He is a member of the Society for Industrial and Applied Mathematics and of Sigma Xi, Tau Beta Pi, Eta Kappa Nu, Phi Kappa Phi, and AAUP.

FAULT-TOLERANT ROUTING ON A CLASS OF REARRANGEABLE NETWORKS

Yao-ming Yeh and Tse-yun Feng

Department of Electrical and Computer Engineering
The Pennsylvania State University
University Park, PA 16802

Abstract — Existing fault-tolerant routing schemes for rearrangeable networks consider switch control faults on the Benes network only. In this paper, we propose a general fault-tolerant routing scheme for a class of $2log_2N$ stage rearrangeable networks. Networks in this class can be either symmetric or asymmetric in their structure, regular or irregular in their inter-stage connections, and with $2log_2N$ or $2log_2N - 1$ stages. Our scheme considers both switch and link faults in the network. For the failure of control line in the switches, a fault-free routing scheme is proposed to tolerate multiple faults on each stage of the network. For the failure of switch data lines and inter-stage links, a graceful degradation routing scheme is developed to configure the network so that the loss is ensured to be minimal for weighted permutation requests.

Key words — *The Benes networks, Fault-free routing schme, Fault-tolerant routing scheme, Graceful degradation routing scheme, Rearrangeable networks*

1. INTRODUCTION

Multistage interconnection networks (MINs) are vulnerable to the failure of switches and links in the network. Two approaches can enhance MINs' fault-tolerant capability: to use extra hardware (such as extra switches or links [1][2][3][9][13]) to provide alternate paths and/or use extra software (such as extra routing passes [15] or special routing operation [8][10]) to bypass the faults. In [18], we proposed a class of $2log_bN$ stage rearrangeable networks, for any b. An interconnection network is rearrangeable [4] if it can realize arbitrary permutation between input and output terminals. This class of networks have multiple paths for every input-output pair, therefore, pure software approach of fault-tolerant routing is possible for these networks. Comparing to the cost of hardware approach, to develop fault-tolerant routing scheme with pure software enhancement is more promising than the hardware approach.

The existing fault-tolerant schemes only apply to the Benes network with very limited capability. Agrawal [3] used an extra switch attached to either side of the network to compensate a faulty switch in the network. Agrawal's scheme can only tolerate single fault in the network. Huang [7][8] also provided a fault-tolerant scheme on the Benes network, which is extended from his routing scheme on the finite state model. Nassimi [10] applied fault-tolerant self-routing to bypass the fault. Nassimi's scheme can tolerate single fault on each stage and no fault on center stage. Wysham and Feng [17] extended the looping algorithm to tolerate the switch control faults on the Benes networks. Above fault-tolerant schemes only consider switch control faults with limited fault-tolerant capability for the Benes network.

In this paper, we develop the fault-tolerant routing scheme for all possible faults in the class of the rearrangeable networks using (2×2) switches. We consider both switch faults and link faults in the network. Our scheme can provide fault-free routing for switch control faults with multiple faults presented in one stage of the network. We

also develop a graceful degradation routing scheme to ensure minimum loss for switch path faults and link faults. Our scheme is extended from our general routing scheme previously proposed in [18].

Feng et.al. [5][6] proposed fault diagnosis schemes for MIN's to pinpoint the faulty spot and distinguish the type of fault. Here, we assume fault diagnosis to be available as needed with respect to the MIN's studied and do not discuss it further.

The remaining sections of this paper are organized as follows: Section 2 describes the notations and concepts in the switch labelling scheme and the original routing algorithm which are related to the fault-tolerant routing scheme. Section 3 introduces the symmetric properties of the network. These properties provide the fault-tolerant capability in the routing scheme. Section 4 describes five algorithms in our fault-tolerant routing scheme. Fault-free routing for switch control faults are given in Algorithms $4 \sim 6$. Minimum-loss routing for switch path faults and link faults are given in Algorithms 7 and 8. Conclusions are given in Section 5.

2. PRELIMINARIES

In this section, a switch labelling scheme and the original routing scheme are briefly described. They are commonly applicable to a class of rearrangeable networks which are equivalent to the Benes network. These equivalent networks can have either regular or irregular inter-stage connections, either symmetry or asymmetry structure, and even, either $2log_bN$ or $2log_bN - 1$ stages.

2.1 Switch labelling scheme

The switch labelling scheme consists of two steps: outside-in decomposition, and inside-out decomposition. These two steps can generate an outside-in code and an inside-out code on every switch in the network.

A. Outside-in decomposition

In a $2log_bN$ stage network, the levels of a network are labelled from 1 to n stage-by-stage from outside-in. A switch is denoted as $S_{ia,j}$ for switch located in input half of the network, or $S_{oa,j}$ for switch in output half. Where the first subscript is the stage index; the second subscript is the switch index within a stage, as shown in Figure 1.

The idea of outside-in decomposition is to label the switches based on the subnetwork decomposition level by level from outside-in till the center stages. To support this mechanism, we can send $2N$ signals simultaneously from both input and output terminals to propagate through stage by stage till they meet in the center of the network. Initially, each signal carry a label with no value. When a signal traverses through one stage, a value i, $0 \leq i \leq b-1$, is attached behind its label according to following rule:

R1: *attach i when the signal goes through the ith port of the switch (i.e., consider the output ports for input half of the network; and input port for output half).*

The label of each switch is derived from the label of all its incoming signals. This label is defined as *outside-in-code* as below.

Definition 1: In a $2log_b N$ stage network, an *outside-in-code*, OC, of a switch in level m (i.e, either switch $S_{im,j}$ or $S_{om,j}$, for $0 \le j \le N-1$), is defined as an m digits base b number: $OC[1:m]$, where $0 \le OC[k] \le b-1$ for $1 \le k \le m-1$. The value of each digit $OC[k]$ is derived from rule R1.

The collection of the switches with the same outside-in-code form a set of *complete residue system module N/b* (i.e., CRS) [18]. These switch sets are defined as below.

Definition 2: In a $2log_b N$ stage network, a *CRS switch set* is the set of switches that have similar outside-in-code. This outside-in-code is called the *code* of this CRS switch set. A CRS switch set with code x is denoted as CRS_x. The *size* of a CRS switch set is the number of switches in the set. It is denoted as $|CRS_x|$.

Lemma 1: In a $2log_b N$ stage network, the size of each CRS switch sets on level a is $2 * b^{n-a}$, for $1 \le a \le log_b N$.

Proof: Refer [18].

B. Inside-out decomposition

The operation of inside-out decomposition is like the reflection of outside-in decomposition. The mechanism of inside-out decomposition is to label the switches level-by-level from center stage to both input and output terminals. Similar procedure is used to derive the *inside-out-code* of each switch except the rule is modified as:

R2: *attach i when the signal goes through the ith port of the switch (i.e., consider the input ports for input half of the network; and output port for output half).*

Definition 3: In a $2log_b N$ stage network, an *inside-out-code* of a switch in level m (i.e, either switch $S_{im,j}$ or $S_{om,j}$, for $0 \le j \le N/b$), is defined as an $n - m$ digits base b number: $IC[1:m]$, where $0 \le IC[k] \le b-1$ for $1 \le k \le n-m$. The value of each digit $IC[k]$ is derived from rule R2.

Lemma 2: In a $2log_b N$ stage network, a CRS switch set with size k contains the switches with unique inside-out-codes values from 0 to $(k/2)-1$ in base b representation on each half of the network.

Proof: Refer [18].

From Lemma 1, labelling the outside-in-code on every switch of a $2log_b N$ stage network reflects the subnetwork construction in the network; furthermore, from Lemma 2, labelling the inside-out-code on the switches indicate their relative location to construct a subnetwork. Figures 1 and 2 show the result of outside-in and inside-out decompositions on baseline-baseline^{-1} and omega-omega^{-1} networks respectively. The outside-in-code and inside-out-code of each switch is indicated within the switch. Two $(N/b) \times (2log_b N)$ matrices are defined to store these codes: *outside-in matrix* and *inside-out matrix*.

2.2 A GENERAL ROUTING SCHEME

With the help of our switch labelling scheme, a general routing scheme is developed for the whole class of $2log_b N$ stage networks.

Two isomorphic trees are used in our routing algorithm. A network tree describes the network configuration, which is constructed from outside-in and inside-out matrices. A permutation tree describes how a permutation request is decomposed to fit in a network. They are defined as below.

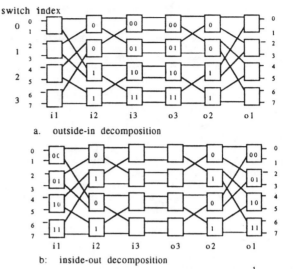

a. outside-in decomposition

b: inside-out decomposition

Figure 1: switch labelling on a baseline-baseline^{-1} network

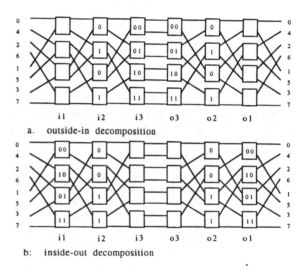

a. outside-in decomposition

b: inside-out decomposition

Figure 2 : switch labelling on an omega-omega^{-1} network

Definition 4: The CRS switch sets in a $2log_b N$ stage network form a *network tree* of depth n and degree b, where $n = log_b N$. A network tree is denoted as $\Phi(n)$, where n is the depth of the tree. A node of the network tree is a CRS switch set. Each node is identified by the code of its CRS switch set. A subtree of the network tree describes a subnetwork of this $2log_b N$ stage network. A subtree is denoted as $\Phi_a(d)$, where subscript a is its root's CRS switch set code and d is its depth.

Definition 5: A $(N \times N)$ permutation request for a $2log_b N$ stage network forms a *permutation tree* of depth n and degree b, where $n = log_b N$. Its root is the permutation request itself. A permutation tree is denoted as $\Psi(n)$, where n is the depth of the tree. A node of the permutation tree is a *reducible sub-permutation* which can be fully assigned to a number of switches. The siblings of a node are the equally decomposed into b sub-permutations from that node.

The outline of the general routing scheme is as below.

Algorithm 1: routing on a $(N \times N)$ network using $(b \times b)$ switches
begin
1: contruct the network tree from outside-in and inside-out matrices;
2: construct the permutation tree by input-output pair permutation;
3: map the permutation tree to the network tree;
4: assign the switch settings in the network tree;
end.

The detail routing procedure for a network using (2×2) switches is shown in Algorithms 2 and 3. In Algorithm 2, a queue (first-in-first-out list) is used to implement breadth-first mechanism in constructing the permutation tree. A procedure $queue(p)$ is used to insert a node to the end of queue and a procedure $dequeue(p)$ to delete a node from the head of the queue. Since the network tree is constructed when a network is specified, Step 1 of Algorithm 1 is not necessary when the same network is used to realize a new permutation request.

In Algorithm 3, the procedure $decompose(P, P_0, P_1)$ decomposes a node in the permutation tree, in other word, it decomposes a reducible subpermutation into two siblings. In this algorithm, the decomposition on a subpermutation is performed on a relation table. In a relation table, the *input buddy* of an input-output pair is the other input-output pair in the same column, meanwhile, its *output buddy* is the other input-output pair in the same row. This algorithm uses $inputbuddy(w)$ and $outputbuddy(w)$ to denote the input and output buddies of an input-output pair w respectively. Since the code assigned to an input-output pair is either 0 or 1, the binary complement operation is applied on variable c.

For example, in an omega-omega^{-1} network, a permutation request is given as following:

$$P = \begin{pmatrix} 0 & 1 & 2 & 3 & 4 & 5 & 6 & 7 \\ 5 & 1 & 2 & 7 & 6 & 3 & 0 & 4 \end{pmatrix}$$

Figure 3 shows the whole routing procedure. The switches are mapped to each column and row of every relation table from their IC and OC as indicated. The switch setting of each switch is derived from the code assigned to its first input-output pair: 0 as "through" and 1 as "cross". This routing scheme needs $O(Nlog_2 N)$ in sequential time and $O((log_2 N)^2)$ in parallel time.

3. ALTERNATE PATHS AND SYMMETRIC PROPERTIES

It is well known that a $log_2 N$ stage interconnection network provides an unique path for every input-output pair. To add an extra stage to the $log_2 N$ stage network will create two alternate paths for every input-output pair. If we keep adding stages to the network, an extra stage doubles the alternate paths in the network. Eventually, a $2log_2 N$ stage interconnection network has N alternate paths for every input-output pair. In this section, we will explore the property of these alternate paths and identify the symmetric property in $2log_2 N$ stage networks

3.1 Redundant switches in $2log_2 N$ stage networks

Waksman [16] pointed out the existence of the redundant switches in a Benes network. It is stemmed from the alternate paths of the Benes network. We can combine his idea with the concept of CRS switch set to identify the redundant switches in every $2log_2 N$ stage network. It is described in the following theorem.

Theorem 1: In a $2log_2 N$ stage network, at least one redundant switch is presented in each CRS switch set.

Proof: refer [19].

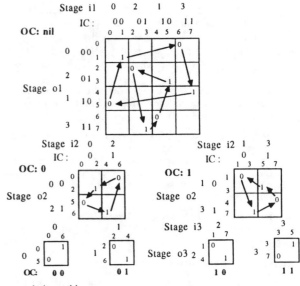

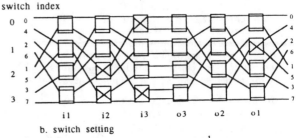

a. relation table

b. switch setting

Figure 3 : Routing on an omega-omega^{-1} network

Algorithm 2: routing on a $(N \times N)$ network using (2×2) switches
begin
  $queue(P)$;
  while queue not empty do
    $dequeue(pptr)$;
    $decompose(pptr, p_0, p_1)$;
    $switchsetting(pptr)$;
    if p_0 decomposable then $queue(p_0)$;
    if p_1 decomposable then $queue(p_1)$;
  endwhile
end.

Algorithm 3: input-output pair decomposition on a $(m \times m)$ sub-permutation P

procedure $decompose(P, P_0, P_1)$;
begin
1: for $i = 0$ to m do { initialization }
    mark "x" on the relation table for $P(i)$;
  endfor
2: map the switches to each row and column of the relation table;
3: while some "x"s remain in the relation table do { code assignment }
    select a "x" as the start point w (i.e., select the first "x" in a column);
    $c \leftarrow 0$; { set code 0 }
    $P(w) \leftarrow c$; { assign code to input-output pair w }
    while $inputbuddy(w)$ is unassigned do
      $w \leftarrow inputbuddy(w)$; $c \leftarrow \bar{c}$
      $P(w) \leftarrow c$;
      if $outputbuddy(w)$ is unassigned then
        $w \leftarrow outputbuddy(w)$; $c \leftarrow \bar{c}$
        $P(w) \leftarrow c$;
      endif;
    endwhile;
  endwhile;
4: for $i = 0$ to m do { collect P_0 and P_1 }
    if $P(i) = 0$ then $P_0(j_0) \leftarrow P(i)$; $j_0 \leftarrow j_0 + 1$;
    if $P(i) = 1$ then $P_1(j_1) \leftarrow P(i)$; $j_1 \leftarrow j_1 + 1$;
  endfor
end.

Note that the redundant switch can be any switch of a CRS switch set. These redundant switches are the resources to provide alternate paths for a given permutation requests. We can achieve fault-tolerant routing with the help of these redundant switches when switch faults and link faults are presented in a network.

For a $2log_2 N$ stage network, since the center level has $N/2$ switch sets, all the switches in one of the center stage can be regarded as redundant switches. Therefore a $2log_2 N - 1$ stage network is a $2log_2 N$ stage network without the redundant center stage.

3.2 Subnetwork symmetry

Here, we will show that different mapping on both network tree and permutation tree creates alternate paths for the same permutation. In addition, different mapping also affects the switch setting of the subnetworks. In order to describe the relationship among them, first, we define the switch settings of a network (and its subnetwork) with a binary matrix as below.

Definition 6: The control matrix of a $2log_2 N$ stage network is a $(2log_2 N) \times (N/2)$ binary matrix and is denoted as $M_{\Phi(n)}$, where $\Phi(n)$ is the network tree which represents this network. Every element in $M_{\Phi(n)}$ represents a switch control bit which is either 0 (through) or 1 (cross). We use a triple-vector to represent the control matrix of a network: $M_{\Phi(n)} = (M_{CRS}, M_{\Phi_0(n-1)}, M_{\Phi_1(n-1)})$, where M_{CRS} is a $2 \times (N/2)$ binary matrix represents the control settings of the switches in its root node $CRS(N,k)$. $M_{\Phi_0(n-1)}$ and $M_{\Phi_1(n-1)}$ are the control matrices of its subnetworks $\Phi_0(n-1)$ and $\Phi_1(n-1)$ respectively.

Above triple-vector defined can also represent the control matrix of a subnetwork $\Phi_a(m)$ by the representation: $M_{\Phi_a(m)} = (M_{CRS_a}, M_{\Phi_{a0}(n-1)}, M_{\Phi_{a1}(n-1)})$, where a is a binary number which represents the index of the subnetwork, and $0 < m < n$.

Theorem 2: Subnetwork symmetry

In a $2log_2 N$ stage network $\Phi(n)$, if a permutation request P is realized by a control matrix $M_{\Phi(n)}$, where $M_{\Phi(n)} = (M_{CRS}, M_{\Phi_0(n-1)}, M_{\Phi_1(n-1)})$, then another control matrix $M'_{\Phi(n)}$ also realize P, where

$$M'_{\Phi(n)} = (\overline{M_{CRS}}, M_{\Phi_1(n-1)}, M_{\Phi_0(n-1)})$$

Proof: refer [19].

Theorem 2 can be applied to any subnetwork $\Phi_a(m)$ within $\Phi(n)$. The property of subnetwork symmetry reveals the concept that each subnetwork within a $2log_2 N$ stage network is an independent unit. Once a fault is presented in the network, we need only change the routing of the smallest subnetwork which contains this faulty switch. In addition, this subnetwork symmetric property is independent of the permutation request, it only depends on the network configuration.

With the subnetwork symmetric property, a network with n level of subnetworks provides 2^n alternate paths for every input-output pair. We can derive these alternate paths by applying the operation defined below.

Definition 7: The operation of *subnetwork-complement-and-swap*, $NCAS(M_{\Phi_a(m)})$, to a subnetwork $\Phi_a(m)$ is defined as

$$NCAS(M_{\Phi_a(m)}) = NCAS(M_{CRS_a}, M_{\Phi_{a0}(m-1)}, M_{\Phi_{a1}(m-1)})$$
$$= (\overline{M_{CRS_a}}, M_{\Phi_{a1}(m-1)}, M_{\Phi_{a0}(m-1)})$$

Consider the code assignment shown in Figure 4, to perform $NCAS(M_{\Phi(n)})$ is equivalent to replace all the assigned indices by applying a mapping $(0 \rightarrow 1 ; 1 \rightarrow 0)$ to CRS table, the decomposed sub-permutations are the same except that they swap the subnetworks assigned to them. Originally, the decomposed sub-permutations are as follows

$$P_0 = \begin{pmatrix} 0 & 2 & 4 & 6 \\ 5 & 2 & 6 & 0 \end{pmatrix} \quad P_1 = \begin{pmatrix} 1 & 3 & 5 & 7 \\ 1 & 7 & 3 & 4 \end{pmatrix}$$

P_0 and P_1 are assigned to Φ_0 and Φ_1 respectively. After applying $NCAS(M_{\Phi(n)})$, P_0 is assigned to Φ_1 and P_1 to Φ_0. For more specific, to perform $NCAS(M_{\Phi_a(m)})$ generates two effects: First, the switch settings of CRS_a table's corresponding switches (include input and output sides) are complemented. Second, the control settings of its subnetworks Φ_{a0} and Φ_{a1} are swapped.

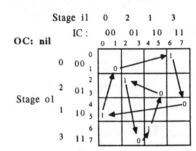

Figure 4: Subnetwork symmetry: complement all codes

3.3 Loop symmetry

Beside subnetwork symmetry, we will explore the symmetric property which depends on permutation requests rather than network configuration.

Opferman and Tsao-Wu [11][12] defined the loop and discussed its properties in their looping algorithm. A loop is defined as follows.

Definition 8: A *loop*, L, is a set of input-output pairs, in which if an input-output pair $\begin{bmatrix} x \\ y \end{bmatrix} \in L$, then its input buddy $\begin{bmatrix} \hat{x} \\ y' \end{bmatrix} \in L$, and also its output buddy $\begin{bmatrix} x' \\ \hat{y} \end{bmatrix} \in L$. Where $\hat{x}$ and $\hat{y}$ are the buddies of x and y respectively, and $x \neq x'$, $y \neq y'$. The number of input-output pairs in a loop is called the *order* of the loop, which is always even.

Lemma 3: A CRS switch set with size $2m$ forms at least one loop and at most m loops.

Proof: Refer [19].

Similar to subnetwork symmetry, the effect to apply a mapping $(0 \rightarrow 1 ; 1 \rightarrow 0)$ to each loop individually in a multiple-loop relation table will form a different decomposed sub-permutation pair for its lower level, as shown in Figure 5.

Theorem 3: Loop symmetry

In a CRS switch set, if m loops are formed from a permutation P, then 2^{m-1} distinct decomposed sub-permutation pairs can be formed from this switch set.

Proof: refer [19].

Loop symmetry depends on the permutation request given, whereas, it is independent of the network configuration. If two different networks are applied with the same permutation request, they have the same loop property. For a multiple-loop CRS switch set, we can derive alternate paths in a loop by applying the operation defined below.

Definition 9: The operation of *loop-complement-and-swap*, $LCAS(M_{\Phi_{La}(m)})$, to a subset $\Phi_{La}(m)$ of subnetwork $\Phi_a(m)$ is defined as

$$LCAS(M_{\Phi_{La}(m)}) = LCAS(M_{CRS_{La}}, M_{\Phi_{La0}(m-1)}, M_{\Phi_{La1}(m-1)})$$
$$= (\overline{M_{CRS_{La}}}, M_{\Phi_{La1}(i-1)}, M_{\Phi_{La0}(i-1)})$$

Since loop symmetry is similar to network symmetry, we can also apply a redundant switch to a loop as in Theorem 1.

Theorem 4: To realize a permutation P in a $2log_2N$ stage network, one redundant switch is presented in every loop of every reducible sub-permutation.

Proof: refer [19]. □

Both subnetwork and loop symmetric properties can provide us to enumerate all the possible switch settings for a given permutation. Investigating these possible cases, we can select the best one to tolerate the faults.

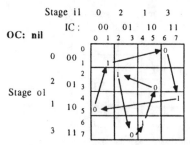

Figure 5: Loop symmetry: complement a loop

4. FAULT-TOLERANT ROUTING

In this section, the fault-tolerant routing scheme for all possible faults in the class of $2log_2N$ stage networks is described. We consider both switch faults and link faults in the network. Our scheme can provide fault-free routing for switch control faults with multiple faults presented in one stage of the network. We also develop a graceful degradation routing scheme to ensure minimum loss for switch path faults and link faults.

4.1 Fault model

Feng and Wu [5] suggested a fault model for the purpose of fault diagnosis on MIN's. In this model, a (2×2) switch is considered as a (2×2) crossbar circuit. A (2×2) crossbar has four cross-points. Two possible cases (i.e. either connected or not connected) are assumed for each crosspoint, therefore, 16 possible states are derived for a (2×2) switch. These possible states consist of 2 valid states (i.e. "through" connection when control signal is 0; "cross" connection when control signal is 1) and 14 faulty states.

To meet our need for fault-tolerant routing, the faults in a switch are classified as *switch control faults* and *switch path faults*. A switch control fault is a switch configuration fault in which a switch is unable to respond to the control signal. The switch control faults are further classified as *stuck-at-0* and *stuck-at-1* as shown in Figure 6.a. A switch path fault is a transmission path fault in which a switch is unable to transmit the data from its input ports to its output ports. Considering the number of paths which can be passed through a (2×2) switch, switch path faults are further classified as *stuck-one-path* and *stuck-two-path* as shown in Figure 6.b.

Beside the switch faults, link faults may also present in an interconnection network. A link fault is that the link can not transmit the data, which can be simulated by the stuck-one-path faults on the two stages of switches to which the faulty link connects. It is shown in Figure 6.c. Above classification covers all possible cases in Feng and Wu's fault model and it will simplify our fault-tolerant routing scheme.

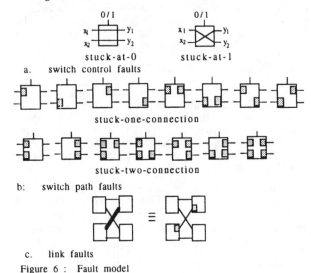

Figure 6 : Fault model

4.2 Fault-tolerant routing for switch control faults

A switch control fault makes the faulty switch as fixed configuration: stuck-at-0 makes "through" connections; and stuck-at-1 makes "cross" connections. The faulty switch can still transmit the data. No path is stuck when switch control fault occurs. However, undesired permutation will happen when the desired control configuration of the faulty switch conflicts with the stuck configuration. Our goal here is to overcome this situation and develop a fault-free configuration with the presence of switch control faults in the class of $2log_2N$ stage network.

From Theorem 1, a redundant switch in a CRS switch set can be selected from arbitrary switch in this set. The function of a faulty switch with switch control fault is just the same as what a redundant switch has. Therefore, the idea of our fault-tolerant routing is to select the faulty switch as the redundant switch. To achieve this mechanism, we should modify two places in our routing scheme. First, locate the faulty switch in the network tree. This can be easily determined from the outside-in-code and inside-out-code of the faulty switch: outside-in-code decides the node (i.e., CRS switch set); inside-out-code decides the position within the node. Through switch mapping, we can locate the input-output pairs which pass through the faulty switch. Second, apply fault-free input-output pair decomposition on the node which contains the faulty switch. The code assignment operation is modified so that the switch setting of the faulty switch is fixed and set at the stuck-at-fault. In other words, the input-output pair on the upper port of the faulty switch (i.e., the first entry on the faulty switch) is set as 0 when stuck-at-0 or set as 1 when stuck-at-1.

The procedure to configure fault free switch settings is shown in Algorithms 4 and 5. From Algorithm 4, a faulty switch only affects the routing on the node which contains this faulty switch. In Algorithm 5, the procedure $faultdecompose(P, P_0, P_1)$ is modified from procedure $decompose(P, P_0, P_1)$. Only the modified Step 3 is shown in this algorithm. To adjust the code assignment so that the switch settings do not conflict with the faults, we start the code assignment from the input-output pair on the faulty switch. This modified operation has the same effect as selecting the faulty switch as the redundant switch. This scheme just adjusts the start point of code assignment according to the location of the faulty switch. There is no extra overhead involved, therefore, its time and space complexity is the same as the original routing scheme.

Algorithm 4: fault-tolerant routing on a $(N \times N)$ network using (2×2) switches

```
begin
  queue(P);
  while queue not empty do
    dequeue(pptr);
    if sub-permutation pptr contains faulty switch
      then faultdecompose(pptr, p_0, p_1);
      else decompose(pptr, p_0, p_1);
    endif;
    switchsetting(pptr);
    if p_0 decomposible then queue(p_0);
    if p_1 decomposible then queue(p_1);
  endwhile
end.
```

For example, fault-free routing for stuck-at-1 faults located at $S_{i1.3}$, $S_{i2.1}$, and $S_{o2.0}$ is shown in Figure 7. This algorithm can tolerate one switch control fault in a loop. From Lemma 3, a CRS switch set with size $2m$ can tolerate at least one fault and at most m faults. If we consider its fault-tolerant capability independent of the permutation request, the number of faults can be tolerated is equal to the number of CRS switch sets in the network if only the faults are evenly distributed to every CRS switch set in the network. There are $N - 1$ CRS switch sets for an $(N \times N)$ network, therefore, $N - 1$ switch control faults can be tolerated in the network.

Algorithm 5: procedure $faultdecompose(P, P_0, P_1)$

```
3:  while some "x"s remain in the relation table do { code assignment }
      if unassigned faulty switch in the relation table
        then select the first "x" of the faulty switch as w;
          if stuck-at-0 then c ← 0;
          if stuck-at-1 then c ← 1;
        else select the first "x" in the column as w;
          c ← 0; { set code 0 }
      endif
      P(w) ← c; { assign code to input-output pair w }
      while inputbuddy(w) is unassigned do
        w ← inputbuddy(w); c ← c̄
        P(w) ← c;
        if outputbuddy(w) is unassigned then
          w ← outputbuddy(w); c ← c̄
          P(w) ← c;
        endif
      endwhile
    endwhile;
```

4.2.1 Fault-free routing for $2log_2 N - 1$ stage networks: center stage fault-tolerance

Algorithms 4 and 5 use the redundant switches in the network to tolerate the switch control fault. This scheme provides the maximum fault-tolerant capacity on the center stages of the $2log_2 N$ stage network, which can tolerate $N/2$ faults on the center stages. However, a $2log_2 N - 1$ stage network, such as the Benes network, does not have the redundant center stage. Thus, this scheme can not provide any fault-tolerant capability to the fault in its single center stage. We develop a different procedure to tolerate the fault located in the center stage of a $2log_2 N - 1$ stage network. This procedure use $NCAS$ operation to relocate the switch settings when a conflict occurred on the faulty switch. In Algorithm 6, the switches on the center stage are numbered as a $n - 1$ bits binary code from

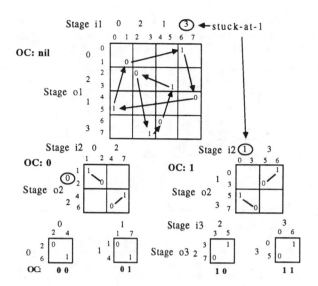

a. relation table

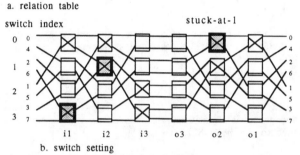

b. switch setting

Figure 7: Fault-free routing for switch control faults

$00 \ldots 0$ to $11 \ldots 1$ with the switch on top as $00 \ldots 0$. Assume the faulty switch is located at $F[1 : n - 1]$. A binary operation $\oplus$ is used in the algorithm, which is bit-wise exclusive-OR on two binary numbers.

Algorithm 6: fault-tolerant routing on the center stage of a $2log_2 N - 1$ stage network

```
begin
  derive the switch setting of whole network by original routing scheme;
  if the faulty switch, F[1 : n - 1], conflicts with its control setting then
    select a substitute switch, S[1 : n - 1], in the center stage;
    D[1 : n - 1] = F[1 : n - 1] ⊕ S[1 : n - 1];
    for i = 1 to n - 1 do
      if D[i] = 1 then NCAS(M_{Φ_{S[1:i-1]}(n-i+1)});
    endfor
  endif
end.
```

For the switch setting in Figure 3.b (i.e., eliminate the redundant stage $o3$), if the faulty switch is stuck-at-0 at $S_{3.0}$, then $F[1 : n - 1]$ is 00. The candidates for the substitute switch are $S_{3.1}$ and $S_{3.2}$. If we select the nearest to the faulty switch as the substitute switch, then the number of switches to be relocated is minimum. It is equivalent to find the candidate switch with the minimum distance code to the faulty switch. $S_{3.1}$ is selected as the substitute switch by this principle, as a result, $S[1 : n - 1]$ is 01. The distance code is $01 = 00 \oplus 01$. Thus, we should perform $NCAS(M_{Φ_{0(1)}})$. The result fault-free control setting is shown in Figure 8.

The shortage of this algorithm is that it fails when we cannot find a substitute switch on the center stage from the initial switch setting. This situation happens when the switch settings of all switches in the center stage are the same and also conflict with the fault.

For the faults in non-center stages of a $2log_2 N - 1$ stage network, we can use the procedure as described in previous section to derive the fault-free routing.

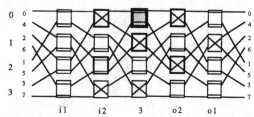

Figure 8: Fault-free routing for fault on center stage

4.3 Fault-tolerant routing for switch path faults

Some input-output pairs will be stuck if a switch path fault happens in the network. Therefore, it is impossible to provide fault-free routing for switch path faults and link faults. However, for weighted connection requests, we can find the best switch settings such that the network can achieve minimum-loss configuration. We define a set of weighted connection as below:

Definition 10: A set of weighted connection requests assigned to a network is described as a weighted permutation:

$$P = \begin{pmatrix} x_1 & x_2 & \dots & x_N \\ y_1 & y_2 & \dots & y_N \\ w(x_1) & w(x_2) & \dots & w(x_N) \end{pmatrix}$$

where $w(x_i)$ is a positive value represents the weight assigned to the input-output pair $\begin{bmatrix} x_i \\ y_i \end{bmatrix}$.

For example, a weighted permutation is shown below

$$P = \begin{pmatrix} 0 & 1 & 2 & 3 & 4 & 5 & 6 & 7 \\ 5 & 1 & 2 & 7 & 6 & 3 & 0 & 4 \\ 5 & 7 & 3 & 1 & 2 & 4 & 6 & 8 \end{pmatrix}$$

In this weighted permutation, a larger weight indicates the higher priority for that input-output pair.

In order to investigate the input-output pairs which are affected by switch path faults, we define the fault projection set as below:

Definition 11: A *fault projection set* of a faulty switch is the set of input-output pairs which are possible to pass through the stuck path of this switch. If the faulty switch is located in input half, the fault is projected to input terminals; and vice versa. Assume the inside-out-code of a faulty switch $S_{a,j}$ is denoted as $IC[1:m]$, where $1 \le m \le n-1$. The fault projection set of this faulty switch is denoted as: $FPS(S_{ia,j}) = \{ \begin{pmatrix} x \\ y \end{pmatrix} \mid \forall\ x[1:n]$ such that $x[1:m] = IC[1:m]\}$ or $FPS(S_{oa,j}) = \{ \begin{pmatrix} x \\ y \end{pmatrix} \mid \forall\ y[1:n]$ such that $y[1:m] = IC[1:m]\}$

Above definition consider a faulty switch as an unit, thus, it can only describe the fault projection set of a stuck-two-path fault. To describe the fault projection set of a stuck-one-path fault, we can project the faulty spot to a switch in its outer level and derive the fault projection set of this switch. Figure 9 shows the fault projection set of both stuck-one-path and stuck-two-path faults. On the input half, a stuck-two-path fault is located at switch $S_{i2.2}$. $S_{i2.2}$ has inside-out-code $IC[1] = 1$ and outside-in-code $OC[1] = 0$. Its fault projection set is $1 \times \times$, which

covers input terminals $4 \sim 7$. And on the output half, a stuck-one-path is located at switch $S_{o2.1}$. Its projected switch on the outer level is $S_{o1.0}$ which has inside-out-code $IC[1:2] = 00$, therefore, its fault projection set is $00\times$, which covers output terminals $0 \sim 1$.

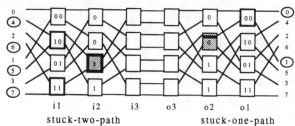

Figure 9: Fault projection set

4.3.1 Routing with the minimum-loss configuration

The criteria to tolerate the switch path faults is to reduce the total weight passing through the stuck paths to minimum. Different scheme should be considered for stuck-one-path and stuck-two-path faults. They are described in Algorithms 7 and 8 respectively.

```
Algorithm 7: fault-tolerant routing for stuck-one-path
faults
begin
  derive the permutation tree;
  derive fault projection set FPS(one path of S_{a,j});
  stuck_path ← minimum weight in FPS(one path of S_{a,j});
  locate the permutation node which contains stuck_path;
  map this node to the network node contains the faulty switch;
  map other nodes accordingly;
  determine the switch settings of all nodes;
end.
```

```
Algorithm 8: fault-tolerant routing for stuck-two-path
faults
begin
  derive fault projection set FPS(S_{a,j});
  while tree_level ≤ a do
    decompose(pptr);
    for all loops covered by FPS(S_{a,j}) do
      apply LCAS on node pptr to form all sub-permutation pairs {P_0, P_1};
    endfor
    if faulty switch S_{a,j} in sub-permutation pptr then
      locate stuck_path;
      calculate weight(stuck_path);
      candidate_set ← candidate_set ∪ stuck_path
    endif
  endwhile
  stuck_pairs ← minimum weight in candidate_set;
  locate the permutation node which contains stuck_pair;
  map this node to the network node contains the faulty switch;
  map other nodes accordingly;
  eliminate the unneeded permutation nodes;
  derive the remaining levels of the permutation tree;
  determine the switch settings of all nodes;
end.
```

In Algorithms 7 and 8, instead of setting the switches of each network node immediately after its corresponding permutation node is decomposed, their switch setting is determined after the whole permutation tree is formed. This is because the mapping between these two trees can not be determined before the node containing the faulty switch is reached. Since the permutation node involved in Algorithm 7 is the same as the original routing algorithm, the extra overhead is small without increasing the time complexity of the routing scheme. Algorithm 8 is a brute force scheme, which evaluates all the possible branches affected by the fault projection set. However, by enumerating all the possible cases covered by the fault projection set, we can always find the minimum-loss configuration when a stuck-two-path fault is presented in the network. The extra overhead involved in Algorithm 8 depends on the location of the faulty switch and the number of loops presented in its upper levels. The more loops and the inner the faulty switch located, the more extra overhead is needed to configure the minimum-loss routing.

5. CONCLUSIONS

The alternate paths and symmetric properties on the class of $2log_2N$ stage rearrangeable networks are introduced. Based on these properties, a general fault-tolerant routing scheme for both switch and link faults for every network in the class is proposed. For switch control faults, a fault-free routing scheme is devised. With the same time and space complexity as the original routing algorithm, the proposed algorithm can tolerate multiple faults on each stage of the network. A fault-free routing scheme for the fault in the center stage of a $2log_2N - 1$ stage network is also developed. For switch path faults and link faults, a minimum-loss routing scheme is introduced. Our scheme considers stuck-one-path and stuck-two-path faults separately. The proposed algorithms select the best configuration among all possible cases so that the loss due to stuck paths is minimal. The extra overhead for this graceful degradation scheme depends on the location of the stuck path. It has more flexibility for the the stuck paths in the inner levels of the network, however, acquiring more extra overhead to derive minimum-loss configuration.

REFERENCES

[1] G.B. Adams, D.P. Agrawal and H.J. Siegel, "A survey and comparison of fault-tolerant multistage interconnection networks," *IEEE Computer Magazine*, June 1987, pp. 14-27.

[2] G.B. Adams, and H.J. Siegel, "The extra stage cube: a fault-tolerant interconnection network for supercomputer," *IEEE Trans. Computers*, vol. C-31, no. 5, May 1982, pp. 443-454.

[3] D.P. Agrawal, "Testing and fault tolerance of multistage interconnection networks," *IEEE Computer*, Apr. 1982, pp. 41-53.

[4] Tse-yun Feng, "A survey of interconnection networks," *IEEE Computer*, Vol. 14, Dec. 1981, pp. 12-27,

[5] T.Y. Feng and C.W. Wu, "Fault diagnosis for a class of multistage interconnection networks," *IEEE Trans. Computers*, vol. C-30, no. 10, Oct. 1981, pp. 743-758.

[6] T.Y. Feng and W. Young, "Fault diagnosis for a class of rearrangeable networks," *J. Paral. Distr. Comp.*, vol. 3, 1986, pp. 23-47.

[7] Shing-tsaan Huang and Satish K. Tripathi, "Finite state model and compatibility theorey: new analysis tools for permutation networks," *IEEE Trans. Computers*, vol. C-35, no. 7, July 1986, pp. 591-601.

[8] Shing-tsaan Huang and Chin-hsiang Tung, "On fault-tolerant routing of Benes network," *Journal of Information Science and Engineering*, vol. 4, July 1988, pp. 1-13.

[9] V.P. Kumar and S.M. Reddy, "Augmented shuffle-exchange multistage interconnection networks," *IEEE Computer Magazine*, June 1987, pp. 30-40.

[10] David Nassimi, "A Fault-tolerant routing algorithm for BPC permutation on multistage interconnection networks," *Proceedings, 1989 International Conference on Parallel Processing*, 1989, pp. I.278-I.287.

[11] D.C. Opferman and N.T. Tsao-Wu, "On a class of rearrangeable switching networks-part I: control algorithm," *Bell System Technical Journal*, Vol. 50, No.5, 1971, pp. 1579-1600.

[12] D.C. Opferman and N.T. Tsao-Wu, "On a class of rearrangeable switching networks-part II: enumeration studies and fault diagnosis," *Bell System Technical Journal*, Vol. 50, No.5, 1971, pp. 1601-1618.

[13] C.S. Raghavendra and A. Varma, "Fault-tolerant multiprocessors with redundant-path interconnection networks," *IEEE Trans. Computers*, vol. C-35, no. 4, April 1986, pp. 307-316.

[14] John Paul Shen and John P. Hayes, "Fault-tolerant of dynamic-full-access interconnection networks," *IEEE Trans. Computers*, vol. C-33, no. 3, March 1984, pp. 241-248.

[15] A. Varma and C.S. Raghavendra, " Fault-tolerant routing in multistage interconnection networks," *IEEE Trans. Computers*, vol. C-38, no. 3, March 1989, pp. 385-393.

[16] A. Waksman, "A permutation network," *J. Ass. Comput. Mach.*, vol. 15, Jan. 1968, pp. 159-163.

[17] S. Wysham and Tse-yun Feng, " On routing a faulty Benes network," *Proceedings, 1986 International Conference on Parallel Processing*, vol. I, 1990, pp. 351-354.

[18] Yao-ming Yeh and Tse-yun Feng, " On a class of rearrangeable networks," Submitted to *IEEE Trans. Computers*.

[19] Yao-ming Yeh, " Fault-tolerance and generalization On a class of multistage interconnection networks," Ph. D. Dissertation, Dept. Electrical & Computer Engineering, The Pennsylvania State University, Aug. 1991.

Fault-Tolerant Routing in Multistage Interconnection Networks

ANUJAN VARMA, MEMBER, IEEE, AND C. S. RAGHAVENDRA, SENIOR MEMBER, IEEE

Abstract—In this paper, we study the fault tolerance of multiprocessor systems with multistage interconnection networks under multiple faults in the network. The fault tolerance is analyzed with respect to the criterion of dynamic full access (DFA) property of the processors in the system. A characterization of multiple faults in the Omega network is introduced and used to develop simple tests for the DFA capability under a given set of faults. It is shown that the DFA capability is maintained under a large number of faults. A maximum of three passes is shown to be sufficient for communication between any two processors in the system when the faults satisfy certain conditions which can be checked easily. For cases in which these conditions do not hold, at most $\log_2 N - 2$ passes through the network are shown to be sufficient if a set of weaker conditions is satisfied. Techniques for routing data between processing elements through the faulty network are described. Extension of the results to general k-stage shuffle/exchange networks with $k < \log_2 N$ is also given. These techniques allow continued operation of a multiprocessor system in the presence of network faults with full connectivity among the processing elements of the system, and with minimal loss of network throughput.

Index Terms—Dynamic full access, fault-tolerant interconnection, fault-tolerant routing, multistage interconnection, Omega network.

I. Introduction

SEVERAL experimental multiprocessor systems with a large number of processors are currently in various stages of development [1]. A vital component of these systems is the interconnection network that enables the processing elements (PE's) to communicate among themselves or with memory units. The performance of the system depends to a great extent on the interprocessor communication possible. The failure of a component in the interconnection network can frequently bring down the entire system or cause a severe degradation in performance, unless sufficient measures are provided to make the network tolerant to such failures.

As a compromise between the costly crossbar network and the linear bus, several interconnection networks with $\log_2 N$ stages of 2×2 switching elements for interconnecting N inputs to N outputs have been proposed in the literature (for a

Manuscript received September 3, 1986; revised January 29, 1987. This work was supported in part by the NSF Presidential Young Investigator Award ECS-8452003 and DARPA/ARO Contract DAAG 29-84-K-0066. A preliminary version of this paper was presented at the Sixteenth International Symposium on Fault-Tolerant Computing, Vienna, Austria, July 1986.

A. Varma is with IBM Thomas J. Watson Research Center, Yorktown Heights, NY 10598.

C. S. Raghavendra is with the Department of Electrical Engineering-Systems, University of Southern California, Los Angeles, CA 90089.

IEEE Log Number 8825674.

survey, see [2]) These networks possess the property of *full access* which implies that data from any input terminal can be transferred to any output terminal in a single pass through the network; in addition, there exists *a unique path* from any input terminal of the network to any output terminal. The unique-path property facilitates the use of simple and efficient routing algorithms for setting up connections through the network. However, the presence of a single fault among the switching elements or the connecting links of these networks destroys the full access property.

Integrated models for the analysis of the fault tolerance and reliability of multiprocessor systems with multistage interconnection networks have been studied in [3] and [4]. In [3] and [4], an Omega network [5] has been used to connect $N = 2^n$ PE's to N memory units. In these models, the failure of a switching element in the interconnection network causes the removal of a number of processors and/or memory units and reconfiguration of the system in a degraded mode. The reconfiguration is such that full access is maintained among the active processors and memory units. This allows the reconfigured system to have the same communication capability as the original system. However, this strategy results in an enormous waste of resources: for example, the failure of a single switching element in the middle stage of the Omega network causes the loss of one-fourth of the processors or memory units from the system, resulting in a substantial degradation in performance. In addition, reconfiguration requires the reassignment of the active tasks on the new system to a reduced number of processors, which is accompanied by the loss of computational effort as well as overhead in moving the tasks among the processors. Lastly, the removal of processors and/or memory units causes a loss of parallelism and might require redesign of the computational algorithm being performed on the system to run on the reconfigured system; this results in a loss of efficiency.

An alternate strategy is to minimize the loss of processors and/or memory units at the expense of routing overhead. Thus, when a multistage network is used for processor-to-processor connection, the effect of the failure of a network component on the system can be reduced by allowing multiple passes through the network. The network is said to possess *dynamic full access* (DFA) capability if every processor in the system can communicate with every other processor in a finite number of passes through the network, routing the data through intermediate PE's if necessary [6]. Even though the failure of a single component destroys the full access capability of the Omega network, a large number of faults does

Reprinted from *IEEE Trans. Computers*, Vol. 38, No. 3, Mar. 1989, pp. 385-393. Copyright © 1989 by The Institute of Electrical and Electronics Engineers, Inc. All rights reserved.

not destroy the DFA capability. Thus, by devising a routing procedure that allows routing through intermediate processors, reconfiguration without the loss of any processors is possible if the faults do not destroy the DFA property of the network. The reconfigured system still operates in a degraded mode owing to the increased latency and the additional blocking and congestion introduced by the loss of paths. However, a large waste of computational effort and resources is prevented. Under this strategy, the successful operation of the system in the presence of network failures requires the solution of the following problems.

1) The effective detection and location of the fault(s) in the network.

2) The characterization of the faults according to whether they destroy the DFA capability or not. Faults which do not destroy the DFA can be sustained without removing any processors from the system. Faults that destroy the DFA cause the loss of processors; in this case, one has the choice of either shutting down the system to invoke a repair process or operating the system in a degraded mode with a fewer number of processors.

3) The formulation of a routing algorithm that is capable of routing data from any processor to any other processor in the faulty network if the network has DFA.

In this paper, we address the problems 2) and 3) above. Efficient techniques for the detection and diagnosis of single and multiple faults in unique-path multistage networks like the Omega network are already available [7]–[9]. We will assume that information on the location of the faulty components in the network is available. Given this information, we are concerned with the problem of determining whether the network has the DFA property, and if so, how to route data between any two processors in the system.

This paper is organized as follows. In Section II, we define equivalence of multiple faults on the Omega network based on their effect on the communication capability of the system and develop tests for the DFA capability under a given fault set. At most three passes through the network, independent of the network size, are shown to be sufficient for routing data under certain conditions which can be tested easily. For the cases in which this test fails, $\log_2 N - 2$ passes are shown to be sufficient if a weaker condition is satisfied. Techniques for routing data between processors through a faulty network that has DFA are outlined in Section III. Extension of our results to shuffle/exchange networks with $k < \log_2 N$ stages is discussed in Section IV. Concluding remarks and ideas for further research are given in Section V.

II. Dynamic Full Accessibility of Omega Networks

In this section, we study multiple faults in the Omega network and characterize them as critical or noncritical depending on whether they destroy the DFA capability of the network or not. We also formulate sufficient conditions for testing the DFA capability of the network under a given set of faults.

The problem of determining the DFA of faulty networks has been studied previously in [6] and [10]. In [6], general techniques are given for checking the DFA property of a faulty

network constructed from 2×2 switching elements, with respect to a fault model that only allows the switching elements to be stuck in one of their valid states. A more general fault model is used in [10]; here the DFA is tested by performing a transitive closure on the adjacency matrix of the connectivity graph of the faulty network. While these techniques are general, they can become unwieldy for large networks. In multistage networks like the Omega network, it is possible to design simpler tests for DFA due to the regular topology of the network.

In this section, we will restrict ourselves to Omega networks built from 2×2 switching elements. This network consists of $n = \log_2 N$ stages of 2×2 switching elements for connecting N inputs to N outputs, each stage consisting of $N/2$ switching elements. The interconnection between stages is the perfect shuffle permutation [5]. Although our analysis is restricted to the Omega network, it is applicable to several other multistage interconnection networks which are known to be topologically equivalent to the Omega network [11]. The following naming conventions are used throughout the paper. The stages of the network are numbered from 0 through $n - 1$ from left to right, and the switching elements in each stage are numbered from 0 through $N/2 - 1$ from top to bottom. Stage 0 of the network is sometimes referred to as the input stage and stage $n - 1$ as the output stage. The terms "switching element" and "switch" are used synonymously in the paper to denote a 2×2 switching element in the Omega network. The Omega network for $N = 16$ is shown in Fig. 1. The corresponding input and output terminals of the network are connected to communication ports on the same processor.

A. Preliminaries

The fault model we consider is one in which only the switching elements fail and the connecting links do not fail. A faulty switch is treated as unusable and no connections can be routed through it. Faults in connecting links can be accommodated in this model by treating them as part of the switching elements. A switching element in the network is represented by an ordered pair (r, s) where r is the stage number in which the element is located and s is the switch number ($0 \le r \le n - 1$ and $0 \le s \le N/2 - 1$).

Definition 1: The fault set F in an Omega network is the set of faulty switching elements in the network under consideration.

Definition 2 [6]: A fault set F in an Omega network is critical if and only if it destroys the dynamic-full-accessibility of the network.

If F is noncritical, data can be routed from any input of the network to any output in a finite number of passes. Hence, there is a need for characterizing faults as critical and noncritical.

Definition 3: Let π be a permutation passable by the Omega network with $N = 2^n$ inputs and outputs. The set of faulty paths $C_{F,\pi}$ of the permutation π under the fault set F is the set of all connections that pass through some switch in F when the network is configured to realize π.

In the special case when π is the identity permutation I, $C_{F,I}$ contains the paths disconnected by the faulty switches while

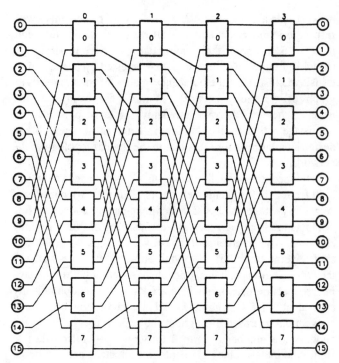

Fig. 1. A multiprocessor system with 16 processors interconnected by an Omega network.

realizing the identity permutation (all the switches set straight).

For example, the fault set $F = \{(1, 0), (2, 2)\}$ in the network of Fig. 1 disconnects the paths $0 \to 0$, $4 \to 4$, $8 \to 8$, and $10 \to 10$ of the identity permutation; hence, $C_{F,I} = \{(0 \to 0), (4 \to 4), (8 \to 8), (10 \to 10)\}$.

Since every switch in the network carries a unique pair of connections of π, no two switches in F disconnect the same pair of paths. However, $C_{F,\pi} = C_{F',\pi}$ does not imply that F and F' are identical, although F and F' have the same effect on the communication capability of the system. Hence, there is a need to define the equivalence of fault sets.

Definition 4: Two fault sets F and F' are *equivalent* if and only if $C_{F,I} = C_{F',I}$. We use the notation $F \equiv F'$ to denote that F and F' are equivalent.

The "$\equiv$" relation is an equivalence relation since it is reflexive, transitive, and symmetric. Hence, it partitions the fault sets into equivalence classes such that fault sets in the same equivalence class disconnect the same set of paths of the identity permutation. It should be noted that any Omega-passable permutation could have been used in Definition 4 instead of identity.

Definition 5: The *maximal fault set* F_{max} corresponding to a fault set F in the Omega network is the set of maximum size that is equivalent to F. That is, $F_{max} \equiv F$ and $F_{max} \supseteq F'$, for all $F' \equiv F$.

A graph model of the Omega network can be constructed as described in [12], with the switching elements represented by nodes and connecting links by directed arcs. When viewed from one of the switching elements in the first stage, the graph has the shape of a binary tree where the leaves are the switching elements in the last stage. Similarly, when viewed from a switching element in the last stage, the network again

looks like a binary tree where the leaves are the switching elements in the first stage. If the fault set contains an element in the first stage, the communication tree rooted on the switching element is completely destroyed so that no transfer of data is possible from the processors connected to the switching element to any of the network outputs. Similarly, a fault in the last stage disrupts all communication to the processors connected to the faulty switch. In the general case, faults can occur anywhere in the tree and we are faced with the problem of determining the criticality of the fault set. This can be checked by constructing the maximal fault set F_{max} from the given fault set F. We now describe how to construct F_{max} from the fault set F.

B. Construction of Maximal Fault Sets

Given a fault set F in the Omega network, the maximal fault set F_{max} is constructed by *propagating* the faults to the input and output sides of the network through the communication trees. It can be observed that the pair of switching elements (i, s), $(i, s + N/4)$ in the ith stage of the network is connected to only one pair $(i + 1, 2s)$ and $(i + 1, 2s + 1)$ of the next stage, for all $0 \leq s < N/4$ and $0 \leq i < n - 1$. This is described as the "buddy property" in [12]. The pair of switching elements in the ith stage is called output buddies and the pair in the $(i + 1)$th stage is called input buddies. If both the elements (i, s) and $(i, s + N/4)$ are in the fault set F, then F can be expanded to include $(i + 1, 2s)$ and $(i + 1, 2s + 1)$ without disconnecting any additional communication paths. Similarly, if both $(i + 1, 2s)$ and $(i + 1, 2s + 1)$ are in F, then both (i, s) and $(i, s + N/4)$ can be included without affecting equivalence in the sense of Definition 4.

Thus, the maximal fault set F_{max} can be constructed by starting from F and scanning the network first from the input side to the output side and then in reverse, including the buddies of all pairs already in F_{max}, until no more additions are possible. In fact, one forward pass and one reverse pass can be shown to be sufficient to attain maximality. The algorithm for the construction of F_{max} from F is shown in Algorithm 1.

Algorithm 1:

(Constructs the maximal fault set F_{max} corresponding to a given fault set F)

```
1.  F_max ← F (Initially F_max = F)
2.  for i : = 0 to n − 2 do (forward pass)
3.    begin
4.    for s : = 0 to N/4 − 1 do
5.      begin
6.      if {(i, s), (i, s + N/4)} ⊆ F_max then
            F_max ← F_max ∪ {(i + 1, 2s), (i + 1, 2s + 1)}
7.      end
8.    end;
9.  for i : = n − 1 downto 1 do (reverse pass)
10.   begin
11.   for s : = 0 to N/4 − 1 do
12.     begin
13.     if {(i, 2s), (i, 2s + 1)} ⊆ F_max then
            F_max ← F_max ∪ {(i − 1, s), (i − 1, s + N/4)}
14.     end
15.   end.
```

A simple proof can be given for the correctness of Algorithm 1. First, the F_{max} constructed by Algorithm 1 is equivalent to F since no additional communication paths are disconnected during the construction process. To show that the construction can be completed in two passes, we use contradiction. Two separate cases need to be considered.

1) At the end of the execution of Algorithm 1, F_{max} contains the elements (i, x) and $(i, x + N/4)$ for some $0 \leq i < n - 1$ and $0 \leq x < N/4$, but does not contain one or both of the elements $(i + 1, 2x)$, $(i + 1, 2x + 1)$. This would imply that at least one of (i, x), $(i, x + N/4)$ was added to F_{max} during the reverse pass. This could have happened only if both $(i + 1, 2x)$ and $(i + 1, 2x + 1)$ were in F_{max}, which is a contradiction.

2) F_{max} contains elements $(i, 2x)$ and $(i, 2x + 1)$ for some $1 \leq i \leq n - 1$ and $0 \leq x < N/4$, but does not contain one or both of the elements $(i - 1, x)$, $(i - 1, x + N/4)$. This is impossible since $(i, 2x)$ and $(i, 2x + 1)$ should have been added to F_{max} before reaching stage $i - 1$ during the reverse pass.

Lastly, to prove that F_{max} is maximal, consider any switch (r, s) not in F_{max}. By the construction of F_{max}, at least one of its input buddies in stage $r + 1$, say $(r + 1, s')$, is fault-free. By the same reasoning, one of the input buddies of $(r + 1, s')$ in stage $r + 2$ is again fault-free, and so on. Thus, a fault-free path exists from (r, s) to the output of the network. Similarly, one can show the existence of a fault-free path from the input side of the network to (r, s). Hence, (r, s) cannot be included in F_{max}. This proves the maximality of F_{max} constructed by Algorithm 1.

C. Checking the DFA Capability

The criticality of a fault set F can be checked from the knowledge of the corresponding maximal fault set F_{max}. In this section, we formulate sufficient conditions for DFA of the Omega network under multiple faults.

A switch in stage i of the network is accessible from a switch in stage i', $i' < i$, if and only if the former is accessible from the output buddy of the latter. The following definition is motivated by this observation.

Definition 6: Let S be a subset of the set of switching elements in some stage i, $0 \leq i \leq n - 1$, of the Omega network. The base set of S, denoted by $\beta(S)$, is defined as

$$\beta(S) = \left\{ s \bmod \frac{N}{4} \,|\, (i, s) \in S \right\}.$$

$\beta(S)$ is obtained by removing every switch (i, s) that has $s \geq N/4$ and replacing with its output buddy, if it is not already present. Thus, $\beta(S)$ defines a mapping from the $2^{N/2}$ subsets of switches in a particular stage to the $2^{N/4}$ subsets of $\{0, 1, \cdots, N/4 - 1\}$.

Lemma 1: Let F be a fault set in the Omega network of size $N = 2^n$ and F_{max} be the corresponding maximal fault set. Let S be a subset of switching elements in the input stage of the network such that $S \cap F_{max} = \varnothing$ and $|\beta(S)| = N/4$. Then any switch in the output stage of the network, not in F_{max}, is reachable from some switch in S in one pass.

Proof: Consider any switching element $(n - 1, x)$ not in F_{max}. Since $(n - 1, x)$ is not in F_{max}, at least one of its predecessor switching elements in stage $n - 2$ is not in F_{max}. By repeating this argument, we can show that $(n - 1, x)$ is reachable from some switching element in the input stage. Also, if a switch in the output stage is reachable from a switch in the input stage, the former is also reachable from the output buddy of the latter. Thus, if S contains one from every pair of output buddies in the input stage, all the switches in the output stage which are not in F_{max} are reachable from some switch in S in one pass.

A fault set F in the Omega network is critical if the corresponding maximal fault set F_{max} contains a switching element from the input or output stages of the network. The absence of such elements, however, does not guarantee DFA of the network, although for small networks this can be shown to be true. The trivial case $N = 4$ has no fault tolerance. For $N = 8$, it is easy to observe that routing is possible between any pair of processing elements in at most two passes if F_{max} does not contain any switching element from the input or output stages. This can also be shown to be true for $N = 16$.

Theorem 1: A fault set F in the Omega network for $N = 16$ is critical if and only if the maximal fault set F_{max} contains a switching element from the input or output stages of the network. Furthermore, data can be routed from any processing element to any other processing element in at most two passes through the network if F is noncritical.

Proof: We will prove only the "only if" part, since the "if" part is obvious. Consider any processing element p. Since F_{max} contains no switching elements in the input stage, there exists at least one switching element $(1, x)$ in stage 1, not in F_{max}, that is accessible from p in the first pass. Now, since $(1, x)$ is not in F_{max}, there exist switching element $(2, x')$ that is not in F_{max} and is accessible from p in the first pass. During the second pass, data from $(2, x')$ can be routed to any of the four switching elements in the set $S = \{(0, 4x' + y \bmod 8)| 0 \leq y \leq 3\}$ in stage 0. Since $S \cap F_{max} = \varnothing$ and $|\beta(S)| = 4$, by Lemma 1, every processing element is accessible from some switch in S during the second pass. Thus, two passes are sufficient.

Beyond $N = 16$, the condition that F_{max} does not contain switching elements from the first and last stages is not, in general, sufficient to conclude that the network has DFA. (The reason for this will become obvious in the discussion following Theorem 3.) Additional conditions need to be tested to ascertain the noncriticality of a fault set. In the following parts of this section, we will formulate sufficient conditions for testing the DFA in the general case. In the rest of this section we assume $N \geq 32$, unless stated explicitly.

Definition 7: The subset of switching elements $A_{i,j}$, $0 \leq i \leq n - 2$ and $0 \leq j \leq 2^{N-4} - 1$, in stage i of the Omega network, is defined as follows:

Stage 0: $A_{0,j} = \{(0, 4j + k), (0, 4j + k + N/4)|0 \leq k \leq 3\}$,

Stage 1: $A_{1,j} = \{(1, 8j + k)|0 \leq k \leq 7\}$,

Stage i, $2 \leq i \leq n - 2$: $A_{i,j} = \{(i, 2^{i+2}j + k \bmod N/2)|0 \leq k \leq 2^{i+2} - 1\}$.

$A_{i,j}$, for $1 \leq i \leq n - 2$, represents the set of switching elements in stage i of the network that is accessible from some switch in $A_{0,j}$ by one pass in the fault-free network. $A_{1,j}$ is the set of eight switching elements in stage 1 that is reachable from a switching element $(n - 2, 2^{n-4}k + j)$, $0 \leq k \leq 3$, in stage $n - 2$ in the next pass through the network.

Definition 8: $A_{i,j}/F$, $1 \leq i \leq n - 2$, denotes the set of fault-free switching elements in stage i of the Omega network which is accessible from some switch in $A_{0,j}$ in one pass under the fault set F. Clearly, $A_{i,j}/F \subseteq A_{i,j}$.

Definitions 7 and 8 were motivated by the following observation. Assume that data from a processing element p can reach a switch $(n - 2, x)$, $0 \leq x \leq N/2 - 1$, in stage $n - 2$ under a fault set F. Assume also that $F_{\max}$ contains neither the switch $(n - 2, x)$ nor any switch in the input or output stages of the network; then data from this switch can be routed to any of the eight switches in the set $\{(1, 8x \bmod 2^{n-4} + y)|0 \leq y \leq 7\}$ in stage 1 of the network in the next pass. This is simply the set $A_{1, x \bmod 2^{n-4}}$. Thus, $A_{1,j}$ represents the set of switching elements in stage 1 that is accessible from a switch $(n - 2, 2^{n-4}k + j)$, $0 \leq k \leq 7$, in stage $n - 2$ in a subsequent pass through the network. The set $A_{0,j}$ is the set of switches in stage 0 which fan out to some element in $A_{1,j}$. Thus, any output terminal of the network that is accessible from some switch in $A_{0,j}$ in one pass through the network is also accessible from a switch $2^{n-4}k + j$, $0 \leq k \leq 7$, in stage $n - 2$ in a second pass.

Example 1: Fig. 2 shows the omega network for $N = 32$ with a maximal fault set F. In this case, $A_{0,0} = \{(0, 0), (0, 1), (0, 2), (0, 3), (0, 8), (0, 9), (0, 10), (0, 11)\}$. Every switch in stage 3 is reachable from some switch in $A_{0,0}$ in the fault-free network; thus, $A_{3,0} = \{(3, 0), (3, 1), \cdots, (3, 15)\}$. However, in the presence of the fault set shown, every switch in $A_{0,0}$ has access to exactly one switch in stage 3 and $A_{3,0}/F = \{(3, 0), (3, 6), (3, 10), (3, 12)\}$.

Some important results on the DFA capability of a faulty network can be determined from the knowledge of the sets $A_{n-2,j}/F$, the set of switching elements in stage $n - 2$ accessible from the group of switches $A_{0,j}$ in stage 0. The sets $A_{n-2,j}/F$ can be constructed in a straightforward manner by examination of the fault set F. Algorithm 2 outlines the procedure for construction of $A_{n-2,j}/F$ from F.

Algorithm 2:

(Constructs $A_{n-2,j}/F$ from the fault set F.)

1. **for** $k := 0$ **to** 3 **do**
2. **begin**
3. $S_k \leftarrow \varnothing$;
4.   **for** every $(r, s) \in F$ **do**
5.   **if** $s \in \{2^{r+2}j + 2^r k + m \bmod N/2|0 \leq m < 2^r\}$ **then**
6. $S_k \leftarrow S_k \cup \{2^{(n-2)-r}s + m \bmod N/2|0 \leq m < 2^{(n-2)-r}\}$
7. **end**;
8. $S_0' = \{0, 1, \cdots, N/4 - 1\} - (S_0 \cap S_2)$;
9. $S_1' = \{N/4, N/4 + 1, \cdots, N/2 - 1\} - (S_1 \cap S_3)$;
10. $A_{n-2,j}/F = \{(n - 2, s)|s \in S_0' \cup S_1'\}$.

The sets S_k, $0 \leq k \leq 3$, in Algorithm 2 are used to accumulate the inaccessible switches in stage $n - 2$ from the switch $(0, 4j + k)$ in stage 0. S_k is the set of inaccessible

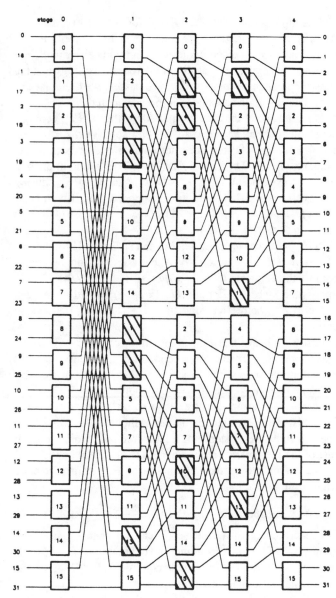

Fig. 2. The Omega network for $N = 32$ with a critical fault set.

switches from the buddy pair $\{(0, 4j + k), (0, 4j + k + N/4)\}$ in $A_{0,j}$. A faulty switch s in stage r disconnects some of the switching paths from the switch $(0, 4j + k)$ in stage 0 if $s = (2^{r+2}j + 2^r k + m) \bmod N/2$, for some $0 \leq m < 2^r$. This makes all the switching elements in the set $\{2^{(n-2)-r}s + m \bmod N/2|0 \leq m < 2^{(n-2)-r}\}$ in stage $n - 2$ inaccessible from the switch $(0, 4j + k)$ in stage 0. The sets S_k are constructed by accumulating such inaccessible sets in stage $n - 2$ for every switch in F. A switching element in stage $n - 2$ is inaccessible from $A_{0,j}$ if and only if 1) it belongs to both S_0 and S_2, or 2) it belongs to both S_1 and S_3. The set $A_{n-2,j}/F$ is obtained by removing such elements from $A_{n-2,j}$.

Definition 9: Let S be a subset of the set of the switching elements in stage $n - 2$ of the Omega network. Then the mapping g is defined as

$$g(S) = \{s \bmod 2^{n-4}|(n - 2, s) \in S\}.$$

The function g groups switching elements in stage $n - 2$ in accordance with their reachable sets in stage 1 during the next pass through the network. Since data can be routed from a switch in the set $\{(n-2, 2^{n-4}k+j), 0 \le k \le 7\}, 0 \le j \le 2^{n-4}-1$, in stage $n-2$ to any switch in $A_{1,j}$ in stage 1 in the next pass, all switches in the set are treated equivalently by the mapping. For example, let $S = \{(3,0), (3,2), (3,4), (3,15)\}$ in the network of Fig. 2. If there are no faulty switches in the input and the output stages, data from $(3,0)$ can be routed to any switch in the set $\{(1,0), (1,1), \cdots, (1,7)\}$ in stage 1 during the next pass; this is simply the set $A_{1,0}$. Similarly $(3,2)$ and $(3,4)$ both have access to every switch in $A_{1,0}$ in the next pass, while $(3,15)$ has access to every switch in $A_{1,1}$. Thus, $g(S) = \{0, 1\}$.

If S is chosen such that $|g(S)| = 2^{n-4}$, then data can be routed through *some* switch in S to *any* switch in the output stage during the second pass, assuming that F_{max} does not contain any switch in the first or last stage. Thus, if data from a PE can reach any switch in S in at most k passes, then it can be routed to any other PE in at most $(k+1)$ passes.

Lemma 2: Let F be a fault set in the Omega network of size $N = 2^n$ such that its maximal fault set F_{max} does not contain any switching element in the input or output stages. Let S be the set of fault-free switching elements in stage $n-2$ that are accessible from a processing element p in one pass, with $(n-2, x) \in S$ for some $0 \le x \le 2^{n-4}-1$. If an output terminal of the network is reachable from some switch in $A_{0,x}$ in at most k passes, it is reachable from the processing element p in at most $k+1$ passes.

Proof: Since the output terminal is accessible from a switch in $A_{0,x}$, there is a switch in $A_{1,x}/F$ that has access to the terminal in one pass. Data from the processing element p can reach the switch $(n-2, x)$ in at most k passes; also, since all the switches in the first and last stages are fault-free, data can be routed from $(n-2, x)$ to any switch in $A_{1,x}$ during the next pass. Hence, the output terminal is reachable from p in at most $k+1$ passes.

Lemmas 1 and 2 directly lead to the following.

Lemma 3: Let F be a fault set in the Omega network of size $N = 2^n$ such that its maximal fault set F_{max} does not contain any switching element in the input or output stages. Let S be the set of fault-free switching elements in stage $n-2$ that are accessible from a processing element p in one pass. Then data can be routed from p to any other processing element in at most two passes through the network if $|g(S)| = 2^{n-4}$.

Proof: Consider any processing element $q \ne p$. By Lemma 1, q is accessible from some switch in $A_{0,x}$, for some $0 \le x \le 2^{n-4}-1$, in one pass through the network. Hence, by Definition 7, q is accessible from some switch in $A_{1,x}$ in one pass. However, since $|g(S)| = 2^{n-4}$, there is at least one switch in the set $\{(n-2, 2^{n-4}k+j) | 0 \le k \le 7\}$, for all $0 \le j \le 2^{n-4}-1$, in stage $n-2$ that is directly accessible from p. Thus, every switch in every set $A_{1,j}, 0 \le j \le 2^{n-4}-1$, is reachable from p during the second pass. Hence, data can be routed from p to q in at most two passes.

The condition in Lemma 3 is not necessary for DFA. However, it is useful when the number of faulty switches in the network is small. In particular, application of Lemma 3 shows that all single and double faults in the network are noncritical if the corresponding maximal fault sets do not include a switch from the input or output stages.

Example 2: In the faulty network shown in Fig. 2, the switching elements $S = \{(3,0), (3,2), (3,3)\}$ in stage 3 are accessible from PE 6 in one pass. Since $|g(S)| = 2$, by Lemma 3, every PE is reachable from PE 6 in at most two passes. However, the only accessible switch in stage 3 from PE 0 in one pass is $(3,0)$ and the condition in Lemma 3 is not satisfied. Although this is not a necessary condition, it may be observed, in this case, that PE 0 is incapable of reaching half the number of PE's in a finite number of passes through the network.

Now we are in a position to state one of the main results of this paper.

Theorem 2: Let F be a fault set in the Omega network of size $N = 2^n$ such that its maximal fault set F_{max} does not contain any switching elements in the input or output stages of the network. The fault set F is noncritical if $|g(A_{n-2,j}/F)| = 2^{n-4}$ for all $0 \le j \le 2^{n-4}-1$. Furthermore, any connection between two processing elements can be routed in at most *three* passes through the network if this condition is satisfied.

Proof: Consider any processing element p connected to the network. By construction of F_{max}, there exists some fault-free switch, say $(n-2, x)$, in stage $n-2$ directly accessible from p. During the second pass, data can be routed from $(n-2, x)$ to any of the eight switches in $A_{1, x \bmod 2^{n-4}}$. Since $|g(A_{n-2, x \bmod 2^{n-4}}/F)| = 2^{n-4}$, it is possible to reach at least one fault-free member of any $A_{n-2,k}, 0 \le k \le 2^{n-4}-1$, during the second pass, Thus, every switch in stage 1 is reachable in the third pass. Hence, by Lemma 1, every output is reachable from p in the third pass.

Example 3: Fig. 3 shows the Omega network for $N = 32$ with a fault set F which is maximal. For this example,

$$A_{3,0}/F = \{(3,0), (3,6), (3,10), (3,12), (3,13)\},$$

$$\text{and } A_{3,1}/F = \{(3,3), (3,5), (3,8), (3,9), (3,15)\}$$

$$g(A_{3,0}/F) = g(A_{3,1}/F) = \{0, 1\}.$$

Thus, the condition in Theorem 2 is satisfied. One can verify that every connection in the network of Fig. 3 can be routed in at most three passes. Some connections require exactly three passes, as evidenced by the connection from PE 0 to PE 4. Every fault-free path from PE 0 to PE 4 makes at least three passes through the network; the only way to route data in exactly three passes is to send it to PE 3 in the first pass, from there to PE 23 in the second pass, and finally to PE 4 in the third pass.

Theorem 2 shows that system operation is possible without the loss of any processing elements in the presence of a large number of network faults. When faults are confined to a single stage, as many as $7N/16$ switch faults can be tolerated without violating the condition in Theorem 2.

The condition in Theorem 2 is only a sufficient condition for DFA. It is possible to develop less stringent conditions on the fault set F under which the DFA of the network is maintained. The following theorem introduces a set of conditions which is weaker than that given by Theorem 2.

Theorem 3: Let F be a fault set in the Omega network for $N = 2^n$ and F_{max} be the corresponding maximal fault set. F is noncritical if the following conditions are satisfied.

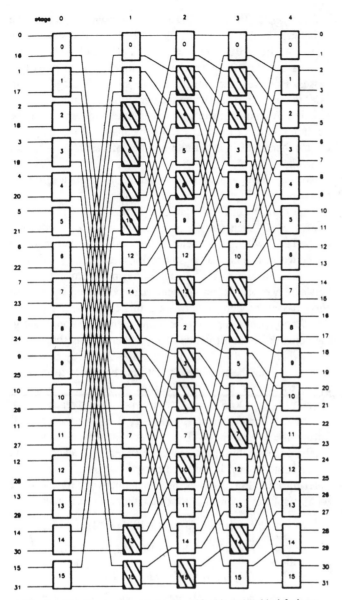

Fig. 3. The Omega network for $N = 32$ with a noncritical fault set.

a) F_{max} does not contain any switching elements in the input or output stages of the network.

b) For every $0 \le k \le n - 5$, and for every $J \subseteq \{0, 1, \cdots, 2^{n-4} - 1\}$ with $|J| = 2^k$, the union $\bigcup_{j \in J} g(A_{n-2,j}/F)$ has at least 2^{k+1} elements.

Furthermore, data can be routed from any PE to any other PE in at most $n - 2$ passes if these conditions are satisfied.

Theorem 3 forms unions of the sets $A_{n-2,j}/F$, $0 \le j \le 2^{n-4} - 1$, in sizes of 2, 4, $\cdots$, 2^{n-5} and checks if every combination is capable of routing data to twice the number of $A_{1,j}$'s in stage 1 in the next pass. Satisfaction of this condition assures the existence of a binary routing tree of depth $n - 2$ from p to the other processing elements.

Proof: Consider any processing element p. There exists at least one fault-free switch, say $(n - 2, x)$, in stage $n - 2$ accessible from p in one pass. During the second pass, data from this switch can be routed to any switch in $A_{1,x \bmod 2^{n-4}}$. Since $|g(A_{n-2,x} \bmod 2^{n-4}/F)| \ge 2$, the data can reach every switch in at least two distinct groups of switches in stage

1, say $A_{1,y}$ and $A_{1,z}$, in the third pass. In general, during the kth pass, $k \ge 2$, data can reach at least 2^{k-2} distinct groups in stage 1. Thus, during the $(n - 2)$th pass, every switch in stage 1 is reachable. Hence, by Lemma 1, every PE is reachable from p in the $(n - 2)$th pass.

The above proof provides a clue to why condition a) is sufficient to establish DFA for $N \le 16$. When $N = 16$, there is exactly one $A_{n-2,j}$, that is $A_{2,0}$, which consists of all the switches in stage 2. When F_{max} does not contain any input or output switches, any fault-free switch in this set can be reached during the second pass.

The practical significance of Theorem 3 is limited because of the difficulty of checking condition b) in large networks, and of the large number of passes that might be needed. However, it is sufficient to check condition b) only on those $A_{n-2,j}/F$'s with $|A_{n-2,j}/F| \le 2^{n-4}$. When the size of the fault set is small, it is probable that the number of such sets is small so that the test can be performed in reasonable time. It should be noted that Theorems 2 and 3 imply the same set of conditions when $N = 32$.

Example 4: Consider the Omega network of size $N = 2^n$ with the following fault set:

$$F = \left\{ (i, 2j), \left(i, 2j + 1 + \frac{N}{4} \right) \,\middle|\, 1 \le i \le n - 2, 0 \le j < \frac{N}{8} \right\}.$$

This set contains exactly $N/4(\log_2 N - 2)$ switching elements and is maximal. It can be shown that, for $N > 32$,

$$|g(A_{n-2,j}/F)| = 4, \qquad 0 \le j < 2^{n-4}$$

and

$$\left| \bigcup_{j \in J} g(A_{n-2,j}/F) \right| = 2^{k+2},$$

for every $J \subseteq \{0, 1, \cdots, 2^{n-4} - 1\}$ with $|J| = 2^k$, $0 \le k \le n - 5$.

Thus, by Theorem 3, the network has DFA and every connection can be routed in at most $\log_2 N - 2$ passes. It is possible to show that some connections in this example need as many as $\log_2 N - 3$ passes. It should be noted that the number of faulty switches in this example, $N/4$ ($\log_2 N - 2$), is an upper bound, since any additional fault would destroy the DFA of the network.

Theorems 2 and 3 state only sufficient conditions for DFA. It is possible that a faulty network not satisfying the condition b) of Theorem 3 has DFA. The general problem of determining the noncriticality of a fault set is as hard as the transitive closure problem. However, certain savings in computation can be obtained by using subsets of switching elements instead of individual switching elements. Algorithm 3 can be used to test if a processing element p has access to every other processing element in a finite number of passes through the network.

Algorithm 3:

(Determines if a PE p has access to every other PE)

1. $S \leftarrow$ Set of accessible switching elements in stage $n - 2$ from p under the fault set F.

2. $P \leftarrow g(S)$; $S^* \leftarrow P$;

3. **while** $|S^*| < 2^{n-4}$ **do**

4.   **begin**

5. $Q \leftarrow \varnothing$;
6.   **for every** $k \in P$ **do** $Q \leftarrow Q \cup g(A_{n-2,k}/F)$;
7.   **if** $Q \subseteq S^*$ **then** return false (no DFA from this PE)
8. $P \leftarrow S^* - S^* \cap Q$;
9. $S^* \leftarrow S^* \cup Q$;
10.   **end**;
11. return true.

Algorithm 3 essentially performs a transitive closure on the connectivity graph of the network, starting from a terminal connected to the processing element p. Each iteration of the loop in the algorithm represents one pass in the network; successful completion of the mth pass of the loop indicates that data from p can reach all $A_{1,j}$'s with $j \in S^*$, in at most $m + 2$ passes. As new elements are added into S^*, the reachable $A_{1,j}$'s in stage 1 increase with every iteration. The algorithm returns false when an iteration produces no new $A_{1,j}$'s and some $A_{1,j}$'s remain unreachable. To check the DFA of the entire network, it is sufficient to apply Algorithm 3 on one out of every 16 PE's.

III. Routing in a Faulty Network

In the last section, we formulated sufficient conditions for the DFA of an Omega network under multiple faults and proved that at most $\log_2 N - 2$ passes are sufficient for routing data from any processor to any other processor if the fault set F satisfies certain conditions. In this section, we will discuss some techniques that could be used for routing in a faulty network that has DFA. We will assume a packet-switched network since routing in multiple passes is more easily implemented in such systems.

A deterministic technique is to use routing tables in every processor. In this method, a communication packet has two routing tags—a final destination tag that specifies the final destination of the data, and an intermediate destination tag that specifies the destination of the packet in the current pass through the network. As the packet travels through the system, every recipient processor of the packet updates the intermediate tag from the knowledge of the final destination of the packet. The routing table in each processor stores the best intermediate destination for each final destination. The path to the intermediate destination is guaranteed to be fault-free; furthermore, due to the unique-path property of the network, the actual routing of data through the network is no different than in the fault-free case.

This technique requires *a priori* knowledge of the exact route to be followed, that is, the intermediate destination during each pass. This needs precomputation of a (shortest) path from every processor to every other processor. However, this information needs to be computed only once during the recovery phase and can be used until new faults occur. The routing table in each processor needs only $N/4$ entries since the path to be followed for the set of destinations $\{4x + y \mid 0 \leq y \leq 3\}$ is identical for all $0 \leq x \leq N/4$. If the conditions in Theorem 2 are satisfied, this information can be computed from knowledge of the set of accessible switches (in one pass) in stage $n - 2$ from each processing element.

Probabilistic techniques can be used when the actual path to be followed from the source to the destination is not known in

advance, which could be suitable for networks of large size. Whenever a processor receives a packet whose ultimate destination is not directly accessible from it, the packet is routed randomly to an intermediate destination that is accessible. Some mechanisms for preventing cycles should be provided, or else the network soon gets saturated with wasteful traffic. This technique does not guarantee a finite communication delay, but may give good results when the number of faulty paths is not large. This technique is similar to the use of a single-stage network to provide communication in multiple passes, as studied in [13] and [14] where conflicts in the network cause packets to be routed to wrong intermediate destinations.

Another technique is to distribute the routing information among the switching elements in the network, thereby making them more intelligent. The information to be stored in each switch can be computed in a relatively simple manner and can be used to avoid wasteful communication.

IV. Extension to k-Stage Shuffle/Exchange Networks

The results derived in Section III are not restricted to the Omega network and can be applied to multistage shuffle/exchange networks in general. When the number of shuffle/exchange stages is $k < n$, the network does not possess the full access property even in the fault-free case, since only 2^k outputs are accessible from any input terminal. However, the fault-free network always has DFA, facilitating data transfer between PE's in multiple passes. Networks with $k < 3$ are not interesting from the fault-tolerance point of view, since a single fault destroys DFA. Hence, we consider only networks of size $N = 2^n$ with $3 \leq k < n$ stages.

For a fault set F in this network, the maximal fault set $F_{\max}$ can be constructed using the same procedure in Algorithm 1. If $F_{\max}$ contains any switching elements from the first or last stage of the network, the network has no DFA. If this is not the case, the condition in Theorem 2 can be applied on the sets $A_{k-2,j}$ in the preultimate stage $k - 2$ to see if the routing can be done in at most three passes. This is possible only when the number of stages k is at least $n - 5$, since even a nonfaulty network will not satisfy the conditions in Theorem 2 if $k < n - 5$. However, Theorem 3 is applicable for all values of k in the range $3 \leq k < n$. Thus, if the conditions set forth by Theorem 3 are met, any connection can be routed in $\log_2 N - 2$ passes, independent of the number of stages in the network. As the number of stages is reduced, the fault tolerance decreases in the sense that the probability of violating the conditions in Theorem 3 increases. However, the rate at which faults occur also diminishes with a decrease in the number of stages, and this may compensate, at least partially, for the reduced fault tolerance. The routing overhead, of course, increases with a reduction in the number of stages.

V. Concluding Remarks

In this paper, we studied the DFA capability of multistage interconnection networks under multiple faults. A characterization of multiple faults in the Omega network was introduced and used to develop simple tests for the DFA capability under a given set of faults. Under certain conditions, a maximum of three passes through the network was shown to be sufficient for communication between any two processors in the system. $\log_2 N - 2$ passes were shown to be sufficient when the fault set satisfies a weaker set of conditions. The results show that a large number of faults can be tolerated without destroying the connectivity of the PE's.

More research is needed on techniques for efficient routing of data between processors in the system when the network has DFA. The objective is to avoid expensive computations in the recovery phase to construct the routing tables. One possible solution is to distribute the routing information in the switching elements of the network to facilitate routing in an adaptive manner. Another possibility is to use incremental techniques whenever a fault occurs to update only those parts of the routing tables that need to be modified. Another interesting and related topic is the development of integrated models for analysis of the fault tolerance and performance degradation of systems employing unique-path multistage interconnection networks, with DFA as the basic fault-tolerance criterion.

In this paper, we have chosen connectivity among all the processing elements in the system as the basic requirement. This eliminates the need for reassignment of processing elements and the resulting movement of data during reconfiguration. With a unique-path multistage network like the Omega network, the model allows no faults to be tolerated in the input or output stages. If full connnectivity is not needed, or if the system is able to tolerate the loss of a subset of processing elements without interrupting operation, faults in the input and output stages can be tolerated. The fault tolerance and performance characteristics of such systems need to be studied in detail.

ACKNOWLEDGMENT

The authors wish to thank an anonymous referee for suggesting several improvements on earlier versions of this paper.

REFERENCES

[1] Special Issue on Multiprocessing Technology, *IEEE Computer*, vol. 18, June 1985.
[2] T. Y. Feng, "A survey of interconnection networks," *IEEE Computer*, vol. 14, pp. 12–27, Dec. 1981.
[3] J. Arlat and J. C. Laprie, "Performance-related dependability evaluation of supercomputer systems," in *Proc. 13th Annu. Int. Symp. Fault-Tolerant Comput.*, June 1983, pp. 276–283.
[4] C. R. Das and L. N. Bhuyan, "Reliability simulation of multiprocessor systems," in *Proc. Int. Conf. Parallel Processing*, Aug. 1985, pp. 764–771.
[5] D. H. Lawrie, "Access and alignment of data in an array processor," *IEEE Trans. Comput.*, vol. C-24, pp. 1145–1155, Dec. 1975.
[6] J. P. Shen, "Fault-tolerance of β-networks in interconnected multicomputer systems," Ph.D. dissertation, Dep. E.E., U.S.C., USCEE Tech. Rep. 510, Aug. 1981.
[7] D. P. Agrawal, "Testing and fault-tolerance of multistage interconnection networks," *IEEE Computer*, vol. 15, pp. 41–53, Apr. 1982.
[8] S. Thanawastien and V. P. Nelson, "Optimal fault detection test sequences for shuffle/exchange networks," in *Proc. 13th Annu. Int. Symp. Fault-Tolerant Comput.*, June 1983, pp. 442–445.
[9] C. L. Wu and T. Y. Feng, "Fault diagnosis for a class of multistage shuffle/exchange networks," *IEEE Trans. Comput.*, vol. C-30, pp. 743–758, Oct. 1981.
[10] D. P. Agrawal and J. S. Leu, "Dynamic accessibility testing and path length optimization of multistage interconnection networks," in *Proc. 4th Int. Conf. Distribut. Comput. Syst.*, May, 1984, pp. 266–277.
[11] C. L Wu and T. Y. Feng, "On a class of multistage interconnection networks," *IEEE Trans. Comput.*, vol. C-29, pp. 694–702, Aug. 1980.
[12] D. P. Agrawal, "Graph theoretical analysis and design of multistage interconnection networks," *IEEE Trans. Comput.*, vol. C-32, pp. 637–648, July 1983.
[13] P.-Y. Chen, P.-C. Yew, and D. H. Lawrie, "Performance of packet switching in buffered single stage shuffle-exchange networks," in *Proc. 3rd Int. Conf. Distribut. Comput. Syst.*, Oct. 1982, pp. 622–629.
[14] D. H. Lawrie and D. A Padua, "Analysis of message switching with shuffle-exchanges in multiprocessors," in *Proc. Workshop Interconnection Networks Parallel Distribut. Processing*, Apr. 1980, pp. 116–123.

Anujan Varma (S'83–M'86) received the B.Sc. degree in electrical engineering from the University of Calicut, India, and the M.E. degree in automation from the Indian Institute of Science, Bangalore, India, and the Ph.D. degree in computer enigneering from the University of Southern California, Los Angeles.

He is a member of the Research Staff in the System Interconnection Structures Department at IBM Thomas J. Watson Research Center, Yorktown Heights, NY. His research interests include computer architecture, fault-tolerant computing, interconnection networks, and optical computing.

Dr. Varma is a member of the Association for Computing Machinery.

C.S. Raghavendra (S'80–M'82–SM'85) was born in India. He received the B.Sc. (Hons) physics degree from Bangalore University in 1973, the B.E. and M.E. degrees in electronics and communication from the Indian Institute of Science, Bangalore, in 1976 and 1978, respectively, and the Ph.D. degree in computer science from University of California at Los Angeles in 1982.

Since September 1982 he has been on the faculty of Electrical Engineering–Systems Department at University of Southern California, Los Angeles where he is currently an Associate Professor. His research interest are computer system architecture, fault-tolerant computing, and reliability analysis of networks and distributed systems.

Dr. Raghavendra is a recipient of the Presidential Young Investigator Award for 1985.

Fault-Tolerant Multiprocessor Link and Bus Network Architectures

DHIRAJ K. PRADHAN, SENIOR MEMBER, IEEE

Abstract — This paper presents a general class of regular networks which provide optimal (near-optimal) fault tolerance.

The proposed networks compare favorably to other regular networks such as leaf-ringed binary trees and cube networks. In particular, the networks proposed possess certain advantages in that the number of connections per node is neither an arbitrarily fixed number (as in leaf-ringed trees) nor does it grow arbitrarily large with the size of the network (as in cube networks). This point has significant relevance to fault tolerance in that the degree of fault tolerance provided by the network can be varied according to the design specification. Also, the networks admit simple self-routing of messages and that routing is adaptable to faults.

Index Terms — Algorithmic routing, circuit switching, connectivity, diameter of graphs, fault-tolerant communication network, multiple bus network, multiprocessor networks, packet switching, regular graphs, regular networks, shared-bus fault tolerance, shuffle-exchange graph.

I. INTRODUCTION

RECENT developments in technology have made it possible to interconnect a large number of computing elements in order to form an integrated system. Various network architectures have been proposed that are suitable for both multiprocessors and VLSI systems [1]–[8], [11]–[14], [19]–[27].

The likelihood increases of one or more elements failing with the increasing number of elements in the system. Consequently, a key consideration in the design of such systems is their overall reliability and fault tolerance. The fault tolerance of a system can be defined in various ways. One measure that possesses relevance to a system which consists of a large number of homogeneous elements is the maximum number of elements which can become faulty without disconnecting the system. That is, the assumption is made that the system can perform in a degraded mode with loss of one or more components, as long as the system is fully connected. Also, more importantly, each element can still be capable of communicating with all of the other elements in the system with ease, in spite of the faults. In the context of communication delays, the performance degradation that is due to faults may be measured in terms of the increase in path lengths, and the associated increase in the routing overhead. So, it is not only important that the system remain fully connected, but also that the nodes be able to communicate

with each other fairly easily — preferably with only minor modification to the original routing procedure. It is precisely in this framework that a class of new fault-tolerant architectures has been developed here.

The proposed class of networks is regular in that all of the system nodes (elements) possess the same number of connections per node. The proposed networks favorably compare to other regular networks such as the binary cube [1], [6], generalized hypercube networks [13], cube-connected cycles [2], leaf-ringed binary tree networks [3], and De Bruijn graph networks [6], [10], [14] as seen from Table I.

In general, the proposed networks possess the following attractive features.

1) Compared to other networks, the proposed networks possess certain advantages in terms of their number of connections per node. Specifically, networks such as the binary cube require that the number of connections per node increases with the number of nodes (whereas cube-connected cycles and binary tree networks use nodes that only have three connections per node). On the other hand, the proposed network of any arbitrarily large size can be built using nodes with any specified number of connections per node. For example, given nodes with 5 connections per node, one can build a network of 256 nodes ($r = 4, m = 4$), or 1024 nodes ($r = 4, m = 5$), or in general, any arbitrarily large 4^m node network.

2) The internode distances are *small*. The maximum internode distances are proportional to only the *logarithm* of the number of nodes; inversely, to the logarithm of the number of connections per node.

3) More importantly, the networks are capable of maximal or near-maximal fault tolerance.

4) Degradation that is due to an increase in the routing distances and communication overhead resulting from faults can be fairly low. A detour technique is presented that allows the network to degrade proportionately to the number of faults.

5) Also of interest is the fact that the network admits self-routing of messages, both when the network is fault free as well as when it is faulty. Self-routing refers to that ability to route messages from node to node by using information such as destination address tag bits contained within the message and where intermediate nodes perform no additional computation for routing. This is possible if the routing path can be determined algorithmically, without using routing tables and directories.

Manuscript received June 24, 1982; revised December 28, 1983 and August 2, 1984. This work was supported by the Air Force Office of Scientific Research under Grant AFOSR 84-0052.

The author is with the Department of Electrical and Computer Engineering, University of Massachusetts, Amherst, MA 01003.

Reprinted from *IEEE Trans. Computers*, Vol. 34, No. 1, Jan. 1985, pp. 33-45.

TABLE I
DIFFERENT INTERCONNECTION NETWORKS

Network	Number of nodes	Number of connections/ node	Routing distance	Fault tolerance
Leaf-ringed binary tree	$(2^m - 1)$	3	$(2m - 1)$	2
Cube-connected cycles	$3 \cdot 2^m$	3	$m^2/2$	2
Binary cube	2^m	m	m	$(m - 1)$
Generalized hybercube	$\prod_{i=1}^{m} x_i$	$\sum_{i=1}^{m} x_i$	m	$\sum_{i=1}^{m} (x_i - 1)$
DeBruijn network	r^m	$2r$	m	$(2r - 3)$
Proposed network	r^m	r or $(r + 1)$	$(2m - 1)$	$(r - 1)$ or r

The next section presents the proposed network. Following this, Section III and Section IV develop the fault tolerance of the networks.

II. PROPOSED NETWORK

First, given a graph structure one can formulate a link network and a bus network based on the graph structure as described below. Let $G = \langle V, E \rangle$ be an undirected graph where V is a set of n vertices represented as 0 through $(n - 1)$. The set E represents the edges denoted as (i, j) where i and j are two neighboring nodes connected by (i, j) in G. Let LA and BA be defined as two mappings of G into a link network and a bus network, as described below.

Let $LA(G) = \langle \text{PE}, C \rangle$ where PE is a set of processing elements, represented as $\text{PE}(0), \text{PE}(1), \cdots, \text{PE}(n - 1)$, which corresponds to the set of vertices in G. Let C be the set of bidirectional communication links. There is a communication link $C(i, j)$ in C which connects $\text{PE}(i)$ with $\text{PE}(j)$ iff $(i, j) \, \varepsilon \, E$.

Let $BA(G) = \langle B, \text{PE} \rangle$ where B represents a set of buses defined as $\text{BUS}(0), \text{BUS}(1), \cdots, \text{BUS}(n - 1)$, corresponding to n vertices. The set PE represents the set of processing elements defined as $\text{PE}(i, j) \, \varepsilon \, \text{PE}$ iff $(i, j) \, \varepsilon \, E$. The processing element $\text{PE}(i, j)$ is connected to buses $\text{BUS}(i)$ and $\text{BUS}(j)$ as shown in Fig. 1. Thus, the link architecture is obtained by using the interpretation that vertices denote processing elements and edges denote communication links. On the other hand, the bus architecture is obtained by using the interpretation that buses are shown as vertices and computing elements as edges in the graph. Thus, the number of processing elements in $BA(G)$ is equal to the number of edges in G. Each processing element is connected to two buses and each bus is connected to a subset of the processing elements. (The number of processing elements connected to $\text{BUS}(i)$ is equal to the degree of node i in G.) This differs from the conventional multiple-bus design where all processing elements are connected to all buses. Since each bus is connected to a subset of processing elements, an inter-PE transfer may require several interbus transfers.

However, if bus load is equated to the number of connections per bus, then the $BA(G)$ network has a much smaller bus load when compared to an equivalent design which uses conventional shared buses. Therefore, a $BA(G)$ type bus net-

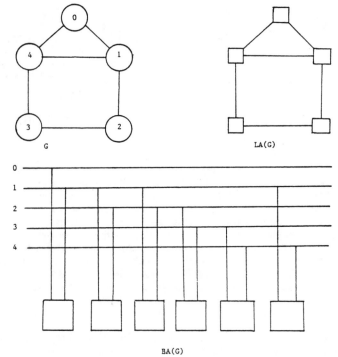

Fig. 1. Link and bus architecture.

work may have certain advantages over the conventional shared multiple-bus design when there are large numbers of processing elements to be connected. Also, it may be noted that one of the advantages of a $BA(G)$ network over $LA(G)$ network is that it can be easily extended by adding more PE's to buses as required and there are well developed bus protocols available.

This alternate multiprocessor multibus architecture can be quite attractive where
1) a processor may not have the hardware capabilities to allow its attachment to more than a certain number of buses, and
2) for reasons of reliability, the buses may be in physically different locations; hence, a processor may not be located next to every bus.

Various relationships between G and the corresponding $LA(G)$ and $BA(G)$ are described in Table II. In describing the FG networks below first the underlying graph structure FG is defined.

FG Network Design: The number of nodes in the graphs defined below is assumed to be equal to r^m. As seen later, the chosen values of r and m will determine the number of connections per PE (or BUS), the routing distance between PE's, and the degree of fault tolerance.

Here, the nodes are assumed to be numbered 0 through $(n - 1)$. Each node i has an m-tuple representation in radix-r; this will be denoted as $(i_{m-1}, \cdots, i_1, i_0)$.

Given $i, j, 0 \le i, j \le (n - 1)$, the following defines certain relationships denoted as g and h.

Here, it is assumed that $i = (i_{m-1}, \cdots, i_1, i_0)$ and $j = (j_{m-1}, \cdots, j_1, j_0)$ in radix-r.

Let $i = g(j)$, if $i_p = j_{p+1}$ for all $p, 0 \le p \le (m - 2)$ and $i_{m-1} = j_0$. Thus, j is an end-around shift of i.

Let $i = h(j)$, if $i_p = j_p$ for all $p, 1 \le p \le (m - 1)$.

(For $r = 2$ the mappings g and h correspond to shuffle and

$LA(G)$ link network	Equivalence in $BA(G)$ bus network
Number of processors	Number of buses
Number of links	Number of processors
Number of connections/processors	Number of connections/bus
Interprocessor transfer	Interbus transfer
Number of processor–processor transfers in a message path	Number of bus–bus transfers in a message path
Processor fault	Bus fault
Link fault	Processor fault

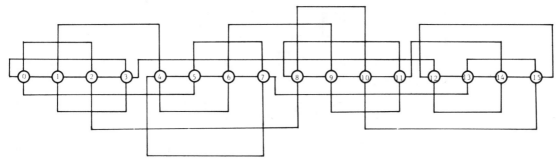

Fig. 2. $FG(4, 2)$ network.

exchange mappings, respectively [8], [9], [18]).

Thus, $i = h(j)$ implies $j = h(i)$, i and j differ only in the last digit.

These graphs are constructed using a two-step approach. First, a skeletal graph SG is constructed, which is then augmented to obtain the fault-tolerant graph FG.

The skeletal graph denoted as $SG(r, m)$ is obtained by connecting every pair of nodes i and j that satisfy the relationship $i = g(j)$ or $i = h(j)$.

In the following, let $k = (r^m - 1)/(r - 1)$. Thus, $k = (1, 1, \cdots, 1)$ in radix-r.

FG(r, m) Design, m = 2:

$r = even$: Construct an $SG(r, 2)$ graph for the specific r; then augment the graph by adding $r/2$ links, defined as $(0, k), (2k, 3k), \cdots, ((r - 2)k, (r - 1)k)$.

Fig. 2 illustrates an $FG(4, 2)$ network.

$r = odd$: Construct an $SG(r, 2)$ graph for the specific r; then augment it by adding an extra node n which is then connected to nodes $0, k, 2k, \cdots, (r - 1)k$ by adding r additional links: $(n, 0), (n, k), \cdots, (n, (r - 1)k)$.[1]

(The resulting graph when $r = odd$ has $(n + 1)$ nodes. This extra node can be used as a spare and as shown later, is useful for routing when faults occur in the system.)

FG(r, m) Design, m $\geq$ 3:

Let $q = \begin{cases} (r^m - 1)/(r^2 - 1) & \text{for } m = even, \\ (r^{m+1} - 1)/(r^2 - 1) & \text{for } m = odd. \end{cases}$

Thus, in radix r,

$q = \begin{matrix} (0, 1, 0, 1, \cdots, 0, 1) & \text{for } m = even \\ (1, 0, 1, 0, \cdots, 1, 0, 1) & \text{for } m = odd. \end{matrix}$

$r = 2$: Construct an $SG(2, m)$ graph for the given m; then add links: $(0, k), (k, k - q),$ and $(q, 0)$. For odd m add an

---

[1]It may be noted that there cannot exist any degree r regular graph of exactly r^2 nodes since $r = odd$. Therefore, one must add an additional node.

additional link $(k - q, q)$.

$FG(2, 4)$ graph is illustrated in Fig. 3.

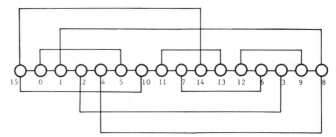

Fig. 3. $FG(2, 4)$ network.

$r \geq 3$: Construct an $SG(r, m)$ graph for the given r, m. Add r links, as defined below: $(0, k), (k, 2k), \cdots, ((r - 2)k, (r - 1)k), ((r - 1)k, 0)$. If $m = even$, add additional $(r^2 - r)/2$ links defined by the following expression for all $a, b, a \neq b$ and $0 \leq a, b \leq (r - 1)$:

$$(arq + bq, (r - 1 - a)rq + (r - 1 - b)q).$$

Fig. 4 illustrates $FG(3, 3)$ graph.

The following basic properties of $FG(r, m)$ networks can be easily proven.

Theorem 1: $FG(r, m)$ is a regular network of degree r if $m = 2$.

Theorem 2: $FG(r, m)$ is a regular network of degree $(r + 1)$ if $r \geq 3$ and $m \geq 3$.

Theorem 3: $FG(2, m), m \geq 3, m = even$ are regular networks of degree 3. For $m = odd$, all nodes are of degree 3 except nodes q and $(k - q)$, which have degree 5.

Thus, the $LA(FG)$ and $BA(FG)$ networks derived from FG will have the following characteristics. Each PE in $LA(FG)$ will have the same number of links connected to it—either r or $(r + 1)$. Analogously, each bus in $BA(FG)$ will be connected to the same number of PE's—either r or $(r + 1)$. Thus, from the point of view of I/O ports and inter-

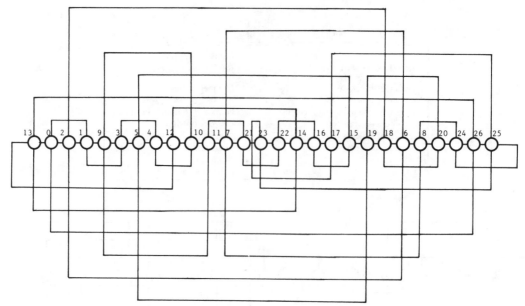

Fig. 4. $FG(3, 3)$ network.

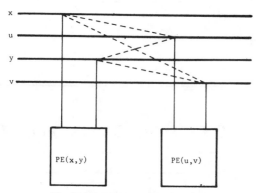

Fig. 5.   Routing on bus architecture.

connections, these networks can be considered regular. The similarities and differences are noted that exist between the link network and the bus network, are described in Table II.

The following shows that a path always exists of length, at most $(2m - 1)$, given any pair of nodes in $FG(r, m)$ networks.

First, it may be noted that in the link architecture $LA(FG)$, transmitting data from one PE to another PE may require one or more hops through other PE's in the path. Similarly, in the bus architectures $BA(FG)$, direct transfer is possible only when both of the processing elements are connected to the same bus; i.e., PE(x, y) can transfer to PE(u, v) if $x = u$ or v or if $y = u$ or v. In other cases, a transfer would require one or more interbus transfer through the connecting PE's. However, the difference between the bus architecture and the link architecture, insofar as formulating a routing path between a source and a destination PE is concerned, is that in the bus architecture various choices exist depending on the various combinations of the source and destination buses. For example, given PE(x, y) as the source and PE(u, v) as the destination, PE(x, y) can initiate the transmission on bus x or y, and PE(u, v) can receive it from bus u or v as illustrated in Fig. 5.

However, topologically, there are certain equivalences between paths in $LA(FG)$ and $BA(FG)$. Given a PE-to-PE path in the link architecture, there is an equivalent BUS-to-BUS

path in the bus architecture. If an inter-PE transfer constitutes a single hop, both of these paths will have the same number of hops. On the other hand, given a PE-to-PE path in $BA(FG)$, there is an equivalent link to the link path in $LA(FG)$. Below, the routing in these networks is described in the context of the link network $LA(FG)$. The formulation below can be adapted for the bus architecture $BA(FG)$ as well.

Consider the following path from the source PE(s) to the destination PE(d). Let $s = (s_{m-1}, \cdots, s_1, s_0)$ and $d = (d_{m-1}, \cdots, d_1, d_0)$ in radix-r.

$$
\begin{aligned}
s = &(s_{m-1}, \cdots\cdots\cdots, s_1, s_0) \\
&(s_{m-2}, \cdots\cdots, s_1, s_0, s_{m-1}) \\
&(s_{m-2}, \cdots\cdots, s_1, s_0, d_{m-1}) \\
&(s_{m-3}, \cdots, s_0, d_{m-1}, s_{m-2}) \\
&\qquad\quad \vdots \\
&(s_0, d_{m-1}, d_{m-2}, \cdots, d_1) \\
&(d_{m-1}, \cdots\cdots\cdots, d_1, s_0) \\
d = &(d_{m-1}, \cdots\cdots\cdots, d_1, d_0) .
\end{aligned}
$$

The above path will be herewith denoted as $pt(s, d)$. This is used below to formulate a simple message routing procedure that routes the message from node to node using only the destination address information.

A message routing algorithm suitable for $LA(FG(r, m))$ is described here. It is assumed that each message carries m tag bits. These m bits denoted as T are initialized at the source PE, equal to d the destination address as shown in Fig. 6(a) and (b). The destination address d is also carried by the message separately.

Although the routing algorithms given below are for $LA(FG)$ networks, they can be used for the bus network $BA(FG)$ as well with some modifications. Each PE(x) in $LA(FG)$ corresponds to a node x in FG and vice versa. Also, every path from PE(x) to PE(y) in $LA(FG)$ has a corresponding path from node x to y in FG and vice versa. Therefore,

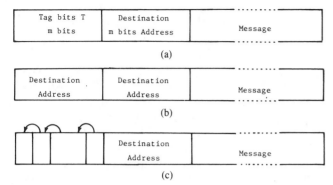

Fig. 6. (a) Message format. (b) Message at source node. (c) Shifting the tagbit at node x.

all the paths and routing actions for $LA(FG)$ will be described by using the graph FG. The remainder of the section will use node x to denote $PE(x)$.

When a message arrives at node x, the following steps are executed to determine the next node in the path. Here, x_0 denotes the least-significant bit of the binary number x.

Step 1: If $x = d$, then the message has reached the destination and is accepted. Otherwise, the message is forwarded to a neighbor of x by using the following steps.

Step 2: Compare x_0 (the least significant bit of x) to the leading bit of T. If they are equal, then go to Step 3; else, forward the message to the neighbor of x, given as $(x_{m-1}, \cdots, x_1, \bar{x}_0)$ in binary.

Step 3: Shift the tag field T left by one bit as shown in Fig. 6(c). Now, if $x = 0$ or $x = (n - 1)$, then go to Step 2; else, forward the message to the neighbor y of x, given as $(x_{m-2}, \cdots, x_1, x_0, x_{m-1})$ in binary.

The following example illustrates the above routing steps further.

Example 1: Consider the 16 node FG $(2, 4)$ network. Let $s = 8$ and $d = 11$. The following table describes the path and the corresponding tag bits at different nodes:

Node	x	8	9	3	2	4	5	10	11
	in binary	1000	1001	0011	0010	0100	0101	1010	1011
T at arrival			1011	0110	0110	1100	1100	1000	1000
T at departure		1011	0110	0110	1100	1100	1000	1000	–

It can be easily seen that the above steps route the message according to the path $pt(s, d)$ described earlier. The routing procedure discussed above is algorithmic and uses only local information contained in the message.

III. FAULT TOLERANCE OF FG$(2, m)$ NETWORKS

This section and the following section exhibit various fault-tolerant features of the network. First, $FG(2, m)$ networks are considered, followed by $FG(r, m)$ networks for any r. Below, routing techniques for $FG(2, m)$ networks are developed which admit routing of messages with all single and double faults. Following this, Section IV considers FG ($r \geqq 3, m$) networks and develops routing techniques based on detours around faulty nodes. The detour technique of routing allows for certain attractive features, such as providing transparency of faults with respect to the global routing strategy. Also, this permits the routing to degrade proportionately to the number of faults; thus, graceful degradation.

In considering the fault tolerance of $LA(FG)$ and $BA(FG)$, the following may be noted regarding the effects of various faults from the point of view of communication and routing, as described in Table II. The effect of a faulty PE in the link architecture is equivalent to the effect of a faulty BUS in the corresponding bus architecture. Similarly, a faulty PE in the bus architecture has an equivalent effect on the routing, as a faulty link in the link architecture. The following discusses fault tolerance in the context of link architecture and this can fairly easily be extended to bus architecture.

Primarily, node failures are considered here since the effect of a link failure can be no worse than a node failure. (The paths affected by a link failure are a subset of the paths affected by the failure of one of the nodes connected by the link. Therefore, the routing and detour techniques can be adapted to link failures easily.)

The fault tolerance of a regular network of degree b can be, at most, equal to $(b - 1)$. This is because any node can always be disconnected from the network by removing the b nodes (links) that are connected to it. Accordingly, we will call a regular network an *optimal* fault-tolerant network if its fault tolerance is equal to $(b - 1)$, the maximum possible.

Later, $FG(2, m)$ networks are shown to be optimally fault tolerant (m = even).

The case of single faults is considered separately first. An algorithm is developed below that routes messages from one node to another, in spite of any single faulty node or link.

Given a binary number x, let the weight of x, $(wt(x))$, represent the number of 1's in x.

Lemma 1: Any node x in the path pt $(i, 0)$ satisfies the relationship given below.

For $x \neq i$,

$$wt(x) \leqq wt(i), \qquad \text{if } i_0 = 0$$
$$wt(x) < wt(i), \qquad \text{if } i_0 = 1 .$$

Proof: Consider any two consecutive nodes u and v in the path pt $(i, 0)$. Let $u = (u_{m-1}, \cdots, u_1, u_0)$ and $v = (v_{m-1}, \cdots, v_1, v_0)$ in binary, and let u precede v in the path.

The following relationship between u and v must be satisfied: v is obtained from u by an end-around shift of u if the least-significant bit of u is 0; or by complementing the least-significant bit of u, if the least significant bit of u is 1. Thus, the number of 1's in v cannot exceed the number of 1's in u. Furthermore, if $u_0 = 1$, then the number of 1's in v is less than the number of 1's in u.

Hence, the Lemma.   Q.E.D.

Lemma 2: Any node x in the path $pt(i, n - 1)$ satisfies the following.

For $x \neq i$,

$$wt(x) \geq wt(i), \qquad \text{if } i_0 = 1$$
$$wt(x) > wt(i), \qquad \text{if } i_0 = 0 .$$

Proof: Proof is similar to Lemma 1.   Q.E.D.

The proofs of the following Lemmas are also similar.

Lemma 3: Any node x in the path $pt(0, i)$ also satisfies Lemma 1.

Lemma 4: Any node x in the path $pt(n - 1, i)$ also satisfies Lemma 2.

The algorithm discussed below is based on the above observations and is useful for routing messages when a node becomes faulty. This also establishes an upper bound on the maximum path length, in the presence of a fault. The algorithm given is shown to be easily implementable.

Let f denote the faulty PE, PE(f).

Let s denote the source PE, PE(s).

Let d denote the destination PE, PE(d).

Routing with a Faulty PE: The following describes different paths from s to d in FG which correspond to different cases of f.

a) $wt(f) > wt(s)$ and $wt(f) > wt(d)$.

$$s \rightarrow \cdots pt(s, 0) \cdots \rightarrow 0 \rightarrow \cdots pt(0, d) \cdots \rightarrow d.$$

b) $wt(f) < wt(s)$ and $wt(f) < wt(d)$.

$$s \rightarrow \cdots pt(s, n-1) \cdots \rightarrow (n-1) \rightarrow$$
$$\cdots pt(n-1, d) \cdots \rightarrow d.$$

c) $wt(f) > wt(s)$ and $wt(f) < wt(d)$.

$$s \rightarrow \cdots pt(s, 0) \cdots \rightarrow 0 \rightarrow (n-1) \rightarrow$$
$$\cdots pt(n-1, d) \cdots \rightarrow d.$$

d) $wt(f) < wt(d)$ and $wt(f) > wt(d)$.

$$s \rightarrow \cdots pt(s, n-1) \cdots \rightarrow (n-1) \rightarrow$$
$$0 \rightarrow \cdots pt(0, d) \cdots \rightarrow d.$$

e) $wt(f) = wt(s)$ and $wt(f) > wt(d)$.

$$\text{If } s_0 = \begin{cases} 1 & \text{path as } a) \\ 0 & \text{path as } d). \end{cases}$$

f) $w(f) = wt(s)$ and $wt(f) < wt(d)$.

$$\text{If } s_0 = \begin{cases} 1 & \text{path as } c) \\ 0 & \text{path as } b). \end{cases}$$

g) $wt(f) = wt(d)$ and $wt(f) > wt(s)$.

$$\text{If } d_0 = \begin{cases} 1 & \text{path as } a) \\ 0 & \text{path as } c). \end{cases}$$

h) $wt(f) = wt(d)$ and $wt(f) < wt(s)$.

$$\text{If } d_0 = \begin{cases} 1 & \text{path as } d) \\ 0 & \text{path as } b). \end{cases}$$

i) $wt(f) = wt(s) = wt(d)$.

$$\text{If } \begin{cases} s_0 = 0, & d_0 = 0 & \text{path as } b) \\ s_0 = 0, & d_0 = 1 & \text{path as } d) \\ s_0 = 1, & d_0 = 0 & \text{path as } c) \\ s_0 = 1, & d_0 = 1 & \text{path as } a). \end{cases}$$

The following Theorem is an immediate consequence of the above routing steps.

Theorem 4: In the presence of any single fault, a message can be routed from any node to any other node using at most $(4m - 1)$ hops.

The earlier described routing procedure is easily adaptable when the network becomes faulty. As an example, assume node 0 is the faulty node. This will correspond to case b),

which describes the following path from s to d:
$$s \rightarrow \cdots pt(s, n-1) \cdots \rightarrow (n-1) \rightarrow \cdots pt(n-1, d)$$
$$\cdots \rightarrow d.$$

This can be implemented as follows. The source s may initialize the tagfield T equal to $(n-1)$. This will route the message to the intermediate destination node $(n-1)$. The node $(n-1)$, upon recognizing that the destination address d is not equal to $(n-1)$, will replace T by d and then forward the message to the final destination d.

Next, we consider the case of double faults in $FG(2, m)$ networks $m \geq 3$. In Appendix A, a technique is exhibited that can route a message from a source node s to a destination node d, despite *two* faulty nodes. The following theorem is a direct consequence of this.

Theorem 5: In the presence of any two faults, a message can be routed from any node s to any node d in $FG(2, m)$, using at most $(4m + 2)$ hops.

Thus, a second fault may cause a small increase in the path length; $(4m + 2)$ versus $(4m - 1)$.

IV. FAULT TOLERANCE OF $FG(r, m)$ NETWORKS

This section considers $FG(r, m)$ networks for all $r, m \geq 3$. Techniques are first formulated that construct detours around the faulty nodes. These detour techniques are applicable when the number of faults does not exceed $(r - 1)/2$. Following this, it is shown that these networks in general can also tolerate a much larger number of faults by showing how to construct paths from s to d when the number of faults is equal to $(r - 1)$.

The detour techniques shown below possess certain attractive features. These detours perform local alterations of paths which connect the two nodes that are adjacent to the faulty node(s). Hence, the faults can be made transparent to the global routing strategy. Other important aspects of these detours include the fact that they are of constant length, independent of m, thus, the size of the network. Furthermore, increases in path length that are due to the use of detours become directly proportional to the number of faults; thus, graceful degradation is made possible.

Definition: Let $F = \{f^1, f^2, \cdots, f^t\}$ represent the set of t faulty nodes.

Definition: Let the m-tuple $(f^i_{m-1}, f^i_{m-2}, \cdots, f^i_1, f^i_0)$ represent the faulty node f^i in radix-r.

Definition: Let e be a radix-r digit that does not belong to the set

$$\{f^1_{m-1}, f^2_{m-1}, \cdots, f^t_{m-1}, f^1_0, f^2_0, \cdots, f^t_0\}.$$

Thus, e is a digit that does *not* appear either in the least- or in the most-significant position of any of the faulty nodes. Since $2t < r$, there always exists such an e. Thus, any node that has e in the least or in the most significant position cannot be faulty. This will be quite useful later.

Here, in constructing these detours, it will be assumed that u, v, and w are three consecutive nodes in the path from s to d. The node v is assumed to be faulty with u and w being fault free. The detour therefore connects u with w without passing through any of the faulty nodes in F, including v. (The case when two or more consecutive nodes are faulty can be treated by successive applications of the given techniques.)

First, it may be seen that there are, altogether, three possible distinct relationships between u, v, and w in the type of path discussed earlier in the section. (This follows from the observation that if v is an h-neighbor of u, then w cannot also be an h-neighbor of v.) These relationships are described in the following:

$$R1: \; v = h(u) \quad \text{and} \quad w = g(v)$$

$$R2: \; v = g(u) \quad \text{and} \quad w = h(v)$$

$$R3: \; v = g(u) \quad \text{and} \quad w = g(v).$$

The following constructs detours that correspond to the above three cases. The detailed construction is described in Appendix B.

Case R1: Here, the original path contains the following sequence of nodes represented in radix-r as

$$u = (u_{m-1}, \cdots\cdots, u_1, u_0)$$

faulty: $\quad v = (u_{m-1}, \cdots\cdots, u_1, c), \qquad c \neq u_0$

$$w = (u_{m-2}, \cdots, u_1, c, u_{m-1}).$$

The following describes construction of an alternate path from u to w that does not pass through any of the nodes in fault set F (which includes the faulty node v):

$$u = (u_{m-1}, \cdots\cdots, u_1, u_0)$$

$(u_{m-2}, \cdots, u_1, x, u_{m-1})$ x as determined per Appendix B

$(u_{m-2}, \cdots\cdots, u_1, x, e)$

$(e, u_{m-2}, \cdots\cdots, u_1, x)$ e as defined earlier

$(e, u_{m-2}, \cdots\cdots, u_1, c)$

$(u_{m-2}, \cdots\cdots, u_1, c, e)$

$w = (u_{m-2}, \cdots, u_1, c, u_{m-1}).$

The above detour is of length 7, and hence will result in a net increase of 5 in the path length.

Case R2: $u \rightarrow v = g(u) \rightarrow w = h(v)$. This corresponds to the following path segment:

$$u = (u_{m-1}, \cdots\cdots, u_1, u_0)$$

faulty: $\quad v = (u_{m-2}, \cdots, u_1, u_0, u_{m-1})$

$$w = (u_{m-2}, \cdots\cdots, u_1, u_0, c) \qquad c \neq u_{m-1}.$$

The following constructs an alternate path from u to w.

$$u = (u_{m-1}, \cdots\cdots, u_1, u_0)$$

$(u_{m-1}, \cdots\cdots, u_1, x)$ x determined as per Appendix B

$(u_{m-2}, \cdots, u_1, x, u_{m-1})$

$(u_{m-2}, \cdots\cdots, u_1, x, e)$ e defined earlier

$(e, u_{m-2}, \cdots\cdots, u_1, x)$

$(e, u_{m-2}, \cdots, u_1, u_0)$

$(u_{m-2}, \cdots\cdots, u_1, u_0, e)$

$w = (u_{m-2}, \cdots\cdots, u_1, u_0, c).$

TABLE III
FAULT-TOLERANT PROPERTIES OF $FG(r, m)$ NETWORKS

r	m	Fault tolerance t	Routing Distance with t faults
2	m	1	$(4m - 1)$
		2	$(4m + 2)$
$r > 3$	2	$(r - 1)$	12
$r \geqq 3$	$m \geqq 3$	$t \leqq (r - 1)/2$	$(2m - 1 + 11t)$
		$t > (r - 1)/2$	$(6m - 3)$

As in Case R1, the detour shown above is of length 7, and thus the path length will increase by at most 5.

Case R3: $u \rightarrow v = g(u) \rightarrow w = g(v)$. This corresponds to the following segment:

$$u = (u_{m-1}, \cdots\cdots\cdots, u_1, u_0)$$

faulty: $\quad v = (u_{m-2}, \cdots\cdots, u_1, u_0, u_{m-1})$

$$w = (u_{m-3}, \cdots, u_0, u_{m-1}, u_{m-2}).$$

One can construct a detour from u to w, as illustrated in the following:

$$u = (u_{m-1}, \cdots\cdots\cdots, u_1, u_0)$$

$(u_{m-1}, \cdots\cdots\cdots, u_1, x)$ x and y determined as per Appendix B

$(u_{m-2}, \cdots\cdots, u_1, x, u_{m-1})$

$(u_{m-2}, \cdots\cdots\cdots, u_1, x, y)$

$(u_{m-3}, \cdots, u_1, x, y, u_{m-1})$

$(u_{m-3}, \cdots\cdots, u_1, x, y, e)$ e defined earlier

$(e, u_{m-3}, \cdots\cdots\cdots, u_1, x, y)$

$(e, u_{m-3}, \cdots\cdots, u_1, x, e)$

$(e, e, u_{m-3}, \cdots\cdots\cdots, u_1, x)$

$(e, e, u_{m-3}, \cdots\cdots\cdots, u_1, u_0)$

$(e, u_{m-3}, \cdots\cdots\cdots, u_0, e)$

$(e, u_{m-3}, \cdots\cdots, u_0, u_{m-1})$

$(u_{m-3}, \cdots\cdots, u_0, u_{m-1}, e)$

$w = (u_{m-3}, \cdots, u_0, u_{m-1}, u_{m-2}).$

The above detour is of length 13; thus, it will result in a net increase of 11 in the path length.

The above corresponds to the worst case increase in the path length. It may be noted that when two or more consecutive nodes are faulty, the above techniques can be applied iteratively, to construct a detour around the faulty nodes. As an example, consider the following path segment:

$$u \rightarrow v = h(u) \rightarrow w = g(v) \rightarrow z = g(w).$$

Assume here that both the nodes v and w are faulty. Thus, one needs to construct a detour from u to z. This can be constructed in two steps: first, by using Case R1, one can construct a detour of length 6 from u to $(u_{m-2}, \cdots, u_1, c, e)$.

Next, by applying Case R2, one can construct a detour of length 11 from $(u_{m-2}, \cdots, u_1, c, e)$ to $z = (u_{m-4}, \cdots, u_1, c, u_{m-1}, u_{m-2}, u_{m-3})$. Thus, the total detour length will be 17 for both the faulty nodes together. The following theorem is a direct consequence of these above discussions.

Theorem 6: A message can be routed from one node to another using at most $(2m - 1 + 11t)$ hops with t faults where $t \leq (r - 1)/2$.

The following exhibits the complete fault tolerance of $FG(r, m)$ networks for all $r, m, r \geq 3 m \geq 2$. It is shown that in spite of any $(r - 1)$ faults, the network remains fully connected and the messages can still be routed easily from node to node.

Definition: Let N denote the set of all n nodes in $FG(r, m)$.

Definition: Let R_k denote the set of r nodes, $0, k, 2k, 3k, \cdots, (r - 1)k$.

Definition: Let $N - R_k$ denote the set of $(n - r)$ nodes consisting of all nodes other than those appearing in the set R_k.

Fault Tolerance of $FG(r, m)$, $m = 2$, Networks: Since $m = 2$, any node i in the network can be represented in radix-r as (i_1, i_0). Now, consider the following r paths from s to the nodes in R_k:

s to 0: $s = (s_1, s_0) \rightarrow (s_1, 0) \rightarrow (0, s_1) \rightarrow (0, 0) = 0$

s to k: $s = (s_1, s_0) \rightarrow (s_1, 1) \rightarrow (1, s_1) \rightarrow (1, 1) = k$

s to $2k$: $s = (s_1, s_0) \rightarrow (s_1, 2) \rightarrow (2, s_1) \rightarrow (2, 2) = 2k$

$$\vdots$$

s to $(r - 1)k$: $s = (s_1, s_0) \rightarrow (s_1, r - 1)$

$$\rightarrow (r - 1, s_1) \rightarrow (r - 1, r - 1)$$
$$= (r - 1)k.$$

These above paths can be seen to be disjoint from the following observation.

Assume that there exists a node in the path from s to ik that also belongs to the path from s to jk where $i \neq j$. This would imply either that $(s_1, i) = (j, s_1)$, or that $(s_1, j) = (i, s_1)$. So, one has $s_1 = i = j$, a contradiction.

It may therefore be deduced that there always exists a node xk for which the path s to xk is fault free, in spite of any $(r - 1)$ faults.

Similarly, it can also be asserted that there always exists a node yk for which the path yk to d is fault free, in spite of any $(r - 1)$ faults. So, in order to establish that the fault tolerance of the network is $(r - 1)$, it will be sufficient to show that there always exist r disjoint paths between any xk and yk. The following shows techniques to construct such r paths from xk to yk.

(The paths are shown here using radix-r representation. Thus, $xk = (x, x)$ and $yk = (y, y)$ in radix-r.)

First, consider the following set of $(r - 1)$ paths denoted as path 1–path $(r - 1)$.

path-1: $(x, x) \rightarrow (x, y) \rightarrow (y, x) \rightarrow (y, y)$.

path-2–path $(r - 1)$: Let $w = 0, 1, \cdots, (r - 1)$ and $w \neq x, y$. There are exactly $(r - 2)$ distinct values of w and these define the following $(r - 2)$ paths:

$$(x, x) \rightarrow (x, w) \rightarrow (w, x) \rightarrow (w, y) \rightarrow (y, w) \rightarrow (y, y).$$

These $(r - 1)$ paths shown above are all disjoint. Paths 2 through $(r - 2)$ are disjoint because of the value of w, distinct

for each path.

Path 1 is disjoint with paths 2 through $(r - 1)$ since $w \neq x$ and $w \neq y$.

Thus, it remains to be shown that there exists one additional path from xk to yk that is disjoint from the above $(r - 1)$ paths. The following constructs such a path, denoted as path-r for $r =$ even and $r =$ odd, separately.

$r =$ even: First, it may be noted that as per the construction procedure, nodes xk and yk are directly connected to some nodes uk and vk (in R_k), respectively.

i) Let $u = y$ (thus, $v = x$). Hence, xk and yk are connected by the link (xk, yk). Path r: $xk \rightarrow yk$.

ii) Let $u \neq y$ (thus, $v \neq x$). Hence, xk and yk are not connected. *Path r:* $(x, x) \rightarrow (u, u) \rightarrow (u, v) \rightarrow (v, v) \rightarrow (y, y)$.

This above path is disjoint from the paths 1 through $(r - 1)$ shown above since $x \neq u$ and $y \neq v$.

$r =$ odd: path r: $xk \rightarrow n \rightarrow yk$.

This path passes through node n which has not been used in any of the above paths.

Since $FG(r, 2)$ networks are of degree r, the following theorem is a direct consequence of the above discussions.

Theorem 7: $FG(r, 2)$ networks are optimally fault tolerant, and failure of any $(r - 1)$ components is tolerated.

Example 2: Consider the network shown in Fig. 2. Here $r = 4$. Hence, the network is 3-fault-tolerant. Let the nodes 0, 5, and 7 be faulty.

Given these nodes as faulty, one can construct the following path from any s to d, which will be fault free:

$$(s_1, s_0) \rightarrow (s_1, 2) \rightarrow (2, s_1) \rightarrow (2, 2)$$
$$\rightarrow (2, d_1) \rightarrow (d_1, 2) \rightarrow (d_1, d_0).$$

Thus, given $s = 4$ and $d = 15$, one has the following path:

$$4 \rightarrow 6 \rightarrow 9 \rightarrow 10 \rightarrow 11 \rightarrow 14 \rightarrow 15.$$

Fault Tolerance of $FG(r, m)$ Networks, $m \geq 3$: The following definitions and lemmas will be useful in constructing the paths.

Definition: Let $wt_i(x)$ represent the number of occurrences of i in radix-r representation of x.

For example, if $x = (0, 1, 1, 2, 1)$ in radix-r, $wt_0(x) = 1$, $wt_1(x) = 3$, $wt_2(x) = 1$, and $wt_3(x) = 0$.

Lemma 3: If $wt_i(x) \neq wt_i(y)$, for any $i, 0 \leq i \leq (r - 1)$, then $x \neq yy$.

Let $pt(i, j)$ represent the path from i to j, as defined in Section II.

The path $pt(i, j)$ denotes a path of length at most $(2m - 1)$.

Lemma 4: Given any node x, $x \neq s$, in $pt(s, ik)$, $ik \, \varepsilon \, R_k$, the following relationship holds:

$$wt_i(x) > wt_i(s) \qquad \text{if } s_0 \neq i$$
$$wt_i(x) \geq wt_i(s) \qquad \text{if } s_0 = i$$
$$wt_j(x) \leq wt_j(s) \qquad \text{if } j \neq i.$$

Lemma 5: Two paths $pt(s, ik)$ and $pt(s, jk)$ are node disjoint if $i \neq j$.

Proof: Let $x \, \varepsilon \, pt(s, ik)$ and $y \, \varepsilon \, pt(s, jk)$ denote any two nodes in paths $pt(s, ik)$ and $pt(s, jk)$, respectively.

Case I: Let $s_0 = i$.

Thus, one has, from Lemma 4, $wt_j(y) > wt_j(s)$, but $wt_j(x) \leq wt_j(s)$. Hence, $x \neq y$.

Case II: Let $s_0 = j$.

Similar to Case I.

Case III: Let $s_0 \neq i$ and $s_0 \neq j$. Here, $wt_i(x) > wt_i(s)$, and $wt_i(y) < wt_i(s)$. Thus, $wt_i(x) \neq wt_i(y)$, and hence $x \neq y$. Q.E.D.

The following Lemmas are direct consequences of the above Lemma.

Lemma 6: Given any $(r - 1)$ faulty nodes, there exists at least one node xk where $xk \, \varepsilon \, R_k$, such that the path $pt(s, xk)$ is fault free.

Lemma 7: Given any $(r - 1)$ faulty nodes, there exists at least one node yk where $uk \, \varepsilon \, R_k$, such that the path $pt(yk, d)$ is fault free.

The following shows it is possible to travel from any s to any d, in spite of faults in any $(r - 1)$ nodes. This is illustrated by considering the following cases separately.

Case I: All of the faulty nodes belong to the subset R_k.

The subset R_k contains r nodes. Since the number of faulty nodes does not exceed $(r - 1)$, there must be at least one node xk which is fault free.

Consider the path **$pt(s, xk)$**. This entire path must be fault free since all of the intermediate nodes in the path pass through nodes in $N - R_k$.

Similarly, the path **$pt(xk, d)$** must also be fault free. Hence, the following path from s to d must be fault free:

$$s \rightarrow \cdots \textbf{\textit{pt}}(s, xk) \cdots \rightarrow xk \rightarrow \cdots \textbf{\textit{pt}}(x, kd) \cdots \rightarrow d .$$

The length of the above path is, at most, equal to $(2m - 1) + (2m - 1) = (4m - 2)$.

Case II: All of the nodes in the subset R_k are fault free.

In this case, the faulty nodes are thus confined to the subset $N - R_k$.

As per Lemmas 4 and 5, one always has two fault-free paths of the type **$pt(s, xk)$** and **$pt(yk, d)$**.

The following constructs a fault-free path from s to d.

If $x = y$, then follow the path given in Case I; else, if

$$x > y, \quad \text{and} \quad x - y \leq r/2 \quad \text{or}$$
$$x < y, \quad \text{and} \quad y - x > r/2 \quad \text{then:}$$

follow the path given below in (1); otherwise, follow the path given in (2)

$$s \rightarrow \cdots \textbf{\textit{pt}}(s, xk) \cdots \rightarrow xk \rightarrow (x - 1)k \rightarrow \cdots$$
$$\rightarrow (y + 1)k \rightarrow yk \rightarrow \cdots \textbf{\textit{pt}}(yk, d) \cdots \rightarrow d \quad (1)$$
$$s \rightarrow \cdots \textbf{\textit{pt}}(s, xk) \cdots \rightarrow xk \rightarrow (x + 1)k \rightarrow \cdots$$
$$\rightarrow (y - 1)k \rightarrow yk \rightarrow \cdots \textbf{\textit{pt}}(yk, d) \cdots \rightarrow d . \quad (2)$$

Here the maximum path length is equal to

$$(4m - 2) + r/2 .$$

Case III: Nodes in both R_k as well as in $N - R_k$ are faulty.

As before, there always exist fault-free paths $pt(s, xk)$ and $pt(yk, d)$.

The following shows that there exist *at least r* disjoint paths between any xk and yk. Consider the following paths:

path-1: $xk \rightarrow (x + 1)k \rightarrow \cdots \rightarrow (y - 1)k \rightarrow yk$

path-2: $xk \rightarrow (x - 1)k \rightarrow \cdots \rightarrow (y + 1)k \rightarrow yk$

path-3 through r: for all w, $0 \leq w, \leq (r - 1)$ and
$$w \neq x \quad \text{and} \quad w \neq y,$$

consider the following $(r \cdot 2)$ paths:

$$xk = (x, \cdots\cdots, x, x)$$
$$(x, \cdots\cdots, x, w)$$
$$(x, \cdots\cdots, x, w, x)$$
$$(x, \cdots\cdots, x, w, y)$$
$$(x, \cdots, x, w, y, x)$$
$$(x, \cdots, x, w, y, y)$$
$$(w, y, y, \cdots\cdots, y)$$
$$(y, y, \cdots\cdots, y, w)$$
$$yk = (y, y, \cdots\cdots, y) .$$

Since $w \neq x$ and $w \neq y$, there are exactly $(r - 2)$ distinct values of w. Each one of these distinct values defines a path and in this set all of the $(r - 2)$ paths are disjoint since the value of w for each path is different. Now it may be seen all of the r paths shown above are disjoint. The intermediate nodes in path-1 and path-2 have only one digit in their representation, whereas the intermediate nodes paths 3–r have at least two digits in their representation. Therefore, there cannot be any intermediate nodes that are common to any two of the above r paths.

The maximum path length here is given as

$$(2m - 1) + (2m - 1) + (2m - 1) = (6m - 3) .$$

The following theorem is based on the above observation.

Theorem 8: Given any $FG(r, m)$ network, there exists a path from any node to any other node in spite of $(r - 1)$ faults of length at most $(6m - 3)$ and this path can be constructed algorithmically.

Example 3: Consider the $FG(4, 3)$ network which has 64 nodes and is of degree 5.

Let $s = 5$ and $d = 22$.

Here, $R_k = \{0, 21, 42, 63\}$. The following illustrates Case I and Case III.

Case I: Let nodes $0, 21$, and 42 be faulty. Using the technique shown in Case I, one constructs the following path:

$$5 \rightarrow \cdots \textbf{\textit{pt}}(5, 63) \cdots \rightarrow 63 \rightarrow \cdots \textbf{\textit{pt}}(63, 22) \cdots \rightarrow 22$$

which is equal to

$$5 \rightarrow 7 \rightarrow 28 \rightarrow 31 \rightarrow 61 \rightarrow 63 \rightarrow 61 \rightarrow 55 \rightarrow 23 \rightarrow 22 .$$

Case III: Let nodes $0, 21$, and 23 be faulty. Using Case III, one has

$$5 \rightarrow \cdots \textbf{\textit{pt}}(5, 63) \cdots \rightarrow 63 \rightarrow 42$$
$$\rightarrow \cdots \textbf{\textit{pt}}(42, 22) \cdots \rightarrow 22$$

which is equal to

$$5 \rightarrow 7 \rightarrow 28 \rightarrow 31 \rightarrow 61 \rightarrow 63$$
$$\rightarrow 42 \rightarrow 41 \rightarrow 38 \rightarrow 37 \rightarrow 22 .$$

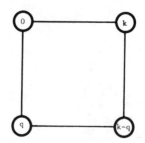

Fig. 7. Nodes in Q.

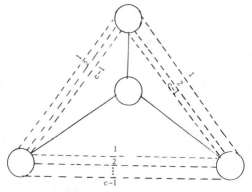

Fig. 8. Detour method of analyzing connectivity.

In the above, the fault tolerance of $FG(r, m)$ networks has been shown to be at least equal to $(r - 1)$. By using an analysis similar to that given for $FG(2, m)$ networks, it can also be shown that the fault tolerance of $FG(r, m)$ networks for m = even is equal to r, and thus is optimally fault tolerant. However, it remains to be seen whether $FG(r, m)$ networks for m = odd are also optimally fault tolerant.

V. CONCLUSION

This paper presents certain regular networks with optimal (near-optimal) fault tolerance. Various fault-tolerant properties of these networks are summarized in Table II. Further research of interest here is the VLSI layout [8], as well as internal testing and self-diagnosis [1], [4]–[6] of these networks. The binary $FG(2, m)$ network can be considered as a supergraph of the shuffle-exchange graphs [8]; this is known to possess efficient VLSI layouts [9], [18]. Also of interest is how best one can utilize the large degree of fault tolerance available in these networks for both yield enhancement as well as for fault tolerance.

It may also be noted that the graphs presented here may be of interest in the context of (d, k) graphs [4]. Specifically, the $FG(2, m)$ graphs with even m and $FG(r, 2)$ graphs provide optimum connectivity and small diameter for both the original graph and the subgraph obtained after deleting faulty nodes [19], [20]. Other recent work in the area [21]–[23] also have addressed these problems.

Finally, it may be added that the detour technique provides a tool for analyzing the connectivity [24] of arbitrary graph. One way to establish that the connectivity of a given graph is c is to prove that there exists at least c disjoint paths between every pair of nodes. But this requires a computation of $O(n^2)$ for an n node graph. However, an alternate approach would

be to establish that there exist at least $(c - 1)$ independent detours around every node (connecting every pair of neighbors) as illustrated in Fig. 8. Such an analysis may be simpler at it would require a computational complexity of $O(n)$ for bounded degree graphs.

APPENDIX A

Let Q represent the set of four nodes $(0, k, q, k - q)$. These four nodes are interconnected, as shown in Fig. 7.

Let $N - Q$ represent the set of $(n - 4)$ nodes which consist of all nodes other than the nodes in Q.

To begin with, it may be seen that given any node s one can construct, from s, three disjoint paths to nodes $0, k$, and q, below.

$$s = (s_{m-1}), \cdots, s_2, 1, 1)$$

$(1, s_{m-1}, \cdots, s_2, 1)$

$(1, s_{m-1}, \cdots, s_2, 0)$

$(s_{m-1}, \cdots, s_2, 0, 1)$

$(s_{m-1}, \cdots, s_2, 0, 0)$ $(s_{m-1}, \cdots, s_2, 1, 0)$

$(s_{m-2}, \cdots, s_2,$ $(s_{m-2}, \cdots, s_2,$ $(s_{m-2}, \cdots, s_2,$

$0, 0, s_{m-1})$ $1, 1, s_{m-1})$ $1, 0, s_{m-1})$

$(s_{m-2}, \cdots, s_2,$ $(s_{m-2}, \cdots, s_2,$ $(s_{m-2}, \cdots, s_2,$

$0, 0, 0)$ $1, 1, 1)$ $1, 0, 1)$

 $\vdots$ $\vdots$ $\vdots$

$(0, 0, \cdots, 0, 0)$ $(1, 1, \cdots, 1)$ $(0, 1, 0, 1, \cdots, 0, 1)$

  0 k q

$$s_1 = s_0 = 1 \quad m = \text{even}$$

other cases are similar.

In constructing these paths, it is assumed that m = even and $s = s_0 = 1$. (Proof of disjointedness can be readily derived.) Similar paths can be constructed for other combinations of (s_1, s_0) as well as when m = odd. Furthermore, it can be seen that there exist three paths from 0, k, and q to any destination node d where the paths are disjoint. The length of these disjoint paths can be seen to be at most equal to $2m$. These observations form the basis for the following path construction procedure, which constructs paths from s to d, given two faulty nodes in the network. This is described by considering various cases which correspond to different distributions of faulty nodes between Q and $N - Q$.

Case I: Both the faulty nodes are in $N - Q$.

This implies that all the four nodes in Q are fault free. Since there are three disjoint paths from s to nodes in Q, one can reach at least one of the nodes in Q with two faulty nodes in $N - Q$. Similarly, one can reach d from one of the nodes in Q. Since all of the nodes in Q are fault free, one can reach d from s through Q by using a path of length at most $2m + 2 + 2m = 4m + 2$ [there exists a path of length 2 between any pair of nodes (Fig. 7)].

Case II: Both the faulty nodes are in Q.

In this case, there must exist at least one node: 0, q, or k, through which a path can be constructed from s to d. For example, assume nodes 0 and q are faulty. Since the paths from s to 0, s to q, and s to dk are disjoint, one can reach k in spite of these two faults. Similarly, from k one can reach d. The total path length here will be equal to $4m$.

Case III: Faulty nodes in both Q and $N - Q$.

In this case, there is a node in Q and a node in $N - Q$, both of which are faulty. Thus, the three remaining nodes in Q are fault free and are connected. With a single faulty node in $N - Q$, one can reach at least two of the three remaining fault-free nodes. Similarly, d can be reached from at least two of these three fault-free nodes. Thus, there must exist one node 0, k, or q through which an entire fault-free path from s to d can be constructed. Thus, this path is of length at most $4m + 2$.

APPENDIX B
CONSTRUCTION OF DETOURS

Case R1: Here, the original path contains the following sequence of nodes represented in radix-r as

$$u = (u_{m-1}, \cdots \cdots, u_1, u_0)$$

faulty: $\quad v = (u_{m-1}, \cdots \cdots, u_1, c) \qquad c \neq u_0$

$$w = (u_{m-2}, \cdots, u_1, c, u_{m-1}).$$

First, it will be shown that there exists a *fault-free* path from u, of the type shown below, for some x. Then, this path will be used as part of the detour from u to w.

$$u = (u_{m-1}, \cdots \cdots, u_1, u_0)$$
$$(u_{m-1}, \cdots \cdots, u_1, x)$$
$$(u_{m-2}, \cdots, u_1, x, u_{m-1}).$$

In order to prove this, we will consider two separate cases. First, we consider the case $r = 3$, and next consider $r \geq 4$.

i) Let $r = 3$: Thus, one has $t = 1$; therefore, there is only one faulty node v. Consider the path

$$u \rightarrow (u_{m-1}, \cdots, u_1, e) \rightarrow (u_{m-2}, \cdots, u_1, e, u_{m-1}).$$

This path must be fault free because the node $(u_{m-1}, \cdots, u_1, e)$ cannot be the faulty node v since $e \neq c$, the least significant digit of v. The other node $(u_{m-1}, \cdots, u_1, e, u_{m-1})$ also cannot be faulty because then one has

$$(u_{m-2}, \cdots, u_1, e, u_{m-1}) = v = (u_{m-1}, \cdots, u_1, c).$$

This would in turn imply $c = e$, a contradiction of the definition of e.

ii) Let $r > 4$: Consider the following two subcases, the first corresponding to all of the t faulty nodes that have the same digit in the least significant position; that is, $f_0^1 = f_0^2 = \cdots = f_0^t = c$, the least significant digit of v. The second case corresponds to when the above is *not* the case.

a) Let $f_0^1 = f_0^2 = \cdots = f_0^t$. Consider all the h-neighbors of u. There are altogether $(r - 1)$ of these. No two of these nodes have the same digit in the least significant position. Since all of the faulty nodes have the same digit in the least significant position, only one of these h-neighbors of u can be faulty and this node is v. Thus, the remaining $(r - 2)$ h-neighbors must be fault free.

Without loss of generality, let us assume these nodes to be

$$(u_{m-1}, \cdots, u_1, u_0), (u_{m-1}, \cdots, u_1, 1), \cdots,$$
$$(u_{m-1}, \cdots, u_1, r - 3) \text{ in radix } r.$$

Consider the following $(r - 2)$ paths from u to the g-neighbors of these $(r - 2)$ nodes shown above:

Fault free   At most t are faulty

$$u \rightarrow (u_{m-1}, \cdots \cdots, u_1, 0) \longrightarrow (u_{m-2}, \cdots \cdots, u_1, 0, u_{m-1})$$
$$(u_{m-1}, \cdots \cdots, u_1, 1) \longrightarrow (u_{m-2}, \cdots \cdots, u_1, 1, u_{m-1})$$
$$\vdots \qquad\qquad\qquad \vdots$$
$$(u_{m-1}, \cdots, u_1, r - 3) \longrightarrow (u_{m-2}, \cdots, u_1, r - 3, u_{m-1}).$$

The $(r - 2)$ nodes shown in the right-hand side are seen to be all distinct. Therefore, at least $(r - 2 - t)$ of these are fault free. For $r \geq 4$, one has $(r - 2 - t) \geq 1$. There must be at least one path of the type $u \rightarrow (u_{m-1}, \cdots, u_1, x) \rightarrow (u_{m-1}, \cdots, u_1, x, u_{m-1})$ that is fault free.

For $r = 3$, one has $t = 1$; therefore, there is only one node that is faulty, the node v.

Now, consider the second case for which all of the t digits appearing in the least-significant position of the faulty nodes are not distinct. Thus, at most $(t - 1)$ distinct digits appear in the least-significant position. Consider the $(r - 1)$ h-neighbors of u. All of these nodes have distinct digits in the least-significant position. So, at most $(t - 2)$ of these h-neighbors can be faulty.

Consequently, there must be at least $(t + 1)$ of these h-neighbors that must be fault free since $(r - 1) \geq 2t$. As before, without loss of generality, we can assume these

$(t + 1)$ neighbors as $(u_{m-1}, \cdots, u_1, 0)$, $(u_{m-1}, \cdots, u_1, 1)$, $\cdots, (u_{m-1}, \cdots, u_1, t)$ in radix-r. Consider the following $(t + 1)$ g-neighbors of these nodes, through these nodes:

Fault free   At most t are faulty

$$u \rightarrow \begin{matrix} (u_{m-1}, \cdots, u_1, 0) \longrightarrow (u_{m-2}, \cdots, u_1, 0, u_{m-1}) \\ (u_{m-1}, \cdots, u_1, 1) \longrightarrow (u_{m-2}, \cdots, u_1, 1, u_{m-1}) \\ \vdots \qquad\qquad\qquad \vdots \\ (u_{m-1}, \cdots, u_1, t) \longrightarrow (u_{m-2}, \cdots, u_1, t, u_{m-1}). \end{matrix}$$

Since the $(t + 1)$ nodes in the right-hand side are all distinct, there can be at most t of these that can be faulty. Thus, there must exist at least one path of the type $u \rightarrow (u_{m-1}, \cdots, u_1, x) \rightarrow (u_{m-2}, \cdots, u_1 x, u_{m-1})$ that is fault free.

Now consider the following path from u to w that uses the fault-free path, as constructed above.

b) Let $f_0^i \neq f_0^j$ for some $i \neq j$, $1 \leq i, j \leq t$. Here, consider the following two separate subcases. First assume that the t-digits $f_0^1, f_0^2, \cdots, f_0^t$ appearing in the least significant position of the faulty nodes are all distinct.

One always has at least $(r - 1 - t)$ of the h-neighbors of u which are fault free. Let these fault-free nodes be represented as

$$(u_{m-1}, \cdots, u_1, 0), (u_{m-1}, \cdots, u_1, 1), \cdots,$$
$$(u_{m-1}, \cdots, u_1, r - 2 - t).$$

Now consider the following g-neighbors of these $(r - 1 - t)$ nodes. These may be represented as

$$(u_{m-2}, \cdots, u_1, 0, u_{m-1}), (u_{m-2}, \cdots, u_1, 1, u_{m-1}),$$
$$\cdots, (u_{m-1}, \cdots, u_1, r - 2 - t, u_{m-1}).$$

Note that these nodes are all distinct and have the same digit in the least-significant position. According to the hypothesis, no two faulty nodes have the same digit in the least-significant position. Thus, only one of the above nodes can be faulty the remaining $(r - 2 - t)$ of these must be fault free. For $r \geq 4$, one has $(r - 2 - t) \geq 1$. Consequently, in this case one has at least one path of the type shown below that is fault free.

$$u \rightarrow (u_{m-1}, \cdots, u_1, x) \rightarrow (u_{m-2}, \cdots, u_1, x, u_{m-1})$$

$$\begin{matrix} u = (u_{m-1}, \cdots, u_1, u_0) & \text{fault-free segment} \\ (u_{m-1}, \cdots, u_1, x) & \text{constructed as above} \\ (u_{m-2}, \cdots, u_1, x, u_{m-1}) & \\ (u_{m-2}, \cdots, u_1, x, e) & e \text{ appears in the least- or} \\ (e, u_{m-2}, \cdots, u_1, x) & \text{most-significant position;} \\ (e, u_{m-2}, \cdots, u_1, c) & \text{hence, the nodes are fault} \\ (m_{m-2}, \cdots, u_1, c, e) & \text{free} \\ (m_{m-2}, \cdots, u_1, c, u_{m-1}). & \end{matrix}$$

Case R2: $u \rightarrow v = g(u) \rightarrow w = h(v)$. This corresponds to the following path segment:

$$u = (u_{m-1}, \cdots, u_1, u_0)$$
faulty:
$$v = (u_{m-2}, \cdots, u_1, u_0, u_{m-1})$$
$$w = (u_{m-2}, \cdots, u_1, u_0, c) \qquad c \neq u_{m-1}.$$

Now, consider the $(r - 1)$ h-neighbors of u. All of these are distinct, and none of these is the faulty node v since this node cannot be both g and h-neighbor simultaneously. Beside v, there are $(t - 1)$ faulty nodes; thus, at most $(t - 1)$ of the h-neighbors of u can be faulty. This therefore implies that there are at least $(t + 1)$ h-neighbors of u that are fault free since $r - 1 \geq 2t$. So, using arguments similar to those given in Case R1 (when the least significant digits of faulty nodes are not distinct), one can assert that there exists a fault-free path of the type

$$u \rightarrow (u_{m-1}, \cdots, u_1, x) \rightarrow (u_{m-2}, \cdots, u_1, x, u_{m-1}).$$

Now, consider the following path from u to v that uses the above-described fault-free path:

$$\begin{matrix} u = (u_{m-1}, \cdots, u_1, u_0) & \\ (u_{m-1}, \cdots, u_1, x) & \\ (u_{m-2}, \cdots, u_1, x, u_{m-1}) & \\ (u_{m-2}, \cdots, u_1, x, e) & \\ (e, u_{m-2}, \cdots, u_1, x) & \text{nodes cannot be faulty, as} \\ (e, u_{m-2}, \cdots, u_1, u_0) & e \text{ appears in the least- or} \\ (u_{m-2}, \cdots, u_1, u_0, e) & \text{most-significant position.} \\ w = (u_{m-2}, \cdots, u_1, u_0, c). & \end{matrix}$$

Case R3: $u \rightarrow v = g(u) \rightarrow w = g(v)$. This corresponds to the following segment:

$$u = (u_{m-1}, \cdots, u_1, u_0)$$
faulty:
$$v = (u_{m-2}, \cdots, u_1, u_0, u_{m-1})$$
$$w = (u_{m-3}, \cdots, u_0, u_{m-1}, u_{m-2}).$$

As in Case R2, one can construct a fault-free path of the type

$$u \rightarrow (u_{m-1}, \cdots, u_1, x) \rightarrow (u_{m-2}, \cdots, u_1, x, u_{m-1}).$$

Consider the $(r - 1)$ h-neighbors of the node $(u_{m-2}, \cdots, u_1, x, u_{m-1})$. None of these nodes has u_{m-1} in the least-significant position; hence, none of these is the faulty node v. Since there are $(t - 1)$ faulty nodes besides v, at most $(t - 1)$ of these h-neighbors can be faulty. Thus, there must be at least $(t + 1)$ of these h-neighbors that are fault free. Without loss of generality, these nodes can be assumed to be $(u_{m-2}, \cdots, u_1, x, 0)$, $(u_{m-2}, \cdots, u_1, x, 1)$, $\cdots$, $(u_{m-2}, \cdots, u_1, x, t)$. Consider the g-neighbors of these nodes, as shown below:

$$(u_{m-3}, \cdots, u_1, x, 0, u_{m-2}), (u_{m-3}, \cdots, u_1, x, 1, u_{m-2}),$$
$$\cdots, (u_{m-2}, \cdots, u_1, x, t, u_{m-2}).$$

These $(t + 1)$ nodes are all distinct; hence, at least one of these must be fault free. Let this fault-free node be $(n_{m-1}, \cdots, u_1, x, y, u_{m-2})$. Thus, a fault-free path of the type shown below is easily constructed:

$$u \to (u_{m-2}, \cdots, u_1, x) \to$$
$$\to (u_{m-2}, \cdots, u_1, x, u_{m-1}) \to (u_{m-2}, \cdots, u, x, y)$$
$$\to (u_{m-3}, \cdots, u_1, x, y, u_{m-2}) \,.$$

Now, using this path, one can construct a detour from u to w, as illustrated in the following:

$$u = (u_{m-1}, \cdots\cdots\cdots, u_1, u_0)$$
$$(u_{m-1}, \cdots\cdots\cdots, u_1, x)$$
$$(u_{m-2}, \cdots\cdots, u_1, x, u_{m-1})$$
$$(u_{m-2}, \cdots\cdots\cdots, u_1, x, y)$$
$$(u_{m-3}, \cdots\cdot, u_1, x, y, u_{m-1})$$
$$(u_{m-3}, \cdots\cdots, u_1, x, y, e)$$
$$(e, u_{m-3}, \cdots\cdots, u_1, x, y)$$
$$(e, u_{m-3}, \cdots\cdots, u_1, x, e)$$
$$(e, e, u_{m-3}, \cdots\cdots, u_1, x)$$
$$(e, e, u_{m-3}, \cdots\cdot, u_1, u_0)$$
$$(e, u_{m-3}, \cdots\cdots\cdots, u_0, e)$$
$$(e, u_{m-3}, \cdots\cdot, u_0, u_{m-1})$$
$$(u_{m-3}, \cdots\cdot, u_0, u_{m-1}, e)$$
$$w = (u_{m-3}, \cdots, u_0, u_{m-1}, u_{m-2}) \,.$$

e appears in the most- or least-significant position; hence, these nodes cannot be faulty

REFERENCES

[1] J. R. Armstrong and F. G. Gray, "Fault diagnosis in Boolean n-cube array of microprocessors," *IEEE Trans. Comput.*, vol. C-30, pp. 590–596, Aug. 1981.

[2] F. P. Preparata and J. Vuillemin, "The cube-connected cycles: A versatile network for parallel computation," in *Proc. 20th Annu. IEEE Symp. Found. Comput. Sci.*, 1979.

[3] E. Horowitz and A. Zorat, "The binary tree as an interconnection network applications to multiprocessor systems and VLSI," *IEEE Trans. Comput.*, vol. C-30, pp. 247–253, Apr. 1981.

[4] S. B. Akers, "On the construction of (d, k) graphs," *IEEE Trans. Comput.*, vol. C-19, 1965.

[5] I. Koren, "A reconfigurable and fault-tolerant VLSI multiprocessor array," in *Proc. 8th Annu. Symp. Comput. Arch.*, Minneapolis, MN, May 1981.

[6] J. Kuhl and S. Reddy, "Distributed fault-tolerance for large multiprocessor systems," in *Proc. 7th Annu. Symp. Comput. Arch.*, May 1980, pp. 23–30.

[7] D. K. Pradhan and S. M. Reddy, "A fault-tolerant communication architecture for distributed systems," *IEEE Trans. Comput.*, vol. C-31, Sept. 1982.

[8] H. S. Stone, "Parallel processing with perfect shuffle," *IEEE Trans. Comput.*, vol. C-20, pp. 153–161, Feb. 1971.

[9] F. T. Leighton, "Layouts for the shuffle-exchange graphs and lowerbound techniques for VLSI," Ph.D. dissertation, Massachusetts Inst. Technol., Cambridge, MA, 1981.

[10] M. L. Schlumberger, "DeBruijn communication networks," Ph.D. dissertation, Stanford Univ., Stanford, CA, 1974.

[11] J. P. Hayes, "A graph model for fault-tolerant computing systems," *IEEE Trans. Comput.*, vol. C-25, pp. 876–884, Sept. 1976.

[12] C. L. Kwan and S. Toida, "Optimal fault-tolerant realizations of some classes of hierarchical tree systems," in *Proc. FTCS-11*, June 1981, pp. 176–178.

[13] L. Bhuyan and D. P. Agrawal, "Generalized hypercube and hyperbus structures for a computer network," *IEEE Trans. Comput.*, vol. C-30, Apr. 1984.

[14] A. H. Esfahanian and S. L. Hakimi, "Fault-tolerant routing in DeBruijn communication networks," *IEEE Trans. Comput.*, to be published.

[15] M. C. Pease, "The indirect binary n-cube microprocessor array," *IEEE Trans. Comput.*, vol. C-26, pp. 458–473, May 1977.

[16] M. Imase and M. Itoh, "Design to minimize a diameter on building block network," *IEEE Trans. Comput.*, vol. C-30, pp. 439–433, June 1981.

[17] M. T. Liu, "Distributed loop computer networks," *Advances Comput.*, vol. 17, pp. 163–221, 1978.

[18] C. D. Thompson, "A complexity theory for VLSI," Ph.D. dissertation, Carnegie-Mellon Univ., Pittsburgh, PA, Aug. 1980.

[19] J. Kuhl, "Fault diagnosis in computing networks," Ph.D. dissertation, Univ. Iowa, Iowa City, IA, 1980.

[20] D. K. Pradhan, "Interconnection topologies for fault-tolerant parallel and distributed architectures," in *Proc. 1981 Int. Conf. Parallel Processing*, Aug. 1981, pp. 238–242.

[21] W. E. Leland, "Density and reliability of interconnection topologies for multicomputers," Ph.D. dissertation, Univ. Wisconsin-Madison, Madison, WI, May 1982.

[22] V. P. Kumar and S. M. Reddy, "A class of fault-tolerant processor interconnections," in *Proc. 4th Int. Conf. Distrib. Comput. Syst.*, San Francisco, CA, May 1984, pp. 448–460.

[23] S. B. Akers and B. Krishnamurthy, "Group graphs as interconnection networks," in *Proc. FTCS-14*, Orlando, FL, June 1984, pp. 422–427.

[24] J. Bondy and U. Murthy, *Graph Theory with Applications*. New York: American Elsevier, 1976.

[25] R. A. Finkel and M. H. Solomon, "The lens interconnection strategy," *IEEE Trans. Comput.*, vol. C-30, pp. 960–965, Dec. 1981.

[26] M. Malek and E. Opper, "Multiple fault-diagnosis of SW-banyan networks," in *Proc. FTCS-13*, Milan, Italy, June 1983.

[27] D. K. Pradhan, Z. Hanquan, and M. L. Schlumberger, "Fault-tolerant multi-bus architectures for multiprocessors," in *Proc. FTCS-14*, Orlando, FL, June 1984, pp. 400–408.

Dhiraj K. Pradhan (S'70–M'72–SM'80) was born in India on December 1, 1948. He received the M.S. degree from Brown University, Providence, RI, in 1969, and the Ph.D. degree from the University of Iowa, Iowa City, in 1972.

He is currently a Professor in the Department of Electrical and Computer Engineering, University of Massachusetts, Amherst. Previously he has held positions with Oakland University, Rochester, MI and the IBM Corporation, NY. He has been actively involved with research in fault-tolerant computing and parallel processing since 1972. He has presented several papers at fault-tolerant computing and parallel processing conferences. He has also published extensively in journals such as the IEEE TRANSACTIONS ON COMPUTERS and *Networks*. His research interests include fault-tolerant computing, computer architecture, graph theory, and flow networks.

Dr. Pradhan has edited the Special Issue on Fault-Tolerant Computing of IEEE COMPUTER (March 1980), and served as Session Chairman and Program Committee Member for various conferences. He is an Editor for the *Journal of VLSI and Digital Systems*. He is also the Editor of a forthcoming book entitled *Fault-tolerant Computing: Theory and Techniques* (Prentice-Hall).

The Design, Analysis and Simulation of a Fault-Tolerant Interconnection Network Supporting the Fetch-and-Add Primitive

PRITHVIRAJ BANERJEE AND ABHIJEET DUGAR, MEMBER, IEEE

Abstract—The paracomputer model of parallel computation permits every processor in a parallel processor system to read or write a shared memory location in one cycle; one way of implementing this model is through the "fetch-and-add" synchronization primitive. The NYU Ultracomputer and the IBM RP3 are two real parallel machines which implement the "fetch-and-add" primitive using a combining multistage interconnection network. This paper addresses the issue of fault tolerance in such a combining network. Basically, the approach uses 4 × 4 switches as switching elements in a multistage network, and introduces an extra stage of such switches and links to create four independent paths between any source–destination pair. Four copies of every message are sent through the network simultaneously in the presence of combining, and the results are voted upon at the end, thereby providing single error correction and double error detection. In a regular network, in the presence of multiple messages and conflicts for output ports, different copies of a message can get delayed by different amounts; hence, the four copies may not arrive simultaneously at the output to allow the voting. It is shown in the paper that by using the property of the omega network, and a rigorous scheduling discipline, it is possible to enforce that all four copies arrive simultaneously at the output for a fault-free network, and that at least three copies arrive simultaneously at the output in the presence of a single fault in a switching element or a line. The scheduling discipline, the design of the switching elements to support the discipline, and the theoretical proof of correctness of the design constitute the key contributions of the paper. We provide estimates of various network parameters as a function of the workload using analytical models and detailed network simulations. We show that the proposed design for fault tolerance is more cost effective than the brute-force technique of having multiple copies of the network.

Index Terms—Fault tolerance, fetch-and-add, omega network, performance evaluation, scheduling discipline, systolic queues.

I. INTRODUCTION

THE *paracomputer* model of computation is an idealized parallel computation model which permits every

Manuscript received July 10, 1986; revised March 1, 1987 and April 6, 1988. This work has been supported in part by the National Science Foundation President Young Investigator Award under Grant NSF MIP 86-57563 PYI, in part by the Semiconductor Research Corporation under Contract 87-DP-109, and in part by the Joint Services Electronics Program (U.S. Army, U.S. Navy, and U.S. Air Force) under Contract N00014-79-C-0424.

P. Banerjee is with the Department of Electrical and Computer Engineering and the Coordinated Science Laboratory, University of Illinois at Urbana-Champaign, Urbana, IL 61801.

A. Dugar is with the Design Automation Group, Texas Instruments, Inc., Dallas, TX.

IEEE Log Number 8823539.

processor in a parallel processor system to read or write a shared memory location in one cycle [1], [2]. The effect of simultaneous accesses to a shared memory can be accomplished by the serialization principle, which states that the effect of simultaneous actions by the PE's is as if the actions occurred in some unspecified serial order. Paracomputers must be regarded as idealized computation models because physical limitations, such as restricted fan-in, prevent their realization.

One simple but effective way of implementing this model is through the *fetch-and-add* synchronization primitive, denoted by F&A (X, e), where X is an integer variable, and e is an integer expression. This indivisible operation is defined to return the old value of X and to replace X by the sum $X + e$. If X is a shared variable and many fetch-and-add operations simultaneously address X, the effect of these operations is exactly what it would be if they occurred in some *unspecified* serial order, which is the serialization principle described above. The advantage of using the fetch-and-add over other operating system synchronization primitives such as test-and-set and compare-and-swap for a variety of commonly useful parallel algorithms has been discussed in [3].

The NYU Ultracomputer [4] and the IBM RP3 [5] are two real parallel machines which implement the "fetch-and-add" primitive using a combining multistage interconnection network which consists of a regular omega network of Lawrie [6] with each 2 × 2 switching element enhanced to include an adder and some local memory. When two fetch-and-adds referencing the same variable, say F&A (X, e) and F&A (X, f), meet at a switch, the switch forms the sum $e + f$, transmits the combined request F&A $(X, e + f)$, and stores the value e in its local memory. When the value Y is returned to the switch in response to F&A $(X, e + f)$, the switch transmits Y to satisfy the original request F&A (X, e) and transmits $Y + e$ to satisfy the request F&A (X, f).

An important criterion for estimating the performance of a multiprocessor system is its reliability. To a large extent the reliability of the system depends on that of the interconnection network. A fault-tolerant interconnection network can tolerate faults to some degree and still provide reliable communication between any input–output pair. Some amount of redundancy has to be present to achieve fault tolerance. In what is known as information redundancy, error detecting/correcting codes are used [7]. Such schemes require minimal additional hardware, but fault tolerance is limited to the data being

Reprinted from *IEEE Trans. Computers,* Vol. 38, No. 1, Jan. 1989, pp. 30-46. Copyright © 1989 by The Institute of Electrical and Electronics Engineers, Inc. All rights reserved.

transferred. Faults in the control portion of the network may not be tolerated. Another approach is hardware redundancy in which multiple paths are created between the inputs and outputs of the network. Multiple paths can be created by the addition of an extra stage to the multistage network as in [8]–[10], or by providing redundant links as in [11] and [12]. The INDRA network [13] uses a redundant stage as well as redundant links. Once a failure of a switch/link in the path of a message is detected, an alternate path is selected. The mechanism of detection of a failure can be performed either off-line through diagnosis [14] or on-line by using error detecting codes [7]. A technique for detecting errors in both the data and control parts of an interconnection network has been proposed in [15]. Off-line diagnosis is not useful in detecting transient or intermittent failures which have been shown to occur more frequently than permanent failures [16], [17].

An on-line fault detection/location mechanism may use coding techniques. Simple algebraic codes, such as Hamming codes or cyclic codes [18], can be used for detecting errors in the address portion X of a message F&A (X, a), but not for the data portion a because the fetch-and-add primitive requires arithmetic operations to be performed on the data portion of the message. For the data portion, arithmetic codes, such as the residue codes and the AN codes, would have to be used [18]. Considering that the encoding/decoding circuits would have to be provided in each switching element of the network, adopting this scheme is not cost efficient. In addition, the arithmetic codes may be used for detecting errors but not for correcting them. Furthermore, such circuits would have to be designed to be fault secure; i.e., faults in these circuits should not produce incorrect codewords; this would increase the cost of the scheme even more.

A less costly technique would be to place the encoding circuitry only at the processor network interface (PNI) and the decoding circuitry only at the memory network interface (MNI) for a message flow in the forward direction. However, in this technique, once an error is detected, the message has to be sent through an alternate path, and it may be impossible to recover from the deleterious effects produced by the erroneous message. Consider what happens if a message F&A (X, a) changes to (Y, c). This could have several effects.

1) A wrong value would be returned to the processor from which F&A (X, a) originated.

2) Memory location X will not be updated.

3) Memory location Y will be written into when it should not have been written into.

4) If there is a message F&A (Y, b) also propagating through the network, combining of F&A (X, a) [changed to F&A (Y, c)] and F&A (Y, b) may take place when no combining should have taken place. As a result, a wrong value would be returned to the processor from which F&A (Y, b) originated and a wrong value would be written into memory location Y.

5) If there are several messages propagating through the network with destination Y, the effect of combining the erroneous message F&A (X, a) [changed to F&A (Y, c)] with all the messages may be disastrous. Recovery from the effects

of combining in this case may be extremely difficult or even impossible since combining of the erroneous message F&A (X, a) with error-free messages may have taken place at various stages of the network.

From the above examples, it is clear that due to a single fault, several errors may be generated which might be impossible to recover from. In the schemes proposed for fault tolerance in interconnection networks so far, the design of the interconnection network is considered at a very high level or on a totally theoretical basis. None of techniques can be directly applied to provide fault tolerance in a combining network.

This paper addresses the important issue of fault tolerance in a combining network. Section II provides an overview and motivation of the proposed design. In Section III, the detailed design of the switching elements constituting the proposed interconnection network is described which supports a rigorous scheduling discipline on the servicing of conflicting messages at the output ports of switches. Various properties of the network under fault-free conditions are discussed in Section IV. The behavior of the network under faults is analyzed in Section V. Section VI provides estimates of various network parameters as a function of the workload using analytical models and detailed network simulations. Finally, Section VII shows that the proposed design for fault tolerance is more cost effective than the brute-force technique of having multiple copies of the network. Section VIII uses some simple probabilistic models to show the reliability improvement of the network using our scheme.

II. Overview of Proposed Fault-Tolerant Network

The proposed interconnection network is based on the omega network [6]. The omega network with N inputs and N outputs consists of $n = \log_B (N)$ stages of $B \times B$ switching elements. A $B^n \times B^n$ omega network is constructed using $B \times B$ switching elements and $B*B^{n-1}$ shuffles interconnecting the stages. A $P*Q$ shuffle is the permutation of PQ elements defined as

$$\pi(i) = \left[Pi + \left\lfloor \frac{i}{Q} \right\rfloor \right]_{\mathrm{mod}\ PQ} \qquad 0 \leq i \leq PQ - 1.$$

In the proposed network, we choose $B = 4$ and use 4×4 switching elements. By adding an extra stage to the omega network, redundant paths between the processors and memory modules are created. By using 4×4 switches instead of 2×2 switches, four paths can be obtained for any given source–destination pair. Hence, the proposed design consists of $(\log_4 N + 1)$ stages. It has been proved in [19] that the four paths created are unique, i.e., they use independent links and independent switching elements at every stage of the network except at stage 0 and stage $n (n = \log_4 N)$ of the network. To make the first and last stages also fault tolerant, the 4×4 switch can be modified as explained in Sections III-B and III-C. The scheme we will propose in this paper can tolerate single faults in the network which is defined as 1) complete failure of one switching element, 2) failure of one link between any two stages of the network.

In the proposed scheme, the processor network interface (PNI) creates four copies of a message from a processor. Four disjoint paths in the network are used to send the four copies simultaneously through the network. Voting is carried out on the four copies in the memory network interface (MNI). This enables correction of message transmission errors due to any number of faults along a single path, or detection of message transmission errors due to any number of faults along two paths, as messages propagate through the network.

In the absence of multiple messages in the network, it is easy to check that the four copies of a message propagate synchronously through the network, one stage at a time, assuming that the link delays and switch cycles are identical. Hence, the four copies can be assumed to arrive at the output port of the last stage after $\log_4(N) + 1$ time units where a unit of time includes the time to process a message and to send it along a link between stages. Hence, under fault-free conditions, the four copies arrive almost simultaneously at the output port, barring minor clock skews. Voting can therefore be performed relatively easily on the four copies.

In the presence of multiple messages through the network where they conflict for the same output ports of switches in intermediate stages, messages are queued up in buffers. Hence, unless special precautions are taken, the four copies of a message may be delayed by different amounts. In such cases, it may be necessary to store all the copies in local memories at the memory network interface (MNI) such that after all the copies arrive, the voter can access them and vote on them. This approach has three limitations.

1) In order to support fast lookup of multiple copies of a message in memory, it may be necessary to have content addressable memories (CAM) which are very expensive.

2) In general, it is not possible to exactly predict how much the last copy of a message will be delayed after the first copies arrives at the output; hence, the size of the memory (CAM) may be unacceptably large.

3) The more serious drawback is that in the presence of faults in the network, certain messages may be garbled, hence the voter may wait forever for the fourth copy of a message but may not realize that it will never arrive. It might be possible to use timeout after waiting for a time period equal to the maximum estimated delay between copies of messages; however, the size of the CAM required to save all messages for such long periods may be too large.

In view of the above, we propose the use of a rigorous scheduling discipline on the queueing and servicing of messages at the output ports of switches such that the four copies of a message proceed *synchronously* through the network in the presence of multiple messages and conflicts for output ports. This is really the key contribution of this paper. A detailed design of the network switching elements and their scheduling disciplines is given in Section III. A formal proof of the synchronous movement of messages is given in Section IV.

III. Detailed Network Design

This section describes in detail the design of the switching elements constituting the network. In the following, we

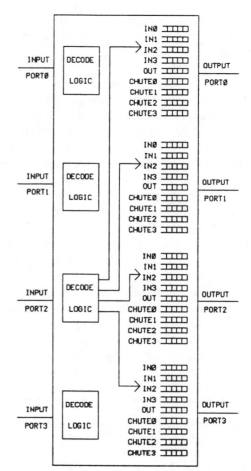

Fig. 1. A 4 × 4 switch in an intermediate stage of the network.

assume that the network consists of N inputs and $n + 1$ stages where $n = \log_4(N)$. Switches in stages 1 through $n - 1$ of the network are identical and are described first. Next we describe the design of switches in stage 0. Finally we will discuss the design of switches in stage n.

A. Stages 1 through $(n - 1)$

Fig. 1 shows a switch in an intermediate stage having four input and four output ports. One queue is associated with each input–output port pair. Hence, there are four IN queues associated with each output port. These are labeled as IN0, IN1, IN2, and IN3: IN0 is connected to input port 0, IN1 to port 1, and so on. When a message arrives at an input port, the decoder determines which output port the message is bound for by looking at the relevant two bits in the destination address of the message. The message is placed in the appropriate IN queue of the particular output port. Messages are sent to the next stage of the network following a rigorous scheduling discipline satisfying two conditions.

1) If a message M arrives at a port at a particular cycle t, then all messages that arrived at that port in cycles $< t$ will be serviced before M.

2) If between one to four messages arrive at the same cycle at the same output port, they will be serviced in the order of their input port addresses. Messages having source addresses such that the input port addresses are low, e.g., 00, will be serviced earlier than messages having input port addresses that

712

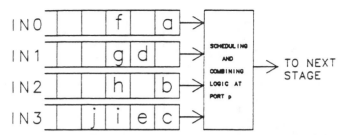

Fig. 2. Round-robin scheduling discipline at an output port of a switch.

are high, e.g., 11. This scheduling scheme is illustrated by the following example.

Example 1: Messages *a, b, c, d, e, f, g, h, i, j* arrive at various input ports of a switch over a period of five cycles and are routed to output port *p* as shown in Fig. 2. For the purpose of this example, assume that none of these messages can be combined. Messages *a, b,* and *c* arrive in the same cycle at input ports 0, 2, and 3, respectively. Suppose this is cycle *C*. Messages *d* and *e* arrive in cycle *C* + 1 at ports 1 and 3, respectively. In cycle *C* + 2, messages *f, g, h,* and *i* arrive at input ports 0, 1, 2, and 3, respectively, and are routed to output port *p*. In cycle *C* + 3, message *j*, arriving at input port 3, is routed to output port *p*. These messages are sent to the next stage in ten cycles in the order *a, b, c, d, e, f, g, h, i,* and *j*. Note that after message *c* is sent to the next stage, message *d* is sent to the next stage and not message *f*. Any blank slots in the IN queues are skipped while following the round-robin scheduling of messages. □

Implementation of the correct ordering of the messages and possible combining of messages is based on the scheme proposed in [20]. For the benefit of the reader, the scheme proposed in [20] is now briefly described. The scheme has been used for a network consisting of 2 × 2 switching elements called ultraswitches. Three columns of shift registers, called the IN column, the OUT column, and the CHUTE column, are associated with each output port of a switch. These columns of shift registers are connected as shown in Fig. 3. Messages arrive in the IN column and shift up one position at each cycle. Similarly, messages shift down one position in the OUT column at each cycle. If a message in the IN column is adjacent to a slot on the OUT column that is empty, then it shifts to that slot. In addition, this scheme detects a message in the IN queue going to the same address as another message already in the OUT queue. The message in the IN queue is then placed in the CHUTE column. The two messages move synchronously and arrive at the combine logic simultaneously. The combine logic detects the possibility of combining and combines the two messages so that only one message is sent to the next stage of the network.

In our proposed scheme, there are four IN queues, labeled IN0, IN1, IN2, and IN3, at each output port. In addition, at each output port there is one OUT queue and four CHUTE queues, labeled CHUTE0, CHUTE 1, CHUTE 2, and CHUTE 3, one corresponding to each IN queue. Fig. 1 shows an overview of the queues and the decoding logic within each switch.

A detailed diagram of the switch is shown in Fig. 4. Possible movements of messages are indicated by the arrows.

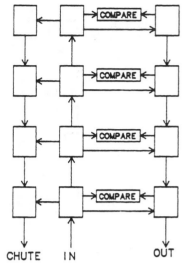

Fig. 3. Design of the output port of the Ultraswitch.

Control signals have been omitted from the figure for the sake of clarity. A message arriving at an input port is placed in the appropriate IN queue of an output port at level 0. Messages in the IN*i* queue then move to the OUT queue, or to the corresponding CHUTE*i* queue (if combining is possible), or one level up in the IN*i* queue. The movements of messages in one cycle can be described by dividing the cycle into three phases.

Phase 1: The messages at level 0 of the OUT queue and the CHUTE queues are sent to the combine logic. The function of the combine logic is the same as in the scheme proposed in [20], except that now it is possible to have a five-way combining by adding the elements of OUT queue with the elements in four of the IN queues. Messages arriving at the four input ports are placed at level 0 of the appropriate IN queues. Messages already in the IN queues move to the OUT queue, the corresponding CHUTE queue, or the next level up in the IN queue. The movement of messages is decided according to the following conditions.

1) If the OUT queue slot is empty at any level, the message in that level in the IN queue *with the smallest label* moves into the OUT queue at that level. The other messages at that level move up one level within the same IN queue.

2) At every level, if the OUT queue slot is occupied and the corresponding CHUTE queue slot is empty, then the messages in the IN queues are compared to the message in the OUT queue at that level to determine if any of the messages in the IN queues can be combined with the message in the OUT queue. If none of the messages in the IN queues can be combined with the message in the OUT queue at a level, then all messages in the IN queue at that level move up one level. If one or more of the messages can be combined, that message(s) is(are) moved to the *corresponding* CHUTE slot(s) at that level. The rest of the messages at that level move up one level.

3) If the OUT queue slot is occupied at a level and the corresponding CHUTE slot is also occupied at that level, then all messages at that level move up one level.

Phase 2: Messages in the OUT queue and the CHUTE queues do not move. Messages in the IN queues move to the OUT queue, the corresponding CHUTE queues, or the next

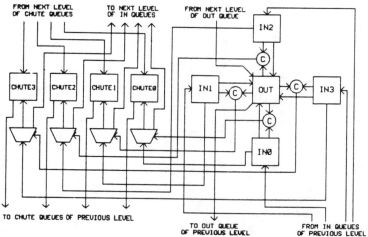

Fig. 4. Design of the output port of a switching element in the proposed network.

level up in the IN queue. Movement of the messages in the IN queues is decided according to the conditions described for phase 1.

Phase 3: Messages in the OUT queue and the CHUTE do not move. Messages in the IN queue may move only within the level they are in; they cannot move to a higher level. If any message in an IN queue can be combined or moved to the OUT queue, it is moved to the appropriate CHUTE queue or the OUT queue ãt its own level.

Example 2: The movement of messages in the three phases is illustrated in Fig. 5(a) and (b). During four clock cycles, messages a, b, c, d, e, f, g, h, i, and j reach an output port p. Assume that none of these messages can be combined. It is easy to extend the example when combining is possible. Hence, only the IN queues and the OUT queue at output port p are shown. Messages a, b, c, and d arrive at the same time at the four input ports of the switch and are all bound for output port p. They are placed in the four IN queues associated with output port p at level 0, in phase 1 of cycle one. In phase 2 of cycle one, message a moves to the OUT queue, and messages b, c, and d move up one level. In phase 3 of cycle one, message b moves to the OUT queue. Messages c and d do not move. This is the end of the first cycle. In phase 1 of the second cycle, message a is sent to the next stage and message b moves one level down in the OUT queue; message c moves to the OUT queue; message d moves up one level and messages e and f at input ports 0 and 3 of the switch are placed in IN queues 0 and 3 at level 0. Further movements of messages are also depicted in Fig. 5. □

B. Stage 0

Logically, switches in stage 0, which is the extra stage of the network, have four inputs and four outputs. A message arriving at any input port in this stage is broadcast to all four output ports of the switch. Thus, a message arriving at input port 2 of a switch in stage 0 is put into queue IN2 of each output port of the switch. It is then sent to stage 1 as described above. We are proposing a design of an interconnection network that can tolerate failure of individual modules or links where a module is a 4×4 switch in stages 1 through $n - 1$.

However, our scheme will not work if a switch in stage 0 is considered as a module, because under failure of the module (switch), there cannot be four independent paths from each source–destination pair. We therefore modify the switches in stage 0 to consist of four modules, only one of which can become faulty.

Therefore, physically the replication of messages should be done by the processor network interface (PNI) logic. There are N 4×1 modules in stage 0 where each module has four inputs and one output. Thus, stage 0 has $4N$ inputs and N outputs overall. The four IN queues associated with each output port are in one module. Thus, each module has four IN queues, one OUT queue, and one CHUTE queue as shown in Fig. 6. The four copies of a message enter stage 0 at different 4×1 modules and are placed in the appropriate IN queues. Movement of messages and any possible combining can proceed as in stages 1 through $n - 1$. Essentially, the 4×4 switch has been broken up into four 4×1 modules so that the failure of any one of them can be tolerated.

C. Stage n

Logically, each switch in the last stage of the network (stage n) receives the four copies of a message, one copy arriving at each input port. The topology of the network and the scheduling of the movement of messages guarantee that the four copies arrive simultaneously at the last stage. Voting is carried out on the four copies. If at most one copy is erroneous, the correct message is routed to the appropriate memory module. If two copies are erroneous, the error is detected. Again if we want to tolerate single module faults, we have to partition each 4×4 switch of stage n into four modules each having one input and four outputs. There will, therefore, be N 1×4 modules in stage n and therefore $4N$ outputs from the network.

In the physical design of the network, voting should be carried out by the memory network interface (MNI). The physical implementation of a logical 4×4 switch in the last stage is identical to Fig. 7. Failure of one such last stage module can be tolerated in our design. In each module, there are four OUT queues, one for each output port. Each output

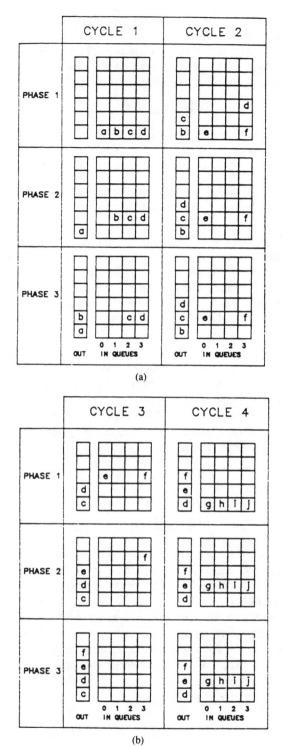

(a)

(b)

Fig. 5. (a) Movement of messages in the three phases of a cycle. (b) Movement of messages in the three phases of a cycle (Cont'd).

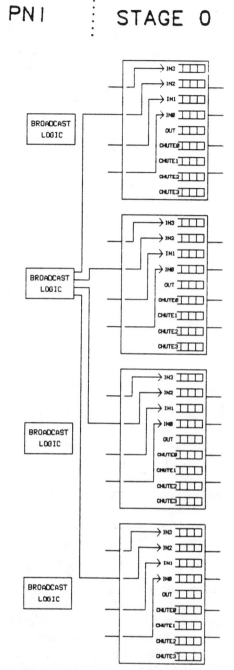

Fig. 6. Physical implementation of a 4 × 4 switch in stage 0 of the network.

port of a switch has one OUT queue, one IN queue, and one CHUTE queue. These queues are connected in a manner similar to those in the ultraswitch shown in Fig. 3 earlier. The four copies of a message arrive at four 1 × 4 switches. A message arriving at the input port of a switch is placed in one of the IN queues depending upon the address of its destination. Two messages in the same queue may combine if their destination address within a module is the same. Each output of the N 1 × 4 switches is hardwired to a voting unit in the MNI. There are N such voting units, each being hardwired to

four outputs of stage n on the network side and to one memory module on the other side. The MNI receives the four copies, carries out the voting, and routes the message to the appropriate memory module.

D. Reverse Network

It is clear that there has to be a reverse path in the switches for the network to be useful. We propose the use of almost identical circuitry for the switches in the forward and reverse directions. The only notable differences will be that the roles of switches in stages 0 and n will be reversed. In the reverse direction, the creation of four copies of a message will be logically performed by the switches in stage n. Physically they will be performed by the MNI. Voting of the messages is

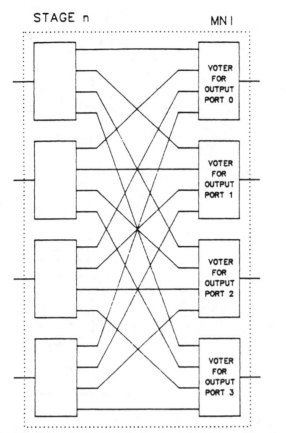

STAGE n   MN I

Fig. 7.   Physical implementation of a 4 × 4 switch in stage n of the network.

logically performed by switches in stage 0. Physically they will be performed by the PNI. Intermediate stage switches have duplicate copies of the circuitry shown in Fig. 1 for the two directions. In addition, there will be four local memories in each switch, one per output port for storing temporary variables during combining in the forward direction that will be needed during decombining in the reverse direction.

IV. Network Properties Under Fault-Free Conditions

In this section, we will first prove that four copies of every message move synchronously through the network in the forward direction for a fault-free network. We will then show that the four copies combine simultaneously in the forward direction and decombine simultaneously in the reverse direction for a fault-free network. In the next section, we will show that in the presence of a single faulty switching element or link, at least three copies of every message move simultaneously in the forward and reverse direction in the presence of combining and blocking of messages due to finite size queues. The simultaneous propagation properties of the network will be proved by making use of the topology of the network and the scheduling discipline described in Section III. For the purpose of this section, the switches in stages 0 and $(n - 1)$ will be considered to be 4 × 4 switches.

Notation: The four copies of a fetch-and-add message originating from processor A for memory module X will be denoted by $(A, X)^0$, $(A, X)^1$, $(A, X)^2$, and $(A, X)^3$.

Notation: A switch i in stage s of the network will be denoted by (s, i).

Lemma 1: In a fault-free network, all copies of a message

enter different switches in stages 1 through $(n - 1)$ at the same input port of the switches.

Proof: The inputs and outputs of all the stages are labeled for 0 to $N - 1$ in binary as m-bit addresses ($m = \log_2 N$). Suppose a message originates at processor

$$A = a_0 a_1 a_2 \cdots a_{m-2} a_{m-1}$$

and the address of its destination is

$$X = x_0 x_1 x_2 \cdots x_{m-2} x_{m-1}.$$

The path of the message through the network is traced in Table I. It can be seen from Table I that for every stage between 1 through $(n - 1)$ of the network, the least two significant bits of the address in the input port address column are the same for all the copies. Since these two bits specify the input port within a switch, the four copies of a message arrive at the same input port of different switches in the same stage.   □

Lemma 2: In an intermediate stage of a fault-free network, if four copies of a message (A, X) enter a stage at switches (s, i), (s, j), (s, k), and (s, l) at port p, and one copy of a message (B, Y) enters switch (s, i) at port q, then the other copies of (B, Y) must enter at switches (s, j), (s, k), and (s, l) at port q.

Proof: This can be proved by first determining the condition under which two messages originating from different processors will meet at a switch in a stage s. Consider a standard omega network (no extra stage). Suppose a message originates at processor

$$A = a_0 a_1 a_2 \cdots a_{m-2} a_{m-1}$$

and the address of its destination is

$$X = x_0 x_1 x_2 \cdots x_{m-2} x_{m-1}.$$

The path of the message can be traced by selecting an m-bit window at each stage from the concatenated source and destination address bits. At successive stages, the window is shifted right by two bits. For two messages to meet at a stage, the most significant $m - 2$ bits in the windows of the two messages for that stage must match. These bits specify the switch at which the two messages meet in the stage. From Table I ("Address of Output Port" column), it can be seen that when an extra stage is added to the network, the m-bit window is chosen from

$$a_0 a_1 \cdots a_{m-1} ** x_0 x_1 \cdots x_{m-1}$$

in any intermediate stage, where ** is 00, 01, 10, and 11. Each value of ** identifies the particular copy of a message. Thus, if one copy of two messages meets at a switch, the other copies must also meet.   □

Lemma 3: In a fault-free network, four copies of every message exit stage 0 of the network simultaneously.

Proof: From the design of stage 0 switches discussed in Section III-B, it is evident that for a message (A, X) arriving at an input port p of switch $(0, i)$, its copies $(A, X)^0$, $(A, X)^1$, $(A, X)^2$, and $(A, X)^3$ will be placed in queue INp at each output port of switch $(0, i)$ at the same time. The scheduling discipline ensures that all the copies have the same priority in

TABLE I
PATH OF MESSAGE THROUGH THE NETWORK

Stage No.	Address of Input Port	Address of Output Port
Stage 0	$a_2a_3a_4a_5 \cdots a_{m-2}a_{m-1}a_0a_1$	$a_2a_3a_4a_5 \cdots a_{m-2}a_{m-1}00$ $a_2a_3a_4a_5 \cdots a_{m-2}a_{m-1}01$ $a_2a_3a_4a_5 \cdots a_{m-2}a_{m-1}10$ $a_2a_3a_4a_5 \cdots a_{m-2}a_{m-1}11$
Stage 1	$a_4a_5a_6 \cdots a_{m-2}a_{m-1}00a_2a_3$ $a_4a_5a_6 \cdots a_{m-2}a_{m-1}01a_2a_3$ $a_4a_5a_6 \cdots a_{m-2}a_{m-1}10a_2a_3$ $a_4a_5a_6 \cdots a_{m-2}a_{m-1}11a_2a_3$	$a_4a_5 \cdots a_{m-2}a_{m-1}00x_0x_1$ $a_4a_5 \cdots a_{m-2}a_{m-1}01x_0x_1$ $a_4a_5 \cdots a_{m-2}a_{m-1}10x_0x_1$ $a_4a_5 \cdots a_{m-2}a_{m-1}11x_0x_1$
...	...	...
Stage n-1	$00x_0x_1x_2x_3 \cdots x_{m-6}x_{m-5}a_{m-2}a_{m-1}$ $01x_0x_1x_2x_3 \cdots x_{m-6}x_{m-5}a_{m-2}a_{m-1}$ $01x_0x_1x_2x_3 \cdots x_{m-6}x_{m-5}a_{m-2}a_{m-1}$ $11x_0x_1x_2x_3 \cdots x_{m-6}x_{m-5}a_{m-2}a_{m-1}$	$00x_0x_1 \cdots x_{m-4}x_{m-3}$ $01x_0x_1 \cdots x_{m-4}x_{m-3}$ $10x_0x_1 \cdots x_{m-4}x_{m-3}$ $11x_0x_1 \cdots x_{m-4}x_{m-3}$
Stage n	$x_0x_1 \cdots x_{m-6}x_{m-5}x_{m-4}x_{m-3}00$ $x_0x_1 \cdots x_{m-6}x_{m-5}x_{m-4}x_{m-3}01$ $x_0x_1 \cdots x_{m-6}x_{m-5}x_{m-4}x_{m-3}10$ $x_0x_1 \cdots x_{m-6}x_{m-5}x_{m-4}x_{m-3}11$	$x_0x_1 \cdots x_{m-3}x_{m-2}x_{m-1}$

being sent to the OUT queue or to the appropriate CHUTE queues of the respective output ports. Hence, the copies will exit stage 0 and enter stage 1 simultaneously. □

Lemma 4: In a fault-free network, if there is a message at level L of the OUT queue at an output port, then there will be messages at all levels less than L in the OUT queue.

Proof: This is proved by considering the movement of messages in the IN queues during the three phases of a cycle as described in Section III-A. The following points are noted about the messages in the IN queues.

1) In all phases of a cycle, messages can move to the OUT queue or to the CHUTE queues.

2) In phases 1 and 2, messages may move to a higher level in the IN queue. However, movement of a message to the OUT queue or to the CHUTE queues is given priority over moving to a higher level. Thus, if a message can move to the OUT queue, it is sent to the OUT queue instead of one level higher in the IN queue.

3) During Phase 3, messages may not move to a higher level. As a result, when messages in the OUT queue and the CHUTE queues move in phase 1 of the next cycle, an empty slot between two messages in an OUT queue will never be created.

Hence, if L is the highest level in the OUT queue in which there is a message, then there are messages in all levels from 0 through $(L - 1)$ of the OUT queue. □

Theorem 1: In a fault-free network, all copies of a message enter/exit any stage between 1 and $(n - 1)$ of the network simultaneously.

Proof: This theorem is proved by induction on the stage number at which copy 0 of a message enters. Consider a message (A, X) entering stage 1 at switches $(1, i)$, $(1, j)$, $(1, k)$, and $(1, l)$. From Lemma 3 it is evident that the four copies of (A, X) enter stage 1 of the network simultaneously. Suppose $(A, X)^0$ enters stage 1 at switch $(1, i)$ at port p at time t. Then, according to Lemma 1, the other copies of (A, X) will enter switches $(1, j)$, $(1, k)$, and $(1, l)$ at port p. Since the destination of all the copies is the same, all copies will be routed to the same output port, say, q. Messages $(A, X)^0$, $(A, X)^1$, $(A, X)^2$, and $(A, X)^3$ will be placed in the IN queues p at output ports q of switches $(1, i)$, $(1, j)$, $(1, k)$, and $(1, l)$ simultaneously. Since all copies are in IN queues with the same label, they have equal priority in being sent to the OUT queue or to the CHUTE.

According to Lemma 4, there are no empty slots between messages in an OUT queue. Hence, one message can be sent to the next stage in every cycle if there is any message at an output port. Suppose at the time when $(A, X)^0$ arrives at $(1, i)$, there are d messages waiting in the IN queues and the OUT queue at output port q. Suppose none of these d messages can be combined with each other. (The case when combining is possible is considered separately in Theorem 2.) If $(A, X)^0$ does not combine with any of the d messages, then $(A, X)^0$ will experience a delay of d cycles before it is sent to the next stage. From Lemma 1 and Lemma 2 it is evident that if there are d messages in the IN queues and the OUT queue at output port q of switch $(1, i)$, then there must be d messages at output port q of switches $(1, j)$, $(1, k)$, and $(1, l)$. Hence, all copies of (A, X) will experience a delay of d cycles before being sent to the next stage. Thus, in all stages, all copies move synchronously, i.e., delays for all copies of a message in any stage will be the same. □

Theorem 2: In a fault-free network, if one copy of a message combines with another message, then all the other copies of the two messages are guaranteed to combine.

Proof: It has been proved in Theorem 1 that all copies of a message are placed at level 0 of the IN queues with the same label. It has also been proved that the four copies are placed in the IN queues simultaneously. Initially, when all queues are empty, if one copy of a message in the IN queue moves to the OUT queue, the other copies would also move to the OUT queue. When there are messages waiting in the OUT queue, if one copy of a message moves up one level in the IN queue, the other copies would also move up one level. Hence, all copies are always at the same level of the IN queue or the OUT queue. All copies of a message in the IN queue will be compared to copies of the same message in the OUT queue. Hence, if one copy of a message moves to a CHUTE, all the copies must also move to the corresponding CHUTEs at the same time. So if one copy of a message combines, then all other copies of the message must combine. □

Theorem 3: In a fault-free network, all copies of a message enter/exit any stage simultaneously in the reverse direction.

Proof: In the following, we give an outline of the proof because a rigorous and detailed proof of this theorem is quite long. Besides, most of the results can be derived from the lemmas and theorems that were proved earlier for the forward path. In Section III-D, we briefly mentioned that the circuitry and scheduling discipline for the switches in the reverse direction are very similar to those in the forward direction. By carrying out an analysis similar to Lemma 1, it can be shown that all copies of a messages enter different switches through the same input port of the switches in the reverse direction. Note that since the network topology in the reverse direction is a $4*4^{n-1}$ inverse shuffle, when a message traverses a link using the $4*4^{n-1}$ inverse shuffle, the message addresses are manipulated as if they are rotated right by two bits instead of being rotated left. Also, the addresses of the input ports are determined by the first two bits of the resultant address instead of the last two bits. It is possible to construct a table similar to Table I to check the exact sequences of address manipulations in the reverse direction. We can extend Lemma 2 for message propagation in the reverse direction by considering m-bit windows starting from the right and sliding it left instead of starting from the left and sliding it right as was the case in the forward direction. Hence, the modified Lemma 2 for the reverse direction would state that in an intermediate stage in the reverse path, if four copies of a message enter four switches of a stage at a certain port, and one copy of another message enters one of those switches at a different port, then the other copies of the second message enter those same switches at those ports. We also mentioned in Section III-D that switches in stage n will perform the broadcast of the four copies of a message. Hence, Lemma 3 may be modified to state that all four copies of a message exit stage n in the reverse direction simultaneously. The only difference in the circuitry for processing messages in the reverse direction is the absence of the CHUTE queues. These are replaced by content addressable memories which store information necessary for decombining. It can be shown by extending Theorem 2 that if a particular copy of a message decombined at a switch in a certain stage, then the other copies of the message also decombine at corresponding switches in the same stage. The four copies of the messages therefore exit stage 0 in the reverse direction simultaneously; hence, voting can be performed on them in this stage. □

Theorem 4: In a fault-free network, all four copies of a message move synchronously in the presence blocking of messages due to finite buffers.

Proof: Until now, we have assumed that each switching element has infinite buffer sizes, which is not a practical assumption. We now address the case when there are finite buffers. We assume that if the queues for a given output port q of a switch (s, i) are full, then a message $(A, X)^0$ from an input port of a network destined for port q will be blocked. From Lemma 4, since there are no empty slots between messages in

the OUT queue for port q of switch (s, i), if there are d messages waiting in the queue for that port, there are d messages waiting in the queues for ports q of three other switches (s, j), (s, k), and (s, l) which receive the other copies of the messages $(A, X)^1$, $(A, X)^2$, and $(X, a)^3$, respectively; these messages will therefore be also blocked. □

V. NETWORK PROPERTIES UNDER FAULTY CONDITIONS

Having characterized the behavior of the network for the fault-free situation, we will now proceed to prove certain properties about the behavior of the network under failure of a single switching element or link. We propose functional level models for faults in the switching elements in various stages of the network in the forward and reverse direction. Functional fault models for various modules in computer systems have been proposed by several researchers in the past. Such models should ideally be verified by fault simulation at the logic gate level. Most functional models proposed by other researchers earlier have been based on what appeared to be realistic and have also not been supported by detailed logic level fault simulations. Since we do not have a gate level implementation of the network at the present, we have also decided to propose some fault models which appear to be reasonable at the functional level.

We first model the effects of faults in switches in the forward direction. Finally, we will consider the effects of faults in switches in the reverse direction as well.

Assumption 1: A faulty switching element or a link in an intermediate stage of the network will result in one of the following in the forward direction: 1) incorrect messages (data or address portion) coming out of one or more output ports of the switch, 2) change in the order of messages, 3) extra messages coming out of one or more output ports, 4) lost messages at one or more output ports.

Discussion: A switching element in an intermediate stage of the network for the forward direction consists of four decoders and four sets of controlling logic for the four output ports, each consisting of four IN queues, four CHUTE queues, and an OUT queue which move synchronously.

Case 1. Faulty Decoder for Input Port i: Let us denote the IN queue corresponding to input port i at the output port j of a switch as $IN_{i,j}$. Then under a decoder fault, a message destined for $IN_{i,j}$ will be sent to

1) $IN_{i,k}$, where $j <> k$, i.e., a different IN queue from the desired one. In this case, the output port k gets an extra message and output port j gets one less message.

2) $IN_{i,j} + IN_{i,k} + \cdots + IN_{i,l}$, i.e., a set of IN queues in addition to the desired one. In this case, the output ports k, $\cdots$, l all get extra messages.

3) $IN_{i,k} + \cdots + IN_{i,l}$, i.e., a set of IN queues other than the desired one. In this case, the output port j gets one less message, and the other ports get extra messages.

4) null queue, i.e., the message is lost.

Case 2. Faulty Logic for an Output Port: Clearly, the fault could result in the corruption of the data or address portion of the message if the fault is in the data path. If the fault is in the control, such as an incorrect scheduling of messages, or improper movement of the queues, it would result in creation of an extra message, deletion of a message, or a change in the order in which the messages came out of the ports; the latter can be viewed as corrupted messages. □

Assumption 2: A faulty module in a switching element in stage 0 of the network will affect only one output port of the switch by either corrupting messages, or creating extra messages, or deleting messages in the forward direction.

Discussion: We mentioned in Section III-B that a logical switch in stage 0 actually corresponds to four physical 4×1 modules, only one of which can become faulty. Each such module controls one output port; hence, a faulty module can only cause corrupted messages, extra messages or lost messages in only one output port of a stage 0 switch. □

Assumption 3: A faulty module in a switching element of the last stage (stage n) of the network will affect only one copy of a message in the forward direction.

Discussion: We mentioned in Section III-C that a logical switch in stage n corresponds to four physical 1×4 modules, each of which is a decoder. A faulty decoder can produce one of the fault effects listed in Assumption 1. For a network having a fault in the last stage, the rest of the network is fault-free; hence, all four copies of the message arrive at the four decoders at the same time. A faulty decoder will therefore affect only one copy. As a result, one MNI will receive three copies, and the other MNI's may receive one copy incorrectly. □

Theorem 5: Under a single fault in the network, at least three copies of all messages move synchronously in the forward direction.

Proof: We will consider three cases of the location of the fault, first in a switch in stage 0, next in a switch in stage n, and finally, in a switch in an intermediate stage.

Case 1. Fault in a Switch in Stage 0: From Assumption 2, a fault in this stage causes only one copy of a message to be either lost, delayed, or move ahead of the rest of the copies when leaving the first stage. The remaining three copies exit the stage 0 simultaneously.

Case 2. Fault in a Switch in Stage n: From Assumption 3, a fault in a switch in this stage causes only one copy to move asynchronously. The remaining three copies arrive synchronously at the MNI.

Case 3. Fault in a Switch in an Intermediate Stage: If the fault exists in a switch in stage i; then all switches are correctly operational for stages 0 through $i - 1$. Hence, the Lemmas 1, 2, 3, and 4 and Theorem 1 are valid up to stage $i - 1$. Messages in all four output ports of the faulty switch in stage i might get lost, delayed, or move ahead. However, from Lemma 1, we note that the four copies of any particular message enter different switches in stage i. Therefore, the faulty switch is going to affect only one copy of any message. We prove this more formally below.

From the proof of Lemma 2 we noted that the path of a message originating at processor A for destination X can be traced by selecting an m-bit window at each stage from the concatenated source and destination address bits with an extra two bits to represent the extra stage:

$$a_0 a_1 \cdots a_{m-1} ** x_0 x_1 \cdots x_{m-1}$$

where ** denotes 00, 01, 10, or 11, and identifies the particular copy of a message. The most significant $m - 2$ bits in the window of a message specify the address of the switch in a particular stage, which always has the subfield ** corresponding to the specific copy of the message. The least significant two bits in the m-bit window specify the output port address within the switch.

The addresses of the output port of a switch in stage i for the four copies of the message in a fault-free environment are

$$a_{2i+2} \cdots a_{m-1} ** x_0 \cdots x_{2i-2} x_{2i-1}$$

where the ** corresponds to 00, 01, 10, 11, respectively, for the four copies of the message.

Let us also consider the concatenated addresses of four copies of two other messages, (B, Y) and (C, Z) which are, respectively,

$$b_{2i+2} \cdots b_{m-1} ** y_0 \cdots y_{2i-2} y_{2i-1}$$

and

$$c_{2i+2} \cdots c_{m-1} ** z_0 \cdots z_{2i-2} z_{2i-1}.$$

For all these messages to enter a particular switch, the $m - 2$ most significant bits have to be identical. Note that this property is still valid for the faulty network since the stages 0 through $i - 1$ are fault-free. Hence, $a_{2i+2} = b_{2i+2} = c_{2i+2}$, etc. Knowing the location of the faulty switch, the appropriate two bits of the extra stage address ** can be determined. Let the two bits be denoted by FF. Hence, this faulty switch received as inputs only copy FF of all messages. Again since the network is fault-free until stage $i - 1$, this property is valid.

Let us now consider the output ports with address $x_{2i-2} x_{2i-1}$ of the faulty switch FF in the stage i, and the three corresponding switches whose $m - 2$ bit addresses are identical to the above except for the two bits corresponding to **. Each of the remaining fault-free switches has d messages waiting in the output queues, i.e., the messages are supposed to incur a delay of d cycles. Hence, those three copies of the message exit stage i simultaneously. From the fault model of Assumption 2, if there is a fault in the output port of a switch, that copy of the message will observe either a smaller or a larger delay, or will get lost. Since the other copies of the message do not intersect any switches or links in the path of this faulty message, the other copies of the message will proceed synchronously through the rest of the network.

Let us now consider the effect of the incorrect propagation of message (A, X) on other messages. We noted earlier that two messages will meet at an output port of a switch if the m-bit windows of the concatenated source and destination addresses are identical. Let us assume that because of a decoder fault in the switch in stage i, the message originally targeted for output port $x_{2i-2} x_{2i-1}$ ends up in output port $\overline{x_{2i-2}}\overline{x_{2i-1}}$, where $\overline{x_{2i-2}}$ and $\overline{x_{2i-1}}$ may or may not equal x_{2i-2} and x_{2i-1}. Then a message (B, Y) supposed to go through the output port $x_{2i-2} x_{2i-1}$ at a later time will suffer one cycle less delay since there is one less message in the output queue. Conversely, the message (C, Z) originally intended to go through output port $\overline{x_{2i-2}}\overline{x_{2i-1}}$ of the switch FF will incur one cycle extra delay because of the extra message in the output port queue. Note, however, that only copy FF of both messages (B, Y) and (C, Z) gets affected by greater or lesser than normal delays. The other three copies will proceed synchronously.

Effect on Subsequent Fault-Free Stages: Let us finally consider the effect of the messages going through the faulty switch on subsequent stages of fault-free switches in the network. All switches in the network can be classified into four disjoint classes, 00, 01, 10, 11, depending on the two-bit field (corresponding to the extra stage) in the m-bit window of the concatenated source and destination addresses. The faulty switch (which has to be of one of four classes, 00, 01, 10, 11, depending on the copy of the message passing through the switch) can potentially affect all four output posts by inserting extra delays, less delays, or removing messages in those ports. However, each of the four ports will go into a different switching element of the next stage of the same class. Assuming that these switches are fault-free, only one output port of the switch will be affected by the corrupted message in the form of extra/reduced delay. Hence, only one copy of any message $(D, Z)^0$ passing through the appropriate output port will be affected. The other three copies of the message, $(D, Z)^1$, $(D, Z)^2$, and $(D, Z)^3$, which pass through switches of the other classes, will proceed synchronously.

Theorem 6: In a network with a single faulty switch in the forward direction, at least three copies of a message will combine and proceed synchronously if one of the uncorrupted copies combines. The corrupted copy may or may not combine.

Proof: This property can be proved in a similar manner by following the proofs of Theorems 2 and 5. □

Theorem 7: In a network with a single faulty switch, at least three copies of a message will proceed synchronously in the forward direction in the presence of finite buffers.

Proof: This property can be proved in a similar manner to Theorems 4 and 5. □

Theorem 8: In a network with a single faulty switch, at least three copies of a message proceed synchronously in the reverse direction.

Proof: In the following, we give an outline of the proof because a rigorous and detailed proof will be quite long. Also, most of the results can be derived from the lemmas and theorems that were proved for the movement of messages in the forward direction in the presence of faults. In Section III-D, we mentioned that a switching element in an intermediate stage of the network for the reverse direction consists of identical circuitry such as a decoder for each input port in the reverse direction, and IN queues and OUT queues corresponding to each of the four output ports in reverse direction. In addition, there will be four local content addressable memories (CAM) in each switch, one per output port, for storing temporary variables during combining in the forward direction that are needed during decombining in the reverse direction. We consider functional fault models for each block. Clearly, the fault in decoders and output port logic (IN queues and OUT queues) in the reverse direction can result in the

corruption of the data or address portion of the message if the fault is in the data path. If the fault is in the control, such as an incorrect scheduling of messages, or improper movement of the queues, it would result in the creation of extra messages, deletion of messages, or incorrect ordering of messages; the latter can be viewed as corrupted messages. A fault in the CAM can cause corruption of data in all four output ports in the reverse direction since it is possible to decombine a message when it should not be done, or vice versa. It can also give rise to extra or less delays in messages or lost messages at all the output ports.

By concatenating the source and destination addresses of messages in the reverse direction and by performing a similar analysis as the one in the forward direction for the identification of switching elements and output ports by viewing a sliding m-bit window, it can be shown that a single faulty switching element can only affect one copy of any message. The other three copies proceed simultaneously and decombine simultaneously in the reverse direction. □

VI. ANALYSIS AND SIMULATION OF NETWORK

By sending four copies of a message instead of one, the network traffic has definitely increased fourfold. This is a penalty that one has to pay for obtaining increased reliability using our scheme. In actual parallel processor implementations such as the RP3, the network traffic through the combining network is not very high because there are separate combining and noncombining networks. Messages that are potential candidates for combining are sent through the combining network, the others through the noncombining network.

Suppose the probability of a message request generated by a processor is p. Then, the probability of a request arriving at stage 1 of the network is $4p$ since each message is replicated four times in stage 0 of the network. If p is less than 0.25, then the switching elements will have finite queue lengths. In a machine such as the IBM RP3 [5], the fetch-and-add instructions are routed to the combining network and all other instructions to the noncombining network. Of all the requests generated by a processor, since the percentage of fetch-and-add instructions is less than 25 percent [21], the increase in traffic by a factor of four may be justified.

To evaluate the performance of the network accurately under the increased traffic, we performed a simple analysis and some detailed simulations.

A. Analytical Modeling

Buffered packet-switching interconnection networks have been analytically studied by several researchers [22]–[25]. We will use a similar approach to model our network and derive analytical expressions for the queue lengths and message delays. We will derive some expressions without combining because it becomes very complicated otherwise.

Consider the buffered 4×4 switch described in Section III-A where there are four IN queues of infinite length for each of the four output ports, such that each port can receive up to four requests per cycle. The scheduling discipline described in

Section III-A satisfies two conditions: 1) if a message M arrives at a port at a particular cycle t, *all* messages that arrived in that port in cycles $<t$ will be serviced before M. 2) If between one to four messages arrive at the same cycle at the same output port, they will be served in the order of their input port addresses. Messages having source addresses such that the input port addresses that are low will be serviced earlier than messages having input port addresses that are high. Since we are trying to estimate statistical averages for various parameters, we will assume that all sources are equally likely to generate messages; hence, on the average, all messages will have an equal share of low and high address labels. In practice, the probability distributions of the delays incurred by messages from various sources will not be exactly uniform, but will be skewed such that messages from lower address sources incur less delay than higher address sources. However, because of condition 1, the distributions will not be grossly skewed. In our analysis, we will model the first and not the second condition.

In a previous analysis of buffered packet-switching networks by other researchers [24], two timing parameters were introduced:

1) t_c was defined to be the cycle time of the switch, i.e., the interval between successive packet intervals, 2) t_τ was defined to be the transit time of a packet from one switch to the next one when the buffers in the path are empty.

In our network, because of the synchronous operation, $t_c = t_\tau$. In general, the transit time for a packet P through a switch is $t_\tau + b \cdot t_c$, where b is the number of packets with the same destination address as P that arrived before P, or arrived at the same time as P but transmitted before P. Even though the servicing of such packets in our network is deterministic, for our analysis we assume that it is random. If at each cycle, a packet arrives at each input of a $k \times k$ switch with probability p satisfying the Bernoulli distribution, then the average number of queueing cycles for a packet (average length of a queue) is

$$c_{\mathrm{av}} = \frac{(1-1/k)p}{2(1-p)} .$$

The average transit time of a packet through a $k \times k$ switch is

$$t_k = t_\tau + t_c \frac{(1-1/k)p}{2(1-p)} .$$

These results have been proved in [24], subject to the following assumptions.

1) Each switch has infinite queues.
2) Message arrivals are independent Bernoulli processes.
3) Memory references are uniformly distributed over all memory modules.

In our network, we assume that the processors generate requests with probability p per cycle of the network. Since stage 0 of the network effectively makes four copies of every message, the resultant probability of message generation becomes $4p$ for switches in stage 0. Assuming uniform network flow, we expect the probability of arrival of messages at input ports of switches in stages 1 through n to be the same,

i.e., $4p$. The last stage of the network receives all four copies of the message simultaneously which are all directed to the same output port. Since the results are voted upon immediately, the queue length for stage n is zero, and the message propagation delay is t_c. The resultant total transit time for a packet through the network is the delay expression shown above, modified for probability $4p$, and multiplied by n for the first n stages, plus the delay in the last stage.

$$T = n \cdot \left(t_c + t_c \cdot \frac{(1-1/4)4p}{2(1-4p)} \right) + t_c.$$

B. Simulation

In practice, messages may arrive quite randomly or may arrive in groups. Traces of large parallel applications show that memory references may be localized instead of being uniformly distributed. Hence, it is necessary to simulate the network to be able to correctly estimate the performance of an interconnection network for a given multiprocessor system.

In view of the above, a simulator for the network was developed with the following objectives:

1) verify the correctness of the proposed design,
2) model different message generation distributions, such as Bernoulli, binomial, geometric, etc.
3) determine the optimal size of queues as a function of the network traffic for different message generation distributions,
4) determine the network delay as a function of the network traffic for different message generation distributions,
5) study the effect of combining messages,
6) model faults in the network.

We developed a general network simulator in Path Pascal, a concurrent programming language developed at the University of Illinois, running on a SUN 3/50 workstation under UNIX. The exact scheduling of the switches was modeled. The simulator allowed a processor to generate several requests before its previous requests are serviced. The message arrivals were modeled as a Bernoulli distribution for various message generation rates (network loads). Both an individual switching element and the complete network were simulated.

C. Switch Simulation

Simulation of a single switching element was carried out and movement of messages in each phase of a cycle was noted. Messages with the same destination address were introduced and combining of messages was verified. It was found that even if two messages with the same destination existed simultaneously in the switch, they may not necessarily combine due to the manner in which the IN queues and OUT queues move in different phases. Whether or not two messages with the same destination address combine depends upon three conditions:

1) the number of messages waiting in the OUT queue as well as the IN queues,
2) the number of cycles after which the second message enters the switch with respect to the first message,
3) the positions of two messages, msg 1 and msg 2 with respect to each other in the different IN queues, as well as with respect to messages that arrived before msg 1.

All possible combinations of two messages with the same destination were introduced in the switch and the above three parameters were varied. Our studies indicated that combining of two messages occurred in over 65 percent of the cases where they could possibly combine.

D. Fault-Free Network Simulation

We next simulated a complete fault-free network for connecting 64 processors to 64 memory modules in the presence of the scheduling disciplines. Owing to computing time and storage limitations, networks of larger size were not simulated because the next higher size of the network for which our scheme is directly applicable is $N = 256$. Also, we feel that the network simulation for $N = 64$ demonstrated all the concepts.

From the simulations, it was verified that the proposed design is correct. Simulation of the complete network confirmed that all four copies of every message exit/enter each stage of the network simultaneously. The simulation was carried out using independent Bernoulli message generation distributions for different rates. The destination module for every message was selected randomly from a uniform distribution. The mean, standard deviation, variance, maximum and minimum values of the length of the OUT queue, and the delay in number of cycles were then determined as a function of the probability. It is generally not enough to have a small average delay for messages in a parallel machine; highly variant return times will impede performance. Hence, we computed the standard deviation in addition to the average of each parameter.

The total simulation time was 500 cycles. In calculating the statistics, the first 100 cycles were ignored to counter the effect of startup and to let the network reach a reasonably steady state.

Table II shows the results of simulations assuming that messages are randomly generated by $N = 64$ processors independently satisfying the Bernoulli distribution. We chose the Bernoulli distribution for its simplicity and because of its memoryless (Markov) property which has been used by numerous researchers in analytically modeling the behavior of computer systems. For every simulation cycle, a random number between 0 and 1 was generated for each source (processor) using the randomizing function in Path Pascal. If the number was less than p, the parameter of the Bernoulli distribution, then a message was generated for a random destination port from a uniform distribution. The maximum OUT queue length was set to 25, and the simulations were performed using finite buffer sizes. The first column shows the parameter p of the Bernoulli distribution which is the probability of a processor generating a request in a particular cycle. The next four columns show the minimum, maximum, average, and the variance of the OUT queue length of any switch between stages 0 and $n - 1$. The length of the OUT queues in the switches in the last stage of the network can never be greater than one. Hence, statistics are taken for OUT queues in stages 0 through $n - 1$ only. From the design of the 4×4 switches in Section III-A, it is clear that it may be possible to have some packets in the IN and CHUTE queues in

TABLE II
SIMULATION RESULTS FOR BERNOULLI DISTRIBUTION

p	OUT queue length				Messages per port				Network delay			
	min	max	avg	sd	min	max	avg	sd	min	max	avg	sd
0.250	0	12	2.10	1.89	0	20	2.87	2.94	5	30	13.86	4.40
0.200	0	8	1.27	1.09	0	16	1.59	1.61	5	20	9.83	2.53
0.166	0	5	0.97	0.97	0	12	1.16	1.38	5	18	8.64	1.98
0.125	0	5	0.68	0.87	0	11	0.79	1.17	5	14	7.71	1.63
0.100	0	5	0.52	0.79	0	11	0.59	1.04	5	14	7.39	1.51

addition to the OUT queues waiting to be serviced by a particular output port. Columns 6–9 show the minimum, maximum, average, and variance of the total number of packets waiting to be serviced at any output port of a switch (IN queues, CHUTE queues, and OUT queue) in stages 0 through $n - 1$. Columns 10–13 show the minimum, maximum, average, and variance of the delay incurred by a packet.

Table III shows a comparison of results obtained from our analytical modeling and the simulation results assuming a Bernoulli distribution for message generation for a 64×64 network. We could not theoretically estimate the OUT queue length because the theoretical models were too complicated for closed form solutions. From the table, it can be seen that there is moderate agreement between our analytical and simulation results.

E. Fault Simulation

The network was simulated with a single fault introduced in the network. The simulation was carried out for a random set of cases representing each of the following cases for a 64×64 network:

1) faulty links between stages,
2) faulty 4×1 module of a switch in stage 0,
3) faulty switch in stage 1 of the network,
4) faulty switch in stage 2 of the network,
5) faulty 1×4 module in stage 3 of the network.

All types of faults listed in Assumptions 1, 2, and 3 were simulated for various network loads, $p = 0.1, 0.125, 0.166, 0.2,$ and $0.25,$ and the simulations were carried out over 500 cycles for each case. The simulation of the network in the presence of single faults confirmed that for messages whose one copy passed through the faulty switch/link, the three other copies of the messages arrived simultaneously at three of the four input ports of the same switch of the last stage. In addition, it was confirmed that for those messages that did not pass through the faulty switch/link but visited the same switch as the faulty message (i.e., the message that passed through the faulty switch/link) in a subsequent stage, three copies of those messages arrived simultaneously at the last stage of the network.

VII. Overhead in Fault-Tolerant Network

It is difficult to quantify exactly the overhead involved in achieving the fault tolerance using the design proposed in this

TABLE III
COMPARISON OF RESULTS OF ANALYSIS FOR BERNOULLI DISTRIBUTION

Request Prob..	Analytical Results		Simulation Results	
p	Avg. messages per port	Avg. network delay	Avg. messages per port	Avg. network delay
0.250	Infinity	Infinity	2.87	13.86
0.200	1.5	8.5	1.59	9.83
0.167	0.75	6.3	1.16	8.64
0.125	0.38	5.1	0.79	7.71
0.100	0.25	4.8	0.59	7.39
0	0	4.0	0	4.0

paper without carrying out a complete design. The latter was clearly beyond the scope of this research. In the following, we provide a rough idea of the overhead by counting the number of extra switches and links required in this scheme, a measure that is used widely by other researchers in the comparison of fault-tolerant interconnection networks [8], [13], [12], [19]. For a network connecting N processors and memories, where N is a power of four, i.e., $N = 4^n$, the number of 4×4 switches in the nonredundant network is $(N/4) \cdot n$. In the redundant network proposed in this paper, there are three types of switches of varying complexities. Stage 0 has N switches of the type 4×1, stage n has N switches of the type 1×4, and stages 1 through $n - 1$ have $(N/4) \cdot (n - 1)$ switches of type 4×4. If we simply count the number of extra switches in the redundant network, the hardware overhead counting switches becomes $= 7N/4$. The relative hardware overhead counting switches (ratio of extra switches to original number of switches) becomes $= 7/\log_4 (N))$.

However, we note that each 4×4 switch is four times as complex as a 4×1 switch, or a 1×4 switch in terms of gate counts. Hence, the hardware overhead counting gates becomes $= 7N$. The relative hardware overhead counting gates becomes $1/n = 1/\log_4 (N)$.

If we count links, the number of links in the original nonredundant network is $(n + 1) \cdot N$. The number of links in the redundant network between stages 1 and $n - 1$ is $(n - 1) \cdot N$. Stage 0 receives $4 \cdot N$ links as input, and stage n provides $4N$ links as outputs. Hence, the hardware overhead counting links is $8N$. The relative overhead counting links therefore becomes $8/(n + 1)$.

Calculation of the time overhead has to be done by estimating the extra message delays in the network under varying network loads. For simplicity, we use our models of network delays assuming infinite queues for various levels of the probability of message generation, p. For a normal interconnection network without fault tolerance with number of stages, $n = \log_4 (N)$, the network delay in the forward direction assuming a probability of request generation p is

$$T_{\text{reg}} = n \cdot \left(t_c + t_c \cdot \frac{(1 - 1/4)4p}{2(1 - p)} \right) .$$

The expression for the delay in our proposed fault-tolerant scheme was shown to be

$$T_{\text{FT}} = n \cdot \left(t_c + t_c \cdot \frac{(1 - 1/4)4p}{2(1 - 4p)} \right) + t_c .$$

The time overhead ratio in the presence of queueing delays is $(T_{\text{FT}} - T_{\text{Reg}})/T_{\text{Reg}}$.

Table IV shows the variation of the time overhead using these simple models for varying network loads for $N = 256$, assuming the cycle time $t_c = 1$. It is clear that our network saturates much quicker and gives very high delay overheads for loads greater than 20 percent. However, as we had mentioned earlier in this section, we assume that such a combining network will be used in conjunction with a noncombining network. Of all the requests generated by a processor, only the fetch-and-add instructions (whose fraction is less than 20 percent) will be sent to the combining network. Hence, in the region of interest for network loads less than 20 percent, the delay overheads may be acceptable (less than 30 percent).

Although our scheme assumes complex 4×4 switches, we make the following observations to show that the complexity might be acceptable. One has to be willing to incur extra complexity in order to support combining in a network switching element. The 2×2 ultraswitch [20] which could support two-way combining was reported to be about 6–32 times more complex than a simple 2×2 switch without combining [26]. We are proposing the use of 4×4 switches that can support four-way combining and is therefore about four times as complex as the ultraswitch. Note that this is purely an architectural decision regarding whether one wishes to take advantage of VLSI technology to implement a four-way combining 4×4 switch instead of a two-way combining 2×2 switch in one VLSI chip in order to reduce the overall chip count for the network. The *only additional requirement* that we are proposing to use in the fault tolerant network is the *logic for synchronous scheduling* which requires little extra overhead over a normal 4×4 switch that can support a four-way combining for which there needs to exist several comparators, adders, multiplexers, and CAM's anyway. In VLSI technology, a queue can be implemented by a shift

Request Prob. (percent)	Normal network delay (cycles)	Redundant network delay (cycles)	Overhead (percent)
0.0	4.00	5.00	25.0
2.5	4.04	5.06	25.2
5.0	4.08	5.13	25.6
7.5	4.12	5.21	26.5
10.0	4.17	5.33	28.0
12.5	4.21	5.5	30.5
15.0	4.26	5.75	34.8
17.5	4.32	6.17	42.8
20.0	4.38	7.0	60.0
22.5	4.43	9.5	114.2
25.0	4.5	Infinity	Infinity
50.0	5.5	Infinity	Infinity
100.0	Infinity	Infinity	Infinity

register [27]. This design has also been used in the NYU ultraswitch [20]. Our scheme needs some globally synchronous clock across the interconnection network. Such clocking is used in synchronizing large systolic arrays [28]. Although we have not performed a detailed design of the proposed 4 × 4 switches for the intermediate stages of the network, we believe that it should be possible to implement all the logic for a 4 × 4 combining switch with the scheduling discipline in a single VLSI chip. The design of the 4 × 1 switches and 1 × 4 switches in the first and last stages of the network is considerably simpler.

Our scheme of fault tolerance is definitely much less expensive than using four copies of the network (where the switches also have to support combining) for providing single error correction and double error detection which requires an overhead of at least 300 percent in hardware with no time overhead. Note, however, that the replicated network can handle a higher bandwidth. It is a matter of trading off the hardware overhead for a performance overhead.

VIII. Reliability Improvements

In this section, we use simple probabilistic models to show the improvement of the reliability of the network using our scheme. We assume that the failure rate of a 4 × 4 switch is exponential with a failure rate of λ_{44}. We include the effect of a faulty link in the fault model of the output port of the switch, so that we need not explicitly consider the effects of faulty links in the analysis. The reliability of a single 4 × 4 switch is

$$R_{44} = e^{-\lambda_{44} t}.$$

For the nonredundant system to be operational, all the $(N/4) \cdot n$ switches must be operational. The reliability of the normal nonredundant network is

$$R_{normal} = (R_{44})^{(N/4) \cdot n}.$$

The redundant network has N switches of type 4 × 1 (having an exponential failure rate λ_{41}) for the first stage, $N/4$ switches of type 4 × 4 (having failure rate λ_{44}) in the intermediate stages, and N switches of type 1 × 4 (having failure rate λ_{14}) in the last stage. The reliability of a single 4 × 1 switch is

$$R_{41} = e^{-\lambda_{41} t}.$$

The reliability of a single 1 × 4 switch is

$$R_{14} = e^{-\lambda_{14} t}.$$

Our scheme can tolerate a single faulty switch in any stage. Hence, the reliability expression of the redundant network is a sum of four expressions which represent four disjoint sets of events.

The first term corresponds to no faults in any switch in the network.

$$R_{term\ 1} = (R_{41})^N \cdot (R_{44})^{(N/4) \cdot (n-1)} \cdot (R_{14})^N.$$

The second term corresponds to tolerance of a single fault in only stage 0; no faults in stages 1 through n.

$$R_{term\ 2} = [N \cdot (R_{41})^{N-1} \cdot (1 - R_{41})]$$
$$\cdot [(R_{44})^{(N/4) \cdot (n-1)}] \cdot [(R_{14})^N].$$

The third term corresponds to tolerance of a single fault in only one of switches in stages 1 through $n - 1$; no faults in stages 0 or n.

$$R_{term\ 3} = [(R_{41})^N] \cdot [(N/4) \cdot (n-1) \cdot (R_{44})^{((N/4) \cdot (n-1)-1)}$$
$$\cdot (1 - R_{44})] \cdot [(R_{14})^N].$$

The fourth term corresponds to tolerance of a single fault in only stage n; no faults in stages 0 through $n - 1$.

$$R_{term\ 4} = [(R_{41})^N] \cdot [(R_{44})^{(N/4) \cdot (n-1)}]$$
$$\cdot [N \cdot (R_{14})^{N-1} \cdot (1 - R_{14})].$$

The reliability of the redundant fault tolerant network is

$$R_{FT} = R_{term\ 1} + R_{term\ 2} + R_{term\ 3} + R_{term\ 4}.$$

Fig. 8 shows the reliability curves for the nonredundant network and the corresponding fault-tolerant network for $N = 64$ (hence $n = 3$). We assumed that $\lambda_{44} = 0.04$ failures per time unit, and $\lambda_{14} = \lambda_{41} = 0.01$ failures per time unit. The failure rate for the 1 × 4 and 4 × 1 switches were chosen as one-fourth of the failure rate of a 4 × 4 switch since they are one-fourth as complex.

IX. Summary and Conclusions

This paper has proposed a technique for achieving fault tolerance in a multistage interconnection network capable of supporting the fetch-and-add and similar combining primitives. The basic idea involves the addition of an extra stage in a network consisting of 4 × 4 switching elements, thereby creating four disjoint paths between every source–destination pair. Four copies of every message are sent through the network simultaneously, and the results are voted upon at the end, thereby providing single error correction and double error detection. In a buffered multistage interconnection network, in the presence of multiple messages and conflicts, different copies of a message may get delayed by different amounts; hence, the four copies may not arrive simultaneously at the output to allow the voting. It was shown in this paper that by using the property of the omega network, and a rigorous scheduling discipline, it is possible to enforce that all four

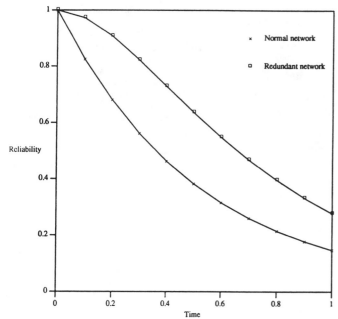

Fig. 8. Reliability curves for normal and redundant network for $N = 64$. $\lambda_{44} = 0.04$, $\lambda_{41} = 0.01$, $\lambda_{14} = 0.01$.

copies arrive simultaneously at the output for a fault-free network. For a network with a single faulty switching element or link, at least three copies arrive simultaneously at the output. The scheduling discipline, the design of the switching elements to support the discipline, and the theoretical proof of the correctness of the design constitute the key contributions of this paper.

We also proposed an analytical model for estimating various network parameters such as packet queue lengths and network latencies as a function of the workload. We verified the results of the analytical modeling with detailed simulations using a network simulator that we have developed.

We have shown that the proposed design for fault tolerance is more cost effective than the brute-force technique of having multiple copies of the network.

Future research involves extending the proposed design to a lower level of implementation. This would give an estimate of the area required to implement a 4×4 switching element in a single chip or several chips using VLSI technology. From our analytical and simulations results of the performance of the network, we have obtained the necessary design parameters for the chip design, such as the maximum length of various queues as a function of the probability of request generation. We would then be able to estimate the speed of the switching elements and the latency in the network.

ACKNOWLEDGMENT

The authors are extremely grateful to the anonymous referees for pointing out some technical deficiencies in the initial versions of the paper and for making numerous suggestions for improving the general quality of presentation.

REFERENCES

[1] J. T. Swartz, "Ultracomputers," *ACM TOPLAS*, pp. 484–521, 1980.

[2] A. Borodin and J. E. Hopcroft, "Routing, merging and sorting on parallel models of computation," in *Proc. 14th Annu. ACM Symp. Theory Comput.*, 1982, pp. 338–344.

[3] H. S. Stone, "Database applications of the fetch-and-add instruction," *IEEE Trans. Comput.*, vol. C-33, pp. 604–612, July 1984.

[4] A. Gottlieb, R. Grishman, C. P. Kruskal, K. P. McAuliffe, L. Rudolph, and M. Snir, "The NYU Ultracomputer—Designing an MIMD shared memory parallel computer," *IEEE Trans. Comput.*, vol. C-32, pp. 175–189, Feb. 1983.

[5] G. F. Pfister, W. C. Brantley, D. A. George, S. L. Harvey, W. J. Kleinfelder, K. P. McAuliffe, E. A. Melton, V. A. Norton, and J. Weiss, "The IBM Research Parallel Processor Prototype (RP3): Introduction and architecture," in *Proc. Int. Conf. Parallel Processing*, 1985, pp. 764–771.

[6] D. H. Lawrie, "Access and alignment of data in an array processor," *IEEE Trans. Comput.*, vol. C-24, pp. 1145–1155, Dec. 1975.

[7] J. E. Lilienkamp, D. H. Lawrie, and P. Yew, "A fault tolerant interconnection network using error correcting codes," in *Proc. Int. Conf. Parallel Processing*, 1982, pp. 123–125.

[8] G. B. Adams, III and H. J. Siegel, "The extra stage cube: A fault tolerant interconnection network for supersystems," *IEEE Trans. Comput.*, vol. C-31, May 1982.

[9] C. L. Wu, T. Y. Feng, and M. C. Lin, "STAR: A local network system for real-time management of imagery data," *IEEE Trans. Comput.*, vol. C-31, pp. 923–933, Oct. 1982.

[10] R. J. McMillen and H. J. Siegel, "Routing schemes for augmented data manipulator network in an MIMD system," *IEEE Trans. Comput.*, vol. C-31, pp. 1202–1214, Dec. 1982.

[11] N-F Tzeng, P-C Yew, and C-Q Zhu, "A fault tolerant scheme for multistage interconnection networks," in *Proc. 12th Int. Conf. Computer Architecture*, June 1985, pp. 368–375.

[12] V. P. Kumar and S. M. Reddy, "Design and analysis of fault-tolerant multistage interconnection networks with low link complexity," in *Proc. 12th Comput. Architecture Conf.*, 1985, pp. 376–386.

[13] C. S. Raghavendra and A. Varma, "INDRA: A class of interconnection networks with redundant paths," in *Proc. Real Time Syst. Symp.*, May 1984, pp. 153–165.

[14] C. Wu and T. Feng, "On a class of multistage interconnection networks," *IEEE Trans. Comput.*, vol. C-29, pp. 694–702, Aug. 1980.

[15] W. K. Fuchs, K. H. Huang, and J. A. Abraham, "Concurrent error detection in VLSI interconnection networks," in *Proc. 10th Int. Symp. Comput. Architecture*, Stockholm, Sweden, June 1983.

[16] R. K. Iyer and D. J. Rossetti, "Permanent CPU errors and system activity: Measurement and modelling," in *Proc. Real-Time Syst. Symp.*, 1983.

[17] X. Castillo, S. R. McConnel, and D. P. Siewiorek, "Derivation and calibration of a transient error reliability model," *IEEE Trans. Comput.*, vol. C-31, pp. 658–671, July 1982.

[18] J. Wakerly, *Error Detecting Codes, Self-Checking Circuits and Applications*. New York: Elsevier North Holland, 1978.

[19] K. Padmanabhan and D. H. Lawrie, "A class of redundant path multistage interconnection networks," *IEEE Trans. Comput.*, vol. C-32, pp. 1099–1108, Dec. 1983.

[20] M. Snir and J. Solworth, "The Ultraswitch—A VLSI network node for parallel processing," NYU Ultracomputer Note 39, 1982.

[21] A. Gottlieb, private communication.

[22] D. M. Dias and J. R. Jump, "Analysis and simulation of buffered delta networks," *IEEE Trans. Comput.*, vol. C-30, pp. 273–282, Apr. 1981.

[23] J. H. Patel, "Performance of processor memory interconnections for multiprocessors," *IEEE Trans. Comput.*, vol. C-30, pp. 771–780, Oct. 1981.

[24] C. Kruskal and M. Snir, "The performance of multistage interconnection networks for multiprocessors," *IEEE Trans. Comput.*, vol. C-32, pp. 1091–1098, Dec. 1983.

[25] C. P. Kruskal, M. Snir, and A. Weiss, "The distribution of waiting times in clocked multistage interconnection networks," in *Proc. Int. Parallel Processing Conf.*, Aug. 1986, pp. 12–19.

[26] G. F. Pfister and V. A. Norton, "Hot spot contention and combining in multistage interconnection networks," in *Proc. Int. Conf. Parallel Processing*, 1985, pp. 790–797.

[27] C. Mead and L. Conway, *Introduction to VLSI Systems*. Reading, MA: Addison-Wesley, 1980, pp. 263–292.

[28] A. L. Fisher and H. T. Kung, "Synchronizing large systolic arrays," *Real Time Signal Processing*, vol. 341, pp. 44–52, 1982.

Prithviraj Banerjee was born in Khartoum, Sudan, on July 17, 1960. He received the B.Tech. degree in electronics and electrical engineering from the Indian Institute of Technology, Kharagpur, in August 1981, and the M.S. and Ph.D. degrees in electrical engineering from the University of Illinois at Urbana-Champaign in December 1982 and December 1984, respectively.

He is currently Assistant Professor of Electrical and Computer Engineering and the Coordinated Science Laboratory at the University of Illinois at Urbana-Champaign. His research interests are in fault tolerance in multiprocessor systems, and parallel algorithms for VLSI design automation, and he is the author of over 30 research papers in these areas.

Dr. Banerjee was the recipient of the IBM Young Faculty Development Award in 1986, and the National Science Foundation's Presidential Young Investigators' Award in 1987.

Abhijeet Dugar (S'85–M'87) received the B.E. degree in electrical engineering from the University of Delhi, India, in 1984 and the M.S. degree in electrical engineering from the University of Illinois, Urbana–Champaign, in 1986.

Since August 1986, he has been working in the Design Automation Division of Texas Instruments Inc., Dallas, TX on logic and timing analysis of VLSI circuits. His research interests include design of algorithms for CAD tools, VLSI, computer architecture, fault-tolerance, and interconnection networks.

Fast Algorithms for Routing Around Faults in Multibutterflies and Randomly-Wired Splitter Networks

F. Thomson Leighton, *Member, IEEE*, and Bruce M. Maggs

Abstract—This paper describes simple deterministic $O(\log N)$-step algorithms for routing permutations of packets in multibutterflies and randomly-wired splitter networks. The algorithms are robust against faults (even in the worst case), and are efficient from a practical point of view. As a consequence, we find that the multibutterfly is an excellent candidate for a high-bandwidth low-diameter switching network underlying a shared-memory machine.

Index Terms—Fault tolerance, interconnection network, multibutterfly, multistage network, routing algorithm.

I. INTRODUCTION

NETWORKS derived from hypercubes form the architectural basis of most parallel computers, including machines such as the BBN Butterfly, the Connection Machine, the IBM RP3 and GF11, the Intel iPSC, and the NCUBE. The butterfly, in particular, is quite popular, and has been demonstrated to perform reasonably well in practice. An example of an 8-input butterfly is illustrated in Fig. 1. The nodes in this graph represent switches, and the edges represent wires. Each node in the network has a distinct label (r, l), where r is the row, and l is the level. In a butterfly with N inputs, the row is a $\log N$-bit binary number[1] and the level is an integer between 0 and $\log N$. The nodes on level 0 and $\log N$ are called the *inputs* and *outputs*, respectively. For $l < \log N$, a node labeled (r, l) is connected to nodes $(r, l+1)$ and $(r^l, l+1)$, where r^l denotes r with bit l complemented (bit 0 is the most significant, bit $\log N - 1$ the least).

The primary duty of the network in a parallel machine is to route messages between its processors and/or memory modules. In a butterfly, messages are typically sent from the switches on level 0, called the *inputs*, to those on level $\log N$, called the *outputs*. In a *one-to-one* routing problem, each input

Manuscript received July 9, 1991; revised December 14, 1991. This work was supported by the Defense Advanced Research Projects Agency under Contracts N00014-87-K-825 and N00014-89-J-1988, the Air Force under Contract OSR–89–0271, and the Army under Contract DAAL-03-86-K-0171. F. T. Leighton was supported by an NSF Presidential Young Investigator Award with matching funds provided by IBM and AT&T. A preliminary version of this paper appeared in the Proceedings of the 30th Annual Symposium on Foundations of Computer Science, October 1989, pp. 384–389.

F. T. Leighton is with the Mathematics Department and the Laboratory for Computer Science, Massachusetts Institute of Technology, Cambridge, MA 02139.

B. M. Maggs is with NEC Research Institute, Princeton, NJ 08540.

IEEE Log Number 9108210.

[1] Throughout this paper, $\log N$ denotes $\log_2 N$.

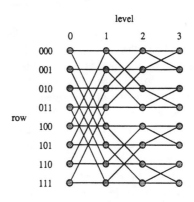

Fig. 1. An 8-input butterfly network.

is the origin of at most one message, and each output is the destination of a most one message. One-to-one routing is also called *permutation routing*. All of the algorithms discussed in this paper route messages in a *store-and-forward* fashion. A store-and-forward algorithm treats messages as indivisible objects. At each step, a message can either remain at a switch or move in its entirety from one switch to another across an edge, provided that no other messages use the same edge at that step. Store-and-forward routing is also called *packet switching*, and messages are often referred to as packets. A related paper [2] extends the results of this paper for a different method of routing called *circuit switching*.

One of the nice features of the butterfly is that there is a simple algorithm for finding a path of length $\log N$ from any input to any output. Upon reaching switch (r, l), $l < \log N$, a packet with destination $(R, \log N)$ compares r with R. If they are equal, the packet takes the edge to $(r, l+1)$. If not, it takes the edge to $(r^l, l+1)$. One problem with the butterfly is that this path is unique. As a consequence, if some switch or edge along the unique path from input i to output j (say) becomes congested or fails, then communication between input i and output j will be disrupted.

A. Dilated Butterflies

Because message congestion is a common occurrence in real networks, the wires in butterfly networks are typically *dilated*, so that each wire is replaced by a *channel* consisting of two or more wires. In a d-dilated butterfly, each channel consists of d wires. Because it is harder to congest a channel than it is to congest a single wire in a butterfly, dilated butterflies are better routing networks than simple butterflies [14], [16], [27].

B. Splitter Networks

Butterfly and dilated butterfly networks belong to a larger class of networks that are often referred to as *splitter networks*. The switches on each level of a splitter network can be partitioned into *blocks*. All of the switches on level 0 belong to the same block. On level 1, there are two blocks, one consisting of the switches that are in the upper $N/2$ rows, and the other consisting of the switches that are in the lower $N/2$ rows. In general, the switches in a block B of size $M = N/2^l$ on level l have neighbors in two blocks, B_u and B_l, on level $l + 1$, where u stands for *upper* and l for *lower*. The upper block, B_u, contains the switches on level $l + 1$ that are in the same rows as the upper $M/2$ switches of B. The lower block, B_l, consists of the switches that are in the same rows as the lower $M/2$ switches of B. The edges from B to B_u are called the *up* edges, and those from B to B_l are called the *down* edges. The three blocks, B, B_u, and B_l, and the edges between them are collectively called a *splitter*. The switches in B are called the *splitter inputs*, and those in B_u and B_l are called the *splitter outputs*. In a splitter network with *multiplicity d*, each splitter input is incident to d outgoing up edges and d outgoing down edges, and each splitter output is incident to $2d$ incoming edges. In a d-dilated butterfly, the d up (and d down) edges incident to each splitter input all lead to the same splitter output, but this need not be the case in general. For example, we have illustrated an 8-input splitter network with multiplicity 2 in Fig. 2.

In a splitter network, each input and output are connected by a single logical (up–down) path through the blocks of the network. For example, Fig. 3 shows the logical path from any input to output 011. In a butterfly, this logical path specifies a unique path through the network, since only one up and one down edge emanate from each switch. (In fact, a splitter network with multiplicity one is very similar to a delta network [17].) In a general splitter network with multiplicity d, however, each switch will have d up and d down edges, and each step of the logical path can be taken on any one of d edges. Hence, one logical path can be realized by a myriad of physical paths in a general splitter network.

C. Randomly-Wired Splitter Networks and Multibutterflies

In this paper, we are primarily concerned with randomly-wired splitter networks. A *randomly-wired splitter network* is a splitter network where the up and down edges within each splitter are chosen at random subject to the constraint that each splitter input is incident to d up and d down edges, and each splitter output is incident to $2d$ incoming edges.

The crucial property that randomly-wired splitter networks are likely to possess is known as *expansion*. In particular, an M-input splitter is said to have (α, β)-expansion if every set of $k \leq \alpha M$ inputs is connected to at least βk up outputs and βk down outputs, where $\alpha > 0$ and $\beta > 1$ are fixed constants. For example, see Fig. 4.

A splitter network is said to have (α, β)-*expansion* if all of its splitters have (α, β)-expansion. More simply, a splitter

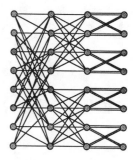

Fig. 2. An 8-input splitter network with multiplicity 2.

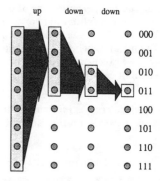

Fig. 3. The logical path from any input to output 011.

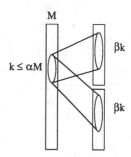

Fig. 4. An M-input splitter with (α, β)-expansion.

or a splitter network is said to have *expansion* if it has (α, β)-expansion for some constants $\alpha > 0$ and $\beta > 1$. A splitter network with expansion is more commonly known as a *multibutterfly* [29], and a *multibutterfly with (α, β)-expansion and multiplicity d* consists of splitters in which each splitter input is incident to d up and d down edges and for which any $k \leq \alpha M$ splitter inputs are adjacent to βk splitter outputs.

Splitters with expansion are known to exist for any $d \geq 3$, and they can be constructed deterministically in polynomial time [23], [11], [29], but randomized wirings typically provide the best possible expansion. In fact, the expansion of a randomly-wired splitter will be close to $d - 1$ with probability close to 1, provided that α is a sufficiently small constant. (For a discussion of the tradeoffs between α and β in randomly-wired splitters, see [20] and [29].)

A multibutterfly with (α, β)-expansion is good at routing because one must block βk splitter outputs in order to block k splitter inputs. In classical networks such as the butterfly, the reverse is true: it is possible to block $2k$ inputs by blocking only k outputs. When this effect is compounded over several levels, the effect is dramatic. In a butterfly, a single fault can block 2^l switches l levels back, whereas in a multibutterfly, it takes β^l faults to block a single switch l levels back.

In 1989, Upfal showed that any N-input multibutterfly can route any one-to-one problem in $O(\log N)$ steps using a simple greedy algorithm [29], and that, by using pipelining, any N-input multibutterfly can route $O(\log N)$ one-to-one problems in $O(\log N)$ steps. Although the proof is complicated and the constants hidden by the Big Oh notation are large, the result is important because the only previously known deterministic on-line linear-hardware $O(\log N)$-step packet routing algorithm [18] requires the use of the AKS sorting circuit [1] (which is even more complicated and has even larger constant factors).

D. Our Results

In this paper, we provide a substantially simpler analysis of the greedy routing algorithm on multibutterflies, and as a consequence, derive much smaller constant factors for the $O(\log N)$ time bound. The analysis uses a potential function argument that may eventually prove to be useful for other routing problems as well.

More importantly, we show that the multibutterfly is highly fault-tolerant. In particular, we prove that no matter how an adversary chooses f switches to fail, there will be at least $N - O(f)$ inputs and $N - O(f)$ outputs between which a simple variant of the greedy algorithm can route any $\log N$ permutations in $O(\log N)$ steps. Note that this is the best that we could hope for in general, since the adversary can always choose to isolate $\Omega(f)$ inputs and $\Omega(f)$ outputs by carefully selecting f faults. In the more commonly studied model of randomly located faults [10], [25], [26], we can do even better. For example, even if $\Theta(N \log N)$ faults are randomly-placed in the multibutterfly, with probability near 1, the network can still deterministically route a permutation on $\Theta(N)$ inputs and outputs. Thus, the multibutterfly becomes the first bounded-degree network known to be able to sustain large numbers of faults with only minimal degradation in performance.

We also consider the experimental performance of the algorithms for $N = 1024$ inputs. Interestingly, we find that randomly-wired splitter networks with multiplicity 2 outperform 2-dilated butterflies with equivalent hardware on random routing problems, even if the splitter network has 100 faults. On worst case routing problems such as transpose and bit reversal, the randomly-wired splitter networks perform substantially better than the dilated butterflies, which take $\Omega(\sqrt{N})$ steps. Hence, randomly-wired splitter networks appear to be good candidates for high-bandwidth, low-diameter switching networks underlying a shared-memory machine such as the BBN butterfly.

E. Related Work

Randomly-wired splitter networks and multibutterflies have appeared in a number of different contexts. In 1974, Bassalygo and Pinsker [3] used (randomly-wired) splitter networks with expansion to construct the first nonblocking network of size $O(N \log N)$ and depth $O(\log N)$. In 1980, Fahlman [7] proposed a randomly-wired network called the *Hashnet*. In 1989,

Upfal [29] studied splitter networks with expansion (which he called multibutterflies—a term attributed to Ron Fagin) and described a simple deterministic algorithm for routing in $O(\log N)$ steps on an N-input multibutterfly. In another paper, Arora, Leighton, and Maggs [2] developed a circuit-switching algorithm for multibutterfly and *multi-Beneš* networks and showed that the algorithm can be used to establish connections in a nonblocking fashion. Most recently, DeHon, Knight, and Minsky [5] designed a 64-processor switching network using a randomly-wired splitter network for processor to memory communications. Experimental work on randomly-wired splitter networks is described in [4], [5], [13], [15], and [21]. See also [8] and [6] for other applications in which expanders are used to tolerate faults.

F. Outline

The remainder of the paper is divided into four sections as follows. The analysis of greedy routing algorithms on multibutterflies without faults is described in Section II. In Section III, we describe how to route around faults in $O(\log N)$ steps. The experimental data are presented in Section IV.

II. ROUTING WITHOUT FAULTS

In this section, we describe several algorithms for routing packets in $O(\log N)$ steps on an N-input multibutterfly. We start by describing and analyzing Upfal's greedy algorithm for routing P permutations in Sections II-A and II-B. This duplicates the result of Upfal, except that the proof is simpler and the constants are better. In Section II-C, we describe variations of the algorithm that allow pipelining and queueing for which the constant factors in the $O(\log N)$ running time bound are substantially smaller. We conclude in Section II-D by mentioning some improvements to the network itself.

Throughout this section, we will assume that, unless stated otherwise, the multibutterflies we are working with have multiplicity d and (α, β)-expansion, where $d \geq 3$, α is an integral power of $1/2$, and $\beta > 1$.

A. The Algorithm

Upfal's greedy algorithm starts by partitioning the packets into *waves* so that at most one packet in each wave is destined for any set of L contiguous outputs, where L is a power of 2. One way to do this is to group packets into the same wave if they are in the same permutation and their destinations are congruent modulo L. If there are P permutations to be routed, this results in the formation of at most PL waves. In general, we will set $L \geq 1/2\alpha$ since then we will be guaranteed that at most $\lceil M/2L \rceil \leq \lceil \alpha M \rceil$ packets in any wave will ever pass through the up (or down) edges of any M-input splitter of the multibutterfly. Since M is a power of 2 and α is a power of $1/2$, αM is an integer unless $\alpha M < 1$, in which case $\lceil \alpha M \rceil = 1$. This will allow us to apply the (α, β)-expansion property to the set of inputs of any splitter occupied by the packets of a single wave at any time. (E.g., if k inputs of a splitter contain packets of a single wave that want to traverse up edges, then these inputs are connected to at least βk up outputs.) This is because packets going through the $M/2$ up (or $M/2$ down) splitter outputs can only be destined for the descendant set of $M/2$ contiguous multibutterfly outputs. For $\alpha M < 1$, an M-input splitter can receive at most one upward or downward destined packet, and we obtain expansion $d \geq \beta$. (Note that for $M/2 \leq d$, we can replace an M-input splitter with an $M \times M$ complete bipartite graph.)

The routing of the packets proceeds in stages, each stage consisting of an even and odd phase, and each phase consisting of $2d$ steps. In even phases, packets are sent from even levels to the next (odd) level, and in odd phases, packets are sent from the odd levels to the next (even) level. The edges within each splitter are colored with $2d$ colors so that exactly one edge of each color is incident on each input and exactly one edge of each color is incident on each output. In each phase, we process the colors in sequence, one step per color. For each color, we move a packet forward along an edge with that color if there is a packet in the switch at the tail of the edge that wants to go in that direction (up or down) and if there is no packet in the switch at the head of the edge. Alternatively, if there is a packet in the switch at the head of the edge and if it is in a later wave than the packet at the tail of the edge, then the two packets are swapped, so that the packet in the earlier wave moves forward. Note that every switch processes and/or contains at most one packet at any step.

If there is only one permutation to route, then each input of the multibutterfly starts with one packet. If there are P permutations to be routed, however, then it will be useful to augment the front-end of the multibutterfly with $P-1$ copies of the first level of the multibutterfly. Each switch on each of these levels starts with one packet. This will preserve the bound of queue size 1 at the input level, and it will ensure that these levels have the same (α, β)-expansion property as the first level. For notational purposes, we will refer to these additional levels as levels $-1, -2, \cdots, -(P-1)$.

B. The Analysis

We will analyze the behavior of the greedy algorithm described in Section II-A by means of a potential function argument. In particular, we will assign each packet in wave i $(0 \leq i < LP)$ *weight* ν^i for some fixed $\nu < 1$ to be determined later, and we will define the *potential of a switch* on level $k(-(P-1) \leq k \leq \log N)$ to be w^k if k is odd, and w^{k+1} if k is even, where $w < 1$ is also a constant to be determined later. Thus, the *potential of a packet* in the ith wave at the kth level is $\nu^i w^k$ if k is odd, and $\nu^i w^{k+1}$ if k is even, and the *potential of the system* is the sum of potentials of the packets. By varying the values of ν and w, we can obtain different bounds on the running time of the algorithm as follows.

Theorem 2.1: The algorithm of Section II-A routes P permutations in at most

$$\frac{4d \log \frac{2}{w}}{\log \frac{1}{\rho}} \log N + \frac{4d \log \frac{1}{\nu}}{\log \frac{1}{\rho}} PL$$

$$+ \frac{4d \log \left(\frac{\nu}{L(1-\nu)(1-\nu^L w^{-1})} \right)}{\log \frac{1}{\rho}} = O(P + \log N)$$

steps, provided that $\beta > 1$ and ν is sufficiently small, where

$$L \geq \frac{1}{2\alpha},$$

$$\sigma = \frac{\beta(1-\nu)}{1+\beta(1-\nu)},$$

$$\rho = [\sigma w + (1-\sigma)w^{-1}]^2.$$

Corollary 2.2: The algorithm in Section II-A routes a single permutation in at most

$$\frac{4d \log \frac{2}{w}}{\log \frac{1}{\rho}} \log N + \frac{4dL \log \frac{1}{\nu}}{\log \frac{1}{\rho}}$$

$$+ \frac{4d \log \left(\frac{\nu}{L(1-\nu)(1-\nu^L w^{-1})} \right)}{\log \frac{1}{\rho}} = O(\log N)$$

steps.

Corollary 2.3: The algorithm in Section II-A routes $\log N$ permutations in at most

$$\frac{4d(\log \frac{2}{w} + L \log \frac{1}{\nu})}{\log \frac{1}{\rho}} \log N$$

$$+ \frac{4d \log \left(\frac{\nu}{L(1-\nu)(1-\nu^L w^{-1})} \right)}{\log \frac{1}{\rho}} = O(\log N)$$

steps.

The key fact necessary to prove Theorem 2.1 is that the potential of the system drops by a constant fraction during each stage. In particular, we will need to prove the following claim.

Claim 2.4: After each stage of the algorithm, the total potential of the system decreases by a factor of at least

$$\rho = [\sigma w + (1-\sigma)w^{-1}]^2$$

where

$$\sigma = \frac{\beta(1-\nu)}{1+\beta(1-\nu)}.$$

The main idea behind proving Claim 2.4 is that during any stage of the algorithm, a reasonable number of the heaviest packets move forward, thereby decreasing the potential of the system by a constant fraction. To formalize this intuition, we will need the following series of lemmas.

Lemma 2.5: After any phase of routing packets through a splitter, the weight of a packet at the head of any edge cannot be less than the weight of the packet at the tail of the edge.

Proof: Consider any edge e. At some step of the phase, the algorithm looks at the head and tail of e, and rearranges packets (if any) so that the heavier weight packet is sent to the head of e. In subsequent steps, only a packet with greater weight can be moved into the head of e, and only packets with lesser weight can move into the tail of e. Hence, at the end of the phase, the weight of the packet at the head of e is at least as great as the weight of the packet at the tail of e, if any. (Nonexistent packets can be considered to have zero weight.) $\square$

In what follows, let W_r^{ui} denote the sum of the weights of the r heaviest upward-destined packets left at the inputs of a splitter after a phase of routing through the splitter. If there are fewer than r upward-destined packets left at the inputs, then W_r^{ui} denotes the weight of all of them. A similar definition holds for W_r^{li} and also for W_r^{uo} and W_r^{lo}, which denote the sum of the weights of the r heaviest packets in the upper and lower outputs, respectively.

Lemma 2.6: For any M-input splitter and any integer $r \leq \lceil \alpha M \rceil$, $W_{\lceil \beta r \rceil}^{uo} \geq \beta W_r^{ui}$ and $W_{\lceil \beta r \rceil}^{lo} \geq \beta W_r^{li}$.

Proof: For simplicity, we will only argue the result for upward-destined packets. The proof for lower-destined packets is identical.

We will prove by induction on r that $W_{\lceil \beta r \rceil}^{uo} \geq \lceil \beta r \rceil / r W_r^{ui}$. For $r = 1$, the result follows from Lemma 2.5 and the fact that every input is adjacent to $d \geq \beta$ upper outputs. Now assume the result is true for $r = k - 1$, and look at the k heaviest upward-destined packets left at the inputs of the splitter. By the expansion property, we know that the inputs containing these packets are incident to at least $\lceil \beta k \rceil$ upper outputs. By Lemma 2.5, each of these outputs contains a packet of weight at least $W_k^{ui} - W_{k-1}^{ui}$ (i.e., the weight of the kth heaviest upper-destined packet left at an input). Hence, there are $\lceil \beta k \rceil$ or more upper outputs containing packets with weight at least $W_k^{ui} - W_{k-1}^{ui}$, and by induction, the $\lceil \beta(k-1) \rceil$ heaviest of these account for at least $\lceil \beta(k-1) \rceil / (k-1) W_{k-1}^{ui}$ weight. Thus,

$$
\begin{aligned}
W_{\lceil \beta k \rceil}^{uo} &\geq \frac{\lceil \beta(k-1) \rceil}{k-1} W_{k-1}^{ui} + (\lceil \beta k \rceil \\
&\quad - \lceil \beta(k-1) \rceil)(W_k^{ui} - W_{k-1}^{ui}) \\
&= (\lceil \beta k \rceil - \lceil \beta(k-1) \rceil) W_k^{ui} \\
&\quad + \left(\lceil \beta(k-1) \rceil \frac{k}{k-1} - \lceil \beta k \rceil \right) W_{k-1}^{ui} \\
&\geq (\lceil \beta k \rceil - \lceil \beta(k-1) \rceil) W_k^{ui} \\
&\quad + \left(\lceil \beta(k-1) \rceil \frac{k}{k-1} - \lceil \beta k \rceil \right) \frac{W_k^{ui}(k-1)}{k} \\
&= \frac{\lceil \beta k \rceil}{k} W_k^{ui},
\end{aligned}
$$

thereby verifying the inductive hypothesis. $\square$

Lemma 2.7: For $L \geq 1/2\alpha$, the total weights of all upper and lower-destined packets left at the inputs of any M-input splitter are at most $W_{\lceil \alpha M \rceil}^{ui}/(1-\nu)$ and $W_{\lceil \alpha M \rceil}^{li}/(1-\nu)$, respectively.

Proof: For simplicity, we will only consider upward-destined packets. The same argument holds for lower-destined packets. Arrange the packets at the inputs in order of decreasing weight. Since $\lceil \alpha M \rceil \geq M/2L$, at most $\lceil \alpha M \rceil$ of these packets can belong to any wave. Hence, the weight of the $(i + \lceil \alpha M \rceil)$th heaviest packet is at most ν times the weight of the ith heaviest packet for all i. Since the weight of the $\lceil \alpha M \rceil$ heaviest packets is $W_{\lceil \alpha M \rceil}^{ui}$ by definition, the total weight of all the upper-destined packets at the inputs is at most

$$
W_{\lceil \alpha M \rceil}^{ui} + \nu W_{\lceil \alpha M \rceil}^{ui} + \nu^2 W_{\lceil \alpha M \rceil}^{ui} + \cdots \leq \frac{W_{\lceil \alpha M \rceil}^{ui}}{1-\nu},
$$

as claimed. $\square$

Lemma 2.8: For $L \geq 1/2\alpha$, after one phase of routing packets through a splitter, a fraction of at least σ of all the packet weight in the splitter is at the outputs, where

$$
\sigma = \frac{\beta(1-\nu)}{1 + \beta(1-\nu)}.
$$

Proof: By Lemma 2.6, the total weight of packets on the upper and lower outputs is at least $\beta(W_{\lceil \alpha M \rceil}^{ui} + W_{\lceil \alpha M \rceil}^{li})$. By Lemma 2.7, the total weight of packets left at the inputs is at most $1/(1-\nu)(W_{\lceil \alpha M \rceil}^{ui} + W_{\lceil \alpha M \rceil}^{li})$. Hence the total weight on the outputs is at least $\beta(1-\nu)$ times the total weight on the inputs, and thus at least a $\beta(1-\nu)/(1 + \beta(1-\nu))$ fraction of the weight is on the outputs. $\square$

Corollary 2.9: After a phase of routing packets from level l to level $l + 1$, at least a total fraction σ of the weight in the two levels is in level $l + 1$.

We are now ready to prove Claim 2.4 and Theorem 2.1.

Proof of Claim 2.4: Let x_l denote the weight at the beginning of the stage in levels l and $l + 1$, where l is even. If V is the potential of the system at the beginning of the stage, then

$$
V = \sum_{\text{even } l} x_l w^{l+1}.
$$

During the first phase of the stage, packets move from even levels to odd levels. This does not change the potential of the system since each even level has the same potential as the next odd level. However, it does ensure that the weight in odd level $l + 1$ is at least σx_l and the weight in even level l is at most $(1 - \sigma)x_l$.

During the second phase, the weight in odd level $l + 1$ is rearranged with the weight in even level $l + 2$ for each l. By Corollary 2.9, and the argument of the previous paragraph, we know that at least $\sigma^2 x_l - (1 - \sigma)^2 x_{l+2}$ weight moves from level $l + 1$ to level $l + 2$ for any l. Hence, the potential at the end of the stage is at most

$$
\begin{aligned}
\sum_{\text{even } l} &[x_l - (\sigma^2 x_l - (1 - \sigma)^2 x_{l+2}) \\
&\quad + (\sigma^2 x_{l-2} - (1 - \sigma)^2 x_l)] w^{l+1} \\
&= \sum_{\text{even } l} x_l w^{l+1} [\sigma^2 w^2 + 2\sigma(1 - \sigma) + (1 - \sigma)^2 w^{-2}] \\
&= \rho V,
\end{aligned}
$$

as claimed. $\square$

Proof of Theorem 2.1: To compute an upper bound on the running time of the algorithm, we now need only to compute the initial potential of the system and the potential at which we will be guaranteed that every packet has reached its destination at level $\log N$.

To compute the initial potential, we will assume without loss of generality that the first L waves start in level 0, the next L waves start in level -1, and so forth. The total weight in the first L waves is at most

$$
\frac{N}{L}(1 + \nu^1 + \nu^2 + \cdots + \nu^{L-1}) \leq \frac{N}{L(1-\nu)}.
$$

Similarly the weight of the ith group ($1 \leq i \leq P$) of L waves is at most

$$\frac{N}{L}\left(\nu^{(i-1)L} + \nu^{(i-1)L+1} + \nu^{(i-1)L+2} + \cdots\right) \leq \frac{N\nu^{(i-1)L}}{L(1-\nu)}.$$

Hence the total initial potential is at most

$$\frac{N}{L(1-\nu)}\left(w + \frac{\nu^L}{w^1} + \frac{\nu^{2L}}{w^1} + \frac{\nu^{3L}}{w^3} + \frac{\nu^{4L}}{w^3} + \cdots\right)$$
$$\leq \frac{N}{L(1-\nu)(1-\nu^L w^{-1})}.$$

The potential of a packet from the last wave on level $\log N$ is at most $\nu^{PL-1} w^{\log N}$. Hence, all of the packets must have reached level $\log N$ (their destinations) once the total potential falls below this amount. Since the total potential drops by a factor of ρ at every stage, the total number of stages can be at most S, where

$$\frac{N\rho^S}{L(1-\nu)(1-\nu^L w^{-1})} = \nu^{PL-1} w^{\log N}.$$

Hence, it suffices to choose

$$S = \frac{\log \frac{2}{w}}{\log \frac{1}{\rho}} \log N + \frac{\log \frac{1}{\nu}}{\log \frac{1}{\rho}} PL + \frac{\log\left(\frac{\nu}{L(1-\nu)(1-\nu^L w^{-1})}\right)}{\log \frac{1}{\rho}}.$$

Since each stage takes $4d$ steps, we can multiply by $4d$ to obtain the bounded stated in the theorem.

In order to show that $S = O(P + \log N)$, we need to show that there exist constants d, α, β, $w < 1$, and $\nu < 1$ such that $\nu^L/w < 1$ and $\rho < 1$. The key, of course, is showing that $\rho < 1$ (i.e., that the potential of the system drops during every stage). If $\sigma > 1/2$, then we can always find a value of $w < 1$ for which $\rho < 1$. (In particular, we can choose $w = \sqrt{(1/\sigma) - 1} < 1$, for then $\rho = 2\sigma(1 - \sigma) < 1$.) In order for σ to be greater than $1/2$, it suffices that $\beta(1 - \nu) > 1$. This can be accomplished for any $\beta > 1$ by setting ν to be sufficiently small. Making ν small also guarantees that $\nu^L/w < 1$. Hence, we only need to choose d, α, and β so that $\beta > 1$, which can be done for any $d \geq 3$ by choosing α to be sufficiently small.

For example, we could choose $d = 11$, $\alpha = 1/32$, $\beta = 4$, $L = 16$, $\nu = 1/2$, $\sigma = 2/3$, $w = 1/\sqrt{2}$, and $\rho = 8/9$, to show that $\log N$ permutations can be routed in at most $4273 \log N$ steps using the algorithm. □

C. Improving the Constant Factors

Although the constant factors derived for the running time bound in Theorem 2.1 are superior to those proved by Upfal [29] (who achieved a bound of $18500 \log N$ steps for $d = 21$), they are very far from what can be considered practical. Fortunately, the constant factors can be substantially improved if we allow each switch to process communications along each incident edge at the same time. In particular, we can handle $4d$ routing problems for the price of one by interleaving and pipelining the $4d$ problems in the standard way. (I.e., every edge will now be active at every step—edges with the jth color will be working on the ith problem during steps

congruent to $i + j \mod 4d$.) Similarly, we can partition a single problem into $4d$ batches, each of which can be handled simultaneously but independently. The number of waves in each batch is $PL/4d$ which means that we can simply reduce PL by a factor of $4d$ in the overall time bound. As long as $PL > 4d$, this means that we can route P permutations in

$$(4d \log \frac{2}{w} / \log \frac{1}{\rho}) \log N + (\log \frac{1}{\nu} / \log \frac{1}{\rho}) PL$$
$$+ 4d \log \left(\frac{\nu}{L(1-\nu)(1-\nu^L w^{-1})}\right) / \log \frac{1}{\rho}$$

steps.

The most interesting application of this procedure is to routing $\log N$ permutations, for which the time bound is $(4d \log (2w) / \log (1/\rho) + L \log (1/\nu) / \log (1/\rho)) \log N + 4d \log \left(\nu/(L(1-\nu)(1-\nu^L w^{-1}))\right) / \log 1/\rho$ steps. For $L = 16$, $\alpha = 1/32$, $\beta = 4$, $d = 11$, $w = 2/3$, $\nu = 1/4$, $\sigma = 3/4$, and $\rho = (7/8)^2$, this gives an absolute bound of $367 \log N - 637$ steps which is substantially better than the previous bound.

Recently, Leighton and Maggs [19] developed an alternative method for analyzing greedy routing algorithms on multibutterflies which allows for another order-of-magnitude improvement in the constant factors. In particular, they have shown that a simple greedy algorithm can routing a single permutation in at most $56 \log N$ steps using $d = 10$ and queues of size 2 at each edge. By increasing d further, the time bound can be decreased to about $5 \log N$. Using a more complicated algorithm, and large d, the time bound can be decreased to nearly $2 \log N$ [2].

Even the best bounds for the constant factors are not very good, however. Fortunately, as we will see in Section IV, randomly-wired splitter networks (even those with $d = 2$) appear to perform much better in practice than would be indicated by the known theoretical upper bounds.

D. Other Improvements

The algorithms described in Sections II-A through II-C can be improved in several ways. For example, by considering the expansion obtained across two or more levels of splitters, it is possible to obtain much larger expansion factors for randomly-wired splitter networks. In fact, it is possible to show that even a splitter network with multiplicity 2 can route any permutation in $O(\log N)$ steps. This is not possible to prove using the previous analysis for splitters with $d = 2$, since they do not have expansion.

One of the nice properties of a d-multibutterfly is that it requires about the same VLSI layout area [28] as a d-dilated butterfly. In particular, the layout area of an N-input d-butterfly or d-dilated butterfly is $\Theta(N^2 d^2)$. In Section II-A we proposed appending a set of levels numbered $-1, -2, \cdots, -(P-1)$ to the multibutterfly, each isomorphic to the first. Unfortunately, each such level requires $\Theta(N^2 d^2)$ area to lay out (as much as the entire multibutterfly), so the total area becomes $\Theta(PN^2 d^2)$. For $P \leq \log N + 1$, however, it can be shown that a more area-efficient network will suffice: the *multi-Beneš* network. The multi-Beneš network consists of back-to-back multibutterflies and requires twice the area of the multibutterfly.

III. Routing Around Faults

In this section, we prove that the multibutterfly is a highly fault-tolerant network. We start by considering worst case faults in Section II-A and then consider the less malevolent case of random faults in Section III-B. For simplicity, we will assume that $d \geq 5$, although similar results can be proved for smaller d. On-line algorithms for reconfiguring around faults are discussed in Section III-C.

A. Worst Case Faults

In this section, we will prove that no matter how an adversary selects f switches to be faulty, there are always at least $N - O(f)$ inputs and $N - O(f)$ outputs through which any permutation on those inputs and outputs can be routed in $O(\log N)$ steps. In fact, the greedy algorithm described in Section II works once we have removed an appropriate set of switches which include at most $O(f)$ inputs and outputs.

We first describe which outputs to remove. Examine each splitter in the multibutterfly and check if more than an ε fraction of the input switches are faulty, where $\varepsilon = 2\alpha(\beta' - 1)$ and $\beta' = \beta - \lfloor d/2 \rfloor$. If so, then "erase" the splitter from the network as well as all descendant switches and outputs. The following lemma bounds the number of erased outputs.

Lemma 3.1: The erasure process removes at most $f/\varepsilon = O(f)$ outputs.

Proof: The erasure of an M-input splitter causes the removal of M multibutterfly outputs, and accounts for at least εM faults. Hence, at most $f/\varepsilon = f/2\alpha(\beta' - 1) = O(f)$ multibutterfly outputs are removed by this process. $\square$

We next describe which inputs to remove. Working from level $\log N$ backward, examine each switch to see if at least half of its upper output edges lead to faulty switches that have not been erased, or if at least half of its lower output edges lead to faulty switches that have not been erased. If so, then declare the switch to be faulty (but do not erase it). In the following lemmas, we will prove that at most $f/(\beta' - 1)$ additional switches are declared to be faulty at each level of this process. Hence, at most $O(f)$ multibutterfly inputs will be faulty (declared or otherwise).

Lemma 3.2: In any splitter, at most a 2α fraction of the inputs are declared to be faulty as a consequence of propagating faults backward. Moreover, at most an α fraction are propagated by faulty upper outputs and at most an α fraction are propagated by faulty lower inputs.

Proof: The proof is by induction on the level, starting at level $\log N$ and working backward. The base case at level $\log N$ is trivial since there are no propagated faults on level $\log N$. Now consider an arbitrary M-input splitter on level i. Let U_i denote the set of faults propagated from the splitter's upper outputs and let L_i denote those propagated from the lower outputs. If the upper outputs were erased, then $|U_i| = 0$. Otherwise, the number of faults placed by the adversary in the upper outputs is at most $\varepsilon M/2$. Since each propagated input fault is connected to at most $\lfloor d/2 \rfloor$ working upper outputs, we

can conclude that $|U_{i+1}| + |L_{i+1}| + \varepsilon M/2 \geq |U_i|(\beta - \lfloor d/2 \rfloor) = |U_i|\beta'$. By induction, $|U_{i+1}| \leq \alpha M/2$ and $|L_{i+1}| \leq \alpha M/2$. For $|U_i| > \alpha M$ and $\varepsilon = 2\alpha(\beta' - 1)$, we have a contradiction. A similar argument shows that $|L_i| \leq \alpha M$. $\square$

Lemma 3.3: Even if we allow the adversary to make f switches fail on every level, there will be at most $\frac{f}{(\beta' - 1)}$ propagated faults on any level.

Proof: The proof is again by induction on the level. Consider some level l and assume that it has more than $\frac{f}{\beta' - 1}$ propagated faults. By Lemma 3.2, we know that these faults are divided among the splitters linking level l to $l+1$ so that we can apply the expansion property to the faults within each splitter. Hence, there must be more than $((\beta - \lfloor d/2 \rfloor)f)/(\beta' - 1)$ faults on level $l + 1$. This is a contradiction, however, since level $l + 1$ can have at most $f + f/(\beta' - 1) = \beta'f/(\beta' - 1)$ total faults by induction. Hence, level l can have at most $f/(\beta' - 1)$ propagated faults. $\square$

We now erase all the remaining faulty switches. This leaves a network with $N - O(f)$ inputs and $N - O(f)$ outputs. Moreover, every input in every splitter is linked to $\lceil d/2 \rceil$ functioning upper outputs (if the descendant multibutterfly outputs exist) and $\lceil d/2 \rceil$ functioning lower outputs (if the corresponding multibutterfly outputs exist). Hence, every splitter has an (α, β') expansion property. Thus, we can apply Theorem 2.1 with β replaced by β' to prove that the greedy algorithm still routes any permutation on the remaining inputs and outputs in $O(\log N)$ steps. This is summarized as Theorem 3.4 below. (Note that we can achieve expansion $\beta > \lfloor d/2 \rfloor + 1$ for $d \geq 5$.)

Theorem 3.4: No matter which f interior switches are made faulty in an N-input multibutterfly, there are at least $N - f/(\beta' - 1)$ inputs and $N - (f/(2\alpha(\beta' - 1)))$ outputs between which any $\log N$ permutations can be routed in at most $O(\log N)$ steps, provided that $\beta > \lfloor d/2 \rfloor + 1$.

Proof: The results follows from Theorem 2.1, Lemmas 3.1 and 3.3, and the fact that $\beta' = \beta - \lfloor d/2 \rfloor > 1$. $\square$

B. Random Faults

Random faults are much easier to tolerate than worst case faults. In fact, any network can be made to tolerate a large number of randomly placed faults simply by making multiple copies of its switches and edges. For example, suppose that an n-switch network G is replaced by a network G' in which for each switch u in G there are a pair of switches u and u' in G', and for each edge $\{u, v\}$ in G there are four edges $\{u, v\}$, $\{u, v'\}$, $\{u', v\}$, and $\{u', v'\}$. Then G' can simulate G provided that there is no pair of switches u and u' in G' that simultaneously fail. If each switch fails independently with probability $1/\sqrt{2n}$, then the expected number of failures is $\sqrt{2n}$, and the probability that any particular pair of switches u and u' both fail is $1/2n$. Since there are n pairs of switches, the probability that *any* pair fails is at most $1/2$. This technique is easily generalized. By making c copies of each switch and c^2 copies of each edge, any n-switch network can be made to tolerate a failure rate of $(cn)^{-1/c}$ with probability $1 - 1/c$.

By a similar argument, even if each switch in G' fails with some fixed constant probability then, with high probability,

G' can simulate a constant fraction of the switches in G. In general, however, there is no guarantee that these switches in G will be connected in a useful fashion. As the following theorem shows, however, even if the switches fail with some constant probability, an N-input multibutterfly will have some set of $\Theta(N)$ inputs and $\Theta(N)$ outputs between which any permutation can be routed in $O(\log N)$ steps, with high probability. Furthermore, an N-input multi-Beneš network can tolerate constant failure probability and still route $\log N$ permutations of $\Theta(N)$ packets in $O(\log N)$ time. The only other networks that are known to tolerate constant failure probability are the N-switch hypercube, which can route any $\log N$ permutations of N packets in $O(\log N)$ time, with high probability, but has degree $\log N$ [10], and the N-switch mesh, which can route $\log N$ permutations of $\Theta(N)$ packets in $O(\sqrt{N} \log N)$ time [12].

The strategy for tolerating random faults is the same as the strategy of Section III-A for tolerating worst case faults. We first examine each splitter to determine if more than an ε fraction of the input switches in that splitter are faulty, where $\varepsilon = 2\alpha(\beta' - 1)$ and $\beta' = \beta - \lfloor d/2 \rfloor$. If so, then we erase the splitter and all of its descendant switches and outputs. Then we propagate faults back from level $\log N$ to level 0. A switch is declared to be faulty if at least half of its upper input edges or output edges lead to faulty switches that have not been erased. The following theorem shows that, with high probability, this strategy leaves a constant fraction of the network intact.

Theorem 3.5: There exist fixed constants $p > 0$, and $\lambda > 0$, such that if each switch fails independently with probability p, then with probability at least $1 - e^{-\Theta(N/\log^2 N)}$ there is some set of λN inputs and λN outputs between which any permutation can be routed in $O(\log N)$ time.

Proof: The hard part of the proof is showing that we do not erase too many outputs.

We begin by deriving an upper bound on the probability that more than εM input switches fail in an M-input splitter. Let S_M denote the number of input switches that fail in an M-input splitter. Then S_M has a binomial distribution, and

$$\Pr\{S_M \geq k\} \leq \binom{M}{k} p^k.$$

Setting $k = \varepsilon M$, we have $\Pr\{S_M \geq \varepsilon M\} \leq \binom{M}{\varepsilon M} p^{\varepsilon M}$. Using the inequality $\binom{a}{b} \leq (ae/b)^b$ and letting $\delta = \varepsilon(\ln(\varepsilon/p) - 1)$, we have $\Pr\{S_M \geq \varepsilon M\} \leq e^{-\delta M}$, where $\delta > 0$ for $p < \varepsilon/e$, and $\delta \to \infty$ as $p \to 0$.

We can analyze the number of erased splitters on each level in a similar fashion. Consider a level of the network that contains N/M M-input splitters. Using the fact that each splitter on this level is erased independently with probability at most $e^{-\delta M}$, we can show that with probability at least $1 - e^{-\Theta(N/\log^2 N)}$, the number of erased splitters is at most $cN/M \log^2 M$ for any constant $c > \log^2 M e^{1-\delta M/2}$. (By making δ large, c can be made arbitrarily close to 0 for all M.) Hence, with probability at least $1 - e^{-\Theta(N/\log^2 N)}$, at most $cN/\log^2 M$ outputs are erased due to faults occurring in splitters with M inputs. Summing over $M = 2, 4, 8, \cdots, N$, we find that with probability at least $1 - e^{-\Theta(N/\log^2 N)}$, at

most $cN(1 + 1/4 + 1/9 + \cdots + 1/\log^2 N) \leq c\pi^2 N/6$ outputs are erased overall. Hence, at least λN outputs remain, where $\lambda = 1 - (c\pi^2/6)$ can be made close to 1 by setting c to be close to zero.

Once all of the blocks containing more than an ε fraction of faulty switches are erased, we can apply Lemmas 3.2 and 3.3 to show that there are not too many propagated faults on any level. In order to apply Lemma 3.3, we must bound the number of switches that fail on any level. To do this, we bound the binomial distribution to show that at most $c'N$ switches fail on a level with probability $1 - e^{\Theta(N)}$, where $c' < 2p$. By Lemma 3.3, if there are at most $c'N$ switch failures on any level, then there are at most $c'N/(\beta'-1)$ propagated faults, and $\beta'c'N/(\beta'-1)$ total faults on any level. Thus, with probability at least $1 - e^{-\Theta(N/\log^2 N)}$, some set of λN inputs and λN outputs remain, where $\lambda = \min\{1 - \beta'c'/(\beta'-1), 1 - c\pi^2/6\}$. (Notice that λ will be close to 1 for small p since c and c' approach 0 as $p \to 0$.) The time to route between these inputs and outputs is given by Theorem 3.4. ☐

C. On-line Reconfiguration

Deciding which switches to remove from the network using the procedure described in Sections III-A and III-B is straightforward if we can reconfigure the network off-line. On-line reconfiguration is more challenging, however. The hard part is deciding locally which splitters contain too many faults at the input, since this calculation must be performed in the presence of faults. Fast on-line algorithms for this task are described by Goldberg, Plotkin, and Maggs in [9].

Once the splitters containing too many faults are erased, then it is a simple matter to propagate faults back through the network. Each switch simply checks its up and down output neighbors to see how many are faulty. As we will see in Section IV, the multibutterfly can tolerate a surprisingly large number of random faults without having to erase any inputs or outputs at all, so this simple fault propagation technique may be sufficient for reconfiguring multibutterflies in practice.

IV. EXPERIMENTS

This section presents data generated by a Pascal program that simulates randomly-wired splitter networks. The experimental data demonstrates that a randomly-wired splitter network with multiplicity 2 is capable of routing efficiently even when many of its switches are faulty. The random numbers used in the simulations were generated using the minimal standard linear congruential generator from [24].

The program tested the ability of a randomly-wired splitter network with multiplicity 2 to tolerate randomly-placed faults. Four types of splitter networks were compared: normal butterflies, a 2-dilated butterfly, randomly-wired splitter networks with multiplicity 2, and randomly-wired splitter networks with multiplicity 2 that were modified to improve their fault tolerance. Each network had $N = 1024$ inputs. The randomly-wired networks were "cleaned up" after their creation to remove parallel edges between the same two switches where possible.

The program primarily simulated store-and-forward routing. Messages were routed according to a simple greedy algorithm. At each time step, a switch was allowed to send a message along an edge provided that at the end of the previous step the number of messages in the switch at the end of the edge was at most 4. The average number of steps required to route all of the messages to their destinations was measured.

We made two modifications to the random networks in order to make them more fault tolerant. First, we removed the last 2 levels and replaced each 4-input splitter on these levels with a 4×4 complete bipartite graph. We then added a level numbered -1 with 4 random matchings to level 0. We use an asterisk (*) in Tables I through III to indicate that the networks were modified.

Faults were placed at random interior (i.e., not input or output) switches of the modified splitter networks. A nonfaulty switch was declared faulty if either both of its up edges or both of its down edges led to faulty switches. Thus, faults could propagate from the last interior level back to the inputs. Because the faults were placed at random, the modified splitter networks could tolerate about $(N \log N)^{3/4}$ faults without any faults propagating back to the inputs. If any faults reached the inputs, then all of the faults were removed, and a new set of random faults was placed in the network. The number of faults in the modified splitter networks varied from 0 to 1000. Table I shows the percentage of trials in which at least one fault reached the inputs.

We first ran a set of trials to compare the performance of the randomly-wired splitter networks to the normal butterflies and the 2-dilated butterflies when routing random and worst case problems. We ran 4 types of trials. The first type consisted of routing a message from each input to a random destination, for a total of $N = 1024$ messages. The second consisted of routing a collection of 10 such random routing problems. The third type was the transpose permutation, a worst case problem for the butterfly and dilated butterfly. In this problem the destination of each message is formed by rotating the binary representation of the origin of the message $1/2 \log N$ positions in a circular fashion. The last type consisted of 10 of these transpose permutations. For each of these types, we varied the number of faults in the modified randomly-wired splitter networks from 0 to 1000.

The data are presented in Table II. There is one column in the table for each type of routing problem: a random problem (1), 10 random problems (10), a transpose problem (1T), and 10 transpose problems (10T). For each type of network tested, there is a row in the table. Each entry in a row shows the average, over 500 trials, of the number of steps required to route all of the packets to their destinations, and the standard deviation, σ. The butterfly rows are labeled 0 (nor), the 2-dilated butterfly rows are labeled 0 (dil), the randomly-wired splitter network rows are labeled 0, and the modified randomly-wired splitter network rows are labeled 0* through 1000* depending on the number of faults in the network.

Surprisingly, a randomly-wired splitter network with up to 100 faults performs nearly as well as the fault-free 2-dilated butterfly on random problems, and much better on transpose problems, even though both networks consist of the same

TABLE I
NETWORK FAILURE RATE.. THE LEFT COLUMN SHOWS THE NUMBER OF RANDOMLY-PLACED FAULTS. THE RIGHT COLUMN SHOWS THE PERCENTAGE OF TRIALS IN WHICH AT LEAST ONE FAULT WAS PROPAGATED BACK TO AN INPUT IN A 1024-INPUT MODIFIED RANDOMLY-WIRED SPLITTER NETWORK WITH MULTIPLICITY 2. EACH BOX REPRESENTS 2000 TRIALS

10*	0.0
100*	0.0
250*	0.3
500*	1.3
750*	9.1
1000*	27.8

TABLE II
STORE-AND-FORWARD COMPLETION TIME. EACH BOX SHOWS THE AVERAGE, OVER 500 TRIALS, OF THE NUMBER OF STEPS FOR ALL OF THE PACKETS TO REACH THEIR DESTINATIONS, AND THE STANDARD DEVIATION

	1	10	1T	10T
0 (nor), σ	14.1, 0.6	26.0, 1.0	38	272
0 (dil), σ	11.8, 0.4	18.7, 0.7	17	160
0, σ	11.1, 0.2	16.4, 0.5	11.8, 0.4	19.8, 0.5
0*, σ	12.0, 0.3	18.0, 0.6	11.8, 0.4	17.2, 0.4
1*. σ	12.0, 0.3	18.0, 0.6	11.8, 0.4	17.4, 0.6
10*, σ	12.0, 0.3	18.3, 0.7	12.0, 0.5	18.4, 0.8
100*. σ	12.2, 0.4	20.1, 1.3	12.7, 0.6	20.6, 1.3
250*, σ	12.4, 0.5	21.8, 1.6	13.3, 0.7	22.7, 1.4
500*, σ	12.9, 0.6	24.7, 3.0	14.0, 0.8	25.7, 2.2
750*, σ	13.1, 0.7	26.6, 4.0	14.5, 1.3	28.2, 4.7
1000*, σ	13.1, 1.0	26.5, 7.7	14.0, 1.9	27.5, 8.8

amount of hardware.

It is also possible to use this program to simulate circuit-switching. In the *circuit-switching* model, the goal of a message is to establish a dedicated path from its source to its destination. This path must be disjoint from the paths of all other messages; an edge can appear on at most one message's path. This model is most appropriate when the messages being transmitted are too long to be considered atomic objects. For circuit-switching we ran the same algorithm but instead measured the percentage of messages that reached their destinations without ever being delayed. These messages can be viewed as having successfully locked down paths from their sources to their destinations. The data are presented in Table III. Here we found that a modified randomly-wired splitter network with 100 faults outperformed a fault-free 2-dilated butterfly! In a related paper [2], we describe more sophisticated circuit-switching algorithms that guarantee that all of the messages succeed in establishing their paths in $O(\log N)$ time.

Additional experimental data on the performance of randomly-wired splitter networks can be found in [4], [5], [13], [15], [21].

V. REMARKS

The fault tolerance and potential function arguments developed in this paper can be applied to other leveled switching networks with local expansion properties. A good example of

TABLE III

AVERAGE THROUGHPUT. EACH BOX SHOWS THE AVERAGE, OVER
500 TRIALS, PERCENTAGE OF MESSAGES THAT SUCCESSFULLY
LOCKED DOWN THEIR PATHS, AND THE STANDARD DEVIATION

	1	1T
0 (nor), σ	44.8, 1.1	3.1
0 (dil), σ	87.0, 1.0	12.5
0, σ	94.1, 0.7	89.9 , 0.8
0*, σ	88.5, 0.9	89.9, 0.9
1*, σ	88.5, 0.9	89.8, 0.9
10*, σ	88.4, 0.9	89.6, 0.9
100*, σ	86.5, 1.0	86.9, 1.0
250*, σ	83.4, 1.1	82.5, 1.2
500*, σ	77.9, 1.5	75.9, 2.2
750*, σ	73.7, 5.1	71.4, 6.5
1000*, σ	74.3, 11.2	73.4, 13.4

such a network is a fat-tree [22] with expander-based switches.
Using the methods described in this paper, it is possible to
devise algorithms for routing around faults in this network,
although the problem of optimally assigning packets to waves
in a deterministic on-line fashion is still unresolved.

ACKNOWLEDGMENT

Thanks to M. Ben-Or, F. Chong, A. DeHon, A. Goldberg,
M. Grigni, J. Kilian, T. Knight, S. Plotkin, S. Rao, J. Rompel,
and E. Upfal for numerous helpful comments.

REFERENCES

[1] M. Ajtai, J. Komlos, and E. Szemeredi, "Sorting in $c \log n$ parallel steps," *Combinatorica*, vol. 3, pp. 1–19, 1983.
[2] S. Arora, T. Leighton, and B. Maggs, "On-line algorithms for path selection in a nonblocking network," in *Proc. 22nd Annu. ACM Symp. Theory Comput.*, May 1990, pp. 149–158.
[3] L. A. Bassalygo and M. S. Pinsker, "Complexity of an optimum non-blocking switching network without reconnections," *Problems Inform. Transmission*, vol. 9, pp. 64–66, 1974.
[4] F. Chong, E. Egozy, and A. DeHon, "Fault tolerance and performance of multipath multistage interconnection networks," in *Advanced Research in VLSI: Proc. MIT/Brown Conf. 1992*, T. F. Knight, Jr. and J. Savage, Eds. Cambridge, MA: MIT Press, Mar. 1992, to be published.
[5] A. DeHon, T. Knight, and H. Minsky, "Fault-tolerant design for multi-stage routing networks," in *Proc. Int. Symp. Shared Memory Multiprocessing*, Inform. Processing Soc. of Japan, Apr. 1991.
[6] C. Dwork, D. Peleg, N. Pippenger, and E. Upfal, "Byzantine agreement in faulty networks," *SIAM J. Comput.*, vol. 17, no. 5, pp. 975–988, 1988.
[7] S. E. Fahlman, "The hashnet interconnection scheme," Tech. Rep. CMU-CS-80-125, Dep. Comput. Sci., Carnegie–Mellon Univ., Pittsburgh, PA, June 1980.
[8] J. Friedman and N. Pippenger, "Expanding graphs contain all small trees," *Combinatorica*, vol. 7, no. 1, pp. 71–76, 1987.
[9] A. V. Goldberg, S. A. Plotkin, and B. M. Maggs, "A parallel algorithm for reconfiguring a multibutterfly network with faults," unpublished manuscript, Dec. 1991.
[10] J. Hastad, T. Leighton, and M. Newman, "Fast computation using faulty hypercubes," in *Proc. 21st Annu. ACM Symp. Theory Comput.*, May 1989, pp. 251–263.
[11] N. Kahale, "Better expansion for ramanujan graphs," in *Proc. 32nd Annu. Symp. Foundations Comput. Sci.*, IEEE, Oct. 1991, pp. 398–404.
[12] C. Kaklamanis, A. R. Karlin, F. T. Leighton, V. Milenkovic, P. Raghavan, S. Rao, C. Thomborson, and A. Tsantilas, "Asymptotically tight bounds for computing with faulty arrays of processors," in *Proc. 31st Annu. Symp. Foundations Comput. Sci.*, IEEE, Oct. 1990, pp. 285–296.
[13] T. F. Knight, Jr., "Technologies for low latency interconnection switches," in *Proc. 1989 ACM Symp. Parallel Algorithms and Architectures*, June 1989, pp. 351–358.
[14] R. R. Koch, "Increasing the size of a network by a constant factor can increase performance by more than a constant factor," in *Proc. 29th Annu. Symp. Foundations Comput. Sci.*, IEEE, Oct. 1988, pp. 221–230.
[15] S. Konstantinidou and E. Upfal, "Experimental comparison of multistage networks," IBM Almaden Research Center, unpublished manuscript, 1991.
[16] C. P. Kruskal and M. Snir, "The performance of multistage interconnection networks for multiprocessors," *IEEE Trans. Comput.*, vol. C-32, pp. 1091–1098, Dec. 1983.
[17] ——, "A unified theory of interconnection network structure," *Theoret. Comput. Sci.*, vol. 48, pp. 75–94, 1986.
[18] F. T. Leighton, "Tight bounds on the complexity of parallel sorting," *IEEE Trans. Comput.*, vol. C-34, pp. 344–354, Apr. 1985.
[19] F. T. Leighton and B. M. Maggs, "Introduction to parallel algorithms and architectures: Expanders, PRAM's, VLSI," manuscript in preparation.
[20] T. Leighton, C. L. Leiserson, and M. Klugerman, "Theory of parallel and VLSI computation," Research Seminar Series Rep. MIT/LCS/RSS 10, MIT Lab. for Comput. Sci., May 1991.
[21] T. Leighton, D. Lisinski, and B. Maggs, "Empirical evaluation of randomly-wired multistage networks," in *Proc. 1990 IEEE Int. Conf. Comput. Design: VLSI in Comput. & Processors*, IEEE, Sept. 1990, pp. 380–385.
[22] C. E. Leiserson, "Fat-trees: Universal networks for hardware-efficient supercomputing," *IEEE Trans. Comput.*, vol. C-34, pp. 892–901, Oct. 1985.
[23] A. Lubotzky, R. Phillips, and P Sarnak, "Ramanujan graphs," *Combinatorica*, vol. 8, no. 3, pp. 261–277, 1988.
[24] S. K. Park and K. W. Miller, "Random number generators: Good ones are hard to find," *Commun. ACM*, vol. 31, no. 10, pp. 1192–1201, Oct. 1988.
[25] M. O. Rabin, "Efficient dispersal of information for security, load balancing, and fault tolerance," *J. ACM*, vol. 36, no. 2, Apr. 1989.
[26] P. Raghavan, "Robust algorithms for packet routing in a mesh," in *Proc. 1989 ACM Symp. Parallel Algorithms and Architectures*, June 1989, pp 344–350,
[27] R. D. Rettberg, W. R. Crowther, P. P. Carvey, and R. S. Tomlinson, "The monarch parallel processor hardware design," *IEEE Comput. Mag.*, vol. 23, no. 4, pp. 18–30, Apr. 1990.
[28] C. D. Thompson, "A complexity theory for VLSI," Ph.D. dissertation, Dep. Comput. Sci., Carnegie-Mellon Univ., Pittsburgh, PA, 1980.
[29] E. Upfal, "An $O(\log N)$ deterministic packet routing scheme," in *Proc. 21st Annu. ACM Symp. Theory Comput.*, May 1989, pp. 241–250,

F. Thomson Leighton (M'81) received the B.S.E. degree in electrical engineering and computer science from Princeton University, Princeton, NJ, in 1978, and the Ph.D. degree in applied mathematics from the Massachusetts Institute of Technology, Cambridge, in 1981.

Currently he is a Professor of Applied Mathematics at the Massachusetts Institute of Technology, Cambridge, and a member of the MIT Laboratory for Computer Science. His research interests include parallel algorithms and architectures, discrete algorithms, VLSI, complexity theory, and combinatorics.

Dr. Leighton was among the first group of scientists to receive the NSF Presidential Young Investigator Award. He is the editor-in-chief of the *Journal of the ACM* and also serves on the editorial boards of *SIAM Journal on Computing, SIAM Journal on Discrete Mathematics, Journal on Graph Theory, Journal of Algorithms, Cominatorica*, and *Algorithmica*.

Bruce M. Maggs received the S.B., S.M., and Ph.D., degrees in computer science from the Massachusetts Institute of Technology in 1985, 1986, and 1989, respectively.

Currently he is a Research Scientist at the NEC Research Institute, Princeton, NJ. His research interests include parallel computing systems and parallel algorithms.

Traffic Routing for Multicomputer Networks with Virtual Cut-Through Capability

Dilip D. Kandlur, *Member, IEEE*, and Kang G. Shin, *Fellow, IEEE*

Abstract—A point-to-point interconnection network can be a good choice for use in distributed real-time systems, since it can provide multiple disjoint paths between nodes to tolerate link and node failures. The major drawback of this type of network has been that full connectivity becomes prohibitively expensive as the number of nodes increases, and partial connectivity implies long store-and-forward delays in the prevalent packet-switching mode of operation. However, this drawback of partially connected point-to-point networks can now be overcome with virtual cut-through, a scheme which is feasible to implement using current VLSI technology.

This paper addresses the problem of selecting routes for inter-process communication in a network with virtual cut-through capability, while balancing the network load and minimizing the number of times that a message gets buffered. The problem is important because the message delivery delay depends upon the number of times that a message gets buffered at intermediate nodes on the route. The approach taken here is to formulate the route selection problem as a minimization problem, with a link cost function that depends upon the traffic through the link. The form of this cost function is derived based on the probability of establishing a virtual cut-through route.

It is shown that this route selection problem is $\mathcal{NP}$-Hard, so an approximate algorithm is developed which tries to incrementally reduce the cost by re-routing traffic. The performance of this algorithm is evaluated for two popular network topologies: the hypercube and the C-wrapped hexagonal mesh—example networks for which virtual cut-through switching support has been developed.

Index Terms— Fault-tolerant networks, $\mathcal{NP}$-Hard, real-time communications, routing, virtual cut-through.

I. INTRODUCTION

THE availability of inexpensive and powerful microprocessors has led to the use of multicomputers in an increasing number of critical real-time applications. Many of these applications have stringent reliability requirements, since a failure of the computer system can lead to a disaster. The network interconnecting processors is an important component in these multicomputer systems. One of the goals in the design of the interconnection network is to provide reliable communication in the presence of component failures. The approach taken in multicomputers like SIFT [1] and MAFT [2] is to provide a fully-connected network. Although this method is extremely reliable, it does not scale and it is difficult to use in large systems.

Another approach to providing fault-tolerant communications is the AIPS *virtual bus* scheme [3], [4]. The AIPS network controllers are connected by multiple redundant point-to-point links, but they are configured under software control to act as a single virtual bus. However, there is a significant delay incurred in traversing through the repeater stages in a controller node, so the end-to-end latency is substantial when multiple links are to be traversed. This results in long bit-holding times for the contention resolution protocol, which can adversely affect the throughput. Also, the virtual bus configuration does not permit simultaneous communication over disjoint paths in the network.

A point-to-point interconnection network with a regular structure is proposed as a good candidate for use in real-time applications. Examples of such networks include hypercubes and meshes [5], [6]. The existence of multiple disjoint paths between nodes in these networks make them robust to link and node failures. Also, since it is possible to support multiple simultaneous conversations in different links, the total throughput achievable is higher. Until recently, one major drawback of such networks was the large delay in communication which was associated with store-and-forward packet switching. Advances in VLSI technology have now made it possible to implement sophisticated switching schemes, like the *virtual cut-through* scheme [7], which reduce the message delivery time significantly. It is therefore feasible to use a multicomputer system based on a point-to-point network with virtual cut-through for many real-time applications. Virtual cut-through, which is pivotal in the discussion that follows, is described below.

Virtual cut-through is a switching technique introduced by Kermani and Kleinrock [7] which has flavors of both circuit switching and packet switching. In this method, messages arriving at an intermediate node are forwarded to the next node in the route without buffering if a circuit can be established to the next node. This differs from conventional packet-switching schemes in the sense that messages do not always get buffered at an intermediate node. It also differs from circuit switching schemes since messages do not wait for the entire circuit to the destination to be established before proceeding along the route. With current VLSI technology, it is now possible to implement this switching scheme for multicomputer interconnection net-

Manuscript received September 11, 1990; revised October 6, 1991. This work was supported in part by the Office of Naval Research under Contract N00014-85-K-0122, NASA under Grant NAG-1-296, and an IBM Graduate Fellowship. Any opinions, findings, and conclusions or recommendations expressed in this paper are those of the authors and do not necessarily reflect the views of the funding agencies.

D. D. Kandlur is with IBM Research Division, T. J. Watson Research Center, Yorktown Heights, NY 10598.

K. G. Shin is with the Real-Time Computing Laboratory, Department of Electrical Engineering and Computer Science, The University of Michigan, Ann Arbor, MI 48109-2122.

IEEE Log Number 9200312.

Reprinted from *IEEE Trans. Computers*, Vol. 41, No. 10, Oct. 1992, pp. 1257-1270. Copyright © 1992 by The Institute of Electrical and Electronics Engineers, Inc. All rights reserved.

works, and network controllers like the Torus routing chip [8], [9] and the HARTS routing controller [10] are examples of such implementations.

The main advantages of a virtual cut-through scheme over a circuit switching scheme are that circuit setup and tear-down delays are not incurred, and network channels are not tied up. On the other hand, since messages do not necessarily get buffered at intermediate nodes, the delays encountered are smaller than those for a packet switching scheme. The automatic forwarding also means that if a cut-through switch is established, the packet is not seen by the processor at that intermediate node. Hence, the load imposed on the processors at the intermediate nodes is much smaller than that for a packet switching scheme.

The problem addressed in this paper is the selection of routes for messages in a multicomputer system of this type. It is assumed that the assignment of tasks to different nodes has already been done and the communication patterns between tasks are known. The reason for this is that, in a real-time system, the placement of tasks depends not only on the communication pattern but also on the peripherals and resources available at the different nodes. The traffic between nodes is specified in terms of mean data rates, which can be determined from the length of the messages and the periodicity of the communication. Given the network topology and this traffic pattern, the objective is to select a route for each pair of communicating processes such that the network load is balanced and the probability of establishing virtual cut-through is enhanced. Route selection is essential in order to reduce message delivery delays and to make full use of the network's cut-through capabilities. It can be considered to be a high-level approach to message scheduling, where the units considered are inter-process traffic patterns and not individual packets.

In the type of network considered here, it is assumed that link capacities are large and the overheads in handling packets at intermediate nodes is a significant factor. This assumption is reasonable considering the Gigabit range bandwidth possible with fiber-optic links. Also, we restrict our attention to finding a single fixed route for each pair of communicating processes. Fixed routing is preferable in real-time systems because it can simplify the computation of bounds for the message delivery time, an issue which is important when messages with delivery time constraints are considered [11].

Variations of this problem have been studied for general wide-area networks, mainly as techniques for building routing tables in packet switched networks [12]. However, most of these studies are based on link capacities, since these are limited for wide-area networks. In the TRANSPAC network, the routing algorithm uses link costs depending upon utilization [12]. The cost function is piecewise continuous with hysteresis. The routing is computed to minimize costs depending upon the current utilization or queue lengths, but future traffic is not considered.

One study relating to multiprocessor networks is by Bianchini and Shen [13], in which a traffic scheduling algorithm is presented. However, they assume that the switching nodes in the network have the ability to implement traffic splitting, which makes the network behave like a fluid-flow pipeline.

They further assume that the delivery cost is not depended on the length of the path and arrive at a link cost which is an exponential function of the link traffic. The properties of the exponential link cost function result in a major simplification for their traffic scheduling algorithm. On the other hand, the message delivery delays in a multicomputer network have a strong dependence on the length of the path and this is taken into account in the cost function derived here.

In this paper, the traffic scheduling problem is formulated as an optimization problem in Section II. The link cost function used in this formulation is derived in Section III. In Section IV it is shown that the optimization problem is $\mathcal{NP}$-Hard and the associated decision problem is $\mathcal{NP}$-Complete. The heuristic algorithms developed to solve this problem and their basis are presented in Section V. The performance of these algorithms is then analyzed using simulation in Section VI. The paper concludes with Section VII.

II. Notation and Problem Formulation

The environment under consideration is a multicomputer system with a point-to-point interconnection structure and a set of assigned tasks. It is assumed that the message communication patterns between the tasks are known in terms of average length of messages and the frequency of communication. From this, one can determine the unidirectional task-to-task communication volume. We call this volume a *flow*, which is measured in bytes/second. The problem is then to determine a route through the network for each flow to meet a global "goodness" criterion. The notation used to describe this problem formally is given below.

DG: A digraph (N, L) representing the multicomputer system which consists of a set, N, of n nodes and a set, L, of m links.

e_{ij}: The directed link/edge from node i to node j.

Q: The set of q flows $\{(s_i, d_i, r_i) :$ flow r_i required from node s_i to node d_i in DG, $\{i = 1, \cdots, q\}$.

P_k: The set of all simple directed paths from s_k to d_k in DG, where $(s_k, d_k, r_k) \in Q$.

p_k: An element of P_k, which can be considered to be an ordered subset of L.

S: $\{p_k : k = 1, \cdots, q\}$, an element of $P_1 \times P_2 \cdots \times P_q$.

f_{ij}: The flow in link e_{ij}. $f_{ij} = \sum_{k=1}^{q} I_{ij}^k r_k$, where $I_{ij}^k = 1$ if $e_{ij} \in p_k$ and 0 otherwise.

C_{ij}: The capacity of link e_{ij}.

c_{ij}: The cost of routing traffic onto link e_{ij}, which can be a function of f_{ij} and/or C_{ij}.

For brevity, the term *path* is used to denote a *simple directed path* in the digraph DG. Also, the terms *path* and *route* are used interchangeably in this paper. Given these definitions, and the condition that there is a unique path for each flow, the routing problem can be stated as follows.

Path Selection Problem: Given N, L, Q, the capacities and the costs of the links, find a set, S, of paths such that for each link $e_{ij} \in L$, $f_{ij} \leq C_{ij}$ and total cost $T = \sum_{k=1}^{q} r_k \cdot (\sum_{e_{ij} \in p_k} c_{ij})$ is minimized.

By changing the order of summation, T can be rewritten as $T = \sum_{e_{ij} \in L} c_{ij} \cdot (\sum_{k=1}^{q} I_{ij}^k r_k)$. The inner summation is seen to be the link flow f_{ij}, so $T = \sum_{e_{ij} \in L} c_{ij} \cdot f_{ij}$.

As formulated above, the objective of route selection is to minimize the total cost over all the flows in the network, while adhering to the capacity constraints for each link. Although this formulation is general, the characteristics of a particular type of network can be incorporated by a suitable choice of the link cost function c_{ij}. The features of virtual cut-through switching make the flow through a link critical to the cost function, since it affects the probability of establishing a cut-through route. Intuitively, it would be better to choose longer than optimal routes so as to avoid heavily used links. However, path lengths remain an important factor because long paths use up more network resources. It will be shown in the next section that the link cost function can be chosen such that minimizing the total cost is equivalent to maximizing the weighted probability of achieving virtual cut-through in the network. The total cost function T then represents a tradeoff between using longer than optimal paths to avoid busy links versus the penalty incurred by the increased path length.

III. DERIVATION OF THE LINK COST FUNCTION

It is our intention to minimize the probability of messages getting buffered at intermediate nodes in the path. When a message gets buffered, it has to be examined by the processor on the communication adapter and then scheduled for onward transmission. Thus, in addition to the message store-and-forward delay, an additional processing cost is incurred. Hence, it is preferable to use a long path with a lower probability of buffering. The link cost function is derived based on this probability.

The network $DG = (N, L)$ is modeled as a network of queues with one (single server) queue for each link. The problem of analyzing a network of queues with arbitrary arrival and service patterns is known to be intractable. To make the analysis tractable, the following assumptions are made in this analysis. It is noted that these assumptions may not be valid for a real-time system where periodic message traffic is predominant. However, their use is justified, since the results obtained are used mainly as a guideline for the choice of the link cost function.

A0: Poisson message generation at the source nodes.
A1: Exponentially distributed message lengths.
A2: Infinite nodal capacity.
A3: A packet loses its identity when it arrives at a node and a new length is chosen for it at random, i.e., the Independence Assumption [14].

This model, and the Independence Assumption, was first used by Kleinrock [14], and simulations and actual measurements have later demonstrated the validity of the model. The model has also been used by other researchers for the analysis of networks [7], [15]. Under these assumptions, the arrival process for a link is independent of the departure process from the link and Jackson's result [16] can be applied to the network of queues. That is, in the steady state the network behaves as if each node were stochastically independent of the other nodes and similar to an M/M/1 system.

Consequently, the probability that a message gets buffered at a particular intermediate node is independent of the probability of it getting buffered at any other intermediate node. Hence, the probability of establishing a source-destination cut-through route can be written as a product form expression. Consider a path $P = \{e_{n_0 n_1}, e_{n_1 n_2}, \cdots, e_{n_{l-1} n_l}\}$ from node $n_0 = i$ to node $n_l = j$. The probability that a message from node i to node j will be delivered without buffering at intermediate nodes is given by

$$\text{Prob(cut-through on } P)$$
$$= \prod_{r=1}^{l-1} (1 - \text{Prob(buffering at node } n_r))$$
$$= \prod_{r=1}^{l-1} (1 - \text{Prob(link } e_{n_r n_{r+1}} \text{ is busy}))$$
$$= \prod_{r=1}^{l-1} (1 - \rho_{n_r n_{r+1}})$$
$$= 1 - \sum_{r=1}^{l-1} \rho_{n_r n_{r+1}} + \text{higher order terms in } \rho$$

where $\rho_{n_r n_{r+1}} = f_{n_r n_{r+1}}/C_{n_r n_{r+1}}$ is the mean utilization of link $c_{n_r n_{r+1}}$.

In the type of high-bandwidth network considered here, the mean utilization of the links would tend to be small. Hence, to a good approximation, the higher order terms can be dropped from the equation. Therefore,

$$\text{Prob(cut-through on } P) \approx 1 - \sum_{r=1}^{l-1} f_{n_r n_{r+1}}/C_{n_r n_{r+1}}.$$

$\text{Prob(cut-through on } P)$ is maximum when $\sum_{r=1}^{l-1} f_{n_r n_{r+1}}/C_{n_r n_{r+1}}$ is minimum.

To consider all flows in Q we have to form a weighted sum over all q flows and maximize this:

$$\sum_{k=1}^{q} r_k \cdot \text{Prob(cut-through on } p_k).$$

In this sum, the utilization of the first link in the path will not be included because the expression for cut-through on p_k includes only intermediate nodes. However, for this analysis, an approximation is used in which the utilization of the first link is also considered, since a lower utilization for the first link would ensure that the delay experienced before the message is transmitted from the source node is small. This then corresponds to finding the minimum of

$$\sum_{k=1}^{q} r_k \cdot \left(\sum_{e_{ij} \in p_k} (f_{ij}/C_{ij}) \right).$$

The form of this function matches the cost function of the Path Selection Problem, with the link cost $c_{ij} \equiv f_{ij}/C_{ij}$. If we restrict our attention to homogeneous networks, the capacity C_{ij} is the same for all links and the cost function can be simplified to $c_{ij} = f_{ij}$. This function can be interpreted as follows. As the number of flows through a link increases, f_{ij}

increases and so does the cost of using the link. This would present a bias toward the choice of longer paths to circumvent heavily used links. On the other hand, the total cost for a flow depends upon the length of the path and so, there is an opposing bias to reduce the length of the paths. With $c_{ij} = f_{ij}$ as the link cost function, the total cost $T = \sum_{e_{ij} \in L} f_{ij}^2$. This is the form of the total cost function used in subsequent sections.

IV. PROBLEM CHARACTERIZATION

In this section it is shown that the Path Selection Problem is $\mathcal{NP}$-Hard and the decision problem associated with it is $\mathcal{NP}$-Complete. The decision problem, shown below as Decision Problem 1, is $\mathcal{NP}$-Complete because it contains the subproblem of finding a feasible set of paths. It can be shown that SATISFIABILITY (SAT) [17] is reducible to this subproblem of finding feasible paths. The reduction relies on capacity constraints which force exclusive use of links. However, even when the capacity constraints are not imposed, the problem remains $\mathcal{NP}$-Complete when the link cost c_{ij} is a function of the link utilization. In particular, it is shown that Decision Problem 2 given below, which has the cost function $c_{ij} = f_{ij}$ and no link capacity constraints, is $\mathcal{NP}$-Complete. The definition of SAT, adapted from [18], is given in Appendix A.

Decision Problem 1: Given N, L, Q, and the link capacities C_{ij}. Is there a feasible set, S, of paths such that for each edge $e_{ij} \in L$, $f_{ij} \leq C_{ij}$ where $f_{ij} = \sum_{e_{ij} \in p_k} r_k$?

Decision Problem 2: Given N, L, Q, link cost function $c_{ij} = f_{ij}$, and a bound B. Is there a feasible set, S, of paths such that total cost $= \sum_{k=1}^{k=q} r_k \cdot \left(\sum_{e_{ij} \in p_k} c_{ij} \right) = \sum_{e_{ij} \in L} f_{ij}^2 \leq B$?

The reduction from SAT is similar for the two problems and it is shown only for the second problem. It is based on the method used in [19] for the Multicommodity Integral Flow problem. The proof is constructive, using graph components shown in Fig. 3, and it shows a polynomial time transformation from an instance of SAT to an instance of Decision Problem 2.

Theorem 1: Decision Problem 2 (DP2) is $\mathcal{NP}$-Complete.

Proof: The proof of this theorem can be found in Appendix B.

Corollary 1: The Path Selection Problem with cost function $c_{ij} = f_{ij}$, and no capacity constraints, is $\mathcal{NP}$-Hard.

The Path Selection Problem is a search problem which has a finite upper bound, so it can be easily shown that it is Turing reducible to DP2 using the "binary search" technique described in [18]. Hence, it follows from the theorem that the Path Selection problem is $\mathcal{NP}$-Hard. Also, from the proof of Theorem 5 it can be seen that a bound, B, can be suitably chosen to accommodate other cost functions where the link cost is a monotone increasing function of the link utilization.

V. SOLUTION ALGORITHM

The problem of finding a minimum cost solution has been shown to be $\mathcal{NP}$-Hard when the link cost function is a function

of the utilization. It is observed that the search space grows as $\prod_{k=1}^{q} |P_k|$, where $|P_k|$ is usually large for the types of regular interconnection networks that are under consideration. This implies that it is impractical to determine the optimal solution by brute-force techniques, even for a small number of flows. Thus, we need to find a good heuristic solution for the problem. We have developed an algorithm which selects paths one at a time, while keeping the other paths fixed. The algorithm begins with an initial assignment of paths to the flows. It then successively tries to improve the paths, considering one flow at a time, until no further cost improvement is possible. An outline of this algorithm, which is called Route_All, is given in Fig. 2. The procedure for determining the path for a single flow, called Route_One, is described in Fig. 1. The theoretical basis for this procedure is given below.

The algorithm required for selection of a single route is one in which we are given the current utilization of the network and the characteristics of the new flow to be established. The objective here is to find a route such that, under the given cost function, the incremental cost is minimized. It is shown that a version of the *shortest path* algorithm with appropriately defined link lengths will yield a solution.

Consider a path p_k for this new flow. When this flow is added to the system, the new flows in the links are given by

$$f'_{ij} = \begin{cases} f_{ij} + r_k & \text{if } e_{ij} \in p_k \\ f_{ij} & \text{otherwise.} \end{cases}$$

The additional cost incurred is then

$$
\begin{aligned}
I &= \sum_{e_{ij} \in L} [(f'_{ij})^2 - f_{ij}^2] \\
&= \sum_{e_{ij} \in p_k} (2 f_{ij} r_k + r_k^2) \\
&= r_k \cdot \sum_{e_{ij} \in p_k} (2 f_{ij} + r_k).
\end{aligned}
$$

This incremental cost, I, is minimum when $\sum_{e_{ij} \in p_k} (2 f_{ij} + r_k)$ is minimum. This minimum can be obtained by using $2 f_{ij} + r_k$ as the *length* of link e_{ij} and finding the shortest path from s_k to d_k. This is the approach used in Algorithm Route_One, in which a greedy algorithm is used to find the shortest path. Since all the link lengths are nonnegative, a greedy algorithm would yield the shortest path. From this discussion, it is clear that Algorithm Route_One is optimal under the condition that routes that are already established cannot be disturbed. This is the case when requests for creation of new flows arrive dynamically and are serviced in order.

Algorithm Route_All starts with an initial flow assignment, F. It then selects each flow in turn, removes it from F, and checks whether a better route is available using Route_One. The function *Incremental_cost* computes I as shown in the derivation above. The solution obtained is not guaranteed to be optimal because it is possible that a better solution may be obtained by the simultaneous re-routing of multiple paths. The algorithm, however, is guaranteed to terminate since the cost function is monotone decreasing with successive re-routing. Algorithm Route_One is essentially a shortest path algorithm and its complexity is $O(N^2)$ for an adjacency

Algorithm Route_One

*/

Given N, L, $F=\{f_{ij} : e_{ij} \in L\}$ and a new flow (s_k,d_k,r_k), find a route p_k with minimum incremental cost.

*/

/* Initialize the distance matrix D_{ij} */
```
for each i, j ∈ N
    if e_ij ∈ L
        D_ij := 2 * f_ij + r_k
    else
        D_ij := 0
    endif
end for
```
Use the Greedy Algorithm to find a path p_k from s_k to d_k with the distance matrix D_{ij}.

end Route_One

Fig. 1.   Single path selection.

Algorithm Route_All

/*

Given N, L, and Q, find a set of paths for each flow in Q with the objective of minimizing the cost function.

*/

```
Assign an initial path for each flow, initialize the flow matrix F.
new_route_found := TRUE
while (new_route_found)
    new_route_found := FALSE
    for each (s_i, d_i, r_i) in Q
        remove p_i from F
        old_cost = Incremental_cost(p_i)

        Route_One (s_i, d_i, r_i) returns path p'_i

        new_cost = Incremental_cost(p'_i)
        if (new_cost < old_cost)
            add p'_i to F
            new_route_found := TRUE
        else
            restore p_i to F
        end if
    end for
end while
end Route_All
```

Fig. 2.   The route selection algorithm.

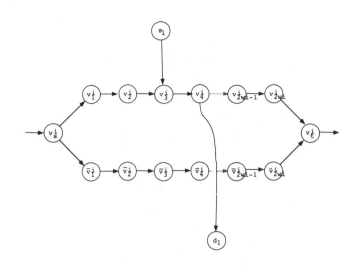

Fig. 3.   Graph component corresponding to a variable.

matrix representation of the network. Algorithm Route_All uses Route_One repeatedly, but the number of iterations is data dependent and cannot be easily determined. The running time of Route_All is bounded below by $q \cdot N^2$, that is, it is $\Omega(qN^2)$. However, the results of experiments with the algorithm on several flow patterns show that the convergence is rapid.

VI. PERFORMANCE EVALUATION

In this section, we evaluate the performance of the algorithms developed in Section V, and study the effectiveness of the cost function derived in Section III. To evaluate the performance of Algorithm Route_All, termed ALLP, it is compared with two other path selection algorithms. One of them, called INC, is a simple extension of Algorithm Route_One in which routes are assigned to the flows in the order of arrival and no further re-routing is employed. The other is a "pure" shortest path algorithm (SP) in which a path of minimum length from source to destination is selected for each flow. The purpose of this comparison is to measure the improvement obtained using the re-routing technique. The

comparison between SP and INC demonstrates the utility of Algorithm Route_One as compared to a simple shortest path algorithm. The complexity of INC is the same as that of the shortest path algorithm, $O(N^2)$ for an adjacency matrix representation of the network. The execution time is slightly higher because it has to update the flow f_{ij} in the links which constitute the route after the route has been selected.

To evaluate the effectiveness of the cost function, we used a discrete-event simulator which models a network with virtual cut-through switching. This simulator was originally developed by the authors of [20] to study the performance of the HARTS network. HARTS is a multicomputer with a C-wrapped hexagonal mesh topology [6], currently being built in the Real-Time Computing Laboratory, The University of Michigan. The C-wrapped hexagonal mesh is a regular, homogeneous graph in which each node is connected to six other nodes (see Fig. 4). Each HARTS node has a network processor which is connected to the network through the routing controller. The simulator models the front-end routing controller [10], which implements virtual cut-through, and its interface to the network processor of each HARTS node. It accurately models the delivery of each packet by emulating the routing hardware along the route of a packet at the microcode level. It also captures the internal bus access overheads in the routing controller experienced by packets as they pass through an intermediate node. We modified the simulator to generate traffic based on each connection (flow), and to collect statistics on the number of *bufferings*, i.e., the number of times packets failed to cut-through and were buffered at intermediate nodes. We chose to measure the number of bufferings because that is what the cost function tries to capture. We did not use the average delivery time as a measure because the overhead cost incurred when a packet is buffered depends upon the processor, and the load on the processor. The simulator did not model this load.

The simulator allows us to relax many of the modeling assumptions used in the derivation of the cost function. In particular, we do not use the Independence assumption, nor do we have exponentially distributed message lengths. In our

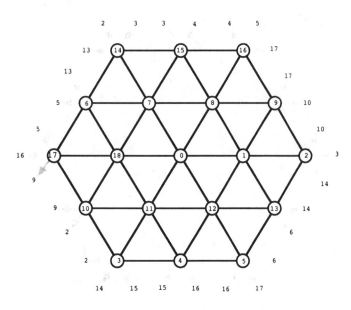

Fig. 4.   A hexagonal mesh of dimension 3 (E-3).

experiments, we configured the simulator for a hexagonal mesh of size 5 (denoted by E-5), which has 61 nodes. We generated sets of flows by selecting the source, destination, and quantity of each flow using independent random number generators. The source node was chosen using a uniform random number generator. For a fixed source, the destination node was chosen using an independent random number generator, with two different types of distributions in different experiments. One was a uniform distribution, where the destination node is chosen to be any other node in the system with equal probability. The second distribution tried to capture the principle of locality, that is, the destination node is more likely to be close to the source. The value of each flow was selected in the range [1, 10] using a third uniform random number generator. Note that in the cost function, it is the *relative* values of the flows which are significant, the units do not affect the results.

We used the SP, INC, and ALLP algorithms to produce 3 different sets of route assignments for each set of flows. These algorithms also returned the "cost" of the route assignments that they produced. We then used the mesh simulator to simulate traffic on these flows and measured the number of bufferings for each of the three sets of routes. The value of a flow was interpreted to be a rate of packet generation, and the packet size was fixed at 128 bytes. On each flow, packets were generated using a Poisson distribution with a mean inter-arrival time specified by the value of the flow. The actual rate of packet generation and the service time for the packets are a function of the link transmission rate. The effective link transmission rate in our simulation was 1.5 μs per byte, and a flow value of 1 was converted into an arrival rate of 1 packet per 180 ms. This value was chosen to ensure that the average link utilization remained low (it was below 0.4 in all our experiments). We note that the number of bufferings observed is a function of link utilization and it would change if we assigned a different rate for the flow value. We could make this arbitrary choice of generation rate because,

in our experiments, we are interested in the relative values of the number of bufferings for the three route assignments. In each simulation, we collected statistics over a period in which 100 000 packets were delivered. This number was chosen by looking at the convergence of the statistic of interest (number of bufferings) in some sample simulations.

Experiment 1: In this experiment, for any source, the destination of the flow was chosen using a uniform distribution. The number of flows was varied from 50 to 500, and this resulted in a change in the observed average link utilization from 0.035 to 0.33. The results of the simulation are shown in Fig. 5, which plots the number of bufferings observed for a particular number of flows with each of the three algorithms. Each data point in the graph represents an average over 50 different data sets. The results here can be compared with the cost figures shown in Fig. 6 for the same sets of flows. This experiment also allows us to compare the performance of the three algorithms. The comparison shows that the computed cost and the observed number of bufferings have similar behavior, except when the number of flows is very small. In this case, INC and ALLP perform better than what the cost function shows. It is seen that there is a modest improvement for INC over SP, and for ALLP over INC. The improvement for INC over SP is higher when there are fewer flows, that is, when the network load is light, because INC is able to locate routes through links that are otherwise unused. Since INC performs quite well in this situation, the additional improvement attainable by using ALLP is small. On the other hand, when the number of flows is very large, because of the uniform communication pattern, most of the links are almost evenly loaded and INC is not able to find much improvement.

Experiment 2: This experiment differs from Experiment 1 in that the destination node was picked by first selecting a hexagonal ring and then selecting the particular node within the ring, considering the source node as the center of the mesh. Since there are more nodes in the outer rings, the probability of selecting a node in an outer hexagon is smaller than that of selecting a node from an inner hexagon. With this distribution, the average source-destination separation in a mesh of size e is $e/2$ as compared to $(2e - 1)/3$ in the case of a uniform distribution. When the number of flows was varied from 50 to 400, the observed average link utilization changed from 0.035 to 0.26. The number of flows could not be increased beyond 400 for the simulation because the routes generated by SP resulted in severe network congestion. The results of the simulation are shown in Fig. 7, while those of the cost function are shown in Fig. 8. Here again, the results for the simulation match well with those given by the cost function. There is an apparent anomaly seen here, in that, the cost for the SP algorithm is vastly increased even though the average distance for a route is reduced as compared to the uniform distribution. The reason for this is that, although the route length is longer in Experiment 1, the number of different paths to nodes in an outer hexagon is substantially larger. Hence, because of the uniform distributions for sources and destinations, the SP algorithm performed quite well. However, for the nonuniform distribution, where the average number of possible shortest paths for a flow is smaller, the effects

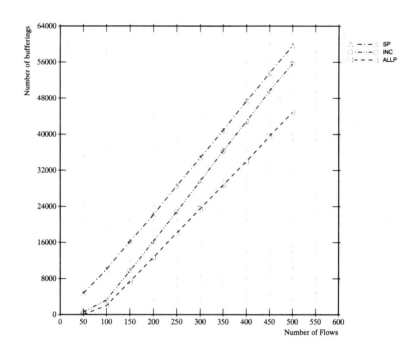

Fig. 5. Comparison using number of bufferings: E-5 mesh, uniform distribution.

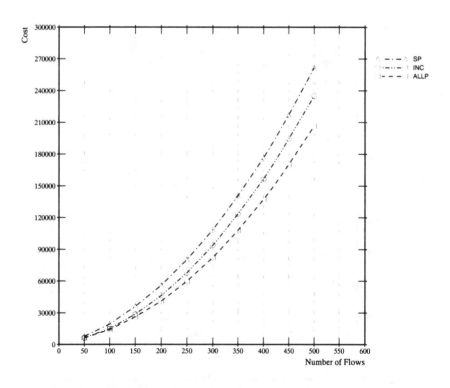

Fig. 6. Comparison using the cost function: E-5 mesh, uniform distribution.

of congestion are more pronounced and so the performance for SP deteriorates. The INC and ALLP algorithms are better equipped to cope with congestion and this is reflected in their vastly better performance than SP.

From these experiments, we can see that a route assignment which reduces the cost function also results in a reduction of the number of bufferings in a hexagonal mesh network.

Other Experiments: To evaluate the performance of the routing algorithms, we have to test them on other topologies and other mesh sizes. However, the computing resources required for comparing the performance using the number of bufferings is prohibitive. The mesh simulator ran on a SUN Sparcstation 1, and the time required for the simulation of a single set of routes was several minutes. Consequently, we

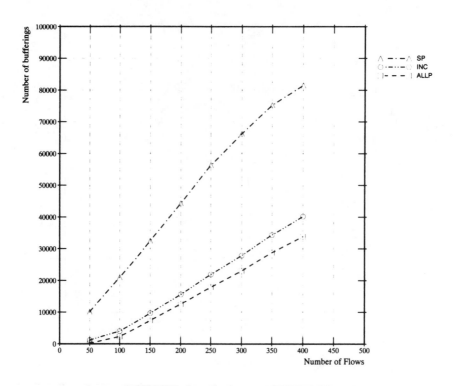

Fig. 7. Comparison using number of bufferings: E-5 mesh, nonuniform distribution.

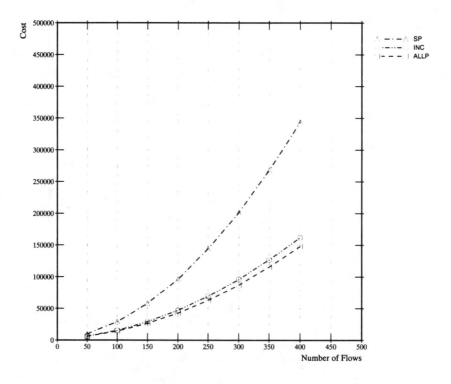

Fig. 8. Comparison using the cost function: E-5 mesh, nonuniform distribution.

evaluate the algorithms based only on the cost function. We have tested the routing algorithms on two network topologies: binary hypercubes and hexagonal meshes, and for different network sizes. This choice was motivated by the fact that variations of virtual cut-through switching have been implemented for these topologies. The binary hypercube is a well-studied topology [5] and is used in many commercially available multicomputer systems, hence its description is omitted.

The performance of these algorithms has been studied using simulated traffic patterns which were generated as described

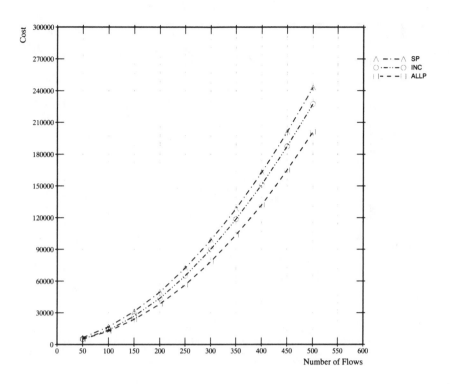

Fig. 9. Cost comparison: E-4 mesh, uniform distribution.

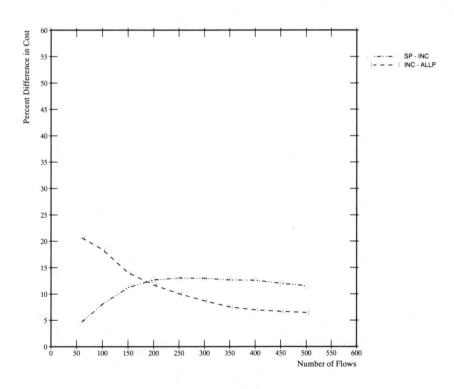

Fig. 10. Performance improvement: E-4 mesh, uniform distribution.

earlier. For each data point, the experiment was repeated with 100 different sets of flows and an average value was obtained. The standard deviation of the mean was found to be less than 5% of the mean for all data points, and less than 3% for most data points.

Figs. 9 and 10 show the results of the simulation on a hexagonal mesh of size 4 (denoted by E-4), having 37 nodes, using a uniform distribution for the selection of the destination node. A comparison of the total cost for the solutions obtained by the three algorithms is shown in Fig. 9, and the percent

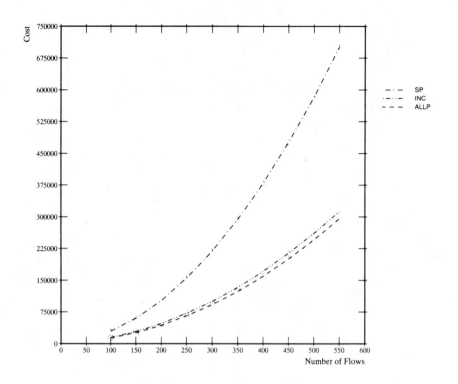

Fig. 11.   Cost comparison: E-4 mesh, nonuniform distribution.

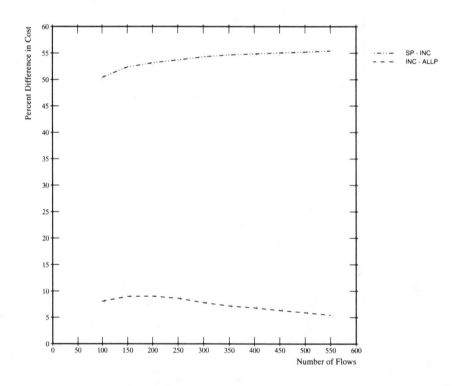

Fig. 12.   Performance improvement: E-4 mesh, nonuniform distribution.

improvement in cost between SP and INC, and between INC and ALLP, is shown in Fig. 10. These results are similar to those obtained for the E-5 mesh in Experiment 1. In the second set of experiments for the hexagonal mesh, the destination node was selected using a nonuniform distribution as in Experiment 2. The simulation results obtained with this nonuniform distribution for an E-4 mesh are shown in Figs. 11 and 12, and they are similar to the results obtained for the E-5 mesh in Experiment 2. We also performed experiments on an E-6 mesh, with similar results.

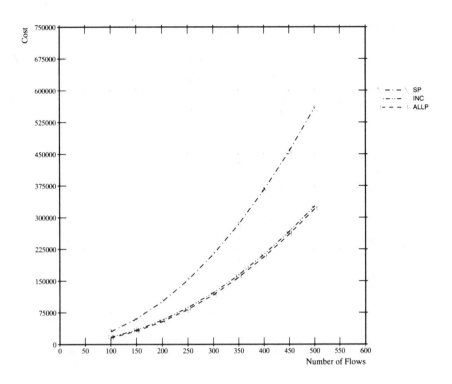

Fig. 13. Cost comparison: Q-5 hypercube, uniform distribution.

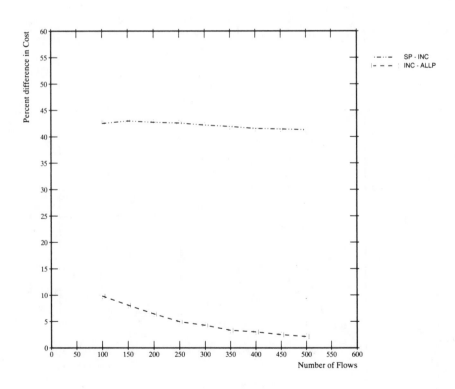

Fig. 14. Performance improvement: Q-5 hypercube, uniform distribution.

The experiments with the binary hypercube used a uniform distribution for the selection of source and destination nodes, but in this case, the average distance between source and destination is $n/2$ for a hypercube of dimension n. The results obtained for hypercubes of dimension 5 (Q-5, 32 nodes) and 6 (Q-6, 64 nodes) are shown in Figs. 13 to 16. These are similar to the results for the hexagonal mesh with a nonuniform source-destination distribution. They also show that the INC and ALLP algorithms perform much better than the SP algorithm. ALLP again shows a modest improvement over INC.

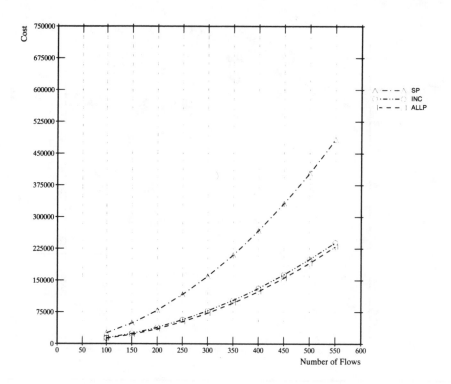

Fig. 15. Cost comparison: Q-6 hypercube, uniform distribution.

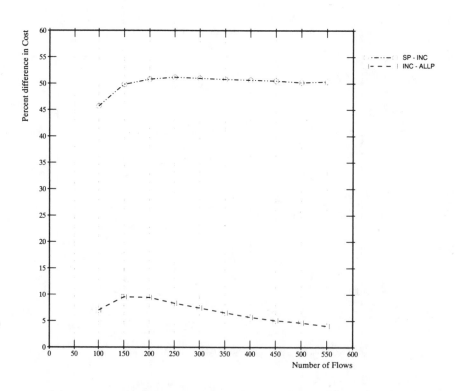

Fig. 16. Performance improvement: Q-6 hypercube, uniform distribution.

In Algorithm Route_All, the final results can depend on the initial state of the network. To study the sensitivity of the results to the initial flow assignment, three different strategies were used to select this assignment. The first method was to select a route using the shortest path algorithm without considering the other routes in the network. The second method used the Route_One algorithm, with routes chosen in the order in which the flows were generated. In the third strategy, the flows were sorted in the order of cost before using the Route_One algorithm for assignment. Both the ascending and the descending order of cost were considered. A comparison of these strategies was made for an E-4 mesh using the same set of flows as input, and the experiment was repeated several times with different sets of flows. The results indicated that, on the average, there was very little difference in the final cost.

VII. CONCLUSIONS

The problem of routing inter-processor message traffic in a point-to-point interconnection network has been formulated as an optimization problem for the total cost, where the cost of a route depends upon the links that are used. The link cost function $c_{ij} = f_{ij}$ was chosen with the objective of maximizing the probability of establishing virtual cut-through routes in the network using analysis based on a queueing model for the network. It is noted that although some of the assumptions made in the queueing analysis may not be valid in a real-time system, the cost function obtained intuitively captures the notion of congestion avoidance. This was verified in our experiments with the hexagonal mesh simulator.

The optimization problem was shown to be $\mathcal{NP}$-Hard, and thus, a heuristic algorithm was developed for the solution. The performance of this algorithm was studied for the binary hypercube and the hexagonal mesh network topologies using simulation. It was found that the extent of the performance improvement depends upon the network topology and the distribution of the source-destination pairs in the network.

The ALLP algorithm can be used for selecting routes off-line in conjunction with an algorithm for assignment of tasks to the nodes. The cost function of ALLP can then be incorporated into the cost of the task assignment to reflect the cost of communication. On the other hand, the INC algorithm can be used to select routes for flows in a dynamic environment when requests are serviced as they arrive. It is optimal for the cost function derived here under the condition that routes that are already established cannot be disturbed. We have used this algorithm to select routes for real-time channels, as described in [21]. One possible extension of this work is to consider routing for multicast communication and to integrate this with the current algorithm. This problem is significantly different from the one treated so far because we are now trying to increase the overlap between paths from a node to different destinations.

APPENDIX

A. THE SATISFIABILITY PROBLEM

Let $U = \{x_1, x_2, \cdots, x_m\}$ be a set of Boolean variables. If u is a variable in U, then u and $\overline{u}$ are *literals* over U. A truth assignment for U is a function $t : U \to \{T, F\}$, which corresponds to *true* and *false*, respectively. The literal u is true under t if and only if the variable u is true under t. Similarly, the literal $\overline{u}$ is true if and only if the variable u is false.

A *clause* over U is a set of literals over U, and represents the disjunction of those literals. It is *satisfied* by a truth assignment if and only if at least one of its members is true under that assignment. A collection C of clauses over U is

satisfiable if and only if there exists some truth assignment for U that simultaneously satisfies all the clauses in C. With this definitions, the SATISFIABILITY problem can be stated as follows. It was shown to be $\mathcal{NP}$-Complete by Cook [17].

SATISFIABILITY: Given a set U of variables and a collection C of clauses over U. Is there a truth assignment for U such that C is satisfiable?

B. PROOF OF THEOREM 1

Theorem: Decision Problem 2 (DP2) is $\mathcal{NP}$-Complete.

Proof: It is easy to see that DP2 is in $\mathcal{NP}$ because given a guess for the set of paths, it is possible to compute and verify that the total cost is within the bound B, in polynomial time. We now show that SAT is reducible to DP2.

Given an instance of SAT with collection $C = \{C_1, C_2, \cdots, C_\ell\}$ of clauses on a finite set U of variables. For each variable x_i, let t_i be the number of occurrences of x_i in the clauses, and u_i be the number of occurrences of $\overline{x_i}$. Let $w_i = \max(t_i, u_i)$. Construct a graph component G_i corresponding to this variable as shown in Fig. 3. The component consists of a start node v_s^i, an end node v_t^i, and two chains of nodes, each with $2w_i$ nodes. The chains represent a choice of truth assignment for the variable. These components are then connected in series with the end node of component G_i connected to the start node of component G_{i+1}, that is, v_t^i connected to v_s^{i+1}. Create special nodes s and d and links from s to v_s^1, $v_t^{|U|}$ to d.

For each clause C_i create two nodes, s_i and d_i. For the jth occurrence of literal x_i, say in clause C_ℓ, create links from from s_ℓ to v_{2j-1}^i and from v_{2j}^i to d_ℓ. A similar construction is used for an occurrence of $\overline{x_i}$, but in that case, the nodes $\overline{v_{2j-1}^i}$ and $\overline{v_{2j}^i}$ would be used. The graph components and the additional links described above, together form the sets N and L. The set of flows is chosen to be $Q = \{(s, d, 1), (s_1, d_1, 1), \cdots, (s_{|C|}, d_{|C|}, 1)\}$. Finally, the bound B is selected to be $3|C| + 1 + \sum_{i=1}^{|U|} (2w_i + 2)$. This bound is in fact the total cost of routing the set of flows Q, where each link has *exactly one* flow. The $3|C|$ part corresponds to the flows associated with the clauses, and the $(1 + \sum_{i=1}^{|U|} (2w_i + 2))$ part corresponds to the $(s, d, 1)$ flow. This gives an instance of DP2.

If the instance of SAT has a feasible solution, there is a truth assignment to the variables which satisfies all the clauses. In the corresponding instance of DP2, the following solution is feasible. The path from s to d is chosen such that if x_i is assigned a FALSE value, the upper trail $(v_1^i, v_2^i, \cdots)$ is chosen through the component G_i, and vice versa. In each clause C_j, there exists a term u_k^j which evaluates to TRUE and the link in the graph component corresponding to this term, say e_j, would be unused. The path for (s_j, d_j) can be chosen to go through this link. It can be verified that this choice of paths gives a feasible solution for DP2.

Similarly, given a solution to DP2, the path from s to d through the component G_i determines the truth assignment for the corresponding variable. The choice of B forces the paths selected to be disjoint. Otherwise, if a link were used in more than one path, its cost will be greater than 1 and the total cost will exceed B. This ensures that a variable cannot be used with conflicting values in different clauses, and the path (s_j, d_j) identifies a term in C_j which has a TRUE value. Thus, it is clear that the instance of SAT has a feasible truth assignment *iff* there is a feasible set of paths for the instance of DP2. □

REFERENCES

[1] J. Goldberg *et al.*, "Development and analysis of SIFT," NASA contractor rep. 172146, NASA Langley Research Center, Feb. 1984.
[2] R. M. Kieckhafer, C. J. Walter, A. M. Finn, and P. M. Thambidurai, "The MAFT architecture for distributed fault tolerance," *IEEE Trans. Comput.*, vol. C-37, pp. 398–405, Apr. 1988.
[3] J. Lala, "AIPS tutorial," tech. rep., The Charles Stark Draper Laboratory, Inc., Jan. 1987.
[4] "Completion of the advanced information processing system," The Charles Stark Draper Laboratory, report in response to NASA Langley Research Center CBD announcement Ref SS017, Issue PSA-9214.
[5] C. L. Seitz, "The cosmic cube," *Commun. ACM*, vol. 28, pp. 22–33, Jan. 1985.
[6] M.-S. Chen, K. G. Shin, and D. D. Kandlur, "Addressing, routing, and broadcasting in hexagonal mesh multiprocessors," *IEEE Trans. Comput.*, vol. C-39, pp. 10–18, Jan. 1990.
[7] P. Kermani and L. Kleinrock, "Virtual cut-through: A new computer communication switching technique," *Comput. Networks*, vol. 3, pp. 267–286, 1979.
[8] W. J. Dally and C. L. Seitz, "The torus routing chip," *J. Distributed Syst.*, vol. 1, no. 3, pp. 187–196, 1986.
[9] W. J. Dally and P. Song, "Design of a self-timed VLSI multicomputer communication controller," in *Proc. IEEE Int. Conf. Comput. Design: VLSI in Comput.*, 1987, pp. 230–234.
[10] J. W. Dolter, P. Ramanathan, and K. G. Shin, "A microprogrammable VLSI routing controller for HARTS," in *Proc. IEEE Int. Conf. Comput. Design: VLSI in Comput.*, IEEE, Oct. 1989, pp. 160–163.
[11] D. Ferrari, "Guaranteeing performance for real-time communication in wide-area networks," Tech. Rep. UCB/CSD 89/485, U.C.B. Computer Science Division, EECS, Berkeley, CA, Jan. 1989.
[12] M. Schwartz and T. E. Stern, "Routing techniques used in computer communication networks," *IEEE Trans. Commun.*, vol. 28, pp. 539–552, Apr. 1980.
[13] R. P. Bianchini and J. P. Shen, "Interprocessor traffic scheduling algorithm for multiple-processor networks," *IEEE Trans. Comput.*, vol. C-36, pp. 396–409, Apr. 1987.
[14] L. Kleinrock, *Communication Nets: Stochastic Message Flow and Delay.* New York: McGraw-Hill, 1964.
[15] M. Ilyas and H. T. Mouftah, "Toward performance improvement of cut-through switching in computer networks," *Perform. Eval.*, vol. 6, pp. 125–133, July 1986.
[16] J. R. Jackson, "Networks of waiting lines," *Oper. Res.*, vol. 5, pp. 518–521, Aug. 1957.
[17] S. A. Cook, "The complexity of theorem-proving procedures," in *Proc. 3rd Annu. ACM Symp. Theory of Comput.*, 1971, pp. 151–158.
[18] M. R. Garey and D. S. Johnson, *Computers and Intractability.* San Francisco, CA: Freeman, 1979.
[19] S. Even, A. Itai, and A. Shamir, "On the complexity of timetable and multicommodity flow problems," *SIAM J. Comput.*, vol. 5, pp. 691–703, Dec. 1976.
[20] J. W. Dolter, P. Ramanathan, and K. G. Shin, "Performance analysis of virtual cut-through switching in HARTS: A hexagonal mesh multicomputer," *IEEE Trans. Comput.*, vol. 40, pp. 669–680, June 1991.
[21] D. D. Kandlur and K. G. Shin, "A communication subsystem for HARTS: An experimental distributed real-time system," Tech. Rep., CSE-TR-109-91, CSE Div., EECS Dep., Unv. of Michigan, Ann Arbor, Oct. 1991.

Dilip D. Kandlur (S'90–M'91) received the B.Tech. degree in computer science and engineering from the Indian Institute of Technology, Bombay, in 1985 and the M.S.E. and Ph.D. degrees, also in computer science and engineering, from the University of Michigan, Ann Arbor, in 1987 and 1991 respectively.

From 1987 to 1991 he was a member of the Real-Time Computing Laboratory at the University of Michigan, involved in the development of the HARTS experimental real-time system. He was also the recipient of an IBM Graduate Fellowship. Currently, he is a research staff member at the IBM Thomas J. Watson Research Center, Yorktown Heights, NY. His research interests include operating systems, real-time systems, and computer networks.

Kang G. Shin (S'75–M'78–SM'83–F'92) received the B.S. degree in electronics engineering from Seoul National University, Seoul, Korea, in 1970, and both the M.S. and Ph.D degrees in electrical engineering from Cornell University, Ithaca, NY in 1976 and 1978, respectively.

He is Professor and Associate Chair of Electrical Engineering and Computer Science (EECS) for Computer Science and Engineering, The University of Michigan, Ann Arbor. He has authored/coauthored over 230 technical papers (about 100 of these in archival journals) and several book chapters in the areas of distributed real-time computing and control, fault-tolerant computing, computer architecture, and robotics and automation. In 1985, he founded the Real-Time Computing Laboratory, where he and his colleagues are currently building a 19-node hexagonal mesh multicomputer, called **HARTS**, to validate various architectures and analytic results in the area of distributed real-time computing. From 1978 to 1982 he was on the faculty of Rensselaer Polytechnic Institute, Troy, NY. He has held visiting positions at the U.S. Airforce Flight Dynamics Laboratory, AT&T Bell Laboratories, Computer Science Division within the Department of Electrical Engineering and Computer Science at U.C. Berkeley, and International Computer Science Institute, Berkeley, CA.

Dr. Shin was the Program Chairman of the 1986 IEEE Real-Time Systems Symposium (RTSS), the General Chairman of the 1987 RTSS, the Guest Editor of the 1987 August special issue of IEEE TRANSACTIONS ON COMPUTERS on Real-Time Systems, and is a Program Co-Chair for the 1992 International Conference on Parallel Processing. He currently chairs the IEEE Technical Committee on Real-Time Systems, is a Distinguished Visitor of the Computer Society of the IEEE, an Editor of IEEE TRANSACTIONS ON PARALLEL AND DISTRIBUTED SYSTEMS, and an Area Editor of *International Journal of Time-Critical Computing Systems*. In 1987, he received the Outstanding IEEE Transactions on Automatic Control Paper Award for a paper on robot trajectory planning. In 1989, he also received the Research Excellence Award from The University of Michigan.

Chapter 11: Fault Diagnosis

Before fault-tolerance schemes can be applied in a given network, *fault detection* and *fault diagnosis* must take place. Normally, fault detection in interconnection networks is accomplished by means of handshaking protocols. Fault diagnosis, which consists of testing and fault location, is more involved. Several network fault-diagnosis mechanisms have been proposed and studied. These mechanisms can be centralized or distributed, in software or in hardware, for circuit-switched or packet-switched networks, for single or multiple faults, and for processor, switch, or link faults.

This chapter includes a selection of papers that covers the whole spectrum of fault-diagnosis methods. The paper by Davis, Hsu, and Siegel (1985) gives distributed software techniques for locating a single link or switch stuck-at fault in circuit-switched multistage networks. The paper by Mourad, Özden, and Malek (1991) gives centralized software techniques for testing multiple stuck-at faults and control circuitry faults in packet-switched multistage networks. Liu and Shin (1989) present a method called *polynomial testing* to test stuck-at faults in packet-switched multistage networks at two levels: the *network level* and the *switch level*. At the network level, the procedure is distributed and implemented in software. At the switch level, the switches are provided with self-testing hardware. The final paper, by Chiang and Wu (1986), describes a distributed software method to test multiple processor faults in general networks.

Fault Location Techniques for Distributed Control Interconnection Networks

NATHANIEL J. DAVIS IV, STUDENT MEMBER, IEEE, WILLIAM TSUN-YUK HSU, AND HOWARD JAY SIEGEL, SENIOR MEMBER, IEEE

Abstract —One class of networks suitable for use in parallel processing systems is the multistage cube network. This paper focuses on fault location procedures suitable for use in networks that employ distributed routing control through the use of routing tags and message transmission protocols. Faults occurring in the data lines can corrupt message routing tags transmitted over them and thereby cause misrouting of messages. Protocol lines (used in handshaking between network sources and destinations), if faulty, can prevent a message path from being established or can cause the path to "lock up" once transmission of data has begun. These faults have more pronounced effects on the network performance than faults previously considered for centralized routing control systems. The single-fault location procedures presented form a logical superset to those of the centralized control systems (where message routing is dictated by the actions of a global control unit) and can be adapted for use in both circuit and packet switching networks.

Index Terms —Circuit switching, cube network, distributed processing, fault location, generalized cube, interconnection networks, multimicroprocessor systems, parallel processing, PASM.

I. INTRODUCTION

WITH the advent of very large scale integrated circuit technology, relatively inexpensive hardware systems and subsystems are now readily available. The result has been the greater use of multiple-processor system designs that employ processing elements, operating in parallel, to achieve high levels of computational power. The ability of these parallel systems to continue operations, despite the occurrence of faults, is of critical importance.

One class of interconnection networks suitable for use in parallel processing systems is the multistage cube network [15]. This class includes the omega [9], the indirect binary n-cube [13], the baseline [6], and the generalized cube [15]. The cube network is not, however, fault tolerant. Any single point failure in the network will prevent some source—destination pair of functional subsystems from communi-

cating. Fault tolerance can be introduced into the network through the use of one or more "extra" stages of switches [1], [3], [12]. Effective use of the redundant paths in the network, available as a result of the extra stages, requires that each source know the exact location of any network faults.

Previous work in fault location has concentrated on networks operating under a centralized control scheme [2], [6], [7], [11]. Systems such as PASM [14] and Ultracomputer [8] implement the network using a distributed control methodology. Network faults in a distributed system, especially faults occurring in the interconnecting links within the network, can cause much more severe errors in network operations than could a similar fault in a centralized control system (a result of message misrouting due to the corruption of data tags). In addition, faulty protocol lines (used in handshaking between network sources and destinations) can prevent a path from being established or can cause the path to "lock up" once the transmission of data has begun. In this paper, the single-fault location procedures necessary for distributed control networks are considered. These procedures form a logical superset to those of the centralized systems. This work has been motivated by the implementation of the PASM system prototype [4].

In Section II, the system and network models are defined and the fault model is presented. Section III overviews the centralized control fault location procedures of [6]. An outline of the testing procedure for use in a distributed control network is presented in Section IV. Potential network faults, their ensuing effects on the network, and the testing procedure outputs they would produce are presented in Section V. Section VI discusses fault location techniques based on the output responses of the testing procedures. Procedures for testing broadcast connections are overviewed in Section VII. Section VIII summarizes these results.

II. THE INTERCONNECTION NETWORK MODEL

Consider a parallel processing system consisting of N functional subsystems where $N = 2^n$. The subsystems will be assumed to be *processing elements (PE's)*, processors paired with their own local memories. The interconnection network will have N inputs (sources) and N outputs (destinations). PE i will be connected to network input i and output i. The multistage cube network [15] consists of n stages with each stage being composed of $N/2$ two-by-two interchange boxes. Interchange boxes in stage i pair I/O lines with link

Manuscript received February 1, 1985; revised May 30, 1985. This work was supported by the Rome Air Development Center under Contract F30602-83-K-0119. A preliminary version of this paper was presented at the IEEE 1985 International Conference on Parallel Processing, St. Charles, IL, Aug. 1985.

N. J. Davis IV was with the PASM Parallel Processing Laboratory, School of Electrical Engineering, Purdue University, West Lafayette, IN 47907. He is now with the Department of Electrical Engineering, Air Force Institute of Technology, Wright-Patterson Air Force Base, OH 45433.

W. T. -Y. Hsu and H. J. Siegel are with the PASM Parallel Processing Laboratory, School of Electrical Engineering, Purdue University, West Lafayette, IN 47907.

Reprinted from *IEEE Trans. Computers*, Vol. C-34, No. 10, Oct. 1985, pp. 902-910. Copyright © 1985 by The Institute of Electrical and Electronics Engineers, Inc. All rights reserved.

labels that differ only in the ith bit position. The same labeling is used for both the input and output lines connected to an interchange box. A multistage cube network is shown in Fig. 1, with $N = 8$. Each data path through the network will be m bits wide where m is a function of the system hardware used. Circuit switched data transmission is assumed, where a complete path linking the source and destination PE's must be established before the actual data transfer can begin.

Two different approaches can be used to govern the manner in which connections are made in the network. Using centralized control, a global network controller mediates between message requests and establishes the desired network connections. In contrast, distributed control removes this serial bottleneck by allowing the individual interchange boxes to establish their own connections based on the use of *routing tags* associated with each message. Distributed routing control using *destination address* routing tags [9] is assumed in this paper. The complete routing information is contained in a $2n$ bit routing tag: an n bit *broadcast mask* and an n bit *destination tag* equal to the binary expansion of the destination address. Interchange boxes in stage i examine bits i of both the broadcast masks and the routing tags for the messages at their input ports and make the switching connections accordingly. If a mask bit is "1," then a broadcast to both outputs is to be performed. If the mask bit is "0," then the routing tag specifies the desired connection pattern. A "0" in bit i of the routing tag indicates a connection to the upper output port is desired, while a "1" indicates connection to the lower output port. Conflicting connection requests can be resolved using conflict resolution schemes such as those discussed in [5], [10]. A message on the data lines will have the following format. The first word of the message will contain the message routing tag. The remaining words constitute the actual data that are to be transmitted. The set of data lines is assumed to include parity bit lines.

Message transmission in the network is controlled through the use of two types of asynchronous protocols. A message request/grant protocol is used to establish a path connecting source and destination PE's. The message request is the combination of the routing tag and a message request signal REQ. "Data available–data received" handshaking signals are used to transmit data between the input/output ports that interface the PE's to the network. The network interface ports are assumed to have the ability to validate message routing and data transmission (e.g., through the use of parity bits or checksum bits and the comparison of the routing tag information to known destination addresses). Thus, the complete information path will consist of the data lines (including the parity bit lines), the message REQ line, the data available line, the message grant line, and the data received line.

Blockages and potential faults in the network are detected by the source PE's when the anticipated return protocol signals are not received. The return protocol signals will not be generated if the message is blocked within the network or if the destination PE detects an error (e.g., a parity error or the destination tag does not match the destination PE's address). This process can be facilitated through the use of watchdog timers and/or nonacknowledge signals. Detection of a pos-

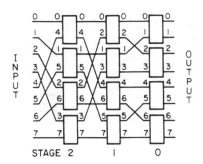

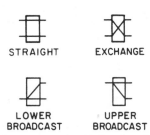

Fig. 1.   A multistage cube network, with $N = 8$, and the allowable box settings.

sible fault can initiate the execution of the fault location diagnostic routine.

A fault within the interconnection network can occur in either an interchange box or in one of the interconnection links within the information paths. All faults will be assumed to be nontransient. As delineated in [6], there are 16 possible ways of connecting the inputs of an interchange box to its outputs, as shown in Table I. A faulty box can become stuck in one particular invalid state, regardless of the routing information at its input ports, or it can respond incorrectly (but consistently) to the routing information. For an example of the latter situation, it is possible for a box to respond correctly when the straight state (S_{10}) is requested, but incorrectly when the exchange state (S_5) is requested. Furthermore, a faulty box may enter one incorrect state (say, S_{11}) in response to a straight state request, and enter a different incorrect state (say, S_{12}) in response to an exchange state request. Thus, a box fault occurs when an interchange box enters an incorrect state.

Any network fault that corrupts data on an information path will be called a link fault. A link fault occurs in an information line when it becomes stuck at either logical "0" or "1," regardless of the actual input signal that is applied to it. The actual location of the fault can be in the link itself, an interchange box, or in the hardware interfaces of the interchange boxes that the link connects. (Depending on the box implementation, some such faults within a box may be detected as box faults.) The fault model will allow link faults to occur in either the data lines themselves or the lines carrying the protocol and parity bit signals. As will be seen in Section IV, link faults in distributed control systems can create a large number of network errors not found in centralized control systems. These errors are due to the corruption of routing tags as they are transmitted over faulty links and the ensuing misrouting and blocking of the messages.

TABLE I
16 POSSIBLE STATES FOR A TWO-BY-TWO INTERCHANGE BOX

State	Interchange Box Setting	State	Interchange Box Setting
S_0		S_8	
S_1		S_9	
S_2		S_{10}	
S_3		S_{11}	
S_4		S_{12}	
S_5		S_{13}	
S_6		S_{14}	
S_7		S_{15}	

III. FAULT LOCATION IN CENTRALIZED CONTROL NETWORKS

In [6], [7], Feng, Wu, and Zhang present a comprehensive method for detecting and locating both link and box faults in a centralized control interconnection network. A three-phase testing strategy is developed to detect faults within the network. The testing of the network is performed in an SIMD (synchronous) operating mode under the direction of a global system control unit.

In phase 1, all interchange boxes are set to the straight connection. A logical "0" and a logical "1" are transmitted over each data link through the network. By comparing the received output words (at the destinations) to the known correct output specified by the system control unit, the presence of a fault can be readily determined. In phase 2, the process is repeated with the interchange boxes set to exchange.

The two-phase process requires the transmission of exactly four data words and has been shown to detect all single faults within the network for the straight and exchange settings. The fault location can be obtained by comparing the paths on which detected errors occurred or through the use of a binary tree search algorithm that can isolate most faults (or, in a few cases, indicate a localized region of two adjacent boxes and their connecting link) in no more than $\max(12, 6 + 2\lceil \log_2(\log_2 N)\rceil)$ tests. Complete details of the testing procedures can be found in [6].

Once the link faults and faults in the straight and exchange box settings have been located, testing for the broadcast settings can be performed. Each stage is individually set to

upper (lower) broadcast, while the remaining stages are set to either straight or exchange. Faults that resulted from the broadcast operation can be quickly pinpointed within the broadcast stage. Including the detection of faults in the broadcast settings in the procedure of [6] requires a total of $\max(28, 4 \log_2 N + 8, 14 + 2\lceil \log_2 N(\log_2 N)\rceil)$ tests to, in most cases, locate the fault or, in a few cases, localize the faulty region to two adjacent boxes and their connecting link [7].

IV. NETWORK FAULT DETECTION IN DISTRIBUTED CONTROL SYSTEMS

The set of possible fault patterns in a distributed control network is more complex than that of a centralized control network. This is because the routing tags which direct the path establishment through the network and the data transmission protocol lines are carried over the same information paths as the data. For example, a link fault may produce an erroneous routing tag which, in turn, may cause the message to be misrouted — an error that is not possible in a centralized control system.

The procedures and methodology described here are for detecting and locating single faults in a distributed control network. They are based on the network model of Section II, but can be adapted for other cube-type interconnection networks and for different formats of the data path and protocol lines. Specific examples will refer to a multistage cube network, with 16 PE's and a 16 bit data path. The routing tag word will contain the 4 bit destination address in bits 3–0 of the word and a 4 bit broadcast mask in bits 11–8. The other bits in the word (bits 7–4 and 15–12) are not used. There are two parity bits, a high-order bit for bits 15–8, and a low-order bit for bits 7–0 of the 16 bit word. This format is similar to the routing tag format used in the PASM prototype network [4].

The fundamental testing procedure remains similar to that described in [6], [7]. To check for link stuck-at faults, each set of links carrying data or parity bits must have two bitwise complementary words transmitted over it. Procedures for isolating these types of faults will be discussed in Section V. To test for faults in the interchange boxes, we shall first attempt to set each box to the valid states S_{10} and S_5 (straight and exchange). Broadcast settings will be evaluated separately. Faults will be detected by examining the test patterns which propagate through the network and are received by the destination PE's, and by combining this information with the blockage/timeout information available from the source PE's.

The basic testing procedure for straight and exchange settings is divided into two phases. In each phase we shall attempt to detect if there are one or more faulty paths and, through their intersection, isolate the faulty component. In phase 1, all boxes are preset to the "straight" setting through the actions of routing tags submitted to the network by the source PE's. Each source PE sends its own address as the destination address tag (bits 4–15 are set to zero). Call the process of sending routing tags through the network to preset all paths the *setup*.

If some block or routing error is detected, all paths are immediately dropped (by negating REQ), and phase 2 of the test is begun. If, however, no block or routing error occurred, each PE will begin the *data transfer* testing subphase of phase 1. The first data word to be transmitted will be the bitwise complement of the routing word. If again no error is detected, a second data word, with different parity, is sent through the network to ensure the links carrying the parity bits have been tested properly. This is necessary because, for a data path with an even number of bits (as assumed here), the parity bit values will remain the same for the routing tag word in setup and the first data word, since complementing a word with an even number of bits does not change its parity bit. The second data word is formed by complementing bits 0 and 8 of the first data word, i.e., the low-order bit from each byte.

As an example of this phase of the testing procedure, consider a 16 PE system. PE 6 would have a phase 1 routing tag word of 0000000000000110 with parity bits 00. The first data word would be 1111111111111001 with parity bits 00. The second data word would be 1111111011111000 with parity bits 11. Every data and parity link in the information path will have had both logical "0" and logical "1" signal levels transmitted over it.

In *phase 2,* the setup procedure involves having each source PE send the complement of its address as the destination tag. This is equivalent to requesting that all interchange boxes be set to exchange (setting S_5). As in phase 1, all unused bits are set to "0" for convenience. If no block or routing error occurs in the setup subphase, the PE's will send as the first data word the bitwise complement of the routing word.

If no error is detected with the transmission of the first data word, an extra data word with different parity is sent through the network to ensure that the links carrying the parity bits have been properly tested. This second data word is formed in the same way as that in phase 1, i.e., by complementing bits 0 and 8 of the first data word. Continuing with the example from phase 1, PE 6 would have a phase 2 routing tag word of 0000000000001001 with parity bits 00. The first data word would be 1111111111110110 with parity bits 00. The second data word would be 1111111011110111 with parity bits 11.

The destination's network interface verifies the message routing during setup (by examining the destination address portion of the setup word) and the parity for every received word. If there are no errors, it then generates the return protocol signals for the source PE.

V. THE EFFECTS OF NETWORK FAULTS

Faults occurring in a network that uses distributed control can cause much more serious operational errors than in a comparable centralized control network. Faults and their concomitant error patterns generated by the two phases of the straight and exchange setting tests are discussed below for both link and box faults.

A. Error Patterns for Link Stuck Faults

Two types of link faults can occur: faults in the data path or parity bit links, or faults in the links which carry the message protocol signals. Table II is a complete listing of the errors caused by each type of link fault. In the table, columns "one phase" and "other phase" record the received error signals (if any) and do not necessarily correspond to the phase 1–phase 2 testing sequence.

1) Type 1: Faults on the Data Path and Parity Bits: Functionally, Type 1 faults can be divided into five cases.

Case 1: A link fault occurs in a bit that is not used by the routing word. No matter how the unused bits are scrambled, messages will still be routed to their correct destinations. Since all unused bits are set to "0" in setup, if a link carrying one of these bits is stuck at "1," there will only be one parity error in each test phase (Type 1, Case 1a of Table II). If a link carrying the bit is stuck at "0," no error will occur during setup. When the first data word is sent through the network, all unused bits are set to "1." Parity checks will then result in one error in each phase (Type 1, Case 1b of Table II).

Case 2: A link fault occurs in a routing bit after that bit has already been examined for routing purposes. For example, if a link carrying bit 3 of the destination tag has a stuck-at fault between stage 1 and stage 0, the message routing will not be affected (for routing purposes, bit 3 would have already been examined at stage 3). This type of fault produces the same fault patterns as Case 1 (Type 1, Case 2a and Type 1, Case 2b of Table II).

Case 3: In this case, a link fault occurs in a routing bit before that bit has been examined in the setup process. Since a link of this nature carries a "1" in the setup of one phase and a "0" in the setup of the other, in one of the phases there will be no setup error, but an error will occur when transferring the first data word. In the other phase, there will be an error in setup. Two routing possibilities may happen. The erroneous bit may successfully request an erroneous path and, in turn, block an otherwise good path — causing a block and a routing error (Type 1, Case 3b of Table II) — or, if the good path has already been established, the erroneous path will be blocked and the only error in that phase would be a block (Type 1, Case 3a of Table II).

Case 4: A fault occurs on a link carrying a parity bit. Here, a link carrying a parity bit is stuck at "1" or "0." In both test phases, this will either be detected during setup or when transmitting one of the two data words. There will either be errors in both phases when doing data transfers (Type 1, Case 4a of Table II), routing errors in setup in both phases (Type 1, Case 4b of Table II), or an error in the setup in one phase and an error in data transfer in the other phase (Type 1, Case 4c of Table II) (routing error here refers to a parity error in the setup word, not a misroute).

Case 5: A link carrying a broadcast bit is stuck so that a broadcast operation is erroneously requested. The erroneous broadcast request may succeed in neither, one, or both of the two test phases (Type 1, Case 5 of Table II). The observed errors depend on whether the broadcast setting is successfully set up (which will result in a parity error detected at a destination and a blockage of the correct path of another mes-

TABLE II
FAULT PATTERNS FOR LINK STUCK FAULTS

Case	Faulty Link	one phase		other phase	
		setup	data transfer	setup	data transfer
TYPE 1					
1a	unused bits	E		E	
1b		OK	E	OK	E
2a	destination bit,	E		E	
2b	does not affect routing	OK	E	OK	E
3a	destination bit,	B		OK	E
3b	affects routing	EB		OK	E
4a		OK	E	OK	E
4b	parity bit	E		E	
4c		E		OK	E
5a	broadcast bit	B		B	
5b	asserted,	EB		EB	
5c	affects routing	EB		B	
TYPE 2					
1	message request stuck negated	B		B	
2	message grant stuck negated	B		B	
3	data available stuck negated	E		E	
4	data received stuck negated	E		E	
5a	message request stuck asserted	OK	OK	EB	
5b		EB		EB	
6	message grant stuck asserted	OK	OK	OK	OK
7	data available stuck asserted, before stage 0	OK	E	OK	E
8	data available stuck asserted, after stage 0	E		E	
9	data received stuck asserted, after stage n-1	OK	E	OK	E
10	data received stuck asserted, before stage n-1	E		E	

Fault pattern notation:
"OK" -- No errors or blocks in that testing subphase.
"E" -- Only 1 PE detects a routing or parity error.
"B" -- Only 1 PE detects a block.
"EB" -- One PE detects a routing error, 1 or more PEs detects blocks.

sage), or if the broadcast request is blocked at the box in which the broadcast would be performed (by the other box input correctly establishing its path first and thus preventing the broadcast setting).

2) Type 2: Link Faults in Control Links: There are four control lines which can be stuck at asserted or negated: message request, message grant, data available, and data received.

Case 1: A link carrying a message request signal is stuck in the negated state. To set up an interchange box, a message's request signal must be asserted. If not, the message will not propagate through the box, causing a perceived blocking error to be detected. This will occur in both test phases (Type 2, Case 1 of Table II).

Case 2: A link carrying a message grant signal is stuck in the negated state. A perceived blocking error will be detected in each phase (Type 2, Case 2 of Table II).

Case 3: A link carrying a data available signal is stuck in the negated state. A routing error will occur in each phase because the assertion of the data available signal is never detected by the destination port, and as a result, the data received signal is never returned to the source PE (Type 2, Case 3 of Table II).

Case 4: A link carrying a data received signal is stuck in the negated state. This will result in one routing error in each phase since no data received signal returns to indicate that the routing tag has been received (Type 2, Case 4 of Table II).

Case 5: A link carrying a message request signal is stuck in the asserted state. Because message request is always asserted, the portion of the last path that is after the fault location (and established before the link failed) will not be dropped and will remain held through the fault isolation procedure. Depending on what this last path was, there are several different fault patterns. If the held path consists of all straight or all exchange box settings, there will be no routing errors or blocks in one phase, but a routing error and a block in the other phase (Type 2, Case 5a of Table II). Note that the new routing tags generated by the source PE will be treated as nontag data items by the incorrectly held path, causing the routing error. If the held path consists of a combination of straights and exchanges, there will be a routing error and one or more blocks in each phase (Type 2, Case 5b of Table II).

Case 6: A link carrying the message grant signal is stuck in the asserted state. This will produce no errors or blocks in the normal fault location procedure. The only way to detect this is to deliberately attempt to set up paths which will be blocked in the network and check for the signal being stuck (Type 2, Case 6 of Table II).

Cases 7 and 8: A link carrying the data available signal is stuck at the asserted state. Assume that the data available signal is edge-sensitive and that active low logic is being used in the network implementation (both reasonable assumptions for typical port handshaking signals). The errors that can be generated will depend on whether the stuck link is before or after stage 0 (i.e., whether it is the network output link or not).

In Case 7, a data available link is stuck at asserted before stage 0 (recall from Fig. 1 that stage 0 is the network output stage). An edge is still produced on subsequent links when the path is first set up. Hence in both phases, no error or block occurs in setup, but errors will occur when transmitting the first data word since the destination port will not receive the required negated-to-asserted edge on the data available line to gate the data word in (Type 2, Case 7 of Table II).

For Case 8, a data available link is stuck at asserted after stage 0 (on the line connecting stage 0 to its respective network–destination interface port). As a result of the fault, the port never detects an edge transition being produced on this control link. In each phase, there will be one routing error only. The fault patterns generated here are identical to those in Case 3 (Type 2, Case 8 of Table II).

Cases 9 and 10: A link carrying the data received signal is stuck at asserted. Similarly to Cases 7 and 8, the errors generated depend on whether the bad link is before stage $n - 1$.

In Case 9, assume that a data received link is stuck at asserted after stage $n - 1$ (the input stage of the network). As with the data available signal, assume that the data received signal is edge-sensitive. An edge will be produced when the path is first established. Hence, in both phases, no error or block occurs in setup, but errors will occur when transmitting the first data word since the source port will not receive the required negated-to-asserted edge on the data received line (Type 2, Case 9 of Table II).

For Case 10, let a data received link be stuck asserted

before stage $n - 1$. Since the stuck link is between stage $n - 1$ and the source port, no edge is ever produced on this bad link. In each phase, there will be one routing error only (Type 2, Case 10 of Table II).

B. Error Patterns for Interchange Box Faults

Interchange box faults in interconnection networks with distributed routing schemes are handled in much the same way as are Feng and Wu's switching element faults in [6]. Differences lie primarily in the additional effects of the m bit data path and the routing and protocol schemes, not addressed in [6]. This class of faults will be described briefly with emphasis being placed on these differences.

Initially, two groups will be considered: a faulty state when S_{10} is the desired state and a faulty state when S_5 is desired (broadcast states are discussed in Section VII). The possible fault patterns for interchange box faults in these states are summarized in Table III. In the analysis, it is assumed that a box fault will affect all lines of an input port in the same way.

1) Faulty State in S_{10}: This refers to the condition where the combination of the routing tag and REQ signals requests setting a box to S_{10}, but, because of a fault in the internal logic of the box, it is set to some other state instead. From Table I, there are 15 possible erroneous states. Erroneous states S_0, S_1, S_2, S_4, S_5, and S_8 are straightforward — messages are either misrouted or blocked, and error-checking hardware at the PE's detects routing errors or blocks. For erroneous states S_3 and S_{12}, one of the messages requesting passage through the faulty box is blocked, while the other message is sent to both output lines. The effect of this will be a blocked message and a routing error signal from the second incorrect output. The box input port hardware is assumed to perform a logical AND operation on the returning protocol signals from each of the box output ports to detect the presence of an error condition (i.e., message received logically 0) from either output link. The error signal is, in turn, propagated towards the respective source PE. The error patterns resulting from these eight erroneous states are similar to those of [6].

The remaining seven erroneous states, S_6, S_7, S_9, S_{11}, S_{13}, S_{14}, and S_{15}, may involve changes to the routing tags, and therefore, new considerations come to bear. The routing tags can become corrupted when one of the messages at the output links of the faulty box is the result of the two input messages overwriting each other. The effect of having two input bits write to the same output bit is defined in a way similar to that of Feng and Wu in [6]. If the two input bits are identical, the output bit will be equal to either one of the inputs. However, if the input bits are different, the output bit will always be a "1" or always a "0," i.e., an overwritten bit position always sticks at the same value. When two m bit routing words are transferred to the same output link, some bits in the resulting tag may be scrambled by the overwrite. Depending on the message at the output link of the faulty box, there are two resultant cases.

In the first case, the message is changed by the overwrite so that an error in the bits of the setup word which specify the destination address is generated. A routing error is detected.

TABLE III
FAULT PATTERNS FOR INTERCHANGE BOX FAULTS

Interchange Box Faults					
Desired Setting is S_{10}			Desired Setting is S_5		
Erroneous	Observed Errors		Erroneous	Observed Errors	
	Setup	Data Transfer		Setup	Data Transfer
S_0	2B		S_0	2B	
S_1	EB		S_1	B	
S_2	B		S_2	EB	
S_3	EB		S_3	EB	
S_4	EB		S_4	B	
S_5	2E		S_6a	2E	
			S_6b	OK	2E
S_6a	2E		S_7a	2E	
S_6b	OK	2E	S_7b	OK	2E
S_7a	2E		S_8	EB	
S_7b	E				
S_8	B		S_9a	2E	
			S_9b	OK	2E
S_9a	2E		S_{10}	2E	
S_9b	OK	2E			
S_{11}a	2E		S_{11}a	2E	
S_{11}b	OK	2E	S_{11}b	E	
S_{12}	EB		S_{12}	EB	
S_{13}a	2E		S_{13}a	2E	
S_{13}b	E		S_{13}b	OK	2E
S_{14}a	2E		S_{14}a	2E	
S_{14}b	OK	2E	S_{14}b	E	
S_{15}a	2E		S_{15}a	2E	
S_{15}b	OK	2E	S_{15}b	OK	2E

Fault pattern notation:
"OK" -- No errors or blocks in that testing subphase.
"E" -- Only 1 PE detects a routing or parity error.
"2E" -- Two PEs detect routing or parity errors.
"B" -- Only 1 PE detects a block.
"2B" -- Two PEs detect a block.
"EB" -- One PE detects a routing error, 1 or more PEs detects blocks.

For example, if a stage i box is in erroneous state S_6, bit i of the setup word using the lower input should be a "1." Assume the two setup words entering the box are merged so that bit i is overwritten and is stuck at "0." Thus, a destination with a "1" in its ith address bit position will receive a setup word with a "0" in the ith bit position. The source PE's requesting a path through the faulty interchange box will detect this error since the error condition is propagated back to both PE's.

In the second case, the message can be changed by the overwrite so that an error in the destination address part of the setup word is not generated as a result of the overwritten bits (e.g., for a stage i box, bit i of the message at the lower output of S_6 in Table I should be "1" and is stuck at the same value because of the overwrite). The proper return protocol signals are propagated back to both of the affected source PE's. In this case, no routing error or block is detected in the setup for S_6, S_9, S_{11}, S_{14}, and S_{15}. However, the first data word is a bitwise complement of the routing tag, while the overwritten bits always stay at the value they took in the setup. An error will result from the parity check, and both source PE's receive the error signal. The result is two routing errors. In the setup for S_7 and S_{13}, one of the messages is misrouted regardless of whether the overwritten message was scrambled. For example, the message at the upper output of S_7 in Table I is misrouted, and the lower input performs a logical AND operation on both returning protocol signals and informs the PE connected to the lower input of the error. In these two states, a single routing error in the setup will result.

2) Faulty State in S_5: This refers to the condition where the combination of the routing tag and REQ signals requests setting the interchange box to S_5, but the box is set to some other state instead. As for the case where the desired state was S_{10}, there are 15 possible erroneous states. The way in which fault patterns are generated is very similar to those of S_{10}. Refer to Table III for a complete description of the fault patterns generated by each type of fault.

VI. ISOLATION OF SINGLE FAULTS

Tables II and III summarize the errors resulting from the different types of faults after the first two phases of the testing procedure. The principle behind the testing procedure is to determine the fault type, i.e., whether a link or an interchange box is faulty, and the location of the fault. This is done by recording the path on which faults are detected in each phase and intersecting the faulty paths.

Notice that in the condition denoted by "EB" in the tables, i.e., one PE detects a routing error with one or more PE's detecting blocks, only the path which resulted in the routing error is considered to be the faulty path. This is because the blocked path may be fault free, but it was blocked by a misrouted message. If no routing errors are detected in a test phase but blocks occurred (i.e., in the conditions denoted by "B" and "$2B$"), paths with blocks are considered faulty paths. This is because there is no detected error in the network which could have caused a fault-free path to be blocked. The exception to this rule is for faults belonging to Group 3, as explained below. In the conditions denoted by "$2E$," two paths are considered to be faulty paths.

Looking over the tables of results for link faults and box faults, the faulty responses can be divided into several groups. These are considered below.

A. Group 1: Two Faulty Paths in Either the Setup or Data Transfer of a Single Phase

This refers to situations where the error conditions denoted by "$2E$" and "$2B$" are detected, either in the setup or in the data transfer. Referring to Tables II and III, these conditions will only be registered if an interchange box is faulty, i.e., if the desired state is S_{10} and the erroneous state is S_0, S_5, S_6, S_7a, $S_9, S_{11}, S_{13}a, S_{14}$, and S_{15} or if the desired state is S_5 and the erroneous state is $S_0, S_6, S_7, S_9, S_{10}, S_{11}a, S_{13}, S_{14}a$, and S_{15}. Since two faulty paths were registered in a single phase, intersection of these two paths will pinpoint the faulty box.

B. Group 2: No Setup Errors in One or Both Phases, Data Transfer Error in Phase(s) Where No Setup Error Occurred

In this group, no setup errors occur in one or both setup subphases. Where the setup is valid, a single error will be detected in the ensuing data transfer. This group includes link faults of Type 1, Cases 1b, 2b, 3, and 4a and c, and Type 2, Cases 7 and 9. Interchange box faults are not in Group 2 since they never generate a single error in data transfer in one or both phases (see Table III).

Referring to Table II, a Group 2 link fault always generates one faulty path in each phase. Since fault patterns of this type can be definitely identified as being caused by link faults, intersection of the faulty path obtained in phase 1 and that obtained in phase 2 will isolate the faulty link.

C. Group 3: No Anomaly in One Phase, Only One Faulty Path in the Other Phase

This group includes all those conditions where no anomaly (i.e., no routing error, parity error, or block) was detected in one phase, but an error and/or block in setup or data transfer was detected in the other phase. Hence, if faulty test patterns of this group were detected, only one faulty path will be registered and further tests are necessary to isolate the fault.

From Table II, only one type of link fault might produce fault patterns of this group: Type 2, Case 5a. The fault pattern produced here is the condition denoted by "EB." If the fault were in an interchange box, several types of faults would generate patterns belonging to this group.

a) The faulty box would work normally if it were set to S_{10} in the phase 1 test, but in the phase 2 test, instead of being set to S_5, it is set to $S_1, S_2, S_3, S_4, S_8, S_{11}b, S_{12}$, or $S_{14}b$. Of these eight possibilities, $S_1, S_4, S_{11}b$, and $S_{14}b$ do not produce the condition denoted by "EB" and are thus easily recognized as box faults instead of a link fault of Type 2, Case 5a.

b) The faulty box would work normally if it were set to S_5 in the phase 2 test, but in the phase 1 test, instead of being set to S_{10}, it is set to $S_1, S_2, S_3, S_4, S_7b, S_8, S_{12}$, or $S_{13}b$. Of these eight possibilities, S_2, S_8, S_7b, and $S_{13}b$ do not produce the condition denoted by "EB" and are thus easily recognized as box faults instead of a link fault of Type 2, Case 5a.

For the "EB" fault conditions in this group, both paths are considered faulty, and the location of the faulty component is exactly pinpointed by the intersection of the two paths on which the routing/parity error and the block lie. If the "EB" condition is caused by link fault Type 2, Case 5a, the intersection of the faulty path and the blocked path will give the interchange box immediately after the stuck link. If more than one block is detected, each blocked path is intersected with the path containing the routing/parity error. The component(s) obtained by the intersection that is closest to the input stage of the network is considered to be the faulty component. Hence, the faulty component is either the interchange box indicated by the intersection of the two bad paths, or an input link on that box.

For the remaining faults in this group (the non-"EB" cases), a binary tree search algorithm can be used to isolate the fault. See the discussion given in [6] under the section on "Switching Element Faults," Case 1.

D. Group 4: Anomalies in the Setup of Both Phases

In this group, one faulty path is generated in the setup of both phase 1 and phase 2. This group covers all the remaining link faults except Type 2, Case 6, and also the interchange box faults in which a particular box is set to an erroneous state(s) in both phase 1 and phase 2. The three error conditions possible in the setup are "E," "EB," and "B." All possible combinations of these conditions are summarized in Table IV. From Table II, it can be observed that link faults which generate fault patterns in the setup of both

TABLE IV
Group 4 Fault Patterns

Fault Patterns for Group 4		
Subgroup	phase 1 setup	phase 2 setup
1	E	E
2	E	EB
3	E	B
4	EB	E
5	EB	EB
6	EB	B
7	B	E
8	B	EB
9	B	B

phases always produce identical fault patterns in both phases. Hence, combinations of fault patterns which are not identical in both phases (Table IV, Subgroups 2, 3, 4, 6, 7, and 8) are immediately identifiable as interchange box faults. Since two faulty paths are obtained after the two-phase test, the intersection of the faulty paths will locate either the faulty box or a pair of interchange boxes connected by a link. The latter condition and subcases 1, 5, and 9 of Table IV require special procedures to further isolate the faulty component. These procedures, which involve trying to pinpoint the fault by setting boxes in different stages to different valid states, are described in detail in [6] and are an abbreviation of their tree search algorithm.

E. Group 5: No Anomalies Detected

In this group, no errors are detected in either the straight, the exchange, or the broadcast testing (discussed in Section VII) phases. This could indicate the presence of one remaining fault type — a Type 2, Case 6 link fault (a message grant protocol line is stuck asserted). Knowing the source PE that requested the diagnostic testing and the path that it was trying to set up when the initial network error was detected (the fault was in that particular path), the location of the fault can be determined. Blocking paths can be systematically established in the network that are known to conflict with the path containing the fault. If the faulty path and a blocking path intersect before the fault location, the grant signal should become negated (as a result of the blockage). If the paths intersect after the fault location, the grant signal will remain asserted, despite the path being blocked. The fault is identified as being in a particular link when a block in the preceding interchange box causes the grant signal to be negated, while a block in the succeeding box does not negate the signal. The search for the fault location can be performed in a binary tree search fashion and will require $O(\log_2 n)$ steps to complete.

F. Fault Location Summary

After the first two phases of the testing, it is possible to detect all link faults and single straight and exchange faults. The location of the component can be determined by examining the combination of error signals or, at worst case, narrowed to a pair of interchange boxes and their connecting links. Group 4 faults present the most difficult combination of error patterns. In those cases where the fault has not been completely isolated, the special procedures described in [6] are necessary to further isolate the fault.

VII. Testing for Broadcasts

If no anomalies are detected in the two-phase test for the straight and exchange settings, the broadcast states will be validated. Since possible link faults have been checked for, only interchange box faults need to be considered.

The basic procedure is very similar to that used in [7]. Each stage will in turn be set to both the upper and the lower broadcast states (S_{12} and S_3), with all other stages being set to straight for simplicity. Since the broadcasting stage is known, any anomaly immediately pinpoints the fault.

The testing procedure is divided into two subphases for each stage. Suppose stage i is being tested. In the setup subphase for upper broadcast testing, all boxes in the stage i are set to S_{12}. Each of the $N/2$ PE's with a "0" in bit i of its address sends its own address as the destination address, and a broadcast tag which is all "0"s except for bit i, which would be a "1." If no anomaly is detected, the PE's perform the data transfer subphase by sending the bitwise complement of the message header in order to check for overwrites (discussed below).

In the setup subphase of lower broadcast testing, all boxes in the stage being tested are set to S_3. Each of the $N/2$ PE's with a "1" in bit i of its address sends its own address as the destination address, and a broadcast tag which is all "0"s except for bit i, which would be a "1." If no anomaly is detected, the PE's perform the data transfer subphase by sending the bitwise complement of the message header.

In either subphase, the presence of an erroneous overwrite state can be detected by having the $N/2$ previously idle PE's attempt to establish paths using all straight connections. An overwrite state would not block the new straight request, as should normally happen. Instead, data from both inputs would be overwritten and the ensuing parity errors would be detected.

In summary, the stagewise validation of the network for broadcasting would take $O(n)$ tests where n is the number of stages. Because the links and the interchange boxes not performing broadcasts are assumed to be fault free, any anomaly would immediately isolate the faulty box.

VIII. Summary

In this paper, an existing fault detection and location procedure for centralized routing control networks has been overviewed and extended for use in distributed routing control systems. Networks that employ distributed routing control transmit both message routing and protocol information and data through the network. The errors that could occur in these networks were analyzed and shown to be a superset of the errors occurring in a centrally controlled system. Faults occurring in the data lines could corrupt the message routing tags transmitted over them and thereby cause the misrouting of messages. Additionally, protocol lines used in the handshaking between source–destination PE pairs, if faulty, could prevent a message path from being established or could cause the path to become "locked up" once the transmission of data has begun. A fault detection and location procedure, patterned after the ones presented in [6], [7], was developed. The procedure is executed in three phases where each phase involves the transmission of routing control information to set up the desired network connections and the transmission of data words to test the integrity of the paths. Response patterns to the test messages were derived for link faults in the data path as well as in the protocol links. Interchange box faults and their associated fault patterns were also investigated. Faults were detected by the source PE's, as perceived routing and/or parity errors, rather than through the inspection of received data at the destinations as in [6], [7].

While the procedures described in this paper were specifically targeted to a circuit switched network implementation, the approach could be modified for packet switched networks using similar control protocol structures. In packet switching, protocol lines connect interchange boxes in adjacent stages rather than the sources and destinations in circuit switching. As a result, the effects of faults in these lines will tend to be more localized than in the circuit switched networks discussed in this paper.

REFERENCES

[1] G. B. Adams III and H. J. Siegel, "The extra stage cube: A fault-tolerant interconnection network for supersystems," *IEEE Trans. Comput.*, vol. C-31, pp. 443–454, May 1982.

[2] D. P. Agrawal, "Testing and fault tolerance of multistage interconnection networks," *IEEE Comput.*, vol. 15, pp. 41–53, Apr. 1982.

[3] C. -Y. Chin and K. Hwang, "Packet switching networks for multiprocessors and data flow computers," *IEEE Trans. Comput.*, vol. C-33, pp. 991–1003, Nov. 1984.

[4] N. J. Davis IV and H. J. Siegel, "The PASM prototype interconnection network," in *Proc. 1985 Nat. Comput. Conf.*, July 1985, pp. 183–190.

[5] ——, "The performance analysis of partitioned circuit switched multistage interconnection networks," in *Proc. 12th Symp. Comput. Architecture*, June 1985, pp. 387–394.

[6] T. -Y. Feng and C. -L. Wu, "Fault-diagnosis for a class of multistage interconnection networks," *IEEE Trans. Comput.*, vol. C-30, pp. 743–758, Oct. 1981.

[7] T. -Y. Feng and Q. Zhang, "Fault diagnosis of multistage interconnection networks with four valid states," in *Proc. Fifth Int. Conf. Distrib. Comput. Syst.*, May 1985, pp. 218–226.

[8] A. Gottlieb, R. Grishman, C. P. Kruskal, K. P. McAuliffe, L. Rudolph, and M. Snir, "The NYU Ultracomputer — Designing an MIMD shared-memory parallel computer," *IEEE Trans. Comput.*, vol. C-32, pp. 175–189, Feb. 1983.

[9] D. H. Lawrie, "Access and alignment of data in an array processor," *IEEE Trans. Comput.*, vol. C-24, pp. 1145–1155, Dec. 1975.

[10] M. Lee and C. -L. Wu, "Performance analysis of circuit switching baseline interconnection networks," in *Proc. 11th Symp. Comput. Architecture*, June 1984, pp. 82–90.

[11] W. Y. -P. Lim, "A test strategy for packet switching networks," in *Proc. 1982 Int. Conf. Parallel Processing*, Aug. 1982, pp. 96–98.

[12] K. Padmanabhan and D. H. Lawrie, "A class of redundant path multistage interconnection networks," *IEEE Trans. Comput.*, vol. C-32, pp. 1099–1108, Dec. 1983.

[13] M. C. Pease III, "The indirect binary *n*-cube microprocessor array," *IEEE Trans. Comput.*, vol. C-26, pp. 458–473, May 1977.

[14] H. J. Siegel, L. J. Siegel, F. C. Kemmerer, P. T. Mueller, Jr., H. E. Smalley, Jr., and S. D. Smith, "PASM: A partitionable SIMD/MIMD system for image processing and pattern recognition," *IEEE Trans. Comput.*, vol. C-30, pp. 934–947, Dec. 1981.

[15] H. J. Siegel, *Interconnection Networks for Large-Scale Parallel Processing: Theory and Case Studies*. Lexington, MA: Lexington Books, 1985.

Nathaniel J. Davis IV (S'82) was born in Alexandria, VA, on February 13, 1954. He received the B.S. degree in 1976 and the M.S. degree in 1977, both in electrical engineering, from Virginia Polytechnic Institute and State University, Blacksburg, and the Ph.D. degree in electrical engineering in 1985 from Purdue University, West Lafayette, IN.

He is currently a Captain in the U.S. Army Signal Corps and is an Assistant Professor with the Department of Electrical Engineering, Air Force Institute of Technology, Wright–Patterson Air Force Base, OH. While attending Purdue University, he was a Graduate Research Assistant and worked on the development of the PASM parallel processing system. His previous assignments within the U.S. Army have been as an Instructor at the Air Force Institute of Technology and as a Communication-Electronics Officer with the 35th Signal Brigade (Corps) (Airborne), Fort Bragg, NC. His research interests include computer architecture, communications networks, interconnection networks, parallel processing, and system modeling and performance analysis.

Dr. Davis is a member of the IEEE Computer Society and the Eta Kappa Nu, Tau Beta Pi, and Sigma Xi honorary societies.

William Tsun-Yuk Hsu was born in Hong Kong on March 6, 1962. He received the B.S. degree in 1983 and the M.S. degree in 1985, both in electrical engineering, from Purdue University, West Lafayette, IN, and is now beginning work towards the Ph.D. degree at Purdue University.

He has worked as a Graduate Research Assistant on the design of the PASM parallel processing system. His research interests include computer architecture, parallel processing, interconnection networks, and graph theory.

Mr. Hsu is a member of the Eta Kappa Nu and Phi Kappa Phi honorary societies.

Howard Jay Siegel (M'77–SM'82) was born in New Jersey on January 16, 1950. He received the B.S. degree in electrical engineering and the B.S. degree in management from the Massachusetts Institute of Technology, Cambridge, MA, in 1972 and the M.A. and M.S.E. degrees in 1974 and the Ph.D. degree in 1977, all in electrical engineering and computer science, from Princeton University, Princeton, NJ.

In 1976 he joined the School of Electrical Engineering, Purdue University, West Lafayette, IN, where he is currently a Professor and Director of the PASM Parallel Processing Laboratory. His research interests include parallel/distributed processing, computer architecture, and image and speech understanding.

Dr. Siegel has published over 100 technical papers and is the author of the book *Interconnection Networks for Large-Scale Parallel Processing: Theory and Case Studies* (Lexington Books, 1985). He has served as Program Co-Chairperson of the 1983 International Conference on Parallel Processing, as the General Chairman of the Third International Conference on Distributed Computing Systems (1982), as an IEEE Computer Society Distinguished Visitor, as Chairman of the IEEE Computer Society Technical Committee on Computer Architecture (TCCA), as Chairman of the ACM Special Interest Group on Computer Architecture (SIGARCH), and as a Guest Editor of the IEEE TRANSACTIONS ON COMPUTERS. He is currently an Area (Associate) Editor of the *Journal of Parallel and Distributed Computing*. He is a member of the Eta Kappa Nu and Sigma Xi honorary societies.

Comprehensive Testing of Multistage Interconnection Networks

Antoine Mourad, *Student Member, IEEE,* Banu Özden, *Student Member, IEEE,* and Miroslaw Malek, *Senior Member, IEEE*

Abstract— We present efficient methods for testing packet-switched multistage interconnection networks. In addition to testing the data paths and routing capabilities, we provide tests for detecting faults in the control circuitry including the conflict resolution capabilities. Using a general model of the switch, we construct testing sequences for the internal functions of the $f \times f$ switch requiring only $O(f^2 2^f)$ tests in the case of round-robin priority and $O(f 2^{f-1})$ in the case of fixed priority (f is usually a constant that is less than or equal to 8). We follow with algorithms to test the entire network using at most twice the number of tests needed to test a switch, independently of the network size, which results in $O(\log N)$ testing time for an N-processor network. It is shown that the method achieves higher coverage and several orders of magnitude reduction in the testing time of complex multiprocessor systems when compared to the previous methods.

Index Terms— Conflict resolution, fault detection, multiprocessor systems, multistage interconnection networks, packet-switching, round-robin priority, testing.

I. Introduction

MULTISTAGE interconnection networks [1] became popular with the advent of multiprocessor systems [2]–[5]. But testing these networks, especially in the case of packet-switching, remains a problem. For example, testing of the multistage interconnection network of a 64-processor computer may take over 22 hours [6].

The multiprocessor system is assumed to be synchronous and packet-switching is used. The objective of the proposed test is to detect stuck-at faults and bridge faults on the data and control lines of the network as well as routing and conflict resolution faults in the switches of the network.

For circuit-switched networks, fault detection and location results were presented in [7]. For packet-switched networks, some work has already been done in [8], [9] where test techniques for detecting and locating faults in the data paths and the routing circuitry, have been developed. In a recent paper [10], a method called polynomial testing was proposed for testing packet-switched multistage interconnection networks using self-testing switches. However, the method does not test the conflict resolution capabilities of the switches which is the most complex part of the testing procedure. In this study, we

focus on this problem and develop efficient test procedures for a comprehensive fault model including control and routing faults where also misrouting of one or more data bits of a packet is considered as opposed to routing faults where the entire packet is misdirected. We use a rectangular SW-banyan [11] to demonstrate our methods. Most of the results can be extended to other topologically equivalent networks [12].

In the following section, the topology and behavior of the network are described and definitions as well as previous results are presented. Section III defines the fault model. In Section IV, the method for testing the switch is given while Section V deals with testing the entire network. In Section VI, the time to test the entire network is evaluated for the proposed method and compared to a pseudo-exhaustive testing approach. In Section VII, the fault coverage of the method is discussed. Section VII also describes how the tests for the control circuitry presented in Sections IV and V can be used to detect faults on data lines. Finally Section VIII presents conclusions.

II. Preliminaries

A. Description of the Network

The number of stages in the network is denoted by L. Each switch has f inputs and f outputs. The number of computers is $N = f^L$. We will use the notation (f, L) *system* to designate such a network. The stages of the network, also called levels, are numbered from 0 to $L - 1$ starting from the processor side of the network. Also switches at the same stage will be numbered from 0 to $f^{L-1} - 1$. Fig. 1 shows the architecture of the network. In some of the tests for control lines, a specific design is needed to describe the test. We will use a switch design based on the RP3 network [3]. Each connection between a computer and a switch or between two switches in the network includes a number of data lines, usually 8, a parity line, a data-valid (DV) line and a clear-to-send (CTS) line. Several other protocols between switches can be used such as the one in [13]. The packet length usually varies between 8 and 64 bytes. A buffer is used at each input of the switch to store the incoming packet and once the transmission from one stage to the next is allowed, the packet is sent byte after byte to a switch at the next stage. Some designs [13] use a larger data bus and a packet size equal to the bus width in which case the entire packet is put on the bus in one cycle. The proposed testing schemes apply to both types of networks.

We will develop two levels of testing to detect the faults in the network. First we will show how to test a single switch for our fault model. Here we assume that all the inputs and

Manuscript received May 22, 1989; revised December 13, 1990. This work was supported by the Office of Naval Research under Grants N00014-86-K-0554 and N00014-88-K-0543.

A. Mourad is with the Center for Reliable and High-Performance Computing, Coordinated Science Laboratory, The University of Illinois, Urbana, IL 61801.

B. Özden and M. Malek are with the Department of Electrical and Computer Engineering, The University of Texas at Austin, Austin, TX 78712.

IEEE Log Number 9101667.

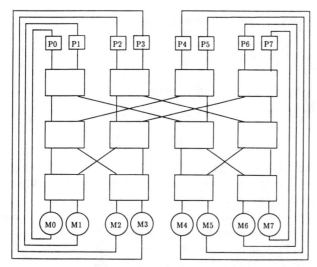

Fig. 1. Example of banyan network with 2 × 2 switches and 3 levels.

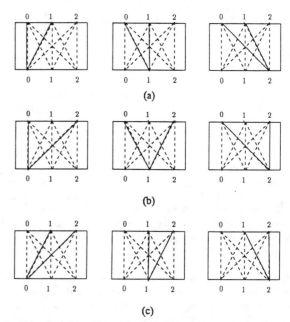

Fig. 2. (a) First 2-conflict, (b) second 2-conflict, (c) third 2-conflict at the output channels 0, 1, and 2 of a 3 × 3 switch.

outputs of the switch are directly accessible either via a tester or scan-paths. Then we will test all the switches in the network through the computers connected to the ports of the network. Testing the processors is beyond the scope of this paper, therefore we will assume that each processor has been tested before incorporating it into the system and functions correctly during the network testing period. The tests are parallelized and instead of $\frac{N}{f} \log_f N$ times the number of tests for a single switch the entire network is tested with at most $\log_f N$ times the number of tests for a single switch. At network level the testing packets that a computer will send and receive are stored in its memory. Each computer sends the testing packets simultaneously and compares the received packets with the expected ones to verify the test results.

B. Basic Definitions

Testing Packet: A packet which contains the necessary test data.

A testing packet is a regular packet with necessary headers, such as routing tag and control information, such as end of packet flag or error detecting, or correcting codes depending on the implementation of the interconnection network. The test data carried in testing packets vary with the type of the faults to be detected during a given test procedure. The necessary test data for each type of fault will be given along with the corresponding test strategies. For example, the test data for conflict resolution faults contains three types of information: destination address, source address, and a time-stamp. Destination address is the network address of the computer, to which the test packet is sent. If the routing tag is carried in the header along the network to the destination computer then destination address can be derived from the routing tag. Source address consists of the network address of the computer, which sends the packet. Each computer time-stamps the testing packet it transmits, just before it sends the packet.

Test Graph: A subgraph of the network graph which is constructed to accomplish a test.

i-conflict: The conflict which occurs at one of the outputs of the switch, when i active input channels of a switch try to get the right of way from an output at the same time.

There are fC_i^f different i-conflicts in an $f \times f$ switch. In Fig. 2 all possible 2-conflicts for a 3×3 switch are enumerated. Note that for $i = 1$, there is no conflict but we still use the notation 1-conflict for the ease of description and generality.

Active Number: There are two sets of input channel numbers for each possible i-conflict of a switch. One set contains the input channel number of the i active inputs, which create the i-conflict at a switch output. The other set consists of the channel numbers of $(f - i)$ passive inputs for the i-conflicts. The numbers in the first set are called active numbers and the numbers in the second set are called passive numbers for a given i-conflict.

In Fig. 2 the active numbers for the first 2-conflict are $(0, 1)$, for the second 2-conflict $(0, 2)$, and for the third 2-conflict $(1, 2)$.

C. Previous Results

A method for diagnosing circuit-switched baseline networks with 2×2 switches was introduced in [7]. A simplified version of this fault model and the testing techniques were presented in [14]. Fault location techniques for distributed control routing networks with 2×2 switches were proposed in [15]. A similar fault model was used to test packet-switched networks with again 2×2 switches in [8]. Concurrent error detection methods were examined with a functional fault model for 2×2 switches and a unidirectional fault model (including bridge faults) for the control and data lines of the network in [16]. In a recent paper [10] testable switch design and corresponding test methods were developed for diagnosing packet-switched networks with switches of arbitrary sizes.

The graph representation of a rectangular SW-banyan contains a Hamiltonian circuit and an efficient way for construct-

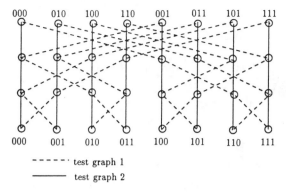

000 010 100 110 001 011 101 111

000 001 010 011 100 101 110 111

----- test graph 1
——— test graph 2

Fig. 3. Graph model of the network and the 2 edge-disjoint test graphs ($f = 2$).

ing such a circuit was shown in [17]. Also since every node in the graph representation has an even degree, an Eulerian circuit can be constructed. These circuits can be used to implement serial on-line tests for detection of stuck-at faults on data lines [9]. Eulerians and Hamiltonians can be used in arbitrary systems for optimized testing of their topology or behavior [18].

It was also shown in [19] that f pairwise edge-disjoint test graphs, each with f^L disjoint paths between pairs of computers, can be constructed. These test graphs contain every edge of the graph exactly once and can be used to apply N tests in parallel. Fig. 3 shows the edge-disjoint test graphs that can be constructed in the network of Fig. 1.

Using the graph model of the network, it was shown in [9] that two parallel tests are sufficient to detect any number of stuck-at-α ($\alpha = 0, 1$) faults in the nodes of the system graph and that $2f$ parallel tests are sufficient to detect any number of stuck-at-α faults in the edges of the graph. The tests simply send the sequence 01 or 10 through every vertex or every edge of the graph. The above results were established for networks in which a packet has only one word (word = data bus width). In the case of networks with packets of larger size, the sequence 01 or 10 can be included in the same packet and therefore the number of tests will be f instead of $2f$. Also fault location was studied and efficient methods were developed for fault location. It was also shown that the routing capabilities of the network can be tested using f tests. The f edge-disjoint test graphs, mentioned in the above section, were used for testing both stuck-at-α faults on the edges and routing faults.

III. FAULT MODEL

The faults in the network can originate either from the switches or links connecting the switches. We model the link faults as stuck-at-α and bridge faults and develop a comprehensive fault model for the switch with the following strategy: The switch is partitioned into modules for which behavioral fault models are constructed while the faults on the connections between these modules are abstracted with stuck-at-α and bridge faults. The partitioning is done in a natural way based on the switch design in [13]. For each input port of the switch, there is a routing and storage block (RSB) which handles the routing of the incoming packets to

that port. Similarly for each output port, there is an arbitration logic block (ALB) which resolves the conflicting requests and selects an input port. Every RSB is connected to every ALB with one SELECT line and one DESELECT line to perform the necessary handshaking between the input and output ports. The data part of the switch consists of a data storage block (DSB) at each input port and a data multiplexing block (DMB) at each output port. Every DSB is connected to every DMB with w data lines where w is the data width of the switch. The necessary control signals for data storage and multiplexing units are generated by the routing and arbitration control units (RSB's and ALB's).

We assume that the switches at only one stage of the network are faulty at a time. The coverage for multiple faults on arbitrary locations will be discussed along with the test procedures. The following types of faults will be considered:

Stuck-at-α faults on data lines and data storage blocks: Stuck-at-0 and stuck-at-1 faults will be considered on data lines in switches and between switches at two different stages as well as in the storage elements in the switches.

Bridge faults on data channels: OR- and AND-bridge faults will be considered between the lines of a data channel as well as different data channels in a switch.

Stuck-at-α faults and bridge faults on control lines: Stuck-at-0 and stuck-at-1 faults as well as OR- and AND-bridge faults will be considered on control lines.

In addition, the following functional fault models will be considered which are the effects of faults occurring in the modules of a switch identified above:

Routing faults: The ability of a switch input to route correctly the incoming packet to the desired output will be tested. We will assume that the faults in the routing logic (RSB) of an input port are independent of the faults in the routing logic of any other input port of the switch. The following functional fault model is used for routing function:

1) When requesting an output, one or more other outputs will be selected instead of, or in addition to, the correct output.
2) When requesting an output, no output will be selected.

Conflict resolution faults: The behavior of a switch under contention at its output will be tested as well as its conformance with the priority scheme used to resolve conflicts. We will assume that the faults in the control logic (ALB) of an output port are independent of the faults in the control logic of any other output port of the switch. The following functional fault model is used for conflict resolution function:

1) When there is one or more requests for an output, one or more other inputs will be selected instead of, or in addition to, the correct input.
2) When there is one or more requests for an output, no inputs will be selected.

Data multiplexing faults: The stuck-at-α and bridge faults in the data multiplexing logic (DMB) at each output port of the switch can produce the following effect in addition to the stuck-at-α faults on the data paths: When connecting one bit of the input port to one bit of the output port, the output will be the logical AND or OR function of one or more inputs.

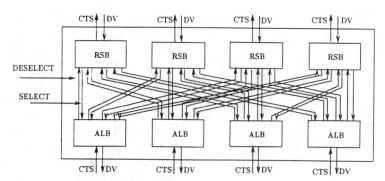

Fig. 4. Design of the control part of a 4×4 switch.

IV. TESTING THE SWITCH

The objective here is to test the correct behavior of each switch under any type of input pattern. The general strategy consists of partitioning the switch into modules for which tests are generated using a behavioral model while the connections between these modules are tested using stuck-at-α and bridge fault model.

The most difficult aspect of the test concerns checking the behavior of the switches under contention on one or more of their outputs. The priority scheme used in case of contention should also be tested. Both fixed priority and round-robin priority schemes are considered in the proposed testing methods. These methods make extensive use of the synchrony of the system especially for testing the behavior of the switches under contention.

As a basis for comparison, we consider first an exhaustive approach that applies all possible patterns to the switch. The possible patterns can be enumerated by classifying them according to the number of switch inputs activated (i.e., inputs receiving data) in the pattern. There are $C_i^f f^i$ patterns that activate i switch inputs since the number of different combinations of i active inputs out of the f inputs is C_i^f and the number of different choices of outputs for i active inputs is f^i. Taking the sum over all values of i, we get the total number n_t of patterns to be applied:

$$n_t = \sum_{i=0}^{f} C_i^f f^i = (1 + f)^f. \tag{1}$$

The above number of tests grows superexponentially with the number of inputs f. For example, for a 4×4 switch, $n_t = 624$, for an 8×8 switch, $n_t = 43,046,720$. Note that the above sequence of tests does not constitute a truly exhaustive test. The switch is a sequential circuit and the above sequence does not guarantee to put the switch in every state and exercise every possible input to the switch in that state. For instance, if the design implements a round-robin priority scheme to resolve conflicts at switch outputs, then the number of different states corresponding to different priority settings is f^f since at each output we have f possible relative priority settings and the number of states grows as the product of all these possible settings for all switch outputs. A truly exhaustive test would have to apply the above patterns in each state of the switch which leads to an unacceptable number of tests. Therefore, the above test will be referred to in the rest of the paper as the

pseudo-exhaustive approach because it is not a truly exhaustive test and does not provide full fault coverage.

In developing our testing procedure we use the design of Fig. 4 for the control part of the switch. The procedure will be applicable to any design as long as the conflict resolution units at the outputs are independent. The control part of an $f \times f$ switch comprises usually one routing and storage block at each input (RSB) and one arbitration logic block (ALB) at each output. Every RSB is connected to every ALB with one SELECT line and one DESELECT line. The SELECT line signals to the ALB that the corresponding RSB has a packet to send to the output of the ALB. The DESELECT line disables the corresponding RSB until the packet in storage has been transmitted. A detailed implementation of each of the above functional blocks is described in [13].

It is possible to test the RSB's using the tests for data paths and routing developed in [9]. The tests for the arbitration units to be presented in Section IV-C will cover misrouting faults. Also the tests for stuck-at-faults on the data lines will cover stuck-at-faults in the storage units. Therefore, we do not generate tests specifically for the RSB's. In the next sections, we look into testing of bridge faults on the data lines in the switch and stuck-at-α faults and bridge faults on the SELECT and DESELECT lines as well as testing of the ALB's and DMB's.

A. Testing of the Internal Data Lines and the Multiplexing Logic

The data plane of the switch is usually designed in such a way that the output of the storage buffer at each input fans out into f branches such that each branch goes to one of the outputs of the switch [10], [13]. Fig. 5 shows the design of the data part of a 4×4 switch. Data coming out of the storage buffer (DSB) will be available at all switch outputs. At each output, a set of multiplexers (DMB) controlled by the ALB of that output, is used to select the right data path and connect it to the output of the switch. The availability of the data coming to a given input in all the branches connected to that input can be used in generating tests for bridge faults between data lines. If the logic value of a data line in one branch is modified due to a bridge fault then all lines connected to that line in other branches belonging to the same data path will be affected and the fault effect can be observed on any one of them [20], [21]. In the following lemma, a test set for all bridge faults between

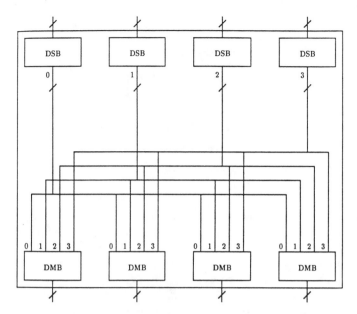

Fig. 5. Design of the data part of a 4 × 4 switch.

data lines belonging to the same data path is generated.

Lemma 1: $\lceil \log_2 w \rceil$ tests are sufficient to detect bridge faults between data lines in the same data path, w being the width in bits of the data path.

Proof: The f data paths connecting the inputs of the switch to its outputs are tested at the same time. Any connection of the inputs to the outputs that does not involve conflicts can be used and that same connection can be used to apply all the tests in the sequence. The data contents of the packets sent to each of the inputs are the same and are constructed as follows.

First, the lines in each data path are divided into two subsets such that the number of lines in each subset is the same or differs by one. Links in the first subset are set to the logic value 0 and lines in the second subset are set to the logic value 1. In the next test, the lines in each subset are again divided into two subsets and complementary logic values are assigned to each subset. The process continues until the size of the subsets is equal to one. The number of steps in the process is $\lceil \log_2 w \rceil$. Each pair of lines in the data path will be assigned complementary values in at least one of the above tests. For example, in the case $w = 8$, the data contents of the sequence of three tests are (11110000, 11001100, 10101010). □

Note that several of the data patterns used to test the data paths for bridge faults could be encapsulated in the same testing packet. Hence, the number of tests can be reduced to $\lceil \log_2 w \rceil / l$ where l is the length of the data part of the packet.

A similar approach can be used to detect bridge faults between lines belonging to different data paths. The only difference is that in this case, the data paths are divided into subsets and all the data paths in a given subset have all their lines set to the same logic value while the data paths in the other subset have all their lines set to the complementary value. The total number of tests is $\lceil \log_2 f \rceil$.

In the following lemma, we generate tests for faults in the data multiplexing logic. We consider faults such that when an input is selected the output of the multiplexer is a logical AND or OR function of one or more inputs.

Lemma 2: $2f^2$ tests are sufficient to detect data multiplexing faults.

Proof: To detect faults in a multiplexer, we need to select each input once with the value 0 and once with the value 1 while all other inputs are set to the complementary value. To do so we proceed as follows. Select one of the f^2 data connections in the switch (e.g., $0 \rightarrow 0$). Set all the data lines in that connection to one. Select $f - 1$ other connections to form a nonconflicting pattern ($i \rightarrow i$, for $1 \leq i \leq f - 1$, for the running example). Set the lines in the $f - 1$ connection to zero. This test will select input 0 of the multiplexer at output 0 with the value 1 while all other inputs to that multiplexer have value 0. Replace the 1's in the connection under test with 0's and the 0's on the other connections with 1's and repeat the test. This second test will select input 0 of the multiplexer at output 0 with the value 0 while all other inputs to that multiplexer have value 1. Repeat the above two tests f^2 times, each time selecting a different data connection as the connection under test. □

The tests for data multiplexing faults will also detect bridge faults across data paths. Hence, there is no need to perform the tests for the latter faults if the sequence of tests of Lemma 2 is applied.

Data for several of the tests for data multiplexing faults can be packed in the same testing packet, thus reducing further the total number of test patterns to be applied to the switch. For a given test pattern, each byte (or word) of the packet transmitted through the switch could be involved in testing a different set of data multiplexing faults. If the size of the packet is sufficiently large, data for up to $2f$ of the tests described in Lemma 2 [e.g., the test for each set of f channels of the form $(i \rightarrow (i + j) \bmod f)$] can be put in the same testing packet thus reducing the total number of testing packets to only f.

B. Testing the Internal Control Lines

The SELECT/DESELECT lines are used according to the following protocol. When a packet comes into the RSB, its address is decoded and the SELECT line connected to the ALB of the desired output will be activated (SELECT ← 1). The ALB will, in turn, activate the DESELECT line to stop the RSB from accepting a new packet (DESELECT ← 1). When the RSB of the next stage is available, the ALB will enable the transmission of the packet and deactivate the DESELECT line. If more than one packet has to be sent through the same output channel, the ALB will enable their transmission one after the other according to a fixed or round-robin priority scheme.

Stuck-at-α faults on SELECT and DESELECT lines have been addressed in [18]. The techniques for detecting bridge faults presented in the following subsection will also detect stuck-at-α faults on those lines.

1) Bridge Faults on SELECT and DESELECT Lines: First we consider bridge faults between SELECT lines. An AND-bridge between two SELECT lines will produce the loss of a message due to the deactivation of a SELECT line that is supposed to be activated, an OR-bridge on the other hand, will produce the transmission of an extra message due to the activation of a SELECT line that is supposed to be idle. To detect these faults, every pair of SELECT lines should be put in the state (active, idle) or in the complementary state (idle, active). The testing scheme will be independent of the layout. If the layout of the lines in the switch was known, then a less complex approach, testing only adjacent lines, could be used to detect bridge faults.

Detection of bridge faults on SELECT lines can be done using a sequence of f^2 tests, such that each test activates one SELECT line while the other lines remain idle. However, as shown in the following lemma, a smaller test set can be obtained.

Lemma 3: $2f$ tests are sufficient to detect bridge faults between SELECT lines, when f is odd, and, $3f$ tests are sufficient when f is even.

Proof: The sequence of tests of the form $i \rightarrow (i + j) \bmod f$, for every input i of the switch and for j taking successively the values $0, 1, \cdots, f - 1$ is applied. These tests produce the activation of every SELECT line in the switch. Assuming that activated SELECT lines have logic value 1 and idle lines have logic value 0, a test pattern that activates a given SELECT line will detect all bridge faults between that line and all lines that remain idle during that test. An AND-bridge fault between the activated line and an idle line would cause the loss of the packet that caused the activation of the line and an OR-bridge fault will activate the idle SELECT line which leads to the creation of a random new packet which would be detected by the receiving computer as an unexpected packet. Hence, a test pattern in which a given SELECT line is activated will detect bridge faults between that line and all other SELECT lines except the $f - 1$ lines activated by the same test pattern because those lines have the same logic value. To cover the remaining faults, some additional tests are necessary. To construct these tests, we need to consider two cases:

a) f is odd: The additional test patterns in this case are: $i \rightarrow (2i + j) \bmod f$, for every input i of the switch and for j taking successively the values $0, 1, \cdots, f - 1$. These tests do not involve conflicts because $2i \bmod f$ is always different from $2j \bmod f$ when f is odd, $0 \leq i, j \leq (f - 1)$ and $i \neq j$. In this sequence of tests, when a SELECT line is activated the SELECT lines that were activated with it in the first sequence of tests will be idle this time, thus sensitizing the bridge faults that were not sensitized by the first sequence.

b) f is even $(f > 2)$: In this case, the test pattern $i \rightarrow (2i + j) \bmod f$ will involve a conflict. To get a nonconflicting test pattern, the following test can be used: we consider the first test pattern of the sequence described in a) for a switch with fan-out $(f - 1)$, i.e., the pattern $(0, 2, \cdots, 2(f - 2) \bmod (f - 1))$, and apply it to the first $f-1$ inputs of the switch, then we slide the pattern by one input to the left and apply it again and repeat the operation for a total of f tests. The SELECT lines that are not activated by the above sequence are the SELECT lines of the form: $i \rightarrow i + f/2$, for $0 \leq i \leq f - 1$. These lines are then activated separately in an additional sequence of f tests. $\square$

For the case $f = 2$, it is preferable to activate each SELECT line separately which leads to a test sequence with four test

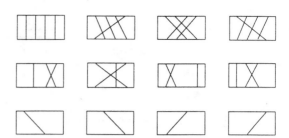

Fig. 6. The 12 tests for bridge faults between SELECT lines in a 4×4 switch.

patterns: $(0 \rightarrow 0)$, $(1 \rightarrow 1)$, $(0 \rightarrow 1)$, and $(1 \rightarrow 0)$, instead of using the sequence generated by the above lemma which would have six patterns. Fig. 6 shows the 12 tests for bridge faults on SELECT lines for a 4×4 switch resulting from the proof of Lemma 3.

For bridge faults between DESELECT lines, we need to distinguish between OR- and AND-bridges. An OR-bridge fault will disable an RSB and will delay the incoming packet or even destroy part of the packet or corrupt it if it occurs during the transmission of the packet into the RSB. An AND-bridge will enable an RSB to receive a new packet while the precedent packet has not yet been completely transmitted thus causing the corruption of the data of the first packet or the complete loss of one of the messages.

The DESELECT line is activated by the ALB as soon as it receives a request from the RSB signaled by the activation of the SELECT line. The activation of the DESELECT line prevents the RSB from receiving new packets. The DESELECT line remains active until the current packet is transmitted out of the switch.

To detect bridge faults on DESELECT lines, we use a scheme in which a packet is loaded into the RSB but its transmission out of the switch is delayed. This is done in order to maintain the DESELECT line in the active stage (logic value 1) so that the effect of a bridge fault can be observed. A method for achieving the delay when the switch is not accessible to the computers running the test will be discussed in Section V-B where the testing scheme is generalized to the entire network.

Lemma 4: f^2 tests are sufficient to detect OR-bridge faults between DESELECT lines.

Proof: One DESELECT line (e.g., $0 \rightarrow 0$) is selected as the line under test, and a test pattern is applied to detect bridge faults between this line and all the other DESELECT lines. The test pattern consists of selecting nonconflicting destinations for the other $f - 1$ inputs of the switch ($i \rightarrow i$, for $1 \leq i \leq f-1$, for the running example), sending a packet along the line under test and blocking its transmission out of the switch and then sending packets to the other $f - 1$ selected connections in the next time step. An OR-bridge fault between the line under test and any DESELECT line connected to some other input will cause the packet incoming to that input to be delayed as long as the packet on the line under test is blocked. This procedure is repeated for every DESELECT line in the switch. In all, f^2 tests will be needed. Blocking the transmission of a packet can be done by the testing computer if it is connected to the output of the switch. Methods for blocking the transmission if the computer is not connected to the output of the switch include either causing the packet to wait by creating a conflict with other packets at the next stage in the network or by filling the data from that output to the receiving computer with waiting packets. These techniques will be discussed further in Section V-B. □

Note that due to the symmetry of bridge faults, some of the above tests are not needed. For example, the last f test patterns of the test set in Lemma 4, i.e., the ones corresponding to the DESELECT lines connected to the last switch input, are not needed because a fault between one of these lines and one of the other $f^2 - f$ DESELECT lines will be detected by the test corresponding to the other line. However, this feature will not be used because it complicates the routing scheme that is used for testing of the entire network.

An OR-bridge fault between two of the f DESELECT lines connected to the same switch input will not produce an observable error because these lines are ORed at the RSB. If one or more of them have value one, then the RSB must be disabled. Hence, an OR-bridge fault between two of these lines does not have an observable effect.

Lemma 5: $4f$ tests are sufficient to detect AND-bridge faults between DESELECT lines when f is odd and $6f$ tests when f is even.

Proof: The same tests as for testing faults on SELECT lines can be used but for each test, two consecutive packets should be sent to the same input, one having all 0's in its data part and the other all 1's. The transmission of the first packet out of the switch is delayed in order to produce an observable error. The occurrence of an AND-bridge fault will cause the corruption or the loss of one or both of the packets because the second packet will be accepted in the buffer before the first one is transmitted out of the switch. In all, $4f$ ($6f$) tests will be needed with this scheme when f is odd (even). □

Note that faults on DESELECT lines will not be handled by the pseudo-exhaustive tests mentioned above, because they involve interaction between successive test patterns.

2) Other Types of Bridge Faults: Bridge faults can also appear on lines of different types. An AND-bridge fault between a SELECT and a DESELECT line will cause the SELECT line to remain idle if the DESELECT line is idle (0 logic value) and vice versa. The fact that the SELECT and DESELECT lines are activated during different time periods (when the SELECT line goes from 0 to 1 the DESELECT lines connected to the same input should be 0) makes that any test that activates the SELECT lines will detect AND-bridge faults between SELECT and DESELECT lines connected to the same switch input. For example, the tests for AND-bridge faults on DESELECT lines of Lemma 5 will detect those faults. The tests will also detect faults between SELECT and DESELECT lines corresponding to different switch inputs because each test pattern activates f SELECT lines in parallel and when those lines are activated all the DESELECT lines in the switch are idle (otherwise the packets would not have been admitted into the RSB's). An OR-bridge fault between a SELECT and a DESELECT line will cause an idle SELECT line to be activated whenever the DESELECT line is activated and vice versa. Therefore, these faults are detected by the tests for bridge faults between SELECT lines described in Lemma 3.

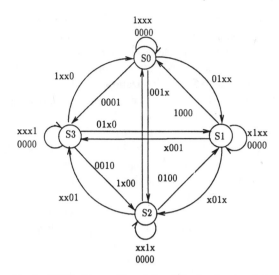

Fig. 7. Finite state machine of the ALB of a 4 × 4 switch.

Theorem 1: $f^2 + 4f$ tests are sufficient to detect all stuck-at-α faults and bridge faults on SELECT and DESELECT lines when f is odd and $f^2 + 6f$ tests when f is even.

Proof: Follows from Lemmas 4 and 5 and the above discussion. □

The control logic and the switching logic are usually physically separated in the switch. Sometimes they are situated on different boards [13] or chips. Therefore, bridge faults between data lines and control lines, such as SELECT/DESELECT, are unlikely to occur.

Stuck-at-α and bridge faults involving the control lines between switches (DV, CTS lines) have the same syndrome as faults involving SELECT/DESELECT lines and therefore they will be detected by the same tests.

C. Testing the Arbitration Logic Blocks

In this section, we generate tests for the conflict resolution functions which are handled by the ALB of each switch output. Fig. 7 shows the finite state machine representation of an ALB implementing the round-robin priority scheme. In state S_i, the relative priority of the inputs is $(i \succ (i+1) \bmod f \succ (i+2) \bmod f \succ (i+3) \bmod f)$, where $i \succ j$ means that input i has higher priority than input j. The four-bit number(s) on each transition arc enumerate(s) the states of the four SELECT lines connected to the ALB, that would produce the transition. A possible implementation for the ALB is shown in [13]. The following result is based on the behavioral model of the ALB and therefore it is independent of the actual design.

Theorem 2: $f2^{f-1}$ tests are sufficient to detect the faults in the conflict resolution functions of a switch, in the fixed priority case, and, $f^2 2^f$ tests are sufficient in the round-robin priority case.

Proof: In the case of fixed priority, the Arbitration Logic Block is a priority encoder which can be tested by applying all possible patterns to its inputs which requires 2^f tests. If the f ALB's are tested serially the total number of tests per switch would be $f2^f$. In the case of round-robin priority, the design of the ALB is more complex. The ALB implements

767

a finite state machine with f states, each state corresponding to a particular setting of the relative priority of the inputs. For each state, 2^f possible transition arcs exist. In all, the finite state machine has $f2^f$ transition arcs. Every transition needs to be tested. Reinitialization will be needed between tests to bring the ALB to the desired state. Testing all the ALB's serially would require $f2 2^f$ tests not including the reinitialization packets. In both cases, the test can proceed by applying 1-conflicts then 2-conflicts, $\cdots$, then f-conflicts to each ALB. There are C_i^f i-conflicts for each i, $1 \leq i \leq f$.

It is possible to test more than one ALB at the same time. While applying a test using i active inputs to one output (i-conflict), another test using $f - i$ active inputs ($(f - i)$-conflict) can be applied to another output. This would reduce the number of tests by a factor of two since $C_i^f = C_{f-i}^f$. In the case of fixed priority, the number of tests becomes $f2^{f-1}$. In the round-robin priority case, the number of tests will be $f2^{f-1}$ not including the reinitialization steps. In the case of round-robin priority, the procedure for reinitializing the ALB depends on what the state of the ALB is after it finishes servicing a given set of requests. If the last serviced request was from input i and there are no outstanding requests, then depending on the implementation, the ALB will either stay in state S_i or go to the next state, i.e., $S_{i+1 \bmod f}$. Under both strategies, reinitializing the ALB to a given state S_k can be done by sending a request to that ALB from input k, for the first implementation, or from input $k - 1 \bmod f$, for the second implementation. The testing of the ALB can proceed as follows: test first all the transitions going out of state S_0, using one reinitializing packet to go back to S_0 between tests if needed, then test all the transitions going out of state S_1 and continue in this fashion until all transitions have been covered. When testing two ALB's at the same time one can start testing one of them in state S_0 and the other in state S_1 in such a fashion that the required reinitialization step does not present a conflict, i.e., the two reinitializing packets come from two different inputs. Since the number of tests to be applied to the ALB is the same in each state, when testing two ALB's at the same time, one can maintain a situation in which the two reinitializing packets are nonconflicting during the entire testing procedure. Hence, there will be at most one reinitialization pattern per test which implies that the number of such patterns is bounded by the number of tests itself. Therefore, the number of patterns required to detect faults in the ALB's, in the case of round-robin priority, is $f2 2^f$ including both the testing patterns and the reinitialization patterns. $\square$

The number of tests in the proposed scheme is still exponential with respect to the number of inputs, but it is several orders of magnitude smaller than the number of tests required in the pseudo-exhaustive method. For an 8×8 switch, $f2 2^f = 16,384$ while, in the pseudo-exhaustive method, more than 43 million tests are needed (see Section IV). Furthermore, in multistage interconnection networks, f is usually less than or equal to eight due to technological and packaging constraints imposed on switches.

The number of initialization steps required in the round-robin priority case may be reduced if the tests are ordered

properly. If a test sequence, such that each test transfers the ALB of each output to the desired priority state for the next test, can be found, then only one initialization step will be sufficient.

The tests for conflict resolution will cover most of the faults on control lines considered in this section except for the stuck-at-1 faults and bridge faults on DESELECT lines which may not be completely covered and would require separate tests. The fault coverage of the tests is discussed in more detail in Section VII.

Next we consider the problem of extending the tests to the entire network. In the case where the test does not involve a conflict, the testing packets can be easily routed such that the test will be applied to the entire network. In the case where the test involves a conflict, a more complex routing scheme needs to be used to ensure that the desired conflicts will occur at every switch of the network. The procedures for generating the routing tags for the testing packets are presented in the next section.

V. Testing the Network

Our objective here is to minimize the number of tests for the entire network. We develop algorithms to generate routing tags for the testing packets in such a fashion that the same packets can be used to detect faults in switches at different stages in the network.

A. Testing of the Internal Data Lines and the Multiplexing Logic

In this section, we present a method for detecting bridge faults between data lines and data multiplexing faults in any switch of the network using the same number of tests as for a single switch. The tests of Lemma 1 can be applied to the entire network in a straightforward manner since in each test the same data are sent to each switch input and the connections involved do not involve any conflicts. Also since those tests do not require any special routing, they can be combined with other tests such as the tests for the internal control lines or the tests for the arbitration logic blocks. The tests of Lemma 2 detect both data multiplexing faults and bridge faults across data paths. In the following, we show how to extend those tests to the entire network. These tests do not involve any conflicts. In each test pattern and for every switch, there is one testing packet that carries all 0's or all 1's in its data part (referred to as packet of type α) and $f - 1$ packets that carry the complementary value in their data parts (referred to as packets of type $\overline{\alpha}$). These packets should be properly routed to create the same configuration (i.e., one packet of type α and the remaining packets of type $\overline{\alpha}$) in each switch traversed. Procedure **DATA_test** generates routing tags for the testing packets to be applied by each computer. A denotes the address of the sending computer, $a_{L-1} a_{L-2} \cdots a_0$ is the f-ary representation of A, $D[\ ]$ is an array with $2f^2$ entries in which the routing tags are stored and $C[\ ]$ is an array with $2f^2$ entries. Each entry in $C[\ ]$ corresponds to one of the tests and its content indicates the value (0 or 1) to be carried in the data part of that test.

DATA_test$(A, f, L, D[\ ], C[\ ])$

```
begin
  for k = 0 to f − 1 do
  begin
    for j = 0 to f − 1 do
    begin
      if ((a_{L−1} + ⋯ + a_1 + k) mod f = a_0) then
      begin
        C[2(j + kf)] ← 1;
        C[2(j + kf) + 1] ← 0;
      end
      else
      begin
        C[2(j + kf)] ← 0;
        C[2(j + kf) + 1] ← 1;
      end
      for s = 0 to L − 1 do
      begin
        temp ← (a_0 + j) mod f;
        a_0 ← a_{L−1−s};
        a_{L−1−s} ← temp;
      end
      D[2(j + kf)] ← A;
      D[2(j + kf) + 1] ← A;
    end
  end
end
```

Theorem 3: $2f^2$ tests are sufficient to detect data multiplexing faults and bridge faults across data paths in the entire network:

Proof: The $2f^2$ tests are the ones described in the proof of Lemma 2. In these tests, one channel in the switch is selected for testing and a packet of type α is sent through this channel while $f − 1$ packets of type $\overline{\alpha}$ are sent to the other inputs of the switch. Note that the $f − 1$ packets of type $\overline{\alpha}$ can be routed to any set of outputs in the switch and therefore a routing that does not produce a conflict can be selected. The problem with applying this type of tests to the entire network is to ensure that the same configuration will occur at each switch in the network. Since the tests do not involve conflicts, the packets will take the same amount of time to traverse a stage. Therefore, to achieve the required configuration, it is sufficient to apply the test to all the switches of the first stage then route the packets in such a way that each switch in the network receives exactly one packet of type α. In the following, we prove that the routing generated by algorithm **Data_test** ensures that two packets of type α will not go to the same switch in the same pattern.

The inputs to the switches at each stage will be numbered from 0 to $f^L − 1$ using the f-ary notation (the inputs at the first stage have the same numbers as the addresses of the computers to which they are connected). In **DATA_test**, at the first stage of the network, packets of type α go to the inputs whose numbers verify the equation

$$a_0 = (a_1 + a_2 + ⋯ + a_{L−1} + k) \bmod f. \qquad (2)$$

A packet that comes to an input numbered $a_{L−1}a_{L−2} \cdots a_0$, in the first stage of the network, will go at the second stage to an input numbered $a'_{L−1}a'_{L−2} \cdots a'_0$ where $a'_{L−1} = (a_0 + j) \bmod f$, $a'_i = a_i$ for $1 \le i \le (L − 2)$ and $a'_0 = a_{L−1}$. At a given stage, two inputs belong to the same switch if their numbers have the same most significant $f − 1$ digits. Two packets of type α coming at the same time to inputs number $A = a_{L−1}a_{L−2} \cdots a_0$ and $B = b_{L−1}b_{L−2} \cdots b_0$ at the first stage will go to the same switch at the next level if an only if $a'_i = b'_i$ for $1 \le i \le (L − 1)$ which implies that $a_i = b_i$ for $0 \le i \le (L − 2)$. But since A and B verify (2), $a_{L−1}$ is also equal to $b_{L−1}$ and hence $A = B$. Therefore, each switch at the second level will receive exactly one packet of type α. Moreover the packets of type α will come, at the second stage, to inputs whose numbers verify an equation similar to (2): $a'_{L−1} = \left(a'_0 + a'_1 + ⋯ + a'_{L−2} + k − j\right) \bmod f$ which implies that the above property can be generalized by induction to all stages of the network. □

These tests cover the multiple bridge faults across data paths under the assumption that depending on the technology used in the design either AND- or OR-bridge faults exist in the system. Since any of these faults can change the data in one direction (either ones become zeros or zeros become ones, but not both) [16], the bridge faults in different switches on the path traversed by a testing packet will not cancel each other. Similarly, with the above assumption, the tests of Lemma 1 will cover multiple bridge faults within a data path in the entire network.

The above test procedure also detects the data multiplexing faults with the assumption that only the switches at one stage are faulty. If there is more than one faulty switch on the path from a source processor to a destination processor, the data multiplexing faults on the data path can mask each other. A test procedure for multiple faults on different stages is to ensure that only one switch on each path, that a testing packet traverses, has a packet of type α packet and $f − 1$ packets of type $\overline{\alpha}$ and all other switches at other stages receive either all α or all $\overline{\alpha}$ packets. Then the switches other than the switch under test on the path will transmit either only α or only $\overline{\alpha}$ packets to all their outputs even if they have data multiplexing faults on their data paths. This can be accomplished by testing each stage of the network separately and applying the test procedure for an $f \times f$ switch, as described in Section IV-A, to the switches at the stage under test. Hence, testing for faults in data multiplexing logic of multiple switches requires $2f^2L$ tests.

B. Testing the Internal Control Lines

In Theorem 1, we showed that faults involving the internal control lines (SELECT/DESELECT) in the switch can be detected using $f^2 + 4f$ or $f^2 + 6f$ tests. In this section, we look into the problem of testing the entire network for these faults.

We need to apply the tests of Lemmas 4 and 5 to the entire network. These tests were developed for bridge faults between DESELECT lines but, as discussed in Section IV-B they will also detect stuck-at-α faults and bridge faults on all SELECT and DESELECT lines and some bridge faults between data lines and control lines. The tests for OR-bridge faults described in the proof of Lemma 4 involve sending packets along the selected connections in the switch while the transmission of the first packet is blocked. To implement the test for the entire network, we use f^2 test graphs. Each test graph consists of $N = f^L$ disjoint paths through the network and f^{L-1} of those paths contain the lines under tests (one line per switch). Packets will be sent along these paths while at the output links of the network the reception of the packets is blocked in such a way that all the buffers along the selected paths are filled and all the DESELECT lines along these paths are activated (logic value 1). Packets are then sent along the remaining $f^L - f^{L-1}$ paths of the test graph, one packet per path. The DESELECT lines under test in a given test graph and the corresponding data channels are referred as lines and channels of type I while all the DESELECT lines and data channels not sharing the same input with a line under test are referred to as lines or channels of type II. If an OR-bridge fault exists between a DESELECT line of type I and a line of type II then the packet incoming to the input of the line of type II will be delayed as long as the packets in the channels of type I remain blocked.

In the case where the computers are handling the reception of the packets at the output links of the network, the above scheme can be implemented by having the computer delay the servicing of the incoming packets while at each input of the network $L + 1$ consecutive packets are sent to fill up the paths under test in the network.

Theorem 4: $f^2(L+1)$ tests are sufficient to detect OR-bridge faults on DESELECT lines in the entire network.

Proof: The test graphs for these faults can be generated using the same technique as in **DATA_test**. In each switch, one line of type I and $f - 1$ lines of type II should be activated. Hence, the routing tags generated by procedure **DATA_test** can be used to achieve the desired pattern at every switch. Since f^2 test graphs need to be generated to cover all OR-bridge faults between DESELECT lines in every switch and for each test graph $L+1$ packets need to be sent along the paths of type I, the total number of steps in this testing procedure will be $f^2(L+1)$. $\square$

In the case where the packets go directly to the memory, the desired delay can still be produced by taking advantage of the large latency of the memory access, but more packets will have to be sent in that case. The number of packets to be sent to fill up the data paths depends on the memory access time T and the time τ it takes to apply a new packet at an input of the network, and is equal to $n_p = \lceil (L+1)/(1 - \frac{\tau}{T}) \rceil$. This number of packets has to be sent along the paths to type I in each of the f^2 test graphs.

The procedure for generating the routing tags for the testing packets for OR-bridge faults on DESELECT lines is similar to **DATA_test**. Hence, it will be omitted. Procedure **AND_test** generates the routing tags for the testing packets that will be used to create at each switch of the network one of the connection patterns presented in the proof of Lemma 3 for testing bridge faults on SELECT lines. It is also used to detect AND-bridge faults on DESLECT lines as well as other types of faults as shown in the proofs of Lemma 5 and Theorem 1. Procedure **AND_test** generates, using the address A of the computer, $2f$ routing tags when f is odd and $3f$ tags when f is even. The tags are stored in the array $D[\,]$. Some of

the test patterns of Lemma 3 do not activate every input in the switch. For those tests, only a subset of the computers will send testing packets. The remaining computers should not apply any packets to the network. The following procedure initializes the array $S[\,]$ which contains the flags that indicate to the computer whether it should skip the test and not send any packets.

```
AND_test (A, f, L, D[ ], S[ ])
begin
    for j = 0 to f − 1 do
    begin
        S[j] ← 0;
        for s = 0 to L − 1 do
        begin
            temp ← (a_0 + j) mod f;
            a_0 ← a_{L−1−s};
            a_{L−1−1} ← temp;
        end
        D[j] ← A;
    end
    if (f is odd) then
        for j = 0 to f − 1 do
        begin
            S[f + j] ← 0;
            for s = 0 to L − 1 do
            begin
                temp ← (2a_0 + j) mod f;
                a_0 ← a_{L−1−s};
                a_{L−1−s} ← temp;
            end
            D[f + j] ← A;
        end
    else                                        ;f is even
    begin
        j_0 ← (a_0 − (a_{L−1} + ··· + a_1)) mod f;    ;from (2)
        for j = 0 to f − 1 do
        begin
            if (j = j_0) then
                S[f + j] ← 1;                       ;Skip
            else
            begin
                S[f + j] ← 0;
                for s = 0 to L − 1 do    ;the following generates the
                                                 sliding test
                begin                    ;with f − 1 active inputs
                    aux ← 2((f − 1) − (j − j_0)) mod (f − 1);
                    temp ← (a_0 + (j − j_0) + 1 + aux) mod f;
                    a_0 ← a_{L−1−s};
                    a_{L−1−s} ← temp;
                end
                D[f + j] ← A;
            end
        end
        for j = 0 to f − 1 do
        begin                            ;this generates the additional f
            if (j = j_0) then                ;tests for the case f even.
            begin
                S[2f + j] ← 0;
```

```
for s = 0 to L − 1 do
begin
    temp ← (a_0 + f/2) mod f;    ;from Lemma 3
    a_0 ← a_{L−1−s};
    a_{L−1−s} ← temp;
end
    D[2f + j] ← A;
end
else
    S[f + j] ← 1;                          ;Skip
end
end
end
```

The tests for AND-bridge faults described in the proof of Lemma 5 involve sending consecutive packets along each connection in the switch while the transmission of the first packet is blocked. To test the entire network, we select a set of disjoint paths through the network and send a sequence of consecutive packets along these paths while at the outputs the reception of the packets is blocked in such a way that all the buffers along the selected paths will be filled. If any one of the DESELECT lines along the paths is not functioning properly then some packets will be lost or their data will be corrupted. To block the reception of the packets at the output of the network, the methods described above for the tests of Theorem 4 can be used.

Theorem 5: $2f(L+1)$ tests are sufficient to detect AND-bridge faults on DESELECT lines in the entire network when f is odd and $3f(L+1)$ tests when f is even.

Proof: Procedure **AND_test** implements the scheme described in Lemma 5. In each test graph generated by the procedure, f, $f−1$ or 1 nonconflicting connections are selected in every switch in the system forming f^L, $(f−1)f^{L−1}$ or $f^{L−1}$ disjoint paths through the network, respectively. As many as $2f$ ($3f$) such test graphs are generated for f odd (even). Each test graph is used to send $L+1$ consecutive testing packets while at the other end of the network the reception of the packets is blocked. In the case where f is even, a special scheme has to be used to generate the second sequence of f test patterns. In these tests one of the inputs of the switch is not activated. The scheme used to select the inputs that will not be activated is the same as that used to send the packets of type α in procedure **DATA_test**. The proof of the correctness of that scheme is provided in the proof of Theorem 3. The last f tests for the case f even activate only one line per switch. The above scheme is also used to select which input links at the first stage of the network will receive testing packets at the same time. □

As was shown in Section IV-B, the tests for bridge faults between DESELECT lines will also detect all other faults involving SELECT and DESELECT lines. This is also true at the network level. In the next section, we present a scheme for detecting conflict resolution faults in the entire network which minimizes the total number of tests.

C. Testing Conflict Resolution

We now proceed to present a method to test the network for conflict resolution faults and a test generation algorithm. It tests the entire network with only twice the number of tests needed to test an $f \times f$ switch, independently of the number of levels L of the (f, L) system. The method is general and can be applied to networks with arbitrary fan-out f and arbitrary number of levels L.

In our discussion, when we refer to an $(f − i)$- and an i-conflict, we will assume that $(f − i)$ is greater than or equal to i, without loss of generality.

To show that an (f, L) system can be tested with only twice the number of tests needed to test an $f \times f$ switch, the following lemmas are introduced.

Lemma 6: One test is sufficient to create an i- and an $(f − i)$-conflict at two outputs of each switch at all even-numbered levels of the (f, L) system.

Proof: The (f, L) system can be divided into f partitions, such that starting from level $l = 1$, each partition itself is an $(f, L − 1)$ subsystem. With the addressing scheme used in this paper, if a computer has an address A labeled in f-ary representation $a_{L−1}a_{L−2} \cdots a_1 a_0$, then it belongs to the partition $p = a_{L−1}$.

Each input of an (f, L) system can be activated with one test, such that an i- and an $(f − i)$-conflict are created at two outputs of each switch at level $l = 0$: Suppose the routing tag of a packet is $D = d_{L−1}d_{L−2} \cdots d_0$. The f-ary digit $d_{L−(l+1)}$ of the routing tag determines which switch output will be taken at level l.

If the computers connected to $(f − i)$ inputs of a switch at level $l = 0$ send testing packets with routing tags which have a common most significant digit $d_{L−1}$, an $(f − i)$-conflict will be created at the switch output $d_{L−1}$.

Similarly, if the computers attached to the remaining i inputs of a switch at level $l = 0$ send testing packets with routing tags which have a common most significant digit $d'_{L−1}$, an i-conflict will be created at the switch output $d'_{L−1}$.

Furthermore, we can assign a unique most significant digit $d_{L−1}$ (from 0 to $f − 1$) to each partition so that all of the $(f − i)$-conflicts in the partition at level $l = 0$ are created at the switch outputs with that unique number. For $i > 0$, we can assign another unique number to each partition and create the i-conflicts in a partition at level $l = 0$ at the switch outputs with that number.

As the outputs with the same number of all switches at level $l = 0$ are connected to the inputs of the same $(f, L − 1)$ subsystem at level $l = 1$, testing packets forming an $(f − i)$-conflict in a partition at level $l = 0$ will reach exactly one $(f, L − 1)$ subsystem. Similarly, testing packets contributing to an i-conflict at level $l = 0$ of a partition will arrive at exactly one $(f, L − 1)$ subsystem. So each $(f, L − 1)$ subsystem will receive only packets which contributed to $(f − i)$-conflicts at level $l = 0$ in exactly one partition. If $i > 0$, the same subsystem will also receive packets which contributed to i-conflicts at level $l = 0$ in another partition.

The testing packets from a conflicting output will arrive to the next level at different times according to their priorities. We will assume that each packet traverses a level in one unit of time, if it has the right of way to pass the desired switch output. Thus, each $(f, L − 1)$ subsystem has $2f^{L−2}$ active inputs at each time t for $0 < t \leq i$ and $f^{L−2}$ active inputs for $i < t \leq (f − i)$.

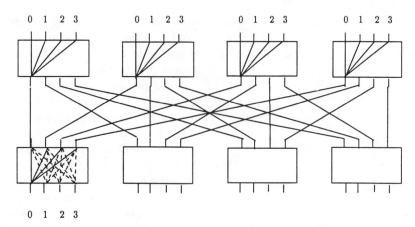

Fig. 8. The 4-conflicts represented with dashed lines at switch outputs 1, 2, and 3 cannot occur at the last level.

Testing packets at each of these f^{L-2} active inputs of an $(f, L-1)$ subsystem can be directed to the inputs of the same $(f, L-2)$ subsystem at level $l = 2$ by assigning the same second most significant routing digit d_{L-2} (same switch output) to these packets. Furthermore, a unique d_{L-2} can be selected for each set of f^{L-2} active inputs of an $(f, L-1)$ subsystem.

As all switch outputs with the same number at level $l = 1$ are connected to inputs of the same $(f, L-2)$ subsystem at level $l = 2$, in each partition there will be two disjoint $(f, L-2)$ subsystems with all their inputs active at each time t, for $1 < t \le i + 1$ and one $(f, L-2)$ subsystem with all its inputs active for $i + 1 < t \le f - i + 1$. Thus, all inputs of all $(f, L-2)$ subsystems of the network are activated with only one test.

The same scheme can be applied recursively to each resulting $(f, L-2s)$ subsystems for $1 \le s \le M$, where $M = \lfloor \frac{L-1}{2} \rfloor$. Hence, Lemma 6 is proved. $\square$

Lemma 7: One test is sufficient to create an i- and an $(f - i)$-conflict at two outputs of each switch at all odd-numbered levels of the (f, L) system.

Proof: It is always possible to activate all inputs of level $l = 1$ of an (f, L) system with one test by sending test packets through each input of the system at the same time, such that there is no conflict at level $l = 0$. Each computer attached to the same switch at level $l = 0$ needs to send a testing packet with a routing tag where the most significant bit d_{L-1} is unique to that computer. This scheme produces f disjoint $(f, L-1)$ systems with all inputs active starting from level $l = 1$. Applying Lemma 6 the same test can be used to generate i- and $(f - i)$-conflicts at two outputs of each switch at the even-numbered levels of these $(f, L-1)$ systems. Hence, Lemma 7 is proved. $\square$

Theorem 6: Only two tests are sufficient to generate an i- and an $(f - i)$-conflict at two outputs of all switches in an (f, L) system.

Proof: Follows from Lemmas 6 and 7. $\square$

Corollary 1: $f2^f$ tests are sufficient to detect faults in the conflict resolution functions of all switches in an (f, L) system in the fixed priority case, and $f^2 2^{f+1}$ tests are sufficient in the round-robin case.

Proof: Follows directly from Theorems 2 and 6. $\square$

Although we can generate i- and $(f - i)$-conflicts in all switches of a level at the same time, some of the testing packets used at one level cannot be used to create i- and $(f - i)$-conflicts in the switches at the next level. If there is an i-conflict created at a switch output, only one of the i active input channels will be selected at a time. The last input, which contributes to the i-conflict, will be selected after i time units. If the same i inputs are reused to generate the i-conflict at another output of the switch at time t, where $1 \le t \le i$, the i-conflict at the second output will not be created. At time t there will be still some lower priority input channels with buffered packets, which wait for the right of way from the first output. Therefore, the packets which are sent for the next i-conflict to these channels will not be transmitted to the switch from the previous level. Thus, they will not form the next i-conflict at the second output of the switch. This case is illustrated in Fig. 8 on a $(4, 2)$ system for a 4-conflict.

The number of tests for the entire network is only twice the number of tests needed for an $f \times f$ switch, but the testing time grows logarithmically with the number of processors, due to the network latency. Testing time can be reduced if the next test is applied before all testing packets of the previous test traverse the network. Instead of waiting $\lfloor \frac{L}{2} \rfloor + \lceil \frac{L}{2} \rceil (f - i)$ and $\lceil \frac{L}{2} \rceil + \lfloor \frac{L}{2} \rfloor (f - i)$ time units to apply the next test after a test which generates $(f - i)$- and i-conflicts at even and at odd-numbered levels of the system, respectively, the next test can be pipelined after only $(f - i)$ time units for the fixed priority case. In the case of round-robin priority, the waiting time between each test and an initialization step is $\lceil \frac{L}{2} \rceil (f - i) - \lceil \frac{L}{2} \rceil + 1$ and $\lfloor \frac{L}{2} \rfloor (f - i) - \lfloor \frac{L}{2} \rfloor + 1$ time units for the tests which create the conflicts at even and odd-numbered levels of the system, respectively. A test can be applied to the system immediately after an initialization step.

It was shown in the proof of Lemma 6 that the $(f, L-2)$ subsystem in a partition can receive only packets with a given priority during a test. We will represent the highest priority by f. So the priority h of a packet, which contributes to an i-conflict can be $f - i + 1 \le h \le f$. Pipelining of the tests after $(f - i)$ time units requires the following condition: If an $(f, L-2)$ subsystems receives the packets with priority h during one test, at the next test it should get packets with a priority h or less. This condition is necessary to avoid the

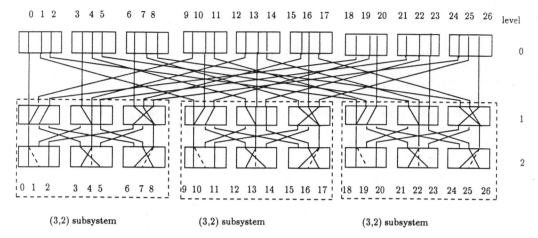

Fig. 9. Testing the odd-numbered stages of a (3,3) system for a 2-conflict and a 1-conflict.

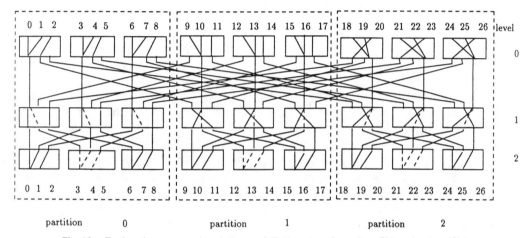

Fig. 10. Testing the even-numbered stages of (3,3) system for a 2-conflict and a 1-conflict.

interaction between any testing packets of two consecutive tests.

A switch in an $(f, L-2)$ subsystem at level $l = 2$ releases the last packet of a test for an i- and $(f-i)$-conflict, at time $t_c = 2 + (f-i) + (f-h)$. Here the testing packets, which arrive at the given $(f, L-2)$ system, passed the conflicts at level $l = 0$ with a priority h, where $i + 1 \leq h \leq f$.

The arrival time of the packets at an $(f, L-2)$ subsystem during the next test is $t_a = 2 + (f-i) + (f-h')$. The priority, with which the arriving packets passed the level $l = 0$ during the next test for an i'-and $(f-i')$-conflicts, is h', where $i' + 1 \leq h' \leq f$. To avoid any interaction between any packets of two consecutive tests, t_a should be greater than or equal to t_c for any $(f, L-2)$ subsystem. This implies, that $h' \leq h$ for any $(f, L-2)$ subsystem. Thus, during each consecutive test an $(f, L-2)$ subsystem should get packets either with equal priority or lower priority than the packets it received at the previous test. It implies that i should be greater than or equal to i'. So the tests need to be applied in a sequence, where i is monotonically decreasing.

Each computer in the system sends $f2^f$ testing packets in the case of fixed priority and $f^2 2^f$ testing packets and $f^2 2^f$ initialization packets in the case of round-robin priority. Each testing packet contains three types of information:

routing tag, source tag, and a time-stamp. These routing packets can be pregenerated and stored in the memory of each computer. Each computer compares the packets it receives to the testing packets it expects. A mismatch between the received and the expected packets signals the presence of a fault. The expected testing packets can be stored in the memory of each computer. Only $f2^f$ and $f^2 2^{f+1}$ packets need to be stored in each computer, independent of the size of the system, for the fixed and round-robin priority case respectively.

Fig. 9 shows testing of the odd-numbered stages in a (3,3) system to activate a 2-conflict and 1-conflict. Fig. 10 illustrates generation of conflicts at even-numbered levels.

VI. TESTING TIME

In the previous section, it has been shown that two tests are sufficient to create an i- and an $(f-i)$-conflict at each switch of the network. Therefore, only twice the number of tests needed to test an $f \times f$ switch is required to test the entire network, independent of its size. The number of tests is $f2^f$ for the fixed priority case and $f^2 2^f + n_i(f)$ for the round-robin priority case, where $n_i(f)$ is the number of initialization steps and its upper bound is $f^2 2^f$.

Although the number of tests is constant, the testing time grows with the number of levels L of the system due to the network latency. We define the interval in which a packet traverses a stage of the network without conflicts as a time unit. For simplicity of calculation, we assume that packets involved in an i-conflict traverse the switch in i time units neglecting the additional time overhead due to the conflict resolution.

The scheme proposed in the previous section generates i and $(f-i)$-conflicts at the same time. The maximum of the numbers i and $(f-i)$ should be taken as the number of time units necessary to traverse a stage with conflicts. A stage with conflicts is followed by a stage with no conflicts which is traversed in one time unit by the testing packets. A test involving an i and an $(f-i)$-conflict on even-numbered stages of the network takes $\lfloor \frac{L}{2} \rfloor + \lceil \frac{L}{2} \rceil \max\{i, (f-i)\}$ time units to traverse the network. A test involving an i and an $(f-i)$-conflict on odd-numbered stages of the network takes $\lceil \frac{L}{2} \rceil + \lfloor \frac{L}{2} \rfloor \max\{i, (f-i)\}$ time units to traverse the network. These two tests take together $L + L \max\{i, (f-i)\}$ time units. The total time is obtained by adding up the times for all i conflicts for $0 \leq i \leq \lfloor \frac{f}{2} \rfloor$. But to get a symmetric expression the sum will be taken for $0 \leq i \leq f$ and then it will be divided by two. In addition to the tests for conflict resolution we need to take into account the time needed to apply the tests of Theorems 3, 4, and 5 since the faults covered by these tests are not necessarily covered by the tests for conflict resolution. The time needed to complete these tests is $2f^2L + f^2(2L+1) + 3f(2L+1)$ when f is even, and $2f^2L + f^2(2L+1) + 2f(2L+1)$ when f is odd. We will use the first number as an upper bound. The tests for bridge faults within a data path can be combined with the tests for the control logic since, for practical values of w, f, and the length l of the packet, it is always possible to fit the $\lceil \log_2 w \rceil$ data patterns of Lemma 1 in the data part of the testing packets of Theorem 4 or the packets for testing conflict resolution faults. Hence, no additional time is required for testing for those faults. The total testing time, in the case where fixed priority is used, is

$$
\begin{aligned}
T_{\text{fix}} &= \frac{1}{2} f \sum_{i=0}^{f} C_i^f (L + L \max\{i, (f-i)\}) \\
&\quad + 2f^2L + f^2(2L+1) + 3f(2L+1) \\
&= Lf2^{f-2}(f+2) + \frac{1}{2} LfC_{\lceil \frac{f}{2} \rceil}^f \left\lceil \frac{f}{2} \right\rceil \\
&\quad + L(4f^2 + 6f) + f^2 + 3f \text{ time units.}
\end{aligned}
$$

In the case of round-robin priority, each initialization step takes L time units. The total time spent for initialization is $T_i = Lf^2 2^f$ time units. Each output of a switch needs to be tested for f different priority states. The total testing time becomes

$$
\begin{aligned}
T_{\text{round}} &= Lf^2 2^{f-2}(f+2) + Lf^2 2^f + \frac{1}{2} Lf^2 C_{\lceil \frac{f}{2} \rceil}^f \left\lceil \frac{f}{2} \right\rceil \\
&\quad + 2f^2L + f^2(2L+1) + 3f(2L+1) \\
&= Lf^2 2^{f-2}(f+6) + \frac{1}{2} Lf^2 C_{\lceil \frac{f}{2} \rceil}^f \left\lceil \frac{f}{2} \right\rceil \\
&\quad + L(4f^2 + 6f) + f^2 + 3f \text{ time units.}
\end{aligned}
$$

The testing time for the network can be further reduced by applying the tests in a pipelined fashion. A test that creates an i-conflict at the switch outputs is followed, $\max\{i, (f-i)\}$ time units later, by another test. The time delay is required to allow the first test to clear the first stage before another test is applied. The routing scheme in the testing algorithm is designed such that packets from pipelined tests do not collide with each other. The testing time for a network with the fixed priority scheme is

$$
\begin{aligned}
T_{\text{fix}}^{(p)} &= 2f \sum_{i=0}^{\lfloor \frac{f}{2} \rfloor} C_i^f \max\{i, (f-i)\} + \left\lfloor \frac{L}{2} \right\rfloor f + \left\lceil \frac{L}{2} \right\rceil \\
&\quad - f + 2f^2 + f^2(L+1) + 3f(L+1) \\
&= f^2 2^{f-1} + fC_{\lceil \frac{f}{2} \rceil}^f \left\lceil \frac{f}{2} \right\rceil + \left\lfloor \frac{L}{2} \right\rfloor f + \left\lceil \frac{L}{2} \right\rceil \\
&\quad + (f^2 + 3f)L + 3f^2 + 2f \text{ time units.}
\end{aligned}
$$

In the case of round-robin priority, a test involving conflict cannot be followed in a pipelined fashion by an initialization step because packets from the initialization step might catch up with the testing packets and create different inputs at the switches than the ones intended. The waiting time is $\lceil \frac{L}{2} \rceil (f-i) - \lceil \frac{L}{2} \rceil + 1$ in the case of a test for even-numbered levels and $\lfloor \frac{L}{2} \rfloor (f-i) - \lfloor \frac{L}{2} \rfloor + 1$ in the case of a test for odd-numbered levels. On the other hand an initialization step can be followed, one time unit later by a testing packet. Therefore the testing time becomes:

$$
\begin{aligned}
T_{\text{round}}^{(p)} &= f^2 \sum_{i=0}^{\lfloor \frac{f}{2} \rfloor} C_i^f (L(f-i) - L + 4) + L - 1 \\
&\quad + 2f^2 + f^2(L+1) + 3f(L+1) \\
&= Lf^2 2^{f-2}(f-2) + 4f^2 2^{f-1} + L \frac{f^2}{2} C_{\lceil \frac{f}{2} \rceil}^f \left\lceil \frac{f}{2} \right\rceil \\
&\quad + L - 1 + (f^2 + 3f)L + 3f^2 + 3f \text{ time units.}
\end{aligned}
$$

Next, we consider the specific multistage network used in the Sigma-I computer [5], which has two stages, $L = 2$, and uses, for fault tolerance purposes, 10×10 switches configured as 8×8's. The network is duplicated and one side is used to write into memory and the other to read from it. We make an estimate of the testing time using first the pseudo-exhaustive method and then our approach. We assume the time taken for traversing the network and accessing the memory is around 120 ns. Therefore, the time unit, as defined above, will be taken to be 60 ns and will be denoted by t. The number of different possible settings of a switch is $s = \left(C_8^{10}\right)^2 = 2025$ and f is equal to 8. The number of tests for the pseudo-exhaustive approach, as derived in Section 4, is $m = \sum_{i=0}^{f} C_i^f f^i$, which can be rewritten as $m = \sum_{i=0}^{f} C_i^f \left(\sum_{i_1+i_2+\cdots+i_f=i} \frac{i!}{i_1! i_2! \cdots i_f!} \right)$, where i is the number of active inputs and i_j is the number of inputs going to output j out of the i active inputs. A test will take $\max(i_1, i_2, \cdots, i_f)$ time units to clear the stage it is testing and will take $L - 1$ time units to clear the rest of the network, therefore the testing time in the exhaustive approach would be

$$T = 2stL\left(\sum_{i=0}^{f} C_i^f \left(\sum_{i_1+i_2+\cdots+i_f=i} \frac{i!}{i_1! \, i_2! \cdots i_f!} \right. \right.$$
$$\left. \left. \cdot \left(\max(i_1, i_2, \cdots, i_f) + L - 1\right) \right) \right)$$
$$= 19.8 \text{ hours.}$$

The testing time in our approach is

$$T = 2st\left(Lf^2 2^{f-2}(f-2) + 4f^2 2^{f-1} + L\frac{f^2}{2} C_{\lceil \frac{f}{2} \rceil}^f \left\lceil \frac{f}{2} \right\rceil \right.$$
$$\left. + L - 1 + \left(f^2 + 3f\right)L + 3f^2 + 3f\right)$$
$$= 24.4 \text{ s.}$$

This represents over three orders of magnitude improvement. In this particular case the testing time for the network is about 2700 times shorter. Note that the only advantage of the exhaustive test is that it would cover faults due to the interference between the arbitration units at the outputs of the switch. Such faults are not completely covered by our test. On the other hand, a truly exhaustive test should test the switch in every priority state which would multiply the number of tests required by a factor of f^f. Our method does test the ALB's in every state without requiring as many tests. Also our method covers such faults as stuck-at-0 faults or bridge faults on DESELECT lines which can be observed only by sending particular *sequences* of packets and therefore will not be detected by the pseudo-exhaustive test.

VII. Test Coverage

The testing packet used in Section IV-C for conflict resolution tests can be expanded to cover the stuck-at-α faults on the data lines by adding the one's complement of the routing tag: All the edges of the network are traversed at least once during an i- and $(f-i)$-conflict test. For example, Fig. 11 illustrates the tests to generate two 2-conflicts at all outputs of a 4×4 switch which cover all the edges of the switch at least once. Stuck-at-α faults on the data paths can change the data and the routing tag in the packets. If the change in the routing tag occurs before the changed bit has been used by the switch at the corresponding level this fault will cause misrouting of the packet. If the change in the routing tag occurs after the changed bit has been used by the switch at the corresponding level the packet will still arrive at the correct destination. In any case any multiple stuck-at-α faults will be detected by the destination processor as the routing tag and its complement in the testing packet will mismatch. Data patterns developed to detect the bridge faults on the data paths in Lemma 1 can be encapsulated in one or more of the testing packets. We assume that depending on the technology used in the design either AND- or OR-bridge faults exist in the system. This type of faults on the data lines will change one of the $\lceil \log_2 w \rceil$ words added for bridge faults and hence will be detected. If any combination of stuck-at-α

Fig. 11. Four tests creating two 2-conflicts and covering all edges of the 4×4 switch.

and bridge faults exists on a data path where the last fault on the path is a stuck-at-α fault it is obviously detected by the mismatch of the routing tag and its complement. If the last fault is a bridge fault, it is detected due to the change of data in at least one of the $\lceil \log_2 w \rceil$ words added for bridge faults. Hence, multiple stuck-at-α and bridge faults on the lines and the data storage elements of the switches are detected if there exists no other type of faults in the network.

In the remaining part of this section, we will discuss the coverage for multiple faults on the same stage of the network. The routing faults are also covered by the tests for conflict resolution since each input channel is connected to each output channel at least once. Thus, the RSB's at the input ports of all switches are exhaustively tested. A misrouting fault will be detected by one or more of the following syndromes:

- A computer does not receive a packet it expects.
- A computer receives a packet with a routing tag that does not match its address. In this case the misrouting was due to an incorrect decoding of the address at one of the switches.
- A computer receives a testing packet in which the source tag does not match the source tag of the expected packet. This check will detect misrouting faults due to a corrupted address.

The arbitration circuitry at each output of a switch (ALB) is tested exhaustively since it is set in every state and in each state all possible input requests are applied. We consider the following faulty behavior which is due to a fault in the control logic of a switch output and we show how they will be detected by our scheme:

- If an active input channel is not selected, at least one computer at the output will not receive one of the test packets it expects and the fault will be detected.
- If an input channel, which does not ask the right of way from an output channel, is selected in addition to the active input channels for that output, then the computer for which the packet in the channel was intended will not receive an expected packet and another computer will receive a packet which it does not expect. Merging faults are a special case of the above faults.
- If an input channel, which does not ask the right of way, is selected by an output instead of an active input, then an unexpected packet will be received by one of the computers.
- The active inputs which try to pass through the same output of the switch at the same time may be selected in the wrong order due to a fault in the priority logic of a switch output. This will be detected because at least one computer will receive a test packet either with longer or shorter delay than it expects.

The bridge faults on the data lines in all the switches and faults in the data multiplexing circuit at switch outputs are tested in Section IV-A. The possible syndromes of these faults are stuck-at-α faults on data paths, misrouting of the one or more data bits of a data channel, or bridging faults between the data lines of different data channels.

The tests described in Section IV-B cover stuck-at-α faults and bridge faults on the control lines that link the control circuitry of the inputs to that of the outputs as well as the faults on the control lines between two switches at consecutive stages.

VIII. CONCLUSIONS

Efficient testing techniques for packet-switched multistage interconnection networks were presented. The tests cover faults in the data paths and the control circuitry including faults in the conflict resolution capabilities of the switches. The approach achieves several orders of magnitude improvement with respect to methods which are based on a pseudo-exhaustive testing of the switches. Algorithms for testing the entire network using at most twice the number of tests required for a switch were presented and the total testing time for the network was evaluated. The most costly part of the test, the one dealing with conflict resolution faults, requires $f2^f$ tests to test the entire network in the case of fixed priority and $f^2 2^{f+1}$ in the case of round-robin priority independently of the number of processors (f is usually not greater than eight). The testing time increases only logarithmically with the growth in the system size.

REFERENCES

[1] H. J. Siegel, *Interconnection Networks for Large-Scale Parallel Processing: Theory and Case Studies.* Lexington, MA, Lexington, 1985.

[2] U. V. Premkumar, R. Kapur, M. Malek, G. J. Lipovski, and P. Horne, "Design and implementation of the banyan network in TRAC," in *Proc. 1980 AFIPS Conf.,* May 1980, pp. 623–629.

[3] G. F. Pfister, W. C. Brantley, D. A. George, S. L. Harvey, W. J. Kleinfelder, K. P. McAuliffe, E. A. Melton, V. A. Norton, and J. Weiss, "The IBM research parallel processor prototype (RP3); Introduction and architecture," in *Proc. 1985 Int. Conf. Parallel Processing,* Chicago, IL, 1985, pp. 764–771.

[4] R. D. Rettberg, "Shared memory parallel processing: The Butterfly and the Monarch," *Advanced Research in VLSI,* C. E. Leiserson, Ed. Cambridge, MA: MIT Press, 1986.

[5] T. Yuba, T. Shimada, K. Hiraki, and H. Kashiwagi, "SIGMA-1: A dataflow computer for scientific computations," *Comput. Phys. Commun.,* vol. 37, pp. 141–148, 1985.

[6] K. Hiraki, private communication, Tokyo, July 1988.

[7] T.-Y. Feng, and C.-L. Wu, "Fault diagnosis for a class of multistage interconnection networks," *IEEE Trans. Comput.,* pp. 743–758, Oct. 1981.

[8] W. Y.-P. Lim, "A test strategy for packet switching networks," in *Proc. Int. Conf. Parallel Processing,* Aug. 1982, pp. 96–98.

[9] M. Malek and E. Opper, "Multiple fault diagnosis of SW-banyan networks," in *Proc. 13th Annu. Int. Symp. Fault Tolerant Comput.,* June 1983, pp. 446–449.

[10] J.-C. Liu and K. G. Shin, "Polynomial testing for packet switching networks," *IEEE Trans. Comput.,* pp. 202–217, Feb. 1989.

[11] L. R. Goke and G. J. Lipovski, "Banyan networks for partitioning multiprocessor systems," in *Proc. First Annu. Comput. Architecture Conf.,* 1973, pp. 21–28.

[12] C.-L. Wu and T.-Y. Feng, "On a class of multistage interconnection networks," *IEEE Trans. Comput.,* pp. 694–702, Aug. 1980.

[13] A. C. Hung and M. Malek, "A 4 × 4 modular crossbar design for the multistage interconnection networks," in *Proc. Real-Time Syst. Symp.,* Dec. 1981, pp. 3–12.

[14] D. P. Agrawal, "Testing and fault tolerance of multistage interconnection networks," *IEEE Comput. Mag.,* pp. 367–379, Apr. 1982.

[15] N. J. Davis IV, W. T.-Y. Hsu, and H. J. Siegel, "Fault location techniques for distributed control interconnection networks," *IEEE Trans. Comput.* pp. 902–910, Oct. 1985.

[16] W. K. Fuchs, J. A. Abraham, and K. H. Huang, "Concurrent error detection in VLSI interconnection networks," in *Proc. 10th Annu. Int. Symp. Comput. Architecture,* 1983, pp. 309–315.

[17] E. Opper and M. Malek, "Resource allocation for a class of problem structures in multistage interconnection network-based systems," in *Proc. 3rd Int. Conf. Distributed Comput., Syst.,* Oct. 1982, pp. 106–113.

[18] M. Malek, A. Mourad, and M. Pandya, "Topological testing," in *Proc. Int. Test Conf.,* Aug. 1989, pp. 103–110.

[19] E. Opper and M. Malek, "Real-time diagnosis of banyan networks," in *Proc. Real-Time Syst. Symp.,* Los Angeles, CA, Dec. 1982, pp. 27–36.

[20] M. Abramovici, M. A. Breuer, and A. D. Friedman, "Testing for bridging faults," in *Digital Systems Testing and Testable Design.* Rockville, MD: Computer Science Press, 1990.

[21] A. D. Friedman, "Diagnosis of short-circuit faults in combinational circuits," *IEEE Trans. Comput.,* pp. 746–752, July 1974.

Antoine Mourad (S'91) was born in Lebanon in 1965. He received the Diplôme d'Ingéniueur from Ecole Polytechnique, Paris, France, in 1986, and the M.S. degree in electrical and computer engineering from The University of Texas at Austin, in 1989.

He is currently working towards the Ph.D. degree in Electrical and Computer Engineering at the University of Illinois at Urbana-Champaign. His areas of interest include computer architecture, fault tolerance, and performance evaluation of computer systems.

Mr. Mourad is a member of the Association for Computing Machinery and the IEEE Computer Society. In 1989, he received the MCC Award for Excellence for research performed at The University of Texas.

Banu Özden (S'89) received the B.S.E.E. degree in 1986 from the Technical University of Istanbul, Turkey, and the M.S.E.E. degree in electrical and computer engineering from The University of Texas at Austin in 1990.

Currently, she is a Ph.D. degree student in Department of Electrical and Computer Engineering, at The University of Texas at Austin. Her research interests include testing, fault-tolerant computing, parallel and distributed computing, and memory systems.

Ms. Özden is a student member of the IEEE Computer Society.

**Miroslaw Malek** (M'78–SM'87) received the M.Sc. degree in electrical engineering in 1970 and the Ph.D. degree in computer science in 1975, both from the Technical University of Wroclaw, Poland.

He is the Bettie Margaret Smith Professor in Engineering at The University of Texas at Austin, where he has served on the faculty since September 1977. In 1977, he was a Visiting Scholar at the Department of Systems Design, University of Waterloo, Waterloo, Ont., Canada. He works in the area of responsive (fault-tolerant, real-time) computer architectures, and has published over 75 papers on a variety of topics germane to this topic. He coauthored a book titled *Parallel Computing: Theory and Comparisons* and participated in the Texas Reconfigurable Array Computer (TRAC) and IBM's Research Parallel Processor Prototype (RP3) projects. He is currently on leave at the Office of Naval Research in London.

Dr. Malek organized, chaired, and was a program committee member of numerous IEEE and ACM international conferences and workshops. Among others, he was Program and General Chairman of the 1983 and 1984 Real-Time Systems Symposium, respectively. He serves on the editorial boards of *Journal of Parallel and Distributed Computing* and *Journal of Real-Time Systems*.

Polynomial Testing of Packet Switching Networks

JYH-CHARN LIU, STUDENT MEMBER, IEEE, AND KANG G. SHIN, SENIOR MEMBER, IEEE

Abstract—A functional testing method called *polynomial testing* is proposed to test packet switching networks (PSN's) used in multiprocessor systems. For the purpose of concreteness, we focus on applying the method to packet switching multistage interconnection networks (PMIN's). A multiple stuck-at (MSA) fault model is developed first, and then faults are diagnosed at two different levels: *network level* and *switch level*. The former uses each processor as a tester and can test part of the network concurrently with the normal operations on the remaining part of the network. On the other hand, the latter uses switches in the network as testers and is inherently an autonomous testing method. To facilitate the network level testing, the routing dynamic in a PMIN is eliminated by synchronizing switch operations. The network is then decomposed into *routes*, each of which is tested after transforming it into a polynomial calculator. For switch level testing, a built-in tester (BIT) is embedded into each switch's structure to provide self-testing capabilities. Network level testing is distributed and suitable for concurrent testing, whereas switch level testing is off-line with a small testing time.

Index Terms—Built-in tester, concurrent testing, linear feedback shift register, multistage interconnection network, packet switching, polynomial generator, polynomial testing, stuck-at routing fault, switch self-testing.

I. INTRODUCTION

DESPITE the continuing improvement in semiconductor device speed, use of multiple processors and memories is an attractive alternative to meet ever-increasing needs of computing speed and reliability. Interconnection networks are one of the most important components of such multiprocessor systems and are made feasible by the advancement in VLSI technology. Since VLSI technology greatly degrades testability, an interconnection network must have a structure that is easily testable.

There are two well-known switching methods for interconnection networks: *circuit switching* and *packet switching*. To distinguish these two methods, a *path* and a *route* for a source–destination pair are defined as follows. A path is a physically-established communication medium between the source and destination to transfer a request/data. A route is a logical path which can transfer a request from a source to its destination without total dedication to it; resources on a route are time-shared among several packets. In a circuit switching network (CSN), the path from a source to its destination is physically set up *a priori* and dedicated to a request until the request is completely serviced. By contrast, no complete physical path is established *a priori* for a request in a packet switching network (PSN). A packet switching multistage interconnection network (PMIN) is composed of a large number of links and switches with buffers. Each PMIN switch is essentially an $r \times r$ crossbar, in which a queue is placed at each input port to store packets. A request/message is decomposed into several packets, each of which is independently transferred through an available route.

Many PSN's have an undesirable effect called the *routing dynamic*: the order of arrival of packets at the destination may be different from the order of their transmission from the source. Although PMIN's can be designed not to have the routing dynamic, the routing dynamic will be considered in our testing method to provide better versatility. Clearly, a PMIN with the routing dynamic is an asynchronous sequential machine. Although a sequential machine can be fully tested with a checking sequence derived from its state-transition table [1], no feasible checking sequence seems to be derivable for large scale asynchronous sequential machines like PMIN's. Functional testing is an alternative to prove the correctness of some of the machine's functions within a finite time period.

Several researchers have proposed functional testing procedures for specific networks. Error control codes are popular for on-line fault detection [2], [3]. A comprehensive method for diagnosing the baseline CSN's with 2×2 switches was introduced by Feng and Wu [4]. A simplified version of the fault model in [4] and the corresponding testing strategy can be found in [5]. Davis *et al*. proposed some fault location techniques for distributed routing control networks [6]. Lee and Shen modeled a CSN using 2×2 switches as an ILA [7]. Low-order switches, e.g., 2×2 switches, can be completely tested with a constant number of patterns. Agrawal and Leu used the dynamic full accessibility of MIN's to test their connectivity [8]. Several high-level testing strategies for general PMIN's have also been studied [9]–[15], most of which are adaptive procedures requiring human assistance.

Most existing methods are centralized and off-line, i.e., the whole network is tested off-line by *one* tester. Since there are $N/r \log_r N$ switches in a PMIN, the complexity of the network testing problem is $O(N/r \log_r N)$. Centralized testing methods are usually very inefficient for large networks, because the problem to be handled by the tester grows exponentially with the size of the network. To improve testing efficiency, we

Manuscript received August 31, 1986; revised February 28, 1987. This work was supported in part by the Office of Naval Research under Contract N00014-85-K-0122 and NASA under Grants NAG-1-296 and NAG-1-492. Any opinions, findings, and conclusions or recommendations expressed in this publication are those of the authors and do not necessarily reflect the views of the funding agencies.

The authors are with the Real Time Computing Laboratory, Department of Electrical Engineering and Computer Science, the University of Michigan, Ann Arbor, MI 48109.

IEEE Log Number 8824535.

Reprinted from *IEEE Trans. Computers,* Vol. 38, No. 2, Feb. 1989, pp. 202–217. Copyright © 1989 by The Institute of Electrical and Electronics Engineers, Inc. All rights reserved.

propose a two-level testing strategy: *network level* and *switch level testing*.[1] In the network level, every processor can serve as a tester to test part of the network; thus, there are N testers for the network. Assuming that testers are homogeneous, the complexity of the testing problem in each tester is reduced to $O(1/r \log_r N)$. In the switch level testing, switches are used as testers and designed to have autonomous testing capability [17]. In other words, the complexity of the testing problem in each tester is independent of the network size and is fixed. The characteristics of the network level testing are that it can test the network concurrently, but may have a lower fault coverage than the switch level testing. On the other hand, the switch level testing is an off-line method with a small testing time but has high fault coverage.

The network level testing is based on the topology and functions of the network, because processors must cooperate to test the network. To eliminate the routing dynamic, network operations are first synchronized. Then, an $N \times N$ blocking network is decomposed into N^2 routes, $NT = \{\text{RT}_{ij} | 1 \leq i, j \leq N\}$, where RT_{ij} is the route from source i to destination j. RUT_{ij} is the route RT_{ij} under test, and the testing processors are the processors connected to the route under test (RUT). In the network level testing, faults in RUT_{ij} are tested without stopping the normal operations on $NT - \{\text{RUT}_{ij}\}$, where $\text{RUT}_{ij} \in NT$ and $\{\text{RUT}_{ij}\} \neq NT$. To test a route without interrupting, or being interrupted by, normal operations, the testing processors should be able to lock/unlock the RUT. A RUT can be locked by activating the busy signals of the switches on the RUT. Locking a route prevents unexpected packets from entering the route. As shown in Fig. 1, a route can be viewed as a cascaded shift register array. The register array can then be easily modified into *divisors, multipliers,* or other similar structures for *polynomial testing.*

In the switch level testing, each switch is a tester and switches are assumed to be homogeneous. Thus, the logic structure, instead of its topology, of the network is the main concern. To obtain high fault coverage with a small testing time, each switch is designed to have self-testing capabilities. A switch is composed of buffers, a routing control unit (RCU), and output ports consisting of multiplexers–demultiplexers (MUDEX's). Since thorough testing of the RCU may require an intractable testing length, an on-line checker is proposed to detect malfunctions in the RCU. For the rest of the network, queues are first self-tested by polynomial generation and comparison. If the queues are fault-free, they are then used to generate test patterns for links and MUDEX's. The testing responses of switches at one stage are verified at the next stage.

The rest of this paper consists of four sections. Section II gives a brief review of the polynomial operations necessary for our testing method. Section III introduces the network fault models which are to be tested with operations on polynomials. Testable designs and the corresponding network and switch level testing are presented in Section IV. The paper concludes with Section V.

---

[1] This term should not be confused with the switch-level fault model for MOS circuits [16].

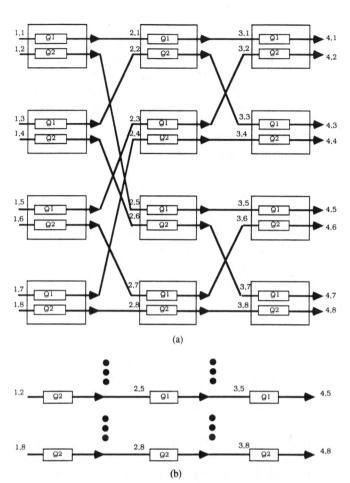

(a)

(b)

Fig. 1. A baseline PMIN with switch permutation E_0 and the corresponding cascaded shift register arrays. (a) A baseline PMIN with switch permutation E_0. (b) The corresponding cascaded shift register array of the PMIN.

II. PRINCIPLES OF POLYNOMIAL TESTING

Basic polynomial operations and their implementations are briefly discussed below. Use of the polynomial ring $GF(2)[x]$ is well-known for error control codes [18]. Only those properties useful for testing PSN's will be introduced below for completeness.

Definition 1: A polynomial $P_b(x) = \sum_{i=0}^{n} b_i x^i$ in $GF(2)[x]$ is said to be a *bit polynomial* if each of its coefficients is a bit, i.e., $b_i \in \{0, 1\}, \forall 0 \leq i \leq n$. A *word polynomial* is the one whose coefficients are words instead of bits, i.e., $P_w(x) = \sum_{i=0}^{n} w_i x^i$, where for every $i \in I_n = \{0, 1, \cdots, n\}$, $w_i = \text{ONE}$ or ZERO, and ONE is a b-bit vector of *arbitrary* pattern and ZERO = $\overline{\text{ONE}}$, i.e., ZERO is bitwise complemented to ONE. Thus, any two words with maximum Hamming distance can be used as ONE and ZERO, respectively.

For notational convenience, let $W_n(x)$ denote a polynomial $\sum_{i=0}^{n} c_i x^i$, $c_i = 1$ or ONE, $\forall i \in I_n$. $\bar{P}(x) = \sum_{i=0}^{n} \bar{c}_i x^i = P(x) \oplus W_n(x)$ is the complement of $P(x)$, and the symbol "$\oplus$" represents the addition in $GF(2)$. Unless otherwise specified, we will use the term "polynomial" to represent both bit and word polynomials. The mechanisms to manipulate polynomials are called their *calculators*. The contents of a calculator before operating on its input are called the *initial state*, which will always be assumed, for clarity of presentation, to be all zeros. A calculator with the zero initial state is called an *inert linear machine* [19]. When a word polynomial operation is applied to a faulty circuit, the closure property of $GF(2)[x]$ may not hold. However, when a word polynomial is applied to a nonfaulty circuit, the resulting polynomial belongs to $GF(2)[x]$. Calculators are more hardware efficient if ONE and ZERO are composed of all 1's and 0's, respectively, because for each operation every bit will require an identical circuit.

A. Operations on Polynomials

A *periodic* polynomial with period p is the series $\sum_{i=1}^{\infty} c_i x^i$ where $c_i = c_{i+p}$, $\forall i \in I$, and I is the set of integers. It can be generated by a linear (or nonlinear) feedback shift register (LFSR) called a *polynomial generator* (PG). Registers in a PG can be implemented by different types of flip-flops, and apparently different test patterns are needed for different implementations. However, as shown in Appendix A, at most two inputs are needed to detect faults in a master–slave SR flip-flop. Since the network level testing deals with the network topology, we will consider only the input and output stuck-at faults of registers, i.e., not the stuck-at faults inside registers. However, the same test patterns can test all the faults in those registers implemented with the master–slave flip-flops shown in Appendix A.

Two polynomials $P_1(x) = \sum_{i=0}^{n} c_{1,i} x^i$ and $P_2(x) = \sum_{i=0}^{n} c_{2,i} x^i$, are *equal* iff $c_{1,i} = c_{2,i}$, $\forall i \in I_n$. Two polynomials can be compared for equality by XOR gates. The following operations are useful for our discussion.

Addition and Boolean: Let $\{P_j(x) = \sum_{i=0}^{n} c_{j,i} x^i\}_{j=1}^{k}$ be k polynomials in $GF(2)[x]$. $P_3(x)$ is the *addition* of $P_1(x)$ and $P_2(x)$, denoted by $P_3(x) = \sum_{i=0}^{n} c_{3,i} x^i = P_1(x) \oplus P_2(x)$, if for each $i \in I_n$ $c_{3,i} = c_{1,i} \oplus c_{2,i}$. Addition can be implemented with XOR gates. If a Boolean operation Δ is applied to $P_1(x)$, $P_2(x), \cdots P_k(x)$, the resulting polynomial $P(x) = \sum_{i=0}^{n} c_i x^i$ is calculated by $c_i = c_i^1 \Delta c_i^2 \Delta \cdots \Delta c_i^k$, $\forall i \in I_n$, and Δ is a bitwise operation when c_i is a word. Only AND and OR, the two most important operations, will be considered in this paper.

Division and Multiplication: Given $P(x) = \sum_{i=0}^{n} p_i x^i$ and $M(x) = \sum_{i=0}^{n} m_i x^i$ in $GF(2)[x]$, the *multiplication* of $M(x)$ (multiplier) to $P(x)$ (multiplicand) is $P_3(x) = P(x)M(x) = \sum_{i=0}^{n} p_{3,i} x^i$, where $\forall i \in I_n$, $p_{3,i} = p_i m_0 \oplus p_{i-1} m_1 \oplus \cdots \oplus p_1 m_{i-1} \oplus p_0 m_i$. On the other hand, given two polynomials $P(x)$ (dividend) and $D(x) = \sum_{i=0}^{r} d_i x^i \neq 0$ (divisor) in $GF(2)[x]$ there exist two polynomials $Q(x)$ and $R(x)$ in $GF(2)[x]$ such that $P(x) = D(x)Q(x) + R(x)$ where $R(x) = 0$ or deg $R(x) <$ deg $D(x)$. In this process, $P(x)$ is said to be *divided* by $D(x)$, yielding a quotient $Q(x)$ and a remainder $R(x)$.

A *bit divisor* (*multiplier*) divides (multiplies) an input stream by a fixed bit polynomial. Similarly, a *word divisor* (*multiplier*) performs divisions (multiplications) between two word polynomials. In a word polynomial divisor/multiplier (PDM), operands are ONE or ZERO instead of 1 or 0. It has logic operations similar to those of a bit PDM, but special mechanisms are necessary to preserve the properties of the polynomial ring.

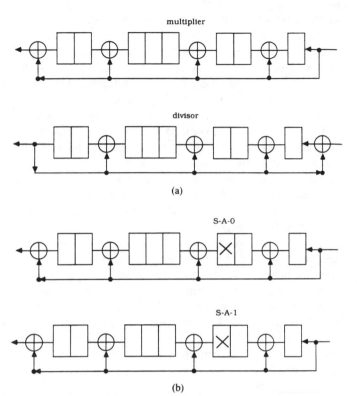

Fig. 2. The structure of faulty and nonfaulty multipliers and divisors. (a) Normal multiplier and divisor. (b) Two faulty multipliers.

The final contents of a PDM will henceforth be represented by $R(x)$, the input stream will be represented by $P(x)$, and the output stream by $Q(x)$. The general structures of a bit divisor and a bit multiplier are shown in Fig. 2(a). $M(x)$ and $D(x)$ in Fig. 2(a) are $1 + x^2 + x^5 + x^7 + x^8$ and $x^8 + x^6 + x^3 + x + 1$, respectively. The lowest order position is located in the input (output) port of the divisor (multiplier). There is an XOR gate, denoted by $\oplus$, at the D-type flip-flop's (DFF's) output of stage i only when m_i or d_i is 1. A *block* B_i is the collection of DFF's between the $(i - 1)$th and ith XOR gates, counting from the lowest order position, in a PDM. Thus, a PDM is composed of a set of blocks $\{B_i\}$. Let the order (the number of stages) of B_i be r_i. In the multiplier of Fig. 2(a), $r_1 = 2$, $r_2 = 3$, $r_3 = 2$, and $r_4 = 1$.

Since a RUT is to be transformed into a polynomial calculator for testing, the effects of DFF's multiple stuck-at (MSA) faults on a PDM are discussed as follows. An MSA fault f_M in a block B_i is composed of multiple single stuck-at (SSA) faults, i.e., $f_M = \{f_s^i\}$, where f_s^i is an SSA fault in B_i. Let k be the faulty position nearest to the output port of B_i. Then, $f_s^k \in f_M$ will block the effects of all the other SSA faults in f_M. Such an f_s^k is called the *leading* SSA fault in B_i. There are $2r_i$ possible leading faults in B_i, and, thus, there are $2r_i$ distinguishable stuck-at faults in the block, where r_i is the number of stages in B_i.

An s-a-0 FL changes the attached XOR gates into null operators. Thus, for a multiplier, $M'(x) = \sum_{i=1}^{k} m_i' x^i$, where $m_i' = 0$ if the FL attached to the XOR gate at x^i is stuck at 0, and $m_i' = m_i$ otherwise. It is shown in Lemma 1 that multiple s-a-0 at the FL-inputs of XOR gates can be tested by the impulse polynomial. On the other hand, when the FL is s-a-1, $M'(x)$ becomes $\Sigma_{i=1, i \neq m_f}^{k} m_i x^i + \Sigma_{\{m_f\}} x^{m_f} W(x)$, where m_f is the location of an XOR gate whose input from the FL is fixed at 1 due to an s-a-1 fault. Thus, when an all zero input stream, i.e., $\Sigma_{i=1}^{k} 0 x^i$, is applied to the PDM, the locations of those XOR gates affected by the FL s-a-1 faults can be uniquely determined by the corresponding output stream.

Lemma 1 [19]: The impulse response of a multiplier is $m_0 m_1 \cdots m_n 0 \cdots 0$, where the impulse polynomial is $P_I(x) = 10 \cdots 0$.

Clearly, an unknown multiplier can be uniquely identified by its impulse response, and the multiplication of $P_I(x)$ to $M(x)$ can be viewed as a discrete convolution between them.

Lemma 2: When a PDM is an inert machine and an s-a-0 fault occurs in B_k, the multiplier $M(x) = \Sigma_{i=0}^{n} m_i x^i$ is changed to a new multiplier $M'(x) = \Sigma_{i=0}^{k-1} m_i x^i$.

Lemma 3: Let l be the number of fault-free DFF's between B_i's output and the leading faulty DFF. Then, when the leading faulty DFF^l in B_k is s-a-1, $Q(x) = M'(x)P(x) \oplus x^{r'} W_n(x)$, where $r' = l + \Sigma_{j<k} r_j$ and $M'(x)$ is the new multiplier whose highest order position is located at the leading faulty DFF in B_k.

Proof: Let the input (or output) of B_i be I_i (or O_i). Then we have $I_{i-1} = O_i \oplus P(x)$ and $O_{i-1} = x^{r_{i-1}} I_{i-1}$. When DFF^l is s-a-1, $O_k = W_n(x)$. Thus, $I_{k-1} = P(x) \oplus x^l W_n(x)$ and $O_{k-1} = x^{r_{k-1}}(P(x) + x^l W_n(x))$. By induction, we can show that $Q(x) = M'(x)P(x) \oplus x^{r'} W_n(x)$. ∎

When x^k of a divisor is s-a-1, the output $Q(x) = P'(x)/D'(x)$, where $P'(x) = \{x^l (\Sigma_{i=k+1}^{r} n_i x^{i-k}) \oplus W_l(x)\}$, $\Sigma_{i=k+1}^{r} n_i x^{i-k}$ is the initial state of the divisor and l is the polynomial length that is sufficient for testing, and $D'(x)$ is the new divisor with its lowest order position at the output of B_k. Similarly, an s-a-0 fault at x^k makes $Q(x)$ periodic, i.e., $Q(x) = x^l (\Sigma_{i=k+1}^{r} n_i x^{i-k})/D'(x)$, where the degree of the faulty divisor is $r_d = \Sigma_{j>k} r_j$. Note that the output $Q(x)$ is independent of the input stream. The structures of s-a-0 and s-a-1 multipliers are shown in Fig. 2(b). The resulting $M_0'(x)$ (for s-a-0) and M_1' (for s-a-1) are $1 + x^2 + x^5$ and $M_0' \oplus x^r W(x)$, respectively.

For testing purposes, it is assumed that every DFF on a route can be simultaneously set to ZERO by an external signal. Signature analysis examines $R(x)$ after the testing polynomial $P(x)$ is applied to a circuit under test. The final contents of each DFF must be directly read out for signature analysis. Unfortunately, this will greatly increase the number of I/O terminals of a network. Thus, signature analysis or other similar methods requiring direct access to DFF's are not followed here and interested readers are referred to other articles, such as [20].

The proposed network level testing is to diagnose the network by appropriate operations on the output stream. After the testing polynomial $P(x)$ is applied to a RUT, a fault f_i changes $Q(x)$ into $Q_i(x)$, where $Q(x)$ [or $Q_i(x)$] is the correct (or faulty) output polynomial of the RUT. The procedure is then to find a testing polynomial $P(x)$ and an operation Θ_{f_i} such that $\Theta_{f_i}(P(x), Q(x)) = Q_i(x)$. The combination of $P(x)$, its output $Q(x)$, and the operation Θ_{f_i} is called a *testing routine* for the fault f_i.

III. FAULT MODELS

A PSN is composed of links and switches. There are $r!$ possible interconnection patterns within an $r \times r$ switch. There are then $(r!)^{(N/r) \log_r N}$ different conflict-free interconnection patterns in an $N \times N$ PMIN. Links' stuck-at faults are equivalent to stuck-at faults of the switches to which they are attached. Thus, only switch faults are considered for the network level testing. That is, link stuck-at faults are implicitly included in the switch fault models.

Permanent *multiple stuck-at, delay, partial setting, blocking, merging, broadcasting,* and *misrouting* faults are all considered in this paper. An MSA fault occurs when one or more signal lines are fixed at 0 or 1. A delay fault occurs when the operation speed of some component(s) is slower than the specified and, thus, erroneous operations result. A partial setting fault occurs when some of the identical components in a unit do not provide the same operation as the others. A blocking fault occurs when an appropriate route within a switch cannot be established for a request. A handshake signal deadlock is an example of blocking fault. A switch has a merging (broadcasting) fault when two or more input (output) ports are connected to one output (input) port. A misrouting fault represents the case when packets are misdirected to incorrect output ports. Stuck-line faults at gate level are tested at the switch level testing.

IV. PMIN DIAGNOSIS

As mentioned earlier, our testing strategy is divided into two levels: network and switch levels. At each of these two levels, we present testable designs and testing methods on the basis of the polynomial operations and the fault models introduced in Sections II and III, respectively. The network is designed such that all signal lines have only two states, i.e., 1 or 0, whether or not they are used to transfer data. The output port of a switch is a combination of multiplexers and demultiplexers (MUDEX's). A MUDEX is basically composed of AND and OR gates. When multiple requests are assigned to an output port, a combination of OR/AND functions among the requests will take place.

A. Network Level Diagnosis

Assume that the PMIN under test connects N sources and N destinations and is built with $r \times r$ switches. The number of stages in the PMIN is $k \equiv \log_r N$. To describe the PMIN's topology and permutation, the input (output) ports of all switches in each stage are vertically indexed. The number assigned to an input (output) port is called its *global index*. For each $r \times r$ switch, there is a one-to-one correspondence between the global index and the input/output port number: $f_i(j) = m$, where j is the port number of the ith switch at a stage, and m is the port's global index. A *link permutation* $T_i, 1 \leq i \leq k$, is a one-to-one mapping from the output ports at stage $i - 1$ to the input ports at stage i. On the other hand, a *switch permutation* $E_m^i: f_i(j) \rightarrow f_i((j + m) \text{ MOD } r)$ is a one-to-one mapping from input ports of a switch to its output ports, $0 \leq m \leq r - 1$. For simplicity, all the switches on the RUT are assumed to have an identical permutation, i.e., $i_1 =$

i_2 for all $E_m^{i_1}$, $E_m^{i_2} \in$ RUT, and E_m will henceforth be used to denote E_m^i. More general cases than this can be easily derived by using the actual permutation at each stage. To allow for simultaneous diagnosis and normal operation at the network level, the testing processors should be equipped with complete information of link and switch permutations.

1) Testable Design: Links are passive components and can be treated as data paths of switches, whereas switches make all switching decisions and also contain memory elements. To make the network easily testable, switches are designed to have two operational modes: *normal* and *testing* modes.

As mentioned in the Introduction, a RUT can be viewed as a cascaded shift register array. FL and XOR gates must be added to transform a 1-bit wide RUT into a bit PDM. Since links are the predominating cost factor of a PMIN, the link overhead in improving testability must be kept as small as possible. A tracer in each switch is thus proposed to minimize the width of FL. A tracer is composed of a testing pattern masker and mapper, a feedback/feedforward selector (F-selector) and a modulo TWO adder, where TWO = {ONE, ZERO}. The masker examines if bits of the testing pattern are identical and maps the testing pattern from ONE (ZERO) to 1(0) for FL. The mapper transforms 1(0) to ONE (ZERO) to use the adder. The F-selector determines the transmission direction of FL.[2] An adder is necessary for each switch to form a block on a route for data path diagnosis.

Four possible operational states, S, A, X, and N, are assigned to a switch when the network is being tested. Once a switch in a RUT is in state S, the switch will not allow any packets, except those from the same RUT, to enter the RUT, and the operations of switches on the route are synchronized. State S can be taken as a suboperation of the other states, because the tracer in the other states is activated *and* switch operations are synchronized. When the switch is in state N, only FL and the F-selector are activated. When a switch at stage i is in state A, the F-selector blocks the FL signals from stage $i + 1$, and the current switch's output is led to FL. When the switch is in state X, the data on FL are mapped, by the mapper, from 1 (0) to ONE (ZERO), and the logic operation $BU_0 \leftarrow P_{in} \oplus$ FL is performed at the input of the queue, where BU_0 is the input of the queue and P_{in} is the input packet. Fig. 3 shows these switch operations in different states. The logic diagram in Fig. 4 shows a switch design example of the network level testing.

A switch can enter/exit the testing mode by command packets. Two formats, *data packets* and *command packets*, are used to control the switch operations. A command packet is composed of routing tags and a command array $\{CA(1), \cdots, CA(k)\}$, where k is the number of stages of the network and $CA(i)$ is a 2-bit command word associated with stage i. A switch at stage i will enter states S, A, N, and X, when $CA(i)$ = 00, 11, 10, and 01, respectively. The type of packets can be identified by a one-bit flag in each packet. As shown below, this testing method can also identify a misinterpreted command array (by a faulty switch).

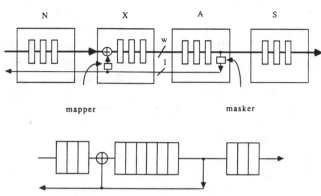

Fig. 3. Switches on a RUT and the corresponding word divisor.

Theorem 1: All misinterpreted command packets can be tested in one testing routine.

Proof: Once a RUT is transformed into a multiplier, the test pattern for misinterpreted command packets becomes an impulse polynomial. From Lemma 1, $M(x)$ of the RUT can be uniquely identified. ∎

2) Data Path Stuck-at Faults: All switches are in state X when data path stuck-at faults are being tested. An SSA fault at the network level represents a stuck-at fault(s) in a *single* switch. But an MSA fault at the network level implies stuck-at faults in more than one switch. In a conventional approach, upon detection of a fault on some route, test patterns must be submitted from processors on different routes to locate the fault. It is shown below that the fault location with the polynomial testing is much easier than that with the conventional approach.

SSA Faults: Every switch is set to an identical permutation. When $r \times r$ switches are used, r different switch permutations $\{E_i | 0 \le i \le r - 1\}$ are necessary to test every data path within a switch. For any input port of a switch, its data paths to all the output ports are included in $\{E_i | 0 \le i \le r - 1\}$. Thus, in these r permutations every data path from each input port to every output port is tested.[3] The procedure can be generalized as follows: in testing routine m, the switch permutation E_m, $0 \le m \le r - 1$, is performed first. Then, the connection of source i to destination j is specified by $j = T_k E_m T_{k-1} E_m \cdots T_2 E_m T_1(i)$. The special case of $r = 2$ allows data path stuck-at faults to be detected in two permutations, each of which is composed of two steps [4].

Theorem 2: When a locked RUT_{ij} is configured as a multiplier, an SSA fault on the data path can be located by processor j in one testing routine.

Proof: The testing polynomial for the data path SSA fault is $W_n(x)$, where n is the total length of buffers on RUT_{ij}. As discussed earlier, RUT_{ij} can be expressed as $M_{ij}(x) = \sum_{i=0}^n m_i x^i$. The output at the destination j becomes $Q(x) = \sum_{l=0}^n m_l x^l W_n(x)$. $Q(x)$ should then have the format of $1 \cdots 10 \cdots 01 \cdots$, where a 0 (1) $\rightarrow$ 1 (0) transition takes place

---

[2] The F-selector can be eliminated if the RUT is to be transformed into either a multiplier or divisor, but not both.

[3] Only r permutations are needed to test a data path, although $r!$ permutations are required to test the routing functions.

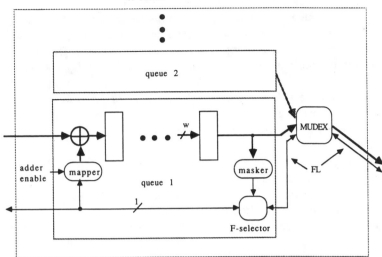

Fig. 4.   A testable design of switches for concurrent testing.

at each position of an XOR gate on RUT_{ij} and the number of consecutive 1's (0's) in the ith block is the size of B_i. For example, the output stream of the multiplier in Fig. 2(a) is 10011100. When M_{ij} changes to $M'_{ij} \neq M_{ij}$ due to an SSA fault, there must be at least one i such that $m_i \neq m'_i$, $1 \leq i \leq k$, by Lemmas 2 and 3. When the number of $0 \to 1$ transitions is m_f, the faulty switch can be located by $s_f = (\Pi_{i=0}^{m_f} E^{-1} T_{m_f-i}^{-1})(j)$, where T_i^{-1} is the inverse of permutation T_i.   ■

MSA Faults: An MSA fault on a data path cannot be determined in one testing routine. However, the polynomial testing can be applied to a sequential repairing procedure which locates and then replaces leading faulty switches/links in each testing routine.

Theorem 3: An MSA fault on a data path can be repaired in k testing routines, where k is the number of stages of the network.

Proof: An MSA fault is the collection of multiple SSA faults. When the testing polynomial $W_n(x)$ is applied to a PDM, $Q(x)$ is uniquely determined by the type (s-a-0 or s-a-1) and the location of the leading stuck-at fault. In other words, the lowest order faulty switch can be located in each testing routine, regardless of the cardinality of the multiple fault. Since there are k switches on a route, at most k steps are required to repair the network.   ■

Delay Faults: A delay fault on a data path is detectable when its operational speed is at least one clock cycle slower than specified.

Theorem 4: A single delay fault of longer than one clock cycle can be located in one testing routine.

Proof: The polynomial $P_E^1(x) = \Sigma_{i=0}^k x^{2i}$ can detect all delay faults. However, a polynomial $P_E^m(x) = \Sigma_{i=0}^k x^{(m+1)i}$ can be used to distinguish a $1 \to 0$ transition delay fault of m clock cycles from delay faults of less than m cycles. When an m unit delay fault occurs and $P_E^m(x)$ is applied, the faulty switch's output becomes $W(x)$. By forming a PDM on RUT_{ij}, a delay fault can be located in one testing routine. A testing polynomial for $0 \to 1$ delay transitions is complemented to become $P_E^m(x)$ and the output is $\bar{W}(x)$.   ■

Like MSA faults, a multiple delay fault composed of different delay lengths can be repaired in k testing routines.

3) Routing Faults: Methods for locating routing faults are studied in this subsection. Switches are set to state S when routing functions are tested.

Merging and Broadcasting Faults: Depending on the implementation details, a merging fault can be located in one testing routine when appropriate polynomials are applied. A Δ-*merging* fault occurs when a Δ (i.e., AND or OR) operation results from the merging of two or more switch input/output ports.

Consider the effect of the OR merging first. For two routes RUT_{i_1} and RUT_{i_2}, they will topologically intersect in at most one switch when the network is not redundant.

Theorem 5: For a given permutation, a multiple OR-merging fault can be located in one testing routine for both distributed and centralized routing control PMIN's.

Proof: The testing polynomial at processor j is $P_j^N(x) = \Sigma_{i=1}^N c_i x^i$, where $c_j = \text{ONE}$ and $c_i = \text{ZERO}$, $\forall i \neq j$. First, consider the case when two RUT's are merged. The two routes from i_1 and i_2 under the given permutation intersect at most once. When the intersecting switch has an OR-merging fault, and the testing polynomials $P_{i_1}^N(x)$ and $P_{i_2}^N(x)$ are applied, there will be an OR operation between these two polynomials. Without loss of generality, $P_{i_1}^N(x)$ can be assumed to be merged into $P_{i_1}^N(x)$, i.e., $P'_{i_1}(x) = P_{i_1}^N(x)$ OR $P_{i_2}^N(x)$. Since there is no overlap of the positions containing 1's in both $P_{i_1}^N(x)$ and $P_{i_2}^N(x)$, new information on the merging fault is added to $P'_{i_1}(x)$. Applying the XOR operation between $P'_{i_2}(x)$ and $P_{i_2}^N(x)$ at the destination of $P_{i_2}^N(x)$, we get $P_{i_2}(x) = P'_{i_2}(x) \oplus P_{i_2}^N(x)$. A nonzero resulting polynomial implies that some polynomial is merged into $P_{i_2}^N(x)$. The switch with the merging fault is determined by the topology. That is, $P_{i_1}^N(x)$ merges with $P_{i_2}^N(x)$ at $S(i_f, j_f)$, where $S(i_f, j_f)$ is the j_fth switch located at stage i_f, when $(j_f - 1)r = \Pi_{i=1}^{i_f} E_m T_i(i_1) - \Pi_{i=1}^{i_f} E_m T_i(i_1) \text{ MOD } r$ and $(j_f - 1)r = \Pi_{i=1}^{i_f} E_m T_i(i_2) - \Pi_{i=1}^{i_f} E_m T_i(i_2) \text{ MOD } r$. It is easy to see that no information will be lost when multiple mergings occur. Thus, all multiple merging faults can be determined in one testing routine.   ■

If merging faults are assumed to be independent of the interconnection pattern, they can be located in one testing routine. Otherwise, we need $r!$ tests to set each switch to every interconnection pattern for fault location. The AND-*merging* fault can be diagnosed by the same method with the testing polynomial $\bar{P}_j^N(x)$.

A broadcasting fault at one input port of a switch implies a merging fault at the output port of the broadcast data path. Thus, broadcasting faults can be located by the same procedure used for testing merging faults.

Misrouting Faults: There are $r!$ possible permutations in an $r \times r$ switch. To locate a misrouting fault, the testing polynomial $P_i(x)$ for source i must be unique.

Theorem 6: One testing routine is sufficient to locate a multiple misrouting fault for both distributed and centralized routing control PMIN's.

Proof: The testing polynomial for merging faults can also be used for testing misrouting faults. $kr!$ permutation calculations are required in each testing routine. Given a permutation $j = T_k ET_{k-1}E \cdots ET_1(i)$, a misrouting fault results when E becomes E', where $E' \neq E$ is a faulty permutation. The fault locating procedure is to find E' of a faulty switch. For a given processor j which receives an incorrect polynomial, all possible permutations have to be calculated to find E' of the faulty switch. Since each switch has $r!$ permutations, we need $kr!$ inverse permutations to locate the faulty switch. ∎

A misrouting fault may be caused by either the misdecoding of a routing tag in the RCU of a faulty switch or a stuck-at link/switch which transmits the routing tag before the routing tag is actually decoded.

Blocking Faults: As mentioned earlier, the network is designed such that there are only two logic values, i.e., 0 and 1, in all signal lines. When a blocking fault occurs, a data path cannot be utilized, even though it is available.

Theorem 7: A blocked data path in a centralized routing control PMIN can be located in one testing routine.

The proof of this theorem is straightforward. In a centralized routing control network, a locked route can be established even when its data path is blocked. Since the output of a blocked switch is fixed at 1 or 0, it has the same output as a stuck-at data path. It is much more difficult to locate a blocking fault in a distributed routing control network, because routing tags and data are blocked at the same time. It can be located by a binary search which requires $\log_2 k$ testing routines.

Partial Setting Faults: When a data path is partially stuck, the testing procedures with multipliers can still be applied. Test patterns, however, must be determined by the design details of the masker and the mapper. In case of a partial fault, unaffected data bits have correct outputs but the stuck-at bit needs the same testing procedures as described above. In such a case, we have to examine a faulty bit(s) instead of a faulty word(s).

4) Pattern Generation: Test patterns are generated by pattern generators $\{G_i\}$ which are processors or dedicated hardware mechanisms. The cost of pattern generators is one of the most important factors for evaluating the performance of a testing method. Only two testing patterns $W_n(x)$ and $\{P_i^N(x)\}$ need to be generated for the network level testing. Both patterns can be easily generated when G_i's are *ringed* through a single bit control line. Denote the input and output of the ring in G_i by $D_{i(\text{in})}$ and $D_{i(\text{out})}$, respectively. $D_{N(\text{out})}$ is connected to $D_{1(\text{in})}$, and $D_{i(\text{out})}$ is connected to $D_{i+1(\text{in})}$, $\forall 1 \leq i \leq N - 1$. To generate $\{P_i^N(x)\}$, the ring is initialized as $D_{1(\text{in})} = 1$, $D_{i(\text{in})} = 0$, $\forall i, i \neq 1$. Operations of G_i at the kth clock cycle are given as

$$OP1. \quad P_i(k) = \begin{cases} \text{ONE when } D_{i(\text{in})} = 1 \\ \text{ZERO when } D_{i(\text{in})} = 0 \end{cases},$$

$$OP2. \quad D_{i(\text{out})}(k) \leftarrow D_{i(\text{in})}(k)$$

where $P_i(k)$ is that the pattern generated by G_i at the kth clock cycle. The other test pattern $W_n(x)$ can be easily generated by the initialization $D_{i(\text{out})} = \text{ONE}$, $\forall i \leq N$, and applying OP1 and OP2 in each pattern generator. For a given permutation, there are only rk possible mergings on a route and the above testing polynomial is thus not optimal for testing OR-merging faults. For testing OR-merging faults, the length of the testing polynomial can be reduced to rk, when $P_k(x) \neq P_j(x)$ for any pair of polynomials $P_j(x)$ and $P_k(x)$ intersecting in a switch under a given permutation. However, the testing polynomial allows merging and misrouting faults to be tested simultaneously, and, thus, simplifies testing procedures. Moreover, G_i has a very simple structure and can be easily applied to various interconnection networks.

5) Testing Complexity: It is important to consider the testing complexity of the network level testing. The length of test patterns for data path stuck-at faults and misinterpreted command packets is km, where m is the queue length in each switch.[4] The calculation of a misinterpreted command packet is straightforward, because the coefficients of the multiplier can be identified directly from the output stream. The stuck-at-1 faults at the inputs of XOR gates, to which the FL are connected to, can be tested by an all zero polynomial, and its testing length is km. To test single data path stuck-at (delay) faults, we need one testing routine which is composed of at most k steps of inverse permutations. At most k testing routines are thus necessary to repair all multiple data path stuck-at faults, and each testing routine needs k inverse permutations. Thus, a total of $k^2 + k + 2$ inverse permutations is needed for data path diagnosis.

For routing faults, the test pattern length is N. One testing routine is sufficient to identify all merging and broadcasting faults. To locate a merging (broadcasting) fault, two RUT's are needed at a time. Since there are k switches on a RUT and each switch needs $r!$ inverse permutations, $k^2 r!$ inverse permutations are required to locate a merging (broadcasting) fault. Finally, $kr!$ inverse permutations are required to locate the misrouting faults.

The network level testing is quite general to handle various circuit implementations and locate faults without completely stopping the normal operations of the network. The testing time varies with the size of the network. Note, however, that

---

[4] The queue lengths need not be identical.

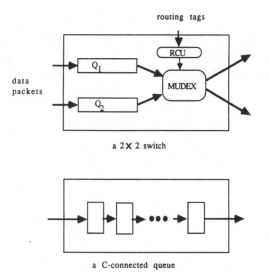

a 2 X 2 switch

a C-connected queue

Fig. 5. The structure of a 2×2 switch and a C-connected queue.

the network level testing may not detect all possible faults for different circuit implementations. When the network level testing fails to locate some faults, a fast off-line testing method with high fault coverage needs to be called for. The switch level testing described below meets this very need.

B. Switch Level Testing

A switch is composed of data paths and a RCU. Data paths consist of links, queues, and MUDEX's. A pool of buffers, BU_i^j, $1 \leq i \leq m$, in a switch constitutes the jth queue of the switch, where m is the number of buffers within the queue. A buffer can store one w-bit packet. There are then at least $Nwm \log_r N$ memory bits in an $N \times N$ PMIN built with $r \times r$ switches, and a CSN is the special case of $m = 0$. Let BU_0^j and BU_{m+1}^j denote, respectively, the input and output ports of a switch. It is shown in Fig. 5 that these buffers are cascaded, or C-connected, and formally described by $CN:BU_i \rightarrow BU_{i+1}$, where "$\rightarrow$" denotes an interconnection within a queue, called an *interlink*.

Different implementations of registers need different test patterns. We use random testing to test the queues. However, when specific test patterns like the one in Appendix A is needed, they are also easy to generate. In each switch, queues are tested by generation and comparison of polynomials. For the generation of a polynomial we can use the natural structure of a queue. The basic idea is to convert the queue into two PG's. A queue can be taken as a $w \times m$ matrix M in which each column is a buffer of w DFF's. Note that DFF's in each row j (collection of the jth DFF's of m buffers), $1 \leq j \leq w$, of the matrix are cascaded by its natural structure. Assuming w to be even, two PG's, PG_1 and PG_2, are formed by properly cascading the rows of M.

Two symmetric PG's can be obtained by 1) horizontally halving the buffers in the queue, 2) connecting $M(i + 1, 1)$ to $M(i, m)$ $\forall i \leq w/2$ for PG_1, and $M(i + 1, m)$ to $M(i, 1)$, $\forall i \geq (w/2) + 1$ for PG_2, 3) identically connecting registers' outputs to the feedback XOR gates in PG_1 and PG_2, and 4) connecting the output of the XOR gate outputs of PG_1 and PG_2 to $M(1, 1)$ and $M((w/2)+1, 1)$, respectively. It is well-known

that the maximum period of the output stream of a PG can be obtained when $2^l - 1$ is a prime number, where l is the PG's length, and the PG's characteristic function is irreducible [18]. A fault is detectable when it yields different output sequences in the two PG's.

The PGs' outputs form a 1-out-of-2 codeword when an inverter is added to one XOR gate's output. An XOR gate with n inputs needs $n + 1$ test patterns when n is odd; on the other hand, three test patterns are sufficient for an XOR gate with an even number of inputs. The test patterns for the XOR gate with an odd and an even number of inputs are $\{0\cdots0, 10\cdots0, 010\cdots0, \cdots, 0\cdots01\}$, and $\{0\cdots0, 1\cdots1, I_s\}$, respectively, where I_s is any input with an odd number of 1's. The test patterns for the XOR gate of a PG can be easily generated by setting the PG's initial state. Since every component in the PG's is tested, there is no hardcore in this design.

When two symmetric PG's are used, unidirectional stuck-at faults in a buffer cannot be detected. To solve this problem, PG_1 can be modified such that the outputs $M(i, m/2)$, $\forall i \leq w/2$, are connected to the XOR gate whose output is then connected to $M(1, (m/2) + 1)$. Although the physical interconnection of $M(1, 1)$ to $M(w/2, m)$ is different from that of $M((w/2) + 1, 1)$ to $M(w, m)$, both PG_1 and PG_2 still have an identical structure. Such a modification can now detect the unidirectional faults mentioned above. Symmetric and asymmetric PG configurations are illustrated in Figs. 6(a) and (b), respectively.

The optimal testing length of a PG and its fault coverage are important performance parameters. Any DFF in the MSA fault model can be s-a-1, s-a-0, or fault-free. To evaluate the MSA fault coverage of the proposed method, we only need to consider the type and position of leading faulty DFF's in a block. Consider a pair of leading faulty DFF's, s_1 and s_2, which are in x^i and x^j positions of PG_1 and PG_2, respectively. The effects of faults in s_1 and s_2 can be distinguished only when they yield different outputs for at least one clock cycle. We begin with the simplest special case of the MSA fault model, i.e., the SSA fault model.

Theorem 8: All SSA faults are detectable, and the maximum testing length is $r + 1$, where r is the order of the PG.

Proof: An SSA fault in a PG is detectable when it generates an output different from that of the other PG. Let the initial state of the PG be $\sum_{i=1}^{r} n_i x^i$, where $n_1 = 1$ and $n_i = 0$, $\forall i \neq 1$. When an s-a-0 is located at output of x^i, n_1 is falsely inverted at the ith shift. The fault cannot be revealed during the first $i - 1$ clock cycles, because the s-a-0 is the same as the preset value of a fault-free circuit. The worst case occurs when the s-a-0 is located at the output of x^r, and, thus, r is the maximum testing length.

When an s-a-1 is located at the output of x^i, it will change the parity of the output immediately when it propagates to a feedback line. The worst case occurs when feedback lines emanate from x^1 and x^r, and the s-a-1 is present at the input of x^1. The output of the faulty PG is the same as the nonfaulty one until the $r + 1$th clock cycle. Thus, the maximum testing length for SSA faults is $r + 1$. ∎

To calculate the MSA fault coverage, the position and type

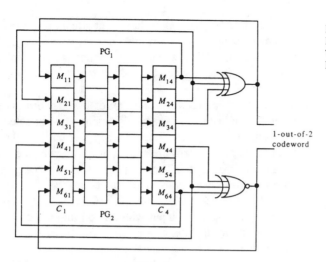

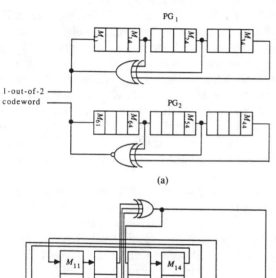

(a)

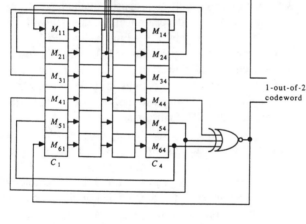

(b)

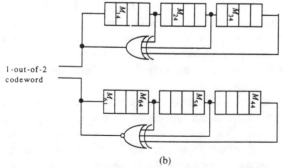

Fig. 6.   A queue transformed into two symmetric and asymmetric PG's. (a) Symmetric PG's. (b) Asymmetric PG's.

TABLE I
MSA FAULT COVERAGES OF PG's. (a) MSA FAULT COVERAGE (C) OF DIFFERENT NUMBERS AND LOCATIONS OF FEEDBACK LINES. (b) $k = 8$ WITH THREE FEEDBACK LINES. (c) PG's TESTED TWICE BY TWO FEEDBACK CONFIGURATIONS. (d) FEEDBACK LINES AT k, 0, AND THE PG's ARE TESTED TWICE WITH TWO DIFFERENT INITIAL STATES.

feedback(f_i)	Stage No.(k)								
	3	4	5	6	7	8	12	16	20
k,0	.728	.715	.710	.709	.708	.708	.708	.708	.708
k,1,0	.780	.788	.793	.794	.794	.795	.795	.795	-
k,2,1,0	*	.827	.828	.831	.831	.832	.831	-	-

(a)

f_1, f_2, f_3	8,1,0	8,2,0	8,3,0	8,4,0	8,5,0	8,6,0
C	.795	.785	.780	.777	.770	.746

(b)

(k, f'_1, f'_2) / C; $f_1 = k, f_2 = 0$									
(3,2,1) .868	(4,2,1) .876	(5,2,1) .877	(6,2,1) .876	(7,2,1) .875	(8,2,1) .875	(9,2,1) .875	(10,2,1) .875	(11,2,1) .875	(12,2,1) .879
(8,1,0) .875	(8,3,1) .876	(8,3,2) .876	(8,4,1) .879	(8,4,3) .877	(8,5,1) .886	(8,5,3) .885	(8,5,4) .879	(8,6,1) .900	(8,6,3) .899
(8,6,5) .874	(8,7,0) .801	(8,7,1) .875	(8,7,5) .883	(8,7,6) .869	(16,1,2) .875	(18,10,9) .875	(19,10,9) .875	(20,11,10) .875	(21,12,11) .875

(c)

$(k, in_2 = 2^n)$ / C; first initial condition $in_1 = 2^0$									
(3,1) .762	(3,2) .809	(4,1) .748	(4,2) .764	(4,3) .805	(5,1) .745	(5,2) .749	(5,3) .764	(5,4) .803	(6,1) .743
(6,2) .745	(6,3) .749	(6,4) .764	(6,5) .803	(7,1) .743	(7,3) .745	(7,5) .764	(7,6) .803	(8,1) .743	(8,2) .745
(8,4) .745	(8,6) .764	(8,7) .803	(9,1) .743	(9,3) .743	(9,5) .745	(9,7) .764	(9,8) .803	(10,1-5) .743	(10,6) .745
(10,7) .749	(10,8) .764	(10,9) .803	(12,1-7) .743	(12,8) .745	(12,9) .749	(12,10) .764	(12,11) .803	(16,1-10) .743	(16,11) .743
(16,12) .745	(16,13) .749	(16,14) .764	(16,15) .803						

(d)

"–": not computed because of excessive simulation time requirements.
"*": not applicable.

of leading faulty DFF's must be considered. Each DFF can be s-a-1, s-a-0, or fault-free, and the number of MSA faults in a queue is $3^{mw} - 1$. Due to the fault masking effect, the actual computing time is $K \prod_{i=1}^{k} (2r_i + 1)^2$, where r_i is the order of block B_i and K is the computing time required for each iteration. As shown in Table I, various testing strategies are simulated to examine their MSA fault coverages. The initial state of each simulation is $n_1 = 1$, $n_i = 0$, $\forall i \neq 1$. From the simulation results, the following three conjectures are made.

Conjecture 1: The fault coverage is dominated by the number of feedback lines. It monotonically increases with the number of feedback lines. The length of a PG has little effect on the fault coverage.

Conjecture 2: For a given PG of length r, and l_f feedback lines, the MSA fault coverage attains a maximum when feedback lines are located at x^1, x^2, $\cdots x^{l_f - 1}$, and x^r.

Conjecture 3: The MSA fault coverage increases with the number of testing routines, each of which uses a different initial state. The optimal testing length for MSA faults is r for a given initial state and a feedback configuration.

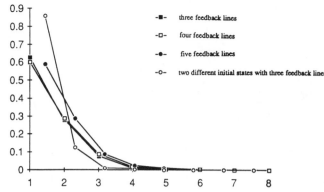

Fig. 7. Detected-faults/detectable-faults versus number of shifts when $r = 8$.

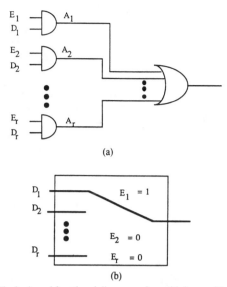

Fig. 8. The logic and functional diagrams of a multiplexer with r data inputs and r enable signals. (a) Logic diagram. (b) Functional diagram.

For a given PG configuration and the initial state, theoretically, 2^r shifts are required to exercise all the states of the PG. However, our simulation results show that testing lengths are rarely required to be longer than the length of the PG. Although the choice of an initial state affects the fault coverage, the number and location of feedback lines are the dominating factors in the fault coverage. It is shown in Fig. 7 that about 65 percent of detectable MSA faults are immediately detected for most cases. From Theorem 8 and the above conjectures, each testing length is found to be $r + 1$.

Unlike the off-line testing of data paths, a faulty RCU can be detected on-line. An *RCU checker* is proposed to detect faults in the RCU using its output signals. An RCU has an r $\log_2 r$-bit input and an r^2-bit output. The RCU output signals are denoted by E_{ij}, $1 \le i, j \le r$, where $E_{ij} = 1$ if queue j is connected to output port i, and $E_{ij} = 0$ otherwise. For any fixed k, $\{E_{ik}\}$ or $\{E_{ki}\}$, $1 \le i \le r$, forms a 1-out-of-r codeword. Thus, $2r$ 1-out-of-r self-checking checkers, one for each $\{E_{ik}\}$ or $\{E_{ki}\}$, are needed to detect all noncodeword outputs.

The outputs of the RCU and queues are the inputs of the MUDEX to which they are connected. The RCU and queues can be tested first using the above procedures. If they are fault-free, then the MUDEX and the links connected to the MUDEX are tested by using the RCU and queues to generate test patterns for the the MUDEX and its links. For output verification, the streams from the MUDEX's of stage i are transmitted through the links and then verified at stage $i + 1$ with special mechanisms.

Before we develop the test method for MUDEX's and links, it is necessary to find the test patterns of the $r \times 1$ multiplexer shown in Fig. 8, where E_i and D_i are the enable and data of the ith input, respectively. The $r \times 1$ multiplexer is implemented by r two-input AND gates and an OR gate.

Lemma 4: All SSA faults in the multiplexer of Fig. 8 can be detected in $r + 2$ steps.

Proof: After fault collapsing, the faults that need to be tested are 1) s-a-0 and s-a-1 primary output, i.e., output of the OR gate in Fig. 8, 2) s-a-0 A_i, $\forall i \le r$ in Fig. 8, and 3) s-a-1 $D_i(E_i)$, $\forall i \le r$. Test patterns can be derived as follows.

PT(1): $E_i D_i = 10$, $\forall i \le r$,

PT(2): $E_i D_i = 01$, $\forall i \le r$,

PT(3): $E_1 D_1 = 11$, and $E_i D_i = e_i d_i$ for $i \ne 1$

PT(4): $E_2 D_2 = 11$, and $E_i D_i = e_i d_i$ for $i \ne 2$

$\cdots \quad \cdots$

PT($r+2$): $E_r D_r = 11$, and $E_i D_i = e_i d_i$ for $i \ne r$,

where $d_i = 0$ or $e_i = 0$, $\forall 1 \le i \le r$.

An $r \times r$ MUDEX connects r queues' outputs to r links. The MUDEX can be implemented by two-level AND and OR gates, where each MUDEX's output port is basically a multiplexer. An example design of MUDEX is shown in Fig. 9, where E_{ij} is the enable signal from the RCU to route the packet at queue j to output port i. E_{ij} fans out to w branches to simultaneously enable the w bits of queue j.

Theorem 9: Any SSA fault on links or MUDEX's can be tested in $r + 2$ clock cycles.

Proof: Since operations to be applied to each of the w bits of a packet are identical, it is sufficient to discuss only one bit of the packet. Each output port of the 1-bit MUDEX is an $r \times 1$ multiplexer, and there are a total of r multiplexers in a MUDEX. Test patterns derived in Lemma 4 can be directly applied to test the MUDEX. However, it is important to minimize the test length when one selects test patterns. The proposed testing procedures are as follows. At clock cycle 1, all the RCU's outputs are set to 1 and the queue outputs to 0. Queue outputs are fixed at 1 for the rest of the procedures. At cycle 2, all the RCU's outputs are set to 0. During the remaining r cycles, the RCU performs permutation $i \rightarrow (i + j - 1)$ MOD r at cycle j, $3 \le j \le r + 2$. When the network uses distributed routing control, the queues for storing routing tags can be used to generate the desired routing requests to the RCU. By this permutation and the data queue setting, the r multiplexers in a MUDEX are tested simultaneously. The testing procedures are shown in Fig. 10. ∎

The MUDEX's output stream is two 0's followed by r 1's. Since both 0 and 1 appear at each switch's output, and thus, at each link, the links can be tested without introducing any

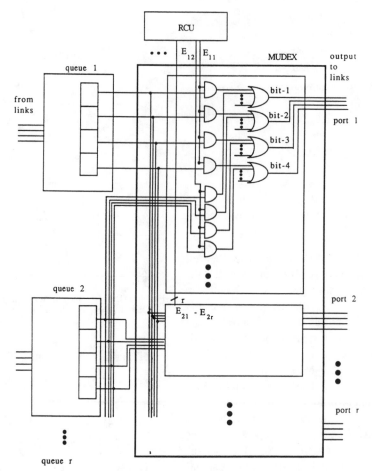

Fig. 9. An example of the MUDEX in an $r \times r$ switch.

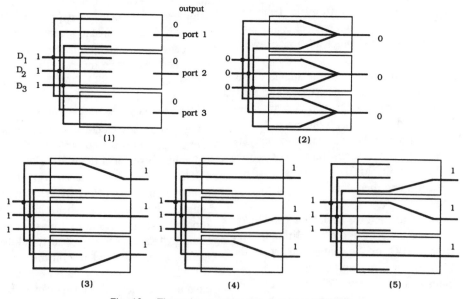

Fig. 10. The testing procedures for a 3×3 MUDEX.

additional cost. For test verification, it should be noted that all links in the network have identical outputs. Thus, the comparison method to verify the test results of queues can be applied similarly. Without loss of generality, the number of links from each switch is assumed to be even. Half of the links are connected to the primary inputs of a fan-out-free XOR tree, and the rest are connected to the primary inputs of the other fan-out-free XNOR tree. The outputs of the two fan-out-free networks form a 1-out-of-2 codeword. A design example for this method is given in Fig. 11(a).

It has been shown in [21] that a linear function implemented by two-input XOR gates needs at most four test patterns. The test patterns can be recursively derived from the primary output of the XOR (XNOR) tree to the primary inputs. Assume

788

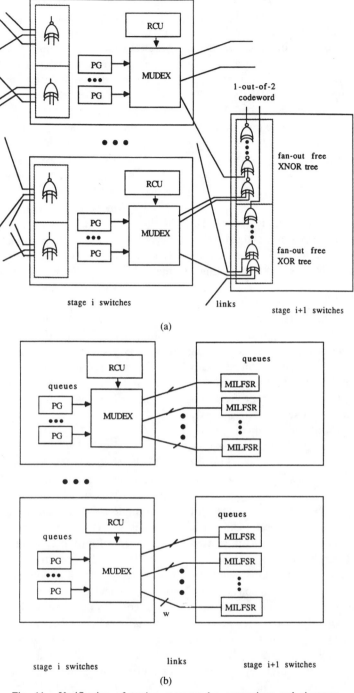

(a)

(b)

Fig. 11. Verification of testing response by comparison and signature analysis.

that a linear function P_n of n variables is implemented by an XOR tree as in Fig. 11(a). Then P_n can be recursively expressed by $P_n = x_n \oplus P_{n-1}$, where x_n is the nth primary input (variable), and P_{n-1} is the linear function implemented by the subnetwork excluding the primary output XOR gate and the primary input x_n. To test the primary output gate, it is sufficient to have $P_{n-1}x_n = 00, 01, 10, 11$. The input stream in x_n is then 0101, and P_{n-1} should be 0011. We want to derive a test pattern which can be easily generated, e.g., all inputs are identical, or, only one or two inputs are different from others. Thus, for $P_{n-1} = 0011$ and $P_{n-1} = P_{n-2} \oplus$

x_{n-1}, we set $x_{n-1} = 0101$ (as x_n), and thus, $P_{n-2} = 0110$. It can be shown by induction that $x_i = 0101$, $\forall i \neq 1$, and $x_1 = 0110$ (0011) when the number of gates is even (odd).

It is now clear that we can eliminate the hardcore in the XOR and XNOR trees when their test patterns are applied. Assume that $w/2$ links are connected to inputs $x_1 \cdots x_{w/2}$ of the XOR tree. To test the XOR (XNOR) tree, we need to add one more input x_0 to the tree, and x_0 is controlled by the BIT. Since the output stream of MUDEX testing is composed of two 0's and r 1's, the XOR (XNOR) tree can be tested simultaneously with the MUDEX's and links when $0011 \cdots (0110 \cdots)$ are simultaneously applied to x_0 by the BIT. It requires wr XOR and XNOR gates in each switch to verify the test response. When the number of XOR (XNOR) gates is too high, the testing method can be decomposed into two phases as follows. In phase one (two), all the queues in even (odd) stage switches serve as pattern generators and those in odd (even)-stage switches serve as multiple input linear feedback shift registers (MILFSR's). To test MUDEX's and links, the outputs of the MILFSR's are compared in a way similar to the case of testing queues. Thus, the network can be tested in two phases, each phase requiring $r + 2$ clock cycles. An example design showing such a strategy is given in Fig. 11(b).

V. CONCLUSION

A two-level testing strategy is developed in this paper. The network level testing uses processors as testers, and the switch level testing uses switches to test the network. The network level testing is concurrent testing and the switch level testing is off-line testing.

The first step to ease the network level testing is to synchronize network operations. Then, the network is tested with different polynomial operations. Although only a small number of functional fault models and the corresponding testing procedures are discussed, this method can be easily extended to detect other faults at the cost of additional testing times. For example, it can be used for *conflict resolving* testing. When two or more requests in a switch requesting the same output port to use, the RCU should grant only one. Using the testing polynomials, $P_i^N(x)$ and conflicting routing requests, testing an $r \times r$ switch can be done in $r^r - r!$ testing routines. Obviously, conflict resolving testing is very expensive, when r is large.

Since testing polynomials can be easily generated by processors or a dedicated hardware, the proposed method can be used for both SIMD and MIMD machines. Most of network faults can be diagnosed in a decentralized manner by processors with the polynomial testing. A processor need not communicate with others except for the simultaneous submission of polynomials. Thus, when the network becomes faulty, the testing method can be used to identify, with different levels of accuracy, fault-free components, i.e., a faulty system can be reconfigured following the testing.

The costs of testable designs are measured by the extra hardware required for links and logic components in switches. When the packet width is more than one bit, one of the data links can be used as a feedforward line (but not as a feedback line). However, when a data line is to be transformed into a feedforward line, a multiplexer should be used to bypass the queue that the link is connected to. One masker, a mapper, and an adder of w bits are required for each data queue. For an $r \times r$ switch, at least r^2 logic gates are needed to implement the

MUDEX, and the overhead, relative to the combinational circuit of the switch to implement the tracer, is $2/r$. It should be noted that the overhead is an upper bound, because hardware for the data buffers is not considered.

The goal of the switch level testing is to obtain high fault coverage with a small testing time. Queues are self-tested first by converting them into polynomial generators. Furthermore, test patterns for the MUDEX can also be generated by the PG's. For a C-connected queue, it needs w extra interlinks to convert a queue into PG's. Testing the RCU by the conventional method is very inefficient. It is proposed to use r 1-out-of-r codeword checkers to monitor the outputs of the RCU. Finally, the MUDEX's and links are tested simultaneously. Testing responses are verified by using XOR and XNOR trees. It is shown that the network testing time is independent of the network size and the design method can be applied to various types of switch. For the switch level testing, comparators in the switches are the predominating overhead, which is $wr/r^2 = 1/r$ for the combinational circuits of switches, and no extra links are needed.

In this paper, we have focused only on the development of testing strategies. To determine an optimal (in some sense) testing period, the tradeoff between the performance penalty and fault-detection time must be studied. This and modifications of the proposed testing method for CSN's are the subject of further inquiry.

APPENDIX A

FAULT COVERAGE OF POLYNOMIAL TESTING

Fault coverage of polynomial testing may vary with different circuit implementations of the network. To obtain a concrete figure on its fault coverage at the logic level, consider an example LFSR design in Fig. 12. The basic structure of a shift register is essentially a master–slave S/R flip-flop. The ith gate in a flip-flop is denoted as G_i, and its output and jth input (indexed from top to bottom) by GO_i and GI_i^j, respectively. It should be noted that latches usually have two outputs Q and $\bar{Q}$. However, since the number of links is a major concern in the network design, only the Q output of the slave latch will be used, and $\bar{Q}$ is ignored. In other words, a fault is detectable only when an erroneous response can be observed at the Q output of the slave latch. During normal operations, the S and R inputs are in the form of $d\bar{d}$, 11, $d\bar{d}$, 11, $\cdots$, where $d \in \{0, 1\}$. It should be noted that the input 11 is inserted automatically when CLK = 0 (1) at the master (slave) latch, and the outputs of a latch are read out when SR = 11. 01, 10, and 11 at the SR inputs are referred to as r, s, and b, respectively.

To derive its test set, the slave latch composed of G_7, G_8 is considered first. Using the D-algorithm, test patterns for faults in the latch are summarized as follows.

faults/nodes	GI_7^1	GI_7^2	GO_7	GI_8^1	GI_8^2	GO_8
s-a-0	sb	sb	rb	rb	rb	sb
s-a-1	sbrb	sbrb	sb	sb	rbsb	rb

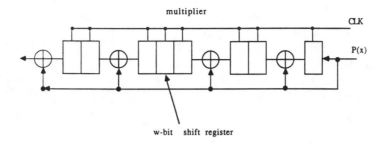

multiplier

w-bit shift register

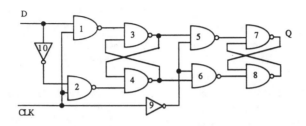

An one-bit shift register implemented by a master-slave S/R flip/flop

Fig. 12. An example LFSR implemented with master–slave *SR* latches.

Testing the master latch is more complicated, because the slave latch must be in an appropriate initial state, i.e., output, to propagate the erroneous response of the master latch to the Q output of the slave latch. For example, when $(Q, \bar{Q}) = (0, \bar{D})$ at the master latch,[5] the initial state of the slave latch must be $(1, 0)$ to obtain D at the output of the slave latch. Otherwise, the slave latch's output is 01, meaning that the fault is not tested. In our case, the master and slave latches have identical test patterns.

Test patterns for G_5 and G_6 are summarized below:

faults/nodes	GI_5^1	GI_5^2	GO_5	GI_6^1	GI_6^2	GO_6
s-a-0	sbrb	sbrb	sb	rbsb	rbsb	rb
s-a-1	rb	rbsb	sbrb	sbrb	sb	rbsb.

It can be shown that the above pattern can test G_1, G_2 simultaneously. GI_{10} s-a-1 and GO_{10} s-a-0 can be tested by *sbrb*. The only undetectable faults are GI_{10} s-a-0 and GO_{10} s-a-1, because the erroneous responses can only propagate to the $\bar{Q}$ output of the slave latch. GI_9 s-a-1 and GO_9 s-a-0 will block the transmission of data, and thus, *sbrb* is sufficient to test them. GI_9 s-a-0 and GO_9 s-a-1 faults do not cause logic faults, and thus, are not detectable by the D-algorithm. However, the *memory* of the register is lost when the above two faults occur, i.e., the latch fails to hold the data for a specific period. Assume that the high (low) period t_T of testing clock is three times slower than the latch's transition time t_d. Then, such faults can be tested by the polynomial testing method. For example, when GO_9 is stuck-at-1, the data at the input of the register will be shifted to the slave latch's output after $2t_d$. At the third t_d, the data are erroneously shifted into the next

register. Thus, the shift register fails to perform the *delay* function. Occurrence of such faults in a queue implies that the length of queue is reduced. Since the polynomial testing can identify the configuration of an LFSR, all such faults can be detected.

Although the polynomial testing is developed as a functional level testing, it can clearly detect all the detectable stuck-at faults at the logic level of registers. Since only two of the 56 faults are undetectable in a register, and all other faults, i.e., stuck-at faults on the XOR gates and feedforward lines, are detectable, the lower bound of the polynomial testing method is 96 percent.

APPENDIX B

LIST OF SYMBOLS

A, N, S, X Four states of a switch on the route under test.

B_i The ith block in a PDM.

BU_i The ith buffer in a queue.

$D_{i(\text{in})}, D_{i(\text{out})}$ The ring link input (output) of the ith pattern generator G_i.

DFF   A D-type flip-flop with a single input and a single output.

E_m Switch permutation, $E_m^{i+1} : f(ir + j) \rightarrow f(ir + j + m \text{ MOD } r)$, where $f(ir + j)$ and $f(ir + j + m \text{ MOD } r)$ are the global indexes of the jth input port and the $(j + m \text{ MOD } r)$th output port of the $(i + 1)$th

---

[5] They are inverted to $(1, D)$ before they enter the slave latch.

switch, respectively, where r is the switch order, and $\rightarrow$ is the interconection. E_m^i is denoted as E_m when all switches have the same permutation.

E_m^{-1} The inverse of the switch permutation E_m.

E_{ij} An RCU output which enables queue j to be connected to output port i.

$GF(2)[x]$ The polynomial ring.

I, I_n I is the set of integers and $I_n = \{0, 1, 2, \cdots, n\}$.

M An $m \times w$ matrix representing m buffers in a queue of w bits each. The ith row of M is the ith bits of all buffers and the jth column of M is the jth buffer in the queue.

$M_{ij}(x)$ The multiplier formed by the route connecting source i to destination j.

MUDEX   An $r \times r$ MUDEX is the combination of r multiplexers and r demultiplexers. It is used to direct packets in a PMIN switch.

ONE, ZERO   Coefficients of a word polynomial, ONE = $\overline{\text{ZERO}}$.

$P(x), \bar{P}(x)$ A polynomial and its complement.

$P_j^N(x)$ $P_j^N(x) = \sum_{i=0}^{N} c_i x^i$, where $c_j = 1$, $c_i = 0$, $i \neq j$, is a test pattern submitted by processor j.

$P_E^m(x)$ $P_E^m(x) = \sum_{i=0}^{k} x^{(m+1)i}$, the test polynomial for m unit delay faults.

PDM   Polynomial multiplier or divisor.

PG   Polynomial generator.

PMIN   Packet switching multistage interconnection network.

$Q(x)$ The product of $P(x)$ and $M(x)$, or the quotient of $P(x)/D(x)$, or the output of a PDM.

$R(x)$ The remainder of the operation that $D(x)$ divides $P(x)$ or the final contents of a PDM.

RCU   Routing control unit.

RUT   Route under test.

r_i The length or order of B_i.

SSA   Single stuck at fault.

T_i The link permutation at stage i.

$W_k(x), W(x)$ $W_k(x) = \sum_{i=0}^{k} x^i$. $W(x) = W_\infty(x)$.

$\sum_{i=0}^{r} n_i x^i$ The initial state of a PDM or a PG.

ACKNOWLEDGMENT

The authors are grateful to N. K. Jha for the valuable comments on the material in Section IV-C. They also want to thank M. H. Woodbury and referee A for numerous suggestions on the initial draft of this paper.

REFERENCES

[1] M. A. Breuer and A. D. Friedman, *Diagnosis and Reliable Design of Digital Systems.* Rockville, MD: Computer Science, 1976.

[2] W. K. Fuchs, J. A. Abraham, and K. H. Huang, "Concurrent error detection in VLSI interconnection networks," in *Dig. Papers, FTCS-13*, 1983, pp. 309–315.

[3] J. E. Lilienkamp, D. H. Lawrie, and P. C. Yew, "A fault tolerant interconnection network using error correcting codes," in *Dig. Papers, FTCS-12*, 1982, pp. 123–125.

[4] T. Y. Feng and C. L. Wu, "Fault-diagnosis of a class of multistage interconnection networks," *IEEE Trans. Comput.*, vol. C-30, pp. 743–758, Oct. 1981.

[5] D. P. Agrawal, "Testing and fault tolerance of multistage interconnection networks," *Computer*, pp. 41–53, Apr. 1982.

[6] N. J. Davis IV, W. T.-Y. Hsu, and H. J. Siegel, "Fault location techniques for distributed control interconnection networks," *IEEE Trans. Comput.*, Vol. C-34, pp. 902–910, Oct. 1985.

[7] D. C. H. Lee and J. P. Shen, "Easily-testable (N, K) shuffle/exchange networks," in *Proc. Int. Conf. Parallel Processing*, 1983, pp. 65–70.

[8] D. P. Agrawal and J.-S. Leu, "Dynamic accessibility testing and path length optimization of multistage interconnection networks," *IEEE Trans. Comput.*, vol. C-34, pp. 255–266, Mar. 1985.

[9] V. Cherkassky, E. Opper, and M. Malek, "Reliability and fault diagnosis analysis of fault-tolerant multistage interconnection networks," in *Dig. Papers, FTCS-14*, 1984, pp. 246–251.

[10] M. Malek and E. Opper, "Multiple fault diagnosis of SW-banyan networks," in *Proc. FTCS-13*, 1983, pp. 446–449.

[11] E. Opper and M. Malek, "Real-time diagnosis of banyan networks," in *Proc. Real Time Syst. Symp.*, 1982, pp. 27–36.

[12] W. Y.-P. Lim, "A test strategy for packet switching networks," in *Proc. Int. Conf. Parallel Processing*, 1982, pp. 96–98.

[13] V. Cherkassky and E. Opper, "Fault diagnosis and permuting properties of CC-banyan networks," in *Proc. Real-Time Syst. Symp.*, 1984, pp. 175–183.

[14] J. Y. Maeng, "Self-diagnosis of multistage network-based computer systems," in *Dig. Papers, FTCS-13*, 1983, pp. 324–331.

[15] S. Thanawastien and V. P. Nelson, "Diagnosis of multiple faults in shuffle/exchange networks," in *Proc. Real Time Syst. Symp.*, 1984, pp. 184–192.

[16] R. E. Bryant, "A switch-level model and simulator for MOS digital systems," *IEEE Trans. Comput.*, vol. C-33, pp. 160–177, Feb. 1984.

[17] E. J. McCluskey and S. Bozorgui-Nesbat, "Design for autonomous test," *IEEE Trans. Comput.*, vol. C-30, pp. 866–875, Nov. 1981.

[18] S. W. Golomb, *Shift Register Sequences.* San Francisco, CA: Holden-Day, 1967.

[19] Z. Kohavi, *Switching and Finite Automata Theory.* New York: McGraw-Hill, 1978.

[20] J. E. Smith, "Measures of effectiveness of fault signature analysis," *IEEE Trans. Comput.*, vol. C-29, pp. 510–514, June 1980.

[21] J. P. Hayes, "On realizations of boolean functions requiring a minimal or near-minimal numbers of tests," *IEEE Trans. Comput.*, Vol. C-20, pp. 1506–1513, Dec. 1971.

Jyh-Charn Liu (S'84) was born in Kaohsiung, Taiwan, on December 6, 1956. He received the B.S. and M.S. degrees in electrical engineering from the National Cheng Kung University, Tainan, Taiwan, in 1979 and 1981, respectively.

He was a system engineer of Siantek Co. Taiwan in 1983. Since 1984 he has been a Research Assistant at the University of Michigan, where he is currently pursuing the Ph.D. degree in electrical and computer engineering. His research interests include fault-tolerant computing and easily testable architectures for real-time applications.

Mr. Liu is a student member of the IEEE Computer Society.

Kang G. Shin (S'74–M'78–SM'83) received the B.S. degree in electronics engineering from Seoul National University, Seoul, Korea in 1970, and the M.S. and Ph.D. degrees in electrical engineering from Cornell University, Ithaca, NY, in 1976 and 1978, respectively.

From 1970 to 1972 he served in the Korean Army as an ROTC officer and from 1972 to 1974 he was on the research staff of the Korea Institute of Science and Technology, Seoul, working on the design of VHF/UHF communication systems. From 1978 to 1982 he was an Assistant Professor at Rensselaer Polytechnic

Institute, Troy, NY. He was also a Visiting Scientist at the U.S. Airforce Flight Dynamics Laboratory in Summer 1979 and at Bell Laboratories, Holmdel, NJ in Summer 1980. Since September 1982, he has been with the Department of Electrical Engineering and Computer Science at The University of Michigan, Ann Arbor, MI, where he is currently a Professor. He has been very active and authored/coauthored over 140 technical papers in the areas of distributed fault-tolerant real-time computing, computer architecture, and robotics and automation. As an initial phase of validation of architectures and analytic results, he and his students are currently building a 19-node hexagonal mesh multiprocessor at the Real-Time Computing Laboratory (RTCL), The University of Michigan.

Dr. Shin is a member of the Association for Computing Machinery, Sigma Xi, and Phi Kappa Phi. He was the Program Chairman of the 1986 IEEE Real-Time Systems Symposium and is the Guest Editor of the special issue of IEEE TRANSACTIONS ON COMPUTERS on Real-Time Systems which appeared in August 1987. In 1987, he also received an Outstanding Paper Award for a paper on robot trajectory planning published in IEEE TRANSACTIONS ON AUTOMATIC CONTROL.

FAIL SAFE DISTRIBUTED FAULT DIAGNOSIS
OF MULTIPROCESSOR SYSTEMS*

Chung Yang Chiang and Chuan-lin Wu
Department of Electrical and Computer Engineering
The University of Texas at Austin
Austin,TX 78712

Abstract -- Techniques for distributively, reliably diagnosing multiprocessor systems are presented in this paper. Based on these techniques,trustworthy diagnostic results on the status,faulty or fault free,of every processor node will be revealed by fault free processors. An assumption which has been commonly made in most papers and might lead to totally incorrect results is eliminated for fail safe purpose. The assumption puts a limit on the number of existing faulty processors. Capabilites of the diagnosis system is analyzed in terms of trustability,diagnosability,coverage and mean diagnosability. Comparison to an existing diagnosis approach is also provided on diagnosing system using a multistage topology. The results single out the uniqueness of our approach on the fail safe diagnosis.

1. Introduction

A general guideline has been established to avoid introducing extra faults which can lead a fault tolerant system to earlier destruction whenever system recovery schemes, such as fault detection,diagnosis, isolation and reconfiguration,for restoring the system to operating mode are called for[1].

A lot of research works have been done to mold processor nodes together to form parallel processing systems. Yet,only a little effort has been exerted on how to reliably manage the system whenever faults occur. Fault detection and location are the first two steps to take to avoid further damages to the system. Basically there are two kinds of fault diagnosis methods. The first is the centralized one in which an external processor takes the responsibility of locating the faulty processors. The second is the distributed one in which every processor involves the execution of the diagnosis procedure. For a large and/or widely dispersed system,centralized diagnosis is not feasible due to the limitation of communication links. Besides,those diagnosis processors will form the hardcore of the system. For nonrepairable and/or autonomous systems,only distributed diagnosis is feasible.

Valid fault detection and location methods should imply one hundred percent reliability in carrying out the job. They should never come up with

----

* This work is supported in part by a grant from IBM Corporation.

false diagnostic results. Otherwise,these methods would be as harmful as those faults which call for these methods since they could introduce more faults into the system. Previous papers in fault diagnosis tend to put a limit on the number of existing faults[2-8]. If more faults than the assumed limit occur,often times it is quite possible,depending on the reliability and size of the system,the system will simply yield false results. This is especially true for a large, distributed system in which only distributed fault diagnosis is feasible. There should be no room at all for uncertainty. A very small percentage of increase of uncertainty will result in dramatic decrease of system reliability as can be observed in [9]. This paper reports new techniques and concepts for reliably diagnosing multiprocessor system.

In section 2,we present a system graphs model and a fault model which forms the basis of a new fault diagnosis algorithm. Section 3 consists of the diagnosis algorithm and proof of the validity of this algorithm. Comparisons of coverage,trustability and mean diagnosability of systems with different diagnosability are presented in section 4. Section 5 concludes the work in this paper.

2. System Graphs and Fault Model

2.1 System Graphs

A system interconnection graph is an undirected graph showing the interconnections among processors of the system. Yet,test graph is a graph which shows the relationship between testing and tested processors. Interconnrction graph is the underlying graph of test graph. An example of these graphs is shown in Fig. 1. A directed test graph is depicted in Fig. 1.a in which the two processors linked by the arrowheaded link are associated with each other with the processor to which the arrowhead is incident defined as the tested processor and the other as the testing processor. Fig. 1.b is an undirected test graph in which every processor is both a testing and tested processor to its neighboring processors. In this particular case,the system test graph is the same as the interconnection graph.

A processor has two roles : it is a tester at one time,and a testee at another time. As a testing processor,it initiates its tested processors to commence self test and monitors the results from its tested processors. As a tested processor,it receives start signals from its testing processors to start self

Reprinted from *Proc. Int'l Conf. Parallel Processing*, 1986, pp. 358-365. Copyright © 1986 by The Institute of Electrical and Electronics Engineers, Inc. All rights reserved.

test,reports its own status and reroutes received fault vectors from its testees to its testers.

2.2 Fault Model

The fault model is similar to most of the ones presented in previous papers[2-8] except one point,that is,no assumption on the number of allowable faults is ever made in order to avoid false diagnostic results and therefore possible system catastrophy.

The fault model is defined as follows :
(1) a faulty processor might modify the fault vectors sent to it by its testees.
(2) only permanent fault is considered. That is,once a processor is identified as faulty by any fault free processor,it will be regarded as faulty even though other processors might identify it as fault free.
(3) a fault free processor can become faulty during diagnosis period.

Link faults will be treated as proceesor faults since it is technically difficult to differentiate between link faults and processor faults. If that happens,the system simply loses those fault free processors which have association with the faulty links.
Since the diagnosis system is based on a distributed algorithm and no global clock has ever been provided as a system wide synchronization mechanism,it is impossible for processors to know the exact time of occurences of any link or processor faults. The only condition for the processors to differentiate link faults from processor faults is that they know exactly when faults have occurred. That implies a global,nonskewed clock should be implemented,which is impossible. The following paragraph explains in a circumstance on how link faults and processor faults can be differentiated by systems adopting distributed diagnosis algorithms.

For instance,we have 2 processors testing a common processor,the first tester identifies it as fault free and the second one identifies it as faulty due to the broken or stuck link between them. Following situations are possible :

(1) If the second tester identifies the link fault before the first one,then every processor will receive time-stamped messages from both the second tester indicating the tested processor as faulty and the first tester indicating it as fault free. Since only permanent fault is considered and fault condition was located first in terms of global clock,processors shall resolve this situation as a link fault. And the faulty link is the one that connects the second tester and the tested processor. In this case,the useful resource in this tested processor will not be dispensed. Only the faulty link will be isolated.

(2) Yet, if the first tester identifies the fault free processor first and the second one identifies the tested processor as faulty due to broken or stuck link between them after the first tester, then it is impossible to tell if it is a link fault or processor fault since the situation is the same as that of a fault free processor becoming faulty later before it is tested by the second testers. Unless the first tester,after receiving this conflicting message,can test this tested processor again and issue a later-time-stamped message indicating this supposedly faulty processor is still fault free.

3. Reliable Distributed Diagnosis Algorithm

3.1 Fail Safe Distributed Algorithm

The initiation and execution of the system fault diagnosis is assumed fully distributed. The following algorithm is for fault diagnosis only. Fault detection at individual processor is assumed. In this diagnosis system,we assume a certain number of processors can periodically initiate fault diagnosis cycles to locate faulty processors. The number of these watchdog-type processors should be greater than the expected degree of system fault tolerance in order to provide the necessary fault tolerance. Whenever the first processor initiates current cycle,every other processors which receive the initiation message,in addition to starting the diagnosis cycle,should also adjust its own internal clock to prepare for initiating next cycle. For the case in which faults did occur before the cycle is started,the effect of faults will be confined to only one cycle.

Definition 1 : Diagnosability -- A system is said to be t-fault self diagnosable if and only if each processor in the system can correctly identify all t faulty processors.

Diagnosability should not be taken as the sole gauge of the system diagnosis capability. The degree of confidence on the yielded results should be seriously taken into consideration in addition to diagnosability. Some might argue that we can always construct a system with diagnosability as high as possible. Yet no matter how complicated the system and therefore how high the diagnosability might be,it is always possible that the number of faults might surmount the diagnosability. On the other hand, for systems in which the diagnosability is low due to physically restricted structure of the system,the possibility of more fatal faults is even higher.
The algorithm is equally applicable to every processor in the system.The algorithm is written in C-like language.

(1) f[i] == fault vector maintained locally by p(i) (processor with logical id of i).

  (a) f[i][k] == kth element in f[i] representing the status of p(k) with the following possible values if k is not equal to i :

    0 : if p(k) is fault free.

    1 : if p(k) is faulty.

    x : status of p(k) is undetermined.

  (b) f[i][i] is the status of p(i) itself with only two possible values of 0 or 1.

(2) F[i] == fault vector sent by p(i) == f[i] ; F[i][k] == kth element in F[i].

Node p(j),j=0,1,....,n-1,after receiving diagnosis initiation messages,will perform following algorithm :

```
{
INITIALIZATION :
/*self test and initialization*/
broadcast diagnosis initiation message to
neighboring(both tested and testing) processors;
SELF_TEST :
if(self test passed)
      {
      f[j] = [i_{n-1},..,i_j,..,i_1,i_0] = [x,x,..,0,..,x,x];
      send self test status to p(j)'s testers;
      }
else {
      f[i] = [x,x,..,1,..,x,x];
      send self test status to p(j)'s testers;
      break;

      }/*faulty processor makes self dormant if
        possible*/
while ((at least one element in f[j] undetermined) and
      (time not up yet))
      {
TEST : /*testing testees p(i)'s of p(j)*/
      for (every p(i) tested by p(j))
          switch (status of p(i)){
          case FAULT_FREE :
              f[j][i] = 0;
              break;
          case FAULTY:
          case NO_RESPONSE and TIMED_OUT :
              f[j][i] =1;
              break;
          case NO_RESPONSE and TIME_NOT_UP :
              break;
          } /*switch*/
BROADCAST : /*broadcast newly modified fault
vector to testers p(k)'s of p(j) if any*/
      while((any F[i] received from fault free p(i))) {
      if(F[i] results in changes of any element in f[j] from
        x to 1 or from 0 to 1)
          {
          initiate self test of p(i);
          if (p(i) is found fault free and F[i][i] ==0)
```

```
              update f[j] with F[i] from p(i);
          else   /*p(i) found faulty*/
              f[j][i]=1;
          }/*if*/
      broadcast newly changed element in f[j] to
      nonfaulty p(k)'s which test p(j);
      }/*while*/
      }/*while*/
if(at least one element in f[j] is undefined)
FAILED:
      for(nonfaulty p(k)'s which test p(j))
          broadcast failure message to p(k);
else{
      for(nonfaulty p(k)'s which test p(j))
          broadcast done message to p(k);
      while(at least one done message not yet received
      from fault free processors and time not up yet and
      no failure message received) ;
      if(timed out)
          go to INITIALIZATION;
      else
          if(failure message received)
              go to FAILED;
      }/*else*/
}/*main*/
```

The failure message indicates some of the fault free processors fail to generate decisive and unanimous result,although other fault free processors can locate all faulty processors.

3.2 Definition and Theorem

Definition 2 : Connectivity -- For an undirected(directed) test graph,the (vertex) connectivity K_v is the minimun number of vertices whose removal from the graph results in a disconnected (weakly connected or disconnected)graph [10].

The test graph of Fig. 1.a is a directed graph with connectivity of 2. Yet ,the test graph of Fig. 1.b is an undirected graph with connectivity of 4.

When the number of faults is equal to the connectivity of the test graph,then the diagnosis system will fail us in some cases as the following paragraphs show. By failing us,we mean the diagnosis system found that current fault situation is undiagnosable due to lack of unanimous and decisive diagnostic result.

Assume the test graph of a multiprocessor system has connectivity of t,then the following cases are the situations in which the diagnosis system fails when the number of faults is not less than t.

case 1: Any processor with all its t testers being faulty. In this situation,the status of this particular processor will be unknown to other processors in the system.

case 2: Any processor with all its t testees being faulty. This particular processor will be totally blocked from the diagnostic information flowing around the system.

case 3 : There are some special cases with not less than t faults which also result in failed system.

As long as the number of faults is less than t, the diagnosis system always comes up with decisive and unanimous result.

From the above cases, we observe that the diagnosability of the system proposed in this paper is always 1 less than the connectivity. The main reason behind this decrease of diagnosability, as compared with that of the diagnosis systems proposed in other papers, is to achieve fail safety. Yet, it doesn't at all imply the system has an inferior capability of locating existing faults. On the contrary, it has a better capability.

The following theorem verifies that when the number of faults is less than the connectivity of the system, the system can always locate all faults by adopting the previous algorithm. And when the number of faults is eqaul to or greater than the system connectivity, the algorithm never comes up with false diagnostic results.

Theorem 1 - Using the above algorithm, a system with test graph T of K_v equals t will either correctly locate all faulty processors or not incorrectly locate any faulty processors.

Proof : We will prove the validity of the algorithm in three cases.

(1) if the number of faults is less than t :

As the system has a test graph with K_v equals t, therefore, it will still be connected (or strongly connected). There will be at least one path between every pair of vertices according to the definition of connected graphs. Therefore, for a directed test graph system, every fault free vertex can receive the diagnostic information from its fault free testees and broadcast new information to its nonfaulty testers. For a directed test graph, the set of testers and the set of testees of a vertex do not have any element in commom. Yet for an undirected test graph, the set of testers is the same as the set of testees for a vertex. There is still at least one path which consists of fault free vertices, and correct diagnostic information can be received and broadcast along this path.

(2) if the number of faults is greater than t :

According to the definition of connected graph, we encounter two situations :

(A) it is possible that the test graph is disconnected (or weakly connected), then there will be no path at all between some pairs of vertices. These vertices will fail to either collect status of other vertices or be known to other vertices of its status. Therefore, we can sort all fault free vertices into two

categories : those which fail to collect status of every vertex and those which can collect status of every vertex. For those which fail, they will broadcast failure message to every other fault free vertex according to the algorithm. And since the other set consists of those which can collect status of every vertex, they will be able to collect this newly broadcast failure message. The result is no vertex in the system will ever go into a faulty state in which it thinks the system yields decisive and unanimous results. We conclude that no vertex will ever incorrectly locate faulty vertices.

(B) if the test graph is still connected (or strongly connected), then the situation is the same as that of (1).

(3) if the number of faults is equal to t :

This case is the same as (2) except the possibility of the test graph being connected is higher than that of (2). The only occassions that the test graph will be disconnected are : (a) when either all testers or all testees of a vertex are faulty, and (b) few special cases.

Q.E.D.

4. System Coverage, Diagnosability, Trustability and Mean Diagnosability

4.1 Analysis of Diagnosis Trustability

Definition 3 : Trustability of Diagnosis -- Trustability of fault diagnosis is the probability that the diagnosis system either yields correct or does not yield incorrect diagnostic results regardless the number of faults in the system.

Trustability is actually a reliability measure. A diagnosis system which guarantees locating up to k faults when the number of faults is not more than k will have diagnosis trustability of 1 when the number of faults is less than or equal to k. Yet, when the number of faults is greater than k, the trustability decreases as the number of faults increases. For example, in [2], the system will yield false results when the number of faults is greater than the assumed one. Take the 5-node completely connected graph system in Fig.1.a as an example. According to the structure of this system, diagnosis algorithm in [2] can diagnose up to 2 faults, yet, if the number of faults is greater than 2, the trustability of the diagnosis system will be the probability of any 3 or more existing faults in the system. According to the algorithm presented in this paper, the diagnosability is 1 instead of 2, which of course is 1 less than that of [2], yet the trustability of diagnosis is still 1 regardless the number of faults in the system. As we can see, the increase in diagnosis trustability is at the expense of diagnosability.

Analysis -- Trustability measures for both fail-safe and non-fail-safe diagnosis systems are analyzed below. We assume there is an exponential failure distribution for every processor in the system and the failure distributions are independent. The reliability function is : $R(t) = e^{-qt}$. We will use R instead of R(t) just for simplicity. Equation for trustability is stated as follows :

$$T(t) = \sum_{i=0}^{n} p_i * C(n,i) R^{n-i} (1-R)^i \qquad (1)$$

where $C(n,i)$ is the number of combinations for choosing r faulty processors out of a total of n processors. The product term of $C(n,i)$, R and (1-R) is the probability of exactly i faulty processors out of n processors. p_i is the probability of correctly locating all i faulty processors or not incorrectly locating any faulty processor.

(1)Fail safe diagnosis system : A system with n processors can correctly locate up to k faults and doesn't incorrectly locate faults if the number of faults is greater than k. Then the trustability of diagnosis will be 1 as described below :

$T_{fs}(t)=$
$1*R^n + 1*C(n,1)R^{n-1}(1-R)^1 + 1*C(n,2)R^{n-2}(1-R)^2 + ... + 1*C(n,k)R^{n-k}(1-R)^k + 1*C(n,k+1)R^{n-k-1}(1-R)^{k+1} + ... + 1*C(n,i)R^{n-i}(1-R)^i + ... + 1*(1-R)^n \qquad (2)$

which is the binomial expansion of $(R + (1-R))^n = 1$. The jth (j <= k) item is the probability of correctly locating all faults if there are j faults. The ith(i > k) item is the probability of not incorrectly locating any faults if there are i faults.

(2)Non-fail-safe diagnosis system : If the system can correctly locate only up to k faults,and can not guarantee the correctness of the results when the number of faults is greater than k,then the trustability will be :

$T_{nfs}(t) = 1*R^n + 1*C(n,1)R^{n-1}(1-R)^1 + 1*C(n,2)R^{n-2}(1-R)^2 + ... + 1*C(n,k)R^{n-k}(1-R)^k + p_{k+1}*C(n,k+1)R^{n-k-1}(1-R)^{k+1} + ... + p_i*C(n,i)R^{n-i}(1-R)^i + ... + p_n*(1-R)^n \qquad (3)$

where p_i's are the probabilities that the diagnosis system yields correct diagnostic results if there are i faults(i > k) in the system. The probability that the system being led to incorrect state is 1 minus the trustability as follows :

$$\overline{T_{nfs}(t)} = (1-p_{k+1})*C(n,k+1)R^{n-k-1}(1-R)^{k+1} + ... + (1-p_n)*(1-R)^n \qquad (4)$$

4.2 Comparison of Trustability , Diagnosability , Coverage and Mean Diagnosability

We will compare the diagnosis system in [2] and the one proposed here. The system in [2] is the first one proposes a fully distributed diagnosis system. We call it R system and ours S system. The comparison is done on the diagnosis of a system employing multistage topology[11],which is also employed for functional language architectures[12]. An example topology is shown in Fig. 2.

(A) Trustability :

(1) R system = $\sum_{i=0}^{2} 1 * C(n,i)R^{n-i}(1-R)^i + \sum_{i=3}^{n} 0 * C(n,i)R^{n-i}(1-R)^i$

(2) S system = 1

p_i's(i >=3) are 0's in R system simply because it assumes there are at most 2 existing faults in the system. If there are more than 2 faults,then,according to its diagnosis algorithm,every processor will conclude that it has already located all faulty processors whenever there are 2 1's in its fault vector even though there are still a few don't care terms. This is especially truly for those processors which fail to determine status of every processor,since they have no way of determining status of some processors. They can yield decisive results only by assuming 2 faults in the system. Trustability of S system is 1 because it determines to yield decisive and unanimous result,no guessing is ever involved.

Remember that part of trustability is just the probability of not incorrectly locating any faults. When the system can correctly locate all faults no matter how many existing faults in the system,it is equal to the probability of correctly locating the faults. Yet,when the system can locate the faults for some of the fault situations and falsely locates the faults in other fault situations,then the trustability is simply the portion in which the system can locate the faults.

(B) Diagnosability :
According to PMC model,we have :
(1) R system = 2 ; and
(2) S system = 1

Even though the diagnosability of the S system is 1,it does not imply that it can't locate 2-fault incidents at all. As the way in which diagnosability is defined,it simply means it can not locate all 2-fault incidents,although it is capable of locating most of the 2-fault incidents as we shall see in the next paragraph. Therefore,it should be coupled with coverage to give a better idea of the probability of correctly locating faults.

(C) Coverage :

Definition 4 : Coverage of Diagnosis -- The percentage of fault incidents in which diagnosis system can correctly locate all faulty processors.

Simulation Features -- Coverage measure for S system is acquired by simulation which is executed in the following manner :

(1) specify size of the system , i.e. , number of stages.

(2) specify number of faulty processing elements (PE's).

(3) for every possible combination of the number of faults , check if every fault free PE can receive fault vector broadcast by other fault free PE's.

If at least one PE is incapable of receiving broadcast fault vectors from at least one other fault free PE, then it is regarded as a failed diagnosis situation since it implies this particular PE has a fault vector with at least one element undertermined. Therefore, the whole system is incapable of coming up with a decisive and unanimous diagnostic results.

According to simulation, we have the following results :

(1) R system =
$$\begin{cases} 1 \text{ for all system size if \# faults} <= 2; \\ 0 \text{ for all system size if \# faults} > 2. \end{cases}$$

(2) S system =
$$\begin{cases} 1.0000 \text{ for 3-stage system if \# faults} = 1; \\ 0.7879 \text{ for 3-stage system if \# faults} = 2; \\ 0.4727 \text{ for 3-stage system if \# faults} = 3. \\[6pt] 1.0000 \text{ for 4-stage system if \# faults} = 1; \\ 0.9395 \text{ for 4-stage system if \# faults} = 2; \\ 0.8218 \text{ for 4-stage system if \# faults} = 3. \end{cases}$$

The numbers shown above for 2-fault cases can be estimated quite easily as following example shows.

Example 1 -- For a 4-stage multistage interconnection network, there are three components which contribute to undiagnosable fault situations : (1) all testers of a particular PE are faulty, (2) all testees of a particular PE are faulty, and (3) special cases, as stated in the proof of Theorem 1.

For stage 0 PE's there are 2*8 such cases. As an example, in Fig. 2, assume PE(0,0) is the faulty PE addressed (0,0) with the first 0 representing its stage address and second 0 representing its address in that stage starting from top. If PE(0,1) is also faulty, then they will block the status of their two common testees in stage 1, PE(1,0) and PE(1,4), from being known to other PE's. Yet, if we assume PE(0,4) instead of PE(0,1) is faulty besides PE(0,0), then they will block their two common testers in stage 3, PE(3,0) and PE(3,1), from receiving diagnostic information. Therefore, for PE(0,0), there are 2 cases in which the diagnosis system fails. It is the same for other PE's in stage 0. Therefore, we have 2*8 cases in stage 0.

The numbers for stage 1 and 2 will still be the same. For stage 3, the number will be 1*8 only. We get 56 for cases covered by (1) and (2) situations stated at the begining of this example. Besides that, there are 4 special cases.

Therefore, there are 56+4 cases in which 2-fault situations make the diagnosis system fail. The total combinations for choosing 2 faulty PE's out of 4*8 PE's is 992. Thus, the coverage is (992-60)/992, which is 0.9395. The same estimation process can be applied to 2-fault cases for 3-stage system.

As the size of the system grows, the difference in coverage diminishes as can be observed in Fig. 3.a and 3.b. That implies S system can correctly locate almost the same number of faulty PE's when the size of system grows, as compared with those of R system, although diagnosability of S system is still 1.

As we pointed out earlier, when one considers the positive capability of a diagnosis system, he should take both coverage and diagnosability into account. We define the next measure accordingly.

Definition 5 : Mean Diagnosability -- The expected value of faults which can be correctly located regardless the number of faults in the system.

The mean diagnosability is as follows.

$$E[D] = \sum_{i=0}^{n} i * c_i \qquad (5)$$

where c_i is the coverage of the diagnosis system provided there are only i faults.

(D) Mean Diagnosability :

$$(1) \text{ R system} = 1 * 1 + 2 * 1 + \sum_{i=3}^{n} 3 * 0$$
$$= 3$$

$$(2) \text{ S system} = 1 * 1 + 2 * 0.9395 + 3 * 0.8218 +$$
$$+ \sum_{i=4}^{n} 3 * c_i$$
$$= 5.3444 + \sum_{i=4}^{n} 3 * c_i$$

It is obvious that the mean diagnosability of S system is better than that of R system.

From the above comparisons, we acquire the following conclusions :

(1) Advantages of S system are :

(a) It either correctly locates all faulty processors or doesn't incorrectly locate any faulty processor, which is the basic requirement for a truly fault tolerant computing machine. This can be perceived from the trustability of S system. Implication of this capability is S system can afford to have a longer diagnosis period since it doesn't set an upper limit on the number of allowable faults. For R system,diagnosis period should be as short as possible in order to avoid extra faults occuring during diagnosis period.

(b) The actual number of fault incidents in which faults can be located by S system is far more better than that of R system. This is justified by coverage and mean diagnosability of S system.

(2) Disadvantage of S system is :

(a) Diagnosability is always 1 less than that of R system. Yet this is not an actual disadvantage as it is a false indicator of diagnosis system capability.

5. Conclusion

We have presented a technique which is suitable for fail safely, distributively,locating faults in multiprocessor systems. That the system is both competent and fail safe is justified by the measures defined in this paper in terms of mean diagnosability and trustability. As we perceived,the assumption which has been widely used in several research papers does not necessarily make diagnosis systems more competent nor reliable. On the other hand,it is always fail safe to make as few assumptions as possible. The simulation and comparison done on a multistage system proves that,by emphasizing fail safety,we improve not only reliability but also capability of the diagnosis system.

6. References

[1] Special Issue on Fault Tolerant Computing,Computer,Vol. 13,Mar. 1980.

[2] J.G. Kuhl and S.M. Reddy."Distributed Fault-Tolerance for Large Multiprocessor Systems",Proc. Symposium on Computer Architecture,1980,pp. 23-30.

[3] J.G. Kuhl and S.M. Reddy,"Fault Diagnosis in Fully Distributed Systems",Proc. Symposium on Fault Tolerant Computing,June 1981,pp 100-105.

[4] F. Preparata,G. Metze and R. Chien,"On the Connection Assignment Problem of Diagnosable Systems",IEEE Trans. on Computers,Vol. EC-16,Dec. 1967,pp 848-854.

[5] F Barsi,F. Grandoni and P. Maestrini,"A Theory of Diagnosability of Digital Systems",IEEE Trans. on Computers,Vol. C-25,June 1976,pp 585-593.

[6] J. Russel and C. Kime,"System Fault Diagnosis",IEEE Trans. on Computers, Vol. C-24, Nov. 1975,pp 1078-1089.

[7] G. Meyer and G. Masson,"An Efficient Fault Diagnosis Algorithm for Symmetric Multiple Processor Architectures",IEEE Trans. on Computers,Vol. C-27,Nov. 1978,pp 1059-1063.

[8] S.N. Maheshwari and S.L. Hakimi,"On Model for Diagnosable Systems and Probabilistic Fault Diagnosis",IEEE Trans. on Computers,Vol. C-25, Mar. 1976,pp 228-236.

[9] K.M. Falavarjani and D.K. Pradhan,"Fault Diagnosis of Parallel Interconnection Network",Proc. Conference on Parallel Processing,1981,pp 209-212.

[10] T.F. Arnold,"The Concept of Coverage and Its Effect on the Reliability Model of a Repairable System",IEEE Trans. on Computers,Vol. C-22,Mar. 1973,pp 251-254.

[11] Narsingh Deo,Graph Theory with Applications to Engineering and Computer Science, Prentice-Hall, Inc,1974,478 pp.

[12] C.L. Wu,T.Y. Feng,"On a Class of Multistage Interconnection Networks",IEEE Trans. on Computers,Vol. C-29,Aug. 1980,pp 694-704.

[13] F.S. Wong and M.R. Ito,"A Loop-Structured Switching Network",IEEE Trans. on Computers,Vol. C-33,May 1984,pp. 450-455.

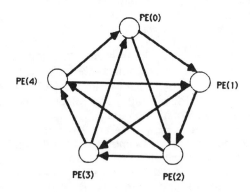

Fig. 1.a Directed Test Graph for a 5-processor System

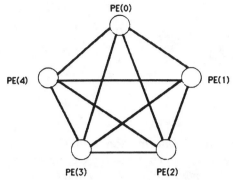

Fig. 1.b Undirected Test Graph for a 5-processor System

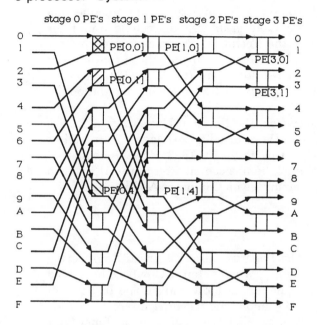

$\boxtimes$ = Faulty PE's which block the communication paths of their testers

$\diagup\!\!\!\!\square$ = Faulty PE's which block the communication paths of their testees

Fig. 2 Two Cases in Which Diagnosis System Fails to Yield Diagnosable Results

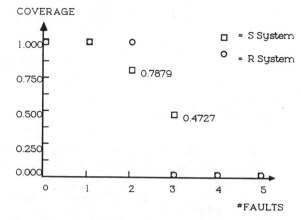

Fig. 3.a Comparison of Coverage as a Function of Number of Faults in a 3-stage MIN System

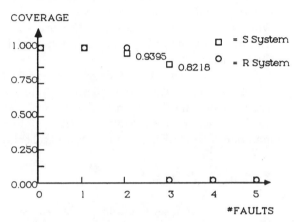

Fig. 3.b Comparison of Coverage as a Function of Number of Faults in a 4-stage MIN System

About the Authors

Isaac D. Scherson

Isaac D. Scherson is a professor with the Department of Information and Computer Science and the Department of Electrical and Computer Engineering at the University of California, Irvine. From 1987 to 1991, he held a faculty position in the Department of Electrical Engineering at Princeton University, Princeton, New Jersey. Prior to this, from 1983 to 1987, he held a faculty position at the University of California, Santa Barbara. His research interests include massively parallel computer architectures, interconnection networks, associative memory and processing, computer graphics, algorithms and their complexity, and VLSI. He has been a member of the Technical Program Committee for several professional conferences. He served as Workshops Chair for the Frontiers '92 Workshop and is the editor of the proceedings that resulted from this workshop. Also, he was guest editor of the June 1990 special issue of *The Visual Computer* on foundations of ray tracing.

Scherson received a BS degree and an MS degree from the National University of Mexico (UNAM), Mexico City, in 1975 and 1977, respectively. He received a PhD degree in computer science from the Weizmann Institute of Science, Rehovot, Israel, in 1983. He is a member of the IEEE Computer Society and the ACM. Since 1992, he has contributed to the IEEE as a member of the IEEE Computer Society Technical Committee on Computer Architecture.

Abdou S. Youssef

Abdou S. Youssef is an associate professor with the Department of Electrical Engineering and Computer Science at George Washington University, Washington, DC, where he served as an assistant professor from 1987 to 1993. In 1982, he taught for a year at The Institute of Applied Sciences, The Lebanese University, Beirut, Lebanon. His research interests include interconnection networks and computer architecture, parallel processing, algorithms, fault tolerance, image processing, and image databases. He has published numerous papers in journals and conference proceedings.

Youssef received a BS degree in mathematics from The Lebanese University in 1981 and an MA degree and a PhD degree in computer science from Princeton University, Princeton, New Jersey, in 1985 and 1988, respectively. He is involved in professional activities and is a senior member of the IEEE and a member of the ACM.